Weiss Ratings' Guide to Stock Mutual Funds

A Quarterly Compilation of Investment Ratings
and Analyses Covering Equity and Balanced Mutual Funds

Summer 2006

P.O. Box 689608
Jupiter, FL 33468-9608
(561) 627-3300

www.WeissRatings.com

Our customer hotline is here to serve you.
Don't hesitate to call us at

(800) 289-9222

ISSN: 1527-7909
ISBN-10: 1-58773-275-0
ISBN-13: 978-1-58773-275-1

Edition No. 32, Summer 2006

Data Source: Thomson Wealth Management
1455 Research Boulevard
Rockville, MD 20850

Date of data analyzed: June 30, 2006

Contents

Terms and Conditions

Welcome to Weiss Ratings'
Guide to Stock Mutual Funds

With the growing popularity of mutual fund investing, consumers need a reliable source to help them track and evaluate the performance of their mutual fund holdings. Plus, they need a way of identifying and monitoring other funds as potential new investments. Unfortunately, the hundreds of performance and risk measures available – multiplied by the vast number of mutual fund investments on the market today – can make this a daunting task for even the most sophisticated investor.

The Weiss Investment Ratings simplify the evaluation process. We condense all of the available mutual fund data into a single composite opinion of each fund's risk-adjusted performance. This allows you to instantly identify those funds that have historically done well and those that have underperformed the market. While there is no guarantee of future performance, the Weiss Investment Ratings provide a solid framework for making informed investment decisions.

Weiss Ratings' Mission Statement

Weiss Ratings' mission is to empower consumers, professionals, and institutions with high quality advisory information for selecting or monitoring a financial services company or financial investment.

In doing so, Weiss Ratings will adhere to the highest ethical standards by maintaining our independent, unbiased outlook and approach to advising our customers.

Why rely on Weiss?

For more than 30 years, Weiss has been recognized as a leader in helping consumers manage their finances. To that end, we provide safety ratings evaluating the financial stability of insurance companies and banks in addition to the Weiss Investment Ratings. Our mission is to provide fair, objective information to help professionals and consumers alike make educated purchasing decisions.

At Weiss, objectivity and total independence are never compromised. We never take a penny from rated companies for issuing our ratings, and we publish them without regard for the companies' preferences. Weiss' ratings are more frequently reviewed and updated than any other ratings, so you can be sure that the information you receive is accurate and current.

Weiss' rating scale, from A to E, is easy to understand as follows:

	Rating	Description
Top 10% of stock mutual funds	A	Excellent
Next 20% of stock mutual funds	B	Good
Middle 40% of stock mutual funds	C	Fair
Next 20% of stock mutual funds	D	Weak
Bottom 10% of stock mutual funds	E	Very Weak

In addition, a plus or minus sign designates that a fund is in the top third or bottom third of funds with the same letter grade.

Thank you for your trust and purchase of this Guide. If you have any comments, or wish to review other products from Weiss Ratings, please call 1-800-289-9222 or visit www.WeissRatings.com. We look forward to hearing from you.

How Others View Weiss Ratings

"Correctly identified"

"Weiss' ratings…correctly identified some of the worst-performing stocks."

L.A. Times

"The first to see the danger"

"Weiss was the first to see the danger and to say so unambiguously."

The New York Times

"A glowing tribute"

"The U.S. General Accounting Office's report is a glowing tribute to Weiss"

Barron's

"Free of any possible conflict of interest"

"The only company [that] provides financial grades free of any possible conflict of interest."

Esquire

"Tougher"

"A tougher service"

Louis Rukeyser, host of CNBC's Wall Street

"So good…[you] need look no further"

"Weiss' record ... is so good compared with that of his competitors...[you] need look no further."

Worth

How to Use This Guide

The purpose of the *Guide to Stock Mutual Funds* is to provide investors with a reliable source of investment ratings and analyses on a timely basis. We realize that past performance is an important factor to consider when making the decision to purchase shares in a mutual fund. The ratings and analyses in this Guide can make that evaluation easier when you are considering:

- growth funds

- index funds

- balanced funds

- sector or international funds

However, this Guide does not include pure bond funds and money market funds since they are not comparable investments to funds invested exclusively or partially in equities. For information on bond and money market funds, refer to *Weiss Ratings' Guide to Bond and Money Market Mutual Funds*. The rating for a particular fund indicates our opinion regarding that fund's past risk-adjusted performance.

When evaluating a specific mutual fund, we recommend you follow these steps:

Step 1 **Confirm the fund name and ticker symbol.** To ensure you evaluate the correct mutual fund, verify the fund's exact name and ticker symbol as it was given to you in its prospectus or appears on your account statement. Many funds have similar names, so you want to make sure the fund you look up is really the one you are interested in evaluating.

Step 2 **Check the fund's Weiss Investment Rating.** Turn to Section I, the Index of Stock Mutual Funds, and locate the fund you are evaluating. This section contains all stock mutual funds analyzed by Weiss including those that did not receive a Weiss Investment Rating. All funds are listed in alphabetical order by the name of the fund with the ticker symbol following the name for additional verification. Once you have located your specific fund, the first column after the ticker symbol shows its Weiss Investment Rating and corresponding percentile. Turn to *About the Weiss Investment Ratings* on page 7 for information about what this rating means.

Step 3 **Analyze the supporting data.** Following the Weiss Investment Rating are some of the various measures we have used in rating the fund. Refer to the Section I introduction (beginning on page 15) to see what each of these factors measures. In most cases, lower rated funds will have a low performance rating and/or a low risk rating (i.e., high volatility). Bear in mind, however, that the Weiss Investment Rating is the result of a complex computer-generated analysis which cannot be reproduced using only the data provided here.

When looking to identify a mutual fund that achieves your specific investing goals, we recommend the following:

Step 4   **Take our Investor Profile Quiz.** Turn to page 631 of the Appendix and take our Investor Profile Quiz to help determine your level of risk tolerance. After you have scored yourself, the last page of the quiz will refer you to the risk category in Section VII (Top-Rated Stock Mutual Funds by Risk Category) that is best for you. There you can choose a fund that has historically provided top notch returns while keeping the risk at a level that is suited to your investment style.

Step 5   **View the 100 top performing funds.** If your priority is to achieve the highest return, regardless of the amount of risk, turn to Section V which lists the top 100 stock mutual funds with the best financial performance. Keep in mind that past performance alone is not always a true indicator of the future since these funds have already experienced a run up in price and could be due for a correction.

Step 6   **View the 100 funds with the lowest risk.** On the other hand, if capital preservation is your top priority, turn to Section VI which lists the top 100 stock mutual funds with the lowest risk. These funds will have lower performance ratings than most other funds, but can provide a safe harbor for your savings.

Step 7   **View the top-rated funds by fund type.** If you are looking to invest in a particular type of mutual fund (e.g., aggressive growth or a balanced fund), turn to Section VIII, Top-Rated Stock Mutual Funds by Fund Type. There you will find the top 100 stock mutual funds with the highest performance rating in each category. Please be careful to also consider the risk component when selecting a fund from one of these lists.

Step 8   **Refer back to Section I.** Once you have identified a particular fund that interests you, refer back to Section I, the Index of Stock Mutual Funds, for a more thorough analysis.

Always remember:

Step 9   **Read our warnings and cautions.** In order to use the Weiss Investment Ratings most effectively, we strongly recommend you consult the Important Warnings and Cautions listed on page 11. These are more than just "standard disclaimers." They are very important factors you should be aware of before using this Guide.

Step 10   **Stay up to date.** Periodically review the latest Weiss Investment Ratings for the funds that you own to make sure they are still in line with your investment goals and level of risk tolerance. For information on how to acquire follow-up reports on a particular mutual fund, call 1-800-289-9222 or visit www.WeissRatings.com.

About the Weiss Investment Ratings

The Weiss Investment Ratings represent a completely independent, unbiased opinion of a mutual fund's historical risk-adjusted performance. Each fund's rating is based on two primary components:

Primary Component #1   A fund's **Performance Rating** is based on its total return to shareholders over the last trailing three years, including share price appreciation and distributions to shareholders. This total return figure is stated net of the expenses and fees charged by the fund, and we also make additional adjustments for any front-end or deferred sales loads.

This adjusted return is then weighted to give more recent performance a slightly greater emphasis. Thus, two mutual funds may have provided identical returns to their shareholders over the last three years, but the one with the better performance in the last 12 months will receive a slightly higher performance rating.

Primary Component #2   The **Risk Rating** is based on the level of volatility in the fund's monthly returns, also over the last trailing three years. We use several statistical measures – standard deviation, semi-deviation and a drawdown factor – as our barometer of volatility. Funds with more volatility relative to other mutual funds are considered riskier, and thus receive a lower risk rating. By contrast, funds with a very stable returns are considered less risky and receive a higher risk rating.

Note that none of the mutual funds listed in this publication have received a risk rating in the A (Excellent) range. This is because all stock investments, by their very nature, involve at least some degree of risk.

Rarely will you ever find a mutual fund that has both a very high Performance Rating plus, at the same time, a very high Risk Rating. Therefore, the funds that receive the highest overall Weiss Investment Ratings are those that combine the ideal combination of both primary components. There is always a tradeoff between risk and reward. That is why we suggest you assess your own personal risk tolerance using the quiz on page 631 as a part of your decision-making process.

Keep in mind that while the Weiss Investment Ratings use the same rating scale as the Weiss Safety Ratings of financial institutions, the two ratings have totally independent meanings. The Weiss Safety Ratings assess the *future* financial stability of an insurer or bank as a way of helping investors place their money with a financially sound company and minimize the risk of loss. These ratings are derived without regard to the performance of the individual investments offered by the insurance companies, banks, or thrifts.

On the other hand, the Weiss Investment Ratings employ a ranking system to evaluate both safety and performance. Based on these measures, funds are divided into percentiles, and an individual performance rating and a risk rating are assigned to each fund. Then these measures are combined to derive a fund's composite percentile ranking. Finally, the Weiss Investment Ratings are assigned to their corresponding percentile rankings as shown on page 3.

How Our Ratings Differ From Those of Other Services

Balanced approach: The Weiss Investment Ratings are designed to meet the needs of aggressive *as well as* conservative investors. We realize that your investment goals can be different from those of other investors based upon your age, income, and tolerance for risk. Therefore, our ratings balance a fund's performance against the amount of risk it poses to identify those funds that have achieved the optimum mix of both factors. Some of these top funds have achieved excellent returns with only average risk. Others have achieved average returns with only moderate risk. Whatever your personal preferences, we can help you identify a top notch fund that meets your investing style.

Other Investment rating firms give a far greater weight to performance and insufficient consideration to risk. In effect, they are betting too heavily on a continuing bull market and not giving enough consideration to the risk of a decline. While performance is obviously a very important factor to consider, we believe that the riskiness of a fund is also very important. Therefore, we weigh these two components more equally when assigning the Weiss Investment Ratings.

But we don't stop there. We also assign a separate performance rating and risk rating to each fund so you can focus on the component that is most important to you. In fact, Sections V, VI, and VII are designed specifically to help you select the best stock mutual funds based on these two factors. No other source gives you the cream of the crop in this manner.

Easy to use: Unlike those of other services, the Weiss Investment Ratings are extremely intuitive and easy to use. Our rating scale (A to E) is easily understood by members of the general public based on their familiarity with school grades. So, there are no stars to count and no numbering systems to interpret.

More funds: Weiss Ratings' *Guide to Stock Mutual Funds* tracks more mutual funds than any other publication – with updates that come out more frequently than those of other rating agencies. We've included more than 8,000 funds in this edition, all of which are updated every three months. Compare that to other investment rating agencies, such as Morningstar, where coverage stops after the top 1,500 funds and it takes five months for a fund to cycle through their publication's update process.

Recency: Recognizing that every fund's performance is going to have its peaks and valleys, superior long-term performance is a major consideration in the Weiss Investment Ratings. Even so, we do not give a fund a top rating solely because it did well 10 or 15 years ago. Times change and the top performing funds in the current economic environment are often very different from those of a decade ago. Thus, our ratings are designed to keep you abreast of the best funds available *today* and in the *near future,* not the distant past.

No bias toward load funds: In keeping with our conservative, consumer-oriented nature, we adjust the performance for so-called "load" funds differently from other rating agencies. We spread the impact to you of front-end loads and back-end loads (a.k.a. deferred sales charges) over a much shorter period in our evaluation of a fund. Thus our performance rating, as well as the overall Weiss Investment Rating, more fully reflects the actual returns the typical investor experiences when placing money in a load fund.

What Our Ratings Mean

A **Excellent**. The mutual fund has an excellent track record for maximizing performance while minimizing risk, thus delivering the best possible combination of total return on investment and reduced volatility. It has made the most of the recent economic environment to maximize risk-adjusted returns compared to other mutual funds. While past performance is just an indication – not a guarantee – we believe this fund is among the most likely to deliver superior performance relative to risk in the future.

B **Good.** The mutual fund has a good track record for balancing performance with risk. Compared to other mutual funds, it has achieved above-average returns given the level of risk in its underlying investments. While the risk-adjusted performance of any mutual fund is subject to change, we believe that this fund has proven to be a good investment in the recent past.

C **Fair.** In the trade-off between performance and risk, the mutual fund has a track record which is about average. It is neither significantly better nor significantly worse than most other mutual funds. With some funds in this category, the total return may be better than average, but this can be misleading since the higher return was achieved with higher than average risk. With other funds, the risk may be lower than average, but the returns are also lower. In short, based on recent history, there is no particular advantage to investing in this fund.

D **Weak.** The mutual fund has underperformed the universe of other funds given the level of risk in its underlying investments, resulting in a weak risk-adjusted performance. Thus, its investment strategy and/or management has not been attuned to capitalize on the recent economic environment. While the risk-adjusted performance of any mutual fund is subject to change, we believe that this fund has proven to be a bad investment over the recent past.

E **Very Weak.** The mutual fund has significantly underperformed most other funds given the level of risk in its underlying investments, resulting in a very weak risk-adjusted performance. Thus, its investment strategy and/or management has done just the opposite of what was needed to maximize returns in the recent economic environment. While the risk-adjusted performance of any mutual fund is subject to change, we believe this fund has proven to be a very bad investment in the recent past.

+ **The plus sign** is an indication that the fund is in the top third of its letter grade.

- **The minus sign** is an indication that the fund is in the bottom third of its letter grade.

U **Unrated.** The mutual fund is unrated because it is too new to make a reliable assessment of its risk-adjusted performance. Typically, a fund must be established for at least three years before it is eligible to receive a Weiss Investment Rating.

Important Warnings and Cautions

1. **A rating alone cannot tell the whole story.** Please read the explanatory information contained here, in the section introductions and in the appendix. It is provided in order to give you an understanding of our rating methodology as well as to paint a more complete picture of a mutual fund's strengths and weaknesses.

2. **Investment ratings shown in this Guide were current as of the publication date.** In the meantime, the rating may have been updated based on more recent data. Weiss offers a notification service for ratings changes on companies that you specify. For more information call 1-800-289-9222, visit www.WeissRatings.com or see the last section of this publication for details.

3. **When deciding to buy or sell shares in a specific mutual fund, your decision must be based on a wide variety of factors in addition to the Weiss Investment Rating.** These include any charges you may incur from switching funds, to what degree it meets your long-term planning needs, and what other choices are available to you.

4. **The Weiss Investment Ratings represent our opinion of a mutual fund's past risk-adjusted performance.** As such, a high rating means we feel that the mutual fund has performed very well for its shareholders compared to other stock mutual funds. A high rating is not a guarantee that a fund will continue to perform well, nor is a low rating a prediction of continued weak performance. The Weiss Investment Ratings are not deemed to be a recommendation concerning the purchase or sale of any mutual fund.

5. **A mutual fund's individual performance is not the only factor in determining its rating.** Since the Weiss Investment Ratings are based on performance relative to other funds, it is possible for a fund's rating to be upgraded or downgraded based strictly on the improved or deteriorated performance of other funds.

6. **All funds that have the same Weiss Investment Rating should be considered to be essentially equal from a risk/reward perspective.** This is true regardless of any differences in the underlying numbers which might appear to indicate greater strengths.

7. **Our rating standards are more consumer-oriented than those used by other rating agencies.** We make more conservative assumptions about the amortization of loads and other fees as we attempt to identify those funds that have historically provided superior returns with only little or moderate risk.

8. **We are an independent rating agency and do not depend on the cooperation of the managers operating the mutual funds we rate**. Our data are derived, for the most part, from price quotes obtained and documented on the open market. This is supplemented by information collected from the mutual fund prospectuses and regulatory filings. Although we seek to maintain an open line of communication with the mutual fund managers, we do not grant them the right to stop or influence publication of the ratings. This policy stems from the fact that this Guide is designed for the information of the consumer.

9. **This Guide does not cover bond and money market funds.** Because bond and money market funds represent a whole separate class of investments with unique risk profiles and performance expectations, they are excluded from this publication.

Section I

Index of
Stock Mutual Funds

An analysis of all rated and selected unrated

Equity Mutual Funds.

Funds are listed in alphabetical order.

Section I Contents

Left Pages

1. **Fund Type**
The mutual fund's peer category based on an analysis of its investment portfolio.

AG	Aggressive Growth	HL	Health
AA	Asset Allocation	IN	Income
BA	Balanced	IX	Index
CV	Convertible	MC	Mid Cap
EM	Emerging Market	OT	Other
EN	Energy/Natural Resources	PM	Precious Metals
FS	Financial Services	RE	Real Estate
FO	Foreign	SC	Small Cap
GL	Global	TC	Technology
GR	Growth	UT	Utilities
GI	Growth and Income		

A blank fund type means that the mutual fund has not yet been categorized.

2. **Fund Name**
The name of the mutual fund as stated in its prospectus, which can sometimes differ slightly from the name that the company uses for advertising. If you cannot find the particular mutual fund you are interested in, or if you have any doubts regarding the precise name, verify the information with your broker or on your account statement. Also, use the fund's ticker symbol for confirmation. (See column 3.)

3. **Ticker Symbol**
The unique alphabetic symbol used for identifying and trading a specific mutual fund. No two funds can have the same ticker symbol, and the ticker symbol for mutual funds always ends with an "X".

A handful of funds currently show no associated ticker symbol. This means that the fund is either small or new since the NASD only assigns a ticker symbol to funds with at least $25 million in assets or 1,000 shareholders.

4. **Overall Weiss Investment Rating**
Our overall rating is measured on a scale from A to E based on each fund's risk-adjusted performance. Please see page 10 for specific descriptions of each letter grade. Also, refer to page 7 for information on how our ratings are derived. Most important, when using this rating, please be sure to consider the warnings beginning on page 11 regarding the ratings' limitations and the underlying assumptions.

5. **Phone**
The telephone number of the company managing the fund. Call this number to receive a prospectus or other information about the fund.

6. **Performance Rating/Points**

A letter grade rating based solely on the mutual fund's financial performance over the trailing three years, without any consideration for the amount of risk the fund poses. Like the overall Weiss Investment Rating, the Performance Rating is measured on a scale from A to E for ease of interpretation. The points score indicates where the Performance Rating falls on a scale of 0 to 10.

7. **3-Month Total Return**

The total return the fund has provided to investors over the preceding three months. This total return figure is computed based on the fund's dividend distributions and share price appreciation/depreciation during the period, net of the expenses and fees it imposes on its shareholders. Although the total return figure does not reflect an adjustment for any loads the fund may carry, such adjustments have been made in deriving the Weiss Investment Ratings. The 3-Month Total Return shown here is not annualized.

8. **6-Month Total Return**

The total return the fund has provided investors over the preceding six months, not annualized.

9. **1-Year Total Return**

The total return the fund has provided investors over the preceding twelve months.

10. **1-Year Total Return Percentile**

The fund's percentile rank based on its one-year performance compared to that of all other equity funds in existence for at least one year. A score of 99 is the best possible, indicating that the fund outperformed 99% of the other mutual funds. Zero is the worst possible percentile score.

11. **3-Year Total Return**

The total annual return the fund has provided investors over the preceding three years.

12. **3-Year Total Return Percentile**

The fund's percentile rank based on its three-year performance compared to that of all other equity funds in existence for at least three years. A score of 99 is the best possible, indicating that the fund outperformed 99% of the other mutual funds. Zero is the worst possible percentile score.

13. **5-Year Total Return**

The total annual return the fund has provided investors over the preceding five years.

14. **5-Year Total Return Percentile**

The fund's percentile rank based on its five-year performance compared to that of all other equity funds in existence for at least five years. A score of 99 is the best possible, indicating that the fund outperformed 99% of the other mutual funds. Zero is the worst possible percentile score.

15. Dividend Yield

Distributions provided to fund investors over the preceding 12 months, expressed as a percent of the fund's current share price. The dividend yield of a fund can have little correlation to the amount of dividends the fund has received from its underlying investments. Rather, dividend distributions are based on a fund's need to pass earnings from both dividends and gains on the sale of investments along to shareholders. Thus, these dividend distributions are included as a part of the fund's total return.

Keep in mind that a higher dividend yield means more current income, as opposed to capital appreciation, which in turn means a higher tax liability in the year of the distribution.

16. Expense Ratio

The expense ratio is taken directly from each fund's annual report with no further calculation. It indicates the percentage of the fund's assets that are deducted each fiscal year to cover its expenses, although for practical purposes, it is actually accrued daily. Typical fund expenses include 12b-1 fees, management fees, administrative fees, operating costs, and all other asset-based costs incurred by the fund. Brokerage costs incurred by the fund to buy or sell shares of the underlying stocks, as well as any sales loads levied on investors, are not included in the expense ratio.

If a mutual fund's net assets are small, its expense ratio can be quite high because the fund must cover its expenses from a smaller asset base. Conversely, as the net assets of the fund grow, the expense percentage should ideally diminish since the expenses are being spread across a larger asset base.

Funds with higher expense ratios are generally less attractive since the expense ratio represents a hurdle that must be met before the investment becomes profitable to its shareholders. Since a fund's expenses affect its total return though, they are already factored into its Weiss Investment Rating.

Right Pages

1. Risk Rating/Points

A letter grade rating based solely on the mutual fund's risk as determined by its monthly performance volatility over the trailing three years. The risk rating does not take into consideration the overall financial performance the fund has achieved or the total return it has provided to its shareholders. Like the overall Weiss Investment Rating, the Risk Rating is measured on a scale from A to E for ease of interpretation. The points score indicates where the Risk Rating falls on a scale of 0 to 10.

2. Standard Deviation

A statistical measure of the amount of volatility in a fund's monthly performance over the last trailing 36 months. In absolute terms, standard deviation provides a historical measure of a fund's deviation from its mean, or average, monthly total return over the period.

A high standard deviation indicates a high degree of volatility in the past, which usually means you should expect to see a high degree of volatility in the future as well. This translates into higher risk since a large negative swing could easily become a sizable loss in the event you need to liquidate your shares.

3.   Beta

The level of correlation between the fund's monthly performance over the last trailing 36 months and the performance of its investment category as a whole.

A beta of 1.00 means that the fund's returns have matched those of the index one for one during the stock market's ups and downs. A beta of 1.10 means that on average the fund has outperformed the index by 10% during rising markets and underperformed it by 10% during falling markets. Conversely, a beta of 0.85 means that the fund has typically perfomed 15% worse than the overall market during up markets and 15% better during down markets.

4.   Net Asset Value (NAV)

The fund's share price as of the date indicated. A fund's NAV is computed by dividing the value of the fund's asset holdings, less accrued fees and expenses, by the number of its shares outstanding.

5.   Net Assets

The total value (stated in millions of dollars) of all of the fund's asset holdings including stocks, bonds, cash, and other financial instruments, less accrued expenses and fees.

Larger funds have the advantage of being able to spread their expenses over a greater asset base so that the effect per share is lessened. On the other hand, if a fund becomes too large, it can be more difficult for the fund manager to buy and sell investments for the benefit of shareholders.

6.   Cash %

The percentage of the fund's assets held in cash or money market funds as of the last reporting period. Investments in this area will tend to hamper the fund's returns while adding to its stability during market swings.

7.   Stocks %

The percentage of the fund's assets held in common or preferred stocks as of the last reporting period. Since stocks are inherently riskier investments than the other categories, it is common for funds invested primarily or exclusively in stocks to receive a lower risk rating.

8.   Bonds %

The percentage of the fund's assets held in bonds as of the last reporting period. This category includes corporate bonds, municipal bonds, and government bonds such as T-bills and T-bonds.

9.   Other %

The percentage of the fund's assets invested as of the last reporting period in other types of financial instruments such as convertible securities, options, and warrants.

10. Portfolio Turnover Ratio

The average annual portion of the fund's holdings that have been moved from one specific investment to another over the past three years. This indicates the amount of buying and selling the fund manager engages in. A portfolio turnover ratio of 100% signifies that on average, the entire value of the fund's assets is turned over once during the course of a year.

A high portfolio turnover ratio has implications for shareholders since the fund is required to pass all realized earnings along to shareholders each year. Thus a high portfolio turnover ratio will result in higher annual distributions for shareholders, effectively increasing their annual taxable income. In contrast, a low turnover ratio means a higher level of unrealized gains that will not be taxable until you sell your shares in the fund.

11. Last Bull Market Return

The fund's performance during the most recent stock bull market. Use this field in combination with the Last Bear Market Return (next column) to assess how well the fund anticipates and reacts to changing market conditions.

Keep in mind that lower risk funds tend to under perform higher risk funds during a bull market due to the risk/reward tradeoff.

12. Last Bear Market Return

The fund's performance during the most recent stock bear market. Use this field in combination with the Last Bull Market Return (previous column) to assess how well the fund anticipates and reacts to changing market conditions.

Keep in mind that lower risk funds tend to fare better than higher risk funds during a bear market although they may still record a net loss.

13. Manager Quality Percentile

The manager quality percentile is based on a ranking of the fund's alpha, a statistical measure representing the difference between a fund's actual returns and its expected performance given its level of risk. Fund managers who have been able to exceed the fund's statistically expected performance receive a high percentile rank with 99 representing the highest possible score. At the other end of the spectrum, fund managers who have actually detracted from the fund's expected performance receive a low percentile rank with 0 representing the lowest possible score.

14. Manager Tenure

The number of years the current manager has been managing the fund. Since fund managers who deliver substandard returns are usually replaced, a long tenure is usually a good sign that shareholders are satisfied that the fund is achieving its stated objectives.

15. Initial Purchase Minimum

The minimum investment amount, stated in dollars, that the fund management company requires in order for you to initially purchase shares in the fund. In theory, funds with high purchase minimums are able to keep expenses down because they have fewer accounts to administer. Don't be mislead, however, by the misconception that a fund with a high purchase minimum will deliver superior results simply because it is designed for "high rollers."

16. Additional Purchase Minimum

The minimum subsequent fund purchase, stated in dollars, that you can make once you have opened an existing account. This minimum may be lowered or waived if you participate in an electronic transfer plan where shares of the fund are automatically purchased at regularly scheduled intervals.

17. Front End Load

A fee charged on all new investments in the fund, stated as a percentage of the initial investment. Thus a fund with a 4% front-end load means that only 96% of your initial investment is working for you while the other 4% is immediately sacrificed to the fund company. It is generally best to avoid funds that charge a front-end load since there is usually a comparable no-load fund available to serve as an alternative.

While a fund's total return does not reflect the expense to shareholders of a front end load, we have factored this fee into our evaluation when deriving its Weiss Investment Rating.

18. Back End Load

Also known as a deferred sales charge, this fee is levied when you sell the fund, and is stated as a percentage of your total sales price. For instance, investing in a fund with a 5% back-end load means that you will only receive 95% of your total investment when you sell the fund. The remaining 5% goes to the fund company. As with front-end loads, it is generally best to avoid funds that charge a back-end load since there is usually a comparable no-load fund available to serve as an alternative.

While a fund's total return does not reflect the expense to shareholders of a back-end load, we have factored this fee into our evaluation when deriving its Weiss Investment Rating.

Fund Type	Fund Name	Ticker Symbol	Overall Weiss Investment Rating	Phone	Performance Rating/Pts	3 Mo	6 Mo	1Yr / Pct	3Yr / Pct	5Yr / Pct	Dividend Yield	Expense Ratio
GR	1st Source Monogram Dvrs Equity	FMDEX	D-	(800) 766-8938	D- / 1.0	-4.93	-3.03	2.10 / 5	6.70 / 9	-1.19 /11	0.01	1.37
IN	1st Source Monogram Income Equity	FMIEX	B	(800) 766-8938	B / 7.7	-0.77	7.82	15.55 /73	18.42 /74	10.10 /81	1.25	1.19
AA	1st Source Monogram Long/Short	FMLSX	U	(800) 766-8938	U /	1.01	5.10	9.63 /44	--	--	2.26	1.72
SC	1st Source Monogram Special Eq	FMSPX	E-	(800) 766-8938	D / 1.7	-7.08	5.31	11.49 /57	6.98 /10	3.88 /45	0.00	1.32
AA	ABN AMRO Balanced Fund N	CHTAX	E+	(800) 443-4725	E / 0.5	-4.09	-2.33	1.43 / 3	4.85 / 4	1.41 /23	1.55	1.09
GI	ABN AMRO Growth Fund I	CTGIX	D-	(800) 443-4725	E+ / 0.9	-6.10	-2.55	2.85 / 7	6.51 / 8	-0.26 /14	0.25	0.81
GI	ABN AMRO Growth Fund N	CHTIX	D-	(800) 443-4725	E+ / 0.8	-6.19	-2.69	2.54 / 6	6.19 / 7	-0.54 /13	0.00	1.10
GI	ABN AMRO Growth Fund R	CCGRX	D-	(800) 443-4725	E+ / 0.7	-6.27	-2.80	2.32 / 5	5.96 / 7	--	0.00	1.32
MC	ABN AMRO Mid Cap Instl	ABMIX	U	(800) 443-4725	U /	-2.32	3.67	9.82 /46	--	--	0.00	0.89
MC	ABN AMRO Mid Cap N	CHTTX	C	(800) 443-4725	C / 5.5	-2.41	3.56	9.50 /43	13.60 /52	9.34 /78	0.00	1.17
BA	ABN AMRO Montag&Caldwell Bal I	MOBIX	D+	(800) 443-4725	E / 0.5	-1.48	-0.27	3.18 / 8	3.93 / 2	1.36 /23	1.81	1.01
BA	ABN AMRO Montag&Caldwell Bal N	MOBAX	D+	(800) 443-4725	E / 0.4	-1.49	-0.39	2.94 / 7	3.69 / 2	1.11 /21	1.51	1.27
GR	ABN AMRO Montag&Caldwell Gr I	MCGIX	D	(800) 443-4725	D- / 1.1	-2.16	0.30	6.56 /24	6.25 / 7	-0.04 /15	0.59	0.76
GR	ABN AMRO Montag&Caldwell Gr N	MCGFX	D	(800) 443-4725	E+ / 0.9	-2.22	0.15	6.28 /22	5.95 / 7	-0.33 /14	0.26	1.03
GR	ABN AMRO Montag&Caldwell Gr R	MCRGX	D-	(800) 443-4725	E+ / 0.8	-2.31	0.04	5.99 /20	5.70 / 6	--	0.00	1.26
RE	ABN AMRO Real Estate I	AARIX	U	(800) 443-4725	U /	-0.38	13.94	--	--	--	0.00	1.12
RE	ABN AMRO Real Estate N	ARFCX	C+	(800) 443-4725	A / 9.4	-0.44	13.88	22.06 /84	27.69 /94	19.94 /96	0.99	1.37
SC	ABN AMRO River Road Sm Cap	ARSVX	U	(800) 443-4725	U /	3.39	14.67	25.10 /89	--	--	0.00	1.50
GR	ABN AMRO TAMRO Lg Cap Val N	ATLVX	C	(800) 443-4725	C- / 3.9	-1.15	2.30	7.41 /29	10.91 /35	5.02 /54	0.55	1.20
SC	ABN AMRO TAMRO Small Cap I	ATSIX	U	(800) 443-4725	U /	-5.36	13.13	18.69 /80	--	--	0.00	1.02
SC	ABN AMRO TAMRO Small Cap N	ATASX	C	(800) 443-4725	B / 7.6	-5.43	12.92	18.33 /80	18.28 /73	12.69 /88	0.00	1.30
GI	ABN AMRO Value I	AAVIX	U	(800) 443-4725	U /	0.91	6.04	--	--	--	0.00	0.69
GI	ABN AMRO Value N	RVALX	A-	(800) 443-4725	C+ / 6.3	0.85	5.92	11.35 /56	14.77 /58	4.66 /51	1.42	0.94
AG	ABN AMRO Veredus Agg Gr I	AVEIX	D-	(800) 443-4725	C / 5.1	-9.62	1.44	7.23 /28	14.06 /54	--	0.00	1.13
AG	ABN AMRO Veredus Agg Gr N	VERDX	D-	(800) 443-4725	C / 4.9	-9.74	1.25	6.87 /25	13.71 /52	-0.94 /12	0.00	1.41
TC	ABN AMRO Veredus SciTech N	AVSTX	E-	(800) 443-4725	D+ / 2.5	-7.53	3.96	15.65 /74	8.92 /20	-0.94 /12	0.00	1.60
GR	ABN AMRO Veredus Select Growth	AVSGX	C+	(800) 443-4725	C+ / 5.9	-6.42	1.20	7.39 /29	15.49 /61	--	0.00	1.30
AG	Accessor Fd-Aggress Gr Alloc Adv	AAGRX	C	(800) 759-3504	C+ / 6.4	-2.42	3.87	12.29 /61	15.26 /60	4.64 /51	0.00	0.20
AG	Accessor Fd-Aggress Gr Alloc C	ACAGX	B	(800) 759-3504	C+ / 5.7	-2.61	3.40	11.54 /57	14.10 /54	--	0.00	1.20
AG	Accessor Fd-Aggress Gr Alloc Inv	ACAIX	C	(800) 759-3504	C+ / 6.1	-2.53	3.63	11.74 /58	14.67 /57	4.11 /47	0.00	0.70
BA	Accessor Fd-Balanced Alloc Adv	ABAAX	C+	(800) 759-3504	D+ / 2.8	-1.04	2.24	6.96 /26	9.10 /21	4.82 /53	2.26	0.20
BA	Accessor Fd-Balanced Alloc C	ABAFX	C	(800) 759-3504	D / 2.0	-1.35	1.68	5.86 /19	8.00 /15	--	1.29	1.20
BA	Accessor Fd-Balanced Alloc Inv	ACBIX	C	(800) 759-3504	D+ / 2.5	-1.16	1.99	6.47 /23	8.56 /18	4.30 /49	1.79	0.70
GI	Accessor Fd-Gr & Inc Alloc Adv	AGWAX	C+	(800) 759-3504	C- / 3.6	-1.49	2.41	7.96 /32	10.42 /30	4.73 /52	1.90	0.20
GI	Accessor Fd-Gr & Inc Alloc C	AGIGX	C	(800) 759-3504	D+ / 2.7	-1.73	1.93	6.83 /25	9.32 /23	--	0.96	1.20
GI	Accessor Fd-Gr & Inc Alloc Inv	AGIIX	C+	(800) 759-3504	C- / 3.3	-1.53	2.18	7.43 /29	9.91 /27	4.23 /48	1.47	0.70
AA	Accessor Fd-Growth Alloc Adv	ACGAX	B	(800) 759-3504	C / 5.3	-2.01	3.15	10.28 /49	13.23 /50	5.05 /55	1.13	0.20
AA	Accessor Fd-Growth Alloc C	AGGGX	B-	(800) 759-3504	C / 4.5	-2.20	2.61	9.22 /41	12.12 /43	--	0.20	1.20
AA	Accessor Fd-Growth Alloc Inv	AGALX	B	(800) 759-3504	C / 5.0	-2.07	2.91	9.80 /46	12.68 /47	4.54 /50	0.69	0.70
GR	Accessor Fd-Growth Portfolio Adv	AGROX	D+	(800) 759-3504	D / 2.2	-4.63	-1.63	5.90 /20	9.40 /23	0.93 /20	0.10	1.18
GR	Accessor Fd-Growth Portfolio C	AGCGX	D	(800) 759-3504	D / 1.6	-4.85	-2.12	4.85 /14	8.32 /17	--	0.00	2.18
GR	Accessor Fd-Growth Portfolio Inv	AGRIX	D	(800) 759-3504	D / 1.9	-4.69	-1.75	5.64 /18	8.96 /20	0.54 /18	0.04	1.68
GL	Accessor Fd-Inc & Gr Alloc Adv	AIGAX	C-	(800) 759-3504	D- / 1.3	-0.51	1.51	4.69 /14	6.27 / 7	4.38 /49	3.02	0.20
GL	Accessor Fd-Inc & Gr Alloc C	AIGMX	C-	(800) 759-3504	E+ / 0.7	-0.76	1.01	3.67 / 9	5.21 / 4	--	2.02	1.20
GL	Accessor Fd-Inc & Gr Alloc Inv	ACIGX	C-	(800) 759-3504	D- / 1.1	-0.63	1.28	4.33 /12	5.77 / 6	3.88 /45	2.60	0.70
AA	Accessor Fd-Income Allocation Adv	AIAAX	D+	(800) 759-3504	E- / 0.2	0.39	0.73	1.81 / 4	2.31 / 1	3.74 /43	4.17	0.20
AA	Accessor Fd-Income Allocation C	AIACX	D+	(800) 759-3504	E- / 0.1	0.15	0.25	0.76 / 2	1.28 / 0	--	3.19	1.20
AA	Accessor Fd-Income Allocation Inv	AIAIX	D+	(800) 759-3504	E- / 0.2	0.26	0.49	1.35 / 3	1.81 / 1	3.22 /39	3.72	0.70
FO	Accessor Fd-Intl Equity Adv	ACIEX	B+	(800) 759-3504	B+ / 8.9	-1.23	11.01	28.77 /93	22.80 /87	8.81 /76	0.20	1.40
FO	Accessor Fd-Intl Equity C	AICIX	A	(800) 759-3504	B+ / 8.6	-1.47	10.45	27.45 /92	21.58 /84	--	0.00	2.42
FO	Accessor Fd-Intl Equity Inv	AIINX	B+	(800) 759-3504	B+ / 8.8	-1.37	10.80	28.40 /93	22.32 /86	8.37 /73	0.00	1.90
SC	Accessor Fd-Small-Mid Cap Adv	ASMCX	A-	(800) 759-3504	B / 8.1	-3.14	6.24	15.50 /73	20.86 /82	10.45 /82	0.00	1.26

RISK			NET ASSETS		ASSET				Portfolio Turnover Ratio	BULL / BEAR		FUND MANAGER		MINIMUMS		LOADS	
Risk Rating/Pts	3 Year Standard Deviation	Beta	NAV As of 6/30/06	Total $(Mil)	Cash %	Stocks %	Bonds %	Other %		Last Bull Market Return	Last Bear Market Return	Manager Quality Pct	Manager Tenure (Years)	Initial Purch. $	Additional Purch. $	Front End Load	Back End Load
B- / 7.4	7.9	0.97	7.33	53	6	93	0	1	57.0	42.4	-8.3	20	N/A	1,000	25	0.0	0.0
C+ / 6.8	9.4	1.12	13.98	130	7	91	0	2	37.0	98.5	-9.3	94	10	1,000	25	0.0	0.0
U /	N/A	N/A	11.23	31	N/A	100	0	N/A	123.0	N/A	N/A	N/A	3	1,000	25	0.0	0.0
D- / 1.2	14.4	0.95	8.93	28	4	95	0	1	54.0	62.2	-10.4	2	N/A	1,000	25	0.0	0.0
C+ / 6.7	6.2	1.14	10.20	66	39	40	20	1	30.0	29.9	-6.5	24	11	2,500	50	0.0	0.0
B- / 7.6	9.6	1.12	22.00	437	2	97	0	1	31.3	43.4	-11.3	12	6	5,000,000	0	0.0	0.0
B- / 7.1	9.6	1.12	21.69	494	2	97	0	1	31.3	42.2	-11.4	11	7	2,500	50	0.0	0.0
B- / 7.1	9.6	1.12	21.53	2	2	97	0	1	31.3	41.2	N/A	10	4	2,500	50	0.0	0.0
U /	N/A	N/A	24.86	79	0	99	0	1	30.0	N/A	N/A	N/A	N/A	2,000,000	0	0.0	0.0
C+ / 6.6	12.7	0.98	24.72	576	0	99	0	1	30.0	87.5	-10.1	21	N/A	2,500	50	0.0	0.0
B+ / 9.5	5.1	0.96	16.43	13	3	63	32	2	34.0	23.7	-4.4	24	8	1,000,000	0	0.0	0.0
B+ / 9.5	5.2	0.97	16.45	31	3	63	32	2	34.0	22.8	-4.5	22	12	2,500	50	0.0	0.0
B- / 7.7	7.9	0.92	23.89	1,346	2	97	0	1	51.0	38.5	-9.0	20	10	5,000,000	0	0.0	0.0
B- / 7.7	7.9	0.91	23.82	846	2	97	0	1	51.0	37.2	-9.0	18	12	2,500	50	0.0	0.0
B- / 7.7	7.9	0.91	23.71	1	2	97	0	1	51.0	36.2	N/A	17	4	2,500	50	0.0	0.0
U /	N/A	N/A	17.23	44	0	99	0	1	43.1	N/A	N/A	N/A	1	2,000,000	0	0.0	2.0
C- / 3.7	16.6	0.99	17.24	62	0	99	0	1	43.1	127.6	0.8	84	9	2,500	50	0.0	2.0
U /	N/A	N/A	12.51	53	6	93	0	1	32.0	N/A	N/A	N/A	N/A	2,500	50	0.0	0.0
B- / 7.7	7.6	0.93	12.99	16	1	98	0	1	46.0	69.6	-9.5	60	6	2,500	50	0.0	0.0
U /	N/A	N/A	18.35	36	2	97	0	1	60.0	N/A	N/A	N/A	N/A	2,000,000	0	0.0	0.0
C- / 4.2	15.0	0.99	18.27	157	2	97	0	1	60.0	126.4	-9.2	54	6	2,500	50	0.0	0.0
U /	N/A	N/A	12.89	226	1	98	0	1	21.8	N/A	N/A	N/A	N/A	2,000,000	0	0.0	0.0
B+ / 9.2	6.9	0.84	12.89	97	1	98	0	1	21.8	76.1	-9.1	92	4	2,500	50	0.0	0.0
D+ / 2.8	19.0	1.89	19.72	174	0	99	0	1	136.0	110.3	-9.2	14	8	2,000,000	0	0.0	0.0
C- / 3.3	19.0	1.89	19.45	506	0	99	0	1	136.0	108.4	-9.2	13	8	2,500	0	0.0	0.0
D+ / 2.4	19.5	1.95	7.61	4	N/A	100	0	N/A	236.0	72.7	-6.0	2	5	2,500	50	0.0	2.0
B- / 7.1	12.8	1.38	12.68	32	1	98	0	1	203.0	98.4	-5.1	63	N/A	2,500	50	0.0	0.0
C+ / 6.0	8.4	1.04	16.90	27	0	99	0	1	2.0	86.1	-9.7	86	N/A	5,000	100	0.0	0.0
B / 8.6	8.4	1.04	16.43	7	0	99	0	1	2.0	80.1	N/A	79	N/A	5,000	100	0.0	1.0
C+ / 6.1	8.3	1.03	16.56	12	0	99	0	1	2.0	83.1	-9.3	83	N/A	5,000	100	0.0	0.0
B+ / 9.9	4.4	0.90	16.05	40	7	49	42	2	3.2	46.4	-4.0	76	6	5,000	100	0.0	0.0
B+ / 9.9	4.4	0.90	16.01	19	7	49	42	2	3.2	41.7	N/A	67	6	5,000	100	0.0	1.0
B+ / 9.9	4.4	0.89	16.04	14	7	49	42	2	3.2	44.1	-4.1	72	6	5,000	100	0.0	0.0
B+ / 9.7	5.2	0.64	16.19	49	2	60	36	2	2.0	54.5	-5.2	79	6	5,000	100	0.0	0.0
B+ / 9.7	5.2	0.65	16.13	42	2	60	36	2	2.0	42.3	N/A	70	N/A	5,000	100	0.0	1.0
B+ / 9.7	5.2	0.65	16.18	10	2	60	36	2	2.0	52.2	-5.3	75	6	5,000	100	0.0	0.0
B+ / 9.1	7.0	1.39	16.54	43	0	80	18	2	1.8	72.8	-7.6	86	6	5,000	100	0.0	0.0
B+ / 9.1	7.0	1.40	16.47	32	0	80	18	2	1.8	67.7	N/A	78	4	5,000	100	0.0	1.0
B+ / 9.1	7.1	1.40	16.53	16	0	80	18	2	1.8	70.2	-7.7	82	6	5,000	100	0.0	0.0
B- / 7.6	7.6	0.91	24.08	143	0	98	0	2	47.4	51.8	-8.2	44	2	5,000	100	0.0	2.0
B- / 7.7	7.6	0.91	23.56	5	0	98	0	2	47.4	47.1	N/A	34	2	5,000	100	0.0	2.0
B- / 7.6	7.6	0.91	23.58	3	0	98	0	2	47.4	49.8	-8.2	40	2	5,000	100	0.0	2.0
B+ / 9.9	2.9	0.59	15.55	15	14	30	55	1	11.5	30.4	-1.6	66	N/A	5,000	100	0.0	0.0
B+ / 9.9	2.9	0.60	15.50	10	14	30	55	1	11.5	26.3	N/A	54	4	5,000	100	0.0	1.0
B+ / 9.9	2.9	0.59	15.55	5	14	30	55	1	11.5	28.5	-1.8	61	6	5,000	100	0.0	0.0
B+ / 9.9	1.8	0.14	14.72	10	24	0	75	1	19.9	9.6	2.4	47	6	5,000	100	0.0	0.0
B+ / 9.9	1.8	0.13	14.69	2	24	0	75	1	19.9	6.1	N/A	36	6	5,000	100	0.0	1.0
B+ / 9.9	1.7	0.13	14.71	3	24	0	75	1	19.9	7.9	2.3	41	6	5,000	100	0.0	0.0
C+ / 5.9	11.3	1.07	19.26	116	0	99	0	1	127.6	133.4	-11.7	28	N/A	5,000	100	0.0	2.0
B- / 7.2	11.3	1.07	18.71	3	0	99	0	1	127.6	126.2	N/A	21	N/A	5,000	100	0.0	2.0
C+ / 5.9	11.3	1.07	18.67	2	0	99	0	1	127.6	130.8	-11.8	25	N/A	5,000	100	0.0	2.0
B- / 7.4	11.7	0.79	29.96	197	2	97	0	1	41.6	124.6	-9.1	93	N/A	5,000	100	0.0	2.0

Fund Type	Fund Name	Ticker Symbol	Overall Weiss Investment Rating	Phone	PERFORMANCE Perfor-mance Rating/Pts	Total Return % through 6/30/06 3 Mo	6 Mo	1Yr / Pct	Annualized 3Yr / Pct	5Yr / Pct	Incl. in Returns Dividend Yield	Expense Ratio
	99 Pct = Best											
	0 Pct = Worst											
SC	Accessor Fd-Small-Mid Cap C	ACSMX	A-	(800) 759-3504	B / 7.8	-3.40	5.69	14.31 /69	19.66 /78	--	0.00	2.26
SC	Accessor Fd-Small-Mid Cap Inv	ACSIX	A-	(800) 759-3504	B / 7.9	-3.25	5.98	15.07 /72	20.33 /81	9.97 /80	0.00	1.76
GR	Accessor Fd-Value Fund Adv	AVAIX	B	(800) 759-3504	C / 5.4	-0.60	4.02	8.64 /38	13.98 /54	2.74 /34	1.20	1.00
GR	Accessor Fd-Value Fund C	AVCVX	B-	(800) 759-3504	C / 4.9	-0.86	3.51	7.52 /29	12.85 /48	--	0.23	2.00
GR	Accessor Fd-Value Fund Inv	AVUIX	B	(800) 759-3504	C / 5.1	-0.74	3.76	8.29 /35	13.52 /51	2.34 /30	0.89	1.50
CV	ACM Convertible Secs	CNCVX	E+	(888) 387-2273	D / 2.2	-9.94	-4.07	11.35 /56	10.58 /32	0.47 /18	0.00	2.25
GR	Activa Growth Fund	AGFDX	D	(800) 346-2670	D+ / 2.6	-4.11	-1.76	6.47 /23	9.46 /24	-3.29 / 5	0.00	1.40
FO	Activa International Fund	AINFX	B-	(800) 346-2670	B / 8.0	-1.21	7.46	22.96 /86	18.82 /76	5.18 /55	0.58	1.60
RE	Adelante US Real Estate Sec K	LLUKX	B-	(877) 563-5327	A / 9.3	-0.63	13.82	20.78 /83	25.76 /92	19.51 /96	1.06	1.25
RE	Adelante US Real Estate Sec Y	LLUYX	B-	(877) 563-5327	A / 9.3	-0.57	13.90	21.09 /83	26.17 /92	19.92 /96	1.35	0.97
EM	● Adv Inn Cir Acadian Emg Mkt I	AEMGX	B-	(866) 777-7818	A+ / 9.9	-2.35	12.46	43.02 /98	42.26 /99	30.72 /99	1.21	1.47
GL	Adv Inn Cir Analytic Glb Lng-Shrt	ANGLX	C+	(866) 777-7818	C / 4.7	-0.46	7.46	8.75 /38	12.19 /44	6.10 /62	0.00	6.13
SC	Adv Inn Cir Champlain Sm Comp	CIPSX	U	(866) 777-7818	U /	-4.08	4.73	11.00 /53	--	--	0.05	1.40
SC	Adv Inn Cir FMA Sm Co I	FMACX	C-	(866) 777-7818	B / 8.0	-3.00	11.05	16.74 /76	19.11 /76	9.20 /77	0.00	1.20
IN	Adv Inn Cir FMC Select Fd		C	(866) 777-7818	D+ / 2.3	-1.40	1.64	1.95 / 4	8.90 /20	6.10 /62	1.02	1.02
GR	Adv Inn Cir HGK Equity Val A	HGKEX	B+	(866) 777-7818	C+ / 6.5	1.87	7.40	15.17 /72	16.26 /65	6.36 /63	0.71	1.50
SC	Adv Inn Cir ICM Sm Co I	ICSCX	B	(866) 777-7818	B / 7.7	-2.62	9.80	14.68 /71	18.40 /74	12.60 /88	0.00	0.87
FO	Adv Inn Cir Japan Smaller Comp I	JSCFX	C-	(866) 777-7818	B / 7.6	-12.41	-13.56	18.12 /79	21.61 /84	11.77 /86	1.09	1.56
GR	Adv Inn Cir LSV Value Equity	LSVEX	A	(866) 777-7818	B / 8.1	1.57	7.59	15.03 /72	19.76 /78	11.26 /85	0.92	0.67
FO	Adv Inn Cir McKee Intl Eqty I	MKIEX	A	(866) 777-7818	A- / 9.1	0.97	10.74	26.03 /90	24.00 /89	10.54 /82	1.37	1.01
GR	Adv Inn Cir Reaves Sel Research I	RSRFX	U	(866) 777-7818	U /	3.62	6.29	9.38 /43	--	--	3.13	1.28
SC	Adv Inn Cir Sterling Cap SmCp Val I	SPSCX	C+	(866) 777-7818	B- / 7.3	-3.30	5.79	15.34 /73	17.44 /70	8.74 /75	0.09	1.25
GR	Adv Inn Cir TS&W Eq Port I	TSWEX	B-	(866) 777-7818	C+ / 5.6	-2.60	3.47	12.74 /63	13.73 /52	4.23 /48	0.72	1.33
FO	Adv Inn Cir TS&W Intl Eq I	TSWIX	B+	(866) 777-7818	B+ / 8.5	-0.29	9.28	26.41 /90	20.58 /81	7.29 /68	0.48	1.63
GR	AdvisorOne Amerigo N	CLSAX	B-	(800) 377-8796	C+ / 5.7	-3.23	2.16	12.54 /62	13.87 /53	4.53 /50	0.42	1.15
SC	Aegis Value Fund	AVALX	B-	(800) 528-3780	C+ / 6.4	1.45	7.20	9.87 /46	15.07 /59	13.73 /90	0.96	1.40
BA	AFBA 5Star Balanced A	AFSAX	B-	(800) 243-9865	C / 4.3	2.23	6.87	11.06 /54	12.47 /46	5.87 /60	2.39	1.33
BA	AFBA 5Star Balanced B	AFSBX	B-	(800) 243-9865	C- / 4.1	2.06	6.49	10.26 /48	11.63 /40	5.20 /56	1.86	2.08
BA	AFBA 5Star Balanced C	AFSCX	B	(800) 243-9865	C / 4.6	2.01	6.50	10.16 /48	11.58 /40	5.17 /55	1.86	2.08
BA	AFBA 5Star Balanced I	AFBAX	B+	(800) 243-9865	C / 5.2	2.29	6.99	11.22 /55	12.70 /47	5.95 /61	2.88	1.08
BA	AFBA 5Star Balanced R	ASBRX	B+	(800) 243-9865	C / 4.9	2.15	6.68	10.64 /51	12.27 /44	5.51 /58	2.45	1.58
GR	AFBA 5Star Large Cap A	AFEAX	D	(800) 243-9865	E+ / 0.8	-3.47	-0.37	5.12 /16	7.66 /13	-0.85 /12	0.00	1.53
GR	AFBA 5Star Large Cap B	AFEBX	D	(800) 243-9865	E+ / 0.8	-3.67	-0.69	4.38 /12	6.86 /10	-1.30 /11	0.00	2.28
GR	AFBA 5Star Large Cap C	AFECX	D	(800) 243-9865	D- / 1.0	-3.67	-0.77	4.30 /12	6.82 /10	-1.30 /11	0.00	2.28
GR	AFBA 5Star Large Cap I	AFBEX	D	(800) 243-9865	D / 1.6	-3.38	-0.22	5.41 /17	7.91 /15	-0.71 /13	0.00	1.28
GR	AFBA 5Star Large Cap R	ASLRX	D	(800) 243-9865	D- / 1.4	-3.55	-0.46	4.90 /15	7.52 /12	-1.15 /11	0.00	1.78
MC	AFBA 5Star Mid Cap A	AFMAX	C	(800) 243-9865	C / 4.7	-8.43	-2.23	8.92 /40	15.72 /62	--	0.00	1.53
MC	AFBA 5Star Mid Cap B	AFMBX	C	(800) 243-9865	C / 4.7	-8.56	-2.57	8.15 /34	14.85 /58	--	0.00	2.28
MC	AFBA 5Star Mid Cap C	AFMCX	C	(800) 243-9865	C / 5.1	-8.62	-2.63	8.07 /33	14.85 /58	--	0.00	2.28
MC	AFBA 5Star Mid Cap I	AFMIX	C+	(800) 243-9865	C+ / 5.8	-8.35	-2.07	9.23 /41	16.02 /64	--	0.00	1.28
MC	AFBA 5Star Mid Cap R	ASPRX	C	(800) 243-9865	C / 5.5	-8.49	-2.37	8.67 /38	15.50 /61	--	0.00	1.78
TC	AFBA 5Star Science & Tech A	AFATX	C	(800) 243-9865	C / 5.5	-7.77	1.62	12.90 /64	16.26 /65	--	0.00	1.53
TC	AFBA 5Star Science & Tech B	AFBTX	C	(800) 243-9865	C / 5.4	-8.04	1.11	12.06 /60	15.36 /60	--	0.00	2.28
TC	AFBA 5Star Science & Tech C	AFCTX	C	(800) 243-9865	C+ / 5.8	-8.04	1.19	12.05 /60	15.39 /61	--	0.00	2.28
TC	AFBA 5Star Science & Tech I	AFITX	C+	(800) 243-9865	C+ / 6.4	-7.75	1.68	13.22 /65	16.50 /66	--	0.00	1.28
TC	AFBA 5Star Science & Tech R	ASNRX	C	(800) 243-9865	C+ / 6.2	-7.90	1.39	12.64 /63	16.07 /64	--	0.00	1.78
SC	AFBA 5Star Small Cap A	AFCAX	C-	(800) 243-9865	C / 4.9	-9.01	2.15	4.11 /11	16.32 /65	--	0.00	1.53
SC	AFBA 5Star Small Cap B	AFCBX	C-	(800) 243-9865	C / 4.8	-9.20	1.72	3.27 / 8	15.44 /61	--	0.00	2.28
SC	AFBA 5Star Small Cap C	AFCCX	C	(800) 243-9865	C / 5.2	-9.20	1.72	3.27 / 8	15.44 /61	--	0.00	2.28
SC	AFBA 5Star Small Cap I	AFCIX	C	(800) 243-9865	C+ / 5.8	-8.96	2.25	4.31 /12	16.60 /66	--	0.00	1.28
SC	AFBA 5Star Small Cap R	ASSRX	C	(800) 243-9865	C+ / 5.6	-9.07	2.04	3.82 /10	16.15 /64	--	0.00	1.78
GR	AFBA 5Star USA Global A	AFUAX	D+	(800) 243-9865	D / 2.0	-3.66	0.54	6.22 /22	10.34 /30	1.31 /22	0.00	1.53

● Denotes fund is closed to new investors
* Denotes fund is included in Section II

RISK	3 Year		NET ASSETS		ASSET					BULL / BEAR		FUND MANAGER		MINIMUMS		LOADS	
Risk Rating/Pts	Standard Deviation	Beta	NAV As of 6/30/06	Total $(Mil)	Cash %	Stocks %	Bonds %	Other %	Portfolio Turnover Ratio	Last Bull Market Return	Last Bear Market Return	Manager Quality Pct	Manager Tenure (Years)	Initial Purch. $	Additional Purch. $	Front End Load	Back End Load
B- / 7.7	11.7	0.79	28.99	3	2	97	0	1	41.6	117.6	N/A	90	N/A	5,000	100	0.0	1.0
B- / 7.4	11.7	0.79	28.87	4	2	97	0	1	41.6	121.5	-9.1	92	N/A	5,000	100	0.0	2.0
B+ / 9.1	8.0	1.00	21.56	120	1	98	0	1	70.0	79.8	-10.2	81	N/A	5,000	100	0.0	2.0
B+ / 9.0	8.0	1.00	21.54	3	1	98	0	1	70.0	74.2	N/A	72	N/A	5,000	100	0.0	1.0
B+ / 9.0	7.9	0.99	21.58	3	1	98	0	1	70.0	77.5	-10.3	78	N/A	5,000	100	0.0	2.0
C / 4.3	16.0	1.53	17.66	5	1	62	0	37	19.8	72.2	-7.4	62	18	1,000	50	0.0	0.0
C+ / 6.1	9.6	1.11	7.24	24	0	100	0	0	79.0	56.6	-10.0	29	N/A	500	50	0.0	0.0
C+ / 5.7	11.7	1.10	9.80	38	0	100	0	0	178.3	105.2	-8.6	8	N/A	500	50	0.0	0.0
C / 4.5	16.2	0.97	20.20	9	1	98	0	1	6.8	119.4	1.0	76	N/A	10,000	250	0.0	0.0
C / 4.5	16.3	0.97	20.02	23	1	98	0	1	6.8	121.9	1.1	78	N/A	250,000	10,000	0.0	0.0
C- / 3.9	20.3	1.20	28.61	808	3	96	0	1	54.0	299.7	-2.4	43	N/A	2,500	1,000	0.0	2.0
B / 8.3	7.8	0.49	10.81	8	10	80	8	2	134.0	68.1	-3.6	50	N/A	2,500	100	0.0	2.0
U /	N/A	N/A	11.52	47	10	89	0	1	N/A	N/A	N/A	N/A	N/A	10,000	0	0.0	0.0
D+ / 2.8	12.2	0.80	21.70	193	5	94	0	1	169.0	104.0	-7.1	87	N/A	2,500	100	0.0	0.0
B+ / 9.3	5.8	0.64	21.06	291	3	80	14	3	18.4	49.5	-5.0	67	11	10,000	1,000	0.0	0.0
B+ / 9.0	7.2	0.89	11.27	14	2	97	0	1	67.4	89.1	-10.7	95	N/A	2,000	0	5.5	0.0
C+ / 6.7	12.0	0.80	39.78	1,464	4	95	0	1	17.0	108.7	-6.5	83	17	2,500,000	1,000	0.0	0.0
C- / 3.6	17.2	0.84	13.13	41	12	88	0	0	63.7	131.7	-3.1	66	5	2,500	500	0.0	2.0
B- / 7.8	9.0	1.09	17.43	2,425	1	98	0	1	12.2	107.4	-7.8	97	7	100,000	0	0.0	0.0
C+ / 6.9	10.1	0.98	14.64	243	1	98	0	1	27.0	129.8	-9.2	57	6	2,500	100	0.0	1.0
U /	N/A	N/A	11.38	68	2	97	0	1	N/A	N/A	N/A	N/A	N/A	1,000,000	0	0.0	0.0
C+ / 5.7	11.6	0.74	16.98	64	2	97	0	1	45.0	104.5	-8.6	83	N/A	2,500	100	0.0	0.0
B / 8.1	8.0	0.91	13.48	49	4	95	0	1	54.0	77.9	-9.6	85	N/A	2,500	100	0.0	1.0
C+ / 6.6	11.3	1.06	17.43	65	6	93	0	1	22.0	118.9	-11.8	17	N/A	2,500	100	0.0	1.0
B / 8.3	9.5	1.15	14.68	571	16	84	0	0	57.0	79.8	-8.6	69	9	2,500	250	0.0	0.0
B- / 7.3	9.8	0.53	18.17	444	20	79	0	1	17.0	85.6	-8.4	89	N/A	10,000	1,000	0.0	0.0
B+ / 9.8	5.0	0.82	13.70	15	20	51	15	14	7.0	65.6	-7.8	95	N/A	500	100	5.5	2.0
B+ / 9.8	5.0	0.82	13.52	1	20	51	15	14	7.0	61.7	-7.9	92	N/A	500	100	0.0	4.8
B+ / 9.8	5.0	0.82	13.53	11	20	51	15	14	7.0	61.6	-7.9	92	N/A	500	100	0.0	2.0
B+ / 9.8	5.0	0.82	13.25	52	20	51	15	14	7.0	66.8	-7.7	95	N/A	500	100	0.0	2.0
B+ / 9.8	5.0	0.82	13.13	N/A	20	51	15	14	7.0	65.1	-7.9	94	N/A	0	0	0.0	2.0
B / 8.1	8.7	1.01	13.34	N/A	7	92	0	1	14.0	59.5	-16.1	23	9	500	100	5.5	2.0
B / 8.0	8.7	1.01	12.86	N/A	7	92	0	1	14.0	55.7	-16.3	18	9	500	100	0.0	4.8
B / 8.1	8.6	1.01	12.86	N/A	7	92	0	1	14.0	55.7	-16.3	19	9	500	100	0.0	2.0
B- / 7.6	8.7	1.01	13.45	21	7	92	0	1	14.0	60.5	-16.0	25	9	500	100	0.0	2.0
B / 8.1	8.7	1.02	13.05	N/A	7	92	0	1	14.0	59.5	-16.4	22	2	0	0	0.0	2.0
C+ / 6.9	13.1	1.12	14.54	14	5	94	0	1	10.0	108.8	-13.4	20	N/A	500	100	5.5	2.0
C+ / 6.8	13.2	1.12	14.08	N/A	5	94	0	1	10.0	103.9	-13.6	16	N/A	500	100	0.0	4.8
C+ / 6.9	13.2	1.12	14.08	6	5	94	0	1	10.0	104.0	-13.6	16	N/A	500	100	0.0	2.0
C+ / 6.9	13.1	1.12	14.69	5	5	94	0	1	10.0	110.4	-13.4	22	N/A	500	100	0.0	2.0
C+ / 6.8	13.4	1.13	14.43	N/A	5	94	0	1	10.0	107.1	-13.4	18	N/A	0	0	0.0	2.0
C+ / 6.3	15.5	1.54	12.54	2	5	94	0	1	29.0	118.9	-17.7	55	9	500	100	5.5	2.0
C+ / 6.2	15.5	1.54	12.06	N/A	5	94	0	1	29.0	113.5	-18.0	44	9	500	100	0.0	4.8
C+ / 6.2	15.5	1.55	12.07	1	5	94	0	1	29.0	113.7	-18.0	45	9	500	100	0.0	2.0
C+ / 6.3	15.5	1.55	12.69	6	5	94	0	1	29.0	120.3	-17.7	57	9	500	100	0.0	2.0
C+ / 6.2	15.8	1.57	12.43	N/A	5	94	0	1	29.0	116.6	-17.7	50	2	0	0	0.0	2.0
C+ / 6.5	14.7	0.94	16.73	184	5	94	0	1	11.0	126.6	-17.4	41	N/A	500	100	5.5	2.0
C+ / 6.5	14.7	0.95	16.15	3	5	94	0	1	11.0	121.4	-17.6	33	N/A	500	100	0.0	4.8
C+ / 6.5	14.7	0.94	16.15	21	5	94	0	1	11.0	121.4	-17.6	34	N/A	500	100	0.0	2.0
C+ / 6.5	14.7	0.94	16.93	10	5	94	0	1	11.0	128.4	-17.3	44	N/A	500	100	0.0	2.0
C+ / 6.4	14.9	0.96	16.61	N/A	5	94	0	1	11.0	124.6	-17.3	37	N/A	0	0	0.0	2.0
B- / 7.9	10.0	1.15	15.02	2	5	94	0	1	8.0	64.7	-13.1	33	9	500	100	5.5	2.0

					PERFORMANCE							
99 Pct = Best / 0 Pct = Worst			Overall Weiss Investment Rating		Perfor-mance Rating/Pts	Total Return % through 6/30/06			Annualized		Incl. in Returns	
Fund Type	Fund Name	Ticker Symbol		Phone		3 Mo	6 Mo	1Yr / Pct	3Yr / Pct	5Yr / Pct	Dividend Yield	Expense Ratio
GR	AFBA 5Star USA Global B	AFUBX	D+	(800) 243-9865	D / 2.0	-3.77	0.14	5.52 /18	9.59 /25	0.79 /19	0.00	2.28
GR	AFBA 5Star USA Global C	AFUCX	D+	(800) 243-9865	D+ / 2.4	-3.84	0.14	5.44 /17	9.56 /24	0.79 /19	0.00	2.28
GR	AFBA 5Star USA Global I	AFGLX	C-	(800) 243-9865	C- / 3.1	-3.62	0.60	6.49 /23	10.66 /32	1.48 /24	0.03	1.28
GR	AFBA 5Star USA Global R	ASURX	C-	(800) 243-9865	D+ / 2.8	-3.71	0.41	5.94 /20	10.26 /29	1.03 /20	0.00	1.78
BA	AHA Balanced Portfolio	AHBPX	C	(800) 445-1341	D+ / 2.9	-0.75	2.20	6.00 /20	9.41 /24	4.35 /49	1.74	1.00
GR	AHA Diversified Equity A	AHADX	B-	(800) 445-1341	C / 5.3	-1.30	3.02	9.24 /42	13.25 /50	--	0.49	1.26
GR	AHA Diversified Equity I	AHDEX	B-	(800) 445-1341	C / 5.5	-1.24	3.15	9.53 /44	13.56 /52	4.64 /51	0.72	1.01
GL	AIM Advantage Health Sciences A	IAGHX	D-	(800) 347-4246	D- / 1.4	-7.87	1.86	12.82 /63	8.76 /19	2.46 /32	0.00	2.26
GL	AIM Advantage Health Sciences B	IGHBX	D-	(800) 347-4246	D- / 1.1	-8.04	1.50	12.00 /59	7.84 /14	1.32 /22	0.00	3.01
GL	AIM Advantage Health Sciences C	IGHCX	D-	(800) 347-4246	D- / 1.4	-8.02	1.49	11.97 /59	7.52 /12	0.96 /20	0.00	3.01
FO	AIM Asia Pacific Growth A	ASIAX	A-	(800) 347-4246	A / 9.3	-2.17	11.40	27.99 /93	28.54 /94	15.23 /92	0.55	1.94
FO	AIM Asia Pacific Growth B	ASIBX	B+	(800) 347-4246	A / 9.3	-2.32	11.03	27.08 /91	27.70 /94	14.50 /91	0.17	2.69
FO	AIM Asia Pacific Growth C	ASICX	A-	(800) 347-4246	A / 9.4	-2.33	10.95	26.98 /91	27.71 /94	14.41 /91	0.17	2.69
BA	AIM Basic Balanced A	BBLAX	C-	(800) 347-4246	D- / 1.4	-2.30	1.15	5.52 /18	8.23 /16	--	1.94	1.08
BA	AIM Basic Balanced B	BBLBX	D+	(800) 347-4246	D- / 1.1	-2.50	0.77	4.66 /13	7.47 /12	--	1.31	1.83
BA	AIM Basic Balanced C	BBLCX	C-	(800) 347-4246	D / 1.6	-2.42	0.77	4.66 /13	7.46 /12	--	1.31	1.83
BA	AIM Basic Balanced Inst	BBLIX	C	(800) 347-4246	D+ / 2.4	-2.18	1.40	5.93 /20	8.62 /19	--	2.53	0.66
BA	AIM Basic Balanced Inv	BBLTX	C	(800) 347-4246	D / 2.1	-2.31	1.07	5.44 /17	8.21 /16	--	2.06	1.08
★ GR	AIM Basic Value A	GTVLX	C-	(800) 347-4246	C- / 3.1	-3.81	0.96	6.80 /25	11.72 /41	2.68 /33	0.00	1.14
GR	AIM Basic Value B	GTVBX	C-	(800) 347-4246	D+ / 2.7	-3.99	0.59	6.01 /20	10.96 /35	1.99 /27	0.00	1.89
GR	AIM Basic Value C	GTVCX	C-	(800) 347-4246	C- / 3.4	-3.99	0.59	5.98 /20	10.96 /35	1.99 /27	0.00	1.89
MC	AIM Capital Development A	ACDAX	C+	(800) 347-4246	C+ / 6.8	-2.66	8.55	17.98 /79	17.53 /70	6.21 /62	0.00	1.29
MC	AIM Capital Development B	ACDBX	C	(800) 347-4246	C+ / 6.5	-2.85	8.14	17.09 /77	16.73 /67	5.49 /58	0.00	2.04
MC	AIM Capital Development C	ACDCX	C+	(800) 347-4246	C+ / 6.9	-2.85	8.15	17.12 /77	16.72 /67	5.48 /58	0.00	2.04
MC	AIM Capital Development Inst	ACDVX	C+	(800) 347-4246	B / 7.6	-2.54	8.83	18.57 /80	18.15 /73	--	0.00	0.81
MC	AIM Capital Development Inv	ACDIX	C+	(800) 347-4246	B- / 7.3	-2.71	8.55	17.97 /79	17.55 /70	6.22 /62	0.00	1.29
★ GI	AIM Charter Fund A	CHTRX	C	(800) 347-4246	D+ / 2.9	-1.85	3.75	10.16 /48	10.28 /29	1.95 /27	0.84	1.20
GI	AIM Charter Fund B	BCHTX	C-	(800) 347-4246	D+ / 2.4	-2.07	3.36	9.32 /42	9.50 /24	1.22 /22	0.07	1.95
GI	AIM Charter Fund C	CHTCX	C	(800) 347-4246	C- / 3.1	-1.99	3.35	9.38 /43	9.50 /24	1.22 /22	0.07	1.95
GI	AIM Charter Fund Inst	CHTVX	C-	(800) 347-4246	C- / 4.2	-1.73	3.96	10.65 /51	10.82 /34	2.43 /31	1.41	0.71
AA	AIM Conservative Alloc A	ACNAX	U	(800) 347-4246	U /	-0.57	1.25	3.73 /10	--	--	1.84	1.11
★ GR	AIM Constellation Fund A	CSTGX	D-	(800) 347-4246	D / 1.7	-6.25	-0.65	10.51 /50	9.96 /27	0.22 /16	0.00	1.26
GR	AIM Constellation Fund B	CSTBX	D-	(800) 347-4246	D- / 1.3	-6.40	-1.00	9.72 /45	9.18 /22	-0.48 /14	0.00	2.01
GR	AIM Constellation Fund C	CSTCX	D-	(800) 347-4246	D / 1.8	-6.44	-1.00	9.67 /45	9.16 /22	-0.49 /14	0.00	2.01
GR	AIM Constellation Fund Inst	CSITX	D-	(800) 347-4246	D+ / 2.8	-6.15	-0.41	11.05 /54	10.52 /31	0.75 /19	0.00	0.76
EM	AIM Developing Markets Fd A	GTDDX	B	(800) 347-4246	A+ / 9.7	-6.27	9.29	39.34 /98	36.22 /98	21.75 /98	0.51	1.75
EM	AIM Developing Markets Fd B	GTDBX	B	(800) 347-4246	A+ / 9.7	-6.46	8.86	38.21 /97	35.37 /98	21.04 /97	0.18	2.50
EM	AIM Developing Markets Fd C	GTDCX	B	(800) 347-4246	A+ / 9.7	-6.42	8.92	38.33 /98	35.40 /98	21.06 /97	0.18	2.50
EM	AIM Developing Markets Fd Inst	GTDIX	C	(800) 347-4246	A+ / 9.8	-6.17	9.49	39.76 /98	36.36 /98	21.82 /98	0.60	1.35
GI	AIM Diversified Dividend A	LCEAX	C+	(800) 347-4246	C / 4.3	-0.61	3.48	8.17 /34	13.03 /49	--	1.18	1.00
GI	AIM Diversified Dividend B	LCEDX	C+	(800) 347-4246	C- / 3.8	-0.86	3.08	7.45 /29	12.26 /44	--	0.62	1.65
GI	AIM Diversified Dividend C	LCEVX	B-	(800) 347-4246	C / 4.6	-0.78	3.09	7.55 /29	12.28 /44	--	0.62	1.65
GI	AIM Diversified Dividend Inst	DDFIX	C	(800) 347-4246	C / 5.2	-0.58	3.58	8.35 /36	13.09 /49	--	1.49	0.76
GI	AIM Diversified Dividend Inv	LCEIX	C	(800) 347-4246	C / 5.2	-0.66	3.45	8.19 /34	13.03 /49	--	1.35	1.00
MC	AIM Dynamics Fund A	IDYAX	C+	(800) 347-4246	C+ / 6.4	-2.87	7.63	17.78 /79	16.51 /66	--	0.00	1.10
MC	AIM Dynamics Fund B	IDYBX	C	(800) 347-4246	C+ / 6.0	-3.06	7.29	16.86 /77	15.70 /62	--	0.00	1.85
MC	AIM Dynamics Fund C	IFDCX	C+	(800) 347-4246	C+ / 6.5	-3.02	7.32	16.95 /77	15.73 /62	0.08 /16	0.00	1.85
MC	AIM Dynamics Fund Inst	IDICX	B-	(800) 347-4246	B- / 7.2	-2.76	7.89	18.31 /80	17.12 /69	1.35 /23	0.00	0.63
MC	● AIM Dynamics Fund Inv	FIDYX	C+	(800) 347-4246	B- / 7.0	-2.87	7.69	17.78 /79	16.57 /66	0.89 /20	0.00	1.10
EN	AIM Energy A	IENAX	A-	(800) 347-4246	A+ / 9.8	5.61	12.26	38.51 /98	38.00 /99	--	0.00	1.37
EN	AIM Energy B	IENBX	A-	(800) 347-4246	A+ / 9.8	5.39	11.83	37.49 /97	37.06 /99	--	0.00	2.12
EN	AIM Energy C	IEFCX	A-	(800) 347-4246	A+ / 9.8	5.39	11.84	37.48 /97	37.06 /99	20.12 /96	0.00	2.12

● Denotes fund is closed to new investors
★ Denotes fund is included in Section II

RISK			NET ASSETS		ASSET					BULL / BEAR		FUND MANAGER		MINIMUMS		LOADS	
	3 Year		NAV						Portfolio	Last Bull	Last Bear	Manager	Manager	Initial	Additional	Front	Back
Risk Rating/Pts	Standard Deviation	Beta	As of 6/30/06	Total $(Mil)	Cash %	Stocks %	Bonds %	Other %	Turnover Ratio	Market Return	Market Return	Quality Pct	Tenure (Years)	Purch. $	Purch. $	End Load	End Load
B- / 7.9	10.1	1.16	14.53	N/A	5	94	0	1	8.0	60.9	-13.2	27	9	500	100	0.0	4.8
B- / 7.9	10.0	1.15	14.53	1	5	94	0	1	8.0	60.9	-13.2	27	9	500	100	0.0	2.0
B- / 7.7	10.1	1.16	15.17	36	5	94	0	1	8.0	66.2	-12.9	35	9	500	100	0.0	2.0
B- / 7.9	10.1	1.16	14.80	N/A	5	94	0	1	8.0	64.9	-13.3	32	2	0	0	0.0	2.0
B+ / 9.0	5.2	1.07	9.43	18	3	64	32	1	32.0	47.6	-4.6	71	N/A	1,000,000	0	0.0	0.0
B / 8.7	8.1	1.04	17.47	10	5	94	0	1	47.0	72.9	N/A	72	N/A	1,000	0	0.0	0.0
B / 8.5	8.2	1.04	17.43	97	5	94	0	1	47.0	74.5	-9.7	75	N/A	1,000,000	0	0.0	0.0
C+ / 6.9	11.1	0.55	16.98	141	N/A	N/A	0	N/A	128.0	62.9	-3.3	16	N/A	1,000	50	5.5	0.0
C+ / 6.8	11.1	0.55	16.24	3	N/A	N/A	0	N/A	128.0	58.1	-3.7	12	N/A	1,000	50	0.0	5.0
C+ / 6.7	11.1	0.54	15.71	2	N/A	N/A	0	N/A	128.0	56.0	-3.9	11	N/A	1,000	50	0.0	1.0
C+ / 5.9	14.1	1.15	20.32	244	9	90	0	1	36.0	158.2	-3.3	59	9	1,000	50	5.5	2.0
C+ / 5.9	14.1	1.15	19.33	49	9	90	0	1	36.0	153.0	-3.4	51	9	1,000	50	0.0	5.0
C+ / 5.9	14.1	1.15	19.25	47	9	90	0	1	36.0	152.7	-3.4	51	9	1,000	50	0.0	2.0
B+ / 9.1	5.8	1.11	12.25	767	0	66	40	0	90.0	48.2	-6.9	57	N/A	1,000	50	5.5	0.0
B+ / 9.1	5.8	1.12	12.22	415	0	66	40	0	90.0	45.0	-7.0	47	N/A	1,000	50	0.0	5.0
B+ / 9.1	5.7	1.11	12.23	175	0	66	40	0	90.0	44.9	-6.9	47	N/A	1,000	50	0.0	1.0
B+ / 9.5	5.8	1.11	12.24	N/A	0	66	40	0	90.0	49.8	-6.9	61	5	10,000,000	0	0.0	0.0
B+ / 9.5	5.8	1.11	12.24	297	0	66	40	0	90.0	48.2	-6.9	57	5	1,000	50	0.0	0.0
B / 8.1	9.0	1.10	34.55	3,354	1	98	0	1	12.0	75.7	-11.7	51	8	1,000	50	5.5	0.0
B / 8.1	9.0	1.10	32.28	1,485	1	98	0	1	12.0	72.0	-11.9	42	8	1,000	50	0.0	5.0
B / 8.0	9.0	1.10	32.27	516	1	98	0	1	12.0	72.0	-11.9	42	8	1,000	50	0.0	1.0
C+ / 5.8	12.0	1.07	19.04	1,004	2	97	0	1	120.0	101.7	-7.0	38	8	1,000	50	5.5	0.0
C+ / 5.6	12.0	1.06	17.40	264	2	97	0	1	120.0	97.4	-7.1	32	8	1,000	50	0.0	5.0
C+ / 5.6	12.0	1.06	17.38	103	2	97	0	1	120.0	97.4	-7.1	32	8	1,000	50	0.0	1.0
C / 5.2	12.3	1.09	19.59	41	2	97	0	1	120.0	105.2	-6.8	40	8	1,000,000	0	0.0	0.0
C / 5.2	12.0	1.06	19.05	8	2	97	0	1	120.0	101.8	-7.0	38	N/A	1,000	50	0.0	0.0
B+ / 9.0	7.2	0.87	13.82	4,701	8	91	0	1	54.0	59.5	-9.5	59	4	1,000	50	5.5	0.0
B / 8.9	7.2	0.87	13.24	1,656	8	91	0	1	54.0	55.9	-9.6	50	11	1,000	50	0.0	5.0
B / 8.9	7.2	0.87	13.28	290	8	91	0	1	54.0	55.8	-9.6	50	4	1,000	50	0.0	1.0
C+ / 6.6	7.2	0.87	14.19	104	8	91	0	1	54.0	62.0	-9.3	65	4	1,000,000	0	0.0	0.0
U /	N/A	N/A	10.54	41	9	90	0	1	24.0	N/A	N/A	N/A	N/A	1,000	50	5.5	0.0
C+ / 6.7	11.1	1.30	24.61	6,657	0	99	0	1	59.0	63.3	-10.0	21	1	1,000	50	5.5	0.0
C+ / 6.6	11.1	1.31	22.80	1,096	0	99	0	1	59.0	59.6	-10.1	17	1	1,000	50	0.0	5.0
C+ / 6.6	11.1	1.31	22.79	289	0	99	0	1	59.0	59.6	-10.1	17	1	1,000	50	0.0	1.0
C / 5.3	11.1	1.30	26.84	194	0	99	0	1	59.0	66.0	-9.8	25	1	10,000,000	0	0.0	0.0
C / 4.5	18.3	1.11	20.94	413	7	92	0	1	40.0	238.0	-5.7	28	3	1,000	50	5.5	2.0
C / 4.4	18.3	1.11	20.40	54	7	92	0	1	40.0	232.1	-5.9	23	3	1,000	50	0.0	5.0
C / 4.4	18.4	1.11	20.39	49	7	92	0	1	40.0	232.3	-6.1	24	3	1,000	50	0.0	2.0
D+ / 2.4	18.3	1.11	20.99	5	7	92	0	1	40.0	238.9	-5.7	29	N/A	10,000,000	0	0.0	2.0
B+ / 9.3	6.6	0.81	12.76	211	3	96	0	1	22.0	70.2	-9.7	86	4	1,000	50	5.5	0.0
B+ / 9.4	6.6	0.81	12.65	88	3	96	0	1	22.0	66.7	-9.8	81	4	1,000	50	0.0	5.0
B+ / 9.4	6.6	0.82	12.64	45	3	96	0	1	22.0	66.7	-9.9	81	4	1,000	50	0.0	1.0
C+ / 6.5	6.6	0.81	12.75	26	3	96	0	1	22.0	70.4	-9.7	86	N/A	1,000,000	0	0.0	0.0
C+ / 6.5	6.6	0.81	12.75	1,450	3	96	0	1	22.0	70.2	-9.7	86	4	1,000	50	0.0	0.0
C+ / 6.4	12.7	1.13	19.61	142	2	97	0	1	87.0	97.8	-9.4	24	2	1,000	50	5.5	0.0
C+ / 6.3	12.8	1.13	18.99	69	2	97	0	1	87.0	93.5	-9.5	19	2	1,000	50	0.0	5.0
C+ / 6.3	12.8	1.13	18.63	34	2	97	0	1	87.0	93.7	-9.7	20	2	1,000	50	0.0	1.0
C+ / 6.4	12.8	1.13	20.10	69	2	97	0	1	87.0	101.0	-9.3	28	2	1,000,000	0	0.0	0.0
C+ / 6.4	12.8	1.13	19.61	1,631	2	97	0	1	87.0	98.2	-9.4	25	2	1,000	50	0.0	0.0
C+ / 5.7	20.8	1.01	45.59	591	4	95	0	1	72.0	185.7	4.4	89	9	1,000	50	5.5	0.0
C+ / 5.7	20.8	1.01	44.16	155	4	95	0	1	72.0	179.6	4.3	85	9	1,000	50	0.0	5.0
C+ / 5.6	20.8	1.01	43.44	186	4	95	0	1	72.0	179.7	4.2	85	9	1,000	50	0.0	1.0

			Overall Weiss Investment Rating		PERFORMANCE							Incl. in Returns	
99 Pct = Best *0 Pct = Worst*					Perfor- mance Rating/Pts	Total Return % through 6/30/06			Annualized			Dividend Yield	Expense Ratio
Fund Type	Fund Name	Ticker Symbol		Phone		3 Mo	6 Mo	1Yr / Pct	3Yr / Pct	5Yr / Pct			
EN	● AIM Energy Inv	FSTEX	A-	(800) 347-4246	A+ / 9.9	5.60	12.24	38.47 /98	38.02 /99	20.95 /97	0.00	1.37
FO	AIM European Growth A	AEDAX	A+	(800) 347-4246	A+ / 9.6	2.52	17.24	31.66 /95	30.63 /96	16.49 /93	0.53	1.64
FO	AIM European Growth B	AEDBX	A+	(800) 347-4246	A / 9.5	2.30	16.78	30.66 /95	29.73 /95	15.70 /93	0.02	2.39
FO	AIM European Growth C	AEDCX	A+	(800) 347-4246	A+ / 9.6	2.30	16.81	30.64 /95	29.73 /95	15.69 /93	0.02	2.39
FO	● AIM European Growth Inv	EGINX	A+	(800) 347-4246	A+ / 9.7	2.52	17.26	31.71 /95	30.70 /96	16.53 /94	0.61	1.63
FO	● AIM European Small Company A	ESMAX	A+	(800) 347-4246	A+ / 9.9	1.54	24.86	49.80 /99	49.86 /99	32.52 /99	0.24	1.90
FO	● AIM European Small Company B	ESMBX	A+	(800) 347-4246	A+ / 9.9	1.32	24.41	48.69 /99	48.76 /99	31.58 /99	0.00	2.65
FO	● AIM European Small Company C	ESMCX	A+	(800) 347-4246	A+ / 9.9	1.36	24.39	48.74 /99	48.83 /99	31.59 /99	0.00	2.65
FS	AIM Financial Services A	IFSAX	D	(800) 347-4246	D+ / 2.8	-1.81	1.28	10.08 /47	10.47 /31	--	1.21	1.28
FS	AIM Financial Services B	IFSBX	D-	(800) 347-4246	D+ / 2.4	-1.99	0.91	9.26 /42	9.71 /25	--	0.55	2.03
FS	AIM Financial Services C	IFSCX	D	(800) 347-4246	C- / 3.0	-2.00	0.90	9.28 /42	9.61 /25	2.58 /33	0.57	2.03
FS	● AIM Financial Services Inv	FSFSX	D+	(800) 347-4246	C- / 3.8	-1.80	1.27	10.07 /47	10.51 /31	3.49 /41	1.30	1.28
GL	AIM Global Aggr Growth Fund A	AGAAX	B+	(800) 347-4246	B+ / 8.8	-3.40	8.97	26.18 /90	25.60 /92	9.83 /80	0.29	1.62
GL	AIM Global Aggr Growth Fund B	AGABX	B+	(800) 347-4246	B+ / 8.8	-3.58	8.56	25.27 /89	24.87 /91	9.21 /77	0.21	2.37
GL	AIM Global Aggr Growth Fund C	AGACX	B+	(800) 347-4246	A- / 9.0	-3.57	8.61	25.25 /89	24.85 /91	9.20 /77	0.21	2.37
GL	AIM Global Equity Fund A	GTNDX	B+	(800) 347-4246	B / 7.7	-0.71	7.59	16.32 /75	20.28 /80	11.21 /84	0.71	1.51
GL	AIM Global Equity Fund B	GNDBX	B+	(800) 347-4246	B / 7.6	-0.87	7.24	15.52 /73	19.56 /78	10.63 /83	0.20	2.26
GL	AIM Global Equity Fund C	GNDCX	A-	(800) 347-4246	B / 7.9	-0.93	7.18	15.46 /73	19.53 /78	10.59 /82	0.20	2.26
GL	AIM Global Equity Fund Inst	GNDIX	B	(800) 347-4246	B / 8.2	-0.59	7.86	16.91 /77	20.78 /82	11.49 /85	1.14	1.02
GL	AIM Global Growth Fund A	AGGAX	C+	(800) 347-4246	C+ / 6.1	-2.02	5.69	18.38 /80	16.52 /66	4.66 /51	0.58	1.72
GL	AIM Global Growth Fund B	AGGBX	C+	(800) 347-4246	C+ / 6.0	-2.19	5.34	17.53 /78	15.80 /63	4.06 /46	0.00	2.47
GL	AIM Global Growth Fund C	AGGCX	B-	(800) 347-4246	C+ / 6.5	-2.19	5.29	17.52 /78	15.82 /63	4.07 /46	0.00	2.47
HL	AIM Global Health Care A	GGHCX	D	(800) 347-4246	D- / 1.4	-7.49	-2.79	7.38 /28	8.93 /20	1.48 /24	0.00	1.25
HL	AIM Global Health Care B	GTHBX	D-	(800) 347-4246	D- / 1.1	-7.65	-3.16	6.57 /24	8.26 /16	0.90 /20	0.00	2.00
HL	AIM Global Health Care C	GTHCX	D	(800) 347-4246	D / 1.7	-7.64	-3.16	6.57 /24	8.27 /16	0.91 /20	0.00	2.00
HL	AIM Global Health Care Inv	GTHIX	D-	(800) 347-4246	D / 2.2	-7.49	-2.82	7.38 /29	8.93 /20	1.48 /24	0.00	1.25
RE	AIM Global Real Estate A	AGREX	U	(800) 347-4246	U /	-0.18	12.87	27.29 /92	--	--	1.66	1.40
RE	AIM Global Real Estate C	CGREX	U	(800) 347-4246	U /	-0.29	12.44	26.45 /90	--	--	1.07	2.15
GL	AIM Global Value A	AWSAX	A	(800) 347-4246	B- / 7.3	-0.46	7.51	15.53 /73	19.40 /77	12.25 /87	0.95	1.90
GL	AIM Global Value B	AWSBX	A	(800) 347-4246	B- / 7.3	-0.61	7.10	14.65 /71	18.54 /75	11.51 /85	0.52	2.65
GL	AIM Global Value C	AWSCX	A+	(800) 347-4246	B / 7.6	-0.61	7.09	14.63 /70	18.56 /75	11.50 /85	0.52	2.65
GL	AIM Global Value I	AWSIX	B	(800) 347-4246	B / 8.0	-0.33	7.79	15.94 /74	19.54 /78	12.33 /87	1.02	1.42
PM	AIM Gold & Prec Met A	IGDAX	C-	(800) 347-4246	A+ / 9.8	0.00	17.88	59.27 /99	29.65 /95	--	0.00	1.59
PM	AIM Gold & Prec Met B	IGDBX	C-	(800) 347-4246	A+ / 9.7	0.00	17.40	58.19 /99	28.87 /95	--	0.00	2.34
PM	AIM Gold & Prec Met C	IGDCX	C-	(800) 347-4246	A+ / 9.8	0.00	17.39	58.40 /99	28.87 /95	28.40 /99	0.00	2.34
PM	● AIM Gold & Prec Met Inv	FGLDX	C-	(800) 347-4246	A+ / 9.8	0.18	17.98	59.50 /99	29.76 /95	29.72 /99	0.00	1.59
AA	AIM Growth Allocation A	AADAX	U	(800) 347-4246	U /	-2.51	4.91	14.74 /71	--	--	0.53	1.42
AA	AIM Growth Allocation B	AAEBX	U	(800) 347-4246	U /	-2.68	4.52	13.93 /68	--	--	0.12	2.17
AA	AIM Growth Allocation C	AADCX	U	(800) 347-4246	U /	-2.76	4.53	13.84 /68	--	--	0.12	2.17
FO	AIM International Allocation A	AINAX	U	(800) 347-4246	U /	-0.25	9.99	--	--	--	0.00	1.58
FO	AIM International Growth A	AIIEX	A-	(800) 347-4246	B+ / 8.7	-0.93	8.94	27.21 /92	23.56 /89	9.29 /78	0.65	1.66
FO	AIM International Growth B	AIEBX	A-	(800) 347-4246	B+ / 8.5	-1.12	8.53	26.26 /90	22.70 /87	8.52 /74	0.08	2.41
FO	AIM International Growth C	AIECX	A-	(800) 347-4246	B+ / 8.8	-1.12	8.52	26.23 /90	22.70 /87	8.53 /74	0.08	2.41
FO	AIM International Growth Inst	AIEVX	B+	(800) 347-4246	A- / 9.0	-0.84	9.18	27.78 /92	24.26 /90	--	1.20	1.07
EM	● AIM International Small Co A	IEGAX	A+	(800) 347-4246	A+ / 9.9	-0.33	19.30	47.00 /99	44.51 /99	30.21 /99	0.19	1.72
EM	● AIM International Small Co B	IEGBX	A+	(800) 347-4246	A+ / 9.9	-0.50	18.90	45.85 /98	43.47 /99	29.30 /99	0.00	2.47
EM	● AIM International Small Co C	IEGCX	A+	(800) 347-4246	A+ / 9.9	-0.50	18.85	45.88 /98	43.45 /99	29.33 /99	0.00	2.47
EM	● AIM International Small Co Inst	IEGIX	B+	(800) 347-4246	A+ / 9.9	-0.24	19.49	47.30 /99	44.61 /99	30.26 /99	0.24	1.35
FO	AIM Intl Core Equity A	IBVAX	A	(800) 347-4246	B / 8.1	1.06	9.62	23.48 /87	20.99 /82	--	0.65	1.50
FO	AIM Intl Core Equity B	IBVBX	A	(800) 347-4246	B / 8.0	0.84	9.25	22.56 /85	20.19 /80	--	0.11	2.25
FO	AIM Intl Core Equity C	IBVCX	A	(800) 347-4246	B+ / 8.3	0.94	9.28	22.58 /85	20.31 /80	7.51 /69	0.11	2.25
FO	AIM Intl Core Equity Inst	IBVIX	U	(800) 347-4246	U /	1.21	9.93	24.18 /87	--	--	1.14	0.98

● Denotes fund is closed to new investors
* Denotes fund is included in Section II

www.WeissRatings.com

RISK			NET ASSETS		ASSET					BULL / BEAR		FUND MANAGER		MINIMUMS		LOADS	
	3 Year		NAV						Portfolio	Last Bull	Last Bear	Manager	Manager	Initial	Additional	Front	Back
Risk	Standard		As of	Total	Cash	Stocks	Bonds	Other	Turnover	Market	Market	Quality	Tenure	Purch.	Purch.	End	End
Rating/Pts	Deviation	Beta	6/30/06	$(Mil)	%	%	%	%	Ratio	Return	Return	Pct	(Years)	$	$	Load	Load
C+ / 5.7	20.8	1.01	45.48	594	4	95	0	1	72.0	185.8	4.4	89	9	1,000	50	0.0	0.0
B- / 7.0	11.5	1.03	36.66	665	3	96	0	1	48.0	172.7	-5.2	91	9	1,000	50	5.5	2.0
B- / 7.0	11.5	1.03	34.72	159	3	96	0	1	48.0	167.1	-5.3	89	9	1,000	50	0.0	5.0
B- / 7.0	11.5	1.03	34.74	84	3	96	0	1	48.0	167.2	-5.4	88	9	1,000	50	0.0	1.0
B- / 7.9	11.5	1.03	36.61	242	3	96	0	1	48.0	173.2	-5.2	92	9	1,000	50	0.0	0.0
C+ / 6.6	14.0	1.15	27.07	323	9	90	0	1	72.0	346.5	-4.7	99	6	1,000	50	5.5	2.0
C+ / 6.5	14.0	1.15	26.15	54	9	90	0	1	72.0	336.5	-4.9	99	6	1,000	50	0.0	5.0
C+ / 6.5	14.0	1.15	26.16	66	9	90	0	1	72.0	336.7	-4.8	99	6	1,000	50	0.0	1.0
C+ / 6.0	9.9	1.06	27.71	67	2	97	0	1	3.0	66.6	-9.3	22	2	1,000	50	5.5	0.0
C+ / 6.0	9.9	1.06	27.59	48	2	97	0	1	3.0	62.9	-9.4	18	2	1,000	50	0.0	5.0
C+ / 6.0	9.9	1.05	26.92	18	2	97	0	1	3.0	62.3	-9.5	17	2	1,000	50	0.0	1.0
C+ / 6.0	9.9	1.06	27.86	522	2	97	0	1	3.0	66.7	-9.3	22	2	1,000	50	0.0	0.0
C+ / 6.3	11.9	1.08	23.33	773	3	96	0	1	67.0	147.8	-6.7	47	7	1,000	50	5.5	2.0
C+ / 6.2	11.9	1.08	21.57	139	3	96	0	1	67.0	143.3	-6.8	40	7	1,000	50	0.0	5.0
C+ / 6.2	11.9	1.08	21.58	27	3	96	0	1	67.0	143.2	-6.9	40	7	1,000	50	0.0	1.0
B- / 7.5	8.9	0.77	16.72	297	2	97	0	1	120.0	108.9	-5.8	68	7	1,000	50	4.8	2.0
B- / 7.5	8.9	0.77	16.00	97	2	97	0	1	120.0	105.2	-5.9	62	9	1,000	50	0.0	5.0
B- / 7.5	8.9	0.77	15.97	37	2	97	0	1	120.0	105.2	-5.9	62	8	1,000	50	0.0	1.0
C+ / 6.0	8.8	0.77	16.87	51	2	97	0	1	120.0	111.4	-5.8	73	7	10,000,000	0	0.0	2.0
B- / 7.3	9.2	0.84	21.36	298	0	99	0	1	51.0	88.7	-7.4	22	7	1,000	50	5.5	2.0
B- / 7.2	9.2	0.84	20.11	95	0	99	0	1	51.0	85.2	-7.6	18	7	1,000	50	0.0	5.0
B- / 7.2	9.1	0.84	20.12	24	0	99	0	1	51.0	85.1	-7.5	19	7	1,000	50	0.0	1.0
B- / 7.4	9.0	0.70	29.28	526	1	98	0	1	92.0	56.0	-10.0	61	N/A	1,000	50	5.5	0.0
B- / 7.4	9.0	0.70	26.33	139	1	98	0	1	92.0	53.1	-10.1	54	N/A	1,000	50	0.0	5.0
B- / 7.4	9.0	0.70	26.35	41	1	98	0	1	92.0	53.1	-10.1	53	N/A	1,000	50	0.0	1.0
C+ / 5.9	9.0	0.70	29.28	736	1	98	0	1	92.0	56.0	-10.0	61	N/A	1,000	50	0.0	0.0
U /	N/A	N/A	13.09	140	5	94	0	1	3.0	N/A	N/A	N/A	1	1,000	50	5.5	0.0
U /	N/A	N/A	13.10	32	5	94	0	1	3.0	N/A	N/A	N/A	1	1,000	50	0.0	1.0
B / 8.6	9.2	0.76	15.03	109	11	88	0	1	51.0	94.2	-5.7	63	4	1,000	50	5.5	2.0
B / 8.6	9.2	0.76	14.64	53	11	88	0	1	51.0	90.1	-5.9	55	4	1,000	50	0.0	5.0
B / 8.6	9.2	0.76	14.65	30	11	88	0	1	51.0	90.0	-5.9	55	4	1,000	50	0.0	1.0
C+ / 6.2	9.2	0.76	15.08	24	11	88	0	1	51.0	94.7	-5.7	65	N/A	10,000,000	0	0.0	0.0
D- / 1.2	29.1	1.36	5.67	50	0	99	0	1	155.0	154.3	14.6	65	7	1,000	50	5.5	0.0
D- / 1.2	29.3	1.37	5.60	22	0	99	0	1	155.0	151.0	15.1	57	7	1,000	50	0.0	5.0
D- / 1.2	29.2	1.37	5.94	17	0	99	0	1	155.0	150.0	14.7	58	7	1,000	50	0.0	1.0
D- / 1.2	29.2	1.37	5.71	143	0	99	0	1	155.0	155.7	15.0	65	7	1,000	50	0.0	0.0
U /	N/A	N/A	12.82	189	N/A	100	0	N/A	14.0	N/A	N/A	N/A	N/A	1,000	50	5.5	0.0
U /	N/A	N/A	12.71	90	N/A	100	0	N/A	14.0	N/A	N/A	N/A	N/A	1,000	50	0.0	5.0
U /	N/A	N/A	12.70	58	N/A	100	0	N/A	14.0	N/A	N/A	N/A	N/A	1,000	50	0.0	1.0
U /	N/A	N/A	11.78	58	N/A	100	0	N/A	N/A	N/A	N/A	N/A	N/A	1,000	50	5.5	1.0
C+ / 6.8	10.6	0.99	25.58	1,721	5	94	0	1	37.0	124.7	-6.1	49	11	1,000	50	5.5	1.0
C+ / 6.8	10.6	0.99	23.79	252	5	94	0	1	37.0	119.7	-6.3	41	11	1,000	50	0.0	5.0
C+ / 6.8	10.6	0.99	23.81	170	5	94	0	1	37.0	119.7	-6.3	41	11	1,000	50	0.0	1.0
C+ / 5.8	10.5	0.99	25.92	227	5	94	0	1	37.0	128.6	-5.9	58	11	1,000,000	0	0.0	2.0
C+ / 6.2	14.3	0.74	24.48	558	6	93	0	1	60.0	302.0	1.2	99	6	1,000	50	5.5	2.0
C+ / 6.2	14.3	0.74	23.72	78	6	93	0	1	60.0	293.4	1.0	99	6	1,000	50	0.0	5.0
C+ / 6.2	14.3	0.74	23.71	114	6	93	0	1	60.0	293.3	1.0	99	6	1,000	50	0.0	1.0
C / 4.9	14.3	0.74	24.52	9	6	93	0	1	60.0	302.7	1.2	99	N/A	10,000,000	0	0.0	0.0
B- / 7.8	9.5	0.92	13.33	104	4	95	0	1	21.0	108.9	-9.1	41	8	1,000	50	5.5	2.0
B- / 7.7	9.5	0.91	13.23	30	4	95	0	1	21.0	104.8	-9.1	35	8	1,000	50	0.0	5.0
B- / 7.7	9.5	0.92	12.95	41	4	95	0	1	21.0	105.5	-9.3	35	8	1,000	50	0.0	1.0
U /	N/A	N/A	13.40	155	4	95	0	1	21.0	N/A	N/A	N/A	N/A	10,000,000	0	0.0	2.0

99 Pct = Best
0 Pct = Worst

Fund Type	Fund Name	Ticker Symbol	Overall Weiss Investment Rating	Phone	Perfor-mance Rating/Pts	3 Mo	6 Mo	1Yr / Pct	3Yr / Pct (Annualized)	5Yr / Pct (Annualized)	Dividend Yield	Expense Ratio
FO	● AIM Intl Core Equity Inv	IIBCX	A+	(800) 347-4246	B+ / 8.4	1.05	9.67	23.42 /86	21.10 /83	8.44 /74	0.72	1.50
GR	AIM Large Cap Basic Value A	LCBAX	C-	(800) 347-4246	C- / 3.2	-3.51	1.67	8.40 /36	11.46 /39	2.70 /34	0.00	1.22
GR	AIM Large Cap Basic Value B	LCBBX	C-	(800) 347-4246	D+ / 2.7	-3.71	1.23	7.60 /30	10.69 /33	2.00 /27	0.00	1.97
GR	AIM Large Cap Basic Value C	LCBCX	C-	(800) 347-4246	C- / 3.4	-3.71	1.23	7.60 /30	10.73 /33	2.00 /27	0.00	1.97
GR	AIM Large Cap Basic Value Inst	LCBIX	C-	(800) 347-4246	C / 4.4	-3.48	1.80	8.84 /39	11.85 /41	2.92 /36	0.18	0.76
GR	● AIM Large Cap Basic Value Inv	LCINX	C+	(800) 347-4246	C- / 4.2	-3.57	1.60	8.39 /36	11.51 /39	2.73 /34	0.00	1.22
GR	AIM Large Cap Growth A	LCGAX	D	(800) 347-4246	D / 2.0	-5.54	-0.47	7.63 /30	9.90 /27	0.23 /16	0.00	1.32
GR	AIM Large Cap Growth B	LCGBX	D	(800) 347-4246	D / 1.7	-5.71	-0.89	6.79 /25	9.12 /21	-0.47 /14	0.00	2.07
GR	AIM Large Cap Growth C	LCGCX	D	(800) 347-4246	D / 2.2	-5.71	-0.89	6.79 /25	9.07 /21	-0.47 /14	0.00	2.07
GR	● AIM Large Cap Growth Inv	LCGIX	C-	(800) 347-4246	C- / 3.1	-5.51	-0.47	7.69 /30	10.11 /28	0.34 /17	0.00	1.26
GR	AIM Leisure Fund A	ILSAX	D	(800) 347-4246	C- / 3.4	0.76	5.90	6.83 /25	11.28 /38	--	0.94	1.32
GR	AIM Leisure Fund B	ILSBX	D	(800) 347-4246	C- / 3.0	0.59	5.54	6.05 /21	10.52 /31	--	0.71	2.07
GR	AIM Leisure Fund C	IVLCX	D+	(800) 347-4246	C- / 3.6	0.60	5.53	6.06 /21	10.47 /31	3.18 /38	0.73	2.07
GR	● AIM Leisure Fund Inv	FLISX	C-	(800) 347-4246	C / 4.4	0.78	5.91	6.84 /25	11.34 /38	4.06 /46	1.01	1.32
MC	AIM Mid Cap Basic Value A	MDCAX	C	(800) 347-4246	C- / 4.1	-6.44	-2.69	5.15 /16	14.24 /55	--	0.00	1.52
MC	AIM Mid Cap Basic Value B	MDCBX	C-	(800) 347-4246	C- / 3.6	-6.63	-3.05	4.27 /12	13.46 /51	--	0.00	2.27
MC	AIM Mid Cap Basic Value C	MDCVX	C	(800) 347-4246	C / 4.3	-6.63	-3.05	4.27 /12	13.43 /51	--	0.00	2.27
MC	AIM Mid Cap Basic Value Inst	MDICX	C-	(800) 347-4246	C / 5.3	-6.30	-2.39	5.70 /19	14.73 /57	--	0.00	1.01
MC	● AIM Mid Cap Core Equity A	GTAGX	C-	(800) 347-4246	C- / 3.6	-3.20	1.61	7.36 /28	12.37 /45	6.26 /63	0.00	1.27
MC	● AIM Mid Cap Core Equity B	GTABX	C-	(800) 347-4246	C- / 3.1	-3.40	1.23	6.54 /23	11.54 /39	5.51 /58	0.00	2.02
MC	● AIM Mid Cap Core Equity C	GTACX	C-	(800) 347-4246	C- / 3.8	-3.41	1.23	6.54 /23	11.54 /39	5.52 /58	0.00	1.95
AA	AIM Moderate Allocation Fund A	AMKAX	U	(800) 347-4246	U /	-1.83	2.61	8.97 /40	--	--	1.46	1.29
AA	AIM Moderate Allocation Fund B	AMKBX	U	(800) 347-4246	U /	-2.09	2.19	8.19 /34	--	--	1.05	2.04
AA	AIM Moderate Allocation Fund C	AMKCX	U	(800) 347-4246	U /	-2.09	2.19	8.19 /34	--	--	1.05	2.04
AA	AIM Moderate Growth Alloc A	AAMGX	U	(800) 347-4246	U /	-2.07	4.05	12.47 /62	--	--	0.76	1.30
AA	AIM Moderate Growth Alloc B	AMBGX	U	(800) 347-4246	U /	-2.33	3.62	11.59 /57	--	--	0.62	2.05
AA	AIM Moderate Growth Alloc C	ACMGX	U	(800) 347-4246	U /	-2.25	3.71	11.70 /58	--	--	0.62	1.90
GR	AIM Multi Sector Fund A	IAMSX	B	(800) 347-4246	C+ / 6.1	-1.39	3.62	14.24 /69	16.01 /64	--	0.00	1.44
GR	AIM Multi Sector Fund B	IBMSX	B-	(800) 347-4246	C+ / 5.8	-1.55	3.25	13.45 /66	15.18 /60	--	0.00	2.19
GR	AIM Multi Sector Fund C	ICMSX	B	(800) 347-4246	C+ / 6.3	-1.55	3.25	13.46 /66	15.19 /60	--	0.00	2.19
GR	AIM Multi Sector Fund Inst	IIMSX	U	(800) 347-4246	U /	-1.30	3.83	14.77 /71	--	--	0.00	1.02
SC	AIM Opportunities I A	ASCOX	E	(800) 347-4246	D+ / 2.5	-1.94	3.44	7.76 /31	10.01 /27	2.36 /31	0.17	2.70
SC	AIM Opportunities I B	SCPBX	E-	(800) 347-4246	D / 2.1	-2.18	3.01	6.93 /26	9.24 /22	1.65 /25	0.00	3.45
SC	AIM Opportunities I C	SCOCX	E	(800) 347-4246	D+ / 2.7	-2.18	3.09	6.92 /26	9.26 /22	1.65 /25	0.00	3.45
MC	AIM Opportunities II A	AMCOX	C	(800) 347-4246	C / 4.4	-1.19	4.57	10.05 /47	12.86 /48	3.77 /43	0.00	3.57
MC	AIM Opportunities II B	MCOVX	C-	(800) 347-4246	C- / 3.9	-1.38	4.18	9.23 /41	12.06 /43	3.04 /37	0.00	4.32
MC	AIM Opportunities II C	MCODX	C	(800) 347-4246	C / 4.6	-1.38	4.18	9.23 /41	12.06 /43	3.04 /37	0.00	4.32
GR	AIM Opportunities III A	LCPAX	D-	(800) 347-4246	E / 0.5	-1.98	1.36	3.59 / 9	5.51 / 5	-3.27 / 5	0.21	3.76
GR	AIM Opportunities III B	LCPBX	D-	(800) 347-4246	E / 0.3	-2.17	0.94	2.76 / 6	4.78 / 4	-3.94 / 4	0.00	4.51
GR	AIM Opportunities III C	LCPCX	D-	(800) 347-4246	E+ / 0.6	-2.17	0.94	2.88 / 7	4.78 / 4	-3.94 / 4	0.00	4.51
RE	● AIM Real Estate Fund A	IARAX	B-	(800) 347-4246	A / 9.5	0.47	15.00	24.73 /88	29.57 /95	22.76 /98	1.47	1.30
RE	● AIM Real Estate Fund B	AARBX	B-	(800) 347-4246	A / 9.4	0.25	14.56	23.81 /87	28.69 /94	21.94 /98	0.87	2.05
RE	● AIM Real Estate Fund C	IARCX	B-	(800) 347-4246	A / 9.5	0.25	14.56	23.78 /87	28.68 /94	21.93 /98	0.87	2.05
RE	● AIM Real Estate Fund Inst	IARIX	B	(800) 347-4246	A+ / 9.6	0.58	15.27	25.32 /89	30.04 /96	23.03 /98	1.96	0.86
RE	● AIM Real Estate Fund Inv	REINX	B+	(800) 347-4246	A+ / 9.6	0.47	15.02	24.72 /88	29.64 /95	22.80 /98	1.55	1.27
IX	AIM S&P 500 Inst	ISIIX	C	(800) 347-4246	C- / 3.7	-1.50	2.62	8.28 /35	10.86 /34	1.93 /27	1.64	0.35
IX	● AIM S&P 500 Inv	ISPIX	C	(800) 347-4246	C- / 3.3	-1.63	2.42	7.97 /32	10.50 /31	1.75 /25	1.39	0.33
GR	AIM Select Equity Fund A	AGWFX	C	(800) 347-4246	C- / 3.6	-3.46	2.16	7.98 /33	12.53 /46	0.17 /16	0.00	1.38
GR	AIM Select Equity Fund B	AGWBX	C-	(800) 347-4246	C- / 3.3	-3.68	1.70	7.17 /27	11.67 /40	-0.58 /13	0.00	2.13
GR	AIM Select Equity Fund C	AGWCX	C	(800) 347-4246	C- / 4.0	-3.63	1.77	7.18 /27	11.69 /40	-0.58 /13	0.00	2.13
SC	AIM Small Cap Equity A	SMEAX	C	(800) 347-4246	C+ / 6.6	-1.47	9.30	17.22 /77	17.15 /69	8.49 /74	0.00	1.41
SC	AIM Small Cap Equity B	SMEBX	C	(800) 347-4246	C+ / 6.6	-1.69	8.84	16.28 /75	16.29 /65	7.72 /70	0.00	2.16

● Denotes fund is closed to new investors
* Denotes fund is included in Section II

RISK			NET ASSETS		ASSET				Portfolio	BULL / BEAR		FUND MANAGER		MINIMUMS		LOADS	
	3 Year		NAV							Last Bull	Last Bear	Manager	Manager	Initial	Additional	Front	Back
Risk Rating/Pts	Standard Deviation	Beta	As of 6/30/06	Total $(Mil)	Cash %	Stocks %	Bonds %	Other %	Turnover Ratio	Market Return	Market Return	Quality Pct	Tenure (Years)	Purch. $	Purch. $	End Load	End Load
B- /7.7	9.5	0.92	13.49	41	4	95	0	1	21.0	109.9	-9.1	41	8	1,000	50	0.0	2.0
B- /7.9	8.8	1.05	14.58	137	1	98	0	1	9.0	74.1	-11.8	53	7	1,000	50	5.5	0.0
B- /7.8	8.8	1.05	14.01	67	1	98	0	1	9.0	70.4	-12.0	45	7	1,000	50	0.0	5.0
B- /7.8	8.8	1.05	14.01	26	1	98	0	1	9.0	70.4	-12.0	45	7	1,000	50	0.0	1.0
C+ /6.0	8.8	1.04	14.71	140	1	98	0	1	9.0	75.9	-11.8	59	7	10,000,000	0	0.0	0.0
B /8.5	8.8	1.05	14.60	61	1	98	0	1	9.0	74.3	-11.8	55	7	1,000	50	0.0	0.0
B- /7.0	10.4	1.15	10.58	961	3	96	0	1	103.0	60.9	-6.2	30	7	1,000	50	5.5	0.0
B- /7.0	10.4	1.15	10.07	683	3	96	0	1	103.0	57.1	-6.2	25	7	1,000	50	0.0	5.0
B- /7.0	10.4	1.16	10.07	180	3	96	0	1	103.0	57.3	-6.3	24	7	1,000	50	0.0	1.0
B- /7.8	10.4	1.15	10.64	348	3	96	0	1	103.0	61.8	-6.2	31	7	1,000	50	0.0	0.0
C+ /6.2	9.8	1.10	43.78	128	1	98	0	1	20.0	67.9	-10.2	46	10	1,000	50	5.5	0.0
C+ /6.5	9.8	1.10	42.71	32	1	98	0	1	20.0	64.3	-10.4	38	10	1,000	50	0.0	5.0
C+ /6.5	9.8	1.10	41.60	32	1	98	0	1	20.0	63.9	-10.5	38	10	1,000	50	0.0	1.0
C+ /6.6	9.8	1.10	43.71	540	1	98	0	1	20.0	68.1	-10.2	46	10	1,000	50	0.0	0.0
B- /7.6	10.4	0.87	14.09	116	2	97	0	1	29.0	93.0	-10.5	38	5	1,000	50	5.5	0.0
B- /7.6	10.4	0.87	13.67	57	2	97	0	1	29.0	89.0	-10.7	32	5	1,000	50	0.0	5.0
B- /7.6	10.4	0.87	13.66	28	2	97	0	1	29.0	88.8	-10.6	32	5	1,000	50	0.0	1.0
C+ /5.6	10.4	0.86	14.27	34	2	97	0	1	29.0	95.3	-10.5	43	N/A	10,000,000	0	0.0	0.0
B- /7.8	8.4	0.71	29.03	1,942	14	85	0	1	61.0	71.5	-8.1	44	8	1,000	50	5.5	0.0
B- /7.4	8.4	0.72	25.54	530	14	85	0	1	61.0	67.6	-8.3	36	8	1,000	50	0.0	5.0
B- /7.4	8.4	0.72	25.51	244	14	85	0	1	61.0	67.6	-8.3	36	8	1,000	50	0.0	1.0
U /	N/A	N/A	11.79	259	0	99	0	1	2.0	N/A	N/A	N/A	1	1,000	50	5.5	0.0
U /	N/A	N/A	11.69	132	0	99	0	1	2.0	N/A	N/A	N/A	1	1,000	50	0.0	5.0
U /	N/A	N/A	11.69	99	0	99	0	1	2.0	N/A	N/A	N/A	1	1,000	50	0.0	1.0
U /	N/A	N/A	11.81	78	0	99	0	1	1.0	N/A	N/A	N/A	1	1,000	50	5.5	0.0
U /	N/A	N/A	11.73	35	0	99	0	1	1.0	N/A	N/A	N/A	1	1,000	50	0.0	5.0
U /	N/A	N/A	11.73	27	0	99	0	1	1.0	N/A	N/A	N/A	1	1,000	50	0.0	1.0
B /8.0	9.6	1.13	25.49	302	5	94	0	1	63.0	89.2	-5.8	86	N/A	1,000	50	5.5	0.0
B- /7.9	9.6	1.13	24.79	69	5	94	0	1	63.0	85.1	-6.0	81	N/A	1,000	50	0.0	5.0
B- /7.9	9.6	1.13	24.78	66	5	94	0	1	63.0	85.0	-6.0	81	N/A	1,000	50	0.0	1.0
U /	N/A	N/A	25.77	82	5	94	0	1	63.0	N/A	N/A	N/A	N/A	10,000,000	0	0.0	0.0
C- /3.0	13.4	0.82	12.64	122	N/A	N/A	0	N/A	190.0	66.6	-12.4	14	6	1,000	50	5.5	0.0
D+ /2.5	13.3	0.81	11.64	62	N/A	N/A	0	N/A	190.0	63.0	-12.4	11	8	1,000	50	0.0	5.0
D+ /2.5	13.3	0.82	11.66	14	N/A	N/A	0	N/A	190.0	63.0	-12.5	11	8	1,000	50	0.0	1.0
B- /7.2	9.8	0.85	22.44	57	N/A	N/A	0	N/A	174.0	71.9	-8.9	30	1	1,000	50	5.5	0.0
B- /7.1	9.8	0.85	21.42	35	N/A	N/A	0	N/A	174.0	68.3	-9.1	25	1	1,000	50	0.0	5.0
B- /7.1	9.8	0.85	21.42	13	N/A	N/A	0	N/A	174.0	68.3	-9.1	25	1	1,000	50	0.0	1.0
B- /7.5	7.7	0.89	8.93	30	N/A	N/A	0	N/A	205.0	36.4	-9.0	17	7	1,000	50	5.5	0.0
B- /7.4	7.7	0.89	8.57	29	N/A	N/A	0	N/A	205.0	33.5	-9.1	13	6	1,000	50	0.0	5.0
B- /7.4	7.6	0.89	8.57	8	N/A	N/A	0	N/A	205.0	33.5	-9.1	13	6	1,000	50	0.0	1.0
C- /4.2	15.5	0.93	31.86	1,058	3	96	0	1	38.0	141.3	0.7	95	N/A	1,000	50	4.8	0.0
C- /4.2	15.5	0.93	31.97	227	3	96	0	1	38.0	136.2	0.5	93	N/A	1,000	50	0.0	5.0
C- /4.2	15.5	0.93	31.90	194	3	96	0	1	38.0	136.1	0.6	93	N/A	1,000	50	0.0	1.0
C /4.5	15.5	0.93	31.85	23	3	96	0	1	38.0	143.7	0.7	96	N/A	10,000,000	0	0.0	0.0
C /5.3	15.5	0.93	31.83	43	3	96	0	1	38.0	141.7	0.7	95	N/A	1,000	50	0.0	1.0
B /8.6	7.7	1.00	12.76	9	3	96	0	1	4.0	62.7	-9.8	52	3	1,000	50	0.0	2.0
B /8.6	7.7	1.00	13.32	211	3	96	0	1	4.0	61.3	-9.9	47	3	1,000	50	5.5	1.0
B /8.0	9.2	1.09	18.95	245	2	97	0	1	91.0	74.0	-10.5	61	7	1,000	50	0.0	5.0
B /8.0	9.2	1.10	16.74	89	2	97	0	1	91.0	69.9	-10.7	51	4	1,000	50	0.0	1.0
B /8.0	9.2	1.09	16.72	20	2	97	0	1	91.0	69.9	-10.6	51	4	1,000	50	5.5	1.0
C /5.5	13.2	0.86	13.40	231	2	97	0	1	52.0	105.4	-9.2	66	2	1,000	50	0.0	5.0
C /5.3	13.2	0.86	12.81	127	2	97	0	1	52.0	101.0	-9.4	57	2	1,000	50		

Data as of June 30, 2006

Fund Type	Fund Name	Ticker Symbol	Overall Weiss Investment Rating	Phone	Performance Rating/Pts	3 Mo	6 Mo	1Yr / Pct	3Yr / Pct	5Yr / Pct	Dividend Yield	Expense Ratio
	99 Pct = Best							**PERFORMANCE**			**Incl. in Returns**	
	0 Pct = Worst							Total Return % through 6/30/06				
									Annualized			
SC	AIM Small Cap Equity C	SMECX	C	(800) 347-4246	C+ / 6.9	-1.61	8.93	16.38 /76	16.34 /65	7.72 /70	0.00	2.16
SC	● AIM Small Cap Growth A	GTSAX	D+	(800) 347-4246	C / 5.1	-4.94	6.43	13.19 /65	13.89 /53	2.86 /35	0.00	1.27
SC	● AIM Small Cap Growth B	GTSBX	D	(800) 347-4246	C / 4.6	-5.13	6.05	12.35 /61	13.04 /49	2.08 /28	0.00	2.02
SC	● AIM Small Cap Growth C	GTSDX	D+	(800) 347-4246	C / 5.2	-5.13	6.05	12.32 /61	13.05 /49	2.09 /28	0.00	2.02
SC	AIM Small Cap Growth Inst	GTSVX	C-	(800) 347-4246	C+ / 6.2	-4.86	6.66	13.73 /67	14.50 /56	--	0.00	0.84
TC	AIM Technology A	ITYAX	E-	(800) 347-4246	D- / 1.3	-8.51	-0.46	8.37 /36	8.48 /18	--	0.00	1.55
TC	AIM Technology B	ITYBX	E-	(800) 347-4246	D- / 1.0	-8.70	-0.83	7.51 /29	7.73 /13	--	0.00	2.30
TC	AIM Technology C	ITHCX	E-	(800) 347-4246	D- / 1.5	-8.71	-0.85	7.54 /29	7.73 /13	-9.32 / 0	0.00	2.30
TC	AIM Technology Inst	FTPIX	E	(800) 347-4246	D+ / 2.6	-8.35	-0.11	9.14 /41	9.35 /23	-7.87 / 1	0.00	0.79
TC	● AIM Technology Inv	FTCHX	E	(800) 347-4246	D / 2.0	-8.55	-0.46	8.32 /35	8.38 /17	-8.66 / 0	0.00	1.55
MC	AIM Trimark Endeavor Fund A	ATDAX	U	(800) 347-4246	U /	-3.06	5.71	12.99 /64	--	--	0.20	1.59
SC	AIM Trimark Small Companies A	ATIAX	U	(800) 347-4246	U /	-4.07	2.31	11.29 /55	--	--	0.00	1.45
SC	AIM Trimark Small Companies C	ATICX	U	(800) 347-4246	U /	-4.27	1.92	10.41 /50	--	--	0.00	2.20
SC	AIM Trimark Small Companies Inst	ATIIX	U	(800) 347-4246	U /	-3.97	2.57	11.84 /59	--	--	0.00	1.01
UT	AIM Utilities Fund A	IAUTX	A	(800) 347-4246	B- / 7.5	5.37	7.60	14.14 /69	19.12 /76	--	2.09	1.30
UT	AIM Utilities Fund B	IBUTX	A	(800) 347-4246	B- / 7.3	5.15	7.17	13.24 /65	18.27 /73	--	1.49	2.05
UT	AIM Utilities Fund C	IUTCX	A	(800) 347-4246	B / 7.6	5.11	7.19	13.22 /65	18.25 /73	1.81 /25	1.47	2.05
UT	● AIM Utilities Fund Inv	FSTUX	A+	(800) 347-4246	B / 8.0	5.33	7.55	14.12 /69	19.21 /77	2.71 /34	2.22	1.30
GR	AI Frank Dividend Value Fd	VALDX	U	(888) 878-3944	U /	-1.93	6.56	11.50 /57	--	--	0.21	1.98
GR	AI Frank Fund (The)	VALUX	B+	(888) 878-3944	B+ / 8.4	-5.20	2.99	12.87 /64	23.63 /89	13.01 /89	0.00	1.65
BA	Alger Fund-Balanced A	ALBAX	D-	(800) 992-3863	E / 0.5	-2.73	-2.40	4.00 /11	6.41 / 8	2.03 /28	1.00	1.31
BA	Alger Fund-Balanced B	ALGBX	D-	(800) 992-3863	E+ / 0.6	-2.93	-2.78	3.24 / 8	5.63 / 5	1.27 /22	0.24	2.06
BA	Alger Fund-Balanced C	ALBCX	D-	(800) 992-3863	E / 0.5	-2.91	-2.77	3.25 / 8	5.61 / 5	1.27 /22	0.26	2.06
BA	Alger Fund-Balanced Instl I	ABLRX	E+	(800) 992-3863	E+ / 0.7	-2.75	-2.50	3.85 /10	5.27 / 4	-1.94 / 8	0.74	1.25
BA	Alger Fund-Balanced Instl R	ABIRX	E+	(800) 992-3863	E / 0.5	-3.17	-3.05	2.98 / 7	4.60 / 3	--	0.27	1.75
GR	Alger Fund-Capital App A	ACAAX	D-	(800) 992-3863	C- / 3.6	-4.28	2.65	16.15 /75	12.41 /45	0.77 /19	0.00	1.63
GR	Alger Fund-Capital App B	ACAPX	D	(800) 992-3863	C- / 3.9	-4.51	2.31	15.35 /73	11.57 /40	--	0.00	2.37
GR	Alger Fund-Capital App C	ALCCX	D	(800) 992-3863	C- / 3.8	-4.41	2.31	15.35 /73	11.63 /40	0.02 /15	0.00	2.37
GR	Alger Fund-Capital App Instl I	ALARX	D+	(800) 992-3863	C / 4.9	-4.06	2.64	16.00 /75	12.51 /46	1.12 /21	0.30	1.17
GR	Alger Fund-Capital App Instl R	ACARX	D	(800) 992-3863	C / 4.4	-4.26	2.31	15.03 /72	11.81 /41	--	0.00	1.69
HL	Alger Fund-Health Sciences A	AHSAX	C-	(800) 992-3863	C / 4.7	-5.87	-2.23	5.26 /16	15.83 /63	--	0.00	1.50
HL	Alger Fund-Health Sciences B	AHSBX	C-	(800) 992-3863	C / 4.5	-6.05	-2.67	4.39 /12	14.96 /59	--	0.00	2.25
HL	Alger Fund-Health Sciences C	AHSCX	C-	(800) 992-3863	C / 5.0	-6.05	-2.67	4.39 /12	14.96 /59	--	0.00	2.25
GR	Alger Fund-Large Cap Gr Instl I	ALGRX	D-	(800) 992-3863	D+ / 2.4	-4.44	-3.27	6.59 /24	9.22 /22	-1.52 /10	0.06	1.08
GR	Alger Fund-Large Cap Gr Instl R	ALGIX	D-	(800) 992-3863	D / 2.1	-4.57	-3.54	6.37 /22	8.80 /20	--	0.00	1.57
GR	Alger Fund-Large Cap Growth A	ALGAX	E+	(800) 992-3863	D / 1.6	-4.39	-3.09	7.03 /26	9.59 /25	-0.93 /12	0.00	1.37
GR	Alger Fund-Large Cap Growth B	AFGPX	E+	(800) 992-3863	D / 1.8	-4.57	-3.44	6.17 /21	8.79 /20	-1.67 / 9	0.00	2.12
GR	Alger Fund-Large Cap Growth C	ALGCX	E+	(800) 992-3863	D / 1.7	-4.48	-3.44	6.28 /22	8.79 /20	-1.67 / 9	0.00	2.12
MC	Alger Fund-MidCap Gr A	AMGAX	D-	(800) 992-3863	C- / 3.9	-8.18	0.12	8.98 /40	13.82 /53	3.78 /44	0.00	1.36
MC	Alger Fund-MidCap Gr B	AMCGX	D-	(800) 992-3863	C / 4.3	-8.41	-0.25	8.07 /33	12.98 /49	3.01 /37	0.00	2.11
MC	Alger Fund-MidCap Gr C	AMGCX	D-	(800) 992-3863	C- / 4.0	-8.43	-0.38	8.09 /33	12.95 /49	2.99 /37	0.00	2.11
MC	Alger Fund-MidCap Gr Instl I	ALMRX	D	(800) 992-3863	C / 5.1	-7.67	0.06	9.73 /45	13.73 /52	4.17 /47	0.00	1.10
MC	Alger Fund-MidCap Gr Instl R	AGIRX	D	(800) 992-3863	C / 4.8	-7.80	-0.18	9.22 /41	13.17 /50	--	0.00	1.60
SC	Alger Fund-Small Cap A	ALSAX	C+	(800) 992-3863	B / 8.1	-3.54	9.51	23.25 /86	21.98 /85	6.08 /62	0.00	1.62
SC	Alger Fund-Small Cap B	ALSCX	C+	(800) 992-3863	B / 8.2	-3.85	8.93	22.27 /85	20.99 /82	5.30 /56	0.00	2.36
SC	Alger Fund-Small Cap C	AGSCX	C+	(800) 992-3863	B / 8.1	-3.68	9.13	22.49 /85	21.06 /83	5.29 /56	0.00	2.37
SC	Alger Fund-Small Cap Instl I	ALSRX	B-	(800) 992-3863	B+ / 8.4	-3.83	8.82	22.69 /85	21.73 /84	6.74 /65	0.00	1.20
SC	Alger Fund-Small Cap Instl R	ASIRX	C+	(800) 992-3863	B+ / 8.3	-3.93	8.59	22.10 /84	21.21 /83	--	0.00	1.68
MC	Alger Fund-SmallCap and MidCap A	ALMAX	C+	(800) 992-3863	B / 8.0	-3.18	8.08	25.64 /89	21.12 /83	--	0.00	1.50
MC	Alger Fund-SmallCap and MidCap B	ALMBX	C+	(800) 992-3863	B / 8.1	-3.36	7.73	24.77 /88	20.29 /80	--	0.00	2.25
MC	Alger Fund-SmallCap and MidCap C	ALMCX	C+	(800) 992-3863	B / 8.1	-3.28	7.72	24.86 /88	20.32 /80	--	0.00	2.25
GR	Alger Fund-Social Resp Gr Instl-I	ASRGX	D+	(800) 992-3863	C / 4.8	-3.97	2.54	16.33 /75	12.25 /44	-1.64 / 9	0.00	1.25

● Denotes fund is closed to new investors

* Denotes fund is included in Section II

RISK Risk Rating/Pts	3 Year Standard Deviation	Beta	NET ASSETS NAV As of 6/30/06	Total $(Mil)	ASSET Cash %	Stocks %	Bonds %	Other %	Portfolio Turnover Ratio	BULL/BEAR Last Bull Market Return	Last Bear Market Return	FUND MANAGER Manager Quality Pct	Manager Tenure (Years)	MINIMUMS Initial Purch. $	Additional Purch. $	LOADS Front End Load	Back End Load
C /5.4	13.1	0.85	12.81	57	2	97	0	1	52.0	100.9	-9.4	58	2	1,000	50	0.0	1.0
C /4.9	14.5	0.95	29.28	1,164	2	97	0	1	41.0	92.7	-11.8	23	8	1,000	50	5.5	0.0
C /4.7	14.5	0.95	26.82	111	2	97	0	1	41.0	88.1	-11.9	18	2	1,000	50	0.0	5.0
C /4.7	14.5	0.95	26.80	32	2	97	0	1	41.0	88.1	-11.9	18	7	1,000	50	0.0	1.0
C /4.6	14.5	0.95	29.95	157	2	97	0	1	41.0	95.9	-11.6	27	N/A	10,000,000	0	0.0	0.0
C- /3.1	17.3	1.84	26.03	291	1	98	0	1	107.0	66.8	-13.6	2	N/A	1,000	50	5.5	0.0
C- /3.0	17.4	1.85	25.19	70	1	98	0	1	107.0	63.0	-13.8	1	N/A	1,000	50	0.0	5.0
C- /3.0	17.4	1.85	24.52	23	1	98	0	1	107.0	62.9	-13.8	1	N/A	1,000	50	0.0	1.0
C- /3.3	17.4	1.84	27.22	N/A	1	98	0	1	107.0	70.7	-13.5	3	N/A	1,000	50	0.0	0.0
C- /3.1	17.4	1.85	25.78	666	1	98	0	1	107.0	66.0	-13.7	2	N/A	1,000	50	0.0	0.0
U /	N/A	N/A	14.25	61	5	94	0	1	15.0	N/A	N/A	N/A	3	1,000	50	5.5	0.0
U /	N/A	N/A	14.61	166	7	92	0	1	20.0	N/A	N/A	N/A	3	1,000	50	5.5	0.0
U /	N/A	N/A	14.35	35	7	92	0	1	20.0	N/A	N/A	N/A	3	1,000	50	0.0	1.0
U /	N/A	N/A	14.76	25	7	92	0	1	20.0	N/A	N/A	N/A	3	10,000,000	0	0.0	0.0
B /8.3	9.1	0.74	14.55	154	1	98	0	1	37.0	91.0	-4.5	76	3	1,000	50	5.5	0.0
B /8.3	9.1	0.74	14.60	41	1	98	0	1	37.0	86.7	-4.5	69	3	1,000	50	0.0	5.0
B /8.3	9.1	0.74	14.71	11	1	98	0	1	37.0	86.4	-5.0	69	3	1,000	50	0.0	1.0
B /8.3	9.1	0.74	14.67	83	1	98	0	1	37.0	91.3	-4.4	77	3	1,000	50	0.0	0.0
U /	N/A	N/A	12.67	28	2	96	0	2	5.0	N/A	N/A	N/A	N/A	1,000	100	0.0	2.0
C+ /6.2	16.2	1.79	31.37	307	2	96	0	2	15.0	161.4	-10.3	90	8	1,000	100	0.0	2.0
B- /7.7	7.6	1.39	20.32	45	1	63	34	2	218.8	41.2	-4.5	26	N/A	1,000	50	5.3	1.0
B- /7.6	7.6	1.39	19.90	76	1	63	34	2	218.8	37.8	-4.6	20	N/A	1,000	50	0.0	2.0
B- /7.6	7.5	1.39	19.99	24	1	63	34	2	218.8	37.9	-4.7	20	N/A	1,000	50	1.0	2.0
C+ /6.5	7.3	1.31	7.42	2	5	61	33	1	211.3	33.0	-3.1	21	N/A	100,000	0	0.0	0.0
C+ /6.4	7.4	1.34	7.32	N/A	5	61	33	1	211.3	31.2	N/A	16	N/A	100,000	0	0.0	0.0
C /4.9	13.5	1.41	10.07	140	N/A	100	0	N/A	144.6	77.9	-6.2	31	N/A	1,000	50	5.3	2.0
C /4.9	13.6	1.42	9.32	179	N/A	100	0	N/A	144.6	74.0	-6.5	25	N/A	1,000	50	0.0	2.0
C /4.9	13.5	1.41	9.32	33	N/A	100	0	N/A	144.6	74.0	-6.3	26	N/A	1,000	50	1.0	2.0
C /5.1	13.3	1.39	14.41	145	1	98	0	1	148.9	77.4	-6.3	33	N/A	100,000	25	0.0	0.0
C /5.0	13.2	1.38	14.16	4	1	98	0	1	148.9	74.3	N/A	28	N/A	100,000	25	0.0	0.0
C+ /5.9	10.6	0.79	16.20	107	6	93	0	1	127.8	92.7	-2.6	95	N/A	1,000	50	5.3	2.0
C+ /5.8	10.6	0.80	15.69	21	6	93	0	1	127.8	88.2	-2.7	93	N/A	1,000	50	0.0	5.0
C+ /5.8	10.6	0.79	15.69	39	6	93	0	1	127.8	88.3	-2.8	94	N/A	1,000	50	0.0	2.0
C+ /5.7	11.6	1.31	12.71	103	3	96	0	1	249.1	64.6	-9.3	17	5	100,000	25	0.0	0.0
C+ /5.6	11.6	1.31	12.53	5	3	96	0	1	249.1	62.4	N/A	15	5	100,000	0	0.0	0.0
C+ /5.7	11.7	1.32	10.66	172	1	98	0	1	249.2	66.0	-8.9	18	5	1,000	50	5.3	2.0
C+ /5.6	11.6	1.31	9.81	235	1	98	0	1	249.2	62.3	-9.1	15	5	1,000	50	0.0	2.0
C+ /5.6	11.7	1.32	9.81	42	1	98	0	1	249.2	62.3	-9.0	14	5	1,000	50	1.0	2.0
C /4.3	15.7	1.34	8.64	332	2	97	0	1	239.3	96.1	-7.8	3	5	1,000	50	5.3	2.0
C- /4.0	15.6	1.33	7.84	240	2	97	0	1	239.3	91.7	-8.0	2	5	1,000	50	0.0	2.0
C- /4.0	15.6	1.33	7.82	77	2	97	0	1	239.3	91.7	-8.1	2	5	1,000	50	1.0	2.0
C /4.4	15.1	1.29	16.73	1,288	3	96	0	1	237.7	95.4	-8.0	4	5	0	25	0.0	0.0
C /4.3	15.1	1.29	16.43	39	3	96	0	1	237.7	92.4	N/A	3	5	100,000	0	0.0	0.0
C /5.3	15.5	1.02	5.99	179	3	96	0	1	104.3	127.1	-8.9	80	5	1,000	50	5.3	2.0
C /5.2	15.5	1.02	5.49	61	3	96	0	1	104.3	121.9	-9.1	73	5	1,000	50	0.0	2.0
C /5.2	15.5	1.02	5.50	13	3	96	0	1	104.3	122.3	-9.1	74	5	1,000	50	1.0	2.0
C /5.3	15.5	1.02	22.82	111	5	94	0	1	116.2	124.7	-8.6	79	5	100,000	25	0.0	0.0
C /5.2	15.5	1.02	22.49	5	5	94	0	1	116.2	121.6	N/A	76	5	100,000	0	0.0	0.0
C /5.0	15.1	1.30	13.38	27	5	94	0	1	80.5	120.6	-9.0	34	4	1,000	50	5.3	2.0
C /4.9	15.0	1.30	12.96	6	5	94	0	1	80.5	115.7	-9.2	29	4	1,000	50	0.0	2.0
C /4.9	15.1	1.30	12.97	8	5	94	0	1	80.5	115.8	-9.2	29	4	1,000	50	1.0	2.0
C /4.9	13.1	1.37	6.05	2	17	82	0	1	152.6	75.7	-6.3	32	N/A	100,000	0	0.0	0.0

Fund Type	Fund Name	Ticker Symbol	Overall Weiss Investment Rating	Phone	Performance Rating/Pts	3 Mo	6 Mo	1Yr / Pct	3Yr / Pct	5Yr / Pct	Dividend Yield	Expense Ratio
								Total Return % through 6/30/06	Annualized		Incl. in Returns	
GR	Alger Fund-Social Resp Gr Instl-R	ASRRX	D	(800) 992-3863	C / 4.5	-4.03	2.41	15.78 /74	11.70 /40	--	0.00	1.75
AG	Alger Spectra Fund A	SPEAX	C-	(800) 992-3863	C- / 4.0	-3.39	3.50	18.13 /79	12.44 /45	0.69 /19	0.00	2.07
AG	Alger Spectra Fund N	SPECX	D+	(800) 992-3863	C / 4.9	-3.53	3.51	18.03 /79	12.43 /45	0.61 /18	0.00	2.07
AA	Allegiant Aggressive Alloc A	ARAAX	C-	(800) 622-3863	D / 1.9	-1.80	2.17	9.44 /43	9.35 /23	2.16 /29	1.91	0.58
AA	Allegiant Aggressive Alloc B	ARABX	C-	(800) 622-3863	D / 1.7	-1.94	1.81	8.77 /39	8.72 /19	1.55 /24	1.67	1.17
AA	Allegiant Aggressive Alloc C	ARACX	C-	(800) 622-3863	D / 2.2	-1.95	1.81	8.75 /38	8.74 /19	1.55 /24	1.67	1.17
AA	Allegiant Aggressive Alloc Inst	ARAIX	C	(800) 622-3863	C- / 3.0	-1.70	2.26	9.74 /45	9.64 /25	2.41 /31	2.21	0.33
BA	Allegiant Balanced Allocation A	ABLLX	C-	(800) 622-3863	D / 1.8	-1.38	1.72	7.68 /30	8.87 /20	3.22 /39	1.32	1.30
BA	Allegiant Balanced Allocation B	ALOBX	C-	(800) 622-3863	D- / 1.5	-1.64	1.26	6.86 /25	8.08 /15	2.46 /32	0.71	1.99
BA	Allegiant Balanced Allocation C	ABACX	C-	(800) 622-3863	D / 2.0	-1.60	1.32	6.87 /25	8.05 /15	2.43 /31	0.68	1.99
BA	Allegiant Balanced Allocation Inst	ABAIX	C	(800) 622-3863	D+ / 2.9	-1.32	1.78	8.00 /33	9.14 /22	3.45 /41	1.65	1.05
AA	Allegiant Conservative Alloc A	AOAAX	D+	(800) 622-3863	E / 0.4	-0.85	1.00	4.23 /12	5.14 / 4	3.04 /37	2.49	0.55
AA	Allegiant Conservative Alloc B	AOABX	D+	(800) 622-3863	E / 0.3	-1.01	0.66	3.69 / 9	4.54 / 3	--	2.09	1.14
AA	Allegiant Conservative Alloc C	AOACX	C-	(800) 622-3863	E / 0.5	-1.02	0.64	3.67 / 9	4.54 / 3	2.45 /32	2.07	1.14
AA	Allegiant Conservative Alloc Inst	AOAIX	C-	(800) 622-3863	D- / 1.0	-0.78	1.11	4.56 /13	5.45 / 5	3.32 /40	2.92	0.30
FO	Allegiant International Equity A	AMIEX	B-	(800) 622-3863	B / 8.2	-1.28	10.74	26.65 /91	21.26 /83	6.91 /66	1.69	1.62
FO	Allegiant International Equity B	AMINX	B-	(800) 622-3863	B / 8.2	-1.53	10.34	25.85 /90	20.31 /80	6.21 /62	1.03	2.29
FO	Allegiant International Equity C	AIUCX	B	(800) 622-3863	B+ / 8.4	-1.53	10.38	25.84 /90	20.40 /81	6.23 /63	0.87	2.29
FO	Allegiant International Equity Inst	AIEIX	B	(800) 622-3863	B+ / 8.6	-1.26	10.88	27.07 /91	21.49 /84	7.21 /68	1.98	1.37
GR	Allegiant Large Cap Core Eq A	ACQAX	D+	(800) 622-3863	D / 2.1	-3.19	1.15	8.16 /34	9.77 /26	2.13 /28	0.12	1.22
GR	Allegiant Large Cap Core Eq B	ARCEX	C-	(800) 622-3863	D+ / 2.4	-3.39	0.78	7.40 /29	9.01 /21	1.42 /23	0.00	1.89
GR	Allegiant Large Cap Core Eq C	ACQCX	C-	(800) 622-3863	D+ / 2.5	-3.39	0.86	7.40 /29	9.02 /21	1.42 /23	0.00	1.89
GR	Allegiant Large Cap Core Eq Inst	ACFIX	C	(800) 622-3863	C- / 3.3	-3.18	1.28	8.43 /36	10.05 /28	2.39 /31	0.37	0.97
GR	Allegiant Large Cap Growth A	AEQRX	E+	(800) 622-3863	E / 0.4	-4.08	-1.33	7.67 /30	6.12 / 7	-2.60 / 6	0.59	1.23
GR	Allegiant Large Cap Growth B	AREGX	E+	(800) 622-3863	E / 0.3	-4.23	-1.66	6.95 /26	5.40 / 5	-3.27 / 5	0.00	1.90
GR	Allegiant Large Cap Growth C	AEWCX	D-	(800) 622-3863	E / 0.5	-4.27	-1.71	6.94 /26	5.38 / 5	-3.26 / 5	0.00	1.90
GR	Allegiant Large Cap Growth Inst	AEQIX	D-	(800) 622-3863	D- / 1.0	-4.02	-1.21	7.95 /32	6.40 / 8	-2.34 / 7	0.93	0.98
GR	Allegiant Large Cap Value A	AEIRX	B-	(800) 622-3863	C+ / 5.8	-0.18	5.37	14.67 /71	15.15 /60	6.24 /63	0.86	1.22
GR	Allegiant Large Cap Value B	AEINX	B-	(800) 622-3863	C+ / 5.6	-0.34	5.05	13.90 /68	14.39 /56	5.49 /58	0.27	1.89
GR	Allegiant Large Cap Value C	ALVCX	B	(800) 622-3863	C+ / 6.1	-0.34	5.01	13.89 /68	14.36 /56	5.48 /58	0.25	1.89
GR	Allegiant Large Cap Value Inst	AEIIX	B	(800) 622-3863	C+ / 6.7	-0.06	5.53	14.96 /72	15.46 /61	6.52 /64	1.13	0.97
MC	Allegiant Mid Cap Growth A	AMGFX	E	(800) 622-3863	D / 2.1	-5.52	1.52	8.55 /37	10.06 /28	-1.36 /10	0.00	1.21
MC	Allegiant Mid Cap Growth B	AQIBX	E	(800) 622-3863	D / 1.9	-5.70	1.19	7.78 /31	9.34 /23	-2.05 / 8	0.00	1.88
MC	Allegiant Mid Cap Growth C	ADWCX	E	(800) 622-3863	D+ / 2.5	-5.77	1.17	7.66 /30	9.34 /23	-2.08 / 8	0.00	1.88
MC	Allegiant Mid Cap Growth Inst	AMCIX	E+	(800) 622-3863	C- / 3.4	-5.40	1.72	8.90 /39	10.34 /30	-1.13 /11	0.00	0.96
MC	Allegiant Mid Cap Value A	ARVAX	C+	(800) 622-3863	B / 8.1	-0.80	7.19	18.31 /80	21.43 /84	--	0.53	1.28
MC	Allegiant Mid Cap Value B	ARVBX	A+	(800) 622-3863	B / 7.9	-0.96	6.80	17.50 /78	20.60 /81	--	0.00	1.95
MC	Allegiant Mid Cap Value C	ARVCX	A+	(800) 622-3863	B / 8.2	-1.03	6.77	17.41 /78	20.56 /81	--	0.00	1.95
MC	Allegiant Mid Cap Value Inst	ARVIX	C+	(800) 622-3863	B+ / 8.5	-0.80	7.27	18.53 /80	21.70 /84	--	0.75	1.03
SC	Allegiant Multi-Factor Sm Cap Val A	AMRRX	D	(800) 622-3863	C+ / 6.3	-4.18	9.21	10.99 /53	17.31 /69	11.25 /85	0.00	1.46
SC	Allegiant Multi-Factor Sm Cap Val B	ASMVX	D	(800) 622-3863	C+ / 6.2	-4.37	8.78	10.25 /48	16.51 /66	10.46 /82	0.00	2.13
SC	Allegiant Multi-Factor Sm Cap Val C	ASVCX	D	(800) 622-3863	C+ / 6.7	-4.38	8.74	10.21 /48	16.50 /66	10.48 /82	0.00	2.13
SC	Allegiant Multi-Factor Sm Cap Val I	AMRIX	D+	(800) 622-3863	B- / 7.1	-4.16	9.28	11.23 /55	17.60 /71	11.51 /85	0.16	1.21
GR	Allegiant S&P 500 Index A	AEXAX	C	(800) 622-3863	C- / 3.2	-1.64	2.40	8.02 /33	10.57 /31	1.88 /26	1.51	0.59
GR	Allegiant S&P 500 Index B	AEXBX	C-	(800) 622-3863	D+ / 2.3	-1.84	2.04	7.18 /27	9.76 /26	1.08 /21	0.83	1.34
GR	Allegiant S&P 500 Index C	AEXCX	C	(800) 622-3863	C- / 3.0	-1.83	2.05	7.12 /27	9.75 /25	1.08 /21	0.79	1.34
GR	Allegiant S&P 500 Index Inst	AQDIX	C+	(800) 622-3863	C- / 3.9	-1.58	2.55	8.26 /35	10.85 /34	2.12 /28	1.78	0.34
SC	Allegiant Small Cap Core I	ACRIX	U	(800) 622-3863	U /	-3.71	8.26	11.56 /57	--	--	0.00	1.21
SC	Allegiant Small Cap Growth A	ASMGX	E-	(800) 622-3863	E+ / 0.9	-6.14	4.75	9.34 /42	7.55 /13	-4.86 / 3	0.00	1.49
SC	Allegiant Small Cap Growth B	ASGRX	E-	(800) 622-3863	E+ / 0.8	-6.29	4.56	8.63 /38	6.84 /10	-5.50 / 2	0.00	2.16
SC	Allegiant Small Cap Growth C	ASGCX	E-	(800) 622-3863	D- / 1.3	-6.18	4.55	8.74 /38	6.83 /10	-5.49 / 2	0.00	2.16
SC	Allegiant Small Cap Growth Inst	ASMIX	E-	(800) 622-3863	D / 1.7	-6.01	4.98	9.73 /45	7.86 /14	-4.62 / 3	0.00	1.24

99 Pct = Best
0 Pct = Worst

● Denotes fund is closed to new investors
* Denotes fund is included in Section II

www.WeissRatings.com

RISK			NET ASSETS		ASSET					BULL / BEAR		FUND MANAGER		MINIMUMS		LOADS	
	3 Year		NAV						Portfolio	Last Bull	Last Bear	Manager	Manager	Initial	Additional	Front	Back
Risk Rating/Pts	Standard Deviation	Beta	As of 6/30/06	Total $(Mil)	Cash %	Stocks %	Bonds %	Other %	Turnover Ratio	Market Return	Market Return	Quality Pct	Tenure (Years)	Purch. $	Purch. $	End Load	End Load
C / 4.8	13.1	1.38	5.95	N/A	17	82	0	1	152.6	73.3	N/A	28	N/A	100,000	0	0.0	0.0
C+ / 6.6	13.5	1.39	7.69	5	5	94	0	1	247.7	76.5	-6.4	32	N/A	1,000	50	5.3	2.0
C / 5.0	13.5	1.39	7.66	187	5	94	0	1	247.7	76.1	-6.4	32	N/A	1,000	50	0.0	2.0
B / 8.9	6.5	1.24	10.35	1	3	79	17	1	14.0	54.7	-7.8	62	N/A	500	0	4.8	1.0
B / 8.9	6.5	1.23	10.13	2	3	79	17	1	14.0	51.7	-8.0	56	N/A	500	0	0.0	5.0
B / 8.9	6.5	1.23	10.15	1	3	79	17	1	14.0	51.9	-8.0	56	N/A	500	0	0.0	1.0
B / 8.9	6.6	1.24	10.41	7	3	79	17	1	14.0	55.8	-7.7	64	N/A	0	0	0.0	0.0
B+ / 9.3	5.6	1.11	10.62	14	N/A	67	33	N/A	114.0	49.2	-5.7	64	N/A	500	0	4.8	1.0
B+ / 9.3	5.6	1.10	10.61	6	N/A	67	33	N/A	114.0	45.9	-5.7	56	N/A	500	0	0.0	5.0
B+ / 9.3	5.5	1.10	10.56	1	N/A	67	33	N/A	114.0	45.8	-5.8	56	N/A	500	0	0.0	1.0
B+ / 9.3	5.5	1.10	10.61	122	N/A	67	33	N/A	114.0	50.5	-5.5	67	N/A	0	0	0.0	0.0
B+ / 9.8	3.4	0.70	10.34	1	3	39	57	1	9.0	28.0	-2.3	45	N/A	500	0	4.8	1.0
B+ / 9.9	3.4	0.69	10.29	1	3	39	57	1	9.0	25.8	-2.5	39	N/A	500	0	0.0	5.0
B+ / 9.9	3.4	0.69	10.30	1	3	39	57	1	9.0	25.9	-2.5	39	N/A	500	0	0.0	1.0
B+ / 9.9	3.4	0.69	10.35	7	3	39	57	1	9.0	29.2	-2.3	50	N/A	0	0	0.0	0.0
C+ / 5.8	11.4	1.10	13.92	14	10	89	0	1	107.0	114.5	-7.7	16	N/A	500	0	5.5	2.0
C+ / 5.8	11.5	1.11	13.55	1	10	89	0	1	107.0	110.2	-7.8	12	N/A	500	0	0.0	5.0
C+ / 5.8	11.4	1.11	13.51	1	10	89	0	1	107.0	110.5	-7.8	12	N/A	500	0	0.0	1.0
C+ / 5.8	11.4	1.10	14.06	264	10	89	0	1	107.0	116.6	-7.6	17	N/A	0	0	0.0	2.0
B / 8.2	8.3	1.05	12.16	6	0	99	0	1	27.0	59.1	-10.5	36	9	500	0	5.5	1.0
B / 8.2	8.3	1.05	11.67	3	0	99	0	1	27.0	55.8	-10.7	30	9	500	0	0.0	1.0
B / 8.2	8.3	1.05	11.67	N/A	0	99	0	1	27.0	55.6	-10.7	30	9	500	0	0.0	1.0
B / 8.2	8.3	1.05	12.30	226	0	99	0	1	27.0	60.4	-10.5	38	9	0	0	0.0	0.0
B- / 7.0	8.6	1.04	19.28	116	1	98	0	1	36.0	41.3	-9.7	14	17	500	0	5.5	1.0
C+ / 6.9	8.6	1.04	18.35	8	1	98	0	1	36.0	38.3	-9.9	11	17	500	0	0.0	5.0
C+ / 6.9	8.6	1.04	18.37	1	1	98	0	1	36.0	38.4	-9.9	11	17	500	0	0.0	1.0
B- / 7.0	8.6	1.04	19.57	445	1	98	0	1	36.0	42.4	-9.7	15	17	0	0	0.0	0.0
B / 8.1	8.1	0.96	18.75	54	0	99	0	1	20.0	80.1	-9.0	89	N/A	500	0	5.5	1.0
B / 8.2	8.1	0.96	18.63	9	0	99	0	1	20.0	76.3	-9.2	85	N/A	500	0	0.0	5.0
B / 8.2	8.1	0.96	18.55	1	0	99	0	1	20.0	76.3	-9.2	86	N/A	500	0	0.0	1.0
B / 8.1	8.1	0.96	18.82	578	0	99	0	1	20.0	81.5	-8.9	90	N/A	0	0	0.0	0.0
C- / 3.5	14.2	1.23	7.36	17	3	96	0	1	42.0	68.9	-8.6	1	18	500	0	5.5	1.0
C- / 3.4	14.2	1.23	5.96	1	3	96	0	1	42.0	64.9	-8.5	1	18	500	0	0.0	5.0
C- / 3.4	14.2	1.23	6.04	N/A	3	96	0	1	42.0	65.1	-8.6	1	18	500	0	0.0	1.0
C- / 3.5	14.2	1.23	7.71	16	3	96	0	1	42.0	69.9	-8.5	2	18	0	0	0.0	0.0
C / 4.5	9.8	0.86	13.57	11	N/A	N/A	0	N/A	23.0	110.6	-6.1	93	N/A	500	0	5.5	1.0
B / 8.2	9.8	0.86	13.35	5	N/A	N/A	0	N/A	23.0	N/A	N/A	91	N/A	500	0	0.0	5.0
B / 8.2	9.8	0.86	13.41	2	N/A	N/A	0	N/A	23.0	N/A	N/A	90	N/A	500	0	0.0	1.0
C / 4.6	9.8	0.86	13.72	97	N/A	N/A	0	N/A	23.0	112.5	-6.2	93	N/A	0	0	0.0	0.0
D+ / 2.9	13.3	0.87	19.93	195	1	98	0	1	46.0	103.7	-9.2	64	N/A	500	0	5.5	2.0
D+ / 2.7	13.3	0.87	18.84	16	1	98	0	1	46.0	99.2	-9.5	56	N/A	500	0	0.0	5.0
D+ / 2.7	13.2	0.87	18.79	19	1	98	0	1	46.0	99.4	-9.5	57	N/A	500	0	0.0	1.0
C- / 3.2	13.3	0.87	20.97	623	1	98	0	1	46.0	105.3	-9.2	67	N/A	0	0	0.0	2.0
B / 8.7	7.7	1.00	10.89	25	2	97	0	1	4.0	61.6	-9.8	48	N/A	500	0	2.5	0.5
B / 8.7	7.7	1.00	10.80	4	2	97	0	1	4.0	57.9	-10.1	39	N/A	500	0	0.0	5.0
B / 8.7	7.7	1.00	10.82	2	2	97	0	1	4.0	58.1	-10.1	39	N/A	500	0	0.0	1.0
B / 8.7	7.6	0.99	10.92	171	2	97	0	1	4.0	63.0	-9.8	52	N/A	0	0	0.0	0.0
U /	N/A	N/A	12.45	223	3	96	0	1	41.0	N/A	N/A	N/A	2	0	0	0.0	2.0
D- / 1.5	20.0	1.29	9.48	17	1	98	0	1	50.0	64.2	-12.3	0	N/A	500	0	5.5	2.0
D- / 1.5	20.0	1.29	8.94	2	1	98	0	1	50.0	61.0	-12.6	0	N/A	500	0	0.0	5.0
D- / 1.5	20.0	1.29	8.96	N/A	1	98	0	1	50.0	60.8	-12.6	0	N/A	500	0	0.0	1.0
D- / 1.5	20.0	1.29	9.70	21	1	98	0	1	50.0	65.8	-12.4	0	N/A	0	0	0.0	2.0

Fund Type	Fund Name	Ticker Symbol	Overall Weiss Investment Rating	Phone	Perfor-mance Rating/Pts	3 Mo	6 Mo	1Yr / Pct	Annualized 3Yr / Pct	Annualized 5Yr / Pct	Dividend Yield	Expense Ratio
BA	AllianceBernstein Bal Wlth Stgy A	ABWAX	U	(800) 221-5672	U /	-1.71	2.92	10.45 /50	--	--	1.77	1.13
BA	AllianceBernstein Bal Wlth Stgy Adv	ABWYX	U	(800) 221-5672	U /	-1.63	3.06	10.83 /52	--	--	2.12	0.84
BA	AllianceBernstein Bal Wlth Stgy B	ABWBX	U	(800) 221-5672	U /	-1.88	2.53	9.67 /45	--	--	1.20	1.84
BA	AllianceBernstein Bal Wlth Stgy C	ABWCX	U	(800) 221-5672	U /	-1.88	2.53	9.76 /45	--	--	1.20	1.83
BA	AllianceBernstein Balanced Shs A	CABNX	D+	(800) 221-5672	D- / 1.4	-1.36	0.76	4.30 /12	8.30 /17	4.69 /52	1.61	1.04
BA	AllianceBernstein Balanced Shs Adv	CBSYX	C-	(800) 221-5672	D+ / 2.3	-1.28	0.96	4.59 /13	8.63 /19	5.00 /54	1.96	0.74
BA	AllianceBernstein Balanced Shs B	CABBX	D+	(800) 221-5672	D- / 1.1	-1.56	0.39	3.44 / 9	7.51 /12	3.92 /45	1.05	1.76
BA	AllianceBernstein Balanced Shs C	CBACX	D+	(800) 221-5672	D- / 1.5	-1.55	0.39	3.49 / 9	7.50 /12	3.93 /45	1.04	1.76
GR	AllianceBernstein Foc Gr & Inc A	ADGAX	D-	(800) 221-5672	D- / 1.0	-4.11	-1.52	1.60 / 3	8.03 /15	1.83 /26	0.00	1.27
GR	AllianceBernstein Foc Gr & Inc B	ADGBX	D-	(800) 221-5672	E+ / 0.8	-4.27	-1.87	0.86 / 2	7.26 /11	1.09 /21	0.00	2.00
GR	AllianceBernstein Foc Gr & Inc C	ADGCX	D-	(800) 221-5672	D- / 1.1	-4.27	-1.94	0.86 / 2	7.26 /11	1.11 /21	0.00	1.99
HL	AllianceBernstein Glb Hlth Care A	AHLAX	D-	(800) 221-5672	D- / 1.1	-4.44	-5.20	5.89 /20	8.16 /16	3.22 /39	0.00	1.89
HL	AllianceBernstein Glb Hlth Care Adv	AHLDX	D+	(800) 221-5672	D / 1.9	-4.39	-5.06	6.21 /22	8.46 /17	3.53 /42	0.00	1.59
HL	AllianceBernstein Glb Hlth Care B	AHLBX	E+	(800) 221-5672	E+ / 0.9	-4.59	-5.53	5.14 /16	7.35 /12	2.45 /32	0.00	2.63
HL	AllianceBernstein Glb Hlth Care C	AHLCX	D-	(800) 221-5672	D- / 1.2	-4.66	-5.52	5.13 /16	7.37 /12	2.48 /32	0.00	2.61
GL	AllianceBernstein Glb Res Gr A	ABZAX	B-	(800) 221-5672	C+ / 6.6	-3.35	3.53	19.24 /81	17.58 /71	--	0.00	1.50
GL	AllianceBernstein Glb Res Gr Adv	ABZYX	B+	(800) 221-5672	B- / 7.2	-3.32	3.68	19.61 /81	17.93 /72	--	0.00	1.20
GL	AllianceBernstein Glb Res Gr B	ABZBX	B-	(800) 221-5672	C+ / 6.3	-3.56	3.17	18.44 /80	16.74 /67	--	0.00	2.20
GL	AllianceBernstein Glb Res Gr C	ABZCX	B-	(800) 221-5672	C+ / 6.7	-3.50	3.17	18.44 /80	16.74 /67	--	0.00	2.20
TC	AllianceBernstein Glb Tech A	ALTFX	E-	(800) 221-5672	D- / 1.0	-9.15	-4.71	4.49 /13	8.70 /19	-5.91 / 2	0.00	1.83
TC	AllianceBernstein Glb Tech Adv	ATEYX	E-	(800) 221-5672	D / 1.9	-9.09	-4.59	4.77 /14	9.03 /21	-5.63 / 2	0.00	1.53
TC	AllianceBernstein Glb Tech B	ATEBX	E-	(800) 221-5672	E+ / 0.8	-9.33	-5.09	3.67 / 9	7.86 /14	-6.63 / 1	0.00	2.60
TC	AllianceBernstein Glb Tech C	ATECX	E-	(800) 221-5672	D- / 1.2	-9.30	-5.06	3.73 /10	7.92 /15	-6.60 / 1	0.00	2.56
GL	AllianceBernstein Global Value A	ABAGX	A	(800) 221-5672	B / 8.1	-0.13	9.31	23.56 /87	20.51 /81	10.46 /82	0.87	1.45
GL	AllianceBernstein Global Value Adv	ABGYX	A+	(800) 221-5672	B+ / 8.5	0.00	9.51	23.95 /87	20.89 /82	10.77 /83	1.13	1.14
GL	AllianceBernstein Global Value B	ABBGX	A-	(800) 221-5672	B / 7.9	-0.27	8.90	22.71 /85	19.64 /78	9.68 /79	0.43	2.19
GL	AllianceBernstein Global Value C	ABCGX	A	(800) 221-5672	B / 8.2	-0.27	8.88	22.68 /85	19.69 /78	9.71 /79	0.43	2.16
GL	AllianceBernstein Global Value I	AGVIX	U	(800) 221-5672	U /	0.00	9.54	24.01 /87	--	--	1.19	1.20
★ GI	AllianceBernstein Gr & Inc A	CABDX	D+	(800) 221-5672	D+ / 2.6	-2.26	1.30	5.97 /20	10.70 /33	1.71 /25	0.76	1.06
GI	AllianceBernstein Gr & Inc Adv	CBBYX	C-	(800) 221-5672	C- / 3.8	-2.01	1.30	6.13 /21	11.10 /36	1.99 /27	0.97	0.75
GI	AllianceBernstein Gr & Inc B	CBBDX	D+	(800) 221-5672	D / 2.2	-2.56	0.53	4.75 /14	9.85 /26	0.90 /20	0.34	1.80
GI	AllianceBernstein Gr & Inc C	CBBCX	C-	(800) 221-5672	D+ / 2.7	-2.56	0.53	5.02 /15	9.82 /26	0.90 /20	0.34	1.79
GR	AllianceBernstein Growth Fund A	AGRFX	E	(800) 221-5672	D- / 1.2	-10.86	-10.27	0.21 / 2	10.45 /30	0.13 /16	0.00	1.60
GR	AllianceBernstein Growth Fund Adv	AGRYX	E	(800) 221-5672	D / 2.1	-10.80	-10.13	0.52 / 2	10.79 /34	0.42 /17	0.00	1.30
GR	AllianceBernstein Growth Fund B	AGBBX	E-	(800) 221-5672	D- / 1.0	-11.03	-10.59	-0.55 / 1	9.62 /25	-0.62 /13	0.00	2.34
GR	AllianceBernstein Growth Fund C	AGRCX	E	(800) 221-5672	D- / 1.3	-11.04	-10.60	-0.51 / 1	9.65 /25	-0.60 /13	0.00	2.31
FO	AllianceBernstein Grtr Chna 97 A	GCHAX	C+	(800) 221-5672	A / 9.5	3.26	23.91	28.93 /94	27.21 /93	12.06 /87	0.38	2.29
FO	AllianceBernstein Grtr Chna 97 Adv	GCHYX	C+	(800) 221-5672	A+ / 9.6	3.26	24.08	29.28 /94	27.59 /94	12.41 /87	0.61	1.97
FO	AllianceBernstein Grtr Chna 97 B	GCHBX	C+	(800) 221-5672	A / 9.4	3.01	23.50	28.06 /93	26.26 /92	11.27 /85	0.00	3.01
FO	AllianceBernstein Grtr Chna 97 C	GCHCX	C+	(800) 221-5672	A / 9.5	3.09	23.55	28.13 /93	26.29 /92	11.23 /84	0.00	2.99
FO	AllianceBernstein Intl Gr A	AWPAX	B+	(800) 221-5672	A- / 9.2	-3.48	6.75	25.11 /89	27.29 /93	14.56 /91	0.51	1.47
FO	AllianceBernstein Intl Gr Adv	AWPYX	A-	(800) 221-5672	A / 9.4	-3.45	6.89	25.48 /89	27.64 /94	14.91 /92	0.72	1.18
FO	AllianceBernstein Intl Gr B	AWPBX	B+	(800) 221-5672	A- / 9.1	-3.63	6.32	24.28 /88	26.30 /92	13.68 /90	0.07	2.22
FO	AllianceBernstein Intl Gr C	AWPCX	B+	(800) 221-5672	A- / 9.2	-3.63	6.38	24.34 /88	26.35 /93	13.71 /90	0.07	2.19
FO	AllianceBernstein Intl Ptf A	AIZAX	U	(800) 221-5672	U /	-1.40	9.02	27.29 /92	--	--	1.08	1.62
FO	AllianceBernstein Intl Res Gr A	AIPAX	B	(800) 221-5672	B / 8.2	-1.62	8.80	29.50 /94	20.31 /80	7.52 /69	0.00	1.65
FO	AllianceBernstein Intl Res Gr Adv	AIPYX	B	(800) 221-5672	B+ / 8.6	-1.51	8.95	29.91 /94	20.65 /82	7.85 /71	0.00	1.35
FO	AllianceBernstein Intl Res Gr B	AIPBX	B-	(800) 221-5672	B / 8.1	-1.80	8.42	28.57 /93	19.41 /77	6.74 /65	0.00	2.35
FO	AllianceBernstein Intl Res Gr C	AIPCX	B	(800) 221-5672	B+ / 8.3	-1.80	8.42	28.57 /93	19.41 /77	6.74 /65	0.00	2.35
★ FO	AllianceBernstein Intl Value A	ABIAX	A+	(800) 221-5672	A / 9.4	0.59	13.66	33.85 /96	27.12 /93	17.74 /94	1.04	1.20
FO	AllianceBernstein Intl Value Adv	ABIYX	A+	(800) 221-5672	A / 9.5	0.68	13.88	34.32 /96	27.51 /94	18.15 /95	1.23	0.90
FO	AllianceBernstein Intl Value B	ABIBX	A	(800) 221-5672	A / 9.3	0.40	13.26	32.96 /96	26.23 /92	16.94 /94	0.59	1.90

● Denotes fund is closed to new investors
★ Denotes fund is included in Section II

Risk Rating/Pts	Standard Deviation	Beta	NAV As of 6/30/06	Total $(Mil)	Cash %	Stocks %	Bonds %	Other %	Portfolio Turnover Ratio	Last Bull Market Return	Last Bear Market Return	Manager Quality Pct	Manager Tenure (Years)	Initial Purch. $	Additional Purch. $	Front End Load	Back End Load
U /	N/A	N/A	12.51	864	0	0	99	1	59.0	N/A	N/A	N/A	N/A	2,500	50	4.3	1.0
U /	N/A	N/A	12.53	76	0	0	99	1	59.0	N/A	N/A	N/A	N/A	0	0	0.0	0.0
U /	N/A	N/A	12.46	426	0	0	99	1	59.0	N/A	N/A	N/A	N/A	2,500	50	0.0	4.0
U /	N/A	N/A	12.47	386	0	0	99	1	59.0	N/A	N/A	N/A	N/A	2,500	50	0.0	1.0
B / 8.6	5.3	1.07	16.61	905	0	74	25	1	57.0	47.5	-4.0	60	N/A	2,500	50	4.3	1.0
B / 8.6	5.2	1.07	16.64	112	0	74	25	1	57.0	48.9	-4.0	63	N/A	0	0	0.0	0.0
B / 8.5	5.2	1.07	15.75	489	0	74	25	1	57.0	44.2	-4.2	50	N/A	2,500	50	0.0	4.0
B / 8.5	5.2	1.07	15.82	169	0	74	25	1	57.0	44.2	-4.2	51	N/A	2,500	50	0.0	1.0
B- / 7.4	8.3	0.98	14.25	135	2	97	0	1	152.0	60.0	-7.0	28	7	2,500	50	4.3	0.0
B- / 7.2	8.3	0.98	13.67	124	2	97	0	1	152.0	56.3	-7.1	23	7	2,500	50	0.0	4.0
B- / 7.3	8.3	0.98	13.66	51	2	97	0	1	152.0	56.3	-7.2	23	7	2,500	50	0.0	1.0
C+ / 6.5	9.8	0.66	13.12	46	1	98	0	1	30.0	49.4	-4.9	57	7	2,500	50	4.3	1.0
B / 8.2	9.8	0.65	13.51	14	1	98	0	1	30.0	50.8	-4.8	61	7	0	0	0.0	0.0
C+ / 6.4	9.8	0.66	12.47	78	1	98	0	1	30.0	45.8	-5.0	47	7	2,500	50	0.0	4.0
C+ / 6.4	9.8	0.66	12.49	22	1	98	0	1	30.0	45.9	-5.0	47	7	2,500	50	0.0	1.0
B- / 7.7	10.3	0.92	16.73	50	1	98	0	1	36.0	103.8	-9.9	18	N/A	2,500	50	4.3	1.0
B- / 7.7	10.3	0.92	16.89	68	1	98	0	1	36.0	105.4	-9.8	20	N/A	0	0	0.0	0.0
B- / 7.6	10.3	0.92	16.26	3	1	98	0	1	36.0	99.1	-10.0	14	N/A	2,500	50	0.0	4.0
B- / 7.6	10.3	0.92	16.26	3	1	98	0	1	36.0	99.1	-10.0	14	N/A	2,500	50	0.0	1.0
D / 2.1	16.3	1.74	57.02	928	0	99	0	1	80.0	65.8	-12.6	3	3	2,500	50	4.3	1.0
D / 2.1	16.3	1.74	58.81	49	0	99	0	1	80.0	67.5	-12.5	4	3	0	0	0.0	0.0
D / 2.0	16.3	1.74	51.11	598	0	99	0	1	80.0	61.9	-12.7	2	3	2,500	50	0.0	4.0
D / 2.0	16.3	1.74	51.19	201	0	99	0	1	80.0	62.1	-12.7	3	3	2,500	50	0.0	1.0
B- / 7.6	9.1	0.86	14.91	46	2	97	0	1	25.0	115.8	-6.1	50	5	2,500	50	4.3	1.0
B- / 7.6	9.1	0.86	14.97	183	2	97	0	1	25.0	117.9	-6.1	55	5	0	0	0.0	0.0
B- / 7.6	9.2	0.86	14.69	21	2	97	0	1	25.0	111.0	-6.3	41	5	2,500	50	0.0	4.0
B- / 7.6	9.1	0.86	14.71	13	2	97	0	1	25.0	111.2	-6.4	41	5	2,500	50	0.0	1.0
U /	N/A	N/A	14.93	32	2	97	0	1	25.0	N/A	N/A	N/A	1	10,000,000	0	0.0	0.0
B- / 7.7	7.4	0.91	3.89	2,345	0	99	0	1	63.0	66.8	-8.0	60	8	2,500	50	4.3	1.0
B- / 7.7	7.3	0.90	3.91	185	0	99	0	1	63.0	67.7	-7.9	65	8	0	0	0.0	0.0
B- / 7.7	7.3	0.90	3.80	1,411	0	99	0	1	63.0	62.7	-8.4	50	8	2,500	50	0.0	4.0
B- / 7.7	7.3	0.90	3.81	570	0	99	0	1	63.0	63.1	-8.4	50	8	2,500	50	0.0	1.0
C- / 4.0	14.2	1.55	33.82	961	0	99	0	1	27.0	77.4	-8.4	12	5	2,500	50	4.3	1.0
C- / 4.0	14.2	1.56	34.95	51	0	99	0	1	27.0	79.1	-8.3	13	5	2,500	50	0.0	0.0
C- / 3.9	14.2	1.56	23.30	354	0	99	0	1	27.0	73.3	-8.5	9	5	2,500	50	0.0	4.0
C- / 3.9	14.2	1.55	23.36	159	0	99	0	1	27.0	73.4	-8.5	9	5	2,500	50	0.0	1.0
C- / 3.6	18.8	1.35	16.17	25	5	94	0	1	15.0	132.8	5.9	15	1	2,500	50	4.3	1.0
C- / 3.6	18.9	1.35	16.49	4	5	94	0	1	15.0	135.1	6.0	17	1	0	0	0.0	0.0
C- / 3.6	18.8	1.35	15.40	17	5	94	0	1	15.0	127.3	5.7	12	1	2,500	50	0.0	4.0
C- / 3.6	18.9	1.36	15.37	15	5	94	0	1	15.0	126.8	5.7	12	1	2,500	50	0.0	1.0
C+ / 5.9	12.1	1.15	16.93	944	5	94	0	1	47.0	159.4	-5.9	47	N/A	2,500	50	4.3	1.0
C+ / 5.9	12.1	1.15	17.07	108	5	94	0	1	47.0	162.6	-5.9	51	N/A	0	0	0.0	0.0
C+ / 5.9	12.2	1.15	15.65	110	5	94	0	1	47.0	153.2	-6.0	37	N/A	2,500	50	0.0	4.0
C+ / 5.9	12.1	1.15	15.67	210	5	94	0	1	47.0	153.4	-6.0	38	N/A	2,500	50	0.0	1.0
U /	N/A	N/A	26.10	31	1	98	0	1	61.0	N/A	N/A	N/A	N/A	2,500	50	4.3	1.0
C+ / 5.9	11.4	1.08	12.73	111	2	97	0	1	40.0	112.3	-12.5	14	N/A	2,500	50	4.3	1.0
C+ / 6.0	11.4	1.07	13.03	54	2	97	0	1	40.0	114.2	-12.4	16	N/A	0	0	0.0	0.0
C+ / 5.9	11.4	1.08	11.97	76	2	97	0	1	40.0	107.5	-12.6	11	N/A	2,500	50	0.0	4.0
C+ / 5.9	11.4	1.08	11.97	31	2	97	0	1	40.0	107.3	-12.6	11	N/A	2,500	50	0.0	1.0
C+ / 6.8	10.7	1.00	20.30	2,107	4	95	0	1	26.0	155.8	-4.6	77	6	2,500	50	4.3	1.0
C+ / 6.8	10.8	1.01	20.59	1,171	4	95	0	1	26.0	158.2	-4.5	80	6	0	0	0.0	0.0
C+ / 6.7	10.7	1.00	19.99	247	4	95	0	1	26.0	150.1	-4.8	71	6	2,500	50	0.0	4.0

					PERFORMANCE							
	99 Pct = Best		Overall					Total Return % through 6/30/06			Incl. in Returns	
	0 Pct = Worst		Weiss		Perfor-					Annualized		
Fund		Ticker	Investment		mance						Dividend	Expense
Type	Fund Name	Symbol	Rating	Phone	Rating/Pts	3 Mo	6 Mo	1Yr / Pct	3Yr / Pct	5Yr / Pct	Yield	Ratio
FO	AllianceBernstein Intl Value C	ABICX	A+	(800) 221-5672	A / 9.4	0.45	13.26	32.96 /96	26.23 /92	16.97 /94	0.59*	1.90
FO	AllianceBernstein Intl Value I	AIVIX	U	(800) 221-5672	U /	0.69	13.89	34.38 /96	--	--	1.35	0.90
GR	AllianceBernstein Lrg Cap Gr A	APGAX	E	(800) 221-5672	D- / 1.0	-8.10	-7.93	5.85 /19	8.45 /17	-3.52 / 4	0.00	1.73
GR	AllianceBernstein Lrg Cap Gr Adv	APGYX	E+	(800) 221-5672	D / 1.8	-8.02	-7.81	6.16 /21	8.79 /20	-3.23 / 5	0.00	1.37
GR	AllianceBernstein Lrg Cap Gr B	APGBX	E	(800) 221-5672	E+ / 0.8	-8.28	-8.28	5.08 /15	7.65 /13	-4.24 / 3	0.00	2.48
GR	AllianceBernstein Lrg Cap Gr C	APGCX	E+	(800) 221-5672	D- / 1.1	-8.30	-8.30	5.06 /15	7.68 /13	-4.22 / 3	0.00	2.45
MC	AllianceBernstein Mid-Cap Gr A	CHCLX	D	(800) 221-5672	C+ / 6.0	-12.50	-1.10	13.75 /67	17.36 /70	5.21 /56	0.00	1.29
MC	AllianceBernstein Mid-Cap Gr Adv	CHCYX	D+	(800) 221-5672	C+ / 6.8	-12.40	-0.92	14.04 /68	17.56 /70	5.45 /57	0.00	1.07
MC	AllianceBernstein Mid-Cap Gr B	CHCBX	D	(800) 221-5672	C+ / 5.7	-12.65	-1.50	12.75 /63	16.39 /65	4.32 /49	0.00	2.10
MC	AllianceBernstein Mid-Cap Gr C	CHCCX	D	(800) 221-5672	C+ / 6.1	-12.50	-1.32	12.97 /64	16.39 /65	4.36 /49	0.00	2.08
GR	AllianceBernstein Premr Gr Instl A	AIPGX	E+	(800) 221-5672	D- / 1.3	-7.88	-7.72	6.72 /25	9.25 /22	-2.31 / 7	0.00	0.90
GR	AllianceBernstein Premr Gr Instl B	APPGX	E+	(800) 221-5672	D- / 1.3	-8.01	-7.85	6.28 /22	8.89 /20	-2.64 / 6	0.00	1.20
RE	AllianceBernstein Real Est Iv A	AREAX	C+	(800) 221-5672	A / 9.3	-1.94	14.04	22.61 /85	27.60 /94	20.05 /96	0.95	1.35
RE	AllianceBernstein Real Est Iv Adv	ARSYX	C+	(800) 221-5672	A / 9.4	-1.87	14.23	22.95 /86	28.01 /94	20.42 /96	1.27	0.95
RE	AllianceBernstein Real Est Iv B	AREBX	C+	(800) 221-5672	A- / 9.2	-2.10	13.74	21.74 /84	26.69 /93	19.21 /95	0.30	2.05
RE	AllianceBernstein Real Est Iv C	ARECX	C+	(800) 221-5672	A / 9.3	-2.10	13.66	21.76 /84	26.72 /93	19.23 /95	0.30	2.04
RE	AllianceBernstein Real Est Iv Inst	ARIIX	C+	(800) 221-5672	A / 9.4	-1.71	14.28	22.98 /86	28.03 /94	20.14 /96	1.73	0.65
SC	AllianceBernstein Sm/Md Cap Val A	ABASX	B-	(800) 221-5672	B- / 7.5	-0.76	6.49	12.19 /61	19.87 /79	14.23 /91	0.00	1.15
SC	AllianceBernstein Sm/Md Cap Val	ABYSX	B	(800) 221-5672	B / 8.0	-0.70	6.68	12.58 /62	20.19 /80	14.54 /91	0.00	0.85
SC	AllianceBernstein Sm/Md Cap Val B	ABBSX	C+	(800) 221-5672	B- / 7.3	-0.91	6.15	11.43 /56	19.00 /76	13.41 /89	0.00	1.85
SC	AllianceBernstein Sm/Md Cap Val C	ABCSX	B-	(800) 221-5672	B / 7.6	-0.91	6.15	11.43 /56	19.00 /76	13.43 /89	0.00	1.85
SC	AllianceBernstein Sml Cap Gr A	QUASX	C-	(800) 221-5672	C+ / 6.2	-9.44	5.03	15.09 /72	16.65 /66	2.41 /31	0.00	1.82
SC	AllianceBernstein Sml Cap Gr Adv	QUAYX	C-	(800) 221-5672	B- / 7.0	-9.35	5.20	15.43 /73	16.98 /68	2.68 /33	0.00	1.55
SC	AllianceBernstein Sml Cap Gr B	QUABX	D+	(800) 221-5672	C+ / 5.9	-9.60	4.63	14.19 /69	15.72 /62	1.58 /24	0.00	2.60
SC	AllianceBernstein Sml Cap Gr C	QUACX	C-	(800) 221-5672	C+ / 6.3	-9.61	4.61	14.21 /69	15.78 /62	1.62 /24	0.00	2.57
SC	AllianceBernstein Sml Cap Gr I	QUAIX	U	(800) 221-5672	U /	-9.31	5.32	15.82 /74	--	--	0.00	1.08
AA	AllianceBernstein T-M Bal W-S A	AGIAX	D+	(800) 221-5672	D- / 1.2	-1.38	0.95	6.94 /26	7.55 /13	1.43 /23	1.35	1.20
AA	AllianceBernstein T-M Bal W-S B	AGIBX	D+	(800) 221-5672	D- / 1.0	-1.55	0.62	6.19 /21	6.75 / 9	0.67 /18	0.71	1.90
AA	AllianceBernstein T-M Bal W-S C	AGICX	D+	(800) 221-5672	D- / 1.4	-1.55	0.62	6.17 /21	6.74 / 9	0.69 /19	0.71	1.90
GR	AllianceBernstein T-M W-A Stgy A	ATWAX	U	(800) 221-5672	U /	-3.06	1.79	14.14 /69	--	--	0.08	1.50
GR	AllianceBernstein T-M W-A Stgy Adv	ATWYX	U	(800) 221-5672	U /	-2.97	2.01	14.51 /70	--	--	0.25	1.20
GR	AllianceBernstein T-M W-A Stgy B	ATWBX	U	(800) 221-5672	U /	-3.18	1.44	13.35 /66	--	--	0.00	2.20
GR	AllianceBernstein T-M W-A Stgy C	ATWCX	U	(800) 221-5672	U /	-3.18	1.51	13.44 /66	--	--	0.00	2.20
AA	AllianceBernstein T-M W-Presv A	ACIAX	D	(800) 221-5672	E- / 0.2	-0.74	0.83	4.56 /13	4.01 / 2	3.22 /39	1.52	1.20
AA	AllianceBernstein T-M W-Presv B	ACIBX	D	(800) 221-5672	E- / 0.2	-0.90	0.53	3.87 /10	3.26 / 1	2.51 /32	0.82	1.90
AA	AllianceBernstein T-M W-Presv C	ACICX	D	(800) 221-5672	E / 0.3	-0.90	0.53	3.87 /10	3.26 / 1	2.50 /32	0.82	1.90
GR	AllianceBernstein US Large Cap A	ABBAX	D	(800) 221-5672	D / 2.0	-4.06	-1.22	8.86 /39	9.45 /24	--	0.00	1.47
GR	AllianceBernstein US Large Cap Adv	ABBYX	C-	(800) 221-5672	C- / 3.1	-3.95	-0.98	9.20 /41	9.80 /26	--	0.00	1.17
GR	AllianceBernstein US Large Cap B	ABBBX	D	(800) 221-5672	D / 1.7	-4.25	-1.56	8.03 /33	8.68 /19	--	0.00	2.19
GR	AllianceBernstein US Large Cap C	ABBCX	D	(800) 221-5672	D / 2.2	-4.25	-1.56	8.03 /33	8.68 /19	--	0.00	2.17
UT	AllianceBernstein Utility Inc A	AUIAX	B+	(800) 221-5672	B- / 7.1	2.01	5.38	10.42 /50	18.42 /74	4.90 /53	2.33	1.44
UT	AllianceBernstein Utility Inc Adv	AUIYX	A	(800) 221-5672	B / 7.6	2.08	5.51	10.80 /52	18.80 /75	5.21 /56	2.70	1.13
UT	AllianceBernstein Utility Inc B	AUIBX	B	(800) 221-5672	C+ / 6.8	1.90	5.01	9.60 /44	17.58 /71	4.15 /47	1.74	2.15
UT	AllianceBernstein Utility Inc C	AUICX	B+	(800) 221-5672	B- / 7.1	1.84	5.00	9.58 /44	17.59 /71	4.15 /47	1.74	2.15
IN	AllianceBernstein Value A	ABVAX	C+	(800) 221-5672	C / 5.0	0.08	5.39	10.35 /49	13.68 /52	6.89 /66	1.36	1.16
IN	AllianceBernstein Value Adv	ABVYX	B	(800) 221-5672	C+ / 5.9	0.08	5.53	10.60 /51	14.00 /54	7.20 /68	1.67	0.83
IN	AllianceBernstein Value B	ABVBX	C+	(800) 221-5672	C / 4.8	0.08	5.41	10.02 /47	13.03 /49	6.21 /62	0.72	1.82
IN	AllianceBernstein Value C	ABVCX	C+	(800) 221-5672	C / 5.1	-0.15	5.01	9.54 /44	12.87 /48	6.11 /62	0.67	1.86
IN	AllianceBernstein Value I	ABVIX	U	(800) 221-5672	U /	0.15	5.57	10.62 /51	--	--	1.87	0.83
GR	AllianceBernstein Wlt Ap Stgy A	AWAAX	U	(800) 221-5672	U /	-2.70	4.23	16.23 /75	--	--	0.36	1.33
GR	AllianceBernstein Wlt Ap Stgy Adv	AWAYX	U	(800) 221-5672	U /	-2.62	4.37	16.60 /76	--	--	0.57	1.02
GR	AllianceBernstein Wlt Ap Stgy B	AWABX	U	(800) 221-5672	U /	-2.93	3.81	15.42 /73	--	--	0.00	2.04

● Denotes fund is closed to new investors
* Denotes fund is included in Section II

RISK			NET ASSETS		ASSET					BULL / BEAR		FUND MANAGER		MINIMUMS		LOADS	
	3 Year		NAV						Portfolio	Last Bull	Last Bear	Manager	Manager	Initial	Additional	Front	Back
Risk	Standard		As of	Total	Cash	Stocks	Bonds	Other	Turnover	Market	Market	Quality	Tenure	Purch.	Purch.	End	End
Rating/Pts	Deviation	Beta	6/30/06	$(Mil)	%	%	%	%	Ratio	Return	Return	Pct	(Years)	$	$	Load	Load
C+ / 6.7	10.7	1.00	19.99	515	4	95	0	1	26.0	150.1	-4.8	71	6	2,500	50	0.0	1.0
U /	N/A	N/A	20.33	378	4	95	0	1	26.0	N/A	N/A	N/A	1	10,000,000	0	0.0	0.0
C / 5.4	11.7	1.31	19.17	1,176	0	99	0	1	56.0	59.3	-13.3	13	N/A	2,500	50	4.3	1.0
C / 5.5	11.7	1.31	19.83	157	0	99	0	1	56.0	60.8	-13.2	15	N/A	0	0	0.0	0.0
C / 5.4	11.7	1.31	17.18	1,199	0	99	0	1	56.0	55.6	-13.5	10	N/A	2,500	50	0.0	4.0
C / 5.4	11.7	1.31	17.23	419	0	99	0	1	56.0	55.7	-13.5	10	N/A	2,500	50	0.0	1.0
C- / 3.3	20.5	1.68	6.30	675	0	99	0	1	66.0	132.0	-10.8	1	N/A	2,500	50	4.3	1.0
C- / 3.3	20.4	1.68	6.43	80	0	99	0	1	66.0	134.1	-11.0	1	N/A	0	0	0.0	0.0
C- / 3.2	20.4	1.68	5.25	60	0	99	0	1	66.0	126.3	-11.2	1	N/A	2,500	50	0.0	4.0
C- / 3.2	20.5	1.68	5.25	30	0	99	0	1	66.0	126.7	-11.2	1	N/A	2,500	50	0.0	1.0
C+ / 5.8	11.7	1.30	10.64	76	2	97	0	1	73.0	62.9	-13.3	18	N/A	2,000,000	0	4.3	1.0
C+ / 5.8	11.7	1.30	10.33	2	2	97	0	1	73.0	61.3	-13.5	16	N/A	2,000,000	0	0.0	4.0
C- / 3.9	16.8	1.01	25.07	159	4	95	0	1	46.0	135.8	N/A	82	N/A	2,500	50	4.3	0.0
C- / 3.9	16.8	1.01	24.92	5	4	95	0	1	46.0	138.1	0.1	84	N/A	0	0	0.0	0.0
C- / 3.9	16.8	1.01	24.91	64	4	95	0	1	46.0	130.6	-0.2	76	N/A	2,500	50	0.0	4.0
C- / 3.9	16.9	1.01	24.95	56	4	95	0	1	46.0	130.7	-0.2	75	N/A	2,500	50	0.0	1.0
C- / 3.8	16.9	1.01	15.88	991	4	95	0	1	46.0	137.9	0.2	83	N/A	2,000,000	0	0.0	0.0
C+ / 6.3	11.1	0.73	16.89	462	5	94	0	1	42.0	108.3	-8.1	94	N/A	2,500	50	4.3	1.0
C+ / 6.4	11.1	0.73	17.10	157	5	94	0	1	42.0	110.2	-8.1	94	4	0	0	0.0	0.0
C+ / 6.1	11.1	0.72	16.39	239	5	94	0	1	42.0	103.4	-8.2	91	4	2,500	50	0.0	4.0
C+ / 6.2	11.1	0.72	16.39	202	5	94	0	1	42.0	103.6	-8.2	91	N/A	2,500	50	0.0	1.0
C / 4.4	16.5	1.09	25.70	226	2	97	0	1	82.0	116.0	-10.2	25	6	2,500	50	4.3	1.0
C / 4.4	16.5	1.09	26.48	22	2	97	0	1	82.0	117.9	-10.2	27	6	0	0	0.0	0.0
C / 4.3	16.5	1.09	21.48	80	2	97	0	1	82.0	110.7	-10.5	20	6	2,500	50	0.0	4.0
C / 4.3	16.5	1.09	21.54	33	2	97	0	1	82.0	110.9	-10.5	20	6	2,500	50	0.0	1.0
U /	N/A	N/A	25.92	26	2	97	0	1	82.0	N/A	N/A	N/A	1	10,000,000	0	0.0	0.0
B / 8.8	4.4	0.90	11.82	195	2	48	49	1	51.0	41.8	-5.8	62	N/A	2,500	50	4.3	1.0
B / 8.8	4.4	0.90	11.84	60	2	48	49	1	51.0	38.6	-6.0	53	N/A	2,500	50	0.0	4.0
B / 8.8	4.5	0.90	11.86	60	2	48	49	1	51.0	38.6	-6.0	52	N/A	2,500	50	0.0	1.0
U /	N/A	N/A	13.63	96	5	94	0	1	51.0	N/A	N/A	N/A	N/A	2,500	50	4.3	1.0
U /	N/A	N/A	13.71	85	5	94	0	1	51.0	N/A	N/A	N/A	N/A	0	0	0.0	0.0
U /	N/A	N/A	13.40	27	5	94	0	1	51.0	N/A	N/A	N/A	N/A	2,500	50	0.0	4.0
U /	N/A	N/A	13.41	45	5	94	0	1	51.0	N/A	N/A	N/A	N/A	2,500	50	0.0	1.0
B+ / 9.2	3.0	0.58	11.32	86	1	29	68	2	63.0	21.7	-0.8	40	N/A	2,500	50	4.3	1.0
B+ / 9.2	3.1	0.60	11.58	39	1	29	68	2	63.0	18.9	-0.9	33	N/A	2,500	50	0.0	4.0
B+ / 9.2	3.1	0.60	11.59	29	1	29	68	2	63.0	19.0	-0.9	33	N/A	2,500	50	0.0	1.0
B- / 7.3	9.1	1.10	12.98	52	N/A	100	0	N/A	44.0	58.6	-8.0	30	N/A	2,500	50	4.3	1.0
B / 8.2	9.1	1.10	13.12	12	N/A	100	0	N/A	44.0	60.4	-8.0	33	N/A	2,500	50	0.0	0.0
B- / 7.2	9.1	1.10	12.62	53	N/A	100	0	N/A	44.0	55.1	-8.2	25	4	2,500	50	0.0	4.0
B- / 7.2	9.1	1.10	12.62	34	N/A	100	0	N/A	44.0	55.2	-8.2	25	4	2,500	50	0.0	1.0
B / 8.1	8.2	0.64	18.60	77	0	93	0	7	47.0	91.4	-3.6	85	5	2,500	50	4.3	0.0
B / 8.1	8.2	0.64	18.69	3	0	93	0	7	47.0	93.3	-3.6	87	5	0	0	0.0	0.0
B / 8.1	8.2	0.64	18.40	100	0	93	0	7	47.0	87.1	-3.7	79	5	2,500	50	0.0	4.0
B / 8.1	8.2	0.64	18.44	39	0	93	0	7	47.0	87.1	-3.7	80	10	2,500	50	0.0	1.0
B / 8.3	7.8	0.98	13.09	248	2	97	0	1	25.0	75.6	-8.9	80	N/A	2,500	50	4.3	1.0
B / 8.3	7.8	0.98	13.16	329	2	97	0	1	25.0	77.3	-8.7	82	N/A	0	0	0.0	0.0
B / 8.3	7.9	0.99	13.05	145	2	97	0	1	25.0	72.2	-9.1	75	N/A	2,500	50	0.0	4.0
B / 8.3	7.8	0.98	13.00	99	2	97	0	1	25.0	71.7	-9.1	73	N/A	2,500	50	0.0	1.0
U /	N/A	N/A	13.08	120	2	97	0	1	25.0	N/A	N/A	N/A	N/A	10,000,000	0	0.0	0.0
U /	N/A	N/A	14.06	484	0	99	0	1	32.0	N/A	N/A	N/A	N/A	2,500	50	4.3	1.0
U /	N/A	N/A	14.10	271	0	99	0	1	32.0	N/A	N/A	N/A	N/A	0	0	0.0	0.0
U /	N/A	N/A	13.90	249	0	99	0	1	32.0	N/A	N/A	N/A	3	2,500	50	0.0	4.0

			Overall Weiss Investment Rating		PERFORMANCE							
					Perfor-mance Rating/Pts	Total Return % through 6/30/06					Incl. in Returns	
									Annualized		Dividend	Expense
Fund Type	Fund Name	Ticker Symbol		Phone		3 Mo	6 Mo	1Yr / Pct	3Yr / Pct	5Yr / Pct	Yield	Ratio
GR	AllianceBernstein Wlt Ap Stgy C	AWACX	U	(800) 221-5672	U /	-2.87	3.89	15.42 /73	--	--	0.00	2.03
AA	AllianceBernstein Wlt Prs Stgy A	ABPAX	U	(800) 221-5672	U /	-0.60	1.95	5.77 /19	--	--	2.05	1.20
AA	AllianceBernstein Wlt Prs Stgy B	ABPBX	U	(800) 221-5672	U /	-0.69	1.63	5.09 /15	--	--	1.49	1.90
AA	AllianceBernstein Wlt Prs Stgy C	ABPCX	U	(800) 221-5672	U /	-0.77	1.64	5.10 /16	--	--	1.49	1.90
AA	Allianz AAM Asset Allocation A	PALAX	C	(800) 628-1237	D+ / 2.7	-1.86	2.49	9.03 /40	10.62 /32	5.96 /61	1.27	1.33
AA	Allianz AAM Asset Allocation B	PALBX	C-	(800) 628-1237	D+ / 2.4	-2.06	2.05	8.20 /34	9.76 /26	5.14 /55	0.55	2.08
AA	Allianz AAM Asset Allocation C	PALCX	C	(800) 628-1237	C- / 3.1	-2.06	2.05	8.21 /34	9.75 /25	5.16 /55	0.56	2.08
AA	Allianz AAM Asset Allocation Inst	PALLX	C+	(800) 628-1237	C- / 4.2	-1.81	2.65	9.56 /44	11.13 /36	6.44 /64	1.83	0.83
GR	Allianz CCM Cap Appreciation A	PCFAX	C-	(800) 628-1237	C- / 3.5	-3.85	2.07	9.96 /47	12.16 /43	2.47 /32	0.02	1.11
GR	Allianz CCM Cap Appreciation Admin	PICAX	C	(800) 628-1237	C / 4.7	-3.84	2.17	10.09 /47	12.32 /44	2.68 /34	0.12	0.96
GR	Allianz CCM Cap Appreciation B	PFCBX	D+	(800) 628-1237	C- / 3.2	-4.03	1.72	9.10 /41	11.33 /38	1.70 /25	0.00	1.86
GR	Allianz CCM Cap Appreciation C	PFCCX	C-	(800) 628-1237	C- / 3.9	-4.02	1.71	9.14 /41	11.33 /38	1.72 /25	0.00	1.86
GR	Allianz CCM Cap Appreciation D	PCADX	C	(800) 628-1237	C / 4.6	-3.88	2.09	9.91 /46	12.17 /43	2.47 /32	0.09	1.11
GR	Allianz CCM Cap Appreciation Inst	PAPIX	C	(800) 628-1237	C / 4.9	-3.81	2.28	10.33 /49	12.59 /46	2.88 /36	0.18	0.71
GR	Allianz CCM Cap Appreciation R	PCARX	C	(800) 628-1237	C / 4.4	-3.98	1.96	9.62 /44	11.82 /41	2.14 /28	0.10	1.36
SC	● Allianz CCM Emerging Co Admin	PMGAX	C-	(800) 628-1237	C+ / 6.7	-6.69	6.70	13.82 /68	16.76 /67	11.46 /85	0.00	1.76
SC	● Allianz CCM Emerging Co Inst	PMCIX	C-	(800) 628-1237	C+ / 6.8	-6.62	6.83	14.08 /68	17.04 /68	11.73 /86	0.00	1.51
GR	Allianz CCM Focused Growth Inst		B+	(800) 628-1237	B / 7.6	-3.11	7.70	19.68 /81	18.29 /74	4.18 /48	0.21	0.71
MC	Allianz CCM Mid Cap A	PFMAX	C+	(800) 628-1237	C+ / 6.2	-3.36	3.69	12.67 /63	16.85 /67	5.73 /59	0.00	1.11
MC	Allianz CCM Mid Cap Admin	PMCGX	C+	(800) 628-1237	B- / 7.0	-3.33	3.76	12.87 /64	17.03 /68	5.84 /60	0.00	0.96
MC	Allianz CCM Mid Cap B	PFMBX	C	(800) 628-1237	C+ / 5.9	-3.53	3.30	11.85 /59	15.98 /63	4.93 /53	0.00	1.86
MC	Allianz CCM Mid Cap C	PFMCX	C+	(800) 628-1237	C+ / 6.4	-3.53	3.30	11.84 /59	15.97 /63	4.93 /54	0.00	1.86
MC	Allianz CCM Mid Cap D	PMCDX	C+	(800) 628-1237	C+ / 6.7	-3.35	3.70	12.68 /63	16.85 /67	5.73 /59	0.00	1.11
MC	Allianz CCM Mid Cap Inst	PMGIX	C+	(800) 628-1237	B- / 7.1	-3.26	3.86	13.10 /65	17.32 /69	6.13 /62	0.00	0.71
MC	Allianz CCM Mid Cap R	PMCRX	B-	(800) 628-1237	C+ / 6.8	-3.41	3.54	12.37 /61	16.49 /66	5.35 /57	0.00	1.36
AG	Allianz NACM Flex-Cap Value A	PNFAX	B	(800) 628-1237	C+ / 6.5	0.70	5.72	14.70 /71	16.68 /67	--	0.17	1.32
AG	Allianz NACM Flex-Cap Value Admin		A	(800) 628-1237	B- / 7.2	0.75	5.80	14.90 /71	16.89 /68	--	0.16	1.17
AG	Allianz NACM Flex-Cap Value B	PNFBX	B	(800) 628-1237	C+ / 6.2	0.48	5.30	13.78 /67	15.80 /63	--	0.00	2.07
AG	Allianz NACM Flex-Cap Value C	PNFCX	B	(800) 628-1237	C+ / 6.7	0.48	5.30	13.78 /67	15.80 /63	--	0.00	2.07
AG	Allianz NACM Flex-Cap Value D	PNFDX	B+	(800) 628-1237	B- / 7.0	0.69	5.71	14.74 /71	16.68 /67	--	0.25	1.32
AG	Allianz NACM Flex-Cap Value Inst		A	(800) 628-1237	B- / 7.3	0.80	5.96	15.14 /72	17.18 /69	--	0.48	0.91
GL	Allianz NACM Global A	NGBAX	B-	(800) 628-1237	B / 7.6	-3.80	4.61	17.85 /79	20.18 /80	--	0.00	1.46
GL	Allianz NACM Global Admin		B	(800) 628-1237	B / 8.0	-3.83	4.64	17.95 /79	20.36 /81	--	0.00	1.31
GL	Allianz NACM Global B	NGBBX	C+	(800) 628-1237	B- / 7.4	-3.97	4.18	16.98 /77	19.29 /77	--	0.00	2.21
GL	Allianz NACM Global C	NGBCX	B-	(800) 628-1237	B / 7.7	-4.01	4.17	16.93 /77	19.30 /77	--	0.00	2.21
GL	Allianz NACM Global D	NGBDX	B	(800) 628-1237	B / 7.9	-3.85	4.61	17.84 /79	20.16 /80	--	0.00	1.45
GL	Allianz NACM Global Inst		B	(800) 628-1237	B / 8.1	-3.69	4.78	18.29 /80	20.68 /82	--	0.00	1.06
GL	Allianz NACM Global R	NGBRX	B+	(800) 628-1237	B / 7.8	-3.89	4.40	17.49 /78	19.87 /79	--	0.00	1.72
GR	Allianz NACM Growth A	NGWAX	D-	(800) 628-1237	D- / 1.5	-3.30	3.62	9.46 /43	8.71 /19	--	0.00	1.17
GR	Allianz NACM Growth Admin		D	(800) 628-1237	D+ / 2.6	-3.28	3.59	9.56 /44	8.87 /20	--	0.00	1.02
GR	Allianz NACM Growth B	NGWBX	D-	(800) 628-1237	D- / 1.2	-3.48	3.14	8.50 /37	7.86 /14	--	0.00	1.92
GR	Allianz NACM Growth C	NGWCX	D-	(800) 628-1237	D / 1.8	-3.48	3.23	8.60 /37	7.87 /14	--	0.00	1.92
GR	Allianz NACM Growth D	NGWDX	D	(800) 628-1237	D+ / 2.4	-3.30	3.54	9.37 /42	8.68 /19	--	0.00	1.17
GR	Allianz NACM Growth Inst		D	(800) 628-1237	D+ / 2.8	-3.24	3.80	9.81 /46	9.16 /22	--	0.00	0.77
FO	Allianz NACM International A	PNIAX	A+	(800) 628-1237	A+ / 9.6	0.83	14.05	39.18 /98	30.99 /96	16.00 /93	0.64	1.45
FO	Allianz NACM International C	PNICX	A+	(800) 628-1237	A+ / 9.7	0.65	13.65	38.19 /97	30.07 /96	15.14 /92	0.43	2.19
FO	Allianz NACM International D	PNIDX	A+	(800) 628-1237	A+ / 9.7	0.78	13.99	39.19 /98	31.01 /96	16.01 /93	0.79	1.44
FO	Allianz NACM International I	NAISX	A+	(800) 628-1237	A+ / 9.7	0.92	14.22	39.76 /98	31.33 /96	16.20 /93	0.64	1.34
FO	Allianz NACM Pacific Rim A	PPRAX	C+	(800) 628-1237	A+ / 9.6	-4.15	5.23	46.50 /99	32.75 /97	14.72 /91	0.28	1.76
FO	Allianz NACM Pacific Rim B	PPRBX	C+	(800) 628-1237	A+ / 9.6	-4.31	4.87	45.39 /98	31.77 /97	13.96 /90	0.00	2.50
FO	Allianz NACM Pacific Rim C	PPRCX	B-	(800) 628-1237	A+ / 9.7	-4.33	4.82	45.31 /98	32.11 /97	14.02 /90	0.00	2.50
FO	Allianz NACM Pacific Rim D	PPRDX	C+	(800) 628-1237	A+ / 9.7	-4.09	5.32	46.55 /99	32.73 /97	14.71 /91	0.45	1.75

● Denotes fund is closed to new investors
* Denotes fund is included in Section II

RISK			NET ASSETS		ASSET					BULL / BEAR		FUND MANAGER		MINIMUMS		LOADS	
Risk Rating/Pts	3 Year Standard Deviation	Beta	NAV As of 6/30/06	Total $(Mil)	Cash %	Stocks %	Bonds %	Other %	Portfolio Turnover Ratio	Last Bull Market Return	Last Bear Market Return	Manager Quality Pct	Manager Tenure (Years)	Initial Purch. $	Additional Purch. $	Front End Load	Back End Load
U /	N/A	N/A	13.90	227	0	99	0	1	32.0	N/A	N/A	N/A	3	2,500	50	0.0	1.0
U /	N/A	N/A	11.35	241	0	0	99	1	81.0	N/A	N/A	N/A	N/A	2,500	50	4.3	1.0
U /	N/A	N/A	11.32	119	0	0	99	1	81.0	N/A	N/A	N/A	N/A	2,500	50	0.0	4.0
U /	N/A	N/A	11.31	127	0	0	99	1	81.0	N/A	N/A	N/A	N/A	2,500	50	0.0	1.0
B /8.9	6.2	1.24	11.78	66	0	64	36	0	25.0	58.2	-4.7	73	4	5,000	100	5.5	1.0
B+/9.0	6.2	1.25	11.71	80	0	64	36	0	25.0	54.5	-4.9	66	4	5,000	100	0.0	5.0
B+/9.0	6.2	1.25	11.71	141	0	64	36	0	25.0	54.7	-4.9	65	4	5,000	100	0.0	1.0
B+/9.0	6.2	1.25	11.79	1	0	64	36	0	25.0	60.5	-4.7	77	4	5,000,000	0	0.0	0.0
B- /7.0	10.0	1.17	19.71	361	1	98	0	1	137.0	71.0	-6.5	48	9	5,000	100	5.5	1.0
B- /7.0	10.0	1.17	19.78	458	1	98	0	1	137.0	71.7	-6.4	50	10	5,000,000	0	0.0	0.0
C+/6.9	10.0	1.17	18.35	75	1	98	0	1	137.0	66.9	-6.7	39	9	5,000	100	0.0	5.0
C+/6.9	10.0	1.17	18.39	138	1	98	0	1	137.0	67.0	-6.7	40	9	5,000	100	0.0	1.0
B- /7.0	10.0	1.17	19.58	34	1	98	0	1	137.0	71.0	-6.5	49	N/A	5,000	100	0.0	0.0
B- /7.0	10.0	1.17	20.22	380	1	98	0	1	137.0	73.2	-6.5	54	14	5,000,000	0	0.0	0.0
B- /7.7	10.1	1.17	19.79	13	1	98	0	1	137.0	69.2	-6.6	44	N/A	2,500	50	0.0	0.0
C- /4.0	16.0	1.06	23.57	63	6	94	0	0	144.0	121.0	-7.7	29	10	5,000,000	0	0.0	2.0
C- /4.1	15.9	1.06	24.55	598	6	94	0	0	144.0	122.8	-7.7	31	13	5,000,000	0	0.0	2.0
B- /7.3	11.9	1.29	9.34	5	7	92	0	1	123.0	101.0	-6.9	89	7	5,000,000	0	0.0	0.0
C+/6.3	12.5	1.11	27.57	353	3	96	0	1	140.0	95.3	-6.0	28	9	5,000	100	5.5	1.0
C+/6.3	12.5	1.11	27.89	304	3	96	0	1	140.0	96.3	-6.0	29	12	5,000,000	0	0.0	0.0
C+/6.3	12.5	1.11	25.68	85	3	96	0	1	140.0	90.7	-6.2	23	9	5,000	100	0.0	5.0
C+/6.3	12.5	1.11	25.69	122	3	96	0	1	140.0	90.6	-6.1	23	9	5,000	100	0.0	1.0
C+/6.3	12.5	1.11	27.73	32	3	96	0	1	140.0	95.3	-6.0	28	N/A	5,000	100	0.0	2.0
C+/6.3	12.5	1.11	28.50	470	3	96	0	1	140.0	97.8	-6.0	31	14	5,000,000	0	0.0	0.0
B- /7.1	12.5	1.11	27.79	41	3	96	0	1	140.0	93.3	-6.1	26	N/A	2,500	100	0.0	0.0
B /8.1	9.2	1.12	17.36	5	7	92	0	1	150.0	93.5	-10.1	89	4	5,000	100	5.5	1.0
B /8.4	9.1	1.12	17.52	N/A	7	92	0	1	150.0	94.5	-10.0	90	4	5,000,000	0	0.0	0.0
B /8.2	9.2	1.12	16.90	5	7	92	0	1	150.0	88.9	-10.3	85	4	5,000	100	0.0	5.0
B /8.2	9.2	1.12	16.90	6	7	92	0	1	150.0	88.8	-10.2	85	4	5,000	100	0.0	1.0
B /8.3	9.2	1.12	17.41	3	7	92	0	1	150.0	93.3	-10.1	89	4	5,000	100	0.0	2.0
B /8.4	9.1	1.12	17.61	33	7	92	0	1	150.0	96.1	-10.0	91	4	5,000,000	0	0.0	0.0
C+/6.1	11.5	1.01	17.47	11	2	97	0	1	148.0	119.6	-12.3	21	3	5,000	100	5.5	1.0
C+/6.1	11.5	1.01	17.59	N/A	2	97	0	1	148.0	120.8	-12.2	22	3	5,000,000	0	0.0	2.0
C+/6.1	11.5	1.01	16.94	15	2	97	0	1	148.0	114.5	-12.4	17	3	5,000	100	0.0	5.0
C+/6.1	11.5	1.01	16.98	10	2	97	0	1	148.0	114.4	-12.4	17	3	5,000	100	0.0	1.0
C+/6.1	11.5	1.01	17.48	1	2	97	0	1	148.0	119.5	-12.2	21	3	5,000	100	0.0	2.0
C+/6.1	11.5	1.01	17.76	N/A	2	97	0	1	148.0	122.3	-12.1	24	3	5,000,000	0	0.0	2.0
C+/6.9	11.5	1.01	17.31	N/A	2	97	0	1	148.0	117.6	-13.2	20	3	2,500	50	0.0	2.0
C+/6.4	10.1	1.11	12.89	1	1	98	0	1	274.0	51.1	-11.6	24	N/A	5,000	100	5.5	1.0
C+/6.4	10.1	1.11	12.98	N/A	1	98	0	1	274.0	51.8	-11.5	26	N/A	5,000,000	0	0.0	0.0
C+/6.3	10.0	1.11	12.47	2	1	98	0	1	274.0	47.5	-11.7	19	N/A	5,000	100	0.0	5.0
C+/6.3	10.1	1.11	12.47	1	1	98	0	1	274.0	47.4	-11.7	19	N/A	5,000	100	0.0	1.0
C+/6.4	10.0	1.11	12.88	N/A	1	98	0	1	274.0	51.0	-11.6	24	N/A	5,000	100	0.0	0.0
C+/6.5	10.1	1.11	13.12	1	1	98	0	1	274.0	53.1	-11.5	27	N/A	5,000,000	0	0.0	0.0
B- /7.7	11.5	1.09	21.84	168	5	94	0	1	107.0	181.7	-9.4	87	N/A	5,000	100	5.5	1.0
B- /7.7	11.5	1.09	21.65	84	5	94	0	1	107.0	175.3	-9.5	83	N/A	5,000	100	0.0	0.0
B- /7.7	11.5	1.09	21.84	4	5	94	0	1	107.0	181.8	-9.4	87	N/A	5,000	100	0.0	2.0
C+/6.8	11.5	1.08	22.01	105	5	94	0	1	107.0	183.8	-9.4	89	N/A	5,000,000	0	0.0	2.0
C- /3.3	42.3	0.34	14.08	80	2	97	0	1	101.0	186.5	-10.1	99	N/A	5,000	100	5.5	1.0
C- /3.3	43.5	0.31	13.77	34	2	97	0	1	101.0	180.2	-10.1	99	N/A	5,000	100	0.0	5.0
C- /4.2	16.6	1.29	13.69	69	2	97	0	1	101.0	182.1	-10.4	59	N/A	5,000	100	0.0	0.0
C- /3.3	42.4	0.34	14.06	21	2	97	0	1	101.0	186.4	-10.1	99	N/A	5,000	100	0.0	2.0

			Overall Weiss Investment Rating		PERFORMANCE							Incl. in Returns	
					Perfor-mance Rating/Pts	Total Return % through 6/30/06						Dividend	Expense
										Annualized			
Fund Type	Fund Name	Ticker Symbol		Phone		3 Mo	6 Mo	1Yr / Pct	3Yr / Pct	5Yr / Pct		Yield	Ratio
FO	Allianz NACM Pacific Rim Inst	NAPRX	B-	(800) 628-1237	A+ / 9.7	-4.03	5.54	47.18 /99	33.65 /97	15.41 /92		0.65	1.47
IN	Allianz NFJ Dividend Value A	PNEAX	A+	(800) 628-1237	B- / 7.0	1.95	8.87	16.73 /76	17.52 /70	10.37 /82		2.37	1.10
IN	Allianz NFJ Dividend Value Admin		A+	(800) 628-1237	B / 7.7	2.00	8.94	16.89 /77	17.73 /71	10.60 /83		2.40	0.96
IN	Allianz NFJ Dividend Value B	PNEBX	B+	(800) 628-1237	C+ / 6.8	1.83	8.56	15.94 /74	16.64 /66	9.56 /79		1.57	1.84
IN	Allianz NFJ Dividend Value C	PNECX	A+	(800) 628-1237	B- / 7.2	1.78	8.51	15.84 /74	16.65 /66	9.54 /79		1.62	1.84
IN	Allianz NFJ Dividend Value D	PEIDX	A+	(800) 628-1237	B- / 7.4	1.97	8.90	16.72 /76	17.53 /70	10.36 /82		2.60	1.10
IN	Allianz NFJ Dividend Value Inst	NFJEX	A+	(800) 628-1237	B / 7.6	2.09	9.18	17.21 /77	18.07 /73	10.90 /84		2.89	0.71
IN	Allianz NFJ Dividend Value R	PNERX	A+	(800) 628-1237	B- / 7.3	1.90	8.77	16.44 /76	17.24 /69	10.10 /81		2.53	1.33
FO	Allianz NFJ Intl Value A	AFJAX	B	(800) 628-1237	A+ / 9.6	-0.91	10.76	28.12 /93	31.94 /97	--		1.04	1.45
FO	Allianz NFJ Intl Value C	AFJCX	B	(800) 628-1237	A+ / 9.6	-1.08	10.38	27.14 /91	31.00 /96	--		0.71	2.18
FO	Allianz NFJ Intl Value D	AFJDX	B	(800) 628-1237	A+ / 9.6	-0.89	10.78	28.09 /93	31.93 /97	--		1.05	1.45
FO	Allianz NFJ Intl Value Inst	ANJIX	A+	(800) 628-1237	A+ / 9.7	-0.82	11.03	28.63 /93	32.44 /97	--		0.90	1.06
GR	Allianz NFJ Large Cap Value A	PNBAX	B+	(800) 628-1237	C+ / 6.8	3.56	8.38	15.23 /72	17.10 /68	10.40 /82		1.54	1.11
GR	Allianz NFJ Large Cap Value B	PNBBX	B+	(800) 628-1237	C+ / 6.6	3.44	7.98	14.41 /70	16.26 /65	9.60 /79		0.76	1.86
GR	Allianz NFJ Large Cap Value C	PNBCX	A+	(800) 628-1237	B- / 7.1	3.39	7.99	14.45 /70	16.24 /64	9.60 /79		0.74	1.86
GR	Allianz NFJ Large Cap Value D	PNBDX	A+	(800) 628-1237	B- / 7.3	3.58	8.32	15.22 /72	17.12 /69	10.40 /82		1.83	1.11
GR	Allianz NFJ Large Cap Value Inst		A+	(800) 628-1237	B- / 7.5	3.70	8.65	15.77 /74	17.64 /71	10.94 /84		2.08	0.71
SC	● Allianz NFJ Small Cap Value A	PCVAX	B+	(800) 628-1237	B / 7.7	-0.35	8.89	14.50 /70	20.54 /81	15.18 /92		1.44	1.25
SC	● Allianz NFJ Small Cap Value Adm	PVADX	B+	(800) 628-1237	B / 8.1	-0.32	8.96	14.65 /71	20.35 /81	15.13 /92		1.68	1.11
SC	● Allianz NFJ Small Cap Value B	PCVBX	B+	(800) 628-1237	B / 7.6	-0.56	8.48	13.64 /67	19.65 /78	14.31 /91		0.85	2.00
SC	● Allianz NFJ Small Cap Value C	PCVCX	B+	(800) 628-1237	B / 7.9	-0.52	8.51	13.67 /67	19.64 /78	14.31 /91		0.90	2.00
SC	● Allianz NFJ Small Cap Value D	PNVDX	A+	(800) 628-1237	B / 8.1	-0.34	8.90	14.51 /70	20.54 /81	15.19 /92		1.43	1.25
SC	● Allianz NFJ Small Cap Value I	PSVIX	A-	(800) 628-1237	B / 8.2	-0.22	9.12	15.00 /72	21.02 /83	15.68 /93		1.79	0.86
SC	● Allianz NFJ Small Cap Value R	PNVRX	A	(800) 628-1237	B / 8.0	-0.38	8.76	14.23 /69	20.19 /80	14.85 /92		1.49	1.49
GI	Allianz OCC Renaissance A	PQNAX	D-	(800) 927-4648	C / 4.3	-5.14	0.65	6.28 /22	14.55 /57	8.32 /73		0.00	1.23
GI	Allianz OCC Renaissance Admin	PRAAX	D+	(800) 927-4648	C / 5.2	-5.08	0.78	6.45 /23	14.71 /57	8.57 /74		0.00	1.11
GI	Allianz OCC Renaissance B	PQNBX	D-	(800) 927-4648	C- / 4.1	-5.30	0.30	5.53 /18	13.70 /52	7.53 /69		0.00	1.99
GI	Allianz OCC Renaissance C	PQNCX	D-	(800) 927-4648	C / 4.6	-5.34	0.31	5.47 /17	13.70 /52	7.51 /69		0.00	1.99
GI	Allianz OCC Renaissance D	PREDX	D	(800) 927-4648	C / 5.1	-5.17	0.65	6.26 /22	14.52 /56	8.31 /73		0.00	1.23
GI	Allianz OCC Renaissance Inst	PRNIX	D+	(800) 927-4648	C / 5.4	-5.05	0.86	6.73 /25	15.00 /59	8.74 /75		0.00	0.86
GI	Allianz OCC Renaissance R	PRNRX	C+	(800) 927-4648	C / 4.9	-5.21	0.55	6.03 /21	14.20 /55	7.97 /71		0.00	1.48
GI	Allianz OCC Value A	PDLAX	C-	(800) 927-4648	C / 4.9	-0.80	2.35	8.11 /33	14.93 /58	7.28 /68		0.87	1.10
GI	Allianz OCC Value Admin	PVLAX	C	(800) 927-4648	C+ / 5.8	-0.74	2.41	8.25 /35	15.09 /59	7.41 /69		1.07	0.96
GI	Allianz OCC Value B	PDLBX	C-	(800) 927-4648	C / 4.7	-0.96	1.91	7.23 /28	14.07 /54	6.48 /64		0.34	1.85
GI	Allianz OCC Value C	PDLCX	C-	(800) 927-4648	C / 5.2	-0.96	1.97	7.31 /28	14.03 /54	6.46 /64		0.24	1.85
GI	Allianz OCC Value D	PVLDX	C	(800) 927-4648	C+ / 5.7	-0.80	2.35	8.13 /34	14.94 /58	7.29 /68		0.82	1.10
GI	Allianz OCC Value Inst	PDLIX	C	(800) 927-4648	C+ / 5.9	-0.66	2.55	8.51 /37	15.37 /61	7.70 /70		1.23	0.72
GI	Allianz OCC Value R	PPVRX	B-	(800) 927-4648	C / 5.5	-0.86	2.22	7.83 /31	14.58 /57	6.95 /66		0.81	1.35
GI	Allianz PEA Eq Pre Str Fd A	PGRAX	C-	(800) 927-4648	D+ / 2.5	-2.17	3.63	8.52 /37	10.55 /31	-0.49 /14		0.03	1.27
GI	Allianz PEA Eq Pre Str Fd Admin	PGOIX	C	(800) 927-4648	C- / 3.6	-2.14	3.70	8.66 /38	10.89 /34	-0.27 /14		0.04	1.12
GI	Allianz PEA Eq Pre Str Fd B	PGRBX	C-	(800) 927-4648	D+ / 2.4	-2.33	3.20	7.84 /31	9.79 /26	-1.23 /11		0.00	2.02
GI	Allianz PEA Eq Pre Str Fd C	PGNCX	C-	(800) 927-4648	D+ / 2.9	-2.34	3.20	7.71 /30	9.73 /25	-1.22 /11		0.00	2.02
GI	Allianz PEA Eq Pre Str Fd D	PGIDX	C-	(800) 927-4648	C- / 3.4	-2.17	3.63	8.52 /37	10.57 /31	-0.51 /13		0.04	1.27
GI	Allianz PEA Eq Pre Str Fd Inst	PMEIX	C	(800) 927-4648	C- / 3.8	-2.13	3.80	8.91 /39	11.11 /36	-0.01 /15		0.06	0.87
GI	Allianz PEA Eq Pre Str Fd R	PGIRX	C	(800) 927-4648	C- / 3.3	-2.28	3.50	8.35 /36	10.26 /29	-0.78 /12		0.02	1.52
GR	Allianz PEA Growth A	PGWAX	D	(800) 927-4648	D+ / 2.6	-2.50	2.12	10.12 /48	10.66 /32	-1.47 /10		0.00	1.16
GR	Allianz PEA Growth Admin	PGFAX	C-	(800) 927-4648	C- / 3.6	-2.45	2.22	10.28 /49	10.82 /34	-1.36 /10		0.00	1.01
GR	Allianz PEA Growth B	PGFBX	D	(800) 927-4648	D+ / 2.5	-2.66	1.76	9.29 /42	9.83 /26	-2.22 / 7		0.00	1.91
GR	Allianz PEA Growth C	PGWCX	D+	(800) 927-4648	C- / 3.0	-2.71	1.76	9.29 /42	9.83 /26	-2.22 / 7		0.00	1.91
GR	Allianz PEA Growth D	PGRDX	D+	(800) 927-4648	C- / 3.5	-2.54	2.09	10.08 /47	10.64 /32	-1.49 /10		0.00	1.16
GR	Allianz PEA Growth Inst	PGFIX	C-	(800) 927-4648	C- / 3.8	-2.40	2.32	10.55 /51	11.09 /36	-1.10 /11		0.00	0.76
GR	Allianz PEA Growth R	PPGRX	C-	(800) 927-4648	C- / 3.3	-2.52	2.06	9.88 /46	10.32 /29	-1.78 / 9		0.00	1.41

● Denotes fund is closed to new investors

* Denotes fund is included in Section II

RISK			NET ASSETS		ASSET				Portfolio Turnover Ratio	BULL / BEAR		FUND MANAGER		MINIMUMS		LOADS	
	3 Year		NAV As of 6/30/06	Total $(Mil)	Cash %	Stocks %	Bonds %	Other %		Last Bull Market Return	Last Bear Market Return	Manager Quality Pct	Manager Tenure (Years)	Initial Purch. $	Additional Purch. $	Front End Load	Back End Load
Risk Rating/Pts	Standard Deviation	Beta															
C- / 4.2	16.5	1.29	14.28	36	2	97	0	1	101.0	193.1	-10.1	72	N/A	5,000,000	0	0.0	2.0
B+ / 9.4	7.6	0.91	15.35	995	6	93	0	1	30.0	90.6	-9.2	96	5	5,000	100	5.5	1.0
B+ / 9.1	7.6	0.91	15.56	10	6	93	0	1	30.0	91.7	-9.1	97	N/A	5,000,000	0	0.0	0.0
B+ / 9.4	7.6	0.92	15.25	279	6	93	0	1	30.0	86.0	-9.2	95	5	5,000	100	0.0	5.0
B+ / 9.4	7.6	0.92	15.23	711	6	93	0	1	30.0	86.1	-9.3	95	5	5,000	100	0.0	1.0
B+ / 9.4	7.6	0.92	15.38	78	6	93	0	1	30.0	90.6	-9.2	96	5	5,000	100	0.0	2.0
B+ / 9.1	7.6	0.92	15.51	321	6	93	0	1	30.0	93.3	-9.0	97	N/A	5,000,000	0	0.0	2.0
B+ / 9.1	7.6	0.92	15.33	19	6	93	0	1	30.0	89.1	-9.3	96	N/A	2,500	50	0.0	2.0
C / 5.0	14.4	1.30	19.28	65	12	88	0	0	61.0	187.7	N/A	57	N/A	5,000	100	5.5	2.0
C / 4.9	14.8	1.31	19.20	35	12	88	0	0	61.0	181.3	N/A	43	N/A	5,000	100	0.0	2.0
C / 4.9	14.8	1.31	19.30	3	12	88	0	0	61.0	187.7	N/A	52	N/A	5,000	100	0.0	2.0
B- / 7.2	14.4	1.30	19.43	3	12	88	0	0	61.0	191.4	N/A	61	N/A	5,000,000	0	0.0	2.0
B+ / 9.1	7.8	0.91	17.69	37	3	96	0	1	35.0	85.4	-8.4	96	N/A	5,000	100	5.5	1.0
B+ / 9.1	7.8	0.91	17.57	23	3	96	0	1	35.0	81.0	-8.5	94	N/A	5,000	100	0.0	5.0
B+ / 9.1	7.8	0.91	17.58	32	3	96	0	1	35.0	81.0	-8.5	94	N/A	5,000	100	0.0	1.0
B+ / 9.1	7.7	0.90	17.73	3	3	96	0	1	35.0	85.4	-8.3	96	N/A	5,000	100	0.0	2.0
B+ / 9.1	7.8	0.91	17.79	20	3	96	0	1	35.0	88.2	-8.3	96	N/A	5,000,000	0	0.0	2.0
B- / 7.0	11.1	0.70	31.47	1,756	5	94	0	1	20.0	104.7	-4.3	96	9	5,000	100	5.5	1.0
B- / 7.0	11.0	0.70	31.51	706	5	94	0	1	20.0	103.7	-4.2	96	11	5,000,000	0	0.0	2.0
B- / 7.1	11.1	0.70	30.45	295	5	94	0	1	20.0	99.9	-4.4	94	9	5,000	100	0.0	5.0
B- / 7.1	11.0	0.70	30.49	580	5	94	0	1	20.0	99.8	-4.4	94	9	5,000	100	0.0	1.0
B / 8.0	11.1	0.70	32.07	5	5	94	0	1	20.0	104.7	-4.3	96	N/A	5,000	100	0.0	2.0
B- / 7.0	11.0	0.70	32.44	644	5	94	0	1	20.0	107.2	-4.2	96	15	5,000,000	0	0.0	2.0
B / 8.0	11.0	0.70	31.80	47	5	94	0	1	20.0	102.6	-4.4	95	N/A	2,500	50	0.0	2.0
C- / 4.2	12.5	1.47	21.58	948	3	96	0	1	101.0	108.8	-16.0	44	1	5,000	100	5.5	2.0
C / 4.5	12.5	1.47	21.86	127	3	96	0	1	101.0	109.5	-15.9	45	1	5,000,000	0	0.0	2.0
C- / 3.9	12.5	1.47	19.83	719	3	96	0	1	101.0	103.8	-16.1	36	1	5,000	100	0.0	5.0
C- / 3.9	12.5	1.47	19.67	753	3	96	0	1	101.0	103.9	-16.1	36	1	5,000	100	0.0	2.0
C / 4.4	12.5	1.47	21.65	47	3	96	0	1	101.0	108.7	-16.0	44	1	5,000	100	0.0	2.0
C / 4.6	12.5	1.47	22.19	52	3	96	0	1	101.0	111.2	-15.9	49	1	5,000,000	0	0.0	2.0
B- / 7.5	12.5	1.47	20.02	38	3	96	0	1	101.0	106.6	-16.0	40	1	2,500	50	0.0	2.0
C+ / 5.9	9.8	1.19	16.09	614	1	98	0	1	101.0	98.5	-13.8	74	1	5,000	100	5.5	2.0
C+ / 5.9	9.9	1.19	16.18	84	1	98	0	1	101.0	99.6	-13.8	75	1	5,000,000	0	0.0	2.0
C+ / 5.9	9.8	1.19	15.47	383	1	98	0	1	101.0	94.0	-13.9	67	1	5,000	100	0.0	5.0
C+ / 5.9	9.8	1.19	15.50	485	1	98	0	1	101.0	93.7	-13.9	67	1	5,000	100	0.0	2.0
C+ / 6.0	9.8	1.19	16.09	157	1	98	0	1	101.0	98.6	-13.8	74	1	5,000	100	0.0	2.0
C+ / 6.0	9.9	1.19	16.49	91	1	98	0	1	101.0	100.9	-13.7	77	1	5,000,000	0	0.0	2.0
B / 8.4	9.8	1.19	16.15	24	1	98	0	1	101.0	96.7	-13.9	71	1	2,500	50	0.0	2.0
B / 8.0	8.1	0.99	8.28	27	1	98	0	1	24.0	59.1	-7.2	49	N/A	5,000	100	5.5	2.0
B / 8.0	8.1	0.99	8.41	1	1	98	0	1	24.0	60.4	-7.0	54	N/A	5,000,000	0	0.0	2.0
B / 8.5	8.1	1.00	8.10	16	1	98	0	1	24.0	55.4	-7.3	40	N/A	5,000	100	0.0	5.0
B / 8.5	8.1	0.99	8.09	19	1	98	0	1	24.0	55.5	-7.4	41	N/A	5,000	100	0.0	2.0
B / 8.0	8.1	1.00	8.28	1	1	98	0	1	24.0	59.2	-7.2	49	N/A	5,000	100	0.0	2.0
B / 8.0	8.1	1.00	8.45	5	1	98	0	1	24.0	61.5	-6.9	56	N/A	5,000,000	0	0.0	2.0
B / 8.6	8.1	0.99	8.29	N/A	1	98	0	1	24.0	57.6	-7.1	46	N/A	2,500	50	0.0	2.0
C+ / 6.7	10.4	1.24	22.63	82	0	99	0	1	39.0	61.7	-9.7	30	N/A	5,000	100	5.5	2.0
C+ / 6.7	10.3	1.23	20.28	N/A	0	99	0	1	39.0	62.3	-9.7	31	N/A	5,000,000	0	0.0	2.0
C+ / 6.7	10.4	1.24	19.05	29	0	99	0	1	39.0	57.9	-9.9	24	N/A	5,000	100	0.0	5.0
C+ / 6.7	10.3	1.23	19.05	412	0	99	0	1	39.0	57.9	-9.9	25	N/A	5,000	100	0.0	2.0
C+ / 6.7	10.3	1.23	19.99	N/A	0	99	0	1	39.0	61.6	-9.7	30	N/A	5,000	100	0.0	2.0
C+ / 6.8	10.4	1.23	20.74	6	0	99	0	1	39.0	63.5	-9.6	33	N/A	5,000,000	0	0.0	2.0
B- / 7.3	10.4	1.24	19.36	1	0	99	0	1	39.0	60.1	-9.8	27	N/A	2,500	50	0.0	2.0

Data as of June 30, 2006

Fund Type	Fund Name	Ticker Symbol	Overall Weiss Investment Rating	Phone	Perfor- mance Rating/Pts	3 Mo	6 Mo	1Yr / Pct	3Yr / Pct	5Yr / Pct	Dividend Yield	Expense Ratio
SC	Allianz PEA Opportunity A	POPAX	C-	(800) 927-4648	C+ / 6.5	-8.94	7.06	14.78 /71	18.03 /73	5.98 /61	0.00	1.31
SC	Allianz PEA Opportunity Admin	POADX	C-	(800) 927-4648	B- / 7.2	-8.88	7.16	14.99 /72	18.23 /73	6.14 /62	0.00	1.16
SC	Allianz PEA Opportunity B	POOBX	C-	(800) 927-4648	C+ / 6.4	-9.10	6.66	13.94 /68	17.14 /69	5.19 /56	0.00	2.06
SC	Allianz PEA Opportunity C	POPCX	C-	(800) 927-4648	C+ / 6.8	-9.10	6.60	13.88 /68	17.12 /69	5.19 /56	0.00	2.06
SC	Allianz PEA Opportunity Inst	POFIX	C	(800) 927-4648	B- / 7.3	-8.85	7.27	15.25 /73	18.48 /74	6.39 /63	0.00	0.91
MC	Allianz PEA Target A	PTAAX	D	(800) 927-4648	C / 4.3	-6.63	2.23	10.48 /50	13.90 /53	0.41 /17	0.00	1.21
MC	Allianz PEA Target Admin	PTADX	D+	(800) 927-4648	C / 5.2	-6.62	2.30	10.61 /51	14.09 /54	0.58 /18	0.00	1.07
MC	Allianz PEA Target B	PTABX	D	(800) 927-4648	C- / 4.1	-6.83	1.85	9.58 /44	13.03 /49	-0.34 /14	0.00	1.96
MC	Allianz PEA Target C	PTACX	D	(800) 927-4648	C / 4.6	-6.78	1.85	9.65 /44	13.06 /49	-0.34 /14	0.00	1.96
MC	Allianz PEA Target D	PTRDX	D+	(800) 927-4648	C / 5.1	-6.63	2.23	10.48 /50	13.90 /53	0.42 /17	0.00	1.21
MC	Allianz PEA Target Inst	PFTIX	C-	(800) 927-4648	C / 5.4	-6.54	2.44	10.89 /53	14.36 /56	0.80 /19	0.00	0.82
HL	Allianz RCM Biotechnology A	RABTX	E-	(800) 628-1237	E- / 0.0	-13.16	-9.09	-5.28 / 0	3.13 / 1	-4.81 / 3	0.00	1.57
HL	Allianz RCM Biotechnology B	RBBTX	E-	(800) 628-1237	E- / 0.0	-13.35	-9.48	-6.05 / 0	2.34 / 1	-5.55 / 2	0.00	2.32
HL	Allianz RCM Biotechnology C	RCBTX	E-	(800) 628-1237	E- / 0.0	-13.31	-9.44	-6.01 / 0	2.35 / 1	-5.54 / 2	0.00	2.32
HL	Allianz RCM Biotechnology D	DRBNX	E-	(800) 628-1237	E- / 0.0	-13.20	-9.13	-5.33 / 0	3.10 / 1	-4.64 / 3	0.00	1.56
GL	Allianz RCM Global Small Cap A	RGSAX	B+	(800) 628-1237	A- / 9.2	-3.76	6.86	24.02 /87	27.19 /93	11.41 /85	0.00	1.76
GL	Allianz RCM Global Small Cap B	RGSBX	B+	(800) 628-1237	A- / 9.1	-3.90	6.49	23.19 /86	26.29 /92	10.68 /83	0.00	2.51
GL	Allianz RCM Global Small Cap C	RGSCX	B+	(800) 628-1237	A- / 9.2	-3.94	6.49	23.16 /86	26.29 /92	10.66 /83	0.00	2.51
GL	Allianz RCM Global Small Cap D	DGSNX	B	(800) 628-1237	A / 9.3	-3.76	6.86	24.08 /87	27.22 /93	11.55 /86	0.00	1.76
GL	Allianz RCM Global Small Cap I	DGSCX	B	(800) 628-1237	A / 9.3	-3.66	7.11	24.61 /88	27.72 /94	11.93 /86	0.00	1.36
HL	Allianz RCM Healthcare A	RAGHX	E+	(800) 628-1237	E- / 0.1	-7.45	-4.76	0.19 / 2	4.43 / 3	0.33 /17	0.00	1.57
HL	Allianz RCM Healthcare B	RBGHX	E+	(800) 628-1237	E- / 0.1	-7.61	-5.13	-0.53 / 1	3.66 / 2	-0.43 /14	0.00	2.31
HL	Allianz RCM Healthcare C	RCGHX	E+	(800) 628-1237	E- / 0.1	-7.56	-5.08	-0.48 / 1	3.66 / 2	-0.42 /14	0.00	2.31
HL	Allianz RCM Healthcare D	DGHCX	E	(800) 628-1237	E- / 0.2	-7.41	-4.76	0.24 / 2	4.43 / 3	0.45 /17	0.00	1.56
FO	Allianz RCM Intl Growth Eqty A	RAIGX	B	(800) 628-1237	B+ / 8.3	-0.70	9.49	29.25 /94	21.02 /83	4.17 /47	1.24	1.37
FO	Allianz RCM Intl Growth Eqty Admin	RAIAX	A-	(800) 628-1237	B+ / 8.6	-0.69	9.61	29.48 /94	21.20 /83	4.34 /49	0.00	1.36
FO	Allianz RCM Intl Growth Eqty B	RBIGX	B	(800) 628-1237	B / 8.2	-0.88	9.20	28.38 /93	20.11 /80	3.40 /40	0.89	2.12
FO	Allianz RCM Intl Growth Eqty C	RCIGX	B	(800) 628-1237	B+ / 8.4	-0.87	9.16	28.36 /93	20.10 /80	3.40 /40	0.60	2.12
FO	Allianz RCM Intl Growth Eqty D	DIENX	B+	(800) 628-1237	B+ / 8.7	-0.70	9.51	29.26 /94	21.01 /83	4.27 /48	1.13	1.37
FO	Allianz RCM Intl Growth Eqty Inst	DRIEX	B+	(800) 628-1237	B+ / 8.7	-0.62	9.78	29.82 /94	21.48 /84	4.78 /52	1.78	1.02
IX	Allianz RCM Large-Cap Growth A	RALGX	D	(800) 628-1237	D- / 1.1	-4.20	-1.64	7.82 /31	8.00 /15	-0.61 /13	0.01	1.11
IX	Allianz RCM Large-Cap Growth	DLGAX	D	(800) 628-1237	D / 2.1	-4.24	-1.68	7.94 /32	8.18 /16	-0.41 /14	0.10	0.96
IX	Allianz RCM Large-Cap Growth B	RBLGX	D-	(800) 628-1237	E+ / 0.9	-4.45	-2.06	6.92 /26	7.19 /11	-1.35 /11	0.01	1.86
IX	Allianz RCM Large-Cap Growth C	RCLGX	D	(800) 628-1237	D- / 1.4	-4.38	-1.98	6.99 /26	7.21 /11	-1.34 /11	0.01	1.86
IX	Allianz RCM Large-Cap Growth D	DLCNX	D	(800) 628-1237	D / 2.0	-4.22	-1.65	7.77 /31	8.01 /15	-0.52 /13	0.01	1.11
IX	Allianz RCM Large-Cap Growth Inst	DRLCX	D+	(800) 628-1237	D / 2.2	-4.16	-1.47	8.25 /35	8.47 /18	-0.19 /15	0.36	0.71
IX	Allianz RCM Large-Cap Growth R	PLCRX	D	(800) 628-1237	D- / 1.5	-4.28	-1.80	7.49 /29	7.74 /14	-0.87 /12	0.10	1.36
MC	Allianz RCM Mid-Cap A	RMDAX	D+	(800) 628-1237	C- / 3.5	-6.47	-0.34	12.02 /60	12.31 /44	0.71 /19	0.00	1.14
MC	Allianz RCM Mid-Cap Admin	DRMAX	C-	(800) 628-1237	C / 4.6	-6.96	-0.68	11.36 /56	12.41 /45	1.13 /21	0.00	0.98
MC	Allianz RCM Mid-Cap B	RMDBX	D-	(800) 628-1237	C- / 3.2	-6.91	-1.05	10.98 /53	11.53 /39	0.21 /16	0.00	1.88
MC	Allianz RCM Mid-Cap C	RMDCX	D+	(800) 628-1237	C- / 3.8	-6.93	-1.05	11.02 /54	11.40 /39	0.14 /16	0.00	1.88
MC	Allianz RCM Mid-Cap D	DMCNX	D+	(800) 628-1237	C / 4.6	-6.71	-0.34	11.88 /59	12.33 /45	1.13 /21	0.00	1.14
MC	Allianz RCM Mid-Cap Inst	DRMCX	C-	(800) 628-1237	C / 4.8	-6.56	-0.33	11.99 /59	12.68 /47	1.47 /23	0.00	0.74
MC	Allianz RCM Mid-Cap R	PRMRX	C-	(800) 628-1237	C- / 4.0	-6.71	-0.68	11.45 /56	11.97 /42	0.77 /19	0.00	1.38
TC	Allianz RCM Technology A	RAGTX	E	(800) 628-1237	C- / 3.3	-13.22	-7.16	7.65 /30	13.89 /53	1.99 /27	0.00	1.63
TC	Allianz RCM Technology Admin		E	(800) 628-1237	C- / 4.2	-13.19	-7.09	7.82 /31	14.07 /54	2.15 /28	0.00	1.48
TC	Allianz RCM Technology B	RBGTX	E-	(800) 628-1237	C- / 3.0	-13.37	-7.48	6.84 /25	13.05 /49	1.22 /22	0.00	2.38
TC	Allianz RCM Technology C	RCGTX	E	(800) 628-1237	C- / 3.6	-13.35	-7.49	6.84 /25	13.06 /49	1.21 /22	0.00	2.38
TC	Allianz RCM Technology D	DGTNX	E	(800) 628-1237	C- / 4.1	-13.22	-7.15	7.66 /30	13.89 /53	2.00 /27	0.00	1.63
TC	Allianz RCM Technology Inst	DRGTX	E+	(800) 628-1237	C / 4.4	-13.13	-6.98	8.08 /33	14.35 /56	2.39 /31	0.00	1.23
AA	Alpha Strategies I Fund (The)	ALPHX	C+	(800) 569-2382	C- / 3.2	0.31	6.92	9.18 /41	9.38 /23	--	0.32	3.99
IN	Alpine Dynamic Dividend Fund	ADVDX	U	(888) 785-5578	U /	-0.22	8.30	15.66 /74	--	--	12.67	1.23

99 Pct = Best
0 Pct = Worst

PERFORMANCE

Total Return % through 6/30/06

Annualized

Incl. in Returns

● Denotes fund is closed to new investors
* Denotes fund is included in Section II

RISK			NET ASSETS		ASSET					BULL / BEAR		FUND MANAGER		MINIMUMS		LOADS	
	3 Year		NAV						Portfolio	Last Bull	Last Bear	Manager	Manager	Initial	Additional	Front	Back
Risk	Standard		As of	Total	Cash	Stocks	Bonds	Other	Turnover	Market	Market	Quality	Tenure	Purch.	Purch.	End	End
Rating/Pts	Deviation	Beta	6/30/06	$(Mil)	%	%	%	%	Ratio	Return	Return	Pct	(Years)	$	$	Load	Load
C- /4.2	17.1	1.13	25.47	56	0	99	0	1	139.0	139.4	-11.7	30	N/A	5,000	100	5.5	2.0
C- /4.2	17.1	1.13	21.55	3	0	99	0	1	139.0	140.5	-11.6	31	N/A	5,000,000	0	0.0	2.0
C- /4.1	17.1	1.13	20.19	19	0	99	0	1	139.0	133.8	-11.8	24	N/A	5,000	100	0.0	5.0
C- /4.1	17.1	1.13	20.18	140	0	99	0	1	139.0	133.8	-11.8	24	N/A	5,000	100	0.0	2.0
C- /4.2	17.1	1.13	21.84	38	0	99	0	1	139.0	142.3	-11.5	33	N/A	5,000,000	0	0.0	2.0
C /4.9	14.9	1.33	19.71	169	N/A	100	0	N/A	103.0	91.2	-8.1	4	N/A	5,000	100	5.5	2.0
C /5.0	14.9	1.33	20.02	N/A	N/A	100	0	N/A	103.0	92.2	-8.0	4	N/A	5,000,000	0	0.0	2.0
C /4.9	14.9	1.33	17.04	62	N/A	100	0	N/A	103.0	86.7	-8.3	3	N/A	5,000	100	0.0	5.0
C /4.9	15.0	1.33	17.04	423	N/A	100	0	N/A	103.0	86.7	-8.3	3	N/A	5,000	100	0.0	2.0
C /4.9	14.9	1.32	19.71	1	N/A	100	0	N/A	103.0	91.2	-8.1	4	N/A	5,000	100	0.0	2.0
C /5.0	14.9	1.32	20.16	7	N/A	100	0	N/A	103.0	93.6	-8.0	4	N/A	5,000,000	0	0.0	2.0
D /2.1	17.7	0.97	23.30	13	0	99	0	1	139.0	56.0	-8.6	6	N/A	5,000	100	5.5	1.0
D /2.1	17.6	0.97	22.53	6	0	99	0	1	139.0	52.3	-8.8	4	N/A	5,000	100	0.0	5.0
D /2.1	17.7	0.97	22.54	7	0	99	0	1	139.0	52.3	-8.8	4	N/A	5,000	100	0.0	1.0
D /1.6	17.7	0.97	23.28	147	0	99	0	1	139.0	56.0	-8.6	6	N/A	5,000	100	0.0	2.0
C+ /6.0	13.3	1.13	27.88	71	5	94	0	1	96.0	174.6	-8.6	52	N/A	5,000	100	5.5	1.0
C+ /6.0	13.3	1.13	27.09	48	5	94	0	1	96.0	168.2	-8.8	43	N/A	5,000	100	0.0	5.0
C+ /6.0	13.3	1.13	27.07	41	5	94	0	1	96.0	168.4	-8.8	43	N/A	5,000	100	0.0	1.0
C /5.0	13.3	1.13	27.88	31	5	94	0	1	96.0	174.8	-8.6	53	N/A	5,000	100	0.0	2.0
C /5.0	13.3	1.13	28.46	24	5	94	0	1	96.0	177.8	-8.6	58	N/A	5,000,000	0	0.0	2.0
B- /7.0	8.8	0.57	21.23	15	1	98	0	1	210.0	45.7	-2.0	28	N/A	5,000	100	5.5	1.0
B- /7.0	8.8	0.57	20.53	8	1	98	0	1	210.0	42.2	-2.2	23	N/A	5,000	100	0.0	5.0
B- /7.0	8.8	0.57	20.54	8	1	98	0	1	210.0	42.3	-2.2	23	N/A	2,500	100	0.0	1.0
C+ /6.1	8.8	0.57	21.23	84	1	98	0	1	210.0	45.6	-2.0	28	N/A	5,000	100	0.0	2.0
C+ /6.0	11.5	1.10	12.69	18	0	99	0	1	138.0	114.0	-9.6	15	N/A	5,000	100	5.5	1.0
B- /7.0	11.5	1.10	13.00	N/A	0	99	0	1	138.0	115.0	-9.5	16	N/A	5,000,000	0	0.0	2.0
C+ /6.0	11.5	1.10	12.46	13	0	99	0	1	138.0	108.9	-9.8	11	N/A	5,000	100	0.0	5.0
C+ /6.0	11.5	1.10	12.51	39	0	99	0	1	138.0	108.9	-9.8	11	N/A	5,000	100	0.0	1.0
C+ /6.0	11.5	1.10	12.78	2	0	99	0	1	138.0	114.1	-9.6	15	N/A	5,000	100	0.0	0.0
C+ /6.1	11.5	1.10	12.91	7	0	99	0	1	138.0	117.5	-9.5	17	N/A	5,000,000	0	0.0	2.0
B- /7.5	8.1	0.91	13.67	56	1	98	0	1	118.0	50.2	-8.5	32	N/A	5,000	100	5.5	1.0
B- /7.5	8.1	0.91	13.77	63	1	98	0	1	118.0	51.1	-8.4	33	N/A	5,000,000	0	0.0	0.0
B- /7.4	8.1	0.91	13.30	11	1	98	0	1	118.0	46.6	-8.7	26	N/A	5,000	100	0.0	5.0
B- /7.4	8.1	0.91	13.33	10	1	98	0	1	118.0	46.8	-8.7	27	N/A	5,000	100	0.0	1.0
B- /7.5	8.1	0.91	13.61	54	1	98	0	1	118.0	50.4	-8.5	32	N/A	5,000	100	0.0	0.0
B- /7.5	8.1	0.91	13.83	349	1	98	0	1	118.0	52.3	-8.4	35	N/A	5,000,000	0	0.0	0.0
B- /7.5	8.1	0.91	13.64	4	1	98	0	1	118.0	49.1	-8.6	30	N/A	2,500	50	0.0	2.0
C+ /6.5	12.4	1.05	2.89	4	1	98	0	1	147.0	75.3	-6.3	10	N/A	5,000	100	5.5	1.0
C+ /6.4	12.6	1.08	2.94	N/A	1	98	0	1	147.0	77.2	-5.8	9	N/A	5,000,000	0	0.0	0.0
C /4.9	12.4	1.07	2.83	3	1	98	0	1	147.0	71.9	-6.3	7	N/A	2,500	100	0.0	5.0
C+ /6.4	12.7	1.08	2.82	4	1	98	0	1	147.0	71.9	-5.8	6	N/A	5,000	100	0.0	1.0
C+ /5.6	12.5	1.06	2.92	1	1	98	0	1	147.0	76.5	-5.8	10	N/A	5,000	100	0.0	0.0
C+ /5.6	12.6	1.08	2.99	102	1	98	0	1	147.0	79.0	-5.7	10	N/A	5,000,000	0	0.0	0.0
C+ /6.4	12.6	1.08	2.92	N/A	1	98	0	1	147.0	74.6	-5.7	8	N/A	2,500	50	0.0	2.0
D /1.9	18.9	1.73	36.18	329	4	95	0	1	238.0	130.0	-14.2	21	N/A	5,000	100	5.5	1.0
D /2.2	18.3	1.62	36.67	25	4	95	0	1	238.0	131.0	-14.1	28	N/A	5,000	100	0.0	2.0
D /1.9	18.9	1.73	34.99	117	4	95	0	1	238.0	124.4	-14.3	16	N/A	5,000	100	0.0	5.0
D /1.9	18.9	1.73	34.97	193	4	95	0	1	238.0	124.6	-14.3	16	N/A	5,000	100	0.0	1.0
D+ /2.3	18.9	1.73	35.84	246	4	95	0	1	238.0	129.9	-14.1	21	N/A	5,000	100	0.0	2.0
D+ /2.4	18.9	1.73	36.78	324	4	95	0	1	238.0	132.8	-14.1	24	N/A	5,000,000	0	0.0	2.0
B+ /9.6	5.6	0.65	12.97	220	2	58	31	9	97.0	32.1	2.2	87	4	10,000	250	0.0	2.0
U /	N/A	N/A	12.35	472	2	97	0	1	216.0	N/A	N/A	N/A	3	1,000	50	0.0	1.0

	99 Pct = Best 0 Pct = Worst		Overall Weiss Investment Rating		PERFORMANCE						Incl. in Returns	
					Perfor-mance Rating/Pts	Total Return % through 6/30/06			Annualized		Dividend Yield	Expense Ratio
Fund Type	Fund Name	Ticker Symbol		Phone		3 Mo	6 Mo	1Yr / Pct	3Yr / Pct	5Yr / Pct		
RE	Alpine Intl Real Estate Y	EGLRX	A	(888) 785-5578	A / 9.5	-5.52	9.18	18.73 /80	31.05 /96	22.11 /98	1.15	1.18
RE	Alpine Realty Inc & Growth Y	AIGYX	A-	(888) 785-5578	B+ / 8.8	-0.21	10.29	14.94 /72	23.66 /89	20.36 /96	3.45	1.18
RE	Alpine U.S. Real Estate Eq Y	EUEYX	D	(888) 785-5578	C+ / 6.1	-13.62	-12.01	-17.88 / 0	21.93 /85	21.67 /97	0.07	1.19
GR	Amana Mutual Fund-Growth Fund	AMAGX	B+	(800) 728-8762	B+ / 8.3	-4.09	3.35	19.81 /82	21.74 /84	8.39 /73	0.00	1.66
IN	Amana Mutual Fund-Income Fund	AMANX	A+	(800) 728-8762	B+ / 8.3	0.49	9.83	19.65 /81	20.62 /82	8.77 /75	1.12	1.61
BA	American Beacon Balance Inst	AADBX	C+	(800) 967-9009	C- / 4.1	-0.48	2.16	5.70 /19	11.53 /39	7.53 /69	2.50	0.56
BA	American Beacon Balance PlanAhd	AABPX	C	(800) 967-9009	C- / 3.9	-0.50	2.07	5.47 /17	11.16 /37	7.25 /68	2.47	0.86
BA	American Beacon Balance Ser	ABLSX	C+	(800) 967-9009	C- / 3.7	-0.58	1.93	4.86 /14	10.94 /35	7.13 /67	2.38	1.09
EM	American Beacon Emerg Mkts Inst	AEMFX	B	(800) 967-9009	A+ / 9.7	-5.09	6.89	32.27 /96	32.43 /97	21.18 /97	1.20	1.52
EM	American Beacon Emerg Mkts	AAEPX	B	(800) 967-9009	A+ / 9.6	-5.19	6.81	32.06 /96	32.16 /97	20.95 /97	1.05	2.00
IN	American Beacon Enhanced Income	AANPX	U	(800) 967-9009	U /	-0.41	0.35	1.16 / 3	--	--	2.87	0.92
FO	American Beacon Intl Eq Index Inst	AIIIX	A+	(800) 967-9009	A- / 9.1	0.89	10.26	26.58 /91	23.88 /89	9.96 /80	2.95	0.23
FO	American Beacon Intl Eq Inst	AAIEX	A+	(800) 967-9009	A- / 9.1	1.32	10.60	25.22 /89	24.47 /90	11.41 /85	1.75	0.70
FO	American Beacon Intl Eq PlanAhd	AAIPX	A+	(800) 967-9009	A- / 9.0	1.25	10.45	24.88 /88	24.18 /90	11.23 /84	1.59	0.95
FO	American Beacon Intl Eq Svc	AAISX	A+	(800) 967-9009	A- / 9.0	1.16	10.35	24.62 /88	23.81 /89	11.03 /84	1.10	1.21
GR	American Beacon Lg Cap Val Inst	AADEX	A+	(800) 967-9009	B- / 7.4	0.28	5.00	11.93 /59	18.20 /73	9.05 /76	1.15	0.60
GR	American Beacon Lg Cap Val	AAGPX	A+	(800) 967-9009	B- / 7.3	0.24	4.86	11.62 /57	17.90 /72	8.75 /75	1.13	0.86
GR	American Beacon Lrg Cap Gr Inst	ALCGX	D+	(800) 967-9009	D+ / 2.4	-4.04	-0.77	6.65 /24	8.99 /21	-0.59 /13	0.50	0.90
MC	American Beacon MidCap Val AMR	AMDIX	U	(800) 967-9009	U /	-1.99	3.47	8.22 /34	--	--	1.10	1.02
IX	American Beacon S&P 500 Index	AASPX	C+	(800) 967-9009	C- / 3.9	-1.49	2.70	7.98 /33	10.86 /34	2.19 /29	1.31	1.28
IX	American Beacon S&P 500 PlanAhd	AAFPX	C	(800) 967-9009	C- / 3.6	-1.56	2.42	7.55 /30	10.51 /31	1.81 /26	1.02	0.62
SC	American Beacon Sm Cap Index Inst	ASCIX	B-	(800) 967-9009	B- / 7.3	-5.22	8.06	12.69 /63	17.82 /72	8.06 /72	1.21	0.18
SC	American Beacon Sm Cap Val AMR	AASVX	A	(800) 967-9009	B / 8.1	-3.03	5.71	10.20 /48	21.31 /83	16.04 /93	0.84	0.58
SC	● American Beacon Sm Cap Val Inst	AVFIX	A	(800) 967-9009	B / 8.1	-3.10	5.59	9.91 /46	21.00 /83	15.73 /93	0.61	0.87
SC	● American Beacon Sm Cap Val	AVPAX	A	(800) 967-9009	B / 8.0	-3.16	5.44	9.60 /44	20.67 /82	15.39 /92	0.42	1.10
SC	● American Beacon Sm Cap Val Svc	AASSX	A-	(800) 967-9009	B / 7.8	-3.23	5.26	9.26 /42	20.33 /81	15.18 /92	0.27	1.40
BA	American Century Balanced Adv	TWBAX	C-	(800) 345-6488	D / 2.0	-0.61	1.11	4.12 /11	7.98 /15	4.04 /46	1.65	1.15
BA	American Century Balanced Inst	ABINX	C	(800) 345-6488	D+ / 2.3	-0.44	1.38	4.64 /13	8.46 /18	4.52 /50	2.08	0.70
BA	American Century Balanced Inv	TWBIX	C-	(800) 345-6488	D / 2.2	-0.49	1.29	4.43 /12	8.24 /16	4.32 /49	1.89	0.90
GI	American Century Capital Val Adv	ACCVX	B-	(800) 345-6488	C / 4.9	0.27	4.04	8.24 /35	12.42 /45	--	1.12	1.35
GI	American Century Capital Val Inst	ACPIX	B	(800) 345-6488	C / 5.3	0.40	4.32	8.85 /39	12.91 /48	--	1.54	0.90
GI	American Century Capital Val Inv	ACTIX	B	(800) 345-6488	C / 5.1	0.40	4.18	8.50 /37	12.71 /47	6.05 /61	1.36	1.10
EM	American Century Emerging Mkt Adv	AEMMX	B-	(800) 345-6488	A+ / 9.8	-3.82	11.49	45.77 /98	34.83 /98	16.13 /93	0.30	2.10
EM	American Century Emerging Mkt C	ACECX	B-	(800) 345-6488	A+ / 9.8	-4.01	10.95	44.70 /98	33.98 /97	--	0.00	2.85
EM	American Century Emerging Mkt Inst	AMKIX	C+	(800) 345-6488	A+ / 9.8	-3.82	11.52	46.14 /98	35.37 /98	16.62 /94	0.69	1.65
EM	American Century Emerging Mkt Inv	TWMIX	B-	(800) 345-6488	A+ / 9.8	-3.76	11.56	45.98 /98	35.18 /98	16.39 /93	0.52	1.85
GR	American Century Equity Growth Adv	BEQAX	C+	(800) 345-6488	C / 5.2	-0.73	2.83	8.48 /37	13.00 /49	3.88 /45	0.63	0.92
GR	American Century Equity Growth C	AEYCX	C+	(800) 345-6488	C / 4.5	-0.92	2.42	7.65 /30	12.22 /44	--	0.08	1.67
GR	American Century Equity Growth Inst	AMEIX	B-	(800) 345-6488	C / 5.4	-0.58	3.04	9.01 /40	13.48 /51	4.37 /49	1.07	0.47
★ GR	American Century Equity Growth Inv	BEQGX	C+	(800) 345-6488	C / 5.3	-0.63	2.95	8.79 /39	13.29 /50	4.16 /47	0.88	0.67
IN	American Century Equity Income Adv	TWEAX	C+	(800) 345-6488	C / 4.4	1.06	5.32	7.30 /28	11.23 /37	8.43 /74	1.84	1.24
IN	American Century Equity Income C	AEYIX	C	(800) 345-6488	C- / 3.6	0.87	4.95	6.50 /23	10.47 /31	--	1.12	1.98
IN	American Century Equity Income Inst	ACIIX	C+	(800) 345-6488	C / 4.7	1.17	5.53	7.78 /31	11.73 /41	8.91 /76	2.26	0.79
★ IN	American Century Equity Income Inv	TWEIX	C+	(800) 345-6488	C / 4.5	1.00	5.31	7.44 /29	11.46 /39	8.67 /75	2.08	0.99
IN	American Century Equity Income R	AEURX	U	(800) 345-6488	U /	0.99	5.07	6.91 /26	--	--	1.60	1.48
IN	American Century Equity Index Inst	ACQIX	C	(800) 345-6488	C- / 4.0	-1.37	2.59	8.50 /37	10.97 /35	2.23 /29	1.62	0.29
IN	American Century Equity Index Inv	ACIVX	C	(800) 345-6488	C- / 3.8	-1.62	2.50	8.07 /33	10.68 /33	1.98 /27	1.42	0.49
SC	American Century Giftrust	TWGTX	C	(800) 345-6488	B / 7.8	-3.14	9.52	27.25 /92	17.44 /70	2.56 /32	0.00	1.00
PM	American Century Global Gold Adv	ACGGX	D+	(800) 345-6488	A+ / 9.8	1.52	20.36	65.85 /99	27.39 /93	31.64 /99	0.04	0.92
PM	American Century Global Gold Inv	BGEIX	D+	(800) 345-6488	A+ / 9.8	1.56	20.49	66.31 /99	27.65 /94	31.93 /99	0.25	0.67
GL	● American Century Global Growth Adv	AGGRX	C+	(800) 345-6488	B- / 7.5	-4.35	4.41	19.99 /82	19.63 /78	6.52 /64	0.44	1.55
GL	● American Century Global Growth C	AGLCX	C+	(800) 345-6488	B- / 7.3	-4.55	4.05	19.07 /81	18.81 /76	--	0.00	2.30

● Denotes fund is closed to new investors
★ Denotes fund is included in Section II

46

RISK			NET ASSETS		ASSET					BULL / BEAR		FUND MANAGER		MINIMUMS		LOADS	
	3 Year		NAV							Last Bull	Last Bear	Manager	Manager	Initial	Additional	Front	Back
Risk Rating/Pts	Standard Deviation	Beta	As of 6/30/06	Total $(Mil)	Cash %	Stocks %	Bonds %	Other %	Portfolio Turnover Ratio	Market Return	Market Return	Quality Pct	Tenure (Years)	Purch. $	Purch. $	End Load	End Load
C+ / 6.4	11.6	0.38	33.18	614	3	96	0	1	10.0	190.9	0.6	99	17	1,000	50	0.0	1.0
C+ / 6.6	13.2	0.78	24.74	727	0	100	0	0	34.0	114.9	-0.5	89	7	1,000	0	0.0	1.0
C- / 3.3	20.2	0.72	36.20	359	0	100	0	0	34.0	186.3	-5.1	88	13	1,000	50	0.0	1.0
C+ / 6.3	10.7	1.26	18.51	210	2	97	0	1	7.0	123.0	-7.2	97	12	250	25	0.0	2.0
B / 8.0	10.7	1.03	25.54	78	6	93	0	1	6.0	106.4	-6.3	98	16	250	25	0.0	2.0
B / 8.6	5.4	1.10	14.65	17	9	60	30	1	58.0	60.4	-4.2	85	N/A	2,000,000	0	0.0	0.0
B / 8.5	5.4	1.10	13.82	92	9	60	30	1	58.0	58.8	-4.3	83	N/A	2,500	50	0.0	0.0
B+ / 9.6	5.4	1.10	13.75	850	9	60	30	1	58.0	58.0	-4.3	82	N/A	2,500	50	0.0	0.0
C / 4.5	17.5	1.07	15.67	14	4	94	0	2	63.0	213.4	-6.0	16	N/A	2,000,000	0	0.0	2.0
C / 4.5	17.5	1.07	15.53	5	4	94	0	2	63.0	211.1	-6.1	15	N/A	2,500	50	0.0	2.0
U /	N/A	N/A	9.96	105	0	4	81	15	41.0	N/A	N/A	N/A	N/A	2,500	50	0.0	0.0
B / 8.1	10.1	1.00	11.39	91	6	93	0	1	11.3	132.0	-9.6	50	6	2,000,000	0	0.0	0.0
B- / 7.8	9.7	0.94	22.96	1,505	4	94	0	2	37.0	139.9	-10.3	70	N/A	2,000,000	0	0.0	2.0
B- / 7.8	9.7	0.94	22.73	696	4	94	0	2	37.0	138.2	-10.3	67	N/A	2,500	50	0.0	2.0
B / 8.4	9.7	0.94	22.61	4	4	94	0	2	37.0	136.1	-10.3	64	N/A	2,500	50	0.0	2.0
B / 8.8	8.1	1.00	21.84	584	5	94	0	1	25.0	102.5	-8.4	96	N/A	2,000,000	0	0.0	0.0
B / 8.8	8.1	1.00	20.91	1,528	5	94	0	1	25.0	100.7	-8.5	95	N/A	2,500	50	0.0	0.0
B- / 7.9	9.3	1.14	6.41	N/A	4	95	0	1	164.0	54.5	-0.1	25	N/A	2,000,000	0	0.0	0.0
U /	N/A	N/A	9.83	42	3	96	0	1	298.0	N/A	N/A	N/A	N/A	2,000,000	0	0.0	2.0
B / 8.7	7.7	1.01	17.27	203	2	96	0	2	8.0	63.2	-9.8	51	N/A	2,000,000	0	0.0	0.0
B / 8.7	7.7	1.01	17.03	51	2	96	0	2	8.0	61.4	-9.9	47	6	2,500	50	0.0	0.0
C+ / 6.5	14.6	1.00	13.81	178	18	81	0	1	36.6	115.6	-10.9	45	N/A	2,000,000	0	0.0	0.0
B- / 7.7	12.4	0.82	21.47	433	5	94	0	1	47.0	137.0	-9.2	93	N/A	0	0	0.0	0.0
B- / 7.7	12.4	0.82	21.54	1,305	5	94	0	1	47.0	135.1	-9.3	92	N/A	2,000,000	0	0.0	0.0
B- / 7.7	12.4	0.82	21.12	1,334	5	94	0	1	47.0	133.1	-9.4	91	N/A	2,500	50	0.0	0.0
B- / 7.7	12.4	0.82	21.00	61	5	94	0	1	47.0	131.1	-9.4	90	N/A	2,500	50	0.0	0.0
B / 8.6	5.1	1.04	16.13	14	1	57	41	1	204.0	41.6	-3.8	58	9	2,500	50	0.0	0.0
B+ / 9.8	5.1	1.04	16.14	1	1	57	41	1	204.0	43.6	-3.7	63	18	5,000,000	0	0.0	0.0
B / 8.6	5.1	1.04	16.14	621	1	57	41	1	204.0	42.7	-3.8	61	18	2,500	50	0.0	0.0
B / 8.8	7.2	0.90	7.46	15	2	98	0	0	29.0	N/A	N/A	76	7	2,500	50	0.0	0.0
B+ / 9.0	7.2	0.91	7.48	32	2	98	0	0	29.0	72.1	-8.5	79	7	5,000,000	0	0.0	0.0
B+ / 9.0	7.2	0.90	7.47	417	2	98	0	0	29.0	71.1	-8.5	79	7	2,500	50	0.0	0.0
C- / 4.0	19.1	1.12	8.05	6	7	92	0	1	155.0	224.6	-6.4	19	N/A	2,500	50	0.0	2.0
C- / 4.0	19.1	1.12	7.90	1	7	92	0	1	155.0	218.4	-6.7	15	N/A	2,500	50	0.0	1.0
C- / 3.6	19.2	1.13	8.32	82	7	92	0	1	155.0	229.6	-6.3	20	N/A	5,000,000	0	0.0	2.0
C- / 4.0	19.1	1.12	8.20	361	7	92	0	1	155.0	227.5	-6.4	20	9	2,500	50	0.0	2.0
B / 8.3	8.4	1.04	23.91	352	0	99	0	1	106.0	71.6	-8.6	70	9	2,500	50	0.0	0.0
B / 8.3	8.4	1.04	23.81	7	0	99	0	1	106.0	67.9	-8.8	62	N/A	2,500	50	0.0	1.0
B / 8.3	8.4	1.04	23.94	377	0	99	0	1	106.0	73.9	-8.4	74	N/A	5,000,000	0	0.0	0.0
B / 8.3	8.4	1.04	23.93	2,211	0	99	0	1	106.0	72.9	-8.5	72	9	2,500	50	0.0	0.0
B / 8.5	6.1	0.70	8.17	890	0	67	0	33	175.0	57.9	-6.9	81	N/A	2,500	50	0.0	0.0
B / 8.5	6.0	0.70	8.17	99	0	67	0	33	175.0	54.4	-7.0	76	N/A	2,500	50	0.0	1.0
B / 8.5	6.0	0.70	8.17	357	0	67	0	33	175.0	60.3	-6.9	84	N/A	5,000,000	0	0.0	0.0
B / 8.5	6.0	0.70	8.16	3,580	0	67	0	33	175.0	59.3	-6.8	83	N/A	2,500	50	0.0	0.0
U /	N/A	N/A	8.15	26	0	67	0	33	175.0	N/A	N/A	N/A	N/A	2,500	50	0.0	0.0
B / 8.3	7.7	1.00	5.07	744	1	98	0	1	4.0	63.2	-9.8	53	N/A	5,000,000	0	0.0	0.0
B / 8.2	7.7	1.01	5.06	210	1	98	0	1	4.0	62.2	-9.8	49	7	10,000	50	0.0	0.0
C- / 4.1	14.2	0.87	20.36	1,029	1	98	0	1	219.0	92.0	-9.9	66	N/A	2,500	50	0.0	0.0
E- / 0.0	34.4	1.67	18.60	6	2	97	0	1	5.0	153.9	17.4	9	15	2,500	50	0.0	1.0
E- / 0.0	34.4	1.67	18.62	1,012	2	97	0	1	5.0	155.7	17.3	10	15	2,500	50	0.0	1.0
C+ / 5.8	11.0	0.96	9.46	5	1	98	0	1	38.0	112.0	-10.6	26	N/A	2,500	50	0.0	2.0
C+ / 5.7	11.0	0.96	9.24	1	1	98	0	1	38.0	107.3	-10.8	20	N/A	2,500	50	0.0	1.0

	99 Pct = Best 0 Pct = Worst		Overall Weiss		PERFORMANCE						Incl. in Returns	
					Perfor-mance	Total Return % through 6/30/06			Annualized		Dividend	Expense
Fund Type	Fund Name	Ticker Symbol	Investment Rating	Phone	Rating/Pts	3 Mo	6 Mo	1Yr / Pct	3Yr / Pct	5Yr / Pct	Yield	Ratio
GL	● American Century Global Growth Inst	AGGIX	B	(800) 345-6488	B / 7.7	-4.28	4.68	20.60 /83	20.16 /80	7.04 /67	0.86	1.10
GL	● American Century Global Growth Inv	TWGGX	C+	(800) 345-6488	B / 7.6	-4.21	4.60	20.36 /82	19.93 /79	6.80 /66	0.67	1.30
GR	American Century Growth Adv	TCRAX	D	(800) 345-6488	D / 2.1	-3.74	-1.38	5.35 /17	8.49 /18	-0.60 /13	0.21	1.25
GR	American Century Growth C	TWGCX	D-	(800) 345-6488	D- / 1.5	-3.89	-1.71	4.55 /13	7.71 /13	--	0.00	2.00
GR	American Century Growth Inst	TWGIX	D+	(800) 345-6488	D+ / 2.3	-3.62	-1.16	5.84 /19	8.97 /21	-0.10 /15	0.59	0.80
★ GR	American Century Growth Inv	TWCGX	D	(800) 345-6488	D / 2.2	-3.65	-1.21	5.66 /18	8.77 /19	-0.31 /14	0.42	1.00
GR	American Century Heritage Adv	ATHAX	C	(800) 345-6488	B / 8.0	-3.30	9.37	27.14 /91	18.30 /74	4.36 /49	0.00	1.25
GR	American Century Heritage C	AHGCX	C	(800) 345-6488	B / 7.7	-3.47	8.93	26.19 /90	17.48 /70	3.60 /42	0.00	2.00
GR	American Century Heritage Inst	ATHIX	C	(800) 345-6488	B / 8.2	-3.15	9.68	27.76 /92	18.83 /76	4.86 /53	0.00	0.80
GR	American Century Heritage Inv	TWHIX	C	(800) 345-6488	B / 8.1	-3.25	9.51	27.41 /92	18.60 /75	4.64 /51	0.00	1.00
GI	American Century Inc & Gr Adv	AMADX	C+	(800) 345-6488	C / 4.4	-0.20	2.67	6.98 /26	11.78 /41	3.69 /43	1.66	0.92
GI	American Century Inc & Gr C	ACGCX	C	(800) 345-6488	C- / 3.7	-0.39	2.32	6.19 /21	11.01 /36	2.92 /36	0.95	1.67
GI	American Century Inc & Gr Inst	AMGIX	C+	(800) 345-6488	C / 4.7	-0.09	2.92	7.45 /29	12.26 /44	4.18 /48	2.09	0.47
★ GI	American Century Inc & Gr Inv	BIGRX	C+	(800) 345-6488	C / 4.6	-0.14	2.82	7.24 /28	12.05 /43	3.97 /46	1.90	0.67
FO	● American Century Intl Disc Adv	ACIDX	C+	(800) 345-6488	A+ / 9.7	-2.19	12.56	46.32 /99	31.07 /96	15.09 /92	0.46	1.72
FO	● American Century Intl Disc Inst	TIDIX	C+	(800) 345-6488	A+ / 9.7	-2.09	12.74	46.98 /99	31.61 /96	15.62 /93	0.84	1.27
FO	● American Century Intl Disc Inv	TWEGX	C+	(800) 345-6488	A+ / 9.7	-2.10	12.69	46.75 /99	31.36 /96	15.39 /92	0.67	1.47
FO	American Century Intl Gr A	CAIGX	B+	(800) 345-6488	B- / 7.4	-2.16	7.63	23.30 /86	18.46 /74	--	1.31	1.48
FO	American Century Intl Gr Adv	TWGAX	B-	(800) 345-6488	B / 7.7	-2.16	7.64	23.33 /86	18.47 /74	4.88 /53	1.39	1.48
FO	American Century Intl Gr B	CBIGX	B	(800) 345-6488	B- / 7.1	-2.35	7.25	22.27 /85	17.57 /70	--	0.70	2.23
FO	American Century Intl Gr C	AIWCX	B+	(800) 345-6488	B- / 7.5	-2.36	7.29	22.40 /85	17.62 /71	--	0.71	2.23
FO	American Century Intl Gr Inst	TGRIX	B	(800) 345-6488	B / 7.8	-2.07	7.82	23.78 /87	18.97 /76	5.39 /57	1.80	1.03
★ FO	● American Century Intl Gr Inv	TWIEX	B-	(800) 345-6488	B / 7.8	-2.16	7.73	23.60 /87	18.72 /75	5.16 /55	1.63	1.23
FO	American Century Intl Opport Inst	ACIOX	A+	(800) 345-6488	A+ / 9.8	-6.49	6.98	34.51 /96	38.09 /99	--	0.28	1.71
FO	American Century Intl Opport Inv	AIOIX	A+	(800) 345-6488	A+ / 9.8	-6.51	6.90	34.22 /96	37.77 /99	25.47 /99	0.10	1.91
FO	American Century Intl Stock Inv	ASKIX	U	(800) 345-6488	U /	-2.09	7.51	22.93 /86	--	--	0.65	1.50
HL	American Century Life Sciences Adv	ALSVX	E+	(800) 345-6488	E+ / 0.9	-7.65	-6.60	-2.94 / 0	7.81 /14	--	0.00	1.75
HL	American Century Life Sciences C	ALFSX	E+	(800) 345-6488	E+ / 0.6	-7.69	-6.98	-3.61 / 0	7.07 /11	--	0.00	2.50
HL	American Century Life Sciences Fd	ALSIX	D-	(800) 345-6488	D- / 1.0	-7.55	-6.52	-2.71 / 0	8.05 /15	-0.66 /13	0.00	1.30
HL	American Century Life Sciences I	AILSX	D-	(800) 345-6488	D- / 1.1	-7.45	-6.26	-2.49 / 0	8.27 /16	-0.43 /14	0.00	1.50
GR	American Century Lrge Comp Val A	ALAVX	C+	(800) 345-6488	C- / 4.2	0.41	4.05	8.57 /37	12.75 /47	--	1.37	1.09
GR	American Century Lrge Comp Val	ALPAX	B-	(800) 345-6488	C / 5.1	0.26	4.05	8.42 /36	12.69 /47	6.10 /62	1.46	1.09
GR	American Century Lrge Comp Val B	ALBVX	C+	(800) 345-6488	C- / 3.8	0.07	3.68	7.75 /31	11.96 /42	--	0.73	1.84
GR	American Century Lrge Comp Val C	ALPCX	C+	(800) 345-6488	C / 4.5	0.07	3.69	7.61 /30	11.93 /42	--	0.73	1.84
GR	American Century Lrge Comp Val Inst	ALVSX	B	(800) 345-6488	C / 5.4	0.52	4.43	9.07 /40	13.18 /50	--	1.89	0.67
GR	● American Century Lrge Comp Val Inv	ALVIX	B	(800) 345-6488	C / 5.3	0.47	4.33	8.85 /39	13.03 /49	6.39 /63	1.70	0.87
AA	American Century LStrong 2015 Inv	ARFIX	U	(800) 345-6488	U /	-0.54	2.03	6.03 /21	--	--	2.80	0.20
AA	American Century LStrong 2025 Inst	ARWFX	U	(800) 345-6488	U /	-1.12	2.50	8.29 /35	--	--	2.89	0.70
MC	American Century Mid Cap Val Inv	ACMVX	U	(800) 345-6488	U /	-1.40	5.20	11.68 /58	--	--	0.98	1.00
SC	American Century New Opps II A	ANOAX	C	(800) 345-6488	B- / 7.5	-3.93	9.86	17.82 /79	19.33 /77	--	0.00	1.75
SC	American Century New Opps II B	ANOBX	C-	(800) 345-6488	B- / 7.3	-4.09	9.33	16.87 /77	18.38 /74	--	0.00	2.50
SC	American Century New Opps II C	ANOCX	C	(800) 345-6488	B / 7.6	-4.08	9.45	16.80 /77	18.36 /74	--	0.00	2.50
SC	● American Century New Opps II Inv	ANOIX	C	(800) 345-6488	B / 8.1	-3.79	9.97	18.14 /79	19.57 /78	9.39 /78	0.00	1.50
SC	● American Century New Opps Inv	TWNOX	C-	(800) 345-6488	C+ / 5.6	-5.01	8.40	16.85 /77	13.77 /53	2.01 /27	0.00	1.50
AA	American Century One Chc Conv Inv	AOCIX	U	(800) 345-6488	U /	-0.36	2.12	5.16 /16	--	--	3.12	0.78
AA	American Century One Chc VryAgg	AOVIX	U	(800) 345-6488	U /	-2.07	4.59	14.41 /70	--	--	2.16	1.03
RE	American Century Real Estate Adv	AREEX	C+	(800) 345-6488	A / 9.4	-0.65	13.31	22.80 /85	27.01 /93	20.40 /96	1.79	1.40
RE	American Century Real Estate Inst	REAIX	C+	(800) 345-6488	A / 9.4	-0.54	13.59	23.34 /86	27.50 /93	20.89 /97	2.17	0.96
RE	American Century Real Estate Inv	REACX	C+	(800) 345-6488	A / 9.4	-0.55	13.50	23.12 /86	27.28 /93	20.65 /97	2.00	1.16
GR	American Century Select A	AASLX	E+	(800) 345-6488	E- / 0.0	-7.01	-7.31	-3.46 / 0	3.21 / 1	--	0.50	1.25
GR	American Century Select Adv	TWCAX	E+	(800) 345-6488	E- / 0.1	-7.01	-7.30	-3.43 / 0	3.23 / 1	-2.44 / 7	0.53	1.25
GR	American Century Select B	ABSLX	E+	(800) 345-6488	E- / 0.0	-7.18	-7.65	-4.16 / 0	2.44 / 1	--	0.00	2.00

● Denotes fund is closed to new investors
★ Denotes fund is included in Section II

48

RISK	3 Year		NET ASSETS		ASSET					BULL / BEAR		FUND MANAGER		MINIMUMS		LOADS	
Risk Rating/Pts	Standard Deviation	Beta	NAV As of 6/30/06	Total $(Mil)	Cash %	Stocks %	Bonds %	Other %	Portfolio Turnover Ratio	Last Bull Market Return	Last Bear Market Return	Manager Quality Pct	Manager Tenure (Years)	Initial Purch. $	Additional Purch. $	Front End Load	Back End Load
C+ / 6.8	11.0	0.96	9.61	8	1	98	0	1	38.0	114.7	-10.4	28	N/A	5,000,000	0	0.0	2.0
C+ / 5.8	11.1	0.96	9.55	396	1	98	0	1	38.0	113.7	-10.6	26	N/A	2,500	50	0.0	2.0
B- / 7.3	8.5	1.04	20.06	80	1	98	0	1	81.0	49.8	-9.8	27	9	2,500	50	0.0	0.0
B- / 7.3	8.5	1.04	19.52	1	1	98	0	1	81.0	46.4	-10.0	22	9	2,500	50	0.0	1.0
B- / 7.3	8.5	1.03	20.50	721	1	98	0	1	81.0	51.9	-9.8	31	9	5,000,000	0	0.0	0.0
B- / 7.3	8.5	1.03	20.33	3,841	1	98	0	1	81.0	51.0	-9.8	30	9	2,500	50	0.0	0.0
C / 4.3	13.9	1.42	15.52	50	2	97	0	1	238.0	95.5	-9.6	83	6	2,500	50	0.0	0.0
C- / 4.2	13.9	1.42	15.00	2	2	97	0	1	238.0	91.3	-9.8	77	6	2,500	50	0.0	1.0
C / 4.3	13.9	1.42	15.98	60	2	97	0	1	238.0	98.2	-9.5	86	N/A	5,000,000	0	0.0	0.0
C / 4.3	13.8	1.41	15.77	1,170	2	97	0	1	238.0	97.1	-9.6	85	6	2,500	50	0.0	0.0
B / 8.1	8.4	1.06	30.71	686	0	99	0	1	70.0	67.0	-9.5	56	N/A	2,500	50	0.0	0.0
B / 8.2	8.5	1.07	30.69	2	0	99	0	1	70.0	63.4	-9.7	46	9	2,500	50	0.0	1.0
B / 8.1	8.4	1.06	30.75	426	0	99	0	1	70.0	69.3	-9.3	61	N/A	5,000,000	0	0.0	0.0
B / 8.1	8.5	1.06	30.74	3,439	0	99	0	1	70.0	68.3	-9.4	59	9	2,500	50	0.0	0.0
C- / 3.3	15.9	1.38	16.09	N/A	2	97	0	1	135.0	190.4	-6.6	31	N/A	10,000	50	0.0	2.0
C- / 3.3	15.9	1.38	16.42	306	2	97	0	1	135.0	194.3	-6.6	34	N/A	5,000,000	0	0.0	2.0
C- / 3.3	16.0	1.39	16.30	1,343	2	97	0	1	135.0	192.3	-6.5	32	12	10,000	50	0.0	2.0
B- / 7.4	10.7	1.02	10.86	26	2	97	0	1	91.0	99.2	N/A	12	4	2,500	50	5.8	0.0
C+ / 6.2	10.7	1.01	10.85	307	2	97	0	1	91.0	99.3	-10.1	13	2	2,500	50	0.0	2.0
B- / 7.4	10.7	1.02	10.80	2	2	97	0	1	91.0	94.3	N/A	10	4	2,500	50	0.0	5.0
B- / 7.4	10.7	1.01	10.75	6	2	97	0	1	91.0	94.6	N/A	10	4	2,500	50	0.0	1.0
C+ / 6.3	10.7	1.01	10.89	112	2	97	0	1	91.0	102.0	-10.1	15	2	5,000,000	0	0.0	2.0
C+ / 6.3	10.7	1.01	10.87	2,195	2	97	0	1	91.0	100.8	-10.1	14	2	2,500	50	0.0	2.0
C+ / 6.2	16.5	1.34	10.81	N/A	0	99	0	1	116.0	271.1	N/A	89	N/A	5,000,000	0	0.0	2.0
C+ / 6.3	16.4	1.33	10.77	189	0	99	0	1	116.0	268.4	-1.4	89	N/A	10,000	0	0.0	2.0
U /	N/A	N/A	12.17	65	1	98	0	1	117.0	N/A	N/A	N/A	N/A	2,500	0	0.0	2.0
C+ / 6.0	9.0	0.76	4.95	N/A	4	94	0	2	150.0	51.5	N/A	42	6	2,500	50	0.0	0.0
C+ / 5.9	9.0	0.75	4.80	N/A	4	94	0	2	150.0	48.1	-3.4	36	6	2,500	50	0.0	1.0
B- / 7.3	8.9	0.76	5.02	125	4	94	0	2	150.0	52.6	-3.4	44	6	2,500	50	0.0	0.0
B- / 7.3	8.9	0.76	5.09	3	4	94	0	2	150.0	53.5	-3.4	47	6	5,000,000	0	0.0	0.0
B / 8.8	7.2	0.90	6.72	219	4	96	0	0	17.0	71.3	N/A	79	7	2,500	50	5.8	0.0
B / 8.9	7.1	0.89	6.71	199	4	96	0	0	17.0	71.0	-8.3	79	6	2,500	50	0.0	0.0
B+ / 9.0	7.0	0.88	6.73	16	4	96	0	0	17.0	67.3	N/A	74	7	2,500	50	0.0	5.0
B / 8.9	7.1	0.89	6.71	62	4	96	0	0	17.0	67.3	-8.5	73	7	2,500	50	0.0	1.0
B / 8.9	7.2	0.90	6.72	491	4	96	0	0	17.0	72.3	-8.2	82	N/A	5,000,000	0	0.0	0.0
B / 8.9	7.2	0.91	6.72	1,165	4	96	0	0	17.0	72.4	-8.3	80	7	2,500	50	0.0	0.0
U /	N/A	N/A	11.04	84	5	54	40	1	15.0	N/A	N/A	N/A	N/A	2,500	50	0.0	0.0
U /	N/A	N/A	11.48	31	4	65	29	2	10.0	N/A	N/A	N/A	N/A	5,000,000	0	0.0	0.0
U /	N/A	N/A	11.90	184	5	94	0	1	223.0	N/A	N/A	N/A	N/A	2,500	0	0.0	0.0
C- / 3.9	16.7	1.06	7.58	60	0	99	0	1	269.0	113.9	N/A	50	N/A	2,500	50	5.8	0.0
C- / 3.9	16.5	1.06	7.50	3	0	99	0	1	269.0	109.3	N/A	42	N/A	2,500	50	0.0	5.0
C- / 3.9	16.6	1.06	7.53	4	0	99	0	1	269.0	109.5	N/A	42	N/A	2,500	50	0.0	1.0
C- / 4.0	16.6	1.06	7.61	48	0	99	0	1	269.0	115.6	-7.9	54	N/A	2,500	50	0.0	0.0
C / 5.0	15.7	1.01	6.45	265	0	99	0	1	256.0	83.4	-8.2	16	N/A	2,500	50	0.0	2.0
U /	N/A	N/A	10.59	97	10	45	44	1	7.0	N/A	N/A	N/A	N/A	2,500	0	0.0	0.0
U /	N/A	N/A	12.30	76	2	96	1	1	5.0	N/A	N/A	N/A	N/A	2,500	0	0.0	0.0
C- / 4.1	15.8	0.94	28.66	346	4	95	0	1	172.0	130.8	1.7	87	5	2,500	50	0.0	0.0
C- / 4.1	15.8	0.94	28.65	243	4	95	0	1	172.0	133.8	1.8	89	5	5,000,000	0	0.0	0.0
C- / 4.1	15.8	0.94	28.63	975	4	95	0	1	172.0	132.5	1.7	88	5	2,500	50	0.0	0.0
C+ / 6.6	8.8	1.02	35.26	35	1	98	0	1	55.0	37.7	N/A	5	N/A	2,500	50	5.8	0.0
C+ / 6.7	8.7	1.02	35.03	24	1	98	0	1	55.0	37.8	-9.4	5	N/A	2,500	50	0.0	0.0
B- / 7.2	8.7	1.02	34.54	7	1	98	0	1	55.0	34.5	N/A	4	N/A	2,500	50	0.0	5.0

					PERFORMANCE							
99 Pct = Best 0 Pct = Worst			Overall Weiss Investment Rating		Perfor- mance Rating/Pts	Total Return % through 6/30/06					Incl. in Returns	
									Annualized		Dividend	Expense
Fund Type	Fund Name	Ticker Symbol		Phone		3 Mo	6 Mo	1Yr / Pct	3Yr / Pct	5Yr / Pct	Yield	Ratio
GR	American Century Select C	ACSLX	E+	(800) 345-6488	E- / 0.1	-7.17	-7.62	-4.16 / 0	2.45 / 1	--	0.00	2.00
GR	American Century Select Inst	TWSIX	E+	(800) 345-6488	E- / 0.1	-6.89	-7.08	-3.00 / 0	3.68 / 2	-1.96 / 8	0.94	0.80
★ GR ●	American Century Select Inv	TWCIX	E+	(800) 345-6488	E- / 0.1	-6.94	-7.16	-3.18 / 0	3.48 / 2	-2.17 / 8	0.74	1.00
SC ●	American Century Sm Cap Val Adv	ACSCX	C+	(800) 345-6488	B- / 7.0	-4.98	3.20	9.03 / 40	17.80 / 72	11.72 / 86	0.33	1.50
SC ●	American Century Sm Cap Val C	ACVCX	C	(800) 345-6488	C+ / 6.5	-5.04	2.89	8.26 / 35	17.02 / 68	10.88 / 83	0.00	2.25
SC ●	American Century Sm Cap Val Inst	ACVIX	B	(800) 345-6488	B- / 7.2	-4.78	3.49	9.50 / 43	18.28 / 73	12.21 / 87	0.74	1.05
SC ●	American Century Sm Cap Val Inv	ASVIX	C+	(800) 345-6488	B- / 7.1	-4.78	3.35	9.30 / 42	18.06 / 73	11.99 / 87	0.56	1.25
SC ●	American Century Small Company	ASQAX	B-	(800) 345-6488	B+ / 8.3	-6.53	3.43	8.49 / 37	22.64 / 86	16.53 / 94	0.00	1.12
SC ●	American Century Small Company	ASCQX	B	(800) 345-6488	B+ / 8.4	-6.46	3.65	8.94 / 40	23.12 / 88	16.98 / 94	0.32	0.67
SC ●	American Century Small Company	ASQIX	B-	(800) 345-6488	B+ / 8.3	-6.48	3.46	8.70 / 38	22.88 / 87	16.77 / 94	0.09	0.87
AA	American Century Str Alloc:Agg A	ALLAX	U	(800) 345-6488	U /	-1.82	3.40	11.51 / 57	--	--	0.78	1.45
AA	American Century Str Alloc:Agg Adv	ACVAX	C+	(800) 345-6488	C / 5.1	-1.82	3.40	11.38 / 56	12.58 / 46	5.32 / 57	0.83	1.45
AA	American Century Str Alloc:Agg C	ASTAX	C	(800) 345-6488	C / 4.5	-1.95	3.02	10.75 / 52	11.83 / 41	--	0.11	2.20
AA ●	American Century Str Alloc:Agg Inv	TWSAX	C+	(800) 345-6488	C / 5.3	-1.69	3.66	11.78 / 58	12.88 / 48	5.57 / 58	1.06	1.20
AA	American Century Str Alloc:Agg R	AAARX	C	(800) 345-6488	C / 5.1	-1.94	3.27	11.14 / 54	12.62 / 46	5.42 / 57	0.74	1.70
AA	American Century Str Alloc:Con Adv	ACCAX	C-	(800) 345-6488	D- / 1.4	-0.65	1.39	4.54 / 13	6.64 / 9	4.22 / 48	1.95	1.24
AA	American Century Str Alloc:Con Inst	ACCIX	C	(800) 345-6488	D / 1.7	-0.54	1.60	5.00 / 15	7.11 / 11	4.69 / 52	2.38	0.79
AA ●	American Century Str Alloc:Con Inv	TWSCX	C-	(800) 345-6488	D / 1.6	-0.59	1.51	4.80 / 14	6.90 / 10	4.48 / 50	2.19	0.99
AA	American Century Str Alloc:Mod A	ASMAX	U	(800) 345-6488	U /	-1.27	2.61	8.64 / 38	--	--	1.28	1.31
AA	American Century Str Alloc:Mod Adv	ACOAX	C	(800) 345-6488	C- / 3.6	-1.27	2.61	8.65 / 38	10.18 / 29	5.26 / 56	1.36	1.31
AA	American Century Str Alloc:Mod B	ASTBX	U	(800) 345-6488	U /	-1.46	2.26	7.84 / 31	--	--	0.65	2.06
AA	American Century Str Alloc:Mod C	ASTCX	C	(800) 345-6488	D+ / 2.9	-1.46	2.25	7.83 / 31	9.41 / 24	--	0.65	2.06
AA	American Century Str Alloc:Mod Inst	ASAMX	C+	(800) 345-6488	C- / 3.9	-1.16	2.82	9.13 / 41	10.66 / 32	5.72 / 59	1.78	0.86
AA ●	American Century Str Alloc:Mod Inv	TWSMX	C	(800) 345-6488	C- / 3.7	-1.21	2.73	8.92 / 40	10.45 / 30	5.48 / 58	1.60	1.06
TC	American Century Technology Adv	ATADX	E-	(800) 345-6488	D / 1.9	-12.65	-1.41	17.63 / 78	8.68 / 19	-4.88 / 3	0.00	1.76
TC	American Century Technology Fd	ATCIX	E-	(800) 345-6488	D / 2.1	-12.57	-1.24	17.97 / 79	8.93 / 20	-4.62 / 3	0.00	1.51
TC	American Century Technology Inst	ATYIX	E-	(800) 345-6488	D / 2.2	-12.54	-1.18	18.18 / 79	9.12 / 21	-4.37 / 3	0.00	1.31
GR	American Century Ultra Adv	TWUAX	E+	(800) 345-6488	E / 0.5	-6.32	-6.13	-0.21 / 2	5.67 / 6	-1.03 / 12	0.00	1.24
GR	American Century Ultra C	TWCCX	E+	(800) 345-6488	E / 0.3	-6.49	-6.49	-0.95 / 1	4.93 / 4	--	0.00	1.99
GR	American Century Ultra Inst	TWUIX	E+	(800) 345-6488	E+ / 0.6	-6.23	-5.95	0.20 / 2	6.13 / 7	-0.55 / 13	0.33	0.79
★ GR	American Century Ultra Inv	TWCUX	E+	(800) 345-6488	E / 0.5	-6.26	-6.02	0.04 / 2	5.93 / 7	-0.76 / 12	0.13	0.99
UT	American Century Utilities Adv	ACUTX	A-	(800) 345-6488	B- / 7.2	3.63	5.81	8.50 / 37	17.53 / 70	3.04 / 37	2.87	0.92
UT	American Century Utilities Inv	BULIX	A-	(800) 345-6488	B- / 7.3	3.69	6.00	8.84 / 39	17.84 / 72	3.33 / 40	3.11	0.67
GI	American Century Value A	ACAVX	C+	(800) 345-6488	C- / 4.0	-0.85	2.90	7.33 / 28	13.13 / 49	--	0.99	1.24
GI	American Century Value Adv	TWADX	C-	(800) 345-6488	C / 5.1	-0.85	2.76	7.34 / 28	13.08 / 49	7.66 / 70	1.04	1.24
GI	American Century Value B	ACBVX	C+	(800) 345-6488	C- / 3.7	-1.04	2.41	6.55 / 24	12.34 / 45	--	0.36	1.99
GI	American Century Value C	ACLCX	C+	(800) 345-6488	C / 4.5	-1.05	2.42	6.59 / 24	12.36 / 45	--	0.36	1.99
GI	American Century Value Inst	AVLIX	C	(800) 345-6488	C / 5.4	-0.74	3.12	7.81 / 31	13.58 / 52	8.16 / 72	1.46	0.79
★ GI ●	American Century Value Inv	TWVLX	C-	(800) 345-6488	C / 5.3	-0.79	2.88	7.61 / 30	13.37 / 51	7.93 / 71	1.27	0.99
AG	American Century Veedot Inst	AVDIX	D+	(800) 345-6488	C / 4.4	-7.73	3.22	10.93 / 53	12.48 / 46	3.33 / 40	0.00	1.30
AG	American Century Veedot Inv	AMVIX	D	(800) 345-6488	C / 4.3	-7.81	3.08	10.66 / 51	12.31 / 44	3.09 / 38	0.00	1.50
GR	American Century Vista Adv	TWVAX	C-	(800) 345-6488	B- / 7.3	-3.10	6.57	16.81 / 77	17.22 / 69	5.49 / 58	0.00	1.25
GR	American Century Vista C	TWVCX	C+	(800) 345-6488	C+ / 6.9	-3.25	6.15	15.96 / 75	16.41 / 65	--	0.00	2.00
GR	American Century Vista Inst	TWVIX	C-	(800) 345-6488	B- / 7.5	-3.00	6.79	17.30 / 78	17.73 / 71	6.03 / 61	0.00	0.80
★ GR	American Century Vista Inv	TWCVX	C-	(800) 345-6488	B- / 7.4	-3.05	6.64	17.08 / 77	17.47 / 70	5.78 / 60	0.00	1.00
GI	American Century VP Inc & Gr II	AVPGX	C+	(800) 345-6488	C / 4.4	-0.26	2.58	6.86 / 25	11.71 / 41	--	1.61	0.95
GI	American Century VP Inc & Gr III	AIGTX	C+	(800) 345-6488	C / 4.4	-0.13	2.84	7.12 / 27	11.97 / 42	--	1.86	0.70
GL	American Century VP Intl I	AVIIX	B-	(800) 345-6488	B / 7.9	-2.13	7.73	23.48 / 87	18.49 / 74	4.28 / 49	1.63	1.23
GL	American Century VP Intl II	ANVPX	B+	(800) 345-6488	B / 7.8	-2.02	7.70	23.30 / 86	18.31 / 74	--	1.48	1.38
GL	American Century VP Intl III	AIVPX	B-	(800) 345-6488	B / 7.8	-2.13	7.73	23.48 / 87	18.49 / 74	--	1.63	1.23
GR	American Century VP Ultra I	AVPUX	D-	(800) 345-6488	E / 0.5	-6.25	-6.07	--	5.94 / 7	--	0.00	1.01
GR	American Century VP Ultra II	AVPSX	D-	(800) 345-6488	E / 0.5	-6.28	-6.10	-0.21 / 2	5.80 / 6	--	0.00	1.16

● Denotes fund is closed to new investors
★ Denotes fund is included in Section II

RISK	3 Year		NET ASSETS		ASSET					BULL / BEAR		FUND MANAGER		MINIMUMS		LOADS	
Risk Rating/Pts	Standard Deviation	Beta	NAV As of 6/30/06	Total $(Mil)	Cash %	Stocks %	Bonds %	Other %	Portfolio Turnover Ratio	Last Bull Market Return	Last Bear Market Return	Manager Quality Pct	Manager Tenure (Years)	Initial Purch. $	Additional Purch. $	Front End Load	Back End Load
B- /7.2	8.7	1.02	34.57	2	1	98	0	1	55.0	34.5	N/A	4	N/A	2,500	50	0.0	1.0
C+ /6.7	8.8	1.02	35.70	216	1	98	0	1	55.0	39.6	-9.2	6	N/A	5,000,000	0	0.0	0.0
C+ /6.7	8.8	1.02	35.42	2,770	1	98	0	1	55.0	38.8	-9.3	5	N/A	2,500	50	0.0	0.0
C /5.5	11.3	0.74	9.93	423	3	96	0	1	56.0	105.0	-7.7	85	7	2,500	50	0.0	0.0
C /5.4	11.3	0.74	9.61	3	3	96	0	1	56.0	100.3	-7.9	80	8	2,500	50	0.0	1.0
B- /7.4	11.2	0.74	9.97	414	3	96	0	1	56.0	107.7	-7.5	87	8	5,000,000	0	0.0	0.0
C /5.5	11.2	0.74	9.95	1,263	3	96	0	1	56.0	106.4	-7.7	87	8	2,500	50	0.0	0.0
C+ /5.7	14.4	0.95	10.02	396	0	99	0	1	132.0	146.6	-8.0	90	N/A	2,500	50	0.0	0.0
C+ /5.7	14.4	0.95	10.14	438	0	99	0	1	132.0	149.7	-7.9	92	N/A	5,000,000	0	0.0	0.0
C+ /5.7	14.5	0.95	10.11	1,038	0	99	0	1	132.0	148.3	-7.8	91	N/A	2,500	50	0.0	0.0
U /	N/A	N/A	8.11	61	5	75	19	1	167.0	N/A	N/A	N/A	2	2,500	0	5.8	0.0
B- /7.9	7.6	1.47	8.10	317	5	75	19	1	167.0	68.8	-6.7	79	10	2,500	0	0.0	0.0
B- /7.9	7.7	1.48	8.06	20	5	75	19	1	167.0	65.2	-6.7	72	N/A	2,500	0	0.0	1.0
B- /7.9	7.7	1.47	8.12	752	5	75	19	1	167.0	70.1	-6.4	81	N/A	2,500	0	0.0	0.0
C+ /6.5	7.7	1.47	8.09	N/A	5	75	19	1	167.0	69.1	-6.4	79	N/A	2,500	50	0.0	0.0
B+ /9.5	3.8	0.81	5.51	155	10	41	47	2	246.0	33.1	-2.5	57	10	2,500	50	0.0	0.0
B+ /9.9	3.9	0.82	5.51	157	10	41	47	2	246.0	35.0	-2.6	62	N/A	5,000,000	0	0.0	0.0
B+ /9.4	3.9	0.81	5.51	388	10	41	47	2	246.0	34.2	-2.6	60	N/A	2,500	50	0.0	0.0
U /	N/A	N/A	6.84	140	8	59	31	2	198.0	N/A	N/A	N/A	2	2,500	50	5.8	0.0
B /8.7	5.9	1.18	6.84	412	8	59	31	2	198.0	53.5	-4.8	72	10	2,500	50	0.0	0.0
U /	N/A	N/A	6.84	31	8	59	31	2	198.0	N/A	N/A	N/A	2	2,500	50	0.0	5.0
B /8.7	6.0	1.20	6.85	25	8	59	31	2	198.0	50.3	-4.8	64	5	2,500	50	0.0	1.0
B+ /9.4	6.0	1.20	6.84	565	8	59	31	2	198.0	55.6	-4.5	76	N/A	5,000,000	0	0.0	0.0
B /8.7	6.0	1.19	6.84	966	8	59	31	2	198.0	54.7	-4.5	74	N/A	2,500	50	0.0	0.0
E+ /0.8	22.4	2.25	19.55	N/A	0	99	0	1	393.0	80.2	-13.3	0	4	2,500	50	0.0	0.0
E+ /0.8	22.4	2.25	19.89	128	0	99	0	1	393.0	81.8	-13.2	0	4	2,500	50	0.0	0.0
E+ /0.8	22.4	2.25	20.15	6	0	99	0	1	393.0	82.8	-13.1	1	N/A	5,000,000	0	0.0	0.0
C+ /6.7	9.5	1.11	27.86	484	1	98	0	1	33.0	46.0	-9.8	9	10	2,500	50	0.0	0.0
C+ /6.6	9.5	1.12	27.10	4	1	98	0	1	33.0	42.7	-9.9	7	5	2,500	50	0.0	1.0
C+ /6.7	9.5	1.11	28.60	1,213	1	98	0	1	33.0	48.0	-9.7	11	10	5,000,000	0	0.0	0.0
C+ /6.7	9.5	1.12	28.28	14,912	1	98	0	1	33.0	47.1	-9.7	10	10	2,500	50	0.0	0.0
B /8.1	8.5	0.67	13.97	4	0	98	0	2	21.0	90.7	-5.2	75	N/A	2,500	50	0.0	0.0
B /8.1	8.5	0.67	13.99	245	0	98	0	2	21.0	91.9	-5.0	78	9	2,500	50	0.0	0.0
B /8.8	7.1	0.87	7.11	63	4	95	0	1	135.0	72.4	N/A	83	3	2,500	50	5.8	1.0
C+ /6.1	7.1	0.87	7.10	213	4	95	0	1	135.0	72.5	-9.6	83	9	2,500	50	0.0	0.0
B /8.8	7.1	0.87	7.10	7	4	95	0	1	135.0	69.0	N/A	78	3	2,500	50	0.0	5.0
B /8.8	7.1	0.87	7.06	19	4	95	0	1	135.0	68.2	N/A	78	3	2,500	50	0.0	1.0
C+ /6.1	7.2	0.88	7.11	236	4	95	0	1	135.0	74.9	-9.5	86	9	5,000,000	0	0.0	0.0
C+ /6.1	7.2	0.87	7.10	2,227	4	95	0	1	135.0	73.6	-9.4	85	13	2,500	50	0.0	0.0
C /5.5	15.3	1.63	6.09	11	1	98	0	1	399.0	86.0	-10.2	19	7	5,000,000	0	0.0	2.0
C /4.6	15.4	1.64	6.02	164	1	98	0	1	399.0	84.6	-10.0	17	7	2,500	50	0.0	2.0
C- /3.8	14.3	1.45	16.54	229	0	99	0	1	284.0	107.6	-10.0	72	N/A	2,500	50	0.0	0.0
C+ /5.6	14.4	1.46	16.06	3	0	99	0	1	284.0	N/A	N/A	65	N/A	2,500	50	0.0	1.0
C- /3.8	14.3	1.46	17.15	139	0	99	0	1	284.0	110.5	-9.8	76	N/A	5,000,000	0	0.0	0.0
C- /3.8	14.3	1.46	16.86	2,118	0	99	0	1	284.0	109.2	-9.8	74	13	2,500	50	0.0	0.0
B /8.6	8.5	1.07	7.57	26	0	100	0	0	76.0	66.3	-9.4	55	4	2,500	0	0.0	0.0
B /8.7	8.4	1.06	7.58	5	0	100	0	0	76.0	67.9	-9.5	59	4	500,000	0	0.0	1.0
C+ /6.1	10.6	1.00	8.72	564	2	98	0	0	97.0	98.8	-10.2	14	4	2,500	0	0.0	0.0
B- /7.3	10.6	1.01	8.72	141	2	98	0	0	97.0	98.0	-10.2	13	4	2,500	0	0.0	0.0
C+ /6.1	10.7	1.01	8.72	112	2	98	0	0	97.0	99.0	N/A	13	4	2,500	0	0.0	1.0
B- /7.4	9.4	1.11	9.75	109	0	99	0	1	58.0	46.0	N/A	10	5	2,500	0	0.0	0.0
B- /7.4	9.5	1.11	9.70	361	0	99	0	1	58.0	45.5	-9.8	10	4	2,500	0	0.0	0.0

Fund Type	Fund Name	Ticker Symbol	Overall Weiss Investment Rating	Phone	Performance Rating/Pts	3 Mo	6 Mo	1Yr / Pct	3Yr / Pct	5Yr / Pct	Dividend Yield	Expense Ratio
GR	American Century VP Ultra III	AVUTX	D-	(800) 345-6488	E / 0.5	-6.26	-6.08	-0.10 / 2	5.95 / 7	--	0.00	1.01
GR	American Century VP Value Cl II	AVPVX	C-	(800) 345-6488	C / 5.2	-0.78	2.99	7.59 /30	13.27 /50	--	1.24	1.08
GR	American Century VP Value Cl III	AVPTX	C-	(800) 345-6488	C / 5.2	-0.78	3.04	7.77 /31	13.40 /51	--	1.40	0.93
GR	American Century VP Vista I	AVSIX	B-	(800) 345-6488	B- / 7.3	-3.02	6.65	16.72 /76	17.08 /68	--	0.00	1.01
AG	American Eagle Capital Apprec Fd	AECAX	E+	(866) 811-0215	E- / 0.1	-6.04	-3.29	1.73 / 4	1.90 / 1	-7.93 / 1	0.00	5.17
GR	American Eagle Twenty Fd	AETWX	D-	(866) 811-0215	E / 0.3	-7.12	-8.33	-4.22 / 0	5.41 / 5	-1.39 /10	0.00	5.39
GR	American Funds AMCAP 529A	CAFAX	D	(800) 421-4120	D / 2.1	-2.59	0.57	7.22 /27	10.07 /28	3.51 /41	0.51	0.72
GR	American Funds AMCAP 529B	CAFBX	D	(800) 421-4120	D / 1.8	-2.78	0.15	6.30 /22	9.10 /21	2.60 /33	0.00	1.58
GR	American Funds AMCAP 529C	CAFCX	D+	(800) 421-4120	D+ / 2.4	-2.77	0.15	6.36 /22	9.14 /22	2.62 /33	0.00	1.56
GR	American Funds AMCAP 529E	CAFEX	C-	(800) 421-4120	C- / 3.0	-2.67	0.42	6.88 /26	9.70 /25	3.15 /38	0.22	1.05
GR	American Funds AMCAP 529F	CAFFX	C-	(800) 421-4120	C- / 3.3	-2.51	0.65	7.44 /29	10.09 /28	3.48 /41	0.64	0.59
★ GR	American Funds AMCAP A	AMCPX	D	(800) 421-4120	D / 2.2	-2.58	0.57	7.30 /28	10.14 /28	3.57 /42	0.54	0.65
GR	American Funds AMCAP B	AMPBX	D	(800) 421-4120	D / 1.9	-2.79	0.21	6.45 /23	9.29 /23	2.77 /34	0.00	1.44
GR	American Funds AMCAP C	AMPCX	D+	(800) 421-4120	D+ / 2.5	-2.75	0.21	6.43 /23	9.23 /22	2.71 /34	0.00	1.49
★ GR	American Funds AMCAP F	AMPFX	C-	(800) 421-4120	C- / 3.3	-2.54	0.63	7.32 /28	10.11 /28	3.51 /41	0.57	0.68
GR	American Funds AMCAP R1	RAFAX	D+	(800) 421-4120	D+ / 2.6	-2.81	0.15	6.38 /22	9.20 /22	2.70 /34	0.00	1.51
GR	American Funds AMCAP R2	RAFBX	D+	(800) 421-4120	D+ / 2.7	-2.76	0.21	6.44 /23	9.26 /22	2.74 /34	0.00	1.48
GR	American Funds AMCAP R3	RAFCX	C-	(800) 421-4120	C- / 3.0	-2.66	0.42	6.87 /25	9.69 /25	3.16 /38	0.27	1.02
GR	American Funds AMCAP R4	RAFEX	C-	(800) 421-4120	C- / 3.2	-2.60	0.57	7.21 /27	10.05 /28	3.49 /41	0.63	0.71
GR	American Funds AMCAP R5	RAFFX	C-	(800) 421-4120	C- / 3.4	-2.53	0.72	7.56 /30	10.41 /30	3.83 /44	0.83	0.41
BA	American Funds Amer Balanced Fd	CLBAX	D+	(800) 421-4120	D- / 1.4	-0.62	2.17	5.05 /15	8.55 /18	6.10 /62	2.18	0.65
BA	American Funds Amer Balancd Fd	CLBBX	C-	(800) 421-4120	D- / 1.2	-0.77	1.81	4.23 /12	7.65 /13	5.25 /56	1.49	1.49
BA	American Funds Amer Balancd Fd	CLBCX	C-	(800) 421-4120	D / 1.7	-0.82	1.76	4.24 /12	7.66 /13	5.27 /56	1.50	1.48
BA	American Funds Amer Balancd Fd	CLBEX	C-	(800) 421-4120	D / 2.2	-0.69	2.01	4.72 /14	8.19 /16	5.76 /60	2.00	0.97
BA	American Funds Amer Balancd Fd	CLBFX	C	(800) 421-4120	D+ / 2.4	-0.57	2.27	5.24 /16	8.59 /18	6.07 /61	2.50	0.55
★ BA	American Funds Amer Balancd Fd A	ABALX	D+	(800) 421-4120	D- / 1.5	-0.55	2.24	5.14 /16	8.63 /19	6.16 /62	2.21	0.59
BA	American Funds Amer Balancd Fd B	BALBX	C-	(800) 421-4120	D- / 1.3	-0.79	1.81	4.31 /12	7.81 /14	5.36 /57	1.61	1.34
BA	American Funds Amer Balancd Fd C	BALCX	C-	(800) 421-4120	D / 1.8	-0.81	1.79	4.26 /12	7.75 /14	5.29 /56	1.56	1.40
BA	American Funds Amer Balancd Fd F	BALFX	C	(800) 421-4120	D+ / 2.4	-0.60	2.20	5.09 /16	8.59 /18	6.13 /62	2.36	0.61
BA	American Funds Amer Balancd Fd R1	RLBAX	C-	(800) 421-4120	D / 1.9	-0.80	1.79	4.20 /11	7.70 /13	5.27 /56	1.56	1.42
BA	American Funds Amer Balancd Fd R2	RLBBX	C-	(800) 421-4120	D / 1.9	-0.81	1.79	4.25 /12	7.75 /14	5.33 /57	1.56	1.40
BA	American Funds Amer Balancd Fd R3	RLBCX	C-	(800) 421-4120	D / 2.2	-0.69	2.04	4.76 /14	8.22 /16	5.77 /60	2.04	0.89
BA	American Funds Amer Balancd Fd R4	RLBEX	C	(800) 421-4120	D+ / 2.4	-0.62	2.17	5.05 /15	8.57 /18	6.11 /62	2.31	0.63
BA	American Funds Amer Balancd Fd R5	RLBFX	C	(800) 421-4120	D+ / 2.6	-0.54	2.32	5.34 /17	8.89 /20	6.44 /64	2.60	0.34
GI	American Funds Amer Mutual Fd	CMLAX	C	(800) 421-4120	C- / 3.1	0.36	4.16	8.77 /39	10.98 /35	5.79 /60	1.74	0.68
GI	American Funds Amer Mutual Fd	CMLBX	C	(800) 421-4120	D+ / 2.7	0.14	3.74	7.89 /32	10.04 /28	4.90 /53	1.05	1.53
GI	American Funds Amer Mutual Fd	CMLCX	C+	(800) 421-4120	C- / 3.4	0.15	3.74	7.90 /32	10.06 /28	4.92 /53	1.06	1.52
GI	American Funds Amer Mutual Fd	CMLEX	C+	(800) 421-4120	C- / 4.0	0.28	4.01	8.45 /36	10.63 /32	5.44 /57	1.55	1.00
GI	American Funds Amer Mutual Fd	CMLFX	B-	(800) 421-4120	C / 4.3	0.40	4.30	9.01 /40	11.02 /36	5.78 /60	2.03	0.62
★ GI	American Funds Amer Mutual Fd A	AMRMX	C	(800) 421-4120	C- / 3.3	0.38	4.23	8.89 /39	11.12 /36	5.90 /60	1.81	0.56
GI	American Funds Amer Mutual Fd B	AMFBX	C	(800) 421-4120	D+ / 2.9	0.18	3.81	8.01 /33	10.23 /29	5.06 /55	1.17	1.36
GI	American Funds Amer Mutual Fd C	AMFCX	C+	(800) 421-4120	C- / 3.5	0.16	3.79	7.97 /32	10.17 /28	4.98 /54	1.13	1.42
GI	American Funds Amer Mutual Fd F	AMFFX	B-	(800) 421-4120	C / 4.3	0.37	4.19	8.82 /39	11.02 /36	5.78 /60	1.89	0.65
GI	American Funds Amer Mutual Fd R1	RMFAX	C+	(800) 421-4120	C- / 3.6	0.15	3.76	7.91 /32	10.12 /28	4.95 /54	1.10	1.45
GI	American Funds Amer Mutual Fd R2	RMFBX	C+	(800) 421-4120	C- / 3.6	0.20	3.81	7.93 /32	10.17 /28	4.97 /54	1.11	1.42
GI	American Funds Amer Mutual Fd R3	RMFCX	C+	(800) 421-4120	C- / 4.0	0.31	4.04	8.45 /36	10.64 /32	5.42 /57	1.54	0.96
GI	American Funds Amer Mutual Fd R4	RMFEX	B-	(800) 421-4120	C / 4.3	0.35	4.14	8.71 /38	10.98 /35	5.77 /60	1.82	0.67
GI	American Funds Amer Mutual Fd R5	RMFFX	B-	(800) 421-4120	C / 4.5	0.43	4.30	9.06 /40	11.33 /38	6.10 /62	2.11	0.36
GL	American Funds Cap Inc Builder	CIRAX	B	(800) 421-4120	C / 5.0	1.68	6.62	11.18 /55	13.78 /53	10.05 /81	3.54	0.68
GL	American Funds Cap Inc Builder	CIRBX	B	(800) 421-4120	C / 4.7	1.45	6.18	10.26 /49	12.81 /48	9.15 /77	2.94	1.53
GL	American Funds Cap Inc Builder	CIRCX	B+	(800) 421-4120	C / 5.3	1.46	6.19	10.28 /49	12.83 /48	9.16 /77	2.95	1.52
GL	American Funds Cap Inc Builder	CIREX	A-	(800) 421-4120	C+ / 5.8	1.59	6.45	10.83 /52	13.40 /51	9.71 /79	3.44	1.00

● Denotes fund is closed to new investors
★ Denotes fund is included in Section II

52

RISK			NET ASSETS		ASSET				BULL / BEAR			FUND MANAGER		MINIMUMS		LOADS	
	3 Year		NAV						Last Bull	Last Bear		Manager	Manager	Initial	Additional	Front	Back
Risk	Standard		As of	Total	Cash	Stocks	Bonds	Other	Market	Market		Quality	Tenure	Purch.	Purch.	End	End
Rating/Pts	Deviation	Beta	6/30/06	$(Mil)	%	%	%	%	Return	Return		Pct	(Years)	$	$	Load	Load
B- / 7.4	9.4	1.11	9.74	2	0	99	0	1	58.0	46.1	-9.7	10	4	2,500	0	0.0	1.0
C+ / 5.7	7.2	0.87	7.59	690	4	95	0	1	133.0	73.2	-9.5	84	5	2,500	0	0.0	0.0
C+ / 5.7	7.1	0.87	7.59	9	4	95	0	1	133.0	73.8	-9.5	85	4	2,500	0	0.0	1.0
C+ / 6.7	14.2	1.44	15.40	41	3	96	0	1	276.0	106.9	-10.0	72	N/A	2,500	0	0.0	0.0
B- / 7.0	12.3	0.67	5.29	2	7	92	0	1	431.0	35.1	-6.1	10	7	1,000	50	0.0	0.0
B- / 7.9	10.2	0.58	7.04	2	25	74	0	1	481.0	44.9	-5.8	34	7	1,000	50	0.0	0.0
B- / 7.3	7.9	0.95	19.02	352	17	82	0	1	19.5	60.1	-7.9	48	N/A	250	50	5.8	1.0
B- / 7.4	7.9	0.95	18.46	75	17	82	0	1	19.5	55.7	-8.1	38	N/A	250	50	0.0	5.0
B- / 7.4	7.9	0.94	18.48	113	17	82	0	1	19.5	55.8	-8.1	38	N/A	250	50	0.0	1.0
B- / 7.4	7.9	0.95	18.85	21	17	82	0	1	19.5	58.4	-8.0	44	N/A	25	25	0.0	0.0
B- / 7.4	7.9	0.94	19.04	11	17	82	0	1	19.5	59.9	-7.9	49	N/A	250	50	0.0	0.0
B- / 7.3	7.9	0.95	19.06	15,986	17	82	0	1	19.5	60.4	-7.8	49	39	250	50	5.8	1.0
B- / 7.4	7.9	0.94	18.39	1,119	17	82	0	1	19.5	56.5	-8.1	40	N/A	250	50	0.0	5.0
B- / 7.4	7.9	0.95	18.28	1,582	17	82	0	1	19.5	56.3	-8.1	39	5	250	50	0.0	1.0
B- / 7.4	7.9	0.95	18.98	2,144	17	82	0	1	19.5	60.1	-7.8	49	5	250	50	0.0	0.0
B- / 7.4	7.9	0.95	18.59	36	17	82	0	1	19.5	56.2	-8.1	39	N/A	0	0	0.0	0.0
B- / 7.4	7.9	0.95	18.58	364	17	82	0	1	19.5	56.2	-8.0	39	N/A	0	0	0.0	0.0
B- / 7.4	7.9	0.94	18.85	680	17	82	0	1	19.5	58.3	-7.9	44	N/A	0	0	0.0	0.0
B- / 7.4	7.9	0.95	18.99	415	17	82	0	1	19.5	60.0	-7.8	47	N/A	0	0	0.0	0.0
B- / 7.5	7.9	0.95	19.13	406	17	82	0	1	19.5	61.7	-7.8	52	N/A	0	0	0.0	0.0
B / 8.7	5.0	1.04	17.98	981	4	66	29	1	35.0	46.6	-5.0	64	N/A	250	50	5.8	1.0
B+ / 9.1	5.1	1.04	17.98	277	4	66	29	1	35.0	42.7	-5.3	54	N/A	250	50	0.0	5.0
B+ / 9.1	5.1	1.04	17.98	446	4	66	29	1	35.0	42.8	-5.3	55	N/A	250	50	0.0	1.0
B+ / 9.1	5.1	1.04	17.97	64	4	66	29	1	35.0	45.0	-5.2	61	N/A	25	25	0.0	0.0
B+ / 9.1	5.0	1.04	17.97	22	4	66	29	1	35.0	46.6	-5.1	65	N/A	250	50	0.0	0.0
B / 8.8	5.1	1.04	18.00	33,072	4	66	29	1	35.0	46.9	-5.1	65	31	250	50	5.8	1.0
B+ / 9.1	5.1	1.04	17.94	5,143	4	66	29	1	35.0	43.5	-5.3	56	N/A	250	50	0.0	5.0
B+ / 9.1	5.0	1.04	17.93	5,468	4	66	29	1	35.0	43.2	-5.2	56	N/A	250	50	0.0	1.0
B+ / 9.1	5.0	1.04	17.99	1,171	4	66	29	1	35.0	46.7	-5.1	65	5	250	50	0.0	0.0
B+ / 9.1	5.1	1.04	17.92	68	4	66	29	1	35.0	43.0	-5.3	55	N/A	0	0	0.0	0.0
B+ / 9.1	5.1	1.04	17.93	953	4	66	29	1	35.0	43.1	-5.3	56	N/A	0	0	0.0	0.0
B+ / 9.1	5.0	1.04	17.94	2,712	4	66	29	1	35.0	45.1	-5.2	61	N/A	0	0	0.0	0.0
B+ / 9.1	5.1	1.04	17.97	1,532	4	66	29	1	35.0	46.7	-5.1	64	N/A	0	0	0.0	0.0
B+ / 9.1	5.1	1.04	18.00	318	4	66	29	1	35.0	48.1	-5.0	68	N/A	0	0	0.0	0.0
B+ / 9.0	6.0	0.76	27.06	181	16	83	0	1	22.0	57.9	-7.2	75	N/A	250	50	5.8	1.0
B+ / 9.5	6.0	0.76	27.00	36	16	83	0	1	22.0	53.6	-7.4	67	N/A	250	50	0.0	5.0
B+ / 9.5	6.0	0.76	27.00	55	16	83	0	1	22.0	53.7	-7.4	67	N/A	250	50	0.0	1.0
B+ / 9.4	6.0	0.76	27.01	10	16	83	0	1	22.0	56.2	-7.3	72	N/A	25	25	0.0	0.0
B+ / 9.4	6.0	0.76	27.09	5	16	83	0	1	22.0	57.8	-7.2	76	N/A	250	50	0.0	0.0
B+ / 9.0	6.0	0.76	27.10	14,808	16	83	0	1	22.0	58.4	-7.2	76	N/A	250	50	5.8	0.0
B+ / 9.4	6.0	0.76	26.93	640	16	83	0	1	22.0	54.5	-7.4	69	N/A	250	50	0.0	5.0
B+ / 9.5	6.0	0.76	26.89	726	16	83	0	1	22.0	54.1	-7.4	68	N/A	250	50	0.0	1.0
B+ / 9.4	6.0	0.76	27.03	458	16	83	0	1	22.0	57.9	-7.2	76	N/A	250	50	0.0	0.0
B+ / 9.5	6.0	0.76	26.96	14	16	83	0	1	22.0	54.0	-7.4	68	N/A	0	0	0.0	0.0
B+ / 9.5	6.0	0.76	26.94	116	16	83	0	1	22.0	54.1	-7.5	68	N/A	0	0	0.0	0.0
B+ / 9.4	6.0	0.76	26.99	204	16	83	0	1	22.0	56.1	-7.3	72	N/A	0	0	0.0	0.0
B+ / 9.4	6.0	0.76	27.05	52	16	83	0	1	22.0	57.8	-7.2	75	N/A	0	0	0.0	0.0
B+ / 9.4	6.0	0.76	27.09	234	16	83	0	1	22.0	59.4	-7.1	78	N/A	0	0	0.0	0.0
B+ / 9.3	6.1	1.05	55.59	614	9	68	20	3	20.0	64.9	-1.1	94	N/A	250	50	5.8	1.0
B+ / 9.6	6.0	1.05	55.59	103	9	68	20	3	20.0	60.3	-1.3	92	N/A	250	50	0.0	5.0
B+ / 9.6	6.0	1.05	55.59	250	9	68	20	3	20.0	60.4	-1.3	92	N/A	250	50	0.0	1.0
B+ / 9.6	6.1	1.05	55.59	34	9	68	20	3	20.0	63.1	-1.2	94	N/A	25	25	0.0	0.0

99 Pct = Best
0 Pct = Worst

Fund Type	Fund Name	Ticker Symbol	Overall Weiss Investment Rating	Phone	Perfor-mance Rating/Pts	Total Return % through 6/30/06			Annualized		Incl. in Returns	
						3 Mo	6 Mo	1Yr / Pct	3Yr / Pct	5Yr / Pct	Dividend Yield	Expense Ratio
GL	American Funds Cap Inc Builder	CIRFX	A-	(800) 421-4120	C+ / 6.0	1.72	6.72	11.38 /56	13.78 /53	10.04 /81	3.92	0.60
★ GL	American Funds Cap Inc Builder A	CAIBX	B	(800) 421-4120	C / 5.1	1.69	6.66	11.26 /55	13.89 /53	10.18 /81	3.60	0.57
GL	American Funds Cap Inc Builder B	CIBBX	B	(800) 421-4120	C / 4.8	1.48	6.24	10.39 /49	13.00 /49	9.32 /78	3.05	1.36
GL	American Funds Cap Inc Builder C	CIBCX	B+	(800) 421-4120	C / 5.4	1.47	6.22	10.34 /49	12.93 /48	9.23 /77	3.01	1.42
GL	American Funds Cap Inc Builder F	CIBFX	A-	(800) 421-4120	C+ / 6.0	1.68	6.63	11.20 /55	13.78 /53	10.06 /81	3.77	0.65
GL	American Funds Cap Inc Builder R1	RIRAX	B+	(800) 421-4120	C / 5.5	1.46	6.20	10.29 /49	12.89 /48	9.22 /77	2.97	1.46
GL	American Funds Cap Inc Builder R2	RIRBX	B+	(800) 421-4120	C / 5.5	1.46	6.20	10.31 /49	12.93 /48	9.26 /78	2.98	1.44
GL	American Funds Cap Inc Builder R3	RIRCX	A-	(800) 421-4120	C+ / 5.8	1.58	6.44	10.80 /52	13.40 /51	9.70 /79	3.41	0.98
GL	American Funds Cap Inc Builder R4	RIREX	A-	(800) 421-4120	C+ / 5.9	1.66	6.60	11.14 /54	13.76 /53	10.05 /81	3.72	0.68
GL	American Funds Cap Inc Builder R5	RIRFX	A	(800) 421-4120	C+ / 6.1	1.74	6.76	11.47 /56	14.11 /54	10.39 /82	4.00	0.37
GL	American Funds Cap Wld Gr&Inc	CWIAX	A	(800) 421-4120	B+ / 8.3	0.41	6.53	21.45 /84	22.07 /85	12.26 /87	2.09	0.80
GL	American Funds Cap Wld Gr&Inc	CWIBX	A	(800) 421-4120	B / 8.2	0.20	6.07	20.42 /82	21.01 /83	11.34 /85	1.40	1.67
GL	American Funds Cap Wld Gr&Inc	CWICX	A	(800) 421-4120	B+ / 8.4	0.23	6.11	20.44 /82	21.02 /83	11.36 /85	1.42	1.65
GL	American Funds Cap Wld Gr&Inc	CWIEX	A+	(800) 421-4120	B+ / 8.6	0.35	6.35	21.03 /83	21.65 /84	11.92 /86	1.90	1.13
GL	American Funds Cap Wld Gr&Inc	CWIFX	A+	(800) 421-4120	B+ / 8.7	0.49	6.65	21.70 /84	22.09 /85	12.26 /87	2.36	0.73
★ GL	American Funds Cap Wld Gr&Inc A	CWGIX	A	(800) 421-4120	B+ / 8.3	0.45	6.57	21.51 /84	22.16 /86	12.37 /87	2.13	0.73
GL	American Funds Cap Wld Gr&Inc B	CWGBX	A	(800) 421-4120	B / 8.2	0.26	6.16	20.57 /83	21.21 /83	11.50 /85	1.52	1.52
GL	American Funds Cap Wld Gr&Inc C	CWGCX	A+	(800) 421-4120	B+ / 8.4	0.24	6.12	20.51 /82	21.15 /83	11.42 /85	1.47	1.57
GL	American Funds Cap Wld Gr&Inc F	CWGFX	A+	(800) 421-4120	B+ / 8.7	0.42	6.54	21.46 /84	22.08 /85	12.28 /87	2.23	0.78
GL	American Funds Cap Wld Gr&Inc R1	RWIAX	A+	(800) 421-4120	B+ / 8.5	0.24	6.12	20.47 /82	21.11 /83	11.41 /85	1.46	1.58
GL	American Funds Cap Wld Gr&Inc R2	RWIBX	A+	(800) 421-4120	B+ / 8.5	0.24	6.12	20.50 /82	21.11 /83	11.44 /85	1.47	1.57
GL	American Funds Cap Wld Gr&Inc R3	RWICX	A+	(800) 421-4120	B+ / 8.6	0.34	6.35	21.00 /83	21.64 /84	11.89 /86	1.89	1.12
GL	American Funds Cap Wld Gr&Inc R4	RWIEX	A+	(800) 421-4120	B+ / 8.7	0.43	6.51	21.40 /83	22.04 /85	12.29 /87	2.18	0.81
GL	American Funds Cap Wld Gr&Inc R5	RWIFX	A+	(800) 421-4120	B+ / 8.8	0.51	6.69	21.80 /84	22.44 /86	12.63 /88	2.45	0.50
FO	American Funds EuroPacific Gr 529A	CEUAX	B+	(800) 421-4120	B+ / 8.8	-0.70	6.80	28.35 /93	24.46 /90	10.78 /83	1.51	0.80
FO	American Funds EuroPacific Gr 529B	CEUBX	B+	(800) 421-4120	B+ / 8.6	-0.90	6.35	27.25 /92	23.38 /88	9.82 /80	0.95	1.67
FO	American Funds EuroPacific Gr 529C	CEUCX	B+	(800) 421-4120	B+ / 8.8	-0.90	6.36	27.26 /92	23.39 /88	9.83 /80	1.01	1.66
FO	American Funds EuroPacific Gr 529E	CEUEX	A-	(800) 421-4120	A- / 9.0	-0.78	6.63	27.93 /93	24.04 /89	10.41 /82	1.38	1.13
FO	American Funds EuroPacific Gr 529F	CEUFX	A-	(800) 421-4120	A- / 9.1	-0.64	6.90	28.58 /93	24.47 /90	10.74 /83	1.67	0.66
★ FO	American Funds EuroPacific Gr A	AEPGX	B+	(800) 421-4120	B+ / 8.8	-0.68	6.81	28.36 /93	24.53 /90	10.85 /83	1.50	0.76
FO	American Funds EuroPacific Gr B	AEGBX	B+	(800) 421-4120	B+ / 8.7	-0.85	6.43	27.46 /92	23.64 /89	10.02 /81	1.03	1.51
FO	American Funds EuroPacific Gr C	AEPCX	A-	(800) 421-4120	B+ / 8.9	-0.90	6.39	27.32 /92	23.51 /88	9.92 /80	1.04	1.60
FO	American Funds EuroPacific Gr F	AEGFX	A-	(800) 421-4120	A- / 9.1	-0.68	6.81	28.36 /93	24.47 /90	10.80 /83	1.59	0.80
FO	American Funds EuroPacific Gr R1	RERAX	A-	(800) 421-4120	B+ / 8.9	-0.88	6.40	27.34 /92	23.49 /88	9.95 /80	1.16	1.65
FO	American Funds EuroPacific Gr R2	RERBX	A-	(800) 421-4120	B+ / 8.9	-0.90	6.36	27.31 /92	23.50 /88	9.95 /80	1.09	1.76
FO	American Funds EuroPacific Gr R3	RERCX	A-	(800) 421-4120	A- / 9.0	-0.78	6.62	27.93 /93	24.09 /90	10.43 /82	1.40	1.15
FO	American Funds EuroPacific Gr R4	REREX	A-	(800) 421-4120	A- / 9.1	-0.71	6.77	28.30 /93	24.47 /90	10.67 /83	1.61	0.87
FO	American Funds EuroPacific Gr R5	RERFX	A	(800) 421-4120	A- / 9.1	-0.61	6.96	28.71 /93	24.85 /91	11.13 /84	1.79	0.58
GI	American Funds Fundamentl Invs	CFNAX	B+	(800) 421-4120	B- / 7.5	1.36	8.80	20.51 /82	18.54 /75	7.28 /68	1.45	0.70
GI	American Funds Fundamentl Invs	CFNBX	B+	(800) 421-4120	B- / 7.2	1.17	8.38	19.51 /81	17.53 /70	6.42 /64	0.75	1.54
GI	American Funds Fundamentl Invs	CFNCX	B+	(800) 421-4120	B- / 7.5	1.17	8.35	19.53 /81	17.54 /70	6.43 /64	0.76	1.53
GI	American Funds Fundamentl Invs	CFNEX	A-	(800) 421-4120	B / 7.8	1.31	8.66	20.14 /82	18.15 /73	6.93 /66	1.25	1.02
GI	American Funds Fundamentl Invs	CFNFX	A-	(800) 421-4120	B / 8.0	1.41	8.91	20.74 /83	18.56 /75	7.26 /68	1.72	0.58
★ GI	American Funds Fundamentl Invs A	ANCFX	B+	(800) 421-4120	B- / 7.5	1.37	8.82	20.56 /83	18.63 /75	7.36 /68	1.50	0.62
GI	American Funds Fundamentl Invs B	AFIBX	B+	(800) 421-4120	B- / 7.2	1.18	8.43	19.65 /81	17.72 /71	6.55 /64	0.87	1.39
GI	American Funds Fundamentl Invs C	AFICX	B+	(800) 421-4120	B / 7.6	1.16	8.37	19.57 /81	17.64 /71	6.47 /64	0.82	1.45
GI	American Funds Fundamentl Invs F	AFIFX	A-	(800) 421-4120	B / 8.0	1.37	8.83	20.60 /83	18.58 /75	7.32 /68	1.59	0.66
GI	American Funds Fundamentl Invs R1	RFNAX	B+	(800) 421-4120	B / 7.6	1.18	8.38	19.56 /81	17.63 /71	6.46 /64	0.79	1.64
GI	American Funds Fundamentl Invs R2	RFNBX	B+	(800) 421-4120	B / 7.7	1.16	8.39	19.56 /81	17.66 /71	6.50 /64	0.81	1.64
GI	American Funds Fundamentl Invs R3	RFNCX	A-	(800) 421-4120	B / 7.8	1.30	8.62	20.10 /82	18.14 /73	6.93 /66	1.24	1.01
GI	American Funds Fundamentl Invs R4	RFNEX	A-	(800) 421-4120	B / 8.0	1.38	8.80	20.51 /82	18.55 /75	7.30 /68	1.54	0.69
GI	American Funds Fundamentl Invs R5	RFNFX	A	(800) 421-4120	B / 8.1	1.43	8.95	20.83 /83	18.90 /76	7.63 /70	1.81	0.39

● Denotes fund is closed to new investors
★ Denotes fund is included in Section II

54

RISK			NET ASSETS		ASSET					BULL / BEAR		FUND MANAGER		MINIMUMS		LOADS	
	3 Year		NAV						Portfolio	Last Bull	Last Bear	Manager	Manager	Initial	Additional	Front	Back
Risk Rating/Pts	Standard Deviation	Beta	As of 6/30/06	Total $(Mil)	Cash %	Stocks %	Bonds %	Other %	Turnover Ratio	Market Return	Market Return	Quality Pct	Tenure (Years)	Purch. $	Purch. $	End Load	End Load
B+ / 9.6	6.1	1.05	55.59	10	9	68	20	3	20.0	64.7	-1.2	95	N/A	250	50	0.0	0.0
B+ / 9.3	6.1	1.05	55.59	49,729	9	68	20	3	20.0	65.4	-1.1	95	N/A	250	50	5.8	1.0
B+ / 9.6	6.0	1.05	55.59	3,842	9	68	20	3	20.0	61.2	-1.3	93	N/A	250	50	0.0	5.0
B+ / 9.6	6.0	1.05	55.59	7,064	9	68	20	3	20.0	60.9	-1.3	92	N/A	250	50	0.0	1.0
B+ / 9.6	6.1	1.05	55.59	2,621	9	68	20	3	20.0	64.8	-1.2	95	N/A	250	50	0.0	0.0
B+ / 9.6	6.0	1.05	55.59	51	9	68	20	3	20.0	60.7	-1.3	92	N/A	0	0	0.0	0.0
B+ / 9.6	6.0	1.05	55.59	321	9	68	20	3	20.0	60.9	-1.3	92	N/A	0	0	0.0	0.0
B+ / 9.6	6.1	1.05	55.59	355	9	68	20	3	20.0	63.0	-1.2	94	N/A	0	0	0.0	0.0
B+ / 9.6	6.1	1.05	55.59	87	9	68	20	3	20.0	64.8	-1.1	94	N/A	0	0	0.0	0.0
B+ / 9.6	6.1	1.05	55.59	379	9	68	20	3	20.0	66.4	-1.1	95	N/A	0	0	0.0	0.0
B- / 7.7	8.9	0.85	38.45	838	9	89	0	2	26.0	120.4	-6.3	67	N/A	250	50	5.8	1.0
B- / 7.6	8.9	0.85	38.37	112	9	89	0	2	26.0	114.4	-6.6	57	N/A	250	50	0.0	5.0
B- / 7.6	8.9	0.86	38.37	233	9	89	0	2	26.0	114.5	-6.5	57	N/A	250	50	0.0	1.0
B- / 7.6	8.9	0.85	38.42	42	9	89	0	2	26.0	117.9	-6.4	63	N/A	25	25	0.0	0.0
B- / 7.7	8.9	0.85	38.47	17	9	89	0	2	26.0	120.3	-6.4	67	N/A	250	50	0.0	0.0
B- / 7.7	8.9	0.85	38.51	50,226	9	89	0	2	26.0	120.9	-6.3	68	N/A	250	50	5.8	1.0
B- / 7.6	8.9	0.85	38.36	2,844	9	89	0	2	26.0	115.5	-6.5	59	N/A	250	50	0.0	5.0
B- / 7.6	8.9	0.85	38.25	5,260	9	89	0	2	26.0	115.1	-6.5	59	N/A	250	50	0.0	1.0
B- / 7.7	8.9	0.85	38.46	3,258	9	89	0	2	26.0	120.4	-6.3	67	N/A	250	50	0.0	0.0
B- / 7.6	8.9	0.86	38.34	64	9	89	0	2	26.0	114.9	-6.5	58	N/A	0	0	0.0	0.0
B- / 7.6	8.9	0.85	38.25	614	9	89	0	2	26.0	115.0	-6.5	58	N/A	0	0	0.0	0.0
B- / 7.6	8.9	0.85	38.37	872	9	89	0	2	26.0	117.9	-6.4	63	N/A	0	0	0.0	0.0
B- / 7.6	8.9	0.85	38.46	615	9	89	0	2	26.0	120.3	-6.4	67	N/A	0	0	0.0	0.0
B- / 7.7	8.9	0.85	38.52	728	9	89	0	2	26.0	122.5	-6.2	70	N/A	0	0	0.0	0.0
C+ / 6.4	10.4	0.98	43.69	406	8	91	0	1	35.0	134.4	-9.5	60	22	250	50	5.8	1.0
C+ / 6.4	10.4	0.99	43.03	67	8	91	0	1	35.0	127.8	-9.8	48	22	250	50	0.0	5.0
C+ / 6.4	10.4	0.99	42.99	172	8	91	0	1	35.0	128.0	-9.8	49	22	250	50	0.0	1.0
C+ / 6.4	10.4	0.99	43.41	25	8	91	0	1	35.0	131.9	-9.7	56	22	25	25	0.0	0.0
C+ / 6.4	10.4	0.99	43.70	25	8	91	0	1	35.0	134.2	-9.6	60	22	250	50	0.0	0.0
C+ / 6.4	10.4	0.99	43.90	49,564	8	91	0	1	35.0	134.8	-9.6	60	22	250	50	5.8	1.0
C+ / 6.4	10.4	0.99	43.34	1,428	8	91	0	1	35.0	129.3	-9.8	51	22	250	50	0.0	5.0
C+ / 6.4	10.4	0.99	42.96	2,822	8	91	0	1	35.0	128.7	-9.7	50	22	250	50	0.0	1.0
C+ / 6.4	10.4	0.99	43.75	6,955	8	91	0	1	35.0	134.4	-9.6	60	22	250	50	0.0	0.0
C+ / 6.4	10.4	0.99	42.91	75	8	91	0	1	35.0	128.6	-9.8	50	22	0	0	0.0	0.0
C+ / 6.4	10.4	0.99	42.97	770	8	91	0	1	35.0	128.7	-9.7	50	22	0	0	0.0	0.0
C+ / 6.4	10.4	0.99	43.30	4,733	8	91	0	1	35.0	132.0	-9.7	N/A	22	0	0	0.0	0.0
C+ / 6.4	10.4	0.99	43.38	5,699	8	91	0	1	35.0	134.3	-9.6	60	22	0	0	0.0	0.0
C+ / 6.5	10.4	0.99	43.95	10,063	8	91	0	1	35.0	136.6	-9.5	63	22	0	0	0.0	0.0
B- / 7.6	9.7	1.14	38.28	305	4	95	0	1	23.7	98.1	-9.7	94	28	250	50	5.8	0.0
B- / 7.6	9.7	1.14	38.28	48	4	95	0	1	23.7	92.8	-10.0	92	28	250	50	0.0	5.0
B- / 7.6	9.7	1.14	38.27	94	4	95	0	1	23.7	92.8	-10.0	92	28	250	50	0.0	1.0
B- / 7.6	9.7	1.14	38.27	15	4	95	0	1	23.7	96.0	-9.8	93	28	25	25	0.0	0.0
B- / 7.5	9.7	1.14	38.26	7	4	95	0	1	23.7	98.0	-9.8	94	28	250	50	0.0	0.0
B- / 7.6	9.7	1.14	38.30	27,883	4	95	0	1	23.7	98.6	-9.7	94	28	250	50	5.8	0.0
B- / 7.6	9.7	1.14	38.23	1,244	4	95	0	1	23.7	93.8	-9.9	92	28	250	50	0.0	5.0
B- / 7.6	9.7	1.14	38.19	1,026	4	95	0	1	23.7	93.4	-9.9	92	28	250	50	0.0	1.0
B- / 7.6	9.7	1.14	38.29	1,050	4	95	0	1	23.7	98.2	-9.8	94	5	250	50	0.0	0.0
B- / 7.6	9.7	1.14	38.21	15	4	95	0	1	23.7	93.3	-9.9	92	28	0	0	0.0	0.0
B- / 7.6	9.7	1.14	38.19	214	4	95	0	1	23.7	93.5	-9.9	92	28	0	0	0.0	0.0
B- / 7.6	9.7	1.14	38.25	325	4	95	0	1	23.7	95.9	-9.8	93	28	0	0	0.0	0.0
B- / 7.6	9.7	1.14	38.26	246	4	95	0	1	23.7	98.1	-9.7	94	28	0	0	0.0	0.0
B- / 7.5	9.7	1.14	38.31	364	4	95	0	1	23.7	100.0	-9.7	95	28	0	0	0.0	0.0

Fund Type	Fund Name	Ticker Symbol	Overall Weiss Investment Rating	Phone	Perfor-mance Rating/Pts	3 Mo	6 Mo	1Yr / Pct	Annualized 3Yr / Pct	5Yr / Pct	Dividend Yield	Expense Ratio
	99 Pct = Best							Total Return % through 6/30/06			Incl. in Returns	
GR	American Funds Gr Fnd of Amer	CGFAX	C+	(800) 421-4120	C / 5.3	-1.59	2.70	15.36 /73	15.12 /59	4.85 /53	0.55	0.71
GR	American Funds Gr Fnd of Amer	CGFBX	C	(800) 421-4120	C / 4.9	-1.79	2.29	14.38 /69	14.12 /55	3.94 /45	0.00	1.57
GR	American Funds Gr Fnd of Amer	CGFCX	C+	(800) 421-4120	C / 5.5	-1.78	2.32	14.41 /70	14.14 /55	3.95 /45	0.00	1.56
GR	American Funds Gr Fnd of Amer	CGFEX	C+	(800) 421-4120	C+/ 5.9	-1.66	2.55	14.97 /72	14.72 /57	4.50 /50	0.34	1.04
GR	American Funds Gr Fnd of Amer	CGFFX	C+	(800) 421-4120	C+/ 6.1	-1.56	2.80	15.56 /73	15.11 /59	4.80 /52	0.67	0.70
★ GR	American Funds Gr Fnd of Amer A	AGTHX	C+	(800) 421-4120	C / 5.4	-1.58	2.72	15.40 /73	15.16 /60	4.88 /53	0.56	0.66
GR	American Funds Gr Fnd of Amer B	AGRBX	C	(800) 421-4120	C / 5.0	-1.73	2.37	14.58 /70	14.31 /55	4.10 /47	0.00	1.41
GR	American Funds Gr Fnd of Amer C	GFACX	C+	(800) 421-4120	C / 5.5	-1.80	2.31	14.47 /70	14.23 /55	4.04 /46	0.00	1.46
GR	American Funds Gr Fnd of Amer F	GFAFX	C+	(800) 421-4120	C+/ 6.1	-1.56	2.74	15.43 /73	15.15 /60	4.87 /53	0.62	0.68
GR	American Funds Gr Fnd of Amer R1	RGAAX	C+	(800) 421-4120	C+/ 5.7	-1.78	2.31	14.46 /70	14.23 /55	4.04 /46	0.14	1.44
★ GR	American Funds Gr Fnd of Amer R2	RGABX	C+	(800) 421-4120	C+/ 5.7	-1.78	2.31	14.45 /70	14.25 /55	4.07 /46	0.00	1.45
GR	American Funds Gr Fnd of Amer R3	RGACX	C+	(800) 421-4120	C+/ 6.0	-1.63	2.59	15.04 /72	14.78 /58	4.52 /50	0.42	0.94
GR	American Funds Gr Fnd of Amer R4	RGAEX	C+	(800) 421-4120	C+/ 6.1	-1.59	2.71	15.36 /73	15.14 /59	4.86 /53	0.62	0.68
GR	American Funds Gr Fnd of Amer R5	RGAFX	C+	(800) 421-4120	C+/ 6.3	-1.49	2.88	15.72 /74	15.47 /61	5.18 /55	0.85	0.38
AA	American Funds Inc Fnd of Amer	CIMAX	C+	(800) 421-4120	C- / 4.1	1.78	6.79	9.59 /44	12.26 /44	8.31 /73	3.59	0.68
AA	American Funds Inc Fnd of Amer	CIMBX	C+	(800) 421-4120	C- / 3.7	1.52	6.31	8.67 /38	11.32 /38	7.42 /69	3.02	1.53
AA	American Funds Inc Fnd of Amer	CIMCX	B-	(800) 421-4120	C / 4.4	1.52	6.31	8.68 /38	11.33 /38	7.43 /69	3.03	1.52
AA	American Funds Inc Fnd of Amer	CIMEX	B	(800) 421-4120	C / 5.0	1.70	6.64	9.28 /42	11.91 /42	7.96 /71	3.52	1.01
AA	American Funds Inc Fnd of Amer	CIMFX	B+	(800) 421-4120	C / 5.2	1.78	6.83	9.75 /45	12.27 /44	8.29 /73	3.99	0.68
★ AA	American Funds Inc Fnd of Amer A	AMECX	C+	(800) 421-4120	C- / 4.1	1.74	6.77	9.62 /44	12.35 /45	8.42 /74	3.66	0.54
AA	American Funds Inc Fnd of Amer B	IFABX	C+	(800) 421-4120	C- / 3.8	1.56	6.39	8.84 /39	11.51 /39	7.59 /70	3.16	1.32
AA	American Funds Inc Fnd of Amer C	IFACX	B-	(800) 421-4120	C / 4.5	1.55	6.38	8.74 /38	11.42 /39	7.49 /69	3.11	1.41
AA	American Funds Inc Fnd of Amer F	IFAFX	B	(800) 421-4120	C / 5.2	1.79	6.75	9.58 /44	12.27 /44	8.31 /73	3.84	0.65
AA	American Funds Inc Fnd of Amer R1	RIDAX	B	(800) 421-4120	C / 4.6	1.58	6.38	8.69 /38	11.40 /39	7.48 /69	3.04	1.45
AA	American Funds Inc Fnd of Amer R2	RIDBX	B	(800) 421-4120	C / 4.6	1.59	6.41	8.74 /38	11.42 /39	7.47 /69	3.07	1.42
AA	American Funds Inc Fnd of Amer R3	RIDCX	B	(800) 421-4120	C / 4.9	1.70	6.62	9.25 /42	11.89 /42	7.95 /71	3.50	0.96
AA	American Funds Inc Fnd of Amer R4	RIDEX	B	(800) 421-4120	C / 5.2	1.77	6.77	9.57 /44	12.24 /44	8.31 /73	3.78	0.65
AA	American Funds Inc Fnd of Amer R5	RIDFX	B+	(800) 421-4120	C / 5.4	1.85	6.93	9.89 /46	12.59 /46	8.64 /75	4.07	0.35
GI	American Funds Inv Co of Amer 529A	CICAX	C+	(800) 421-4120	C / 4.4	1.49	5.72	12.77 /63	12.61 /46	5.24 /56	1.96	0.67
GI	American Funds Inv Co of Amer 529B	CICBX	C+	(800) 421-4120	C- / 4.0	1.29	5.27	11.80 /58	11.64 /40	4.37 /49	1.29	1.51
GI	American Funds Inv Co of Amer	CICCX	B-	(800) 421-4120	C / 4.7	1.29	5.31	11.85 /59	11.67 /40	4.39 /50	1.30	1.50
GI	American Funds Inv Co of Amer 529E	CICEX	B	(800) 421-4120	C / 5.2	1.39	5.54	12.38 /62	12.23 /44	4.89 /53	1.79	0.99
GI	American Funds Inv Co of Amer 529F	CICFX	B+	(800) 421-4120	C / 5.5	1.54	5.82	12.98 /64	12.63 /46	5.22 /56	2.25	0.56
★ GI	American Funds Inv Co of Amer A	AIVSX	C+	(800) 421-4120	C / 4.4	1.51	5.72	12.80 /63	12.71 /47	5.33 /57	2.02	0.57
GI	American Funds Inv Co of Amer B	AICBX	C+	(800) 421-4120	C- / 4.2	1.32	5.33	11.95 /59	11.85 /41	4.51 /50	1.41	1.35
GI	American Funds Inv Co of Amer C	AICCX	B-	(800) 421-4120	C / 4.7	1.30	5.31	11.87 /59	11.76 /41	4.43 /50	1.35	1.42
GI	American Funds Inv Co of Amer F	AICFX	B+	(800) 421-4120	C / 5.4	1.50	5.74	12.77 /63	12.63 /47	5.24 /56	2.11	0.64
GI	American Funds Inv Co of Amer R1	RICAX	B	(800) 421-4120	C / 4.9	1.30	5.28	11.90 /59	11.74 /41	4.43 /50	1.36	1.42
GI	American Funds Inv Co of Amer R2	RICBX	B	(800) 421-4120	C / 4.9	1.30	5.30	11.87 /59	11.76 /41	4.47 /50	1.35	1.57
GI	American Funds Inv Co of Amer R3	RICCX	B	(800) 421-4120	C / 5.2	1.41	5.56	12.39 /62	12.25 /44	4.89 /53	1.77	0.95
GI	American Funds Inv Co of Amer R4	RICEX	B	(800) 421-4120	C / 5.4	1.49	5.71	12.74 /63	12.61 /46	5.24 /56	2.07	0.65
GI	American Funds Inv Co of Amer R5	RICFX	B+	(800) 421-4120	C+/ 5.6	1.56	5.86	13.08 /65	12.95 /49	5.56 /58	2.34	0.36
GR	American Funds New Economy 529A	CNGAX	C	(800) 421-4120	C / 5.0	-3.65	0.51	13.98 /68	14.42 /56	2.69 /34	0.61	0.87
GR	American Funds New Economy 529B	CNGBX	C	(800) 421-4120	C / 4.6	-3.83	0.09	13.04 /64	13.42 /51	1.80 /25	0.00	1.76
GR	American Funds New Economy 529C	CNGCX	C	(800) 421-4120	C / 5.3	-3.82	0.09	13.04 /64	13.42 /51	1.81 /26	0.00	1.75
GR	American Funds New Economy 529E	CNGEX	C+	(800) 421-4120	C+/ 5.7	-3.71	0.34	13.58 /67	14.01 /54	2.36 /31	0.39	1.22
GR	American Funds New Economy 529F	CNGFX	C+	(800) 421-4120	C+/ 5.9	-3.61	0.60	14.16 /69	14.41 /56	2.66 /33	0.74	0.81
★ GR	American Funds New Economy A	ANEFX	C	(800) 421-4120	C / 5.0	-3.60	0.55	14.03 /68	14.47 /56	2.74 /34	0.60	0.83
GR	American Funds New Economy B	ANFBX	C	(800) 421-4120	C / 4.7	-3.78	0.13	13.14 /65	13.58 /52	1.94 /27	0.00	1.60
GR	American Funds New Economy C	ANFCX	C	(800) 421-4120	C / 5.3	-3.80	0.13	13.13 /65	13.54 /52	1.90 /26	0.04	1.65
GR	American Funds New Economy F	ANFFX	C+	(800) 421-4120	C+/ 5.9	-3.66	0.51	14.00 /68	14.41 /56	2.69 /34	0.68	0.86
GR	American Funds New Economy R1	RNGAX	C+	(800) 421-4120	C / 5.5	-3.84	0.09	13.10 /65	13.55 /52	1.92 /26	0.14	1.70

● Denotes fund is closed to new investors
★ Denotes fund is included in Section II

RISK			NET ASSETS		ASSET					BULL / BEAR		FUND MANAGER		MINIMUMS		LOADS	
	3 Year		NAV						Portfolio	Last Bull	Last Bear	Manager	Manager	Initial	Additional	Front	Back
Risk	Standard		As of	Total	Cash	Stocks	Bonds	Other	Turnover	Market	Market	Quality	Tenure	Purch.	Purch.	End	End
Rating/Pts	Deviation	Beta	6/30/06	$(Mil)	%	%	%	%	Ratio	Return	Return	Pct	(Years)	$	$	Load	Load
B- /7.2	9.3	1.11	31.59	1,868	9	90	0	1	20.4	85.5	-10.2	82	33	250	50	5.8	0.0
B- /7.1	9.3	1.11	30.80	409	9	90	0	1	20.4	80.4	-10.4	74	33	250	50	0.0	5.0
B- /7.1	9.3	1.11	30.82	593	9	90	0	1	20.4	80.5	-10.4	74	33	250	50	0.0	1.0
B- /7.1	9.3	1.11	31.38	102	9	90	0	1	20.4	83.4	-10.3	79	33	25	25	0.0	0.0
B- /7.2	9.3	1.11	31.57	47	9	90	0	1	20.4	85.3	-10.3	82	33	250	50	0.0	0.0
B- /7.2	9.3	1.11	31.70	77,843	9	90	0	1	20.4	85.7	-10.2	82	33	250	50	5.8	0.0
B- /7.1	9.3	1.11	30.66	6,813	9	90	0	1	20.4	81.3	-10.4	76	33	250	50	0.0	5.0
B- /7.1	9.3	1.11	30.55	8,795	9	90	0	1	20.4	81.0	-10.4	75	33	250	50	0.0	1.0
B- /7.2	9.3	1.11	31.54	16,391	9	90	0	1	20.4	85.6	-10.2	82	33	250	50	0.0	0.0
B- /7.1	9.3	1.11	30.95	219	9	90	0	1	20.4	80.9	-10.3	75	33	0	0	0.0	0.0
B- /7.1	9.3	1.11	30.98	2,080	9	90	0	1	20.4	81.1	-10.4	75	33	0	0	0.0	0.0
B- /7.2	9.3	1.10	31.29	9,090	9	90	0	1	20.4	83.7	-10.3	79	33	0	0	0.0	0.0
B- /7.2	9.3	1.10	31.51	11,825	9	90	0	1	20.4	85.6	-10.2	82	33	0	0	0.0	0.0
B- /7.2	9.3	1.11	31.74	6,165	9	90	0	1	20.4	87.3	-10.1	84	33	0	0	0.0	0.0
B+ /9.2	5.9	1.10	18.96	426	6	66	23	5	23.9	58.1	-2.0	89	33	250	50	5.8	1.0
B+ /9.4	5.8	1.10	18.91	88	6	66	23	5	23.9	54.0	-2.3	84	33	250	50	0.0	5.0
B+ /9.4	5.8	1.10	18.92	191	6	66	23	5	23.9	54.0	-2.3	84	33	250	50	0.0	1.0
B+ /9.4	5.9	1.10	18.93	22	6	66	23	5	23.9	56.3	-2.1	87	33	25	25	0.0	0.0
B+ /9.4	5.9	1.10	18.95	9	6	66	23	5	23.9	57.9	-2.0	89	33	250	50	0.0	0.0
B+ /9.2	5.9	1.10	18.97	51,236	6	66	23	5	23.9	58.5	-2.0	89	33	250	50	5.8	1.0
B+ /9.4	5.8	1.10	18.87	4,313	6	66	23	5	23.9	54.8	-2.2	85	33	250	50	0.0	5.0
B+ /9.4	5.8	1.10	18.84	6,399	6	66	23	5	23.9	54.4	-2.2	85	5	250	50	0.0	1.0
B+ /9.4	5.9	1.10	18.95	1,819	6	66	23	5	23.9	58.1	-2.0	89	5	250	50	0.0	0.0
B+ /9.4	5.8	1.10	18.92	33	6	66	23	5	23.9	54.3	-2.2	85	33	0	0	0.0	0.0
B+ /9.4	5.8	1.10	18.87	353	6	66	23	5	23.9	54.2	-2.2	85	33	0	0	0.0	0.0
B+ /9.4	5.9	1.11	18.94	536	6	66	23	5	23.9	56.4	-2.1	87	33	0	0	0.0	0.0
B+ /9.4	5.9	1.10	18.96	227	6	66	23	5	23.9	57.9	-2.0	89	33	0	0	0.0	0.0
B+ /9.4	6.0	1.11	18.97	147	6	66	23	5	23.9	59.5	-2.0	90	33	0	0	0.0	0.0
B+ /9.0	6.9	0.86	32.83	937	15	83	0	2	19.1	64.3	-7.7	81	73	250	50	5.8	1.0
B+ /9.2	6.9	0.86	32.76	208	15	83	0	2	19.1	59.8	-8.0	73	73	250	50	0.0	5.0
B+ /9.3	6.9	0.86	32.77	275	15	83	0	2	19.1	59.9	-7.9	73	73	250	50	0.0	1.0
B+ /9.1	6.9	0.86	32.77	40	15	83	0	2	19.1	62.6	-7.9	78	73	25	25	0.0	0.0
B+ /9.2	6.9	0.86	32.82	9	15	83	0	2	19.1	64.3	-7.8	81	73	250	50	0.0	0.0
B+ /9.0	6.9	0.86	32.85	68,759	15	83	0	2	19.1	64.8	-7.7	82	73	250	50	5.8	1.0
B+ /9.2	6.9	0.86	32.73	3,956	15	83	0	2	19.1	60.8	-7.9	75	73	250	50	0.0	5.0
B+ /9.2	6.9	0.86	32.67	3,036	15	83	0	2	19.1	60.4	-7.9	74	73	250	50	0.0	1.0
B+ /9.2	6.9	0.86	32.82	1,422	15	83	0	2	19.1	64.4	-7.7	81	5	250	50	0.0	0.0
B+ /9.2	6.9	0.86	32.74	36	15	83	0	2	19.1	60.3	-7.9	74	73	0	0	0.0	0.0
B+ /9.2	6.9	0.86	32.75	538	15	83	0	2	19.1	60.4	-7.9	74	73	0	0	0.0	0.0
B+ /9.2	6.9	0.86	32.80	754	15	83	0	2	19.1	62.6	-7.9	78	73	0	0	0.0	0.0
B+ /9.2	6.9	0.86	32.82	267	15	83	0	2	19.1	64.4	-7.8	81	73	0	0	0.0	0.0
B+ /9.2	6.9	0.86	32.85	1,665	15	83	0	2	19.1	65.9	-7.7	83	73	0	0	0.0	0.0
B- /7.2	10.6	1.26	23.50	62	8	90	0	2	32.0	94.7	-13.8	64	N/A	250	50	5.8	1.0
B- /7.1	10.6	1.26	22.88	11	8	90	0	2	32.0	89.3	-14.0	54	N/A	250	50	0.0	5.0
B- /7.1	10.6	1.26	22.89	19	8	90	0	2	32.0	89.2	-14.0	54	N/A	250	50	0.0	1.0
B- /7.2	10.6	1.26	23.33	4	8	90	0	2	32.0	92.4	-13.9	60	N/A	25	25	0.0	0.0
B- /7.2	10.6	1.26	23.49	1	8	90	0	2	32.0	94.4	-13.9	64	N/A	250	50	0.0	0.0
B- /7.2	10.6	1.26	23.57	7,086	8	90	0	2	32.0	94.8	-13.9	65	N/A	250	50	5.8	1.0
B- /7.1	10.6	1.26	22.65	188	8	90	0	2	32.0	90.1	-14.0	56	N/A	250	50	0.0	5.0
B- /7.1	10.6	1.26	22.55	113	8	90	0	2	32.0	89.9	-14.0	55	N/A	250	50	0.0	1.0
B- /7.2	10.6	1.26	23.45	149	8	90	0	2	32.0	94.6	-13.8	64	N/A	250	50	0.0	0.0
B- /7.1	10.6	1.26	23.04	5	8	90	0	2	32.0	90.0	-14.0	56	N/A	0	0	0.0	0.0

					PERFORMANCE							
99 Pct = Best			**Overall Weiss Investment Rating**					Total Return % through 6/30/06			Incl. in Returns	
0 Pct = Worst					**Perfor-mance Rating/Pts**				Annualized		Dividend Yield	Expense Ratio
Fund Type	Fund Name	Ticker Symbol		Phone		3 Mo	6 Mo	1Yr / Pct	3Yr / Pct	5Yr / Pct		
GR	American Funds New Economy R2	RNGBX	C+	(800) 421-4120	C / 5.5	-3.79	0.13	13.14 /65	13.59 /52	1.95 /27	0.05	1.91
GR	American Funds New Economy R3	RNGCX	C+	(800) 421-4120	C+ / 5.7	-3.71	0.34	13.55 /66	14.01 /54	2.35 /31	0.36	1.24
GR	American Funds New Economy R4	RNGEX	C+	(800) 421-4120	C+ / 5.9	-3.61	0.51	13.96 /68	14.42 /56	2.72 /34	0.68	0.86
GR	American Funds New Economy R5	RNGFX	C+	(800) 421-4120	C+ / 6.1	-3.55	0.68	14.35 /69	14.80 /58	3.04 /37	0.91	0.55
GL	American Funds New Perspective	CNPAX	A-	(800) 421-4120	B- / 7.2	0.36	6.14	20.48 /82	18.69 /75	7.87 /71	1.14	0.85
GL	American Funds New Perspective	CNPBX	B+	(800) 421-4120	B- / 7.0	0.13	5.70	19.46 /81	17.66 /71	6.95 /66	0.51	1.71
GL	American Funds New Perspective	CNPCX	A	(800) 421-4120	B- / 7.4	0.13	5.71	19.48 /81	17.69 /71	6.96 /66	0.55	1.70
GL	American Funds New Perspective	CNPEX	A	(800) 421-4120	B / 7.7	0.27	5.96	20.08 /82	18.30 /74	7.52 /69	0.96	1.18
GL	American Funds New Perspective	CNPFX	A+	(800) 421-4120	B / 7.8	0.40	6.25	20.73 /83	18.71 /75	7.85 /71	1.29	0.82
★ GL	American Funds New Perspective A	ANWPX	B+	(800) 421-4120	B- / 7.3	0.36	6.15	20.55 /83	18.78 /75	7.94 /71	1.16	0.77
GL	American Funds New Perspective B	NPFBX	B+	(800) 421-4120	B- / 7.1	0.17	5.74	19.64 /81	17.87 /72	7.12 /67	0.59	1.54
GL	American Funds New Perspective C	NPFCX	B+	(800) 421-4120	B- / 7.4	0.17	5.73	19.56 /81	17.80 /72	7.06 /67	0.58	1.60
GL	American Funds New Perspective F	NPFFX	A-	(800) 421-4120	B / 7.8	0.36	6.16	20.57 /83	18.74 /75	7.90 /71	1.20	0.82
GL	American Funds New Perspective R1	RNPAX	B+	(800) 421-4120	B- / 7.5	0.13	5.72	19.59 /81	17.79 /72	7.04 /67	0.74	1.66
GL	American Funds New Perspective R2	RNPBX	B+	(800) 421-4120	B- / 7.5	0.13	5.71	19.54 /81	17.81 /72	7.08 /67	0.65	1.76
GL	American Funds New Perspective R3	RNPCX	A-	(800) 421-4120	B / 7.7	0.27	5.96	20.11 /82	18.33 /74	7.54 /69	1.01	1.10
GL	American Funds New Perspective R4	RNPEX	A-	(800) 421-4120	B / 7.8	0.33	6.15	20.53 /82	18.74 /75	7.90 /71	1.25	0.79
GL	American Funds New Perspective R5	RNPFX	A-	(800) 421-4120	B / 7.9	0.40	6.29	20.82 /83	19.06 /76	8.22 /72	1.45	0.52
GL	American Funds New World 529A	CNWAX	B+	(800) 421-4120	A- / 9.0	-3.02	8.32	26.56 /91	26.53 /93	15.50 /92	1.64	1.21
GL	American Funds New World 529B	CNWBX	B	(800) 421-4120	B+ / 8.9	-3.20	7.88	25.48 /89	25.44 /92	14.50 /91	1.16	2.09
GL	American Funds New World 529C	CNWCX	B+	(800) 421-4120	A- / 9.1	-3.23	7.87	25.49 /89	25.45 /92	14.52 /91	1.21	2.08
GL	American Funds New World 529E	CNWEX	B+	(800) 421-4120	A- / 9.2	-3.08	8.17	26.16 /90	26.10 /92	15.12 /92	1.55	1.55
GL	American Funds New World 529F	CNWFX	B+	(800) 421-4120	A- / 9.2	-2.97	8.41	26.77 /91	26.55 /93	15.47 /92	1.78	1.17
★ GL	American Funds New World A	NEWFX	B+	(800) 421-4120	A- / 9.0	-3.01	8.35	26.63 /91	26.60 /93	15.56 /93	1.64	1.18
GL	American Funds New World B	NEWBX	B+	(800) 421-4120	A- / 9.1	-3.19	7.96	25.64 /89	25.64 /92	14.66 /91	1.25	1.94
GL	American Funds New World C	NEWCX	B+	(800) 421-4120	A- / 9.2	-3.22	7.90	25.55 /89	25.57 /92	14.61 /91	1.32	1.98
GL	American Funds New World F	NWFFX	B+	(800) 421-4120	A- / 9.2	-3.00	8.36	26.61 /91	26.57 /93	15.51 /92	1.75	1.19
GL	American Funds New World R1	RNWAX	B+	(800) 421-4120	A- / 9.2	-3.23	7.90	25.56 /89	25.57 /92	14.63 /91	1.34	2.06
GL	American Funds New World R2	RNWBX	B+	(800) 421-4120	A- / 9.1	-3.20	7.93	25.61 /89	25.60 /92	14.68 /91	1.32	2.27
GL	American Funds New World R3	RNWCX	B+	(800) 421-4120	A / 9.3	-3.12	8.13	26.08 /90	26.08 /92	15.21 /92	1.48	1.60
GL	American Funds New World R4	RNWEX	B+	(800) 421-4120	A / 9.3	-3.03	8.32	26.53 /91	26.53 /93	15.52 /93	1.77	1.21
GL	American Funds New World R5	RNWFX	B+	(800) 421-4120	A / 9.3	-2.93	8.52	26.95 /91	26.94 /93	15.89 /93	1.92	0.89
GL	American Funds SMALLCAP World	CSPAX	B+	(800) 421-4120	B+ / 8.6	-3.88	7.79	22.88 /86	23.71 /89	9.77 /80	1.02	1.08
GL	American Funds SMALLCAP World	CSPBX	B	(800) 421-4120	B+ / 8.4	-4.07	7.36	21.87 /84	22.64 /86	8.80 /76	0.60	1.96
GL	American Funds SMALLCAP World	CSPCX	B+	(800) 421-4120	B+ / 8.7	-4.09	7.36	21.87 /84	22.64 /86	8.81 /76	0.65	1.95
GL	American Funds SMALLCAP World	CSPEX	B+	(800) 421-4120	B+ / 8.9	-3.96	7.64	22.50 /85	23.30 /88	9.39 /78	0.92	1.42
GL	American Funds SMALLCAP World	CSPFX	B+	(800) 421-4120	A- / 9.0	-3.83	7.91	23.11 /86	23.74 /89	9.73 /79	1.10	1.06
★ GL	American Funds SMALLCAP World A	SMCWX	B+	(800) 421-4120	B+ / 8.6	-3.87	7.83	22.93 /86	23.76 /89	9.79 /80	1.00	1.04
GL	American Funds SMALLCAP World B	SCWBX	B+	(800) 421-4120	B+ / 8.5	-4.06	7.41	22.01 /84	22.80 /87	8.94 /76	0.66	1.81
GL	American Funds SMALLCAP World C	SCWCX	B+	(800) 421-4120	B+ / 8.7	-4.08	7.39	21.93 /84	22.77 /87	8.91 /76	0.71	1.85
GL	American Funds SMALLCAP World F	SCWFX	B+	(800) 421-4120	A- / 9.0	-3.86	7.81	22.95 /86	23.73 /89	9.76 /80	1.10	1.07
GL	American Funds SMALLCAP World	RSLAX	B+	(800) 421-4120	B+ / 8.8	-4.08	7.37	21.93 /84	22.76 /87	8.93 /76	0.76	1.85
GL	American Funds SMALLCAP World	RSLBX	B+	(800) 421-4120	B+ / 8.8	-4.05	7.39	21.97 /84	22.79 /87	8.96 /76	0.74	1.82
GL	American Funds SMALLCAP World	RSLCX	B+	(800) 421-4120	B+ / 8.9	-3.99	7.60	22.39 /85	23.26 /88	9.38 /78	0.93	1.44
GL	American Funds SMALLCAP World	RSLEX	B+	(800) 421-4120	A- / 9.0	-3.88	7.79	22.91 /86	23.73 /89	9.78 /80	1.12	1.06
GL	American Funds SMALLCAP World	RSLFX	A-	(800) 421-4120	A- / 9.0	-3.82	7.97	23.27 /86	24.12 /90	10.13 /81	1.23	0.76
GI	American Funds Wash Mutl Invs	CWMAX	C	(800) 421-4120	C- / 3.1	0.67	5.10	8.87 /39	10.86 /34	4.80 /52	1.77	0.70
GI	American Funds Wash Mutl Invs	CWMBX	C	(800) 421-4120	D+ / 2.7	0.47	4.66	7.98 /33	9.92 /27	3.93 /45	1.08	1.57
GI	American Funds Wash Mutl Invs	CWMCX	C	(800) 421-4120	C- / 3.4	0.47	4.67	7.97 /32	9.92 /27	3.94 /45	1.10	1.56
GI	American Funds Wash Mutl Invs	CWMEX	C+	(800) 421-4120	C- / 4.0	0.57	4.93	8.54 /37	10.48 /31	4.45 /50	1.59	1.04
GI	American Funds Wash Mutl Invs	CWMFX	C+	(800) 421-4120	C / 4.3	0.73	5.21	9.08 /41	10.88 /34	4.77 /52	2.08	0.79
★ GI	American Funds Wash Mutl Invs A	AWSHX	C	(800) 421-4120	C- / 3.1	0.69	5.16	8.97 /40	10.96 /35	4.88 /53	1.83	0.60

● Denotes fund is closed to new investors
★ Denotes fund is included in Section II

RISK			NET ASSETS		ASSET					BULL / BEAR		FUND MANAGER		MINIMUMS		LOADS	
Risk Rating/Pts	3 Year		NAV As of 6/30/06	Total $(Mil)	Cash %	Stocks %	Bonds %	Other %	Portfolio Turnover Ratio	Last Bull Market Return	Last Bear Market Return	Manager Quality Pct	Manager Tenure (Years)	Initial Purch. $	Additional Purch. $	Front End Load	Back End Load
	Standard Deviation	Beta															
B- / 7.1	10.6	1.26	23.07	70	8	90	0	2	32.0	90.0	-13.9	56	N/A	0	0	0.0	0.0
B- / 7.2	10.6	1.26	23.34	63	8	90	0	2	32.0	92.3	-13.9	60	N/A	0	0	0.0	0.0
B- / 7.2	10.6	1.26	23.51	34	8	90	0	2	32.0	94.7	-13.8	64	N/A	0	0	0.0	0.0
B- / 7.3	10.6	1.26	23.66	86	8	90	0	2	32.0	96.6	-13.8	68	N/A	0	0	0.0	0.0
B / 8.3	10.0	0.92	30.26	543	9	90	0	1	30.0	103.7	-10.2	24	N/A	250	50	5.8	1.0
B / 8.2	10.0	0.92	29.84	97	9	90	0	1	30.0	98.1	-10.4	19	N/A	250	50	0.0	5.0
B / 8.2	10.0	0.92	29.83	148	9	90	0	1	30.0	98.1	-10.4	19	N/A	250	50	0.0	1.0
B / 8.2	10.0	0.92	30.06	32	9	90	0	1	30.0	101.5	-10.3	22	N/A	25	25	0.0	0.0
B / 8.3	10.0	0.92	30.25	8	9	90	0	1	30.0	103.6	-10.2	24	N/A	250	50	0.0	0.0
B- / 7.6	10.0	0.92	30.39	38,995	9	90	0	1	30.0	104.1	-10.2	25	N/A	250	50	5.8	1.0
B- / 7.6	10.0	0.92	29.86	1,660	9	90	0	1	30.0	99.2	-10.4	19	6	250	50	0.0	5.0
B- / 7.6	10.0	0.92	29.71	1,436	9	90	0	1	30.0	98.8	-10.4	19	5	250	50	0.0	1.0
B- / 7.6	10.0	0.92	30.31	867	9	90	0	1	30.0	103.8	-10.2	25	5	250	50	0.0	0.0
B- / 7.6	10.0	0.92	29.75	25	9	90	0	1	30.0	98.8	-10.4	19	N/A	0	0	0.0	0.0
B- / 7.6	10.0	0.92	29.79	426	9	90	0	1	30.0	98.9	-10.4	19	N/A	0	0	0.0	0.0
B- / 7.6	10.0	0.92	30.03	815	9	90	0	1	30.0	101.6	-10.3	22	N/A	0	0	0.0	0.0
B- / 7.6	10.0	0.92	30.21	625	9	90	0	1	30.0	103.9	-10.2	25	N/A	0	0	0.0	0.0
B- / 7.6	10.0	0.92	30.42	1,800	9	90	0	1	30.0	105.7	-10.1	27	N/A	0	0	0.0	0.0
C+ / 5.8	12.4	1.08	41.77	135	15	76	8	1	26.0	156.5	-4.5	57	N/A	250	50	5.8	1.0
C+ / 5.7	12.4	1.08	41.09	18	15	76	8	1	26.0	149.3	-4.7	45	N/A	250	50	0.0	5.0
C+ / 5.7	12.4	1.08	41.10	34	15	76	8	1	26.0	149.4	-4.8	45	N/A	250	50	0.0	1.0
C+ / 5.8	12.4	1.08	41.55	8	15	76	8	1	26.0	153.5	-4.6	52	N/A	25	25	0.0	0.0
C+ / 5.8	12.4	1.08	41.76	7	15	76	8	1	26.0	156.3	-4.5	57	N/A	250	50	0.0	0.0
C+ / 5.8	12.4	1.08	41.93	6,626	15	76	8	1	26.0	156.6	-4.5	57	N/A	250	50	5.8	1.0
C+ / 5.7	12.5	1.09	41.24	285	15	76	8	1	26.0	150.5	-4.7	47	N/A	250	50	0.0	5.0
C+ / 5.7	12.5	1.08	40.86	452	15	76	8	1	26.0	150.2	-4.7	46	5	250	50	0.0	1.0
C+ / 5.8	12.4	1.08	41.72	549	15	76	8	1	26.0	156.5	-4.6	57	5	250	50	0.0	0.0
C+ / 5.7	12.4	1.08	41.09	6	15	76	8	1	26.0	150.2	-4.7	46	N/A	0	0	0.0	0.0
C+ / 5.7	12.4	1.08	41.10	85	15	76	8	1	26.0	150.4	-4.7	47	N/A	0	0	0.0	0.0
C+ / 5.8	12.4	1.08	41.64	71	15	76	8	1	26.0	153.4	-4.6	52	N/A	0	0	0.0	0.0
C+ / 5.8	12.4	1.08	41.92	28	15	76	8	1	26.0	156.4	-4.6	57	N/A	0	0	0.0	0.0
C+ / 5.8	12.4	1.08	42.05	279	15	76	8	1	26.0	158.9	-4.4	61	N/A	0	0	0.0	0.0
C+ / 6.2	12.4	1.04	37.92	264	8	91	0	1	45.5	152.3	-8.8	40	N/A	250	50	5.8	1.0
C+ / 6.2	12.4	1.04	37.04	45	8	91	0	1	45.5	145.3	-9.0	32	N/A	250	50	0.0	5.0
C+ / 6.2	12.4	1.04	37.03	108	8	91	0	1	45.5	145.3	-9.0	32	N/A	250	50	0.0	1.0
C+ / 6.2	12.4	1.04	37.60	17	8	91	0	1	45.5	149.6	-8.9	36	N/A	25	25	0.0	0.0
C+ / 6.2	12.4	1.04	37.92	18	8	91	0	1	45.5	152.2	-8.9	40	N/A	250	50	0.0	0.0
C+ / 6.2	12.4	1.04	38.03	15,140	8	91	0	1	45.5	152.6	-8.9	40	N/A	250	50	5.8	1.0
C+ / 6.2	12.4	1.04	36.67	576	8	91	0	1	45.5	146.4	-9.0	33	N/A	250	50	0.0	5.0
C+ / 6.2	12.4	1.04	36.48	667	8	91	0	1	45.5	146.2	-9.0	33	N/A	250	50	0.0	1.0
C+ / 6.2	12.4	1.04	37.81	402	8	91	0	1	45.5	152.3	-8.8	40	5	250	50	0.0	0.0
C+ / 6.2	12.4	1.04	37.15	20	8	91	0	1	45.5	146.2	-9.0	33	N/A	0	0	0.0	0.0
C+ / 6.2	12.4	1.04	37.18	383	8	91	0	1	45.5	146.3	-9.0	33	N/A	0	0	0.0	0.0
C+ / 6.2	12.4	1.04	37.54	297	8	91	0	1	45.5	149.4	-8.9	36	N/A	0	0	0.0	0.0
C+ / 6.2	12.4	1.04	37.90	109	8	91	0	1	45.5	152.3	-8.8	40	N/A	0	0	0.0	0.0
C+ / 6.3	12.4	1.04	38.22	207	8	91	0	1	45.5	155.0	-8.8	43	N/A	0	0	0.0	0.0
B / 8.5	6.8	0.85	32.08	825	2	96	0	2	13.0	61.1	-9.1	67	54	250	50	5.8	1.0
B / 8.8	6.9	0.85	31.97	177	2	96	0	2	13.0	56.7	-9.3	57	54	250	50	0.0	5.0
B / 8.8	6.8	0.85	31.96	291	2	96	0	2	13.0	56.8	-9.3	57	54	250	50	0.0	1.0
B / 8.8	6.8	0.85	31.98	46	2	96	0	2	13.0	59.3	-9.2	63	54	25	25	0.0	0.0
B / 8.8	6.8	0.85	32.04	32	2	96	0	2	13.0	61.0	-9.1	67	54	250	50	0.0	0.0
B / 8.5	6.9	0.86	32.11	62,498	2	96	0	2	13.0	61.5	-9.1	68	54	250	50	5.8	1.0

						PERFORMANCE							
	99 Pct = Best 0 Pct = Worst			Overall Weiss Investment Rating		Perfor- mance Rating/Pts	Total Return % through 6/30/06					Incl. in Returns	
										Annualized		Dividend	Expense
Fund Type	Fund Name	Ticker Symbol			Phone		3 Mo	6 Mo	1Yr / Pct	3Yr / Pct	5Yr / Pct	Yield	Ratio
GI	American Funds Wash Mutl Invs B	WSHBX	C		(800) 421-4120	D+ / 2.9	0.50	4.76	8.13 /34	10.12 /28	4.08 /47	1.21	1.37
GI	American Funds Wash Mutl Invs C	WSHCX	C		(800) 421-4120	C- / 3.5	0.48	4.69	8.04 /33	10.02 /27	4.00 /46	1.15	1.45
GI	American Funds Wash Mutl Invs F	WSHFX	C+		(800) 421-4120	C / 4.3	0.66	5.10	8.90 /39	10.88 /34	4.80 /52	1.92	0.68
GI	American Funds Wash Mutl Invs R1	RWMAX	C		(800) 421-4120	C- / 3.6	0.48	4.68	8.00 /33	9.98 /27	3.98 /46	1.12	1.47
GI	American Funds Wash Mutl Invs R2	RWMBX	C		(800) 421-4120	C- / 3.6	0.45	4.70	8.01 /33	10.02 /28	4.00 /46	1.15	1.44
GI	American Funds Wash Mutl Invs R3	RWMCX	C+		(800) 421-4120	C- / 4.0	0.60	4.96	8.54 /37	10.52 /31	4.47 /50	1.58	0.94
GI	American Funds Wash Mutl Invs R4	RWMEX	C+		(800) 421-4120	C / 4.3	0.67	5.10	8.88 /39	10.87 /34	4.80 /52	1.87	0.67
GI	American Funds Wash Mutl Invs R5	RWMFX	C+		(800) 421-4120	C / 4.5	0.75	5.28	9.22 /41	11.20 /37	5.12 /55	2.16	0.37
GR	American Growth Fund A	AMRAX	E-		(800) 525-2406	E- / 0.1	-6.05	-5.14	7.27 /28	4.98 / 4	-6.24 / 2	0.00	3.57
GR	American Growth Fund B	AMRBX	E-		(800) 525-2406	E- / 0.1	-6.53	-5.56	6.25 /22	4.12 / 2	-7.10 / 1	0.00	4.35
GR	American Growth Fund C	AMRCX	E-		(800) 525-2406	E- / 0.2	-6.53	-5.56	6.25 /22	4.12 / 2	-7.10 / 1	0.00	4.30
GR	American Growth Fund D	AMRGX	E-		(800) 525-2406	E- / 0.1	-6.21	-5.03	7.47 /29	5.12 / 4	-6.03 / 2	0.00	3.35
AG	American Heritage Fund	AHERX	E-		(212) 397-3900	E- / 0.1	-11.11	0.00	-11.11 / 0	4.55 / 3	-12.94 / 0	0.00	10.85
FO	American Ind Intl Multi-Mgr Sv	IMSSX	A+		(800) 342-1223	B+ / 8.5	0.33	9.06	23.16 /86	22.78 /87	10.44 /82	1.57	1.26
GR	American Ind Stock Svc	ISISX	B-		(800) 342-1223	C / 4.7	0.20	3.10	4.78 /14	14.19 /55	5.90 /60	1.38	1.29
GI	American Perf US T/Eff Lg Cp Eq Inv	APEQX	B+		(800) 762-7085	C+ / 5.8	-1.87	2.62	10.75 /52	14.26 /55	1.96 /27	0.30	0.99
SC	American Perf US T/Eff SmCp Eq Inst	AISMX	C+		(800) 762-7085	B / 7.6	-4.38	6.04	12.29 /61	18.85 /76	9.56 /79	0.15	0.93
SC	American Perf US T/Eff SmCp Eq Inv	APSMX	C		(800) 762-7085	B- / 7.5	-4.44	5.81	12.06 /60	18.77 /75	9.51 /79	0.24	1.18
BA	American Performance Balanced	APBAX	C+		(800) 762-7085	C- / 3.4	-1.09	3.28	9.23 /41	9.77 /26	4.90 /53	1.81	0.87
GR	American Performance Growth Equity	APGEX	C		(800) 762-7085	C / 4.8	0.00	10.61	17.98 /79	9.45 /24	1.11 /21	0.95	1.01
GR	American Trust Allegiance Fd	ATAFX	D+		(800) 385-7003	C- / 3.4	-4.45	-0.06	6.69 /24	10.68 /33	1.75 /25	0.07	1.45
GI	Ameriprime Adv Monteagle Value	MVRGX	A-		(800) 934-5550	B+ / 8.5	0.59	10.80	18.65 /80	21.05 /83	9.15 /77	0.84	1.37
GI	Ameristock Mutual Fund	AMSTX	D+		(800) 394-5064	D- / 1.5	0.87	5.04	4.27 /12	6.28 / 8	1.15 /21	2.15	0.79
AG	Ameritor Investment	AIVTX	E-		(800) 424-8570	E- / 0.0	-40.00	-57.14	-75.00 / 0	-56.72 / 0	-47.61 / 0	0.00	21.57
AG	Ameritor Security Trust 1	ASTRX	E-		(800) 424-8570	E- / 0.0	-4.65	2.50	10.81 /52	-3.06 / 0	-10.15 / 0	0.00	18.72
GI	AMF Large Cap Equity Inst	IICAX	E+		(800) 982-1846	E+ / 0.7	-2.40	1.00	2.76 / 6	5.25 / 4	1.18 /21	0.12	1.20
FO	Amidex 35 Israel Fund A	AMDAX	E-		(888) 876-3566	E+ / 0.9	-6.62	-6.94	10.49 /50	9.43 /24	-2.29 / 7	0.00	3.38
FO	Amidex 35 Israel Fund C	AMDCX	E		(888) 876-3566	D- / 1.2	-6.63	-7.05	9.93 /46	8.68 /19	-2.97 / 5	0.00	4.13
FO	Amidex 35 Israel Fund Fd	AMDEX	E		(888) 876-3566	D- / 1.4	-6.60	-6.84	10.59 /51	9.48 /24	-2.22 / 7	0.00	3.53
HL	Amidex Cancer Innov & Healthcare A	CNCRX	E+		(888) 876-3566	D- / 1.3	-3.57	-2.21	5.94 /20	8.70 /19	--	0.00	4.45
MC	Apex Mid-Cap Growth Fund	BMCGX	E-		(877) 593-8637	E- / 0.0	-12.34	-0.74	2.27 / 5	-3.24 / 0	-1.82 / 9	0.00	5.88
GL	API Trust-Capital Income D	APIGX	C		(800) 544-6060	C / 5.0	-1.58	3.43	8.60 /37	13.22 /50	4.87 /53	0.00	2.15
GL	API Trust-Growth C	APITX	C-		(800) 544-6060	C+ / 5.8	-6.47	2.09	12.95 /64	14.73 /57	3.26 /39	0.00	2.73
GL	API Trust-Multiple Index Adv	APIMX	C		(800) 544-6060	C+ / 6.7	-3.29	4.05	17.60 /78	16.62 /66	4.81 /53	0.00	1.52
GR	API Trust-Value C	YCVTX	C-		(800) 544-6060	B- / 7.1	-3.45	1.67	12.24 /61	18.00 /72	2.67 /33	0.00	2.62
GR	Aquila Rocky Mountain Equity A	ROCAX	C+		(800) 437-1020	C / 5.5	-4.72	3.40	9.97 /47	15.12 /59	8.52 /74	0.00	1.50
GR	Aquila Rocky Mountain Equity C	ROCCX	C+		(800) 437-1020	C / 5.5	-4.93	3.01	9.12 /41	14.28 /55	7.72 /70	0.00	2.25
GR	Aquila Rocky Mountain Equity Y	ROCYX	B-		(800) 437-1020	C+ / 5.9	-4.68	3.49	10.19 /48	15.41 /61	8.80 /76	0.00	1.25
GI	Arbitrage Fund (The) - Instl	ARBNX	U		(800) 295-4485	U /	1.34	4.39	7.36 /28	--	--	0.00	1.70
GI	Arbitrage Fund (The) - Retail	ARBFX	C-		(800) 295-4485	E+ / 0.9	1.35	4.34	7.14 /27	4.64 / 3	6.00 /61	0.00	1.95
* MC	Ariel Appreciation Fund	CAAPX	C-		(800) 292-7435	D+ / 2.6	-3.03	-1.22	1.79 / 4	9.97 /27	7.23 /68	0.27	1.13
* SC	Ariel Fund	ARGFX	C		(800) 292-7435	C- / 4.2	-6.21	1.40	0.97 / 2	12.87 /48	9.94 /80	0.28	1.05
GR	Armstrong Associates	ARMSX	D			D / 2.0	-1.50	1.30	5.69 /19	7.78 /14	1.87 /26	0.24	1.26
* FO	Artisan International Fund Inv	ARTIX	A-		(800) 344-1770	B+ / 8.8	-1.04	9.48	29.81 /94	22.36 /86	8.18 /72	1.48	1.19
FO	Artisan International Small Cap Inv	ARTJX	A+		(800) 344-1770	A+ / 9.6	-4.63	10.20	34.99 /97	32.51 /97	--	0.84	1.53
FO	Artisan International Value Inv	ARTKX	A+		(800) 344-1770	A / 9.5	0.92	14.78	30.13 /94	28.71 /94	--	1.83	1.31
* MC	● Artisan Mid Cap Fund	ARTMX	C		(800) 344-1770	C+ / 6.0	-4.85	2.20	11.92 /59	14.76 /58	4.52 /50	0.00	1.18
* MC	● Artisan Mid Cap Value Inv	ARTQX	A+		(800) 344-1770	B / 8.1	-2.37	3.04	7.32 /28	21.61 /84	13.56 /90	0.05	1.22
SC	● Artisan Small Cap Fund	ARTSX	C+		(800) 344-1770	C+ / 6.4	-9.25	2.30	8.59 /37	16.77 /67	6.49 /64	0.00	1.18
SC	● Artisan Small Cap Value	ARTVX	B+		(800) 344-1770	B / 8.1	-3.81	5.45	12.45 /62	20.71 /82	14.47 /91	0.00	1.18
FO	AssetMark International Equity	AFIEX	A+		(800) 664-5345	B+ / 8.9	-1.64	9.24	27.63 /92	22.97 /87	8.94 /76	1.04	1.34
GR	AssetMark Large-Cap Growth	AFLGX	D-		(800) 664-5345	E+ / 0.6	-7.54	-7.54	--	6.62 / 9	-1.65 / 9	0.00	1.32

● Denotes fund is closed to new investors

* Denotes fund is included in Section II

RISK			NET ASSETS		ASSET					BULL / BEAR		FUND MANAGER		MINIMUMS		LOADS	
	3 Year		NAV						Portfolio	Last Bull	Last Bear	Manager	Manager	Initial	Additional	Front	Back
Risk	Standard		As of	Total	Cash	Stocks	Bonds	Other	Turnover	Market	Market	Quality	Tenure	Purch.	Purch.	End	End
Rating/Pts	Deviation	Beta	6/30/06	$(Mil)	%	%	%	%	Ratio	Return	Return	Pct	(Years)	$	$	Load	Load
B /8.8	6.9	0.85	31.94	2,971	2	96	0	2	13.0	57.6	-9.2	59	54	250	50	0.0	5.0
B /8.8	6.9	0.85	31.88	3,033	2	96	0	2	13.0	57.2	-9.3	58	54	250	50	0.0	1.0
B /8.8	6.9	0.85	32.04	2,596	2	96	0	2	13.0	61.2	-9.1	67	54	250	50	0.0	0.0
B /8.8	6.9	0.85	31.95	47	2	96	0	2	13.0	57.1	-9.3	58	54	0	0	0.0	0.0
B /8.8	6.9	0.85	31.87	798	2	96	0	2	13.0	57.2	-9.3	58	54	0	0	0.0	0.0
B /8.8	6.9	0.85	31.97	1,838	2	96	0	2	13.0	59.5	-9.2	63	54	0	0	0.0	0.0
B /8.8	6.8	0.85	32.03	970	2	96	0	2	13.0	61.0	-9.1	67	54	0	0	0.0	0.0
B /8.8	6.8	0.85	32.10	867	2	96	0	2	13.0	62.6	-9.0	70	54	0	0	0.0	0.0
D+ /2.9	15.6	1.71	2.95	7	2	97	0	1	4.9	49.1	-12.9	1	10	0	0	5.8	1.0
D+ /2.6	15.1	1.49	2.72	6	2	97	0	1	4.9	45.2	-13.1	1	10	0	0	0.0	5.0
D+ /2.9	15.6	1.71	2.72	6	2	97	0	1	4.9	46.0	-13.5	0	10	0	0	0.0	1.0
C- /3.0	15.6	1.71	3.02	14	2	97	0	1	4.9	49.5	-12.7	1	10	0	0	5.8	1.0
D /1.9	49.8	1.28	0.08	1	16	82	0	2	912.5	28.6	-12.5	3	16	1,000	500	0.0	0.0
B /8.2	9.6	0.93	15.41	106	9	90	0	1	37.0	131.5	-10.4	57	N/A	1,000	50	5.0	0.0
B+ /9.2	7.6	0.81	14.96	100	0	93	6	1	15.0	81.9	-6.0	91	N/A	1,000	50	5.0	0.0
B /8.8	8.1	1.00	9.97	3	0	99	0	1	N/A	80.7	-10.1	83	N/A	1,000	100	0.0	0.0
C /4.9	13.3	0.89	13.80	13	0	99	0	1	35.2	106.2	-9.3	75	N/A	100,000	100	0.0	0.0
C /4.9	13.3	0.89	13.78	N/A	0	99	0	1	35.2	105.8	-9.3	74	N/A	1,000	100	0.0	0.0
B+ /9.2	5.8	1.14	13.60	28	0	47	51	2	96.4	51.0	-4.8	71	N/A	1,000	100	0.0	0.0
B- /7.0	8.7	0.94	11.04	N/A	2	97	0	1	375.9	48.6	-10.0	42	N/A	1,000	100	0.0	0.0
C+ /6.8	9.5	1.13	16.76	21	3	96	0	1	27.1	61.9	-11.0	37	9	2,500	250	0.0	0.0
C+ /6.9	13.5	1.41	17.13	22	2	97	0	1	25.0	112.2	-13.9	94	N/A	0	0	0.0	0.0
B /8.5	6.6	0.76	40.45	639	2	97	0	1	4.6	40.7	-10.9	29	11	1,000	100	0.0	0.0
D- /1.3	27.8	1.34	0.03	N/A	N/A	N/A	0	N/A	61.0	-88.6	-10.3	0	9	1,000	25	0.0	0.0
D+ /2.7	15.0	1.37	0.41	1	9	90	0	1	104.0	10.0	-4.8	0	9	1,000	25	0.0	0.0
C+ /6.6	6.4	0.71	143.96	62	2	97	0	1	6.9	33.6	-12.3	25	15	20,000	0	0.0	0.0
C- /4.0	16.1	0.88	8.32	2	N/A	100	0	N/A	10.4	114.5	-10.7	1	N/A	500	250	5.5	1.0
C- /4.0	16.1	0.89	6.20	1	N/A	100	0	N/A	10.4	109.9	-11.0	1	N/A	500	250	0.0	1.0
C- /4.0	16.1	0.88	10.76	9	N/A	100	0	N/A	10.4	115.1	-10.7	1	N/A	500	250	0.0	2.0
C /5.5	11.9	0.57	11.06	1	9	90	0	1	2.1	63.7	-7.0	70	5	500	250	5.5	1.0
E- /0.0	32.2	2.10	1.35	N/A	5	94	0	1	161.0	96.1	-19.0	0	13	1,000	100	0.0	0.0
C+ /6.5	10.2	0.83	18.69	9	N/A	89	10	N/A	137.0	76.5	-7.0	9	18	500	100	0.0	1.5
C+ /5.6	13.7	1.06	12.73	53	N/A	100	0	N/A	174.0	103.2	-12.5	2	21	500	100	0.0	1.0
C /5.3	14.3	1.13	14.39	4	0	98	1	1	298.0	103.7	-12.2	3	9	500	100	0.0	0.0
C /4.3	17.6	2.07	17.07	32	1	98	0	1	159.0	123.3	-11.8	26	14	500	100	0.0	1.0
B- /7.8	11.5	1.24	30.45	21	13	86	0	1	9.8	88.7	-6.9	72	7	1,000	50	4.3	0.0
B- /7.7	11.5	1.24	28.37	3	13	86	0	1	9.8	84.4	-7.1	64	7	1,000	50	0.0	1.0
B- /7.8	11.5	1.24	31.13	1	13	86	0	1	9.8	90.3	-6.9	74	7	1,000	50	0.0	2.0
U /	N/A	N/A	12.83	88	2	97	0	1	336.0	N/A	N/A	N/A	6	100,000	0	0.0	2.0
B+ /9.7	5.4	0.48	12.75	90	2	97	0	1	336.0	18.1	2.2	35	6	2,000	0	0.0	2.0
B /8.3	8.1	0.66	46.15	2,900	0	99	0	1	12.0	71.5	-13.7	32	N/A	1,000	50	0.0	0.0
B- /7.5	9.4	0.57	50.77	4,600	1	98	0	1	10.0	83.4	-10.3	70	20	1,000	50	0.0	0.0
B- /7.5	6.2	0.73	12.46	18	7	92	0	1	7.0	45.7	-9.7	44	38	250	0	0.0	0.0
C+ /6.7	11.1	1.05	27.71	9,288	1	98	0	1	56.2	131.5	-14.7	27	11	1,000	50	0.0	2.0
B- /7.2	13.9	1.26	21.83	974	1	98	0	1	57.3	228.2	-1.5	70	5	1,000	50	0.0	2.0
B /8.1	10.5	0.96	25.32	948	8	91	0	1	53.2	183.1	-2.7	91	4	1,000	50	0.0	2.0
C+ /6.4	12.3	1.07	31.60	5,756	2	97	0	1	83.0	86.0	-10.5	19	9	1,000	50	0.0	0.0
B /8.4	10.1	0.81	19.32	2,773	2	96	0	2	51.6	118.4	-4.1	95	5	1,000	50	0.0	0.0
C+ /6.4	14.8	0.97	17.76	1,333	4	95	0	1	78.6	116.4	-9.0	40	11	1,000	50	0.0	0.0
C+ /6.9	12.9	0.75	18.19	1,922	7	92	0	1	56.0	117.7	-6.0	94	9	1,000	50	0.0	0.0
B- /7.7	10.8	1.04	13.83	647	2	97	0	1	67.0	129.2	-11.0	34	5	0	0	0.0	0.0
B- /7.2	11.4	1.33	9.20	616	1	98	0	1	21.6	53.7	-10.6	7	N/A	0	0	0.0	0.0

Fund Type	Fund Name	Ticker Symbol	Overall Weiss Investment Rating	Phone	Perfor-mance Rating/Pts	3 Mo	6 Mo	1Yr / Pct	3Yr / Pct	5Yr / Pct	Dividend Yield	Expense Ratio
GR	AssetMark Large-Cap Value	AFLVX	B	(800) 664-5345	C+ / 5.7	2.04	6.85	10.04 /47	13.32 /50	5.23 /56	0.59	1.30
RE	AssetMark Real Estate Securities	AFREX	A-	(800) 664-5345	A / 9.3	-0.92	14.17	21.81 /84	26.33 /92	19.36 /95	1.57	1.49
MC	AssetMark Small Mid-Cap Growth	AFSGX	C-	(800) 664-5345	C- / 4.1	-7.08	4.23	12.27 /61	12.00 /42	1.43 /23	0.00	1.38
MC	AssetMark Small Mid-Cap Value	AFSVX	B	(800) 664-5345	C+ / 6.5	-1.18	6.35	9.87 /46	15.74 /62	9.45 /78	0.00	1.53
IN	Atlantic Whitehall Equity Inc Inst	AWEIX	U	(800) 994-2533	U /	-0.69	1.31	--	--	--	0.00	1.10
GR	Atlantic Whitehall Growth Dist	WHGFX	E-	(800) 994-2533	E / 0.4	-5.23	-4.41	1.50 / 3	4.65 / 3	-3.25 / 5	0.00	1.35
GR	Atlantic Whitehall Growth Inst	AWGFX	U	(800) 994-2533	U /	-5.11	-4.30	1.79 / 4	--	--	0.00	1.10
GL	Atlantic Whitehall Internatl Inst	AWIFX	U	(800) 994-2533	U /	1.07	9.98	24.90 /88	--	--	0.95	1.53
MC	Atlantic Whitehall Mid-Cap Gr Inst	AWMCX	U	(800) 994-2533	U /	-3.79	2.14	10.25 /48	--	--	0.00	1.23
BA	Atlas Dual Focus Fund	ATBAX	C-	(800) 933-2852	D / 1.9	-0.80	2.10	5.45 /17	7.47 /12	0.83 /19	1.48	1.27
SC	Atlas Emerging Growth Fund A	ATEAX	B+	(800) 933-2852	B / 8.1	-5.85	8.12	14.85 /71	20.39 /81	3.68 /43	0.00	1.45
GL	Atlas Global Growth Fund A	AGRAX	B	(800) 933-2852	B / 7.9	-3.40	3.26	17.76 /79	20.12 /80	7.42 /69	0.44	1.31
GI	Atlas Growth Opportunities Fund	ASGIX	D+	(800) 933-2852	D+ / 2.9	-4.92	-0.72	6.14 /21	10.06 /28	2.67 /33	0.07	1.14
GR	Atlas Strategic Growth Fund A	ASGAX	D	(800) 933-2852	D+ / 2.8	-5.15	-1.73	7.24 /28	9.80 /26	-1.10 /11	0.00	1.28
GL	Austin Global Equity Fund	AGEQX	B-	(800) 754-8759	B+ / 8.9	-2.32	8.77	18.33 /80	23.92 /89	8.49 /74	2.19	2.52
AA	Auxier Focus Inv	AUXFX	C	(877) 328-9437	D+ / 2.7	-1.99	0.20	3.44 / 9	10.35 /30	7.29 /68	1.17	1.35
GR	AXA Enterprise Cap Apprec A	ENCAX	D+	(800) 432-4320	D / 2.2	-4.34	-1.44	5.52 /18	10.78 /33	3.38 /40	0.00	1.65
GR	AXA Enterprise Cap Apprec B	ECABX	D	(800) 432-4320	D / 2.1	-4.48	-1.71	4.95 /15	10.17 /28	2.80 /35	0.00	2.20
GR	AXA Enterprise Cap Apprec C	ENACX	D+	(800) 432-4320	D+ / 2.4	-4.44	-1.69	4.97 /15	10.18 /29	2.81 /35	0.00	2.20
GR	AXA Enterprise Cap Apprec Y	ECAYX	C-	(800) 432-4320	C- / 3.3	-4.22	-1.19	6.03 /21	11.30 /38	3.85 /44	0.00	1.20
GR	AXA Enterprise Equity Fund A	ENEAX	E	(800) 432-4320	E+ / 0.8	-5.56	-7.09	1.94 / 4	8.83 /20	1.38 /23	0.00	1.60
GR	AXA Enterprise Equity Fund B	ENEBX	E-	(800) 432-4320	E+ / 0.8	-5.81	-7.41	1.35 / 3	8.17 /16	0.84 /19	0.00	2.15
GR	AXA Enterprise Equity Fund C	ENQCX	E	(800) 432-4320	D- / 1.0	-5.65	-7.40	1.52 / 3	8.23 /16	0.84 /19	0.00	2.15
GR	AXA Enterprise Equity Fund Y	EEQYX	E	(800) 432-4320	D / 1.6	-5.52	-6.88	2.52 / 6	9.29 /23	1.84 /26	0.00	1.15
FO	AXA Enterprise International Gr A	ENIGX	B+	(800) 432-4320	B+ / 8.6	1.74	12.88	35.14 /97	20.04 /79	5.87 /60	0.34	1.85
FO	AXA Enterprise International Gr B	EIGBX	B+	(800) 432-4320	B+ / 8.5	1.67	12.62	34.58 /97	19.42 /77	5.20 /56	0.00	2.40
FO	AXA Enterprise International Gr C	ENICX	B+	(800) 432-4320	B+ / 8.7	1.60	12.60	34.49 /96	19.32 /77	5.17 /55	0.00	2.40
FO	AXA Enterprise International Gr Y	ENIYX	B+	(800) 432-4320	B+ / 8.9	1.87	13.19	35.77 /97	20.59 /81	6.28 /63	0.75	1.40
GR	AXA Enterprise Multimgr Core Eqty B	AERBX	C-	(800) 432-4320	D+ / 2.5	-3.32	0.56	6.72 /25	9.44 /24	--	0.00	2.20
GR	AXA Enterprise Multimgr Core Eqty C	AERCX	C-	(800) 432-4320	D+ / 2.5	-3.32	0.56	6.72 /25	9.44 /24	--	0.00	2.20
GR	AXA Enterprise Multimgr Core Eqty P	AERPX	D+	(800) 432-4320	D / 2.1	-3.16	0.91	7.48 /29	10.23 /29	--	0.01	1.45
GR	AXA Enterprise Multimgr Core Eqty Y	AERYX	C-	(800) 432-4320	C- / 3.2	-3.15	1.09	7.74 /31	10.54 /31	--	0.26	1.20
GR	AXA Enterprise Multimgr Growth B	AEMBX	E+	(800) 432-4320	E / 0.4	-6.91	-6.91	2.99 / 7	6.31 / 8	--	0.00	2.20
GR	AXA Enterprise Multimgr Growth C	AEMCX	E+	(800) 432-4320	E+ / 0.6	-6.81	-6.81	3.10 / 8	6.31 / 8	--	0.00	2.20
GR	AXA Enterprise Multimgr Growth P	AEGPX	E+	(800) 432-4320	E / 0.4	-6.73	-6.45	3.91 /10	7.15 /11	--	0.00	1.45
GR	AXA Enterprise Multimgr Growth Y	AEMYX	E+	(800) 432-4320	E+ / 0.9	-6.60	-6.32	4.11 /11	7.39 /12	--	0.00	1.20
HL	AXA Enterprise Multimgr Hlth Care B	AEABX	D	(800) 432-4320	D- / 1.1	-5.77	-2.46	6.04 /21	8.15 /16	--	0.00	2.70
HL	AXA Enterprise Multimgr Hlth Care C	AEACX	D	(800) 432-4320	D- / 1.5	-5.86	-2.56	5.93 /20	8.13 /16	--	0.00	2.70
HL	AXA Enterprise Multimgr Hlth Care P	AEAPX	D	(800) 432-4320	D- / 1.2	-5.69	-2.12	6.79 /25	8.90 /20	--	0.00	1.95
HL	AXA Enterprise Multimgr Hlth Care Y	AEAYX	D+	(800) 432-4320	D / 2.1	-5.56	-2.01	7.03 /26	9.22 /22	--	0.00	1.70
FO	AXA Enterprise Multimgr Intl Eq B	AENBX	B+	(800) 432-4320	B+ / 8.4	-1.26	9.09	27.30 /92	21.47 /84	--	0.00	2.55
FO	AXA Enterprise Multimgr Intl Eq C	AENCX	B+	(800) 432-4320	B+ / 8.6	-1.26	9.16	27.27 /92	21.49 /84	--	0.00	2.55
FO	AXA Enterprise Multimgr Intl Eq P	AENPX	B-	(800) 432-4320	B+ / 8.4	-1.12	9.52	28.22 /93	22.38 /86	--	0.66	1.80
FO	AXA Enterprise Multimgr Intl Eq Y	AENYX	A-	(800) 432-4320	B+ / 8.8	-1.06	9.66	28.57 /93	22.70 /87	--	0.92	1.55
MC	AXA Enterprise Multimgr Mid Cp Gr B	AEBWX	D	(800) 432-4320	C / 4.7	-7.12	4.19	14.68 /71	14.54 /56	--	0.00	2.45
MC	AXA Enterprise Multimgr Mid Cp Gr C	AECWX	D+	(800) 432-4320	C / 5.2	-7.12	4.19	14.70 /71	14.61 /57	--	0.00	2.45
MC	AXA Enterprise Multimgr Mid Cp Gr P	AESPX	D+	(800) 432-4320	C / 4.9	-6.97	4.53	15.55 /73	15.42 /61	--	0.00	1.70
MC	AXA Enterprise Multimgr Mid Cp Gr Y	AEYWX	C-	(800) 432-4320	C+ / 6.4	-6.98	4.68	15.72 /74	15.73 /62	--	0.00	1.45
SC	AXA Enterprise Multimgr Mid Cp Vl B	AEUBX	C+	(800) 432-4320	C+ / 6.6	-2.19	6.08	12.29 /61	17.20 /69	--	0.00	2.45
SC	AXA Enterprise Multimgr Mid Cp Vl C	AEUCX	C+	(800) 432-4320	C+ / 6.9	-2.28	6.00	12.21 /61	17.16 /69	--	0.00	2.45
SC	AXA Enterprise Multimgr Mid Cp Vl P	AEUPX	C+	(800) 432-4320	C+ / 6.7	-2.06	6.36	12.99 /64	17.99 /72	--	0.00	1.70
SC	AXA Enterprise Multimgr Mid Cp Vl Y	AEUYX	B-	(800) 432-4320	B- / 7.3	-2.04	6.49	13.28 /65	18.30 /74	--	0.00	1.45

● Denotes fund is closed to new investors
* Denotes fund is included in Section II

www.WeissRatings.com

RISK			NET ASSETS		ASSET				Portfolio	BULL / BEAR		FUND MANAGER		MINIMUMS		LOADS	
	3 Year		NAV							Last Bull	Last Bear	Manager	Manager	Initial	Additional	Front	Back
Risk Rating/Pts	Standard Deviation	Beta	As of 6/30/06	Total $(Mil)	Cash %	Stocks %	Bonds %	Other %	Turnover Ratio	Market Return	Market Return	Quality Pct	Tenure (Years)	Purch. $	Purch. $	End Load	End Load
B / 8.6	8.6	1.06	12.01	621	2	97	0	1	20.1	77.6	-12.1	71	N/A	0	0	0.0	0.0
C+ / 6.0	16.2	0.97	18.29	81	2	93	0	5	77.6	121.5	1.0	80	5	0	0	0.0	0.0
C+ / 6.4	14.3	1.22	9.85	186	1	98	0	1	99.4	88.8	-11.5	3	5	0	0	0.0	0.0
B / 8.1	9.9	0.86	14.24	186	5	94	0	1	92.4	91.9	-9.0	56	N/A	0	0	0.0	0.0
U /	N/A	N/A	10.04	32	4	95	0	1	N/A	N/A	N/A	N/A	1	1,000,000	0	0.0	0.0
D / 1.6	9.6	1.09	12.14	38	5	94	0	1	36.0	37.4	-10.0	7	N/A	1,000	50	0.0	0.0
U /	N/A	N/A	12.25	26	5	94	0	1	36.0	N/A	N/A	N/A	N/A	1,000,000	0	0.0	0.0
U /	N/A	N/A	14.11	184	1	98	0	1	34.0	N/A	N/A	N/A	3	1,000,000	0	0.0	0.0
U /	N/A	N/A	11.94	110	1	98	0	1	25.0	N/A	N/A	N/A	2	1,000,000	0	0.0	0.0
B+ / 9.5	5.6	1.02	11.45	63	1	59	39	1	95.5	39.3	-6.6	53	2	2,500	250	0.0	0.0
C+ / 6.7	14.2	0.93	17.71	106	4	95	0	1	173.0	120.4	-14.5	81	4	2,500	250	0.0	0.0
C+ / 6.2	10.7	0.96	24.42	376	4	95	0	1	27.6	117.3	-12.4	27	2	2,500	250	0.0	2.0
B- / 7.1	8.8	1.08	23.60	418	1	98	0	1	40.0	62.3	-7.3	35	6	2,500	250	0.0	0.0
C+ / 6.7	10.1	1.19	13.63	105	1	98	0	1	70.9	62.2	-11.3	27	2	2,500	250	0.0	0.0
C / 5.0	11.2	0.98	21.45	41	0	99	0	1	56.0	132.0	-8.9	56	13	10,000	2,500	0.0	0.0
B+ / 9.0	6.6	1.24	14.76	104	0	99	0	1	28.0	58.0	-6.0	71	7	10,000	100	0.0	2.0
B- / 7.5	9.7	1.11	35.01	194	4	94	0	2	74.0	69.5	-8.7	40	N/A	2,000	50	4.8	2.0
B- / 7.4	9.7	1.11	32.23	74	4	94	0	2	74.0	66.5	-8.8	35	N/A	2,000	50	0.0	5.0
B- / 7.4	9.7	1.10	33.17	67	4	94	0	2	74.0	66.6	-8.8	35	N/A	2,000	50	1.0	2.0
B- / 7.5	9.7	1.11	36.56	64	4	94	0	2	74.0	72.0	-8.6	45	N/A	1,000,000	0	0.0	2.0
C / 4.3	14.3	1.51	6.29	53	0	100	0	0	13.0	71.5	-11.2	8	N/A	2,000	50	4.8	2.0
C- / 4.2	14.3	1.52	6.00	39	0	100	0	0	13.0	68.5	-11.5	6	N/A	2,000	50	0.0	5.0
C- / 4.2	14.4	1.53	6.01	27	0	100	0	0	13.0	68.3	-11.2	6	N/A	2,000	50	1.0	2.0
C / 4.3	14.3	1.52	6.50	8	0	100	0	0	13.0	74.0	-11.2	9	N/A	1,000,000	0	0.0	2.0
C+ / 6.2	12.6	1.11	18.67	73	10	88	0	2	136.0	105.3	-14.1	10	N/A	2,000	50	4.8	2.0
C+ / 6.2	12.5	1.11	17.67	27	10	88	0	2	136.0	101.8	-14.2	9	N/A	2,000	50	0.0	5.0
C+ / 6.2	12.5	1.11	17.78	29	10	88	0	2	136.0	101.4	-14.2	9	N/A	2,000	50	0.0	2.0
C+ / 6.3	12.6	1.11	19.05	26	10	88	0	2	136.0	108.5	-14.1	12	N/A	1,000,000	0	0.0	2.0
B / 8.2	8.1	1.03	10.78	N/A	0	100	0	0	48.0	60.9	-9.4	34	N/A	2,000	50	0.0	2.0
B / 8.1	8.1	1.03	10.78	N/A	0	100	0	0	48.0	60.9	-9.4	35	N/A	2,000	50	0.0	2.0
B / 8.2	8.0	1.03	11.05	4	0	100	0	0	48.0	64.8	-9.2	42	N/A	2,000	50	5.5	2.0
B / 8.2	8.1	1.03	11.08	7	0	100	0	0	48.0	66.0	-9.1	45	N/A	1,000,000	0	0.0	2.0
C+ / 6.2	12.1	1.36	9.30	N/A	2	98	0	0	40.0	50.7	-10.6	5	N/A	2,000	50	0.0	5.0
C+ / 6.4	11.3	1.27	9.30	N/A	2	98	0	0	40.0	50.5	-10.4	7	N/A	2,000	50	0.0	2.0
C+ / 6.5	11.3	1.27	9.57	3	2	98	0	0	40.0	54.3	-10.3	9	N/A	2,000	50	5.5	2.0
C+ / 6.5	11.3	1.27	9.63	6	2	98	0	0	40.0	55.5	-10.2	10	N/A	1,000,000	0	0.0	2.0
B- / 7.6	8.3	0.66	10.29	N/A	4	96	0	0	115.0	57.0	-7.6	57	N/A	2,000	50	0.0	5.0
B- / 7.6	8.3	0.66	10.29	N/A	4	96	0	0	115.0	57.1	-7.7	57	N/A	2,000	50	0.0	2.0
B- / 7.8	8.3	0.66	10.60	2	4	96	0	0	115.0	60.6	-7.4	65	N/A	2,000	50	5.5	2.0
B- / 7.8	8.3	0.65	10.71	6	4	96	0	0	115.0	62.0	-7.4	68	N/A	1,000,000	0	0.0	2.0
C+ / 6.4	10.8	1.05	14.88	3	0	100	0	0	73.0	126.5	-11.8	23	N/A	2,000	50	0.0	5.0
C+ / 6.4	10.8	1.05	14.89	1	0	100	0	0	73.0	126.6	-11.8	24	N/A	2,000	50	0.0	2.0
C / 5.4	10.8	1.05	14.95	4	0	100	0	0	73.0	131.9	-11.7	29	N/A	2,000	50	5.5	2.0
C+ / 6.5	10.8	1.05	14.99	30	0	100	0	0	73.0	133.8	-11.6	31	N/A	1,000,000	0	0.0	2.0
C / 4.4	14.7	1.30	10.70	1	2	96	0	2	80.0	100.3	-12.9	6	N/A	2,000	50	0.0	5.0
C / 4.4	14.7	1.30	10.69	1	2	96	0	2	80.0	100.9	-13.0	6	N/A	2,000	50	0.0	2.0
C / 4.8	14.7	1.29	11.07	5	2	96	0	2	80.0	105.5	-12.8	8	N/A	2,000	50	5.5	2.0
C / 4.9	14.7	1.30	11.19	7	2	96	0	2	80.0	107.0	-12.7	9	N/A	1,000,000	0	0.0	2.0
C+ / 6.4	11.7	0.77	12.04	1	2	96	0	2	72.0	99.8	-8.8	78	N/A	2,000	50	0.0	5.0
C+ / 6.4	11.7	0.77	12.01	1	2	96	0	2	72.0	99.6	-8.8	78	N/A	2,000	50	0.0	2.0
C+ / 6.5	11.7	0.77	12.38	6	2	96	0	2	72.0	104.2	-8.5	83	N/A	2,000	50	5.5	2.0
C+ / 6.6	11.7	0.78	12.47	9	2	96	0	2	72.0	105.8	-8.5	85	N/A	1,000,000	0	0.0	2.0

			Overall Weiss Investment Rating		PERFORMANCE						Incl. in Returns	
	99 Pct = Best *0 Pct = Worst*				Perfor-mance Rating/Pts	Total Return % through 6/30/06			Annualized		Dividend Yield	Expense Ratio
Fund Type	Fund Name	Ticker Symbol		Phone		3 Mo	6 Mo	1Yr / Pct	3Yr / Pct	5Yr / Pct		
TC	AXA Enterprise Multimgr Tech B	AEHBX	E-	(800) 432-4320	D / 2.2	-9.15	-4.00	8.84 /39	10.63 /32	--	0.00	2.70
TC	AXA Enterprise Multimgr Tech C	AEHCX	E	(800) 432-4320	D+ / 2.7	-9.06	-4.00	8.84 /39	10.63 /32	--	0.00	2.70
TC	AXA Enterprise Multimgr Tech P	AEHPX	E-	(800) 432-4320	D+ / 2.4	-8.96	-3.57	9.75 /45	11.49 /39	--	0.00	1.95
TC	AXA Enterprise Multimgr Tech Y	AEHYX	E	(800) 432-4320	C- / 3.4	-8.90	-3.55	9.91 /46	11.73 /41	--	0.00	1.70
GI	AXA Enterprise Multimgr Value B	AEVBX	C+	(800) 432-4320	C / 4.7	-0.89	4.35	10.05 /47	13.40 /51	--	0.00	2.45
GI	AXA Enterprise Multimgr Value C	AEVCX	B-	(800) 432-4320	C / 5.2	-0.89	4.35	10.04 /47	13.38 /51	--	0.00	2.45
GI	AXA Enterprise Multimgr Value P	AEVPX	B-	(800) 432-4320	C / 4.9	-0.72	4.76	10.84 /53	14.20 /55	--	0.33	1.70
GI	AXA Enterprise Multimgr Value Y	AEYVX	B	(800) 432-4320	C+ / 5.8	-0.64	4.92	11.19 /55	14.55 /57	--	0.59	1.45
SC	AXA Enterprise Small Co Value A	ENSPX	C	(800) 432-4320	C+ / 6.2	-2.47	8.02	9.72 /45	16.91 /68	9.22 /77	0.00	1.64
SC	AXA Enterprise Small Co Value B	ESCBX	C-	(800) 432-4320	C+ / 6.1	-2.58	7.69	9.02 /40	16.26 /65	8.60 /75	0.00	2.19
SC	AXA Enterprise Small Co Value C	ESCVX	C	(800) 432-4320	C+ / 6.4	-2.51	7.67	9.16 /41	16.25 /64	8.61 /75	0.00	2.19
SC	AXA Enterprise Small Co Value Y	EIGYX	C	(800) 432-4320	B- / 7.0	-2.33	8.24	10.21 /48	17.42 /70	9.68 /79	0.00	1.19
GR	AXA Enterprise-Deep Value A	EDVAX	C-	(800) 432-4320	C- / 3.4	-0.09	2.90	5.68 /19	12.21 /44	3.84 /44	0.96	1.50
GR	AXA Enterprise-Deep Value B	EDVBX	C-	(800) 432-4320	C- / 3.3	-0.19	2.63	5.09 /15	11.60 /40	3.62 /42	0.46	2.05
GR	AXA Enterprise-Deep Value C	EDVCX	C-	(800) 432-4320	C- / 3.8	-0.19	2.63	5.00 /15	11.61 /40	3.27 /39	0.46	2.05
GR	AXA Enterprise-Deep Value Y	EDVYX	C	(800) 432-4320	C / 4.5	0.00	3.09	5.96 /20	12.65 /47	4.62 /51	1.45	1.05
IN	AXA Enterprise-Equity Income A	ENGIX	C+	(800) 432-4320	C+ / 5.7	-0.73	4.91	9.53 /44	15.89 /63	6.09 /62	1.07	1.50
IN	AXA Enterprise-Equity Income B	ENIBX	C+	(800) 432-4320	C+ / 5.6	-0.86	4.61	8.88 /39	15.24 /60	5.51 /58	0.59	2.05
IN	AXA Enterprise-Equity Income C	ENECX	B-	(800) 432-4320	C+ / 6.0	-0.85	4.61	8.93 /40	15.26 /60	5.51 /58	0.58	2.05
IN	AXA Enterprise-Equity Income Y	ENEYX	B-	(800) 432-4320	C+ / 6.5	-0.62	5.14	9.99 /47	16.41 /65	6.58 /65	1.56	1.05
GR	AXA Enterprise-Grow A	ENGRX	D-	(800) 432-4320	E / 0.3	-2.32	-0.17	5.83 /19	5.43 / 5	-0.81 /12	0.00	1.60
GR	AXA Enterprise-Grow B	ENGBX	E+	(800) 432-4320	E / 0.3	-2.48	-0.43	5.29 /16	4.87 / 4	-1.36 /10	0.00	2.15
GR	AXA Enterprise-Grow C	ENGCX	D-	(800) 432-4320	E / 0.4	-2.51	-0.49	5.22 /16	4.84 / 4	-1.36 /10	0.00	2.15
GR	AXA Enterprise-Grow Y	ENGYX	D-	(800) 432-4320	E+ / 0.7	-2.26	0.06	6.32 /22	5.92 / 6	-0.37 /14	0.00	1.15
GI	AXA Enterprise-Growth and Income A	EGNAX	C	(800) 432-4320	C- / 3.6	-2.31	1.13	8.36 /36	12.60 /46	2.01 /27	0.53	1.50
GI	AXA Enterprise-Growth and Income B	EGNBX	C	(800) 432-4320	C- / 3.5	-2.45	0.86	7.77 /31	11.98 /42	1.45 /23	0.00	2.05
GI	AXA Enterprise-Growth and Income	EGRCX	C+	(800) 432-4320	C- / 4.0	-2.45	0.86	7.76 /31	11.99 /42	1.44 /23	0.00	2.05
GI	AXA Enterprise-Growth and Income Y	ENCEX	C+	(800) 432-4320	C / 4.8	-2.19	1.38	8.87 /39	13.11 /49	2.48 /32	1.01	1.05
GR	AXA Enterprise-Merg & Acquisition A	EMAAX	D+	(800) 432-4320	D+ / 2.5	1.83	7.57	9.97 /47	9.02 /21	5.80 /60	0.79	1.71
GR	AXA Enterprise-Merg & Acquisition B	EMABX	D+	(800) 432-4320	D+ / 2.4	1.79	7.39	9.41 /43	8.45 /17	5.23 /56	0.32	2.26
GR	AXA Enterprise-Merg & Acquisition C	EMACX	D+	(800) 432-4320	D+ / 2.7	1.71	7.30	9.41 /43	8.45 /17	5.25 /56	0.31	2.26
GR	AXA Enterprise-Merg & Acquisition Y	EMAYX	C-	(800) 432-4320	C- / 3.6	1.96	7.87	10.46 /50	9.55 /24	6.30 /63	1.26	1.26
GL	AXA Entp Socially Resp A	EGSAX	C+	(800) 432-4320	C / 4.6	-1.41	5.85	15.31 /73	13.26 /50	3.51 /41	0.00	1.75
GL	AXA Entp Socially Resp B	EGSBX	C+	(800) 432-4320	C / 4.5	-1.63	5.52	14.75 /71	12.64 /47	2.89 /36	0.00	2.30
GL	AXA Entp Socially Resp C	EGCCX	C+	(800) 432-4320	C / 5.0	-1.54	5.63	14.75 /71	12.69 /47	2.94 /36	0.00	2.30
GL	AXA Entp Socially Resp Y	EGCYX	B-	(800) 432-4320	C+ / 5.7	-1.29	6.11	15.86 /74	13.78 /53	4.00 /46	0.00	1.30
FS	AXA Entp-Global Financial Serv A	EGFAX	B+	(800) 432-4320	B- / 7.5	-1.12	6.00	23.79 /87	19.44 /77	10.95 /84	1.21	1.75
FS	AXA Entp-Global Financial Serv B	EGFBX	B+	(800) 432-4320	B- / 7.3	-1.24	5.69	22.47 /85	18.54 /75	10.23 /81	0.74	2.30
FS	AXA Entp-Global Financial Serv C	EGFCX	A-	(800) 432-4320	B / 7.7	-1.25	5.58	22.96 /86	18.65 /75	10.31 /82	0.74	2.30
FS	AXA Entp-Global Financial Serv Y	EGFYX	A	(800) 432-4320	B / 8.1	-1.00	6.23	24.24 /88	19.92 /79	11.44 /85	1.70	1.30
GR	AXA Entp-Moderate Plus Allocation A	APLAX	C-	(800) 432-4320	D / 2.2	-1.03	3.93	10.26 /49	9.71 /25	0.98 /20	1.77	1.18
GR	AXA Entp-Moderate Plus Allocation B	APLBX	C-	(800) 432-4320	D / 2.1	-1.19	3.60	9.56 /44	9.12 /21	0.44 /17	1.32	1.73
GR	AXA Entp-Moderate Plus Allocation C	APLCX	C	(800) 432-4320	D+ / 2.5	-1.19	3.62	9.60 /44	9.08 /21	0.39 /17	1.33	1.73
GR	AXA Entp-Moderate Plus Allocation Y	APLYX	C	(800) 432-4320	C- / 3.3	-1.02	4.18	10.69 /51	10.17 /28	1.40 /23	2.31	0.73
SC	AXA Entp-Small Co Growth A	ENSAX	E	(800) 432-4320	C- / 3.4	-6.02	8.43	13.27 /65	11.83 /41	1.86 /26	0.00	1.65
SC	AXA Entp-Small Co Growth B	ENSBX	E	(800) 432-4320	C- / 3.3	-6.19	8.10	12.58 /62	11.19 /37	1.29 /22	0.00	2.20
SC	AXA Entp-Small Co Growth C	ESGCX	E	(800) 432-4320	C- / 3.8	-6.16	8.14	12.65 /63	11.22 /37	1.30 /22	0.00	2.20
SC	AXA Entp-Small Co Growth Y	ENGEX	E+	(800) 432-4320	C / 4.6	-5.95	8.67	13.74 /67	12.33 /45	2.32 /30	0.00	1.20
MC	Azzad Ethical Mid Cap Fund	ADJEX	D+	(888) 350-3369	C / 4.7	-3.21	1.79	11.04 /54	12.10 /43	2.01 /27	0.00	2.25
GR	Baird Large Cap Inst	BHGIX	D-	(800) 338-1579	E+ / 0.6	-4.82	-2.88	1.53 / 3	5.66 / 6	-0.98 /12	0.94	0.75
GR	Baird Large Cap Inv	BHGSX	D-	(800) 338-1579	E+ / 0.6	-4.85	-3.02	1.41 / 3	5.44 / 5	-1.23 /11	0.68	1.00
MC	Baird Midcap Inst	BMDIX	C	(800) 338-1579	C / 5.0	-6.94	3.69	12.13 /60	12.78 /47	4.98 /54	0.00	0.85

• Denotes fund is closed to new investors

* Denotes fund is included in Section II

| RISK | 3 Year | | NET ASSETS | | ASSET | | | | Portfolio | BULL / BEAR | | FUND MANAGER | | MINIMUMS | | LOADS | |
Risk Rating/Pts	Standard Deviation	Beta	NAV As of 6/30/06	Total $(Mil)	Cash %	Stocks %	Bonds %	Other %	Turnover Ratio	Last Bull Market Return	Last Bear Market Return	Manager Quality Pct	Manager Tenure (Years)	Initial Purch. $	Additional Purch. $	Front End Load	Back End Load
D+ / 2.7	17.6	1.82	9.13	25	2	98	0	0	252.0	92.2	-13.7	6	N/A	2,000	50	0.0	5.0
D+ / 2.7	17.6	1.82	9.13	7	2	98	0	0	252.0	92.2	-13.7	6	N/A	2,000	50	0.0	2.0
D / 2.2	17.6	1.82	9.45	1	2	98	0	0	252.0	96.8	-13.6	8	N/A	2,000	50	5.5	2.0
D+ / 2.9	17.6	1.81	9.52	6	2	98	0	0	252.0	98.0	-13.5	9	N/A	1,000,000	0	0.0	2.0
B / 8.7	7.5	0.93	12.23	1	2	98	0	0	72.0	74.9	-7.4	82	N/A	2,000	50	0.0	5.0
B / 8.8	7.5	0.93	12.24	1	2	98	0	0	72.0	75.0	-7.4	82	N/A	2,000	50	0.0	2.0
B / 8.8	7.5	0.93	12.33	4	2	98	0	0	72.0	78.9	-7.3	86	N/A	2,000	50	5.5	2.0
B / 8.8	7.5	0.93	12.38	40	2	98	0	0	72.0	80.7	-7.2	88	N/A	1,000,000	0	0.0	2.0
C / 5.4	10.5	0.69	12.26	256	0	98	0	2	4.0	97.7	-7.9	85	N/A	2,000	50	4.8	2.0
C / 5.3	10.5	0.69	11.34	188	0	98	0	2	4.0	94.1	-7.9	82	N/A	2,000	50	0.0	5.0
C / 5.3	10.5	0.69	11.65	96	0	98	0	2	4.0	94.1	-8.0	82	N/A	2,000	50	1.0	2.0
C / 5.4	10.5	0.69	13.01	23	0	98	0	2	4.0	100.4	-7.7	88	N/A	1,000,000	0	0.0	2.0
B- / 7.4	7.6	0.91	10.63	27	2	98	0	0	101.0	70.4	-10.5	74	N/A	2,000	50	4.8	2.0
B- / 7.5	7.5	0.91	10.55	17	2	98	0	0	101.0	67.4	-10.7	69	N/A	2,000	50	0.0	5.0
B- / 7.5	7.6	0.91	10.55	7	2	98	0	0	101.0	67.2	-10.6	69	N/A	2,000	50	0.0	2.0
B- / 7.3	7.5	0.91	10.69	8	2	98	0	0	101.0	72.3	-10.3	77	N/A	1,000,000	0	0.0	2.0
B- / 7.8	9.2	1.07	27.14	113	4	94	0	2	96.0	82.3	-9.3	88	N/A	2,000	50	4.8	2.0
B- / 7.8	9.2	1.07	26.56	47	4	94	0	2	96.0	79.2	-9.5	85	N/A	2,000	50	0.0	5.0
B- / 7.8	9.2	1.07	26.77	16	4	94	0	2	96.0	79.2	-9.5	85	N/A	2,000	50	0.0	2.0
B- / 7.7	9.2	1.07	27.19	13	4	94	0	2	96.0	84.9	-9.3	90	N/A	1,000,000	0	0.0	2.0
B- / 7.2	7.9	0.91	17.24	760	2	98	0	0	51.0	34.9	-9.2	16	N/A	2,000	50	4.8	2.0
B- / 7.1	7.9	0.91	16.11	247	2	98	0	0	51.0	32.5	-9.4	13	N/A	2,000	50	0.0	5.0
B- / 7.1	7.9	0.92	16.33	141	2	98	0	0	51.0	32.7	-9.4	13	N/A	2,000	50	1.0	2.0
B- / 7.2	7.9	0.91	18.17	46	2	98	0	0	51.0	36.9	-9.1	18	N/A	1,000,000	0	0.0	2.0
B / 8.7	7.3	0.90	37.63	84	0	98	0	2	42.0	69.6	-9.5	78	N/A	2,000	50	4.8	2.0
B / 8.7	7.2	0.90	36.21	65	0	98	0	2	42.0	66.6	-9.5	72	N/A	2,000	50	0.0	5.0
B / 8.7	7.3	0.90	36.25	17	0	98	0	2	42.0	66.6	-9.5	72	N/A	2,000	50	0.0	2.0
B / 8.7	7.2	0.90	38.81	24	0	98	0	2	42.0	72.0	-9.3	82	N/A	1,000,000	0	0.0	2.0
B- / 7.6	3.8	0.42	12.22	233	24	74	0	2	183.0	39.3	-1.3	84	N/A	2,000	50	4.8	2.0
B- / 7.6	3.8	0.41	11.91	51	24	74	0	2	183.0	36.8	-1.5	80	N/A	2,000	50	0.0	5.0
B- / 7.6	3.8	0.41	11.91	121	24	74	0	2	183.0	36.8	-1.5	80	N/A	2,000	50	1.0	2.0
B- / 7.5	3.8	0.42	12.48	61	24	74	0	2	183.0	41.4	-1.2	87	N/A	1,000,000	0	0.0	2.0
B / 8.2	8.4	0.77	11.22	8	2	96	0	2	45.0	73.8	-8.9	14	N/A	2,000	50	4.8	2.0
B / 8.1	8.4	0.76	10.89	3	2	96	0	2	45.0	70.7	-9.1	12	N/A	2,000	50	0.0	5.0
B / 8.1	8.3	0.76	10.89	5	2	96	0	2	45.0	70.9	-9.2	12	N/A	2,000	50	0.0	2.0
B / 8.2	8.4	0.76	11.47	1	2	96	0	2	45.0	76.0	-8.9	17	N/A	1,000,000	0	0.0	2.0
B- / 7.7	9.9	0.88	8.83	17	2	98	0	0	25.0	119.0	-7.4	96	N/A	2,000	50	4.8	2.0
B- / 7.7	9.8	0.88	8.73	15	2	98	0	0	25.0	114.2	-7.6	94	N/A	2,000	50	0.0	5.0
B- / 7.7	9.9	0.89	8.70	5	2	98	0	0	25.0	115.1	-7.6	95	N/A	2,000	50	0.0	1.0
B- / 7.6	9.9	0.89	8.87	12	2	98	0	0	25.0	122.1	-7.3	97	N/A	1,000,000	0	0.0	2.0
B+ / 9.0	6.1	0.76	7.67	74	0	70	30	0	153.0	51.4	-6.1	64	N/A	2,000	50	4.8	2.0
B+ / 9.0	6.1	0.75	7.48	40	0	70	30	0	153.0	48.9	-6.1	58	N/A	2,000	50	0.0	5.0
B+ / 9.0	6.1	0.76	7.45	9	0	70	30	0	153.0	48.8	-6.2	57	N/A	2,000	50	0.0	2.0
B+ / 9.0	6.2	0.76	7.73	N/A	0	70	30	0	153.0	53.5	-5.9	68	N/A	1,000,000	0	0.0	2.0
D+ / 2.3	17.3	1.10	30.74	47	2	98	0	0	146.0	69.8	-9.5	5	N/A	2,000	50	4.8	2.0
D / 2.2	17.3	1.10	28.97	33	2	98	0	0	146.0	66.8	-9.7	4	N/A	2,000	50	0.0	5.0
D / 2.2	17.3	1.10	29.09	14	2	98	0	0	146.0	66.9	-9.7	4	N/A	2,000	50	0.0	2.0
D+ / 2.3	17.3	1.10	32.10	16	2	98	0	0	146.0	72.2	-9.4	7	N/A	1,000,000	0	0.0	2.0
C / 5.2	12.1	0.92	9.65	3	6	93	0	1	144.9	68.8	-7.7	18	N/A	1,000	50	0.0	0.0
B- / 7.7	8.2	0.96	8.09	24	N/A	100	0	N/A	23.0	40.6	-11.6	15	6	100,000	0	0.0	0.0
B- / 7.7	8.3	0.97	8.04	2	N/A	100	0	N/A	23.0	39.5	-11.7	13	6	2,500	250	0.0	0.0
C+ / 6.8	11.2	0.94	11.53	92	2	97	0	1	67.3	70.4	-8.6	20	N/A	100,000	0	0.0	0.0

			Overall Weiss		PERFORMANCE						Incl. in Returns	
					Perfor-	Total Return % through 6/30/06						
			Investment		mance				Annualized		Dividend	Expense
Fund Type	Fund Name	Ticker Symbol	Rating	Phone	Rating/Pts	3 Mo	6 Mo	1Yr / Pct	3Yr / Pct	5Yr / Pct	Yield	Ratio
MC	Baird Midcap Inv	BMDSX	C	(800) 338-1579	C / 4.9	-7.03	3.55	11.76 /58	12.48 /46	4.74 /52	0.00	1.10
SC	Baird Small Cap Fund Inst	BSMIX	U	(800) 338-1579	U /	-6.06	3.84	7.59 /30	--	--	0.00	0.95
BA	Barclays Gbl Inv - Ret Port Inst	STLAX	C-	(800) 474-2737	D- / 1.2	-0.39	1.53	4.49 /13	5.98 / 7	4.72 /52	3.14	0.85
BA	Barclays Gbl Inv - Ret Port R	LPRAX	C-	(800) 474-2737	D- / 1.0	-0.47	1.41	4.23 /12	5.63 / 5	4.38 /49	3.09	1.10
AA	Barclays Gbl Inv LifePath 2010 Fd I	STLBX	C	(800) 474-2737	D / 2.0	-0.47	2.15	6.26 /22	7.66 /13	4.23 /48	2.69	0.85
AA	Barclays Gbl Inv LifePath 2010 Fd R	LPRBX	C	(800) 474-2737	D / 1.8	-0.54	1.99	5.94 /20	7.28 /12	3.89 /45	2.49	1.10
AA	Barclays Gbl Inv LifePath 2020 Fd I	STLCX	C+	(800) 474-2737	C- / 3.6	-0.66	3.33	9.20 /41	10.09 /28	4.33 /49	2.22	0.85
AA	Barclays Gbl Inv LifePath 2020 Fd R	LPRCX	C+	(800) 474-2737	C- / 3.4	-0.69	3.22	8.91 /39	9.73 /25	3.85 /44	2.09	1.10
AA	Barclays Gbl Inv LifePath 2030 Fd I	STLDX	C+	(800) 474-2737	C / 4.8	-0.79	4.12	11.40 /56	11.75 /41	4.38 /49	1.58	0.85
GR	Barclays Gbl Inv LifePath 2040 Fd I	STLEX	B-	(800) 474-2737	C+ / 5.6	-0.88	4.83	13.00 /64	13.17 /50	4.25 /48	1.28	0.85
GR	Barclays Gbl Inv LifePath 2040 Fd R	LPREX	B	(800) 474-2737	C / 5.5	-0.98	4.67	12.64 /63	12.89 /48	4.15 /47	1.10	1.10
IX	Barclays Gbl Inv S&P500 Stock Fd	WFSPX	C+	(800) 474-2737	C- / 4.0	-1.48	2.62	8.43 /36	11.01 /36	2.29 /30	1.61	0.20
GL	Barclays Glbl Inv LifePath 2030 R	LPRDX	B-	(800) 474-2737	C / 4.6	-0.86	4.00	11.11 /54	11.46 /39	3.99 /46	1.38	1.10
★ SC	Baron Asset Fund	BARAX	B	(800) 992-2766	B+ / 8.3	-2.62	6.47	17.35 /78	21.01 /83	8.86 /76	0.00	1.34
GR	Baron Fifth Avenue Growth Fd	BFTHX	U	(800) 992-2766	U /	-4.20	-0.25	6.08 /21	--	--	0.00	1.40
★ GR ●	Baron Growth Fund	BGRFX	C+	(800) 992-2766	B- / 7.2	-3.88	6.92	9.72 /45	17.90 /72	11.25 /85	0.00	1.31
TC	Baron iOpportunity Fund	BIOPX	C	(800) 992-2766	B / 7.6	-6.13	0.82	15.02 /72	19.66 /78	8.29 /73	0.00	1.50
GR	Baron Partners Fund	BPTRX	A+	(800) 992-2766	A / 9.5	-2.65	9.82	20.06 /82	29.89 /95	14.37 /91	0.00	1.62
★ SC ●	Baron Small Cap	BSCFX	C+	(800) 992-2766	C+ / 6.3	-7.41	3.06	7.52 /29	16.48 /66	10.56 /82	0.00	1.33
GR	Barrett Growth Fund	BGRWX	C-		D+ / 2.6	-4.71	0.48	8.33 /35	9.05 /21	0.35 /17	0.00	1.25
SC ●	Battery March US Small Cap I	LMSIX	C-	(888) 425-6432	C+ / 6.3	-5.77	6.67	10.47 /50	16.00 /63	9.19 /77	0.14	0.75
GI	BB&T Capital Manager Conserv Gr A	BCGAX	D+	(800) 228-1872	E / 0.5	-0.89	1.03	3.53 / 9	5.75 / 6	3.04 /37	2.81	0.34
GI	BB&T Capital Manager Conserv Gr B	BCGBX	D+	(800) 228-1872	E / 0.4	-1.18	0.65	2.75 / 6	4.97 / 4	2.34 /30	2.22	1.09
GI	BB&T Capital Manager Conserv Gr C	BCCCX	C-	(800) 228-1872	E+ / 0.6	-1.18	0.66	2.74 / 6	4.95 / 4	2.28 /30	2.21	1.09
GI	BB&T Capital Manager Conserv Gr Tr	BMGTX	C-	(800) 228-1872	E+ / 0.9	-0.92	1.15	3.75 /10	5.99 / 7	3.33 /40	3.21	0.20
AG	BB&T Capital Manager Eqty A	BCAAX	C	(800) 228-1872	C- / 3.8	-1.85	4.01	10.30 /49	12.29 /44	2.78 /35	1.24	1.12
AG	BB&T Capital Manager Eqty B	BCABX	C	(800) 228-1872	C- / 3.5	-1.97	3.60	9.52 /43	11.49 /39	2.00 /27	0.76	1.11
AG	BB&T Capital Manager Eqty C	BCACX	C	(800) 228-1872	C- / 4.2	-1.98	3.61	9.33 /42	11.45 /39	1.93 /27	0.76	1.11
AG	BB&T Capital Manager Eqty Tr	BCATX	B-	(800) 228-1872	C / 4.8	-1.79	4.10	10.58 /51	12.59 /46	3.00 /37	1.52	0.22
GI	BB&T Capital Manager Growth A	BCMAX	C-	(800) 228-1872	D+ / 2.4	-1.61	2.96	7.71 /30	10.31 /29	2.70 /34	1.73	0.37
GI	BB&T Capital Manager Growth B	BCMBX	C-	(800) 228-1872	D / 2.2	-1.72	2.63	6.95 /26	9.54 /24	1.92 /26	1.13	1.12
GI	BB&T Capital Manager Growth C	BCGCX	C	(800) 228-1872	D+ / 2.8	-1.82	2.53	6.81 /25	9.48 /24	1.91 /26	1.21	1.12
GI	BB&T Capital Manager Growth Tr	BCMTX	C	(800) 228-1872	C- / 3.4	-1.54	3.08	7.96 /32	10.60 /32	2.97 /36	2.07	0.23
GI	BB&T Capital Manager Mod Gr A	BAMGX	C-	(800) 228-1872	D- / 1.4	-1.38	2.20	5.91 /20	8.51 /18	3.12 /38	2.13	0.49
GI	BB&T Capital Manager Mod Gr B	BBMGX	C-	(800) 228-1872	D- / 1.2	-1.59	1.74	5.11 /16	7.64 /13	2.33 /30	1.55	1.24
GI	BB&T Capital Manager Mod Gr C	BCMCX	C-	(800) 228-1872	D / 1.8	-1.48	1.85	5.16 /16	7.72 /13	2.39 /31	1.51	1.24
GI	BB&T Capital Manager Mod Gr Tr	BCGTX	C	(800) 228-1872	D / 2.2	-1.31	2.31	6.15 /21	8.73 /19	3.35 /40	2.50	0.23
IN	BB&T Equity Income A	BAEIX	U	(800) 228-1872	U /	2.81	8.44	14.11 /69	--	--	2.41	1.19
GR	BB&T Equity Index A	BAEQX	C-	(800) 228-1872	D+ / 2.6	-1.61	2.37	7.85 /31	10.67 /32	1.99 /27	1.19	0.57
GR	BB&T Equity Index B	BBEQX	C-	(800) 228-1872	D+ / 2.3	-1.82	2.03	7.05 /26	9.82 /26	1.21 /22	0.54	1.32
GR	BB&T Equity Index C		C	(800) 228-1872	D+ / 2.9	-1.69	1.24	6.72 /25	9.73 /25	1.37 /23	0.17	1.32
FO	BB&T International Equity A	BIQAX	B	(800) 228-1872	B- / 7.3	-0.54	7.68	20.45 /82	18.80 /76	5.10 /55	0.96	1.41
FO	BB&T International Equity B	BIQBX	B	(800) 228-1872	B- / 7.1	-0.67	7.23	19.52 /81	17.91 /72	4.33 /49	0.71	2.16
FO	BB&T International Equity C	BIQCX	A-	(800) 228-1872	B- / 7.5	-0.70	7.32	19.62 /81	17.86 /72	4.33 /49	0.65	2.16
FO	BB&T International Equity Tr	BBTIX	B+	(800) 228-1872	B / 8.0	-0.38	7.84	20.73 /83	19.07 /76	5.35 /57	1.22	1.20
GR	BB&T Large Company Growth A	BLGAX	D+	(800) 228-1872	D+ / 2.8	-4.31	-1.91	16.87 /77	11.29 /38	1.06 /20	0.43	1.13
GR	BB&T Large Company Growth B	BLRBX	D+	(800) 228-1872	D+ / 2.8	-4.47	-2.23	16.90 /77	10.74 /33	0.43 /17	0.24	1.88
GR	BB&T Large Company Growth C	BLGCX	C-	(800) 228-1872	C- / 3.4	-4.58	-2.34	16.76 /76	10.69 /33	0.39 /17	0.26	1.87
GR	BB&T Large Company Growth Tr	BLCTX	C-	(800) 228-1872	C- / 4.1	-4.22	-1.74	16.97 /77	11.50 /39	1.21 /22	0.63	0.89
GI	BB&T Large Company Value A	BBTGX	C+	(800) 228-1872	C / 4.7	0.03	6.00	11.78 /58	13.27 /50	4.95 /54	1.40	1.13
GI	BB&T Large Company Value B	BGISX	C+	(800) 228-1872	C / 4.4	-0.16	5.59	10.92 /53	12.43 /45	4.16 /47	0.78	1.88
GI	BB&T Large Company Value Tr	BBISX	B-	(800) 228-1872	C+ / 5.6	0.04	6.12	12.02 /60	13.56 /52	5.20 /56	1.70	0.89

● Denotes fund is closed to new investors

★ Denotes fund is included in Section II

RISK			NET ASSETS		ASSET					BULL / BEAR		FUND MANAGER		MINIMUMS		LOADS	
	3 Year		NAV						Portfolio	Last Bull	Last Bear	Manager	Manager	Initial	Additional	Front	Back
Risk	Standard		As of	Total	Cash	Stocks	Bonds	Other	Turnover	Market	Market	Quality	Tenure	Purch.	Purch.	End	End
Rating/Pts	Deviation	Beta	6/30/06	$(Mil)	%	%	%	%	Ratio	Return	Return	Pct	(Years)	$	$	Load	Load
C+ / 6.8	11.3	0.94	11.38	5	2	97	0	1	67.3	69.3	-8.8	18	N/A	2,500	250	0.0	0.0
U /	N/A	N/A	11.63	56	2	97	0	1	61.4	N/A	N/A	N/A	N/A	100,000	0	0.0	0.0
B+ / 9.8	3.6	0.70	11.22	103	N/A	27	72	N/A	11.0	29.2	-2.4	56	N/A	100,000	0	0.0	0.0
B+ / 9.9	3.6	0.69	10.55	10	N/A	27	72	N/A	11.0	32.3	-2.3	53	N/A	0	0	0.0	0.0
B+ / 9.7	4.3	0.88	13.03	359	0	30	71	0	12.0	38.5	-4.5	64	N/A	1,000,000	0	0.0	0.0
B+ / 9.9	4.3	0.88	12.83	37	0	30	71	0	12.0	37.1	-4.6	60	N/A	0	0	0.0	0.0
B+ / 9.3	5.6	1.14	16.21	631	N/A	34	66	N/A	17.0	52.0	-6.1	73	N/A	1,000,000	0	0.0	0.0
B+ / 9.6	5.5	1.13	15.56	73	N/A	34	66	N/A	17.0	50.4	-6.1	71	N/A	0	0	0.0	0.0
B / 8.7	6.6	1.33	15.89	399	N/A	37	63	N/A	24.0	62.8	-7.2	79	N/A	1,000,000	0	0.0	0.0
B / 8.4	7.5	0.93	18.94	248	N/A	39	61	N/A	38.0	72.0	-8.1	80	N/A	1,000,000	0	0.0	0.0
B+ / 9.0	7.5	0.93	18.19	45	N/A	39	61	N/A	38.0	70.6	-8.1	78	N/A	0	0	0.0	0.0
B / 8.7	7.7	1.00	152.25	274	1	98	0	1	10.0	63.8	-9.8	54	N/A	1,000,000	0	0.0	0.0
B+ / 9.2	6.6	1.34	15.64	50	6	0	93	1	17.0	61.4	-7.4	76	N/A	0	0	0.0	0.0
C+ / 5.7	10.4	0.63	59.93	3,207	1	98	0	1	11.5	117.0	-10.8	98	19	2,000	0	0.0	0.0
U /	N/A	N/A	11.87	148	8	91	0	1	46.7	N/A	N/A	N/A	N/A	2,000	0	0.0	0.0
C+ / 5.9	11.1	1.11	48.54	5,584	6	91	1	2	15.5	107.4	-7.5	93	12	2,000	0	0.0	0.0
C / 4.5	16.2	1.65	9.80	167	20	79	0	1	83.6	163.2	-12.0	77	N/A	2,000	0	0.0	1.0
B- / 7.2	12.9	1.26	20.24	1,670	N/A	N/A	1	N/A	37.6	182.3	-16.5	99	14	2,000	0	0.0	0.0
C+ / 6.2	13.2	0.75	23.88	3,185	5	94	0	1	24.7	109.1	-6.4	76	9	2,000	0	0.0	0.0
B / 8.1	9.3	1.08	10.53	20	1	98	0	1	56.4	55.7	-9.0	28	8	2,500	50	0.0	0.0
C / 4.4	15.2	1.01	11.64	849	0	99	0	1	50.2	97.4	-6.0	29	N/A	1,000	100	0.0	2.0
B+ / 9.7	3.7	0.41	9.72	9	3	39	56	2	2.7	29.3	-3.0	55	N/A	1,000	0	5.8	1.0
B+ / 9.9	3.7	0.40	9.72	5	3	39	56	2	2.7	26.5	-3.2	45	N/A	1,000	0	0.0	5.0
B+ / 9.9	3.7	0.41	9.69	N/A	3	39	56	2	2.7	26.5	-3.2	45	N/A	1,000	0	0.0	1.0
B+ / 9.9	3.7	0.40	9.79	71	3	39	56	2	2.7	30.4	-2.9	58	N/A	1,500,000	0	0.0	2.0
B / 8.2	7.6	0.97	11.23	7	3	96	0	1	1.1	68.1	-9.5	70	N/A	1,000	0	5.8	1.0
B / 8.2	7.6	0.97	10.93	8	3	96	0	1	1.1	64.3	-9.7	62	N/A	1,000	0	0.0	5.0
B / 8.1	7.6	0.97	10.90	N/A	3	96	0	1	1.1	64.2	-9.7	62	N/A	1,000	0	0.0	1.0
B / 8.9	7.6	0.97	11.30	30	3	96	0	1	1.1	69.4	-9.4	73	N/A	1,500,000	0	0.0	2.0
B / 8.9	6.4	0.81	9.94	22	3	79	16	2	5.6	56.3	-7.9	66	N/A	1,000	0	5.8	1.0
B / 8.8	6.4	0.81	9.77	19	3	79	16	2	5.6	52.8	-8.1	57	N/A	1,000	0	0.0	5.0
B / 8.8	6.5	0.82	9.76	N/A	3	79	16	2	5.6	52.9	-8.1	56	N/A	1,000	0	0.0	1.0
B / 8.9	6.4	0.81	9.95	42	3	79	16	2	5.6	57.7	-7.9	68	N/A	1,500,000	0	0.0	2.0
B+ / 9.4	5.2	0.65	9.94	33	3	59	37	1	37.8	45.3	-6.1	61	N/A	1,000	0	5.8	1.0
B+ / 9.4	5.2	0.65	9.77	22	3	59	37	1	37.8	41.7	-6.2	52	N/A	1,000	0	0.0	5.0
B+ / 9.4	5.3	0.66	9.83	N/A	3	59	37	1	37.8	42.1	-6.0	51	N/A	1,000	0	0.0	1.0
B+ / 9.4	5.3	0.65	9.97	48	3	59	37	1	37.8	46.3	-6.0	63	N/A	1,500,000	0	0.0	2.0
U /	N/A	N/A	12.84	53	6	93	0	1	25.7	N/A	N/A	N/A	6	1,000	0	5.8	1.0
B / 8.8	7.7	1.01	8.53	52	1	98	0	1	10.0	62.2	-9.8	49	N/A	1,000	0	5.8	1.0
B / 8.8	7.7	1.00	8.39	8	1	98	0	1	10.0	58.3	-10.0	40	N/A	1,000	0	0.0	5.0
B / 8.6	7.7	1.00	8.47	12	1	98	0	1	10.0	58.0	-9.9	40	N/A	1,000	0	0.0	1.0
B- / 7.0	9.3	0.89	10.61	4	1	98	0	1	23.6	95.6	-13.3	30	N/A	1,000	0	5.8	1.0
B- / 7.0	9.2	0.89	10.04	2	1	98	0	1	23.6	90.7	-13.6	25	N/A	1,000	0	0.0	5.0
B / 8.0	9.2	0.88	10.03	N/A	1	98	0	1	23.6	90.8	-13.6	25	N/A	1,000	0	0.0	1.0
B- / 7.1	9.2	0.89	10.78	239	1	98	0	1	23.6	97.0	-13.5	32	N/A	1,500,000	0	0.0	0.0
B- / 7.2	11.5	0.98	8.87	9	0	98	0	2	78.2	67.0	-8.3	59	1	1,000	0	5.8	1.0
B- / 7.1	11.9	0.97	8.33	10	0	98	0	2	78.2	64.3	-8.5	53	1	1,000	0	0.0	5.0
B- / 7.5	11.9	0.97	8.33	N/A	0	98	0	2	78.2	64.2	-8.5	53	1	1,000	0	0.0	1.0
B- / 7.2	11.5	0.98	9.02	337	0	98	0	2	78.2	68.0	-8.2	61	1	1,500,000	0	0.0	0.0
B / 8.4	7.0	0.87	19.20	47	2	97	0	1	12.6	71.5	-9.5	84	13	1,000	0	5.8	1.0
B / 8.3	7.0	0.88	19.03	16	2	97	0	1	12.6	67.3	-9.6	78	13	1,000	0	0.0	5.0
B / 8.4	7.0	0.87	19.24	625	2	97	0	1	12.6	72.9	-9.4	86	13	1,500,000	0	0.0	2.0

Fund Type	Fund Name	Ticker Symbol	Overall Weiss Investment Rating	Phone	Performance Rating/Pts	3 Mo	6 Mo	1Yr / Pct	3Yr / Pct	5Yr / Pct	Dividend Yield	Expense Ratio
MC	BB&T Mid Cap Growth A	OVCBX	D+	(800) 228-1872	C+ / 6.4	-7.11	2.03	15.43 /73	17.68 /71	5.70 /59	0.14	1.13
MC	BB&T Mid Cap Growth B	OVMBX	D+	(800) 228-1872	C+ / 6.2	-7.31	1.70	14.62 /70	16.81 /67	4.93 /54	0.00	1.88
MC	BB&T Mid Cap Growth C	OVMCX	D+	(800) 228-1872	C+ / 6.7	-7.23	1.78	14.61 /70	16.84 /67	4.94 /54	0.00	1.87
MC	BB&T Mid Cap Growth Tr	OCAAX	C-	(800) 228-1872	B- / 7.3	-7.05	2.19	15.75 /74	17.99 /72	5.99 /61	0.24	0.91
MC	BB&T Mid Cap Value A	OVEAX	D-	(800) 228-1872	C+ / 6.6	-1.64	5.68	13.18 /65	17.64 /71	9.45 /78	0.22	1.13
MC	BB&T Mid Cap Value B	OVEBX	D-	(800) 228-1872	C+ / 6.4	-1.78	5.33	12.37 /61	16.78 /67	8.61 /75	0.01	1.88
MC	BB&T Mid Cap Value C	OVECX	D-	(800) 228-1872	C+ / 6.9	-1.78	5.42	12.46 /62	16.79 /67	8.59 /75	0.01	1.89
MC	BB&T Mid Cap Value Tr	OVEIX	D	(800) 228-1872	B- / 7.4	-1.58	5.88	13.53 /66	17.92 /72	9.74 /79	0.38	0.89
SC	BB&T Small Cap Fund A	BTVAX	B	(800) 228-1872	C+ / 6.9	-4.54	5.58	9.61 /44	19.34 /77	--	0.15	1.26
SC	BB&T Small Cap Fund B	BTVBX	B-	(800) 228-1872	C+ / 6.7	-4.80	5.14	8.87 /39	18.45 /74	--	0.05	2.07
SC	BB&T Small Cap Fund C	BTVCX	B+	(800) 228-1872	B- / 7.2	-4.74	5.20	8.86 /39	18.45 /74	--	0.03	1.99
SC	BB&T Small Cap Fund Inst	BTVIX	A	(800) 228-1872	B / 7.7	-4.52	5.65	9.92 /46	19.63 /78	--	0.27	1.01
IN	BB&T Special Opport Eqty A	BOPAX	B	(800) 228-1872	C+ / 6.9	1.96	6.79	8.55 /37	18.60 /75	--	0.00	1.28
IN	BB&T Special Opport Eqty B	BOPBX	B	(800) 228-1872	C+ / 6.7	1.74	6.37	7.79 /31	17.67 /71	--	0.00	2.03
IN	BB&T Special Opport Eqty C	BOPCX	A	(800) 228-1872	B- / 7.1	1.74	6.36	7.79 /31	17.69 /71	--	0.00	2.03
IN	BB&T Special Opport Eqty Inst	BOPIX	A+	(800) 228-1872	B / 7.6	2.01	6.95	8.84 /39	18.89 /76	--	0.00	1.03
FO	BBH International Equity I	BBHLX	A+	(800) 625-5759	B+ / 8.7	1.11	9.39	25.78 /89	21.78 /85	6.86 /66	1.54	0.98
FO	BBH International Equity N	BBHEX	A+	(800) 625-5759	B+ / 8.6	1.04	9.25	25.38 /89	21.49 /84	6.47 /64	1.35	1.23
GR	BBH Tax Efficient Equity N	BBTEX	C-	(800) 625-5759	D / 2.1	-2.16	2.26	8.89 /39	8.63 /19	-0.46 /14	0.07	1.22
GR	Becker Value Equity Fund	BVEFX	U	(800) 551-3998	U /	-0.68	3.20	10.39 /49	--	--	0.61	1.20
GR	Berkshire Focus Fund	BFOCX	E-	(877) 526-0707	C- / 3.0	-12.85	-6.44	18.86 /80	11.69 /40	-13.99 / 0	0.00	2.02
GR	Berwyn Cornerstone Fund	BERCX	C	(800) 992-6757	C- / 3.7	-0.50	5.34	6.67 /24	10.75 /33	--	0.00	2.00
GR	● Berwyn Fund	BERWX	B-	(800) 992-6757	B / 7.6	-7.53	-1.48	7.62 /30	20.87 /82	14.51 /91	0.06	1.28
GI	Bishop Street Large Cap Growth	BSEQX	D-	(800) 262-9565	D- / 1.3	-3.13	0.47	5.69 /19	6.43 / 8	-2.15 / 8	0.57	1.00
GR	Bishop Street Strategic Growth Inst	BSRIX	C	(800) 262-9565	C- / 4.1	-6.13	-1.74	10.51 /50	11.61 /40	--	0.00	1.07
SC	Bjurman Barry Small Cap Growth	BBSFX	E-	(800) 227-7264	D / 2.1	-7.87	3.58	8.34 /35	8.58 /18	--	0.00	1.80
SC	● Bjurman Micro-Cap Growth Fund	BMCFX	D-	(800) 227-7264	C+ / 6.3	-7.42	1.69	14.52 /70	16.06 /64	10.62 /83	0.00	1.80
GR	Bjurman Mid Cap Growth Fund	BACFX	C-	(800) 227-7264	C+ / 5.7	-4.78	4.84	17.38 /78	14.44 /56	3.85 /44	0.00	1.80
GI	BlackRock Invst Trust Prtf A	CEIAX	C-	(888) 825-2257	D+ / 2.4	-2.24	1.31	5.31 /17	11.21 /37	0.15 /16	0.49	1.16
GI	BlackRock Invst Trust Prtf B	CINBX	C-	(888) 825-2257	D+ / 2.9	-2.50	0.89	4.47 /13	10.40 /30	-0.59 /13	0.00	1.91
GI	BlackRock Invst Trust Prtf C	BSECX	C-	(888) 825-2257	D+ / 2.9	-2.42	0.97	4.55 /13	10.41 /30	-0.58 /13	0.00	1.91
GI	BlackRock Invst Trust Prtf Inst	PNEIX	C	(888) 825-2257	C- / 3.7	-2.21	1.45	5.67 /18	11.68 /40	0.58 /18	0.77	0.81
GI	BlackRock Invst Trust Prtf Ser	PCESX	C	(888) 825-2257	C- / 3.5	-2.20	1.37	5.44 /17	11.37 /38	0.29 /17	0.42	1.01
GR	BlackRock-All Cap Glb Resrces Inst	BACIX	U	(888) 825-2257	U /	4.74	15.71	44.99 /98	--	--	0.00	1.04
GR	BlackRock-All Cap Glb Resrces Inv A	BACAX	U	(888) 825-2257	U /	4.70	15.55	44.14 /98	--	--	0.00	1.34
GR	BlackRock-All Cap Glb Resrces Inv B	BACBX	U	(888) 825-2257	U /	4.53	15.12	43.27 /98	--	--	0.00	2.04
GR	BlackRock-All Cap Glb Resrces Inv C	BACCX	U	(888) 825-2257	U /	4.52	15.18	43.33 /98	--	--	0.00	2.04
BA	BlackRock-Asset Allo A	PCBAX	C-	(888) 825-2257	D+ / 2.6	-2.21	1.98	7.85 /31	10.99 /35	5.44 /57	1.36	1.20
BA	BlackRock-Asset Allo B	CBIBX	C-	(888) 825-2257	C- / 3.0	-2.37	1.60	7.04 /26	10.17 /28	4.80 /52	0.72	1.98
BA	BlackRock-Asset Allo C	BRBCX	C-	(888) 825-2257	C- / 3.0	-2.32	1.68	7.13 /27	10.19 /29	4.82 /53	0.80	1.87
BA	BlackRock-Asset Allo Inst	PBAIX	C	(888) 825-2257	C- / 3.8	-2.10	2.25	8.33 /35	11.38 /38	5.92 /61	1.83	0.80
SC	BlackRock-Aurora Investor A	SSRAX	D	(888) 825-2257	C+ / 5.7	-4.59	2.78	6.75 /25	17.08 /68	7.99 /72	0.00	1.44
SC	BlackRock-Aurora Investor B	SSRPX	D-	(888) 825-2257	C+ / 6.0	-4.77	2.39	5.92 /20	16.24 /64	7.22 /68	0.00	2.17
SC	BlackRock-Aurora Investor C	SSRDX	D-	(888) 825-2257	C+ / 6.0	-4.77	2.39	5.95 /20	16.24 /64	7.22 /68	0.00	2.13
SC	BlackRock-Aurora Investor Inst	SSRCX	D+	(888) 825-2257	C+ / 6.6	-4.49	2.96	7.12 /27	17.45 /70	8.35 /73	0.00	0.97
SC	BlackRock-Aurora Investor Svc	SSRSX	C-	(888) 825-2257	C+ / 6.4	-4.59	2.78	6.77 /25	17.08 /68	7.99 /72	0.00	1.44
TC	BlackRock-Glb Science & Tech A	BGSAX	E	(888) 825-2257	D+ / 2.9	-8.44	-0.74	15.64 /74	12.79 /47	-0.18 /15	0.00	1.75
TC	BlackRock-Glb Science & Tech B	BGSBX	E+	(888) 825-2257	C- / 3.2	-8.68	-1.23	14.64 /70	11.83 /41	-0.94 /12	0.00	2.65
TC	BlackRock-Glb Science & Tech C	BGSCX	E+	(888) 825-2257	C- / 3.3	-8.53	-1.08	14.82 /71	11.89 /42	-0.94 /12	0.00	2.65
TC	BlackRock-Glb Science & Tech Inst	BGSIX	E+	(888) 825-2257	C / 4.3	-8.34	-0.43	16.30 /75	13.28 /50	0.26 /17	0.00	1.35
TC	BlackRock-Glb Science & Tech Svc	BSTSX	E+	(888) 825-2257	C- / 3.9	-8.48	-0.73	15.84 /74	12.94 /48	-0.03 /15	0.00	1.73
EN	● BlackRock-Global Resources A	SSGRX	B-	(888) 825-2257	A+ / 9.9	3.89	14.53	50.16 /99	52.19 /99	33.45 /99	0.54	1.33

● Denotes fund is closed to new investors
* Denotes fund is included in Section II

RISK			NET ASSETS		ASSET				Portfolio Turnover Ratio	BULL / BEAR		FUND MANAGER		MINIMUMS		LOADS	
Risk Rating/Pts	3 Year		NAV As of 6/30/06	Total $(Mil)	Cash %	Stocks %	Bonds %	Other %		Last Bull Market Return	Last Bear Market Return	Manager Quality Pct	Manager Tenure (Years)	Initial Purch. $	Additional Purch. $	Front End Load	Back End Load
	Standard Deviation	Beta															
C- /3.7	16.2	1.41	13.06	11	2	97	0	1	51.2	110.1	-9.8	9	13	1,000	0	5.8	1.0
C- /3.6	16.2	1.41	12.56	3	2	97	0	1	51.2	105.2	-10.0	6	13	1,000	0	0.0	5.0
C- /3.6	16.2	1.41	12.57	N/A	2	97	0	1	51.2	105.2	-10.0	7	13	1,000	0	0.0	1.0
C- /3.7	16.3	1.41	13.72	139	2	97	0	1	51.2	111.9	-9.8	9	13	1,500,000	0	0.0	0.0
D- /1.3	8.6	0.75	12.92	13	4	96	0	0	25.5	95.9	-6.7	85	N/A	1,000	0	5.8	1.0
D- /1.3	8.7	0.75	12.69	5	4	96	0	0	25.5	91.4	-6.8	80	N/A	1,000	0	0.0	5.0
D- /1.3	8.7	0.75	12.69	1	4	96	0	0	25.5	91.2	-6.9	80	N/A	1,000	0	0.0	1.0
D- /1.3	8.7	0.76	12.96	200	4	96	0	0	25.5	97.4	-6.6	87	N/A	1,500,000	0	0.0	0.0
B /8.0	11.3	0.75	15.04	10	20	79	0	1	24.5	N/A	N/A	91	3	1,000	0	5.8	1.0
B- /7.9	11.4	0.75	14.68	5	20	79	0	1	24.5	N/A	N/A	88	3	1,000	0	0.0	5.0
B /8.0	11.3	0.74	14.67	N/A	20	79	0	1	24.5	N/A	N/A	88	3	1,000	0	0.0	1.0
B /8.0	11.3	0.74	15.11	110	20	79	0	1	24.5	N/A	N/A	92	3	1,500,000	0	0.0	0.0
B /8.7	8.3	0.89	15.58	79	13	86	0	1	28.7	N/A	N/A	98	3	1,000	0	5.8	1.0
B /8.7	8.3	0.88	15.20	22	13	86	0	1	28.7	N/A	N/A	97	3	1,000	50	0.0	5.0
B /8.7	8.3	0.88	15.21	32	13	86	0	1	28.7	N/A	N/A	97	3	1,000	0	0.0	1.0
B /8.7	8.4	0.89	15.70	62	13	86	0	1	28.7	N/A	N/A	98	3	1,500,000	0	0.0	0.0
B /8.0	9.6	0.92	14.56	42	2	97	0	1	5.0	108.7	-9.3	48	N/A	5,000,000	25,000	0.0	2.0
B- /7.5	9.6	0.92	14.53	467	2	97	0	1	5.0	107.1	-9.4	45	N/A	100,000	25,000	0.0	2.0
B /8.5	7.9	0.92	10.87	38	12	87	0	1	65.0	54.7	-12.3	36	N/A	100,000	25,000	0.0	2.0
U /	N/A	N/A	13.21	42	8	91	0	1	26.1	N/A	N/A	N/A	3	2,500	100	0.0	1.0
E- /0.0	31.0	2.72	7.12	20	N/A	100	0	N/A	284.1	106.6	-20.7	0	9	5,000	500	0.0	0.0
B /8.7	8.1	0.86	13.81	6	9	90	0	1	18.0	49.8	0.4	64	4	3,000	250	0.0	1.0
C+ /6.1	12.4	1.30	29.23	174	10	89	0	1	31.0	126.5	-6.3	95	22	3,000	250	0.0	1.0
C+ /6.3	8.6	1.09	9.90	30	0	98	0	2	40.0	45.5	-10.4	13	N/A	1,000	0	0.0	0.0
B- /7.6	11.2	1.24	14.10	139	1	98	0	1	55.0	78.6	-7.7	37	4	1,000	0	0.0	0.0
D /1.8	20.5	1.27	14.16	27	0	99	0	1	144.0	N/A	N/A	0	3	1,000	500	0.0	2.0
D- /1.4	20.3	1.29	31.21	524	0	99	0	1	62.0	126.8	-10.4	8	9	1,000	500	0.0	2.0
C /5.5	16.2	1.38	12.56	8	0	99	0	1	76.0	93.6	-13.9	53	N/A	1,000	500	0.0	2.0
B /8.5	7.8	1.00	13.10	478	0	99	0	1	105.0	64.0	-9.9	56	1	500	50	5.8	2.0
B /8.5	7.8	1.00	12.48	204	0	99	0	1	105.0	60.4	-10.1	46	1	500	50	0.0	2.0
B /8.5	7.8	1.00	12.50	19	0	99	0	1	105.0	60.3	-10.1	46	1	500	50	0.0	2.0
B /8.5	7.8	1.01	13.28	479	0	99	0	1	105.0	66.2	-9.9	61	1	2,000,000	0	0.0	2.0
B /8.5	7.8	1.01	13.32	1	0	99	0	1	105.0	64.9	-9.9	57	1	5,000	0	0.0	2.0
U /	N/A	N/A	15.47	364	11	88	0	1	12.0	N/A	N/A	N/A	N/A	2,000,000	0	0.0	2.0
U /	N/A	N/A	15.38	282	11	88	0	1	12.0	N/A	N/A	N/A	N/A	500	50	5.8	2.0
U /	N/A	N/A	15.23	46	11	88	0	1	12.0	N/A	N/A	N/A	N/A	500	50	0.0	2.0
U /	N/A	N/A	15.25	147	11	88	0	1	12.0	N/A	N/A	N/A	N/A	500	50	0.0	2.0
B /8.4	6.8	1.31	15.19	480	4	68	27	1	90.0	60.9	-6.5	73	1	500	50	5.8	2.0
B /8.4	6.7	1.30	15.05	177	4	68	27	1	90.0	57.1	-6.6	67	1	500	50	0.0	2.0
B /8.4	6.8	1.31	15.04	78	4	68	27	1	90.0	57.3	-6.7	66	1	500	50	0.0	2.0
B /8.4	6.8	1.30	15.23	31	4	68	27	1	90.0	62.6	-6.4	77	1	2,000,000	0	0.0	2.0
C- /3.2	13.7	0.89	35.14	1,325	2	98	0	0	73.0	108.1	-13.3	59	1	500	50	5.8	2.0
D+ /2.4	13.8	0.89	31.31	356	2	98	0	0	73.0	103.4	-13.5	50	1	500	50	0.0	2.0
D+ /2.4	13.8	0.89	31.31	315	2	98	0	0	73.0	103.4	-13.4	50	1	500	50	0.0	2.0
C- /3.5	13.8	0.89	36.83	162	2	98	0	0	73.0	110.1	-13.3	62	1	2,000,000	0	0.0	2.0
C /4.8	13.7	0.89	35.14	N/A	2	98	0	0	73.0	108.1	-13.3	59	1	5,000	0	0.0	2.0
D+ /2.9	17.0	1.77	6.73	14	7	92	0	1	113.0	99.7	-15.4	14	N/A	500	50	5.8	2.0
C- /3.9	17.1	1.78	6.42	11	7	92	0	1	113.0	95.0	-15.7	10	N/A	500	50	0.0	2.0
C- /3.9	17.1	1.78	6.43	6	7	92	0	1	113.0	95.3	-15.7	10	N/A	500	50	0.0	2.0
D+ /2.9	17.1	1.78	6.92	2	7	92	0	1	113.0	103.0	-15.7	15	N/A	2,000,000	0	0.0	2.0
D+ /2.9	17.1	1.78	6.80	N/A	7	92	0	1	113.0	100.8	-15.5	14	N/A	5,000	0	0.0	2.0
C- /3.8	22.9	1.05	75.84	885	N/A	100	0	N/A	9.0	335.7	8.4	99	1	500	50	5.8	2.0

				Overall Weiss Investment Rating		PERFORMANCE							
	99 Pct = Best							Total Return % through 6/30/06				Incl. in Returns	
	0 Pct = Worst					Perfor-					Annualized	Dividend	Expense
Fund Type	Fund Name	Ticker Symbol	Phone			mance Rating/Pts	3 Mo	6 Mo	1Yr / Pct	3Yr / Pct	5Yr / Pct	Yield	Ratio
EN	● BlackRock-Global Resources B	SSGPX	(888) 825-2257	B-		A+ / 9.9	3.70	14.12	49.06 /99	51.19 /99	32.57 /99	0.49	2.04
EN	● BlackRock-Global Resources C	SSGDX	(888) 825-2257	B-		A+ / 9.9	3.70	14.13	49.09 /99	51.16 /99	32.57 /99	0.49	2.04
EN	● BlackRock-Global Resources Inst	SGLSX	(888) 825-2257	C+		A+ / 9.9	3.97	14.72	50.63 /99	52.62 /99	33.96 /99	0.60	0.99
HL	BlackRock-Health Sciences A	SHSAX	(888) 825-2257	B-		C+ / 6.0	-5.67	-0.33	11.97 /59	17.60 /71	12.44 /87	0.00	1.55
HL	BlackRock-Health Sciences B	SHSPX	(888) 825-2257	B		C+ / 6.3	-5.89	-0.73	11.13 /54	16.76 /67	11.64 /86	0.00	2.25
HL	BlackRock-Health Sciences C	SHSCX	(888) 825-2257	B		C+ / 6.3	-5.86	-0.69	11.16 /55	16.78 /67	11.65 /86	0.00	2.21
HL	BlackRock-Health Sciences Inst	SHSSX	(888) 825-2257	B-		C+ / 6.9	-5.62	-0.20	12.31 /61	17.93 /72	12.76 /88	0.00	1.15
HL	BlackRock-Health Sciences Svc	SHISX	(888) 825-2257	C		C+ / 6.7	-5.66	-0.29	12.05 /60	17.68 /71	12.49 /88	0.00	1.55
IX	BlackRock-Index Eq Inst	PNIEX	(888) 825-2257	C		C- / 3.7	-1.48	2.69	8.56 /37	11.09 /36	2.35 /31	1.77	0.18
IX	BlackRock-Index Eq Inv A	CIEAX	(888) 825-2257	C		D+ / 2.9	-1.54	2.55	8.24 /35	10.62 /32	1.84 /26	1.47	0.38
IX	● BlackRock-Index Eq Inv B	CIEBX	(888) 825-2257	C		D+ / 2.9	-1.72	2.13	7.43 /29	9.78 /26	1.08 /21	0.71	1.24
IX	● BlackRock-Index Eq Inv C	CIECX	(888) 825-2257	C		D+ / 2.9	-1.75	2.10	7.41 /29	9.78 /26	1.07 /21	0.73	1.22
IX	BlackRock-Index Eq Svc	PNESX	(888) 825-2257	C		C- / 3.4	-1.55	2.53	8.23 /35	10.68 /33	1.95 /27	1.51	0.43
FO	● BlackRock-Intl Opp Inst	BISIX	(888) 825-2257	B+		A+ / 9.8	-1.62	10.47	42.50 /98	34.35 /98	19.63 /96	0.88	1.36
FO	● BlackRock-Intl Opp Inv A	BREAX	(888) 825-2257	B+		A+ / 9.7	-1.72	10.32	42.10 /98	33.88 /97	19.14 /95	0.82	1.75
FO	● BlackRock-Intl Opp Inv B	BREBX	(888) 825-2257	B+		A+ / 9.7	-1.93	9.85	40.99 /98	32.85 /97	18.24 /95	0.75	2.55
FO	● BlackRock-Intl Opp Inv C	BRECX	(888) 825-2257	B+		A+ / 9.7	-1.88	9.89	41.06 /98	32.89 /97	18.28 /95	0.77	2.49
FO	● BlackRock-Intl Opp Serv	BRESX	(888) 825-2257	B+		A+ / 9.8	-1.68	10.34	42.13 /98	33.99 /98	19.33 /95	0.88	1.69
GR	BlackRock-Large Cap Gr Inst	PNAPX	(888) 825-2257	D+		D+ / 2.3	-3.21	0.00	5.32 /17	9.38 /23	-2.89 / 6	0.91	0.82
GR	BlackRock-Large Cap Gr Inv A	PGIAX	(888) 825-2257	D		D- / 1.2	-3.34	-0.30	4.77 /14	8.88 /20	-3.33 / 5	0.49	1.29
GR	BlackRock-Large Cap Gr Inv B	BLGBX	(888) 825-2257	D		D / 1.6	-3.43	-0.55	4.04 /11	8.11 /16	-4.05 / 4	0.00	2.04
GR	BlackRock-Large Cap Gr Inv C	BGECX	(888) 825-2257	D		D- / 1.5	-3.54	-0.66	4.05 /11	8.08 /15	-4.06 / 4	0.00	2.04
GR	BlackRock-Large Cap Gr Svc	PNGEX	(888) 825-2257	D+		D / 2.1	-3.28	-0.20	4.99 /15	9.02 /21	-3.19 / 5	0.29	1.12
GR	BlackRock-Large Cap Val Eq Inst	PNVEX	(888) 825-2257	B+		C+ / 6.0	-0.12	5.52	10.98 /53	14.79 /58	3.32 /40	1.61	0.78
GR	BlackRock-Large Cap Val Eq Inv A	PNVIX	(888) 825-2257	B-		C / 4.9	-0.23	5.31	10.53 /50	14.30 /55	2.87 /35	1.14	1.25
GR	BlackRock-Large Cap Val Eq Inv B	CLCVX	(888) 825-2257	B		C / 5.2	-0.45	4.89	9.61 /44	13.40 /51	2.09 /28	0.44	2.00
GR	BlackRock-Large Cap Val Eq Inv C	BLVCX	(888) 825-2257	B		C / 5.3	-0.36	4.93	9.72 /45	13.45 /51	2.11 /28	0.47	1.96
GR	BlackRock-Large Cap Val Eq Svc	PNVSX	(888) 825-2257	B+		C+ / 5.8	-0.20	5.33	10.59 /51	14.42 /56	3.01 /37	1.29	1.09
GR	BlackRock-Legacy Inst	SRLSX	(888) 825-2257	D		D+ / 2.6	-4.33	-2.01	6.89 /26	10.01 /27	1.50 /24	0.00	0.90
GR	BlackRock-Legacy Inv A	SRLAX	(888) 825-2257	D-		D- / 1.5	-4.45	-2.21	6.55 /24	9.69 /25	1.20 /21	0.00	1.35
GR	BlackRock-Legacy Inv B	SRLPX	(888) 825-2257	D		D / 1.9	-4.66	-2.64	5.64 /18	8.86 /20	0.47 /18	0.00	2.10
GR	BlackRock-Legacy Inv C	SRLCX	(888) 825-2257	D		D / 1.9	-4.66	-2.56	5.72 /19	8.89 /20	0.47 /18	0.00	2.03
GR	BlackRock-Legacy Svc	SSSLX	(888) 825-2257	D-		D+ / 2.4	-4.45	-2.21	6.55 /24	9.69 /25	1.20 /21	0.00	1.35
MC	BlackRock-Mid Cap Growth Eq A	BMGAX	(888) 825-2257	D+		C- / 4.1	-5.12	1.69	9.81 /46	13.75 /53	2.02 /27	0.00	1.58
MC	BlackRock-Mid Cap Growth Eq B	BMGBX	(888) 825-2257	C-		C / 4.5	-5.30	1.31	9.06 /40	12.89 /48	1.26 /22	0.00	2.33
MC	BlackRock-Mid Cap Growth Eq C	BMGCX	(888) 825-2257	C-		C / 4.5	-5.30	1.31	9.06 /40	12.95 /49	1.29 /22	0.00	2.33
MC	BlackRock-Mid Cap Growth Eq Inst	CMGIX	(888) 825-2257	C		C / 5.3	-4.97	1.96	10.34 /49	14.24 /55	2.48 /32	0.00	1.04
MC	BlackRock-Mid Cap Growth Eq Svc	CMGSX	(888) 825-2257	C-		C / 5.1	-5.08	1.65	9.88 /46	13.88 /53	2.18 /29	0.00	1.50
MC	BlackRock-Mid Cap Value Eq A	BMCAX	(888) 825-2257	C-		B- / 7.3	-1.30	4.79	12.25 /61	20.14 /80	9.80 /80	0.17	1.25
MC	BlackRock-Mid Cap Value Eq B	BMCVX	(888) 825-2257	C-		B / 7.6	-1.47	4.51	11.45 /56	19.53 /78	9.17 /77	0.00	2.00
MC	BlackRock-Mid Cap Value Eq C	BMCCX	(888) 825-2257	C-		B / 7.9	-1.47	17.89	11.45 /56	19.53 /78	9.20 /77	0.00	2.00
MC	BlackRock-Mid Cap Value Eq Inst	CMVIX	(888) 825-2257	C		B / 8.0	-1.20	5.02	12.62 /63	20.73 /82	10.27 /81	0.25	1.00
SC	BlackRock-Small Cap Core Eq A	BSQAX	(888) 825-2257	B-		B- / 7.2	-4.93	4.01	10.25 /48	20.44 /81	--	0.00	1.77
SC	BlackRock-Small Cap Core Eq B	BSQBX	(888) 825-2257	B		B- / 7.4	-5.07	3.61	9.47 /43	19.65 /78	--	0.00	2.52
SC	BlackRock-Small Cap Core Eq C	BSQCX	(888) 825-2257	B		B- / 7.4	-5.07	3.67	9.47 /43	19.65 /78	--	0.00	2.52
SC	BlackRock-Small Cap Core Eq Inst	BSQIX	(888) 825-2257	B		B / 7.8	-4.83	4.20	10.66 /51	20.87 /82	--	0.00	1.30
SC	BlackRock-Small Cap Core Eq Svc	BSQSX	(888) 825-2257	B		B / 7.8	-4.84	4.10	10.37 /49	20.72 /82	--	0.00	1.60
SC	BlackRock-Small Cap Gr A	CSGEX	(888) 825-2257	C-		C+ / 6.7	-4.58	7.10	16.06 /75	17.80 /72	2.45 /32	0.00	1.27
SC	BlackRock-Small Cap Gr B	CSGBX	(888) 825-2257	C-		C+ / 6.9	-4.89	6.50	15.06 /72	16.87 /67	1.65 /25	0.00	2.21
SC	BlackRock-Small Cap Gr C	CGICX	(888) 825-2257	C-		C+ / 6.9	-4.83	6.63	15.12 /72	16.88 /67	1.67 /25	0.00	2.12
SC	BlackRock-Small Cap Gr Inst	PSGIX	(888) 825-2257	C		B- / 7.4	-4.52	7.24	16.41 /76	18.18 /73	2.84 /35	0.00	0.83
SC	BlackRock-Small Cap Gr Svc	PCGEX	(888) 825-2257	C-		B- / 7.3	-4.52	7.16	16.17 /75	17.90 /72	2.57 /32	0.00	1.05

● Denotes fund is closed to new investors
* Denotes fund is included in Section II

www.WeissRatings.com

RISK			NET ASSETS		ASSET					BULL / BEAR		FUND MANAGER		MINIMUMS		LOADS	
	3 Year		NAV						Portfolio	Last Bull	Last Bear	Manager	Manager	Initial	Additional	Front	Back
Risk Rating/Pts	Standard Deviation	Beta	As of 6/30/06	Total $(Mil)	Cash %	Stocks %	Bonds %	Other %	Turnover Ratio	Market Return	Market Return	Quality Pct	Tenure (Years)	Purch. $	Purch. $	End Load	End Load
C- / 3.6	22.9	1.05	68.13	110	N/A	100	0	N/A	9.0	326.8	8.3	99	1	500	50	0.0	2.0
C- / 3.6	22.9	1.05	68.07	190	N/A	100	0	N/A	9.0	326.4	8.2	99	1	500	50	0.0	2.0
D+ / 2.7	22.9	1.05	80.06	43	N/A	100	0	N/A	9.0	339.8	8.5	99	1	2,000,000	0	0.0	2.0
B- / 7.8	11.2	0.88	24.13	366	6	93	0	1	77.0	136.3	-7.7	97	1	500	50	5.8	2.0
B- / 7.8	11.2	0.88	23.17	71	6	93	0	1	77.0	131.1	-7.9	95	1	500	50	0.0	2.0
B- / 7.8	11.2	0.88	23.13	220	6	93	0	1	77.0	131.2	-7.9	96	1	500	50	0.0	2.0
B- / 7.8	11.2	0.88	24.53	98	6	93	0	1	77.0	138.5	-7.7	97	1	2,000,000	0	0.0	2.0
C+ / 5.6	11.1	0.86	24.18	3	6	93	0	1	77.0	136.7	-9.2	97	1	5,000	0	0.0	2.0
B / 8.6	7.7	1.00	24.42	492	N/A	100	0	N/A	7.0	64.2	-9.7	55	8	2,000,000	0	0.0	2.0
B / 8.6	7.6	1.00	24.24	283	N/A	100	0	N/A	7.0	61.9	-9.9	49	8	500	50	3.0	2.0
B / 8.6	7.6	1.00	23.84	101	N/A	100	0	N/A	7.0	58.0	-10.1	40	8	500	50	0.0	2.0
B / 8.6	7.6	1.00	23.82	180	N/A	100	0	N/A	7.0	58.0	-10.0	40	8	500	50	0.0	2.0
B / 8.6	7.6	1.00	24.26	73	N/A	100	0	N/A	7.0	62.2	-9.9	50	8	5,000	0	0.0	2.0
C / 5.4	13.7	1.27	40.71	329	1	98	0	1	86.0	196.7	-5.3	80	6	2,000,000	0	0.0	2.0
C / 5.4	13.7	1.27	39.45	401	1	98	0	1	86.0	193.4	-5.4	77	6	500	50	5.0	2.0
C / 5.3	13.7	1.27	37.58	92	1	98	0	1	86.0	186.2	-5.6	70	6	500	50	0.0	2.0
C / 5.3	13.7	1.27	37.55	205	1	98	0	1	86.0	186.4	-5.6	70	8	500	50	0.0	2.0
C / 5.4	13.7	1.27	39.68	124	1	98	0	1	86.0	194.0	-5.4	78	6	5,000	0	0.0	2.0
B- / 7.7	8.4	1.03	10.26	18	1	98	0	1	63.0	55.5	-10.9	34	N/A	2,000,000	0	0.0	2.0
B- / 7.7	8.4	1.03	9.85	16	1	98	0	1	63.0	53.4	-11.0	30	N/A	500	50	5.8	2.0
B- / 7.6	8.4	1.03	9.01	8	1	98	0	1	63.0	49.7	-11.1	25	N/A	500	50	0.0	2.0
B- / 7.6	8.4	1.03	8.99	3	1	98	0	1	63.0	49.8	-11.1	25	N/A	500	50	0.0	2.0
B- / 7.7	8.4	1.03	10.04	5	1	98	0	1	63.0	54.1	-10.9	31	N/A	5,000	0	0.0	2.0
B+ / 9.0	7.4	0.91	15.37	116	0	99	0	1	93.0	80.1	-11.1	90	1	2,000,000	0	0.0	2.0
B+ / 9.0	7.4	0.90	15.37	156	0	99	0	1	93.0	77.7	-11.1	88	1	500	50	5.8	2.0
B+ / 9.0	7.4	0.91	15.08	38	0	99	0	1	93.0	73.4	-11.4	83	1	500	50	0.0	2.0
B+ / 9.0	7.4	0.91	15.10	10	0	99	0	1	93.0	73.6	-11.4	83	1	500	50	0.0	2.0
B+ / 9.0	7.4	0.91	15.41	24	0	99	0	1	93.0	78.3	-11.1	88	1	5,000	0	0.0	2.0
C+ / 6.8	9.8	1.15	14.59	48	1	98	0	1	70.0	60.3	-9.8	30	1	2,000,000	0	0.0	2.0
C+ / 6.8	9.8	1.15	14.16	113	1	98	0	1	70.0	58.7	-9.8	28	1	500	50	5.8	2.0
C+ / 6.7	9.8	1.16	13.30	74	1	98	0	1	70.0	55.2	-10.0	23	1	500	50	0.0	2.0
C+ / 6.8	9.8	1.16	13.31	18	1	98	0	1	70.0	55.3	-10.1	23	1	500	50	0.0	2.0
C+ / 5.6	9.7	1.13	14.16	N/A	1	98	0	1	70.0	58.7	-9.8	30	N/A	5,000	0	0.0	2.0
C+ / 6.2	11.9	1.02	10.20	275	1	98	0	1	85.0	85.6	-6.8	18	1	500	50	5.8	2.0
C+ / 6.1	12.0	1.03	9.29	53	1	98	0	1	85.0	81.3	-6.9	14	1	500	50	0.0	2.0
C+ / 6.1	11.9	1.02	9.29	19	1	98	0	1	85.0	81.3	-6.9	14	1	500	50	0.0	2.0
C+ / 6.2	11.9	1.02	10.90	80	1	98	0	1	85.0	88.0	-6.6	21	1	2,000,000	0	0.0	2.0
C+ / 6.2	11.9	1.02	10.47	1	1	98	0	1	85.0	86.6	-6.8	19	1	5,000	0	0.0	2.0
C- / 3.9	10.6	0.91	12.91	478	3	96	0	1	60.0	112.6	-13.4	84	1	500	50	5.8	2.0
C- / 3.4	10.5	0.90	12.06	125	3	96	0	1	60.0	109.3	-13.6	82	1	500	50	0.0	2.0
C- / 3.4	15.3	1.08	12.06	130	3	96	0	1	60.0	109.4	-13.6	56	1	500	50	0.0	2.0
C- / 3.8	10.5	0.91	13.19	76	3	96	0	1	60.0	116.0	-13.3	88	1	2,000,000	0	0.0	2.0
C+ / 6.7	13.6	0.90	18.14	21	2	97	0	1	118.0	134.6	-8.0	85	N/A	500	50	5.8	2.0
C+ / 6.7	13.6	0.90	17.78	9	2	97	0	1	118.0	130.3	-8.0	80	N/A	500	50	0.0	2.0
C+ / 6.7	13.7	0.90	17.78	27	2	97	0	1	118.0	130.3	-8.0	79	N/A	500	50	0.0	2.0
C+ / 6.7	13.7	0.90	18.34	24	2	97	0	1	118.0	137.0	-8.0	87	N/A	2,000,000	0	0.0	2.0
C+ / 6.7	13.6	0.90	18.27	3	2	97	0	1	118.0	136.2	-8.0	86	N/A	5,000	0	0.0	2.0
C- / 4.1	15.7	1.02	17.49	170	4	95	0	1	91.0	118.9	-10.4	43	N/A	500	50	5.8	2.0
C- / 4.1	15.7	1.02	15.74	12	4	95	0	1	91.0	113.6	-10.7	34	N/A	500	50	0.0	2.0
C- / 4.1	15.7	1.02	15.76	16	4	95	0	1	91.0	113.6	-10.6	34	N/A	500	50	0.0	2.0
C- / 4.2	15.7	1.02	18.80	410	4	95	0	1	91.0	121.3	-10.4	46	N/A	2,000,000	0	0.0	2.0
C- / 4.1	15.7	1.02	17.96	25	4	95	0	1	91.0	119.5	-10.5	44	N/A	5,000	0	0.0	2.0

Fund Type	Fund Name	Ticker Symbol	Overall Weiss Investment Rating	Phone	Perfor- mance Rating/Pts	3 Mo	6 Mo	1Yr / Pct	3Yr / Pct	5Yr / Pct	Dividend Yield	Expense Ratio
	99 Pct = Best 0 Pct = Worst				**PERFORMANCE** Total Return % through 6/30/06 — Annualized						Incl. in Returns	
SC	● BlackRock-Small Cap Val A	PSEIX	E+	(888) 825-2257	C+ / 6.7	-3.39	6.13	9.10 /41	18.76 /75	9.89 /80	1.03	1.32
SC	● BlackRock-Small Cap Val B	CCVBX	E+	(888) 825-2257	C+ / 6.9	-3.57	5.64	8.19 /34	17.84 /72	9.07 /77	1.08	2.11
SC	● BlackRock-Small Cap Val Blrk	BSEBX	B	(888) 825-2257	B- / 7.4	-3.31	6.31	9.32 /42	19.13 /76	10.31 /82	1.10	1.05
SC	● BlackRock-Small Cap Val C	BSCCX	E+	(888) 825-2257	C+ / 6.9	-3.57	5.73	8.29 /35	17.87 /72	9.06 /77	1.09	2.03
SC	● BlackRock-Small Cap Val Inst	PNSEX	D-	(888) 825-2257	B- / 7.4	-3.23	6.38	9.51 /43	19.21 /77	10.35 /82	1.12	0.80
SC	● BlackRock-Small Cap Val Svc	PSESX	E+	(888) 825-2257	B- / 7.3	-3.37	6.17	9.15 /41	18.81 /76	10.00 /80	1.11	1.27
SC	BlackRock-Small/Mid Gro A	SCGAX	E	(888) 825-2257	C- / 3.4	-5.53	3.70	14.87 /71	12.57 /46	5.92 /61	0.00	1.35
SC	BlackRock-Small/Mid Gro B	SRCBX	E+	(888) 825-2257	C- / 3.8	-5.70	3.28	14.00 /68	11.78 /41	5.21 /56	0.00	2.10
SC	BlackRock-Small/Mid Gro Inst	SSEGX	D-	(888) 825-2257	C / 4.6	-5.38	3.92	15.28 /73	12.92 /48	6.26 /63	0.00	0.96
SC	BlackRock-Small/Mid Gro Svc	SSPSX	D	(888) 825-2257	C / 4.4	-5.53	3.70	14.96 /72	12.57 /46	5.92 /61	0.00	1.35
AG	BlackRock-U.S Opportunities A	BMEAX	B+	(888) 825-2257	B+ / 8.4	-3.45	10.91	24.05 /87	23.66 /89	4.13 /47	0.00	1.60
AG	BlackRock-U.S Opportunities B	BRMBX	B+	(888) 825-2257	B+ / 8.6	-3.62	10.50	23.17 /86	22.74 /87	3.35 /40	0.00	2.25
AG	BlackRock-U.S Opportunities C	BMECX	B+	(888) 825-2257	B+ / 8.6	-3.59	10.51	23.19 /86	22.74 /87	3.34 /40	0.00	2.25
AG	BlackRock-U.S Opportunities Inst	BMCIX	A-	(888) 825-2257	B+ / 8.9	-3.33	11.16	24.60 /88	24.15 /90	4.58 /51	0.00	1.09
AG	BlackRock-U.S Opportunities Svc	BMCSX	A-	(888) 825-2257	B+ / 8.8	-3.42	10.93	24.22 /87	23.78 /89	4.35 /49	0.00	1.55
GR	Blue Chip Investor Fund	BCIFX	C	(800) 710-5777	C- / 3.1	-0.40	1.81	6.27 /22	9.61 /25	--	0.02	1.45
FO	BNY Hamilton Intl Equity Inst	BNUIX	B+	(800) 426-9363	B+ / 8.5	-0.07	9.11	25.90 /90	21.46 /84	6.16 /62	1.36	0.84
GR	BNY Hamilton Large Cap Value Inst	BCPVX	B	(800) 426-9363	C+ / 6.1	1.29	7.32	13.93 /68	13.74 /53	6.74 /65	1.52	0.80
IN	BNY Hamilton Lrg Cap Equity A	BNEIX	C	(800) 426-9363	D+ / 2.9	-1.48	3.98	9.28 /42	10.57 /31	2.52 /32	0.88	1.04
IN	BNY Hamilton Lrg Cap Equity Inst	BNQIX	C+	(800) 426-9363	C- / 4.2	-1.41	4.17	9.52 /43	10.87 /34	2.78 /35	1.16	0.79
GR	BNY Hamilton Lrg Cap Gr A	BLCGX	E-	(800) 426-9363	E- / 0.1	-5.58	-2.75	1.38 / 3	4.01 / 2	-2.75 / 6	0.00	1.08
GR	BNY Hamilton Lrg Cap Gr Inst	BNLIX	E-	(800) 426-9363	E / 0.3	-5.65	-2.72	1.47 / 3	3.84 / 2	-2.75 / 6	0.19	0.82
IN	BNY Hamilton Multi-Cap Equity Fd	BKMCX	C+		C / 4.4	-1.25	4.14	7.73 /31	13.38 /51	0.75 /19	0.61	1.25
GR	BNY Hamilton S&P 500 Index Inst	BNSPX	C	(800) 426-9363	C- / 3.8	-1.54	2.55	8.26 /35	10.78 /33	2.08 /28	1.54	0.35
SC	BNY Hamilton Small Cap Gr A	BNSVX	E	(800) 426-9363	D- / 1.4	-6.02	4.05	1.75 / 4	9.30 /23	0.92 /20	0.00	1.16
SC	BNY Hamilton Small Cap Gr Inst	BNSIX	E	(800) 426-9363	D+ / 2.5	-5.98	4.12	1.99 / 4	9.45 /24	1.02 /20	0.00	0.91
SC	● Bogle Small Cap Inst	BOGIX	B	(877) 264-5346	B+ / 8.7	-6.24	8.42	25.14 /89	22.99 /87	12.83 /88	0.00	1.25
SC	● Bogle Small Cap Inv	BOGLX	B	(877) 264-5346	B+ / 8.6	-6.31	8.32	24.97 /88	22.87 /87	12.73 /88	0.00	1.35
BA	Boston Balanced Fund	BMGFX	C-	(866) 811-0215	D / 1.7	-0.69	1.90	4.84 /14	7.24 /11	5.39 /57	1.77	1.00
IN	Boston Equity Fund	BEQFX	U	(866) 811-0215	U /	-1.45	2.35	5.94 /20	--	--	0.69	1.00
GR	Boston Ptrs All Cap Value Inst	BPAIX	A	(800) 261-4073	B- / 7.2	-1.42	3.30	8.40 /36	18.29 /74	--	0.50	0.95
GR	Boston Ptrs All Cap Value Inv	BPAVX	A	(800) 261-4073	B- / 7.0	-1.55	3.18	8.03 /33	18.00 /72	--	0.34	1.20
AA	● Boston Ptrs Long/Short Equity Inst	BPLSX	C-	(888) 261-4073	C- / 3.5	8.52	1.71	9.24 /42	9.48 /24	6.59 /65	0.00	2.50
AA	● Boston Ptrs Long/Short Equity Inv	BPLEX	D+	(888) 261-4073	C- / 3.4	8.55	1.61	9.07 /40	9.23 /22	6.33 /63	0.00	2.75
GI	Boston Ptrs Lrg Cap Value Inst	BPLAX	C+	(888) 261-4073	C+ / 6.5	-0.92	4.32	13.95 /68	15.41 /61	6.51 /64	0.98	0.75
GI	Boston Ptrs Lrg Cap Value Inv	BPLIX	C+	(888) 261-4073	C+ / 6.3	-0.97	4.24	13.72 /67	15.13 /59	6.24 /63	0.78	1.00
MC	Boston Ptrs Mid Cp Val Inst	BPMIX	C	(888) 261-4073	C+ / 6.9	-2.85	2.37	9.11 /41	17.66 /71	10.18 /81	0.15	1.00
MC	Boston Ptrs Mid Cp Val Inv	BPMCX	C	(888) 261-4073	C+ / 6.8	-2.90	2.33	8.92 /40	17.40 /70	9.93 /80	0.00	1.25
SC	● Boston Ptrs Sm Cap Value II Inst	BPSIX	C	(888) 261-4073	B- / 7.0	-4.44	3.21	10.08 /47	17.80 /72	12.07 /87	0.27	1.55
SC	● Boston Ptrs Sm Cap Value II Inv	BPSCX	C	(888) 261-4073	C+ / 6.8	-4.48	3.08	9.77 /45	17.51 /70	11.79 /86	0.03	1.80
MC	Boyar Value Fund	BOYAX	D+	(800) 266-5566	E+ / 0.8	-0.32	3.90	2.94 / 7	6.92 /10	4.51 /50	0.26	1.75
GR	Boyle Marathon Fund	BFUNX	E-	(888) 882-6953	E+ / 0.7	-8.46	-3.24	-0.80 / 1	6.52 / 8	-4.33 / 3	0.00	3.00
FO	Brandes Instl Intl Equity Fund	BIIEX	A+	(800) 237-7119	A / 9.3	0.21	9.36	25.82 /89	26.07 /92	12.09 /87	1.12	1.14
MC	Brandywine Advisors	BWAFX	D+	(800) 656-3017	C+ / 5.7	-5.99	2.20	13.28 /65	13.98 /54	4.82 /53	0.00	1.20
GR	Brandywine Blue Fund Inc.	BLUEX	C+	(800) 656-3017	C+ / 5.9	-4.31	2.94	10.22 /48	14.71 /57	5.54 /58	0.00	1.10
★ GR	Brandywine Fund Inc.	BRWIX	C+	(800) 656-3017	C+ / 6.5	-5.24	3.57	14.10 /68	15.57 /62	4.16 /47	0.00	1.07
GR	Brazos Growth Portfolio B	BMUBX	E+	(800) 426-9157	D / 2.1	-7.00	2.05	10.54 /51	10.21 /29	-2.25 / 7	0.00	2.20
GR	Brazos Growth Portfolio N	BMUAX	D-	(800) 426-9157	C- / 3.3	-6.84	2.38	11.24 /55	10.92 /35	-1.64 / 9	0.00	1.55
GR	Brazos Growth Portfolio Y	BJGRX	D	(800) 426-9157	C- / 3.5	-6.74	2.51	11.62 /57	11.31 /38	-1.16 /11	0.00	1.20
SC	Brazos Micro Cap Portfolio B	BMCBX	D	(800) 426-9157	C+ / 5.8	-7.65	7.98	13.47 /66	15.17 /60	0.78 /19	0.00	2.53
SC	Brazos Micro Cap Portfolio N	BMIAX	D+	(800) 426-9157	C+ / 6.7	-7.49	8.33	14.18 /69	15.90 /63	1.45 /23	0.00	1.88
SC	Brazos Micro Cap Portfolio Y	BJMIX	D+	(800) 426-9157	C+ / 6.8	-7.42	8.50	14.57 /70	16.29 /65	1.75 /25	0.00	1.58

● Denotes fund is closed to new investors
★ Denotes fund is included in Section II

RISK			NET ASSETS		ASSET					BULL / BEAR		FUND MANAGER		MINIMUMS		LOADS	
	3 Year		NAV						Portfolio	Last Bull	Last Bear	Manager	Manager	Initial	Additional	Front	Back
Risk	Standard		As of	Total	Cash	Stocks	Bonds	Other	Turnover	Market	Market	Quality	Tenure	Purch.	Purch.	End	End
Rating/Pts	Deviation	Beta	6/30/06	$(Mil)	%	%	%	%	Ratio	Return	Return	Pct	(Years)	$	$	Load	Load
E- /0.1	12.5	0.82	12.81	29	4	96	0	0	133.0	116.8	-6.8	83	4	500	50	5.8	2.0
E- /0.0	12.6	0.83	11.06	9	4	96	0	0	133.0	111.8	-7.0	76	4	500	50	0.0	2.0
B- /7.2	12.6	0.83	13.15	5	4	96	0	0	133.0	118.9	-6.7	84	4	5,000,000	0	0.0	2.0
E- /0.0	12.6	0.83	11.07	5	4	96	0	0	133.0	112.0	-7.0	76	4	500	50	0.0	2.0
E- /0.2	12.6	0.83	13.17	50	4	96	0	0	133.0	119.3	-6.7	85	4	2,000,000	0	0.0	2.0
E- /0.1	12.6	0.83	12.90	4	4	96	0	0	133.0	117.4	-6.8	82	4	5,000	0	0.0	2.0
D+ /2.8	15.9	0.99	14.86	216	2	97	0	1	122.0	99.2	-12.3	13	1	500	50	5.8	2.0
D+ /2.8	15.9	0.99	13.24	25	2	97	0	1	122.0	95.0	-12.6	10	1	500	50	0.0	2.0
C- /3.4	15.9	0.98	15.64	28	2	97	0	1	122.0	101.0	-12.2	15	1	2,000,000	0	0.0	2.0
C- /4.2	15.9	0.99	14.86	N/A	2	97	0	1	122.0	99.2	-12.3	13	1	5,000	0	0.0	2.0
C+ /6.5	13.4	1.53	28.27	67	6	93	0	1	94.0	139.9	-11.4	96	8	500	50	5.8	2.0
C+ /6.5	13.4	1.53	26.63	37	6	93	0	1	94.0	134.2	-11.6	95	N/A	500	50	0.0	2.0
C+ /6.5	13.4	1.53	26.61	35	6	93	0	1	94.0	134.1	-11.6	95	8	500	50	0.0	2.0
C+ /6.5	13.4	1.53	29.28	17	6	93	0	1	94.0	143.0	-11.3	97	N/A	2,000,000	0	0.0	2.0
C+ /6.5	13.4	1.53	28.52	2	6	93	0	1	94.0	140.5	-11.4	96	N/A	5,000	0	0.0	2.0
B /8.7	8.2	0.85	106.34	24	6	93	0	1	93.8	54.2	-11.0	54	N/A	5,000	100	0.0	0.0
C+ /6.1	10.3	1.01	13.77	367	0	99	0	1	17.0	115.4	-8.9	28	N/A	1,000,000	0	0.0	2.0
B /8.2	9.0	1.06	11.91	343	0	99	0	1	43.0	73.1	-6.4	74	6	1,000,000	0	0.0	0.0
B /8.6	7.1	0.87	13.84	28	0	99	0	1	52.0	57.1	-5.4	62	N/A	2,000	100	5.3	1.0
B /8.6	7.1	0.87	13.88	355	0	99	0	1	52.0	58.4	-5.3	65	N/A	1,000,000	0	0.0	0.0
C- /3.1	8.1	0.99	7.44	8	0	99	0	1	101.0	35.8	-8.6	8	N/A	2,000	100	5.3	1.0
C- /3.2	8.1	0.98	7.52	172	0	99	0	1	101.0	35.3	-8.5	8	N/A	1,000,000	0	0.0	0.0
B /8.7	8.2	0.96	15.85	66	0	99	0	1	10.0	75.9	-9.5	79	N/A	2,000	100	5.3	1.0
B- /7.8	7.7	1.00	8.11	124	2	97	0	1	49.0	63.0	-9.8	51	6	1,000,000	0	0.0	0.0
C- /3.8	15.3	1.02	15.15	15	3	96	0	1	77.0	63.1	-11.2	3	N/A	2,000	100	5.3	1.0
C- /3.8	15.3	1.02	15.40	246	3	96	0	1	77.0	63.9	-11.1	4	N/A	1,000,000	0	0.0	0.0
C+ /5.9	16.1	1.05	28.83	208	2	97	0	1	66.4	155.1	-7.2	84	7	1,000,000	5,000	0.0	0.0
C+ /5.9	16.2	1.05	28.64	157	2	97	0	1	66.4	154.3	-7.3	83	7	1,000	250	0.0	0.0
B+ /9.5	5.0	0.98	28.91	160	4	73	21	2	29.8	33.2	-1.0	53	11	100,000	1,000	0.0	0.0
U /	N/A	N/A	12.21	49	2	97	0	1	20.4	N/A	N/A	N/A	N/A	100,000	1,000	0.0	0.0
B /8.7	8.5	1.01	15.32	9	6	93	0	1	28.7	105.4	-7.9	96	4	100,000	5,000	0.0	1.0
B /8.7	8.6	1.02	15.26	4	6	93	0	1	28.7	104.1	-8.0	95	4	2,500	100	0.0	1.0
C+ /6.9	6.4	-0.17	17.20	83	32	67	0	1	107.1	20.6	-2.2	98	N/A	100,000	5,000	0.0	1.0
C+ /6.8	6.4	-0.17	17.02	19	32	67	0	1	107.1	19.6	-2.3	98	N/A	2,500	100	0.0	1.0
C+ /6.4	8.2	0.97	14.01	28	0	99	0	1	76.9	83.6	-8.8	90	9	100,000	5,000	0.0	1.0
C+ /6.5	8.2	0.98	14.25	20	0	99	0	1	76.9	82.3	-9.0	89	9	2,500	100	0.0	1.0
C /4.8	10.4	0.92	12.94	28	4	95	0	1	74.1	101.0	-7.6	64	N/A	100,000	5,000	0.0	1.0
C /4.7	10.4	0.92	12.71	5	4	95	0	1	74.1	99.4	-7.6	62	N/A	2,500	100	0.0	1.0
C /5.3	12.0	0.78	22.81	128	5	94	0	1	37.6	127.7	-9.4	81	8	100,000	5,000	0.0	1.0
C /5.2	12.0	0.78	22.40	260	5	94	0	1	37.6	125.9	-9.4	79	8	2,500	100	0.0	1.0
B+ /9.5	5.9	0.49	15.44	30	23	76	0	1	9.0	47.0	-7.9	28	8	5,000	1,000	5.0	2.0
C- /4.2	15.7	1.61	7.47	2	1	98	0	1	65.7	49.5	-10.2	2	8	500	100	0.0	0.0
B- /7.3	10.4	0.97	23.48	776	0	99	0	1	20.9	153.3	-11.6	76	N/A	1,000,000	0	0.0	0.0
C- /4.0	14.0	1.15	10.67	191	2	97	0	1	206.8	89.8	-6.8	10	6	10,000	1,000	0.0	0.0
C+ /6.8	12.4	1.34	30.45	1,665	2	97	0	1	180.5	84.8	-4.8	59	15	10,000	1,000	0.0	0.0
C+ /6.3	13.6	1.45	32.20	4,128	2	97	0	1	183.4	95.9	-8.1	57	N/A	10,000	1,000	0.0	0.0
C /5.2	14.3	1.46	15.42	2	9	90	0	1	310.0	66.3	-6.0	15	10	2,500	100	0.0	4.0
C /5.2	14.3	1.46	15.94	43	9	90	0	1	310.0	69.7	-5.8	19	10	2,500	100	0.0	0.0
C /5.2	14.3	1.46	16.33	17	9	90	0	1	310.0	71.7	-5.7	21	10	1,000,000	1,000	0.0	0.0
D+ /2.9	19.6	1.22	21.37	3	7	92	0	1	235.0	114.4	-7.8	9	9	2,500	100	0.0	4.0
D+ /2.9	19.6	1.22	22.11	8	7	92	0	1	235.0	118.4	-7.6	11	9	2,500	100	0.0	0.0
C- /3.0	19.6	1.22	22.46	84	7	92	0	1	235.0	121.0	-7.6	12	9	1,000,000	1,000	0.0	0.0

Fund Type	Fund Name	Ticker Symbol	Overall Weiss Investment Rating	Phone	Perfor-mance Rating/Pts	3 Mo	6 Mo	1Yr / Pct	3Yr / Pct	5Yr / Pct	Dividend Yield	Expense Ratio
								Total Return % through 6/30/06			Incl. in Returns	
									Annualized			
GR	Brazos Mid Cap Portfolio N	BMCNX	D-	(800) 426-9157	C- / 3.2	-6.30	1.50	8.01 /33	10.24 /29	0.89 /20	0.00	1.55
GR	Brazos Mid Cap Portfolio Y	BJMCX	D-	(800) 426-9157	C- / 3.4	-6.30	1.64	8.26 /35	10.60 /32	1.27 /22	0.00	1.20
SC	Brazos Small Cap Portfolio B		E+	(800) 426-9157	D+ / 2.3	-6.26	4.70	11.14 /54	9.78 /26	-0.95 /12	0.00	2.30
SC	Brazos Small Cap Portfolio N	BSMAX	E+	(800) 426-9157	C- / 3.4	-6.11	5.07	11.92 /59	10.46 /30	-0.32 /14	0.00	1.65
SC	Brazos Small Cap Portfolio Y	BJSCX	D-	(800) 426-9157	C- / 3.6	-6.07	5.20	12.23 /61	10.80 /34	0.14 /16	0.00	1.35
GR	Bremer Growth Stock Fund	BSTKX	D	(800) 595-5552	D / 1.9	-3.19	0.55	5.67 /18	7.95 /15	-0.96 /12	0.44	1.00
GI	Bridges Investment Fund	BRGIX	E+	(800) 939-8401	D / 1.8	-4.67	-3.39	3.19 / 8	8.47 /18	0.90 /20	0.73	0.84
AG	● Bridgeway Aggressive Investor 1	BRAGX	C-	(800) 661-3550	B / 8.2	-1.35	9.91	21.81 /84	19.96 /79	10.45 /82	0.00	1.66
AG	Bridgeway Aggressive Investor 2	BRAIX	C-	(800) 661-3550	B / 8.0	-4.83	7.01	21.65 /84	20.32 /80	--	0.00	1.23
BA	Bridgeway Balanced Fund	BRBPX	C+	(800) 661-3550	C- / 3.2	1.12	4.03	7.83 /31	9.33 /23	5.87 /60	0.85	0.94
GR	Bridgeway Blue-Chip 35 Index Fund	BRLIX	D+	(800) 661-3550	D / 1.7	-0.41	1.84	6.64 /24	6.89 /10	1.28 /22	1.47	0.15
GR	Bridgeway Large Cap Growth N	BRLGX	U	(800) 661-3550	U /	-5.17	0.33	10.09 /47	--	--	0.00	0.84
GR	Bridgeway Large Cap Value N	BRLVX	U	(800) 661-3550	U /	-1.50	6.35	14.69 /71	--	--	1.03	0.84
SC	● Bridgeway Micro-Cap Ltd	BRMCX	D	(800) 661-3550	B / 7.6	-8.78	1.37	12.97 /64	19.96 /79	13.50 /89	0.00	1.67
SC	Bridgeway Small Cap Growth N	BRSGX	U	(800) 661-3550	U /	-4.16	8.86	22.20 /85	--	--	0.00	0.82
SC	Bridgeway Small Cap Value N	BRSVX	U	(800) 661-3550	U /	-1.78	11.79	25.25 /89	--	--	0.00	0.76
SC	● Bridgeway Ultra Small Company	BRUSX	C-	(800) 661-3550	A / 9.4	-2.17	18.00	25.58 /89	26.85 /93	25.83 /99	0.00	1.08
SC	Bridgeway Ultra SmComp Market	BRSIX	C+	(800) 661-3550	B / 8.2	-6.52	5.52	15.08 /72	21.65 /84	22.39 /98	0.15	0.66
GR	Brown Advisory Growth Equity Inst	BIAGX	D+	(800) 540-6807	D- / 1.5	-3.86	1.01	4.80 /14	7.24 /11	-0.38 /14	0.00	1.13
FO	Brown Advisory International Inst	BIANX	A+	(800) 540-6807	B+ / 8.8	0.07	9.00	26.22 /90	22.18 /86	--	0.89	1.33
SC	Brown Advisory Small Cp Val	BIACX	U	(800) 540-6807	U /	-6.10	5.71	12.72 /63	--	--	0.02	1.30
SC	Brown Advisory Small-Cap Gr A	BIAAX	D-	(800) 540-6807	C- / 3.5	-8.15	0.47	7.52 /29	12.20 /44	--	0.00	1.85
SC	Brown Advisory Small-Cap Gr Inst	BIASX	D-	(800) 540-6807	C / 4.4	-8.07	0.62	7.96 /32	12.50 /46	-1.70 / 9	0.00	1.23
GR	Brown Advisory Value Equity Inst	BIAVX	B-	(800) 540-6807	C / 4.6	-2.20	2.49	7.24 /28	12.40 /45	--	1.29	1.02
BA	Brown Capital Mgmt-Balanced	BCBIX	D-	(800) 525-3683	E / 0.5	-5.92	-2.67	1.90 / 4	5.18 / 4	-0.67 /13	0.47	1.20
AG	Brown Capital Mgmt-Equity	BCEIX	E+	(800) 525-3683	E+ / 0.7	-7.72	-3.49	2.18 / 5	6.24 / 7	-2.44 / 7	0.00	1.20
MC	Brown Capital Mgmt-Mid Cap Inv	BCMVX	D-	(800) 525-3683	C- / 3.1	-7.37	0.00	6.26 /22	10.50 /31	--	0.00	1.55
SC	Brown Capital Mgmt-Small Company	BCSIX	D-	(800) 525-3683	C / 4.4	-4.27	6.95	13.91 /68	11.03 /36	0.61 /18	0.00	1.18
GR	Bruce Fund		A+	(800) 872-7823	A+ / 9.7	0.07	12.52	18.36 /80	33.71 /97	29.74 /99	0.10	0.93
BA	Buffalo Balanced Fund	BUFBX	B+	(800) 492-8332	C+ / 5.6	2.31	7.71	11.82 /58	13.24 /50	5.76 /59	2.79	1.03
GR	Buffalo Large Cap Fund	BUFEX	D	(800) 492-8332	D- / 1.5	-3.57	-0.39	5.31 /17	7.75 /14	-0.50 /14	0.09	1.04
SC	Buffalo Micro Cap Fund	BUFOX	U	(800) 492-8332	U /	-8.23	1.39	11.22 /55	--	--	0.00	1.51
MC	Buffalo Mid Cap Fund	BUFMX	C+	(800) 492-8332	C+ / 6.1	-8.21	-2.00	9.93 /46	16.62 /66	--	0.00	1.02
TC	Buffalo Science & Technology Fund	BUFTX	C	(800) 492-8332	C+ / 6.9	-7.76	1.68	13.59 /67	17.79 /72	3.35 /40	0.00	1.03
SC	● Buffalo Small Cap Fund	BUFSX	C	(800) 492-8332	C+ / 6.9	-9.40	2.24	6.34 /22	19.17 /76	10.55 /82	0.00	1.01
GL	Buffalo USA Global Fund	BUFGX	C-	(800) 492-8332	C- / 3.3	-3.43	0.92	7.14 /27	10.84 /34	1.92 /26	0.23	1.04
MC	Bull Moose Growth Fund	BULLX	C+	(877) 322-0576	B- / 7.0	-2.66	2.81	12.87 /64	17.10 /68	--	0.13	1.32
FS	Burnham Financial Industries A	BURFX	U	(800) 874-3863	U /	0.83	5.73	11.34 /56	--	--	0.75	1.81
FS	Burnham Financial Services A	BURKX	E+	(800) 874-3863	C / 4.6	1.40	5.96	10.53 /50	13.37 /51	15.57 /93	0.89	1.60
FS	Burnham Financial Services B	BURMX	E+	(800) 874-3863	C / 4.9	1.18	5.55	9.65 /44	12.54 /46	14.71 /91	0.20	2.35
GI	Burnham Fund A	BURHX	E	(800) 874-3863	E+ / 0.7	-1.46	-2.30	4.93 /15	7.08 /11	-0.68 /13	0.32	1.39
GI	Burnham Fund B	BURIX	E	(800) 874-3863	E+ / 0.9	-1.63	-2.64	4.20 /11	6.30 / 8	-1.40 /10	0.00	2.14
GR	C & B Core Equity Fd Inst	CBCEX	C+	(866) 777-7818	C- / 4.2	-2.14	2.56	9.25 /42	11.26 /37	--	0.64	0.94
GI	C/Fund		C-	(800) 338-9477	D / 1.6	0.81	3.32	7.92 /32	6.24 / 7	4.90 /53	0.31	2.00
GR	Calamos Blue Chip Fund A	CBCAX	U	(800) 823-7386	U /	-2.39	0.94	7.06 /27	--	--	0.00	1.46
CV	● Calamos Convertible Fund A	CCVIX	D-	(800) 823-7386	D / 1.8	-0.99	2.92	8.80 /39	8.75 /19	6.11 /62	4.76	1.12
CV	Calamos Convertible Fund B	CALBX	D-	(800) 823-7386	D- / 1.4	-1.17	2.60	8.05 /33	7.96 /15	5.33 /57	3.60	1.87
CV	Calamos Convertible Fund C	CCVCX	D-	(800) 823-7386	D / 2.0	-1.17	2.58	8.06 /33	7.96 /15	5.32 /57	4.23	1.87
CV	Calamos Convertible Fund I	CICVX	D	(800) 823-7386	D+ / 2.8	-0.97	3.05	9.08 /41	9.03 /21	6.36 /63	5.48	0.87
GL	Calamos Global Growth & Income A	CVLOX	C+	(800) 823-7386	C+ / 5.6	-2.06	3.53	21.35 /83	14.13 /55	8.63 /75	3.23	1.44
GL	Calamos Global Growth & Income B	CVLDX	C+	(800) 823-7386	C / 5.0	-2.36	3.11	20.33 /82	13.19 /50	7.77 /70	2.71	2.19
GL	Calamos Global Growth & Income C	CVLCX	C+	(800) 823-7386	C+ / 5.7	-2.27	3.21	20.43 /82	13.22 /50	7.80 /71	2.90	2.19

● Denotes fund is closed to new investors
* Denotes fund is included in Section II

www.WeissRatings.com

RISK			NET ASSETS		ASSET				Portfolio Turnover Ratio	BULL / BEAR		FUND MANAGER		MINIMUMS		LOADS	
Risk Rating/Pts	3 Year Standard Deviation	Beta	NAV As of 6/30/06	Total $(Mil)	Cash %	Stocks %	Bonds %	Other %		Last Bull Market Return	Last Bear Market Return	Manager Quality Pct	Manager Tenure (Years)	Initial Purch. $	Additional Purch. $	Front End Load	Back End Load
C /4.8	13.7	1.41	10.85	35	10	89	0	1	285.0	67.4	-5.1	17	7	2,500	100	0.0	0.0
C /4.8	13.7	1.40	11.16	19	10	89	0	1	285.0	69.1	-5.0	20	7	1,000,000	1,000	0.0	0.0
C /5.0	16.6	1.04	18.26	1	10	89	0	1	204.0	69.3	-8.5	3	10	2,500	100	0.0	4.0
C- /4.0	16.4	1.03	19.06	4	10	89	0	1	204.0	72.5	-8.3	5	10	2,500	100	0.0	0.0
C- /4.0	16.4	1.03	19.64	25	10	89	0	1	204.0	74.4	-8.3	6	10	1,000,000	1,000	0.0	0.0
C+ /6.9	7.6	0.95	14.55	67	1	98	0	1	16.0	50.7	-9.5	29	9	2,000	100	0.0	0.0
C /5.5	8.7	1.04	33.71	80	2	92	4	2	23.7	63.6	-9.0	27	9	1,000	250	0.0	0.0
C- /3.2	19.3	1.92	61.91	439	0	99	0	1	75.9	143.6	-10.7	55	11	2,000	500	0.0	0.0
C- /3.0	19.4	1.91	17.55	585	0	99	0	1	75.9	144.7	-10.8	60	11	2,000	500	0.0	0.0
B+ /9.9	4.2	0.67	12.65	85	N/A	54	46	N/A	21.6	39.6	1.4	86	5	2,000	500	0.0	0.0
B /8.1	8.0	0.97	7.21	43	0	99	0	1	25.9	45.8	-11.0	21	N/A	2,000	500	0.0	0.0
U /	N/A	N/A	12.11	104	0	100	0	0	17.7	N/A	N/A	N/A	N/A	2,000	500	0.0	0.0
U /	N/A	N/A	14.41	88	3	96	0	1	18.6	N/A	N/A	N/A	N/A	2,000	500	0.0	0.0
D- /1.2	20.6	1.22	11.12	81	1	98	0	1	51.0	161.6	-8.4	32	N/A	2,000	500	0.0	0.0
U /	N/A	N/A	14.75	275	2	97	0	1	23.9	N/A	N/A	N/A	N/A	2,000	500	0.0	0.0
U /	N/A	N/A	16.02	359	5	94	0	1	27.8	N/A	N/A	N/A	N/A	2,000	500	0.0	0.0
D- /1.0	19.2	1.21	42.42	132	2	97	0	1	52.7	200.0	-2.5	88	12	2,000	500	0.0	0.0
C /5.2	15.6	1.03	18.93	1,086	10	89	0	1	8.4	157.8	-1.6	77	9	2,000	500	0.0	2.0
B /8.1	8.9	1.07	8.96	54	0	100	0	0	40.0	51.3	-10.8	18	N/A	5,000	100	0.0	0.0
B- /7.9	10.3	0.97	15.52	290	0	99	0	1	21.0	125.3	N/A	39	N/A	5,000	100	0.0	0.0
U /	N/A	N/A	14.12	114	0	100	0	0	28.0	N/A	N/A	N/A	3	2,000	100	0.0	0.0
C- /4.1	18.0	1.13	21.30	14	0	100	0	0	22.0	96.4	-17.2	5	N/A	2,000	100	3.5	0.0
C- /4.2	17.9	1.12	11.39	122	0	100	0	0	22.0	98.2	-17.2	6	N/A	5,000	100	0.0	0.0
B /8.9	8.2	1.00	13.57	157	0	100	0	0	78.0	77.3	N/A	68	N/A	5,000	100	0.0	0.0
B- /7.8	7.5	1.34	14.90	12	2	73	24	1	65.6	38.8	-6.2	19	14	10,000	500	0.0	0.0
C+ /6.4	10.3	1.21	16.85	12	2	97	0	1	65.6	49.0	-9.8	8	14	10,000	500	0.0	0.0
C /4.6	13.7	1.18	14.58	5	2	97	0	1	80.7	71.8	-9.1	2	4	10,000	500	0.0	0.0
C- /3.3	15.9	0.99	33.41	393	5	94	0	1	10.0	73.7	-11.6	8	14	10,000	500	0.0	0.0
B /8.4	13.0	0.84	408.85	215	28	42	29	1	10.1	207.8	5.4	99	23	1,000	500	0.0	0.0
B+ /9.7	5.3	0.82	10.96	149	6	61	19	14	18.0	71.3	-10.7	96	N/A	2,500	100	0.0	2.0
B- /7.5	8.6	1.01	18.74	50	3	96	0	1	40.0	60.9	-16.1	24	11	2,500	100	0.0	2.0
U /	N/A	N/A	12.37	56	11	88	0	1	50.0	N/A	N/A	N/A	N/A	2,500	100	0.0	2.0
C+ /6.9	13.6	1.15	14.19	351	7	92	0	1	19.0	112.1	-13.6	22	5	2,500	100	0.0	2.0
C /4.7	15.0	1.51	12.13	110	5	94	0	1	46.0	125.1	-18.1	73	5	2,500	100	0.0	2.0
C /5.0	14.9	0.95	26.01	1,879	1	98	0	1	27.0	143.6	-17.2	69	8	2,500	100	0.0	2.0
B- /7.5	10.0	0.63	20.63	68	1	98	0	1	11.0	66.0	-12.6	17	11	2,500	100	0.0	2.0
C+ /5.6	11.4	0.94	14.99	11	9	89	0	2	N/A	N/A	N/A	56	N/A	1,000	500	0.0	0.0
U /	N/A	N/A	12.18	27	0	99	0	1	57.8	N/A	N/A	N/A	N/A	2,500	500	5.0	2.0
D /2.0	8.8	0.79	22.41	100	1	98	0	1	29.2	66.1	2.5	76	7	2,500	500	5.0	2.0
D /1.9	8.8	0.79	21.48	26	1	98	0	1	29.2	62.3	2.3	69	7	2,500	500	0.0	2.0
C /5.2	7.7	0.90	26.35	101	4	95	0	1	25.1	41.6	-6.0	26	11	2,500	500	5.0	2.0
C /5.3	7.7	0.90	26.51	2	4	95	0	1	25.1	38.3	-6.2	21	11	2,500	500	0.0	2.0
B /8.5	8.7	1.05	12.98	55	2	97	0	1	38.6	N/A	N/A	51	3	2,500	500	0.0	0.0
B+ /9.5	6.5	0.78	16.19	4	10	89	0	1	17.6	35.1	-9.0	28	21	0	0	0.0	0.0
U /	N/A	N/A	11.83	96	0	98	0	2	27.7	N/A	N/A	N/A	N/A	2,500	50	4.8	0.5
C+ /5.9	7.6	1.15	19.34	367	0	17	0	83	63.4	46.1	-3.3	63	19	2,500	50	4.8	0.5
C+ /6.3	7.7	1.15	22.29	160	0	17	0	83	63.4	42.7	-3.4	55	6	2,500	50	0.0	5.0
C+ /5.9	7.7	1.15	19.40	323	0	17	0	83	63.4	42.7	-3.5	55	10	2,500	50	0.0	1.0
C+ /6.0	7.6	1.15	18.37	25	0	17	0	83	63.4	47.2	-3.2	66	9	5,000,000	50	0.0	0.0
B- /7.8	8.2	1.31	9.87	408	3	41	0	56	59.0	73.5	-3.3	92	10	2,500	50	4.8	0.5
B- /7.7	8.2	1.32	10.24	54	3	41	0	56	59.0	69.3	-3.4	88	6	2,500	50	0.0	5.0
B- /7.7	8.2	1.30	9.68	238	3	41	0	56	59.0	69.2	-3.4	88	10	2,500	50	0.0	1.0

99 Pct = Best
0 Pct = Worst

Fund Type	Fund Name	Ticker Symbol	Overall Weiss Investment Rating	Phone	Performance Rating/Pts	3 Mo	6 Mo	1Yr / Pct	3Yr / Pct	5Yr / Pct	Dividend Yield	Expense Ratio
GL	Calamos Global Growth & Income I	CGCIX	B-	(800) 823-7386	C+ / 6.4	-2.00	3.68	21.74 /84	14.39 /56	8.91 /76	3.56	1.19
★ GI	Calamos Growth & Income A	CVTRX	C-	(800) 823-7386	C- / 3.2	-3.35	2.30	10.32 /49	11.05 /36	8.30 /73	2.20	1.06
GI	Calamos Growth & Income B	CVTYX	C-	(800) 823-7386	D+ / 2.7	-3.53	1.94	9.50 /43	10.23 /29	7.49 /69	1.32	1.81
★ GI	Calamos Growth & Income C	CVTCX	C-	(800) 823-7386	C- / 3.3	-3.56	1.91	9.45 /43	10.21 /29	7.48 /69	1.57	1.81
GI	Calamos Growth & Income I	CGIIX	C	(800) 823-7386	C / 4.3	-3.32	2.43	10.57 /51	11.34 /38	8.65 /75	2.59	0.81
★ MC	Calamos Growth Fund A	CVGRX	D+	(800) 823-7386	C / 5.3	-6.96	-1.47	11.41 /56	15.55 /62	7.61 /70	0.00	1.20
MC	Calamos Growth Fund B	CVGBX	D	(800) 823-7386	C / 4.8	-7.14	-1.84	10.56 /51	14.69 /57	6.81 /66	0.00	1.95
MC	Calamos Growth Fund C	CVGCX	D+	(800) 823-7386	C / 5.4	-7.14	-1.85	10.57 /51	14.69 /57	6.81 /66	0.00	1.95
MC	Calamos Growth Fund I	CGRIX	C-	(800) 823-7386	C+ / 6.2	-6.90	-1.35	11.69 /58	15.84 /63	7.88 /71	0.00	0.95
FO	Calamos International Growth A	CIGRX	U	(800) 823-7386	U /	-4.05	5.99	26.05 /90	--	--	0.43	1.62
FO	Calamos International Growth C	CIGCX	U	(800) 823-7386	U /	-4.23	5.60	25.13 /89	--	--	0.38	2.37
IN	● Calamos Market Neutral Fund A	CVSIX	E+	(800) 823-7386	E / 0.3	-0.14	3.37	4.95 /15	3.57 / 2	4.84 /53	5.63	1.57
IN	● Calamos Market Neutral Fund B	CAMNX	E+	(800) 823-7386	E- / 0.2	-0.33	2.95	4.12 /11	2.80 / 1	4.06 /46	4.91	2.32
IN	● Calamos Market Neutral Fund C	CVSCX	E+	(800) 823-7386	E / 0.3	-0.32	2.97	4.17 /11	2.81 / 1	4.07 /46	5.14	2.32
IN	● Calamos Market Neutral Fund I	CMNIX	E+	(800) 823-7386	E+ / 0.6	-0.05	3.50	5.34 /17	3.88 / 2	5.39 /57	6.21	1.32
MC	Calamos Value Fund A	CVAAX	C-	(800) 823-7386	C- / 3.3	-3.76	1.54	6.62 /24	11.84 /41	--	0.00	1.47
MC	Calamos Value Fund B	CVABX	C-	(800) 823-7386	D+ / 2.7	-3.97	1.09	5.77 /19	11.03 /36	--	0.00	2.22
MC	Calamos Value Fund C	CVACX	C-	(800) 823-7386	C- / 3.4	-3.97	1.09	5.77 /19	11.00 /35	--	0.00	2.22
MC	Calamos Value Fund I	CVAIX	C+	(800) 823-7386	C / 4.4	-3.72	1.60	6.89 /26	12.15 /43	--	0.00	1.22
AA	Caldwell & Orkin Mkt Opportunity	COAGX	E	(800) 237-7073	E- / 0.0	-0.71	-0.65	0.51 / 2	-1.24 / 0	-0.65 /13	1.11	2.01
IN	California Inv Tr-Eqty Inc Fd	EQTIX	C+	(800) 225-8778	C / 4.4	-1.54	3.00	4.62 /13	12.17 /43	6.18 /62	1.67	0.83
FO	California Inv Tr-Euro Gr&Inc Fd	EUGIX	B	(800) 225-8778	B / 7.9	2.63	9.96	19.42 /81	17.88 /72	6.92 /66	1.97	1.00
GR	California Inv Tr-NASDAQ 100 Ind Fd	NASDX	E+	(800) 225-8778	D / 2.1	-7.49	-4.11	5.33 /17	9.11 /21	-3.21 / 5	0.28	0.74
IX	California Inv Tr-S&P 500 Index Fd	SPFIX	C	(800) 225-8778	C- / 4.0	-1.54	2.54	8.29 /35	10.97 /35	2.40 /31	1.57	0.36
MC	California Inv Tr-S&P MidCp Indx Fd	SPMIX	C+	(800) 225-8778	B- / 7.1	-3.42	3.69	11.96 /59	17.48 /70	8.99 /76	0.84	0.57
SC	California Inv Tr-S&P SmCp Index Fd	SMCIX	B-	(800) 225-8778	B- / 7.2	-4.61	7.48	8.38 /36	18.11 /73	9.49 /79	0.52	0.74
MC	Calvert Capital Accumulation A	CCAFX	E+	(800) 368-2745	D- / 1.4	-5.34	3.61	3.09 / 8	9.12 /21	-0.87 /12	0.00	1.68
MC	Calvert Capital Accumulation B	CWCBX	E+	(800) 368-2745	D- / 1.5	-5.56	3.13	2.20 / 5	8.18 /16	-1.76 / 9	0.00	2.54
MC	Calvert Capital Accumulation C	CCACX	E+	(800) 368-2745	D / 1.6	-5.52	3.18	2.27 / 5	8.24 /16	-1.68 / 9	0.00	2.49
GR	Calvert Large Cap Growth A	CLGAX	C-	(800) 368-2745	C / 4.8	-5.67	-0.66	12.02 /60	14.69 /57	5.28 /56	0.00	1.56
GR	Calvert Large Cap Growth B	CLGBX	C-	(800) 368-2745	C / 4.9	-5.90	-1.11	11.01 /54	13.62 /52	4.27 /48	0.00	1.56
GR	Calvert Large Cap Growth C	CLGCX	C-	(800) 368-2745	C / 4.9	-5.84	-1.03	11.20 /55	13.68 /52	4.29 /49	0.00	2.39
GR	Calvert Large Cap Growth I	CLCIX	C	(800) 368-2745	C+ / 6.1	-5.58	-0.38	12.63 /63	15.36 /60	5.90 /60	0.00	0.97
MC	Calvert Mid Cap Value A	CMVAX	U	(800) 368-2745	U /	-2.04	3.61	6.73 /25	--	--	0.00	1.59
AA	Calvert Moderate Allocation A	CMAAX	U	(800) 368-2745	U /	-1.90	1.81	6.61 /24	--	--	0.85	1.75
SC	Calvert New Vision Small Cap A	CNVAX	E	(800) 368-2745	D / 1.9	-3.46	4.85	5.01 /15	9.65 /25	2.36 /31	0.00	1.74
SC	Calvert New Vision Small Cap B	CNVBX	E	(800) 368-2745	D / 2.0	-3.74	4.32	4.00 /11	8.64 /19	1.38 /23	0.00	2.65
SC	Calvert New Vision Small Cap C	CNVCX	E	(800) 368-2745	D / 2.1	-3.64	4.41	4.16 /11	8.78 /19	1.51 /24	0.00	2.53
SC	Calvert New Vision Small Cap I	CVSMX	C-	(800) 368-2745	C- / 4.0	-3.25	5.27	5.88 /20	11.26 /37	2.80 /35	0.00	0.92
SC	Calvert Small Cap Value A	CCVAX	U	(800) 368-2745	U /	-5.53	4.92	3.76 /10	--	--	0.00	1.69
BA	Calvert Social-Balanced Portf A	CSIFX	C-	(800) 368-2745	E+ / 0.8	-1.59	0.39	4.17 /11	7.38 /12	2.35 /31	1.36	1.22
BA	Calvert Social-Balanced Portf B	CSLBX	C-	(800) 368-2745	E+ / 0.9	-1.85	-0.09	3.15 / 8	6.30 / 8	1.31 /22	0.45	2.20
BA	Calvert Social-Balanced Portf C	CSGCX	C-	(800) 368-2745	E+ / 0.9	-1.96	-0.18	3.07 / 7	6.31 / 8	1.32 /22	0.50	2.16
BA	Calvert Social-Balanced Portf I	CBAIX	C	(800) 368-2745	D / 1.9	-1.51	0.62	4.66 /13	7.82 /14	2.82 /35	1.59	0.72
AA	Calvert Social-Enhanced Eq A	CMIFX	D	(800) 368-2745	D / 1.7	-2.70	0.86	6.87 /25	9.32 /23	2.88 /36	0.32	1.38
AA	Calvert Social-Enhanced Eq B	CDXBX	D+	(800) 368-2745	D / 1.8	-2.92	0.35	5.92 /20	8.30 /17	1.83 /26	0.00	2.32
AA	Calvert Social-Enhanced Eq C	CMICX	D	(800) 368-2745	D / 1.8	-2.91	0.40	5.89 /20	8.33 /17	1.85 /26	0.00	2.28
GR	Calvert Social-Equity A	CSIEX	D+	(800) 368-2745	D- / 1.1	-2.46	1.25	5.22 /16	7.96 /15	3.21 /39	0.00	1.25
GR	Calvert Social-Equity B	CSEBX	D+	(800) 368-2745	D- / 1.2	-2.69	0.80	4.32 /12	7.06 /11	2.31 /30	0.00	2.09
GR	Calvert Social-Equity C	CSECX	D+	(800) 368-2745	D- / 1.3	-2.63	0.85	4.43 /12	7.13 /11	2.38 /31	0.00	2.01
GR	Calvert Social-Equity I	CEYIX	C-	(800) 368-2745	D+ / 2.3	-2.33	1.51	5.81 /19	8.57 /18	3.75 /43	0.00	0.68
AG	Calvert Social-Index A	CSXAX	D-	(800) 368-2745	D- / 1.2	-3.67	-0.17	6.47 /23	8.32 /17	0.31 /17	0.72	0.75

● Denotes fund is closed to new investors
★ Denotes fund is included in Section II

76

RISK			NET ASSETS		ASSET					BULL / BEAR		FUND MANAGER		MINIMUMS		LOADS	
	3 Year		NAV						Portfolio	Last Bull	Last Bear	Manager	Manager	Initial	Additional	Front	Back
Risk	Standard		As of	Total	Cash	Stocks	Bonds	Other	Turnover	Market	Market	Quality	Tenure	Purch.	Purch.	End	End
Rating/Pts	Deviation	Beta	6/30/06	$(Mil)	%	%	%	%	Ratio	Return	Return	Pct	(Years)	$	$	Load	Load
B- / 7.6	8.2	1.31	9.92	33	3	41	0	56	59.0	74.6	-3.0	92	9	5,000,000	50	0.0	0.0
B- / 7.8	8.9	0.96	31.17	3,384	2	41	1	56	73.1	60.6	-1.4	59	18	2,500	50	4.8	0.5
B- / 7.8	8.9	0.96	34.63	716	2	41	1	56	73.1	56.9	-1.6	49	6	2,500	50	0.0	5.0
B- / 7.8	8.9	0.96	31.36	2,082	2	41	1	56	73.1	56.8	-1.6	49	10	2,500	50	0.0	1.0
B- / 7.8	8.9	0.96	30.59	138	2	41	1	56	73.1	61.9	-1.4	62	9	5,000,000	50	0.0	0.0
C / 4.8	15.7	1.35	54.25	13,291	0	99	0	1	74.7	100.7	-8.5	6	16	2,500	50	4.8	0.5
C / 4.8	15.7	1.35	55.63	1,322	0	99	0	1	74.7	96.0	-8.6	4	6	2,500	50	0.0	5.0
C / 4.8	15.7	1.35	51.60	3,909	0	99	0	1	74.7	96.0	-8.6	4	10	2,500	50	0.0	1.0
C / 4.9	15.7	1.35	57.78	185	0	99	0	1	74.7	102.3	-8.4	6	N/A	5,000,000	50	0.0	0.0
U /	N/A	N/A	12.57	148	4	95	0	1	49.3	N/A	N/A	N/A	N/A	2,500	50	4.8	0.5
U /	N/A	N/A	12.45	51	4	95	0	1	49.3	N/A	N/A	N/A	N/A	2,500	50	0.0	1.0
C+ / 6.8	4.0	0.34	12.43	370	5	30	0	65	137.1	15.2	1.6	36	16	2,500	50	4.8	0.5
B- / 7.1	4.0	0.34	12.96	42	5	30	0	65	137.1	12.4	1.4	30	6	2,500	50	0.0	5.0
C+ / 6.9	4.0	0.34	12.60	244	5	30	0	65	137.1	12.5	1.5	30	6	2,500	50	0.0	1.0
C+ / 6.7	4.0	0.34	12.33	80	5	30	0	65	137.1	16.1	1.7	39	6	5,000,000	50	0.0	0.0
B / 8.0	8.8	0.74	12.54	92	2	96	0	2	63.3	79.4	-11.9	36	4	2,500	50	4.8	0.5
B- / 7.9	8.9	0.74	12.11	9	2	96	0	2	63.3	75.1	-12.1	30	4	2,500	50	0.0	5.0
B / 8.0	8.8	0.73	12.10	14	2	96	0	2	63.3	75.0	-12.0	30	4	2,500	50	0.0	1.0
B / 8.3	8.8	0.73	12.69	41	2	96	0	2	63.3	80.8	-11.7	39	N/A	5,000,000	50	0.0	0.0
C+ / 6.3	4.4	-0.36	16.82	144	3	96	0	1	226.0	-7.9	-0.5	36	14	25,000	100	0.0	2.0
B / 8.1	7.7	0.91	16.07	17	13	86	0	1	3.3	68.4	-5.9	73	4	1,000	250	0.0	0.0
C+ / 6.4	10.3	0.92	9.47	5	2	97	0	1	1.5	98.0	-9.9	20	4	10,000	250	0.0	0.0
C / 5.0	14.8	1.67	3.95	12	3	96	0	1	9.9	67.5	-10.2	5	4	10,000	250	0.0	0.0
B- / 7.7	7.6	1.00	25.55	99	1	98	0	1	3.4	63.9	-9.9	53	4	10,000	250	0.0	0.0
C+ / 6.3	10.8	1.00	23.31	168	1	98	0	1	18.1	100.4	-9.0	49	4	10,000	250	0.0	0.0
C+ / 6.6	13.4	0.89	19.73	25	2	97	0	1	7.3	107.1	-9.7	69	4	10,000	250	0.0	0.0
C / 5.5	13.0	1.10	24.65	108	0	99	0	1	157.0	62.8	-9.1	2	N/A	2,000	250	4.8	2.0
C / 5.4	13.0	1.10	22.75	15	0	99	0	1	157.0	58.4	-9.3	1	N/A	2,000	250	0.0	2.0
C / 5.4	13.0	1.10	22.08	14	0	99	0	1	157.0	58.6	-9.2	1	N/A	2,000	250	0.0	2.0
C+ / 5.8	12.5	1.42	30.11	739	2	97	0	1	61.0	90.7	-5.9	50	6	2,000	250	4.8	2.0
C+ / 5.8	12.5	1.42	28.53	41	2	97	0	1	61.0	85.0	-6.1	39	6	2,000	250	0.0	2.0
C+ / 5.8	12.5	1.42	28.69	82	2	97	0	1	61.0	85.2	-6.1	39	6	2,000	250	0.0	2.0
C+ / 5.9	12.5	1.42	31.13	216	2	97	0	1	61.0	94.2	-5.8	58	12	1,000,000	0	0.0	0.0
U /	N/A	N/A	17.81	30	1	98	0	1	78.0	N/A	N/A	N/A	N/A	1,000	250	4.8	2.0
U /	N/A	N/A	16.29	27	6	66	28	0	1.0	N/A	N/A	N/A	N/A	2,000	250	4.8	0.8
C- / 4.1	13.7	0.88	17.30	139	0	98	0	2	76.0	60.9	-14.2	9	N/A	2,000	250	4.8	2.0
C- / 3.6	13.6	0.88	15.70	17	0	98	0	2	76.0	56.4	-14.5	7	N/A	2,000	250	0.0	2.0
C- / 3.6	13.6	0.88	15.87	20	0	98	0	2	76.0	56.9	-14.5	7	N/A	2,000	250	0.0	2.0
C+ / 6.9	13.8	0.89	18.17	16	0	98	0	2	76.0	67.8	-14.2	15	N/A	1,000,000	0	0.0	0.0
U /	N/A	N/A	16.22	26	2	96	0	2	39.0	N/A	N/A	N/A	N/A	1,000	250	4.8	2.0
B+ / 9.7	4.7	0.97	28.46	511	4	63	32	1	70.0	39.4	-4.7	56	11	1,000	250	4.8	2.0
B+ / 9.9	4.7	0.98	28.25	28	4	63	32	1	70.0	35.0	-5.0	42	11	1,000	250	0.0	2.0
B+ / 9.8	4.7	0.98	27.96	27	4	63	32	1	70.0	35.1	-4.9	43	11	1,000	250	0.0	2.0
B+ / 9.9	4.6	0.94	28.69	6	4	63	32	1	70.0	41.3	-4.6	62	11	1,000,000	0	0.0	0.0
B- / 7.8	7.6	1.48	18.73	54	2	98	0	0	38.0	55.6	-9.5	46	N/A	5,000	250	4.8	2.0
B- / 7.8	7.6	1.48	17.30	8	2	98	0	0	38.0	51.1	-9.7	36	N/A	5,000	250	0.0	2.0
B- / 7.8	7.6	1.48	17.37	8	2	98	0	0	38.0	51.2	-9.7	36	N/A	5,000	250	0.0	2.0
B / 8.8	7.7	0.95	35.74	898	0	98	0	2	31.0	48.9	-9.4	29	8	1,000	250	4.8	2.0
B / 8.6	7.7	0.95	32.92	98	0	98	0	2	31.0	44.9	-9.6	23	8	1,000	250	0.0	2.0
B / 8.7	7.7	0.94	30.74	107	0	98	0	2	31.0	45.2	-9.6	24	8	1,000	250	0.0	2.0
B / 8.9	7.7	0.95	36.94	153	0	98	0	2	31.0	51.5	-9.2	34	8	1,000,000	0	0.0	0.0
B- / 7.1	8.9	1.11	11.55	46	2	98	0	0	7.0	55.4	-10.0	22	6	5,000	250	4.8	2.0

	99 Pct = Best 0 Pct = Worst				PERFORMANCE							
			Overall Weiss Investment Rating		Perfor-mance Rating/Pts	Total Return % through 6/30/06			Annualized		Incl. in Returns	
Fund Type	Fund Name	Ticker Symbol		Phone		3 Mo	6 Mo	1Yr / Pct	3Yr / Pct	5Yr / Pct	Dividend Yield	Expense Ratio
AG	Calvert Social-Index B	CSXBX	D-	(800) 368-2745	D- / 1.2	-3.98	-0.80	5.31 /17	7.21 /11	-0.71 /13	0.00	1.75
AG	Calvert Social-Index C	CSXCX	D-	(800) 368-2745	D- / 1.3	-3.89	-0.72	5.41 /17	7.25 /11	-0.67 /13	0.00	1.75
AG	Calvert Social-Index I	CISIX	D	(800) 368-2745	D / 2.2	-3.55	0.00	6.89 /26	8.71 /19	0.70 /19	0.76	0.75
FO	Calvert World Values Intl Eqty A	CWVGX	B+	(800) 368-2745	B / 7.8	-0.35	9.22	24.94 /88	19.59 /78	7.51 /69	0.70	1.86
FO	Calvert World Values Intl Eqty B	CWVBX	A-	(800) 368-2745	B / 7.8	-0.62	8.70	23.66 /87	18.27 /73	6.19 /62	0.02	2.92
FO	Calvert World Values Intl Eqty C	CWVCX	B+	(800) 368-2745	B / 7.9	-0.58	8.76	23.91 /87	18.57 /75	6.48 /64	0.13	2.75
FO	Calvert World Values Intl Eqty I	CWVIX	A+	(800) 368-2745	B+ / 8.5	-0.21	9.56	25.75 /89	20.51 /81	8.39 /73	1.04	1.77
FO	Cambiar International Equity Inv	CAMIX	A+	(866) 777-8227	B+ / 8.5	0.65	14.40	22.80 /85	20.86 /82	7.79 /71	0.12	1.63
GR	Cambiar Opportunity Fund Inv	CAMOX	B	(866) 777-8227	C+ / 6.0	-1.77	3.61	8.85 /39	14.90 /58	6.89 /66	0.19	1.20
GR	CAN SLIM Select Growth Fund	CSSGX	U	(800) 558-9105	U /	-6.39	4.90	--	--	--	0.00	1.70
GR	Capital Management Mid-Cap Inst	CMEIX	C	(800) 525-3863	C+ / 6.3	-3.30	2.45	11.63 /57	15.36 /60	7.06 /67	0.00	1.50
GR	Capital Management Mid-Cap Inv	CMCIX	C-	(800) 525-3863	C / 5.5	-3.39	2.23	10.86 /53	14.53 /56	6.31 /63	0.00	2.25
GI	Capital One Capital Apprn Fund A	CWRSX	D+	(800) 999-0124	D+ / 2.6	-2.60	1.13	6.77 /25	10.44 /30	1.68 /25	0.39	1.26
GI	Capital One Capital Apprn Fund B	TCABX	D	(800) 999-0124	D / 2.0	-2.75	0.80	5.98 /20	9.61 /25	0.92 /20	0.00	2.01
MC	Capital One Mid Cap Equity Fund A	CMCEX	B-	(800) 999-0124	C+ / 6.7	-3.02	4.05	11.28 /55	17.96 /72	8.42 /74	0.21	1.36
MC	Capital One Mid Cap Equity Fund B	CMCPX	B-	(800) 999-0124	C+ / 6.3	-3.15	3.74	10.49 /50	17.09 /68	7.63 /70	0.00	2.11
IX	Catholic Equity Fund A	CTHQX	C	(877) 222-2402	C- / 3.2	-1.52	3.38	9.41 /43	10.90 /35	1.81 /26	0.81	0.60
IX	Catholic Equity Fund I	CTHRX	C+	(877) 222-2402	C / 4.3	-1.42	3.58	9.76 /45	11.20 /37	--	1.08	0.35
FO	Causeway International Value Inst	CIVIX	A+	(866) 947-7000	A- / 9.0	1.84	10.37	20.08 /82	24.04 /89	--	1.97	0.93
FO	Causeway International Value Inv	CIVVX	A+	(866) 947-7000	B+ / 8.9	1.84	10.29	19.87 /82	23.79 /89	--	1.79	1.15
FS	Century Shares Trust	CENSX	D+	(800) 321-1928	C- / 3.1	-1.78	-0.40	5.06 /15	10.41 /30	4.94 /54	2.16	1.15
SC	● Century Small Cap Select Inst	CSMCX	C	(800) 321-1928	C / 5.3	-5.08	2.96	5.00 /15	14.66 /57	12.74 /88	0.35	1.13
SC	● Century Small Cap Select Inv	CSMVX	C	(800) 321-1928	C / 5.2	-5.17	2.78	4.64 /13	14.30 /55	12.26 /87	0.12	1.12
EM	CG Cap Mkt Fds-Emerging Mkts	TEMUX	C+	(800) 446-1013	A+ / 9.7	-3.18	7.82	35.28 /97	32.92 /97	19.75 /96	0.91	1.44
FO	CG Cap Mkt Fds-Intl Equity Invts	TIEUX	A	(800) 446-1013	A- / 9.0	-1.06	8.98	26.74 /91	23.42 /88	9.34 /78	1.27	0.99
GR	CG Cap Mkt Fds-Large Cap Grwth	TLGUX	C-	(800) 446-1013	C- / 3.5	-3.96	-2.32	8.10 /33	10.98 /35	0.36 /17	0.00	0.88
GR	CG Cap Mkt Fds-Large Cap Val Eq	TLVUX	B	(800) 446-1013	C+ / 5.9	0.17	5.82	12.08 /60	13.65 /52	4.54 /50	1.52	0.86
SC	CG Cap Mkt Fds-Small Cap Growth	TSGUX	C-	(800) 446-1013	C+ / 6.3	-6.66	5.86	16.30 /75	15.94 /63	2.77 /34	0.00	1.24
SC	CG Cap Mkt Fds-Small Cap Val Eq	TSVUX	D	(800) 446-1013	B+ / 8.6	-2.09	8.75	15.38 /73	22.66 /86	13.16 /89	0.50	1.17
GR	● CGM Capital Development	LOMCX	C	(800) 345-4048	A+ / 9.6	2.19	11.36	27.79 /92	30.60 /96	13.19 /89	0.00	1.12
★ AG	CGM Focus Fund	CGMFX	C+	(800) 345-4048	A+ / 9.6	4.53	15.32	26.45 /90	29.43 /95	21.11 /97	1.06	1.07
BA	CGM Mutual Fund	LOMMX	B-	(800) 345-4048	B / 7.7	1.33	6.52	13.62 /67	18.67 /75	9.11 /77	1.28	1.09
RE	CGM Realty Fund	CGMRX	C	(800) 345-4048	A+ / 9.8	-1.25	13.31	31.65 /95	37.79 /99	31.43 /99	1.28	0.92
GL	Chaconia Income & Growth Fund	CHIGX	D	(800) 368-3322	D- / 1.0	-2.58	-0.73	1.43 / 3	6.91 /10	1.06 /20	0.51	3.10
SC	Chartwell Small Cap Value Adv	CASVX	B+	(610) 296-1430	B- / 7.3	-3.98	5.91	11.18 /55	18.00 /72	--	0.03	1.35
SC	Chartwell Small Cap Value I	CHSVX	B+	(610) 296-1430	B- / 7.4	-3.78	6.15	11.50 /57	18.33 /74	9.52 /79	0.22	1.10
GR	● Chartwell US Equity Adv	CALVX	C-	(610) 296-1430	D+ / 2.5	-1.24	2.58	7.63 /30	8.38 /17	--	0.44	1.00
GR	● Chartwell US Equity I	CHLVX	C	(610) 296-1430	D+ / 2.7	-1.14	2.77	7.86 /32	8.63 /19	0.78 /19	0.68	0.75
GR	Chase Growth Fund	CHASX	C	(888) 861-7556	C- / 4.2	-3.19	0.00	7.18 /27	12.54 /46	4.42 /50	0.00	1.16
AG	● Chesapeake Aggressive Growth	CPGRX	E-	(800) 525-3863	D+ / 2.5	-2.11	15.91	9.26 /42	7.93 /15	-1.56 /10	0.00	2.34
GR	Chesapeake Core Growth Fund	CHCGX	D	(800) 525-3863	D+ / 2.9	-4.26	-0.30	2.98 / 7	10.37 /30	2.34 /30	0.00	1.40
GR	Chesapeake Growth Fund A	CHEAX	D+	(800) 525-3863	C / 5.1	-3.32	2.67	9.24 /42	14.04 /54	-0.81 /12	0.00	2.22
GR	Chesapeake Growth Fund Inst	CHESX	C-	(800) 525-3863	C+ / 5.6	-3.73	2.26	8.96 /40	14.22 /55	-0.42 /14	0.00	1.97
FO	China U.S. Growth Fund (The)	CHUSX	U	(800) 544-4774	U /	-0.53	20.42	37.64 /97	--	--	0.00	2.20
FO	CitiStreet International Stock R	CISRX	A+		B+ / 8.7	-0.36	10.16	28.87 /94	20.58 /81	--	0.85	1.25
GR	CitiStreet Large Company Stock R	CLCRX	C		C- / 3.3	-2.99	0.74	6.60 /24	10.26 /29	--	0.78	0.99
SC	CitiStreet Small Company Stock R	CSCRX	B-		B- / 7.0	-4.82	5.70	13.15 /65	16.90 /68	--	0.00	1.13
BA	Citizens Balanced Fund	CFBLX	C-	(800) 223-7010	D / 1.6	-3.86	-2.04	4.17 /11	7.70 /13	--	1.04	1.30
GR	Citizens Core Growth Admin	CGADX	E+	(800) 223-7010	D- / 1.4	-6.80	-3.94	3.92 /10	7.91 /15	-1.21 /11	0.00	1.09
GR	Citizens Core Growth Fd	WAIDX	D-	(800) 223-7010	D- / 1.2	-6.89	-4.13	3.50 / 9	7.48 /12	-1.60 /10	0.00	1.52
GR	Citizens Core Growth Inst	WINIX	D	(800) 223-7010	D / 1.7	-6.74	-3.76	4.26 /12	8.28 /16	-0.90 /12	0.00	0.80
MC	Citizens Emerg Growth Admin	CGRDX	C-	(800) 223-7010	C+ / 6.0	-5.63	5.54	16.70 /76	14.71 /57	1.11 /21	0.00	1.58

● Denotes fund is closed to new investors
★ Denotes fund is included in Section II

RISK			NET ASSETS		ASSET				Portfolio Turnover Ratio	BULL / BEAR		FUND MANAGER		MINIMUMS		LOADS	
Risk Rating/Pts	3 Year		NAV As of 6/30/06	Total $(Mil)	Cash %	Stocks %	Bonds %	Other %		Last Bull Market Return	Last Bear Market Return	Manager Quality Pct	Manager Tenure (Years)	Initial Purch. $	Additional Purch. $	Front End Load	Back End Load
	Standard Deviation	Beta															
B- / 7.2	8.9	1.11	11.11	5	2	98	0	0	7.0	50.5	-10.2	16	6	5,000	250	0.0	2.0
B- / 7.2	8.8	1.11	11.11	6	2	98	0	0	7.0	50.6	-10.2	16	6	5,000	250	0.0	2.0
B- / 7.3	8.8	1.10	11.68	10	2	98	0	0	7.0	57.3	-9.9	25	6	1,000,000	0	0.0	1.0
C+ / 6.9	10.3	0.99	22.87	369	0	98	0	2	53.0	103.7	-7.7	20	N/A	2,000	250	4.8	2.0
B- / 7.7	10.3	0.99	20.98	17	0	98	0	2	53.0	96.5	-8.0	14	N/A	2,000	250	0.0	2.0
C+ / 6.9	10.3	0.99	20.49	30	0	98	0	2	53.0	98.0	-7.9	15	N/A	2,000	250	0.0	2.0
B- / 7.8	10.3	0.99	24.06	117	0	98	0	2	53.0	108.8	-7.5	26	N/A	1,000,000	0	0.0	0.0
B- / 7.5	11.3	0.96	24.86	38	1	98	0	1	63.0	127.8	-14.4	32	9	2,500	100	0.0	2.0
B / 8.3	9.0	1.08	18.35	989	3	96	0	1	43.0	87.5	-10.2	82	9	2,500	100	0.0	0.0
U /	N/A	N/A	10.70	93	2	97	0	1	117.7	N/A	N/A	N/A	1	2,500	100	0.0	2.0
C+ / 5.9	9.9	1.04	18.78	16	31	68	0	1	72.8	87.3	-11.1	87	11	250,000	500	0.0	0.0
C+ / 5.8	9.9	1.04	17.40	1	31	68	0	1	72.8	82.6	-11.2	82	11	2,500	500	3.0	0.0
B- / 7.2	7.4	0.94	18.72	231	0	99	0	1	20.0	58.9	-9.6	54	11	1,000	100	4.5	0.0
B- / 7.4	7.4	0.93	17.65	7	0	99	0	1	20.0	55.2	-9.8	44	10	1,000	100	0.0	5.5
B- / 7.4	10.5	0.95	17.98	137	2	97	0	1	15.0	94.1	-6.8	63	N/A	1,000	100	4.5	1.0
B- / 7.4	10.5	0.95	16.91	5	2	97	0	1	15.0	89.6	-7.0	54	N/A	1,000	100	0.0	5.5
B / 8.9	7.6	0.99	10.39	13	0	99	0	1	56.0	62.6	-9.8	54	N/A	1,000	50	5.0	0.0
B / 8.9	7.6	0.99	10.41	44	0	99	0	1	56.0	64.1	-9.7	57	N/A	2,000,000	1,000	0.0	0.0
B / 8.2	9.5	0.88	18.31	3,240	2	98	0	0	22.4	146.3	-12.4	77	5	1,000,000	0	0.0	2.0
B / 8.1	9.5	0.88	18.22	1,354	2	98	0	0	22.4	144.4	-12.4	76	5	5,000	0	0.0	2.0
B- / 7.0	7.0	0.63	33.36	294	3	96	0	1	19.0	61.4	-8.8	67	7	250,000	0	0.0	1.0
C+ / 6.9	11.1	0.70	25.06	750	3	96	0	1	96.0	91.3	-4.8	67	7	250,000	0	0.0	1.0
C+ / 6.9	11.1	0.70	24.76	393	3	96	0	1	96.0	89.0	-4.9	63	7	2,500	50	0.0	1.0
D+ / 2.9	18.9	1.14	13.18	283	2	97	0	1	70.0	213.0	-6.7	9	N/A	10,000	0	0.0	0.0
C+ / 6.8	10.5	1.01	13.10	1,422	5	94	0	1	57.0	138.9	-11.6	42	N/A	10,000	0	0.0	0.0
B- / 7.2	10.9	1.25	13.08	1,590	2	97	0	1	77.0	71.7	-10.9	31	15	10,000	0	0.0	0.0
B / 8.6	8.0	1.02	11.81	1,548	3	96	0	1	67.0	75.4	-9.2	77	N/A	10,000	0	0.0	0.0
C / 4.4	16.1	1.06	16.27	383	2	97	0	1	70.0	112.8	-10.8	25	7	10,000	0	0.0	0.0
E / 0.5	13.2	0.86	14.04	352	5	94	0	1	64.0	126.5	-7.3	94	13	10,000	0	0.0	0.0
D / 2.0	22.7	1.85	31.75	476	0	99	0	1	211.0	161.5	-7.0	99	30	2,500	50	0.0	0.0
C- / 3.8	21.2	1.43	38.53	2,270	N/A	N/A	0	N/A	282.0	206.3	-15.7	99	9	2,500	50	0.0	0.0
C+ / 6.1	14.2	1.83	29.61	533	0	58	40	2	336.0	94.8	-5.0	95	25	2,500	50	0.0	0.0
D / 1.9	20.1	0.69	30.69	1,249	0	99	0	1	136.0	269.2	1.3	99	12	2,500	50	0.0	0.0
B / 8.0	6.0	0.45	10.93	19	0	75	23	2	26.4	44.0	-4.8	17	N/A	250	100	0.0	2.0
B- / 7.5	12.5	0.82	15.94	N/A	3	96	0	1	102.9	99.9	-10.6	78	7	2,500	500	0.0	0.0
B- / 7.5	12.5	0.82	16.05	23	3	96	0	1	102.9	101.6	-10.5	80	7	2,500	500	0.0	0.0
B / 8.8	6.9	0.81	10.35	N/A	1	98	0	1	66.2	50.7	-10.5	43	N/A	2,500	500	0.0	0.0
B / 8.9	6.8	0.80	10.39	11	1	98	0	1	66.2	51.7	-10.5	47	N/A	2,500	500	0.0	0.0
B- / 7.8	9.8	1.00	19.40	651	4	95	0	1	86.7	65.1	-5.9	69	9	2,000	250	0.0	2.0
D- / 1.1	19.6	2.06	10.20	7	1	98	0	1	88.6	66.6	-14.5	1	13	25,000	500	3.0	0.0
C+ / 6.3	11.2	1.27	16.87	708	2	98	0	0	90.1	72.4	-9.2	26	9	25,000	500	0.0	0.0
C / 4.7	14.6	1.57	11.94	5	0	99	0	1	78.0	89.9	-13.0	32	12	25,000	500	3.0	0.0
C / 4.7	14.7	1.57	12.65	12	0	99	0	1	78.0	92.3	-12.7	33	12	1,000,000	5,000	0.0	0.0
U /	N/A	N/A	14.98	61	2	97	0	1	288.5	N/A	N/A	N/A	N/A	1,000	50	5.3	0.0
B- / 7.9	10.1	0.97	16.80	22	0	99	0	1	93.0	113.1	-12.4	28	N/A	1,000	50	0.0	0.0
B / 8.6	8.0	1.03	12.32	34	2	97	0	1	35.2	61.4	-9.6	41	N/A	1,000	50	0.0	0.0
C+ / 6.9	13.5	0.92	15.02	15	N/A	100	0	N/A	69.8	104.0	-11.3	52	N/A	1,000	50	0.0	0.0
B / 8.8	6.1	1.12	12.24	11	7	65	27	1	31.8	40.3	N/A	50	N/A	2,500	50	0.0	0.0
C+ / 5.6	9.4	1.09	20.96	2	2	97	0	1	71.1	53.5	-10.2	21	2	1,000,000	0	0.0	0.0
B- / 7.0	9.4	1.08	20.41	269	2	97	0	1	71.1	51.5	-10.2	18	2	2,500	50	0.0	0.0
B- / 7.0	9.4	1.09	17.15	45	2	97	0	1	71.1	55.0	-10.1	23	2	1,000,000	0	0.0	0.0
C / 4.8	13.2	1.13	16.77	5	1	98	0	1	63.0	87.3	-9.6	15	1	1,000,000	0	0.0	0.0

					PERFORMANCE							
						Total Return % through 6/30/06					Incl. in Returns	
			Overall Weiss Investment Rating		Perfor-mance Rating/Pts				Annualized		Dividend Yield	Expense Ratio
Fund Type	Fund Name	Ticker Symbol		Phone		3 Mo	6 Mo	1Yr / Pct	3Yr / Pct	5Yr / Pct		
MC	Citizens Emerg Growth Fd	WAEGX	C-	(800) 223-7010	C+ / 5.8	-5.64	5.47	16.31 /75	14.38 /56	0.76 /19	0.00	1.92
MC	Citizens Emerg Growth Inst	CEGIX	C	(800) 223-7010	C+ / 6.1	-5.52	5.68	17.03 /77	15.07 /59	1.40 /23	0.00	1.35
GL	Citizens Global Eq Admin	CEADX	D+	(800) 223-7010	C / 4.7	-0.32	6.20	15.83 /74	11.37 /38	0.30 /17	0.00	1.74
GL	Citizens Global Eq Fd	WAGEX	C	(800) 223-7010	C / 4.5	-0.38	6.08	15.57 /73	11.04 /36	0.02 /15	0.00	2.03
GL	Citizens Global Eq Inst	CGEIX	C	(800) 223-7010	C / 4.9	-0.26	6.31	16.23 /75	11.75 /41	0.63 /18	0.00	1.40
SC	Citizens Small Cap Core Growth Fd	CSCSX	C-	(800) 223-7010	C+ / 6.2	-5.17	6.94	13.45 /66	14.64 /57	6.53 /64	0.00	1.44
GR	Citizens Value Fund	MYPVX	C+	(800) 410-3337	C / 5.5	-0.55	5.12	9.83 /46	13.82 /53	-1.33 /11	0.00	1.29
★ GR	Clipper Fund	CFIMX	D	(800) 432-2504	D- / 1.3	-0.11	1.33	3.04 / 7	6.62 / 9	5.03 /54	1.45	0.70
GR	CM Advisers Fund	CMAFX	C	(800) 664-4888	D / 2.2	-0.41	2.98	7.20 /27	8.14 /16	--	1.51	1.50
GR	CMG Enhanced S&P 500 Index Fund	CESPX	C-	(800) 426-3750	C / 4.7	-1.83	2.92	10.53 /50	11.97 /42	--	1.78	0.25
FO	CMG International Stock Fund	COISX	B-	(800) 426-3750	B+ / 8.5	0.00	9.78	26.91 /91	20.31 /80	8.40 /73	1.66	0.75
GR	CMG Large Cap Growth Fund	CLCGX	U	(800) 426-3750	U /	-3.63	0.53	7.89 /32	--	--	0.64	0.50
GR	CMG Large Cap Value Fund	CLCPX	U	(800) 426-3750	U /	-0.76	5.27	11.69 /58	--	--	2.12	0.50
MC	CMG Mid Cap Growth Fund	CMCGX	C-	(800) 426-3750	C+ / 6.1	-5.11	4.91	20.36 /82	14.28 /55	--	0.00	0.52
MC	CMG Mid Cap Value Fund	CMCVX	C+	(800) 426-3750	B- / 7.4	-1.61	6.09	15.01 /72	17.73 /71	--	0.97	0.47
SC	CMG Small Cap Value Fund	CSCPX	C+	(800) 426-3750	B+ / 8.5	-2.97	9.57	16.99 /77	21.88 /85	--	0.72	0.68
MC	CMG Small/Mid Cap Fund	COSMX	C+	(800) 426-3750	B / 7.6	-5.72	9.20	22.77 /85	18.01 /72	6.56 /64	0.00	0.75
IN	CMG Strategic Equity Fund	COSTX	B	(800) 426-3750	C+ / 6.0	-1.93	2.85	11.48 /57	14.63 /57	--	3.68	0.40
GR	CNI Charter Large Cap Growth Eq A	CLEAX	D	(888) 889-0799	E+ / 0.8	-4.17	-2.11	3.17 / 8	5.83 / 6	-0.29 /14	0.05	1.23
GR	CNI Charter Large Cap Growth Eq I	CNGIX	D	(888) 889-0799	E+ / 0.9	-4.19	-1.98	3.34 / 8	6.05 / 7	-0.04 /15	0.25	0.98
GR	CNI Charter Large Cap Value Eq A	CVEAX	B	(888) 889-0799	C+ / 6.5	0.48	6.23	12.32 /61	15.00 /59	5.04 /55	0.95	1.20
GR	CNI Charter Large Cap Value Eq I	CNLIX	B	(888) 889-0799	C+ / 6.6	0.55	6.36	12.57 /62	15.30 /60	5.31 /56	1.17	0.95
SC	CNI Charter RCB Small Cap Value A	RCBAX	C	(888) 889-0799	C- / 3.9	-4.74	-0.80	-1.29 / 1	12.84 /48	9.13 /77	0.01	1.44
SC	CNI Charter RCB Small Cap Value I	RCBIX	C	(888) 889-0799	C- / 4.1	-4.70	-0.68	-1.04 / 1	13.11 /49	9.37 /78	0.24	1.19
SC	CNI Charter RCB Small Cap Value R	RCBSX	C-	(888) 889-0799	C- / 3.3	-4.75	-0.80	-1.28 / 1	12.83 /48	9.12 /77	0.02	1.44
TC	CNI Charter Technology Growth A	CTGAX	E-	(888) 889-0799	D / 1.6	-8.10	-1.98	7.01 /26	7.68 /13	-6.75 / 1	0.00	1.50
TC	CNI Charter Technology Growth I	CTEIX	E-	(888) 889-0799	D / 1.7	-8.22	-1.95	7.26 /28	8.02 /15	-6.45 / 1	0.33	1.20
RE	Cohen & Steers Reality Income A	CSEIX	C	(800) 437-9912	B / 7.9	-1.48	10.91	12.83 /63	20.88 /82	16.23 /93	4.18	1.26
RE	Cohen & Steers Reality Income B	CSBIX	C	(800) 437-9912	B / 7.7	-1.58	10.64	12.14 /60	20.09 /80	15.48 /92	3.95	1.91
RE	Cohen & Steers Reality Income C	CSCIX	C	(800) 437-9912	B / 8.0	-1.64	10.57	12.07 /60	20.07 /79	15.47 /92	3.95	1.91
RE	Cohen & Steers Reality Income I	CSDIX	A-	(800) 437-9912	B+ / 8.4	-1.39	11.17	13.21 /65	21.26 /83	16.64 /94	4.52	0.91
RE	Cohen & Steers Realty Focus I	CSSPX	B+	(800) 437-9912	A / 9.5	-1.11	11.21	17.59 /78	30.22 /96	22.16 /98	2.59	1.30
★ RE	Cohen & Steers Realty Shrs Fd	CSRSX	B	(800) 437-9912	A / 9.5	-0.51	14.54	22.77 /85	30.16 /96	20.65 /97	2.59	0.97
RE	Cohen & Steers Realty Shrs Inst	CSRIX	A	(800) 437-9912	A+ / 9.6	-0.41	14.53	22.64 /85	30.21 /96	20.76 /97	2.76	0.75
UT	Cohen & Steers Utility A	CSUAX	U	(800) 437-9912	U /	4.00	3.10	4.98 /15	--	--	2.02	1.49
SC	Columbia Acorn 529A		C+	(800) 426-3750	B / 7.8	-3.85	5.55	15.86 /74	21.24 /83	--	0.00	N/A
SC	Columbia Acorn 529B		C+	(800) 426-3750	B / 7.6	-4.05	5.11	14.93 /72	20.21 /80	--	0.00	N/A
SC	Columbia Acorn 529C		C+	(800) 426-3750	B / 8.0	-4.04	5.16	14.95 /72	20.32 /80	--	0.00	N/A
SC	Columbia Acorn 529Z		B-	(800) 426-3750	B+ / 8.4	-3.77	5.67	16.12 /75	21.59 /84	--	0.00	N/A
SC	Columbia Acorn Fund A	LACAX	B	(800) 426-3750	B / 8.0	-3.81	5.64	16.11 /75	21.49 /84	11.81 /86	0.22	1.01
SC	Columbia Acorn Fund B	LACBX	B-	(800) 426-3750	B / 7.7	-3.96	5.32	15.31 /73	20.64 /82	11.05 /84	0.00	1.72
SC	Columbia Acorn Fund C	LIACX	B	(800) 426-3750	B / 8.0	-4.00	5.25	15.20 /72	20.57 /81	11.01 /84	0.00	1.80
SC	Columbia Acorn Fund Z	ACRNX	B	(800) 426-3750	B / 8.0	-3.73	5.81	16.44 /76	21.94 /85	12.31 /87	0.45	0.73
FO	Columbia Acorn International Fund A	LAIAX	B+	(800) 426-3750	A+ / 9.6	-1.16	14.11	34.74 /97	32.29 /97	14.90 /92	0.49	1.23
FO	Columbia Acorn International Fund B	LIABX	B+	(800) 426-3750	A+ / 9.6	-1.34	13.74	33.83 /96	31.38 /96	14.11 /90	0.00	1.93
FO	Columbia Acorn International Fund C	LAICX	B+	(800) 426-3750	A+ / 9.6	-1.34	13.72	33.73 /96	31.35 /96	14.10 /90	0.00	2.01
★ FO	Columbia Acorn International Fund Z	ACINX	B+	(800) 426-3750	A+ / 9.7	-1.11	14.27	35.18 /97	32.82 /97	15.42 /92	0.95	0.94
FO	Columbia Acorn Intl 529A		B+	(800) 426-3750	A+ / 9.6	-1.24	13.96	34.46 /96	31.97 /97	--	0.00	N/A
FO	Columbia Acorn Intl 529B		B+	(800) 426-3750	A+ / 9.6	-1.43	13.57	33.52 /96	31.00 /96	--	0.00	N/A
FO	Columbia Acorn Intl 529C		B+	(800) 426-3750	A+ / 9.6	-1.43	13.62	33.50 /96	31.02 /96	--	0.00	N/A
FO	Columbia Acorn Intl 529Z		B+	(800) 426-3750	A+ / 9.7	-1.15	14.17	34.91 /97	32.38 /97	--	0.00	N/A
FO	Columbia Acorn Intl Select Fund A	LAFAX	A	(800) 426-3750	A / 9.3	0.41	12.74	29.75 /94	27.47 /93	11.45 /85	0.01	1.62

● Denotes fund is closed to new investors
★ Denotes fund is included in Section II

RISK			NET ASSETS		ASSET					BULL / BEAR		FUND MANAGER		MINIMUMS		LOADS	
	3 Year		NAV						Portfolio	Last Bull	Last Bear	Manager	Manager	Initial	Additional	Front	Back
Risk	Standard		As of	Total	Cash	Stocks	Bonds	Other	Turnover	Market	Market	Quality	Tenure	Purch.	Purch.	End	End
Rating/Pts	Deviation	Beta	6/30/06	$(Mil)	%	%	%	%	Ratio	Return	Return	Pct	(Years)	$	$	Load	Load
C+ / 5.6	13.1	1.13	16.40	171	1	98	0	1	63.0	85.2	-9.7	13	1	2,500	50	0.0	0.0
C+ / 5.7	13.1	1.13	17.11	1	1	98	0	1	63.0	88.9	-9.6	16	1	1,000,000	0	0.0	0.0
C / 5.4	9.0	0.80	18.66	1	1	98	0	1	12.6	59.0	-10.2	6	2	1,000,000	0	0.0	2.0
B- / 7.3	9.0	0.80	18.33	80	1	98	0	1	12.6	57.6	-10.2	5	2	2,500	50	0.0	2.0
B- / 7.4	9.0	0.80	19.05	1	1	98	0	1	12.6	60.8	-10.2	7	2	1,000,000	0	0.0	2.0
C / 4.4	16.1	1.03	12.48	38	3	96	0	1	77.6	88.6	-12.6	20	7	2,500	50	0.0	0.0
B / 8.0	9.5	1.16	12.74	33	3	96	0	1	102.2	81.2	-12.6	68	N/A	2,500	50	0.0	2.0
B- / 7.9	6.4	0.65	84.88	3,250	4	95	0	1	13.0	40.9	-11.5	40	N/A	25,000	1,000	0.0	0.0
B+ / 9.9	3.7	0.33	12.07	213	13	64	22	1	18.9	N/A	N/A	83	3	100,000	1,000	0.0	1.0
C+ / 6.3	7.7	1.00	13.41	100	4	96	0	0	49.0	N/A	N/A	64	1	3,000,000	2,500	0.0	0.0
C / 5.4	10.5	1.01	14.48	104	1	98	0	1	68.0	111.3	-9.1	22	1	3,000,000	2,500	0.0	0.0
U /	N/A	N/A	11.40	37	4	95	0	1	120.0	N/A	N/A	N/A	1	3,000,000	2,500	0.0	0.0
U /	N/A	N/A	11.79	37	2	97	0	1	45.0	N/A	N/A	N/A	N/A	3,000,000	2,500	0.0	0.0
C / 4.6	14.4	1.24	15.61	24	4	96	0	0	141.0	N/A	N/A	7	2	3,000,000	2,500	0.0	0.0
C+ / 6.0	9.0	0.80	14.10	18	4	94	0	2	59.0	N/A	N/A	82	1	3,000,000	2,500	0.0	0.0
C / 5.0	13.0	0.88	15.69	34	0	99	0	1	41.0	N/A	N/A	92	3	3,000,000	2,500	0.0	0.0
C+ / 5.7	15.5	1.35	11.87	9	1	98	0	1	170.0	110.5	-6.9	13	6	3,000,000	2,500	0.0	0.0
B / 8.4	8.3	1.02	11.20	138	3	96	0	1	64.0	84.5	-9.7	84	N/A	3,000,000	2,500	0.0	0.0
B- / 7.8	8.3	1.04	7.27	10	2	97	0	1	15.0	40.3	-9.2	12	7	0	0	0.0	0.0
B- / 7.8	8.2	1.04	7.34	34	2	97	0	1	15.0	41.5	-9.1	13	N/A	0	0	0.0	0.0
B / 8.7	7.9	0.97	9.90	13	2	97	0	1	14.0	84.3	-10.1	88	7	0	0	0.0	0.0
B / 8.7	7.8	0.97	9.91	88	2	97	0	1	14.0	85.8	-10.0	89	N/A	0	0	0.0	0.0
B- / 7.7	10.1	0.60	27.32	11	5	91	3	1	37.0	94.0	-11.3	66	N/A	0	0	0.0	0.0
B- / 7.8	9.9	0.59	27.56	13	5	91	3	1	37.0	95.6	-11.2	71	N/A	0	0	0.0	0.0
B- / 7.7	9.9	0.59	27.27	47	5	91	3	1	37.0	94.0	-11.3	68	N/A	25,000	1,000	3.5	0.0
D+ / 2.4	16.0	1.73	3.97	1	4	95	0	1	11.0	63.0	-14.8	2	N/A	0	0	0.0	0.0
D+ / 2.4	16.1	1.74	4.02	1	4	95	0	1	11.0	64.6	-14.7	3	N/A	0	0	0.0	0.0
C / 4.4	14.8	0.89	16.56	1,606	0	98	0	2	25.0	99.6	-0.3	48	N/A	1,000	250	4.5	1.0
C / 4.3	14.8	0.89	15.95	133	0	98	0	2	25.0	95.6	-0.5	40	N/A	1,000	250	0.0	5.0
C / 4.3	14.8	0.89	15.94	229	0	98	0	2	25.0	95.6	-0.5	40	N/A	1,000	250	0.0	1.0
B- / 7.0	14.8	0.89	16.89	37	0	98	0	2	25.0	101.9	-0.3	52	N/A	100,000	500	0.0	0.0
C+ / 5.6	14.7	0.88	64.79	165	2	96	0	2	158.0	162.2	-0.2	98	9	10,000	500	0.0	1.0
C / 4.8	16.2	0.97	82.00	2,464	2	96	0	2	28.0	149.7	-0.9	94	15	10,000	500	0.0	1.0
C+ / 6.1	16.3	0.97	51.30	1,011	2	96	0	2	28.0	149.3	-0.7	94	15	3,000,000	10,000	0.0	0.0
U /	N/A	N/A	15.58	174	2	98	0	0	45.0	N/A	N/A	N/A	N/A	1,000	250	4.5	1.0
C / 5.5	11.4	0.77	19.21	1	6	93	0	1	20.0	N/A	N/A	95	3	1,000	50	5.8	1.0
C / 5.5	11.4	0.78	18.71	1	6	93	0	1	20.0	N/A	N/A	92	3	1,000	50	0.0	5.0
C / 5.5	11.4	0.77	18.76	1	6	93	0	1	20.0	N/A	N/A	93	3	1,000	50	0.0	1.0
C / 5.5	11.4	0.77	19.38	2	6	93	0	1	20.0	N/A	N/A	95	3	1,000	50	0.0	0.0
C+ / 6.2	11.4	0.78	28.81	3,809	7	92	0	1	20.0	128.4	-7.1	95	6	75,000	50	5.8	1.0
C+ / 6.2	11.4	0.78	27.71	1,407	7	92	0	1	20.0	123.5	-7.2	93	6	75,000	50	0.0	5.0
C+ / 6.2	11.4	0.78	27.66	1,301	7	92	0	1	20.0	123.1	-7.2	93	6	75,000	50	0.0	1.0
C+ / 6.3	11.4	0.77	29.49	11,396	7	92	0	1	20.0	131.3	-6.9	96	6	75,000	50	5.8	1.0
C / 5.2	12.4	1.15	37.33	211	3	96	0	1	27.0	198.8	-5.1	86	3	1,000	50	5.8	2.0
C / 5.2	12.4	1.15	36.65	82	3	96	0	1	27.0	192.2	-5.3	80	3	1,000	50	0.0	5.0
C / 5.2	12.4	1.15	36.61	77	3	96	0	1	27.0	192.0	-5.2	80	3	1,000	50	0.0	2.0
C / 5.2	12.4	1.15	37.58	3,221	3	96	0	1	27.0	202.8	-5.3	88	3	1,000	50	0.0	2.0
C / 5.1	12.4	1.16	24.66	1	0	99	0	1	40.0	N/A	N/A	84	3	1,000	50	5.8	1.0
C / 5.1	12.4	1.15	24.10	N/A	0	99	0	1	40.0	N/A	N/A	78	3	1,000	50	0.0	5.0
C / 5.1	12.4	1.15	24.11	N/A	0	99	0	1	40.0	N/A	N/A	78	3	1,000	50	0.0	1.0
C / 5.1	12.4	1.16	24.89	1	0	99	0	1	40.0	N/A	N/A	86	3	1,000	50	0.0	0.0
C+ / 6.3	11.7	1.10	22.95	14	2	97	0	1	39.0	165.1	-8.3	62	5	1,000	50	5.8	2.0

Fund Type	Fund Name	Ticker Symbol	Overall Weiss Investment Rating	Phone	PERFORMANCE Performance Rating/Pts	Total Return % through 6/30/06 3 Mo	6 Mo	1Yr / Pct	Annualized 3Yr / Pct	5Yr / Pct	Incl. in Returns Dividend Yield	Expense Ratio
	99 Pct = Best											
	0 Pct = Worst											
FO	Columbia Acorn Intl Select Fund B	LFFBX	A-	(800) 426-3750	A- / 9.2	0.23	12.32	28.93 /94	26.63 /93	10.73 /83	0.00	2.29
FO	Columbia Acorn Intl Select Fund C	LFFCX	A	(800) 426-3750	A / 9.3	0.23	12.27	28.79 /94	26.51 /93	10.69 /83	0.00	2.41
FO	Columbia Acorn Intl Select Fund Z	ACFFX	A	(800) 426-3750	A / 9.4	0.48	12.83	30.10 /94	27.82 /94	11.83 /86	0.21	1.32
GR	Columbia Acorn Select 529A		C-	(800) 426-3750	C / 5.4	-2.40	5.09	16.60 /76	15.03 /59	--	0.00	N/A
GR	Columbia Acorn Select 529B		C-	(800) 426-3750	C / 5.2	-2.51	4.81	15.78 /74	14.13 /55	--	0.00	N/A
GR	Columbia Acorn Select 529C		C	(800) 426-3750	C+ / 5.7	-2.56	4.72	15.74 /74	14.22 /55	--	0.00	N/A
GR	Columbia Acorn Select 529Z		C	(800) 426-3750	C+ / 6.4	-2.31	5.24	16.96 /77	15.38 /61	--	0.00	N/A
MC	Columbia Acorn Select Fund A	LTFAX	C	(800) 426-3750	C+ / 5.8	-2.27	5.30	16.96 /77	15.51 /61	11.34 /85	0.09	1.23
MC	Columbia Acorn Select Fund B	LTFBX	C	(800) 426-3750	C / 5.4	-2.41	4.91	16.14 /75	14.67 /57	10.56 /82	0.00	1.95
MC	Columbia Acorn Select Fund C	LTFCX	C+	(800) 426-3750	C+ / 5.9	-2.46	4.87	16.04 /75	14.62 /57	10.55 /82	0.00	2.04
MC	Columbia Acorn Select Fund Z	ACTWX	C+	(800) 426-3750	C+ / 6.7	-2.22	5.43	17.28 /78	15.89 /63	11.75 /86	0.20	0.96
SC	Columbia Acorn USA 529A		C	(800) 426-3750	C+ / 6.5	-4.56	1.79	8.72 /38	18.53 /74	--	0.00	N/A
SC	Columbia Acorn USA 529B		C	(800) 426-3750	C+ / 6.3	-4.71	1.43	7.95 /32	17.67 /71	--	0.00	N/A
SC	Columbia Acorn USA 529C		C	(800) 426-3750	C+ / 6.7	-4.72	1.48	7.95 /32	17.64 /71	--	0.00	N/A
SC	Columbia Acorn USA 529Z		C+	(800) 426-3750	B- / 7.3	-4.47	2.00	9.09 /41	18.89 /76	--	0.00	N/A
SC	Columbia Acorn USA Fund A	LAUAX	C+	(800) 426-3750	C+ / 6.8	-4.44	2.04	9.12 /41	19.07 /76	9.07 /77	0.00	1.25
SC	Columbia Acorn USA Fund B	LAUBX	C+	(800) 426-3750	C+ / 6.5	-4.61	1.73	8.38 /36	18.24 /73	8.34 /73	0.00	1.95
SC	Columbia Acorn USA Fund C	LAUCX	C+	(800) 426-3750	B- / 7.0	-4.61	1.69	8.30 /35	18.20 /73	8.31 /73	0.00	2.05
SC	Columbia Acorn USA Fund Z	AUSAX	C+	(800) 426-3750	C+ / 6.9	-4.39	2.19	9.45 /43	19.51 /78	9.58 /79	0.16	0.96
AA	Columbia Agg Gr Ass Alloc 529A		C	(800) 426-3750	D+ / 2.8	-2.75	3.72	11.72 /58	11.05 /36	--	0.00	N/A
AA	Columbia Agg Gr Ass Alloc 529B		C-	(800) 426-3750	D+ / 2.5	-3.02	3.29	10.82 /52	10.16 /28	--	0.00	N/A
AA	Columbia Agg Gr Ass Alloc 529C		C	(800) 426-3750	C- / 3.2	-2.95	3.29	10.90 /53	10.19 /29	--	0.00	N/A
AA	Columbia Agg Gr Ass Alloc 529Z		C+	(800) 426-3750	C- / 4.2	-2.73	3.84	12.03 /60	11.38 /38	--	0.00	N/A
AG	Columbia Agg Gr NY 529A		U	(800) 426-3750	U /	-1.76	4.88	13.31 /65	--	--	0.00	0.97
AG	Columbia Agg Gr NY 529B		U	(800) 426-3750	U /	-1.95	4.51	12.42 /62	--	--	0.00	0.97
AA	Columbia Asset Alloc Fund II A	PHAAX	C-	(800) 426-3750	D- / 1.3	-1.30	1.23	4.64 /13	8.18 /16	2.48 /32	1.56	1.13
AA	Columbia Asset Alloc Fund II B	NBASX	C-	(800) 426-3750	D- / 1.0	-1.45	0.86	3.84 /10	7.39 /12	1.69 /25	0.91	1.88
AA	Columbia Asset Alloc Fund II C	NAACX	C-	(800) 426-3750	D- / 1.5	-1.45	0.86	3.84 /10	7.39 /12	1.69 /25	0.91	1.88
AA	Columbia Asset Alloc Fund II Z	NPRAX	C	(800) 426-3750	D+ / 2.3	-1.19	1.41	4.86 /14	8.45 /17	2.70 /34	1.90	0.88
AA	Columbia Asset Allocation Fund A	LAAAX	D+	(800) 426-3750	D / 2.0	-1.55	2.33	7.89 /32	8.91 /20	2.93 /36	1.68	1.30
AA	Columbia Asset Allocation Fund B	LAABX	D	(800) 426-3750	D- / 1.5	-1.74	1.95	7.08 /27	8.10 /16	2.21 /29	1.04	2.05
AA	Columbia Asset Allocation Fund C	LAACX	D+	(800) 426-3750	D / 2.1	-1.74	2.01	7.15 /27	8.11 /16	2.21 /29	1.04	2.05
AA	Columbia Asset Allocation Fund G	GBAAX	D	(800) 426-3750	D / 1.6	-1.72	2.04	7.20 /27	8.18 /16	2.23 /29	1.09	2.00
AA	Columbia Asset Allocation Fund T	GAAAX	D+	(800) 426-3750	D / 1.9	-1.56	2.37	7.89 /32	8.90 /20	2.92 /36	1.62	1.35
AA	Columbia Asset Allocation Fund Z	GAATX	C-	(800) 426-3750	C- / 3.0	-1.48	2.46	8.15 /34	9.21 /22	3.22 /39	1.99	1.05
AA	Columbia Bal Ass Alloc 529A		C-	(800) 426-3750	E / 0.5	-1.29	1.57	5.14 /16	5.97 / 7	--	0.00	N/A
AA	Columbia Bal Ass Alloc 529B		C-	(800) 426-3750	E / 0.5	-1.56	1.10	4.26 /12	5.13 / 4	--	0.00	N/A
AA	Columbia Bal Ass Alloc 529C		C-	(800) 426-3750	E+ / 0.7	-1.56	1.10	4.26 /12	5.16 / 4	--	0.00	N/A
AA	Columbia Bal Ass Alloc 529Z		C-	(800) 426-3750	D- / 1.3	-1.27	1.64	5.36 /17	6.25 / 7	--	0.00	N/A
BA	Columbia Bal NY 529A		U	(800) 426-3750	U /	-0.79	2.27	6.04 /21	--	--	0.00	0.84
BA	Columbia Bal NY 529C		U	(800) 426-3750	U /	-0.99	1.85	5.25 /16	--	--	0.00	0.84
BA	Columbia Balanced A	CBLAX	D+	(800) 426-3750	E+ / 0.9	-2.35	-0.05	6.38 /22	7.15 /11	2.31 /30	1.74	0.94
BA	Columbia Balanced B	CBLBX	D+	(800) 426-3750	E+ / 0.7	-2.49	-0.39	5.57 /18	6.36 / 8	1.76 /25	1.08	1.69
BA	● Columbia Balanced D	CBLDX	D+	(800) 426-3750	D- / 1.1	-2.53	-0.43	5.58 /18	6.37 / 8	--	1.08	1.69
BA	Columbia Balanced Z	CBALX	C-	(800) 426-3750	D / 1.8	-2.29	0.11	6.63 /24	7.46 /12	2.56 /32	2.09	0.69
AA	Columbia College Asset Alloc 529A		D+	(800) 426-3750	E- / 0.1	-0.36	0.82	2.31 / 5	2.87 / 1	--	0.00	N/A
AA	Columbia College Asset Alloc 529B		D+	(800) 426-3750	E- / 0.1	-0.46	0.46	1.60 / 3	2.12 / 1	--	0.00	N/A
AA	Columbia College Asset Alloc 529C		D+	(800) 426-3750	E- / 0.2	-0.46	0.56	1.69 / 4	2.25 / 1	--	0.00	N/A
AA	Columbia College Asset Alloc 529Z		D+	(800) 426-3750	E / 0.4	-0.27	0.99	2.66 / 6	3.21 / 1	--	0.00	N/A
GR	Columbia Common Stock Fund A	LCCAX	D+	(800) 426-3750	D / 1.9	-3.57	0.30	10.83 /53	9.55 /24	0.75 /19	0.05	1.14
GR	Columbia Common Stock Fund B	LCCBX	D	(800) 426-3750	D- / 1.5	-3.71	0.00	10.05 /47	8.71 /19	0.01 /15	0.00	1.89
GR	Columbia Common Stock Fund C	LCCCX	D+	(800) 426-3750	D / 2.0	-3.79	-0.08	10.05 /47	8.74 /19	--	0.00	1.89

● Denotes fund is closed to new investors

* Denotes fund is included in Section II

RISK			NET ASSETS		ASSET					BULL / BEAR		FUND MANAGER		MINIMUMS		LOADS	
	3 Year		NAV						Portfolio	Last Bull	Last Bear	Manager	Manager	Initial	Additional	Front	Back
Risk Rating/Pts	Standard Deviation	Beta	As of 6/30/06	Total $(Mil)	Cash %	Stocks %	Bonds %	Other %	Turnover Ratio	Market Return	Market Return	Quality Pct	Tenure (Years)	Purch. $	Purch. $	End Load	End Load
C+ / 6.3	11.7	1.09	22.24	8	2	97	0	1	39.0	159.5	-8.3	N/A	5	1,000	50	0.0	5.0
C+ / 6.3	11.7	1.09	22.23	5	2	97	0	1	39.0	159.2	-8.4	54	5	1,000	50	0.0	2.0
C+ / 6.3	11.7	1.09	23.16	92	2	97	0	1	39.0	168.0	-8.2	66	5	1,000	50	0.0	2.0
C+ / 5.8	10.1	1.06	16.30	1	5	94	0	1	34.0	N/A	N/A	84	3	1,000	50	5.8	1.0
C+ / 5.8	10.1	1.06	15.92	1	5	94	0	1	34.0	N/A	N/A	78	3	1,000	50	0.0	5.0
C+ / 5.8	10.1	1.06	15.96	1	5	94	0	1	34.0	N/A	N/A	79	3	1,000	50	0.0	1.0
C+ / 5.8	10.0	1.05	16.48	N/A	5	94	0	1	34.0	N/A	N/A	86	3	1,000	50	0.0	0.0
C+ / 6.5	10.1	0.81	23.55	790	2	97	0	1	19.0	85.2	-4.6	62	N/A	50,000	50	5.8	0.0
C+ / 6.6	10.1	0.81	22.69	204	2	97	0	1	19.0	81.0	-4.7	53	N/A	50,000	50	0.0	5.0
C+ / 6.6	10.1	0.81	22.66	155	2	97	0	1	19.0	80.7	-4.7	53	N/A	50,000	50	0.0	1.0
C+ / 6.7	10.1	0.81	23.87	790	2	97	0	1	19.0	87.1	-4.4	66	N/A	50,000	50	0.0	0.0
C / 5.5	12.1	0.79	18.20	N/A	9	90	0	1	13.0	N/A	N/A	85	3	1,000	50	5.8	1.0
C / 5.5	12.1	0.79	17.79	N/A	9	90	0	1	13.0	N/A	N/A	79	3	1,000	50	0.0	5.0
C / 5.4	12.2	0.79	17.78	N/A	9	90	0	1	13.0	N/A	N/A	79	3	1,000	50	0.0	1.0
C / 5.5	12.1	0.79	18.37	N/A	9	90	0	1	13.0	N/A	N/A	87	3	1,000	50	0.0	0.0
C+ / 6.6	12.2	0.79	26.96	219	9	90	0	1	13.0	117.9	-7.8	87	10	75,000	50	5.8	0.0
C+ / 6.5	12.2	0.79	25.95	68	9	90	0	1	13.0	113.1	-7.9	83	10	75,000	50	0.0	5.0
C+ / 6.5	12.2	0.79	25.92	51	9	90	0	1	13.0	113.0	-7.9	83	10	75,000	50	0.0	1.0
C+ / 6.6	12.2	0.79	27.52	1,131	9	90	0	1	13.0	120.5	-7.6	89	10	75,000	50	5.8	1.0
B / 8.8	8.7	1.64	14.49	6	0	0	0	100	N/A	N/A	N/A	56	N/A	1,000	50	5.8	1.0
B / 8.7	8.8	1.65	14.13	8	0	0	0	100	N/A	N/A	N/A	45	N/A	1,000	50	0.0	5.0
B / 8.7	8.7	1.63	14.14	2	0	0	0	100	N/A	N/A	N/A	46	N/A	1,000	50	0.0	1.0
B / 8.8	8.7	1.65	14.62	2	0	0	0	100	N/A	N/A	N/A	59	N/A	1,000	50	0.0	0.0
U /	N/A	N/A	12.26	52	0	0	0	100	N/A	N/A	N/A	N/A	3	1,000	50	5.8	1.0
U /	N/A	N/A	12.04	36	0	0	0	100	N/A	N/A	N/A	N/A	3	1,000	50	0.0	5.0
B+ / 9.4	5.1	1.08	21.82	114	0	64	34	2	102.0	42.6	-5.6	58	1	1,000	50	5.8	0.0
B+ / 9.7	5.1	1.08	21.65	19	0	64	34	2	102.0	39.0	-5.8	49	8	1,000	50	0.0	5.0
B+ / 9.7	5.1	1.08	21.63	3	0	64	34	2	102.0	39.0	-5.7	49	10	1,000	50	0.0	1.0
B+ / 9.7	5.1	1.08	21.78	22	0	64	34	2	102.0	43.4	-5.5	61	7	250,000	50	0.0	0.0
B / 8.0	5.8	1.17	15.67	6	5	61	32	2	86.0	48.9	-6.1	61	N/A	1,000	50	4.8	0.0
B / 8.0	5.8	1.17	15.67	7	5	61	32	2	86.0	45.6	-6.2	51	N/A	1,000	50	0.0	5.0
B / 8.0	5.8	1.18	15.68	1	5	61	32	2	86.0	45.4	-6.1	51	N/A	1,000	50	0.0	1.0
B / 8.0	5.8	1.17	15.67	13	5	61	32	2	86.0	45.7	-6.2	53	N/A	1,000	50	0.0	5.0
B / 8.0	5.8	1.17	15.69	176	5	61	32	2	86.0	48.8	-6.1	61	N/A	1,000	50	5.8	0.0
B / 8.0	5.8	1.17	15.68	152	5	61	32	2	86.0	50.2	-5.9	64	N/A	1,000	50	0.0	0.0
B+ / 9.9	4.1	0.84	12.28	5	0	0	0	100	N/A	N/A	N/A	46	3	1,000	50	5.8	1.0
B+ / 9.9	4.1	0.85	11.99	2	0	0	0	100	N/A	N/A	N/A	37	3	1,000	50	0.0	5.0
B+ / 9.9	4.1	0.85	11.99	5	0	0	0	100	N/A	N/A	N/A	38	3	1,000	50	0.0	1.0
B+ / 9.9	4.1	0.84	12.39	1	0	0	0	100	N/A	N/A	N/A	50	3	1,000	50	0.0	0.0
U /	N/A	N/A	11.24	39	0	0	0	100	N/A	N/A	N/A	N/A	3	1,000	50	5.8	1.0
U /	N/A	N/A	11.02	28	0	0	0	100	N/A	N/A	N/A	N/A	3	1,000	50	0.0	1.0
B / 8.8	6.0	1.20	21.86	4	2	60	36	2	63.0	37.7	-5.4	38	4	1,000	50	5.8	1.0
B / 8.9	6.0	1.20	21.86	7	2	60	36	2	63.0	34.4	-5.5	32	4	1,000	50	0.0	5.0
B / 8.9	6.0	1.20	21.85	N/A	2	60	36	2	63.0	34.7	-5.5	33	4	1,000	50	0.0	1.0
B / 8.9	6.0	1.20	21.84	236	2	60	36	2	63.0	39.1	-5.2	42	15	1,000	50	0.0	0.0
B+ / 9.9	2.0	0.40	11.07	N/A	0	0	0	100	N/A	N/A	N/A	38	3	1,000	50	5.8	1.0
B+ / 9.9	2.1	0.41	10.82	N/A	0	0	0	100	N/A	N/A	N/A	31	3	1,000	50	0.0	5.0
B+ / 9.9	2.1	0.41	10.86	N/A	0	0	0	100	N/A	N/A	N/A	33	3	1,000	50	0.0	1.0
B+ / 9.9	2.1	0.40	11.18	N/A	0	0	0	100	N/A	N/A	N/A	41	3	1,000	50	0.0	0.0
B- / 7.7	8.3	1.00	13.25	11	1	98	0	1	105.0	55.7	-9.8	37	1	1,000	50	4.8	0.0
B- / 7.6	8.3	1.00	12.71	6	1	98	0	1	105.0	52.1	-10.1	31	1	1,000	50	0.0	5.0
B- / 7.6	8.3	1.00	12.71	1	1	98	0	1	105.0	52.2	N/A	31	1	1,000	50	0.0	1.0

Fund Type	Fund Name	Ticker Symbol	Overall Weiss Investment Rating	Phone	Performance Rating/Pts	3 Mo	6 Mo	1Yr / Pct	3Yr / Pct	5Yr / Pct	Dividend Yield	Expense Ratio
GR	Columbia Common Stock Fund G	GGRBX	D	(800) 426-3750	D- / 1.5	-3.75	0.00	10.15 /48	8.74 /19	-0.01 /15	0.00	1.84
GR	Columbia Common Stock Fund T	SGIEX	D	(800) 426-3750	D / 1.8	-3.58	0.30	10.84 /53	9.48 /24	0.70 /19	0.01	1.19
GR	Columbia Common Stock Fund Z	SMGIX	C-	(800) 426-3750	D+ / 2.9	-3.48	0.45	11.12 /54	9.84 /26	1.04 /20	0.28	0.89
AA	Columbia Conser Asset Alloc 529A		D+	(800) 426-3750	E / 0.3	-0.76	1.21	3.64 / 9	4.45 / 3	--	0.00	N/A
AA	Columbia Conser Asset Alloc 529B		D+	(800) 426-3750	E- / 0.2	-0.87	0.80	2.89 / 7	3.64 / 2	--	0.00	N/A
AA	Columbia Conser Asset Alloc 529C		C-	(800) 426-3750	E / 0.4	-0.87	0.88	3.06 / 7	3.79 / 2	--	0.00	N/A
AA	Columbia Conser Asset Alloc 529Z		C-	(800) 426-3750	E+ / 0.7	-0.68	1.29	3.88 /10	4.72 / 3	--	0.00	N/A
CV	Columbia Convertible Sec Fund A	PACIX	D+	(800) 426-3750	D+ / 2.9	-0.46	3.10	9.17 /41	10.44 /30	5.48 /58	2.78	1.09
CV	Columbia Convertible Sec Fund B	NCVBX	C	(800) 426-3750	D+ / 2.4	-0.66	2.68	8.33 /35	9.61 /25	4.69 /52	2.23	1.84
CV	Columbia Convertible Sec Fund C	PHIKX	C-	(800) 426-3750	C- / 3.1	-0.65	2.65	8.30 /35	9.60 /25	4.68 /52	2.21	1.84
CV	Columbia Convertible Sec Fund Z	NCIAX	C+	(800) 426-3750	C- / 4.0	-0.46	3.16	9.37 /42	10.71 /33	5.73 /59	3.19	0.84
GR	Columbia Disciplined Value Fund A	LEVAX	B	(800) 426-3750	C+ / 6.0	0.50	6.99	15.57 /73	15.31 /60	--	1.04	1.20
GR	Columbia Disciplined Value Fund B	LEVBX	B-	(800) 426-3750	C+ / 5.6	0.32	6.69	14.78 /71	14.45 /56	--	0.43	1.95
GR	Columbia Disciplined Value Fund C	LEVCX	B	(800) 426-3750	C+ / 6.1	0.32	6.62	14.72 /71	14.42 /56	--	0.43	1.95
GR	Columbia Disciplined Value Fund G	GEVBX	B-	(800) 426-3750	C+ / 5.6	0.34	6.63	14.84 /71	14.50 /56	2.77 /34	0.48	1.90
GR	Columbia Disciplined Value Fund T	GALEX	B	(800) 426-3750	C+ / 5.9	0.42	6.96	15.51 /73	15.25 /60	3.51 /41	1.00	1.25
GR	Columbia Disciplined Value Fund Z	GEVTX	B	(800) 426-3750	C+ / 6.8	0.56	7.12	15.85 /74	15.59 /62	3.88 /45	1.31	0.95
IN	Columbia Dividend Income Fund A	LBSAX	C+	(800) 426-3750	C- / 4.1	0.42	3.95	8.87 /39	12.15 /43	--	2.02	0.95
IN	Columbia Dividend Income Fund B	LBSBX	C+	(800) 426-3750	C- / 3.4	0.32	3.64	8.06 /33	11.29 /38	--	1.41	1.70
IN	Columbia Dividend Income Fund C	LBSCX	C+	(800) 426-3750	C- / 4.2	0.32	3.64	8.06 /33	11.31 /38	--	1.42	1.70
IN	Columbia Dividend Income Fund G	GEQBX	C+	(800) 426-3750	C- / 3.5	0.25	3.58	8.12 /34	11.35 /38	3.20 /39	1.47	1.65
IN	Columbia Dividend Income Fund T	GEQAX	C+	(800) 426-3750	C- / 3.8	0.40	3.92	8.82 /39	12.08 /43	3.95 /45	1.95	1.00
IN	Columbia Dividend Income Fund Z	GSFTX	B	(800) 426-3750	C / 5.0	0.48	4.07	9.14 /41	12.42 /45	4.36 /49	2.36	0.70
AG	Columbia FS Agg Gr Portfolio A		B+	(800) 426-3750	C+ / 6.0	-1.84	5.54	15.67 /74	15.77 /62	--	0.00	N/A
AG	Columbia FS Agg Gr Portfolio B		B	(800) 426-3750	C+ / 5.8	-1.99	5.15	14.74 /71	14.88 /58	--	0.00	N/A
AG	Columbia FS Agg Gr Portfolio BX		B+	(800) 426-3750	C+ / 6.3	-1.89	5.33	15.16 /72	15.25 /60	--	0.00	N/A
AG	Columbia FS Agg Gr Portfolio C		B+	(800) 426-3750	C+ / 6.3	-1.97	5.18	14.80 /71	14.89 /58	--	0.00	N/A
AG	Columbia FS Agg Gr Portfolio CX		B	(800) 426-3750	C+ / 6.7	-1.81	5.51	15.38 /73	15.50 /61	--	0.00	N/A
AG	Columbia FS Agg Gr Portfolio Dir		B+	(800) 426-3750	C+ / 6.2	-1.85	4.41	12.67 /63	14.79 /58	--	0.00	N/A
AG	Columbia FS Agg Gr Portfolio E		B	(800) 426-3750	C+ / 6.7	-1.80	5.37	15.31 /73	15.60 /62	--	0.00	N/A
AG	Columbia FS Agg Gr Portfolio Z		B	(800) 426-3750	C+ / 6.9	-1.59	5.84	15.94 /74	16.05 /64	--	0.00	N/A
BA	Columbia FS Bal Gr Portfolio A		C+	(800) 426-3750	C- / 4.1	-1.22	4.43	11.82 /58	12.43 /45	--	0.00	N/A
BA	Columbia FS Bal Gr Portfolio B		C+	(800) 426-3750	C- / 3.8	-1.37	4.07	11.05 /54	11.57 /40	--	0.00	N/A
BA	Columbia FS Bal Gr Portfolio BX		B-	(800) 426-3750	C / 4.4	-1.33	4.20	11.35 /56	11.88 /42	--	0.00	N/A
BA	Columbia FS Bal Gr Portfolio C		B-	(800) 426-3750	C / 4.4	-1.44	3.95	10.94 /53	11.53 /39	--	0.00	N/A
BA	Columbia FS Bal Gr Portfolio CX		B	(800) 426-3750	C / 5.0	-1.24	4.33	11.64 /57	12.13 /43	--	0.00	N/A
BA	Columbia FS Bal Gr Portfolio Dir		B-	(800) 426-3750	C- / 4.2	-1.29	3.34	9.26 /42	11.00 /35	--	0.00	N/A
BA	Columbia FS Bal Gr Portfolio E		B	(800) 426-3750	C / 4.9	-1.27	4.16	11.41 /56	12.05 /43	--	0.00	N/A
BA	Columbia FS Bal Gr Portfolio Z		B	(800) 426-3750	C / 5.2	-1.13	4.17	11.73 /58	12.54 /46	--	0.00	N/A
BA	Columbia FS Balanced Portfolio A		C	(800) 426-3750	D / 2.1	-0.78	3.43	8.86 /39	9.41 /24	--	0.00	N/A
BA	Columbia FS Balanced Portfolio B		C	(800) 426-3750	D / 1.9	-0.88	3.06	8.11 /33	8.59 /18	--	0.00	N/A
BA	Columbia FS Balanced Portfolio BX		C	(800) 426-3750	D+ / 2.5	-0.87	3.12	8.36 /36	8.87 /20	--	0.00	N/A
BA	Columbia FS Balanced Portfolio C		C	(800) 426-3750	D+ / 2.5	-1.01	2.94	8.07 /33	8.55 /18	--	0.00	N/A
BA	Columbia FS Balanced Portfolio CX		C+	(800) 426-3750	C- / 3.0	-0.79	3.22	8.60 /37	9.12 /21	--	0.00	N/A
BA	Columbia FS Balanced Portfolio Dir		C	(800) 426-3750	D+ / 2.4	-0.79	2.53	6.80 /25	8.28 /16	--	0.00	N/A
BA	Columbia FS Balanced Portfolio E		C+	(800) 426-3750	C- / 3.1	-0.77	3.26	8.61 /38	9.14 /22	--	0.00	N/A
BA	Columbia FS Balanced Portfolio Z		C+	(800) 426-3750	C- / 3.5	-0.69	3.89	9.57 /44	9.81 /26	--	0.00	N/A
CV	Columbia FS Convertible Sec Port A		D+	(800) 426-3750	D / 2.0	-0.57	2.87	8.80 /39	9.23 /22	--	0.00	1.39
CV	Columbia FS Convertible Sec Port B		D+	(800) 426-3750	D / 2.2	-0.79	2.46	7.92 /32	9.28 /23	--	0.00	2.14
CV	Columbia FS Convertible Sec Port C		C-	(800) 426-3750	D+ / 2.9	-0.80	2.57	7.94 /32	9.29 /23	--	0.00	2.14
GR	Columbia FS Foc Eq Port A		D-	(800) 426-3750	D+ / 2.7	-4.80	-0.76	10.18 /48	11.11 /36	--	0.00	1.53
GR	Columbia FS Foc Eq Port B		D-	(800) 426-3750	D+ / 2.5	-4.94	-1.06	9.38 /43	10.30 /29	--	0.00	2.28

● Denotes fund is closed to new investors
* Denotes fund is included in Section II

84

RISK			NET ASSETS		ASSET					BULL / BEAR		FUND MANAGER		MINIMUMS		LOADS	
Risk Rating/Pts	3 Year Standard Deviation	Beta	NAV As of 6/30/06	Total $(Mil)	Cash %	Stocks %	Bonds %	Other %	Portfolio Turnover Ratio	Last Bull Market Return	Last Bear Market Return	Manager Quality Pct	Manager Tenure (Years)	Initial Purch. $	Additional Purch. $	Front End Load	Back End Load
B- / 7.6	8.3	1.00	12.59	4	1	98	0	1	105.0	51.8	-10.0	31	1	1,000	50	0.0	5.0
B- / 7.7	8.3	1.00	13.18	167	1	98	0	1	105.0	55.3	-9.8	37	1	1,000	50	5.8	0.0
B- / 7.7	8.2	1.00	13.32	254	1	98	0	1	105.0	56.9	-9.8	41	1	1,000	50	0.0	0.0
B+ / 9.9	2.9	0.60	11.68	3	0	0	0	100	N/A	N/A	N/A	44	N/A	1,000	50	5.8	1.0
B+ / 9.9	3.0	0.60	11.40	N/A	0	0	0	100	N/A	N/A	N/A	35	N/A	1,000	50	0.0	5.0
B+ / 9.9	3.0	0.61	11.45	3	0	0	0	100	N/A	N/A	N/A	36	N/A	1,000	50	0.0	1.0
B+ / 9.9	2.9	0.60	11.77	N/A	0	0	0	100	N/A	N/A	N/A	47	N/A	1,000	50	0.0	0.0
C+ / 6.9	6.6	1.01	16.41	335	2	27	0	71	40.0	50.8	-1.2	84	1	1,000	50	5.8	0.0
B+ / 9.2	6.6	1.01	16.20	109	2	27	0	71	40.0	47.2	-1.4	78	1	1,000	50	0.0	5.0
B- / 7.5	6.6	1.00	16.39	54	2	27	0	71	40.0	47.1	-1.4	78	1	1,000	50	0.0	1.0
B+ / 9.2	6.7	1.01	16.40	672	2	27	0	71	40.0	51.8	-1.0	85	1	250,000	50	0.0	0.0
B / 8.4	7.9	0.97	14.79	7	N/A	100	0	N/A	94.0	84.1	-9.6	89	1	1,000	50	5.8	0.0
B / 8.3	7.9	0.97	14.10	4	N/A	100	0	N/A	94.0	79.5	-9.9	86	1	1,000	50	0.0	5.0
B / 8.3	7.9	0.97	14.07	1	N/A	100	0	N/A	94.0	79.2	-9.9	85	1	1,000	50	0.0	1.0
B / 8.3	7.9	0.97	14.10	2	N/A	100	0	N/A	94.0	79.5	-9.7	86	1	1,000	50	0.0	5.0
B / 8.4	7.9	0.97	14.79	134	N/A	100	0	N/A	94.0	83.5	-9.6	89	1	1,000	50	5.8	0.0
B / 8.4	7.9	0.97	15.09	270	N/A	100	0	N/A	94.0	85.6	-9.5	91	1	1,000	50	0.0	0.0
B+ / 9.1	6.9	0.80	12.51	29	2	91	0	7	18.0	70.2	-12.1	82	26	1,000	50	4.8	0.0
B+ / 9.1	6.9	0.79	12.26	16	2	91	0	7	18.0	66.1	-12.1	75	26	1,000	50	0.0	5.0
B+ / 9.1	6.9	0.79	12.25	4	2	91	0	7	18.0	66.4	-12.3	76	26	1,000	50	0.0	1.0
B+ / 9.1	6.9	0.79	12.24	2	2	91	0	7	18.0	66.4	-12.3	76	26	1,000	50	0.0	5.0
B+ / 9.1	6.9	0.79	12.51	93	2	91	0	7	18.0	69.9	-12.1	81	26	1,000	50	5.8	0.0
B+ / 9.1	6.9	0.79	12.51	407	2	91	0	7	18.0	71.9	-12.0	83	26	1,000	50	0.0	0.0
B / 8.7	9.1	1.14	12.77	60	0	0	0	100	N/A	88.8	-10.3	83	N/A	250	50	5.8	1.0
B / 8.7	9.2	1.15	16.74	33	0	0	0	100	N/A	N/A	N/A	77	N/A	250	50	0.0	5.0
B / 8.7	9.2	1.15	12.46	11	0	0	0	100	N/A	85.9	-10.3	79	N/A	250	50	0.0	2.5
B / 8.7	9.2	1.15	16.44	21	0	0	0	100	N/A	N/A	N/A	77	N/A	250	50	0.0	1.0
B / 8.7	9.2	1.15	12.45	4	0	0	0	100	N/A	87.3	-10.3	82	N/A	250	50	0.0	0.0
B / 8.8	8.7	1.10	13.25	43	0	0	0	100	N/A	84.1	-9.8	80	N/A	250	50	0.0	0.0
B / 8.7	9.1	1.14	16.87	1	0	0	0	100	N/A	87.5	-10.3	83	N/A	250	50	0.0	0.0
B / 8.7	9.2	1.15	16.66	2	0	0	0	100	N/A	90.2	N/A	85	N/A	250	50	0.0	0.0
B+ / 9.3	6.9	1.36	12.96	39	0	0	0	100	N/A	65.7	-6.0	82	N/A	250	50	5.8	1.0
B+ / 9.3	6.9	1.36	15.07	21	0	0	0	100	N/A	N/A	N/A	76	N/A	250	50	0.0	5.0
B+ / 9.3	6.8	1.35	12.66	10	0	0	0	100	N/A	63.2	-6.1	78	N/A	250	50	0.0	2.5
B+ / 9.3	6.8	1.35	15.01	21	0	0	0	100	N/A	N/A	N/A	76	N/A	250	50	0.0	1.0
B+ / 9.3	6.8	1.35	12.76	6	0	0	0	100	N/A	64.2	-5.9	81	N/A	250	50	0.0	0.0
B+ / 9.5	6.2	1.25	12.98	28	0	0	0	100	N/A	58.1	-5.7	76	N/A	250	50	0.0	0.0
B+ / 9.3	6.9	1.36	15.53	1	0	0	0	100	N/A	64.0	-6.1	79	N/A	250	50	0.0	0.0
B+ / 9.3	6.9	1.36	15.72	1	0	0	0	100	N/A	66.2	N/A	83	N/A	250	50	0.0	0.0
B+ / 9.8	5.1	1.03	12.65	34	0	0	0	100	N/A	47.3	-3.4	73	N/A	250	50	5.8	1.0
B+ / 9.8	5.0	1.02	13.47	14	0	0	0	100	N/A	N/A	N/A	66	N/A	250	50	0.0	5.0
B+ / 9.8	5.1	1.03	12.57	8	0	0	0	100	N/A	45.2	-3.6	68	N/A	250	50	0.0	2.5
B+ / 9.8	5.1	1.03	13.66	24	0	0	0	100	N/A	N/A	N/A	65	N/A	250	50	0.0	1.0
B+ / 9.8	5.1	1.03	12.50	10	0	0	0	100	N/A	46.4	-3.4	71	N/A	250	50	0.0	0.0
B+ / 9.9	4.5	0.94	12.57	23	0	0	0	100	N/A	41.3	-3.3	68	N/A	250	50	0.0	0.0
B+ / 9.8	5.1	1.03	14.25	1	0	0	0	100	N/A	46.2	-3.6	70	N/A	250	50	0.0	0.0
B+ / 9.8	5.1	1.03	14.42	1	0	0	0	100	N/A	49.1	N/A	76	N/A	250	50	0.0	0.0
B / 8.0	6.8	1.02	13.97	1	2	27	0	71	N/A	N/A	N/A	74	N/A	250	50	5.8	1.0
B / 8.1	6.7	1.01	13.77	N/A	2	27	0	71	N/A	N/A	N/A	75	N/A	250	50	0.0	5.0
B / 8.1	6.7	1.01	13.59	1	2	27	0	71	N/A	N/A	N/A	75	N/A	250	50	0.0	1.0
C / 5.5	10.4	1.17	13.10	3	0	99	0	1	89.0	69.6	-8.9	38	N/A	250	50	5.8	1.0
C / 5.5	10.3	1.16	12.13	2	0	99	0	1	89.0	65.6	-9.1	32	N/A	250	50	0.0	5.0

Data as of June 30, 2006

Fund Type	Fund Name	Ticker Symbol	Overall Weiss Investment Rating	Phone	PERFORMANCE Perfor-mance Rating/Pts	3 Mo	6 Mo	1Yr / Pct	3Yr / Pct	5Yr / Pct	Dividend Yield	Expense Ratio
GR	Columbia FS Foc Eq Port C		D-	(800) 426-3750	C- / 3.1	-4.95	-1.21	9.35 /42	10.26 /29	--	0.00	2.28
GR	Columbia FS Foc Eq Port E		D	(800) 426-3750	C- / 3.6	-4.83	-0.86	9.93 /46	10.85 /34	--	0.00	1.78
GR	Columbia FS Foc Eq Port Z		D	(800) 426-3750	C- / 4.1	-4.68	-0.60	10.48 /50	11.40 /39	--	0.00	N/A
GR	Columbia FS Growth Eq A		D-	(800) 426-3750	D+ / 2.4	-4.60	-1.01	6.51 /23	11.18 /37	--	0.00	1.42
GR	Columbia FS Growth Eq B		D-	(800) 426-3750	D / 2.2	-4.75	-1.39	5.80 /19	10.35 /30	--	0.00	2.17
GR	Columbia FS Growth Eq C		D-	(800) 426-3750	D+ / 2.9	-4.77	-1.38	5.76 /19	10.34 /30	--	0.00	2.17
GR	Columbia FS Growth Port A		B	(800) 426-3750	C / 5.5	-1.60	5.21	14.32 /69	14.69 /57	--	0.00	1.42
GR	Columbia FS Growth Port B		B	(800) 426-3750	C / 5.2	-1.76	4.85	13.44 /66	13.83 /53	--	0.00	2.17
GR	Columbia FS Growth Port BX		B+	(800) 426-3750	C+ / 5.8	-1.67	5.00	13.79 /68	14.16 /55	--	0.00	1.87
GR	Columbia FS Growth Port C		B+	(800) 426-3750	C+ / 5.8	-1.74	4.84	13.51 /66	13.84 /53	--	0.00	2.17
GR	Columbia FS Growth Port CX		B+	(800) 426-3750	C+ / 6.2	-1.62	5.18	14.09 /68	14.41 /56	--	0.00	1.67
GR	Columbia FS Growth Port Dir		B+	(800) 426-3750	C+ / 5.7	-1.72	4.11	11.61 /57	13.66 /52	--	0.00	0.51
GR	Columbia FS Growth Port E		B+	(800) 426-3750	C+ / 6.2	-1.62	5.13	13.66 /67	14.36 /56	--	0.00	1.67
GR	Columbia FS Growth Port Z		B+	(800) 426-3750	C+ / 6.3	-1.47	5.37	13.63 /67	14.64 /57	--	0.00	N/A
GI	Columbia FS Inc & Gr Port A		C-	(800) 426-3750	E+ / 0.8	0.08	2.98	6.33 /22	6.49 / 8	--	0.00	1.12
GI	Columbia FS Inc & Gr Port B		C-	(800) 426-3750	E+ / 0.7	-0.16	2.51	5.51 /18	5.67 / 6	--	0.00	1.87
GI	Columbia FS Inc & Gr Port BX		C-	(800) 426-3750	D- / 1.0	-0.08	2.76	5.87 /20	6.03 / 7	--	0.00	1.57
GI	Columbia FS Inc & Gr Port C		C-	(800) 426-3750	D- / 1.0	-0.16	2.50	5.49 /18	5.68 / 6	--	0.00	1.87
GI	Columbia FS Inc & Gr Port CX		C-	(800) 426-3750	D- / 1.4	0.00	2.84	6.04 /21	6.24 / 7	--	0.00	1.37
GI	Columbia FS Inc & Gr Port Dir		C-	(800) 426-3750	D- / 1.1	-0.17	2.05	4.92 /15	5.73 / 6	--	0.00	0.57
GI	Columbia FS Inc & Gr Port E		C-	(800) 426-3750	D- / 1.4	0.00	2.77	6.06 /21	6.23 / 7	--	0.00	1.37
GI	Columbia FS Inc & Gr Port Z		C	(800) 426-3750	D / 1.7	0.08	3.04	6.63 /24	6.78 /10	--	0.00	N/A
FO	Columbia FS Intl Opport Port A		A+	(800) 426-3750	B+ / 8.3	-3.12	6.26	31.23 /95	21.92 /85	--	0.00	1.67
FO	Columbia FS Intl Opport Port B		A	(800) 426-3750	B+ / 8.3	-3.35	6.05	31.09 /95	21.33 /83	--	0.00	2.42
FO	Columbia FS Intl Opport Port C		A+	(800) 426-3750	B+ / 8.7	-3.39	6.13	31.57 /95	21.88 /85	--	0.00	2.42
FO	Columbia FS Intl Opport Port E		A	(800) 426-3750	B / 7.9	-2.89	5.55	26.78 /91	18.50 /74	--	0.00	1.92
FO	Columbia FS Intl Opport Port Z		A+	(800) 426-3750	B+ / 8.5	-2.91	5.67	29.83 /94	20.95 /82	--	0.00	N/A
FO	● Columbia FS Intl Value Port A		A+	(800) 426-3750	A- / 9.0	0.21	10.91	26.68 /91	25.66 /92	--	0.00	1.72
FO	● Columbia FS Intl Value Port B		A+	(800) 426-3750	B+ / 8.9	0.00	10.48	25.66 /89	24.72 /90	--	0.00	2.47
FO	● Columbia FS Intl Value Port C		A+	(800) 426-3750	A- / 9.1	0.06	10.53	25.76 /89	24.74 /90	--	0.00	2.47
GR	Columbia FS Large Cap Core Port A		D	(800) 426-3750	C- / 3.0	0.09	4.49	10.19 /48	10.58 /32	--	0.00	1.31
GR	Columbia FS Large Cap Core Port B		D	(800) 426-3750	D+ / 2.7	-0.19	4.00	9.33 /42	9.72 /25	--	0.00	2.06
GR	Columbia FS Large Cap Core Port C		D	(800) 426-3750	C- / 3.4	-0.18	4.10	9.30 /42	9.74 /25	--	0.00	2.06
GR	Columbia FS Large Cap Value Port A		C	(800) 426-3750	C+ / 5.6	-0.74	5.12	12.18 /60	15.25 /60	--	0.00	N/A
GR	Columbia FS Large Cap Value Port B		C-	(800) 426-3750	C / 5.4	-0.84	4.78	11.36 /56	14.37 /56	--	0.00	N/A
GR	Columbia FS Large Cap Value Port C		C	(800) 426-3750	C+ / 5.9	-0.93	4.73	11.35 /56	14.37 /56	--	0.00	N/A
GR	Columbia FS Large Cap Value Port Z		C+	(800) 426-3750	C+ / 6.5	-0.62	5.14	12.30 /61	15.46 /61	--	0.00	N/A
GR	Columbia FS Lrg Cap Idx Port Dir		C+	(800) 426-3750	C- / 3.9	-1.60	2.46	8.26 /35	10.80 /34	--	0.00	N/A
MC	Columbia FS Mid Cap Growth Port A		C	(800) 426-3750	C+ / 6.6	-1.16	11.87	23.27 /86	15.30 /60	--	0.00	N/A
MC	Columbia FS Mid Cap Growth Port B		C	(800) 426-3750	C+ / 6.4	-1.34	11.47	22.30 /85	14.35 /56	--	0.00	N/A
MC	Columbia FS Mid Cap Growth Port C		C	(800) 426-3750	C+ / 6.8	-1.35	11.44	22.28 /85	14.34 /56	--	0.00	N/A
MC	Columbia FS Mid Cap Growth Port Z		C+	(800) 426-3750	B- / 7.4	-1.11	11.93	23.48 /87	15.50 /61	--	0.00	N/A
MC	Columbia FS Mid Cap Indx Port Dir		A-	(800) 426-3750	B- / 7.2	-3.26	4.14	12.67 /63	17.78 /71	--	0.00	N/A
MC	Columbia FS Mid Cap Value Port A		B-	(800) 426-3750	B / 7.8	-1.51	5.94	15.17 /72	20.99 /83	--	0.00	N/A
MC	Columbia FS Mid Cap Value Port B		C+	(800) 426-3750	B- / 7.5	-1.71	5.58	14.32 /69	19.81 /79	--	0.00	N/A
MC	Columbia FS Mid Cap Value Port C		B-	(800) 426-3750	B / 8.1	-1.72	5.55	14.21 /69	20.60 /81	--	0.00	N/A
FO	Columbia FS Mul Adv Intl Eq Port A		A+	(800) 426-3750	B / 8.2	-0.67	8.60	25.92 /90	21.17 /83	--	0.00	N/A
FO	Columbia FS Mul Adv Intl Eq Port B		A+	(800) 426-3750	B / 8.1	-0.87	8.21	25.00 /88	20.39 /81	--	0.00	N/A
FO	Columbia FS Mul Adv Intl Eq Port C		A+	(800) 426-3750	B+ / 8.3	-0.84	8.16	24.98 /88	20.39 /81	--	0.00	N/A
FO	Columbia FS Mul Adv Intl Eq Port E		A+	(800) 426-3750	B+ / 8.5	-0.72	8.48	25.53 /89	20.96 /82	--	0.00	N/A
FO	Columbia FS Mul Adv Intl Eq Port Z		A+	(800) 426-3750	B+ / 8.7	-0.58	8.78	26.57 /91	21.70 /84	--	0.00	N/A
SC	Columbia FS Small Cap Growth Port		D+	(800) 426-3750	C+ / 5.7	-5.77	9.52	17.91 /79	15.48 /61	--	0.00	N/A

● Denotes fund is closed to new investors
★ Denotes fund is included in Section II

www.WeissRatings.com

RISK			NET ASSETS		ASSET					BULL / BEAR		FUND MANAGER		MINIMUMS		LOADS	
	3 Year		NAV						Portfolio	Last Bull	Last Bear	Manager	Manager	Initial	Additional	Front	Back
Risk Rating/Pts	Standard Deviation	Beta	As of 6/30/06	Total $(Mil)	Cash %	Stocks %	Bonds %	Other %	Turnover Ratio	Market Return	Market Return	Quality Pct	Tenure (Years)	Purch. $	Purch. $	End Load	End Load
C / 5.5	10.3	1.17	12.28	3	0	99	0	1	89.0	65.6	-9.1	31	N/A	250	50	0.0	1.0
C / 5.5	10.4	1.17	16.17	N/A	0	99	0	1	89.0	N/A	N/A	35	N/A	250	50	0.0	0.0
C / 5.5	10.3	1.16	14.86	N/A	0	99	0	1	89.0	70.9	-8.9	41	N/A	250	50	0.0	0.0
C+ / 5.7	9.5	1.10	14.72	1	0	99	0	1	62.0	N/A	N/A	45	N/A	250	50	5.8	1.0
C+ / 5.7	9.5	1.10	14.23	1	0	99	0	1	62.0	N/A	N/A	36	N/A	250	50	0.0	5.0
C+ / 5.7	9.5	1.10	13.58	1	0	99	0	1	62.0	N/A	N/A	36	N/A	250	50	0.0	1.0
B / 8.9	8.4	1.05	12.93	38	0	0	0	100	N/A	80.8	-8.9	83	N/A	250	50	5.8	1.0
B / 8.9	8.4	1.05	16.21	21	0	0	0	100	N/A	N/A	N/A	77	N/A	250	50	0.0	5.0
B / 8.9	8.4	1.05	12.38	10	0	0	0	100	N/A	78.3	-9.0	79	N/A	250	50	0.0	2.5
B / 8.9	8.3	1.04	15.80	16	0	0	0	100	N/A	N/A	N/A	77	N/A	250	50	0.0	1.0
B / 8.9	8.4	1.05	12.79	5	0	0	0	100	N/A	79.4	-8.9	81	N/A	250	50	0.0	0.0
B+ / 9.0	7.9	1.00	13.17	23	0	0	0	100	N/A	75.7	-8.4	78	N/A	250	50	0.0	0.0
B / 8.9	8.3	1.04	16.39	1	0	0	0	100	N/A	79.2	-8.9	81	N/A	250	50	0.0	0.0
B / 8.9	8.4	1.05	16.09	1	0	0	0	100	N/A	80.7	N/A	82	N/A	250	50	0.0	0.0
B+ / 9.9	3.2	0.39	12.10	12	0	0	0	100	N/A	29.7	-1.9	65	N/A	250	50	5.8	1.0
B+ / 9.9	3.2	0.39	12.26	2	0	0	0	100	N/A	N/A	N/A	56	N/A	250	50	0.0	5.0
B+ / 9.9	3.2	0.39	11.91	2	0	0	0	100	N/A	27.9	-2.1	60	N/A	250	50	0.0	2.5
B+ / 9.9	3.2	0.39	12.30	10	0	0	0	100	N/A	N/A	N/A	56	N/A	250	50	0.0	1.0
B+ / 9.9	3.2	0.39	11.93	5	0	0	0	100	N/A	28.6	-1.9	62	N/A	250	50	0.0	0.0
B+ / 9.9	2.8	0.33	11.95	9	0	0	0	100	N/A	26.1	-1.8	62	N/A	250	50	0.0	0.0
B+ / 9.9	3.2	0.40	12.60	N/A	0	0	0	100	N/A	28.5	-2.1	61	N/A	250	50	0.0	0.0
B+ / 9.9	3.2	0.39	12.87	N/A	0	0	0	100	N/A	30.9	N/A	68	N/A	250	50	0.0	0.0
B- / 7.8	11.9	1.11	18.32	2	0	0	0	100	165.0	135.1	-11.4	18	N/A	250	50	5.8	1.0
B- / 7.7	12.2	1.13	17.88	1	0	0	0	100	165.0	131.9	-11.6	13	N/A	250	50	0.0	5.0
B- / 7.6	12.4	1.15	17.67	2	0	0	0	100	165.0	136.3	-11.8	14	N/A	250	50	0.0	1.0
B / 8.1	10.5	0.98	20.17	N/A	0	0	0	100	165.0	N/A	N/A	17	N/A	250	50	0.0	0.0
B- / 7.9	11.4	1.06	19.02	N/A	0	0	0	100	165.0	125.8	-10.6	19	N/A	250	50	0.0	0.0
B / 8.2	10.9	1.02	18.71	N/A	0	0	0	100	15.0	153.8	-10.4	63	N/A	250	50	5.8	1.0
B / 8.2	10.9	1.02	17.19	N/A	0	0	0	100	15.0	148.0	-10.8	54	N/A	250	50	0.0	5.0
B / 8.2	10.9	1.02	17.43	N/A	0	0	0	100	15.0	147.9	-10.8	55	N/A	250	50	0.0	1.0
C+ / 6.2	7.6	0.97	10.71	1	N/A	100	0	N/A	122.0	60.2	-10.3	52	N/A	250	50	5.8	1.0
C+ / 6.1	7.6	0.97	10.66	1	N/A	100	0	N/A	122.0	56.5	-10.5	41	N/A	250	50	0.0	5.0
C+ / 6.1	7.6	0.97	10.93	1	N/A	100	0	N/A	122.0	56.4	-10.4	42	N/A	250	50	0.0	1.0
C+ / 6.0	8.7	1.07	13.35	3	1	98	0	1	52.0	84.0	-9.6	84	N/A	250	50	5.8	1.0
C+ / 6.0	8.6	1.07	12.94	2	1	98	0	1	52.0	79.4	-9.8	79	N/A	250	50	0.0	5.0
C+ / 6.0	8.7	1.07	12.85	3	1	98	0	1	52.0	79.8	-9.8	78	N/A	250	50	0.0	1.0
C+ / 6.0	8.6	1.07	16.16	N/A	1	98	0	1	52.0	85.1	-9.6	86	N/A	250	50	0.0	0.0
B+ / 9.0	7.6	1.00	11.67	7	0	0	0	100	N/A	63.0	-9.9	51	N/A	250	50	0.0	0.0
C / 5.1	12.8	1.06	11.97	2	8	91	0	1	148.0	81.9	-10.8	24	N/A	250	50	5.8	1.0
C / 5.1	12.8	1.06	11.08	1	8	91	0	1	148.0	77.4	-11.0	18	N/A	250	50	0.0	5.0
C / 5.1	12.8	1.06	11.69	1	8	91	0	1	148.0	77.4	-10.9	18	N/A	250	50	0.0	1.0
C / 5.2	12.7	1.06	16.04	N/A	8	91	0	1	148.0	83.1	-10.8	25	N/A	250	50	0.0	0.0
B / 8.2	10.9	1.01	14.85	6	0	0	0	100	N/A	102.6	-9.3	51	N/A	250	50	0.0	0.0
C+ / 5.8	9.7	0.85	18.90	1	3	96	0	1	61.0	N/A	N/A	92	N/A	250	50	5.8	1.0
C+ / 5.9	9.6	0.85	18.92	1	3	96	0	1	61.0	N/A	N/A	88	N/A	250	50	0.0	5.0
C+ / 5.8	10.0	0.86	17.68	1	3	96	0	1	61.0	N/A	N/A	91	N/A	250	50	0.0	1.0
B / 8.2	10.5	1.02	16.42	1	0	0	0	100	153.0	118.6	-10.6	25	N/A	250	50	5.8	1.0
B / 8.1	10.5	1.02	15.95	1	0	0	0	100	153.0	114.3	-10.8	21	N/A	250	50	0.0	5.0
B / 8.1	10.5	1.02	16.56	1	0	0	0	100	153.0	114.0	-10.7	21	N/A	250	50	0.0	1.0
B / 8.1	10.5	1.02	20.60	N/A	0	0	0	100	153.0	117.7	N/A	24	N/A	250	50	0.0	0.0
B / 8.2	10.5	1.02	18.96	N/A	0	0	0	100	153.0	121.4	-9.8	28	N/A	250	50	0.0	0.0
C / 4.3	15.4	1.02	13.23	1	N/A	100	0	N/A	59.0	100.4	-10.8	26	N/A	250	50	5.8	1.0

Fund Type	Fund Name	Ticker Symbol	Overall Weiss Investment Rating	Phone	PERFORMANCE Perfor-mance Rating/Pts	3 Mo	6 Mo	1Yr / Pct	Annualized 3Yr / Pct	5Yr / Pct	Incl. in Returns Dividend Yield	Expense Ratio
			99 Pct = Best *0 Pct = Worst*					Total Return % through 6/30/06				
SC	Columbia FS Small Cap Growth Port		D+	(800) 426-3750	C / 5.5	-5.91	9.15	17.08 /77	14.58 /57	--	0.00	N/A
SC	Columbia FS Small Cap Growth Port		C-	(800) 426-3750	C+ / 6.0	-5.94	9.10	17.06 /77	14.58 /57	--	0.00	N/A
SC	Columbia FS Small Cap Growth Port		C-	(800) 426-3750	C+ / 6.7	-5.72	9.61	18.17 /79	15.74 /62	--	0.00	N/A
SC	Columbia FS Small Cap Value Port A		C+	(800) 426-3750	B+ / 8.3	-3.22	9.15	15.65 /74	22.94 /87	--	0.00	N/A
SC	Columbia FS Small Cap Value Port B		C+	(800) 426-3750	B / 8.0	-3.41	8.77	14.87 /71	21.45 /84	--	0.00	N/A
SC	Columbia FS Small Cap Value Port C		B-	(800) 426-3750	B+ / 8.5	-3.39	8.79	14.87 /71	22.66 /86	--	0.00	N/A
GL	● Columbia Global Value Fund A	NVVAX	B	(800) 426-3750	B- / 7.4	1.00	8.09	17.56 /78	19.11 /76	9.44 /78	1.17	1.45
GL	● Columbia Global Value Fund B	NGLBX	B-	(800) 426-3750	B- / 7.3	0.77	7.62	16.58 /76	18.22 /73	8.61 /75	0.57	2.20
GL	● Columbia Global Value Fund C	NCGLX	B	(800) 426-3750	B / 7.6	0.69	7.62	16.58 /76	18.22 /73	8.61 /75	0.57	2.20
GL	● Columbia Global Value Fund Z	NVPAX	B+	(800) 426-3750	B / 8.0	1.01	8.15	17.75 /79	19.40 /77	9.69 /79	1.47	1.20
FO	Columbia Greater China A	NGCAX	B	(800) 426-3750	A / 9.5	4.29	22.82	30.39 /95	28.38 /94	13.27 /89	1.39	1.63
FO	Columbia Greater China B	NGCBX	B	(800) 426-3750	A / 9.5	4.10	22.36	29.41 /94	27.43 /93	12.44 /87	0.91	2.38
FO	Columbia Greater China C	NGCCX	B	(800) 426-3750	A / 9.5	4.12	22.35	29.41 /94	27.41 /93	12.40 /87	0.90	2.38
FO	Columbia Greater China Z	LNGZX	B	(800) 426-3750	A+ / 9.6	4.37	22.96	30.71 /95	28.78 /95	14.14 /90	1.61	1.38
AA	Columbia Growth Asset Alloc 529A		C-	(800) 426-3750	D / 2.1	-2.41	2.84	9.28 /42	9.48 /24	--	0.00	N/A
AA	Columbia Growth Asset Alloc 529B		C-	(800) 426-3750	D / 1.9	-2.54	2.52	8.47 /37	8.67 /19	--	0.00	N/A
AA	Columbia Growth Asset Alloc 529C		C	(800) 426-3750	D+ / 2.5	-2.61	2.44	8.47 /37	8.67 /19	--	0.00	N/A
AA	Columbia Growth Asset Alloc 529Z		C+	(800) 426-3750	C- / 3.4	-2.32	2.97	9.63 /44	9.78 /26	--	0.00	N/A
GR	Columbia Growth NY 529A		U	(800) 426-3750	U /	-1.49	3.92	10.57 /51	--	--	0.00	0.93
GR	Columbia Growth NY 529B		U	(800) 426-3750	U /	-1.68	3.45	9.64 /44	--	--	0.00	0.93
GR	Columbia Growth Stock Fund 529A		E	(800) 426-3750	E- / 0.0	-6.65	-3.27	1.67 / 4	1.99 / 1	--	0.00	N/A
GR	Columbia Growth Stock Fund 529B		E-	(800) 426-3750	E- / 0.0	-10.45	-7.39	-3.11 / 0	-0.10 / 0	--	0.00	N/A
GR	Columbia Growth Stock Fund 529C		E-	(800) 426-3750	E- / 0.0	-10.45	-7.39	-3.02 / 0	-0.10 / 0	--	0.00	N/A
GR	Columbia Growth Stock Fund 529Z		E	(800) 426-3750	E- / 0.1	-5.49	-2.02	3.04 / 7	2.67 / 1	--	0.00	N/A
GR	Columbia Growth Stock Fund A	CGSAX	E	(800) 426-3750	E- / 0.0	-5.52	-1.97	3.11 / 8	2.46 / 1	-1.51 /10	0.00	1.35
GR	Columbia Growth Stock Fund B	CGSBX	E	(800) 426-3750	E- / 0.0	-5.69	-2.37	2.29 / 5	1.68 / 0	--	0.00	2.10
GR	Columbia Growth Stock Fund C	CGSCX	E	(800) 426-3750	E- / 0.1	-5.69	-2.37	2.29 / 5	1.71 / 0	--	0.00	2.10
GR	Columbia Growth Stock Fund Z	SRFSX	E	(800) 426-3750	E- / 0.1	-5.41	-1.87	3.40 / 8	3.01 / 1	-5.44 / 2	0.28	1.07
FO	Columbia International Stk 529A		A+	(800) 426-3750	B / 8.0	-0.11	9.47	26.59 /91	19.88 /79	--	0.00	N/A
FO	Columbia International Stk 529B		A	(800) 426-3750	B / 7.9	-0.28	9.09	25.69 /89	19.07 /76	--	0.00	N/A
FO	Columbia International Stk 529C		A+	(800) 426-3750	B / 8.2	-0.28	9.15	25.74 /89	19.12 /76	--	0.00	N/A
FO	Columbia International Stk 529Z		A+	(800) 426-3750	B+ / 8.5	-0.11	9.62	26.90 /91	20.30 /80	--	0.00	N/A
FO	Columbia International Stock A	CISAX	B+	(800) 426-3750	B / 8.0	-0.05	9.43	26.63 /91	20.09 /80	--	0.63	1.18
FO	Columbia International Stock B	CISBX	B+	(800) 426-3750	B / 7.9	-0.22	9.06	25.89 /90	19.21 /77	--	0.04	1.93
FO	Columbia International Stock C	CSKCX	U	(800) 426-3750	U /	-0.22	9.02	25.94 /90	--	--	0.04	1.93
FO	● Columbia International Stock D	CISDX	B+	(800) 426-3750	B / 8.1	-0.28	9.00	25.85 /90	19.36 /77	--	0.04	1.93
FO	Columbia International Stock Z	CMISX	A-	(800) 426-3750	B+ / 8.4	0.00	9.61	27.11 /91	20.59 /81	7.84 /71	0.87	0.93
FO	● Columbia International Value Fd A	NIVLX	A-	(800) 426-3750	A- / 9.0	0.32	11.04	26.96 /91	25.98 /92	12.18 /87	1.26	1.27
FO	● Columbia International Value Fd B	NBIVX	A-	(800) 426-3750	A- / 9.0	0.16	10.67	26.10 /90	25.05 /91	11.35 /85	0.71	2.02
FO	● Columbia International Value Fd C	NVICX	A-	(800) 426-3750	A- / 9.1	0.12	10.68	26.07 /90	25.02 /91	11.35 /85	0.71	2.02
FO	● Columbia International Value Fd Z	EMIEX	A	(800) 426-3750	A / 9.3	0.36	11.22	27.28 /92	26.30 /92	12.46 /88	1.54	1.02
GR	Columbia Large Cap Core Fund A	NSGAX	C	(800) 426-3750	C- / 3.2	0.17	4.64	10.63 /51	10.87 /34	0.80 /19	0.86	1.03
GR	Columbia Large Cap Core Fund B	NSIBX	C	(800) 426-3750	D+ / 2.9	-0.08	4.19	9.74 /45	10.03 /28	0.01 /15	0.15	1.78
GR	Columbia Large Cap Core Fund C	NSGCX	C	(800) 426-3750	C- / 3.5	0.00	4.19	9.74 /45	10.02 /28	--	0.15	1.78
GR	Columbia Large Cap Core Fund Z	NSEPX	C+	(800) 426-3750	C / 4.5	0.19	4.73	10.87 /53	11.15 /37	1.01 /20	1.38	0.78
GR	Columbia Large Cap Enh Core Fd A	NMIAX	C	(800) 426-3750	C / 4.4	-2.19	2.22	8.46 /36	11.72 /41	3.02 /37	1.14	0.75
GR	Columbia Large Cap Enh Core Fd Z	NMIMX	C	(800) 426-3750	C / 4.6	-2.15	2.40	8.81 /39	11.98 /42	3.29 /39	1.62	0.50
GR	Columbia Large Cap Growth Fund A	LEGAX	D-	(800) 426-3750	D- / 1.1	-3.69	0.32	7.37 /28	7.59 /13	-1.17 /11	0.18	0.98
GR	Columbia Large Cap Growth Fund B	LEGBX	D-	(800) 426-3750	E+ / 0.8	-3.84	-0.05	6.60 /24	6.77 / 9	-1.97 / 8	0.00	1.73
GR	Columbia Large Cap Growth Fund C	LEGCX	D-	(800) 426-3750	D- / 1.3	-3.84	-0.05	6.59 /24	6.80 /10	--	0.00	1.73
GR	Columbia Large Cap Growth Fund G	GBEGX	D-	(800) 426-3750	E+ / 0.9	-3.82	-0.05	6.65 /24	6.82 /10	-2.04 / 8	0.00	1.68
GR	Columbia Large Cap Growth Fund T	GAEGX	D-	(800) 426-3750	D- / 1.1	-3.67	0.28	7.37 /28	7.54 /13	-1.32 /11	0.13	1.03

● Denotes fund is closed to new investors
* Denotes fund is included in Section II

RISK			NET ASSETS		ASSET					BULL / BEAR		FUND MANAGER		MINIMUMS		LOADS	
	3 Year		NAV						Portfolio	Last Bull	Last Bear	Manager	Manager	Initial	Additional	Front	Back
Risk	Standard		As of	Total	Cash	Stocks	Bonds	Other	Turnover	Market	Market	Quality	Tenure	Purch.	Purch.	End	End
Rating/Pts	Deviation	Beta	6/30/06	$(Mil)	%	%	%	%	Ratio	Return	Return	Pct	(Years)	$	$	Load	Load
C /4.3	15.5	1.03	11.93	1	N/A	100	0	N/A	59.0	95.6	-11.0	20	N/A	250	50	0.0	5.0
C /4.3	15.4	1.02	12.35	1	N/A	100	0	N/A	59.0	95.6	-10.9	20	N/A	250	50	0.0	1.0
C /4.3	15.5	1.02	16.65	N/A	N/A	100	0	N/A	59.0	102.0	-11.5	27	N/A	250	50	0.0	0.0
C /5.1	12.8	0.86	19.81	1	3	96	0	1	61.0	N/A	N/A	95	N/A	250	50	5.8	1.0
C /5.1	12.8	0.87	19.85	1	3	96	0	1	61.0	N/A	N/A	91	N/A	250	50	0.0	5.0
C /5.1	13.0	0.87	19.93	1	3	96	0	1	61.0	N/A	N/A	94	N/A	250	50	0.0	1.0
C+/6.7	10.0	0.89	11.82	115	0	99	0	1	16.0	115.7	-14.0	32	5	1,000	50	5.8	2.0
C+/6.6	9.9	0.88	11.55	30	0	99	0	1	16.0	110.7	-14.2	27	5	1,000	50	0.0	5.0
C+/6.6	10.0	0.88	11.55	90	0	99	0	1	16.0	110.8	-14.2	27	5	1,000	50	0.0	2.0
C+/6.7	10.0	0.88	11.90	107	0	99	0	1	16.0	117.6	-14.0	34	5	250,000	50	0.0	2.0
C /4.8	16.6	1.16	30.62	74	3	96	0	1	24.0	138.7	-4.5	56	N/A	1,000	50	5.8	2.0
C /4.8	16.6	1.16	29.93	16	3	96	0	1	24.0	133.0	-4.7	45	N/A	1,000	50	0.0	5.0
C /4.8	16.6	1.16	30.33	21	3	96	0	1	24.0	132.9	-4.7	46	N/A	1,000	50	0.0	2.0
C /4.8	16.6	1.16	31.76	17	3	96	0	1	24.0	147.1	-4.4	59	N/A	1,000	50	0.0	2.0
B+/9.2	7.1	1.38	13.78	5	0	0	0	100	N/A	N/A	N/A	55	N/A	1,000	50	5.8	1.0
B+/9.0	7.1	1.38	13.45	9	0	0	0	100	N/A	N/A	N/A	45	N/A	1,000	50	0.0	5.0
B+/9.0	7.1	1.38	13.45	3	0	0	0	100	N/A	N/A	N/A	45	N/A	1,000	50	0.0	1.0
B+/9.3	7.1	1.38	13.89	3	0	0	0	100	N/A	N/A	N/A	58	N/A	1,000	50	0.0	0.0
U /	N/A	N/A	11.93	51	0	0	0	100	N/A	N/A	N/A	N/A	3	1,000	50	5.8	1.0
U /	N/A	N/A	11.71	29	0	0	0	100	N/A	N/A	N/A	N/A	3	1,000	50	0.0	5.0
C /5.1	10.1	1.19	10.95	N/A	1	98	0	1	2.0	N/A	N/A	2	N/A	1,000	50	5.8	1.0
C /5.0	10.4	1.20	10.28	N/A	1	98	0	1	2.0	N/A	N/A	1	N/A	1,000	50	0.0	5.0
C /5.0	10.5	1.21	10.28	N/A	1	98	0	1	2.0	N/A	N/A	1	N/A	1,000	50	0.0	1.0
C /5.2	10.0	1.17	11.18	N/A	1	98	0	1	2.0	N/A	N/A	2	N/A	1,000	50	0.0	0.0
C+/6.1	10.1	1.18	10.95	49	1	98	0	1	2.0	31.6	-10.5	2	N/A	1,000	50	5.8	0.0
C+/6.0	10.1	1.18	10.28	132	1	98	0	1	2.0	28.7	-10.7	1	3	1,000	50	0.0	5.0
C+/6.0	10.1	1.18	10.28	11	1	98	0	1	2.0	28.7	-10.7	1	3	1,000	50	0.0	1.0
C+/6.2	10.1	1.18	8.91	226	1	98	0	1	2.0	34.1	-10.4	3	3	1,000	50	0.0	0.0
B /8.1	10.5	1.02	18.14	N/A	0	0	0	100	66.0	N/A	N/A	19	N/A	1,000	50	5.8	1.0
B /8.1	10.5	1.01	17.76	N/A	0	0	0	100	66.0	N/A	N/A	15	N/A	1,000	50	0.0	5.0
B /8.1	10.5	1.01	17.78	N/A	0	0	0	100	66.0	N/A	N/A	15	N/A	1,000	50	0.0	1.0
B /8.1	10.5	1.02	18.35	N/A	0	0	0	100	66.0	N/A	N/A	21	N/A	1,000	50	0.0	0.0
C+/6.9	10.5	1.01	18.34	272	2	97	0	1	66.0	108.6	-8.7	20	N/A	1,000	50	5.8	2.0
C+/6.9	10.5	1.01	17.93	47	2	97	0	1	66.0	103.9	-9.1	16	N/A	1,000	50	0.0	5.0
U /	N/A	N/A	18.00	28	2	97	0	1	66.0	N/A	N/A	N/A	3	1,000	50	0.0	2.0
C+/6.8	10.5	1.02	18.05	1	2	97	0	1	66.0	105.2	-9.0	16	N/A	1,000	50	1.0	2.0
C+/6.9	10.4	1.01	18.47	1,000	2	97	0	1	66.0	111.9	-8.7	23	14	1,000	50	0.0	2.0
C+/6.5	10.9	1.02	23.49	992	N/A	100	0	N/A	15.0	155.9	-10.5	66	N/A	1,000	50	5.8	2.0
C+/6.4	10.9	1.02	23.02	109	N/A	100	0	N/A	15.0	149.8	-10.6	58	N/A	1,000	50	0.0	5.0
C+/6.4	10.9	1.02	22.99	162	N/A	100	0	N/A	15.0	149.9	-10.7	58	N/A	1,000	50	0.0	2.0
C+/6.5	10.9	1.02	23.62	2,461	N/A	100	0	N/A	15.0	157.9	-10.4	69	N/A	250,000	50	0.0	2.0
B /8.6	7.6	0.98	13.36	194	N/A	100	0	N/A	122.0	61.8	-10.2	55	N/A	1,000	50	5.8	1.0
B /8.6	7.6	0.98	12.94	30	N/A	100	0	N/A	122.0	57.8	-10.4	45	N/A	1,000	50	0.0	5.0
B /8.5	7.7	0.98	12.94	14	N/A	100	0	N/A	122.0	57.7	-10.3	44	N/A	1,000	50	0.0	1.0
B /8.6	7.6	0.97	13.37	1,349	N/A	100	0	N/A	122.0	62.9	-10.2	58	N/A	250,000	50	0.0	0.0
B- /7.5	7.9	1.02	13.22	18	4	95	0	1	269.0	67.1	-9.4	60	N/A	1,000	50	0.0	0.0
B- /7.5	7.9	1.02	13.24	469	4	95	0	1	269.0	68.5	-9.4	62	N/A	250,000	50	0.0	0.0
C+/6.8	9.4	1.13	21.66	10	0	99	0	1	113.0	48.8	-10.3	17	1	1,000	50	5.8	0.0
C+/6.8	9.4	1.13	20.51	8	0	99	0	1	113.0	45.1	-10.4	13	1	1,000	50	0.0	5.0
C+/6.8	9.4	1.13	20.54	2	0	99	0	1	113.0	45.2	-10.4	13	1	1,000	50	0.0	1.0
C+/6.8	9.4	1.13	19.89	29	0	99	0	1	113.0	45.2	-10.5	13	1	1,000	50	0.0	5.0
C+/6.8	9.4	1.13	21.53	210	0	99	0	1	113.0	48.4	-10.3	16	1	1,000	50	5.8	0.0

Fund Type	Fund Name	Ticker Symbol	Overall Weiss Investment Rating	Phone	Performance Rating/Pts	3 Mo	6 Mo	1Yr / Pct	3Yr / Pct	5Yr / Pct	Dividend Yield	Expense Ratio
GR	Columbia Large Cap Growth Fund Z	GEGTX	D	(800) 426-3750	D / 2.0	-3.63	0.41	7.63 /30	7.86 /14	-0.95 /12	0.41	0.73
IX	Columbia Large Cap Index Fund A	NEIAX	C+	(800) 426-3750	C- / 3.8	-1.55	2.52	8.22 /34	10.78 /33	2.00 /27	1.48	0.39
IX	Columbia Large Cap Index Fund Z	NINDX	D+	(800) 426-3750	C- / 4.1	-1.49	2.63	8.50 /37	11.05 /36	2.25 /30	1.70	0.14
GR	Columbia Large Cap Value 529A		C+	(800) 426-3750	C- / 3.6	-0.66	5.18	10.76 /52	11.68 /40	--	0.00	N/A
GR	Columbia Large Cap Value 529B		C	(800) 426-3750	C- / 3.3	-0.88	4.78	9.96 /47	10.84 /34	--	0.00	N/A
GR	Columbia Large Cap Value 529C		C+	(800) 426-3750	C- / 4.1	-0.88	4.78	9.96 /47	10.87 /34	--	0.00	N/A
GR	Columbia Large Cap Value 529Z		B	(800) 426-3750	C / 5.0	-0.59	5.34	11.05 /54	12.02 /43	--	0.00	N/A
GI	Columbia Large Cap Value Fund A	NVLEX	B	(800) 426-3750	C+ / 5.9	-0.70	5.33	12.46 /62	15.59 /62	6.14 /62	1.10	0.96
GI	Columbia Large Cap Value Fund B	NVLNX	B-	(800) 426-3750	C / 5.5	-0.85	4.94	11.56 /57	14.68 /57	5.31 /56	0.47	1.71
GI	Columbia Large Cap Value Fund C	NVALX	B	(800) 426-3750	C+ / 6.1	-0.85	4.94	11.65 /58	14.69 /57	5.32 /57	0.47	1.71
GI	Columbia Large Cap Value Fund Z	NVLUX	B	(800) 426-3750	C+ / 6.7	-0.57	5.45	12.80 /63	15.84 /63	6.38 /63	1.41	0.71
BA	Columbia Liberty Fund A	COLFX	C-	(800) 426-3750	D- / 1.4	-1.68	1.96	7.54 /29	8.34 /17	3.24 /39	1.97	1.07
BA	Columbia Liberty Fund B	CCFBX	C-	(800) 426-3750	D- / 1.3	-1.76	1.70	6.87 /25	7.58 /13	2.49 /32	1.35	1.82
BA	Columbia Liberty Fund C	CTCCX	C-	(800) 426-3750	D / 1.8	-1.76	1.70	6.88 /26	7.59 /13	2.49 /32	1.35	1.82
BA	Columbia Liberty Fund Z	CTCFX	C	(800) 426-3750	D+ / 2.6	-1.64	2.07	7.80 /31	8.60 /18	3.49 /41	2.18	0.84
AA	Columbia Life Goal Bal Growth Fd A	NBIAX	C	(800) 426-3750	D+ / 2.8	-1.06	3.08	8.78 /39	10.46 /31	5.88 /60	2.36	1.29
AA	Columbia Life Goal Bal Growth Fd B	NLBBX	C	(800) 426-3750	D+ / 2.4	-1.25	2.72	8.02 /33	9.66 /25	5.10 /55	1.78	2.04
AA	Columbia Life Goal Bal Growth Fd C	NBICX	C	(800) 426-3750	C- / 3.1	-1.15	2.78	8.03 /33	9.68 /25	5.11 /55	1.76	2.04
AA	Columbia Life Goal Bal Growth Fd Z	NBGPX	C+	(800) 426-3750	C- / 4.0	-0.99	3.22	9.07 /40	10.75 /33	6.16 /62	2.74	1.04
GR	Columbia Life Goal Growth Fund A	NLGIX	C+	(800) 426-3750	C+ / 6.5	-1.79	5.73	16.05 /75	16.51 /66	5.76 /59	1.02	1.39
GR	Columbia Life Goal Growth Fund B	NLGBX	C+	(800) 426-3750	C+ / 6.1	-1.99	5.30	15.18 /72	15.62 /62	4.96 /54	0.77	2.14
GR	Columbia Life Goal Growth Fund C	NLGCX	C+	(800) 426-3750	C+ / 6.6	-2.00	5.25	15.09 /72	15.57 /62	4.95 /54	0.77	2.14
GR	Columbia Life Goal Growth Fund Z	NGPAX	B	(800) 426-3750	B- / 7.2	-1.79	5.84	16.27 /75	16.77 /67	6.00 /61	1.19	1.14
AA	Columbia Life Goal Inc & Gr Fund A	NLGAX	D	(800) 426-3750	E+ / 0.9	-0.30	2.33	5.97 /20	6.81 /10	4.93 /54	2.91	1.16
AA	Columbia Life Goal Inc & Gr Fund B	NLIBX	D+	(800) 426-3750	E+ / 0.7	-0.49	1.96	5.10 /16	6.02 / 7	4.13 /47	2.35	1.91
AA	Columbia Life Goal Inc & Gr Fund C	NIICX	C-	(800) 426-3750	D- / 1.1	-0.49	1.88	5.12 /16	5.99 / 7	4.13 /47	2.37	1.91
AA	Columbia Life Goal Inc & Gr Fund Z	NIPAX	C-	(800) 426-3750	D / 1.8	-0.34	2.38	6.07 /21	7.04 /10	5.17 /55	3.35	0.91
GR	Columbia Marsico 21st Century Fd A	NMTAX	B+	(800) 426-3750	B / 7.8	-2.70	7.96	22.62 /85	20.47 /81	12.52 /88	0.03	1.31
GR	Columbia Marsico 21st Century Fd B	NMTBX	B	(800) 426-3750	B / 7.6	-2.90	7.53	21.75 /84	19.56 /78	11.68 /86	0.00	2.06
GR	Columbia Marsico 21st Century Fd C	NMYCX	B+	(800) 426-3750	B / 7.9	-2.90	7.53	21.75 /84	19.56 /78	11.68 /86	0.00	2.06
GR	Columbia Marsico 21st Century Fd R	CMTRX	C+	(800) 426-3750	B / 8.1	-2.84	7.80	22.45 /85	20.42 /81	12.48 /88	0.04	1.39
GR	Columbia Marsico 21st Century Fd Z	NMYAX	B+	(800) 426-3750	B+ / 8.3	-2.66	8.10	22.97 /86	20.74 /82	12.81 /88	0.24	1.06
GR	Columbia Marsico Focus 529A		C-	(800) 426-3750	D+ / 2.8	-4.73	-0.81	10.12 /48	11.28 /38	--	0.00	N/A
GR	Columbia Marsico Focus 529B		C-	(800) 426-3750	D+ / 2.6	-4.90	-1.10	9.36 /42	10.50 /31	--	0.00	N/A
GR	Columbia Marsico Focus 529C		C	(800) 426-3750	C- / 3.3	-4.83	-1.10	9.36 /42	10.50 /31	--	0.00	N/A
GR	Columbia Marsico Focus 529Z		C+	(800) 426-3750	C- / 4.2	-4.63	-0.60	10.50 /50	11.66 /40	--	0.00	N/A
★ GR	Columbia Marsico Focused Eq Fd A	NFEAX	C-	(800) 426-3750	C- / 3.1	-4.69	-0.59	10.56 /51	11.42 /39	4.68 /52	0.00	1.22
GR	Columbia Marsico Focused Eq Fd B	NFEBX	D+	(800) 426-3750	D+ / 2.6	-4.87	-0.99	9.67 /45	10.60 /32	3.89 /45	0.00	1.97
GR	Columbia Marsico Focused Eq Fd C	NFECX	C-	(800) 426-3750	C- / 3.3	-4.91	-0.99	9.64 /44	10.59 /32	3.89 /45	0.00	1.97
GR	Columbia Marsico Focused Eq Fd Z	NFEPX	C	(800) 426-3750	C / 4.3	-4.66	-0.49	10.78 /52	11.71 /41	4.94 /54	0.00	0.97
GR	Columbia Marsico Growth 529A		C-	(800) 426-3750	D+ / 2.3	-4.60	-1.54	5.89 /20	11.13 /36	--	0.00	N/A
GR	Columbia Marsico Growth 529B		C-	(800) 426-3750	D / 2.1	-4.82	-1.91	5.03 /15	10.27 /29	--	0.00	N/A
GR	Columbia Marsico Growth 529C		C-	(800) 426-3750	D+ / 2.8	-4.76	-1.91	5.11 /16	10.29 /29	--	0.00	N/A
GR	Columbia Marsico Growth 529Z		C	(800) 426-3750	C- / 3.7	-4.49	-1.39	6.13 /21	11.50 /39	--	0.00	N/A
★ GR	Columbia Marsico Growth Fund A	NMGIX	C-	(800) 426-3750	D+ / 2.8	-4.51	-0.85	6.88 /26	11.48 /39	3.89 /45	0.00	1.21
GR	Columbia Marsico Growth Fund B	NGIBX	D+	(800) 426-3750	D+ / 2.4	-4.67	-1.24	6.05 /21	10.64 /32	3.11 /38	0.00	1.96
GR	Columbia Marsico Growth Fund C	NMICX	C-	(800) 426-3750	C- / 3.1	-4.67	-1.18	6.10 /21	10.68 /33	3.12 /38	0.00	1.96
GR	Columbia Marsico Growth Fund R	CMWRX	D	(800) 426-3750	C- / 3.4	-4.57	-1.12	6.59 /24	11.38 /38	3.83 /44	0.00	1.54
GR	Columbia Marsico Growth Fund Z	NGIPX	C	(800) 426-3750	C- / 4.0	-4.44	-0.73	7.13 /27	11.75 /41	4.14 /47	0.00	0.96
FO	Columbia Marsico Intl Opp Fund A	MAIOX	B-	(800) 426-3750	B+ / 8.4	-3.12	6.54	32.25 /96	22.66 /86	13.01 /89	0.69	1.34
FO	Columbia Marsico Intl Opp Fund B	MBIOX	C+	(800) 426-3750	B+ / 8.4	-3.31	6.13	31.27 /95	21.74 /84	12.17 /87	0.11	2.09
FO	Columbia Marsico Intl Opp Fund C	MCIOX	B-	(800) 426-3750	B+ / 8.6	-3.30	6.21	31.37 /95	21.77 /85	12.19 /87	0.11	2.09

● Denotes fund is closed to new investors
★ Denotes fund is included in Section II

Risk Rating/Pts	3 Year Standard Deviation	Beta	NAV As of 6/30/06	Total $(Mil)	Cash %	Stocks %	Bonds %	Other %	Portfolio Turnover Ratio	Last Bull Market Return	Last Bear Market Return	Manager Quality Pct	Manager Tenure (Years)	Initial Purch. $	Additional Purch. $	Front End Load	Back End Load
C+ / 6.9	9.4	1.13	22.05	952	0	99	0	1	113.0	50.0	-10.2	18	1	1,000	50	0.0	0.0
B / 8.7	7.7	1.00	24.47	69	2	97	0	1	12.0	62.7	-9.9	51	N/A	1,000	50	0.0	0.0
C+ / 5.8	7.6	1.00	24.66	2,280	2	97	0	1	12.0	63.9	-9.8	55	N/A	250,000	50	0.0	0.0
B+ / 9.1	7.6	0.89	15.03	1	0	0	0	100	52.0	N/A	N/A	71	N/A	1,000	50	5.8	1.0
B+ / 9.1	7.6	0.90	14.68	1	0	0	0	100	52.0	N/A	N/A	62	N/A	1,000	50	0.0	5.0
B+ / 9.1	7.6	0.90	14.69	N/A	0	0	0	100	52.0	N/A	N/A	62	N/A	1,000	50	0.0	1.0
B+ / 9.1	7.6	0.89	15.18	N/A	0	0	0	100	52.0	N/A	N/A	73	N/A	1,000	50	0.0	0.0
B / 8.2	8.6	1.07	14.02	1,119	1	97	0	2	59.0	85.7	-9.6	86	N/A	1,000	50	5.8	0.0
B / 8.2	8.6	1.07	13.62	626	1	97	0	2	59.0	81.0	-9.7	81	N/A	1,000	50	0.0	5.0
B / 8.2	8.7	1.08	13.62	94	1	97	0	2	59.0	81.2	-9.8	80	N/A	1,000	50	0.0	1.0
B / 8.2	8.7	1.08	14.04	2,005	1	97	0	2	59.0	87.0	-9.5	87	N/A	250,000	50	0.0	0.0
B+ / 9.2	5.6	1.13	8.55	514	5	61	32	2	83.0	46.5	-6.0	57	1	1,000	50	5.8	1.0
B+ / 9.1	5.6	1.14	8.55	95	5	61	32	2	83.0	43.2	-6.2	47	1	1,000	50	0.0	5.0
B+ / 9.2	5.5	1.12	8.53	5	5	61	32	2	83.0	43.0	-6.2	48	1	1,000	50	0.0	1.0
B+ / 9.2	5.5	1.13	9.09	1	5	61	32	2	83.0	47.7	-6.1	60	1	1,000	50	0.0	0.0
B / 8.9	5.7	1.16	11.50	221	3	53	42	2	23.0	55.6	-4.4	76	N/A	1,000	50	5.8	0.0
B+ / 9.1	5.7	1.16	11.45	311	3	53	42	2	23.0	52.0	-4.7	69	N/A	1,000	50	0.0	5.0
B+ / 9.0	5.7	1.16	11.57	102	3	53	42	2	23.0	52.1	-4.6	69	N/A	1,000	50	0.0	1.0
B+ / 9.0	5.7	1.16	11.48	251	3	53	42	2	23.0	56.7	-4.3	78	N/A	250,000	50	0.0	0.0
C+ / 6.9	9.5	1.19	13.41	152	0	99	0	1	22.0	93.4	-9.6	85	N/A	1,000	50	5.8	0.0
C+ / 6.8	9.5	1.18	12.78	152	0	99	0	1	22.0	88.7	-9.8	80	N/A	1,000	50	0.0	5.0
C+ / 6.8	9.5	1.18	12.70	72	0	99	0	1	22.0	88.6	-9.7	80	N/A	1,000	50	0.0	1.0
C+ / 6.9	9.5	1.18	13.49	192	0	99	0	1	22.0	94.9	-9.5	87	N/A	250,000	50	0.0	0.0
B / 8.6	3.5	0.71	10.54	49	2	30	66	2	16.0	32.8	-1.4	65	N/A	1,000	50	5.8	0.0
B+ / 9.3	3.5	0.73	10.51	78	2	30	66	2	16.0	29.6	-1.6	55	N/A	1,000	50	0.0	5.0
B+ / 9.2	3.5	0.72	10.45	22	2	30	66	2	16.0	29.6	-1.6	55	N/A	1,000	50	0.0	1.0
B+ / 9.2	3.5	0.72	10.46	66	2	30	66	2	16.0	33.8	-1.3	67	N/A	250,000	50	0.0	0.0
C+ / 6.9	13.1	1.40	13.00	948	12	87	0	1	141.0	125.5	-8.8	93	N/A	1,000	50	5.8	0.0
C+ / 6.9	13.2	1.40	12.49	107	12	87	0	1	141.0	120.3	-8.9	90	N/A	1,000	50	0.0	5.0
C+ / 6.9	13.1	1.40	12.49	226	12	87	0	1	141.0	120.3	-8.9	90	N/A	1,000	50	0.0	1.0
C / 5.3	13.2	1.40	13.02	N/A	12	87	0	1	141.0	125.5	-8.8	92	N/A	1,000	50	0.0	2.0
C+ / 6.9	13.1	1.40	13.15	342	12	87	0	1	141.0	127.5	-8.8	93	N/A	250,000	50	0.0	0.0
B / 8.3	10.3	1.16	14.69	N/A	0	0	0	100	N/A	N/A	N/A	41	3	1,000	50	5.8	1.0
B / 8.3	10.2	1.15	14.37	N/A	0	0	0	100	N/A	N/A	N/A	34	3	1,000	50	0.0	5.0
B / 8.3	10.3	1.16	14.37	N/A	0	0	0	100	N/A	N/A	N/A	34	3	1,000	50	0.0	1.0
B / 8.3	10.3	1.16	14.84	N/A	0	0	0	100	N/A	N/A	N/A	44	3	1,000	50	0.0	0.0
B- / 7.3	10.3	1.16	20.11	2,060	0	99	0	1	89.0	71.0	-8.8	41	9	1,000	50	5.8	0.0
B- / 7.2	10.3	1.16	18.94	449	0	99	0	1	89.0	67.1	-9.0	34	9	1,000	50	0.0	5.0
B- / 7.2	10.3	1.16	18.99	529	0	99	0	1	89.0	67.0	-9.0	34	9	1,000	50	0.0	1.0
B- / 7.3	10.3	1.16	20.45	1,019	0	99	0	1	89.0	72.4	-8.8	44	9	250,000	50	0.0	0.0
B / 8.6	9.5	1.08	14.74	1	0	0	0	100	N/A	N/A	N/A	46	3	1,000	50	5.8	1.0
B / 8.5	9.5	1.08	14.40	1	0	0	0	100	N/A	N/A	N/A	37	3	1,000	50	0.0	5.0
B / 8.5	9.6	1.09	14.41	N/A	0	0	0	100	N/A	N/A	N/A	37	3	1,000	50	0.0	1.0
B / 8.6	9.5	1.08	14.90	N/A	0	0	0	100	N/A	N/A	N/A	50	3	1,000	50	0.0	0.0
B- / 7.6	9.5	1.10	18.65	2,066	0	99	0	1	62.0	69.6	-8.0	49	N/A	1,000	50	5.8	0.0
B- / 7.6	9.5	1.09	17.54	178	0	99	0	1	62.0	65.7	-8.3	40	N/A	1,000	50	0.0	5.0
B- / 7.6	9.5	1.10	17.57	693	0	99	0	1	62.0	65.6	-8.2	39	N/A	1,000	50	0.0	1.0
C+ / 5.7	9.5	1.10	18.60	N/A	0	99	0	1	62.0	69.2	-8.0	47	N/A	1,000	50	0.0	2.0
B- / 7.6	9.5	1.10	18.94	1,511	0	99	0	1	62.0	71.0	-8.0	52	N/A	250,000	50	0.0	0.0
C / 5.3	12.2	1.13	13.42	194	5	94	0	1	118.0	140.2	-11.4	19	N/A	1,000	50	5.8	2.0
C / 5.1	12.2	1.13	12.91	32	5	94	0	1	118.0	134.5	-11.5	15	N/A	1,000	50	0.0	5.0
C / 5.1	12.2	1.13	12.92	58	5	94	0	1	118.0	134.7	-11.5	15	N/A	1,000	50	0.0	2.0

Fund Type	Fund Name	Ticker Symbol	Overall Weiss Investment Rating	Phone	Performance Rating/Pts	3 Mo	6 Mo	1Yr / Pct	3Yr / Pct	5Yr / Pct	Dividend Yield	Expense Ratio
								Total Return % through 6/30/06	Annualized		Incl. in Returns	
FO	Columbia Marsico Intl Opp Fund R	CMORX	B-	(800) 426-3750	B+ / 8.8	-3.19	6.46	32.16 /96	22.62 /86	--	0.73	1.64
FO	Columbia Marsico Intl Opp Fund Z	NMOAX	B	(800) 426-3750	B+ / 8.9	-3.02	6.70	32.65 /96	23.01 /87	13.31 /89	0.92	1.09
MC	Columbia Marsico Mid Cap Gr Fund	NEGAX	C+	(800) 426-3750	C+ / 6.8	-1.13	12.02	23.50 /87	15.53 /61	-0.80 /12	0.00	1.18
MC	Columbia Marsico Mid Cap Gr Fund	NEGNX	C+	(800) 426-3750	C+ / 6.5	-1.30	11.56	22.56 /85	14.56 /57	-1.62 / 9	0.00	1.93
MC	Columbia Marsico Mid Cap Gr Fund	NEMGX	C+	(800) 426-3750	C+ / 6.9	-1.29	11.58	22.62 /85	14.57 /57	-1.61 /10	0.00	1.93
MC	Columbia Marsico Mid Cap Gr Fund Z	NEGRX	B-	(800) 426-3750	B- / 7.5	-1.02	12.12	23.82 /87	15.83 /63	-0.57 /13	0.00	0.93
MC	Columbia Mid Cap Growth 529A		D	(800) 426-3750	C / 4.7	-5.17	4.85	20.11 /82	13.38 /51	--	0.00	N/A
MC	Columbia Mid Cap Growth 529B		D	(800) 426-3750	C / 4.4	-5.35	4.48	19.21 /81	12.46 /45	--	0.00	N/A
MC	Columbia Mid Cap Growth 529C		D	(800) 426-3750	C / 5.0	-5.35	4.48	19.21 /81	12.46 /45	--	0.00	N/A
MC	Columbia Mid Cap Growth 529Z		D+	(800) 426-3750	C+ / 5.9	-5.07	5.08	20.51 /82	13.70 /52	--	0.00	N/A
MC	Columbia Mid Cap Growth Fund A	CBSAX	D+	(800) 426-3750	C / 5.2	-5.04	5.02	20.42 /82	14.08 /54	3.62 /42	0.00	1.18
MC	Columbia Mid Cap Growth Fund B	CBSBX	D	(800) 426-3750	C / 4.8	-5.21	4.67	19.57 /81	13.21 /50	2.10 /28	0.00	1.93
MC ●	Columbia Mid Cap Growth Fund D	CBSDX	D+	(800) 426-3750	C / 5.4	-5.25	4.62	19.50 /81	13.25 /50	--	0.00	1.93
MC	Columbia Mid Cap Growth Fund G	CBSGX	D	(800) 426-3750	C / 4.8	-5.19	4.68	19.57 /81	13.14 /50	--	0.00	1.88
MC	Columbia Mid Cap Growth Fund T	CBSTX	D+	(800) 426-3750	C / 5.2	-5.07	4.97	20.35 /82	14.07 /54	--	0.00	1.23
MC	Columbia Mid Cap Growth Fund Z	CLSPX	C-	(800) 426-3750	C+ / 6.2	-5.02	5.13	20.70 /83	14.43 /56	3.89 /45	0.00	0.93
MC	Columbia Mid Cap Index Fund A	NTIAX	B	(800) 426-3750	B- / 7.2	-3.22	4.12	12.64 /63	17.71 /71	8.76 /75	1.00	0.39
MC	Columbia Mid Cap Index Fund Z	NMPAX	B	(800) 426-3750	B- / 7.3	-3.21	4.29	12.88 /64	18.02 /73	9.03 /76	1.46	0.14
MC	Columbia Mid Cap Value 529A		C+	(800) 426-3750	C+ / 6.5	-1.52	5.93	14.36 /69	17.18 /69	--	0.00	N/A
MC	Columbia Mid Cap Value 529B		C	(800) 426-3750	C+ / 6.3	-1.68	5.60	13.49 /66	16.31 /65	--	0.00	N/A
MC	Columbia Mid Cap Value 529C		C+	(800) 426-3750	C+ / 6.7	-1.74	5.54	13.43 /66	16.24 /64	--	0.00	N/A
MC	Columbia Mid Cap Value 529Z		C+	(800) 426-3750	B- / 7.3	-1.45	6.07	14.69 /71	17.47 /70	--	0.00	N/A
MC	Columbia Mid Cap Value Fund A	CMUAX	B+	(800) 426-3750	B / 8.0	-1.55	6.02	15.44 /73	21.44 /84	--	0.51	1.08
MC	Columbia Mid Cap Value Fund B	CMUBX	B+	(800) 426-3750	B / 7.7	-1.69	5.66	14.61 /70	20.50 /81	--	0.10	1.84
MC	Columbia Mid Cap Value Fund C	CMUCX	B+	(800) 426-3750	B / 8.1	-1.69	5.65	14.56 /70	20.52 /81	--	0.10	1.84
MC	Columbia Mid Cap Value Fund Z	NAMAX	A+	(800) 426-3750	B+ / 8.4	-1.41	6.22	15.78 /74	21.76 /85	--	0.77	0.84
AA	Columbia Mod Gr Asset Alloc 529A		C-	(800) 426-3750	D- / 1.0	-1.90	1.89	6.51 /23	7.47 /12	--	0.00	N/A
AA	Columbia Mod Gr Asset Alloc 529B		C-	(800) 426-3750	E+ / 0.9	-2.02	1.53	5.79 /19	6.67 / 9	--	0.00	N/A
AA	Columbia Mod Gr Asset Alloc 529C		C-	(800) 426-3750	D- / 1.3	-2.02	1.53	5.78 /19	6.66 / 9	--	0.00	N/A
AA	Columbia Mod Gr Asset Alloc 529Z		C	(800) 426-3750	D / 2.1	-1.81	2.03	6.89 /26	7.80 /14	--	0.00	N/A
GI	Columbia Moderate Gr NY 529A		U	(800) 426-3750	U /	-1.20	2.67	7.56 /30	--	--	0.00	0.88
GI	Columbia Moderate Gr NY 529B		U	(800) 426-3750	U /	-1.39	2.35	6.79 /25	--	--	0.00	0.88
FO	Columbia Multi Adv Intl Eq Fd A	NIIAX	B+	(800) 426-3750	B / 8.2	-0.58	8.70	26.26 /90	21.62 /84	9.04 /76	1.66	1.14
FO	Columbia Multi Adv Intl Eq Fd B	NIENX	B+	(800) 426-3750	B / 8.2	-0.80	8.25	25.27 /89	20.71 /82	8.05 /72	1.10	1.89
FO	Columbia Multi Adv Intl Eq Fd C	NITRX	B+	(800) 426-3750	B+ / 8.3	-0.74	8.26	25.36 /89	20.70 /82	8.37 /73	1.11	1.89
FO	Columbia Multi Adv Intl Eq Fd Z	NIEQX	B+	(800) 426-3750	B+ / 8.6	-0.53	8.86	26.61 /91	21.91 /85	9.13 /77	2.16	0.89
GL	Columbia Oppenheimer Global 529A		A	(800) 426-3750	B / 7.8	-3.57	3.45	18.15 /79	20.99 /83	--	0.00	N/A
GL	Columbia Oppenheimer Global 529B		A-	(800) 426-3750	B / 7.6	-3.75	3.02	17.25 /78	20.10 /80	--	0.00	N/A
GL	Columbia Oppenheimer Global 529C		A	(800) 426-3750	B / 7.9	-3.80	3.02	17.19 /77	20.08 /80	--	0.00	N/A
GL	Columbia Oppenheimer Global 529Z		A+	(800) 426-3750	B+ / 8.3	-3.48	3.58	18.52 /80	21.35 /83	--	0.00	N/A
GR	Columbia Oppenheimer Main St.		C	(800) 426-3750	D+ / 2.6	-2.08	2.69	8.96 /40	10.54 /31	--	0.00	N/A
GR	Columbia Oppenheimer Main St.		C-	(800) 426-3750	D+ / 2.4	-2.27	2.30	8.16 /34	9.76 /26	--	0.00	N/A
GR	Columbia Oppenheimer Main St.		C	(800) 426-3750	C- / 3.1	-2.27	2.30	8.16 /34	9.73 /25	--	0.00	N/A
GR	Columbia Oppenheimer Main St.		C+	(800) 426-3750	C- / 4.1	-1.99	2.89	9.44 /43	10.95 /35	--	0.00	N/A
RE	Columbia Real Estate Equity A	CREAX	C	(800) 426-3750	B+ / 8.7	-0.83	12.76	17.24 /78	23.95 /89	--	2.41	1.17
RE	Columbia Real Estate Equity B	CREBX	C	(800) 426-3750	B+ / 8.5	-1.04	12.38	16.35 /75	23.04 /87	--	1.88	1.92
RE ●	Columbia Real Estate Equity D	CREDX	C	(800) 426-3750	B+ / 8.8	-1.04	12.34	16.35 /75	23.04 /87	--	1.88	1.92
RE	Columbia Real Estate Equity Fd 529A		A	(800) 426-3750	B+ / 8.5	-0.91	12.63	16.88 /77	23.53 /88	--	0.00	N/A
RE	Columbia Real Estate Equity Fd 529B		A	(800) 426-3750	B+ / 8.4	-1.09	12.24	16.06 /75	22.62 /86	--	0.00	N/A
RE	Columbia Real Estate Equity Fd 529C		A+	(800) 426-3750	B+ / 8.7	-1.09	12.24	16.00 /75	22.63 /86	--	0.00	N/A
RE	Columbia Real Estate Equity Fd 529Z		A+	(800) 426-3750	A- / 9.0	-0.81	12.82	17.25 /78	23.91 /89	--	0.00	N/A
RE	Columbia Real Estate Equity Z	CREEX	C	(800) 426-3750	A- / 9.1	-0.77	12.94	17.52 /78	24.26 /90	17.16 /94	2.76	0.92

99 Pct = Best
0 Pct = Worst

● Denotes fund is closed to new investors
* Denotes fund is included in Section II

www.WeissRatings.com

Risk Rating/Pts	Standard Deviation	Beta	NAV As of 6/30/06	Total $(Mil)	Cash %	Stocks %	Bonds %	Other %	Portfolio Turnover Ratio	Last Bull Market Return	Last Bear Market Return	Manager Quality Pct	Manager Tenure (Years)	Initial Purch. $	Additional Purch. $	Front End Load	Back End Load
C /5.2	12.2	1.13	13.41	N/A	5	94	0	1	118.0	140.1	-11.4	19	N/A	1,000	50	0.0	2.0
C /5.2	12.2	1.13	13.59	1,728	5	94	0	1	118.0	142.0	-11.3	21	N/A	250,000	50	0.0	2.0
C+ /6.3	12.7	1.06	14.82	32	2	97	0	1	148.0	83.0	-10.6	26	N/A	1,000	50	5.8	0.0
C+ /6.2	12.8	1.06	12.93	15	2	97	0	1	148.0	78.4	-10.9	19	N/A	1,000	50	0.0	5.0
C+ /6.2	12.7	1.06	13.01	2	2	97	0	1	148.0	78.5	-10.9	20	N/A	1,000	50	0.0	1.0
C+ /6.3	12.7	1.06	15.54	558	2	97	0	1	148.0	84.7	-10.7	27	N/A	250,000	50	0.0	0.0
C /4.4	14.4	1.24	15.77	N/A	0	100	0	0	104.0	N/A	N/A	5	N/A	1,000	50	5.8	1.0
C /4.4	14.4	1.24	15.39	N/A	0	100	0	0	104.0	N/A	N/A	4	N/A	1,000	50	0.0	5.0
C /4.4	14.4	1.24	15.39	N/A	0	100	0	0	104.0	N/A	N/A	4	N/A	1,000	50	0.0	1.0
C /4.4	14.4	1.24	15.92	N/A	0	100	0	0	104.0	N/A	N/A	6	N/A	1,000	50	0.0	0.0
C /4.8	14.5	1.25	24.67	13	2	97	0	1	20.0	84.2	-7.4	6	2	1,000	50	5.8	0.0
C /4.7	14.5	1.25	24.00	8	2	97	0	1	20.0	79.8	-7.5	4	2	1,000	50	0.0	5.0
C /4.7	14.5	1.25	24.01	N/A	2	97	0	1	20.0	79.9	-7.5	5	2	1,000	50	0.0	1.0
C /4.7	14.5	1.25	23.94	1	2	97	0	1	20.0	79.3	-7.5	4	2	1,000	50	0.0	5.0
C /4.8	14.5	1.25	24.70	28	2	97	0	1	20.0	84.2	-7.3	6	2	1,000	50	5.8	0.0
C /4.8	14.5	1.25	25.00	843	2	97	0	1	20.0	86.2	-7.2	7	21	1,000	50	0.0	0.0
C+ /6.8	10.8	1.00	11.73	29	1	98	0	1	18.0	102.2	-9.3	51	N/A	1,000	50	0.0	0.0
C+ /6.8	10.9	1.00	11.73	1,847	1	98	0	1	18.0	103.8	-9.2	54	N/A	250,000	50	0.0	0.0
C+ /6.0	9.2	0.82	16.80	1	3	96	0	1	61.0	N/A	N/A	75	N/A	1,000	50	5.8	1.0
C+ /5.9	9.2	0.82	16.41	1	3	96	0	1	61.0	N/A	N/A	68	N/A	1,000	50	0.0	5.0
C+ /6.0	9.2	0.82	16.38	1	3	96	0	1	61.0	N/A	N/A	68	N/A	1,000	50	0.0	1.0
C+ /6.0	9.2	0.81	16.94	N/A	3	96	0	1	61.0	N/A	N/A	78	N/A	1,000	50	0.0	0.0
B- /7.1	9.6	0.84	13.84	920	3	96	0	1	41.0	116.3	-7.7	93	N/A	1,000	50	5.8	0.0
B- /7.1	9.6	0.85	13.64	279	3	96	0	1	41.0	111.0	-7.8	91	N/A	1,000	50	0.0	5.0
B- /7.1	9.6	0.84	13.68	155	3	96	0	1	41.0	111.2	-7.8	91	N/A	1,000	50	0.0	1.0
B /8.3	9.7	0.85	13.87	1,391	3	96	0	1	41.0	118.0	-7.7	94	N/A	250,000	50	0.0	0.0
B+ /9.7	5.3	1.09	12.92	5	0	0	0	100	N/A	N/A	N/A	49	3	1,000	50	5.8	1.0
B+ /9.7	5.4	1.09	12.61	8	0	0	0	100	N/A	N/A	N/A	40	3	1,000	50	0.0	5.0
B+ /9.7	5.4	1.09	12.62	2	0	0	0	100	N/A	N/A	N/A	39	3	1,000	50	0.0	1.0
B+ /9.7	5.4	1.09	13.04	2	0	0	0	100	N/A	N/A	N/A	53	3	1,000	50	0.0	0.0
U /	N/A	N/A	11.53	49	0	0	0	100	N/A	N/A	N/A	N/A	3	1,000	50	5.8	1.0
U /	N/A	N/A	11.33	26	0	0	0	100	N/A	N/A	N/A	N/A	3	1,000	50	0.0	5.0
C+ /6.6	10.5	1.02	15.55	39	3	96	0	1	74.0	121.0	-10.6	28	N/A	1,000	50	5.8	2.0
C+ /6.5	10.5	1.02	14.46	5	3	96	0	1	74.0	116.0	-10.8	23	N/A	1,000	50	0.0	5.0
C+ /6.5	10.5	1.02	14.32	3	3	96	0	1	74.0	119.2	-10.8	23	N/A	1,000	50	0.0	2.0
C+ /6.5	10.5	1.02	15.71	1,873	3	96	0	1	74.0	122.7	-10.5	30	N/A	250,000	50	0.0	2.0
B /8.0	11.2	1.01	19.20	N/A	0	0	0	100	N/A	N/A	N/A	26	3	1,000	50	5.8	1.0
B /8.0	11.2	1.01	18.76	N/A	0	0	0	100	N/A	N/A	N/A	21	3	1,000	50	0.0	5.0
B /8.0	11.2	1.01	18.75	N/A	0	0	0	100	N/A	N/A	N/A	21	3	1,000	50	0.0	1.0
B /8.0	11.2	1.01	19.39	N/A	0	0	0	100	N/A	N/A	N/A	28	3	1,000	50	0.0	0.0
B+ /9.1	7.6	0.97	14.10	N/A	0	0	0	100	N/A	N/A	N/A	51	3	1,000	50	5.8	1.0
B+ /9.0	7.5	0.97	13.79	N/A	0	0	0	100	N/A	N/A	N/A	42	3	1,000	50	0.0	5.0
B /8.9	7.6	0.98	13.78	N/A	0	0	0	100	N/A	N/A	N/A	41	3	1,000	50	0.0	1.0
B+ /9.1	7.5	0.97	14.26	N/A	0	0	0	100	N/A	N/A	N/A	56	3	1,000	50	0.0	0.0
C- /3.3	14.4	0.86	27.42	42	1	98	0	1	10.0	111.4	-0.7	81	N/A	1,000	50	5.8	0.0
C- /3.3	14.4	0.86	27.47	13	1	98	0	1	10.0	106.5	-0.8	75	N/A	1,000	50	0.0	5.0
C- /3.3	14.4	0.86	27.46	4	1	98	0	1	10.0	106.7	-0.9	75	N/A	1,000	50	0.0	1.0
B- /7.4	14.1	0.84	19.53	N/A	0	0	0	100	10.0	N/A	N/A	82	N/A	1,000	50	5.8	1.0
B- /7.4	14.1	0.84	19.08	N/A	0	0	0	100	10.0	N/A	N/A	75	N/A	1,000	50	0.0	5.0
B- /7.4	14.1	0.84	19.07	N/A	0	0	0	100	10.0	N/A	N/A	75	N/A	1,000	50	0.0	1.0
B- /7.4	14.1	0.84	19.71	N/A	0	0	0	100	10.0	N/A	N/A	84	N/A	1,000	50	0.0	0.0
C- /3.3	14.4	0.86	27.43	567	1	98	0	1	10.0	113.4	-0.6	83	N/A	1,000	50	0.0	0.0

					PERFORMANCE								
99 Pct = Best *0 Pct = Worst*							Total Return % through 6/30/06					Incl. in Returns	
			Overall Weiss Investment Rating		Perfor-mance Rating/Pts					Annualized		Dividend Yield	Expense Ratio
Fund Type	Fund Name	Ticker Symbol		Phone		3 Mo	6 Mo	1Yr / Pct	3Yr / Pct	5Yr / Pct			
SC	Columbia Small Cap Core 529A		B	(800) 426-3750	C+ / 6.3	-4.24	6.25	13.10 /65	16.92 /68	--	0.00	N/A
SC	Columbia Small Cap Core 529B		B-	(800) 426-3750	C+ / 6.0	-4.44	5.87	12.25 /61	16.01 /64	--	0.00	N/A
SC	Columbia Small Cap Core 529C		B-	(800) 426-3750	C+ / 6.5	-4.44	5.80	12.25 /61	16.01 /64	--	0.00	N/A
SC	Columbia Small Cap Core 529Z		B+	(800) 426-3750	B- / 7.1	-4.16	6.46	13.52 /66	17.15 /69	--	0.00	N/A
SC	● Columbia Small Cap Core Fd A	LSMAX	C+	(800) 426-3750	C+ / 6.4	-4.18	6.45	13.44 /66	17.15 /69	11.40 /85	0.00	1.13
SC	● Columbia Small Cap Core Fd B	LSMBX	C+	(800) 426-3750	C+ / 6.2	-4.39	6.01	12.56 /62	16.29 /65	10.52 /82	0.00	1.88
SC	● Columbia Small Cap Core Fd C	LSMCX	C+	(800) 426-3750	C+ / 6.6	-4.38	6.00	12.55 /62	16.25 /64	--	0.00	1.88
SC	● Columbia Small Cap Core Fd G	GBSMX	C+	(800) 426-3750	C+ / 6.2	-4.38	6.00	12.62 /63	16.30 /65	10.52 /82	0.00	1.83
SC	● Columbia Small Cap Core Fd T	SSCEX	C+	(800) 426-3750	C+ / 6.5	-4.17	6.40	13.37 /66	17.09 /68	11.32 /85	0.00	1.18
SC	● Columbia Small Cap Core Fd Z	SMCEX	B-	(800) 426-3750	B- / 7.2	-4.14	6.55	13.72 /67	17.44 /70	11.71 /86	0.00	0.88
SC	Columbia Small Cap Growth Fd I A	CGOAX	C-	(800) 426-3750	B- / 7.2	-4.84	11.28	23.38 /86	18.02 /73	5.88 /60	0.00	1.40
SC	Columbia Small Cap Growth Fd I B	CGOBX	C-	(800) 426-3750	B- / 7.2	-5.03	10.86	22.87 /86	17.86 /72	5.80 /60	0.00	2.15
SC	Columbia Small Cap Growth Fd I C	CGOCX	C	(800) 426-3750	B / 7.6	-5.03	10.86	22.87 /86	17.86 /72	5.80 /60	0.00	2.15
SC	● Columbia Small Cap Growth Fd I Z	CMSCX	C	(800) 426-3750	B / 7.8	-4.77	11.46	23.61 /87	18.09 /73	5.92 /61	0.00	1.13
SC	Columbia Small Cap Growth Fund II	NSCGX	D-	(800) 426-3750	C+ / 6.0	-5.73	9.70	18.22 /79	15.79 /63	3.97 /46	0.00	1.24
SC	Columbia Small Cap Growth Fund II	NCPBX	E+	(800) 426-3750	C+ / 5.7	-5.85	9.24	17.42 /78	14.91 /58	3.18 /38	0.00	1.99
SC	Columbia Small Cap Growth Fund II	NCPCX	D-	(800) 426-3750	C+ / 6.2	-5.88	9.32	17.38 /78	14.91 /58	3.19 /39	0.00	1.99
SC	Columbia Small Cap Growth Fund II	PSCPX	D-	(800) 426-3750	C+ / 6.8	-5.66	9.78	18.52 /80	16.06 /64	4.22 /48	0.00	0.99
SC	Columbia Small Cap Index Fd A	NMSAX	B-	(800) 426-3750	B / 7.9	-4.72	7.44	13.31 /65	19.88 /79	10.38 /82	0.40	0.46
SC	Columbia Small Cap Index Fd Z	NMSCX	B	(800) 426-3750	B / 8.0	-4.63	7.58	13.68 /67	20.20 /80	10.68 /83	0.81	0.21
SC	Columbia Small Cap Value Fund I A	CSMIX	B	(800) 426-3750	B / 8.0	-3.26	9.11	16.25 /75	21.37 /83	13.24 /89	0.00	1.31
SC	Columbia Small Cap Value Fund I B	CSSBX	B-	(800) 426-3750	B / 7.8	-3.45	8.70	15.36 /73	20.48 /81	12.39 /87	0.00	2.06
SC	Columbia Small Cap Value Fund I C	CSSCX	B	(800) 426-3750	B / 8.1	-3.45	8.70	15.37 /73	20.48 /81	12.40 /87	0.00	2.06
SC	Columbia Small Cap Value Fund I Z	CSCZX	B+	(800) 426-3750	B+ / 8.5	-3.23	9.24	16.51 /76	21.70 /84	13.56 /90	0.01	1.06
SC	Columbia Small Cap Value Fund II A	COVAX	B	(800) 426-3750	B+ / 8.4	-3.16	9.39	16.09 /75	23.13 /88	--	0.18	1.23
SC	Columbia Small Cap Value Fund II B	COVBX	B-	(800) 426-3750	B / 8.2	-3.32	8.96	15.17 /72	22.22 /86	--	0.00	1.98
SC	Columbia Small Cap Value Fund II C	COVCX	B	(800) 426-3750	B+ / 8.4	-3.32	8.97	15.19 /72	22.19 /86	--	0.00	1.98
SC	Columbia Small Cap Value Fund II Z	NSVAX	B	(800) 426-3750	B+ / 8.8	-3.09	9.47	16.32 /75	23.47 /88	--	0.46	0.98
SC	Columbia Small Company Equity A	LSEAX	D	(800) 426-3750	C / 5.4	-5.88	9.35	15.59 /73	14.81 /58	--	0.00	1.34
SC	Columbia Small Company Equity B	LSEBX	D-	(800) 426-3750	C / 5.0	-6.08	8.89	14.71 /71	13.92 /53	--	0.00	2.09
SC	Columbia Small Company Equity C	LSECX	D	(800) 426-3750	C / 5.5	-6.05	8.92	14.76 /71	13.85 /53	--	0.00	2.09
SC	Columbia Small Company Equity G	GERBX	D-	(800) 426-3750	C / 5.0	-6.04	8.98	14.81 /71	13.94 /54	1.25 /22	0.00	2.04
SC	Columbia Small Company Equity T	GASEX	D	(800) 426-3750	C / 5.3	-5.90	9.31	15.56 /73	14.74 /58	2.03 /28	0.00	1.39
SC	Columbia Small Company Equity Z	GSETX	D+	(800) 426-3750	C+ / 6.3	-5.81	9.50	15.88 /74	15.10 /59	2.41 /31	0.00	1.09
GR	Columbia Strategic Investor Fund A	CSVAX	C+	(800) 426-3750	C / 5.3	-2.08	2.89	9.85 /46	15.07 /59	--	0.60	1.21
GR	Columbia Strategic Investor Fund B	CSVBX	C+	(800) 426-3750	C / 4.9	-2.31	2.53	9.02 /40	14.23 /55	--	0.00	1.96
GR	Columbia Strategic Investor Fund C	CSRCX	U	(800) 426-3750	U /	-2.26	2.52	9.02 /40	--	--	0.00	1.96
GR	● Columbia Strategic Investor Fund D	CSVDX	C+	(800) 426-3750	C / 5.4	-2.26	2.53	9.07 /40	14.26 /55	--	0.00	1.96
GR	Columbia Strategic Investor Fund Z	CSVFX	B	(800) 426-3750	C+ / 6.3	-2.03	3.03	10.15 /48	15.38 /61	10.75 /83	0.86	0.96
GR	Columbia Tax-Managed Growth Fund	STMAX	D-	(800) 426-3750	E+ / 0.7	-4.29	-2.71	3.51 / 9	7.16 /11	-0.28 /14	0.00	1.26
GR	Columbia Tax-Managed Growth Fund	CTMBX	D-	(800) 426-3750	E / 0.5	-4.46	-3.11	2.77 / 7	6.37 / 8	-1.02 /12	0.00	2.01
GR	Columbia Tax-Managed Growth Fund	CTMCX	D-	(800) 426-3750	E+ / 0.8	-4.46	-3.11	2.77 / 7	6.37 / 8	-1.02 /12	0.00	2.01
GR	Columbia Tax-Managed Growth Fund	LTGEX	D-	(800) 426-3750	E+ / 0.7	-4.32	-2.79	3.40 / 8	7.05 /10	-0.38 /14	0.00	1.36
GR	Columbia Tax-Managed Growth Fund	STMFX	D-	(800) 426-3750	E / 0.5	-4.45	-3.11	2.77 / 7	6.36 / 8	-1.02 /12	0.00	2.01
GR	Columbia Tax-Managed Growth Fund	LMGZX	D	(800) 426-3750	D- / 1.5	-4.20	-2.59	4.15 /11	7.54 /13	0.04 /15	0.00	1.01
TC	Columbia Technology A	CTCAX	C	(800) 426-3750	A- / 9.1	-7.71	5.59	30.29 /95	27.78 /94	--	0.00	1.73
TC	Columbia Technology B	CTCBX	C	(800) 426-3750	A- / 9.0	-7.88	5.27	29.49 /94	26.89 /93	--	0.00	2.48
TC	Columbia Technology D	CTCDX	C	(800) 426-3750	A- / 9.1	-7.83	5.23	29.43 /94	26.88 /93	--	0.00	2.48
TC	Columbia Technology Z	CMTFX	C	(800) 426-3750	A / 9.3	-7.63	5.76	30.68 /95	28.11 /94	7.64 /70	0.00	1.48
GI	Columbia Thermostat A	CTFAX	C	(800) 426-3750	D / 1.8	-0.65	2.37	6.29 /22	8.77 /19	--	2.85	0.50
GI	Columbia Thermostat B	CTFBX	C-	(800) 426-3750	D- / 1.5	-0.76	2.10	5.71 /19	8.10 /16	--	2.32	1.10
GI	Columbia Thermostat C	CTFDX	C	(800) 426-3750	D / 2.0	-0.84	2.02	5.55 /18	8.00 /15	--	2.18	1.25

● Denotes fund is closed to new investors
* Denotes fund is included in Section II

RISK			NET ASSETS		ASSET				Portfolio Turnover Ratio	BULL / BEAR		FUND MANAGER		MINIMUMS		LOADS	
Risk Rating/Pts	3 Year		NAV As of 6/30/06	Total $(Mil)	Cash %	Stocks %	Bonds %	Other %		Last Bull Market Return	Last Bear Market Return	Manager Quality Pct	Manager Tenure (Years)	Initial Purch. $	Additional Purch. $	Front End Load	Back End Load
	Standard Deviation	Beta															
B- / 7.9	12.0	0.81	17.18	N/A	0	0	0	100	16.0	N/A	N/A	71	N/A	1,000	50	5.8	1.0
B- / 7.9	12.0	0.81	16.77	N/A	0	0	0	100	16.0	N/A	N/A	63	N/A	1,000	50	0.0	5.0
B- / 7.9	12.0	0.81	16.77	N/A	0	0	0	100	16.0	N/A	N/A	63	N/A	1,000	50	0.0	1.0
B- / 7.9	12.0	0.81	17.30	N/A	0	0	0	100	16.0	N/A	N/A	73	N/A	1,000	50	0.0	0.0
C+ / 6.7	12.0	0.81	19.47	197	2	98	0	0	16.0	101.5	-7.1	72	14	1,000	50	5.8	1.0
C+ / 6.7	12.0	0.81	18.53	41	2	98	0	0	16.0	96.6	-7.3	65	14	1,000	50	0.0	5.0
C+ / 6.7	12.0	0.81	18.54	48	2	98	0	0	16.0	96.6	-7.2	64	14	1,000	50	0.0	1.0
C+ / 6.7	12.0	0.81	18.36	7	2	98	0	0	16.0	96.9	-7.4	65	14	1,000	50	0.0	5.0
C+ / 6.7	12.0	0.81	19.28	140	2	98	0	0	16.0	101.0	-7.2	72	14	1,000	50	5.8	0.0
C+ / 6.7	12.0	0.81	19.69	934	2	98	0	0	16.0	103.1	-7.1	75	14	1,000	50	0.0	0.0
C- / 4.2	16.3	1.05	31.46	2	0	99	0	1	114.0	115.8	-7.1	39	N/A	1,000	50	5.8	1.0
C- / 4.2	16.3	1.05	31.33	1	0	99	0	1	114.0	115.2	-7.1	38	N/A	1,000	50	0.0	5.0
C- / 4.2	16.3	1.05	31.33	N/A	0	99	0	1	114.0	115.2	-7.1	38	N/A	1,000	50	0.0	1.0
C- / 3.9	16.3	1.05	31.52	208	0	99	0	1	114.0	116.1	-7.1	40	2	1,000	50	0.0	0.0
D- / 1.5	15.4	1.02	14.12	140	N/A	100	0	N/A	59.0	102.1	-10.8	27	N/A	1,000	50	5.8	0.0
D- / 1.3	15.4	1.02	12.96	14	N/A	100	0	N/A	59.0	97.4	-10.9	22	N/A	1,000	50	0.0	5.0
D- / 1.4	15.4	1.02	13.20	4	N/A	100	0	N/A	59.0	97.4	-10.9	22	N/A	1,000	50	0.0	1.0
D- / 1.5	15.4	1.02	14.56	252	N/A	100	0	N/A	59.0	103.7	-10.7	29	N/A	250,000	50	0.0	0.0
C+ / 6.1	13.6	0.92	21.14	47	0	99	0	1	16.0	117.9	-9.9	78	N/A	1,000	50	0.0	0.0
C+ / 6.1	13.6	0.92	21.22	1,466	0	99	0	1	16.0	119.6	-9.8	81	N/A	250,000	50	0.0	0.0
C+ / 6.1	13.0	0.88	48.03	505	0	99	0	1	31.0	123.9	-10.5	90	4	1,000	50	5.8	0.0
C+ / 5.9	13.0	0.88	41.75	136	0	99	0	1	31.0	118.7	-10.7	87	4	1,000	50	0.0	5.0
C+ / 6.0	13.0	0.88	43.60	68	0	99	0	1	31.0	118.7	-10.7	87	4	1,000	50	0.0	1.0
C+ / 6.2	13.0	0.88	49.79	114	0	99	0	1	31.0	125.8	-10.5	91	4	1,000	50	0.0	0.0
C+ / 5.9	12.8	0.87	13.09	24	3	96	0	1	80.0	132.5	-9.1	95	N/A	1,000	50	5.8	0.0
C+ / 5.8	12.8	0.86	12.72	3	3	96	0	1	80.0	127.0	-9.3	93	N/A	1,000	50	0.0	5.0
C+ / 5.8	12.8	0.87	12.71	4	3	96	0	1	80.0	127.0	-9.4	93	N/A	1,000	50	0.0	1.0
C+ / 5.7	12.8	0.86	13.18	241	3	96	0	1	80.0	134.4	-9.1	96	N/A	250,000	50	0.0	0.0
C- / 3.4	16.0	1.07	18.72	6	1	98	0	1	110.0	103.9	-13.5	17	N/A	1,000	50	5.8	0.0
C- / 3.3	16.0	1.07	17.14	2	1	98	0	1	110.0	99.0	-13.8	13	N/A	1,000	50	0.0	5.0
C- / 3.3	16.1	1.07	17.09	1	1	98	0	1	110.0	98.4	-13.8	13	N/A	1,000	50	0.0	1.0
C- / 3.3	16.0	1.07	17.12	2	1	98	0	1	110.0	98.9	-13.8	13	N/A	1,000	50	0.0	5.0
C- / 3.4	16.1	1.07	18.67	68	1	98	0	1	110.0	103.5	-13.6	17	N/A	1,000	50	5.8	0.0
C- / 3.5	16.1	1.07	19.94	136	1	98	0	1	110.0	105.7	-13.5	19	N/A	1,000	50	0.0	0.0
B- / 7.9	8.1	0.97	20.67	170	17	80	1	2	80.0	88.1	-10.3	88	N/A	1,000	50	5.8	0.0
B / 8.0	8.1	0.97	20.30	52	17	80	1	2	80.0	83.6	-10.6	84	N/A	1,000	50	0.0	5.0
U /	N/A	N/A	20.31	44	17	80	1	2	80.0	N/A	N/A	N/A	N/A	1,000	50	0.0	1.0
B / 8.0	8.1	0.97	20.30	N/A	17	80	1	2	80.0	83.6	-10.6	84	N/A	1,000	50	1.0	1.0
B- / 7.9	8.0	0.97	20.73	179	17	80	1	2	80.0	89.5	-10.2	90	N/A	1,000	50	0.0	0.0
B- / 7.5	8.6	1.08	14.73	65	3	96	0	1	31.0	45.5	-8.6	17	10	1,000	50	5.8	0.0
B- / 7.5	8.5	1.07	13.71	109	3	96	0	1	31.0	42.2	-8.9	13	10	1,000	50	0.0	5.0
B- / 7.5	8.5	1.07	13.71	21	3	96	0	1	31.0	42.1	-8.8	13	10	1,000	50	0.0	1.0
B- / 7.6	8.5	1.07	14.61	12	3	96	0	1	31.0	45.0	-8.6	17	10	1,000	50	4.5	0.0
B- / 7.5	8.6	1.08	13.73	6	3	96	0	1	31.0	42.1	-8.8	13	10	1,000	50	0.0	5.0
B- / 7.6	8.5	1.07	15.05	N/A	3	96	0	1	31.0	47.1	-8.6	20	10	1,000	50	0.0	0.0
C- / 3.0	21.3	2.16	9.82	73	6	93	0	1	328.0	201.3	-10.6	91	1	1,000	50	5.8	0.0
D+ / 2.9	21.2	2.15	9.59	8	6	93	0	1	328.0	193.9	-10.8	88	1	1,000	50	0.0	5.0
D+ / 2.9	21.3	2.15	9.65	N/A	6	93	0	1	328.0	195.5	-10.8	88	1	1,000	50	1.0	1.0
C- / 3.0	21.3	2.16	9.92	80	6	93	0	1	328.0	204.1	-10.5	92	1	1,000	50	0.0	0.0
B+ / 9.9	4.5	0.55	12.53	64	0	40	59	1	96.0	46.8	N/A	73	N/A	1,000	50	5.8	0.0
B+ / 9.9	4.6	0.56	12.53	74	0	40	59	1	96.0	43.8	N/A	66	N/A	1,000	50	0.0	5.0
B+ / 9.9	4.5	0.55	12.52	27	0	40	59	1	96.0	43.4	N/A	66	N/A	1,000	50	0.0	1.0

Fund Type	Fund Name	Ticker Symbol	Overall Weiss Investment Rating	Phone	Performance Rating/Pts	3 Mo	6 Mo	1Yr / Pct	Annualized 3Yr / Pct	5Yr / Pct	Dividend Yield	Expense Ratio
GI	Columbia Thermostat Z	COTZX	C-	(800) 426-3750	D+ / 2.8	-0.55	2.56	6.65 /24	9.08 /21	--	3.50	0.25
UT	Columbia Utilities Fund A	CUTLX	B	(800) 426-3750	C+ / 5.6	3.48	5.58	7.19 /27	14.93 /58	-1.51 /10	2.54	1.21
UT	Columbia Utilities Fund B	CUTBX	B-	(800) 426-3750	C / 5.1	3.29	5.19	6.40 /23	14.08 /54	-2.24 / 7	1.93	1.96
UT	Columbia Utilities Fund C	CUTFX	B	(800) 426-3750	C+ / 5.7	3.29	5.19	6.39 /23	14.07 /54	-2.22 / 8	1.93	1.96
UT	Columbia Utilities Fund Z	LUFZX	B	(800) 426-3750	C+ / 6.4	3.48	5.65	7.39 /29	15.22 /60	-1.28 /11	2.91	1.00
UT	Columbia World Equity Fund A	CGUAX	B	(800) 426-3750	C+ / 6.1	-0.18	6.44	17.56 /78	15.60 /62	3.52 /41	0.63	1.51
UT	Columbia World Equity Fund B	CGUBX	B-	(800) 426-3750	C+ / 5.8	-0.37	6.03	16.73 /76	14.77 /58	2.76 /34	0.00	2.26
UT	Columbia World Equity Fund C	CGUCX	B	(800) 426-3750	C+ / 6.3	-0.38	6.04	16.66 /76	14.75 /58	2.72 /34	0.00	2.26
GR	Columbia Young Investor Fund A	LYIAX	C-	(800) 426-3750	D+ / 2.7	-2.35	2.01	8.89 /39	10.55 /31	--	0.14	1.35
GR	Columbia Young Investor Fund B	LYIBX	C-	(800) 426-3750	D+ / 2.4	-2.47	1.74	8.22 /34	9.78 /26	--	0.00	2.05
GR	Columbia Young Investor Fund C	LYICX	C-	(800) 426-3750	C- / 3.0	-2.47	1.67	8.22 /35	9.78 /26	--	0.00	2.05
GR	Columbia Young Investor Fund Z	SRYIX	C	(800) 426-3750	C- / 3.8	-2.21	2.22	9.23 /42	10.69 /33	-0.61 /13	0.45	1.05
AA	Commerce Asset Allocation Inst	CAAIX	D	(800) 995-6365	D+ / 2.8	-1.55	1.66	7.39 /29	9.09 /21	--	1.93	1.05
GI	Commerce Core Equity Inst	CEFIX	C-	(800) 995-6365	D+ / 2.9	-3.10	-0.01	4.65 /13	9.90 /27	1.69 /25	0.56	1.09
GR	Commerce Growth Fd	CFGRX	D-	(800) 995-6365	D / 1.9	-4.93	-1.48	6.14 /21	8.20 /16	-0.17 /15	0.51	1.13
FO	Commerce Intl Equity Fd	CFIEX	B	(800) 995-6365	B / 8.1	-1.69	8.68	24.36 /88	19.59 /78	6.40 /63	0.82	1.72
MC	Commerce Mid Cap Growth Fd	CFAGX	C-	(800) 995-6365	C+ / 6.2	-5.18	3.53	15.90 /74	15.85 /63	2.39 /31	0.00	1.29
GI	Commerce Value Fund Inst	CFVLX	B-	(800) 995-6365	C / 5.2	-0.72	5.29	11.00 /53	12.56 /46	4.03 /46	1.20	1.19
FO	Commonwealth-Australia/New	CNZLX	C-	(888) 345-1898	C / 5.3	1.37	0.78	4.77 /14	13.92 /53	18.48 /95	2.93	2.12
FO	Commonwealth-Japan Fund	CNJFX	E+	(888) 345-1898	D+ / 2.6	-7.89	-4.00	23.86 /87	8.22 /16	-0.17 /15	0.00	3.07
GR	Concorde Value Fund	CONVX	C+	(800) 294-1699	C / 5.0	-0.41	5.08	9.51 /43	12.29 /44	4.10 /47	0.00	2.12
SC	Conestoga Small Cap Fund	CCASX	C-	(800) 344-2716	C+ / 6.5	-6.69	6.14	10.73 /52	15.95 /63	--	0.00	1.35
FO	Const Pitcairn Intl Equity Fund	PTIEX	A+	(800) 214-6744	B+ / 8.7	-0.79	7.89	25.20 /89	23.00 /87	7.19 /68	1.23	1.44
GR	Constellation Clover Core Val Fd I	CCEVX	B	(800) 224-6312	B- / 7.1	-1.06	3.22	9.68 /45	18.30 /74	9.91 /80	0.26	1.13
SC	Constellation Clover Sm Cap Val I	TCSVX	C+	(800) 224-6312	B / 8.0	-4.13	8.81	13.79 /68	20.53 /81	8.99 /76	0.00	1.23
GR	Constellation HLAM Lg Cp Qty Gr	HLGRX	E-	(800) 444-1854	E+ / 0.9	-2.45	0.45	7.11 /27	6.16 / 7	-1.50 /10	0.15	1.25
GR	Constellation Pitcairn Div Gr Fund	PTDGX	D	(800) 214-6744	D / 1.6	-3.08	0.38	5.22 /16	7.87 /14	-2.12 / 8	0.08	1.10
GR	Constellation Pitcairn Div Val Fund	PTDVX	B	(800) 214-6744	C / 5.3	-0.89	4.79	9.42 /43	13.58 /52	6.14 /62	1.18	1.09
GR	Constellation Pitcairn Fy Hg Fund	PTFMX	C-	(800) 214-6744	D+ / 2.3	-1.07	0.04	4.82 /14	9.22 /22	2.45 /32	0.27	1.29
GR	Constellation Pitcairn Sel Val Fund	PTSVX	C+	(800) 214-6744	C / 4.4	-1.67	4.19	8.23 /35	12.18 /43	2.40 /31	1.10	1.14
SC	Constellation Pitcairn Sm Cap Fund	PTMVX	C	(800) 214-6744	C+ / 5.8	-5.93	4.32	8.44 /36	15.49 /61	8.12 /72	0.00	1.09
GR	Constellation Sands Cap Inst Gr Ptf	CISGX	U	(800) 214-6744	U /	-7.84	-9.33	1.91 / 4	--	--	0.00	0.79
GR	Constellation Sands Cap Sel Gr I	CFSIX	D-	(800) 214-6744	D / 2.1	-7.95	-9.71	1.48 / 3	10.91 /35	2.70 /34	0.00	1.11
GR	Constellation Sands Cap Sel Gr II	PTSGX	D-	(800) 214-6744	D / 2.0	-7.98	-9.75	1.21 / 3	10.76 /33	2.62 /33	0.00	1.36
GI	Constellation Strg Val & Hgh Inc I	TSVIX	C	(800) 224-6312	C+ / 5.9	-2.43	5.00	10.84 /53	14.87 /58	--	1.69	3.83
HL	Constellation TIP Hlth & Bio Fd II	THBCX	D	(800) 224-6312	D / 2.0	-6.62	-7.15	-0.84 / 1	10.79 /34	7.02 /67	0.00	1.88
SC	Constellation TIP Sm Cap Val opp II	TSVOX	A+	(800) 224-6312	A- / 9.1	-4.07	8.19	17.30 /78	25.87 /92	--	0.10	1.46
IN	Copley Fund	COPLX	C	(800) 424-8570	C- / 3.0	1.66	4.50	4.13 /11	9.96 /27	3.34 /40	0.00	1.09
BA	CornerCap Balanced Fund	CBLFX	C	(888) 813-8637	D / 2.2	-0.86	0.43	3.30 / 8	8.92 /20	5.87 /60	0.00	1.30
SC	CornerCap Contrarian Fund	CMCRX	B-	(888) 813-8637	C+ / 6.9	-3.96	1.66	5.52 /18	18.65 /75	3.96 /45	0.46	1.50
GR	CornerCap Sm. Cap Value Fd	CSCVX	E+	(888) 813-8637	C- / 3.0	-6.35	-0.95	1.06 / 3	11.45 /39	7.72 /70	0.00	1.50
BA	Country Trust Balanced A	CTAAX	C-	(800) 245-2100	E+ / 0.7	-1.13	1.35	3.76 /10	6.43 / 8	--	1.60	1.37
BA	Country Trust Balanced Y	CTYAX	C-	(800) 245-2100	D- / 1.3	-1.13	1.35	3.77 /10	6.43 / 8	2.84 /35	1.70	1.37
GR	Country Trust Growth A	CGRAX	C-	(800) 245-2100	D / 2.0	-1.87	1.72	6.10 /21	9.51 /24	--	0.75	1.23
GR	Country Trust Growth Y	CTYGX	C-	(800) 245-2100	D+ / 2.9	-1.87	1.73	6.10 /21	9.52 /24	2.56 /32	0.80	1.23
GR	Credit Suisse Capital Apprec A	CUAAX	E+	(800) 222-8977	E / 0.4	-6.06	-4.09	2.75 / 6	6.30 / 8	--	0.00	1.50
GR	Credit Suisse Capital Apprec Adv	WCATX	D-	(800) 222-8977	E+ / 0.7	-6.11	-4.12	2.52 / 6	6.05 / 7	-4.44 / 3	0.00	1.75
GR	Credit Suisse Capital Apprec B	CUCBX	E+	(800) 222-8977	E / 0.3	-6.26	-4.39	1.99 / 4	5.51 / 5	--	0.00	2.25
GR	Credit Suisse Capital Apprec C	CUCCX	E+	(800) 222-8977	E / 0.5	-6.26	-4.46	1.93 / 4	5.51 / 5	--	0.00	2.25
GR	Credit Suisse Capital Apprec Com	CUCAX	D-	(800) 222-8977	E+ / 0.9	-6.00	-3.93	3.01 / 7	6.59 / 9	-3.97 / 4	0.10	1.25
EM	Credit Suisse Emerg Markets A	CUMKX	C+	(800) 222-8977	A / 9.5	-3.50	7.18	35.12 /97	30.70 /96	--	0.54	1.95
EM	Credit Suisse Emerg Markets Adv	WPEAX	C+	(800) 222-8977	A / 9.5	-3.48	7.25	35.40 /97	30.96 /96	14.42 /91	0.89	1.70

● Denotes fund is closed to new investors
* Denotes fund is included in Section II

RISK			NET ASSETS		ASSET					BULL / BEAR		FUND MANAGER		MINIMUMS		LOADS	
Risk Rating/Pts	3 Year		NAV As of 6/30/06	Total $(Mil)	Cash %	Stocks %	Bonds %	Other %	Portfolio Turnover Ratio	Last Bull Market Return	Last Bear Market Return	Manager Quality Pct	Manager Tenure (Years)	Initial Purch. $	Additional Purch. $	Front End Load	Back End Load
	Standard Deviation	Beta															
B /8.1	4.6	0.56	12.53	27	0	40	59	1	96.0	48.0	-5.6	75	N/A	1,000	50	0.0	0.0
B /8.8	7.6	0.61	14.24	296	14	84	0	2	16.0	79.3	-10.7	63	N/A	1,000	50	4.8	0.0
B /8.9	7.7	0.62	14.24	40	14	84	0	2	16.0	75.1	-10.9	54	N/A	1,000	50	0.0	5.0
B /8.8	7.7	0.62	14.25	6	14	84	0	2	16.0	75.0	-10.9	52	N/A	1,000	50	0.0	1.0
B /8.8	7.7	0.62	14.21	32	14	84	0	2	16.0	80.7	-10.6	66	N/A	1,000	50	0.0	0.0
B /8.0	8.6	0.14	13.97	80	1	98	0	1	62.0	82.4	-5.4	99	1	1,000	50	5.8	0.0
B- /7.9	8.7	0.14	13.42	12	1	98	0	1	62.0	78.3	-5.6	99	1	1,000	50	0.0	5.0
B- /7.9	8.6	0.14	13.40	1	1	98	0	1	62.0	78.1	-5.6	99	1	1,000	50	0.0	1.0
B /8.2	8.2	1.02	13.71	84	4	95	0	1	79.0	60.8	-10.1	46	1	1,000	50	5.8	0.0
B /8.2	8.2	1.02	13.43	5	4	95	0	1	79.0	57.3	-10.2	38	1	1,000	50	0.0	5.0
B /8.2	8.2	1.02	13.43	1	4	95	0	1	79.0	57.5	-10.3	38	1	1,000	50	0.0	1.0
B /8.2	8.2	1.03	11.95	639	4	95	0	1	79.0	61.4	-10.0	47	1	1,000	50	0.0	0.0
C+ /6.4	5.6	1.12	19.63	16	3	58	38	1	39.0	45.7	-4.7	65	N/A	1,000	250	0.0	0.0
B- /7.9	7.4	0.92	16.66	210	1	98	0	1	19.0	58.0	-9.3	49	6	1,000	250	0.0	0.0
C+ /6.4	9.3	1.11	23.32	146	2	97	0	1	40.0	50.0	-8.9	21	9	1,000	250	0.0	0.0
C+ /6.2	10.5	1.00	25.54	79	3	96	0	1	103.0	115.1	-12.8	19	N/A	1,000	250	0.0	2.0
C /5.2	12.1	1.08	31.64	85	4	95	0	1	87.0	93.2	-7.5	25	N/A	1,000	250	0.0	0.0
B /8.5	7.4	0.89	26.90	113	4	95	0	1	37.0	68.4	-8.2	78	N/A	1,000	250	0.0	0.0
C /5.4	10.6	0.76	15.51	35	5	63	30	2	32.0	78.6	6.8	18	15	200	0	0.0	0.0
C- /4.0	16.3	0.89	4.32	9	12	80	6	2	47.0	41.7	0.3	1	9	200	0	0.0	0.0
B- /7.8	8.2	0.96	17.17	17	5	94	0	1	22.0	60.5	-10.5	70	19	500	100	0.0	0.0
C /4.8	13.7	0.88	17.99	17	0	99	0	1	24.0	102.0	-9.9	48	4	2,500	0	0.0	0.0
B /8.0	10.3	0.99	9.86	146	2	97	0	1	53.0	134.1	-13.4	44	N/A	2,500	50	0.0	2.0
B- /7.4	9.4	1.10	18.19	97	N/A	N/A	0	N/A	75.0	103.6	-11.3	94	15	2,500	50	0.0	2.0
C /4.6	13.0	0.87	25.32	290	N/A	N/A	0	N/A	78.0	131.7	-13.8	87	10	2,500	50	0.0	2.0
D- /1.3	9.2	1.07	15.66	14	0	99	0	1	37.0	35.4	-13.4	13	N/A	2,500	50	0.0	2.0
B- /7.8	9.0	1.09	5.94	116	0	99	0	1	56.0	48.4	-10.4	20	N/A	2,500	50	0.0	2.0
B /8.8	7.9	0.97	12.12	163	0	99	0	1	64.0	77.0	-11.1	80	N/A	2,500	50	0.0	2.0
B /8.1	8.3	1.03	10.13	82	0	100	0	0	25.0	58.0	-10.7	33	N/A	2,500	50	0.0	2.0
B /8.3	9.8	1.13	10.90	60	1	98	0	1	94.0	71.7	-13.2	54	N/A	2,500	50	0.0	2.0
C+ /5.9	14.8	0.97	15.23	84	N/A	N/A	0	N/A	100.0	103.4	-11.4	31	N/A	2,500	50	0.0	2.0
U /	N/A	N/A	10.69	1,074	3	96	0	1	15.6	N/A	N/A	N/A	1	1,000,000	0	0.0	0.0
C+ /5.6	12.2	1.23	7.53	182	16	83	0	1	24.0	72.1	-7.2	32	N/A	250,000	50	0.0	2.0
C+ /6.5	12.1	1.23	7.50	323	16	83	0	1	24.0	71.5	-7.2	31	N/A	2,500	50	0.0	2.0
C+ /6.2	8.4	0.91	14.63	2	N/A	60	40	N/A	90.0	79.2	-2.1	90	N/A	2,500	50	0.0	2.0
B- /7.2	10.3	0.86	14.80	58	4	95	0	1	169.0	67.5	1.1	66	N/A	2,500	50	0.0	2.0
B- /7.1	13.6	0.89	19.55	251	5	94	0	1	193.0	149.8	-6.7	98	4	2,500	50	0.0	2.0
B /8.6	7.3	0.56	47.15	74	2	97	0	1	0.7	50.1	-4.4	82	28	1,000	100	0.0	2.0
B+ /9.5	5.9	1.14	13.88	16	6	59	33	2	19.9	48.0	-4.8	63	N/A	2,000	250	0.0	1.0
B- /7.0	13.5	0.82	10.44	5	2	93	4	1	49.1	118.4	-14.3	82	N/A	2,000	250	0.0	2.0
C- /3.5	13.3	1.44	12.54	20	2	97	0	1	27.2	79.4	-7.5	23	14	2,000	250	0.0	1.0
B+ /9.8	4.8	1.00	15.46	5	1	62	35	2	15.3	34.7	-4.3	43	N/A	1,000	100	5.5	0.0
B+ /9.5	4.8	1.00	15.41	20	1	62	35	2	15.3	34.8	-4.4	43	N/A	1,000	100	0.0	0.0
B /8.8	7.3	0.92	24.18	13	15	84	0	1	16.1	54.0	-8.2	44	N/A	1,000	100	5.5	0.0
B /8.5	7.3	0.93	24.16	199	15	84	0	1	16.1	53.9	-8.2	44	N/A	1,000	100	0.0	0.0
B- /7.0	10.1	1.19	16.43	2	2	97	0	1	97.0	46.9	-8.6	9	5	2,500	100	5.8	0.0
C+ /6.9	10.1	1.19	15.84	4	2	97	0	1	97.0	45.7	-8.6	9	6	0	0	0.0	0.0
C+ /6.9	10.1	1.19	15.88	1	2	97	0	1	97.0	43.5	-8.8	7	5	2,500	100	0.0	4.0
C+ /6.9	10.1	1.19	15.87	N/A	2	97	0	1	97.0	43.5	-8.7	7	5	2,500	100	0.0	1.0
B- /7.0	10.1	1.19	16.61	246	2	97	0	1	97.0	48.1	-8.5	10	6	2,500	100	0.0	0.0
C- /3.1	17.8	1.08	15.98	1	1	98	0	1	90.0	189.7	-8.4	10	5	2,500	100	5.8	0.0
C- /3.2	17.8	1.07	15.54	1	1	98	0	1	90.0	191.4	-8.1	11	6	0	0	0.0	2.0

99 Pct = Best
0 Pct = Worst

Fund Type	Fund Name	Ticker Symbol	Overall Weiss Investment Rating	Phone	PERFORMANCE Perfor-mance Rating/Pts	Total Return % through 6/30/06			Annualized		Incl. in Returns Dividend Yield	Expense Ratio
						3 Mo	6 Mo	1Yr / Pct	3Yr / Pct	5Yr / Pct		
EM	● Credit Suisse Emerg Markets Com	WPEMX	C+	(800) 222-8977	A / 9.5	-3.54	7.13	35.05 /97	30.78 /96	14.44 /91	0.57	1.95
GL	Credit Suisse Global Small Cap A	CPVAX	C+	(800) 222-8977	B / 7.6	-6.11	4.94	15.25 /73	20.78 /82	--	0.00	1.65
GL	Credit Suisse Global Small Cap Adv	WPVAX	C+	(800) 222-8977	B / 7.8	-6.14	4.83	14.94 /72	20.36 /81	3.71 /43	0.00	1.90
GL	Credit Suisse Global Small Cap B	CPVBX	C+	(800) 222-8977	B- / 7.4	-6.25	4.58	14.39 /70	19.74 /78	--	0.00	2.40
GL	Credit Suisse Global Small Cap C	CPVCX	C+	(800) 222-8977	B / 7.7	-6.28	4.57	14.37 /69	19.76 /78	--	0.00	2.40
GL	Credit Suisse Global Small Cap Com	WVCCX	C+	(800) 222-8977	B / 7.9	-6.11	4.94	15.25 /73	20.66 /82	4.00 /46	0.00	1.65
GR	Credit Suisse Inst Cap Apprec	CSCAX	D-	(800) 222-8977	D- / 1.0	-5.89	-3.66	3.05 / 7	6.76 / 9	--	0.10	0.75
FO	Credit Suisse Inst Intl Focus Fd	WPIEX	B+	(800) 222-8977	B+ / 8.4	-0.94	6.83	24.93 /88	20.73 /82	8.37 /73	2.03	0.95
GR	Credit Suisse Inst Large Cap Val	WPIVX	B+	(800) 222-8977	C+ / 5.6	1.77	4.55	9.89 /46	13.42 /51	5.34 /57	1.24	0.75
FO	● Credit Suisse Internatl Focus A	CUIAX	B	(800) 222-8977	B / 7.7	-1.52	5.96	23.73 /87	19.90 /79	--	0.64	1.81
FO	Credit Suisse Internatl Focus Adv	CUFAX	B	(800) 222-8977	B / 7.9	-1.53	5.84	23.53 /87	19.63 /78	--	0.47	2.07
FO	● Credit Suisse Internatl Focus B	CUIBX	B-	(800) 222-8977	B / 7.6	-1.67	5.60	22.84 /85	19.01 /76	--	0.04	2.57
FO	● Credit Suisse Internatl Focus C	CUICX	B	(800) 222-8977	B / 7.8	-1.74	5.55	22.85 /86	19.03 /76	--	0.04	2.57
FO	● Credit Suisse Internatl Focus Com	WPMFX	B+	(800) 222-8977	B / 8.1	-1.45	6.12	24.06 /87	20.22 /80	6.91 /66	0.89	1.57
FO	Credit Suisse Japan Equity A	CUJAX	C	(800) 222-8977	B- / 7.4	-7.74	-2.68	30.62 /95	20.09 /80	--	0.00	1.75
FO	Credit Suisse Japan Equity Adv	WPJAX	C	(800) 222-8977	B / 7.7	-7.73	-2.58	30.77 /95	20.26 /80	0.69 /19	0.00	1.50
FO	● Credit Suisse Japan Equity Com	WPJGX	C	(800) 222-8977	B / 7.6	-7.84	-2.80	30.45 /95	20.06 /79	0.83 /19	0.00	1.75
GR	Credit Suisse Large Cap Blend A	CFFAX	D-	(800) 222-8977	E+ / 0.7	-2.96	-1.06	2.92 / 7	6.97 /10	--	0.51	1.30
GR	Credit Suisse Large Cap Blend B	CFFBX	D-	(800) 222-8977	E+ / 0.6	-3.13	-1.43	2.13 / 5	6.14 / 7	--	0.05	2.05
GR	Credit Suisse Large Cap Blend C	CFFCX	D-	(800) 222-8977	E+ / 0.8	-3.22	-1.51	2.05 / 4	6.16 / 7	--	0.05	2.05
GR	Credit Suisse Large Cap Blend Com	WFDCX	D	(800) 222-8977	D- / 1.3	-2.97	-1.06	2.93 / 7	6.95 /10	-1.55 /10	0.54	1.30
GR	Credit Suisse Large Cap Value A	WFGIX	C-	(800) 222-8977	C / 4.5	0.94	4.17	9.51 /43	13.01 /49	5.09 /55	0.79	1.30
GR	Credit Suisse Large Cap Value Adv	CSLVX	C+	(800) 222-8977	C / 5.2	0.88	4.03	9.22 /41	12.63 /47	--	0.61	1.41
GR	Credit Suisse Large Cap Value B	WGIBX	C-	(800) 222-8977	C- / 4.2	0.77	3.79	8.72 /38	12.06 /43	4.26 /48	0.17	2.05
GR	Credit Suisse Large Cap Value C	CVUCX	C-	(800) 222-8977	C / 4.7	0.77	3.82	8.72 /38	12.10 /43	4.27 /48	0.17	2.05
GR	Credit Suisse Large Cap Value Com	CSWVX	C	(800) 222-8977	C / 5.4	1.01	4.32	9.82 /46	13.09 /49	5.13 /55	1.06	1.05
MC	Credit Suisse Mid Cap Growth A	CUWAX	D-	(800) 222-8977	C- / 3.2	-6.64	-1.16	4.04 /11	12.77 /47	--	0.00	1.70
MC	Credit Suisse Mid Cap Growth Adv	WEGTX	D	(800) 222-8977	C- / 4.0	-6.70	-1.26	3.74 /10	12.47 /46	2.28 /30	0.00	1.95
MC	● Credit Suisse Mid Cap Growth Com	CUEGX	D	(800) 222-8977	C / 4.4	-6.61	-1.05	4.28 /12	13.04 /49	2.80 /35	0.00	1.45
SC	Credit Suisse Small Cap Gr A	CUSLX	E	(800) 222-8977	D+ / 2.3	-10.64	3.71	1.27 / 3	11.46 /39	--	0.00	1.40
SC	● Credit Suisse Small Cap Gr Com	WSCGX	E+	(800) 222-8977	C- / 3.2	-10.68	3.66	1.28 / 3	11.42 /39	2.15 /28	0.00	1.40
SC	Credit Suisse Small Cap Gr Tr	WTSGX	E+	(800) 222-8977	C- / 3.5	-11.00	3.83	1.71 / 4	11.88 /42	1.43 /23	0.00	1.13
SC	Credit Suisse Small Cap Val A	WFAGX	C+	(800) 222-8977	C+ / 6.3	-3.07	4.70	8.62 /38	17.50 /70	10.27 /81	0.00	1.55
SC	Credit Suisse Small Cap Val B	WSCBX	C	(800) 222-8977	C+ / 6.2	-3.20	4.44	7.87 /32	16.66 /67	9.43 /78	0.00	2.30
SC	Credit Suisse Small Cap Val C	CCPCX	C	(800) 222-8977	C+ / 6.5	-3.26	4.36	7.80 /31	16.62 /66	9.42 /78	0.00	2.13
SC	Credit Suisse Small Cap Val Com	CSWCX	C+	(800) 222-8977	B- / 7.0	-3.04	4.73	8.62 /38	17.50 /70	10.24 /81	0.00	1.55
SC	Credit Suisse Small Cap Val Tr	CUSVX	A	(800) 222-8977	B+ / 8.3	-3.16	5.01	23.41 /86	21.44 /84	--	0.00	1.29
GR	Credit Suisse Tr-Blue Chip	CUBCX	C	(800) 222-8977	C- / 3.6	-1.57	2.59	9.41 /43	10.13 /28	--	0.66	0.95
EM	Credit Suisse Tr-Emerg Markets	WPETX	C+	(800) 222-8977	A / 9.5	-3.88	6.12	33.25 /96	30.03 /96	14.30 /91	0.59	1.38
GL	Credit Suisse Tr-Glb Small Cp	WTVCX	C	(800) 222-8977	B / 8.1	-5.94	3.86	14.96 /72	21.01 /83	4.22 /48	0.00	1.40
FO	Credit Suisse Tr-Intl Focus	WTIEX	B+	(800) 222-8977	B+ / 8.3	-1.19	6.41	24.47 /88	20.59 /81	7.16 /68	0.77	1.42
GR	Credit Suisse Tr-Large Cap Value	WGICX	B	(800) 222-8977	C / 5.4	1.01	4.24	9.62 /44	13.02 /49	3.39 /40	0.72	1.00
EM	Credit Suisse Tr-Mid Cap Growth	WPEGX	C-	(800) 222-8977	C / 4.3	-6.37	-0.76	4.47 /13	12.80 /48	3.26 /39	0.00	1.20
GR	CRM Large Cap Value Inv	CRMLX	B	(800) 276-2883	C+ / 5.6	1.13	7.07	14.00 /68	12.64 /47	1.66 /25	0.53	1.50
MC	● CRM Mid Cap Value Instl	CRIMX	A+	(800) 276-2883	B / 8.0	-2.33	5.33	11.82 /58	20.44 /81	12.73 /88	0.79	0.85
MC	● CRM Mid Cap Value Inv A	CRMMX	A	(800) 276-2883	B / 7.9	-2.43	5.17	11.55 /57	20.12 /80	12.44 /87	0.59	1.09
SC	CRM Small Cap Value Inst	CRISX	B+	(800) 276-2883	B / 7.6	-4.10	4.11	14.60 /70	18.86 /76	11.23 /84	0.00	0.87
SC	CRM Small Cap Value Inv	CRMSX	C+	(800) 276-2883	B- / 7.5	-4.18	3.95	14.28 /69	18.56 /75	10.95 /84	0.00	1.12
GR	Croft-Leominster Value	CLVFX	B-	(800) 551-0990	C+ / 6.9	1.59	1.16	17.99 /79	17.25 /69	5.29 /56	0.26	1.50
GR	CSI Equity Fund Inv	CSIIX	B+	(800) 527-9500	C / 5.2	0.24	5.30	12.08 /60	12.84 /48	4.33 /49	1.63	1.45
GI	Cullen High Dividend Equity I	CHDVX	U	(877) 485-8586	U /	-0.07	6.86	12.25 /61	--	--	2.75	0.75
GI	Cutler Value Fund	CALEX	C	(888) 288-5374	C- / 3.7	1.25	4.41	8.86 /39	9.93 /27	1.69 /25	1.43	1.27

● Denotes fund is closed to new investors
* Denotes fund is included in Section II

RISK	3 Year		NET ASSETS		ASSET				Portfolio Turnover Ratio	BULL / BEAR		FUND MANAGER		MINIMUMS		LOADS	
Risk Rating/Pts	Standard Deviation	Beta	NAV As of 6/30/06	Total $(Mil)	Cash %	Stocks %	Bonds %	Other %		Last Bull Market Return	Last Bear Market Return	Manager Quality Pct	Manager Tenure (Years)	Initial Purch. $	Additional Purch. $	Front End Load	Back End Load
C- /3.2	17.7	1.07	16.08	33	1	98	0	1	90.0	190.5	-8.0	10	5	2,500	100	0.0	2.0
C /5.4	13.2	1.04	22.29	94	3	96	0	1	73.0	142.1	-14.7	20	N/A	2,500	100	5.8	0.0
C /5.3	13.2	1.04	21.69	2	3	96	0	1	73.0	138.7	-14.4	18	N/A	0	0	0.0	2.0
C /5.3	13.2	1.05	21.46	1	3	96	0	1	73.0	135.0	-14.5	15	N/A	2,500	100	0.0	4.0
C /5.3	13.3	1.05	21.49	1	3	96	0	1	73.0	135.2	-14.5	15	N/A	2,500	100	0.0	1.0
C /5.4	13.3	1.04	22.29	46	3	96	0	1	73.0	140.8	-14.3	19	N/A	2,500	100	0.0	2.0
B- /7.1	10.0	1.18	9.75	9	3	96	0	1	104.0	47.7	-8.2	11	6	1,000,000	0	0.0	0.0
C+ /6.7	10.2	0.96	12.67	30	3	96	0	1	55.0	117.2	-8.8	31	N/A	3,000,000	50,000	0.0	0.0
B+ /9.0	7.9	0.93	1.15	28	2	97	0	1	60.0	69.1	-8.1	82	N/A	1,000,000	0	0.0	0.0
C+ /6.5	10.3	0.97	14.94	15	3	96	0	1	50.0	113.7	-8.6	25	N/A	2,500	100	5.8	0.0
C+ /6.5	10.3	0.97	14.85	20	3	96	0	1	50.0	111.6	-8.6	23	N/A	0	0	0.0	2.0
C+ /6.5	10.3	0.97	14.71	2	3	96	0	1	50.0	108.2	-8.8	20	N/A	2,500	100	0.0	4.0
C+ /6.5	10.3	0.97	14.65	2	3	96	0	1	50.0	108.2	-8.8	20	N/A	2,500	100	0.0	1.0
C+ /6.6	10.3	0.97	14.91	218	3	96	0	1	50.0	114.9	-8.5	27	N/A	2,500	100	0.0	2.0
C /4.3	17.9	1.09	6.91	2	3	96	0	1	42.0	107.9	-10.0	12	1	2,500	100	5.8	0.0
C- /4.2	17.9	1.09	6.80	N/A	3	96	0	1	42.0	108.3	-10.0	13	1	2,500	0	0.0	2.0
C- /4.2	18.1	1.10	6.94	65	3	96	0	1	42.0	107.6	-9.7	11	1	2,500	100	0.0	2.0
B- /7.7	7.5	0.94	12.13	51	N/A	100	0	N/A	101.0	43.2	-10.0	23	2	2,500	100	5.8	0.0
B- /7.5	7.4	0.94	11.75	7	N/A	100	0	N/A	101.0	39.9	-10.2	18	2	2,500	100	0.0	4.0
B- /7.5	7.5	0.94	11.71	1	N/A	100	0	N/A	101.0	39.9	-10.1	18	2	2,500	100	0.0	1.0
B- /7.7	7.5	0.94	12.10	3	N/A	100	0	N/A	101.0	43.2	-10.0	23	2	2,500	100	0.0	0.0
C+ /6.6	7.7	0.93	20.02	300	0	99	0	1	57.8	68.2	-7.5	78	3	2,500	100	5.8	0.0
B /8.4	7.7	0.93	20.07	8	0	99	0	1	57.8	N/A	N/A	76	3	0	0	0.0	0.0
C+ /6.5	7.7	0.93	19.74	16	0	99	0	1	57.8	63.7	-7.6	71	3	2,500	100	0.0	4.0
C+ /6.5	7.7	0.93	19.63	3	0	99	0	1	57.8	64.0	-7.7	71	3	2,500	100	0.0	1.0
C+ /6.5	7.7	0.93	19.93	1	0	99	0	1	57.8	68.3	-7.4	79	3	2,500	100	0.0	0.0
C /4.8	13.8	1.18	32.48	1	2	97	0	1	79.0	86.2	-7.2	6	N/A	2,500	100	5.8	0.0
C /4.8	13.8	1.18	30.49	21	2	97	0	1	79.0	84.8	-7.2	5	N/A	0	0	0.0	0.0
C /4.9	13.8	1.18	32.92	264	2	97	0	1	79.0	87.6	-7.0	7	N/A	2,500	100	0.0	0.0
C- /3.5	17.3	1.14	20.66	1	5	94	0	1	90.0	86.1	-10.5	4	N/A	2,500	100	5.8	0.0
C- /3.5	17.3	1.14	20.65	17	5	94	0	1	90.0	86.0	-10.5	4	N/A	2,500	100	0.0	0.0
C- /3.4	17.6	1.15	15.46	522	5	94	0	1	90.0	89.2	-9.8	4	N/A	0	0	0.0	0.0
C+ /6.3	11.2	0.69	23.38	269	5	94	0	1	72.1	86.6	-6.9	88	3	2,500	100	5.8	0.0
C+ /5.9	11.2	0.70	21.17	15	5	94	0	1	72.1	82.3	-7.1	83	3	2,500	100	0.0	4.0
C+ /5.9	11.2	0.69	21.07	18	5	94	0	1	72.1	82.2	-7.0	83	3	2,500	100	0.0	1.0
C+ /6.3	11.2	0.69	23.27	65	5	94	0	1	72.1	86.5	-6.9	88	3	2,500	100	0.0	0.0
B- /7.5	13.6	0.64	15.92	30	5	94	0	1	72.1	107.6	-7.1	98	3	0	0	0.0	0.0
B /8.9	7.4	0.94	10.68	11	5	94	0	1	114.0	58.8	-10.5	50	N/A	0	0	0.0	0.0
C- /3.2	17.5	1.06	17.85	210	3	96	0	1	77.0	185.3	-8.3	9	N/A	0	0	0.0	0.0
C- /4.1	12.8	1.01	13.45	141	8	91	0	1	75.0	144.9	-14.3	26	N/A	0	0	0.0	0.0
C+ /6.6	10.3	0.97	12.45	97	2	97	0	1	47.0	116.2	-9.3	29	7	0	0	0.0	0.0
B+ /9.2	7.6	0.92	14.99	58	1	98	0	1	81.0	65.9	-8.2	80	N/A	0	0	0.0	0.0
C+ /6.7	13.6	0.55	13.09	35	5	94	0	1	95.0	86.0	-7.1	10	N/A	2,500	100	0.0	0.0
B /8.8	7.7	0.93	13.48	26	3	96	0	1	12.0	69.6	-10.8	76	4	2,500	100	0.0	0.0
B /8.1	9.5	0.78	28.47	1,753	3	92	3	2	65.0	118.3	-5.7	94	3	1,000,000	100	0.0	0.0
B /8.1	9.5	0.78	28.07	1,137	3	92	3	2	65.0	116.6	-5.7	93	3	2,500	100	0.0	0.0
B- /7.5	12.3	0.80	27.58	538	2	97	0	1	37.0	132.1	-14.4	85	N/A	1,000,000	20,000	0.0	0.0
C+ /5.7	12.3	0.80	26.56	305	2	97	0	1	37.0	130.4	-14.5	84	N/A	2,500	100	0.0	0.0
B- /7.9	10.9	1.04	21.72	11	10	89	0	1	22.3	91.6	-8.4	93	11	2,000	200	0.0	2.0
B+ /9.7	7.2	0.87	16.71	45	0	99	0	1	17.5	66.6	-8.4	82	9	1,000	50	0.0	2.0
U /	N/A	N/A	13.55	186	0	84	14	2	11.0	N/A	N/A	N/A	2	1,000,000	100	0.0	0.0
B /8.5	7.8	0.89	10.46	38	0	98	0	2	29.0	54.2	-11.7	52	3	25,000	0	0.0	0.0

Data as of June 30, 2006

			Overall Weiss Investment Rating		PERFORMANCE							
					Perfor-mance Rating/Pts	Total Return % through 6/30/06					Incl. in Returns	
									Annualized		Dividend	Expense
Fund Type	Fund Name	Ticker Symbol		Phone		3 Mo	6 Mo	1Yr / Pct	3Yr / Pct	5Yr / Pct	Yield	Ratio
GR	Davenport Equity Fund (The)	DAVPX	C+		C- / 3.7	-1.23	2.17	7.96 /32	10.66 /32	4.08 /47	0.53	0.98
CV	Davis Appreciation & Income A	RPFCX	C+	(800) 279-0279	C / 4.5	0.89	5.84	10.06 /47	12.46 /45	8.27 /73	1.94	1.08
CV	Davis Appreciation & Income B	DCSBX	C	(800) 279-0279	C- / 3.9	0.68	5.38	9.09 /41	11.44 /39	7.27 /68	1.21	1.99
CV	Davis Appreciation & Income C	DCSCX	C+	(800) 279-0279	C / 4.4	0.68	5.38	9.10 /41	11.45 /39	7.29 /68	1.22	1.98
CV	Davis Appreciation & Income Y	DCSYX	B-	(800) 279-0279	C / 5.4	0.96	5.96	10.33 /49	12.71 /47	8.46 /74	2.26	0.86
FS	Davis Financial A	RPFGX	C+	(800) 279-0279	C / 5.0	-0.83	1.30	12.99 /64	13.74 /53	4.82 /53	0.00	1.01
FS	Davis Financial B	DFIBX	C	(800) 279-0279	C / 4.5	-1.06	0.85	11.99 /59	12.74 /47	3.92 /45	0.00	1.88
FS	Davis Financial C	DFFCX	C+	(800) 279-0279	C / 5.0	-1.04	0.86	12.00 /59	12.73 /47	3.92 /45	0.00	1.89
FS	Davis Financial Y	DVFYX	B-	(800) 279-0279	C+ / 5.8	-0.79	1.37	13.15 /65	13.92 /53	5.01 /54	0.00	0.85
★ GR	Davis New York Venture Fund A	NYVTX	B	(800) 279-0279	C+ / 5.6	0.00	3.20	12.15 /60	14.89 /58	6.11 /62	0.74	0.89
GR	Davis New York Venture Fund B	NYVBX	B	(800) 279-0279	C / 5.3	-0.18	2.81	11.29 /55	13.98 /54	5.26 /56	0.04	1.69
GR	Davis New York Venture Fund C	NYVCX	B+	(800) 279-0279	C+ / 5.7	-0.18	2.83	11.27 /55	14.00 /54	5.28 /56	0.06	1.68
GR	Davis New York Venture Fund R	NYVRX	U	(800) 279-0279	U /	-0.06	3.05	11.85 /59	--	--	0.55	1.15
GR	Davis New York Venture Fund Y	DNVYX	B+	(800) 279-0279	C+ / 6.4	0.06	3.32	12.42 /62	15.25 /60	6.43 /64	1.05	0.58
GR	Davis Opportunity A	RPEAX	B-	(800) 279-0279	C+ / 6.2	-2.54	6.01	13.04 /64	16.04 /64	8.18 /72	0.85	1.20
GR	Davis Opportunity B	RPFEX	C+	(800) 279-0279	C+ / 5.9	-2.71	5.60	12.19 /61	15.17 /60	7.31 /68	0.19	1.97
GR	Davis Opportunity C	DGOCX	B-	(800) 279-0279	C+ / 6.2	-2.72	5.63	12.17 /60	15.17 /60	7.32 /68	0.19	1.97
GR	Davis Opportunity Y	DGOYX	B-	(800) 279-0279	C+ / 6.9	-2.47	6.13	13.36 /66	16.46 /65	8.53 /74	1.19	0.86
RE	Davis Real Estate A	RPFRX	B-	(800) 279-0279	A- / 9.2	-2.54	12.55	22.31 /85	26.61 /93	19.83 /96	1.62	1.26
RE	Davis Real Estate B	DREBX	B-	(800) 279-0279	A- / 9.1	-2.75	12.06	21.31 /83	25.68 /92	19.24 /95	1.02	1.94
RE	Davis Real Estate C	DRECX	B-	(800) 279-0279	A- / 9.2	-2.75	12.10	21.34 /83	25.69 /92	18.96 /95	1.03	1.93
RE	Davis Real Estate Y	DREYX	B-	(800) 279-0279	A / 9.4	-2.46	12.72	22.72 /85	27.12 /93	20.30 /96	1.98	0.80
OT	● Davis Research Fund Class A		C-	(800) 279-0279	C / 5.0	-1.99	1.61	7.19 /27	14.81 /58	--	1.96	0.93
OT	● Davis Research Fund Class B		D+	(800) 279-0279	C- / 4.1	-2.36	0.78	5.47 /17	13.03 /49	--	0.07	2.02
OT	● Davis Research Fund Class C		C-	(800) 279-0279	C / 4.6	-2.35	0.78	5.54 /18	13.08 /49	--	0.07	2.02
AA	DE 100% Equity Portfolio		C+	(800) 522-7297	C / 5.1	-3.12	2.23	11.89 /59	12.65 /47	3.15 /38	0.00	0.30
AA	DE 70% Equity Portfolio		C+	(800) 522-7297	C- / 3.4	-2.17	1.84	8.76 /38	10.09 /28	4.28 /49	0.00	0.30
AA	DE College Portfolio		C-	(800) 522-7297	E / 0.4	-0.36	0.72	2.73 / 6	3.54 / 2	3.59 /42	0.00	0.30
AA	DE Conservative Portfolio		D+	(800) 522-7297	E- / 0.1	0.44	0.61	1.14 / 3	1.67 / 0	--	0.00	0.30
AA	DE Portfolio 2006		C-	(800) 522-7297	E+ / 0.8	-0.57	0.87	3.43 / 9	5.30 / 5	2.75 /34	0.00	0.30
AA	DE Portfolio 2009		C	(800) 522-7297	D / 1.7	-0.93	0.87	4.76 /14	7.23 /11	2.98 /37	0.00	0.30
AA	DE Portfolio 2012		C	(800) 522-7297	D+ / 2.4	-1.29	1.25	6.32 /22	8.62 /19	3.01 /37	0.00	0.30
AA	DE Portfolio 2015		C+	(800) 522-7297	C- / 3.5	-1.82	1.51	7.84 /31	10.43 /30	2.98 /37	0.00	0.30
AA	DE Portfolio 2018		C+	(800) 522-7297	C- / 3.9	-2.29	1.77	8.80 /39	10.98 /35	3.13 /38	0.00	0.30
AA	DE Portfolio 2021		C+	(800) 522-7297	C / 4.5	-2.65	2.15	10.40 /49	11.70 /40	--	0.00	0.30
BA	Dean Balanced Fund A	DABVX	C-	(888) 899-8343	D / 2.2	-0.11	2.63	7.44 /29	9.69 /25	1.62 /24	0.75	1.85
BA	Dean Balanced Fund C	DBVCX	C	(888) 899-8343	D+ / 2.7	-0.30	2.52	6.97 /26	9.01 /21	1.02 /20	0.23	2.60
FO	Dean International Value A	DAIVX	B-	(888) 899-8343	B+ / 8.5	-4.53	7.27	21.44 /84	23.25 /88	10.11 /81	0.25	2.10
FO	Dean International Value C	DCIVX	B-	(888) 899-8343	B+ / 8.6	-4.76	6.84	20.58 /83	22.62 /86	9.32 /78	0.44	2.85
GR	Dean Large Cap Value A	DALCX	C+	(888) 899-8343	C / 4.4	0.35	4.67	11.50 /57	12.71 /47	-0.04 /15	0.00	1.85
GR	Dean Large Cap Value C	DCLCX	C+	(888) 899-8343	C / 4.6	0.09	4.24	10.58 /51	11.83 /41	-0.82 /12	0.00	2.60
SC	Dean Small Cap Value A	DASCX	C-	(888) 899-8343	C+ / 5.8	-6.00	3.94	8.93 /40	16.57 /66	9.40 /78	0.00	1.85
SC	Dean Small Cap Value C	DACCX	C-	(888) 899-8343	C+ / 6.1	-6.16	3.62	8.28 /35	15.99 /63	8.92 /76	0.00	2.36
SC	Delafield Fund Inc	DEFIX	C+	(800) 221-3079	B- / 7.4	-2.84	7.15	15.18 /72	18.40 /74	13.71 /90	0.10	1.44
GR	Delaware Aggressive Alloc Port A	DFGAX	C-	(800) 362-3863	C- / 3.2	-2.56	1.68	8.86 /39	11.80 /41	4.92 /53	0.92	0.80
GR	Delaware Aggressive Alloc Port B	DFGDX	C-	(800) 362-3863	C- / 3.1	-2.78	1.30	7.96 /32	10.96 /35	4.13 /47	0.27	1.55
GR	Delaware Aggressive Alloc Port C	DFGCX	C	(800) 362-3863	C- / 3.6	-2.77	1.29	8.06 /33	10.94 /35	4.15 /47	0.27	1.55
GR	Delaware Aggressive Alloc Port I	DFGIX	C+	(800) 362-3863	C / 4.6	-2.46	1.88	9.21 /41	12.08 /43	5.19 /56	1.21	0.55
GR	Delaware Aggressive Alloc Port R	DFGRX	C+	(800) 362-3863	C- / 4.2	-2.66	1.59	8.58 /37	11.47 /39	--	0.70	1.05
FS	Delaware American Services Fund A	DASAX	C+	(800) 362-3863	C+ / 6.3	-2.54	4.86	11.35 /56	17.32 /69	14.37 /91	0.00	1.38
FS	Delaware American Services Fund B	DASBX	C+	(800) 362-3863	C+ / 6.2	-2.76	4.48	10.47 /50	16.42 /65	13.53 /89	0.00	2.07
FS	Delaware American Services Fund C	DAMCX	B-	(800) 362-3863	C+ / 6.6	-2.76	4.48	10.47 /50	16.42 /65	13.53 /89	0.00	2.07

● Denotes fund is closed to new investors
★ Denotes fund is included in Section II

RISK			NET ASSETS		ASSET					BULL / BEAR		FUND MANAGER		MINIMUMS		LOADS	
	3 Year		NAV							Last Bull	Last Bear	Manager	Manager	Initial	Additional	Front	Back
Risk	Standard		As of	Total	Cash	Stocks	Bonds	Other	Portfolio	Market	Market	Quality	Tenure	Purch.	Purch.	End	End
Rating/Pts	Deviation	Beta	6/30/06	$(Mil)	%	%	%	%	Turnover Ratio	Return	Return	Pct	(Years)	$	$	Load	Load
B / 8.8	7.8	0.96	13.80	144	0	98	0	2	39.0	61.3	-8.0	55	N/A	10,000	100	0.0	0.0
B / 8.3	5.7	0.72	29.40	277	25	24	0	51	16.6	59.2	2.1	96	13	1,000	25	4.8	0.0
B / 8.3	5.7	0.73	29.05	63	25	24	0	51	16.6	54.6	1.9	94	13	1,000	25	0.0	4.0
B / 8.3	5.7	0.72	29.46	65	25	24	0	51	16.6	54.7	1.9	94	13	1,000	25	0.0	1.0
B / 8.3	5.7	0.73	29.53	42	25	24	0	51	16.6	60.3	2.1	96	13	5,000,000	0	0.0	0.0
B- / 7.8	9.1	0.83	42.95	639	0	99	0	1	5.2	81.5	-8.5	76	15	1,000	25	4.8	0.0
B- / 7.6	9.1	0.82	39.16	135	0	99	0	1	5.2	76.6	-8.7	68	15	1,000	25	0.0	4.0
B- / 7.7	9.1	0.82	39.80	88	0	99	0	1	5.2	76.5	-8.7	68	15	1,000	25	0.0	1.0
B- / 7.8	9.1	0.82	43.69	11	0	99	0	1	5.2	82.5	-8.5	77	15	5,000,000	0	0.0	0.0
B+ / 9.0	7.4	0.91	34.78	22,272	0	99	0	1	3.0	81.1	-8.2	90	11	1,000	25	4.8	0.8
B / 9.0	7.4	0.90	33.24	4,291	0	99	0	1	3.0	76.6	-8.4	86	11	1,000	25	0.0	4.0
B+ / 9.0	7.4	0.90	33.45	6,144	0	99	0	1	3.0	76.6	-8.4	86	11	1,000	25	0.0	1.0
U /	N/A	N/A	34.78	265	0	99	0	1	3.0	N/A	N/A	N/A	11	500,000	0	0.0	0.0
B+ / 9.0	7.4	0.91	35.20	4,059	0	99	0	1	3.0	83.0	-8.2	91	11	5,000,000	0	0.0	0.0
B- / 7.6	10.3	1.19	25.75	545	5	93	0	2	35.8	103.5	-11.6	82	N/A	1,000	25	4.8	0.0
B- / 7.5	10.3	1.19	22.64	90	5	93	0	2	35.8	98.5	-11.8	76	N/A	1,000	25	0.0	4.0
B- / 7.5	10.3	1.19	23.63	193	5	93	0	2	35.8	98.8	-11.8	76	N/A	1,000	25	0.0	1.0
B- / 7.6	10.3	1.19	26.48	58	5	93	0	2	35.8	105.8	-11.6	85	N/A	5,000,000	0	0.0	0.0
C / 4.7	15.2	0.91	45.09	450	6	93	0	1	24.9	131.1	1.4	89	12	1,000	25	4.8	0.0
C / 4.7	15.2	0.91	44.78	74	6	93	0	1	24.9	127.3	1.2	85	12	1,000	25	0.0	4.0
C / 4.7	15.2	0.91	45.13	103	6	93	0	1	24.9	126.0	1.2	85	9	1,000	25	0.0	1.0
C / 4.7	15.2	0.91	45.46	90	6	93	0	1	24.9	134.1	1.6	91	10	5,000,000	0	0.0	0.0
C+ / 5.9	8.9	0.91	13.27	45	0	99	0	1	54.0	76.7	-2.1	90	5	1,000	25	4.8	0.8
C+ / 5.9	8.9	0.90	12.85	N/A	0	99	0	1	54.0	68.5	-2.5	81	5	1,000	25	0.0	4.0
C+ / 5.9	8.9	0.90	12.87	N/A	0	99	0	1	54.0	68.7	-2.5	81	5	1,000	25	0.0	1.0
B / 8.5	8.8	1.70	11.48	31	0	100	0	0	3.0	73.9	-9.6	69	5	1,000	50	0.0	0.0
B+ / 9.3	6.5	1.31	12.17	14	0	70	30	0	9.0	56.3	-5.0	65	5	1,000	50	0.0	0.0
B+ / 9.9	2.3	0.43	13.91	10	40	20	40	0	29.0	16.6	-0.1	44	8	1,000	50	0.0	0.0
B+ / 9.9	2.2	0.11	11.54	7	54	0	44	2	19.0	6.5	2.5	41	5	1,000	50	0.0	0.0
B+ / 9.9	3.2	0.65	13.86	28	13	24	61	2	18.0	27.4	-2.8	51	8	1,000	50	0.0	0.0
B+ / 9.9	4.4	0.93	13.86	39	5	48	46	1	16.0	38.7	-4.3	57	8	1,000	50	0.0	0.0
B+ / 9.6	5.4	1.13	13.79	44	6	58	34	2	14.0	47.2	-5.2	60	8	1,000	50	0.0	0.0
B+ / 9.2	6.7	1.35	13.48	46	0	70	30	0	19.0	60.7	-7.3	66	8	1,000	50	0.0	0.0
B+ / 9.0	7.2	1.43	13.23	53	0	71	28	1	16.0	64.1	-7.3	67	7	1,000	50	0.0	0.0
B / 8.8	7.9	1.54	12.85	25	0	84	14	2	3.0	68.6	-7.7	68	5	1,000	50	0.0	0.0
B+ / 9.2	5.8	1.18	10.52	8	3	63	33	1	56.0	58.6	-9.0	68	9	1,000	0	5.3	1.0
B+ / 9.6	5.9	1.18	9.83	N/A	3	63	33	1	56.0	55.4	-9.3	61	9	1,000	0	0.0	1.0
C / 5.4	12.2	1.14	14.75	16	0	99	0	1	87.0	145.3	-10.8	20	9	1,000	0	5.3	1.0
C / 5.4	12.2	1.14	14.21	1	0	99	0	1	87.0	141.1	-11.0	18	9	1,000	0	0.0	1.0
B / 8.6	7.8	0.97	11.44	8	7	92	0	1	62.0	82.5	-15.7	73	9	1,000	0	5.3	1.0
B / 8.7	7.9	0.98	10.56	N/A	7	92	0	1	62.0	77.5	-15.8	65	9	1,000	0	0.0	1.0
C / 4.9	13.5	0.85	15.05	18	1	98	0	1	48.0	106.8	-12.9	62	N/A	1,000	0	5.3	1.0
C / 4.8	13.5	0.84	14.32	N/A	1	98	0	1	48.0	104.2	-13.0	57	N/A	1,000	0	0.0	1.0
C / 5.5	11.3	0.71	25.32	427	16	82	0	2	71.0	108.1	-10.3	90	13	5,000	0	0.0	2.0
B / 8.2	7.0	0.88	10.27	36	7	79	13	1	15.0	67.9	-7.1	73	2	1,000	100	5.8	1.0
B / 8.2	7.0	0.88	10.16	8	7	79	13	1	15.0	63.9	-7.3	65	2	1,000	100	0.0	4.0
B / 8.2	7.0	0.88	10.17	5	7	79	13	1	15.0	64.1	-7.4	65	2	1,000	100	0.0	1.0
B / 8.2	7.0	0.88	10.29	N/A	7	79	13	1	15.0	69.5	-7.3	75	2	1,000,000	0	0.0	0.0
B / 8.3	7.1	0.89	10.24	1	7	79	13	1	15.0	N/A	N/A	69	2	1,000	100	0.0	0.0
B- / 7.1	12.3	1.00	17.27	237	2	97	0	1	128.0	117.1	-5.4	86	N/A	1,000	100	5.8	1.0
B- / 7.1	12.3	0.99	16.57	59	2	97	0	1	128.0	112.0	-5.6	80	N/A	1,000	100	0.0	4.0
B- / 7.1	12.3	0.99	16.57	101	2	97	0	1	128.0	112.0	-5.5	80	N/A	1,000	100	0.0	1.0

					PERFORMANCE							
99 Pct = Best			Overall			Total Return % through 6/30/06					Incl. in Returns	
0 Pct = Worst			Weiss		Perfor-mance				Annualized		Dividend	Expense
Fund		Ticker	Investment		Rating/Pts	3 Mo	6 Mo	1Yr / Pct	3Yr / Pct	5Yr / Pct	Yield	Ratio
Type	Fund Name	Symbol	Rating	Phone								
FS	Delaware American Services Fund I	DASIX	B	(800) 362-3863	B- / 7.2	-2.51	4.98	11.61 /57	17.58 /71	14.66 /91	0.00	1.07
BA	Delaware Balanced A	DELFX	C-	(800) 362-3863	D- / 1.1	0.04	3.72	6.17 /21	7.45 /12	1.66 /25	2.44	1.20
BA	Delaware Balanced B	DELBX	C-	(800) 362-3863	D- / 1.1	-0.11	3.30	5.33 /17	6.60 / 9	0.88 /20	1.81	1.98
BA	Delaware Balanced C	DEDCX	C-	(800) 362-3863	D- / 1.4	-0.11	3.31	5.34 /17	6.58 / 9	0.88 /20	1.81	1.98
BA	Delaware Balanced I	DEICX	C-	(800) 362-3863	D / 2.1	0.09	3.76	6.33 /22	7.64 /13	1.89 /26	2.80	0.98
BA	Delaware Balanced R	DELRX	C	(800) 362-3863	D / 1.8	0.02	3.57	5.86 /19	7.02 /10	--	2.29	1.48
GI	Delaware Conservative Alloc Port A	DFIAX	C-	(800) 362-3863	E+ / 0.6	-1.32	0.90	3.90 /10	6.55 / 9	4.66 /51	2.25	0.80
GI	Delaware Conservative Alloc Port B	DFIDX	C-	(800) 362-3863	E+ / 0.6	-1.54	0.56	3.14 / 8	5.75 / 6	3.88 /45	1.64	1.55
GI	Delaware Conservative Alloc Port C	DFICX	C-	(800) 362-3863	E+ / 0.8	-1.55	0.56	3.15 / 8	5.78 / 6	3.84 /44	1.65	1.55
GI	Delaware Conservative Alloc Port I	DFIIX	C-	(800) 362-3863	D- / 1.4	-1.21	1.13	4.15 /11	6.84 /10	4.94 /54	2.62	0.55
GI	Delaware Conservative Alloc Port R	DFIRX	C-	(800) 362-3863	D- / 1.1	-1.33	0.79	3.60 / 9	6.25 / 7	--	2.08	1.05
IN	Delaware Dividend Income A	DDIAX	C	(800) 362-3863	D+ / 2.6	0.17	5.90	7.84 /31	10.15 /28	8.46 /74	3.71	1.00
IN	Delaware Dividend Income B	DDDBX	U	(800) 362-3863	U /	-0.01	5.50	7.02 /26	--	--	3.19	1.75
IN	Delaware Dividend Income C	DDICX	U	(800) 362-3863	U /	-0.02	5.50	7.02 /26	--	--	3.19	1.75
IN	Delaware Dividend Income I	DDIIX	C+	(800) 362-3863	C- / 3.9	0.23	5.93	8.11 /33	10.41 /30	8.61 /75	4.18	1.25
EM	● Delaware Emerging Markets A	DEMAX	B+	(800) 362-3863	A+ / 9.6	-5.99	2.85	22.77 /85	34.18 /98	22.30 /98	1.34	1.97
EM	● Delaware Emerging Markets B	DEMBX	B+	(800) 362-3863	A+ / 9.6	-6.14	2.49	21.86 /84	33.18 /97	21.39 /97	0.79	2.72
EM	● Delaware Emerging Markets C	DEMCX	B+	(800) 362-3863	A+ / 9.6	-6.15	2.43	21.89 /84	33.19 /97	21.40 /97	0.80	2.72
EM	● Delaware Emerging Markets I	DEMIX	B+	(800) 362-3863	A+ / 9.7	-5.92	2.95	23.10 /86	34.51 /98	22.60 /98	1.63	1.72
FO	Delaware Global Value A	DABAX	A	(800) 362-3863	A- / 9.1	0.08	11.69	21.71 /84	25.76 /92	13.66 /90	1.71	1.89
FO	Delaware Global Value B	DABBX	A	(800) 362-3863	A- / 9.0	0.00	11.29	20.83 /83	24.87 /91	--	1.18	2.64
FO	Delaware Global Value C	DABCX	A+	(800) 362-3863	A- / 9.1	0.00	11.28	20.81 /83	24.85 /91	--	1.18	2.64
FO	Delaware Global Value I	DABIX	A	(800) 362-3863	A / 9.3	0.25	11.85	22.04 /84	26.11 /92	13.95 /90	2.01	1.20
MC	Delaware Growth Opportunities A	DFCIX	C-	(800) 362-3863	C / 5.0	-6.02	2.48	13.11 /65	14.63 /57	4.89 /53	0.00	1.44
MC	Delaware Growth Opportunities B	DFBIX	C-	(800) 362-3863	C / 4.9	-6.15	2.13	12.37 /61	13.82 /53	4.15 /47	0.00	2.14
MC	Delaware Growth Opportunities C	DEEVX	C-	(800) 362-3863	C / 5.4	-6.18	2.13	12.33 /61	13.83 /53	4.15 /47	0.00	2.14
MC	Delaware Growth Opportunities I	DFDIX	C	(800) 362-3863	C+ / 6.1	-5.94	2.62	13.47 /66	14.97 /59	5.20 /56	0.00	1.14
MC	Delaware Growth Opportunities R	DFRIX	C+	(800) 362-3863	C+ / 5.8	-6.06	2.36	12.91 /64	14.33 /56	--	0.00	1.64
FO	Delaware Intl Value Equity A	DEGIX	D+	(800) 362-3863	B / 7.9	-1.29	6.63	18.68 /80	20.66 /82	11.15 /84	2.01	1.40
FO	Delaware Intl Value Equity B	DEIEX	D	(800) 362-3863	B / 7.8	-1.48	6.26	17.81 /79	19.81 /79	10.37 /82	1.50	2.10
FO	Delaware Intl Value Equity C	DEGCX	D+	(800) 362-3863	B / 8.0	-1.43	6.26	17.83 /79	19.84 /79	10.36 /82	1.51	2.10
FO	Delaware Intl Value Equity I	DEQIX	D+	(800) 362-3863	B+ / 8.4	-1.17	6.80	19.04 /81	21.03 /83	11.48 /85	2.36	1.10
FO	Delaware Intl Value Equity R	DIVRX	A+	(800) 362-3863	B+ / 8.3	-1.30	6.59	18.46 /80	20.40 /81	--	1.88	1.60
GR	Delaware Large Cap Growth A	DGDAX	D-	(800) 362-3863	D- / 1.1	-6.06	-2.77	6.84 /25	8.36 /17	-1.25 /11	0.00	1.00
GR	Delaware Large Cap Growth B	DGDBX	D-	(800) 362-3863	D- / 1.0	-6.35	-3.13	5.99 /20	7.50 /12	--	0.00	1.75
GR	Delaware Large Cap Growth C	DGDCX	D-	(800) 362-3863	D- / 1.3	-6.34	-3.13	5.99 /20	7.55 /13	--	0.00	1.75
GR	Delaware Large Cap Growth I	DGDIX	D	(800) 362-3863	D / 2.1	-6.06	-2.63	7.01 /26	8.59 /18	-1.02 /12	0.17	0.75
IN	Delaware Large Cap Value Fund A	DELDX	C	(800) 362-3863	C- / 3.4	0.11	6.34	10.49 /50	11.23 /37	4.00 /46	1.44	1.12
IN	Delaware Large Cap Value Fund B	DEIBX	C	(800) 362-3863	C- / 3.4	-0.08	5.94	9.68 /45	10.40 /30	3.22 /39	0.83	1.85
IN	Delaware Large Cap Value Fund C	DECCX	C	(800) 362-3863	C- / 3.8	-0.08	5.96	9.67 /45	10.40 /30	3.22 /39	0.83	1.85
IN	Delaware Large Cap Value Fund I	DEDIX	C+	(800) 362-3863	C / 4.8	0.18	6.48	10.80 /52	11.53 /39	4.26 /48	1.78	0.85
IN	Delaware Large Cap Value Fund R	DECRX	C+	(800) 362-3863	C / 4.4	0.05	6.22	10.25 /48	10.91 /35	--	1.32	1.45
AA	Delaware Moderate Allocation Port A	DFBAX	C-	(800) 362-3863	D / 1.7	-1.98	1.22	6.22 /22	9.10 /21	5.02 /54	1.11	0.80
AA	Delaware Moderate Allocation Port B	DFBBX	C-	(800) 362-3863	D / 1.6	-2.08	1.02	5.58 /18	8.31 /17	4.24 /48	0.47	1.55
AA	Delaware Moderate Allocation Port C	DFBCX	C	(800) 362-3863	D / 2.0	-2.07	0.92	5.46 /17	8.29 /17	4.24 /48	0.46	1.55
AA	Delaware Moderate Allocation Port I	DFFIX	C+	(800) 362-3863	D+ / 2.9	-1.78	1.43	6.57 /24	9.38 /23	5.30 /56	1.42	0.55
AA	Delaware Moderate Allocation Port R	DFBRX	C	(800) 362-3863	D+ / 2.5	-1.98	1.23	6.03 /21	8.80 /20	--	0.89	1.05
GR	Delaware Pooled Tr-All Cap Gr Eq	DPCEX	E+	(800) 362-3863	D / 1.6	-7.41	-3.77	5.05 /15	8.17 /16	-1.10 /11	0.00	0.89
EM	● Delaware Pooled Tr-Emerging Mkts	DPEMX	C	(800) 362-3863	A+ / 9.8	-5.52	3.74	23.89 /87	36.76 /98	24.45 /98	2.92	1.28
FO	● Delaware Pooled Tr-Intl Equity	DPIEX	A+	(800) 362-3863	A- / 9.0	2.97	11.38	24.51 /88	23.20 /88	13.26 /89	2.27	0.88
FO	Delaware Pooled Tr-Labor Intl Eq	DELPX	A+	(800) 362-3863	B+ / 8.9	3.45	11.42	23.31 /86	22.69 /87	13.39 /89	2.25	0.89
GI	Delaware Pooled Tr-Lg Cap Val	DPDEX	B-	(800) 362-3863	C / 4.8	0.87	5.13	9.90 /46	11.74 /41	5.11 /55	1.36	0.68

● Denotes fund is closed to new investors
* Denotes fund is included in Section II

RISK			NET ASSETS		ASSET					BULL / BEAR		FUND MANAGER		MINIMUMS		LOADS	
	3 Year		NAV						Portfolio	Last Bull	Last Bear	Manager	Manager	Initial	Additional	Front	Back
	Standard		As of	Total	Cash	Stocks	Bonds	Other	Turnover	Market	Market	Quality	Tenure	Purch.	Purch.	End	End
Risk Rating/Pts	Deviation	Beta	6/30/06	$(Mil)	%	%	%	%	Ratio	Return	Return	Pct	(Years)	$	$	Load	Load
B- / 7.1	12.2	0.99	17.50	18	2	97	0	1	128.0	118.6	-5.3	87	N/A	1,000,000	0	0.0	0.0
B+ / 9.3	4.8	0.95	16.91	209	3	60	36	1	203.0	38.0	-5.0	58	N/A	1,000	100	5.8	1.0
B+ / 9.3	4.8	0.96	16.93	18	3	60	36	1	203.0	34.6	-5.2	47	N/A	1,000	100	0.0	4.0
B+ / 9.3	4.8	0.96	16.91	5	3	60	36	1	203.0	34.6	-5.2	47	N/A	1,000	100	0.0	1.0
B+ / 9.3	4.8	0.96	16.92	2	3	60	36	1	203.0	39.0	-5.0	60	N/A	1,000,000	0	0.0	0.0
B+ / 9.8	4.8	0.95	16.89	N/A	3	60	36	1	203.0	N/A	N/A	53	N/A	1,000	100	0.0	0.0
B+ / 9.8	4.0	0.45	8.94	32	5	43	50	2	8.0	35.2	-2.2	59	2	1,000	100	5.8	1.0
B+ / 9.9	4.0	0.46	8.96	1	5	43	50	2	8.0	32.1	-2.5	49	2	1,000	100	0.0	4.0
B+ / 9.8	4.1	0.47	8.92	1	5	43	50	2	8.0	32.1	-2.5	49	2	1,000	100	0.0	1.0
B+ / 9.8	4.0	0.46	8.96	N/A	5	43	50	2	8.0	36.3	-2.3	62	2	1,000,000	0	0.0	0.0
B+ / 9.9	4.0	0.45	8.93	N/A	5	43	50	2	8.0	N/A	N/A	56	2	1,000	100	0.0	0.0
B+ / 9.4	6.2	0.68	11.40	318	7	59	22	12	85.0	54.0	-2.4	75	N/A	1,000	100	5.8	1.0
U /	N/A	N/A	11.41	64	7	59	22	12	85.0	N/A	N/A	N/A	N/A	1,000	100	0.0	4.0
U /	N/A	N/A	11.41	198	7	59	22	12	85.0	N/A	N/A	N/A	N/A	1,000	100	0.0	1.0
B+ / 9.4	6.2	0.68	11.40	1	7	59	22	12	85.0	55.1	-2.4	77	N/A	1,000,000	0	0.0	0.0
C / 5.5	15.6	0.92	18.06	653	3	96	0	1	25.0	218.2	0.8	68	10	50,000	100	5.8	1.0
C / 5.5	15.6	0.92	17.73	35	3	96	0	1	25.0	210.5	0.8	59	10	50,000	100	0.0	4.0
C / 5.5	15.6	0.92	17.71	193	3	96	0	1	25.0	210.7	0.8	59	10	50,000	100	0.0	1.0
C / 5.5	15.6	0.92	18.13	299	3	96	0	1	25.0	220.8	0.9	70	10	1,000,000	0	0.0	0.0
C+ / 6.8	9.7	0.83	11.85	20	4	95	0	1	51.0	153.5	-3.4	92	N/A	1,000	100	5.8	1.0
C+ / 6.9	9.7	0.83	11.73	5	4	95	0	1	51.0	147.6	-3.6	89	N/A	1,000	100	0.0	4.0
C+ / 6.9	9.7	0.83	11.74	9	4	95	0	1	51.0	147.4	-3.5	89	N/A	1,000	100	0.0	1.0
C+ / 6.7	9.7	0.83	11.89	4	4	95	0	1	51.0	155.3	-3.1	92	N/A	1,000,000	0	0.0	0.0
C+ / 6.1	13.5	1.17	23.59	549	6	92	0	2	84.0	92.7	-10.0	11	N/A	1,000	100	5.8	1.0
C+ / 6.0	13.6	1.18	20.60	19	6	92	0	2	84.0	88.6	-10.2	9	N/A	1,000	100	0.0	4.0
C+ / 6.0	13.5	1.17	21.12	9	6	92	0	2	84.0	88.6	-10.2	9	N/A	1,000	100	0.0	1.0
C+ / 6.1	13.5	1.17	25.48	8	6	92	0	2	84.0	94.6	-10.0	12	N/A	1,000,000	0	0.0	0.0
C+ / 6.8	13.6	1.17	23.40	4	6	92	0	2	84.0	N/A	N/A	10	N/A	1,000	100	0.0	0.0
D / 1.7	10.0	0.93	14.35	472	4	95	0	1	14.0	126.7	-7.4	35	N/A	1,000	100	5.8	0.0
D / 1.7	10.0	0.93	14.16	38	4	95	0	1	14.0	122.0	-7.7	30	N/A	1,000	100	0.0	4.0
D / 1.7	10.0	0.93	14.14	141	4	95	0	1	14.0	122.0	-7.6	30	N/A	1,000	100	0.0	1.0
D / 1.7	10.0	0.93	14.42	381	4	95	0	1	14.0	129.0	-7.4	38	N/A	1,000,000	0	0.0	0.0
B / 8.1	10.0	0.93	14.30	5	4	95	0	1	14.0	N/A	N/A	33	N/A	1,000	100	0.0	0.0
C+ / 6.8	9.1	1.08	6.66	7	0	99	0	1	124.0	54.3	-9.3	24	1	1,000	100	5.8	1.0
C+ / 6.7	9.1	1.07	6.49	2	0	99	0	1	124.0	50.9	-9.5	19	1	1,000	100	0.0	4.0
C+ / 6.7	9.1	1.07	6.50	2	0	99	0	1	124.0	50.9	-9.7	19	1	1,000	100	0.0	1.0
C+ / 6.8	9.1	1.08	6.67	106	0	99	0	1	124.0	55.6	-9.3	26	1	1,000,000	0	0.0	0.0
B / 8.4	7.4	0.91	18.73	1,141	1	98	0	1	117.0	64.4	-9.5	65	N/A	1,000	100	5.8	1.0
B / 8.4	7.4	0.91	18.62	105	1	98	0	1	117.0	60.7	-9.7	56	N/A	1,000	100	0.0	4.0
B / 8.4	7.4	0.91	18.74	33	1	98	0	1	117.0	60.7	-9.7	56	N/A	1,000	100	0.0	1.0
B / 8.4	7.4	0.91	18.72	40	1	98	0	1	117.0	65.9	-9.5	68	N/A	1,000,000	0	0.0	0.0
B+ / 9.0	7.4	0.92	18.72	1	1	98	0	1	117.0	N/A	N/A	61	N/A	1,000	100	0.0	0.0
B+ / 9.7	5.4	1.08	9.92	32	5	65	28	2	3.0	51.6	-4.9	68	2	1,000	100	5.8	1.0
B+ / 9.7	5.4	1.08	9.90	4	5	65	28	2	3.0	48.0	-5.0	59	2	1,000	100	0.0	4.0
B+ / 9.7	5.4	1.09	9.92	4	5	65	28	2	3.0	48.0	-5.0	59	2	1,000	100	0.0	1.0
B+ / 9.7	5.4	1.10	9.94	N/A	5	65	28	2	3.0	52.9	-4.8	69	2	1,000,000	0	0.0	0.0
B+ / 9.6	5.4	1.09	9.90	1	5	65	28	2	3.0	N/A	N/A	64	2	1,000	100	0.0	0.0
C / 5.4	11.8	1.26	5.62	15	9	90	0	1	220.0	67.1	-9.3	14	1	1,000,000	0	0.0	0.0
D / 1.9	15.7	0.92	13.87	659	1	98	0	1	48.0	238.7	1.2	84	9	1,000,000	0	0.0	0.0
B / 8.4	9.3	0.87	22.91	2,107	2	97	0	1	10.0	132.7	-7.1	73	N/A	1,000,000	0	0.0	0.0
B / 8.1	9.0	0.83	20.10	866	1	98	0	1	7.0	129.9	-7.5	76	11	1,000,000	0	0.0	0.0
B+ / 9.0	7.3	0.90	18.64	15	1	98	0	1	49.0	66.0	-9.4	70	N/A	1,000,000	0	0.0	0.0

	99 Pct = Best 0 Pct = Worst		Overall Weiss		PERFORMANCE						Incl. in Returns	
					Perfor-mance	Total Return % through 6/30/06			Annualized		Dividend	Expense
Fund Type	Fund Name	Ticker Symbol	Investment Rating	Phone	Rating/Pts	3 Mo	6 Mo	1Yr / Pct	3Yr / Pct	5Yr / Pct	Yield	Ratio
GR	Delaware Pooled Tr-Lg Cp Gr Eq	DPLGX	U	(800) 362-3863	U /	-6.10	-2.60	--	--	--	0.00	0.91
MC	Delaware Pooled Tr-Mid Cap Gr	DPAGX	C	(800) 362-3863	C+ / 6.1	-5.97	2.60	13.63 /67	14.88 /58	5.10 /55	0.00	0.93
RE	● Delaware Pooled Tr-REIT Port I	DPRIX	C	(800) 362-3863	B+ / 8.7	-2.12	10.73	13.35 /66	23.23 /88	17.26 /94	2.18	1.09
RE	● Delaware Pooled Tr-REIT Port II	DPRTX	C	(800) 362-3863	B+ / 8.7	-1.92	11.12	13.61 /67	23.14 /88	17.40 /94	3.77	0.86
SC	Delaware Pooled Tr-Sm Cap Growth	DPSGX	D	(800) 362-3863	C- / 4.1	-9.57	0.97	11.23 /55	11.67 /40	3.44 /41	0.00	0.86
RE	Delaware REIT A	DPREX	C	(800) 362-3863	B+ / 8.3	-2.18	10.60	13.07 /65	22.94 /87	16.96 /94	1.86	1.34
RE	Delaware REIT B	DPRBX	C	(800) 362-3863	B / 8.2	-2.36	10.21	12.24 /61	22.03 /85	16.09 /93	1.30	2.09
RE	Delaware REIT C	DPRCX	C+	(800) 362-3863	B+ / 8.4	-2.36	10.21	12.28 /61	22.02 /85	16.10 /93	1.29	2.09
RE	Delaware REIT I	DPRSX	C+	(800) 362-3863	B+ / 8.7	-2.12	10.73	13.35 /66	23.24 /88	17.26 /94	2.18	1.09
RE	Delaware REIT R	DPRRX	B+	(800) 362-3863	B+ / 8.6	-2.29	10.47	12.77 /63	22.57 /86	--	1.72	1.59
AG	Delaware Select Growth A	DVEAX	E+	(800) 362-3863	D / 2.1	-7.64	-4.15	14.63 /70	11.13 /36	0.06 /16	0.00	1.50
AG	Delaware Select Growth B	DVEBX	E+	(800) 362-3863	D / 1.8	-7.81	-4.50	13.76 /67	10.28 /29	-0.69 /13	0.00	2.25
AG	Delaware Select Growth C	DVECX	E+	(800) 362-3863	D+ / 2.3	-7.81	-4.50	13.76 /67	10.29 /29	-0.69 /13	0.00	2.25
AG	Delaware Select Growth I	VAGGX	D-	(800) 362-3863	C- / 3.2	-7.57	-4.02	14.89 /71	11.39 /38	0.31 /17	0.00	1.25
AG	Delaware Select Growth R	DFSRX	D	(800) 362-3863	D+ / 2.8	-7.70	-4.26	14.36 /69	10.79 /34	--	0.00	1.75
SC	Delaware Small Cap Core A	DCCAX	C	(800) 362-3863	B- / 7.4	-3.42	9.37	14.49 /70	19.48 /78	14.14 /90	0.00	1.25
SC	Delaware Small Cap Core I	DCCIX	C+	(800) 362-3863	B / 8.0	-3.34	9.57	14.79 /71	19.58 /78	14.20 /90	0.24	1.00
SC	● Delaware Small Cap Value A	DEVLX	C+	(800) 362-3863	B- / 7.4	-3.05	7.99	14.15 /69	19.91 /79	13.90 /90	0.00	1.39
SC	● Delaware Small Cap Value B	DEVBX	C+	(800) 362-3863	B- / 7.4	-3.23	7.59	13.35 /66	19.06 /76	13.10 /89	0.00	2.14
SC	● Delaware Small Cap Value C	DEVCX	C+	(800) 362-3863	B / 7.6	-3.25	7.59	13.32 /65	19.08 /76	13.11 /89	0.00	2.14
SC	● Delaware Small Cap Value I	DEVIX	B-	(800) 362-3863	B / 8.1	-2.97	8.14	14.47 /70	20.27 /80	14.25 /91	0.00	1.14
SC	● Delaware Small Cap Value R	DVLRX	A	(800) 362-3863	B / 7.9	-3.10	7.86	13.90 /68	19.60 /78	--	0.00	1.64
SC	Delaware Small-Cap Growth A	DSCAX	E+	(800) 362-3863	C- / 3.0	-9.44	3.03	10.70 /52	11.33 /38	--	0.00	1.60
SC	Delaware Small-Cap Growth B	DSCBX	E+	(800) 362-3863	D+ / 2.7	-9.69	2.59	9.87 /46	10.47 /31	--	0.00	2.35
SC	Delaware Small-Cap Growth C	DSCCX	E+	(800) 362-3863	C- / 3.2	-9.69	2.59	9.87 /46	10.47 /31	--	0.00	2.35
SC	Delaware Small-Cap Growth I	DSCIX	D-	(800) 362-3863	C- / 4.1	-9.42	3.00	10.88 /53	11.55 /39	--	0.00	1.35
SC	Delaware Small-Cap Growth R	DSCRX	D+	(800) 362-3863	C- / 3.7	-9.60	2.79	10.41 /50	10.97 /35	--	0.00	1.85
SC	Delaware Trend Fund A	DELTX	D-	(800) 362-3863	D+ / 2.9	-9.67	0.76	11.15 /55	11.41 /39	3.09 /38	0.00	1.38
SC	Delaware Trend Fund B	DERBX	E+	(800) 362-3863	D+ / 2.7	-9.85	0.40	10.36 /49	10.60 /32	2.36 /31	0.00	2.08
SC	Delaware Trend Fund C	DETCX	D-	(800) 362-3863	C- / 3.2	-9.82	0.44	10.34 /49	10.61 /32	2.36 /31	0.00	2.08
SC	Delaware Trend Fund I	DGTIX	D	(800) 362-3863	C- / 4.2	-9.59	0.94	11.50 /57	11.73 /41	3.39 /40	0.00	1.08
SC	Delaware Trend Fund R	DETRX	D+	(800) 362-3863	C- / 3.7	-9.74	0.68	10.87 /53	11.10 /36	--	0.00	1.58
GR	Delaware US Growth A	DUGAX	E+	(800) 362-3863	D- / 1.0	-6.12	-2.50	10.75 /52	8.73 /19	-1.96 / 8	0.00	1.05
GR	Delaware US Growth B	DEUBX	E+	(800) 362-3863	E+ / 0.9	-6.30	-2.85	9.94 /47	7.99 /15	-2.64 / 6	0.00	1.75
GR	Delaware US Growth C	DEUCX	E+	(800) 362-3863	D- / 1.3	-6.26	-2.86	9.97 /47	7.99 /15	-2.64 / 6	0.00	1.75
GR	Delaware US Growth I	DEUIX	D-	(800) 362-3863	D / 2.0	-6.06	-2.39	11.03 /54	9.06 /21	-1.68 / 9	0.00	0.75
GR	Delaware US Growth R	DEURX	D	(800) 362-3863	D / 1.7	-6.17	-2.59	10.46 /50	8.45 /17	--	0.00	1.25
IN	Delaware Value A	DDVAX	B-	(800) 362-3863	C / 4.8	0.34	6.60	10.57 /51	13.55 /52	5.09 /55	0.96	1.00
IN	Delaware Value B	DDVBX	B-	(800) 362-3863	C / 4.7	0.08	6.16	9.75 /45	12.69 /47	--	0.34	1.75
IN	Delaware Value C	DDVCX	B	(800) 362-3863	C / 5.2	0.17	6.24	9.74 /45	12.72 /47	--	0.34	1.75
IN	Delaware Value I	DDVIX	B+	(800) 362-3863	C+ / 5.9	0.34	6.69	10.76 /52	13.79 /53	5.29 /56	1.26	0.75
GR	DF Dent Premier Growth	DFDPX	A	(866) 233-3368	B / 7.6	-2.70	4.78	15.77 /74	18.46 /74	--	0.00	1.25
FO	DFA Continental Small Company	DFCSX	B+	(800) 984-9472	A+ / 9.8	-0.21	19.67	34.90 /97	35.91 /98	24.74 /98	1.66	0.71
EM	DFA Emerging Markets	DFEMX	B-	(800) 984-9472	A+ / 9.6	-6.45	3.53	28.84 /94	31.79 /97	20.50 /97	2.45	0.69
FO	DFA Emerging Markets Small Cap	DEMSX	B	(800) 984-9472	A+ / 9.6	-7.53	4.33	28.16 /93	32.21 /97	24.65 /98	1.78	0.97
EM	DFA Emerging Markets Value	DFEVX	B	(800) 984-9472	A+ / 9.9	-3.95	9.20	37.52 /97	41.16 /99	28.82 /99	2.10	0.70
GL	DFA Global 60/40 Inst	DGSIX	U	(800) 984-9472	U /	-0.63	4.59	10.90 /53	--	--	2.08	0.41
GL	DFA Global Equity Inst	DGEIX	U	(800) 984-9472	U /	-1.96	6.59	17.35 /78	--	--	1.65	0.44
FO	DFA International Small Cap Value	DISVX	A+	(800) 984-9472	A+ / 9.7	-2.70	9.65	28.16 /93	33.59 /97	23.77 /98	1.81	0.75
FO	DFA International Small Company	DFISX	A+	(800) 984-9472	A+ / 9.6	-2.46	8.40	27.97 /93	30.60 /96	20.00 /96	1.82	0.64
FO	DFA International Value I	DFIVX	A+	(800) 984-9472	A+ / 9.6	0.10	12.46	31.08 /95	30.05 /96	15.74 /93	2.64	0.48
FO	DFA International Value IV	DFVFX	A+	(800) 984-9472	A+ / 9.6	0.18	12.63	31.38 /95	30.29 /96	15.88 /93	2.39	0.32

● Denotes fund is closed to new investors
* Denotes fund is included in Section II

RISK			NET ASSETS		ASSET				Portfolio Turnover Ratio	BULL / BEAR		FUND MANAGER		MINIMUMS		LOADS	
Risk Rating/Pts	3 Year		NAV As of 6/30/06	Total $(Mil)	Cash %	Stocks %	Bonds %	Other %		Last Bull Market Return	Last Bear Market Return	Manager Quality Pct	Manager Tenure (Years)	Initial Purch. $	Additional Purch. $	Front End Load	Back End Load
	Standard Deviation	Beta															
U /	N/A	N/A	8.62	197	1	98	0	1	N/A	N/A	N/A	N/A	N/A	1,000,000	0	0.0	0.0
C+ / 6.1	13.5	1.16	3.94	17	8	91	0	1	84.0	93.8	-9.6	13	10	1,000,000	0	0.0	0.0
C- / 3.4	16.2	0.98	21.03	21	5	94	0	1	41.0	107.7	-0.2	52	7	1,000,000	0	0.0	0.0
C- / 3.5	16.1	0.97	26.58	26	5	94	0	1	41.0	107.4	-0.3	54	9	1,000,000	0	0.0	0.0
C / 4.9	14.8	0.95	16.64	64	4	95	0	1	61.0	82.8	-9.4	12	6	1,000,000	0	0.0	0.0
C- / 4.1	16.3	0.98	21.02	220	2	97	0	1	37.0	106.1	-0.3	48	9	1,000	100	5.8	1.0
C- / 4.1	16.2	0.98	21.01	67	2	97	0	1	37.0	101.2	-0.4	40	9	1,000	100	0.0	4.0
C- / 4.1	16.3	0.98	21.02	68	2	97	0	1	37.0	101.3	-0.4	39	9	1,000	100	0.0	1.0
C- / 4.1	16.3	0.98	21.04	37	2	97	0	1	37.0	107.6	-0.2	52	9	1,000,000	0	0.0	0.0
C+ / 6.4	16.3	0.98	21.02	5	2	97	0	1	37.0	N/A	N/A	44	9	1,000	100	0.0	0.0
C / 5.1	12.5	1.29	25.39	176	0	97	2	1	72.0	83.2	-10.1	29	N/A	1,000	100	5.8	0.0
C / 5.1	12.5	1.29	23.15	173	0	97	2	1	72.0	78.8	-10.2	24	N/A	1,000	100	0.0	4.0
C / 5.0	12.5	1.29	22.90	76	0	97	2	1	72.0	78.7	-10.2	24	N/A	1,000	100	0.0	1.0
C / 5.1	12.5	1.30	26.00	43	0	97	2	1	72.0	84.5	-10.0	31	N/A	1,000,000	0	0.0	0.0
C+ / 6.4	12.6	1.30	25.16	1	0	97	2	1	72.0	N/A	N/A	27	N/A	1,000	100	0.0	0.0
C / 5.0	13.2	0.88	12.14	15	2	97	0	1	104.0	119.0	-7.1	81	N/A	1,000	100	5.8	0.0
C / 5.0	13.1	0.88	12.14	13	2	97	0	1	104.0	119.2	-7.1	82	N/A	1,000,000	0	0.0	0.0
C+ / 5.8	12.1	0.80	39.07	473	7	92	0	1	33.0	118.8	-7.4	90	9	1,000	100	5.8	1.0
C / 5.5	12.1	0.80	36.29	99	7	92	0	1	33.0	113.9	-7.5	86	9	1,000	100	0.0	4.0
C / 5.5	12.1	0.80	36.27	144	7	92	0	1	33.0	113.9	-7.5	86	9	1,000	100	0.0	1.0
C+ / 5.9	12.1	0.80	40.12	40	7	92	0	1	33.0	120.9	-7.3	91	9	1,000,000	0	0.0	0.0
B- / 7.7	12.1	0.80	38.72	17	7	92	0	1	33.0	N/A	N/A	89	9	1,000	100	0.0	0.0
C- / 4.1	15.9	1.01	11.89	15	1	94	3	2	87.0	92.4	-9.4	8	N/A	1,000	100	5.8	0.0
C- / 4.0	15.9	1.02	11.47	5	1	94	3	2	87.0	87.9	-9.5	5	N/A	1,000	100	0.0	4.0
C- / 4.0	15.9	1.02	11.47	10	1	94	3	2	87.0	87.9	-9.5	5	N/A	1,000	100	0.0	1.0
C- / 4.1	15.9	1.01	12.02	N/A	1	94	3	2	87.0	93.8	-9.3	8	N/A	1,000,000	0	0.0	0.0
C+ / 6.0	15.9	1.01	11.77	2	1	94	3	2	87.0	N/A	N/A	7	N/A	1,000	100	0.0	0.0
C / 4.8	15.1	0.97	22.43	679	3	96	0	1	44.0	82.9	-9.8	10	N/A	1,000	100	5.8	0.0
C / 4.8	15.2	0.97	20.13	114	3	96	0	1	44.0	78.8	-10.0	8	N/A	1,000	100	0.0	4.0
C / 4.8	15.2	0.97	20.49	123	3	96	0	1	44.0	78.8	-9.9	8	N/A	1,000	100	0.0	1.0
C / 4.9	15.2	0.97	23.56	264	3	96	0	1	44.0	84.6	-9.7	11	N/A	1,000,000	0	0.0	0.0
C+ / 6.3	15.1	0.97	22.24	3	3	96	0	1	44.0	N/A	N/A	9	N/A	1,000	100	0.0	0.0
C+ / 6.0	10.9	1.22	12.88	106	2	97	0	1	65.0	49.0	-9.0	19	N/A	1,000	100	5.8	1.0
C+ / 5.9	10.9	1.21	11.61	24	2	97	0	1	65.0	45.8	-9.2	15	N/A	1,000	100	0.0	4.0
C+ / 5.9	10.9	1.21	12.58	20	2	97	0	1	65.0	45.7	-9.1	15	N/A	1,000	100	0.0	1.0
C+ / 6.0	10.8	1.21	13.49	446	2	97	0	1	65.0	50.3	-8.9	21	N/A	1,000,000	0	0.0	0.0
B- / 7.1	10.8	1.21	12.78	1	2	97	0	1	65.0	N/A	N/A	18	N/A	1,000	100	0.0	0.0
B+ / 9.1	8.0	0.94	11.96	160	4	95	0	1	26.0	73.2	-8.6	82	N/A	1,000	100	5.8	1.0
B+ / 9.0	7.9	0.93	11.90	8	4	95	0	1	26.0	69.1	-8.7	76	N/A	1,000	100	0.0	4.0
B+ / 9.0	7.9	0.94	11.91	28	4	95	0	1	26.0	69.3	-8.8	76	N/A	1,000	100	0.0	1.0
B+ / 9.1	7.9	0.93	11.96	189	4	95	0	1	26.0	74.5	-8.5	84	N/A	1,000,000	0	0.0	0.0
B / 8.3	9.5	1.10	15.11	78	0	100	0	0	13.0	99.8	-8.5	95	5	100,000	2,000	0.0	0.0
C / 5.0	13.1	1.15	17.67	75	0	100	0	0	18.0	236.0	-1.9	96	N/A	2,000,000	0	0.0	0.0
C- / 4.2	17.0	1.01	21.35	2,359	0	100	0	0	9.0	222.4	-5.6	25	N/A	2,000,000	0	0.0	0.0
C / 4.7	17.3	1.46	14.35	685	0	100	0	0	8.0	239.2	-2.7	27	N/A	2,000,000	0	0.0	0.0
C- / 4.2	18.8	1.09	25.82	2,920	0	100	0	0	7.0	295.1	-1.9	70	N/A	2,000,000	0	0.0	0.0
U /	N/A	N/A	11.79	413	0	100	0	0	54.0	N/A	N/A	N/A	3	2,000,000	0	0.0	0.0
U /	N/A	N/A	13.36	634	0	100	0	0	15.0	N/A	N/A	N/A	3	2,000,000	0	0.0	0.0
C+ / 6.7	11.7	1.00	19.30	5,412	0	100	0	0	13.0	221.9	2.1	98	N/A	2,000,000	0	0.0	0.0
B- / 7.6	11.4	0.98	17.55	3,848	0	100	0	0	10.0	194.3	0.9	94	N/A	2,000,000	0	0.0	0.0
B- / 7.0	10.8	1.04	20.01	3,398	0	100	0	0	10.0	177.3	-7.7	89	N/A	2,000,000	0	0.0	0.0
B / 8.0	10.8	1.04	16.41	481	0	100	0	0	10.0	178.6	-7.7	89	N/A	2,000,000	0	0.0	0.0

Fund Type	Fund Name	Ticker Symbol	Overall Weiss Investment Rating	Phone	Performance Rating/Pts	3 Mo	6 Mo	1Yr / Pct	3Yr / Pct	5Yr / Pct	Dividend Yield	Expense Ratio
								Total Return % through 6/30/06	Annualized		Incl. in Returns	
FO	DFA Japanese Small Co	DFJSX	B-	(800) 984-9472	A- / 9.1	-8.94	-6.88	22.02 /84	26.53 /93	14.18 /90	1.10	0.68
FO	DFA Large Cap International	DFALX	A+	(800) 984-9472	B+ / 8.9	0.67	9.74	26.58 /91	22.87 /87	9.76 /80	2.40	0.37
GR	DFA Large Cap Value I	DFLVX	A+	(800) 984-9472	B / 8.1	1.79	8.10	15.77 /74	19.45 /78	8.87 /76	1.66	0.30
FO	DFA Pacific Rim Small Company	DFRSX	B+	(800) 984-9472	A / 9.4	-0.99	12.60	21.37 /83	27.50 /93	21.13 /97	3.36	0.74
RE	DFA Real Estate Securities Port	DFREX	C	(800) 984-9472	A / 9.3	-1.49	13.68	20.48 /82	26.57 /93	19.78 /96	2.96	0.37
SC	DFA Small Cap Value I	DFSVX	A-	(800) 984-9472	A / 9.3	-3.40	11.14	19.77 /82	26.50 /93	16.66 /94	1.22	0.55
FO	DFA Tax Managed Intl Value	DTMIX	A+	(800) 984-9472	A / 9.5	-0.01	12.07	31.05 /95	29.32 /95	14.73 /91	2.79	0.60
SC	DFA Tax Managed Sm Co Fd	DFTSX	B+	(800) 984-9472	B / 8.1	-5.61	7.00	16.17 /75	20.21 /80	10.11 /81	0.28	0.55
MC	DFA Tax Managed US MktWide Val	DTMMX	A+	(800) 984-9472	B+ / 8.3	0.21	7.99	17.94 /79	20.18 /80	6.17 /62	1.47	0.40
SC	DFA Tax Mgd Sm Cap Val Fd	DTMVX	A	(800) 984-9472	A- / 9.0	-3.46	9.85	19.23 /81	23.95 /89	13.68 /90	0.52	0.55
IN	DFA Tax-Managed U.S. Equity	DTMEX	C+	(800) 984-9472	C / 4.8	-2.17	2.71	9.16 /41	12.34 /45	--	1.35	0.25
FO	DFA United Kingdom Small Co	DFUKX	A+	(800) 984-9472	A / 9.4	2.71	14.04	28.30 /93	27.28 /93	17.47 /94	2.52	0.70
IX	DFA US Large Company	DFLCX	C+	(800) 984-9472	C- / 4.1	-1.46	2.69	8.58 /37	11.10 /36	2.37 /31	1.78	0.15
SC	DFA US Micro Cap Portfolio	DFSCX	C+	(800) 984-9472	B / 8.0	-7.11	6.26	15.48 /73	20.45 /81	13.14 /89	2.18	0.55
SC	DFA US Small Cap Portfolio	DFSTX	B-	(800) 984-9472	B / 7.8	-5.79	7.28	15.28 /73	19.35 /77	10.04 /81	1.74	0.40
GR	Diamond Hill Financial Lng-Sht A	BANCX	B-		C / 5.5	1.09	5.25	8.06 /33	14.88 /58	15.46 /92	1.44	1.65
GR	Diamond Hill Financial Lng-Sht C	BSGCX	B-		C+ / 5.6	0.92	4.82	7.22 /27	14.01 /54	--	0.64	2.40
GR	Diamond Hill Large Cap A	DHLAX	A+		B / 7.8	0.93	4.99	16.76 /76	20.40 /81	9.24 /78	0.36	1.25
GR	Diamond Hill Large Cap C	DHLCX	A+		B / 7.9	0.75	4.59	15.93 /74	19.50 /78	8.36 /73	0.00	2.00
GR	Diamond Hill Large Cap I	DHLRX	B		B+ / 8.3	1.06	5.18	17.22 /78	20.65 /82	9.37 /78	0.53	0.80
GR	Diamond Hill Long-Short Fd Cl A	DIAMX	A+		B / 7.7	2.14	7.41	21.57 /84	19.23 /77	8.28 /73	0.54	1.55
GR	Diamond Hill Long-Short Fd Cl C	DHFCX	A+		B / 7.8	1.92	6.97	20.70 /83	18.33 /74	7.44 /69	0.15	2.30
GR	Diamond Hill Long-Short Fd Cl I	DHLSX	B+		B / 8.2	2.19	7.64	22.08 /84	19.49 /78	8.42 /74	0.78	1.10
SC	● Diamond Hill Small Cap A	DHSCX	A		B+ / 8.6	-2.94	3.34	14.06 /68	24.58 /90	15.20 /92	0.03	1.41
SC	● Diamond Hill Small Cap C	DHSMX	A		B+ / 8.6	-3.10	2.95	13.22 /65	23.68 /89	14.33 /91	0.00	2.16
SC	● Diamond Hill Small Cap I	DHSIX	B+		B+ / 8.9	-2.82	3.54	14.56 /70	24.78 /91	15.32 /92	0.15	0.98
GI	Direxion Dow 30 Plus Fd	PDOWX	C-	(800) 851-0511	C- / 3.4	0.27	4.86	10.52 /50	9.36 /23	0.76 /19	0.68	1.75
GR	Direxion Evolution All Equity Inv	PEVEX	U	(800) 851-0511	U /	-2.87	6.32	18.74 /80	--	--	0.00	1.85
BA	Direxion HCM Freedom Fund Adv	HCMFX	U	(800) 851-0511	U /	-0.93	-3.32	-4.34 / 0	--	--	0.67	2.08
GR	Direxion OTC Plus Inv	POTCX	E	(800) 851-0511	D / 1.7	-10.04	-6.54	3.97 /10	9.08 /21	-6.94 / 1	0.00	1.75
IX	Direxion PSI Calender Effects Inv	PCALX	U	(800) 851-0511	U /	1.66	5.52	9.52 /43	--	--	0.61	1.91
SC	Direxion Small Cap Bull 2.5X Fd	DXRLX	E	(800) 851-0511	C / 4.6	-15.68	-1.61	3.06 / 7	14.65 /57	3.73 /43	0.00	1.75
SC	Direxion Small Cp Bear 2.5X	DXRSX	E-	(800) 851-0511	E- / 0.0	10.37	-14.50	-24.02 / 0	-22.65 / 0	-14.36 / 0	4.73	1.95
EM	Direxion Spectrum Equity Opp Adv	SFEOX	U	(800) 851-0511	U /	-1.59	5.00	11.08 /54	--	--	0.00	2.50
GR	Direxion U.S. Short Inv	PSPSX	E-	(800) 851-0511	E- / 0.0	2.96	0.15	-3.48 / 0	-9.61 / 0	-4.46 / 3	0.00	1.95
AG	Diversified Inst Aggress Equity	DIAEX	D-	(800) 926-0044	C- / 4.2	-7.61	-0.09	10.93 /53	11.67 /40	-0.88 /12	0.09	0.80
BA	Diversified Inst Balanced	DIBFX	C	(800) 926-0044	D / 2.1	-1.00	1.63	6.06 /21	7.94 /15	3.62 /42	1.81	0.50
GR	Diversified Inst Equity Growth	DIEGX	D-	(800) 926-0044	D / 1.6	-5.57	-3.11	5.46 /17	7.82 /14	-0.04 /15	0.12	0.65
GI	Diversified Inst Growth & Income	DIGIX	C-	(800) 926-0044	C- / 3.6	-2.62	0.97	8.25 /35	10.53 /31	0.83 /19	1.65	0.64
AA	Diversified Inst Interm Horizon	DIIHX	C	(800) 926-0044	D / 2.0	-1.19	1.75	6.04 /21	7.69 /13	4.31 /49	2.65	1.29
FO	Diversified Inst International Eq	DIIEX	A	(800) 926-0044	B+ / 8.7	-0.71	9.55	25.07 /89	21.79 /85	8.22 /72	2.27	0.88
AA	Diversified Inst Intrm-Long Hor SAF	DILHX	C	(800) 926-0044	C- / 3.3	-1.79	2.11	8.19 /34	9.78 /26	3.92 /45	2.15	0.20
AA	Diversified Inst Long Horizon SAF	DILSX	C+	(800) 926-0044	C / 4.5	-2.48	2.42	9.96 /47	11.82 /41	3.19 /39	1.62	0.20
MC	Diversified Inst Mid-Cap Growth	DIMGX	D	(800) 926-0044	C+ / 5.6	-7.35	0.82	11.95 /59	14.25 /55	--	2.45	0.75
MC	Diversified Inst Mid-Cap Value	DIMVX	A-	(800) 926-0044	B+ / 8.4	-1.01	6.78	14.04 /68	21.56 /84	--	5.62	0.70
OT	Diversified Inst Money Market	DFINX	D+	(800) 926-0044	E / 0.3	1.12	2.12	3.85 /10	2.08 / 1	1.92 /26	3.69	0.28
AA	Diversified Inst Short Horizon SAF	DISHX	C-	(800) 926-0044	E / 0.4	0.04	0.64	1.94 / 4	3.52 / 2	4.39 /50	3.72	1.10
AA	Diversified Inst Shrt-Intrm Hor SAF	DIHSX	C-	(800) 926-0044	D- / 1.0	-0.56	1.23	4.03 /11	5.57 / 5	4.36 /49	3.18	0.20
GL	Diversified Inst Small Cap Value	DIVSX	C	(800) 926-0044	C / 5.5	-5.05	4.91	6.74 /25	14.25 /55	--	0.07	0.85
GR	Diversified Inst Special Equity	DISEX	C	(800) 926-0044	C+ / 6.8	-6.12	3.61	11.45 /56	17.05 /68	5.27 /56	1.41	0.85
IX	Diversified Inst Stock Index	DISFX	C	(800) 926-0044	C- / 3.9	-1.57	2.57	8.24 /35	10.92 /35	2.19 /29	1.59	0.38
IN	Diversified Inst Value & Income	DIVIX	B-	(800) 926-0044	C+ / 5.8	0.12	5.62	11.65 /58	13.71 /52	5.79 /60	1.76	0.48

RISK			NET ASSETS		ASSET					BULL / BEAR		FUND MANAGER		MINIMUMS		LOADS	
	3 Year		NAV						Portfolio	Last Bull	Last Bear	Manager	Manager	Initial	Additional	Front	Back
Risk	Standard		As of	Total	Cash	Stocks	Bonds	Other	Turnover	Market	Market	Quality	Tenure	Purch.	Purch.	End	End
Rating/Pts	Deviation	Beta	6/30/06	$(Mil)	%	%	%	%	Ratio	Return	Return	Pct	(Years)	$	$	Load	Load
C /4.6	18.6	0.84	18.43	203	0	100	0	0	6.0	172.8	6.5	93	N/A	2,000,000	0	0.0	0.0
B- /7.1	10.0	0.98	21.48	1,372	0	100	0	0	4.0	124.9	-9.3	45	N/A	2,000,000	0	0.0	0.0
B /8.7	9.6	1.18	23.38	4,726	0	100	0	0	9.0	101.8	-9.5	95	N/A	2,000,000	0	0.0	0.0
C+ /5.8	13.8	1.01	16.93	55	0	100	0	0	10.0	157.0	5.1	79	13	2,000,000	0	0.0	0.0
C- /3.1	16.5	0.99	28.27	2,077	0	100	0	0	3.0	126.8	0.5	77	N/A	2,000,000	0	0.0	0.0
C+ /6.2	15.0	1.01	29.37	7,922	0	100	0	0	27.0	170.4	-10.7	96	13	2,000,000	0	0.0	0.0
B /8.0	10.8	1.03	17.58	1,967	0	100	0	0	11.0	171.5	-7.4	86	N/A	2,000,000	0	0.0	0.0
C+ /6.7	14.9	1.02	24.51	1,476	0	100	0	0	15.0	135.0	-11.0	68	14	2,000,000	0	0.0	0.0
B /8.3	10.1	0.88	16.34	2,830	0	100	0	0	12.0	112.1	-10.3	87	8	2,000,000	0	0.0	0.0
C+ /6.9	14.6	0.99	25.68	3,000	0	100	0	0	21.0	154.7	-10.8	92	8	2,000,000	0	0.0	0.0
B /8.5	8.5	1.08	13.47	1,209	0	100	0	0	10.0	71.3	-9.8	60	5	2,000,000	0	0.0	0.0
B- /7.2	11.6	0.90	27.37	24	0	100	0	0	12.0	170.1	-5.9	91	N/A	2,000,000	0	0.0	0.0
B /8.7	7.6	1.00	37.28	2,370	0	100	0	0	6.0	64.2	-9.8	55	15	2,000,000	0	0.0	0.0
C /5.5	15.4	1.04	15.67	4,571	0	100	0	0	24.0	141.2	-9.1	67	15	2,000,000	0	0.0	0.0
C+ /5.9	14.8	1.01	20.85	3,471	0	100	0	0	21.0	129.6	-11.0	61	14	2,000,000	0	0.0	0.0
B /8.3	8.2	0.78	19.45	23	9	88	1	2	15.0	79.5	-3.4	94	5	10,000	100	5.0	0.0
B /8.3	8.2	0.78	18.70	3	9	88	1	2	15.0	75.3	-3.5	91	5	10,000	100	0.0	1.0
B /8.3	9.8	1.06	15.16	265	15	84	0	1	15.0	107.5	-6.7	98	4	10,000	100	5.0	0.0
B /8.3	9.9	1.06	14.80	17	15	84	0	1	15.0	102.8	-6.7	97	4	10,000	100	0.0	1.0
C+ /6.2	9.8	1.06	15.22	19	15	84	0	1	15.0	108.6	-6.7	98	4	500,000	100	0.0	0.0
B /8.9	7.7	0.46	17.68	508	19	80	0	1	12.0	99.7	-4.7	99	6	10,000	100	5.0	0.0
B /8.9	7.7	0.46	17.03	117	19	80	0	1	12.0	95.1	-4.9	99	6	10,000	100	0.0	1.0
C+ /6.8	7.8	0.46	17.75	146	19	80	0	1	12.0	100.9	-4.7	99	6	500,000	100	0.0	0.0
B- /7.4	11.4	0.71	24.75	427	31	68	0	1	15.0	155.5	-9.9	99	6	10,000	100	5.0	0.0
B- /7.4	11.4	0.71	23.76	39	31	68	0	1	15.0	149.6	-10.1	99	5	10,000	100	0.0	1.0
C+ /6.3	11.4	0.71	24.84	55	31	68	0	1	15.0	156.6	-9.9	99	5	500,000	100	0.0	0.0
B- /7.5	10.6	1.28	33.90	9	3	93	2	2	103.0	56.6	-13.9	19	7	10,000	1,000	0.0	0.0
U /	N/A	N/A	23.39	112	20	77	1	2	536.0	N/A	N/A	N/A	N/A	10,000	1,000	0.0	0.0
U /	N/A	N/A	18.03	60	0	48	56	0	1,236.0	N/A	N/A	N/A	N/A	10,000	1,000	0.0	0.0
C- /3.4	18.8	2.11	42.90	11	6	94	0	0	135.0	76.3	-12.9	1	6	10,000	1,000	0.0	0.0
U /	N/A	N/A	21.40	55	1	98	0	1	705.0	N/A	N/A	N/A	N/A	10,000	1,000	0.0	0.0
D- /1.3	20.4	1.36	55.65	4	10	0	89	1	N/A	129.1	-14.9	3	6	10,000	1,000	0.0	0.0
E- /0.2	23.7	-1.50	15.86	16	3	0	96	1	N/A	-67.0	11.0	11	7	10,000	1,000	0.0	0.0
U /	N/A	N/A	22.26	53	52	47	0	1	1,152.0	N/A	N/A	N/A	N/A	10,000	1,000	0.0	0.0
C- /3.2	7.9	-1.01	27.46	6	4	95	0	1	N/A	-39.8	9.0	19	9	10,000	1,000	0.0	0.0
C /4.3	13.9	1.44	5.83	68	0	99	0	1	187.0	74.6	-9.6	24	N/A	5,000	0	0.0	0.0
B+ /9.8	4.9	1.03	9.63	57	0	59	46	0	367.0	40.8	-4.7	58	5	5,000	0	0.0	0.0
C+ /6.5	9.3	1.14	7.06	760	1	98	0	1	76.0	53.0	-8.8	18	N/A	5,000	0	0.0	0.0
B- /7.8	8.4	1.06	6.59	176	0	99	0	1	79.0	59.6	-9.5	42	17	5,000	0	0.0	0.0
B+ /9.8	4.5	0.92	9.76	468	2	49	48	1	57.0	39.2	-3.2	62	10	5,000	0	0.0	0.0
B- /7.1	10.7	1.02	9.66	464	2	97	0	1	94.0	116.9	-10.3	29	N/A	5,000	0	0.0	0.0
B+ /9.1	6.0	1.21	9.52	374	5	74	20	1	147.0	52.1	-5.7	68	10	5,000	0	0.0	0.0
B /8.2	7.7	1.50	9.08	223	N/A	92	7	N/A	96.0	67.5	-9.2	71	8	5,000	0	0.0	0.0
C- /3.6	13.5	1.16	12.36	70	2	97	0	1	142.0	84.7	-5.9	11	N/A	5,000	0	0.0	0.0
B- /7.0	9.4	0.80	15.77	166	3	96	0	1	112.0	121.4	-5.7	95	5	5,000	0	0.0	0.0
B+ /9.9	0.4	N/A	10.06	201	100	0	0	0	N/A	5.8	0.4	53	N/A	5,000	0	0.0	0.0
B+ /9.9	2.5	0.33	10.11	74	18	18	62	2	142.0	15.3	1.2	50	10	5,000	0	0.0	0.0
B+ /9.9	3.1	0.63	9.61	66	7	31	61	1	135.0	27.2	-0.8	N/A	8	5,000	0	0.0	0.0
C+ /6.2	12.8	0.93	15.80	43	4	95	0	1	143.0	104.4	-12.7	6	N/A	5,000	0	0.0	0.0
C /5.4	14.1	1.50	11.20	246	2	97	0	1	92.0	110.4	-11.0	67	N/A	5,000	0	0.0	0.0
B /8.2	7.6	1.00	8.48	675	1	98	0	1	10.0	63.4	-9.9	53	N/A	5,000	0	0.0	0.0
B /8.0	7.6	0.96	12.22	717	2	97	0	1	89.0	72.0	-8.2	82	N/A	5,000	0	0.0	0.0

					PERFORMANCE							
99 Pct = Best 0 Pct = Worst		Overall Weiss Investment Rating		Perfor- mance	Total Return % through 6/30/06					Incl. in Returns		
								Annualized		Dividend	Expense
Fund Type	Fund Name	Ticker Symbol		Phone	Rating/Pts	3 Mo	6 Mo	1Yr / Pct	3Yr / Pct	5Yr / Pct	Yield	Ratio
AG	Diversified Inv Aggress Equity	DVAEX	D-	(800) 926-0044	C- / 3.9	-7.62	-0.12	10.69 /51	11.34 /38	-1.12 /11	0.03	1.30
BA	Diversified Inv Balanced	DVIBX	C	(800) 926-0044	D / 1.9	-1.06	1.41	5.77 /19	7.58 /13	3.28 /39	2.00	1.08
GR	Diversified Inv Equity Growth	DVEGX	D-	(800) 926-0044	D- / 1.5	-5.63	-3.27	5.51 /18	7.57 /13	-0.81 /12	0.06	1.21
GI	Diversified Inv Growth & Income	DVGIX	C-	(800) 926-0044	C- / 3.4	-2.67	0.94	8.04 /33	10.27 /29	0.61 /18	0.52	1.15
GL	Diversified Inv Inst SmCap Growth	DISGX	D+	(800) 926-0044	C- / 4.1	-8.90	2.48	8.55 /37	11.79 /41	--	0.00	0.90
AA	Diversified Inv Interm Horizon SAF	DVMSX	C-	(800) 926-0044	D / 1.7	-1.13	1.55	5.68 /19	7.12 /11	3.80 /44	2.73	1.19
FO	Diversified Inv International Eq	DVIEX	A	(800) 926-0044	B+ / 8.6	-0.69	9.46	24.87 /88	21.50 /84	7.99 /72	4.61	1.40
AA	Diversified Inv Intrm-Long Horizon	DVASX	C	(800) 926-0044	C- / 3.0	-1.79	1.94	7.77 /31	9.38 /23	3.77 /44	2.28	1.23
AA	Diversified Inv Long Horizon SAF	DVLSX	C+	(800) 926-0044	C / 4.4	-2.39	2.44	9.88 /46	11.50 /39	2.67 /33	1.82	1.28
MC	Diversified Inv Mid-Cap Growth	DVMGX	D	(800) 926-0044	C / 5.3	-7.48	0.63	11.47 /56	13.81 /53	--	4.34	1.35
MC	Diversified Inv Mid-Cap Value	DVMVX	A-	(800) 926-0044	B+ / 8.3	-1.12	6.64	13.60 /67	21.12 /83	--	5.91	1.25
OT	Diversified Inv Money Market	DVMKX	D+	(800) 926-0044	E- / 0.2	0.99	1.94	3.43 / 9	1.76 / 1	1.63 /24	3.38	0.80
AA	Diversified Inv Short Horizon SAF	DVCSX	D+	(800) 926-0044	E / 0.3	0.01	0.49	1.65 / 4	3.13 / 1	3.96 /46	3.63	1.20
AA	Diversified Inv Shrt-Intrm Horizon	DVSIX	C-	(800) 926-0044	E+ / 0.8	-0.59	1.02	3.63 / 9	5.22 / 4	4.13 /47	3.18	1.14
SC	Diversified Inv Small Cap Growth	DVSGX	D-	(800) 926-0044	C- / 3.3	-9.03	2.28	8.11 /33	10.60 /32	--	0.00	1.55
SC	Diversified Inv Small Cap Value	DVSVX	D+	(800) 926-0044	C / 5.2	-5.12	4.75	6.17 /21	13.69 /52	--	0.10	1.49
GR	Diversified Inv Special Equity	DVPEX	C	(800) 926-0044	C+ / 6.7	-6.23	3.40	11.06 /54	16.70 /67	4.92 /53	1.77	1.41
IX	Diversified Inv Stock Index	DSKIX	C	(800) 926-0044	C- / 3.6	-1.67	2.39	7.87 /32	10.53 /31	1.83 /26	1.31	0.65
IN	Diversified Inv Value & Income	DVEIX	C+	(800) 926-0044	C+ / 5.7	0.10	5.48	11.39 /56	13.41 /51	5.53 /58	1.93	1.00
GR	Diversified Inv Value Fd Inv	DVVLX	U	(800) 926-0044	U /	-2.71	-0.77	4.76 /14	--	--	0.80	1.05
GR	Dividend Growth Tr Cap Appr A	ICTWX	E	(877) 423-8637	D- / 1.4	-2.20	8.46	11.88 /59	6.74 / 9	2.91 /36	0.00	1.75
★ BA ●	Dodge & Cox Balanced Fund	DODBX	B+	(800) 621-3979	C / 5.3	0.53	4.09	9.88 /46	12.76 /47	9.27 /78	2.34	0.53
★ FO	Dodge & Cox International Stock	DODFX	A+	(800) 621-3979	A+ / 9.7	1.19	11.22	27.64 /92	33.39 /97	16.39 /93	0.89	0.70
★ GI ●	Dodge & Cox Stock Fund	DODGX	A+	(800) 621-3979	B / 7.7	0.81	6.15	15.30 /73	18.36 /74	10.58 /82	1.20	0.52
FO	Domini European Social Equity Inv	DEUFX	U	(800) 762-6814	U /	1.38	18.06	--	--	--	0.00	1.60
GR	Domini Institutional Social Eq	DIEQX	D+	(800) 762-6814	D / 2.1	-3.36	-0.05	5.98 /20	8.99 /21	1.67 /25	1.23	0.40
GR	Domini Social Equity	DSEFX	D+	(800) 762-6814	D / 1.8	-3.50	-0.30	5.43 /17	8.39 /17	1.15 /21	0.76	0.95
GR	Domini Social Equity R	DSFRX	U	(800) 762-6814	U /	-3.42	-0.18	5.74 /19	--	--	1.05	0.63
GR	Dow Jones Islamic Index Fd	IMANX	C-	(877) 417-6161	D / 2.2	-3.80	1.10	6.10 /21	8.45 /17	0.22 /16	0.18	1.53
★ GR	Dreyfus Appreciation Fund	DGAGX	C-	(800) 242-8671	D / 2.2	0.87	2.57	6.11 /21	7.88 /14	1.64 /25	1.34	0.91
IX	Dreyfus Basic S&P 500 Stock Idx	DSPIX	C+	(800) 242-8671	C- / 4.0	-1.51	2.60	8.40 /36	11.00 /35	2.28 /30	1.66	0.20
GI	Dreyfus Disciplined Stock Fund	DDSTX	C	(800) 242-8671	C- / 3.4	-2.27	2.34	8.67 /38	10.01 /27	0.83 /19	0.75	0.90
BA	Dreyfus Founders Balanced Fund A	FRIDX	D	(800) 242-8671	E+ / 0.6	-2.88	0.45	4.27 /12	6.39 / 8	0.28 /17	0.93	1.66
BA	Dreyfus Founders Balanced Fund B	FRIBX	D	(800) 242-8671	E / 0.5	-2.96	0.16	3.52 / 9	5.64 / 6	-0.39 /14	0.12	2.45
BA	Dreyfus Founders Balanced Fund C	FRICX	D+	(800) 242-8671	E+ / 0.7	-2.97	0.22	3.50 / 9	5.54 / 5	-0.73 /13	0.17	2.51
BA	Dreyfus Founders Balanced Fund F	FRINX	D+	(800) 242-8671	D- / 1.3	-2.86	0.51	4.44 /12	6.64 / 9	0.63 /18	1.16	1.40
BA	Dreyfus Founders Balanced Fund R	FRIRX	C-	(800) 242-8671	D- / 1.3	-2.84	0.59	4.65 /13	6.64 / 9	0.29 /17	1.35	1.17
BA	Dreyfus Founders Balanced Fund T	FRIUX	D	(800) 242-8671	E+ / 0.6	-2.94	0.38	4.07 /11	6.04 / 7	0.47 /18	0.73	1.87
SC	Dreyfus Founders Discovery Fund A	FDIDX	E+	(800) 242-8671	D / 2.1	-9.75	1.47	3.75 /10	10.85 /34	-1.84 / 9	0.00	1.45
SC	Dreyfus Founders Discovery Fund B	FDIEX	E	(800) 242-8671	D / 1.7	-10.00	1.00	2.74 / 6	9.78 /26	-2.76 / 6	0.00	2.43
SC	Dreyfus Founders Discovery Fund C	FDICX	E+	(800) 242-8671	D / 2.2	-9.95	1.03	2.85 / 7	9.84 /26	-2.72 / 6	0.00	2.35
SC	Dreyfus Founders Discovery Fund F	FDISX	E+	(800) 242-8671	C- / 3.0	-9.77	1.47	3.72 / 9	10.85 /34	-1.84 / 9	0.00	1.45
SC	Dreyfus Founders Discovery Fund R	FDIRX	D-	(800) 242-8671	C- / 3.2	-9.68	1.61	4.05 /11	11.17 /37	-1.55 /10	0.00	1.17
SC	Dreyfus Founders Discovery Fund T	FDITX	E	(800) 242-8671	D / 2.1	-9.82	1.29	3.40 / 8	10.47 /31	-2.29 / 7	0.00	1.76
GI	Dreyfus Founders Equity Growth A	FRMAX	D-	(800) 242-8671	D / 1.8	-4.14	0.39	8.21 /34	9.15 /22	0.77 /19	0.12	1.33
GI	Dreyfus Founders Equity Growth B	FRMEX	D-	(800) 242-8671	D / 1.6	-4.29	0.00	7.21 /27	8.26 /16	0.34 /17	0.00	2.18
GI	Dreyfus Founders Equity Growth C	FRMDX	D	(800) 242-8671	D / 2.1	-4.17	0.21	7.59 /30	8.41 /17	0.01 /15	0.24	1.96
GI	Dreyfus Founders Equity Growth F	FRMUX	D+	(800) 242-8671	D+ / 2.9	-4.05	0.58	8.53 /37	9.46 /24	1.47 /23	0.20	1.12
GI	Dreyfus Founders Equity Growth R	FRMRX	D+	(800) 242-8671	C- / 3.0	-3.90	0.78	8.70 /38	9.56 /24	1.03 /20	0.29	1.09
GI	Dreyfus Founders Equity Growth T	FRMVX	D-	(800) 242-8671	D- / 1.5	-4.14	0.21	8.00 /33	8.07 /15	-0.03 /15	0.00	2.15
GR	Dreyfus Founders Growth Fund A	FRGDX	E+	(800) 242-8671	D- / 1.5	-4.11	0.46	8.15 /34	8.42 /17	-0.52 /13	0.34	1.47
GR	Dreyfus Founders Growth Fund B	FRGEX	E+	(800) 242-8671	D- / 1.2	-4.30	0.00	7.17 /27	7.54 /13	-1.30 /11	0.00	2.30

RISK			NET ASSETS		ASSET				BULL / BEAR		FUND MANAGER		MINIMUMS		LOADS	
	3 Year		NAV						Last Bull	Last Bear	Manager	Manager	Initial	Additional	Front	Back
Risk	Standard		As of	Total	Cash	Stocks	Bonds	Other	Market	Market	Quality	Tenure	Purch.	Purch.	End	End
Rating/Pts	Deviation	Beta	6/30/06	$(Mil)	%	%	%	%	Return	Return	Pct	(Years)	$	$	Load	Load
C / 4.3	13.8	1.42	13.70	179	0	99	0	1	187.0	73.0	-9.6	23	N/A	5,000	0	0.0	0.0
B+ / 9.8	4.9	1.04	14.92	165	0	59	53	0	367.0	39.2	-4.7	54	7	5,000	0	0.0	0.0
C+ / 6.5	9.3	1.14	19.71	855	1	98	0	1	74.0	52.1	-8.9	16	6	5,000	0	0.0	0.0
B- / 7.9	8.4	1.06	20.53	534	0	99	0	1	79.0	58.5	-9.7	39	5	5,000	0	0.0	0.0
C+ / 5.7	16.4	0.98	13.21	27	1	98	0	1	183.0	67.1	-11.4	1	N/A	5,000	0	0.0	0.0
B+ / 9.7	4.5	0.92	11.61	706	14	51	34	1	57.0	36.8	-3.4	56	10	5,000	0	0.0	0.0
B- / 7.1	10.7	1.03	17.18	667	2	97	0	1	94.0	115.1	-10.3	27	14	5,000	0	0.0	0.0
B+ / 9.1	6.1	1.23	12.47	672	23	68	8	1	147.0	50.7	-5.8	62	10	5,000	0	0.0	0.0
B / 8.3	7.8	1.51	11.03	410	N/A	92	7	N/A	96.0	65.3	-9.1	68	8	5,000	0	0.0	0.0
C- / 3.6	13.5	1.16	11.13	141	2	97	0	1	142.0	82.5	-6.0	9	2	5,000	0	0.0	0.0
B- / 7.2	9.4	0.80	14.57	444	3	96	0	1	112.0	118.9	-5.8	95	5	5,000	0	0.0	0.0
B+ / 9.9	0.4	-0.01	10.64	410	100	0	0	0	N/A	4.8	0.3	49	N/A	5,000	0	0.0	0.0
B+ / 9.9	2.6	0.33	10.55	158	0	9	89	2	142.0	13.9	1.2	45	10	5,000	0	0.0	0.0
B+ / 9.9	3.1	0.63	9.82	169	0	31	68	1	135.0	26.1	-1.0	51	8	5,000	0	0.0	0.0
C / 4.8	16.5	1.06	14.81	54	1	98	0	1	183.0	87.1	-11.4	4	N/A	5,000	0	0.0	0.0
C / 5.1	12.9	0.84	12.78	114	4	95	0	1	143.0	92.3	-9.1	34	4	5,000	0	0.0	0.0
C / 4.8	14.1	1.51	25.57	467	2	97	0	1	92.0	108.4	-11.1	63	21	5,000	0	0.0	0.0
B / 8.2	7.6	1.00	9.88	588	1	98	0	1	10.0	61.5	-9.8	48	7	5,000	0	0.0	0.0
B- / 7.6	7.6	0.96	24.88	1,137	2	97	0	1	89.0	70.7	-8.2	80	6	5,000	0	0.0	0.0
U /	N/A	N/A	10.56	26	1	98	0	1	21.0	N/A	N/A	N/A	N/A	2,000,000	0	0.0	0.0
C / 4.9	12.8	1.36	12.43	2	3	96	0	1	396.0	48.9	-9.8	6	1	250	50	5.8	1.0
B+ / 9.7	5.5	1.09	83.57	24,683	4	62	32	2	18.0	63.0	-4.7	91	75	2,500	100	0.0	0.0
B- / 7.7	11.7	1.06	38.96	20,665	5	94	0	1	7.0	197.6	-11.9	95	N/A	2,500	100	0.0	0.0
B / 8.8	8.3	1.03	144.48	57,086	6	93	0	1	12.0	96.5	-8.6	96	41	2,500	100	0.0	0.0
U /	N/A	N/A	12.14	51	2	97	0	1	N/A	N/A	N/A	N/A	1	2,500	100	0.0	2.0
B / 8.2	8.3	1.05	18.03	241	0	99	0	1	9.0	56.3	-10.3	30	10	2,000,000	0	0.0	2.0
B / 8.2	8.3	1.05	29.72	1,105	0	99	0	1	9.0	53.6	-10.5	26	15	2,500	100	0.0	2.0
U /	N/A	N/A	11.24	45	0	99	0	1	9.0	N/A	N/A	N/A	3	2,500	100	0.0	2.0
B / 8.2	8.7	1.07	7.35	27	3	96	0	1	0.2	53.0	-9.8	25	N/A	250	50	0.0	0.0
B+ / 9.1	6.5	0.75	40.72	4,015	0	99	0	1	6.8	45.2	-9.1	44	16	2,500	100	0.0	0.0
B / 8.7	7.7	1.00	26.48	1,466	2	97	0	1	9.0	63.8	-9.8	53	11	10,000	1,000	0.0	0.0
B / 8.4	7.7	0.99	34.46	905	N/A	100	0	N/A	68.4	56.1	-9.0	43	2	2,500	100	0.0	0.0
B+ / 9.0	6.1	1.16	8.58	2	9	57	33	1	181.0	37.4	-4.2	34	4	1,000	100	5.8	0.0
B+ / 9.0	6.1	1.16	8.51	1	9	57	33	1	181.0	34.2	-4.5	29	4	1,000	100	0.0	4.0
B+ / 9.0	6.1	1.17	8.37	N/A	9	57	33	1	181.0	33.5	-4.4	28	4	1,000	100	0.0	1.0
B+ / 9.0	6.2	1.17	8.59	61	9	57	33	1	181.0	38.5	-4.2	35	4	1,000	100	0.0	0.0
B+ / 9.0	6.1	1.16	8.56	N/A	9	57	33	1	181.0	38.0	-4.3	36	4	1,000	100	0.0	0.0
B+ / 9.0	6.1	1.17	8.81	N/A	9	57	33	1	181.0	35.7	-4.6	31	4	1,000	100	4.5	0.0
C / 4.4	16.0	1.05	29.05	45	1	98	0	1	160.0	82.6	-14.0	5	2	1,000	100	5.8	0.0
C / 4.3	16.0	1.05	27.37	8	1	98	0	1	160.0	77.2	-14.2	3	2	1,000	100	0.0	4.0
C / 4.3	16.0	1.05	27.43	4	1	98	0	1	160.0	77.5	-14.2	3	2	1,000	100	0.0	1.0
C / 4.4	16.0	1.05	29.00	289	1	98	0	1	160.0	82.7	-14.0	5	2	1,000	100	0.0	0.0
C / 4.4	16.0	1.05	29.58	10	1	98	0	1	160.0	84.4	-13.9	6	2	1,000	100	0.0	0.0
C / 4.4	16.0	1.05	28.27	N/A	1	98	0	1	160.0	80.8	-14.1	4	2	1,000	100	4.5	0.0
C+ / 6.7	8.9	1.08	5.09	2	5	94	0	1	126.0	58.9	-7.9	29	5	1,000	100	5.8	0.0
C+ / 6.7	8.8	1.05	4.91	1	5	94	0	1	126.0	54.8	-8.2	25	5	1,000	100	0.0	4.0
C+ / 6.7	8.8	1.07	4.83	2	5	94	0	1	126.0	55.2	-8.1	25	5	1,000	100	0.0	1.0
C+ / 6.8	8.8	1.06	5.21	204	5	94	0	1	126.0	60.1	-8.0	32	5	1,000	100	0.0	0.0
C+ / 6.8	8.9	1.07	5.17	N/A	5	94	0	1	126.0	60.1	-7.8	33	5	1,000	100	0.0	0.0
C+ / 6.6	8.9	1.07	4.86	N/A	5	94	0	1	126.0	53.9	-8.3	22	5	1,000	100	4.5	0.0
C+ / 6.0	9.0	1.08	10.96	9	4	96	0	0	120.0	57.9	-8.5	24	5	1,000	100	5.8	0.0
C+ / 5.9	9.0	1.07	10.46	5	4	96	0	0	120.0	53.8	-8.7	19	5	1,000	100	0.0	4.0

					PERFORMANCE							
	99 Pct = Best				Perfor-	Total Return % through 6/30/06					Incl. in Returns	
	0 Pct = Worst		Overall Weiss		mance				Annualized		Dividend	Expense
Fund		Ticker	Investment		Rating/Pts						Yield	Ratio
Type	Fund Name	Symbol	Rating	Phone		3 Mo	6 Mo	1Yr / Pct	3Yr / Pct	5Yr / Pct		
GR	Dreyfus Founders Growth Fund C	FRGFX	D-	(800) 242-8671	D / 1.7	-4.30	0.10	7.28 /28	7.63 /13	-1.30 /11	0.00	2.22
GR	● Dreyfus Founders Growth Fund F	FRGRX	D-	(800) 242-8671	D+ / 2.3	-4.17	0.46	8.13 /34	8.54 /18	-0.43 /14	0.38	1.37
GR	Dreyfus Founders Growth Fund R	FRGYX	D	(800) 242-8671	D+ / 2.6	-4.03	0.72	8.75 /38	8.96 /21	-0.17 /15	0.58	1.04
GR	Dreyfus Founders Growth Fund T	FRGZX	E+	(800) 242-8671	D- / 1.3	-4.28	0.10	7.25 /28	7.81 /14	-1.39 /10	0.00	2.20
FO	Dreyfus Founders Intl Equity A	FOIAX	B+	(800) 242-8671	A- / 9.0	0.48	9.75	26.42 /90	25.26 /91	5.61 /59	0.75	1.40
FO	Dreyfus Founders Intl Equity B	FOIDX	B+	(800) 242-8671	B+ / 8.9	0.35	9.38	25.55 /89	24.31 /90	4.82 /53	0.17	2.15
FO	Dreyfus Founders Intl Equity C	FOICX	B+	(800) 242-8671	A- / 9.1	0.35	9.40	25.62 /89	24.34 /90	4.82 /53	0.25	2.15
FO	● Dreyfus Founders Intl Equity F	FOIEX	A-	(800) 242-8671	A- / 9.2	0.54	9.81	26.46 /90	25.27 /91	5.65 /59	0.80	1.40
FO	Dreyfus Founders Intl Equity R	FOIRX	A-	(800) 242-8671	A- / 9.2	0.61	9.95	26.85 /91	25.73 /92	5.94 /61	0.99	1.15
FO	Dreyfus Founders Intl Equity T	FOIUX	B+	(800) 242-8671	A- / 9.0	0.48	9.65	26.22 /90	24.93 /91	5.38 /57	0.56	1.65
MC	Dreyfus Founders Mid-Cap Growth A	FRSDX	B-	(800) 242-8671	B / 8.0	-3.55	10.26	25.85 /90	20.35 /81	5.49 /58	0.00	1.55
MC	Dreyfus Founders Mid-Cap Growth B	FRSFX	C+	(800) 242-8671	B / 7.7	-3.91	9.60	24.30 /88	19.19 /77	4.82 /53	0.00	2.41
MC	Dreyfus Founders Mid-Cap Growth C	FRSCX	B-	(800) 242-8671	B / 8.1	-3.57	9.95	24.62 /88	19.33 /77	4.61 /51	0.00	2.32
MC	● Dreyfus Founders Mid-Cap Growth F	FRSPX	B	(800) 242-8671	B+ / 8.4	-3.48	10.25	25.78 /89	20.53 /81	6.04 /61	0.00	1.39
MC	Dreyfus Founders Mid-Cap Growth R	FRSRX	B	(800) 242-8671	B+ / 8.4	-3.33	10.36	26.09 /90	20.28 /80	5.73 /59	0.00	1.34
MC	Dreyfus Founders Mid-Cap Growth T	FRSVX	C+	(800) 242-8671	B / 7.7	-3.76	9.71	24.62 /88	19.19 /77	4.39 /50	0.00	2.57
GL	● Dreyfus Founders Passport Fund A	FPSAX	C+	(800) 242-8671	A+ / 9.6	-1.13	13.18	34.06 /96	31.61 /96	15.52 /93	0.00	2.12
GL	● Dreyfus Founders Passport Fund B	FPSBX	C+	(800) 242-8671	A / 9.5	-1.33	12.70	32.92 /96	30.50 /96	14.53 /91	0.00	2.97
GL	● Dreyfus Founders Passport Fund C	FPSCX	C+	(800) 242-8671	A+ / 9.6	-1.28	12.76	33.09 /96	30.59 /96	14.57 /91	0.00	2.92
GL	● Dreyfus Founders Passport Fund F	FPSSX	C+	(800) 242-8671	A+ / 9.7	-1.09	13.18	34.12 /96	31.67 /96	15.57 /93	0.00	2.08
GL	● Dreyfus Founders Passport Fund R	FPSRX	C+	(800) 242-8671	A+ / 9.7	-1.07	13.32	34.44 /96	31.98 /97	14.86 /92	0.00	1.89
GL	● Dreyfus Founders Passport Fund T	FPSTX	C+	(800) 242-8671	A+ / 9.6	-1.19	13.00	33.56 /96	31.05 /96	14.46 /91	0.00	2.54
GL	Dreyfus Founders Worldwide Grwth A	FWWAX	C+	(800) 242-8671	C+ / 6.6	-1.64	5.77	18.44 /80	17.10 /68	2.85 /35	0.00	1.92
GL	Dreyfus Founders Worldwide Grwth B	FWWBX	C+	(800) 242-8671	C+ / 6.4	-1.85	5.30	17.50 /78	16.26 /65	2.18 /29	0.00	2.66
GL	Dreyfus Founders Worldwide Grwth C	FWWCX	C+	(800) 242-8671	C+ / 6.7	-1.89	5.26	17.53 /78	16.20 /64	1.78 /25	0.00	2.66
GL	● Dreyfus Founders Worldwide Grwth F	FWWGX	C+	(800) 242-8671	B- / 7.2	-1.69	5.75	18.46 /80	17.15 /69	3.04 /37	0.00	1.91
GL	Dreyfus Founders Worldwide Grwth R	FWWRX	B-	(800) 242-8671	B- / 7.4	-1.58	5.92	19.42 /81	17.79 /72	3.57 /42	0.00	1.44
GL	Dreyfus Founders Worldwide Grwth T	FWWTX	C+	(800) 242-8671	C+ / 6.6	-1.68	5.63	18.15 /79	16.82 /67	1.67 /25	0.00	2.30
GI	Dreyfus Fund	DREVX	C-	(800) 242-8671	C- / 3.2	-2.02	1.82	8.98 /40	9.64 /25	1.63 /24	1.30	0.80
SC	● Dreyfus Gr & Value-Emerg Leaders	DRELX	C-	(800) 242-8671	C+ / 6.4	-7.75	2.37	11.45 /56	16.55 /66	5.89 /60	0.00	1.15
MC	● Dreyfus Gr & Value-Midcap Val	DMCVX	C+	(800) 242-8671	C+ / 6.9	-4.34	0.92	9.46 /43	17.91 /72	6.10 /62	0.00	1.17
SC	● Dreyfus Gr & Value-Sm Co Val	DSCVX	D	(800) 242-8671	C+ / 6.0	-10.88	-6.24	5.27 /16	17.59 /71	3.82 /44	0.00	1.21
GI	Dreyfus Growth & Income	DGRIX	D+	(800) 242-8671	D / 1.9	-3.44	-0.21	5.26 /16	8.08 /15	-0.30 /14	1.03	1.01
GR	Dreyfus Growth Opportunity	DREQX	D	(800) 242-8671	D- / 1.5	-5.14	-2.32	5.91 /20	7.44 /12	0.40 /17	0.21	1.01
FO	Dreyfus Intl Stock Index	DIISX	A	(800) 242-8671	B+ / 8.9	0.72	9.99	25.84 /90	23.28 /88	8.94 /76	1.64	0.60
GR	Dreyfus Inv Core Value I		B-	(800) 242-8671	C+ / 5.6	0.84	5.14	11.43 /56	13.15 /50	3.75 /43	1.34	0.86
GR	Dreyfus Inv Core Value S		B-	(800) 242-8671	C / 5.5	0.77	5.09	11.30 /55	13.00 /49	3.60 /42	1.18	1.00
GR	● Dreyfus Inv Emerging Leaders I		D+	(800) 242-8671	C+ / 6.2	-7.81	2.70	9.68 /45	15.82 /63	7.95 /71	0.00	1.03
GR	● Dreyfus Inv Emerging Leaders S		C-	(800) 242-8671	C+ / 6.0	-7.93	2.54	9.30 /42	15.50 /61	7.68 /70	0.00	1.28
SC	● Dreyfus Inv Founders Discovery I		D	(800) 242-8671	C- / 3.1	-9.36	1.84	4.40 /12	10.80 /34	-1.77 / 9	0.00	1.16
SC	Dreyfus Inv Founders Discovery S		D	(800) 242-8671	D+ / 2.9	-9.45	1.65	4.22 /11	10.53 /31	-1.95 / 8	0.00	1.39
GR	Dreyfus Inv Founders Growth I		D-	(800) 242-8671	D+ / 2.7	-3.87	0.85	8.87 /39	8.93 /20	0.53 /18	0.29	1.00
GR	Dreyfus Inv Founders Growth S		C-	(800) 242-8671	D+ / 2.7	-3.80	0.93	8.88 /39	8.91 /20	0.50 /18	0.29	1.00
FO	Dreyfus Inv Founders Intl Eqty I		A+	(800) 242-8671	A- / 9.2	0.56	9.81	26.25 /90	24.95 /91	5.87 /60	0.64	1.49
FO	Dreyfus Inv Founders Intl Eqty S		B+	(800) 242-8671	A- / 9.2	0.56	9.81	26.32 /90	24.97 /91	5.88 /60	0.64	1.49
MC	Dreyfus Inv MidCap Stock I		B	(800) 242-8671	C+ / 6.5	-2.48	4.71	12.03 /60	15.52 /61	8.20 /72	0.37	0.79
MC	Dreyfus Inv MidCap Stock S		B-	(800) 242-8671	C+ / 6.4	-2.49	4.63	11.78 /58	15.28 /60	8.00 /72	0.18	1.00
GR	Dreyfus Inv Tech Growth Fund I		E+	(800) 242-8671	E+ / 0.8	-7.48	-2.98	7.33 /28	6.94 /10	-3.55 / 4	0.00	0.81
GR	Dreyfus Inv Tech Growth Fund S		E+	(800) 242-8671	E+ / 0.7	-7.59	-3.03	7.05 /27	6.70 / 9	-3.80 / 4	0.00	1.06
AA	Dreyfus Lifetime Gr & Inc Inv	DGIIX	C-	(800) 242-8671	D / 2.2	-1.29	2.55	6.64 /24	8.01 /15	3.16 /38	4.66	1.30
AA	Dreyfus Lifetime Gr & Inc Rest	DGIRX	C	(800) 242-8671	D+ / 2.5	-1.17	2.76	6.85 /25	8.42 /17	3.58 /42	5.08	1.23
AA	Dreyfus Lifetime Growth Inv	DLGIX	C+	(800) 242-8671	C / 5.1	-2.04	4.28	11.63 /57	12.47 /46	2.49 /32	2.01	1.39

RISK			NET ASSETS		ASSET					BULL / BEAR		FUND MANAGER		MINIMUMS		LOADS	
	3 Year		NAV						Portfolio	Last Bull	Last Bear	Manager	Manager	Initial	Additional	Front	Back
Risk Rating/Pts	Standard Deviation	Beta	As of 6/30/06	Total $(Mil)	Cash %	Stocks %	Bonds %	Other %	Turnover Ratio	Market Return	Market Return	Quality Pct	Tenure (Years)	Purch. $	Purch. $	End Load	End Load
C+ / 5.9	9.0	1.07	10.46	1	4	96	0	0	120.0	54.0	-8.7	20	5	1,000	100	0.0	1.0
C+ / 6.0	9.0	1.07	11.02	295	4	96	0	0	120.0	58.5	-8.5	26	5	1,000	100	0.0	0.0
C+ / 6.0	9.0	1.08	11.19	2	4	96	0	0	120.0	60.5	-8.5	28	5	1,000	100	0.0	0.0
C+ / 5.9	9.0	1.08	10.50	N/A	4	96	0	0	120.0	55.1	-8.7	21	5	1,000	100	4.5	0.0
C+ / 6.2	10.8	1.04	14.75	28	2	97	0	1	54.0	137.7	-13.3	54	3	1,000	100	5.8	0.0
C+ / 6.2	10.9	1.05	14.35	1	2	97	0	1	54.0	132.0	-13.4	43	3	1,000	100	0.0	4.0
C+ / 6.2	10.9	1.04	14.32	1	2	97	0	1	54.0	132.2	-13.6	44	3	1,000	100	0.0	1.0
C+ / 6.2	10.8	1.04	14.78	13	2	97	0	1	54.0	138.0	-13.2	54	3	1,000	100	0.0	0.0
C+ / 6.2	10.8	1.04	14.92	N/A	2	97	0	1	54.0	140.2	-13.2	60	3	1,000	100	0.0	0.0
C+ / 6.2	10.8	1.04	14.66	N/A	2	97	0	1	54.0	135.6	-13.3	50	3	1,000	100	4.5	1.0
C+ / 5.7	11.9	1.02	5.16	21	4	95	0	1	211.0	120.7	-8.6	73	2	1,000	100	5.8	0.0
C+ / 5.7	11.8	1.02	4.91	2	4	95	0	1	211.0	115.4	-9.1	62	2	1,000	100	0.0	4.0
C+ / 5.7	11.9	1.03	4.86	1	4	95	0	1	211.0	115.1	-8.8	63	2	1,000	100	0.0	1.0
C+ / 5.7	11.9	1.03	5.27	125	4	95	0	1	211.0	122.0	-8.4	73	2	1,000	100	0.0	0.0
C+ / 5.7	11.8	1.02	5.22	1	4	95	0	1	211.0	121.4	-8.8	72	2	1,000	100	0.0	0.0
C+ / 5.7	11.9	1.03	4.86	N/A	4	95	0	1	211.0	114.6	-8.4	61	2	1,000	100	4.5	0.0
C- / 3.8	17.6	1.35	22.75	34	1	98	0	1	729.0	205.9	-7.6	39	1	1,000	100	5.8	0.0
C- / 3.7	17.6	1.36	21.56	5	1	98	0	1	729.0	197.8	-7.9	31	1	1,000	100	0.0	4.0
C- / 3.7	17.6	1.36	21.56	7	1	98	0	1	729.0	198.1	-7.8	32	1	1,000	100	0.0	1.0
C- / 3.8	17.6	1.36	22.76	64	1	98	0	1	729.0	206.4	-7.6	39	1	1,000	100	0.0	0.0
C- / 3.8	17.6	1.36	22.21	N/A	1	98	0	1	729.0	208.5	-8.1	42	1	1,000	100	0.0	0.0
C- / 3.8	17.6	1.36	21.65	1	1	98	0	1	729.0	201.4	-7.8	35	1	1,000	100	0.0	0.0
C+ / 6.4	9.6	0.84	15.03	1	0	99	0	1	120.0	97.6	-10.4	26	3	1,000	100	5.8	0.0
C+ / 6.3	9.6	0.84	14.30	1	0	99	0	1	120.0	93.2	-10.6	22	3	1,000	100	0.0	4.0
C+ / 6.3	9.5	0.83	14.01	N/A	0	99	0	1	120.0	93.3	-10.6	22	3	1,000	100	0.0	1.0
C+ / 6.4	9.6	0.84	15.08	52	0	99	0	1	120.0	98.1	-10.4	27	3	1,000	100	0.0	0.0
C+ / 6.4	9.6	0.84	15.56	2	0	99	0	1	120.0	101.5	-10.3	30	3	1,000	100	0.0	0.0
C+ / 6.4	9.6	0.84	14.06	N/A	0	99	0	1	120.0	96.0	-11.3	25	3	1,000	100	4.5	0.0
B- / 7.3	7.7	0.99	10.25	1,340	N/A	100	0	N/A	58.5	58.5	-10.9	39	N/A	2,500	100	0.0	0.0
C / 4.7	13.7	0.90	42.39	629	15	84	0	1	42.1	103.0	-10.8	52	N/A	2,500	100	0.0	1.0
C+ / 6.0	13.9	1.17	31.98	1,187	0	99	0	1	128.6	119.5	-11.4	28	3	2,500	100	0.0	1.0
C- / 3.2	20.0	1.27	23.60	144	2	97	0	1	107.1	153.1	-17.0	14	1	2,500	100	0.0	1.0
B / 8.4	8.2	1.05	15.64	729	1	98	0	1	72.2	54.6	-11.3	24	1	2,500	100	0.0	0.0
B- / 7.2	8.3	1.04	8.42	208	0	99	0	1	85.4	52.6	-10.1	21	1	2,500	100	0.0	0.0
C+ / 6.7	10.2	1.00	16.74	295	3	96	0	1	3.5	127.0	-9.9	43	9	2,500	100	0.0	1.0
B / 8.3	7.9	0.99	16.90	32	1	98	0	1	55.4	70.2	-10.5	75	N/A	1,000,000	1,000	0.0	0.0
B / 8.3	7.9	0.99	16.94	38	1	98	0	1	55.4	69.4	-10.5	74	N/A	1,000	100	0.0	0.0
C- / 3.9	14.2	1.61	20.41	20	N/A	N/A	0	N/A	68.8	102.4	-7.1	42	N/A	1,000,000	1,000	0.0	0.0
C / 4.6	14.2	1.61	20.08	14	N/A	N/A	0	N/A	68.8	100.8	-7.2	39	N/A	1,000	100	0.0	0.0
C+ / 6.0	15.7	1.03	9.97	24	1	98	0	1	199.9	80.9	-13.4	6	2	1,000,000	1,000	0.0	0.0
C+ / 6.0	15.7	1.03	9.87	3	1	98	0	1	199.9	79.8	-13.5	5	2	1,000	100	0.0	0.0
C+ / 5.8	8.9	1.07	12.42	13	3	96	0	1	125.1	59.0	-8.5	28	5	1,000,000	1,000	0.0	0.0
B / 8.2	8.9	1.06	12.41	4	3	96	0	1	125.1	58.9	-8.5	29	5	1,000	100	0.0	0.0
B- / 7.9	10.7	1.03	17.85	9	1	98	0	1	62.5	137.3	-13.6	54	3	1,000,000	1,000	0.0	0.0
C / 5.5	10.7	1.04	17.86	2	1	98	0	1	62.5	137.2	-13.5	52	3	1,000	100	0.0	0.0
B- / 7.6	11.0	1.00	16.90	357	0	99	0	1	99.3	87.7	-6.8	31	12	1,000,000	1,000	0.0	0.0
B- / 7.6	11.0	1.00	16.83	90	0	99	0	1	99.3	86.5	-6.8	30	12	1,000	100	0.0	0.0
C+ / 5.9	15.7	1.64	8.78	74	4	95	0	1	49.1	66.3	-13.0	2	N/A	1,000,000	1,000	0.0	0.0
C+ / 5.9	15.7	1.64	8.65	59	4	95	0	1	49.1	65.0	-13.1	2	N/A	1,000	100	0.0	0.0
B+ / 9.1	5.5	1.12	16.90	49	19	45	21	15	58.3	43.3	-4.9	54	3	2,500	100	0.0	0.0
B+ / 9.2	5.5	1.12	16.00	50	19	45	21	15	58.3	45.2	-4.8	59	3	2,500	100	0.0	0.0
B- / 7.8	8.5	1.63	16.34	17	31	68	0	1	75.9	70.9	-9.6	71	3	2,500	100	0.0	0.0

					PERFORMANCE						Incl. in Returns	
						Total Return % through 6/30/06						
									Annualized			
99 Pct = Best / 0 Pct = Worst Fund Type	Fund Name	Ticker Symbol	Overall Weiss Investment Rating	Phone	Performance Rating/Pts	3 Mo	6 Mo	1Yr / Pct	3Yr / Pct	5Yr / Pct	Dividend Yield	Expense Ratio
AA	Dreyfus Lifetime Growth Rest	DLGRX	C+	(800) 242-8671	C / 5.3	-1.99	4.50	11.78 /58	12.90 /48	2.94 /36	2.43	1.36
★ MC	Dreyfus MidCap Index Fund	PESPX	B-	(800) 242-8671	B- / 7.1	-3.26	4.08	12.57 /62	17.61 /71	8.78 /75	0.86	0.50
SC	Dreyfus Prem New Lead Strat Fd A	DNLDX	C+	(800) 782-6620	C+ / 6.7	-2.13	3.50	15.95 /74	17.37 /70	8.45 /74	0.18	1.16
SC	Dreyfus Prem New Lead Strat Fd B	DNLBX	C+	(800) 782-6620	C+ / 6.5	-2.30	3.13	15.05 /72	16.46 /65	--	0.00	1.99
SC	Dreyfus Prem New Lead Strat Fd C	DNLCX	C+	(800) 782-6620	C+ / 6.8	-2.28	3.15	15.08 /72	16.50 /66	--	0.00	1.93
SC	Dreyfus Prem New Lead Strat Fd R	DNLRX	C+	(800) 782-6620	B- / 7.3	-2.14	3.47	15.95 /74	17.57 /70	--	0.33	1.11
SC	Dreyfus Prem New Lead Strat Fd T	DNLTX	C+	(800) 782-6620	C+ / 6.7	-2.14	3.44	15.75 /74	17.08 /68	--	0.29	1.38
GR	Dreyfus Premier Alpha Growth A	DPWAX	C-	(800) 782-6620	C / 4.7	-4.31	2.08	17.19 /77	13.97 /54	8.01 /72	0.00	1.08
GR	Dreyfus Premier Alpha Growth B	BSFBX	E+	(800) 782-6620	C / 4.5	-4.53	1.68	16.28 /75	13.18 /50	7.41 /69	0.00	1.86
GR	Dreyfus Premier Alpha Growth C	BSFCX	E+	(800) 782-6620	C / 5.0	-4.47	1.72	16.35 /76	13.23 /50	7.45 /69	0.00	1.86
GR	Dreyfus Premier Alpha Growth R	DPARX	C	(800) 782-6620	C+ / 5.6	-4.23	2.26	17.39 /78	14.03 /54	8.05 /72	0.00	0.78
GR	Dreyfus Premier Alpha Growth T	BSFAX	E+	(800) 782-6620	C / 4.8	-4.37	1.96	16.93 /77	13.79 /53	7.91 /71	0.00	1.34
BA	Dreyfus Premier Balanced Fd A	PRBAX	D	(800) 782-6620	E / 0.4	-2.17	-0.33	3.06 / 7	5.40 / 5	-0.08 /15	1.90	1.10
BA	Dreyfus Premier Balanced Fd B	PRBBX	D+	(800) 782-6620	E / 0.3	-2.33	-0.64	2.31 / 5	4.62 / 3	-0.82 /12	1.19	1.85
BA	Dreyfus Premier Balanced Fd C	DPBCX	D+	(800) 782-6620	E / 0.5	-2.39	-0.72	2.30 / 5	4.61 / 3	-0.83 /12	1.19	1.85
BA	Dreyfus Premier Balanced Fd R	PDBLX	D+	(800) 782-6620	E+ / 0.9	-2.08	-0.16	3.33 / 8	5.69 / 6	0.18 /16	2.43	0.85
BA	Dreyfus Premier Balanced Fd T	DBFTX	D+	(800) 782-6620	E / 0.4	-2.25	-0.42	2.83 / 7	5.14 / 4	-0.31 /14	1.55	1.35
BA	Dreyfus Premier Balanced Opport A	DBOAX	D+	(800) 782-6620	E / 0.3	-2.55	0.76	0.89 / 2	5.05 / 4	4.04 /46	1.45	1.18
BA	Dreyfus Premier Balanced Opport B	DBOBX	D+	(800) 782-6620	E / 0.3	-2.72	0.39	0.12 / 2	4.39 / 3	3.64 /42	0.82	1.96
BA	Dreyfus Premier Balanced Opport C	DBOCX	E-	(800) 782-6620	E / 0.4	-2.72	0.39	0.17 / 2	4.45 / 3	3.68 /43	0.82	1.91
BA	● Dreyfus Premier Balanced Opport J	THPBX	D+	(800) 782-6620	E+ / 0.7	-2.44	0.92	1.15 / 3	5.26 / 4	4.17 /47	1.73	0.95
BA	Dreyfus Premier Balanced Opport R	DBORX	D+	(800) 782-6620	E+ / 0.6	-2.50	0.87	1.05 / 3	5.17 / 4	4.11 /47	1.74	1.06
BA	Dreyfus Premier Balanced Opport T	DBOTX	D+	(800) 782-6620	E / 0.3	-2.61	0.60	0.58 / 2	4.82 / 4	3.90 /45	1.17	1.44
BA	Dreyfus Premier Balanced Opport Z	DBOZX	D+	(800) 782-6620	E+ / 0.6	-2.50	0.82	0.98 / 2	5.13 / 4	4.09 /47	1.68	1.07
GR	Dreyfus Premier Blue Chip Fd A	DBCAX	D-	(800) 782-6620	E / 0.3	-4.59	-0.08	-1.37 / 1	5.66 / 6	--	0.31	1.12
GR	Dreyfus Premier Blue Chip Fd B	DBCBX	D-	(800) 782-6620	E / 0.3	-4.79	-0.42	-2.22 / 1	5.24 / 4	--	0.12	1.73
GR	Dreyfus Premier Blue Chip Fd C	DBUCX	D	(800) 782-6620	E+ / 0.7	-4.76	0.58	0.01 / 2	6.09 / 7	--	0.34	1.39
GR	Dreyfus Premier Blue Chip Fd J	TPBCX	D-	(800) 782-6620	E+ / 0.6	-4.51	-0.08	-1.27 / 1	5.75 / 6	--	0.42	1.19
GR	Dreyfus Premier Blue Chip Fd R	DBCRX	D-	(800) 782-6620	E+ / 0.6	-4.51	0.00	-1.48 / 1	5.73 / 6	--	0.29	0.99
GR	Dreyfus Premier Blue Chip Fd T	DBCTX	D-	(800) 782-6620	E / 0.3	-4.53	-0.17	-1.87 / 1	5.48 / 5	--	0.22	1.50
GR	Dreyfus Premier Core Equity A	DLTSX	D+	(800) 782-6620	E+ / 0.8	0.60	2.16	5.00 /15	6.38 / 8	0.22 /16	0.72	1.35
GR	Dreyfus Premier Core Equity B	DPEBX	D	(800) 782-6620	E+ / 0.6	0.41	1.78	4.16 /11	5.57 / 5	--	0.52	2.10
GR	Dreyfus Premier Core Equity C	DPECX	D+	(800) 782-6620	E+ / 0.9	0.47	1.85	4.24 /12	5.59 / 5	--	0.52	2.10
GR	Dreyfus Premier Core Equity R	DPERX	C-	(800) 782-6620	D / 1.8	0.65	2.33	5.26 /16	7.24 /11	--	0.82	1.10
GR	Dreyfus Premier Core Equity T	DCETX	D	(800) 782-6620	E+ / 0.8	0.54	2.04	4.73 /14	6.12 / 7	--	0.64	1.60
GR	Dreyfus Premier Core Value A	DCVIX	C+	(800) 782-6620	C / 4.6	0.69	4.98	11.25 /55	12.87 /48	3.07 /37	1.14	1.15
GR	Dreyfus Premier Core Value B	DBCVX	C+	(800) 782-6620	C / 4.3	0.51	4.59	10.45 /50	12.06 /43	2.32 /30	0.48	1.90
GR	Dreyfus Premier Core Value C	DCVCX	C+	(800) 782-6620	C / 4.8	0.51	4.56	10.42 /50	12.04 /43	2.30 /30	0.48	1.90
GR	Dreyfus Premier Core Value Inst	DCVFX	B-	(800) 782-6620	C / 5.5	0.72	5.01	11.37 /56	12.99 /49	3.18 /39	1.30	1.05
GR	Dreyfus Premier Core Value R	DTCRX	B-	(800) 782-6620	C+ / 5.6	0.77	5.09	11.51 /57	13.15 /50	3.33 /40	1.46	0.90
GR	Dreyfus Premier Core Value T	DCVTX	C+	(800) 782-6620	C / 4.6	0.63	4.82	10.97 /53	12.58 /46	2.81 /35	0.92	1.40
EM	● Dreyfus Premier Emerging Mrkts A	DRFMX	B-	(800) 782-6620	A / 9.4	-5.27	5.64	28.24 /93	30.35 /96	20.42 /96	1.15	1.77
EM	● Dreyfus Premier Emerging Mrkts B	DBPEX	B-	(800) 782-6620	A / 9.4	-5.48	5.21	27.28 /92	29.36 /95	--	0.55	2.53
EM	● Dreyfus Premier Emerging Mrkts C	DCPEX	B-	(800) 782-6620	A / 9.5	-5.46	5.24	27.33 /92	29.41 /95	--	0.59	2.50
EM	● Dreyfus Premier Emerging Mrkts R	DRPEX	B	(800) 782-6620	A+ / 9.6	-5.21	5.77	28.65 /93	30.81 /96	--	1.49	1.44
EM	● Dreyfus Premier Emerging Mrkts T	DTPEX	B-	(800) 782-6620	A / 9.4	-5.32	5.46	27.87 /92	29.89 /95	--	0.86	2.07
SC	● Dreyfus Premier Enterprise Fund A	DPMGX	C+	(800) 782-6620	B+ / 8.7	-3.13	9.38	25.46 /89	24.39 /90	15.47 /92	0.00	2.27
SC	● Dreyfus Premier Enterprise Fund B	DMCGX	C+	(800) 782-6620	B+ / 8.6	-3.33	8.99	24.53 /88	23.44 /88	14.60 /91	0.00	3.05
SC	● Dreyfus Premier Enterprise Fund C	DMCCX	C+	(800) 782-6620	B+ / 8.8	-3.33	8.98	24.62 /88	23.45 /88	14.62 /91	0.00	3.04
SC	● Dreyfus Premier Enterprise Fund T	DMCTX	C+	(800) 782-6620	B+ / 8.7	-3.23	9.22	25.15 /89	24.05 /89	15.16 /92	0.00	2.55
FS	Dreyfus Premier Financial Svcs A	DFSFX	C+	(800) 782-6620	C / 4.6	-1.72	3.91	9.78 /45	13.49 /51	--	1.17	1.30
GR	Dreyfus Premier Future Leaders A	DFLAX	D+	(800) 782-6620	C / 5.2	-4.83	3.06	11.19 /55	14.77 /58	6.09 /62	0.00	1.25

● Denotes fund is closed to new investors
★ Denotes fund is included in Section II

www.WeissRatings.com

RISK			NET ASSETS		ASSET					Portfolio	BULL / BEAR		FUND MANAGER		MINIMUMS		LOADS	
	3 Year		NAV								Last Bull	Last Bear	Manager	Manager	Initial	Additional	Front	Back
Risk	Standard		As of	Total	Cash	Stocks	Bonds	Other		Turnover	Market	Market	Quality	Tenure	Purch.	Purch.	End	End
Rating/Pts	Deviation	Beta	6/30/06	$(Mil)	%	%	%	%		Ratio	Return	Return	Pct	(Years)	$	$	Load	Load
B- / 7.8	8.5	1.62	16.27	36	31	68	0	1		75.9	73.0	-9.5	75	3	2,500	100	0.0	0.0
C+ / 6.8	10.8	1.00	29.08	2,267	2	97	0	1		19.5	101.8	-9.2	50	11	2,500	100	0.0	1.0
C+ / 6.2	10.4	0.66	47.68	1,103	0	99	0	1		37.9	95.4	-8.8	90	N/A	2,500	100	5.8	0.0
C+ / 6.1	10.4	0.66	46.32	22	0	99	0	1		37.9	90.7	-8.9	86	N/A	1,000	100	0.0	4.0
C+ / 6.1	10.4	0.66	46.37	24	0	99	0	1		37.9	91.0	-8.9	86	N/A	1,000	100	0.0	1.0
C+ / 6.2	10.4	0.65	47.99	14	0	99	0	1		37.9	96.6	-8.7	91	N/A	1,000	100	0.0	0.0
C+ / 6.1	10.4	0.65	47.13	20	0	99	0	1		37.9	93.9	-8.8	89	N/A	1,000	100	4.5	0.0
C+ / 6.5	14.6	1.53	22.40	721	0	99	0	1		128.6	80.6	-6.9	34	2	1,000	100	5.8	0.0
D / 2.2	14.6	1.53	21.24	75	0	99	0	1		128.6	77.0	-6.8	28	2	1,000	100	0.0	4.0
D+ / 2.3	14.6	1.54	21.30	170	0	99	0	1		128.6	77.2	-6.8	28	2	1,000	100	0.0	1.0
C+ / 6.5	14.6	1.53	22.44	46	0	99	0	1		128.6	80.9	-6.9	34	2	1,000	100	0.0	0.0
D+ / 2.4	14.6	1.53	22.29	130	0	99	0	1		128.6	79.9	-6.9	32	2	1,000	100	4.5	0.0
B+ / 9.1	5.4	1.14	12.72	81	3	62	15	20		246.5	34.8	-7.1	28	1	1,000	100	5.8	0.0
B+ / 9.3	5.4	1.14	12.69	20	3	62	15	20		246.5	31.7	-7.3	22	1	1,000	100	0.0	4.0
B+ / 9.4	5.4	1.14	12.73	10	3	62	15	20		246.5	31.7	-7.2	23	1	1,000	100	0.0	1.0
B+ / 9.4	5.4	1.14	12.71	23	3	62	15	20		246.5	35.9	-7.0	30	1	1,000	100	0.0	0.0
B+ / 9.3	5.4	1.14	12.73	N/A	3	62	15	20		246.5	33.8	-7.1	26	1	1,000	100	4.5	0.0
B+ / 9.5	6.0	1.19	18.96	233	0	71	6	23		39.4	36.4	-6.4	24	19	1,000	100	5.8	0.0
B+ / 9.4	6.0	1.20	18.80	172	0	71	6	23		39.4	34.0	-6.4	19	19	1,000	100	0.0	4.0
E- / 0.0	6.0	1.20	18.84	131	0	71	6	23		39.4	34.2	-6.4	19	19	1,000	100	0.0	1.0
B+ / 9.3	6.0	1.18	19.02	180	0	71	6	23		39.4	37.1	-6.4	25	19	1,000	100	0.0	0.0
B+ / 9.5	6.0	1.19	18.96	1	0	71	6	23		39.4	36.7	-6.4	24	19	1,000	100	0.0	0.0
B+ / 9.5	6.0	1.19	18.92	3	0	71	6	23		39.4	35.5	-6.4	22	19	1,000	100	4.5	0.0
B+ / 9.5	5.9	1.18	18.95	88	0	71	6	23		39.4	36.7	-6.4	25	N/A	1,000	100	0.0	0.0
B- / 7.9	9.2	1.07	12.05	1	N/A	100	0	N/A		37.3	52.7	-13.1	11	N/A	1,000	100	5.8	0.0
B- / 7.9	9.2	1.08	11.93	N/A	N/A	100	0	N/A		37.3	51.1	-13.1	9	N/A	1,000	100	0.0	4.0
B- / 7.9	9.3	1.07	12.20	N/A	N/A	100	0	N/A		37.3	54.8	-13.1	12	N/A	1,000	100	0.0	1.0
B- / 7.9	9.2	1.07	12.07	24	N/A	100	0	N/A		37.3	52.9	-13.1	11	4	1,000	100	0.0	0.0
B- / 7.9	9.2	1.07	12.08	N/A	N/A	100	0	N/A		37.3	52.9	-13.1	11	N/A	1,000	100	0.0	0.0
B- / 7.9	9.2	1.06	12.00	N/A	N/A	100	0	N/A		37.3	51.7	-13.1	10	N/A	1,000	100	4.5	0.0
B / 8.9	6.5	0.73	15.12	82	0	99	0	1		80.0	36.4	-8.3	32	8	1,000	100	5.8	0.0
B / 8.8	6.5	0.73	14.86	40	0	99	0	1		80.0	33.3	-8.5	26	8	1,000	100	0.0	4.0
B / 8.7	6.5	0.73	14.86	61	0	99	0	1		80.0	33.2	-8.5	27	8	1,000	100	0.0	1.0
B / 8.9	6.4	0.70	15.40	N/A	0	99	0	1		80.0	39.8	-8.2	42	8	1,000	100	0.0	0.0
B / 8.8	6.5	0.73	14.99	3	0	99	0	1		80.0	35.3	-8.3	30	8	1,000	100	4.5	0.0
B / 8.3	7.9	0.99	31.41	540	N/A	N/A	0	N/A		56.0	69.1	-10.5	73	2	1,000	100	5.8	0.0
B / 8.2	7.9	1.00	30.88	56	N/A	N/A	0	N/A		56.0	65.3	-10.7	66	2	1,000	100	0.0	4.0
B / 8.2	7.9	0.99	30.86	19	N/A	N/A	0	N/A		56.0	65.2	-10.7	66	2	1,000	100	0.0	1.0
B / 8.2	8.0	1.00	31.39	41	N/A	N/A	0	N/A		56.0	69.7	-10.4	73	2	1,000	100	0.0	0.0
B / 8.2	7.9	1.00	31.39	5	N/A	N/A	0	N/A		56.0	70.4	-10.4	75	2	1,000	100	0.0	0.0
B / 8.3	7.9	0.99	31.40	3	N/A	N/A	0	N/A		56.0	67.7	-10.5	70	2	1,000	100	4.5	0.0
C / 4.5	16.8	1.01	22.84	1,265	2	97	0	1		41.4	200.6	-5.5	16	10	1,000	100	5.8	1.0
C / 4.5	16.8	1.01	22.43	4	2	97	0	1		41.4	193.2	-5.7	12	10	1,000	100	0.0	4.0
C / 4.5	16.8	1.01	22.49	7	2	97	0	1		41.4	193.7	-5.6	13	10	1,000	100	0.0	1.0
C / 4.5	16.8	1.01	22.92	49	2	97	0	1		41.4	203.9	-5.5	19	10	1,000	100	0.0	0.0
C / 4.5	16.8	1.01	22.60	N/A	2	97	0	1		41.4	196.8	-5.7	15	10	1,000	100	4.5	1.0
C / 4.5	15.6	0.99	24.72	159	3	96	0	1		156.6	166.2	-5.3	93	2	1,000	100	5.8	0.0
C / 4.4	15.6	0.99	23.52	47	3	96	0	1		156.6	159.7	-5.5	90	2	1,000	100	0.0	4.0
C / 4.4	15.6	0.99	23.55	72	3	96	0	1		156.6	159.9	-5.5	90	2	1,000	100	0.0	1.0
C / 4.4	15.6	0.99	24.28	2	3	96	0	1		156.6	163.7	-5.3	92	2	1,000	100	4.5	0.0
B / 8.1	10.9	1.14	15.41	3	N/A	100	0	N/A		175.8	81.9	-8.6	35	4	1,000	100	5.8	0.0
C / 4.6	14.2	1.57	18.52	96	1	98	0	1		80.0	101.9	-11.3	36	N/A	1,000	100	5.8	0.0

Fund Type	Fund Name	Ticker Symbol	Overall Weiss Investment Rating	Phone	Performance Rating/Pts	3 Mo	6 Mo	1Yr / Pct	3Yr / Pct	5Yr / Pct	Dividend Yield	Expense Ratio
					PERFORMANCE			Total Return % through 6/30/06	Annualized		Incl. in Returns	
GR	Dreyfus Premier Future Leaders B	DFLBX	D	(800) 782-6620	C / 4.9	-4.96	2.68	10.41 /50	13.98 /54	5.31 /56	0.00	2.00
GR	Dreyfus Premier Future Leaders C	DPFCX	D+	(800) 782-6620	C / 5.4	-5.01	2.68	10.39 /49	13.98 /54	5.33 /57	0.00	2.00
GR	Dreyfus Premier Future Leaders R	DFLRX	C-	(800) 782-6620	C+ / 6.2	-4.76	3.20	11.73 /58	15.28 /60	6.51 /64	0.00	1.00
GR	Dreyfus Premier Future Leaders T	DFLTX	D+	(800) 782-6620	C / 5.2	-4.88	2.95	11.00 /53	14.39 /56	5.70 /59	0.00	1.50
FO	Dreyfus Premier Greater China A	DPCAX	B-	(800) 782-6620	A / 9.5	-0.59	32.66	38.55 /98	25.99 /92	16.03 /93	0.04	1.78
FO	Dreyfus Premier Greater China B	DPCBX	C+	(800) 782-6620	A / 9.5	-0.83	32.10	37.39 /97	25.02 /91	15.12 /92	0.00	2.55
FO	Dreyfus Premier Greater China C	DPCCX	C+	(800) 782-6620	A+ / 9.6	-0.79	32.12	37.47 /97	25.05 /91	15.14 /92	0.00	2.55
FO	Dreyfus Premier Greater China R	DPCRX	B-	(800) 782-6620	A+ / 9.7	-0.55	32.86	38.88 /98	26.33 /92	16.39 /93	0.21	1.49
FO	Dreyfus Premier Greater China T	DPCTX	B-	(800) 782-6620	A / 9.5	-0.71	32.31	38.03 /97	25.62 /92	15.77 /93	0.00	2.13
GI	Dreyfus Premier Growth & Inc A	PEGAX	D	(800) 782-6620	E+ / 0.9	-3.64	-0.37	4.61 /13	7.48 /12	-0.93 /12	0.63	1.63
GI	Dreyfus Premier Growth & Inc B	PEGBX	D	(800) 782-6620	E+ / 0.7	-3.84	-0.82	3.78 /10	6.57 / 9	-1.75 / 9	0.00	2.44
GI	Dreyfus Premier Growth & Inc C	DGICX	D	(800) 782-6620	D- / 1.1	-3.71	-0.75	3.88 /10	6.69 / 9	-1.67 / 9	0.00	2.37
GI	Dreyfus Premier Growth & Inc R	DRERX	D	(800) 782-6620	D- / 1.2	-3.60	-0.41	4.32 /12	6.61 / 9	-1.40 /10	0.52	1.75
GI	Dreyfus Premier Growth & Inc T	DGITX	D	(800) 782-6620	E+ / 0.8	-3.83	-0.58	4.21 /11	6.80 /10	-1.72 / 9	0.53	2.11
HL	Dreyfus Premier Health Care A	DHCAX	E+	(800) 782-6620	E+ / 0.6	-5.89	-4.49	1.14 / 3	7.40 /12	3.76 /43	0.00	1.65
HL	Dreyfus Premier Health Care B	DHCBX	E+	(800) 782-6620	E / 0.5	-6.12	-4.87	0.32 / 2	6.47 / 8	--	0.00	2.40
HL	Dreyfus Premier Health Care C	DHCCX	E+	(800) 782-6620	E+ / 0.6	-6.13	-4.88	0.32 / 2	6.45 / 8	--	0.00	2.40
HL	Dreyfus Premier Health Care R	DHCRX	D-	(800) 782-6620	D- / 1.2	-5.84	-4.32	1.47 / 3	7.65 /13	--	0.00	1.40
HL	Dreyfus Premier Health Care T	DHCTX	E+	(800) 782-6620	E / 0.5	-6.00	-4.70	0.67 / 2	6.75 / 9	--	0.00	1.90
FO	Dreyfus Premier Intl Equity A	DIEAX	A+	(800) 782-6620	A- / 9.2	0.34	10.83	27.94 /93	26.31 /92	13.77 /90	0.09	1.50
FO	Dreyfus Premier Intl Equity B	DIEBX	A+	(800) 782-6620	A- / 9.1	0.13	10.46	27.00 /91	25.53 /92	13.31 /89	0.00	2.25
FO	Dreyfus Premier Intl Equity C	DIECX	A+	(800) 782-6620	A- / 9.2	0.13	10.43	27.02 /91	25.49 /92	13.29 /89	0.02	2.25
FO	Dreyfus Premier Intl Equity R	DIERX	A+	(800) 782-6620	A / 9.3	0.39	11.00	28.26 /93	26.78 /93	14.08 /90	0.13	1.25
FO	Dreyfus Premier Intl Equity T	DIETX	A+	(800) 782-6620	A- / 9.2	0.23	10.71	27.59 /92	26.15 /92	13.69 /90	0.00	1.75
FO	Dreyfus Premier Intl Growth A	DRGLX	B+	(800) 782-6620	B+ / 8.8	0.52	9.88	27.09 /91	23.83 /89	6.54 /64	0.63	1.53
FO	Dreyfus Premier Intl Growth B	DGLBX	B	(800) 782-6620	B+ / 8.7	0.37	9.51	26.01 /90	22.82 /87	5.58 /58	0.12	2.35
FO	Dreyfus Premier Intl Growth C	DIGCX	B	(800) 782-6620	B+ / 8.8	0.30	9.45	25.99 /90	22.84 /87	5.57 /58	0.36	2.27
FO	Dreyfus Premier Intl Growth R	DIGRX	B+	(800) 782-6620	A- / 9.1	0.51	9.96	27.43 /92	23.77 /89	6.63 /65	0.91	1.21
FO	Dreyfus Premier Intl Growth T	DPITX	B	(800) 782-6620	B+ / 8.7	0.45	9.62	26.48 /90	22.69 /87	5.47 /58	0.31	1.98
FO	● Dreyfus Premier Intl Small Cap A	DSMAX	A+	(800) 782-6620	A+ / 9.8	-1.28	12.43	37.42 /97	35.64 /98	22.32 /98	0.11	1.63
FO	● Dreyfus Premier Intl Small Cap B	DSMBX	A+	(800) 782-6620	A+ / 9.7	-1.46	11.98	36.45 /97	34.71 /98	21.72 /97	0.00	2.38
FO	● Dreyfus Premier Intl Small Cap C	DSMCX	A+	(800) 782-6620	A+ / 9.8	-1.42	12.02	36.45 /97	34.74 /98	21.72 /98	0.00	2.38
FO	● Dreyfus Premier Intl Small Cap R	DSMRX	A+	(800) 782-6620	A+ / 9.8	-1.24	12.59	37.95 /97	36.13 /98	22.58 /98	0.15	1.38
FO	● Dreyfus Premier Intl Small Cap T	DSMTX	A+	(800) 782-6620	A+ / 9.8	-1.33	12.31	37.16 /97	35.34 /98	22.11 /98	0.00	1.88
FO	Dreyfus Premier Intl Value A	DVLAX	A-	(800) 782-6620	B+ / 8.5	0.59	9.36	23.43 /86	22.83 /87	10.95 /84	0.99	1.49
FO	Dreyfus Premier Intl Value B	DIBVX	B+	(800) 782-6620	B+ / 8.4	0.40	8.92	22.45 /85	21.85 /85	--	0.53	2.23
FO	Dreyfus Premier Intl Value C	DICVX	A-	(800) 782-6620	B+ / 8.6	0.40	8.94	22.56 /85	21.92 /85	--	0.52	2.21
FO	Dreyfus Premier Intl Value R	DIRVX	A	(800) 782-6620	B+ / 8.9	0.69	9.52	23.82 /87	23.25 /88	--	1.39	1.14
FO	Dreyfus Premier Intl Value T	DITVX	A-	(800) 782-6620	B+ / 8.4	0.46	9.08	22.85 /86	22.28 /86	--	0.84	1.86
GR	Dreyfus Premier Intrinsic Value A	DPVAX	C	(800) 782-6620	D+ / 2.7	-1.03	2.60	6.03 /21	10.63 /32	4.18 /48	1.24	1.09
GR	Dreyfus Premier Intrinsic Value B	BLCBX	D+	(800) 782-6620	D+ / 2.4	-1.26	2.15	5.07 /15	9.85 /26	3.51 /41	0.00	1.84
GR	Dreyfus Premier Intrinsic Value C	BLCCX	C-	(800) 782-6620	D+ / 2.9	-1.25	2.19	5.09 /16	9.85 /26	3.54 /42	0.00	1.84
GR	Dreyfus Premier Intrinsic Value R	BSLYX	C	(800) 782-6620	C- / 3.8	-0.97	2.69	6.16 /21	10.99 /35	4.70 /52	1.62	0.84
GR	Dreyfus Premier Intrinsic Value T	BLCAX	C-	(800) 782-6620	D+ / 2.7	-1.08	2.44	5.64 /18	10.41 /30	4.06 /46	0.45	1.34
IN	Dreyfus Premier Large Co Stock A	DRDEX	D	(800) 782-6620	D+ / 2.5	-2.33	2.27	8.48 /37	10.07 /28	0.79 /19	0.32	1.05
IN	Dreyfus Premier Large Co Stock B	DRLBX	D	(800) 782-6620	D / 2.2	-2.49	1.85	7.63 /30	9.26 /22	0.05 /16	0.01	1.80
IN	Dreyfus Premier Large Co Stock C	DLCCX	D+	(800) 782-6620	D+ / 2.7	-2.49	1.90	7.68 /30	9.28 /23	0.05 /16	0.01	1.80
IN	Dreyfus Premier Large Co Stock R	DEIRX	C-	(800) 782-6620	C- / 3.6	-2.25	2.39	8.73 /38	10.38 /30	1.06 /20	0.57	0.80
IN	Dreyfus Premier Large Co Stock T	DLSTX	D+	(800) 782-6620	D+ / 2.5	-2.37	2.14	8.21 /34	9.81 /26	0.54 /18	0.18	1.30
MC	Dreyfus Premier Midcap Stock A	DPMAX	E+	(800) 782-6620	C / 5.5	-2.59	4.50	11.56 /57	15.06 /59	7.62 /70	0.00	1.35
MC	Dreyfus Premier Midcap Stock B	DMSBX	E+	(800) 782-6620	C / 5.3	-2.71	4.16	10.74 /52	14.23 /55	6.83 /66	0.00	2.10
MC	Dreyfus Premier Midcap Stock C	DMSCX	E+	(800) 782-6620	C+ / 5.7	-2.77	4.07	10.72 /52	14.20 /55	6.82 /66	0.00	2.10

99 Pct = Best
0 Pct = Worst

● Denotes fund is closed to new investors
* Denotes fund is included in Section II

RISK			NET ASSETS		ASSET					BULL / BEAR		FUND MANAGER		MINIMUMS		LOADS	
	3 Year		NAV						Portfolio	Last Bull	Last Bear	Manager	Manager	Initial	Additional	Front	Back
Risk	Standard		As of	Total	Cash	Stocks	Bonds	Other	Turnover	Market	Market	Quality	Tenure	Purch.	Purch.	End	End
Rating/Pts	Deviation	Beta	6/30/06	$(Mil)	%	%	%	%	Ratio	Return	Return	Pct	(Years)	$	$	Load	Load
C /4.3	14.2	1.57	17.62	41	1	98	0	1	80.0	97.4	-11.5	31	N/A	1,000	100	0.0	4.0
C /4.3	14.2	1.57	17.65	38	1	98	0	1	80.0	97.5	-11.5	31	N/A	1,000	100	0.0	1.0
C /4.7	14.2	1.57	19.00	10	1	98	0	1	80.0	104.6	-11.2	41	N/A	1,000	100	0.0	0.0
C /4.5	14.2	1.57	18.12	2	1	98	0	1	80.0	99.6	-11.4	34	N/A	1,000	100	4.5	0.0
C- /4.1	19.2	1.32	28.76	144	4	95	0	1	178.3	140.1	6.5	14	3	1,000	100	5.8	0.0
C- /4.0	19.2	1.31	27.45	33	4	95	0	1	178.3	134.3	6.4	11	3	1,000	100	0.0	4.0
C- /4.0	19.2	1.31	27.48	75	4	95	0	1	178.3	134.6	6.3	11	3	1,000	100	0.0	1.0
C- /4.1	19.2	1.32	29.11	16	4	95	0	1	178.3	142.4	6.7	15	3	1,000	100	0.0	0.0
C- /4.1	19.2	1.32	28.09	1	4	95	0	1	178.3	138.5	6.4	12	3	1,000	100	4.5	0.0
B /8.3	8.3	1.06	18.26	24	1	98	0	1	78.0	51.9	-11.3	20	2	1,000	100	5.8	0.0
B /8.2	8.3	1.06	17.03	4	1	98	0	1	78.0	48.0	-11.6	15	2	1,000	100	0.0	4.0
B /8.2	8.3	1.06	17.14	2	1	98	0	1	78.0	48.3	-11.5	15	2	1,000	100	0.0	1.0
B /8.2	8.2	1.05	18.06	N/A	1	98	0	1	78.0	48.3	-11.3	15	2	1,000	100	0.0	0.0
B /8.3	8.2	1.05	17.34	N/A	1	98	0	1	78.0	48.8	-11.7	16	2	1,000	100	4.5	0.0
C+ /6.9	8.7	0.72	14.69	7	3	96	0	1	88.9	55.1	-6.0	41	N/A	1,000	100	5.8	0.0
C+ /6.8	8.7	0.72	14.26	2	3	96	0	1	88.9	50.9	-6.0	33	N/A	1,000	100	0.0	4.0
C+ /6.8	8.7	0.73	14.24	1	3	96	0	1	88.9	50.9	-6.1	33	N/A	1,000	100	0.0	1.0
C+ /6.9	8.7	0.72	14.83	1	3	96	0	1	88.9	56.2	-5.9	44	N/A	1,000	100	0.0	0.0
C+ /6.9	8.6	0.72	14.41	N/A	3	96	0	1	88.9	52.2	-6.0	35	N/A	1,000	100	4.5	0.0
B- /7.3	10.5	1.01	38.58	90	1	98	0	1	N/A	143.3	-5.2	71	3	1,000	100	5.8	0.0
B- /7.3	10.5	1.01	38.02	12	1	98	0	1	N/A	138.9	-5.3	64	3	1,000	100	0.0	4.0
B- /7.3	10.5	1.01	38.02	47	1	98	0	1	N/A	138.7	-5.3	64	3	1,000	100	0.0	1.0
B- /7.3	10.6	1.02	39.05	8	1	98	0	1	N/A	146.4	-5.2	73	3	1,000	100	0.0	0.0
B- /7.3	10.5	1.01	38.57	1	1	98	0	1	N/A	142.6	-5.2	69	3	1,000	100	4.5	0.0
C+ /5.8	10.8	1.03	11.57	38	2	97	0	1	64.3	136.6	-10.5	42	2	1,000	100	5.8	0.0
C+ /5.8	10.8	1.03	10.71	3	2	97	0	1	64.3	130.3	-10.9	34	2	1,000	100	0.0	4.0
C+ /5.8	10.7	1.03	10.19	2	2	97	0	1	64.3	130.9	-10.8	34	2	1,000	100	0.0	1.0
C+ /5.8	10.8	1.04	11.81	N/A	2	97	0	1	64.3	136.8	-11.3	41	2	1,000	100	0.0	0.0
C+ /5.8	10.7	1.03	11.28	N/A	2	97	0	1	64.3	128.6	-10.7	34	2	1,000	100	4.5	0.0
C+ /6.4	12.0	1.09	26.14	243	4	95	0	1	N/A	220.3	-3.1	97	3	1,000	100	5.8	0.0
C+ /6.3	12.0	1.09	25.62	18	4	95	0	1	N/A	213.3	-3.2	96	3	1,000	100	0.0	4.0
C+ /6.3	12.0	1.09	25.62	72	4	95	0	1	N/A	213.1	-3.2	96	3	1,000	100	0.0	1.0
C+ /6.4	12.0	1.09	26.38	12	4	95	0	1	N/A	223.5	-3.1	98	3	1,000	100	0.0	0.0
C+ /6.3	12.0	1.09	26.00	1	4	95	0	1	N/A	217.9	-3.2	97	3	1,000	100	4.5	0.0
C+ /6.9	9.6	0.93	20.33	649	3	96	0	1	43.1	131.0	-11.6	58	4	1,000	100	5.8	0.0
C+ /6.9	9.6	0.93	19.91	22	3	96	0	1	43.1	125.2	-11.8	47	4	1,000	100	0.0	4.0
C+ /6.9	9.6	0.93	19.98	72	3	96	0	1	43.1	125.6	-11.7	48	4	1,000	100	0.0	1.0
C+ /6.8	9.6	0.93	20.36	78	3	96	0	1	43.1	133.6	-11.7	62	4	1,000	100	0.0	0.0
C+ /6.8	9.6	0.92	19.82	2	3	96	0	1	43.1	126.7	-11.9	53	4	1,000	100	4.5	0.0
B+ /9.0	7.2	0.88	20.69	12	0	99	0	1	62.4	69.6	-11.9	62	N/A	1,000	100	5.8	0.0
B- /7.8	7.2	0.88	20.22	25	0	99	0	1	62.4	66.2	-12.1	54	N/A	1,000	100	0.0	4.0
B- /7.8	7.2	0.88	20.35	23	0	99	0	1	62.4	66.2	-12.1	54	N/A	1,000	100	0.0	1.0
B- /7.6	7.2	0.87	21.01	92	0	99	0	1	62.4	72.1	-11.8	66	N/A	1,000	100	0.0	0.0
B- /7.8	7.2	0.88	20.81	30	0	99	0	1	62.4	68.7	-11.9	60	N/A	1,000	100	4.5	0.0
B- /7.2	7.8	0.99	22.12	44	N/A	100	0	N/A	70.1	56.4	-9.1	43	2	1,000	100	5.8	0.0
B- /7.1	7.7	0.99	21.06	18	N/A	100	0	N/A	70.1	52.8	-9.2	36	2	1,000	100	0.0	4.0
B- /7.1	7.8	0.99	21.07	7	N/A	100	0	N/A	70.1	52.7	-9.2	36	2	1,000	100	0.0	1.0
B- /7.2	7.8	0.99	22.37	8	N/A	100	0	N/A	70.1	57.6	-9.0	47	2	1,000	100	0.0	0.0
B- /7.1	7.8	0.99	21.83	N/A	N/A	100	0	N/A	70.1	55.1	-9.1	41	2	1,000	100	4.5	0.0
D- /1.3	11.1	1.01	16.20	88	0	99	0	1	87.4	85.0	-7.0	27	12	1,000	100	5.8	0.0
D- /1.2	11.1	1.01	14.73	30	0	99	0	1	87.4	80.6	-7.1	22	8	1,000	100	0.0	4.0
D- /1.2	11.1	1.01	14.76	15	0	99	0	1	87.4	80.5	-7.1	22	8	1,000	100	0.0	1.0

Fund Type	Fund Name	Ticker Symbol	Overall Weiss Investment Rating	Phone	Perfor-mance Rating/Pts	PERFORMANCE Total Return % through 6/30/06					Incl. in Returns	
						3 Mo	6 Mo	1Yr / Pct	3Yr / Pct (Annualized)	5Yr / Pct (Annualized)	Dividend Yield	Expense Ratio
MC	Dreyfus Premier Midcap Stock R	DDMRX	D-	(800) 782-6620	C+ / 6.4	-2.51	4.61	11.86 /59	15.36 /60	7.89 /71	0.00	1.10
MC	Dreyfus Premier Midcap Stock T	DMSTX	E+	(800) 782-6620	C / 5.5	-2.65	4.34	11.29 /55	14.79 /58	7.36 /68	0.00	1.60
MC	Dreyfus Premier Midcap Value A	DMVPX	C	(800) 782-6620	C+ / 5.8	-2.13	2.62	9.66 /45	16.20 /64	5.11 /55	0.00	1.50
GR	Dreyfus Premier S&P STARS Fd A	DPPAX	C+	(800) 782-6620	C / 4.8	-6.86	0.46	8.76 /38	14.86 /58	-1.00 /12	0.00	1.19
GR	Dreyfus Premier S&P STARS Fd B	BSPBX	C	(800) 782-6620	C / 4.6	-7.04	0.04	7.93 /32	14.11 /54	-1.58 /10	0.00	2.00
GR	Dreyfus Premier S&P STARS Fd C	BSPCX	C+	(800) 782-6620	C / 5.0	-7.04	0.04	7.89 /32	14.10 /54	-1.58 /10	0.00	2.00
GR	Dreyfus Premier S&P STARS Fd R	BSSPX	C+	(800) 782-6620	C+ / 5.9	-6.78	0.60	9.13 /41	15.37 /61	-0.53 /13	0.00	0.91
GR	Dreyfus Premier S&P STARS Fd T	BSPAX	C	(800) 782-6620	C / 4.9	-6.95	0.28	8.44 /36	14.67 /57	-1.12 /11	0.00	1.19
MC	Dreyfus Premier S&P STARS Opp A	DPOAX	A-	(800) 782-6620	B / 8.1	-5.16	7.80	23.38 /86	22.20 /86	--	0.00	1.28
MC	Dreyfus Premier S&P STARS Opp B	BSOBX	B	(800) 782-6620	B / 8.0	-5.33	7.47	22.63 /85	21.58 /84	--	0.00	2.00
MC	Dreyfus Premier S&P STARS Opp C	BSOCX	B+	(800) 782-6620	B / 8.2	-5.37	7.47	22.63 /85	21.58 /84	--	0.00	2.00
MC	Dreyfus Premier S&P STARS Opp R	DSORX	A	(800) 782-6620	B+ / 8.6	-5.10	8.00	23.81 /87	22.74 /87	--	0.00	1.00
MC	Dreyfus Premier S&P STARS Opp T	BSOAX	B+	(800) 782-6620	B / 8.2	-5.23	7.68	23.19 /86	22.27 /86	--	0.00	1.50
GR	Dreyfus Premier Select A	DSLAX	D	(800) 782-6620	D- / 1.1	-5.37	1.48	-1.88 / 1	9.13 /22	--	0.11	1.52
GR	Dreyfus Premier Select B	DSLBX	D	(800) 782-6620	D- / 1.2	-5.57	1.14	-2.62 / 0	8.77 /19	--	0.03	2.30
GR	Dreyfus Premier Select C	DSLCX	D	(800) 782-6620	D / 1.6	-5.56	1.14	-2.57 / 0	8.79 /20	--	0.00	2.30
GR	Dreyfus Premier Select J	THPSX	D+	(800) 782-6620	D / 2.0	-5.35	1.57	-1.66 / 1	9.24 /22	--	0.18	1.28
MC	Dreyfus Premier Select Mid-Cap Gr A	DASMX	B-	(800) 782-6620	C+ / 6.7	-1.96	8.92	20.01 /82	16.64 /66	--	0.00	1.50
MC	Dreyfus Premier Select Mid-Cap Gr B	DBSMX	C+	(800) 782-6620	C+ / 6.5	-2.10	8.55	19.15 /81	15.76 /62	--	0.00	2.25
MC	Dreyfus Premier Select Mid-Cap Gr C	DCSMX	B-	(800) 782-6620	C+ / 6.8	-2.19	8.48	19.12 /81	15.81 /63	--	0.00	2.25
MC	Dreyfus Premier Select Mid-Cap Gr R	DRSMX	B	(800) 782-6620	B- / 7.4	-1.99	8.99	20.30 /82	16.98 /68	--	0.00	1.50
MC	Dreyfus Premier Select Mid-Cap Gr T	DMGTX	B-	(800) 782-6620	C+ / 6.7	-2.02	8.76	19.78 /82	16.41 /65	--	0.00	1.75
GR	Dreyfus Premier Select R	DSLRX	D+	(800) 782-6620	D / 1.9	-5.51	1.39	-1.77 / 1	9.20 /22	--	0.15	1.30
GR	Dreyfus Premier Select T	DSLTX	D	(800) 782-6620	D- / 1.1	-5.37	1.48	-2.02 / 1	9.05 /21	--	0.05	1.80
SC	● Dreyfus Premier Small Cap Eqty A	DSEAX	A	(800) 782-6620	B+ / 8.5	-1.11	10.46	15.73 /74	23.54 /88	15.47 /92	0.00	1.35
SC	● Dreyfus Premier Small Cap Eqty B	DSEBX	A	(800) 782-6620	B+ / 8.4	-1.34	10.07	14.83 /71	22.60 /86	14.87 /92	0.00	2.10
SC	● Dreyfus Premier Small Cap Eqty C	DSECX	A	(800) 782-6620	B+ / 8.6	-1.34	10.03	14.79 /71	22.57 /86	14.85 /92	0.00	2.10
SC	● Dreyfus Premier Small Cap Eqty R	DSERX	A+	(800) 782-6620	B+ / 8.9	-1.07	10.60	15.96 /75	23.84 /89	15.66 /93	0.00	1.10
SC	● Dreyfus Premier Small Cap Eqty T	DSETX	A	(800) 782-6620	B+ / 8.5	-1.19	10.33	15.42 /73	23.17 /88	15.25 /92	0.00	1.60
SC	● Dreyfus Premier Small Cap Val A	DSVAX	B	(800) 782-6620	B- / 7.3	-4.21	5.95	10.79 /52	20.07 /79	14.29 /91	0.00	1.50
SC	● Dreyfus Premier Small Cap Val B	DSVBX	B	(800) 782-6620	B- / 7.2	-4.40	5.58	9.93 /46	19.22 /77	13.46 /89	0.00	2.25
SC	● Dreyfus Premier Small Cap Val C	DSVCX	B	(800) 782-6620	B- / 7.5	-4.39	5.62	9.98 /47	19.22 /77	13.46 /89	0.00	2.25
SC	● Dreyfus Premier Small Cap Val R	DSVRX	B+	(800) 782-6620	B / 7.9	-4.15	6.10	11.09 /54	20.40 /81	14.59 /91	0.00	1.25
SC	● Dreyfus Premier Small Cap Val T	DSVTX	B	(800) 782-6620	B- / 7.4	-4.23	5.85	10.54 /51	19.79 /79	14.02 /90	0.00	1.75
IN	Dreyfus Premier Small Co Growth A	DSGAX	B-	(800) 782-6620	B- / 7.0	-5.12	5.64	13.73 /67	18.66 /75	--	0.00	1.65
IN	Dreyfus Premier Small Co Growth B	DSGBX	C+	(800) 782-6620	C+ / 6.8	-5.31	5.27	12.93 /64	17.79 /72	--	0.00	2.40
IN	Dreyfus Premier Small Co Growth C	DSGCX	B-	(800) 782-6620	B- / 7.1	-5.32	5.21	12.80 /63	17.73 /71	--	0.00	2.40
IN	Dreyfus Premier Small Co Growth R	DSGRX	B	(800) 782-6620	B / 7.7	-5.09	5.73	14.16 /69	19.05 /76	--	0.00	1.40
IN	Dreyfus Premier Small Co Growth T	DSGTX	B-	(800) 782-6620	B- / 7.0	-4.82	5.81	13.45 /66	18.38 /74	--	0.00	1.90
AG	Dreyfus Premier Strategic Value A	DAGVX	B-	(800) 782-6620	C+ / 6.6	-0.40	5.07	13.82 /68	17.02 /68	7.18 /68	0.33	1.21
AG	Dreyfus Premier Strategic Value B	DBGVX	B-	(800) 782-6620	C+ / 6.4	-0.58	4.66	12.99 /64	16.17 /64	6.44 /64	0.14	1.96
AG	Dreyfus Premier Strategic Value C	DCGVX	B-	(800) 782-6620	C+ / 6.7	-0.55	4.69	13.07 /65	16.19 /64	6.47 /64	0.18	1.91
AG	Dreyfus Premier Strategic Value R	DRGVX	B+	(800) 782-6620	B- / 7.3	-0.30	5.21	14.17 /69	17.24 /69	7.24 /68	0.44	0.92
AG	Dreyfus Premier Strategic Value T	DTGVX	B-	(800) 782-6620	C+ / 6.6	-0.44	4.93	13.57 /67	16.67 /67	6.72 /65	0.30	1.40
MC	Dreyfus Premier Structure Mid Cap A	DPSAX	B-	(800) 782-6620	C+ / 6.8	-1.95	6.30	13.76 /67	18.08 /73	9.95 /80	0.00	1.29
MC	Dreyfus Premier Structure Mid Cap B	DPSBX	B-	(800) 782-6620	C+ / 6.7	-2.18	5.81	12.83 /63	17.12 /69	9.08 /77	0.00	2.14
MC	Dreyfus Premier Structure Mid Cap C	DPSCX	B	(800) 782-6620	B- / 7.1	-2.18	5.88	12.90 /64	17.16 /69	9.09 /77	0.00	2.07
MC	Dreyfus Premier Structure Mid Cap R	DPSRX	B+	(800) 782-6620	B- / 7.5	-1.84	6.13	13.58 /67	18.19 /73	10.12 /81	0.00	1.25
MC	Dreyfus Premier Structure Mid Cap T	DPSTX	B-	(800) 782-6620	C+ / 6.9	-1.97	6.18	13.58 /67	17.83 /72	9.71 /79	0.00	1.51
GR	Dreyfus Premier Tax Mgd Grwth A	DTMGX	D-	(800) 782-6620	E+ / 0.8	0.72	2.12	5.55 /18	6.71 / 9	0.64 /18	0.69	1.25
GR	Dreyfus Premier Tax Mgd Grwth B	DPTMX	D-	(800) 782-6620	E+ / 0.8	0.50	1.71	4.73 /14	5.93 / 7	-0.11 /15	0.63	2.00
GR	Dreyfus Premier Tax Mgd Grwth C	DPTAX	D	(800) 782-6620	D- / 1.1	0.50	1.65	4.68 /14	5.91 / 6	-0.12 /15	0.64	2.00

● Denotes fund is closed to new investors
* Denotes fund is included in Section II

www.WeissRatings.com

RISK			NET ASSETS		ASSET					BULL / BEAR		FUND MANAGER		MINIMUMS		LOADS	
	3 Year		NAV						Portfolio	Last Bull	Last Bear	Manager	Manager	Initial	Additional	Front	Back
Risk Rating/Pts	Standard Deviation	Beta	As of 6/30/06	Total $(Mil)	Cash %	Stocks %	Bonds %	Other %	Turnover Ratio	Market Return	Market Return	Quality Pct	Tenure (Years)	Purch. $	Purch. $	End Load	End Load
D- / 1.4	11.1	1.01	16.72	33	0	99	0	1	87.4	86.3	-7.0	29	13	1,000	100	0.0	0.0
D- / 1.3	11.2	1.02	15.81	2	0	99	0	1	87.4	83.5	-7.1	25	7	1,000	100	4.5	0.0
C+ / 6.5	11.6	0.95	13.31	15	2	97	0	1	122.6	97.0	-10.7	44	3	1,000	100	5.8	0.0
B- / 7.9	10.7	1.23	28.67	41	N/A	100	0	N/A	123.1	98.9	-12.7	70	N/A	1,000	100	5.8	0.0
B- / 7.5	10.7	1.24	27.22	313	N/A	100	0	N/A	123.1	95.1	-12.8	63	N/A	1,000	100	0.0	4.0
B- / 7.5	10.8	1.24	27.20	230	N/A	100	0	N/A	123.1	95.1	-12.8	63	N/A	1,000	100	0.0	1.0
B- / 7.6	10.8	1.24	30.11	143	N/A	100	0	N/A	123.1	102.0	-12.5	74	N/A	1,000	100	0.0	0.0
B- / 7.5	10.7	1.24	28.53	390	N/A	100	0	N/A	123.1	98.1	-12.7	69	N/A	1,000	100	4.5	0.0
B- / 7.3	12.4	1.08	21.37	58	6	93	0	1	32.8	122.0	-10.0	79	2	1,000	100	5.8	0.0
C+ / 6.5	12.4	1.08	20.82	24	6	93	0	1	32.8	118.4	-10.0	74	2	1,000	100	0.0	4.0
C+ / 6.5	12.4	1.08	20.82	39	6	93	0	1	32.8	118.4	-10.1	74	2	1,000	100	0.0	1.0
B- / 7.3	12.4	1.08	21.83	13	6	93	0	1	32.8	125.0	-9.8	82	2	1,000	100	0.0	0.0
C+ / 6.6	12.4	1.08	21.41	23	6	93	0	1	32.8	122.5	-10.0	79	2	1,000	100	4.5	0.0
B- / 7.7	11.4	1.24	11.64	2	0	99	0	1	35.3	82.7	-16.5	20	N/A	1,000	100	5.8	1.0
B- / 7.7	11.4	1.25	11.53	N/A	0	99	0	1	35.3	81.0	-16.5	18	N/A	1,000	100	0.0	4.0
B- / 7.6	11.4	1.25	11.54	N/A	0	99	0	1	35.3	81.2	-16.5	18	N/A	1,000	100	0.0	1.0
B- / 7.7	11.4	1.24	11.67	27	0	99	0	1	35.3	83.3	-16.5	20	5	1,000	100	0.0	0.0
B- / 7.0	12.7	1.09	21.50	1	0	99	0	1	45.1	N/A	N/A	29	N/A	1,000	100	5.8	0.0
B- / 7.0	12.7	1.09	20.95	1	0	99	0	1	45.1	N/A	N/A	24	N/A	1,000	100	0.0	4.0
B- / 7.0	12.8	1.09	20.98	1	0	99	0	1	45.1	N/A	N/A	24	N/A	1,000	100	0.0	1.0
B- / 7.0	12.8	1.09	21.71	N/A	0	99	0	1	45.1	N/A	N/A	31	N/A	1,000	100	0.0	0.0
B- / 7.0	12.7	1.09	21.35	N/A	0	99	0	1	45.1	N/A	N/A	27	N/A	1,000	100	4.5	0.0
B- / 7.7	11.4	1.24	11.66	N/A	0	99	0	1	35.3	83.1	-16.5	20	N/A	1,000	100	0.0	0.0
B- / 7.7	11.4	1.24	11.62	N/A	0	99	0	1	35.3	82.2	-16.5	19	N/A	1,000	100	4.5	1.0
B- / 7.3	12.7	0.86	30.21	39	1	98	0	1	N/A	138.8	-10.7	96	3	1,000	100	5.8	0.0
B- / 7.3	12.7	0.85	29.41	4	1	98	0	1	N/A	133.1	-10.8	95	3	1,000	100	0.0	4.0
B- / 7.3	12.7	0.86	29.39	11	1	98	0	1	N/A	133.0	-10.8	94	3	1,000	100	0.0	1.0
B- / 7.3	12.7	0.86	30.47	14	1	98	0	1	N/A	140.7	-10.7	96	3	1,000	100	0.0	0.0
B- / 7.3	12.7	0.85	29.91	1	1	98	0	1	N/A	136.6	-10.7	96	3	1,000	100	4.5	0.0
B- / 7.1	12.7	0.85	22.73	409	1	98	0	1	100.6	126.3	-10.1	87	1	1,000	100	5.8	0.0
B- / 7.0	12.7	0.86	21.53	28	1	98	0	1	100.6	121.2	-10.2	82	1	1,000	100	0.0	4.0
B- / 7.0	12.7	0.85	21.56	57	1	98	0	1	100.6	121.0	-10.3	82	1	1,000	100	0.0	1.0
B- / 7.2	12.7	0.85	23.07	240	1	98	0	1	100.6	128.1	-10.1	88	1	1,000	100	0.0	0.0
B- / 7.1	12.7	0.85	22.39	21	1	98	0	1	100.6	124.6	-10.2	85	1	1,000	100	4.5	0.0
C+ / 6.8	13.6	1.44	18.72	6	3	96	0	1	253.3	113.0	-11.8	84	3	1,000	100	5.8	0.0
C+ / 6.8	13.7	1.44	18.18	1	3	96	0	1	253.3	108.4	-12.0	78	3	1,000	100	0.0	4.0
C+ / 6.8	13.6	1.44	18.17	1	3	96	0	1	253.3	108.3	-12.1	77	3	1,000	100	0.0	1.0
C+ / 6.8	13.7	1.44	19.01	N/A	3	96	0	1	253.3	115.8	-11.7	85	3	1,000	100	0.0	0.0
C+ / 6.8	13.6	1.44	18.58	N/A	3	96	0	1	253.3	110.8	-11.8	82	3	1,000	100	4.5	0.0
B- / 7.4	9.1	1.11	30.06	229	0	99	0	1	106.1	97.5	-9.5	91	3	1,000	100	5.8	0.0
B- / 7.4	9.1	1.11	28.99	14	0	99	0	1	106.1	93.0	-9.7	87	3	1,000	100	0.0	4.0
B- / 7.4	9.0	1.11	29.02	20	0	99	0	1	106.1	93.1	-9.6	87	3	1,000	100	0.0	1.0
B- / 7.4	9.0	1.11	30.08	2	0	99	0	1	106.1	98.6	-9.5	91	3	1,000	100	0.0	0.0
B- / 7.4	9.1	1.11	29.38	3	0	99	0	1	106.1	95.7	-9.6	89	3	1,000	100	4.5	0.0
B- / 7.5	11.0	0.98	19.08	35	0	99	0	1	160.5	105.6	-8.2	58	5	1,000	100	5.8	1.0
B- / 7.5	11.0	0.98	18.38	6	0	99	0	1	160.5	100.3	-8.3	48	5	1,000	100	0.0	4.0
B- / 7.5	11.0	0.99	18.38	22	0	99	0	1	160.5	100.5	-8.4	47	5	1,000	100	0.0	1.0
B- / 7.6	11.0	0.99	19.22	5	0	99	0	1	160.5	105.8	-8.0	59	5	1,000	100	0.0	0.0
B- / 7.5	11.0	0.99	18.89	5	0	99	0	1	160.5	104.2	-8.2	55	5	1,000	100	4.5	1.0
B- / 7.7	6.7	0.73	16.85	95	0	99	0	1	1.1	39.4	-9.1	34	9	1,000	100	5.8	1.0
B- / 7.6	6.6	0.72	16.09	39	0	99	0	1	1.1	36.2	-9.3	29	9	1,000	100	0.0	4.0
B- / 7.6	6.7	0.73	16.05	34	0	99	0	1	1.1	36.2	-9.3	28	9	1,000	100	0.0	1.0

	99 Pct = Best 0 Pct = Worst		Overall Weiss Investment Rating		PERFORMANCE						Incl. in Returns	
					Perfor-mance	Total Return % through 6/30/06			Annualized		Dividend	Expense
Fund Type	Fund Name	Ticker Symbol		Phone	Rating/Pts	3 Mo	6 Mo	1Yr / Pct	3Yr / Pct	5Yr / Pct	Yield	Ratio
GR	Dreyfus Premier Tax Mgd Grwth T	DPMTX	D-	(800) 782-6620	E+ / 0.8	0.67	1.97	5.23 /16	6.46 / 8	0.38 /17	0.69	1.50
TC	Dreyfus Premier Tech Growth A	DTGRX	E-	(800) 782-6620	E / 0.3	-8.12	-3.51	7.00 /26	6.91 /10	-3.80 / 4	0.00	1.41
TC	Dreyfus Premier Tech Growth B	DTGBX	E-	(800) 782-6620	E- / 0.2	-8.40	-4.09	5.83 /19	5.82 / 6	-4.73 / 3	0.00	2.52
TC	Dreyfus Premier Tech Growth C	DTGCX	E-	(800) 782-6620	E / 0.4	-8.30	-3.95	5.97 /20	5.88 / 6	-4.68 / 3	0.00	2.44
TC	Dreyfus Premier Tech Growth R	DGVRX	E-	(800) 782-6620	E+ / 0.8	-8.02	-3.38	7.37 /28	7.35 /12	-3.36 / 5	0.00	1.08
TC	Dreyfus Premier Tech Growth T	DPTGX	E-	(800) 782-6620	E / 0.3	-8.24	-3.70	6.57 /24	6.43 / 8	-4.23 / 3	0.00	1.83
GR	Dreyfus Premier Third Century A	DTCAX	E+	(800) 782-6620	E+ / 0.7	-4.51	-1.17	4.57 /13	7.13 /11	-3.03 / 5	0.00	1.51
GR	Dreyfus Premier Third Century B	DTCBX	E+	(800) 782-6620	E+ / 0.6	-4.76	-1.72	3.49 / 9	6.24 / 7	-3.83 / 4	0.00	2.46
GR	Dreyfus Premier Third Century C	DTCCX	E+	(800) 782-6620	E+ / 0.9	-4.63	-1.59	3.61 / 9	6.33 / 8	-3.80 / 4	0.00	2.27
GR	Dreyfus Premier Third Century R	DRTCX	D-	(800) 782-6620	D- / 1.5	-4.45	-0.46	5.23 /16	7.32 /12	-2.77 / 6	0.58	1.24
GR	Dreyfus Premier Third Century T	DTCTX	E+	(800) 782-6620	E+ / 0.6	-4.66	-1.56	3.94 /10	6.72 / 9	-3.47 / 4	0.00	1.94
GR	● Dreyfus Premier Third Century Z	DRTHX	D-	(800) 782-6620	D- / 1.5	-4.46	-1.15	4.64 /13	7.37 /12	-2.85 / 6	0.37	1.18
GR	Dreyfus Premier Value A	DRSIX	D+	(800) 782-6620	C / 4.7	-0.42	4.96	13.75 /67	13.70 /52	4.88 /53	0.63	1.26
GR	Dreyfus Premier Value B	DSTBX	D	(800) 782-6620	C / 4.5	-0.61	4.51	12.81 /63	12.72 /47	3.99 /46	0.00	2.18
GR	Dreyfus Premier Value C	DPVCX	D+	(800) 782-6620	C / 5.0	-0.62	4.47	12.77 /63	12.69 /47	3.96 /46	0.00	2.25
GR	Dreyfus Premier Value R	DPVRX	C-	(800) 782-6620	C+ / 5.7	-0.38	5.06	13.90 /68	13.68 /52	4.67 /52	0.80	1.22
GR	Dreyfus Premier Value T	DTPVX	D	(800) 782-6620	C / 4.5	-0.54	4.71	13.12 /65	12.97 /49	3.97 /46	0.17	2.06
GL	Dreyfus Premier Wrldwde Growth A	PGROX	C	(800) 782-6620	C / 4.3	1.70	6.06	12.54 /62	12.48 /46	3.93 /45	1.44	1.22
GL	Dreyfus Premier Wrldwde Growth B	PGWBX	C	(800) 782-6620	C- / 4.2	1.45	5.56	11.57 /57	11.53 /39	3.12 /38	0.44	2.09
GL	Dreyfus Premier Wrldwde Growth C	PGRCX	C	(800) 782-6620	C / 4.7	1.47	5.64	11.67 /58	11.61 /40	3.17 /38	0.88	1.97
GL	Dreyfus Premier Wrldwde Growth R	DPWRX	C+	(800) 782-6620	C+ / 5.6	1.74	6.19	12.68 /63	12.79 /47	4.24 /48	1.71	0.98
GL	Dreyfus Premier Wrldwde Growth T	DPWTX	C	(800) 782-6620	C / 4.3	1.61	5.89	12.24 /61	12.18 /43	3.70 /43	1.21	1.46
★ IX	Dreyfus S&P 500 Index Fund	PEOPX	C-	(800) 242-8671	C- / 3.6	-1.56	2.48	8.14 /34	10.69 /33	2.00 /27	1.30	0.50
SC	Dreyfus Small Cap Stock Index Fd	DISSX	B+	(800) 242-8671	B / 7.8	-4.60	7.50	13.44 /66	19.93 /79	10.58 /82	0.48	0.50
GR	Dreyfus Socially Resp Growth I		E+	(800) 242-8671	D / 1.6	-4.38	-1.01	4.86 /14	7.57 /13	-2.54 / 6	0.11	0.81
GR	● Dreyfus Socially Resp Growth S		D	(800) 242-8671	D- / 1.4	-4.44	-1.12	4.57 /13	7.32 /12	-2.79 / 6	0.00	1.06
GI	Dreyfus Stock Index Fund I		C+	(800) 242-8671	C- / 4.0	-1.49	2.57	8.38 /36	10.96 /35	2.22 /29	1.66	0.27
GI	Dreyfus Stock Index Fund S		C+	(800) 242-8671	C- / 3.8	-1.55	2.44	8.10 /33	10.68 /33	1.95 /27	1.41	0.52
EM	Driehaus Emerging Markets Growth	DREGX	C+	(800) 560-6111	A+ / 9.9	-1.59	13.86	55.77 /99	38.46 /99	24.86 /98	0.22	2.00
FO	Driehaus International Discovery Fd	DRIDX	B-	(800) 560-6111	A+ / 9.6	-5.11	6.26	42.17 /98	31.09 /96	18.50 /95	7.30	1.77
BA	DWS Balanced Fund A	KTRAX	D+	(800) 621-1048	E+ / 0.6	-1.48	1.53	4.97 /15	6.53 / 8	1.32 /22	2.18	0.68
BA	DWS Balanced Fund AARP	KTRPX	U	(800) 621-1048	U /	-1.54	1.53	5.08 /15	--	--	2.53	0.75
BA	DWS Balanced Fund B	KTRBX	D+	(800) 621-1048	E+ / 0.7	-1.62	1.34	4.59 /13	5.81 / 6	0.55 /18	1.74	0.88
BA	DWS Balanced Fund C	KTRCX	D+	(800) 621-1048	E+ / 0.7	-1.69	1.12	4.12 /11	5.64 / 5	0.46 /17	1.49	0.81
BA	DWS Balanced Fund Inst	KTRIX	C-	(800) 621-1048	D- / 1.3	-1.50	1.70	5.32 /17	6.88 /10	1.65 /25	2.66	0.60
BA	DWS Balanced Fund S	KTRSX	U	(800) 621-1048	U /	-1.43	1.64	5.32 /17	--	--	2.54	0.74
GI	DWS Blue Chip Fund A	KBCAX	C	(800) 621-1048	C / 4.7	-1.87	2.76	10.14 /48	14.40 /56	2.77 /35	0.27	1.19
GI	DWS Blue Chip Fund B	KBCBX	C	(800) 621-1048	C / 4.7	-2.04	2.34	9.21 /41	13.44 /51	1.91 /26	0.00	1.01
GI	DWS Blue Chip Fund C	KBCCX	C	(800) 621-1048	C / 5.1	-1.97	2.42	9.34 /42	13.50 /51	1.95 /27	0.00	1.00
GI	DWS Blue Chip Fund Inst	KBCIX	C+	(800) 621-1048	C+ / 5.8	-1.72	2.97	10.62 /51	14.90 /58	3.21 /39	0.72	0.73
GR	DWS Capital Growth Fund A	SDGAX	D+	(800) 621-1048	D / 1.6	-3.76	-0.92	6.21 /22	8.99 /21	-1.48 /10	0.00	1.06
GR	DWS Capital Growth Fund AARP	ACGFX	C-	(800) 621-1048	D+ / 2.3	-3.71	-0.81	6.46 /23	9.32 /23	-1.20 /11	0.26	0.80
GR	DWS Capital Growth Fund B	SDGBX	D	(800) 621-1048	D- / 1.3	-3.99	-1.40	5.20 /16	8.06 /15	-2.29 / 7	0.00	2.00
GR	DWS Capital Growth Fund C	SDGCX	D+	(800) 621-1048	D / 1.7	-3.94	-1.31	5.31 /17	8.12 /16	-2.25 / 7	0.00	1.94
GR	DWS Capital Growth Fund Inst	SDGTX	C-	(800) 621-1048	D+ / 2.7	-3.67	-0.77	6.59 /24	9.44 /24	--	0.41	0.72
GR	● DWS Capital Growth Fund S	SCGSX	C-	(800) 621-1048	D / 2.2	-3.71	-0.85	6.39 /23	9.23 /22	-1.24 /11	0.15	0.91
EN	DWS Commodity Securities A	SKNRX	U	(800) 621-1048	U /	3.63	8.93	22.36 /85	--	--	0.16	1.51
EN	DWS Commodity Securities C	SKCRX	U	(800) 621-1048	U /	3.49	8.54	21.40 /83	--	--	0.00	2.25
TC	DWS Communication Fund A	TISHX	C	(800) 621-1048	C+ / 6.0	-1.17	4.61	15.97 /75	16.07 /64	-2.02 / 8	0.00	1.64
TC	DWS Communication Fund B	FTEBX	C	(800) 621-1048	C+ / 6.1	-1.32	4.29	15.12 /72	15.20 /60	-2.88 / 6	0.00	2.55
TC	DWS Communication Fund C	FTICX	C+	(800) 621-1048	C+ / 6.3	-1.32	4.28	15.10 /72	15.21 /60	-2.88 / 6	0.00	2.51
TC	DWS Communication Fund Inst	FLICX	C+	(800) 621-1048	C+ / 6.8	-1.06	4.78	16.32 /75	16.38 /65	-1.72 / 9	0.00	1.31

● Denotes fund is closed to new investors
★ Denotes fund is included in Section II

RISK			NET ASSETS		ASSET				Portfolio Turnover Ratio	BULL / BEAR		FUND MANAGER		MINIMUMS		LOADS	
Risk Rating/Pts	3 Year Standard Deviation	Beta	NAV As of 6/30/06	Total $(Mil)	Cash %	Stocks %	Bonds %	Other %		Last Bull Market Return	Last Bear Market Return	Manager Quality Pct	Manager Tenure (Years)	Initial Purch. $	Additional Purch. $	Front End Load	Back End Load
B- / 7.7	6.6	0.73	16.59	3	0	99	0	1	1.1	38.3	-9.2	33	9	1,000	100	4.5	1.0
D+ / 2.5	16.2	1.69	23.08	404	3	96	0	1	47.2	68.2	-13.5	2	9	1,000	100	5.8	1.0
D+ / 2.4	16.2	1.69	21.60	57	3	96	0	1	47.2	63.0	-13.8	1	7	1,000	100	0.0	4.0
D+ / 2.4	16.2	1.69	21.65	54	3	96	0	1	47.2	63.2	-13.7	1	7	1,000	100	0.0	1.0
D+ / 2.6	16.2	1.69	23.74	5	3	96	0	1	47.2	70.4	-13.4	2	7	1,000	100	0.0	0.0
D+ / 2.5	16.2	1.69	22.39	4	3	96	0	1	47.2	65.8	-13.6	2	7	1,000	100	4.5	1.0
C+ / 6.7	8.9	1.08	8.46	12	0	99	0	1	67.2	45.9	-9.9	17	1	1,000	100	5.8	1.0
C+ / 6.6	8.9	1.08	8.01	9	0	99	0	1	67.2	42.2	-10.0	12	1	1,000	100	0.0	4.0
C+ / 6.6	8.9	1.08	8.03	3	0	99	0	1	67.2	42.4	-10.0	13	1	1,000	100	0.0	1.0
C+ / 6.6	9.1	1.11	8.58	1	0	99	0	1	67.2	47.0	-9.8	16	1	1,000	100	0.0	0.0
C+ / 6.6	8.9	1.08	8.18	1	0	99	0	1	67.2	44.3	-10.1	14	1	1,000	100	4.5	1.0
C+ / 6.7	8.9	1.08	8.56	326	0	99	0	1	67.2	46.8	-9.8	18	1	2,500	100	0.0	0.0
C / 5.0	7.9	0.98	19.04	116	0	99	0	1	155.0	76.2	-11.5	80	2	1,000	100	5.8	1.0
C / 4.8	7.9	0.98	17.85	4	0	99	0	1	155.0	71.5	-11.7	73	2	1,000	100	0.0	4.0
C / 4.7	7.9	0.98	17.54	1	0	99	0	1	155.0	71.3	-11.7	73	2	1,000	100	0.0	1.0
C / 4.8	7.9	0.98	18.47	N/A	0	99	0	1	155.0	75.9	-11.6	80	2	1,000	100	0.0	0.0
C / 4.9	8.0	0.98	18.45	N/A	0	99	0	1	155.0	72.3	-11.9	74	2	1,000	100	4.5	1.0
B- / 7.5	8.0	0.66	37.60	530	N/A	100	0	N/A	0.5	65.7	-9.3	22	13	1,000	100	5.8	1.0
B- / 7.5	8.0	0.66	35.72	108	N/A	100	0	N/A	0.5	61.4	-9.5	17	13	1,000	100	0.0	4.0
B- / 7.5	8.1	0.66	35.19	85	N/A	100	0	N/A	0.5	61.8	-9.5	17	11	1,000	100	0.0	1.0
B- / 7.5	8.0	0.66	37.94	1	N/A	100	0	N/A	0.5	67.2	-9.3	24	10	1,000	100	0.0	0.0
B- / 7.5	8.0	0.66	37.20	4	N/A	100	0	N/A	0.5	64.4	-9.4	20	7	1,000	100	4.5	1.0
B- / 7.7	7.7	1.00	37.25	3,368	0	99	0	1	7.2	62.4	-9.8	50	11	2,500	100	0.0	1.0
C+ / 6.8	13.5	0.91	23.04	895	N/A	100	0	N/A	13.6	117.8	-9.7	80	9	2,500	100	0.0	1.0
C+ / 5.6	8.9	1.08	25.79	386	0	99	0	1	56.0	47.8	-9.8	19	N/A	1,000,000	1,000	0.0	0.0
B / 8.0	8.9	1.08	25.61	12	0	99	0	1	56.0	46.7	-9.8	18	1	1,000	100	0.0	0.0
B+ / 9.2	7.7	1.00	32.37	3,497	0	99	0	1	6.1	63.6	-9.8	53	N/A	5,000	500	0.0	0.0
B / 8.8	7.6	1.00	32.38	531	0	99	0	1	6.1	62.3	-9.8	50	N/A	5,000	500	0.0	0.0
C- / 3.0	19.0	1.11	32.21	488	3	96	0	1	349.7	265.2	-4.3	41	9	10,000	2,000	0.0	2.0
C- / 4.2	16.6	1.35	43.78	767	5	94	0	1	180.4	210.7	-3.7	35	8	10,000	2,000	0.0	2.0
B+ / 9.1	5.0	1.03	9.19	1,363	0	42	56	2	158.0	35.7	-5.0	42	4	1,000	50	5.8	2.0
U /	N/A	N/A	9.18	275	0	42	56	2	158.0	N/A	N/A	N/A	N/A	1,000	50	0.0	2.0
B+ / 9.4	5.0	1.03	9.23	85	0	42	56	2	158.0	32.7	-5.2	35	4	1,000	50	0.0	4.0
B+ / 9.4	5.0	1.03	9.17	34	0	42	56	2	158.0	32.1	-5.3	34	4	1,000	50	1.0	2.0
B+ / 9.7	5.0	1.01	9.20	N/A	0	42	56	2	158.0	37.1	-5.0	47	4	1,000,000	0	0.0	2.0
U /	N/A	N/A	9.19	136	0	42	56	2	158.0	N/A	N/A	N/A	N/A	2,500	50	0.0	2.0
B- / 7.4	8.2	1.05	20.47	408	0	98	0	2	329.0	77.2	-9.5	81	3	1,000	50	5.8	2.0
B- / 7.3	8.2	1.05	19.21	78	0	98	0	2	329.0	72.5	-9.7	73	3	1,000	50	0.0	4.0
B- / 7.3	8.2	1.05	19.43	41	0	98	0	2	329.0	72.6	-9.6	73	3	1,000	50	0.0	2.0
B- / 7.4	8.2	1.04	21.15	51	0	98	0	2	329.0	79.5	-9.4	84	3	1,000,000	0	0.0	2.0
B / 8.4	7.8	0.98	46.34	780	1	98	0	1	20.0	54.3	-10.0	34	4	1,000	50	5.8	0.0
B / 8.4	7.8	0.98	46.67	806	1	98	0	1	20.0	55.8	-9.9	37	4	1,000	50	0.0	2.0
B / 8.3	7.9	0.98	44.52	61	1	98	0	1	20.0	50.2	-10.1	28	4	1,000	50	0.0	4.0
B / 8.3	7.8	0.98	44.60	32	1	98	0	1	20.0	50.4	-10.1	28	4	1,000	50	0.0	1.0
B / 8.4	7.9	0.98	46.67	28	1	98	0	1	20.0	56.3	-9.9	38	4	1,000,000	0	0.0	2.0
B / 8.4	7.9	0.98	46.69	90	1	98	0	1	20.0	55.4	-9.9	36	4	2,500	50	0.0	2.0
U /	N/A	N/A	12.56	166	18	47	34	1	76.0	N/A	N/A	N/A	1	1,000	50	5.8	0.0
U /	N/A	N/A	12.46	47	18	47	34	1	76.0	N/A	N/A	N/A	N/A	1,000	50	0.0	2.0
C+ / 6.3	12.1	1.22	20.19	291	0	98	0	2	21.0	102.1	-14.7	81	22	1,000	50	5.8	2.0
C+ / 6.2	12.2	1.22	18.73	15	0	98	0	2	21.0	97.5	-15.5	74	11	1,000	50	0.0	4.0
C+ / 6.2	12.1	1.22	18.75	13	0	98	0	2	21.0	97.5	-15.5	74	11	1,000	50	0.0	2.0
C+ / 6.3	12.1	1.22	20.60	4	0	98	0	2	21.0	103.9	-14.6	83	4	1,000,000	0	0.0	2.0

			Overall Weiss Investment Rating		PERFORMANCE							
99 Pct = Best 0 Pct = Worst					Perfor-mance Rating/Pts	Total Return % through 6/30/06					Incl. in Returns	
									Annualized		Dividend	Expense
Fund Type	Fund Name	Ticker Symbol		Phone		3 Mo	6 Mo	1Yr / Pct	3Yr / Pct	5Yr / Pct	Yield	Ratio
AA	DWS Conserv Alloc Fd A	SUCAX	D+	(800) 621-1048	E+ / 0.8	-0.72	1.90	5.45 /17	6.69 / 9	3.69 /43	2.61	1.10
AA	DWS Conserv Alloc Fd AARP	APWCX	C	(800) 621-1048	D / 1.7	-0.66	2.02	5.72 /19	7.00 /10	3.96 /46	3.03	0.85
AA	DWS Conserv Alloc Fd B	SUCBX	C-	(800) 621-1048	E+ / 0.7	-0.91	1.52	4.66 /14	5.92 / 6	2.91 /36	2.01	1.85
AA	DWS Conserv Alloc Fd C	SUCCX	C-	(800) 621-1048	E+ / 0.9	-0.99	1.52	4.66 /14	5.90 / 6	2.92 /36	1.99	1.85
AA	● DWS Conserv Alloc Fd S	SCPCX	C	(800) 621-1048	D / 1.7	-0.66	2.02	5.72 /19	6.99 /10	3.95 /45	3.03	0.85
GR	DWS Dreman Concen Value A	LOPEX	U	(800) 621-1048	U /	1.28	4.68	9.00 /40	--	--	1.12	1.25
FS	DWS Dreman Financial Srvcs A	KDFAX	D	(800) 621-1048	D / 2.0	-0.34	3.01	6.80 /25	9.23 /22	4.26 /48	1.45	1.61
FS	DWS Dreman Financial Srvcs B	KDFBX	D	(800) 621-1048	D / 1.8	-0.63	2.58	5.92 /20	8.36 /17	3.40 /40	0.75	2.39
FS	DWS Dreman Financial Srvcs C	KDFCX	D+	(800) 621-1048	D / 2.2	-0.58	2.63	5.90 /20	8.38 /17	3.42 /40	0.75	2.39
★ GR	DWS Dreman High Ret Eqty A	KDHAX	C+	(800) 621-1048	C / 4.7	1.04	4.03	9.25 /42	13.84 /53	5.63 /59	1.31	1.12
GR	DWS Dreman High Ret Eqty B	KDHBX	C+	(800) 621-1048	C / 4.6	0.86	3.63	8.40 /36	12.91 /48	4.78 /52	0.58	1.95
GR	DWS Dreman High Ret Eqty C	KDHCX	B-	(800) 621-1048	C / 5.1	0.85	3.67	8.45 /36	12.97 /49	4.83 /53	0.66	1.88
GR	DWS Dreman High Ret Eqty Inst	KDHIX	B+	(800) 621-1048	C+ / 5.9	1.10	4.18	9.59 /44	14.20 /55	--	1.73	0.79
GR	DWS Dreman High Ret Eqty Inv		B+	(800) 621-1048	C+ / 5.8	1.09	4.23	9.62 /44	14.03 /54	5.94 /61	1.71	0.81
GR	DWS Dreman High Ret Eqty R	KDHRX	U	(800) 621-1048	U /	0.98	3.96	9.02 /40	--	--	1.22	1.36
GR	● DWS Dreman High Ret Eqty S	KDHSX	U	(800) 621-1048	U /	1.09	4.20	9.60 /44	--	--	1.69	0.84
SC	DWS Dreman Small Cap Val A	KDSAX	A-	(800) 621-1048	B+ / 8.8	-1.12	13.45	21.19 /83	24.38 /90	14.40 /91	0.94	1.27
SC	DWS Dreman Small Cap Val B	KDSBX	A-	(800) 621-1048	B+ / 8.8	-1.31	12.94	20.08 /82	23.29 /88	13.43 /89	0.00	2.19
SC	DWS Dreman Small Cap Val C	KDSCX	A-	(800) 621-1048	B+ / 8.9	-1.27	13.02	20.31 /82	23.46 /88	13.55 /89	0.00	2.05
SC	DWS Dreman Small Cap Val I		A	(800) 621-1048	B+ / 8.7	-5.24	8.83	16.49 /76	23.06 /87	13.94 /90	0.82	0.91
SC	DWS Dreman Small Cap Val Inst	KDSIX	A	(800) 621-1048	A- / 9.2	-1.02	13.62	21.61 /84	24.86 /91	--	0.80	0.95
SC	DWS Dreman Small Cap Val R	KDSRX	A+	(800) 621-1048	A- / 9.0	-1.16	13.32	20.94 /83	24.11 /90	14.25 /91	0.02	1.60
FO	DWS EAFE Equity Index Fund Inst	BTAEX	A+	(800) 621-1048	B+ / 8.9	0.56	9.89	27.04 /91	23.12 /88	9.23 /77	2.35	0.59
EM	DWS Emerg Mkts Eqty Fd A	SEKAX	C+	(800) 621-1048	A / 9.5	-5.69	4.78	31.17 /95	32.31 /97	19.98 /96	0.00	1.75
EM	DWS Emerg Mkts Eqty Fd AARP	SEMMX	C+	(800) 621-1048	A+ / 9.6	-5.68	4.84	31.35 /95	32.55 /97	20.26 /96	0.00	1.75
EM	DWS Emerg Mkts Eqty Fd B	SEKBX	C+	(800) 621-1048	A / 9.5	-5.89	4.27	30.04 /94	31.22 /96	18.97 /95	0.00	1.75
EM	DWS Emerg Mkts Eqty Fd C	SEKCX	C+	(800) 621-1048	A+ / 9.6	-5.88	4.36	30.10 /94	31.23 /96	19.03 /95	0.00	1.75
EM	● DWS Emerg Mkts Eqty Fd S	SEMGX	C+	(800) 621-1048	A+ / 9.7	-5.64	4.89	31.44 /95	32.58 /97	20.26 /96	0.00	1.75
GR	DWS Enhac S&P 500 Indx A	OUTDX	C-	(800) 621-1048	D+ / 2.3	-1.00	3.14	7.71 /31	10.39 /30	--	0.59	1.25
GR	DWS Enhac S&P 500 Indx AARP	SSLFX	C	(800) 621-1048	C- / 3.5	-0.89	3.29	7.94 /32	10.68 /33	2.05 /28	0.79	1.01
GR	DWS Enhac S&P 500 Indx B	OUTBX	C-	(800) 621-1048	D+ / 2.5	-1.10	2.78	6.89 /26	9.58 /24	--	0.18	2.00
GR	DWS Enhac S&P 500 Indx C	OUTCX	C	(800) 621-1048	D+ / 2.8	-1.18	2.77	6.79 /25	9.57 /24	--	0.18	1.99
GR	● DWS Enhac S&P 500 Indx S	SSFFX	C	(800) 621-1048	C- / 3.5	-0.97	3.29	7.85 /32	10.65 /32	2.03 /28	0.79	1.01
IX	DWS Equity 500 Index Inst	BTIIX	C	(800) 621-1048	C- / 3.7	-1.46	2.68	8.57 /37	11.11 /36	2.39 /31	1.74	0.10
IX	DWS Equity 500 Index Inv	BTIEX	C	(800) 621-1048	C- / 3.6	-1.49	2.60	8.40 /36	10.95 /35	2.25 /30	1.59	0.25
GI	DWS Equity Income A	SDDAX	U	(800) 621-1048	U /	-0.65	4.25	7.25 /28	--	--	2.20	1.34
GI	DWS Equity Income C	SDDCX	U	(800) 621-1048	U /	-0.85	3.91	6.37 /22	--	--	1.54	2.10
GI	DWS Equity Part A	FLEPX	C+	(800) 621-1048	C / 4.5	0.31	4.24	8.87 /39	13.85 /53	5.35 /57	0.42	1.22
GI	DWS Equity Part B	FEPBX	C+	(800) 621-1048	C / 4.6	0.15	3.83	8.10 /33	13.01 /49	4.56 /51	0.00	1.97
GI	DWS Equity Part C	FEPCX	C+	(800) 621-1048	C / 4.9	0.11	3.83	8.06 /33	13.00 /49	4.56 /51	0.00	1.97
GI	DWS Equity Part Inst	FLIPX	B	(800) 621-1048	C+ / 5.6	0.38	4.32	9.12 /41	14.15 /55	5.61 /58	0.69	0.97
FO	DWS Europe Equity Fund A	SERAX	B+	(800) 621-1048	B+ / 8.5	-0.56	14.17	28.40 /93	22.04 /85	7.19 /68	2.16	1.17
FO	DWS Europe Equity Fund AARP	SGEGX	B+	(800) 621-1048	B+ / 8.9	-0.53	14.19	28.46 /93	22.19 /86	7.38 /69	2.28	1.42
FO	DWS Europe Equity Fund B	SERBX	B+	(800) 621-1048	B+ / 8.5	-0.80	13.58	27.06 /91	20.94 /82	6.27 /63	1.37	1.45
FO	DWS Europe Equity Fund C	SERCX	B+	(800) 621-1048	B+ / 8.7	-0.74	13.68	27.24 /92	21.04 /83	6.36 /63	1.48	1.29
FO	● DWS Europe Equity Fund S	SCGEX	B+	(800) 621-1048	B+ / 8.9	-0.53	14.25	28.60 /93	22.26 /86	7.42 /69	2.35	1.28
GL	DWS Global Opportunities Fund A	KGDAX	B	(800) 621-1048	B+ / 8.6	-4.88	6.07	19.93 /82	24.77 /91	10.65 /83	0.40	1.50
GL	DWS Global Opportunities Fund	SGDPX	B+	(800) 621-1048	A- / 9.0	-4.84	6.17	20.23 /82	25.06 /91	10.93 /84	0.65	1.50
GL	DWS Global Opportunities Fund B	KGDBX	B	(800) 621-1048	B+ / 8.6	-5.06	5.66	19.02 /80	23.79 /89	9.78 /80	0.00	1.50
GL	DWS Global Opportunities Fund C	KGDCX	B	(800) 621-1048	B+ / 8.7	-5.04	5.69	19.07 /81	23.82 /89	9.81 /80	0.00	1.50
GL	● DWS Global Opportunities Fund S	SGSCX	B+	(800) 621-1048	A- / 9.0	-4.82	6.25	20.35 /82	25.13 /91	10.96 /84	0.73	1.42
GL	DWS Global Thematic Fund A	SGQAX	A-	(800) 621-1048	B+ / 8.9	-1.77	11.19	33.07 /96	24.15 /90	9.32 /78	0.28	1.59

● Denotes fund is closed to new investors
★ Denotes fund is included in Section II

RISK			NET ASSETS		ASSET				Portfolio Turnover Ratio	BULL / BEAR		FUND MANAGER		MINIMUMS		LOADS	
Risk Rating/Pts	3 Year Standard Deviation	Beta	NAV As of 6/30/06	Total $(Mil)	Cash %	Stocks %	Bonds %	Other %		Last Bull Market Return	Last Bear Market Return	Manager Quality Pct	Manager Tenure (Years)	Initial Purch. $	Additional Purch. $	Front End Load	Back End Load
B+ / 9.5	3.8	0.79	11.90	40	18	46	35	1	82.0	32.7	-2.5	59	N/A	1,000	50	5.8	1.0
B+ / 9.9	3.8	0.79	11.90	49	18	46	35	1	82.0	33.8	-2.4	63	N/A	1,000	50	0.0	0.0
B+ / 9.9	3.8	0.79	11.92	8	18	46	35	1	82.0	29.6	-2.6	50	N/A	1,000	50	0.0	4.0
B+ / 9.9	3.8	0.79	11.91	11	18	46	35	1	82.0	29.7	-2.7	49	N/A	1,000	50	1.0	1.0
B+ / 9.9	3.8	0.79	11.90	31	18	46	35	1	82.0	33.8	-2.4	62	N/A	2,500	50	0.0	0.0
U /	N/A	N/A	10.79	30	0	100	0	0	5.0	N/A	N/A	N/A	N/A	1,000	50	5.8	2.0
C+ / 6.8	9.3	0.96	12.56	68	N/A	99	0	N/A	25.0	56.8	-7.7	22	8	1,000	50	5.8	0.0
B- / 7.5	9.3	0.96	12.44	13	N/A	99	0	N/A	25.0	52.7	-7.9	16	8	1,000	50	0.0	4.0
B- / 7.5	9.3	0.96	12.48	9	N/A	99	0	N/A	25.0	53.0	-7.9	16	8	1,000	50	0.0	1.0
B / 8.7	8.1	0.86	46.81	5,201	10	85	3	2	9.0	75.8	-5.1	88	N/A	1,000	50	5.8	1.0
B / 8.8	8.1	0.86	46.70	729	10	85	3	2	9.0	71.3	-5.3	83	N/A	1,000	50	0.0	4.0
B / 8.7	8.1	0.86	46.74	961	10	85	3	2	9.0	71.7	-5.3	83	N/A	1,000	50	0.0	1.0
B / 8.7	8.0	0.86	46.78	672	10	85	3	2	9.0	77.6	-5.0	89	N/A	1,000,000	0	0.0	0.0
B+ / 9.0	8.0	0.86	46.77	24	10	85	3	2	9.0	76.9	-5.0	89	N/A	1,000	0	0.0	0.0
U /	N/A	N/A	46.74	29	10	85	3	2	9.0	N/A	N/A	N/A	3	0	0	0.0	0.0
U /	N/A	N/A	46.79	135	10	85	3	2	9.0	N/A	N/A	N/A	N/A	2,500	50	0.0	0.0
C+ / 6.8	12.6	0.80	36.46	908	6	94	0	0	67.0	141.7	-4.3	98	4	1,000	50	5.8	2.0
C+ / 6.7	12.6	0.80	33.83	111	6	94	0	0	67.0	135.2	-4.5	97	4	1,000	50	0.0	2.0
C+ / 6.7	12.6	0.80	34.26	211	6	94	0	0	67.0	136.1	-4.5	97	4	1,000	50	0.0	2.0
B- / 7.1	12.8	0.81	36.89	1	6	94	0	0	67.0	134.3	-4.2	96	4	1,000	50	0.0	0.0
C+ / 6.8	12.6	0.80	36.89	58	6	94	0	0	67.0	144.7	-4.3	98	N/A	1,000,000	0	0.0	0.0
B- / 7.5	12.6	0.80	36.86	7	6	94	0	0	67.0	140.2	-4.3	98	4	0	0	0.0	2.0
B- / 7.7	9.9	0.98	14.45	333	3	96	0	1	16.0	126.2	-9.5	48	N/A	1,000,000	0	0.0	2.0
C- / 3.1	17.7	1.07	22.56	84	2	96	0	2	126.0	216.5	-6.0	15	5	1,000	50	5.8	2.0
C- / 3.1	17.7	1.07	22.75	14	2	96	0	2	126.0	218.5	-5.8	16	6	1,000	50	0.0	2.0
C- / 3.1	17.7	1.07	21.72	6	2	96	0	2	126.0	208.6	-6.2	11	5	1,000	50	0.0	4.0
C- / 3.1	17.7	1.07	21.77	11	2	96	0	2	126.0	208.5	-6.1	11	5	1,000	50	0.0	1.0
C- / 3.1	17.7	1.07	22.74	183	2	96	0	2	126.0	218.6	-5.9	16	10	2,500	50	0.0	2.0
B / 8.6	7.7	0.99	12.80	32	0	98	0	2	85.0	59.9	-9.9	47	N/A	1,000	50	5.8	2.0
B / 8.9	7.7	1.00	12.71	5	0	98	0	2	85.0	61.1	-9.8	50	N/A	1,000	50	0.0	2.0
B / 8.9	7.7	0.99	12.58	12	0	98	0	2	85.0	56.1	-10.1	38	N/A	1,000	50	0.0	4.0
B / 8.9	7.7	1.00	12.60	9	0	98	0	2	85.0	56.3	-10.1	38	N/A	1,000	50	0.0	2.0
B / 8.9	7.6	0.99	12.70	35	0	98	0	2	85.0	61.0	-9.8	50	N/A	2,500	50	0.0	2.0
B / 8.6	7.6	1.00	143.86	1,833	0	98	0	2	9.0	64.2	-9.8	55	7	1,000,000	0	0.0	2.0
B / 8.6	7.7	1.00	142.38	748	0	98	0	2	9.0	63.5	-9.8	53	7	1,000	50	0.0	2.0
U /	N/A	N/A	11.91	69	2	88	10	0	28.0	N/A	N/A	N/A	3	1,000	50	5.8	2.0
U /	N/A	N/A	11.91	40	2	88	10	0	28.0	N/A	N/A	N/A	3	1,000	50	0.0	2.0
B / 8.6	8.5	0.97	29.03	251	6	94	0	0	11.0	80.3	-10.3	82	11	1,000	50	5.8	2.0
B / 8.6	8.5	0.97	27.38	8	6	94	0	0	11.0	76.1	-10.5	76	11	1,000	50	0.0	4.0
B / 8.6	8.5	0.96	27.37	13	6	94	0	0	11.0	76.0	-10.5	76	11	1,000	50	0.0	2.0
B / 8.6	8.5	0.96	29.25	161	6	94	0	0	11.0	81.7	-10.3	84	11	1,000,000	0	0.0	2.0
C+ / 6.2	11.7	1.03	34.01	133	0	100	0	0	168.0	130.7	-12.0	29	N/A	1,000	50	5.8	2.0
C+ / 6.3	11.7	1.03	34.03	6	0	100	0	0	168.0	131.7	-12.0	30	N/A	1,000	50	0.0	2.0
C+ / 6.2	11.7	1.03	33.53	8	0	100	0	0	168.0	124.3	-12.2	23	N/A	1,000	50	0.0	4.0
C+ / 6.2	11.7	1.03	33.58	7	0	100	0	0	168.0	124.8	-12.2	24	N/A	1,000	50	1.0	1.0
C+ / 6.3	11.7	1.03	34.08	363	0	100	0	0	168.0	132.0	-12.0	31	N/A	2,500	50	0.0	2.0
C+ / 5.8	12.4	1.11	40.57	202	0	98	0	2	12.0	157.4	-6.7	35	8	1,000	50	5.8	2.0
C+ / 5.8	12.4	1.11	41.48	11	0	98	0	2	12.0	159.3	-6.7	37	5	1,000	50	0.0	2.0
C+ / 5.8	12.4	1.11	37.90	37	0	98	0	2	12.0	151.2	-7.0	29	8	1,000	50	0.0	4.0
C+ / 5.8	12.4	1.11	38.06	32	0	98	0	2	12.0	151.2	-7.0	29	8	1,000	50	1.0	1.0
C+ / 5.8	12.4	1.11	41.50	412	0	98	0	2	12.0	159.8	-6.7	37	15	2,500	50	0.0	2.0
C+ / 6.5	11.5	1.04	33.78	83	5	94	0	1	133.0	127.8	-5.3	42	N/A	1,000	50	5.8	2.0

						PERFORMANCE						
								Total Return % through 6/30/06			Incl. in Returns	
99 Pct = Best			Overall Weiss		Perfor-				Annualized		Dividend	Expense
0 Pct = Worst		Ticker	Investment		mance						Yield	Ratio
Fund Type	Fund Name	Symbol	Rating	Phone	Rating/Pts	3 Mo	6 Mo	1Yr / Pct	3Yr / Pct	5Yr / Pct		
GL	DWS Global Thematic Fund AARP	ACOBX	A	(800) 621-1048	A- / 9.2	-1.75	11.30	33.36 /96	24.45 /90	9.58 /79	0.55	1.37
GL	DWS Global Thematic Fund B	SGQBX	A-	(800) 621-1048	B+ / 8.9	-2.03	10.66	31.89 /96	23.13 /88	8.43 /74	0.00	2.47
GL	DWS Global Thematic Fund C	SGQCX	A-	(800) 621-1048	A- / 9.0	-1.97	10.79	32.09 /96	23.21 /88	8.47 /74	0.00	2.39
GL	● DWS Global Thematic Fund S	SCOBX	A	(800) 621-1048	A- / 9.2	-1.72	11.36	33.54 /96	24.58 /90	9.65 /79	0.76	1.27
PM	DWS Gold & Prec Metals Fund A	SGDAX	D+	(800) 621-1048	A+ / 9.8	1.53	19.98	57.64 /99	34.79 /98	34.41 /99	1.18	1.50
PM	DWS Gold & Prec Metals Fund AARP	SGLDX	D+	(800) 621-1048	A+ / 9.9	1.57	20.16	57.98 /99	35.10 /98	34.70 /99	1.43	1.40
PM	DWS Gold & Prec Metals Fund B	SGDBX	D+	(800) 621-1048	A+ / 9.8	1.32	19.54	56.42 /99	33.76 /97	33.35 /99	0.65	1.38
PM	DWS Gold & Prec Metals Fund C	SGDCX	D+	(800) 621-1048	A+ / 9.9	1.32	19.57	56.47 /99	33.80 /97	33.38 /99	0.67	1.38
PM	● DWS Gold & Prec Metals Fund S	SCGDX	D+	(800) 621-1048	A+ / 9.9	1.61	20.13	58.04 /99	35.10 /98	34.68 /99	1.45	1.37
GI	DWS Growth & Income A	SUWAX	D	(800) 621-1048	D / 1.6	-3.10	-0.38	5.80 /19	9.56 /24	0.89 /20	0.53	0.99
★ GI	DWS Growth & Income AARP	ACDGX	C-	(800) 621-1048	C- / 3.0	-3.03	-0.18	6.17 /21	9.98 /27	1.25 /22	0.94	0.64
GI	DWS Growth & Income B	SUWBX	D	(800) 621-1048	D / 1.6	-3.34	-0.85	4.79 /14	8.59 /18	0.04 /15	0.00	1.97
GI	DWS Growth & Income C	SUWCX	D	(800) 621-1048	D / 2.0	-3.25	-0.70	4.98 /15	8.68 /19	0.08 /16	0.00	1.78
GI	DWS Growth & Income Inst	SUWIX	D+	(800) 621-1048	D+ / 2.7	-2.98	-0.16	6.25 /22	10.06 /28	--	1.01	0.58
GI	● DWS Growth & Income S	SCDGX	D+	(800) 621-1048	D+ / 2.6	-3.03	-0.19	6.16 /21	9.93 /27	1.21 /22	0.92	0.67
GR	DWS Growth Alloc Fd A	SUPAX	C	(800) 621-1048	D+ / 2.9	-1.55	2.87	8.63 /38	11.05 /36	2.50 /32	1.85	1.12
GR	DWS Growth Alloc Fd AARP	APWGX	C+	(800) 621-1048	C / 4.3	-1.55	3.02	8.90 /39	11.30 /38	2.73 /34	2.22	0.87
GR	DWS Growth Alloc Fd B	SUPBX	C	(800) 621-1048	D+ / 2.8	-1.70	2.52	7.86 /32	10.24 /29	1.73 /25	1.21	1.87
GR	DWS Growth Alloc Fd C	SUPCX	C+	(800) 621-1048	C- / 3.3	-1.77	2.52	7.86 /32	10.23 /29	1.71 /25	1.21	1.87
GR	● DWS Growth Alloc Fd S	SPGRX	C+	(800) 621-1048	C- / 3.9	-1.48	3.02	8.97 /40	11.33 /38	2.75 /34	2.22	0.87
HL	DWS Health Care Fund A	SUHAX	E+	(800) 621-1048	E+ / 0.7	-6.43	-3.26	3.45 / 9	8.33 /17	2.72 /34	0.00	1.39
HL	DWS Health Care Fund AARP	SHCAX	D-	(800) 621-1048	D- / 1.5	-6.39	-3.14	3.67 / 9	8.53 /18	2.94 /36	0.00	1.36
HL	DWS Health Care Fund B	SUHBX	E+	(800) 621-1048	E+ / 0.8	-6.60	-3.66	2.58 / 6	7.39 /12	1.83 /26	0.00	1.41
HL	DWS Health Care Fund C	SUHCX	E+	(800) 621-1048	D- / 1.0	-6.59	-3.57	2.67 / 6	7.45 /12	1.85 /26	0.00	1.41
HL	DWS Health Care Fund Inst	SUHIX	D-	(800) 621-1048	D / 1.6	-6.34	-3.08	3.81 /10	8.67 /19	3.10 /38	0.00	1.30
HL	● DWS Health Care Fund S	SCHLX	D-	(800) 621-1048	D / 1.7	-6.35	-3.14	3.71 / 9	8.56 /18	2.93 /36	0.00	1.33
FO	DWS International Fd A	SUIAX	B-	(800) 621-1048	B / 8.2	-1.19	9.50	27.56 /92	21.25 /83	6.60 /65	1.49	1.26
FO	DWS International Fd AARP	AINTX	B	(800) 621-1048	B+ / 8.6	-1.16	9.54	27.62 /92	21.37 /83	6.76 /65	1.59	1.19
FO	DWS International Fd B	SUIBX	B-	(800) 621-1048	B / 8.1	-1.45	8.91	26.14 /90	20.07 /79	5.64 /59	0.61	2.37
FO	DWS International Fd C	SUICX	B	(800) 621-1048	B+ / 8.3	-1.38	9.08	26.48 /90	20.22 /80	5.72 /59	0.72	2.12
FO	DWS International Fd Inst	SUIIX	B	(800) 621-1048	B+ / 8.7	-1.11	9.67	28.02 /93	21.83 /85	7.12 /67	2.03	0.95
FO	● DWS International Fd S	SCINX	B	(800) 621-1048	B+ / 8.6	-1.11	9.66	27.93 /93	21.67 /84	6.93 /66	1.91	0.98
FO	DWS Internatl Eqty A	DBAIX	B+	(800) 621-1048	B / 8.2	-1.21	9.42	27.27 /92	21.25 /83	6.59 /65	1.47	1.50
FO	DWS Internatl Eqty B	DBBIX	B+	(800) 621-1048	B / 8.2	-1.37	9.06	26.41 /90	20.33 /81	5.81 /60	0.86	2.25
FO	DWS Internatl Eqty C	DBCIX	B+	(800) 621-1048	B / 8.2	-1.39	9.00	26.24 /90	20.29 /80	5.81 /60	0.85	2.25
FO	● DWS Internatl Eqty Inst	BEIIX	B+	(800) 621-1048	B+ / 8.7	-1.02	9.90	28.08 /93	21.96 /85	7.49 /69	6.15	0.95
FO	DWS Internatl Eqty Inv	BTEQX	B+	(800) 621-1048	B+ / 8.5	-1.21	9.43	27.29 /92	21.20 /83	6.61 /65	1.56	1.50
FO	DWS Internatl Sel Eqty A	DBISX	B	(800) 621-1048	B+ / 8.4	-1.57	9.59	27.16 /92	22.27 /86	9.24 /78	2.44	1.42
FO	DWS Internatl Sel Eqty B	DBIBX	B	(800) 621-1048	B+ / 8.3	-1.77	9.08	26.18 /90	21.33 /83	8.34 /73	2.04	2.25
FO	DWS Internatl Sel Eqty C	DBICX	B	(800) 621-1048	B+ / 8.4	-1.85	9.09	26.08 /90	21.35 /83	8.29 /73	2.02	2.16
FO	DWS Internatl Sel Eqty Inst	MGINX	C-	(800) 621-1048	B+ / 8.7	-1.53	9.59	27.37 /92	22.53 /86	9.37 /78	2.58	1.02
FO	DWS Internatl Sel Eqty Inv	MGIVX	C-	(800) 621-1048	B+ / 8.9	-1.60	9.51	29.53 /94	23.03 /87	9.55 /79	2.55	1.17
FO	DWS Internatl Sel Eqty Prem	MGIPX	C-	(800) 621-1048	B+ / 8.8	-1.52	9.68	27.68 /92	22.79 /87	9.63 /79	2.89	0.90
FO	DWS Japan Equity A	FJEAX	B-	(800) 621-1048	B+ / 8.9	-7.89	-0.86	42.03 /98	25.63 /92	8.49 /74	0.00	1.75
FO	DWS Japan Equity B	FJEBX	B-	(800) 621-1048	B+ / 8.9	-8.03	-1.26	40.97 /98	24.71 /90	7.71 /70	0.00	2.50
FO	DWS Japan Equity C	FJECX	B-	(800) 621-1048	B+ / 8.9	-8.03	-1.21	41.07 /98	24.76 /91	7.71 /70	0.00	2.50
FO	● DWS Japan Equity S	FJESX	B-	(800) 621-1048	A- / 9.2	-7.83	-0.75	42.39 /98	25.96 /92	--	0.00	1.15
GR	DWS Large Cap Value Fund A	KDCAX	C-	(800) 621-1048	D+ / 2.6	-0.56	3.88	8.00 /33	10.74 /33	5.04 /55	1.32	1.05
GR	DWS Large Cap Value Fund AARP	KDCPX	U	(800) 621-1048	U /	-0.52	3.96	8.17 /34	--	--	1.54	0.89
GR	DWS Large Cap Value Fund B	KDCBX	C-	(800) 621-1048	D+ / 2.7	-0.77	3.44	7.11 /27	9.86 /26	4.20 /48	0.56	1.89
GR	DWS Large Cap Value Fund C	KDCCX	C-	(800) 621-1048	C- / 3.1	-0.74	3.49	7.21 /27	9.92 /27	4.23 /48	0.66	1.81
GR	DWS Large Cap Value Fund Inst	KDCIX	C	(800) 621-1048	C- / 3.7	-0.46	4.03	8.41 /36	10.87 /34	5.30 /56	1.76	0.65

● Denotes fund is closed to new investors
★ Denotes fund is included in Section II

Risk Rating/Pts	Standard Deviation	Beta	NAV As of 6/30/06	Total $(Mil)	Cash %	Stocks %	Bonds %	Other %	Portfolio Turnover Ratio	Last Bull Market Return	Last Bear Market Return	Manager Quality Pct	Manager Tenure (Years)	Initial Purch. $	Additional Purch. $	Front End Load	Back End Load
C+ / 6.5	11.5	1.04	33.78	134	5	94	0	1	133.0	129.7	-5.2	45	N/A	1,000	50	0.0	2.0
C+ / 6.4	11.5	1.04	33.32	12	5	94	0	1	133.0	122.1	-5.4	34	N/A	1,000	50	0.0	4.0
C+ / 6.4	11.5	1.04	33.36	26	5	94	0	1	133.0	122.4	-5.4	34	N/A	1,000	50	1.0	1.0
C+ / 6.5	11.5	1.04	33.73	986	5	94	0	1	133.0	130.3	-5.2	47	N/A	2,500	50	0.0	2.0
E- / 0.0	35.1	1.57	23.30	188	0	98	0	2	53.0	188.0	20.4	69	5	1,000	50	5.8	2.0
E- / 0.0	35.0	1.57	23.36	33	0	98	0	2	53.0	190.0	20.5	71	5	1,000	50	0.0	2.0
E- / 0.0	35.1	1.57	23.06	47	0	98	0	2	53.0	181.2	20.0	61	5	1,000	50	0.0	4.0
E- / 0.0	35.1	1.57	23.03	101	0	98	0	2	53.0	181.3	20.2	61	5	1,000	50	0.0	1.0
E- / 0.0	35.1	1.57	23.33	276	0	98	0	2	53.0	190.1	20.3	71	5	2,500	50	0.0	2.0
B- / 7.5	8.1	1.04	21.51	79	0	99	0	1	102.0	57.6	-9.8	35	N/A	1,000	50	5.8	2.0
B- / 7.5	8.1	1.03	21.67	2,298	0	99	0	1	102.0	59.6	-9.7	39	N/A	1,000	50	0.0	0.0
B- / 7.4	8.1	1.03	21.10	15	0	99	0	1	102.0	53.2	-9.9	28	N/A	1,000	50	0.0	4.0
B- / 7.4	8.1	1.03	21.15	9	0	99	0	1	102.0	53.6	-10.0	29	N/A	1,000	50	0.0	1.0
B- / 7.5	8.1	1.03	21.66	44	0	99	0	1	102.0	59.9	-9.7	39	N/A	1,000,000	0	0.0	2.0
B- / 7.5	8.1	1.03	21.64	1,972	0	99	0	1	102.0	59.3	-9.7	38	N/A	2,500	50	0.0	2.0
B+ / 9.2	6.6	0.85	13.96	83	9	77	12	2	57.0	60.5	-8.1	69	N/A	1,000	50	5.8	1.0
B+ / 9.2	6.6	0.85	13.98	62	9	77	12	2	57.0	61.8	-8.0	70	N/A	1,000	50	0.0	0.0
B+ / 9.2	6.6	0.85	13.84	29	9	77	12	2	57.0	56.7	-8.3	61	N/A	1,000	50	0.0	4.0
B+ / 9.1	6.6	0.85	13.84	34	9	77	12	2	57.0	56.8	-8.3	60	N/A	1,000	50	0.0	1.0
B+ / 9.2	6.6	0.85	13.99	92	9	77	12	2	57.0	61.8	-8.1	71	N/A	2,500	50	0.0	2.0
C+ / 6.2	9.2	0.72	23.72	37	2	98	0	0	61.0	56.5	-3.6	52	6	1,000	50	5.8	2.0
C+ / 6.2	9.2	0.72	24.03	36	2	98	0	0	61.0	57.5	-3.5	55	6	1,000	50	0.0	2.0
C+ / 6.1	9.2	0.72	22.63	13	2	98	0	0	61.0	52.2	-3.8	41	6	1,000	50	0.0	4.0
C+ / 6.1	9.2	0.71	22.69	8	2	98	0	0	61.0	52.5	-3.8	42	6	1,000	50	1.0	1.0
C+ / 6.3	9.2	0.72	24.24	3	2	98	0	0	61.0	58.0	-3.5	57	6	1,000,000	0	0.0	2.0
C+ / 6.2	9.2	0.72	24.04	127	2	98	0	0	61.0	57.5	-3.5	56	6	2,500	50	0.0	1.0
C+ / 5.8	11.2	1.07	54.99	237	0	99	0	1	61.0	116.6	-10.3	19	1	1,000	50	5.8	2.0
C+ / 5.8	11.2	1.07	55.21	32	0	99	0	1	61.0	117.4	-10.3	19	1	1,000	50	0.0	2.0
C+ / 5.7	11.2	1.07	54.26	29	0	99	0	1	61.0	110.2	-10.5	14	1	1,000	50	0.0	4.0
C+ / 5.8	11.2	1.07	54.30	23	0	99	0	1	61.0	110.9	-10.5	14	1	1,000	50	1.0	1.0
C+ / 5.8	11.2	1.07	55.03	6	0	99	0	1	61.0	120.1	-10.2	22	1	1,000,000	0	0.0	2.0
C+ / 5.8	11.2	1.07	55.28	1,331	0	99	0	1	61.0	119.0	-10.3	21	1	2,500	50	0.0	2.0
C+ / 6.5	11.8	1.13	14.64	7	1	98	0	1	54.0	118.3	-9.4	13	N/A	1,000	50	5.8	2.0
C+ / 6.4	11.8	1.13	14.44	1	1	98	0	1	54.0	112.9	-10.4	10	N/A	1,000	50	0.0	4.0
C+ / 6.4	11.8	1.13	14.17	1	1	98	0	1	54.0	113.2	-10.5	9	N/A	1,000	50	1.0	2.0
C+ / 6.5	11.8	1.13	13.65	6	1	98	0	1	54.0	123.0	-10.1	16	N/A	1,000,000	0	0.0	2.0
C+ / 6.5	11.8	1.13	28.56	302	1	98	0	1	54.0	118.0	-10.3	12	N/A	1,000	50	0.0	2.0
C+ / 6.0	11.5	1.09	12.38	76	1	98	0	1	122.0	125.0	-12.6	22	N/A	1,000	50	5.8	2.0
C+ / 6.0	11.4	1.09	12.08	10	1	98	0	1	122.0	120.0	-12.7	17	N/A	1,000	50	0.0	4.0
C+ / 6.0	11.5	1.09	12.07	15	1	98	0	1	122.0	119.8	-12.8	17	N/A	1,000	50	1.0	2.0
D / 1.9	11.5	1.09	12.15	104	1	98	0	1	122.0	126.6	-12.6	23	N/A	1,000,000	0	0.0	2.0
D / 1.9	11.6	1.11	12.13	36	1	98	0	1	122.0	129.6	-12.7	23	N/A	1,000	50	0.0	2.0
D / 1.9	11.5	1.09	12.16	9	1	98	0	1	122.0	128.3	-12.6	25	N/A	5,000,000	1,000,000	0.0	2.0
C / 4.9	17.7	1.16	17.28	72	1	98	0	1	103.0	131.6	-5.7	32	N/A	1,000	50	5.8	2.0
C / 4.9	17.8	1.16	17.19	14	1	98	0	1	103.0	126.2	-5.8	26	N/A	1,000	50	0.0	4.0
C / 4.9	17.7	1.16	17.19	60	1	98	0	1	103.0	126.1	-5.8	26	N/A	1,000	50	1.0	2.0
C / 4.9	17.7	1.16	17.31	67	1	98	0	1	103.0	133.4	-5.6	33	N/A	2,500	50	0.0	2.0
B- / 7.9	7.9	0.98	22.33	338	4	95	0	1	56.0	63.7	-8.8	52	9	1,000	50	5.8	2.0
U /	N/A	N/A	22.32	26	4	95	0	1	56.0	N/A	N/A	N/A	2	1,000	50	0.0	0.0
B / 8.1	7.9	0.99	22.37	39	4	95	0	1	56.0	59.6	-9.0	42	9	1,000	50	0.0	4.0
B / 8.1	7.9	0.99	22.36	36	4	95	0	1	56.0	59.9	-9.0	42	9	1,000	50	0.0	2.0
B / 8.1	8.0	0.99	22.35	49	4	95	0	1	56.0	64.4	-8.6	53	6	1,000,000	0	0.0	2.0

Fund Type	Fund Name	Ticker Symbol	Overall Weiss Investment Rating	Phone	Performance Rating/Pts	3 Mo	6 Mo	1Yr / Pct	3Yr / Pct	5Yr / Pct	Dividend Yield	Expense Ratio
GR	DWS Large Cap Value Fund S	KDCSX	U	(800) 621-1048	U /	-0.47	4.07	8.39 /36	--	--	1.74	0.68
GR	DWS Large Company Growth A	SGGAX	D	(800) 621-1048	E+ / 0.9	-4.21	-1.68	5.93 /20	7.79 /14	-2.73 / 6	0.27	1.34
GR	DWS Large Company Growth AARP	SLGRX	D	(800) 621-1048	D / 1.6	-4.12	-1.54	6.20 /22	8.05 /15	-2.48 / 7	0.47	1.06
GR	DWS Large Company Growth B	SGGBX	D-	(800) 621-1048	E+ / 0.9	-4.38	-2.03	5.17 /16	6.95 /10	-3.48 / 4	0.00	2.21
GR	DWS Large Company Growth C	SGGCX	D	(800) 621-1048	D- / 1.2	-4.37	-2.03	5.16 /16	6.96 /10	-3.45 / 4	0.00	2.21
GR	DWS Large Company Growth Inst	SGGIX	D+	(800) 621-1048	D / 2.0	-4.10	-1.46	6.41 /23	8.25 /16	-2.31 / 7	0.74	0.91
GR	● DWS Large Company Growth S	SCQGX	D	(800) 621-1048	D / 1.6	-4.15	-1.58	6.15 /21	8.03 /15	-2.49 / 7	0.47	1.06
FO	DWS Latin America Eq Fund A	SLANX	C-	(800) 621-1048	A+ / 9.9	-3.37	12.36	52.33 /99	43.41 /99	21.67 /97	0.83	1.83
FO	DWS Latin America Eq Fund AARP	SLAMX	C-	(800) 621-1048	A+ / 9.9	-3.33	12.49	52.61 /99	43.70 /99	22.00 /98	1.64	1.64
FO	DWS Latin America Eq Fund B	SLAOX	C-	(800) 621-1048	A+ / 9.9	-3.62	11.87	51.00 /99	42.21 /99	20.70 /97	0.04	2.74
FO	DWS Latin America Eq Fund C	SLAPX	C-	(800) 621-1048	A+ / 9.9	-3.58	11.93	51.13 /99	42.29 /99	20.69 /97	0.16	2.62
FO	● DWS Latin America Eq Fund S	SLAFX	C-	(800) 621-1048	A+ / 9.9	-3.34	12.48	52.65 /99	43.72 /99	21.97 /98	1.07	1.60
AA	DWS Lifecycle Long Range Inst	BTAMX	C	(800) 621-1048	D+ / 2.5	-0.67	2.09	6.53 /23	8.56 /18	4.24 /48	2.63	0.55
AA	DWS Lifecycle Long Range Inv	BTILX	C	(800) 621-1048	D / 2.2	-0.83	1.81	6.01 /20	8.03 /15	3.76 /43	2.18	1.00
SC	DWS Micro Cap Fd A	SMFAX	D-	(800) 621-1048	C / 5.0	-10.32	2.73	9.40 /43	15.80 /63	4.68 /52	0.00	1.74
SC	DWS Micro Cap Fd B	SMFBX	D-	(800) 621-1048	C / 5.3	-10.55	2.24	8.48 /37	14.90 /58	3.88 /45	0.00	2.49
SC	DWS Micro Cap Fd C	SMFCX	D-	(800) 621-1048	C / 5.2	-10.50	2.30	8.58 /37	14.92 /58	3.89 /45	0.00	2.49
SC	DWS Micro Cap Fd Inst	MGMCX	D	(800) 621-1048	C+ / 5.9	-10.25	2.81	9.65 /44	16.06 /64	4.91 /53	0.00	1.49
SC	DWS Micro Cap Fd Inv	MMFSX	D	(800) 621-1048	C+ / 5.8	-10.33	2.68	9.36 /42	15.79 /63	4.66 /51	0.00	1.74
MC	DWS Mid Cap Growth A	SMCAX	D	(800) 621-1048	C- / 3.5	-9.47	1.17	8.94 /40	13.30 /50	3.34 /40	0.00	1.25
MC	DWS Mid Cap Growth B	SMCBX	D	(800) 621-1048	C- / 3.9	-9.68	0.73	8.08 /33	12.43 /45	2.50 /32	0.00	2.00
MC	DWS Mid Cap Growth C	SMCCX	D	(800) 621-1048	C- / 3.7	-9.62	0.73	8.08 /33	12.43 /45	2.50 /32	0.00	2.00
MC	DWS Mid Cap Growth Inst	BTEAX	D+	(800) 621-1048	C / 4.6	-9.44	1.22	9.18 /41	13.57 /52	3.59 /42	0.00	1.00
MC	DWS Mid Cap Growth Inv	BTCAX	D+	(800) 621-1048	C / 4.5	-9.41	1.17	8.94 /40	13.29 /50	3.35 /40	0.00	1.12
MC	DWS Mid Cap Growth S	SMCSX	U	(800) 621-1048	U /	-9.40	1.23	9.08 /41	--	--	0.00	1.05
BA	DWS Moderate Alloc Fd A	SPDAX	C-	(800) 621-1048	D- / 1.4	-1.28	2.11	6.59 /24	8.67 /19	3.13 /38	2.58	0.64
BA	DWS Moderate Alloc Fd AARP	SPWBX	C	(800) 621-1048	D+ / 2.4	-1.20	2.28	6.87 /25	9.00 /21	3.37 /40	3.09	0.81
BA	DWS Moderate Alloc Fd B	SPDBX	C-	(800) 621-1048	D- / 1.5	-1.46	1.73	5.78 /19	7.85 /14	2.33 /30	1.97	1.39
BA	DWS Moderate Alloc Fd C	SPDCX	C-	(800) 621-1048	D / 1.8	-1.45	1.74	5.81 /19	7.87 /14	2.34 /30	2.01	1.39
BA	● DWS Moderate Alloc Fd S	SPBAX	C	(800) 621-1048	D+ / 2.4	-1.22	2.24	6.78 /25	8.91 /20	3.34 /40	3.00	0.87
FO	DWS Pacific Opp Eq A	SPAOX	B	(800) 621-1048	A- / 9.2	-1.96	9.50	30.39 /95	27.23 /93	15.34 /92	0.72	1.90
FO	DWS Pacific Opp Eq AARP	SPOPX	B	(800) 621-1048	A / 9.3	-1.89	9.67	30.70 /95	27.50 /93	15.62 /93	0.84	1.75
FO	DWS Pacific Opp Eq B	SBPOX	B	(800) 621-1048	A- / 9.2	-2.16	8.99	29.28 /94	26.19 /92	14.40 /91	0.00	2.74
FO	DWS Pacific Opp Eq C	SPCCX	B	(800) 621-1048	A- / 9.2	-2.16	9.11	29.43 /94	26.19 /92	14.42 /91	0.00	2.75
FO	● DWS Pacific Opp Eq S	SCOPX	B	(800) 621-1048	A / 9.3	-1.89	9.62	30.71 /95	27.51 /94	15.62 /93	0.95	1.63
RE	DWS RREEF Real Est Sec A	RRRAX	C+	(800) 621-1048	A- / 9.1	-0.64	13.66	19.04 /81	26.57 /93	21.45 /97	2.61	1.07
RE	DWS RREEF Real Est Sec B	RRRBX	C+	(800) 621-1048	A- / 9.1	-0.87	13.19	17.99 /79	25.41 /91	20.35 /96	1.93	1.78
RE	DWS RREEF Real Est Sec C	RRRCX	B-	(800) 621-1048	A- / 9.1	-0.88	13.23	18.05 /79	25.54 /92	20.46 /96	2.04	1.75
RE	DWS RREEF Real Est Sec Inst	RRRRX	B-	(800) 621-1048	A / 9.3	-0.62	13.82	19.37 /81	26.91 /93	21.42 /97	3.00	0.67
IX	DWS S&P 500 Index Fund A	SXPAX	U	(800) 621-1048	U /	-1.66	2.32	7.90 /32	--	--	1.16	0.66
IX	DWS S&P 500 Index Fund AARP	ASPIX	C	(800) 621-1048	C- / 3.5	-1.61	2.50	8.14 /34	10.72 /33	2.05 /28	1.44	0.48
IX	● DWS S&P 500 Index Fund S	SCPIX	C	(800) 621-1048	C- / 3.5	-1.55	2.50	8.14 /34	10.72 /33	2.07 /28	1.44	0.48
SC	DWS Small Cap Core A	SZCAX	D-	(800) 621-1048	C+ / 5.7	-5.61	6.08	8.46 /36	16.72 /67	10.37 /82	0.00	1.55
SC	DWS Small Cap Core AARP	ASCSX	D	(800) 621-1048	C+ / 6.5	-5.53	6.22	8.79 /39	16.95 /68	10.63 /83	0.00	1.29
SC	DWS Small Cap Core B	SZCBX	D-	(800) 621-1048	C+ / 5.7	-5.82	5.62	7.51 /29	15.75 /62	9.44 /78	0.00	2.35
SC	DWS Small Cap Core C	SZCCX	D-	(800) 621-1048	C+ / 6.0	-5.76	5.71	7.68 /30	15.84 /63	9.49 /79	0.00	2.35
SC	● DWS Small Cap Core S	SSLCX	D	(800) 621-1048	C+ / 6.6	-5.55	6.25	8.90 /39	17.07 /68	10.68 /83	0.00	1.19
SC	DWS Small Cap Growth Fund A	SSDAX	D	(800) 621-1048	C- / 4.0	-7.49	3.20	9.41 /43	13.67 /52	1.47 /23	0.00	1.25
SC	DWS Small Cap Growth Fund B	SSDBX	D	(800) 621-1048	C / 4.4	-7.68	2.82	8.59 /37	12.83 /48	0.71 /19	0.00	2.00
SC	DWS Small Cap Growth Fund C	SSDCX	D	(800) 621-1048	C- / 4.2	-7.68	2.82	8.59 /37	12.81 /48	0.71 /19	0.00	2.00
SC	DWS Small Cap Growth Fund Inv	BTSCX	D+	(800) 621-1048	C / 4.9	-7.49	3.24	9.41 /43	13.69 /52	1.47 /23	0.00	1.12
SC	DWS Small Cap Growth Fund S	SSDSX	U	(800) 621-1048	U /	-7.43	3.36	9.69 /45	--	--	0.00	1.04

● Denotes fund is closed to new investors
* Denotes fund is included in Section II

RISK			NET ASSETS		ASSET					BULL / BEAR		FUND MANAGER		MINIMUMS		LOADS	
	3 Year		NAV						Portfolio	Last Bull	Last Bear	Manager	Manager	Initial	Additional	Front	Back
Risk Rating/Pts	Standard Deviation	Beta	As of 6/30/06	Total $(Mil)	Cash %	Stocks %	Bonds %	Other %	Turnover Ratio	Market Return	Market Return	Quality Pct	Tenure (Years)	Purch. $	Purch. $	End Load	End Load
U /	N/A	N/A	22.33	1,396	4	95	0	1	56.0	N/A	N/A	N/A	2	2,500	50	0.0	0.0
B- / 7.8	8.3	1.01	24.55	25	2	98	0	0	21.0	47.0	-8.9	24	4	1,000	50	5.8	1.0
B- / 7.8	8.3	1.01	24.93	7	2	98	0	0	21.0	48.2	-9.0	26	4	1,000	50	0.0	2.0
B- / 7.7	8.3	1.01	23.60	3	2	98	0	0	21.0	43.5	-9.1	19	4	1,000	50	0.0	4.0
B- / 7.7	8.3	1.02	23.63	3	2	98	0	0	21.0	43.5	-9.1	19	4	1,000	50	0.0	1.0
B- / 7.8	8.3	1.02	25.04	30	2	98	0	0	21.0	49.1	-8.9	27	4	1,000,000	0	0.0	0.0
B- / 7.8	8.3	1.01	24.93	267	2	98	0	0	21.0	48.2	-8.9	26	4	2,500	50	0.0	2.0
D- / 1.4	23.4	1.70	51.35	45	0	100	0	0	73.0	322.9	-3.2	63	5	1,000	50	5.8	2.0
D- / 1.4	23.4	1.70	51.62	18	0	100	0	0	73.0	325.7	-3.1	65	6	1,000	50	0.0	2.0
D- / 1.4	23.4	1.70	50.89	6	0	100	0	0	73.0	312.1	-3.5	52	5	1,000	50	0.0	2.0
D- / 1.4	23.4	1.70	50.85	12	0	100	0	0	73.0	312.8	-3.4	52	5	1,000	50	1.0	2.0
D- / 1.4	23.4	1.70	51.48	621	0	100	0	0	73.0	325.8	-3.1	66	10	2,500	50	0.0	2.0
B+ / 9.6	5.1	1.07	11.59	705	4	55	39	2	108.0	45.1	-4.6	63	6	1,000,000	0	0.0	0.0
B+ / 9.7	5.1	1.08	11.15	30	4	55	39	2	108.0	43.1	-4.7	57	13	1,000	50	0.0	0.0
C- / 3.1	14.7	0.89	20.34	32	4	95	0	1	97.0	102.0	-9.6	45	N/A	1,000	50	5.8	2.0
D+ / 2.9	14.6	0.89	19.59	5	4	95	0	1	97.0	97.3	-9.8	37	N/A	1,000	50	0.0	2.0
D+ / 2.9	14.6	0.89	19.60	9	4	95	0	1	97.0	97.3	-9.8	37	N/A	1,000	50	1.0	2.0
C- / 3.3	14.6	0.89	20.85	35	4	95	0	1	97.0	103.6	-9.5	48	N/A	1,000,000	0	0.0	2.0
C- / 3.1	14.6	0.89	20.32	20	4	95	0	1	97.0	102.0	-9.6	45	N/A	1,000	50	0.0	2.0
C / 5.3	13.5	1.18	15.59	544	1	98	0	1	50.0	82.1	-8.2	7	N/A	1,000	50	5.8	2.0
C / 5.3	13.5	1.18	15.12	44	1	98	0	1	50.0	77.9	-8.4	5	N/A	1,000	50	0.0	2.0
C / 5.3	13.5	1.18	15.12	30	1	98	0	1	50.0	77.9	-8.4	5	N/A	1,000	50	1.0	2.0
C / 5.3	13.6	1.18	15.82	437	1	98	0	1	50.0	83.6	-8.1	8	N/A	1,000,000	0	0.0	2.0
C / 5.3	13.6	1.18	15.60	31	1	98	0	1	50.0	82.3	-8.2	7	N/A	1,000	50	0.0	2.0
U /	N/A	N/A	15.62	215	1	98	0	1	50.0	N/A	N/A	N/A	N/A	2,500	50	0.0	2.0
B+ / 9.4	5.1	1.07	11.70	101	8	62	29	1	53.0	44.9	-5.0	64	N/A	1,000	50	5.8	2.0
B+ / 9.6	5.1	1.07	11.68	25	8	62	29	1	53.0	46.2	-5.0	67	N/A	1,000	50	0.0	2.0
B+ / 9.6	5.1	1.07	11.71	24	8	62	29	1	53.0	41.5	-5.2	56	N/A	1,000	50	0.0	4.0
B+ / 9.6	5.1	1.07	11.71	33	8	62	29	1	53.0	41.7	-5.2	56	N/A	1,000	50	0.0	2.0
B+ / 9.6	5.0	1.06	11.68	118	8	62	29	1	53.0	46.0	-5.0	67	N/A	2,500	50	0.0	2.0
C / 5.0	15.3	1.18	17.52	22	2	98	0	0	100.0	152.1	-9.4	39	N/A	1,000	50	5.8	2.0
C / 5.1	15.3	1.19	17.69	4	2	98	0	0	100.0	153.9	-9.4	39	N/A	1,000	50	0.0	2.0
C / 4.9	15.3	1.18	17.22	5	2	98	0	0	100.0	145.8	-9.7	32	N/A	1,000	50	0.0	2.0
C / 4.9	15.3	1.18	17.24	5	2	98	0	0	100.0	145.7	-9.5	32	N/A	1,000	50	1.0	2.0
C / 5.0	15.3	1.19	17.67	106	2	98	0	0	100.0	154.0	-9.4	41	N/A	2,500	50	0.0	2.0
C / 4.5	15.5	0.93	23.32	872	1	98	0	1	66.0	126.7	0.5	86	N/A	1,000	50	5.8	2.0
C / 4.5	15.5	0.93	23.33	30	1	98	0	1	66.0	120.1	0.3	80	N/A	1,000	50	0.0	4.0
C / 4.5	15.5	0.93	23.38	105	1	98	0	1	66.0	120.9	0.4	81	N/A	1,000	50	0.0	2.0
C / 4.5	15.6	0.93	23.30	544	1	98	0	1	66.0	128.5	0.6	88	N/A	1,000,000	0	0.0	2.0
U /	N/A	N/A	16.84	83	0	98	0	2	9.0	N/A	N/A	N/A	N/A	1,000	50	4.5	2.0
B / 8.8	7.6	1.00	16.85	320	0	98	0	2	9.0	62.5	-9.8	51	N/A	1,000	50	0.0	2.0
B / 8.8	7.7	1.00	16.85	283	0	98	0	2	9.0	62.5	-9.8	50	N/A	2,500	50	0.0	2.0
D+ / 2.5	14.4	0.98	23.56	13	0	99	0	1	194.0	111.7	-10.3	39	N/A	1,000	50	5.8	2.0
D+ / 2.6	14.5	0.98	23.92	62	0	99	0	1	194.0	112.9	-10.2	41	N/A	1,000	50	0.0	2.0
D / 1.9	14.5	0.98	22.35	3	0	99	0	1	194.0	106.2	-10.4	32	N/A	1,000	50	0.0	4.0
D / 2.0	14.5	0.98	22.41	2	0	99	0	1	194.0	106.6	-10.4	32	N/A	1,000	50	1.0	1.0
D+ / 2.6	14.5	0.98	23.98	92	0	99	0	1	194.0	113.6	-10.2	42	N/A	2,500	50	0.0	2.0
C / 4.9	14.7	0.95	24.82	95	3	96	0	1	80.0	77.7	-15.1	22	N/A	1,000	50	5.8	2.0
C / 4.8	14.7	0.95	24.04	7	3	96	0	1	80.0	73.5	-15.3	17	N/A	1,000	50	0.0	2.0
C / 4.8	14.7	0.95	24.04	10	3	96	0	1	80.0	73.5	-15.3	18	N/A	1,000	50	1.0	2.0
C / 4.9	14.7	0.95	24.82	337	3	96	0	1	80.0	77.8	-15.2	22	N/A	1,000	50	0.0	2.0
U /	N/A	N/A	24.93	72	3	96	0	1	80.0	N/A	N/A	N/A	N/A	2,500	50	0.0	2.0

Fund Type	Fund Name	Ticker Symbol	Overall Weiss Investment Rating	Phone	Performance Rating/Pts	3 Mo	6 Mo	1Yr / Pct	3Yr / Pct	5Yr / Pct	Dividend Yield	Expense Ratio
	99 Pct = Best 0 Pct = Worst							Total Return % through 6/30/06	Annualized		Incl. in Returns	
SC	DWS Small Cap Value A	SAAUX	D+	(800) 621-1048	B- / 7.0	-2.40	8.91	10.41 / 50	19.16 / 76	--	0.00	1.45
SC	DWS Small Cap Value B	SABUX	D+	(800) 621-1048	B- / 7.0	-2.61	8.45	9.43 / 43	18.13 / 73	--	0.00	2.24
SC	DWS Small Cap Value C	SACUX	D+	(800) 621-1048	B- / 7.2	-2.56	8.51	9.54 / 44	18.22 / 73	--	0.00	2.23
SC	● DWS Small Cap Value S	SCSUX	C-	(800) 621-1048	B / 7.6	-2.33	9.09	10.73 / 52	19.51 / 78	12.69 / 88	0.46	1.04
BA	● DWS Target 2008 Fd A	KRFGX	D	(800) 621-1048	E- / 0.0	-0.57	-0.19	0.62 / 2	1.57 / 0	3.12 / 38	4.16	1.31
AA	● DWS Target 2010	KRFAX	D-	(800) 621-1048	E- / 0.0	-1.21	-1.43	-1.28 / 1	1.93 / 1	3.51 / 41	5.32	1.10
AA	● DWS Target 2011	KRFBX	D-	(800) 621-1048	E- / 0.1	-1.05	-1.43	-1.09 / 1	2.27 / 1	3.53 / 42	5.25	1.03
AA	● DWS Target 2012	KRFCX	D	(800) 621-1048	E- / 0.1	-1.34	-1.78	-1.04 / 1	2.77 / 1	2.29 / 30	3.02	1.07
AA	● DWS Target 2013 Fund	KRFDX	D	(800) 621-1048	E- / 0.1	-1.32	-2.08	-1.77 / 1	2.75 / 1	1.08 / 21	2.55	1.15
BA	DWS Target 2014 Fd A	KRFEX	D-	(800) 621-1048	E- / 0.1	-1.60	-2.90	-2.95 / 0	3.38 / 2	1.15 / 21	7.07	1.18
TC	DWS Technology Fd A	KTCAX	E-	(800) 621-1048	E- / 0.1	-11.93	-10.12	-0.38 / 1	5.64 / 5	-6.25 / 1	0.00	1.11
TC	DWS Technology Fd B	KTCBX	E-	(800) 621-1048	E- / 0.1	-12.15	-10.64	-1.45 / 1	4.45 / 3	-7.25 / 1	0.00	2.17
TC	DWS Technology Fd C	KTCCX	E-	(800) 621-1048	E- / 0.1	-12.03	-10.38	-1.20 / 1	4.67 / 3	-7.10 / 1	0.00	2.01
TC	DWS Technology Fd S	KTCSX	U	(800) 621-1048	U /	-11.85	-10.11	-0.29 / 1	--	--	0.00	1.05
BA	DWS Value Builder Fund A	FLVBX	D	(800) 621-1048	D- / 1.1	-0.58	1.32	2.43 / 5	8.08 / 15	2.29 / 30	2.16	1.22
BA	DWS Value Builder Fund B	FVBBX	D	(800) 621-1048	D- / 1.0	-0.77	0.89	1.65 / 4	7.27 / 11	1.52 / 24	1.54	2.02
BA	DWS Value Builder Fund C	FVBCX	D	(800) 621-1048	D- / 1.3	-0.77	0.90	1.66 / 4	7.27 / 11	1.51 / 24	1.54	1.95
BA	DWS Value Builder Fund I	FLIVX	D+	(800) 621-1048	D / 2.1	-0.55	1.40	2.65 / 6	8.34 / 17	2.54 / 32	2.54	0.91
FO	E*TRADE International Index Fund	ETINX	A+	(800) 786-2575	A- / 9.0	0.57	9.93	26.75 / 91	23.38 / 88	9.48 / 79	2.34	0.09
SC	E*TRADE Russell 2000 Index Fund	ETRUX	C+	(800) 786-2575	B- / 7.3	-5.09	8.10	14.14 / 69	17.99 / 72	7.77 / 71	0.92	0.22
IX	E*TRADE S & P 500 Index Fund	ETSPX	C	(800) 786-2575	C- / 3.8	-1.51	2.62	8.45 / 36	10.98 / 35	2.22 / 29	1.76	0.09
TC	E*TRADE Technology Index Fund	ETTIX	E-	(800) 786-2575	E+ / 0.9	-9.43	-5.57	3.67 / 9	7.35 / 12	-5.31 / 2	0.00	0.60
GR	Eagle Growth Shares	EGRWX	D-	(800) 749-9933	C- / 3.3	-1.30	5.73	6.73 / 25	12.18 / 44	5.26 / 56	0.00	3.58
FO	● Eaton Vance Asian Small Co A	EVASX	C-	(800) 225-6265	A+ / 9.7	-4.56	16.08	40.82 / 98	34.16 / 98	25.65 / 99	0.05	2.16
FO	● Eaton Vance Asian Small Co B	EBASX	C-	(800) 225-6265	A+ / 9.7	-4.72	15.77	40.10 / 98	33.48 / 97	25.00 / 98	0.00	2.66
GR	Eaton Vance Atlanta Cap LrgCap Gr	EAALX	D	(800) 225-6265	E+ / 0.9	-3.30	-0.18	5.06 / 15	7.22 / 11	--	0.00	0.86
GR	Eaton Vance Atlanta Cap LrgCap Gr I	EILGX	D+	(800) 225-6265	D / 1.7	-3.18	-0.09	5.21 / 16	7.51 / 12	--	0.30	1.00
SC	Eaton Vance Atlanta Cap SmCap A	EAASX	C+	(800) 225-6265	C+ / 5.6	-2.99	6.85	12.62 / 63	14.97 / 59	--	0.00	1.35
SC	Eaton Vance Atlanta Cap SmCap I	EISMX	B-	(800) 225-6265	C+ / 6.5	-2.95	7.09	13.02 / 64	15.35 / 60	--	0.00	1.35
BA	Eaton Vance Balanced A	EVIFX	D+	(800) 225-6265	D / 1.9	-2.73	2.86	8.71 / 38	8.96 / 21	4.45 / 50	1.35	1.20
BA	Eaton Vance Balanced B	EMIFX	E-	(800) 225-6265	D / 1.6	-2.91	2.47	7.79 / 31	8.10 / 16	3.65 / 42	0.56	1.95
BA	Eaton Vance Balanced C	ECIFX	E-	(800) 225-6265	D / 2.1	-2.91	2.61	7.88 / 32	8.11 / 16	3.66 / 42	0.56	1.95
GL	Eaton Vance Diversified Income A	EADDX	U	(800) 225-6265	U /	0.60	2.43	4.38 / 12	--	--	6.21	1.17
GL	Eaton Vance Diversified Income B	EBDDX	U	(800) 225-6265	U /	0.52	2.15	3.71 / 9	--	--	5.76	1.92
GL	Eaton Vance Diversified Income C	ECDDX	U	(800) 225-6265	U /	0.52	2.15	3.71 / 9	--	--	5.76	1.92
EM	Eaton Vance Emerging Mkts A	ETEMX	B-	(800) 225-6265	A / 9.3	-6.23	3.67	29.07 / 94	29.45 / 95	20.34 / 96	0.40	2.41
EM	Eaton Vance Emerging Mkts B	EMEMX	B-	(800) 225-6265	A / 9.3	-6.31	3.43	28.44 / 93	28.81 / 95	19.65 / 96	0.05	2.91
GL	Eaton Vance Eqty Resrch A	EAERX	D+	(800) 225-6265	C- / 4.0	-2.05	2.81	11.41 / 56	12.27 / 44	--	0.15	1.25
GL	Eaton Vance Global Growth Equity A	ETIAX	D-	(800) 225-6265	C- / 3.5	-4.44	4.81	13.48 / 66	12.30 / 44	2.79 / 35	0.00	2.52
GL	Eaton Vance Global Growth Equity B	EMIAX	D-	(800) 225-6265	C- / 3.4	-4.53	4.59	12.93 / 64	11.75 / 41	2.19 / 29	0.00	3.02
GL	Eaton Vance Global Growth Equity C	ECIAX	D	(800) 225-6265	C- / 4.2	-4.58	4.57	12.93 / 64	11.73 / 41	2.19 / 29	0.00	3.02
FO	Eaton Vance Greater China A	EVCGX	B-	(800) 225-6265	A- / 9.1	-0.06	14.70	22.60 / 85	25.77 / 92	11.88 / 86	0.62	2.36
FO	Eaton Vance Greater China B	EMCGX	B-	(800) 225-6265	A- / 9.1	-0.17	14.39	22.02 / 84	25.20 / 91	11.25 / 85	0.23	2.86
FO	Eaton Vance Greater China C	ECCGX	B-	(800) 225-6265	A- / 9.2	-0.17	14.41	22.04 / 84	25.13 / 91	11.20 / 84	0.33	2.86
FO	Eaton Vance Greater India A	ETGIX	C-	(800) 225-6265	A+ / 9.9	-15.08	6.32	39.32 / 98	47.36 / 99	28.71 / 99	0.00	2.35
FO	Eaton Vance Greater India B	EMGIX	C-	(800) 225-6265	A+ / 9.9	-15.18	6.12	38.64 / 98	47.04 / 99	28.24 / 99	0.00	2.85
GR	Eaton Vance Growth Fund A	EVGFX	E+	(800) 225-6265	D+ / 2.3	-8.07	3.01	12.45 / 62	10.92 / 35	2.97 / 36	0.00	1.27
GR	Eaton Vance Growth Fund B	EMGFX	E-	(800) 225-6265	D / 2.0	-8.22	2.62	11.57 / 57	10.09 / 28	2.18 / 29	0.00	2.02
GR	Eaton Vance Growth Fund C	ECGFX	E-	(800) 225-6265	D+ / 2.6	-8.22	2.62	11.56 / 57	10.06 / 28	2.18 / 29	0.00	2.02
GR	Eaton Vance Large Cap Core A	EALCX	C-	(800) 225-6265	D+ / 2.7	-3.45	1.13	9.41 / 43	10.62 / 32	--	0.00	1.40
GR	Eaton Vance Large Cap Core B	EBLCX	C-	(800) 225-6265	D+ / 2.3	-3.62	0.80	8.62 / 38	9.79 / 26	--	0.00	2.15
GR	Eaton Vance Large Cap Core C	ECLCX	C-	(800) 225-6265	D+ / 2.9	-3.62	0.80	8.62 / 38	9.76 / 26	--	0.00	2.15

● Denotes fund is closed to new investors
* Denotes fund is included in Section II

RISK			NET ASSETS		ASSET					BULL / BEAR		FUND MANAGER		MINIMUMS		LOADS	
	3 Year		NAV						Portfolio	Last Bull	Last Bear	Manager	Manager	Initial	Additional	Front	Back
Risk Rating/Pts	Standard Deviation	Beta	As of 6/30/06	Total $(Mil)	Cash %	Stocks %	Bonds %	Other %	Turnover Ratio	Market Return	Market Return	Quality Pct	Tenure (Years)	Purch. $	Purch. $	End Load	End Load
C- / 3.1	13.4	0.88	26.40	13	2	98	0	0	98.0	110.8	-8.1	78	N/A	1,000	50	5.8	2.0
D+ / 2.8	13.4	0.89	25.42	3	2	98	0	0	98.0	105.1	-8.2	70	N/A	1,000	50	0.0	4.0
D+ / 2.8	13.4	0.89	25.49	5	2	98	0	0	98.0	105.6	-8.2	71	N/A	1,000	50	1.0	1.0
D+ / 2.9	13.4	0.89	26.40	311	2	98	0	0	98.0	112.6	-8.0	80	N/A	2,500	50	0.0	2.0
B / 8.8	3.4	0.45	10.47	21	0	22	78	0	21.0	10.7	1.9	26	N/A	1,000	50	5.0	1.0
B- / 7.7	5.0	0.55	8.95	50	0	24	74	2	22.0	13.1	2.4	25	1	1,000	50	5.0	0.0
B / 8.3	5.3	0.60	10.36	79	0	26	72	2	23.0	14.8	2.5	26	1	1,000	50	5.0	0.0
B+ / 9.4	5.4	0.68	8.81	62	0	32	66	2	28.0	17.2	1.8	26	1	1,000	50	5.0	0.0
B+ / 9.2	6.1	0.69	8.95	44	0	32	68	0	32.0	17.6	-1.4	26	1	1,000	50	5.0	0.0
B- / 7.7	4.0	0.50	7.37	45	0	26	72	2	98.0	17.9	-2.8	38	1	1,000	50	5.0	2.0
D+ / 2.7	16.8	1.85	10.48	828	2	98	0	0	114.0	58.0	-13.4	1	N/A	1,000	50	5.8	2.0
D+ / 2.6	16.8	1.84	8.82	80	2	98	0	0	114.0	52.5	-13.6	0	N/A	1,000	50	0.0	4.0
D+ / 2.6	16.8	1.85	9.07	42	2	98	0	0	114.0	53.4	-13.6	0	N/A	1,000	50	0.0	1.0
U /	N/A	N/A	10.49	116	2	98	0	0	114.0	N/A	N/A	N/A	N/A	2,500	50	0.0	2.0
B / 8.2	7.4	1.30	23.54	377	2	74	22	2	19.0	54.8	-7.9	43	14	1,000	50	5.8	1.0
B / 8.2	7.4	1.30	23.55	13	2	74	22	2	19.0	51.2	-8.1	35	14	1,000	50	0.0	4.0
B / 8.2	7.4	1.31	23.56	21	2	74	22	2	19.0	51.2	-8.1	35	14	1,000	50	0.0	1.0
B / 8.2	7.4	1.30	23.76	83	2	74	22	2	19.0	56.0	-7.9	45	14	1,000,000	0	0.0	0.0
B- / 7.1	9.9	0.98	11.78	85	0	99	0	1	42.0	128.7	-9.7	50	N/A	5,000	250	0.0	1.0
C+ / 5.8	14.6	1.00	13.35	105	1	98	0	1	29.6	114.8	-11.2	47	6	5,000	250	0.0	1.0
B / 8.6	7.7	1.00	10.07	282	0	99	0	1	3.9	63.6	-9.7	53	7	5,000	250	0.0	1.0
C- / 3.2	16.9	1.85	5.09	43	1	98	0	1	3.6	63.7	-14.3	1	7	5,000	250	0.0	1.0
C / 4.7	8.9	0.64	13.65	4	9	90	0	1	23.0	56.4	-6.4	89	19	500	0	8.5	0.0
E+ / 0.6	16.0	1.13	25.34	194	3	96	0	1	17.0	222.8	-0.4	93	2	1,000	50	5.8	1.0
E+ / 0.6	16.0	1.13	25.26	39	3	96	0	1	17.0	217.7	-0.5	92	2	1,000	50	0.0	5.0
B / 8.1	8.1	1.00	11.13	13	1	98	0	1	45.0	48.5	-10.5	21	4	1,000	50	5.8	0.0
B / 8.1	8.0	1.00	10.64	13	1	98	0	1	45.0	50.0	-10.3	23	4	1,000	0	0.0	0.0
B- / 7.7	11.3	0.75	12.32	6	1	98	0	1	38.0	82.8	-10.0	62	4	1,000	50	5.8	0.0
B- / 7.7	11.4	0.75	12.84	12	1	98	0	1	38.0	84.8	-10.0	66	4	1,000	0	0.0	0.0
B / 8.3	7.7	1.27	7.04	153	5	66	28	1	32.0	58.6	-8.9	55	6	1,000	50	5.8	0.0
E- / 0.0	7.7	1.28	7.04	33	5	66	28	1	32.0	55.0	-9.0	44	6	1,000	50	0.0	5.0
E- / 0.0	7.7	1.28	7.06	15	5	66	28	1	32.0	55.0	-9.0	44	6	1,000	50	0.0	1.0
U /	N/A	N/A	9.68	121	7	1	88	4	71.0	N/A	N/A	N/A	2	1,000	50	4.8	0.0
U /	N/A	N/A	9.68	29	7	1	88	4	71.0	N/A	N/A	N/A	2	1,000	50	0.0	5.0
U /	N/A	N/A	9.68	119	7	1	88	4	71.0	N/A	N/A	N/A	2	1,000	50	0.0	1.0
C / 4.4	18.4	1.09	24.82	121	4	95	0	1	32.0	185.1	-0.5	5	6	1,000	50	5.8	1.0
C / 4.4	18.4	1.09	23.76	29	4	95	0	1	32.0	180.4	-0.6	4	6	1,000	50	0.0	5.0
C+ / 5.7	8.1	0.66	12.44	2	1	98	0	1	93.0	69.2	-9.0	22	1	1,000	50	5.8	0.0
C / 4.8	12.8	1.11	17.01	49	3	96	0	1	90.0	77.2	-12.2	1	11	1,000	50	5.8	1.0
C / 4.8	12.8	1.12	16.86	24	3	96	0	1	90.0	74.4	-12.5	0	11	1,000	50	0.0	5.0
C / 4.8	12.8	1.12	16.25	11	3	96	0	1	90.0	74.4	-12.4	0	11	1,000	50	0.0	1.0
C / 4.7	15.0	1.16	17.79	129	5	94	0	1	27.0	134.0	0.5	33	4	1,000	50	5.8	1.0
C / 4.6	15.0	1.16	17.81	23	5	94	0	1	27.0	130.4	0.3	30	4	1,000	50	0.0	5.0
C / 4.6	15.0	1.16	17.78	31	5	94	0	1	27.0	130.1	0.4	29	4	1,000	50	0.0	1.0
D- / 1.2	26.6	1.74	20.55	575	5	94	0	1	29.0	378.8	1.9	80	1	1,000	50	5.8	1.0
D- / 1.2	26.6	1.74	19.27	138	5	94	0	1	29.0	375.2	1.8	78	1	1,000	50	0.0	5.0
C- / 4.1	16.7	1.65	7.86	105	4	95	0	1	112.0	95.2	-16.4	11	6	1,000	50	5.8	0.0
E+ / 0.7	16.7	1.65	7.82	11	4	95	0	1	112.0	90.7	-16.6	8	6	1,000	50	0.0	5.0
E+ / 0.7	16.7	1.66	7.82	6	4	95	0	1	112.0	90.7	-16.7	8	6	1,000	50	0.0	1.0
B / 8.1	8.4	1.05	14.26	22	2	97	0	1	55.0	61.8	-9.0	44	4	1,000	50	5.8	0.0
B / 8.1	8.4	1.05	13.84	11	2	97	0	1	55.0	58.0	-9.3	36	4	1,000	50	0.0	5.0
B / 8.1	8.4	1.04	13.84	8	2	97	0	1	55.0	57.9	-9.2	36	4	1,000	50	0.0	1.0

Fund Type	Fund Name	Ticker Symbol	Overall Weiss Investment Rating	Phone	Performance Rating/Pts	3 Mo	6 Mo	1Yr / Pct	3Yr / Pct	5Yr / Pct	Dividend Yield	Expense Ratio
*GI	Eaton Vance Large Cap Value A	EHSTX	B	(800) 225-6265	C+ / 6.3	1.19	5.89	13.86 /68	16.14 /64	7.04 /67	1.19	1.07
GI	Eaton Vance Large Cap Value B	EMSTX	C+	(800) 225-6265	C+ / 6.0	1.00	5.49	13.06 /64	15.29 /60	6.24 /63	0.50	1.82
GI	Eaton Vance Large Cap Value C	ECSTX	B	(800) 225-6265	C+ / 6.5	1.00	5.49	13.04 /64	15.28 /60	6.23 /63	0.58	1.82
GI	Eaton Vance Large Cap Value I	EILVX	A	(800) 225-6265	B- / 7.0	1.26	6.03	14.13 /69	16.19 /64	7.06 /67	1.49	0.88
GI	Eaton Vance Large Cap Value R	ERSTX	B	(800) 225-6265	C+ / 6.9	1.13	5.79	13.62 /67	15.93 /63	6.92 /66	1.12	1.38
GL	Eaton Vance Medallion Strtgc Inc A	EAMSX	U	(800) 225-6265	U /	-0.46	1.23	--	--	--	0.00	2.00
GL	Eaton Vance Medallion Strtgc Inc C	ECMSX	U	(800) 225-6265	U /	-0.46	1.04	--	--	--	0.00	N/A
SC	Eaton Vance Small Cap Growth A	ETEGX	E	(800) 225-6265	C- / 3.2	-5.86	5.74	16.85 /77	10.70 /33	-2.64 / 6	0.00	2.00
SC	Eaton Vance Small Cap Growth B	EBSMX	E+	(800) 225-6265	D+ / 2.8	-6.06	5.42	15.96 /75	9.85 /26	-3.45 / 4	0.00	3.44
SC	Eaton Vance Small Cap Growth C	ECSMX	D-	(800) 225-6265	C- / 3.5	-5.97	5.47	16.10 /75	9.91 /27	-3.29 / 5	0.00	2.75
SC	Eaton Vance Small Cap Value A	EAVSX	B	(800) 225-6265	C+ / 6.4	-1.84	7.81	11.41 /56	16.80 /67	--	0.00	1.75
SC	Eaton Vance Small Cap Value B	EBVSX	B-	(800) 225-6265	C+ / 6.1	-2.01	7.42	10.61 /51	15.97 /63	--	0.00	2.50
SC	Eaton Vance Small Cap Value C	ECVSX	B-	(800) 225-6265	C+ / 6.6	-1.96	7.44	10.64 /51	15.95 /63	--	0.00	2.50
SC	Eaton Vance Special Eq A	EVSEX	D-	(800) 225-6265	C- / 3.8	-5.85	6.44	18.08 /79	11.53 /39	-1.70 / 9	0.00	1.76
SC	Eaton Vance Special Eq B	EMSEX	D-	(800) 225-6265	C- / 3.4	-6.03	6.11	17.26 /78	10.67 /32	-2.43 / 7	0.00	2.51
SC	Eaton Vance Special Eq C	ECSEX	D	(800) 225-6265	C- / 4.1	-6.03	6.11	17.27 /78	10.71 /33	-2.43 / 7	0.00	2.51
SC ●	Eaton Vance Tax Mgd SmCap Gr A	ETMGX	D-	(800) 225-6265	C- / 3.6	-5.88	5.89	17.49 /78	11.43 /39	-1.38 /10	0.00	1.44
SC ●	Eaton Vance Tax Mgd SmCap Gr B	EMMGX	D-	(800) 225-6265	C- / 3.2	-6.09	5.50	16.51 /76	10.58 /32	-2.11 / 8	0.00	2.19
SC ●	Eaton Vance Tax Mgd SmCap Gr C	ECMGX	D-	(800) 225-6265	C- / 3.9	-6.03	5.52	16.58 /76	10.59 /32	-2.12 / 8	0.00	2.19
GR	Eaton Vance Tax-Managed Div Inc A	EADIX	B-	(800) 225-6265	C / 4.7	0.94	6.62	11.02 /54	13.06 /49	--	5.07	1.25
GR	Eaton Vance Tax-Managed Div Inc B	EBDIX	C+	(800) 225-6265	C / 4.4	0.67	6.14	10.22 /48	12.24 /44	--	4.66	2.00
GR	Eaton Vance Tax-Managed Div Inc C	ECDIX	B	(800) 225-6265	C / 5.0	0.75	6.22	10.22 /48	12.27 /44	--	4.66	2.00
FO	Eaton Vance Tax-Mgd Emg Mkt Fd I	EITEX	A+	(800) 225-6265	A+ / 9.8	-3.39	9.26	35.45 /97	37.77 /99	25.58 /99	2.08	0.95
AA	Eaton Vance Tax-Mgd Eqty A-Alloc A	EAEAX	C+	(800) 225-6265	C / 5.2	-2.01	6.05	15.43 /73	14.31 /55	--	0.00	1.43
AA	Eaton Vance Tax-Mgd Eqty A-Alloc B	EBEAX	C	(800) 225-6265	C / 4.9	-2.15	5.72	14.64 /70	13.48 /51	--	0.00	2.18
AA	Eaton Vance Tax-Mgd Eqty A-Alloc C	ECEAX	C+	(800) 225-6265	C / 5.5	-2.15	5.65	14.57 /70	13.48 /51	--	0.00	2.18
GR ●	Eaton Vance Tax-Mgd Growth 1.0	CAPEX	C+	(800) 225-6265	C- / 3.9	-1.34	2.93	9.40 /43	10.60 /32	2.57 /33	1.21	0.46
GR ●	Eaton Vance Tax-Mgd Growth 1.1 A	ETTGX	C-	(800) 225-6265	D+ / 2.7	-1.40	2.79	9.03 /40	10.23 /29	2.22 /29	0.82	0.83
GR ●	Eaton Vance Tax-Mgd Growth 1.1 B	EMTGX	C-	(800) 225-6265	D / 2.2	-1.65	2.39	8.23 /35	9.40 /23	1.44 /23	0.03	1.58
GR ●	Eaton Vance Tax-Mgd Growth 1.1 C	ECTGX	C	(800) 225-6265	D+ / 2.9	-1.63	2.35	8.20 /34	9.39 /23	1.44 /23	0.18	1.58
GR ●	Eaton Vance Tax-Mgd Growth 1.1 I	EITMX	C+	(800) 225-6265	C- / 3.8	-1.39	2.86	9.27 /42	10.49 /31	2.56 /32	1.17	0.58
GR	Eaton Vance Tax-Mgd Growth 1.2 A	EXTGX	C-	(800) 225-6265	D+ / 2.5	-1.46	2.67	8.94 /40	10.03 /28	2.09 /28	0.60	0.97
GR	Eaton Vance Tax-Mgd Growth 1.2 B	EYTGX	C-	(800) 225-6265	D+ / 2.8	-1.69	2.25	8.06 /33	9.21 /22	1.31 /22	0.00	1.72
GR	Eaton Vance Tax-Mgd Growth 1.2 C	EZTGX	C-	(800) 225-6265	D+ / 2.8	-1.69	2.35	8.05 /33	9.20 /22	1.31 /22	0.00	1.72
GR	Eaton Vance Tax-Mgd Growth 1.2 I	EITGX	C	(800) 225-6265	C- / 3.7	-1.37	2.85	9.18 /41	10.30 /29	2.35 /31	0.89	0.72
FO	Eaton Vance Tax-Mgd Intl Equity A	ETIGX	A-	(800) 225-6265	B+ / 8.8	0.20	11.76	31.77 /95	22.92 /87	2.19 /29	0.69	1.89
FO	Eaton Vance Tax-Mgd Intl Equity B	EMIGX	A-	(800) 225-6265	B+ / 8.7	0.00	11.42	30.79 /95	22.00 /85	1.41 /23	0.09	2.64
FO	Eaton Vance Tax-Mgd Intl Equity C	ECIGX	A-	(800) 225-6265	B+ / 8.9	0.00	11.31	30.62 /95	22.03 /85	1.43 /23	0.16	2.64
MC	Eaton Vance Tax-Mgd Mid-Cap Core	EXMCX	C	(800) 225-6265	C- / 4.0	-0.81	6.06	11.25 /55	11.91 /42	--	0.00	1.70
MC	Eaton Vance Tax-Mgd Mid-Cap Core	EBMCX	C-	(800) 225-6265	C- / 3.5	-1.06	5.59	10.44 /50	11.06 /36	--	0.00	2.45
MC	Eaton Vance Tax-Mgd Mid-Cap Core	ECMCX	C	(800) 225-6265	C / 4.3	-0.99	5.67	10.44 /50	11.06 /36	--	0.00	2.45
GR	Eaton Vance Tax-Mgd MultiCap Opp	EACPX	E+	(800) 225-6265	D+ / 2.3	-7.56	3.35	12.31 /61	10.60 /32	3.42 /40	0.00	1.55
GR	Eaton Vance Tax-Mgd MultiCap Opp	EBCPX	E	(800) 225-6265	D / 1.9	-7.78	2.96	11.48 /57	9.76 /26	2.64 /33	0.00	2.30
GR	Eaton Vance Tax-Mgd MultiCap Opp	ECCPX	E+	(800) 225-6265	D+ / 2.5	-7.77	2.95	11.46 /56	9.78 /26	2.66 /33	0.00	2.30
SC	Eaton Vance Tax-Mgd Small-Cap Val	ESVAX	B-	(800) 225-6265	C+ / 6.5	-2.38	7.58	11.78 /58	17.05 /68	--	0.00	1.75
SC	Eaton Vance Tax-Mgd Small-Cap Val	ESVBX	B-	(800) 225-6265	C+ / 6.2	-2.52	7.23	10.98 /53	16.19 /64	--	0.00	2.50
SC	Eaton Vance Tax-Mgd Small-Cap Val	ESVCX	B-	(800) 225-6265	C+ / 6.6	-2.52	7.14	10.97 /53	16.21 /64	--	0.00	2.50
GR	Eaton Vance Tax-Mgd Value A	EATVX	B+	(800) 225-6265	C+ / 6.3	0.92	6.63	15.27 /73	15.81 /63	6.74 /65	0.77	1.21
GR	Eaton Vance Tax-Mgd Value B	EBTVX	B+	(800) 225-6265	C+ / 5.9	0.67	6.18	14.33 /69	14.95 /59	5.93 /61	0.19	1.96
GR	Eaton Vance Tax-Mgd Value C	ECTVX	B	(800) 225-6265	C+ / 6.4	0.65	6.21	14.40 /70	14.95 /59	5.94 /61	0.21	1.96
UT	Eaton Vance Utilities A	EVTMX	A+	(800) 225-6265	B+ / 8.3	2.78	7.70	17.10 /77	22.03 /85	9.88 /80	2.21	1.08
UT	Eaton Vance Utilities B	EMTMX	C	(800) 225-6265	B / 8.1	2.59	7.29	16.28 /75	21.12 /83	9.05 /76	1.43	1.83

● Denotes fund is closed to new investors
* Denotes fund is included in Section II

RISK			NET ASSETS		ASSET				BULL / BEAR		FUND MANAGER		MINIMUMS		LOADS	
	3 Year		NAV						Last Bull	Last Bear	Manager	Manager	Initial	Additional	Front	Back
Risk	Standard		As of	Total	Cash	Stocks	Bonds	Other	Market	Market	Quality	Tenure	Purch.	Purch.	End	End
Rating/Pts	Deviation	Beta	6/30/06	$(Mil)	%	%	%	%	Return	Return	Pct	(Years)	$	$	Load	Load
B / 8.9	7.4	0.90	19.22	2,331	4	95	0	1	72.0	80.8	-8.7	94	6	1,000	50	5.8	0.0
C+ / 6.5	7.5	0.91	19.22	222	4	95	0	1	72.0	76.7	-8.9	92	6	1,000	50	0.0	5.0
B / 8.9	7.5	0.91	19.22	328	4	95	0	1	72.0	76.6	-8.9	92	6	1,000	50	0.0	1.0
B / 8.8	7.4	0.90	19.22	22	4	95	0	1	72.0	81.0	-8.7	94	2	250,000	0	0.0	0.0
B / 8.8	7.4	0.90	19.22	27	4	95	0	1	72.0	79.8	-8.7	93	2	1,000	50	0.0	0.0
U /	N/A	N/A	9.86	32	0	0	0	100	N/A	N/A	N/A	N/A	N/A	5,000	2,000	6.0	0.0
U /	N/A	N/A	9.85	31	0	0	0	100	N/A	N/A	N/A	N/A	N/A	5,000	2,000	0.0	1.0
D+ / 2.8	15.3	0.97	11.24	8	1	98	0	1	218.0	68.5	-10.0	8	1	1,000	50	5.8	0.0
C / 4.7	15.3	0.97	11.48	3	1	98	0	1	218.0	64.5	-10.2	6	1	1,000	50	0.0	5.0
C / 4.7	15.3	0.97	11.18	2	1	98	0	1	218.0	64.5	-10.2	6	1	1,000	50	0.0	1.0
B / 8.0	11.1	0.72	16.01	11	6	92	0	2	28.0	90.6	-7.3	82	4	1,000	50	5.8	0.0
B- / 7.7	11.0	0.71	16.06	5	6	92	0	2	28.0	86.2	-7.5	77	4	1,000	50	0.0	5.0
B- / 7.7	11.0	0.71	16.02	6	6	92	0	2	28.0	86.1	-7.5	76	N/A	1,000	50	0.0	1.0
C / 4.8	15.5	0.99	12.23	38	3	96	0	1	207.0	73.2	-10.4	9	1	1,000	50	5.8	0.0
C / 4.7	15.5	0.99	12.16	2	3	96	0	1	207.0	69.1	-10.7	7	1	1,000	50	0.0	5.0
C / 4.7	15.5	0.99	12.16	2	3	96	0	1	207.0	69.2	-10.8	7	1	1,000	50	0.0	1.0
C / 4.8	15.5	0.99	11.69	43	5	94	0	1	282.0	71.3	-10.2	9	N/A	1,000	50	5.8	0.0
C / 4.7	15.5	0.99	10.94	48	5	94	0	1	282.0	67.5	-10.5	7	N/A	1,000	50	0.0	5.0
C / 4.7	15.5	0.99	10.90	27	5	94	0	1	282.0	67.3	-10.4	7	N/A	1,000	50	0.0	1.0
B+ / 9.0	6.8	0.69	12.60	480	3	96	0	1	118.0	N/A	N/A	91	3	1,000	50	5.8	0.0
B+ / 9.1	6.7	0.68	12.57	120	3	96	0	1	118.0	N/A	N/A	88	3	1,000	50	0.0	5.0
B+ / 9.1	6.7	0.67	12.58	367	3	96	0	1	118.0	N/A	N/A	89	3	1,000	50	0.0	1.0
C+ / 6.7	15.9	1.36	31.61	557	0	99	0	1	6.0	248.3	-0.9	85	8	50,000	0	0.0	2.0
B- / 7.5	9.6	1.69	13.14	219	1	98	0	1	40.0	81.0	-9.8	82	4	1,000	50	5.8	0.0
B- / 7.4	9.5	1.69	12.75	135	1	98	0	1	40.0	76.8	-9.9	76	4	1,000	50	0.0	5.0
B- / 7.4	9.5	1.69	12.72	195	1	98	0	1	40.0	76.9	-10.0	77	4	1,000	50	0.0	1.0
B / 8.6	7.4	0.95	559.64	973	0	99	0	1	N/A	58.5	-9.7	54	16	25,000	0	0.0	0.0
B / 8.5	7.4	0.96	23.96	1,264	0	99	0	1	N/A	56.8	-9.8	49	10	1,000	50	5.8	0.0
B / 8.6	7.4	0.95	22.70	1,021	0	99	0	1	N/A	53.2	-9.9	40	10	1,000	50	0.0	5.0
B / 8.6	7.4	0.95	21.74	587	0	99	0	1	N/A	53.2	-9.9	40	10	1,000	50	0.0	1.0
B / 8.7	7.4	0.96	22.62	1	0	99	0	1	N/A	58.0	-9.6	52	7	250,000	0	0.0	0.0
B / 8.5	7.5	0.96	10.78	609	0	99	0	1	N/A	55.9	-9.7	46	5	1,000	50	5.8	0.0
B / 8.6	7.5	0.96	10.46	326	0	99	0	1	N/A	52.3	-9.9	38	5	1,000	50	0.0	1.0
B / 8.6	7.4	0.95	10.47	334	0	99	0	1	N/A	52.3	-9.9	38	5	1,000	50	0.0	1.0
B / 8.7	7.4	0.95	10.81	7	0	99	0	1	N/A	57.1	-9.7	51	5	250,000	0	0.0	0.0
C+ / 6.6	11.3	1.08	10.26	47	1	98	0	1	39.0	120.3	-12.0	27	2	1,000	50	5.8	1.0
C+ / 6.6	11.3	1.08	9.76	30	1	98	0	1	39.0	115.2	-12.2	22	2	1,000	50	0.0	5.0
C+ / 6.6	11.3	1.08	9.74	25	1	98	0	1	39.0	114.9	-12.1	22	2	1,000	50	0.0	1.0
B- / 7.9	9.0	0.79	13.47	16	2	97	0	1	42.0	66.5	-7.1	30	4	1,000	50	5.8	0.0
B- / 7.8	9.0	0.79	13.04	7	2	97	0	1	42.0	62.7	-7.3	24	4	1,000	50	0.0	5.0
B- / 7.8	9.1	0.79	13.04	7	2	97	0	1	42.0	62.7	-7.3	24	4	1,000	50	0.0	1.0
C / 4.5	16.0	1.59	11.74	24	4	95	0	1	217.0	91.7	-14.8	12	6	1,000	50	5.8	0.0
C / 4.5	16.0	1.59	11.14	18	4	95	0	1	217.0	87.4	-15.0	9	6	1,000	50	0.0	5.0
C / 4.5	16.0	1.59	11.16	18	4	95	0	1	217.0	87.4	-15.0	9	6	1,000	50	0.0	1.0
B- / 7.5	11.7	0.76	15.18	16	4	94	0	2	24.0	92.1	-7.2	78	4	1,000	50	5.8	0.0
B- / 7.5	11.7	0.76	14.69	8	4	94	0	2	24.0	87.7	-7.4	71	4	1,000	50	0.0	5.0
B- / 7.5	11.7	0.76	14.70	8	4	94	0	2	24.0	88.0	-7.4	72	4	1,000	50	0.0	1.0
B / 8.7	7.7	0.92	17.53	466	0	99	0	1	40.0	81.6	-8.6	93	7	1,000	50	5.8	0.0
B / 8.7	7.7	0.92	16.50	244	0	99	0	1	40.0	77.3	-8.8	90	6	1,000	50	0.0	5.0
B / 8.7	7.7	0.92	16.94	276	0	99	0	1	40.0	77.4	-8.8	90	6	1,000	50	0.0	1.0
B / 8.4	8.5	0.60	12.02	782	N/A	100	0	N/A	54.0	115.8	-4.9	97	7	1,000	50	5.8	0.0
C- / 3.8	8.5	0.60	12.03	109	N/A	100	0	N/A	54.0	110.5	-5.0	96	7	1,000	50	0.0	5.0

					PERFORMANCE							
99 Pct = Best						Total Return % through 6/30/06					Incl. in Returns	
0 Pct = Worst			Overall Weiss		Perfor-				Annualized		Dividend	Expense
Fund Type	Fund Name	Ticker Symbol	Investment Rating	Phone	mance Rating/Pts	3 Mo	6 Mo	1Yr / Pct	3Yr / Pct	5Yr / Pct	Yield	Ratio
UT	Eaton Vance Utilities C	ECTMX	C-	(800) 225-6265	B+ / 8.4	2.59	7.20	16.24 /75	21.10 /83	9.05 /76	1.36	1.83
UT	Eaton Vance Utilities I	EIUTX	B+	(800) 225-6265	B+ / 8.7	2.85	7.84	17.39 /78	22.13 /85	9.94 /80	2.58	0.83
HL	Eaton Vance WW Health Sciences A	ETHSX	E-	(800) 225-6265	E- / 0.2	-5.95	-6.36	6.86 /25	5.67 / 6	1.19 /21	0.00	1.56
HL	Eaton Vance WW Health Sciences B	EMHSX	E-	(800) 225-6265	E- / 0.1	-6.07	-6.69	6.01 /20	4.90 / 4	0.43 /17	0.00	2.31
HL	Eaton Vance WW Health Sciences C	ECHSX	E-	(800) 225-6265	E- / 0.2	-6.15	-6.69	5.99 /20	4.90 / 4	0.43 /17	0.00	2.31
HL	Eaton Vance WW Health Sciences R	ERHSX	E	(800) 225-6265	E / 0.3	-5.99	-6.47	6.60 /24	5.49 / 5	1.09 /21	0.00	1.81
GR	Edgar Lomax Value Fund	LOMAX	C+	(888) 263-6443	C / 5.1	-0.49	4.84	8.01 /33	12.73 /47	4.82 /53	1.93	0.99
AA	Elfun Diversified Fund	ELDFX	C-	(800) 242-0134	D+ / 2.8	-1.08	3.09	8.58 /37	8.74 /19	5.16 /55	2.14	0.22
FO	Elfun International Fund	EGLBX	A	(800) 242-0134	A- / 9.2	-0.79	9.90	31.75 /95	24.91 /91	9.72 /79	1.71	0.23
★ GR	Elfun Trusts	ELFNX	E+	(800) 242-0134	D- / 1.3	-2.57	0.89	4.48 /13	6.73 / 9	1.45 /23	1.16	0.11
GI	Elite Growth & Income Fund	ELGIX	C-	(800) 423-1068	C / 4.5	-3.65	1.86	14.79 /71	11.91 /42	0.45 /17	0.96	1.42
GR	Emerald Growth A	HSPGX	D+	(800) 232-0224	C+ / 6.9	-4.07	11.27	22.63 /85	17.02 /68	5.53 /58	0.00	1.40
FS	Emerald Select Banking & Finance A	HSSAX	C+	(800) 232-0224	C+ / 6.2	-2.41	3.98	9.50 /43	17.37 /70	16.50 /94	0.00	1.57
TC	Emerald Select Technology C	HSYCX	D-	(800) 232-0224	B- / 7.0	-3.14	5.50	25.62 /89	15.78 /62	-5.72 / 2	0.00	3.22
GI	Endowments Growth & Income Fund	ENDIX	C-	(800) 421-4120	C- / 3.1	-0.76	2.57	6.48 /23	9.51 /24	5.85 /60	1.51	0.66
FO	Epoch Global Eq Shrhld Yield I	EPSYX	U	(800) 527-9500	U /	-0.46	6.43	--	--	--	0.00	1.10
GR	Epoch U.S. All Cap Equity Inst	EPACX	U	(800) 527-9500	U /	-2.51	1.74		--	--	0.00	1.29
GI	EquiTrust Blue Chip Fund Trad	FBBLX	D+	(877) 860-2904	D- / 1.2	-0.20	2.59	6.15 /21	7.19 /11	0.46 /17	0.80	1.46
BA	EquiTrust Managed Fund Trad	FBMGX	C-	(877) 860-2904	D- / 1.4	-0.95	2.30	3.73 /10	8.08 /16	5.52 /58	0.52	1.80
GR	EquiTrust Value Growth Trad	FABUX	C	(877) 860-2904	C- / 3.0	-2.93	0.14	4.17 /11	11.78 /41	6.65 /65	0.35	1.60
GR	Everest America Fund	EVAMX	C	(866) 232-3837	C+ / 5.9	-2.01	1.94	9.47 /43	14.70 /57	--	0.47	2.10
AG	Evergreen Aggressive Growth A	EAGAX	E	(800) 343-2898	D- / 1.0	-9.46	-4.01	4.81 /14	8.91 /20	0.58 /18	0.00	1.42
AG	Evergreen Aggressive Growth B	EAGBX	E	(800) 343-2898	E+ / 0.8	-9.66	-4.34	4.05 /11	8.14 /16	-0.14 /15	0.00	2.12
AG	Evergreen Aggressive Growth C	EAGCX	E	(800) 343-2898	D- / 1.3	-9.64	-4.36	4.06 /11	8.12 /16	-0.14 /15	0.00	2.12
AG	Evergreen Aggressive Growth I	EAGYX	E+	(800) 343-2898	D / 2.0	-9.36	-3.84	5.14 /16	9.25 /22	0.88 /20	0.00	1.12
GL	Evergreen Asset Allocation A	EAAFX	C	(800) 343-2898	C- / 3.4	-1.04	2.50	8.37 /36	11.95 /42	9.37 /78	2.20	0.93
GL	Evergreen Asset Allocation B	EABFX	C	(800) 343-2898	C- / 3.2	-1.27	2.09	7.62 /30	11.15 /37	8.82 /76	1.72	1.63
★ GL	Evergreen Asset Allocation C	EACFX	C+	(800) 343-2898	C- / 3.8	-1.29	2.13	7.65 /30	11.15 /37	8.84 /76	1.80	1.63
GL	Evergreen Asset Allocation I	EAIFX	B-	(800) 343-2898	C / 4.7	-1.04	2.63	8.68 /38	12.25 /44	9.61 /79	2.51	0.63
GL	Evergreen Asset Allocation R	EAXFX	B-	(800) 343-2898	C / 4.5	-1.12	2.37	8.16 /34	11.79 /41	9.27 /78	2.40	1.68
BA	Evergreen Balanced A	EKBAX	D+	(800) 343-2898	E+ / 0.7	-2.02	0.74	4.65 /13	6.96 /10	2.98 /37	1.77	0.99
BA	Evergreen Balanced B	EKBBX	D+	(800) 343-2898	E+ / 0.6	-2.22	0.46	3.97 /10	6.25 / 7	2.19 /29	1.10	1.69
BA	Evergreen Balanced C	EKBCX	D+	(800) 343-2898	D- / 1.0	-2.20	0.38	3.79 /10	6.21 / 7	2.22 /29	1.17	1.69
BA	Evergreen Balanced I	EKBYX	C-	(800) 343-2898	D / 1.7	-1.96	0.89	4.97 /15	7.30 /12	3.22 /39	2.18	0.69
IN	Evergreen Disciplined Value A	EDSAX	C	(800) 343-2898	C+ / 6.1	1.45	5.96	11.02 /54	16.20 /64	5.77 /60	1.07	1.12
IN	Evergreen Disciplined Value B	EDSBX	C	(800) 343-2898	C+ / 6.0	1.16	5.49	9.98 /47	15.81 /63	5.56 /58	0.65	1.87
IN	Evergreen Disciplined Value C	EDSCX	C+	(800) 343-2898	C+ / 6.5	1.14	5.48	9.95 /47	15.78 /62	5.54 /58	0.67	1.87
IN	Evergreen Disciplined Value I	EDSIX	B	(800) 343-2898	C+ / 6.9	1.44	6.03	11.16 /55	16.27 /65	5.81 /60	1.44	0.87
EM	Evergreen Emerging Market Growth	EMGAX	B-	(800) 343-2898	A+ / 9.8	-2.09	14.53	45.90 /98	34.79 /98	22.39 /98	0.59	1.96
EM	Evergreen Emerging Market Growth	EMGBX	B-	(800) 343-2898	A+ / 9.8	-2.31	14.10	44.81 /98	33.91 /97	21.58 /97	0.13	2.66
EM	Evergreen Emerging Market Growth	EMGCX	B-	(800) 343-2898	A+ / 9.8	-2.32	14.09	44.79 /98	33.83 /97	21.53 /97	0.24	2.66
EM	Evergreen Emerging Market Growth I	EMGYX	B-	(800) 343-2898	A+ / 9.8	-2.09	14.68	46.31 /99	35.19 /98	22.75 /98	0.86	1.66
IN	Evergreen Equity Income A	ETRAX	C-	(800) 343-2898	C- / 3.2	-0.94	3.87	7.68 /30	11.52 /39	5.02 /54	1.14	1.23
IN	Evergreen Equity Income B	ETRBX	C-	(800) 343-2898	C- / 3.0	-1.14	3.52	6.95 /26	10.72 /33	4.25 /48	0.50	1.93
IN	Evergreen Equity Income C	ETRCX	C	(800) 343-2898	C- / 3.8	-1.14	3.53	6.93 /26	10.72 /33	4.26 /48	0.52	1.93
IN	Evergreen Equity Income I	EVTRX	C	(800) 343-2898	C / 4.6	-0.90	4.04	8.01 /33	11.84 /41	5.30 /56	1.50	0.93
IN	Evergreen Equity Income R	ETRRX	C+	(800) 343-2898	C- / 4.2	-1.03	3.74	7.43 /29	11.28 /38	4.98 /54	0.98	1.41
IX	Evergreen Equity Index Fund A	ESINX	C-	(800) 343-2898	D+ / 2.8	-1.58	2.43	8.05 /33	10.60 /32	1.90 /26	1.30	0.57
IX	Evergreen Equity Index Fund B	ESIOX	C-	(800) 343-2898	D+ / 2.3	-1.76	2.06	7.26 /28	9.78 /26	1.15 /21	0.60	1.32
IX	Evergreen Equity Index Fund C	ESECX	C	(800) 343-2898	C- / 3.0	-1.77	2.05	7.24 /28	9.78 /26	1.14 /21	0.61	1.32
IX	Evergreen Equity Index Fund I	EVIIX	C+	(800) 343-2898	C- / 3.9	-1.51	2.56	8.32 /35	10.88 /34	2.16 /29	1.61	0.31
IX	Evergreen Equity Index Fund IS	EVISX	C	(800) 343-2898	C- / 3.7	-1.58	2.43	8.05 /33	10.60 /32	1.90 /26	1.36	0.57

● Denotes fund is closed to new investors
★ Denotes fund is included in Section II

RISK			NET ASSETS		ASSET					BULL / BEAR		FUND MANAGER		MINIMUMS		LOADS	
	3 Year		NAV						Portfolio	Last Bull	Last Bear	Manager	Manager	Initial	Additional	Front	Back
Risk	Standard		As of	Total	Cash	Stocks	Bonds	Other	Turnover	Market	Market	Quality	Tenure	Purch.	Purch.	End	End
Rating/Pts	Deviation	Beta	6/30/06	$(Mil)	%	%	%	%	Ratio	Return	Return	Pct	(Years)	$	$	Load	Load
D+ / 2.3	8.5	0.60	12.03	128	N/A	100	0	N/A	54.0	110.7	-5.1	96	7	1,000	50	0.0	1.0
C+ / 6.0	8.5	0.60	12.02	5	N/A	100	0	N/A	54.0	116.2	-4.9	97	1	250,000	0	0.0	0.0
C / 4.4	10.9	0.74	10.75	1,266	3	96	0	1	4.0	53.3	-7.8	26	17	1,000	50	5.8	1.0
C / 4.4	10.9	0.74	11.29	553	3	96	0	1	4.0	49.8	-8.1	21	10	1,000	50	0.0	5.0
C / 4.4	11.0	0.74	11.29	425	3	96	0	1	4.0	49.5	-7.9	21	8	1,000	50	0.0	1.0
C / 5.5	10.9	0.73	11.14	5	3	96	0	1	4.0	52.8	-32.4	26	6	1,000	0	0.0	1.0
B / 8.4	8.7	1.00	12.14	16	5	94	0	1	48.0	71.1	-11.7	71	9	2,500	100	0.0	0.0
B- / 7.6	5.7	1.13	19.32	265	3	74	21	2	118.0	48.2	-4.9	62	N/A	500	100	0.0	0.0
C+ / 6.6	11.5	1.10	23.98	336	2	96	0	2	42.0	141.7	-9.6	37	15	500	100	0.0	0.0
C+ / 6.1	7.3	0.85	51.19	2,233	2	97	0	1	13.0	45.2	-9.4	27	18	500	100	0.0	0.0
C+ / 6.0	8.7	1.01	21.67	62	N/A	100	0	N/A	86.3	69.0	-8.3	63	N/A	10,000	100	0.0	0.0
C- / 3.2	16.8	1.78	15.10	180	2	97	0	1	34.0	118.3	-13.4	39	14	4,000	100	4.8	2.0
B- / 7.1	10.3	0.80	28.71	167	3	96	0	1	15.0	86.4	0.9	94	9	4,000	100	4.8	2.0
D- / 1.4	22.7	2.24	8.63	2	9	90	0	1	297.0	120.2	-15.6	9	1	4,000	100	0.0	1.0
B / 8.3	6.7	0.85	14.69	103	16	83	0	1	11.0	54.6	-7.3	52	36	50,000	0	0.0	0.0
U /	N/A	N/A	15.55	142	2	97	0	1	N/A	N/A	N/A	N/A	N/A	100,000	10,000	0.0	2.0
U /	N/A	N/A	15.17	27	7	92	0	1	65.0	N/A	N/A	N/A	N/A	100,000	10,000	0.0	1.0
B / 8.5	7.2	0.90	40.80	16	4	95	0	1	N/A	45.1	-10.8	27	N/A	250	0	0.0	5.0
B+ / 9.6	5.9	1.12	15.56	9	19	64	16	1	12.0	44.7	-2.8	55	6	250	0	0.0	5.0
B / 8.9	8.1	1.00	13.91	14	13	86	0	1	16.0	69.8	-6.1	63	6	250	0	0.0	5.0
C+ / 6.6	7.5	0.84	13.14	11	10	89	0	1	78.6	73.0	-6.3	92	5	5,000	250	0.0	0.0
C / 4.7	14.7	1.55	17.22	130	3	96	0	1	108.0	73.7	-10.9	8	7	1,000	0	5.8	1.0
C / 4.6	14.7	1.55	15.43	25	3	96	0	1	108.0	69.9	-11.0	6	7	1,000	0	0.0	5.0
C / 4.6	14.7	1.55	15.37	5	3	96	0	1	108.0	69.9	-11.1	6	7	1,000	0	0.0	1.0
C / 4.7	14.6	1.55	18.01	9	3	96	0	1	108.0	75.3	-10.8	9	7	1,000,000	0	0.0	0.0
B+ / 9.1	5.9	1.15	14.24	3,485	7	57	35	1	15.0	61.2	-1.8	86	10	1,000	0	5.8	1.0
B+ / 9.0	5.9	1.17	14.04	1,866	7	57	35	1	15.0	57.8	-2.0	81	10	1,000	0	0.0	5.0
B+ / 9.0	5.9	1.17	13.80	3,619	7	57	35	1	15.0	57.7	-2.0	81	10	1,000	0	0.0	1.0
B+ / 9.1	5.9	1.16	14.33	231	7	57	35	1	15.0	62.9	-1.9	87	10	1,000,000	0	0.0	0.0
B+ / 9.5	5.9	1.16	14.15	8	7	57	35	1	15.0	60.6	-1.8	85	3	1,000	0	0.0	0.0
B+ / 9.1	5.3	1.11	8.68	938	11	66	22	1	77.0	38.4	-4.9	42	5	1,000	0	5.8	1.0
B+ / 9.3	5.3	1.12	8.68	153	11	66	22	1	77.0	35.5	-5.1	35	5	1,000	0	0.0	5.0
B+ / 9.2	5.4	1.12	8.68	79	11	66	22	1	77.0	35.3	-5.0	34	5	1,000	0	0.0	1.0
B+ / 9.2	5.3	1.10	8.65	240	11	66	22	1	77.0	39.7	-4.8	46	5	1,000,000	0	0.0	0.0
C+ / 6.3	8.1	0.99	16.39	13	5	94	0	1	62.0	87.0	-7.9	92	1	1,000	0	5.8	1.0
C+ / 6.3	8.1	0.98	16.33	5	5	94	0	1	62.0	85.5	-7.9	91	1	1,000	0	0.0	5.0
C+ / 6.3	8.1	0.99	16.31	2	5	94	0	1	62.0	85.4	-7.9	91	1	1,000	0	0.0	1.0
B / 8.9	8.1	0.98	16.36	669	5	94	0	1	62.0	87.3	-7.9	92	1	1,000,000	0	0.0	0.0
C- / 3.9	19.0	1.14	19.63	72	0	99	0	1	120.0	229.2	-6.3	15	7	1,000	0	5.8	1.0
C- / 3.8	19.0	1.14	18.21	15	0	99	0	1	120.0	222.3	-6.4	12	7	1,000	0	0.0	5.0
C- / 3.8	19.0	1.14	18.14	31	0	99	0	1	120.0	222.2	-6.4	12	7	1,000	0	0.0	1.0
C- / 3.9	19.0	1.14	20.15	280	0	99	0	1	120.0	232.4	-6.2	16	12	1,000,000	0	0.0	0.0
B- / 7.8	8.7	1.07	23.64	417	0	99	0	1	95.0	65.4	-7.3	52	5	1,000	0	5.8	1.0
B- / 7.9	8.7	1.07	23.46	60	0	99	0	1	95.0	61.8	-7.5	43	5	1,000	0	0.0	5.0
B- / 7.9	8.7	1.07	23.42	29	0	99	0	1	95.0	61.8	-7.5	43	5	1,000	0	0.0	0.0
B- / 7.8	8.7	1.07	23.63	606	0	99	0	1	95.0	67.0	-7.3	56	5	1,000,000	0	0.0	0.0
B / 8.5	8.7	1.07	23.67	N/A	0	99	0	1	95.0	64.7	-7.3	49	5	0	0	0.0	0.0
B / 8.4	7.6	1.00	47.45	242	1	98	0	1	5.0	61.7	-9.8	49	6	25,000	0	4.8	1.0
B / 8.6	7.6	1.00	47.22	145	1	98	0	1	5.0	57.9	-10.0	40	6	25,000	0	0.0	5.0
B / 8.6	7.6	1.00	47.27	175	1	98	0	1	5.0	57.9	-10.0	40	6	25,000	0	0.0	1.0
B / 8.6	7.6	1.00	47.48	260	1	98	0	1	5.0	63.0	-9.8	52	6	1,000,000	0	0.0	0.0
B / 8.6	7.6	1.00	47.45	15	1	98	0	1	5.0	61.7	-9.8	49	6	1,000,000	0	0.0	0.0

Fund Type	Fund Name	Ticker Symbol	Overall Weiss Investment Rating	Phone	Perfor-mance Rating/Pts	3 Mo	6 Mo	1Yr / Pct	3Yr / Pct	5Yr / Pct	Dividend Yield	Expense Ratio
								Total Return % through 6/30/06	Annualized		Incl. in Returns	
GI	Evergreen Fundamental Large Cap A	EGIAX	C-	(800) 343-2898	D+ / 2.9	-2.86	1.38	7.08 /27	11.55 /40	3.17 /38	0.31	1.39
GI	Evergreen Fundamental Large Cap B	EGIBX	C-	(800) 343-2898	D+ / 2.7	-3.01	1.06	6.38 /22	10.77 /33	2.43 /31	0.00	2.10
GI	Evergreen Fundamental Large Cap C	EGICX	C-	(800) 343-2898	C- / 3.4	-3.05	1.06	6.38 /22	10.78 /33	2.43 /31	0.00	2.10
GI	Evergreen Fundamental Large Cap I	EVVTX	C	(800) 343-2898	C / 4.3	-2.81	1.52	7.39 /29	11.88 /42	3.45 /41	0.64	1.08
GL	Evergreen Global Large Cap Eq Fd A	EAGLX	C+	(800) 343-2898	C / 4.7	-0.45	6.41	16.48 /76	12.82 /48	2.65 /33	0.65	1.84
GL	Evergreen Global Large Cap Eq Fd B	EBGLX	C+	(800) 343-2898	C / 5.1	-0.60	6.00	15.60 /74	12.05 /43	1.91 /26	0.00	2.54
GL	Evergreen Global Large Cap Eq Fd C	ECGLX	C+	(800) 343-2898	C / 5.1	-0.66	5.95	15.56 /73	12.02 /43	1.90 /26	0.00	2.54
GL	Evergreen Global Large Cap Eq Fd I	EYGLX	B-	(800) 343-2898	C+ / 5.7	-0.38	6.49	16.75 /76	13.15 /50	2.94 /36	0.98	1.54
GL	Evergreen Global Opportunities A	EKGAX	B+	(800) 343-2898	A- / 9.2	-3.58	9.32	29.16 /94	28.61 /94	12.90 /88	0.00	1.78
GL	Evergreen Global Opportunities B	EKGBX	B+	(800) 343-2898	A / 9.3	-3.76	8.96	28.27 /93	27.69 /94	12.06 /87	0.00	2.48
GL	Evergreen Global Opportunities C	EKGCX	B+	(800) 343-2898	A / 9.3	-3.77	8.91	28.23 /93	27.72 /94	12.07 /87	0.00	2.48
GL	Evergreen Global Opportunities I	EKGYX	B+	(800) 343-2898	A / 9.4	-3.49	9.51	29.57 /94	29.00 /95	13.15 /89	0.00	1.48
SC	Evergreen Growth A	EGWAX	D+	(800) 343-2898	C / 5.2	-7.59	6.05	12.74 /63	14.95 /59	4.89 /53	0.00	1.25
SC	Evergreen Growth B	EGRBX	D	(800) 343-2898	C / 5.0	-7.73	5.66	11.96 /59	14.16 /55	4.13 /47	0.00	1.95
SC	Evergreen Growth C	EGRTX	D+	(800) 343-2898	C+ / 5.6	-7.80	5.60	11.91 /59	14.12 /55	4.12 /47	0.00	1.95
SC	Evergreen Growth I	EGRYX	C-	(800) 343-2898	C+ / 6.3	-7.54	6.12	13.02 /64	15.29 /60	5.17 /55	0.00	0.95
HL	Evergreen Health Care Fund A	EHABX	D	(800) 343-2898	C- / 3.3	-4.63	1.56	11.09 /54	11.75 /41	7.42 /69	0.00	1.61
HL	Evergreen Health Care Fund B	EHCBX	D	(800) 343-2898	C- / 3.0	-4.84	1.15	10.29 /49	10.95 /35	6.64 /65	0.00	2.31
HL	Evergreen Health Care Fund C	EHCCX	D+	(800) 343-2898	C- / 3.7	-4.79	1.20	10.30 /49	10.96 /35	6.65 /65	0.00	2.31
HL	Evergreen Health Care Fund I	EHCYX	C-	(800) 343-2898	C / 4.6	-4.55	1.68	11.47 /56	12.09 /43	7.73 /70	0.00	1.31
FO	Evergreen International Equity A	EKZAX	A-	(800) 343-2898	B+ / 8.4	-0.38	8.64	26.64 /91	22.53 /86	10.45 /82	2.04	1.03
FO	Evergreen International Equity B	EKZBX	A	(800) 343-2898	B+ / 8.6	-0.58	8.22	25.72 /89	21.65 /84	9.67 /79	1.55	1.73
FO	Evergreen International Equity C	EKZCX	A	(800) 343-2898	B+ / 8.6	-0.58	8.22	25.78 /89	21.65 /84	9.67 /79	1.59	1.73
FO	Evergreen International Equity I	EKZYX	A	(800) 343-2898	B+ / 8.9	-0.19	8.89	27.09 /91	22.93 /87	10.81 /83	2.36	0.73
FO	Evergreen International Equity R	EKZRX	A+	(800) 343-2898	B+ / 8.8	-0.38	8.52	26.44 /90	22.17 /86	9.95 /80	2.21	1.23
GI	Evergreen Large Cap Equity A	EVSAX	C+	(800) 343-2898	C- / 4.0	-1.47	3.17	9.53 /44	12.52 /46	3.27 /39	0.99	0.86
GI	Evergreen Large Cap Equity B	EVSBX	C	(800) 343-2898	C- / 3.5	-1.72	2.75	8.71 /38	11.70 /40	2.49 /32	0.40	1.61
GI	Evergreen Large Cap Equity C	EVSTX	C+	(800) 343-2898	C / 4.3	-1.68	2.75	8.68 /38	11.71 /41	2.50 /32	0.45	1.60
GI	Evergreen Large Cap Equity I	EVSYX	B-	(800) 343-2898	C / 5.2	-1.46	3.29	9.79 /45	12.83 /48	3.53 /42	1.30	0.60
GI	Evergreen Large Cap Equity IS	EVSSX	B-	(800) 343-2898	C / 5.0	-1.53	3.17	9.55 /44	12.57 /46	3.28 /39	1.05	0.85
GI	Evergreen Large Cap Value A	EILAX	D+	(800) 343-2898	D- / 1.1	-3.46	-0.97	0.98 / 2	9.03 /21	2.90 /36	0.94	1.12
GI	Evergreen Large Cap Value B	EILBX	D+	(800) 343-2898	D- / 1.0	-3.66	-1.36	0.17 / 2	8.15 /16	2.32 /30	0.18	1.94
GI	Evergreen Large Cap Value C	EILCX	C-	(800) 343-2898	D- / 1.4	-3.58	-1.28	0.25 / 2	8.16 /16	2.33 /30	0.16	1.94
GI	Evergreen Large Cap Value I	EILIX	C-	(800) 343-2898	D / 2.2	-3.32	-0.86	1.19 / 3	9.20 /22	3.01 /37	1.21	0.94
GR	Evergreen Large Comp Growth A	EKJAX	E+	(800) 343-2898	E+ / 0.8	-6.15	-2.75	6.47 /23	7.68 /13	-0.96 /12	0.14	1.13
GR	Evergreen Large Comp Growth B	EKJBX	E+	(800) 343-2898	E+ / 0.7	-6.29	-2.95	5.74 /19	6.93 /10	-1.67 / 9	0.00	1.83
GR	Evergreen Large Comp Growth C	EKJCX	E+	(800) 343-2898	D- / 1.1	-6.29	-2.95	5.74 /19	6.93 /10	-1.67 / 9	0.00	1.83
GR	Evergreen Large Comp Growth I	EKJYX	D-	(800) 343-2898	D / 1.8	-6.15	-2.61	6.80 /25	7.99 /15	-0.67 /13	0.46	0.83
MC	Evergreen Mid Cap Growth A	EKAAX	E+	(800) 343-2898	D / 2.2	-8.16	1.31	6.72 /25	10.89 /34	2.82 /35	0.00	1.09
MC	Evergreen Mid Cap Growth B	EKABX	E+	(800) 343-2898	D / 2.1	-8.24	1.01	5.92 /20	10.14 /28	2.03 /28	0.00	1.79
MC	Evergreen Mid Cap Growth C	EKACX	E+	(800) 343-2898	D+ / 2.7	-8.23	1.01	6.13 /21	10.11 /28	2.12 /28	0.00	1.79
MC	Evergreen Mid Cap Growth I	EKAYX	D-	(800) 343-2898	C- / 3.6	-7.95	1.65	7.13 /27	11.23 /37	3.11 /38	0.00	0.79
AG	Evergreen Omega A	EKOAX	E	(800) 343-2898	E+ / 0.6	-9.02	-4.39	3.03 / 7	8.01 /15	-0.48 /14	0.00	1.43
AG	Evergreen Omega B	EKOBX	E	(800) 343-2898	E / 0.5	-9.22	-4.75	2.29 / 5	7.25 /11	-1.20 /11	0.00	2.13
AG	Evergreen Omega C	EKOCX	E	(800) 343-2898	E+ / 0.9	-9.20	-4.74	2.33 / 5	7.25 /11	-1.20 /11	0.00	2.13
AG	Evergreen Omega I	EOMYX	E+	(800) 343-2898	D- / 1.5	-8.95	-4.25	3.37 / 8	8.34 /17	-0.20 /15	0.00	1.13
AG	Evergreen Omega R	EKORX	D-	(800) 343-2898	D- / 1.2	-9.09	-4.52	2.83 / 7	7.83 /14	-0.58 /13	0.00	1.63
PM	Evergreen Precious Metals A	EKWAX	D+	(800) 343-2898	A+ / 9.9	3.62	25.59	75.57 /99	37.63 /99	37.06 /99	0.54	1.30
PM	Evergreen Precious Metals B	EKWBX	D+	(800) 343-2898	A+ / 9.9	3.44	25.14	74.33 /99	36.66 /98	36.06 /99	0.14	2.00
PM	Evergreen Precious Metals C	EKWCX	D+	(800) 343-2898	A+ / 9.9	3.44	25.14	74.33 /99	36.68 /98	36.05 /99	0.17	2.00
PM	Evergreen Precious Metals I	EKWYX	D+	(800) 343-2898	A+ / 9.9	3.72	25.77	76.08 /99	38.03 /99	37.41 /99	0.75	1.00
SC	● Evergreen Small Cap Value A	ESKAX	B-	(800) 343-2898	C+ / 6.5	-3.77	6.20	13.15 /65	17.45 /70	11.14 /84	0.00	1.53

● Denotes fund is closed to new investors
* Denotes fund is included in Section II

www.WeissRatings.com

Risk Rating/Pts	Standard Deviation	Beta	NAV As of 6/30/06	Total $(Mil)	Cash %	Stocks %	Bonds %	Other %	Portfolio Turnover Ratio	Last Bull Market Return	Last Bear Market Return	Manager Quality Pct	Manager Tenure (Years)	Initial Purch. $	Additional Purch. $	Front End Load	Back End Load
B- /7.9	8.5	1.09	23.43	652	0	99	0	1	22.0	66.8	-9.1	50	5	1,000	0	5.8	1.0
B- /7.8	8.5	1.09	21.94	222	0	99	0	1	22.0	63.2	-9.3	41	5	1,000	0	0.0	5.0
B- /7.8	8.5	1.09	21.94	88	0	99	0	1	22.0	63.1	-9.2	42	5	1,000	0	0.0	1.0
B /8.0	8.5	1.09	23.81	267	0	99	0	1	22.0	68.4	-9.0	55	5	1,000,000	0	0.0	0.0
B- /7.9	8.8	0.82	17.75	98	0	99	0	1	39.0	68.6	-10.1	9	5	1,000	0	5.8	1.0
B- /7.9	8.8	0.82	16.60	18	0	99	0	1	39.0	65.0	-10.4	7	N/A	1,000	0	0.0	1.0
B- /7.9	8.8	0.82	16.56	17	0	99	0	1	39.0	65.0	-10.3	7	N/A	1,000	0	0.0	1.0
B- /7.9	8.7	0.82	18.21	3	0	99	0	1	39.0	70.0	-10.0	10	N/A	1,000,000	0	0.0	1.0
C+ /5.6	13.3	1.12	30.97	229	2	96	0	2	107.0	184.0	-11.1	67	9	1,000	0	5.8	1.0
C /5.5	13.3	1.12	26.40	48	2	96	0	2	107.0	177.7	-11.2	58	9	1,000	0	0.0	1.0
C /5.5	13.3	1.12	26.52	54	2	96	0	2	107.0	177.9	-11.3	59	9	1,000	0	0.0	1.0
C+ /5.6	13.4	1.12	31.77	11	2	96	0	2	107.0	186.7	-11.0	69	9	1,000,000	0	0.0	1.0
C /4.4	15.6	1.03	17.89	99	3	96	0	1	90.0	100.2	-9.2	21	11	1,000	0	5.8	1.0
C- /4.2	15.6	1.03	15.88	21	3	96	0	1	90.0	95.7	-9.5	17	7	1,000	0	0.0	5.0
C- /4.2	15.6	1.03	15.85	184	3	96	0	1	90.0	95.6	-9.4	17	21	1,000	0	0.0	1.0
C /4.4	15.6	1.03	18.39	731	3	96	0	1	90.0	102.1	-9.2	23	9	1,000,000	0	0.0	0.0
C+ /6.2	9.7	0.85	19.56	132	0	99	0	1	68.0	88.7	-5.5	75	7	1,000	0	5.8	1.0
C+ /6.1	9.7	0.85	18.50	94	0	99	0	1	68.0	84.6	-5.8	68	7	1,000	0	0.0	5.0
C+ /6.1	9.7	0.85	18.49	61	0	99	0	1	68.0	84.5	-5.8	68	7	1,000	0	0.0	1.0
C+ /6.2	9.7	0.85	19.94	12	0	99	0	1	68.0	90.5	-5.6	78	7	1,000,000	0	0.0	0.0
B- /7.1	10.6	1.01	10.56	586	2	97	0	1	67.0	118.6	-7.3	35	8	1,000	0	5.8	1.0
B- /7.1	10.7	1.02	10.27	68	2	97	0	1	67.0	113.7	-7.5	29	15	1,000	0	0.0	1.0
B- /7.1	10.6	1.01	10.27	95	2	97	0	1	67.0	114.1	-7.7	30	8	1,000	0	0.0	1.0
B- /7.1	10.6	1.01	10.66	2,311	2	97	0	1	67.0	120.7	-7.4	38	8	1,000,000	0	0.0	1.0
B- /7.8	10.7	1.01	10.45	4	2	97	0	1	67.0	116.3	-7.5	32	3	0	0	0.0	0.0
B /8.8	7.8	1.00	16.15	113	1	98	0	1	53.0	70.8	-7.8	69	6	25,000	0	4.8	1.0
B /8.7	7.9	1.01	15.45	30	1	98	0	1	53.0	66.9	-8.0	61	6	25,000	0	0.0	5.0
B /8.8	7.8	1.00	15.72	8	1	98	0	1	53.0	66.9	-8.0	62	6	25,000	0	0.0	1.0
B /8.8	7.8	1.00	16.21	1,652	1	98	0	1	53.0	72.3	-7.7	72	6	1,000,000	0	0.0	0.0
B /8.8	7.8	1.00	16.15	68	1	98	0	1	53.0	70.9	-7.8	70	6	1,000,000	0	0.0	0.0
B /8.8	7.8	0.94	11.21	49	0	97	2	1	85.0	56.8	-7.7	37	N/A	1,000	0	5.8	1.0
B+ /9.0	7.7	0.94	11.19	21	0	97	2	1	85.0	52.6	-7.7	31	N/A	1,000	0	0.0	5.0
B+ /9.0	7.8	0.95	11.21	9	0	97	2	1	85.0	52.6	-7.7	31	N/A	1,000	0	0.0	1.0
B+ /9.1	7.7	0.94	11.21	3	0	97	2	1	85.0	57.4	-7.7	40	N/A	1,000,000	0	0.0	0.0
C+ /6.3	10.9	1.29	6.72	341	1	98	0	1	95.0	54.4	-10.0	11	8	1,000	0	5.8	1.0
C+ /6.2	10.9	1.29	6.26	19	1	98	0	1	95.0	51.1	-10.3	8	11	1,000	0	0.0	5.0
C+ /6.2	10.8	1.29	6.26	9	1	98	0	1	95.0	51.1	-10.3	9	8	1,000	0	0.0	1.0
C+ /6.3	10.8	1.29	6.72	15	1	98	0	1	95.0	56.0	-10.1	12	7	1,000,000	0	0.0	0.0
C /4.8	14.9	1.31	5.40	510	0	99	0	1	127.0	87.9	-6.3	1	8	1,000	0	5.8	1.0
C /4.7	14.9	1.31	5.01	22	0	99	0	1	127.0	84.2	-6.6	1	10	1,000	0	0.0	5.0
C /4.7	14.8	1.30	5.02	6	0	99	0	1	127.0	84.2	-6.6	1	8	1,000	0	0.0	1.0
C /4.7	15.0	1.32	5.56	116	0	99	0	1	127.0	89.7	-6.2	1	8	1,000,000	0	0.0	0.0
C /5.3	13.1	1.45	24.82	400	0	99	0	1	105.0	63.1	-9.5	7	17	1,000	0	5.8	1.0
C /5.3	13.1	1.46	21.86	318	0	99	0	1	105.0	59.5	-9.7	5	13	1,000	0	0.0	5.0
C /5.3	13.1	1.45	21.92	65	0	99	0	1	105.0	59.5	-9.7	5	13	1,000	0	0.0	1.0
C /5.4	13.1	1.46	25.43	9	0	99	0	1	105.0	64.7	-9.5	8	9	1,000,000	0	0.0	0.0
C+ /6.4	13.1	1.46	24.70	N/A	0	99	0	1	105.0	62.4	-9.5	7	3	0	0	0.0	0.0
E- /0.2	33.1	1.56	55.56	401	2	94	3	1	39.2	206.5	18.3	87	N/A	1,000	0	5.8	1.0
E- /0.2	33.2	1.56	53.26	74	2	94	3	1	39.2	199.8	18.1	83	N/A	1,000	0	0.0	1.0
E- /0.2	33.1	1.56	52.96	202	2	94	3	1	39.2	199.8	18.1	83	N/A	1,000	0	0.0	1.0
E- /0.2	33.1	1.56	55.24	6	2	94	3	1	39.2	209.1	18.4	89	N/A	1,000,000	0	0.0	1.0
B- /7.8	11.7	0.77	24.99	91	5	94	0	1	33.0	100.6	-8.4	81	N/A	1,000	0	5.8	1.0

					PERFORMANCE							
	99 Pct = Best		**Overall**				Total Return % through 6/30/06				Incl. in Returns	
	0 Pct = Worst		**Weiss**		**Perfor-**				Annualized		Dividend	Expense
Fund		Ticker	**Investment**		**mance**							
Type	Fund Name	Symbol	**Rating**	Phone	**Rating/Pts**	3 Mo	6 Mo	1Yr / Pct	3Yr / Pct	5Yr / Pct	Yield	Ratio
SC	● Evergreen Small Cap Value B	ESKBX	B	(800) 343-2898	C+ / 6.3	-3.98	5.79	12.28 /61	16.64 /66	10.80 /83	0.00	2.24
SC	● Evergreen Small Cap Value C	ESKCX	B-	(800) 343-2898	C+ / 6.8	-4.02	5.74	12.23 /61	16.65 /66	10.81 /83	0.00	2.24
SC	● Evergreen Small Cap Value I	ESKIX	B+	(800) 343-2898	B- / 7.3	-3.71	6.33	13.39 /66	17.81 /72	11.49 /85	0.00	1.23
SC	Evergreen Special Equity A	ESEAX	D	(800) 343-2898	C / 4.9	-5.62	3.71	13.25 /65	14.17 /55	4.87 /53	0.00	1.62
SC	Evergreen Special Equity B	ESEBX	D	(800) 343-2898	C / 4.6	-5.76	3.42	12.50 /62	13.40 /51	4.15 /47	0.00	2.32
SC	Evergreen Special Equity C	ESQCX	D+	(800) 343-2898	C / 5.3	-5.76	3.42	12.50 /62	13.40 /51	4.15 /47	0.00	2.32
SC	Evergreen Special Equity I	ESDDX	C-	(800) 343-2898	C+ / 6.0	-5.50	3.94	13.62 /67	14.54 /56	5.21 /56	0.00	1.31
SC	Evergreen Special Equity IS	ESSEX	C-	(800) 343-2898	C+ / 5.9	-5.53	3.84	13.36 /66	14.27 /55	4.94 /54	0.00	1.57
SC	● Evergreen Special Values A	ESPAX	B	(800) 343-2898	B / 7.8	-3.09	9.01	15.75 /74	20.76 /82	13.57 /90	0.60	1.31
SC	● Evergreen Special Values B	ESPBX	B	(800) 343-2898	B / 7.6	-3.28	8.59	14.91 /71	19.91 /79	12.75 /88	0.00	2.06
SC	● Evergreen Special Values C	ESPCX	B+	(800) 343-2898	B / 8.0	-3.24	8.61	14.93 /72	19.90 /79	12.76 /88	0.00	2.06
SC	● Evergreen Special Values I	ESPIX	B+	(800) 343-2898	B+ / 8.3	-3.01	9.14	16.11 /75	21.11 /83	13.88 /90	0.83	1.06
SC	● Evergreen Special Values R	ESPRX	A	(800) 343-2898	B / 8.2	-3.14	8.86	15.49 /73	20.52 /81	13.44 /89	0.49	1.57
GR	Evergreen Strategic Growth A	ESGAX	E+	(800) 343-2898	E / 0.4	-6.66	-4.40	2.24 / 5	6.96 /10	-1.16 /11	0.07	1.06
GR	Evergreen Strategic Growth B	ESGBX	E+	(800) 343-2898	E / 0.4	-6.83	-4.75	1.50 / 3	6.20 / 7	-1.86 / 9	0.00	1.76
GR	Evergreen Strategic Growth C	ESGTX	E+	(800) 343-2898	E+ / 0.6	-6.82	-4.71	1.50 / 3	6.20 / 7	-1.86 / 9	0.00	1.76
GR	Evergreen Strategic Growth I	ESGIX	D-	(800) 343-2898	D- / 1.1	-6.57	-4.23	2.55 / 6	7.29 /12	-0.87 /12	0.22	0.77
GR	Evergreen Strategic Growth IS	ESGSX	D-	(800) 343-2898	D- / 1.0	-6.66	-4.39	2.26 / 5	7.01 /10	-1.11 /11	0.09	1.02
GR	Evergreen Strategic Growth R	ESGRX	D-	(800) 343-2898	E+ / 0.9	-6.71	-4.50	2.04 / 4	6.87 /10	-1.09 /11	0.04	1.26
UT	Evergreen Utility and Telecom A	EVUAX	A+	(800) 343-2898	A- / 9.1	6.28	11.80	16.61 /76	25.92 /92	6.62 /65	5.80	1.08
UT	Evergreen Utility and Telecom B	EVUBX	A+	(800) 343-2898	A- / 9.0	6.08	11.38	15.77 /74	24.98 /91	5.85 /60	5.45	1.77
UT	Evergreen Utility and Telecom C	EVUCX	A+	(800) 343-2898	A- / 9.1	6.08	11.38	15.76 /74	25.01 /91	5.85 /60	5.45	1.79
UT	Evergreen Utility and Telecom I	EVUYX	A+	(800) 343-2898	A / 9.3	6.35	11.93	16.95 /77	26.25 /92	6.93 /66	6.44	0.81
GR	Excelsior Blended Equity Fd	UMEQX	C	(800) 446-1012	C- / 4.0	-2.44	4.39	6.73 /25	11.13 /36	2.24 /29	0.54	1.08
EM	Excelsior Emerging Markets Fd	UMEMX	C+	(800) 446-1012	A+ / 9.7	-4.36	7.69	36.50 /97	35.23 /98	22.04 /98	0.65	1.81
EM	Excelsior Emerging Markets I	EXEMX	U	(800) 446-1012	U /	-4.36	7.76	36.63 /97	--	--	0.77	1.59
EN	Excelsior Energy & Nat Resrc Fd	UMESX	C+	(800) 446-1012	A+ / 9.8	-0.21	7.97	34.61 /97	36.56 /98	19.13 /95	0.02	1.13
IN	Excelsior Equity Core Fd	UMECX	U	(800) 446-1012	U /	-1.71	7.98	11.57 /57	--	--	0.44	1.05
IN	Excelsior Equity Core I	EXECX	U	(800) 446-1012	U /	-1.68	8.10	11.91 /59	--	--	0.65	0.79
IN	Excelsior Equity Income Fd	UMEIX	U	(800) 446-1012	U /	-0.52	3.85	5.01 /15	--	--	2.27	1.10
FO	Excelsior Instl Intl Equity I	EXIIX	A	(800) 446-1012	A / 9.3	-0.94	9.00	26.82 /91	26.70 /93	9.10 /77	0.76	1.04
FO	Excelsior International Fd	UMINX	A	(800) 446-1012	A- / 9.2	-0.84	8.50	25.75 /89	26.15 /92	8.70 /75	0.48	1.50
GR	Excelsior Large Cap Growth Retail	UMLGX	C-	(800) 446-1012	C / 4.3	-5.95	-2.20	10.69 /51	12.02 /43	-3.17 / 5	0.00	1.20
MC	Excelsior Mid Cap Value & Restr Fd	UMVEX	B-	(800) 446-1012	C+ / 6.7	-3.23	5.41	10.25 /48	16.32 /65	9.59 /79	0.09	1.11
MC	Excelsior Mid Cap Value & Restr I	EXVAX	B-	(800) 446-1012	C+ / 6.8	-3.16	5.52	10.56 /51	16.58 /66	9.87 /80	0.27	0.86
FO	Excelsior Pacific/Asia Retail	USPAX	C	(800) 446-1012	B / 7.9	-6.34	0.77	24.69 /88	21.45 /84	10.84 /83	1.00	1.59
RE	Excelsior Real Estate Fd	UMREX	C+	(800) 446-1012	A- / 9.1	-1.73	11.39	17.62 /78	24.68 /90	18.18 /95	1.74	1.23
SC	Excelsior Small Cap Retail	UMLCX	B-	(800) 446-1012	B+ / 8.3	-5.10	10.01	18.03 /79	20.67 /82	11.97 /87	0.00	1.23
★ GR	Excelsior Value & Restructg Fd	UMBIX	B+	(800) 446-1012	B / 8.0	-1.35	5.44	13.26 /65	20.05 /79	8.62 /75	1.08	1.04
GR	Excelsior Value & Restructg I	EXBIX	A	(800) 446-1012	B / 8.1	-1.31	5.53	13.47 /66	20.33 /81	--	1.27	0.83
AA	Exeter Pro Blend Extend Term Series	MNBAX	B-	(800) 466-3863	C / 4.8	0.00	5.25	10.22 /48	11.74 /41	7.07 /67	0.81	1.17
AA	Exeter Pro-Blend Consrv Term Series	EXDAX	C-	(800) 466-3863	E+ / 0.8	-0.08	1.73	3.65 / 9	4.97 / 4	5.36 /57	1.65	1.00
AA	Exeter Pro-Blend Max Term Series	EXHAX	B-	(800) 466-3863	C+ / 6.4	-0.83	6.36	12.19 /61	14.99 /59	6.59 /65	0.46	1.20
AA	Exeter Pro-Blend Mod Term Series	EXBAX	C+	(800) 466-3863	C- / 3.2	-0.15	3.93	7.92 /32	9.37 /23	6.22 /62	1.02	1.20
★ MC	Fairholme Fund	FAIRX	A+	(800) 417-5525	B+ / 8.4	2.43	8.93	16.90 /77	21.49 /84	14.55 /91	0.78	1.00
IN	FAM Equity-Income Fund	FAMEX	D+	(800) 932-3271	D+ / 2.3	-7.56	-0.85	1.32 / 3	9.78 /26	8.85 /76	0.71	1.26
SC	FAM Value Fund	FAMVX	C	(800) 932-3271	C- / 3.8	-6.17	0.06	3.84 /10	12.06 /43	8.48 /74	0.77	1.18
BA	FBP Contrarian Balanced Fund	FBPBX	C-	(800) 443-4249	D+ / 2.9	-0.54	2.61	6.41 /23	9.15 /22	5.04 /55	1.75	0.99
GR	FBP Contrarian Value Fund	FBPEX	C	(800) 443-4249	C / 4.8	-1.20	3.01	8.17 /34	12.34 /45	4.84 /53	1.14	1.01
EN	FBR Gas Utility Index Fund	GASFX	B+	(888) 888-0025	B- / 7.0	4.94	5.69	7.49 /29	17.17 /69	5.38 /57	2.37	0.79
FS	FBR Large Cap Financial Fd	FBRFX	D-	(888) 888-0025	C- / 4.1	-0.35	2.03	4.59 /13	11.92 /42	6.20 /62	0.69	1.74
TC	FBR Large Cap Technology Fd	FBRTX	C-	(888) 888-0025	C / 4.8	-7.13	-0.91	12.41 /62	13.13 /49	--	0.00	1.93

● Denotes fund is closed to new investors

★ Denotes fund is included in Section II

RISK Risk Rating/Pts	3 Year Standard Deviation	Beta	NET ASSETS NAV As of 6/30/06	Total $(Mil)	ASSET Cash %	Stocks %	Bonds %	Other %	Portfolio Turnover Ratio	BULL Last Bull Market Return	BEAR Last Bear Market Return	FUND MANAGER Manager Quality Pct	Manager Tenure (Years)	MINIMUMS Initial Purch. $	Additional Purch. $	LOADS Front End Load	Back End Load
B- / 7.8	11.7	0.77	24.85	11	5	94	0	1	33.0	96.6	-8.3	75	N/A	1,000	0	0.0	5.0
B- / 7.8	11.7	0.77	24.86	11	5	94	0	1	33.0	96.8	-8.3	75	N/A	1,000	0	0.0	1.0
B- / 7.9	11.7	0.77	25.70	369	5	94	0	1	33.0	102.5	-8.3	83	9	1,000,000	0	0.0	0.0
C / 4.5	15.9	1.03	14.27	43	0	98	2	0	125.0	101.2	-10.9	17	N/A	1,000	0	5.8	1.0
C / 4.4	15.9	1.03	13.59	27	0	98	2	0	125.0	96.7	-11.0	13	N/A	1,000	0	0.0	5.0
C / 4.4	15.9	1.03	13.59	13	0	98	2	0	125.0	96.9	-11.1	13	N/A	1,000	0	0.0	1.0
C / 4.5	15.9	1.03	14.77	103	0	98	2	0	125.0	103.2	-10.8	19	N/A	1,000,000	0	0.0	0.0
C / 4.5	15.9	1.03	14.34	3	0	98	2	0	125.0	101.5	-10.8	18	N/A	1,000,000	0	0.0	0.0
C+ / 6.8	11.8	0.77	29.17	954	4	95	0	1	43.0	117.6	-9.8	94	9	1,000	0	5.8	1.0
C+ / 6.7	11.8	0.77	28.32	187	4	95	0	1	43.0	112.6	-10.0	92	6	1,000	0	0.0	5.0
C+ / 6.7	11.8	0.77	28.38	143	4	95	0	1	43.0	112.6	-10.0	92	4	1,000	0	0.0	1.0
C+ / 6.8	11.8	0.77	29.36	1,086	4	95	0	1	43.0	119.6	-9.8	95	9	1,000,000	0	0.0	0.0
B- / 7.6	11.8	0.77	28.99	7	4	95	0	1	43.0	116.4	-9.8	93	3	0	0	0.0	0.0
C+ / 6.8	9.6	1.13	26.49	5	0	98	1	1	133.0	49.7	-6.6	14	9	1,000	0	5.8	1.0
C+ / 6.7	9.6	1.13	25.66	3	0	98	1	1	133.0	46.4	-6.7	11	9	1,000	0	0.0	5.0
C+ / 6.7	9.6	1.13	25.67	2	0	98	1	1	133.0	46.4	-6.7	11	9	1,000	0	0.0	1.0
C+ / 6.8	9.6	1.13	26.73	1,465	0	98	1	1	133.0	51.1	-6.6	15	9	1,000,000	0	0.0	0.0
C+ / 6.8	9.6	1.13	26.33	16	0	98	1	1	133.0	50.0	-6.6	14	8	1,000,000	0	0.0	0.0
B- / 7.3	9.6	1.13	26.54	N/A	0	98	1	1	133.0	49.6	-6.6	13	3	0	0	0.0	0.0
B / 8.1	9.0	0.64	12.84	278	4	88	2	6	141.0	127.7	-5.9	99	N/A	1,000	0	5.8	1.0
B / 8.1	9.0	0.65	12.84	65	4	88	2	6	141.0	122.7	-6.1	99	N/A	1,000	0	0.0	5.0
B / 8.1	9.0	0.64	12.85	23	4	88	2	6	141.0	122.9	-6.3	99	N/A	1,000	0	0.0	1.0
B / 8.1	9.0	0.64	12.85	2	4	88	2	6	141.0	130.0	-5.9	99	N/A	1,000,000	0	0.0	0.0
B- / 7.8	7.8	0.98	36.25	435	0	98	0	2	21.7	63.4	-9.8	58	N/A	500	50	0.0	0.0
C- / 3.2	17.8	1.07	12.01	874	7	92	0	1	7.0	228.4	-3.1	29	N/A	500	50	0.0	2.0
U /	N/A	N/A	12.02	26	7	92	0	1	7.0	N/A	N/A	N/A	N/A	0	0	0.0	2.0
D+ / 2.9	21.1	1.00	25.94	560	1	98	0	1	234.0	204.2	1.0	84	11	500	50	0.0	0.0
U /	N/A	N/A	12.44	147	6	93	0	1	17.0	N/A	N/A	N/A	N/A	500	50	0.0	0.0
U /	N/A	N/A	12.45	55	6	93	0	1	17.0	N/A	N/A	N/A	N/A	0	0	0.0	0.0
U /	N/A	N/A	8.43	200	0	99	0	1	45.7	N/A	N/A	N/A	3	500	50	0.0	0.0
C+ / 6.3	11.3	1.09	9.70	60	2	97	0	1	34.0	152.3	-9.2	57	N/A	0	0	0.0	0.0
C+ / 6.5	11.2	1.08	16.29	535	2	97	0	1	26.0	148.8	-9.7	54	N/A	500	50	0.0	2.0
C+ / 6.2	11.7	1.21	9.32	566	6	93	0	1	24.5	71.3	-11.5	43	N/A	500	50	0.0	0.0
B- / 7.2	12.2	1.07	19.00	226	0	99	0	1	23.2	98.6	-8.7	29	N/A	500	50	0.0	0.0
B- / 7.7	12.2	1.07	19.05	31	0	99	0	1	23.2	100.0	-8.7	31	N/A	0	0	0.0	0.0
C- / 4.1	15.2	1.22	10.63	219	2	97	0	1	68.0	128.7	-7.5	7	8	500	50	0.0	2.0
C- / 4.0	15.3	0.92	9.86	108	0	99	0	1	14.0	113.0	-0.8	77	9	500	50	0.0	0.0
C / 5.5	14.8	0.97	18.25	570	1	98	0	1	65.0	140.9	-15.1	78	N/A	500	50	0.0	0.0
C+ / 6.7	11.5	1.34	48.43	6,581	4	95	0	1	12.0	120.8	-7.1	93	14	500	50	0.0	0.0
B- / 7.6	11.5	1.34	48.40	320	4	95	0	1	12.0	122.4	-7.3	94	14	0	0	0.0	0.0
B+ / 9.0	5.9	1.05	15.80	424	3	67	28	2	71.0	57.7	-5.2	88	13	2,000	100	0.0	0.0
B+ / 9.9	2.9	0.45	11.73	60	4	25	70	1	60.0	21.4	0.4	60	11	2,000	100	0.0	0.0
B- / 7.2	7.9	1.45	16.71	228	3	82	13	2	61.0	80.2	-8.0	92	11	2,000	100	0.0	0.0
B+ / 9.5	4.6	0.83	12.65	263	2	54	42	2	77.0	43.8	-3.6	81	13	2,000	100	0.0	0.0
B / 8.9	7.7	0.50	27.44	2,629	5	63	31	1	37.4	107.1	-7.2	99	7	2,500	1,000	0.0	2.0
B- / 7.9	8.8	0.92	21.26	161	8	91	0	1	14.1	61.0	-7.2	47	10	2,000	50	0.0	0.0
B / 8.4	7.8	0.44	48.03	1,053	14	85	0	1	14.3	71.4	-7.4	81	19	500	50	0.0	0.0
B / 8.2	5.5	1.05	18.20	62	0	70	29	1	24.0	51.0	-6.0	70	17	25,000	100	0.0	0.0
B- / 7.7	7.6	0.93	26.20	58	0	99	0	1	15.0	72.4	-10.1	73	13	25,000	100	0.0	0.0
B / 8.2	8.6	0.25	18.19	256	7	92	0	1	20.0	95.3	-5.8	97	N/A	2,000	100	0.0	1.0
C / 4.5	10.1	0.97	20.11	26	6	93	0	1	41.0	56.2	-2.0	40	9	2,000	100	0.0	1.0
C+ / 6.5	14.9	1.65	10.94	21	1	98	0	1	100.0	97.9	-10.3	21	4	2,000	100	0.0	1.0

Fund Type	Fund Name	Ticker Symbol	Overall Weiss Investment Rating	Phone	Performance Rating/Pts	3 Mo	6 Mo	1Yr / Pct	3Yr / Pct	5Yr / Pct	Dividend Yield	Expense Ratio
FS	FBR Small Cap Financial Fd	FBRSX	D+	(888) 888-0025	C+ / 6.3	2.56	7.21	7.05 /27	15.29 /60	16.55 /94	0.40	1.48
SC	● FBR Small Cap Fund	FBRVX	B+	(888) 888-0025	B / 7.8	-3.76	11.32	10.49 /50	19.76 /78	17.92 /94	0.00	1.40
GI	Federated American Leaders A	FALDX	D	(800) 341-7400	D / 2.1	-1.64	0.88	5.04 /15	10.17 /28	2.22 /29	1.03	1.16
GI	Federated American Leaders B	FALBX	D	(800) 341-7400	D / 1.8	-1.82	0.49	4.20 /11	9.32 /23	1.44 /23	0.30	1.92
GI	Federated American Leaders C	FALCX	D+	(800) 341-7400	D+ / 2.3	-1.80	0.51	4.25 /12	9.34 /23	1.45 /23	0.34	1.93
GI	Federated American Leaders F	FALFX	D+	(800) 341-7400	D+ / 2.8	-1.64	0.88	5.06 /15	10.19 /29	2.21 /29	1.08	1.94
GI	Federated American Leaders K	FALKX	C-	(800) 341-7400	D+ / 2.8	-1.71	0.66	4.59 /13	9.69 /25	1.71 /25	0.68	1.63
GR	Federated Capital Appreciation A	FEDEX	D	(800) 341-7400	D- / 1.2	-2.30	1.44	5.42 /17	7.93 /15	1.37 /23	0.68	1.22
GR	Federated Capital Appreciation B	CPABX	D-	(800) 341-7400	E+ / 0.9	-2.53	1.02	4.54 /13	7.09 /11	0.59 /18	0.00	2.01
GR	Federated Capital Appreciation C	CPACX	D	(800) 341-7400	D- / 1.2	-2.49	1.02	4.54 /13	7.07 /11	0.59 /18	0.00	2.02
GR	Federated Capital Appreciation K	CPAKX	D	(800) 341-7400	D / 1.7	-2.42	1.20	4.95 /15	7.43 /12	1.03 /20	0.19	1.67
AA	Federated Capital Income Fund A	CAPAX	D+	(800) 341-7400	D+ / 2.5	0.61	3.70	8.23 /35	9.95 /27	0.04 /15	4.76	1.31
AA	Federated Capital Income Fund B	CAPBX	D	(800) 341-7400	D / 2.1	0.35	3.23	7.33 /28	9.09 /21	-0.73 /13	4.21	2.06
AA	Federated Capital Income Fund C	CAPCX	D+	(800) 341-7400	D+ / 2.7	0.36	3.25	7.35 /28	9.11 /21	-0.73 /13	4.19	2.06
AA	Federated Capital Income Fund F	CAPFX	C-	(800) 341-7400	C- / 3.3	0.62	3.84	8.39 /36	9.96 /27	0.04 /15	5.00	1.27
AA	Federated Conserv Allocation Inst	FMCGX	C-	(800) 341-7400	E+ / 0.8	-1.13	0.50	2.78 / 7	5.29 / 5	3.85 /44	2.41	1.37
AA	Federated Conserv Allocation Sel	FCGSX	D+	(800) 341-7400	E+ / 0.6	-1.22	0.23	2.15 / 5	4.58 / 3	3.12 /38	1.69	2.07
IN	Federated Equity Income A	LEIFX	C	(800) 341-7400	C / 4.5	2.20	6.97	11.64 /58	12.52 /46	3.88 /45	2.17	1.11
IN	Federated Equity Income B	LEIBX	C	(800) 341-7400	C- / 4.0	1.88	6.44	10.69 /52	11.65 /40	3.08 /38	1.48	1.89
IN	Federated Equity Income C	LEICX	C+	(800) 341-7400	C / 4.6	1.89	6.45	10.71 /52	11.65 /40	3.08 /38	1.48	1.89
IN	Federated Equity Income F	LFEIX	C+	(800) 341-7400	C / 5.0	2.06	6.75	11.30 /55	12.22 /44	3.60 /42	1.99	1.39
AA	Federated Growth Allocation Inst	FMGPX	D+	(800) 341-7400	D+ / 2.4	-1.95	1.67	6.33 /22	8.54 /18	2.27 /30	0.87	1.53
AA	Federated Growth Allocation Sel	FMGSX	D	(800) 341-7400	D / 1.9	-2.11	1.27	5.57 /18	7.78 /14	1.55 /24	0.20	2.23
GL	Federated International Cap App A	IGFAX	B	(800) 341-7400	B / 7.8	-1.11	8.11	24.64 /88	20.45 /81	7.16 /68	0.79	1.55
GL	Federated International Cap App B	IGFBX	B	(800) 341-7400	B / 8.0	-1.34	7.59	23.49 /87	19.45 /78	6.31 /63	0.04	2.40
GL	Federated International Cap App C	IGFCX	B	(800) 341-7400	B / 7.9	-1.34	7.70	23.53 /87	19.43 /77	6.31 /63	0.27	2.40
FO	Federated International Equity A	FTITX	B-	(800) 341-7400	B- / 7.5	-1.14	8.56	25.02 /88	18.92 /76	3.60 /42	0.00	1.71
FO	Federated International Equity B	FIEBX	B	(800) 341-7400	B / 7.6	-1.32	8.17	23.89 /87	17.94 /72	2.78 /35	0.00	2.52
FO	Federated International Equity C	FIECX	B-	(800) 341-7400	B / 7.6	-1.34	8.17	23.89 /87	17.95 /72	2.78 /35	0.00	2.52
FO	Federated International Sm Co A	ISCAX	B	(800) 341-7400	A / 9.4	-1.90	9.74	34.85 /97	29.33 /95	12.75 /88	0.41	1.88
FO	Federated International Sm Co B	ISCBX	B	(800) 341-7400	A / 9.4	-2.07	9.35	33.86 /96	28.37 /94	11.91 /86	0.00	2.63
FO	Federated International Sm Co C	ISCCX	B	(800) 341-7400	A / 9.4	-2.04	9.37	33.86 /96	28.37 /94	11.92 /86	0.00	2.63
FO	Federated International Value A	FGFAX	B+	(800) 341-7400	B / 8.0	-0.14	11.21	27.55 /92	19.59 /78	9.28 /78	0.38	1.95
FO	Federated International Value B	FGFBX	B+	(800) 341-7400	B / 8.1	-0.25	10.86	26.67 /91	18.70 /75	8.47 /74	0.00	2.70
FO	Federated International Value C	FGFCX	B+	(800) 341-7400	B / 8.1	-0.30	10.83	26.67 /91	18.70 /75	8.48 /74	0.00	2.70
MC	Federated Kaufmann A	KAUAX	C	(800) 341-7400	C+ / 5.8	-6.19	2.86	14.65 /71	15.99 /63	8.33 /73	0.00	1.93
MC	Federated Kaufmann B	KAUBX	C	(800) 341-7400	C / 5.5	-6.37	2.57	13.78 /68	15.30 /60	7.73 /70	0.00	2.49
MC	Federated Kaufmann C	KAUCX	C	(800) 341-7400	C+ / 6.0	-6.37	2.57	13.77 /67	15.30 /60	7.73 /70	0.00	2.49
★ MC	Federated Kaufmann K	KAUFX	C+	(800) 341-7400	C+ / 6.5	-6.19	2.86	14.43 /70	15.98 /63	8.32 /73	0.00	1.95
SC	Federated Kaufmann Sm Cap A	FKASX	B-	(800) 341-7400	B+ / 8.7	-4.18	7.22	17.72 /79	24.77 /91	--	0.00	1.95
SC	Federated Kaufmann Sm Cap B	FKBSX	B-	(800) 341-7400	B+ / 8.5	-4.37	6.92	17.04 /77	24.07 /89	--	0.00	2.50
SC	Federated Kaufmann Sm Cap C	FKCSX	B	(800) 341-7400	B+ / 8.7	-4.37	6.92	17.04 /77	24.07 /89	--	0.00	2.50
GR	Federated Large Cap Gr A	FLGAX	E+	(800) 341-7400	E / 0.5	-4.84	-3.17	2.74 / 6	6.97 /10	-3.17 / 5	0.00	1.45
GR	Federated Large Cap Gr B	FLGBX	E+	(800) 341-7400	E / 0.4	-5.09	-3.45	1.95 / 4	6.18 / 7	-3.89 / 4	0.00	2.20
GR	Federated Large Cap Gr C	FLGCX	E+	(800) 341-7400	E+ / 0.6	-5.09	-3.45	1.95 / 4	6.18 / 7	-3.89 / 4	0.00	2.20
AA	Federated Market Opportunity A	FMAAX	D+	(800) 341-7400	D / 1.7	5.41	4.83	7.84 /31	7.89 /14	7.92 /71	1.84	1.24
AA	Federated Market Opportunity B	FMBBX	D+	(800) 341-7400	D- / 1.4	5.15	4.46	6.99 /26	7.09 /11	7.11 /67	1.24	1.99
AA	Federated Market Opportunity C	FMRCX	C-	(800) 341-7400	D / 1.9	5.16	4.47	7.02 /26	7.11 /11	7.10 /67	1.25	1.99
GR	Federated Max-Cap Index C	MXCCX	D+	(800) 341-7400	C- / 3.0	-1.74	2.16	7.41 /29	9.93 /27	1.20 /21	0.58	1.32
GR	Federated Max-Cap Index Inst	FISPX	C-	(800) 341-7400	C- / 4.1	-1.47	2.67	8.43 /36	11.03 /36	2.22 /29	1.54	0.35
GR	Federated Max-Cap Index Instl-Svc	FMXSX	C-	(800) 341-7400	C- / 3.8	-1.51	2.56	8.16 /34	10.70 /33	1.92 /27	1.25	0.65
GR	Federated Max-Cap Index K	FMXKX	C-	(800) 341-7400	C- / 3.5	-1.63	2.30	7.65 /30	10.22 /29	1.47 /23	0.87	1.10

● Denotes fund is closed to new investors
★ Denotes fund is included in Section II

RISK			NET ASSETS		ASSET					Portfolio	BULL / BEAR		FUND MANAGER		MINIMUMS		LOADS	
	3 Year		NAV								Last Bull	Last Bear	Manager	Manager	Initial	Additional	Front	Back
Risk	Standard		As of	Total	Cash	Stocks	Bonds	Other		Turnover	Market	Market	Quality	Tenure	Purch.	Purch.	End	End
Rating/Pts	Deviation	Beta	6/30/06	$(Mil)	%	%	%	%		Ratio	Return	Return	Pct	(Years)	$	$	Load	Load
C- /4.0	10.9	0.88	32.11	361	2	97	0	1		15.0	73.7	0.1	82	9	2,000	100	0.0	1.0
B- /7.2	11.4	0.67	46.82	846	5	94	0	1		20.0	129.5	-3.3	95	9	2,000	100	0.0	1.0
B- /7.4	7.9	0.99	23.56	1,455	1	98	0	1		49.0	61.3	-8.5	45	5	1,500	100	5.5	0.8
B- /7.4	7.9	0.99	23.63	506	1	98	0	1		49.0	57.4	-8.7	36	5	1,500	100	0.0	5.5
B- /7.4	7.9	0.99	23.64	108	1	98	0	1		49.0	57.4	-8.7	36	5	1,500	100	1.0	1.0
B- /7.4	7.9	0.99	23.52	51	1	98	0	1		49.0	61.4	-8.5	45	5	1,500	100	1.0	1.0
B /8.1	7.9	0.99	23.56	54	1	98	0	1		49.0	59.1	-9.1	39	5	1,500	100	0.0	0.0
B- /7.7	7.6	0.97	25.44	1,655	3	96	0	1		43.0	49.8	-9.7	27	6	1,500	100	5.5	0.8
B- /7.7	7.6	0.98	24.70	445	3	96	0	1		43.0	46.1	-9.8	22	6	1,500	100	0.0	5.5
B- /7.7	7.6	0.98	24.68	146	3	96	0	1		43.0	46.1	-9.9	22	6	1,500	100	1.0	1.0
B- /7.6	7.6	0.98	25.38	12	3	96	0	1		43.0	48.1	-9.8	24	6	1,500	100	0.0	0.0
B- /7.3	4.5	0.84	7.47	326	3	40	55	2		46.0	52.7	-3.4	85	N/A	1,500	100	5.5	0.8
B- /7.5	4.6	0.85	7.48	53	3	40	55	2		46.0	49.3	-3.8	78	N/A	1,500	100	0.0	5.5
B- /7.5	4.5	0.85	7.47	28	3	40	55	2		46.0	49.1	-3.6	79	N/A	1,500	100	1.0	1.0
B- /7.4	4.6	0.86	7.47	96	3	40	55	2		46.0	52.7	-3.4	84	N/A	1,500	100	1.0	1.0
B+ /9.7	4.1	0.85	10.97	52	1	45	53	1		10.0	29.7	-2.3	39	8	25,000	0	0.0	0.0
B+ /9.8	4.1	0.85	10.98	28	1	45	53	1		10.0	26.8	-2.4	33	8	1,500	0	0.0	0.0
B- /7.9	7.3	0.88	18.91	680	1	94	0	5		33.0	66.8	-10.5	78	9	1,500	100	5.5	0.8
B /8.0	7.3	0.88	18.90	244	1	94	0	5		33.0	62.7	-10.6	71	9	1,500	100	0.0	5.5
B /8.0	7.3	0.88	18.91	68	1	94	0	5		33.0	62.8	-10.6	71	9	1,500	100	1.0	1.0
B- /7.9	7.3	0.89	18.92	38	1	94	0	5		33.0	65.5	-10.5	76	9	1,500	100	1.0	1.0
B- /7.7	6.8	1.37	13.06	34	1	85	12	2		5.0	52.4	-8.6	44	8	25,000	0	0.0	0.0
B- /7.6	6.8	1.37	12.98	32	1	85	12	2		5.0	49.1	-8.7	36	8	1,500	0	0.0	0.0
C+ /6.5	10.6	1.63	11.60	150	7	92	0	1		129.0	115.7	-8.7	99	4	1,500	100	5.5	2.0
C+ /6.4	10.6	1.64	11.05	22	7	92	0	1		129.0	110.0	-8.9	98	4	1,500	100	0.0	2.0
C+ /6.4	10.6	1.64	11.05	31	7	92	0	1		129.0	110.1	-8.9	98	4	1,500	100	1.0	2.0
C+ /6.5	11.0	1.02	20.79	198	1	98	0	1		113.0	103.1	-11.4	14	1	1,500	100	5.5	2.0
C+ /6.4	11.0	1.02	18.67	34	1	98	0	1		113.0	98.0	-11.6	11	1	1,500	100	0.0	2.0
C+ /6.4	11.0	1.02	18.41	63	1	98	0	1		113.0	98.0	-11.6	11	1	1,500	100	1.0	2.0
C /5.1	14.2	1.28	38.30	316	2	97	0	1		79.0	188.1	-4.7	37	7	1,500	100	5.5	2.0
C /5.0	14.2	1.28	35.54	142	2	97	0	1		79.0	181.3	-4.8	30	7	1,500	100	0.0	2.0
C /5.0	14.2	1.28	35.50	68	2	97	0	1		79.0	181.3	-4.8	31	7	1,500	100	1.0	2.0
B- /7.0	10.3	0.95	21.04	72	4	95	0	1		28.0	120.3	-13.0	27	8	1,500	100	5.5	2.0
B- /7.0	10.3	0.95	19.90	40	4	95	0	1		28.0	115.0	-13.2	21	8	1,500	100	0.0	2.0
B- /7.0	10.3	0.95	19.95	10	4	95	0	1		28.0	115.1	-13.2	21	8	1,500	100	1.0	2.0
C+ /6.4	12.1	1.04	5.76	2,777	6	92	0	2		71.0	115.6	-10.5	30	20	1,500	100	5.5	0.8
C+ /6.4	12.1	1.05	5.59	1,176	6	92	0	2		71.0	111.5	-10.3	25	20	1,500	100	0.0	5.5
C+ /6.4	12.1	1.04	5.59	865	6	92	0	2		71.0	111.5	-10.3	26	20	1,500	100	1.0	1.0
C+ /6.5	12.1	1.04	5.76	4,178	6	92	0	2		71.0	114.9	-10.3	30	20	1,500	100	0.0	0.2
C /5.3	15.2	0.99	24.07	582	5	94	0	1		42.0	193.0	N/A	94	20	1,500	100	5.5	0.8
C /5.3	15.2	0.98	23.65	159	5	94	0	1		42.0	188.5	N/A	93	20	1,500	100	0.0	5.5
C /5.3	15.2	0.98	23.65	243	5	94	0	1		42.0	188.5	N/A	93	20	1,500	100	1.0	1.0
C+ /6.1	9.2	1.13	8.25	97	0	99	0	1		128.0	46.1	-12.0	14	3	1,500	100	5.5	0.8
C+ /6.0	9.2	1.13	7.83	64	0	99	0	1		128.0	42.8	-12.1	11	8	1,500	100	0.0	5.5
C+ /6.0	9.1	1.12	7.83	11	0	99	0	1		128.0	42.6	-12.1	11	8	1,500	100	1.0	1.0
B /8.3	4.7	0.13	13.14	1,496	13	26	59	2		61.0	36.2	1.8	93	6	1,500	100	5.5	1.0
B /8.5	4.7	0.13	13.08	444	13	26	59	2		61.0	32.9	1.6	90	6	1,500	100	0.0	5.5
B /8.5	4.7	0.12	13.05	949	13	26	59	2		61.0	33.0	1.6	90	6	1,500	100	1.0	1.0
B- /7.3	7.7	1.01	25.13	75	3	96	0	1		30.0	58.4	-10.0	41	N/A	1,500	100	1.0	1.0
B- /7.2	7.7	1.01	25.23	617	3	96	0	1		30.0	63.6	-9.8	54	N/A	25,000	0	0.0	0.0
B- /7.3	7.7	1.01	25.19	499	3	96	0	1		30.0	62.0	-9.9	49	N/A	25,000	0	0.0	0.0
B- /7.2	7.7	1.00	25.20	67	3	96	0	1		30.0	59.7	-9.9	44	N/A	1,500	100	0.0	0.0

Fund Type	Fund Name	Ticker Symbol	Overall Weiss Investment Rating	Phone	Perfor- mance Rating/Pts	3 Mo	6 Mo	1Yr / Pct	3Yr / Pct	5Yr / Pct	Dividend Yield	Expense Ratio
GR	Federated MidCap Gr Strategies A	FGSAX	C-	(800) 341-7400	C+ / 6.1	-6.82	2.08	12.02 /60	17.11 /68	4.38 /49	0.00	0.99
GR	Federated MidCap Gr Strategies B	FGSBX	C-	(800) 341-7400	C+ / 5.7	-7.01	1.67	11.07 /54	16.17 /64	3.57 /42	0.00	1.74
GR	Federated MidCap Gr Strategies C	FGSCX	C-	(800) 341-7400	C+ / 6.1	-7.00	1.65	11.07 /54	16.17 /64	3.57 /42	0.00	1.74
MC	Federated Mid-Cap Index Fund	FMDCX	B	(800) 341-7400	B- / 7.2	-3.35	4.03	12.41 /62	17.54 /70	8.69 /75	1.23	0.49
SC	Federated Mini-Cap Index C	MNCCX	C+	(800) 341-7400	C+ / 6.8	-5.35	7.46	13.02 /64	16.82 /67	6.77 /65	0.00	1.72
SC	Federated Mini-Cap Index Inst	FMCPX	C+	(800) 341-7400	B- / 7.4	-5.12	7.87	13.87 /68	17.83 /72	7.66 /70	0.18	0.91
AA	Federated Moderate Allocation Inst	FMMGX	C-	(800) 341-7400	D / 1.6	-1.52	1.09	4.68 /14	7.09 /11	3.42 /41	1.84	1.26
AA	Federated Moderate Allocation Sel	FMMSX	C-	(800) 341-7400	D- / 1.2	-1.70	0.74	3.94 /10	6.32 / 8	2.72 /34	1.13	1.96
BA	Federated Stock and Bond Fund A	FSTBX	D	(800) 341-7400	E+ / 0.7	-1.59	1.27	4.87 /14	6.53 / 8	3.01 /37	1.71	1.16
BA	Federated Stock and Bond Fund B	FSBBX	D	(800) 341-7400	E / 0.5	-1.75	0.86	4.03 /11	5.70 / 6	2.23 /29	1.01	1.95
BA	Federated Stock and Bond Fund C	FSBCX	D	(800) 341-7400	E+ / 0.8	-1.80	0.84	4.02 /11	5.73 / 6	2.24 /29	1.03	1.93
BA	Federated Stock and Bond Fund K	FSBKX	D+	(800) 341-7400	D- / 1.1	-1.72	1.02	4.34 /12	6.08 / 7	2.57 /33	1.26	1.65
GI	Federated Stock Trust	FSTKX	E+	(800) 341-7400	C- / 3.6	-1.43	1.62	6.17 /21	10.69 /33	3.48 /41	1.02	0.99
IN	Federated Strategic Value A	SVAAX	U	(800) 341-7400	U /	1.40	8.92	11.17 /55	--	--	3.64	1.00
IN	Federated Strategic Value C	SVACX	U	(800) 341-7400	U /	1.14	8.43	10.25 /48	--	--	3.03	1.75
IN	Federated Strategic Value Inst	SVAIX	U	(800) 341-7400	U /	1.49	9.27	11.44 /56	--	--	4.10	0.75
TC	Federated Technology A	FCTAX	E-	(800) 341-7400	E+ / 0.6	-10.05	-5.90	--	8.34 /17	-6.38 / 1	0.00	2.00
TC	Federated Technology B	FCTEX	E-	(800) 341-7400	E / 0.5	-10.19	-6.19	-0.61 / 1	7.63 /13	-7.08 / 1	0.00	2.75
TC	Federated Technology C	FCTYX	E-	(800) 341-7400	E+ / 0.7	-10.19	-6.19	-0.61 / 1	7.63 /13	-7.08 / 1	0.00	2.75
GR	Fidelity Adv 529 100% Equity A		C	(800) 522-7297	C- / 3.3	-3.26	2.36	12.92 /64	12.25 /44	--	0.00	1.38
GR	Fidelity Adv 529 100% Equity B		C	(800) 522-7297	C- / 3.1	-3.44	1.99	12.07 /60	11.48 /39	--	0.00	2.13
GR	Fidelity Adv 529 100% Equity C		C	(800) 522-7297	C- / 3.7	-3.45	1.99	11.99 /59	11.42 /39	--	0.00	2.13
GR	● Fidelity Adv 529 100% Equity D		C+	(800) 522-7297	C / 4.4	-3.35	2.28	12.63 /63	12.02 /43	--	0.00	1.63
GR	● Fidelity Adv 529 100% Equity Old-A		C	(800) 522-7297	C- / 3.7	-3.19	2.45	12.94 /64	12.28 /44	--	0.00	1.38
GR	● Fidelity Adv 529 100% Equity Old-B		C	(800) 522-7297	C- / 3.7	-3.42	2.15	12.30 /61	11.73 /41	--	0.00	1.88
GR	Fidelity Adv 529 100% Equity P		C+	(800) 522-7297	C- / 4.2	-3.37	2.12	12.32 /61	11.75 /41	--	0.00	1.88
AA	Fidelity Adv 529 2007 A		C-	(800) 522-7297	E / 0.5	-0.68	0.86	4.37 /12	6.05 / 7	--	0.00	0.55
AA	Fidelity Adv 529 2007 B		C-	(800) 522-7297	E / 0.5	-0.87	0.53	3.56 / 9	5.34 / 5	--	0.00	1.30
AA	Fidelity Adv 529 2007 C		C-	(800) 522-7297	E+ / 0.7	-0.87	0.53	3.56 / 9	5.27 / 4	--	0.00	1.30
AA	● Fidelity Adv 529 2007 D		C-	(800) 522-7297	D- / 1.0	-0.86	0.70	4.05 /11	5.81 / 6	--	0.00	0.80
AA	● Fidelity Adv 529 2007 Old-A		C-	(800) 522-7297	E+ / 0.7	-0.76	0.86	4.37 /12	6.08 / 7	--	0.00	0.55
AA	● Fidelity Adv 529 2007 Old-B		C-	(800) 522-7297	E+ / 0.7	-0.87	0.62	3.81 /10	5.55 / 5	--	0.00	1.05
AA	Fidelity Adv 529 2007 P		C-	(800) 522-7297	E+ / 0.9	-0.87	0.62	3.72 / 9	5.55 / 5	--	0.00	1.05
AA	Fidelity Adv 529 2010 A		C-	(800) 522-7297	D- / 1.2	-1.15	1.18	6.20 /22	7.92 /15	--	0.00	0.55
AA	Fidelity Adv 529 2010 B		C-	(800) 522-7297	D- / 1.0	-1.27	0.78	5.42 /17	7.14 /11	--	0.00	1.30
AA	Fidelity Adv 529 2010 C		C-	(800) 522-7297	D- / 1.5	-1.35	0.78	5.33 /17	7.11 /11	--	0.00	1.30
AA	● Fidelity Adv 529 2010 D		C	(800) 522-7297	D / 1.9	-1.17	1.02	5.90 /20	7.65 /13	--	0.00	0.80
AA	● Fidelity Adv 529 2010 Old-A		C-	(800) 522-7297	D- / 1.5	-1.16	1.18	6.21 /22	7.92 /15	--	0.00	0.55
AA	● Fidelity Adv 529 2010 Old-B		C-	(800) 522-7297	D- / 1.4	-1.26	0.86	5.58 /18	7.39 /12	--	0.00	1.05
AA	Fidelity Adv 529 2010 P		C	(800) 522-7297	D / 1.8	-1.26	0.95	5.69 /19	7.37 /12	--	0.00	1.05
AA	Fidelity Adv 529 2013 A		C-	(800) 522-7297	D / 1.9	-1.55	1.68	7.96 /32	9.28 /23	--	0.00	0.55
AA	Fidelity Adv 529 2013 B		C-	(800) 522-7297	D / 1.7	-1.76	1.21	7.12 /27	8.51 /18	--	0.00	1.30
AA	Fidelity Adv 529 2013 C		C-	(800) 522-7297	D+ / 2.3	-1.76	1.21	7.13 /27	8.48 /18	--	0.00	1.30
AA	● Fidelity Adv 529 2013 D		C	(800) 522-7297	D+ / 2.8	-1.65	1.54	7.70 /30	9.04 /21	--	0.00	0.80
AA	● Fidelity Adv 529 2013 Old-A		C	(800) 522-7297	D+ / 2.3	-1.47	1.68	8.04 /33	9.33 /23	--	0.00	0.55
AA	● Fidelity Adv 529 2013 Old-B		C-	(800) 522-7297	D / 2.2	-1.66	1.37	7.36 /28	8.75 /19	--	0.00	1.05
AA	Fidelity Adv 529 2013 P		C	(800) 522-7297	D+ / 2.6	-1.59	1.46	7.48 /29	8.79 /20	--	0.00	1.05
AA	Fidelity Adv 529 2016 A		C	(800) 522-7297	D+ / 2.6	-2.17	1.84	9.34 /42	10.54 /31	--	0.00	0.55
AA	Fidelity Adv 529 2016 B		C-	(800) 522-7297	D+ / 2.4	-2.38	1.45	8.49 /37	9.78 /26	--	0.00	1.30
AA	Fidelity Adv 529 2016 C		C	(800) 522-7297	C- / 3.1	-2.38	1.45	8.49 /37	9.82 /26	--	0.00	1.30
AA	● Fidelity Adv 529 2016 D		C+	(800) 522-7297	C- / 3.6	-2.19	1.69	9.14 /41	10.33 /30	--	0.00	0.80
AA	● Fidelity Adv 529 2016 Old-A		C	(800) 522-7297	C- / 3.0	-2.17	1.84	9.33 /42	10.60 /32	--	0.00	0.55

● Denotes fund is closed to new investors
* Denotes fund is included in Section II

RISK	3 Year		NET ASSETS		ASSET				Portfolio	BULL / BEAR		FUND MANAGER		MINIMUMS		LOADS	
Risk Rating/Pts	Standard Deviation	Beta	NAV As of 6/30/06	Total $(Mil)	Cash %	Stocks %	Bonds %	Other %	Turnover Ratio	Last Bull Market Return	Last Bear Market Return	Manager Quality Pct	Manager Tenure (Years)	Initial Purch. $	Additional Purch. $	Front End Load	Back End Load
C / 5.2	13.4	1.46	34.85	511	0	99	0	1	139.0	107.7	-9.2	70	11	1,500	100	5.5	0.8
C / 5.2	13.4	1.47	31.70	107	0	99	0	1	139.0	102.6	-9.3	62	11	1,500	100	0.0	5.5
C / 5.2	13.4	1.47	32.01	31	0	99	0	1	139.0	102.7	-9.3	62	11	1,500	100	1.0	1.0
B- / 7.3	10.9	1.00	22.91	1,200	14	85	0	1	14.0	101.6	-9.2	49	N/A	25,000	0	0.0	0.0
C+ / 5.9	14.5	1.00	16.28	18	0	99	0	1	20.0	109.1	-11.1	37	N/A	1,500	100	1.0	1.0
C+ / 6.0	14.5	0.99	16.85	86	0	99	0	1	20.0	114.4	-11.0	47	N/A	25,000	0	0.0	0.0
B+ / 9.2	5.3	1.11	12.22	66	1	65	32	2	7.0	41.9	-5.2	43	8	25,000	0	0.0	0.0
B+ / 9.2	5.3	1.11	12.21	44	1	65	32	2	7.0	38.8	-5.3	36	8	1,500	0	0.0	0.0
B / 8.3	5.3	1.10	18.81	205	11	62	26	1	50.0	36.2	-3.7	38	12	1,500	100	5.5	0.8
B / 8.4	5.3	1.10	18.78	53	11	62	26	1	50.0	32.9	-3.8	31	10	1,500	100	0.0	5.5
B / 8.4	5.4	1.11	18.72	26	11	62	26	1	50.0	33.0	-3.8	31	10	1,500	100	1.0	1.0
B / 8.7	5.3	1.11	18.83	6	11	62	26	1	50.0	34.5	-3.8	34	7	1,500	100	0.0	0.0
C- / 3.7	7.8	0.97	31.60	742	0	99	0	1	43.0	62.0	-8.2	53	7	25,000	0	0.0	0.0
U /	N/A	N/A	5.59	235	3	96	0	1	16.0	N/A	N/A	N/A	1	1,500	100	5.5	0.0
U /	N/A	N/A	5.60	52	3	96	0	1	16.0	N/A	N/A	N/A	1	1,500	100	1.0	1.0
U /	N/A	N/A	5.60	44	3	96	0	1	16.0	N/A	N/A	N/A	1	50,000	0	0.0	0.0
D+ / 2.4	18.2	1.93	5.10	22	5	94	0	1	71.0	75.3	-15.0	1	6	1,500	100	5.5	0.8
D / 2.2	18.2	1.93	4.85	40	5	94	0	1	71.0	71.2	-15.1	1	6	1,500	100	0.0	5.5
D / 2.2	18.2	1.94	4.85	8	5	94	0	1	71.0	71.2	-15.1	1	6	1,500	100	1.0	1.0
B / 8.5	8.7	1.10	12.15	30	0	100	0	0	4.0	72.2	-9.6	57	1	1,000	50	5.8	1.0
B / 8.4	8.8	1.11	11.79	9	0	100	0	0	4.0	67.9	-9.6	48	1	1,000	50	0.0	5.0
B / 8.5	8.7	1.10	11.77	17	0	100	0	0	4.0	67.7	-9.6	47	1	1,000	50	0.0	1.0
B / 8.5	8.7	1.10	12.13	20	0	100	0	0	4.0	70.3	-9.5	55	1	1,000	50	0.0	0.0
B / 8.5	8.7	1.10	12.13	17	0	100	0	0	4.0	71.8	-9.6	58	1	1,000	50	3.5	1.0
B / 8.5	8.7	1.10	11.87	18	0	100	0	0	4.0	69.1	-9.6	51	1	1,000	50	0.0	2.5
B / 8.5	8.7	1.10	12.03	1	0	100	0	0	4.0	69.3	-9.5	52	1	1,000	50	0.0	0.0
B+ / 9.9	4.1	0.85	11.70	44	15	36	47	2	27.0	32.5	-4.0	47	1	1,000	50	5.8	1.0
B+ / 9.9	4.0	0.84	11.35	3	15	36	47	2	27.0	29.5	-4.0	40	1	1,000	50	0.0	5.0
B+ / 9.9	4.0	0.84	11.34	44	15	36	47	2	27.0	29.5	-4.0	39	1	1,000	50	0.0	1.0
B+ / 9.9	4.0	0.84	11.55	35	15	36	47	2	27.0	31.5	-4.0	45	1	1,000	50	0.0	0.0
B+ / 9.9	4.1	0.85	11.71	23	15	36	47	2	27.0	32.6	-4.0	48	1	1,000	50	3.5	1.0
B+ / 9.9	4.0	0.84	11.43	18	15	36	47	2	27.0	30.4	-4.0	42	1	1,000	50	0.0	2.5
B+ / 9.9	4.1	0.85	11.44	2	15	36	47	2	27.0	30.6	-4.1	42	1	1,000	50	0.0	0.0
B+ / 9.7	5.3	1.09	11.99	82	9	51	39	1	27.0	43.6	-5.0	54	1	1,000	50	5.8	1.0
B+ / 9.7	5.3	1.10	11.67	27	9	51	39	1	27.0	40.2	-5.1	44	1	1,000	50	0.0	5.0
B+ / 9.7	5.3	1.10	11.66	48	9	51	39	1	27.0	40.2	-5.1	44	1	1,000	50	0.0	1.0
B+ / 9.7	5.3	1.08	11.84	29	9	51	39	1	27.0	42.4	-5.2	52	1	1,000	50	0.0	0.0
B+ / 9.7	5.3	1.09	11.98	28	9	51	39	1	27.0	43.4	-5.0	55	1	1,000	50	3.5	1.0
B+ / 9.7	5.3	1.09	11.74	36	9	51	39	1	27.0	41.0	-5.1	48	1	1,000	50	0.0	2.5
B+ / 9.7	5.3	1.09	11.71	2	9	51	39	1	27.0	41.2	-5.2	47	1	1,000	50	0.0	0.0
B+ / 9.3	6.3	1.28	12.07	91	4	62	32	2	21.0	52.4	-6.0	58	1	1,000	50	5.8	1.0
B / 8.8	6.3	1.27	11.73	39	4	62	32	2	21.0	49.1	-6.1	50	1	1,000	50	0.0	5.0
B / 8.7	6.3	1.27	11.72	36	4	62	32	2	21.0	48.9	-6.1	50	1	1,000	50	0.0	1.0
B+ / 9.3	6.4	1.28	11.89	23	4	62	32	2	21.0	51.5	-6.1	56	1	1,000	50	0.0	0.0
B+ / 9.3	6.3	1.27	12.10	27	4	62	32	2	21.0	52.7	-6.0	59	1	1,000	50	3.5	1.0
B+ / 9.0	6.3	1.27	11.82	39	4	62	32	2	21.0	50.2	-6.1	52	1	1,000	50	0.0	2.5
B+ / 9.0	6.4	1.29	11.78	2	4	62	32	2	21.0	50.3	-6.1	52	1	1,000	50	0.0	0.0
B+ / 9.0	7.4	1.47	12.17	89	0	73	26	1	19.0	61.5	-6.7	61	1	1,000	50	5.8	1.0
B / 8.9	7.5	1.47	11.88	35	0	73	26	1	19.0	58.3	-6.9	52	1	1,000	50	0.0	5.0
B / 8.9	7.4	1.45	11.88	27	0	73	26	1	19.0	58.3	-6.9	54	1	1,000	50	0.0	1.0
B+ / 9.0	7.4	1.46	12.06	20	0	73	26	1	19.0	60.5	-6.8	59	1	1,000	50	0.0	0.0
B+ / 9.0	7.4	1.47	12.19	24	0	73	26	1	19.0	61.7	-6.7	61	1	1,000	50	3.5	1.0

						PERFORMANCE							
99 Pct = Best *0 Pct = Worst*				**Overall Weiss Investment Rating**		**Perfor-mance Rating/Pts**	Total Return % through 6/30/06					Incl. in Returns	
										Annualized		Dividend Expense	
Fund Type	Fund Name		Ticker Symbol		Phone		3 Mo	6 Mo	1Yr / Pct	3Yr / Pct	5Yr / Pct	Yield	Ratio
AA	● Fidelity Adv 529 2016 Old-B			C	(800) 522-7297	C- / 3.0	-2.29	1.53	8.73 /38	10.02 /28	--	0.00	1.05
AA	Fidelity Adv 529 2016 P			C	(800) 522-7297	C- / 3.4	-2.29	1.62	8.85 /39	10.05 /28	--	0.00	1.05
AA	Fidelity Adv 529 2019 A			C	(800) 522-7297	C- / 3.0	-2.69	2.07	10.70 /52	11.13 /36	--	0.00	0.55
AA	Fidelity Adv 529 2019 B			C	(800) 522-7297	D+ / 2.8	-2.84	1.78	9.91 /46	10.33 /30	--	0.00	1.30
AA	Fidelity Adv 529 2019 C			C	(800) 522-7297	C- / 3.5	-2.84	1.78	9.90 /46	10.36 /30	--	0.00	1.30
AA	● Fidelity Adv 529 2019 D			C+	(800) 522-7297	C- / 4.0	-2.72	2.02	10.45 /50	10.89 /34	--	0.00	0.80
AA	● Fidelity Adv 529 2019 Old-A			C	(800) 522-7297	C- / 3.4	-2.69	2.07	10.69 /52	11.16 /37	--	0.00	0.55
AA	● Fidelity Adv 529 2019 Old-B			C	(800) 522-7297	C- / 3.4	-2.82	1.86	10.13 /48	10.61 /32	--	0.00	1.05
AA	Fidelity Adv 529 2019 P			C+	(800) 522-7297	C- / 3.8	-2.75	1.86	10.16 /48	10.64 /32	--	0.00	1.05
AA	Fidelity Adv 529 2022 A			C	(800) 522-7297	C- / 3.1	-2.99	2.21	11.22 /55	11.23 /37	--	0.00	0.55
AA	Fidelity Adv 529 2022 B			C	(800) 522-7297	D+ / 2.9	-3.24	1.84	10.36 /49	10.44 /30	--	0.00	2.08
AA	Fidelity Adv 529 2022 C			C	(800) 522-7297	C- / 3.6	-3.18	1.91	10.43 /50	10.49 /31	--	0.00	1.30
AA	● Fidelity Adv 529 2022 D			C+	(800) 522-7297	C- / 4.2	-3.07	2.16	10.98 /53	11.02 /36	--	0.00	0.80
AA	● Fidelity Adv 529 2022 Old-A			C	(800) 522-7297	C- / 3.5	-2.98	2.28	11.21 /55	11.27 /38	--	0.00	0.55
AA	● Fidelity Adv 529 2022 Old-B			C	(800) 522-7297	C- / 3.5	-3.10	2.04	10.69 /52	10.71 /33	--	0.00	1.05
AA	Fidelity Adv 529 2022 P			C+	(800) 522-7297	C- / 3.9	-3.09	2.04	10.67 /51	10.72 /33	--	0.00	1.05
AA	Fidelity Adv 529 70% Equity A			C	(800) 522-7297	D+ / 2.3	-2.52	1.75	9.50 /43	10.07 /28	--	0.00	0.55
AA	Fidelity Adv 529 70% Equity B			C-	(800) 522-7297	D / 2.1	-2.68	1.40	8.73 /38	9.16 /22	--	0.00	1.30
AA	Fidelity Adv 529 70% Equity C			C	(800) 522-7297	D+ / 2.7	-2.68	1.40	8.73 /38	9.16 /22	--	0.00	1.30
AA	● Fidelity Adv 529 70% Equity D			C+	(800) 522-7297	C- / 3.3	-2.54	1.69	9.25 /42	9.72 /25	--	0.00	0.80
AA	● Fidelity Adv 529 70% Equity Old-A			C	(800) 522-7297	D+ / 2.7	-2.51	1.83	9.49 /43	9.98 /27	--	0.00	0.55
AA	● Fidelity Adv 529 70% Equity Old-B			C	(800) 522-7297	D+ / 2.6	-2.66	1.55	8.95 /40	9.42 /24	--	0.00	1.05
AA	Fidelity Adv 529 70% Equity P			C	(800) 522-7297	C- / 3.1	-2.64	1.54	8.96 /40	9.44 /24	--	0.00	1.05
AA	Fidelity Adv 529 College A			D+	(800) 522-7297	E- / 0.1	-0.34	0.69	2.81 / 7	3.12 / 1	--	0.00	0.55
AA	Fidelity Adv 529 College B			D+	(800) 522-7297	E- / 0.1	-0.53	0.27	2.00 / 4	2.37 / 1	--	0.00	1.30
AA	Fidelity Adv 529 College C			D+	(800) 522-7297	E- / 0.2	-0.62	0.27	1.91 / 4	2.34 / 1	--	0.00	1.30
AA	● Fidelity Adv 529 College D			D+	(800) 522-7297	E / 0.3	-0.43	0.52	2.49 / 6	2.85 / 1	--	0.00	0.80
AA	● Fidelity Adv 529 College Old-A			D+	(800) 522-7297	E- / 0.2	-0.34	0.69	2.81 / 7	3.12 / 1	--	0.00	0.55
AA	● Fidelity Adv 529 College Old-B			D+	(800) 522-7297	E- / 0.2	-0.53	0.45	2.27 / 5	2.61 / 1	--	0.00	1.05
AA	Fidelity Adv 529 College P			D+	(800) 522-7297	E / 0.3	-0.44	0.44	2.33 / 5	2.64 / 1	--	0.00	1.05
FO	Fidelity Adv 529 Diversified Intl A			A	(800) 522-7297	B+ / 8.3	-3.53	5.71	25.48 /89	23.06 /87	--	0.00	0.55
FO	Fidelity Adv 529 Diversified Intl B			A	(800) 522-7297	B+ / 8.4	-3.67	5.38	24.60 /88	22.16 /86	--	0.00	1.30
FO	Fidelity Adv 529 Diversified Intl C			A	(800) 522-7297	B+ / 8.4	-3.67	5.32	24.51 /88	22.16 /86	--	0.00	1.30
FO	● Fidelity Adv 529 Diversified Intl D			A+	(800) 522-7297	B+ / 8.6	-3.51	5.65	25.19 /89	22.82 /87	--	0.00	0.80
FO	Fidelity Adv 529 Diversified Intl P			A	(800) 522-7297	B+ / 8.5	-3.59	5.52	24.95 /88	22.46 /86	--	0.00	1.05
GR	Fidelity Adv 529 Dividend Growth A			D	(800) 522-7297	E+ / 0.6	-3.47	0.78	6.27 /22	6.30 / 8	--	0.00	0.55
GR	Fidelity Adv 529 Dividend Growth B			D-	(800) 522-7297	E / 0.4	-3.64	0.44	5.56 /18	5.50 / 5	--	0.00	1.30
GR	Fidelity Adv 529 Dividend Growth C			D	(800) 522-7297	E+ / 0.6	-3.64	0.44	5.56 /18	5.50 / 5	--	0.00	1.30
GR	● Fidelity Adv 529 Dividend Growth D			D	(800) 522-7297	E+ / 0.9	-3.50	0.70	6.14 /21	6.11 / 7	--	0.00	0.80
GR	Fidelity Adv 529 Dividend Growth P			D	(800) 522-7297	D- / 1.0	-3.69	0.53	5.71 /19	5.75 / 6	--	0.00	1.05
GR	Fidelity Adv 529 Equity Growth A			D	(800) 522-7297	D- / 1.1	-4.28	-0.26	7.39 /29	7.93 /15	--	0.00	0.55
GR	Fidelity Adv 529 Equity Growth B			D-	(800) 522-7297	E+ / 0.9	-4.43	-0.62	6.56 /24	7.08 /11	--	0.00	1.30
GR	Fidelity Adv 529 Equity Growth C			D	(800) 522-7297	D- / 1.4	-4.41	-0.62	6.62 /24	7.12 /11	--	0.00	1.30
GR	● Fidelity Adv 529 Equity Growth D			D	(800) 522-7297	D / 1.8	-4.34	-0.43	7.10 /27	7.67 /13	--	0.00	0.80
GR	Fidelity Adv 529 Equity Growth P			D	(800) 522-7297	D / 1.7	-4.37	-0.44	6.95 /26	7.38 /12	--	0.00	1.05
IN	Fidelity Adv 529 Equity Income A			C+	(800) 522-7297	C- / 4.0	-1.32	3.37	9.94 /47	12.76 /47	--	0.00	0.55
IN	Fidelity Adv 529 Equity Income B			C+	(800) 522-7297	C- / 3.8	-1.43	3.07	9.17 /41	11.95 /42	--	0.00	1.30
IN	Fidelity Adv 529 Equity Income C			C+	(800) 522-7297	C / 4.5	-1.50	2.99	9.08 /41	11.90 /42	--	0.00	1.30
IN	● Fidelity Adv 529 Equity Income D			B-	(800) 522-7297	C / 5.0	-1.33	3.25	9.70 /45	12.54 /46	--	0.00	0.80
IN	Fidelity Adv 529 Equity Income P			C+	(800) 522-7297	C / 4.8	-1.34	3.20	9.52 /43	12.23 /44	--	0.00	1.05
MC	Fidelity Adv 529 Mid Cap A			C	(800) 522-7297	C / 5.1	-8.13	1.31	12.08 /60	15.28 /60	--	0.00	0.55
MC	Fidelity Adv 529 Mid Cap B			C-	(800) 522-7297	C / 4.8	-8.34	0.87	11.23 /55	14.40 /56	--	0.00	1.30

● Denotes fund is closed to new investors
* Denotes fund is included in Section II

www.WeissRatings.com

RISK			NET ASSETS		ASSET					BULL / BEAR		FUND MANAGER		MINIMUMS		LOADS	
	3 Year		NAV						Portfolio	Last Bull	Last Bear	Manager	Manager	Initial	Additional	Front	Back
Risk Rating/Pts	Standard Deviation	Beta	As of 6/30/06	Total $(Mil)	Cash %	Stocks %	Bonds %	Other %	Turnover Ratio	Market Return	Market Return	Quality Pct	Tenure (Years)	Purch. $	Purch. $	End Load	End Load
B+ / 9.0	7.4	1.47	11.96	36	0	73	26	1	19.0	59.3	-6.9	55	1	1,000	50	0.0	2.5
B+ / 9.0	7.4	1.46	11.93	3	0	73	26	1	19.0	59.2	-6.8	56	1	1,000	50	0.0	0.0
B / 8.9	7.8	1.52	12.31	88	0	82	17	1	9.0	65.7	-6.8	64	1	1,000	50	5.8	1.0
B / 8.8	7.8	1.53	11.98	35	0	82	17	1	9.0	62.1	-6.9	55	1	1,000	50	0.0	5.0
B / 8.9	7.8	1.52	11.99	24	0	82	17	1	9.0	62.2	-6.9	56	1	1,000	50	0.0	1.0
B / 8.8	7.8	1.53	12.15	18	0	82	17	1	9.0	64.7	-6.9	61	1	1,000	50	0.0	0.0
B / 8.9	7.8	1.52	12.32	28	0	82	17	1	9.0	65.8	-6.8	64	1	1,000	50	3.5	1.0
B / 8.8	7.8	1.53	12.07	35	0	82	17	1	9.0	63.2	-6.9	58	1	1,000	50	0.0	2.5
B / 8.8	7.8	1.53	12.04	3	0	82	17	1	9.0	63.5	-6.9	58	1	1,000	50	0.0	0.0
B / 8.8	7.9	1.55	15.26	89	0	86	13	1	1.0	67.1	-7.2	63	1	1,000	50	5.8	1.0
B / 8.8	8.0	1.56	14.91	34	0	86	13	1	1.0	63.7	-7.3	54	1	1,000	50	0.0	5.0
B / 8.8	7.9	1.56	14.93	24	0	86	13	1	1.0	63.8	-7.3	55	1	1,000	50	0.0	1.0
B / 8.8	7.9	1.55	15.16	1	0	86	13	1	1.0	65.9	-7.2	61	1	1,000	50	0.0	0.0
B / 8.8	7.9	1.55	15.28	2	0	86	13	1	1.0	67.3	-7.2	64	1	1,000	50	3.5	1.0
B / 8.8	7.9	1.54	15.02	2	0	86	13	1	1.0	64.7	-7.3	58	1	1,000	50	0.0	2.5
B / 8.8	7.9	1.55	15.04	1	0	86	13	1	1.0	64.8	-7.2	58	1	1,000	50	0.0	0.0
B+ / 9.2	6.7	1.33	12.79	25	0	71	28	1	5.0	56.4	-5.1	64	1	1,000	50	5.8	1.0
B+ / 9.1	6.7	1.34	12.33	5	0	71	28	1	5.0	53.0	-5.1	53	1	1,000	50	0.0	5.0
B+ / 9.1	6.7	1.34	12.33	16	0	71	28	1	5.0	53.0	-5.1	54	1	1,000	50	0.0	1.0
B+ / 9.2	6.6	1.33	12.64	18	0	71	28	1	5.0	55.2	-5.1	60	1	1,000	50	0.0	0.0
B+ / 9.2	6.7	1.34	12.81	16	0	71	28	1	5.0	56.5	-5.1	63	1	1,000	50	3.5	1.0
B+ / 9.2	6.6	1.33	12.42	15	0	71	28	1	5.0	54.1	-5.1	57	1	1,000	50	0.0	2.5
B+ / 9.2	6.7	1.34	12.53	N/A	0	71	28	1	5.0	54.0	-5.1	57	1	1,000	50	0.0	0.0
B+ / 9.9	2.2	0.41	11.69	13	39	21	39	1	20.0	14.9	-0.2	40	1	1,000	50	5.8	1.0
B+ / 9.9	2.2	0.41	11.20	2	39	21	39	1	20.0	12.3	-0.3	33	1	1,000	50	0.0	5.0
B+ / 9.9	2.3	0.42	11.18	13	39	21	39	1	20.0	12.2	-0.3	33	1	1,000	50	0.0	1.0
B+ / 9.9	2.2	0.41	11.52	23	39	21	39	1	20.0	14.0	-0.2	37	1	1,000	50	0.0	0.0
B+ / 9.9	2.3	0.42	11.69	13	39	21	39	1	20.0	14.9	-0.2	39	1	1,000	50	3.5	1.0
B+ / 9.9	2.3	0.42	11.28	4	39	21	39	1	20.0	13.1	-0.3	35	1	1,000	50	0.0	2.5
B+ / 9.9	2.3	0.43	11.42	1	39	21	39	1	20.0	13.2	-0.4	35	1	1,000	50	0.0	0.0
B- / 7.5	11.3	1.08	18.32	24	1	98	0	1	1.0	136.3	-5.5	28	1	1,000	50	5.8	1.0
B- / 7.5	11.3	1.08	17.83	7	1	98	0	1	1.0	130.7	-5.8	23	1	1,000	50	0.0	1.0
B- / 7.5	11.3	1.08	17.83	13	1	98	0	1	1.0	130.6	-5.7	23	1	1,000	50	0.0	1.0
B- / 7.5	11.4	1.08	18.14	1	1	98	0	1	1.0	134.6	-5.7	27	1	1,000	50	0.0	1.0
B- / 7.5	11.4	1.08	17.98	N/A	1	98	0	1	1.0	132.7	-5.7	25	1	1,000	50	0.0	1.0
B / 8.2	7.5	0.89	11.70	10	1	98	0	1	3.0	44.1	-11.1	22	1	1,000	50	5.8	1.0
B / 8.0	7.5	0.89	11.39	5	1	98	0	1	3.0	40.6	-11.0	17	1	1,000	50	0.0	5.0
B / 8.0	7.5	0.89	11.39	6	1	98	0	1	3.0	40.8	-11.1	17	1	1,000	50	0.0	1.0
B / 8.1	7.6	0.90	11.59	N/A	1	98	0	1	3.0	43.0	-11.1	20	1	1,000	50	0.0	0.0
B / 8.0	7.5	0.89	11.47	N/A	1	98	0	1	3.0	41.7	-11.1	18	1	1,000	50	0.0	0.0
B- / 7.6	10.4	1.25	11.63	10	0	99	0	1	4.0	55.0	-11.5	13	1	1,000	50	5.8	1.0
B- / 7.5	10.4	1.26	11.21	4	0	99	0	1	4.0	51.1	-11.5	10	1	1,000	50	0.0	5.0
B- / 7.5	10.4	1.26	11.27	5	0	99	0	1	4.0	51.3	-11.1	10	1	1,000	50	0.0	1.0
B- / 7.6	10.4	1.26	11.47	N/A	0	99	0	1	4.0	53.6	-11.5	12	1	1,000	50	0.0	0.0
B- / 7.6	10.4	1.25	11.38	N/A	0	99	0	1	4.0	52.3	-11.5	11	1	1,000	50	0.0	0.0
B / 8.7	8.1	1.04	13.49	15	3	95	0	2	1.0	73.2	-10.6	68	1	1,000	50	5.8	1.0
B / 8.7	8.1	1.04	13.09	5	3	95	0	2	1.0	69.0	-10.6	60	1	1,000	50	0.0	5.0
B / 8.7	8.2	1.04	13.10	9	3	95	0	2	1.0	68.8	-10.4	59	1	1,000	50	0.0	1.0
B / 8.7	8.1	1.04	13.34	1	3	95	0	2	1.0	71.7	-10.6	66	1	1,000	50	0.0	0.0
B / 8.7	8.1	1.04	13.23	N/A	3	95	0	2	1.0	70.3	-10.6	63	1	1,000	50	0.0	0.0
C+ / 6.6	13.8	1.13	15.49	19	0	99	0	1	1.0	103.4	-4.6	17	1	1,000	50	5.8	1.0
C+ / 6.6	13.8	1.13	15.06	7	0	99	0	1	1.0	98.5	-4.8	13	1	1,000	50	0.0	5.0

					PERFORMANCE							
	99 Pct = Best					Total Return % through 6/30/06					Incl. in Returns	
	0 Pct = Worst		Overall Weiss Investment Rating		Perfor-mance Rating/Pts				Annualized		Dividend	Expense
Fund Type	Fund Name	Ticker Symbol		Phone		3 Mo	6 Mo	1Yr / Pct	3Yr / Pct	5Yr / Pct	Yield	Ratio
MC	Fidelity Adv 529 Mid Cap C		C	(800) 522-7297	C / 5.4	-8.27	0.94	11.28 /55	14.43 /56	--	0.00	1.30
MC	● Fidelity Adv 529 Mid Cap D		C+	(800) 522-7297	C+ / 5.8	-8.21	1.18	11.81 /58	14.95 /59	--	0.00	0.80
MC	Fidelity Adv 529 Mid Cap P		C	(800) 522-7297	C+ / 5.7	-8.20	1.05	11.57 /57	14.70 /57	--	0.00	1.05
SC	Fidelity Adv 529 Small Cap A		B-	(800) 522-7297	B- / 7.0	-2.28	4.62	11.27 /55	18.99 /76	--	0.00	0.55
SC	Fidelity Adv 529 Small Cap B		B-	(800) 522-7297	C+ / 6.8	-2.40	4.28	10.39 /49	18.10 /73	--	0.00	1.30
SC	Fidelity Adv 529 Small Cap C		B	(800) 522-7297	B- / 7.2	-2.46	4.21	10.39 /49	18.10 /73	--	0.00	1.30
SC	● Fidelity Adv 529 Small Cap D		B	(800) 522-7297	B- / 7.5	-2.36	4.47	10.94 /53	18.72 /75	--	0.00	0.80
SC	Fidelity Adv 529 Small Cap P		B	(800) 522-7297	B- / 7.4	-2.43	4.29	10.70 /52	18.50 /74	--	0.00	1.05
GR	Fidelity Adv 529 Value Strat A		C	(800) 522-7297	C+ / 5.8	-3.55	3.41	10.28 /49	16.40 /65	--	0.00	0.55
GR	Fidelity Adv 529 Value Strat B		C-	(800) 522-7297	C+ / 5.6	-3.74	3.00	9.43 /43	15.52 /61	--	0.00	1.30
GR	Fidelity Adv 529 Value Strat C		C	(800) 522-7297	C+ / 6.1	-3.72	2.98	9.52 /43	15.54 /61	--	0.00	1.30
GR	● Fidelity Adv 529 Value Strat D		C	(800) 522-7297	C+ / 6.4	-3.59	3.32	10.04 /47	15.96 /63	--	0.00	0.80
GR	Fidelity Adv 529 Value Strat P		C	(800) 522-7297	C+ / 6.4	-3.66	3.13	9.77 /45	15.83 /63	--	0.00	1.05
AG	Fidelity Adv Aggressive Growth A	FGVAX	E	(800) 522-7297	D- / 1.4	-8.65	-3.03	5.69 /19	9.74 /25	-0.98 /12	0.00	1.30
AG	Fidelity Adv Aggressive Growth B	FGVBX	E	(800) 522-7297	D- / 1.2	-8.80	-3.47	4.82 /14	8.95 /20	-1.73 / 9	0.00	2.05
AG	Fidelity Adv Aggressive Growth C	FGECX	E	(800) 522-7297	D / 1.8	-8.78	-3.35	4.94 /15	8.98 /21	-1.70 / 9	0.00	2.05
AG	Fidelity Adv Aggressive Growth I	FRVIX	E+	(800) 522-7297	D+ / 2.6	-8.51	-2.87	5.93 /20	10.09 /28	-0.68 /13	0.00	1.05
AG	Fidelity Adv Aggressive Growth T	FGVTX	E	(800) 522-7297	D / 1.7	-8.67	-3.07	5.41 /17	9.54 /24	-1.22 /11	0.00	1.55
AA	Fidelity Adv Asset Allocation A	FLOAX	C-	(800) 522-7297	C- / 3.4	-1.94	1.61	8.15 /34	12.12 /43	4.97 /54	0.87	1.25
AA	Fidelity Adv Asset Allocation B	FLLBX	C-	(800) 522-7297	C- / 3.1	-2.06	1.25	7.37 /28	11.22 /37	4.12 /47	0.18	2.00
AA	Fidelity Adv Asset Allocation C	FLOCX	C	(800) 522-7297	C- / 3.8	-2.13	1.18	7.40 /29	11.26 /37	4.16 /47	0.20	2.00
AA	Fidelity Adv Asset Allocation I	FAVIX	C+	(800) 522-7297	C / 4.8	-1.87	1.84	8.53 /37	12.55 /46	5.30 /56	1.26	1.00
AA	Fidelity Adv Asset Allocation T	FAATX	C-	(800) 522-7297	C- / 3.7	-2.02	1.45	7.83 /31	11.82 /41	4.67 /52	0.59	1.50
GI	Fidelity Adv Balanced Fund A	FABLX	D+	(800) 522-7297	D- / 1.0	-1.42	2.98	10.74 /52	6.88 /10	4.09 /47	1.76	1.00
GI	Fidelity Adv Balanced Fund B	FAISX	D+	(800) 522-7297	E+ / 0.8	-1.65	2.56	9.81 /46	5.99 / 7	3.22 /39	1.04	1.85
GI	Fidelity Adv Balanced Fund C	FABCX	D+	(800) 522-7297	D- / 1.3	-1.62	2.59	9.89 /46	6.04 / 7	3.25 /39	1.11	1.81
GI	Fidelity Adv Balanced Fund I	FAIOX	C-	(800) 522-7297	D / 2.1	-1.33	3.21	11.09 /54	7.16 /11	4.36 /49	2.06	0.75
GI	Fidelity Adv Balanced Fund T	FAIGX	D+	(800) 522-7297	D- / 1.3	-1.47	2.90	10.52 /50	6.61 / 9	3.81 /44	1.54	1.24
HL	Fidelity Adv Biotechnology A	FBTAX	E-	(800) 522-7297	E+ / 0.8	-8.33	-2.81	11.24 /55	8.60 /18	-2.41 / 7	0.00	1.40
HL	Fidelity Adv Biotechnology B	FBTBX	E-	(800) 522-7297	D- / 1.1	-8.54	-3.21	10.48 /50	7.74 /14	-3.17 / 5	0.00	2.15
HL	Fidelity Adv Biotechnology C	FBTCX	E-	(800) 522-7297	D- / 1.1	-8.54	-3.21	10.48 /50	7.74 /14	-3.17 / 5	0.00	2.15
HL	Fidelity Adv Biotechnology I	FBTIX	E-	(800) 522-7297	D / 1.6	-8.34	-2.77	11.59 /57	8.92 /20	-2.16 / 8	0.00	1.10
HL	Fidelity Adv Biotechnology T	FBTTX	E-	(800) 522-7297	E+ / 0.9	-8.45	-2.98	11.06 /54	8.28 /17	-2.67 / 6	0.00	1.65
GR	Fidelity Adv Consumer Indust A	FCNAX	D-	(800) 522-7297	D- / 1.5	-2.51	1.71	5.11 /16	8.85 /20	3.08 /38	0.00	1.40
GR	Fidelity Adv Consumer Indust B	FCIBX	D-	(800) 522-7297	D / 1.8	-2.69	1.30	4.24 /12	8.01 /15	2.30 /30	0.00	2.15
GR	Fidelity Adv Consumer Indust C	FCECX	D-	(800) 522-7297	D / 1.8	-2.69	1.37	4.30 /12	8.02 /15	2.31 /30	0.00	2.15
GR	Fidelity Adv Consumer Indust I	FCNIX	D	(800) 522-7297	D+ / 2.5	-2.39	1.84	5.36 /17	9.13 /22	2.85 /35	0.00	1.15
GR	Fidelity Adv Consumer Indust T	FACPX	D-	(800) 522-7297	D / 1.6	-2.57	1.56	4.83 /14	8.56 /18	2.82 /35	0.00	1.65
GR	Fidelity Adv Cyclical Indust A	FCLAX	A	(800) 522-7297	B+ / 8.8	-2.39	9.34	22.33 /85	24.34 /90	11.55 /86	0.00	1.34
GR	Fidelity Adv Cyclical Indust B	FCLBX	A	(800) 522-7297	B+ / 8.9	-2.56	8.91	21.38 /83	23.37 /88	10.70 /83	0.00	2.11
GR	Fidelity Adv Cyclical Indust C	FCLCX	A	(800) 522-7297	B+ / 8.9	-2.54	8.95	21.52 /84	23.43 /88	10.73 /83	0.00	2.07
GR	Fidelity Adv Cyclical Indust I	FCLIX	A+	(800) 522-7297	A- / 9.1	-2.29	9.52	22.78 /85	24.68 /90	11.85 /86	0.00	1.06
GR	Fidelity Adv Cyclical Indust T	FCLTX	A	(800) 522-7297	B+ / 8.8	-2.42	9.22	22.10 /84	24.04 /89	11.29 /85	0.00	1.57
GR	Fidelity Adv Destiny I CL B	FDTBX	D-	(800) 522-7297	D+ / 2.7	-3.30	0.64	13.44 /66	10.55 /31	0.36 /17	0.38	1.84
GR	Fidelity Adv Destiny I CL C	FDTCX	D	(800) 522-7297	C- / 3.4	-3.23	0.79	13.53 /66	10.58 /32	0.37 /17	0.46	1.84
TC	Fidelity Adv Developing Comm A	FDMAX	E	(800) 522-7297	C / 4.5	-14.57	-1.59	10.15 /48	15.29 /60	-1.86 / 9	0.00	2.55
TC	Fidelity Adv Developing Comm B	FDMBX	E	(800) 522-7297	C / 4.8	-14.71	-2.03	9.36 /42	14.40 /56	-2.59 / 6	0.00	3.30
TC	Fidelity Adv Developing Comm C	FDMCX	E	(800) 522-7297	C / 4.8	-14.71	-1.91	9.36 /42	14.40 /56	-2.59 / 6	0.00	3.28
TC	Fidelity Adv Developing Comm I	FDMIX	E	(800) 522-7297	C / 5.5	-14.48	-1.45	10.43 /50	15.57 /62	-1.59 /10	0.00	2.08
TC	Fidelity Adv Developing Comm T	FDMTX	E	(800) 522-7297	C / 4.6	-14.55	-1.61	9.99 /47	14.96 /59	-2.10 / 8	0.00	2.91
★ FO	Fidelity Adv Diversified Intl A	FDVAX	B	(800) 522-7297	B+ / 8.3	-3.46	5.88	25.78 /89	23.35 /88	13.01 /89	0.58	1.20
FO	Fidelity Adv Diversified Intl B	FDIBX	B	(800) 522-7297	B+ / 8.4	-3.68	5.40	24.64 /88	22.27 /86	12.02 /87	0.35	2.10

● Denotes fund is closed to new investors
★ Denotes fund is included in Section II

142

Risk Rating/Pts	3 Year Standard Deviation	Beta	NAV As of 6/30/06	Total $(Mil)	Cash %	Stocks %	Bonds %	Other %	Portfolio Turnover Ratio	Last Bull Market Return	Last Bear Market Return	Manager Quality Pct	Manager Tenure (Years)	Initial Purch. $	Additional Purch. $	Front End Load	Back End Load
C+ / 6.6	13.8	1.13	15.09	11	0	99	0	1	1.0	98.3	-4.5	13	1	1,000	50	0.0	1.0
C+ / 6.6	13.8	1.13	15.43	1	0	99	0	1	1.0	103.2	-4.8	15	1	1,000	50	0.0	0.0
C+ / 6.6	13.8	1.13	15.33	N/A	0	99	0	1	1.0	101.8	-4.8	14	1	1,000	50	0.0	0.0
C+ / 6.9	13.5	0.88	16.29	13	0	99	0	1	1.0	112.2	-12.5	77	1	1,000	50	5.8	1.0
B- / 7.0	13.5	0.88	15.83	5	0	99	0	1	1.0	107.2	-12.6	70	1	1,000	50	0.0	5.0
C+ / 6.9	13.5	0.88	15.83	7	0	99	0	1	1.0	107.1	-12.5	70	1	1,000	50	0.0	1.0
C+ / 6.9	13.5	0.88	16.13	N/A	0	99	0	1	1.0	110.3	-12.5	75	1	1,000	50	0.0	0.0
B- / 7.0	13.5	0.88	16.04	N/A	0	99	0	1	1.0	109.2	-12.5	74	1	1,000	50	0.0	0.0
C+ / 5.9	16.6	1.77	15.77	8	4	96	0	0	5.0	116.2	-16.8	34	1	1,000	50	5.8	1.0
C+ / 5.8	16.6	1.77	15.43	4	4	96	0	0	5.0	111.2	-17.0	29	1	1,000	50	0.0	5.0
C+ / 5.8	16.6	1.76	15.53	4	4	96	0	0	5.0	111.2	-16.6	29	1	1,000	50	0.0	1.0
C+ / 5.9	16.6	1.76	15.56	N/A	4	96	0	0	5.0	113.4	-16.9	32	1	1,000	50	0.0	0.0
C+ / 5.9	16.5	1.76	15.51	N/A	4	96	0	0	5.0	112.8	-16.9	31	1	1,000	50	0.0	0.0
C / 4.6	12.4	1.33	9.29	9	1	98	0	1	213.0	67.9	-6.5	19	1	2,500	100	5.8	1.0
C / 4.5	12.3	1.32	8.91	8	1	98	0	1	213.0	64.1	-6.8	15	1	2,500	100	0.0	5.0
C / 4.5	12.4	1.33	8.93	7	1	98	0	1	213.0	64.2	-6.7	15	1	2,500	100	0.0	1.0
C / 4.6	12.4	1.33	9.46	1	1	98	0	1	213.0	69.3	-6.4	21	1	2,500	100	0.0	0.0
C / 4.6	12.4	1.33	9.16	15	1	98	0	1	213.0	66.6	-6.5	18	1	2,500	100	3.5	0.3
B- / 7.7	7.5	1.45	11.74	68	4	73	22	1	125.0	64.8	-6.2	76	8	2,500	100	5.8	1.0
B- / 7.7	7.6	1.45	11.62	39	4	73	22	1	125.0	60.6	-6.4	68	8	2,500	100	0.0	5.0
B- / 7.7	7.6	1.46	11.61	38	4	73	22	1	125.0	60.8	-6.4	69	8	2,500	100	0.0	1.0
B- / 7.7	7.6	1.47	11.78	2	4	73	22	1	125.0	66.7	-6.2	79	8	2,500	100	0.0	0.0
B- / 7.7	7.6	1.46	11.68	70	4	73	22	1	125.0	63.3	-6.3	73	8	2,500	100	3.5	0.3
B / 8.6	5.6	0.61	16.16	192	1	67	30	2	145.0	40.8	-3.6	46	5	2,500	100	5.8	1.0
B / 8.8	5.6	0.62	16.09	83	1	67	30	2	145.0	37.2	-3.8	36	5	2,500	100	0.0	5.0
B / 8.8	5.6	0.62	16.09	72	1	67	30	2	145.0	37.4	-3.8	37	5	2,500	100	0.0	1.0
B / 8.8	5.6	0.62	16.36	17	1	67	30	2	145.0	41.9	-3.5	49	5	2,500	100	0.0	0.0
B / 8.8	5.6	0.61	16.25	967	1	67	30	2	145.0	39.6	-3.6	43	5	2,500	100	3.5	0.3
D+ / 2.9	16.3	0.88	6.93	13	0	98	0	2	88.0	61.1	-6.8	39	1	2,500	100	5.8	1.0
D+ / 2.9	16.2	0.87	6.64	16	0	98	0	2	88.0	57.4	-7.1	33	1	2,500	100	0.0	1.0
D+ / 2.8	16.2	0.88	6.64	14	0	98	0	2	88.0	57.6	-7.1	32	1	2,500	100	0.0	1.0
D+ / 2.9	16.2	0.87	7.03	1	0	98	0	2	88.0	62.9	-6.8	43	1	2,500	100	0.0	1.0
D+ / 2.9	16.3	0.88	6.83	14	0	98	0	2	88.0	60.2	-6.8	36	1	2,500	100	3.5	1.0
C+ / 6.7	9.8	1.08	16.69	20	0	99	0	1	35.0	54.9	-10.4	27	2	2,500	100	5.8	1.0
C+ / 6.6	9.8	1.08	15.54	15	0	99	0	1	35.0	51.2	-10.5	22	2	2,500	100	0.0	1.0
C+ / 6.6	9.8	1.07	15.57	7	0	99	0	1	35.0	51.3	-10.5	22	2	2,500	100	0.0	1.0
C+ / 6.7	9.8	1.07	17.13	1	0	99	0	1	35.0	56.1	-10.3	29	2	2,500	100	0.0	1.0
C+ / 6.7	9.8	1.08	16.32	15	0	99	0	1	35.0	53.7	-10.5	26	2	2,500	100	3.5	1.0
B- / 7.2	12.5	1.43	23.30	97	7	92	0	1	139.0	135.1	-9.6	98	N/A	2,500	100	5.8	1.0
B- / 7.1	12.4	1.42	22.12	39	7	92	0	1	139.0	129.4	-9.7	97	N/A	2,500	100	0.0	1.0
B- / 7.1	12.4	1.42	22.27	42	7	92	0	1	139.0	129.7	-9.7	97	N/A	2,500	100	0.0	1.0
B- / 7.2	12.4	1.42	23.94	17	7	92	0	1	139.0	137.1	-9.5	98	N/A	2,500	100	0.0	1.0
B- / 7.1	12.4	1.42	22.99	57	7	92	0	1	139.0	133.4	-9.6	98	N/A	2,500	100	3.5	1.0
C+ / 5.8	9.2	1.11	14.07	1	2	97	0	1	130.0	60.1	-9.3	37	N/A	2,500	100	0.0	5.0
C+ / 5.8	9.2	1.11	14.07	1	2	97	0	1	130.0	60.1	-9.3	37	N/A	2,500	100	0.0	1.0
E+ / 0.8	24.1	2.36	8.03	4	1	98	0	1	191.0	120.7	-10.2	5	3	2,500	100	5.8	1.0
E+ / 0.8	24.1	2.34	7.71	3	1	98	0	1	191.0	115.7	-10.5	4	3	2,500	100	0.0	1.0
E+ / 0.7	24.1	2.36	7.71	3	1	98	0	1	191.0	115.7	-10.5	3	3	2,500	100	0.0	1.0
E+ / 0.8	24.1	2.35	8.15	N/A	1	98	0	1	191.0	122.0	-10.1	6	3	2,500	100	0.0	1.0
E+ / 0.8	24.1	2.35	7.93	3	1	98	0	1	191.0	118.9	-10.2	4	3	2,500	100	3.5	1.0
C+ / 6.2	11.3	1.08	22.34	4,237	0	99	0	1	59.0	138.0	-5.4	30	2	2,500	100	5.8	1.0
C+ / 6.2	11.3	1.08	21.48	484	0	99	0	1	59.0	131.4	-5.7	24	2	2,500	100	0.0	1.0

Fund Type	Fund Name	Ticker Symbol	Overall Weiss Investment Rating	Phone	Performance Rating/Pts	3 Mo	6 Mo	1Yr / Pct	3Yr / Pct	5Yr / Pct	Dividend Yield	Expense Ratio
FO	Fidelity Adv Diversified Intl C	FADCX	B+	(800) 522-7297	B+ / 8.4	-3.67	5.43	24.79 /88	22.37 /86	12.11 /87	0.37	1.99
FO	Fidelity Adv Diversified Intl I	FDVIX	B+	(800) 522-7297	B+ / 8.8	-3.37	6.04	26.15 /90	23.73 /89	13.37 /89	0.75	0.91
★ FO	Fidelity Adv Diversified Intl T	FADIX	B	(800) 522-7297	B+ / 8.4	-3.49	5.74	25.51 /89	23.04 /87	12.69 /88	0.57	1.45
GR	Fidelity Adv Dividend Growth A	FADAX	D-	(800) 522-7297	E / 0.5	-3.47	0.91	6.52 /23	6.50 / 8	0.79 /19	0.16	1.15
GR	Fidelity Adv Dividend Growth B	FADBX	D-	(800) 522-7297	E / 0.4	-3.65	0.59	5.70 /19	5.66 / 6	0.02 /15	0.00	1.95
GR	Fidelity Adv Dividend Growth C	FDGCX	D	(800) 522-7297	E+ / 0.7	-3.65	0.59	5.78 /19	5.72 / 6	0.07 /16	0.00	1.88
GR	Fidelity Adv Dividend Growth I	FDGIX	D	(800) 522-7297	D- / 1.3	-3.36	1.06	6.90 /26	6.87 /10	1.14 /21	0.50	0.80
GR	Fidelity Adv Dividend Growth T	FDGTX	D	(800) 522-7297	E+ / 0.8	-3.57	0.83	6.29 /22	6.29 / 8	0.60 /18	0.00	1.31
GR	Fidelity Adv Dynamic Cap App A	FARAX	D	(800) 522-7297	C / 5.0	-3.35	5.35	22.13 /84	12.72 /47	4.90 /53	0.00	1.18
GR	Fidelity Adv Dynamic Cap App B	FRMBX	D-	(800) 522-7297	C / 4.6	-3.53	4.98	21.25 /83	11.87 /42	4.11 /47	0.00	1.93
GR	Fidelity Adv Dynamic Cap App C	FRECX	D	(800) 522-7297	C / 5.2	-3.52	4.97	21.28 /83	11.93 /42	4.20 /48	0.00	1.93
GR	Fidelity Adv Dynamic Cap App I	FDCIX	D+	(800) 522-7297	C+ / 6.0	-3.24	5.51	22.53 /85	13.10 /49	5.31 /56	0.00	0.93
GR	Fidelity Adv Dynamic Cap App T	FRGTX	D	(800) 522-7297	C / 5.2	-3.39	5.24	21.91 /84	12.46 /45	4.66 /51	0.00	1.43
TC	Fidelity Adv Electronics A	FELAX	E-	(800) 522-7297	D- / 1.3	-8.46	-2.83	5.90 /20	9.48 /24	-4.62 / 3	0.00	1.31
TC	Fidelity Adv Electronics B	FELBX	E-	(800) 522-7297	D / 1.7	-8.65	-3.18	5.12 /16	8.68 /19	-5.32 / 2	0.00	2.07
TC	Fidelity Adv Electronics C	FELCX	E-	(800) 522-7297	D / 1.7	-8.55	-3.19	4.98 /15	8.70 /19	-5.31 / 2	0.00	2.07
TC	Fidelity Adv Electronics I	FELIX	E-	(800) 522-7297	D+ / 2.4	-8.32	-2.66	6.21 /22	9.88 /27	-4.31 / 3	0.00	1.07
TC	Fidelity Adv Electronics T	FELTX	E-	(800) 522-7297	D- / 1.5	-8.44	-2.86	5.68 /19	9.25 /22	-4.82 / 3	0.00	1.56
FO	Fidelity Adv Emerging Asia A	FEAAX	B	(800) 522-7297	A / 9.4	0.15	10.40	31.30 /95	30.08 /96	16.01 /93	0.70	1.44
FO	Fidelity Adv Emerging Asia B	FERBX	B	(800) 522-7297	A / 9.4	-0.05	10.01	30.33 /95	29.13 /95	15.14 /92	0.20	2.19
FO	Fidelity Adv Emerging Asia C	FERCX	B	(800) 522-7297	A / 9.5	-0.05	10.08	30.34 /95	29.12 /95	15.14 /92	0.33	2.19
FO	Fidelity Adv Emerging Asia I	FERIX	B	(800) 522-7297	A+ / 9.6	0.24	10.51	31.56 /95	30.42 /96	16.24 /93	0.92	1.19
FO	Fidelity Adv Emerging Asia T	FEATX	B	(800) 522-7297	A / 9.4	0.10	10.27	30.96 /95	29.78 /95	15.71 /93	0.55	1.69
EM	Fidelity Adv Emerging Markets A	FAMKX	U	(800) 522-7297	U /	-5.36	7.97	44.90 /98	--	--	0.58	1.49
EM	Fidelity Adv Emerging Markets C	FMCKX	U	(800) 522-7297	U /	-5.48	7.68	43.89 /98	--	--	0.29	2.23
EM	Fidelity Adv Emerging Markets T	FTMKX	U	(800) 522-7297	U /	-5.44	7.88	44.58 /98	--	--	0.50	1.73
GR	Fidelity Adv Equity Growth A	EPGAX	E+	(800) 522-7297	D- / 1.2	-4.20	-0.15	7.64 /30	8.10 /16	-2.03 / 8	0.00	1.14
GR	Fidelity Adv Equity Growth B	EPGBX	E+	(800) 522-7297	D- / 1.0	-4.39	-0.55	6.79 /25	7.24 /11	-2.79 / 6	0.00	1.96
GR	Fidelity Adv Equity Growth C	EPGCX	D-	(800) 522-7297	D- / 1.4	-4.39	-0.55	6.78 /25	7.25 /11	-2.77 / 6	0.00	1.94
GR	Fidelity Adv Equity Growth I	EQPGX	D-	(800) 522-7297	D+ / 2.3	-4.11	0.02	8.01 /33	8.50 /18	-1.64 / 9	0.00	0.79
★ GR	Fidelity Adv Equity Growth T	FAEGX	D-	(800) 522-7297	D- / 1.4	-4.25	-0.25	7.44 /29	7.90 /14	-2.20 / 8	0.00	1.33
IN	Fidelity Adv Equity Income A	FEIAX	C+	(800) 522-7297	C / 4.4	-1.23	3.55	10.27 /49	13.03 /49	5.42 /57	0.91	1.00
IN	Fidelity Adv Equity Income B	FEIBX	C	(800) 522-7297	C- / 3.9	-1.42	3.12	9.37 /42	12.08 /43	4.54 /50	0.10	1.85
IN	Fidelity Adv Equity Income C	FEICX	C+	(800) 522-7297	C+ / 4.6	-1.39	3.18	9.44 /43	12.15 /43	4.59 /51	0.21	1.79
IN	Fidelity Adv Equity Income I	EQPIX	B-	(800) 522-7297	C / 5.5	-1.13	3.71	10.60 /51	13.39 /51	5.75 /59	1.20	0.68
★ IN	Fidelity Adv Equity Income T	FEIRX	C+	(800) 522-7297	C / 4.6	-1.27	3.44	10.03 /47	12.79 /47	5.18 /55	0.70	1.22
GR	Fidelity Adv Equity Value A	FAVAX	C	(800) 522-7297	C- / 3.5	-2.16	2.72	10.20 /48	11.97 /42	5.76 /59	0.64	1.18
GR	Fidelity Adv Equity Value B	FAVBX	C-	(800) 522-7297	C- / 3.2	-2.36	2.31	9.42 /43	11.09 /36	4.98 /54	0.00	1.93
GR	Fidelity Adv Equity Value C	FAVCX	C	(800) 522-7297	C- / 3.9	-2.36	2.32	9.37 /42	11.11 /36	4.97 /54	0.00	1.93
GR	Fidelity Adv Equity Value I	FAIVX	C+	(800) 522-7297	C / 4.9	-2.14	2.78	10.47 /50	12.33 /45	6.09 /62	0.91	0.92
GR	Fidelity Adv Equity Value T	FAVTX	C	(800) 522-7297	C- / 3.8	-2.25	2.55	9.91 /46	11.65 /40	5.48 /58	0.37	1.43
FO	Fidelity Adv Europe Cap App A	FAEAX	B+	(800) 522-7297	B+ / 8.7	-2.08	13.44	29.03 /94	22.95 /87	11.04 /84	0.76	1.39
FO	Fidelity Adv Europe Cap App B	FBEAX	B+	(800) 522-7297	B+ / 8.7	-2.08	13.26	28.36 /93	22.13 /85	10.25 /81	0.04	2.14
FO	Fidelity Adv Europe Cap App C	FCEAX	B+	(800) 522-7297	B+ / 8.8	-2.27	13.11	28.21 /93	22.07 /85	10.22 /81	0.12	2.14
FO	Fidelity Adv Europe Cap App I	FIEAX	B+	(800) 522-7297	A- / 9.1	-1.99	13.58	29.47 /94	23.21 /88	11.30 /85	1.04	1.14
FO	Fidelity Adv Europe Cap App T	FAECX	B+	(800) 522-7297	B+ / 8.8	-2.15	13.31	28.85 /94	22.66 /86	10.80 /83	0.50	1.64
GL	Fidelity Adv Fifty A	FFYAX	D	(800) 522-7297	D+ / 2.8	-2.94	3.67	18.02 /79	9.75 /26	7.03 /67	0.00	1.21
GL	Fidelity Adv Fifty B	FFYBX	D	(800) 522-7297	D+ / 2.5	-3.15	3.22	16.93 /77	8.83 /20	6.21 /62	0.00	1.96
GL	Fidelity Adv Fifty C	FFYCX	D	(800) 522-7297	C- / 3.2	-3.15	3.22	16.93 /77	8.87 /20	6.24 /63	0.00	1.96
GL	Fidelity Adv Fifty I	FFYIX	C-	(800) 522-7297	C- / 4.2	-2.88	3.76	18.23 /79	10.10 /28	7.44 /69	0.00	0.98
GL	Fidelity Adv Fifty T	FFYTX	D	(800) 522-7297	C- / 3.1	-3.07	3.47	17.51 /78	9.38 /23	6.71 /65	0.00	1.46
FS	Fidelity Adv Financial Serv A	FAFDX	C-	(800) 522-7297	C- / 3.8	-3.08	1.59	11.88 /59	12.55 /46	5.84 /60	0.99	1.23

● Denotes fund is closed to new investors
★ Denotes fund is included in Section II

144

RISK			NET ASSETS		ASSET				BULL / BEAR		FUND MANAGER		MINIMUMS		LOADS	
	3 Year		NAV						Last Bull	Last Bear	Manager	Manager	Initial	Additional	Front	Back
Risk	Standard		As of	Total	Cash	Stocks	Bonds	Other	Portfolio	Market	Market	Quality	Tenure	Purch.	Purch.	End	End
Rating/Pts	Deviation	Beta	6/30/06	$(Mil)	%	%	%	%	Turnover Ratio	Return	Return	Pct	(Years)	$	$	Load	Load
C+ / 6.2	11.3	1.08	21.54	1,275	0	99	0	1	59.0	132.2	-5.7	24	2	2,500	100	0.0	1.0
C+ / 6.2	11.3	1.08	22.66	3,894	0	99	0	1	59.0	140.3	-5.4	33	2	2,500	100	0.0	1.0
C+ / 6.2	11.3	1.08	22.11	3,407	0	99	0	1	59.0	136.0	-5.5	28	2	2,500	100	3.5	1.0
B / 8.1	7.5	0.89	12.24	489	2	97	0	1	32.0	44.7	-10.9	23	8	2,500	100	5.8	1.0
B / 8.2	7.6	0.89	11.87	333	2	97	0	1	32.0	41.2	-11.0	18	8	2,500	100	0.0	5.0
B / 8.2	7.6	0.90	11.89	306	2	97	0	1	32.0	41.4	-11.0	18	8	2,500	100	0.0	1.0
B / 8.3	7.5	0.89	12.37	979	2	97	0	1	32.0	46.5	-10.8	25	8	2,500	100	0.0	0.0
B / 8.2	7.6	0.89	12.17	1,232	2	97	0	1	32.0	43.8	-10.9	22	8	2,500	100	3.5	0.3
C- / 3.8	14.8	1.49	17.33	88	6	93	0	1	204.0	74.4	-5.4	27	8	2,500	100	5.8	0.0
C- / 3.7	14.9	1.49	16.66	59	6	93	0	1	204.0	70.2	-5.5	22	8	2,500	100	0.0	5.0
C- / 3.7	14.8	1.49	16.70	53	6	93	0	1	204.0	70.6	-5.5	23	8	2,500	100	0.0	1.0
C- / 3.8	14.8	1.49	17.62	29	6	93	0	1	204.0	76.3	-5.3	30	8	2,500	100	0.0	0.0
C- / 3.7	14.9	1.50	17.08	166	6	93	0	1	204.0	73.2	-5.4	26	8	2,500	100	3.5	0.3
E / 0.5	24.6	2.42	7.90	9	1	98	0	1	106.0	81.3	-18.4	0	2	2,500	100	5.8	1.0
E / 0.4	24.7	2.42	7.60	7	1	98	0	1	106.0	77.1	-18.6	0	2	2,500	100	0.0	1.0
E / 0.4	24.7	2.42	7.59	8	1	98	0	1	106.0	77.3	-18.7	0	2	2,500	100	0.0	1.0
E / 0.5	24.6	2.41	8.04	1	1	98	0	1	106.0	83.2	-18.5	0	2	2,500	100	0.0	1.0
E / 0.5	24.6	2.42	7.81	10	1	98	0	1	106.0	80.0	-18.5	0	2	2,500	100	3.5	1.0
C / 4.8	16.8	1.20	20.60	48	6	93	0	1	66.0	161.1	-12.0	62	2	2,500	100	5.8	1.5
C / 4.8	16.8	1.20	19.68	18	6	93	0	1	66.0	155.2	-12.2	53	2	2,500	100	0.0	5.0
C / 4.8	16.8	1.20	19.65	29	6	93	0	1	66.0	155.1	-12.2	54	2	2,500	100	0.0	1.5
C / 4.8	16.8	1.20	20.92	5	6	93	0	1	66.0	162.9	-12.0	66	2	2,500	100	0.0	1.5
C / 4.8	16.8	1.20	20.30	24	6	93	0	1	66.0	159.2	-12.1	60	2	2,500	100	3.5	1.5
U /	N/A	N/A	17.47	54	3	96	0	1	54.0	N/A	N/A	N/A	2	2,500	100	5.8	1.5
U /	N/A	N/A	17.24	31	3	96	0	1	54.0	N/A	N/A	N/A	2	2,500	100	0.0	1.5
U /	N/A	N/A	17.38	30	3	96	0	1	54.0	N/A	N/A	N/A	2	2,500	100	3.5	1.5
C+ / 6.2	10.4	1.25	47.91	1,548	1	98	0	1	80.0	55.6	-11.4	14	9	2,500	100	5.8	1.0
C+ / 6.1	10.4	1.26	44.85	551	1	98	0	1	80.0	51.7	-11.6	10	9	2,500	100	0.0	5.0
C+ / 6.1	10.4	1.25	45.54	306	1	98	0	1	80.0	51.8	-11.6	11	9	2,500	100	0.0	1.0
C+ / 6.2	10.4	1.25	50.82	1,259	1	98	0	1	80.0	57.5	-11.3	16	9	2,500	100	0.0	0.0
C+ / 6.2	10.4	1.25	47.96	3,206	1	98	0	1	80.0	54.7	-11.5	13	9	2,500	100	3.5	0.2
B / 8.4	8.1	1.04	28.71	1,303	0	99	0	1	45.0	74.4	-10.5	71	10	2,500	100	5.8	0.0
B / 8.5	8.1	1.04	28.75	423	0	99	0	1	45.0	69.8	-10.6	61	10	2,500	100	0.0	5.0
B / 8.5	8.1	1.04	28.80	348	0	99	0	1	45.0	70.1	-10.7	62	9	2,500	100	0.0	1.0
B / 8.5	8.1	1.04	29.45	1,724	0	99	0	1	45.0	76.1	-10.4	74	10	2,500	100	0.0	0.0
B / 8.5	8.1	1.04	29.06	2,848	0	99	0	1	45.0	73.2	-10.5	69	10	2,500	100	3.5	0.3
B / 8.1	8.5	1.06	11.80	24	0	99	0	1	190.0	74.2	-11.0	58	5	2,500	100	5.8	1.0
B / 8.1	8.5	1.06	11.60	20	0	99	0	1	190.0	70.1	-11.2	48	5	2,500	100	0.0	5.0
B / 8.1	8.5	1.06	11.59	16	0	99	0	1	190.0	70.2	-11.2	48	5	2,500	100	0.0	1.0
B / 8.0	8.5	1.05	11.91	5	0	99	0	1	190.0	76.1	-11.0	63	5	2,500	100	0.0	0.0
B / 8.1	8.5	1.06	11.74	50	0	99	0	1	190.0	72.9	-11.2	55	5	2,500	100	3.5	0.3
C+ / 6.0	13.5	1.19	16.04	14	12	87	0	1	200.0	145.5	-10.2	14	N/A	2,500	100	5.8	1.0
C+ / 6.0	13.5	1.18	15.55	7	12	87	0	1	200.0	139.5	-10.3	12	N/A	2,500	100	0.0	5.0
C+ / 6.0	13.5	1.19	15.53	6	12	87	0	1	200.0	139.7	-10.4	11	N/A	2,500	100	0.0	1.0
C+ / 6.0	13.5	1.19	16.23	1	12	87	0	1	200.0	146.9	-10.1	15	N/A	2,500	100	0.0	1.0
C+ / 6.0	13.5	1.19	15.92	24	12	87	0	1	200.0	143.5	-10.2	13	N/A	2,500	100	3.5	1.0
C+ / 6.4	11.6	0.83	12.54	32	7	92	0	1	115.0	57.1	-9.4	2	3	2,500	100	5.8	1.0
C+ / 6.3	11.5	0.84	11.99	19	7	92	0	1	115.0	53.1	-9.6	2	3	2,500	100	0.0	5.0
C+ / 6.3	11.5	0.84	11.99	14	7	92	0	1	115.0	53.3	-9.6	2	3	2,500	100	0.0	1.0
C+ / 6.4	11.5	0.83	12.81	3	7	92	0	1	115.0	58.8	-9.3	3	3	2,500	100	0.0	0.0
C+ / 6.4	11.5	0.83	12.32	29	7	92	0	1	115.0	55.4	-9.4	2	3	2,500	100	3.5	0.3
C+ / 6.8	9.6	1.02	23.00	83	0	99	0	1	39.0	76.6	-9.2	40	N/A	2,500	100	5.8	1.0

			Overall		PERFORMANCE							
	99 Pct = Best 0 Pct = Worst		Weiss		Perfor-		Total Return % through 6/30/06					Incl. in Returns	
		Ticker	Investment		mance					Annualized		Dividend	Expense
Fund Type	Fund Name	Symbol	Rating	Phone	Rating/Pts	3 Mo	6 Mo	1Yr / Pct	3Yr / Pct	5Yr / Pct	Yield	Ratio
FS	Fidelity Adv Financial Serv B	FAFBX	C-	(800) 522-7297	C / 4.3	-3.28	1.17	11.01 /54	11.72 /41	5.05 /55	0.04	1.98
FS	Fidelity Adv Financial Serv C	FAFCX	C-	(800) 522-7297	C / 4.4	-3.28	1.22	11.08 /54	11.77 /41	5.11 /55	0.06	1.92
FS	Fidelity Adv Financial Serv I	FFSIX	C	(800) 522-7297	C / 5.1	-3.04	1.75	12.28 /61	13.00 /49	6.25 /63	1.48	0.84
FS	Fidelity Adv Financial Serv T	FAFSX	C-	(800) 522-7297	C- / 4.1	-3.13	1.46	11.62 /57	12.32 /44	5.60 /58	0.58	1.46
AA	Fidelity Adv Freedom 2010 A	FACFX	U	(800) 522-7297	U /	-1.53	1.39	6.27 /22	--	--	1.87	0.99
AA	Fidelity Adv Freedom 2010 B	FCFBX	U	(800) 522-7297	U /	-1.64	1.03	5.53 /18	--	--	1.26	1.74
AA	Fidelity Adv Freedom 2010 C	FCFCX	U	(800) 522-7297	U /	-1.64	1.04	5.48 /17	--	--	1.30	1.74
AA	Fidelity Adv Freedom 2010 T	FCFTX	U	(800) 522-7297	U /	-1.60	1.24	5.94 /20	--	--	1.69	1.24
AA	Fidelity Adv Freedom 2015 A	FFVAX	U	(800) 522-7297	U /	-1.92	1.78	8.29 /35	--	--	1.47	1.02
AA	Fidelity Adv Freedom 2015 B	FFVBX	U	(800) 522-7297	U /	-2.02	1.43	7.52 /29	--	--	0.90	1.77
AA	Fidelity Adv Freedom 2015 C	FFVCX	U	(800) 522-7297	U /	-2.09	1.35	7.45 /29	--	--	0.93	1.77
AA	Fidelity Adv Freedom 2015 I	FFVIX	U	(800) 522-7297	U /	-1.86	1.91	8.54 /37	--	--	1.73	0.77
AA	Fidelity Adv Freedom 2015 T	FFVTX	U	(800) 522-7297	U /	-1.89	1.63	8.07 /33	--	--	1.30	1.27
AA	Fidelity Adv Freedom 2020 A	FDAFX	U	(800) 522-7297	U /	-2.31	1.97	9.46 /43	--	--	1.30	1.04
AA	Fidelity Adv Freedom 2020 B	FDBFX	U	(800) 522-7297	U /	-2.42	1.63	8.66 /38	--	--	0.69	1.79
AA	Fidelity Adv Freedom 2020 C	FDCFX	U	(800) 522-7297	U /	-2.42	1.56	8.69 /38	--	--	0.71	1.79
AA	Fidelity Adv Freedom 2020 T	FDTFX	U	(800) 522-7297	U /	-2.38	1.75	9.12 /41	--	--	1.10	1.29
AA	Fidelity Adv Freedom 2025 A	FATWX	U	(800) 522-7297	U /	-2.39	2.08	10.16 /48	--	--	1.14	1.05
AA	Fidelity Adv Freedom 2025 B	FBTWX	U	(800) 522-7297	U /	-2.58	1.73	9.32 /42	--	--	0.60	1.80
AA	Fidelity Adv Freedom 2025 T	FTTWX	U	(800) 522-7297	U /	-2.45	2.02	9.91 /46	--	--	0.95	1.30
AA	Fidelity Adv Freedom 2030 A	FAFEX	U	(800) 522-7297	U /	-2.70	2.39	11.34 /56	--	--	0.96	1.06
AA	Fidelity Adv Freedom 2030 B	FBFEX	U	(800) 522-7297	U /	-2.89	1.99	10.49 /50	--	--	0.35	1.81
AA	Fidelity Adv Freedom 2030 C	FCFEX	U	(800) 522-7297	U /	-2.88	2.00	10.53 /50	--	--	0.39	1.81
AA	Fidelity Adv Freedom 2030 T	FTFEX	U	(800) 522-7297	U /	-2.77	2.26	11.01 /54	--	--	0.76	1.31
AA	Fidelity Adv Freedom 2035 A	FATHX	U	(800) 522-7297	U /	-2.76	2.41	11.61 /57	--	--	0.86	1.07
AA	Fidelity Adv Freedom 2035 T	FTTHX	U	(800) 522-7297	U /	-2.91	2.28	11.35 /56	--	--	0.76	1.32
AA	Fidelity Adv Freedom 2040 A	FAFFX	U	(800) 522-7297	U /	-2.84	2.65	12.15 /60	--	--	0.93	1.07
AA	Fidelity Adv Freedom 2040 B	FBFFX	U	(800) 522-7297	U /	-3.02	2.21	11.28 /55	--	--	0.43	1.82
AA	Fidelity Adv Freedom 2040 C	FCFFX	U	(800) 522-7297	U /	-3.09	2.21	11.21 /55	--	--	0.44	1.82
AA	Fidelity Adv Freedom 2040 T	FTFFX	U	(800) 522-7297	U /	-2.90	2.45	11.84 /59	--	--	0.73	1.32
BA	Fidelity Adv Freedom Income T	FTAFX	U	(800) 522-7297	U /	-0.36	0.80	2.90 / 7	--	--	2.59	0.51
GL	Fidelity Adv Global Cap App-Cl A	FGEAX	C-	(800) 522-7297	C / 4.6	-5.52	-1.64	11.33 /56	14.50 /56	5.50 /58	0.24	1.48
GL	Fidelity Adv Global Cap App-Cl B	FGEBX	C-	(800) 522-7297	C / 5.0	-5.66	-2.08	10.43 /50	13.63 /52	4.69 /52	0.00	2.23
GL	Fidelity Adv Global Cap App-Cl C	FEUCX	C-	(800) 522-7297	C / 5.0	-5.72	-2.15	10.42 /50	13.62 /52	4.69 /52	0.00	2.23
GL	Fidelity Adv Global Cap App-Cl I	FEUIX	C	(800) 522-7297	C+ / 5.6	-5.49	-1.61	11.53 /57	14.76 /58	5.81 /60	0.47	1.23
GL	Fidelity Adv Global Cap App-Cl T	FGETX	C-	(800) 522-7297	C / 4.8	-5.60	-1.80	11.03 /54	14.20 /55	5.21 /56	0.04	1.73
GR	Fidelity Adv Gr Opportunity A	FAGAX	E+	(800) 522-7297	D- / 1.0	-6.54	-4.54	4.81 /14	8.38 /17	0.85 /19	0.27	1.13
GR	Fidelity Adv Gr Opportunity B	FABGX	E+	(800) 522-7297	E+ / 0.7	-6.73	-4.89	4.04 /11	7.54 /13	0.05 /16	0.00	1.88
GR	Fidelity Adv Gr Opportunity C	FACGX	E+	(800) 522-7297	D- / 1.2	-6.72	-4.89	4.02 /11	7.58 /13	0.09 /16	0.00	1.88
GR	Fidelity Adv Gr Opportunity I	FAGCX	D-	(800) 522-7297	D / 1.9	-6.41	-4.32	5.24 /16	8.81 /20	1.25 /22	0.48	0.73
★ GR	Fidelity Adv Gr Opportunity T	FAGOX	D-	(800) 522-7297	D- / 1.2	-6.59	-4.59	4.66 /14	8.24 /16	0.71 /19	0.02	1.26
GI	Fidelity Adv Growth & Income A	FGIRX	D+	(800) 522-7297	D / 1.6	-3.10	1.51	13.44 /66	8.06 /15	1.87 /26	0.39	1.09
GI	Fidelity Adv Growth & Income B	FGISX	D	(800) 522-7297	D- / 1.2	-3.27	1.10	12.52 /62	7.22 /11	1.08 /21	0.00	1.87
GI	Fidelity Adv Growth & Income C	FGIUX	D+	(800) 522-7297	D / 1.8	-3.27	1.16	12.57 /62	7.25 /11	1.13 /21	0.00	1.83
GI	Fidelity Adv Growth & Income I	FGIOX	C-	(800) 522-7297	D+ / 2.6	-3.03	1.67	13.79 /68	8.41 /17	2.22 /29	0.74	0.77
GI	Fidelity Adv Growth & Income T	FGITX	D+	(800) 522-7297	D / 1.7	-3.17	1.41	13.17 /65	7.82 /14	1.63 /24	0.09	1.32
HL	Fidelity Adv Health Care A	FACDX	D-	(800) 522-7297	E+ / 0.8	-5.66	-3.97	5.01 /15	7.86 /14	3.12 /38	0.00	1.26
HL	Fidelity Adv Health Care B	FAHTX	D-	(800) 522-7297	D- / 1.0	-5.84	-4.37	4.16 /11	7.04 /10	2.36 /31	0.00	2.01
HL	Fidelity Adv Health Care C	FHCCX	D-	(800) 522-7297	D- / 1.1	-5.82	-4.31	4.24 /12	7.13 /11	2.42 /31	0.00	1.94
HL	Fidelity Adv Health Care I	FHCIX	D	(800) 522-7297	D / 1.6	-5.60	-3.83	5.33 /17	8.27 /16	3.51 /41	0.00	0.85
HL	Fidelity Adv Health Care T	FACTX	D-	(800) 522-7297	E+ / 0.9	-5.74	-4.13	4.68 /14	7.58 /13	2.86 /35	0.00	1.51
FO	Fidelity Adv International Disc A	FAIDX	A+	(800) 522-7297	B+ / 8.8	-1.65	7.93	26.61 /91	25.27 /91	13.00 /89	0.82	1.36

RISK			NET ASSETS		ASSET					BULL / BEAR		FUND MANAGER		MINIMUMS		LOADS	
	3 Year		NAV						Portfolio	Last Bull	Last Bear	Manager	Manager	Initial	Additional	Front	Back
Risk Rating/Pts	Standard Deviation	Beta	As of 6/30/06	Total $(Mil)	Cash %	Stocks %	Bonds %	Other %	Turnover Ratio	Market Return	Market Return	Quality Pct	Tenure (Years)	Purch. $	Purch. $	End Load	End Load
C+ / 6.7	9.6	1.02	22.42	115	0	99	0	1	39.0	72.5	-9.4	33	N/A	2,500	100	0.0	1.0
C+ / 6.7	9.6	1.02	22.41	63	0	99	0	1	39.0	72.8	-9.4	33	N/A	2,500	100	0.0	1.0
C+ / 6.8	9.6	1.03	23.27	12	0	99	0	1	39.0	79.0	-9.1	44	N/A	2,500	100	0.0	1.0
C+ / 6.8	9.6	1.02	22.92	112	0	99	0	1	39.0	75.4	-9.3	37	N/A	2,500	100	3.5	1.0
U /	N/A	N/A	11.41	153	10	48	40	2	7.0	N/A	N/A	N/A	3	2,500	100	5.8	1.0
U /	N/A	N/A	11.34	33	10	48	40	2	7.0	N/A	N/A	N/A	3	2,500	100	0.0	5.0
U /	N/A	N/A	11.32	39	10	48	40	2	7.0	N/A	N/A	N/A	3	2,500	100	0.0	1.0
U /	N/A	N/A	11.37	150	10	48	40	2	7.0	N/A	N/A	N/A	3	2,500	100	3.5	0.0
U /	N/A	N/A	11.43	149	4	58	36	2	4.0	N/A	N/A	N/A	3	2,500	100	5.8	1.0
U /	N/A	N/A	11.37	35	4	58	36	2	4.0	N/A	N/A	N/A	3	2,500	100	0.0	5.0
U /	N/A	N/A	11.36	39	4	58	36	2	4.0	N/A	N/A	N/A	3	2,500	100	0.0	1.0
U /	N/A	N/A	11.48	29	4	58	36	2	4.0	N/A	N/A	N/A	3	2,500	100	0.0	0.0
U /	N/A	N/A	11.41	136	4	58	36	2	4.0	N/A	N/A	N/A	3	2,500	100	3.5	0.3
U /	N/A	N/A	12.30	320	0	68	30	2	6.0	N/A	N/A	N/A	3	2,500	100	5.8	1.0
U /	N/A	N/A	12.24	73	0	68	30	2	6.0	N/A	N/A	N/A	3	2,500	100	0.0	5.0
U /	N/A	N/A	12.23	65	0	68	30	2	6.0	N/A	N/A	N/A	3	2,500	100	0.0	1.0
U /	N/A	N/A	12.28	312	0	68	30	2	6.0	N/A	N/A	N/A	3	2,500	100	3.5	0.3
U /	N/A	N/A	11.83	150	0	73	26	1	5.0	N/A	N/A	N/A	3	2,500	100	5.8	1.0
U /	N/A	N/A	11.75	29	0	73	26	1	5.0	N/A	N/A	N/A	3	2,500	100	0.0	5.0
U /	N/A	N/A	11.84	94	0	73	26	1	5.0	N/A	N/A	N/A	3	2,500	100	3.5	0.3
U /	N/A	N/A	12.86	181	0	82	17	1	4.0	N/A	N/A	N/A	3	2,500	100	5.8	1.0
U /	N/A	N/A	12.76	45	0	82	17	1	4.0	N/A	N/A	N/A	3	2,500	100	0.0	5.0
U /	N/A	N/A	12.76	41	0	82	17	1	4.0	N/A	N/A	N/A	3	2,500	100	0.0	1.0
U /	N/A	N/A	12.82	197	0	82	17	1	4.0	N/A	N/A	N/A	3	2,500	100	3.5	0.3
U /	N/A	N/A	12.11	62	0	82	16	2	4.0	N/A	N/A	N/A	3	2,500	100	5.8	1.0
U /	N/A	N/A	12.05	52	0	82	16	2	4.0	N/A	N/A	N/A	3	2,500	100	3.5	0.3
U /	N/A	N/A	13.19	155	0	85	14	1	4.0	N/A	N/A	N/A	3	2,500	100	5.8	1.0
U /	N/A	N/A	13.06	35	0	85	14	1	4.0	N/A	N/A	N/A	3	2,500	100	0.0	5.0
U /	N/A	N/A	13.05	41	0	85	14	1	4.0	N/A	N/A	N/A	3	2,500	100	0.0	1.0
U /	N/A	N/A	13.15	145	0	85	14	1	4.0	N/A	N/A	N/A	3	2,500	100	3.5	0.3
U /	N/A	N/A	10.33	34	40	20	38	2	21.0	N/A	N/A	N/A	3	2,500	100	3.5	0.3
C+ / 6.4	10.2	0.92	14.38	13	6	92	0	2	52.0	87.4	-8.2	7	N/A	2,500	100	5.8	1.0
C+ / 6.3	10.3	0.93	13.66	7	6	92	0	2	52.0	83.1	-8.4	5	N/A	2,500	100	0.0	1.0
C+ / 6.4	10.3	0.93	13.67	6	6	92	0	2	52.0	83.1	-8.4	5	N/A	2,500	100	0.0	1.0
C+ / 6.4	10.2	0.93	14.63	3	6	92	0	2	52.0	89.2	-8.0	8	N/A	2,500	100	0.0	1.0
C+ / 6.4	10.2	0.93	14.15	29	6	92	0	2	52.0	86.0	-8.3	6	N/A	2,500	100	3.5	1.0
C+ / 6.3	9.7	1.15	31.13	374	0	99	0	1	110.0	58.2	-9.5	20	1	2,500	100	5.8	0.0
C+ / 6.3	9.7	1.16	30.37	158	0	99	0	1	110.0	54.4	-9.7	15	1	2,500	100	0.0	5.0
C+ / 6.3	9.7	1.16	30.52	78	0	99	0	1	110.0	54.6	-9.7	16	1	2,500	100	0.0	1.0
C+ / 6.4	9.7	1.16	31.68	88	0	99	0	1	110.0	60.2	-9.4	23	1	2,500	100	0.0	0.0
C+ / 6.3	9.7	1.16	31.59	2,285	0	99	0	1	110.0	57.6	-9.5	19	1	2,500	100	3.5	1.0
B / 8.1	7.2	0.85	18.11	217	1	98	0	1	187.0	52.5	-8.4	36	1	2,500	100	5.8	1.0
B / 8.2	7.2	0.85	17.43	166	1	98	0	1	187.0	48.7	-8.5	30	1	2,500	100	0.0	5.0
B / 8.2	7.2	0.85	17.46	120	1	98	0	1	187.0	48.9	-8.6	30	1	2,500	100	0.0	1.0
B / 8.2	7.2	0.86	18.23	466	1	98	0	1	187.0	54.1	-8.3	39	1	2,500	100	0.0	0.0
B / 8.2	7.2	0.85	18.00	514	1	98	0	1	187.0	51.3	-8.5	34	1	2,500	100	3.5	0.0
B- / 7.0	9.0	0.61	23.00	188	0	99	0	1	71.0	46.6	-5.1	59	1	2,500	100	5.8	1.0
C+ / 6.9	9.0	0.61	21.46	183	0	99	0	1	71.0	43.2	-5.2	48	1	2,500	100	0.0	1.0
C+ / 6.9	9.0	0.61	21.53	113	0	99	0	1	71.0	43.5	-5.2	50	1	2,500	100	0.0	1.0
B- / 7.0	9.0	0.61	23.62	20	0	99	0	1	71.0	48.5	-5.0	63	1	2,500	100	0.0	1.0
C+ / 6.9	9.0	0.61	22.50	214	0	99	0	1	71.0	45.5	-5.1	56	1	2,500	100	3.5	1.0
B- / 7.5	11.7	1.13	34.03	104	2	96	0	2	75.0	146.7	-9.0	34	1	2,500	100	5.8	1.0

Fund Type	Fund Name	Ticker Symbol	Overall Weiss Investment Rating	Phone	Perfor-mance Rating/Pts	3 Mo	6 Mo	1Yr / Pct	3Yr / Pct	5Yr / Pct	Dividend Yield	Expense Ratio
								Total Return % through 6/30/06	Annualized		Incl. in Returns	
FO	Fidelity Adv International Disc B	FADDX	A+	(800) 522-7297	A- / 9.0	-1.86	7.47	25.61 /89	24.76 /91	12.73 /88	0.32	2.18
FO	Fidelity Adv International Disc C	FCADX	A+	(800) 522-7297	A- / 9.0	-1.88	7.42	25.67 /89	24.83 /91	12.76 /88	0.34	1.98
FO	Fidelity Adv International Disc I	FIADX	A+	(800) 522-7297	A- / 9.1	-1.55	8.05	27.15 /92	25.54 /92	13.15 /89	0.93	0.90
FO	Fidelity Adv International Disc T	FTADX	A+	(800) 522-7297	B+ / 8.9	-1.74	7.65	26.16 /90	25.06 /91	12.89 /88	0.66	1.69
FO	● Fidelity Adv International Sm Cap A	FIASX	B	(800) 522-7297	A+ / 9.7	-5.33	7.16	29.89 /94	36.63 /98	--	0.14	1.62
FO	● Fidelity Adv International Sm Cap B	FIBSX	B	(800) 522-7297	A+ / 9.8	-5.51	6.75	28.89 /94	35.46 /98	--	0.00	2.37
FO	● Fidelity Adv International Sm Cap C	FICSX	B	(800) 522-7297	A+ / 9.8	-5.50	6.74	28.92 /94	35.64 /98	--	0.00	2.37
FO	● Fidelity Adv International Sm Cap I	FIXIX	B	(800) 522-7297	A+ / 9.8	-5.24	7.35	30.35 /95	37.12 /99	--	0.45	1.27
FO	● Fidelity Adv International Sm Cap T	FTISX	B	(800) 522-7297	A+ / 9.8	-5.39	7.03	29.59 /94	36.28 /98	--	0.00	1.87
FO	Fidelity Adv Intl Cap Apprec A	FCPAX	C-	(800) 522-7297	C+ / 5.7	-3.22	1.85	17.94 /79	16.20 /64	9.64 /79	0.99	1.30
FO	Fidelity Adv Intl Cap Apprec B	FCPBX	C-	(800) 522-7297	C+ / 5.9	-3.41	1.38	16.95 /77	15.23 /60	8.75 /75	0.28	2.12
FO	Fidelity Adv Intl Cap Apprec C	FCPCX	C	(800) 522-7297	C+ / 6.0	-3.40	1.44	17.04 /77	15.37 /61	8.87 /76	0.35	2.04
FO	Fidelity Adv Intl Cap Apprec I	FCPIX	C	(800) 522-7297	C+ / 6.6	-3.11	2.07	18.37 /80	16.56 /66	10.05 /81	0.00	1.09
FO	Fidelity Adv Intl Cap Apprec T	FIATX	C-	(800) 522-7297	C+ / 5.8	-3.26	1.74	17.69 /78	15.92 /63	9.41 /78	0.77	1.53
FO	Fidelity Adv Japan A	FJPAX	C	(800) 522-7297	B / 7.7	-8.58	-6.80	26.54 /91	23.92 /89	5.95 /61	0.00	1.49
FO	Fidelity Adv Japan B	FAJBX	C	(800) 522-7297	B / 7.9	-8.81	-7.22	25.55 /89	22.98 /87	5.11 /55	0.00	2.24
FO	Fidelity Adv Japan C	FAJCX	C	(800) 522-7297	B / 7.9	-8.71	-7.12	25.63 /89	23.02 /87	5.15 /55	0.00	2.24
FO	Fidelity Adv Japan I	FAJIX	C	(800) 522-7297	B+ / 8.3	-8.51	-6.67	27.02 /91	24.34 /90	6.28 /63	0.00	1.17
FO	Fidelity Adv Japan T	FAJTX	C	(800) 522-7297	B / 7.8	-8.70	-7.00	26.11 /90	23.57 /89	5.63 /59	0.00	1.74
FO	Fidelity Adv Korea A	FAKAX	C	(800) 522-7297	A+ / 9.7	-1.33	-0.30	53.08 /99	34.48 /98	26.14 /99	0.12	1.55
FO	Fidelity Adv Korea B	FAKBX	C	(800) 522-7297	A+ / 9.7	-1.52	-0.68	51.83 /99	33.48 /97	25.21 /98	0.00	2.30
FO	Fidelity Adv Korea C	FAKCX	C	(800) 522-7297	A+ / 9.7	-1.52	-0.72	51.76 /99	33.45 /97	25.18 /98	0.00	2.30
FO	Fidelity Adv Korea I	FKRIX	C	(800) 522-7297	A+ / 9.8	-1.27	-0.17	53.42 /99	34.89 /98	26.46 /99	0.16	1.30
FO	Fidelity Adv Korea T	FAKTX	C	(800) 522-7297	A+ / 9.7	-1.44	-0.44	52.59 /99	34.16 /98	25.79 /99	0.00	1.80
GR	Fidelity Adv Large Cap Fund A	FALAX	D+	(800) 522-7297	D+ / 2.6	-3.49	1.44	14.44 /70	10.73 /33	0.49 /18	0.00	1.23
GR	Fidelity Adv Large Cap Fund B	FALHX	D+	(800) 522-7297	D+ / 2.4	-3.65	1.07	13.56 /66	9.88 /27	-0.26 /14	0.00	1.98
GR	Fidelity Adv Large Cap Fund C	FLCCX	C-	(800) 522-7297	C- / 3.1	-3.66	1.07	13.59 /67	9.90 /27	-0.24 /15	0.00	1.98
GR	Fidelity Adv Large Cap Fund I	FALIX	C	(800) 522-7297	C- / 4.1	-3.39	1.64	14.84 /71	11.15 /37	0.88 /20	0.12	0.87
GR	Fidelity Adv Large Cap Fund T	FALGX	C-	(800) 522-7297	C- / 3.0	-3.50	1.39	14.29 /69	10.57 /31	0.34 /17	0.00	1.39
FO	Fidelity Adv Latin America A	FLTAX	C+	(800) 522-7297	A+ / 9.9	-3.27	13.78	56.82 /99	49.18 /99	23.94 /98	0.94	1.45
FO	Fidelity Adv Latin America B	FLTBX	C+	(800) 522-7297	A+ / 9.9	-3.46	13.25	55.53 /99	48.10 /99	23.02 /98	0.52	2.20
FO	Fidelity Adv Latin America C	FLACX	C+	(800) 522-7297	A+ / 9.9	-3.44	13.30	55.72 /99	48.10 /99	23.03 /98	0.63	2.20
FO	Fidelity Adv Latin America I	FLNIX	C+	(800) 522-7297	A+ / 9.9	-3.21	13.84	57.17 /99	49.53 /99	24.28 /98	1.09	1.20
FO	Fidelity Adv Latin America T	FLTTX	C+	(800) 522-7297	A+ / 9.9	-3.32	13.57	56.36 /99	48.81 /99	23.63 /98	0.79	1.68
GR	Fidelity Adv Leveraged Co Stk A	FLSAX	A	(800) 522-7297	A- / 9.1	-0.16	9.42	18.65 /80	27.14 /93	24.67 /98	0.22	1.26
GR	Fidelity Adv Leveraged Co Stk B	FLCBX	A	(800) 522-7297	A- / 9.1	-0.36	9.00	17.73 /79	26.15 /92	23.78 /98	0.00	2.03
GR	Fidelity Adv Leveraged Co Stk C	FLSCX	A	(800) 522-7297	A- / 9.2	-0.33	9.05	17.85 /79	26.25 /92	23.76 /98	0.00	2.00
GR	Fidelity Adv Leveraged Co Stk I	FLVIX	A	(800) 522-7297	A / 9.3	-0.10	9.56	19.03 /81	27.54 /94	25.00 /98	0.40	0.93
GR	Fidelity Adv Leveraged Co Stk T	FLSTX	A	(800) 522-7297	A- / 9.2	-0.23	9.28	18.36 /80	26.78 /93	24.29 /98	0.10	1.52
MC	● Fidelity Adv Mid Cap Fund A	FMCDX	D+	(800) 522-7297	C / 5.2	-8.10	1.42	12.35 /61	15.50 /61	6.88 /66	0.00	1.11
MC	● Fidelity Adv Mid Cap Fund B	FMCBX	D+	(800) 522-7297	C / 4.9	-8.27	0.98	11.42 /56	14.58 /57	6.06 /61	0.00	1.90
MC	● Fidelity Adv Mid Cap Fund C	FMCEX	C-	(800) 522-7297	C+ / 5.6	-8.22	1.06	11.51 /57	14.65 /57	6.12 /62	0.00	1.85
MC	● Fidelity Adv Mid Cap Fund I	FMCCX	C-	(800) 522-7297	C+ / 6.3	-7.99	1.59	12.73 /63	15.92 /63	7.32 /68	0.00	0.73
★ MC	● Fidelity Adv Mid Cap Fund T	FMCAX	C-	(800) 522-7297	C / 5.5	-8.10	1.32	12.16 /60	15.31 /60	6.72 /65	0.00	1.25
GR	Fidelity Adv Mid Cap II A	FIIAX	U	(800) 522-7297	U /	-2.27	6.33	21.43 /83	--	--	0.00	1.25
GR	Fidelity Adv Mid Cap II B	FIIBX	U	(800) 522-7297	U /	-2.48	5.90	20.50 /82	--	--	0.00	2.00
GR	Fidelity Adv Mid Cap II C	FIICX	U	(800) 522-7297	U /	-2.48	5.97	20.49 /82	--	--	0.00	2.00
GR	Fidelity Adv Mid Cap II I	FIIMX	U	(800) 522-7297	U /	-2.27	6.45	21.71 /84	--	--	0.00	1.00
GR	Fidelity Adv Mid Cap II T	FITIX	U	(800) 522-7297	U /	-2.34	6.27	21.25 /83	--	--	0.00	1.50
EN	Fidelity Adv Natural Resources A	FANAX	B+	(800) 522-7297	A+ / 9.8	3.96	18.23	46.08 /98	36.31 /98	18.29 /95	0.00	1.16
EN	Fidelity Adv Natural Resources B	FANRX	B+	(800) 522-7297	A+ / 9.8	3.76	17.75	45.02 /98	35.33 /98	17.44 /94	0.00	1.91
EN	Fidelity Adv Natural Resources C	FNRCX	B+	(800) 522-7297	A+ / 9.9	3.77	17.77	45.09 /98	35.39 /98	17.49 /94	0.00	1.87

● Denotes fund is closed to new investors
★ Denotes fund is included in Section II

RISK			NET ASSETS		ASSET					BULL / BEAR		FUND MANAGER		MINIMUMS		LOADS	
	3 Year		NAV						Portfolio	Last Bull	Last Bear	Manager	Manager	Initial	Additional	Front	Back
Risk Rating/Pts	Standard Deviation	Beta	As of 6/30/06	Total $(Mil)	Cash %	Stocks %	Bonds %	Other %	Turnover Ratio	Market Return	Market Return	Quality Pct	Tenure (Years)	Purch. $	Purch. $	End Load	End Load
B- / 7.4	11.8	1.13	33.82	2	2	96	0	2	75.0	144.1	-9.0	30	1	2,500	100	0.0	1.0
B- / 7.4	11.8	1.13	33.87	4	2	96	0	2	75.0	144.5	-9.0	31	1	2,500	100	0.0	1.0
B- / 7.5	11.7	1.13	34.23	22	2	96	0	2	75.0	148.2	-9.0	36	1	2,500	100	0.0	1.0
B- / 7.5	11.8	1.13	33.93	6	2	96	0	2	75.0	145.6	-9.0	33	1	2,500	2,500	3.5	1.0
C / 4.6	15.5	1.33	28.75	40	0	98	0	2	79.0	264.3	-1.5	84	4	2,500	100	5.8	2.0
C / 4.6	15.5	1.33	28.29	14	0	98	0	2	79.0	255.1	-1.5	78	4	2,500	100	0.0	2.0
C / 4.6	15.5	1.33	28.36	27	0	98	0	2	79.0	256.6	-1.5	79	4	2,500	100	0.0	2.0
C / 4.6	15.5	1.33	28.92	10	0	98	0	2	79.0	268.2	-1.5	86	4	2,500	100	0.0	2.0
C / 4.6	15.5	1.33	28.63	49	0	98	0	2	79.0	261.6	-1.5	83	4	2,500	100	3.5	2.0
C / 5.5	12.4	1.12	17.11	116	1	98	0	1	176.0	107.3	-10.4	3	N/A	2,500	100	5.8	1.0
C / 5.5	12.4	1.12	16.13	55	1	98	0	1	176.0	102.0	-10.6	2	N/A	2,500	100	0.0	1.0
C / 5.5	12.4	1.12	16.20	68	1	98	0	1	176.0	102.6	-10.6	2	N/A	2,500	100	0.0	1.0
C+ / 5.6	12.4	1.12	17.74	37	1	98	0	1	176.0	109.3	-10.3	3	N/A	2,500	100	0.0	1.0
C / 5.5	12.4	1.12	16.91	210	1	98	0	1	176.0	105.9	-10.5	2	N/A	2,500	100	3.5	1.0
C- / 4.0	19.9	1.03	17.26	43	1	98	0	1	89.0	128.5	-7.9	42	N/A	2,500	100	5.8	1.5
C- / 4.0	19.9	1.04	16.46	21	1	98	0	1	89.0	123.2	-8.1	34	N/A	2,500	100	0.0	1.5
C- / 4.0	19.8	1.03	16.57	64	1	98	0	1	89.0	123.2	-8.0	35	N/A	2,500	100	0.0	1.5
C- / 4.1	19.9	1.03	17.63	16	1	98	0	1	89.0	130.9	-7.8	47	N/A	2,500	100	0.0	1.5
C- / 4.0	19.9	1.03	17.00	24	1	98	0	1	89.0	126.5	-7.9	39	N/A	2,500	100	3.5	1.5
D / 1.9	23.4	1.39	22.99	32	0	98	0	2	97.0	214.0	-20.0	57	N/A	2,500	100	5.8	1.5
D / 1.8	23.5	1.40	22.00	8	0	98	0	2	97.0	206.7	-20.2	46	N/A	2,500	100	0.0	1.5
D / 1.8	23.5	1.39	22.00	12	0	98	0	2	97.0	206.5	-20.2	46	N/A	2,500	100	0.0	1.5
D / 1.9	23.5	1.40	23.34	5	0	98	0	2	97.0	217.1	-20.0	60	N/A	2,500	100	0.0	1.5
D / 1.9	23.5	1.39	22.65	6	0	98	0	2	97.0	211.7	-20.1	54	N/A	2,500	100	3.5	1.5
B- / 7.5	9.0	1.09	16.88	95	0	99	0	1	188.0	60.3	-9.3	41	1	2,500	100	5.8	1.0
B- / 7.4	9.1	1.10	16.08	69	0	99	0	1	188.0	56.7	-9.6	33	1	2,500	100	0.0	5.0
B- / 7.4	9.0	1.10	16.05	41	0	99	0	1	188.0	56.6	-9.5	33	1	2,500	100	0.0	1.0
B- / 7.6	9.0	1.10	17.39	414	0	99	0	1	188.0	62.3	-9.3	45	1	2,500	100	0.0	0.0
B- / 7.5	9.0	1.09	16.80	139	0	99	0	1	188.0	59.7	-9.4	39	1	2,500	100	3.5	0.3
C- / 3.3	22.2	1.67	33.45	43	4	95	0	1	42.0	381.7	-4.3	94	1	2,500	100	5.8	1.5
C- / 3.3	22.2	1.67	32.66	14	4	95	0	1	42.0	371.3	-4.4	91	1	2,500	100	0.0	1.5
C- / 3.3	22.2	1.67	32.55	23	4	95	0	1	42.0	370.8	-4.4	91	1	2,500	100	0.0	1.5
C- / 3.3	22.2	1.67	34.05	5	4	95	0	1	42.0	386.1	-4.1	94	1	2,500	100	0.0	1.5
C- / 3.3	22.2	1.67	33.22	19	4	95	0	1	42.0	378.2	-4.4	93	1	2,500	100	3.5	1.5
C+ / 6.6	14.0	1.46	31.02	523	6	92	0	2	20.0	216.7	-4.3	99	3	10,000	1,000	5.8	1.0
C+ / 6.6	14.0	1.46	30.14	125	6	92	0	2	20.0	209.5	-4.6	99	3	10,000	1,000	0.0	5.0
C+ / 6.6	14.0	1.46	30.11	309	6	92	0	2	20.0	209.5	-4.5	99	3	10,000	1,000	0.0	1.0
C+ / 6.7	14.0	1.46	31.29	113	6	92	0	2	20.0	219.9	-4.3	99	3	10,000	1,000	0.0	0.0
C+ / 6.6	14.0	1.46	30.61	340	6	92	0	2	20.0	213.8	-4.5	99	3	10,000	1,000	3.5	0.3
C / 4.8	13.9	1.13	23.61	1,604	0	99	0	1	138.0	104.5	-4.6	18	5	2,500	100	5.8	1.0
C / 4.9	13.8	1.13	22.75	777	0	99	0	1	138.0	99.4	-4.7	14	5	2,500	100	0.0	5.0
C / 4.9	13.8	1.13	22.78	524	0	99	0	1	138.0	99.7	-4.7	14	5	2,500	100	0.0	1.0
C / 4.9	13.8	1.13	24.31	732	0	99	0	1	138.0	106.8	-4.4	20	5	2,500	100	0.0	0.0
C / 4.9	13.8	1.13	23.82	4,019	0	99	0	1	138.0	103.5	-4.6	17	5	2,500	100	3.5	0.3
U /	N/A	N/A	15.48	334	5	94	0	1	111.0	N/A	N/A	N/A	2	2,500	100	5.8	1.0
U /	N/A	N/A	15.32	79	5	94	0	1	111.0	N/A	N/A	N/A	2	2,500	100	0.0	5.0
U /	N/A	N/A	15.33	171	5	94	0	1	111.0	N/A	N/A	N/A	2	2,500	100	0.0	1.0
U /	N/A	N/A	15.53	231	5	94	0	1	111.0	N/A	N/A	N/A	2	2,500	100	0.0	0.0
U /	N/A	N/A	15.44	482	5	94	0	1	111.0	N/A	N/A	N/A	2	2,500	100	3.5	0.3
C / 4.8	19.9	0.97	47.03	199	2	98	0	0	157.0	184.2	1.3	88	N/A	2,500	100	5.8	1.0
C / 4.8	19.9	0.97	45.77	134	2	98	0	0	157.0	177.8	1.1	83	N/A	2,500	100	0.0	5.0
C / 4.8	19.9	0.97	46.00	122	2	98	0	0	157.0	178.1	1.2	84	N/A	2,500	100	0.0	1.0

99 Pct = Best
0 Pct = Worst

Fund Type	Fund Name	Ticker Symbol	Overall Weiss Investment Rating	Phone	Performance Rating/Pts	3 Mo	6 Mo	1Yr / Pct	Annualized 3Yr / Pct	Annualized 5Yr / Pct	Dividend Yield	Expense Ratio
EN	Fidelity Adv Natural Resources I	FANIX	B+	(800) 522-7297	A+ / 9.9	4.06	18.37	46.62 /99	36.85 /98	18.75 /95	0.00	0.80
EN	Fidelity Adv Natural Resources T	FAGNX	B+	(800) 522-7297	A+ / 9.9	3.93	18.09	45.80 /98	36.07 /98	18.08 /95	0.00	1.37
GR	● Fidelity Adv New Insights A	FNIAX	U	(800) 522-7297	U /	-0.75	3.84	18.51 /80	--	--	0.00	1.17
GR	● Fidelity Adv New Insights B	FNIBX	U	(800) 522-7297	U /	-0.94	3.42	17.51 /78	--	--	0.00	1.98
GR	● Fidelity Adv New Insights C	FNICX	U	(800) 522-7297	U /	-0.94	3.48	17.64 /78	--	--	0.00	1.89
GR	● Fidelity Adv New Insights I	FINSX	U	(800) 522-7297	U /	-0.68	3.99	18.87 /80	--	--	0.00	0.84
GR	● Fidelity Adv New Insights T	FNITX	U	(800) 522-7297	U /	-0.81	3.74	18.23 /79	--	--	0.00	1.38
FO	Fidelity Adv Overseas Fund A	FAOAX	B	(800) 522-7297	B / 8.0	-1.75	6.53	24.12 /87	21.45 /84	7.32 /68	0.86	1.15
FO	Fidelity Adv Overseas Fund B	FAOBX	B+	(800) 522-7297	B / 8.2	-2.01	6.11	23.10 /86	20.45 /81	6.42 /64	0.09	1.94
FO	Fidelity Adv Overseas Fund C	FAOCX	B+	(800) 522-7297	B / 8.2	-1.98	6.11	23.17 /86	20.54 /81	6.52 /64	0.18	1.90
FO	Fidelity Adv Overseas Fund I	FAOIX	B+	(800) 522-7297	B+ / 8.5	-1.68	6.73	24.57 /88	21.93 /85	7.74 /70	1.00	0.73
FO	Fidelity Adv Overseas Fund T	FAERX	B+	(800) 522-7297	B / 8.1	-1.81	6.45	23.95 /87	21.30 /83	7.18 /68	0.56	1.27
RE	Fidelity Adv Real Estate A	FHEAX	B-	(800) 522-7297	A / 9.3	-0.45	14.12	24.03 /87	28.36 /94	--	1.05	1.23
RE	Fidelity Adv Real Estate B	FHEBX	B-	(800) 522-7297	A / 9.3	-0.66	13.71	23.09 /86	27.35 /93	--	0.75	1.98
RE	Fidelity Adv Real Estate C	FHECX	B-	(800) 522-7297	A / 9.4	-0.66	13.69	23.06 /86	27.39 /93	--	0.75	1.98
RE	Fidelity Adv Real Estate I	FHEIX	B-	(800) 522-7297	A / 9.5	-0.40	14.29	24.32 /88	28.80 /95	--	1.27	0.90
RE	Fidelity Adv Real Estate T	FHETX	B-	(800) 522-7297	A / 9.4	-0.56	13.95	23.67 /87	27.97 /94	--	0.96	1.48
SC	Fidelity Adv Small Cap A	FSCDX	C	(800) 522-7297	B- / 7.0	-2.21	4.73	11.46 /56	19.23 /77	7.91 /71	0.00	1.38
SC	Fidelity Adv Small Cap B	FSCBX	C	(800) 522-7297	C+ / 6.8	-2.41	4.34	10.60 /51	18.30 /74	7.07 /67	0.00	2.13
SC	Fidelity Adv Small Cap C	FSCEX	C	(800) 522-7297	B- / 7.3	-2.39	4.35	10.67 /51	18.35 /74	7.11 /67	0.00	2.10
SC	Fidelity Adv Small Cap I	FSCIX	C+	(800) 522-7297	B / 7.8	-2.14	4.89	11.85 /59	19.65 /78	8.33 /73	0.00	0.98
SC	Fidelity Adv Small Cap T	FSCTX	C	(800) 522-7297	B- / 7.2	-2.30	4.64	11.26 /55	18.98 /76	7.66 /70	0.00	1.51
SC	Fidelity Adv Small Cap Value A	FCVAX	U	(800) 522-7297	U /	-5.00	7.47	18.53 /80	--	--	0.00	1.34
SC	Fidelity Adv Small Cap Value C	FCVCX	U	(800) 522-7297	U /	-5.10	7.10	17.70 /78	--	--	0.00	2.09
SC	Fidelity Adv Small Cap Value T	FCVTX	U	(800) 522-7297	U /	-5.01	7.40	18.26 /80	--	--	0.00	1.59
GI	Fidelity Adv Strat Div & Inc A	FASDX	U	(800) 522-7297	U /	-1.59	4.08	12.23 /61	--	--	1.27	1.13
GI	Fidelity Adv Strat Div & Inc C	FCSDX	U	(800) 522-7297	U /	-1.78	3.74	11.36 /56	--	--	0.66	1.87
GI	Fidelity Adv Strat Div & Inc T	FTSDX	U	(800) 522-7297	U /	-1.65	3.95	12.00 /60	--	--	1.11	1.35
RE	Fidelity Adv Strat Real Return I	FSIRX	U	(800) 522-7297	U /	2.22	2.02	--	--	--	0.00	0.85
GR	Fidelity Adv Strategic Growth A	FTQAX	E	(800) 522-7297	E- / 0.2	-8.61	-5.71	0.79 / 2	6.09 / 7	-5.87 / 2	0.00	1.20
GR	Fidelity Adv Strategic Growth B	FTQBX	E	(800) 522-7297	E- / 0.2	-8.76	-5.91	0.12 / 2	5.34 / 5	-6.53 / 1	0.00	1.95
GR	Fidelity Adv Strategic Growth C	FTQCX	E	(800) 522-7297	E / 0.4	-8.79	-5.93	0.12 / 2	5.32 / 5	-6.57 / 1	0.00	1.95
GR	Fidelity Adv Strategic Growth I	FTQIX	E+	(800) 522-7297	E+ / 0.6	-8.59	-5.53	1.00 / 3	6.37 / 8	-5.63 / 2	0.00	0.95
GR	Fidelity Adv Strategic Growth T	FTQTX	E+	(800) 522-7297	E / 0.3	-8.57	-5.71	0.57 / 2	5.84 / 6	-6.09 / 2	0.00	1.45
GR	Fidelity Adv Tax Mgd Stock Fund A	FTAMX	C+	(800) 522-7297	C / 5.3	-0.47	4.22	11.91 /59	14.81 /58	--	0.00	1.19
GR	Fidelity Adv Tax Mgd Stock Fund B	FTBMX	C+	(800) 522-7297	C / 5.1	-0.65	3.85	11.07 /54	13.93 /54	--	0.00	1.94
GR	Fidelity Adv Tax Mgd Stock Fund C	FTCMX	C+	(800) 522-7297	C+ / 5.7	-0.65	3.85	11.07 /54	13.93 /54	--	0.00	1.94
GR	Fidelity Adv Tax Mgd Stock Fund I	FTIMX	B	(800) 522-7297	C+ / 6.4	-0.39	4.34	12.05 /60	15.08 /59	--	0.00	0.94
GR	Fidelity Adv Tax Mgd Stock Fund T	FTMSX	C+	(800) 522-7297	C+ / 5.6	-0.48	4.10	11.66 /58	14.56 /57	--	0.00	1.44
TC	Fidelity Adv Technology A	FADTX	E-	(800) 522-7297	D- / 1.3	-13.97	-3.93	9.12 /41	9.56 /24	-2.60 / 6	0.00	1.33
TC	Fidelity Adv Technology B	FABTX	E-	(800) 522-7297	D / 1.6	-14.11	-4.24	8.34 /35	8.74 /19	-3.31 / 5	0.00	2.08
TC	Fidelity Adv Technology C	FTHCX	E-	(800) 522-7297	D / 1.7	-14.11	-4.28	8.38 /36	8.78 /20	-3.28 / 5	0.00	2.08
TC	Fidelity Adv Technology I	FATIX	E-	(800) 522-7297	D+ / 2.4	-13.87	-3.76	9.59 /44	10.08 /28	-2.13 / 8	0.00	0.91
TC	Fidelity Adv Technology T	FATEX	E-	(800) 522-7297	D- / 1.5	-14.03	-4.06	8.88 /39	9.30 /23	-2.83 / 6	0.00	1.57
UT	Fidelity Adv Telecom & Util Gr A	FUGAX	B	(800) 522-7297	C+ / 6.7	2.42	11.10	14.68 /71	16.66 /67	3.04 /37	1.52	1.38
UT	Fidelity Adv Telecom & Util Gr B	FAUBX	B	(800) 522-7297	C+ / 6.9	2.21	10.64	13.80 /68	15.76 /62	2.29 /30	0.50	2.12
UT	Fidelity Adv Telecom & Util Gr C	FUGCX	A-	(800) 522-7297	B- / 7.0	2.20	10.71	13.86 /68	15.87 /63	2.36 /31	0.62	2.04
UT	Fidelity Adv Telecom & Util Gr I	FUGIX	A	(800) 522-7297	B- / 7.4	2.46	11.28	15.20 /72	17.12 /69	3.52 /41	1.96	0.93
UT	Fidelity Adv Telecom & Util Gr T	FAUFX	B	(800) 522-7297	C+ / 6.8	2.30	10.90	14.37 /69	16.35 /65	2.77 /35	1.11	1.64
GR	Fidelity Adv Value A	FAVFX	U	(800) 522-7297	U /	-2.94	3.20	12.14 /60	--	--	0.00	1.23
IN	Fidelity Adv Value Leaders A	FVLAX	C+	(800) 522-7297	C / 5.1	-2.43	3.01	12.60 /63	14.44 /56	--	0.26	1.21
IN	Fidelity Adv Value Leaders B	FVLBX	C+	(800) 522-7297	C / 4.8	-2.61	2.67	11.78 /58	13.54 /52	--	0.00	1.96

● Denotes fund is closed to new investors
* Denotes fund is included in Section II

RISK			NET ASSETS		ASSET				BULL / BEAR		FUND MANAGER		MINIMUMS		LOADS	
	3 Year		NAV						Last Bull	Last Bear	Manager	Manager	Initial	Additional	Front	Back
Risk Rating/Pts	Standard Deviation	Beta	As of 6/30/06	Total $(Mil)	Cash %	Stocks %	Bonds %	Other %	Portfolio Turnover Ratio	Market Return	Market Return	Quality Pct	Tenure (Years)	Purch. $	Purch. $	End Load	End Load
C /4.8	19.8	0.97	48.14	20	2	98	0	0	157.0	187.8	1.4	90	N/A	2,500	100	0.0	0.0
C /4.8	19.9	0.97	47.86	367	2	98	0	0	157.0	182.6	1.3	87	N/A	2,500	100	3.5	0.3
U /	N/A	N/A	17.24	1,683	8	90	0	2	65.0	N/A	N/A	N/A	3	2,500	100	5.8	1.0
U /	N/A	N/A	16.86	449	8	90	0	2	65.0	N/A	N/A	N/A	3	2,500	100	0.0	5.0
U /	N/A	N/A	16.89	1,514	8	90	0	2	65.0	N/A	N/A	N/A	3	2,500	100	0.0	1.0
U /	N/A	N/A	17.40	1,278	8	90	0	2	65.0	N/A	N/A	N/A	3	2,500	100	0.0	0.0
U /	N/A	N/A	17.14	2,013	8	90	0	2	65.0	N/A	N/A	N/A	3	2,500	100	3.5	0.3
C+ /6.6	11.8	1.11	20.73	111	1	98	0	1	120.0	124.9	-13.0	16	1	2,500	100	5.8	1.0
C+ /6.5	11.8	1.10	19.96	42	1	98	0	1	120.0	118.7	-13.2	12	1	2,500	100	0.0	1.0
C+ /6.5	11.8	1.10	20.32	40	1	98	0	1	120.0	119.3	-13.2	13	1	2,500	100	0.0	1.0
C+ /6.6	11.8	1.11	21.08	292	1	98	0	1	120.0	127.5	-12.9	19	1	2,500	100	0.0	1.0
C+ /6.6	11.8	1.10	21.11	597	1	98	0	1	120.0	123.9	-13.0	16	1	2,500	100	3.5	1.0
C /4.4	16.2	0.97	19.72	78	4	95	0	1	68.0	129.5	0.3	90	2	2,500	100	5.8	1.0
C /4.4	16.2	0.97	19.58	27	4	95	0	1	68.0	123.8	0.2	85	2	2,500	100	0.0	5.0
C /4.4	16.2	0.97	19.60	34	4	95	0	1	68.0	124.0	0.2	86	2	2,500	100	0.0	1.0
C /4.4	16.2	0.97	19.84	7	4	95	0	1	68.0	132.0	0.4	91	2	2,500	100	0.0	0.0
C /4.4	16.2	0.97	19.69	88	4	95	0	1	68.0	127.4	0.3	88	2	2,500	100	3.5	0.3
C /5.2	13.5	0.88	23.44	706	0	99	0	1	30.0	113.2	-12.3	79	1	2,500	100	5.8	1.0
C /4.9	13.5	0.88	21.85	259	0	99	0	1	30.0	108.0	-12.5	72	1	2,500	100	0.0	5.0
C /4.9	13.5	0.88	22.01	317	0	99	0	1	30.0	108.3	-12.5	72	1	2,500	100	0.0	1.0
C /5.4	13.5	0.88	24.18	467	0	99	0	1	30.0	115.8	-12.3	82	1	2,500	100	0.0	0.0
C /5.2	13.5	0.88	22.95	1,567	0	99	0	1	30.0	111.9	-12.4	77	1	2,500	100	3.5	0.3
U /	N/A	N/A	13.67	41	5	94	0	1	60.0	N/A	N/A	N/A	N/A	2,500	100	5.8	1.5
U /	N/A	N/A	13.58	27	5	94	0	1	60.0	N/A	N/A	N/A	N/A	2,500	100	0.0	1.5
U /	N/A	N/A	13.64	46	5	94	0	1	60.0	N/A	N/A	N/A	N/A	2,500	100	3.5	1.5
U /	N/A	N/A	12.60	54	4	77	0	19	55.0	N/A	N/A	N/A	N/A	2,500	100	5.8	0.0
U /	N/A	N/A	12.55	62	4	77	0	19	55.0	N/A	N/A	N/A	N/A	2,500	100	0.0	1.0
U /	N/A	N/A	12.58	98	4	77	0	19	55.0	N/A	N/A	N/A	N/A	2,500	100	3.5	0.3
U /	N/A	N/A	10.15	67	2	0	98	0	78.0	N/A	N/A	N/A	1	2,500	100	0.0	0.8
C+ /6.1	10.1	1.17	8.92	5	N/A	100	0	N/A	115.0	49.7	-11.0	9	3	2,500	100	5.8	1.0
C+ /6.1	10.1	1.17	8.44	4	N/A	100	0	N/A	115.0	46.2	-11.2	7	3	2,500	100	0.0	5.0
C+ /6.0	10.1	1.18	8.40	3	N/A	100	0	N/A	115.0	46.0	-11.1	7	3	2,500	100	0.0	1.0
C+ /6.1	10.1	1.18	9.05	N/A	N/A	100	0	N/A	115.0	50.8	-11.0	10	3	2,500	100	0.0	0.0
C+ /6.1	10.1	1.17	8.75	9	N/A	100	0	N/A	115.0	48.4	-11.0	8	3	2,500	100	3.5	0.3
B- /7.9	10.4	1.23	12.59	8	0	99	0	1	236.0	77.1	-10.9	70	2	2,500	100	5.8	1.0
B- /7.9	10.4	1.23	12.14	4	0	99	0	1	236.0	72.9	-11.0	62	2	2,500	100	0.0	5.0
B- /7.9	10.4	1.23	12.14	5	0	99	0	1	236.0	72.9	-11.0	62	2	2,500	100	0.0	1.0
B- /7.9	10.4	1.23	12.74	1	0	99	0	1	236.0	78.6	-10.9	72	2	2,500	100	0.0	0.0
B- /7.9	10.4	1.23	12.45	6	0	99	0	1	236.0	75.8	-11.0	68	2	2,500	100	3.5	0.3
D- /1.2	19.8	2.00	16.63	191	0	99	0	1	180.0	86.8	-13.4	2	1	2,500	100	5.8	1.0
D- /1.2	19.8	2.00	15.58	218	0	99	0	1	180.0	82.5	-13.5	1	1	2,500	100	0.0	1.0
D- /1.2	19.8	2.00	15.65	91	0	99	0	1	180.0	82.7	-13.6	1	1	2,500	100	0.0	1.0
D- /1.2	19.7	2.00	17.14	13	0	99	0	1	180.0	89.7	-13.2	2	1	2,500	100	0.0	1.0
D- /1.2	19.8	2.00	16.30	284	0	99	0	1	180.0	85.5	-13.5	2	1	2,500	100	3.5	1.0
B /8.2	8.5	0.43	16.51	36	0	99	0	1	44.0	96.4	-6.9	95	3	2,500	100	5.8	1.0
B /8.3	8.5	0.43	16.22	66	0	99	0	1	44.0	92.0	-7.1	92	3	2,500	100	0.0	1.0
B /8.3	8.5	0.43	16.23	32	0	99	0	1	44.0	92.4	-7.1	93	3	2,500	100	0.0	1.0
B /8.2	8.5	0.42	16.67	2	0	99	0	1	44.0	99.1	-6.8	96	3	2,500	100	0.0	1.0
B /8.3	8.5	0.42	16.48	50	0	99	0	1	44.0	95.0	-7.0	94	3	2,500	100	3.5	1.0
U /	N/A	N/A	13.88	39	6	92	0	2	25.0	N/A	N/A	N/A	3	2,500	100	5.8	1.0
B /8.3	9.1	1.13	14.04	9	0	99	0	1	86.0	N/A	N/A	75	3	2,500	100	5.8	1.0
B /8.3	9.1	1.13	13.82	5	0	99	0	1	86.0	N/A	N/A	68	3	2,500	100	0.0	5.0

Fund Type	Fund Name	Ticker Symbol	Overall Weiss Investment Rating	Phone	Performance Rating/Pts	3 Mo	6 Mo	1Yr / Pct	Annualized 3Yr / Pct	Annualized 5Yr / Pct	Dividend Yield	Expense Ratio
IN	Fidelity Adv Value Leaders C	FVLCX	B-	(800) 522-7297	C / 5.4	-2.61	2.68	11.78 /58	13.55 /52	--	0.00	1.96
IN	Fidelity Adv Value Leaders I	FVLIX	B	(800) 522-7297	C+ / 6.2	-2.35	3.22	12.94 /64	14.71 /57	--	0.47	1.00
IN	Fidelity Adv Value Leaders T	FVLTX	B-	(800) 522-7297	C / 5.3	-2.45	2.87	12.32 /61	14.12 /55	--	0.04	1.46
GR	Fidelity Adv Value Strategies A	FSOAX	D	(800) 522-7297	C+ / 5.9	-3.51	3.49	10.46 /50	16.58 /66	5.95 /61	0.03	1.19
GR	Fidelity Adv Value Strategies B	FASBX	D-	(800) 522-7297	C+ / 5.6	-3.70	3.08	9.61 /44	15.64 /62	5.10 /55	0.00	1.98
GR	Fidelity Adv Value Strategies C	FVCSX	D	(800) 522-7297	C+ / 6.2	-3.69	3.10	9.60 /44	15.67 /62	5.13 /55	0.00	1.98
GR	Fidelity Adv Value Strategies Fd	FSLSX	C-	(800) 522-7297	C+ / 6.8	-3.43	3.62	10.78 /52	16.94 /68	6.33 /63	0.29	0.85
GR	Fidelity Adv Value Strategies I	FASOX	D+	(800) 522-7297	C+ / 6.9	-3.42	3.67	10.88 /53	17.02 /68	6.35 /63	0.38	0.80
GR	Fidelity Adv Value Strategies T	FASPX	D	(800) 522-7297	C+ / 6.2	-3.56	3.41	10.26 /49	16.36 /65	5.74 /59	0.00	1.37
GR	Fidelity Adv Value T	FTVFX	U	(800) 522-7297	U /	-2.95	3.13	11.87 /59	--	--	0.00	1.48
FO	Fidelity Advisor Intl Sm Opp Fd A	FOPAX	U	(800) 522-7297	U /	-4.40	10.59	--	--	--	0.00	1.65
★ AG	Fidelity Aggressive Growth Fund	FDEGX	D-	(800) 544-8888	D+ / 2.7	-8.51	-2.70	6.32 /22	10.61 /32	-6.73 / 1	0.00	0.70
FO	Fidelity Aggressive Int'l Fd	FIVFX	C	(800) 544-8888	C+ / 6.8	-2.46	2.71	18.74 /80	16.79 /67	10.54 /82	1.20	0.97
★ AA	Fidelity Asset Manager	FASMX	C-	(800) 544-8888	D- / 1.2	-1.28	1.49	5.89 /20	5.90 / 6	3.42 /41	2.47	0.72
GR	Fidelity Asset Manager Aggressive	FAMRX	C+	(800) 544-8888	C+ / 5.9	-2.06	2.15	13.15 /65	14.12 /55	1.20 /22	0.49	0.92
★ AA	Fidelity Asset Manager Growth	FASGX	C-	(800) 544-8888	D- / 1.3	-2.30	1.46	6.79 /25	6.76 / 9	2.63 /33	1.89	0.81
★ GI	Fidelity Balanced Fund	FBALX	B-	(800) 544-8888	C / 5.3	-1.28	3.14	11.64 /58	12.93 /48	8.16 /72	1.56	0.64
★ GR	Fidelity Blue Chip Growth	FBGRX	D	(800) 544-8888	D- / 1.0	-5.03	-2.80	3.27 / 8	6.45 / 8	-1.53 /10	0.55	0.64
GR	Fidelity Blue Chip Value	FBCVX	B	(800) 544-8888	C+ / 6.1	-2.32	3.11	12.77 /63	14.56 /57	--	0.57	0.93
★ FO	Fidelity Canada Fund	FICDX	A	(800) 544-8888	A / 9.4	-0.85	5.77	27.34 /92	27.87 /94	18.98 /95	0.35	1.04
★ GR	Fidelity Capital Appreciation	FDCAX	C+	(800) 544-8888	C+ / 6.6	-2.89	5.70	15.33 /73	15.36 /60	6.43 /64	0.00	0.90
FO	Fidelity China Region Fund	FHKCX	B	(800) 544-8888	B+ / 8.8	1.01	9.02	19.66 /81	23.17 /88	10.35 /82	1.05	1.12
GI	● Fidelity Congress Street	CNGRX	C-	(800) 544-8888	D+ / 2.6	-0.66	3.66	7.95 /32	8.38 /17	2.59 /33	1.62	0.65
★ GR	● Fidelity Contrafund	FCNTX	B+	(800) 544-8888	B- / 7.4	-0.77	3.95	16.96 /77	17.58 /71	9.36 /78	0.34	0.91
CV	Fidelity Convertible Securities	FCVSX	C+	(800) 544-8888	C / 5.3	0.21	7.08	15.64 /74	11.63 /40	6.36 /63	1.88	0.69
GR	Fidelity Destiny I Class A	FDTOX	C	(800) 544-8888	C- / 3.8	-3.07	1.14	14.38 /69	10.85 /34	0.52 /18	0.35	1.03
GR	Fidelity Destiny I Class O	FDESX	C	(800) 544-8888	C / 4.4	-2.95	1.40	14.92 /71	11.60 /40	1.28 /22	0.78	0.44
GR	Fidelity Destiny II Class A	FDTTX	D	(800) 522-7297	D / 1.7	-5.20	1.46	9.22 /41	7.76 /14	0.73 /19	0.60	1.06
★ GR	Fidelity Destiny II Class O	FDETX	D+	(800) 522-7297	D / 2.0	-5.10	1.68	9.71 /45	8.38 /17	1.46 /23	1.03	0.61
★ GR	Fidelity Disciplined Equity	FDEQX	B-	(800) 544-8888	C / 5.5	-1.03	3.54	11.35 /56	13.39 /51	4.56 /51	0.63	0.87
GR	Fidelity Discovery Fund	FDSVX	D+	(800) 544-8888	D / 1.9	-5.15	1.67	9.67 /45	8.29 /17	1.14 /21	1.12	0.70
★ FO	● Fidelity Diversified Intl Fund	FDIVX	A	(800) 544-8888	A- / 9.0	-1.26	8.27	26.21 /90	24.21 /90	13.51 /89	0.78	1.07
★ GR	Fidelity Dividend Growth Fund	FDGFX	D	(800) 544-8888	D- / 1.3	-3.38	1.22	7.01 /26	6.97 /10	1.18 /21	1.05	0.66
★ EM	Fidelity Emerging Markets	FEMKX	B-	(800) 544-8888	A+ / 9.8	-5.36	8.30	45.90 /98	36.75 /98	21.38 /97	1.05	1.07
IN	Fidelity Equity Income I	FEQIX	B	(800) 544-8888	C+ / 5.7	-0.15	5.06	12.59 /62	13.29 /50	5.02 /54	1.51	0.69
IN	Fidelity Equity Income-II	FEQTX	C	(800) 544-8888	C- / 4.1	-2.12	2.31	8.75 /38	11.11 /36	4.79 /52	1.32	0.62
★ FO	Fidelity Europe	FIEUX	A+	(800) 544-8888	A / 9.4	-1.50	9.34	25.28 /89	28.65 /94	12.56 /88	0.69	1.07
FO	Fidelity European Cap Apprec	FECAX	B+	(800) 544-8888	A- / 9.2	-1.84	14.08	30.20 /94	24.00 /89	12.34 /87	1.08	0.84
GR	● Fidelity Exchange Fund	FDLEX	C+	(800) 544-8888	C / 4.4	-1.79	3.54	9.14 /41	11.47 /39	4.03 /46	1.17	0.58
★ GR	Fidelity Export Fund	FEXPX	B-	(800) 544-8888	C+ / 6.6	-1.69	1.51	15.03 /72	15.82 /63	7.24 /68	0.26	0.82
AG	Fidelity Fifty Fund	FFTYX	C-	(800) 544-8888	C- / 4.2	-2.80	3.92	18.56 /80	10.16 /28	7.61 /70	0.04	0.92
GR	Fidelity Focused Stock Fund	FTQGX	A-	(800) 544-8888	B- / 7.5	1.88	4.96	16.14 /75	17.89 /72	0.08 /16	0.32	0.98
AA	Fidelity Four In One Index Fund	FFNOX	B-	(800) 544-8888	C / 5.1	-1.28	3.71	10.50 /50	12.72 /47	5.02 /54	1.72	0.08
AA	Fidelity Freedom 2000 Fd	FFFBX	C-	(800) 544-8888	E+ / 0.7	-0.58	1.05	3.79 /10	4.60 / 3	3.39 /40	3.02	0.58
AA	Fidelity Freedom 2005 Fd	FFFVX	U	(800) 544-8888	U /	-1.26	1.58	6.36 /22	--	--	2.13	0.68
AA	Fidelity Freedom 2010 Fd	FFFCX	C	(800) 544-8888	D / 2.0	-1.43	1.59	6.65 /24	7.68 /13	4.39 /50	2.39	0.69
AA	Fidelity Freedom 2015 Fd	FFVFX	U	(800) 544-8888	U /	-1.72	1.94	8.39 /36	--	--	1.61	0.71
★ AA	Fidelity Freedom 2020 Fd	FFFDX	C	(800) 544-8888	C- / 3.9	-2.13	2.27	9.82 /46	10.78 /33	4.53 /50	1.73	0.75
AA	Fidelity Freedom 2025 Fd	FFTWX	U	(800) 544-8888	U /	-2.23	2.34	10.42 /50	--	--	1.30	0.75
AA	Fidelity Freedom 2030 Fd	FFFEX	C+	(800) 544-8888	C / 4.9	-2.58	2.61	11.52 /57	12.30 /44	4.37 /49	1.36	0.77
AA	Fidelity Freedom 2035 Fd	FFTHX	U	(800) 522-7297	U /	-2.53	2.73	11.91 /59	--	--	1.19	0.78
AA	Fidelity Freedom 2040 Fd	FFFFX	C+	(800) 522-7297	C / 5.5	-2.63	2.88	12.25 /61	13.29 /50	4.23 /48	1.21	0.79

● Denotes fund is closed to new investors
★ Denotes fund is included in Section II

152

RISK			NET ASSETS		ASSET					BULL / BEAR		FUND MANAGER		MINIMUMS		LOADS	
	3 Year		NAV						Portfolio	Last Bull	Last Bear	Manager	Manager	Initial	Additional	Front	Back
Risk	Standard		As of	Total	Cash	Stocks	Bonds	Other	Turnover	Market	Market	Quality	Tenure	Purch.	Purch.	End	End
Rating/Pts	Deviation	Beta	6/30/06	$(Mil)	%	%	%	%	Ratio	Return	Return	Pct	(Years)	$	$	Load	Load
B /8.2	9.1	1.13	13.81	5	0	99	0	1	86.0	N/A	N/A	67	3	2,500	100	0.0	1.0
B /8.3	9.1	1.13	14.11	2	0	99	0	1	86.0	N/A	N/A	77	3	2,500	100	0.0	0.0
B /8.3	9.0	1.12	13.96	26	0	99	0	1	86.0	N/A	N/A	73	3	2,500	100	3.5	0.3
C- /3.2	16.6	1.76	29.67	306	5	94	0	1	105.0	117.3	-16.8	36	N/A	2,500	100	5.8	1.0
D+ /2.9	16.6	1.77	28.10	212	5	94	0	1	105.0	111.7	-17.0	29	N/A	2,500	100	0.0	5.0
D+ /2.9	16.6	1.77	27.91	97	5	94	0	1	105.0	111.9	-17.0	29	N/A	2,500	100	0.0	1.0
C- /3.6	16.6	1.76	32.11	166	5	94	0	1	105.0	119.4	-16.7	39	N/A	2,500	100	0.0	0.0
C- /3.4	16.6	1.77	31.11	75	5	94	0	1	105.0	120.0	-16.7	40	N/A	2,500	100	0.0	0.0
C- /3.3	16.6	1.77	30.36	828	5	94	0	1	105.0	116.0	-16.8	34	N/A	2,500	100	3.5	0.3
U /	N/A	N/A	13.83	40	6	92	0	2	25.0	N/A	N/A	N/A	3	2,500	100	3.5	0.3
U /	N/A	N/A	13.89	33	1	98	0	1	46.0	N/A	N/A	N/A	1	2,500	100	5.8	2.0
C /5.2	12.6	1.36	17.32	3,798	2	97	0	1	192.0	72.5	-9.8	22	1	2,500	250	0.0	1.5
C+ /5.7	12.3	1.10	17.45	473	3	96	0	1	185.0	109.6	-10.4	4	N/A	2,500	250	0.0	1.0
B+ /9.6	4.6	0.91	16.19	9,283	8	54	36	2	32.0	33.7	-4.1	42	10	2,500	250	0.0	0.0
B- /7.4	10.4	1.22	12.34	426	10	83	5	2	71.0	85.9	-6.5	65	7	2,500	250	0.0	0.0
B+ /9.1	6.0	1.19	15.30	3,107	4	74	21	1	37.0	42.3	-6.8	36	10	2,500	250	0.0	0.0
B /8.5	7.6	0.90	19.27	19,707	1	66	32	1	82.0	70.4	-4.7	80	4	2,500	250	0.0	0.0
B- /7.7	8.2	1.03	41.95	20,139	1	98	0	1	29.0	45.6	-9.2	15	10	2,500	250	0.0	0.0
B /8.3	9.0	1.13	13.92	273	1	98	0	1	81.0	N/A	N/A	76	3	2,500	250	0.0	0.0
C+ /6.3	13.8	1.04	45.62	2,826	0	97	1	2	24.0	155.3	4.6	76	4	2,500	250	0.0	1.5
C+ /6.1	11.6	1.33	26.53	8,018	7	92	0	1	109.0	97.3	-8.3	67	1	2,500	250	0.0	0.0
C+ /5.6	13.8	1.00	21.04	582	7	92	0	1	44.0	116.6	-7.9	43	2	2,500	250	0.0	1.5
B /8.5	7.6	0.87	412.86	65	1	98	0	1	N/A	48.7	-8.1	38	9	2,500	250	0.0	0.0
B- /7.4	9.3	1.04	66.03	64,904	8	90	0	2	60.0	91.9	-4.9	94	16	2,500	250	0.0	0.0
B /8.0	8.3	1.22	23.93	2,036	2	18	0	80	81.0	60.5	0.4	84	N/A	2,500	250	0.0	0.0
B- /7.6	9.2	1.12	14.19	110	0	99	0	1	130.0	61.2	-9.3	40	6	2,500	100	0.0	0.0
B- /7.7	9.2	1.12	14.46	2,940	0	99	0	1	130.0	64.7	-9.1	47	6	50	50	0.0	0.0
B- /7.8	8.2	0.91	11.85	338	7	92	0	1	244.0	44.1	-6.5	30	6	2,500	100	0.0	0.0
B- /7.8	8.2	0.91	12.09	4,807	7	92	0	1	244.0	46.9	-6.2	35	6	50	50	0.0	0.0
B /8.5	8.6	1.06	28.69	6,925	2	97	0	1	80.0	72.2	-7.8	71	6	2,500	250	0.0	0.8
B- /7.8	8.3	0.92	11.60	412	6	92	0	2	220.0	46.6	-6.4	33	6	2,500	250	0.0	0.0
C+ /6.7	10.8	1.03	35.23	39,868	3	96	0	1	41.0	139.4	-5.6	45	5	2,500	250	0.0	1.0
B- /7.6	7.7	0.91	29.14	15,540	1	97	0	2	33.0	46.9	-10.8	25	9	2,500	250	0.0	0.0
C- /3.9	19.8	1.19	19.97	2,700	3	96	0	1	68.0	239.9	-7.6	15	2	2,500	250	0.0	1.5
B /8.5	8.3	1.04	54.40	26,229	2	96	0	2	21.0	75.2	-10.2	72	13	2,500	250	0.0	0.0
B- /7.6	8.5	1.07	23.13	11,412	0	98	0	2	143.0	68.6	-10.8	47	6	2,500	250	0.0	0.0
C+ /6.7	12.4	1.09	39.33	3,373	3	96	0	1	99.0	185.5	-15.2	73	3	2,500	250	0.0	1.0
C+ /5.9	13.6	1.20	25.12	751	10	89	0	1	133.0	151.3	-9.9	18	6	2,500	250	0.0	1.0
B /8.2	7.3	0.92	284.40	229	2	97	0	1	N/A	64.6	-8.6	67	9	2,500	250	0.0	0.0
B- /7.0	10.3	1.21	21.56	4,661	4	94	0	2	68.0	91.1	-9.0	80	1	2,500	250	0.0	0.8
C+ /6.4	11.5	1.31	23.62	1,194	36	26	37	1	91.0	59.1	-9.1	22	3	2,500	250	0.0	0.8
B- /7.9	10.9	1.14	12.49	100	1	98	0	1	158.0	83.0	-8.9	93	2	2,500	250	0.0	0.8
B /8.9	7.1	1.44	27.05	1,188	0	85	14	1	3.0	70.0	-7.7	81	7	10,000	1,000	0.0	0.5
B+ /9.9	2.6	0.52	12.21	1,568	36	26	37	1	7.0	21.4	-0.7	51	10	2,500	250	0.0	0.0
U /	N/A	N/A	11.15	587	13	47	39	1	3.0	N/A	N/A	N/A	3	2,500	250	0.0	0.0
B+ /9.5	4.6	0.94	14.07	10,825	9	49	40	2	4.0	39.5	-2.5	61	10	2,500	250	0.0	0.0
U /	N/A	N/A	11.62	3,066	4	59	36	1	1.0	N/A	N/A	N/A	3	2,500	250	0.0	0.0
B /8.4	6.6	1.32	14.77	14,282	0	70	29	1	4.0	59.1	-5.2	71	10	2,500	250	0.0	0.0
U /	N/A	N/A	12.06	2,437	0	73	26	1	1.0	N/A	N/A	N/A	3	2,500	250	0.0	0.0
B- /7.8	7.7	1.51	15.14	8,777	0	83	16	1	5.0	69.5	-6.8	75	10	2,500	250	0.0	0.0
U /	N/A	N/A	12.37	1,349	0	83	16	1	1.0	N/A	N/A	N/A	3	2,500	250	0.0	0.0
B- /7.6	8.3	1.61	8.91	4,112	0	85	14	1	4.0	76.3	-7.8	78	5	2,500	250	0.0	0.0

					PERFORMANCE							
	99 Pct = Best *0 Pct = Worst*		**Overall** **Weiss** **Investment** **Rating**					Total Return % through 6/30/06			Incl. in Returns	
					Perfor- **mance**				Annualized		Dividend	Expense
Fund Type	Fund Name	Ticker Symbol		Phone	**Rating/Pts**	3 Mo	6 Mo	1Yr / Pct	3Yr / Pct	5Yr / Pct	Yield	Ratio
★ BA	Fidelity Freedom Income Fd	FFFAX	C-	(800) 522-7297	E / 0.5	-0.27	1.14	3.66 / 9	4.02 / 2	3.41 / 40	3.25	0.56
★ GI	Fidelity Fund	FFIDX	C	(800) 544-8888	C- / 4.2	-2.34	2.51	10.40 / 49	11.11 / 36	1.40 / 23	0.83	0.60
GL	Fidelity Global Balanced Fund	FGBLX	B	(800) 544-8888	C+ / 6.6	-0.32	4.51	13.21 / 65	15.68 / 62	9.20 / 77	0.59	1.15
★ GI ●	Fidelity Growth & Income	FGRIX	D-	(800) 544-8888	D / 1.9	-2.94	0.95	5.37 / 17	7.89 / 14	1.32 / 22	1.08	0.69
GI	Fidelity Growth & Income II	FGRTX	C-	(800) 544-8888	D+ / 2.5	-3.01	1.57	13.63 / 67	8.23 / 16	2.60 / 33	0.57	0.87
★ GR ●	Fidelity Growth Company	FDGRX	C	(800) 544-8888	C+ / 6.2	-5.75	0.71	14.76 / 71	15.06 / 59	1.81 / 26	0.00	0.96
★ GR	Fidelity Independence Fund	FDFFX	C	(800) 544-8888	C / 5.5	-3.16	4.48	17.08 / 77	13.02 / 49	3.89 / 45	0.24	0.72
★ FO	Fidelity International Discovery Fd	FIGRX	A	(800) 544-8888	A- / 9.1	-1.61	7.99	26.99 / 91	25.46 / 92	13.10 / 89	0.86	1.01
GL	Fidelity International Real Estate	FIREX	U	(800) 544-8888	U /	-2.38	11.56	27.90 / 93	--	--	1.62	1.23
★ FO ●	Fidelity International Small Cap	FISMX	B	(800) 544-8888	A+ / 9.8	-5.27	7.34	30.35 / 95	37.11 / 99	--	0.44	1.25
FO	Fidelity Intl Sm Cp Opp Fd	FSCOX	U	(800) 544-8888	U /	-4.33	10.75	--	--	--	0.00	1.37
FO	Fidelity Japan Fund	FJPNX	C+	(800) 544-8888	B+ / 8.9	-8.40	-5.54	40.60 / 98	24.91 / 91	6.74 / 65	0.12	1.02
FO	Fidelity Japan Small Companies	FJSCX	C-	(800) 544-8888	A / 9.3	-10.94	-13.85	19.40 / 81	30.39 / 96	14.18 / 90	0.13	1.01
GR	Fidelity Large Cap Stock Fund	FLCSX	C-	(800) 544-8888	C- / 3.1	-3.36	1.53	11.73 / 58	9.91 / 27	0.15 / 16	0.57	0.75
★ EM	Fidelity Latin American Fund	FLATX	C+	(800) 544-8888	A+ / 9.9	-3.72	13.35	56.63 / 99	50.37 / 99	24.99 / 98	1.26	1.04
★ GR	Fidelity Leveraged Company Stock	FLVCX	A	(800) 544-8888	A / 9.3	-0.35	9.30	20.58 / 83	27.77 / 94	24.27 / 98	0.73	0.86
★ SC ●	Fidelity Low-Priced Stock	FLPSX	A-	(800) 544-8888	B / 7.7	-3.27	5.07	11.80 / 58	19.92 / 79	14.77 / 92	0.57	0.85
★ GR ●	Fidelity Magellan Fund	FMAGX	E-	(800) 544-8888	D+ / 2.6	-3.99	1.75	9.61 / 44	9.40 / 23	0.86 / 19	0.84	0.59
★ MC ●	Fidelity Mid-Cap Stock Fund	FMCSX	C+	(800) 544-8888	B / 7.7	-3.70	9.21	25.20 / 89	17.83 / 72	4.14 / 47	0.00	0.62
GR	Fidelity NASDAQ Composite Index	FNCMX	U	(800) 544-8888	U /	-7.00	-1.32	6.15 / 21	--	--	0.27	0.45
★ AG ●	Fidelity New Millennium	FMILX	C	(800) 544-8888	B- / 7.2	-3.67	10.00	27.04 / 91	14.90 / 58	5.56 / 58	0.00	0.86
FO	Fidelity Nordic Fund	FNORX	A-	(800) 544-8888	A+ / 9.7	-0.93	14.60	27.23 / 92	32.00 / 97	13.76 / 90	0.95	1.13
★ SC	Fidelity OTC Portfolio	FOCPX	D-	(800) 544-8888	C- / 3.1	-9.08	-3.76	6.53 / 23	11.07 / 36	0.86 / 20	0.00	0.72
★ FO	Fidelity Overseas Fund	FOSFX	B+	(800) 544-8888	B+ / 8.9	-1.01	6.42	29.13 / 94	23.35 / 88	8.53 / 74	0.92	0.86
FO	Fidelity Pacific Basin	FPBFX	B	(800) 544-8888	A- / 9.2	-4.84	3.31	34.40 / 96	26.30 / 92	11.54 / 85	0.67	1.05
★ GI	Fidelity Puritan Fund	FPURX	C	(800) 544-8888	C- / 3.5	-0.10	3.26	8.24 / 35	9.89 / 27	5.59 / 58	2.63	0.62
RE	Fidelity Real Estate High Income Fd		C	(800) 544-8888	C- / 3.4	1.65	2.18	-0.46 / 1	10.90 / 35	12.12 / 87	7.14	0.86
RE	Fidelity Real Estate Income	FRIFX	C+	(800) 544-8888	D+ / 2.9	0.94	3.57	5.40 / 17	9.41 / 24	--	5.61	0.85
★ RE	Fidelity Real Estate Investment	FRESX	C	(800) 544-8888	A / 9.3	-1.33	12.11	21.02 / 83	27.47 / 93	19.81 / 96	1.60	0.81
SC	Fidelity Small Cap Growth Fund	FCPGX	U	(800) 544-8888	U /	-6.45	5.99	13.57 / 67	--	--	0.00	1.07
★ SC	Fidelity Small Cap Independence	FDSCX	C+	(800) 544-8888	C+ / 6.9	-5.21	4.93	13.50 / 66	17.21 / 69	9.50 / 79	0.31	0.75
SC	Fidelity Small Cap Retirement Fd	FSCRX	C+	(800) 544-8888	C+ / 6.2	-5.43	3.37	10.12 / 48	15.90 / 63	8.51 / 74	0.00	1.00
★ SC	Fidelity Small Cap Stock Fund	FSLCX	C	(800) 544-8888	B- / 7.5	-7.14	5.95	15.22 / 72	19.27 / 77	10.64 / 83	0.00	1.00
SC	Fidelity Small Cap Value Fund	FCPVX	U	(800) 544-8888	U /	-4.92	7.61	18.88 / 80	--	--	0.08	0.99
FO	Fidelity Southeast Asia Fund	FSEAX	B	(800) 544-8888	A+ / 9.6	-1.66	8.63	34.29 / 96	30.95 / 96	17.65 / 94	1.11	1.09
IX	Fidelity Spartan 500 Idx Adv	FSMAX	D+	(800) 544-8888	C- / 4.0	-1.44	2.70	8.59 / 37	11.11 / 36	2.34 / 30	1.58	0.07
★ IX	Fidelity Spartan 500 Idx Fd	FSMKX	C+	(800) 544-8888	C- / 4.0	-1.46	2.68	8.55 / 37	11.10 / 36	2.33 / 30	1.56	0.10
GR	Fidelity Spartan Ext Mkt Idx Adv	FSEVX	C+	(800) 544-8888	B- / 7.5	-3.60	5.62	14.11 / 69	18.74 / 75	8.88 / 76	1.02	0.07
GR	Fidelity Spartan Ext Mkt Idx Inv	FSEMX	B	(800) 544-8888	B- / 7.5	-3.60	5.61	14.10 / 68	18.73 / 75	8.88 / 76	1.01	0.10
FO	Fidelity Spartan Intl Index Adv	FSIVX	B	(800) 544-8888	A- / 9.0	0.65	9.89	26.66 / 91	23.51 / 88	9.66 / 79	1.62	0.07
FO	Fidelity Spartan Intl Index Inv	FSIIX	A+	(800) 544-8888	A- / 9.0	0.67	9.88	26.64 / 91	23.51 / 88	9.66 / 79	1.61	0.10
GR	Fidelity Spartan Total Mkt Idx Adv	FSTVX	C-	(800) 544-8888	C / 5.0	-1.94	3.41	9.97 / 47	12.82 / 48	3.87 / 45	1.49	0.07
★ GR	Fidelity Spartan Total Mkt Idx Inv	FSTMX	C+	(800) 544-8888	C / 5.1	-1.95	3.40	9.96 / 47	12.82 / 48	3.86 / 44	1.48	0.07
IX	Fidelity Spartan US Equity Idx Adv	FUSVX	C-	(800) 544-8888	C- / 4.1	-1.45	2.70	8.59 / 37	11.11 / 36	2.33 / 30	1.74	0.07
IX	Fidelity Spartan US Equity Idx Inv	FUSEX	C+	(800) 544-8888	C- / 4.1	-1.44	2.69	8.57 / 37	11.11 / 36	2.32 / 30	1.73	0.07
GR	Fidelity Stock Selector	FDSSX	C+	(800) 544-8888	C / 4.5	-3.03	2.06	11.42 / 56	11.57 / 40	3.13 / 38	0.48	0.79
GI	Fidelity Strategic Div & Inc	FSDIX	U	(800) 544-8888	U /	-1.51	4.32	12.60 / 63	--	--	1.61	0.82
IN	Fidelity Strategic Real Return Fund	FSRRX	U	(800) 544-8888	U /	2.32	2.01	--	--	--	0.00	0.85
GR	Fidelity Structured Lg Cap Growth	FSLGX	C-	(800) 544-8888	C- / 4.0	-6.42	-2.11	6.60 / 24	12.42 / 45	--	0.09	0.94
GR	Fidelity Structured Lg Cap Value	FSLVX	A-	(800) 522-7297	B- / 7.0	-0.51	5.34	13.76 / 67	16.83 / 67	--	0.85	0.89
MC	Fidelity Structured Mid Cap Growth	FSMGX	C	(800) 522-7297	B- / 7.1	-6.63	3.30	13.28 / 65	17.75 / 71	--	0.00	1.04
MC	Fidelity Structured Mid Cap Value	FSMVX	A	(800) 522-7297	B / 8.2	0.77	6.27	15.50 / 73	20.70 / 82	--	0.65	0.86

● Denotes fund is closed to new investors
★ Denotes fund is included in Section II

RISK			NET ASSETS		ASSET					BULL / BEAR		FUND MANAGER		MINIMUMS		LOADS	
Risk Rating/Pts	3 Year Standard Deviation	Beta	NAV As of 6/30/06	Total $(Mil)	Cash %	Stocks %	Bonds %	Other %	Portfolio Turnover Ratio	Last Bull Market Return	Last Bear Market Return	Manager Quality Pct	Manager Tenure (Years)	Initial Purch. $	Additional Purch. $	Front End Load	Back End Load
B+ / 9.9	2.2	0.44	11.32	2,167	40	21	38	1	18.0	17.9	-0.4	49	10	2,500	250	0.0	0.0
B- / 7.9	8.0	1.00	32.55	8,297	1	98	0	1	71.0	63.7	-8.9	55	4	2,500	250	0.0	0.0
B / 8.1	7.5	1.34	22.01	236	8	61	30	1	95.0	79.9	-4.9	95	N/A	2,500	250	0.0	1.0
C+ / 6.2	6.8	0.85	34.66	29,366	0	98	0	2	31.0	47.1	-6.9	35	1	2,500	250	0.0	0.0
B / 8.2	7.3	0.86	10.31	183	2	96	0	2	235.0	53.4	-7.7	37	N/A	2,500	250	0.0	0.0
C / 5.3	12.3	1.36	64.08	28,297	0	99	0	1	50.0	95.9	-12.2	61	9	2,500	250	0.0	0.0
C+ / 6.8	11.6	1.35	20.53	4,468	0	98	0	2	119.0	72.5	-7.2	39	3	2,500	250	0.0	0.0
C+ / 6.5	11.7	1.13	34.19	6,835	1	98	0	1	75.0	147.7	-9.0	35	2	2,500	250	0.0	1.0
U /	N/A	N/A	14.38	434	3	96	0	1	36.0	N/A	N/A	N/A	2	2,500	250	0.0	1.5
C / 4.7	15.5	1.33	28.95	2,250	1	98	0	1	79.0	268.1	-1.5	86	4	2,500	250	0.0	2.0
U /	N/A	N/A	13.91	1,096	1	98	0	1	46.0	N/A	N/A	N/A	N/A	2,500	250	0.0	2.0
C- / 3.6	19.4	1.19	17.22	1,806	2	97	0	1	74.0	133.4	-5.7	23	6	2,500	250	0.0	1.5
D / 2.0	23.6	1.05	14.49	1,557	2	97	0	1	65.0	169.3	-1.6	89	10	2,500	250	0.0	1.5
B- / 7.5	8.8	1.10	15.82	721	0	99	0	1	221.0	56.8	-9.1	34	N/A	2,500	250	0.0	0.0
C- / 3.3	22.2	1.27	36.25	2,545	3	96	0	1	40.0	393.3	-3.9	83	N/A	2,500	250	0.0	1.5
C+ / 6.4	14.5	1.51	28.44	4,177	2	96	0	2	16.0	222.1	-2.1	99	3	10,000	1,000	0.0	1.5
B- / 7.8	11.1	0.73	42.91	36,659	9	90	0	1	23.0	119.7	-9.4	94	17	2,500	250	0.0	1.5
D / 2.0	8.4	1.03	87.61	46,615	1	98	0	1	9.0	60.5	-10.1	34	10	2,500	250	0.0	0.0
C+ / 5.8	13.4	1.17	28.40	12,027	N/A	100	0	N/A	0.7	99.6	-9.1	27	1	2,500	250	0.0	0.8
U /	N/A	N/A	29.35	118	0	100	0	0	10.0	N/A	N/A	N/A	3	10,000	1,000	0.0	0.8
C / 4.5	15.5	1.63	37.56	2,763	1	98	0	1	120.0	93.5	-12.0	34	N/A	2,500	250	0.0	0.0
C+ / 5.6	15.5	1.28	34.23	315	3	96	0	1	76.0	201.8	-19.2	62	8	2,500	250	0.0	1.5
C / 4.4	14.6	0.92	36.37	7,795	0	99	0	1	154.0	76.7	-12.9	12	N/A	2,500	250	0.0	0.0
C+ / 6.3	12.3	1.15	44.28	6,492	5	94	0	1	87.0	135.9	-12.7	20	N/A	2,500	250	0.0	1.0
C / 5.2	14.6	1.14	26.52	1,087	0	99	0	1	78.0	147.5	-7.7	41	2	2,500	250	0.0	1.5
B / 8.9	5.7	0.70	19.21	23,404	0	64	34	2	75.0	51.5	-5.0	71	6	2,500	250	0.0	0.0
B / 8.1	6.9	0.03	11.00	566	5	7	86	2	27.0	42.1	4.3	98	11	5,000,000	0	0.0	0.0
B+ / 9.9	3.9	0.20	11.67	518	8	42	46	4	26.0	40.6	N/A	84	3	2,500	250	0.0	0.8
C- / 3.1	15.9	0.95	34.82	6,659	2	97	0	1	57.0	127.6	0.7	88	8	2,500	250	0.0	0.8
U /	N/A	N/A	13.63	424	3	96	0	1	90.0	N/A	N/A	N/A	1	2,500	250	0.0	1.5
C+ / 5.6	13.1	0.85	21.49	2,509	2	97	0	1	61.0	105.2	-9.2	68	1	2,500	250	0.0	1.5
B- / 7.2	12.2	0.79	15.14	235	0	99	0	1	60.0	96.5	-9.1	65	6	2,500	250	0.0	1.5
C / 4.6	13.0	0.86	18.17	4,789	4	94	0	2	78.0	120.7	-10.3	82	1	2,500	250	0.0	2.0
U /	N/A	N/A	13.72	993	5	94	0	1	74.0	N/A	N/A	N/A	2	2,500	250	0.0	1.5
C / 4.7	17.5	1.31	23.04	1,296	2	97	0	1	1.2	186.2	-12.2	43	13	2,500	250	0.0	1.5
C+ / 6.2	7.6	1.00	87.90	6,630	0	100	0	0	6.0	64.3	-9.8	55	3	100,000	1,000	0.0	0.5
B / 8.7	7.6	1.00	87.89	6,928	0	100	0	0	6.0	64.3	-9.8	55	3	10,000	1,000	0.0	0.5
C / 5.2	11.8	1.35	36.30	711	0	100	0	0	13.0	114.2	-8.8	88	3	1,000,000	1,000	0.0	0.8
C+ / 6.9	11.8	1.36	36.30	1,588	0	100	0	0	13.0	114.2	-8.8	88	3	10,000	1,000	0.0	0.8
C+ / 5.6	10.1	0.99	39.15	735	0	99	0	1	2.0	130.0	-9.5	48	3	1,000,000	1,000	0.0	1.0
B- / 7.3	10.1	0.99	39.15	1,702	0	99	0	1	2.0	130.0	-9.5	47	3	10,000	1,000	0.0	1.0
C+ / 6.1	8.3	1.07	35.73	1,926	0	100	0	0	6.0	74.4	-9.6	66	3	1,000,000	1,000	0.0	0.5
B / 8.4	8.3	1.07	35.73	2,123	0	100	0	0	6.0	74.3	-9.6	66	3	10,000	1,000	0.0	0.5
C+ / 6.2	7.6	1.00	45.15	3,405	0	100	0	0	6.0	64.3	-9.8	55	3	1,000,000	2,500	0.0	0.0
B / 8.6	7.6	1.00	45.15	20,420	0	100	0	0	6.0	64.3	-9.8	55	3	100,000	2,500	0.0	0.0
B / 8.2	8.2	1.05	25.25	803	N/A	100	0	N/A	136.0	68.3	-9.8	56	5	2,500	250	0.0	0.0
U /	N/A	N/A	12.64	1,025	4	77	0	19	64.0	N/A	N/A	N/A	3	2,500	250	0.0	0.0
U /	N/A	N/A	10.16	1,936	2	9	87	2	78.0	N/A	N/A	N/A	1	2,500	250	0.0	0.8
C+ / 6.4	11.2	1.30	10.94	167	0	99	0	1	268.0	75.8	-10.2	38	2	2,500	250	0.0	0.8
B / 8.5	8.3	1.00	13.61	753	0	99	0	1	175.0	87.9	-10.3	93	N/A	2,500	250	0.0	0.8
C / 5.1	14.5	1.28	13.37	467	1	98	0	1	173.0	111.5	-9.0	17	2	2,500	250	0.0	0.8
B- / 7.8	9.8	0.85	15.75	435	0	99	0	1	207.0	106.0	-6.8	91	N/A	2,500	250	0.0	0.8

					PERFORMANCE							
	99 Pct = Best 0 Pct = Worst		Overall Weiss Investment Rating			Total Return % through 6/30/06					Incl. in Returns	
									Annualized			
Fund Type	Fund Name	Ticker Symbol		Phone	Perfor-mance Rating/Pts	3 Mo	6 Mo	1Yr / Pct	3Yr / Pct	5Yr / Pct	Dividend Yield	Expense Ratio
GR	Fidelity Tax Managed Stock Fund	FTXMX	B-	(800) 544-8888	C+ / 6.4	-0.08	4.74	12.71 /63	15.42 /61	3.61 /42	0.38	0.86
GR	Fidelity Trend Fund	FTRNX	C	(800) 544-8888	C- / 4.2	-2.79	1.80	10.04 /47	11.16 /37	2.72 /34	0.72	0.83
UT	Fidelity Utilities Fund	FIUIX	B+	(800) 544-8888	B- / 7.0	3.20	10.23	14.71 /71	15.59 /62	2.84 /35	1.49	0.87
GI	Fidelity Value Discovery Fund	FVDFX	B+	(800) 544-8888	B / 7.8	-1.13	5.94	19.55 /81	19.09 /76	--	0.18	0.99
★ GI	Fidelity Value Fund	FDVLX	A-	(800) 544-8888	B / 7.8	-2.84	3.58	13.28 /65	19.82 /79	11.92 /86	0.51	0.72
FO	Fidelity Worldwide Fund	FWWFX	B	(800) 544-8888	B- / 7.2	-1.31	4.29	20.15 /82	17.51 /70	7.70 /70	0.47	1.01
BA	Fifth Third Balanced A	FSBFX	D	(800) 282-5706	E- / 0.2	-2.67	-0.44	0.27 / 2	4.80 / 4	-0.01 /15	1.65	1.21
BA	Fifth Third Balanced Adv	FTBAX	D+	(800) 282-5706	E / 0.3	-2.73	-0.57	0.02 / 2	4.54 / 3	-0.30 /14	1.44	1.46
BA	Fifth Third Balanced B	FBFBX	D	(800) 282-5706	E- / 0.2	-2.89	-0.83	-0.49 / 1	4.01 / 2	-0.74 /13	0.98	1.96
BA	Fifth Third Balanced C	FTBCX	D	(800) 282-5706	E / 0.3	-2.90	-0.83	-0.49 / 1	4.01 / 2	-0.76 /12	0.99	1.96
BA	Fifth Third Balanced Inst	FBFIX	D+	(800) 282-5706	E+ / 0.6	-2.59	-0.30	0.55 / 2	5.08 / 4	0.26 /17	2.01	0.96
IN	Fifth Third Discpl Lrge Cap Val A	FSSIX	C+	(800) 282-5706	C+ / 5.8	1.27	7.16	11.64 /58	15.16 /60	7.24 /68	0.96	1.32
IN	Fifth Third Discpl Lrge Cap Val B	FBEQX	B	(800) 282-5706	C / 5.5	1.07	6.78	10.77 /52	14.30 /55	6.48 /64	0.37	2.07
IN	Fifth Third Discpl Lrge Cap Val C	FEQCX	C+	(800) 282-5706	C+ / 6.0	1.08	6.74	10.80 /52	14.24 /55	6.43 /64	0.37	2.07
IN	Fifth Third Discpl Lrge Cap Val I	FEINX	B-	(800) 282-5706	C+ / 6.7	1.34	7.29	11.96 /59	15.44 /61	7.51 /69	1.22	1.07
GR	Fifth Third Dividend Growth A	FSPIX	E+	(800) 282-5706	D- / 1.3	-1.34	1.96	10.17 /48	7.74 /14	-3.03 / 5	1.03	0.98
GR	Fifth Third Dividend Growth B	FTPBX	D-	(800) 282-5706	D- / 1.0	-1.62	1.51	9.26 /42	6.92 /10	-3.89 / 4	0.75	1.73
GR	Fifth Third Dividend Growth C	FTPCX	E+	(800) 282-5706	D / 1.6	-1.53	1.57	9.33 /42	6.93 /10	-3.75 / 4	0.75	1.73
GR	Fifth Third Dividend Growth I	FPFIX	D-	(800) 282-5706	D / 2.2	-1.43	1.92	10.24 /48	7.96 /15	-2.82 / 6	1.19	0.73
GI	Fifth Third Equity Index A	KNIDX	C	(800) 282-5706	D+ / 2.8	-1.53	2.51	8.20 /34	10.69 /33	1.96 /27	1.48	0.44
GI	Fifth Third Equity Index Adv	FVINX	C	(800) 282-5706	C- / 3.1	-1.58	2.40	7.93 /32	10.41 /30	--	1.26	0.69
GI	Fifth Third Equity Index B	FBINX	C-	(800) 282-5706	D+ / 2.4	-1.74	2.13	7.39 /29	9.86 /26	--	0.82	1.19
GI	Fifth Third Equity Index C	FCINX	C	(800) 282-5706	C- / 3.1	-1.70	2.16	7.42 /29	9.87 /26	--	0.81	1.19
GI	Fifth Third Equity Index Inst	KNIEX	C+	(800) 282-5706	C- / 4.0	-1.51	2.63	8.44 /36	10.94 /35	2.21 /29	1.80	0.19
GI	Fifth Third Equity Index Pfd	KNIPX	U	(800) 282-5706	U /	-1.50	2.55	8.33 /35	--	--	1.65	0.34
GI	Fifth Third Equity Index Tr	KNITX	U	(800) 282-5706	U /	-1.57	2.50	8.17 /34	--	--	1.55	0.34
FO	Fifth Third Internatl Equity A	FSIEX	B	(800) 282-5706	B / 8.2	-0.86	8.07	25.76 /89	21.15 /83	8.69 /75	1.24	1.60
FO	Fifth Third Internatl Equity B	FBIEX	A-	(800) 282-5706	B / 8.0	-1.03	7.65	24.80 /88	20.23 /80	7.77 /71	0.81	2.35
FO	Fifth Third Internatl Equity C	FTECX	B+	(800) 282-5706	B+ / 8.3	-1.05	7.68	24.88 /88	20.24 /80	7.80 /71	0.84	2.35
FO	Fifth Third Internatl Equity Inst	FIEIX	B+	(800) 282-5706	B+ / 8.6	-0.86	8.18	26.11 /90	21.43 /84	8.86 /76	1.53	1.35
GR	Fifth Third Large Cap Core A	KNVIX	C	(800) 282-5706	C- / 3.1	-1.84	3.03	8.00 /33	11.17 /37	1.50 /24	0.74	1.17
GR	Fifth Third Large Cap Core B	FBLVX	C-	(800) 282-5706	D+ / 2.6	-2.04	2.63	7.20 /27	10.32 /29	--	0.21	1.92
GR	Fifth Third Large Cap Core C	FCLVX	C	(800) 282-5706	C- / 3.3	-2.04	2.63	7.12 /27	10.31 /29	--	0.20	1.92
GR	Fifth Third Large Cap Core Inst	KNVEX	C+	(800) 282-5706	C / 4.3	-1.81	3.13	8.18 /34	11.41 /39	1.75 /25	1.03	0.92
AG	Fifth Third LifeModel Agg A	LASAX	C	(800) 282-5706	C / 4.4	-2.47	4.03	10.67 /51	12.99 /49	--	1.00	1.42
AG	Fifth Third LifeModel Agg B	LAXBX	C	(800) 282-5706	C- / 3.9	-2.63	3.67	9.86 /46	12.17 /43	--	0.68	2.17
AG	Fifth Third LifeModel Agg C	LASCX	C	(800) 282-5706	C / 4.6	-2.63	3.67	9.87 /46	12.16 /43	--	0.69	2.17
AG	Fifth Third LifeModel Agg Inst	LASIX	C+	(800) 282-5706	C / 5.5	-2.39	4.15	10.99 /53	13.29 /50	--	1.30	1.17
AA	Fifth Third LifeModel Conserv A	LCVAX	D+	(800) 282-5706	E- / 0.2	-0.53	1.11	2.89 / 7	4.18 / 3	--	3.26	1.12
AA	Fifth Third LifeModel Conserv B	LCVBX	D+	(800) 282-5706	E- / 0.2	-0.72	0.73	2.11 / 5	3.41 / 2	--	2.66	1.87
AA	Fifth Third LifeModel Conserv C	LCVCX	D+	(800) 282-5706	E / 0.3	-0.72	0.73	2.09 / 5	3.39 / 2	--	2.64	1.87
AA	Fifth Third LifeModel Conserv Inst	LCVIX	C-	(800) 282-5706	E+ / 0.6	-0.56	1.24	3.06 / 7	4.43 / 3	--	3.69	0.87
AG	Fifth Third LifeModel Mod Agg A	LMAAX	C-	(800) 282-5706	D+ / 2.7	-1.85	3.34	8.47 /37	10.43 /30	--	1.66	1.33
AG	Fifth Third LifeModel Mod Agg B	LMABX	C-	(800) 282-5706	D+ / 2.3	-2.05	2.90	7.64 /30	9.59 /25	--	1.05	2.08
AG	Fifth Third LifeModel Mod Agg C	LMACX	C	(800) 282-5706	C- / 3.2	-2.06	2.96	7.62 /30	9.60 /25	--	1.03	2.08
AG	Fifth Third LifeModel Mod Agg Inst	LMAIX	C	(800) 282-5706	C- / 3.9	-1.79	3.47	8.72 /38	10.71 /33	--	1.98	1.08
AA	Fifth Third LifeModel Mod Cons A	LAMVX	D+	(800) 282-5706	E+ / 0.8	-1.07	1.91	4.86 /14	6.56 / 9	--	2.56	1.21
AA	Fifth Third LifeModel Mod Cons B	LBMVX	D+	(800) 282-5706	E+ / 0.6	-1.36	1.44	4.09 /11	5.75 / 6	--	1.96	1.96
AA	Fifth Third LifeModel Mod Cons C	LCMVX	D+	(800) 282-5706	E+ / 0.9	-1.29	1.51	4.05 /11	5.74 / 6	--	1.93	1.96
AA	Fifth Third LifeModel Mod Cons Inst	LIMVX	C-	(800) 282-5706	D- / 1.5	-1.10	1.95	5.11 /16	6.82 /10	--	2.94	0.96
GR	Fifth Third LifeModel Moderate A	LMDAX	C-	(800) 282-5706	D- / 1.3	-1.50	2.30	6.20 /22	7.99 /15	--	2.24	1.25
GR	Fifth Third LifeModel Moderate B	LMDBX	D+	(800) 282-5706	D- / 1.1	-1.69	1.93	5.36 /17	7.14 /11	--	1.64	2.00

● Denotes fund is closed to new investors
★ Denotes fund is included in Section II

RISK			NET ASSETS		ASSET				BULL / BEAR		FUND MANAGER		MINIMUMS		LOADS	
	3 Year		NAV						Last Bull	Last Bear	Manager	Manager	Initial	Additional	Front	Back
Risk	Standard		As of	Total	Cash	Stocks	Bonds	Other	Market	Market	Quality	Tenure	Purch.	Purch.	End	End
Rating/Pts	Deviation	Beta	6/30/06	$(Mil)	%	%	%	%	Return	Return	Pct	(Years)	$	$	Load	Load
B- / 7.9	10.4	1.22	13.27	66	0	99	0	1	179.0	80.1	-10.9	76	2	10,000	1,000	0.0	1.0
B / 8.2	8.0	1.03	58.24	866	0	99	0	1	64.0	67.3	-9.6	52	6	2,500	250	0.0	0.0
B / 8.1	9.0	0.56	16.14	1,038	2	97	0	1	66.0	83.8	-4.9	78	2	2,500	250	0.0	0.0
B- / 7.3	10.9	1.28	16.58	614	1	98	0	1	113.0	102.1	N/A	92	4	2,500	250	0.0	0.0
B- / 7.7	10.3	1.24	78.60	15,805	6	93	0	1	29.0	110.3	-8.0	95	10	2,500	250	0.0	0.0
B- / 7.1	10.1	0.93	20.41	1,282	2	98	0	0	93.0	103.3	-11.2	17	N/A	2,500	250	0.0	1.0
B+ / 9.1	4.6	0.91	12.41	41	2	61	36	1	146.0	27.8	-5.2	32	N/A	1,000	50	5.0	1.0
B+ / 9.4	4.6	0.91	12.38	N/A	2	61	36	1	146.0	26.8	-5.3	30	N/A	1,000	50	3.3	0.0
B+ / 9.4	4.6	0.91	12.27	8	2	61	36	1	146.0	24.9	-5.4	27	N/A	1,000	50	0.0	5.0
B+ / 9.2	4.6	0.91	12.25	2	2	61	36	1	146.0	24.8	-5.5	27	N/A	1,000	50	0.0	1.0
B+ / 9.2	4.6	0.90	12.48	39	2	61	36	1	146.0	28.9	-5.2	34	N/A	1,000	50	0.0	0.0
B- / 7.5	8.7	1.05	14.46	23	1	98	0	1	31.0	85.7	-11.3	85	N/A	1,000	50	5.0	1.0
B / 8.8	8.7	1.05	14.59	6	1	98	0	1	31.0	81.4	-11.5	79	N/A	1,000	50	0.0	5.0
B- / 7.5	8.7	1.05	14.34	2	1	98	0	1	31.0	81.3	-11.6	79	N/A	1,000	50	0.0	1.0
B- / 7.5	8.8	1.05	14.49	568	1	98	0	1	31.0	87.1	-11.3	86	N/A	1,000	50	0.0	0.0
C / 5.4	13.0	1.35	21.79	5	0	100	0	0	28.0	44.8	-10.5	9	N/A	1,000	50	5.0	1.0
B- / 7.1	13.0	1.35	21.17	N/A	0	100	0	0	28.0	41.3	-10.7	7	N/A	1,000	50	0.0	5.0
C / 5.3	13.0	1.35	20.62	N/A	0	100	0	0	28.0	41.4	-10.8	7	N/A	1,000	50	0.0	1.0
C / 5.5	13.0	1.35	22.16	15	0	100	0	0	28.0	45.7	-10.5	10	N/A	1,000	50	0.0	0.0
B / 8.7	7.7	1.00	24.02	65	3	96	0	1	4.0	62.2	-9.9	50	14	1,000	50	5.0	1.0
B / 8.8	7.6	1.00	24.00	2	3	96	0	1	4.0	61.0	-9.9	47	N/A	1,000	50	3.3	0.0
B / 8.7	7.6	1.00	23.89	4	3	96	0	1	4.0	58.5	-10.0	41	N/A	1,000	50	0.0	5.0
B / 8.7	7.6	1.00	23.91	2	3	96	0	1	4.0	58.5	-10.1	41	N/A	1,000	50	0.0	1.0
B / 8.8	7.6	1.00	24.09	183	3	96	0	1	4.0	63.6	-9.8	53	14	1,000	50	0.0	0.0
U /	N/A	N/A	24.09	66	3	96	0	1	4.0	N/A	N/A	N/A	5	1,000	50	0.0	0.0
U /	N/A	N/A	24.09	68	3	96	0	1	4.0	N/A	N/A	N/A	5	1,000	50	0.0	0.0
C+ / 6.4	10.8	1.05	12.72	28	5	94	0	1	21.0	114.3	-8.6	21	12	1,000	50	5.0	1.0
B- / 7.3	10.8	1.05	12.53	2	5	94	0	1	21.0	108.9	-8.7	16	N/A	1,000	50	0.0	5.0
C+ / 6.4	10.8	1.05	12.20	1	5	94	0	1	21.0	109.1	-8.9	16	10	1,000	50	0.0	1.0
C+ / 6.4	10.8	1.05	12.70	429	5	94	0	1	21.0	115.6	-8.5	23	8	1,000	50	0.0	0.0
B / 8.7	8.1	1.04	14.82	21	1	98	0	1	102.0	62.4	-10.0	52	N/A	1,000	50	5.0	1.0
B / 8.7	8.1	1.04	14.85	1	1	98	0	1	102.0	58.6	-10.1	42	N/A	1,000	50	0.0	5.0
B / 8.7	8.1	1.03	14.85	N/A	1	98	0	1	102.0	58.5	-10.1	42	N/A	1,000	50	0.0	1.0
B / 8.6	8.1	1.04	15.01	160	1	98	0	1	102.0	63.7	-9.9	55	N/A	1,000	50	0.0	0.0
B- / 7.4	9.9	1.22	14.70	51	8	91	0	1	35.0	75.9	-10.2	53	4	1,000	50	5.0	1.0
B / 8.4	9.9	1.22	14.42	17	8	91	0	1	35.0	71.8	-10.5	44	4	1,000	50	0.0	5.0
B- / 7.3	9.9	1.22	14.42	3	8	91	0	1	35.0	72.0	-10.4	44	4	1,000	50	0.0	1.0
B- / 7.4	9.9	1.22	14.75	102	8	91	0	1	35.0	77.4	-10.1	57	4	1,000	50	0.0	0.0
B+ / 9.7	3.0	0.60	10.65	16	3	24	71	2	46.0	20.8	-0.5	41	4	1,000	50	5.0	1.0
B+ / 9.9	3.0	0.60	10.63	10	3	24	71	2	46.0	18.0	-0.6	34	4	1,000	50	0.0	5.0
B+ / 9.9	3.0	0.60	10.63	4	3	24	71	2	46.0	17.9	-0.7	34	4	1,000	50	0.0	1.0
B+ / 9.8	3.0	0.59	10.66	24	3	24	71	2	46.0	21.8	-0.5	44	4	1,000	50	0.0	0.0
B / 8.2	7.7	0.95	14.05	130	6	72	21	1	35.0	58.0	-7.3	52	4	1,000	50	5.0	1.0
B / 8.2	7.7	0.95	13.99	54	6	72	21	1	35.0	54.2	-7.4	42	4	1,000	50	0.0	5.0
B / 8.6	7.7	0.95	13.99	8	6	72	21	1	35.0	54.2	-7.4	42	4	1,000	50	0.0	0.0
B / 8.2	7.7	0.95	14.07	140	6	72	21	1	35.0	59.1	-7.2	56	4	1,000	50	0.0	0.0
B+ / 9.3	4.6	0.94	11.34	37	4	43	51	2	38.0	34.2	-3.3	48	4	1,000	50	5.0	0.0
B+ / 9.3	4.6	0.93	11.30	21	4	43	51	2	38.0	31.1	-3.5	39	4	1,000	50	0.0	5.0
B+ / 9.3	4.7	0.94	11.31	3	4	43	51	2	38.0	31.1	-3.5	38	4	1,000	50	0.0	1.0
B+ / 9.3	4.6	0.93	11.35	42	4	43	51	2	38.0	35.4	-3.2	51	4	1,000	50	0.0	0.0
B+ / 9.1	5.7	0.70	12.43	101	4	54	40	2	41.0	42.3	-4.4	51	4	1,000	50	5.0	1.0
B+ / 9.1	5.7	0.70	12.37	44	4	54	40	2	41.0	39.1	-4.6	41	4	1,000	50	0.0	5.0

					PERFORMANCE						
	99 Pct = Best 0 Pct = Worst		**Overall Weiss Investment Rating**		Perfor- mance Rating/Pts	Total Return % through 6/30/06			Annualized		Incl. in Returns
Fund Type	Fund Name	Ticker Symbol		Phone		3 Mo	6 Mo	1Yr / Pct	3Yr / Pct	5Yr / Pct	Dividend Expense Yield Ratio
GR	Fifth Third LifeModel Moderate C	LMDCX	C-	(800) 282-5706	D / 1.6	-1.70	1.91	5.33 /17	7.17 /11	--	1.62 2.00
GR	Fifth Third LifeModel Moderate Inst	LMDIX	C-	(800) 282-5706	D+ / 2.3	-1.44	2.43	6.37 /22	8.23 /16	--	2.60 1.00
SC	Fifth Third Micro Cap Value A	MXCAX	D	(800) 282-5706	B / 7.7	-4.59	5.89	15.28 /73	20.77 /82	--	1.42 1.60
SC	Fifth Third Micro Cap Value Adv	MXSAX	B-	(800) 282-5706	B- / 7.2	-4.86	5.10	13.22 /65	18.64 /75	15.73 /93	0.00 1.85
SC	Fifth Third Micro Cap Value B	MXCBX	C+	(800) 282-5706	C+ / 6.9	-4.98	4.82	12.59 /62	18.32 /74	--	0.00 2.35
SC	Fifth Third Micro Cap Value C	MXCSX	B-	(800) 282-5706	B- / 7.3	-4.98	4.82	12.59 /63	18.32 /74	--	0.00 2.35
SC	Fifth Third Micro Cap Value Inst	MXAIX	D	(800) 282-5706	B / 7.6	-4.78	5.27	13.74 /67	19.06 /76	16.21 /93	0.08 1.35
MC	Fifth Third Mid Cap Growth A	FSMCX	C-	(800) 282-5706	C / 5.3	-5.65	5.76	14.16 /69	14.51 /56	2.76 /34	0.04 1.34
MC	Fifth Third Mid Cap Growth Adv	FTMVX	C	(800) 282-5706	C / 5.5	-5.76	5.56	13.81 /68	14.23 /55	--	0.00 1.59
MC	Fifth Third Mid Cap Growth B	FBMBX	C	(800) 282-5706	C / 4.9	-5.87	5.34	13.27 /65	13.67 /52	--	0.00 2.09
MC	Fifth Third Mid Cap Growth C	FCMCX	C-	(800) 282-5706	C+ / 5.6	-5.79	5.40	13.34 /66	13.69 /52	1.99 /27	0.00 2.09
MC	Fifth Third Mid Cap Growth Inst	FMCIX	C	(800) 282-5706	C+ / 6.2	-5.63	5.82	14.39 /70	14.80 /58	3.01 /37	0.10 1.09
GI	Fifth Third Multi Cap Value A	MXLAX	B-	(800) 282-5706	C+ / 6.6	-1.42	6.70	12.81 /63	17.16 /69	--	0.61 1.54
GI	Fifth Third Multi Cap Value Adv	MXSEX	B-	(800) 282-5706	C+ / 6.7	-1.49	6.56	12.53 /62	16.90 /68	9.63 /79	0.42 1.79
GI	Fifth Third Multi Cap Value B	MXLBX	B	(800) 282-5706	C+ / 6.2	-1.62	6.29	11.92 /59	16.27 /65	--	0.22 2.29
GI	Fifth Third Multi Cap Value C	MXLCX	B	(800) 282-5706	C+ / 6.7	-1.61	6.29	11.97 /59	16.24 /64	--	0.21 2.29
GI	Fifth Third Multi Cap Value Inst	MXEIX	B+	(800) 282-5706	B- / 7.3	-1.38	6.80	13.08 /65	17.44 /70	10.16 /81	0.86 1.29
GR	Fifth Third Quality Growth A	FSQGX	E	(800) 282-5706	E / 0.5	-5.66	-2.20	5.19 /16	6.32 / 8	-2.38 / 7	0.00 1.33
GR	Fifth Third Quality Growth Adv	FQGVX	D-	(800) 282-5706	E+ / 0.6	-5.72	-2.28	4.97 /15	6.05 / 7	--	0.00 1.58
GR	Fifth Third Quality Growth B	FSBQX	E+	(800) 282-5706	E / 0.4	-5.82	-2.54	4.42 /12	5.53 / 5	-3.11 / 5	0.00 2.08
GR	Fifth Third Quality Growth C	FSQCX	E	(800) 282-5706	E+ / 0.6	-5.85	-2.54	4.39 /12	5.53 / 5	-3.12 / 5	0.00 2.08
GR	Fifth Third Quality Growth Inst	FQGIX	E+	(800) 282-5706	D- / 1.1	-5.61	-2.04	5.50 /18	6.59 / 9	-2.13 / 8	0.01 1.08
SC	Fifth Third Small Cap Growth A	KNEMX	E	(800) 282-5706	C / 4.6	-7.53	8.13	14.23 /69	14.01 /54	4.11 /47	0.00 1.26
SC	Fifth Third Small Cap Growth Adv	FTGVX	D-	(800) 282-5706	C / 4.9	-7.53	8.05	13.96 /68	13.75 /53	--	0.00 1.51
SC	Fifth Third Small Cap Growth B	FTGBX	D-	(800) 282-5706	C- / 4.2	-7.64	7.75	13.33 /66	13.17 /50	--	0.00 2.01
SC	Fifth Third Small Cap Growth C	FTGCX	D-	(800) 282-5706	C / 4.8	-7.69	7.74	13.31 /65	13.18 /50	--	0.00 2.01
SC	Fifth Third Small Cap Growth Inst	KNEEX	E+	(800) 282-5706	C+ / 5.7	-7.43	8.25	14.50 /70	14.33 /56	4.42 /50	0.00 1.01
SC	Fifth Third Small Cap Value A	FTVAX	B	(800) 282-5706	C+ / 6.4	-1.34	5.39	10.33 /49	17.27 /69	--	0.00 1.45
SC	Fifth Third Small Cap Value Adv	FTVVX	B-	(800) 282-5706	C+ / 6.6	-1.40	5.23	10.05 /47	17.00 /68	--	0.00 1.70
SC	Fifth Third Small Cap Value B	FTVBX	B-	(800) 282-5706	C+ / 6.1	-1.52	5.01	9.52 /43	16.45 /65	--	0.00 2.20
SC	Fifth Third Small Cap Value C	FTVCX	B-	(800) 282-5706	C+ / 6.6	-1.52	4.97	9.54 /44	16.39 /65	--	0.00 2.20
SC	Fifth Third Small Cap Value Inst	FTVIX	B+	(800) 282-5706	B- / 7.2	-1.29	5.51	10.66 /51	17.59 /71	--	0.19 1.20
TC	Fifth Third Technology A	FTTAX	E-	(800) 282-5706	D- / 1.2	-12.85	-0.57	14.12 /69	9.48 /24	-1.54 /10	0.00 1.88
TC	Fifth Third Technology Adv	FTTVX	E-	(800) 282-5706	D- / 1.3	-13.00	-0.77	13.71 /67	9.17 /22	--	0.00 2.13
TC	Fifth Third Technology B	FTCBX	E-	(800) 282-5706	E+ / 0.9	-13.05	-0.98	13.29 /65	8.67 /19	--	0.00 2.63
TC	Fifth Third Technology C	FTTCX	E-	(800) 282-5706	D- / 1.4	-13.08	-0.99	13.21 /65	8.70 /19	-2.29 / 7	0.00 2.63
TC	Fifth Third Technology Inst	FTTIX	E-	(800) 282-5706	D / 2.1	-12.91	-0.56	14.38 /70	9.72 /25	-1.30 /11	0.00 1.63
BA	First American Balanced A	FABAX	C-	(800) 677-3863	D / 1.6	-2.21	0.70	6.38 /23	8.97 /21	3.47 /41	1.50 1.10
BA	First American Balanced B	FANBX	C-	(800) 677-3863	D- / 1.4	-2.35	0.38	5.66 /18	8.18 /16	2.67 /33	0.78 1.85
BA	First American Balanced C	FCBAX	C-	(800) 677-3863	D / 1.9	-2.35	0.36	5.63 /18	8.14 /16	--	0.50 1.85
BA	First American Balanced R	FBGYX	C	(800) 677-3863	D+ / 2.4	-2.35	0.60	6.09 /21	8.77 /19	3.33 /40	0.87 1.35
BA	First American Balanced Y	FBAIX	C	(800) 677-3863	D+ / 2.7	-2.23	0.78	6.57 /24	9.23 /22	3.69 /43	1.87 0.85
IN	First American Eqty Inc A	FFEIX	C	(800) 677-3863	D+ / 2.7	-1.49	3.70	9.25 /42	10.33 /30	3.57 /42	1.23 1.19
IN	First American Eqty Inc B	FAEBX	C-	(800) 677-3863	D+ / 2.3	-1.64	3.34	8.43 /36	9.49 /24	2.81 /35	0.72 1.94
IN	First American Eqty Inc C	FFECX	C	(800) 677-3863	C- / 3.1	-1.64	3.40	8.48 /37	9.52 /24	2.79 /35	0.71 1.94
IN	First American Eqty Inc R	FEISX	C+	(800) 677-3863	C- / 3.6	-1.55	3.57	9.01 /40	10.10 /28	--	1.08 1.35
IN	First American Eqty Inc Y	FAQIX	C+	(800) 677-3863	C- / 3.9	-1.41	3.80	9.52 /43	10.60 /32	3.82 /44	1.52 0.94
IX	First American Eqty Indx A	FAEIX	C-	(800) 677-3863	D+ / 2.6	-1.52	2.50	8.16 /34	10.60 /32	1.95 /27	1.25 0.62
IX	First American Eqty Indx B	FAEQX	C-	(800) 677-3863	D+ / 2.3	-1.72	2.11	7.32 /28	9.77 /26	1.19 /21	0.64 1.37
IX	First American Eqty Indx C	FCEIX	C	(800) 677-3863	C- / 3.0	-1.72	2.14	7.32 /28	9.78 /26	1.18 /21	0.63 1.37
IX	First American Eqty Indx R	FADSX	C	(800) 677-3863	C- / 3.6	-1.58	2.43	7.88 /32	10.40 /30	--	1.10 0.87
IX	First American Eqty Indx Y	FEIIX	C+	(800) 677-3863	C- / 3.9	-1.46	2.63	8.39 /36	10.87 /34	2.21 /29	1.57 0.37

● Denotes fund is closed to new investors
★ Denotes fund is included in Section II

RISK			NET ASSETS		ASSET					BULL / BEAR		FUND MANAGER		MINIMUMS		LOADS	
Risk Rating/Pts	3 Year		NAV As of 6/30/06	Total $(Mil)	Cash %	Stocks %	Bonds %	Other %	Portfolio Turnover Ratio	Last Bull Market Return	Last Bear Market Return	Manager Quality Pct	Manager Tenure (Years)	Initial Purch. $	Additional Purch. $	Front End Load	Back End Load
	Standard Deviation	Beta															
B+ / 9.1	5.7	0.70	12.38	7	4	54	40	2	41.0	39.2	-4.7	41	4	1,000	50	0.0	1.0
B+ / 9.1	5.7	0.70	12.44	310	4	54	40	2	41.0	43.6	-4.4	54	4	1,000	50	0.0	0.0
D- / 1.5	14.8	0.93	8.11	19	3	96	0	1	12.0	150.5	-5.2	83	N/A	1,000	50	5.0	1.0
C+ / 6.7	14.8	0.93	8.03	18	3	96	0	1	12.0	136.2	-5.7	67	N/A	1,000	50	3.3	0.0
C+ / 6.8	14.7	0.93	7.83	6	3	96	0	1	12.0	133.8	-5.7	65	N/A	1,000	50	0.0	5.0
C+ / 6.7	14.7	0.93	7.83	5	3	96	0	1	12.0	133.8	-5.9	64	N/A	1,000	50	0.0	1.0
D- / 1.5	14.7	0.93	8.37	78	3	96	0	1	12.0	139.0	-5.6	71	N/A	1,000	50	0.0	0.0
C+ / 5.9	14.0	1.23	16.88	37	5	94	0	1	54.0	91.6	-12.5	8	N/A	1,000	50	5.0	1.0
C+ / 6.6	14.0	1.23	16.70	1	5	94	0	1	54.0	90.0	-12.4	8	N/A	1,000	50	3.3	0.0
C+ / 6.6	14.0	1.23	16.19	7	5	94	0	1	54.0	87.2	-12.6	6	N/A	1,000	50	0.0	5.0
C+ / 5.8	14.0	1.23	15.61	1	5	94	0	1	54.0	87.0	-12.6	6	N/A	1,000	50	0.0	1.0
C+ / 5.9	14.0	1.23	17.27	333	5	94	0	1	54.0	93.0	-12.4	9	N/A	1,000	50	0.0	0.0
B- / 7.6	10.0	1.22	25.34	39	1	98	0	1	24.0	102.8	-10.5	87	N/A	1,000	50	5.0	1.0
B- / 7.6	10.0	1.22	25.21	34	1	98	0	1	24.0	101.4	-10.5	86	3	1,000	50	3.3	0.0
B / 8.3	10.0	1.22	24.57	22	1	98	0	1	24.0	98.1	-10.6	82	N/A	1,000	50	0.0	5.0
B / 8.3	10.0	1.22	24.55	4	1	98	0	1	24.0	97.9	-10.6	82	N/A	1,000	50	0.0	1.0
B- / 7.7	10.0	1.22	25.62	222	1	98	0	1	24.0	104.5	-10.4	88	3	1,000	50	0.0	0.0
C / 5.5	12.1	1.37	16.00	122	0	99	0	1	71.0	46.2	-11.8	5	14	1,000	50	5.0	1.0
B- / 7.1	12.1	1.38	15.83	2	0	99	0	1	71.0	45.1	-11.8	4	N/A	1,000	50	3.3	0.0
B- / 7.1	12.1	1.38	15.37	14	0	99	0	1	71.0	42.9	-12.0	4	N/A	1,000	50	0.0	5.0
C / 5.4	12.1	1.38	14.97	3	0	99	0	1	71.0	42.8	-11.9	4	N/A	1,000	50	0.0	1.0
C / 5.5	12.1	1.38	16.33	641	0	99	0	1	71.0	47.4	-11.6	6	4	1,000	50	0.0	0.0
D- / 1.4	17.9	1.17	14.36	19	3	96	0	1	65.0	89.8	-10.4	8	N/A	1,000	50	5.0	1.0
C- / 3.7	18.0	1.18	14.37	1	3	96	0	1	65.0	88.2	-10.4	7	N/A	1,000	50	3.3	0.0
C- / 3.7	18.0	1.18	13.91	2	3	96	0	1	65.0	85.3	-10.5	6	N/A	1,000	50	0.0	5.0
C- / 3.7	18.0	1.18	13.92	N/A	3	96	0	1	65.0	85.3	-10.5	6	N/A	1,000	50	0.0	1.0
D- / 1.5	18.0	1.18	14.83	132	3	96	0	1	65.0	91.3	-10.3	8	N/A	1,000	100	0.0	0.0
B- / 7.8	11.9	0.74	21.30	3	6	92	0	2	105.0	N/A	N/A	82	3	1,000	50	5.0	1.0
B- / 7.8	11.9	0.74	21.12	1	6	92	0	2	105.0	N/A	N/A	80	3	1,000	50	3.3	0.0
B- / 7.8	11.9	0.74	20.74	1	6	92	0	2	105.0	N/A	N/A	76	3	1,000	50	0.0	5.0
B- / 7.8	11.8	0.74	20.70	1	6	92	0	2	105.0	N/A	N/A	77	3	1,000	50	0.0	1.0
B- / 7.8	11.8	0.74	21.45	121	6	92	0	2	105.0	N/A	N/A	84	3	1,000	50	0.0	0.0
D- / 1.0	26.9	2.55	10.51	4	1	98	0	1	367.0	105.8	-13.9	0	6	1,000	50	5.0	1.0
D- / 1.0	26.9	2.56	10.37	2	1	98	0	1	367.0	104.3	-13.9	0	5	1,000	50	3.3	0.0
D- / 1.0	26.9	2.56	10.06	1	1	98	0	1	367.0	101.1	-14.0	0	6	1,000	50	0.0	5.0
D- / 1.0	26.9	2.56	10.03	1	1	98	0	1	367.0	101.2	-14.0	0	6	1,000	50	0.0	1.0
D- / 1.0	27.0	2.56	10.66	52	1	98	0	1	367.0	107.7	-13.9	0	6	1,000	50	0.0	0.0
B+ / 9.1	6.0	1.20	11.56	106	1	69	29	1	132.0	48.6	-5.7	60	N/A	1,000	100	5.5	1.0
B+ / 9.1	6.0	1.20	11.48	15	1	69	29	1	132.0	45.0	-5.7	50	N/A	1,000	100	0.0	5.0
B+ / 9.0	6.1	1.21	11.55	4	1	69	29	1	132.0	44.9	-5.8	49	N/A	1,000	100	0.0	1.0
B+ / 9.1	6.0	1.20	11.63	N/A	1	69	29	1	132.0	47.8	-5.6	58	N/A	0	0	0.0	0.0
B+ / 9.1	6.0	1.20	11.58	241	1	69	29	1	132.0	49.7	-5.5	62	N/A	0	0	0.0	0.0
B / 8.9	7.0	0.89	14.40	163	0	99	0	1	22.0	62.4	-9.4	58	12	1,000	100	5.5	1.0
B+ / 9.0	7.0	0.89	14.28	19	0	99	0	1	22.0	58.5	-9.5	47	12	1,000	100	0.0	5.0
B+ / 9.0	7.0	0.89	14.31	12	0	99	0	1	22.0	58.6	-9.6	47	12	1,000	100	0.0	1.0
B+ / 9.0	7.0	0.90	14.39	1	0	99	0	1	22.0	61.4	-9.3	54	N/A	0	0	0.0	0.0
B+ / 9.0	7.0	0.89	14.50	1,083	0	99	0	1	22.0	63.6	-9.4	61	12	0	0	0.0	0.0
B / 8.5	7.6	1.00	23.79	228	0	99	0	1	4.0	61.8	-9.8	49	N/A	1,000	100	5.5	1.0
B / 8.7	7.6	1.00	23.48	45	0	99	0	1	4.0	58.0	-10.0	40	N/A	1,000	100	0.0	5.0
B / 8.7	7.6	1.00	23.62	22	0	99	0	1	4.0	58.0	-10.0	40	N/A	1,000	100	0.0	1.0
B / 8.7	7.6	1.00	23.77	3	0	99	0	1	4.0	61.1	-9.8	47	N/A	0	0	0.0	0.0
B / 8.7	7.6	1.00	23.78	1,827	0	99	0	1	4.0	63.1	-9.8	53	N/A	0	0	0.0	0.0

Fund Type	Fund Name	Ticker Symbol	Overall Weiss Investment Rating	Phone	Perfor-mance Rating/Pts	3 Mo	6 Mo	1Yr / Pct	3Yr / Pct	5Yr / Pct	Dividend Yield	Expense Ratio
								Total Return % through 6/30/06	(Annualized)		Incl. in Returns	

99 Pct = Best
0 Pct = Worst

Fund Type	Fund Name	Ticker Symbol	Overall Weiss Investment Rating	Phone	Performance Rating/Pts	3 Mo	6 Mo	1Yr / Pct	3Yr / Pct	5Yr / Pct	Dividend Yield	Expense Ratio
FO	First American International A	FAIAX	B+	(800) 677-3863	B / 7.8	-0.22	9.06	24.60 /88	19.49 /78	5.82 /60	0.89	1.52
FO	First American International B	FNABX	B	(800) 677-3863	B / 7.6	-0.39	8.65	23.59 /87	18.59 /75	5.01 /54	0.31	2.27
FO	First American International C	FIACX	B+	(800) 677-3863	B / 8.0	-0.30	8.77	23.66 /87	18.60 /75	--	0.25	2.27
FO	First American International R	ARQIX	B+	(800) 677-3863	B / 8.2	-0.29	8.86	24.26 /88	18.99 /76	5.53 /58	0.00	1.77
FO	First American International Y	FAICX	B+	(800) 677-3863	B+ / 8.3	-0.14	9.28	24.95 /88	19.76 /79	6.06 /61	1.14	1.27
GR	First American Lrg Cap Gr Opp A	FRGWX	D-	(800) 677-3863	E+ / 0.7	-6.00	-4.61	2.55 / 6	8.01 /15	-1.17 /11	0.00	1.20
GR	First American Lrg Cap Gr Opp B	FETBX	D-	(800) 677-3863	E+ / 0.6	-6.20	-4.98	1.78 / 4	7.19 /11	-1.92 / 8	0.00	1.95
GR	First American Lrg Cap Gr Opp C	FAWCX	D-	(800) 677-3863	E+ / 0.9	-6.21	-4.99	1.78 / 4	7.19 /11	--	0.00	1.95
GR	First American Lrg Cap Gr Opp R	FLCYX	D	(800) 677-3863	D- / 1.3	-6.06	-4.76	2.30 / 5	7.80 /14	-1.28 /11	0.00	1.45
GR	First American Lrg Cap Gr Opp Y	FIGWX	D	(800) 677-3863	D / 1.6	-5.93	-4.48	2.81 / 7	8.28 /17	-0.92 /12	0.00	0.95
GR	First American Lrg Cap Select A	FLRAX	D+	(800) 677-3863	D+ / 2.3	-3.42	-0.59	5.82 /19	10.70 /33	--	0.39	1.22
GR	First American Lrg Cap Select B	FLPBX	D+	(800) 677-3863	D / 2.0	-3.63	-0.97	5.10 /16	9.89 /27	--	0.04	1.97
GR	First American Lrg Cap Select C	FLYCX	C-	(800) 677-3863	D+ / 2.6	-3.63	-1.00	4.99 /15	9.90 /27	--	0.08	1.97
GR	First American Lrg Cap Select R	FLSSX	C-	(800) 677-3863	C- / 3.2	-3.50	-0.72	5.55 /18	10.47 /31	--	0.22	1.47
GR	First American Lrg Cap Select Y	FLRYX	C	(800) 677-3863	C- / 3.5	-3.42	-0.54	6.10 /21	10.99 /35	--	0.61	0.97
GI	First American Lrg Cap Val A	FASKX	C+	(800) 677-3863	C / 4.9	-0.14	5.41	11.43 /56	13.66 /52	3.75 /43	0.89	1.20
GI	First American Lrg Cap Val B	FATBX	C+	(800) 677-3863	C / 4.6	-0.30	5.01	10.58 /51	12.81 /48	2.98 /37	0.54	1.95
GI	First American Lrg Cap Val C	FALVX	B-	(800) 677-3863	C / 5.2	-0.35	5.00	10.56 /51	12.79 /47	2.96 /36	0.53	1.95
GI	First American Lrg Cap Val R	FAVSX	B	(800) 677-3863	C+ / 5.7	-0.21	5.24	11.08 /54	13.44 /51	--	0.73	1.45
GI	First American Lrg Cap Val Y	FSKIX	B	(800) 677-3863	C+ / 5.9	-0.06	5.53	11.66 /58	13.93 /54	4.01 /46	1.17	0.95
MC	First American Mid Cap Gr Opp A	FRSLX	C	(800) 677-3863	C+ / 6.8	-6.20	3.33	12.52 /62	18.97 /76	8.48 /74	0.00	1.24
MC	First American Mid Cap Gr Opp B	FMQBX	C-	(800) 677-3863	C+ / 6.6	-6.40	2.92	11.65 /58	18.08 /73	7.67 /70	0.00	1.99
MC	First American Mid Cap Gr Opp C	FMECX	C	(800) 677-3863	B- / 7.1	-6.38	2.95	11.65 /58	18.08 /73	--	0.00	1.99
MC	First American Mid Cap Gr Opp R	FMEYX	C	(800) 677-3863	B- / 7.4	-6.26	3.19	12.24 /61	18.79 /75	8.40 /73	0.00	1.49
MC	First American Mid Cap Gr Opp Y	FISGX	C+	(800) 677-3863	B / 7.6	-6.15	3.44	12.80 /63	19.28 /77	8.76 /75	0.00	0.99
MC	First American Mid Cap Index A	FDXAX	B-	(800) 677-3863	C+ / 6.4	-3.33	3.97	12.37 /61	17.36 /70	8.48 /74	0.67	0.75
MC	First American Mid Cap Index B	FMDBX	C+	(800) 677-3863	C+ / 6.2	-3.45	3.58	11.59 /57	16.50 /66	7.72 /70	0.08	1.50
MC	First American Mid Cap Index C	FDXCX	B-	(800) 677-3863	C+ / 6.6	-3.50	3.58	11.47 /56	16.48 /66	--	0.09	1.50
MC	First American Mid Cap Index R	FMCYX	B	(800) 677-3863	B- / 7.0	-3.45	3.75	12.00 /60	17.10 /68	8.36 /73	0.64	1.00
MC	First American Mid Cap Index Y	FIMEX	B	(800) 677-3863	B- / 7.2	-3.27	4.10	12.65 /63	17.63 /71	8.78 /75	0.95	0.50
MC	First American Mid Cap Val A	FASEX	A+	(800) 677-3863	B / 7.8	-0.41	6.74	14.41 /70	20.85 /82	12.30 /87	0.52	1.25
MC	First American Mid Cap Val B	FAESX	A+	(800) 677-3863	B / 7.6	-0.61	6.32	13.56 /66	19.95 /79	11.46 /85	0.14	2.00
MC	First American Mid Cap Val C	FACSX	A+	(800) 677-3863	B / 7.9	-0.60	6.31	13.55 /66	19.93 /79	11.46 /85	0.17	2.00
MC	First American Mid Cap Val R	FMVSX	A+	(800) 677-3863	B / 8.2	-0.47	6.59	14.16 /69	20.66 /82	--	0.47	1.50
MC	First American Mid Cap Val Y	FSEIX	A+	(800) 677-3863	B+ / 8.3	-0.34	6.83	14.69 /71	21.15 /83	12.58 /88	0.75	1.00
RE	First American Real Est Secs A	FREAX	B-	(800) 677-3863	A / 9.4	0.38	15.69	25.90 /90	28.72 /94	21.43 /97	2.30	1.25
RE	First American Real Est Secs B	FREBX	B-	(800) 677-3863	A / 9.3	0.20	15.26	24.94 /88	27.77 /94	20.54 /97	1.80	2.00
RE	First American Real Est Secs C	FRLCX	B-	(800) 677-3863	A / 9.4	0.17	15.20	24.91 /88	27.73 /94	20.52 /97	1.80	2.00
RE	First American Real Est Secs R	FRSSX	B	(800) 677-3863	A / 9.5	0.37	15.55	25.60 /89	28.48 /94	--	2.30	1.50
RE	First American Real Est Secs Y	FARCX	B	(800) 677-3863	A / 9.5	0.44	15.83	26.21 /90	29.04 /95	21.74 /98	2.58	1.00
SC	First American Sm Cap Gr Opp A	FRMPX	E-	(800) 677-3863	D+ / 2.9	-10.89	-0.30	8.55 /37	12.15 /43	4.12 /47	0.00	1.47
SC	First American Sm Cap Gr Opp B	FROBX	E-	(800) 677-3863	D+ / 2.6	-11.06	-0.66	7.73 /31	11.32 /38	3.35 /40	0.00	2.22
SC	First American Sm Cap Gr Opp C	FMPCX	E-	(800) 677-3863	C- / 3.3	-11.05	-0.68	7.71 /31	11.33 /38	--	0.00	2.22
SC	First American Sm Cap Gr Opp R	FMPYX	E-	(800) 677-3863	C- / 3.9	-10.97	-0.40	8.21 /34	12.02 /43	4.04 /46	0.00	1.72
SC	First American Sm Cap Gr Opp Y	FIMPX	E	(800) 677-3863	C- / 4.2	-10.83	-0.19	8.77 /39	12.41 /45	4.37 /49	0.00	1.22
SC	First American Sm Cap Index A	FMDAX	C	(800) 677-3863	C+ / 6.7	-5.23	7.82	13.74 /67	17.74 /71	8.27 /73	0.46	0.83
SC	First American Sm Cap Index B	FPXBX	C	(800) 677-3863	C+ / 6.4	-5.38	7.40	12.89 /64	16.72 /67	7.40 /69	0.00	1.58
SC	First American Sm Cap Index C	FPXCX	C	(800) 677-3863	C+ / 6.8	-5.40	7.41	12.85 /64	16.72 /67	--	0.00	1.58
SC	First American Sm Cap Index R	ARSCX	C+	(800) 677-3863	B- / 7.2	-5.27	7.66	13.49 /66	17.41 /70	8.05 /72	0.35	1.08
SC	First American Sm Cap Index Y	ASETX	C+	(800) 677-3863	B- / 7.4	-5.16	7.96	14.02 /68	17.88 /72	8.49 /74	0.72	0.58
SC	First American Sm Cap Select A	EMGRX	D	(800) 677-3863	B / 7.6	-4.13	10.34	21.71 /84	19.96 /79	10.87 /83	0.00	1.25
SC	First American Sm Cap Select B	ARSBX	D	(800) 677-3863	B- / 7.4	-4.35	9.92	20.74 /83	19.08 /76	10.04 /81	0.00	2.00

• Denotes fund is closed to new investors
* Denotes fund is included in Section II

| RISK | 3 Year | | NET ASSETS | | ASSET | | | | Portfolio | BULL / BEAR | | FUND MANAGER | | MINIMUMS | | LOADS | |
Risk Rating/Pts	Standard Deviation	Beta	NAV As of 6/30/06	Total $(Mil)	Cash %	Stocks %	Bonds %	Other %	Turnover Ratio	Last Bull Market Return	Last Bear Market Return	Manager Quality Pct	Manager Tenure (Years)	Initial Purch. $	Additional Purch. $	Front End Load	Back End Load
C+ / 6.9	10.4	0.99	13.85	51	0	99	0	1	74.0	107.9	-11.0	20	12	1,000	100	5.5	1.0
C+ / 6.8	10.4	0.99	12.81	7	0	99	0	1	74.0	102.9	-11.2	15	12	1,000	100	0.0	5.0
C+ / 6.8	10.3	0.99	13.27	8	0	99	0	1	74.0	103.0	-11.2	16	12	1,000	100	0.0	1.0
C+ / 6.8	10.4	1.00	13.88	N/A	0	99	0	1	74.0	105.4	-11.0	17	12	0	0	0.0	0.0
C+ / 6.9	10.4	0.99	14.02	1,657	0	99	0	1	74.0	109.7	-11.1	22	12	0	0	0.0	0.0
B- / 7.7	9.0	1.09	27.75	90	1	98	0	1	103.0	53.4	-11.2	21	N/A	1,000	100	5.5	1.0
B- / 7.6	8.9	1.09	26.34	15	1	98	0	1	103.0	49.8	-11.3	17	N/A	1,000	100	0.0	5.0
B- / 7.6	9.0	1.09	26.87	9	1	98	0	1	103.0	49.8	-11.3	16	N/A	1,000	100	0.0	1.0
B- / 7.7	9.0	1.09	27.61	1	1	98	0	1	103.0	52.6	-11.1	20	N/A	0	0	0.0	0.0
B- / 7.7	8.9	1.09	28.57	828	1	98	0	1	103.0	54.6	-11.1	23	N/A	0	0	0.0	0.0
B- / 7.9	8.6	1.08	13.99	7	2	97	0	1	176.0	64.6	N/A	42	N/A	1,000	100	5.5	1.0
B- / 7.9	8.6	1.07	13.79	1	2	97	0	1	176.0	60.6	N/A	35	N/A	1,000	100	0.0	5.0
B- / 7.9	8.6	1.07	13.79	N/A	2	97	0	1	176.0	60.7	N/A	35	N/A	1,000	100	0.0	1.0
B- / 7.9	8.6	1.08	13.94	N/A	2	97	0	1	176.0	63.3	N/A	40	N/A	0	0	0.0	0.0
B- / 7.9	8.6	1.07	14.02	436	2	97	0	1	176.0	65.9	N/A	46	N/A	0	0	0.0	0.0
B / 8.6	8.2	1.02	20.43	111	1	98	0	1	61.0	74.0	-10.1	77	N/A	1,000	100	5.5	1.0
B / 8.6	8.3	1.02	19.91	10	1	98	0	1	61.0	70.0	-10.2	70	N/A	1,000	100	0.0	5.0
B / 8.6	8.2	1.01	20.15	5	1	98	0	1	61.0	70.0	-10.3	70	N/A	1,000	100	0.0	1.0
B / 8.6	8.3	1.02	20.41	N/A	1	98	0	1	61.0	73.3	-10.1	75	N/A	0	0	0.0	0.0
B / 8.6	8.3	1.02	20.49	761	1	98	0	1	61.0	75.5	-10.1	79	N/A	0	0	0.0	0.0
C / 5.0	12.7	1.12	40.07	300	0	99	0	1	107.0	108.4	-7.4	42	N/A	1,000	100	5.5	1.0
C / 4.7	12.7	1.12	36.99	16	0	99	0	1	107.0	103.5	-7.6	34	N/A	1,000	100	0.0	5.0
C / 4.8	12.7	1.12	38.44	19	0	99	0	1	107.0	103.5	-7.6	35	N/A	1,000	100	0.0	1.0
C / 5.0	12.7	1.12	39.83	16	0	99	0	1	107.0	107.5	-7.4	41	N/A	0	0	0.0	0.0
C / 5.2	12.7	1.12	42.15	1,272	0	99	0	1	107.0	110.0	-7.3	45	N/A	0	0	0.0	0.0
B- / 7.3	10.8	1.00	13.89	15	0	99	0	1	15.0	100.3	-9.3	47	6	1,000	100	5.5	1.0
B- / 7.3	10.8	1.00	13.64	3	0	99	0	1	15.0	95.6	-9.5	39	6	1,000	100	0.0	5.0
B- / 7.3	10.8	1.00	13.68	4	0	99	0	1	15.0	95.5	-9.5	39	N/A	1,000	100	0.0	1.0
B- / 7.3	10.8	1.00	13.83	1	0	99	0	1	15.0	99.1	-9.3	45	5	0	0	0.0	0.0
B- / 7.3	10.8	1.00	13.90	334	0	99	0	1	15.0	102.0	-9.3	50	6	0	0	0.0	0.0
B / 8.5	9.6	0.83	25.55	106	2	97	0	1	101.0	106.2	-5.7	93	7	1,000	100	5.5	1.0
B / 8.4	9.6	0.83	24.47	9	2	97	0	1	101.0	101.4	-5.9	90	2	1,000	100	0.0	5.0
B / 8.5	9.6	0.83	24.97	14	2	97	0	1	101.0	101.3	-5.8	90	2	1,000	100	0.0	1.0
B / 8.5	9.6	0.83	25.47	10	2	97	0	1	101.0	105.2	-5.7	92	2	0	0	0.0	0.0
B / 8.5	9.6	0.83	25.66	684	2	97	0	1	101.0	107.8	-5.6	93	N/A	0	0	0.0	0.0
C / 4.6	16.2	0.97	22.82	177	2	97	0	1	118.0	134.5	0.2	91	7	1,000	100	5.5	1.0
C / 4.6	16.2	0.97	22.49	5	2	97	0	1	118.0	129.2	-0.1	87	7	1,000	100	0.0	5.0
C / 4.6	16.2	0.97	22.57	6	2	97	0	1	118.0	129.2	-0.1	87	7	1,000	100	0.0	1.0
C / 4.6	16.2	0.97	23.03	4	2	97	0	1	118.0	133.4	0.2	90	7	0	0	0.0	0.0
C / 4.6	16.3	0.97	22.97	602	2	97	0	1	118.0	136.4	0.2	92	7	0	0	0.0	0.0
D- / 1.1	17.1	1.09	19.80	78	2	97	0	1	190.0	113.5	-17.9	7	2	1,000	100	5.5	1.0
E+ / 0.9	17.1	1.09	18.18	7	2	97	0	1	190.0	108.5	-18.1	5	2	1,000	100	0.0	5.0
D- / 1.0	17.1	1.09	18.92	3	2	97	0	1	190.0	108.4	-18.0	5	2	1,000	100	0.0	1.0
D- / 1.1	17.1	1.09	19.72	1	2	97	0	1	190.0	112.9	-17.9	6	2	0	0	0.0	0.0
D- / 1.2	17.1	1.09	20.91	212	2	97	0	1	190.0	115.1	-17.9	7	2	0	0	0.0	0.0
C+ / 5.6	14.6	1.00	15.35	10	0	100	0	0	23.0	114.2	-11.3	45	6	1,000	100	5.5	1.0
C+ / 5.6	14.5	1.00	14.94	1	0	100	0	0	23.0	108.5	-11.4	36	5	1,000	100	0.0	5.0
C+ / 5.6	14.5	1.00	15.07	2	0	100	0	0	23.0	108.5	-11.5	36	N/A	1,000	100	0.0	1.0
C+ / 5.6	14.5	1.00	15.18	N/A	0	100	0	0	23.0	112.6	-11.5	42	6	0	0	0.0	0.0
C+ / 5.6	14.5	1.00	15.35	137	0	100	0	0	23.0	115.3	-11.3	47	6	0	0	0.0	0.0
D- / 1.4	13.8	0.91	14.41	141	3	96	0	1	122.0	122.7	-11.5	80	2	1,000	100	5.5	1.0
D- / 1.4	13.9	0.92	12.30	15	3	96	0	1	122.0	117.4	-11.7	73	2	1,000	100	0.0	5.0

							PERFORMANCE						
	99 Pct = Best 0 Pct = Worst			Overall Weiss Investment Rating		Perfor- mance Rating/Pts	Total Return % through 6/30/06					Incl. in Returns	
										Annualized		Dividend	Expense
Fund Type	Fund Name	Ticker Symbol			Phone		3 Mo	6 Mo	1Yr / Pct	3Yr / Pct	5Yr / Pct	Yield	Ratio
SC	First American Sm Cap Select C	FHMCX	D		(800) 677-3863	B / 7.8	-4.33	9.94	20.79 /83	19.06 /76	--	0.00	2.00
SC	First American Sm Cap Select R	ASEIX	D		(800) 677-3863	B / 8.1	-4.23	10.19	21.37 /83	19.78 /79	10.78 /83	0.00	1.50
SC	First American Sm Cap Select Y	ARSTX	D+		(800) 677-3863	B / 8.2	-4.14	10.40	21.93 /84	20.24 /80	11.15 /84	0.00	1.00
SC	First American Sm Cap Val A	FSCAX	D		(800) 677-3863	B / 7.6	-2.48	8.51	13.77 /67	20.33 /81	10.32 /82	0.21	1.26
SC	First American Sm Cap Val B	FCSBX	D		(800) 677-3863	B- / 7.4	-2.65	8.11	12.86 /64	19.41 /77	9.49 /79	0.00	2.01
SC	First American Sm Cap Val C	FSCVX	D		(800) 677-3863	B / 7.7	-2.68	8.13	12.90 /64	19.44 /77	9.50 /79	0.00	2.01
SC	First American Sm Cap Val R	FSVSX	D+		(800) 677-3863	B / 8.1	-2.57	8.34	13.40 /66	20.16 /80	--	0.40	1.51
SC	First American Sm Cap Val Y	FSCCX	D+		(800) 677-3863	B / 8.2	-2.43	8.64	13.96 /68	20.61 /81	10.59 /82	0.40	1.01
TC	First American Sm Mid Cap Core A	FATAX	E+		(800) 677-3863	C / 4.6	-3.02	8.89	14.80 /71	12.90 /48	-5.39 / 2	0.00	1.32
TC	First American Sm Mid Cap Core B	FITBX	E+		(800) 677-3863	C / 4.3	-3.10	8.53	14.01 /68	12.09 /43	-6.12 / 2	0.00	2.25
TC	First American Sm Mid Cap Core C	FTACX	D-		(800) 677-3863	C / 4.9	-3.17	8.57	13.86 /68	12.08 /43	-6.10 / 2	0.00	2.25
TC	First American Sm Mid Cap Core Y	FATCX	D-		(800) 677-3863	C+ / 5.7	-2.91	9.13	15.10 /72	13.16 /50	-5.15 / 2	0.00	1.25
AA	First American Strat-Agg Gr Alloc A	FAAGX	C+		(800) 677-3863	C / 5.1	-2.12	3.71	12.67 /63	14.24 /55	--	1.36	0.40
AA	First American Strat-Agg Gr Alloc B	FSGBX	C+		(800) 677-3863	C / 4.8	-2.30	3.42	11.88 /59	13.43 /51	--	1.14	1.15
AA	First American Strat-Agg Gr Alloc C	FSACX	C+		(800) 677-3863	C / 5.4	-2.38	3.33	11.77 /58	13.38 /51	--	1.15	1.15
AA	First American Strat-Agg Gr Alloc R	FSASX	B-		(800) 677-3863	C+ / 5.9	-2.19	3.65	12.44 /62	14.09 /54	4.24 /48	1.38	0.65
AA	First American Strat-Agg Gr Alloc Y	FSAYX	B		(800) 677-3863	C+ / 6.1	-2.06	3.94	12.96 /64	14.54 /56	--	1.68	0.15
AA	First American Strat-Gr Alloc A	FAGSX	C		(800) 677-3863	C- / 3.6	-1.79	3.00	10.47 /50	12.01 /42	--	1.74	0.40
AA	First American Strat-Gr Alloc B	FSNBX	C		(800) 677-3863	C- / 3.3	-1.99	2.58	9.61 /44	11.18 /37	--	1.19	1.15
AA	First American Strat-Gr Alloc C	FSNCX	C+		(800) 677-3863	C- / 4.0	-1.98	2.57	9.66 /45	11.15 /37	--	1.16	1.15
AA	First American Strat-Gr Alloc R	FSNSX	C+		(800) 677-3863	C / 4.6	-1.86	2.79	10.16 /48	11.82 /41	4.13 /47	1.63	0.65
AA	First American Strat-Gr Alloc Y	FSGYX	B-		(800) 677-3863	C / 4.9	-1.72	3.13	10.75 /52	12.31 /44	--	2.09	0.15
AA	First American Strat-Gr&Inc Allc A	FSGNX	C		(800) 677-3863	D+ / 2.3	-1.31	2.57	8.68 /38	9.93 /27	--	2.21	0.40
AA	First American Strat-Gr&Inc Allc B	FSKBX	C-		(800) 677-3863	D / 2.1	-1.48	2.23	7.88 /32	9.10 /21	--	1.67	1.15
AA	First American Strat-Gr&Inc Allc C	FSKCX	C		(800) 677-3863	D+ / 2.7	-1.58	2.22	7.84 /31	9.09 /21	--	1.64	1.15
AA	First American Strat-Gr&Inc Allc R	FSKSX	C+		(800) 677-3863	C- / 3.3	-1.43	2.43	8.37 /36	9.72 /25	4.20 /48	2.22	0.65
AA	First American Strat-Gr&Inc Allc Y	FSKYX	C+		(800) 677-3863	C- / 3.6	-1.25	2.71	8.87 /39	10.19 /29	--	2.60	0.15
AA	First American Strat-Inc Alloc A	FSFIX	D+		(800) 677-3863	E / 0.5	-0.60	1.00	3.87 /10	5.86 / 6	--	3.36	0.40
AA	First American Strat-Inc Alloc B	FSFBX	D+		(800) 677-3863	E / 0.4	-0.87	0.55	3.04 / 7	5.03 / 4	--	2.84	1.15
AA	First American Strat-Inc Alloc C	FSJCX	C-		(800) 677-3863	E+ / 0.6	-0.87	0.58	3.07 / 7	5.04 / 4	--	2.87	1.15
AA	First American Strat-Inc Alloc R	FSJSX	C-		(800) 677-3863	E+ / 0.9	-0.79	0.78	3.48 / 9	5.62 / 5	4.56 /51	3.36	0.65
AA	First American Strat-Inc Alloc Y	FSFYX	C-		(800) 677-3863	D- / 1.1	-0.63	1.04	4.04 /11	6.09 / 7	--	3.81	0.15
MC	First Eagle Fund of America A	FEFAX	C+		(800) 334-2143	C / 4.8	-1.39	4.50	10.88 /53	13.93 /54	7.70 /70	0.00	1.41
MC	First Eagle Fund of America C	FEAMX	C+		(800) 334-2143	C / 5.0	-1.56	4.14	10.09 /47	13.13 /49	7.00 /67	0.00	2.17
MC	● First Eagle Fund of America Y	FEAFX	C+		(800) 334-2143	C / 5.5	-1.37	4.52	10.87 /53	13.96 /54	7.80 /71	0.00	1.43
★ GL	● First Eagle Global Fund A	SGENX	A+		(800) 334-2143	B / 8.2	1.30	9.18	22.33 /85	21.75 /85	18.11 /95	1.69	1.20
GL	● First Eagle Global Fund C	FESGX	A+		(800) 334-2143	B+ / 8.3	1.11	8.77	21.43 /83	20.84 /82	17.26 /94	1.21	1.95
GL	● First Eagle Global Fund I	SGIIX	A+		(800) 334-2143	B+ / 8.6	1.36	9.30	22.62 /85	22.04 /85	18.42 /95	1.98	0.95
PM	● First Eagle Gold Fund A	SGGDX	D+		(800) 334-2143	A / 9.5	1.84	16.76	54.82 /99	25.01 /91	35.05 /99	1.97	1.29
PM	● First Eagle Gold Fund C	FEGOX	D		(800) 334-2143	A / 9.5	1.69	16.34	53.69 /99	24.13 /90	--	1.61	2.04
PM	● First Eagle Gold Fund I	FEGIX	D		(800) 334-2143	A+ / 9.6	1.97	16.94	55.27 /99	25.32 /91	--	2.27	1.04
★ FO	● First Eagle Overseas Fund A	SGOVX	A+		(800) 334-2143	A- / 9.0	2.10	11.59	26.35 /90	25.26 /91	20.35 /96	2.84	1.18
FO	● First Eagle Overseas Fund C	FESOX	A+		(800) 334-2143	A- / 9.1	1.92	11.20	25.40 /89	24.36 /90	19.50 /96	2.39	1.93
FO	● First Eagle Overseas Fund I	SGOIX	A+		(800) 334-2143	A- / 9.2	2.21	11.72	26.68 /91	25.58 /92	20.66 /97	3.17	0.93
SC	First Eagle U.S. Value A	FEVAX	B		(800) 334-2143	C / 4.9	1.25	4.33	9.73 /45	14.07 /54	--	1.48	1.28
SC	First Eagle U.S. Value C	FEVCX	B+		(800) 334-2143	C / 5.1	0.99	3.92	8.84 /39	13.20 /50	--	1.21	2.02
SC	First Eagle U.S. Value I	FEVIX	A-		(800) 334-2143	C+ / 5.7	1.30	4.43	9.98 /47	14.32 /55	--	1.71	1.04
BA	First Focus Balanced Fund Inst	FOBAX	C+		(800) 662-4203	C / 4.3	-2.73	2.54	8.08 /33	11.63 /40	7.88 /71	0.36	1.35
AA	First Focus Core Equity Inst	FOEQX	B-		(800) 662-4203	C / 5.3	-0.44	5.04	9.94 /47	12.90 /48	5.08 /55	0.87	1.20
GR	First Focus Growth Opp Inst	FOGRX	C+		(800) 662-4203	C+ / 6.7	-4.03	4.95	13.08 /65	16.11 /64	8.46 /74	0.00	1.24
AA	First Focus Sh Inter Bond Inst	FOSIX	D		(800) 662-4203	E- / 0.1	0.45	0.61	0.89 / 2	1.12 / 0	3.37 /40	4.44	0.84
SC	First Focus Small Company Inst	FOSCX	C+		(800) 662-4203	C+ / 6.2	-1.37	8.38	16.42 /76	14.14 /55	9.41 /78	0.25	1.36

● Denotes fund is closed to new investors
★ Denotes fund is included in Section II

Risk Rating/Pts	Standard Deviation	Beta	NAV As of 6/30/06	Total $(Mil)	Cash %	Stocks %	Bonds %	Other %	Portfolio Turnover Ratio	Last Bull Market Return	Last Bear Market Return	Manager Quality Pct	Manager Tenure (Years)	Initial Purch. $	Additional Purch. $	Front End Load	Back End Load
D- / 1.4	13.9	0.92	13.71	16	3	96	0	1	122.0	117.4	-11.7	73	2	1,000	100	0.0	1.0
D- / 1.4	13.8	0.92	14.28	2	3	96	0	1	122.0	121.7	-11.5	78	2	0	0	0.0	0.0
D / 1.8	13.8	0.91	15.28	709	3	96	0	1	122.0	124.5	-11.5	82	2	0	0	0.0	0.0
D / 1.8	12.3	0.83	14.54	54	3	96	0	1	72.0	116.2	-7.9	90	1	1,000	100	5.5	1.0
D / 1.7	12.3	0.83	13.20	8	3	96	0	1	72.0	111.1	-8.1	86	1	1,000	100	0.0	5.0
D / 1.7	12.3	0.83	13.43	4	3	96	0	1	72.0	111.2	-8.2	86	1	1,000	100	0.0	1.0
D / 1.7	12.3	0.83	14.42	1	3	96	0	1	72.0	115.4	-8.0	89	1	0	0	0.0	0.0
D / 1.9	12.3	0.83	14.84	351	3	96	0	1	72.0	118.1	-8.0	91	1	0	0	0.0	0.0
D+ / 2.7	19.5	1.98	9.31	27	1	98	0	1	197.0	91.7	-17.0	8	1	1,000	100	5.5	1.0
D+ / 2.6	19.5	1.97	8.14	9	1	98	0	1	197.0	87.4	-17.3	6	1	1,000	100	0.0	5.0
D+ / 2.6	19.4	1.96	8.87	5	1	98	0	1	197.0	87.3	-17.2	6	1	1,000	100	0.0	1.0
D+ / 2.7	19.4	1.97	9.68	64	1	98	0	1	197.0	93.1	-17.0	8	1	0	0	0.0	0.0
B / 8.1	8.5	1.63	11.68	63	1	96	1	2	17.0	78.8	-8.5	84	N/A	1,000	100	5.5	1.0
B / 8.0	8.4	1.62	11.49	3	1	96	1	2	17.0	74.7	-8.8	79	N/A	1,000	100	0.0	5.0
B / 8.0	8.4	1.63	11.49	3	1	96	1	2	17.0	74.6	-8.8	78	N/A	1,000	100	0.0	1.0
B / 8.1	8.5	1.63	11.63	N/A	1	96	1	2	17.0	77.9	-8.5	83	N/A	0	0	0.0	0.0
B / 8.1	8.4	1.62	11.67	57	1	96	1	2	17.0	80.1	-8.5	86	N/A	0	0	0.0	0.0
B / 8.7	7.1	1.40	11.32	68	0	84	14	2	18.0	64.4	-6.7	77	N/A	1,000	100	5.5	1.0
B / 8.6	7.1	1.41	11.22	7	0	84	14	2	18.0	60.5	-6.9	70	N/A	1,000	100	0.0	5.0
B / 8.7	7.0	1.40	11.26	5	0	84	14	2	18.0	60.3	-6.9	70	N/A	1,000	100	0.0	1.0
B / 8.7	7.1	1.41	11.28	N/A	0	84	14	2	18.0	63.4	-6.6	76	N/A	0	0	0.0	0.0
B / 8.7	7.1	1.40	11.32	78	0	84	14	2	18.0	65.5	-6.5	80	N/A	0	0	0.0	0.0
B+ / 9.3	5.7	1.16	10.71	126	1	69	29	1	17.0	51.2	-4.7	71	N/A	1,000	100	5.5	1.0
B+ / 9.3	5.7	1.16	10.65	7	1	69	29	1	17.0	47.6	-4.9	63	N/A	1,000	100	0.0	5.0
B+ / 9.2	5.7	1.15	10.66	5	1	69	29	1	17.0	47.6	-4.8	64	N/A	1,000	100	0.0	1.0
B+ / 9.3	5.7	1.16	10.65	N/A	1	69	29	1	17.0	50.4	-4.6	69	N/A	0	0	0.0	0.0
B+ / 9.3	5.7	1.17	10.68	131	1	69	29	1	17.0	52.3	-4.5	73	N/A	0	0	0.0	0.0
B+ / 9.7	3.6	0.68	11.10	30	1	38	60	1	16.0	29.2	-0.7	56	8	1,000	100	5.5	1.0
B+ / 9.9	3.6	0.68	11.05	3	1	38	60	1	16.0	26.3	-0.9	46	8	1,000	100	0.0	5.0
B+ / 9.7	3.6	0.68	11.07	2	1	38	60	1	16.0	26.1	-0.8	46	8	1,000	100	0.0	1.0
B+ / 9.9	3.6	0.68	11.09	N/A	1	38	60	1	16.0	28.6	-0.8	53	8	0	0	0.0	0.0
B+ / 9.9	3.6	0.68	11.09	59	1	38	60	1	16.0	30.2	-0.6	59	8	0	0	0.0	0.0
B / 8.8	7.2	0.60	26.26	40	5	94	0	1	54.5	63.9	-3.5	78	8	2,500	100	5.0	2.0
B- / 7.6	7.2	0.60	24.63	45	5	94	0	1	54.5	60.3	-3.6	71	8	2,500	100	0.0	2.0
B- / 7.8	7.2	0.60	26.60	663	5	94	0	1	54.5	64.1	-3.5	78	8	2,500	100	0.0	2.0
B / 8.8	7.1	0.66	45.92	11,148	16	74	8	2	12.3	112.7	-0.7	92	7	2,500	100	5.0	2.0
B / 8.8	7.1	0.66	45.53	4,626	16	74	8	2	12.3	107.8	-0.9	89	7	2,500	100	0.0	2.0
B / 8.8	7.1	0.66	46.07	2,392	16	74	8	2	12.3	114.5	-0.6	93	7	1,000,000	100	0.0	2.0
E+ / 0.7	26.5	1.37	23.75	848	4	60	35	1	21.7	119.8	20.5	26	7	2,500	100	5.0	2.0
E- / 0.0	26.5	1.37	23.50	182	4	60	35	1	21.7	N/A	N/A	21	7	2,500	100	0.0	2.0
E- / 0.0	26.5	1.37	23.88	145	4	60	35	1	21.7	N/A	N/A	27	7	1,000,000	100	0.0	2.0
B / 8.0	7.8	0.71	25.71	5,646	23	68	8	1	19.4	133.5	1.5	96	7	2,500	100	5.0	2.0
B / 8.1	7.8	0.71	25.42	1,128	23	68	8	1	19.4	128.1	1.3	95	7	2,500	100	0.0	2.0
B / 8.1	7.7	0.71	25.93	3,733	23	68	8	1	19.4	135.3	1.6	97	7	1,000,000	100	0.0	2.0
B+ / 9.6	5.9	0.34	15.43	208	40	50	9	1	17.2	72.6	-4.7	95	5	2,500	100	5.0	2.0
B+ / 9.7	5.9	0.34	15.36	137	40	50	9	1	17.2	68.3	-4.9	94	5	2,500	100	0.0	2.0
B+ / 9.6	5.9	0.34	15.56	103	40	50	9	1	17.2	73.8	-4.7	96	5	1,000,000	100	0.0	2.0
B / 8.6	8.5	1.55	13.74	33	0	72	54	0	44.0	61.9	-4.5	68	10	1,000	50	0.0	0.0
B / 8.3	7.8	1.42	10.38	99	N/A	97	3	N/A	18.0	64.0	-8.1	83	14	1,000	50	0.0	0.0
C+ / 6.2	12.4	1.41	15.47	72	0	99	0	1	28.0	93.5	-10.6	67	8	1,000	50	0.0	0.0
B+ / 9.0	3.1	0.13	9.29	57	2	0	98	0	41.0	5.5	3.0	34	14	1,000	50	0.0	0.0
B- / 7.3	11.5	0.74	19.79	49	0	97	18	0	15.0	76.7	-8.6	56	10	1,000	50	0.0	0.0

Fund Type	Fund Name	Ticker Symbol	Overall Weiss Investment Rating	Phone	Perfor-mance Rating/Pts	3 Mo	6 Mo	1Yr / Pct	3Yr / Pct	5Yr / Pct	Dividend Yield	Expense Ratio
			99 Pct = Best 0 Pct = Worst					Total Return % through 6/30/06	Annualized		Incl. in Returns	
AG	First Inv All Cap Growth A	FICGX	D	(800) 423-4026	C- / 3.0	-4.99	-1.08	8.17 /34	11.63 /40	2.65 /33	0.00	1.58
AG	First Inv All Cap Growth B	FIGBX	D	(800) 423-4026	D+ / 2.8	-5.08	-1.35	7.46 /29	10.87 /34	1.93 /27	0.00	2.28
GR	First Inv Blue Chip A	FIBCX	D	(800) 423-4026	D / 1.7	-2.00	1.76	6.70 /24	8.67 /19	-1.68 / 9	0.65	1.45
GR	First Inv Focused Equity A	FIFEX	D	(800) 423-4026	D- / 1.0	-2.76	0.23	4.76 /14	7.53 /12	-0.90 /12	0.11	1.79
GL	First Inv Global A	FIISX	C+	(800) 423-4026	C+ / 5.9	0.00	6.15	15.95 /74	15.39 /61	4.53 /50	0.19	1.76
GL	First Inv Global B	FIBGX	C	(800) 423-4026	C+ / 5.7	-0.14	5.75	15.16 /72	14.55 /57	3.79 /44	0.00	2.46
GI	First Inv Growth & Income A	FGINX	C-	(800) 423-4026	C- / 3.3	-3.55	2.10	7.57 /30	11.89 /42	2.03 /28	0.33	1.38
MC	First Inv Mid-Cap Opp A	FIUSX	C	(800) 423-4026	C / 5.5	-5.77	0.25	8.08 /33	16.38 /65	4.82 /53	0.00	1.47
MC	First Inv Mid-Cap Opp B	FIMBX	C	(800) 423-4026	C / 5.3	-5.92	-0.08	7.34 /28	15.57 /62	4.09 /47	0.00	2.17
SC	First Inv Special Situations A	FISSX	C-	(800) 423-4026	C+ / 5.8	-3.65	7.71	12.81 /63	15.43 /61	1.95 /27	0.00	1.57
SC	First Inv Special Situations B	FISBX	D+	(800) 423-4026	C+ / 5.6	-3.80	7.36	12.00 /60	14.62 /57	1.05 /20	0.00	2.27
AA	First Inv Total Return A	FITRX	D+	(800) 423-4026	D- / 1.2	-2.36	1.26	4.80 /14	8.00 /15	2.61 /33	1.46	1.42
MC	First Inv Value A	FIUTX	B	(800) 423-4026	C / 5.4	-0.14	6.89	10.68 /51	14.44 /56	2.49 /32	1.06	1.37
TC	Firsthand-E-Commerce Fund (The)	TEFQX	E	(888) 884-2675	C / 4.6	-3.55	3.82	15.74 /74	11.74 /41	-1.15 /11	0.00	1.95
TC	Firsthand-Global Technology	GTFQX	E-	(888) 884-2675	E- / 0.1	-9.74	-0.51	4.01 /11	3.10 / 1	-6.69 / 1	0.00	1.95
TC	Firsthand-Technology Innovators	TIFQX	E-	(888) 884-2675	E / 0.3	-12.66	8.78	14.86 /71	1.27 / 0	-10.52 / 0	0.00	1.95
TC	Firsthand-Technology Leaders Fund	TLFQX	E	(888) 884-2675	C- / 3.5	-8.25	-1.42	15.24 /72	11.71 /41	-4.74 / 3	0.00	1.95
TC	Firsthand-Technology Value Fund	TVFQX	E	(888) 884-2675	C+ / 5.7	-9.77	4.56	24.17 /87	13.46 /51	-6.56 / 1	0.00	1.92
AG	Flex-funds Aggressive Growth	FLAGX	D+	(800) 325-3539	C- / 3.9	-3.79	2.50	9.22 /41	10.98 /35	0.73 /19	0.32	1.88
GR	Flex-funds Dynamic Growth	FLDGX	C-	(800) 325-3539	C / 4.5	-2.15	4.59	10.74 /52	11.36 /38	2.02 /27	0.74	1.41
GR	Flex-funds Muirfield	FLMFX	D	(800) 325-3539	C- / 3.2	-3.11	2.91	8.06 /33	9.72 /25	3.81 /44	1.30	1.42
GR	Flex-funds The Quantex Fund	FLCGX	D+	(800) 325-3539	C- / 3.5	-5.18	2.93	7.72 /31	10.57 /31	1.15 /21	0.06	1.75
UT	Flex-funds Total Return Utilities	FLRUX	B	(800) 325-3539	C+ / 6.8	1.54	5.47	10.90 /53	16.03 /64	1.61 /24	1.15	2.03
GI	FMC Strategic Value Fund		A+	(866) 777-7818	B+ / 8.6	1.54	10.70	19.52 /81	21.41 /83	15.28 /92	0.47	1.25
GR	● FMI Common Stock Fund	FMIMX	C+	(800) 811-5311	C+ / 6.4	-4.31	3.98	12.87 /64	15.44 /61	10.14 /81	0.06	1.22
SC	FMI Focus Fund	FMIOX	C-	(800) 811-5311	C+ / 5.6	-3.84	3.91	11.76 /58	13.56 /52	6.40 /63	0.00	1.44
GR	FMI Large Cap Fund	FMIHX	B	(800) 811-5311	C+ / 6.8	0.36	4.48	12.50 /62	16.19 /64	--	0.24	1.00
GR	FMI Provident Trust Strategy Fd	FMIRX	B	(800) 811-5311	B- / 7.0	-3.78	2.79	10.33 /49	17.50 /70	5.94 /61	0.00	1.00
FO	Forester Discovery Fund	INTLX	D+	(800) 388-0365	E- / 0.1	0.99	1.90	1.54 / 3	1.09 / 0	1.27 /22	0.64	N/A
IN	Forester Value Fund	FVALX	D	(800) 388-0365	D+ / 2.4	0.09	0.54	5.45 /17	8.61 /18	6.50 /64	0.58	1.35
EM	Forward Global Emerg Markets Inst	PTEMX	B	(800) 999-6809	A+ / 9.7	-5.00	3.60	31.25 /95	34.91 /98	24.37 /98	1.54	1.39
EM	Forward Global Emerg Markets Inv	PGERX	C	(800) 999-6809	A+ / 9.7	-5.02	3.51	30.96 /95	34.55 /98	--	1.35	1.69
GI	Forward Hoover Mini Cap Fd	FFHMX	C+	(800) 999-6809	C+ / 6.8	-8.47	6.18	18.78 /80	17.95 /72	--	0.00	1.79
GI	Forward Hoover Mini Cap Inst	FFMIX	U	(800) 999-6809	U /	-8.30	6.48	19.44 /81	--	--	0.00	1.23
SC	Forward Hoover Small Cap Eq A	FFHAX	U	(800) 999-6809	U /	-8.55	4.74	12.02 /60	--	--	0.00	1.69
SC	Forward Hoover Small Cap Eq Fd	FFSCX	B-	(800) 999-6809	B- / 7.3	-8.55	4.74	11.97 /59	19.28 /77	9.78 /80	0.00	1.69
SC	Forward Hoover Small Cap Eq Inst	FFHIX	B+	(800) 999-6809	B- / 7.5	-8.47	4.91	12.36 /61	19.76 /79	--	0.00	1.34
FO	Forward International Equity Fund	FFINX	B+	(800) 999-6809	A- / 9.0	-0.71	11.79	31.46 /95	22.87 /87	9.65 /79	0.04	1.69
FO	Forward Intl Small Comp Eq Inst	PTSCX	A-	(800) 999-6809	A+ / 9.8	-1.98	11.10	33.92 /96	35.08 /98	17.49 /94	0.59	1.26
RE	Forward Uniplan Real Estate Ret	FFREX	B-	(800) 999-6809	B+ / 8.8	-1.71	11.62	17.92 /79	23.51 /88	17.07 /94	0.80	1.59
MC	Fountainhead Special Value Fund	KINGX	C+	(800) 868-9535	C+ / 6.3	-4.18	-2.23	7.13 /27	17.06 /68	-0.61 /13	0.13	1.50
★ GR	● FPA Capital Fund Inc	FPPTX	C+	(800) 982-4372	C+ / 6.0	-3.60	1.14	9.79 /45	17.22 /69	14.20 /90	0.53	0.83
BA	● FPA Crescent Fund	FPACX	B+	(800) 982-4372	C / 5.5	0.57	5.76	12.35 /61	13.29 /50	13.08 /89	1.21	1.39
GI	FPA Paramount Fund Inc	FPRAX	B-	(800) 982-4372	C+ / 5.9	-5.01	1.03	11.04 /54	17.07 /68	11.49 /85	0.30	0.62
GR	FPA Perennial Fund Inc	FPPFX	B-	(800) 982-4372	C+ / 5.8	-5.38	0.79	10.71 /52	16.83 /67	11.56 /86	0.27	0.90
AG	Franklin Aggressive Growth Fd A	FGRAX	C	(800) 342-5236	C+ / 6.1	-7.13	3.08	18.46 /80	17.92 /72	2.43 /31	0.00	1.51
AG	Franklin Aggressive Growth Fd Adv	FRAAX	C+	(800) 321-8563	B- / 7.0	-7.04	3.20	18.72 /80	18.28 /73	2.72 /34	0.00	1.22
AG	Franklin Aggressive Growth Fd B	FKABX	C	(800) 342-5236	C+ / 6.1	-7.27	2.64	17.57 /78	17.10 /68	1.71 /25	0.00	2.21
AG	Franklin Aggressive Growth Fd C	FKACX	C	(800) 342-5236	C+ / 6.4	-7.28	2.71	17.60 /78	17.10 /68	1.72 /25	0.00	2.22
AG	Franklin Aggressive Growth Fd R	FKARX	C+	(800) 342-5236	C+ / 6.8	-7.14	2.92	18.18 /79	17.68 /71	2.21 /29	0.00	1.72
★ GI	● Franklin Balance Sheet Investmt A	FRBSX	A+	(800) 342-5236	B / 8.2	-0.74	8.73	17.11 /77	21.91 /85	13.55 /90	0.63	1.00
GI	● Franklin Balance Sheet Investmt Adv	FBSAX	A+	(800) 321-8563	B+ / 8.6	-0.69	8.86	17.39 /78	22.20 /86	13.81 /90	0.89	1.00

● Denotes fund is closed to new investors
★ Denotes fund is included in Section II

164

RISK	3 Year		NET ASSETS		ASSET					BULL / BEAR		FUND MANAGER		MINIMUMS		LOADS	
Risk Rating/Pts	Standard Deviation	Beta	NAV As of 6/30/06	Total $(Mil)	Cash %	Stocks %	Bonds %	Other %	Portfolio Turnover Ratio	Last Bull Market Return	Last Bear Market Return	Manager Quality Pct	Manager Tenure (Years)	Initial Purch. $	Additional Purch. $	Front End Load	Back End Load
C+ / 6.3	11.5	1.29	9.14	193	4	95	0	1	91.0	79.3	-11.4	33	6	1,000	0	5.8	0.0
C+ / 6.3	11.5	1.28	8.79	24	4	95	0	1	91.0	75.5	-11.5	28	6	1,000	0	0.0	4.0
B- / 7.0	7.8	1.00	21.33	427	0	99	0	1	55.0	52.5	-9.8	30	N/A	1,000	0	5.8	0.0
B / 8.4	7.2	0.91	8.81	46	1	98	0	1	60.0	51.8	-11.9	29	N/A	1,000	0	5.8	0.0
C+ / 6.7	9.0	0.83	7.59	258	2	97	0	1	104.0	84.1	-11.4	18	12	1,000	0	5.8	0.0
C+ / 6.7	9.0	0.83	6.99	14	2	97	0	1	104.0	79.7	-11.4	14	12	1,000	0	0.0	4.0
B- / 7.1	9.0	1.10	14.30	654	0	98	0	2	42.0	72.1	-9.2	53	N/A	1,000	0	5.8	0.0
C+ / 6.4	11.3	1.02	27.93	439	1	98	0	1	4.0	98.6	-11.1	35	N/A	1,000	0	5.8	0.0
C+ / 6.3	11.3	1.02	25.58	55	1	98	0	1	4.0	94.3	-11.3	30	N/A	1,000	0	0.0	4.0
C / 4.6	13.1	0.85	21.93	243	2	97	0	1	112.0	93.2	-12.4	48	N/A	1,000	0	5.8	0.0
C / 4.6	13.1	0.85	19.98	19	2	97	0	1	112.0	88.9	-12.5	39	N/A	1,000	0	0.0	4.0
B+ / 9.1	5.8	1.17	14.20	304	2	66	30	2	52.0	45.9	-4.7	50	N/A	1,000	0	5.8	0.0
B+ / 9.0	7.3	0.60	7.10	311	6	92	0	2	17.0	76.2	-5.7	82	10	1,000	0	5.8	0.0
D- / 1.2	20.1	1.91	3.53	38	13	86	0	1	55.0	88.8	-15.9	6	7	10,000	50	0.0	0.0
E / 0.3	23.7	2.50	3.89	14	8	91	0	1	23.0	86.8	-19.0	0	6	10,000	50	0.0	0.0
E / 0.3	26.6	2.47	9.66	35	18	79	0	3	41.0	70.4	-25.4	0	8	10,000	50	0.0	0.0
D / 1.9	18.9	1.95	18.68	84	N/A	N/A	0	N/A	43.0	98.3	-15.0	5	9	10,000	50	0.0	0.0
E+ / 0.7	23.3	2.16	34.63	452	3	96	0	1	42.0	130.2	-23.0	5	12	10,000	50	0.0	0.0
C+ / 6.0	11.9	1.29	7.37	18	4	94	1	1	181.0	71.2	-12.6	28	6	2,500	100	0.0	0.0
C+ / 6.4	10.9	1.20	8.66	17	11	85	2	2	202.0	69.5	-11.5	37	6	2,500	100	0.0	0.0
C+ / 6.4	8.4	1.00	5.30	49	5	92	1	2	145.0	56.8	-10.5	39	N/A	2,500	100	0.0	0.0
C+ / 6.3	10.1	1.19	17.59	16	1	97	1	1	171.0	65.9	-9.9	32	N/A	2,500	100	0.0	0.0
B / 8.0	9.1	0.49	19.99	22	0	99	0	1	28.0	85.8	-8.9	89	11	2,500	100	0.0	0.0
B- / 7.7	11.2	1.18	22.32	181	0	80	18	2	13.3	110.8	-9.0	98	8	10,000	1,000	0.0	0.0
C+ / 6.3	10.0	1.08	25.33	452	7	92	0	1	34.2	88.6	-8.4	85	25	1,000	100	0.0	0.0
C / 5.1	13.6	0.90	33.77	948	2	97	0	1	43.1	91.4	-12.6	27	9	1,000	100	0.0	0.0
B / 8.9	7.5	0.81	13.99	120	10	89	0	1	39.5	84.5	-8.0	96	5	1,000	100	0.0	0.0
B- / 7.6	9.4	0.99	7.38	34	8	91	0	1	8.3	92.7	-4.3	95	7	1,000	100	0.0	0.0
B+ / 9.9	1.1	-0.01	10.18	3	100	0	0	0	N/A	2.9	0.2	43	7	25,000	100	0.0	0.0
C+ / 6.3	11.4	-0.24	11.27	4	17	82	0	1	24.0	29.6	-0.2	98	7	2,500	100	0.0	0.0
C / 4.6	18.6	1.11	19.56	35	0	98	0	2	62.0	237.6	-5.0	20	11	100,000	100	0.0	2.0
D / 1.9	18.6	1.12	19.49	12	0	98	0	2	62.0	N/A	N/A	18	N/A	2,500	100	0.0	2.0
C+ / 6.7	14.3	1.41	18.91	13	5	94	0	1	277.0	125.0	N/A	81	3	2,500	100	0.0	2.0
U /	N/A	N/A	19.22	34	5	94	0	1	277.0	N/A	N/A	N/A	3	100,000	100	0.0	2.0
U /	N/A	N/A	20.33	25	2	96	0	2	190.0	N/A	N/A	N/A	N/A	2,500	100	4.8	2.0
C+ / 6.5	14.5	0.96	20.32	420	2	96	0	2	190.0	116.6	-7.2	69	8	2,500	100	0.0	2.0
B- / 7.3	14.5	0.96	20.74	53	2	96	0	2	190.0	119.6	-6.9	73	8	100,000	100	0.0	2.0
C+ / 6.1	12.2	1.13	16.78	29	1	98	0	1	138.0	130.2	-11.2	20	1	2,500	100	0.0	2.0
C / 5.5	14.2	1.24	16.82	242	4	95	0	1	91.0	228.9	-9.5	88	10	100,000	100	0.0	2.0
C / 4.9	15.6	0.93	18.53	45	1	98	0	1	21.0	104.1	-0.1	65	7	2,500	100	0.0	2.0
C+ / 6.6	11.4	0.76	21.13	17	0	100	0	0	95.0	124.1	-5.5	81	10	5,000	1,000	0.0	1.0
B- / 7.1	11.9	1.16	43.37	2,240	23	56	20	1	26.0	111.0	-13.5	90	22	1,500	100	5.3	2.0
B+ / 9.4	6.5	0.91	26.62	1,369	22	45	32	1	24.0	70.8	-4.3	95	13	1,500	100	0.0	2.0
B / 8.1	11.2	1.14	15.74	537	32	67	0	1	19.0	112.0	-16.5	90	6	1,500	100	5.3	2.0
B- / 7.9	10.9	1.11	34.66	588	31	68	0	1	9.0	105.9	-13.7	90	11	1,500	100	5.3	2.0
C+ / 5.8	13.9	1.56	17.07	105	4	96	0	0	94.3	109.9	-11.0	69	7	1,000	50	5.8	1.0
C+ / 5.8	13.9	1.56	17.44	70	4	96	0	0	94.3	111.8	-11.0	72	7	5,000,000	50	0.0	0.0
C+ / 5.8	13.9	1.56	16.33	18	4	96	0	0	94.3	105.3	-11.2	62	7	1,000	50	0.0	4.0
C+ / 5.8	14.0	1.56	16.30	29	4	96	0	0	94.3	105.0	-11.2	62	7	1,000	50	0.0	1.0
C+ / 5.8	13.9	1.56	16.90	5	4	96	0	0	94.3	108.5	-11.2	68	7	1,000	50	0.0	0.0
B / 8.3	10.1	1.15	67.12	4,421	14	86	0	0	3.9	111.9	-8.3	98	N/A	1,000	50	5.8	1.0
B / 8.3	10.1	1.15	67.22	305	14	86	0	0	3.9	113.5	-8.2	99	N/A	5,000,000	50	0.0	0.0

Fund Type	Fund Name	Ticker Symbol	Overall Weiss Investment Rating	Phone	Perfor-mance Rating/Pts	3 Mo	6 Mo	1Yr / Pct	3Yr / Pct (Annualized)	5Yr / Pct (Annualized)	Dividend Yield	Expense Ratio
GI	● Franklin Balance Sheet Investmt B	FBSBX	A+	(800) 342-5236	B / 8.1	-0.93	8.32	16.23 /75	20.98 /82	12.68 /88	0.00	2.00
GI	● Franklin Balance Sheet Investmt C	FCBSX	A+	(800) 342-5236	B+ / 8.3	-0.93	8.32	16.22 /75	20.98 /82	12.69 /88	0.00	2.00
GI	Franklin Balance Sheet Investmt R	FBSRX	A+	(800) 342-5236	B+ / 8.5	-0.82	8.57	16.79 /77	21.58 /84	13.25 /89	0.52	1.00
HL	Franklin Biotechnology Discovery A	FBDIX	E-	(800) 342-5236	E+ / 0.6	-12.70	-6.67	4.67 /14	8.21 /16	-3.46 / 4	0.00	1.29
GR	Franklin Blue Chip A	FKBCX	D	(800) 342-5236	D- / 1.1	-2.84	-0.40	4.28 /12	8.42 /17	0.80 /19	0.78	1.22
GR	● Franklin Blue Chip B	FKBBX	D	(800) 342-5236	D- / 1.1	-3.07	-0.75	3.48 / 9	7.65 /13	0.11 /16	0.06	2.07
GR	Franklin Blue Chip C	FBCCX	D	(800) 342-5236	D- / 1.5	-3.13	-0.75	3.50 / 9	7.63 /13	0.10 /16	0.08	1.92
GR	Franklin Blue Chip R	FBCRX	D	(800) 342-5236	D / 1.9	-2.99	-0.53	3.98 /10	8.18 /16	0.60 /18	0.58	1.42
GR	Franklin Capital Growth A	FKREX	D-	(800) 342-5236	E+ / 0.9	-3.45	0.54	6.74 /25	7.47 /12	-1.22 /11	0.33	0.98
GR	Franklin Capital Growth Adv	FEACX	D	(800) 321-8563	D / 1.9	-3.42	0.62	6.97 /26	7.72 /13	-0.97 /12	0.63	0.73
GR	● Franklin Capital Growth B	FKEQX	D-	(800) 342-5236	E+ / 0.9	-3.61	0.19	5.96 /20	6.67 / 9	-1.94 / 8	0.00	1.72
GR	Franklin Capital Growth C	FREQX	D	(800) 342-5236	D- / 1.2	-3.65	0.19	5.92 /20	6.67 / 9	-1.94 / 8	0.00	1.71
GR	Franklin Capital Growth R	FKIRX	D	(800) 342-5236	D / 1.6	-3.57	0.36	6.42 /23	7.21 /11	-1.45 /10	0.19	1.23
CV	Franklin Convertible Securities A	FISCX	C	(800) 342-5236	C / 4.6	-1.43	3.23	9.02 /40	13.73 /52	7.79 /71	3.32	1.00
CV	Franklin Convertible Securities C	FROTX	C+	(800) 342-5236	C / 4.9	-1.56	2.88	8.24 /35	12.88 /48	6.98 /67	2.83	2.00
TC	Franklin DynaTech A	FKDNX	E+	(800) 342-5236	D- / 1.5	-6.38	-3.90	6.26 /22	9.43 /24	3.41 /40	0.00	0.99
TC	● Franklin DynaTech B	FDNBX	E+	(800) 342-5236	D- / 1.3	-6.55	-4.28	5.46 /17	8.60 /18	2.63 /33	0.00	1.73
TC	Franklin DynaTech C	FDYNX	E+	(800) 342-5236	D / 1.7	-6.57	-4.29	5.48 /17	8.61 /19	2.64 /33	0.00	1.73
IN	Franklin Equity Inc A	FISEX	C	(800) 342-5236	C- / 3.3	0.70	4.09	7.66 /30	11.22 /37	4.34 /49	2.25	1.00
IN	● Franklin Equity Inc B	FBEIX	C-	(800) 342-5236	C- / 3.0	0.47	3.67	6.84 /25	10.39 /30	3.57 /42	1.67	2.00
IN	Franklin Equity Inc C	FRETX	C	(800) 342-5236	C- / 3.5	0.47	3.67	6.84 /25	10.38 /30	3.56 /42	1.67	2.00
IN	Franklin Equity Inc R	FREIX	C+	(800) 342-5236	C- / 4.1	0.59	3.96	7.39 /29	10.94 /35	4.09 /47	2.14	1.00
GR	Franklin Flex Cap Growth A	FKCGX	C-	(800) 342-5236	C- / 4.1	-5.18	0.65	10.07 /47	13.51 /51	3.62 /42	0.00	0.96
GR	Franklin Flex Cap Growth Adv		C	(800) 321-8563	C / 5.3	-5.12	0.77	10.32 /49	13.68 /52	3.71 /43	0.00	0.71
GR	Franklin Flex Cap Growth B	FKCBX	C-	(800) 342-5236	C- / 4.0	-5.35	0.29	9.24 /42	12.66 /47	2.85 /35	0.00	1.70
GR	Franklin Flex Cap Growth C	FCIIX	C-	(800) 342-5236	C / 4.5	-5.34	0.29	9.25 /42	12.67 /47	2.85 /35	0.00	1.71
GR	Franklin Flex Cap Growth R	FRCGX	C	(800) 342-5236	C / 5.0	-5.24	0.53	9.80 /46	13.22 /50	3.37 /40	0.00	1.21
TC	Franklin Global Communications A	FRGUX	C	(800) 342-5236	C+ / 6.7	-4.79	4.88	23.17 /86	17.61 /71	1.40 /23	0.86	1.47
TC	● Franklin Global Communications B		C	(800) 342-5236	C+ / 6.6	-5.01	4.47	22.25 /85	16.70 /67	0.65 /18	0.20	2.21
TC	Franklin Global Communications C	FRUTX	C	(800) 342-5236	C+ / 6.9	-5.01	4.47	22.16 /84	16.71 /67	0.62 /18	0.27	2.22
HL	Franklin Global Health Care A	FKGHX	E+	(800) 342-5236	D- / 1.4	-5.57	0.63	5.58 /18	9.12 /21	-1.27 /11	0.00	1.32
HL	● Franklin Global Health Care B	FGHBX	E+	(800) 342-5236	D- / 1.4	-5.75	0.24	4.77 /14	8.31 /17	-2.00 / 8	0.00	2.06
HL	Franklin Global Health Care C	FGIIX	E+	(800) 342-5236	D / 1.8	-5.76	0.24	4.76 /14	8.30 /17	-2.01 / 8	0.00	2.07
PM	Franklin Gold & Prec Metals A	FKRCX	D+	(800) 342-5236	A+ / 9.9	1.78	20.44	72.23 /99	33.32 /97	27.46 /99	0.48	0.96
PM	Franklin Gold & Prec Metals Adv	FGADX	D+	(800) 321-8563	A+ / 9.9	1.86	20.62	72.57 /99	33.63 /97	27.75 /99	0.63	0.71
PM	● Franklin Gold & Prec Metals B	FAGPX	D+	(800) 342-5236	A+ / 9.9	1.60	20.02	70.90 /99	32.30 /97	26.49 /99	0.06	0.96
PM	Franklin Gold & Prec Metals C	FRGOX	D+	(800) 342-5236	A+ / 9.9	1.58	20.04	70.95 /99	32.29 /97	26.51 /99	0.11	1.71
GR	Franklin Growth A	FKGRX	C	(800) 342-5236	C- / 3.7	-1.98	2.71	12.99 /64	12.75 /47	2.97 /36	0.16	0.93
GR	Franklin Growth Adv	FCGAX	C+	(800) 321-8563	C / 5.1	-1.93	2.84	13.28 /65	13.04 /49	3.23 /39	0.40	0.68
GR	● Franklin Growth B	FKGBX	C	(800) 342-5236	C- / 3.6	-2.16	2.34	12.17 /60	11.92 /42	2.21 /29	0.00	1.67
GR	Franklin Growth C	FRGSX	C	(800) 342-5236	C- / 4.2	-2.18	2.34	12.15 /60	11.91 /42	2.20 /29	0.00	1.67
GR	Franklin Growth R	FGSRX	C-	(800) 342-5236	C / 4.7	-2.05	2.61	12.73 /63	12.48 /46	2.72 /34	0.00	1.18
★ IN	Franklin Income A	FKINX	C	(800) 342-5236	C- / 3.4	1.88	6.42	5.95 /20	11.16 /37	9.29 /78	5.66	0.64
IN	Franklin Income Adv	FRIAX	C+	(800) 321-8563	C / 4.3	1.51	6.10	5.62 /18	11.20 /37	9.39 /78	6.03	0.49
IN	● Franklin Income B	FBICX	C	(800) 342-5236	D+ / 2.9	1.66	5.99	5.08 /15	10.11 /28	8.20 /72	5.10	1.48
IN	Franklin Income C	FCISX	C+	(800) 342-5236	C- / 3.6	1.75	6.13	4.97 /15	10.55 /31	8.70 /75	5.40	1.14
IN	Franklin Income R	FISRX	C+	(800) 342-5236	C- / 3.9	1.39	5.86	5.21 /16	10.73 /33	8.70 /75	5.64	0.99
FO	Franklin Intl Smaller Co Grw Adv	FKSCX	B+	(800) 321-8563	A+ / 9.9	-0.04	15.26	53.40 /99	40.64 /99	--	0.37	0.95
GI	Franklin Large Cap Value A	FLVAX	C	(800) 342-5236	C- / 3.1	-0.33	2.50	8.97 /40	10.99 /35	5.04 /55	0.92	1.31
GI	Franklin Large Cap Value Adv		D+	(800) 342-5236	C- / 3.5	-0.26	2.64	6.85 /25	10.19 /29	4.42 /50	1.34	0.96
GI	● Franklin Large Cap Value B	FBLCX	C	(800) 342-5236	D+ / 2.9	-0.53	2.11	8.26 /35	10.27 /29	4.38 /49	0.32	1.95
GI	Franklin Large Cap Value C	FLCVX	C+	(800) 342-5236	C- / 3.4	-0.53	2.11	8.28 /35	10.28 /29	4.37 /49	0.33	1.94

● Denotes fund is closed to new investors
★ Denotes fund is included in Section II

www.WeissRatings.com

RISK			NET ASSETS		ASSET				BULL / BEAR		FUND MANAGER		MINIMUMS		LOADS	
	3 Year		NAV													
	Standard		As of	Total	Cash	Stocks	Bonds	Other	Portfolio Turnover	Last Bull Market	Last Bear Market	Manager Quality	Manager Tenure	Initial Purch.	Additional Purch.	Front End	Back End
Risk Rating/Pts	Deviation	Beta	6/30/06	$(Mil)	%	%	%	%	Ratio	Return	Return	Pct	(Years)	$	$	Load	Load
B /8.3	10.1	1.15	66.16	129	14	86	0	0	3.9	106.9	-8.5	98	N/A	1,000	50	0.0	4.0
B /8.3	10.1	1.15	66.25	142	14	86	0	0	3.9	106.6	-8.3	98	N/A	1,000	50	0.0	1.0
B /8.3	10.1	1.15	66.73	48	14	86	0	0	3.9	110.3	-8.4	98	N/A	1,000	50	0.0	0.0
D /2.2	15.7	1.05	52.86	462	2	98	0	0	16.4	75.1	-11.4	24	9	1,000	50	5.8	1.0
B- /7.6	7.3	0.93	15.02	152	2	98	0	0	7.6	53.7	-9.2	33	8	1,000	50	5.8	1.0
B- /7.6	7.4	0.93	14.50	20	2	98	0	0	7.6	50.3	-9.3	28	N/A	1,000	50	0.0	4.0
B- /7.6	7.3	0.93	14.54	32	2	98	0	0	7.6	50.4	-9.3	28	N/A	1,000	50	0.0	1.0
B- /7.7	7.4	0.93	14.93	6	2	98	0	0	7.6	52.6	-9.2	32	N/A	1,000	50	0.0	0.0
B- /7.1	9.3	1.14	11.19	908	2	96	0	2	20.7	51.4	-9.3	16	N/A	1,000	50	5.8	1.0
B- /7.6	9.3	1.14	11.29	333	2	96	0	2	20.7	52.6	-9.2	17	N/A	5,000,000	50	0.0	0.0
B- /7.6	9.2	1.13	10.67	65	2	96	0	2	20.7	47.9	-9.5	12	N/A	1,000	50	0.0	4.0
B- /7.6	9.3	1.14	10.56	135	2	96	0	2	20.7	47.8	-9.5	12	N/A	1,000	50	0.0	1.0
B- /7.6	9.3	1.14	11.09	37	2	96	0	2	20.7	50.3	-9.3	14	N/A	1,000	50	0.0	0.0
B- /7.4	7.0	1.04	16.43	671	4	4	0	92	35.3	75.6	-2.0	95	8	1,000	50	5.8	0.0
B- /7.9	7.0	1.04	16.30	256	4	4	0	92	35.3	71.4	-2.2	93	8	1,000	50	0.0	1.0
C /5.3	12.4	1.41	25.11	591	0	100	0	0	17.3	63.5	-7.9	14	38	1,000	50	5.8	0.0
C /5.2	12.4	1.41	24.13	20	0	100	0	0	17.3	59.5	-8.0	10	N/A	1,000	50	0.0	4.0
C /5.2	12.4	1.41	23.88	71	0	100	0	0	17.3	59.6	-8.0	11	N/A	1,000	50	0.0	1.0
B /8.3	7.2	0.86	21.07	666	2	94	4	0	38.1	63.5	-11.2	69	18	1,000	50	5.8	0.0
B /8.4	7.2	0.86	20.97	50	2	94	4	0	38.1	59.7	-11.3	61	7	1,000	50	0.0	4.0
B /8.4	7.2	0.86	20.98	166	2	94	4	0	38.1	59.7	-11.4	61	11	1,000	50	0.0	1.0
B /8.4	7.2	0.86	21.08	19	2	94	4	0	38.1	62.2	-11.2	67	N/A	1,000	50	0.0	0.0
C+ /6.7	11.3	1.31	40.44	1,972	6	92	0	2	32.8	78.7	-6.8	49	N/A	1,000	50	5.8	1.0
B- /7.1	11.3	1.31	40.62	261	6	92	0	2	32.8	79.4	-6.8	52	N/A	5,000,000	50	0.0	0.0
C+ /6.6	11.3	1.31	38.19	132	6	92	0	2	32.8	74.5	-7.0	40	N/A	1,000	50	0.0	4.0
C+ /6.6	11.3	1.31	38.27	366	6	92	0	2	32.8	74.5	-6.9	40	N/A	1,000	50	0.0	1.0
C+ /6.7	11.3	1.31	40.00	86	6	92	0	2	32.8	77.2	-6.8	46	N/A	1,000	50	0.0	0.0
C /5.3	13.9	1.48	10.53	63	0	98	0	2	72.0	115.6	-11.4	73	N/A	1,000	50	5.8	1.0
C /5.2	13.9	1.48	10.04	3	0	98	0	2	72.0	110.6	-11.4	66	N/A	1,000	50	0.0	4.0
C /5.2	13.9	1.48	10.05	9	0	98	0	2	72.0	110.5	-11.5	66	N/A	1,000	50	0.0	1.0
C /5.2	9.1	0.85	22.53	100	8	92	0	0	21.7	64.6	-9.3	47	12	1,000	50	5.8	1.0
C /5.2	9.1	0.85	21.32	13	8	92	0	0	21.7	60.8	-9.5	38	7	1,000	50	0.0	4.0
C /5.2	9.1	0.85	21.11	26	8	92	0	0	21.7	60.8	-9.5	38	10	1,000	50	0.0	1.0
E- /0.0	31.0	1.48	30.88	855	4	94	0	2	11.3	183.8	10.3	73	9	1,000	50	5.8	1.0
E- /0.0	31.1	1.48	31.71	61	4	94	0	2	11.3	186.0	10.3	75	9	5,000,000	50	0.0	0.0
E- /0.0	31.0	1.48	29.85	61	4	94	0	2	11.3	177.0	10.1	66	9	1,000	50	0.0	4.0
E- /0.0	31.1	1.48	30.13	219	4	94	0	2	11.3	177.1	10.1	66	9	1,000	50	0.0	1.0
B /8.1	9.4	1.12	37.55	1,650	1	98	0	1	1.2	73.5	-10.9	60	41	1,000	50	5.8	1.0
B /8.1	9.4	1.12	37.60	258	1	98	0	1	1.2	74.8	-10.9	63	41	5,000,000	50	0.0	0.0
B /8.0	9.4	1.12	36.23	123	1	98	0	1	1.2	69.4	-11.1	51	41	1,000	50	0.0	4.0
B /8.0	9.4	1.12	35.91	271	1	98	0	1	1.2	69.4	-11.1	51	41	1,000	50	0.0	1.0
C+ /5.9	9.4	1.12	37.29	36	1	98	0	1	1.2	72.1	-11.0	57	41	1,000	50	0.0	0.0
B /8.8	5.9	0.50	2.48	23,999	2	37	47	14	28.5	59.5	0.2	91	49	1,000	50	4.3	1.0
B+ /9.1	6.0	0.52	2.46	3,327	2	37	47	14	28.5	59.6	0.7	90	49	5,000,000	50	0.0	0.0
B+ /9.1	5.8	0.50	2.47	3,658	2	37	47	14	28.5	54.8	0.5	86	N/A	1,000	50	0.0	4.0
B+ /9.2	5.9	0.49	2.49	10,862	2	37	47	14	28.5	56.6	0.1	88	11	1,000	50	0.0	1.0
B+ /9.1	6.0	0.52	2.45	160	2	37	47	14	28.5	57.6	0.6	88	49	1,000	50	0.0	0.0
C /4.9	13.9	1.14	26.43	48	4	95	0	1	30.9	250.3	-3.3	99	4	5,000,000	50	0.0	0.0
B /8.8	6.4	0.78	15.19	168	10	89	0	1	25.3	62.9	-8.8	73	6	1,000	50	5.8	0.0
C+ /6.8	6.6	0.80	15.18	2	10	89	0	1	25.3	59.3	-8.8	65	1	5,000,000	50	0.0	0.0
B+ /9.3	6.4	0.79	15.02	21	10	89	0	1	25.3	59.6	-9.0	67	6	1,000	50	0.0	4.0
B+ /9.3	6.4	0.79	15.02	58	10	89	0	1	25.3	59.3	-8.8	67	6	1,000	50	0.0	1.0

Fund Type	Fund Name	Ticker Symbol	Overall Weiss Investment Rating	Phone	Performance Rating/Pts	3 Mo	6 Mo	1Yr / Pct	Annualized 3Yr / Pct	5Yr / Pct	Dividend Yield	Expense Ratio
GI	Franklin Large Cap Value R	FLCRX	C+	(800) 342-5236	C- / 4.0	-0.40	2.38	8.75 /38	10.83 /34	4.88 /53	0.92	1.46
SC ●	Franklin MicroCap Value A	FRMCX	A+	(800) 342-5236	B+ / 8.3	-2.01	9.41	19.63 /81	22.28 /86	16.26 /93	0.42	1.00
SC	Franklin MicroCap Value Adv		B+	(800) 342-5236	B+ / 8.7	-1.96	9.54	19.53 /81	22.15 /85	16.18 /93	0.44	0.87
MC	Franklin MidCap Value A	FMVAX	U	(800) 342-5236	U /	-1.37	4.85	--	--	--	0.00	1.40
EN	Franklin Natural Resources A	FRNRX	B-	(800) 342-5236	A+ / 9.7	2.51	11.09	34.56 /96	33.23 /97	16.17 /93	0.26	1.08
EN	Franklin Natural Resources Adv	FNRAX	B-	(800) 321-8563	A+ / 9.8	2.60	11.28	35.01 /97	33.70 /97	16.60 /94	0.35	0.73
RE	Franklin Real Estate Sec A	FREEX	C	(800) 342-5236	B / 7.6	-5.23	2.39	8.12 /34	21.93 /85	16.69 /94	2.09	0.92
RE	Franklin Real Estate Sec Adv	FRLAX	C	(800) 321-8563	B / 8.2	-5.21	2.51	8.36 /36	22.24 /86	16.97 /94	2.36	0.67
RE ●	Franklin Real Estate Sec B	FBREX	C-	(800) 342-5236	B- / 7.5	-5.42	2.00	7.32 /28	21.02 /83	15.82 /93	1.74	1.66
RE	Franklin Real Estate Sec C	FRRSX	C	(800) 342-5236	B / 7.8	-5.41	2.01	7.32 /28	21.04 /83	15.81 /93	1.76	1.67
IN	Franklin Real Return A	FRRAX	U	(800) 342-5236	U /	1.49	2.71	5.30 /17	--	--	4.09	1.00
GI	Franklin Rising Dividends A	FRDPX	C	(800) 342-5236	C- / 3.3	-2.07	5.10	10.67 /51	11.01 /36	8.52 /74	0.96	1.09
GI	Franklin Rising Dividends Adv	FRDAX	C-	(800) 321-8563	C / 4.4	-2.05	5.20	10.82 /52	11.06 /36	8.55 /74	1.26	0.78
GI ●	Franklin Rising Dividends B	FRDBX	C	(800) 342-5236	C- / 3.1	-2.27	4.70	9.83 /46	10.29 /29	7.87 /71	0.28	1.77
GI	Franklin Rising Dividends C	FRDTX	C	(800) 342-5236	C- / 3.8	-2.27	4.71	9.84 /46	10.30 /29	7.87 /71	0.31	1.75
GI	Franklin Rising Dividends R	FRDRX	C+	(800) 342-5236	C- / 4.2	-2.14	4.95	10.41 /50	10.85 /34	8.41 /73	0.79	1.28
SC ●	Franklin Small Cap Growth II A	FSGRX	C-	(800) 342-5236	C+ / 5.6	-7.17	4.69	10.78 /52	15.84 /63	4.26 /48	0.00	1.15
SC ●	Franklin Small Cap Growth II Adv	FSSAX	C-	(800) 321-8563	C+ / 6.3	-7.11	4.77	11.03 /54	16.09 /64	4.55 /51	0.00	0.91
SC ●	Franklin Small Cap Growth II B	FBSGX	D+	(800) 342-5236	C / 5.4	-7.32	4.29	9.93 /46	14.97 /59	3.52 /41	0.00	1.91
SC ●	Franklin Small Cap Growth II C	FCSGX	C-	(800) 342-5236	C+ / 5.9	-7.32	4.20	9.93 /46	14.92 /58	3.50 /41	0.00	1.91
SC ●	Franklin Small Cap Growth II R	FSSRX	C-	(800) 342-5236	C+ / 6.2	-7.25	4.49	10.44 /50	15.53 /61	4.00 /46	0.00	1.41
SC	Franklin Small Cap Value A	FRVLX	A-	(800) 342-5236	B+ / 8.3	-2.16	10.46	17.99 /79	21.99 /85	12.65 /88	0.20	1.29
SC	Franklin Small Cap Value Adv	FVADX	A	(800) 321-8563	B+ / 8.7	-2.06	10.64	18.39 /80	22.41 /86	13.04 /89	0.50	1.00
SC ●	Franklin Small Cap Value B	FBVAX	A-	(800) 342-5236	B / 8.2	-2.31	10.10	17.22 /78	21.20 /83	11.93 /86	0.00	2.00
SC	Franklin Small Cap Value C	FRVFX	A	(800) 342-5236	B+ / 8.4	-2.31	10.10	17.23 /78	21.20 /83	11.91 /86	0.00	2.00
SC	Franklin Small Cap Value R	FVFRX	A	(800) 342-5236	B+ / 8.6	-2.19	10.34	17.79 /79	21.81 /85	12.47 /88	0.01	1.00
★ MC	Franklin Small-Mid Cap Growth A	FRSGX	C-	(800) 342-5236	C / 4.7	-5.97	1.06	11.55 /57	14.46 /56	2.70 /34	0.11	0.97
MC	Franklin Small-Mid Cap Growth Adv	FSGAX	C	(800) 321-8563	C+ / 5.9	-5.92	1.18	11.83 /59	14.74 /58	2.95 /36	0.37	0.72
MC	Franklin Small-Mid Cap Growth B	FBSMX	C-	(800) 342-5236	C / 4.6	-6.18	0.68	10.71 /52	13.59 /52	--	0.00	1.72
MC	Franklin Small-Mid Cap Growth C	FRSIX	C	(800) 342-5236	C / 5.1	-6.17	0.67	10.73 /52	13.61 /52	1.94 /27	0.00	1.72
MC	Franklin Small-Mid Cap Growth R	FSMRX	C	(800) 342-5236	C+ / 5.6	-6.06	0.91	11.25 /55	14.17 /55	2.43 /31	0.06	1.22
TC	Franklin Technology A	FTCAX	E+	(800) 342-5236	C- / 3.7	-10.54	-0.20	10.41 /50	13.08 /49	-3.65 / 4	0.00	1.73
TC	Franklin Technology Adv	FRTCX	D-	(800) 321-8563	C / 4.9	-10.52	0.00	10.90 /53	13.39 /51	-3.34 / 5	0.00	1.42
TC ●	Franklin Technology B		E+	(800) 342-5236	C- / 3.5	-10.58	-0.41	9.87 /46	12.30 /44	-4.26 / 3	0.00	2.40
TC	Franklin Technology C	FFTCX	E+	(800) 342-5236	C- / 4.0	-10.79	-0.61	9.66 /45	12.25 /44	-4.30 / 3	0.00	2.42
TC	Franklin Technology R	FTERX	D-	(800) 342-5236	C / 4.6	-10.44	-0.20	10.48 /50	12.86 /48	-3.78 / 4	0.00	1.92
GL	Franklin Templeton Conserv Tgt A	FTCIX	C-	(800) 342-5236	D / 1.6	-0.92	3.20	7.86 /32	8.45 /17	5.44 /57	2.57	1.31
GL	Franklin Templeton Conserv Tgt Adv		C+	(800) 321-8563	D+ / 2.6	-0.85	3.39	7.98 /33	8.49 /18	5.46 /58	2.91	1.28
GL	Franklin Templeton Conserv Tgt C	FTCCX	C	(800) 342-5236	D / 1.9	-1.11	2.92	7.09 /27	7.64 /13	4.67 /52	2.04	2.06
GL	Franklin Templeton Conserv Tgt R	FTCRX	C	(800) 342-5236	D+ / 2.5	-0.99	3.16	7.67 /30	8.20 /16	5.19 /56	2.46	1.56
GL	Franklin Templeton Corefl Allc A	FTCOX	U	(800) 342-5236	U /	-1.44	3.60	11.74 /58	--	--	0.77	1.30
GL ●	Franklin Templeton Corefl Allc B	FBCOX	U	(800) 342-5236	U /	-1.61	3.31	11.02 /54	--	--	0.18	1.90
GL	Franklin Templeton Corefl Allc C	FTCLX	U	(800) 342-5236	U /	-1.61	3.23	10.98 /53	--	--	0.29	1.95
GL	Franklin Templeton Foundng Allc A	FFALX	U	(800) 342-5236	U /	0.39	5.76	10.82 /52	--	--	2.23	1.25
GL ●	Franklin Templeton Foundng Allc B	FFABX	U	(800) 342-5236	U /	0.23	5.45	10.17 /48	--	--	1.68	1.90
GL	Franklin Templeton Foundng Allc C	FFACX	U	(800) 342-5236	U /	0.16	5.41	10.19 /48	--	--	2.42	1.90
GL	Franklin Templeton Growth Tgt A	FGTIX	C+	(800) 342-5236	C / 5.0	-2.38	4.88	13.50 /66	14.08 /54	5.76 /59	1.29	1.00
GL	Franklin Templeton Growth Tgt Adv		C	(800) 321-8563	C+ / 6.0	-2.25	5.07	13.71 /67	14.15 /55	5.80 /60	1.48	1.44
GL	Franklin Templeton Growth Tgt C	FTGTX	C+	(800) 342-5236	C / 5.4	-2.54	4.52	12.70 /63	13.22 /50	4.96 /54	0.99	2.00
GL	Franklin Templeton Growth Tgt R	FGTRX	B-	(800) 342-5236	C+ / 5.8	-2.40	4.80	13.23 /65	13.82 /53	5.50 /58	1.21	1.00
FS	Franklin Templeton Hard Curr A	ICPHX	D	(800) 342-5236	D / 1.9	4.05	6.67	7.93 /32	6.60 / 9	10.28 /81	6.80	1.00
FS	Franklin Templeton Hard Curr Adv	ICHHX	D+	(800) 321-8563	D+ / 2.6	4.23	6.78	8.28 /35	7.00 /10	10.68 /83	7.16	1.00

● Denotes fund is closed to new investors
★ Denotes fund is included in Section II

RISK			NET ASSETS		ASSET				Portfolio Turnover Ratio	BULL / BEAR		FUND MANAGER		MINIMUMS		LOADS	
Risk Rating/Pts	3 Year Standard Deviation	Beta	NAV As of 6/30/06	Total $(Mil)	Cash %	Stocks %	Bonds %	Other %		Last Bull Market Return	Last Bear Market Return	Manager Quality Pct	Manager Tenure (Years)	Initial Purch. $	Additional Purch. $	Front End Load	Back End Load
B+ / 9.3	6.5	0.79	15.07	8	10	89	0	1	25.3	62.1	-8.8	71	N/A	1,000	50	0.0	0.0
B / 8.7	9.0	0.54	40.47	477	16	80	2	2	13.9	106.9	-3.3	99	11	1,000	50	5.8	1.0
C+ / 6.4	9.0	0.54	40.54	6	16	80	2	2	13.9	106.2	-3.3	99	1	5,000,000	50	0.0	0.0
U /	N/A	N/A	10.81	32	2	96	0	2	N/A	N/A	N/A	N/A	1	1,000	50	5.8	1.0
C- / 4.1	20.1	0.99	34.67	429	4	96	0	0	32.5	170.1	-2.5	65	11	1,000	50	5.8	1.0
C- / 4.2	20.1	0.99	36.29	42	4	96	0	0	32.5	173.4	-2.4	69	N/A	5,000,000	50	0.0	0.0
C- / 3.9	14.5	0.86	26.20	765	6	94	0	0	8.2	117.7	0.2	66	N/A	1,000	50	5.8	0.0
C- / 3.9	14.5	0.86	26.30	45	6	94	0	0	8.2	119.5	0.2	69	N/A	5,000,000	50	0.0	0.0
C- / 3.8	14.5	0.86	25.88	66	6	94	0	0	8.2	112.5	N/A	57	N/A	1,000	50	0.0	4.0
C- / 3.8	14.5	0.86	25.76	177	6	94	0	0	8.2	112.6	N/A	57	N/A	1,000	50	0.0	0.0
U /	N/A	N/A	10.05	31	2	12	84	2	8.9	N/A	N/A	N/A	N/A	1,000	50	4.3	0.0
B / 8.2	7.6	0.88	34.03	1,594	2	98	0	0	3.6	60.3	-7.3	65	19	1,000	50	5.8	0.0
C+ / 6.3	7.6	0.88	33.99	28	2	98	0	0	3.6	60.5	-7.3	66	N/A	5,000,000	50	0.0	0.0
B / 8.6	7.6	0.89	33.65	280	2	98	0	0	3.6	57.2	-7.5	58	10	1,000	50	0.0	4.0
B / 8.6	7.6	0.88	33.60	530	2	98	0	0	3.6	57.1	-7.5	58	11	1,000	50	0.0	0.0
B / 8.6	7.6	0.88	33.91	43	2	98	0	0	3.6	59.7	-7.4	64	19	1,000	50	0.0	0.0
C / 5.1	16.4	1.06	12.95	628	0	100	0	0	18.6	100.0	-9.3	23	6	1,000	50	5.8	0.0
C / 5.1	16.4	1.06	13.19	312	0	100	0	0	18.6	101.3	-9.2	25	6	5,000,000	50	0.0	1.0
C / 4.9	16.5	1.07	12.40	100	0	100	0	0	18.6	95.0	-9.4	18	6	1,000	50	0.0	4.0
C / 4.9	16.4	1.06	12.40	148	0	100	0	0	18.6	95.2	-9.5	18	6	1,000	50	0.0	0.0
C / 5.0	16.4	1.06	12.80	6	0	100	0	0	18.6	98.4	-9.4	21	6	1,000	50	0.0	0.0
B- / 7.3	13.0	0.80	44.45	663	14	86	0	0	12.7	123.9	-10.0	95	10	1,000	50	5.8	0.0
B- / 7.3	13.0	0.80	45.56	50	14	86	0	0	12.7	126.3	-10.0	96	10	5,000,000	50	0.0	0.0
B- / 7.3	13.0	0.80	42.74	83	14	86	0	0	12.7	119.4	-10.2	94	7	1,000	50	0.0	4.0
B- / 7.3	13.0	0.80	42.31	231	14	86	0	0	12.7	119.2	-10.1	94	10	1,000	50	0.0	0.0
B- / 7.3	13.0	0.80	44.28	48	14	86	0	0	12.7	122.7	-10.1	95	10	1,000	50	0.0	0.0
C+ / 6.6	12.5	1.11	38.12	5,937	2	96	0	2	18.5	89.1	-9.5	15	14	1,000	50	5.8	1.0
C+ / 6.6	12.5	1.11	38.62	770	2	96	0	2	18.5	90.6	-9.4	16	14	5,000,000	50	0.0	0.0
C+ / 6.5	12.5	1.11	37.02	33	2	96	0	2	18.5	84.6	-9.6	11	4	1,000	50	0.0	4.0
C+ / 6.5	12.5	1.11	36.03	668	2	96	0	2	18.5	84.8	-9.7	11	11	1,000	50	0.0	1.0
C+ / 6.6	12.5	1.11	37.69	96	2	96	0	2	18.5	87.6	-9.5	13	14	1,000	50	0.0	0.0
C- / 3.5	18.6	1.94	5.09	29	10	90	0	0	41.2	90.3	-9.9	9	N/A	1,000	50	5.8	0.0
C- / 3.6	18.6	1.94	5.19	3	10	90	0	0	41.2	92.1	-9.6	10	N/A	5,000,000	50	0.0	0.0
C- / 3.3	18.8	1.97	4.90	4	10	90	0	0	41.2	86.7	-10.1	6	N/A	1,000	50	0.0	4.0
C- / 3.4	18.5	1.93	4.88	9	10	90	0	0	41.2	86.7	-10.1	7	N/A	1,000	50	0.0	1.0
C- / 3.5	18.6	1.95	5.06	4	10	90	0	0	41.2	89.9	-10.0	8	N/A	1,000	50	0.0	0.0
B+ / 9.5	4.6	0.89	12.92	174	18	41	39	2	8.2	40.6	-1.3	71	10	1,000	50	5.8	1.0
B+ / 9.9	4.6	0.89	12.91	1	18	41	39	2	8.2	40.7	-1.3	72	10	5,000,000	50	0.0	0.0
B+ / 9.6	4.7	0.89	12.78	69	18	41	39	2	8.2	37.2	-1.5	64	10	1,000	50	0.0	1.0
B+ / 9.6	4.6	0.89	12.90	12	18	41	39	2	8.2	39.6	-1.4	69	10	1,000	50	0.0	0.0
U /	N/A	N/A	12.98	396	N/A	100	0	N/A	2.5	N/A	N/A	N/A	3	1,000	50	5.8	1.0
U /	N/A	N/A	12.85	72	N/A	100	0	N/A	2.5	N/A	N/A	N/A	3	1,000	50	0.0	4.0
U /	N/A	N/A	12.83	147	N/A	100	0	N/A	2.5	N/A	N/A	N/A	3	1,000	50	0.0	1.0
U /	N/A	N/A	12.99	5,252	0	66	33	1	0.7	N/A	N/A	N/A	3	1,000	50	5.8	1.0
U /	N/A	N/A	12.91	703	0	66	33	1	0.7	N/A	N/A	N/A	3	1,000	50	0.0	4.0
U /	N/A	N/A	12.80	2,639	0	66	33	1	0.7	N/A	N/A	N/A	3	1,000	50	0.0	1.0
B / 8.0	8.3	1.51	14.75	285	4	80	14	2	10.5	75.5	-5.9	87	10	1,000	50	5.8	1.0
C+ / 6.3	8.3	1.50	14.76	4	4	80	14	2	10.5	75.7	-5.9	87	10	5,000,000	50	0.0	0.0
B / 8.0	8.3	1.50	14.57	105	4	80	14	2	10.5	71.2	-5.9	82	10	1,000	50	0.0	1.0
B / 8.0	8.4	1.51	14.65	22	4	80	14	2	10.5	74.1	-5.8	85	10	1,000	50	0.0	0.0
B- / 7.1	6.6	0.24	9.39	292	88	0	12	0	N/A	27.8	8.8	73	8	1,000	50	2.3	1.0
B- / 7.0	6.6	0.24	9.41	28	88	0	12	0	N/A	29.2	9.0	77	8	5,000,000	50	0.0	0.0

Data as of June 30, 2006

Fund Type	Fund Name	Ticker Symbol	Overall Weiss Investment Rating	Phone	Perfor-mance Rating/Pts	3 Mo	6 Mo	1Yr / Pct	3Yr / Pct	5Yr / Pct	Dividend Yield	Expense Ratio
								Total Return % through 6/30/06	Annualized		Incl. in Returns	
GL	Franklin Templeton Moderate Tgt A	FMTIX	C	(800) 342-5236	D+ / 2.9	-1.49	3.83	9.86 /46	10.68 /33	5.83 /60	2.20	1.38
GL	Franklin Templeton Moderate Tgt Adv		C+	(800) 321-8563	C- / 4.2	-1.35	4.04	10.14 /48	10.78 /33	5.88 /60	2.51	1.34
GL	● Franklin Templeton Moderate Tgt B	FBMTX	U	(800) 342-5236	U /	-1.62	3.45	8.98 /40	--	--	1.61	2.13
GL	Franklin Templeton Moderate Tgt C	FTMTX	C	(800) 342-5236	C- / 3.3	-1.63	3.43	9.05 /40	9.88 /27	5.05 /55	1.66	2.13
GL	Franklin Templeton Moderate Tgt R	FTMRX	C+	(800) 342-5236	C- / 3.8	-1.49	3.76	9.57 /44	10.43 /30	5.58 /58	2.07	1.63
GL	Franklin Templeton Persptv Allc A	FPAAX	U	(800) 342-5236	U /	-1.87	3.96	12.41 /62	--	--	0.99	1.31
GL	Franklin Templeton Persptv Allc C	FPCAX	U	(800) 342-5236	U /	-1.96	3.63	11.71 /58	--	--	0.71	1.96
GR	Franklin U.S. Long-Short A	FUSLX	D	(800) 342-5236	E- / 0.0	-2.61	-2.43	0.63 / 2	0.56 / 0	-1.33 /11	0.86	1.75
UT	Franklin Utilities A	FKUTX	B-	(800) 342-5236	C+ / 5.8	4.51	5.55	5.45 /17	15.60 /62	8.11 /72	3.21	0.80
UT	Franklin Utilities Adv	FRUAX	B	(800) 321-8563	C+ / 6.5	4.52	5.60	5.56 /18	15.75 /62	8.27 /73	3.46	0.65
UT	● Franklin Utilities B	FRUBX	B-	(800) 342-5236	C+ / 5.6	4.30	5.21	4.84 /14	14.99 /59	7.55 /69	2.86	1.28
UT	Franklin Utilities C	FRUSX	B	(800) 342-5236	C+ / 6.0	4.31	5.23	4.87 /14	15.01 /59	7.57 /70	2.88	1.28
UT	Franklin Utilities R	FRURX	B+	(800) 342-5236	C+ / 6.2	4.34	5.31	4.97 /15	15.20 /60	7.73 /70	3.06	1.13
CV	Froley Revy Convertible Sec A	FRCVX	E+	(888) 823-2867	E / 0.3	-4.06	-0.65	5.31 /17	4.55 / 3	2.23 /29	3.94	1.50
SC	Frontegra IronBridge Small Cap Fund	IBSCX	C	(888) 825-2100	C+ / 6.6	-4.45	6.29	14.20 /69	15.46 /61	--	0.00	1.10
EM	Frontegra New Star Intl Equity Fd	FRNSX	U	(888) 825-2100	U /	-0.38	7.74	19.36 /81	--	--	0.54	0.75
SC	Frontier Fund-Equity	FEFPX	E-	(800) 231-2901	E- / 0.0	-20.83	5.56	-17.39 / 0	-15.06 / 0	-35.18 / 0	0.00	10.97
FO	FTI European Smaller Companies	FESCX	B+	(888) 343-8242	A+ / 9.9	1.17	25.21	45.14 /98	34.94 /98	13.74 /90	0.21	1.43
GI	FTI Large Cap Growth and Income	FLCIX	C-	(888) 343-8242	C- / 4.0	-3.11	1.61	7.95 /32	11.24 /37	3.23 /39	0.51	1.01
SC	FTI Small Capitalization Equity	FTSCX	E+	(888) 343-8242	C- / 4.2	-11.49	4.16	10.65 /51	11.75 /41	-0.37 /14	0.00	1.30
GR	Fund *X Aggressive Upgrader Fund	HOTFX	B	(866) 455-3863	B / 7.6	-3.35	5.76	20.20 /82	19.37 /77	--	0.91	1.50
GR	Fund *X Conservative Upgrader Fund	RELAX	B-	(866) 455-3863	C+ / 5.7	-2.25	4.63	11.21 /55	14.28 /55	--	1.08	1.50
GR	Fund *X Flexible Income Fund	INCMX	C-	(866) 455-3863	E+ / 0.9	-0.07	2.26	3.92 /10	5.74 / 6	--	3.84	0.99
GR	Fund *X Upgrader Fund	FUNDX	B+	(866) 455-3863	B- / 7.4	-2.38	6.28	17.87 /79	17.97 /72	--	0.42	1.27
AA	Gabelli ABC Fund	GABCX	C	(800) 422-3554	D / 2.1	2.43	6.90	10.32 /49	5.77 / 6	4.29 /49	1.38	0.62
GR	Gabelli Asset A	GATAX	B	(800) 422-3554	C+ / 5.9	0.91	8.29	11.48 /57	15.50 /61	7.12 /67	0.34	1.38
GR	Gabelli Asset B	GATBX	B	(800) 422-3554	C+ / 5.8	0.73	7.95	10.72 /52	14.89 /58	6.78 /66	0.00	2.13
GR	Gabelli Asset C	GATCX	B+	(800) 422-3554	C+ / 6.2	0.71	7.89	10.63 /51	14.84 /58	6.75 /65	0.13	2.13
★ GR	Gabelli Asset Fd	GABAX	B	(800) 422-3554	C+ / 6.5	0.93	8.29	11.47 /56	15.56 /62	7.15 /67	0.25	1.38
GR	Gabelli Blue Chip Value A	GBCAX	C+	(800) 422-3554	C / 5.1	0.00	5.38	11.01 /54	14.23 /55	1.69 /25	0.00	1.38
GR	Gabelli Blue Chip Value AAA	GABBX	B	(800) 422-3554	C+ / 5.9	-0.08	5.32	10.86 /53	14.09 /54	1.62 /24	0.00	1.89
GR	Gabelli Blue Chip Value B	GBCBX	C+	(800) 422-3554	C / 4.9	-0.30	4.97	10.09 /48	13.47 /51	1.29 /22	0.00	2.13
GR	Gabelli Blue Chip Value C	GBCCX	B-	(800) 422-3554	C / 5.5	-0.30	4.89	10.10 /48	13.44 /51	1.27 /22	0.00	2.13
MC	Gabelli Capital Asset Fund		B	(800) 422-3554	C+ / 6.6	0.32	8.79	11.80 /58	15.22 /60	7.26 /68	0.25	1.10
AG	Gabelli Comstck Partners Cap Val A	DRCVX	E-	(800) 422-3554	E- / 0.0	4.27	-1.21	-8.86 / 0	-13.99 / 0	-4.56 / 3	1.88	1.97
AG	Gabelli Comstck Partners Cap Val B	DCVBX	E-	(800) 422-3554	E- / 0.0	3.93	-1.24	-9.35 / 0	-14.59 / 0	-5.27 / 2	1.32	2.67
AG	Gabelli Comstock Partners Cap Val C	CPCCX	E-	(800) 422-3554	E- / 0.0	4.11	-1.30	-9.35 / 0	-14.59 / 0	-5.27 / 2	1.39	2.71
AG	Gabelli Comstock Partners Cap Val R	CPCRX	E-	(800) 422-3554	E- / 0.0	4.27	-0.81	-8.67 / 0	-13.78 / 0	-4.44 / 3	2.18	1.66
AG	Gabelli Comstock Partners Strat A	CPFAX	E-	(800) 422-3554	E- / 0.0	0.18	-4.29	-10.77 / 0	-11.71 / 0	-5.88 / 2	2.10	2.34
AG	Gabelli Comstock Partners Strat C	CPFCX	E-	(800) 422-3554	E- / 0.0	0.05	-4.70	-11.71 / 0	-12.47 / 0	-6.61 / 1	1.26	3.08
AG	● Gabelli Comstock Partners Strat O	CPSFX	E-	(800) 422-3554	E- / 0.0	0.23	-4.29	-10.66 / 0	-11.47 / 0	-5.62 / 2	2.74	1.10
IN	Gabelli Equity Income A	GCAEX	B	(800) 422-3554	C / 5.0	1.35	6.93	11.60 /57	13.77 /53	8.13 /72	1.73	1.41
IN	Gabelli Equity Income B	GCBEX	B-	(800) 422-3554	C / 4.9	1.16	6.58	10.79 /52	13.09 /49	7.74 /70	1.86	2.16
IN	Gabelli Equity Income C	GCCEX	B	(800) 422-3554	C / 5.5	1.16	6.58	10.85 /53	13.14 /50	7.77 /71	1.86	2.16
IN	Gabelli Equity Income Fd	GABEX	B+	(800) 422-3554	C+ / 6.0	1.35	6.97	11.62 /57	13.82 /53	8.16 /72	1.83	1.41
SC	Gabelli Small Cap Growth A	GCASX	B+	(800) 422-3554	B- / 7.1	-2.70	7.25	12.03 /60	19.21 /77	11.53 /85	0.00	1.42
SC	Gabelli Small Cap Growth B	GCBSX	B+	(800) 422-3554	B- / 7.0	-2.81	6.94	11.27 /55	18.50 /74	11.13 /84	0.00	2.17
SC	Gabelli Small Cap Growth C	GCCSX	B+	(800) 422-3554	B- / 7.4	-2.81	6.94	11.28 /55	18.49 /74	11.12 /84	0.00	2.17
SC	Gabelli Small Cap Growth Fd	GABSX	B+	(800) 422-3554	B / 7.7	-2.63	7.33	12.11 /60	19.23 /77	11.54 /85	0.00	1.42
UT	Gabelli Utilities A	GAUAX	C	(800) 422-3554	C / 5.3	3.76	8.16	7.75 /31	14.45 /56	6.46 /64	9.20	1.50
UT	Gabelli Utilities AAA	GABUX	B+	(800) 422-3554	C+ / 6.2	3.77	8.19	7.65 /30	14.45 /56	6.41 /64	9.80	1.50
UT	Gabelli Utilities B	GAUBX	C-	(800) 422-3554	C / 5.0	3.52	7.79	6.85 /25	13.64 /52	5.82 /60	10.13	2.25

RISK			NET ASSETS		ASSET					Portfolio	BULL / BEAR		FUND MANAGER		MINIMUMS		LOADS	
	3 Year		NAV								Last Bull	Last Bear	Manager	Manager	Initial	Additional	Front	Back
Risk	Standard		As of	Total	Cash	Stocks	Bonds	Other		Turnover	Market	Market	Quality	Tenure	Purch.	Purch.	End	End
Rating/Pts	Deviation	Beta	6/30/06	$(Mil)	%	%	%	%		Ratio	Return	Return	Pct	(Years)	$	$	Load	Load
B+ / 9.1	6.1	1.15	13.48	357	9	56	34	1		10.6	53.5	-2.8	78	10	1,000	50	5.8	1.0
B+ / 9.4	6.1	1.15	13.49	6	9	56	34	1		10.6	53.8	-2.8	79	10	5,000,000	50	0.0	0.0
U /	N/A	N/A	13.44	495	9	56	34	1		10.6	N/A	N/A	N/A	10	1,000	50	0.0	4.0
B+ / 9.1	6.1	1.15	13.27	124	9	56	34	1		10.6	50.0	-3.1	71	10	1,000	50	0.0	1.0
B+ / 9.1	6.0	1.14	13.46	27	9	56	34	1		10.6	52.4	-2.9	77	10	1,000	50	0.0	0.0
U /	N/A	N/A	12.08	150	0	99	0	1		0.7	N/A	N/A	N/A	2	1,000	50	5.8	1.0
U /	N/A	N/A	11.99	56	0	99	0	1		0.7	N/A	N/A	N/A	2	1,000	50	0.0	1.0
B / 8.7	4.3	0.29	16.06	40	N/A	N/A	0	N/A		156.2	4.6	1.7	18	6	10,000	50	5.8	0.0
B / 8.2	8.0	0.67	12.22	1,828	6	94	0	0		13.5	78.2	-3.6	58	14	1,000	50	4.3	1.0
B / 8.3	8.0	0.67	12.27	90	6	94	0	0		13.5	79.0	-3.7	60	14	5,000,000	50	0.0	0.0
B / 8.3	8.0	0.67	12.20	132	6	94	0	0		13.5	75.4	-3.7	52	7	1,000	50	0.0	4.0
B / 8.2	8.0	0.66	12.18	372	6	94	0	0		13.5	75.3	-3.7	53	11	1,000	50	0.0	1.0
B / 8.8	8.0	0.67	12.19	19	6	94	0	0		13.5	76.2	-3.7	54	4	1,000	50	0.0	0.0
C+ / 6.2	8.5	1.26	9.10	1	4	10	0	86		60.0	28.9	-1.3	20	6	10,000	1,000	4.0	0.0
C / 5.3	14.1	0.94	18.25	405	4	95	0	1		29.0	108.0	-6.4	34	4	100,000	1,000	0.0	0.0
U /	N/A	N/A	13.09	532	4	95	0	1		23.0	N/A	N/A	N/A	2	100,000	1,000	0.0	2.0
E / 0.5	26.2	0.82	0.19	N/A	26	73	0	1		26.9	-44.2	-28.3	0	4	500	50	0.0	2.0
C / 4.8	16.2	1.33	14.65	97	4	95	0	1		22.7	222.1	-7.1	75	5	1,000	0	0.0	0.0
C+ / 6.9	8.9	1.10	6.69	99	1	98	0	1		29.5	64.0	-9.3	46	8	1,000	0	0.0	0.0
C- / 3.0	18.0	1.17	18.80	46	2	97	0	1		62.3	97.0	-14.1	3	6	1,000	0	0.0	0.0
C+ / 6.8	13.8	1.43	41.87	161	1	98	0	1		116.0	123.1	-11.1	88	4	2,500	100	0.0	2.0
B / 8.3	9.5	1.11	33.41	63	0	99	0	1		107.0	79.7	-8.1	76	4	2,500	100	0.0	2.0
B+ / 9.9	4.1	0.35	28.43	56	0	99	0	1		83.0	26.4	3.0	60	4	2,500	100	0.0	2.0
B- / 7.5	11.8	1.29	38.20	513	0	99	0	1		129.0	106.9	-9.4	88	5	2,500	100	0.0	2.0
B+ / 9.8	2.0	0.18	10.53	178	0	58	41	1		127.0	18.7	0.4	80	13	10,000	0	0.0	0.0
B / 8.5	8.8	1.06	44.41	3	0	99	0	1		6.0	85.0	-10.4	86	20	1,000	0	5.8	1.0
B / 8.5	8.9	1.07	43.87	N/A	0	99	0	1		6.0	82.4	-10.4	83	20	1,000	0	0.0	5.0
B / 8.5	8.9	1.06	43.74	3	0	99	0	1		6.0	82.1	-10.4	83	20	1,000	0	0.0	1.0
B / 8.3	8.9	1.06	44.54	2,331	0	99	0	1		6.0	85.3	-10.4	87	20	1,000	0	0.0	2.0
B / 8.5	8.8	1.07	13.31	N/A	0	98	1	1		37.0	91.7	-11.2	77	7	1,000	0	5.8	1.0
B / 8.6	8.8	1.07	13.27	38	0	98	1	1		37.0	91.0	-11.2	77	7	1,000	0	0.0	0.0
B / 8.5	8.8	1.07	13.09	N/A	0	98	1	1		37.0	88.2	-11.2	72	7	1,000	0	0.0	5.0
B / 8.5	8.8	1.07	13.08	N/A	0	98	1	1		37.0	88.1	-11.2	71	7	1,000	0	0.0	1.0
B / 8.4	9.1	0.74	18.93	228	0	98	1	1		25.0	86.2	-9.5	69	11	1,000	0	0.0	0.0
D+ / 2.3	10.6	-1.25	2.44	50	0	1	98	1		N/A	-50.1	9.7	7	10	1,000	0	4.5	1.0
D+ / 2.3	10.4	-1.23	2.38	5	0	1	98	1		N/A	-51.3	9.1	5	10	1,000	0	0.0	4.0
D+ / 2.3	10.3	-1.21	2.28	14	0	1	98	1		N/A	-51.1	9.2	4	10	1,000	0	0.0	1.0
D+ / 2.3	10.4	-1.22	2.44	N/A	0	1	98	1		N/A	-49.7	9.4	7	10	1,000	0	0.0	0.0
C- / 3.2	7.5	-0.62	2.77	3	0	3	96	1		1.0	-39.5	6.2	2	10	1,000	0	4.5	1.0
C- / 3.2	7.3	-0.60	2.80	N/A	0	3	96	1		1.0	-41.0	6.1	1	10	1,000	0	0.0	1.0
C- / 3.2	7.5	-0.62	2.69	11	0	3	96	1		1.0	-39.0	6.3	2	10	1,000	0	0.0	0.0
B+ / 9.1	7.0	0.85	19.45	1	1	92	5	2		10.0	72.5	-5.4	88	3	1,000	0	5.8	1.0
B+ / 9.1	7.1	0.85	19.14	N/A	1	92	5	2		10.0	69.7	-5.4	84	3	1,000	0	0.0	5.0
B+ / 9.1	7.1	0.85	19.14	1	1	92	5	2		10.0	69.8	-5.4	84	3	1,000	0	0.0	1.0
B+ / 9.2	7.0	0.85	19.51	727	1	92	5	2		10.0	72.8	-5.4	88	3	1,000	0	0.0	0.0
B- / 7.7	11.2	0.74	30.31	1	0	93	6	1		2.0	109.4	-8.6	91	N/A	1,000	0	5.8	1.0
B- / 7.7	11.2	0.74	29.73	N/A	0	93	6	1		2.0	105.9	-8.6	89	N/A	1,000	0	0.0	5.0
B- / 7.7	11.2	0.74	29.72	1	0	93	6	1		2.0	105.8	-8.6	89	N/A	1,000	0	0.0	1.0
B- / 7.2	11.2	0.74	30.32	809	0	93	6	1		2.0	109.4	-8.6	91	N/A	1,000	0	0.0	0.0
C+ / 6.4	7.4	0.55	8.47	1	0	87	11	2		18.0	86.5	-4.5	70	N/A	1,000	0	5.8	1.0
B+ / 9.0	7.4	0.55	8.44	124	0	87	11	2		18.0	86.3	-4.7	71	N/A	1,000	0	0.0	0.0
C+ / 6.4	7.4	0.55	8.16	N/A	0	87	11	2		18.0	81.8	-4.8	64	N/A	1,000	0	0.0	5.0

					PERFORMANCE							
99 Pct = Best 0 Pct = Worst			Overall Weiss		Perfor-	Total Return % through 6/30/06					Incl. in Returns	
			Investment		mance				Annualized		Dividend	Expense
Fund Type	Fund Name	Ticker Symbol	Rating	Phone	Rating/Pts	3 Mo	6 Mo	1Yr / Pct	3Yr / Pct	5Yr / Pct	Yield	Ratio
UT	Gabelli Utilities C	GAUCX	C	(800) 422-3554	C+ / 5.6	3.50	7.76	6.82 /25	13.64 /52	5.88 /60	10.09	2.25
AG	Gabelli Value Fund A	GABVX	C-	(800) 422-3554	C / 4.4	1.03	8.23	8.22 /35	12.56 /46	5.43 /57	0.06	1.40
AG	Gabelli Value Fund B	GVCBX	D+	(800) 422-3554	C- / 3.9	0.81	7.81	7.45 /29	11.73 /41	4.64 /51	0.00	2.15
AG	Gabelli Value Fund C	GVCCX	C-	(800) 422-3554	C / 4.6	0.81	7.81	7.44 /29	11.72 /41	4.64 /51	0.00	2.15
BA	Gabelli Westwood Balanced Fd A	WEBCX	C	(800) 422-3554	D+ / 2.9	0.77	4.73	10.18 /48	10.11 /28	4.74 /52	1.08	1.55
BA	Gabelli Westwood Balanced Fd AAA	WEBAX	C+	(800) 422-3554	C- / 4.0	0.81	4.82	10.53 /50	10.36 /30	5.32 /57	1.57	1.30
GR	Gabelli Westwood Equity Fund A	WEECX	B	(800) 422-3554	C+ / 6.3	1.01	7.14	16.17 /75	15.78 /62	5.02 /54	0.36	1.76
GR	Gabelli Westwood Equity Fund AAA	WESWX	A	(800) 422-3554	B- / 7.0	1.01	7.21	16.49 /76	16.04 /64	5.30 /56	0.41	1.51
RE	Gabelli Westwood Income AAA	WESRX	E+	(800) 422-3554	B- / 7.0	-1.38	2.93	3.07 / 7	18.33 /74	14.79 /92	1.84	1.50
SC	Gabelli Westwood Mighty Mites AAA	WEMMX	C	(800) 422-3554	C+ / 6.3	-2.32	5.63	13.72 /67	14.66 /57	10.21 /81	0.00	1.50
SC	Gabelli Westwood Mighty Mites C	WMMCX	C	(800) 422-3554	C+ / 5.7	-2.48	5.20	12.86 /64	13.77 /53	9.43 /78	0.00	2.25
SC	Gabelli Westwood Sm Cap Equity	WESCX	C+	(800) 422-3554	B / 7.8	-2.23	11.66	21.45 /84	17.97 /72	2.41 /31	0.00	1.50
SC	Gabelli Woodland Small Cap Val A		C-	(800) 422-3554	C / 5.1	-5.96	1.19	5.38 /17	16.12 /64	--	0.00	2.00
SC	Gabelli Woodland Small Cap Val AAA	GWSVX	B-	(800) 422-3554	C+ / 6.0	-5.90	1.19	5.39 /17	16.10 /64	--	0.00	2.01
SC	Gabelli Woodland Small Cap Val B		C-	(800) 422-3554	C / 5.3	-6.06	0.59	3.18 / 8	16.30 /65	--	0.00	2.75
SC	Gabelli Woodland Small Cap Val C		C-	(800) 422-3554	C / 5.5	-6.10	0.84	4.64 /13	15.32 /60	--	0.00	2.75
FO	GAM Asia-Pacific Equity A	GAPCX	B+	(800) 426-4685	A- / 9.1	-4.71	3.41	33.68 /96	26.88 /93	10.78 /83	0.90	2.00
FO	GAM European Equity A	GEURX	A+	(800) 426-4685	B+ / 8.8	1.14	12.92	23.29 /86	23.54 /88	9.48 /79	0.37	2.01
GR	GAM Gabelli Long/Short A	GFLAX	C-	(800) 426-4685	D+ / 2.4	2.21	8.73	8.13 /34	9.23 /22	--	0.00	2.60
GR	● GAM Gabelli Long/Short B	GFLBX	C-	(800) 426-4685	D+ / 2.3	2.03	8.40	7.42 /29	8.58 /18	--	0.00	3.19
GR	GAM Gabelli Long/Short C	GFLCX	C-	(800) 426-4685	D+ / 2.9	2.14	8.42	7.44 /29	8.55 /18	--	0.00	3.33
FO	GAM International Equity Fund A	GAMNX	A-	(800) 426-4685	B / 8.2	-1.35	6.64	21.15 /83	21.54 /84	7.73 /70	0.70	1.95
FO	● GAM International Equity Fund B	GAIBX	A-	(800) 426-4685	B / 8.1	-1.52	6.30	20.93 /83	20.94 /82	7.10 /67	0.01	2.59
FO	GAM International Equity Fund C	GAICX	A	(800) 426-4685	B+ / 8.3	-1.55	6.15	20.73 /83	20.83 /82	7.01 /67	0.00	2.86
CV	GAMCO Global Convertible A		C	(800) 422-3554	D+ / 2.8	-2.89	3.04	14.13 /69	10.62 /32	5.52 /58	1.33	2.00
CV	GAMCO Global Convertible AAA	GAGCX	D	(800) 422-3554	C- / 3.9	-2.88	3.06	14.17 /69	10.61 /32	5.48 /58	1.41	2.00
CV	GAMCO Global Convertible B		C-	(800) 422-3554	D+ / 2.5	-2.89	2.69	13.35 /66	9.77 /26	4.72 /52	1.49	2.75
CV	GAMCO Global Convertible C		C	(800) 422-3554	C- / 3.2	-3.01	2.66	13.36 /66	9.78 /26	--	1.47	2.75
GL	GAMCO Global Growth A	GGGAX	C+	(800) 422-3554	C / 5.3	-2.08	3.57	17.72 /79	14.67 /57	3.07 /38	0.18	1.71
GL	GAMCO Global Growth B	GGGBX	C+	(800) 422-3554	C / 5.0	-2.27	3.16	16.83 /77	13.78 /53	2.30 /30	0.00	2.46
GL	GAMCO Global Growth C	GGGCX	C+	(800) 422-3554	C+ / 5.6	-2.32	3.12	16.77 /76	13.77 /53	2.27 /30	0.00	2.46
GL	GAMCO Global Growth Fd	GICPX	C+	(800) 422-3554	C+ / 6.2	-2.13	3.52	17.66 /78	14.64 /57	3.06 /37	0.08	1.82
GL	GAMCO Global Opportunity AAA	GABOX	A	(800) 422-3554	B / 8.2	-1.28	6.79	23.20 /86	19.86 /79	7.11 /67	0.14	1.84
TC	GAMCO Global Telecom A	GTCAX	B-	(800) 422-3554	C+ / 5.6	-0.22	5.03	10.56 /51	15.39 /61	2.85 /35	1.01	1.59
TC	GAMCO Global Telecom AAA	GABTX	B-	(800) 422-3554	C+ / 6.4	-0.22	5.02	10.51 /50	15.38 /61	2.85 /35	1.03	1.62
TC	GAMCO Global Telecom B	GTCBX	C+	(800) 422-3554	C / 5.3	-0.44	4.62	9.68 /45	14.51 /56	2.08 /28	0.00	2.33
TC	GAMCO Global Telecom C	GTCCX	B-	(800) 422-3554	C+ / 5.9	-0.45	4.64	9.66 /45	14.51 /56	2.07 /28	0.06	2.34
PM	GAMCO Gold A	GLDAX	D+	(800) 422-3554	A+ / 9.9	3.47	24.77	76.43 /99	30.54 /96	35.10 /99	0.29	1.54
PM	GAMCO Gold AAA	GOLDX	D+	(800) 422-3554	A+ / 9.9	3.47	24.81	76.37 /99	30.54 /96	35.10 /99	0.43	1.52
PM	GAMCO Gold B	GLDBX	D+	(800) 422-3554	A+ / 9.9	3.26	24.31	75.03 /99	29.52 /95	34.38 /99	0.02	2.27
PM	GAMCO Gold C	GLDCX	D+	(800) 422-3554	A+ / 9.9	3.30	24.32	75.05 /99	29.56 /95	34.40 /99	0.00	2.27
GR	GAMCO Growth A	GGCAX	C-	(800) 422-3554	D+ / 2.5	-3.98	-0.49	10.05 /47	10.70 /33	-1.65 / 9	0.00	1.47
GR	GAMCO Growth B	GGCBX	D+	(800) 422-3554	D+ / 2.3	-4.16	-0.85	9.20 /41	10.00 /27	-2.03 / 8	0.00	2.24
GR	GAMCO Growth C	GGCCX	C-	(800) 422-3554	C- / 3.0	-4.12	-0.85	9.20 /41	10.00 /27	-2.03 / 8	0.00	2.23
GR	GAMCO Growth Fd	GABGX	C-	(800) 422-3554	C- / 3.6	-3.95	-0.49	10.02 /47	10.69 /33	-1.66 / 9	0.00	1.49
FO	GAMCO International Growth A	GAIGX	C+	(800) 422-3554	B / 8.2	-0.13	7.77	23.17 /86	21.44 /84	8.20 /72	0.31	1.89
FO	GAMCO International Growth AAA	GIGRX	B+	(800) 422-3554	B+ / 8.5	-0.09	7.80	23.19 /86	21.46 /84	7.91 /71	0.39	1.89
FO	GAMCO International Growth B	GBIGX	C+	(800) 422-3554	B / 8.0	-0.28	7.38	22.22 /85	20.55 /81	7.06 /67	0.00	2.63
FO	GAMCO International Growth C	GCIGX	C+	(800) 422-3554	B / 8.2	-0.32	7.35	22.26 /85	20.23 /80	6.91 /66	0.21	2.62
GR	GAMCO Mathers Fund	MATRX	D+	(800) 422-3554	E- / 0.1	1.14	1.92	2.48 / 6	0.28 / 0	-2.18 / 8	1.67	2.14
SC	GAMerica A	GCFAX	E	(800) 426-4685	E+ / 0.8	-7.88	-3.84	10.67 /51	8.74 /19	3.93 /45	0.65	1.83
SC	● GAMerica B	GUSBX	E	(800) 426-4685	E+ / 0.7	-8.06	-4.18	9.81 /46	7.99 /15	3.21 /39	0.00	2.54

● Denotes fund is closed to new investors
* Denotes fund is included in Section II

RISK			NET ASSETS		ASSET					BULL / BEAR		FUND MANAGER		MINIMUMS		LOADS	
	3 Year		NAV						Portfolio	Last Bull	Last Bear	Manager	Manager	Initial	Additional	Front	Back
Risk	Standard		As of	Total	Cash	Stocks	Bonds	Other	Turnover	Market	Market	Quality	Tenure	Purch.	Purch.	End	End
Rating/Pts	Deviation	Beta	6/30/06	$(Mil)	%	%	%	%	Ratio	Return	Return	Pct	(Years)	$	$	Load	Load
C+ / 6.4	7.4	0.55	8.19	1	0	87	11	2	18.0	82.0	-4.7	64	N/A	1,000	0	0.0	1.0
C+ / 6.5	9.5	1.09	19.60	1,048	0	99	0	1	3.0	71.7	-10.5	62	17	1,000	0	5.5	0.0
C+ / 5.8	9.5	1.08	18.63	18	0	99	0	1	3.0	67.7	-10.7	53	6	1,000	0	0.0	5.0
C+ / 5.8	9.5	1.08	18.64	14	0	99	0	1	3.0	67.6	-10.7	54	6	1,000	0	0.0	1.0
B / 8.8	5.2	0.95	12.50	5	1	61	36	2	38.0	46.6	-3.9	82	13	1,000	0	4.0	1.0
B / 8.8	5.2	0.94	12.48	144	1	61	36	2	38.0	47.7	-4.0	84	15	1,000	0	0.0	0.0
B / 8.9	8.5	0.95	12.00	3	1	98	0	1	40.0	78.1	-7.8	92	12	1,000	0	4.0	1.0
B / 8.9	8.5	0.96	12.04	181	1	98	0	1	40.0	79.5	-7.6	92	19	1,000	0	0.0	0.0
E- / 0.0	13.9	0.79	11.71	15	0	0	0	100	N/A	88.7	0.4	45	9	1,000	0	0.0	0.0
C+ / 5.7	9.5	0.56	15.57	113	0	98	1	1	1.0	75.9	-2.2	86	N/A	50,000	0	0.0	0.0
C+ / 5.9	9.5	0.56	14.96	N/A	0	98	1	1	1.0	71.8	-2.4	80	N/A	1,000	0	0.0	1.0
C / 5.4	13.8	0.86	12.74	9	5	94	0	1	42.0	94.1	-13.5	72	N/A	1,000	0	0.0	0.0
C+ / 5.6	10.5	0.67	13.57	N/A	N/A	98	2	N/A	35.0	83.3	N/A	83	4	1,000	0	5.8	1.0
B- / 7.9	10.5	0.67	13.56	11	N/A	98	2	N/A	35.0	83.4	N/A	82	4	1,000	0	0.0	0.0
C / 5.4	11.4	0.71	13.63	N/A	N/A	98	2	N/A	35.0	84.1	N/A	79	4	1,000	0	0.0	5.0
C+ / 5.6	10.5	0.67	13.23	N/A	N/A	98	2	N/A	35.0	79.4	N/A	77	4	1,000	0	0.0	1.0
C+ / 5.7	13.5	1.09	13.96	29	2	97	0	1	92.0	136.7	-6.7	59	N/A	5,000	100	5.5	1.0
B- / 7.9	10.6	0.95	15.91	30	0	94	0	6	83.0	125.6	-10.3	58	13	5,000	100	5.5	1.0
B / 8.4	7.3	0.61	9.71	15	6	93	0	1	60.0	40.6	-3.6	72	4	5,000	100	5.5	1.0
B / 8.3	7.3	0.62	9.55	4	6	93	0	1	60.0	38.8	-3.6	66	4	5,000	100	0.0	5.0
B / 8.3	7.3	0.62	9.53	9	6	93	0	1	60.0	38.6	-3.8	65	4	5,000	100	0.0	1.0
B- / 7.3	10.4	0.99	23.44	84	10	89	0	1	81.0	112.6	-9.5	31	2	5,000	100	5.5	1.0
B- / 7.3	10.4	1.00	23.30	7	10	89	0	1	81.0	109.1	-9.6	27	2	5,000	100	0.0	5.0
B- / 7.3	10.4	0.99	23.47	4	10	89	0	1	81.0	108.5	-9.7	27	2	5,000	100	0.0	1.0
B / 8.9	7.7	0.97	6.36	N/A	0	0	8	92	58.0	54.5	3.5	86	N/A	1,000	0	5.8	1.0
C / 4.9	7.7	0.96	6.35	14	0	0	8	92	58.0	54.0	3.5	86	N/A	1,000	0	0.0	0.0
B / 8.9	7.7	0.96	6.01	N/A	0	0	8	92	58.0	50.5	3.4	81	N/A	1,000	0	0.0	5.0
B / 8.9	7.7	0.97	6.09	19	0	0	8	92	58.0	50.8	3.3	81	N/A	1,000	0	0.0	1.0
B- / 7.8	9.6	0.83	21.16	1	1	98	0	1	33.0	99.8	-8.9	14	N/A	1,000	0	5.8	1.0
B- / 7.7	9.6	0.83	20.27	N/A	1	98	0	1	33.0	95.1	-9.1	11	N/A	1,000	0	0.0	5.0
B- / 7.7	9.6	0.84	20.19	N/A	1	98	0	1	33.0	95.1	-9.1	11	N/A	1,000	0	0.0	1.0
B- / 7.2	9.6	0.83	21.15	108	1	98	0	1	33.0	99.7	-8.8	14	N/A	1,000	0	0.0	0.0
B- / 7.5	11.1	1.02	16.99	22	0	100	0	0	26.0	118.6	-7.5	18	8	1,000	0	0.0	0.0
B / 8.1	10.0	1.10	18.39	1	0	99	0	1	4.0	100.1	-7.9	84	6	1,000	0	5.8	1.0
B- / 7.4	10.0	1.09	18.41	188	0	99	0	1	4.0	100.1	-7.8	84	6	1,000	0	0.0	0.0
B / 8.1	9.9	1.09	17.90	N/A	0	99	0	1	4.0	95.5	-8.0	78	6	1,000	0	0.0	5.0
B / 8.1	10.0	1.10	17.82	N/A	0	99	0	1	4.0	95.5	-8.1	78	6	1,000	0	0.0	1.0
E- / 0.0	33.0	1.55	25.94	12	1	98	0	1	4.0	154.9	21.1	35	12	1,000	0	5.8	1.0
E- / 0.0	33.0	1.56	25.96	370	1	98	0	1	4.0	154.9	21.1	35	12	1,000	0	0.0	0.0
E- / 0.0	33.0	1.55	25.67	1	1	98	0	1	4.0	148.7	20.9	29	12	1,000	0	0.0	5.0
E- / 0.0	33.0	1.55	25.66	4	1	98	0	1	4.0	149.2	20.8	29	12	1,000	0	0.0	1.0
B- / 7.9	10.0	1.21	28.68	N/A	1	98	0	1	39.0	67.2	-15.4	32	11	1,000	0	5.8	1.0
B- / 7.9	10.1	1.22	28.14	N/A	1	98	0	1	39.0	64.3	-15.4	27	11	1,000	0	0.0	5.0
B- / 7.9	10.1	1.22	28.14	1	1	98	0	1	39.0	64.3	-15.4	27	11	1,000	0	0.0	1.0
B- / 7.4	10.0	1.21	28.67	1,133	1	98	0	1	39.0	67.1	-15.4	32	11	1,000	0	0.0	0.0
C / 5.3	11.1	1.05	22.46	N/A	1	98	0	1	19.0	115.3	-8.1	23	11	1,000	0	5.8	0.0
C+ / 6.5	11.1	1.05	22.24	55	1	98	0	1	19.0	115.3	-8.2	24	11	1,000	0	0.0	0.0
C / 5.3	11.1	1.05	21.67	N/A	1	98	0	1	19.0	110.4	-8.4	18	11	1,000	0	0.0	5.0
C / 5.3	11.0	1.04	21.47	65	1	98	0	1	19.0	108.9	-8.4	18	11	1,000	0	0.0	1.0
B+ / 9.7	1.9	-0.13	10.64	35	83	16	0	1	149.0	-0.2	-0.1	44	N/A	1,000	0	0.0	0.0
C / 4.9	14.3	0.79	25.82	33	0	100	0	0	6.0	70.7	-7.6	11	11	5,000	100	5.5	1.0
C / 4.8	14.3	0.79	24.76	7	0	100	0	0	6.0	67.0	-7.7	9	8	5,000	100	0.0	5.0

Fund Type	Fund Name	Ticker Symbol	Overall Weiss Investment Rating	Phone	Perfor-mance Rating/Pts	3 Mo	6 Mo	1Yr / Pct	3Yr / Pct	5Yr / Pct	Dividend Yield	Expense Ratio
								Total Return % through 6/30/06			Incl. in Returns	
									Annualized			
SC	GAMerica C	GUSCX	E	(800) 426-4685	D- / 1.0	-8.08	-4.31	9.55 /44	7.82 /14	3.11 /38	0.00	2.83
CV	Gartmore Convertible Inst	GRVIX	U	(800) 848-0920	U /	-1.36	1.77	6.45 /23	--	--	2.82	0.95
EM	Gartmore Emerging Markets A	GEGAX	C+	(800) 848-0920	A+ / 9.6	-6.21	6.53	32.57 /96	33.36 /97	20.92 /97	0.35	1.88
EM	Gartmore Emerging Markets B	GEGBX	C+	(800) 848-0920	A+ / 9.6	-6.37	6.13	31.58 /95	32.49 /97	20.09 /96	0.03	2.55
EM	Gartmore Emerging Markets C	GEGCX	C+	(800) 848-0920	A+ / 9.6	-6.38	6.10	31.60 /95	32.48 /97	20.18 /96	0.03	2.55
EM	Gartmore Emerging Markets Inst	GEGIX	C+	(800) 848-0920	A+ / 9.7	-6.13	6.71	32.98 /96	33.81 /97	21.32 /97	0.57	1.55
EM	Gartmore Emerging Markets Instl-Svc	GEGSX	B-	(800) 848-0920	A+ / 9.7	-6.13	6.71	32.98 /96	33.81 /97	21.32 /97	0.57	1.55
EM	Gartmore Emerging Markets R	GEMRX	C+	(800) 848-0920	A+ / 9.7	-6.24	6.42	32.37 /96	33.10 /97	20.42 /96	0.40	2.15
HL	Gartmore Glbl Health Sci A	GLSAX	E	(800) 848-0920	E- / 0.2	-7.55	-4.81	-0.14 / 2	6.31 / 8	5.28 /56	0.00	1.73
HL	Gartmore Glbl Health Sci B	GLSBX	E	(800) 848-0920	E / 0.4	-7.66	-5.09	-0.71 / 1	5.65 / 6	4.60 /51	0.00	2.39
HL	Gartmore Glbl Health Sci C	GMSCX	E	(800) 848-0920	E / 0.4	-7.66	-5.09	-0.81 / 1	5.61 / 5	4.60 /51	0.00	2.39
HL	Gartmore Glbl Health Sci Inst	GGHIX	D-	(800) 848-0920	E+ / 0.6	-7.43	-4.56	0.23 / 2	6.64 / 9	5.60 /58	0.00	1.39
HL	Gartmore Glbl Health Sci Instl-Svc	GLSIX	E	(800) 848-0920	E / 0.5	-7.54	-4.75	0.05 / 2	6.49 / 8	5.51 /58	0.00	1.59
HL	Gartmore Glbl Health Sci R	GGHRX	D-	(800) 848-0920	E / 0.5	-7.56	-4.84	-0.05 / 2	6.14 / 7	4.89 /53	0.00	1.99
TC	Gartmore Glob Tech & Comm A	GAGTX	E-	(800) 848-0920	E- / 0.1	-11.24	-5.12	6.61 /24	6.17 / 7	-7.61 / 1	0.00	2.21
TC	Gartmore Glob Tech & Comm B	GBGTX	E-	(800) 848-0920	E- / 0.2	-11.47	-5.58	5.97 /20	5.42 / 5	-8.22 / 0	0.00	2.90
TC	Gartmore Glob Tech & Comm C	GCGTX	E-	(800) 848-0920	E- / 0.2	-11.39	-5.54	5.92 /20	5.49 / 5	-8.13 / 0	0.00	2.90
TC	Gartmore Glob Tech & Comm Inst	GGTIX	E-	(800) 848-0920	E / 0.3	-11.22	-4.76	7.34 /28	6.45 / 8	-7.23 / 1	0.00	1.90
TC	Gartmore Glob Tech & Comm	GIGTX	E-	(800) 848-0920	E / 0.3	-11.27	-5.03	6.78 /25	6.27 / 8	-7.33 / 1	0.00	2.11
TC	Gartmore Glob Tech & Comm R	GGTRX	E-	(800) 848-0920	E- / 0.2	-11.33	-5.01	6.83 /25	5.91 / 6	-7.96 / 0	0.00	2.50
FS	Gartmore Global Finan Svc A	GLFAX	A	(800) 848-0920	B / 7.7	-1.78	6.71	21.48 /84	20.91 /82	--	1.34	1.65
FS	Gartmore Global Finan Svc B	GLFBX	A+	(800) 848-0920	B / 7.9	-1.99	6.28	20.68 /83	20.01 /79	--	0.83	2.40
FS	Gartmore Global Finan Svc C	GLFCX	A	(800) 848-0920	B / 7.8	-2.00	6.31	20.62 /83	20.00 /79	--	0.85	2.40
FS	Gartmore Global Finan Svc Inst	GLFIX	A+	(800) 848-0920	B / 8.2	-1.71	6.87	21.83 /84	21.22 /83	--	1.63	1.40
FS	Gartmore Global Finan Svc Instl-Svc	GFISX	A+	(800) 848-0920	B / 8.2	-1.78	6.80	21.83 /84	21.22 /83	--	1.63	1.40
FS	Gartmore Global Finan Svc R	GLFRX	A+	(800) 848-0920	B / 8.0	-1.84	6.63	21.43 /84	20.59 /81	--	1.38	2.00
UT	Gartmore Global Utilities A	GGUAX	C+	(800) 848-0920	B / 7.7	3.35	11.22	14.82 /71	20.13 /80	--	1.48	1.50
UT	Gartmore Global Utilities B	GGUBX	C+	(800) 848-0920	B / 7.9	3.10	10.80	13.89 /68	19.25 /77	--	0.94	2.23
UT	Gartmore Global Utilities C	GGUCX	C+	(800) 848-0920	B / 7.9	3.01	10.80	13.88 /68	19.25 /77	--	0.92	2.23
UT	Gartmore Global Utilities Inst	GLUIX	A+	(800) 848-0920	B / 8.2	3.31	11.32	14.97 /72	20.42 /81	--	1.79	1.23
UT	Gartmore Global Utilities R	GLURX	A+	(800) 848-0920	B / 8.1	3.23	11.03	14.45 /70	19.81 /79	--	1.40	1.83
GR	Gartmore Growth Fund A	NMFAX	D-	(800) 848-0920	E+ / 0.7	-6.49	-3.29	2.27 / 5	8.49 /18	-0.94 /12	0.00	1.34
GR	Gartmore Growth Fund B	NMFBX	D-	(800) 848-0920	E+ / 0.8	-6.49	-3.58	1.81 / 4	7.79 /14	-1.77 / 9	0.00	1.98
GR	Gartmore Growth Fund C	GCGRX	D-	(800) 848-0920	D- / 1.0	-6.63	-3.58	1.64 / 3	7.72 /13	-1.80 / 9	0.00	1.98
GR	Gartmore Growth Fund D	MUIGX	D-	(800) 848-0920	D- / 1.1	-6.24	-3.09	2.83 / 7	8.90 /20	-0.64 /13	0.00	0.99
GR	Gartmore Growth Fund Inst	GGFIX	D	(800) 848-0920	D / 1.6	-6.25	-3.09	2.68 / 6	8.85 /20	-0.66 /13	0.00	0.98
GR	Gartmore Growth Fund Instl-Svc	GWISX	D	(800) 848-0920	D / 1.6	-6.37	-3.22	2.52 / 6	8.84 /20	-0.63 /13	0.00	0.98
GR	Gartmore Growth Fund R	GGFRX	D	(800) 848-0920	D- / 1.4	-6.42	-3.25	2.39 / 5	8.52 /18	-0.85 /12	0.00	1.58
FO	Gartmore Internatl Index A	GIIAX	A-	(800) 848-0920	B+ / 8.7	0.63	9.82	26.58 /91	23.22 /88	8.77 /75	0.99	0.77
FO	Gartmore Internatl Index B	GIIBX	A-	(800) 848-0920	B+ / 8.6	0.47	9.55	25.75 /89	22.46 /86	8.08 /72	0.67	1.37
FO	Gartmore Internatl Index Inst	GIXIX	A	(800) 848-0920	A- / 9.1	0.73	10.12	27.03 /91	23.72 /89	9.19 /77	1.30	0.37
FO	Gartmore Intl Growth A	GIGAX	B+	(800) 848-0920	A / 9.4	-1.49	9.96	38.50 /98	28.19 /94	11.38 /85	0.29	1.65
FO	Gartmore Intl Growth B	GIGBX	B+	(800) 848-0920	A / 9.4	-1.70	9.57	37.60 /97	27.27 /93	10.56 /82	0.10	2.40
FO	Gartmore Intl Growth C	GIGCX	A+	(800) 848-0920	A / 9.4	-1.61	9.61	37.73 /97	27.32 /93	10.58 /82	0.17	2.40
FO	Gartmore Intl Growth Inst	GIGIX	A+	(800) 848-0920	A / 9.5	-1.41	10.08	38.94 /98	28.54 /94	11.67 /86	0.43	1.40
FO	Gartmore Intl Growth Instl-Svc	GIGSX	A-	(800) 848-0920	A / 9.5	-1.41	10.08	38.94 /98	28.54 /94	11.67 /86	0.43	1.40
GL	Gartmore Inv Dest Aggressive A	NDAAX	B-	(800) 848-0920	C+ / 5.8	-1.85	4.79	13.63 /67	15.38 /61	5.63 /59	1.38	0.77
GL	Gartmore Inv Dest Aggressive B	NDABX	B-	(800) 848-0920	C / 5.5	-1.96	4.57	12.94 /64	14.59 /57	4.93 /54	0.98	1.50
GL	Gartmore Inv Dest Aggressive C	NDACX	B	(800) 848-0920	C+ / 6.0	-1.87	4.58	12.97 /64	14.58 /57	4.91 /53	0.98	1.50
GL	Gartmore Inv Dest Aggressive Inst	GAIDX	B	(800) 848-0920	C+ / 6.6	-1.93	4.82	14.01 /68	15.53 /61	5.72 /59	1.64	0.50
GL	Gartmore Inv Dest Aggressive R	GAFRX	B	(800) 848-0920	C+ / 6.4	-1.86	4.79	13.53 /66	15.18 /60	5.25 /56	1.41	1.10
GL	Gartmore Inv Dest Aggressive Svc	NDASX	B	(800) 848-0920	C+ / 6.5	-1.84	4.74	13.48 /66	15.24 /60	5.57 /58	1.37	0.90

● Denotes fund is closed to new investors
* Denotes fund is included in Section II

RISK			NET ASSETS		ASSET						BULL / BEAR		FUND MANAGER		MINIMUMS		LOADS	
	3 Year		NAV						Portfolio		Last Bull	Last Bear	Manager	Manager	Initial	Additional	Front	Back
Risk	Standard		As of	Total	Cash	Stocks	Bonds	Other	Turnover		Market	Market	Quality	Tenure	Purch.	Purch.	End	End
Rating/Pts	Deviation	Beta	6/30/06	$(Mil)	%	%	%	%	Ratio		Return	Return	Pct	(Years)	$	$	Load	Load
C /4.8	14.3	0.79	24.45	3	0	100	0	0	6.0		66.3	-7.8	8	8	5,000	100	0.0	1.0
U /	N/A	N/A	10.28	38	4	0	0	96	169.5		N/A	N/A	N/A	N/A	1,000,000	0	0.0	0.0
C- /3.9	19.8	1.19	16.21	33	0	98	0	2	129.0		222.9	-5.4	6	N/A	2,000	100	5.8	2.0
C- /3.8	19.8	1.20	15.66	6	0	98	0	2	129.0		216.3	-5.6	4	N/A	2,000	100	0.0	5.0
C- /3.8	19.8	1.20	15.91	7	0	98	0	2	129.0		216.4	-5.7	4	N/A	2,000	100	0.0	2.0
C- /3.6	19.8	1.19	16.49	7	0	98	0	2	129.0		226.2	-5.3	7	N/A	1,000,000	0	0.0	2.0
C- /3.9	19.8	1.19	16.49	7	0	98	0	2	129.0		226.2	-5.3	7	N/A	50,000	0	0.0	2.0
C- /3.5	19.8	1.20	15.77	N/A	0	98	0	2	129.0		220.5	-5.6	5	N/A	1,000,000	0	0.0	2.0
C+ /5.6	9.2	0.68	10.28	11	0	100	0	0	401.4		59.5	-4.1	35	5	2,000	100	5.8	2.0
C /5.4	9.3	0.68	9.88	1	0	100	0	0	401.4		56.2	-4.3	29	5	2,000	100	0.0	2.0
C /5.4	9.3	0.69	9.88	4	0	100	0	0	401.4		56.1	-4.3	29	4	2,000	100	0.0	2.0
B- /7.9	9.3	0.68	10.47	9	0	100	0	0	401.4		60.8	-4.1	37	2	1,000,000	0	0.0	2.0
C+ /5.6	9.3	0.68	10.42	1	0	100	0	0	401.4		60.2	-4.1	36	5	50,000	0	0.0	2.0
B- /7.8	9.3	0.67	10.03	N/A	0	100	0	0	401.4		58.4	-4.3	34	6	1,000,000	0	0.0	2.0
D+ /2.5	20.0	2.00	3.71	3	6	94	0	0	443.0		63.2	-14.8	0	N/A	2,000	100	5.8	2.0
D+ /2.4	20.1	2.02	3.55	1	6	94	0	0	443.0		59.7	-14.8	0	N/A	2,000	100	0.0	2.0
D+ /2.4	20.1	2.00	3.58	N/A	6	94	0	0	443.0		59.6	-14.7	0	N/A	2,000	100	0.0	2.0
D+ /2.8	20.1	2.01	3.80	6	6	94	0	0	443.0		64.2	-14.3	0	N/A	1,000,000	0	0.0	2.0
D+ /2.5	20.1	2.01	3.78	1	6	94	0	0	443.0		63.8	-14.3	0	N/A	50,000	0	0.0	2.0
D+ /2.8	20.0	2.01	3.60	N/A	6	94	0	0	443.0		61.7	-14.8	0	N/A	1,000,000	0	0.0	2.0
B /8.0	9.3	0.88	14.54	14	6	94	0	0	210.0		120.3	-9.4	98	4	2,000	100	5.8	2.0
B /8.6	9.3	0.88	14.26	3	6	94	0	0	210.0		115.3	-9.7	97	4	2,000	100	0.0	2.0
B /8.0	9.3	0.88	14.25	4	6	94	0	0	210.0		115.2	-9.7	97	4	2,000	100	0.0	2.0
B /8.6	9.3	0.88	14.62	14	6	94	0	0	210.0		121.9	-9.4	98	2	1,000,000	0	0.0	2.0
B /8.0	9.3	0.88	14.62	1	6	94	0	0	210.0		122.1	-9.4	98	4	50,000	0	0.0	2.0
B /8.6	9.3	0.88	14.30	N/A	6	94	0	0	210.0		118.2	-9.7	97	3	1,000,000	0	0.0	2.0
C /5.0	9.1	0.53	11.36	3	0	98	0	2	260.0		103.4	-7.7	97	N/A	2,000	100	5.8	2.0
C /4.9	9.1	0.52	11.19	1	0	98	0	2	260.0		98.7	-7.8	96	N/A	2,000	100	0.0	2.0
C /4.9	9.1	0.52	11.19	2	0	98	0	2	260.0		98.7	-7.8	96	N/A	2,000	100	0.0	2.0
B /8.4	9.1	0.52	11.40	12	0	98	0	2	260.0		105.1	-7.6	97	N/A	1,000,000	0	0.0	2.0
B /8.4	9.1	0.52	11.23	N/A	0	98	0	2	260.0		101.2	-7.8	96	N/A	1,000,000	0	0.0	2.0
B- /7.1	10.1	1.22	6.77	27	0	98	0	2	275.0		60.3	-10.0	18	6	2,000	100	5.8	2.0
B- /7.0	10.2	1.23	6.20	5	0	98	0	2	275.0		57.1	-10.1	13	6	2,000	100	0.0	5.0
B- /7.5	10.2	1.22	6.20	1	0	98	0	2	275.0		57.4	-10.6	13	5	2,000	100	0.0	2.0
B- /7.2	10.1	1.22	6.91	181	0	98	0	2	275.0		61.9	-9.9	20	6	2,000	100	4.5	2.0
B- /7.6	10.1	1.21	6.90	N/A	0	98	0	2	275.0		61.7	-9.9	20	2	1,000,000	0	0.0	2.0
B- /7.6	10.1	1.21	6.91	N/A	0	98	0	2	275.0		62.2	-9.9	20	4	50,000	0	0.0	2.0
B- /7.5	10.1	1.22	6.85	N/A	0	98	0	2	275.0		60.5	-9.9	18	3	1,000,000	0	0.0	2.0
C+ /6.8	10.2	1.00	9.85	63	0	100	0	0	12.0		127.6	-10.0	43	7	2,000	100	5.8	0.0
C+ /6.9	10.2	1.00	9.70	1	0	100	0	0	12.0		123.2	-10.0	37	7	2,000	100	0.0	5.0
C+ /6.9	10.2	1.00	9.87	1,680	0	100	0	0	12.0		130.5	-9.9	48	7	1,000,000	0	0.0	0.0
C+ /5.8	13.4	1.20	12.01	17	4	96	0	0	254.0		158.1	-9.0	44	N/A	2,000	100	5.8	2.0
C+ /5.7	13.4	1.20	11.56	5	4	96	0	0	254.0		152.7	-10.5	36	N/A	2,000	100	0.0	2.0
C+ /6.9	13.4	1.20	11.63	6	4	96	0	0	254.0		152.5	-10.3	36	N/A	2,000	100	0.0	2.0
B- /7.0	13.4	1.20	12.17	3	4	96	0	0	254.0		160.2	-10.1	46	N/A	1,000,000	0	0.0	2.0
C+ /5.8	13.5	1.20	12.17	4	4	96	0	0	254.0		160.2	-10.1	46	N/A	50,000	0	0.0	2.0
B /8.2	8.5	1.64	10.09	50	0	94	4	2	6.5		86.6	-9.3	89	N/A	2,000	100	5.8	0.2
B /8.2	8.4	1.63	9.99	15	0	94	4	2	6.5		82.7	-9.5	86	N/A	2,000	100	0.0	5.0
B /8.2	8.4	1.63	9.97	85	0	94	4	2	6.5		82.5	-9.6	86	N/A	2,000	100	0.0	1.0
B /8.6	8.5	1.63	10.15	1	0	94	4	2	6.5		87.5	-9.3	90	N/A	1,000,000	0	0.0	0.0
B /8.6	8.4	1.63	10.03	1	0	94	4	2	6.5		85.3	-9.5	89	N/A	1,000,000	0	0.0	0.0
B /8.2	8.5	1.64	10.12	574	0	94	4	2	6.5		85.8	-9.3	89	N/A	50,000	0	0.0	0.0

Fund Type	Fund Name	Ticker Symbol	Overall Weiss Investment Rating	Phone	Perfor-mance Rating/Pts	3 Mo	6 Mo	1Yr / Pct	3Yr / Pct	5Yr / Pct	Dividend Yield	Expense Ratio
	99 Pct = Best				PERFORMANCE		Total Return % through 6/30/06				Incl. in Returns	
	0 Pct = Worst								Annualized			
GL	Gartmore Inv Dest Conservative A	NDCAX	D+	(800) 848-0920	E- / 0.2	-0.79	0.51	2.57 / 6	4.12 / 2	3.58 /42	2.02	0.79
GL	Gartmore Inv Dest Conservative B	NDCBX	D+	(800) 848-0920	E- / 0.2	-0.79	0.35	2.02 / 4	3.46 / 2	2.89 /36	1.70	1.49
GL	Gartmore Inv Dest Conservative C	NDCCX	D+	(800) 848-0920	E / 0.3	-0.79	0.35	2.02 / 4	3.48 / 2	2.88 /36	1.70	1.49
GL	Gartmore Inv Dest Conservative Inst	GIMCX	C-	(800) 848-0920	E+ / 0.6	-0.68	0.68	2.97 / 7	4.37 / 3	3.69 /43	2.43	0.49
GL	Gartmore Inv Dest Conservative R	GCFRX	C-	(800) 848-0920	E / 0.5	-0.78	0.50	2.47 / 6	3.97 / 2	3.19 /39	2.24	1.09
GL	Gartmore Inv Dest Conservative Svc	NDCSX	C-	(800) 848-0920	E / 0.5	-0.88	0.39	2.37 / 5	4.03 / 2	3.49 /41	2.14	0.89
GL	Gartmore Inv Dest Mod Aggr A	NDMAX	C+	(800) 848-0920	C / 4.4	-1.61	3.69	11.01 /54	12.97 /49	5.37 /57	1.49	0.77
GL	Gartmore Inv Dest Mod Aggr B	NDMBX	C+	(800) 848-0920	C- / 4.1	-1.63	3.58	10.47 /50	12.21 /44	4.64 /51	1.10	1.49
GL	Gartmore Inv Dest Mod Aggr C	NDMCX	C+	(800) 848-0920	C / 4.7	-1.63	3.58	10.47 /50	12.23 /44	4.69 /52	1.10	1.49
GL	Gartmore Inv Dest Mod Aggr Inst	GMIAX	B	(800) 848-0920	C / 5.4	-1.61	3.76	11.24 /55	13.07 /49	5.39 /57	1.78	0.49
GL	Gartmore Inv Dest Mod Aggr R	GMARX	B	(800) 848-0920	C / 5.2	-1.63	3.70	11.04 /54	12.73 /47	4.93 /54	1.51	1.09
GL	Gartmore Inv Dest Mod Aggr Svc	NDMSX	B	(800) 848-0920	C / 5.3	-1.61	3.67	10.94 /53	12.86 /48	5.27 /56	1.50	0.89
GL	Gartmore Inv Dest Mod Conserv A	NADCX	C-	(800) 848-0920	E+ / 0.8	-1.16	1.16	4.70 /14	6.76 / 9	4.21 /48	1.87	0.82
GL	Gartmore Inv Dest Mod Conserv B	NBDCX	C-	(800) 848-0920	E+ / 0.6	-1.25	1.01	4.07 /11	6.09 / 7	3.54 /42	1.49	1.50
GL	Gartmore Inv Dest Mod Conserv C	NCDCX	C-	(800) 848-0920	D- / 1.0	-1.16	1.02	4.19 /11	6.08 / 7	3.55 /42	1.50	1.50
GL	Gartmore Inv Dest Mod Conserv Inst	GMIMX	C	(800) 848-0920	D / 1.6	-1.25	1.23	5.01 /15	6.93 /10	4.31 /49	2.20	0.50
GL	Gartmore Inv Dest Mod Conserv R	GMMRX	C-	(800) 848-0920	D- / 1.4	-1.25	1.16	4.69 /14	6.68 / 9	3.89 /45	1.89	1.10
GL	Gartmore Inv Dest Mod Conserv Svc	NSDCX	C-	(800) 848-0920	D- / 1.4	-1.15	1.24	4.72 /14	6.69 / 9	4.17 /47	1.92	0.90
GL	Gartmore Inv Dest Moderate A	NADMX	C	(800) 848-0920	D / 2.2	-1.51	2.34	7.50 /29	9.59 /25	4.68 /52	1.64	0.76
GL	Gartmore Inv Dest Moderate B	NBDMX	C	(800) 848-0920	D / 1.9	-1.52	2.21	6.90 /26	8.86 /20	3.95 /45	1.24	1.48
GL	Gartmore Inv Dest Moderate C	NCDMX	C	(800) 848-0920	D+ / 2.5	-1.52	2.21	6.92 /26	8.86 /20	3.92 /45	1.24	1.48
GL	Gartmore Inv Dest Moderate Inst	GMDIX	C+	(800) 848-0920	C- / 3.3	-1.51	2.51	7.83 /31	9.76 /26	4.72 /52	1.94	0.48
GL	Gartmore Inv Dest Moderate R	GMDRX	C+	(800) 848-0920	C- / 3.0	-1.52	2.43	7.43 /29	9.35 /23	4.23 /48	1.74	1.08
GL	Gartmore Inv Dest Moderate Svc	NSDMX	C+	(800) 848-0920	C- / 3.1	-1.51	2.33	7.34 /28	9.49 /24	4.56 /51	1.67	0.88
GR	Gartmore Large Cap Value A	NPVAX	B+	(800) 848-0920	C+ / 5.8	0.90	6.68	13.03 /64	15.24 /60	6.52 /64	0.96	1.46
GR	Gartmore Large Cap Value B	NLVBX	B+	(800) 848-0920	C+ / 6.0	0.73	6.28	12.36 /61	14.51 /56	5.82 /60	0.45	2.08
GR	Gartmore Large Cap Value C	NLVAX	B+	(800) 848-0920	C+ / 6.0	0.69	6.25	12.30 /61	14.50 /56	5.82 /60	0.43	2.08
GR	Gartmore Large Cap Value R	GLVRX	B+	(800) 848-0920	C+ / 6.3	0.87	6.54	13.01 /64	15.12 /59	6.15 /62	1.00	1.68
GR	Gartmore Long-Short Equity Plus A	MLSAX	E-	(800) 848-0920	D / 1.9	-1.92	1.74	8.16 /34	9.25 /22	2.76 /34	0.21	2.79
GR	Gartmore Long-Short Equity Plus B	MLSBX	E-	(800) 848-0920	D / 2.1	-2.03	1.41	7.51 /29	8.51 /18	2.18 /29	0.07	3.54
GR	Gartmore Long-Short Equity Plus C	MLSCX	E-	(800) 848-0920	D / 2.1	-2.07	1.39	7.37 /28	8.48 /18	0.96 /20	0.17	3.54
SC	● Gartmore Micro Cap Equity A	GMEAX	B	(800) 848-0920	A / 9.3	-4.67	12.42	20.78 /83	29.02 /95	--	0.00	1.86
SC	● Gartmore Micro Cap Equity B	GMEBX	B	(800) 848-0920	A / 9.3	-4.81	12.11	19.98 /82	28.12 /94	--	0.00	2.61
SC	● Gartmore Micro Cap Equity C	GMECX	B	(800) 848-0920	A / 9.3	-4.81	12.09	19.96 /82	28.16 /94	--	0.00	2.61
SC	● Gartmore Micro Cap Equity Inst	GMEIX	B	(800) 848-0920	A / 9.4	-4.58	12.64	21.17 /83	29.39 /95	--	0.00	1.63
SC	● Gartmore Micro Cap Equity Instl-Svc	GMESX	B	(800) 848-0920	A / 9.4	-4.58	12.64	21.17 /83	29.39 /95	--	0.00	1.62
SC	● Gartmore Micro Cap Equity R	GCERX	C+	(800) 848-0920	A / 9.3	-4.83	12.26	20.53 /82	28.27 /94	--	0.00	1.94
MC	Gartmore Mid Cap Gr Leaders A	NMGAX	C-	(800) 848-0920	C / 4.7	-3.10	0.27	9.86 /46	14.46 /56	1.46 /23	0.00	1.52
MC	Gartmore Mid Cap Gr Leaders B	NMGBX	C-	(800) 848-0920	C / 5.0	-3.28	-0.07	9.17 /41	13.71 /52	0.60 /18	0.00	2.22
MC	Gartmore Mid Cap Gr Leaders C	GMGCX	C	(800) 848-0920	C / 5.0	-3.28	-0.07	9.16 /41	13.70 /52	0.60 /18	0.00	2.23
MC	Gartmore Mid Cap Gr Leaders D	NMCGX	C-	(800) 848-0920	C / 5.0	-2.96	0.47	10.24 /48	14.84 /58	1.82 /26	0.00	1.22
MC	Gartmore Mid Cap Gr Leaders R	GMGRX	C	(800) 848-0920	C / 5.4	-3.05	0.34	9.95 /47	14.46 /56	1.62 /24	0.00	1.60
MC	Gartmore Mid Cap Growth A	GMCAX	C-	(800) 848-0920	C- / 4.2	-5.76	3.16	11.13 /54	13.07 /49	--	0.00	1.42
MC	Gartmore Mid Cap Growth B	GCPBX	C	(800) 848-0920	C / 4.4	-5.93	2.75	10.38 /49	12.33 /45	--	0.00	2.15
MC	Gartmore Mid Cap Growth C	GCPCX	C	(800) 848-0920	C / 4.4	-5.93	2.75	10.38 /49	12.33 /45	--	0.00	2.15
MC	Gartmore Mid Cap Growth Inst	GMCGX	C	(800) 848-0920	C / 5.0	-5.71	3.32	11.53 /57	13.39 /51	--	0.00	1.15
MC	Gartmore Mid Cap Growth R	GMCRX	C	(800) 848-0920	C / 4.7	-5.84	3.03	11.02 /54	12.93 /48	--	0.00	1.49
MC	Gartmore Mid Cap Market Index A	GMXAX	B-	(800) 848-0920	C+ / 6.4	-3.32	3.91	12.17 /60	17.25 /69	8.46 /74	0.96	0.70
MC	Gartmore Mid Cap Market Index B	GMCBX	B	(800) 848-0920	C+ / 6.2	-3.45	3.59	11.45 /56	16.57 /66	7.79 /71	0.48	1.31
MC	Gartmore Mid Cap Market Index Inst	GMXIX	B+	(800) 848-0920	B- / 7.2	-3.20	4.07	12.59 /63	17.73 /71	8.91 /76	1.37	0.31
GI	Gartmore Nationwide A	NWFAX	D-	(800) 848-0920	D+ / 2.8	-2.12	2.28	9.38 /43	10.67 /32	3.72 /43	0.65	1.14
GI	Gartmore Nationwide B	NWFBX	D-	(800) 848-0920	C- / 3.0	-2.24	1.98	8.65 /38	9.97 /27	3.00 /37	0.07	1.79

● Denotes fund is closed to new investors
* Denotes fund is included in Section II

176

RISK			NET ASSETS		ASSET					BULL / BEAR		FUND MANAGER		MINIMUMS		LOADS	
	3 Year		NAV						Portfolio	Last Bull	Last Bear	Manager	Manager	Initial	Additional	Front	Back
Risk Rating/Pts	Standard Deviation	Beta	As of 6/30/06	Total $(Mil)	Cash %	Stocks %	Bonds %	Other %	Turnover Ratio	Market Return	Market Return	Quality Pct	Tenure (Years)	Purch. $	Purch. $	End Load	End Load
B+ / 9.8	2.3	0.42	10.11	9	44	20	34	2	13.4	19.2	-0.4	51	N/A	2,000	100	5.8	0.2
B+ / 9.9	2.2	0.41	10.10	4	44	20	34	2	13.4	16.6	-0.6	43	N/A	2,000	100	0.0	5.0
B+ / 9.9	2.2	0.41	10.07	19	44	20	34	2	13.4	16.6	-0.6	44	N/A	2,000	100	0.0	1.0
B+ / 9.9	2.2	0.41	10.17	N/A	44	20	34	2	13.4	20.0	-0.5	55	N/A	1,000,000	0	0.0	0.0
B+ / 9.9	2.2	0.41	10.12	N/A	44	20	34	2	13.4	18.4	-0.6	50	N/A	1,000,000	0	0.0	0.0
B+ / 9.9	2.2	0.42	10.12	152	44	20	34	2	13.4	19.0	-0.5	50	N/A	50,000	0	0.0	0.0
B / 8.9	7.0	1.39	10.37	70	4	80	14	2	5.5	70.3	-7.4	84	N/A	2,000	100	5.8	0.2
B / 8.8	7.0	1.38	10.25	36	4	80	14	2	5.5	66.2	-7.6	79	N/A	2,000	100	0.0	5.0
B / 8.8	7.0	1.38	10.25	181	4	80	14	2	5.5	66.5	-7.6	80	N/A	2,000	100	0.0	1.0
B+ / 9.1	7.0	1.37	10.37	2	4	80	14	2	5.5	70.6	-7.5	85	N/A	1,000,000	0	0.0	0.0
B+ / 9.1	7.0	1.38	10.27	1	4	80	14	2	5.5	68.6	-7.6	83	N/A	1,000,000	0	0.0	0.0
B / 8.9	7.0	1.38	10.36	927	4	80	14	2	5.5	69.7	-7.5	84	N/A	50,000	0	0.0	0.0
B+ / 9.8	3.6	0.74	10.24	26	24	40	34	2	8.4	33.3	-2.7	62	N/A	2,000	100	5.8	0.2
B+ / 9.9	3.5	0.73	10.24	7	24	40	34	2	8.4	30.5	-2.8	56	N/A	2,000	100	0.0	5.0
B+ / 9.9	3.5	0.74	10.21	42	24	40	34	2	8.4	30.5	-2.7	55	N/A	2,000	100	0.0	1.0
B+ / 9.9	3.6	0.74	10.30	1	24	40	34	2	8.4	34.1	-2.7	64	N/A	1,000,000	0	0.0	0.0
B+ / 9.9	3.6	0.74	10.29	N/A	24	40	34	2	8.4	32.6	-2.8	62	N/A	1,000,000	0	0.0	0.0
B+ / 9.9	3.6	0.74	10.28	220	24	40	34	2	8.4	33.1	-2.7	62	N/A	50,000	0	0.0	0.0
B+ / 9.5	5.2	1.07	10.44	62	14	60	24	2	5.9	49.8	-5.1	73	N/A	2,000	100	5.8	0.2
B+ / 9.6	5.2	1.07	10.37	34	14	60	24	2	5.9	46.4	-5.2	66	N/A	2,000	100	0.0	5.0
B+ / 9.6	5.2	1.08	10.34	169	14	60	24	2	5.9	46.5	-5.3	66	N/A	2,000	100	0.0	1.0
B+ / 9.7	5.2	1.07	10.45	1	14	60	24	2	5.9	50.4	-5.1	74	N/A	1,000,000	0	0.0	0.0
B+ / 9.7	5.2	1.06	10.38	3	14	60	24	2	5.9	48.3	-5.2	71	N/A	1,000,000	0	0.0	0.0
B+ / 9.7	5.2	1.07	10.42	1,051	14	60	24	2	5.9	49.3	-5.1	72	N/A	50,000	0	0.0	0.0
B / 8.8	7.9	0.96	13.76	28	0	98	0	2	73.0	81.5	-8.8	90	N/A	2,000	100	5.8	0.5
B / 8.8	8.0	0.96	13.56	1	0	98	0	2	73.0	78.1	-9.0	86	N/A	2,000	100	0.0	2.0
B+ / 9.0	8.0	0.96	13.51	4	0	98	0	2	73.0	78.0	-9.0	86	N/A	2,000	100	0.0	2.0
B+ / 9.0	8.0	0.96	13.57	N/A	0	98	0	2	73.0	80.8	-9.0	89	N/A	1,000,000	0	0.0	2.0
E+ / 0.8	5.9	0.56	10.09	45	38	61	0	1	777.0	52.5	-7.7	77	N/A	2,000	100	5.8	1.0
E+ / 0.8	5.8	0.56	9.82	1	38	61	0	1	777.0	48.6	-7.7	70	N/A	2,000	100	0.0	2.0
E- / 0.0	5.9	0.56	7.45	34	38	61	0	1	777.0	48.7	-7.7	70	N/A	2,000	100	0.0	2.0
C / 4.8	17.4	1.06	23.89	65	6	94	0	0	93.0	206.3	-2.6	98	4	2,000	100	5.8	1.0
C / 4.7	17.4	1.06	23.15	8	6	94	0	0	93.0	199.3	-2.8	97	4	2,000	100	0.0	2.0
C / 4.8	17.4	1.06	23.17	39	6	94	0	0	93.0	199.6	-2.8	97	4	2,000	100	0.0	2.0
C / 4.9	17.4	1.06	24.15	14	6	94	0	0	93.0	208.8	-2.5	98	4	1,000,000	0	0.0	2.0
C / 4.9	17.4	1.06	24.15	N/A	6	94	0	0	93.0	208.8	-2.5	98	4	50,000	0	0.0	2.0
C- / 3.5	17.4	1.06	23.44	N/A	6	94	0	0	93.0	200.9	-2.6	97	4	1,000,000	0	0.0	2.0
C+ / 5.9	12.4	1.04	14.71	7	8	90	0	2	137.0	92.4	-9.1	20	N/A	2,000	100	5.8	1.0
C+ / 5.9	12.4	1.05	13.57	3	8	90	0	2	137.0	88.4	-9.2	16	N/A	2,000	100	0.0	2.0
C+ / 6.6	12.4	1.05	13.58	1	8	90	0	2	137.0	88.4	-9.2	16	N/A	2,000	100	0.0	2.0
C+ / 6.0	12.4	1.05	15.07	11	8	90	0	2	137.0	94.2	-9.0	22	N/A	2,000	100	4.5	2.0
C+ / 6.7	12.4	1.05	14.92	N/A	8	90	0	2	137.0	92.4	-9.0	20	N/A	1,000,000	0	0.0	2.0
C+ / 6.3	12.4	1.09	16.02	2	8	92	0	0	56.0	91.8	-6.8	11	3	2,000	100	5.8	0.5
B- / 7.2	12.4	1.09	15.70	N/A	8	92	0	0	56.0	88.4	-6.8	8	3	2,000	100	0.0	2.0
B- / 7.2	12.4	1.09	15.70	1	8	92	0	0	56.0	88.4	-6.8	8	3	2,000	100	0.0	2.0
B- / 7.2	12.4	1.09	16.18	17	8	92	0	0	56.0	93.4	-6.8	12	4	1,000,000	0	0.0	2.0
B- / 7.2	12.4	1.09	15.96	N/A	8	92	0	0	56.0	91.2	-6.8	10	3	1,000,000	0	0.0	2.0
B- / 7.4	10.8	1.00	15.26	195	0	100	0	0	17.0	99.7	-9.2	46	N/A	2,000	100	5.8	0.0
B- / 7.9	10.8	1.00	15.08	1	0	100	0	0	17.0	96.2	-9.3	39	N/A	2,000	100	0.0	5.0
B- / 7.4	10.8	1.00	15.36	1,029	0	100	0	0	17.0	102.3	-9.1	52	N/A	1,000,000	0	0.0	0.0
C / 5.3	8.6	1.08	19.33	113	0	98	0	2	176.0	63.4	-9.3	42	N/A	2,000	100	5.8	0.5
C / 5.2	8.6	1.08	18.70	22	0	98	0	2	176.0	59.9	-9.4	35	N/A	2,000	100	0.0	2.0

					PERFORMANCE							
	99 Pct = Best						Total Return % through 6/30/06				Incl. in Returns	
	0 Pct = Worst		Overall Weiss Investment Rating		Perfor-mance Rating/Pts				Annualized		Dividend Yield	Expense Ratio
Fund Type	Fund Name	Ticker Symbol		Phone		3 Mo	6 Mo	1Yr / Pct	3Yr / Pct	5Yr / Pct		
GI	Gartmore Nationwide C	GTRCX	D-	(800) 848-0920	D+ / 2.8	-2.28	1.90	8.63 /38	9.94 /27	2.99 /37	0.09	1.79
GI	Gartmore Nationwide D	MUIFX	D-	(800) 848-0920	C- / 3.0	-2.04	2.42	9.65 /45	10.99 /35	3.99 /46	0.89	0.85
GI	Gartmore Nationwide Inst	GNWIX	C	(800) 848-0920	C- / 3.7	-2.03	2.45	9.71 /45	11.04 /36	4.01 /46	0.98	0.81
GR	Gartmore Nationwide Ldrs A	GULAX	C	(800) 848-0920	C+ / 6.2	-0.40	4.50	13.64 /67	16.58 /66	--	1.57	1.51
GR	Gartmore Nationwide Ldrs B	GULBX	C	(800) 848-0920	C+ / 6.4	-0.54	4.16	12.84 /63	15.75 /62	--	1.19	2.20
GR	Gartmore Nationwide Ldrs C	GULCX	C	(800) 848-0920	C+ / 6.4	-0.54	4.17	12.94 /64	15.75 /62	--	1.26	2.20
GR	Gartmore Nationwide Ldrs Inst	GNLIX	B-	(800) 848-0920	C+ / 6.9	-0.26	4.71	14.02 /68	16.81 /67	--	1.92	1.20
GR	Gartmore Nationwide Ldrs Instl-Svc	GULIX	C+	(800) 848-0920	C+ / 6.8	-0.39	4.52	13.76 /67	16.64 /66	--	0.89	1.43
GR	Gartmore Nationwide Ldrs R	GNLRX	B-	(800) 848-0920	C+ / 6.7	-0.38	4.40	13.58 /67	16.33 /65	--	1.60	1.45
GI	Gartmore Nationwide R	GNWRX	C-	(800) 848-0920	C- / 3.5	-2.09	2.36	9.54 /44	10.71 /33	3.83 /44	0.71	0.96
GR	Gartmore Northpt SmCap Gr Inst	GNSIX	U	(800) 848-0920	U /	-4.13	12.23	18.87 /80		--	0.00	N/A
IX	Gartmore S&P 500 Index A	GRMAX	C-	(800) 848-0920	D+ / 2.8	-1.55	2.50	8.11 /33	10.70 /33	1.97 /27	1.37	0.50
IX	Gartmore S&P 500 Index B	GRMBX	C-	(800) 848-0920	D+ / 2.4	-1.75	2.14	7.32 /28	9.89 /27	1.25 /22	0.72	1.23
IX	Gartmore S&P 500 Index C	GRMCX	C	(800) 848-0920	C- / 3.1	-1.74	2.17	7.36 /28	9.90 /27	1.25 /22	0.73	1.23
IX	Gartmore S&P 500 Index Inst	GRMIX	C+	(800) 848-0920	C- / 4.0	-1.48	2.62	8.43 /36	11.01 /36	2.29 /30	1.68	0.23
IX	Gartmore S&P 500 Index Instl-Svc	GRISX	C	(800) 848-0920	C- / 3.8	-1.54	2.50	8.17 /34	10.69 /33	2.01 /27	1.44	0.48
IX	Gartmore S&P 500 Index L	GRMLX	C+	(800) 848-0920	C- / 3.9	-1.50	2.58	8.34 /35	10.90 /35	2.19 /29	1.61	0.30
IX	Gartmore S&P 500 Index Svc	GRMSX	C	(800) 848-0920	C- / 3.7	-1.59	2.43	7.94 /32	10.54 /31	1.86 /26	1.30	0.63
SC	Gartmore Small Cap Fd A	GSXAX	B+	(800) 848-0920	A / 9.4	-5.09	10.75	26.72 /91	29.04 /95	14.56 /91	0.06	1.71
SC	Gartmore Small Cap Fd B	GSXBX	B+	(800) 848-0920	A / 9.4	-5.24	10.40	26.05 /90	28.28 /94	13.82 /90	0.00	2.29
SC	Gartmore Small Cap Fd C	GSXCX	B	(800) 848-0920	A / 9.4	-5.23	10.38	26.00 /90	28.25 /94	13.81 /90	0.00	2.32
SC	Gartmore Small Cap Fd Inst	GSCIX	A+	(800) 848-0920	A / 9.5	-5.02	10.92	27.15 /92	29.43 /95	14.85 /92	0.13	1.32
SC	Gartmore Small Cap Fd R	GNSRX	A+	(800) 848-0920	A / 9.4	-5.09	10.72	26.75 /91	28.85 /95	14.13 /90	0.07	1.74
SC	Gartmore Small Cap Index A	GMRAX	C+	(800) 848-0920	C+ / 6.8	-5.30	7.66	13.96 /68	18.00 /72	7.82 /71	0.93	0.69
SC	Gartmore Small Cap Index B	GMRBX	C+	(800) 848-0920	C+ / 6.6	-5.51	7.29	13.10 /65	17.17 /69	7.16 /68	0.41	1.29
SC	Gartmore Small Cap Index Inst	GMRIX	B-	(800) 848-0920	B / 7.6	-5.24	7.88	14.39 /70	18.47 /74	8.29 /73	1.34	0.29
GR	Gartmore U.S. Gr Leaders A	GXXAX	E+	(800) 848-0920	D+ / 2.8	-7.41	-4.53	4.70 /14	12.70 /47	6.77 /65	0.00	1.56
GR	Gartmore U.S. Gr Leaders B	GXXBX	D-	(800) 848-0920	C- / 3.1	-7.63	-4.92	3.99 /10	11.94 /42	6.03 /61	0.00	2.24
GR	Gartmore U.S. Gr Leaders C	GXXCX	D-	(800) 848-0920	C- / 3.1	-7.58	-4.89	4.08 /11	11.90 /42	6.05 /61	0.00	2.22
GR	Gartmore U.S. Gr Leaders Inst	GGLIX	D	(800) 848-0920	C- / 3.8	-7.38	-4.45	5.06 /15	12.96 /49	7.05 /67	0.00	1.23
GR	Gartmore U.S. Gr Leaders Instl-Svc	GXXIX	D-	(800) 848-0920	C- / 3.7	-7.41	-4.47	4.85 /14	12.81 /48	6.96 /66	0.00	1.48
GR	Gartmore U.S. Gr Leaders R	GGLRX	D	(800) 848-0920	C- / 3.5	-7.52	-4.65	4.72 /14	12.52 /46	6.36 /63	0.00	1.54
SC	Gartmore Value Opp Fund A	GVOAX	D+	(800) 848-0920	C+ / 6.9	-3.79	9.50	15.21 /72	17.87 /72	8.31 /73	0.00	1.49
SC	Gartmore Value Opp Fund B	GVOBX	C-	(800) 848-0920	B- / 7.0	-4.03	9.08	14.36 /69	17.09 /68	7.60 /70	0.00	2.14
SC	Gartmore Value Opp Fund C	GVOCX	B	(800) 848-0920	B- / 7.1	-3.98	9.11	14.40 /70	17.11 /68	7.60 /70	0.00	2.14
SC	Gartmore Value Opp Fund Inst	GVAIX	B+	(800) 848-0920	B- / 7.4	-3.79	9.65	15.51 /73	18.20 /73	8.59 /75	0.00	1.08
SC	Gartmore Value Opp Fund R	GVORX	B	(800) 848-0920	B- / 7.3	-3.91	9.42	15.12 /72	17.66 /71	7.91 /71	0.00	1.61
GL	Gartmore Worldwd Leaders A	GLLAX	B	(800) 848-0920	B+ / 8.4	-1.14	7.74	27.44 /92	22.45 /86	7.72 /70	0.23	1.69
GL	Gartmore Worldwd Leaders B	GLLBX	B	(800) 848-0920	B+ / 8.5	-1.36	7.42	26.65 /91	21.57 /84	6.97 /66	0.08	2.41
GL	Gartmore Worldwd Leaders C	GLLCX	B	(800) 848-0920	B+ / 8.4	-1.33	7.41	26.55 /91	21.62 /84	6.98 /67	0.10	2.41
GL	Gartmore Worldwd Leaders Inst	GWLIX	A	(800) 848-0920	B+ / 8.7	-1.15	7.92	27.80 /92	22.66 /86	7.99 /72	0.31	1.40
GL	Gartmore Worldwd Leaders Instl-Svc	GLLSX	B+	(800) 848-0920	B+ / 8.7	-1.22	7.77	27.54 /92	22.46 /86	7.89 /71	0.24	1.64
GL	Gartmore Worldwd Leaders R	GWLRX	A-	(800) 848-0920	B+ / 8.6	-1.31	7.58	27.23 /92	22.13 /85	7.26 /68	0.20	1.75
* GI	Gateway Fund	GATEX	C-	(800) 354-6339	D / 1.9	0.88	4.15	6.25 /22	7.13 /11	3.89 /45	2.20	0.95
GL	GE Global Equity A	GEGEX	C+	(800) 242-0134	C+ / 6.1	-1.82	6.16	21.75 /84	15.61 /62	4.70 /52	0.53	1.45
GL	GE Global Equity B	GGEBX	C+	(800) 242-0134	C+ / 6.4	-2.01	5.74	20.83 /83	14.76 /58	3.93 /45	0.00	2.20
GL	GE Global Equity Y	GGEDX	B-	(800) 242-0134	C+ / 6.9	-1.77	6.28	22.06 /84	15.90 /63	4.98 /54	0.78	1.20
FO	GE Institutional Intl Equity Inv	GIEIX	A	(800) 242-0134	A- / 9.2	-0.88	9.69	31.20 /95	24.32 /90	9.30 /78	1.23	0.57
IX	GE Institutional S&P 500 Index Inv	GIDIX	C+	(800) 242-0134	C- / 4.0	-1.54	2.62	8.43 /36	11.02 /36	2.27 /30	1.79	0.15
SC	GE Institutional Sm-Cap Val Eq Inv	GSVIX	C+	(800) 242-0134	C+ / 6.7	-6.69	5.35	11.02 /54	16.78 /67	8.42 /74	0.37	0.61
GI	GE Institutional Strategic Invmnt	GSIVX	D+	(800) 242-0134	D+ / 2.4	-1.48	3.01	8.51 /37	8.44 /17	4.79 /52	1.65	0.61
GR	GE Institutional US Equity Inv	GUSIX	C-	(800) 242-0134	D+ / 2.4	-0.95	3.47	7.52 /29	8.11 /16	1.51 /24	1.38	0.37

● Denotes fund is closed to new investors

* Denotes fund is included in Section II

RISK			NET ASSETS		ASSET					BULL / BEAR		FUND MANAGER		MINIMUMS		LOADS	
	3 Year		NAV						Portfolio	Last Bull	Last Bear	Manager	Manager	Initial	Additional	Front	Back
Risk	Standard		As of	Total	Cash	Stocks	Bonds	Other	Turnover	Market	Market	Quality	Tenure	Purch.	Purch.	End	End
Rating/Pts	Deviation	Beta	6/30/06	$(Mil)	%	%	%	%	Ratio	Return	Return	Pct	(Years)	$	$	Load	Load
C / 5.2	8.6	1.08	18.67	1	0	98	0	2	176.0	59.9	-9.4	35	N/A	2,000	100	1.0	2.0
C / 5.3	8.6	1.08	19.14	1,106	0	98	0	2	176.0	64.7	-9.2	45	N/A	2,000	100	4.5	2.0
B- / 7.7	8.6	1.07	19.14	7	0	98	0	2	176.0	64.9	-9.2	46	N/A	1,000,000	0	0.0	2.0
C+ / 6.0	11.0	1.13	13.32	6	8	90	0	2	476.0	84.4	-8.0	88	N/A	2,000	100	5.8	1.0
C+ / 5.9	11.0	1.13	12.99	1	8	90	0	2	476.0	80.3	-8.0	84	N/A	2,000	100	0.0	2.0
C+ / 5.9	11.1	1.13	12.98	3	8	90	0	2	476.0	80.3	-8.1	84	N/A	2,000	100	0.0	2.0
B- / 7.8	11.1	1.13	13.37	N/A	8	90	0	2	476.0	85.4	-7.9	89	N/A	1,000,000	0	0.0	2.0
C+ / 6.2	11.1	1.13	13.48	N/A	8	90	0	2	476.0	84.8	-7.9	89	N/A	50,000	0	0.0	2.0
B- / 7.8	11.1	1.14	13.11	N/A	8	90	0	2	476.0	82.9	-8.0	87	N/A	1,000,000	0	0.0	2.0
B- / 7.7	8.6	1.07	19.18	N/A	0	98	0	2	176.0	63.5	-9.2	42	N/A	1,000,000	0	0.0	2.0
U /	N/A	N/A	12.76	50	3	96	0	1	N/A	N/A	N/A	N/A	N/A	1,000,000	0	0.0	2.0
B / 8.3	7.6	1.00	10.82	36	0	100	0	0	5.0	62.4	-9.9	50	N/A	2,000	100	5.8	0.0
B / 8.6	7.6	1.00	10.79	6	0	100	0	0	5.0	58.6	-10.0	41	N/A	2,000	100	0.0	5.0
B / 8.4	7.6	1.00	10.74	1	0	100	0	0	5.0	58.6	-10.0	41	N/A	2,000	100	0.0	1.0
B / 8.4	7.7	1.00	10.87	2,429	0	100	0	0	5.0	63.7	-9.8	54	N/A	1,000,000	0	0.0	0.0
B / 8.4	7.7	1.00	10.86	76	0	100	0	0	5.0	62.3	-9.8	50	N/A	50,000	0	0.0	0.0
B / 8.5	7.7	1.00	10.89	N/A	0	100	0	0	5.0	63.4	-9.8	52	N/A	2,000	100	0.0	0.0
B / 8.6	7.6	0.99	10.82	581	0	100	0	0	5.0	61.5	-9.8	49	N/A	25,000	100	0.0	0.0
C+ / 5.7	14.7	0.98	19.30	141	2	96	0	2	252.0	183.8	-10.3	99	N/A	2,000	100	5.8	0.5
C / 5.5	14.8	0.98	18.26	8	2	96	0	2	252.0	178.4	-10.4	98	N/A	2,000	100	0.0	2.0
C / 4.6	14.8	0.98	18.29	55	2	96	0	2	252.0	178.6	-11.4	98	N/A	2,000	100	0.0	1.0
C+ / 6.9	14.8	0.98	19.66	29	2	96	0	2	252.0	186.3	-10.3	99	N/A	1,000,000	0	0.0	2.0
C+ / 6.9	14.8	0.98	18.53	N/A	2	96	0	2	252.0	182.0	-10.4	99	N/A	1,000,000	0	0.0	2.0
C+ / 6.1	14.6	1.00	12.76	99	0	100	0	0	23.0	115.4	-10.9	48	6	2,000	100	5.8	0.0
C+ / 6.7	14.5	1.00	12.66	1	0	100	0	0	23.0	111.0	-11.1	40	6	2,000	100	0.0	5.0
C+ / 6.2	14.5	1.00	12.86	452	0	100	0	0	23.0	118.5	-11.0	54	7	1,000,000	0	0.0	0.0
C / 4.5	12.4	1.37	9.49	102	4	94	0	2	408.0	99.0	-10.2	35	6	2,000	100	5.8	1.0
C / 4.4	12.4	1.37	9.08	6	4	94	0	2	408.0	94.7	-10.4	30	6	2,000	100	0.0	2.0
C / 5.4	12.5	1.38	9.14	38	4	94	0	2	408.0	94.5	-10.3	29	6	2,000	100	0.0	2.0
C / 5.5	12.5	1.38	9.66	4	4	94	0	2	408.0	100.1	-10.1	37	2	1,000,000	0	0.0	2.0
C / 4.5	12.4	1.37	9.62	1	4	94	0	2	408.0	99.4	-10.1	36	6	50,000	0	0.0	2.0
C / 5.4	12.5	1.37	9.23	1	4	94	0	2	408.0	97.5	-10.4	34	3	1,000,000	0	0.0	2.0
C- / 3.4	12.5	0.84	14.98	13	2	96	0	2	170.0	103.6	-9.3	74	6	2,000	100	5.8	1.0
C- / 3.3	12.6	0.85	14.53	3	2	96	0	2	170.0	99.4	-9.4	67	6	2,000	100	0.0	2.0
B- / 7.3	12.6	0.85	14.49	1	2	96	0	2	170.0	99.4	-9.3	67	5	2,000	100	0.0	2.0
B- / 7.3	12.6	0.85	15.22	N/A	2	96	0	2	170.0	105.3	-9.2	76	2	1,000,000	0	0.0	2.0
B- / 7.3	12.6	0.85	14.75	N/A	2	96	0	2	170.0	102.1	-9.4	72	3	1,000,000	0	0.0	2.0
C+ / 6.1	11.6	1.02	10.64	40	0	98	0	2	347.0	128.7	-12.9	33	N/A	2,000	100	5.8	1.0
C+ / 6.0	11.6	1.02	10.25	1	0	98	0	2	347.0	123.9	-13.1	28	N/A	2,000	100	0.0	2.0
C+ / 6.0	11.6	1.02	10.29	3	0	98	0	2	347.0	124.1	-13.2	27	N/A	2,000	100	1.0	2.0
C+ / 6.9	11.6	1.02	10.79	N/A	0	98	0	2	347.0	130.2	-12.9	34	N/A	1,000,000	0	0.0	2.0
C+ / 6.1	11.6	1.02	10.75	N/A	0	98	0	2	347.0	129.3	-12.9	33	N/A	50,000	0	0.0	2.0
C+ / 6.9	11.6	1.02	10.36	N/A	0	98	0	2	347.0	126.9	-13.1	31	N/A	1,000,000	0	0.0	2.0
B+ / 9.3	2.8	0.32	25.91	2,934	1	98	0	1	15.0	33.9	-4.4	76	12	1,000	100	0.0	0.0
B- / 7.1	9.4	0.87	23.77	34	4	95	0	1	61.0	87.3	-9.5	14	13	500	100	5.8	2.0
B- / 7.1	9.4	0.87	21.93	1	4	95	0	1	61.0	83.0	-9.6	11	13	500	100	0.0	2.0
B- / 7.1	9.4	0.87	23.86	19	4	95	0	1	61.0	88.8	-9.4	16	13	500	100	0.0	2.0
C+ / 6.6	11.5	1.10	14.72	1,142	3	96	0	1	40.0	138.2	-9.3	33	9	5,000,000	0	0.0	0.0
B / 8.7	7.6	1.00	12.13	102	2	97	0	1	12.0	63.8	-9.7	54	9	5,000,000	0	0.0	0.0
C+ / 6.4	12.3	0.81	15.35	577	3	96	0	1	33.0	97.3	-9.6	69	8	5,000,000	0	0.0	0.0
B- / 7.3	5.8	0.69	11.28	305	4	73	22	1	131.0	47.1	-4.8	57	9	5,000,000	0	0.0	0.0
B / 8.7	6.5	0.82	12.51	511	2	97	0	1	42.0	49.4	-10.0	39	N/A	5,000,000	0	0.0	0.0

	99 Pct = Best 0 Pct = Worst		Overall Weiss		PERFORMANCE							
					Perfor- mance		Total Return % through 6/30/06				Incl. in Returns	
			Investment						Annualized		Dividend	Expense
Fund Type	Fund Name	Ticker Symbol	Rating	Phone	Rating/Pts	3 Mo	6 Mo	1Yr / Pct	3Yr / Pct	5Yr / Pct	Yield	Ratio
GI	GE Institutional Value Equity Inv	GEIVX	C+	(800) 242-0134	C- / 4.0	-0.46	3.95	8.60 /38	10.67 /32	3.41 /40	1.70	0.44
FO	GE International Equity Fd A	GEICX	B+	(800) 242-0134	B+ / 8.5	-1.35	8.92	29.91 /94	22.59 /86	5.69 /59	0.71	1.39
FO	GE International Equity Fd B	GEIBX	B+	(800) 242-0134	B+ / 8.6	-1.50	8.52	28.97 /94	21.60 /84	4.85 /53	0.17	2.14
FO	GE International Equity Fd Y	GEIDX	A-	(800) 242-0134	B+ / 8.9	-1.28	9.21	30.45 /95	22.85 /87	5.94 /61	0.94	1.14
GR	GE Premier Growth Equity A	GEPCX	D-	(800) 242-0134	E / 0.5	-4.29	-1.37	2.73 / 6	6.65 / 9	0.74 /19	0.00	0.98
GR	GE Premier Growth Equity B	GEPBX	D-	(800) 242-0134	E / 0.5	-4.52	-1.75	1.93 / 4	5.85 / 6	-0.01 /15	0.00	1.73
GR	GE Premier Growth Equity Y	GEPDX	D-	(800) 242-0134	D- / 1.2	-4.26	-1.28	2.98 / 7	6.92 /10	0.99 /20	0.21	0.73
★ GI	GE S&S Program Mutual Fund	GESSX	C-	(800) 242-0134	C- / 3.0	-0.87	3.59	7.72 /31	9.12 /22	2.36 /31	1.60	0.09
SC	GE Small Cap Equity A	GASCX	C+	(800) 242-0134	C+ / 5.7	-6.88	4.88	10.50 /50	16.44 /65	7.92 /71	0.10	1.19
SC	GE Small Cap Equity B	GBSCX	C-	(800) 242-0134	C+ / 5.7	-7.02	4.57	9.70 /45	15.57 /62	7.17 /68	0.00	1.94
SC	GE Small Cap Equity C	GESCX	C+	(800) 242-0134	C+ / 6.0	-7.04	4.51	9.66 /45	15.56 /62	7.10 /67	0.00	1.94
AA	GE Strategic Investment Fd A	GESIX	D	(800) 242-0134	D / 1.6	-1.71	2.86	8.10 /33	8.14 /16	4.58 /51	1.52	0.92
AA	GE Strategic Investment Fd B	GESBX	D	(800) 242-0134	D- / 1.4	-1.89	2.51	7.30 /28	7.35 /12	3.81 /44	0.88	1.67
AA	GE Strategic Investment Fd Y	GESDX	C-	(800) 242-0134	D+ / 2.5	-1.62	3.58	8.99 /40	8.62 /19	4.97 /54	1.85	0.67
GR	GE US Equity A	GEEQX	D+	(800) 242-0134	D / 1.6	-1.05	3.18	6.95 /26	8.51 /18	1.70 /25	1.47	0.79
GR	GE US Equity B	GEEBX	D+	(800) 242-0134	D- / 1.5	-1.24	2.82	6.17 /21	7.70 /13	0.94 /20	0.58	1.55
GR	GE US Equity Y	GEEDX	C-	(800) 242-0134	D+ / 2.7	-0.98	3.34	7.25 /28	8.78 /20	1.96 /27	1.83	0.54
IN	GE Value Equity Fund A	ITVAX	D+	(800) 242-0134	D+ / 2.3	-0.62	3.60	7.80 /31	9.81 /26	2.67 /33	0.74	1.20
IN	GE Value Equity Fund B	ITVBX	D+	(800) 242-0134	D / 2.2	-0.83	3.17	7.03 /26	9.00 /21	1.89 /26	0.00	1.95
IN	GE Value Equity Fund Y	ITVYX	C	(800) 242-0134	C- / 3.5	-0.50	3.83	8.18 /34	10.02 /28	2.87 /36	0.99	0.95
HL	Genomics Fund	GENEX	E	(800) 527-9500	D- / 1.4	-14.64	-5.79	4.39 /12	9.40 /23	-9.85 / 0	0.00	1.90
FO	Glenmede International Equity	GTCIX	B-	(800) 442-8299	A+ / 9.6	0.16	11.50	41.75 /98	28.79 /95	14.24 /91	1.21	1.10
GR	Glenmede Large Cap Growth Fund	GTLLX	U	(800) 442-8299	U /	-1.76	1.37	12.43 /62	--	--	0.39	0.93
GI	Glenmede Large Cap Value Fd	GTMEX	C+	(800) 442-8299	C+ / 6.4	-1.12	2.69	10.13 /48	15.65 /62	6.68 /65	1.34	0.88
FO	Glenmede Philadelphia Intl Fund	GTIIX	A+	(800) 442-8299	A- / 9.0	0.03	11.10	26.84 /91	23.02 /87	10.47 /82	0.96	0.85
SC	Glenmede Small Cap Equity Adv	GTCSX	D+	(800) 442-8299	B- / 7.0	-4.11	7.91	11.80 /58	16.71 /67	10.17 /81	0.00	0.92
SC	Glenmede Small Cap Equity I	GTSCX	C-	(800) 442-8299	B- / 7.0	-4.06	8.06	12.04 /60	16.95 /68	10.41 /82	0.00	0.72
GR	Glenmede Strategic Equity	GTCEX	C	(800) 442-8299	C- / 3.7	-1.24	3.07	6.40 /23	10.69 /33	1.31 /22	0.70	0.85
SC	Glenmede U.S. Emerging Growth	GTGSX	C-	(800) 442-8299	C+ / 6.5	-5.49	7.62	21.10 /83	14.77 /58	0.09 /16	0.00	0.93
GL	Globalt Growth Fund	GROWX	D	(800) 408-4682	D- / 1.5	-5.87	-3.58	1.73 / 4	8.20 /16	-1.01 /12	0.07	1.17
GL	GMO Alpha Only Fund III	GGHEX	D+		E / 0.4	0.10	0.88	2.33 / 5	3.23 / 1	5.36 /57	3.58	0.75
AA	GMO Benchmark Free Allocation III	GBMFX	U		U /	-0.82	3.36	14.66 /71	--	--	5.18	0.65
EM	GMO Emerging Countries Fund M	GECMX	B-		A+ / 9.8	-3.48	6.71	37.61 /97	37.08 /99	--	1.38	1.10
EM	GMO Emerging Markets Fund IV	GMEFX	B-		A+ / 9.9	-3.58	6.50	37.75 /97	39.36 /99	26.52 /99	1.77	1.07
EM	GMO Emerging Markets Fund V	GEMVX	U		U /	-3.58	6.50	25.83 /89	--	--	2.01	1.05
EM	GMO Emerging Markets Fund VI	GEMMX	B-		A+ / 9.9	-3.58	6.55	37.82 /97	39.46 /99	--	1.83	1.02
FO	GMO Foreign Fund II	GMFRX	B+		A- / 9.1	0.00	10.06	27.69 /92	24.26 /90	14.02 /90	1.80	0.82
FO	GMO Foreign Fund III	GMOFX	A+		A- / 9.1	0.06	10.15	27.80 /92	24.36 /90	14.10 /90	1.84	0.75
FO	GMO Foreign Fund IV	GMFFX	A+		A- / 9.2	0.06	10.15	27.87 /92	24.46 /90	14.19 /90	1.89	0.69
FO	GMO Foreign Fund M	GMFMX	A+		A- / 9.1	0.00	10.03	27.46 /92	24.03 /89	--	1.64	1.82
FO	GMO Foreign Small Companies IV	GFSFX	A+		A+ / 9.7	0.05	12.86	30.86 /95	31.51 /96	--	1.55	0.80
GL	GMO Glb Bal Asset Allocation III	GMWAX	B+		C+ / 5.6	-0.93	2.90	10.09 /47	13.67 /52	10.59 /83	3.02	0.53
GR	● GMO Growth M	GMGMX	D-		E- / 0.2	-9.04	-7.91	-4.18 / 0	4.42 / 3	--	0.13	0.78
FO	GMO International Core Eqty III	GMIEX	U		U /	0.52	10.70	--	--	--	0.00	0.54
FO	GMO International Core Eqty IV	GMIRX	U		U /	0.57	10.77	--	--	--	0.00	0.48
GL	GMO International Eq Alloc III	GIEAX	A+		A / 9.3	-0.40	9.63	27.70 /92	27.38 /93	18.12 /95	2.57	0.73
FO	GMO International Growth Eqty III	GMIGX	U		U /	0.32	9.72	--	--	--	0.00	0.70
FO	GMO International Intrinsic Val III	GMOIX	B+		A- / 9.2	0.62	11.05	26.71 /91	25.46 /92	16.06 /93	1.03	0.69
FO	GMO International Intrinsic Val IV	GMCFX	A+		A- / 9.2	0.65	11.12	26.76 /91	25.53 /92	16.13 /93	1.07	0.63
FO	GMO International Small Co III	GMISX	B+		A+ / 9.7	-2.37	8.85	30.74 /95	32.45 /97	21.10 /97	2.02	0.75
RE	GMO Real Estate III	GMORX	B		A- / 9.1	-1.80	12.92	18.37 /80	24.88 /91	17.38 /94	2.49	0.69
BA	GMO Strategic Balanced Allc III	GBATX	U		U /	-0.26	5.68	14.51 /70	--	--	2.08	0.54

● Denotes fund is closed to new investors
★ Denotes fund is included in Section II

www.WeissRatings.com

RISK			NET ASSETS		ASSET				BULL / BEAR		FUND MANAGER		MINIMUMS		LOADS	
	3 Year		NAV						Last Bull	Last Bear	Manager	Manager	Initial	Additional	Front	Back
Risk Rating/Pts	Standard Deviation	Beta	As of 6/30/06	Total $(Mil)	Cash %	Stocks %	Bonds %	Other %	Portfolio Turnover Ratio	Market Return	Market Return	Quality Pct	Tenure (Years)	Purch. $	Purch. $	End Load	End Load
B / 8.8	7.1	0.89	10.78	82	0	99	0	1	36.0	60.0	-8.7	61	8	5,000,000	0	0.0	0.0
C+ / 6.5	11.6	1.10	18.31	35	0	99	0	1	66.0	116.5	-9.2	22	12	500	100	5.8	2.0
C+ / 6.4	11.6	1.10	17.07	1	0	99	0	1	66.0	110.6	-9.3	17	12	500	100	0.0	2.0
C+ / 6.5	11.5	1.10	18.49	7	0	99	0	1	66.0	117.8	-9.2	24	12	500	100	0.0	2.0
B- / 7.3	8.5	1.00	26.55	245	3	96	0	1	34.0	46.6	-9.5	18	10	500	100	5.8	1.0
B- / 7.2	8.5	0.99	24.70	18	3	96	0	1	34.0	43.2	-9.7	14	10	500	100	0.0	4.0
B- / 7.3	8.5	0.99	26.98	76	3	96	0	1	34.0	47.8	-9.5	20	10	500	100	0.0	1.0
B- / 7.7	6.8	0.87	44.39	3,934	1	98	0	1	42.0	53.5	-9.0	46	26	100	25	0.0	0.0
B- / 7.3	12.4	0.82	16.11	57	2	97	0	1	34.0	96.1	-11.8	64	8	500	100	5.8	1.0
C / 5.2	12.4	0.82	15.10	10	2	97	0	1	34.0	91.5	-11.9	56	8	500	100	0.0	4.0
B- / 7.3	12.4	0.82	15.05	7	2	97	0	1	34.0	91.5	-11.9	56	8	500	100	0.0	1.0
B- / 7.8	5.8	1.14	24.09	126	3	74	21	2	119.0	46.4	-4.8	54	N/A	500	100	5.8	0.0
B- / 7.9	5.8	1.14	23.30	15	3	74	21	2	119.0	43.1	-5.0	44	13	500	100	0.0	4.0
B- / 7.9	5.8	1.14	24.28	2	3	74	21	2	119.0	48.4	-4.7	60	13	500	100	0.0	0.0
B / 8.3	6.8	0.87	28.27	279	5	94	0	1	36.0	50.8	-9.2	39	N/A	500	100	5.8	1.0
B / 8.4	6.8	0.87	27.02	7	5	94	0	1	36.0	47.3	-9.4	33	N/A	500	100	0.0	4.0
B / 8.3	6.8	0.86	28.17	108	5	94	0	1	36.0	52.1	-9.2	42	N/A	500	100	0.0	0.0
B- / 7.8	7.0	0.89	11.22	44	4	95	0	1	35.0	56.2	-8.8	52	N/A	500	100	5.8	1.0
B- / 7.9	7.0	0.88	10.73	4	4	95	0	1	35.0	52.2	-8.9	43	N/A	500	100	0.0	4.0
B- / 7.9	7.1	0.90	11.92	N/A	4	95	0	1	35.0	57.0	-8.7	54	N/A	500	100	0.0	0.0
C- / 3.7	16.5	1.10	3.09	6	12	87	0	1	159.8	111.8	-11.1	29	3	5,000	100	0.0	2.0
C- / 4.0	12.7	1.03	21.15	902	1	98	0	1	47.0	166.4	-11.0	84	18	25,000	1,000	0.0	0.0
U /	N/A	N/A	12.04	32	0	0	0	100	N/A	N/A	N/A	N/A	2	25,000	1,000	0.0	0.0
C+ / 6.9	7.5	0.88	10.88	43	3	96	0	1	76.0	83.6	-8.3	93	5	25,000	1,000	0.0	0.0
B- / 7.3	9.8	0.93	20.95	856	4	94	0	2	47.0	130.8	-10.9	60	14	1,000,000	1,000	0.0	0.0
C- / 3.4	12.6	0.82	18.68	240	2	97	0	1	51.0	101.6	-6.5	68	14	25,000	1,000	0.0	0.0
C- / 3.4	12.6	0.82	18.90	N/A	2	97	0	1	51.0	103.0	-6.4	70	8	10,000,000	0	0.0	0.0
B / 8.3	7.3	0.91	17.91	82	0	98	0	2	89.0	58.1	-10.0	60	N/A	25,000	1,000	0.0	0.0
C / 4.3	16.3	1.05	7.06	33	6	93	0	1	45.0	103.8	-13.1	19	7	25,000	1,000	0.0	0.0
B- / 7.4	10.4	0.77	13.47	7	0	99	0	1	123.8	57.5	-7.4	2	11	25,000	5,000	0.0	0.0
B+ / 9.9	2.0	0.05	10.33	205	11	88	0	1	40.0	11.4	2.9	N/A	N/A	5,000,000	0	0.0	0.1
U /	N/A	N/A	27.65	1,203	0	46	53	1	47.0	N/A	N/A	N/A	N/A	5,000,000	0	0.0	0.0
C- / 4.2	18.5	1.12	18.61	32	3	96	0	1	35.0	243.4	N/A	29	3	5,000,000	0	0.0	0.0
C- / 4.1	18.7	1.13	21.80	2,823	2	97	0	1	41.0	258.1	-3.6	43	N/A	125,000,000	0	0.0	0.0
U /	N/A	N/A	21.79	1,244	2	97	0	1	41.0	N/A	N/A	N/A	N/A	250,000,000	0	0.0	0.0
C- / 4.0	18.8	1.13	21.81	3,016	2	97	0	1	41.0	N/A	N/A	43	N/A	300,000,000	0	0.0	0.0
C+ / 5.8	10.2	0.99	17.29	1,154	5	94	0	1	25.0	135.2	-5.7	56	10	5,000,000	0	0.0	0.0
B- / 7.1	10.2	0.99	17.36	3,783	5	94	0	1	25.0	135.9	-5.8	57	10	5,000,000	0	0.0	0.0
B- / 7.1	10.2	0.99	17.37	2,576	5	94	0	1	25.0	136.4	-5.8	58	8	250,000,000	0	0.0	0.0
B- / 7.1	10.1	0.99	17.34	6	5	94	0	1	25.0	133.5	-5.8	54	3	5,000,000	0	0.0	0.0
B- / 7.8	11.0	1.03	18.78	605	6	93	0	1	40.0	187.5	-2.9	93	N/A	125,000,000	0	0.0	0.0
B+ / 9.4	6.1	1.21	11.72	2,040	0	73	26	1	16.0	70.9	-1.8	92	N/A	5,000,000	0	0.0	0.0
B- / 7.5	9.4	1.11	17.00	N/A	2	98	0	0	49.0	42.8	-7.3	6	4	5,000,000	0	0.0	0.0
U /	N/A	N/A	36.92	872	5	94	0	1	43.0	N/A	N/A	N/A	N/A	5,000,000	0	0.0	0.0
U /	N/A	N/A	36.92	812	5	94	0	1	43.0	N/A	N/A	N/A	N/A	125,000,000	0	0.0	0.0
B- / 7.6	11.6	1.94	17.64	676	0	100	0	0	7.0	162.3	-3.8	99	10	5,000,000	0	0.0	0.0
U /	N/A	N/A	31.27	3,180	5	94	0	1	33.0	N/A	N/A	N/A	N/A	5,000,000	0	0.0	0.0
C+ / 5.8	10.0	0.96	34.07	2,368	3	96	0	1	38.0	146.9	-3.8	73	N/A	5,000,000	0	0.0	0.0
B / 8.4	10.0	0.96	34.07	3,828	3	96	0	1	38.0	147.4	-3.8	74	N/A	250,000,000	0	0.0	0.0
C / 5.1	13.0	1.20	15.25	866	1	98	0	1	49.0	221.9	-4.1	80	N/A	5,000,000	0	0.0	0.0
C / 5.2	16.4	0.99	10.94	33	3	96	0	1	52.0	118.7	-0.6	66	N/A	5,000,000	0	0.0	0.0
U /	N/A	N/A	22.70	407	3	70	26	1	10.0	N/A	N/A	N/A	1	5,000,000	0	0.0	0.0

			Overall Weiss		PERFORMANCE							Incl. in Returns	
					Perfor-	Total Return % through 6/30/06							
					mance					Annualized		Dividend	Expense
Fund		Ticker	Investment		Rating/Pts	3 Mo	6 Mo	1Yr / Pct	3Yr / Pct	5Yr / Pct		Yield	Ratio
Type	Fund Name	Symbol	Rating	Phone									
FO	GMO Tax Managed Intl Equities III	GTMIX	A+		A / 9.3	0.58	10.53	28.56 /93	26.24 /92	15.83 /93		1.60	0.69
SC	GMO Tax Managed Small Co Fd III	GTMSX	B-		C+ / 6.6	-6.10	2.03	6.66 /24	17.31 /69	11.38 /85		0.58	0.70
IN	GMO Tax Managed US Equities Fd III	GTMUX	D+		D / 2.1	-3.92	-0.59	2.92 / 7	8.84 /20	1.94 /27		1.50	0.48
IN	GMO Tobacco Free Core IV	GMTFX	D		D / 1.8	-3.93	-0.58	1.51 / 3	8.39 /17	--		1.55	0.44
IN	GMO U.S. Quality Equity III	GQETX	U		U /	-3.53	0.20	1.25 / 3	--	--		1.41	0.48
IN	GMO U.S. Quality Equity IV	GQEFX	U		U /	-3.51	0.22	1.29 / 3	--	--		1.45	0.44
GR	GMO US Core Eqty Fund III	GMUEX	U		U /	-3.89	-0.96	--	--	--		0.00	0.47
GR	GMO US Core Eqty Fund IV	GMRTX	U		U /	-3.88	-0.94	--	--	--		0.00	0.43
GR	GMO US Core Eqty Fund M	GMTMX	U		U /	-3.97	-1.10	--	--	--		0.00	0.77
GR	GMO US Core Eqty Fund VI	GMCQX	U		U /	-3.87	-0.86	--	--	--		0.00	0.38
GR	GMO US Growth Fund III	GMGWX	U		U /	-6.39	-4.93	--	--	--		0.00	0.48
GR	GMO US Growth Fund M	GMWMX	U		U /	-6.43	-5.07	--	--	--		0.00	0.77
GR	GMO US Intrinsic Value Fund III	GMVUX	U		U /	-2.72	0.62	--	--	--		0.00	0.48
GR	GMO US S/M Cap Gwth Fd III	GMSPX	U		U /	-7.05	2.53	--	--	--		0.00	0.48
GR	GMO US S/M cap Value Fd III	GMSUX	U		U /	-4.89	2.44	--	--	--		0.00	0.49
GR	GMO US Value Fund III	GMLUX	U		U /	-3.14	-0.54	--	--	--		0.00	0.61
IN	GMO World Opp Equity Alloc - III	GWOAX	U		U /	-1.34	6.31	17.76 /79	--	--		2.03	0.58
AA	Goldman Sachs Aggr Gr Strat A	GAPAX	B+	(800) 292-4726	B / 7.8	-1.40	6.73	19.64 /81	20.31 /80	8.46 /74		0.15	1.36
AA	Goldman Sachs Aggr Gr Strat B	GAPBX	B+	(800) 292-4726	B / 7.6	-1.59	6.33	18.82 /80	19.42 /77	7.65 /70		0.00	2.11
AA	Goldman Sachs Aggr Gr Strat C	GAXCX	A-	(800) 292-4726	B / 8.0	-1.66	6.27	18.67 /80	19.40 /77	7.64 /70		0.00	2.11
AA	Goldman Sachs Aggr Gr Strat Inst	GAPIX	A	(800) 292-4726	B+ / 8.4	-1.39	6.89	20.06 /82	20.78 /82	8.89 /76		0.45	1.12
AA	Goldman Sachs Aggr Gr Strat Svc	GAPSX	A	(800) 292-4726	B / 8.2	-1.48	6.69	19.57 /81	20.16 /80	8.34 /73		0.09	1.62
FO	Goldman Sachs Asia Equity A	GSAGX	C+	(800) 292-4726	B+ / 8.7	-4.22	3.19	20.11 /82	25.26 /91	12.71 /88		0.97	1.60
FO	Goldman Sachs Asia Equity B	GSABX	C+	(800) 292-4726	B+ / 8.6	-4.45	2.82	19.10 /81	24.43 /90	12.00 /87		0.54	2.35
FO	Goldman Sachs Asia Equity C	GSACX	B-	(800) 292-4726	B+ / 8.8	-4.41	2.83	19.20 /81	24.43 /90	11.98 /87		0.68	2.35
FO	Goldman Sachs Asia Equity Inst	GSAIX	B-	(800) 292-4726	A- / 9.1	-4.13	3.42	20.57 /83	25.86 /92	13.41 /89		1.14	1.20
BA	Goldman Sachs Balanced A	GSBFX	C-	(800) 292-4726	D- / 1.0	-0.67	1.79	4.64 /13	7.53 /12	3.50 /41		1.89	1.15
BA	Goldman Sachs Balanced B	GSBBX	C-	(800) 292-4726	E+ / 0.8	-0.87	1.41	3.88 /10	6.74 / 9	2.73 /34		1.26	1.90
BA	Goldman Sachs Balanced C	GSBCX	C-	(800) 292-4726	D- / 1.3	-0.86	1.37	3.85 /10	6.72 / 9	2.72 /34		1.28	1.90
BA	Goldman Sachs Balanced Inst	GSBIX	C	(800) 292-4726	D+ / 2.3	-0.61	1.97	6.10 /21	8.30 /17	4.11 /47		2.36	0.75
AA	Goldman Sachs Balanced Strat A	GIPAX	C	(800) 292-4726	D+ / 2.6	-0.01	4.04	9.20 /41	10.12 /28	5.95 /61		2.13	1.21
AA	Goldman Sachs Balanced Strat B	GIPBX	C	(800) 292-4726	D+ / 2.4	-0.11	3.65	8.47 /37	9.33 /23	5.16 /55		1.50	1.96
AA	Goldman Sachs Balanced Strat C	GIPCX	C+	(800) 292-4726	C- / 3.0	-0.19	3.59	8.33 /35	9.29 /23	5.15 /55		1.56	1.96
AA	Goldman Sachs Balanced Strat Inst	GIPIX	B-	(800) 292-4726	C- / 4.1	0.08	4.23	9.60 /44	10.57 /32	6.39 /63		2.61	0.90
AA	Goldman Sachs Balanced Strat Svc	GIPSX	C+	(800) 292-4726	C- / 3.6	0.05	3.98	9.16 /41	10.01 /27	5.85 /60		2.13	1.40
BA	Goldman Sachs Balanced Svc	GSBSX	C	(800) 292-4726	D / 1.8	-0.72	1.66	4.41 /12	7.36 /12	3.38 /40		1.84	1.25
GR	Goldman Sachs Capital Growth A	GSCGX	D-	(800) 292-4726	E+ / 0.8	-4.89	-0.68	5.11 /16	7.56 /13	-1.17 /11		0.06	1.40
GR	Goldman Sachs Capital Growth B	GSCBX	D-	(800) 292-4726	E+ / 0.7	-5.04	-1.05	4.31 /12	6.76 / 9	-1.91 / 8		0.00	2.15
GR	Goldman Sachs Capital Growth C	GSPCX	D-	(800) 292-4726	D- / 1.1	-5.09	-1.05	4.32 /12	6.77 / 9	-1.91 / 8		0.00	2.15
GR	Goldman Sachs Capital Growth Inst	GSPIX	D	(800) 292-4726	D / 1.8	-4.76	-0.47	5.57 /18	8.00 /15	-0.77 /12		0.45	1.00
GR	Goldman Sachs Capital Growth Svc	GSPSX	D	(800) 292-4726	D- / 1.5	-4.95	-0.74	4.98 /15	7.45 /12	-1.27 /11		0.14	1.50
AG	Goldman Sachs Concentrated Gr A	GCGAX	E+	(800) 292-4726	E / 0.4	-5.48	-1.01	5.69 /19	5.77 / 6	--		0.00	1.48
AG	Goldman Sachs Concentrated Gr B	GCGBX	E+	(800) 292-4726	E / 0.3	-5.63	-1.35	4.98 /15	5.02 / 4	--		0.00	2.24
AG	Goldman Sachs Concentrated Gr C	GCGCX	E+	(800) 292-4726	E / 0.5	-5.64	-1.28	4.99 /15	5.00 / 4	--		0.00	2.23
AG	Goldman Sachs Concentrated Gr Inst	GCRIX	D-	(800) 292-4726	D- / 1.1	-5.42	-0.77	6.12 /21	6.22 / 7	--		0.31	1.08
AG	Goldman Sachs Concentrated Gr Svc	GCGSX	D-	(800) 292-4726	E+ / 0.9	-5.49	-1.01	5.70 /19	5.75 / 6	--		0.00	1.50
EM	Goldman Sachs Emerg Mkts Eq A	GEMAX	C+	(800) 292-4726	A+ / 9.6	-7.71	5.10	35.15 /97	35.02 /98	19.92 /96		0.14	1.87
EM	Goldman Sachs Emerg Mkts Eq B	GEKBX	C+	(800) 292-4726	A+ / 9.7	-7.84	4.71	34.16 /96	34.20 /98	19.24 /95		0.00	2.61
EM	Goldman Sachs Emerg Mkts Eq C	GEMCX	C+	(800) 292-4726	A+ / 9.6	-7.88	4.71	34.14 /96	34.09 /98	19.15 /95		0.00	2.64
EM	Goldman Sachs Emerg Mkts Eq Inst	GEMIX	C+	(800) 292-4726	A+ / 9.7	-7.59	5.33	35.71 /97	35.67 /98	20.56 /97		0.33	1.46
EM	Goldman Sachs Emerg Mkts Eq Svc	GEMSX	C+	(800) 292-4726	A+ / 9.7	-7.70	5.05	35.00 /97	34.98 /98	20.00 /96		0.00	1.94
FO	Goldman Sachs European Equity A	GSEAX	A-	(800) 292-4726	B / 8.0	-0.21	9.55	21.44 /84	21.02 /83	9.10 /77		0.82	1.54

RISK			NET ASSETS		ASSET					BULL / BEAR		FUND MANAGER		MINIMUMS		LOADS	
	3 Year		NAV						Portfolio	Last Bull	Last Bear	Manager	Manager	Initial	Additional	Front	Back
Risk	Standard		As of	Total	Cash	Stocks	Bonds	Other	Turnover	Market	Market	Quality	Tenure	Purch.	Purch.	End	End
Rating/Pts	Deviation	Beta	6/30/06	$(Mil)	%	%	%	%	Ratio	Return	Return	Pct	(Years)	$	$	Load	Load
B / 8.1	10.6	1.02	19.10	946	2	97	0	1	39.0	147.3	-5.1	68	N/A	5,000,000	0	0.0	0.0
B- / 7.3	12.9	0.85	18.60	28	N/A	100	0	N/A	78.0	109.3	-8.9	68	N/A	5,000,000	0	0.0	0.0
B / 8.2	8.4	1.04	12.32	114	1	98	0	1	62.0	54.6	-9.0	29	N/A	5,000,000	0	0.0	0.0
B- / 7.2	8.4	1.04	11.89	144	2	96	0	2	63.0	52.8	-9.1	26	N/A	125,000,000	0	0.0	0.0
U /	N/A	N/A	19.86	979	5	94	0	1	52.0	N/A	N/A	N/A	N/A	5,000,000	0	0.0	0.0
U /	N/A	N/A	19.87	2,412	5	94	0	1	52.0	N/A	N/A	N/A	N/A	125,000,000	0	0.0	0.0
U /	N/A	N/A	13.90	2,102	4	95	0	1	65.0	N/A	N/A	N/A	N/A	5,000,000	0	0.0	0.0
U /	N/A	N/A	13.88	638	4	95	0	1	65.0	N/A	N/A	N/A	N/A	125,000,000	0	0.0	0.0
U /	N/A	N/A	13.87	134	4	95	0	1	65.0	N/A	N/A	N/A	N/A	5,000,000	0	0.0	0.0
U /	N/A	N/A	13.88	3,211	4	95	0	1	65.0	N/A	N/A	N/A	N/A	300,000,000	0	0.0	0.0
U /	N/A	N/A	17.07	287	3	96	0	1	94.0	N/A	N/A	N/A	N/A	5,000,000	0	0.0	0.0
U /	N/A	N/A	17.00	243	3	96	0	1	94.0	N/A	N/A	N/A	N/A	5,000,000	0	0.0	0.0
U /	N/A	N/A	10.48	91	1	98	0	1	62.0	N/A	N/A	N/A	N/A	5,000,000	0	0.0	0.0
U /	N/A	N/A	19.09	28	1	98	0	1	43.0	N/A	N/A	N/A	N/A	5,000,000	0	0.0	0.0
U /	N/A	N/A	10.30	62	2	97	0	1	31.0	N/A	N/A	N/A	N/A	5,000,000	0	0.0	0.0
U /	N/A	N/A	9.96	30	3	96	0	1	103.0	N/A	N/A	N/A	N/A	5,000,000	0	0.0	0.0
U /	N/A	N/A	22.76	529	4	95	0	1	5.0	N/A	N/A	N/A	1	5,000,000	0	0.0	0.0
B- / 7.4	9.5	1.78	14.75	193	4	95	0	1	32.0	111.7	-8.7	98	8	1,000	50	5.5	1.0
B- / 7.4	9.6	1.79	14.27	32	4	95	0	1	32.0	106.5	-8.7	97	8	1,000	50	0.0	5.0
B- / 7.4	9.6	1.79	14.24	106	4	95	0	1	32.0	106.5	-8.9	97	8	1,000	50	0.0	1.0
B- / 7.4	9.6	1.79	14.90	15	4	95	0	1	32.0	114.1	-8.5	98	8	1,000,000	0	0.0	0.0
B- / 7.4	9.5	1.78	14.67	1	4	95	0	1	32.0	110.8	-8.6	98	8	0	0	0.0	0.0
C / 4.8	17.0	1.30	15.22	94	3	96	0	1	26.0	132.8	-11.3	13	N/A	1,000	50	5.5	1.0
C / 4.8	17.0	1.30	14.59	4	3	96	0	1	26.0	128.2	-11.5	10	N/A	1,000	50	0.0	5.0
C / 4.8	17.0	1.30	14.51	4	3	96	0	1	26.0	128.0	-11.5	10	N/A	1,000	50	0.0	1.0
C / 4.8	17.0	1.30	16.01	41	3	96	0	1	26.0	137.4	-11.2	15	N/A	1,000,000	0	0.0	2.0
B+ / 9.4	4.6	0.96	20.04	178	0	56	43	1	101.0	38.7	-3.7	59	12	1,000	50	5.5	1.0
B+ / 9.9	4.6	0.95	19.91	20	0	56	43	1	101.0	35.5	-3.8	49	10	1,000	50	0.0	5.0
B+ / 9.9	4.6	0.95	19.88	6	0	56	43	1	101.0	35.5	-3.8	49	N/A	1,000	50	0.0	1.0
B+ / 9.9	4.7	0.97	20.27	2	0	56	43	1	101.0	41.9	-3.6	66	9	1,000,000	0	0.0	0.0
B+ / 9.6	4.3	0.85	11.19	152	7	40	51	2	90.0	44.4	-2.1	85	N/A	1,000	50	5.5	1.0
B+ / 9.8	4.3	0.85	11.19	32	7	40	51	2	90.0	40.9	-2.3	80	N/A	1,000	50	0.0	5.0
B+ / 9.8	4.3	0.85	11.19	62	7	40	51	2	90.0	40.9	-2.3	80	N/A	1,000	50	0.0	1.0
B+ / 9.8	4.3	0.84	11.19	73	7	40	51	2	90.0	46.1	-2.0	88	8	1,000,000	0	0.0	0.0
B+ / 9.8	4.3	0.85	11.21	2	7	40	51	2	90.0	43.8	-2.2	85	N/A	0	0	0.0	0.0
B+ / 9.9	4.6	0.95	20.04	N/A	0	56	43	1	101.0	38.2	-3.7	57	9	0	0	0.0	0.0
C+ / 6.9	8.7	1.04	20.42	1,305	N/A	100	0	N/A	21.0	51.1	-11.0	22	N/A	1,000	50	5.5	1.0
B- / 7.1	8.6	1.03	18.86	100	N/A	100	0	N/A	21.0	47.6	-11.2	17	10	1,000	50	0.0	5.0
B- / 7.1	8.7	1.04	18.83	70	N/A	100	0	N/A	21.0	47.6	-11.1	17	N/A	1,000	50	0.0	1.0
B- / 7.2	8.7	1.04	21.02	267	N/A	100	0	N/A	21.0	53.1	-10.9	24	9	1,000,000	0	0.0	0.0
B- / 7.2	8.7	1.04	20.18	10	N/A	100	0	N/A	21.0	50.7	-11.0	21	9	0	0	0.0	0.0
C+ / 6.6	9.8	1.13	12.76	72	3	96	0	1	29.0	47.8	-12.3	9	N/A	1,000	50	5.5	1.0
C+ / 6.6	9.7	1.13	12.40	N/A	3	96	0	1	29.0	44.3	-12.5	7	N/A	1,000	50	0.0	5.0
C+ / 6.6	9.8	1.14	12.38	1	3	96	0	1	29.0	44.2	-12.5	7	N/A	1,000	50	0.0	1.0
C+ / 6.6	9.7	1.13	12.92	108	3	96	0	1	29.0	49.6	-12.2	11	N/A	1,000,000	0	0.0	0.0
C+ / 6.6	9.8	1.13	12.75	N/A	3	96	0	1	29.0	47.7	-12.3	9	N/A	0	0	0.0	0.0
C- / 3.5	20.0	1.21	19.16	370	8	91	0	1	38.0	233.5	-7.9	8	N/A	1,000	50	5.5	1.0
C- / 3.5	20.0	1.21	18.45	12	8	91	0	1	38.0	227.3	-8.0	7	N/A	1,000	50	0.0	5.0
C- / 3.5	20.0	1.20	18.46	20	8	91	0	1	38.0	226.9	-8.0	7	N/A	1,000	50	0.0	1.0
C- / 3.5	20.0	1.20	19.96	456	8	91	0	1	38.0	238.9	-7.7	10	N/A	1,000,000	0	0.0	2.0
C- / 3.5	20.0	1.20	18.93	1	8	91	0	1	38.0	233.7	-7.9	8	N/A	0	0	0.0	2.0
B- / 7.3	10.5	0.94	14.00	17	3	96	0	1	45.0	126.2	-14.4	37	N/A	1,000	50	5.5	1.0

	99 Pct = Best				PERFORMANCE						Incl. in Returns	
	0 Pct = Worst		Overall Weiss		Perfor-			Total Return % through 6/30/06				
					mance				Annualized		Dividend	Expense
Fund		Ticker	Investment		Rating/Pts				3Yr / Pct	5Yr / Pct	Yield	Ratio
Type	Fund Name	Symbol	Rating	Phone		3 Mo	6 Mo	1Yr / Pct				
FO	Goldman Sachs European Equity B	GSUBX	B+	(800) 292-4726	B / 7.9	-0.37	9.20	20.69 /83	20.24 /80	8.44 /74	0.15	2.29
FO	Goldman Sachs European Equity C	GSUCX	A-	(800) 292-4726	B / 8.2	-0.37	9.18	20.65 /83	20.30 /80	8.45 /74	0.25	2.29
FO	Goldman Sachs European Equity Inst	GSEIX	A	(800) 292-4726	B+/ 8.4	-0.14	9.77	21.97 /84	21.66 /84	9.68 /79	1.24	1.14
FO	Goldman Sachs European Equity Svc	GEESX	A	(800) 292-4726	B+/ 8.3	-0.14	9.57	21.53 /84	21.09 /83	9.19 /77	1.21	1.64
AA	Goldman Sachs Gr & Inc Strat A	GOIAX	B	(800) 292-4726	C / 5.2	-0.95	4.38	12.48 /62	14.41 /56	7.42 /69	1.93	1.28
AA	Goldman Sachs Gr & Inc Strat B	GOIBX	B-	(800) 292-4726	C / 4.9	-1.22	3.98	11.65 /58	13.58 /52	6.61 /65	1.29	2.03
AA	Goldman Sachs Gr & Inc Strat C	GOICX	B	(800) 292-4726	C / 5.5	-1.13	4.04	11.74 /58	13.57 /52	6.61 /65	1.36	2.03
AA	Goldman Sachs Gr & Inc Strat Inst	GOIIX	A-	(800) 292-4726	C+/ 6.3	-0.94	4.55	12.94 /64	14.88 /58	7.85 /71	2.38	0.19
AA	Goldman Sachs Gr & Inc Strat Svc	GOISX	B+	(800) 292-4726	C+/ 6.1	-0.98	4.32	12.46 /62	14.31 /55	7.32 /68	1.92	0.69
GI	Goldman Sachs Growth & Income A	GSGRX	B	(800) 292-4726	C / 5.0	1.21	5.84	9.29 /42	14.19 /55	6.47 /64	1.47	1.19
GI	Goldman Sachs Growth & Income B	GSGBX	B-	(800) 292-4726	C / 4.8	1.02	5.51	8.55 /37	13.35 /51	5.69 /59	0.86	1.94
GI	Goldman Sachs Growth & Income C	GSGCX	B	(800) 292-4726	C / 5.4	1.02	5.45	8.51 /37	13.34 /51	5.67 /59	0.87	1.94
GI	Goldman Sachs Growth & Income	GSIIX	A-	(800) 292-4726	C+/ 6.2	1.29	6.02	9.69 /45	14.64 /57	6.89 /66	1.92	0.79
GI	Goldman Sachs Growth & Income	GSGSX	B+	(800) 292-4726	C+/ 5.9	1.18	5.79	9.17 /41	14.08 /54	6.37 /63	1.45	1.29
MC	Goldman Sachs Growth Opp A	GGOAX	D	(800) 292-4726	D+/ 2.6	-6.97	-0.88	5.74 /19	11.80 /41	2.20 /29	0.00	1.46
MC	Goldman Sachs Growth Opp B	GGOBX	D-	(800) 292-4726	D+/ 2.3	-7.17	-1.26	4.92 /15	10.96 /35	1.45 /23	0.00	2.21
MC	Goldman Sachs Growth Opp C	GGOCX	D	(800) 292-4726	C-/ 3.0	-7.13	-1.27	4.95 /15	10.98 /35	1.45 /23	0.00	2.22
MC	Goldman Sachs Growth Opp Inst	GGOIX	D+	(800) 292-4726	C-/ 4.1	-6.90	-0.72	6.12 /21	12.24 /44	2.61 /33	0.00	1.07
MC	Goldman Sachs Growth Opp Svc	GGOSX	D	(800) 292-4726	C-/ 3.6	-6.98	-0.94	5.64 /18	11.69 /40	2.11 /28	0.00	1.57
AA	Goldman Sachs Growth Strategy A	GGSAX	B	(800) 292-4726	C+/ 6.9	-1.15	5.54	15.85 /74	17.82 /72	7.86 /71	0.96	1.30
AA	Goldman Sachs Growth Strategy B	GGSBX	B	(800) 292-4726	C+/ 6.7	-1.30	5.15	15.02 /72	16.96 /68	7.05 /67	0.30	2.05
AA	Goldman Sachs Growth Strategy C	GGSCX	A-	(800) 292-4726	B-/ 7.1	-1.38	5.18	14.96 /72	16.96 /68	7.05 /67	0.50	2.05
AA	Goldman Sachs Growth Strategy Inst	GGSIX	A	(800) 292-4726	B / 7.6	-1.01	5.76	16.37 /76	18.29 /74	8.31 /73	1.26	0.19
AA	Goldman Sachs Growth Strategy Svc	GGSSX	A	(800) 292-4726	B-/ 7.4	-1.23	5.48	15.76 /74	17.71 /71	7.73 /70	0.89	0.69
TC	Goldman Sachs Internet Tollkp A	GITAX	E+	(800) 292-4726	D / 1.7	-9.71	-1.50	4.64 /13	10.47 /31	-4.98 / 3	0.00	1.50
TC	Goldman Sachs Internet Tollkp B	GITBX	E+	(800) 292-4726	D-/ 1.4	-9.96	-1.96	3.73 /10	9.58 /24	-5.70 / 2	0.00	2.25
TC	Goldman Sachs Internet Tollkp C	GITCX	E+	(800) 292-4726	D / 2.0	-9.86	-1.83	3.73 /10	9.64 /25	-5.70 / 2	0.00	2.25
TC	Goldman Sachs Internet Tollkp I	GITIX	D-	(800) 292-4726	C-/ 3.0	-9.58	-1.34	4.91 /15	10.92 /35	-4.61 / 3	0.00	1.10
TC	Goldman Sachs Internet Tollkp Svc	GITSX	D-	(800) 292-4726	D+/ 2.7	-9.76	-1.63	4.38 /12	10.41 /30	-5.04 / 2	0.00	1.60
FO	Goldman Sachs Intl Equity A	GSIFX	C+	(800) 292-4726	B-/ 7.3	-3.51	6.05	23.96 /87	18.81 /76	6.06 /61	0.68	1.54
FO	Goldman Sachs Intl Equity B	GSEBX	C+	(800) 292-4726	B-/ 7.1	-3.68	5.65	22.98 /86	18.02 /73	5.42 /57	0.00	2.29
FO	Goldman Sachs Intl Equity C	GSICX	C+	(800) 292-4726	B-/ 7.5	-3.66	5.71	23.06 /86	18.02 /73	5.42 /57	0.21	2.29
FO	Goldman Sachs Intl Equity Inst	GSIEX	B-	(800) 292-4726	B / 7.8	-3.39	6.29	24.44 /88	19.38 /77	6.64 /65	1.05	1.14
FO	Goldman Sachs Intl Equity Svc	GSISX	B-	(800) 292-4726	B / 7.6	-3.53	6.01	23.75 /87	18.78 /75	6.10 /62	0.61	1.64
FO	Goldman Sachs Intl Sm Cap A	GISAX	B+	(800) 292-4726	A / 9.5	-3.78	8.40	26.68 /91	30.63 /96	12.53 /88	0.48	1.64
FO	Goldman Sachs Intl Sm Cap B	GISBX	B+	(800) 292-4726	A / 9.4	-3.97	8.03	25.70 /89	29.76 /95	11.81 /86	0.00	2.39
FO	Goldman Sachs Intl Sm Cap C	GISCX	B+	(800) 292-4726	A / 9.5	-3.88	8.06	25.81 /89	29.72 /95	11.82 /86	0.00	2.39
FO	Goldman Sachs Intl Sm Cap Inst	GISIX	B+	(800) 292-4726	A+/ 9.6	-3.66	8.64	27.22 /92	31.23 /96	13.11 /89	0.66	1.24
FO	Goldman Sachs Intl Sm Cap Serv	GISSX	B+	(800) 292-4726	A / 9.5	-3.78	8.35	26.59 /91	30.60 /96	12.56 /88	0.41	1.74
FO	Goldman Sachs Japanese Equity A	GSJAX	C+	(800) 292-4726	B / 8.0	-6.81	-2.00	36.26 /97	21.48 /84	2.96 /36	0.62	1.55
FO	Goldman Sachs Japanese Equity B	GSJBX	C+	(800) 292-4726	B / 7.9	-7.00	-2.34	35.22 /97	20.61 /81	2.30 /30	0.23	2.30
FO	Goldman Sachs Japanese Equity C	GSJCX	C+	(800) 292-4726	B / 8.2	-7.02	-2.43	35.17 /97	20.63 /82	2.31 /30	0.31	2.30
FO	Goldman Sachs Japanese Equity Inst	GSJIX	C+	(800) 292-4726	B+/ 8.4	-6.73	-1.77	36.77 /97	22.08 /85	3.49 /41	0.95	1.15
FO	Goldman Sachs Japanese Equity Svc	GSJSX	C+	(800) 292-4726	B+/ 8.3	-6.88	-2.06	36.13 /97	21.68 /84	3.14 /38	0.87	1.65
GI	Goldman Sachs Large Cap Value A	GSLAX	B-	(800) 292-4726	C / 5.3	0.15	4.25	10.35 /49	14.79 /58	6.96 /66	0.59	1.24
GI	Goldman Sachs Large Cap Value B	GSVBX	C+	(800) 292-4726	C / 5.0	-0.08	3.86	9.42 /43	13.89 /53	6.13 /62	0.00	1.99
GI	Goldman Sachs Large Cap Value C	GSVCX	B-	(800) 292-4726	C+/ 5.6	0.00	3.95	9.57 /44	13.95 /54	6.17 /62	0.10	1.99
GI	Goldman Sachs Large Cap Value Inst	GSLIX	B	(800) 292-4726	C+/ 6.4	0.22	4.45	10.81 /52	15.22 /60	7.38 /69	0.94	0.84
GI	Goldman Sachs Large Cap Value Svc	GSVSX	B	(800) 292-4726	C+/ 6.1	0.15	4.27	10.23 /48	14.68 /57	6.91 /66	0.64	1.34
★ MC	● Goldman Sachs Mid Cap Value A	GCMAX	A-	(800) 292-4726	B-/ 7.4	-1.43	4.49	10.87 /53	20.27 /80	13.09 /89	0.33	1.17
MC	● Goldman Sachs Mid Cap Value B	GCMBX	B+	(800) 292-4726	B-/ 7.2	-1.63	4.10	10.02 /47	19.38 /77	12.23 /87	0.00	1.92
MC	● Goldman Sachs Mid Cap Value C	GCMCX	A-	(800) 292-4726	B-/ 7.5	-1.62	4.10	10.02 /47	19.37 /77	12.22 /87	0.00	1.92

● Denotes fund is closed to new investors
★ Denotes fund is included in Section II

www.WeissRatings.com

RISK			NET ASSETS		ASSET					BULL / BEAR		FUND MANAGER		MINIMUMS		LOADS	
	3 Year		NAV						Portfolio	Last Bull	Last Bear	Manager	Manager	Initial	Additional	Front	Back
Risk Rating/Pts	Standard Deviation	Beta	As of 6/30/06	Total $(Mil)	Cash %	Stocks %	Bonds %	Other %	Turnover Ratio	Market Return	Market Return	Quality Pct	Tenure (Years)	Purch. $	Purch. $	End Load	End Load
B- / 7.2	10.6	0.94	13.53	2	3	96	0	1	45.0	121.6	-14.5	31	N/A	1,000	50	0.0	5.0
B- / 7.2	10.6	0.94	13.56	1	3	96	0	1	45.0	122.2	-14.6	31	N/A	1,000	50	0.0	1.0
B- / 7.3	10.6	0.94	14.16	23	3	96	0	1	45.0	130.0	-14.3	42	N/A	1,000,000	0	0.0	2.0
B- / 7.3	10.6	0.94	13.85	N/A	3	96	0	1	45.0	126.3	-14.4	38	N/A	0	0	0.0	2.0
B+ / 9.1	6.4	1.26	12.59	809	8	60	30	2	53.0	70.5	-3.6	93	N/A	1,000	50	5.5	1.0
B+ / 9.0	6.4	1.26	12.57	102	8	60	30	2	53.0	66.6	-3.7	91	N/A	1,000	50	0.0	5.0
B+ / 9.0	6.4	1.26	12.55	243	8	60	30	2	53.0	66.6	-3.8	91	N/A	1,000	50	0.0	1.0
B+ / 9.1	6.4	1.26	12.62	172	8	60	30	2	53.0	72.7	-3.5	94	N/A	1,000,000	0	0.0	0.0
B+ / 9.0	6.4	1.26	12.57	4	8	60	30	2	53.0	70.1	-3.6	93	N/A	0	0	0.0	0.0
B+ / 9.1	6.6	0.80	27.00	1,000	1	98	0	1	27.0	72.8	-6.8	91	13	1,000	50	5.5	1.0
B+ / 9.1	6.6	0.79	26.31	61	1	98	0	1	27.0	68.8	-7.0	88	10	1,000	50	0.0	5.0
B+ / 9.1	6.6	0.80	26.22	17	1	98	0	1	27.0	68.7	-7.0	88	N/A	1,000	50	0.0	1.0
B+ / 9.2	6.6	0.80	27.31	18	1	98	0	1	27.0	75.0	-6.7	93	10	1,000,000	0	0.0	0.0
B+ / 9.2	6.6	0.79	27.00	1	1	98	0	1	27.0	72.3	-6.9	91	10	0	0	0.0	0.0
C+ / 6.0	11.1	0.98	21.36	1,001	1	98	0	1	31.0	78.1	-10.3	13	N/A	1,000	50	5.5	1.0
C+ / 5.9	11.1	0.98	20.34	76	1	98	0	1	31.0	74.0	-10.6	10	N/A	1,000	50	0.0	5.0
C+ / 5.9	11.1	0.98	20.20	121	1	98	0	1	31.0	73.9	-10.5	10	N/A	1,000	50	0.0	1.0
C+ / 6.0	11.1	0.97	21.99	978	1	98	0	1	31.0	80.5	-10.3	15	N/A	1,000,000	0	0.0	0.0
C+ / 6.0	11.1	0.98	21.18	11	1	98	0	1	31.0	77.6	-10.4	12	N/A	0	0	0.0	0.0
B / 8.3	8.1	1.56	13.72	591	8	78	12	2	48.0	92.2	-6.1	96	8	1,000	50	5.5	1.0
B / 8.3	8.1	1.56	13.69	106	8	78	12	2	48.0	87.7	-6.3	95	8	1,000	50	0.0	5.0
B / 8.3	8.1	1.56	13.61	319	8	78	12	2	48.0	87.7	-6.3	95	8	1,000	50	0.0	1.0
B / 8.4	8.1	1.56	13.77	98	8	78	12	2	48.0	94.6	-6.0	97	8	1,000,000	0	0.0	0.0
B / 8.3	8.1	1.56	13.66	4	8	78	12	2	48.0	91.7	-6.1	96	8	0	0	0.0	0.0
C / 5.4	14.7	1.66	7.90	112	0	99	0	1	48.0	82.9	-11.0	9	N/A	1,000	50	5.5	1.0
C / 5.4	14.6	1.64	7.50	99	0	99	0	1	48.0	78.4	-11.1	7	N/A	1,000	50	0.0	5.0
C / 5.3	14.7	1.66	7.50	52	0	99	0	1	48.0	78.8	-11.1	7	N/A	1,000	50	0.0	1.0
C / 5.4	14.7	1.65	8.12	11	0	99	0	1	48.0	85.2	-10.8	11	N/A	1,000,000	0	0.0	0.0
C / 5.4	14.7	1.65	7.86	N/A	0	99	0	1	48.0	82.8	-11.0	9	N/A	0	0	0.0	0.0
C+ / 6.1	11.6	1.09	20.32	363	2	97	0	1	27.0	111.4	-11.1	8	14	1,000	50	5.5	1.0
C+ / 6.1	11.6	1.09	19.64	12	2	97	0	1	27.0	107.0	-11.2	6	10	1,000	50	0.0	5.0
C+ / 6.1	11.6	1.09	19.24	22	2	97	0	1	27.0	107.1	-11.2	6	N/A	1,000	50	0.0	1.0
C+ / 6.1	11.6	1.09	20.78	75	2	97	0	1	27.0	114.7	-11.0	10	10	1,000,000	0	0.0	2.0
C+ / 6.1	11.6	1.09	20.47	1	2	97	0	1	27.0	111.4	-11.1	8	10	0	0	0.0	2.0
C / 5.4	13.4	1.15	18.59	106	5	94	0	1	28.0	203.5	-6.7	77	8	1,000	50	5.5	1.0
C / 5.3	13.4	1.15	17.90	5	5	94	0	1	28.0	196.9	-6.8	69	8	1,000	50	0.0	5.0
C / 5.3	13.4	1.15	17.84	9	5	94	0	1	28.0	197.1	-6.8	69	8	1,000	50	0.0	1.0
C / 5.4	13.4	1.15	19.23	91	5	94	0	1	28.0	208.1	-6.7	80	8	1,000,000	0	0.0	2.0
C / 5.4	13.4	1.16	18.56	1	5	94	0	1	28.0	203.4	-6.8	75	8	0	0	0.0	2.0
C / 4.8	16.5	1.10	11.76	42	1	98	0	1	37.0	101.7	-7.7	17	N/A	1,000	50	5.5	1.0
C / 4.7	16.5	1.10	11.29	3	1	98	0	1	37.0	97.2	-7.7	13	N/A	1,000	50	0.0	5.0
C / 4.7	16.6	1.10	11.25	5	1	98	0	1	37.0	97.3	-7.8	13	N/A	1,000	50	0.0	1.0
C / 4.8	16.5	1.10	12.20	15	1	98	0	1	37.0	104.8	-7.5	20	N/A	1,000,000	0	0.0	2.0
C / 4.7	16.6	1.10	11.91	N/A	1	98	0	1	37.0	103.0	-7.7	18	N/A	0	0	0.0	2.0
B / 8.4	7.2	0.88	13.24	650	2	97	0	1	34.0	77.4	-7.1	91	N/A	1,000	50	5.5	1.0
B / 8.4	7.2	0.89	12.92	24	2	97	0	1	34.0	73.2	-7.3	86	7	1,000	50	0.0	5.0
B / 8.4	7.3	0.89	12.88	48	2	97	0	1	34.0	73.3	-7.3	87	N/A	1,000	50	0.0	1.0
B / 8.3	7.2	0.89	13.37	491	2	97	0	1	34.0	79.8	-7.1	92	7	1,000,000	0	0.0	0.0
B / 8.3	7.2	0.89	13.20	4	2	97	0	1	34.0	77.0	-7.2	90	7	0	0	0.0	0.0
B- / 7.9	9.3	0.80	36.57	3,375	2	96	0	2	23.0	101.7	-6.7	92	N/A	1,000	50	5.5	1.0
B- / 7.9	9.3	0.80	35.51	211	2	96	0	2	23.0	97.0	-6.8	90	N/A	1,000	50	0.0	5.0
B- / 7.9	9.3	0.80	35.30	360	2	96	0	2	23.0	97.0	-6.8	90	N/A	1,000	50	0.0	1.0

Data as of June 30, 2006

Fund Type	Fund Name	Ticker Symbol	Overall Weiss Investment Rating	Phone	Performance Rating/Pts	3 Mo	6 Mo	1Yr / Pct	3Yr / Pct	5Yr / Pct	Dividend Yield	Expense Ratio
MC	● Goldman Sachs Mid Cap Value Inst	GSMCX	A	(800) 292-4726	B / 8.1	-1.34	4.68	11.31 /55	20.75 /82	13.54 /89	0.64	0.77
MC	● Goldman Sachs Mid Cap Value Svc	GSMSX	A	(800) 292-4726	B / 7.9	-1.47	4.43	10.74 /52	20.21 /80	13.00 /89	0.38	1.27
RE	Goldman Sachs Real Estate Sec A	GREAX	B-	(800) 292-4726	A / 9.3	-0.44	13.68	21.44 /84	27.89 /94	19.54 /96	1.54	1.44
RE	Goldman Sachs Real Estate Sec B	GREBX	B-	(800) 292-4726	A- / 9.2	-0.58	13.32	20.57 /83	26.94 /93	18.66 /95	0.96	2.19
RE	Goldman Sachs Real Estate Sec C	GRECX	B-	(800) 292-4726	A / 9.3	-0.62	13.22	20.52 /82	26.91 /93	18.68 /95	0.99	2.19
RE	Goldman Sachs Real Estate Sec Inst	GREIX	B	(800) 292-4726	A / 9.5	-0.34	13.90	21.96 /84	28.40 /94	20.01 /96	1.97	1.04
RE	Goldman Sachs Real Estate Sec Svc	GRESX	B-	(800) 292-4726	A / 9.4	-0.45	13.62	21.36 /83	27.77 /94	19.45 /96	1.54	1.54
GR	Goldman Sachs Res Select A	GSRAX	C-	(800) 292-4726	D+ / 2.7	-1.85	2.91	9.26 /42	10.48 /31	-1.52 /10	0.00	1.45
GR	Goldman Sachs Res Select B	GSRBX	C-	(800) 292-4726	D+ / 2.4	-1.93	2.45	8.40 /36	9.62 /25	-2.26 / 7	0.00	2.20
GR	Goldman Sachs Res Select C	GSRCX	C-	(800) 292-4726	C- / 3.1	-1.93	2.60	8.55 /37	9.67 /25	-2.23 / 7	0.00	2.20
GR	Goldman Sachs Res Select Inst	GSRIX	C	(800) 292-4726	C- / 4.1	-1.68	3.12	9.59 /44	10.87 /34	-1.13 /11	0.07	1.05
GR	Goldman Sachs Res Select Svc	GSRSX	C	(800) 292-4726	C- / 3.9	-1.72	2.91	9.75 /45	10.55 /31	-1.52 /10	0.00	1.55
SC	● Goldman Sachs Small Cap Value A	GSSMX	C+	(800) 292-4726	C+ / 6.3	-4.50	6.17	11.96 /59	17.23 /69	12.40 /87	0.00	1.48
SC	● Goldman Sachs Small Cap Value B	GSQBX	C	(800) 292-4726	C+ / 6.1	-4.68	5.78	11.13 /54	16.36 /65	11.55 /86	0.00	2.23
SC	● Goldman Sachs Small Cap Value C	GSSCX	C+	(800) 292-4726	C+ / 6.6	-4.68	5.78	11.12 /54	16.35 /65	11.51 /85	0.00	2.23
SC	● Goldman Sachs Small Cap Value Inst	GSSIX	C+	(800) 292-4726	B- / 7.2	-4.38	6.39	12.44 /62	17.70 /71	12.85 /88	0.00	1.08
SC	● Goldman Sachs Small Cap Value Svc	GSSSX	C+	(800) 292-4726	B- / 7.0	-4.51	6.13	11.88 /59	17.11 /69	12.28 /87	0.00	1.58
MC	Goldman Sachs Small/Mid-Cap Gr A	GSMAX	U	(800) 292-4726	U /	-8.84	2.68	8.42 /36	--	--	0.97	1.50
GR	Goldman Sachs Strategic Gr A	GGRAX	E+	(800) 292-4726	E / 0.4	-5.24	-1.45	3.99 /11	5.81 / 6	-2.82 / 6	0.00	1.44
GR	Goldman Sachs Strategic Gr B	GSWBX	E+	(800) 292-4726	E / 0.3	-5.51	-1.87	3.19 / 8	5.03 / 4	-3.55 / 4	0.00	2.19
GR	Goldman Sachs Strategic Gr C	GGRCX	D-	(800) 292-4726	E / 0.5	-5.39	-1.75	3.19 / 8	5.02 / 4	-3.53 / 4	0.00	2.19
GR	Goldman Sachs Strategic Gr Inst	GSTIX	D-	(800) 292-4726	D- / 1.0	-5.13	-1.20	4.35 /12	6.25 / 7	-2.42 / 7	0.09	1.04
GR	Goldman Sachs Strategic Gr Svc	GSTSX	D-	(800) 292-4726	E+ / 0.8	-5.22	-1.44	4.10 /11	5.83 / 6	-2.78 / 6	0.00	1.43
FO	Goldman Sachs Stru Intl Eq A	GCIAX	A	(800) 292-4726	B+ / 8.9	0.22	10.82	27.20 /92	24.84 /91	10.48 /82	0.72	1.31
FO	Goldman Sachs Stru Intl Eq B	GCIBX	A	(800) 292-4726	B+ / 8.8	0.07	10.43	26.23 /90	24.03 /89	9.82 /80	0.11	2.06
FO	Goldman Sachs Stru Intl Eq C	GCICX	A	(800) 292-4726	A- / 9.0	0.00	10.34	26.14 /90	24.03 /89	9.80 /80	0.13	2.06
FO	Goldman Sachs Stru Intl Eq Inst	GCIIX	A+	(800) 292-4726	A- / 9.2	0.29	10.93	27.59 /92	25.41 /91	11.07 /84	1.02	0.91
FO	Goldman Sachs Stru Intl Eq Svc	GCISX	A+	(800) 292-4726	A- / 9.1	0.22	10.79	27.12 /91	24.88 /91	10.55 /82	0.76	1.41
GR	Goldman Sachs Stru Lrg Cp Gr A	GLCGX	D	(800) 292-4726	D / 2.2	-3.74	-0.08	8.28 /35	10.22 /29	0.36 /17	0.03	1.06
GR	Goldman Sachs Stru Lrg Cp Gr B	GCLCX	D	(800) 292-4726	D / 1.9	-3.92	-0.49	7.54 /29	9.40 /23	-0.40 /14	0.00	1.81
GR	Goldman Sachs Stru Lrg Cp Gr C	GLCCX	D+	(800) 292-4726	D+ / 2.6	-3.84	-0.41	7.53 /29	9.40 /23	-0.39 /14	0.00	1.81
GR	Goldman Sachs Stru Lrg Cp Gr Inst	GCGIX	C-	(800) 292-4726	C- / 3.6	-3.65	0.07	8.76 /38	10.65 /32	0.75 /19	0.29	0.66
GR	Goldman Sachs Stru Lrg Cp Gr Svc	GSCLX	C-	(800) 292-4726	C- / 3.3	-3.77	-0.15	8.50 /37	10.20 /29	0.29 /17	0.00	1.16
GI	Goldman Sachs Stru Lrg Cp Val A	GCVAX	B	(800) 292-4726	C+ / 6.4	-0.85	4.84	14.00 /68	16.75 /67	6.42 /64	0.93	1.05
GI	Goldman Sachs Stru Lrg Cp Val B	GCVBX	B+	(800) 292-4726	C+ / 6.1	-0.97	4.46	13.21 /65	15.88 /63	5.62 /59	0.23	1.80
GI	Goldman Sachs Stru Lrg Cp Val C	GCVCX	B	(800) 292-4726	C+ / 6.6	-1.04	4.47	13.22 /65	15.85 /63	5.62 /59	0.25	1.80
GI	Goldman Sachs Stru Lrg Cp Val Inst	GCVIX	A	(800) 292-4726	B- / 7.2	-0.75	5.03	14.52 /70	17.21 /69	6.83 /66	1.34	0.65
GI	Goldman Sachs Stru Lrg Cp Val Svc	GCLSX	A	(800) 292-4726	B- / 7.0	-0.83	4.80	13.94 /68	16.62 /66	6.33 /63	0.74	1.15
SC	Goldman Sachs Stru Sm Cap Eq A	GCSAX	C+	(800) 292-4726	C+ / 6.6	-5.50	5.70	11.79 /58	18.08 /73	9.64 /79	0.00	1.29
SC	Goldman Sachs Stru Sm Cap Eq B	GCSBX	C	(800) 292-4726	C+ / 6.3	-5.73	5.28	10.80 /52	17.15 /69	8.80 /76	0.00	2.04
SC	Goldman Sachs Stru Sm Cap Eq C	GCSCX	C+	(800) 292-4726	C+ / 6.8	-5.71	5.25	10.85 /53	17.16 /69	8.80 /76	0.00	2.04
SC	Goldman Sachs Stru Sm Cap Eq Inst	GCSIX	C+	(800) 292-4726	B- / 7.4	-5.39	5.89	12.07 /60	18.53 /74	10.05 /81	0.00	0.89
SC	Goldman Sachs Stru Sm Cap Eq Svc	GCSSX	C+	(800) 292-4726	B- / 7.2	-5.56	5.54	11.48 /57	17.91 /72	9.50 /79	0.00	1.39
GI	Goldman Sachs Stru US Equity A	GSSQX	C	(800) 292-4726	C / 4.3	-2.37	1.74	11.24 /55	13.24 /50	3.66 /42	0.32	1.04
GI	Goldman Sachs Stru US Equity B	GSSBX	C	(800) 292-4726	C- / 4.0	-2.57	1.39	10.41 /50	12.40 /45	2.89 /36	0.00	1.79
GI	Goldman Sachs Stru US Equity C	GSUSX	C+	(800) 292-4726	C / 4.6	-2.58	1.36	10.38 /49	12.40 /45	2.90 /36	0.00	1.79
GI	Goldman Sachs Stru US Equity Inst	GSELX	B-	(800) 292-4726	C+ / 5.6	-2.29	1.97	11.69 /58	13.70 /52	4.07 /46	0.58	0.64
GI	Goldman Sachs Stru US Equity Svc	GSESX	C+	(800) 292-4726	C / 5.3	-2.42	1.69	11.08 /54	13.13 /50	3.55 /42	0.29	1.14
GR	Goldman Sachs Struct T/M Eq A	GCTAX	B	(800) 292-4726	C+ / 5.9	-2.09	3.75	12.97 /64	16.01 /64	5.44 /57	0.07	1.09
GR	Goldman Sachs Struct T/M Eq B	GCTBX	B-	(800) 292-4726	C+ / 5.6	-2.26	3.39	12.09 /60	15.14 /59	4.63 /51	0.00	1.84
GR	Goldman Sachs Struct T/M Eq C	GCTCX	B	(800) 292-4726	C+ / 6.2	-2.27	3.29	12.01 /60	15.14 /59	4.64 /51	0.00	1.84
GR	Goldman Sachs Struct T/M Eq Inst	GCTIX	B	(800) 292-4726	C+ / 6.9	-1.97	3.88	13.37 /66	16.49 /66	5.84 /60	0.34	0.79

● Denotes fund is closed to new investors
* Denotes fund is included in Section II

RISK Rating/Pts	3 Year Standard Deviation	Beta	NAV As of 6/30/06	Total $(Mil)	Cash %	Stocks %	Bonds %	Other %	Portfolio Turnover Ratio	Last Bull Market Return	Last Bear Market Return	Manager Quality Pct	Manager Tenure (Years)	Initial Purch. $	Additional Purch. $	Front End Load	Back End Load
B- / 7.9	9.3	0.80	36.88	1,747	2	96	0	2	23.0	104.3	-6.6	93	11	1,000,000	0	0.0	0.0
B- / 7.9	9.3	0.80	36.30	148	2	96	0	2	23.0	101.4	-6.7	92	9	0	0	0.0	0.0
C / 4.6	15.6	0.93	20.30	370	2	97	0	1	19.0	135.5	0.2	91	N/A	1,000	50	5.5	1.0
C / 4.6	15.5	0.93	20.38	22	2	97	0	1	19.0	129.9	N/A	88	N/A	1,000	50	0.0	5.0
C / 4.6	15.6	0.93	20.20	22	2	97	0	1	19.0	129.8	N/A	88	N/A	1,000	50	0.0	1.0
C / 4.7	15.6	0.93	20.37	453	2	97	0	1	19.0	138.5	0.3	93	N/A	1,000,000	0	0.0	0.0
C / 4.6	15.6	0.93	20.40	8	2	97	0	1	19.0	134.7	0.1	91	N/A	0	0	0.0	0.0
B- / 7.7	7.8	0.95	7.43	47	1	98	0	1	25.0	64.2	-10.7	54	N/A	1,000	50	5.5	1.0
B / 8.1	7.9	0.95	7.10	68	1	98	0	1	25.0	60.2	-10.7	43	N/A	1,000	50	0.0	5.0
B / 8.1	7.9	0.95	7.11	26	1	98	0	1	25.0	60.4	-10.7	44	N/A	1,000	50	0.0	1.0
B / 8.2	7.8	0.94	7.60	2	1	98	0	1	25.0	66.4	-10.6	58	N/A	1,000,000	0	0.0	0.0
B / 8.3	7.8	0.93	7.43	N/A	1	98	0	1	25.0	64.5	-10.7	56	N/A	0	0	0.0	0.0
C+ / 6.2	12.8	0.84	43.34	1,044	4	95	0	1	20.0	103.1	-6.5	69	14	1,000	50	5.5	1.0
C+ / 6.0	12.8	0.84	39.74	86	4	95	0	1	20.0	98.4	-6.7	62	10	1,000	50	0.0	5.0
C+ / 6.0	12.8	0.84	39.70	113	4	95	0	1	20.0	98.4	-6.7	61	N/A	1,000	50	0.0	1.0
C+ / 6.3	12.8	0.84	44.77	698	4	95	0	1	20.0	105.7	-6.4	73	9	1,000,000	0	0.0	0.0
C+ / 6.2	12.8	0.84	42.78	45	4	95	0	1	20.0	102.4	-6.5	69	9	0	0	0.0	0.0
U /	N/A	N/A	10.73	78	5	94	0	1	22.0	N/A	N/A	N/A	N/A	1,000	50	5.5	1.0
C+ / 6.6	8.7	1.04	8.86	127	1	98	0	1	34.0	45.9	-11.4	12	N/A	1,000	50	5.5	1.0
B- / 7.0	8.7	1.04	8.40	8	1	98	0	1	34.0	42.5	-11.6	9	N/A	1,000	50	0.0	5.0
B- / 7.0	8.7	1.04	8.42	11	1	98	0	1	34.0	42.5	-11.7	9	N/A	1,000	50	0.0	1.0
B- / 7.1	8.7	1.04	9.07	184	1	98	0	1	34.0	47.7	-11.4	14	N/A	1,000,000	0	0.0	0.0
B- / 7.1	8.8	1.05	8.89	N/A	1	98	0	1	34.0	45.8	-11.4	12	N/A	0	0	0.0	0.0
C+ / 6.9	10.7	1.04	13.73	646	0	100	0	0	38.0	133.6	-9.9	51	9	1,000	50	5.5	1.0
C+ / 6.9	10.7	1.03	13.55	10	0	100	0	0	38.0	128.7	-10.0	43	9	1,000	50	0.0	5.0
C+ / 6.9	10.8	1.04	13.55	7	0	100	0	0	38.0	128.7	-10.0	42	9	1,000	50	0.0	1.0
C+ / 6.9	10.8	1.04	14.01	1,479	0	100	0	0	38.0	137.3	-9.8	56	N/A	1,000,000	0	0.0	2.0
C+ / 6.9	10.8	1.04	13.76	37	0	100	0	0	38.0	133.7	-10.0	51	N/A	0	0	0.0	2.0
B- / 7.3	9.0	1.09	13.12	260	0	99	0	1	55.0	62.9	-9.4	36	9	1,000	50	5.5	1.0
B- / 7.3	9.1	1.10	12.27	44	0	99	0	1	55.0	59.3	-9.6	30	9	1,000	50	0.0	5.0
B- / 7.3	9.1	1.09	12.28	24	0	99	0	1	55.0	59.3	-9.6	30	9	1,000	50	0.0	1.0
B- / 7.4	9.1	1.09	13.48	434	0	99	0	1	55.0	65.0	-9.3	40	N/A	1,000,000	0	0.0	0.0
B- / 7.4	9.1	1.09	13.02	N/A	0	99	0	1	55.0	62.9	-9.4	36	9	0	0	0.0	0.0
B / 8.7	8.0	0.99	13.54	357	0	99	0	1	63.0	88.1	-8.1	93	N/A	1,000	50	5.5	1.0
B / 8.7	8.1	1.00	13.45	19	0	99	0	1	63.0	83.5	-8.2	90	N/A	1,000	50	0.0	5.0
B / 8.7	8.2	1.01	13.46	22	0	99	0	1	63.0	83.7	-8.2	90	N/A	1,000	50	0.0	1.0
B / 8.7	8.0	0.99	13.53	680	0	99	0	1	63.0	90.3	-7.9	95	N/A	1,000,000	0	0.0	0.0
B / 8.7	8.0	0.98	13.60	N/A	0	99	0	1	63.0	87.5	-8.1	93	N/A	0	0	0.0	0.0
C+ / 5.9	14.4	0.96	14.27	196	0	99	0	1	60.0	116.5	-9.6	56	9	1,000	50	5.5	1.0
C+ / 5.8	14.4	0.97	13.17	17	0	99	0	1	60.0	111.3	-9.8	45	9	1,000	50	0.0	5.0
C+ / 5.8	14.3	0.96	13.22	28	0	99	0	1	60.0	111.4	-9.9	46	9	1,000	50	0.0	1.0
C+ / 6.0	14.4	0.97	14.75	520	0	99	0	1	60.0	119.0	-9.6	60	9	1,000,000	0	0.0	0.0
C+ / 5.9	14.4	0.96	14.09	37	0	99	0	1	60.0	115.7	-9.8	55	9	0	0	0.0	0.0
B / 8.0	8.4	1.06	30.96	595	0	99	0	1	47.0	73.1	-8.4	70	N/A	1,000	50	5.5	1.0
B / 8.3	8.4	1.07	29.17	79	0	99	0	1	47.0	69.1	-8.5	62	N/A	1,000	50	0.0	5.0
B / 8.3	8.4	1.07	29.03	37	0	99	0	1	47.0	69.0	-8.4	62	9	1,000	50	0.0	1.0
B / 8.3	8.4	1.07	31.61	596	0	99	0	1	47.0	75.3	-8.2	74	N/A	1,000,000	0	0.0	0.0
B / 8.3	8.5	1.07	30.68	11	0	99	0	1	47.0	72.5	-8.3	69	N/A	0	0	0.0	0.0
B / 8.3	9.1	1.13	10.78	109	0	99	0	1	92.0	87.7	-9.1	85	N/A	1,000	50	5.5	1.0
B / 8.3	9.1	1.14	10.38	25	0	99	0	1	92.0	83.1	-9.1	80	N/A	1,000	50	0.0	5.0
B / 8.3	9.1	1.14	10.35	25	0	99	0	1	92.0	83.3	-9.2	79	N/A	1,000	50	0.0	1.0
B / 8.3	9.1	1.14	10.97	44	0	99	0	1	92.0	89.9	-8.9	88	N/A	1,000,000	0	0.0	0.0

Fund Type	Fund Name	Ticker Symbol	Overall Weiss Investment Rating	Phone	Perfor-mance Rating/Pts	3 Mo	6 Mo	1Yr / Pct	3Yr / Pct	5Yr / Pct	Dividend Yield	Expense Ratio
								Total Return % through 6/30/06	Annualized		Incl. in Returns	
GR	Goldman Sachs Struct T/M Eq Svc	GCTSX	B	(800) 292-4726	C+ / 6.6	-2.19	3.57	12.70 /63	15.89 /63	5.34 /57	0.00	1.29
GR	Government Street Equity Fund	GVEQX	C-	(800) 443-4249	C- / 3.6	-2.02	1.75	8.64 /38	10.44 /30	2.61 /33	0.93	0.76
MC	Government Street Mid-Cap Fund	GVMCX	U	(800) 443-4249	U /	-4.10	3.04	11.49 /57	--	--	0.14	1.10
GR	Granum Value Fund	GRVFX	D	(888) 547-2686	D- / 1.1	-1.75	-1.21	-3.23 / 0	8.07 /15	3.03 /37	0.00	2.96
BA	Green Century Balanced	GCBLX	E+	(800) 934-7336	D- / 1.3	-3.14	-0.98	2.48 / 6	7.74 /14	-0.78 /12	0.17	2.00
GR	Green Century Equity	GCEQX	D	(800) 934-7336	D- / 1.5	-3.58	-0.60	4.85 /14	7.82 /14	0.59 /18	0.16	1.50
BA	Greenspring Fund	GRSPX	C+	(800) 366-3863	C / 5.0	-0.91	6.35	13.55 /66	12.52 /46	8.85 /76	1.91	1.10
AA	Guardian Asset Allocation A	GUAAX	C-	(800) 343-0817	D+ / 2.7	-1.01	2.75	7.74 /31	10.38 /30	2.90 /36	1.20	0.86
AA	Guardian Asset Allocation B	GAABX	D+	(800) 343-0817	D+ / 2.5	-1.26	2.18	6.72 /25	9.40 /24	2.01 /27	0.46	1.68
AA	Guardian Asset Allocation C		C-	(800) 343-0817	D+ / 2.7	-1.34	2.19	6.63 /24	9.26 /22	1.80 /25	0.22	1.87
EM	Guardian Baillie Giff Emerg Mkts A	GBEMX	C+	(800) 343-0817	A+ / 9.8	-1.26	10.51	42.91 /98	36.94 /99	22.20 /98	0.33	1.78
EM	Guardian Baillie Giff Emerg Mkts B		B	(800) 343-0817	A+ / 9.8	-1.47	9.99	41.58 /98	35.55 /98	20.91 /97	0.00	2.74
EM	Guardian Baillie Giff Emerg Mkts C		B	(800) 343-0817	A+ / 9.8	-1.47	10.00	41.65 /98	35.61 /98	21.00 /97	0.00	2.68
FO	Guardian Baillie Giff Intl Growth A	GUBGX	B	(800) 343-0817	B / 8.1	-0.86	8.94	26.20 /90	20.31 /80	6.28 /63	0.56	1.86
FO	Guardian Baillie Giff Intl Growth B	GBGBX	B	(800) 343-0817	B / 7.9	-1.20	8.22	24.64 /88	18.93 /76	5.02 /54	0.00	3.05
FO	Guardian Baillie Giff Intl Growth C		A	(800) 343-0817	B / 8.1	-1.12	8.39	25.04 /88	19.09 /76	5.14 /55	0.00	2.81
GR	Guardian Park Avenue Fund A	GPAFX	D-	(800) 343-0817	D- / 1.2	-1.75	2.02	8.88 /39	7.70 /13	-0.56 /13	0.91	0.91
GR	Guardian Park Avenue Fund B	GUPBX	D-	(800) 343-0817	D- / 1.0	-2.03	1.46	7.69 /30	6.61 / 9	-1.55 /10	0.00	1.92
GR	Guardian Park Avenue Fund C		D	(800) 343-0817	D- / 1.2	-2.03	1.45	7.64 /30	6.45 / 8	-1.73 / 9	0.00	2.08
SC	Guardian Park Avenue Small Cap A	GPSCX	D-	(800) 343-0817	C / 5.4	-7.34	6.35	10.67 /51	15.16 /60	7.47 /69	0.00	1.25
SC	Guardian Park Avenue Small Cap B	GUCBX	D-	(800) 343-0817	C / 5.1	-7.58	5.84	9.54 /44	14.04 /54	6.44 /64	0.00	2.21
SC	Guardian Park Avenue Small Cap C		D-	(800) 343-0817	C / 5.4	-7.53	5.89	9.62 /44	13.98 /54	6.33 /63	0.00	2.23
IX	Guardian S&P 500 Index A	GUSPX	C	(800) 343-0817	D+ / 2.9	-1.46	2.58	8.19 /34	10.69 /33	2.02 /27	1.28	0.53
IX	Guardian S&P 500 Index B		D+	(800) 343-0817	D+ / 2.7	-1.75	2.05	7.31 /28	9.82 /26	1.17 /21	0.63	1.28
IX	Guardian S&P 500 Index C		C-	(800) 343-0817	C- / 3.1	-1.65	2.15	7.43 /29	9.87 /26	1.17 /21	0.61	1.28
GI	Guardian UBS Large Cap Value A		B	(800) 343-0817	C / 5.2	-0.54	4.03	11.70 /58	14.24 /55	--	0.64	1.44
GI	Guardian UBS Large Cap Value B		B	(800) 343-0817	C / 5.1	-0.66	3.69	10.86 /53	13.41 /51	--	0.00	2.19
GI	Guardian UBS Large Cap Value C		B	(800) 343-0817	C / 5.4	-0.73	3.69	10.86 /53	13.41 /51	--	0.00	2.19
SC	Guardian UBS Small Cap Value A		C	(800) 343-0817	C- / 4.2	-5.37	1.61	6.48 /23	13.65 /52	--	0.00	1.92
SC	Guardian UBS Small Cap Value B		C	(800) 343-0817	C- / 3.9	-5.61	1.13	5.69 /19	12.75 /47	--	0.00	2.68
SC	Guardian UBS Small Cap Value C		C	(800) 343-0817	C / 4.3	-5.61	1.13	5.70 /19	12.75 /47	--	0.00	2.69
FO	Guinness Atkinson Asia Focus Fund	IASMX	B-	(800) 915-6565	A / 9.3	-3.78	11.07	24.17 /87	27.33 /93	19.09 /95	1.31	1.87
FO	Guinness Atkinson China & HK Fund	ICHKX	C+	(800) 915-6565	B+ / 8.7	-3.15	11.97	14.08 /68	23.60 /89	10.84 /83	3.90	1.63
EN	Guinness Atkinson Glob Energy Fund	GAGEX	U	(800) 915-6565	U /	3.64	13.36	41.39 /98	--	--	0.00	1.45
TC	Guinness Atkinson Glob Innov Fund	IWIRX	C	(800) 915-6565	C+ / 6.4	-2.68	5.48	20.17 /82	14.93 /58	0.72 /19	0.00	1.66
GR	Hallmark Capital Appreciation R	HCARX	E	(800) 637-1700	E- / 0.1	-2.52	-2.63	1.88 / 4	1.83 / 1	-6.98 / 1	0.00	1.45
GR	Hallmark First Mutual Fund I	HMFIX	E+	(800) 637-1700	D- / 1.1	-2.07	-1.68	2.37 / 5	6.64 / 9	-2.46 / 7	0.00	1.00
GR	Hallmark Informed Investors Gr I	HIIIX	C+	(800) 637-1700	C / 5.5	-6.00	2.72	8.59 /37	14.27 /55	--	0.18	1.56
GR	Hallmark Informed Investors Gr R	HIIRX	C+	(800) 637-1700	C / 5.1	-6.12	2.36	7.82 /31	13.56 /52	3.92 /45	0.18	1.00
FO	Hallmark International Equity R	HIERX	C-	(800) 637-1700	C+ / 6.0	-4.49	3.55	20.44 /82	14.14 /55	1.89 /26	0.00	1.80
GR	Hallmark Large Cap Growth I	HLCGX	C-	(800) 637-1700	D+ / 2.4	0.86	2.63	8.93 /40	8.01 /15	--	0.85	1.46
GR	Hallmark Large Cap Growth R	HLVAX	D+	(800) 637-1700	D / 2.2	0.84	2.36	8.35 /36	7.61 /13	-2.24 / 7	0.85	0.90
SC	Hallmark Small Cap Growth R	HEGAX	E	(800) 637-1700	C / 4.5	-12.75	-5.56	6.88 /26	13.95 /54	0.90 /20	0.00	1.55
IN	Hancock Horizon Burnkenroad A	HHBUX	B+	(888) 346-6300	B / 8.1	-2.82	11.69	17.92 /79	20.94 /82	--	0.00	1.40
IN	Hancock Horizon Burnkenroad D	HYBUX	B+	(888) 346-6300	B+ / 8.3	-2.84	11.63	17.76 /79	20.68 /82	--	0.00	1.65
GR	Hancock Horizon Growth A	HHRAX	C	(888) 346-6300	C / 4.9	-4.46	-0.42	7.84 /31	14.95 /59	6.78 /66	0.00	1.35
GR	Hancock Horizon Growth C	HHRCX	C	(888) 346-6300	C / 5.1	-4.69	-0.82	6.98 /26	14.09 /54	5.98 /61	0.00	2.10
GR	Hancock Horizon Growth Tr	HHRTX	C+	(888) 346-6300	C+ / 5.8	-4.41	-0.31	8.10 /33	15.23 /60	7.02 /67	0.00	1.10
IN	Hancock Horizon Value A	HHGAX	A-	(888) 346-6300	B / 7.8	1.72	9.16	15.80 /74	19.84 /79	11.53 /85	0.57	1.34
IN	Hancock Horizon Value C	HHGCX	A-	(888) 346-6300	B / 7.8	1.57	8.77	14.97 /72	18.93 /76	10.72 /83	0.10	2.09
IN	Hancock Horizon Value Tr	HHGTX	A+	(888) 346-6300	B / 8.2	1.78	9.31	16.12 /75	20.12 /80	11.80 /86	0.81	1.09
EM	Hansberger Instl-Emerging Markets	HEMGX	C+	(800) 414-6927	A- / 9.1	-9.42	0.22	28.32 /93	28.26 /94	19.37 /95	1.68	1.25

99 Pct = Best
0 Pct = Worst

● Denotes fund is closed to new investors
* Denotes fund is included in Section II

www.WeissRatings.com

RISK			NET ASSETS		ASSET				Portfolio Turnover Ratio	BULL / BEAR		FUND MANAGER		MINIMUMS		LOADS	
Risk Rating/Pts	3 Year Standard Deviation	Beta	NAV As of 6/30/06	Total $(Mil)	Cash %	Stocks %	Bonds %	Other %		Last Bull Market Return	Last Bear Market Return	Manager Quality Pct	Manager Tenure (Years)	Initial Purch. $	Additional Purch. $	Front End Load	Back End Load
B / 8.3	9.1	1.14	10.74	N/A	0	99	0	1	92.0	87.2	-9.0	84	N/A	0	0	0.0	0.0
C+ / 6.9	8.2	1.04	48.63	93	0	99	0	1	17.0	61.7	-9.2	43	15	5,000	100	0.0	0.0
U /	N/A	N/A	12.83	34	0	98	0	2	28.0	N/A	N/A	N/A	N/A	5,000	100	0.0	0.0
B / 8.4	7.6	0.77	35.97	113	16	83	0	1	12.3	42.8	-3.7	44	N/A	5,000	1,000	0.0	2.0
C / 5.5	12.3	1.76	16.41	52	2	67	29	2	86.0	81.1	-10.7	21	1	2,500	0	0.0	2.0
B- / 7.3	8.3	1.04	19.91	33	0	100	0	0	9.0	50.9	-10.6	23	11	2,500	0	0.0	2.0
B / 8.3	6.5	0.98	22.94	200	14	46	0	40	36.0	63.5	2.1	92	19	2,000	100	0.0	2.0
B- / 7.7	7.3	1.45	12.03	94	4	94	0	2	3.0	59.8	-9.8	60	11	1,000	100	4.5	1.0
B- / 7.7	7.3	1.45	11.96	17	4	94	0	2	3.0	55.4	-10.0	48	10	1,000	100	0.0	3.0
B / 8.1	7.3	1.45	11.98	9	4	94	0	2	3.0	54.6	-10.1	47	6	1,000	100	0.0	1.0
C- / 3.6	19.1	1.14	20.73	132	2	97	0	1	38.0	237.0	-6.9	24	9	1,000	100	4.5	1.0
C / 4.3	19.1	1.14	18.56	14	2	97	0	1	38.0	225.9	-7.1	18	9	1,000	100	0.0	3.0
C / 4.3	19.1	1.14	18.64	21	2	97	0	1	38.0	226.7	-7.1	18	6	1,000	100	0.0	1.0
C+ / 6.4	10.7	1.01	16.54	45	1	98	0	1	28.0	111.4	-7.7	21	13	1,000	100	4.5	1.0
C+ / 6.4	10.7	1.02	14.87	5	1	98	0	1	28.0	103.6	-7.8	14	10	1,000	100	0.0	3.0
B- / 7.8	12.1	1.11	14.98	8	1	98	0	1	28.0	104.6	-7.9	8	6	1,000	100	0.0	1.0
C+ / 6.8	7.8	1.00	32.59	747	0	99	0	1	101.0	46.8	-9.9	24	1	1,000	100	4.5	1.0
C+ / 6.8	8.0	1.01	31.36	43	0	99	0	1	101.0	42.2	-10.2	17	1	1,000	100	0.0	3.0
B- / 7.5	7.9	1.00	30.86	7	0	99	0	1	101.0	41.4	-10.2	17	1	1,000	100	0.0	1.0
C- / 3.1	15.3	1.03	16.85	139	2	97	0	1	124.0	99.5	-10.4	22	4	1,000	100	4.5	1.0
D+ / 2.7	15.3	1.03	15.03	9	2	97	0	1	124.0	93.5	-10.6	16	4	1,000	100	0.0	3.0
D+ / 2.6	15.2	1.03	14.90	10	2	97	0	1	124.0	93.1	-10.7	16	4	1,000	100	0.0	1.0
B / 8.8	7.6	0.99	8.72	142	1	98	0	1	4.0	62.2	-9.8	51	6	1,000	100	4.5	1.0
B- / 7.4	7.6	0.99	8.69	12	1	98	0	1	4.0	58.3	-10.3	41	6	1,000	100	0.0	3.0
B- / 7.4	7.6	0.99	8.69	9	1	98	0	1	4.0	58.2	-10.3	41	6	1,000	100	0.0	1.0
B+ / 9.0	7.2	0.88	13.30	27	3	96	0	1	35.0	79.8	N/A	89	N/A	1,000	100	4.5	1.0
B+ / 9.0	7.2	0.87	13.26	22	3	96	0	1	35.0	75.7	N/A	85	N/A	1,000	100	0.0	3.0
B+ / 9.0	7.2	0.87	13.26	21	3	96	0	1	35.0	75.7	N/A	85	N/A	1,000	100	0.0	1.0
B- / 7.7	11.1	0.73	11.84	13	2	97	0	1	67.0	87.9	N/A	52	N/A	1,000	100	4.5	1.0
B- / 7.7	11.1	0.73	11.45	10	2	97	0	1	67.0	83.5	N/A	42	N/A	1,000	100	0.0	3.0
B- / 7.7	11.1	0.72	11.45	10	2	97	0	1	67.0	83.4	N/A	43	N/A	1,000	100	0.0	1.0
C / 4.6	17.8	1.38	13.75	42	2	97	0	1	18.3	166.6	-7.4	13	N/A	2,500	250	0.0	2.0
C- / 3.9	16.5	1.13	21.24	120	0	99	0	1	12.5	128.2	-1.8	24	N/A	2,500	250	0.0	2.0
U /	N/A	N/A	27.92	95	0	99	0	1	89.2	N/A	N/A	N/A	2	5,000	250	0.0	1.0
C+ / 5.9	12.3	1.43	15.97	35	1	98	0	1	27.8	92.3	-13.0	52	N/A	2,500	250	0.0	1.0
C+ / 5.8	9.9	1.14	8.14	2	1	98	0	1	139.0	27.8	-6.9	2	1	1,000	100	0.0	0.0
C / 5.3	15.0	1.56	9.92	13	4	95	0	1	22.0	46.4	-11.5	3	N/A	250,000	10,000	0.0	0.0
B- / 7.8	10.9	1.31	10.97	1	0	99	0	1	116.0	83.9	-7.6	58	1	250,000	10,000	0.0	0.0
B- / 7.4	10.9	1.32	12.57	3	0	99	0	1	116.0	80.3	-7.7	49	1	1,000	100	0.0	0.0
C / 5.0	13.4	1.23	12.55	1	3	96	0	1	113.0	87.7	-10.2	0	11	1,000	100	0.0	0.0
B- / 7.9	7.8	0.92	3.51	1	2	97	0	1	63.0	52.0	-13.1	32	N/A	250,000	10,000	0.0	0.0
B- / 7.6	7.9	0.93	9.55	1	2	97	0	1	63.0	50.2	-13.2	28	N/A	1,000	100	0.0	0.0
D / 1.7	18.3	1.13	39.76	29	0	99	0	1	129.0	104.7	-14.4	9	12	1,000	100	0.0	0.0
C+ / 6.7	13.5	1.26	29.61	16	5	94	0	1	32.0	126.9	-7.6	96	5	1,000	500	5.3	0.0
C+ / 6.7	13.5	1.25	29.37	7	5	94	0	1	32.0	125.2	-7.7	96	6	1,000	500	0.0	1.0
C+ / 6.7	11.9	1.22	18.83	30	0	99	0	1	67.0	92.2	-6.6	72	5	1,000	500	5.3	0.0
C+ / 6.7	11.9	1.22	18.08	1	0	99	0	1	67.0	87.7	-6.8	65	5	1,000	500	0.0	1.0
C+ / 6.7	11.8	1.22	19.06	47	0	99	0	1	67.0	93.7	-6.5	75	5	1,000	500	0.0	0.0
B- / 7.8	9.7	1.03	25.23	41	1	98	0	1	77.0	102.2	-4.2	98	6	1,000	500	5.3	0.0
B- / 7.8	9.7	1.03	24.85	1	1	98	0	1	77.0	97.5	-4.4	97	4	1,000	500	0.0	1.0
B- / 7.8	9.7	1.03	25.29	71	1	98	0	1	77.0	103.9	-4.2	98	6	1,000	500	0.0	0.0
C- / 4.1	18.4	1.11	9.23	330	5	94	0	1	45.0	194.3	-4.0	3	N/A	1,000,000	100,000	0.0	2.0

	99 Pct = Best 0 Pct = Worst		Overall Weiss Investment Rating		PERFORMANCE						Incl. in Returns	
					Perfor- mance Rating/Pts	Total Return % through 6/30/06			Annualized		Dividend Yield	Expense Ratio
Fund Type	Fund Name	Ticker Symbol		Phone		3 Mo	6 Mo	1Yr / Pct	3Yr / Pct	5Yr / Pct		
FO	Hansberger Instl-Intl Growth Fund	HITGX	A-	(800) 414-6927	B / 8.2	-1.89	5.47	23.57 /87	21.00 /83	--	0.63	1.00
GR	Harbor Capital Appreciation Inst	HACAX	D	(800) 422-1050	C- / 3.0	-7.32	-6.15	6.67 /24	10.87 /34	-0.08 /15	0.10	0.68
GR	Harbor Capital Appreciation Inv	HCAIX	D	(800) 422-1050	D+ / 2.7	-7.41	-6.35	6.23 /22	10.40 /30	--	0.00	1.10
GR	Harbor Capital Appreciation Retire	HRCAX	D	(800) 422-1050	D+ / 2.8	-7.38	-6.27	6.42 /23	10.63 /32	--	0.00	0.92
FO	Harbor International Growth Fd	HAIGX	B	(800) 422-1050	B+ / 8.6	-2.98	6.92	32.63 /96	21.20 /83	2.80 /35	0.29	1.00
FO	Harbor International Growth Inv	HIIGX	A-	(800) 422-1050	B+ / 8.5	-3.06	6.74	32.12 /96	20.85 /82	--	0.10	1.41
FO	Harbor International Growth Retire	HRIGX	B	(800) 422-1050	B+ / 8.5	-3.06	6.83	32.27 /96	21.00 /83	--	0.12	1.24
FO	Harbor International Inst	HAINX	A	(800) 422-1050	A / 9.4	-0.98	12.15	35.48 /97	27.13 /93	15.12 /92	1.82	0.87
FO	Harbor International Inv	HIINX	A-	(800) 422-1050	A / 9.4	-1.08	11.93	34.91 /97	26.60 /93	--	1.57	1.30
FO	Harbor International Retire	HRINX	A	(800) 422-1050	A / 9.4	-1.04	12.02	35.16 /97	26.83 /93	--	1.69	1.12
GI	Harbor Large Cap Value Inst	HAVLX	C+	(800) 422-1050	C- / 4.2	-0.67	1.84	3.50 / 9	12.06 /43	4.45 /50	1.09	0.70
GI	Harbor Large Cap Value Inv	HILVX	C+	(800) 422-1050	C- / 3.9	-0.73	1.60	3.12 / 8	11.59 /40	--	0.83	1.10
GI	Harbor Large Cap Value Retire	HRLVX	C+	(800) 422-1050	C- / 4.1	-0.64	1.75	3.33 / 8	11.89 /42	--	0.87	0.95
MC	Harbor Mid Cap Growth Inst	HAMGX	C-	(800) 422-1050	B- / 7.2	-4.18	3.24	23.07 /86	17.18 /69	1.99 /27	0.00	0.95
MC	Harbor Mid Cap Growth Inv	HIMGX	C-	(800) 422-1050	B- / 7.0	-4.34	2.97	22.51 /85	16.88 /67	--	0.00	1.38
MC	Harbor Mid Cap Growth Retire	HRMGX	C-	(800) 422-1050	B- / 7.1	-4.31	3.09	22.90 /86	17.12 /69	--	0.00	1.20
MC	Harbor Mid Cap Value Inst	HAMVX	B	(800) 422-1050	C+ / 6.8	-0.08	5.87	11.55 /57	16.07 /64	--	1.04	0.95
MC	Harbor Mid Cap Value Inv	HIMVX	B-	(800) 422-1050	C+ / 6.6	-0.24	5.62	11.02 /54	15.82 /63	--	0.82	1.38
MC	Harbor Mid Cap Value Retire	HRMVX	B-	(800) 422-1050	C+ / 6.7	-0.16	5.70	11.29 /55	15.96 /63	--	0.97	1.20
SC ●	Harbor Small Cap Growth Inst	HASGX	D+	(800) 422-1050	C+ / 6.4	-7.16	7.07	13.73 /67	15.44 /61	1.26 /22	0.00	0.84
SC ●	Harbor Small Cap Growth Inv	HISGX	D	(800) 422-1050	C+ / 6.2	-7.20	6.84	13.31 /65	14.97 /59	--	0.00	1.27
SC ●	Harbor Small Cap Growth Retire	HRSGX	D+	(800) 422-1050	C+ / 6.3	-7.22	6.87	13.39 /66	15.16 /60	--	0.00	1.09
SC ●	Harbor Small Cap Value Inst	HASCX	A	(800) 422-1050	B / 8.2	-3.80	4.69	7.23 /28	22.14 /85	--	0.10	0.83
SC ●	Harbor Small Cap Value Inv	HISVX	A	(800) 422-1050	B / 8.1	-3.88	4.48	6.76 /25	21.68 /84	--	0.00	1.26
SC ●	Harbor Small Cap Value Retire	HSVRX	A	(800) 422-1050	B / 8.2	-3.86	4.55	6.92 /26	21.99 /85	--	0.00	1.08
GL	Harding Loevner Global Equity	HLMGX	B-	(877) 435-8105	B- / 7.0	-2.43	5.93	22.39 /85	16.48 /66	6.05 /61	0.27	1.25
FO	Harding Loevner Intl Equity Inst	HLMIX	B+	(877) 435-8105	B+ / 8.4	-1.19	7.66	25.83 /90	21.19 /83	8.13 /72	0.44	1.05
AA	Hartford Advisers A	ITTAX	D+	(800) 523-7798	E+ / 0.7	-2.15	-0.11	6.28 /22	6.49 / 8	2.20 /29	1.58	1.18
AA	Hartford Advisers B	IHABX	D+	(800) 523-7798	E+ / 0.6	-2.23	-0.37	5.59 /18	5.75 / 6	1.49 /24	1.02	1.92
AA	Hartford Advisers C	HAFCX	C-	(800) 523-7798	E+ / 0.9	-2.33	-0.46	5.54 /18	5.81 / 6	1.54 /24	0.97	1.84
AA	Hartford Advisers Y	IHAYX	C-	(800) 523-7798	D / 1.6	-2.07	0.13	6.71 /24	6.93 /10	2.69 /34	2.12	0.68
AA	Hartford Aggressive Growth Alloc A	HAAAX	U	(800) 523-7798	U /	-2.95	3.31	12.30 /61	--	--	0.68	1.55
AA	Hartford Aggressive Growth Alloc B	HAABX	U	(800) 523-7798	U /	-3.04	3.07	11.60 /57	--	--	0.13	2.20
AA	Hartford Aggressive Growth Alloc C	HAACX	U	(800) 523-7798	U /	-3.12	3.07	11.51 /57	--	--	0.13	2.20
AA	Hartford Balanced Alloc A	HBAAX	U	(800) 523-7798	U /	-1.53	2.30	8.53 /37	--	--	1.68	1.45
AA	Hartford Balanced Alloc B	HBABX	U	(800) 523-7798	U /	-1.69	1.96	7.69 /30	--	--	1.09	2.15
AA	Hartford Balanced Alloc C	HBACX	U	(800) 523-7798	U /	-1.69	1.96	7.79 /31	--	--	1.10	2.15
GR	Hartford Capital App II A	HCTAX	U	(800) 523-7798	U /	-1.75	5.63	18.48 /80	--	--	0.00	1.60
GR	Hartford Capital App II C	HFCCX	U	(800) 523-7798	U /	-2.00	5.23	17.64 /78	--	--	0.00	2.35
★ GR	Hartford Capital Apprec A	ITHAX	B+	(800) 523-7798	B / 7.7	-2.07	3.50	19.97 /82	20.27 /80	6.73 /65	0.00	1.26
GR	Hartford Capital Apprec B	IHCAX	B+	(800) 523-7798	B- / 7.5	-2.25	3.07	19.05 /81	19.38 /77	5.93 /61	0.00	2.03
GR	Hartford Capital Apprec C	HCACX	A-	(800) 523-7798	B / 7.9	-2.24	3.12	19.13 /81	19.48 /78	6.03 /61	0.00	1.94
GR	Hartford Capital Apprec Y	HCAYX	A	(800) 523-7798	B+ / 8.3	-1.97	3.70	20.50 /82	20.88 /82	7.31 /68	0.00	0.78
AA	Hartford Conservative Alloc A	HCVAX	U	(800) 523-7798	U /	-0.86	1.62	5.86 /19	--	--	2.55	1.40
AA	Hartford Conservative Alloc C	HCVCX	U	(800) 523-7798	U /	-1.03	1.38	5.15 /16	--	--	2.03	2.05
GI	Hartford Disciplined Equity A	HAIAX	C-	(800) 523-7798	D+ / 2.5	-1.83	1.48	6.62 /24	10.72 /33	0.94 /20	0.14	1.40
GI	Hartford Disciplined Equity B	HGIBX	C-	(800) 523-7798	D+ / 2.3	-1.92	1.20	5.94 /20	9.95 /27	0.23 /16	0.00	2.15
GI	Hartford Disciplined Equity C	HGICX	C	(800) 523-7798	D+ / 2.9	-2.00	1.12	5.84 /19	9.96 /27	0.26 /17	0.00	2.15
GI	Hartford Disciplined Equity Y	HGIYX	C+	(800) 523-7798	C- / 4.0	-1.70	1.68	7.13 /27	11.28 /38	1.48 /24	0.63	0.90
★ IN	Hartford Dividend & Growth A	IHGIX	C+	(800) 523-7798	C / 4.5	0.52	5.13	11.93 /59	12.82 /48	5.38 /57	1.14	1.17
IN	Hartford Dividend & Growth B	ITDGX	C+	(800) 523-7798	C- / 4.2	0.59	4.99	11.28 /55	11.96 /42	4.61 /51	0.58	2.01
IN	Hartford Dividend & Growth C	HDGCX	B-	(800) 523-7798	C / 4.9	0.34	4.77	11.14 /54	12.05 /43	4.67 /52	0.54	1.89

● Denotes fund is closed to new investors
★ Denotes fund is included in Section II

| RISK | | | NET ASSETS | | ASSET | | | | Portfolio | BULL / BEAR | | FUND MANAGER | | MINIMUMS | | LOADS | |
| Risk Rating/Pts | 3 Year | | NAV As of 6/30/06 | Total $(Mil) | Cash % | Stocks % | Bonds % | Other % | Turnover Ratio | Last Bull Market Return | Last Bear Market Return | Manager Quality Pct | Manager Tenure (Years) | Initial Purch. $ | Additional Purch. $ | Front End Load | Back End Load |
	Standard Deviation	Beta															
B- / 7.4	11.5	1.07	16.66	376	22	77	0	1	38.0	N/A	N/A	18	3	1,000,000	100,000	0.0	2.0
C+ / 6.2	11.4	1.32	30.65	7,562	4	95	0	1	69.0	70.8	-12.2	26	16	50,000	100	0.0	0.0
C+ / 6.2	11.4	1.32	30.37	521	4	95	0	1	69.0	68.5	-12.2	23	16	2,500	100	0.0	0.0
C+ / 6.2	11.4	1.32	30.51	174	4	95	0	1	69.0	69.8	-12.2	24	16	0	0	0.0	0.0
C+ / 5.8	12.3	1.13	11.74	221	3	96	0	1	183.0	112.7	-13.7	13	N/A	50,000	100	0.0	2.0
B- / 7.0	12.3	1.13	11.72	20	3	96	0	1	183.0	110.9	-13.7	12	N/A	2,500	100	0.0	2.0
C+ / 5.8	12.3	1.13	11.73	N/A	3	96	0	1	183.0	111.7	-13.7	12	N/A	0	0	0.0	2.0
C+ / 6.2	11.9	1.12	55.31	13,783	2	97	0	1	13.0	156.5	-8.0	53	19	50,000	100	0.0	2.0
C+ / 6.2	11.9	1.12	54.88	702	2	97	0	1	13.0	152.9	-8.0	48	19	2,500	100	0.0	2.0
C+ / 6.2	11.9	1.12	55.09	126	2	97	0	1	13.0	154.5	-8.0	50	19	0	0	0.0	2.0
B+ / 9.2	7.0	0.85	17.26	583	3	96	0	1	24.0	67.5	-9.2	77	5	50,000	100	0.0	0.0
B+ / 9.1	7.0	0.85	17.20	254	3	96	0	1	24.0	65.3	-9.3	74	5	2,500	100	0.0	0.0
B+ / 9.2	7.0	0.85	17.26	7	3	96	0	1	24.0	66.7	-9.2	76	5	0	0	0.0	0.0
C- / 3.9	14.8	1.27	7.34	104	8	91	0	1	177.0	106.8	-8.5	15	N/A	50,000	100	0.0	0.0
C- / 3.9	14.8	1.27	7.28	7	8	91	0	1	177.0	105.6	-8.5	14	N/A	2,500	100	0.0	0.0
C- / 3.9	14.8	1.27	7.33	N/A	8	91	0	1	177.0	106.5	-8.5	15	N/A	0	0	0.0	0.0
B / 8.3	10.0	0.85	12.62	21	3	96	0	1	20.0	79.4	-11.7	60	N/A	50,000	100	0.0	0.0
B- / 7.5	9.9	0.85	12.59	3	3	96	0	1	20.0	78.4	-11.7	58	N/A	2,500	100	0.0	0.0
B- / 7.5	10.0	0.85	12.60	N/A	3	96	0	1	20.0	79.1	-11.7	59	N/A	0	0	0.0	0.0
C- / 3.4	14.7	0.94	13.48	650	0	100	0	0	69.0	107.3	-9.2	34	N/A	50,000	100	0.0	0.0
C- / 3.3	14.7	0.94	13.28	47	0	100	0	0	69.0	104.7	-9.2	31	N/A	2,500	100	0.0	0.0
C- / 3.4	14.7	0.94	13.37	50	0	100	0	0	69.0	105.9	-9.2	32	N/A	0	0	0.0	0.0
B- / 7.6	12.3	0.77	20.76	1,988	3	96	0	1	20.0	131.7	-7.2	96	5	50,000	100	0.0	0.0
B- / 7.6	12.3	0.77	20.54	154	3	96	0	1	20.0	129.3	-7.2	96	5	2,500	100	0.0	0.0
B- / 7.6	12.3	0.77	20.70	63	3	96	0	1	20.0	130.9	-7.2	96	5	0	0	0.0	0.0
C+ / 6.8	10.1	0.92	22.51	29	0	99	0	1	35.0	92.5	-9.2	14	N/A	100,000	0	0.0	2.0
C+ / 6.6	11.1	1.04	17.42	346	3	96	0	1	38.0	109.5	-10.4	23	N/A	100,000	0	0.0	2.0
B+ / 9.2	5.5	1.09	15.71	1,117	2	64	32	2	66.0	37.3	-5.5	38	N/A	1,000	50	5.5	1.0
B+ / 9.4	5.5	1.09	15.56	366	2	64	32	2	66.0	34.3	-5.7	32	N/A	1,000	50	0.0	5.0
B+ / 9.4	5.5	1.09	15.71	224	2	64	32	2	66.0	34.6	-5.7	33	N/A	1,000	50	0.0	1.0
B+ / 9.4	5.5	1.09	15.86	17	2	64	32	2	66.0	39.2	-5.4	42	N/A	1,000,000	0	0.0	0.0
U /	N/A	N/A	12.49	102	N/A	100	0	N/A	9.0	N/A	N/A	N/A	2	1,000	50	5.5	1.0
U /	N/A	N/A	12.42	30	N/A	100	0	N/A	9.0	N/A	N/A	N/A	2	1,000	50	0.0	5.0
U /	N/A	N/A	12.41	47	N/A	100	0	N/A	9.0	N/A	N/A	N/A	2	1,000	50	0.0	1.0
U /	N/A	N/A	11.50	394	8	60	32	0	2.0	N/A	N/A	N/A	N/A	1,000	50	5.5	1.0
U /	N/A	N/A	11.48	98	8	60	32	0	2.0	N/A	N/A	N/A	N/A	1,000	50	0.0	5.0
U /	N/A	N/A	11.48	151	8	60	32	0	2.0	N/A	N/A	N/A	N/A	1,000	50	0.0	1.0
U /	N/A	N/A	12.38	168	2	98	0	0	46.0	N/A	N/A	N/A	N/A	1,000	50	5.5	1.0
U /	N/A	N/A	12.28	64	2	98	0	0	46.0	N/A	N/A	N/A	N/A	1,000	50	0.0	1.0
B- / 7.6	11.1	1.33	36.96	8,089	4	94	0	2	93.0	114.7	-10.5	94	10	1,000	50	5.5	1.0
B- / 7.4	11.1	1.33	33.87	1,755	4	94	0	2	93.0	109.7	-10.7	91	10	1,000	50	0.0	5.0
B- / 7.5	11.1	1.33	34.00	2,549	4	94	0	2	93.0	110.3	-10.6	92	10	1,000	50	0.0	1.0
B- / 7.6	11.1	1.33	39.25	190	4	94	0	2	93.0	118.3	-10.4	95	10	1,000,000	0	0.0	0.0
U /	N/A	N/A	10.74	85	2	46	50	2	23.0	N/A	N/A	N/A	N/A	1,000	50	5.5	1.0
U /	N/A	N/A	10.74	33	2	46	50	2	23.0	N/A	N/A	N/A	N/A	1,000	50	0.0	1.0
B / 8.7	7.9	1.01	12.36	190	2	96	0	2	61.0	60.9	-10.3	49	8	1,000	50	5.5	1.0
B / 8.6	7.9	1.01	11.77	36	2	96	0	2	61.0	57.3	-10.4	41	8	1,000	50	0.0	5.0
B / 8.6	8.0	1.02	11.78	30	2	96	0	2	61.0	57.5	-10.4	40	8	1,000	50	0.0	1.0
B / 8.7	8.0	1.01	12.70	1	2	96	0	2	61.0	63.5	-10.1	56	8	1,000,000	0	0.0	0.0
B+ / 9.0	7.7	0.94	19.77	2,362	2	98	0	0	26.0	68.3	-9.4	77	5	1,000	50	5.5	1.0
B+ / 9.0	7.7	0.94	19.50	343	2	98	0	0	26.0	64.4	-9.6	70	5	1,000	50	0.0	5.0
B+ / 9.0	7.7	0.94	19.47	290	2	98	0	0	26.0	64.7	-9.6	70	5	1,000	50	0.0	1.0

					PERFORMANCE							
99 Pct = Best 0 Pct = Worst			Overall Weiss Investment Rating				Total Return % through 6/30/06				Incl. in Returns	
					Perfor- mance				Annualized		Dividend	Expense
Fund Type	Fund Name	Ticker Symbol		Phone	Rating/Pts	3 Mo	6 Mo	1Yr / Pct	3Yr / Pct	5Yr / Pct	Yield	Ratio
IN	Hartford Dividend & Growth Y	HDGYX	B+	(800) 523-7798	C+ / 5.8	0.68	5.40	12.45 /62	13.35 /51	5.92 /61	1.59	0.73
IN	Hartford Equity Income A	HQIAX	U	(800) 523-7798	U /	2.26	6.89	11.68 /58	--	--	2.04	1.34
IN	Hartford Equity Income B	HQIBX	U	(800) 523-7798	U /	2.05	6.46	10.66 /51	--	--	1.34	2.18
IN	Hartford Equity Income C	HQICX	U	(800) 523-7798	U /	2.08	6.53	10.89 /53	--	--	1.47	2.03
GR	Hartford Focus A	HFFAX	D	(800) 523-7798	D- / 1.2	-4.26	-2.73	7.14 /27	8.44 /17	1.40 /23	0.60	1.65
GR	Hartford Focus B	HFFBX	D	(800) 523-7798	D- / 1.0	-4.38	-3.09	6.46 /23	7.68 /13	0.67 /18	0.00	2.45
GR	Hartford Focus C	HFFCX	D+	(800) 523-7798	D- / 1.5	-4.38	-3.09	6.46 /23	7.72 /13	0.67 /19	0.00	2.36
GR	Hartford Focus Y	HFFYX	C-	(800) 523-7798	D+ / 2.4	-4.10	-2.50	7.67 /30	8.96 /21	2.01 /27	1.06	1.16
GL	Hartford Global Comm A	HGCAX	C+	(800) 523-7798	C+ / 6.9	-9.74	-4.09	9.62 /44	20.72 /82	3.63 /42	1.34	2.01
GL	Hartford Global Comm B	HGCBX	C	(800) 523-7798	C+ / 6.8	-9.87	-4.33	9.06 /40	20.02 /79	2.96 /36	0.99	3.22
GL	Hartford Global Comm C	HGCCX	C+	(800) 523-7798	B- / 7.2	-10.00	-4.47	8.71 /38	19.89 /79	2.90 /36	0.80	2.94
GL	Hartford Global Comm Y	HGCYX	C+	(800) 523-7798	B / 7.7	-9.56	-3.88	10.13 /48	21.36 /83	4.14 /47	1.78	1.36
FS	Hartford Global Finan Serv A	HGFAX	B	(800) 523-7798	C+ / 6.1	-0.46	5.86	18.28 /80	15.78 /63	4.92 /53	0.81	1.43
FS	Hartford Global Finan Serv B	HGFBX	B-	(800) 523-7798	C+ / 5.8	-0.70	5.45	17.36 /78	14.96 /59	4.19 /48	0.34	2.46
FS	Hartford Global Finan Serv C	HGFCX	B	(800) 523-7798	C+ / 6.3	-0.70	5.45	17.37 /78	14.93 /58	4.17 /48	0.26	2.32
FS	Hartford Global Finan Serv Y	HGFYX	A-	(800) 523-7798	B- / 7.1	-0.38	6.06	18.73 /80	16.30 /65	5.39 /57	1.20	0.91
HL	Hartford Global Health A	HGHAX	D+	(800) 523-7798	C- / 3.4	-2.52	0.79	14.58 /70	12.06 /43	7.13 /67	0.00	1.60
HL	Hartford Global Health B	HGHBX	D+	(800) 523-7798	C- / 3.2	-2.64	0.51	13.88 /68	11.29 /38	6.37 /63	0.00	2.35
HL	Hartford Global Health C	HGHCX	C-	(800) 523-7798	C- / 3.8	-2.70	0.44	13.73 /67	11.24 /37	6.35 /63	0.00	2.35
HL	Hartford Global Health Y	HGHYX	C	(800) 523-7798	C / 4.9	-2.43	1.05	15.23 /72	12.61 /46	7.76 /70	0.00	1.08
GL	Hartford Global Leaders A	HALAX	C	(800) 523-7798	C / 5.1	-2.14	4.82	15.40 /73	14.46 /56	5.03 /54	0.08	1.48
GL	Hartford Global Leaders B	HGLBX	C-	(800) 523-7798	C / 4.7	-2.32	4.37	14.48 /70	13.57 /52	4.23 /48	0.00	2.35
GL	Hartford Global Leaders C	HGLCX	C	(800) 523-7798	C / 5.4	-2.26	4.41	14.54 /70	13.67 /52	4.32 /49	0.00	2.35
GL	Hartford Global Leaders Y	HGLYX	C-	(800) 523-7798	C+ / 6.3	-1.97	5.08	16.03 /75	15.13 /59	5.64 /59	0.53	0.97
TC	Hartford Global Technology A	HGTAX	E	(800) 523-7798	D / 2.0	-8.57	-2.06	12.23 /61	11.43 /39	-1.53 /10	0.00	1.60
TC	Hartford Global Technology B	HGTBX	E-	(800) 523-7798	D / 1.8	-8.59	-2.34	11.36 /56	10.66 /32	-2.24 / 7	0.00	2.35
TC	Hartford Global Technology C	HGTCX	E	(800) 523-7798	D / 2.2	-8.78	-2.54	11.14 /54	10.58 /32	-2.28 / 7	0.00	2.35
TC	Hartford Global Technology Y	HGTYX	E+	(800) 523-7798	C- / 3.3	-8.36	-1.83	12.58 /62	11.92 /42	-1.12 /11	0.00	1.22
AA	Hartford Growth Alloc A	HRAAX	U	(800) 523-7798	U /	-2.43	2.56	10.23 /48	--	--	1.00	1.55
AA	Hartford Growth Alloc B	HRABX	U	(800) 523-7798	U /	-2.60	2.13	9.52 /44	--	--	0.46	2.20
AA	Hartford Growth Alloc C	HRACX	U	(800) 523-7798	U /	-2.60	2.22	9.52 /44	--	--	0.46	2.20
GR	Hartford Growth Fund A	HGWAX	D-	(800) 523-7798	D- / 1.1	-5.05	-2.96	2.85 / 7	9.01 /21	0.81 /19	0.00	1.33
GR	Hartford Growth Fund B	HGWBX	D-	(800) 523-7798	D- / 1.0	-5.16	-3.28	2.09 / 5	8.23 /16	0.10 /16	0.00	2.15
GR	Hartford Growth Fund C	HGWCX	D-	(800) 523-7798	D- / 1.5	-5.15	-3.27	2.15 / 5	8.30 /17	0.13 /16	0.00	2.15
GR	Hartford Growth Fund H	FECHX	D-	(800) 523-7798	D- / 1.2	-5.16	-3.25	2.33 / 5	8.50 /18	0.29 /17	0.00	1.81
GR	Hartford Growth Fund L	FECLX	D-	(800) 523-7798	D- / 1.4	-4.94	-2.82	3.11 / 8	9.35 /23	1.06 /21	0.00	1.06
GR	Hartford Growth Fund M	FECBX	D-	(800) 523-7798	D- / 1.2	-5.11	-3.19	2.40 / 5	8.54 /18	0.30 /17	0.00	1.81
GR	Hartford Growth Fund N	FECCX	D-	(800) 523-7798	D / 1.6	-5.17	-3.25	2.33 / 5	8.51 /18	0.29 /17	0.00	1.81
GR	Hartford Growth Fund Y	HGWYX	D	(800) 523-7798	D+ / 2.3	-4.89	-2.69	3.37 / 8	9.58 /24	--	0.00	0.85
GR	Hartford Growth Opportunity A	HGOAX	C	(800) 523-7798	C+ / 6.4	-5.25	1.33	15.95 /75	17.33 /69	5.20 /56	0.00	1.36
GR	Hartford Growth Opportunity B	HGOBX	C	(800) 523-7798	C+ / 6.2	-5.53	0.83	14.95 /72	16.45 /65	4.45 /50	0.00	2.15
GR	Hartford Growth Opportunity C	HGOCX	C	(800) 523-7798	C+ / 6.6	-5.52	0.87	15.00 /72	16.47 /66	4.44 /50	0.00	2.15
GR	Hartford Growth Opportunity H	FGRHX	C	(800) 523-7798	C+ / 6.4	-5.46	0.99	15.26 /73	16.77 /67	4.67 /52	0.00	1.84
GR	Hartford Growth Opportunity L	FGRWX	C+	(800) 523-7798	C+ / 6.6	-5.28	1.35	16.13 /75	17.64 /71	5.46 /58	0.00	1.09
GR	Hartford Growth Opportunity M	FGRBX	C	(800) 523-7798	C+ / 6.4	-5.47	0.99	15.29 /73	16.76 /67	4.67 /52	0.00	1.84
GR	Hartford Growth Opportunity N	FGRCX	C+	(800) 523-7798	C+ / 6.8	-5.43	0.99	15.29 /73	16.78 /67	4.67 /52	0.00	1.84
GR	Hartford Growth Opportunity Y	HGOYX	C+	(800) 523-7798	B- / 7.3	-5.23	1.48	16.42 /76	17.91 /72	--	0.00	0.88
GR	Hartford Growth Opportunity Z	FGRZX	B	(800) 523-7798	B- / 7.3	-5.23	1.49	16.44 /76	17.95 /72	5.79 /60	0.00	0.84
AA	Hartford Income Alloc A	HINAX	U	(800) 523-7798	U /	0.26	0.26	0.78 / 2	--	--	4.22	1.25
FO	Hartford Intl Capital Apprec A	HNCAX	B-	(800) 523-7798	B / 7.7	-1.75	7.25	22.32 /85	20.29 /80	10.21 /81	0.33	1.60
FO	Hartford Intl Capital Apprec B	HNCBX	B-	(800) 523-7798	B- / 7.5	-1.95	6.92	21.54 /84	19.44 /78	9.42 /78	0.00	2.35
FO	Hartford Intl Capital Apprec C	HNCCX	B	(800) 523-7798	B / 7.9	-1.95	6.92	21.44 /84	19.44 /78	9.42 /78	0.00	2.35

● Denotes fund is closed to new investors
* Denotes fund is included in Section II

RISK			NET ASSETS		ASSET				Portfolio Turnover Ratio	BULL / BEAR		FUND MANAGER		MINIMUMS		LOADS	
Risk Rating/Pts	3 Year Standard Deviation	Beta	NAV As of 6/30/06	Total $(Mil)	Cash %	Stocks %	Bonds %	Other %		Last Bull Market Return	Last Bear Market Return	Manager Quality Pct	Manager Tenure (Years)	Initial Purch. $	Additional Purch. $	Front End Load	Back End Load
B+ / 9.0	7.7	0.94	19.99	101	2	98	0	0	26.0	70.8	-9.3	80	5	1,000,000	0	0.0	0.0
U /	N/A	N/A	12.97	447	0	100	0	0	23.0	N/A	N/A	N/A	N/A	1,000	50	5.5	1.0
U /	N/A	N/A	12.95	37	0	100	0	0	23.0	N/A	N/A	N/A	N/A	1,000	50	0.0	5.0
U /	N/A	N/A	12.96	53	0	100	0	0	23.0	N/A	N/A	N/A	N/A	1,000	50	0.0	1.0
B / 8.2	9.1	1.06	10.35	43	0	98	0	2	112.0	55.0	-11.9	26	1	1,000	50	5.5	1.0
B / 8.1	9.0	1.05	10.05	14	0	98	0	2	112.0	51.2	-12.0	21	1	1,000	50	0.0	5.0
B / 8.1	9.1	1.06	10.05	14	0	98	0	2	112.0	51.6	-12.0	21	1	1,000	50	0.0	1.0
B / 8.3	9.1	1.06	10.53	1	0	98	0	2	112.0	57.2	-11.8	29	1	1,000,000	0	0.0	0.0
C+ / 5.7	17.0	1.36	7.04	16	2	96	0	2	45.0	146.3	-7.5	2	N/A	1,000	50	5.5	1.0
C+ / 5.6	16.9	1.35	6.85	4	2	96	0	2	45.0	140.8	-7.6	1	N/A	1,000	50	0.0	5.0
C+ / 5.6	16.9	1.35	6.84	5	2	96	0	2	45.0	140.3	-7.6	1	N/A	1,000	50	0.0	1.0
C+ / 5.7	16.9	1.35	7.19	1	2	96	0	2	45.0	149.6	-7.4	2	N/A	1,000,000	0	0.0	0.0
B / 8.2	9.6	0.94	13.00	17	2	96	0	2	33.0	89.8	-12.2	80	N/A	1,000	50	5.5	1.0
B / 8.2	9.6	0.94	12.77	4	2	96	0	2	33.0	85.5	-12.3	74	N/A	1,000	50	0.0	5.0
B / 8.2	9.6	0.94	12.77	3	2	96	0	2	33.0	85.4	-12.3	74	N/A	1,000	50	0.0	1.0
B / 8.2	9.6	0.94	13.12	1	2	96	0	2	33.0	92.6	-12.2	83	N/A	1,000,000	0	0.0	0.0
C+ / 6.8	8.8	0.71	16.65	271	2	98	0	0	50.0	76.0	-9.4	86	N/A	1,000	50	5.5	1.0
C+ / 6.7	8.8	0.71	15.84	75	2	98	0	0	50.0	72.0	-9.5	81	N/A	1,000	50	0.0	5.0
C+ / 6.7	8.8	0.71	15.83	83	2	98	0	0	50.0	72.0	-9.5	80	N/A	1,000	50	0.0	1.0
C+ / 6.9	8.8	0.71	17.30	183	2	98	0	0	50.0	78.7	-9.3	88	N/A	1,000,000	0	0.0	0.0
C+ / 6.4	12.6	1.00	18.71	427	0	100	0	0	270.0	87.8	-13.0	4	8	1,000	50	5.5	1.0
C+ / 6.3	12.7	1.00	17.66	77	0	100	0	0	270.0	83.3	-13.1	3	8	1,000	50	0.0	5.0
C+ / 6.3	12.6	0.99	17.75	69	0	100	0	0	270.0	83.8	-13.1	3	8	1,000	50	0.0	1.0
C / 4.8	12.7	1.00	19.44	65	0	100	0	0	270.0	91.4	-12.8	5	N/A	1,000,000	0	0.0	0.0
C- / 3.1	18.1	1.90	5.23	31	0	98	0	2	132.0	89.8	-12.9	6	N/A	1,000	50	5.5	1.0
C- / 3.1	18.0	1.88	5.00	13	0	98	0	2	132.0	85.9	-12.9	5	N/A	1,000	50	0.0	5.0
C- / 3.0	18.2	1.90	4.99	11	0	98	0	2	132.0	85.3	-12.8	4	N/A	1,000	50	0.0	1.0
C- / 3.2	18.1	1.89	5.37	1	0	98	0	2	132.0	92.2	-12.5	7	N/A	1,000,000	0	0.0	0.0
U /	N/A	N/A	12.04	322	0	80	20	0	1.0	N/A	N/A	N/A	2	1,000	50	5.5	1.0
U /	N/A	N/A	11.97	96	0	80	20	0	1.0	N/A	N/A	N/A	2	1,000	50	0.0	5.0
U /	N/A	N/A	11.97	161	0	80	20	0	1.0	N/A	N/A	N/A	2	1,000	50	0.0	1.0
C+ / 6.6	11.2	1.21	17.68	702	2	98	0	0	77.0	68.1	-9.8	20	5	1,000	50	5.5	1.0
C+ / 6.6	11.3	1.22	15.63	45	2	98	0	0	77.0	64.4	-10.0	16	5	1,000	50	0.0	5.0
C+ / 6.6	11.2	1.22	15.66	87	2	98	0	0	77.0	64.7	-10.0	16	5	1,000	50	0.0	1.0
C+ / 6.6	11.2	1.21	15.80	17	2	98	0	0	77.0	65.8	-9.9	18	5	1,000	50	0.0	4.0
C+ / 6.7	11.2	1.21	17.90	277	2	98	0	0	77.0	69.7	-9.7	23	5	1,000	50	4.8	1.0
C+ / 6.6	11.2	1.21	15.79	17	2	98	0	0	77.0	65.8	-9.9	18	5	1,000	50	0.0	4.0
C+ / 6.6	11.2	1.21	15.78	4	2	98	0	0	77.0	65.8	-9.9	18	5	1,000	50	0.0	1.0
C+ / 6.7	11.2	1.21	18.08	90	2	98	0	0	77.0	70.9	-9.7	24	5	1,000,000	0	0.0	0.0
C+ / 5.8	12.7	1.36	28.15	350	2	96	0	2	156.0	115.5	-9.7	80	5	1,000	50	5.5	1.0
C+ / 5.8	12.8	1.36	24.28	32	2	96	0	2	156.0	110.8	-9.9	74	5	1,000	50	0.0	5.0
C+ / 5.8	12.8	1.36	24.29	43	2	96	0	2	156.0	110.8	-9.8	74	5	1,000	50	0.0	1.0
C+ / 5.8	12.8	1.35	24.59	35	2	96	0	2	156.0	112.6	-9.8	77	5	1,000	50	0.0	4.0
C+ / 5.9	12.7	1.35	28.52	568	2	96	0	2	156.0	117.6	-9.6	83	5	1,000	50	4.8	1.0
C+ / 5.8	12.7	1.35	24.55	21	2	96	0	2	156.0	112.5	-9.8	77	5	1,000	50	0.0	4.0
C+ / 5.8	12.8	1.36	24.56	5	2	96	0	2	156.0	112.6	-9.8	77	5	1,000	50	0.0	1.0
C+ / 5.9	12.8	1.36	28.79	14	2	96	0	2	156.0	119.2	-9.6	84	5	1,000,000	0	0.0	0.0
C+ / 6.7	12.8	1.36	29.89	35	2	96	0	2	156.0	119.4	-9.6	84	5	1,000	50	0.0	0.0
U /	N/A	N/A	9.72	26	6	0	92	2	30.0	N/A	N/A	N/A	2	1,000	50	4.5	1.0
C+ / 6.3	12.8	1.10	14.05	188	3	96	0	1	183.0	125.2	-10.2	12	5	1,000	50	5.5	1.0
C+ / 6.3	12.8	1.10	13.60	30	3	96	0	1	183.0	120.2	-10.3	9	5	1,000	50	0.0	5.0
C+ / 6.3	12.8	1.10	13.60	39	3	96	0	1	183.0	119.8	-10.3	9	5	1,000	50	0.0	1.0

Fund Type	Fund Name	Ticker Symbol	Overall Weiss Investment Rating	Phone	Perfor-mance Rating/Pts	3 Mo	6 Mo	1Yr / Pct	3Yr / Pct	5Yr / Pct	Dividend Yield	Expense Ratio
	99 Pct = Best				PERFORMANCE			Total Return % through 6/30/06			Incl. in Returns	
	0 Pct = Worst								Annualized			
FO	Hartford Intl Capital Apprec Y	HNCYX	B+	(800) 523-7798	B+ / 8.3	-1.66	7.54	22.95 /86	20.84 /82	10.72 /83	0.72	1.20
FO	Hartford Intl Opportunity A	IHOAX	A-	(800) 523-7798	B+ / 8.3	0.46	8.92	24.88 /88	21.78 /85	7.46 /69	0.28	1.57
FO	Hartford Intl Opportunity B	HIOBX	B+	(800) 523-7798	B+ / 8.3	0.63	8.93	24.48 /88	21.01 /83	6.75 /65	0.25	2.35
FO	Hartford Intl Opportunity C	HIOCX	A-	(800) 523-7798	B+ / 8.4	0.35	8.54	23.93 /87	20.84 /82	6.63 /65	0.00	2.35
FO	Hartford Intl Opportunity Y	HAOYX	A	(800) 523-7798	B+ / 8.8	0.64	9.23	25.61 /89	22.35 /86	7.97 /71	0.72	1.05
FO	Hartford Intl Small Company A	HNSAX	B+	(800) 523-7798	B+ / 8.9	-1.25	10.19	27.32 /92	25.04 /91	16.31 /93	1.43	1.60
FO	Hartford Intl Small Company B	HNSBX	B	(800) 523-7798	B+ / 8.8	-1.42	9.84	26.33 /90	24.15 /90	15.64 /93	1.02	2.35
FO	Hartford Intl Small Company C	HNSCX	B+	(800) 523-7798	A- / 9.0	-1.43	9.79	26.31 /90	24.11 /90	15.44 /92	0.94	2.35
FO	Hartford Intl Small Company Y	HNSYX	B+	(800) 523-7798	A- / 9.2	-1.17	10.41	27.72 /92	25.52 /92	16.82 /94	1.82	1.20
MC	● Hartford MidCap Fd A	HFMCX	C+	(800) 523-7798	C+ / 6.5	-4.29	3.07	14.30 /69	17.60 /71	9.53 /79	0.00	1.30
MC	● Hartford MidCap Fd B	HAMBX	C	(800) 523-7798	C+ / 6.3	-4.46	2.72	13.45 /66	16.70 /67	8.72 /75	0.00	2.08
MC	● Hartford MidCap Fd C	HMDCX	C+	(800) 523-7798	C+ / 6.8	-4.44	2.75	13.59 /67	16.82 /67	8.81 /76	0.00	1.99
MC	● Hartford MidCap Fd Y	HMDYX	B-	(800) 523-7798	B- / 7.4	-4.19	3.32	14.86 /71	18.18 /73	10.10 /81	0.00	0.83
MC	● Hartford MidCap Value A	HMVAX	B	(800) 523-7798	B- / 7.1	-1.50	6.17	14.88 /71	18.62 /75	10.28 /81	0.00	1.40
MC	● Hartford MidCap Value B	HMVBX	B-	(800) 523-7798	C+ / 6.9	-1.71	5.77	13.97 /68	17.78 /71	9.50 /79	0.00	2.15
MC	● Hartford MidCap Value C	HMVCX	B	(800) 523-7798	B- / 7.3	-1.71	5.77	13.96 /68	17.74 /71	9.49 /79	0.00	2.15
MC	● Hartford MidCap Value Y	HMVYX	A-	(800) 523-7798	B / 7.9	-1.39	6.39	15.42 /73	19.18 /77	10.79 /83	0.00	0.96
MC	Hartford Sel MidCap Value A	HFVAX	U	(800) 523-7798	U /	-1.95	4.53	10.75 /52	--	--	0.06	1.55
SC	Hartford Small Company A	IHSAX	C	(800) 523-7798	B / 7.7	-5.78	6.43	23.40 /86	21.06 /83	7.98 /72	0.00	1.40
SC	Hartford Small Company B	HSCBX	C	(800) 523-7798	B- / 7.5	-5.98	5.99	22.50 /85	20.17 /80	7.22 /68	0.00	2.15
SC	Hartford Small Company C	HSMCX	C+	(800) 523-7798	B / 7.9	-5.97	6.04	22.54 /85	20.18 /80	7.21 /68	0.00	2.15
SC	Hartford Small Company Y	HSCYX	C+	(800) 523-7798	B+ / 8.3	-5.71	6.65	23.96 /87	21.59 /84	8.47 /74	0.00	1.00
SC	Hartford SmallCap Growth A	HSLAX	C-	(800) 523-7798	C+ / 5.6	-8.25	-0.13	7.25 /28	17.14 /69	4.48 /50	0.00	1.40
SC	Hartford SmallCap Growth B	HSLBX	C-	(800) 523-7798	C / 5.4	-8.44	-0.48	6.50 /23	16.36 /65	3.79 /44	0.00	2.15
SC	Hartford SmallCap Growth C	HSLCX	C-	(800) 523-7798	C+ / 5.9	-8.48	-0.55	6.43 /23	16.32 /65	3.75 /43	0.00	2.15
SC	Hartford SmallCap Growth H	FACHX	C-	(800) 523-7798	C+ / 5.6	-8.39	-0.40	6.71 /24	16.54 /66	3.90 /45	0.00	1.96
SC	Hartford SmallCap Growth L	FACAX	C-	(800) 523-7798	C+ / 5.8	-8.22	-0.03	7.52 /29	17.32 /69	4.56 /51	0.00	1.21
SC	Hartford SmallCap Growth M	FACBX	C-	(800) 523-7798	C+ / 5.6	-8.40	-0.40	6.64 /24	16.51 /66	3.89 /45	0.00	1.96
SC	Hartford SmallCap Growth N	FACCX	C	(800) 523-7798	C+ / 6.0	-8.40	-0.40	6.67 /24	16.53 /66	3.89 /45	0.00	1.96
SC	Hartford SmallCap Growth Y	HSLYX	C	(800) 523-7798	C+ / 6.7	-8.19	0.07	7.71 /31	17.67 /71	--	0.00	0.98
GR	Hartford Stock A	IHSTX	D+	(800) 523-7798	D- / 1.4	-3.20	0.52	10.22 /48	8.96 /21	0.20 /16	0.20	1.36
GR	Hartford Stock B	ITSBX	D+	(800) 523-7798	D- / 1.3	-3.23	0.31	9.45 /43	8.15 /16	-0.56 /13	0.14	2.17
GR	Hartford Stock C	HSFCX	D+	(800) 523-7798	D / 1.8	-3.39	0.16	9.36 /42	8.21 /16	-0.44 /14	0.00	2.03
GR	Hartford Stock Y	HASYX	C	(800) 523-7798	D+ / 2.8	-3.12	0.80	10.71 /52	9.54 /24	0.75 /19	0.67	0.78
GI	Hartford Value Fd A	HVFAX	B	(800) 523-7798	C / 5.0	1.10	7.39	13.82 /68	13.35 /51	4.12 /47	0.64	1.40
GI	Hartford Value Fd B	HVFBX	B-	(800) 523-7798	C / 4.7	0.94	7.01	13.09 /65	12.53 /46	3.38 /40	0.00	2.15
GI	Hartford Value Fd C	HVFCX	B	(800) 523-7798	C / 5.3	0.94	7.01	12.98 /64	12.49 /46	3.36 /40	0.00	2.15
GI	Hartford Value Fd Y	HVFYX	B+	(800) 523-7798	C+ / 6.1	1.28	7.60	14.36 /69	13.61 /52	4.60 /51	1.11	0.93
GR	Hartford Value Opportunities A	HVOAX	B+	(800) 523-7798	C+ / 6.3	-1.17	4.00	10.25 /48	17.31 /69	5.24 /56	0.00	1.40
GR	Hartford Value Opportunities B	HVOBX	B	(800) 523-7798	C+ / 6.1	-1.32	3.70	9.50 /43	16.49 /66	4.49 /50	0.00	2.15
GR	Hartford Value Opportunities C	HVOCX	B	(800) 523-7798	C+ / 6.6	-1.32	3.63	9.43 /43	16.45 /65	4.47 /50	0.00	2.15
GR	Hartford Value Opportunities H	FVAHX	B	(800) 523-7798	C+ / 6.3	-1.25	3.75	9.70 /45	16.55 /66	4.53 /50	0.00	2.06
GR	Hartford Value Opportunities L	FVAAX	B	(800) 523-7798	C+ / 6.5	-1.05	4.18	10.51 /50	17.43 /70	5.30 /56	0.12	1.30
GR	Hartford Value Opportunities M	FVABX	B	(800) 523-7798	C+ / 6.3	-1.25	3.76	9.71 /45	16.56 /66	4.53 /50	0.00	2.06
GR	Hartford Value Opportunities N	FRVCX	B	(800) 523-7798	C+ / 6.6	-1.32	3.75	9.63 /44	16.55 /66	4.53 /50	0.00	2.06
GR	Hartford Value Opportunities Y	HVOYX	A-	(800) 523-7798	B- / 7.2	-1.04	4.27	10.71 /52	17.62 /71	--	0.32	1.07
MC	Heartland Select Value Fd	HRSVX	A	(888) 505-5180	B / 8.0	-2.42	7.08	16.35 /76	19.81 /79	12.65 /88	0.20	1.27
SC	Heartland Value Fund	HRTVX	C	(888) 505-5180	B+ / 8.3	-2.44	14.24	23.43 /86	19.27 /77	14.29 /91	0.00	1.10
GI	Heartland Value Plus Fund	HRVIX	C	(888) 505-5180	C+ / 6.1	-5.47	0.77	6.24 /22	16.09 /64	14.76 /91	0.84	1.25
FO	Henderson European Focus A	HFEAX	B	(866) 443-6337	A+ / 9.7	0.58	15.34	31.53 /95	34.77 /98	--	0.00	1.73
FO	Henderson European Focus B	HFEBX	B	(866) 443-6337	A+ / 9.7	0.42	14.94	30.61 /95	33.82 /97	--	0.00	2.48
FO	Henderson European Focus C	HFECX	B	(866) 443-6337	A+ / 9.8	0.42	14.94	30.61 /95	33.82 /97	--	0.00	2.48

● Denotes fund is closed to new investors
* Denotes fund is included in Section II

RISK	3 Year		NET ASSETS		ASSET				Portfolio	BULL / BEAR		FUND MANAGER		MINIMUMS		LOADS	
Risk Rating/Pts	Standard Deviation	Beta	NAV As of 6/30/06	Total $(Mil)	Cash %	Stocks %	Bonds %	Other %	Portfolio Turnover Ratio	Last Bull Market Return	Last Bear Market Return	Manager Quality Pct	Manager Tenure (Years)	Initial Purch. $	Additional Purch. $	Front End Load	Back End Load
C+ / 6.3	12.8	1.10	14.26	6	3	96	0	1	183.0	128.2	-10.0	14	5	1,000,000	0	0.0	0.0
B- / 7.0	11.0	1.05	15.26	147	2	98	0	0	119.0	117.0	-11.5	24	10	1,000	50	5.5	1.0
B- / 7.0	11.0	1.05	14.35	28	2	98	0	0	119.0	112.6	-11.7	20	10	1,000	50	0.0	5.0
B- / 7.0	11.0	1.05	14.24	20	2	98	0	0	119.0	111.6	-11.6	20	8	1,000	50	0.0	1.0
B- / 7.0	10.9	1.05	15.74	7	2	98	0	0	119.0	120.4	-11.4	28	10	1,000,000	0	0.0	0.0
C+ / 5.8	11.3	0.96	15.03	59	2	97	0	1	112.0	154.8	-0.4	70	N/A	1,000	50	5.5	1.0
C+ / 5.7	11.3	0.96	14.62	10	2	97	0	1	112.0	149.4	-0.7	62	N/A	1,000	50	0.0	5.0
C+ / 5.6	11.3	0.96	14.47	16	2	97	0	1	112.0	149.0	-0.7	62	N/A	1,000	50	0.0	1.0
C+ / 5.8	11.3	0.96	15.17	35	2	97	0	1	112.0	158.2	-0.4	74	N/A	1,000,000	0	0.0	0.0
C+ / 6.2	10.9	0.96	24.53	1,815	0	98	0	2	74.0	104.4	-8.4	57	9	1,000	50	5.5	1.0
C+ / 5.8	10.9	0.96	22.69	463	0	98	0	2	74.0	99.6	-8.5	47	9	1,000	50	0.0	5.0
C+ / 5.8	10.9	0.96	22.80	510	0	98	0	2	74.0	100.2	-8.5	48	8	1,000	50	0.0	1.0
C+ / 6.4	10.9	0.96	25.83	182	0	98	0	2	74.0	107.6	-8.3	63	9	1,000,000	0	0.0	0.0
B- / 7.4	11.3	1.00	13.77	300	1	98	0	1	49.0	108.2	-9.0	61	21	1,000	50	5.5	1.0
B- / 7.3	11.3	1.00	13.20	62	1	98	0	1	49.0	103.6	-9.2	53	21	1,000	50	0.0	5.0
B- / 7.3	11.3	1.00	13.20	63	1	98	0	1	49.0	103.7	-9.2	52	21	1,000	50	0.0	1.0
B- / 7.5	11.3	1.00	14.16	1	1	98	0	1	49.0	111.5	-8.9	67	N/A	1,000,000	0	0.0	0.0
U /	N/A	N/A	11.54	41	1	98	0	1	30.0	N/A	N/A	N/A	N/A	1,000	50	5.5	1.0
C / 4.7	15.7	1.00	21.36	188	0	99	0	1	104.0	152.0	-13.0	77	6	1,000	50	5.5	1.0
C / 4.6	15.7	1.00	19.82	55	0	99	0	1	104.0	146.3	-13.2	70	6	1,000	50	0.0	5.0
C / 4.6	15.7	1.00	19.84	46	0	99	0	1	104.0	146.2	-13.1	70	6	1,000	50	0.0	1.0
C / 4.7	15.7	1.00	22.45	13	0	99	0	1	104.0	155.9	-12.9	80	6	1,000,000	0	0.0	0.0
C / 5.5	14.9	0.99	30.04	164	2	96	0	2	81.0	119.3	-15.0	42	5	1,000	50	5.5	1.0
C / 5.4	14.9	0.99	27.02	19	2	96	0	2	81.0	114.8	-15.2	35	5	1,000	50	0.0	5.0
C / 5.4	15.0	0.99	26.99	23	2	96	0	2	81.0	114.6	-15.2	34	5	1,000	50	0.0	1.0
C / 5.4	15.0	0.99	27.18	14	2	96	0	2	81.0	115.6	-15.1	36	5	1,000	50	0.0	4.0
C / 5.5	14.9	0.99	30.15	118	2	96	0	2	81.0	120.2	-15.0	43	5	1,000	50	4.8	1.0
C / 5.4	15.0	0.99	27.14	15	2	96	0	2	81.0	115.7	-15.2	36	5	1,000	50	0.0	4.0
C / 5.4	14.9	0.99	27.17	6	2	96	0	2	81.0	115.7	-15.2	36	5	1,000	50	0.0	1.0
C+ / 5.6	14.9	0.99	30.60	8	2	96	0	2	81.0	122.4	-14.9	47	5	1,000,000	0	0.0	0.0
B / 8.6	8.1	1.00	19.38	675	0	99	0	1	62.0	55.9	-10.9	33	1	1,000	50	5.5	1.0
B / 8.5	8.1	1.00	18.09	236	0	99	0	1	62.0	52.1	-11.0	27	1	1,000	50	0.0	5.0
B / 8.5	8.1	1.00	18.22	162	0	99	0	1	62.0	52.6	-11.1	27	1	1,000	50	0.0	1.0
B / 8.7	8.1	1.00	20.18	105	0	99	0	1	62.0	58.7	-10.8	37	1	1,000,000	0	0.0	0.0
B+ / 9.2	7.6	0.95	11.91	70	0	98	0	2	29.0	72.9	-10.6	80	5	1,000	50	5.5	1.0
B+ / 9.1	7.6	0.95	11.75	11	0	98	0	2	29.0	69.1	-10.9	74	5	1,000	50	0.0	5.0
B+ / 9.2	7.6	0.94	11.75	11	0	98	0	2	29.0	68.9	-10.7	73	5	1,000	50	0.0	1.0
B+ / 9.2	7.7	0.95	11.89	N/A	0	98	0	2	29.0	74.3	-10.5	82	5	1,000,000	0	0.0	0.0
B / 8.3	10.0	1.21	16.91	97	0	98	0	2	38.0	104.3	-11.1	88	N/A	1,000	50	5.5	1.0
B / 8.3	10.0	1.21	15.71	17	0	98	0	2	38.0	99.9	-11.2	84	N/A	1,000	50	0.0	5.0
B / 8.3	10.0	1.21	15.71	18	0	98	0	2	38.0	99.9	-11.3	84	N/A	1,000	50	0.0	1.0
B / 8.3	10.0	1.22	15.75	4	0	98	0	2	38.0	100.2	-11.2	84	N/A	1,000	50	0.0	4.0
B / 8.3	10.0	1.21	16.94	31	0	98	0	2	38.0	104.8	-11.1	89	N/A	1,000	50	4.8	1.0
B / 8.3	10.0	1.21	15.74	7	0	98	0	2	38.0	100.2	-11.3	84	N/A	1,000	50	0.0	4.0
B / 8.3	10.0	1.21	15.75	2	0	98	0	2	38.0	100.2	-11.2	84	N/A	1,000	50	0.0	1.0
B / 8.3	9.9	1.21	17.10	97	0	98	0	2	38.0	106.1	-11.1	89	N/A	1,000,000	0	0.0	0.0
B- / 7.9	10.7	0.92	27.37	322	11	88	0	1	42.0	110.6	-10.3	82	N/A	1,000	100	0.0	0.0
C- / 4.1	14.3	0.93	51.18	1,780	6	93	0	1	38.0	138.0	-8.2	72	N/A	1,000	100	0.0	0.0
C+ / 6.1	13.7	1.48	25.93	242	7	92	0	1	36.0	112.2	-8.2	60	N/A	1,000	100	0.0	0.0
C / 4.8	14.5	1.21	29.40	356	4	95	0	1	51.0	231.7	-5.0	90	N/A	500	50	5.8	2.0
C / 4.8	14.5	1.21	28.47	37	4	95	0	1	51.0	224.5	-5.2	86	N/A	500	50	0.0	5.0
C / 4.8	14.5	1.20	28.47	110	4	95	0	1	51.0	224.5	-5.2	86	N/A	500	50	0.0	1.0

Fund Type	Fund Name	Ticker Symbol	Overall Weiss Investment Rating	Phone	Performance Rating/Pts	3 Mo	6 Mo	1Yr / Pct	3Yr / Pct	5Yr / Pct	Dividend Yield	Expense Ratio
	99 Pct = Best							Total Return % through 6/30/06			Incl. in Returns	
TC	Henderson Global Technology A	HFGAX	D-	(866) 443-6337	C / 5.3	-8.87	1.65	18.52 /80	16.73 /67	--	0.00	2.00
TC	Henderson Global Technology B	HFGBX	D-	(866) 443-6337	C / 5.2	-9.07	1.21	17.59 /78	15.86 /63	--	0.00	2.75
TC	Henderson Global Technology C	HFGCX	D	(866) 443-6337	C+ / 5.7	-9.02	1.21	17.64 /78	15.82 /63	--	0.00	2.75
FO	Henderson Internatl Opport A	HFOAX	A+	(866) 443-6337	A- / 9.2	1.36	11.82	32.31 /96	26.03 /92	--	0.00	1.84
FO	Henderson Internatl Opport B	HFOBX	A	(866) 443-6337	A- / 9.2	1.16	11.36	31.24 /95	25.11 /91	--	0.00	2.59
FO	Henderson Internatl Opport C	HFOCX	A+	(866) 443-6337	A- / 9.2	1.16	11.43	31.27 /95	25.09 /91	--	0.00	2.59
BA	Hennessy Balanced Fund	HBFBX	D+	(800) 966-4354	E+ / 0.8	2.47	5.84	5.93 /20	3.82 / 2	1.68 /25	2.30	1.49
MC	Hennessy Cornerstone Gr Fd Ser 2	HENLX	B	(866) 880-0032	A- / 9.1	-5.57	9.53	16.48 /76	26.27 /92	13.80 /90	0.00	1.25
GR	Hennessy Cornerstone Growth	HFCGX	C	(800) 966-4354	B+ / 8.3	-7.49	7.80	20.24 /82	21.31 /83	14.93 /92	0.00	1.20
GL	Hennessy Cornerstone Value	HFCVX	B-	(800) 966-4354	C / 5.0	1.55	6.08	10.73 /52	12.35 /45	4.33 /49	2.49	1.16
GR	Hennessy Focus 30 Fund	HFTFX	U	(800) 966-4354	U /	-1.79	15.86	34.91 /97	--	--	0.00	1.20
GR	Hennessy Total Return Fund	HDOGX	C-	(800) 966-4354	C- / 3.0	3.55	8.01	9.54 /44	7.92 /15	3.44 /41	2.61	1.23
GR	Henssler Equity Fd	HEQFX	C-	(800) 936-3863	D / 2.1	-2.96	-0.55	2.91 / 7	8.74 /19	2.94 /36	0.28	1.30
GR	Heritage Capital Appreciation A	HRCPX	D-	(800) 421-4184	C- / 3.2	-1.79	3.45	13.29 /65	10.78 /34	0.74 /19	0.00	1.20
GR	● Heritage Capital Appreciation B	HRCBX	D-	(800) 421-4184	D+ / 2.6	-1.99	3.04	12.25 /61	9.90 /27	-0.02 /15	0.00	1.95
GR	Heritage Capital Appreciation C	HRCCX	D	(800) 421-4184	C- / 3.3	-1.95	3.08	12.25 /61	9.90 /27	-0.02 /15	0.00	1.95
AG	Heritage Diversified Growth A	HAGAX	D-	(800) 421-4184	D+ / 2.9	-6.06	1.59	8.03 /33	11.08 /36	7.20 /68	0.00	1.34
AG	● Heritage Diversified Growth B	HAGBX	E+	(800) 421-4184	D+ / 2.3	-6.22	1.23	7.25 /28	10.26 /29	6.40 /63	0.00	2.09
AG	Heritage Diversified Growth C	HAGCX	D-	(800) 421-4184	C- / 3.0	-6.22	1.23	7.21 /27	10.26 /29	6.39 /63	0.00	2.09
IN	Heritage Growth and Income Trust A	HRCVX	C-	(800) 421-4184	C- / 4.2	-0.48	4.71	10.99 /53	12.00 /42	4.76 /52	1.80	1.35
IN	● Heritage Growth and Income Trust B	HIGBX	C-	(800) 421-4184	C- / 3.5	-0.68	4.31	10.01 /47	11.12 /36	3.96 /46	1.24	2.10
IN	Heritage Growth and Income Trust C	HIGCX	C-	(800) 421-4184	C- / 4.2	-0.68	4.39	10.09 /48	11.14 /37	3.97 /46	1.23	2.10
MC	Heritage Mid Cap Stock A	HMCAX	C+	(800) 421-4184	C+ / 6.1	-2.06	5.01	15.11 /72	15.52 /61	7.70 /70	0.00	1.15
MC	● Heritage Mid Cap Stock B	HMCBX	C+	(800) 421-4184	C+ / 5.6	-2.26	4.59	14.23 /69	14.65 /57	6.89 /66	0.00	1.90
MC	Heritage Mid Cap Stock C	HMCCX	C+	(800) 421-4184	C+ / 6.2	-2.22	4.63	14.26 /69	14.68 /57	6.91 /66	0.00	1.90
FO	Heritage Ser Tr-Intl Equity A	HEIAX	B+	(800) 421-4184	B+ / 8.8	-1.92	9.76	29.17 /94	24.43 /90	8.72 /75	0.53	1.81
FO	● Heritage Ser Tr-Intl Equity B	HEIBX	B+	(800) 421-4184	B+ / 8.9	-2.10	9.37	28.22 /93	23.49 /88	7.92 /71	0.05	2.53
FO	Heritage Ser Tr-Intl Equity C	HEICX	B+	(800) 421-4184	B+ / 8.9	-2.10	9.33	28.22 /93	23.49 /88	7.92 /71	0.05	2.53
SC	Heritage Ser Tr-Small Cap Stk A	HRSCX	C	(800) 421-4184	C+ / 5.9	-6.14	5.34	10.55 /51	16.05 /64	7.55 /69	0.00	1.30
SC	● Heritage Ser Tr-Small Cap Stk B	HRSBX	C-	(800) 421-4184	C / 5.4	-6.31	4.96	9.73 /45	15.19 /60	6.74 /65	0.00	2.05
SC	Heritage Ser Tr-Small Cap Stk C	HSCCX	C	(800) 421-4184	C+ / 5.9	-6.34	4.95	9.73 /45	15.18 /60	6.74 /65	0.00	2.05
GR	Hester Total Return Fund	AHTRX	C-	(866) 811-0215	C / 4.3	-1.96	1.72	5.90 /20	11.88 /42	4.42 /50	0.00	1.70
GR	High Pointe Select Value Fund	HPSVX	U	(800) 984-1099	U /	-2.82	0.10	2.75 / 6	--	--	0.14	1.50
IN	Highbridge Stat Mkt Neutral Sel	HSKSX	U	(800) 358-4782	U /	3.78	4.06	--	--	--	0.00	1.70
BA	HighMark Balanced Fund Fid	HMBAX	C-	(800) 433-6884	D / 1.7	-0.89	2.54	5.23 /16	7.03 /10	2.39 /31	1.89	0.94
BA	HighMark Balanced Fund Ret A	HMBRX	D+	(800) 433-6884	E+ / 0.9	-0.89	2.42	4.98 /15	6.78 /10	2.13 /28	1.56	1.22
BA	● HighMark Balanced Fund Ret B	HMBBX	D+	(800) 433-6884	E+ / 0.7	-1.04	2.06	4.35 /12	6.10 / 7	1.48 /24	1.04	1.82
BA	HighMark Balanced Fund Ret C	HMBCX	C-	(800) 433-6884	D- / 1.1	-1.05	2.06	4.29 /12	6.07 / 7	1.45 /23	1.06	1.82
AA	HighMark Capital Growth Alloc A	HMAAX	U	(800) 433-6884	U /	-1.68	3.82	8.98 /40	--	--	0.37	1.57
GR	HighMark Cognitive Value Fund M	HCLMX	B+	(800) 433-6884	B / 8.1	-2.06	11.94	15.55 /73	19.56 /78	10.63 /83	0.22	1.05
GL	HighMark Core Equity Fund Fid	HMCFX	C+	(800) 433-6884	C / 4.5	-0.27	6.09	12.46 /62	11.08 /36	1.86 /26	0.98	1.15
GL	HighMark Core Equity Fund Ret A	HCEAX	C	(800) 433-6884	C- / 3.4	-0.34	5.99	12.23 /61	10.85 /34	1.63 /24	0.72	1.40
GL	● HighMark Core Equity Fund Ret B	HCEBX	C	(800) 433-6884	C- / 3.0	-0.49	5.59	11.48 /57	10.09 /28	0.95 /20	0.30	1.90
GR	HighMark Enhanced Growth Fund M	HEGMX	D-	(800) 433-6884	D- / 1.4	-8.09	-5.33	4.16 /11	8.11 /16	-3.27 / 5	0.00	0.98
GI	HighMark Growth & Inc Alloc A	HMRAX	U	(800) 433-6884	U /	-1.27	2.85	6.92 /26	--	--	1.01	1.57
FO	HighMark International Opp Fund M	HIOMX	A-	(800) 433-6884	A / 9.3	-1.17	10.35	31.38 /95	26.28 /92	12.85 /88	1.69	1.35
IN	HighMark Large Cap Value Fid	HMIEX	A-	(800) 433-6884	B- / 7.1	-0.39	5.59	12.74 /63	16.93 /68	4.86 /53	1.13	0.95
IN	HighMark Large Cap Value Ret A	HMERX	B	(800) 433-6884	C+ / 6.4	-0.46	5.45	12.52 /62	16.69 /67	4.60 /51	0.85	1.42
IN	● HighMark Large Cap Value Ret B	HIEBX	B	(800) 433-6884	C+ / 6.1	-0.59	5.10	11.74 /58	15.91 /63	3.91 /45	0.38	1.92
IN	HighMark Large Cap Value Ret C	HIECX	B	(800) 433-6884	C+ / 6.6	-0.58	5.05	11.70 /58	15.95 /63	3.93 /45	0.40	1.92
GR	HighMark Large Growth Fund Fid	HMGRX	D+	(800) 433-6884	C- / 3.1	-1.92	1.43	11.35 /56	9.69 /25	0.29 /17	0.21	0.97
GR	HighMark Large Growth Fund Ret A	HMRGX	D	(800) 433-6884	D / 2.0	-1.95	1.23	11.10 /54	9.42 /24	0.05 /16	0.04	1.22

RISK	3 Year		NET ASSETS		ASSET				Portfolio	BULL / BEAR		FUND MANAGER		MINIMUMS		LOADS	
Risk Rating/Pts	Standard Deviation	Beta	NAV As of 6/30/06	Total $(Mil)	Cash %	Stocks %	Bonds %	Other %	Portfolio Turnover Ratio	Last Bull Market Return	Last Bear Market Return	Manager Quality Pct	Manager Tenure (Years)	Initial Purch. $	Additional Purch. $	Front End Load	Back End Load
C- / 3.2	17.8	1.85	12.95	26	6	93	0	1	164.0	124.8	-11.7	32	5	500	50	5.8	2.0
C- / 3.1	17.8	1.85	12.53	1	6	93	0	1	164.0	119.7	-11.6	26	5	500	50	0.0	5.0
C- / 3.1	17.8	1.84	12.50	11	6	93	0	1	164.0	119.1	-11.5	26	5	500	50	0.0	1.0
C+ / 6.8	11.1	0.99	21.66	978	9	90	0	1	79.0	152.9	-10.8	72	N/A	500	50	5.8	2.0
C+ / 6.8	11.1	0.99	20.97	77	9	90	0	1	79.0	147.2	-10.9	65	N/A	500	50	0.0	5.0
C+ / 6.8	11.1	0.99	20.96	489	9	90	0	1	79.0	147.2	-11.0	64	N/A	500	50	0.0	2.0
B+ / 9.1	4.8	0.70	11.07	26	N/A	47	53	N/A	21.3	19.9	-5.9	33	10	2,500	100	0.0	1.5
C / 5.0	18.7	1.46	32.19	279	3	96	0	1	195.2	166.2	-6.0	57	N/A	2,500	100	0.0	1.5
C- / 3.2	18.4	1.83	20.87	1,354	0	96	3	1	89.0	140.5	-10.9	75	6	2,500	100	0.0	1.5
B+ / 9.0	7.9	0.62	13.78	178	0	98	1	1	32.2	65.8	-8.4	27	6	2,500	100	0.0	1.5
U /	N/A	N/A	13.15	293	0	94	8	0	155.3	N/A	N/A	N/A	3	2,500	100	0.0	1.5
B / 8.0	7.3	0.70	11.44	84	1	75	23	1	25.7	39.5	-7.6	50	8	2,500	100	0.0	1.5
B / 8.4	7.9	0.99	14.41	128	0	99	0	1	34.0	54.0	-10.3	32	8	2,000	200	0.0	0.0
C / 5.3	10.4	1.17	28.48	381	0	99	0	1	42.0	72.7	-11.9	35	19	1,000	0	4.8	0.0
C+ / 5.6	10.4	1.17	26.12	42	0	99	0	1	42.0	68.5	-12.0	28	19	1,000	0	0.0	5.0
C+ / 5.6	10.4	1.17	26.11	146	0	99	0	1	42.0	68.5	-12.1	28	19	1,000	0	0.0	1.0
C / 4.8	13.3	1.49	27.43	141	1	98	0	1	75.0	84.2	-10.0	18	8	1,000	0	4.8	0.0
C / 4.7	13.3	1.49	25.61	15	1	98	0	1	75.0	79.9	-10.1	14	8	1,000	0	0.0	5.0
C / 4.7	13.3	1.49	25.61	67	1	98	0	1	75.0	79.9	-10.1	14	8	1,000	0	0.0	1.0
B- / 7.2	7.3	0.84	13.76	59	4	92	0	4	73.0	74.4	-7.3	77	5	1,000	0	4.8	0.0
B- / 7.2	7.3	0.85	13.45	10	4	92	0	4	73.0	70.3	-7.4	70	5	1,000	0	0.0	5.0
B- / 7.2	7.3	0.85	13.46	47	4	92	0	4	73.0	70.3	-7.4	70	5	1,000	0	0.0	1.0
B- / 7.0	9.3	0.79	28.52	822	1	98	0	1	146.0	80.7	-6.2	65	9	1,000	0	4.8	0.0
C+ / 6.9	9.2	0.79	26.41	58	1	98	0	1	146.0	76.4	-6.4	56	8	1,000	0	0.0	5.0
C+ / 6.9	9.2	0.79	26.43	326	1	98	0	1	146.0	76.4	-6.4	57	9	1,000	0	0.0	1.0
C+ / 5.8	12.3	1.15	27.55	77	1	98	0	1	78.0	132.7	-6.5	26	4	1,000	0	4.8	2.0
C+ / 5.8	12.3	1.16	25.67	5	1	98	0	1	78.0	127.2	-6.6	20	4	1,000	0	0.0	2.0
C+ / 5.8	12.3	1.16	25.67	103	1	98	0	1	78.0	127.3	-6.6	20	4	1,000	0	0.0	2.0
C+ / 5.8	13.7	0.91	35.14	257	6	93	0	1	50.0	103.6	-11.9	43	13	1,000	0	4.8	0.0
C+ / 5.6	13.8	0.92	31.77	11	6	93	0	1	50.0	98.8	-12.1	35	11	1,000	0	0.0	5.0
C+ / 5.6	13.8	0.91	31.78	95	6	93	0	1	50.0	98.8	-12.0	36	11	1,000	0	0.0	1.0
C+ / 6.1	8.4	1.00	32.52	12	11	88	0	1	24.5	63.1	-7.0	63	18	1,000	250	0.0	0.0
U /	N/A	N/A	10.35	42	0	100	0	0	28.2	N/A	N/A	N/A	N/A	10,000	2,000	0.0	1.0
U /	N/A	N/A	15.63	118	8	64	27	1	78.0	N/A	N/A	N/A	N/A	1,000,000	0	0.0	0.0
B+ / 9.4	5.2	1.03	14.00	38	1	70	28	1	57.0	38.0	-5.7	47	N/A	1,000	100	0.0	0.0
B+ / 9.4	5.2	1.03	13.98	7	1	70	28	1	57.0	36.8	-5.6	44	N/A	1,000	100	5.5	0.0
B+ / 9.4	5.1	1.02	13.94	3	1	70	28	1	57.0	34.1	-5.9	38	N/A	1,000	100	0.0	5.0
B+ / 9.4	5.1	1.02	13.92	N/A	1	70	28	1	57.0	34.0	-5.9	37	N/A	1,000	100	0.0	1.0
U /	N/A	N/A	23.27	29	3	87	9	1	24.0	N/A	N/A	N/A	N/A	1,000	100	5.5	0.0
B- / 7.0	13.5	1.45	13.31	93	2	97	0	1	59.0	112.2	-10.6	88	N/A	5,000	100	0.0	0.0
B / 8.2	7.8	0.60	8.75	110	0	99	0	1	31.0	60.8	-9.8	22	N/A	1,000	100	0.0	0.0
B / 8.5	7.9	0.60	8.73	3	0	99	0	1	31.0	59.6	-10.0	21	N/A	1,000	100	5.5	0.0
B / 8.5	7.9	0.61	8.58	3	0	99	0	1	31.0	56.5	-10.2	16	N/A	1,000	100	0.0	5.0
C+ / 6.3	14.6	1.64	8.52	126	1	98	0	1	8.0	60.2	-8.5	4	N/A	5,000	100	0.0	0.0
U /	N/A	N/A	22.30	30	3	68	28	1	29.0	N/A	N/A	N/A	N/A	1,000	100	5.5	0.0
C+ / 6.1	12.1	1.16	8.42	199	5	94	0	1	74.0	155.3	-6.3	36	N/A	5,000	100	0.0	2.0
B / 8.4	8.7	0.99	13.46	164	2	97	0	1	99.0	89.4	-11.1	94	15	1,000	100	0.0	0.0
B / 8.4	8.7	0.99	13.49	132	2	97	0	1	99.0	87.9	-11.1	93	15	1,000	100	5.5	0.0
B / 8.4	8.7	0.99	13.29	3	2	97	0	1	99.0	84.1	-11.3	91	7	1,000	100	0.0	5.0
B / 8.4	8.7	0.99	13.26	6	2	97	0	1	99.0	84.4	-11.4	91	15	1,000	100	0.0	1.0
C+ / 6.8	10.2	1.11	9.19	108	0	99	0	1	73.0	51.8	-7.8	31	5	1,000	100	0.0	0.0
C+ / 6.7	10.1	1.10	9.04	17	0	99	0	1	73.0	50.6	-8.0	30	5	1,000	100	5.5	0.0

Data as of June 30, 2006

						PERFORMANCE							
	99 Pct = Best 0 Pct = Worst			Overall Weiss		Perfor- mance	Total Return % through 6/30/06					Incl. in Returns	
Fund Type	Fund Name	Ticker Symbol	Investment Rating	Phone	Rating/Pts	3 Mo	6 Mo	1Yr / Pct	Annualized		Dividend Yield	Expense Ratio
										3Yr / Pct	5Yr / Pct		
GR	● HighMark Large Growth Fund Ret B	HMGBX	D-	(800) 433-6884	D / 1.7	-2.18	0.95	10.36 /49	8.72 /19	-0.60 /13	0.00	1.82
GR	HighMark Large Growth Fund Ret C	HGRCX	D	(800) 433-6884	D+ / 2.3	-2.18	0.95	10.36 /49	8.72 /19	-0.60 /13	0.00	1.82
SC	HighMark Sm Cap Value Fid	HMSCX	B-	(800) 433-6884	B- / 7.4	-2.04	8.19	8.58 /37	18.39 /74	12.89 /88	0.40	1.37
SC	HighMark Sm Cap Value Ret A	HASVX	C+	(800) 433-6884	C+ / 6.7	-2.13	8.05	8.35 /36	18.10 /73	12.60 /88	0.26	0.37
SC	● HighMark Sm Cap Value Ret B	HBSVX	C+	(800) 433-6884	C+ / 6.5	-2.28	7.71	7.57 /30	17.35 /69	11.82 /86	0.00	2.27
SC	HighMark Sm Cap Value Ret C	HSVCX	C+	(800) 433-6884	C+ / 6.9	-2.23	7.74	7.66 /30	17.37 /70	11.84 /86	0.00	2.27
SC	HighMark Small Cap Growth Fid	HSRFX	D	(800) 433-6884	C- / 3.3	-8.93	2.07	9.48 /43	10.27 /29	--	0.00	1.52
SC	HighMark Small Cap Growth Ret A	HSRAX	D-	(800) 433-6884	D / 2.2	-8.99	1.94	9.15 /41	10.00 /27	--	0.00	2.13
SC	● HighMark Small Cap Growth Ret B	HSRBX	D-	(800) 433-6884	D / 1.8	-9.16	1.61	8.52 /37	9.31 /23	--	0.00	2.63
SC	HighMark Small Cap Growth Ret C	HSRCX	D-	(800) 433-6884	D+ / 2.4	-9.16	1.61	8.44 /36	9.28 /23	--	0.00	2.63
GI	HighMark Value Momentum Fid	HMVMX	C+	(800) 433-6884	C+ / 5.9	-0.08	5.34	11.55 /57	13.96 /54	5.07 /55	1.24	0.97
GI	HighMark Value Momentum Ret A	HMVLX	C	(800) 433-6884	C / 5.0	-0.10	5.22	11.29 /55	13.68 /52	4.81 /53	0.97	1.36
GI	● HighMark Value Momentum Ret B	HVMBX	C-	(800) 433-6884	C / 4.6	-0.25	4.89	10.61 /51	12.96 /49	4.14 /47	0.51	1.86
GI	HighMark Value Momentum Ret C	HVMCX	C	(800) 433-6884	C / 5.2	-0.29	4.87	10.60 /51	12.94 /48	4.11 /47	0.53	1.86
FS	Hilliard-Lyons Senbanc Fund	SENBX	D-	(800) 444-1854	D / 1.7	-2.40	1.88	3.32 / 8	8.62 /19	12.55 /88	0.68	1.40
GR	Hodges Fund	HDPMX	A+	(877) 232-1222	A / 9.3	-3.04	8.56	23.29 /86	28.05 /94	16.52 /94	0.00	1.47
SC	Homestead Funds-Small Company	HSCSX	B+	(800) 258-3030	B- / 7.5	-3.71	9.82	17.58 /78	18.08 /73	13.00 /89	0.28	1.30
GI	Homestead Funds-Value Fund	HOVLX	A	(800) 258-3030	B- / 7.1	1.64	7.93	15.76 /74	16.64 /66	9.14 /77	1.34	0.76
IN	● Hotchkis and Wiley All Cap Value A	HWAAX	C-	(800) 796-5606	C / 5.2	-9.05	-2.81	-0.50 / 1	17.36 /70	--	1.07	1.19
IN	● Hotchkis and Wiley All Cap Value C	HWACX	C	(800) 796-5606	C / 5.3	-9.22	-3.14	-1.25 / 1	16.36 /65	--	0.51	1.94
IN	● Hotchkis and Wiley All Cap Value I	HWAIX	C+	(800) 796-5606	C+ / 6.0	-8.98	-2.65	-0.24 / 2	17.54 /70	--	1.34	0.94
IN	Hotchkis and Wiley Core Value A	HWCAX	U	(800) 796-5606	U /	-2.66	-0.47	5.01 /15	--	--	0.30	1.18
IN	Hotchkis and Wiley Core Value C	HWCCX	U	(800) 796-5606	U /	-2.84	-0.86	4.24 /12	--	--	0.11	1.93
IN	Hotchkis and Wiley Core Value I	HWCIX	U	(800) 796-5606	U /	-2.58	-0.31	5.31 /17	--	--	0.38	0.94
★ GI	● Hotchkis and Wiley Large Cap Val A	HWLAX	B	(800) 796-5606	C+ / 5.7	-3.95	-0.09	2.82 / 7	17.12 /69	10.88 /83	0.80	1.18
GI	● Hotchkis and Wiley Large Cap Val C	HWLCX	B	(800) 796-5606	C+ / 5.8	-4.13	-0.43	2.08 / 5	16.27 /65	10.04 /81	0.27	1.92
GI	● Hotchkis and Wiley Large Cap Val I	HWLIX	B	(800) 796-5606	C+ / 6.5	-3.90	0.04	3.10 / 8	17.44 /70	11.11 /84	1.03	0.93
GI	● Hotchkis and Wiley Large Cap Val R	HWLRX	B+	(800) 796-5606	C+ / 6.3	-4.01	-0.21	2.59 / 6	17.05 /68	10.67 /83	0.72	1.43
MC	● Hotchkis and Wiley Mid-Cap Val A	HWMAX	A	(800) 796-5606	B / 7.8	-4.64	2.42	8.27 /35	22.47 /86	15.36 /92	0.14	1.25
MC	● Hotchkis and Wiley Mid-Cap Val C	HWMCX	A	(800) 796-5606	B / 7.9	-4.82	2.02	7.46 /29	21.56 /84	14.48 /91	0.00	1.98
MC	● Hotchkis and Wiley Mid-Cap Val I	HWMIX	A+	(800) 796-5606	B+ / 8.3	-4.59	2.52	8.53 /37	22.79 /87	15.61 /93	0.41	0.98
MC	● Hotchkis and Wiley Mid-Cap Val R	HWMRX	A+	(800) 796-5606	B+ / 8.3	-4.72	2.29	7.99 /33	22.77 /87	15.36 /92	0.04	1.48
SC	● Hotchkis and Wiley Small Cap Val A	HWSAX	C	(800) 796-5606	B / 7.6	-8.59	-1.73	4.86 /14	22.95 /87	19.44 /96	0.13	1.28
SC	● Hotchkis and Wiley Small Cap Val C	HWSCX	C	(800) 796-5606	B / 7.7	-8.76	-2.11	4.07 /11	22.03 /85	18.48 /95	0.00	2.01
SC	● Hotchkis and Wiley Small Cap Val I	HWSIX	C+	(800) 796-5606	B / 8.1	-8.53	-1.61	5.13 /16	23.26 /88	19.65 /96	0.26	1.01
GI	HSBC Investor Growth & Income A	HSGAX	D	(800) 782-8183	C- / 3.0	-2.31	2.82	15.39 /73	10.73 /33	0.70 /19	0.00	1.16
GI	HSBC Investor Growth & Income B	HSGBX	D	(800) 782-8183	D+ / 2.9	-2.45	2.47	14.59 /70	9.91 /27	-0.03 /15	0.00	1.91
GI	HSBC Investor Growth & Income Y	HSGYX	C-	(800) 782-8183	C / 4.4	-2.22	3.02	15.80 /74	11.03 /36	0.96 /20	0.06	0.77
FO	HSBC Investor Intl Equity Adv	RINEX	A	(800) 782-8183	A / 9.3	-0.30	12.20	31.44 /95	25.35 /91	9.74 /80	1.75	0.92
MC	HSBC Investor Mid Cap A	HMIAX	C-	(800) 782-8183	C+ / 5.9	-4.08	6.23	12.03 /60	16.18 /64	2.87 /36	0.00	1.35
MC	HSBC Investor Mid Cap B	HMIBX	C-	(800) 782-8183	C+ / 5.8	-4.31	5.80	11.21 /55	15.26 /60	2.11 /28	0.00	2.10
MC	HSBC Investor Mid Cap C	HSMIX	C-	(800) 782-8183	C+ / 6.3	-4.28	5.75	11.12 /54	15.51 /61	2.22 /29	0.00	2.10
MC	HSBC Investor Mid Cap Y	HMCTX	C	(800) 782-8183	C+ / 6.8	-4.13	6.27	12.22 /61	16.37 /65	3.09 /38	0.00	1.10
SC	HSBC Investor Opportunity A	HSOAX	C	(800) 782-8183	C+ / 6.1	-3.77	7.07	18.88 /80	16.30 /65	3.59 /42	0.00	1.65
SC	HSBC Investor Opportunity B	HOPBX	C-	(800) 782-8183	C+ / 6.0	-3.90	6.74	18.04 /79	15.44 /61	2.69 /34	0.00	2.40
SC	HSBC Investor Opportunity C	HOPCX	C-	(800) 782-8183	C+ / 6.3	-3.86	6.76	18.06 /79	15.47 /61	2.70 /34	0.00	2.40
FO	HSBC Investor Overseas Equity A	HOEAX	A-	(800) 782-8183	A- / 9.1	-0.52	11.83	30.47 /95	25.22 /91	9.38 /78	1.27	1.66
FO	HSBC Investor Overseas Equity B	HOEBX	B	(800) 782-8183	A- / 9.0	-0.72	11.37	29.50 /94	24.23 /90	8.53 /74	0.79	2.41
FO	HSBC Investor Overseas Equity C	HOECX	B	(800) 782-8183	A- / 9.1	-0.65	11.40	29.54 /94	24.26 /90	8.55 /74	0.79	2.41
SC	HSBC Investor Small Cap Equity Y	RESCX	C	(800) 782-8183	B- / 7.0	-3.59	7.35	19.52 /81	16.93 /68	4.17 /47	0.00	0.98
MC	Huntington Dividend Capture A	HDCAX	C-	(800) 253-0412	D+ / 2.5	-1.33	3.53	5.70 /19	10.30 /29	8.13 /72	3.31	1.58
MC	Huntington Dividend Capture B	HDCBX	D+	(800) 253-0412	D / 2.2	-1.55	3.29	5.09 /16	9.71 /25	7.58 /70	3.03	2.08

● Denotes fund is closed to new investors

★ Denotes fund is included in Section II

RISK			NET ASSETS		ASSET					Portfolio	BULL / BEAR		FUND MANAGER		MINIMUMS		LOADS	
	3 Year		NAV								Last Bull	Last Bear	Manager	Manager	Initial	Additional	Front	Back
Risk	Standard		As of	Total	Cash	Stocks	Bonds	Other		Turnover	Market	Market	Quality	Tenure	Purch.	Purch.	End	End
Rating/Pts	Deviation	Beta	6/30/06	$(Mil)	%	%	%	%		Ratio	Return	Return	Pct	(Years)	$	$	Load	Load
C+ / 6.6	10.1	1.10	8.52	8	0	99	0	1		73.0	47.3	-8.0	25	5	1,000	100	0.0	5.0
C+ / 6.6	10.2	1.11	8.52	1	0	99	0	1		73.0	47.5	-8.0	25	5	1,000	100	0.0	1.0
C+ / 6.5	12.4	0.82	18.75	167	2	97	0	1		27.0	109.5	-4.5	81	5	1,000	100	0.0	0.0
C+ / 6.5	12.4	0.81	18.39	65	2	97	0	1		27.0	107.9	-4.6	79	5	1,000	100	5.5	0.0
C+ / 6.3	12.4	0.82	17.60	14	2	97	0	1		27.0	103.6	-4.7	73	5	1,000	100	0.0	5.0
C+ / 6.3	12.4	0.81	17.54	20	2	97	0	1		27.0	103.6	-4.7	74	5	1,000	100	0.0	1.0
C+ / 5.8	16.3	1.04	14.28	28	2	98	0	0		181.0	N/A	N/A	4	N/A	1,000	100	0.0	0.0
C+ / 5.7	16.3	1.04	14.17	5	2	98	0	0		181.0	N/A	N/A	4	N/A	1,000	100	5.5	0.0
C+ / 5.7	16.3	1.04	13.88	1	2	98	0	0		181.0	N/A	N/A	3	N/A	1,000	100	0.0	5.0
C+ / 5.7	16.3	1.04	13.88	1	2	98	0	0		181.0	N/A	N/A	3	N/A	1,000	100	0.0	1.0
C+ / 6.6	7.7	0.93	22.98	432	2	97	0	1		18.0	80.1	-8.3	85	14	1,000	100	0.0	0.0
C+ / 6.6	7.7	0.93	22.96	30	2	97	0	1		18.0	78.7	-8.4	83	14	1,000	100	5.5	0.0
C+ / 6.5	7.7	0.93	22.67	8	2	97	0	1		18.0	75.0	-8.5	78	14	1,000	100	0.0	5.0
C+ / 6.5	7.7	0.93	22.61	1	2	97	0	1		18.0	74.9	-8.5	78	14	1,000	100	0.0	1.0
C+ / 6.2	8.4	0.79	16.24	192	0	99	0	1		43.2	46.0	7.2	30	N/A	250	100	2.3	1.0
C+ / 6.8	14.4	1.54	24.86	536	16	83	0	1		50.9	229.0	-20.3	99	14	250	50	0.0	2.0
B- / 7.5	12.1	0.71	18.67	37	6	93	0	1		9.0	103.6	-9.3	89	8	500	0	0.0	2.0
B / 8.7	7.6	0.88	35.12	507	7	92	0	1		8.0	90.2	-12.0	95	16	500	0	0.0	2.0
C+ / 6.2	14.1	1.41	19.40	93	2	98	0	0		39.0	128.4	N/A	77	N/A	2,500	100	5.3	0.0
C+ / 6.8	14.0	1.41	19.00	60	2	98	0	0		39.0	121.7	N/A	69	N/A	2,500	100	0.0	1.0
C+ / 6.8	14.0	1.41	19.36	60	2	98	0	0		39.0	128.9	N/A	78	N/A	1,000,000	100	0.0	0.0
U /	N/A	N/A	12.80	673	2	98	0	0		13.0	N/A	N/A	N/A	N/A	2,500	100	5.3	0.0
U /	N/A	N/A	12.66	163	2	98	0	0		13.0	N/A	N/A	N/A	N/A	2,500	100	0.0	1.0
U /	N/A	N/A	12.85	764	2	98	0	0		13.0	N/A	N/A	N/A	N/A	1,000,000	100	0.0	0.0
B / 8.8	9.4	1.06	23.32	2,956	2	98	0	0		14.0	106.3	-9.9	93	N/A	2,500	100	5.3	0.0
B / 8.7	9.4	1.06	22.96	489	2	98	0	0		14.0	101.6	-10.1	90	N/A	2,500	100	0.0	1.0
B / 8.8	9.4	1.06	23.42	2,110	2	98	0	0		14.0	108.0	-9.9	93	N/A	1,000,000	100	0.0	0.0
B / 8.6	9.4	1.07	23.47	83	2	98	0	0		14.0	105.8	-10.0	92	N/A	2,500	100	0.0	0.0
B / 8.0	11.3	0.95	28.77	1,089	2	96	0	2		27.0	143.5	-9.5	91	N/A	2,500	100	5.3	0.0
B / 8.0	11.3	0.95	27.83	246	2	96	0	2		27.0	137.7	-9.7	88	N/A	2,500	100	0.0	1.0
B / 8.0	11.3	0.95	28.91	2,858	2	96	0	2		27.0	145.4	-9.5	92	N/A	1,000,000	100	0.0	0.0
B / 8.0	11.4	0.96	29.05	23	2	96	0	2		27.0	145.1	-9.6	92	N/A	2,500	100	0.0	0.0
C / 4.8	14.4	0.92	48.30	185	2	98	0	0		49.0	159.0	-7.4	93	N/A	2,500	100	5.3	0.0
C / 4.5	14.4	0.92	45.83	21	2	98	0	0		49.0	152.9	-7.6	90	N/A	2,500	100	0.0	1.0
C / 4.8	14.4	0.92	48.13	553	2	98	0	0		49.0	161.0	-7.4	93	N/A	1,000,000	100	0.0	0.0
C+ / 6.0	8.4	1.05	10.57	1	0	99	0	1		106.5	63.1	-8.5	45	N/A	1,000	100	5.0	2.0
C+ / 5.9	8.4	1.04	10.37	5	0	99	0	1		106.5	59.3	-8.8	37	N/A	1,000	100	0.0	4.0
C+ / 6.0	8.4	1.05	10.59	40	0	99	0	1		106.5	64.4	-8.6	49	N/A	1,000,000	0	0.0	0.0
C+ / 6.6	10.9	1.04	20.23	248	2	97	0	1		31.3	135.0	-10.7	56	N/A	1,000	100	0.0	2.0
C / 5.0	12.5	1.10	8.69	3	0	99	0	1		169.6	91.3	-10.1	25	N/A	1,000	100	5.0	2.0
C / 5.0	12.4	1.10	8.21	8	0	99	0	1		169.6	86.9	-10.3	20	N/A	1,000	100	0.0	4.0
C / 5.0	12.5	1.11	8.28	N/A	0	99	0	1		169.6	87.8	-10.1	20	N/A	1,000	100	0.0	1.0
C / 5.0	12.4	1.10	8.82	16	0	99	0	1		169.6	92.7	-10.0	26	N/A	1,000,000	0	0.0	0.0
C+ / 5.8	12.8	0.82	13.79	24	1	98	0	1		64.0	102.1	-8.9	63	N/A	1,000	100	5.0	2.0
C / 5.1	12.8	0.83	12.83	5	1	98	0	1		64.0	97.4	-9.1	54	N/A	1,000	100	0.0	4.0
C / 5.1	12.8	0.83	12.95	N/A	1	98	0	1		64.0	97.6	-9.1	54	N/A	1,000	100	0.0	2.0
C+ / 6.4	11.0	1.05	17.30	22	1	98	0	1		31.3	131.2	-11.4	52	N/A	1,000	100	5.0	2.0
C / 5.4	11.0	1.05	16.56	3	1	98	0	1		31.3	125.5	-11.5	42	N/A	1,000	100	0.0	4.0
C / 5.4	10.9	1.04	16.90	N/A	1	98	0	1		31.3	125.6	-11.5	43	N/A	1,000	100	0.0	2.0
C / 4.8	12.8	0.82	16.65	186	0	100	0	0		64.0	106.1	-8.7	69	N/A	1,000	100	0.0	2.0
B / 8.1	6.1	0.42	11.07	10	1	98	0	1		131.0	50.3	-1.6	72	5	1,000	50	5.8	0.0
B / 8.1	6.1	0.42	11.04	17	1	98	0	1		131.0	48.0	-1.7	67	5	1,000	50	0.0	5.0

Fund Type	Fund Name	Ticker Symbol	Overall Weiss Investment Rating	Phone	PERFORMANCE						Incl. in Returns	
	99 Pct = Best / 0 Pct = Worst				Perfor-mance Rating/Pts	Total Return % through 6/30/06			Annualized		Dividend Yield	Expense Ratio
						3 Mo	6 Mo	1Yr / Pct	3Yr / Pct	5Yr / Pct		
MC	Huntington Dividend Capture Tr	HDCTX	C	(800) 253-0412	C- / 3.6	-1.27	3.66	5.96 /20	10.55 /31	8.39 /73	3.73	1.32
GR	Huntington Growth A	HGWIX	E	(800) 253-0412	E- / 0.1	-8.59	-5.38	-3.19 / 0	4.84 / 4	-1.62 / 9	0.00	1.40
GR	Huntington Growth B	HUGBX	E	(800) 253-0412	E- / 0.1	-8.86	-5.77	-3.82 / 0	4.26 / 3	-2.14 / 8	0.00	1.90
GR	Huntington Growth Tr	HGWTX	E	(800) 253-0412	E / 0.3	-8.48	-5.21	-2.88 / 0	5.12 / 4	-1.36 /10	0.08	1.15
IN	Huntington Income Equity A	HUINX	D	(800) 253-0412	D / 2.0	-0.78	2.03	3.93 /10	9.79 /26	3.70 /43	1.52	1.40
IN	Huntington Income Equity B	HUIEX	D	(800) 253-0412	D / 1.8	-0.91	1.79	3.40 / 8	9.25 /22	3.18 /39	1.14	1.90
IN	Huntington Income Equity Tr	HIEFX	D+	(800) 253-0412	C- / 3.2	-0.69	2.19	4.19 /11	10.05 /28	3.96 /46	1.84	1.15
FO	Huntington International Equity A	HIEAX	B+	(800) 253-0412	B+ / 8.6	-0.92	10.65	26.27 /90	23.08 /87	8.62 /75	0.47	1.83
FO	Huntington International Equity B	HUIBX	B+	(800) 253-0412	B+ / 8.5	-1.09	10.30	25.68 /89	22.41 /86	8.05 /72	0.07	2.33
FO	Huntington International Equity Tr	HIETX	A-	(800) 253-0412	A- / 9.0	-0.91	10.68	26.56 /91	23.31 /88	8.86 /76	0.57	1.58
MC	Huntington Mid Corp America A	HUMIX	C+	(800) 253-0412	C / 5.1	-4.67	0.33	6.69 /24	15.61 /62	8.30 /73	0.00	1.57
MC	Huntington Mid Corp America B	HMABX	C	(800) 253-0412	C / 4.9	-4.84	0.00	6.11 /21	15.01 /59	7.75 /70	0.00	2.07
MC	Huntington Mid Corp America Tr	HMATX	B-	(800) 253-0412	C+ / 6.1	-4.61	0.39	6.95 /26	15.89 /63	8.57 /74	0.06	1.32
TC	Huntington New Economy A	HNEAX	C	(800) 253-0412	C+ / 6.3	-6.08	2.10	11.84 /59	17.55 /70	9.22 /77	0.00	1.71
TC	Huntington New Economy B	HNEBX	C	(800) 253-0412	C+ / 6.1	-6.24	1.76	11.26 /55	16.96 /68	8.57 /74	0.00	2.21
TC	Huntington New Economy Tr	HNETX	C+	(800) 253-0412	B- / 7.1	-6.01	2.20	12.21 /61	17.87 /72	9.45 /78	0.00	1.46
GR	Huntington Rotating Markets A	HRIAX	C+	(800) 253-0412	C+ / 6.2	-1.71	6.61	17.71 /79	14.57 /57	4.71 /52	0.27	1.42
GR	Huntington Rotating Markets Tr	HRITX	B-	(800) 253-0412	C+ / 6.5	-1.53	6.84	18.05 /79	14.90 /58	4.99 /54	0.49	1.17
SC	Huntington Situs Small Cap A	HSUAX	A-	(800) 253-0412	B / 8.0	-4.37	3.20	13.50 /66	22.30 /86	--	0.00	1.61
SC	Huntington Situs Small Cap B	HSUBX	B	(800) 253-0412	B / 7.8	-4.50	2.88	12.88 /64	21.66 /84	--	0.00	2.11
SC	Huntington Situs Small Cap Tr	HSUTX	B+	(800) 253-0412	B+ / 8.4	-4.29	3.33	13.80 /68	22.61 /86	--	0.00	1.36
★ GR	Hussman Strategic Growth	HSGFX	C-	(800) 487-7626	D / 2.2	1.19	2.87	5.05 /15	8.30 /17	11.52 /85	0.33	1.16
GR	ICAP Equity Fund	ICAEX	C	(888) 221-4227	C+ / 6.3	-0.17	6.35	14.79 /71	14.75 /58	4.88 /53	1.14	0.80
FO	ICAP International Fund	ICEUX	A+	(888) 221-4227	A / 9.4	1.72	10.28	31.53 /95	28.02 /94	13.98 /90	1.37	0.80
GR	ICAP Select Equity Fund	ICSLX	A+	(888) 221-4227	B- / 7.4	-0.71	6.32	12.86 /64	17.95 /72	7.03 /67	1.02	0.80
FO	ICON Asia Region	ICARX	C+	(800) 764-0442	A- / 9.2	-3.26	-2.39	38.52 /98	26.05 /92	8.64 /75	0.10	1.93
GR	ICON Consumer Discretionary	ICCCX	E-	(800) 764-0442	D / 1.6	-5.20	2.51	-1.85 / 1	8.25 /16	4.96 /54	0.00	1.25
IN	ICON Core Equity C	ICNCX	C	(800) 764-0442	C+ / 6.5	-4.07	4.51	13.20 /65	15.84 /63	4.88 /53	0.00	2.04
IN	ICON Core Equity I	ICNIX	C+	(800) 764-0442	B- / 7.0	-3.90	4.86	14.16 /69	16.75 /67	5.70 /59	0.00	1.27
GR	ICON Covered Call C	IOCCX	D	(800) 764-0442	D- / 1.5	-2.68	0.22	3.14 / 8	7.71 /13	--	0.00	2.20
GR	ICON Covered Call I	IOCIX	D+	(800) 764-0442	D / 2.1	-2.40	0.66	3.97 /10	8.53 /18	--	0.00	1.45
EN	ICON Energy	ICENX	C+	(800) 764-0442	A+ / 9.9	1.74	13.65	38.56 /98	40.72 /99	23.86 /98	0.22	1.15
IN	ICON Equity Income C	IOECX	C-	(800) 764-0442	C- / 3.9	-4.40	2.39	6.03 /21	11.79 /41	--	1.25	2.20
IN	ICON Equity Income I	IOEIX	C-	(800) 764-0442	C / 4.7	-4.24	2.77	6.94 /26	12.78 /47	--	2.11	1.23
FS	ICON Financial	ICFSX	C+	(800) 764-0442	C+ / 6.7	-1.43	5.42	13.56 /66	15.77 /62	7.27 /68	0.63	1.20
HL	ICON Healthcare	ICHCX	C-	(800) 764-0442	C / 4.6	-6.64	-2.63	1.56 / 3	14.10 /54	7.96 /71	0.00	1.17
GR	ICON Industrials	ICTRX	A	(800) 764-0442	A- / 9.2	-0.68	15.84	29.19 /94	23.24 /88	8.49 /74	0.00	1.19
TC	ICON Information Technology	ICTEX	E-	(800) 764-0442	E / 0.5	-8.63	-3.09	2.29 / 5	5.27 / 4	-5.43 / 2	0.00	1.21
FO	ICON International Equity I	IIQIX	U	(800) 764-0442	U /	-2.07	5.86	39.93 /98	--	--	0.09	1.73
FO	ICON International Equity Z	ICNEX	B	(800) 764-0442	A+ / 9.7	-2.06	6.04	40.59 /98	31.92 /97	14.94 /92	0.22	1.41
GR	ICON Leisure & Consumer Staple	ICLEX	E-	(800) 764-0442	E+ / 0.7	-6.01	1.02	-8.00 / 0	7.17 /11	6.05 /61	0.00	1.68
AG	ICON Long/Short C	IOLCX	B+	(800) 764-0442	B- / 7.4	-2.84	8.30	16.18 /75	17.63 /71	--	0.00	2.30
AG	ICON Long/Short I	IOLIX	B+	(800) 764-0442	B / 7.8	-2.71	8.73	17.06 /77	18.51 /74	--	0.00	1.55
EN	ICON Materials	ICBMX	B+	(800) 764-0442	A+ / 9.7	-1.42	14.92	35.29 /97	31.37 /96	16.63 /94	0.16	1.26
FO	ICON South Europe Region	ICSEX	B	(800) 764-0442	A+ / 9.7	0.95	22.04	39.56 /98	28.97 /95	17.18 /94	0.00	1.85
UT	ICON Telecommunications & Utilities	ICTUX	C-	(800) 764-0442	C+ / 6.1	-2.45	4.83	7.27 /28	15.23 /60	5.39 /57	2.26	1.33
GR	IMS Capital Value	IMSCX	B	(800) 934-5550	B- / 7.0	-3.09	5.23	12.35 /61	17.21 /69	13.53 /89	0.00	1.48
GR	Industry Leaders D	ILFDX	C-	(866) 280-1952	C / 5.0	0.00	4.39	10.08 /47	12.32 /45	5.09 /55	0.99	0.79
GR	Industry Leaders I	ILFIX	C-	(866) 280-1952	C / 5.1	0.00	4.34	10.06 /47	12.42 /45	5.24 /56	0.98	0.79
GR	Industry Leaders L	ILFLX	C	(866) 280-1952	C / 5.3	0.09	4.52	10.49 /50	12.80 /48	--	1.66	0.38
MC	ING Alliance Berns Mid Cap Gr I		U	(800) 992-0180	U /	-12.15	-0.58	14.71 /71	--	--	0.00	0.81
MC	ING Alliance Berns Mid Cap Gr S	IALSX	D-	(800) 992-0180	C+ / 6.9	-12.22	-0.68	14.41 /70	17.81 /72	6.25 /63	0.00	1.01

● Denotes fund is closed to new investors
★ Denotes fund is included in Section II

RISK			NET ASSETS		ASSET				Portfolio Turnover Ratio	BULL / BEAR		FUND MANAGER		MINIMUMS		LOADS	
Risk Rating/Pts	3 Year Standard Deviation	Beta	NAV As of 6/30/06	Total $(Mil)	Cash %	Stocks %	Bonds %	Other %		Last Bull Market Return	Last Bear Market Return	Manager Quality Pct	Manager Tenure (Years)	Initial Purch. $	Additional Purch. $	Front End Load	Back End Load
B /8.1	6.1	0.42	11.07	99	1	98	0	1	131.0	51.5	-1.6	75	5	1,000	50	0.0	0.0
C /5.5	8.6	1.02	36.91	10	0	99	0	1	20.0	41.0	-11.6	9	5	1,000	50	5.8	0.0
C /5.3	8.7	1.03	35.58	6	0	99	0	1	20.0	38.8	-11.7	8	13	1,000	50	0.0	5.0
C /5.5	8.6	1.02	37.46	220	0	99	0	1	20.0	42.1	-11.5	10	13	1,000	50	0.0	0.0
B- /7.1	7.4	0.83	31.64	6	N/A	100	0	N/A	33.0	63.3	-10.7	58	N/A	1,000	50	5.8	0.0
B- /7.1	7.5	0.83	31.52	8	N/A	100	0	N/A	33.0	60.8	-10.9	51	N/A	1,000	50	0.0	5.0
B- /7.1	7.5	0.83	31.64	189	N/A	100	0	N/A	33.0	64.6	-10.7	60	N/A	1,000	50	0.0	0.0
C+ /6.5	10.4	0.99	12.99	4	6	93	0	1	21.0	129.3	-8.6	45	5	1,000	50	5.8	0.0
C+ /6.5	10.4	0.99	12.74	2	6	93	0	1	21.0	125.4	-8.7	38	5	1,000	50	0.0	5.0
C+ /6.6	10.4	0.99	13.06	235	6	93	0	1	21.0	130.7	-8.4	48	5	1,000	50	0.0	0.0
B- /7.6	9.8	0.88	15.32	5	4	95	0	1	7.0	89.2	-8.2	50	5	1,000	50	5.8	0.0
B- /7.5	9.8	0.88	14.93	8	4	95	0	1	7.0	86.2	-8.2	43	5	1,000	50	0.0	5.0
B- /7.6	9.8	0.89	15.53	144	4	95	0	1	7.0	90.7	-8.1	52	5	1,000	50	0.0	0.0
C+ /5.9	12.6	1.37	16.07	8	8	91	0	1	61.0	110.9	-8.2	81	5	1,000	50	5.8	0.0
C+ /5.9	12.6	1.37	15.62	4	8	91	0	1	61.0	107.5	-8.3	77	5	1,000	50	0.0	5.0
C+ /5.9	12.6	1.38	16.27	90	8	91	0	1	61.0	112.5	-8.1	83	5	1,000	50	0.0	0.0
B- /7.3	9.8	1.16	12.10	3	4	95	0	1	48.0	80.7	-10.2	74	5	1,000	50	1.5	0.0
B- /7.3	9.9	1.17	12.19	37	4	95	0	1	48.0	82.3	-10.2	76	5	1,000	50	0.0	0.0
B- /7.5	12.0	0.77	19.69	10	2	97	0	1	14.0	131.7	-9.0	97	N/A	1,000	50	5.8	0.0
C+ /6.5	12.0	0.77	19.30	3	2	97	0	1	14.0	127.9	-9.1	96	N/A	1,000	50	0.0	5.0
C+ /6.6	12.0	0.77	19.88	87	2	97	0	1	14.0	133.3	-8.9	97	N/A	1,000	50	0.0	0.0
B+ /9.2	5.1	0.42	16.13	2,816	2	97	0	1	58.0	41.1	1.1	78	6	1,000	100	0.0	1.5
C+ /6.0	7.6	0.93	43.50	862	1	98	0	1	86.0	77.0	-6.3	89	9	1,000	1,000	0.0	0.0
B- /7.5	11.0	1.01	36.05	398	3	96	0	1	139.0	162.9	-9.3	83	9	1,000	1,000	0.0	2.0
B /8.8	8.5	1.00	38.25	1,008	0	99	0	1	170.0	98.1	-3.3	95	9	1,000	1,000	0.0	0.0
C- /4.0	18.0	1.35	13.05	163	0	99	0	1	87.6	142.9	-2.0	11	N/A	1,000	100	0.0	0.0
C- /3.0	15.9	1.52	11.85	236	N/A	100	0	N/A	86.8	70.1	-14.2	7	N/A	1,000	100	0.0	0.0
C+ /5.9	13.2	1.36	15.07	97	1	98	0	1	60.1	99.1	-14.1	68	6	1,000	100	0.0	1.0
C+ /6.0	13.2	1.36	15.76	111	1	98	0	1	60.1	103.7	-13.9	76	6	1,000	100	0.0	0.0
B- /7.7	9.5	0.95	13.43	3	N/A	N/A	0	N/A	65.0	49.1	-6.1	27	N/A	1,000	100	0.0	1.0
B- /7.7	9.6	0.96	13.83	59	N/A	N/A	0	N/A	65.0	52.5	-5.8	32	N/A	1,000	100	0.0	0.0
C- /3.3	22.5	1.08	36.31	1,003	0	99	0	1	15.6	219.0	-0.5	89	N/A	1,000	100	0.0	0.0
C+ /6.5	10.3	1.18	14.78	5	1	90	6	3	73.5	76.5	-7.4	44	4	1,000	100	0.0	1.0
C+ /6.5	10.3	1.18	14.86	134	1	90	6	3	73.5	81.6	-7.3	55	4	1,000	100	0.0	0.0
C+ /6.0	12.2	1.19	13.81	258	N/A	100	0	N/A	83.8	104.3	-13.1	53	9	1,000	100	0.0	0.0
C+ /6.1	11.1	0.82	17.43	587	6	93	0	1	32.2	81.9	-5.3	90	9	1,000	100	0.0	0.0
C+ /6.6	13.6	1.37	14.70	240	0	99	0	1	38.3	120.3	-13.3	98	9	1,000	100	0.0	0.0
D+ /2.4	19.3	1.85	8.47	284	N/A	100	0	N/A	46.7	68.2	-20.8	0	9	1,000	100	0.0	0.0
U /	N/A	N/A	14.63	63	3	96	0	1	81.9	N/A	N/A	N/A	1	1,000	100	0.0	0.0
C /4.4	16.4	1.36	14.75	24	3	96	0	1	81.9	208.2	-2.4	41	1	1,000,000	100	0.0	0.0
D- /1.4	12.4	1.17	8.91	59	N/A	100	0	N/A	126.3	49.3	-13.4	13	9	1,000	100	0.0	0.0
B- /7.5	12.4	1.25	17.09	21	1	98	0	1	112.1	109.8	-15.0	88	N/A	1,000	100	0.0	1.0
B- /7.5	12.4	1.26	17.57	125	1	98	0	1	112.1	114.8	-14.8	91	N/A	1,000	100	0.0	0.0
C /5.1	18.9	0.69	12.48	175	2	97	0	1	76.6	169.6	-11.3	98	9	1,000	100	0.0	0.0
C /4.9	14.3	1.21	18.11	90	5	94	0	1	57.7	174.9	-9.1	49	N/A	1,000	100	0.0	0.0
C /5.3	11.2	0.53	7.16	63	0	99	0	1	70.9	99.2	-9.6	80	N/A	1,000	100	0.0	0.0
B- /7.5	10.2	1.13	19.73	165	5	94	0	1	20.9	118.9	-6.6	91	10	5,000	100	0.0	0.5
C+ /6.2	7.7	0.96	10.94	3	0	99	0	1	43.8	67.4	-9.5	70	7	5,000	100	0.0	0.0
C+ /6.2	7.7	0.96	10.83	8	0	99	0	1	43.8	68.2	-9.5	71	7	5,000	100	0.0	0.0
C+ /6.2	7.6	0.96	11.10	3	0	99	0	1	43.8	69.8	-9.4	75	5	250,000	100	0.0	0.0
U /	N/A	N/A	18.95	108	2	97	0	1	103.0	N/A	N/A	N/A	1	0	0	0.0	0.0
D- /1.2	20.5	1.68	18.90	528	2	97	0	1	103.0	135.0	-10.6	2	1	0	0	0.0	0.0

					PERFORMANCE							
	99 Pct = Best *0 Pct = Worst*			Overall Weiss Investment Rating		Perfor- mance	Total Return % through 6/30/06					Incl. in Returns	
										Annualized		Dividend	Expense
Fund Type	Fund Name	Ticker Symbol			Phone	Rating/Pts	3 Mo	6 Mo	1Yr / Pct	3Yr / Pct	5Yr / Pct	Yield	Ratio
MC	ING Alliance Berns Mid Cap Gr S2	IALTX	D-		(800) 992-0180	C+ / 6.8	-12.23	-0.74	14.22 /69	17.63 /71	--	0.00	N/A
GR	ING Amer Cen Co Val ADV	ISVAX	C		(800) 992-0180	C- / 3.4	0.27	3.91	7.88 /32	9.77 /26	--	0.81	1.50
GR	ING Amer Cen Co Val I	ISVIX	C		(800) 992-0180	C- / 3.8	0.41	4.21	8.46 /36	10.32 /29	--	1.27	1.00
GR	ING Amer Cen Co Val S	ISVSX	C		(800) 992-0180	C- / 3.6	0.34	4.08	8.14 /34	10.05 /28	--	0.97	1.25
GR	ING American Century Select ADV	IGOAX	E+		(800) 992-0180	E- / 0.1	-7.16	-7.36	-3.49 / 0	3.86 / 2	--	0.00	1.16
GR	ING American Century Select I	IGOIX	E+		(800) 992-0180	E- / 0.2	-7.00	-7.10	-2.99 / 0	4.43 / 3	--	0.00	0.66
GR	ING American Century Select S	IGOSX	E+		(800) 992-0180	E- / 0.2	-6.98	-7.18	-3.24 / 0	4.17 / 2	--	0.00	0.91
SC	ING American Century SmCap Val	IASAX	B-		(800) 992-0180	C+ / 6.8	-4.91	3.27	8.75 /38	17.28 /69	--	0.08	1.80
SC	ING American Century SmCap Val I	IACIX	B+		(800) 992-0180	B- / 7.1	-4.77	3.57	9.35 /42	17.87 /72	--	0.39	1.30
SC	ING American Century SmCap Val S	IASSX	B-		(800) 992-0180	C+ / 6.9	-4.86	3.41	9.03 /40	17.55 /70	--	0.17	1.55
GI	ING American FD Growth & Income	IAFGX	U		(800) 992-0180	U /	-0.30	3.69	9.69 /45	--	--	0.32	0.52
GR	ING American Funds Growth Portfolio	IAFSX	U		(800) 992-0180	U /	-1.56	2.16	14.53 /70	--	--	0.00	0.52
FO	ING American Funds Int Portfolio	IFSTX	U		(800) 992-0180	U /	-0.34	5.56	26.30 /90	--	--	0.43	0.52
BA	ING Balanced A	AETAX	D		(800) 992-0180	E+ / 0.7	-1.90	1.11	3.72 / 9	6.66 / 9	3.25 /39	1.23	1.37
BA	ING Balanced B	ABFBX	D		(800) 992-0180	E / 0.5	-2.09	0.78	2.95 / 7	5.90 / 6	2.49 /32	0.65	2.12
BA	ING Balanced C	ACBLX	D		(800) 992-0180	E+ / 0.8	-2.09	0.69	2.89 / 7	5.86 / 6	2.47 /32	0.60	2.12
BA	ING Balanced I	AETFX	D+		(800) 992-0180	D- / 1.4	-1.82	1.20	3.91 /10	6.92 /10	3.49 /41	1.55	1.12
SC	ING Baron Small Cap Growth ADV	IBSAX	B+		(800) 992-0180	B / 7.7	-4.31	7.55	11.04 /54	19.58 /78	--	0.00	1.58
SC	ING Baron Small Cap Growth I	IBGIX	A-		(800) 992-0180	B / 7.9	-4.22	7.71	11.57 /57	20.18 /80	--	0.00	1.20
SC	ING Baron Small Cap Growth S	IBSSX	B+		(800) 992-0180	B / 7.8	-4.27	7.60	11.27 /55	19.88 /79	--	0.00	1.33
SC	ING Cap Guardian Sm/Mid Cp S	ICSMX	D-		(800) 992-0180	C- / 3.3	-4.11	4.03	6.88 /26	10.12 /28	1.73 /25	0.16	0.91
SC	ING Cap Guardian Sm/Mid Cp S2	ICSNX	D-		(800) 992-0180	C- / 3.2	-4.13	3.96	6.71 /24	9.96 /27	--	0.16	1.06
IN	ING Capital Guardian U.S. Equ S	ICGTX	D+		(800) 992-0180	C / 4.4	-1.81	2.05	9.99 /47	11.42 /39	3.73 /43	0.41	1.00
IN	ING Capital Guardian U.S. Equ S2		D+		(800) 992-0180	C / 4.3	-1.82	1.97	9.84 /46	11.26 /38	--	0.35	1.15
CV	ING Convertible A	NAKSX	D		(800) 992-0180	D / 2.1	0.40	4.94	10.86 /53	8.57 /18	4.78 /52	2.71	1.33
CV	ING Convertible B	NANBX	D+		(800) 992-0180	D / 1.8	0.20	4.59	10.06 /47	7.83 /14	4.08 /47	1.81	2.08
CV	ING Convertible C	NRTLX	C-		(800) 992-0180	D+ / 2.4	0.20	4.60	10.06 /47	7.84 /14	4.07 /46	2.05	2.08
CV	ING Convertible Q	NAIQX	C-		(800) 992-0180	C- / 3.2	0.43	5.00	10.99 /53	8.75 /19	5.03 /54	3.03	1.33
GI	ING Corp Leaders Trust A	LEXCX	A		(800) 992-0180	B- / 7.4	1.34	7.09	13.65 /67	17.36 /70	8.32 /73	1.93	0.50
GR	ING Davis Venture Value ADV	ISBAX	C		(800) 992-0180	C- / 4.1	-0.11	2.49	8.64 /38	11.02 /36	--	0.03	1.57
GR	ING Davis Venture Value I	ISFIX	C+		(800) 992-0180	C / 4.5	0.00	2.77	9.06 /40	11.53 /39	--	0.12	1.07
GR	ING Davis Venture Value S	ISCSX	C+		(800) 992-0180	C / 4.3	-0.05	2.62	8.92 /40	11.30 /38	--	0.00	1.32
GR	ING Direct Index Plus Large Cap O	IDLOX	C		(800) 992-0180	C- / 3.4	-2.28	1.75	7.16 /27	10.23 /29	--	0.84	0.93
MC	ING Direct Index Plus Mid Cap O	IDMOX	B-		(800) 992-0180	C+ / 6.8	-3.06	3.93	11.52 /57	16.51 /66	--	0.22	1.00
SC	ING Direct Index Plus Small Cap O	IDSOX	B		(800) 992-0180	B / 7.7	-4.72	7.60	13.28 /65	19.31 /77	--	0.00	1.00
FO	ING Direct International O	IDIOX	A+		(800) 992-0180	B+ / 8.7	-0.29	8.08	27.39 /92	21.95 /85	--	1.23	1.68
TC	ING Direct Technology O	IDTOX	E		(800) 992-0180	C- / 3.0	-8.57	-0.95	15.24 /72	10.54 /31	--	0.00	1.75
GR	ING Disciplined LargeCap A	NREIX	C-		(800) 992-0180	D+ / 2.6	-2.08	2.07	7.33 /28	10.49 /31	1.59 /24	0.36	1.36
GR	ING Disciplined LargeCap B	NBEIX	C-		(800) 992-0180	D / 2.2	-2.28	1.65	6.37 /22	9.71 /25	0.81 /19	0.00	2.11
GR	ING Disciplined LargeCap C	NEICX	C-		(800) 992-0180	C- / 3.0	-2.28	1.65	6.49 /23	9.71 /25	0.81 /19	0.00	2.11
GR	ING Disciplined LargeCap I	NEIIX	D+		(800) 992-0180	D+ / 2.6	-5.13	-1.05	4.44 /12	9.83 /26	1.33 /22	0.00	1.04
FO	ING Diversified International A	IFFAX	U		(800) 992-0180	U /	-1.19	7.59	--	--	--	0.00	0.35
IN	ING Eagle Asset Capital App S	IEASX	D+		(800) 992-0180	C- / 3.4	-2.07	2.44	4.29 /12	10.68 /33	3.09 /38	1.20	0.91
IN	ING Eagle Asset Capital App S2	IEATX	D+		(800) 992-0180	C- / 3.3	-2.13	2.33	4.11 /11	10.51 /31	--	1.23	1.06
EM	ING Emerging Countries A	NECAX	B-		(800) 992-0180	B+ / 8.5	-3.31	3.59	19.98 /82	23.92 /89	13.47 /89	0.49	2.00
EM	ING Emerging Countries B	NACBX	C+		(800) 992-0180	B+ / 8.4	-3.51	3.21	19.10 /81	23.08 /87	12.79 /88	0.00	2.74
EM	ING Emerging Countries C	NAEMX	B-		(800) 992-0180	B+ / 8.6	-3.51	3.18	19.01 /80	23.06 /87	12.50 /88	0.29	2.74
EM	ING Emerging Countries M		B+		(800) 992-0180	B+ / 8.5	-3.43	3.32	19.27 /81	23.32 /88	--	0.00	2.49
EM	ING Emerging Countries Q	NACQX	B-		(800) 992-0180	B+ / 8.9	-3.31	3.62	20.10 /82	24.13 /90	13.59 /90	0.59	1.85
GI	ING Equity Income A	AAGIX	C+		(800) 992-0180	C / 4.3	2.02	6.42	10.70 /52	12.11 /43	0.86 /20	1.52	1.27
GI	ING Equity Income B	AGINX	C+		(800) 992-0180	C- / 3.8	1.86	6.01	9.95 /47	11.34 /38	0.13 /16	1.02	2.02
GI	ING Equity Income C	AEICX	C+		(800) 992-0180	C / 4.5	1.87	6.03	9.99 /47	11.35 /38	0.13 /16	0.94	2.02

RISK	3 Year		NET ASSETS		ASSET					BULL / BEAR		FUND MANAGER		MINIMUMS		LOADS	
Risk Rating/Pts	Standard Deviation	Beta	NAV As of 6/30/06	Total $(Mil)	Cash %	Stocks %	Bonds %	Other %	Portfolio Turnover Ratio	Last Bull Market Return	Last Bear Market Return	Manager Quality Pct	Manager Tenure (Years)	Initial Purch. $	Additional Purch. $	Front End Load	Back End Load
D- / 1.2	20.5	1.68	18.80	20	2	97	0	1	103.0	133.9	-10.7	1	1	0	0	0.0	0.0
B / 8.2	8.2	1.01	14.63	14	17	82	0	1	105.0	61.6	-11.8	39	N/A	0	0	0.0	0.0
B / 8.3	8.2	1.01	14.84	73	17	82	0	1	105.0	64.2	-11.7	44	N/A	0	0	0.0	0.0
B / 8.2	8.2	1.01	14.78	26	17	82	0	1	105.0	63.0	-11.8	42	N/A	0	0	0.0	0.0
B- / 7.2	11.0	1.23	8.56	14	3	96	0	1	133.0	41.7	-9.3	3	5	0	0	0.0	0.0
B- / 7.3	11.0	1.23	8.77	337	3	96	0	1	133.0	44.3	-9.3	4	3	0	0	0.0	0.0
B- / 7.2	11.0	1.24	8.66	5	3	96	0	1	133.0	43.0	-9.3	3	5	0	0	0.0	0.0
B- / 7.7	11.2	0.74	12.01	13	4	96	0	0	101.0	102.2	-7.8	83	N/A	0	0	0.0	0.0
B- / 7.7	11.2	0.74	12.19	63	4	96	0	0	101.0	105.5	-7.7	86	N/A	0	0	0.0	0.0
B- / 7.7	11.2	0.74	12.14	44	4	96	0	0	101.0	103.8	-7.6	84	N/A	0	0	0.0	0.0
U /	N/A	N/A	40.15	1,205	12	87	0	1	1.0	N/A	N/A	N/A	3	0	0	0.0	0.0
U /	N/A	N/A	60.08	1,770	8	91	0	1	1.0	N/A	N/A	N/A	3	0	0	0.0	0.0
U /	N/A	N/A	20.31	914	16	83	0	1	2.0	N/A	N/A	N/A	3	0	0	0.0	0.0
B / 8.3	5.3	1.09	11.86	89	2	69	27	2	239.0	39.3	-3.9	40	4	1,000	100	5.8	0.0
B / 8.4	5.3	1.09	11.70	34	2	69	27	2	239.0	36.0	-3.9	33	4	1,000	100	0.0	5.0
B / 8.4	5.3	1.09	11.71	13	2	69	27	2	239.0	36.1	-4.0	33	4	1,000	100	0.0	1.0
B / 8.4	5.3	1.08	11.85	35	2	69	27	2	239.0	40.5	-3.9	43	4	1,000,000	0	0.0	0.0
B- / 7.4	12.2	0.77	17.10	41	6	92	0	2	11.0	117.1	-7.8	90	4	0	0	0.0	0.0
B- / 7.4	12.2	0.78	17.46	124	6	92	0	2	11.0	120.4	-7.5	92	3	0	0	0.0	0.0
B- / 7.4	12.2	0.77	17.28	268	6	92	0	2	11.0	118.8	-7.6	91	4	0	0	0.0	0.0
C / 4.3	15.4	1.00	12.12	467	2	97	0	1	87.0	77.3	-12.4	5	6	0	0	0.0	0.0
C / 4.3	15.4	1.00	12.07	10	2	97	0	1	87.0	76.5	-12.4	5	6	0	0	0.0	0.0
C+ / 5.8	9.4	1.18	12.45	574	1	98	0	1	33.0	72.6	-9.6	39	6	0	0	0.0	0.0
C+ / 5.7	9.4	1.18	12.42	11	1	98	0	1	33.0	71.8	-9.6	38	6	0	0	0.0	0.0
B- / 7.2	7.3	1.10	19.36	48	1	6	1	92	27.0	42.7	1.1	64	N/A	1,000	100	5.8	0.0
B / 8.1	7.3	1.09	21.41	37	1	6	1	92	27.0	39.6	0.9	57	N/A	1,000	100	0.0	5.0
B / 8.0	7.3	1.10	19.87	48	1	6	1	92	27.0	39.6	0.9	57	N/A	1,000	100	0.0	1.0
B- / 7.9	7.3	1.09	18.76	2	1	6	1	92	27.0	43.3	1.2	66	N/A	250,000	10,000	0.0	0.0
B / 8.4	8.7	0.92	19.79	364	0	100	0	0	N/A	84.1	-7.2	96	N/A	1,000	100	0.0	0.0
B / 8.1	9.6	1.17	18.92	11	4	94	0	2	110.0	64.8	-8.0	37	1	0	0	0.0	0.0
B / 8.1	9.6	1.17	19.31	13	4	94	0	2	110.0	67.2	-7.9	41	1	0	0	0.0	0.0
B / 8.1	9.6	1.17	19.18	80	4	94	0	2	110.0	66.0	-7.9	39	1	0	0	0.0	0.0
B / 8.2	7.6	0.99	16.26	61	0	99	0	1	78.0	58.3	-9.6	45	N/A	1,000	100	0.0	0.0
B- / 7.2	10.6	0.98	17.74	51	1	98	0	1	93.0	92.8	-8.1	42	N/A	1,000	100	0.0	0.0
C+ / 6.7	13.4	0.91	18.97	41	0	99	0	1	83.0	112.3	-9.4	76	N/A	1,000	100	0.0	0.0
B- / 7.7	10.6	1.02	10.17	60	0	99	0	1	90.0	118.7	-10.8	29	N/A	1,000	100	0.0	0.0
D+ / 2.4	17.6	1.83	4.16	26	2	97	0	1	18.0	75.5	-15.8	5	N/A	1,000	100	0.0	0.0
B / 8.1	7.8	0.99	10.36	5	0	99	0	1	92.0	59.2	-9.7	48	N/A	1,000	100	5.8	0.0
B / 8.3	7.7	0.99	9.85	24	0	99	0	1	92.0	55.6	-9.8	40	N/A	1,000	100	0.0	5.0
B / 8.3	7.7	0.99	9.85	9	0	99	0	1	92.0	55.6	-10.0	40	N/A	1,000	100	0.0	5.0
B- / 7.7	8.5	1.07	10.36	N/A	0	99	0	1	92.0	61.6	-9.6	35	N/A	1,000,000	10,000	0.0	0.0
U /	N/A	N/A	10.77	109	0	99	0	1	N/A	N/A	N/A	N/A	N/A	1,000	0	5.8	1.0
C+ / 6.3	8.1	0.99	18.49	178	8	90	0	2	54.0	62.1	-11.0	51	2	0	0	0.0	0.0
C+ / 6.3	8.1	0.99	18.41	3	8	90	0	2	54.0	61.4	-11.0	49	2	0	0	0.0	0.0
C / 5.0	15.9	0.93	26.85	110	1	98	0	1	124.0	150.4	-7.2	7	12	1,000	100	5.8	0.0
C / 5.0	15.9	0.93	26.38	14	1	98	0	1	124.0	145.0	-7.4	5	11	1,000	100	0.0	5.0
C / 5.0	15.9	0.93	25.01	32	1	98	0	1	124.0	144.9	-7.3	5	12	1,000	100	0.0	1.0
C+ / 6.5	15.9	0.93	26.43	1	1	98	0	1	124.0	146.7	-7.3	5	N/A	1,000	100	3.3	0.0
C / 5.0	15.9	0.93	27.74	15	1	98	0	1	124.0	151.9	-7.1	7	11	250,000	0	0.0	0.0
B / 8.7	7.3	0.84	11.11	51	0	99	0	1	12.0	64.8	-10.1	78	N/A	1,000	100	5.8	0.0
B / 8.7	7.2	0.84	10.93	9	0	99	0	1	12.0	61.1	-10.3	72	N/A	1,000	100	0.0	5.0
B / 8.7	7.2	0.84	10.90	2	0	99	0	1	12.0	61.0	-10.3	72	N/A	1,000	100	0.0	1.0

Fund Type	Fund Name	Ticker Symbol	Overall Weiss Investment Rating	Phone	Performance Rating/Pts	3 Mo	6 Mo	1Yr / Pct	3Yr / Pct	5Yr / Pct	Dividend Yield	Expense Ratio
GI	ING Equity Income I	AEGIX	B-	(800) 992-0180	C / 5.3	2.11	6.60	11.06 /54	12.33 /45	1.13 /21	1.85	1.01
HL	ING Evergreen Health Sciences S	IEHSX	U	(800) 992-0180	U /	-2.90	3.18	12.57 /62	--	--	0.00	1.01
GR	ING Evergreen Omega Port Cl I		U	(800) 992-0180	U /	-8.73	-3.91	3.46 / 9	--	--	0.03	0.60
GR	ING Fidelity VIP Contrafund Port S	VPCSX	U	(800) 992-0180	U /	-0.95	3.74	16.74 /76	--	--	0.00	1.21
FS	ING Financial Services A	PBTAX	C	(800) 992-0180	C / 4.7	-1.79	1.94	10.97 /53	13.75 /53	7.36 /68	0.84	1.18
FS	ING Financial Services B	PBTBX	C	(800) 992-0180	C / 4.3	-1.99	1.52	10.15 /48	12.89 /48	6.53 /64	0.07	1.93
MC	ING FMR Div Mid Cap I		U	(800) 992-0180	U /	-2.22	6.57	--	--	--	0.00	0.74
MC	ING FMR Div Mid Cap S	IFDSX	B-	(800) 992-0180	B+ / 8.7	-2.29	6.42	21.06 /83	22.39 /86	9.93 /80	0.00	0.99
MC	ING FMR Div Mid Cap S2	IFDTX	B-	(800) 992-0180	B+ / 8.7	-2.30	6.44	21.02 /83	22.20 /86	--	0.00	1.14
GR	ING FMR Earnings Gr I	FEGJX	U	(800) 992-0180	U /	-7.00	-4.81	-1.27 / 1	--	--	0.18	0.73
GR	ING FMR Earnings Gr S	FEGSX	U	(800) 992-0180	U /	-7.02	-4.91	-1.43 / 1	--	--	0.13	0.98
FO	ING Foreign Fund A	IAFAX	U	(800) 992-0180	U /	-1.38	10.29	29.40 /94	--	--	0.00	1.68
FO	ING Foreign Fund B	IAFBX	U	(800) 992-0180	U /	-1.58	9.89	28.46 /93	--	--	0.00	2.43
FO	ING Foreign Fund C	ICFCX	U	(800) 992-0180	U /	-1.58	9.88	28.42 /93	--	--	0.00	2.43
FO	ING Foreign Fund I	IAFIX	U	(800) 992-0180	U /	-1.37	10.31	29.58 /94	--	--	0.00	1.35
GR	ING Fundamental Res Port ADV	IDIAX	C	(800) 992-0180	C- / 3.2	-3.81	0.78	8.28 /35	9.94 /27	--	0.72	1.30
GR	ING Fundamental Res Port I	IDIIX	C	(800) 992-0180	C- / 3.6	-3.66	1.10	8.94 /40	10.54 /31	--	1.25	0.80
GR	ING Fundamental Res Port S	IDISX	C	(800) 992-0180	C- / 3.4	-3.77	0.88	8.64 /38	10.25 /29	--	0.98	1.05
GR	ING GET Series N		D+	(800) 992-0180	E / 0.3	0.62	1.94	3.56 / 9	2.22 / 1	--	7.99	0.55
GR	ING GET Series P		D+	(800) 992-0180	E- / 0.2	0.57	1.49	2.55 / 6	1.59 / 0	--	8.00	0.80
GR	ING GET Series Q	IGFQX	D+	(800) 992-0180	E- / 0.2	0.21	1.30	2.61 / 6	1.98 / 1	--	8.29	0.80
GR	ING GET Series R		D+	(800) 992-0180	E- / 0.2	-0.09	1.28	2.78 / 7	2.45 / 1	--	7.02	0.80
GR	ING GET Series S	IGFSX	D+	(800) 992-0180	E- / 0.2	-0.42	1.16	2.86 / 7	2.40 / 1	--	5.64	0.80
GR	ING GET Series T	IGFTX	D+	(800) 992-0180	E- / 0.2	-0.35	0.94	2.34 / 5	2.24 / 1	--	5.79	0.80
GR	ING GET Series U	IFGUX	D+	(800) 992-0180	E / 0.3	-0.69	0.74	2.27 / 5	2.75 / 1	--	4.86	0.80
GR	ING GET Series V	IGFVX	D+	(800) 992-0180	E- / 0.1	0.14	0.64	1.12 / 3	1.49 / 0	--	4.42	0.80
IN	ING GET U.S. Core Portfolio -Ser 1	IGUAX	U	(800) 992-0180	U /	-0.70	0.68	2.27 / 5	--	--	4.94	0.96
IN	ING GET U.S. Core Portfolio -Ser 10	IGUBX	U	(800) 992-0180	U /	-1.94	-0.08	--	--	--	0.00	0.76
IN	ING GET U.S. Core Portfolio -Ser 2	IGUDX	U	(800) 992-0180	U /	-0.58	0.52	1.42 / 3	--	--	5.71	0.97
IN	ING GET U.S. Core Portfolio -Ser 3	IGUEX	U	(800) 992-0180	U /	-0.82	0.27	1.17 / 3	--	--	4.78	0.97
IN	ING GET U.S. Core Portfolio -Ser 4	IGUFX	U	(800) 992-0180	U /	-0.89	0.45	1.84 / 4	--	--	4.55	1.00
IN	ING GET U.S. Core Portfolio -Ser 5	IGUGX	U	(800) 992-0180	U /	-2.08	0.42	3.11 / 8	--	--	3.03	1.00
IN	ING GET U.S. Core Portfolio -Ser 6	IGUHX	U	(800) 992-0180	U /	-1.87	0.31	2.59 / 6	--	--	2.86	0.97
IN	ING GET U.S. Core Portfolio -Ser 7	IGUIX	U	(800) 992-0180	U /	-1.96	0.15	2.00 / 4	--	--	2.51	0.94
IN	ING GET U.S. Core Portfolio -Ser 8	IGUJX	U	(800) 992-0180	U /	-2.00	0.39	2.50 / 6	--	--	1.97	0.91
IN	ING GET U.S. Core Portfolio -Ser 9	IGUKX	U	(800) 992-0180	U /	-1.91	0.13	--	--	--	0.00	0.87
GL	ING Global Equity Dividend A	IAGEX	U	(800) 992-0180	U /	1.30	8.86	16.78 /77	--	--	2.56	1.40
GL	ING Global Equity Dividend B	IBGEX	U	(800) 992-0180	U /	1.13	8.46	15.88 /74	--	--	2.11	2.15
GL	ING Global Equity Dividend C	ICGEX	U	(800) 992-0180	U /	1.13	8.47	15.91 /74	--	--	2.11	2.15
RE	ING Global Real Estate A	IGLAX	B+	(800) 992-0180	A / 9.4	-1.39	13.18	25.96 /90	29.35 /95	--	2.12	1.59
RE	ING Global Real Estate B	IGBAX	B+	(800) 992-0180	A / 9.4	-1.53	12.76	25.02 /88	28.39 /94	--	2.02	2.34
RE	ING Global Real Estate C	IGCAX	B+	(800) 992-0180	A / 9.5	-1.57	12.70	25.02 /88	28.49 /94	--	1.92	2.34
TC	ING Global Science And Technology	ATNAX	E	(800) 992-0180	D / 2.0	-8.59	-0.95	15.28 /73	10.45 /30	-3.73 / 4	0.00	1.75
TC	ING Global Science And Technology	ATCBX	E-	(800) 992-0180	D / 1.8	-8.55	-1.25	14.78 /71	9.70 /25	-4.44 / 3	0.00	2.50
TC	ING Global Science And Technology	ATHCX	E	(800) 992-0180	D+ / 2.3	-8.82	-1.26	14.58 /70	9.66 /25	-4.59 / 3	0.00	2.50
TC	ING Global Science And Technology I	ATEIX	E	(800) 992-0180	C- / 3.2	-8.46	-0.94	15.62 /74	10.83 /34	-3.49 / 4	0.00	1.50
GL	ING Global Value Choice A	NAWGX	C+	(800) 992-0180	C+ / 6.2	-0.39	6.51	18.72 /80	15.55 /62	2.32 /30	0.65	1.85
GL	ING Global Value Choice B	NAWBX	C+	(800) 992-0180	C+ / 5.9	-0.54	6.11	17.88 /79	14.79 /58	1.63 /24	0.00	2.50
GL	ING Global Value Choice C	NAWCX	C+	(800) 992-0180	C+ / 6.4	-0.55	6.13	17.90 /79	14.79 /58	1.63 /24	0.10	2.50
GL	ING Global Value Choice Q	NAWQX	B-	(800) 992-0180	B- / 7.0	-0.29	6.63	19.06 /81	15.87 /63	2.62 /33	0.81	1.55
GR	ING Goldman Sachs Capital Gr ADV	IGSAX	D	(800) 992-0180	D- / 1.4	-4.86	-0.70	4.51 /13	7.17 /11	--	0.00	1.55
GR	ING Goldman Sachs Capital Gr I	IGGIX	D+	(800) 992-0180	D / 1.7	-4.75	-0.44	5.07 /15	7.69 /13	--	0.55	1.05

• Denotes fund is closed to new investors
* Denotes fund is included in Section II

RISK			NET ASSETS		ASSET					BULL / BEAR		FUND MANAGER		MINIMUMS		LOADS	
	3 Year		NAV						Portfolio	Last Bull	Last Bear	Manager	Manager	Initial	Additional	Front	Back
Risk	Standard		As of	Total	Cash	Stocks	Bonds	Other	Turnover	Market	Market	Quality	Tenure	Purch.	Purch.	End	End
Rating/Pts	Deviation	Beta	6/30/06	$(Mil)	%	%	%	%	Ratio	Return	Return	Pct	(Years)	$	$	Load	Load
B / 8.7	7.3	0.84	11.15	31	0	99	0	1	12.0	66.0	-10.1	80	N/A	250,000	10,000	0.0	0.0
U /	N/A	N/A	11.03	173	3	96	0	1	118.0	N/A	N/A	N/A	N/A	0	0	0.0	0.0
U /	N/A	N/A	10.56	186	2	98	0	0	140.0	N/A	N/A	N/A	5	0	0	0.0	0.0
U /	N/A	N/A	12.48	133	0	100	0	0	5.0	N/A	N/A	N/A	2	0	0	0.0	0.0
B- / 7.0	9.4	1.01	23.08	217	3	96	0	1	13.0	80.2	-9.9	55	5	1,000	100	5.8	0.0
B- / 7.2	9.4	1.01	22.70	58	3	96	0	1	13.0	75.9	-10.0	45	5	1,000	100	0.0	5.0
U /	N/A	N/A	14.12	84	5	94	0	1	186.0	N/A	N/A	N/A	2	0	0	0.0	0.0
C / 5.2	12.5	1.03	14.08	650	5	94	0	1	186.0	127.6	-8.5	85	2	0	0	0.0	0.0
C / 5.2	12.5	1.03	14.04	37	5	94	0	1	186.0	126.5	-8.5	84	2	0	0	0.0	0.0
U /	N/A	N/A	10.09	486	1	98	0	1	N/A	N/A	N/A	N/A	1	0	0	0.0	0.0
U /	N/A	N/A	10.07	191	1	98	0	1	N/A	N/A	N/A	N/A	1	0	0	0.0	0.0
U /	N/A	N/A	17.15	197	6	93	0	1	81.0	N/A	N/A	N/A	N/A	1,000	100	5.8	1.0
U /	N/A	N/A	16.78	36	6	93	0	1	81.0	N/A	N/A	N/A	N/A	1,000	100	0.0	5.0
U /	N/A	N/A	16.80	139	6	93	0	1	81.0	N/A	N/A	N/A	N/A	1,000	100	0.0	1.0
U /	N/A	N/A	17.33	45	6	93	0	1	81.0	N/A	N/A	N/A	N/A	1,000,000	0	0.0	0.0
B / 8.6	7.9	1.00	9.09	4	2	97	0	1	220.0	63.2	-10.2	41	3	0	0	0.0	0.0
B / 8.6	8.1	1.03	9.20	60	2	97	0	1	220.0	65.7	-10.0	45	5	0	0	0.0	0.0
B / 8.6	8.0	1.03	9.18	42	2	97	0	1	220.0	64.6	-10.2	42	5	0	0	0.0	0.0
B+ / 9.9	2.1	0.09	9.71	58	3	7	88	2	N/A	9.7	1.6	45	N/A	0	0	0.0	0.0
B+ / 9.9	2.4	0.05	9.58	90	3	7	88	2	N/A	7.4	2.5	42	N/A	0	0	0.0	0.0
B+ / 9.9	2.6	0.12	9.83	104	3	7	88	2	N/A	9.9	1.8	39	N/A	0	0	0.0	0.0
B+ / 9.9	2.9	0.19	9.71	96	3	7	88	2	N/A	12.2	2.5	38	N/A	0	0	0.0	0.0
B+ / 9.9	3.2	0.19	9.78	132	3	7	88	2	N/A	12.5	1.9	37	N/A	0	0	0.0	0.0
B+ / 9.9	3.3	0.20	9.58	112	3	7	88	2	N/A	12.0	N/A	35	N/A	0	0	0.0	0.0
B+ / 9.9	3.6	0.27	9.43	114	0	42	56	2	42.0	N/A	N/A	35	N/A	0	0	0.0	0.0
B+ / 9.9	3.7	0.09	9.71	179	3	7	88	2	N/A	N/A	N/A	37	N/A	0	0	0.0	0.0
U /	N/A	N/A	9.72	137	0	43	56	1	49.0	N/A	N/A	N/A	1	0	0	0.0	0.0
U /	N/A	N/A	9.93	32	0	73	25	2	80.0	N/A	N/A	N/A	1	0	0	0.0	0.0
U /	N/A	N/A	9.68	105	0	43	56	1	49.0	N/A	N/A	N/A	3	0	0	0.0	0.0
U /	N/A	N/A	9.75	148	0	43	56	1	49.0	N/A	N/A	N/A	1	0	0	0.0	0.0
U /	N/A	N/A	9.99	63	0	43	56	1	49.0	N/A	N/A	N/A	1	0	0	0.0	0.0
U /	N/A	N/A	9.94	38	0	82	16	2	111.0	N/A	N/A	N/A	1	0	0	0.0	0.0
U /	N/A	N/A	10.06	101	0	75	23	2	81.0	N/A	N/A	N/A	1	0	0	0.0	0.0
U /	N/A	N/A	10.00	72	0	74	24	2	126.0	N/A	N/A	N/A	1	0	0	0.0	0.0
U /	N/A	N/A	10.03	42	0	78	20	2	131.0	N/A	N/A	N/A	1	0	0	0.0	0.0
U /	N/A	N/A	9.94	36	1	75	22	2	188.0	N/A	N/A	N/A	1	0	0	0.0	0.0
U /	N/A	N/A	14.65	81	2	97	0	1	57.0	N/A	N/A	N/A	N/A	1,000	100	5.8	0.0
U /	N/A	N/A	14.60	38	2	97	0	1	57.0	N/A	N/A	N/A	N/A	1,000	100	0.0	5.0
U /	N/A	N/A	14.58	63	2	97	0	1	57.0	N/A	N/A	N/A	N/A	1,000	100	0.0	1.0
C+ / 5.8	12.9	0.71	19.44	257	2	98	0	0	91.0	149.9	0.6	99	N/A	1,000	100	5.8	0.0
C+ / 5.7	12.9	0.71	16.80	21	2	98	0	0	91.0	144.2	0.4	99	N/A	1,000	100	0.0	5.0
C+ / 5.7	12.9	0.71	17.58	58	2	98	0	0	91.0	144.5	0.4	99	N/A	1,000	100	0.0	1.0
C- / 3.0	17.7	1.84	4.15	34	7	92	0	1	128.0	75.8	-15.9	5	N/A	1,000	100	5.8	0.0
C- / 3.0	17.6	1.83	3.96	11	7	92	0	1	128.0	71.0	-15.8	4	N/A	1,000	100	0.0	5.0
C- / 3.0	17.7	1.83	3.93	4	7	92	0	1	128.0	71.5	-16.2	4	N/A	1,000	100	0.0	1.0
C- / 3.0	17.7	1.84	4.22	2	7	92	0	1	128.0	77.5	-15.8	6	N/A	250,000	10,000	0.0	0.0
B- / 7.0	8.9	0.83	20.46	46	4	95	0	1	129.0	83.6	-10.8	19	13	1,000	100	5.8	0.0
B- / 7.0	8.9	0.83	22.22	22	4	95	0	1	129.0	79.8	-10.9	15	11	1,000	100	0.0	5.0
B- / 7.0	8.9	0.83	19.75	31	4	95	0	1	129.0	79.8	-11.0	15	13	1,000	100	0.0	1.0
B- / 7.0	8.9	0.83	23.95	5	4	95	0	1	129.0	85.2	-10.8	20	11	250,000	10,000	0.0	0.0
B / 8.1	8.6	1.03	11.35	3	24	75	0	1	34.0	49.4	-11.1	20	5	0	0	0.0	0.0
B / 8.1	8.6	1.02	11.44	3	24	75	0	1	34.0	51.8	-11.0	23	3	0	0	0.0	0.0

					PERFORMANCE							
	99 Pct = Best					Total Return % through 6/30/06					Incl. in Returns	
	0 Pct = Worst		Overall Weiss		Perfor-				Annualized		Dividend	Expense
Fund Type	Fund Name	Ticker Symbol	Investment Rating	Phone	mance Rating/Pts	3 Mo	6 Mo	1Yr / Pct	3Yr / Pct	5Yr / Pct	Yield	Ratio
GR	ING Goldman Sachs Capital Gr S	IGGSX	D+	(800) 992-0180	D- / 1.5	-4.77	-0.52	4.81 /14	7.43 /12	--	0.29	1.30
GR	ING Goldman Sachs Core Equity	ISPAX	C+	(800) 992-0180	C / 4.6	-2.79	1.87	11.07 /54	11.89 /42	--	1.01	1.40
GR	ING Goldman Sachs Core Equity I	IGCIX	C+	(800) 992-0180	C / 4.8	-3.13	1.60	11.13 /54	12.28 /44	--	1.02	0.90
GR	ING Goldman Sachs Core Equity S	IGCSX	C+	(800) 992-0180	C / 4.8	-2.76	2.01	11.32 /55	12.15 /43	--	0.80	1.15
GR	ING Goldman Sachs Tolkp Pr S	IGSSX	E+	(800) 992-0180	D+ / 2.3	-9.54	-1.52	4.55 /13	9.74 /25	-5.15 / 2	0.00	1.40
GR	ING Goldman Sachs Tolkp Pr S2	IGSTX	E+	(800) 992-0180	D+ / 2.3	-9.46	-1.53	4.57 /13	9.59 /25	--	0.00	1.55
GR	ING Growth A	AEGAX	E+	(800) 992-0180	D- / 1.1	-6.70	-3.90	5.91 /20	8.35 /17	-2.11 / 8	0.20	1.30
GR	ING Growth B	AGRWX	E+	(800) 992-0180	E+ / 0.8	-6.91	-4.28	5.03 /15	7.53 /13	-2.84 / 6	0.00	2.05
GR	ING Growth C	ACGRX	E+	(800) 992-0180	D- / 1.2	-6.84	-4.25	5.08 /15	7.58 /13	-2.87 / 6	0.00	2.05
GR	ING Growth I	AEGRX	D-	(800) 992-0180	D / 2.0	-6.61	-3.70	6.22 /22	8.67 /19	-1.85 / 9	0.32	1.05
FO	ING Index Plus Int Eq I	IFIIX	U	(800) 992-0180	U /	0.28	8.85	--	--	--	0.00	0.90
IX	ING Index Plus Large Cap A	AELAX	C-	(800) 992-0180	D+ / 2.9	-2.29	1.82	7.19 /27	10.22 /29	1.42 /23	0.75	0.95
IX	ING Index Plus Large Cap B	ATLBX	D+	(800) 992-0180	D / 2.0	-2.48	1.39	6.39 /23	9.40 /24	0.66 /18	0.04	1.70
IX	ING Index Plus Large Cap C	AELCX	C-	(800) 992-0180	D+ / 2.9	-2.41	1.57	6.72 /25	9.70 /25	0.92 /20	0.27	1.45
IX	ING Index Plus Large Cap I	AELIX	C	(800) 992-0180	C- / 3.5	-2.21	1.93	7.48 /29	10.49 /31	1.67 /25	1.03	0.70
MC	ING Index Plus Mid Cap A	AIMAX	C+	(800) 992-0180	C+ / 6.4	-3.02	3.94	11.56 /57	16.52 /66	8.56 /74	0.20	1.00
MC	ING Index Plus Mid Cap B	APMBX	C	(800) 992-0180	C+ / 5.7	-3.25	3.54	10.62 /51	15.64 /62	7.73 /70	0.00	1.75
MC	ING Index Plus Mid Cap C	APMCX	C+	(800) 992-0180	C+ / 6.4	-3.15	3.74	11.03 /54	15.94 /63	8.02 /72	0.00	1.50
MC	ING Index Plus Mid Cap I	AIMIX	C+	(800) 992-0180	C+ / 6.9	-2.98	4.07	11.82 /58	16.81 /67	8.84 /76	0.38	0.75
MC	ING Index Plus Mid Cap R	AIMRX	U	(800) 992-0180	U /	-3.09	3.78	11.26 /55	--	--	0.12	1.25
SC	ING Index Plus Small Cap A	AISAX	B-	(800) 992-0180	B- / 7.5	-4.70	7.60	13.31 /65	19.26 /77	10.65 /83	0.00	1.00
SC	ING Index Plus Small Cap B	AISBX	C+	(800) 992-0180	B- / 7.0	-4.86	7.22	12.47 /62	18.36 /74	9.84 /80	0.00	1.75
SC	ING Index Plus Small Cap C	APSCX	B-	(800) 992-0180	B- / 7.5	-4.83	7.41	12.86 /64	18.72 /75	10.11 /81	0.00	1.50
SC	ING Index Plus Small Cap I	AISIX	B	(800) 992-0180	B / 7.8	-4.66	7.79	13.67 /67	19.55 /78	10.96 /84	0.00	0.75
FO	ING International Cap Appr Fd I	ICAIX	U	(800) 992-0180	U /	-1.60	5.34	--	--	--	0.00	1.25
FO	ING International Fd A	LEXIX	C+	(800) 992-0180	C+ / 6.8	-4.01	5.26	21.25 /83	18.46 /74	6.69 /65	1.33	1.65
FO	ING International Fd B	LBXIX	B-	(800) 992-0180	C+ / 6.7	-4.15	4.90	20.31 /82	17.54 /70	5.76 /59	0.75	2.40
FO	ING International Fd C	LCXIX	B	(800) 992-0180	B- / 7.1	-4.15	4.90	20.34 /82	17.47 /70	5.75 /59	0.69	2.40
FO	ING International Fd I	LIXIX	B+	(800) 992-0180	B / 7.7	-3.87	5.46	21.70 /84	18.88 /76	--	1.78	1.26
FO	ING International Fd Q	LQXIX	C+	(800) 992-0180	B / 7.6	-3.97	5.30	21.38 /83	18.63 /75	6.77 /65	1.64	1.51
FO	ING International Growth A	AEIAX	A-	(800) 992-0180	B+ / 8.4	-0.29	8.07	27.38 /92	21.94 /85	3.72 /43	1.07	1.60
FO	ING International Growth B	ANTLX	B+	(800) 992-0180	B+ / 8.3	-0.40	7.70	26.49 /91	21.06 /83	2.98 /37	0.70	2.35
FO	ING International Growth C	AIFCX	A-	(800) 992-0180	B+ / 8.5	-0.40	7.70	26.40 /90	21.00 /83	3.01 /37	0.52	2.35
FO	ING International Growth I	AEIGX	A	(800) 992-0180	B+ / 8.8	-0.19	8.13	27.51 /92	22.22 /86	3.96 /46	1.37	1.35
FO	ING International Portfolio Cl S	IIPSX	C+	(800) 992-0180	B / 7.7	-3.90	6.12	21.89 /84	18.82 /76	--	2.18	1.26
FO	ING International Portfolio Cl S2	IIPTX	C+	(800) 992-0180	B / 7.6	-4.00	6.05	21.59 /84	18.61 /75	--	2.18	1.41
FO	ING International Small Cap A	NTKLX	B+	(800) 992-0180	A / 9.3	-3.96	8.27	32.72 /96	29.21 /95	11.97 /87	0.70	1.74
FO	ING International Small Cap B	NAPBX	B+	(800) 992-0180	A / 9.3	-4.11	7.95	31.91 /96	28.36 /94	11.26 /85	0.09	2.39
FO	ING International Small Cap C	NARCX	B+	(800) 992-0180	A / 9.4	-4.12	7.91	31.89 /96	28.35 /94	11.26 /85	0.27	2.39
FO	ING International Small Cap I	NAPIX	U	(800) 992-0180	U /	-3.85	8.54	--	--	--	0.00	1.24
FO	ING International Small Cap Q	NAGUX	B+	(800) 992-0180	A / 9.5	-3.93	8.37	33.02 /96	29.53 /95	12.31 /87	0.86	1.49
FO	● ING International Value A	NIVAX	A+	(800) 992-0180	A- / 9.2	0.46	10.68	27.69 /92	26.23 /92	11.51 /85	0.69	1.60
FO	● ING International Value B	NIVBX	A	(800) 992-0180	A- / 9.1	0.26	10.34	26.76 /91	25.34 /91	10.74 /83	0.04	2.30
FO	● ING International Value C	NIVCX	A+	(800) 992-0180	A- / 9.2	0.26	10.33	26.79 /91	25.34 /91	10.73 /83	0.14	2.30
FO	ING International Value Choice I	IVCIX	U	(800) 992-0180	U /	-0.67	6.40	--	--	--	0.00	1.45
FO	● ING International Value I	NIIVX	A+	(800) 992-0180	A / 9.3	0.51	10.91	28.16 /93	26.70 /93	11.98 /87	1.09	1.23
FO	● ING International Value Q	NQGVX	A+	(800) 992-0180	A / 9.3	0.51	10.78	27.88 /92	26.41 /93	11.71 /86	0.85	1.48
GR	ING Janus Contrarian Port S	IJCSX	C+	(800) 992-0180	B / 7.9	-3.56	4.48	20.35 /82	20.14 /80	8.92 /76	0.06	1.05
GR	ING Janus Contrarian Port S2	IJCTX	C+	(800) 992-0180	B / 7.8	-3.57	4.42	20.17 /82	19.98 /79	--	0.07	1.20
EM	ING JPMorgan Emrg Mkt Eq Port I		U	(800) 992-0180	U /	-2.58	7.98	--	--	--	0.00	1.30
EM	ING JPMorgan Emrg Mkt Eq Port S	IJPIX	C	(800) 992-0180	A+ / 9.6	-2.65	7.84	36.96 /97	30.81 /96	16.94 /94	0.06	1.50
EM	ING JPMorgan Emrg Mkt Eq Port S2	IJPTX	C	(800) 992-0180	A+ / 9.6	-2.66	7.82	36.83 /97	30.62 /96		0.07	1.65

● Denotes fund is closed to new investors
* Denotes fund is included in Section II

RISK			NET ASSETS		ASSET				Portfolio Turnover Ratio	BULL / BEAR		FUND MANAGER		MINIMUMS		LOADS	
Risk Rating/Pts	3 Year		NAV As of 6/30/06	Total $(Mil)	Cash %	Stocks %	Bonds %	Other %		Last Bull Market Return	Last Bear Market Return	Manager Quality Pct	Manager Tenure (Years)	Initial Purch. $	Additional Purch. $	Front End Load	Back End Load
	Standard Deviation	Beta															
B / 8.1	8.6	1.03	11.38	37	24	75	0	1	34.0	50.7	-11.1	21	5	0	0	0.0	0.0
B / 8.6	8.5	1.06	12.54	1	1	98	0	1	108.0	N/A	N/A	58	3	0	0	0.0	0.0
B / 8.6	8.5	1.07	12.70	N/A	1	98	0	1	108.0	N/A	N/A	61	3	0	0	0.0	0.0
B / 8.6	8.4	1.06	12.70	57	1	98	0	1	108.0	N/A	N/A	61	3	0	0	0.0	0.0
C / 4.5	14.3	1.61	7.11	70	0	99	0	1	76.0	74.6	-10.9	8	5	0	0	0.0	0.0
C / 4.5	14.2	1.60	7.08	6	0	99	0	1	76.0	73.7	-10.7	8	N/A	0	0	0.0	0.0
C+ / 5.8	10.4	1.24	12.81	45	2	97	0	1	44.0	55.5	-9.1	16	9	1,000	100	5.8	0.0
C+ / 5.7	10.4	1.24	12.52	8	2	97	0	1	44.0	51.9	-9.3	12	9	1,000	100	0.0	5.0
C+ / 5.7	10.4	1.25	12.40	2	2	97	0	1	44.0	52.0	-9.4	12	9	1,000	100	0.0	1.0
C+ / 5.8	10.4	1.24	13.28	22	2	97	0	1	44.0	57.1	-9.1	17	9	1,000,000	10,000	0.0	0.0
U /	N/A	N/A	10.82	57	9	90	0	1	N/A	N/A	N/A	N/A	1	1,000,000	0	0.0	0.0
B / 8.3	7.6	0.99	16.21	218	0	99	0	1	44.0	58.4	-9.6	45	5	1,000	0	3.0	0.0
B / 8.2	7.6	0.99	16.10	33	0	99	0	1	44.0	54.6	-9.8	37	5	1,000	0	0.0	5.0
B / 8.3	7.6	0.99	16.22	15	0	99	0	1	44.0	56.0	-9.8	40	5	1,000	0	0.0	1.0
B / 8.3	7.6	0.99	16.34	92	0	99	0	1	44.0	59.5	-9.6	48	5	1,000,000	10,000	0.0	0.0
C+ / 6.6	10.6	0.98	17.68	184	0	99	0	1	56.0	93.0	-8.2	42	N/A	1,000	0	3.0	0.0
C+ / 6.6	10.6	0.98	16.96	33	0	99	0	1	56.0	88.2	-8.4	34	N/A	1,000	0	0.0	5.0
C+ / 6.6	10.6	0.98	17.19	20	0	99	0	1	56.0	89.8	-8.3	37	N/A	1,000	0	0.0	1.0
C+ / 6.6	10.6	0.98	17.90	29	0	99	0	1	56.0	94.4	-8.2	45	N/A	1,000,000	10,000	0.0	0.0
U /	N/A	N/A	17.55	30	0	99	0	1	56.0	N/A	N/A	N/A	N/A	250,000	10,000	0.0	0.0
C+ / 6.4	13.4	0.91	18.84	70	1	98	0	1	38.0	112.1	-9.4	76	N/A	1,000	0	3.0	0.0
C+ / 6.3	13.4	0.91	17.81	16	1	98	0	1	38.0	107.2	-9.6	69	N/A	1,000	0	0.0	5.0
C+ / 6.3	13.4	0.91	18.11	8	1	98	0	1	38.0	109.1	-9.5	71	N/A	1,000	0	0.0	1.0
C+ / 6.4	13.4	0.91	19.24	14	1	98	0	1	38.0	113.8	-9.3	78	N/A	1,000,000	10,000	0.0	0.0
U /	N/A	N/A	10.45	40	19	80	0	1	N/A	N/A	N/A	N/A	1	1,000,000	0	0.0	0.0
C+ / 6.2	11.2	1.06	12.21	57	3	96	0	1	116.0	104.1	-9.8	9	N/A	1,000	0	5.8	2.0
B- / 7.0	11.1	1.06	11.77	17	3	96	0	1	116.0	99.0	-10.3	7	N/A	1,000	0	0.0	5.0
B- / 7.0	11.1	1.06	11.78	16	3	96	0	1	116.0	98.9	-10.3	7	N/A	1,000	0	0.0	1.0
B- / 7.1	11.1	1.06	12.16	12	3	96	0	1	116.0	106.1	-9.9	11	N/A	1,000,000	0	0.0	0.0
C / 5.2	11.1	1.06	12.11	27	3	96	0	1	116.0	105.0	-10.0	10	N/A	250,000	0	0.0	0.0
C+ / 6.9	10.7	1.03	10.18	33	3	96	0	1	102.0	119.0	-10.8	28	N/A	1,000	0	5.8	0.0
C+ / 6.8	10.6	1.03	9.93	4	3	96	0	1	102.0	114.2	-11.0	24	N/A	1,000	0	0.0	5.0
C+ / 6.8	10.6	1.02	9.93	2	3	96	0	1	102.0	113.9	-11.0	24	N/A	1,000	0	0.0	1.0
C+ / 6.9	10.6	1.03	10.24	7	3	96	0	1	102.0	120.2	-10.6	30	N/A	1,000,000	0	0.0	0.0
C / 5.1	11.3	1.07	11.10	176	1	98	0	1	123.0	105.8	-9.8	10	5	0	0	0.0	0.0
C / 5.1	11.3	1.07	11.05	10	1	98	0	1	123.0	104.9	-9.8	9	N/A	0	0	0.0	0.0
C / 5.4	13.4	1.23	44.37	236	2	97	0	1	124.0	177.0	-6.5	46	N/A	1,000	0	5.8	0.0
C / 5.4	13.4	1.23	45.77	60	2	97	0	1	124.0	171.3	-6.7	38	N/A	1,000	0	0.0	5.0
C / 5.4	13.4	1.23	41.87	64	2	97	0	1	124.0	171.3	-6.7	38	N/A	1,000	0	0.0	1.0
U /	N/A	N/A	44.50	85	2	97	0	1	124.0	N/A	N/A	N/A	N/A	100,000	0	0.0	0.0
C / 5.4	13.4	1.23	47.64	78	2	97	0	1	124.0	179.2	-6.5	49	N/A	250,000	0	0.0	0.0
C+ / 6.9	11.2	1.04	19.79	1,904	0	99	0	1	21.0	152.0	-10.6	65	N/A	1,000	0	5.8	0.0
C+ / 6.9	11.2	1.04	19.42	376	0	99	0	1	21.0	146.5	-10.7	56	N/A	1,000	0	0.0	5.0
C+ / 6.9	11.2	1.04	19.34	699	0	99	0	1	21.0	146.5	-10.6	56	N/A	1,000	0	0.0	1.0
U /	N/A	N/A	11.80	26	13	86	0	1	24.0	N/A	N/A	N/A	N/A	1,000,000	0	0.0	0.0
B- / 7.4	11.2	1.04	19.82	1,532	0	99	0	1	21.0	155.2	-10.4	69	N/A	1,000,000	0	0.0	0.0
B- / 7.4	11.2	1.04	19.83	27	0	99	0	1	21.0	153.1	-10.5	66	N/A	250,000	0	0.0	0.0
C / 5.4	11.5	1.30	13.29	109	2	97	0	1	47.0	132.3	-10.6	94	6	0	0	0.0	0.0
C / 5.4	11.5	1.29	13.22	5	2	97	0	1	47.0	131.1	-10.6	94	N/A	0	0	0.0	0.0
U /	N/A	N/A	15.84	125	5	94	0	1	85.0	N/A	N/A	N/A	1	0	0	0.0	0.0
D / 2.2	18.5	1.12	15.82	425	5	94	0	1	85.0	189.0	-8.5	6	1	0	0	0.0	0.0
D / 2.2	18.5	1.12	15.72	26	5	94	0	1	85.0	188.0	-8.6	6	1	0	0	0.0	0.0

					PERFORMANCE							
99 Pct = Best							Total Return % through 6/30/06				Incl. in Returns	
0 Pct = Worst		Overall Weiss			Perfor-					Annualized	Dividend	Expense
Fund		Investment	Ticker		mance						Dividend	Expense
Type	Fund Name	Rating	Symbol	Phone	Rating/Pts	3 Mo	6 Mo	1Yr / Pct	3Yr / Pct	5Yr / Pct	Yield	Ratio
FO	ING JPMorgan Fleming Intl ADV	A+	IIGAX	(800) 992-0180	B+ / 8.3	0.00	9.35	23.19 /86	20.09 /80	--	0.41	1.50
FO	ING JPMorgan Fleming Intl I	A+	ISGIX	(800) 992-0180	B+ / 8.5	0.07	9.61	23.73 /87	20.67 /82	6.04 /61	0.63	1.00
FO	ING JPMorgan Fleming Intl S	A+	ISGSX	(800) 992-0180	B+ / 8.4	0.14	9.52	23.58 /87	20.40 /81	--	0.60	1.25
MC	ING JPMorgan MidCap Val Port ADV	A+	IJMAX	(800) 992-0180	B- / 7.0	-0.27	6.05	9.66 /45	17.03 /68	--	0.16	1.60
MC	ING JPMorgan MidCap Val Port I	A+	IJMIX	(800) 992-0180	B- / 7.2	-0.13	6.28	10.23 /48	17.60 /71	--	0.48	1.10
MC	ING JPMorgan MidCap Val Port S	B-	IJMSX	(800) 992-0180	B- / 7.1	-0.20	6.15	10.01 /47	17.33 /69	--	0.26	1.35
SC	ING JPMorgan Sm Cap Eq Port I	U	IJSIX	(800) 992-0180	U /	-5.38	7.72	12.53 /62	--	--	0.00	0.89
SC	ING JPMorgan Sm Cap Eq Port S	C+	IJSSX	(800) 992-0180	B / 7.8	-5.48	7.59	12.15 /60	19.64 /78	--	0.00	1.14
SC	ING JPMorgan Sm Cap Eq Port S2	C+	IJSTX	(800) 992-0180	B / 7.7	-5.51	7.48	11.96 /59	19.43 /77	--	0.00	1.29
GR	ING JPMorgan Val Opp I	U	IJVIX	(800) 992-0180	U /	0.71	4.83	8.88 /39	--	--	0.00	N/A
GR	ING JPMorgan Val Opp S	U	IJVSX	(800) 992-0180	U /	0.54	4.66	8.49 /37	--	--	0.00	N/A
FO	ING Julius Baer Foreign Port I	U		(800) 992-0180	U /	-1.37	10.41	28.05 /93	--	--	0.12	0.92
FO	ING Julius Baer Foreign Port S	B-	IJBSX	(800) 992-0180	B+ / 8.8	-1.51	10.18	27.72 /92	21.98 /85	--	0.06	1.17
FO	ING Julius Baer Foreign Port S2	B-	IJBTX	(800) 992-0180	B+ / 8.8	-1.51	10.20	27.60 /92	21.82 /85	--	0.03	1.32
GR	ING Large Cap Gr A	E+	NLCAX	(800) 992-0180	D- / 1.3	-5.11	-3.03	2.82 / 7	9.21 /22	-4.02 / 4	0.00	1.44
GR	ING Large Cap Gr B	E	NLCBX	(800) 992-0180	D- / 1.1	-5.25	-3.30	2.17 / 5	8.50 /18	-4.65 / 3	0.00	2.09
GR	ING Large Cap Gr C	E+	NLCCX	(800) 992-0180	D / 1.6	-5.31	-3.31	2.18 / 5	8.49 /18	-4.65 / 3	0.00	2.09
GR	ING Large Cap Gr I	D	PLCIX	(800) 992-0180	D+ / 2.4	-5.02	-2.77	3.32 / 8	9.73 /25	--	0.00	0.99
GR	ING Large Cap Gr Q	D-	NLCQX	(800) 992-0180	D / 2.2	-5.12	-2.95	3.02 / 7	9.42 /24	-3.74 / 4	0.00	1.23
GR	ING Large Cap Value Fd A	U	IVLAX	(800) 992-0180	U /	0.87	10.21	8.27 /35	--	--	0.76	1.45
GR	ING Legg Mason Value Port I	U	ILVIX	(800) 992-0180	U /	-5.50	-4.70	3.26 / 8	--	--	0.00	0.79
GR	ING Legg Mason Value Port S	E+	ILVSX	(800) 992-0180	D / 1.9	-5.52	-4.81	3.06 / 7	9.03 /21	1.42 /23	0.00	1.04
GR	ING Legg Mason Value Port S2	E+	ILVTX	(800) 992-0180	D / 1.8	-5.54	-4.91	2.86 / 7	8.84 /20	--	0.00	1.19
AA	ING Life Style Moderate Portf S1	U	ILOSX	(800) 992-0180	U /	-1.10	2.73	7.74 /31	--	--	0.77	0.14
AG	ING Lifestyle Agg Growth S	U	ILSGX	(800) 992-0180	U /	-2.28	5.32	15.95 /75	--	--	0.07	N/A
AA	ING Lifestyle Growth Portfolio S	U	ILGSX	(800) 992-0180	U /	-2.04	4.44	13.05 /64	--	--	0.29	N/A
AA	ING Lifestyle Moderate Growth S	U	ILMSX	(800) 992-0180	U /	-1.40	3.37	9.76 /45	--	--	0.59	N/A
GI	ING Liquid Assets I	U	IPLXX	(800) 992-0180	U /	1.18	2.26	4.08 /11	--	--	4.00	0.29
GI	ING Liquid Assets S	D+	ISPXX	(800) 992-0180	E / 0.3	1.12	2.13	3.82 /10	2.05 / 1	1.89 /26	3.75	0.54
GI	ING Liquid Assets S2	D+	ITLXX	(800) 992-0180	E / 0.3	1.08	2.06	3.66 / 9	1.90 / 1	--	3.60	0.69
GI	ING Lord Abbett Affiliated I	C-		(800) 992-0180	C / 5.2	-0.47	5.59	12.03 /60	12.29 /44	--	1.33	0.75
GI	ING Lord Abbett Affiliated S	C-	ISLSX	(800) 992-0180	C / 5.0	-0.55	5.43	11.70 /58	12.00 /42	3.62 /42	1.12	1.00
GI	ING Lord Abbett Affiliated S2	C-	ILATX	(800) 992-0180	C / 4.9	-0.47	5.36	11.54 /57	11.85 /41	--	1.13	1.15
GI	ING MagnaCap A	C	PMCFX	(800) 992-0180	C / 4.4	-0.08	3.66	12.23 /61	12.58 /46	2.84 /35	0.95	1.06
GI	ING MagnaCap B	C	PMGBX	(800) 992-0180	C- / 3.9	-0.34	3.25	11.29 /55	11.72 /41	2.07 /28	0.20	1.87
GI	ING MagnaCap C	C+	PMGCX	(800) 992-0180	C / 4.6	-0.34	3.25	11.25 /55	11.70 /40	2.08 /28	0.18	1.87
GI	ING MagnaCap I	C	PMIGX	(800) 992-0180	C / 5.5	0.00	3.86	12.55 /62	12.95 /49	--	1.23	0.81
GI	ING MagnaCap M	C	PMCMX	(800) 992-0180	C / 4.4	-0.25	3.43	11.54 /57	12.03 /43	2.34 /30	0.50	1.62
FO	ING Marsico Intl Opp I	U		(800) 992-0180	U /	-3.23	6.54	30.83 /95	--	--	0.16	N/A
FO	ING Marsico Intl Opp S	U	IMISX	(800) 992-0180	U /	-3.24	6.47	30.59 /95	--	--	0.11	N/A
GR	ING Mercury Large Cap Growth S	D	IMLSX	(800) 992-0180	C- / 4.2	-6.44	-1.90	6.58 /24	12.45 /45	--	0.00	1.01
GR	ING Mercury Large Cap Growth S2	D	IMLTX	(800) 992-0180	C- / 3.9	-7.18	-2.68	6.23 /22	12.21 /44	--	0.00	N/A
GR	ING Mercury Large Cap Value I	U	IMVVX	(800) 992-0180	U /	-1.42	6.64	13.74 /67	--	--	0.00	0.80
GR	ING Mercury Large Cap Value S	C-	IMVSX	(800) 992-0180	C / 5.5	-1.50	6.50	13.51 /66	13.20 /50	--	0.00	1.05
GR	ING Mercury Large Cap Value S2	C-	IMVTX	(800) 992-0180	C / 5.4	-1.51	6.53	13.38 /66	13.04 /49	--	0.00	1.20
GR	ING MFS Capital Opportunities ADV	C-	ICAAX	(800) 992-0180	D+ / 2.5	-2.14	1.55	5.35 /17	8.94 /20	--	0.38	1.40
GR	ING MFS Capital Opportunities I	C-	IMOIX	(800) 992-0180	D+ / 2.9	-2.04	1.79	5.87 /20	9.46 /24	-2.16 / 8	0.77	0.90
GR	ING MFS Capital Opportunities S	C-	IMOSX	(800) 992-0180	D+ / 2.7	-2.09	1.69	5.58 /18	9.20 /22	--	0.48	1.15
MC	ING MFS Mid Cap Growth I	D-	IMMIX	(800) 992-0180	C- / 3.2	-7.49	-1.82	5.80 /19	11.02 /36	--	0.00	N/A
MC	ING MFS Mid Cap Growth S	D-	IMMSX	(800) 992-0180	C- / 3.1	-7.55	-1.92	5.57 /18	10.75 /33	-7.77 / 1	0.00	N/A
MC	ING MFS Mid Cap Growth S2	D-	IMMTX	(800) 992-0180	D+ / 2.9	-7.59	-2.01	5.41 /17	10.56 /31	--	0.00	N/A
IN	ING MFS Total Return A	C-	IMTAX	(800) 992-0180	D- / 1.1	-0.60	1.27	3.27 / 8	7.68 /13	--	2.06	1.25

● Denotes fund is closed to new investors
* Denotes fund is included in Section II

RISK			NET ASSETS		ASSET				Portfolio Turnover Ratio	BULL / BEAR		FUND MANAGER		MINIMUMS		LOADS	
	3 Year		NAV		Cash	Stocks	Bonds	Other		Last Bull	Last Bear	Manager	Manager	Initial	Additional	Front	Back
Risk Rating/Pts	Standard Deviation	Beta	As of 6/30/06	Total $(Mil)	%	%	%	%		Market Return	Market Return	Quality Pct	Tenure (Years)	Purch. $	Purch. $	End Load	End Load
B / 8.0	9.7	0.94	14.50	5	5	94	0	1	8.0	108.8	-11.4	30	5	0	0	0.0	0.0
B / 8.0	9.7	0.94	14.72	850	5	94	0	1	8.0	111.4	-11.2	34	5	0	0	0.0	0.0
B / 8.0	9.7	0.94	14.61	119	5	94	0	1	8.0	110.2	-11.3	32	5	0	0	0.0	0.0
B+ / 9.1	7.1	0.61	14.73	16	4	95	0	1	52.0	86.1	-5.1	93	4	0	0	0.0	0.0
B+ / 9.1	7.1	0.61	14.90	97	4	95	0	1	52.0	88.9	-5.0	94	3	0	0	0.0	0.0
C+ / 6.5	7.1	0.61	14.84	80	4	95	0	1	52.0	87.5	-5.0	93	3	0	0	0.0	0.0
U /	N/A	N/A	13.54	136	3	96	0	1	57.0	N/A	N/A	N/A	2	0	0	0.0	0.0
C / 4.9	13.6	0.91	13.46	219	3	96	0	1	57.0	109.1	-7.3	79	2	0	0	0.0	0.0
C / 4.9	13.7	0.91	13.37	50	3	96	0	1	57.0	108.2	-7.5	77	2	0	0	0.0	0.0
U /	N/A	N/A	11.28	212	2	97	0	1	N/A	N/A	N/A	N/A	N/A	1,000,000	0	0.0	0.0
U /	N/A	N/A	11.24	49	2	97	0	1	N/A	N/A	N/A	N/A	N/A	0	0	0.0	0.0
U /	N/A	N/A	14.43	593	2	97	0	1	92.0	N/A	N/A	N/A	3	0	0	0.0	0.0
C / 5.1	12.2	1.15	14.39	521	2	97	0	1	92.0	128.0	-10.5	14	3	0	0	0.0	0.0
C / 5.1	12.2	1.14	14.37	67	2	97	0	1	92.0	127.0	-10.5	14	3	0	0	0.0	0.0
C / 5.4	11.4	1.23	18.57	93	2	97	0	1	43.0	66.3	-11.0	21	N/A	1,000	0	5.8	0.0
C / 5.3	11.4	1.24	17.88	81	2	97	0	1	43.0	62.9	-11.1	17	N/A	1,000	0	0.0	5.0
C / 5.3	11.4	1.23	17.82	42	2	97	0	1	43.0	62.9	-11.2	17	N/A	1,000	0	0.0	1.0
C+ / 6.2	11.4	1.24	19.29	66	2	97	0	1	43.0	68.8	-10.8	24	N/A	1,000,000	0	0.0	0.0
C / 5.4	11.4	1.24	19.10	1	2	97	0	1	43.0	67.5	-10.9	22	N/A	250,000	0	0.0	0.0
U /	N/A	N/A	10.47	31	1	98	0	1	17.0	N/A	N/A	N/A	N/A	1,000	0	5.8	1.0
U /	N/A	N/A	10.13	243	0	98	0	2	11.0	N/A	N/A	N/A	2	0	0	0.0	0.0
C / 5.2	11.5	1.32	10.10	415	0	98	0	2	11.0	50.8	-7.7	16	2	0	0	0.0	0.0
C / 5.1	11.5	1.33	10.06	27	0	98	0	2	11.0	50.0	-7.7	14	2	0	0	0.0	0.0
U /	N/A	N/A	11.68	711	7	54	38	1	44.0	N/A	N/A	N/A	2	0	0	0.0	0.0
U /	N/A	N/A	12.87	918	0	100	0	0	48.0	N/A	N/A	N/A	2	0	0	0.0	0.0
U /	N/A	N/A	12.47	1,980	0	82	17	1	43.0	N/A	N/A	N/A	2	0	0	0.0	0.0
U /	N/A	N/A	11.97	1,637	0	66	33	1	41.0	N/A	N/A	N/A	2	0	0	0.0	0.0
U /	N/A	N/A	1.00	210	40	0	59	1	N/A	N/A	N/A	N/A	2	0	0	0.0	0.0
B+ / 9.9	0.4	N/A	1.00	884	40	0	59	1	N/A	5.8	0.3	53	2	0	0	0.0	0.0
B+ / 9.9	0.4	N/A	1.00	17	40	0	59	1	N/A	5.3	0.2	51	2	0	0	0.0	0.0
C+ / 6.2	8.0	0.99	12.65	68	3	96	0	1	141.0	N/A	N/A	68	1	0	0	0.0	0.0
C+ / 6.2	8.1	0.99	12.61	134	3	96	0	1	141.0	72.4	-11.8	65	1	0	0	0.0	0.0
C+ / 6.2	8.1	0.99	12.58	3	3	96	0	1	141.0	71.6	-11.8	64	1	0	0	0.0	0.0
B / 8.0	8.3	1.01	12.17	315	2	97	0	1	31.0	70.0	-10.9	69	N/A	1,000	0	5.8	0.0
B / 8.0	8.3	1.01	11.76	28	2	97	0	1	31.0	66.1	-11.0	61	N/A	1,000	0	0.0	5.0
B / 8.3	8.3	1.01	11.77	7	2	97	0	1	31.0	66.2	-11.0	60	N/A	1,000	0	0.0	1.0
C+ / 6.1	8.3	1.01	12.12	3	2	97	0	1	31.0	72.2	-10.8	72	N/A	1,000,000	0	0.0	0.0
B / 8.0	8.3	1.00	12.07	4	2	97	0	1	31.0	67.4	-10.9	64	N/A	1,000	0	3.5	0.0
U /	N/A	N/A	13.19	89	5	94	0	1	73.0	N/A	N/A	N/A	1	1,000,000	0	0.0	0.0
U /	N/A	N/A	13.16	189	5	94	0	1	73.0	N/A	N/A	N/A	1	0	0	0.0	0.0
C / 5.4	10.9	1.25	11.34	148	N/A	100	0	N/A	155.0	66.3	-8.5	43	4	0	0	0.0	0.0
C / 5.4	11.0	1.26	11.25	N/A	N/A	100	0	N/A	155.0	66.5	-8.6	40	4	0	0	0.0	0.0
U /	N/A	N/A	13.17	45	0	99	0	1	170.0	N/A	N/A	N/A	1	0	0	0.0	0.0
C / 5.4	10.9	1.30	13.11	58	0	99	0	1	170.0	76.4	-12.2	46	1	0	0	0.0	0.0
C / 5.4	11.0	1.31	13.06	4	0	99	0	1	170.0	75.6	-12.3	44	1	0	0	0.0	0.0
B / 8.3	8.6	1.06	27.45	N/A	2	97	0	1	95.0	59.4	-11.7	29	1	0	0	0.0	0.0
B / 8.3	8.6	1.06	27.89	177	2	97	0	1	95.0	62.0	-11.6	33	1	0	0	0.0	0.0
B / 8.3	8.6	1.06	27.70	N/A	2	97	0	1	95.0	60.7	-11.7	31	1	0	0	0.0	0.0
C / 4.6	13.5	1.15	11.85	7	0	99	0	1	N/A	N/A	N/A	3	N/A	1,000,000	0	0.0	0.0
C / 4.6	13.6	1.15	11.75	568	0	99	0	1	N/A	77.5	-7.0	3	N/A	0	0	0.0	0.0
C / 4.6	13.5	1.15	11.69	19	0	99	0	1	N/A	76.6	-7.0	3	N/A	0	0	0.0	0.0
B+ / 9.9	4.6	0.52	18.35	6	0	60	38	2	51.0	N/A	N/A	65	2	1,000	100	5.8	0.0

Fund Type	Fund Name	Ticker Symbol	Overall Weiss Investment Rating	Phone	Perfor-mance Rating/Pts	3 Mo	6 Mo	1Yr / Pct	3Yr / Pct	5Yr / Pct	Dividend Yield	Expense Ratio
IN	ING MFS Total Return I	IMTIX	C	(800) 992-0180	D / 2.2	-0.43	1.97	4.28 /12	8.31 /17	--	2.38	0.65
IN	ING MFS Total Return S	IMSRX	C	(800) 992-0180	D / 2.1	-0.48	1.87	3.99 /11	8.04 /15	5.26 /56	2.16	0.89
IN	ING MFS Total Return S2	IMTRX	C	(800) 992-0180	D / 2.0	-0.54	1.82	3.83 /10	7.88 /14	--	2.17	1.04
GI	ING MFS Utilities S	IMUSX	U	(800) 992-0180	U /	4.92	8.48	16.64 /76	--	--	0.64	0.93
MC	ING Mid Cap Opportunities A	NMCAX	D	(800) 992-0180	C / 4.6	-5.95	4.62	15.10 /72	14.18 /55	1.66 /25	0.00	1.50
MC	ING Mid Cap Opportunities B	NMCBX	D	(800) 992-0180	C / 4.3	-6.08	4.28	14.33 /69	13.39 /51	0.96 /20	0.00	2.25
MC	ING Mid Cap Opportunities C	NMCCX	D	(800) 992-0180	C / 4.9	-6.11	4.23	14.24 /69	13.33 /50	0.92 /20	0.00	2.25
MC	ING Mid Cap Opportunities I	NMCIX	C-	(800) 992-0180	C+ / 5.7	-5.84	4.90	15.59 /73	14.57 /57	2.09 /28	0.00	1.25
MC	ING Mid Cap Opportunities Q	NMCQX	C-	(800) 992-0180	C+ / 5.6	-5.88	4.70	15.32 /73	14.40 /56	1.86 /26	0.00	1.50
MC	ING Mid Cap Value A	IMVAX	C-	(800) 992-0180	C / 4.5	1.67	6.20	3.12 / 8	13.67 /52	--	0.00	1.75
MC	ING Mid Cap Value B	IMVBX	D+	(800) 992-0180	C- / 4.0	1.50	5.82	2.38 / 5	12.78 /47	--	0.00	2.50
MC	ING Mid Cap Value C	IMVCX	C-	(800) 992-0180	C / 4.7	1.50	5.94	2.40 / 5	12.83 /48	--	0.00	2.50
GR	ING Mid Cap Value Choice A	PAVAX	U	(800) 992-0180	U /	1.29	12.43	31.07 /95	--	--	0.28	1.50
MC	ING Mid Cap Value I	IMVIX	C	(800) 992-0180	C+ / 5.6	1.74	6.43	3.37 / 8	14.02 /54	--	0.00	1.50
MC	ING Mid Cap Value Q	IMVQX	C	(800) 992-0180	C / 5.3	1.67	6.33	3.22 / 8	13.56 /52	--	0.00	1.75
BA	ING OpCap Balanced Value ADV	IOBAX	C-	(800) 992-0180	D / 2.0	-1.87	0.00	2.46 / 5	8.41 /17	--	0.20	1.50
BA	ING OpCap Balanced Value I	ICBIX	C-	(800) 992-0180	D+ / 2.3	-1.78	0.22	2.97 / 7	8.93 /20	--	0.64	1.00
BA	ING OpCap Balanced Value S	IOBSX	C-	(800) 992-0180	D / 2.1	-1.85	0.15	2.77 / 7	8.66 /19	--	0.37	1.25
GL	ING Oppenheimer Glb Port ADV	IGMAX	B+	(800) 992-0180	B- / 7.0	-3.36	3.75	18.65 /80	17.34 /69	--	0.25	1.15
GL	ING Oppenheimer Glb Port I	IGMIX	B+	(800) 992-0180	B- / 7.4	-3.22	4.02	19.26 /81	18.30 /74	--	0.79	0.66
GL	ING Oppenheimer Glb Port S	IGMSX	B+	(800) 992-0180	B- / 7.2	-3.28	3.88	18.99 /80	17.62 /71	--	0.69	0.91
GR	ING Oppenheimer Main Street I	IOMIX	C-	(800) 992-0180	C / 4.5	-1.91	3.04	9.77 /45	11.70 /40	--	1.11	0.64
GR	ING Oppenheimer Main Street S	IOMSX	C-	(800) 992-0180	C / 4.4	-1.97	2.92	9.48 /43	11.42 /39	0.74 /19	0.86	0.89
GR	ING Oppenheimer Main Street S2	IOMTX	C-	(800) 992-0180	C / 4.3	-1.97	2.88	9.33 /42	11.26 /38	--	0.88	1.04
GI	ING PIMCO Total Return ADV	IPRAX	D+	(800) 992-0180	E- / 0.1	-0.28	-0.93	-1.41 / 1	1.67 / 0	--	1.48	1.35
GI	ING PIMCO Total Return I	IPTIX	D+	(800) 992-0180	E- / 0.1	-0.18	-0.73	-1.00 / 1	2.18 / 1	--	1.85	0.85
GI	ING PIMCO Total Return S	IPTSX	D+	(800) 992-0180	E- / 0.1	-0.28	-0.83	-1.20 / 1	1.93 / 1	--	1.66	1.10
GI	ING Pioneer I	IPPIX	U	(800) 992-0180	U /	0.09	5.16	12.48 /62	--	--	0.43	N/A
MC	ING Pioneer Mid Cap Value I	IPVIX	U	(800) 992-0180	U /	-3.29	1.27	4.79 /14	--	--	0.00	N/A
GI	ING Pioneer S	IPPSX	U	(800) 992-0180	U /	0.00	5.07	12.31 /61	--	--	0.37	N/A
PM	ING Precious Metals A	LEXMX	D+	(800) 992-0180	A+ / 9.7	-2.29	20.11	67.59 /99	27.11 /93	30.19 /99	0.13	1.56
RE	ING Real Estate Fd A	CLARX	C+	(800) 992-0180	A / 9.3	-0.60	15.08	23.44 /86	27.41 /93	--	2.50	1.45
RE	ING Real Estate Fd B	CRBCX	C+	(800) 992-0180	A- / 9.2	-0.77	14.62	22.59 /85	26.50 /93	--	2.02	2.20
RE	ING Real Estate Fd C	CRCRX	C+	(800) 992-0180	A / 9.3	-0.74	14.69	22.58 /85	26.44 /93	--	1.92	2.20
RE	ING Real Estate Fd I	CRARX	C	(800) 992-0180	A / 9.4	-0.45	15.24	23.83 /87	27.77 /94	19.97 /96	2.73	0.87
RE	ING Real Estate Fd O	IDROX	U	(800) 992-0180	U /	-0.53	15.10	23.49 /87	--	--	2.67	1.23
EM	ING Russia A	LETRX	C	(800) 992-0180	A+ / 9.9	3.32	27.84	91.70 /99	41.58 /99	42.61 /99	0.00	2.13
AG	ING Salomon Bros Aggressive Gr	IMEAX	C	(800) 992-0180	C- / 4.1	-3.62	0.64	14.67 /71	11.42 /39	--	0.00	1.31
AG	ING Salomon Bros Aggressive Gr I	IMEIX	C	(800) 992-0180	C / 4.5	-3.50	0.90	15.24 /72	11.98 /42	-0.78 /12	0.00	0.81
AG	ING Salomon Bros Aggressive Gr S	IMESX	C	(800) 992-0180	C / 4.3	-3.58	0.75	14.93 /72	11.71 /41	--	0.00	1.06
GR	ING Salomon Bros All Cap S	ISASX	C-	(800) 992-0180	C / 5.0	-1.14	4.59	11.49 /57	12.13 /43	3.35 /40	0.46	1.00
GR	ING Salomon Bros All Cap S2	ISATX	C-	(800) 992-0180	C / 4.9	-1.21	4.45	11.28 /55	11.95 /42	--	0.53	1.15
GR	ING Salomon Bros Lg Cap Gr ADV	IAPPX	E+	(800) 992-0180	E / 0.4	-6.79	-6.79	2.11 / 5	5.01 / 4	--	0.00	1.34
GR	ING Salomon Bros Lg Cap Gr I	IAAIX	E+	(800) 992-0180	E / 0.5	-6.60	-6.52	2.65 / 6	5.54 / 5	--	0.00	0.84
GR	ING Salomon Bros Lg Cap Gr S	IACSX	E+	(800) 992-0180	E / 0.5	-6.74	-6.74	2.38 / 5	5.25 / 4	--	0.00	1.09
SC	ING Small Cap Value A	IVSAX	D-	(800) 992-0180	C / 5.1	-3.14	1.50	1.04 / 3	16.12 /64	--	0.00	1.75
SC	ING Small Cap Value B	IVSBX	D-	(800) 992-0180	C / 4.7	-3.35	1.14	0.27 / 2	15.24 /60	--	0.00	2.50
SC	ING Small Cap Value C	IVSCX	D-	(800) 992-0180	C / 5.3	-3.36	1.14	0.37 / 2	15.26 /60	--	0.00	2.50
SC	ING Small Cap Value I	IVSIX	D	(800) 992-0180	C+ / 6.1	-3.10	1.67	1.38 / 3	16.47 /66	--	0.00	1.50
SC	ING Small Cap Value Q	IVSQX	D	(800) 992-0180	C+ / 6.0	-3.17	1.57	1.12 / 3	16.25 /65	--	0.00	1.75
SC	ING Small Company A	AESAX	C	(800) 992-0180	B- / 7.1	-3.99	8.73	17.79 /79	18.02 /73	7.02 /67	0.00	1.50
SC	ING Small Company B	ASMLX	C	(800) 992-0180	C+ / 6.8	-4.19	8.34	16.92 /77	17.16 /69	6.22 /62	0.00	2.25

● Denotes fund is closed to new investors
* Denotes fund is included in Section II

www.WeissRatings.com

Risk Rating/Pts	3 Year Standard Deviation	Beta	NAV As of 6/30/06	Total $(Mil)	Cash %	Stocks %	Bonds %	Other %	Portfolio Turnover Ratio	Last Bull Market Return	Last Bear Market Return	Manager Quality Pct	Manager Tenure (Years)	Initial Purch. $	Additional Purch. $	Front End Load	Back End Load
B+ / 9.9	4.6	0.53	18.62	163	0	60	38	2	51.0	N/A	N/A	70	2	0	0	0.0	0.0
B+ / 9.9	4.6	0.52	18.57	1,378	0	60	38	2	51.0	42.0	-4.7	69	2	1,000	100	0.0	0.0
B+ / 9.9	4.6	0.53	18.45	50	0	60	38	2	51.0	41.1	-4.7	66	2	0	0	0.0	0.0
U /	N/A	N/A	12.15	168	2	92	4	2	152.0	N/A	N/A	N/A	N/A	0	0	0.0	0.0
C / 4.6	13.7	1.21	15.17	121	0	99	0	1	55.0	87.4	-11.2	8	N/A	1,000	0	5.8	0.0
C / 4.6	13.7	1.20	14.36	104	0	99	0	1	55.0	83.1	-11.2	7	N/A	1,000	0	0.0	5.0
C / 4.6	13.7	1.21	14.28	89	0	99	0	1	55.0	83.2	-11.4	6	N/A	1,000	0	0.0	1.0
C / 5.5	13.6	1.20	15.64	3	0	99	0	1	55.0	89.3	-11.1	10	N/A	1,000,000	10,000	0.0	0.0
C / 5.5	13.7	1.21	15.36	5	0	99	0	1	55.0	88.6	-11.2	9	N/A	250,000	10,000	0.0	0.0
C+ / 6.2	16.3	1.22	9.76	41	3	96	0	1	24.0	106.5	-15.8	7	N/A	1,000	0	5.8	0.0
C+ / 6.2	16.3	1.22	9.46	25	3	96	0	1	24.0	101.7	-16.0	5	N/A	1,000	0	0.0	5.0
C+ / 6.2	16.3	1.22	9.46	25	3	96	0	1	24.0	101.8	-16.0	5	N/A	1,000	0	0.0	1.0
U /	N/A	N/A	13.39	46	12	73	14	1	23.0	N/A	N/A	N/A	N/A	1,000	100	5.8	1.0
C+ / 6.2	16.4	1.22	9.93	1	3	96	0	1	24.0	108.9	-15.7	7	N/A	1,000,000	10,000	0.0	0.0
C+ / 6.2	16.3	1.22	9.74	N/A	3	96	0	1	24.0	106.4	-15.9	6	N/A	250,000	10,000	0.0	0.0
B / 8.7	7.5	1.40	13.62	3	20	57	21	2	80.0	53.0	-5.7	41	5	0	0	0.0	0.0
B / 8.8	7.5	1.40	13.81	5	20	57	21	2	80.0	55.3	-5.5	46	3	0	0	0.0	0.0
B / 8.7	7.5	1.40	13.76	84	20	57	21	2	80.0	54.1	-5.6	43	5	0	0	0.0	0.0
B- / 7.7	10.2	0.93	14.37	118	0	99	0	1	53.0	95.4	-8.8	17	N/A	0	0	0.0	0.0
B- / 7.7	10.3	0.93	14.74	2,315	0	99	0	1	53.0	100.7	-8.7	22	N/A	0	0	0.0	0.0
B- / 7.7	10.2	0.92	14.44	88	0	99	0	1	53.0	97.0	-8.8	18	N/A	0	0	0.0	0.0
C+ / 6.1	8.2	1.04	17.97	4	0	99	0	1	80.0	N/A	N/A	58	2	0	0	0.0	0.0
C+ / 6.1	8.2	1.04	17.95	538	0	99	0	1	80.0	65.6	-9.0	55	2	0	0	0.0	0.0
C+ / 6.1	8.2	1.03	17.88	5	0	99	0	1	80.0	64.8	-9.0	53	2	0	0	0.0	0.0
B+ / 9.9	3.8	-0.04	10.71	26	8	0	91	1	926.0	7.7	3.5	52	N/A	0	0	0.0	0.0
B+ / 9.9	3.9	-0.04	10.84	224	8	0	91	1	926.0	9.4	3.7	59	N/A	0	0	0.0	0.0
B+ / 9.9	3.9	-0.04	10.78	85	8	0	91	1	926.0	8.6	3.6	55	N/A	0	0	0.0	0.0
U /	N/A	N/A	11.61	28	0	99	0	1	N/A	N/A	N/A	N/A	N/A	1,000,000	0	0.0	0.0
U /	N/A	N/A	11.16	98	1	98	0	1	N/A	N/A	N/A	N/A	N/A	1,000,000	0	0.0	0.0
U /	N/A	N/A	11.60	80	0	99	0	1	N/A	N/A	N/A	N/A	N/A	0	0	0.0	0.0
E- / 0.0	31.8	1.51	10.69	129	4	95	0	1	78.1	150.2	13.3	21	8	1,000	0	5.8	0.0
C- / 4.1	16.8	1.00	17.41	111	1	98	0	1	24.0	128.9	N/A	82	N/A	1,000	0	5.8	0.0
C- / 4.1	16.8	1.00	17.44	5	1	98	0	1	24.0	123.8	N/A	77	N/A	1,000	0	0.0	5.0
C- / 4.1	16.8	1.00	18.00	3	1	98	0	1	24.0	123.4	N/A	76	N/A	1,000	0	0.0	1.0
D+ / 2.7	16.8	1.00	18.30	151	1	98	0	1	24.0	131.0	0.6	84	N/A	1,000,000	0	0.0	0.8
U /	N/A	N/A	17.40	29	1	98	0	1	24.0	N/A	N/A	N/A	N/A	0	0	0.0	0.0
D / 1.6	27.9	1.19	50.15	630	5	94	0	1	26.0	304.0	9.4	42	5	1,000	0	5.8	2.0
B- / 7.9	10.4	1.18	43.92	12	4	95	0	1	10.0	79.6	-9.9	40	N/A	0	0	0.0	0.0
B- / 7.9	10.4	1.18	44.92	975	4	95	0	1	10.0	82.4	-9.8	46	N/A	0	0	0.0	0.0
B- / 7.9	10.4	1.18	44.41	179	4	95	0	1	10.0	81.0	-9.8	43	N/A	0	0	0.0	0.0
C+ / 5.9	9.6	1.17	13.91	369	4	95	0	1	37.0	77.1	-12.9	48	6	0	0	0.0	0.0
C+ / 5.9	9.5	1.16	13.84	23	4	95	0	1	37.0	76.3	-13.0	47	4	0	0	0.0	0.0
C+ / 6.6	13.5	1.34	10.71	20	0	99	0	1	27.0	N/A	N/A	3	N/A	0	0	0.0	0.0
C+ / 6.6	13.5	1.34	10.90	18	0	99	0	1	27.0	N/A	N/A	4	N/A	0	0	0.0	0.0
C+ / 6.6	13.5	1.33	10.79	12	0	99	0	1	27.0	N/A	N/A	4	N/A	0	0	0.0	0.0
C- / 3.2	18.8	1.07	10.18	32	0	99	0	1	14.0	115.0	-19.0	25	N/A	1,000	0	5.8	0.0
C- / 3.2	18.8	1.07	9.80	15	0	99	0	1	14.0	109.9	-19.2	19	N/A	1,000	0	0.0	5.0
C- / 3.2	18.8	1.07	9.79	20	0	99	0	1	14.0	109.9	-19.2	20	N/A	1,000	0	0.0	1.0
C- / 3.2	18.8	1.07	10.33	N/A	0	99	0	1	14.0	117.2	-19.0	27	N/A	1,000,000	0	0.0	0.0
C- / 3.2	18.8	1.07	10.38	N/A	0	99	0	1	14.0	115.9	-19.1	26	N/A	250,000	0	0.0	0.0
C / 5.1	13.8	0.91	18.31	88	5	94	0	1	47.0	111.3	-10.3	65	N/A	1,000	0	5.8	0.0
C / 5.1	13.8	0.91	18.05	8	5	94	0	1	47.0	106.3	-10.4	56	N/A	1,000	0	0.0	5.0

						PERFORMANCE							
	99 Pct = Best							Total Return % through 6/30/06				Incl. in Returns	
	0 Pct = Worst		Overall Weiss		Perfor- mance					Annualized		Dividend	Expense
Fund Type	Fund Name	Ticker Symbol	Investment Rating	Phone	Rating/Pts	3 Mo	6 Mo	1Yr / Pct	3Yr / Pct	5Yr / Pct		Yield	Ratio
SC	ING Small Company C	ASCCX	C	(800) 992-0180	B- / 7.2	-4.22	8.33	16.89 /77	17.16 /69	6.19 /62		0.00	2.25
SC	ING Small Company I	AESGX	C+	(800) 992-0180	B / 7.7	-3.96	8.80	18.01 /79	18.30 /74	7.27 /68		0.00	1.25
SC	● ING SmallCap Opportunities A	NSPAX	C-	(800) 992-0180	C+ / 5.9	-6.47	5.98	14.54 /70	15.81 /63	-4.77 / 3		0.00	1.50
SC	● ING SmallCap Opportunities B	NSPBX	D+	(800) 992-0180	C+ / 5.6	-6.65	5.60	13.70 /67	15.00 /59	-5.45 / 2		0.00	2.25
SC	● ING SmallCap Opportunities C	NSPCX	C-	(800) 992-0180	C+ / 6.1	-6.63	5.57	13.68 /67	14.98 /59	-5.44 / 2		0.00	2.25
SC	ING SmallCap Opportunities I	NSPIX	C+	(800) 992-0180	C+ / 6.9	-6.35	6.27	15.10 /72	16.34 /65	-4.39 / 3		0.00	1.05
SC	ING SmallCap Opportunities Q	NSPQX	C	(800) 992-0180	C+ / 6.7	-6.41	6.08	14.79 /71	16.04 /64	-4.61 / 3		0.00	1.30
AA	ING Solution 2025 Portfolio Class S	ISZSX	U	(800) 992-0180	U /	-1.48	2.73	8.34 /35	--	--		0.00	1.04
GR	ING Stock Index Portfolio Class I	INGIX	U	(800) 992-0180	U /	-1.43	2.63	8.33 /35	--	--		0.00	N/A
AA	ING Strategic Allocation Consv A	ATLAX	D+	(800) 992-0180	E+ / 0.6	-1.22	1.06	3.33 / 8	6.13 / 7	3.25 /39		1.93	1.15
AA	ING Strategic Allocation Consv B	ALYBX	D+	(800) 992-0180	E / 0.4	-1.41	0.67	2.55 / 6	5.32 / 5	2.49 /32		1.58	1.90
AA	ING Strategic Allocation Consv C	ACLGX	D+	(800) 992-0180	E+ / 0.7	-1.40	0.67	2.57 / 6	5.32 / 5	2.47 /32		1.41	1.90
AA	ING Strategic Allocation Consv I	ALEGX	C-	(800) 992-0180	D- / 1.2	-1.21	1.14	3.55 / 9	6.38 / 8	3.50 /41		2.27	0.90
AA	ING Strategic Allocation Growth A	ATAAX	C-	(800) 992-0180	D+ / 2.9	-1.98	2.66	8.38 /36	10.76 /33	3.39 /40		0.78	1.25
AA	ING Strategic Allocation Growth B	AAFBX	C-	(800) 992-0180	D+ / 2.5	-2.17	2.27	7.63 /30	9.94 /27	2.64 /33		0.38	2.00
AA	ING Strategic Allocation Growth C	AAFCX	C-	(800) 992-0180	C- / 3.1	-2.15	2.34	7.67 /30	9.95 /27	2.62 /33		0.38	2.00
AA	ING Strategic Allocation Growth I	ASCEX	C	(800) 992-0180	C- / 4.1	-1.89	2.80	8.74 /38	11.06 /36	3.65 /42		1.04	1.00
BA	ING Strategic Allocation Moderate A	ATCAX	C-	(800) 992-0180	D- / 1.5	-1.80	1.78	5.62 /18	8.41 /17	3.29 /39		1.30	1.20
BA	ING Strategic Allocation Moderate B	ACFBX	C-	(800) 992-0180	D- / 1.2	-1.99	1.46	4.83 /14	7.64 /13	2.55 /32		0.93	1.95
BA	ING Strategic Allocation Moderate C	ACCRX	C-	(800) 992-0180	D / 1.7	-1.96	1.44	4.88 /14	7.65 /13	2.55 /32		0.86	1.95
BA	ING Strategic Allocation Moderate I	ACROX	C	(800) 992-0180	D+ / 2.5	-1.70	1.94	5.89 /20	8.71 /19	3.58 /42		1.59	0.95
AA	ING T. Rowe Price Cap App A	ITRAX	U	(800) 992-0180	U /	-0.97	2.98	9.36 /42	--	--		1.35	N/A
AA	ING T. Rowe Price Cap App I	ITRIX	B+	(800) 992-0180	C+ / 5.9	-0.80	3.26	10.02 /47	14.38 /56	--		1.39	N/A
AA	ING T. Rowe Price Cap App S2		B+	(800) 992-0180	C+ / 5.7	-0.88	3.08	9.60 /44	13.97 /54	--		1.22	N/A
AG	ING T. Rowe Price Div Mid Cap ADV	IAXAX	C	(800) 992-0180	C / 4.7	-5.29	1.42	11.58 /57	12.34 /45	--		0.00	1.15
AG	ING T. Rowe Price Div Mid Cap I	IAXIX	C	(800) 992-0180	C / 5.1	-5.08	1.62	12.14 /60	12.89 /48	--		0.00	0.66
AG	ING T. Rowe Price Div Mid Cap S	IAXSX	C	(800) 992-0180	C / 4.9	-5.24	1.52	11.88 /59	12.61 /46	--		0.00	0.91
IN	ING T. Rowe Price Eq Income A	IRPAX	C+	(800) 992-0180	C- / 4.0	-0.42	4.30	8.87 /39	12.43 /45	--		1.13	1.10
IN	ING T. Rowe Price Eq Income I		C	(800) 992-0180	C / 5.4	-0.21	5.22	9.87 /46	13.04 /49	--		1.24	N/A
IN	ING T. Rowe Price Eq Income S	IRPSX	B	(800) 992-0180	C / 5.3	-0.28	5.08	9.68 /45	12.78 /47	6.12 /62		1.07	0.95
IN	ING T. Rowe Price Eq Income S2	ITETX	C	(800) 992-0180	C / 5.2	-0.35	5.03	9.44 /43	12.62 /46	--		1.04	N/A
GR	ING T. Rowe Price Growth Eq ADV	IGEAX	C	(800) 992-0180	C- / 3.2	-3.12	0.50	7.86 /32	9.93 /27	--		0.09	1.25
GR	ING T. Rowe Price Growth Eq I	ITGIX	C	(800) 992-0180	C- / 3.5	-3.00	0.76	8.42 /36	10.47 /31	2.82 /35		0.47	0.75
GR	ING T. Rowe Price Growth Eq S	ITGSX	C	(800) 992-0180	C- / 3.3	-3.05	0.63	8.14 /34	10.20 /29	--		0.44	1.00
GL	ING Templeton Glb Gr S		C+	(800) 992-0180	B- / 7.3	1.12	6.47	19.67 /81	16.44 /65	5.56 /58		0.64	N/A
GL	ING Templeton Glb Gr S2	ICGGX	C+	(800) 992-0180	B- / 7.2	1.05	6.35	19.45 /81	16.26 /65	--		0.66	N/A
AA	ING UBS U.S. Allocation S		C+	(800) 992-0180	D+ / 2.8	-1.56	1.00	6.03 /21	9.28 /23	3.11 /38		1.24	N/A
AA	ING UBS U.S. Allocation S2		C+	(800) 992-0180	D+ / 2.7	-1.56	1.00	5.96 /20	9.19 /22	--		1.26	N/A
GR	ING UBS U.S. Large Cap Eq ADV	IMRAX	C+	(800) 992-0180	C / 4.6	-2.21	1.31	8.56 /37	12.14 /43	--		0.69	1.35
GR	ING UBS U.S. Large Cap Eq I	IMRIX	B-	(800) 992-0180	C / 4.9	-2.18	1.40	9.00 /40	12.66 /47	1.61 /24		0.84	0.85
GR	ING UBS U.S. Large Cap Eq S	IMRSX	B-	(800) 992-0180	C / 4.7	-2.20	1.30	8.75 /38	12.42 /45	--		0.76	1.10
AA	ING Van Kamp Eq & Inc Port ADV	IUAAX	B-	(800) 992-0180	C / 4.3	0.03	2.00	7.91 /32	11.39 /38	--		0.02	1.07
AA	ING Van Kamp Eq & Inc Port I	IUAIX	B-	(800) 992-0180	C / 4.6	0.14	2.24	8.44 /36	11.95 /42	--		0.08	0.57
AA	ING Van Kamp Eq & Inc Port S	IUASX	B-	(800) 992-0180	C / 4.5	0.08	2.12	8.17 /34	11.67 /40	--		0.00	0.82
GR	ING Van Kampen ComStock ADV	IVKAX	B	(800) 992-0180	C / 5.1	0.73	3.48	8.48 /37	12.68 /47	--		0.33	1.37
GR	ING Van Kampen ComStock I	IVKIX	B	(800) 992-0180	C / 5.4	0.79	3.76	9.06 /40	13.25 /50	--		0.60	0.87
GR	ING Van Kampen ComStock S	IVKSX	B	(800) 992-0180	C / 5.3	0.80	3.62	8.81 /39	12.96 /49	--		0.50	1.12
GI	ING Van Kampen Eq Gr Port I	IVKEX	U	(800) 992-0180	U /	-3.60	-2.95	12.04 /60	--	--		0.48	0.66
GI	ING Van Kampen Eq Gr Port S	IVKGX	D-	(800) 992-0180	D+ / 2.9	-3.61	-2.96	11.74 /58	10.43 /30	--		0.31	0.91
GI	ING Van Kampen Eq Gr Port S2	IVKTX	D-	(800) 992-0180	D+ / 2.8	-3.71	-3.14	11.60 /57	10.24 /29	--		0.23	1.06
GI	ING Van Kampen Glb Franch S	IVGTX	B-	(800) 992-0180	B- / 7.5	2.32	8.00	15.89 /74	17.13 /69	--		0.18	1.25
GI	ING Van Kampen Glb Franch S2		B-	(800) 992-0180	B- / 7.4	2.26	7.88	15.72 /74	16.95 /68	--		0.12	1.40

● Denotes fund is closed to new investors
* Denotes fund is included in Section II

www.WeissRatings.com

RISK	NET ASSETS				ASSET					BULL / BEAR		FUND MANAGER		MINIMUMS		LOADS	
	3 Year		NAV						Portfolio	Last Bull	Last Bear	Manager	Manager	Initial	Additional	Front	Back
Risk Rating/Pts	Standard Deviation	Beta	As of 6/30/06	Total $(Mil)	Cash %	Stocks %	Bonds %	Other %	Turnover Ratio	Market Return	Market Return	Quality Pct	Tenure (Years)	Purch. $	Purch. $	End Load	End Load
C / 5.0	13.8	0.92	17.94	4	5	94	0	1	47.0	106.0	-10.3	56	N/A	1,000	0	0.0	1.0
C / 5.2	13.8	0.91	19.16	17	5	94	0	1	47.0	112.8	-10.2	67	N/A	1,000,000	0	0.0	0.0
C / 4.4	14.8	0.95	29.06	88	5	94	0	1	52.0	97.1	-16.0	36	N/A	1,000	0	5.8	0.0
C / 4.4	14.8	0.95	26.40	30	5	94	0	1	52.0	92.7	-16.1	30	N/A	1,000	0	0.0	5.0
C / 4.4	14.8	0.95	26.34	38	5	94	0	1	52.0	92.7	-16.1	30	N/A	1,000	0	0.0	1.0
C+ / 5.7	14.8	0.95	29.65	3	5	94	0	1	52.0	99.9	-15.9	40	N/A	1,000,000	0	0.0	0.0
C+ / 5.7	14.8	0.95	29.33	N/A	5	94	0	1	52.0	98.4	-16.0	37	N/A	250,000	0	0.0	0.0
U /	N/A	N/A	11.30	31	0	66	33	1	47.0	N/A	N/A	N/A	1	0	0	0.0	0.0
U /	N/A	N/A	11.70	390	3	96	0	1	N/A	N/A	N/A	N/A	1	0	0	0.0	0.0
B+ / 9.1	4.2	0.84	10.50	30	8	49	41	2	197.0	30.1	-1.5	48	4	1,000	0	5.8	0.0
B+ / 9.4	4.2	0.84	10.47	5	8	49	41	2	197.0	27.1	-1.6	39	4	1,000	0	0.0	5.0
B+ / 9.4	4.2	0.85	10.57	1	8	49	41	2	197.0	27.2	-1.8	39	4	1,000	0	0.0	1.0
B+ / 9.3	4.2	0.84	10.62	9	8	49	41	2	197.0	31.3	-1.5	52	4	1,000,000	0	0.0	0.0
B / 8.0	7.3	1.43	12.36	59	2	88	9	1	127.0	60.3	-7.1	65	4	1,000	0	5.8	0.0
B / 8.0	7.3	1.44	12.19	17	2	88	9	1	127.0	56.6	-7.2	56	4	1,000	0	0.0	5.0
B / 8.0	7.3	1.43	12.27	2	2	88	9	1	127.0	56.4	-7.2	57	4	1,000	0	0.0	1.0
B / 8.0	7.2	1.43	12.47	23	2	88	9	1	127.0	61.4	-7.0	68	4	1,000,000	0	0.0	0.0
B+ / 9.2	5.8	1.17	11.98	71	5	74	20	1	162.0	45.1	-4.7	55	4	1,000	0	5.8	0.0
B+ / 9.2	5.7	1.16	11.85	18	5	74	20	1	162.0	41.8	-4.8	46	4	1,000	0	0.0	5.0
B+ / 9.2	5.8	1.18	12.01	2	5	74	20	1	162.0	41.9	-4.8	45	4	1,000	0	0.0	1.0
B+ / 9.2	5.7	1.17	12.11	17	5	74	20	1	162.0	46.5	-4.6	59	4	1,000,000	0	0.0	0.0
U /	N/A	N/A	25.60	61	17	69	0	14	N/A	N/A	N/A	N/A	5	0	0	0.0	0.0
B+ / 9.1	6.9	1.32	25.99	85	17	69	0	14	N/A	N/A	N/A	92	5	0	0	0.0	0.0
B+ / 9.1	6.9	1.33	25.80	103	17	69	0	14	N/A	69.3	-3.6	91	5	0	0	0.0	0.0
C+ / 6.7	13.8	1.46	8.59	67	2	97	0	1	94.0	83.1	-8.5	27	N/A	0	0	0.0	0.0
C+ / 6.7	13.9	1.46	8.79	1,105	2	97	0	1	94.0	86.2	-8.5	31	N/A	0	0	0.0	0.0
C+ / 6.7	13.8	1.46	8.68	24	2	97	0	1	94.0	84.7	-8.5	29	N/A	0	0	0.0	0.0
B / 8.9	7.4	0.93	14.31	30	4	95	0	1	4.0	69.9	-10.3	74	N/A	1,000	100	5.8	0.0
C+ / 6.4	7.4	0.92	14.52	49	4	95	0	1	4.0	N/A	N/A	79	7	0	0	0.0	0.0
B / 8.9	7.4	0.92	14.48	1,092	4	95	0	1	4.0	71.5	-10.2	77	N/A	1,000	100	0.0	0.0
C+ / 6.4	7.4	0.92	14.41	47	4	95	0	1	4.0	70.5	-10.2	76	7	0	0	0.0	0.0
B / 8.3	8.6	1.08	52.13	96	2	96	0	2	41.0	62.2	-8.9	34	5	0	0	0.0	0.0
B / 8.4	8.6	1.08	53.02	1,087	2	96	0	2	41.0	64.8	-8.8	39	9	0	0	0.0	0.0
B / 8.4	8.6	1.08	52.49	45	2	96	0	2	41.0	63.5	-8.8	37	5	0	0	0.0	0.0
C+ / 5.8	8.9	0.81	14.49	392	4	95	0	1	N/A	89.5	-10.6	26	1	0	0	0.0	0.0
C+ / 5.8	8.9	0.82	14.40	7	4	95	0	1	N/A	88.8	-10.6	25	1	0	0	0.0	0.0
B+ / 9.8	4.9	0.99	10.12	116	2	67	29	2	N/A	48.4	-6.0	73	1	0	0	0.0	0.0
B+ / 9.8	5.0	1.01	10.08	5	2	67	29	2	N/A	N/A	N/A	72	1	0	0	0.0	0.0
B+ / 9.0	7.3	0.90	9.31	1	2	98	0	0	51.0	68.4	-9.2	74	9	0	0	0.0	0.0
B+ / 9.0	7.3	0.90	9.43	273	2	98	0	0	51.0	71.3	-9.1	78	9	0	0	0.0	0.0
B+ / 9.0	7.4	0.90	9.33	13	2	98	0	0	51.0	69.8	-9.1	76	9	0	0	0.0	0.0
B+ / 9.4	6.1	1.19	36.26	15	5	64	19	12	125.0	62.8	-10.0	82	N/A	0	0	0.0	0.0
B+ / 9.4	6.2	1.19	36.90	867	5	64	19	12	125.0	65.4	-9.9	85	N/A	0	0	0.0	0.0
B+ / 9.4	6.2	1.19	36.69	84	5	64	19	12	125.0	64.1	-10.0	83	N/A	0	0	0.0	0.0
B+ / 9.1	7.1	0.82	12.50	32	8	91	0	1	27.0	69.0	-7.3	83	4	0	0	0.0	0.0
B+ / 9.1	7.0	0.82	12.68	414	8	91	0	1	27.0	71.6	-7.2	87	3	0	0	0.0	0.0
B+ / 9.1	7.1	0.82	12.60	389	8	91	0	1	27.0	70.2	-7.1	85	4	0	0	0.0	0.0
U /	N/A	N/A	11.50	38	1	98	0	1	84.0	N/A	N/A	N/A	2	0	0	0.0	0.0
C / 5.3	11.2	1.27	11.47	54	1	98	0	1	84.0	61.3	-10.8	27	2	0	0	0.0	0.0
C / 5.3	11.2	1.27	11.42	13	1	98	0	1	84.0	60.4	-10.7	25	2	0	0	0.0	0.0
C+ / 6.3	8.0	0.67	14.99	241	5	94	0	1	17.0	84.4	-5.5	98	3	0	0	0.0	0.0
C+ / 6.3	8.0	0.67	14.92	76	5	94	0	1	17.0	83.4	-5.3	98	3	0	0	0.0	0.0

Fund Type	Fund Name	Ticker Symbol	Overall Weiss Investment Rating	Phone	Perfor-mance Rating/Pts	3 Mo	6 Mo	1Yr / Pct	3Yr / Pct	5Yr / Pct	Dividend Yield	Expense Ratio
GI	ING Van Kampen Gr and Inc S	IVGSX	C+	(800) 992-0180	C+ / 6.0	0.04	2.92	10.70 /52	14.43 /56	6.53 /64	0.95	0.90
GI	ING Van Kampen Gr and Inc S2	IVITX	C	(800) 992-0180	C+ / 5.9	0.00	2.86	10.58 /51	14.25 /55	--	0.95	N/A
RE	ING Van Kampen Real Estate I	IVRIX	B	(800) 992-0180	A+ / 9.6	0.76	15.11	25.25 /89	31.05 /96	--	0.95	0.65
RE	ING Van Kampen Real Estate S	IVRSX	B	(800) 992-0180	A+ / 9.6	0.68	14.98	24.91 /88	30.71 /96	20.98 /97	0.85	0.90
RE	ING Van Kampen Real Estate S2	IVRTX	B	(800) 992-0180	A+ / 9.6	0.65	14.91	24.75 /88	30.54 /96	--	0.81	1.05
BA	ING VP Balanced Portfolio Inc Cl I		C	(800) 992-0180	D / 2.0	-1.66	1.58	4.64 /13	7.91 /15	4.07 /46	4.81	0.60
BA	ING VP Balanced Portfolio Inc Cl S		C	(800) 992-0180	D / 1.8	-1.83	1.35	4.22 /11	7.62 /13	--	4.40	0.85
FS	ING VP Financial Services Port S		U	(800) 992-0180	U /	-1.72	2.03	10.62 /51	--	--	0.93	1.05
GL	ING VP Global Equity Dividend Port		C	(800) 992-0180	C+ / 6.4	1.25	9.05	17.44 /78	13.57 /52	1.94 /27	2.96	1.16
TC	ING VP Global Science and Tech CL		E	(800) 992-0180	C- / 3.4	-8.42	-0.70	15.85 /74	11.12 /36	-3.40 / 4	0.00	1.06
TC	ING VP Global Science and Tech CL		E	(800) 992-0180	C- / 3.4	-8.44	-0.94	15.57 /73	11.16 /37	--	0.00	1.31
GI	ING VP Growth and Income Port I		D+	(800) 992-0180	C- / 4.2	-2.92	2.33	10.43 /50	11.14 /37	0.55 /18	1.04	0.59
GI	ING VP Growth and Income Port S		D+	(800) 992-0180	C- / 4.0	-3.03	2.13	10.16 /48	10.88 /34	--	0.93	0.84
GR	ING VP Growth Portfolio Class I		D-	(800) 992-0180	D / 2.1	-6.59	-3.71	6.55 /24	8.88 /20	-1.69 / 9	0.75	0.69
GR	ING VP Growth Portfolio Class S		E+	(800) 992-0180	D / 2.0	-6.68	-3.78	6.26 /22	8.66 /19	--	0.45	0.94
GL	ING VP Index Plus Intl Eq I		U	(800) 992-0180	U /	-0.08	9.06	--	--	--	0.00	0.55
GL	ING VP Index Plus Intl Eq S		U	(800) 992-0180	U /	-0.25	8.88	--	--	--	0.00	0.80
GR	ING VP Index Plus Large Cap Port I	IPLIX	D+	(800) 992-0180	C- / 3.7	-2.13	2.06	7.77 /31	10.79 /34	2.02 /27	2.31	0.45
GR	ING VP Index Plus Large Cap Port S		D+	(800) 992-0180	C- / 3.5	-2.28	1.87	7.41 /29	10.50 /31	--	2.14	0.70
MC	ING VP Index Plus MidCap Port I	IPMIX	C+	(800) 992-0180	B- / 7.0	-2.95	4.17	12.06 /60	17.08 /68	9.17 /77	0.97	0.49
MC	ING VP Index Plus MidCap Port S	IPMSX	C	(800) 992-0180	C+ / 6.9	-2.97	4.05	11.79 /58	16.81 /67	--	0.77	0.74
SC	ING VP Index Plus SmallCap Port I	IPSIX	C+	(800) 992-0180	B / 7.9	-4.66	7.74	13.87 /68	19.85 /79	10.84 /83	0.65	0.49
SC	ING VP Index Plus SmallCap Port S		C+	(800) 992-0180	B / 7.8	-4.67	7.61	13.58 /67	19.55 /78	--	0.47	0.74
FO	ING VP International Equity Port I		B	(800) 992-0180	B+ / 8.9	0.01	8.71	28.67 /93	22.51 /86	5.34 /57	2.41	1.14
FO	ING VP International Equity Port S		B	(800) 992-0180	B+ / 8.8	-0.14	8.51	28.21 /93	22.14 /85	--	2.15	1.39
FO	ING VP International Value Port I		B	(800) 992-0180	B+ / 8.6	0.67	11.11	26.28 /90	20.50 /81	7.97 /72	1.39	1.00
FO	ING VP International Value Port S		B-	(800) 992-0180	B+ / 8.5	0.61	10.92	25.64 /89	20.14 /80	--	1.24	1.20
GR	ING VP LargeCap Growth Port S		E+	(800) 992-0180	D / 2.1	-5.31	-3.19	2.60 / 6	9.31 /23	--	0.00	1.35
MC	ING VP MidCap Opportunities Port I		C-	(800) 992-0180	C+ / 5.7	-5.82	4.76	15.43 /73	14.59 /57	2.97 /36	0.00	0.90
MC	ING VP MidCap Opportunities Port S		C-	(800) 992-0180	C+ / 5.6	-5.78	4.68	15.32 /73	14.33 /56	2.74 /34	0.00	1.10
EN	ING VP Natural Resources Trust		C-	(800) 992-0180	A+ / 9.8	2.19	15.24	45.72 /98	31.59 /96	17.37 /94	0.03	1.18
RE	ING VP Real Estate Portfolio Cl I		U	(800) 992-0180	U /	-0.49	15.21	23.57 /87	--	--	2.39	1.04
RE	ING VP Real Estate Portfolio Cl S		U	(800) 992-0180	U /	-0.60	15.03	23.30 /86	--	--	2.29	1.21
SC	ING VP Small Company Portfolio I		C	(800) 992-0180	B- / 7.5	-4.01	8.76	18.85 /80	18.31 /74	7.37 /69	0.50	0.85
SC	ING VP Small Company Portfolio S		C	(800) 992-0180	B- / 7.4	-4.10	8.56	18.51 /80	17.99 /72	--	0.20	1.10
SC	ING VP SmallCap Opp Port I		C-	(800) 992-0180	C+ / 6.6	-6.57	5.81	14.52 /70	15.86 /63	-3.80 / 4	0.00	0.90
SC	ING VP SmallCap Opp Port S		C-	(800) 992-0180	C+ / 6.5	-6.59	5.69	14.28 /69	15.60 /62	-4.00 / 4	0.00	1.10
AA	ING VP Strt Alloc Consv Port I		C-	(800) 992-0180	D- / 1.3	-1.14	1.17	3.78 /10	6.58 / 9	3.90 /45	4.72	0.65
AA	ING VP Strt Alloc Gr Port Cl I		C-	(800) 992-0180	C / 4.3	-1.91	2.91	9.14 /41	11.28 /38	4.19 /48	2.57	0.73
AA	ING VP Strt Alloc Mod Port Cl I		C	(800) 992-0180	D+ / 2.6	-1.74	2.03	6.14 /21	8.93 /20	3.98 /46	3.32	0.70
GR	ING VP Value Opportunity Port Cl I		C-	(800) 992-0180	C / 4.6	-0.03	3.94	12.44 /62	11.64 /40	0.43 /17	3.20	0.70
GR	ING VP Value Opportunity Port Cl S		C-	(800) 992-0180	C / 4.5	-0.08	3.84	12.14 /60	11.37 /38	--	2.97	0.95
MC	ING Wells Fargo MdCp Discpl S	IJETX	C	(800) 992-0180	C+ / 6.2	-0.31	4.71	13.75 /67	14.43 /56	1.49 /24	0.57	0.91
MC	ING Wells Fargo MdCp Discpl S2	IJPSX	C	(800) 992-0180	C+ / 6.2	-0.37	4.60	13.49 /66	14.28 /55	--	0.56	1.06
SC	ING Wells Fargo SmCp Discpl I		U	(800) 992-0180	U /	-3.07	10.28	--	--	--	0.00	4.03
SC	ING Wells Fargo SmCp Discpl S	IWSSX	U	(800) 992-0180	U /	-3.16	10.07	--	--	--	0.00	1.12
GI	Integrity Fund of Funds	IFOFX	B-	(701) 852-5292	C / 5.0	-1.30	3.24	11.81 /58	12.79 /47	2.31 /30	0.00	1.65
GI	Integrity Growth & Income A	IGIAX	C+	(701) 852-5292	C / 4.8	-3.34	3.31	10.44 /50	13.93 /54	-2.18 / 8	0.70	1.50
HL	Integrity Health Sciences Fund A	IHLAX	E+	(701) 852-5292	E / 0.4	-8.54	-6.50	0.80 / 2	6.78 /10	-0.46 /14	0.00	2.65
SC	Integrity Small Cap Growth Fund A	ICPAX	C	(701) 852-5292	C / 4.6	-6.58	1.39	10.61 /51	14.09 /54	2.68 /34	0.00	2.65
TC	Integrity Technology Fund A	ITKAX	D+	(701) 852-5292	C- / 4.0	-8.96	-0.67	6.68 /24	14.03 /54	-5.30 / 2	0.00	2.65
GR	Integrity Value Fund A	IVUAX	D	(701) 852-5292	D- / 1.5	-7.81	-0.77	5.99 /20	9.28 /23	1.44 /23	0.00	2.65

• Denotes fund is closed to new investors
* Denotes fund is included in Section II

214

RISK			NET ASSETS		ASSET				Portfolio	BULL / BEAR		FUND MANAGER		MINIMUMS		LOADS	
	3 Year		NAV		Cash	Stocks	Bonds	Other	Portfolio	Last Bull	Last Bear	Manager	Manager	Initial	Additional	Front	Back
Risk Rating/Pts	Standard Deviation	Beta	As of 6/30/06	Total $(Mil)	%	%	%	%	Turnover Ratio	Market Return	Market Return	Quality Pct	Tenure (Years)	Purch. $	Purch. $	End Load	End Load
C+ / 6.5	7.3	0.90	27.86	897	6	93	0	1	39.0	77.9	-6.9	89	3	0	0	0.0	0.0
C+ / 6.5	7.4	0.90	27.73	73	6	93	0	1	39.0	77.0	-6.9	88	3	0	0	0.0	0.0
C / 4.7	14.8	0.89	35.81	171	5	94	0	1	24.0	N/A	N/A	98	5	0	0	0.0	0.0
C / 4.7	14.8	0.89	35.62	804	5	94	0	1	24.0	150.6	-0.6	98	5	0	0	0.0	0.0
C / 4.7	14.8	0.89	35.52	35	5	94	0	1	24.0	149.5	-0.7	98	5	0	0	0.0	0.0
B+ / 9.7	5.2	1.08	13.53	1,242	2	72	24	2	308.0	43.1	-3.7	56	1	0	0	0.0	0.0
B+ / 9.7	5.3	1.08	13.47	11	2	72	24	2	308.0	N/A	N/A	52	1	0	0	0.0	0.0
U /	N/A	N/A	11.75	71	4	94	0	2	N/A	N/A	N/A	N/A	2	0	0	0.0	0.0
C+ / 5.6	8.4	0.79	8.28	62	0	100	0	0	183.0	72.8	-10.5	14	N/A	0	0	0.0	0.0
D / 2.1	18.2	1.86	4.24	84	4	95	0	1	118.0	74.9	-15.8	6	2	0	0	0.0	0.0
D / 2.0	18.3	1.87	4.23	N/A	4	95	0	1	118.0	74.5	-15.5	6	2	0	0	0.0	0.0
C+ / 6.0	8.6	1.08	21.19	3,004	2	97	0	1	80.0	65.6	-10.1	46	2	0	0	0.0	0.0
C+ / 6.0	8.6	1.08	21.13	3	2	97	0	1	80.0	N/A	N/A	43	2	0	0	0.0	0.0
C / 5.4	10.4	1.24	9.99	195	1	98	0	1	119.0	57.8	-9.0	19	8	0	0	0.0	0.0
C / 5.4	10.4	1.24	9.92	N/A	1	98	0	1	119.0	56.8	-9.1	17	8	0	0	0.0	0.0
U /	N/A	N/A	11.80	174	4	95	0	1	N/A	N/A	N/A	N/A	1	0	0	0.0	0.0
U /	N/A	N/A	11.77	86	4	95	0	1	N/A	N/A	N/A	N/A	1	0	0	0.0	0.0
C+ / 6.2	7.6	0.99	15.57	1,977	1	98	0	1	89.0	61.1	-9.6	52	5	0	0	0.0	0.0
C+ / 6.2	7.6	0.99	15.44	180	1	98	0	1	89.0	59.8	-9.6	49	5	0	0	0.0	0.0
C / 5.5	10.6	0.98	17.98	1,109	0	99	0	1	100.0	96.2	-8.3	49	5	0	0	0.0	0.0
C / 5.5	10.6	0.98	17.82	212	0	99	0	1	100.0	94.8	-8.4	45	5	0	0	0.0	0.0
C / 4.9	13.4	0.91	17.03	654	1	98	0	1	71.0	115.6	-9.2	80	5	0	0	0.0	0.0
C / 4.9	13.4	0.91	16.87	183	1	98	0	1	71.0	114.0	-9.4	78	5	0	0	0.0	0.0
C / 5.5	10.6	1.03	10.82	70	2	97	0	1	97.0	122.4	-10.5	33	4	0	0	0.0	0.0
C / 5.5	10.6	1.03	10.75	1	2	97	0	1	97.0	120.2	-10.5	30	4	1,000	0	0.0	0.0
C / 5.5	10.4	0.99	14.08	428	1	98	0	1	125.0	105.2	-9.2	26	4	0	0	0.0	0.0
C / 5.5	10.3	0.98	14.23	4	1	98	0	1	125.0	103.3	-9.4	25	4	0	0	0.0	0.0
C / 5.1	11.6	1.26	9.09	2	0	99	0	1	76.0	65.7	-11.9	20	3	0	0	0.0	0.0
C / 4.8	13.3	1.17	7.93	78	3	96	0	1	90.0	88.2	-11.4	11	1	0	0	0.0	0.0
C / 4.8	13.3	1.17	7.83	39	3	96	0	1	90.0	87.2	-11.3	10	1	1,000	0	0.0	0.0
E+ / 0.7	22.3	1.01	27.53	130	0	99	0	1	122.0	159.8	-1.1	42	6	1,000	0	0.0	0.0
U /	N/A	N/A	17.13	82	2	97	0	1	48.0	N/A	N/A	N/A	4	0	0	0.0	0.0
U /	N/A	N/A	17.10	26	2	97	0	1	48.0	N/A	N/A	N/A	4	0	0	0.0	0.0
C / 4.8	13.9	0.92	20.21	491	2	97	0	1	72.0	112.6	-10.0	66	1	0	0	0.0	0.0
C / 4.8	13.9	0.92	20.15	2	2	97	0	1	72.0	111.8	-10.0	63	1	0	0	0.0	0.0
C / 4.7	14.5	0.94	18.77	84	4	95	0	1	83.0	97.2	-15.1	38	1	0	0	0.0	0.0
C / 4.7	14.5	0.94	18.57	126	4	95	0	1	83.0	95.9	-15.2	36	1	1,000	0	0.0	0.0
B+ / 9.9	4.1	0.84	12.65	147	0	0	0	100	364.0	32.3	-1.5	55	5	0	0	0.0	0.0
C+ / 6.4	7.2	1.43	15.51	287	0	91	10	0	232.0	62.9	-7.0	70	5	0	0	0.0	0.0
B+ / 9.5	5.7	1.16	14.06	289	5	73	20	2	301.0	47.8	-4.6	62	5	0	0	0.0	0.0
C+ / 6.2	7.9	0.95	14.19	169	2	97	0	1	94.0	64.5	-9.2	66	1	0	0	0.0	0.0
C+ / 6.2	7.9	0.94	14.10	28	2	97	0	1	94.0	63.4	-9.3	63	1	0	0	0.0	0.0
C+ / 5.8	10.1	0.80	16.24	278	5	94	0	1	176.0	78.8	-12.4	52	1	0	0	0.0	0.0
C+ / 5.8	10.0	0.79	16.16	4	5	94	0	1	176.0	77.9	-12.5	51	1	0	0	0.0	0.0
U /	N/A	N/A	10.73	85	10	90	0	0	1.0	N/A	N/A	N/A	1	0	0	0.0	0.0
U /	N/A	N/A	10.71	47	10	90	0	0	1.0	N/A	N/A	N/A	1	0	100	0.0	0.0
B / 8.6	8.3	1.03	12.12	6	8	90	0	2	1.7	72.1	-9.7	70	11	1,000	50	0.0	1.5
B / 8.7	8.3	0.89	33.04	48	22	76	0	2	9.7	72.1	-9.5	87	1	1,000	50	5.8	0.0
B- / 7.1	12.4	1.03	10.07	6	4	94	0	2	30.1	53.8	-3.4	17	N/A	1,000	50	5.8	0.0
B- / 7.2	12.7	0.80	12.36	12	4	96	0	0	28.6	82.9	-12.1	44	N/A	1,000	50	5.8	0.0
C+ / 5.9	16.2	1.69	8.94	7	2	96	0	2	33.5	105.7	-17.5	24	N/A	1,000	50	5.8	0.0
B- / 7.3	11.6	1.36	10.27	4	2	96	0	2	30.0	61.1	-11.8	15	N/A	1,000	50	5.8	0.0

Fund Type	Fund Name	Ticker Symbol	Overall Weiss Investment Rating	Phone	Perfor-mance Rating/Pts	3 Mo	6 Mo	1Yr / Pct	3Yr / Pct	5Yr / Pct	Dividend Yield	Expense Ratio
	99 Pct = Best / 0 Pct = Worst				PERFORMANCE — Total Return % through 6/30/06 — Annualized — Incl. in Returns							
GR	IPO Plus Aftermarket Fund	IPOSX	D	(888) 476-3863	C / 5.4	-6.62	1.34	6.47 /23	15.12 /59	2.48 /32	0.00	2.50
SC	Ironwood Isabelle Sm-Co Stk Fd Inst	IZZIX	C	(800) 472-6114	B / 8.0	-9.04	8.92	17.83 /79	20.05 /79	6.63 /65	0.00	1.70
SC	Ironwood Isabelle Sm-Co Stk Fd Inv	IZZYX	C	(800) 472-6114	B / 7.9	-9.09	8.70	17.53 /78	19.62 /78	6.21 /62	0.00	1.95
AA	ISI Strategy A	STRTX	C	(800) 955-7175	D+ / 2.8	-2.18	2.32	8.89 /39	9.78 /26	4.55 /51	1.07	0.94
AA	Ivy Fund-Asset Strategy A	WASAX	B+	(800) 777-6472	B+ / 8.8	3.57	15.59	37.01 /97	19.78 /79	12.46 /88	0.22	1.25
AA	Ivy Fund-Asset Strategy B	WASBX	B+	(800) 777-6472	B+ / 8.6	3.41	15.17	35.95 /97	18.75 /75	11.47 /85	0.01	2.09
AA	Ivy Fund-Asset Strategy C	WASCX	B	(800) 777-6472	B+ / 8.9	3.40	15.20	36.08 /97	18.88 /76	11.60 /86	0.03	1.97
AA	Ivy Fund-Asset Strategy Y	WASYX	B+	(800) 777-6472	A- / 9.1	3.58	15.64	37.07 /97	19.85 /79	12.55 /88	0.25	1.20
BA	Ivy Fund-Balanced Fund A	IBNAX	C	(800) 777-6472	D / 2.2	0.13	3.63	7.87 /32	9.30 /23	4.27 /48	0.91	1.42
BA	Ivy Fund-Balanced Fund Y	IBNYX	U	(800) 777-6472	U /	0.16	3.70	8.03 /33	--	--	1.11	1.26
IN	Ivy Fund-Capital Appreciation A	WMEAX	C-	(800) 777-6472	C- / 3.0	-3.17	-0.45	6.74 /25	11.61 /40	3.94 /45	0.00	1.35
IN	Ivy Fund-Capital Appreciation B	WMEBX	D	(800) 777-6472	D+ / 2.4	-3.35	-0.95	5.69 /19	10.54 /31	2.98 /37	0.00	2.42
IN	Ivy Fund-Capital Appreciation C	WMECX	C-	(800) 777-6472	C- / 3.2	-3.24	-0.83	6.09 /21	10.60 /32	2.92 /36	0.00	2.11
GR	Ivy Fund-Core Equity A	WCEAX	C	(800) 777-6472	C- / 4.1	0.98	6.60	13.01 /64	11.65 /40	1.69 /25	0.00	1.40
GR	Ivy Fund-Core Equity B	WCEBX	C-	(800) 777-6472	C- / 3.5	0.72	6.20	12.04 /60	10.66 /32	0.76 /19	0.00	2.30
GR	Ivy Fund-Core Equity C	WTRCX	C	(800) 777-6472	C / 4.3	0.72	6.15	12.07 /60	10.77 /33	0.88 /20	0.00	2.15
GR	Ivy Fund-Core Equity Y	WCEYX	C+	(800) 777-6472	C / 5.2	1.03	6.64	13.26 /65	11.85 /41	1.84 /26	0.00	1.23
GL	Ivy Fund-Cundill Global Value A	ICDAX	B+	(800) 777-6472	B- / 7.1	-2.00	1.81	14.40 /70	19.47 /78	--	0.94	1.58
GL	● Ivy Fund-Cundill Global Value Adv	ICDVX	A+	(800) 777-6472	B / 7.9	-1.87	2.07	14.96 /72	20.03 /79	9.89 /80	1.22	1.08
GL	Ivy Fund-Cundill Global Value B	ICDBX	B+	(800) 777-6472	B- / 7.0	-2.17	1.43	13.41 /66	18.45 /74	--	0.12	2.46
GL	Ivy Fund-Cundill Global Value C	ICDCX	A-	(800) 777-6472	B- / 7.3	-2.11	1.50	13.65 /67	18.69 /75	--	0.35	2.25
GL	● Ivy Fund-Cundill Global Value I		A	(800) 777-6472	B / 7.9	-1.88	2.02	14.82 /71	19.83 /79	--	1.35	1.21
GI	Ivy Fund-Dividend Income A	IVDAX	B+	(800) 777-6472	C+ / 6.2	2.09	8.36	18.96 /80	14.68 /57	--	0.83	1.41
GI	Ivy Fund-Dividend Income B	IVDBX	B	(800) 777-6472	C+ / 5.8	1.86	7.88	17.85 /79	13.71 /52	--	0.13	2.28
GI	Ivy Fund-Dividend Income C	IVDCX	B	(800) 777-6472	C+ / 6.3	1.89	7.91	17.89 /79	13.73 /53	--	0.17	2.22
GI	Ivy Fund-Dividend Income Y	IVDYX	B	(800) 777-6472	C+ / 6.9	2.12	8.42	19.11 /81	14.83 /58	--	1.00	1.31
FO	Ivy Fund-European Opport A	IEOAX	A-	(800) 777-6472	A+ / 9.6	-0.83	12.01	23.48 /87	32.48 /97	19.45 /96	0.57	1.71
FO	● Ivy Fund-European Opport Adv	IEOVX	A	(800) 777-6472	A+ / 9.7	-0.74	12.25	24.07 /87	33.07 /97	19.78 /96	1.00	1.26
FO	Ivy Fund-European Opport B	IEOBX	A-	(800) 777-6472	A / 9.5	-1.05	11.59	22.60 /85	31.50 /96	18.41 /95	0.00	2.42
FO	Ivy Fund-European Opport C	IEOCX	A-	(800) 777-6472	A+ / 9.6	-1.01	11.62	22.63 /85	31.52 /96	18.42 /95	0.00	2.42
★ EN	Ivy Fund-Global Nat Resource A	IGNAX	A	(800) 777-6472	A+ / 9.9	3.95	20.23	46.52 /99	39.05 /99	24.20 /98	0.00	1.37
EN	● Ivy Fund-Global Nat Resource Adv	IGNVX	A+	(800) 777-6472	A+ / 9.9	4.01	20.48	46.95 /99	39.19 /99	24.29 /98	0.00	1.17
EN	Ivy Fund-Global Nat Resource B	IGNBX	A-	(800) 777-6472	A+ / 9.9	3.75	19.76	45.42 /98	37.92 /99	23.17 /98	0.00	2.20
EN	Ivy Fund-Global Nat Resource C	IGNCX	A-	(800) 777-6472	A+ / 9.9	3.78	19.85	45.48 /98	38.01 /99	23.19 /98	0.00	2.12
EN	Ivy Fund-Global Nat Resource Y	IGNYX	U	(800) 777-6472	U /	4.00	20.34	46.84 /99	--	--	0.00	1.20
GL	Ivy Fund-International Balanced A	IVBAX	B	(800) 777-6472	C+ / 6.8	2.67	8.52	14.17 /69	17.70 /71	11.59 /86	2.69	1.47
FO	Ivy Fund-International Fd A	IVINX	C+	(800) 777-6472	B / 7.7	-1.34	7.91	27.38 /92	19.51 /78	5.91 /61	0.55	1.54
FO	● Ivy Fund-International Fd Adv		B-	(800) 777-6472	B- / 7.4	-2.21	6.15	23.24 /86	16.94 /68	--	0.00	4.69
FO	Ivy Fund-International Fd B	IVIBX	C+	(800) 777-6472	B- / 7.5	-1.63	7.36	26.01 /90	18.17 /73	4.68 /52	0.00	2.58
FO	Ivy Fund-International Fd C	IVNCX	C+	(800) 777-6472	B / 7.8	-1.64	7.42	26.20 /90	18.33 /74	4.78 /52	0.00	2.28
FO	● Ivy Fund-International Fd I	IVIIX	B	(800) 777-6472	B+ / 8.3	-1.26	8.04	27.69 /92	19.72 /78	6.06 /61	0.78	1.37
FO	Ivy Fund-International Value A	IVIAX	A	(800) 777-6472	A- / 9.0	-1.08	10.20	32.88 /96	24.67 /90	10.12 /81	0.00	1.76
FO	● Ivy Fund-International Value Adv	IVIVX	A	(800) 777-6472	A / 9.3	-1.09	10.26	33.22 /96	24.98 /91	9.94 /80	0.00	1.63
FO	Ivy Fund-International Value B	IIFBX	A	(800) 777-6472	B+ / 8.9	-1.30	9.78	31.88 /96	23.65 /89	8.77 /75	0.00	2.48
FO	Ivy Fund-International Value C	IVIFX	A	(800) 777-6472	A- / 9.0	-1.30	9.71	31.81 /96	23.59 /89	8.74 /75	0.00	2.46
GR	Ivy Fund-Large Cap Gr A	WLGAX	D+	(800) 777-6472	C- / 3.6	-1.81	1.60	13.32 /65	12.16 /43	3.13 /38	0.00	1.37
GR	Ivy Fund-Large Cap Gr B	WLGBX	D	(800) 777-6472	D+ / 2.9	-2.12	1.05	12.05 /60	10.91 /35	1.79 /25	0.00	2.42
GR	Ivy Fund-Large Cap Gr C	WLGCX	D+	(800) 777-6472	C- / 3.8	-2.07	1.21	12.42 /62	11.28 /38	2.24 /30	0.00	2.18
GR	Ivy Fund-Large Cap Gr Y	WLGYX	C-	(800) 777-6472	C / 4.7	-1.79	1.68	13.48 /66	12.44 /45	3.37 /40	0.00	1.20
MC	Ivy Fund-Mid Cap Growth A	WMGAX	C+	(800) 777-6472	C / 5.5	-4.85	2.39	14.10 /68	15.18 /60	4.38 /49	0.00	1.59
MC	Ivy Fund-Mid Cap Growth B	WMGBX	C+	(800) 777-6472	C / 4.9	-5.06	1.90	12.95 /64	13.92 /53	3.14 /38	0.00	2.64
MC	Ivy Fund-Mid Cap Growth C	WMGCX	C+	(800) 777-6472	C+ / 5.7	-5.04	1.95	13.20 /65	14.27 /55	3.51 /41	0.00	2.35

● Denotes fund is closed to new investors
★ Denotes fund is included in Section II

RISK			NET ASSETS		ASSET					BULL / BEAR		FUND MANAGER		MINIMUMS		LOADS	
	3 Year		NAV						Portfolio	Last Bull	Last Bear	Manager	Manager	Initial	Additional	Front	Back
Risk Rating/Pts	Standard Deviation	Beta	As of 6/30/06	Total $(Mil)	Cash %	Stocks %	Bonds %	Other %	Turnover Ratio	Market Return	Market Return	Quality Pct	Tenure (Years)	Purch. $	Purch. $	End Load	End Load
C- / 4.0	14.2	1.31	12.83	19	6	93	0	1	121.0	116.1	-10.3	67	9	5,000	100	0.0	2.0
C / 4.3	16.2	0.98	15.99	4	0	100	0	0	65.7	144.9	-20.8	72	8	500,000	50,000	0.0	0.0
C- / 4.2	16.2	0.98	15.50	88	0	100	0	0	65.7	142.1	-20.8	69	8	1,000	100	0.0	0.0
B / 8.8	5.9	1.17	12.73	66	0	77	22	1	30.0	53.1	-6.1	70	9	5,000	1,250	3.0	0.0
C+ / 6.2	11.9	1.48	19.42	476	5	88	6	1	64.0	82.7	2.7	99	7	500	0	5.8	0.0
C+ / 6.2	12.0	1.48	19.13	52	5	88	6	1	64.0	77.8	2.4	98	7	500	0	0.0	5.0
C+ / 5.7	12.0	1.48	19.17	417	5	88	6	1	64.0	78.5	2.4	98	7	500	0	0.0	1.0
C+ / 5.7	12.0	1.49	19.44	47	5	88	6	1	64.0	83.1	2.7	99	9	10,000,000	0	0.0	0.0
B+ / 9.5	5.7	1.10	15.20	57	4	72	22	2	60.0	45.9	-4.6	69	3	500	0	5.8	0.0
U /	N/A	N/A	15.20	34	4	72	22	2	60.0	N/A	N/A	N/A	3	10,000,000	0	0.0	0.0
B- / 7.4	9.7	1.13	8.87	36	1	98	0	1	60.0	63.6	-5.3	46	6	500	0	5.8	0.0
B- / 7.2	9.6	1.12	8.36	2	1	98	0	1	60.0	58.8	-5.6	37	6	500	0	0.0	5.0
B- / 7.3	9.6	1.12	8.36	7	1	98	0	1	60.0	58.6	-5.4	37	6	500	0	0.0	1.0
B- / 7.7	8.2	0.92	10.34	74	5	94	0	1	56.0	58.4	-9.1	69	N/A	500	0	5.8	0.0
B- / 7.7	8.1	0.91	9.77	11	5	94	0	1	56.0	54.0	-9.5	59	N/A	500	0	0.0	5.0
B- / 7.6	8.1	0.91	9.84	167	5	94	0	1	56.0	54.4	-9.3	61	N/A	500	0	0.0	1.0
B- / 7.7	8.0	0.90	10.76	2	5	94	0	1	56.0	59.2	-9.1	71	N/A	10,000,000	0	0.0	0.0
B / 8.2	6.8	0.40	15.21	634	20	79	0	1	6.0	98.8	-6.3	98	6	500	0	5.8	2.0
B / 8.2	6.8	0.41	15.25	3	20	79	0	1	6.0	101.9	-6.1	98	6	500	50	0.0	0.0
B / 8.2	6.8	0.40	14.90	55	20	79	0	1	6.0	93.5	-6.3	97	5	500	0	0.0	5.0
B / 8.2	6.7	0.40	14.84	221	20	79	0	1	6.0	94.4	-6.4	97	5	500	0	0.0	2.0
B / 8.0	7.0	0.41	15.12	N/A	20	79	0	1	6.0	101.4	-6.3	98	4	500	50	0.0	0.0
B / 8.8	7.9	0.87	14.67	68	4	95	0	1	24.0	N/A	N/A	91	3	500	0	5.8	0.0
B / 8.8	8.0	0.88	14.60	8	4	95	0	1	24.0	N/A	N/A	86	3	500	0	0.0	5.0
B / 8.8	7.9	0.87	14.60	15	4	95	0	1	24.0	N/A	N/A	87	3	500	0	0.0	1.0
B / 8.8	7.9	0.87	14.67	1	4	95	0	1	24.0	N/A	N/A	91	3	10,000,000	0	0.0	0.0
C+ / 6.0	13.7	1.14	33.30	249	3	96	0	1	47.0	209.1	-13.1	88	7	500	0	5.8	2.0
C+ / 6.0	13.7	1.14	33.63	2	3	96	0	1	47.0	213.2	-13.3	90	7	500	50	0.0	0.0
C+ / 5.9	13.7	1.14	32.06	42	3	96	0	1	47.0	201.9	-13.4	83	7	500	0	0.0	5.0
C+ / 6.0	13.7	1.13	32.19	50	3	96	0	1	47.0	202.0	-13.5	84	7	500	0	0.0	2.0
C+ / 5.7	16.7	0.72	31.32	2,645	5	94	0	1	107.0	202.6	2.4	99	9	500	0	5.8	2.0
C+ / 6.2	16.7	0.72	31.12	N/A	5	94	0	1	107.0	203.9	2.3	99	8	500	50	0.0	0.0
C+ / 5.7	16.7	0.72	29.64	244	5	94	0	1	107.0	195.2	2.1	99	9	500	0	0.0	5.0
C+ / 5.7	16.7	0.72	29.10	915	5	94	0	1	107.0	195.7	2.1	99	9	500	0	0.0	2.0
U /	N/A	N/A	31.48	164	5	94	0	1	107.0	N/A	N/A	N/A	9	10,000,000	0	0.0	2.0
B / 8.6	8.4	1.39	15.40	125	8	64	27	1	24.0	93.3	-3.7	97	N/A	500	0	5.8	2.0
C+ / 5.8	11.6	1.09	29.34	150	1	98	0	1	79.0	99.9	-10.0	10	6	500	0	5.8	2.0
C+ / 6.6	11.6	1.09	28.32	N/A	1	98	0	1	79.0	88.0	-10.1	4	6	500	50	0.0	0.0
C+ / 5.8	11.6	1.09	27.13	12	1	98	0	1	79.0	93.0	-10.3	7	6	500	0	0.0	5.0
C+ / 5.8	11.6	1.09	27.07	54	1	98	0	1	79.0	93.9	-10.3	7	6	500	0	0.0	2.0
C+ / 5.8	11.6	1.10	29.69	N/A	1	98	0	1	79.0	100.9	-10.0	11	6	500	50	0.0	0.0
C+ / 6.8	11.6	1.08	15.56	83	9	90	0	1	95.0	127.6	-8.6	39	4	500	0	5.8	2.0
C+ / 6.8	11.6	1.08	15.48	N/A	9	90	0	1	95.0	130.0	-8.6	41	4	500	50	0.0	0.0
C+ / 6.7	11.7	1.08	14.48	13	9	90	0	1	95.0	122.1	-8.8	31	4	500	0	0.0	5.0
C+ / 6.7	11.6	1.08	14.46	18	9	90	0	1	95.0	121.7	-8.8	31	4	500	0	0.0	2.0
C+ / 6.2	11.6	1.15	11.40	162	3	96	0	1	73.0	62.8	-4.7	51	6	500	0	5.8	0.0
C+ / 6.0	11.6	1.15	10.60	11	3	96	0	1	73.0	56.7	-5.0	38	6	500	0	0.0	5.0
C+ / 6.1	11.6	1.15	10.86	18	3	96	0	1	73.0	58.3	-4.8	41	6	500	0	0.0	1.0
C+ / 6.2	11.6	1.16	11.53	65	3	96	0	1	73.0	63.8	-4.5	54	6	10,000,000	0	0.0	0.0
B- / 7.6	10.2	0.85	11.98	101	6	93	0	1	23.0	87.0	-4.3	50	5	500	0	5.8	0.0
B- / 7.6	10.1	0.85	11.25	11	6	93	0	1	23.0	80.7	-4.8	38	5	500	0	0.0	5.0
B- / 7.6	10.1	0.85	11.49	13	6	93	0	1	23.0	82.5	-4.6	42	5	500	0	0.0	1.0

Fund Type	Fund Name	Ticker Symbol	Overall Weiss Investment Rating	Phone	Performance Rating/Pts	PERFORMANCE Total Return % through 6/30/06			Annualized		Incl. in Returns	
	99 Pct = Best / 0 Pct = Worst					3 Mo	6 Mo	1Yr / Pct	3Yr / Pct	5Yr / Pct	Dividend Yield	Expense Ratio
MC	Ivy Fund-Mid Cap Growth Y	WMGYX	B	(800) 777-6472	C+ / 6.4	-4.80	2.46	14.49 / 70	15.48 / 61	4.68 / 52	0.00	1.25
FO	Ivy Fund-Pacific Opportunities A	IPOAX	C+	(800) 777-6472	A / 9.4	-2.30	8.11	29.34 / 94	29.60 / 95	16.17 / 93	0.29	1.89
FO	● Ivy Fund-Pacific Opportunities Adv	IPOVX	C+	(800) 777-6472	A+ / 9.6	-2.21	8.39	29.98 / 94	30.22 / 96	16.19 / 93	0.80	1.38
FO	Ivy Fund-Pacific Opportunities B	IPOBX	C+	(800) 777-6472	A- / 9.2	-2.56	7.56	28.17 / 93	28.12 / 94	14.66 / 91	0.00	2.84
FO	Ivy Fund-Pacific Opportunities C	IPOCX	C+	(800) 777-6472	A / 9.4	-2.53	7.72	28.36 / 93	28.64 / 94	15.01 / 92	0.00	2.67
RE	Ivy Fund-Real Estate Securities A	IRSAX	A-	(800) 777-6472	A- / 9.1	-0.82	11.96	17.64 / 78	26.47 / 93	20.51 / 97	0.68	1.62
RE	Ivy Fund-Real Estate Securities Y	IRSYX	U	(800) 777-6472	U /	-0.80	12.10	17.94 / 79	--	--	0.96	1.38
TC	Ivy Fund-Science & Tech A	WSTAX	C	(800) 777-6472	C+ / 6.5	-5.17	0.27	12.93 / 64	17.97 / 72	5.89 / 60	0.00	1.48
TC	Ivy Fund-Science & Tech B	WSTBX	C	(800) 777-6472	C+ / 6.0	-5.43	-0.25	11.71 / 58	16.64 / 66	4.70 / 52	0.00	2.53
TC	Ivy Fund-Science & Tech C	WSTCX	C-	(800) 777-6472	C+ / 6.6	-5.38	-0.12	11.95 / 59	16.96 / 68	5.01 / 54	0.00	2.34
TC	Ivy Fund-Science & Tech Y	WSTYX	C	(800) 777-6472	B- / 7.2	-5.16	0.34	13.07 / 65	18.24 / 73	6.19 / 62	0.00	1.36
SC	Ivy Fund-Small Cap Growth A	WSGAX	C-	(800) 777-6472	C / 5.2	-5.92	2.27	9.17 / 41	15.34 / 60	4.90 / 53	0.00	1.48
SC	Ivy Fund-Small Cap Growth B	WSGBX	C-	(800) 777-6472	C / 4.6	-6.15	1.78	8.13 / 34	14.23 / 55	3.82 / 44	0.00	2.43
SC	Ivy Fund-Small Cap Growth C	WRGCX	C-	(800) 777-6472	C / 5.4	-6.06	1.91	8.43 / 36	14.48 / 56	4.10 / 47	0.00	2.18
SC	Ivy Fund-Small Cap Growth Y	WSCYX	C	(800) 777-6472	C+ / 6.1	-5.88	2.29	9.31 / 42	15.52 / 61	5.06 / 55	0.00	1.33
SC	Ivy Fund-Small Cap Value Fund A	IYSAX	C+	(800) 777-6472	C+ / 6.8	-3.69	5.39	8.60 / 38	18.77 / 75	8.90 / 76	0.00	1.79
GR	Ivy Fund-Value Fund A	IYVAX	C	(800) 777-6472	C- / 3.2	-1.02	2.69	5.17 / 16	11.77 / 41	3.79 / 44	0.60	1.50
RE	IXIS AEW Real Estate A	NRFAX	C	(800) 225-5478	A / 9.3	-1.15	14.22	22.45 / 85	28.02 / 94	20.74 / 97	1.65	1.44
RE	IXIS AEW Real Estate B	NRFBX	C	(800) 225-5478	A- / 9.2	-1.38	13.71	21.50 / 84	27.05 / 93	19.82 / 96	1.13	2.19
RE	IXIS AEW Real Estate C	NRCFX	C	(800) 225-5478	A / 9.3	-1.34	13.80	21.52 / 84	27.05 / 93	19.85 / 96	1.12	2.19
RE	IXIS AEW Real Estate Y	NRFYX	C+	(800) 225-5478	A / 9.5	-1.10	14.38	22.78 / 85	28.35 / 94	21.03 / 97	2.06	1.14
GR	IXIS CGM Advisor Trgt Eqty A	NEFGX	C+	(800) 225-5478	C+ / 6.5	0.86	4.41	14.24 / 69	17.22 / 69	5.33 / 57	0.69	1.20
GR	IXIS CGM Advisor Trgt Eqty B	NEBGX	C+	(800) 225-5478	C+ / 6.4	0.72	4.12	13.46 / 66	16.39 / 65	4.53 / 50	0.68	1.95
GR	IXIS CGM Advisor Trgt Eqty C	NEGCX	C+	(800) 225-5478	C+ / 6.8	0.72	4.12	13.46 / 66	16.39 / 65	4.53 / 50	0.68	1.95
GR	IXIS CGM Advisor Trgt Eqty Y	NEGYX	B-	(800) 225-5478	B- / 7.2	0.93	4.51	14.52 / 70	17.62 / 71	5.78 / 60	0.94	1.07
FO	IXIS Hansberger Intl A	NEFDX	B	(800) 225-5478	B / 8.1	-0.73	7.95	26.09 / 90	20.88 / 82	9.61 / 79	0.72	1.60
FO	IXIS Hansberger Intl B	NEDBX	B	(800) 225-5478	B / 8.0	-0.95	7.56	25.17 / 89	19.97 / 79	8.81 / 76	0.83	2.35
FO	IXIS Hansberger Intl C	NEDCX	B+	(800) 225-5478	B / 8.2	-0.90	7.55	25.23 / 89	19.99 / 79	8.80 / 76	0.82	2.35
MC	IXIS Harris Assoc Foc Val A	NRSAX	E+	(800) 225-5478	D / 1.9	-2.18	-0.07	2.83 / 7	10.10 / 28	4.66 / 51	0.00	1.59
MC	IXIS Harris Assoc Foc Val B	NRSBX	E+	(800) 225-5478	D / 1.6	-2.36	-0.42	2.03 / 4	9.26 / 22	3.87 / 45	0.00	2.34
MC	IXIS Harris Assoc Foc Val C	NRSCX	E+	(800) 225-5478	D / 2.2	-2.44	-0.42	2.02 / 4	9.25 / 22	3.87 / 45	0.00	2.34
GI	IXIS Harris Assoc Large Cap Value A	NEFOX	D	(800) 225-5478	D- / 1.0	-1.80	1.00	4.78 / 14	7.54 / 13	0.99 / 20	0.23	1.30
GI	IXIS Harris Assoc Large Cap Value B	NEGBX	D	(800) 225-5478	E+ / 0.8	-2.00	0.59	3.92 / 10	6.69 / 9	0.24 / 16	0.26	2.05
GI	IXIS Harris Assoc Large Cap Value C	NECOX	D+	(800) 225-5478	D- / 1.2	-2.01	0.51	3.84 / 10	6.71 / 9	0.24 / 16	0.26	2.05
GI	IXIS Harris Assoc Large Cap Value Y	NEOYX	D+	(800) 225-5478	D / 1.6	-1.82	1.05	4.95 / 15	7.83 / 14	1.43 / 23	0.24	0.92
GR	IXIS Loomis Sayles Growth Fund A	LGRRX	E	(800) 225-5478	D- / 1.3	-10.31	-8.89	0.70 / 2	10.62 / 32	2.08 / 28	0.00	1.16
GR	IXIS Loomis Sayles Growth Fund B	LGRBX	E+	(800) 225-5478	D- / 1.0	-10.51	-9.21	--	9.79 / 26	1.36 / 23	0.00	1.90
GR	IXIS Loomis Sayles Growth Fund C	LGRCX	D-	(800) 225-5478	D- / 1.5	-10.51	-9.21	-0.18 / 2	9.79 / 26	1.36 / 23	0.00	1.91
GR	IXIS Loomis Sayles Growth Fund Y	LSGRX	D-	(800) 225-5478	D+ / 2.3	-10.09	-8.72	1.02 / 3	10.96 / 35	2.41 / 31	0.00	0.85
GR	IXIS Loomis Sayles Research Fund A	LSRRX	C	(800) 225-5478	C- / 3.2	-4.15	-0.11	6.83 / 25	12.02 / 43	3.05 / 37	0.28	1.25
GR	IXIS Loomis Sayles Research Fund B	LSCBX	C-	(800) 225-5478	D+ / 2.7	-4.32	-0.45	6.00 / 20	11.14 / 37	2.21 / 29	0.00	2.00
GR	IXIS Loomis Sayles Research Fund C	LSCCX	C	(800) 225-5478	C- / 3.1	-4.34	-0.56	6.01 / 21	10.98 / 35	2.12 / 28	0.11	2.00
GR	IXIS Loomis Sayles Research Fund Y	LISRX	C+	(800) 225-5478	C / 4.4	-4.03	0.11	7.16 / 27	12.34 / 45	2.88 / 36	0.52	0.85
GL	● IXIS Moderate Divers A	AMDPX	U	(800) 225-5478	U /	-3.23	-0.40	4.43 / 12	--	--	1.13	1.45
GL	IXIS Moderate Divers C	CMDPX	U	(800) 225-5478	U /	-3.43	-0.68	3.68 / 9	--	--	0.56	2.20
GR	IXIS U.S. Diversified Portfolio A	NEFSX	C+	(800) 225-5478	C / 5.2	-2.67	4.71	13.06 / 64	14.26 / 55	5.01 / 54	0.00	1.51
GR	IXIS U.S. Diversified Portfolio B	NESBX	C	(800) 225-5478	C / 4.8	-2.89	4.33	12.18 / 60	13.39 / 51	4.22 / 48	0.00	2.26
GR	IXIS U.S. Diversified Portfolio C	NECCX	C+	(800) 225-5478	C / 5.4	-2.89	4.33	12.16 / 60	13.40 / 51	4.22 / 48	0.00	2.35
GR	IXIS U.S. Diversified Portfolio Y	NESYX	B-	(800) 225-5478	C+ / 6.3	-2.60	4.86	13.44 / 66	14.77 / 58	5.60 / 58	0.00	1.14
GR	IXIS Value A	NEFVX	C-	(800) 225-5478	C- / 4.2	-0.64	4.50	9.33 / 42	12.57 / 46	5.01 / 54	0.04	1.44
GR	IXIS Value B	NEVBX	D	(800) 225-5478	D+ / 2.7	-0.84	3.92	8.41 / 36	11.71 / 41	4.23 / 48	0.04	2.19
GR	IXIS Value C	NECVX	C-	(800) 225-5478	C / 4.4	-0.84	4.06	8.41 / 36	11.71 / 41	4.23 / 48	0.04	2.19

● Denotes fund is closed to new investors
* Denotes fund is included in Section II

www.WeissRatings.com

Risk Rating/Pts	Std Dev	Beta	NAV 6/30/06	Total $(Mil)	Cash %	Stocks %	Bonds %	Other %	Portfolio Turnover Ratio	Last Bull Return	Last Bear Return	Mgr Quality Pct	Mgr Tenure (Yrs)	Initial Purch. $	Additional Purch. $	Front End Load	Back End Load
B- /7.6	10.2	0.86	12.09	10	6	93	0	1	23.0	88.6	-4.3	53	5	10,000,000	0	0.0	0.0
C- /3.3	16.2	1.40	13.99	219	5	94	0	1	87.0	163.2	-8.3	20	N/A	500	0	5.8	2.0
C- /3.3	16.2	1.40	13.70	N/A	5	94	0	1	87.0	165.7	-7.8	24	N/A	500	50	0.0	0.0
C- /3.2	16.2	1.39	12.95	13	5	94	0	1	87.0	152.8	-8.5	15	N/A	500	0	0.0	5.0
C- /3.3	16.2	1.40	13.11	21	5	94	0	1	87.0	155.8	-8.5	16	N/A	500	0	0.0	2.0
C+ /6.4	15.2	0.91	22.88	263	2	97	0	1	35.0	129.6	2.1	88	N/A	500	0	5.8	0.0
U /	N/A	N/A	22.88	205	2	97	0	1	35.0	N/A	N/A	N/A	3	10,000,000	0	0.0	0.0
C+ /5.6	13.5	1.40	25.68	151	6	93	0	1	110.0	87.4	-3.6	82	5	500	0	5.8	0.0
C+ /5.6	13.5	1.40	24.04	16	6	93	0	1	110.0	80.6	-3.9	72	5	500	0	0.0	5.0
C /4.7	13.5	1.39	24.45	105	6	93	0	1	110.0	82.3	-3.8	75	5	500	0	0.0	1.0
C /4.8	13.5	1.39	26.48	56	6	93	0	1	110.0	88.7	-3.6	84	5	10,000,000	0	0.0	0.0
C+ /6.2	13.7	0.88	13.99	137	9	90	0	1	78.0	88.0	-5.7	43	N/A	500	0	5.8	0.0
C+ /6.1	13.7	0.87	13.13	18	9	90	0	1	78.0	82.0	-6.0	33	N/A	500	0	0.0	5.0
C /5.5	13.7	0.87	13.34	296	9	90	0	1	78.0	83.5	-6.0	35	N/A	500	0	0.0	1.0
C+ /5.6	13.7	0.87	15.20	162	9	90	0	1	78.0	89.0	-5.7	45	N/A	10,000,000	0	0.0	0.0
C+ /6.8	13.9	0.91	15.64	86	4	95	0	1	157.0	118.3	-13.7	71	N/A	500	0	5.8	0.0
B /8.9	7.6	0.95	16.97	59	1	98	0	1	63.0	65.5	-9.2	67	N/A	500	0	5.8	0.0
C- /3.0	16.6	1.00	21.53	79	2	96	0	2	15.0	133.6	0.6	85	6	2,500	100	5.8	0.0
C- /3.0	16.6	0.99	21.51	16	2	96	0	2	15.0	128.1	0.4	80	N/A	2,500	100	0.0	5.0
C- /3.0	16.6	0.99	21.55	18	2	96	0	2	15.0	128.1	0.4	80	6	2,500	100	1.0	1.0
C- /3.0	16.6	0.99	20.96	24	2	96	0	2	15.0	135.3	0.7	87	N/A	1,000,000	10,000	0.0	0.0
C+ /6.6	13.5	1.11	10.60	692	0	99	0	1	196.0	101.0	-7.4	91	N/A	2,500	100	5.8	2.0
C+ /6.6	13.5	1.11	9.80	50	0	99	0	1	196.0	95.9	-7.6	88	N/A	2,500	100	0.0	5.0
C+ /6.6	13.5	1.11	9.80	8	0	99	0	1	196.0	96.3	-7.6	88	N/A	2,500	100	0.0	1.0
C+ /6.7	13.5	1.11	10.83	12	0	99	0	1	196.0	102.5	-7.0	93	N/A	1,000,000	10,000	0.0	2.0
C+ /6.5	10.9	1.04	21.02	100	2	97	0	1	45.0	121.4	-10.2	21	N/A	2,500	100	5.8	1.0
C+ /6.4	10.9	1.04	19.21	32	2	97	0	1	45.0	116.5	-10.5	16	N/A	2,500	100	0.0	5.0
C+ /6.4	10.9	1.04	19.22	21	2	97	0	1	45.0	116.2	-10.4	16	N/A	2,500	100	1.0	1.0
C /5.5	8.5	0.67	11.68	65	5	94	0	1	39.0	61.6	-6.1	31	5	2,500	100	5.8	0.0
C /5.2	8.5	0.67	11.15	82	5	94	0	1	39.0	58.0	-6.3	25	5	2,500	100	0.0	5.0
C /5.2	8.5	0.67	11.15	97	5	94	0	1	39.0	58.0	-6.3	26	5	2,500	100	0.0	1.0
B /8.3	7.4	0.84	13.42	178	1	98	0	1	39.0	55.0	-9.2	33	N/A	2,500	100	5.8	0.0
B /8.6	7.5	0.85	12.51	46	1	98	0	1	39.0	51.4	-9.4	27	4	2,500	100	0.0	5.0
B /8.6	7.4	0.84	12.49	18	1	98	0	1	39.0	51.4	-9.4	27	N/A	2,500	100	0.0	1.0
B /8.7	7.4	0.84	13.83	13	1	98	0	1	39.0	55.7	-8.4	35	4	1,000,000	10,000	0.0	2.0
C /5.1	13.4	1.46	5.74	216	1	98	0	1	70.0	70.1	-8.5	17	N/A	2,500	100	5.8	0.0
C+ /6.4	13.1	1.47	5.62	34	1	98	0	1	70.0	66.2	-8.6	12	N/A	2,500	100	0.0	5.0
C+ /6.4	13.0	1.47	5.62	46	1	98	0	1	70.0	66.2	-8.6	13	N/A	2,500	100	1.0	1.0
C /5.3	13.0	1.46	5.97	126	1	98	0	1	70.0	71.8	-8.2	19	7	250,000	10,000	0.0	0.0
B /8.4	9.0	1.11	9.00	1	0	99	0	1	83.0	70.4	-8.6	54	N/A	2,500	100	5.8	0.0
B /8.3	9.1	1.11	8.85	N/A	0	99	0	1	83.0	66.1	-8.7	43	N/A	2,500	100	0.0	5.0
B /8.3	9.0	1.10	8.82	1	0	99	0	1	83.0	65.4	-8.7	42	N/A	2,500	100	1.0	1.0
B /8.5	8.9	1.09	9.05	23	0	99	0	1	83.0	71.1	-8.7	59	N/A	250,000	50	0.0	0.0
U /	N/A	N/A	10.76	31	1	67	30	2	88.0	N/A	N/A	N/A	N/A	10,000	100	5.8	0.0
U /	N/A	N/A	10.73	80	1	67	30	2	88.0	N/A	N/A	N/A	N/A	10,000	100	0.0	0.0
B- /7.3	10.0	1.18	21.12	385	1	98	0	1	97.0	82.6	-8.7	70	12	2,500	100	5.8	0.0
B- /7.3	10.2	1.19	18.79	157	1	98	0	1	97.0	78.2	-8.9	60	12	2,500	100	0.0	5.0
B- /7.3	10.2	1.19	18.81	46	1	98	0	1	97.0	78.4	-9.0	61	12	2,500	100	0.0	1.0
B- /7.3	10.1	1.18	22.45	20	1	98	0	1	97.0	85.5	-8.5	74	12	1,000,000	10,000	0.0	0.0
B- /7.0	7.7	0.97	8.53	99	2	97	0	1	62.0	75.5	-10.1	72	N/A	2,500	100	5.8	0.0
C+ /6.6	7.7	0.97	7.64	19	2	97	0	1	62.0	71.5	-10.4	65	N/A	2,500	100	5.8	5.0
C+ /6.6	7.7	0.97	7.64	3	2	97	0	1	62.0	71.5	-10.2	65	N/A	2,500	100	0.0	1.0

					PERFORMANCE							
99 Pct = Best *0 Pct = Worst*			Overall Weiss Investment Rating		Perfor- mance	Total Return % through 6/30/06					Incl. in Returns	
									Annualized		Dividend	Expense
Fund Type	Fund Name	Ticker Symbol		Phone	Rating/Pts	3 Mo	6 Mo	1Yr / Pct	3Yr / Pct	5Yr / Pct	Yield	Ratio
SC	IXIS Vaug Nel Sm Cp Val A	NEFJX	B	(800) 225-5478	B- / 7.1	-3.21	8.99	16.50 /76	18.76 /75	4.09 /47	0.00	1.60
SC	IXIS Vaug Nel Sm Cp Val B	NEJBX	B	(800) 225-5478	B- / 7.1	-3.37	8.62	15.69 /74	17.87 /72	3.31 /40	0.00	2.35
SC	IXIS Vaug Nel Sm Cp Val C	NEJCX	B+	(800) 225-5478	B- / 7.4	-3.37	8.61	15.68 /74	17.90 /72	3.32 /40	0.00	2.35
GR	IXIS Westpeak Capital Growth A	NEFCX	D-	(800) 225-5478	D- / 1.0	-3.70	1.44	5.36 /17	7.44 /12	-2.51 / 6	0.00	1.50
GR	IXIS Westpeak Capital Growth B	NECBX	D-	(800) 225-5478	E+ / 0.6	-3.83	1.08	4.67 /14	6.65 / 9	-3.23 / 5	0.00	2.25
GR	IXIS Westpeak Capital Growth C	NECGX	D	(800) 225-5478	D- / 1.2	-3.84	1.08	4.68 /14	6.67 / 9	-3.26 / 5	0.00	2.25
BA	J Hancock Balanced A	SVBAX	B-	(800) 257-3336	C / 4.3	1.17	5.88	14.18 /69	11.63 /40	4.05 /46	1.22	1.35
BA	J Hancock Balanced B	SVBBX	C+	(800) 257-3336	C- / 3.7	0.99	5.50	13.38 /66	10.87 /34	3.32 /40	0.63	2.05
BA	J Hancock Balanced C	SVBCX	B-	(800) 257-3336	C / 4.5	0.99	5.50	13.38 /66	10.86 /34	3.32 /40	0.63	2.05
BA	J Hancock Balanced I	SVBIX	B+	(800) 257-3336	C / 5.5	1.30	6.15	14.82 /71	12.26 /44	--	1.74	0.84
GI	J Hancock Classic Value A	PZFVX	B-	(800) 257-3336	C / 5.1	-2.80	1.58	8.00 /33	14.81 /58	10.94 /84	0.37	1.32
GI	J Hancock Classic Value B	JCVBX	C+	(800) 257-3336	C / 4.6	-2.98	1.19	7.16 /27	13.94 /54	--	0.00	2.07
GI	J Hancock Classic Value C	JCVCX	B	(800) 257-3336	C / 5.2	-3.02	1.19	7.16 /27	13.94 /54	--	0.00	2.07
GI	J Hancock Classic Value I	JCVIX	B+	(800) 257-3336	C+ / 6.0	-2.71	1.78	8.45 /36	15.28 /60	--	0.79	0.98
GI	J Hancock Core Equity A	JHDCX	C-	(800) 257-3336	D+ / 2.9	-2.05	1.41	7.60 /30	10.90 /35	1.13 /21	0.00	1.48
GI	J Hancock Core Equity B	JHIDX	D+	(800) 257-3336	D+ / 2.4	-2.22	1.07	6.86 /25	10.13 /28	0.43 /17	0.00	2.18
GI	J Hancock Core Equity C	JHCEX	C-	(800) 257-3336	C- / 3.1	-2.22	1.08	6.86 /25	10.13 /28	0.43 /17	0.00	2.18
GI	J Hancock Core Equity I	JHCIX	C	(800) 257-3336	C / 4.3	-1.97	1.68	8.16 /34	11.53 /39	--	0.00	0.90
FS	J Hancock Financial Indust A	FIDAX	C	(800) 257-3336	C- / 3.8	-2.10	2.56	13.15 /65	12.35 /45	3.38 /40	0.29	1.44
FS	J Hancock Financial Indust B	FIDBX	C-	(800) 257-3336	C- / 3.3	-2.25	2.19	12.35 /61	11.57 /40	2.66 /33	0.00	2.14
FS	J Hancock Financial Indust C	FIDCX	C	(800) 257-3336	C- / 4.2	-2.25	2.24	12.35 /61	11.56 /40	2.66 /33	0.00	2.14
FS	J Hancock Financial Indust I	FIDIX	C+	(800) 257-3336	C / 5.0	-1.92	2.83	13.82 /68	12.84 /48	3.91 /45	0.75	0.91
AG	J Hancock Focused Equity A	JFVAX	C-	(800) 257-3336	C / 4.8	-7.61	-1.08	11.47 /56	14.45 /56	-6.65 / 1	0.00	1.50
AG	J Hancock Focused Equity B	JFVBX	C-	(800) 257-3336	C / 4.3	-7.78	-1.49	10.58 /51	13.64 /52	-7.30 / 1	0.00	2.20
AG	J Hancock Focused Equity C	JFVCX	C-	(800) 257-3336	C / 4.9	-7.77	-1.36	10.72 /52	13.69 /52	-7.28 / 1	0.00	2.20
FO	J Hancock Greater China Opp A	JCOAX	U	(800) 257-3336	U /	3.26	26.51	39.26 /98	--	--	0.07	1.98
GR	J Hancock Growth Trends A	JGTAX	D-	(800) 257-3336	D- / 1.2	-6.29	-1.69	7.19 /27	7.99 /15	-2.46 / 7	0.00	1.65
GR	J Hancock Growth Trends B	JGTBX	E+	(800) 257-3336	E+ / 0.8	-6.38	-1.91	6.39 /23	7.20 /11	-3.15 / 5	0.00	2.35
GR	J Hancock Growth Trends C	JGTCX	D-	(800) 257-3336	D- / 1.3	-6.38	-1.91	6.39 /23	7.20 /11	-3.15 / 5	0.00	2.35
HL	J Hancock Health Sciences A	JHGRX	E	(800) 257-3336	D- / 1.2	-7.74	-3.91	3.19 / 8	9.07 /21	3.55 /42	0.00	1.56
HL	J Hancock Health Sciences B	JHRBX	E-	(800) 257-3336	E+ / 0.9	-7.90	-4.24	2.46 / 5	8.30 /17	2.83 /35	0.00	2.26
HL	J Hancock Health Sciences C	JHRCX	E	(800) 257-3336	D- / 1.3	-7.90	-4.26	2.46 / 6	8.30 /17	2.83 /35	0.00	2.26
GR	J Hancock II All Cap Growth 1	JICGX	U	(800) 257-3336	U /	-5.89	0.06	--	--	--	0.00	1.01
GR	J Hancock II All Cap Growth Fd	JHCGX	U	(800) 257-3336	U /	-5.89	0.00	--	--	--	0.00	0.96
GR	J Hancock II All Cap Value Fd	JHCVX	U	(800) 257-3336	U /	-0.44	7.29	--	--	--	0.00	0.95
GR	J Hancock II Blue Chip Grwth 1	JIBCX	U	(800) 257-3336	U /	-4.00	-1.19	--	--	--	0.00	0.89
GR	J Hancock II Blue Chip Grwth Fd	JHBCX	U	(800) 257-3336	U /	-4.01	-1.19	--	--	--	0.00	0.84
GI	J Hancock II Capital Appr 1	JICPX	U	(800) 257-3336	U /	-7.29	-6.18	--	--	--	0.00	0.93
GI	J Hancock II Capital Appr Fd	JHCPX	U	(800) 257-3336	U /	-7.28	-6.08	--	--	--	0.00	0.88
IN	J Hancock II Core Equity Fd	JHCRX	U	(800) 257-3336	U /	-5.46	-4.77	--	--	--	0.00	0.84
GR	J Hancock II Emer Grwth 1	JIEGX	U	(800) 257-3336	U /	-4.37	8.88	--	--	--	0.00	0.92
GR	J Hancock II Emer Grwth Fd	JHEGX	U	(800) 257-3336	U /	-4.37	8.88	--	--	--	0.00	0.87
EM	J Hancock II Emer Sm Comp 1	JIEOX	U	(800) 257-3336	U /	-9.61	1.79	--	--	--	0.00	1.18
IN	J Hancock II Eqty-Inc 1	JIEMX	U	(800) 257-3336	U /	-0.34	5.00	--	--	--	0.00	0.89
IN	J Hancock II Eqty-Inc Fd	JHEIX	U	(800) 257-3336	U /	-0.34	5.01	--	--	--	0.00	0.84
GR	J Hancock II Fundamental Value 1	JIFVX	U	(800) 257-3336	U /	0.51	3.03	--	--	--	0.00	0.87
GR	J Hancock II Fundamental Value Fd	JHFLX	U	(800) 257-3336	U /	0.52	3.04	--	--	--	0.00	0.82
FO	J Hancock II Intl Oppty Fd	JHIOX	U	(800) 257-3336	U /	-3.40	6.54	--	--	--	0.00	1.06
FO	J Hancock II Intl Small Cap 1	JIIMX	U	(800) 257-3336	U /	-3.30	8.94	--	--	--	0.00	1.17
FO	J Hancock II Intl Small Cap Fd	JHISX	U	(800) 257-3336	U /	-3.26	8.94	--	--	--	0.00	1.12
FO	J Hancock II Intl Stock 1	JIILX	U	(800) 257-3336	U /	0.00	10.23	--	--	--	0.00	1.09
FO	J Hancock II Intl Stock Fd	JHILX	U	(800) 257-3336	U /	0.00	10.24	--	--	--	0.00	1.04

● Denotes fund is closed to new investors
* Denotes fund is included in Section II

RISK			NET ASSETS		ASSET					BULL / BEAR		FUND MANAGER		MINIMUMS		LOADS	
	3 Year		NAV						Portfolio	Last Bull	Last Bear	Manager	Manager	Initial	Additional	Front	Back
Risk Rating/Pts	Standard Deviation	Beta	As of 6/30/06	Total $(Mil)	Cash %	Stocks %	Bonds %	Other %	Turnover Ratio	Market Return	Market Return	Quality Pct	Tenure (Years)	Purch. $	Purch. $	End Load	End Load
B- / 7.3	12.5	0.84	19.28	72	4	95	0	1	80.0	118.3	-14.9	81	N/A	2,500	100	5.8	2.0
B- / 7.2	12.5	0.84	17.77	36	4	95	0	1	80.0	113.2	-14.9	74	N/A	2,500	100	0.0	5.0
B- / 7.2	12.5	0.84	17.78	16	4	95	0	1	80.0	113.3	-15.0	75	N/A	2,500	100	0.0	1.0
B- / 7.5	8.9	1.07	11.98	47	1	98	0	1	132.0	48.2	-8.5	19	N/A	2,500	100	5.8	0.0
B- / 7.4	8.9	1.08	10.30	9	1	98	0	1	132.0	44.7	-8.8	14	N/A	2,500	100	5.8	1.0
B- / 7.4	8.9	1.07	10.28	1	1	98	0	1	132.0	44.7	-8.8	15	N/A	2,500	100	0.0	1.0
B+ / 9.5	5.9	0.96	13.24	97	16	63	20	1	88.0	54.7	-4.8	90	3	1,000	0	5.0	0.0
B+ / 9.5	5.9	0.97	13.24	26	16	63	20	1	88.0	51.3	-5.0	86	3	1,000	0	0.0	5.0
B+ / 9.5	5.9	0.97	13.24	8	16	63	20	1	88.0	51.3	-5.0	86	3	1,000	0	0.0	1.0
B+ / 9.5	5.8	0.96	13.25	8	16	63	20	1	88.0	57.3	-4.7	92	3	10,000	0	0.0	0.0
B / 8.8	8.1	1.00	25.03	4,331	2	97	0	1	27.0	87.7	-9.7	86	10	50,000	0	5.0	0.0
B / 8.9	8.2	1.01	24.71	311	2	97	0	1	27.0	83.4	-9.9	80	10	50,000	0	0.0	5.0
B / 8.9	8.2	1.01	24.71	1,015	2	97	0	1	27.0	83.4	-9.9	80	10	50,000	0	0.0	1.0
B / 8.9	8.2	1.00	25.13	1,138	2	97	0	1	27.0	90.2	-9.6	88	10	50,000	0	0.0	0.0
B- / 7.6	8.2	1.05	30.14	189	0	99	0	1	54.0	58.6	-10.2	47	15	1,000	0	5.0	0.0
B- / 7.5	8.2	1.05	28.21	113	0	99	0	1	54.0	55.0	-10.3	38	11	1,000	0	0.0	5.0
B- / 7.5	8.2	1.05	28.20	14	0	99	0	1	54.0	55.1	-10.3	39	8	1,000	0	0.0	1.0
B- / 7.6	8.2	1.05	30.88	N/A	0	99	0	1	54.0	61.3	-9.9	55	15	10,000	0	0.0	0.0
B- / 7.8	8.9	0.94	19.61	642	3	96	0	1	14.0	73.5	-9.9	48	10	1,000	0	5.0	0.0
B- / 7.9	8.9	0.94	18.70	202	3	96	0	1	14.0	69.6	-10.1	39	9	1,000	0	0.0	5.0
B- / 7.8	9.0	0.94	18.69	22	3	96	0	1	14.0	69.7	-10.1	39	7	1,000	0	0.0	0.0
B / 8.0	8.9	0.94	19.97	N/A	3	96	0	1	14.0	75.9	-9.7	55	5	10,000	0	0.0	0.0
C+ / 6.5	13.3	1.44	8.26	9	2	97	0	1	62.0	92.2	-6.1	46	4	1,000	0	5.0	0.0
C+ / 6.4	13.3	1.44	7.94	6	2	97	0	1	62.0	87.9	-6.2	37	4	1,000	0	0.0	5.0
C+ / 6.4	13.4	1.44	7.95	2	2	97	0	1	62.0	88.1	-6.2	38	4	1,000	0	0.0	1.0
U /	N/A	N/A	13.98	48	5	94	0	1	28.0	N/A	N/A	N/A	1	1,000	0	5.0	0.0
C+ / 6.6	9.6	1.11	6.41	41	3	96	0	1	27.0	59.7	-10.3	20	5	1,000	0	5.0	0.0
C+ / 6.5	9.5	1.10	6.16	55	3	96	0	1	27.0	56.3	-10.6	16	5	1,000	0	0.0	5.0
C+ / 6.5	9.5	1.10	6.16	19	3	96	0	1	27.0	56.3	-10.6	16	5	1,000	0	0.0	1.0
C- / 4.2	10.1	0.83	43.53	149	13	86	0	1	50.0	58.5	-3.8	49	N/A	1,000	0	5.0	0.0
C- / 3.9	10.1	0.83	39.08	90	13	86	0	1	50.0	55.1	-3.9	40	N/A	1,000	0	0.0	5.0
C- / 3.9	10.2	0.83	39.08	14	13	86	0	1	50.0	55.1	-3.9	40	N/A	1,000	0	0.0	1.0
U /	N/A	N/A	16.62	33	2	97	0	1	N/A	N/A	N/A	N/A	N/A	1,000	0	0.0	0.0
U /	N/A	N/A	16.63	114	2	97	0	1	N/A	N/A	N/A	N/A	N/A	1,000	0	0.0	0.0
U /	N/A	N/A	15.74	184	3	96	0	1	N/A	N/A	N/A	N/A	N/A	1,000	0	0.0	0.0
U /	N/A	N/A	17.51	122	1	98	0	1	N/A	N/A	N/A	N/A	N/A	1,000	0	0.0	0.0
U /	N/A	N/A	17.49	1,025	1	98	0	1	N/A	N/A	N/A	N/A	N/A	1,000	0	0.0	0.0
U /	N/A	N/A	9.41	65	1	98	0	1	N/A	N/A	N/A	N/A	N/A	1,000	0	0.0	0.0
U /	N/A	N/A	9.42	370	1	98	0	1	N/A	N/A	N/A	N/A	N/A	1,000	0	0.0	0.0
U /	N/A	N/A	14.36	544	N/A	100	0	N/A	N/A	N/A	N/A	N/A	N/A	1,000	0	0.0	0.0
U /	N/A	N/A	19.26	130	4	95	0	1	N/A	N/A	N/A	N/A	N/A	1,000	0	0.0	0.0
U /	N/A	N/A	19.26	48	4	95	0	1	N/A	N/A	N/A	N/A	N/A	1,000	0	0.0	0.0
U /	N/A	N/A	30.74	54	2	97	0	1	80.0	N/A	N/A	N/A	N/A	1,000	0	0.0	0.0
U /	N/A	N/A	17.64	173	4	95	0	1	N/A	N/A	N/A	N/A	N/A	1,000	0	0.0	0.0
U /	N/A	N/A	17.62	505	4	95	0	1	N/A	N/A	N/A	N/A	N/A	1,000	0	0.0	0.0
U /	N/A	N/A	15.62	63	3	94	1	2	N/A	N/A	N/A	N/A	N/A	1,000	0	0.0	0.0
U /	N/A	N/A	15.59	662	3	94	1	2	N/A	N/A	N/A	N/A	N/A	1,000	0	0.0	0.0
U /	N/A	N/A	15.64	526	1	98	0	1	N/A	N/A	N/A	N/A	N/A	1,000	0	0.0	0.0
U /	N/A	N/A	20.48	36	9	90	0	1	N/A	N/A	N/A	N/A	N/A	1,000	0	0.0	0.0
U /	N/A	N/A	20.47	340	9	90	0	1	N/A	N/A	N/A	N/A	N/A	1,000	0	0.0	0.0
U /	N/A	N/A	13.79	38	5	94	0	1	N/A	N/A	N/A	N/A	N/A	1,000	0	0.0	0.0
U /	N/A	N/A	13.78	955	5	94	0	1	N/A	N/A	N/A	N/A	N/A	1,000	0	0.0	0.0

Fund Type	Fund Name	Ticker Symbol	Overall Weiss Investment Rating	Phone	Performance Rating/Pts	3 Mo	6 Mo	1Yr / Pct	3Yr / Pct	5Yr / Pct	Dividend Yield	Expense Ratio
	99 Pct = Best							**Total Return % through 6/30/06**	**Annualized**		**Incl. in Returns**	
GL	J Hancock II Intl Value 1	JIVIX	U	(800) 257-3336	U /	2.12	10.04	--	--	--	0.00	1.00
GL	J Hancock II Intl Value Fd	JHVIX	U	(800) 257-3336	U /	2.13	10.13	--	--	--	0.00	0.95
GR	J Hancock II Large Cap Fd	JHLPX	U	(800) 257-3336	U /	-2.12	1.42	--	--	--	0.00	0.90
GR	J Hancock II Large Cap Value Fd	JHCLX	U	(800) 257-3336	U /	-0.35	5.89	--	--	--	0.00	0.91
MC	J Hancock II Mid Cap Core Fd	JHMRX	U	(800) 257-3336	U /	-2.93	1.95	--	--	--	0.00	0.94
MC	J Hancock II Mid Cap Stock 1	JIMSX	U	(800) 257-3336	U /	-4.37	3.84	--	--	--	0.00	0.95
MC	J Hancock II Mid Cap Stock Fd	JHMSX	U	(800) 257-3336	U /	-4.37	3.90	--	--	--	0.00	0.90
MC	J Hancock II Mid Cap Value 1	JIMVX	U	(800) 257-3336	U /	-3.39	0.21	--	--	--	0.00	0.97
MC	J Hancock II Mid Cap Value Fd	JHMVX	U	(800) 257-3336	U /	-3.34	0.27	--	--	--	0.00	0.92
EN	J Hancock II Natural Resources 1	JINRX	U	(800) 257-3336	U /	2.72	16.32	--	--	--	0.00	1.13
EN	J Hancock II Natural Resources Fd	JHNRX	U	(800) 257-3336	U /	2.73	16.34	--	--	--	0.00	1.08
MC	J Hancock II Quantitative MdCp 1	JIQMX	U	(800) 257-3336	U /	-6.33	0.96	--	--	--	0.00	0.84
MC	J Hancock II Quantitative MdCp Fd	JHQMX	U	(800) 257-3336	U /	-6.33	0.96	--	--	--	0.00	0.79
GR	J Hancock II Quantitative Val 1	JIQVX	U	(800) 257-3336	U /	0.19	5.49	--	--	--	0.00	0.80
GR	J Hancock II Quantitative Val Fd	JHQVX	U	(800) 257-3336	U /	0.19	5.49	--	--	--	0.00	0.75
RE	J Hancock II Real Estate Sec 1		U	(800) 257-3336	U /	-1.03	13.31	--	--	--	0.00	0.79
SC	J Hancock II Sm Cap Oppty 1	JISOX	U	(800) 257-3336	U /	-2.76	7.09	--	--	--	0.00	1.09
SC	J Hancock II Sm Cap Oppty Fd	JHSOX	U	(800) 257-3336	U /	-2.73	7.13	--	--	--	0.00	1.04
GR	J Hancock II Sm Comp Fd	JHSNX	U	(800) 257-3336	U /	-6.55	3.34	--	--	--	0.00	1.31
SC	J Hancock II Small Cap Fd	JHSPX	U	(800) 257-3336	U /	-8.75	0.49	--	--	--	0.00	0.90
SC	J Hancock II Small Comp Grwth Fd	JHSRX	U	(800) 257-3336	U /	-4.79	6.48	--	--	--	0.00	1.09
SC	J Hancock II Small Val Company 1	JISVX	U	(800) 257-3336	U /	-2.92	10.68	--	--	--	0.00	1.10
SC	J Hancock II Small Val Company Fd	JHSVX	U	(800) 257-3336	U /	-2.93	10.69	--	--	--	0.00	1.05
GR	J Hancock II Special Value Fd	JHPEX	U	(800) 257-3336	U /	-2.53	5.25	--	--	--	0.00	1.07
GR	J Hancock II Spectrum Fd	JHSTX	U	(800) 257-3336	U /	0.01	1.20	--	--	--	0.00	0.93
GR	J Hancock II Strategic Value Fd	JHSLX	U	(800) 257-3336	U /	-3.42	1.23	--	--	--	0.00	0.91
GI	J Hancock II Total Return 1	JITRX	U	(800) 257-3336	U /	-0.29	-0.95	--	--	--	0.00	0.83
GI	J Hancock II Total Return Fd	JHTRX	U	(800) 257-3336	U /	-0.27	-0.92	--	--	--	0.00	0.78
GL	J Hancock II US Glbl Ldr Grw Fd	JHGUX	U	(800) 257-3336	U /	-7.19	-6.01	--	--	--	0.00	0.74
IN	J Hancock II US Multi Sector Fd	JHUMX	U	(800) 257-3336	U /	-4.78	-1.74	--	--	--	0.00	0.82
GI	J Hancock II Value & Recons Fd	JHVSX	U	(800) 257-3336	U /	-1.50	5.27	--	--	--	0.00	0.90
GR	J Hancock II Vista Fd	JHVTX	U	(800) 257-3336	U /	-3.07	6.67	--	--	--	0.00	0.99
GI	J Hancock Indep Div Core II I	COREX	E+	(800) 257-3336	C / 5.5	-1.69	2.63	9.78 /45	13.76 /53	3.13 /38	0.67	0.95
FO	J Hancock International A	FINAX	C+	(800) 257-3336	B / 8.1	-2.28	5.15	28.63 /93	20.46 /81	5.79 /60	0.00	2.08
FO	J Hancock International B	FINBX	C+	(800) 257-3336	B / 7.8	-2.38	4.70	27.70 /92	19.68 /78	5.06 /55	0.00	2.78
FO	J Hancock International C	JINCX	C+	(800) 257-3336	B / 8.1	-2.38	4.70	27.70 /92	19.68 /78	5.03 /54	0.00	2.78
FO	J Hancock International I	JINIX	B	(800) 257-3336	B+ / 8.6	-2.09	5.44	29.44 /94	21.45 /84	--	0.00	1.32
GI	J Hancock Large Cap Equity A	TAGRX	C+	(800) 257-3336	C+ / 6.6	1.84	9.63	23.55 /87	14.46 /56	-1.59 /10	0.00	1.25
GI	J Hancock Large Cap Equity B	TSGWX	C+	(800) 257-3336	C+ / 6.2	1.68	9.24	22.63 /85	13.60 /52	-2.32 / 7	0.00	2.01
GI	J Hancock Large Cap Equity C	JHLVX	C+	(800) 257-3336	C+ / 6.7	1.68	9.24	22.63 /85	13.60 /52	-2.32 / 7	0.00	2.01
GI	J Hancock Large Cap Equity I	JLVIX	B-	(800) 257-3336	B- / 7.4	2.01	9.92	24.16 /87	15.30 /60	-1.00 /12	0.00	0.78
GR	J Hancock Large Cap Select A	MSBFX	D-	(800) 257-3336	E / 0.5	-2.36	0.97	3.09 / 8	5.39 / 5	1.36 /23	0.19	1.36
AG	J Hancock Lifestyle Aggressive 1	JILAX	U	(800) 257-3336	U /	-2.58	4.57	--	--	--	0.00	N/A
AG	J Hancock Lifestyle Aggressive A	JALAX	U	(800) 257-3336	U /	-2.72	4.33	--	--	--	0.00	1.60
BA	J Hancock Lifestyle Balanced 1	JILBX	U	(800) 257-3336	U /	-1.53	2.76	--	--	--	0.00	N/A
BA	J Hancock Lifestyle Balanced A	JALBX	U	(800) 257-3336	U /	-1.66	2.46	--	--	--	0.00	0.66
BA	J Hancock Lifestyle Balanced C	JCLBX	U	(800) 257-3336	U /	-1.87	2.09	--	--	--	0.00	1.36
GI	J Hancock Lifestyle Cons 1	JILCX	U	(800) 257-3336	U /	-0.37	1.13	--	--	--	0.00	0.88
GR	J Hancock Lifestyle Growth 1	JILGX	U	(800) 257-3336	U /	-2.11	3.30	--	--	--	0.00	N/A
GR	J Hancock Lifestyle Growth A	JALGX	U	(800) 257-3336	U /	-2.17	3.15	--	--	--	0.00	0.66
GR	J Hancock Lifestyle Growth C	JCLGX	U	(800) 257-3336	U /	-2.31	2.79	--	--	--	0.00	1.36
AA	J Hancock Lifestyle Mode 1	JILMX	U	(800) 257-3336	U /	-1.03	1.81	--	--	--	0.00	0.92

● Denotes fund is closed to new investors
★ Denotes fund is included in Section II

RISK			NET ASSETS		ASSET				Portfolio Turnover Ratio	BULL / BEAR		FUND MANAGER		MINIMUMS		LOADS	
Risk Rating/Pts	3 Year		NAV As of 6/30/06	Total $(Mil)	Cash %	Stocks %	Bonds %	Other %		Last Bull Market Return	Last Bear Market Return	Manager Quality Pct	Manager Tenure (Years)	Initial Purch. $	Additional Purch. $	Front End Load	Back End Load
	Standard Deviation	Beta															
U /	N/A	N/A	17.32	124	5	94	0	1	N/A	N/A	N/A	N/A	N/A	1,000	0	0.0	0.0
U /	N/A	N/A	17.29	799	5	94	0	1	N/A	N/A	N/A	N/A	N/A	1,000	0	0.0	0.0
U /	N/A	N/A	14.29	180	3	96	0	1	N/A	N/A	N/A	N/A	N/A	1,000	0	0.0	0.0
U /	N/A	N/A	22.84	222	0	99	0	1	N/A	N/A	N/A	N/A	N/A	1,000	0	0.0	0.0
U /	N/A	N/A	17.25	277	18	80	0	2	N/A	N/A	N/A	N/A	N/A	1,000	0	0.0	0.0
U /	N/A	N/A	15.96	107	3	96	0	1	N/A	N/A	N/A	N/A	N/A	1,000	0	0.0	0.0
U /	N/A	N/A	15.98	179	3	96	0	1	N/A	N/A	N/A	N/A	N/A	1,000	0	0.0	0.0
U /	N/A	N/A	18.83	91	5	94	0	1	N/A	N/A	N/A	N/A	N/A	1,000	0	0.0	0.0
U /	N/A	N/A	18.82	48	5	94	0	1	N/A	N/A	N/A	N/A	N/A	1,000	0	0.0	0.0
U /	N/A	N/A	36.21	74	3	96	0	1	N/A	N/A	N/A	N/A	N/A	1,000	0	0.0	0.0
U /	N/A	N/A	36.09	704	3	96	0	1	N/A	N/A	N/A	N/A	N/A	1,000	0	0.0	0.0
U /	N/A	N/A	14.79	140	2	97	0	1	N/A	N/A	N/A	N/A	N/A	1,000	0	0.0	0.0
U /	N/A	N/A	14.79	47	2	97	0	1	N/A	N/A	N/A	N/A	N/A	1,000	0	0.0	0.0
U /	N/A	N/A	15.94	86	1	98	0	1	N/A	N/A	N/A	N/A	N/A	1,000	0	0.0	0.0
U /	N/A	N/A	15.94	345	1	98	0	1	N/A	N/A	N/A	N/A	N/A	1,000	0	0.0	0.0
U /	N/A	N/A	27.92	151	1	98	0	1	24.0	N/A	N/A	N/A	N/A	1,000	0	0.0	0.0
U /	N/A	N/A	24.31	31	5	94	0	1	N/A	N/A	N/A	N/A	N/A	1,000	0	0.0	0.0
U /	N/A	N/A	24.20	220	5	94	0	1	N/A	N/A	N/A	N/A	N/A	1,000	0	0.0	0.0
U /	N/A	N/A	16.41	84	0	99	0	1	N/A	N/A	N/A	N/A	N/A	1,000	0	0.0	0.0
U /	N/A	N/A	14.39	220	3	96	0	1	N/A	N/A	N/A	N/A	N/A	1,000	0	0.0	0.0
U /	N/A	N/A	11.34	68	1	98	0	1	N/A	N/A	N/A	N/A	N/A	1,000	0	0.0	0.0
U /	N/A	N/A	24.57	153	3	96	0	1	N/A	N/A	N/A	N/A	N/A	1,000	0	0.0	0.0
U /	N/A	N/A	24.54	223	3	96	0	1	N/A	N/A	N/A	N/A	N/A	1,000	0	0.0	0.0
U /	N/A	N/A	20.84	116	5	94	0	1	N/A	N/A	N/A	N/A	N/A	1,000	0	0.0	0.0
U /	N/A	N/A	10.02	724	9	17	72	2	59.0	N/A	N/A	N/A	N/A	1,000	0	0.0	0.0
U /	N/A	N/A	10.72	129	1	98	0	1	N/A	N/A	N/A	N/A	N/A	1,000	0	0.0	0.0
U /	N/A	N/A	13.38	113	8	0	91	1	N/A	N/A	N/A	N/A	N/A	1,000	0	0.0	0.0
U /	N/A	N/A	13.35	993	8	0	91	1	N/A	N/A	N/A	N/A	N/A	1,000	0	0.0	0.0
U /	N/A	N/A	12.52	421	0	99	0	1	N/A	N/A	N/A	N/A	N/A	1,000	0	0.0	0.0
U /	N/A	N/A	10.17	1,154	5	94	0	1	N/A	N/A	N/A	N/A	N/A	1,000	0	0.0	0.0
U /	N/A	N/A	11.19	282	1	98	0	1	6.0	N/A	N/A	N/A	N/A	1,000	0	0.0	0.0
U /	N/A	N/A	11.36	117	1	98	0	1	79.0	N/A	N/A	N/A	N/A	1,000	0	0.0	0.0
D- / 1.1	8.5	1.06	3.16	26	0	98	0	2	95.0	69.7	-9.2	75	11	10,000	0	0.0	0.0
C / 5.5	13.0	1.18	8.57	88	9	90	0	1	176.0	115.3	-8.8	7	N/A	1,000	0	5.0	0.0
C / 5.4	13.0	1.18	7.79	26	9	90	0	1	176.0	110.6	-9.1	5	N/A	1,000	0	0.0	5.0
C / 5.4	13.0	1.19	7.79	5	9	90	0	1	176.0	110.9	-9.1	5	N/A	1,000	0	0.0	1.0
C+ / 5.6	13.0	1.18	8.91	2	9	90	0	1	176.0	120.9	-8.4	10	N/A	10,000	0	0.0	0.0
C+ / 6.4	10.3	0.94	19.36	386	5	94	0	1	74.0	73.2	-9.8	87	N/A	1,000	0	5.0	0.0
C+ / 6.3	10.2	0.94	18.21	126	5	94	0	1	74.0	69.1	-10.0	82	N/A	1,000	0	0.0	5.0
C+ / 6.3	10.2	0.94	18.21	23	5	94	0	1	74.0	69.1	-10.0	82	N/A	1,000	0	0.0	1.0
C+ / 6.4	10.3	0.95	19.84	N/A	5	94	0	1	74.0	77.1	-9.7	90	N/A	10,000	0	0.0	0.0
B / 8.0	6.4	0.72	17.77	57	9	90	0	1	23.0	34.4	-12.4	26	13	1,000	0	5.0	0.0
U /	N/A	N/A	13.96	2,333	0	100	0	0	2.0	N/A	N/A	N/A	N/A	1,000	0	0.0	0.0
U /	N/A	N/A	13.96	28	0	100	0	0	2.0	N/A	N/A	N/A	N/A	1,000	0	5.0	0.0
U /	N/A	N/A	14.17	6,417	0	60	38	2	3.0	N/A	N/A	N/A	N/A	1,000	0	0.0	0.0
U /	N/A	N/A	14.18	60	0	60	38	2	3.0	N/A	N/A	N/A	N/A	1,000	0	5.0	0.0
U /	N/A	N/A	14.14	61	0	60	38	2	3.0	N/A	N/A	N/A	N/A	1,000	0	0.0	1.0
U /	N/A	N/A	13.47	1,047	0	20	80	0	3.0	N/A	N/A	N/A	N/A	1,000	0	0.0	0.0
U /	N/A	N/A	14.40	6,778	0	80	20	0	3.0	N/A	N/A	N/A	N/A	1,000	0	0.0	0.0
U /	N/A	N/A	14.42	80	0	80	20	0	3.0	N/A	N/A	N/A	N/A	1,000	0	5.0	0.0
U /	N/A	N/A	14.38	73	0	80	20	0	3.0	N/A	N/A	N/A	N/A	1,000	0	0.0	1.0
U /	N/A	N/A	13.48	1,728	0	40	60	0	3.0	N/A	N/A	N/A	N/A	1,000	0	0.0	0.0

Data as of June 30, 2006

Fund Type	Fund Name	Ticker Symbol	Overall Weiss Investment Rating	Phone	Perfor-mance Rating/Pts	3 Mo	6 Mo	1Yr / Pct	3Yr / Pct	5Yr / Pct	Dividend Yield	Expense Ratio
	99 Pct = Best 0 Pct = Worst				**PERFORMANCE** Total Return % through 6/30/06 Annualized Incl. in Returns							
MC	J Hancock Mid Cap Growth A	SPOAX	E	(800) 257-3336	D / 2.0	-10.55	-0.49	12.75 /63	10.93 /35	0.28 /17	0.00	1.74
MC	J Hancock Mid Cap Growth B	SPOBX	E	(800) 257-3336	D- / 1.5	-10.72	-0.87	11.84 /59	10.17 /28	-0.45 /14	0.00	2.44
MC	J Hancock Mid Cap Growth C	SPOCX	E	(800) 257-3336	D / 2.1	-10.71	-0.76	11.97 /59	10.16 /28	-0.41 /14	0.00	2.44
MC	J Hancock Mid Cap Growth I	SPOIX	E+	(800) 257-3336	C- / 3.3	-10.41	-0.19	13.51 /66	11.77 /41	--	0.00	1.04
GR	J Hancock Multi Cap Growth A	JMGAX	C	(800) 257-3336	C / 4.8	-3.13	6.91	11.90 /59	13.15 /50	3.68 /43	0.00	1.40
GR	J Hancock Multi Cap Growth B	JMGBX	C-	(800) 257-3336	C / 4.3	-3.23	6.53	11.11 /54	12.40 /45	2.97 /37	0.00	2.10
GR	J Hancock Multi Cap Growth C	JMGCX	C	(800) 257-3336	C / 4.9	-3.23	6.53	11.24 /55	12.40 /45	2.98 /37	0.00	2.10
RE	J Hancock Real Estate A	JREAX	C+	(800) 257-3336	B+ / 8.8	-2.03	12.17	18.16 /79	24.34 /90	17.59 /94	1.68	1.60
RE	J Hancock Real Estate B	JREBX	C+	(800) 257-3336	B+ / 8.6	-2.20	11.80	17.36 /78	23.46 /88	16.78 /94	1.12	2.30
RE	J Hancock Real Estate C	JRECX	C+	(800) 257-3336	B+ / 8.8	-2.20	11.80	17.36 /78	23.46 /88	16.78 /94	1.12	2.30
FS	J Hancock Regional Bank A	FRBAX	D+	(800) 257-3336	C / 4.7	1.17	5.81	10.35 /49	12.94 /48	8.24 /73	1.51	1.33
FS	J Hancock Regional Bank B	FRBFX	D	(800) 257-3336	C- / 4.2	0.97	5.44	9.57 /44	12.15 /43	7.49 /69	0.95	2.03
FS	J Hancock Regional Bank C	FRBCX	D+	(800) 257-3336	C / 4.9	0.97	5.44	9.59 /44	12.15 /43	7.49 /69	0.95	2.03
SC	J Hancock Small Cap Equity A	SPVAX	C-	(800) 257-3336	C+ / 6.4	-9.24	3.40	14.10 /68	17.42 /70	-1.03 /12	0.00	1.42
SC	J Hancock Small Cap Equity B	SPVBX	C-	(800) 257-3336	C+ / 6.0	-9.38	3.06	13.30 /65	16.59 /66	-1.72 / 9	0.00	2.12
SC	J Hancock Small Cap Equity C	SPVCX	C-	(800) 257-3336	C+ / 6.5	-9.42	3.06	13.30 /65	16.59 /66	-1.72 / 9	0.00	2.12
SC	J Hancock Small Cap Equity I	SPVIX	C	(800) 257-3336	B- / 7.3	-9.09	3.72	14.77 /71	18.15 /73	--	0.00	0.87
SC	J Hancock Small Cap Fund A	DSISX	C-	(800) 257-3336	C / 5.2	-8.99	0.25	5.91 /20	16.15 /64	7.30 /68	0.00	1.58
SC	J Hancock Small Cap Fund C	DSCSX	U	(800) 257-3336	U /	-9.15	-0.08	5.15 /16	--	--	0.00	2.28
SC	J Hancock Small Cap Fund I	DSIIX	U	(800) 257-3336	U /	-8.87	0.49	6.42 /23	--	--	0.00	1.10
IN	J Hancock Sovereign Investors A	SOVIX	D	(800) 257-3336	D- / 1.5	-0.46	3.61	8.69 /38	7.69 /13	1.16 /21	0.86	1.19
IN	J Hancock Sovereign Investors B	SOVBX	D	(800) 257-3336	D- / 1.1	-0.58	3.31	7.95 /32	6.95 /10	0.46 /17	0.24	1.89
IN	J Hancock Sovereign Investors C	SOVCX	D	(800) 257-3336	D / 1.7	-0.58	3.30	7.94 /32	6.96 /10	0.47 /18	0.24	1.89
GR	J Hancock Tech Leaders A	LUXRX	E	(800) 257-3336	D- / 1.4	-7.97	-2.81	8.59 /37	8.75 /19	-3.11 / 5	0.00	1.80
TC	J Hancock Technology A	NTTFX	E-	(800) 257-3336	E- / 0.0	-11.47	-4.87	--	2.09 / 1	-12.30 / 0	0.00	1.90
TC	J Hancock Technology B	FGTBX	E-	(800) 257-3336	E- / 0.0	-11.73	-5.05	-0.66 / 1	1.48 / 0	-12.89 / 0	0.00	2.60
TC	J Hancock Technology C	JHTCX	E-	(800) 257-3336	E- / 0.0	-11.73	-5.05	-0.66 / 1	1.48 / 0	-12.89 / 0	0.00	2.60
TC	J Hancock Technology I	JHTIX	E-	(800) 257-3336	E- / 0.2	-11.49	-4.49	0.84 / 2	4.09 / 2	-10.83 / 0	0.00	0.96
GR	J Hancock US Glob Lead Gr A	USGLX	D-	(800) 257-3336	E- / 0.1	-7.20	-6.19	-0.15 / 2	4.60 / 3	1.38 /23	0.00	1.28
GR	J Hancock US Glob Lead Gr B	USLBX	D-	(800) 257-3336	E- / 0.1	-7.39	-6.56	-0.92 / 1	3.82 / 2	--	0.00	2.03
GR	J Hancock US Glob Lead Gr C	USLCX	D-	(800) 257-3336	E- / 0.1	-7.39	-6.56	-0.92 / 1	3.82 / 2	--	0.00	2.03
GR	J Hancock US Glob Lead Gr I	USLIX	D-	(800) 257-3336	E / 0.4	-7.12	-6.02	0.26 / 2	5.07 / 4	--	0.00	0.85
TC	Jacob Internet Fund	JAMFX	D+	(888) 522-6239	A- / 9.0	-7.46	5.08	28.50 /93	26.33 /92	14.69 /91	0.00	2.43
GI	Jacobs & Co Mutual Fund	JACOX	E+	(877) 560-6823	E- / 0.1	-1.26	-1.60	1.99 / 4	1.45 / 0	-1.30 /11	1.42	1.70
BA	James Advantage Bal Goldn Rainbow	GLRBX	B-	(888) 426-7640	C- / 4.2	0.18	2.77	6.48 /23	11.39 /38	8.71 /75	1.90	1.21
GR	James Advantage Equity A	JALCX	A+	(888) 426-7640	B+ / 8.7	0.27	12.65	24.45 /88	21.58 /84	7.90 /71	0.19	1.50
GR	James Advantage Market Neutral A	JAMNX	C+	(888) 426-7640	D+ / 2.8	4.27	4.09	4.94 /15	8.90 /20	5.02 /54	1.42	1.95
SC	James Advantage Small Cap Value A	JASCX	A-	(888) 426-7640	B+ / 8.7	-0.85	10.65	15.59 /73	22.98 /87	18.01 /94	0.18	1.50
BA	Jamestown Balanced Fund	JAMBX	D	(866) 738-1126	D- / 1.0	-3.24	-0.80	4.31 /12	6.14 / 7	2.40 /31	1.77	0.89
GR	Jamestown Equity Fund	JAMEX	D	(866) 738-1126	D / 2.2	-4.69	-1.00	6.56 /24	8.67 /19	0.98 /20	0.32	0.92
FO	Jamestown Intl Equity Fund	JAMIX	B	(866) 738-1126	B+ / 8.3	-0.71	8.01	27.62 /92	19.98 /79	5.34 /57	0.75	1.44
BA	Janus Adviser Balanced C	JABCX	D+	(800) 525-3713	D / 1.9	-2.29	1.29	7.51 /29	7.82 /14	--	1.00	1.57
BA	Janus Adviser Balanced S	JABRX	C-	(800) 525-3713	D+ / 2.4	-2.19	1.57	8.02 /33	8.36 /17	4.51 /50	1.46	1.07
FO	Janus Adviser Foreign Stock C	JGVCX	B+	(800) 525-3713	B / 7.6	-0.07	5.65	14.54 /70	18.48 /74	--	0.00	2.27
FO	Janus Adviser Foreign Stock S	JADVX	A-	(800) 525-3713	B / 7.7	0.00	5.89	15.06 /72	19.04 /76	8.67 /75	0.24	1.74
GR	Janus Adviser Forty C	JACCX	C-	(800) 525-3713	C / 4.9	-3.43	-0.52	8.02 /33	13.53 /51	--	0.00	1.67
GR	Janus Adviser Forty S	JARTX	C-	(800) 525-3713	C / 5.4	-3.31	-0.28	8.56 /37	14.09 /54	4.12 /47	0.00	1.17
GR	Janus Adviser Fundamental Equity C	JADCX	C	(800) 525-3713	C+ / 6.0	-3.36	3.11	17.19 /77	15.13 /59	--	0.00	1.70
GR	Janus Adviser Fundamental Equity S	JADEX	C+	(800) 525-3713	C+ / 6.4	-3.24	3.36	17.75 /79	15.71 /62	5.23 /56	0.12	1.20
IN	Janus Adviser Growth & Income C	JGICX	C-	(800) 525-3713	C / 4.6	-4.28	0.88	11.33 /56	12.34 /45	--	0.49	1.81
IN	Janus Adviser Growth & Income S	JADGX	C-	(800) 525-3713	C / 5.1	-4.30	0.98	11.86 /59	12.92 /48	3.31 /40	0.88	1.21
GR	Janus Adviser INTECH Rsk Mgd	JLCCX	D	(800) 525-3713	C+ / 5.8	-2.76	1.40	9.09 /41	14.94 /58	--	0.04	1.61

RISK			NET ASSETS		ASSET					Portfolio	BULL / BEAR		FUND MANAGER		MINIMUMS		LOADS	
	3 Year		NAV								Last Bull	Last Bear	Manager	Manager	Initial	Additional	Front	Back
Risk Rating/Pts	Standard Deviation	Beta	As of 6/30/06	Total $(Mil)	Cash %	Stocks %	Bonds %	Other %		Turnover Ratio	Market Return	Market Return	Quality Pct	Tenure (Years)	Purch. $	Purch. $	End Load	End Load
C- /4.0	15.1	1.27	10.17	103	3	96	0	1		71.0	86.1	-10.0	2	N/A	1,000	25	5.0	0.0
C- /3.9	15.1	1.27	9.16	24	3	96	0	1		71.0	82.1	-10.1	1	N/A	1,000	0	0.0	5.0
C- /3.9	15.1	1.27	9.17	4	3	96	0	1		71.0	82.1	-10.2	1	N/A	1,000	25	0.0	1.0
C- /4.1	15.2	1.27	10.50	3	3	96	0	1		71.0	90.4	-9.8	2	N/A	10,000	0	0.0	0.0
B- /7.1	11.3	1.24	9.59	7	5	94	0	1		56.0	85.4	-12.7	52	N/A	1,000	0	5.0	0.0
B- /7.0	11.4	1.25	9.30	4	5	94	0	1		56.0	81.7	-13.0	43	N/A	1,000	0	0.0	5.0
B- /7.0	11.3	1.24	9.30	2	5	94	0	1		56.0	81.5	-13.0	44	N/A	1,000	0	0.0	1.0
C /4.4	16.0	0.96	20.84	38	1	98	0	1		13.0	117.1	0.2	67	8	1,000	0	5.0	0.0
C /4.4	15.9	0.96	20.82	22	1	98	0	1		13.0	112.3	0.1	59	6	1,000	0	0.0	5.0
C /4.4	16.0	0.96	20.82	13	1	98	0	1		13.0	112.3	0.1	59	6	1,000	0	0.0	1.0
C /5.1	9.4	0.89	40.26	1,692	0	99	0	1		3.0	63.5	-4.5	61	14	1,000	0	5.0	0.0
C /5.1	9.4	0.89	39.87	282	0	99	0	1		3.0	59.9	-4.6	53	21	1,000	0	0.0	5.0
C /5.1	9.4	0.89	39.88	44	0	99	0	1		3.0	59.9	-4.6	53	7	1,000	0	0.0	1.0
C /4.9	15.2	0.99	21.61	647	2	97	0	1		22.0	109.6	-8.8	44	4	1,000	0	5.0	0.0
C /4.8	15.2	0.99	20.19	210	2	97	0	1		22.0	105.1	-9.0	36	4	1,000	0	0.0	5.0
C /4.8	15.2	0.99	20.19	59	2	97	0	1		22.0	105.1	-9.0	36	4	1,000	0	0.0	1.0
C /5.0	15.2	0.99	22.30	31	2	97	0	1		22.0	113.9	-8.7	52	4	1,000	0	0.0	0.0
C /5.6	14.5	0.95	12.15	154	2	97	0	1		39.0	103.3	-9.5	39	N/A	1,000	0	5.0	0.0
U /	N/A	N/A	12.02	44	2	97	0	1		39.0	N/A	N/A	N/A	N/A	1,000	0	0.0	1.0
U /	N/A	N/A	12.23	40	2	97	0	1		39.0	N/A	N/A	N/A	N/A	1,000	0	0.0	0.0
B- /7.9	6.3	0.80	19.08	783	7	92	0	1		30.0	42.6	-8.5	37	12	1,000	0	5.0	0.0
B- /7.9	6.3	0.80	19.04	124	7	92	0	1		30.0	39.5	-8.6	32	12	1,000	0	0.0	5.0
B- /7.9	6.3	0.80	19.07	16	7	92	0	1		30.0	39.5	-8.6	32	8	1,000	0	0.0	1.0
C /4.5	14.6	1.66	9.35	4	17	82	0	1		31.0	66.2	-13.0	5	N/A	10,000	0	5.0	0.0
D- /1.4	20.6	2.12	3.32	152	6	93	0	1		25.0	51.6	-16.6	0	N/A	10,000	0	5.0	0.0
D- /1.4	20.7	2.13	3.01	68	6	93	0	1		25.0	48.3	-16.8	0	N/A	1,000	0	0.0	5.0
D- /1.4	20.7	2.12	3.01	11	6	93	0	1		25.0	48.3	-16.8	0	N/A	1,000	0	0.0	1.0
D- /1.4	21.0	2.18	3.62	N/A	6	93	0	1		25.0	61.1	-16.3	0	N/A	1,000	0	0.0	0.0
B- /7.9	8.5	0.83	26.68	1,249	0	99	0	1		28.0	36.4	-10.2	15	N/A	1,000	0	5.0	0.0
B- /7.9	8.5	0.83	25.93	170	0	99	0	1		28.0	33.2	-10.3	12	N/A	1,000	0	0.0	5.0
B- /7.9	8.5	0.83	25.93	216	0	99	0	1		28.0	33.2	-10.3	12	N/A	1,000	0	0.0	1.0
B /8.1	8.5	0.83	27.01	18	0	99	0	1		28.0	38.3	-10.2	18	N/A	10,000	0	0.0	0.0
D- /1.2	23.1	2.03	2.48	97	8	91	0	1		57.3	246.3	-4.8	91	10	2,500	100	0.0	2.0
B- /7.3	7.3	0.69	8.61	5	9	50	40	1		148.8	10.5	-5.7	8	5	2,000	100	0.0	0.0
B+ /9.7	5.1	0.84	17.32	267	19	38	42	1		77.0	52.9	-1.9	91	9	2,000	0	0.0	0.0
B- /7.6	12.2	1.24	11.04	34	4	95	0	1		37.0	107.5	-4.9	97	7	2,000	0	0.0	1.0
B+ /9.8	6.3	-0.16	12.69	75	41	58	0	1		18.0	19.4	4.2	98	8	2,000	100	0.0	1.0
C+ /6.8	15.6	0.95	23.28	170	5	94	0	1		42.0	146.6	-3.8	91	8	2,000	100	0.0	1.0
B- /7.6	5.1	1.02	14.42	53	1	68	29	2		49.0	35.5	-3.0	38	4	5,000	0	0.0	0.0
B- /7.0	7.7	0.94	17.57	40	N/A	100	0	N/A		60.0	54.1	-6.8	34	14	5,000	0	0.0	0.0
C+ /6.2	10.7	1.02	12.66	22	3	96	0	1		13.0	107.7	-10.9	19	2	5,000	0	0.0	2.0
B /8.3	5.4	1.06	26.74	18	1	65	33	1		52.0	38.2	-3.3	55	8	2,500	100	0.0	1.0
B /8.3	5.4	1.06	26.39	533	1	65	33	1		52.0	40.3	-3.2	61	N/A	2,500	100	0.0	0.0
B- /7.5	9.1	0.73	14.97	N/A	18	81	0	1		N/A	105.4	-17.5	61	9	2,500	100	0.0	1.0
B- /7.9	9.1	0.73	14.92	3	18	81	0	1		N/A	109.0	-17.4	65	N/A	2,500	100	0.0	2.0
C+ /5.7	9.7	1.07	28.43	49	5	94	0	1		39.0	68.2	-8.5	72	4	2,500	100	0.0	1.0
C+ /5.7	9.7	1.07	28.65	1,413	5	94	0	1		39.0	70.9	-8.4	77	9	2,500	100	0.0	0.0
C+ /6.3	9.8	1.13	19.55	12	4	95	0	1		61.0	80.1	-8.2	80	N/A	2,500	100	0.0	1.0
C+ /6.3	9.8	1.13	19.68	53	4	95	0	1		61.0	83.0	-8.1	84	N/A	2,500	100	0.0	0.0
C+ /6.3	10.1	1.17	18.29	10	0	99	0	1		37.0	68.2	-8.0	51	N/A	2,500	100	0.0	1.0
C+ /6.3	10.1	1.16	18.26	271	0	99	0	1		37.0	71.2	-7.9	58	N/A	2,500	100	0.0	0.0
C- /3.6	8.1	0.98	13.06	11	1	98	0	1		125.0	78.2	N/A	87	3	2,500	100	0.0	1.0

| | 99 Pct = Best
0 Pct = Worst | | **Overall Weiss Investment Rating** | | **PERFORMANCE** | | | | | | | |
| | | | | | **Perfor-mance Rating/Pts** | Total Return % through 6/30/06 | | | Annualized | | Incl. in Returns | |
Fund Type	Fund Name	Ticker Symbol		Phone		3 Mo	6 Mo	1Yr / Pct	3Yr / Pct	5Yr / Pct	Dividend Yield	Expense Ratio
GR	Janus Adviser INTECH Rsk Mgd	JRMCX	U	(800) 525-3713	U /	-2.50	1.85	--	--	--	0.00	0.60
GR	Janus Adviser INTECH Rsk Mgd	JLCIX	C+	(800) 525-3713	C+ / 5.7	-2.57	1.69	8.47 /37	15.09 /59	--	0.55	1.10
GR	Janus Adviser INTECH Rsk Mgd Gr A	JDRAX	U	(800) 525-3713	U /	-4.12	-0.76	6.50 /23	--	--	2.01	0.86
GR	Janus Adviser INTECH Rsk Mgd Gr	JCGCX	D+	(800) 525-3713	D+ / 2.9	-4.36	-1.17	5.66 /18	10.38 /30	--	0.00	1.60
GR	Janus Adviser INTECH Rsk Mgd Gr I	JRMGX	U	(800) 525-3713	U /	-4.14	-0.69	--	--	--	0.00	0.60
GR	Janus Adviser INTECH Rsk Mgd Gr S	JCGIX	D	(800) 525-3713	C- / 3.1	-4.22	-0.92	6.17 /21	10.95 /35	--	0.02	1.10
FO	Janus Adviser International Gr C	JIGCX	C+	(800) 525-3713	A+ / 9.8	-2.28	16.27	49.73 /99	32.33 /97	--	0.27	1.73
FO	Janus Adviser International Gr S	JIGRX	C+	(800) 525-3713	A+ / 9.8	-2.17	16.53	50.49 /99	32.79 /97	10.95 /84	0.50	1.23
GR	Janus Adviser Large Cap Growth C	JGOCX	D-	(800) 525-3713	D / 1.8	-4.81	-0.09	5.84 /19	8.04 /15	--	0.00	1.66
GR	Janus Adviser Large Cap Growth S	JGORX	D-	(800) 525-3713	D / 2.2	-4.65	0.14	6.42 /23	8.57 /18	-2.47 / 7	0.00	1.16
MC	Janus Adviser Mid Cap Growth C	JGRCX	C	(800) 525-3713	C+ / 6.6	-5.42	2.23	13.93 /68	16.50 /66	--	0.00	1.65
MC	Janus Adviser Mid Cap Growth S	JGRTX	C	(800) 525-3713	B- / 7.0	-5.27	2.49	14.49 /70	17.06 /68	1.95 /27	0.00	1.15
MC	Janus Adviser Mid Cap Value A	JDPAX	U	(800) 525-3713	U /	-1.25	4.33	12.04 /60	--	--	2.30	1.00
MC	Janus Adviser Mid Cap Value C	JMVCX	B+	(800) 525-3713	B- / 7.4	-1.44	3.93	12.39 /62	18.46 /74	--	0.48	1.74
MC	Janus Adviser Mid Cap Value S	JMVIX	B+	(800) 525-3713	B- / 7.5	-1.31	4.20	11.72 /58	18.47 /74	--	2.15	1.24
SC	Janus Adviser Small Company Value	JCSCX	C	(800) 525-3713	B- / 7.3	-4.59	9.42	12.54 /62	17.93 /72	--	0.00	2.25
SC	Janus Adviser Small Company Value	JISCX	C+	(800) 525-3713	B / 7.6	-4.46	9.73	13.06 /64	18.51 /74	--	0.00	1.75
GL	Janus Adviser Worldwide C	JWWCX	D-	(800) 525-3713	D / 1.8	-4.09	0.27	9.43 /43	8.38 /17	--	0.20	1.65
GL	Janus Adviser Worldwide S	JWGRX	D-	(800) 525-3713	D / 2.0	-3.99	0.52	10.01 /47	8.93 /20	-1.79 / 9	0.80	1.15
BA	Janus Aspen Balanced Inst	JABLX	C-	(800) 525-3713	D+ / 2.6	-2.08	1.73	8.36 /36	8.54 /18	4.65 /51	2.14	0.56
GR	Janus Aspen Fdmtl Equity Inst	JEIIX	B-	(800) 525-3713	C+ / 6.3	-3.31	3.13	17.40 /78	15.53 /61	5.11 /55	0.17	1.20
GR	Janus Aspen Forty Instl	JACAX	C-	(800) 525-3713	C / 5.0	-4.02	-0.90	6.72 /25	13.60 /52	4.01 /46	0.29	0.67
HL	Janus Aspen Global Life Sci Inst	JGLIX	C	(800) 525-3713	C+ / 6.0	-8.37	4.14	12.99 /64	14.76 /58	3.52 /41	0.00	0.95
TC	Janus Aspen Global Technology Inst	JGLTX	E	(800) 525-3713	C- / 3.1	-8.29	-1.57	13.94 /68	11.13 /36	-3.98 / 4	0.00	0.73
GI	Janus Aspen Growth & Income Inst	JGIIX	C	(800) 525-3713	C / 5.5	-3.88	1.86	13.01 /64	13.49 /51	2.91 /36	1.32	0.74
FO	Janus Aspen International Gr Inst	JAIGX	A-	(800) 525-3713	A+ / 9.8	-1.69	18.20	53.08 /99	33.07 /97	11.13 /84	1.84	0.70
GR	Janus Aspen Large Cap Growth Inst	JAGRX	D	(800) 525-3713	D+ / 2.7	-4.54	1.09	7.80 /31	9.12 /22	-1.91 / 8	0.41	0.66
AG	Janus Aspen Mid Cap Gr Inst	JAAGX	C+	(800) 525-3713	B- / 7.1	-5.13	2.58	14.68 /71	17.37 /70	2.22 /29	0.00	0.67
MC	Janus Aspen MidCap Value Inst	JAMVX	B-	(800) 525-3713	C+ / 6.9	-4.33	0.98	8.30 /35	17.71 /71	--	1.38	0.86
GL	Janus Aspen Worldwide Growth	JAWGX	D+	(800) 525-3713	D+ / 2.6	-3.42	1.17	10.36 /49	9.28 /23	-1.45 /10	1.70	0.61
★ GR	Janus Contrarian Fund	JSVAX	B-	(800) 525-3713	B+ / 8.9	-4.72	5.28	22.05 /84	23.56 /89	9.73 /79	0.23	0.93
★ BA	Janus Fd Inc-Balanced Fund	JABAX	C-	(800) 525-3713	D+ / 2.5	-2.21	1.70	8.20 /34	8.47 /18	4.54 /50	1.83	0.79
IN	Janus Fd Inc-Core Equity Fund	JAEIX	C+	(800) 525-3713	C+ / 6.5	-3.22	3.09	17.76 /79	15.92 /63	5.32 /57	0.29	0.89
MC	Janus Fd Inc-Enterprise Fund	JAENX	C	(800) 525-3713	C+ / 6.9	-5.17	2.31	13.77 /67	17.00 /68	1.97 /27	0.00	0.95
HL	Janus Fd Inc-Global Life Sciences	JAGLX	D-	(800) 525-3713	C- / 4.1	-6.34	-1.30	6.63 /24	12.77 /47	2.08 /28	0.00	0.96
TC	Janus Fd Inc-Global Technology	JAGTX	E-	(800) 525-3713	D+ / 2.8	-8.68	-1.85	13.92 /68	11.24 /37	-4.30 / 3	0.07	1.03
★ GI	Janus Fd Inc-Growth & Income	JAGIX	C	(800) 525-3713	C / 5.3	-4.12	1.35	12.36 /61	13.34 /51	2.86 /35	1.24	0.87
★ GR	Janus Fd Inc-Janus Fund	JANSX	D	(800) 525-3713	D+ / 2.4	-4.60	0.63	7.07 /27	8.80 /20	-2.52 / 6	0.07	0.87
★ GR	Janus Fd Inc-Mercury Fund	JAMRX	D	(800) 525-3713	C- / 3.1	-5.57	-1.96	7.62 /30	10.27 /29	-1.60 /10	0.28	0.92
MC ●	Janus Fd Inc-Mid Cap Value Inst	JMIVX	A-	(800) 525-3713	B- / 7.5	-1.19	4.11	11.74 /58	18.76 /75	11.39 /85	1.11	0.77
★ MC	Janus Fd Inc-Mid Cap Value Inv	JMCVX	B	(800) 525-3713	B- / 7.5	-1.23	4.03	11.57 /57	18.54 /75	11.19 /84	0.97	0.92
★ GR	Janus Fd Inc-Olympus Fund	JAOLX	D	(800) 525-3713	C- / 4.2	-7.17	-2.54	10.54 /51	12.05 /43	0.39 /17	0.03	0.96
GL	Janus Fd Inc-Orion Fund	JORNX	C+	(800) 525-3713	B+ / 8.5	-3.03	7.68	24.65 /88	21.57 /84	9.58 /79	0.70	1.01
★ FO	Janus Fd Inc-Overseas Fund	JAOSX	C+	(800) 525-3713	A+ / 9.8	-2.12	17.34	52.33 /99	33.29 /97	11.83 /86	0.75	0.89
OT	Janus Fd Inc-Research Fund	JARFX	U	(800) 525-3713	U /	-3.32	5.44	21.64 /84	--	--	0.32	1.25
GR	Janus Fd Inc-Risk-Managed Stock	JRMSX	B-	(800) 525-3713	C+ / 6.1	-2.53	1.79	9.77 /45	15.70 /62	--	0.83	0.88
SC ●	Janus Fd Inc-Small Cap Val Inst	JSIVX	D	(800) 525-3713	C+ / 6.1	-4.47	1.61	7.73 /31	15.80 /63	8.78 /75	1.09	0.79
SC ●	Janus Fd Inc-Small Cap Val Inv	JSCVX	D	(800) 525-3713	C+ / 6.0	-4.54	1.51	7.48 /29	15.53 /61	8.50 /74	0.92	0.99
OT	Janus Fd Inc-Triton Fund	JATTX	U	(800) 525-3713	U /	-10.64	3.48	20.53 /83	--	--	0.25	1.25
★ GR ●	Janus Fd Inc-Twenty Fund	JAVLX	C	(800) 525-3713	C+ / 6.2	-2.06	0.86	11.73 /58	15.13 /59	2.74 /34	0.20	0.86
SC ●	Janus Fd Inc-Venture Fund	JAVTX	D+	(800) 525-3713	B- / 7.1	-8.12	6.86	10.65 /51	17.92 /72	5.58 /58	0.00	0.87
★ GL ●	Janus Fd Inc-Worldwide Fund	JAWWX	D	(800) 525-3713	D+ / 2.4	-3.54	1.13	10.45 /50	9.60 /25	-1.47 /10	1.13	0.85

● Denotes fund is closed to new investors
★ Denotes fund is included in Section II

226

RISK			NET ASSETS		ASSET					Portfolio Turnover Ratio	BULL / BEAR		FUND MANAGER		MINIMUMS		LOADS	
	3 Year		NAV As of 6/30/06	Total $(Mil)	Cash %	Stocks %	Bonds %	Other %		Last Bull Market Return	Last Bear Market Return	Manager Quality Pct	Manager Tenure (Years)	Initial Purch. $	Additional Purch. $	Front End Load	Back End Load
Risk Rating/Pts	Standard Deviation	Beta															
U /	N/A	N/A	13.24	41	1	98	0	1	125.0	N/A	N/A	N/A	N/A	1,000,000	0	0.0	2.0
B- /7.7	8.0	0.98	13.27	16	1	98	0	1	125.0	79.0	N/A	88	4	2,500	100	0.0	2.0
U /	N/A	N/A	13.02	30	13	86	0	1	115.0	N/A	N/A	N/A	N/A	2,500	100	5.8	1.0
B- /7.0	8.4	1.01	12.71	13	13	86	0	1	115.0	59.9	N/A	45	3	2,500	100	0.0	1.0
U /	N/A	N/A	12.96	173	13	86	0	1	115.0	N/A	N/A	N/A	N/A	1,000,000	0	0.0	2.0
C+ /6.3	8.4	1.00	12.95	96	13	86	0	1	115.0	62.5	N/A	53	3	2,500	100	0.0	2.0
C- /3.0	15.4	1.32	44.94	25	N/A	100	0	N/A	61.0	183.5	-12.0	56	4	2,500	100	0.0	1.0
C- /3.1	15.5	1.32	44.12	556	N/A	100	0	N/A	61.0	186.9	-11.9	60	9	2,500	100	0.0	2.0
C+ /6.1	10.3	1.23	21.55	2	N/A	100	0	N/A	99.5	51.0	-10.4	15	N/A	2,500	100	0.0	1.0
C+ /6.2	10.3	1.23	21.54	172	N/A	100	0	N/A	99.5	53.3	-10.3	18	N/A	2,500	100	0.0	0.0
C /5.3	11.7	1.03	28.46	4	4	95	0	1	37.1	95.9	-6.1	34	4	2,500	100	0.0	1.0
C /5.3	11.7	1.03	28.76	98	4	95	0	1	37.1	98.9	-6.0	38	9	2,500	100	0.0	0.0
U /	N/A	N/A	16.64	174	14	85	0	1	60.9	N/A	N/A	N/A	N/A	2,500	100	5.8	1.0
B- /7.8	9.1	0.81	16.41	28	14	85	0	1	60.9	97.3	N/A	85	N/A	2,500	100	0.0	1.0
B- /7.7	9.2	0.81	16.62	72	14	85	0	1	60.9	97.4	N/A	84	N/A	2,500	100	0.0	0.0
C /5.1	12.8	0.85	14.75	1	2	97	0	1	48.9	N/A	N/A	74	3	1,000	100	0.0	1.0
C /5.1	12.8	0.85	15.00	23	2	97	0	1	48.9	110.6	-7.1	78	4	2,500	100	0.0	0.0
C+ /6.5	9.1	0.79	29.52	1	2	97	0	1	50.5	52.5	-11.6	2	4	2,500	100	0.0	1.0
C+ /6.5	9.1	0.79	29.13	163	2	97	0	1	50.5	55.1	-11.5	3	9	2,500	100	0.0	2.0
B /8.3	5.3	1.05	25.88	1,518	1	64	33	2	45.4	41.1	-3.1	64	N/A	2,500	100	0.0	0.0
B- /7.4	9.7	1.12	21.94	14	3	96	0	1	88.3	82.5	-8.9	84	N/A	2,500	100	0.0	0.0
C+ /6.3	9.8	1.10	27.38	436	2	97	0	1	54.7	72.9	-8.9	71	9	2,500	100	0.0	0.0
C+ /5.6	11.5	0.82	9.31	4	4	95	0	1	100.3	78.6	-3.6	93	6	2,500	100	0.0	0.0
D+ /2.6	17.4	1.88	3.76	3	4	95	0	1	177.3	84.4	-14.5	5	N/A	2,500	100	0.0	0.0
C+ /6.9	10.2	1.17	17.71	42	0	99	0	1	50.7	73.6	-8.9	64	8	2,500	100	0.0	0.0
C /5.5	15.6	1.33	41.36	639	N/A	100	0	N/A	57.9	190.4	-11.8	60	12	2,500	100	0.0	0.0
C+ /6.6	10.4	1.23	21.03	683	N/A	100	0	N/A	130.8	57.1	-11.0	20	N/A	2,500	100	0.0	0.0
C+ /5.6	11.5	1.32	29.77	519	1	98	0	1	47.5	100.7	-5.8	83	13	2,500	100	0.0	0.0
B- /7.4	9.9	0.87	15.08	9	7	92	0	1	82.3	N/A	N/A	73	3	2,500	100	0.0	0.0
B- /7.1	8.7	0.75	27.96	1,299	4	95	0	1	77.8	56.1	-11.3	4	N/A	2,500	100	0.0	0.0
C /5.2	12.6	1.35	15.94	3,642	1	98	0	1	40.1	148.2	-7.9	98	6	2,500	100	0.0	0.0
B /8.5	5.3	1.05	22.68	2,474	1	65	33	1	47.0	40.7	-3.1	63	N/A	2,500	100	0.0	0.0
B- /7.0	9.8	1.12	24.35	1,010	3	96	0	1	74.0	83.7	-8.7	85	N/A	2,500	100	0.0	0.0
C /5.4	11.5	1.02	42.88	1,757	2	97	0	1	28.0	100.4	-6.1	41	N/A	2,500	100	0.0	0.0
C /4.3	10.4	0.81	19.79	1,036	0	99	0	1	77.0	66.8	-3.5	85	8	2,500	100	0.0	2.0
D /2.0	17.4	1.90	11.68	969	2	96	0	2	117.8	85.0	-14.6	5	N/A	2,500	100	0.0	2.0
C+ /6.3	10.2	1.17	36.16	6,867	0	99	0	1	32.3	73.9	-8.5	62	N/A	2,500	100	0.0	0.0
C+ /6.2	10.4	1.23	25.69	10,967	2	97	0	1	117.5	55.8	-10.6	18	N/A	2,500	100	0.0	0.0
C+ /5.8	10.1	1.22	22.53	3,767	2	97	0	1	212.3	67.9	-9.7	28	N/A	2,500	100	0.0	0.0
B- /7.7	9.0	0.80	23.32	956	10	89	0	1	84.0	100.5	-7.6	87	8	2,500	100	0.0	0.0
C+ /6.7	9.0	0.80	23.22	4,891	10	89	0	1	84.0	99.3	-7.7	86	8	2,500	100	0.0	0.0
C /4.5	11.6	1.27	31.86	2,229	1	98	0	1	101.8	74.8	-8.4	37	9	2,500	100	0.0	0.0
C /4.5	12.5	0.97	8.97	1,010	5	94	0	1	61.5	137.0	-11.2	36	6	2,500	100	0.0	0.0
D+ /2.9	15.8	1.34	37.35	4,241	0	99	0	1	92.5	192.8	-12.4	58	6	2,500	100	0.0	2.0
U /	N/A	N/A	12.22	84	4	95	0	1	193.3	N/A	N/A	N/A	1	2,500	100	0.0	0.0
B- /7.8	8.0	0.99	15.38	430	4	95	0	1	92.7	80.5	N/A	90	N/A	2,500	100	0.0	2.0
D+ /2.7	10.4	0.67	28.40	1,091	12	87	0	1	61.9	89.1	-8.9	81	N/A	2,500	100	0.0	0.0
D+ /2.7	10.4	0.67	28.18	1,229	12	87	0	1	61.9	87.8	-8.9	79	9	2,500	100	0.0	0.0
U /	N/A	N/A	12.18	147	16	83	0	1	217.4	N/A	N/A	N/A	N/A	2,500	100	0.0	0.0
C+ /5.8	11.0	1.17	49.34	9,218	11	88	0	1	19.6	82.1	-8.5	77	9	2,500	100	0.0	0.0
D+ /2.9	16.2	1.04	60.46	1,355	0	99	0	1	52.3	135.3	-12.4	41	9	2,500	100	0.0	0.0
C+ /6.5	9.1	0.78	43.83	4,424	1	98	0	1	53.6	57.9	-11.6	4	N/A	2,500	100	0.0	2.0

					PERFORMANCE							
99 Pct = Best *0 Pct = Worst*			Overall Weiss Investment Rating		Perfor-mance Rating/Pts	Total Return % through 6/30/06					Incl. in Returns	
									Annualized		Dividend	Expense
Fund Type	Fund Name	Ticker Symbol		Phone		3 Mo	6 Mo	1Yr / Pct	3Yr / Pct	5Yr / Pct	Yield	Ratio
GL	Janus Global Opportunities Fund	JGVAX	C+	(800) 525-3713	C+ / 5.9	-3.02	0.27	8.39 /36	15.73 /62	8.49 /74	0.75	1.02
AA	Janus SMART Portfolio Growth	JSPGX	U	(800) 525-3713	U /	-2.23	5.20	--	--	--	0.00	1.07
AA	Janus SMART Portfolio Moderate	JSPMX	U	(800) 525-3713	U /	-1.80	3.60	--	--	--	0.00	1.00
BA	JennDry Dryden Active Allocation A	PIBAX	C-	(800) 257-3893	D / 2.1	-1.16	2.18	5.67 /18	9.90 /27	4.64 /51	1.46	1.09
BA	JennDry Dryden Active Allocation B	PBFBX	C-	(800) 257-3893	D / 1.8	-1.31	1.80	4.92 /15	9.07 /21	3.88 /45	0.77	1.84
BA	JennDry Dryden Active Allocation C	PABCX	C-	(800) 257-3893	D+ / 2.5	-1.31	1.87	4.92 /15	9.07 /21	3.88 /45	0.77	1.84
BA	JennDry Dryden Active Allocation Z	PABFX	C	(800) 257-3893	C- / 3.3	-1.16	2.32	5.91 /20	10.17 /28	4.88 /53	1.78	0.84
FO	JennDry Dryden Intl Equity A	PJRAX	A	(800) 257-3893	A- / 9.0	0.51	10.72	26.29 /90	25.24 /91	7.78 /71	0.47	1.57
FO	JennDry Dryden Intl Equity B	PJRBX	A	(800) 257-3893	B+ / 8.9	0.39	10.36	25.33 /89	24.25 /90	6.98 /67	0.00	2.32
FO	JennDry Dryden Intl Equity C	PJRCX	A	(800) 257-3893	A- / 9.1	0.39	10.36	25.33 /89	24.25 /90	6.98 /67	0.00	2.32
FO	JennDry Dryden Intl Equity Z	PJIZX	A+	(800) 257-3893	A- / 9.2	0.63	10.77	26.45 /90	25.47 /92	8.02 /72	0.67	1.32
GR	JennDry Dryden Large Cap Core Eq	PTMAX	C	(800) 257-3893	C- / 3.1	-1.98	2.85	8.14 /34	11.36 /38	2.62 /33	0.31	1.22
GR	JennDry Dryden Large Cap Core Eq	PTMBX	C-	(800) 257-3893	D+ / 2.7	-2.23	2.34	7.25 /28	10.51 /31	1.84 /26	0.00	1.97
GR	JennDry Dryden Large Cap Core Eq	PTMCX	C	(800) 257-3893	C- / 3.4	-2.23	2.34	7.25 /28	10.51 /31	1.84 /26	0.00	1.97
GR	JennDry Dryden Large Cap Core Eq	PTEZX	C+	(800) 257-3893	C / 4.4	-1.87	2.98	8.36 /36	11.67 /40	2.89 /36	0.55	0.97
AA	JennDry Dryden Moderate Alloc B	JDMBX	U	(800) 257-3893	U /	-1.59	2.44	10.24 /48	--	--	0.62	1.50
SC	JennDry Dryden Small Cap Core Eq	PQVAX	B	(800) 257-3893	B / 7.8	-4.37	7.06	14.35 /69	21.11 /83	12.11 /87	0.00	1.40
SC	JennDry Dryden Small Cap Core Eq	PQVBX	B-	(800) 257-3893	B / 7.6	-4.50	6.65	13.52 /66	20.21 /80	11.26 /85	0.00	2.15
SC	JennDry Dryden Small Cap Core Eq	PQVCX	B	(800) 257-3893	B / 7.9	-4.50	6.72	13.52 /66	20.21 /80	11.26 /85	0.00	2.15
SC	JennDry Dryden Small Cap Core Eq	PSQZX	B+	(800) 257-3893	B+ / 8.3	-4.28	7.20	14.69 /71	21.35 /83	12.33 /87	0.00	1.15
IX	JennDry Dryden Stock Index A	PSIAX	C	(800) 257-3893	C- / 3.2	-1.52	2.49	8.04 /33	10.57 /32	1.90 /26	1.28	0.64
IX	JennDry Dryden Stock Index B	PBSIX	C-	(800) 257-3893	D+ / 2.3	-1.71	2.10	7.24 /28	9.75 /26	1.14 /21	0.50	1.40
IX	JennDry Dryden Stock Index C	PSICX	C	(800) 257-3893	C- / 3.0	-1.71	2.10	7.24 /28	9.75 /26	1.14 /21	0.50	1.40
IX	JennDry Dryden Stock Index I	PDSIX	C+	(800) 257-3893	C- / 4.0	-1.45	2.63	8.40 /36	10.94 /35	2.24 /30	1.64	0.30
IX	JennDry Dryden Stock Index Z	PSIFX	C+	(800) 257-3893	C- / 3.9	-1.45	2.63	8.33 /35	10.85 /34	2.15 /28	1.53	0.40
GR	JennDry Dryden Strategic Value A	SUVAX	C+	(800) 257-3893	C / 4.4	0.56	5.77	10.56 /51	12.85 /48	4.07 /47	0.00	1.57
GR	JennDry Dryden Strategic Value B	SUVBX	C	(800) 257-3893	C- / 4.1	0.42	5.33	9.75 /45	12.03 /43	3.27 /39	0.00	2.32
GR	JennDry Dryden Strategic Value C	SUVCX	C+	(800) 257-3893	C / 4.8	0.42	5.42	9.75 /45	12.03 /43	3.27 /39	0.00	2.32
GR	JennDry Dryden Strategic Value Z	SUVZX	B-	(800) 257-3893	C+ / 5.6	0.64	5.88	10.82 /52	13.14 /50	4.32 /49	0.00	1.32
GR	JennDry Jennison 20/20 Focus Fd A	PTWAX	B+	(800) 257-3893	B- / 7.3	-2.65	1.91	18.21 /79	19.34 /77	6.61 /65	0.00	1.28
GR	JennDry Jennison 20/20 Focus Fd B	PTWBX	B+	(800) 257-3893	B- / 7.1	-2.88	1.47	17.29 /78	18.44 /74	5.81 /60	0.00	2.03
GR	JennDry Jennison 20/20 Focus Fd C	PTWCX	B+	(800) 257-3893	B- / 7.5	-2.81	1.54	17.37 /78	18.46 /74	5.82 /60	0.00	2.03
GR	JennDry Jennison 20/20 Focus Fd Z	PTWZX	A-	(800) 257-3893	B / 8.0	-2.60	2.01	18.45 /80	19.62 /78	6.88 /66	0.00	1.03
GR	JennDry Jennison Blend A	PBQAX	C	(800) 257-3893	C / 4.8	-3.47	0.17	16.58 /76	14.85 /58	4.15 /47	0.49	0.93
GR	JennDry Jennison Blend B	PBQFX	C	(800) 257-3893	C / 4.5	-3.69	-0.26	15.67 /74	13.98 /54	3.36 /40	0.09	1.68
GR	JennDry Jennison Blend C	PRECX	C	(800) 257-3893	C / 5.2	-3.69	-0.26	15.67 /74	13.98 /54	3.36 /40	0.09	1.68
GR	JennDry Jennison Blend Z	PEQZX	C+	(800) 257-3893	C+ / 5.9	-3.44	0.26	16.83 /77	15.14 /59	4.40 /50	0.72	0.68
GR	JennDry Jennison Conservative Gr A	TBDAX	E	(800) 257-3893	D- / 1.1	-5.73	-4.25	7.64 /30	8.42 /17	-2.23 / 7	0.00	1.58
GR	JennDry Jennison Conservative Gr B	TBDBX	E	(800) 257-3893	E+ / 0.9	-6.02	-4.70	6.84 /25	7.60 /13	-2.97 / 5	0.00	2.33
GR	JennDry Jennison Conservative Gr C	TBDCX	E	(800) 257-3893	D- / 1.4	-6.02	-4.70	6.84 /25	7.60 /13	-2.97 / 5	0.00	2.33
GR	JennDry Jennison Equity Opp A	PJIAX	C-	(800) 257-3893	C / 5.3	-1.82	5.74	14.17 /69	14.26 /55	5.45 /57	0.43	1.12
GR	JennDry Jennison Equity Opp B	PJIBX	C-	(800) 257-3893	C / 5.0	-1.97	5.37	13.39 /66	13.42 /51	4.68 /52	0.00	1.87
GR	JennDry Jennison Equity Opp C	PJGCX	C-	(800) 257-3893	C+ / 5.6	-1.97	5.37	13.39 /66	13.42 /51	4.68 /52	0.00	1.87
GR	JennDry Jennison Equity Opp Z	PJGZX	C	(800) 257-3893	C+ / 6.3	-1.73	5.84	14.50 /70	14.55 /57	5.72 /59	0.77	0.87
FS	JennDry Jennison Financial Svcs A	PFSAX	D	(800) 257-3893	C- / 3.5	-4.25	2.57	9.19 /41	12.19 /44	5.84 /60	0.00	1.56
FS	JennDry Jennison Financial Svcs B	PUFBX	D	(800) 257-3893	C- / 3.1	-4.48	2.16	8.24 /35	11.32 /38	5.03 /54	0.00	2.31
FS	JennDry Jennison Financial Svcs C	PUFCX	D	(800) 257-3893	C- / 3.8	-4.48	2.16	8.24 /35	11.32 /38	5.03 /54	0.00	2.31
FS	JennDry Jennison Financial Svcs Z	PFSZX	D+	(800) 257-3893	C / 4.7	-4.21	2.63	9.28 /42	12.41 /45	6.09 /62	0.00	1.31
GL	JennDry Jennison Global Growth A	PRGAX	C	(800) 257-3893	C+ / 5.6	-3.26	2.58	20.71 /83	15.10 /59	3.40 /40	0.07	1.47
GL	JennDry Jennison Global Growth B	PRGLX	C	(800) 257-3893	C / 5.4	-3.38	2.34	20.09 /82	14.51 /56	2.88 /36	0.00	1.97
GL	JennDry Jennison Global Growth C	PRGCX	C	(800) 257-3893	C+ / 5.8	-3.47	2.17	19.78 /82	14.23 /55	2.68 /34	0.00	2.22
GL	JennDry Jennison Global Growth Z	PWGZX	C+	(800) 257-3893	C+ / 6.5	-3.22	2.66	20.97 /83	15.34 /60	3.69 /43	0.30	1.22

● Denotes fund is closed to new investors
* Denotes fund is included in Section II

RISK			NET ASSETS		ASSET				BULL / BEAR		FUND MANAGER		MINIMUMS		LOADS	
	3 Year		NAV													
Risk Rating/Pts	Standard Deviation	Beta	As of 6/30/06	Total $(Mil)	Cash %	Stocks %	Bonds %	Other %	Portfolio Turnover Ratio	Last Bull Market Return	Last Bear Market Return	Manager Quality Pct	Manager Tenure (Years)	Initial Purch. $	Additional Purch. $	Front End Load	Back End Load
B- / 7.5	9.8	0.76	14.75	157	0	99	0	1	63.2	95.4	-15.4	29	N/A	2,500	100	0.0	2.0
U /	N/A	N/A	10.52	39	0	80	20	0	N/A	N/A	N/A	N/A	1	2,500	100	0.0	2.0
U /	N/A	N/A	10.36	27	0	60	40	0	N/A	N/A	N/A	N/A	1	2,500	100	0.0	2.0
B / 8.5	6.0	1.23	13.61	423	8	64	26	2	119.0	54.5	-5.1	68	N/A	1,000	100	5.5	1.0
B / 8.6	6.0	1.23	13.59	64	8	64	26	2	119.0	50.9	-5.3	59	N/A	1,000	100	0.0	5.0
B / 8.6	6.0	1.23	13.59	14	8	64	26	2	119.0	50.9	-5.3	59	N/A	2,500	100	0.0	1.0
B / 8.5	6.0	1.23	13.68	169	8	64	26	2	119.0	55.6	-5.0	70	N/A	0	0	0.0	0.0
B- / 7.0	10.4	1.01	7.95	52	3	96	0	1	41.0	146.0	-11.4	62	3	1,000	100	5.5	1.0
C+ / 6.9	10.5	1.02	7.67	46	3	96	0	1	41.0	140.4	-11.6	50	3	1,000	100	0.0	5.0
C+ / 6.9	10.5	1.02	7.67	14	3	96	0	1	41.0	140.4	-11.6	49	3	2,500	100	0.0	1.0
B- / 7.0	10.4	1.01	8.02	217	3	96	0	1	41.0	147.7	-11.3	63	3	0	0	0.0	0.0
B / 8.6	7.8	1.01	11.91	72	0	99	0	1	74.0	66.1	-8.3	57	N/A	1,000	100	5.5	1.0
B / 8.6	7.9	1.02	11.39	49	0	99	0	1	74.0	62.1	-8.4	46	N/A	1,000	100	0.0	5.0
B / 8.6	7.9	1.02	11.39	41	0	99	0	1	74.0	62.1	-8.4	46	N/A	2,500	100	0.0	1.0
B / 8.6	7.9	1.02	12.09	16	0	99	0	1	74.0	67.3	-8.2	59	N/A	0	0	0.0	0.0
U /	N/A	N/A	11.75	28	3	96	0	1	5.0	N/A	N/A	N/A	2	1,000	100	0.0	5.0
C+ / 6.4	13.9	0.94	18.81	110	0	99	0	1	90.0	126.3	-8.9	84	6	1,000	100	5.5	0.0
C+ / 6.4	13.9	0.94	17.63	19	0	99	0	1	90.0	121.2	-9.2	79	6	1,000	100	0.0	5.0
C+ / 6.4	13.9	0.94	17.63	17	0	99	0	1	90.0	121.1	-9.2	79	6	2,500	100	0.0	1.0
C+ / 6.4	13.9	0.94	19.21	9	0	99	0	1	90.0	128.1	-8.9	86	6	0	0	0.0	0.0
B / 8.9	7.7	1.00	28.42	85	1	98	0	1	3.0	61.7	-9.8	48	N/A	1,000	100	3.3	0.0
B / 8.8	7.6	1.00	28.21	90	1	98	0	1	3.0	57.9	-10.0	40	N/A	1,000	100	0.0	5.0
B / 8.8	7.6	1.00	28.21	46	1	98	0	1	3.0	57.9	-10.0	40	N/A	2,500	100	0.0	1.0
B / 8.9	7.6	1.00	28.49	844	1	98	0	1	3.0	63.5	-9.8	53	N/A	0	0	0.0	0.0
B / 8.9	7.6	1.00	28.48	716	1	98	0	1	3.0	62.9	-9.7	52	N/A	0	0	0.0	0.0
B / 8.3	8.7	1.05	12.46	15	N/A	100	0	N/A	9.0	77.0	-9.7	68	1	1,000	100	5.5	1.0
B / 8.2	8.7	1.05	12.05	60	N/A	100	0	N/A	9.0	72.7	-9.8	60	1	1,000	100	0.0	5.0
B / 8.2	8.7	1.05	12.05	41	N/A	100	0	N/A	9.0	72.7	-9.8	60	1	2,500	100	0.0	1.0
B / 8.3	8.7	1.05	12.60	4	N/A	100	0	N/A	9.0	78.4	-9.6	70	1	0	0	0.0	0.0
B- / 7.6	10.5	1.21	15.45	586	2	97	0	1	106.0	103.3	-11.9	94	8	1,000	100	5.5	1.0
B- / 7.5	10.5	1.21	14.52	215	2	97	0	1	106.0	98.7	-12.1	92	2	1,000	100	0.0	5.0
B- / 7.5	10.5	1.21	14.53	143	2	97	0	1	106.0	98.7	-12.1	92	8	2,500	100	0.0	1.0
B- / 7.6	10.5	1.21	15.73	130	2	97	0	1	106.0	104.9	-11.8	95	8	0	0	0.0	0.0
C+ / 6.9	10.1	1.20	17.98	1,553	1	98	0	1	102.0	86.2	-9.9	73	6	1,000	100	5.5	1.0
C+ / 6.9	10.1	1.20	17.59	187	1	98	0	1	102.0	81.8	-10.0	66	6	1,000	100	0.0	5.0
C+ / 6.9	10.1	1.20	17.59	38	1	98	0	1	102.0	81.9	-10.0	66	6	2,500	100	0.0	1.0
C+ / 6.9	10.0	1.19	17.96	77	1	98	0	1	102.0	87.8	-9.8	76	6	0	0	0.0	0.0
C / 5.0	12.5	1.43	7.89	16	0	99	0	1	133.0	60.0	-11.0	9	1	1,000	100	5.5	1.0
C / 4.9	12.5	1.43	7.50	23	0	99	0	1	133.0	56.3	-11.1	7	1	1,000	100	0.0	5.0
C / 4.9	12.5	1.42	7.50	31	0	99	0	1	133.0	56.3	-11.1	7	1	2,500	100	0.0	1.0
C+ / 5.7	10.4	1.28	16.87	332	4	95	0	1	93.0	82.9	-12.4	61	6	1,000	100	5.5	1.0
C+ / 5.6	10.4	1.28	15.90	166	4	95	0	1	93.0	78.6	-12.4	51	6	1,000	100	0.0	5.0
C+ / 5.6	10.4	1.28	15.90	55	4	95	0	1	93.0	78.6	-12.4	51	6	2,500	100	0.0	1.0
C+ / 5.8	10.5	1.29	17.13	172	4	95	0	1	93.0	84.4	-12.2	63	6	0	0	0.0	0.0
C / 5.5	11.6	1.14	12.61	31	0	99	0	1	78.0	79.8	-10.4	27	4	1,000	100	5.5	1.0
C / 5.5	11.6	1.14	12.15	53	0	99	0	1	78.0	75.6	-10.6	21	4	1,000	100	0.0	5.0
C / 5.5	11.6	1.14	12.15	22	0	99	0	1	78.0	75.6	-10.6	21	4	2,500	100	0.0	1.0
C / 5.5	11.6	1.15	12.73	4	0	99	0	1	78.0	81.1	-10.3	28	4	0	0	0.0	0.0
C+ / 6.6	10.4	0.94	17.49	349	3	96	0	1	57.0	90.6	-9.6	8	N/A	1,000	100	5.5	1.0
C+ / 6.6	10.4	0.94	15.72	49	3	96	0	1	57.0	87.4	-9.7	6	N/A	1,000	100	0.0	5.0
C+ / 6.5	10.4	0.94	15.56	13	3	96	0	1	57.0	86.1	-9.8	5	N/A	2,500	100	0.0	1.0
C+ / 6.6	10.4	0.94	17.74	16	3	96	0	1	57.0	92.2	-9.6	8	N/A	0	0	0.0	0.0

					PERFORMANCE							
99 Pct = Best 0 Pct = Worst			Overall Weiss Investment Rating		Perfor-mance Rating/Pts	Total Return % through 6/30/06			Annualized		Incl. in Returns	
Fund Type	Fund Name	Ticker Symbol		Phone		3 Mo	6 Mo	1Yr / Pct	3Yr / Pct	5Yr / Pct	Dividend Yield	Expense Ratio
GR	JennDry Jennison Growth A	PJFAX	E+	(800) 257-3893	D / 1.6	-7.75	-6.67	5.96 /20	10.27 /29	-0.66 /13	0.00	1.06
GR	JennDry Jennison Growth B	PJFBX	E+	(800) 257-3893	D- / 1.3	-7.92	-6.99	5.17 /16	9.44 /24	-1.40 /10	0.00	1.81
GR	JennDry Jennison Growth C	PJFCX	E+	(800) 257-3893	D / 1.9	-7.92	-7.06	5.17 /16	9.44 /24	-1.40 /10	0.00	1.81
GR	JennDry Jennison Growth Z	PJFZX	D-	(800) 257-3893	D+ / 2.7	-7.72	-6.61	6.22 /22	10.52 /31	-0.42 /14	0.00	0.81
HL	● JennDry Jennison Health Sciences A	PHLAX	C	(800) 257-3893	C+ / 6.7	-9.58	-2.20	8.82 /39	19.99 /79	9.12 /77	0.00	1.17
HL	● JennDry Jennison Health Sciences B	PHLBX	C-	(800) 257-3893	C+ / 6.5	-9.76	-2.54	8.01 /33	19.10 /76	8.31 /73	0.00	1.92
HL	● JennDry Jennison Health Sciences C	PHLCX	C	(800) 257-3893	C+ / 6.9	-9.76	-2.60	7.95 /32	19.08 /76	8.29 /73	0.00	1.92
HL	● JennDry Jennison Health Sciences Z	PHSZX	C+	(800) 257-3893	B- / 7.5	-9.51	-2.05	9.12 /41	20.32 /80	9.41 /78	0.00	0.92
EN	JennDry Jennison Nat Resources A	PGNAX	B	(800) 257-3893	A+ / 9.9	2.73	16.97	54.75 /99	42.75 /99	28.68 /99	0.56	1.11
EN	JennDry Jennison Nat Resources B	PRGNX	B	(800) 257-3893	A+ / 9.9	2.55	16.55	53.57 /99	41.67 /99	27.72 /99	0.20	1.86
EN	JennDry Jennison Nat Resources C	PNRCX	B	(800) 257-3893	A+ / 9.9	2.52	16.53	53.54 /99	41.66 /99	27.71 /99	0.20	1.86
EN	JennDry Jennison Nat Resources Z	PNRZX	B	(800) 257-3893	A+ / 9.9	2.78	17.11	55.09 /99	43.11 /99	29.00 /99	0.72	0.86
GR	JennDry Jennison Select Growth A	SPFAX	E+	(800) 257-3893	D- / 1.0	-8.02	-9.03	4.89 /15	9.32 /23	-1.22 /11	0.00	1.82
GR	JennDry Jennison Select Growth B	SPFBX	E	(800) 257-3893	E+ / 0.9	-8.09	-9.40	4.09 /11	8.57 /18	-1.93 / 8	0.00	2.57
GR	JennDry Jennison Select Growth C	SPFCX	E+	(800) 257-3893	D- / 1.3	-8.09	-9.40	4.09 /11	8.57 /18	-1.93 / 8	0.00	2.57
GR	JennDry Jennison Select Growth Z	SPFZX	D-	(800) 257-3893	D / 2.1	-7.90	-8.89	5.30 /17	9.63 /25	-0.95 /12	0.00	1.57
SC	JennDry Jennison Small Company A	PGOAX	B	(800) 257-3893	B / 7.9	-4.99	8.02	18.36 /80	21.11 /83	10.87 /83	0.00	1.23
SC	JennDry Jennison Small Company B	CHNDX	C+	(800) 257-3893	B / 7.7	-5.12	7.61	17.48 /78	20.22 /80	10.05 /81	0.00	1.98
SC	JennDry Jennison Small Company C	PSCCX	C+	(800) 257-3893	B / 8.1	-5.12	7.61	17.48 /78	20.22 /80	10.05 /81	0.00	1.98
SC	JennDry Jennison Small Company Z	PSCZX	B+	(800) 257-3893	B+ / 8.4	-4.91	8.10	18.65 /80	21.42 /84	11.15 /84	0.00	0.98
TC	JennDry Jennison Technology A	PTYAX	E	(800) 257-3893	C- / 3.4	-11.01	-3.96	12.46 /62	12.92 /48	-1.64 / 9	0.00	1.83
TC	JennDry Jennison Technology B	PTYBX	E	(800) 257-3893	C- / 3.1	-11.22	-4.29	11.52 /57	12.13 /43	-2.38 / 7	0.00	2.58
TC	JennDry Jennison Technology C	PTYCX	E	(800) 257-3893	C- / 3.8	-11.22	-4.29	11.52 /57	12.13 /43	-2.38 / 7	0.00	2.58
TC	JennDry Jennison Technology Z	PTFZX	E+	(800) 257-3893	C / 4.7	-10.94	-3.89	12.70 /63	13.17 /50	-1.38 /10	0.00	1.58
MC	JennDry Jennison US Emerging Grth	PEEAX	C-	(800) 257-3893	C+ / 6.5	-5.77	2.59	20.35 /82	18.14 /73	3.07 /38	0.00	1.21
MC	JennDry Jennison US Emerging Grth	PEEBX	D+	(800) 257-3893	C+ / 6.2	-5.94	2.21	19.43 /81	17.25 /69	2.30 /30	0.00	1.96
MC	JennDry Jennison US Emerging Grth	PEGCX	C-	(800) 257-3893	C+ / 6.7	-5.94	2.21	19.43 /81	17.25 /69	2.30 /30	0.00	1.96
MC	JennDry Jennison US Emerging Grth	PEGZX	C-	(800) 257-3893	B- / 7.2	-5.72	2.73	20.64 /83	18.41 /74	3.32 /40	0.00	0.96
★ UT	JennDry Jennison Utility A	PRUAX	A+	(800) 257-3893	A / 9.4	4.08	11.38	25.73 /89	28.91 /95	9.90 /80	1.99	0.80
UT	JennDry Jennison Utility B	PRUTX	A+	(800) 257-3893	A / 9.4	3.89	10.98	24.82 /88	27.93 /94	9.07 /77	1.41	1.55
UT	JennDry Jennison Utility C	PCUFX	A+	(800) 257-3893	A / 9.4	3.90	10.91	24.75 /88	27.91 /94	9.06 /77	1.41	1.55
UT	JennDry Jennison Utility Z	PRUZX	A+	(800) 257-3893	A / 9.5	4.14	11.44	25.94 /90	29.17 /95	10.13 /81	2.32	0.55
GR	JennDry Jennison Value A	PBEAX	B+	(800) 257-3893	B- / 7.1	0.00	6.50	18.85 /80	18.39 /74	6.65 /65	0.59	1.04
GR	JennDry Jennison Value B	PBQIX	B	(800) 257-3893	C+ / 6.9	-0.14	6.20	18.02 /79	17.50 /70	5.87 /60	0.00	1.79
GR	JennDry Jennison Value C	PEICX	A-	(800) 257-3893	B- / 7.3	-0.19	6.15	18.02 /79	17.50 /70	5.87 /60	0.00	1.79
GR	JennDry Jennison Value Z	PEIZX	A	(800) 257-3893	B / 7.7	0.05	6.65	19.11 /81	18.68 /75	6.92 /66	0.85	0.79
GR	Jensen Portfolio I	JENIX	U	(800) 992-4144	U /	-1.23	1.39	3.01 / 7	--	--	1.12	0.67
GR	Jensen Portfolio J	JENSX	D	(800) 992-4144	D- / 1.0	-1.25	1.27	2.82 / 7	5.79 / 6	2.98 /37	0.89	0.84
GR	Jhaveri Value Fund		D		D- / 1.2	-4.45	-1.18	0.54 / 2	7.39 /12	-1.49 /10	0.00	2.50
FO	JohnsonFamily Intl Value	JFIEX	A+	(800) 276-8272	B+ / 8.7	0.26	10.38	23.26 /86	22.85 /87	12.18 /87	1.39	1.41
GR	JohnsonFamily Large Cap Value	JFLCX	B	(800) 276-8272	C+ / 6.0	-0.38	5.81	9.90 /46	14.87 /58	6.73 /65	1.55	1.07
SC	JohnsonFamily Small Cap Value	JFSCX	D	(800) 276-8272	C+ / 6.1	-1.58	9.96	9.89 /46	14.99 /59	9.16 /77	0.33	1.22
GR	Jordan Opportunity Fund	JORDX	D+	(800) 441-7013	C / 4.8	-4.68	1.60	11.59 /57	13.02 /49	3.96 /46	0.00	1.82
FO	JPMorgan Asia Eq A	JAEAX	C	(800) 358-4782	B / 7.8	-1.68	4.16	18.83 /80	21.09 /83	--	0.44	1.75
FO	JPMorgan Asia Eq Inst	JPAIX	C+	(800) 358-4782	B+ / 8.3	-1.54	4.39	19.34 /81	21.58 /84	--	0.57	1.35
FO	JPMorgan Asia Eq Sel	JPASX	C+	(800) 358-4782	B+ / 8.3	-1.63	4.31	19.14 /81	21.40 /83	--	0.61	1.50
MC	JPMorgan Capital Growth A	VCAGX	C	(800) 358-4782	C+ / 6.0	-5.53	3.96	11.51 /57	16.46 /66	5.25 /56	0.00	1.35
MC	JPMorgan Capital Growth B	VCGBX	C-	(800) 358-4782	C+ / 5.8	-5.63	3.71	10.95 /53	15.88 /63	4.72 /52	0.00	1.85
MC	JPMorgan Capital Growth C	VCGCX	C	(800) 358-4782	C+ / 6.3	-5.67	3.68	10.95 /53	15.89 /63	4.69 /52	0.00	1.85
MC	JPMorgan Capital Growth Sel	VCGIX	C+	(800) 358-4782	C+ / 6.8	-5.47	4.11	11.81 /58	16.86 /67	5.64 /59	0.00	0.93
GI	JPMorgan Disciplined Eq A	JDEAX	C-	(800) 358-4782	D+ / 2.5	-1.92	1.78	6.21 /22	10.30 /29	0.94 /20	0.95	0.95
GI	JPMorgan Disciplined Eq I	JPIEX	C	(800) 358-4782	C- / 3.6	-1.88	1.89	6.55 /24	10.78 /34	1.39 /23	1.40	0.45

● Denotes fund is closed to new investors
★ Denotes fund is included in Section II

www.WeissRatings.com

RISK			NET ASSETS		ASSET					BULL / BEAR		FUND MANAGER		MINIMUMS		LOADS	
	3 Year		NAV						Portfolio	Last Bull	Last Bear	Manager	Manager	Initial	Additional	Front	Back
Risk	Standard		As of	Total	Cash	Stocks	Bonds	Other	Turnover	Market	Market	Quality	Tenure	Purch.	Purch.	End	End
Rating/Pts	Deviation	Beta	6/30/06	$(Mil)	%	%	%	%	Ratio	Return	Return	Pct	(Years)	$	$	Load	Load
C+ / 5.6	11.5	1.33	15.11	1,412	1	98	0	1	57.0	68.6	-12.5	22	N/A	1,000	100	5.5	1.0
C+ / 5.6	11.5	1.33	13.83	329	1	98	0	1	57.0	64.6	-12.6	17	N/A	1,000	100	0.0	5.0
C+ / 5.6	11.5	1.33	13.83	91	1	98	0	1	57.0	64.6	-12.6	17	N/A	2,500	100	0.0	1.0
C+ / 5.7	11.5	1.33	15.54	1,229	1	98	0	1	57.0	69.9	-12.4	23	N/A	0	0	0.0	0.0
C / 5.0	12.8	0.65	19.70	397	4	94	0	2	122.0	125.3	-0.5	99	7	1,000	100	5.5	1.0
C / 4.9	12.8	0.66	18.48	228	4	94	0	2	122.0	120.0	-0.7	99	7	1,000	100	0.0	5.0
C / 4.9	12.8	0.65	18.47	141	4	94	0	2	122.0	120.0	-0.7	99	7	2,500	100	0.0	1.0
C / 5.0	12.8	0.66	20.16	302	4	94	0	2	122.0	127.2	-0.5	99	7	0	0	0.0	0.0
C / 4.7	21.3	0.97	48.25	757	4	95	0	1	30.0	226.9	8.1	98	3	1,000	100	5.5	1.0
C / 4.7	21.3	0.97	42.67	251	4	95	0	1	30.0	219.2	7.9	98	3	1,000	100	0.0	5.0
C / 4.7	21.3	0.97	42.66	355	4	95	0	1	30.0	219.2	7.9	98	3	2,500	100	0.0	1.0
C / 4.7	21.3	0.97	49.14	232	4	95	0	1	30.0	229.4	8.1	99	3	0	0	0.0	0.0
C+ / 5.6	12.5	1.40	6.65	11	N/A	100	0	N/A	123.0	63.5	-14.2	13	N/A	1,000	100	5.5	1.0
C / 5.5	12.5	1.40	6.36	42	N/A	100	0	N/A	123.0	59.4	-14.3	10	N/A	1,000	100	0.0	5.0
C / 5.5	12.5	1.41	6.36	23	N/A	100	0	N/A	123.0	59.4	-14.3	10	N/A	2,500	100	0.0	1.0
C+ / 5.7	12.5	1.41	6.76	2	N/A	100	0	N/A	123.0	64.5	-13.9	15	N/A	0	0	0.0	0.0
C+ / 6.2	12.1	0.80	19.80	567	3	96	0	1	78.0	140.9	-9.2	93	N/A	1,000	100	5.5	1.0
C / 5.4	12.1	0.80	16.12	67	3	96	0	1	78.0	135.3	-9.4	91	N/A	1,000	100	0.0	5.0
C / 5.4	12.0	0.80	16.12	45	3	96	0	1	78.0	135.3	-9.4	91	N/A	2,500	100	0.0	1.0
C+ / 6.3	12.1	0.80	20.55	62	3	96	0	1	78.0	142.9	-9.2	94	N/A	0	0	0.0	0.0
D+ / 2.3	19.2	1.96	7.76	54	0	99	0	1	125.0	94.9	-12.8	8	1	1,000	100	5.5	1.0
D / 2.2	19.2	1.96	7.36	67	0	99	0	1	125.0	90.2	-12.8	6	1	1,000	100	0.0	5.0
D / 2.2	19.2	1.96	7.36	23	0	99	0	1	125.0	90.2	-12.8	6	1	2,500	100	0.0	1.0
D+ / 2.3	19.3	1.97	7.90	6	0	99	0	1	125.0	96.0	-12.7	9	1	0	0	0.0	0.0
C- / 4.0	15.0	1.24	20.58	356	1	98	0	1	136.0	126.8	-10.9	22	1	1,000	100	5.5	1.0
C- / 4.0	14.9	1.24	18.99	110	1	98	0	1	136.0	121.5	-11.1	18	1	1,000	100	0.0	5.0
C- / 4.0	15.0	1.25	18.99	36	1	98	0	1	136.0	121.5	-11.1	17	1	2,500	100	0.0	1.0
C- / 4.1	15.0	1.24	21.10	172	1	98	0	1	136.0	128.4	-10.8	24	1	0	0	0.0	0.0
B- / 7.9	9.7	0.63	15.42	3,595	0	99	0	1	40.0	163.1	-4.7	99	6	1,000	100	5.5	1.0
B- / 7.9	9.8	0.63	15.41	303	0	99	0	1	40.0	156.7	-4.8	99	6	1,000	100	0.0	5.0
B- / 7.9	9.8	0.63	15.40	103	0	99	0	1	40.0	156.5	-4.8	99	6	2,500	100	0.0	1.0
B- / 7.9	9.8	0.63	15.42	90	0	99	0	1	40.0	164.8	-4.6	99	6	0	0	0.0	0.0
B / 8.1	9.1	1.06	21.13	881	2	97	0	1	56.0	95.9	-9.0	95	3	1,000	100	5.5	1.0
B / 8.1	9.1	1.06	20.90	113	2	97	0	1	56.0	91.5	-9.2	93	3	1,000	100	0.0	5.0
B / 8.1	9.1	1.06	20.90	24	2	97	0	1	56.0	91.5	-9.2	93	3	2,500	100	0.0	1.0
B / 8.1	9.1	1.06	21.18	61	2	97	0	1	56.0	97.5	-8.9	96	3	0	0	0.0	0.0
U /	N/A	N/A	24.00	310	1	98	0	1	5.5	N/A	N/A	N/A	14	1,000,000	100	0.0	0.0
B / 8.1	6.5	0.70	24.01	1,765	1	98	0	1	5.5	36.1	-11.6	29	14	2,500	100	0.0	0.0
B- / 7.4	8.5	0.94	9.24	8	12	87	0	1	258.0	51.3	-9.3	26	11	10,000	1,000	0.0	0.0
B- / 7.7	9.3	0.90	15.63	102	4	95	0	1	16.0	124.0	-6.5	63	8	2,500	50	0.0	2.0
B / 8.1	7.0	0.86	10.21	122	3	96	0	1	54.0	84.5	-9.7	92	8	2,500	50	0.0	2.0
C- / 3.1	11.6	0.74	11.81	42	3	96	0	1	71.0	89.0	-10.5	65	8	2,500	50	0.0	2.0
C / 5.5	12.4	1.11	10.79	22	0	88	11	1	307.0	97.1	-7.7	64	1	10,000	500	0.0	2.0
C / 4.5	15.7	1.17	24.02	7	5	94	0	1	78.0	115.6	-10.2	9	N/A	1,000	25	5.3	2.0
C / 4.5	15.7	1.17	24.25	19	5	94	0	1	78.0	118.2	-10.0	11	N/A	3,000,000	0	0.0	2.0
C / 4.5	15.7	1.17	24.19	265	5	94	0	1	78.0	117.2	-10.1	10	N/A	1,000,000	0	0.0	2.0
C+ / 5.7	12.6	1.12	40.68	470	3	96	0	1	119.0	100.7	-8.7	24	N/A	1,000	25	5.3	0.0
C / 5.5	12.6	1.12	37.22	29	3	96	0	1	119.0	97.5	-8.8	21	N/A	1,000	25	0.0	5.0
C / 5.4	12.6	1.12	36.62	21	3	96	0	1	119.0	97.2	-8.9	21	N/A	1,000	25	0.0	1.0
C+ / 5.8	12.6	1.12	43.05	320	3	96	0	1	119.0	102.9	-8.6	27	N/A	1,000,000	0	0.0	0.0
B / 8.7	7.8	1.01	15.33	1	1	98	0	1	44.0	60.8	-9.8	44	N/A	1,000	25	5.3	0.0
B / 8.8	7.8	1.01	15.33	220	1	98	0	1	44.0	63.2	-9.8	50	N/A	3,000,000	0	0.0	0.0

					PERFORMANCE							
	99 Pct = Best 0 Pct = Worst			Overall Weiss		Perfor- mance	Total Return % through 6/30/06					Incl. in Returns	
				Investment		Rating/Pts				Annualized		Dividend	Expense
Fund Type	Fund Name	Ticker Symbol	Rating	Phone			3 Mo	6 Mo	1Yr / Pct	3Yr / Pct	5Yr / Pct	Yield	Ratio
GI	JPMorgan Disciplined Eq Sel	JDESX	C	(800) 358-4782		C- / 3.5	-1.90	1.85	6.42 /23	10.61 /32	1.20 /22	1.28	0.75
GI	JPMorgan Disciplined Eq Ultra	JDEUX	C+	(800) 358-4782		C- / 3.7	-1.86	1.95	6.66 /24	10.89 /34	1.46 /23	1.50	0.35
MC	JPMorgan Divers Mid Cap Gr A	OSGIX	C-	(800) 358-4782		C / 5.0	-5.41	4.41	12.20 /61	14.04 /54	4.54 /50	0.00	1.24
MC	JPMorgan Divers Mid Cap Gr B	OGOBX	C-	(800) 358-4782		C / 4.5	-5.56	4.05	11.45 /56	13.22 /50	3.78 /44	0.00	1.99
MC	JPMorgan Divers Mid Cap Gr C	OMGCX	C-	(800) 358-4782		C / 5.2	-5.57	4.06	11.49 /57	13.23 /50	3.78 /44	0.00	1.99
MC	JPMorgan Divers Mid Cap Gr Sel	HLGEX	C	(800) 358-4782		C+ / 5.9	-5.32	4.54	12.51 /62	14.32 /56	4.80 /52	0.00	0.99
MC	JPMorgan Divers Mid Cap Gr Ultra	JDGUX	C+	(800) 358-4782		C+ / 5.9	-5.31	4.57	12.63 /63	14.38 /56	4.83 /53	0.00	0.89
MC	● JPMorgan Divers Mid Cap Val A	OGDIX	D	(800) 358-4782		C+ / 6.5	-0.79	5.30	9.50 /43	17.29 /69	8.53 /74	0.59	1.24
MC	● JPMorgan Divers Mid Cap Val B	OGDBX	D	(800) 358-4782		C+ / 6.2	-0.97	4.96	8.82 /39	16.51 /66	7.75 /70	0.26	1.99
MC	● JPMorgan Divers Mid Cap Val C	OMVCX	D	(800) 358-4782		C+ / 6.6	-0.97	4.96	8.82 /39	16.50 /66	7.76 /70	0.27	1.99
MC	● JPMorgan Divers Mid Cap Val Sel	HLDEX	D+	(800) 358-4782		B- / 7.2	-0.79	5.39	9.72 /45	17.58 /71	8.79 /75	0.82	0.99
MC	● JPMorgan Divers Mid Cap Val Ultra	JDVUX	C+	(800) 358-4782		B- / 7.2	-0.69	5.54	9.89 /46	17.68 /71	8.85 /76	0.94	0.84
AA	JPMorgan Diversified Fd A	JDVAX	C-	(800) 358-4782		D / 1.9	-0.72	2.51	7.02 /26	8.85 /20	3.36 /40	1.78	1.14
AA	JPMorgan Diversified Fd B	JDVBX	C-	(800) 358-4782		D / 1.6	-0.86	2.24	6.44 /23	8.20 /16	2.95 /36	1.35	1.65
AA	JPMorgan Diversified Fd C	JDVCX	C	(800) 358-4782		D / 2.2	-0.79	2.31	6.52 /23	8.23 /16	2.97 /37	1.35	1.65
AA	JPMorgan Diversified Fd Inst	JPDVX	C+	(800) 358-4782		C- / 3.1	-0.60	2.76	7.46 /29	9.45 /24	3.84 /44	2.37	0.65
AA	JPMorgan Diversified Fd Sel	JDVSX	C	(800) 358-4782		D+ / 2.9	-0.66	2.63	7.26 /28	9.17 /22	3.57 /42	2.12	0.89
SC	JPMorgan Dynamic Small Cap A	VSCOX	C-	(800) 358-4782		C / 5.5	-8.38	6.73	14.36 /69	14.91 /58	4.63 /51	0.00	1.50
SC	JPMorgan Dynamic Small Cap B	VSCBX	D+	(800) 358-4782		C / 5.2	-8.51	6.42	13.66 /67	14.22 /55	3.99 /46	0.00	2.12
SC	JPMorgan Dynamic Small Cap C	VSCCX	C-	(800) 358-4782		C+ / 5.8	-8.47	6.49	13.75 /67	14.24 /55	4.00 /46	0.00	2.12
SC	JPMorgan Dynamic Small Cap Sel	JDSCX	C	(800) 358-4782		C+ / 6.4	-8.28	6.97	14.89 /71	15.39 /61	5.04 /55	0.00	1.10
EM	JPMorgan Emerg Mkt Eq A	JFAMX	B	(800) 358-4782		A+ / 9.7	-4.95	6.41	30.94 /95	34.58 /98	19.18 /95	0.16	2.00
EM	JPMorgan Emerg Mkt Eq B	JFBMX	B	(800) 358-4782		A+ / 9.7	-5.05	6.31	30.42 /95	33.98 /98	18.70 /95	0.00	2.50
EM	JPMorgan Emerg Mkt Eq C	JEMCX	C	(800) 358-4782		A+ / 9.7	-5.05	6.24	30.33 /95	33.95 /97	18.68 /95	0.00	2.50
EM	JPMorgan Emerg Mkt Eq Inst	JMIEX	B	(800) 358-4782		A+ / 9.8	-4.85	6.73	31.62 /95	35.26 /98	19.85 /96	0.34	1.45
EM	JPMorgan Emerg Mkt Eq Sel	JEMSX	B	(800) 358-4782		A+ / 9.8	-4.89	6.64	31.32 /95	34.97 /98	19.47 /96	0.27	1.75
IN	JPMorgan Equity Income A	OIEIX	E	(800) 358-4782		C- / 3.7	1.67	5.27	7.94 /32	11.64 /40	3.92 /45	1.79	1.24
IN	JPMorgan Equity Income B	OGIBX	E	(800) 358-4782		C- / 3.3	1.53	5.02	7.43 /29	10.93 /35	3.21 /39	1.45	1.99
IN	JPMorgan Equity Income C	OINCX	E	(800) 358-4782		C- / 4.0	1.45	5.02	7.36 /28	10.92 /35	3.22 /39	1.45	1.99
IN	JPMorgan Equity Income Sel	HLIEX	E+	(800) 358-4782		C / 4.8	1.74	5.48	8.28 /35	11.94 /42	4.20 /48	2.08	0.89
IX	JPMorgan Equity Index A	OGEAX	C	(800) 358-4782		D+ / 2.9	-1.56	2.50	8.19 /34	10.65 /32	1.96 /27	1.42	0.45
IX	JPMorgan Equity Index B	OGEIX	C-	(800) 358-4782		D+ / 2.4	-1.74	2.11	7.35 /28	9.82 /26	1.19 /21	0.74	1.20
IX	JPMorgan Equity Index C	OEICX	C	(800) 358-4782		C- / 3.1	-1.73	2.11	7.36 /28	9.83 /26	1.19 /21	0.76	1.20
IX	JPMorgan Equity Index Sel	HLEIX	C+	(800) 358-4782		C- / 4.0	-1.50	2.62	8.45 /36	10.93 /35	2.21 /29	1.74	0.20
GI	JPMorgan Growth & Income A	VGRIX	C+	(800) 358-4782		C- / 3.6	0.26	3.73	7.33 /28	11.75 /41	3.28 /39	0.78	1.30
GI	JPMorgan Growth & Income B	VINBX	C+	(800) 358-4782		C- / 3.3	0.16	3.50	6.81 /25	11.20 /37	2.76 /34	0.32	1.80
GI	JPMorgan Growth & Income C	VGICX	C+	(800) 358-4782		C- / 4.0	0.15	3.50	6.83 /25	11.19 /37	2.76 /34	0.40	1.80
GI	JPMorgan Growth & Income Sel	VGIIX	B	(800) 358-4782		C / 4.8	0.37	3.95	7.72 /31	12.18 /44	3.68 /43	1.12	0.90
GR	JPMorgan Growth Advantage A	VHIAX	C	(800) 358-4782		C+ / 6.2	-6.88	4.41	12.95 /64	16.90 /68	2.96 /36	0.00	1.35
GR	JPMorgan Growth Advantage B	VHIBX	C	(800) 358-4782		C+ / 5.9	-7.05	4.11	12.04 /60	16.05 /64	2.23 /29	0.00	2.05
FO	JPMorgan International Eq A	JSEAX	A-	(800) 358-4782		B / 8.1	0.08	9.83	24.96 /88	20.64 /82	9.76 /80	1.57	1.31
FO	JPMorgan International Eq B	JSEBX	A-	(800) 358-4782		B / 8.0	-0.09	9.46	24.16 /87	19.99 /79	9.24 /78	1.06	2.00
FO	JPMorgan International Eq C	JIECX	A-	(800) 358-4782		B / 8.2	-0.08	9.44	24.14 /87	19.98 /79	9.24 /78	1.20	2.00
FO	JPMorgan International Eq Sel	VSIEX	A	(800) 358-4782		B+ / 8.5	0.11	9.91	25.25 /89	21.06 /83	10.10 /81	1.89	1.06
FO	JPMorgan Intl Equity Index A	OEIAX	A	(800) 358-4782		B+ / 8.8	-0.89	8.97	27.41 /92	24.81 /91	9.91 /80	1.36	1.18
FO	JPMorgan Intl Equity Index B	OGEBX	A	(800) 358-4782		B+ / 8.7	-1.07	8.63	26.54 /91	23.88 /89	9.12 /77	1.07	1.93
FO	JPMorgan Intl Equity Index C	OIICX	A	(800) 358-4782		B+ / 8.9	-1.07	8.61	26.48 /91	23.87 /89	9.11 /77	0.82	1.93
FO	JPMorgan Intl Equity Index Sel	OIEAX	A+	(800) 358-4782		A- / 9.1	-0.84	9.11	27.74 /92	25.09 /91	10.20 /81	1.60	0.93
FO	JPMorgan Intl Growth A	VAIGX	B-	(800) 358-4782		B- / 7.3	-1.53	7.90	24.57 /88	18.31 /74	6.97 /66	0.00	2.00
FO	JPMorgan Intl Growth B	VBIGX	B-	(800) 358-4782		B / 7.6	-1.73	7.59	24.07 /87	17.73 /71	6.44 /64	0.00	2.50
FO	JPMorgan Intl Opps A	JIOAX	A	(800) 358-4782		B+ / 8.6	1.02	11.43	29.20 /94	22.32 /86	7.89 /71	1.17	1.42
FO	JPMorgan Intl Opps B	JIOBX	A	(800) 358-4782		B+ / 8.6	0.88	11.08	28.52 /93	21.72 /84	7.39 /69	0.90	1.92

● Denotes fund is closed to new investors
* Denotes fund is included in Section II

RISK			NET ASSETS		ASSET				BULL / BEAR		FUND MANAGER		MINIMUMS		LOADS	
	3 Year		NAV						Last Bull	Last Bear	Manager	Manager	Initial	Additional	Front	Back
Risk Rating/Pts	Standard Deviation	Beta	As of 6/30/06	Total $(Mil)	Cash %	Stocks %	Bonds %	Other %	Portfolio Turnover Ratio	Market Return	Market Return	Quality Pct	Tenure (Years)	Purch. $	Purch. $	End Load	End Load
B / 8.8	7.8	1.01	15.34	229	1	98	0	1	44.0	62.4	-9.8	47	N/A	1,000,000	0	0.0	0.0
B / 8.8	7.8	1.01	15.33	154	1	98	0	1	44.0	63.7	-9.8	52	N/A	20,000,000	0	0.0	0.0
C+ / 6.3	11.2	1.00	24.85	456	1	98	0	1	119.0	82.9	-8.9	22	N/A	1,000	25	5.3	0.0
C+ / 6.1	11.2	1.00	21.58	157	1	98	0	1	119.0	78.9	-9.1	17	N/A	1,000	25	0.0	5.0
C+ / 6.2	11.2	1.00	23.56	43	1	98	0	1	119.0	78.9	-9.1	18	N/A	1,000	25	0.0	1.0
C+ / 6.3	11.2	1.00	25.81	771	1	98	0	1	119.0	84.4	-8.8	23	N/A	1,000,000	0	0.0	0.0
B- / 7.3	11.2	1.00	25.85	18	1	98	0	1	119.0	84.7	-8.8	24	N/A	5,000,000	0	0.0	0.0
C- / 3.1	9.0	0.80	15.92	226	2	97	0	1	67.0	89.4	-8.8	78	N/A	1,000	25	5.3	0.0
D+ / 2.8	9.0	0.80	15.23	60	2	97	0	1	67.0	85.1	-8.8	73	N/A	1,000	25	0.0	5.0
D+ / 2.8	9.0	0.80	15.23	33	2	97	0	1	67.0	85.2	-8.8	72	N/A	1,000	25	0.0	1.0
C- / 3.0	9.0	0.80	15.84	604	2	97	0	1	67.0	90.9	-8.7	80	N/A	1,000,000	0	0.0	0.0
C+ / 6.0	9.0	0.80	15.85	10	2	97	0	1	67.0	91.2	-8.7	82	1	5,000,000	0	0.0	0.0
B+ / 9.2	5.6	1.17	14.24	140	N/A	73	27	N/A	214.0	46.7	-5.8	60	4	1,000	25	5.3	0.0
B+ / 9.4	5.5	1.16	14.23	112	N/A	73	27	N/A	214.0	44.0	-5.8	54	6	1,000	25	0.0	5.0
B+ / 9.4	5.6	1.17	14.24	5	N/A	73	27	N/A	214.0	44.0	-5.8	53	6	1,000	25	0.0	1.0
B+ / 9.4	5.6	1.17	14.25	207	N/A	73	27	N/A	214.0	49.2	-5.7	67	6	3,000,000	0	0.0	0.0
B+ / 9.4	5.6	1.16	14.26	98	N/A	73	27	N/A	214.0	48.1	-5.8	64	4	1,000,000	0	0.0	0.0
C / 5.1	15.5	1.03	19.34	82	0	99	0	1	143.0	97.6	-10.2	21	N/A	1,000	25	5.3	0.0
C / 5.0	15.5	1.03	18.06	41	0	99	0	1	143.0	93.9	-10.3	17	N/A	1,000	25	0.0	5.0
C / 5.1	15.5	1.03	18.04	55	0	99	0	1	143.0	93.9	-10.3	17	N/A	1,000	25	0.0	1.0
C / 5.1	15.5	1.03	19.95	28	0	99	0	1	143.0	100.1	-10.1	24	N/A	1,000,000	0	0.0	0.0
C / 4.6	18.3	1.10	14.60	22	0	98	0	2	149.0	220.4	-6.3	20	N/A	1,000	25	5.3	2.0
C / 4.6	18.3	1.10	14.49	8	0	98	0	2	149.0	215.3	-6.2	18	N/A	1,000	25	0.0	5.0
D / 2.2	18.4	1.10	14.48	1	0	98	0	2	149.0	215.3	-6.2	17	N/A	1,000	25	0.0	2.0
C / 4.7	18.4	1.11	14.91	78	0	98	0	2	149.0	225.6	-6.2	23	N/A	3,000,000	0	0.0	2.0
C / 4.6	18.3	1.10	14.77	221	0	98	0	2	149.0	222.9	-6.3	22	N/A	1,000,000	0	0.0	2.0
D / 1.8	6.5	0.78	12.10	123	N/A	99	0	N/A	68.0	61.4	-8.5	79	N/A	1,000	25	5.3	0.0
D / 1.8	6.5	0.78	12.05	35	N/A	99	0	N/A	68.0	58.0	-8.6	73	N/A	1,000	25	0.0	5.0
D / 1.8	6.4	0.78	12.04	6	N/A	99	0	N/A	68.0	58.1	-8.6	73	N/A	1,000	25	0.0	1.0
D / 1.8	6.5	0.78	12.19	131	N/A	99	0	N/A	68.0	62.6	-8.3	81	N/A	1,000,000	0	0.0	0.0
B / 8.6	7.6	1.00	28.90	450	1	98	0	1	11.0	62.1	-9.8	50	12	1,000	25	5.3	0.0
B / 8.8	7.7	1.00	28.78	171	1	98	0	1	11.0	58.3	-10.0	40	12	1,000	25	0.0	5.0
B / 8.8	7.7	1.00	28.81	82	1	98	0	1	11.0	58.3	-10.0	40	9	1,000	25	0.0	1.0
B / 8.8	7.6	1.00	28.90	1,293	1	98	0	1	11.0	63.5	-9.8	53	12	1,000,000	0	0.0	0.0
B+ / 9.1	6.8	0.84	34.66	526	1	98	0	1	41.0	66.2	-10.0	75	19	1,000	25	5.3	0.0
B+ / 9.4	6.8	0.84	34.05	30	1	98	0	1	41.0	63.6	-10.1	70	13	1,000	25	0.0	5.0
B+ / 9.4	6.8	0.84	32.86	5	1	98	0	1	41.0	63.6	-10.1	71	N/A	1,000	25	0.0	1.0
B+ / 9.4	6.8	0.84	35.71	3	1	98	0	1	41.0	68.3	-9.9	79	10	1,000,000	0	0.0	0.0
C+ / 6.2	13.2	1.48	6.63	72	2	97	0	1	140.0	107.6	-8.8	68	N/A	1,000	25	5.3	0.0
C+ / 6.1	13.1	1.47	6.33	1	2	97	0	1	140.0	103.3	-9.2	60	N/A	1,000	25	0.0	5.0
B- / 7.4	9.9	0.95	35.06	125	2	97	0	1	22.0	115.2	-11.3	32	4	1,000	25	5.3	2.0
B- / 7.3	9.9	0.96	34.87	11	2	97	0	1	22.0	111.5	-11.3	27	4	1,000	25	0.0	5.0
B- / 7.3	9.9	0.96	34.73	39	2	97	0	1	22.0	111.6	-11.4	27	N/A	1,000	25	0.0	2.0
B- / 7.4	9.9	0.96	35.14	3,906	2	97	0	1	22.0	117.6	-11.2	34	N/A	1,000,000	0	0.0	2.0
B- / 7.1	11.1	1.08	24.55	82	1	98	0	1	14.0	137.9	-8.2	39	N/A	1,000	25	5.3	2.0
B- / 7.0	11.1	1.09	23.04	20	1	98	0	1	14.0	132.2	-8.2	32	N/A	1,000	25	0.0	5.0
B- / 7.0	11.1	1.08	23.97	13	1	98	0	1	14.0	132.3	-8.3	33	N/A	1,000	25	0.0	2.0
B- / 7.1	11.1	1.08	24.67	1,169	1	98	0	1	14.0	139.7	-8.1	42	N/A	1,000,000	0	0.0	2.0
C+ / 6.4	10.6	1.00	11.61	5	0	99	0	1	37.0	109.8	-12.5	13	N/A	1,000	25	5.3	2.0
C+ / 6.4	10.5	1.00	11.34	1	0	99	0	1	37.0	106.6	-12.7	12	N/A	1,000	25	0.0	2.0
B- / 7.1	10.9	1.05	13.84	10	0	100	0	0	58.0	119.5	-11.8	29	N/A	1,000	25	5.3	2.0
B- / 7.1	10.9	1.04	13.73	1	0	100	0	0	58.0	116.1	-11.9	26	N/A	1,000	25	0.0	5.0

Data as of June 30, 2006

					PERFORMANCE							
						Total Return % through 6/30/06					Incl. in Returns	
			Overall Weiss Investment Rating		Perfor- mance				Annualized		Dividend	Expense
Fund Type	Fund Name	Ticker Symbol		Phone	Rating/Pts	3 Mo	6 Mo	1Yr / Pct	3Yr / Pct	5Yr / Pct	Yield	Ratio
FO	JPMorgan Intl Opps Inst	JPIOX	A+	(800) 358-4782	A- / 9.1	1.15	11.69	29.81 /94	23.25 /88	8.84 /76	1.70	0.92
FO	JPMorgan Intl Opps Sel	JIOSX	A+	(800) 358-4782	A- / 9.0	1.09	11.49	29.43 /94	22.92 /87	8.52 /74	1.54	1.17
FO	JPMorgan Intl Value A	JFEAX	A+	(800) 358-4782	A / 9.5	2.28	12.94	34.50 /96	28.89 /95	12.25 /87	1.01	1.45
FO	JPMorgan Intl Value B	JFEBX	A+	(800) 358-4782	A / 9.5	2.18	12.67	33.84 /96	28.26 /94	11.75 /86	0.79	1.95
FO	JPMorgan Intl Value Inst	JNUSX	A+	(800) 358-4782	A+ / 9.6	2.39	13.23	35.15 /97	29.53 /95	12.79 /88	1.29	0.95
FO	JPMorgan Intl Value Sel	JIESX	A+	(800) 358-4782	A+ / 9.6	2.33	13.03	34.87 /97	29.07 /95	12.45 /87	1.15	1.41
GR	JPMorgan Intrepid America A	JIAAX	C	(800) 358-4782	C+ / 5.7	-0.67	4.04	10.82 /52	15.26 /60	--	0.39	1.25
GR	JPMorgan Intrepid America C	JIACX	C	(800) 358-4782	C+ / 6.1	-0.79	3.76	10.26 /49	14.98 /59	--	0.28	1.75
GR	JPMorgan Intrepid America Sel	JPIAX	B	(800) 358-4782	C+ / 6.4	-0.59	4.20	11.13 /54	15.38 /61	--	0.41	1.00
FO	JPMorgan Intrepid Euro A	VEUAX	A	(800) 358-4782	A / 9.5	2.42	17.59	35.29 /97	28.38 /94	18.39 /95	0.46	1.75
FO	JPMorgan Intrepid Euro B	VEUBX	A	(800) 358-4782	A / 9.5	2.25	17.24	34.49 /96	27.70 /94	17.65 /94	0.16	2.50
FO	JPMorgan Intrepid Euro C	VEUCX	A	(800) 358-4782	A / 9.5	2.30	17.28	34.61 /97	27.74 /94	17.66 /94	0.26	2.50
FO	JPMorgan Intrepid Euro Inst	JFEIX	A	(800) 358-4782	A+ / 9.6	2.50	17.81	35.87 /97	29.19 /95	19.11 /95	0.83	1.00
FO	JPMorgan Intrepid Euro Sel	JFESX	A	(800) 358-4782	A+ / 9.6	2.44	17.73	35.61 /97	28.78 /95	18.67 /95	0.72	1.50
GR	JPMorgan Intrepid Growth A	JIGAX	C	(800) 358-4782	C- / 4.1	-3.16	0.82	8.76 /38	12.94 /48	--	0.08	1.25
GR	JPMorgan Intrepid Growth C	JCICX	C+	(800) 358-4782	C / 4.6	-3.27	0.53	8.17 /34	12.68 /47	--	0.05	1.75
GR	JPMorgan Intrepid Growth Sel	JPGSX	C+	(800) 358-4782	C / 5.0	-3.06	0.92	8.99 /40	13.06 /49	--	0.16	1.00
FO	JPMorgan Intrepid Int A	JFTAX	B	(800) 358-4782	B+ / 8.3	-0.88	9.15	26.63 /91	21.88 /85	8.17 /72	0.81	1.80
FO	JPMorgan Intrepid Int C	JIICX	B-	(800) 358-4782	B+ / 8.6	-1.08	8.93	26.38 /90	21.80 /85	8.12 /72	0.86	2.00
FO	JPMorgan Intrepid Int Inst	JFTIX	B+	(800) 358-4782	B+ / 8.8	-0.83	9.37	27.20 /92	22.60 /86	8.90 /76	1.35	1.00
FO	JPMorgan Intrepid Int Sel	JISIX	B-	(800) 358-4782	B+ / 8.8	-0.83	9.31	27.13 /91	22.58 /86	8.89 /76	1.35	1.25
MC	JPMorgan Intrepid Mid Cap A	PECAX	D	(800) 358-4782	B- / 7.2	-2.11	6.06	16.32 /75	18.36 /74	7.92 /71	0.21	1.24
MC	JPMorgan Intrepid Mid Cap B	ODMBX	D	(800) 358-4782	C+ / 6.9	-2.29	5.75	15.59 /73	17.56 /70	7.16 /68	0.00	1.99
MC	JPMorgan Intrepid Mid Cap C	ODMCX	D	(800) 358-4782	B- / 7.3	-2.29	5.68	15.56 /73	17.52 /70	7.14 /67	0.00	1.99
MC	JPMorgan Intrepid Mid Cap Sel	WOOPX	D+	(800) 358-4782	B / 7.7	-2.12	6.15	16.61 /76	18.64 /75	8.19 /72	0.38	0.99
MC	JPMorgan Intrepid Mid Cap Ultra	JDMUX	C+	(800) 358-4782	B / 7.8	-2.02	6.29	16.77 /76	18.74 /75	8.24 /73	0.50	0.83
GR	JPMorgan Intrepid Multi Cap A	JICAX	C	(800) 358-4782	C / 5.5	-0.80	4.25	9.96 /47	15.02 /59	--	0.75	1.25
GR	JPMorgan Intrepid Multi Cap C	JICCX	C	(800) 358-4782	C+ / 5.9	-0.94	3.99	9.42 /43	14.75 /58	--	0.67	1.75
GR	JPMorgan Intrepid Multi Cap Sel	JIISX	B+	(800) 358-4782	C+ / 6.3	-0.75	4.34	10.18 /48	15.13 /59	--	0.86	1.00
GR	JPMorgan Intrepid Value A	JIVAX	A+	(800) 358-4782	B- / 7.3	1.69	8.55	15.64 /74	18.40 /74	--	1.24	1.25
GR	JPMorgan Intrepid Value C	JIVCX	A+	(800) 358-4782	B / 7.6	1.57	8.26	15.04 /72	18.12 /73	--	1.10	1.75
GR	JPMorgan Intrepid Value Sel	JPIVX	A+	(800) 358-4782	B / 7.8	1.72	8.66	15.87 /74	18.53 /74	--	1.43	1.00
AA	JPMorgan Investor Balanced A	OGIAX	C-	(800) 358-4782	D / 1.6	-0.33	2.45	6.26 /22	8.21 /16	4.63 /51	2.68	1.33
AA	JPMorgan Investor Balanced B	OGBBX	C-	(800) 358-4782	D- / 1.2	-0.48	2.15	5.63 /18	7.50 /12	3.89 /45	2.23	2.04
AA	JPMorgan Investor Balanced C	OGBCX	C	(800) 358-4782	D / 1.8	-0.48	2.17	5.69 /19	7.51 /12	3.90 /45	2.26	2.04
AA	JPMorgan Investor Balanced Sel	OIBFX	C	(800) 358-4782	D+ / 2.5	-0.35	2.50	6.52 /23	8.46 /18	4.88 /53	3.07	1.08
AA	JPMorgan Investor Conserv Gr A	OICAX	C-	(800) 358-4782	E / 0.5	0.08	1.55	3.63 / 9	5.44 / 5	4.18 /48	3.16	1.26
AA	JPMorgan Investor Conserv Gr B	OICGX	C-	(800) 358-4782	E / 0.4	-0.05	1.28	3.03 / 7	4.74 / 3	3.45 /41	2.76	2.00
AA	JPMorgan Investor Conserv Gr C	OCGCX	C-	(800) 358-4782	E+ / 0.6	-0.05	1.28	3.03 / 7	4.76 / 4	3.45 /41	2.76	2.00
AA	JPMorgan Investor Conserv Gr Sel	ONCFX	C-	(800) 358-4782	D- / 1.1	0.14	1.67	3.97 /10	5.73 / 6	4.44 /50	3.58	1.01
GI	JPMorgan Investor Gr & Inc A	ONGIX	C	(800) 358-4782	D+ / 2.9	-0.70	3.48	8.79 /39	10.62 /32	4.46 /50	2.11	1.41
GI	JPMorgan Investor Gr & Inc B	ONEBX	C	(800) 358-4782	D+ / 2.6	-0.85	3.13	8.19 /34	9.87 /26	3.74 /43	1.65	2.14
GI	JPMorgan Investor Gr & Inc C	ONECX	C+	(800) 358-4782	C- / 3.2	-0.85	3.10	8.15 /34	9.86 /26	3.72 /43	1.69	2.15
GI	JPMorgan Investor Gr & Inc Sel	ONGFX	C+	(800) 358-4782	C- / 4.1	-0.72	3.49	9.07 /40	10.87 /34	4.73 /52	2.49	1.16
GR	JPMorgan Investor Growth A	ONGAX	C+	(800) 358-4782	C / 4.6	-1.04	4.32	11.31 /55	12.93 /48	4.27 /49	1.41	1.46
GR	JPMorgan Investor Growth B	OGIGX	C	(800) 358-4782	C- / 4.1	-1.19	4.08	10.70 /52	12.18 /44	3.54 /42	0.98	2.27
GR	JPMorgan Investor Growth C	OGGCX	C+	(800) 358-4782	C / 4.8	-1.13	4.07	10.70 /52	12.18 /44	3.54 /42	1.01	2.27
GR	JPMorgan Investor Growth Sel	ONIFX	C+	(800) 358-4782	C / 5.5	-0.97	4.47	11.60 /57	13.21 /50	4.52 /50	1.71	1.21
FO	JPMorgan Japan Fund A	CVJAX	C	(800) 358-4782	B+ / 8.5	-8.91	-4.94	33.62 /96	25.74 /92	8.41 /74	0.00	1.75
FO	JPMorgan Japan Fund B	CVJBX	C	(800) 358-4782	B+ / 8.4	-9.01	-5.16	32.82 /96	24.89 /91	7.58 /70	0.00	2.50
FO	JPMorgan Japan Fund C	JPCNX	D+	(800) 358-4782	B+ / 8.6	-8.92	-5.16	32.82 /96	24.89 /91	7.58 /70	0.00	2.50
FO	JPMorgan Japan Fund Sel	JPNSX	D+	(800) 358-4782	B+ / 8.8	-8.82	-4.94	33.62 /96	25.74 /92	8.41 /74	0.00	1.50

● Denotes fund is closed to new investors
* Denotes fund is included in Section II

99 Pct = Best
0 Pct = Worst

RISK			NET ASSETS		ASSET				BULL / BEAR		FUND MANAGER		MINIMUMS		LOADS	
	3 Year		NAV						Last Bull	Last Bear	Manager	Manager	Initial	Additional	Front	Back
Risk Rating/Pts	Standard Deviation	Beta	As of 6/30/06	Total $(Mil)	Cash %	Stocks %	Bonds %	Other %	Portfolio Turnover Ratio	Market Return	Market Return	Quality Pct	Tenure (Years)	Purch. $	Purch. $	End Load	End Load
B- / 7.1	10.9	1.04	14.05	56	0	100	0	0	58.0	125.4	-11.7	35	9	3,000,000	0	0.0	2.0
B- / 7.1	10.9	1.05	13.97	53	0	100	0	0	58.0	123.3	-11.7	32	N/A	1,000,000	0	0.0	2.0
B- / 7.3	10.4	0.99	15.27	10	N/A	N/A	0	N/A	76.0	157.8	-9.8	89	9	1,000	25	5.3	2.0
B- / 7.3	10.4	0.99	15.03	6	N/A	N/A	0	N/A	76.0	153.8	-9.9	86	9	1,000	25	0.0	5.0
B- / 7.3	10.4	0.99	15.41	44	N/A	N/A	0	N/A	76.0	161.9	-9.7	91	9	3,000,000	0	0.0	2.0
B- / 7.3	10.4	0.99	15.35	202	N/A	N/A	0	N/A	76.0	159.0	-9.7	90	9	1,000,000	0	0.0	2.0
C+ / 5.8	9.6	1.13	25.25	40	1	98	0	1	109.0	83.5	N/A	81	3	1,000	25	5.3	0.0
C+ / 5.8	9.6	1.13	25.10	8	1	98	0	1	109.0	82.2	N/A	79	3	1,000	25	0.0	1.0
B / 8.5	9.6	1.13	25.33	4,416	1	98	0	1	109.0	83.9	N/A	82	3	1,000,000	0	0.0	0.0
C+ / 6.4	12.0	1.06	25.40	89	0	100	0	0	281.0	159.9	-12.1	76	6	1,000	25	5.3	2.0
C+ / 6.3	12.0	1.06	23.67	19	0	100	0	0	281.0	155.5	-12.3	71	6	1,000	25	0.0	5.0
C+ / 6.3	12.0	1.06	23.62	13	0	100	0	0	281.0	155.5	-12.3	72	6	1,000	25	0.0	2.0
C+ / 6.4	12.0	1.06	25.87	92	0	100	0	0	281.0	165.3	-12.0	82	N/A	3,000,000	0	0.0	2.0
C+ / 6.4	12.0	1.06	25.56	191	0	100	0	0	281.0	162.3	-12.1	79	N/A	1,000,000	0	0.0	2.0
B / 8.1	10.4	1.21	20.84	15	2	98	0	0	130.0	69.5	N/A	54	3	1,000	25	5.3	0.0
B / 8.0	10.5	1.07	20.70	7	2	98	0	0	130.0	68.4	N/A	64	3	1,000	25	0.0	1.0
B / 8.1	10.3	1.21	20.89	1,226	2	98	0	0	130.0	70.0	N/A	55	3	1,000,000	0	0.0	0.0
C+ / 6.3	11.1	1.07	20.16	8	0	99	0	1	56.0	119.3	-12.4	23	N/A	1,000	25	5.3	2.0
C / 5.3	11.1	1.07	20.12	N/A	0	99	0	1	56.0	119.2	-12.4	23	N/A	1,000	25	0.0	2.0
C+ / 6.3	11.1	1.07	20.43	437	0	99	0	1	56.0	123.7	-12.1	27	N/A	3,000,000	0	0.0	2.0
C / 5.3	11.1	1.07	20.42	219	0	99	0	1	56.0	123.7	-12.1	27	N/A	1,000,000	0	0.0	2.0
D / 1.9	11.1	0.98	17.33	166	0	99	0	1	131.0	98.8	-8.1	62	2	1,000	25	5.3	0.0
D / 1.8	11.1	0.98	16.18	24	0	99	0	1	131.0	94.5	-8.3	54	2	1,000	25	0.0	5.0
D / 1.8	11.0	0.97	16.18	23	0	99	0	1	131.0	94.3	-8.3	54	2	1,000	25	0.0	1.0
D / 1.9	11.1	0.98	17.75	628	0	99	0	1	131.0	100.3	-8.0	65	2	1,000,000	0	0.0	0.0
C / 5.4	11.0	0.97	17.76	35	0	99	0	1	131.0	100.7	-8.0	66	2	5,000,000	0	0.0	0.0
C+ / 6.0	9.2	1.09	22.30	4	3	96	0	1	177.0	82.9	N/A	82	3	1,000	25	5.3	0.0
C+ / 6.0	9.2	1.09	22.16	1	3	96	0	1	177.0	81.9	N/A	80	3	1,000	25	0.0	1.0
B / 8.5	9.1	1.09	22.35	16	3	96	0	1	177.0	83.4	N/A	83	3	1,000,000	0	0.0	0.0
B / 8.8	8.8	1.01	24.78	17	6	94	0	0	112.0	97.4	N/A	96	3	1,000	25	5.3	0.0
B / 8.8	8.8	1.01	24.69	6	6	94	0	0	112.0	96.2	N/A	96	3	1,000	25	0.0	1.0
B / 8.8	8.8	1.01	24.82	43	6	94	0	0	112.0	98.0	N/A	96	3	1,000,000	0	0.0	0.0
B+ / 9.6	4.2	0.87	12.36	924	1	52	46	1	22.0	41.2	-3.3	70	10	500	25	5.3	0.0
B+ / 9.8	4.2	0.87	12.34	670	1	52	46	1	22.0	38.2	-3.4	63	10	500	25	0.0	5.0
B+ / 9.8	4.2	0.87	12.26	111	1	52	46	1	22.0	38.1	-3.4	63	9	500	25	0.0	1.0
B+ / 9.9	4.2	0.87	12.36	116	1	52	46	1	22.0	42.2	-3.1	72	10	1,000,000	0	0.0	0.0
B+ / 9.8	2.8	0.55	10.98	395	0	32	66	2	20.0	25.7	-0.9	59	10	500	25	5.3	0.0
B+ / 9.9	2.8	0.55	10.98	277	0	32	66	2	20.0	23.1	-1.0	51	10	500	25	0.0	5.0
B+ / 9.9	2.8	0.56	10.96	70	0	32	66	2	20.0	23.2	-1.1	50	9	500	25	0.0	1.0
B+ / 9.9	2.8	0.55	11.01	29	0	32	66	2	20.0	26.7	-0.8	62	10	1,000,000	0	0.0	0.0
B+ / 9.1	5.9	0.74	13.81	895	0	72	26	2	27.0	55.9	-5.8	73	10	500	25	5.3	1.0
B+ / 9.3	5.9	0.74	13.75	798	0	72	26	2	27.0	52.6	-6.1	67	10	500	25	0.0	5.0
B+ / 9.3	5.9	0.74	13.59	110	0	72	26	2	27.0	52.5	-6.0	67	9	500	25	0.0	1.0
B+ / 9.3	5.9	0.75	13.67	119	0	72	26	2	27.0	57.2	-5.8	75	10	1,000,000	0	0.0	0.0
B- / 7.9	7.5	0.95	15.10	553	0	91	7	2	23.0	70.4	-8.2	77	10	500	25	5.3	0.0
B- / 7.9	7.6	0.95	14.92	614	0	91	7	2	23.0	66.9	-8.4	70	10	500	25	0.0	5.0
B- / 7.9	7.5	0.95	14.73	87	0	91	7	2	23.0	66.9	-8.5	70	9	500	25	0.0	1.0
B- / 7.9	7.5	0.95	15.27	48	0	91	7	2	23.0	71.9	-8.2	79	10	1,000,000	0	0.0	0.0
C- / 3.7	20.4	1.16	9.82	609	0	100	0	0	164.0	147.9	-4.5	33	N/A	1,000	25	5.3	2.0
C- / 3.7	20.3	1.16	9.19	7	0	100	0	0	164.0	142.7	-4.7	28	N/A	1,000	25	0.0	5.0
D- / 1.4	20.3	1.16	9.19	4	0	100	0	0	164.0	142.5	-4.7	28	N/A	1,000	25	0.0	2.0
D- / 1.3	20.4	1.16	9.82	319	0	100	0	0	164.0	147.9	-4.5	32	N/A	1,000,000	0	0.0	2.0

Data as of June 30, 2006

						Total Return % through 6/30/06			Annualized		Incl. in Returns	
Fund Type	Fund Name	Ticker Symbol	Overall Weiss Investment Rating	Phone	Performance Rating/Pts	3 Mo	6 Mo	1Yr / Pct	3Yr / Pct	5Yr / Pct	Dividend Yield	Expense Ratio
GR	JPMorgan Large Cap Growth A	OLGAX	D-	(800) 358-4782	D- / 1.1	-3.67	-0.99	7.09 /27	7.47 /12	-1.79 / 9	0.00	1.24
GR	JPMorgan Large Cap Growth B	OGLGX	D-	(800) 358-4782	E+ / 0.8	-3.75	-1.21	6.55 /24	6.77 / 9	-2.46 / 7	0.00	1.78
GR	JPMorgan Large Cap Growth C	OLGCX	D-	(800) 358-4782	D- / 1.2	-3.78	-1.29	6.53 /23	6.77 / 9	-2.46 / 7	0.00	1.78
GR	JPMorgan Large Cap Growth Sel	SEEGX	D	(800) 358-4782	D / 1.9	-3.54	-0.82	7.41 /29	7.74 /14	-1.54 /10	0.00	0.99
GR	JPMorgan Large Cap Growth Ultra	JLGUX	D-	(800) 358-4782	D / 1.9	-3.53	-0.75	7.61 /30	7.84 /14	-1.48 /10	0.00	0.80
GR	JPMorgan Large Cap Value A	OLVAX	B-	(800) 358-4782	C / 4.6	0.58	4.72	8.93 /40	13.21 /50	2.11 /28	1.24	1.24
GR	JPMorgan Large Cap Value B	OLVBX	C+	(800) 358-4782	C- / 4.2	0.39	4.43	8.31 /35	12.49 /46	1.43 /23	0.82	1.99
GR	JPMorgan Large Cap Value C	OLVCX	B-	(800) 358-4782	C / 4.9	0.39	4.45	8.37 /36	12.48 /46	1.42 /23	0.85	1.99
GR	JPMorgan Large Cap Value Sel	HLQVX	B+	(800) 358-4782	C+ / 5.6	0.64	4.82	9.16 /41	13.52 /51	2.38 /31	1.57	0.99
GR	JPMorgan Large Cap Value Ultra	JLVUX	C	(800) 358-4782	C+ / 5.7	0.65	4.95	9.43 /43	13.64 /52	2.44 /32	1.81	0.59
MC	JPMorgan Market Expansion Index A	OMEAX	B	(800) 358-4782	B- / 7.2	-3.17	6.48	13.63 /67	18.94 /76	9.92 /80	0.58	0.82
MC	JPMorgan Market Expansion Index B	OMEBX	C+	(800) 358-4782	C+ / 6.9	-3.38	6.04	12.81 /63	18.11 /73	9.14 /77	0.00	1.57
MC	JPMorgan Market Expansion Index C	OMECX	B	(800) 358-4782	B- / 7.3	-3.31	6.12	12.88 /64	18.10 /73	9.13 /77	0.01	1.57
MC	JPMorgan Market Expansion Index	PGMIX	B+	(800) 358-4782	B / 7.8	-3.10	6.59	13.96 /68	19.25 /77	10.20 /81	0.83	0.57
IN	JPMorgan Market Neutral Fund A	JMNAX	D	(800) 358-4782	E- / 0.1	2.63	3.40	2.76 / 6	1.27 / 0	0.15 /16	4.02	1.50
IN	JPMorgan Market Neutral Fund B	JMNBX	D+	(800) 358-4782	E- / 0.1	2.50	3.19	2.18 / 5	0.77 / 0	-0.29 /14	3.85	2.00
IN	JPMorgan Market Neutral Fund Inst	JPMNX	D+	(800) 358-4782	E- / 0.2	2.74	3.68	3.23 / 8	1.76 / 1	0.49 /18	4.69	1.00
GR	● JPMorgan Mid Cap Equity Sel	VSNGX	B-	(800) 358-4782	B- / 7.0	-2.64	5.42	11.33 /56	17.09 /68	9.36 /78	0.54	1.00
★ MC	● JPMorgan Mid Cap Value A	JAMCX	B+	(800) 358-4782	C+ / 6.6	-0.12	6.23	10.21 /48	17.30 /69	13.43 /89	0.44	1.25
MC	● JPMorgan Mid Cap Value B	JBMCX	A-	(800) 358-4782	C+ / 6.3	-0.25	5.95	9.64 /44	16.62 /66	12.70 /88	0.00	2.00
MC	● JPMorgan Mid Cap Value C	JCMVX	B+	(800) 358-4782	C+ / 6.8	-0.25	5.94	9.67 /45	16.61 /66	12.75 /88	0.00	2.00
MC	● JPMorgan Mid Cap Value Inst	FLMVX	A+	(800) 358-4782	B- / 7.3	0.00	6.45	10.71 /52	17.87 /72	13.99 /90	0.82	0.75
MC	● JPMorgan Mid Cap Value Sel	JMVSX	A+	(800) 358-4782	B- / 7.2	-0.08	6.31	10.42 /50	17.57 /70	13.72 /90	0.63	1.00
AA	JPMorgan Multi-Cap Mrkt Netral A	OGNAX	C-	(800) 358-4782	E+ / 0.7	3.20	4.27	5.14 /16	5.07 / 4	--	1.41	1.75
AA	JPMorgan Multi-Cap Mrkt Netral B	OGNBX	C-	(800) 358-4782	E / 0.5	2.96	3.85	4.33 /12	4.29 / 3	--	0.78	2.50
AA	JPMorgan Multi-Cap Mrkt Netral C	OGNCX	C-	(800) 358-4782	E+ / 0.7	2.96	3.85	4.25 /12	4.29 / 3	--	0.79	2.50
AA	JPMorgan Multi-Cap Mrkt Netral Sel	OGNIX	C-	(800) 358-4782	D- / 1.3	3.27	4.45	5.36 /17	5.33 / 5	--	1.69	1.50
SC	JPMorgan Multi-Manager SmCap	JMSGX	C-	(800) 358-4782	C / 4.6	-7.41	3.50	10.44 /50	12.24 /44	--	0.00	1.40
SC	JPMorgan Multi-Manager SmCap	JMSVX	A-	(800) 358-4782	B+ / 8.3	-3.19	7.63	11.23 /55	21.54 /84	--	0.00	1.40
RE	JPMorgan Realty Income Fund Cl A	URTAX	A-	(800) 358-4782	A / 9.3	-0.77	13.32	22.50 /85	28.03 /94	20.46 /96	2.39	1.40
RE	JPMorgan Realty Income Fund Cl B	URTBX	A-	(800) 358-4782	A / 9.3	-0.92	12.98	21.87 /84	27.58 /94	20.21 /96	2.17	1.90
RE	JPMorgan Realty Income Fund Cl C	URTCX	A-	(800) 358-4782	A / 9.4	-0.86	13.03	21.92 /84	27.59 /94	20.21 /96	2.17	1.90
RE	JPMorgan Realty Income Fund Cl I	URTLX	D	(800) 358-4782	A / 9.5	-0.67	13.53	22.99 /86	28.38 /94	20.66 /97	2.77	1.00
SC	● JPMorgan Small Cap Core Fund Sel	VSSCX	C-	(800) 358-4782	B- / 7.5	-6.05	7.34	11.95 /59	18.59 /75	8.98 /76	0.40	1.00
SC	JPMorgan Small Cap Equity A	VSEAX	B-	(800) 358-4782	B+ / 8.4	-4.10	7.60	17.30 /78	23.36 /88	11.24 /84	0.00	1.38
SC	JPMorgan Small Cap Equity B	VSEBX	C+	(800) 358-4782	B+ / 8.3	-4.23	7.34	16.75 /76	22.59 /86	10.50 /82	0.00	2.12
SC	JPMorgan Small Cap Equity C	JSECX	B-	(800) 358-4782	B+ / 8.5	-4.23	7.30	16.71 /76	22.57 /86	10.49 /82	0.00	2.12
SC	JPMorgan Small Cap Equity Sel	VSEIX	B	(800) 358-4782	B+ / 8.9	-4.01	7.85	17.88 /79	24.00 /89	11.82 /86	0.00	0.85
SC	JPMorgan Small Cap Growth A	PGSGX	C-	(800) 358-4782	B- / 7.2	-6.81	7.88	16.96 /77	18.93 /76	7.24 /68	0.00	1.25
SC	JPMorgan Small Cap Growth B	OGFBX	D+	(800) 358-4782	B- / 7.0	-6.92	7.60	16.25 /75	18.13 /73	6.47 /64	0.00	1.87
SC	JPMorgan Small Cap Growth C	OSGCX	D+	(800) 358-4782	B- / 7.4	-6.98	7.58	16.20 /75	18.12 /73	6.48 /64	0.00	1.87
SC	JPMorgan Small Cap Growth Inst	JISGX	C	(800) 358-4782	B / 7.9	-6.71	8.13	17.42 /78	19.30 /77	7.54 /69	0.00	0.85
SC	JPMorgan Small Cap Growth Sel	OGGFX	C-	(800) 358-4782	B / 7.9	-6.72	8.05	17.34 /78	19.25 /77	7.51 /69	0.00	1.00
SC	JPMorgan Small Cap Value A	PSOAX	C+	(800) 358-4782	B- / 7.5	-3.00	8.58	14.12 /69	20.07 /79	13.03 /89	0.45	1.25
SC	JPMorgan Small Cap Value B	PSOBX	C	(800) 358-4782	B- / 7.4	-3.17	8.24	13.41 /66	19.25 /77	12.24 /87	0.08	2.00
SC	JPMorgan Small Cap Value C	OSVCX	C	(800) 358-4782	B / 7.7	-3.13	8.29	13.43 /66	19.26 /77	12.23 /87	0.08	2.00
SC	JPMorgan Small Cap Value Sel	PSOPX	C+	(800) 358-4782	B / 8.1	-2.98	8.69	14.37 /69	20.33 /81	13.28 /89	0.66	1.00
SC	JPMorgan Small Cap Value Ultra	JSVUX	C+	(800) 358-4782	B / 8.2	-2.95	8.77	14.52 /70	20.45 /81	13.35 /89	0.78	0.86
GI	JPMorgan Tax Aware Disc Eq I	JPDEX	C+	(800) 358-4782	C- / 3.7	-1.79	1.91	6.77 /25	10.89 /34	1.72 /25	1.29	0.55
GR	JPMorgan Tax Aware Lrg Cap Gr Sel	VSLGX	E+	(800) 358-4782	E+ / 0.8	-3.47	-0.76	7.52 /29	5.79 / 6	-2.41 / 7	0.09	0.85
IN	JPMorgan Tax Aware Lrg Cap Val	VEISX	C+	(800) 358-4782	C+ / 5.6	0.45	5.46	10.45 /50	13.37 /51	4.78 /52	1.40	0.85
IX	JPMorgan Tax Aware US Equity A	JTEAX	C-	(800) 358-4782	D / 1.8	-1.00	3.01	6.41 /23	9.03 /21	0.84 /19	0.85	1.10

● Denotes fund is closed to new investors
★ Denotes fund is included in Section II

www.WeissRatings.com

RISK Risk Rating/Pts	3 Year Standard Deviation	Beta	NET ASSETS NAV As of 6/30/06	Total $(Mil)	ASSET Cash %	Stocks %	Bonds %	Other %	Portfolio Turnover Ratio	BULL / BEAR Last Bull Market Return	Last Bear Market Return	FUND MANAGER Manager Quality Pct	Manager Tenure (Years)	MINIMUMS Initial Purch. $	Additional Purch. $	LOADS Front End Load	Back End Load
B- / 7.3	8.9	1.07	16.02	211	0	99	0	1	112.0	50.1	-9.3	19	N/A	1,000	25	5.3	0.0
B- / 7.3	8.9	1.07	14.65	163	0	99	0	1	112.0	46.9	-9.5	15	N/A	1,000	25	0.0	5.0
B- / 7.3	8.9	1.07	14.52	11	0	99	0	1	112.0	46.9	-9.5	15	N/A	1,000	25	0.0	1.0
B- / 7.3	9.0	1.08	15.80	826	0	99	0	1	112.0	51.2	-9.2	20	N/A	1,000,000	0	0.0	0.0
C+ / 5.6	9.0	1.08	15.83	16	0	99	0	1	112.0	51.6	-9.2	21	1	5,000,000	0	0.0	0.0
B+ / 9.0	7.6	0.95	16.55	44	0	99	0	1	112.0	73.4	-9.9	79	N/A	1,000	25	5.3	0.0
B+ / 9.2	7.6	0.94	16.41	16	0	99	0	1	112.0	69.9	-10.0	73	N/A	1,000	25	0.0	5.0
B+ / 9.2	7.6	0.94	16.37	5	0	99	0	1	112.0	69.8	-10.0	74	N/A	1,000	25	0.0	1.0
B+ / 9.2	7.6	0.95	16.42	899	0	99	0	1	112.0	74.8	-9.8	81	N/A	1,000,000	0	0.0	0.0
C+ / 6.2	7.6	0.95	16.42	14	0	99	0	1	112.0	75.4	-9.8	82	1	5,000,000	0	0.0	0.0
B- / 7.0	11.6	1.06	12.47	75	1	98	0	1	64.0	109.9	-9.7	55	8	1,000	25	5.3	0.0
C+ / 6.9	11.6	1.05	12.28	29	1	98	0	1	64.0	105.0	-9.6	45	8	1,000	25	0.0	5.0
C+ / 6.9	11.6	1.06	11.96	22	1	98	0	1	64.0	105.2	-9.7	45	7	1,000	25	0.0	1.0
C+ / 6.9	11.6	1.06	12.50	542	1	98	0	1	64.0	111.5	-9.5	57	8	1,000,000	0	0.0	0.0
B+ / 9.2	2.9	-0.04	13.71	4	9	90	0	1	313.0	2.4	-0.8	47	N/A	1,000	25	5.3	0.0
B+ / 9.7	2.9	-0.04	13.52	N/A	9	90	0	1	313.0	0.8	-0.8	41	N/A	1,000	25	0.0	5.0
B+ / 9.8	2.9	-0.04	13.86	15	9	90	0	1	313.0	3.8	-0.7	53	N/A	3,000,000	0	0.0	0.0
C+ / 6.9	9.3	1.10	34.51	298	3	96	0	1	99.0	94.5	-6.1	91	N/A	1,000,000	0	0.0	0.0
B+ / 9.1	7.0	0.60	24.73	3,006	3	96	0	1	45.0	87.2	-4.5	94	N/A	1,000	25	5.3	0.0
B+ / 9.1	7.0	0.60	24.21	231	3	96	0	1	45.0	83.6	-4.6	92	N/A	1,000	25	0.0	5.0
B+ / 9.1	7.0	0.60	24.26	791	3	96	0	1	45.0	83.6	-4.7	92	N/A	1,000	25	0.0	1.0
B+ / 9.2	7.0	0.60	25.10	2,012	3	96	0	1	45.0	90.1	-4.3	95	N/A	3,000,000	0	0.0	0.0
B+ / 9.1	7.0	0.60	24.92	1,257	3	96	0	1	45.0	88.6	-4.4	94	N/A	1,000,000	0	0.0	0.0
B+ / 9.9	3.5	0.17	10.98	180	6	93	0	1	198.0	N/A	N/A	75	N/A	1,000	25	5.3	0.0
B+ / 9.9	3.5	0.18	10.80	28	6	93	0	1	198.0	N/A	N/A	68	N/A	1,000	25	0.0	5.0
B+ / 9.9	3.6	0.18	10.80	200	6	93	0	1	198.0	N/A	N/A	68	N/A	1,000	25	0.0	1.0
B+ / 9.9	3.5	0.19	11.04	1,451	6	93	0	1	198.0	N/A	N/A	77	N/A	1,000,000	0	0.0	0.0
C+ / 6.1	15.4	1.02	15.38	340	3	96	0	1	132.0	87.2	N/A	10	3	1,000,000	0	0.0	0.0
B- / 7.2	12.7	0.86	18.19	424	1	98	0	1	113.0	129.2	N/A	92	3	1,000,000	0	0.0	0.0
C+ / 6.1	16.1	0.96	17.31	5	4	95	0	1	179.0	132.7	N/A	89	N/A	1,000	25	5.3	0.0
C+ / 6.1	16.1	0.96	17.26	1	4	95	0	1	179.0	130.5	N/A	87	N/A	1,000	25	0.0	5.0
C+ / 6.1	16.1	0.96	17.22	1	4	95	0	1	179.0	130.4	N/A	87	N/A	1,000	25	0.0	1.0
E- / 0.0	16.1	0.96	17.30	142	4	95	0	1	179.0	134.4	N/A	90	N/A	3,000,000	0	0.0	0.0
C- / 3.3	14.3	0.95	47.22	1,104	1	98	0	1	37.0	106.2	-7.8	64	N/A	1,000,000	0	0.0	0.0
C / 5.5	12.6	0.83	28.30	284	2	96	0	2	70.0	128.8	-7.8	96	N/A	1,000	25	5.3	1.0
C / 5.1	12.6	0.83	25.16	22	2	96	0	2	70.0	124.2	-8.0	95	N/A	1,000	25	0.0	5.0
C / 5.1	12.6	0.83	25.14	21	2	96	0	2	70.0	124.2	-8.0	95	N/A	1,000	25	0.0	1.0
C+ / 5.7	12.6	0.83	30.38	359	2	96	0	2	70.0	132.7	-7.7	97	N/A	1,000,000	0	0.0	0.0
C- / 3.4	14.7	0.98	11.91	91	N/A	100	0	N/A	129.0	111.2	-10.7	63	N/A	1,000	25	5.3	1.0
D+ / 2.8	14.6	0.97	10.62	25	N/A	100	0	N/A	129.0	106.8	-10.9	55	N/A	1,000	25	0.0	5.0
D+ / 2.9	14.7	0.98	10.93	17	N/A	100	0	N/A	129.0	106.7	-10.8	54	N/A	1,000	25	0.0	1.0
C / 4.6	14.7	0.98	12.23	67	N/A	100	0	N/A	129.0	113.1	-10.6	66	1	3,000,000	0	0.0	0.0
C- / 3.5	14.7	0.98	12.21	382	N/A	100	0	N/A	129.0	113.0	-10.6	66	N/A	1,000,000	0	0.0	0.0
C / 5.0	11.9	0.80	23.90	165	2	97	0	1	57.0	113.2	-10.8	91	N/A	1,000	25	5.3	1.0
C / 4.6	11.9	0.80	22.14	34	2	97	0	1	57.0	108.6	-11.0	87	N/A	1,000	25	0.0	5.0
C / 4.6	11.9	0.80	22.03	47	2	97	0	1	57.0	108.5	-10.9	87	N/A	1,000	25	0.0	1.0
C / 5.1	11.9	0.80	24.55	588	2	97	0	1	57.0	114.6	-10.8	91	N/A	1,000,000	0	0.0	0.0
C / 5.3	11.9	0.80	24.55	61	2	97	0	1	57.0	115.2	-10.8	92	1	5,000,000	0	0.0	0.0
B / 8.8	7.9	1.03	16.98	570	0	99	0	1	24.0	63.6	-9.9	49	9	3,000,000	0	0.0	0.0
C+ / 6.2	9.4	1.09	16.48	58	0	99	0	1	75.0	40.3	-10.4	10	N/A	1,000,000	0	0.0	0.0
B- / 7.9	7.6	0.93	24.30	416	0	98	0	2	77.0	72.1	-9.7	81	N/A	1,000,000	0	0.0	0.0
B / 8.8	7.0	0.89	17.61	7	0	99	0	1	46.0	51.5	-9.7	43	N/A	1,000	25	5.3	1.0

Fund Type	Fund Name	Ticker Symbol	Overall Weiss Investment Rating	Phone	Perfor- mance Rating/Pts	3 Mo	6 Mo	1Yr / Pct	3Yr / Pct	5Yr / Pct	Dividend Yield	Expense Ratio
	99 Pct = Best 0 Pct = Worst				PERFORMANCE Total Return % through 6/30/06 Annualized						Incl. in Returns	
IX	JPMorgan Tax Aware US Equity B	JTEBX	C-	(800) 358-4782	D / 1.7	-1.09	2.77	5.93 /20	8.48 /18	0.27 /17	0.41	1.60
IX	JPMorgan Tax Aware US Equity C	JTECX	C-	(800) 358-4782	D+ / 2.3	-1.09	2.79	5.90 /20	8.51 /18	0.27 /17	0.43	1.60
IX	JPMorgan Tax Aware US Equity Inst	JTUIX	C	(800) 358-4782	C- / 3.1	-0.89	3.25	6.84 /25	9.45 /24	1.24 /22	1.88	0.70
IX	JPMorgan Tax Aware US Equity Sel	JPTAX	C	(800) 358-4782	C- / 3.0	-0.92	3.15	6.68 /24	9.31 /23	1.07 /21	1.11	0.84
GI	JPMorgan US Equity A	JUEAX	C-	(800) 358-4782	D+ / 2.5	-1.16	3.10	7.61 /30	10.27 /29	1.56 /24	0.78	1.05
GI	JPMorgan US Equity B	JUEBX	C-	(800) 358-4782	D+ / 2.3	-1.31	2.76	7.01 /26	9.61 /25	0.92 /20	0.31	1.57
GI	JPMorgan US Equity C	JUECX	C	(800) 358-4782	C- / 3.0	-1.30	2.77	7.04 /26	9.62 /25	0.93 /20	0.33	1.57
GI	JPMorgan US Equity I	JMUEX	C+	(800) 358-4782	C- / 3.9	-1.05	3.31	8.07 /33	10.73 /33	2.00 /27	1.23	0.64
GI	JPMorgan US Equity Sel	JUESX	C	(800) 358-4782	C- / 3.7	-1.18	3.14	7.80 /31	10.52 /31	1.82 /26	1.07	0.79
GR	JPMorgan US LgCap Core Plus Sel	JLPSX	U	(800) 358-4782	U /	-0.48	5.03	--	--	--	0.00	1.25
RE	JPMorgan US Real Estate A	SUSIX	B+	(800) 358-4782	A / 9.5	-0.04	16.14	26.77 /91	29.99 /95	20.34 /96	1.90	1.18
RE	JPMorgan US Real Estate C	JPRCX	B-	(800) 358-4782	A+ / 9.6	-0.15	15.89	26.16 /90	29.71 /95	20.18 /96	1.78	1.68
RE	JPMorgan US Real Estate Sel	SUIEX	B-	(800) 358-4782	A+ / 9.6	0.07	16.32	27.19 /92	30.18 /96	20.44 /96	2.22	0.93
SC	JPMorgan US Small Company I	JUSSX	C-	(800) 358-4782	C+ / 6.9	-5.95	7.67	12.41 /62	16.64 /66	5.72 /59	0.19	0.83
SC	● JPMorgan US Small Company Sel	JSCSX	C-	(800) 358-4782	C+ / 6.8	-6.02	7.59	12.15 /60	16.44 /65	5.55 /58	0.04	1.01
GI	JPMorgan Value Advtg A	JVAAX	U	(800) 358-4782	U /	0.59	8.12	12.65 /63	--	--	0.33	1.25
GI	JPMorgan Value Advtg C	JVACX	U	(800) 358-4782	U /	0.41	7.82	12.12 /60	--	--	0.16	1.75
GR	JPMorgan Value Opportunity A	JVOAX	D+	(800) 358-4782	C / 5.0	0.56	4.66	8.81 /39	14.29 /55	--	0.87	1.14
GR	JPMorgan Value Opportunity B	JVOBX	D+	(800) 358-4782	C / 4.7	0.46	4.44	8.25 /35	13.49 /51	--	0.35	1.64
GR	JPMorgan Value Opportunity C	JVOCX	C	(800) 358-4782	C / 5.3	0.45	4.43	8.25 /35	13.49 /51	--	0.30	1.64
GR	JPMorgan Value Opportunity Inst	JVOIX	B+	(800) 358-4782	C+ / 6.1	0.67	4.90	9.34 /42	14.54 /56	--	1.39	0.65
GL	Julius Baer Global Equity A	BJGQX	U	(800) 435-4659	U /	-2.26	6.27	20.51 /82	--	--	0.00	1.40
GL	Julius Baer Global Equity I	JGEIX	U	(800) 435-4659	U /	-2.22	6.39	20.82 /83	--	--	0.03	1.15
★ FO	● Julius Baer International Equity A	BJBIX	A-	(800) 435-4659	A / 9.3	-1.15	11.65	30.90 /95	26.73 /93	15.40 /92	0.00	1.31
FO	● Julius Baer International Equity I	JIEIX	A+	(800) 435-4659	A / 9.3	-1.08	11.77	31.22 /95	27.08 /93	15.84 /93	0.00	1.04
GL	Julius Baer Intl Equity II cl A	JETAX	U	(800) 435-4659	U /	-1.67	9.75	27.84 /92	--	--	0.00	1.32
GL	Julius Baer Intl Equity II cl I	JETIX	U	(800) 435-4659	U /	-1.59	9.89	28.33 /93	--	--	0.00	1.05
GR	Jundt Growth Fund A	JGFHX	E	(800) 370-0612	E- / 0.0	-2.47	-1.80	3.49 / 9	2.15 / 1	-3.31 / 5	0.00	3.37
GR	Jundt Growth Fund B	JGFBX	E	(800) 370-0612	E- / 0.0	-2.59	-2.14	2.73 / 6	1.39 / 0	-4.03 / 4	0.00	4.12
GR	Jundt Growth Fund C	JGFCX	E	(800) 370-0612	E- / 0.1	-2.58	-1.98	2.72 / 6	1.39 / 0	-4.03 / 4	0.00	4.12
GR	Jundt Growth Fund I	JGFIX	E	(800) 370-0612	E- / 0.0	-2.39	-1.74	3.66 / 9	2.37 / 1	-3.07 / 5	0.00	3.12
AG	Jundt Opportunity Fund A	JOPHX	E	(800) 370-0612	E+ / 0.9	-5.16	-1.34	5.76 /19	8.15 /16	-0.55 /13	0.00	3.51
AG	Jundt Opportunity Fund B	JOPBX	E-	(800) 370-0612	E+ / 0.8	-5.30	-1.68	5.12 /16	7.31 /12	-1.28 /11	0.00	4.26
AG	Jundt Opportunity Fund C	JOPCX	E	(800) 370-0612	D- / 1.2	-5.33	-1.76	4.97 /15	7.28 /12	-1.30 /11	0.00	4.26
AG	Jundt Opportunity Fund I	JOPIX	D	(800) 370-0612	D / 2.0	-5.10	-1.24	6.10 /21	8.38 /17	-0.29 /14	0.00	3.26
GR	Jundt Twenty Five Fund A	JTFHX	E-	(800) 370-0612	E- / 0.0	-6.75	-6.10	-0.74 / 1	0.25 / 0	-6.64 / 1	0.00	4.04
GR	Jundt Twenty Five Fund B	JTFBX	E-	(800) 370-0612	E- / 0.0	-6.92	-6.45	-1.46 / 1	-0.49 / 0	-7.35 / 1	0.00	4.79
GR	Jundt Twenty Five Fund C	JTFCX	E-	(800) 370-0612	E- / 0.0	-6.99	-6.52	-1.59 / 1	-0.53 / 0	-7.36 / 1	0.00	4.79
GR	Jundt US Emerging Growth A	JEGHX	E-	(800) 370-0612	E- / 0.1	-10.06	-3.94	3.09 / 8	3.73 / 2	-0.74 /13	0.00	3.49
GR	Jundt US Emerging Growth B	JEGBX	E-	(800) 370-0612	E- / 0.1	-10.21	-4.26	2.36 / 5	2.96 / 1	-1.47 /10	0.00	4.24
GR	Jundt US Emerging Growth C	JEGCX	E-	(800) 370-0612	E- / 0.1	-10.15	-4.26	2.36 / 5	2.96 / 1	-1.47 /10	0.00	4.24
GR	Jundt US Emerging Growth I	JEGIX	E	(800) 370-0612	E / 0.3	-9.95	-3.78	3.44 / 9	4.04 / 2	-0.26 /14	0.00	3.24
SC	Kalmar Growth With Value Small Cap	KGSCX	C-	(800) 282-2319	C / 5.4	-7.97	2.00	8.70 /38	14.83 /58	7.60 /70	0.00	1.29
MC	Keeley Mid Cap Value Fund	KMCVX	U	(800) 533-5344	U /	-2.27	6.26	--	--	--	0.00	2.00
★ SC	Keeley Small Cap Value Fund	KSCVX	A	(800) 533-5344	A / 9.5	-0.52	14.00	31.10 /95	29.79 /95	18.02 /94	0.00	1.52
IN	Kelmoore Strategy Eagle A	KSEAX	E-	(877) 328-9456	E- / 0.1	-10.91	-5.87	-0.87 / 1	4.38 / 3	-3.59 / 4	16.29	2.00
IN	Kelmoore Strategy Eagle C	KSECX	E-	(877) 328-9456	E- / 0.1	-11.08	-6.14	-1.63 / 1	3.46 / 2	-4.35 / 3	18.64	2.75
IN	Kelmoore Strategy Fund A	KSAIX	E	(877) 328-9456	E- / 0.2	-1.81	1.71	7.58 /30	3.65 / 2	-3.43 / 4	12.43	2.13
IN	Kelmoore Strategy Fund C	KSOIX	E	(877) 328-9456	E / 0.4	-1.99	1.31	6.74 /25	2.92 / 1	-4.18 / 3	14.25	2.75
GI	Kelmoore Strategy Liberty A	KSLAX	E+	(877) 328-9456	E- / 0.2	-1.70	2.27	3.38 / 8	3.93 / 2	-1.26 /11	9.04	2.25
GI	Kelmoore Strategy Liberty C	KSLCX	E	(877) 328-9456	E / 0.3	-1.88	2.00	2.71 / 6	3.15 / 1	-2.02 / 8	10.07	2.75
RE	Kensington Real Estate Secs A	KREAX	C+	(800) 253-2949	A- / 9.1	0.14	14.57	21.80 /84	25.84 /92	--	2.12	1.45

● Denotes fund is closed to new investors
★ Denotes fund is included in Section II

RISK			NET ASSETS		ASSET						BULL / BEAR		FUND MANAGER		MINIMUMS		LOADS	
	3 Year		NAV							Portfolio	Last Bull	Last Bear	Manager	Manager	Initial	Additional	Front	Back
Risk	Standard		As of	Total	Cash	Stocks	Bonds	Other		Turnover	Market	Market	Quality	Tenure	Purch.	Purch.	End	End
Rating/Pts	Deviation	Beta	6/30/06	$(Mil)	%	%	%	%		Ratio	Return	Return	Pct	(Years)	$	$	Load	Load
B / 8.9	7.0	0.89	17.45	2	0	99	0	1		46.0	49.1	-9.8	37	N/A	1,000	25	0.0	5.0
B / 8.9	7.0	0.89	17.41	1	0	99	0	1		46.0	49.1	-9.8	37	N/A	1,000	25	0.0	1.0
B / 8.9	7.0	0.89	12.32	74	0	99	0	1		46.0	53.3	-9.6	47	N/A	3,000,000	0	0.0	0.0
B / 8.9	7.0	0.89	17.64	319	0	99	0	1		46.0	52.7	-9.7	45	N/A	1,000,000	0	0.0	0.0
B / 8.4	7.9	1.01	11.28	137	0	100	0	0		83.0	64.6	-10.1	44	N/A	1,000	25	5.3	1.0
B / 8.6	7.9	1.01	11.18	29	0	100	0	0		83.0	61.3	-10.1	37	N/A	1,000	25	0.0	5.0
B / 8.6	7.9	1.01	11.18	9	0	100	0	0		83.0	61.3	-10.1	37	N/A	1,000	25	0.0	1.0
B / 8.7	7.9	1.01	11.27	222	0	100	0	0		83.0	66.7	-10.0	49	N/A	3,000,000	0	0.0	0.0
B / 8.6	7.9	1.01	11.26	1,050	0	100	0	0		83.0	65.9	-9.9	47	N/A	1,000,000	0	0.0	0.0
U /	N/A	N/A	16.50	60	0	99	0	1		N/A	N/A	N/A	N/A	1	1,000,000	0	0.0	0.0
C / 5.3	16.1	0.95	22.10	351	1	98	0	1		27.0	141.0	0.5	95	N/A	1,000	25	5.3	1.0
C / 4.3	16.1	0.95	22.01	4	1	98	0	1		27.0	139.6	0.5	94	N/A	1,000	25	0.0	1.0
C / 4.3	16.1	0.95	22.12	342	1	98	0	1		27.0	141.9	0.5	95	N/A	1,000,000	0	0.0	0.0
C / 4.5	14.7	0.99	13.90	55	2	97	0	1		32.0	109.1	-12.0	37	N/A	3,000,000	0	0.0	0.0
C / 4.5	14.7	0.99	13.89	95	2	97	0	1		32.0	107.9	-12.0	35	N/A	1,000,000	0	0.0	0.0
U /	N/A	N/A	17.17	72	4	95	0	1		36.0	N/A	N/A	N/A	N/A	1,000	25	5.3	1.0
U /	N/A	N/A	17.09	77	4	95	0	1		36.0	N/A	N/A	N/A	N/A	1,000	25	0.0	1.0
C / 5.2	7.7	0.95	17.95	77	0	99	0	1		70.0	79.7	-6.1	85	20	1,000	25	5.3	1.0
C / 5.2	7.7	0.95	17.66	9	0	99	0	1		70.0	75.4	-6.3	81	N/A	1,000	25	0.0	5.0
C+ / 6.2	7.7	0.95	17.67	8	0	99	0	1		70.0	75.5	-6.3	81	1	1,000	25	0.0	1.0
B+ / 9.0	7.7	0.95	17.98	692	0	99	0	1		70.0	80.6	-6.1	87	2	3,000,000	0	0.0	0.0
U /	N/A	N/A	35.43	29	2	98	0	0		118.0	N/A	N/A	N/A	N/A	2,500	1,000	0.0	2.0
U /	N/A	N/A	35.63	27	2	98	0	0		118.0	N/A	N/A	N/A	N/A	1,000,000	0	0.0	2.0
C+ / 6.1	12.5	1.18	39.57	8,467	0	98	0	2		57.0	146.8	-6.2	36	13	1,000	1,000	0.0	2.0
B- / 7.2	12.5	1.18	40.35	10,132	0	98	0	2		57.0	148.9	-5.9	38	13	1,000,000	0	0.0	2.0
U /	N/A	N/A	12.95	501	2	96	0	2		N/A	N/A	N/A	N/A	N/A	2,500	1,000	0.0	2.0
U /	N/A	N/A	13.00	1,668	2	96	0	2		N/A	N/A	N/A	N/A	N/A	2,000,000	0	0.0	2.0
C+ / 6.4	8.9	0.60	7.11	N/A	28	71	0	1		460.0	20.1	-6.6	13	11	1,000	50	5.8	2.0
C+ / 6.3	8.9	0.61	6.39	N/A	28	71	0	1		460.0	17.1	-6.8	10	11	1,000	50	0.0	6.0
C+ / 6.3	8.9	0.61	6.43	N/A	28	71	0	1		460.0	17.2	-6.7	10	11	1,000	50	0.0	1.5
C+ / 6.4	8.9	0.61	7.36	14	28	71	0	1		460.0	21.0	-6.5	13	11	1,000	50	5.8	2.0
C- / 4.2	13.8	0.78	13.23	5	13	86	0	1		414.0	62.3	-5.5	44	10	1,000	50	5.8	2.0
C- / 4.2	13.8	0.77	12.32	6	13	86	0	1		414.0	58.5	-5.7	36	10	1,000	50	0.0	6.0
C- / 4.2	13.8	0.77	12.26	3	13	86	0	1		414.0	58.3	-5.7	36	10	1,000	50	0.0	1.5
C+ / 6.7	13.8	0.77	13.57	8	13	86	0	1		414.0	63.6	-5.4	47	10	1,000	50	0.0	0.0
C / 4.7	12.8	0.73	8.01	1	33	66	0	1		409.0	18.0	-2.5	4	9	1,000	50	5.8	2.0
C / 4.7	12.8	0.72	7.40	1	33	66	0	1		409.0	15.4	-2.8	3	9	1,000	50	0.0	6.0
C / 4.6	12.9	0.73	7.45	1	33	66	0	1		409.0	15.5	-2.8	3	9	1,000	50	0.0	1.5
C- / 3.1	15.9	1.01	12.69	4	24	75	0	1		174.0	47.6	-5.2	7	10	1,000	50	5.8	0.0
C- / 3.0	15.9	1.01	11.70	5	24	75	0	1		174.0	44.3	-5.3	5	10	1,000	50	0.0	6.0
C- / 3.0	15.9	1.01	11.69	3	24	75	0	1		174.0	44.3	-5.8	5	10	1,000	50	0.0	0.0
C+ / 6.0	15.9	1.01	13.22	2	24	75	0	1		174.0	49.0	-5.5	8	10	1,000	50	0.0	0.0
C / 5.5	14.6	0.96	16.86	448	5	94	0	1		29.5	95.3	-6.3	28	N/A	10,000	1,000	0.0	2.0
U /	N/A	N/A	11.20	54	0	100	0	0		17.0	N/A	N/A	N/A	1	1,000	50	4.5	0.0
C+ / 6.3	14.6	0.86	49.74	2,377	4	95	0	1		6.7	169.9	-7.7	99	13	1,000	50	4.5	0.0
D- / 1.3	13.9	1.55	11.17	106	N/A	100	0	N/A		139.1	50.5	-10.1	1	6	1,000	50	5.5	1.0
D- / 1.1	13.9	1.54	10.33	73	N/A	100	0	N/A		139.1	46.4	-10.3	1	6	1,000	50	0.0	0.0
C / 5.3	8.1	0.86	30.82	64	0	99	0	1		224.6	31.2	-7.9	10	7	1,000	50	5.5	1.0
C / 5.0	8.1	0.86	28.43	62	0	99	0	1		224.6	28.2	-8.1	8	7	1,000	50	0.0	0.0
C+ / 6.2	7.5	0.76	50.19	28	0	99	0	1		104.7	29.5	-6.2	14	6	1,000	50	5.5	1.0
C+ / 6.0	7.5	0.77	47.67	20	0	99	0	1		104.7	26.4	-6.6	11	6	1,000	50	0.0	0.0
C / 4.3	15.1	0.91	43.91	43	2	97	0	1		122.2	119.1	N/A	85	4	2,000	25	5.8	1.0

Fund Type	Fund Name	Ticker Symbol	Overall Weiss Investment Rating	Phone	Perfor-mance Rating/Pts	3 Mo	6 Mo	1Yr / Pct	3Yr / Pct	5Yr / Pct	Dividend Yield	Expense Ratio
	99 Pct = Best				PERFORMANCE			Total Return % through 6/30/06	Annualized		Incl. in Returns	
RE	Kensington Real Estate Secs B	KREBX	C+	(800) 253-2949	A- / 9.0	-0.14	13.98	20.79 /83	24.82 /91	--	1.61	2.20
RE	Kensington Real Estate Secs C	KRECX	C+	(800) 253-2949	A- / 9.1	-0.12	14.03	20.75 /83	24.81 /91	--	1.57	2.20
RE	Kensington Select Income A	KIFAX	D-	(800) 253-2949	D- / 1.1	1.14	5.18	1.11 / 3	7.90 /14	12.68 /88	6.83	2.13
RE	Kensington Select Income B	KIFBX	D-	(800) 253-2949	E+ / 0.9	0.85	4.69	0.25 / 2	7.05 /11	11.79 /86	6.48	2.88
RE	Kensington Select Income C	KIFCX	D-	(800) 253-2949	D- / 1.4	0.85	4.70	0.27 / 2	7.06 /11	11.81 /86	6.49	2.88
RE	Kensington Strategic Realty A	KSRAX	C	(800) 253-2949	B / 7.9	1.70	13.61	13.29 /65	20.61 /82	17.03 /94	3.58	3.62
RE	Kensington Strategic Realty B	KSRBX	C-	(800) 253-2949	B / 7.7	1.53	13.20	12.44 /62	19.71 /78	16.16 /93	3.15	4.37
RE	Kensington Strategic Realty C	KSRCX	C	(800) 253-2949	B / 8.0	1.51	13.19	12.43 /62	19.71 /78	16.15 /93	3.15	4.37
TC	Kinetics Internet Emerg Growth NL	WWWEX	E+	(800) 930-3828	D+ / 2.6	-2.58	2.48	10.10 /48	9.53 /24	3.99 /46	4.17	2.69
TC	Kinetics Internet Fund A	KINAX	D	(800) 930-3828	C- / 3.3	-1.39	10.57	17.28 /78	9.64 /25	2.14 /28	0.50	2.60
TC	Kinetics Internet Fund NL	WWWFX	D+	(800) 930-3828	C / 4.3	-2.33	10.71	17.13 /77	9.80 /26	2.61 /33	0.75	2.35
HL	Kinetics Medical Fund A	KRXAX	D-	(800) 930-3828	E / 0.5	-4.23	5.20	12.87 /64	4.98 / 4	-1.95 / 8	0.00	2.69
HL	Kinetics Medical Fund NL	MEDRX	D	(800) 930-3828	D- / 1.2	-4.21	5.35	13.17 /65	5.31 / 5	-1.59 /10	0.00	2.44
GL	Kinetics Paradigm Fund A	KNPAX	A-	(800) 930-3828	B+ / 8.6	-1.15	11.60	20.37 /82	23.85 /89	16.19 /93	0.00	1.94
GL	Kinetics Paradigm Fund C	KNPCX	A-	(800) 930-3828	B+ / 8.8	-1.26	11.39	19.77 /82	23.27 /88	--	0.00	2.44
GL	Kinetics Paradigm Fund I	KNPYX	U	(800) 930-3828	U /	-1.00	11.87	20.76 /83	--	--	0.15	1.49
GL	Kinetics Paradigm Fund NL	WWNPX	A	(800) 930-3828	A- / 9.0	-1.09	11.81	20.67 /83	24.31 /90	16.56 /94	0.05	1.69
SC	Kinetics Small Cap Opport A	KSOAX	A	(800) 930-3828	B+ / 8.6	-3.92	10.20	20.52 /82	23.97 /89	--	0.02	1.94
SC	Kinetics Small Cap Opport NL	KSCOX	A+	(800) 930-3828	A- / 9.0	-3.81	10.37	20.95 /83	24.32 /90	11.91 /86	0.02	1.66
MC	Kirr Marbach Value Fund	KMVAX	C		C / 5.1	-2.59	4.15	8.76 /38	13.24 /50	6.68 /65	0.29	1.45
GR	Kobren Growth	KOGRX	C+	(800) 456-2736	C / 5.3	-1.97	3.54	12.21 /61	12.75 /47	5.76 /59	1.12	0.98
SC	KOPP Emerging Growth Fund A	KOPPX	E-	(888) 533-5677	E- / 0.2	-20.29	-4.55	13.81 /68	6.46 / 8	-8.33 / 0	0.00	1.73
SC	KOPP Emerging Growth Fund C	KEGCX	E-	(888) 533-5677	E- / 0.2	-20.43	-4.86	13.11 /65	5.80 / 6	-8.92 / 0	0.00	2.38
SC	KOPP Emerging Growth Fund I	KEGIX	E-	(888) 533-5677	E / 0.3	-20.20	-4.30	14.22 /69	6.84 /10	-7.99 / 0	0.00	1.38
FO	Laudus Internatl MarketMasters Inv	SWOIX	A	(866) 855-9102	A- / 9.0	-2.23	7.75	26.33 /90	25.30 /91	10.98 /84	0.84	1.65
FO	Laudus Internatl MarketMasters Sel	SWMIX	U	(866) 855-9102	U /	-2.17	7.80	26.50 /91	--	--	0.99	1.47
GL	Laudus Rosenberg Glb Lg/Sht Eq Inst	MSMNX	D	(800) 447-3332	E / 0.4	0.16	2.84	5.53 /18	3.35 / 2	7.16 /68	0.89	3.82
GL	Laudus Rosenberg Glb Lg/Sht Eq Inv	RMSIX	D	(800) 447-3332	E / 0.3	0.08	2.70	5.29 /17	2.99 / 1	--	0.69	4.27
FO	Laudus Rosenberg Intl Eq Inst	REQIX	A	(800) 447-3332	B+ / 8.6	-0.59	9.12	24.81 /88	22.19 /86	9.56 /79	0.99	1.34
FO	Laudus Rosenberg Intl Eq Inv	RIEIX	A	(800) 447-3332	B+ / 8.5	-0.59	8.94	24.36 /88	21.80 /85	9.21 /77	0.70	1.72
FO	● Laudus Rosenberg Intl SmCp Inst	ICSIX	A	(800) 447-3332	A+ / 9.7	-2.24	10.81	30.92 /95	33.13 /97	20.57 /97	0.39	1.25
FO	● Laudus Rosenberg Intl SmCp Inv	RISIX	A	(800) 447-3332	A+ / 9.7	-2.31	10.65	30.50 /95	32.70 /97	20.26 /96	0.19	1.60
MC	Laudus Rosenberg US Disc Inst	RDISX	B+	(800) 447-3332	B / 8.0	-2.70	8.84	15.22 /72	20.08 /80	--	0.00	1.09
MC	Laudus Rosenberg US Disc Inv	RDIVX	B+	(800) 447-3332	B / 7.8	-2.78	8.68	14.88 /71	19.70 /78	--	0.00	1.43
GI	Laudus Rosenberg US LgMdCp L/S	SSMNX	C-	(800) 447-3332	D- / 1.2	2.57	4.47	9.38 /43	4.82 / 4	6.50 /64	1.52	2.71
GI	Laudus Rosenberg US LgMdCp L/S	RMNIX	D+	(800) 447-3332	D- / 1.0	2.39	4.29	8.98 /40	4.50 / 3	6.15 /62	1.19	3.02
IX	Laudus Rosenberg US LrgCap Gr	REDIX	C-	(800) 447-3332	D+ / 2.7	-3.89	-0.11	7.07 /27	9.95 /27	2.62 /33	0.09	0.99
GR	Laudus Rosenberg US LrgCap Inst	AXLIX	C+	(800) 447-3332	C / 4.8	-1.70	2.45	11.25 /55	12.70 /47	--	0.70	1.01
GR	Laudus Rosenberg US LrgCap Inv	AXLVX	C+	(800) 447-3332	C / 4.6	-1.78	2.27	10.84 /53	12.34 /45	--	0.51	1.34
SC	● Laudus Rosenberg US SmCap Adv	LIFUX	C-	(800) 447-3332	B- / 7.1	-5.12	6.38	11.34 /56	18.08 /73	11.76 /86	0.00	1.32
SC	● Laudus Rosenberg US SmCap Inst	USCIX	C	(800) 447-3332	B- / 7.2	-5.12	6.54	11.82 /58	18.46 /74	12.09 /87	0.26	1.04
SC	● Laudus Rosenberg US SmCap Inv	BRSCX	C-	(800) 447-3332	B- / 7.1	-5.16	6.35	11.18 /55	17.97 /72	11.64 /86	0.00	1.39
GR	Laudus Rosenberg Value Lg/Shrt Inst	BMNIX	D+	(800) 447-3332	D- / 1.0	4.03	5.12	7.05 /27	4.26 / 3	8.76 /75	0.92	2.89
GR	Laudus Rosenberg Value Lg/Shrt Inv	BRMIX	D+	(800) 447-3332	E+ / 0.8	3.89	4.88	6.76 /25	3.94 / 2	8.42 /74	0.69	3.22
SC	Laudus Small-Cap MarketMasters Inv	SWOSX	C+	(866) 855-9102	C+ / 6.8	-7.07	5.29	11.56 /57	17.60 /71	7.03 /67	0.00	1.55
AA	Laudus U.S. MarketMasters Fund Inv	SWOGX	D	(866) 855-9102	D+ / 2.7	-2.70	2.15	7.17 /27	9.54 /24	2.53 /32	0.13	1.25
EM	Lazard Emerging Markets Inst	LZEMX	B+	(800) 823-6300	A+ / 9.8	-5.87	4.32	35.04 /97	38.12 /99	23.42 /98	0.91	1.32
EM	Lazard Emerging Markets Open	LZOEX	B+	(800) 823-6300	A+ / 9.8	-5.92	4.17	34.65 /97	37.87 /99	23.14 /98	0.67	1.00
GR	Lazard Equity Inst	LZEQX	C+	(800) 823-6300	C- / 4.0	-0.76	2.96	8.16 /34	11.22 /37	3.10 /38	0.95	0.98
GR	Lazard Equity Open	LZEOX	C+	(800) 823-6300	C- / 3.7	-0.93	2.72	7.69 /30	10.79 /34	2.74 /34	0.52	1.32
FO	Lazard Intl Equity Inst	LZIEX	A-	(800) 823-6300	B / 8.1	-0.07	9.29	24.57 /88	19.08 /76	7.36 /69	2.16	0.90
FO	Lazard Intl Equity Open	LZIOX	A-	(800) 823-6300	B / 8.0	-0.13	9.12	24.22 /87	18.70 /75	7.12 /67	1.94	1.20

● Denotes fund is closed to new investors
* Denotes fund is included in Section II

| RISK | | | NET ASSETS | | ASSET | | | | BULL / BEAR | | FUND MANAGER | | MINIMUMS | | LOADS | |
| Risk Rating/Pts | 3 Year | | NAV As of 6/30/06 | Total $(Mil) | Cash % | Stocks % | Bonds % | Other % | Portfolio Turnover Ratio | Last Bull Market Return | Last Bear Market Return | Manager Quality Pct | Manager Tenure (Years) | Initial Purch. $ | Additional Purch. $ | Front End Load | Back End Load |
	Standard Deviation	Beta															
C- / 4.2	15.1	0.91	43.63	7	2	97	0	1	122.2	113.6	N/A	79	4	2,000	25	0.0	5.0
C- / 4.2	15.1	0.91	43.58	24	2	97	0	1	122.2	113.4	N/A	79	4	2,000	25	0.0	1.0
B- / 7.0	6.9	0.34	34.17	416	N/A	N/A	4	N/A	35.7	38.3	5.0	39	5	2,000	25	5.8	1.0
B- / 7.1	6.9	0.34	33.90	69	N/A	N/A	4	N/A	35.7	35.0	4.8	32	5	2,000	25	0.0	5.0
B- / 7.1	6.9	0.34	33.84	210	N/A	N/A	4	N/A	35.7	35.0	4.8	32	5	2,000	25	0.0	1.0
C- / 3.7	15.1	0.88	51.59	425	N/A	N/A	0	N/A	206.2	93.7	0.9	48	7	2,000	25	5.8	1.0
C- / 3.7	15.1	0.88	51.06	63	N/A	N/A	0	N/A	206.2	89.1	0.7	39	7	2,000	25	5.0	1.0
C- / 3.7	15.1	0.88	51.02	163	N/A	N/A	0	N/A	206.2	89.2	0.7	39	7	2,000	25	0.0	1.0
C / 4.8	12.0	0.79	4.54	3	4	87	5	4	2.0	63.1	-4.8	59	N/A	2,500	100	0.0	2.0
C+ / 5.9	10.2	0.91	26.98	N/A	1	93	2	4	12.0	71.9	-4.4	47	N/A	2,500	100	5.8	2.0
C+ / 5.8	10.4	0.92	27.30	145	1	93	2	4	12.0	72.8	-3.8	49	7	2,500	100	0.0	2.0
B- / 7.3	8.6	0.61	17.19	1	2	97	0	1	2.0	45.2	-5.6	29	N/A	2,500	100	5.8	2.0
B- / 7.8	8.6	0.61	17.53	13	2	97	0	1	2.0	46.6	-5.4	32	N/A	2,500	100	0.0	2.0
C+ / 6.7	10.5	0.85	22.41	109	11	88	0	1	5.0	144.2	-2.0	81	N/A	2,500	100	5.8	2.0
C+ / 6.7	10.5	0.85	22.01	69	11	88	0	1	5.0	140.8	-2.2	78	N/A	2,500	100	0.0	2.0
U /	N/A	N/A	22.72	398	11	88	0	1	5.0	N/A	N/A	N/A	N/A	1,000,000	0	0.0	2.0
C+ / 6.8	10.5	0.85	22.73	817	11	88	0	1	5.0	147.1	-1.9	84	N/A	2,500	100	0.0	2.0
B- / 7.1	11.4	0.65	23.02	9	14	84	0	2	4.0	145.8	1.3	99	N/A	2,500	100	5.8	2.0
B- / 7.2	11.4	0.65	23.20	118	14	84	0	2	4.0	147.9	1.4	99	N/A	2,500	100	0.0	2.0
C+ / 6.9	9.6	0.82	15.05	46	3	96	0	1	32.7	81.3	-11.4	36	8	1,000	100	0.0	1.0
B / 8.1	7.9	0.95	14.93	68	0	99	0	1	29.0	71.4	-6.0	75	10	2,500	500	0.0	0.0
E- / 0.0	27.3	1.59	9.23	205	1	98	0	1	19.3	111.5	-21.7	0	9	5,000	100	3.5	1.0
E- / 0.0	27.4	1.59	8.80	17	1	98	0	1	19.3	106.9	-21.7	0	9	5,000	100	0.0	1.0
E- / 0.0	27.3	1.59	9.56	89	1	98	0	1	19.3	113.9	-21.7	0	9	5,000,000	0	0.0	2.0
C+ / 6.7	11.0	1.03	19.33	1,332	9	90	0	1	53.0	156.3	-10.7	57	9	2,500	500	0.0	2.0
U /	N/A	N/A	19.35	564	9	90	0	1	53.0	N/A	N/A	N/A	1	50,000	1,000	0.0	2.0
B / 8.9	4.3	0.14	12.33	28	7	92	0	1	178.4	5.8	9.2	35	6	50,000	0	0.0	2.0
B / 8.9	4.2	0.13	12.17	11	7	92	0	1	178.4	4.8	9.1	33	6	2,500	0	0.0	2.0
B- / 7.2	9.9	0.96	11.73	22	5	94	0	1	59.4	125.5	-7.8	42	6	50,000	0	0.0	2.0
B- / 7.2	9.9	0.96	11.70	47	5	94	0	1	59.4	123.3	-7.8	38	6	2,500	0	0.0	2.0
C+ / 6.1	11.7	1.04	20.50	759	3	96	0	1	101.9	208.0	0.6	96	10	50,000	0	0.0	2.0
C+ / 6.1	11.6	1.04	20.26	809	3	96	0	1	101.9	205.2	0.6	95	10	2,500	0	0.0	2.0
B- / 7.2	13.2	1.16	18.71	667	1	98	0	1	88.6	114.9	-5.5	46	5	50,000	0	0.0	2.0
B- / 7.2	13.2	1.16	18.54	288	1	98	0	1	88.6	112.7	-5.6	43	5	2,500	0	0.0	2.0
B+ / 9.2	5.4	0.01	12.39	19	5	94	0	1	212.6	9.6	5.6	79	8	50,000	0	0.0	2.0
B+ / 9.3	5.3	0.02	12.41	13	5	94	0	1	212.6	8.6	5.5	77	8	2,500	0	0.0	2.0
B- / 7.9	8.8	1.11	8.90	46	1	98	0	1	78.7	59.3	-8.4	33	6	50,000	0	0.0	2.0
B / 8.6	8.7	1.03	12.14	74	2	97	0	1	144.3	71.4	-6.4	69	4	50,000	0	0.0	2.0
B / 8.6	8.7	1.04	12.14	10	2	97	0	1	144.3	69.9	-6.6	65	4	2,500	0	0.0	2.0
C- / 4.2	14.2	0.96	13.17	48	0	99	0	1	69.3	108.0	-7.2	57	17	100,000	1,000	0.0	2.0
C / 4.3	14.3	0.96	13.35	832	0	99	0	1	69.3	110.2	-7.2	60	17	50,000	0	0.0	2.0
C- / 4.2	14.2	0.96	13.06	300	0	99	0	1	69.3	107.3	-7.2	55	17	2,500	0	0.0	2.0
B+ / 9.1	5.1	0.04	11.09	197	5	94	0	1	121.8	3.4	9.9	73	9	50,000	0	0.0	2.0
B+ / 9.0	5.2	0.03	10.96	66	5	94	0	1	121.8	2.5	9.9	71	9	2,500	0	0.0	2.0
C+ / 6.2	15.6	1.05	13.53	106	4	95	0	1	94.0	124.6	-9.5	37	1	2,500	500	0.0	2.0
C+ / 6.8	9.7	1.77	11.88	139	3	96	0	1	83.0	69.4	-9.7	33	1	2,500	500	0.0	2.0
C / 4.8	17.4	1.04	18.61	1,851	3	96	0	1	53.1	255.8	-5.9	62	12	1,000,000	0	0.0	1.0
C / 4.8	17.4	1.04	18.74	234	3	96	0	1	53.1	253.8	-5.7	61	9	10,000	0	0.0	1.0
B / 8.9	7.3	0.93	17.02	51	2	97	0	1	64.9	60.8	-8.4	63	3	1,000,000	0	0.0	1.0
B / 8.9	7.3	0.94	17.00	11	2	97	0	1	64.9	59.2	-8.6	58	3	10,000	1,000	0.0	1.0
B- / 7.4	9.5	0.93	15.30	952	1	98	0	1	59.9	102.3	-8.0	26	3	1,000,000	0	0.0	1.0
B- / 7.4	9.6	0.93	15.31	44	1	98	0	1	59.9	100.7	-8.1	24	3	10,000	0	0.0	1.0

Data as of June 30, 2006

Fund Type	Fund Name	Ticker Symbol	Overall Weiss Investment Rating	Phone	Performance Rating/Pts	3 Mo	6 Mo	1Yr / Pct	3Yr / Pct	5Yr / Pct	Dividend Yield	Expense Ratio
FO	Lazard Intl Small Cap Inst	LZISX	B	(800) 823-6300	A / 9.4	-1.37	9.42	23.84 /87	27.86 /94	17.05 /94	0.96	0.94
FO	Lazard Intl Small Cap Open	LZSMX	B	(800) 823-6300	A / 9.3	-1.43	9.25	23.45 /87	27.50 /93	16.63 /94	0.67	1.36
MC	Lazard Mid Cap Inst	LZMIX	B	(800) 823-6300	B- / 7.2	-0.36	3.17	10.34 /49	18.03 /73	9.88 /80	0.49	1.05
SC	Lazard Small Cap Inst	LZSCX	D-	(800) 823-6300	C+ / 6.7	-5.90	6.69	11.58 /57	16.66 /67	9.57 /79	0.10	0.86
SC	Lazard Small Cap Open	LZCOX	D-	(800) 823-6300	C+ / 6.5	-6.00	6.54	11.20 /55	16.26 /65	9.33 /78	0.00	1.18
GI	Legg Mason American Lead Co Prim	LMALX	C-	(800) 822-5544	C- / 3.4	-3.89	-2.22	5.98 /20	10.89 /35	3.79 /44	0.06	1.86
IX	Legg Mason Balanced Tr Prim	LMBTX	D+	(800) 822-5544	D / 1.7	-0.95	0.63	5.45 /17	7.22 /11	2.59 /33	0.72	1.85
GR	Legg Mason Classic Valuation Prim	LMCVX	C-	(800) 822-5544	C- / 4.2	-2.41	3.13	12.09 /60	11.52 /39	2.82 /35	0.00	1.95
EM	Legg Mason Emerg Mkts Prim	LMEMX	C	(800) 822-5544	A+ / 9.8	-4.32	7.23	41.98 /98	36.95 /99	21.19 /97	0.08	2.25
FS	Legg Mason Financial Services Prim	LMFNX	C-	(800) 822-5544	C+ / 6.2	-2.05	3.07	11.09 /54	15.02 /59	10.10 /81	0.00	2.25
GR	Legg Mason Growth Tr Prim	LMGTX	E-	(800) 822-5544	E+ / 0.7	-8.53	-8.53	0.97 / 2	6.81 /10	7.14 /67	0.00	1.87
FO	Legg Mason Intl Eq Tr Prim	LMGEX	A-	(800) 822-5544	A- / 9.2	-0.96	10.08	30.59 /95	25.44 /92	12.29 /87	0.27	2.00
★ GR	Legg Mason Opport Tr Prim	LMOPX	D	(800) 822-5544	C / 4.6	-8.53	0.88	11.92 /59	12.71 /47	8.52 /74	0.00	2.18
★ AG	Legg Mason Prt Aggr Growth A	SHRAX	D+	(866) 890-4247	C- / 3.4	-4.58	-0.07	14.74 /71	12.41 /45	0.92 /20	0.00	1.16
AG	Legg Mason Prt Aggr Growth B	SAGBX	D+	(866) 890-4247	D+ / 2.9	-4.77	-0.48	13.83 /68	11.50 /39	0.19 /16	0.00	1.98
AG	Legg Mason Prt Aggr Growth C	SAGCX	C-	(866) 890-4247	C- / 3.7	-4.71	-0.38	13.98 /68	11.62 /40	0.20 /16	0.00	1.90
AG	Legg Mason Prt Aggr Growth Y	SAGYX	C+	(866) 890-4247	C / 4.7	-4.48	0.13	15.21 /72	12.88 /48	1.34 /22	0.00	0.75
GR	Legg Mason Prt Appr Fund A	SHAPX	C-	(866) 890-4247	D+ / 2.6	-0.67	3.47	9.07 /41	10.00 /27	3.20 /39	0.33	0.95
GR	Legg Mason Prt Appr Fund B	SAPBX	C-	(866) 890-4247	D / 2.2	-0.91	3.03	8.14 /34	9.08 /21	2.34 /30	0.00	1.78
GR	Legg Mason Prt Appr Fund C	SAPCX	C-	(866) 890-4247	D+ / 2.8	-0.91	3.09	8.20 /34	9.13 /22	2.39 /31	0.00	1.76
GR	Legg Mason Prt Appr Fund Y	SAPYX	C+	(866) 890-4247	C- / 3.9	-0.65	3.64	9.45 /43	10.42 /30	3.59 /42	0.73	0.57
AA	Legg Mason Prt Cap & Inc SB Sh Y	SOLYX	B-	(800) 725-6666	C / 4.6	-1.53	2.55	7.89 /32	12.24 /44	6.80 /66	3.04	0.79
IN	Legg Mason Prt Cap & Inc SmB Sh A	SOPAX	C+	(866) 890-4247	C- / 3.4	-1.57	2.76	7.89 /32	11.92 /42	6.45 /64	2.89	1.93
IN	Legg Mason Prt Cap & Inc SmB Sh B	SOPTX	C	(866) 890-4247	C- / 3.2	-1.72	2.43	7.27 /28	11.33 /38	5.90 /60	2.55	1.63
IN	Legg Mason Prt Cap & Inc SmB Sh C	SBPLX	C+	(866) 890-4247	C- / 3.7	-1.77	2.37	7.01 /26	11.05 /36	5.63 /59	2.32	1.86
IN	Legg Mason Prt Cap & Inc SmB Sh Y		B-	(866) 890-4247	C / 4.7	-1.53	2.83	8.19 /34	12.34 /45	6.86 /66	3.33	N/A
GR	Legg Mason Prt Classic Values A	SCLAX	C-	(866) 890-4247	C- / 3.4	-4.89	0.13	5.23 /16	12.79 /47	--	0.00	1.75
GR	Legg Mason Prt Classic Values B	SCLBX	C-	(866) 890-4247	C- / 3.0	-5.08	-0.26	4.47 /13	11.92 /42	--	0.00	2.53
GR	Legg Mason Prt Classic Values C	SCLLX	C	(866) 890-4247	C- / 3.7	-5.02	-0.20	4.48 /13	11.94 /42	--	0.00	2.52
CV	Legg Mason Prt Con SmB Cl A	SCRAX	D+	(866) 890-4247	D+ / 2.7	-3.48	3.31	8.58 /37	10.52 /31	7.18 /68	1.87	1.18
CV	Legg Mason Prt Con SmB Cl B	SCVSX	D	(866) 890-4247	D+ / 2.4	-3.62	2.98	7.96 /32	9.92 /27	6.61 /65	1.45	1.74
CV	Legg Mason Prt Con SmB Cl C	SMCLX	C-	(866) 890-4247	C- / 3.0	-3.65	2.88	7.74 /31	9.70 /25	6.43 /64	1.29	1.93
CV	Legg Mason Prt Con SmB Cl Y	SCVYX	C-	(866) 890-4247	C- / 4.0	-3.41	3.48	8.98 /40	10.95 /35	7.62 /70	2.30	0.80
IN	● Legg Mason Prt Cp Pres A	SPNAX	D	(866) 890-4247	E- / 0.0	0.09	0.46	1.15 / 3	0.21 / 0	--	2.40	1.95
IN	● Legg Mason Prt Cp Pres B	SPRBX	D	(866) 890-4247	E- / 0.0	-0.09	0.09	0.45 / 2	-0.52 / 0	--	1.74	2.70
IN	● Legg Mason Prt Cp Pres C	SPRLX	D	(866) 890-4247	E- / 0.0	-0.09	0.09	0.44 / 2	-0.53 / 0	--	1.73	2.70
IN	● Legg Mason Prt Cp Pres II A	SMPRX	D	(866) 890-4247	E- / 0.0	-0.53	0.90	1.98 / 4	0.99 / 0	--	1.27	1.12
IN	● Legg Mason Prt Cp Pres II B	SPCBX	D+	(866) 890-4247	E- / 0.0	-0.71	0.54	1.21 / 3	0.25 / 0	--	0.58	2.70
IN	● Legg Mason Prt Cp Pres II C	SMPLX	D	(866) 890-4247	E- / 0.1	-0.63	0.54	1.28 / 3	0.27 / 0	--	0.56	1.87
BA	Legg Mason Prt Div & Inc A	SUTAX	C-	(866) 890-4247	D- / 1.5	0.08	3.36	6.19 /21	8.11 /16	2.94 /36	2.89	0.93
BA	Legg Mason Prt Div & Inc B	SLSUX	C-	(866) 890-4247	D- / 1.3	-0.06	3.09	5.66 /18	7.57 /13	2.43 /31	2.53	1.33
BA	Legg Mason Prt Div & Inc C	SBBLX	C	(866) 890-4247	D / 1.8	-0.11	2.99	5.44 /17	7.33 /12	2.18 /29	2.33	1.66
GR	Legg Mason Prt Div Lg Cp Gr A	CFLGX	D-	(866) 890-4247	E / 0.3	-1.20	2.48	7.13 /27	3.94 / 2	-1.94 / 8	0.53	1.04
GR	Legg Mason Prt Div Lg Cp Gr B	CLCBX	D-	(866) 890-4247	E- / 0.2	-1.32	2.13	6.32 /22	3.16 / 1	-2.67 / 6	0.00	1.79
GR	Legg Mason Prt Div Lg Cp Gr C	SMDLX	D-	(866) 890-4247	E / 0.4	-1.33	2.18	6.34 /22	3.31 / 2	-2.59 / 6	0.00	1.79
GR	Legg Mason Prt Dividend Strategy 1	CSGWX	D-	(866) 890-4247	E+ / 0.8	-0.07	4.96	7.31 /28	6.73 / 9	-1.72 / 9	1.67	0.94
GR	Legg Mason Prt Dividend Strategy A	GROAX	D-	(866) 890-4247	E+ / 0.8	-0.16	4.70	6.95 /26	6.22 / 7	-2.29 / 7	1.47	1.25
GR	Legg Mason Prt Dividend Strategy B	GROBX	D-	(866) 890-4247	E+ / 0.6	-0.35	4.38	6.15 /21	5.41 / 5	-3.06 / 5	0.91	2.00
GR	Legg Mason Prt Dividend Strategy C	SCPLX	D	(866) 890-4247	D- / 1.2	-0.18	4.55	6.36 /22	5.89 / 6	-2.51 / 6	0.95	1.75
FS	Legg Mason Prt Financial Svc A	SBFAX	C	(866) 890-4247	C / 5.3	-1.86	3.41	13.78 /68	14.38 /56	6.30 /63	0.87	1.45
FS	Legg Mason Prt Financial Svc B	SBFBX	C-	(866) 890-4247	C / 4.9	-1.97	3.11	13.01 /64	13.53 /51	5.51 /58	0.25	2.19
FS	Legg Mason Prt Financial Svc C	SFSLX	C	(866) 890-4247	C+ / 5.6	-1.91	3.17	13.18 /65	13.59 /52	5.54 /58	0.28	2.19

● Denotes fund is closed to new investors
★ Denotes fund is included in Section II

www.WeissRatings.com

RISK			NET ASSETS		ASSET				Portfolio Turnover Ratio	BULL / BEAR		FUND MANAGER		MINIMUMS		LOADS	
Risk Rating/Pts	3 Year		NAV As of 6/30/06	Total $(Mil)	Cash %	Stocks %	Bonds %	Other %		Last Bull Market Return	Last Bear Market Return	Manager Quality Pct	Manager Tenure (Years)	Initial Purch. $	Additional Purch. $	Front End Load	Back End Load
	Standard Deviation	Beta															
C /5.2	10.7	0.97	18.71	587	1	98	0	1	32.8	169.4	-5.7	86	13	1,000,000	0	0.0	1.0
C /5.2	10.9	0.97	18.67	73	1	98	0	1	32.8	166.9	-5.8	84	13	10,000	0	0.0	1.0
B- /7.2	9.3	0.83	13.65	184	2	97	0	1	77.9	91.9	-8.2	80	9	1,000,000	0	0.0	1.0
D- /1.4	13.4	0.90	16.43	202	2	97	0	1	91.1	97.7	-10.6	53	5	1,000,000	0	0.0	1.0
D- /1.4	13.4	0.90	16.29	38	2	97	0	1	91.1	95.7	-10.5	48	5	10,000	0	0.0	1.0
B- /7.8	8.9	1.06	23.20	733	1	98	0	1	14.3	71.1	-11.2	45	8	1,000	100	0.0	0.0
B /8.4	4.7	0.56	10.81	38	3	58	37	2	23.0	36.6	-5.1	57	10	1,000	100	0.0	0.0
C+ /6.9	10.2	1.25	14.19	83	1	98	0	1	65.0	83.4	-12.2	35	N/A	1,000	100	0.0	0.0
D+ /2.5	20.1	1.21	20.81	285	4	95	0	1	132.6	249.8	-6.8	13	10	1,000	100	0.0	2.0
C /5.2	8.5	0.72	14.24	56	3	96	0	1	24.8	74.7	-0.2	90	8	1,000	100	0.0	0.0
C- /4.2	15.4	1.69	27.98	538	2	97	0	1	19.7	77.0	-11.3	2	N/A	1,000	100	0.0	0.0
C+ /6.2	10.9	1.05	17.67	362	2	97	0	1	118.0	144.8	-4.8	54	N/A	1,000	100	0.0	2.0
C /4.4	18.1	1.82	16.86	4,291	2	92	1	5	29.7	125.6	-8.8	12	N/A	1,000	100	0.0	1.0
C+ /6.8	10.7	1.19	107.03	4,214	0	99	0	1	2.0	83.1	-9.6	49	23	1,000	50	5.0	1.0
C+ /6.7	10.7	1.19	95.34	2,310	0	99	0	1	2.0	78.5	-9.8	39	14	1,000	50	0.0	5.0
C+ /6.7	10.7	1.19	96.10	1,906	0	99	0	1	2.0	79.0	-9.8	40	13	1,000	50	0.0	1.0
B- /7.8	10.7	1.19	111.49	1,772	0	99	0	1	2.0	85.5	-9.5	55	10	15,000,000	50	0.0	0.0
B /8.5	6.3	0.80	14.72	3,578	5	94	0	1	53.0	53.5	-7.8	63	N/A	1,000	50	5.0	1.0
B /8.6	6.3	0.80	14.32	924	5	94	0	1	53.0	49.5	-7.9	53	N/A	1,000	50	0.0	5.0
B /8.6	6.3	0.80	14.35	636	5	94	0	1	53.0	49.8	-7.9	54	N/A	1,000	50	0.0	1.0
B /8.6	6.3	0.80	14.70	666	5	94	0	1	53.0	55.3	-7.6	68	10	15,000,000	50	0.0	0.0
B+ /9.3	6.5	1.23	17.57	3	7	54	25	14	64.0	66.7	-0.8	86	3	2,500,000	1,000	0.0	0.0
B+ /9.1	6.5	0.77	17.33	1,725	7	56	36	1	49.0	65.1	-0.9	82	4	1,000	50	5.0	1.0
B+ /9.1	6.5	0.77	17.19	576	7	56	36	1	49.0	62.4	-1.0	77	4	1,000	50	0.0	5.0
B+ /9.3	6.5	0.77	17.23	457	7	56	36	1	49.0	61.0	-1.0	75	4	1,000	50	0.0	1.0
B+ /9.3	6.5	0.77	17.57	4	7	56	36	1	49.0	67.2	-0.8	84	4	15,000,000	50	0.0	0.0
B- /7.8	11.0	1.26	15.57	3	10	89	0	1	71.0	N/A	N/A	45	N/A	1,000	50	5.0	1.0
B- /7.8	11.0	1.27	15.14	30	10	89	0	1	71.0	N/A	N/A	37	N/A	1,000	50	0.0	5.0
B- /7.8	11.0	1.27	15.15	59	10	89	0	1	71.0	69.7	0.7	37	N/A	1,000	50	0.0	1.0
B- /7.1	8.2	1.18	16.89	39	2	8	0	90	79.0	61.3	0.5	78	N/A	1,000	50	5.0	1.0
B- /7.1	8.3	1.18	16.82	20	2	8	0	90	79.0	58.7	0.4	73	N/A	1,000	50	0.0	5.0
B- /7.5	8.3	1.18	16.90	30	2	8	0	90	79.0	57.7	0.3	71	N/A	1,000	50	0.0	1.0
B- /7.1	8.3	1.18	17.03	9	2	8	0	90	79.0	63.4	0.6	81	N/A	15,000,000	50	0.0	0.0
B+ /9.5	2.8	0.06	10.95	35	6	12	80	2	16.0	3.2	2.3	28	N/A	1,000	50	5.0	1.0
B+ /9.5	2.8	0.06	10.90	217	6	12	80	2	16.0	0.9	2.1	23	N/A	1,000	50	0.0	5.0
B+ /9.5	2.8	0.07	10.90	23	6	12	80	2	16.0	0.9	2.1	23	N/A	1,000	50	0.0	1.0
B /8.8	3.3	0.18	11.23	21	4	28	68	0	4.0	7.2	1.2	27	N/A	1,000	50	5.0	1.0
B+ /9.6	3.4	0.19	11.12	234	4	28	68	0	4.0	4.8	1.0	22	N/A	1,000	50	0.0	5.0
B /8.8	3.4	0.18	11.13	18	4	28	68	0	4.0	4.8	1.0	22	N/A	1,000	50	0.0	1.0
B+ /9.7	4.1	0.83	12.72	456	5	58	35	2	35.0	44.1	-4.3	71	N/A	1,000	50	5.0	1.0
B+ /9.9	4.2	0.83	12.68	46	5	58	35	2	35.0	41.7	-4.3	66	N/A	1,000	50	0.0	5.0
B+ /9.9	4.2	0.83	12.69	48	5	58	35	2	35.0	40.7	-4.4	63	N/A	1,000	50	0.0	1.0
B- /7.7	6.9	0.84	14.05	147	3	96	0	1	111.0	30.9	-9.3	12	1	1,000	50	5.0	1.0
B- /7.7	6.9	0.84	13.45	8	3	96	0	1	111.0	27.8	-9.4	9	1	1,000	50	0.0	5.0
B- /7.2	7.0	0.84	14.08	N/A	3	96	0	1	111.0	28.3	-9.4	9	1	1,000	50	0.0	1.0
B- /7.4	7.2	0.88	16.96	1,970	4	96	0	0	122.0	43.2	-10.6	25	N/A	0	0	8.5	0.0
B- /7.6	7.1	0.87	16.55	372	4	96	0	0	122.0	41.0	-10.8	22	N/A	1,000	50	5.0	1.0
B- /7.5	7.2	0.88	15.60	249	4	96	0	0	122.0	37.5	-11.0	17	N/A	1,000	50	0.0	5.0
B /8.0	7.2	0.87	16.53	10	4	96	0	0	122.0	39.7	-10.8	20	N/A	1,000	50	0.0	1.0
C+ /6.3	8.6	0.91	16.39	20	1	98	0	1	29.0	82.4	-8.6	72	N/A	1,000	50	5.0	1.0
C+ /6.4	8.6	0.91	15.92	25	1	98	0	1	29.0	78.1	-8.7	65	N/A	1,000	50	0.0	5.0
C+ /6.4	8.6	0.91	15.94	13	1	98	0	1	29.0	78.3	-8.7	66	N/A	1,000	50	0.0	1.0

Fund Type	Fund Name	Ticker Symbol	Overall Weiss Investment Rating	Phone	Performance Rating/Pts	3 Mo	6 Mo	1Yr / Pct	3Yr / Pct	5Yr / Pct	Dividend Yield	Expense Ratio
	99 Pct = Best											
	0 Pct = Worst				PERFORMANCE			Total Return % through 6/30/06	Annualized		Incl. in Returns	
★ GR	Legg Mason Prt Fundamental Value	SHFVX	C-	(866) 890-4247	C- / 3.7	-1.42	4.10	11.13 /54	11.82 /41	2.42 /31	0.42	1.05
GR	Legg Mason Prt Fundamental Value	SFVBX	C-	(866) 890-4247	C- / 3.3	-1.59	3.72	10.25 /48	10.95 /35	1.61 /24	0.00	1.84
GR	Legg Mason Prt Fundamental Value	SFVCX	C-	(866) 890-4247	C- / 4.1	-1.59	3.80	10.41 /50	10.97 /35	1.64 /25	0.00	1.83
GR	Legg Mason Prt Fundamental Value	SFVYX	C	(866) 890-4247	C / 5.1	-1.32	4.41	11.64 /58	12.29 /44	2.84 /35	0.81	0.66
GI	Legg Mason Prt Grow & Inc SmB 1	CGINX	D	(866) 890-4247	D- / 1.3	-3.24	0.84	6.43 /23	9.09 /21	1.62 /24	0.51	0.95
GI	Legg Mason Prt Grow & Inc SmB A	GRIAX	D+	(866) 890-4247	D- / 1.5	-3.30	0.70	6.12 /21	8.76 /19	2.32 /30	0.26	1.25
GI	Legg Mason Prt Grow & Inc SmB B	GRIBX	D	(866) 890-4247	D- / 1.1	-3.52	0.33	5.31 /17	7.78 /14	0.35 /17	0.00	2.00
GI	Legg Mason Prt Grow & Inc SmB C	SGAIX	D+	(866) 890-4247	D / 1.8	-3.45	0.38	5.45 /17	8.11 /16	0.73 /19	0.00	1.82
GI	Legg Mason Prt Grow & Inc SmB Y	SGTYX	D	(866) 890-4247	D+ / 2.8	-3.24	0.89	6.61 /24	9.35 /23	1.90 /26	0.80	0.69
GL	Legg Mason Prt Hbgr Glbl Val A	SGLAX	B-	(866) 890-4247	C+ / 6.2	-2.48	6.06	18.58 /80	16.39 /65	5.94 /61	4.38	1.66
GL	Legg Mason Prt Hbgr Glbl Val B	SGLBX	C+	(866) 890-4247	C+ / 6.0	-2.61	5.66	17.85 /79	15.54 /61	5.14 /55	4.00	2.41
GL	Legg Mason Prt Hbgr Glbl Val C	SGLCX	B-	(866) 890-4247	C+ / 6.4	-2.76	5.52	17.54 /78	15.41 /61	5.07 /55	3.93	2.49
HL	Legg Mason Prt Hlth Sciences A	SBIAX	D-	(866) 890-4247	E / 0.5	-2.51	-1.93	1.38 / 3	6.37 / 8	0.94 /20	0.00	1.46
HL	Legg Mason Prt Hlth Sciences B	SBHBX	E+	(866) 890-4247	E / 0.4	-2.71	-2.33	0.56 / 2	5.59 / 5	0.16 /16	0.00	2.21
HL	Legg Mason Prt Hlth Sciences C	SBHLX	D-	(866) 890-4247	E+ / 0.6	-2.63	-2.18	0.72 / 2	5.64 / 6	0.19 /16	0.00	2.21
FO	● Legg Mason Prt International 1	CSQIX	B+	(866) 890-4247	B / 7.7	-0.40	9.37	23.33 /86	20.15 /80	1.19 /21	1.13	1.71
FO	● Legg Mason Prt International A	CSQAX	B+	(866) 890-4247	B / 7.8	-0.50	9.23	23.02 /86	19.63 /78	0.61 /18	0.96	2.00
FO	● Legg Mason Prt International B	CSQBX	B+	(866) 890-4247	B / 7.6	-0.66	8.86	22.08 /84	18.69 /75	-0.25 /14	0.40	2.75
FO	Legg Mason Prt International C	SIALX	B-	(866) 890-4247	B / 8.1	-0.61	9.05	22.55 /85	19.59 /78	0.96 /20	0.66	2.36
FO	Legg Mason Prt Intl All Cap Grth A	SBIEX	C+	(866) 890-4247	B / 7.7	-1.36	8.11	22.98 /86	19.66 /78	4.84 /53	1.07	1.36
FO	Legg Mason Prt Intl All Cap Grth B	SBIBX	C+	(866) 890-4247	B- / 7.4	-1.63	7.63	21.88 /84	18.66 /75	3.95 /45	0.49	2.18
FO	Legg Mason Prt Intl All Cap Grth C	SBICX	C+	(866) 890-4247	B / 7.7	-1.59	7.68	21.82 /84	18.54 /75	3.86 /44	0.50	2.31
GL	Legg Mason Prt Intl Lg Cp A	CFIPX	B+	(866) 890-4247	B / 7.8	-0.74	9.36	22.96 /86	19.87 /79	7.68 /70	1.13	1.62
GL	Legg Mason Prt Intl Lg Cp B	SILCX	C+	(866) 890-4247	B- / 7.5	-1.00	8.79	21.68 /84	18.83 /76	6.89 /66	0.37	2.48
GL	Legg Mason Prt Intl Lg Cp C	SILLX	A+	(866) 890-4247	B / 7.9	-1.03	8.74	21.64 /84	18.86 /76	6.95 /66	0.34	2.50
GL	Legg Mason Prt Intl Lg Cp Y	SMYIX	A+	(866) 890-4247	B+ / 8.4	-0.66	9.53	23.49 /87	20.26 /80	--	1.60	1.21
★ GR	Legg Mason Prt Large Cap Growth A	SBLGX	E	(866) 890-4247	E- / 0.2	-6.66	-6.66	2.53 / 6	5.43 / 5	0.56 /18	0.00	1.17
GR	Legg Mason Prt Large Cap Growth B	SBLBX	E	(866) 890-4247	E- / 0.2	-6.82	-6.99	1.77 / 4	4.67 / 3	-0.18 /15	0.00	1.90
GR	Legg Mason Prt Large Cap Growth C	SLCCX	E	(866) 890-4247	E / 0.3	-6.82	-6.99	1.77 / 4	4.65 / 3	-0.20 /15	0.00	1.90
GR	Legg Mason Prt Large Cap Growth Y	SBLYX	E+	(866) 890-4247	E+ / 0.6	-6.57	-6.45	2.92 / 7	5.85 / 6	0.95 /20	0.00	0.79
GI	Legg Mason Prt Large Cap Value Fd	SBCIX	C+	(866) 890-4247	C- / 4.2	-0.17	4.74	11.53 /57	12.27 /44	2.04 /28	1.08	0.88
GI	Legg Mason Prt Large Cap Value Fd	SBCCX	C	(866) 890-4247	C- / 3.6	-0.36	4.35	10.58 /51	11.33 /38	1.17 /21	0.33	1.79
GI	Legg Mason Prt Large Cap Value Fd	SBGCX	C+	(866) 890-4247	C / 4.4	-0.36	4.37	10.67 /51	11.38 /38	1.21 /22	0.41	1.74
GI	Legg Mason Prt Large Cap Value Fd	SBCYX	C+	(866) 890-4247	C / 5.3	-0.11	4.89	11.85 /59	12.60 /46	2.36 /31	1.41	0.61
AA	Legg Mason Prt Lifestyle Bal Fund A	SBBAX	D+	(866) 890-4247	E / 0.5	-1.80	-0.49	2.66 / 6	6.09 / 7	3.55 /42	1.96	0.72
AA	Legg Mason Prt Lifestyle Bal Fund B	SCBBX	D+	(866) 890-4247	E / 0.4	-2.03	-0.87	1.86 / 4	5.22 / 4	2.75 /34	1.20	1.51
AA	Legg Mason Prt Lifestyle Bal Fund C	SCBCX	D+	(866) 890-4247	E+ / 0.6	-1.91	-0.71	2.10 / 5	5.40 / 5	2.88 /36	1.36	1.40
AA	Legg Mason Prt Lifestyle Cons Fd A	SBCPX	D+	(866) 890-4247	E / 0.3	-1.25	-0.68	1.35 / 3	4.97 / 4	4.08 /47	2.77	0.72
AA	Legg Mason Prt Lifestyle Cons Fd B	SBCBX	D+	(866) 890-4247	E- / 0.2	-1.37	-0.94	0.77 / 2	4.41 / 3	3.52 /42	2.29	1.26
AA	Legg Mason Prt Lifestyle Cons Fd C	SBCLX	C-	(866) 890-4247	E / 0.4	-1.26	-0.80	0.96 / 2	4.51 / 3	3.60 /42	2.40	1.22
GR	Legg Mason Prt Lifestyle Growth A	SCGRX	D	(866) 890-4247	D- / 1.3	-2.96	-0.40	5.41 /17	8.50 /18	2.38 /31	0.96	0.78
GR	Legg Mason Prt Lifestyle Growth B	SGRBX	D	(866) 890-4247	D- / 1.1	-3.17	-0.79	4.65 /13	7.68 /13	1.61 /24	0.23	1.54
GR	Legg Mason Prt Lifestyle Growth C	SCGCX	D+	(866) 890-4247	D / 1.6	-3.16	-0.71	4.79 /14	7.85 /14	1.75 /25	0.37	1.37
GR	Legg Mason Prt Lifestyle High Gr A	SCHAX	D+	(866) 890-4247	D+ / 2.6	-3.88	-0.53	7.83 /31	10.93 /35	2.37 /31	0.00	0.79
GR	Legg Mason Prt Lifestyle High Gr B	SCHBX	D	(866) 890-4247	D+ / 2.3	-4.04	-0.83	7.06 /27	10.12 /28	1.61 /24	0.00	1.54
GR	Legg Mason Prt Lifestyle High Gr C	SCHCX	D+	(866) 890-4247	C- / 3.0	-4.01	-0.76	7.16 /27	10.33 /30	1.75 /25	0.00	1.36
MC	Legg Mason Prt Md Cp Cr 1	SMCPX	D+	(866) 890-4247	C / 4.3	-2.23	5.03	13.92 /68	13.78 /53	5.15 /55	0.00	1.10
MC	Legg Mason Prt Md Cp Cr A	SBMAX	D+	(866) 890-4247	C / 4.6	-2.29	4.92	13.73 /67	13.68 /52	4.57 /51	0.00	1.22
MC	Legg Mason Prt Md Cp Cr B	SBMDX	D	(866) 890-4247	C- / 4.2	-2.45	4.54	12.86 /64	12.81 /48	3.78 /44	0.00	1.98
MC	Legg Mason Prt Md Cp Cr C	SBMLX	D+	(866) 890-4247	C / 4.9	-2.40	4.59	12.92 /64	12.83 /48	3.79 /44	0.00	2.00
MC	Legg Mason Prt Md Cp Cr D	SMBYX	C-	(866) 890-4247	C+ / 5.7	-2.18	5.15	14.22 /69	14.03 /54	5.11 /55	0.00	0.75
GR	Legg Mason Prt MDF AlCp Gr&VI A	SPAAX	D+	(866) 890-4247	D / 2.2	-2.68	1.11	9.01 /40	9.81 /26	-0.07 /15	0.00	1.20

● Denotes fund is closed to new investors
★ Denotes fund is included in Section II

244

Risk Rating/Pts	Standard Deviation	Beta	NAV As of 6/30/06	Total $(Mil)	Cash %	Stocks %	Bonds %	Other %	Portfolio Turnover Ratio	Last Bull Market Return	Last Bear Market Return	Manager Quality Pct	Manager Tenure (Years)	Initial Purch. $	Additional Purch. $	Front End Load	Back End Load
B- /7.3	10.0	1.22	15.22	2,293	2	96	0	2	30.0	77.4	-12.9	39	16	1,000	50	5.0	1.0
B- /7.2	10.0	1.23	14.21	1,177	2	96	0	2	30.0	73.0	-13.1	32	14	1,000	50	0.0	5.0
B- /7.3	10.0	1.22	14.22	780	2	96	0	2	30.0	73.3	-13.1	33	13	1,000	50	0.0	1.0
B- /7.4	10.0	1.22	15.64	170	2	96	0	2	30.0	79.7	-12.8	44	10	15,000,000	50	0.0	0.0
B- /7.6	8.4	1.08	15.95	466	1	98	0	1	57.0	61.4	-10.1	29	N/A	0	0	8.5	0.0
B /8.2	8.4	1.08	15.95	270	1	98	0	1	57.0	59.7	-10.2	27	N/A	1,000	50	5.0	1.0
B /8.2	8.4	1.07	15.06	97	1	98	0	1	57.0	55.1	-10.5	21	N/A	1,000	50	0.0	5.0
B /8.2	8.4	1.07	15.67	4	1	98	0	1	57.0	56.9	-10.3	23	6	1,000	50	0.0	1.0
C+ /5.8	8.4	1.08	15.97	87	1	98	0	1	57.0	62.7	-10.0	31	N/A	15,000,000	50	0.0	0.0
B- /7.5	9.7	0.89	14.18	13	0	99	0	1	13.0	96.5	-11.6	16	N/A	1,000	50	5.0	1.0
B- /7.4	9.7	0.89	13.81	4	0	99	0	1	13.0	92.0	-11.8	12	N/A	1,000	50	0.0	5.0
B- /7.4	9.7	0.89	13.76	4	0	99	0	1	13.0	91.6	-11.8	12	N/A	1,000	50	0.0	1.0
B- /7.1	8.6	0.51	13.18	22	1	98	0	1	32.0	39.3	-5.0	52	N/A	1,000	50	5.0	1.0
B- /7.0	8.6	0.50	12.56	24	1	98	0	1	32.0	36.2	-5.3	43	N/A	1,000	50	0.0	5.0
B- /7.0	8.5	0.50	12.58	14	1	98	0	1	32.0	36.3	-5.3	43	N/A	1,000	50	0.0	1.0
B- /7.4	9.5	0.92	27.20	4	1	98	0	1	30.0	109.2	-14.3	34	N/A	1,000	50	8.5	0.0
B- /7.3	9.5	0.92	26.03	72	1	98	0	1	30.0	106.1	-14.4	31	N/A	1,000	50	5.0	1.0
B- /7.3	9.5	0.92	23.96	54	1	98	0	1	30.0	100.9	-14.7	26	N/A	1,000	50	0.0	5.0
C+ /5.7	9.5	0.92	26.27	2	1	98	0	1	30.0	106.6	-14.2	30	N/A	1,000	50	0.0	1.0
C /5.5	9.9	0.94	13.73	128	0	100	0	0	14.0	107.5	-11.7	27	20	1,000	50	5.0	1.0
C /5.4	9.9	0.94	12.70	21	0	100	0	0	14.0	102.1	-11.9	22	12	1,000	50	0.0	5.0
C /5.3	10.0	0.94	12.34	56	0	100	0	0	14.0	101.4	-11.9	21	12	1,000	50	0.0	1.0
B- /7.3	9.4	0.91	13.01	40	2	97	0	1	29.0	107.8	-11.1	34	N/A	1,000	50	5.0	1.0
C+ /5.7	9.4	0.90	12.54	7	2	97	0	1	29.0	102.6	-11.1	28	N/A	1,000	50	0.0	5.0
B /8.3	9.3	0.90	13.11	51	2	97	0	1	29.0	102.7	-11.2	29	N/A	1,000	50	0.0	1.0
B /8.4	9.4	0.90	13.02	2	2	97	0	1	29.0	N/A	N/A	37	N/A	15,000,000	50	0.0	0.0
C /5.4	12.4	1.33	21.46	2,045	0	100	0	0	9.0	52.6	-10.8	4	9	1,000	50	5.0	1.0
C /5.3	12.4	1.33	20.10	545	0	100	0	0	9.0	49.1	-10.9	3	9	1,000	50	0.0	5.0
C /5.3	12.4	1.33	20.09	741	0	100	0	0	9.0	49.1	-10.9	3	9	1,000	50	0.0	1.0
C+ /6.7	12.4	1.33	22.18	2,369	0	100	0	0	9.0	54.5	-10.7	5	9	15,000,000	50	0.0	0.0
B /8.4	8.3	1.02	17.37	370	3	96	0	1	55.0	73.8	-11.1	66	2	1,000	50	5.0	1.0
B /8.3	8.3	1.02	17.31	33	3	96	0	1	55.0	69.1	-11.3	56	2	1,000	50	0.0	5.0
B /8.3	8.3	1.02	17.31	74	3	96	0	1	55.0	69.4	-11.3	56	2	1,000	50	0.0	1.0
B /8.2	8.3	1.02	17.36	371	3	96	0	1	55.0	75.4	-11.0	68	2	15,000,000	50	0.0	0.0
B+ /9.3	4.8	1.00	11.99	236	0	52	47	1	48.0	33.7	-2.4	39	N/A	1,000	50	5.0	1.0
B+ /9.6	4.8	1.01	12.27	90	0	52	47	1	48.0	30.5	-2.7	31	N/A	1,000	50	0.0	5.0
B+ /9.6	4.8	1.01	12.30	30	0	52	47	1	48.0	30.9	-2.5	33	N/A	1,000	50	0.0	1.0
B+ /9.6	3.7	0.74	11.19	76	0	31	68	1	56.0	26.5	0.3	41	N/A	1,000	50	4.5	1.0
B+ /9.9	3.7	0.73	11.36	27	0	31	68	1	56.0	24.3	0.2	36	N/A	1,000	50	0.0	4.5
B+ /9.9	3.7	0.73	11.35	7	0	31	68	1	56.0	24.6	0.2	37	N/A	1,000	50	0.0	1.0
B /8.3	7.3	0.91	12.44	387	0	72	27	1	53.0	52.8	-6.9	35	N/A	1,000	50	5.0	1.0
B /8.2	7.3	0.91	12.54	157	0	72	27	1	53.0	49.2	-7.0	29	N/A	1,000	50	0.0	5.0
B /8.2	7.3	0.91	12.56	32	0	72	27	1	53.0	50.0	-7.1	31	N/A	1,000	50	0.0	1.0
B- /7.3	9.6	1.18	14.88	452	0	92	6	2	50.0	70.8	-9.9	35	N/A	1,000	50	5.0	1.0
B- /7.1	9.6	1.19	14.26	176	0	92	6	2	50.0	67.0	-10.2	29	N/A	1,000	50	0.0	5.0
B- /7.1	9.6	1.19	14.37	32	0	92	6	2	50.0	67.8	-10.1	31	N/A	1,000	50	0.0	1.0
C /5.5	11.0	0.98	22.34	7	0	99	0	1	93.0	76.1	-9.0	23	N/A	1,000	50	8.5	0.0
C /5.4	11.0	0.98	22.19	394	0	99	0	1	93.0	75.7	-9.1	22	N/A	1,000	50	5.0	1.0
C /5.2	11.0	0.98	20.74	340	0	99	0	1	93.0	71.6	-9.2	18	N/A	1,000	50	0.0	5.0
C /5.3	11.0	0.98	20.75	290	0	99	0	1	93.0	71.6	-9.2	18	N/A	1,000	50	0.0	1.0
C /5.3	10.9	0.97	22.86	2	0	99	0	1	93.0	77.4	-8.9	25	N/A	15,000,000	50	0.0	0.0
B- /7.8	9.2	1.10	9.07	88	0	99	0	1	16.0	62.1	-11.3	33	N/A	1,000	50	5.0	1.0

Fund Type	Fund Name	Ticker Symbol	Overall Weiss Investment Rating	Phone	Performance Rating/Pts	3 Mo	6 Mo	1Yr / Pct	3Yr / Pct	5Yr / Pct	Dividend Yield	Expense Ratio
GR	Legg Mason Prt MDF AlCp Gr&VI B	SPBBX	D	(866) 890-4247	D / 1.9	-3.02	0.70	8.11 /33	8.98 /21	-0.77 /12	0.00	1.97
GR	Legg Mason Prt MDF AlCp Gr&VI C	SPBLX	D-	(866) 890-4247	D+ / 2.5	-2.91	0.81	8.23 /35	9.01 /21	-0.70 /13	0.00	1.95
GL	Legg Mason Prt MDF GI AC Gr&VI A	SPGAX	D	(866) 890-4247	C / 4.5	-2.33	2.55	11.68 /58	13.30 /50	0.40 /17	0.00	1.30
GL	Legg Mason Prt MDF GI AC Gr&VI B	SPGGX	C	(866) 890-4247	C- / 3.9	-2.53	2.21	10.80 /52	12.17 /43	-0.51 /13	0.00	2.08
GL	Legg Mason Prt MDF GI AC Gr&VI C	SPGLX	D+	(866) 890-4247	C / 4.6	-2.42	2.32	11.03 /54	12.18 /44	-0.43 /14	0.00	2.07
GR	Legg Mason Prt MDF Lrg Cap Gr&VI	SPSAX	D	(866) 890-4247	D- / 1.2	-2.33	0.22	5.71 /19	8.16 /16	-2.83 / 6	0.41	1.26
GR	Legg Mason Prt MDF Lrg Cap Gr&VI	SPSBX	D	(866) 890-4247	D- / 1.0	-2.51	-0.11	4.82 /14	7.38 /12	-3.57 / 4	0.00	2.01
GR	Legg Mason Prt MDF Lrg Cap Gr&VI	SPSLX	E+	(866) 890-4247	D- / 1.5	-2.51	-0.11	4.82 /14	7.38 /12	-3.57 / 4	0.00	2.01
GR	Legg Mason Prt S&P 500 Index A	SBSPX	C	(866) 890-4247	C- / 3.6	-1.52	2.53	8.15 /34	10.61 /32	1.92 /27	1.28	0.58
GR	Legg Mason Prt S&P 500 Index D	SBSDX	C+	(866) 890-4247	C- / 4.0	-1.51	2.84	8.59 /37	10.87 /34	2.18 /29	1.47	0.39
SC	Legg Mason Prt Sm Cap Gwth Opp A	CFSGX	D+	(866) 890-4247	C / 5.5	-10.45	2.64	7.68 /30	16.60 /66	4.10 /47	0.00	1.35
SC	Legg Mason Prt Sm Cap Gwth Opp B	SMOBX	C	(866) 890-4247	C / 5.1	-10.63	2.28	6.85 /25	15.74 /62	3.31 /40	0.00	2.10
SC	Legg Mason Prt Sm Cap Gwth Opp C	SGOLX	C	(866) 890-4247	C+ / 5.7	-10.63	2.23	6.81 /25	15.74 /62	3.32 /40	0.00	2.10
SC	Legg Mason Prt Sm Cap Gwth Opp Y	SGOYX	C+	(866) 890-4247	C+ / 6.4	-10.40	2.77	7.93 /32	16.92 /68	--	0.00	1.10
SC	Legg Mason Prt Sm Cp Core A	SBDSX	E	(866) 890-4247	D / 1.6	-4.96	7.34	-4.01 / 0	9.97 /27	3.69 /43	0.00	1.27
SC	Legg Mason Prt Sm Cp Core B	SBDBX	E-	(866) 890-4247	D- / 1.0	-5.11	6.89	-6.27 / 0	8.54 /18	2.70 /34	0.00	2.09
SC	Legg Mason Prt Sm Cp Core C	SBDLX	E	(866) 890-4247	D- / 1.5	-5.11	6.97	-6.20 / 0	8.56 /18	2.71 /34	0.00	2.09
SC	Legg Mason Prt Sm Cp Core Y		C	(866) 890-4247	B- / 7.0	-4.90	7.56	13.79 /68	16.72 /67	7.66 /70	0.00	0.82
SC	Legg Mason Prt Small Cap Growth 1	SBCFX	E	(866) 890-4247	D / 2.1	-10.34	-0.09	9.27 /42	11.08 /36	-1.09 /11	0.00	1.31
SC	Legg Mason Prt Small Cap Growth A	SBSGX	E	(866) 890-4247	D+ / 2.4	-10.47	-0.28	9.04 /40	11.00 /35	-1.05 /12	0.00	1.52
SC	Legg Mason Prt Small Cap Growth B	SBYBX	E	(866) 890-4247	D / 2.0	-10.70	-0.67	8.15 /34	10.17 /28	-1.78 / 9	0.00	2.25
SC	Legg Mason Prt Small Cap Growth C	SBSLX	E+	(866) 890-4247	D+ / 2.8	-10.57	-0.47	8.48 /37	10.38 /30	-1.49 /10	0.00	2.00
SC	Legg Mason Prt Small Cap Value A	SBVAX	B-	(866) 890-4247	C+ / 6.8	-2.54	5.58	12.17 /60	18.14 /73	12.15 /87	0.00	1.13
SC	Legg Mason Prt Small Cap Value B	SBVBX	B-	(866) 890-4247	C+ / 6.5	-2.74	5.21	11.37 /56	17.24 /69	11.30 /85	0.00	1.88
SC	Legg Mason Prt Small Cap Value C	SBVLX	B-	(866) 890-4247	C+ / 6.9	-2.75	5.13	11.19 /55	17.16 /69	11.26 /85	0.00	1.98
SC	Legg Mason Prt Small Cap Value Y	SMCYX	A-	(866) 890-4247	B- / 7.5	-2.48	5.76	12.60 /63	18.54 /75	--	0.00	0.77
AA	Legg Mason Prt Social Awareness A	SSIAX	D-	(866) 890-4247	E / 0.5	-2.69	-0.39	2.63 / 6	6.11 / 7	1.04 /20	1.29	1.18
AA	Legg Mason Prt Social Awareness B	SESIX	D-	(866) 890-4247	E / 0.4	-2.92	-0.80	1.75 / 4	5.23 / 4	0.21 /16	0.45	1.99
AA	Legg Mason Prt Social Awareness C	SESLX	D-	(866) 890-4247	E+ / 0.6	-2.82	-0.60	1.96 / 4	5.38 / 5	0.33 /17	0.66	1.92
TC	Legg Mason Prt Technology A	SBTAX	E-	(866) 890-4247	E / 0.3	-7.67	-2.70	-0.25 / 2	6.14 / 7	-6.52 / 1	0.00	1.50
TC	Legg Mason Prt Technology B	SBTBX	E-	(866) 890-4247	E- / 0.2	-8.03	-3.08	-1.05 / 1	5.38 / 5	-7.23 / 1	0.00	2.25
TC	Legg Mason Prt Technology C	SBQLX	E-	(866) 890-4247	E / 0.4	-8.03	-3.08	-1.05 / 1	5.38 / 5	-7.23 / 1	0.00	2.25
★ MC	Legg Mason Special Invest Prim	LMASX	E+	(800) 822-5544	C- / 4.2	-9.43	-2.95	6.29 /22	12.86 /48	9.81 /80	0.00	1.76
SC	Legg Mason US Sm-Cap Value Tr	LMSVX	C+	(800) 822-5544	C+ / 6.4	-2.78	4.50	4.69 /14	16.51 /66	10.93 /84	0.00	2.00
GR	Legg Mason Value Trust Fin-Intrm	LMVFX	D+	(800) 822-5544	D+ / 2.6	-5.50	-4.74	3.38 / 8	10.40 /30	3.28 /39	0.00	1.02
GR	Legg Mason Value Trust Navig	LMNVX	D-	(800) 822-5544	D+ / 2.9	-5.43	-4.59	3.72 /10	10.76 /33	3.62 /42	0.00	0.69
★ GR	Legg Mason Value Trust Prim	LMVTX	D	(800) 822-5544	D / 2.2	-5.67	-5.07	2.69 / 6	9.67 /25	2.58 /33	0.00	1.68
BA	Leonetti Balanced Fund	LEONX	D	(866) 811-0215	E / 0.4	-4.95	-1.41	3.36 / 8	4.20 / 3	0.42 /17	0.34	2.31
GI	● Leuthold Core Investment Fund	LCORX	A-	(888) 200-0409	B- / 7.5	0.60	4.49	17.40 /78	17.51 /70	9.99 /80	1.83	1.35
AG	Leuthold Grizzly Short Fund	GRZZX	E-	(888) 200-0409	E- / 0.0	1.72	-1.50	-10.38 / 0	-12.67 / 0	-6.49 / 1	3.84	2.91
GR	● Leuthold Select Industries Fund	LSLTX	C+	(888) 200-0409	B+ / 8.6	-2.82	3.56	24.00 /87	23.08 /88	7.10 /67	0.19	1.30
AA	Lifetime Achievement Fund	LFTAX	B	(414) 299-2120	B- / 7.1	-2.97	9.04	23.52 /87	16.16 /64	8.15 /72	0.00	1.59
GR	Lighthouse Opportunity Fund	LGFTX	C+	(866) 811-0215	C+ / 6.2	-4.46	5.40	11.56 /57	15.65 /62	6.99 /67	2.68	2.00
GR	LKCM Aquinas Growth Fund	AQEGX	E+	(800) 688-5526	E+ / 0.7	-6.68	-5.96	-1.74 / 1	7.30 /12	-1.08 /12	0.00	1.47
SC	LKCM Aquinas Small-Cap Fund	AQBLX	E+	(800) 688-5526	C- / 3.2	-8.22	7.39	13.64 /67	9.97 /27	-0.16 /15	0.00	1.50
IN	LKCM Aquinas Value Fund	AQEIX	C+	(800) 688-5526	C+ / 5.6	-0.78	4.17	9.25 /42	14.11 /54	3.87 /45	0.00	1.50
BA	LKCM Balanced Fd	LKBAX	C	(800) 688-5526	D / 2.1	-0.51	2.06	5.76 /19	8.23 /16	3.81 /44	1.21	0.80
GR	LKCM Equity Fd	LKEQX	C-	(800) 688-5526	D+ / 2.7	-1.81	1.73	6.37 /22	9.39 /23	2.96 /36	0.90	0.80
SC	LKCM Small Cap Equity Adv	LKSAX	A-	(800) 688-5526	B+ / 8.5	-6.80	7.97	19.56 /81	22.27 /86	--	0.00	1.21
SC	LKCM Small Cap Equity Inst	LKSCX	C+	(800) 688-5526	B+ / 8.6	-6.74	8.10	19.83 /82	22.58 /86	13.25 /89	0.00	0.96
GR	● Longleaf Partners Fund	LLPFX	B-	(800) 445-9469	C / 5.4	-1.26	8.98	14.16 /69	12.20 /44	8.27 /73	0.83	0.91
FO	● Longleaf Partners Intl Fd	LLINX	A-	(800) 445-9469	B- / 7.0	-1.69	3.69	15.34 /73	16.57 /66	7.80 /71	0.00	1.64

● Denotes fund is closed to new investors
★ Denotes fund is included in Section II

RISK			NET ASSETS		ASSET				Portfolio Turnover Ratio	BULL / BEAR		FUND MANAGER		MINIMUMS		LOADS	
Risk Rating/Pts	3 Year Standard Deviation	Beta	NAV As of 6/30/06	Total $(Mil)	Cash %	Stocks %	Bonds %	Other %		Last Bull Market Return	Last Bear Market Return	Manager Quality Pct	Manager Tenure (Years)	Initial Purch. $	Additional Purch. $	Front End Load	Back End Load
B- /7.6	9.3	1.11	8.66	69	0	99	0	1	16.0	58.3	-11.4	26	N/A	1,000	50	0.0	5.0
C+ /5.7	9.1	1.10	8.68	180	0	99	0	1	16.0	58.4	-11.4	27	N/A	1,000	50	0.0	1.0
C /4.8	9.6	0.72	9.66	44	3	96	0	1	20.0	80.9	-11.6	19	N/A	1,000	50	5.0	1.0
B- /7.6	9.5	0.72	9.23	26	3	96	0	1	20.0	75.4	-11.8	14	N/A	1,000	50	0.0	5.0
C+ /5.6	9.5	0.72	9.26	54	3	96	0	1	20.0	75.7	-11.8	14	N/A	1,000	50	0.0	1.0
B /8.0	8.3	1.03	9.22	39	3	96	0	1	13.0	53.6	-11.9	26	N/A	1,000	50	5.0	1.0
B /8.0	8.3	1.03	8.92	53	3	96	0	1	13.0	49.7	-11.9	21	N/A	1,000	50	0.0	5.0
C+ /5.8	8.3	1.03	8.92	41	3	96	0	1	13.0	49.8	-11.9	21	N/A	1,000	50	0.0	1.0
B /8.8	7.7	1.00	12.95	442	0	100	0	0	8.0	61.5	-9.8	48	N/A	1,000	50	0.0	1.0
B /8.8	7.7	1.00	13.02	38	0	100	0	0	8.0	63.1	-9.8	52	N/A	1,000	50	0.0	0.0
C /4.7	15.6	1.01	20.22	30	6	93	0	1	125.0	107.6	-11.3	34	2	1,000	50	5.0	1.0
C+ /6.4	15.6	1.01	18.83	3	6	93	0	1	125.0	102.8	-11.6	28	2	1,000	50	0.0	5.0
C+ /6.4	15.6	1.01	19.25	35	6	93	0	1	125.0	102.9	-11.5	29	2	1,000	50	0.0	1.0
C+ /6.4	15.5	1.01	20.42	4	6	93	0	1	125.0	N/A	N/A	37	2	15,000,000	50	0.0	0.0
C /4.3	18.2	1.04	14.93	39	1	98	0	1	86.0	71.8	-10.0	4	N/A	1,000	50	5.0	1.0
C- /3.8	18.7	1.04	13.53	13	1	98	0	1	86.0	65.1	-10.2	2	N/A	1,000	50	0.0	5.0
C- /3.8	18.8	1.04	13.54	18	1	98	0	1	86.0	65.0	-10.1	2	N/A	1,000	50	0.0	1.0
C /4.6	14.4	0.98	15.53	158	1	98	0	1	86.0	105.7	-9.9	39	N/A	15,000,000	50	0.0	0.0
C- /4.1	16.5	1.07	10.84	6	1	98	0	1	41.0	81.5	-11.7	5	6	1,000	50	8.5	0.0
C- /4.0	16.5	1.08	10.86	140	1	98	0	1	41.0	81.6	-11.8	5	7	1,000	50	5.0	1.0
C- /4.0	16.5	1.08	10.35	90	1	98	0	1	41.0	77.5	-11.9	3	7	1,000	50	0.0	5.0
C- /4.0	16.5	1.08	10.49	14	1	98	0	1	41.0	78.7	-11.8	4	7	1,000	50	0.0	1.0
B- /7.9	10.7	0.71	24.21	269	8	91	0	1	13.0	103.8	-10.1	90	8	1,000	50	5.0	1.0
B- /7.8	10.8	0.71	23.42	141	8	91	0	1	13.0	98.8	-10.2	85	8	1,000	50	0.0	5.0
B- /7.8	10.7	0.71	23.37	183	8	91	0	1	13.0	98.4	-10.2	85	8	1,000	50	0.0	1.0
B- /7.9	10.7	0.71	24.43	184	8	91	0	1	13.0	N/A	N/A	91	8	15,000,000	50	0.0	0.0
B- /7.2	6.3	1.24	19.96	206	2	71	25	2	42.0	39.1	-6.0	29	11	1,000	50	5.0	1.0
B- /7.6	6.3	1.24	20.06	66	2	71	25	2	42.0	35.5	-6.2	23	10	1,000	50	0.0	5.0
B- /7.6	6.3	1.24	20.13	15	2	71	25	2	42.0	35.9	-6.1	24	11	1,000	50	0.0	1.0
C- /3.9	15.8	1.75	3.97	19	0	98	0	2	16.0	52.7	-13.5	1	N/A	1,000	50	5.0	1.0
C- /3.8	15.8	1.75	3.78	26	0	98	0	2	16.0	49.6	-13.8	1	N/A	1,000	50	0.0	5.0
C- /3.8	15.9	1.76	3.78	14	0	98	0	2	16.0	49.6	-13.8	1	N/A	1,000	50	0.0	1.0
D+ /2.4	14.8	1.23	39.56	3,388	0	99	0	1	37.9	107.7	-10.1	5	N/A	1,000	100	0.0	0.0
C+ /6.4	11.3	0.74	13.71	222	2	97	0	1	30.9	102.5	-9.3	77	8	1,000	100	0.0	0.0
B- /7.3	11.9	1.38	70.94	2,086	0	99	0	1	12.7	76.4	-9.9	20	N/A	1,000,000	0	0.0	0.0
C /5.1	11.9	1.39	72.16	5,695	0	99	0	1	12.7	78.3	-9.9	22	N/A	1,000,000	0	0.0	0.0
C+ /6.4	11.9	1.39	65.22	11,192	0	99	0	1	12.7	72.8	-10.1	16	N/A	1,000	100	0.0	0.0
B /8.3	6.6	1.23	14.01	11	4	69	25	2	90.6	28.8	-5.4	17	11	100	25	0.0	0.0
B- /7.8	9.0	0.89	17.79	1,595	42	42	14	2	163.9	92.4	-2.1	97	11	10,000	100	0.0	0.0
D /2.2	11.4	-1.32	6.08	110	100	0	0	0	N/A	-47.1	10.3	14	6	10,000	100	0.0	0.0
C /4.5	13.3	1.35	17.48	88	1	98	0	1	156.1	133.6	-6.4	98	6	10,000	100	0.0	0.0
B- /7.3	12.4	2.06	21.22	117	N/A	N/A	0	N/A	27.5	98.8	-10.1	80	6	10,000	500	2.5	0.0
C+ /6.8	11.6	1.29	17.37	11	22	77	0	1	44.0	110.1	-12.2	72	3	2,000	100	0.0	2.0
C+ /6.2	10.0	1.09	14.68	64	2	97	0	1	114.0	50.5	-8.2	17	12	5,000	500	0.0	1.0
C- /3.7	17.2	1.09	6.25	8	2	97	0	1	148.0	70.4	-8.5	3	12	5,000	500	0.0	1.0
B- /7.7	8.9	1.10	12.75	42	N/A	100	0	N/A	71.0	74.0	-10.5	74	12	5,000	500	0.0	1.0
B+ /9.8	4.8	0.94	12.55	9	1	71	27	1	24.0	41.0	-4.8	67	9	10,000	1,000	0.0	1.0
B /8.5	7.7	0.98	13.53	48	5	94	0	1	21.0	51.8	-9.2	37	12	10,000	1,000	0.0	1.0
C+ /6.8	13.9	0.90	22.62	12	4	95	0	1	57.0	N/A	N/A	92	12	10,000	1,000	0.0	1.0
C- /4.2	13.8	0.90	22.83	525	4	95	0	1	57.0	133.8	-8.9	93	12	10,000	1,000	0.0	1.0
B /8.2	8.4	0.88	33.75	10	0	96	2	2	6.6	71.4	-7.5	76	19	10,000	0	0.0	0.0
B /8.4	8.8	0.58	18.00	3	12	88	0	0	16.9	108.6	-17.0	75	8	10,000	0	0.0	0.0

Data as of June 30, 2006

Fund Type	Fund Name	Ticker Symbol	Overall Weiss Investment Rating	Phone	Perfor-mance Rating/Pts	3 Mo	6 Mo	1Yr / Pct	3Yr / Pct	5Yr / Pct	Dividend Yield	Expense Ratio
SC	● Longleaf Partners Small-Cap Fund	LLSCX	C	(800) 445-9469	C+ / 6.6	-2.17	3.26	9.37 /42	16.24 /64	11.84 /86	1.72	0.93
AG	Loomis Sayles Aggressive Gr Inst	LSAIX	C-	(800) 633-3330	B / 7.9	-6.00	5.81	22.25 /85	20.21 /80	-0.10 /15	0.00	1.00
AG	Loomis Sayles Aggressive Gr Ret	LAGRX	C-	(800) 633-3330	B / 7.8	-6.03	5.67	21.98 /84	19.91 /79	-0.36 /14	0.00	1.25
GI	Loomis Sayles Core Value Inst	LSGIX	A+	(800) 633-3330	B- / 7.3	0.46	7.71	17.92 /79	16.98 /68	6.92 /66	1.32	0.85
GL	Loomis Sayles Global Markets Y	LSWWX	C	(800) 225-5478	C / 4.7	-4.81	-1.15	9.11 /41	13.47 /51	10.11 /81	1.36	1.00
SC	Loomis Sayles Small Cap Gr Inst	LSSIX	D+	(800) 633-3330	C+ / 6.8	-7.57	8.05	15.71 /74	16.55 /66	-3.97 / 4	0.00	1.00
SC	Loomis Sayles Small Cap Gr Ret	LCGRX	D+	(800) 633-3330	C+ / 6.7	-7.52	7.96	15.46 /73	16.31 /65	-4.20 / 3	0.00	1.25
SC	Loomis Sayles Small Cap Val Inst	LSSCX	B	(800) 633-3330	B / 7.9	-2.53	10.01	16.61 /76	19.52 /78	11.69 /86	0.48	0.90
SC	Loomis Sayles Small Cap Val Ret	LSCRX	B	(800) 633-3330	B / 7.8	-2.59	9.83	16.29 /75	19.20 /77	11.40 /85	0.28	1.15
★ GI	Lord Abbett Affiliated Fund A	LAFFX	C	(800) 201-6984	C / 4.6	-0.54	5.31	12.27 /61	12.78 /47	4.69 /52	1.20	0.82
GI	Lord Abbett Affiliated Fund B	LAFBX	C	(800) 201-6984	C- / 4.2	-0.70	4.95	11.58 /57	12.04 /43	4.01 /46	0.66	1.47
GI	Lord Abbett Affiliated Fund C	LAFCX	C+	(800) 201-6984	C / 4.9	-0.64	5.04	11.61 /57	12.07 /43	4.01 /46	0.67	1.47
GI	Lord Abbett Affiliated Fund P	LAFPX	C+	(800) 201-6984	C / 5.4	-0.56	5.27	12.18 /61	12.65 /47	4.59 /51	1.18	0.92
GI	Lord Abbett Affiliated Fund Y	LAFYX	C+	(800) 201-6984	C+ / 5.7	-0.38	5.58	12.72 /63	13.19 /50	5.06 /55	1.59	0.48
★ GI	Lord Abbett All Value A	LDFVX	B-	(800) 201-6984	C+ / 6.0	-0.24	7.38	15.77 /74	15.50 /61	7.84 /71	0.40	1.17
GI	Lord Abbett All Value B	GILBX	B-	(800) 201-6984	C+ / 5.7	-0.41	7.00	14.99 /72	14.74 /58	7.16 /68	0.00	1.81
GI	Lord Abbett All Value C	GILAX	B	(800) 201-6984	C+ / 6.2	-0.41	7.02	15.04 /72	14.76 /58	7.19 /68	0.00	1.81
GI	Lord Abbett All Value P	LAVPX	B	(800) 201-6984	C+ / 6.6	-0.24	7.35	15.62 /74	15.39 /61	--	0.44	1.26
GI	Lord Abbett All Value Y	LAVYX	B	(800) 201-6984	C+ / 6.9	-0.08	7.61	16.26 /75	15.92 /63	--	0.71	0.81
IN	Lord Abbett America's Value A	LAMAX	C+	(800) 201-6984	C- / 4.1	0.64	2.97	5.82 /19	13.00 /49	--	2.55	1.33
IN	Lord Abbett America's Value B	LAMBX	C	(800) 201-6984	C- / 3.7	0.48	2.66	5.09 /16	12.26 /44	--	2.09	1.98
IN	Lord Abbett America's Value C	LAMCX	C+	(800) 201-6984	C / 4.4	0.47	2.65	5.16 /16	12.31 /44	--	2.08	1.98
IN	Lord Abbett America's Value P	LAMPX	B-	(800) 201-6984	C / 5.0	0.62	2.93	5.72 /19	12.95 /49	--	2.62	1.43
IN	Lord Abbett America's Value Y	LAMYX	B-	(800) 201-6984	C / 5.3	0.72	3.14	6.16 /21	13.43 /51	--	3.04	0.99
CV	Lord Abbett Convertible Fund A	LACFX	C-	(800) 201-6984	D / 1.7	-2.19	3.68	8.94 /40	8.53 /18	--	1.87	1.28
CV	Lord Abbett Convertible Fund B	LBCFX	C-	(800) 201-6984	D- / 1.3	-2.35	3.37	8.27 /35	7.81 /14	--	1.34	1.93
CV	Lord Abbett Convertible Fund C	LACCX	C-	(800) 201-6984	D / 1.9	-2.35	3.37	8.18 /34	7.80 /14	--	1.34	1.93
CV	Lord Abbett Convertible Fund P	LCFPX	C	(800) 201-6984	D+ / 2.4	-2.19	3.64	8.88 /39	8.49 /18	--	1.83	1.38
CV	Lord Abbett Convertible Fund Y	LCFYX	C	(800) 201-6984	D+ / 2.7	-2.08	3.86	9.31 /42	8.97 /21	--	2.31	0.93
SC	Lord Abbett Developing Growth A	LAGWX	D+	(800) 201-6984	C+ / 6.1	-6.23	8.76	22.21 /85	15.46 /61	4.33 /49	0.00	1.19
SC	Lord Abbett Developing Growth B	LADBX	D+	(800) 201-6984	C+ / 5.8	-6.37	8.41	21.37 /83	14.71 /57	3.69 /43	0.00	1.84
SC	Lord Abbett Developing Growth C	LADCX	C-	(800) 201-6984	C+ / 6.4	-6.35	8.44	21.43 /84	14.73 /57	3.75 /43	0.00	1.84
SC	Lord Abbett Developing Growth P	LADPX	C-	(800) 201-6984	C+ / 6.7	-6.23	8.72	22.06 /84	15.36 /60	4.27 /49	0.00	1.29
SC	Lord Abbett Developing Growth Y	LADYX	C-	(800) 201-6984	B- / 7.0	-6.14	8.95	22.66 /85	15.86 /63	4.73 /52	0.00	0.84
GL	Lord Abbett Global-Equity A	LAGEX	C-	(800) 201-6984	C- / 4.2	-2.37	4.58	15.63 /74	12.30 /44	4.20 /48	0.35	1.60
GL	Lord Abbett Global-Equity B	LAGBX	C-	(800) 201-6984	C- / 3.8	-2.49	4.21	14.91 /71	11.60 /40	3.51 /41	0.00	2.25
GL	Lord Abbett Global-Equity C	LAGCX	C	(800) 201-6984	C / 4.5	-2.49	4.20	14.99 /72	11.62 /40	3.50 /41	0.00	2.25
MC	Lord Abbett Growth Opportunities A	LMGAX	E+	(800) 201-6984	D+ / 2.6	-5.91	2.34	8.04 /33	10.83 /34	1.82 /26	0.00	1.55
MC	Lord Abbett Growth Opportunities B	LMGBX	E+	(800) 201-6984	D+ / 2.3	-6.00	2.04	7.37 /28	10.15 /28	1.20 /22	0.00	2.20
MC	Lord Abbett Growth Opportunities C	LMGCX	E+	(800) 201-6984	C- / 3.0	-6.05	1.98	7.32 /28	10.15 /28	1.19 /21	0.00	2.20
MC	Lord Abbett Growth Opportunities P	LGOPX	D-	(800) 201-6984	C- / 3.5	-5.95	2.24	7.93 /32	10.73 /33	1.77 /25	0.00	1.65
MC	Lord Abbett Growth Opportunities Y	LMGYX	D-	(800) 201-6984	C- / 3.9	-5.78	2.53	8.44 /36	11.23 /37	2.15 /28	0.00	1.20
FO	Lord Abbett Intl Core Equity A	LICAX	U	(800) 201-6984	U /	-2.50	6.53	24.10 /87	--	--	0.35	1.65
FO	Lord Abbett Intl Core Equity B	LICBX	U	(800) 201-6984	U /	-2.67	6.13	23.28 /86	--	--	0.14	2.30
FO	Lord Abbett Intl Core Equity C	LICCX	U	(800) 201-6984	U /	-2.67	6.13	23.29 /86	--	--	0.14	2.30
FO	Lord Abbett Intl Core Equity Y	LICYX	U	(800) 201-6984	U /	-2.49	6.58	24.48 /88	--	--	0.52	1.30
BA	Lord Abbett Invt Tr-Balanced A	LABFX	C-	(800) 201-6984	D / 2.1	-0.68	3.08	7.26 /28	9.34 /23	5.08 /55	3.19	0.93
BA	Lord Abbett Invt Tr-Balanced B	LABBX	C-	(800) 201-6984	D / 1.8	-0.83	2.76	6.60 /24	8.65 /19	4.43 /50	2.77	1.58
BA	Lord Abbett Invt Tr-Balanced C	BFLAX	C	(800) 201-6984	D+ / 2.4	-0.83	2.77	6.53 /23	8.61 /19	4.46 /50	2.79	1.58
BA	Lord Abbett Invt Tr-Balanced P	LABPX	C	(800) 201-6984	C- / 3.0	-0.70	3.06	7.12 /27	9.21 /22	--	3.33	1.03
GR	Lord Abbett Large Cap Core A	LRLCX	C-	(800) 201-6984	D+ / 2.9	-2.04	2.43	7.69 /30	10.94 /35	3.01 /37	0.33	1.30
GR	Lord Abbett Large Cap Core B	LARBX	D+	(800) 201-6984	D+ / 2.5	-2.20	2.11	7.00 /26	10.23 /29	2.36 /31	0.00	1.95

● Denotes fund is closed to new investors
★ Denotes fund is included in Section II

RISK	3 Year		NET ASSETS		ASSET				Portfolio	BULL / BEAR		FUND MANAGER		MINIMUMS		LOADS	
Risk Rating/Pts	Standard Deviation	Beta	NAV As of 6/30/06	Total $(Mil)	Cash %	Stocks %	Bonds %	Other %	Turnover Ratio	Last Bull Market Return	Last Bear Market Return	Manager Quality Pct	Manager Tenure (Years)	Initial Purch. $	Additional Purch. $	Front End Load	Back End Load
C+ / 5.9	9.1	0.53	27.90	4	7	82	10	1	17.3	111.0	-11.6	93	15	10,000	0	0.0	0.0
C- / 3.2	16.4	1.58	21.32	18	3	96	0	1	95.0	122.2	-13.7	84	7	100,000	50	0.0	0.0
C- / 3.2	16.4	1.58	20.87	29	3	96	0	1	95.0	120.5	-13.8	83	7	2,500	50	0.0	0.0
B / 8.8	7.3	0.89	19.69	47	6	93	0	1	19.0	92.4	-9.8	96	6	100,000	50	0.0	0.0
B- / 7.6	8.2	0.69	12.07	65	4	66	28	2	41.0	72.6	2.4	25	10	1,000,000	10,000	0.0	2.0
C- / 3.2	17.4	1.09	12.08	21	2	97	0	1	53.0	112.4	-14.0	25	1	100,000	50	0.0	2.0
C- / 3.1	17.4	1.09	11.80	3	2	97	0	1	53.0	110.4	-13.9	23	1	2,500	50	0.0	2.0
C+ / 6.5	11.6	0.78	27.70	447	5	94	0	1	33.0	107.1	-6.5	90	6	100,000	50	0.0	2.0
C+ / 6.5	11.5	0.78	27.49	296	5	94	0	1	33.0	105.5	-6.6	89	6	2,500	50	0.0	2.0
B- / 7.6	8.6	1.06	14.72	15,078	2	98	0	0	49.4	74.4	-11.2	67	10	250	50	5.8	0.0
B- / 7.6	8.6	1.06	14.76	1,306	2	98	0	0	49.4	70.8	-11.3	59	10	250	50	0.0	5.0
B- / 7.6	8.6	1.06	14.74	1,554	2	98	0	0	49.4	70.9	-11.4	59	10	250	50	0.0	1.0
B- / 7.6	8.6	1.06	14.70	416	2	98	0	0	49.4	73.9	-11.3	66	9	1,000	50	0.0	0.0
B- / 7.6	8.6	1.06	14.76	1,054	2	98	0	0	49.4	76.3	-11.1	70	8	1,000,000	0	0.0	0.0
B / 8.0	9.4	1.16	12.66	2,068	3	96	0	1	52.2	83.5	-8.1	81	10	1,000	50	5.8	0.0
B / 8.0	9.3	1.16	12.23	269	3	96	0	1	52.2	79.8	-8.3	76	9	1,000	50	0.0	5.0
B / 8.0	9.4	1.16	12.19	592	3	96	0	1	52.2	79.8	-8.2	75	12	1,000	50	0.0	1.0
B / 8.0	9.3	1.16	12.56	20	3	96	0	1	52.2	82.9	-8.0	80	5	1,000	50	0.0	0.0
B / 8.2	9.4	1.16	12.72	4	3	96	0	1	52.2	N/A	N/A	83	3	1,000,000	0	0.0	0.0
B / 8.4	6.9	0.83	12.41	1,004	1	76	21	2	31.7	63.1	-8.2	85	5	1,000	50	5.8	0.0
B / 8.7	7.0	0.83	12.33	58	1	76	21	2	31.7	60.0	-8.3	80	5	1,000	50	0.0	5.0
B / 8.7	6.9	0.83	12.35	73	1	76	21	2	31.7	59.8	-8.4	80	5	1,000	50	0.0	1.0
B / 8.7	7.0	0.83	12.44	2	1	76	21	2	31.7	62.7	-8.2	84	N/A	0	50	0.0	0.0
B / 8.7	7.0	0.83	12.46	7	1	76	21	2	31.7	65.1	-8.2	87	5	1,000,000	0	0.0	0.0
B+ / 9.1	6.9	1.04	11.95	98	2	2	0	96	78.3	N/A	N/A	67	3	1,000	50	4.8	0.0
B+ / 9.1	7.0	1.04	11.92	18	2	2	0	96	78.3	N/A	N/A	59	3	1,000	50	0.0	5.0
B+ / 9.1	7.0	1.05	11.91	70	2	2	0	96	78.3	N/A	N/A	59	3	1,000	50	0.0	1.0
B+ / 9.1	7.0	1.05	11.98	N/A	2	2	0	96	78.3	N/A	N/A	66	3	1,000	50	0.0	0.0
B+ / 9.1	6.9	1.04	11.98	86	2	2	0	96	78.3	N/A	N/A	71	3	1,000,000	0	0.0	0.0
C- / 4.2	16.6	1.08	19.12	498	2	97	0	1	123.8	107.5	-12.0	19	N/A	1,000	50	5.8	0.0
C- / 4.1	16.6	1.08	17.92	82	2	97	0	1	123.8	103.5	-12.2	15	N/A	1,000	50	0.0	5.0
C- / 4.1	16.6	1.08	17.99	60	2	97	0	1	123.8	103.4	-12.2	15	N/A	1,000	50	0.0	1.0
C- / 4.2	16.6	1.08	18.95	65	2	97	0	1	123.8	107.0	-12.1	19	N/A	1,000	50	0.0	0.0
C- / 4.2	16.6	1.08	19.73	107	2	97	0	1	123.8	109.9	-11.9	22	N/A	1,000,000	0	0.0	0.0
B- / 7.0	8.8	0.82	12.79	74	0	99	0	1	97.6	73.5	-5.1	7	5	1,000	50	5.8	0.0
B- / 7.0	8.7	0.82	12.14	10	0	99	0	1	97.6	70.0	-5.4	6	5	1,000	50	0.0	5.0
B- / 7.0	8.7	0.82	12.16	10	0	99	0	1	97.6	70.1	-5.1	6	10	1,000	50	0.0	1.0
C- / 4.2	12.4	1.09	21.02	642	7	92	0	1	97.4	73.5	-7.2	5	N/A	1,000	50	5.8	0.0
C- / 4.1	12.4	1.08	20.05	104	7	92	0	1	97.4	70.2	-7.4	4	N/A	1,000	50	0.0	5.0
C- / 4.1	12.4	1.09	20.04	82	7	92	0	1	97.4	70.2	-7.4	4	N/A	1,000	50	0.0	1.0
C- / 4.2	12.4	1.08	21.03	16	7	92	0	1	97.4	73.1	-7.3	5	N/A	1,000	50	0.0	0.0
C- / 4.2	12.4	1.09	21.50	16	7	92	0	1	97.4	75.4	-7.1	6	N/A	1,000,000	0	0.0	0.0
U /	N/A	N/A	14.02	547	4	95	0	1	100.9	N/A	N/A	N/A	N/A	1,000	50	5.8	0.0
U /	N/A	N/A	13.84	43	4	95	0	1	100.9	N/A	N/A	N/A	N/A	1,000	50	0.0	5.0
U /	N/A	N/A	13.84	120	4	95	0	1	100.9	N/A	N/A	N/A	N/A	1,000	50	0.0	1.0
U /	N/A	N/A	14.09	55	4	95	0	1	100.9	N/A	N/A	N/A	N/A	1,000,000	0	0.0	0.0
B / 8.6	5.7	1.13	11.38	928	1	57	40	2	N/A	51.4	-5.7	68	N/A	1,000	50	5.8	0.0
B+ / 9.3	5.7	1.14	11.37	109	1	57	40	2	N/A	48.4	-5.8	60	N/A	1,000	50	0.0	5.0
B+ / 9.3	5.7	1.14	11.35	135	1	57	40	2	N/A	48.4	-5.9	59	N/A	1,000	50	0.0	1.0
B+ / 9.3	5.7	1.14	11.35	3	1	57	40	2	N/A	50.8	N/A	66	N/A	1,000	50	0.0	0.0
B- / 7.5	8.4	1.05	28.28	589	4	95	0	1	44.9	67.4	-11.5	48	N/A	1,000	50	5.8	0.0
B- / 7.7	8.4	1.04	27.15	76	4	95	0	1	44.9	64.0	-11.6	41	N/A	1,000	50	0.0	5.0

						PERFORMANCE						
	99 Pct = Best 0 Pct = Worst		Overall Weiss Investment Rating			Perfor- mance Rating/Pts	Total Return % through 6/30/06			Annualized		Incl. in Returns	
											Dividend Yield	Expense Ratio
Fund Type	Fund Name	Ticker Symbol		Phone			3 Mo	6 Mo	1Yr / Pct	3Yr / Pct	5Yr / Pct		
GR	Lord Abbett Large Cap Core C	LLRCX	C-	(800) 201-6984		C- / 3.2	-2.22	2.10	7.01 /26	10.23 /29	2.40 /31	0.00	1.95
GR	Lord Abbett Large Cap Core P	LRLPX	C	(800) 201-6984		C- / 3.8	-2.08	2.39	7.59 /30	10.83 /34	2.99 /37	0.37	1.40
GR	Lord Abbett Large Cap Core Y	LARYX	C	(800) 201-6984		C- / 4.2	-1.94	2.61	8.08 /33	11.34 /38	3.36 /40	0.62	0.95
GR	Lord Abbett Large Cap Value A	LALAX	C+	(800) 201-6984		C- / 4.1	-0.46	5.06	11.38 /56	12.02 /43	--	0.82	0.95
GR	Lord Abbett Large Cap Value B	LLCBX	C	(800) 201-6984		C- / 3.6	-0.62	4.79	10.62 /51	11.24 /37	--	0.32	1.60
GR	Lord Abbett Large Cap Value C	LLCCX	C+	(800) 201-6984		C / 4.4	-0.62	4.79	10.63 /51	11.27 /38	--	0.41	1.60
GR	Lord Abbett Large Cap Value P	LALPX	C+	(800) 201-6984		C / 4.9	-0.46	5.05	11.22 /55	11.91 /42	--	0.74	1.05
GR	Lord Abbett Large Cap Value Y	LLCYX	B-	(800) 201-6984		C / 5.2	-0.38	5.28	11.75 /58	12.42 /45	--	1.14	0.60
GR	Lord Abbett Lg Cap Growth A	LALCX	E	(800) 201-6984		E / 0.5	-6.21	-2.22	7.74 /31	7.07 /11	-4.42 / 3	0.00	1.50
GR	Lord Abbett Lg Cap Growth B	LALBX	E	(800) 201-6984		E / 0.4	-6.46	-2.69	6.96 /26	6.31 / 8	-5.02 / 2	0.00	2.15
GR	Lord Abbett Lg Cap Growth C	LACGX	E	(800) 201-6984		E+ / 0.6	-6.28	-2.50	6.96 /26	6.39 / 8	-5.02 / 2	0.00	2.15
GR	Lord Abbett Lg Cap Growth P	LLCPX	E	(800) 201-6984		D- / 1.0	-6.16	-2.20	7.90 /32	7.17 /11	-4.24 / 3	0.00	1.60
GR	Lord Abbett Lg Cap Growth Y	LALYX	E	(800) 201-6984		D- / 1.2	-6.03	-2.03	8.16 /34	7.55 /13	-4.35 / 3	0.00	1.15
★ MC	● Lord Abbett Mid-Cap Value A	LAVLX	C	(800) 201-6984		C+ / 5.7	-2.85	0.70	6.72 /25	16.67 /67	9.79 /80	0.43	1.02
MC	● Lord Abbett Mid-Cap Value B	LMCBX	C	(800) 201-6984		C / 5.4	-3.05	0.34	5.95 /20	15.90 /63	9.09 /77	0.04	1.72
MC	● Lord Abbett Mid-Cap Value C	LMCCX	C+	(800) 201-6984		C+ / 5.9	-3.06	0.34	5.92 /20	15.89 /63	9.08 /77	0.05	1.72
MC	● Lord Abbett Mid-Cap Value P	LMCPX	C+	(800) 201-6984		C+ / 6.4	-2.91	0.62	6.55 /24	16.57 /66	9.70 /79	0.41	1.17
MC	● Lord Abbett Mid-Cap Value Y	LMCYX	C+	(800) 201-6984		C+ / 6.6	-2.80	0.84	7.03 /26	17.06 /68	10.18 /81	0.78	0.72
GL	Lord Abbett Sec Tr-Alpha Series A	ALFAX	B	(800) 201-6984		B+ / 8.6	-3.24	10.58	27.77 /92	23.27 /88	9.78 /80	0.00	0.35
GL	Lord Abbett Sec Tr-Alpha Series B	ALFBX	B	(800) 201-6984		B+ / 8.5	-3.40	10.23	26.93 /91	22.49 /86	9.07 /77	0.00	1.00
GL	Lord Abbett Sec Tr-Alpha Series C	ALFCX	B	(800) 201-6984		B+ / 8.7	-3.40	10.28	26.99 /91	22.51 /86	9.10 /77	0.00	1.00
FO	Lord Abbett Sec Tr-Intl A	LAIEX	B	(800) 201-6984		A / 9.3	-2.93	9.64	33.33 /96	28.47 /94	9.84 /80	0.00	1.74
FO	Lord Abbett Sec Tr-Intl B	LINBX	B	(800) 201-6984		A / 9.3	-3.11	9.35	32.58 /96	27.65 /94	9.10 /77	0.00	2.39
FO	Lord Abbett Sec Tr-Intl C	LINCX	B	(800) 201-6984		A / 9.4	-3.05	9.31	32.54 /96	27.67 /94	9.22 /77	0.00	2.39
FO	Lord Abbett Sec Tr-Intl P	LINPX	B	(800) 201-6984		A / 9.5	-2.97	9.61	33.21 /96	28.57 /94	9.91 /80	0.00	1.84
FO	Lord Abbett Sec Tr-Intl Y	LINYX	B	(800) 201-6984		A / 9.5	-2.87	9.82	33.81 /96	28.93 /95	10.20 /81	0.00	1.38
SC	● Lord Abbett Small Cap Blend A	LSBAX	B-	(800) 201-6984		B- / 7.3	-8.62	1.01	9.41 /43	21.17 /83	12.89 /88	0.00	1.46
SC	● Lord Abbett Small Cap Blend B	LSBBX	B-	(800) 201-6984		B- / 7.2	-8.75	0.73	8.78 /39	20.43 /81	12.21 /87	0.00	2.11
SC	● Lord Abbett Small Cap Blend C	LSBCX	B-	(800) 201-6984		B- / 7.5	-8.76	0.67	8.72 /38	20.41 /81	12.19 /87	0.00	2.11
SC	● Lord Abbett Small Cap Blend P	LSBPX	B	(800) 201-6984		B / 7.8	-8.70	0.95	9.31 /42	21.07 /83	12.90 /88	0.00	1.56
SC	● Lord Abbett Small Cap Blend Y	LSBYX	B	(800) 201-6984		B / 8.0	-8.56	1.18	9.82 /46	21.61 /84	13.22 /89	0.00	1.11
★ SC	● Lord Abbett Small Cap Value A	LRSCX	B+	(800) 201-6984		A- / 9.1	-1.13	14.32	27.89 /93	25.30 /91	15.26 /92	0.00	1.30
SC	● Lord Abbett Small Cap Value B	LRSBX	B	(800) 201-6984		A- / 9.0	-1.29	13.97	27.05 /91	24.50 /90	14.53 /91	0.00	1.95
SC	● Lord Abbett Small Cap Value C	LSRCX	B	(800) 201-6984		A- / 9.2	-1.29	13.95	27.06 /91	24.50 /90	14.54 /91	0.00	1.95
SC	● Lord Abbett Small Cap Value P	LRSPX	B+	(800) 201-6984		A- / 9.2	-1.13	14.28	27.76 /92	25.19 /91	15.16 /92	0.00	1.40
SC	● Lord Abbett Small Cap Value Y	LRSYX	B+	(800) 201-6984		A / 9.3	-1.06	14.51	28.32 /93	25.74 /92	15.67 /93	0.00	0.96
MC	Lord Abbett Value Opportunities A	LVOAX	U	(800) 201-6984		U /	2.35	18.43	--	--	--	0.00	1.30
GL	Lord Abbett World Gr & Inc Strat A	LWSAX	U	(800) 201-6984		U /	-2.59	1.90	8.60 /38	--	--	1.20	1.73
GL	Lord Abbett World Gr & Inc Strat C	LWSCX	U	(800) 201-6984		U /	-2.77	1.50	7.89 /32	--	--	0.99	2.38
IN	Lotsoff Capital Mgmt Active Income	LCMAX	U	(877) 568-7633		U /	1.18	2.60	--	--	--	0.00	1.27
SC	Lotsoff Capital Mgmt Micro Cap	LCMMX	U	(877) 568-7633		U /	-7.08	5.99	15.06 /72	--	--	0.00	1.76
GI	Lou Holland Growth Fund	LHGFX	D	(800) 522-2711		D- / 1.2	-3.31	-2.45	1.68 / 4	7.09 /11	1.32 /22	0.00	1.35
AA	MA 100% Equity Portfolio		B-	(800) 522-7297		C / 5.2	-3.27	2.04	11.94 /59	12.86 /48	3.26 /39	0.00	0.30
AA	MA 70% Equity Portfolio		C+	(800) 522-7297		C- / 3.6	-2.32	1.58	8.83 /39	10.35 /30	4.39 /50	0.00	0.30
AA	MA College Portfolio		D+	(800) 522-7297		E / 0.4	-0.38	0.61	2.39 / 5	3.32 / 2	3.38 /40	0.00	0.30
AA	MA Conservative Portfolio		D+	(800) 522-7297		E- / 0.1	0.44	0.61	1.14 / 3	1.64 / 0	--	0.00	0.30
AA	MA Portfolio 2006		C-	(800) 522-7297		E+ / 0.9	-0.69	0.62	3.04 / 7	5.40 / 5	3.04 /37	0.00	0.30
AA	MA Portfolio 2009		C	(800) 522-7297		D- / 1.5	-1.02	0.64	4.12 /11	7.03 /10	3.14 /38	0.00	0.30
AA	MA Portfolio 2012		C	(800) 522-7297		D / 2.1	-1.42	0.97	5.57 /18	8.16 /16	3.06 /37	0.00	0.30
AA	MA Portfolio 2015		C	(800) 522-7297		C- / 3.1	-1.91	1.23	6.93 /26	9.77 /26	3.18 /39	0.00	0.30
AA	MA Portfolio 2018		C+	(800) 522-7297		C- / 3.4	-2.40	1.41	7.96 /32	10.26 /29	3.26 /39	0.00	0.30
AA	MA Portfolio 2021		C+	(800) 522-7297		C- / 3.9	-2.74	1.83	9.32 /42	10.89 /35	--	0.00	0.30

● Denotes fund is closed to new investors
★ Denotes fund is included in Section II

RISK			NET ASSETS		ASSET				BULL / BEAR		FUND MANAGER		MINIMUMS		LOADS	
Risk Rating/Pts	Standard Deviation	Beta	NAV As of 6/30/06	Total $(Mil)	Cash %	Stocks %	Bonds %	Other %	Portfolio Turnover Ratio	Last Bull Market Return	Last Bear Market Return	Manager Quality Pct	Manager Tenure (Years)	Initial Purch. $	Additional Purch. $	Front End Load	Back End Load
B- /7.7	8.4	1.05	27.25	79	4	95	0	1	44.9	64.0	-11.6	40	N/A	1,000	50	0.0	1.0
B- /7.7	8.4	1.05	28.30	7	4	95	0	1	44.9	66.9	-11.4	46	N/A	1,000	50	0.0	0.0
B- /7.7	8.4	1.04	28.35	171	4	95	0	1	44.9	69.3	-11.4	53	N/A	1,000,000	0	0.0	0.0
B /8.6	8.5	1.05	13.09	17	3	96	0	1	54.1	N/A	N/A	60	N/A	1,000	50	5.8	0.0
B /8.6	8.4	1.04	12.91	2	3	96	0	1	54.1	N/A	N/A	52	N/A	1,000	50	0.0	5.0
B /8.6	8.4	1.04	12.90	4	3	96	0	1	54.1	N/A	N/A	52	N/A	1,000	50	0.0	1.0
B /8.6	8.4	1.05	13.10	N/A	3	96	0	1	54.1	N/A	N/A	59	N/A	1,000	50	0.0	0.0
B /8.6	8.4	1.05	13.15	30	3	96	0	1	54.1	N/A	N/A	64	N/A	1,000,000	0	0.0	0.0
C /5.2	10.1	1.18	5.29	116	4	95	0	1	103.1	51.3	-9.4	12	N/A	1,000	50	5.8	0.0
C /5.1	10.0	1.17	5.07	32	4	95	0	1	103.1	48.4	-9.6	10	N/A	1,000	50	0.0	5.0
C /5.1	10.0	1.18	5.07	34	4	95	0	1	103.1	48.4	-9.6	10	N/A	1,000	50	0.0	1.0
C /5.2	10.1	1.18	5.33	N/A	4	95	0	1	103.1	52.0	-9.4	13	N/A	1,000	50	0.0	0.0
C /5.2	10.1	1.19	5.30	26	4	95	0	1	103.1	53.0	-9.8	14	N/A	1,000,000	0	0.0	0.0
C+ /6.7	9.8	0.81	21.85	6,858	2	97	0	1	26.0	89.1	-11.1	72	11	1,000	50	5.8	0.0
C+ /6.6	9.8	0.81	21.01	844	2	97	0	1	26.0	85.3	-11.2	66	9	1,000	50	0.0	5.0
C+ /6.6	9.8	0.81	20.94	1,005	2	97	0	1	26.0	85.4	-11.3	66	9	1,000	50	0.0	1.0
C+ /6.7	9.8	0.81	21.38	796	2	97	0	1	26.0	88.6	-11.1	72	9	1,000	50	0.0	0.0
C+ /6.7	9.8	0.81	21.84	816	2	97	0	1	26.0	91.3	-11.0	76	7	1,000,000	0	0.0	0.0
C+ /5.8	13.1	1.08	22.68	182	2	97	0	1	6.9	141.1	-7.9	29	8	1,000	50	5.8	0.0
C+ /5.8	13.1	1.08	21.87	51	2	97	0	1	6.9	136.3	-8.1	25	8	1,000	50	0.0	5.0
C+ /5.8	13.1	1.08	21.88	59	2	97	0	1	6.9	136.1	-8.0	25	8	1,000	50	0.0	1.0
C /5.0	13.5	1.17	14.56	138	2	97	0	1	78.7	173.3	-6.6	55	N/A	1,000	50	5.8	0.0
C /5.0	13.5	1.17	14.04	35	2	97	0	1	78.7	167.7	-7.1	46	N/A	1,000	50	0.0	5.0
C /5.0	13.4	1.16	13.97	28	2	97	0	1	78.7	167.4	-6.5	48	N/A	1,000	50	0.0	1.0
C /5.0	13.5	1.17	14.72	1	2	97	0	1	78.7	174.3	-6.8	N/A	N/A	1,000	50	0.0	0.0
C /5.0	13.5	1.17	14.88	119	2	97	0	1	78.7	176.0	-6.7	60	N/A	1,000,000	0	0.0	0.0
C+ /6.5	12.3	0.76	16.96	825	4	95	0	1	58.7	152.6	-12.2	95	N/A	1,000	50	5.8	0.0
C+ /6.4	12.3	0.77	16.47	96	4	95	0	1	58.7	147.5	-12.3	93	N/A	1,000	50	0.0	5.0
C+ /6.4	12.3	0.77	16.45	340	4	95	0	1	58.7	147.4	-12.3	93	N/A	1,000	50	0.0	1.0
C+ /6.5	12.3	0.77	17.00	81	4	95	0	1	58.7	152.4	-12.2	95	N/A	1,000	50	0.0	0.0
C+ /6.5	12.3	0.77	17.19	257	4	95	0	1	58.7	155.2	-12.1	96	N/A	1,000,000	0	0.0	0.0
C+ /5.7	14.0	0.91	32.42	2,182	6	93	0	1	71.3	146.2	-5.9	97	N/A	1,000	50	5.8	0.0
C /5.4	14.0	0.91	29.86	78	6	93	0	1	71.3	141.2	-6.1	96	N/A	1,000	50	0.0	5.0
C /5.5	14.0	0.91	29.90	94	6	93	0	1	71.3	141.2	-6.1	96	N/A	1,000	50	0.0	1.0
C+ /5.7	14.0	0.91	32.26	430	6	93	0	1	71.3	145.4	-5.9	97	N/A	1,000	50	0.0	0.0
C+ /5.9	14.0	0.91	33.69	880	6	93	0	1	71.3	149.0	-5.9	98	N/A	1,000,000	0	0.0	0.0
U /	N/A	N/A	11.76	31	21	78	0	1	N/A	N/A	N/A	N/A	N/A	1,000	0	5.8	1.0
U /	N/A	N/A	16.05	116	0	74	24	2	0.1	N/A	N/A	N/A	N/A	1,000	50	5.8	1.0
U /	N/A	N/A	15.99	29	0	74	24	2	0.1	N/A	N/A	N/A	N/A	1,000	50	0.0	1.0
U /	N/A	N/A	10.26	59	58	0	42	0	N/A	N/A	N/A	N/A	N/A	25,000	5,000	0.0	0.0
U /	N/A	N/A	12.20	114	1	98	0	1	19.3	N/A	N/A	N/A	3	25,000	5,000	0.0	0.0
B- /7.8	7.7	0.95	17.55	62	2	96	0	2	30.6	46.1	-8.8	24	N/A	250	0	0.0	0.0
B /8.5	8.9	1.70	11.53	184	0	100	0	0	1.0	75.2	-9.6	71	5	1,000	50	0.0	0.0
B+ /9.2	6.6	1.33	12.20	96	0	70	30	0	3.0	58.2	-5.5	67	5	1,000	50	0.0	0.0
B+ /9.9	2.3	0.42	13.27	73	40	19	40	1	12.0	15.7	N/A	41	7	1,000	50	0.0	0.0
B+ /9.9	2.3	0.11	11.54	34	54	0	44	2	10.0	6.4	2.5	41	5	1,000	50	0.0	0.0
B+ /9.9	3.3	0.69	12.89	202	26	27	45	2	17.0	28.4	-3.3	50	7	1,000	50	0.0	0.0
B+ /9.9	4.4	0.94	12.64	294	11	47	41	1	9.0	38.5	-4.4	54	7	1,000	50	0.0	0.0
B+ /9.7	5.4	1.13	12.50	310	5	58	35	2	8.0	46.1	-5.5	55	7	1,000	50	0.0	0.0
B+ /9.3	6.5	1.34	12.34	332	0	69	29	2	10.0	57.4	-7.2	60	7	1,000	50	0.0	0.0
B+ /9.1	7.0	1.42	12.21	346	N/A	72	28	N/A	11.0	61.0	-7.2	61	7	1,000	50	0.0	0.0
B /8.9	7.5	1.49	12.79	182	0	84	14	2	1.0	64.6	-7.6	63	5	1,000	50	0.0	0.0

					PERFORMANCE							
99 Pct = Best			**Overall**					Total Return % through 6/30/06			Incl. in Returns	
0 Pct = Worst			**Weiss**		**Perfor-**					Annualized		
Fund		Ticker	**Investment**		**mance**						Dividend	Expense
Type	Fund Name	Symbol	**Rating**	Phone	**Rating/Pts**	3 Mo	6 Mo	1Yr / Pct	3Yr / Pct	5Yr / Pct	Yield	Ratio
GR	MainStay All Cap Growth A	MAAAX	C-	(800) 624-6782	C- / 3.3	-4.37	0.17	10.52 /50	11.88 /42	-0.25 /15	0.00	1.42
GR	MainStay All Cap Growth B	MAWBX	C-	(800) 624-6782	C- / 3.0	-4.48	-0.18	9.72 /45	11.07 /36	-0.99 /12	0.00	2.17
GR	MainStay All Cap Growth C	MAWCX	C-	(800) 624-6782	C- / 3.7	-4.52	-0.22	9.77 /45	11.09 /36	-0.98 /12	0.00	2.17
GR	MainStay All Cap Growth I	MATIX	C-	(800) 624-6782	C / 4.7	-4.20	0.42	11.17 /55	12.42 /45	0.13 /16	0.00	0.93
GI	MainStay All Cap Value A	MALAX	C+	(800) 624-6782	C- / 4.1	-0.69	4.56	8.64 /38	12.77 /47	3.75 /43	0.34	1.55
GI	MainStay All Cap Value B	MALBX	C	(800) 624-6782	C- / 3.8	-0.83	4.23	7.84 /31	11.98 /42	3.03 /37	0.00	2.30
GI	MainStay All Cap Value C	MALCX	C+	(800) 624-6782	C / 4.5	-0.83	4.23	7.84 /31	11.98 /42	3.03 /37	0.00	2.30
GI	MainStay All Cap Value I	MALIX	B	(800) 624-6782	C / 5.5	-0.61	4.98	9.50 /43	13.39 /51	4.20 /48	0.96	0.94
BA	MainStay Balanced A	MBNAX	C	(800) 624-6782	D+ / 2.5	-0.27	2.75	5.52 /18	10.64 /32	8.34 /73	1.32	1.27
BA	MainStay Balanced B	MBNBX	C	(800) 624-6782	D+ / 2.3	-0.50	2.38	4.74 /14	9.84 /26	7.55 /69	0.70	2.02
BA	MainStay Balanced C	MBACX	C	(800) 624-6782	D+ / 2.9	-0.50	2.38	4.74 /14	9.83 /26	7.54 /69	0.70	2.02
BA	MainStay Balanced I	MBAIX	C+	(800) 624-6782	C- / 3.9	-0.19	2.98	6.04 /21	11.08 /36	8.71 /75	1.83	0.82
BA	MainStay Balanced R1	MBNRX	C+	(800) 624-6782	C- / 3.9	-0.18	2.97	5.94 /20	10.96 /35	8.60 /75	1.74	0.92
BA	MainStay Balanced R2	MBCRX	C+	(800) 624-6782	C- / 3.7	-0.24	2.84	5.65 /18	10.68 /33	8.33 /73	1.51	1.17
BA	MainStay Balanced R3	MBDRX	C-	(800) 624-6782	C- / 3.5	-0.36	2.65	5.38 /17	10.39 /30	8.05 /72	0.38	0.94
GR	MainStay Capital Appreciation A	MCSAX	E+	(800) 624-6782	D- / 1.1	-3.72	-1.20	6.78 /25	8.03 /15	-2.52 / 6	0.00	1.24
GR	MainStay Capital Appreciation B	MCSCX	E+	(800) 624-6782	E+ / 0.9	-3.90	-1.55	6.01 /21	7.24 /11	-3.27 / 5	0.00	1.99
GR	MainStay Capital Appreciation C	MCACX	E+	(800) 624-6782	D- / 1.4	-3.90	-1.55	6.01 /21	7.22 /11	-3.28 / 5	0.00	1.99
GR	MainStay Capital Appreciation I	MCPIX	D	(800) 624-6782	D / 2.2	-3.57	-0.91	7.20 /27	8.38 /17	-2.27 / 7	0.00	0.80
GI	MainStay Common Stock A	MSOAX	C	(800) 624-6782	D+ / 2.9	-2.04	2.60	8.75 /38	11.07 /36	0.53 /18	0.15	1.30
GI	MainStay Common Stock B	MOPBX	C-	(800) 624-6782	D+ / 2.6	-2.24	2.26	7.94 /32	10.25 /29	-0.20 /15	0.00	2.05
GI	MainStay Common Stock C	MGOCX	C	(800) 624-6782	C- / 3.3	-2.17	2.26	8.03 /33	10.25 /29	-0.20 /15	0.00	2.05
GI	MainStay Common Stock I	MSOIX	C-	(800) 624-6782	C / 4.4	-1.90	2.91	9.44 /43	11.54 /39	0.88 /20	0.80	0.64
AA	MainStay Conservative Allocation A	MCKAX	U	(800) 624-6782	U /	-0.99	0.98	4.02 /11	--	--	2.91	1.25
CV	MainStay Convertible Fund A	MCOAX	D+	(800) 624-6782	D / 2.0	-1.49	3.37	10.60 /51	9.37 /23	4.85 /53	1.27	1.20
CV	MainStay Convertible Fund B	MCSVX	D	(800) 624-6782	D / 1.8	-1.67	3.04	9.90 /46	8.61 /19	4.09 /47	0.60	1.95
CV	MainStay Convertible Fund C	MCCVX	D+	(800) 624-6782	D+ / 2.4	-1.68	3.04	9.82 /46	8.59 /18	4.07 /47	0.60	1.95
IX	● MainStay Equity Index A	MCSEX	C	(800) 624-6782	C- / 3.6	-1.59	2.44	9.46 /43	11.36 /38	3.93 /45	1.15	0.65
AA	MainStay Growth Allocation A	MGXAX	U	(800) 624-6782	U /	-2.27	3.23	11.39 /56	--	--	0.78	1.47
AA	MainStay Income Manager A	MATAX	C	(800) 624-6782	D / 1.7	-0.67	2.97	6.72 /25	8.67 /19	3.42 /41	3.08	1.14
AA	MainStay Income Manager B	MAMBX	C-	(800) 624-6782	D- / 1.4	-0.80	2.62	6.01 /21	7.88 /14	2.67 /33	2.24	1.89
AA	MainStay Income Manager C	MAMCX	C	(800) 624-6782	D / 2.0	-0.80	2.62	5.93 /20	7.90 /15	2.65 /33	2.24	1.89
AA	MainStay Income Manager I	MASIX	C+	(800) 624-6782	D+ / 2.8	-0.57	3.08	7.01 /26	8.93 /20	3.67 /43	3.63	0.92
FO	MainStay Intl Equity A	MSEAX	A-	(800) 624-6782	B- / 7.3	1.70	10.31	19.05 /81	17.95 /72	11.18 /84	0.25	1.64
FO	MainStay Intl Equity B	MINEX	B+	(800) 624-6782	B- / 7.1	1.50	9.91	18.14 /79	17.07 /68	10.33 /82	0.00	2.39
FO	MainStay Intl Equity C	MIECX	A-	(800) 624-6782	B- / 7.4	1.50	9.91	18.06 /79	17.04 /68	10.34 /82	0.00	2.39
FO	MainStay Intl Equity I	MSIIX	A+	(800) 624-6782	B / 7.9	1.83	10.66	19.66 /81	18.57 /75	11.62 /86	0.73	1.08
FO	MainStay Intl Equity R1	MIERX	A+	(800) 624-6782	B / 8.0	1.84	10.64	19.32 /81	18.35 /74	11.43 /85	0.67	1.18
FO	MainStay Intl Equity R2	MIRRX	A+	(800) 624-6782	B / 7.9	1.76	10.46	19.30 /81	18.20 /73	11.22 /84	0.48	1.43
FO	MainStay Intl Equity R3	MIFRX	B-	(800) 624-6782	B / 7.7	1.63	10.14	18.69 /80	17.54 /70	10.77 /83	0.00	1.75
GR	MainStay Large Cap Growth Fd A	MLAAX	C-	(800) 624-6782	D+ / 2.9	-5.16	-0.72	8.95 /40	11.66 /40	1.73 /25	0.00	1.40
GR	MainStay Large Cap Growth Fd B	MLABX	D-	(800) 624-6782	D+ / 2.7	-5.20	-0.91	8.16 /34	10.90 /35	0.97 /20	0.00	2.15
GR	MainStay Large Cap Growth Fd C	MLACX	D	(800) 624-6782	C- / 3.3	-5.37	-1.09	8.18 /34	10.83 /34	0.95 /20	0.00	2.15
GR	MainStay Large Cap Growth Fd I	MLAIX	D+	(800) 624-6782	C / 4.4	-4.96	-0.36	9.72 /45	12.16 /43	2.06 /28	0.00	0.65
GI	MainStay MAP Fund A	MAPAX	B-	(800) 624-6782	C+ / 6.1	-1.68	4.88	13.65 /67	16.12 /64	7.28 /68	0.00	1.35
GI	MainStay MAP Fund B	MAPBX	C+	(800) 624-6782	C+ / 5.8	-1.88	4.49	12.79 /63	15.26 /60	6.47 /64	0.00	2.10
GI	MainStay MAP Fund C	MMPCX	B-	(800) 624-6782	C+ / 6.3	-1.88	4.49	12.79 /63	15.26 /60	6.47 /64	0.00	2.10
GI	MainStay MAP Fund I	MUBFX	B+	(800) 624-6782	B- / 7.0	-1.63	5.08	14.12 /69	16.55 /66	7.62 /70	0.18	0.92
GI	MainStay MAP Fund R1	MAPRX	B	(800) 624-6782	C+ / 6.9	-1.64	5.01	13.99 /68	16.39 /65	7.49 /69	0.10	1.02
GI	MainStay MAP Fund R2	MPRRX	B	(800) 624-6782	C+ / 6.8	-1.71	4.88	13.72 /67	16.10 /64	7.23 /68	0.00	1.27
GI	MainStay MAP Fund R3	MMAPX	C+	(800) 624-6782	C+ / 6.6	-1.76	4.70	13.26 /65	15.72 /62	6.90 /66	0.00	1.35
MC	MainStay Mid Cap Growth Fund A	MMCPX	B-	(800) 624-6782	B / 7.7	-3.22	5.17	14.73 /71	21.13 /83	6.43 /64	0.00	1.50

● Denotes fund is closed to new investors
* Denotes fund is included in Section II

RISK			NET ASSETS		ASSET				Portfolio	BULL / BEAR		FUND MANAGER		MINIMUMS		LOADS	
	3 Year		NAV							Last Bull	Last Bear	Manager	Manager	Initial	Additional	Front	Back
Risk Rating/Pts	Standard Deviation	Beta	As of 6/30/06	Total $(Mil)	Cash %	Stocks %	Bonds %	Other %	Turnover Ratio	Market Return	Market Return	Quality Pct	Tenure (Years)	Purch. $	Purch. $	End Load	End Load
B- /7.4	11.6	1.35	23.22	30	1	98	0	1	16.5	71.2	-9.5	31	15	1,000	50	5.5	1.0
B- /7.4	11.7	1.35	22.80	11	1	98	0	1	16.5	67.2	-9.6	26	15	1,000	50	0.0	5.0
B- /7.4	11.6	1.35	22.81	5	1	98	0	1	16.5	67.3	-9.6	26	15	1,000	50	0.0	1.0
C+ /6.4	11.6	1.34	24.18	297	1	98	0	1	16.5	73.5	-9.4	35	15	5,000,000	0	0.0	0.0
B /8.5	8.8	1.08	14.45	18	2	95	1	2	20.6	67.7	-9.9	64	7	1,000	50	5.5	1.0
B /8.5	8.9	1.09	14.30	7	2	95	1	2	20.6	63.9	-10.1	56	7	1,000	50	0.0	5.0
B /8.5	8.9	1.09	14.30	2	2	95	1	2	20.6	63.9	-10.1	56	7	1,000	50	0.0	1.0
B /8.7	8.8	1.08	14.55	117	2	95	1	2	20.6	70.7	-9.9	70	7	5,000,000	0	0.0	0.0
B+ /9.2	6.8	1.20	26.80	397	1	59	38	2	9.8	55.2	-2.9	76	17	1,000	50	5.5	1.0
B+ /9.2	6.8	1.20	26.74	159	1	59	38	2	9.8	51.7	-3.0	69	17	1,000	50	0.0	5.0
B /8.7	6.8	1.19	26.73	163	1	59	38	2	9.8	51.8	-3.1	69	17	1,000	50	0.0	1.0
B /8.7	6.8	1.20	26.83	329	1	59	38	2	9.8	57.0	-2.8	79	17	5,000,000	0	0.0	0.0
B+ /9.2	6.8	1.20	26.82	104	1	59	38	2	9.8	56.5	-2.8	78	17	0	0	0.0	0.0
B+ /9.2	6.8	1.20	26.80	96	1	59	38	2	9.8	55.3	-2.9	76	17	0	0	0.0	0.0
B- /7.5	6.8	1.19	26.79	N/A	1	59	38	2	9.8	54.0	-2.9	74	17	0	0	0.0	0.0
C+ /5.9	10.3	1.22	31.32	695	1	98	0	1	6.8	52.2	-9.7	15	15	1,000	50	5.5	1.0
C+ /5.9	10.3	1.22	28.56	453	1	98	0	1	6.8	48.6	-9.9	12	15	1,000	50	0.0	5.0
C+ /5.9	10.3	1.22	28.56	7	1	98	0	1	6.8	48.6	-9.9	12	15	1,000	50	0.0	1.0
C+ /6.7	10.3	1.22	31.57	1	1	98	0	1	6.8	53.5	-9.6	17	14	5,000,000	0	0.0	0.0
B /8.6	8.3	1.06	13.42	35	0	99	0	1	51.9	60.3	-8.3	48	2	1,000	50	5.5	1.0
B /8.6	8.3	1.06	12.65	39	0	99	0	1	51.9	56.7	-8.5	39	2	1,000	50	0.0	5.0
B /8.5	8.2	1.05	12.65	3	0	99	0	1	51.9	56.6	-8.5	39	2	1,000	50	0.0	1.0
C+ /6.1	8.2	1.06	13.45	135	0	99	0	1	51.9	62.3	-8.2	54	2	5,000,000	0	0.0	0.0
U /	N/A	N/A	10.29	32	5	40	54	1	3.0	N/A	N/A	N/A	N/A	1,000	50	5.5	1.0
B- /7.6	7.2	1.01	14.05	348	0	8	0	92	42.4	46.6	-1.8	76	7	1,000	50	5.5	1.0
B- /7.6	7.2	1.02	14.09	132	0	8	0	92	42.4	43.2	-1.9	69	7	1,000	50	0.0	5.0
B- /7.6	7.2	1.02	14.08	25	0	8	0	92	42.4	43.1	-1.9	69	7	1,000	50	0.0	1.0
B- /7.9	7.8	1.02	43.22	509	6	92	1	1	2.2	65.1	-5.6	N/A	10	1,000	50	3.0	1.0
U /	N/A	N/A	11.20	37	3	96	0	1	21.0	N/A	N/A	N/A	5	1,000	50	5.5	1.0
B+ /9.8	4.8	0.98	13.72	73	7	54	37	2	87.7	42.1	-3.7	69	N/A	1,000	50	5.5	1.0
B+ /9.8	4.9	0.99	13.59	28	7	54	37	2	87.7	38.8	-3.8	60	N/A	1,000	50	0.0	5.0
B+ /9.8	4.8	0.99	13.59	7	7	54	37	2	87.7	38.8	-3.8	61	N/A	1,000	50	0.0	1.0
B+ /9.8	4.8	0.99	13.81	238	7	54	37	2	87.7	43.2	-3.6	71	N/A	5,000,000	0	0.0	0.0
B /8.1	8.4	0.78	14.98	140	5	94	0	1	21.1	98.6	-7.9	44	5	1,000	50	5.5	1.0
B /8.1	8.3	0.78	14.20	61	5	94	0	1	21.1	94.1	-8.2	35	5	1,000	50	0.0	5.0
B /8.1	8.4	0.78	14.19	14	5	94	0	1	21.1	94.0	-8.2	35	5	1,000	50	0.0	1.0
B /8.2	8.3	0.78	15.05	436	5	94	0	1	21.1	102.1	-8.0	50	5	5,000,000	0	0.0	2.0
B /8.2	8.4	0.78	14.98	4	5	94	0	1	21.1	100.6	-8.0	45	5	0	0	0.0	0.0
B /8.2	8.3	0.78	15.00	N/A	5	94	0	1	21.1	99.8	-8.1	46	5	0	0	0.0	0.0
C+ /6.1	8.3	0.78	14.99	N/A	5	94	0	1	21.1	96.7	-8.2	40	N/A	0	0	0.0	0.0
B- /7.8	10.6	1.18	5.51	174	2	97	0	1	24.6	73.5	-7.5	42	N/A	1,000	50	5.5	1.0
C /5.5	10.5	1.18	5.47	136	2	97	0	1	24.6	69.6	-7.7	35	N/A	1,000	50	0.0	5.0
C /5.5	10.6	1.19	5.46	12	2	97	0	1	24.6	69.6	-7.6	34	N/A	1,000	50	0.0	1.0
C+ /5.6	10.6	1.18	5.56	157	2	97	0	1	24.6	75.6	-7.5	47	N/A	5,000,000	0	0.0	0.0
B- /7.8	9.3	1.15	36.30	483	5	94	0	1	39.8	95.5	-9.1	85	4	1,000	50	5.5	1.0
B- /7.7	9.3	1.15	34.44	346	5	94	0	1	39.8	90.9	-9.2	80	4	1,000	50	0.0	5.0
B- /7.7	9.3	1.15	34.44	218	5	94	0	1	39.8	91.0	-9.2	80	4	1,000	50	0.0	1.0
B- /7.8	9.3	1.15	36.84	336	5	94	0	1	39.8	97.8	-9.1	87	4	5,000,000	0	0.0	0.0
B /8.3	9.3	1.16	36.50	15	5	94	0	1	39.8	97.1	-9.1	86	4	0	0	0.0	0.0
B /8.3	9.3	1.15	36.30	3	5	94	0	1	39.8	95.4	-9.1	85	4	0	0	0.0	0.0
C+ /6.0	9.3	1.16	36.29	N/A	5	94	0	1	39.8	93.4	-9.2	83	N/A	0	0	0.0	0.0
C+ /6.0	14.2	1.25	12.62	126	5	94	0	1	13.1	137.7	-10.3	42	5	1,000	50	5.5	1.0

			Overall Weiss Investment Rating		PERFORMANCE							
99 Pct = Best					Perfor- mance Rating/Pts	Total Return % through 6/30/06					Incl. in Returns	
0 Pct = Worst									Annualized		Dividend	Expense
Fund Type	Fund Name	Ticker Symbol		Phone		3 Mo	6 Mo	1Yr / Pct	3Yr / Pct	5Yr / Pct	Yield	Ratio
MC	MainStay Mid Cap Growth Fund B	MMGBX	C+	(800) 624-6782	B / 7.6	-3.35	4.84	14.02 /68	20.31 /80	5.67 /59	0.00	2.25
MC	MainStay Mid Cap Growth Fund C	MMGCX	B-	(800) 624-6782	B / 7.9	-3.43	4.76	13.92 /68	20.28 /80	5.65 /59	0.00	2.25
MC	MainStay Mid Cap Growth Fund I	MMGOX	C+	(800) 624-6782	B+ / 8.3	-3.20	5.31	15.26 /73	21.53 /84	6.75 /65	0.00	1.11
MC	MainStay Mid Cap Growth Fund R3	MMGRX	C+	(800) 624-6782	B / 8.1	-3.30	5.00	14.32 /69	20.71 /82	6.05 /61	0.00	1.50
MC	MainStay Mid Cap Opportunity A	MMOAX	B	(800) 624-6782	C+ / 6.4	-1.50	3.86	9.95 /47	17.61 /71	11.25 /85	0.25	1.35
MC	MainStay Mid Cap Opportunity B	MMOBX	B-	(800) 624-6782	C+ / 6.2	-1.68	3.46	9.15 /41	16.73 /67	10.43 /82	0.00	2.10
MC	MainStay Mid Cap Opportunity C	MMOCX	B-	(800) 624-6782	C+ / 6.6	-1.72	3.42	9.11 /41	16.68 /67	10.43 /82	0.00	2.10
MC	MainStay Mid Cap Opportunity I	MMOIX	B+	(800) 624-6782	B- / 7.3	-1.45	3.99	10.37 /49	18.00 /72	11.58 /86	0.55	1.04
MC	MainStay Mid Cap Opportunity R3	MMORX	C	(800) 624-6782	B- / 7.0	-1.61	3.66	9.71 /45	17.30 /69	10.91 /84	0.00	1.04
MC	MainStay Mid Cap Value A	MYIAX	C+	(800) 624-6782	C+ / 5.8	-1.01	5.57	10.04 /47	15.92 /63	7.47 /69	0.00	1.35
MC	MainStay Mid Cap Value B	MEIBX	C	(800) 624-6782	C+ / 5.6	-1.16	5.19	9.24 /42	15.07 /59	6.69 /65	0.00	2.10
MC	MainStay Mid Cap Value C	MCEIX	C+	(800) 624-6782	C+ / 6.1	-1.16	5.19	9.24 /42	15.04 /59	6.69 /65	0.00	2.10
MC	MainStay Mid Cap Value I	MMVIX	C	(800) 624-6782	C+ / 6.8	-0.95	5.76	10.52 /50	16.35 /65	7.81 /71	0.00	0.85
MC	MainStay Mid Cap Value R1	MMIRX	B-	(800) 624-6782	C+ / 6.8	-0.89	5.83	10.48 /50	16.28 /65	7.73 /70	0.00	0.95
MC	MainStay Mid Cap Value R2	MMRRX	B-	(800) 624-6782	C+ / 6.6	-1.01	5.57	10.10 /48	15.91 /63	7.43 /69	0.00	1.20
AA	MainStay Moderate Allocation A	MMRAX	U	(800) 624-6782	U /	-1.26	1.96	6.55 /24	--	--	2.00	1.27
AA	MainStay Moderate Allocation B	MMRBX	U	(800) 624-6782	U /	-1.43	1.54	5.72 /19	--	--	1.41	2.02
AA	MainStay Moderate Gr Allocation A	MGDAX	U	(800) 624-6782	U /	-1.87	2.54	8.85 /39	--	--	2.09	1.36
AA	MainStay Moderate Gr Allocation B	MGDBX	U	(800) 624-6782	U /	-2.05	2.23	8.12 /34	--	--	1.70	2.11
GR	MainStay S&P 500 Index A	MSXAX	C	(800) 624-6782	C- / 3.0	-1.65	2.42	7.95 /32	10.52 /31	1.96 /27	1.07	0.68
GR	MainStay S&P 500 Index I	MSPIX	C+	(800) 624-6782	C- / 4.0	-1.50	2.61	8.38 /36	10.92 /35	2.27 /30	1.53	0.29
SC	MainStay Small Cap Growth A	MSMAX	D	(800) 624-6782	C / 4.5	-4.97	6.05	9.47 /43	13.34 /51	1.34 /22	0.00	1.48
SC	MainStay Small Cap Growth B	MSOBX	D-	(800) 624-6782	C- / 3.9	-5.22	5.61	8.54 /37	12.46 /45	0.59 /18	0.00	2.23
SC	MainStay Small Cap Growth C	MSCCX	D	(800) 624-6782	C / 4.8	-5.15	5.68	8.69 /38	12.48 /46	0.60 /18	0.00	2.23
SC	● MainStay Small Cap Opp A	MOPAX	B+	(800) 624-6782	B+ / 8.4	-3.51	5.54	9.46 /43	24.94 /91	16.53 /94	0.00	1.42
SC	● MainStay Small Cap Opp B	MOTBX	B+	(800) 624-6782	B+ / 8.5	-3.71	5.12	8.58 /37	23.95 /89	15.66 /93	0.00	2.17
SC	● MainStay Small Cap Opp C	MOPCX	C	(800) 624-6782	B+ / 8.6	-3.66	5.11	8.64 /38	23.97 /89	15.70 /93	0.00	2.17
SC	● MainStay Small Cap Opp I	MOPIX	C+	(800) 624-6782	B+ / 8.9	-3.37	5.75	9.91 /46	25.41 /91	16.92 /94	0.00	1.07
SC	MainStay Small Cap Value A	MSPAX	E+	(800) 624-6782	C / 5.2	-3.22	5.49	5.26 /16	15.51 /61	8.34 /73	0.00	1.53
SC	MainStay Small Cap Value B	MSPBX	E+	(800) 624-6782	C / 5.5	-3.41	5.02	4.45 /13	14.61 /57	7.52 /69	0.00	2.28
SC	MainStay Small Cap Value C	MSMCX	E+	(800) 624-6782	C+ / 5.6	-3.41	5.02	4.45 /13	14.61 /57	7.52 /69	0.00	2.28
SC	MainStay Small Cap Value I	MSVVX	C-	(800) 624-6782	C+ / 6.3	-3.20	5.61	5.76 /19	15.90 /63	8.67 /75	0.00	0.90
BA	MainStay Total Return A	MTRAX	D	(800) 624-6782	D- / 1.2	-1.27	1.62	6.17 /21	7.95 /15	1.85 /26	1.08	1.19
BA	MainStay Total Return B	MKTRX	D	(800) 624-6782	D- / 1.0	-1.46	1.23	5.42 /17	7.16 /11	1.10 /21	0.40	1.94
BA	MainStay Total Return C	MCTRX	D	(800) 624-6782	D- / 1.5	-1.46	1.23	5.31 /17	7.12 /11	1.08 /21	0.40	1.94
BA	MainStay Total Return I	MTOIX	C-	(800) 624-6782	D+ / 2.5	-1.17	1.91	7.25 /28	8.58 /18	2.30 /30	1.62	0.69
GI	MainStay Value Fund A	MVAAX	C+	(800) 624-6782	C / 4.7	0.28	6.12	10.61 /51	13.48 /51	3.76 /43	0.99	1.17
GI	MainStay Value Fund B	MKVAX	C+	(800) 624-6782	C / 4.5	0.08	5.76	9.78 /45	12.62 /46	2.98 /37	0.32	1.92
GI	MainStay Value Fund C	MSCVX	C+	(800) 624-6782	C / 5.1	0.08	5.76	9.78 /45	12.62 /46	2.98 /37	0.32	1.92
GI	MainStay Value Fund I	MVAIX	B	(800) 624-6782	C+ / 5.9	0.39	6.39	10.89 /53	13.74 /53	4.04 /46	1.39	0.83
GI	MainStay Value Fund R1	MVARX	B	(800) 624-6782	C+ / 5.8	0.37	6.29	10.79 /52	13.66 /52	3.96 /46	1.29	0.93
GI	MainStay Value Fund R2	MVRTX	B	(800) 624-6782	C+ / 5.7	0.30	6.16	10.57 /51	13.45 /51	3.71 /43	1.04	1.18
BA	Mairs & Power Balanced Fund	MAPOX	B-	(800) 304-7404	C- / 3.9	-0.66	5.04	8.95 /40	10.48 /31	7.08 /67	2.61	0.84
★ GR	Mairs & Power Growth Fund	MPGFX	B-	(800) 304-7404	C / 5.1	-2.46	2.52	8.03 /33	13.14 /50	9.13 /77	1.05	0.70
GR	Managers 20 Fund A	MTWAX	E-	(800) 835-3879	E- / 0.0	-8.48	-8.11	-2.79 / 0	0.98 / 0	-10.11 / 0	0.00	1.50
GR	Managers 20 Fund B	MTWBX	E-	(800) 835-3879	E- / 0.0	-8.72	-8.53	-3.60 / 0	0.39 / 0	-10.64 / 0	0.00	2.25
GR	Managers 20 Fund C	MTWCX	E-	(800) 835-3879	E- / 0.0	-8.69	-8.49	-3.58 / 0	0.39 / 0	-10.63 / 0	0.00	2.25
GR	Managers 20 Fund Y	MTWYX	E-	(800) 835-3879	E- / 0.0	-8.51	-7.97	-2.74 / 0	1.41 / 0	-9.74 / 0	0.00	1.25
GR	Managers AMG Essex LrgCap	MELCX	D-	(800) 835-3879	E+ / 0.6	-7.85	-3.61	3.30 / 8	5.65 / 6	--	0.13	1.10
GI	Managers AMG Rorer Large Cap	MRLCX	E-	(800) 835-3879	D- / 1.3	-3.86	0.00	4.11 /11	6.97 /10	--	0.43	1.40
GR	Managers AMG Systematic Value	MSYSX	C	(800) 835-3879	C+ / 6.7	-0.18	5.27	12.73 /63	15.82 /63	--	0.91	0.90
SC	● Managers AMG Times Sqr SmCap Gr	TSCIX	C+	(800) 835-3879	B- / 7.5	-3.70	9.85	19.51 /81	17.95 /72	8.53 /74	0.00	1.05

● Denotes fund is closed to new investors
★ Denotes fund is included in Section II

RISK	3 Year		NET ASSETS		ASSET				Portfolio	BULL / BEAR		FUND MANAGER		MINIMUMS		LOADS	
Risk Rating/Pts	Standard Deviation	Beta	NAV As of 6/30/06	Total $(Mil)	Cash %	Stocks %	Bonds %	Other %	Portfolio Turnover Ratio	Last Bull Market Return	Last Bear Market Return	Manager Quality Pct	Manager Tenure (Years)	Initial Purch. $	Additional Purch. $	Front End Load	Back End Load
C+ / 6.0	14.1	1.25	12.12	62	5	94	0	1	13.1	132.7	-10.6	36	5	1,000	50	0.0	5.0
C+ / 5.9	14.1	1.25	12.11	39	5	94	0	1	13.1	132.5	-10.6	35	5	1,000	50	0.0	1.0
C / 4.8	14.2	1.25	12.69	1	5	94	0	1	13.1	140.4	-10.3	46	5	5,000,000	0	0.0	0.0
C / 4.8	14.2	1.25	12.61	N/A	5	94	0	1	13.1	135.2	-10.4	38	N/A	0	0	0.0	0.0
B- / 7.7	11.2	0.96	26.90	62	0	99	0	1	134.0	101.7	-6.5	58	12	1,000	50	5.5	1.0
B- / 7.7	11.2	0.96	26.31	21	0	99	0	1	134.0	97.0	-6.6	48	12	1,000	50	0.0	5.0
B- / 7.6	11.2	0.96	26.29	33	0	99	0	1	134.0	96.9	-6.6	47	12	1,000	50	0.0	1.0
B- / 7.7	11.2	0.96	27.13	32	0	99	0	1	134.0	103.8	-6.4	62	12	5,000,000	0	0.0	0.0
C / 5.4	11.2	0.95	26.89	N/A	0	99	0	1	134.0	99.9	-6.6	55	N/A	0	0	0.0	0.0
C+ / 6.7	11.7	0.85	17.62	172	3	96	0	1	20.4	81.6	-9.3	60	7	1,000	50	5.5	1.0
C+ / 6.6	11.7	0.85	17.03	163	3	96	0	1	20.4	77.4	-9.5	50	7	1,000	50	0.0	5.0
C+ / 6.6	11.7	0.85	17.03	41	3	96	0	1	20.4	77.4	-9.5	50	7	1,000	50	0.0	1.0
C / 5.4	11.7	0.85	17.80	1	3	96	0	1	20.4	83.7	-9.2	64	7	5,000,000	0	0.0	0.0
B- / 7.6	11.7	0.85	17.78	N/A	3	96	0	1	20.4	83.4	-9.3	63	7	0	0	0.0	0.0
B- / 7.6	11.7	0.85	17.63	2	3	96	0	1	20.4	81.6	-9.4	60	7	0	0	0.0	0.0
U /	N/A	N/A	10.68	77	4	59	36	1	2.0	N/A	N/A	N/A	1	1,000	50	5.5	1.0
U /	N/A	N/A	10.65	30	4	59	36	1	2.0	N/A	N/A	N/A	1	1,000	50	0.0	5.0
U /	N/A	N/A	10.90	77	4	77	18	1	2.0	N/A	N/A	N/A	1	1,000	50	5.5	1.0
U /	N/A	N/A	10.86	36	4	77	18	1	2.0	N/A	N/A	N/A	1	1,000	50	0.0	5.0
B / 8.8	7.7	1.00	29.25	310	2	97	0	1	2.2	61.7	-9.8	48	10	1,000	50	3.0	1.0
B / 8.9	7.7	1.00	29.51	1,294	2	97	0	1	2.2	63.6	-9.8	53	10	5,000,000	0	0.0	0.0
C / 4.4	16.4	1.07	16.64	111	3	96	0	1	9.4	89.2	-11.5	11	8	1,000	50	5.5	0.0
C / 4.3	16.4	1.07	15.63	125	3	96	0	1	9.4	84.8	-11.7	8	8	1,000	50	0.0	5.0
C / 4.3	16.4	1.07	15.64	7	3	96	0	1	9.4	84.8	-11.7	8	8	1,000	50	0.0	0.0
C+ / 6.5	14.8	0.93	19.25	508	1	98	0	1	50.9	141.2	-3.3	96	19	1,000	50	5.5	1.0
C+ / 6.5	14.7	0.93	18.70	48	1	98	0	1	50.9	135.2	-3.5	94	19	1,000	50	0.0	1.0
C- / 3.7	14.7	0.93	18.71	133	1	98	0	1	50.9	135.5	-3.5	94	19	1,000	50	0.0	0.0
C- / 3.9	14.7	0.93	19.51	634	1	98	0	1	50.9	143.9	-3.3	97	19	5,000,000	0	0.0	0.0
D / 2.1	13.6	0.87	13.84	56	2	97	0	1	19.5	89.2	-10.9	45	2	1,000	50	5.5	1.0
D / 1.7	13.6	0.87	12.76	50	2	97	0	1	19.5	84.7	-11.0	36	2	1,000	50	0.0	1.0
D / 1.7	13.5	0.87	12.76	12	2	97	0	1	19.5	84.7	-11.0	37	2	1,000	50	0.0	0.0
C / 4.9	13.6	0.87	13.93	25	2	97	0	1	19.5	91.4	-10.8	50	2	5,000,000	0	0.0	0.0
B- / 7.8	6.1	1.19	18.95	498	2	70	26	2	28.3	42.3	-3.9	48	15	1,000	50	5.5	1.0
B- / 7.8	6.1	1.19	19.00	228	2	70	26	2	28.3	39.1	-4.1	40	15	1,000	50	0.0	5.0
B- / 7.7	6.1	1.19	18.98	3	2	70	26	2	28.3	38.9	-4.1	39	15	1,000	50	0.0	1.0
B / 8.3	6.1	1.18	19.02	N/A	2	70	26	2	28.3	44.8	-3.8	57	15	5,000,000	0	0.0	0.0
B / 8.5	8.3	1.01	21.77	482	1	97	0	2	21.7	70.4	-10.1	77	7	1,000	50	5.5	1.0
B / 8.5	8.3	1.00	21.65	212	1	97	0	2	21.7	66.4	-10.2	70	7	1,000	50	0.0	5.0
B / 8.5	8.3	1.00	21.65	13	1	97	0	2	21.7	66.4	-10.2	70	7	1,000	50	0.0	1.0
B / 8.4	8.2	1.00	21.74	N/A	1	97	0	2	21.7	71.9	-10.1	79	7	5,000,000	0	0.0	0.0
B / 8.4	8.2	1.00	21.73	N/A	1	97	0	2	21.7	71.6	-10.1	79	7	0	0	0.0	0.0
B / 8.3	8.3	1.00	21.71	13	1	97	0	2	21.7	70.2	-10.1	77	7	0	0	0.0	0.0
B+ / 9.9	5.2	1.01	60.66	131	2	62	34	2	13.5	54.4	-2.4	82	14	2,500	100	0.0	0.0
B / 8.8	7.5	0.86	73.19	2,589	2	97	0	1	2.8	71.4	-6.7	84	7	2,500	100	0.0	0.0
D+ / 2.6	15.9	1.76	4.53	3	N/A	100	0	N/A	20.0	38.9	-14.0	0	6	2,000	100	5.8	0.0
D+ / 2.5	16.0	1.77	4.29	6	N/A	100	0	N/A	20.0	36.4	-14.0	0	6	2,000	100	0.0	5.0
D+ / 2.5	16.0	1.77	4.31	5	N/A	100	0	N/A	20.0	36.2	-14.0	0	6	2,000	100	0.0	1.0
D+ / 2.6	16.1	1.77	4.62	3	N/A	100	0	N/A	20.0	40.9	-14.0	0	6	2,500,000	1,000	0.0	0.0
C+ / 6.9	10.0	1.15	7.87	4	2	97	0	1	76.0	N/A	N/A	8	N/A	100,000	1,000	0.0	0.0
D / 2.0	8.2	1.02	7.98	1	3	96	0	1	70.0	46.8	-9.7	19	5	5,000	1,000	0.0	0.0
C / 5.2	8.8	1.06	10.99	24	2	97	0	1	108.0	87.9	-8.7	88	N/A	2,500,000	1,000	0.0	0.0
C / 5.3	12.3	0.79	13.27	424	6	93	0	1	76.0	110.3	-8.6	81	N/A	5,000,000	100,000	0.0	0.0

			Overall Weiss Investment Rating		PERFORMANCE							
					Perfor-mance Rating/Pts	Total Return % through 6/30/06			Annualized		Incl. in Returns	
Fund Type	Fund Name	Ticker Symbol		Phone		3 Mo	6 Mo	1Yr / Pct	3Yr / Pct	5Yr / Pct	Dividend Yield	Expense Ratio
SC	● Managers AMG Times Sqr SmCap Gr	TSCPX	C+	(800) 835-3879	B- / 7.5	-3.73	9.83	19.35 /81	17.78 /72	8.38 /73	0.00	1.25
BA	Managers Balanced Fund A	MBEAX	D	(800) 835-3879	D / 1.9	-0.72	2.78	5.83 /19	9.14 /22	4.08 /47	1.56	1.25
BA	Managers Balanced Fund B	MBEBX	D	(800) 835-3879	D / 1.6	-0.93	2.35	4.95 /15	8.45 /17	3.53 /42	0.94	2.00
BA	Managers Balanced Fund C	MBECX	D	(800) 835-3879	D / 2.2	-0.92	2.32	4.90 /15	8.43 /17	3.51 /41	0.93	2.00
BA	Managers Balanced Fund Y	MBEYX	D+	(800) 835-3879	C- / 3.0	-0.74	2.80	5.97 /20	9.52 /24	4.53 /50	1.91	1.00
GR	Managers Capital Appreciation	MGCAX	E+	(800) 835-3879	E+ / 0.7	-7.68	-3.09	3.90 /10	5.92 / 6	-3.16 / 5	0.00	1.29
EM	Managers Emerging Markets Eq	MEMEX	B-	(800) 835-3879	A+ / 9.6	-4.97	5.57	34.30 /96	33.20 /97	19.72 /96	0.24	1.72
MC	Managers Essex Growth	MEAGX	E-	(800) 835-3879	D- / 1.1	-7.07	1.34	10.04 /47	6.34 / 8	-2.41 / 7	0.00	1.52
MC	● Managers Essex Growth I	MEAIX	E	(800) 835-3879	D- / 1.2	-7.07	1.52	10.26 /49	6.59 / 9	--	0.00	1.27
SC	Managers Essex Sm/MicroCap Gr Fd	MBRSX	C	(800) 835-3879	B+ / 8.5	-9.78	6.81	25.96 /90	23.10 /88	--	0.00	1.49
GI	Managers First Quad Tax-Managed	MFQTX	B	(800) 835-3879	C+ / 6.6	-1.66	4.25	14.45 /70	15.55 /62	5.94 /61	0.18	0.99
GL	Managers Fremont Global Fund	MMAFX	C+	(800) 835-3879	C- / 4.0	-1.74	2.56	9.68 /45	10.87 /34	4.80 /52	5.34	1.06
SC	● Managers Fremont US Micro-Cap Fd	MMCFX	E+	(800) 835-3879	C / 4.3	-8.50	4.13	10.68 /51	11.60 /40	2.62 /33	0.00	1.53
SC	● Managers Fremont US Micro-Cap	MIMFX	E+	(800) 835-3879	C / 4.4	-8.52	4.39	11.03 /54	11.79 /41	3.27 /39	0.00	1.35
FO	Managers International Eq	MGITX	B+	(800) 835-3879	B+ / 8.9	-1.14	10.84	31.55 /95	22.26 /86	7.85 /71	0.82	1.45
FO	Managers International Growth Fund	MIGGX	C+	(800) 835-3879	B / 7.8	-1.85	7.74	22.98 /86	18.93 /76	4.36 /49	3.30	1.50
GR	Managers Mid-Cap A	MKPAX	C+	(800) 835-3879	C+ / 6.2	-2.86	3.27	10.57 /51	16.93 /68	8.70 /75	0.00	1.25
GR	Managers Mid-Cap B	MKPBX	C+	(800) 835-3879	C+ / 5.9	-3.01	2.89	9.73 /45	16.23 /64	8.09 /72	0.00	2.00
GR	Managers Mid-Cap C	MKPCX	C+	(800) 835-3879	C+ / 6.4	-3.01	2.88	9.82 /46	16.21 /64	8.11 /72	0.00	2.00
GR	Managers Mid-Cap Y	MKPYX	B	(800) 835-3879	B- / 7.0	-2.79	3.39	10.89 /53	17.36 /70	9.17 /77	0.00	1.00
RE	Managers Real Estate Sec Fund	MRESX	C+	(800) 835-3879	A / 9.3	-2.07	12.29	20.10 /82	26.37 /93	18.95 /95	1.49	1.47
SC	● Managers Small Cap Fund	MSSCX	E+	(800) 835-3879	B- / 7.1	-4.32	8.64	17.23 /78	17.00 /68	0.19 /16	0.00	1.53
SC	Managers Small Company	MSCFX	C	(800) 835-3879	C+ / 5.9	-6.45	2.95	8.98 /40	15.09 /59	4.99 /54	0.00	1.45
★ SC	Managers Special Equity Fd	MGSEX	C+	(800) 835-3879	C+ / 6.8	-4.66	5.14	11.55 /57	16.66 /67	5.07 /55	0.00	1.40
SC	Managers Special Equity I	MSEIX	U	(800) 835-3879	U /	-4.59	5.26	11.78 /58	--	--	0.00	1.20
GI	Managers Value	MGIEX	C	(800) 835-3879	C / 4.6	-1.98	2.64	5.87 /20	12.42 /45	3.07 /38	0.77	1.19
SC	Marketocracy Masters 100 Fund	MOFQX	C-	(888) 884-8482	C+ / 6.1	-0.88	8.36	21.55 /84	12.49 /46	--	0.00	1.95
FO	Marshall International Stock Adv	MRIAX	B	(800) 236-8554	B / 8.1	-0.13	9.35	29.82 /94	19.89 /79	7.53 /69	0.03	1.50
FO	Marshall International Stock Inst	MRIIX	B+	(800) 236-8554	B+ / 8.6	-0.06	9.46	31.11 /95	20.45 /81	7.96 /71	0.95	1.25
FO	Marshall International Stock Inv	MRISX	B+	(800) 236-8554	B+ / 8.5	-0.13	9.35	30.80 /95	20.16 /80	7.70 /70	0.72	1.50
GI	Marshall Large-Cap Gr & Inc Inv	MASTX	E	(800) 236-8554	D / 1.8	-4.51	-2.06	5.35 /17	8.62 /19	-1.48 /10	0.10	1.26
GI	Marshall Large-Cap Growth	MLCAX	E	(800) 236-8554	D- / 1.1	-4.51	-2.06	5.35 /17	8.62 /19	-1.48 /10	0.10	1.26
IN	Marshall Large-Cap Value Fund-Y	MREIX	C-	(800) 236-8554	C / 4.3	-0.15	5.48	12.35 /61	11.39 /38	4.25 /48	1.27	1.22
IN	Marshall Lrg Cap Value Fd	MAEIX	D+	(800) 236-8554	C- / 3.5	-0.15	5.48	12.35 /61	11.39 /38	4.25 /48	1.21	1.22
MC	Marshall Mid-Cap Growth Adv	MMSAX	D-	(800) 236-8554	D+ / 2.6	-5.18	5.25	12.78 /63	10.67 /32	-0.80 /12	0.00	1.30
MC	Marshall Mid-Cap Growth Inv	MRMSX	D	(800) 236-8554	C- / 3.4	-5.18	5.25	12.78 /63	10.67 /33	-0.80 /12	0.00	1.30
MC	Marshall Mid-Cap Value Adv	MVEAX	C+	(800) 236-8554	C+ / 5.6	-1.31	3.42	7.91 /32	16.02 /64	10.03 /81	0.27	1.19
MC	Marshall Mid-Cap Value Inv	MRVEX	C+	(800) 236-8554	C+ / 6.2	-1.31	3.42	7.91 /32	16.02 /64	10.03 /81	0.29	1.19
SC	Marshall Small-Cap Growth Adv	MASCX	C	(800) 236-8554	B / 7.6	-7.18	9.07	24.19 /87	20.34 /81	6.90 /66	0.00	1.54
SC	Marshall Small-Cap Growth Inv	MRSCX	C	(800) 236-8554	B / 8.0	-7.18	9.07	24.19 /87	20.34 /81	6.90 /66	0.00	1.54
MC	Marsico 21ST Century Fund	MXXIX	B+	(888) 860-8686	B / 8.2	-2.64	8.34	23.41 /86	20.65 /82	12.93 /88	0.01	1.35
★ GR	Marsico Focus Fund	MFOCX	C-	(888) 860-8686	C- / 4.1	-4.58	-0.49	10.75 /52	11.93 /42	4.35 /49	0.00	1.20
★ GR	Marsico Growth Fund	MGRIX	C-	(888) 860-8686	C- / 3.5	-4.47	-1.27	6.40 /23	11.74 /41	3.88 /45	0.00	1.24
FO	Marsico International Oppt	MIOFX	B+	(888) 860-8686	B+ / 8.8	-3.07	6.61	31.62 /95	22.94 /87	12.97 /89	0.64	1.43
IN	MassMutual Prem Enhnd Idx Core Eq	DLBQX	C+	(888) 722-2766	C / 4.4	-1.55	3.15	9.21 /41	11.42 /39	2.61 /33	1.18	0.69
GR	MassMutual Prem Enhnd Idx Growth	DEIGX	D+	(888) 722-2766	D / 2.1	-4.38	-0.93	5.62 /18	8.62 /19	-0.61 /13	0.43	0.69
GR	MassMutual Prem Enhnd Idx Val Y	DENVX	B-	(888) 722-2766	C+ / 6.8	0.41	6.37	12.05 /60	15.85 /63	7.67 /70	1.42	0.69
SC	MassMutual Prem Small Cap Value S	DSMVX	C+	(888) 722-2766	B- / 7.3	-4.92	7.85	9.57 /44	18.40 /74	10.53 /82	0.00	0.85
BA	MassMutual Premier Balanced N	MMBNX	C-	(800) 542-6767	D- / 1.4	-1.24	1.17	4.52 /13	6.91 /10	--	1.89	1.47
BA	MassMutual Premier Balanced S	MBLDX	C	(800) 542-6767	D / 2.1	-0.91	1.66	5.61 /18	7.89 /14	3.45 /41	2.66	0.60
BA	MassMutual Premier Balanced Y	MBAYX	C	(800) 542-6767	D / 1.9	-1.08	1.52	5.38 /17	7.69 /14	3.27 /39	2.41	0.76
GR	MassMutual Premier Capital Apprec	MACAX	U	(800) 542-6767	U /	-4.76	-0.48	6.66 /24	--	--	0.00	1.09

● Denotes fund is closed to new investors
★ Denotes fund is included in Section II

256

RISK			NET ASSETS		ASSET					BULL / BEAR		FUND MANAGER		MINIMUMS		LOADS	
Risk Rating/Pts	3 Year		NAV As of 6/30/06	Total $(Mil)	Cash %	Stocks %	Bonds %	Other %	Portfolio Turnover Ratio	Last Bull Market Return	Last Bear Market Return	Manager Quality Pct	Manager Tenure (Years)	Initial Purch. $	Additional Purch. $	Front End Load	Back End Load
	Standard Deviation	Beta															
C / 5.3	12.3	0.79	13.18	181	7	92	0	1	74.0	109.5	-8.6	80	N/A	1,000,000	10,000	0.0	0.0
B- / 7.0	5.5	1.13	11.77	2	2	0	95	3	53.0	48.3	-2.9	65	N/A	2,000	100	5.8	0.0
B- / 7.0	5.6	1.15	11.57	9	2	0	95	3	53.0	45.6	-2.9	57	N/A	2,000	100	0.0	5.0
B- / 7.1	5.5	1.13	11.67	5	2	0	95	3	53.0	45.6	-2.9	58	N/A	2,000	100	0.0	1.0
B- / 7.1	5.5	1.13	11.85	7	2	0	95	3	53.0	50.3	-2.7	69	N/A	2,500,000	1,000	0.0	0.0
C+ / 6.5	9.7	1.15	26.94	67	3	96	0	1	130.0	47.5	-10.7	9	N/A	2,000	100	0.0	0.0
C- / 4.2	18.4	1.12	21.22	126	3	96	0	1	38.0	215.1	-4.9	12	8	2,000	100	0.0	2.0
C- / 3.6	14.4	1.14	9.86	N/A	1	98	0	1	80.0	57.3	-9.5	0	N/A	5,000	1,000	0.0	0.0
C / 4.3	14.4	1.15	9.99	24	1	98	0	1	80.0	58.5	-9.5	1	N/A	100,000	1,000	0.0	0.0
C- / 3.9	18.4	1.17	18.81	65	3	96	0	1	128.0	170.6	-9.9	69	N/A	2,000	100	0.0	0.0
B / 8.1	9.2	1.04	13.00	73	0	99	0	1	86.0	82.2	-7.6	87	6	2,500,000	1,000	0.0	0.0
B / 8.7	6.5	1.28	13.47	183	4	66	28	2	108.0	59.7	-4.2	73	N/A	2,000	100	0.0	0.0
D+ / 2.7	18.1	1.16	33.05	392	13	86	0	1	63.0	100.1	-11.7	3	N/A	2,000	100	0.0	0.0
D / 2.1	18.1	1.16	14.50	280	13	86	0	1	63.0	99.9	-11.2	4	N/A	250,000	1,000	0.0	0.0
C+ / 6.4	11.8	1.10	59.59	216	1	98	0	1	69.0	120.7	-8.9	21	N/A	2,000	100	0.0	2.0
C / 5.3	10.9	0.99	10.56	26	3	96	0	1	248.0	109.8	-10.9	17	N/A	2,000	100	0.0	2.0
B- / 7.2	11.4	1.25	13.91	9	2	97	0	1	88.0	94.2	-4.9	84	6	2,000	100	5.8	0.0
B- / 7.2	11.3	1.24	13.19	15	2	97	0	1	88.0	90.8	-5.0	80	6	2,000	100	0.0	5.0
B- / 7.2	11.4	1.26	13.20	13	2	97	0	1	88.0	90.7	-5.0	79	6	2,000	100	0.0	1.0
B- / 7.2	11.4	1.25	14.66	55	2	97	0	1	88.0	97.0	-4.8	86	6	2,500,000	0	0.0	0.0
C / 4.3	16.0	0.96	12.77	24	0	99	0	1	70.0	124.2	N/A	81	9	2,000	100	0.0	0.0
E- / 0.0	25.5	0.57	14.83	88	2	97	0	1	58.0	114.7	-13.8	93	N/A	2,000	100	0.0	0.0
C+ / 5.8	14.6	0.95	11.16	36	5	94	0	1	106.0	95.7	-6.4	30	N/A	2,000	100	0.0	0.0
C+ / 6.0	13.6	0.92	91.23	2,789	8	91	0	1	62.0	103.8	-12.1	49	21	2,000	100	0.0	0.0
U /	N/A	N/A	91.68	548	8	91	0	1	62.0	N/A	N/A	N/A	N/A	2,500,000	1,000	0.0	0.0
B- / 7.2	7.6	0.95	28.72	86	4	95	0	1	44.0	71.9	-11.1	72	6	2,000	100	0.0	0.0
C / 4.4	16.6	0.99	13.48	44	12	87	0	1	647.0	76.9	-0.4	12	5	2,000	50	0.0	0.0
C+ / 6.4	12.2	1.11	15.91	7	3	96	0	1	150.0	114.7	-12.0	10	N/A	1,000	50	5.8	1.0
C+ / 6.4	12.3	1.12	16.09	186	3	96	0	1	150.0	117.9	-12.0	11	N/A	1,000,000	50	0.0	2.0
C+ / 6.4	12.2	1.11	15.91	241	3	96	0	1	150.0	116.1	-12.0	11	N/A	1,000	50	0.0	2.0
C- / 4.1	8.7	1.09	11.87	231	2	97	0	1	145.9	51.9	-11.1	25	5	1,000	50	0.0	2.0
C / 5.1	8.7	1.09	11.87	10	2	97	0	1	146.0	51.9	-11.1	25	5	1,000	50	5.8	1.0
C+ / 6.2	7.5	0.84	13.55	329	0	99	0	1	103.0	64.5	-9.7	72	N/A	1,000	50	0.0	2.0
C+ / 6.6	7.5	0.84	13.55	13	0	99	0	1	103.3	64.5	-9.7	72	N/A	1,000	50	5.8	1.0
C / 5.5	13.3	1.14	14.83	5	4	95	0	1	188.0	70.5	-8.7	3	N/A	1,000	50	5.8	1.0
C / 5.5	13.3	1.14	14.83	191	4	95	0	1	188.0	70.5	-8.7	3	N/A	1,000	50	0.0	2.0
B- / 7.3	9.3	0.80	15.10	14	4	94	0	2	37.0	90.3	-7.5	68	8	1,000	50	5.8	1.0
B- / 7.3	9.3	0.80	15.10	698	4	94	0	2	37.0	90.3	-7.5	68	13	1,000	50	0.0	2.0
C / 4.3	16.5	1.05	17.20	8	7	92	0	1	195.0	145.6	-15.4	64	N/A	1,000	50	5.8	1.0
C / 4.3	16.5	1.05	17.20	198	7	92	0	1	195.0	145.6	-15.4	64	N/A	1,000	50	0.0	2.0
C+ / 6.8	13.3	1.07	14.03	632	10	89	0	1	175.0	126.5	-9.0	69	6	2,500	100	0.0	2.0
B- / 7.2	10.3	1.16	18.13	4,485	7	92	0	1	80.0	72.5	-9.1	47	9	2,500	100	0.0	2.0
B- / 7.3	9.5	1.08	18.61	2,420	3	96	0	1	72.0	73.3	-8.5	53	9	2,500	100	0.0	2.0
C+ / 5.8	12.1	1.12	15.15	512	5	94	0	1	154.0	142.0	-11.7	22	6	2,500	100	0.0	2.0
B / 8.8	7.7	0.99	11.46	37	N/A	N/A	0	N/A	154.0	64.6	-9.1	59	6	0	0	0.0	0.0
B- / 7.8	8.6	1.07	8.52	43	N/A	N/A	0	N/A	127.0	55.3	-9.4	26	6	0	0	0.0	0.0
B- / 7.6	7.8	0.96	12.35	90	0	99	0	1	150.0	84.3	-8.5	92	6	0	0	0.0	0.0
C+ / 5.8	13.4	0.87	15.67	109	N/A	N/A	0	N/A	32.0	105.2	-7.4	74	6	0	0	0.0	0.0
B+ / 9.9	4.8	1.01	9.55	N/A	8	61	29	2	139.0	37.3	N/A	47	N/A	0	0	0.0	1.0
B+ / 9.8	4.8	1.01	9.77	210	8	61	29	2	139.0	41.5	-4.8	59	12	0	0	0.0	0.0
B+ / 9.9	4.7	1.00	10.05	2	8	61	29	2	139.0	40.5	-4.9	58	12	0	0	0.0	0.0
U /	N/A	N/A	10.41	302	1	98	0	1	59.0	N/A	N/A	N/A	1	0	0	5.8	0.0

Fund Type	Fund Name	Ticker Symbol	Overall Weiss Investment Rating	Phone	Perfor-mance Rating/Pts	3 Mo	6 Mo	1Yr / Pct	3Yr / Pct	5Yr / Pct	Dividend Yield	Expense Ratio
	99 Pct = Best				PERFORMANCE			Total Return % through 6/30/06			Incl. in Returns	
	0 Pct = Worst								Annualized			
GR	MassMutual Premier Capital Apprec	MCASX	U	(800) 542-6767	U /	-4.66	-0.29	6.76 /25	--	--	0.00	0.71
GR	MassMutual Premier Capital Apprec	MCAYX	U	(800) 542-6767	U /	-4.76	-0.38	7.00 /26	--	--	0.42	0.82
GR	MassMutual Premier Core Growth S	DLBRX	D	(800) 542-6767	E+ / 0.8	-9.02	-6.67	1.74 / 4	7.10 /11	-2.34 / 7	0.61	0.75
GL	MassMutual Premier Global L	MGFLX	U	(800) 542-6767	U /	-3.64	3.28	18.30 /80	--	--	0.63	1.14
GL	MassMutual Premier Global S	MGFSX	U	(800) 542-6767	U /	-3.55	3.45	18.66 /80	--	--	0.77	0.89
FO	MassMutual Premier Intl Equity L	MIELX	A	(800) 542-6767	B+ / 8.8	-2.69	7.21	25.77 /89	23.55 /89	6.97 /67	0.90	1.27
FO	MassMutual Premier Intl Equity N	MIENX	A-	(800) 542-6767	B+ / 8.6	-2.88	6.90	25.07 /89	22.62 /86	--	0.45	1.82
FO	MassMutual Premier Intl Equity S	MIEDX	B+	(800) 542-6767	B+ / 8.9	-2.66	7.30	26.07 /90	23.56 /89	5.54 /58	1.03	1.09
GR	MassMutual Premier Main Street L	MMSLX	U	(800) 542-6767	U /	-2.01	2.87	9.31 /42	--	--	1.06	0.93
GR	MassMutual Premier Main Street S	MMSSX	U	(800) 542-6767	U /	-1.91	3.15	9.82 /46	--	--	1.24	0.60
SC	MassMutual Premier Small Co Opp A	DLBMX	D+	(800) 542-6767	D+ / 2.9	-6.65	2.43	7.33 /28	11.51 /39	5.72 /59	0.00	1.14
SC	MassMutual Premier Small Co Opp N	MSCNX	D	(800) 542-6767	B- / 7.0	-6.69	2.32	6.97 /26	18.56 /75	--	0.00	1.49
SC	MassMutual Premier Small Co Opp S	MSCDX	C+	(800) 542-6767	B- / 7.1	-6.55	2.73	7.81 /31	18.58 /75	10.18 /81	0.00	0.69
GR	MassMutual Premier Value L	DLBVX	C	(888) 722-2766	C- / 3.9	-0.69	1.96	5.19 /16	11.35 /38	4.94 /54	1.56	0.80
AG	MassMutual Select Aggres Gr A	MMAAX	D	(800) 542-6767	D- / 1.5	-8.02	-9.58	1.56 / 3	10.89 /35	-0.24 /15	0.00	1.35
AG	MassMutual Select Aggres Gr N	MMANX	D	(800) 542-6767	D / 2.0	-7.99	-9.58	1.23 / 3	10.58 /32	--	0.00	1.66
AG	MassMutual Select Aggres Gr S	MGRSX	D+	(800) 542-6767	D+ / 2.7	-7.80	-9.32	2.03 / 4	11.41 /39	0.27 /17	0.00	0.86
GI	MassMutual Select Blue Chip Gr A	MBCGX	D-	(800) 542-6767	E / 0.4	-3.71	-2.11	3.52 / 9	5.86 / 6	-2.07 / 8	0.00	1.38
GI	MassMutual Select Blue Chip Gr L	MBCLX	D	(800) 542-6767	E+ / 0.9	-3.67	-1.98	3.74 /10	6.14 / 7	-1.81 / 9	0.02	1.13
GI	MassMutual Select Blue Chip Gr N	MBCNX	D-	(800) 542-6767	E+ / 0.6	-3.86	-2.24	3.20 / 8	5.56 / 5	--	0.00	1.68
GI	MassMutual Select Blue Chip Gr S	MBCSX	D	(800) 542-6767	D- / 1.1	-3.55	-1.86	3.99 /11	6.44 / 8	-1.55 /10	0.28	0.88
GI	MassMutual Select Blue Chip Gr Y	MBCYX	D	(800) 542-6767	D- / 1.0	-3.56	-1.87	3.88 /10	6.28 / 8	-1.68 / 9	0.17	1.01
AA	MassMutual Select Dest Ret 2020 A	MRTAX	U	(800) 542-6767	U /	-1.62	0.46	5.12 /16	--	--	2.31	1.25
AA	MassMutual Select Dest Ret 2020 L	MRTLX	U	(800) 542-6767	U /	-1.52	0.55	5.39 /17	--	--	2.53	1.00
AA	MassMutual Select Dest Ret 2020 S	MRTSX	U	(800) 542-6767	U /	-1.52	0.64	5.54 /18	--	--	2.67	0.85
AA	MassMutual Select Dest Ret 2020 Y	MRTYX	U	(800) 542-6767	U /	-1.52	0.64	5.52 /18	--	--	2.65	0.90
AA	MassMutual Select Dest Ret 2030 A	MRYAX	U	(800) 542-6767	U /	-2.35	1.22	7.96 /32	--	--	1.44	1.34
AA	MassMutual Select Dest Ret 2030 L	MYRLX	U	(800) 542-6767	U /	-2.34	1.30	8.21 /34	--	--	1.61	1.09
AA	MassMutual Select Dest Ret 2030 S	MRYSX	U	(800) 542-6767	U /	-2.34	1.39	8.37 /36	--	--	1.77	0.94
AA	MassMutual Select Dest Ret 2030 Y	MRYYX	U	(800) 542-6767	U /	-2.26	1.39	8.35 /36	--	--	1.75	0.99
GR	MassMutual Select Dest Ret 2040 A	MRFAX	U	(800) 542-6767	U /	-2.84	1.78	9.97 /47	--	--	0.88	1.38
GR	MassMutual Select Dest Ret 2040 L	MRFLX	U	(800) 542-6767	U /	-2.75	1.95	10.23 /48	--	--	1.04	1.13
GR	MassMutual Select Dest Ret 2040 S	MFRSX	U	(800) 542-6767	U /	-2.74	1.95	10.39 /49	--	--	1.19	0.98
GR	MassMutual Select Emerging Growth	MMEGX	E+	(800) 542-6767	C- / 4.2	-7.16	3.22	9.53 /44	13.28 /50	-2.07 / 8	0.00	1.47
GR	MassMutual Select Emerging Growth	MEGLX	D-	(800) 542-6767	C / 5.3	-7.06	3.34	9.95 /47	13.62 /52	-1.78 / 9	0.00	1.22
GR	MassMutual Select Emerging Growth	MEGNX	D-	(800) 542-6767	C / 4.7	-7.26	2.92	9.29 /42	12.89 /48	--	0.00	1.77
GR	MassMutual Select Emerging Growth	MEESX	D	(800) 542-6767	C / 5.4	-6.94	3.45	10.14 /48	13.84 /53	-1.49 /10	0.00	0.97
GR	MassMutual Select Emerging Growth	MEGYX	D	(800) 542-6767	C / 5.3	-6.99	3.48	10.04 /47	13.72 /52	-1.64 / 9	0.00	1.07
GR	MassMutual Select Focused Value A	MFVAX	C-	(800) 542-6767	D+ / 2.7	-2.07	2.09	3.85 /10	11.18 /37	10.43 /82	0.05	1.30
GR	MassMutual Select Focused Value L	MMFVX	C	(800) 542-6767	C- / 3.9	-1.98	2.25	4.19 /11	11.47 /39	10.72 /83	0.29	1.05
GR	MassMutual Select Focused Value N	MFVNX	C	(800) 542-6767	C- / 3.3	-2.10	2.00	3.61 / 9	10.79 /34	--	0.00	1.60
GR	MassMutual Select Focused Value S	MFVSX	C	(800) 542-6767	C- / 4.1	-1.96	2.39	4.43 /12	11.72 /41	10.98 /84	0.51	0.80
GR	MassMutual Select Focused Value Y	MMFYX	C	(800) 542-6767	C- / 4.0	-1.97	2.29	4.30 /12	11.61 /40	10.87 /83	0.42	0.90
IN	MassMutual Select Fundamental Val	MFUAX	B-	(800) 542-6767	C / 5.0	1.02	6.91	13.95 /68	13.24 /50	--	0.84	1.23
IN	MassMutual Select Fundamental Val	MFULX	B+	(800) 542-6767	C+ / 6.0	1.18	7.16	14.33 /69	13.51 /51	--	1.09	0.98
IN	MassMutual Select Fundamental Val	MFUNX	B	(800) 542-6767	C / 5.5	0.85	6.68	13.58 /67	12.88 /48	--	0.66	1.53
IN	MassMutual Select Fundamental Val	MVUSX	B+	(800) 542-6767	C+ / 6.1	1.10	7.14	14.40 /70	13.74 /53	--	1.27	0.79
IN	MassMutual Select Fundamental Val	MFUYX	B+	(800) 542-6767	C+ / 6.0	1.10	7.15	14.39 /70	13.68 /52	--	1.16	0.83
GI	MassMutual Select Growth Equity A	MGQAX	D-	(800) 542-6767	E- / 0.1	-6.54	-5.38	-1.79 / 1	3.55 / 2	-4.07 / 4	0.03	1.25
GI	MassMutual Select Growth Equity L	MGELX	D-	(800) 542-6767	E- / 0.2	-6.58	-5.19	-1.65 / 1	3.83 / 2	-3.82 / 4	0.30	1.00
GI	MassMutual Select Growth Equity N	MGENX	D-	(800) 542-6767	E- / 0.1	-6.63	-5.45	-2.10 / 1	3.29 / 1	--	0.00	1.55
GI	MassMutual Select Growth Equity S	MGESX	D-	(800) 542-6767	E- / 0.2	-6.51	-5.14	-1.44 / 1	4.01 / 2	-3.63 / 4	0.50	0.79

● Denotes fund is closed to new investors
★ Denotes fund is included in Section II

Risk Rating/Pts	Std Dev	Beta	NAV 6/30/06	Total $(Mil)	Cash %	Stocks %	Bonds %	Other %	Portfolio Turnover Ratio	Last Bull Return	Last Bear Return	Mgr Quality Pct	Mgr Tenure	Initial Purch $	Additional Purch $	Front End Load	Back End Load
U /	N/A	N/A	10.43	498	1	98	0	1	59.0	N/A	N/A	N/A	1	0	0	0.0	0.0
U /	N/A	N/A	10.40	41	1	98	0	1	59.0	N/A	N/A	N/A	1	0	0	0.0	0.0
B / 8.2	8.4	0.96	8.67	75	1	98	0	1	35.0	47.3	-8.4	23	N/A	0	0	0.0	0.0
U /	N/A	N/A	11.66	277	2	97	0	1	25.0	N/A	N/A	N/A	N/A	0	0	0.0	0.0
U /	N/A	N/A	11.69	419	2	97	0	1	25.0	N/A	N/A	N/A	N/A	0	0	0.0	0.0
B- / 7.0	12.7	1.17	13.38	110	1	98	0	1	26.0	159.4	-13.6	19	12	0	0	0.0	0.0
B- / 7.0	12.7	1.16	13.17	N/A	1	98	0	1	26.0	153.7	N/A	16	3	0	0	0.0	1.0
C+ / 6.1	12.7	1.16	13.53	715	1	98	0	1	26.0	159.7	-16.0	20	12	0	0	0.0	0.0
U /	N/A	N/A	10.75	102	0	99	0	1	78.0	N/A	N/A	N/A	4	0	0	0.0	0.0
U /	N/A	N/A	10.79	225	0	99	0	1	78.0	N/A	N/A	N/A	4	0	0	0.0	0.0
C+ / 6.8	13.3	0.87	16.42	285	3	96	0	1	45.0	71.6	-5.4	17	N/A	0	0	5.8	0.0
D+ / 2.4	19.5	1.09	16.33	N/A	3	96	0	1	45.0	111.6	N/A	38	N/A	0	0	0.0	1.0
C+ / 5.7	18.5	1.06	16.56	348	3	96	0	1	45.0	112.0	-7.1	43	N/A	0	0	0.0	0.0
B- / 7.9	7.5	0.87	17.20	71	6	93	0	1	53.0	65.8	-9.1	69	N/A	0	0	0.0	0.0
B- / 7.2	12.3	1.26	5.85	119	0	99	0	1	24.0	68.4	-8.4	30	N/A	0	0	5.8	0.0
B- / 7.2	12.2	1.25	5.76	1	0	99	0	1	24.0	67.0	N/A	28	N/A	0	0	0.0	1.0
B- / 7.2	12.3	1.26	6.03	236	0	99	0	1	24.0	71.4	-8.6	34	N/A	0	0	0.0	0.0
B / 8.0	8.0	1.01	8.82	35	0	99	0	1	28.0	42.0	-10.2	13	N/A	0	0	5.8	0.0
B / 8.0	8.0	1.02	8.92	268	0	99	0	1	28.0	43.3	-9.4	14	N/A	0	0	0.0	0.0
B- / 7.9	8.0	1.01	8.72	3	0	99	0	1	28.0	41.0	N/A	12	N/A	0	0	0.0	1.0
B / 8.0	8.0	1.01	8.97	60	0	99	0	1	28.0	44.3	-9.3	16	N/A	0	0	0.0	0.0
B / 8.0	8.0	1.01	8.94	41	0	99	0	1	28.0	43.9	-9.7	15	N/A	0	0	0.0	0.0
U /	N/A	N/A	10.96	114	N/A	57	42	N/A	23.0	N/A	N/A	N/A	3	0	0	5.8	0.0
U /	N/A	N/A	11.02	253	N/A	57	42	N/A	23.0	N/A	N/A	N/A	3	0	0	0.0	0.0
U /	N/A	N/A	11.03	50	N/A	57	42	N/A	23.0	N/A	N/A	N/A	3	0	0	0.0	0.0
U /	N/A	N/A	11.02	81	N/A	57	42	N/A	23.0	N/A	N/A	N/A	3	0	0	0.0	0.0
U /	N/A	N/A	11.64	85	N/A	82	17	N/A	17.0	N/A	N/A	N/A	3	0	0	5.8	0.0
U /	N/A	N/A	11.70	194	N/A	82	17	N/A	17.0	N/A	N/A	N/A	3	0	0	0.0	0.0
U /	N/A	N/A	11.71	32	N/A	82	17	N/A	17.0	N/A	N/A	N/A	3	0	0	0.0	0.0
U /	N/A	N/A	11.70	46	N/A	82	17	N/A	17.0	N/A	N/A	N/A	3	0	0	0.0	0.0
U /	N/A	N/A	11.98	35	N/A	99	0	N/A	18.0	N/A	N/A	N/A	3	0	0	5.8	0.0
U /	N/A	N/A	12.04	124	N/A	99	0	N/A	18.0	N/A	N/A	N/A	3	0	0	0.0	0.0
U /	N/A	N/A	12.05	33	N/A	99	0	N/A	18.0	N/A	N/A	N/A	3	0	0	0.0	0.0
C- / 3.2	17.5	1.75	6.09	16	4	95	0	1	124.0	101.2	-17.1	17	5	0	0	5.8	0.0
C- / 3.3	17.5	1.75	6.19	51	4	95	0	1	124.0	102.7	-17.0	19	N/A	0	0	0.0	0.0
C- / 3.2	17.5	1.75	6.00	N/A	4	95	0	1	124.0	99.7	N/A	15	3	0	0	0.0	1.0
C- / 3.3	17.5	1.74	6.30	51	4	95	0	1	124.0	104.5	-16.8	20	6	0	0	0.0	0.0
C- / 3.3	17.5	1.75	6.25	5	4	95	0	1	124.0	103.6	-16.9	19	N/A	0	0	0.0	0.0
B / 8.2	9.4	1.10	17.06	240	4	95	0	1	31.0	79.8	-6.0	45	N/A	0	0	5.8	0.0
B / 8.3	9.4	1.09	17.30	186	4	95	0	1	31.0	81.2	-5.9	49	N/A	0	0	0.0	0.0
B / 8.2	9.4	1.10	16.81	2	4	95	0	1	31.0	77.8	N/A	41	N/A	0	0	0.0	1.0
B / 8.3	9.4	1.10	17.53	343	4	95	0	1	31.0	82.8	-5.9	52	N/A	0	0	0.0	0.0
B / 8.3	9.4	1.09	17.42	117	4	95	0	1	31.0	82.1	-5.8	51	N/A	0	0	0.0	0.0
B / 8.7	8.1	1.01	11.91	261	1	98	0	1	33.0	73.0	-10.9	75	4	0	0	5.8	0.0
B / 8.7	8.1	1.01	11.97	292	1	98	0	1	33.0	74.2	-10.9	77	4	0	0	0.0	0.0
B / 8.7	8.1	1.01	11.81	1	1	98	0	1	33.0	71.4	N/A	71	3	0	0	0.0	1.0
B / 8.7	8.1	1.00	12.00	473	1	98	0	1	33.0	75.2	-10.7	79	N/A	0	0	0.0	0.0
B / 8.8	8.1	1.00	11.99	96	1	98	0	1	33.0	75.0	-10.8	79	4	0	0	0.0	0.0
B- / 7.6	9.2	1.10	7.57	146	1	98	0	1	92.0	35.6	-10.1	4	N/A	0	0	5.8	0.0
B- / 7.6	9.1	1.09	7.67	339	1	98	0	1	92.0	36.6	-10.0	5	N/A	0	0	0.0	0.0
B- / 7.6	9.1	1.09	7.46	N/A	1	98	0	1	92.0	34.2	N/A	4	N/A	0	0	0.0	1.0
B- / 7.6	9.1	1.10	7.75	281	1	98	0	1	92.0	37.5	-9.9	5	N/A	0	0	0.0	0.0

					PERFORMANCE							
	99 Pct = Best 0 Pct = Worst					Total Return % through 6/30/06					Incl. in Returns	
			Overall Weiss		Perfor- mance				Annualized		Dividend	Expense
Fund Type	Fund Name	Ticker Symbol	Investment Rating	Phone	Rating/Pts	3 Mo	6 Mo	1Yr / Pct	3Yr / Pct	5Yr / Pct	Yield	Ratio
GI	MassMutual Select Growth Equity Y	MGEYX	D-	(800) 542-6767	E- / 0.2	-6.54	-5.16	-1.51 / 1	3.94 / 2	-3.69 / 4	0.43	0.85
GR	MassMutual Select Indexed Equity A	MIEAX	C-	(800) 542-6767	D+ / 2.6	-1.59	2.35	7.88 /32	10.36 /30	1.67 /25	0.92	0.65
GR	MassMutual Select Indexed Equity L	MMILX	C+	(800) 542-6767	C- / 3.7	-1.50	2.52	8.11 /33	10.63 /32	1.93 /27	1.30	0.40
GR	MassMutual Select Indexed Equity N	MMINX	C	(800) 542-6767	C- / 3.2	-1.69	2.20	7.51 /29	9.99 /27	--	0.82	0.95
GR	MassMutual Select Indexed Equity S	MMIEX	C+	(800) 542-6767	C- / 3.8	-1.57	2.49	8.12 /34	10.74 /33	2.04 /28	1.31	0.42
GR	MassMutual Select Indexed Equity Z	MIEZX	C+	(800) 542-6767	C- / 3.7	-1.48	2.66	8.46 /36	10.55 /31	3.81 /44	1.54	0.20
GR	MassMutual Select Large Cap Gr A	MLGAX	D-	(800) 542-6767	E+ / 0.7	-7.83	-7.39	6.72 /25	7.60 /13	--	0.00	1.38
GR	MassMutual Select Large Cap Gr L	MLGLX	D	(800) 542-6767	D / 1.6	-7.75	-7.31	6.90 /26	8.33 /17	--	0.00	1.09
GR	MassMutual Select Large Cap Gr N	MLGNX	D	(800) 542-6767	D- / 1.2	-7.83	-7.57	6.36 /22	7.79 /14	--	0.00	1.66
GR	MassMutual Select Large Cap Gr S	MLGSX	D	(800) 542-6767	D- / 1.5	-7.70	-7.17	7.17 /27	8.05 /15	--	0.00	0.94
GR	MassMutual Select Large Cap Gr Y	MLGYX	D	(800) 542-6767	D- / 1.5	-7.82	-7.29	7.10 /27	7.97 /15	--	0.00	0.98
GR	MassMutual Select Large Cap Value	MMLAX	B-	(800) 542-6767	C / 4.5	0.35	2.84	10.97 /53	13.30 /50	5.13 /55	0.41	1.25
GR	MassMutual Select Large Cap Value	MLVLX	B+	(800) 542-6767	C+ / 5.7	0.34	2.92	11.26 /55	13.55 /52	5.41 /57	0.65	1.00
GR	MassMutual Select Large Cap Value	MLVNX	B	(800) 542-6767	C / 5.2	0.35	2.78	10.70 /52	12.95 /49	--	0.09	1.55
GR	MassMutual Select Large Cap Value	MLVSX	B+	(800) 542-6767	C+ / 5.8	0.43	3.08	11.45 /56	13.82 /53	5.65 /59	0.86	0.76
GR	MassMutual Select Large Cap Value	MMLYX	B+	(800) 542-6767	C+ / 5.7	0.43	3.09	11.46 /56	13.69 /52	5.58 /58	0.77	0.85
MC	MassMutual Select Mid Cap Gr Eq A	MMMAX	C	(800) 542-6767	C+ / 5.6	-5.87	6.10	16.28 /75	15.90 /63	1.69 /25	0.00	1.30
MC	MassMutual Select Mid Cap Gr Eq L	MMGLX	C+	(800) 542-6767	C+ / 6.5	-5.85	6.20	16.45 /76	16.19 /64	1.96 /27	0.00	1.05
MC	MassMutual Select Mid Cap Gr Eq N	MMGNX	C	(800) 542-6767	C+ / 6.1	-5.94	5.97	15.88 /74	15.55 /62	--	0.00	1.60
MC	MassMutual Select Mid Cap Gr Eq S	MCGSX	C+	(800) 542-6767	C+ / 6.6	-5.77	6.42	16.81 /77	16.45 /65	2.19 /29	0.00	0.83
MC	MassMutual Select Mid Cap Gr Eq Y	MCGYX	C+	(800) 542-6767	C+ / 6.6	-5.71	6.34	16.76 /76	16.36 /65	2.10 /28	0.00	0.90
MC	MassMutual Select Mid Cp Gr Eq II A	MEFAX	C+	(800) 542-6767	C+ / 5.8	-4.92	1.13	13.11 /65	16.02 /64	7.48 /69	0.00	1.35
MC	MassMutual Select Mid Cp Gr Eq II L	MMELX	B-	(800) 542-6767	C+ / 6.6	-4.91	1.26	13.40 /66	16.29 /65	7.75 /70	0.00	1.10
MC	MassMutual Select Mid Cp Gr Eq II N	MEFNX	B-	(800) 542-6767	C+ / 6.2	-4.99	1.00	12.50 /62	15.62 /62	--	0.00	1.65
MC	MassMutual Select Mid Cp Gr Eq II S	MGRFX	B-	(800) 542-6767	C+ / 6.7	-4.84	1.38	13.60 /67	16.57 /66	8.00 /72	0.00	0.86
MC	MassMutual Select Mid Cp Gr Eq II Y	MEFYX	B-	(800) 542-6767	C+ / 6.7	-4.86	1.31	13.51 /66	16.48 /66	7.92 /71	0.00	0.95
IN	MassMutual Select OTC 100 A	MOTAX	E+	(800) 542-6767	D- / 1.0	-7.75	-4.61	4.80 /14	8.62 /19	-3.74 / 4	0.00	1.11
IN	MassMutual Select OTC 100 L	MOTLX	D-	(800) 542-6767	D / 1.8	-7.66	-4.56	5.01 /15	8.89 /20	-3.51 / 4	0.00	0.86
IN	MassMutual Select OTC 100 N	MOTNX	D-	(800) 542-6767	D- / 1.5	-7.62	-4.67	4.58 /13	8.38 /17	--	0.00	1.41
IN	MassMutual Select OTC 100 S	MOTCX	D-	(800) 542-6767	D / 2.1	-7.55	-4.27	5.21 /16	9.18 /22	-3.25 / 5	0.00	0.61
IN	MassMutual Select OTC 100 Y	MOTYX	D-	(800) 542-6767	D / 2.0	-7.60	-4.30	5.25 /16	9.12 /22	-3.37 / 5	0.00	0.71
FO	MassMutual Select Overseas A	MOSAX	B-	(800) 542-6767	B / 8.2	1.17	10.78	23.94 /87	20.49 /81	8.15 /72	1.26	1.52
FO	MassMutual Select Overseas L	MOSLX	A+	(800) 542-6767	B+ / 8.6	1.24	10.90	24.16 /87	20.82 /82	8.40 /73	1.52	1.27
FO	MassMutual Select Overseas N	MOSNX	A+	(800) 542-6767	B+ / 8.4	1.09	10.59	23.51 /87	20.12 /80	--	1.10	1.82
FO	MassMutual Select Overseas S	MOSSX	A+	(800) 542-6767	B+ / 8.7	1.32	11.03	24.50 /88	21.05 /83	8.63 /75	1.71	1.17
FO	MassMutual Select Overseas Y	MOSYX	B	(800) 542-6767	B+ / 8.6	1.24	10.96	24.39 /88	20.98 /82	8.56 /74	1.66	1.22
SC	MassMutual Select Small Cap Gr Eq	MMGEX	C+	(800) 542-6767	C+ / 6.1	-5.59	4.13	14.48 /70	16.59 /66	5.04 /55	0.00	1.51
SC	MassMutual Select Small Cap Gr Eq	MSGLX	B	(800) 542-6767	B- / 7.0	-5.56	4.20	14.76 /71	16.85 /67	5.31 /56	0.00	1.26
SC	MassMutual Select Small Cap Gr Eq	MSGNX	B-	(800) 542-6767	C+ / 6.6	-5.68	3.87	14.08 /68	16.22 /64	--	0.00	1.81
SC	MassMutual Select Small Cap Gr Eq	MSGSX	B	(800) 542-6767	B- / 7.1	-5.52	4.31	15.07 /72	17.20 /69	5.61 /59	0.00	0.97
SC	MassMutual Select Small Cap Gr Eq	MSCYX	B	(800) 542-6767	B- / 7.1	-5.51	4.28	14.98 /72	17.06 /68	5.47 /58	0.00	1.11
SC	MassMutual Select Small Comp Gr A	MRWAX	E-	(800) 542-6767	D+ / 2.8	-9.61	3.92	10.85 /53	11.21 /37	--	0.00	1.54
SC	MassMutual Select Small Comp Gr L	MMCLX	E	(800) 542-6767	C- / 4.2	-9.49	4.08	11.17 /55	11.50 /39	--	0.00	1.29
SC	MassMutual Select Small Comp Gr N	MMCNX	E-	(800) 542-6767	C- / 3.5	-9.67	3.77	10.44 /50	10.90 /35	--	0.00	1.84
SC	MassMutual Select Small Comp Gr S	MSCSX	E	(800) 542-6767	C / 4.4	-9.40	4.14	11.41 /56	11.75 /41	--	0.00	1.10
SC	MassMutual Select Small Comp Gr Y	MMCYX	E	(800) 542-6767	C / 4.3	-9.43	4.15	11.32 /55	11.69 /40	--	0.00	1.14
SC	MassMutual Select Small Comp Val A	MMYAX	B+	(800) 542-6767	B- / 7.5	-3.53	8.96	15.31 /73	19.76 /79	--	0.00	1.49
SC	MassMutual Select Small Comp Val L	MMYLX	A-	(800) 542-6767	B / 8.1	-3.45	9.14	15.62 /74	20.06 /79	--	0.00	1.24
SC	MassMutual Select Small Comp Val	MSVNX	B+	(800) 542-6767	B / 7.8	-3.58	8.79	14.95 /72	19.43 /77	--	0.00	1.79
SC	MassMutual Select Small Comp Val S	MSVSX	A-	(800) 542-6767	B / 8.2	-3.43	9.13	15.81 /74	20.30 /80	--	0.00	1.05
SC	MassMutual Select Small Comp Val Y	MMVYX	B+	(800) 542-6767	B / 8.2	-3.44	9.16	15.78 /74	20.25 /80	--	0.00	1.09
IN	MassMutual Select Value Equity L	MMVLX	B	(800) 542-6767	C+ / 6.5	-2.25	3.24	12.99 /64	15.47 /61	5.46 /58	0.53	1.05

● Denotes fund is closed to new investors
★ Denotes fund is included in Section II

www.WeissRatings.com

RISK			NET ASSETS		ASSET				BULL / BEAR		FUND MANAGER		MINIMUMS		LOADS	
	3 Year		NAV						Last Bull	Last Bear	Manager	Manager	Initial	Additional	Front	Back
Risk	Standard		As of	Total	Cash	Stocks	Bonds	Other	Market	Market	Quality	Tenure	Purch.	Purch.	End	End
Rating/Pts	Deviation	Beta	6/30/06	$(Mil)	%	%	%	%	Return	Return	Pct	(Years)	$	$	Load	Load
B- / 7.6	9.1	1.09	7.72	69	1	98	0	1	92.0	37.3	-10.0	5	N/A	0	0	0.0	0.0
B / 8.8	7.6	0.99	11.74	270	1	98	0	1	6.0	60.6	-9.8	47	N/A	0	0	5.8	0.0
B / 8.8	7.7	1.00	11.79	302	1	98	0	1	6.0	62.1	-9.9	49	3	0	0	0.0	0.0
B / 8.7	7.6	1.00	11.60	5	1	98	0	1	6.0	59.3	N/A	42	N/A	0	0	0.0	1.0
B / 8.8	7.7	1.01	11.94	642	1	98	0	1	6.0	62.6	-9.9	50	N/A	0	0	0.0	0.0
B / 8.9	7.5	0.97	11.96	309	1	98	0	1	6.0	61.8	-6.4	52	N/A	0	0	0.0	0.0
B- / 7.4	11.3	1.26	9.53	6	1	98	0	1	83.0	54.9	-13.1	12	3	0	0	5.8	0.0
B- / 7.4	11.2	1.26	9.76	2	1	98	0	1	83.0	58.3	-12.9	14	3	0	0	0.0	0.0
B- / 7.4	11.2	1.26	9.53	N/A	1	98	0	1	83.0	55.6	N/A	12	3	0	0	0.0	1.0
B- / 7.4	11.2	1.25	9.71	18	1	98	0	1	83.0	56.9	-12.6	14	N/A	0	0	0.0	0.0
B- / 7.4	11.2	1.25	9.66	9	1	98	0	1	83.0	56.8	-12.7	13	3	0	0	0.0	0.0
B+ / 9.2	6.9	0.84	11.60	370	0	99	0	1	7.0	71.5	-7.5	86	6	0	0	5.8	1.0
B+ / 9.1	6.9	0.84	11.65	346	0	99	0	1	7.0	72.7	-7.3	87	6	0	0	0.0	0.0
B+ / 9.1	6.9	0.84	11.48	2	0	99	0	1	7.0	69.8	N/A	84	3	0	0	0.0	1.0
B+ / 9.2	6.8	0.83	11.71	567	0	99	0	1	7.0	74.0	-7.3	89	6	0	0	0.0	0.0
B+ / 9.2	6.9	0.84	11.69	193	0	99	0	1	7.0	73.4	-7.2	88	6	0	0	0.0	0.0
C+ / 6.4	14.6	1.24	10.43	39	0	99	0	1	117.0	99.8	-11.0	12	N/A	0	0	5.8	0.0
C+ / 6.4	14.7	1.24	10.62	44	0	99	0	1	117.0	101.4	-10.9	13	N/A	0	0	0.0	0.0
C+ / 6.3	14.7	1.24	10.29	N/A	0	99	0	1	117.0	97.9	N/A	11	N/A	0	0	0.0	1.0
C+ / 6.4	14.7	1.24	10.77	85	0	99	0	1	117.0	102.6	-10.7	14	N/A	0	0	0.0	0.0
C+ / 6.4	14.7	1.24	10.73	26	0	99	0	1	117.0	102.2	-10.9	14	N/A	0	0	0.0	0.0
B- / 7.7	10.9	0.96	14.29	324	2	97	0	1	28.0	100.8	-8.2	40	N/A	0	0	5.8	0.0
B- / 7.7	10.9	0.96	14.52	550	2	97	0	1	28.0	102.4	-8.0	43	N/A	0	0	0.0	0.0
B- / 7.7	11.0	0.97	14.09	2	2	97	0	1	28.0	98.6	N/A	36	N/A	0	0	0.0	1.0
B- / 7.7	10.9	0.96	14.74	285	2	97	0	1	28.0	104.0	-8.0	45	N/A	0	0	0.0	0.0
B- / 7.7	10.9	0.96	14.67	164	2	97	0	1	28.0	103.4	-8.0	45	N/A	0	0	0.0	0.0
C+ / 6.2	14.9	1.68	3.93	22	N/A	N/A	0	N/A	17.0	64.3	-9.8	4	3	0	0	5.8	0.0
C+ / 6.2	14.9	1.68	3.98	11	N/A	N/A	0	N/A	17.0	65.2	-9.7	5	3	0	0	0.0	1.0
C+ / 6.2	15.0	1.68	3.88	N/A	N/A	N/A	0	N/A	17.0	62.5	N/A	4	3	0	0	0.0	1.0
C+ / 6.2	14.9	1.68	4.04	16	N/A	N/A	0	N/A	17.0	66.6	-9.6	5	6	0	0	0.0	0.0
C+ / 6.2	15.0	1.69	4.01	2	N/A	N/A	0	N/A	17.0	66.0	-9.7	5	6	0	0	0.0	0.0
C+ / 5.8	9.4	0.89	12.13	247	3	96	0	1	88.0	113.2	-12.1	43	N/A	0	0	5.8	0.0
B / 8.3	9.4	0.89	12.21	266	3	96	0	1	88.0	115.0	-12.1	46	5	0	0	0.0	0.0
B / 8.2	9.3	0.88	12.01	2	3	96	0	1	88.0	111.4	N/A	40	N/A	0	0	0.0	1.0
B / 8.3	9.4	0.89	12.28	374	3	96	0	1	88.0	116.3	-12.1	48	5	0	0	0.0	0.0
C+ / 5.9	9.4	0.89	12.25	187	3	96	0	1	88.0	116.1	-12.1	47	N/A	0	0	0.0	0.0
B- / 7.1	13.0	0.86	16.37	116	8	91	0	1	59.0	102.4	-8.9	60	N/A	0	0	5.8	1.0
B- / 7.1	12.9	0.86	16.64	98	8	91	0	1	59.0	104.0	-8.8	63	N/A	0	0	0.0	0.0
B- / 7.1	12.9	0.86	16.12	1	8	91	0	1	59.0	100.7	N/A	57	3	0	0	0.0	1.0
B- / 7.1	12.9	0.85	16.95	323	8	91	0	1	59.0	105.8	-8.8	67	4	0	0	0.0	0.0
B- / 7.1	12.9	0.86	16.81	133	8	91	0	1	59.0	105.0	-8.8	65	N/A	0	0	0.0	0.0
D- / 1.4	20.8	1.35	10.07	68	3	96	0	1	149.0	99.2	-14.9	1	N/A	0	0	5.8	1.0
E+ / 0.9	20.8	1.35	10.21	35	3	96	0	1	149.0	101.0	-14.6	1	N/A	0	0	0.0	0.0
D- / 1.4	20.8	1.35	9.90	1	3	96	0	1	149.0	97.3	N/A	1	N/A	0	0	0.0	0.0
D- / 1.4	20.8	1.35	10.31	35	3	96	0	1	149.0	102.0	-18.1	1	N/A	0	0	0.0	0.0
E+ / 0.9	20.8	1.35	10.28	21	3	96	0	1	149.0	101.8	-14.5	1	3	0	0	0.0	0.0
B- / 7.4	12.1	0.82	15.56	153	5	94	0	1	56.0	120.1	-10.7	88	N/A	0	0	5.8	1.0
B- / 7.4	12.1	0.82	15.65	152	5	94	0	1	56.0	121.8	-10.5	89	N/A	0	0	0.0	0.0
B- / 7.4	12.1	0.82	15.35	1	5	94	0	1	56.0	118.1	N/A	86	3	0	0	0.0	1.0
B- / 7.4	12.1	0.82	15.78	295	5	94	0	1	56.0	123.3	-10.3	90	N/A	0	0	0.0	0.0
C+ / 6.8	12.1	0.83	15.73	164	5	94	0	1	56.0	122.9	-10.3	90	3	0	0	0.0	0.0
B / 8.3	9.5	1.17	10.85	9	0	100	0	0	94.0	86.0	-11.3	80	2	0	0	0.0	0.0

					PERFORMANCE							
	99 Pct = Best 0 Pct = Worst					Total Return % through 6/30/06					Incl. in Returns	
			Overall Weiss		Perfor- mance				Annualized		Dividend	Expense
Fund Type	Fund Name	Ticker Symbol	Investment Rating	Phone	Rating/Pts	3 Mo	6 Mo	1Yr / Pct	3Yr / Pct	5Yr / Pct	Yield	Ratio
IN	MassMutual Select Value Equity N	MMVNX	B-	(800) 542-6767	C+ / 5.6	-2.34	3.04	12.53 /62	13.75 /53	--	0.04	1.59
IN	MassMutual Select Value Equity S	MVESX	B	(800) 542-6767	C+ / 6.1	-2.16	3.32	13.26 /65	14.52 /56	5.34 /57	0.71	0.85
IN	MassMutual Select Value Equity Y	MVEYX	B	(800) 542-6767	C+ / 6.1	-2.15	3.41	13.29 /65	14.47 /56	5.31 /56	0.66	0.90
BA	MassMutual Strategic Balanced A	MTSAX	U	(800) 542-6767	U /	-1.01	1.80	5.69 /19	--	--	1.55	1.21
BA	MassMutual Strategic Balanced L	MTSLX	U	(800) 542-6767	U /	-1.01	1.80	5.89 /20	--	--	2.03	0.96
BA	MassMutual Strategic Balanced Y	MSTYX	U	(800) 542-6767	U /	-1.01	1.89	6.03 /21	--	--	2.16	0.81
IN	MassMutual Strategic Income L	MISLX	U	(800) 542-6767	U /	-1.61	-0.41	0.98 / 2	--	--	3.99	0.89
GR	● Masters Select Equity Fund	MSEFX	C-	(800) 960-0188	C- / 4.0	-4.09	-0.07	9.56 /44	11.98 /42	3.67 /43	0.00	1.19
FO	● Masters Select International Fund	MSILX	A+	(800) 960-0188	A- / 9.0	-0.26	7.89	29.63 /94	24.09 /90	11.49 /85	1.35	1.08
SC	● Masters Select Smaller Companies	MSSFX	C+	(800) 960-0188	C+ / 6.2	-6.27	3.97	8.53 /37	16.44 /65	--	0.00	1.30
GR	Mastrapasqua Growth Fund	MAGVX	E+	(800) 448-0982	D / 1.9	-8.46	-3.50	5.34 /17	8.85 /20	-2.55 / 6	0.00	1.25
GI	Matrix Advisor Value Fund	MAVFX	D-	(866) 811-0215	D- / 1.5	-3.87	-1.52	4.09 /11	7.76 /14	4.59 /51	0.64	0.99
GR	Matthew 25 Fund	MXXVX	C-	(888) 625-3863	C / 4.8	-6.68	-2.29	1.92 / 4	14.69 /57	10.54 /82	0.28	1.17
FO	● Matthews Asian Growth & Income Fd	MACSX	A+	(800) 892-0382	B+ / 8.8	0.80	7.10	18.16 /79	23.73 /89	19.10 /95	2.36	1.27
TC	Matthews Asian Technology Fund	MATFX	C+	(800) 892-0382	B+ / 8.8	-6.36	1.38	21.02 /83	24.29 /90	10.09 /81	0.00	1.48
FO	Matthews Asia-Pacific Fund	MPACX	U	(800) 892-0382	U /	-4.07	2.89	20.92 /83	--	--	0.37	1.34
FO	Matthews China Fund	MCHFX	C+	(800) 892-0382	A- / 9.2	-0.28	19.72	26.98 /91	24.50 /90	11.37 /85	1.23	1.30
FO	Matthews India Fund	MINDX	U	(800) 892-0382	U /	-15.79	0.80	--	--	--	0.00	2.00
FO	Matthews Japan Fund	MJFOX	C+	(800) 892-0382	B+ / 8.9	-7.01	-2.38	17.33 /78	26.20 /92	7.38 /69	0.17	1.28
FO	Matthews Korea Fund	MAKOX	C+	(800) 892-0382	A+ / 9.6	-5.56	-1.26	40.57 /98	32.77 /97	29.71 /99	0.00	1.35
★ FO	● Matthews Pacific Tiger Fund	MAPTX	B+	(800) 892-0382	A / 9.4	-3.51	4.05	23.58 /87	29.64 /95	18.97 /95	0.60	1.31
GR	McCarthy Multi-Cap Stk Fund	MGAMX	C+	(888) 263-6443	C- / 3.8	-3.99	-1.03	6.27 /22	11.57 /40	--	0.00	1.15
GL	McIntyre Global Equity Fund	DGLEX	C-	(800) 560-0086	C- / 4.1	-4.57	1.53	9.82 /46	11.36 /38	-5.18 / 2	0.00	0.30
BA	McMorgan Balanced Fd	MCMBX	C-	(800) 788-9485	D / 1.8	-1.22	1.64	5.62 /18	7.24 /11	2.83 /35	2.29	0.60
BA	McMorgan Balanced Z	MCBZX	C-	(800) 788-9485	D / 1.6	-1.29	1.47	5.36 /17	6.97 /10	2.56 /32	2.05	0.85
GR	McMorgan Equity Investment Fd	MCMEX	C	(800) 788-9485	C- / 3.6	-1.93	2.88	9.33 /42	10.29 /29	0.52 /18	1.11	0.75
GR	McMorgan Equity Investment Z	MCEZX	C	(800) 788-9485	C- / 3.5	-1.99	2.71	9.01 /40	10.00 /27	0.26 /17	0.90	1.00
GR	MDT All Cap Core A	QAACX	C+	(866) 784-6867	C / 5.0	-2.12	2.36	10.71 /52	14.89 /58	--	0.03	1.50
GR	MDT All Cap Core C	QCACX	U	(866) 784-6867	U /	-2.26	1.96	--	--	--	0.00	2.25
GR	MDT All Cap Core Instl	QIACX	B	(866) 784-6867	C+ / 6.0	-1.99	2.48	11.05 /54	15.15 /60	--	0.10	1.25
BA	MDT Balanced Growth A	QABGX	B-	(866) 784-6867	C / 4.3	-0.67	3.19	9.40 /43	12.97 /49	--	1.14	1.50
BA	MDT Balanced Growth C	QCBGX	B	(866) 784-6867	C / 4.9	-0.83	2.80	8.73 /38	12.74 /47	--	1.05	2.25
BA	MDT Balanced Growth Instl	QIBGX	B	(866) 784-6867	C / 5.0	-0.60	3.26	9.56 /44	13.02 /49	--	1.27	1.25
GR	Meeder Defensive Equity Portfolio	MPDEX	U	(800) 325-3539	U /	-3.20	2.37	4.68 /14	--	--	1.40	0.75
BA	Mellon Balanced Inv	MIBLX	C	(800) 499-3327	C- / 3.0	-1.71	2.00	7.50 /29	9.41 /24	--	1.92	0.85
BA	Mellon Balanced M	MPBLX	C	(800) 499-3327	C- / 3.2	-1.58	2.14	7.87 /32	9.72 /25	5.14 /55	2.17	0.58
EM	Mellon Emerging Markets Inv	MIEGX	C+	(800) 499-3327	A+ / 9.6	-5.29	5.78	28.96 /94	30.71 /96	--	1.44	1.72
EM	Mellon Emerging Markets M	MEMKX	C+	(800) 499-3327	A+ / 9.6	-5.28	5.86	29.23 /94	31.02 /96	21.09 /97	1.64	1.51
GI	Mellon Income Stock Inv	MIISX	C+	(800) 499-3327	C / 5.2	-0.40	3.78	9.24 /42	12.96 /49	--	1.70	1.07
GI	Mellon Income Stock M	MPISX	C+	(800) 499-3327	C / 5.5	-0.25	4.03	9.66 /45	13.37 /51	4.12 /47	1.94	0.82
FO	Mellon International Inv	MIINX	B+	(800) 499-3327	B+ / 8.9	0.79	9.56	23.92 /87	22.85 /87	--	1.02	1.34
★ FO	Mellon International M	MPITX	A	(800) 499-3327	B+ / 8.9	0.88	9.74	24.20 /87	23.28 /88	11.39 /85	1.24	1.09
GR	Mellon Large Cap Stock Inv	MILCX	D	(800) 499-3327	D+ / 2.8	-2.59	1.17	6.57 /24	9.33 /23	--	0.68	1.05
GR	Mellon Large Cap Stock M	MPLCX	C-	(800) 499-3327	C- / 3.0	-2.53	1.30	6.84 /25	9.62 /25	0.69 /19	0.92	0.80
MC	Mellon Mid Cap Stock Inv	MIMSX	A-	(800) 499-3327	B / 7.9	-3.98	6.24	17.20 /77	19.38 /77	--	0.00	1.15
MC	Mellon Mid Cap Stock M	MPMCX	C+	(800) 499-3327	B / 8.0	-3.83	6.46	17.63 /78	19.73 /78	8.65 /75	0.03	0.91
MC	● Mellon Mid Cap Stock Prem	MMSPX	B+	(800) 499-3327	B- / 7.3	-4.09	5.95	16.45 /76	18.56 /75	--	0.00	1.88
SC	Mellon Small Cap Stock Inv	MISCX	C+	(800) 499-3327	C+ / 6.8	-4.95	7.23	10.30 /49	16.63 /66	--	0.00	1.26
SC	Mellon Small Cap Stock M	MPSSX	C-	(800) 499-3327	C+ / 6.9	-4.87	7.39	10.62 /51	16.94 /68	8.66 /75	0.00	1.01
BA	MEMBERS Balanced Fd A	MBLAX	D+	(800) 877-6089	E+ / 0.6	-1.64	0.07	2.98 / 7	6.95 /10	3.03 /37	1.79	1.10
BA	MEMBERS Balanced Fd B	MBLNX	C-	(800) 877-6089	E+ / 0.6	-1.82	-0.38	2.21 / 5	6.15 / 7	2.26 /30	1.15	1.85
FO	MEMBERS International Fd A	MINAX	A-	(800) 877-6089	B+ / 8.6	-1.49	8.17	25.86 /90	24.25 /90	12.15 /87	0.88	1.60

● Denotes fund is closed to new investors
★ Denotes fund is included in Section II

RISK			NET ASSETS		ASSET					BULL / BEAR		FUND MANAGER		MINIMUMS		LOADS	
Risk Rating/Pts	3 Year		NAV As of 6/30/06	Total $(Mil)	Cash %	Stocks %	Bonds %	Other %	Portfolio Turnover Ratio	Last Bull Market Return	Last Bear Market Return	Manager Quality Pct	Manager Tenure (Years)	Initial Purch. $	Additional Purch. $	Front End Load	Back End Load
	Standard Deviation	Beta															
B / 8.4	9.1	1.13	10.83	N/A	0	100	0	0	94.0	77.7	N/A	69	2	0	0	0.0	1.0
B / 8.4	9.0	1.13	10.89	56	0	100	0	0	94.0	81.5	-10.1	76	2	0	0	0.0	0.0
B / 8.4	9.0	1.13	10.91	5	0	100	0	0	94.0	81.3	-10.1	76	2	0	0	0.0	0.0
U /	N/A	N/A	10.75	28	7	57	34	2	211.0	N/A	N/A	N/A	N/A	0	0	5.8	0.0
U /	N/A	N/A	10.77	91	7	57	34	2	211.0	N/A	N/A	N/A	N/A	0	0	0.0	0.0
U /	N/A	N/A	10.78	87	7	57	34	2	211.0	N/A	N/A	N/A	N/A	0	0	0.0	0.0
U /	N/A	N/A	9.78	203	4	3	91	2	159.0	N/A	N/A	N/A	N/A	0	0	0.0	0.0
B- / 7.2	11.3	1.35	15.23	885	2	97	0	1	46.1	75.4	-11.9	31	10	5,000	250	0.0	2.0
B- / 7.6	11.3	1.04	18.86	1,598	5	94	0	1	160.1	148.4	-14.7	43	N/A	5,000	250	0.0	2.0
B- / 7.3	12.6	0.80	14.66	297	14	85	0	1	118.8	N/A	N/A	68	N/A	5,000	250	0.0	2.0
C / 5.3	13.6	1.52	5.52	16	0	100	0	0	50.0	68.1	-6.5	8	N/A	2,000	250	0.0	0.0
C+ / 6.9	10.5	1.27	51.89	161	1	98	0	1	18.0	63.2	-13.4	12	10	1,000	100	0.0	1.0
C+ / 6.0	14.7	1.38	17.46	106	0	99	0	1	19.5	88.4	-10.9	56	11	10,000	100	0.0	1.0
B- / 7.4	9.6	0.78	18.13	1,771	1	72	3	24	20.2	117.3	-1.3	89	12	2,500	250	0.0	2.0
C / 4.7	16.9	1.44	6.62	82	1	98	0	1	29.8	166.5	-15.1	98	7	2,500	250	0.0	2.0
U /	N/A	N/A	15.32	397	1	98	0	1	15.8	N/A	N/A	N/A	N/A	2,500	250	0.0	2.0
C- / 4.2	16.9	1.16	17.67	549	0	99	0	1	11.8	118.0	3.0	25	8	2,500	250	0.0	2.0
U /	N/A	N/A	11.41	392	0	97	2	1	N/A	N/A	N/A	N/A	1	2,500	250	0.0	2.0
C / 4.3	18.1	0.95	18.04	399	2	97	0	1	20.9	148.1	-7.6	81	8	2,500	250	0.0	2.0
D+ / 2.9	19.4	1.22	6.29	262	3	93	3	1	10.1	216.2	-18.2	78	11	2,500	250	0.0	2.0
C+ / 5.8	15.5	1.23	20.05	2,736	1	98	0	1	3.0	182.5	-7.1	50	12	2,500	250	0.0	2.0
B / 8.7	8.3	0.90	11.55	40	3	96	0	1	61.0	78.2	-13.1	69	5	1,000	100	0.0	0.0
B- / 7.1	13.2	0.91	7.94	10	1	98	0	1	34.1	108.1	-16.9	2	9	1,000	100	0.0	0.0
B+ / 9.4	5.3	1.10	17.92	50	1	65	32	2	120.3	36.2	-4.2	45	12	5,000	250	0.0	0.0
B+ / 9.4	5.3	1.10	17.91	7	1	65	32	2	120.3	35.2	-4.2	43	5	5,000	250	0.0	0.0
B / 8.5	7.9	1.02	23.45	157	0	99	0	1	76.9	55.1	-9.7	44	N/A	5,000	250	0.0	0.0
B / 8.5	7.9	1.02	23.43	13	0	99	0	1	76.9	53.9	-9.7	41	5	5,000	250	0.0	0.0
B- / 7.6	9.2	1.09	15.20	94	3	96	0	1	180.8	80.5	-5.4	81	16	1,000	50	5.8	2.0
U /	N/A	N/A	15.12	45	3	96	0	1	180.8	N/A	N/A	N/A	N/A	1,000	50	0.0	0.0
B / 8.6	9.2	1.10	15.29	43	3	96	0	1	180.8	81.8	-5.4	83	18	1,000,000	2,500	0.0	2.0
B+ / 9.3	6.4	1.26	13.28	1	2	63	33	2	134.3	63.5	-3.8	88	N/A	1,000	50	5.8	0.0
B+ / 9.3	6.4	1.26	13.22	4	2	63	33	2	134.3	62.6	-3.8	87	N/A	1,000	50	0.0	1.0
B+ / 9.3	6.4	1.26	13.29	75	2	63	33	2	134.3	63.6	-3.8	89	16	1,000,000	2,500	0.0	2.0
U /	N/A	N/A	9.08	28	16	81	1	2	82.0	N/A	N/A	N/A	N/A	0	0	0.0	0.0
B+ / 9.1	6.1	1.24	13.00	3	22	37	39	2	62.6	46.6	-3.3	62	2	10,000	100	0.0	0.0
B+ / 9.2	6.1	1.24	12.96	342	22	37	39	2	62.6	48.0	-3.4	66	2	10,000	100	0.0	0.0
C- / 3.1	16.9	1.02	23.97	9	1	98	0	1	44.0	202.6	-5.1	17	5	10,000	100	0.0	0.0
C- / 3.1	16.9	1.02	23.84	1,311	1	98	0	1	44.0	205.3	-5.3	19	6	10,000	100	0.0	0.0
B- / 7.8	7.3	0.88	10.20	1	0	99	0	1	34.6	67.9	-8.1	82	4	10,000	100	0.0	0.0
B- / 7.7	7.3	0.88	10.15	404	0	99	0	1	34.6	69.5	-7.9	84	4	10,000	100	0.0	0.0
C+ / 5.9	9.6	0.92	17.87	7	4	95	0	1	44.9	130.7	-11.4	59	4	10,000	100	0.0	0.0
B- / 7.0	9.6	0.92	17.24	2,436	4	95	0	1	44.9	133.1	-11.5	64	4	10,000	100	0.0	0.0
C+ / 6.0	8.0	1.02	10.13	7	3	96	0	1	23.5	52.8	-8.9	34	2	10,000	100	0.0	0.0
B / 8.3	8.1	1.04	10.11	1,780	3	96	0	1	23.5	54.0	-8.9	35	2	10,000	100	0.0	0.0
B- / 7.5	11.7	1.06	14.47	30	1	98	0	1	83.6	108.8	-7.9	59	2	10,000	100	0.0	0.0
C / 5.5	11.7	1.06	14.58	1,608	1	98	0	1	83.6	110.5	-7.9	62	2	10,000	100	0.0	0.0
B- / 7.5	11.8	1.06	14.07	7	1	98	0	1	83.6	104.2	-8.2	49	2	10,000	100	0.0	4.0
C+ / 6.6	14.3	0.96	15.57	6	2	97	0	1	148.5	99.8	-9.4	41	4	10,000	100	0.0	0.0
C- / 3.8	14.3	0.96	15.83	697	2	97	0	1	148.5	101.2	-9.2	44	4	10,000	100	0.0	0.0
B+ / 9.5	4.6	0.97	12.40	86	0	66	32	2	34.0	37.1	-5.0	50	N/A	1,000	150	5.8	1.0
B+ / 9.9	4.6	0.97	12.41	86	0	66	32	2	34.0	33.8	-5.2	41	N/A	1,000	150	0.0	4.5
C+ / 6.8	10.5	1.01	14.57	73	2	97	0	1	64.0	139.1	-7.4	51	N/A	1,000	150	5.8	2.0

Fund Type	Fund Name	Ticker Symbol	Overall Weiss Investment Rating	Phone	Perfor-mance Rating/Pts	3 Mo	6 Mo	1Yr / Pct	3Yr / Pct	5Yr / Pct	Dividend Yield	Expense Ratio
	99 Pct = Best				**PERFORMANCE**							
	0 Pct = Worst							Total Return % through 6/30/06			Incl. in Returns	
									Annualized			
FO	MEMBERS International Fd B	MINBX	A-	(800) 877-6089	B+ / 8.6	-1.64	7.78	24.93 /88	23.38 /88	11.34 /85	0.24	2.35
GR	MEMBERS Large Cap Growth Fd A	MCAAX	D-	(800) 877-6089	E+ / 0.7	-4.66	-1.51	1.27 / 3	7.78 /14	-2.17 / 8	0.51	1.20
GR	MEMBERS Large Cap Growth Fd B	MCPBX	D-	(800) 877-6089	E+ / 0.6	-4.84	-1.89	0.54 / 2	7.02 /10	-2.88 / 6	0.00	1.95
GI	MEMBERS Large Cap Value Fd A	MGWAX	C+	(800) 877-6089	C- / 4.1	0.50	4.77	10.17 /48	12.56 /46	3.50 /41	1.19	1.00
GI	MEMBERS Large Cap Value Fd B	MGWBX	C	(800) 877-6089	C- / 3.9	0.29	4.37	9.33 /42	11.74 /41	2.71 /34	0.55	1.75
GR	MEMBERS Mid Cap Growth A	MERAX	D+	(800) 877-6089	C- / 4.1	-4.42	2.46	12.31 /61	13.26 /50	1.28 /22	0.00	1.20
GR	MEMBERS Mid Cap Growth B	MERBX	D+	(800) 877-6089	C- / 4.1	-4.62	2.20	11.40 /56	12.42 /45	0.51 /18	0.00	1.95
MC	MEMBERS Mid Cap Value A	MICAX	C	(800) 877-6089	C+ / 6.0	-1.16	5.67	12.42 /62	16.31 /65	8.21 /72	0.05	1.40
MC	MEMBERS Mid Cap Value B	MICBX	C	(800) 877-6089	C+ / 5.9	-1.34	5.33	11.63 /57	15.36 /60	7.37 /69	0.00	2.15
GR	Memorial Growth Equity Inst	MFGIX	E	(888) 263-5593	E+ / 0.7	-4.08	-1.77	3.19 / 8	5.36 / 5	-1.16 /11	0.00	1.25
SC	Mercantile Capital Opport A	MPPAX	C-	(800) 551-2145	C+ / 5.6	-6.81	5.12	12.14 /60	15.16 /60	5.84 /60	0.00	1.78
SC	Mercantile Capital Opport C	MPPCX	C	(800) 551-2145	C+ / 5.8	-6.86	4.93	11.63 /57	14.60 /57	5.42 /57	0.00	2.28
SC	Mercantile Capital Opport Inst	MCOPX	C	(800) 551-2145	C+ / 6.5	-6.68	5.41	12.64 /63	15.73 /62	6.24 /63	0.00	1.28
RE	Mercantile Divers Real Estate A	MDRAX	C+	(800) 551-2145	B+ / 8.8	-0.95	13.41	19.34 /81	24.11 /90	18.45 /95	2.22	1.55
RE	Mercantile Divers Real Estate C	MDRCX	B-	(800) 551-2145	B+ / 8.9	-1.06	13.12	18.84 /80	23.53 /88	18.02 /94	1.86	2.05
RE	Mercantile Divers Real Estate Inst	MDVRX	B-	(800) 551-2145	A- / 9.2	-0.78	13.70	19.96 /82	24.73 /90	18.89 /95	2.77	1.05
GR	Mercantile Equity Growth A	MEWAX	D-	(800) 551-2145	E / 0.3	-6.04	-3.66	1.33 / 3	5.77 / 6	-4.73 / 3	0.00	1.28
GR	Mercantile Equity Growth C	MEWCX	D-	(800) 551-2145	E / 0.4	-6.26	-3.85	0.90 / 2	5.30 / 5	-5.08 / 2	0.00	1.78
GR	Mercantile Equity Growth Inst	MEQGX	D-	(800) 551-2145	E+ / 0.8	-5.98	-3.35	1.88 / 4	6.37 / 8	-4.35 / 3	0.12	0.78
IN	Mercantile Equity Income A	MEYAX	C	(800) 551-2145	D+ / 2.8	-0.18	3.52	6.28 /22	10.36 /30	2.76 /34	1.49	1.28
IN	Mercantile Equity Income C	MEYCX	C	(800) 551-2145	C- / 3.1	-0.42	3.11	5.71 /19	9.91 /27	2.44 /32	1.05	1.78
IN	Mercantile Equity Income Inst	MEQIX	C+	(800) 551-2145	C- / 4.0	-0.14	3.67	6.68 /24	11.02 /36	3.17 /38	1.94	0.78
GI	Mercantile Growth & Income A	MIFAX	D+	(800) 551-2145	D / 1.7	-3.21	-0.39	5.37 /17	9.04 /21	2.43 /31	0.24	1.28
GI	Mercantile Growth & Income C	MIFCX	D+	(800) 551-2145	D / 1.9	-3.37	-0.64	4.88 /14	8.47 /18	2.03 /28	0.00	1.78
GI	Mercantile Growth & Income Inst	MVAEX	C-	(800) 551-2145	D+ / 2.8	-3.13	-0.15	5.85 /19	9.60 /25	2.81 /35	0.72	0.78
FO	Mercantile Internatl Equity A	MIAEX	B+	(800) 551-2145	B / 7.8	0.00	8.24	18.98 /80	19.43 /77	11.05 /84	0.43	1.78
FO	Mercantile Internatl Equity C	MICEX	A-	(800) 551-2145	B / 7.9	-0.13	8.05	18.44 /80	18.92 /76	10.64 /83	0.22	2.28
FO	Mercantile Internatl Equity Inst	MEQUX	A+	(800) 551-2145	B+ / 8.3	0.12	8.52	19.54 /81	20.03 /79	11.46 /85	0.63	1.28
GR	Mercury Basic Value A	MAVAX	D+	(866) 637-2879	C- / 4.0	-0.54	5.26	10.91 /53	12.13 /43	4.65 /51	0.39	1.64
GR	Mercury Basic Value B	MAVBX	C-	(866) 637-2879	C / 4.5	-0.46	5.33	11.01 /54	12.34 /45	4.76 /52	0.37	1.66
GR	Mercury Basic Value C	MAVCX	C-	(866) 637-2879	C / 4.9	-0.47	5.22	10.89 /53	12.12 /43	4.54 /51	0.40	1.65
GR	Mercury Basic Value I	MAVIX	D+	(866) 637-2879	C- / 4.2	-0.46	5.39	11.20 /55	12.42 /45	4.92 /53	0.61	1.42
AG	Merger Fund	MERFX	D	(800) 343-8959	D- / 1.2	2.29	6.48	6.85 /25	5.12 / 4	2.86 /35	0.06	1.41
IN	Meridian Equity Income Fund	MEIFX	U	(800) 446-6662	U /	-1.52	5.54	10.86 /53	--	--	1.09	1.25
SC	Meridian Growth Fund	MERDX	C	(800) 446-6662	C+ / 5.7	-4.46	5.39	10.08 /47	14.73 /58	6.49 /64	0.00	0.85
GR	Meridian Value Fund	MVALX	D+	(800) 446-6662	C / 5.1	-4.74	4.36	7.35 /28	13.91 /53	8.59 /75	0.78	1.09
FS	Merk Hard Currency Fund Investor	MERKX	U	(866) 637-5386	U /	5.67	7.84	9.40 /43	--	--	0.23	1.30
GI	Merrill Lynch Bal Capital A	MDCPX	D+	(800) 543-6217	D / 2.0	-0.19	3.25	7.84 /31	8.80 /20	3.52 /42	1.87	0.83
GI	Merrill Lynch Bal Capital B	MBCPX	D+	(800) 543-6217	D / 1.7	-0.39	2.85	7.00 /26	7.98 /15	2.70 /34	1.14	1.61
GI	Merrill Lynch Bal Capital C	MCCPX	D+	(800) 543-6217	D / 2.1	-0.40	2.84	7.01 /26	7.96 /15	2.69 /34	1.29	1.61
GI	Merrill Lynch Bal Capital I	MACPX	C-	(800) 543-6217	C- / 3.0	-0.11	3.39	8.10 /33	9.08 /21	3.75 /43	2.21	0.58
GI	Merrill Lynch Bal Capital R	MRBPX	C-	(800) 543-6217	D+ / 2.7	-0.23	3.14	7.56 /30	8.62 /19	--	1.82	1.08
GR	Merrill Lynch Basic Val Prin Prot A	MDPVX	E+	(800) 543-6217	D- / 1.1	-0.79	4.61	8.93 /40	6.70 / 9	--	0.00	1.95
GR	Merrill Lynch Basic Val Prin Prot B	MBPVX	E+	(800) 543-6217	E+ / 0.9	-0.97	4.27	8.12 /34	5.88 / 6	--	0.00	2.71
GR	Merrill Lynch Basic Val Prin Prot C	MCPVX	E+	(800) 543-6217	D- / 1.3	-0.88	4.26	8.15 /34	5.89 / 6	--	0.00	2.72
GR	Merrill Lynch Basic Val Prin Prot I	MAPVX	D-	(800) 543-6217	D / 2.0	-0.70	4.80	9.22 /41	6.94 /10	--	0.00	1.70
★ GI	Merrill Lynch Basic Value A	MDBAX	C	(800) 543-6217	C / 4.8	-0.30	5.72	11.89 /59	13.09 /49	5.06 /55	1.08	0.82
GI	Merrill Lynch Basic Value B	MBBAX	C	(800) 543-6217	C / 4.5	-0.50	5.30	11.01 /54	12.23 /44	4.26 /48	0.36	1.59
GI	Merrill Lynch Basic Value C	MCBAX	C	(800) 543-6217	C / 4.9	-0.48	5.31	11.01 /54	12.21 /44	4.24 /48	0.49	1.59
GI	Merrill Lynch Basic Value I	MABAX	C	(800) 543-6217	C / 5.0	-0.21	5.86	12.17 /60	13.39 /51	5.33 /57	1.29	0.57
GI	Merrill Lynch Basic Value R	MRBVX	C+	(800) 543-6217	C / 5.4	-0.34	5.58	11.59 /57	12.81 /48	--	0.95	1.07
AA	Merrill Lynch Core Principal Prot A	MAPWX	D-	(800) 543-6217	D+ / 2.6	-3.31	3.82	11.99 /59	10.45 /30	--	0.00	1.58

● Denotes fund is closed to new investors

★ Denotes fund is included in Section II

RISK			NET ASSETS		ASSET					BULL / BEAR		FUND MANAGER		MINIMUMS		LOADS	
	3 Year		NAV						Portfolio	Last Bull	Last Bear	Manager	Manager	Initial	Additional	Front	Back
Risk	Standard		As of	Total	Cash	Stocks	Bonds	Other	Turnover	Market	Market	Quality	Tenure	Purch.	Purch.	End	End
Rating/Pts	Deviation	Beta	6/30/06	$(Mil)	%	%	%	%	Ratio	Return	Return	Pct	(Years)	$	$	Load	Load
C+ / 6.7	10.6	1.01	14.41	16	2	97	0	1	64.0	133.4	-7.6	42	N/A	1,000	150	0.0	4.5
B- / 7.8	7.8	0.97	13.71	76	0	99	0	1	18.0	53.2	-10.3	27	N/A	1,000	150	5.8	1.0
B- / 7.8	7.8	0.97	12.98	46	0	99	0	1	18.0	49.9	-10.6	22	N/A	1,000	150	0.0	4.5
B / 8.4	7.2	0.91	14.07	102	0	99	0	1	12.0	68.9	-11.5	77	N/A	1,000	150	5.8	1.0
B / 8.4	7.2	0.91	13.86	66	0	99	0	1	12.0	64.8	-11.5	70	N/A	1,000	150	0.0	4.5
C+ / 6.0	11.4	1.25	5.84	33	1	98	0	1	92.0	86.7	-11.3	52	N/A	1,000	150	5.8	2.0
C+ / 6.0	11.4	1.26	5.57	15	1	98	0	1	92.0	82.4	-11.2	42	N/A	1,000	150	0.0	4.5
C+ / 5.9	9.3	0.84	14.54	32	1	98	0	1	37.0	89.3	-9.4	65	N/A	1,000	150	5.8	2.0
C+ / 5.9	9.3	0.84	14.03	24	1	98	0	1	37.0	84.6	-9.5	56	N/A	1,000	150	0.0	4.5
C+ / 5.6	8.8	1.08	7.76	19	4	95	0	1	92.0	36.2	-9.2	9	8	2,000	0	0.0	0.0
C+ / 5.8	13.6	0.91	11.09	2	2	97	0	1	58.3	102.8	-6.4	36	N/A	1,000	100	4.8	0.0
C+ / 5.7	13.7	0.91	10.86	1	2	97	0	1	58.3	99.1	-6.5	31	N/A	1,000	100	0.0	1.0
C+ / 5.9	13.6	0.91	11.31	225	2	97	0	1	58.3	105.7	-6.2	41	N/A	1,000,000	100	0.0	0.0
C / 4.6	16.5	0.99	18.62	3	0	99	0	1	24.5	111.2	-0.2	58	N/A	1,000	100	4.8	0.0
C / 4.7	16.5	0.99	18.57	1	0	99	0	1	24.5	107.9	-0.4	52	N/A	1,000	100	0.0	1.0
C / 4.7	16.5	0.99	18.74	211	0	99	0	1	24.5	114.4	-0.2	64	N/A	1,000,000	100	0.0	0.0
B- / 7.5	8.9	1.11	6.84	N/A	1	98	0	1	59.7	44.4	-10.6	10	N/A	1,000	100	4.8	0.0
B- / 7.5	8.9	1.11	6.74	N/A	1	98	0	1	59.7	42.4	-10.9	8	N/A	1,000	100	0.0	1.0
B- / 7.8	8.9	1.11	6.92	42	1	98	0	1	59.7	46.9	-10.7	12	N/A	1,000,000	100	0.0	0.0
B+ / 9.2	7.3	0.89	5.01	1	1	98	0	1	56.8	60.0	-10.1	58	1	1,000	100	4.8	0.0
B+ / 9.3	7.2	0.88	5.02	N/A	1	98	0	1	56.8	58.0	-10.2	54	1	1,000	100	0.0	1.0
B+ / 9.2	7.2	0.88	5.02	91	1	98	0	1	56.8	62.6	-9.8	66	1	1,000,000	100	0.0	0.0
B / 8.3	7.9	1.00	18.90	9	1	98	0	1	38.6	52.2	-8.7	34	N/A	1,000	100	4.8	0.0
B / 8.2	7.9	1.00	18.66	3	1	98	0	1	38.6	49.6	-8.8	29	N/A	1,000	100	0.0	1.0
B / 8.6	7.9	1.00	19.00	449	1	98	0	1	38.6	54.7	-8.6	38	N/A	1,000,000	100	0.0	0.0
B- / 7.4	10.1	0.98	16.15	4	2	97	0	1	56.8	104.6	-8.2	21	N/A	1,000	100	4.8	0.0
B- / 7.4	10.0	0.97	15.98	1	2	97	0	1	56.8	101.7	-8.4	19	N/A	1,000	100	0.0	1.0
B / 8.1	10.1	0.98	16.31	698	2	97	0	1	56.8	107.9	-8.1	24	N/A	1,000,000	100	0.0	0.0
C+ / 5.9	9.1	1.13	12.81	2	1	98	0	1	21.7	69.5	-11.9	53	6	1,000	100	5.3	1.0
C+ / 5.9	9.1	1.14	12.85	3	1	98	0	1	21.7	70.5	-11.8	55	6	1,000	100	0.0	4.0
C+ / 5.9	9.1	1.14	12.71	1	1	98	0	1	21.7	69.5	-11.8	52	6	1,000	100	0.0	1.0
C+ / 5.9	9.2	1.14	12.90	N/A	1	98	0	1	21.7	71.0	-11.9	55	6	1,000	100	5.3	1.0
B / 8.1	3.4	0.26	15.62	1,426	N/A	N/A	4	N/A	312.0	19.5	0.5	62	17	2,000	0	0.0	2.0
U /	N/A	N/A	11.05	25	3	96	0	1	N/A	N/A	N/A	N/A	1	1,000	50	0.0	2.0
C+ / 6.3	12.7	0.82	38.54	1,689	5	94	0	1	32.0	98.6	-12.0	47	22	1,000	50	0.0	2.0
C / 4.5	10.4	1.21	36.14	1,688	4	95	0	1	59.0	83.6	-5.1	64	N/A	1,000	50	0.0	2.0
U /	N/A	N/A	10.49	31	0	0	100	0	N/A	N/A	N/A	N/A	1	2,500	100	0.0	0.0
B / 8.2	5.4	0.66	26.40	908	1	64	34	1	15.0	46.5	-6.0	64	10	1,000	50	5.3	0.0
B / 8.2	5.6	0.68	25.60	193	1	64	34	1	15.0	43.0	-6.3	52	10	1,000	50	0.0	4.0
B / 8.1	5.6	0.68	24.96	101	1	64	34	1	15.0	43.0	-6.3	52	10	1,000	50	0.0	1.0
B / 8.1	5.6	0.68	26.50	1,209	1	64	34	1	15.0	47.7	-6.1	65	10	1,000	50	0.0	0.0
B / 8.0	5.6	0.68	25.61	4	1	64	34	1	15.0	46.2	N/A	59	10	1,000	50	0.0	0.0
C+ / 5.9	7.3	0.84	11.34	7	1	93	5	1	45.0	33.9	-4.9	27	4	1,000	50	5.3	1.0
C+ / 5.7	7.3	0.83	11.23	104	1	93	5	1	45.0	30.6	-5.0	22	4	1,000	50	0.0	4.0
C+ / 5.7	7.2	0.83	11.25	66	1	93	5	1	45.0	30.7	-5.0	22	4	1,000	50	0.0	1.0
C+ / 5.9	7.3	0.83	11.35	8	1	93	5	1	45.0	34.9	-4.8	29	4	1,000	50	0.0	0.0
B- / 7.3	9.1	1.14	32.69	2,294	0	99	0	1	45.1	74.1	-11.8	62	7	1,000	50	5.3	0.0
B- / 7.3	9.1	1.14	32.00	899	0	99	0	1	45.1	70.0	-11.9	53	7	1,000	50	0.0	4.0
B- / 7.2	9.1	1.14	31.15	768	0	99	0	1	45.1	69.9	-11.9	53	7	1,000	50	0.0	1.0
B- / 7.3	9.1	1.14	32.87	3,689	0	99	0	1	45.1	75.6	-11.7	65	7	1,000	50	5.3	0.0
B- / 7.2	9.1	1.14	31.98	27	0	99	0	1	45.1	73.3	N/A	60	7	1,000	50	0.0	0.0
C+ / 5.8	9.5	1.54	11.96	7	0	100	0	0	94.0	49.6	N/A	56	3	1,000	50	5.3	1.0

	99 Pct = Best 0 Pct = Worst		Overall		PERFORMANCE							
			Weiss		Perfor-		Total Return % through 6/30/06				Incl. in Returns	
Fund		Ticker	Investment		mance					Annualized		Dividend	Expense
Type	Fund Name	Symbol	Rating	Phone	Rating/Pts	3 Mo	6 Mo	1Yr / Pct	3Yr / Pct	5Yr / Pct	Yield	Ratio
AA	Merrill Lynch Core Principal Prot B	MBPWX	D-	(800) 543-6217	D+ / 2.3	-3.66	3.23	10.96 /53	9.57 /24	--	0.00	2.59
AA	Merrill Lynch Core Principal Prot C	MCPWX	D-	(800) 543-6217	D+ / 2.8	-3.57	3.31	10.99 /53	9.58 /25	--	0.00	2.59
AA	Merrill Lynch Core Principal Prot D	MDPWX	D-	(800) 543-6217	D+ / 2.6	-3.48	3.65	11.94 /59	10.61 /32	--	0.00	1.83
EM	Merrill Lynch Dev Cap Market A	MDDCX	C+	(800) 543-6217	A / 9.5	-6.29	5.48	36.46 /97	32.45 /97	18.18 /95	0.25	1.85
EM	Merrill Lynch Dev Cap Market B	MBDCX	C+	(800) 543-6217	A / 9.5	-6.47	5.09	35.42 /97	31.40 /96	17.23 /94	0.00	2.65
EM	Merrill Lynch Dev Cap Market C	MCDCX	C+	(800) 543-6217	A / 9.5	-6.46	5.06	35.45 /97	31.41 /96	17.23 /94	0.00	2.65
EM	Merrill Lynch Dev Cap Market I	MADCX	C+	(800) 543-6217	A / 9.5	-6.22	5.65	36.80 /97	32.83 /97	18.48 /95	0.41	1.60
GI	Merrill Lynch Disciplined Eq A	MDDGX	C-	(800) 543-6217	C- / 4.2	-2.11	3.85	12.08 /60	12.21 /44	2.64 /33	0.00	1.63
GI	Merrill Lynch Disciplined Eq B	MBDGX	C-	(800) 543-6217	C- / 3.7	-2.23	3.49	11.25 /55	11.36 /38	1.84 /26	0.00	2.41
GI	Merrill Lynch Disciplined Eq C	MCDGX	C	(800) 543-6217	C / 4.3	-2.32	3.49	11.14 /55	11.33 /38	1.82 /26	0.00	2.42
GI	Merrill Lynch Disciplined Eq I	MADGX	D+	(800) 543-6217	C- / 4.2	-1.99	4.05	12.37 /61	12.52 /46	2.89 /36	0.00	1.38
IN	Merrill Lynch Equity Dividend A	MDDVX	A-	(800) 543-6217	B- / 7.3	2.82	8.96	17.74 /79	17.84 /72	9.19 /77	1.42	1.12
IN	Merrill Lynch Equity Dividend B	MBDVX	A-	(800) 543-6217	B- / 7.1	2.68	8.59	16.87 /77	16.96 /68	8.49 /74	0.78	1.89
IN	Merrill Lynch Equity Dividend C	MCDVX	A	(800) 543-6217	B- / 7.4	2.63	8.51	16.77 /76	16.93 /68	8.36 /73	0.87	1.89
IN	Merrill Lynch Equity Dividend I	MADVX	A	(800) 543-6217	B- / 7.4	2.94	9.08	18.07 /79	18.13 /73	9.47 /78	1.62	0.87
IN	Merrill Lynch Equity Dividend R	MRDVX	A	(800) 543-6217	B / 7.7	2.76	8.79	17.43 /78	17.65 /71	--	1.34	1.29
FO	Merrill Lynch Eurofund A	MDEFX	A	(800) 543-6217	B+ / 8.7	2.27	14.70	25.61 /89	22.87 /87	11.32 /85	1.61	1.24
FO	Merrill Lynch Eurofund B	MBEFX	A	(800) 543-6217	B+ / 8.7	2.05	14.20	24.64 /88	21.88 /85	10.46 /82	1.31	2.01
FO	Merrill Lynch Eurofund C	MCEFX	A+	(800) 543-6217	B+ / 8.8	2.13	14.22	24.67 /88	21.91 /85	10.47 /82	1.51	2.02
FO	Merrill Lynch Eurofund I	MAEFX	A+	(800) 543-6217	A- / 9.1	2.34	14.82	25.93 /90	23.17 /88	11.61 /86	1.86	0.99
FO	Merrill Lynch Eurofund R	MREFX	A+	(800) 543-6217	A- / 9.0	2.21	14.54	25.35 /89	22.89 /87	--	2.01	1.48
GR	Merrill Lynch Focus 20 Fd A	MDFOX	D	(800) 543-6217	C- / 3.9	-0.52	5.52	20.13 /82	10.39 /30	-9.69 / 0	0.00	1.92
GR	Merrill Lynch Focus 20 Fd B	MBFOX	D-	(800) 543-6217	C- / 3.6	-0.55	5.23	19.08 /81	9.46 /24	-10.09 / 0	0.00	2.78
GR	Merrill Lynch Focus 20 Fd C	MCFOX	D	(800) 543-6217	C- / 4.2	-0.55	5.23	19.08 /81	9.46 /24	-10.09 / 0	0.00	2.80
GR	Merrill Lynch Focus 20 Fd I	MAFOX	D	(800) 543-6217	C / 5.1	-0.51	5.43	20.50 /82	10.70 /33	-9.07 / 0	0.00	1.67
GR	Merrill Lynch Focus Value A	MDPNX	C	(800) 543-6217	C / 4.8	-2.83	5.18	11.59 /57	13.75 /53	5.80 /60	0.13	1.26
GR	Merrill Lynch Focus Value B	MBPNX	C-	(800) 543-6217	C / 4.6	-2.95	4.86	10.85 /53	12.90 /48	4.99 /54	0.00	2.03
GR	Merrill Lynch Focus Value C	MCPNX	C	(800) 543-6217	C / 5.1	-2.94	4.81	10.74 /52	12.89 /48	4.99 /54	0.00	2.04
GR	Merrill Lynch Focus Value I	MAPNX	C	(800) 543-6217	C / 5.0	-2.74	5.35	11.89 /59	14.02 /54	6.06 /61	0.35	1.01
GR	Merrill Lynch Focus Value R	MRPNX	C	(800) 543-6217	C+ / 5.6	-2.81	5.15	11.40 /56	13.54 /52	--	0.03	1.51
GR	Merrill Lynch Fundamental Gr A	MDFGX	D+	(800) 543-6217	C- / 3.2	-2.38	0.59	10.45 /50	11.46 /39	0.37 /17	0.62	1.16
GR	Merrill Lynch Fundamental Gr B	MBFGX	D	(800) 543-6217	C- / 3.0	-2.60	0.17	9.61 /44	10.59 /32	-0.41 /14	0.00	1.94
GR	Merrill Lynch Fundamental Gr C	MCFGX	D+	(800) 543-6217	C- / 3.5	-2.59	0.23	9.58 /44	10.59 /32	-0.43 /14	0.03	1.95
GR	Merrill Lynch Fundamental Gr I	MAFGX	C-	(800) 543-6217	C / 4.5	-2.38	0.68	10.72 /52	11.72 /41	0.61 /18	0.88	0.91
GR	Merrill Lynch Fundamental Gr R	MRFGX	C-	(800) 543-6217	C- / 4.1	-2.45	0.46	10.18 /48	11.21 /37	--	0.58	1.41
AA	Merrill Lynch Fundmntl Gr Pr Pro A	MDPUX	D+	(800) 543-6217	E- / 0.1	-1.86	-0.35	3.26 / 8	3.38 / 2	--	0.04	1.16
AA	Merrill Lynch Fundmntl Gr Pr Pro C	MCPUX	D+	(800) 543-6217	E- / 0.2	-2.06	-0.73	2.50 / 6	2.59 / 1	--	0.04	1.95
AA	Merrill Lynch Fundmntl Gr Pr Pro I	MAPUX	D+	(800) 543-6217	E / 0.4	-1.86	-0.25	3.50 / 9	3.62 / 2	--	0.04	0.91
★ GL	Merrill Lynch Glbl Allocation A	MDLOX	B	(800) 543-6217	C+ / 6.4	0.45	6.63	16.17 /75	16.45 /65	10.53 /82	1.79	1.09
★ GL	Merrill Lynch Glbl Allocation B	MBLOX	B	(800) 543-6217	C+ / 6.6	0.28	6.22	15.34 /73	15.57 /62	9.69 /79	1.20	1.86
GL	Merrill Lynch Glbl Allocation C	MCLOX	B	(800) 543-6217	C+ / 6.6	0.29	6.23	15.33 /73	15.55 /62	9.69 /79	1.38	1.86
GL	Merrill Lynch Glbl Allocation I	MALOX	A	(800) 543-6217	B- / 7.1	0.50	6.73	16.45 /76	16.73 /67	10.80 /83	2.09	0.84
GL	Merrill Lynch Glbl Allocation R	MRLOX	B	(800) 543-6217	C+ / 6.9	0.40	6.48	15.92 /74	16.16 /64	--	1.80	1.35
GL	Merrill Lynch Global Eq Opport Fd A	MDEGX	U	(800) 543-6217	U /	-0.71	7.86	--	--	--	0.00	1.50
FS	Merrill Lynch Global Finan Svc A	MDFNX	C	(800) 543-6217	A- / 9.1	-2.74	4.83	25.39 /89	26.72 /93	16.50 /94	1.86	1.62
FS	Merrill Lynch Global Finan Svc B	MBFNX	C	(800) 543-6217	A- / 9.1	-2.90	4.45	24.47 /88	25.74 /92	15.61 /93	1.20	2.39
FS	Merrill Lynch Global Finan Svc C	MCFNX	C	(800) 543-6217	A- / 9.1	-2.91	4.48	24.49 /88	25.77 /92	15.60 /93	1.24	2.40
FS	Merrill Lynch Global Finan Svc I	MAFNX	C	(800) 543-6217	A / 9.3	-2.66	5.00	25.75 /89	27.05 /93	16.83 /94	2.09	1.32
FS	Merrill Lynch Global Finan Svc R	MRFNX	C+	(800) 543-6217	A- / 9.2	-2.78	4.72	25.11 /89	26.44 /93	--	1.80	1.62
GL	Merrill Lynch Global Growth A	MDGGX	B-	(800) 543-6217	B / 7.8	-2.86	6.71	22.77 /85	21.29 /83	3.78 /44	1.07	1.38
GL	Merrill Lynch Global Growth B	MBGGX	B-	(800) 543-6217	B / 7.9	-3.05	6.32	21.73 /84	20.35 /81	2.97 /37	0.37	2.16
GL	Merrill Lynch Global Growth C	MCGGX	B-	(800) 543-6217	B / 7.9	-3.05	6.33	21.81 /84	20.34 /81	2.94 /36	0.41	2.18

● Denotes fund is closed to new investors
★ Denotes fund is included in Section II

www.WeissRatings.com

RISK Rating/Pts	3 Year Standard Deviation	Beta	NAV As of 6/30/06	Total $(Mil)	Cash %	Stocks %	Bonds %	Other %	Portfolio Turnover Ratio	Last Bull Market Return	Last Bear Market Return	Manager Quality Pct	Manager Tenure (Years)	Initial Purch. $	Additional Purch. $	Front End Load	Back End Load
C+ / 5.7	9.5	1.53	11.84	114	0	100	0	0	94.0	46.0	N/A	45	3	1,000	50	0.0	4.0
C+ / 5.7	9.5	1.53	11.87	66	0	100	0	0	94.0	46.0	N/A	45	3	1,000	50	0.0	1.0
C+ / 5.8	9.5	1.53	11.94	6	0	100	0	0	94.0	50.6	N/A	58	3	1,000	50	5.3	1.0
C- / 3.4	19.2	1.16	23.68	127	1	98	0	1	110.1	211.3	-5.9	6	N/A	1,000	50	5.3	0.0
C- / 3.4	19.2	1.16	22.10	19	1	98	0	1	110.1	203.6	-6.1	4	N/A	1,000	50	0.0	4.0
C- / 3.4	19.2	1.16	22.01	26	1	98	0	1	110.1	203.4	-6.0	5	N/A	1,000	50	0.0	1.0
C- / 3.4	19.2	1.16	24.14	78	1	98	0	1	110.1	213.7	-5.8	7	N/A	1,000	50	5.3	0.0
B- / 7.2	9.7	1.13	11.60	10	1	98	0	1	47.0	70.7	-7.8	53	N/A	1,000	50	5.3	0.0
B- / 7.2	9.7	1.14	10.98	10	1	98	0	1	47.0	66.6	-8.1	43	N/A	1,000	50	0.0	4.0
B- / 7.2	9.7	1.13	10.97	5	1	98	0	1	47.0	66.6	-8.0	43	N/A	1,000	50	0.0	1.0
C+ / 5.8	9.7	1.13	11.81	3	1	98	0	1	47.0	72.2	-7.9	57	N/A	1,000	50	5.3	1.0
B / 8.2	8.7	0.89	17.09	263	9	90	0	1	4.0	86.0	-5.2	97	N/A	1,000	50	5.3	0.0
B / 8.2	8.7	0.90	17.13	83	9	90	0	1	4.0	81.6	-5.4	96	N/A	1,000	50	0.0	4.0
B / 8.2	8.7	0.89	16.80	119	9	90	0	1	4.0	81.5	-5.4	96	N/A	1,000	50	0.0	1.0
B / 8.2	8.7	0.89	17.11	263	9	90	0	1	4.0	87.4	-5.0	97	N/A	1,000	50	5.3	0.0
B / 8.2	8.7	0.89	17.19	9	9	90	0	1	4.0	85.9	N/A	97	N/A	1,000	50	0.0	0.0
B- / 7.3	11.1	0.98	20.75	373	2	97	0	1	72.3	128.1	-11.8	45	6	1,000	50	5.3	2.0
B- / 7.2	11.1	0.98	17.93	102	2	97	0	1	72.3	122.4	-12.0	37	6	1,000	50	0.0	4.0
B- / 7.2	11.0	0.97	17.27	53	2	97	0	1	72.3	122.3	-12.0	37	6	1,000	50	0.0	2.0
B- / 7.3	11.1	0.98	21.00	285	2	97	0	1	72.3	129.9	-11.8	49	6	1,000	50	0.0	0.0
B- / 7.3	11.1	0.98	18.04	2	2	97	0	1	72.3	128.8	N/A	45	6	1,000	50	0.0	2.0
C / 5.5	15.3	1.52	1.91	9	2	97	0	1	143.2	73.7	-10.2	13	N/A	1,000	50	5.3	1.0
C / 4.4	15.3	1.53	1.81	39	2	97	0	1	143.2	69.4	-10.5	9	N/A	1,000	50	0.0	4.0
C / 4.4	15.0	1.50	1.81	23	2	97	0	1	143.2	68.5	-10.5	11	N/A	1,000	50	0.0	1.0
C / 4.4	15.3	1.55	1.94	15	2	97	0	1	143.2	74.8	-10.2	13	N/A	1,000	50	0.0	0.0
C+ / 6.8	10.9	1.29	14.42	128	0	99	0	1	72.4	79.6	-13.8	54	N/A	1,000	50	5.3	1.0
C+ / 6.7	11.0	1.29	13.15	29	0	99	0	1	72.4	75.1	-14.0	44	N/A	1,000	50	0.0	4.0
C+ / 6.7	10.9	1.29	12.86	24	0	99	0	1	72.4	75.1	-13.9	44	N/A	1,000	50	0.0	1.0
C+ / 6.8	10.9	1.29	14.58	159	0	99	0	1	72.4	80.8	-13.7	57	N/A	1,000	50	5.3	1.0
C+ / 6.8	10.9	1.29	13.48	1	0	99	0	1	72.4	78.9	N/A	52	N/A	1,000	50	0.0	0.0
C+ / 6.5	9.4	1.03	18.85	1,689	0	99	0	1	87.7	60.9	-9.0	56	N/A	1,000	50	5.3	1.0
C+ / 6.4	9.4	1.03	17.23	977	0	99	0	1	87.7	57.0	-9.2	46	N/A	1,000	50	0.0	4.0
C+ / 6.4	9.4	1.03	17.32	837	0	99	0	1	87.7	57.1	-9.3	46	N/A	1,000	50	0.0	1.0
C+ / 6.5	9.4	1.03	19.28	1,375	0	99	0	1	87.7	62.2	-8.9	59	N/A	1,000	50	0.0	0.0
C+ / 6.4	9.4	1.03	17.55	32	0	99	0	1	87.7	60.4	N/A	54	N/A	1,000	50	0.0	0.0
B+ / 9.6	5.5	0.97	10.33	4	1	62	36	1	58.2	19.3	-1.3	20	4	1,000	50	5.3	1.0
B+ / 9.6	5.4	0.96	10.27	43	1	62	36	1	58.2	16.4	-1.5	16	4	1,000	50	0.0	1.0
B+ / 9.6	5.4	0.96	10.33	6	1	62	36	1	58.2	20.3	-1.2	22	4	1,000	50	0.0	0.0
B / 8.6	6.8	1.20	18.01	5,334	18	59	21	2	49.1	91.1	-4.4	97	N/A	1,000	50	5.3	2.0
B / 8.6	6.8	1.19	17.60	2,100	18	59	21	2	49.1	86.5	-4.6	96	17	1,000	50	0.0	2.0
B / 8.5	6.8	1.19	17.06	3,944	18	59	21	2	49.1	86.5	-4.6	96	N/A	1,000	50	0.0	2.0
B / 8.5	6.8	1.19	18.08	3,163	18	59	21	2	49.1	92.7	-4.4	98	17	1,000	50	0.0	2.0
B / 8.5	6.8	1.19	17.58	112	18	59	21	2	49.1	90.2	N/A	97	N/A	1,000	50	0.0	2.0
U /	N/A	N/A	11.25	71	8	89	0	3	N/A	N/A	N/A	N/A	N/A	1,000	50	5.3	2.0
D+ / 2.9	17.4	1.33	16.70	26	14	85	0	1	80.1	204.6	-15.6	98	N/A	1,000	50	5.3	2.0
D+ / 2.8	17.5	1.33	16.42	32	14	85	0	1	80.1	197.4	-15.7	97	N/A	1,000	50	0.0	2.0
D+ / 2.9	17.4	1.34	16.33	25	14	85	0	1	80.1	197.3	-15.7	97	N/A	1,000	50	0.0	2.0
D+ / 2.9	17.4	1.33	16.81	55	14	85	0	1	80.1	207.2	-15.4	98	N/A	1,000	50	0.0	2.0
C- / 4.2	17.5	1.34	16.41	5	14	85	0	1	80.1	203.4	N/A	97	N/A	100	1	0.0	2.0
C+ / 6.1	13.1	1.15	12.24	226	0	99	0	1	109.0	119.7	-10.3	11	N/A	1,000	50	5.3	2.0
C+ / 6.0	13.1	1.16	11.77	76	0	99	0	1	109.0	114.3	-10.5	8	N/A	1,000	50	0.0	2.0
C+ / 6.0	13.1	1.15	11.76	58	0	99	0	1	109.0	114.0	-10.5	8	N/A	1,000	50	0.0	2.0

Fund Type	Fund Name	Ticker Symbol	Overall Weiss Investment Rating	Phone	PERFORMANCE							
	99 Pct = Best *0 Pct = Worst*				Performance Rating/Pts	Total Return % through 6/30/06			Annualized		Incl. in Returns	
						3 Mo	6 Mo	1Yr / Pct	3Yr / Pct	5Yr / Pct	Dividend Yield	Expense Ratio
GL	Merrill Lynch Global Growth I	MAGGX	B	(800) 543-6217	B+ / 8.3	-2.75	6.82	23.05 /86	21.58 /84	4.03 /46	1.35	1.13
GL	Merrill Lynch Global Growth R	MRGWX	C+	(800) 543-6217	B / 8.2	-2.91	6.58	22.52 /85	21.27 /83	--	1.27	1.79
GL	Merrill Lynch Global Small Cap A	MDGCX	C	(800) 543-6217	C+ / 6.8	-5.63	3.66	16.51 /76	18.27 /73	9.12 /77	0.00	1.42
GL	Merrill Lynch Global Small Cap B	MBGCX	C	(800) 543-6217	C+ / 6.9	-5.84	3.22	15.60 /74	17.34 /69	8.27 /73	0.00	2.21
GL	Merrill Lynch Global Small Cap C	MCGCX	C	(800) 543-6217	C+ / 6.9	-5.79	3.24	15.62 /74	17.34 /69	8.27 /73	0.00	2.21
GL	Merrill Lynch Global Small Cap I	MAGCX	C+	(800) 543-6217	B- / 7.4	-5.57	3.74	16.80 /77	18.57 /75	9.39 /78	0.11	1.17
GL	Merrill Lynch Global Small Cap R	MRGSX	C+	(800) 543-6217	B- / 7.2	-5.70	3.50	16.22 /75	18.01 /73	--	0.00	1.65
TC	Merrill Lynch Global Technology A	MDGTX	E-	(800) 543-6217	E / 0.5	-8.49	-3.88	5.38 /17	6.96 /10	-7.25 / 1	0.00	1.79
TC	Merrill Lynch Global Technology B	MBGTX	E-	(800) 543-6217	E / 0.5	-8.76	-4.38	4.49 /13	6.00 / 7	-8.03 / 0	0.00	2.63
TC	Merrill Lynch Global Technology C	MCGTX	E-	(800) 543-6217	E / 0.5	-8.78	-4.40	4.35 /12	5.96 / 7	-8.09 / 0	0.00	2.67
TC	Merrill Lynch Global Technology I	MAGTX	E-	(800) 543-6217	D- / 1.0	-8.45	-3.81	5.57 /18	7.22 /11	-7.02 / 1	0.00	1.54
TC	Merrill Lynch Global Technology R	MRGTX	E-	(800) 543-6217	E+ / 0.8	-8.63	-4.13	5.11 /16	6.86 /10	--	0.00	2.03
GL	Merrill Lynch Global Value A	MDVLX	C+	(800) 543-6217	B+ / 8.9	-2.59	4.74	35.51 /97	24.68 /90	9.07 /77	0.14	1.62
GL	Merrill Lynch Global Value B	MBVLX	C+	(800) 543-6217	A- / 9.0	-2.80	4.29	34.39 /96	23.70 /89	8.21 /72	0.00	2.37
GL	Merrill Lynch Global Value C	MCVLX	C+	(800) 543-6217	A- / 9.0	-2.80	4.30	34.47 /96	23.68 /89	8.21 /72	0.00	2.39
GL	Merrill Lynch Global Value I	MAVLX	C+	(800) 543-6217	A- / 9.2	-2.52	4.82	35.85 /97	24.99 /91	9.33 /78	0.34	1.37
GL	Merrill Lynch Global Value R	MRVLX	C+	(800) 543-6217	A- / 9.1	-2.67	4.60	35.20 /97	24.69 /90	--	0.12	1.98
HL	Merrill Lynch Healthcare A	MDHCX	E-	(800) 543-6217	E+ / 0.9	-8.38	-4.30	6.92 /26	8.03 /15	3.06 /37	0.00	1.58
HL	Merrill Lynch Healthcare B	MBHCX	E-	(800) 543-6217	E+ / 0.8	-8.48	-4.62	6.15 /21	7.20 /11	2.27 /30	0.00	2.36
HL	Merrill Lynch Healthcare C	MCHCX	E-	(800) 543-6217	D- / 1.1	-8.49	-4.63	6.22 /22	7.15 /11	2.24 /30	0.00	2.37
HL	Merrill Lynch Healthcare I	MAHCX	E-	(800) 543-6217	D / 1.8	-8.21	-4.22	7.26 /28	8.31 /17	3.33 /40	0.00	1.33
HL	Merrill Lynch Healthcare R	MRHCX	E-	(800) 543-6217	D- / 1.5	-8.30	-4.33	6.91 /26	7.83 /14	--	0.00	1.83
FO	Merrill Lynch International A	MDILX	B	(800) 543-6217	B- / 7.1	-2.25	6.76	22.02 /84	18.30 /74	6.16 /62	0.78	1.97
FO	Merrill Lynch International B	MBILX	B+	(800) 543-6217	B- / 7.2	-2.51	6.30	20.97 /83	17.37 /70	5.34 /57	0.25	2.75
FO	Merrill Lynch International C	MCILX	B+	(800) 543-6217	B- / 7.2	-2.51	6.30	20.92 /83	17.35 /69	5.33 /57	0.22	2.76
FO	Merrill Lynch International I	MAILX	B+	(800) 543-6217	B / 7.6	-2.23	6.88	22.34 /85	18.56 /75	6.46 /64	1.15	1.72
FO	Merrill Lynch Intl Index A	MDIIX	A	(800) 543-6217	B+ / 8.9	0.66	9.91	25.79 /89	23.16 /88	8.78 /75	1.21	0.80
FO	Merrill Lynch Intl Index I	MAIIX	A	(800) 543-6217	B+ / 8.9	0.73	10.02	26.12 /90	23.50 /88	9.06 /77	1.40	0.55
FO	Merrill Lynch Intl Value A	MDIVX	A+	(800) 543-6217	A- / 9.0	1.98	12.84	26.67 /91	24.62 /90	10.78 /83	1.62	1.27
FO	Merrill Lynch Intl Value B	MBIVX	B+	(800) 543-6217	A- / 9.0	1.77	12.40	25.63 /89	23.65 /89	9.92 /80	1.25	2.06
FO	Merrill Lynch Intl Value C	MCIVX	B+	(800) 543-6217	A- / 9.0	1.79	12.40	25.68 /89	23.63 /89	9.94 /80	1.31	2.06
FO	Merrill Lynch Intl Value I	MAIVX	A+	(800) 543-6217	A- / 9.2	2.04	12.96	26.97 /91	24.92 /91	11.05 /84	1.90	1.02
FO	Merrill Lynch Intl Value R	MRIVX	A+	(800) 543-6217	A- / 9.1	1.92	12.69	26.36 /90	24.34 /90	--	1.57	1.52
GR	Merrill Lynch Large Cap Core A	MDLRX	C	(800) 543-6217	C+ / 6.3	-3.22	4.00	12.93 /64	16.91 /68	7.31 /68	0.00	1.16
GR	Merrill Lynch Large Cap Core B	MBLRX	C	(800) 543-6217	C+ / 6.1	-3.44	3.61	12.12 /60	16.04 /64	6.47 /64	0.00	1.93
GR	Merrill Lynch Large Cap Core C	MCLRX	C	(800) 543-6217	C+ / 6.5	-3.44	3.61	12.11 /60	16.04 /64	6.47 /64	0.00	1.94
GR	Merrill Lynch Large Cap Core I	MALRX	C	(800) 543-6217	B- / 7.1	-3.24	4.09	13.21 /65	17.22 /69	7.57 /70	0.00	0.91
GR	Merrill Lynch Large Cap Growth A	MDLHX	C-	(800) 543-6217	C- / 3.9	-6.40	-0.60	9.35 /42	13.43 /51	2.72 /34	0.00	1.33
GR	Merrill Lynch Large Cap Growth B	MBLHX	D+	(800) 543-6217	C- / 3.7	-6.62	-1.05	8.50 /37	12.48 /46	1.90 /26	0.00	2.11
GR	Merrill Lynch Large Cap Growth C	MCLHX	C-	(800) 543-6217	C / 4.3	-6.63	-1.05	8.51 /37	12.50 /46	1.91 /26	0.00	2.11
GR	Merrill Lynch Large Cap Growth I	MALHX	C	(800) 543-6217	C / 5.2	-6.30	-0.49	9.65 /45	13.69 /52	2.98 /37	0.00	1.08
GR	Merrill Lynch Large Cap Growth R	MRLHX	C-	(800) 543-6217	C / 4.8	-6.47	-0.72	9.12 /41	13.20 /50	--	0.00	1.58
GR	Merrill Lynch Large Cap Value A	MDLVX	C+	(800) 543-6217	B / 7.7	-0.33	6.28	16.34 /75	20.45 /81	10.80 /83	0.00	1.23
GR	Merrill Lynch Large Cap Value B	MBLVX	C+	(800) 543-6217	B / 7.6	-0.52	5.86	15.46 /73	19.50 /78	9.95 /80	0.00	2.00
GR	Merrill Lynch Large Cap Value C	MCLVX	C+	(800) 543-6217	B / 7.9	-0.52	5.88	15.45 /73	19.50 /78	10.14 /81	0.00	2.00
GR	Merrill Lynch Large Cap Value I	MALVX	C+	(800) 543-6217	B / 7.9	-0.22	6.42	16.67 /76	20.75 /82	11.28 /85	0.00	0.98
GR	Merrill Lynch Large Cap Value R	MRLVX	A	(800) 543-6217	B / 8.2	-0.34	6.20	16.10 /75	20.21 /80	--	0.00	1.48
FO	Merrill Lynch Latin America A	MDLTX	C+	(800) 543-6217	A+ / 9.9	-3.96	13.41	55.40 /99	51.54 /99	25.05 /98	1.16	1.68
FO	Merrill Lynch Latin America B	MBLTX	C+	(800) 543-6217	A+ / 9.9	-4.14	12.99	54.23 /99	50.38 /99	24.07 /98	0.56	2.46
FO	Merrill Lynch Latin America C	MCLTX	C+	(800) 543-6217	A+ / 9.9	-4.14	12.98	54.28 /99	50.38 /99	24.07 /98	1.02	2.45
FO	Merrill Lynch Latin America I	MALTX	C+	(800) 543-6217	A+ / 9.9	-3.90	13.55	55.80 /99	51.91 /99	25.37 /99	1.37	1.43
MC	Merrill Lynch Mid Cp VI Opp A	MDRFX	C	(800) 543-6217	C+ / 6.9	-2.57	4.99	16.88 /77	17.76 /71	8.32 /73	0.00	1.26

● Denotes fund is closed to new investors
★ Denotes fund is included in Section II

RISK			NET ASSETS		ASSET					BULL / BEAR		FUND MANAGER		MINIMUMS		LOADS	
Risk Rating/Pts	3 Year		NAV As of 6/30/06	Total $(Mil)	Cash %	Stocks %	Bonds %	Other %	Portfolio Turnover Ratio	Last Bull Market Return	Last Bear Market Return	Manager Quality Pct	Manager Tenure (Years)	Initial Purch. $	Additional Purch. $	Front End Load	Back End Load
	Standard Deviation	Beta															
C+ / 6.1	13.1	1.15	12.37	148	0	99	0	1	109.0	121.2	-10.2	12	N/A	1,000	50	0.0	2.0
C / 4.8	13.2	1.16	11.99	2	0	99	0	1	109.0	120.1	N/A	11	N/A	1,000	50	0.0	2.0
C / 5.1	13.1	1.14	25.50	288	3	96	0	1	97.0	120.8	-5.5	5	N/A	1,000	50	5.3	2.0
C / 5.0	13.1	1.14	24.67	149	3	96	0	1	97.0	115.3	-5.7	3	N/A	1,000	50	0.0	2.0
C / 5.0	13.1	1.13	24.25	424	3	96	0	1	97.0	115.4	-5.7	3	N/A	1,000	50	0.0	2.0
C / 5.1	13.1	1.13	25.77	362	3	96	0	1	97.0	122.4	-5.4	5	N/A	1,000	50	0.0	2.0
C+ / 5.9	13.1	1.13	24.83	24	3	96	0	1	97.0	120.2	N/A	4	N/A	1,000	50	0.0	2.0
D / 1.7	19.0	1.94	7.44	62	3	96	0	1	166.1	67.8	-15.1	1	N/A	1,000	50	5.3	2.0
D / 1.8	18.9	1.94	6.98	86	3	96	0	1	166.1	63.6	-15.3	0	N/A	1,000	50	0.0	2.0
D / 1.7	19.0	1.95	6.96	31	3	96	0	1	166.1	63.2	-15.3	0	N/A	1,000	50	0.0	2.0
D / 1.7	18.9	1.94	7.58	80	3	96	0	1	166.1	69.1	-15.0	1	N/A	1,000	50	0.0	2.0
D / 1.9	18.9	1.95	7.20	1	3	96	0	1	166.1	68.2	N/A	1	N/A	1,000	50	0.0	2.0
C / 4.3	12.0	0.94	17.69	453	4	95	0	1	87.7	150.9	-8.8	72	4	1,000	50	5.3	2.0
C / 4.3	12.0	0.93	17.02	122	4	95	0	1	87.7	144.6	-8.9	65	4	1,000	50	0.0	2.0
C / 4.3	12.0	0.93	16.99	109	4	95	0	1	87.7	144.5	-8.9	64	4	1,000	50	0.0	2.0
C / 4.3	12.0	0.93	17.82	119	4	95	0	1	87.7	152.8	-8.6	75	4	1,000	50	0.0	2.0
C / 4.3	12.0	0.94	17.52	2	4	95	0	1	87.7	152.1	N/A	72	4	1,000	50	0.0	2.0
C- / 3.0	11.3	0.84	6.45	163	2	97	0	1	126.8	51.3	-1.8	37	12	1,000	50	5.3	1.0
D+ / 2.8	11.3	0.82	4.75	97	2	97	0	1	126.8	47.3	-2.0	32	14	1,000	50	0.0	4.0
D+ / 2.7	11.3	0.84	4.74	79	2	97	0	1	126.8	47.4	-2.0	30	12	1,000	50	0.0	1.0
C- / 3.1	11.3	0.83	7.04	149	2	97	0	1	126.8	52.5	-1.6	41	14	1,000	50	0.0	0.0
D+ / 2.8	11.3	0.84	4.86	5	2	97	0	1	126.8	50.7	N/A	36	14	1,000	50	0.0	0.0
B- / 7.5	10.4	1.00	12.16	22	0	99	0	1	48.8	103.8	-8.3	14	N/A	1,000	50	5.3	2.0
B- / 7.5	10.4	0.99	11.64	72	0	99	0	1	48.8	98.8	-8.5	11	N/A	1,000	50	0.0	2.0
B- / 7.5	10.4	0.99	11.64	24	0	99	0	1	48.8	98.7	-8.5	11	N/A	1,000	50	0.0	2.0
B- / 7.5	10.4	0.99	12.28	13	0	99	0	1	48.8	105.4	-8.2	15	N/A	1,000	50	0.0	2.0
B- / 7.0	10.1	1.00	13.64	182	5	94	0	1	11.3	128.0	-9.8	43	N/A	1,000	50	0.0	2.0
B- / 7.0	10.1	1.00	13.72	104	5	94	0	1	11.3	129.5	-9.6	46	N/A	1,000	50	0.0	2.0
B- / 7.1	10.3	0.99	30.40	324	2	97	0	1	70.0	135.1	-10.8	61	5	1,000	50	5.3	2.0
C+ / 5.7	10.3	0.99	29.83	80	2	97	0	1	70.0	129.4	-9.1	51	5	1,000	50	0.0	2.0
C+ / 5.7	10.3	0.99	29.55	244	2	97	0	1	70.0	129.3	-9.1	51	5	1,000	50	0.0	2.0
B- / 7.1	10.3	0.99	30.50	966	2	97	0	1	70.0	137.2	-10.7	63	5	1,000	50	0.0	2.0
B- / 7.8	10.3	0.99	30.20	35	2	97	0	1	70.0	134.4	N/A	58	3	1,000	50	0.0	2.0
C / 5.3	11.4	1.21	13.53	845	0	99	0	1	94.0	94.0	-7.0	86	N/A	1,000	50	5.3	1.0
C / 5.3	11.4	1.21	12.93	457	0	99	0	1	94.0	89.0	-7.2	81	N/A	1,000	50	0.0	4.0
C / 5.3	11.4	1.21	12.90	1,005	0	99	0	1	94.0	89.0	-7.2	81	N/A	1,000	50	0.0	1.0
C / 5.3	11.4	1.21	13.73	829	0	99	0	1	94.0	95.5	-7.0	88	N/A	1,000	50	0.0	0.0
C+ / 6.6	12.2	1.33	9.94	165	N/A	100	0	N/A	131.8	79.1	-6.8	46	N/A	1,000	50	5.3	1.0
C+ / 6.5	12.2	1.32	9.45	102	N/A	100	0	N/A	131.8	74.7	-7.1	37	N/A	1,000	50	0.0	4.0
C+ / 6.5	12.2	1.32	9.44	161	N/A	100	0	N/A	131.8	74.8	-7.1	37	N/A	1,000	50	0.0	1.0
C+ / 6.6	12.1	1.32	10.11	202	N/A	100	0	N/A	131.8	80.4	-6.8	51	N/A	1,000	50	0.0	0.0
C+ / 6.5	12.2	1.33	9.69	43	N/A	100	0	N/A	131.8	78.6	N/A	44	N/A	1,000	50	0.0	0.0
C / 5.4	11.2	1.20	17.94	733	0	99	0	1	95.0	107.5	-5.8	96	N/A	1,000	50	5.3	1.0
C / 5.4	11.2	1.19	17.15	269	0	99	0	1	95.0	102.5	-6.0	95	N/A	1,000	50	0.0	4.0
C / 5.4	11.2	1.19	17.11	610	0	99	0	1	95.0	102.4	-6.0	95	N/A	1,000	50	0.0	1.0
C / 5.4	11.2	1.20	18.23	759	0	99	0	1	95.0	109.1	-5.7	97	N/A	1,000	50	5.3	0.0
B- / 7.5	11.2	1.20	17.48	86	0	99	0	1	95.0	106.7	N/A	96	N/A	100	1	0.0	0.0
C- / 3.0	22.8	1.71	41.82	162	0	99	0	1	47.4	405.1	-3.8	96	N/A	1,000	50	5.3	2.0
D+ / 2.9	22.8	1.71	40.14	14	0	99	0	1	47.4	392.8	-4.0	94	N/A	1,000	50	0.0	2.0
D+ / 2.9	22.8	1.71	39.63	42	0	99	0	1	47.4	393.1	-4.0	94	N/A	1,000	50	0.0	2.0
C- / 3.0	22.8	1.71	42.19	166	0	99	0	1	47.4	408.9	-3.7	96	N/A	1,000	50	0.0	2.0
C+ / 5.6	10.6	0.91	19.34	105	1	98	0	1	110.0	105.2	-9.7	68	N/A	1,000	50	5.3	1.0

Fund Type	Fund Name	Ticker Symbol	Overall Weiss Investment Rating	Phone	PERFORMANCE Performance Rating/Pts	Total Return % through 6/30/06 3 Mo	6 Mo	1Yr / Pct	Annualized 3Yr / Pct	5Yr / Pct	Incl. in Returns Dividend Yield	Expense Ratio
MC	Merrill Lynch Mid Cp VI Opp I	MARFX	C+	(800) 543-6217	B / 7.6	-2.53	5.14	17.19 /77	18.06 /73	8.59 /75	0.00	1.01
MC	Merrill Lynch Mid Cp VI Opp R	MRRFX	B+	(800) 543-6217	B- / 7.5	-2.63	4.87	17.85 /79	17.87 /72	--	0.96	1.51
EN	Merrill Lynch Natural Resource A	MDGRX	B	(800) 543-6217	A+ / 9.8	2.02	8.65	35.07 /97	35.94 /98	22.64 /98	0.00	1.16
EN	Merrill Lynch Natural Resource B	MBGRX	B	(800) 543-6217	A+ / 9.8	1.82	8.24	34.07 /96	34.89 /98	21.70 /97	0.00	1.93
EN	Merrill Lynch Natural Resource C	MCGRX	B	(800) 543-6217	A+ / 9.8	1.82	8.24	34.06 /96	34.89 /98	21.69 /97	0.00	1.93
EN	Merrill Lynch Natural Resource I	MAGRX	B	(800) 543-6217	A+ / 9.8	2.06	8.77	35.40 /97	36.28 /98	22.95 /98	0.00	0.91
FO	Merrill Lynch Pacific A	MDPCX	B+	(800) 543-6217	A- / 9.2	-1.25	9.14	33.53 /96	26.18 /92	10.26 /81	1.79	1.13
FO	Merrill Lynch Pacific B	MBPCX	B+	(800) 543-6217	A- / 9.2	-1.44	8.74	32.54 /96	25.21 /91	9.40 /78	1.30	1.90
FO	Merrill Lynch Pacific C	MCPCX	B+	(800) 543-6217	A- / 9.2	-1.46	8.69	32.53 /96	25.20 /91	9.40 /78	1.69	1.90
FO	Merrill Lynch Pacific I	MAPCX	B+	(800) 543-6217	A / 9.3	-1.21	9.25	33.85 /96	26.48 /93	10.53 /82	2.06	0.88
FO	Merrill Lynch Pacific R	MRPCX	B+	(800) 543-6217	A / 9.3	-1.28	9.00	33.21 /96	26.19 /92	--	2.00	1.35
EN	Merrill Lynch Real Investment C	MCCDX	U	(800) 543-6217	U /	6.20	4.53	11.51 /57	--	--	15.76	2.92
IX	Merrill Lynch S & P Index A	MDSRX	C	(800) 543-6217	C- / 3.5	-1.57	2.49	8.08 /33	10.15 /28	1.61 /24	1.29	0.60
IX	Merrill Lynch S & P Index I	MASRX	C	(800) 543-6217	C- / 3.6	-1.51	2.62	8.31 /35	10.34 /30	1.81 /26	1.53	0.35
SC	Merrill Lynch Small Cap Growth A	MDSWX	C+	(800) 543-6217	C+ / 6.7	-7.44	7.01	20.37 /82	18.49 /74	6.70 /65	0.00	1.50
SC	Merrill Lynch Small Cap Growth B	MBSWX	C-	(800) 543-6217	C+ / 6.8	-7.61	6.60	19.43 /81	17.57 /70	5.86 /60	0.00	2.28
SC	Merrill Lynch Small Cap Growth C	MCSWX	C-	(800) 543-6217	C+ / 6.9	-7.62	6.61	19.46 /81	17.56 /70	5.85 /60	0.00	2.30
SC	Merrill Lynch Small Cap Growth I	MASWX	C	(800) 543-6217	B- / 7.3	-7.34	7.11	20.65 /83	18.80 /76	6.95 /66	0.00	1.25
SC	Merrill Lynch Small Cap Growth R	MRUSX	C+	(800) 543-6217	B- / 7.2	-7.48	6.87	20.14 /82	18.41 /74	--	0.00	1.76
SC	Merrill Lynch Small Cap Index A	MDSKX	C	(800) 543-6217	B- / 7.1	-5.38	7.73	13.68 /67	17.75 /71	7.75 /70	0.43	0.79
SC	Merrill Lynch Small Cap Index I	MASKX	C+	(800) 543-6217	B- / 7.2	-5.26	7.94	13.96 /68	18.06 /73	8.03 /72	0.69	0.53
GR	Merrill Lynch Strategy All Equity A	MDAEX	D+	(800) 543-6217	C- / 3.6	-1.58	3.44	9.67 /45	12.05 /43	2.69 /34	0.02	1.42
GR	Merrill Lynch Strategy All Equity B	MBAEX	D	(800) 543-6217	C- / 3.5	-1.66	3.13	8.94 /40	11.16 /37	1.90 /26	0.00	2.19
GR	Merrill Lynch Strategy All Equity C	MCAEX	D+	(800) 543-6217	C- / 3.9	-1.77	3.01	8.84 /39	11.12 /36	1.88 /26	0.02	2.19
GR	Merrill Lynch Strategy All Equity I	MAAEX	C-	(800) 543-6217	C / 4.9	-1.46	3.63	9.92 /46	12.33 /45	2.94 /36	0.22	1.18
GI	Merrill Lynch Strategy Growth&Inc A	MDTGX	C-	(800) 543-6217	E+ / 0.9	-1.22	1.36	4.62 /13	7.35 /12	3.45 /41	1.30	1.50
GI	Merrill Lynch Strategy Growth&Inc B	MBTGX	C-	(800) 543-6217	E+ / 0.8	-1.43	0.94	3.67 / 9	6.51 / 8	2.64 /33	0.55	2.23
GI	Merrill Lynch Strategy Growth&Inc C	MCTGX	C-	(800) 543-6217	D- / 1.1	-1.43	0.94	3.70 / 9	6.51 / 8	2.64 /33	0.47	2.26
GI	Merrill Lynch Strategy Growth&Inc I	MATGX	C	(800) 543-6217	D / 1.8	-1.22	1.46	4.76 /14	7.62 /13	3.64 /42	1.60	1.26
GR	Merrill Lynch Strategy L/T Growth A	MDYLX	D	(800) 543-6217	D+ / 2.4	-1.53	2.55	7.68 /30	10.12 /28	3.44 /41	1.01	1.25
GR	Merrill Lynch Strategy L/T Growth B	MBYLX	D	(800) 543-6217	D+ / 2.3	-1.64	2.23	6.89 /26	9.31 /23	2.66 /33	0.22	2.02
GR	Merrill Lynch Strategy L/T Growth C	MCYLX	D	(800) 543-6217	D+ / 2.7	-1.74	2.13	6.79 /25	9.25 /22	2.62 /33	0.22	2.02
GR	Merrill Lynch Strategy L/T Growth I	MAYLX	D+	(800) 543-6217	C- / 3.6	-1.43	2.66	7.92 /32	10.40 /30	3.69 /43	1.30	1.00
UT	Merrill Lynch Utilities/Telecom A	MDGUX	B+	(800) 543-6217	B- / 7.2	3.70	7.17	11.64 /58	18.30 /74	6.01 /61	1.87	1.23
UT	Merrill Lynch Utilities/Telecom B	MBGUX	B+	(800) 543-6217	B- / 7.0	3.52	6.81	10.97 /53	17.66 /71	5.44 /57	1.43	1.75
UT	Merrill Lynch Utilities/Telecom C	MCGUX	B+	(800) 543-6217	B- / 7.3	3.55	6.88	10.99 /53	17.66 /71	5.39 /57	1.44	1.80
UT	Merrill Lynch Utilities/Telecom I	MAGUX	A-	(800) 543-6217	B / 7.7	3.71	7.27	11.83 /59	18.61 /75	6.26 /63	2.19	0.98
SC	Merrill Lynch Value Opportunities A	MDSPX	C-	(800) 543-6217	C+ / 6.6	-4.37	5.20	16.11 /75	17.60 /71	8.76 /75	0.00	1.27
SC	Merrill Lynch Value Opportunities B	MBSPX	C-	(800) 543-6217	C+ / 6.8	-4.53	4.81	15.22 /72	16.70 /67	7.93 /71	0.00	2.03
SC	Merrill Lynch Value Opportunities C	MCSPX	C-	(800) 543-6217	C+ / 6.8	-4.59	4.77	15.20 /72	16.66 /67	7.91 /71	0.00	2.05
SC	Merrill Lynch Value Opportunities I	MASPX	C	(800) 543-6217	B- / 7.3	-4.32	5.34	16.38 /76	17.89 /72	9.03 /76	0.00	1.02
SC	Merrill Lynch Value Opportunities R	MRSPX	B-	(800) 543-6217	B- / 7.0	-4.43	5.08	15.84 /74	17.30 /69	--	0.00	1.51
GR	Metropolitan West Alpha Trak 500	MWATX	C	(800) 441-6580	C / 4.6	-1.59	3.05	9.02 /40	11.94 /42	2.38 /31	4.66	0.36
EM	Metzler/Payden European Emrg Mkts	MPYMX	C+	(888) 409-8007	A+ / 9.9	2.55	17.73	50.99 /99	45.63 /99	--	0.00	1.20
FO	Metzler/Payden European Growth	MPYGX	A-	(888) 409-8007	A- / 9.2	2.36	18.03	29.25 /94	23.54 /88	--	0.06	1.20
AG	MFS Aggressive Gr Alloc 529A	EAGTX	C+	(800) 343-2829	C / 4.6	-4.02	1.92	10.74 /52	13.86 /53	--	1.10	0.70
AG	MFS Aggressive Gr Alloc 529B	EBAAX	C+	(800) 343-2829	C / 4.5	-4.16	1.59	10.05 /47	13.08 /49	--	0.61	1.35
AG	MFS Aggressive Gr Alloc 529C	ECAAX	C+	(800) 343-2829	C / 4.9	-4.15	1.59	10.09 /48	13.13 /50	--	0.73	1.35
AG	MFS Aggressive Gr Alloc A	MAAGX	C+	(800) 343-2829	C / 4.8	-3.94	1.98	11.02 /54	14.13 /55	--	1.23	0.45
AG	MFS Aggressive Gr Alloc B	MBAGX	C+	(800) 343-2829	C / 4.6	-4.12	1.65	10.28 /49	13.35 /51	--	0.82	1.10
AG	MFS Aggressive Gr Alloc C	MCAGX	C+	(800) 343-2829	C / 5.1	-4.12	1.72	10.36 /49	13.37 /51	--	0.81	1.10
AG	MFS Aggressive Gr Alloc I	MIAGX	B-	(800) 343-2829	C+ / 5.9	-3.90	2.18	11.43 /56	14.52 /56	--	1.61	0.10

RISK			NET ASSETS		ASSET				BULL / BEAR		FUND MANAGER		MINIMUMS		LOADS	
	3 Year		NAV						Last Bull	Last Bear	Manager	Manager	Initial	Additional	Front	Back
Risk	Standard		As of	Total	Cash	Stocks	Bonds	Other	Portfolio	Market	Market	Quality	Tenure	Purch.	Purch.	End	End
Rating/Pts	Deviation	Beta	6/30/06	$(Mil)	%	%	%	%	Turnover Ratio	Return	Return	Pct	(Years)	$	$	Load	Load
C+ / 5.6	10.6	0.91	19.62	117	1	98	0	1	110.0	106.8	-9.7	70	N/A	1,000	50	0.0	0.0
B- / 7.5	10.7	0.92	18.52	22	1	98	0	1	110.0	106.6	N/A	67	N/A	1,000	50	0.0	0.0
C / 4.6	20.8	1.00	54.66	204	9	90	0	1	11.1	184.3	6.3	80	N/A	1,000	50	5.3	1.0
C / 4.5	20.9	1.00	52.00	60	9	90	0	1	11.1	177.6	6.1	73	9	1,000	50	0.0	4.0
C / 4.5	20.9	1.00	51.34	97	9	90	0	1	11.1	177.4	6.1	73	N/A	1,000	50	0.0	1.0
C / 4.6	20.8	1.00	55.55	76	9	90	0	1	11.1	186.7	6.3	82	N/A	1,000	50	0.0	0.0
C+ / 5.6	13.1	1.06	26.76	301	2	97	0	1	21.8	131.4	-4.8	58	4	1,000	50	5.3	2.0
C+ / 5.6	13.1	1.06	24.63	77	2	97	0	1	21.8	125.7	-5.0	48	4	1,000	50	0.0	2.0
C+ / 5.6	13.1	1.06	23.64	142	2	97	0	1	21.8	125.7	-5.0	47	4	1,000	50	0.0	2.0
C+ / 5.6	13.1	1.06	26.93	529	2	97	0	1	21.8	133.1	-4.7	61	4	1,000	50	0.0	2.0
C+ / 5.6	13.1	1.07	24.71	3	2	97	0	1	21.8	132.3	N/A	57	4	100	1	0.0	2.0
U /	N/A	N/A	11.30	49	10	0	89	1	50.0	N/A	N/A	N/A	N/A	1,000	50	0.0	2.0
B / 8.2	7.5	0.98	15.64	892	1	98	0	1	10.8	59.9	-9.9	46	N/A	1,000	50	0.0	0.0
B / 8.2	7.5	0.98	15.69	1,537	1	98	0	1	10.8	60.8	-9.8	48	N/A	1,000	50	0.0	0.0
C+ / 5.9	16.4	1.08	15.42	154	3	96	0	1	129.4	115.5	-7.3	40	N/A	1,000	50	5.3	2.0
C- / 4.2	16.5	1.08	14.69	72	3	96	0	1	129.4	110.3	-7.4	32	N/A	1,000	50	0.0	2.0
C- / 4.2	16.5	1.08	14.67	76	3	96	0	1	129.4	110.3	-7.4	32	N/A	1,000	50	0.0	1.0
C / 4.3	16.4	1.08	15.66	168	3	96	0	1	129.4	117.1	-7.1	43	N/A	1,000	50	0.0	2.0
C+ / 5.9	16.5	1.08	15.09	11	3	96	0	1	129.4	115.7	N/A	38	N/A	100	1	0.0	2.0
C / 5.3	14.5	1.00	15.47	52	18	81	0	1	36.6	114.6	-11.0	46	N/A	1,000	50	0.0	2.0
C / 5.3	14.5	1.00	15.50	75	18	81	0	1	36.6	116.4	-10.9	49	N/A	1,000	50	0.0	2.0
C+ / 6.1	8.2	1.05	9.32	1	N/A	N/A	0	N/A	11.0	69.7	-10.1	60	6	1,000	50	5.3	1.0
C+ / 6.0	8.2	1.07	8.90	10	N/A	N/A	0	N/A	11.0	65.7	-10.3	48	6	1,000	50	0.0	4.0
C+ / 6.0	8.2	1.06	8.89	13	N/A	N/A	0	N/A	11.0	65.5	-10.3	49	6	1,000	50	0.0	1.0
C+ / 6.1	8.2	1.06	9.42	16	N/A	N/A	0	N/A	11.0	71.3	-10.1	62	6	1,000	50	0.0	0.0
B+ / 9.8	5.0	0.62	9.71	2	5	58	36	1	N/A	38.4	-4.1	51	6	1,000	50	5.3	1.0
B+ / 9.8	5.1	0.63	9.64	12	5	58	36	1	N/A	34.9	-4.2	41	6	1,000	50	0.0	4.0
B+ / 9.8	5.1	0.63	9.64	13	5	58	36	1	N/A	35.0	-4.1	40	6	1,000	50	0.0	1.0
B+ / 9.7	5.1	0.63	9.70	12	5	58	36	1	N/A	39.5	-4.0	53	6	1,000	50	0.0	0.0
C+ / 6.7	6.8	0.87	9.64	2	5	82	11	2	1.8	55.4	-7.0	57	N/A	1,000	50	5.3	1.0
C+ / 6.5	6.8	0.88	9.62	8	5	82	11	2	1.8	51.5	-7.1	47	N/A	1,000	50	0.0	4.0
C+ / 6.4	6.8	0.87	9.59	18	5	82	11	2	1.8	51.5	-7.2	46	N/A	1,000	50	0.0	1.0
C+ / 6.7	6.8	0.87	9.65	37	5	82	11	2	1.8	56.5	-6.8	60	N/A	1,000	50	0.0	0.0
B- / 7.6	8.9	0.69	12.74	79	1	97	0	2	25.5	93.1	-4.6	78	4	1,000	50	4.0	1.0
B- / 7.7	8.9	0.69	12.69	25	1	97	0	2	25.5	90.0	-4.8	73	4	1,000	50	0.0	4.0
B- / 7.7	8.9	0.68	12.57	15	1	97	0	2	25.5	89.6	-4.7	74	4	1,000	50	0.0	1.0
B- / 7.6	8.9	0.69	12.73	25	1	97	0	2	25.5	94.5	-4.4	81	4	1,000	50	0.0	0.0
C / 4.5	12.6	0.83	26.92	745	1	98	0	1	77.3	108.9	-10.6	73	N/A	1,000	50	5.3	2.0
C / 4.5	12.6	0.84	24.21	713	1	98	0	1	77.3	103.9	-10.9	65	N/A	1,000	50	0.0	2.0
C / 4.4	12.6	0.84	23.49	565	1	98	0	1	77.3	103.8	-10.8	65	N/A	1,000	50	0.0	2.0
C / 4.5	12.6	0.84	27.23	866	1	98	0	1	77.3	110.5	-10.6	75	N/A	1,000	50	0.0	2.0
C+ / 6.6	12.6	0.83	24.19	42	1	98	0	1	77.3	107.9	N/A	70	N/A	100	1	0.0	2.0
B- / 7.7	8.0	1.04	7.94	168	11	0	88	1	64.0	71.1	-8.6	60	8	3,000,000	50,000	0.0	0.0
C- / 3.6	21.4	1.13	27.36	87	0	100	0	0	178.0	308.9	N/A	86	N/A	5,000	1,000	0.0	2.0
C+ / 6.3	13.8	1.18	17.41	13	6	94	0	0	211.0	134.8	N/A	18	N/A	5,000	1,000	0.0	2.0
B / 8.1	10.0	1.23	14.33	32	0	100	0	0	1.0	82.8	-8.4	62	4	250	50	5.8	0.0
B / 8.1	10.0	1.23	14.07	23	0	100	0	0	1.0	79.1	-8.7	53	4	250	50	0.0	4.0
B / 8.1	10.0	1.23	14.08	9	0	100	0	0	1.0	79.1	-8.6	53	4	250	50	0.0	1.0
B / 8.1	10.0	1.23	14.39	397	0	100	0	0	1.0	84.3	-8.5	64	4	1,000	50	5.8	0.0
B / 8.1	10.0	1.23	14.19	220	0	100	0	0	1.0	80.5	-8.6	N/A	4	1,000	50	0.0	4.0
B / 8.1	10.0	1.23	14.19	163	0	100	0	0	1.0	80.5	-8.6	57	4	1,000	50	0.0	1.0
B / 8.1	10.0	1.23	14.53	50	0	100	0	0	1.0	86.3	-8.4	68	4	10,000,000	0	0.0	0.0

Data as of June 30, 2006

99 Pct = Best 0 Pct = Worst					PERFORMANCE							
			Overall		Perfor-		Total Return % through 6/30/06					Incl. in Returns	
			Weiss		mance					Annualized		Dividend	Expense
Fund		Ticker	Investment		Rating/Pts	3 Mo	6 Mo	1Yr / Pct	3Yr / Pct	5Yr / Pct	Yield	Ratio
Type	Fund Name	Symbol	Rating	Phone								
AG	MFS Aggressive Gr Alloc R	MAARX	C+	(800) 343-2829	C+ / 5.6	-3.95	1.99	10.87 /53	13.99 /54	--	1.22	0.60
AG	MFS Aggressive Gr Alloc R1	MAAFX	C-	(800) 343-2829	C / 5.2	-4.15	1.66	10.19 /48	13.32 /50	--	1.36	1.24
AG	MFS Aggressive Gr Alloc R2	MAAMX	C-	(800) 343-2829	C / 5.3	-4.00	1.80	10.57 /51	13.48 /51	--	1.36	1.83
AG	MFS Aggressive Gr Alloc R3	MAWAX	B-	(800) 343-2829	C / 5.5	-4.04	1.86	10.68 /51	13.85 /53	--	1.28	0.81
AG	MFS Aggressive Gr Alloc R4	MAAHX	C-	(800) 343-2829	C+ / 5.7	-3.95	1.99	10.97 /53	14.12 /55	--	1.54	0.50
AG	MFS Aggressive Gr Alloc R5	MAALX	C-	(800) 343-2829	C+ / 5.8	-3.87	2.13	11.30 /55	14.26 /55	--	1.63	0.20
GR	MFS Capital Opportunities 529A	EACOX	D	(800) 343-2829	D / 1.6	-2.16	1.64	5.50 /18	8.87 /20	-2.74 / 6	0.00	1.56
GR	MFS Capital Opportunities 529B	EBCOX	D	(800) 343-2829	D- / 1.5	-2.27	1.38	4.88 /14	8.18 /16	-3.38 / 4	0.00	2.21
GR	MFS Capital Opportunities 529C	ECCOX	D	(800) 343-2829	D / 1.9	-2.21	1.39	4.91 /15	8.20 /16	-3.49 / 4	0.00	2.22
GR	MFS Capital Opportunities A	MCOFX	D	(800) 343-2829	D / 1.9	-1.99	1.85	5.92 /20	9.26 /22	-2.48 / 7	0.00	1.21
GR	MFS Capital Opportunities B	MCOBX	D	(800) 343-2829	D / 1.7	-2.18	1.45	5.10 /16	8.46 /18	-3.21 / 5	0.00	1.96
GR	MFS Capital Opportunities C	MCOCX	D	(800) 343-2829	D / 2.1	-2.27	1.46	5.04 /15	8.44 /17	-3.21 / 5	0.00	1.96
GR	MFS Capital Opportunities I	MCOIX	D+	(800) 343-2829	C- / 3.0	-1.97	2.05	6.24 /22	9.57 /24	-2.21 / 8	0.00	0.96
GR	MFS Capital Opportunities R	MFCRX	D	(800) 343-2829	D+ / 2.6	-2.08	1.71	5.65 /18	8.99 /21	-2.64 / 6	0.00	1.45
GR	MFS Capital Opportunities R1	MCOGX	D-	(800) 343-2829	D / 2.2	-2.26	1.37	5.02 /15	8.40 /17	-3.24 / 5	0.00	2.16
GR	MFS Capital Opportunities R2	MCOKX	D-	(800) 343-2829	D+ / 2.3	-2.17	1.61	5.35 /17	8.55 /18	-3.17 / 5	0.00	1.82
GR	MFS Capital Opportunities R3	MCOTX	C-	(800) 343-2829	C- / 3.9	-2.09	1.65	5.44 /17	11.42 /39	-1.64 / 9	0.00	1.67
GR	MFS Capital Opportunities R4	MCOUX	D-	(800) 343-2829	D+ / 2.7	-2.07	1.78	5.77 /19	9.20 /22	-2.50 / 6	0.00	1.31
GR	MFS Capital Opportunities R5	MCOJX	D	(800) 343-2829	D+ / 2.8	-1.99	1.92	6.07 /21	9.33 /23	-2.43 / 7	0.00	0.97
BA	MFS Conservative Alloc 529A	ECLAX	C-	(800) 343-2829	E+ / 0.6	-0.60	1.39	4.49 /13	5.96 / 7	--	2.16	0.70
BA	MFS Conservative Alloc 529B	EBCAX	C-	(800) 343-2829	E / 0.5	-0.77	1.05	3.79 /10	5.25 / 4	--	1.60	1.35
BA	MFS Conservative Alloc 529C	ECACX	C-	(800) 343-2829	E+ / 0.8	-0.78	1.05	3.83 /10	5.29 / 5	--	1.80	1.35
BA	MFS Conservative Alloc A	MACFX	C-	(800) 343-2829	E+ / 0.7	-0.60	1.48	4.74 /14	6.22 / 7	--	2.31	0.45
BA	MFS Conservative Alloc B	MACBX	C-	(800) 343-2829	E+ / 0.6	-0.77	1.14	4.03 /11	5.53 / 5	--	1.84	1.10
BA	MFS Conservative Alloc C	MACVX	C-	(800) 343-2829	E+ / 0.9	-0.69	1.14	4.08 /11	5.52 / 5	--	1.88	1.10
BA	MFS Conservative Alloc I	MACIX	C-	(800) 343-2829	D- / 1.4	-0.51	1.64	5.05 /15	6.57 / 9	--	2.76	0.10
BA	MFS Conservative Alloc R	MACRX	C-	(800) 343-2829	D- / 1.2	-0.51	1.39	4.57 /13	6.09 / 7	--	2.37	0.60
BA	MFS Conservative Alloc R1	MACKX	C-	(800) 343-2829	E+ / 0.9	-0.78	1.06	4.03 /11	5.49 / 5	--	2.54	1.24
BA	MFS Conservative Alloc R2	MACLX	C-	(800) 343-2829	D- / 1.0	-0.69	1.23	4.30 /12	5.62 / 5	--	2.45	0.92
BA	MFS Conservative Alloc R3	MCARX	C-	(800) 343-2829	D- / 1.1	-0.60	1.32	4.36 /12	5.77 / 6	--	2.50	0.80
BA	MFS Conservative Alloc R4	MACNX	C-	(800) 343-2829	D- / 1.3	-0.51	1.48	4.72 /14	6.24 / 7	--	2.69	0.50
BA	MFS Conservative Alloc R5	MACJX	C-	(800) 343-2829	D- / 1.3	-0.43	1.65	4.99 /15	6.36 / 8	--	2.78	0.20
GR	MFS Core Equity A	MRGAX	C-	(800) 343-2829	D+ / 2.7	-3.01	0.11	5.93 /20	11.18 /37	3.18 /39	0.00	1.38
GR	MFS Core Equity B	MRGBX	D+	(800) 343-2829	D+ / 2.5	-3.18	-0.24	5.24 /16	10.45 /30	2.50 /32	0.00	2.03
GR	MFS Core Equity C	MRGCX	C-	(800) 343-2829	C- / 3.1	-3.14	-0.24	5.26 /16	10.47 /31	2.50 /32	0.00	2.03
GR	MFS Core Equity R	MGIRX	C-	(800) 343-2829	C- / 3.5	-3.08	0.00	5.72 /19	10.99 /35	3.05 /37	0.00	1.53
GR	MFS Core Equity R3	MRERX	C-	(800) 343-2829	C- / 3.4	-3.10	-0.11	5.56 /18	10.78 /34	2.95 /36	0.00	1.70
GR	MFS Core Equity R4	MRGHX	D+	(800) 343-2829	C- / 3.6	-3.01	0.06	5.87 /20	11.14 /37	3.15 /38	0.00	1.44
GR	MFS Core Equity R5	MRGJX	D+	(800) 343-2829	C- / 3.7	-2.95	0.17	6.16 /21	11.29 /38	3.23 /39	0.00	1.14
GR	MFS Core Growth Fund A	MFCAX	D-	(800) 343-2829	D- / 1.3	-3.95	-0.28	7.94 /32	8.22 /16	-1.77 / 9	0.00	1.37
GR	MFS Core Growth Fund B	MFCBX	D-	(800) 343-2829	D- / 1.2	-4.10	-0.59	7.27 /28	7.52 /12	-2.40 / 7	0.00	2.02
GR	MFS Core Growth Fund C	MFCCX	D-	(800) 343-2829	D / 1.6	-4.10	-0.65	7.27 /28	7.52 /12	-2.41 / 7	0.00	2.01
GR	MFS Core Growth Fund I	MFCIX	D	(800) 343-2829	D+ / 2.4	-3.80	-0.11	8.38 /36	8.60 /18	-1.42 /10	0.00	1.03
GR	MFS Core Growth Fund R	MCFRX	D	(800) 343-2829	D / 2.1	-3.96	-0.34	7.84 /31	8.08 /16	-1.85 / 9	0.00	1.53
GR	MFS Core Growth Fund R3	MCRRX	D	(800) 343-2829	D / 2.0	-3.98	-0.46	7.63 /30	7.87 /14	-1.96 / 8	0.00	1.69
GR	MFS Emerging Growth Fund 529A	EAGRX	D	(800) 343-2829	D / 2.2	-7.11	-1.40	8.99 /40	10.26 /29	-2.65 / 6	0.00	1.62
GR	MFS Emerging Growth Fund 529B	EBEGX	D	(800) 343-2829	D / 2.0	-7.26	-1.70	8.30 /35	9.56 /24	-3.30 / 5	0.00	2.27
GR	MFS Emerging Growth Fund 529C	ECEGX	D+	(800) 343-2829	D+ / 2.5	-7.27	-1.71	8.28 /35	9.55 /24	-3.30 / 5	0.00	2.30
★ GR	MFS Emerging Growth Fund A	MFEGX	D-	(800) 343-2829	D+ / 2.4	-7.02	-1.21	9.37 /42	10.67 /32	-2.38 / 7	0.00	1.27
GR	MFS Emerging Growth Fund B	MEGBX	D-	(800) 343-2829	D / 2.2	-7.19	-1.59	8.55 /37	9.82 /26	-3.12 / 5	0.00	2.02
GR	MFS Emerging Growth Fund C	MFECX	D-	(800) 343-2829	D+ / 2.7	-7.18	-1.57	8.57 /37	9.82 /26	-3.11 / 5	0.00	2.02
GR	MFS Emerging Growth Fund I	MFEIX	C-	(800) 343-2829	C- / 3.5	-6.97	-1.07	9.65 /45	10.93 /35	-2.13 / 8	0.00	1.02

RISK			NET ASSETS		ASSET				Portfolio Turnover Ratio	BULL / BEAR		FUND MANAGER		MINIMUMS		LOADS	
Risk Rating/Pts	3 Year		NAV As of 6/30/06	Total $(Mil)	Cash %	Stocks %	Bonds %	Other %		Last Bull Market Return	Last Bear Market Return	Manager Quality Pct	Manager Tenure (Years)	Initial Purch. $	Additional Purch. $	Front End Load	Back End Load
	Standard Deviation	Beta															
B- /7.2	10.0	1.22	14.35	31	0	100	0	0	1.0	83.6	-8.5	63	4	1,000	50	0.0	0.0
C+ /5.7	10.0	1.23	14.10	4	0	100	0	0	1.0	80.4	-8.6	56	N/A	1,000	50	0.0	0.0
C+ /5.7	10.0	1.23	14.16	2	0	100	0	0	1.0	81.0	-8.6	58	N/A	1,000	50	0.0	0.0
B /8.1	10.1	1.24	14.24	12	0	100	0	0	1.0	82.7	-8.6	61	3	1,000	50	0.0	0.0
C+ /5.7	10.0	1.23	14.35	6	0	100	0	0	1.0	84.3	-8.5	64	N/A	1,000	50	0.0	0.0
C+ /5.7	10.0	1.23	14.39	67	0	100	0	0	1.0	84.9	-8.5	66	N/A	1,000	50	0.0	0.0
B- /7.3	8.7	1.07	13.61	N/A	1	98	0	1	62.0	59.1	-12.1	28	N/A	250	50	5.8	0.0
B- /7.2	8.7	1.07	12.47	N/A	1	98	0	1	62.0	55.9	-12.2	23	N/A	250	50	0.0	4.0
B- /7.2	8.6	1.07	12.40	N/A	1	98	0	1	62.0	55.8	-12.3	24	N/A	250	50	0.0	1.0
B- /7.1	8.7	1.07	13.77	766	1	98	0	1	62.0	60.7	-12.0	31	N/A	1,000	50	5.8	0.0
B- /7.0	8.7	1.07	12.58	414	1	98	0	1	62.0	57.2	-12.2	26	N/A	1,000	50	0.0	4.0
B- /7.0	8.7	1.07	12.51	107	1	98	0	1	62.0	57.1	-12.2	25	N/A	1,000	50	0.0	1.0
B- /7.3	8.7	1.07	13.96	21	1	98	0	1	62.0	62.2	-11.9	33	N/A	10,000,000	0	0.0	0.0
B- /7.0	8.7	1.07	13.65	7	1	98	0	1	62.0	59.5	-12.0	29	N/A	1,000	50	0.0	0.0
C+ /5.7	8.7	1.07	12.56	1	1	98	0	1	62.0	57.0	-12.2	25	N/A	1,000	50	0.0	0.0
C+ /5.8	8.7	1.07	12.61	N/A	1	98	0	1	62.0	57.4	-12.2	26	N/A	1,000	50	0.0	0.0
B- /7.0	10.6	1.26	13.57	2	1	98	0	1	62.0	70.2	-12.2	33	N/A	1,000	50	0.0	0.0
C+ /5.8	8.7	1.07	13.75	1	1	98	0	1	62.0	60.6	-12.0	30	N/A	1,000	50	0.0	0.0
C+ /5.8	8.7	1.07	13.80	N/A	1	98	0	1	62.0	61.1	-12.0	31	N/A	1,000	50	0.0	0.0
B+ /9.9	3.4	0.71	11.65	18	10	40	50	0	2.0	29.1	-2.3	56	4	250	50	5.8	0.0
B+ /9.9	3.4	0.70	11.55	2	10	40	50	0	2.0	26.4	-2.4	47	4	250	50	0.0	4.0
B+ /9.9	3.4	0.71	11.50	11	10	40	50	0	2.0	26.5	-2.5	47	4	250	50	0.0	1.0
B+ /9.9	3.4	0.70	11.69	252	10	40	50	0	2.0	30.1	-2.2	59	4	1,000	50	5.8	0.0
B+ /9.9	3.4	0.71	11.58	163	10	40	50	0	2.0	27.4	-2.4	50	4	1,000	50	0.0	4.0
B+ /9.9	3.4	0.70	11.57	131	10	40	50	0	2.0	27.5	-2.5	50	4	1,000	50	0.0	1.0
B+ /9.9	3.4	0.70	11.77	18	10	40	50	0	2.0	31.5	-2.2	63	4	10,000,000	0	0.0	0.0
B+ /9.9	3.4	0.71	11.64	17	10	40	50	0	2.0	29.5	-2.3	57	4	1,000	50	0.0	0.0
B+ /9.9	3.4	0.70	11.49	1	10	40	50	0	2.0	27.4	-2.4	50	N/A	1,000	50	0.0	0.0
B+ /9.9	3.4	0.70	11.54	1	10	40	50	0	2.0	27.7	-2.4	52	N/A	1,000	50	0.0	0.0
B+ /9.9	3.4	0.70	11.53	3	10	40	50	0	2.0	28.4	-2.4	54	3	1,000	50	0.0	0.0
B+ /9.9	3.4	0.70	11.67	1	10	40	50	0	2.0	30.0	-2.2	59	N/A	1,000	50	0.0	0.0
B+ /9.9	3.4	0.70	11.70	11	10	40	50	0	2.0	30.5	-2.2	61	N/A	1,000	50	0.0	0.0
B- /7.6	8.2	1.04	17.72	151	1	98	0	1	60.0	69.5	-9.1	52	1	1,000	50	5.8	0.0
B- /7.6	8.2	1.04	16.74	54	1	98	0	1	60.0	66.1	-9.3	43	1	1,000	50	0.0	4.0
B- /7.6	8.2	1.04	16.68	18	1	98	0	1	60.0	65.9	-9.3	43	1	1,000	50	0.0	1.0
B- /7.6	8.2	1.04	17.61	5	1	98	0	1	60.0	68.6	-9.1	49	1	1,000	50	0.0	0.0
B- /7.9	8.2	1.03	17.52	1	1	98	0	1	60.0	67.8	-9.1	47	1	1,000	50	0.0	0.0
C+ /6.1	8.2	1.04	17.70	23	1	98	0	1	60.0	69.4	-9.1	51	N/A	1,000	50	0.0	0.0
C+ /6.1	8.2	1.03	17.77	N/A	1	98	0	1	60.0	69.9	-9.1	53	N/A	1,000	50	0.0	0.0
C+ /6.9	8.7	1.04	17.53	554	2	97	0	1	123.0	53.4	-10.9	26	10	1,000	50	5.8	0.0
C+ /6.9	8.7	1.04	16.83	173	2	97	0	1	123.0	50.3	-11.0	21	7	1,000	50	0.0	4.0
C+ /6.9	8.7	1.04	16.83	64	2	97	0	1	123.0	50.3	-11.0	21	7	1,000	50	0.0	1.0
B- /7.2	8.7	1.04	17.97	4	2	97	0	1	123.0	55.0	-10.8	28	10	10,000,000	0	0.0	0.0
C+ /6.9	8.7	1.04	17.46	6	2	97	0	1	123.0	52.8	-10.9	25	10	1,000	50	0.0	0.0
B- /7.2	8.7	1.04	17.36	2	2	97	0	1	123.0	52.0	-10.9	23	3	1,000	50	0.0	0.0
B- /7.2	12.1	1.34	33.83	1	0	99	0	1	88.0	75.3	-8.5	21	4	250	50	5.8	0.0
B- /7.2	12.1	1.34	31.18	N/A	0	99	0	1	88.0	71.8	-8.6	17	4	250	50	0.0	4.0
B- /7.2	12.1	1.34	31.00	N/A	0	99	0	1	88.0	71.8	-8.6	17	4	250	50	0.0	1.0
C+ /5.9	12.1	1.34	34.31	2,208	0	99	0	1	88.0	77.4	-8.4	24	4	1,000	50	5.8	0.0
C+ /5.8	12.1	1.34	31.48	814	0	99	0	1	88.0	73.1	-8.6	19	6	1,000	50	0.0	4.0
C+ /5.8	12.1	1.34	31.30	162	0	99	0	1	88.0	73.1	-8.6	19	6	1,000	50	0.0	1.0
B- /7.2	12.1	1.34	35.11	81	0	99	0	1	88.0	78.7	-8.4	26	6	10,000,000	0	0.0	0.0

					PERFORMANCE							
	99 Pct = Best 0 Pct = Worst		Overall Weiss Investment Rating		Perfor- mance Rating/Pts	Total Return % through 6/30/06					Incl. in Returns	
									Annualized		Dividend	Expense
Fund Type	Fund Name	Ticker Symbol		Phone		3 Mo	6 Mo	1Yr / Pct	3Yr / Pct	5Yr / Pct	Yield	Ratio
GR	MFS Emerging Growth Fund R	MFERX	D	(800) 343-2829	C- / 3.2	-7.08	-1.33	9.11 /41	10.38 /30	-2.55 / 6	0.00	1.53
GR	MFS Emerging Growth Fund R1	MFELX	D-	(800) 343-2829	D+ / 2.8	-7.23	-1.63	8.42 /36	9.76 /26	-3.15 / 5	0.00	2.21
GR	MFS Emerging Growth Fund R2	MFEMX	D-	(800) 343-2829	D+ / 2.9	-7.15	-1.47	8.79 /39	9.91 /27	-3.07 / 5	0.00	1.88
GR	MFS Emerging Growth Fund R3	MEGRX	C-	(800) 343-2829	C / 4.4	-7.12	-1.43	8.89 /39	12.45 /45	-1.73 / 9	0.00	1.76
GR	MFS Emerging Growth Fund R4	MFEHX	D-	(800) 343-2829	C- / 3.3	-7.06	-1.30	9.22 /41	10.61 /32	-2.41 / 7	0.00	1.41
GR	MFS Emerging Growth Fund R5	MFEJX	D-	(800) 343-2829	C- / 3.4	-6.98	-1.12	9.56 /44	10.75 /33	-2.34 / 7	0.00	1.10
EM	MFS Emerging Mkt Equity Fund A	MEMAX	B	(800) 343-2829	A+ / 9.6	-4.58	6.70	34.86 /97	34.84 /98	20.99 /97	0.45	1.88
EM	MFS Emerging Mkt Equity Fund B	MEMBX	B	(800) 343-2829	A+ / 9.7	-4.71	6.38	34.05 /96	34.06 /98	20.33 /96	0.04	2.53
EM	MFS Emerging Mkt Equity Fund C	MEMCX	B	(800) 343-2829	A+ / 9.7	-4.72	6.34	34.01 /96	34.04 /98	20.31 /96	0.27	2.53
EM	● MFS Emerging Mkt Equity Fund I	MEMIX	B	(800) 343-2829	A+ / 9.8	-4.47	6.87	35.34 /97	35.38 /98	21.52 /97	0.66	1.53
GL	MFS Global Equity Fund A	MWEFX	A-	(800) 343-2829	B- / 7.3	1.69	9.12	20.51 /82	17.83 /72	8.72 /75	0.00	1.55
GL	MFS Global Equity Fund B	MWEBX	A-	(800) 343-2829	B- / 7.2	1.52	8.73	19.65 /81	16.95 /68	7.90 /71	0.00	2.30
GL	MFS Global Equity Fund C	MWECX	A	(800) 343-2829	B- / 7.4	1.51	8.73	19.61 /81	16.93 /68	7.89 /71	0.00	2.30
GL	MFS Global Equity Fund I	MWEIX	A+	(800) 343-2829	B / 7.9	1.77	9.29	20.86 /83	18.12 /73	8.97 /76	0.00	1.30
GL	MFS Global Equity Fund R	MGERX	A	(800) 343-2829	B / 7.7	1.67	9.00	20.23 /82	17.52 /70	8.52 /74	0.00	1.81
GL	MFS Global Equity Fund R1	MWEGX	B-	(800) 343-2829	B- / 7.5	1.52	8.66	19.48 /81	16.88 /67	7.87 /71	0.00	2.47
GL	MFS Global Equity Fund R2	MWEKX	B-	(800) 343-2829	B / 7.6	1.59	8.88	19.91 /82	17.04 /68	7.95 /71	0.00	2.17
GL	MFS Global Equity Fund R3	MEQRX	A+	(800) 343-2829	B / 7.9	1.61	8.93	20.01 /82	18.35 /74	8.68 /75	0.00	2.05
GL	MFS Global Equity Fund R4	MWEHX	B-	(800) 343-2829	B / 7.8	1.70	9.05	20.35 /82	17.76 /71	8.68 /75	0.00	1.73
GL	MFS Global Equity Fund R5	MWELX	B	(800) 343-2829	B / 7.8	1.73	9.19	20.72 /83	17.90 /72	8.76 /75	0.00	1.44
GL	MFS Global Growth Fund A	MWOFX	C+	(800) 343-2829	C+ / 6.1	-2.54	3.97	17.34 /78	16.44 /65	4.99 /54	0.00	1.59
GL	MFS Global Growth Fund B	MWOBX	C	(800) 343-2829	C+ / 5.8	-2.74	3.57	16.43 /76	15.56 /62	4.20 /48	0.00	2.34
GL	MFS Global Growth Fund C	MWOCX	C+	(800) 343-2829	C+ / 6.2	-2.77	3.55	16.47 /76	15.55 /62	4.20 /48	0.00	2.34
GL	MFS Global Growth Fund I	MWOIX	B-	(800) 343-2829	C+ / 6.9	-2.49	4.08	17.68 /78	16.73 /67	5.26 /56	0.00	1.34
GL	MFS Global Growth Fund R	MGLRX	C+	(800) 343-2829	C+ / 6.6	-2.65	3.81	16.98 /77	16.13 /64	4.79 /52	0.00	1.85
GL	MFS Global Growth Fund R1	MWOGX	C	(800) 343-2829	C+ / 6.3	-2.75	3.52	16.32 /75	15.50 /61	4.17 /48	0.00	2.52
GL	MFS Global Growth Fund R2	MWOKX	C	(800) 343-2829	C+ / 6.4	-2.69	3.66	16.70 /76	15.65 /62	4.25 /48	0.00	2.20
GL	MFS Global Growth Fund R3	MGWRX	B	(800) 343-2829	B- / 7.3	-2.66	3.74	16.84 /77	17.39 /70	5.19 /56	0.00	2.09
GL	MFS Global Growth Fund R4	MWOHX	C	(800) 343-2829	C+ / 6.7	-2.59	3.88	17.14 /77	16.35 /65	4.94 /54	0.00	1.75
GL	MFS Global Growth Fund R5	MWOJX	C	(800) 343-2829	C+ / 6.8	-2.49	4.06	17.55 /78	16.51 /66	5.03 /54	0.00	1.45
GL	MFS Global Total Return Fund A	MFWTX	C	(800) 343-2829	C / 5.1	2.22	7.03	12.19 /61	13.03 /49	9.11 /77	1.08	1.48
GL	MFS Global Total Return Fund B	MFWBX	C	(800) 343-2829	C / 4.7	2.08	6.67	11.44 /56	12.30 /44	8.40 /73	0.46	2.13
GL	MFS Global Total Return Fund C	MFWCX	C	(800) 343-2829	C / 5.2	2.03	6.66	11.35 /56	12.30 /44	8.39 /73	0.52	2.12
GL	● MFS Global Total Return Fund I	MFWIX	B+	(800) 343-2829	C+ / 5.9	2.33	7.21	12.52 /62	13.43 /51	9.48 /79	1.47	1.12
GL	MFS Global Total Return Fund R	MGRRX	C	(800) 343-2829	C+ / 5.7	2.19	6.98	11.99 /59	12.88 /48	9.01 /76	0.99	1.61
GL	MFS Global Total Return Fund R1	MFWGX	C+	(800) 343-2829	C / 5.3	2.02	6.59	11.30 /55	12.24 /44	8.37 /73	0.54	2.28
GL	MFS Global Total Return Fund R3	MGBRX	C+	(800) 343-2829	C / 5.4	2.17	6.88	11.82 /58	12.42 /45	8.47 /74	0.92	1.87
GL	MFS Global Total Return Fund R4	MFWHX	B	(800) 343-2829	C+ / 5.7	2.23	7.04	12.10 /60	13.01 /49	9.09 /77	1.11	1.50
GL	MFS Global Total Return Fund R5	MFWJX	B	(800) 343-2829	C+ / 5.8	2.29	7.19	12.32 /61	13.11 /49	9.15 /77	1.37	1.20
AA	MFS Growth Allocation 529A	EAGWX	C+	(800) 343-2829	C- / 3.6	-2.61	2.07	9.53 /44	12.10 /43	--	1.98	0.70
AA	MFS Growth Allocation 529B	EBGWX	C	(800) 343-2829	C- / 3.4	-2.79	1.72	8.79 /39	11.37 /38	--	1.55	1.35
AA	MFS Growth Allocation 529C	ECGWX	C+	(800) 343-2829	C- / 4.0	-2.79	1.80	8.83 /39	11.40 /39	--	1.60	1.35
AA	MFS Growth Allocation A	MAGWX	C+	(800) 343-2829	C- / 3.8	-2.60	2.21	9.77 /45	12.39 /45	--	2.15	0.45
AA	MFS Growth Allocation B	MBGWX	C+	(800) 343-2829	C- / 3.6	-2.70	1.94	9.13 /41	11.68 /40	--	1.75	1.10
AA	MFS Growth Allocation C	MCGWX	C+	(800) 343-2829	C- / 4.2	-2.70	1.94	9.16 /41	11.68 /40	--	1.78	1.10
AA	MFS Growth Allocation R	MGARX	C+	(800) 343-2829	C / 4.7	-2.61	2.14	9.67 /45	12.22 /44	--	2.17	0.60
AA	MFS Growth Allocation R1	MAGMX	C-	(800) 343-2829	C / 4.3	-2.73	1.88	9.02 /40	11.61 /40	--	2.45	1.22
AA	MFS Growth Allocation R2	MAGNX	C-	(800) 343-2829	C / 4.5	-2.65	2.02	9.37 /42	11.76 /41	--	2.49	0.89
AA	MFS Growth Allocation R3	MGALX	C+	(800) 343-2829	C / 4.6	-2.70	2.01	9.37 /42	12.10 /43	--	2.21	0.81
AA	MFS Growth Allocation R4	MAGEX	C-	(800) 343-2829	C / 4.8	-2.61	2.14	9.68 /45	12.36 /45	--	2.48	0.50
AA	MFS Growth Allocation R5	MAGJX	C-	(800) 343-2829	C / 4.9	-2.53	2.36	10.10 /48	12.53 /46	--	2.57	0.20
GR	MFS Growth Opportunities Fund A	MGOFX	D-	(800) 343-2829	E / 0.4	-5.53	-2.35	1.02 / 3	6.51 / 8	-2.26 / 7	0.09	0.95

● Denotes fund is closed to new investors
* Denotes fund is included in Section II

RISK			NET ASSETS		ASSET					BULL / BEAR		FUND MANAGER		MINIMUMS		LOADS	
	3 Year		NAV						Portfolio	Last Bull	Last Bear	Manager	Manager	Initial	Additional	Front	Back
Risk Rating/Pts	Standard Deviation	Beta	As of 6/30/06	Total $(Mil)	Cash %	Stocks %	Bonds %	Other %	Turnover Ratio	Market Return	Market Return	Quality Pct	Tenure (Years)	Purch. $	Purch. $	End Load	End Load
C+ / 5.9	12.1	1.34	34.01	14	0	99	0	1	88.0	76.0	-8.4	22	4	1,000	50	0.0	0.0
C / 5.0	12.1	1.34	31.43	2	0	99	0	1	88.0	72.9	-8.6	18	N/A	1,000	50	0.0	0.0
C / 5.1	12.1	1.33	31.56	1	0	99	0	1	88.0	73.5	-8.6	19	N/A	1,000	50	0.0	0.0
C+ / 6.8	13.5	1.51	33.80	5	0	99	0	1	88.0	85.8	-8.6	25	3	1,000	50	0.0	0.0
C / 5.1	12.1	1.33	34.25	2	0	99	0	1	88.0	77.1	-8.4	24	N/A	1,000	50	0.0	0.0
C / 5.1	12.1	1.33	34.38	N/A	0	99	0	1	88.0	77.7	-8.4	24	N/A	1,000	50	0.0	0.0
C / 4.4	17.6	1.08	32.49	193	4	95	0	1	34.0	221.7	-7.8	27	N/A	1,000	50	5.8	1.0
C / 4.4	17.6	1.08	31.19	66	4	95	0	1	34.0	215.8	-7.9	23	N/A	1,000	50	0.0	4.0
C / 4.4	17.6	1.07	30.86	53	4	95	0	1	34.0	215.8	-7.9	23	N/A	1,000	50	0.0	1.0
C / 4.5	17.6	1.07	33.59	97	4	95	0	1	34.0	225.8	-7.7	30	9	10,000,000	0	0.0	0.0
B / 8.2	7.8	0.73	28.24	434	2	97	0	1	39.0	92.5	-9.0	55	13	1,000	50	5.8	0.0
B / 8.2	7.8	0.73	26.79	145	2	97	0	1	39.0	88.0	-9.2	45	14	1,000	50	0.0	4.0
B / 8.2	7.8	0.73	26.28	37	2	97	0	1	39.0	88.0	-9.2	45	12	1,000	50	0.0	1.0
B / 8.4	7.8	0.73	28.71	53	2	97	0	1	39.0	94.1	-8.9	58	9	10,000,000	0	0.0	0.0
B / 8.2	7.8	0.73	27.97	13	2	97	0	1	39.0	91.0	-9.0	51	13	1,000	50	0.0	0.0
C+ / 6.1	7.8	0.73	26.74	1	2	97	0	1	39.0	87.8	-9.2	44	N/A	1,000	50	0.0	0.0
C+ / 6.2	7.8	0.73	26.85	1	2	97	0	1	39.0	88.4	-9.2	46	N/A	1,000	50	0.0	0.0
B / 8.2	8.4	0.76	27.81	6	2	97	0	1	39.0	94.8	-9.2	51	3	1,000	50	0.0	0.0
C+ / 6.2	7.8	0.73	28.19	1	2	97	0	1	39.0	92.2	-9.0	53	N/A	1,000	50	0.0	0.0
C+ / 6.2	7.8	0.73	28.29	N/A	2	97	0	1	39.0	92.8	-9.0	55	N/A	1,000	50	0.0	0.0
C+ / 6.6	9.9	0.92	22.26	294	0	99	0	1	92.0	94.1	-8.7	14	N/A	1,000	50	5.8	0.0
C+ / 6.6	9.9	0.92	20.91	81	0	99	0	1	92.0	89.5	-8.9	11	N/A	1,000	50	0.0	4.0
C+ / 6.6	9.9	0.92	20.72	20	0	99	0	1	92.0	89.6	-8.9	10	N/A	1,000	50	0.0	1.0
B- / 7.2	9.9	0.91	22.70	7	0	99	0	1	92.0	95.7	-8.7	15	N/A	10,000,000	0	0.0	0.0
C+ / 6.6	9.9	0.92	22.05	4	0	99	0	1	92.0	92.6	-8.8	12	N/A	1,000	50	0.0	0.0
C / 5.3	9.9	0.92	20.88	N/A	0	99	0	1	92.0	89.3	-8.9	10	N/A	1,000	50	0.0	0.0
C / 5.3	9.9	0.92	20.96	N/A	0	99	0	1	92.0	90.0	-8.9	11	N/A	1,000	50	0.0	0.0
B- / 7.0	10.9	0.98	21.92	1	0	99	0	1	92.0	98.6	-8.9	12	3	1,000	50	0.0	0.0
C / 5.4	9.9	0.92	22.21	1	0	99	0	1	92.0	93.8	-8.7	13	N/A	1,000	50	0.0	0.0
C / 5.4	9.9	0.92	22.30	N/A	0	99	0	1	92.0	94.5	-8.7	14	N/A	1,000	50	0.0	0.0
C+ / 6.8	6.3	0.55	14.32	369	12	58	29	1	82.0	63.1	-1.4	45	6	1,000	50	4.8	0.0
B- / 7.1	6.3	0.55	14.55	115	12	58	29	1	82.0	59.8	-1.5	38	6	1,000	50	0.0	4.0
B- / 7.0	6.3	0.55	14.45	83	12	58	29	1	82.0	59.8	-1.5	38	6	1,000	50	0.0	1.0
B / 8.9	6.3	0.55	14.22	3	12	58	29	1	82.0	64.8	-1.3	50	9	10,000,000	0	0.0	0.0
C+ / 6.7	6.3	0.55	14.26	2	12	58	29	1	82.0	62.4	-1.4	44	3	1,000	50	0.0	0.0
B- / 7.8	6.3	0.55	14.45	N/A	12	58	29	1	82.0	59.6	-1.5	38	N/A	1,000	50	0.0	0.0
B / 8.0	6.3	0.54	14.26	1	12	58	29	1	82.0	60.2	-1.5	41	3	1,000	50	0.0	0.0
B / 8.5	6.3	0.55	14.30	1	12	58	29	1	82.0	62.9	-1.4	45	N/A	1,000	50	0.0	0.0
B / 8.6	6.3	0.55	14.30	N/A	12	58	29	1	82.0	63.4	-1.4	47	N/A	1,000	50	0.0	0.0
B / 8.9	7.6	1.50	13.79	36	0	80	20	0	N/A	67.4	-6.2	74	4	250	50	5.8	0.0
B / 8.9	7.6	1.49	13.59	26	0	80	20	0	N/A	64.0	-6.4	68	4	250	50	0.0	4.0
B / 8.9	7.6	1.49	13.59	15	0	80	20	0	N/A	64.0	-6.4	68	4	250	50	0.0	1.0
B / 8.9	7.6	1.50	13.86	881	0	80	20	0	N/A	68.8	-6.1	76	4	1,000	50	5.8	0.0
B / 8.9	7.6	1.50	13.68	595	0	80	20	0	N/A	65.5	-6.4	70	4	1,000	50	0.0	4.0
B / 8.9	7.6	1.49	13.67	448	0	80	20	0	N/A	65.5	-6.4	71	4	1,000	50	0.0	1.0
B / 8.3	7.6	1.50	13.83	60	0	80	20	0	N/A	68.2	-6.1	75	4	1,000	50	0.0	0.0
C+ / 6.4	7.6	1.50	13.56	5	0	80	20	0	N/A	65.2	-6.4	70	N/A	1,000	50	0.0	0.0
C+ / 6.4	7.6	1.49	13.61	7	0	80	20	0	N/A	65.8	-6.4	71	N/A	1,000	50	0.0	0.0
B / 8.9	7.7	1.52	13.70	20	0	80	20	0	N/A	67.3	-6.4	73	3	1,000	50	0.0	0.0
C+ / 6.4	7.6	1.50	13.82	11	0	80	20	0	N/A	68.7	-6.1	76	N/A	1,000	50	0.0	0.0
C+ / 6.4	7.6	1.49	13.87	33	0	80	20	0	N/A	69.3	-6.1	77	N/A	1,000	50	0.0	0.0
B- / 7.0	8.9	1.10	8.71	352	2	97	0	1	133.0	53.0	-10.0	13	1	1,000	50	5.8	0.0

Fund Type	Fund Name	Ticker Symbol	Overall Weiss Investment Rating	Phone	Performance Rating/Pts	3 Mo	6 Mo	1Yr / Pct	3Yr / Pct	5Yr / Pct	Dividend Yield	Expense Ratio
	99 Pct = Best				PERFORMANCE							
	0 Pct = Worst							Total Return % through 6/30/06	Annualized		Incl. in Returns	
GR	MFS Growth Opportunities Fund B	MGOBX	E+	(800) 343-2829	E / 0.4	-5.72	-2.64	0.26 / 2	5.71 / 6	-2.99 / 5	0.00	1.71
GR	● MFS Growth Opportunities Fund I		D-	(800) 343-2829	E+ / 0.9	-5.50	-2.23	0.92 / 2	6.67 / 9	-2.06 / 8	0.00	0.71
FO	MFS Inst Intl Equity Fund	MIEIX	A+	(800) 343-2829	A- / 9.0	1.48	11.55	28.80 /94	22.05 /85	11.94 /86	1.02	0.75
FO	MFS Inst Intl Research Equity Fund	MIREX	A+	(800) 343-2829	A / 9.3	-0.74	11.09	32.87 /96	24.88 /91	--	1.12	0.85
GR	MFS Inst Large Cap Growth Fund	ILGRX	D-	(800) 343-2829	E+ / 0.6	-5.30	-3.10	1.51 / 3	5.57 / 5	-2.96 / 6	0.39	0.55
FO	MFS International Diversifictn A	MDIDX	U	(800) 343-2829	U /	-0.70	10.05	29.52 /94	--	--	2.16	1.69
FO	MFS International Diversifictn B	MDIFX	U	(800) 343-2829	U /	-0.84	9.70	28.62 /93	--	--	1.97	2.34
FO	MFS International Diversifictn C	MDIGX	U	(800) 343-2829	U /	-0.84	9.71	28.66 /93	--	--	1.99	2.34
FO	MFS International Diversifictn I	MDIJX	U	(800) 343-2829	U /	-0.63	10.27	30.00 /94	--	--	2.47	1.34
FO	MFS International Growth Fund A	MGRAX	B+	(800) 343-2829	B+ / 8.4	-1.08	9.10	27.32 /92	22.45 /86	9.85 /80	0.02	1.65
FO	MFS International Growth Fund B	MGRBX	B+	(800) 343-2829	B+ / 8.4	-1.21	8.74	26.55 /91	21.73 /84	9.23 /77	0.00	2.30
FO	MFS International Growth Fund C	MGRCX	B+	(800) 343-2829	B+ / 8.6	-1.22	8.76	26.52 /91	21.72 /84	9.23 /78	0.00	2.30
FO	● MFS International Growth Fund I	MQGIX	A+	(800) 343-2829	A- / 9.0	-1.00	9.28	27.82 /92	23.19 /88	10.89 /84	0.15	1.30
FO	MFS Intl New Discovery 529A	EAIDX	A+	(800) 343-2829	A / 9.3	-2.71	7.60	27.75 /92	28.73 /94	16.35 /93	0.31	1.83
FO	MFS Intl New Discovery 529B	EBIDX	A+	(800) 343-2829	A / 9.4	-2.88	7.28	26.91 /91	27.88 /94	15.56 /93	0.00	2.49
FO	MFS Intl New Discovery 529C	ECIDX	A+	(800) 343-2829	A / 9.4	-2.88	7.29	26.95 /91	27.90 /94	15.57 /93	0.00	2.48
★ FO	MFS Intl New Discovery A	MIDAX	A-	(800) 343-2829	A / 9.4	-2.69	7.72	28.04 /93	29.05 /95	16.57 /94	0.44	1.58
FO	MFS Intl New Discovery B	MIDBX	A-	(800) 343-2829	A / 9.4	-2.81	7.42	27.25 /92	28.21 /94	15.82 /93	0.00	2.23
FO	MFS Intl New Discovery C	MIDCX	A-	(800) 343-2829	A / 9.4	-2.82	7.39	27.26 /92	28.22 /94	15.83 /93	0.01	2.23
FO	MFS Intl New Discovery R	MINRX	A-	(800) 343-2829	A / 9.5	-2.70	7.67	27.84 /92	28.89 /95	16.47 /93	0.39	1.73
FO	MFS Intl New Discovery R3	MIDRX	A+	(800) 343-2829	A / 9.4	-2.73	7.60	27.62 /92	28.60 /94	16.33 /93	0.50	1.89
FO	MFS Intl New Discovery R4	MIDHX	B+	(800) 343-2829	A / 9.5	-2.69	7.76	28.06 /93	29.06 /95	16.57 /94	0.48	1.62
FO	MFS Intl New Discovery R5	MIDJX	B+	(800) 343-2829	A / 9.5	-2.58	7.89	28.38 /93	29.20 /95	16.65 /94	0.65	1.33
FO	MFS Intl Value Fund A	MGIAX	A+	(800) 343-2829	A- / 9.1	1.36	12.40	28.10 /93	25.50 /92	13.11 /89	0.66	1.65
FO	MFS Intl Value Fund B	MGIBX	A+	(800) 343-2829	A- / 9.1	1.19	12.08	27.29 /92	24.76 /91	12.48 /88	0.23	2.30
FO	MFS Intl Value Fund C	MGICX	A+	(800) 343-2829	A- / 9.2	1.18	12.01	27.26 /92	24.76 /91	12.48 /88	0.55	2.30
FO	MFS Intl Value Fund I	MINIX	A-	(800) 343-2829	A / 9.3	1.43	12.59	28.53 /93	26.04 /92	13.62 /90	0.83	1.30
GR	MFS Mass Investors Gr Stk 529A	EISTX	D-	(800) 343-2829	E+ / 0.6	-4.78	-1.34	4.93 /15	6.73 / 9	-2.49 / 7	0.00	1.17
GR	MFS Mass Investors Gr Stk 529B	EMIVX	D-	(800) 343-2829	E+ / 0.6	-4.90	-1.55	4.28 /12	6.05 / 7	-3.07 / 5	0.00	1.82
GR	MFS Mass Investors Gr Stk 529C	EMICX	D	(800) 343-2829	E+ / 0.8	-4.92	-1.55	4.30 /12	6.08 / 7	-3.15 / 5	0.00	1.82
★ GR	MFS Mass Investors Gr Stk A	MIGFX	D-	(800) 343-2829	E+ / 0.7	-4.73	-1.17	5.22 /16	7.00 /10	-2.27 / 7	0.00	0.92
GR	MFS Mass Investors Gr Stk B	MIGBX	D-	(800) 343-2829	E+ / 0.6	-4.94	-1.53	4.52 /13	6.32 / 8	-2.90 / 6	0.00	1.57
GR	MFS Mass Investors Gr Stk C	MIGDX	D-	(800) 343-2829	E+ / 0.9	-4.88	-1.46	4.55 /13	6.32 / 8	-2.91 / 6	0.00	1.57
GR	● MFS Mass Investors Gr Stk I	MGTIX	D	(800) 343-2829	D / 1.6	-4.65	-1.00	5.55 /18	7.40 /12	-1.92 / 8	0.00	0.57
GR	MFS Mass Investors Gr Stk R	MIGRX	D	(800) 343-2829	D- / 1.3	-4.74	-1.25	5.06 /15	6.90 /10	-2.32 / 7	0.00	1.07
GR	MFS Mass Investors Gr Stk R1	MIGMX	E+	(800) 343-2829	D- / 1.0	-4.95	-1.62	4.25 /12	6.23 / 7	-2.95 / 6	0.00	1.77
GR	MFS Mass Investors Gr Stk R2	MIGLX	E+	(800) 343-2829	D- / 1.1	-4.85	-1.36	4.70 /14	6.41 / 8	-2.85 / 6	0.00	1.47
GR	MFS Mass Investors Gr Stk R3	MIRGX	D+	(800) 343-2829	D+ / 2.5	-4.78	-1.26	4.94 /15	9.51 /24	-1.16 /11	0.00	1.32
GR	MFS Mass Investors Gr Stk R4	MIGHX	E+	(800) 343-2829	D- / 1.3	-4.73	-1.17	5.14 /16	6.97 /10	-2.28 / 7	0.00	0.97
GR	MFS Mass Investors Gr Stk R5	MIGKX	E+	(800) 343-2829	D- / 1.4	-4.72	-1.09	5.47 /17	7.12 /11	-2.21 / 8	0.00	0.67
GI	MFS Mass Investors Trust 529A	EAMTX	C-	(800) 343-2829	D+ / 2.6	-2.86	0.62	8.39 /36	10.53 /31	1.43 /23	0.16	1.18
GI	MFS Mass Investors Trust 529B	EBMTX	D+	(800) 343-2829	D+ / 2.3	-2.95	0.34	7.77 /31	9.65 /25	0.60 /18	0.00	1.83
GI	MFS Mass Investors Trust 529C	ECITX	C-	(800) 343-2829	D+ / 2.8	-2.98	0.34	7.71 /31	9.67 /25	0.51 /18	0.00	1.83
★ GI	MFS Mass Investors Trust A	MITTX	C-	(800) 343-2829	D+ / 2.7	-2.77	0.79	8.67 /38	10.65 /32	1.43 /23	0.34	0.93
GI	MFS Mass Investors Trust B	MITBX	D+	(800) 343-2829	D+ / 2.5	-2.95	0.44	8.00 /33	9.92 /27	0.77 /19	0.00	1.58
GI	MFS Mass Investors Trust C	MITCX	C-	(800) 343-2829	C- / 3.0	-2.96	0.39	7.97 /32	9.92 /27	0.77 /19	0.00	1.58
GI	● MFS Mass Investors Trust I	MITIX	C	(800) 343-2829	C- / 3.9	-2.71	0.95	9.06 /40	11.03 /36	1.79 /25	0.72	0.58
GI	MFS Mass Investors Trust R	MITRX	C-	(800) 343-2829	C- / 3.5	-2.81	0.69	8.55 /37	10.48 /31	1.26 /22	0.27	1.08
GI	MFS Mass Investors Trust R1	MITGX	D	(800) 343-2829	C- / 3.1	-2.96	0.39	7.88 /32	9.86 /26	0.74 /19	0.28	1.78
GI	MFS Mass Investors Trust R2	MITKX	D	(800) 343-2829	C- / 3.3	-2.85	0.60	8.29 /35	10.02 /28	0.83 /19	0.49	1.48
GI	MFS Mass Investors Trust R4	MITHX	D+	(800) 343-2829	C- / 3.6	-2.83	0.77	8.62 /38	10.63 /32	1.42 /23	0.54	0.98
GI	MFS Mass Investors Trust R5	MITDX	D+	(800) 343-2829	C- / 3.7	-2.72	0.92	8.96 /40	10.77 /33	1.49 /24	0.64	0.68

● Denotes fund is closed to new investors
★ Denotes fund is included in Section II

RISK			NET ASSETS		ASSET				BULL / BEAR		FUND MANAGER		MINIMUMS		LOADS	
	3 Year		NAV						Last Bull	Last Bear	Manager	Manager	Initial	Additional	Front	Back
Risk Rating/Pts	Standard Deviation	Beta	As of 6/30/06	Total $(Mil)	Cash %	Stocks %	Bonds %	Other %	Portfolio Turnover Ratio	Market Return	Market Return	Quality Pct	Tenure (Years)	Purch. $	Purch. $	End Load	End Load
B- / 7.0	8.9	1.09	7.75	19	2	97	0	1	133.0	49.5	-10.2	10	1	1,000	50	0.0	4.0
B- / 7.2	8.9	1.09	8.76	4	2	97	0	1	133.0	53.7	-10.0	14	1	10,000,000	0	0.0	0.0
B / 8.2	9.6	0.91	19.22	1,868	5	94	0	1	45.0	116.5	-7.7	53	N/A	3,000,000	0	0.0	0.0
B- / 7.9	10.6	1.01	16.13	181	N/A	N/A	0	N/A	93.0	134.3	-7.9	57	N/A	3,000,000	0	0.0	0.0
B- / 7.8	9.0	1.07	6.25	35	0	99	0	1	89.0	44.0	-10.1	10	N/A	3,000,000	0	0.0	0.0
U /	N/A	N/A	14.23	590	0	100	0	0	N/A	N/A	N/A	N/A	N/A	1,000	50	5.8	0.0
U /	N/A	N/A	14.13	151	0	100	0	0	N/A	N/A	N/A	N/A	N/A	1,000	50	0.0	4.0
U /	N/A	N/A	14.12	375	0	100	0	0	N/A	N/A	N/A	N/A	N/A	1,000	50	0.0	1.0
U /	N/A	N/A	14.28	34	0	100	0	0	N/A	N/A	N/A	N/A	N/A	10,000,000	0	0.0	0.0
C+ / 6.6	10.9	1.05	23.86	207	3	96	0	1	40.0	124.9	-8.7	29	N/A	1,000	50	5.8	1.0
C+ / 6.6	11.0	1.05	22.77	53	3	96	0	1	40.0	120.8	-8.9	24	N/A	1,000	50	0.0	4.0
C+ / 6.6	10.9	1.05	22.60	33	3	96	0	1	40.0	120.8	-8.9	25	N/A	1,000	50	0.0	1.0
B- / 7.6	10.9	1.05	25.68	357	3	96	0	1	40.0	130.4	-8.6	34	9	10,000,000	0	0.0	0.0
B- / 7.4	12.1	1.12	25.47	3	1	98	0	1	36.0	170.2	-7.0	67	4	250	50	5.8	1.0
B- / 7.4	12.1	1.12	24.62	1	1	98	0	1	36.0	164.4	-7.1	60	4	250	50	0.0	1.0
B- / 7.4	12.1	1.12	24.59	1	1	98	0	1	36.0	164.6	-7.2	60	4	250	50	0.0	1.0
C+ / 5.9	12.1	1.12	25.68	2,644	1	98	0	1	36.0	172.2	-7.0	70	9	1,000	50	5.8	1.0
C+ / 5.9	12.1	1.12	24.89	327	1	98	0	1	36.0	166.7	-7.1	63	6	1,000	50	0.0	1.0
C+ / 5.9	12.1	1.12	24.85	438	1	98	0	1	36.0	166.7	-7.1	63	N/A	1,000	50	0.0	1.0
C+ / 5.9	12.1	1.12	25.56	41	1	98	0	1	36.0	171.1	-7.0	69	9	1,000	50	0.0	1.0
B- / 7.4	12.1	1.12	25.34	21	1	98	0	1	36.0	169.5	-7.0	67	3	1,000	50	0.0	1.0
C / 5.2	12.1	1.12	25.68	5	1	98	0	1	36.0	172.4	-7.0	70	N/A	1,000	50	0.0	1.0
C / 5.2	12.1	1.12	25.72	6	1	98	0	1	36.0	173.1	-7.0	71	N/A	1,000	50	0.0	1.0
B- / 7.3	9.3	0.88	29.01	242	3	96	0	1	28.0	138.4	-6.8	86	N/A	1,000	50	5.8	0.0
B- / 7.3	9.3	0.88	28.03	71	3	96	0	1	28.0	133.8	-6.8	81	N/A	1,000	50	0.0	4.0
B- / 7.2	9.3	0.89	27.51	63	3	96	0	1	28.0	134.0	-6.9	81	N/A	1,000	50	0.0	1.0
C+ / 5.9	9.3	0.88	29.79	303	3	96	0	1	28.0	141.7	-6.6	88	N/A	10,000,000	0	0.0	0.0
B- / 7.9	8.9	1.07	12.55	4	3	96	0	1	125.0	48.1	-10.3	15	4	250	50	5.8	0.0
B- / 7.9	8.9	1.07	11.45	1	3	96	0	1	125.0	45.1	-10.4	12	4	250	50	0.0	4.0
B- / 7.9	8.9	1.08	11.40	1	3	96	0	1	125.0	45.2	-10.4	12	4	250	50	0.0	1.0
B- / 7.5	8.9	1.07	12.69	4,152	3	96	0	1	125.0	49.3	-10.2	16	7	1,000	50	5.8	0.0
B- / 7.3	8.9	1.07	11.55	1,609	3	96	0	1	125.0	46.3	-10.5	13	1	1,000	50	0.0	4.0
B- / 7.4	8.9	1.07	11.50	487	3	96	0	1	125.0	46.2	-10.4	13	1	1,000	50	0.0	1.0
B / 8.0	8.9	1.07	12.93	95	3	96	0	1	125.0	51.0	-10.1	19	1	10,000,000	0	0.0	0.0
B- / 7.5	8.9	1.08	12.66	52	3	96	0	1	125.0	49.0	-10.2	16	7	1,000	50	0.0	0.0
C+ / 5.6	8.9	1.07	11.52	2	3	96	0	1	125.0	46.0	-10.5	13	1	1,000	50	0.0	0.0
C+ / 5.6	8.9	1.07	11.58	N/A	3	96	0	1	125.0	46.6	-10.5	13	1	1,000	50	0.0	0.0
B- / 7.5	11.2	1.29	12.54	7	3	96	0	1	125.0	59.7	-10.5	19	7	1,000	50	0.0	0.0
C+ / 5.7	8.9	1.08	12.68	7	3	96	0	1	125.0	49.3	-10.2	16	1	1,000	50	0.0	0.0
C+ / 5.7	8.9	1.07	12.73	126	3	96	0	1	125.0	49.7	-10.2	17	1	1,000	50	0.0	0.0
B- / 7.8	7.6	0.95	18.34	1	1	98	0	1	41.0	61.3	-9.3	54	N/A	250	50	5.8	0.0
B- / 7.7	7.5	0.94	17.76	N/A	1	98	0	1	41.0	57.1	-9.8	44	N/A	250	50	0.0	4.0
B- / 7.7	7.5	0.94	17.61	1	1	98	0	1	41.0	57.2	-9.8	44	N/A	250	50	0.0	1.0
B- / 7.7	7.5	0.94	18.59	3,227	1	98	0	1	41.0	61.7	-9.6	56	N/A	1,000	50	5.8	0.0
B- / 7.7	7.5	0.94	18.10	1,208	1	98	0	1	41.0	58.2	-9.7	47	N/A	1,000	50	0.0	4.0
B- / 7.7	7.5	0.94	18.01	312	1	98	0	1	41.0	58.3	-9.7	47	N/A	1,000	50	0.0	1.0
B- / 7.9	7.5	0.94	18.32	117	1	98	0	1	41.0	63.3	-9.5	60	N/A	10,000,000	0	0.0	0.0
B- / 7.7	7.5	0.94	18.34	19	1	98	0	1	41.0	60.9	-9.9	54	N/A	1,000	50	0.0	0.0
C+ / 6.2	7.5	0.94	18.02	2	1	98	0	1	41.0	58.0	-9.7	46	N/A	1,000	50	0.0	0.0
C+ / 6.2	7.5	0.94	18.06	1	1	98	0	1	41.0	58.6	-9.7	48	N/A	1,000	50	0.0	0.0
C+ / 6.3	7.5	0.94	18.55	6	1	98	0	1	41.0	61.6	-9.6	56	N/A	1,000	50	0.0	0.0
C+ / 6.3	7.5	0.94	18.60	N/A	1	98	0	1	41.0	62.1	-9.6	58	N/A	1,000	50	0.0	0.0

| | | | | | | Total Return % through 6/30/06 | | | Annualized | | Incl. in Returns | |
| | | | 99 Pct = Best 0 Pct = Worst Overall Weiss Investment Rating | | Perfor-mance | | | | | | Dividend | Expense |
Fund Type	Fund Name	Ticker Symbol		Phone	Rating/Pts	3 Mo	6 Mo	1Yr / Pct	3Yr / Pct	5Yr / Pct	Yield	Ratio
MC	MFS Mid Cap Value Fund 529A	EACVX	C+	(800) 343-2829	C / 5.4	-3.83	0.31	6.98 / 26	15.95 / 63	--	0.00	1.59
MC	MFS Mid Cap Value Fund 529B	EBCVX	C+	(800) 343-2829	C / 5.2	-4.02	-0.08	6.28 / 22	15.18 / 60	--	0.00	2.24
MC	MFS Mid Cap Value Fund 529C	ECCVX	C+	(800) 343-2829	C+ / 5.6	-4.02	-0.08	6.26 / 22	15.21 / 60	--	0.00	2.24
MC	MFS Mid Cap Value Fund A	MVCAX	C-	(800) 343-2829	C / 5.5	-3.78	0.46	7.23 / 28	16.27 / 65	--	0.00	1.34
MC	MFS Mid Cap Value Fund B	MCBVX	C-	(800) 343-2829	C / 5.3	-3.98	0.08	6.46 / 23	15.49 / 61	--	0.00	1.99
MC	MFS Mid Cap Value Fund C	MVCCX	C-	(800) 343-2829	C+ / 5.8	-3.98	0.08	6.54 / 23	15.48 / 61	--	0.00	1.99
MC	● MFS Mid Cap Value Fund I	MCVIX	B-	(800) 343-2829	C+ / 6.5	-3.72	0.60	7.58 / 30	16.65 / 67	--	0.00	0.99
MC	MFS Mid Cap Value Fund R	MMVRX	C	(800) 343-2829	C+ / 6.2	-3.80	0.38	7.10 / 27	16.17 / 64	--	0.00	1.49
MC	MFS Mid Cap Value Fund R4	MVCHX	C	(800) 343-2829	C+ / 6.2	-3.78	0.38	7.14 / 27	16.24 / 64	--	0.00	1.39
MC	MFS Mid Cap Value Fund R5	MVCJX	C	(800) 343-2829	C+ / 6.3	-3.77	0.45	7.45 / 29	16.37 / 65	--	0.00	1.09
MC	MFS Mid-Cap Growth Fund 529A	EAMCX	E+	(800) 343-2829	D / 1.6	-7.89	-2.53	4.60 / 13	9.80 / 26	--	0.00	1.65
MC	MFS Mid-Cap Growth Fund 529B	EBCGX	E+	(800) 343-2829	D- / 1.4	-8.10	-2.78	3.83 / 10	8.98 / 21	-7.60 / 1	0.00	2.30
MC	MFS Mid-Cap Growth Fund 529C	ECGRX	E+	(800) 343-2829	D / 1.8	-8.05	-2.72	3.92 / 10	9.04 / 21	-7.59 / 1	0.00	2.30
MC	MFS Mid-Cap Growth Fund A	OTCAX	E	(800) 343-2829	D / 1.7	-7.81	-2.29	4.91 / 15	10.11 / 28	-6.74 / 1	0.00	1.30
MC	MFS Mid-Cap Growth Fund B	OTCBX	E	(800) 343-2829	D- / 1.5	-8.03	-2.76	4.05 / 11	9.23 / 22	-7.45 / 1	0.00	2.05
MC	MFS Mid-Cap Growth Fund C	OTCCX	E	(800) 343-2829	D / 1.9	-8.00	-2.70	4.15 / 11	9.25 / 22	-7.46 / 1	0.00	2.05
MC	● MFS Mid-Cap Growth Fund I	OTCIX	D-	(800) 343-2829	D+ / 2.8	-7.79	-2.25	5.20 / 16	10.35 / 30	-6.49 / 1	0.00	1.05
MC	MFS Mid-Cap Growth Fund R	MMCRX	E+	(800) 343-2829	D+ / 2.4	-7.88	-2.41	4.59 / 13	9.83 / 26	-6.91 / 1	0.00	1.55
MC	MFS Mid-Cap Growth Fund R1	OTCGX	E+	(800) 343-2829	D / 2.0	-8.04	-2.76	4.06 / 11	9.18 / 22	-7.47 / 1	0.00	2.17
MC	MFS Mid-Cap Growth Fund R2	OTCKX	E+	(800) 343-2829	D / 2.1	-7.92	-2.53	4.30 / 12	9.31 / 23	-7.40 / 1	0.00	1.83
MC	MFS Mid-Cap Growth Fund R3	MCPRX	D-	(800) 343-2829	C- / 3.0	-7.91	-2.53	4.49 / 13	10.83 / 34	-6.63 / 1	0.00	1.72
MC	MFS Mid-Cap Growth Fund R4	OTCHX	E+	(800) 343-2829	D+ / 2.5	-7.92	-2.40	4.80 / 14	10.02 / 28	-6.78 / 1	0.00	1.46
MC	MFS Mid-Cap Growth Fund R5	OTCJX	E+	(800) 343-2829	D+ / 2.6	-7.80	-2.29	5.03 / 15	10.15 / 28	-6.72 / 1	0.00	1.16
AA	MFS Moderate Allocation 529A	EAMDX	C-	(800) 343-2829	D / 1.7	-1.70	1.44	6.36 / 22	8.78 / 20	--	2.10	0.70
AA	MFS Moderate Allocation 529B	EBMDX	C-	(800) 343-2829	D- / 1.5	-1.88	1.13	5.67 / 18	8.06 / 15	--	1.78	1.35
AA	MFS Moderate Allocation 529C	ECMAX	C	(800) 343-2829	D / 1.9	-1.87	1.05	5.67 / 18	8.08 / 16	--	1.71	1.35
AA	MFS Moderate Allocation A	MAMAX	C	(800) 343-2829	D / 1.8	-1.69	1.51	6.63 / 24	9.06 / 21	--	2.28	0.45
AA	MFS Moderate Allocation B	MMABX	C-	(800) 343-2829	D / 1.7	-1.79	1.28	5.97 / 20	8.34 / 17	--	1.85	1.10
AA	MFS Moderate Allocation C	MMACX	C	(800) 343-2829	D / 2.1	-1.79	1.20	5.94 / 20	8.33 / 17	--	1.89	1.10
AA	● MFS Moderate Allocation I	MMAIX	C+	(800) 343-2829	C- / 3.0	-1.53	1.74	6.99 / 26	9.46 / 24	--	2.71	0.10
AA	MFS Moderate Allocation R	MAMRX	C	(800) 343-2829	D+ / 2.6	-1.70	1.44	6.46 / 23	8.87 / 20	--	2.32	0.60
AA	MFS Moderate Allocation R1	MAMFX	C	(800) 343-2829	D / 2.2	-1.80	1.21	5.88 / 20	8.28 / 17	--	2.56	1.23
AA	MFS Moderate Allocation R2	MAMKX	C	(800) 343-2829	D+ / 2.3	-1.77	1.35	6.27 / 22	8.44 / 17	--	1.42	0.96
AA	MFS Moderate Allocation R3	MARRX	C	(800) 343-2829	D+ / 2.4	-1.71	1.36	6.23 / 22	8.65 / 19	--	2.33	0.81
AA	MFS Moderate Allocation R4	MAMHX	C	(800) 343-2829	D+ / 2.7	-1.62	1.60	6.63 / 24	9.06 / 21	--	2.65	0.50
AA	MFS Moderate Allocation R5	MAMJX	C	(800) 343-2829	D+ / 2.8	-1.54	1.67	6.88 / 26	9.18 / 22	--	2.74	0.20
SC	MFS New Discovery Fund 529A	EANDX	E+	(800) 343-2829	D / 1.6	-9.19	1.53	11.48 / 57	10.23 / 29	-0.68 / 13	0.00	1.76
SC	MFS New Discovery Fund 529B	EBNDX	D-	(800) 343-2829	D / 2.0	-9.33	1.29	10.79 / 52	9.53 / 24	-1.57 / 10	0.00	2.42
SC	MFS New Discovery Fund 529C	ECNDX	D-	(800) 343-2829	D / 2.0	-9.32	1.22	10.78 / 52	9.52 / 24	-1.56 / 10	0.00	2.42
SC	MFS New Discovery Fund A	MNDAX	E-	(800) 343-2829	D / 1.7	-9.16	1.69	11.79 / 58	10.48 / 31	-0.50 / 14	0.00	1.50
SC	MFS New Discovery Fund B	MNDBX	E-	(800) 343-2829	D / 2.2	-9.30	1.34	10.98 / 53	9.77 / 26	-1.14 / 11	0.00	2.16
SC	MFS New Discovery Fund C	MNDCX	E-	(800) 343-2829	D / 2.1	-9.34	1.33	11.04 / 54	9.76 / 26	-1.14 / 11	0.00	2.17
SC	MFS New Discovery Fund I	MNDIX	D-	(800) 343-2829	D+ / 2.9	-9.05	1.87	12.16 / 60	10.88 / 34	-0.13 / 15	0.00	1.18
SC	● MFS New Discovery Fund R	MFNRX	E	(800) 343-2829	D+ / 2.5	-9.21	1.58	11.57 / 57	10.32 / 29	-0.60 / 13	0.00	1.67
SC	MFS New Discovery Fund R3	MNDRX	D-	(800) 343-2829	D+ / 2.4	-9.20	1.53	11.41 / 56	10.12 / 28	-0.69 / 13	0.00	1.85
SC	MFS New Discovery Fund R4	MNDHX	E+	(800) 343-2829	D+ / 2.6	-9.12	1.69	11.72 / 58	10.46 / 31	-0.51 / 13	0.00	1.57
SC	MFS New Discovery Fund R5	MNDJX	E+	(800) 343-2829	D+ / 2.7	-9.09	1.80	12.04 / 60	10.59 / 32	-0.44 / 14	0.00	1.27
MC	MFS New Endeavor Fund A	MECAX	D-	(800) 343-2829	C- / 3.3	-6.60	-0.65	7.80 / 31	12.46 / 45	9.48 / 79	0.00	1.40
MC	MFS New Endeavor Fund B	MECBX	D-	(800) 343-2829	C- / 3.1	-6.83	-1.04	6.99 / 26	11.73 / 41	8.85 / 76	0.00	2.05
MC	MFS New Endeavor Fund C	MECCX	D-	(800) 343-2829	C- / 3.6	-6.76	-0.96	7.07 / 27	11.75 / 41	8.85 / 76	0.00	2.05
MC	● MFS New Endeavor Fund I	MECIX	C-	(800) 343-2829	C / 4.6	-6.57	-0.50	8.09 / 33	12.85 / 48	-4.44 / 3	0.00	1.05
MC	MFS New Endeavor Fund R	MNERX	D	(800) 343-2829	C / 4.3	-6.63	-0.73	7.59 / 30	12.30 / 44	9.37 / 78	0.00	1.55

● Denotes fund is closed to new investors
* Denotes fund is included in Section II

RISK			NET ASSETS		ASSET				Portfolio	BULL / BEAR		FUND MANAGER		MINIMUMS		LOADS	
	3 Year		NAV							Last Bull	Last Bear	Manager	Manager	Initial	Additional	Front	Back
Risk Rating/Pts	Standard Deviation	Beta	As of 6/30/06	Total $(Mil)	Cash %	Stocks %	Bonds %	Other %	Turnover Ratio	Market Return	Market Return	Quality Pct	Tenure (Years)	Purch. $	Purch. $	End Load	End Load
B- /7.6	11.3	0.98	13.06	1	0	98	0	2	55.0	93.7	-8.2	37	4	250	50	5.8	0.0
B- /7.5	11.3	0.98	12.64	N/A	0	98	0	2	55.0	89.6	-8.3	32	4	250	50	0.0	4.0
B- /7.5	11.3	0.98	12.67	N/A	0	98	0	2	55.0	89.8	-8.4	32	4	250	50	0.0	1.0
C+ /5.8	11.3	0.98	13.23	157	0	98	0	2	55.0	95.3	-8.1	39	5	1,000	50	5.8	0.0
C+ /5.6	11.3	0.98	12.79	101	0	98	0	2	55.0	91.4	-8.3	34	5	1,000	50	0.0	4.0
C+ /5.6	11.3	0.98	12.80	42	0	98	0	2	55.0	91.1	-8.3	34	5	1,000	50	0.0	1.0
B- /7.5	11.5	1.00	13.46	474	0	98	0	2	55.0	97.3	-8.0	41	N/A	10,000,000	0	0.0	0.0
C+ /5.8	11.3	0.98	13.16	7	0	98	0	2	55.0	94.6	-8.1	39	5	1,000	50	0.0	0.0
C /5.3	11.3	0.98	13.22	1	0	98	0	2	55.0	95.1	-8.1	39	N/A	1,000	50	0.0	0.0
C /5.3	11.3	0.98	13.27	N/A	0	98	0	2	55.0	95.8	-8.1	41	N/A	1,000	50	0.0	0.0
C /5.1	13.6	1.16	8.87	1	1	98	0	1	42.0	72.8	-7.1	2	1	250	50	5.8	0.0
C /5.1	13.6	1.16	8.40	N/A	1	98	0	1	42.0	68.7	-7.3	1	1	250	50	0.0	4.0
C /5.1	13.6	1.16	8.22	N/A	1	98	0	1	42.0	69.1	-7.3	1	1	250	50	0.0	1.0
C- /4.2	13.5	1.16	8.97	614	1	98	0	1	42.0	74.2	-7.0	2	1	1,000	50	5.8	0.0
C- /4.1	13.5	1.16	8.47	313	1	98	0	1	42.0	70.2	-7.2	2	1	1,000	50	0.0	4.0
C- /4.1	13.6	1.16	8.28	92	1	98	0	1	42.0	70.1	-7.2	2	1	1,000	50	0.0	1.0
C /5.2	13.5	1.15	9.11	466	1	98	0	1	42.0	75.6	-6.9	3	1	10,000,000	0	0.0	0.0
C- /4.1	13.5	1.15	8.89	7	1	98	0	1	42.0	72.7	-7.0	2	1	1,000	50	0.0	0.0
C /4.6	13.6	1.16	8.46	N/A	1	98	0	1	42.0	70.0	-7.2	1	1	1,000	50	0.0	0.0
C /4.6	13.6	1.16	8.49	N/A	1	98	0	1	42.0	70.4	-7.2	2	1	1,000	50	0.0	0.0
C /5.0	14.3	1.22	8.85	1	1	98	0	1	42.0	77.5	-7.2	2	1	1,000	50	0.0	0.0
C /4.6	13.6	1.16	8.95	2	1	98	0	1	42.0	73.8	-7.0	2	1	1,000	50	0.0	0.0
C /4.6	13.5	1.16	8.98	41	1	98	0	1	42.0	74.2	-7.0	2	1	1,000	50	0.0	0.0
B+ /9.6	5.4	1.11	12.71	29	4	60	34	2	N/A	46.5	-4.2	63	4	250	50	5.8	0.0
B+ /9.6	5.5	1.12	12.55	16	4	60	34	2	N/A	43.5	-4.3	55	4	250	50	0.0	4.0
B+ /9.6	5.5	1.12	12.57	14	4	60	34	2	N/A	43.7	-4.3	55	4	250	50	0.0	1.0
B+ /9.6	5.5	1.11	12.76	774	4	60	34	2	N/A	47.7	-4.1	66	4	1,000	50	5.8	0.0
B+ /9.6	5.5	1.12	12.64	526	4	60	34	2	N/A	44.7	-4.2	58	4	1,000	50	0.0	4.0
B+ /9.6	5.5	1.12	12.62	409	4	60	34	2	N/A	44.7	-4.3	58	4	1,000	50	0.0	1.0
B+ /9.6	5.4	1.11	12.88	41	4	60	34	2	N/A	49.4	-4.1	69	4	10,000,000	0	0.0	0.0
B+ /9.4	5.4	1.11	12.70	57	4	60	34	2	N/A	46.9	-4.1	64	4	1,000	50	0.0	0.0
B+ /9.6	5.5	1.12	12.53	5	4	60	34	2	N/A	44.5	-4.2	57	N/A	1,000	50	0.0	0.0
B+ /9.6	5.4	1.11	12.73	2	4	60	34	2	N/A	45.1	-4.2	59	N/A	1,000	50	0.0	0.0
B+ /9.6	5.5	1.12	12.63	18	4	60	34	2	N/A	46.0	-4.2	61	4	1,000	50	0.0	0.0
B+ /9.6	5.4	1.11	12.73	34	4	60	34	2	N/A	47.6	-4.1	66	N/A	1,000	50	0.0	0.0
B+ /9.6	5.5	1.11	12.76	28	4	60	34	2	N/A	48.1	-4.1	67	N/A	1,000	50	0.0	0.0
C+ /5.6	16.9	1.09	17.29	2	0	99	0	1	21.0	75.9	-10.7	3	N/A	250	50	5.8	1.0
C /5.5	16.9	1.09	16.53	N/A	0	99	0	1	21.0	72.2	-10.9	2	N/A	250	50	0.0	1.0
C /5.5	16.9	1.09	16.54	N/A	0	99	0	1	21.0	72.2	-10.9	2	N/A	250	50	0.0	1.0
D+ /2.9	16.9	1.09	17.45	460	0	99	0	1	21.0	77.0	-10.6	3	N/A	1,000	50	5.8	1.0
D+ /2.8	16.9	1.09	16.68	161	0	99	0	1	21.0	73.5	-10.8	3	N/A	1,000	50	0.0	1.0
D+ /2.8	16.9	1.09	16.70	53	0	99	0	1	21.0	73.6	-10.9	3	N/A	1,000	50	0.0	1.0
C+ /5.6	16.9	1.09	17.98	126	0	99	0	1	21.0	79.2	-10.6	4	N/A	10,000,000	0	0.0	1.0
D+ /2.9	16.9	1.09	17.36	15	0	99	0	1	21.0	76.2	-10.6	3	N/A	1,000	50	0.0	1.0
C+ /5.6	16.9	1.09	17.28	3	0	99	0	1	21.0	75.4	-10.6	3	N/A	1,000	50	0.0	1.0
C- /3.9	16.9	1.09	17.44	2	0	99	0	1	21.0	76.9	-10.6	3	N/A	1,000	50	0.0	1.0
C- /3.9	16.9	1.09	17.50	65	0	99	0	1	21.0	77.5	-10.6	4	N/A	1,000	50	0.0	1.0
C /4.8	15.0	1.28	13.73	180	0	99	0	1	91.0	90.0	-6.9	3	N/A	1,000	50	5.8	0.0
C /4.7	15.0	1.28	13.37	56	0	99	0	1	91.0	86.0	-6.9	2	N/A	1,000	50	0.0	4.0
C /4.7	15.1	1.28	13.38	32	0	99	0	1	91.0	86.2	-7.0	2	N/A	1,000	50	0.0	1.0
C+ /6.1	15.0	1.28	13.94	4	0	99	0	1	91.0	92.0	-6.8	3	N/A	10,000,000	0	0.0	0.0
C /4.7	15.0	1.28	13.65	14	0	99	0	1	91.0	89.1	-6.9	3	N/A	1,000	50	0.0	0.0

99 Pct = Best
0 Pct = Worst

Fund Type	Fund Name	Ticker Symbol	Overall Weiss Investment Rating	Phone	PERFORMANCE Perfor-mance Rating/Pts	3 Mo	6 Mo	Total Return % through 6/30/06 1Yr / Pct	Annualized 3Yr / Pct	5Yr / Pct	Incl. in Returns Dividend Yield	Expense Ratio
MC	MFS New Endeavor Fund R3	MENRX	D+	(800) 343-2829	C- / 4.1	-6.68	-0.80	7.39 / 29	12.03 / 43	9.23 / 78	0.00	1.70
MC	MFS New Endeavor Fund R4	MECHX	D	(800) 343-2829	C / 4.4	-6.60	-0.65	7.80 / 31	12.46 / 45	9.48 / 79	0.00	1.45
MC	MFS New Endeavor Fund R5	MECJX	D	(800) 343-2829	C / 4.4	-6.58	-0.58	8.02 / 33	12.57 / 46	9.54 / 79	0.00	1.15
GR	MFS Research Fund 529A	EARFX	C-	(800) 343-2829	D+ / 2.7	-3.96	-0.70	6.01 / 21	11.33 / 38	0.71 / 19	0.00	1.28
GR	MFS Research Fund 529B	EBRFX	C-	(800) 343-2829	D+ / 2.5	-4.10	-1.00	5.36 / 17	10.60 / 32	0.04 / 16	0.00	1.93
GR	MFS Research Fund 529C	ECRFX	C-	(800) 343-2829	C- / 3.0	-4.11	-1.05	5.31 / 17	10.59 / 32	0.04 / 16	0.00	1.93
GR	MFS Research Fund A	MFRFX	C-	(800) 343-2829	D+ / 2.9	-3.88	-0.60	6.25 / 22	11.60 / 40	0.89 / 20	0.13	1.03
GR	MFS Research Fund B	MFRBX	C-	(800) 343-2829	D+ / 2.7	-4.06	-0.89	5.57 / 18	10.87 / 34	0.23 / 16	0.00	1.68
GR	MFS Research Fund C	MFRCX	C-	(800) 343-2829	C- / 3.2	-4.06	-0.94	5.56 / 18	10.88 / 34	0.23 / 16	0.00	1.68
GR	MFS Research Fund I	MRFIX	C+	(800) 343-2829	C- / 4.2	-3.81	-0.41	6.63 / 24	11.99 / 42	1.24 / 22	0.47	0.68
GR	MFS Research Fund R	MFRRX	C	(800) 343-2829	C- / 3.7	-3.92	-0.65	6.13 / 21	11.42 / 39	0.77 / 19	0.11	1.18
GR	MFS Research Fund R1	MFRLX	D	(800) 343-2829	C- / 3.3	-4.08	-0.94	5.49 / 18	10.82 / 34	0.21 / 16	0.38	1.78
GR	MFS Research Fund R2	MFRKX	D	(800) 343-2829	C- / 3.4	-3.97	-0.79	5.78 / 19	10.96 / 35	0.29 / 17	0.46	1.43
GR	MFS Research Fund R3	MSRRX	C+	(800) 343-2829	C / 4.8	-3.98	-0.75	5.92 / 20	13.38 / 51	1.59 / 24	0.07	1.33
GR	MFS Research Fund R4	MFRHX	D+	(800) 343-2829	C- / 3.8	-3.89	-0.60	6.21 / 22	11.58 / 40	0.88 / 20	0.29	1.08
GR	MFS Research Fund R5	MFRJX	D+	(800) 343-2829	C- / 4.0	-3.84	-0.46	6.55 / 24	11.72 / 41	0.96 / 20	0.43	0.78
FO	MFS Research International 529A	EARSX	A+	(800) 343-2829	B+ / 8.9	-0.81	10.23	31.36 / 95	23.82 / 89	10.45 / 82	0.46	1.75
FO	MFS Research International 529B	EBRIX	A+	(800) 343-2829	B+ / 8.8	-1.01	9.84	30.45 / 95	22.98 / 87	9.37 / 78	0.04	2.40
FO	MFS Research International 529C	ECRIX	A+	(800) 343-2829	A- / 9.0	-0.96	9.86	30.44 / 95	22.99 / 87	9.34 / 78	0.00	2.39
FO	MFS Research International A	MRSAX	A-	(800) 343-2829	A- / 9.0	-0.80	10.34	31.61 / 95	24.09 / 90	10.65 / 83	0.59	1.50
FO	MFS Research International B	MRIBX	B+	(800) 343-2829	B+ / 8.9	-0.94	10.00	30.83 / 95	23.31 / 88	9.94 / 80	0.13	2.14
FO	MFS Research International C	MRICX	A-	(800) 343-2829	A- / 9.0	-0.95	9.97	30.77 / 95	23.33 / 88	9.96 / 80	0.19	2.15
FO	MFS Research International I	MRSIX	A+	(800) 343-2829	A- / 9.2	-0.68	10.52	32.09 / 96	24.53 / 90	11.04 / 84	0.86	1.15
FO	MFS Research International R	MRIRX	A-	(800) 343-2829	A- / 9.2	-0.81	10.29	31.49 / 95	23.88 / 89	10.54 / 82	0.54	1.65
FO	MFS Research International R3	MRSRX	A+	(800) 343-2829	A- / 9.1	-0.81	10.19	31.20 / 95	23.64 / 89	10.41 / 82	0.59	1.83
FO	MFS Research International R4	MRSHX	B+	(800) 343-2829	A- / 9.2	-0.75	10.30	31.55 / 95	24.07 / 89	10.64 / 83	0.77	1.55
FO	MFS Research International R5	MRSJX	B+	(800) 343-2829	A- / 9.2	-0.69	10.46	31.95 / 96	24.22 / 90	10.72 / 83	0.82	1.25
GR	MFS Strategic Growth Fund 529A	EASGX	E+	(800) 343-2829	E / 0.4	-5.58	-1.90	2.87 / 7	5.67 / 6	-3.45 / 4	0.00	1.54
GR	MFS Strategic Growth Fund 529B	EBSGX	E+	(800) 343-2829	E / 0.3	-5.76	-2.27	2.20 / 5	4.94 / 4	-4.48 / 3	0.00	2.19
GR	MFS Strategic Growth Fund 529C	ECSGX	E+	(800) 343-2829	E / 0.5	-5.71	-2.21	2.26 / 5	4.96 / 4	-4.46 / 3	0.00	2.19
GR	MFS Strategic Growth Fund A	MFSGX	E	(800) 343-2829	E / 0.4	-5.53	-1.83	3.13 / 8	5.90 / 6	-3.29 / 5	0.00	1.28
GR	MFS Strategic Growth Fund B	MSBGX	E	(800) 343-2829	E / 0.3	-5.66	-2.14	2.47 / 6	5.21 / 4	-3.90 / 4	0.00	1.93
GR	MFS Strategic Growth Fund C	MFGCX	E	(800) 343-2829	E / 0.5	-5.71	-2.14	2.47 / 6	5.20 / 4	-3.91 / 4	0.00	1.93
GR	MFS Strategic Growth Fund I	MSGIX	E+	(800) 343-2829	E+ / 0.9	-5.43	-1.63	3.54 / 9	6.27 / 8	-2.93 / 6	0.00	0.94
GR	MFS Strategic Growth Fund R	MSGRX	E	(800) 343-2829	E+ / 0.7	-5.56	-1.89	3.03 / 7	5.76 / 6	-3.38 / 4	0.00	1.43
GR	MFS Strategic Growth Fund R3	MSTRX	E+	(800) 343-2829	E+ / 0.7	-5.59	-1.95	2.82 / 7	5.53 / 5	-3.49 / 4	0.00	1.60
GR	MFS Strategic Growth Fund R4	MFSHX	E	(800) 343-2829	E+ / 0.8	-5.53	-1.83	3.13 / 8	5.88 / 6	-3.30 / 5	0.00	1.34
GR	MFS Strategic Growth Fund R5	MFSJX	E	(800) 343-2829	E+ / 0.8	-5.47	-1.67	3.40 / 8	6.02 / 7	-3.22 / 5	0.00	1.04
GR	MFS Strategic Value 529A	EASVX	D+	(800) 343-2829	D- / 1.5	-3.70	0.50	1.35 / 3	9.41 / 24	3.89 / 45	0.12	1.53
GR	MFS Strategic Value 529B	EBSVX	D+	(800) 343-2829	D- / 1.4	-3.82	0.22	0.70 / 2	8.70 / 19	3.18 / 39	0.00	2.18
GR	MFS Strategic Value 529C	ECSVX	D+	(800) 343-2829	D / 1.8	-3.89	0.22	0.62 / 2	8.68 / 19	3.16 / 38	0.00	2.18
GR	MFS Strategic Value A	MSVTX	E+	(800) 343-2829	D / 1.6	-3.67	0.64	1.59 / 3	9.67 / 25	4.10 / 47	0.28	1.28
GR	MFS Strategic Value B	MSVLX	E+	(800) 343-2829	D- / 1.5	-3.78	0.29	0.89 / 2	8.96 / 21	3.43 / 41	0.00	1.93
GR	MFS Strategic Value C	MQSVX	E+	(800) 343-2829	D / 1.9	-3.78	0.36	0.96 / 2	8.96 / 21	3.43 / 41	0.00	1.93
GR	MFS Strategic Value I	MISVX	D	(800) 343-2829	D+ / 2.7	-3.52	0.85	1.97 / 4	10.05 / 28	4.46 / 50	0.64	0.93
GR	MFS Strategic Value R	MSVRX	D-	(800) 343-2829	D+ / 2.4	-3.69	0.57	1.42 / 3	9.51 / 24	4.00 / 46	0.20	1.43
GR	MFS Strategic Value R3	MVSRX	C-	(800) 343-2829	D / 2.2	-3.72	0.50	1.26 / 3	9.26 / 22	3.87 / 45	0.16	1.58
GR	MFS Strategic Value R4	MSVHX	D-	(800) 343-2829	D+ / 2.5	-3.68	0.64	1.50 / 3	9.63 / 25	4.08 / 47	0.40	1.33
GR	MFS Strategic Value R5	MSVJX	D-	(800) 343-2829	D+ / 2.6	-3.54	0.78	1.83 / 4	9.78 / 26	4.17 / 48	0.58	1.03
TC	MFS Technology Fund A	MTCAX	E-	(800) 343-2829	D / 1.7	-9.00	0.72	14.20 / 69	9.61 / 25	-6.84 / 1	0.00	1.50
TC	MFS Technology Fund B	MTCBX	E-	(800) 343-2829	D / 1.6	-9.06	0.43	13.60 / 67	8.95 / 20	-7.43 / 1	0.00	2.15
TC	MFS Technology Fund C	MTCCX	E-	(800) 343-2829	D / 1.9	-9.16	0.32	13.49 / 66	8.87 / 20	-7.46 / 1	0.00	2.15

● Denotes fund is closed to new investors
* Denotes fund is included in Section II

RISK			NET ASSETS		ASSET					BULL / BEAR		FUND MANAGER		MINIMUMS		LOADS	
	3 Year		NAV						Portfolio	Last Bull	Last Bear	Manager	Manager	Initial	Additional	Front	Back
Risk Rating/Pts	Standard Deviation	Beta	As of 6/30/06	Total $(Mil)	Cash %	Stocks %	Bonds %	Other %	Turnover Ratio	Market Return	Market Return	Quality Pct	Tenure (Years)	Purch. $	Purch. $	End Load	End Load
C+ / 6.1	15.0	1.28	13.56	3	0	99	0	1	91.0	88.0	-6.9	2	N/A	1,000	50	0.0	0.0
C / 4.3	15.0	1.28	13.73	2	0	99	0	1	91.0	90.0	-6.9	3	N/A	1,000	50	0.0	0.0
C / 4.3	15.0	1.28	13.77	N/A	0	99	0	1	91.0	90.5	-6.9	3	N/A	1,000	50	0.0	0.0
B / 8.3	9.2	1.11	21.35	N/A	1	98	0	1	55.0	69.4	-9.1	45	4	250	50	5.8	0.0
B / 8.3	9.1	1.11	19.86	N/A	1	98	0	1	55.0	65.8	-9.2	38	4	250	50	0.0	4.0
B / 8.2	9.1	1.11	19.84	N/A	1	98	0	1	55.0	65.9	-9.2	38	4	250	50	0.0	1.0
B- / 7.9	9.1	1.11	21.55	1,515	1	98	0	1	55.0	70.7	-9.1	49	N/A	1,000	50	5.8	0.0
B- / 7.8	9.1	1.11	20.10	380	1	98	0	1	55.0	67.2	-9.2	41	N/A	1,000	50	0.0	4.0
B- / 7.8	9.1	1.11	20.11	182	1	98	0	1	55.0	67.1	-9.1	41	N/A	1,000	50	0.0	1.0
B / 8.4	9.1	1.11	21.96	710	1	98	0	1	55.0	72.5	-9.0	53	N/A	10,000,000	0	0.0	0.0
B- / 7.9	9.2	1.11	21.33	6	1	98	0	1	55.0	69.6	-9.1	46	N/A	1,000	50	0.0	0.0
C+ / 5.8	9.1	1.11	20.00	2	1	98	0	1	55.0	66.9	-9.2	40	N/A	1,000	50	0.0	0.0
C+ / 5.8	9.1	1.11	20.06	N/A	1	98	0	1	55.0	67.5	-9.2	42	N/A	1,000	50	0.0	0.0
B- / 7.9	10.5	1.27	21.21	2	1	98	0	1	55.0	78.7	-9.2	52	3	1,000	50	0.0	0.0
C+ / 5.9	9.1	1.11	21.51	2	1	98	0	1	55.0	70.6	-9.1	49	N/A	1,000	50	0.0	0.0
C+ / 5.9	9.1	1.11	21.56	N/A	1	98	0	1	55.0	71.1	-9.1	50	N/A	1,000	50	0.0	0.0
B- / 7.9	10.5	1.01	18.42	1	3	96	0	1	42.0	128.0	-8.1	48	4	250	50	5.8	0.0
B- / 7.8	10.5	1.01	17.63	N/A	3	96	0	1	42.0	123.5	-8.3	40	4	250	50	0.0	4.0
B- / 7.8	10.5	1.01	17.61	1	3	96	0	1	42.0	123.5	-8.4	40	4	250	50	0.0	1.0
C+ / 6.4	10.5	1.01	18.57	1,286	3	96	0	1	42.0	129.8	-8.0	51	9	1,000	50	5.8	0.0
C+ / 6.3	10.5	1.01	17.82	178	3	96	0	1	42.0	125.3	-8.3	43	8	1,000	50	0.0	4.0
C+ / 6.3	10.5	1.01	17.76	149	3	96	0	1	42.0	125.2	-8.2	43	8	1,000	50	0.0	1.0
B- / 7.9	10.5	1.01	19.02	1,221	3	96	0	1	42.0	132.4	-8.0	56	10	10,000,000	0	0.0	0.0
C+ / 6.3	10.5	1.01	18.44	66	3	96	0	1	42.0	128.7	-8.0	48	9	1,000	50	0.0	0.0
B- / 7.9	10.4	1.00	18.27	8	3	96	0	1	42.0	127.4	-8.0	47	3	1,000	50	0.0	0.0
C+ / 5.6	10.5	1.01	18.53	6	3	96	0	1	42.0	129.7	-8.0	51	1	1,000	50	0.0	0.0
C+ / 5.6	10.5	1.01	18.59	104	3	96	0	1	42.0	130.5	-8.0	52	1	1,000	50	0.0	0.0
C+ / 6.3	11.1	1.28	18.63	1	1	98	0	1	100.0	48.0	-10.4	5	1	250	50	5.8	0.0
C+ / 6.3	11.1	1.28	17.66	N/A	1	98	0	1	100.0	44.8	-10.5	4	1	250	50	0.0	4.0
C+ / 6.3	11.2	1.28	17.68	N/A	1	98	0	1	100.0	44.8	-10.6	4	1	250	50	0.0	1.0
C / 5.4	11.1	1.28	18.79	427	1	98	0	1	100.0	49.0	-10.4	6	1	1,000	50	5.8	0.0
C / 5.4	11.1	1.28	17.82	277	1	98	0	1	100.0	46.0	-10.5	4	1	1,000	50	0.0	4.0
C / 5.4	11.1	1.28	17.85	71	1	98	0	1	100.0	46.0	-10.5	4	1	1,000	50	0.0	1.0
C+ / 6.3	11.1	1.28	19.32	757	1	98	0	1	100.0	50.6	-10.3	7	1	10,000,000	0	0.0	0.0
C / 5.4	11.1	1.28	18.70	3	1	98	0	1	100.0	48.3	-10.4	6	1	1,000	50	0.0	0.0
C+ / 6.3	11.1	1.28	18.59	1	1	98	0	1	100.0	47.4	-10.4	5	1	1,000	50	0.0	0.0
C / 5.1	11.1	1.28	18.78	N/A	1	98	0	1	100.0	48.9	-10.4	6	1	1,000	50	0.0	0.0
C / 5.1	11.1	1.28	18.85	N/A	1	98	0	1	100.0	49.4	-10.4	6	1	1,000	50	0.0	0.0
B / 8.4	8.6	1.01	14.07	1	0	99	0	1	60.0	65.4	-12.7	35	4	250	50	5.8	0.0
B / 8.3	8.6	1.01	13.60	N/A	0	99	0	1	60.0	62.1	-12.9	31	4	250	50	0.0	4.0
B / 8.3	8.6	1.01	13.60	1	0	99	0	1	60.0	62.1	-12.9	30	4	250	50	0.0	1.0
C / 5.2	8.6	1.01	14.17	610	0	99	0	1	60.0	66.7	-12.7	38	8	1,000	50	5.8	0.0
C / 5.2	8.6	1.01	13.75	285	0	99	0	1	60.0	63.4	-12.8	32	6	1,000	50	0.0	4.0
C / 5.2	8.6	1.01	13.76	116	0	99	0	1	60.0	63.4	-12.9	33	6	1,000	50	0.0	1.0
C+ / 5.9	8.6	1.01	14.26	58	0	99	0	1	60.0	68.7	-12.6	42	8	10,000,000	0	0.0	0.0
C / 5.3	8.6	1.02	14.10	16	0	99	0	1	60.0	66.1	-12.7	36	N/A	1,000	50	0.0	0.0
B / 8.3	8.6	1.01	13.98	3	0	99	0	1	60.0	65.0	-12.7	35	3	1,000	50	0.0	0.0
C+ / 5.9	8.6	1.01	14.14	2	0	99	0	1	60.0	66.6	-12.7	37	N/A	1,000	50	0.0	0.0
C+ / 5.9	8.6	1.01	14.17	N/A	0	99	0	1	60.0	67.1	-12.7	39	N/A	1,000	50	0.0	0.0
D / 2.1	18.4	1.88	9.81	47	1	98	0	1	105.0	78.9	-15.3	3	N/A	1,000	50	5.8	0.0
D / 2.0	18.4	1.89	9.44	41	1	98	0	1	105.0	75.5	-15.6	2	N/A	1,000	50	0.0	4.0
D / 2.0	18.4	1.88	9.42	12	1	98	0	1	105.0	75.2	-15.5	2	N/A	1,000	50	0.0	1.0

99 Pct = Best 0 Pct = Worst				PERFORMANCE							
		Overall Weiss Investment Rating		**Perfor-mance Rating/Pts**	Total Return % through 6/30/06					Incl. in Returns	
								Annualized		Dividend	Expense
Fund Type	Fund Name		Ticker Symbol	Phone	3 Mo	6 Mo	1Yr / Pct	3Yr / Pct	5Yr / Pct	Yield	Ratio
TC	● MFS Technology Fund I	MTCIX	E	(800) 343-2829	D+ / 2.8	-8.88	0.90	14.58 /70	9.99 /27	-6.52 / 1	0.00	1.15
TC	MFS Technology Fund R	MTQRX	E-	(800) 343-2829	D+ / 2.4	-9.06	0.62	14.05 /68	9.44 /24	-6.97 / 1	0.00	1.65
TC	MFS Technology Fund R3	MTERX	E	(800) 343-2829	D+ / 2.3	-9.01	0.52	13.87 /68	9.16 /22	-7.07 / 1	0.00	1.80
TC	MFS Technology Fund R4	MTCHX	E-	(800) 343-2829	D+ / 2.5	-9.00	0.72	14.20 /69	9.61 /25	-6.84 / 1	0.00	1.55
TC	MFS Technology Fund R5	MTCJX	E-	(800) 343-2829	D+ / 2.7	-8.88	0.92	14.54 /70	9.76 /26	-6.76 / 1	0.00	1.25
BA	MFS Total Return Fund 529A	EATRX	C-	(800) 343-2829	D- / 1.4	-0.69	1.60	3.85 /10	8.12 /16	4.99 /54	2.25	1.16
BA	MFS Total Return Fund 529B	EBTRX	C-	(800) 343-2829	D- / 1.1	-0.85	1.33	3.24 / 8	7.42 /12	4.35 /49	1.72	1.81
BA	MFS Total Return Fund 529C	ECTRX	C-	(800) 343-2829	D- / 1.5	-0.84	1.27	3.17 / 8	7.42 /12	4.35 /49	1.72	1.81
★ BA	MFS Total Return Fund A	MSFRX	C-	(800) 343-2829	D / 1.6	-0.56	1.79	4.11 /11	8.41 /17	5.23 /56	2.48	0.91
BA	MFS Total Return Fund B	MTRBX	C-	(800) 343-2829	D- / 1.3	-0.72	1.46	3.50 / 9	7.71 /13	4.55 /51	1.97	1.56
BA	MFS Total Return Fund C	MTRCX	C-	(800) 343-2829	D / 1.7	-0.72	1.46	3.50 / 9	7.72 /13	4.55 /51	1.97	1.56
BA	MFS Total Return Fund I	MTRIX	C	(800) 343-2829	D+ / 2.5	-0.47	1.97	4.54 /13	8.79 /20	5.59 /58	2.94	0.56
BA	MFS Total Return Fund R	MFTRX	C	(800) 343-2829	D / 2.1	-0.60	1.71	4.02 /11	8.24 /16	5.13 /55	2.45	1.06
BA	MFS Total Return Fund R1	MSFFX	C	(800) 343-2829	D / 1.8	-0.74	1.41	3.37 / 8	7.65 /13	4.51 /50	1.84	1.66
BA	MFS Total Return Fund R2	MSFKX	C	(800) 343-2829	D / 1.9	-0.72	1.52	3.59 / 9	7.76 /14	4.57 /51	2.17	1.31
BA	MFS Total Return Fund R3	MTRRX	C	(800) 343-2829	D / 2.0	-0.63	1.64	3.77 /10	8.01 /15	4.72 /52	2.28	1.21
BA	MFS Total Return Fund R4	MSFHX	C	(800) 343-2829	D / 2.2	-0.57	1.77	4.14 /11	8.41 /17	5.23 /56	2.57	0.96
BA	MFS Total Return Fund R5	MSFJX	C	(800) 343-2829	D+ / 2.3	-0.56	1.85	4.37 /12	8.52 /18	5.29 /56	2.85	0.68
GR	MFS Union Standard Equity Fund A	MUEAX	C	(800) 343-2829	C / 4.4	0.38	5.04	11.35 /56	12.59 /46	2.72 /34	0.76	1.30
GR	MFS Union Standard Equity Fund B	MUSBX	C	(800) 343-2829	C- / 4.2	0.23	4.70	10.53 /51	11.87 /42	2.02 /27	0.08	1.95
GR	MFS Union Standard Equity Fund C	MUECX	C+	(800) 343-2829	C / 4.7	0.16	4.65	10.45 /50	11.83 /41	2.05 /28	0.29	1.95
GR	MFS Union Standard Equity Fund I	MUSEX	C+	(800) 343-2829	C / 5.5	0.46	5.17	11.60 /57	12.94 /48	3.05 /37	1.09	0.95
UT	MFS Utilities Fund A	MMUFX	A+	(800) 343-2829	B+ / 8.5	4.98	8.43	16.88 /77	22.69 /87	7.19 /68	1.30	1.13
UT	MFS Utilities Fund B	MMUBX	A+	(800) 343-2829	B+ / 8.4	4.72	7.97	15.99 /75	21.77 /85	6.39 /63	0.66	1.89
UT	MFS Utilities Fund C	MMUCX	A+	(800) 343-2829	B+ / 8.5	4.79	8.04	16.07 /75	21.78 /85	6.40 /63	0.66	1.88
UT	MFS Utilities Fund I	MMUIX	A+	(800) 343-2829	B+ / 8.9	5.03	8.55	17.24 /78	22.95 /87	7.47 /69	1.59	0.88
UT	MFS Utilities Fund R	MMURX	A+	(800) 343-2829	B+ / 8.7	4.84	8.22	16.53 /76	22.32 /86	6.97 /67	1.13	1.38
UT	MFS Utilities Fund R1	MMUGX	B+	(800) 343-2829	B+ / 8.6	4.77	7.91	16.04 /75	21.74 /84	6.37 /63	0.55	2.05
UT	MFS Utilities Fund R2	MMUKX	B+	(800) 343-2829	B+ / 8.6	4.87	8.10	16.34 /75	21.87 /85	6.44 /64	0.86	1.71
UT	MFS Utilities Fund R3	MURRX	A+	(800) 343-2829	B+ / 8.7	4.88	8.14	16.43 /76	22.09 /85	6.56 /64	0.97	1.60
UT	MFS Utilities Fund R4	MMUHX	B+	(800) 343-2829	B+ / 8.8	4.86	8.27	16.63 /76	22.58 /86	7.13 /67	1.22	1.26
UT	MFS Utilities Fund R5	MMUJX	B+	(800) 343-2829	B+ / 8.8	5.01	8.42	17.07 /77	22.76 /87	7.23 /68	1.51	0.96
IN	MFS Value Fund 529A	EAVLX	B	(800) 343-2829	C / 5.3	0.86	5.88	11.16 /55	14.33 /56	5.89 /60	0.87	1.44
IN	MFS Value Fund 529B	EBVLX	B	(800) 343-2829	C / 5.2	0.66	5.51	10.43 /50	13.59 /52	5.35 /57	0.36	2.09
IN	MFS Value Fund 529C	ECVLX	B+	(800) 343-2829	C+ / 5.6	0.66	5.55	10.42 /50	13.59 /52	5.37 /57	0.35	2.09
★ IN	MFS Value Fund A	MEIAX	B	(800) 343-2829	C / 5.5	0.91	6.03	11.46 /56	14.62 /57	6.12 /62	1.08	1.19
IN	MFS Value Fund B	MFEBX	B	(800) 343-2829	C / 5.3	0.74	5.66	10.75 /52	13.88 /53	5.43 /57	0.53	1.83
IN	MFS Value Fund C	MEICX	B+	(800) 343-2829	C+ / 5.8	0.75	5.67	10.74 /52	13.87 /53	5.43 /57	0.55	1.84
IN	● MFS Value Fund I	MEIIX	B+	(800) 343-2829	C+ / 6.4	0.96	6.19	11.84 /59	15.01 /59	6.48 /64	1.46	0.84
IN	MFS Value Fund R	MFVRX	B+	(800) 343-2829	C+ / 6.2	0.87	5.91	11.27 /55	14.45 /56	6.01 /61	1.00	1.34
IN	MFS Value Fund R3	MVRRX	B+	(800) 343-2829	C+ / 6.1	0.82	5.85	11.12 /54	14.23 /55	5.91 /61	0.94	1.50
IN	MFS Value Fund R4	MEIHX	C+	(800) 343-2829	C+ / 6.2	0.86	5.96	11.38 /56	14.60 /57	6.11 /62	1.23	1.24
IN	MFS Value Fund R5	MEIJX	C+	(800) 343-2829	C+ / 6.3	0.98	6.16	11.74 /58	14.75 /58	6.19 /62	1.38	0.95
PM	Midas Fund	MIDSX	C-	(800) 400-6432	A+ / 9.9	7.43	35.45	104.55 /99	39.25 /99	35.70 /99	0.00	2.78
AG	Midas Special Equities Fund	MISEX	D	(800) 400-6432	D- / 1.3	0.47	0.88	3.97 /10	6.64 / 9	0.39 /17	0.00	4.03
GR	MMA Praxis Core Stock Fund A	MMPAX	D+	(800) 977-2947	D- / 1.4	-0.61	1.11	6.38 /23	8.04 /15	1.14 /21	0.16	1.43
GR	MMA Praxis Core Stock Fund B	MMPGX	C-	(800) 977-2947	D- / 1.5	-0.71	0.79	5.73 /19	7.35 /12	0.51 /18	0.00	2.08
FO	MMA Praxis International A	MPIAX	B+	(800) 977-2947	B- / 7.5	-0.64	7.52	23.15 /86	18.89 /76	5.37 /57	0.81	1.67
FO	MMA Praxis International B	MMPNX	B+	(800) 977-2947	B / 7.6	-0.78	7.14	22.43 /85	18.11 /73	4.72 /52	0.40	2.32
GI	MMA Praxis Value Index A	MVIAX	C+	(800) 977-2947	C / 4.6	0.22	-2.27	11.89 /59	13.71 /52	2.86 /35	1.36	0.96
GI	MMA Praxis Value Index B	MPVBX	B	(800) 977-2947	C / 5.3	0.18	5.45	11.43 /56	13.17 /50	2.34 /30	0.97	1.51
SC	Monetta Fund	MONTX	C-	(800) 666-3882	C / 4.8	-3.33	4.09	13.04 /64	12.48 /46	3.50 /41	0.00	1.65

● Denotes fund is closed to new investors
★ Denotes fund is included in Section II

RISK			NET ASSETS		ASSET					Portfolio	BULL / BEAR		FUND MANAGER		MINIMUMS		LOADS	
	3 Year		NAV								Last Bull	Last Bear	Manager	Manager	Initial	Additional	Front	Back
Risk	Standard		As of	Total	Cash	Stocks	Bonds	Other		Turnover	Market	Market	Quality	Tenure	Purch.	Purch.	End	End
Rating/Pts	Deviation	Beta	6/30/06	$(Mil)	%	%	%	%		Ratio	Return	Return	Pct	(Years)	$	$	Load	Load
D+ / 2.9	18.4	1.88	10.06	3	1	98	0	1		105.0	80.7	-15.3	3	9	10,000,000	0	0.0	0.0
D / 2.1	18.3	1.87	9.74	3	1	98	0	1		105.0	78.1	-15.5	3	N/A	1,000	50	0.0	0.0
D+ / 2.9	18.3	1.87	9.69	1	1	98	0	1		105.0	76.8	-15.3	3	3	1,000	50	0.0	0.0
D / 1.9	18.4	1.88	9.81	N/A	1	98	0	1		105.0	78.9	-15.3	3	N/A	1,000	50	0.0	0.0
D / 1.9	18.4	1.88	9.85	N/A	1	98	0	1		105.0	79.4	-15.3	3	N/A	1,000	50	0.0	0.0
B+ / 9.9	4.7	0.97	15.43	12	1	57	39	3		23.0	41.6	-4.2	64	4	250	50	4.8	0.0
B+ / 9.9	4.7	0.97	15.46	5	1	57	39	3		23.0	38.7	-4.3	57	4	250	50	0.0	4.0
B+ / 9.9	4.7	0.97	15.52	4	1	57	39	3		23.0	38.6	-4.3	57	4	250	50	0.0	1.0
B+ / 9.1	4.7	0.97	15.46	7,182	1	57	39	3		23.0	42.8	-4.1	67	N/A	1,000	50	4.8	0.0
B+ / 9.3	4.7	0.97	15.46	2,379	1	57	39	3		23.0	39.9	-4.3	60	N/A	1,000	50	0.0	4.0
B+ / 9.3	4.7	0.97	15.52	1,552	1	57	39	3		23.0	39.8	-4.3	60	N/A	1,000	50	0.0	1.0
B+ / 9.9	4.7	0.97	15.46	217	1	57	39	3		23.0	44.3	-4.0	70	N/A	10,000,000	0	0.0	0.0
B+ / 9.3	4.7	0.97	15.47	102	1	57	39	3		23.0	42.1	-4.1	65	N/A	1,000	50	0.0	0.0
B+ / 9.9	4.7	0.97	15.46	4	1	57	39	3		23.0	39.7	-4.3	59	N/A	1,000	50	0.0	0.0
B+ / 9.9	4.7	0.96	15.44	2	1	57	39	3		23.0	40.0	-4.3	61	N/A	1,000	50	0.0	0.0
B+ / 9.9	4.7	0.96	15.50	41	1	57	39	3		23.0	41.0	-4.3	63	3	1,000	50	0.0	0.0
B+ / 9.9	4.7	0.97	15.47	24	1	57	39	3		23.0	42.8	-4.1	67	N/A	1,000	50	0.0	0.0
B+ / 9.9	4.7	0.96	15.46	10	1	57	39	3		23.0	43.2	-4.1	68	N/A	1,000	50	0.0	0.0
B- / 7.9	7.9	1.00	13.14	11	1	98	0	1		24.0	67.9	-9.0	70	N/A	1,000	50	5.8	0.0
B- / 7.9	7.8	0.99	12.91	2	1	98	0	1		24.0	64.4	-9.2	64	N/A	1,000	50	0.0	4.0
B- / 7.9	7.9	1.00	12.84	1	1	98	0	1		24.0	64.7	-9.2	63	N/A	1,000	50	0.0	1.0
B- / 7.9	7.9	1.00	13.23	36	1	98	0	1		24.0	69.8	-8.9	72	N/A	10,000,000	0	0.0	0.0
B / 8.3	8.4	0.58	13.63	994	3	91	4	2		101.0	123.5	-0.5	98	14	1,000	50	4.8	0.0
B / 8.3	8.4	0.57	13.58	585	3	91	4	2		101.0	118.1	-0.7	97	13	1,000	50	0.0	4.0
B / 8.3	8.4	0.58	13.60	225	3	91	4	2		101.0	118.4	-0.8	97	12	1,000	50	0.0	1.0
B / 8.1	8.4	0.58	13.65	7	3	91	4	2		101.0	125.2	-0.4	98	14	10,000,000	0	0.0	0.0
B / 8.3	8.4	0.57	13.61	8	3	91	4	2		101.0	121.4	-0.5	98	14	1,000	50	0.0	0.0
C+ / 6.2	8.4	0.57	13.59	1	3	91	4	2		101.0	117.9	-0.7	97	1	1,000	50	0.0	0.0
C+ / 6.2	8.4	0.57	13.58	1	3	91	4	2		101.0	118.5	-0.7	98	1	1,000	50	0.0	0.0
B / 8.1	8.4	0.57	13.61	6	3	91	4	2		101.0	119.7	-0.7	98	3	1,000	50	0.0	0.0
C+ / 6.2	8.4	0.58	13.62	2	3	91	4	2		101.0	122.9	-0.5	98	1	1,000	50	0.0	0.0
C+ / 6.2	8.4	0.58	13.63	N/A	3	91	4	2		101.0	123.8	-0.5	98	1	1,000	50	0.0	0.0
B+ / 9.1	6.9	0.84	24.31	4	0	99	0	1		11.0	73.5	-9.0	91	4	250	50	5.8	0.0
B+ / 9.1	6.9	0.84	24.12	1	0	99	0	1		11.0	70.6	-9.1	87	4	250	50	0.0	4.0
B+ / 9.1	6.9	0.84	24.11	1	0	99	0	1		11.0	70.8	-9.1	87	4	250	50	0.0	1.0
B / 8.9	6.9	0.84	24.41	4,819	0	99	0	1		11.0	75.1	-9.0	91	4	1,000	50	5.8	0.0
B / 8.9	6.9	0.85	24.28	1,162	0	99	0	1		11.0	71.6	-9.2	89	4	1,000	50	0.0	4.0
B / 8.9	6.9	0.84	24.25	867	0	99	0	1		11.0	71.5	-9.2	89	4	1,000	50	0.0	1.0
B+ / 9.1	6.9	0.84	24.50	1,063	0	99	0	1		11.0	77.1	-8.9	93	4	10,000,000	0	0.0	0.0
B / 8.9	6.9	0.84	24.36	104	0	99	0	1		11.0	74.4	-9.1	91	4	1,000	50	0.0	0.0
B+ / 9.1	6.9	0.84	24.30	23	0	99	0	1		11.0	73.4	-9.0	90	3	1,000	50	0.0	0.0
C+ / 6.4	6.9	0.84	24.38	22	0	99	0	1		11.0	75.0	-9.0	91	4	1,000	50	0.0	0.0
C+ / 6.4	6.9	0.84	24.42	55	0	99	0	1		11.0	75.6	-9.0	92	4	1,000	50	0.0	0.0
D- / 1.1	31.8	1.60	4.05	131	N/A	N/A	0	N/A		63.0	210.0	9.4	90	N/A	1,000	100	0.0	1.0
B- / 7.3	8.4	0.73	14.93	15	N/A	N/A	0	N/A		118.0	37.0	-19.7	34	7	1,000	100	0.0	1.0
B / 8.7	6.7	0.84	14.58	81	4	95	0	1		32.7	42.9	-9.2	37	N/A	500	50	5.3	0.5
B / 8.8	6.7	0.84	14.03	76	4	95	0	1		32.7	40.0	-9.3	32	N/A	500	50	0.0	2.0
B- / 7.2	10.3	0.98	12.77	39	0	99	0	1		71.9	99.3	-10.3	18	3	500	50	5.3	0.5
B- / 7.1	10.3	0.98	12.56	24	0	99	0	1		71.9	95.1	-10.4	15	3	500	50	0.0	2.0
B / 8.9	9.0	0.82	10.58	17	0	99	0	1		25.3	78.1	-10.6	89	7	500	50	5.3	0.5
B+ / 9.3	7.5	0.92	10.56	12	0	99	0	1		25.3	75.2	-10.6	80	7	500	50	0.0	2.0
C+ / 6.1	12.6	0.75	12.48	58	2	97	0	1		40.8	75.3	-12.7	37	20	1,000	0	0.0	0.0

Fund Type	Fund Name	Ticker Symbol	Overall Weiss Investment Rating	Phone	Perfor-mance Rating/Pts	3 Mo	6 Mo	1Yr / Pct	3Yr / Pct	5Yr / Pct	Dividend Yield	Expense Ratio
BA	Monetta Trust-Balanced A	MBALX	D	(800) 666-3882	D- / 1.2	-1.43	1.52	4.67 / 14	6.07 / 7	1.80 / 25	0.37	2.29
MC	Monetta Trust-Mid-Cap Equity A	MMCEX	E+	(800) 666-3882	C- / 3.4	-6.97	3.76	13.42 / 66	10.42 / 30	-0.16 / 15	0.00	2.13
TC	Monetta Trust-Select Technology A	MSCEX	E-	(800) 666-3882	E- / 0.0	-15.41	-12.32	-3.23 / 0	2.69 / 1	-9.83 / 0	0.00	4.20
GR	Monteagle Large Cap Grw Fund	MEHRX	D	(877) 272-9746	D / 1.6	-8.50	-6.87	4.70 / 14	8.64 / 19	-3.00 / 5	0.00	1.21
AG	Morgan Stanley Aggr Equity A	AEQAX	C+	(800) 869-6397	C+ / 6.5	-2.87	2.27	22.93 / 86	17.20 / 69	3.75 / 43	0.00	1.40
AG	Morgan Stanley Aggr Equity B	AEQBX	C+	(800) 869-6397	C+ / 6.3	-3.04	1.86	22.10 / 84	16.32 / 65	2.98 / 37	0.00	2.15
AG	Morgan Stanley Aggr Equity C	AEQCX	C+	(800) 869-6397	C+ / 6.8	-3.12	1.86	22.08 / 84	16.36 / 65	2.99 / 37	0.00	2.15
AG	Morgan Stanley Aggr Equity D	AEQDX	B-	(800) 869-6397	B- / 7.3	-2.82	2.40	23.28 / 86	17.49 / 70	4.00 / 46	0.00	1.15
IN	Morgan Stanley Allocator A	ALRAX	D	(800) 869-6397	E+ / 0.9	-2.88	2.50	8.01 / 33	7.16 / 11	--	0.00	1.38
IN	Morgan Stanley Allocator B	ALRBX	D	(800) 869-6397	E+ / 0.7	-3.02	2.17	7.23 / 28	6.38 / 8	--	0.00	2.13
IN	Morgan Stanley Allocator C	ALRCX	D	(800) 869-6397	D- / 1.1	-2.93	2.17	7.23 / 28	6.40 / 8	--	0.00	2.13
IN	Morgan Stanley Allocator D	ALRDX	D+	(800) 869-6397	D / 1.8	-2.78	2.58	8.27 / 35	7.44 / 12	--	0.00	1.13
BA	Morgan Stanley Balance Growth A	BGRAX	C	(800) 869-6397	D+ / 2.4	-0.09	1.53	6.77 / 25	9.97 / 27	4.56 / 51	1.76	1.13
BA	Morgan Stanley Balance Growth B	BGRBX	C-	(800) 869-6397	D / 2.0	-0.21	1.20	5.93 / 20	9.15 / 22	3.76 / 43	1.08	1.89
BA	Morgan Stanley Balance Growth C	BGRCX	C	(800) 869-6397	D+ / 2.6	-0.21	1.21	6.02 / 21	9.15 / 22	3.78 / 44	1.09	1.89
BA	Morgan Stanley Balance Growth D	BGRDX	C+	(800) 869-6397	C- / 3.5	0.05	1.73	7.03 / 26	10.26 / 29	4.83 / 53	2.09	0.89
BA	Morgan Stanley Balance Income A	BINAX	D	(800) 869-6397	E / 0.5	-0.25	0.09	2.50 / 6	5.61 / 5	4.31 / 49	3.18	1.08
BA	Morgan Stanley Balance Income B	BINBX	D	(800) 869-6397	E / 0.3	-0.44	-0.31	1.79 / 4	4.80 / 4	3.53 / 42	2.58	1.84
BA	Morgan Stanley Balance Income C	BINCX	D	(800) 869-6397	E / 0.5	-0.45	-0.29	1.73 / 4	4.81 / 4	3.53 / 42	2.60	1.77
BA	Morgan Stanley Balance Income D	BINDX	D	(800) 869-6397	D- / 1.0	-0.18	0.13	2.76 / 6	5.84 / 6	4.55 / 51	3.60	0.84
MC	Morgan Stanley Capital Opp Trust A	CPOAX	C+	(800) 869-6397	B / 8.0	-2.70	2.03	22.58 / 85	22.40 / 86	-1.40 / 10	0.00	1.48
MC	Morgan Stanley Capital Opp Trust B	CPOBX	C+	(800) 869-6397	B / 7.7	-2.87	1.64	21.71 / 84	21.47 / 84	-2.16 / 8	0.00	2.23
MC	Morgan Stanley Capital Opp Trust C	CPOCX	C+	(800) 869-6397	B / 8.1	-2.88	1.71	21.73 / 84	21.51 / 84	-2.11 / 8	0.00	2.19
MC	Morgan Stanley Capital Opp Trust D	CPODX	C+	(800) 869-6397	B+ / 8.4	-2.60	2.20	22.92 / 86	22.70 / 87	-1.17 / 11	0.00	1.23
CV	Morgan Stanley Convertbl Sec Tr A	CNSAX	D	(800) 869-6397	D- / 1.4	-1.74	3.79	8.86 / 39	8.18 / 16	5.35 / 57	2.35	1.11
CV	Morgan Stanley Convertbl Sec Tr B	CNSBX	D+	(800) 869-6397	D- / 1.2	-1.87	3.43	8.05 / 33	7.34 / 12	4.55 / 51	1.69	1.86
CV	Morgan Stanley Convertbl Sec Tr C	CNSCX	C-	(800) 869-6397	D / 1.7	-1.94	3.49	8.15 / 34	7.39 / 12	4.58 / 51	1.87	1.85
CV	Morgan Stanley Convertbl Sec Tr D	CNSDX	C-	(800) 869-6397	D+ / 2.5	-1.67	3.85	9.06 / 40	8.41 / 17	5.59 / 58	2.73	0.86
SC	Morgan Stanley Devlp Growth Sec A	DGRAX	B	(800) 869-6397	B / 8.0	-4.98	4.14	19.52 / 81	21.64 / 84	6.45 / 64	0.00	1.09
SC	Morgan Stanley Devlp Growth Sec B	DGRBX	B	(800) 869-6397	B / 7.8	-5.14	3.75	18.58 / 80	20.70 / 82	5.62 / 59	0.00	1.85
SC	Morgan Stanley Devlp Growth Sec C	DGRCX	B	(800) 869-6397	B / 8.1	-5.16	3.78	18.62 / 80	20.73 / 82	5.65 / 59	0.00	1.81
SC	Morgan Stanley Devlp Growth Sec D	DGRDX	B+	(800) 869-6397	B+ / 8.5	-4.90	4.30	19.77 / 82	21.90 / 85	6.69 / 65	0.00	0.85
GI	Morgan Stanley Dividend Gr Sec A ★	DIVAX	E-	(800) 869-6397	D / 1.7	-2.46	-0.25	6.24 / 22	9.27 / 22	2.00 / 27	1.17	0.80
GI	Morgan Stanley Dividend Gr Sec B	DIVBX	E-	(800) 869-6397	D / 1.9	-2.45	-0.20	6.41 / 23	9.25 / 22	1.67 / 25	1.36	0.75
GI	Morgan Stanley Dividend Gr Sec C	DIVCX	E-	(800) 869-6397	D / 2.0	-2.63	-0.60	5.50 / 18	8.47 / 18	1.24 / 22	0.49	1.52
GI	Morgan Stanley Dividend Gr Sec D	DIVDX	E-	(800) 869-6397	D+ / 2.9	-2.39	-0.13	6.54 / 23	9.54 / 24	2.24 / 30	1.46	0.56
GI	Morgan Stanley Equal-Wgtd S&P500	VADAX	B-	(800) 869-6397	C+ / 5.8	-2.20	3.78	11.22 / 55	15.92 / 63	7.74 / 70	0.83	0.63
GI	Morgan Stanley Equal-Wgtd S&P500	VADBX	B-	(800) 869-6397	C / 5.5	-2.39	3.40	10.38 / 49	15.07 / 59	6.93 / 66	0.00	1.38
GI	Morgan Stanley Equal-Wgtd S&P500	VADCX	B	(800) 869-6397	C+ / 6.0	-2.38	3.45	10.44 / 50	15.08 / 59	6.94 / 66	0.17	1.38
GI	Morgan Stanley Equal-Wgtd S&P500	VADDX	B	(800) 869-6397	C+ / 6.7	-2.14	3.92	11.49 / 57	16.22 / 64	8.01 / 72	1.03	0.38
FO	Morgan Stanley European Growth A	EUGAX	B+	(800) 869-6397	B / 7.6	1.55	11.24	23.89 / 87	17.93 / 72	6.50 / 64	1.29	1.47
FO	Morgan Stanley European Growth B	EUGBX	B+	(800) 869-6397	B / 7.7	1.55	11.26	24.04 / 87	18.11 / 73	6.25 / 63	1.27	1.34
FO	Morgan Stanley European Growth C	EUGCX	B+	(800) 869-6397	B / 7.7	1.35	10.83	22.93 / 86	17.06 / 68	5.70 / 59	0.48	2.21
FO	Morgan Stanley European Growth D	EUGDX	B+	(800) 869-6397	B / 8.2	1.61	11.35	24.15 / 87	18.23 / 73	6.75 / 65	1.44	1.22
FS	Morgan Stanley Financl Serv Tr A	FSVAX	E+	(800) 869-6397	D+ / 2.9	-2.15	1.49	10.86 / 53	10.98 / 35	5.00 / 54	0.92	1.27
FS	Morgan Stanley Financl Serv Tr B	FSVBX	E+	(800) 869-6397	D+ / 2.7	-2.33	1.04	10.03 / 47	10.13 / 28	4.19 / 48	0.00	2.02
FS	Morgan Stanley Financl Serv Tr C	FSVCX	E+	(800) 869-6397	C- / 3.2	-2.32	1.12	10.08 / 47	10.18 / 29	4.29 / 49	0.00	1.95
FS	Morgan Stanley Financl Serv Tr D	FSVDX	D-	(800) 869-6397	C- / 3.9	-2.12	1.54	11.06 / 54	11.21 / 37	5.24 / 56	0.99	1.02
GR	Morgan Stanley Focus Growth A	AMOAX	D-	(800) 869-6397	D- / 1.3	-4.35	-4.59	10.60 / 51	9.68 / 25	0.20 / 16	0.00	1.01
GR	Morgan Stanley Focus Growth B	AMOBX	E+	(800) 869-6397	D- / 1.1	-4.53	-4.93	9.76 / 45	8.85 / 20	-0.57 / 13	0.00	1.76
GR	Morgan Stanley Focus Growth C	AMOCX	D-	(800) 869-6397	D / 1.6	-4.54	-4.94	9.77 / 45	8.87 / 20	-0.54 / 13	0.00	1.73
GR	Morgan Stanley Focus Growth D	AMODX	D	(800) 869-6397	D+ / 2.4	-4.29	-4.45	10.87 / 53	9.94 / 27	0.43 / 17	0.00	0.76

● Denotes fund is closed to new investors
★ Denotes fund is included in Section II

www.WeissRatings.com

RISK			NET ASSETS		ASSET					BULL / BEAR		FUND MANAGER		MINIMUMS		LOADS	
	3 Year		NAV						Portfolio	Last Bull	Last Bear	Manager	Manager	Initial	Additional	Front	Back
Risk Rating/Pts	Standard Deviation	Beta	As of 6/30/06	Total $(Mil)	Cash %	Stocks %	Bonds %	Other %	Turnover Ratio	Market Return	Market Return	Quality Pct	Tenure (Years)	Purch. $	Purch. $	End Load	End Load
B /8.3	6.2	1.09	11.18	4	0	62	36	2	1.4	34.6	-5.1	34	10	1,000	0	0.0	0.0
C- /3.7	14.0	1.16	8.28	7	0	99	0	1	41.8	85.1	-10.9	3	10	1,000	0	0.0	0.0
D- /1.4	21.5	2.19	7.19	1	3	96	0	1	29.2	56.4	-14.9	0	9	1,000	0	0.0	0.0
B- /7.8	11.5	1.27	6.24	30	0	0	0	100	59.5	61.2	-11.5	16	3	25,000	0	0.0	0.0
C+ /6.4	12.8	1.40	12.17	51	0	100	0	0	123.0	87.9	-9.3	76	N/A	1,000	100	5.3	1.0
C+ /6.3	12.9	1.41	11.49	209	0	100	0	0	123.0	83.2	-9.4	68	N/A	1,000	100	0.0	5.0
C+ /6.3	12.8	1.41	11.50	29	0	100	0	0	123.0	83.4	-9.5	69	N/A	1,000	100	0.0	1.0
C+ /6.4	12.8	1.40	12.39	4	0	100	0	0	123.0	89.2	-9.2	78	N/A	5,000,000	0	0.0	0.0
B /8.2	6.9	0.85	11.26	12	1	88	7	4	64.0	36.4	N/A	30	3	10,000	100	5.3	1.0
B /8.0	6.9	0.85	11.06	67	1	88	7	4	64.0	33.1	N/A	25	3	10,000	100	0.0	5.0
B /8.0	6.9	0.85	11.06	10	1	88	7	4	64.0	33.2	N/A	25	3	10,000	100	0.0	1.0
B /8.3	6.9	0.85	11.32	2	1	88	7	4	64.0	37.4	N/A	32	3	5,000,000	0	0.0	0.0
B+ /9.0	5.1	1.02	14.05	34	3	67	29	1	52.0	51.4	-4.0	78	4	1,000	100	5.3	0.0
B+ /9.1	5.1	1.01	14.06	74	3	67	29	1	52.0	47.8	-4.2	72	4	1,000	100	0.0	5.0
B+ /9.1	5.1	1.02	14.07	73	3	67	29	1	52.0	47.9	-4.3	71	4	1,000	100	0.0	1.0
B+ /9.0	5.1	1.01	14.05	1	3	67	29	1	52.0	52.5	-3.9	81	4	5,000,000	0	0.0	0.0
B /8.1	3.3	0.59	12.20	23	2	34	63	1	78.0	27.4	-0.5	59	4	1,000	100	5.3	0.0
B /8.4	3.4	0.59	12.16	87	2	34	63	1	78.0	24.4	-0.7	49	4	1,000	100	0.0	5.0
B /8.4	3.4	0.59	12.17	35	2	34	63	1	78.0	24.5	-0.7	49	4	1,000	100	0.0	1.0
B /8.3	3.4	0.59	12.16	1	2	34	63	1	78.0	28.5	-0.5	61	4	5,000,000	0	0.0	0.0
C /5.1	12.3	1.04	19.11	137	0	99	0	1	88.0	128.6	-8.5	85	N/A	1,000	100	5.3	1.0
C /5.1	12.4	1.05	17.94	112	0	99	0	1	88.0	123.1	-8.6	78	N/A	1,000	100	0.0	5.0
C /5.1	12.4	1.05	17.87	16	0	99	0	1	88.0	123.2	-8.6	78	N/A	1,000	100	0.0	1.0
C /5.1	12.4	1.05	19.47	88	0	99	0	1	88.0	130.4	-8.4	86	N/A	5,000,000	0	0.0	0.0
B- /7.9	6.7	1.04	16.87	113	2	0	0	98	47.0	42.2	0.3	63	5	1,000	100	5.3	1.0
B /8.6	6.7	1.04	16.89	55	2	0	0	98	47.0	39.0	0.1	54	5	1,000	100	0.0	5.0
B /8.6	6.7	1.04	16.78	9	2	0	0	98	47.0	39.2	0.1	55	5	1,000	100	0.0	1.0
B /8.7	6.7	1.04	16.86	4	2	0	0	98	47.0	43.3	0.4	66	5	5,000,000	0	0.0	0.0
C+ /6.3	12.6	0.81	27.68	275	0	99	0	1	115.0	128.4	-8.5	94	3	1,000	100	5.3	1.0
C+ /6.3	12.6	0.81	25.46	152	0	99	0	1	115.0	122.8	-8.7	92	3	1,000	100	0.0	5.0
C+ /6.3	12.5	0.81	25.55	28	0	99	0	1	115.0	123.0	-8.6	92	3	1,000	100	0.0	1.0
C+ /6.4	12.5	0.81	28.35	24	0	99	0	1	115.0	130.1	-8.5	95	3	5,000,000	0	0.0	0.0
D- /1.0	7.4	0.93	27.61	3,114	0	99	0	1	38.0	59.0	-8.2	41	3	1,000	100	5.3	1.0
D- /1.1	7.4	0.94	27.74	1,055	0	99	0	1	38.0	58.5	-8.4	41	3	1,000	100	0.0	5.0
D- /1.1	7.4	0.93	27.57	72	0	99	0	1	38.0	55.3	-8.4	34	3	1,000	100	0.0	1.0
D- /1.0	7.4	0.93	27.63	458	0	99	0	1	38.0	60.2	-8.2	44	3	5,000,000	0	0.0	0.0
B- /7.9	9.7	1.23	40.04	851	1	98	0	1	18.0	91.2	-8.6	79	3	1,000	100	5.3	1.0
B /8.2	9.7	1.23	39.57	675	1	98	0	1	18.0	86.7	-8.7	73	3	1,000	100	0.0	5.0
B /8.2	9.7	1.23	38.97	102	1	98	0	1	18.0	86.8	-8.7	73	3	1,000	100	0.0	1.0
B /8.3	9.7	1.23	40.28	509	1	98	0	1	18.0	92.7	-8.5	81	3	5,000,000	0	0.0	0.0
B- /7.0	10.5	0.95	19.60	435	1	98	0	1	64.0	99.6	-12.7	17	N/A	1,000	100	5.3	1.0
B- /7.1	10.5	0.95	18.97	151	1	98	0	1	64.0	99.8	-12.9	18	N/A	1,000	100	0.0	5.0
C+ /6.9	10.5	0.95	18.83	14	1	98	0	1	64.0	94.8	-12.9	13	N/A	1,000	100	0.0	1.0
B- /7.0	10.6	0.95	20.21	5	1	98	0	1	64.0	101.1	-12.6	18	N/A	5,000,000	0	0.0	0.0
C /4.5	9.2	0.98	13.66	86	3	96	0	1	58.0	71.2	-9.3	31	N/A	1,000	100	5.3	2.0
C- /3.9	9.2	0.98	12.58	68	3	96	0	1	58.0	67.3	-9.6	26	N/A	1,000	100	0.0	5.0
C- /4.0	9.2	0.98	12.64	8	3	96	0	1	58.0	67.4	-9.5	26	N/A	1,000	100	0.0	2.0
C /4.6	9.2	0.98	13.88	8	3	96	0	1	58.0	72.4	-9.3	33	N/A	5,000,000	0	0.0	2.0
C+ /6.3	11.0	1.23	26.61	1,146	9	90	0	1	65.0	53.0	-8.6	24	N/A	1,000	100	5.3	1.0
C+ /6.2	11.0	1.23	24.85	995	9	90	0	1	65.0	49.4	-8.8	19	N/A	1,000	100	0.0	5.0
C+ /6.2	11.0	1.23	24.61	108	9	90	0	1	65.0	49.4	-8.8	19	N/A	1,000	100	0.0	1.0
C+ /6.3	11.0	1.23	27.24	502	9	90	0	1	65.0	54.1	-8.6	25	N/A	5,000,000	0	0.0	0.0

99 Pct = Best
0 Pct = Worst

Fund Type	Fund Name	Ticker Symbol	Overall Weiss Investment Rating	Phone	PERFORMANCE							
					Performance Rating/Pts	Total Return % through 6/30/06			Annualized		Incl. in Returns	
						3 Mo	6 Mo	1Yr / Pct	3Yr / Pct	5Yr / Pct	Dividend Yield	Expense Ratio
IN	Morgan Stanley Fundamental Value	FVFAX	C	(800) 869-6397	C / 4.8	0.07	3.67	11.10 /54	13.61 /52	--	0.77	1.36
IN	Morgan Stanley Fundamental Value	FVFBX	C	(800) 869-6397	C / 4.7	0.15	3.69	11.09 /54	13.06 /49	--	0.25	2.03
IN	Morgan Stanley Fundamental Value	FVFCX	C	(800) 869-6397	C / 5.1	-0.15	3.23	10.22 /48	12.80 /48	--	0.20	1.98
IN	Morgan Stanley Fundamental Value	FVFDX	C+	(800) 869-6397	C+ / 5.8	0.07	3.75	11.32 /55	13.89 /53	--	1.00	1.11
GL	Morgan Stanley Glb Divnd Gr Sec A	GLBAX	C+	(800) 869-6397	C+ / 5.7	0.08	4.87	12.70 /63	15.47 /61	7.37 /69	1.38	1.22
GL	Morgan Stanley Glb Divnd Gr Sec B	GLBBX	C+	(800) 869-6397	C+ / 5.8	0.10	4.90	12.78 /63	15.06 /59	6.80 /66	1.36	1.19
GL	Morgan Stanley Glb Divnd Gr Sec C	GLBCX	B-	(800) 869-6397	C+ / 5.9	-0.08	4.50	11.85 /59	14.61 /57	6.55 /64	0.74	1.93
GL	Morgan Stanley Glb Divnd Gr Sec D	GLBDX	B-	(800) 869-6397	C+ / 6.5	0.21	5.07	13.01 /64	15.74 /62	7.62 /70	1.67	0.97
UT	Morgan Stanley Glbl Utilities A	GUTAX	B	(800) 869-6397	C+ / 5.7	3.15	4.69	6.63 /24	16.04 /64	3.84 /44	2.06	1.16
UT	Morgan Stanley Glbl Utilities B	GUTBX	B-	(800) 869-6397	C / 5.5	2.95	4.32	5.81 /19	15.20 /60	3.07 /38	0.71	1.92
UT	Morgan Stanley Glbl Utilities C	GUTCX	B	(800) 869-6397	C+ / 5.9	3.02	4.30	5.82 /19	15.20 /60	3.11 /38	1.03	1.89
UT	Morgan Stanley Glbl Utilities D	GUTDX	B	(800) 869-6397	C+ / 6.5	3.18	4.78	6.85 /25	16.35 /65	4.09 /47	2.40	0.92
GL	Morgan Stanley Global Advantage A	GADAX	C	(800) 869-6397	C / 4.5	-3.09	3.06	12.95 /64	13.52 /51	2.81 /35	0.00	1.29
GL	Morgan Stanley Global Advantage B	GADBX	C-	(800) 869-6397	C / 4.3	-3.39	2.67	12.06 /60	12.63 /47	2.04 /28	0.00	2.04
GL	Morgan Stanley Global Advantage C	GADCX	C	(800) 869-6397	C / 4.8	-3.28	2.67	12.15 /60	12.64 /47	2.06 /28	0.00	2.04
GL	Morgan Stanley Global Advantage D	GADDX	C+	(800) 869-6397	C / 5.5	-3.13	3.23	13.21 /65	13.76 /53	3.08 /38	0.00	1.04
GR	Morgan Stanley Growth Fund A	GRTAX	D	(800) 869-6397	D / 2.1	-3.58	-3.19	11.84 /59	10.50 /31	0.86 /20	0.00	1.05
GR	Morgan Stanley Growth Fund B	GRTBX	D	(800) 869-6397	D+ / 2.3	-3.80	-3.59	10.91 /53	9.65 /25	0.09 /16	0.00	1.80
GR	Morgan Stanley Growth Fund C	GRTCX	D	(800) 869-6397	D+ / 2.4	-3.78	-3.57	10.97 /53	9.65 /25	0.14 /16	0.00	1.77
GR	Morgan Stanley Growth Fund D	GRTDX	D+	(800) 869-6397	C- / 3.1	-3.57	-3.12	12.06 /60	10.72 /33	1.09 /21	0.00	0.80
HL	Morgan Stanley Health Sci Tr A	HCRAX	E-	(800) 869-6397	E+ / 0.7	-4.20	-3.27	9.16 /41	8.04 /15	2.96 /36	0.00	1.53
HL	Morgan Stanley Health Sci Tr B	HCRBX	E-	(800) 869-6397	E+ / 0.6	-4.42	-3.70	8.34 /35	7.23 /11	2.18 /29	0.00	2.29
HL	Morgan Stanley Health Sci Tr C	HCRCX	E-	(800) 869-6397	E+ / 0.9	-4.41	-3.63	8.40 /36	7.27 /11	2.21 /29	0.00	2.23
HL	Morgan Stanley Health Sci Tr D	HCRDX	E	(800) 869-6397	D- / 1.4	-4.15	-3.13	9.49 /43	8.33 /17	3.22 /39	0.00	1.29
IN	Morgan Stanley Income Builder A	INBAX	C+	(800) 869-6397	D+ / 2.8	0.30	2.73	7.93 /32	10.38 /30	5.66 /59	2.89	1.26
IN	Morgan Stanley Income Builder B	INBBX	C	(800) 869-6397	D+ / 2.3	0.09	2.30	7.06 /27	9.53 /24	4.85 /53	2.25	2.01
IN	Morgan Stanley Income Builder C	INBCX	C+	(800) 869-6397	C- / 3.0	0.10	2.35	7.13 /27	9.53 /24	4.87 /53	2.30	2.00
IN	Morgan Stanley Income Builder D	INBDX	C+	(800) 869-6397	C- / 3.9	0.44	2.85	8.19 /34	10.64 /32	5.92 /61	3.29	1.01
TC	Morgan Stanley Information Fd A	IFOAX	E-	(800) 869-6397	E- / 0.1	-10.77	-7.74	-1.14 / 1	6.05 / 7	-8.50 / 0	0.00	1.67
TC	Morgan Stanley Information Fd B	IFOBX	E-	(800) 869-6397	E- / 0.1	-10.99	-8.21	-2.00 / 1	5.17 / 4	-9.27 / 0	0.00	2.45
TC	Morgan Stanley Information Fd C	IFOCX	E-	(800) 869-6397	E- / 0.2	-10.99	-8.21	-1.89 / 1	5.17 / 4	-9.22 / 0	0.00	2.45
TC	Morgan Stanley Information Fd D	IFODX	E-	(800) 869-6397	E / 0.4	-10.72	-7.68	-0.92 / 1	6.30 / 8	-8.33 / 0	0.00	1.45
FO	Morgan Stanley International A	INLAX	B+	(800) 869-6397	B+ / 8.3	-0.65	8.49	26.88 /91	21.77 /85	8.81 /76	1.72	1.30
FO	Morgan Stanley International B	INLBX	B	(800) 869-6397	B / 8.2	-0.90	8.01	25.90 /90	20.80 /82	7.93 /71	1.01	2.05
FO	Morgan Stanley International C	INLCX	B+	(800) 869-6397	B+ / 8.4	-0.82	8.03	26.06 /90	20.83 /82	7.98 /72	1.19	2.05
FO	Morgan Stanley International D	INLDX	B+	(800) 869-6397	B+ / 8.8	-0.64	8.54	27.24 /92	22.01 /85	9.02 /76	1.99	1.05
FO	Morgan Stanley Intl Small Cap A	ISMAX	C+	(800) 869-6397	B+ / 8.9	-3.38	6.54	17.88 /79	26.29 /92	15.37 /92	0.71	1.81
FO	Morgan Stanley Intl Small Cap B	ISMBX	C+	(800) 869-6397	B+ / 8.8	-3.59	6.11	16.94 /77	25.33 /91	14.39 /91	0.00	2.55
FO	Morgan Stanley Intl Small Cap C	ISMCX	C+	(800) 869-6397	A- / 9.0	-3.65	6.35	17.23 /78	25.43 /91	14.52 /91	0.00	2.55
FO	Morgan Stanley Intl Small Cap D	ISMDX	C+	(800) 869-6397	A- / 9.2	-3.36	6.65	18.17 /79	26.58 /93	15.54 /93	0.81	1.55
FO	Morgan Stanley Intl Value Equity A	IVQAX	B+	(800) 869-6397	B- / 7.3	0.82	8.01	16.50 /76	18.85 /76	10.38 /82	1.18	1.37
FO	Morgan Stanley Intl Value Equity B	IVQBX	B	(800) 869-6397	B- / 7.2	0.60	7.66	15.65 /74	17.96 /72	9.53 /79	0.36	2.13
FO	Morgan Stanley Intl Value Equity C	IVQCX	B+	(800) 869-6397	B- / 7.5	0.68	7.78	15.81 /74	18.04 /73	9.56 /79	0.50	1.96
FO	Morgan Stanley Intl Value Equity D	IVQDX	B+	(800) 869-6397	B / 7.9	0.89	8.23	16.87 /77	19.15 /76	10.66 /83	1.36	1.13
FO	Morgan Stanley Japan Fund A	JPNAX	B-	(800) 869-6397	B / 8.2	-1.33	1.58	32.60 /96	21.76 /85	5.40 /57	0.00	1.88
FO	Morgan Stanley Japan Fund B	JPNBX	B-	(800) 869-6397	B / 8.2	-1.52	1.22	31.74 /95	20.85 /82	4.54 /51	0.00	2.63
FO	Morgan Stanley Japan Fund C	JPNCX	B-	(800) 869-6397	B+ / 8.4	-1.53	1.24	31.82 /96	20.88 /82	4.54 /51	0.00	2.63
FO	Morgan Stanley Japan Fund D	JPNDX	B	(800) 869-6397	B+ / 8.6	-1.31	1.66	32.97 /96	22.05 /85	5.61 /59	0.00	1.63
MC	Morgan Stanley Mid Cap Value A	MDFAX	C-	(800) 869-6397	C+ / 6.6	-2.06	4.40	14.12 /69	17.37 /70	--	0.00	1.40
MC	Morgan Stanley Mid Cap Value B	MDFBX	C-	(800) 869-6397	C+ / 6.3	-2.15	4.10	13.35 /66	16.53 /66	--	0.00	2.16
MC	Morgan Stanley Mid Cap Value C	MDFCX	C-	(800) 869-6397	C+ / 6.8	-2.23	3.99	13.33 /66	16.59 /66	--	0.00	2.04
MC	Morgan Stanley Mid Cap Value D	MDFDX	C	(800) 869-6397	B- / 7.3	-1.95	4.53	14.45 /70	17.66 /71	--	0.00	1.16

● Denotes fund is closed to new investors
* Denotes fund is included in Section II

www.WeissRatings.com

RISK			NET ASSETS		ASSET				Portfolio Turnover Ratio	BULL / BEAR		FUND MANAGER		MINIMUMS		LOADS	
Risk Rating/Pts	3 Year		NAV As of 6/30/06	Total $(Mil)	Cash %	Stocks %	Bonds %	Other %		Last Bull Market Return	Last Bear Market Return	Manager Quality Pct	Manager Tenure (Years)	Initial Purch. $	Additional Purch. $	Front End Load	Back End Load
	Standard Deviation	Beta															
B- /7.1	7.1	0.86	13.56	36	5	85	0	10	37.0	73.1	-6.0	86	4	1,000	100	5.3	1.0
B- /7.3	7.2	0.86	13.50	58	5	85	0	10	37.0	69.9	-6.1	83	4	1,000	100	0.0	5.0
B- /7.2	7.2	0.86	13.43	6	5	85	0	10	37.0	69.3	-6.2	82	4	1,000	100	0.0	1.0
B- /7.0	7.2	0.87	13.57	2	5	85	0	10	37.0	74.4	-5.9	87	4	5,000,000	0	0.0	0.0
B- /7.7	8.1	0.76	14.62	847	2	97	0	1	21.0	87.4	-10.6	28	N/A	1,000	100	5.3	2.0
B- /7.7	8.1	0.76	14.80	178	2	97	0	1	21.0	84.9	-10.7	26	N/A	1,000	100	0.0	5.0
B- /7.7	8.1	0.76	14.55	18	2	97	0	1	21.0	83.0	-10.7	22	N/A	1,000	100	0.0	2.0
B- /7.7	8.1	0.76	14.66	276	2	97	0	1	21.0	88.7	-10.5	29	N/A	5,000,000	0	0.0	2.0
B /8.5	8.3	0.66	15.79	156	1	98	0	1	18.0	80.5	-3.5	65	9	1,000	100	5.3	2.0
B /8.5	8.3	0.66	16.25	81	1	98	0	1	18.0	76.4	-3.7	57	12	1,000	100	0.0	5.0
B /8.5	8.3	0.66	15.79	4	1	98	0	1	18.0	76.3	-3.6	57	9	1,000	100	0.0	2.0
B /8.5	8.3	0.66	15.84	2	1	98	0	1	18.0	82.0	-3.4	68	9	5,000,000	0	0.0	2.0
B- /7.0	9.5	0.86	9.42	181	3	96	0	1	47.0	82.9	-10.8	8	N/A	1,000	100	5.3	2.0
C+ /6.9	9.5	0.86	8.83	60	3	96	0	1	47.0	78.7	-10.9	6	N/A	1,000	100	0.0	5.0
C+ /6.9	9.6	0.86	8.86	23	3	96	0	1	47.0	78.7	-11.1	6	N/A	1,000	100	0.0	2.0
B- /7.0	9.5	0.86	9.60	4	3	96	0	1	47.0	84.4	-10.7	9	N/A	5,000,000	0	0.0	2.0
C+ /6.6	11.3	1.28	14.26	341	1	98	0	1	75.0	65.9	-10.8	26	N/A	1,000	100	5.3	0.0
C+ /6.4	11.3	1.28	13.42	199	1	98	0	1	75.0	61.9	-11.1	21	N/A	1,000	100	0.0	0.0
C+ /6.5	11.3	1.27	13.25	28	1	98	0	1	75.0	61.9	-11.0	21	N/A	1,000	100	0.0	0.0
C+ /6.6	11.3	1.27	14.59	40	1	98	0	1	75.0	67.2	-10.8	28	N/A	5,000,000	0	0.0	0.0
C- /3.9	11.1	0.89	16.88	163	4	95	0	1	32.0	56.1	-9.8	34	1	1,000	100	5.3	2.0
C- /3.2	11.1	0.89	15.37	157	4	95	0	1	32.0	52.5	-10.0	28	1	1,000	100	0.0	5.0
C- /3.2	11.1	0.89	15.40	16	4	95	0	1	32.0	52.8	-10.0	28	1	1,000	100	0.0	2.0
C- /4.1	11.1	0.89	17.34	8	4	95	0	1	32.0	57.4	-9.8	36	1	5,000,000	0	0.0	2.0
B+ /9.6	5.1	0.62	11.88	62	8	62	11	19	33.0	52.1	-3.1	81	4	1,000	100	5.3	0.0
B+ /9.6	5.1	0.62	11.90	52	8	62	11	19	33.0	48.6	-3.4	74	4	1,000	100	0.0	5.0
B+ /9.7	5.1	0.62	11.86	19	8	62	11	19	33.0	48.6	-3.4	74	4	1,000	100	0.0	1.0
B+ /9.7	5.0	0.62	11.88	1	8	62	11	19	33.0	53.3	-3.1	83	4	5,000,000	0	0.0	0.0
D /1.6	18.7	1.93	9.53	94	5	94	0	1	177.0	56.2	-14.0	0	N/A	1,000	100	5.3	2.0
D /1.6	18.8	1.93	8.83	193	5	94	0	1	177.0	52.2	-14.2	0	N/A	1,000	100	0.0	5.0
D /1.6	18.7	1.92	8.83	25	5	94	0	1	177.0	52.2	-14.2	0	N/A	1,000	100	0.0	2.0
D /1.6	18.7	1.93	9.74	3	5	94	0	1	177.0	57.3	-14.0	1	N/A	5,000,000	0	0.0	2.0
C+ /6.4	10.7	1.04	12.27	135	2	97	0	1	22.0	116.7	-8.3	26	7	1,000	100	5.3	1.0
C+ /6.4	10.6	1.04	12.13	167	2	97	0	1	22.0	111.6	-8.6	21	7	1,000	100	0.0	5.0
C+ /6.4	10.7	1.04	12.11	29	2	97	0	1	22.0	111.6	-8.5	21	7	1,000	100	0.0	1.0
C+ /6.4	10.7	1.04	12.33	23	2	97	0	1	22.0	118.3	-8.3	27	7	5,000,000	0	0.0	0.0
C- /4.2	11.1	0.89	15.14	34	0	99	0	1	16.0	164.0	-3.1	89	N/A	1,000	100	5.3	2.0
C- /4.0	11.0	0.88	14.24	26	0	99	0	1	16.0	156.9	-3.3	85	N/A	1,000	100	0.0	5.0
C- /4.0	11.1	0.88	14.24	4	0	99	0	1	16.0	157.8	-3.3	85	N/A	1,000	100	0.0	2.0
C /4.3	11.0	0.88	15.24	9	0	99	0	1	16.0	165.1	-2.9	90	N/A	5,000,000	0	0.0	2.0
B- /7.4	9.1	0.87	13.49	108	1	98	0	1	11.0	101.9	-9.0	33	5	1,000	100	5.3	2.0
B- /7.4	9.1	0.87	13.35	209	1	98	0	1	11.0	96.9	-9.2	28	5	1,000	100	0.0	5.0
B- /7.4	9.1	0.87	13.30	66	1	98	0	1	11.0	97.3	-9.3	28	5	1,000	100	0.0	2.0
B- /7.4	9.1	0.87	13.55	443	1	98	0	1	11.0	103.5	-9.1	35	5	5,000,000	0	0.0	2.0
C /5.5	15.0	0.93	9.64	33	3	96	0	1	101.0	102.4	-3.1	46	N/A	1,000	100	5.3	2.0
C /5.4	14.9	0.93	9.09	22	3	96	0	1	101.0	97.7	-3.4	38	N/A	1,000	100	0.0	5.0
C /5.4	15.0	0.93	8.99	15	3	96	0	1	101.0	97.7	-3.4	37	N/A	1,000	100	0.0	2.0
C /5.5	15.0	0.93	9.80	8	3	96	0	1	101.0	104.2	-3.3	49	N/A	5,000,000	0	0.0	2.0
C /4.8	10.1	0.84	11.39	14	3	96	0	1	72.0	107.4	-11.1	73	N/A	1,000	100	5.3	1.0
C /4.5	10.0	0.84	10.92	49	3	96	0	1	72.0	102.5	-11.3	67	N/A	1,000	100	0.0	5.0
C /4.5	10.1	0.84	10.94	8	3	96	0	1	72.0	102.9	-11.3	67	N/A	1,000	100	0.0	1.0
C /4.9	10.1	0.85	11.54	240	3	96	0	1	72.0	108.9	-11.1	75	N/A	5,000,000	0	0.0	0.0

Fund Type	Fund Name	Ticker Symbol	Overall Weiss Investment Rating	Phone	Performance Rating/Pts	3 Mo	6 Mo	1Yr / Pct	3Yr / Pct	5Yr / Pct	Dividend Yield	Expense Ratio
								Total Return % through 6/30/06 (Annualized)			Incl. in Returns	
GI	Morgan Stanley Multi-Asst Cl FD A	MAFAX	C	(800) 869-6397	C- / 4.2	-3.43	1.23	9.75 /45	13.26 /50	2.56 /32	1.02	0.24
GI	Morgan Stanley Multi-Asst Cl FD B	MAFBX	C	(800) 869-6397	C- / 3.8	-3.58	0.89	9.01 /40	12.40 /45	1.78 /25	0.04	1.00
GI	Morgan Stanley Multi-Asst Cl FD C	MAFCX	C+	(800) 869-6397	C / 4.5	-3.58	0.89	9.00 /40	12.41 /45	1.79 /25	0.32	0.95
GI	Morgan Stanley Multi-Asst Cl FD D	MAFDX	B-	(800) 869-6397	C / 5.3	-3.33	1.39	10.13 /48	13.53 /51	2.82 /35	1.21	N/A
GI	Morgan Stanley NASDAQ 100 A	NSQAX	E+	(800) 869-6397	D- / 1.2	-7.53	-4.38	5.29 /17	9.20 /22	--	0.00	0.64
GI	Morgan Stanley NASDAQ 100 B	NSQBX	E	(800) 869-6397	D- / 1.0	-7.71	-4.65	4.48 /13	8.39 /17	--	0.00	1.40
GI	Morgan Stanley NASDAQ 100 C	NSQCX	E+	(800) 869-6397	D- / 1.5	-7.80	-4.64	4.48 /13	8.37 /17	--	0.00	1.32
GI	Morgan Stanley NASDAQ 100 D	NSQDX	D-	(800) 869-6397	D / 2.2	-7.66	-4.34	5.36 /17	9.37 /23	--	0.00	0.40
EN	Morgan Stanley Natural Res Dev A	NREAX	B	(800) 869-6397	A+ / 9.7	2.05	10.41	36.93 /97	34.71 /98	15.15 /92	0.00	1.11
EN	Morgan Stanley Natural Res Dev B	NREBX	B-	(800) 869-6397	A+ / 9.7	1.88	9.98	35.90 /97	33.69 /97	14.22 /91	0.00	1.87
EN	Morgan Stanley Natural Res Dev C	NRECX	B-	(800) 869-6397	A+ / 9.7	1.84	9.96	35.82 /97	33.69 /97	14.21 /90	0.00	1.87
EN	Morgan Stanley Natural Res Dev D	NREDX	B	(800) 869-6397	A+ / 9.8	2.13	10.54	37.22 /97	35.03 /98	15.37 /92	0.00	0.87
FO	Morgan Stanley Pacific Growth A	TGRAX	B	(800) 869-6397	B+ / 8.8	-2.32	7.00	27.96 /93	24.99 /91	11.09 /84	0.00	1.81
FO	Morgan Stanley Pacific Growth B	TGRBX	B-	(800) 869-6397	B+ / 8.7	-2.53	6.55	26.93 /91	23.93 /89	10.17 /81	0.00	2.56
FO	Morgan Stanley Pacific Growth C	TGRCX	B	(800) 869-6397	B+ / 8.8	-2.53	6.61	27.01 /91	24.00 /89	10.24 /81	0.00	2.55
FO	Morgan Stanley Pacific Growth D	TGRDX	B	(800) 869-6397	A- / 9.1	-2.24	7.08	28.25 /93	25.22 /91	11.32 /85	0.00	1.56
RE	Morgan Stanley Real Estate A	REFAX	D+	(800) 869-6397	A / 9.5	0.03	14.69	24.02 /87	30.33 /96	20.41 /96	1.49	1.50
RE	Morgan Stanley Real Estate B	REFBX	D+	(800) 869-6397	A / 9.4	-0.23	14.16	22.99 /86	29.32 /95	19.49 /96	0.92	2.26
RE	Morgan Stanley Real Estate C	REFCX	D+	(800) 869-6397	A / 9.5	-0.22	14.20	23.05 /86	29.33 /95	19.52 /96	0.96	2.23
RE	Morgan Stanley Real Estate D	REFDX	D+	(800) 869-6397	A+ / 9.6	0.03	14.80	24.36 /88	30.63 /96	20.70 /97	1.75	1.26
IX	Morgan Stanley S&P 500 Index A	SPIAX	C-	(800) 869-6397	D+ / 2.6	-1.57	2.38	7.95 /32	10.52 /31	1.82 /26	1.28	0.63
IX	Morgan Stanley S&P 500 Index B	SPIBX	C-	(800) 869-6397	D+ / 2.3	-1.77	1.99	7.13 /27	9.64 /25	1.04 /20	0.39	1.40
IX	Morgan Stanley S&P 500 Index C	SPICX	C	(800) 869-6397	C- / 3.0	-1.77	1.99	7.14 /27	9.68 /25	1.06 /21	0.62	1.32
IX	Morgan Stanley S&P 500 Index D	SPIDX	C+	(800) 869-6397	C- / 3.8	-1.56	2.51	8.18 /34	10.75 /33	2.04 /28	1.55	0.40
IN	Morgan Stanley Sm-Mid Special Val	JBJAX	C	(800) 869-6397	C+ / 6.6	-2.77	4.51	11.76 /58	17.83 /72	--	0.00	1.30
IN	Morgan Stanley Sm-Mid Special Val	JBJBX	C-	(800) 869-6397	C+ / 6.3	-2.95	4.11	10.92 /53	16.94 /68	--	0.00	2.06
IN	Morgan Stanley Sm-Mid Special Val	JBJCX	C	(800) 869-6397	C+ / 6.8	-2.95	4.11	10.99 /53	16.97 /68	--	0.00	2.01
IN	Morgan Stanley Sm-Mid Special Val	JBJDX	C+	(800) 869-6397	B- / 7.3	-2.67	4.61	12.03 /60	18.10 /73	--	0.00	1.06
SC	Morgan Stanley Special Growth A	SMPAX	C-	(800) 869-6397	C+ / 6.6	-8.91	2.95	10.36 /49	19.10 /76	-5.68 / 2	0.00	1.77
SC	Morgan Stanley Special Growth B	SMPBX	C-	(800) 869-6397	C+ / 6.5	-9.09	2.61	9.50 /43	18.22 /73	-6.40 / 1	0.00	2.53
SC	Morgan Stanley Special Growth C	SMPCX	C	(800) 869-6397	C+ / 6.8	-9.10	2.61	9.57 /44	18.26 /73	-6.34 / 1	0.00	2.49
SC	Morgan Stanley Special Growth D	SMPDX	C	(800) 869-6397	B- / 7.4	-8.83	3.15	10.66 /51	19.42 /77	-5.45 / 2	0.00	1.53
SC	Morgan Stanley Special Value A	SVFAX	C	(800) 869-6397	B- / 7.0	-2.67	8.52	13.38 /66	18.56 /75	9.58 /79	0.00	1.32
SC	Morgan Stanley Special Value B	SVFBX	C	(800) 869-6397	C+ / 6.8	-2.84	8.11	12.55 /62	17.65 /71	8.74 /75	0.00	2.07
SC	Morgan Stanley Special Value C	SVFCX	C	(800) 869-6397	B- / 7.2	-2.83	8.16	12.54 /62	17.72 /71	8.77 /75	0.00	2.07
SC	Morgan Stanley Special Value D	SVFDX	C+	(800) 869-6397	B / 7.6	-2.57	8.69	13.67 /67	18.83 /76	9.83 /80	0.00	1.07
AA	Morgan Stanley Strategist Fund A	SRTAX	B-	(800) 869-6397	C / 4.4	0.40	5.36	12.23 /61	12.46 /45	5.16 /55	1.52	0.93
AA	Morgan Stanley Strategist Fund B	SRTBX	C+	(800) 869-6397	C- / 4.0	0.20	4.99	11.38 /56	11.62 /40	4.35 /49	0.84	1.68
AA	Morgan Stanley Strategist Fund C	SRTCX	B-	(800) 869-6397	C / 4.7	0.20	5.02	11.41 /56	11.64 /40	4.35 /49	0.90	1.68
AA	Morgan Stanley Strategist Fund D	SRTDX	B+	(800) 869-6397	C / 5.5	0.46	5.49	12.50 /62	12.74 /47	5.40 /57	1.84	0.68
GR	Morgan Stanley Total Mkt Index A	TMIAX	C	(800) 869-6397	C- / 3.6	-2.02	3.05	9.23 /42	12.13 /43	3.17 /38	1.11	0.64
GR	Morgan Stanley Total Mkt Index B	TMIBX	C	(800) 869-6397	C- / 3.3	-2.16	2.65	8.50 /37	11.32 /38	2.40 /31	0.30	1.40
GR	Morgan Stanley Total Mkt Index C	TMICX	C+	(800) 869-6397	C- / 4.0	-2.25	2.65	8.44 /36	11.30 /38	2.41 /31	0.44	1.39
GR	Morgan Stanley Total Mkt Index D	TMIDX	C+	(800) 869-6397	C / 4.9	-2.01	3.21	9.59 /44	12.45 /45	3.44 /41	1.37	0.40
GI	Morgan Stanley Total Return Tr A	TRFAX	C-	(800) 869-6397	C- / 3.8	-0.17	5.95	13.81 /68	11.53 /39	0.32 /17	0.00	1.42
GI	Morgan Stanley Total Return Tr B	TRFBX	C-	(800) 869-6397	C- / 3.5	-0.30	5.57	13.01 /64	10.72 /33	-0.44 /14	0.00	2.17
GI	Morgan Stanley Total Return Tr C	TRFCX	C	(800) 869-6397	C- / 4.2	-0.36	5.51	12.96 /64	10.71 /33	-0.46 /14	0.00	2.17
GI	Morgan Stanley Total Return Tr D	TRFDX	C+	(800) 869-6397	C / 5.1	-0.05	6.13	14.12 /69	11.82 /41	0.56 /18	0.00	1.17
MC	Morgan Stanley U.S Mid Cap Value I	UMCVX	C+	(800) 869-6397	B- / 7.3	-2.05	4.48	14.57 /70	17.67 /71	5.62 /59	0.28	1.05
UT	Morgan Stanley Utilities Fund A	UTLAX	C	(800) 869-6397	C / 5.4	3.69	4.54	7.09 /27	15.08 /59	3.56 /42	2.11	1.03
UT	Morgan Stanley Utilities Fund B	UTLBX	C	(800) 869-6397	C+ / 5.6	3.70	4.56	7.25 /28	15.14 /59	3.28 /39	2.33	0.94
UT	Morgan Stanley Utilities Fund C	UTLCX	C	(800) 869-6397	C+ / 5.7	3.47	4.13	6.32 /22	14.24 /55	2.79 /35	1.48	1.71

● Denotes fund is closed to new investors
* Denotes fund is included in Section II

RISK			NET ASSETS		ASSET					BULL / BEAR		FUND MANAGER		MINIMUMS		LOADS	
	3 Year		NAV						Portfolio	Last Bull	Last Bear	Manager	Manager	Initial	Additional	Front	Back
Risk Rating/Pts	Standard Deviation	Beta	As of 6/30/06	Total $(Mil)	Cash %	Stocks %	Bonds %	Other %	Turnover Ratio	Market Return	Market Return	Quality Pct	Tenure (Years)	Purch. $	Purch. $	End Load	End Load
B / 8.1	8.6	1.05	11.53	13	0	99	0	1	12.0	78.3	-10.0	71	9	1,000	100	5.3	1.0
B / 8.4	8.6	1.06	11.30	19	0	99	0	1	12.0	74.3	-10.3	63	9	1,000	100	0.0	5.0
B / 8.4	8.5	1.05	11.30	4	0	99	0	1	12.0	74.2	-10.2	64	9	1,000	100	0.0	1.0
B / 8.5	8.6	1.05	11.63	1	0	99	0	1	12.0	79.9	-10.0	73	9	5,000,000	0	0.0	0.0
C / 5.3	14.9	1.67	8.96	11	8	91	0	1	8.0	67.0	-9.5	6	5	1,000	100	5.3	1.0
C / 5.2	15.0	1.69	8.62	21	8	91	0	1	8.0	63.2	-9.8	4	5	1,000	100	0.0	5.0
C / 5.2	14.9	1.67	8.63	8	8	91	0	1	8.0	63.1	-9.6	4	5	1,000	100	0.0	1.0
C / 5.3	15.0	1.69	9.04	1	8	91	0	1	8.0	68.2	-9.5	6	5	5,000,000	0	0.0	0.0
C / 4.4	20.6	1.00	26.76	115	0	99	0	1	21.0	165.3	-2.8	72	1	1,000	100	5.3	2.0
C / 4.3	20.6	1.00	24.96	91	0	99	0	1	21.0	158.9	-3.0	65	1	1,000	100	0.0	5.0
C / 4.3	20.6	1.00	24.89	16	0	99	0	1	21.0	159.1	-3.1	65	1	1,000	100	0.0	2.0
C / 4.4	20.6	1.00	27.19	44	0	99	0	1	21.0	167.4	-2.9	75	1	5,000,000	0	0.0	2.0
C / 5.4	13.4	1.12	18.49	134	2	97	0	1	25.0	135.9	-7.4	35	9	1,000	100	5.3	2.0
C / 5.4	13.4	1.12	17.72	46	2	97	0	1	25.0	129.1	-7.6	28	11	1,000	100	0.0	5.0
C / 5.3	13.4	1.11	17.73	8	2	97	0	1	25.0	129.5	-7.6	29	9	1,000	100	0.0	2.0
C / 5.4	13.4	1.11	18.75	2	2	97	0	1	25.0	137.1	-7.5	37	9	5,000,000	0	0.0	2.0
E+ / 0.6	15.3	0.92	16.73	27	2	97	0	1	21.0	149.4	-0.6	97	7	1,000	100	5.3	0.0
E+ / 0.6	15.3	0.92	16.66	86	2	97	0	1	21.0	143.4	-0.7	95	7	1,000	100	0.0	5.0
E+ / 0.6	15.3	0.91	16.66	16	2	97	0	1	21.0	143.6	-0.7	95	7	1,000	100	0.0	2.0
E+ / 0.6	15.3	0.91	16.75	16	2	97	0	1	21.0	151.4	-0.5	97	7	5,000,000	0	0.0	2.0
B / 8.7	7.6	1.00	13.77	440	2	97	0	1	2.0	61.5	-9.9	48	8	1,000	100	5.3	1.0
B / 8.8	7.6	1.00	13.35	560	2	97	0	1	2.0	57.7	-10.1	39	8	1,000	100	0.0	5.0
B / 8.8	7.7	1.00	13.32	133	2	97	0	1	2.0	57.7	-10.0	39	8	1,000	100	0.0	1.0
B / 8.9	7.6	1.00	13.90	157	2	97	0	1	2.0	62.6	-9.8	51	8	5,000,000	0	0.0	0.0
C / 5.4	10.1	1.11	13.68	39	2	97	0	1	78.0	104.2	-6.2	93	4	1,000	100	5.3	1.0
C / 5.1	10.1	1.11	13.17	134	2	97	0	1	78.0	99.3	-6.5	91	4	1,000	100	0.0	5.0
C / 5.1	10.1	1.11	13.18	28	2	97	0	1	78.0	99.3	-6.5	91	4	1,000	100	0.0	1.0
C / 5.5	10.1	1.11	13.84	9	2	97	0	1	78.0	105.8	-6.2	94	4	5,000,000	0	0.0	0.0
C / 4.7	14.4	0.93	20.24	58	1	98	0	1	80.0	131.2	-11.3	72	8	1,000	100	5.3	2.0
C / 4.7	14.5	0.93	18.90	48	1	98	0	1	80.0	125.8	-11.5	64	8	1,000	100	0.0	5.0
C / 4.7	14.4	0.93	18.89	6	1	98	0	1	80.0	126.2	-11.5	65	8	1,000	100	0.0	2.0
C / 4.7	14.4	0.93	20.66	9	1	98	0	1	80.0	133.1	-11.3	74	8	5,000,000	0	0.0	0.0
C / 5.3	11.6	0.73	20.76	284	3	96	0	1	14.0	109.1	-8.1	90	N/A	1,000	100	5.3	2.0
C / 4.8	11.6	0.73	19.19	258	3	96	0	1	14.0	104.2	-8.4	85	N/A	1,000	100	0.0	5.0
C / 4.8	11.6	0.73	19.21	37	3	96	0	1	14.0	104.4	-8.3	86	N/A	1,000	100	0.0	2.0
C / 5.4	11.6	0.73	21.26	57	3	96	0	1	14.0	110.7	-8.1	91	N/A	5,000,000	0	0.0	2.0
B+ / 9.4	6.1	1.21	19.64	487	13	67	18	2	24.0	65.3	-6.7	87	9	1,000	100	5.3	1.0
B+ / 9.4	6.1	1.21	19.70	309	13	67	18	2	24.0	61.4	-6.9	82	16	1,000	100	0.0	5.0
B+ / 9.4	6.1	1.21	19.57	40	13	67	18	2	24.0	61.5	-6.9	82	9	1,000	100	0.0	1.0
B+ / 9.4	6.1	1.21	19.66	58	13	67	18	2	24.0	66.5	-6.7	88	9	5,000,000	0	0.0	0.0
B / 8.6	8.2	1.06	11.14	25	1	98	0	1	2.0	70.1	-9.7	60	7	1,000	100	5.3	1.0
B / 8.6	8.2	1.06	10.86	116	1	98	0	1	2.0	66.0	-9.8	51	7	1,000	100	0.0	5.0
B / 8.5	8.2	1.06	10.84	30	1	98	0	1	2.0	66.3	-9.9	50	7	1,000	100	0.0	1.0
B / 8.6	8.2	1.06	11.24	18	1	98	0	1	2.0	71.5	-9.7	63	7	5,000,000	0	0.0	0.0
B- / 7.6	8.2	0.96	17.80	43	2	97	0	1	82.0	58.4	-9.7	63	N/A	1,000	100	5.3	1.0
B- / 7.6	8.2	0.96	16.68	54	2	97	0	1	82.0	54.6	-9.8	55	N/A	1,000	100	0.0	5.0
B- / 7.6	8.2	0.97	16.65	6	2	97	0	1	82.0	54.7	-9.8	54	N/A	1,000	100	0.0	1.0
B- / 7.6	8.2	0.96	18.19	11	2	97	0	1	82.0	59.6	-9.6	66	N/A	5,000,000	0	0.0	0.0
C+ / 5.8	10.1	0.85	19.59	364	5	94	0	1	77.0	110.5	-10.8	76	N/A	0	0	0.0	0.0
C+ / 6.0	8.3	0.69	14.44	630	1	97	0	2	20.0	75.9	-5.0	47	9	1,000	100	5.3	1.0
C+ / 6.1	8.3	0.69	14.52	152	1	97	0	2	20.0	75.7	-5.2	48	18	1,000	100	0.0	5.0
C+ / 6.1	8.3	0.69	14.50	8	1	97	0	2	20.0	71.9	-5.2	39	9	1,000	100	0.0	1.0

					PERFORMANCE							
99 Pct = Best 0 Pct = Worst			Overall Weiss		Perfor- mance	Total Return % through 6/30/06					Incl. in Returns	
Fund Type	Fund Name	Ticker Symbol	Investment Rating	Phone	Rating/Pts	3 Mo	6 Mo	1Yr / Pct	Annualized 3Yr / Pct	5Yr / Pct	Dividend Yield	Expense Ratio
UT	Morgan Stanley Utilities Fund D	UTLDX	C	(800) 869-6397	C+ / 6.4	3.76	4.75	7.44 /29	15.39 /61	3.82 /44	2.47	0.78
GI	Morgan Stanley Value Fund A	VLUAX	B	(800) 869-6397	C / 4.9	1.08	3.84	9.37 /42	13.94 /54	3.81 /44	1.89	0.97
GI	Morgan Stanley Value Fund B	VLUBX	B-	(800) 869-6397	C / 4.5	0.82	3.42	8.46 /36	13.06 /49	3.03 /37	1.09	1.72
GI	Morgan Stanley Value Fund C	VLUCX	B	(800) 869-6397	C / 5.2	0.82	3.50	8.55 /37	13.08 /49	3.04 /37	1.17	1.71
GI	Morgan Stanley Value Fund D	VLUDX	B+	(800) 869-6397	C+ / 5.9	1.07	3.94	9.53 /44	14.21 /55	4.06 /46	2.15	0.72
BA	Mosaic Balanced Fund	BHBFX	D-	(800) 336-3063	E+ / 0.7	-0.94	1.75	1.69 / 4	4.96 / 4	2.65 /33	1.07	1.21
GI	Mosaic Foresight Fund	GEWWX	D	(800) 336-3063	E+ / 0.7	-1.44	2.85	3.62 / 9	4.60 / 3	1.27 /22	0.24	1.25
GR	Mosaic Investors Fund	MINVX	D	(800) 336-3063	D / 1.8	-1.38	2.92	3.36 / 8	7.45 /12	2.39 /31	0.29	0.94
MC	Mosaic Mid-Cap Growth Fd	GTSGX	C	(800) 336-3063	C / 4.5	-2.52	3.42	5.08 /15	12.42 /45	8.27 /73	0.00	1.25
GR	MP 63 Fund	DRIPX	D	(877) 676-3386	C- / 3.1	-1.65	2.04	4.00 /11	10.77 /33	4.93 /54	0.00	1.02
GI	MSIF Inc Lrge Cap Rel Value Port A	MSIVX	B+	(800) 354-8185	C+ / 6.0	0.13	3.02	10.85 /53	15.03 /59	4.37 /49	1.27	0.68
GI	MSIF Inc Lrge Cap Rel Value Port B	IVABX	C	(800) 354-8185	C+ / 5.8	-0.02	2.86	10.59 /51	14.68 /57	4.12 /47	1.04	0.93
GR	MSIF Inc US Large Cap Growth Port	MSEQX	D+	(800) 354-8185	C- / 3.2	-3.47	-2.98	12.08 /60	10.86 /34	1.07 /21	0.22	0.65
GR	MSIF Inc US Large Cap Growth Port	MSEGX	D	(800) 354-8185	C- / 3.0	-3.52	-3.07	11.87 /59	10.59 /32	0.82 /19	0.14	0.90
FO	MSIF Inc. Active Intl Allocation A	MSACX	A-	(800) 354-8185	B+ / 8.7	-0.51	8.85	27.34 /92	22.07 /85	9.74 /80	1.07	0.80
FO	MSIF Inc. Active Intl Allocation B	MSIBX	A-	(800) 354-8185	B+ / 8.6	-0.58	8.62	27.07 /91	21.74 /84	9.43 /78	0.80	1.05
EM	MSIF Inc. Emerging Markets A	MGEMX	C+	(800) 354-8185	A+ / 9.7	-4.83	8.75	38.49 /98	35.21 /98	21.23 /97	1.26	1.41
EM	MSIF Inc. Emerging Markets B	MMKBX	C+	(800) 354-8185	A+ / 9.7	-4.89	8.61	38.13 /97	34.87 /98	20.94 /97	1.07	1.66
AG	MSIF Inc. Focus Equity A	MSAGX	D+	(800) 354-8185	C- / 3.8	-3.27	-1.83	14.00 /68	11.56 /40	1.91 /26	0.15	0.79
AG	MSIF Inc. Focus Equity B	MAEBX	D+	(800) 354-8185	C- / 3.6	-3.41	-2.01	13.66 /67	11.29 /38	1.66 /25	0.16	1.04
GL	MSIF Inc. Global Franchise B	MSFBX	A	(800) 354-8185	B- / 7.4	2.32	7.85	16.25 /75	17.36 /70	--	1.51	1.32
GL	MSIF Inc. Global Value Equity A	MSGEX	B	(800) 354-8185	C+ / 6.2	-0.11	4.71	12.12 /60	15.25 /60	5.08 /55	1.61	0.90
GL	MSIF Inc. Global Value Equity B	MIGEX	B	(800) 354-8185	C+ / 6.1	-0.22	4.52	11.84 /59	14.94 /58	4.80 /52	1.32	1.15
FO	● MSIF Inc. International Equity A	MSIQX	A-	(800) 354-8185	B / 8.0	0.92	8.26	17.03 /77	19.62 /78	11.46 /85	1.48	0.93
FO	● MSIF Inc. International Equity B	MIQBX	A-	(800) 354-8185	B / 7.9	0.83	8.12	16.73 /76	19.32 /77	11.22 /84	1.27	1.18
FO	MSIF Inc. International Magnum A	MSIMX	B+	(800) 354-8185	B / 8.2	-0.21	8.22	22.68 /85	20.34 /81	7.72 /70	1.11	1.00
FO	MSIF Inc. International Magnum B	MIMBX	B+	(800) 354-8185	B / 8.1	-0.21	8.17	22.51 /85	20.07 /79	7.44 /69	0.90	1.25
FO	MSIF Inc. International Sm-Cap A	MSISX	B+	(800) 354-8185	A- / 9.2	-3.34	6.84	18.07 /79	26.87 /93	17.22 /94	1.59	1.10
RE	MSIF Inc. Intl Real Estate A	MSUAX	A+	(800) 354-8185	A+ / 9.8	-1.19	16.07	29.15 /94	35.81 /98	27.26 /99	1.20	1.00
RE	MSIF Inc. Intl Real Estate B	IERBX	A+	(800) 354-8185	A+ / 9.8	-1.26	15.96	28.87 /94	35.44 /98	26.95 /99	1.15	1.25
SC	MSIF Inc. Small Company Growth A	MSSGX	C	(800) 354-8185	B- / 7.3	-8.55	2.95	11.03 /54	19.38 /77	8.00 /72	0.00	1.04
SC	MSIF Inc. Small Company Growth B	MSSMX	C	(800) 354-8185	B- / 7.2	-8.60	2.76	10.77 /52	19.10 /76	7.64 /70	0.00	1.29
RE	MSIF Inc. US Real Estate A	MSUSX	B+	(800) 354-8185	A+ / 9.6	0.76	15.22	25.08 /89	30.91 /96	21.16 /97	1.43	0.89
RE	MSIF Inc. US Real Estate B	MUSDX	B+	(800) 354-8185	A+ / 9.6	0.67	15.07	24.77 /88	30.59 /96	20.81 /97	1.24	1.14
BA	MSIF Trust Balanced Adv	MBAAX	C	(800) 354-8185	D+ / 2.7	-1.48	0.80	7.76 /31	8.93 /20	3.57 /42	1.96	0.84
BA	MSIF Trust Balanced Inst	MPBAX	C	(800) 354-8185	D+ / 2.9	-1.42	1.02	8.10 /33	9.20 /22	3.85 /44	2.20	0.59
BA	MSIF Trust Balanced Inv	MABIX	C	(800) 354-8185	D+ / 2.8	-1.46	0.90	7.95 /32	9.05 /21	3.63 /42	2.06	0.74
MC	MSIF Trust Mid Cap Growth Adv	MACGX	B	(800) 354-8185	B+ / 8.3	-4.99	3.59	18.61 /80	21.18 /83	4.53 /50	0.00	0.89
MC	MSIF Trust Mid Cap Growth Inst	MPEGX	B	(800) 354-8185	B+ / 8.4	-4.94	3.70	18.91 /80	21.48 /84	4.79 /52	0.00	0.64
MC	MSIF Trust Mid Cap Value Adv	MMCAX	A-	(800) 354-8185	B- / 7.5	-1.82	5.51	15.86 /74	18.02 /73	5.46 /58	0.37	1.15
MC	MSIF Trust Mid Cap Value Inst	MPMVX	A	(800) 354-8185	B / 7.6	-1.77	5.65	16.11 /75	18.31 /74	5.74 /59	0.72	0.90
MC	MSIF Trust Mid Cap Value Inv	MPMIX	A	(800) 354-8185	B / 7.6	-1.82	5.56	15.94 /74	18.13 /73	5.56 /58	0.59	1.05
SC	MSIF Trust U.S Small Cap Value Adv	MCVAX	A-	(800) 354-8185	B / 7.7	-2.59	8.57	13.62 /67	19.27 /77	9.13 /77	0.42	1.06
SC	● MSIF Trust U.S Small Cap Value Inst	MPSCX	B	(800) 354-8185	B / 7.8	-2.50	8.72	13.91 /68	19.58 /78	9.41 /78	0.66	0.81
GR	MSIF Trust Value Adv	MPVAX	B	(800) 354-8185	C+ / 6.1	1.04	3.94	9.60 /44	14.58 /57	5.52 /58	1.69	0.86
GR	MSIF Trust Value Inst	MPVLX	B	(800) 354-8185	C+ / 6.2	1.11	4.07	9.81 /46	14.84 /58	5.78 /60	1.93	0.65
GR	MSIF Trust Value Inv	MPVIX	B	(800) 354-8185	C+ / 6.1	1.07	4.02	9.70 /45	14.70 /57	5.64 /59	1.79	0.80
BA	MTB Balanced A	ARBAX	D-	(800) 836-2211	E- / 0.1	-3.18	-0.38	2.54 / 6	3.93 / 2	0.27 /17	1.60	1.11
BA	MTB Balanced B	ABLDX	D-	(800) 836-2211	E- / 0.1	-3.29	-0.67	1.87 / 4	3.22 / 1	-0.44 /14	0.96	1.81
BA	MTB Balanced I	ARGIX	D-	(800) 836-2211	E / 0.5	-3.06	-0.30	2.73 / 6	4.14 / 2	0.43 /17	1.96	0.95
GI	MTB Equity Income A	ARERX	E+	(800) 836-2211	C- / 3.3	-0.12	5.88	11.67 /58	10.70 /33	2.48 /32	1.47	1.23
GI	MTB Equity Income I	AREIX	D-	(800) 836-2211	C / 4.5	0.07	6.05	12.01 /60	10.94 /35	2.67 /33	1.76	1.94

● Denotes fund is closed to new investors
* Denotes fund is included in Section II

Risk Rating/Pts	Standard Deviation	Beta	NAV As of 6/30/06	Total $(Mil)	Cash %	Stocks %	Bonds %	Other %	Portfolio Turnover Ratio	Last Bull Market Return	Last Bear Market Return	Manager Quality Pct	Manager Tenure (Years)	Initial Purch. $	Additional Purch. $	Front End Load	Back End Load
C+ / 6.0	8.3	0.69	14.42	6	1	97	0	2	20.0	77.2	-4.9	52	9	5,000,000	0	0.0	0.0
B+ / 9.2	7.8	0.92	14.05	74	2	97	0	1	31.0	80.1	-9.6	85	3	1,000	100	5.3	1.0
B+ / 9.2	7.8	0.93	13.59	200	2	97	0	1	31.0	75.8	-9.7	79	3	1,000	100	0.0	5.0
B+ / 9.2	7.8	0.92	13.59	21	2	97	0	1	31.0	76.0	-9.7	79	3	1,000	100	0.0	1.0
B+ / 9.2	7.8	0.92	14.23	12	2	97	0	1	31.0	81.4	-9.5	87	3	5,000,000	0	0.0	0.0
B- / 7.4	4.7	0.89	17.60	16	1	64	33	2	34.0	29.0	-5.9	34	14	1,000	50	0.0	0.0
B / 8.7	5.9	0.67	12.97	4	3	96	0	1	122.0	29.6	-6.5	23	10	1,000	50	0.0	0.0
B- / 7.6	6.8	0.82	19.36	124	2	97	0	1	34.0	45.9	-11.3	34	N/A	1,000	50	0.0	0.0
B- / 7.7	8.3	0.69	12.40	135	3	96	0	1	46.0	69.9	-7.9	49	N/A	1,000	50	0.0	0.0
C+ / 6.4	7.0	0.82	12.48	38	0	99	0	1	6.6	61.1	-9.4	69	N/A	1,000	100	0.0	2.0
B+ / 9.0	7.6	0.92	11.40	187	3	96	0	1	46.0	86.2	-9.7	90	3	500,000	1,000	0.0	2.0
C+ / 6.3	7.6	0.93	11.38	60	3	96	0	1	46.0	84.9	-9.9	89	3	100,000	1,000	0.0	2.0
C+ / 6.5	11.2	1.27	18.91	901	2	97	0	1	106.0	65.9	-10.5	29	N/A	500,000	1,000	0.0	0.0
C+ / 6.4	11.2	1.27	18.62	37	2	97	0	1	106.0	64.6	-10.6	27	N/A	100,000	1,000	0.0	2.0
C+ / 6.9	10.6	1.03	13.53	871	8	91	0	1	24.0	119.4	-8.2	29	14	500,000	1,000	0.0	2.0
C+ / 6.9	10.6	1.03	13.73	3	8	91	0	1	24.0	117.3	-8.3	27	14	100,000	1,000	0.0	2.0
C- / 3.6	19.0	1.16	27.58	1,845	0	98	0	2	59.0	228.1	-7.9	13	5	500,000	1,000	0.0	2.0
C- / 3.6	19.0	1.16	27.24	157	0	98	0	2	59.0	225.1	-8.0	12	5	100,000	1,000	0.0	2.0
C+ / 6.3	11.6	1.30	14.51	53	0	99	0	1	78.0	74.1	-9.8	32	N/A	500,000	1,000	0.0	0.0
C+ / 6.2	11.6	1.30	14.16	13	0	99	0	1	78.0	72.9	-10.0	30	N/A	100,000	1,000	0.0	2.0
B / 8.4	8.2	0.59	16.77	4	4	94	0	2	19.0	88.4	-5.2	79	4	100,000	1,000	0.0	2.0
B / 8.3	8.0	0.75	18.69	87	2	97	0	1	29.0	86.8	-12.8	28	14	500,000	1,000	0.0	2.0
B / 8.3	8.0	0.75	18.49	23	2	97	0	1	29.0	85.2	-12.9	26	14	100,000	1,000	0.0	2.0
B- / 7.5	9.1	0.87	22.02	106	2	97	0	1	28.0	106.5	-9.0	38	11	500,000	1,000	0.0	2.0
B- / 7.5	9.1	0.87	21.83	1,208	2	97	0	1	28.0	104.9	-9.1	36	17	100,000	1,000	0.0	2.0
C+ / 6.8	9.9	0.96	14.08	106	8	90	0	2	32.0	109.1	-10.0	29	10	500,000	1,000	0.0	2.0
C+ / 6.8	9.9	0.96	14.03	2	8	90	0	2	32.0	107.3	-10.0	27	10	100,000	1,000	0.0	2.0
C+ / 5.8	10.9	0.87	25.79	1,482	2	98	0	0	47.0	168.7	-2.5	92	14	500,000	1,000	0.0	2.0
B- / 7.5	12.6	0.44	27.44	472	5	94	0	1	57.0	201.1	-0.4	99	7	500,000	1,000	0.0	2.0
B- / 7.6	12.5	0.44	27.46	25	5	94	0	1	57.0	198.6	-0.4	99	7	100,000	1,000	0.0	2.0
C / 5.0	14.1	0.91	13.26	1,071	2	97	0	1	73.0	132.1	-11.2	77	2	500,000	1,000	0.0	2.0
C / 5.0	14.0	0.90	12.65	910	2	97	0	1	73.0	130.1	-11.3	75	2	100,000	1,000	0.0	2.0
C / 5.5	15.1	0.90	26.88	1,392	3	96	0	1	33.0	150.8	N/A	98	11	500,000	1,000	0.0	2.0
C / 5.5	15.1	0.90	26.63	178	3	96	0	1	33.0	148.8	-0.1	97	10	100,000	1,000	0.0	2.0
B+ / 9.2	5.5	1.12	12.15	36	4	65	30	1	38.0	48.8	-6.2	64	4	500,000	1,000	0.0	0.0
B+ / 9.3	5.5	1.12	12.18	255	4	65	30	1	38.0	50.0	-6.2	67	4	5,000,000	1,000	0.0	0.0
B+ / 9.2	5.5	1.12	12.16	4	4	65	30	1	38.0	49.3	-6.3	65	4	1,000,000	1,000	0.0	0.0
C+ / 6.0	12.5	1.09	25.11	1,048	2	98	0	0	29.0	128.3	-8.8	70	4	500,000	1,000	0.0	0.0
C+ / 6.0	12.5	1.09	25.78	982	2	98	0	0	29.0	130.1	-8.8	72	4	5,000,000	1,000	0.0	0.0
B / 8.1	10.2	0.85	27.56	13	4	95	0	1	33.0	112.7	-11.1	78	8	500,000	1,000	0.0	0.0
B / 8.1	10.2	0.85	27.68	114	4	95	0	1	33.0	114.3	-11.1	79	12	5,000,000	1,000	0.0	0.0
B / 8.1	10.2	0.85	27.54	2	4	95	0	1	33.0	113.5	-11.1	78	10	1,000,000	1,000	0.0	0.0
B- / 7.6	12.1	0.78	25.21	26	3	96	0	1	28.0	114.9	-10.7	89	3	500,000	1,000	0.0	2.0
C+ / 6.7	12.0	0.77	25.32	744	3	96	0	1	28.0	116.6	-10.7	91	3	5,000,000	1,000	0.0	2.0
B / 8.4	7.9	0.93	17.70	175	2	96	0	2	13.0	84.4	-10.0	88	N/A	500,000	1,000	0.0	0.0
B / 8.3	7.9	0.93	17.72	297	2	96	0	2	13.0	86.0	-10.0	89	22	5,000,000	1,000	0.0	0.0
B / 8.4	7.9	0.93	17.75	60	2	96	0	2	13.0	85.1	-10.0	89	N/A	1,000,000	1,000	0.0	0.0
B- / 7.8	6.3	1.22	13.26	20	0	74	27	0	22.0	32.5	-5.8	16	N/A	500	25	5.5	1.0
B- / 7.8	6.2	1.21	13.28	8	0	74	27	0	22.0	29.6	-5.9	13	N/A	500	25	0.0	5.0
B- / 7.8	6.2	1.21	13.30	19	0	74	27	0	22.0	33.3	-5.8	18	N/A	100,000	150,000	0.0	0.0
C- / 3.4	7.5	0.90	8.39	5	2	97	0	1	46.0	60.8	-9.7	61	3	500	25	5.5	0.0
C- / 3.6	7.5	0.90	8.35	50	2	97	0	1	46.0	61.8	-9.7	63	3	100,000	150,000	0.0	0.0

Fund Type	Fund Name	Ticker Symbol	Overall Weiss Investment Rating	Phone	Performance Rating/Pts	3 Mo	6 Mo	1Yr / Pct	Annualized 3Yr / Pct	5Yr / Pct	Dividend Yield	Expense Ratio
GR	MTB Equity Index A	ARKAX	C-	(800) 836-2211	D+ / 2.8	-1.53	2.58	8.01 /33	10.51 /31	1.87 /26	1.26	0.56
GR	MTB Equity Index I	ARKEX	C	(800) 836-2211	C- / 3.9	-1.45	2.72	8.39 /36	10.81 /34	2.18 /29	1.58	0.28
FO	MTB International Equity A	GVIEX	B	(800) 836-2211	B / 7.7	-0.34	9.07	23.30 /86	19.27 /77	8.95 /76	1.28	1.55
FO	MTB International Equity B	VIEFX	B-	(800) 836-2211	B- / 7.5	-0.52	8.60	22.49 /85	18.40 /74	8.07 /72	0.93	2.26
FO	MTB International Equity I	MVIEX	U	(800) 836-2211	U /	-0.26	9.13	23.53 /87	--	--	1.40	1.46
GR	MTB Large Cap Growth A	VLCPX	D-	(800) 836-2211	E / 0.3	-3.86	-0.25	4.12 /11	4.75 / 3	-1.05 /12	0.07	1.31
GR	MTB Large Cap Growth B	VLGRX	D-	(800) 836-2211	E- / 0.2	-3.93	-0.53	3.42 / 9	3.95 / 2	-1.87 / 9	0.00	2.07
GR	MTB Large Cap Growth I	MLGIX	U	(800) 836-2211	U /	-3.74	-0.13	4.36 /12	--	--	0.18	1.14
GR	MTB Large Cap Stock A	AVERX	E+	(800) 836-2211	E+ / 0.7	-3.73	-0.84	2.24 / 5	7.54 /13	0.23 /16	1.23	1.26
GR	MTB Large Cap Stock B	AVEBX	E+	(800) 836-2211	E+ / 0.6	-3.81	-1.14	1.55 / 3	6.71 / 9	-0.51 /14	0.71	2.00
GR	MTB Large Cap Stock I	MVEFX	E	(800) 836-2211	D / 1.6	-3.52	-0.60	2.50 / 6	7.71 /13	0.39 /17	1.42	1.10
GR	MTB Large Cap Value A	VEINX	C+	(800) 836-2211	C / 5.2	0.76	5.14	15.36 /73	13.74 /53	3.08 /38	0.79	1.12
GR	MTB Large Cap Value B	VLCVX	C+	(800) 836-2211	C / 4.6	0.50	4.60	14.22 /69	12.75 /47	2.14 /28	0.00	1.92
GR	MTB Large Cap Value I	MLCVX	U	(800) 836-2211	U /	0.74	5.03	15.29 /73	--	--	0.78	1.03
MC	MTB Mid Cap Growth A	AMCRX	C-	(800) 836-2211	C / 5.1	-6.01	2.22	9.98 /47	15.32 /60	5.41 /57	0.00	1.29
MC	MTB Mid Cap Growth I	ARMEX	C	(800) 836-2211	C+ / 6.1	-5.95	2.33	10.17 /48	15.51 /61	5.56 /58	0.00	1.13
MC	MTB Mid Cap Stock A	VMCSX	C-	(800) 836-2211	C+ / 5.7	-2.71	4.78	12.05 /60	15.60 /62	6.36 /63	0.00	1.19
MC	MTB Mid Cap Stock B	VMCPX	D+	(800) 836-2211	C / 5.3	-2.89	4.31	11.04 /54	14.60 /57	5.42 /57	0.00	2.03
MC	MTB Mid Cap Stock I	MMCIX	U	(800) 836-2211	U /	-2.71	4.71	11.97 /59	--	--	0.00	1.15
AA	MTB Mngd Alloc-Aggressive Gr A	VMAGX	D+	(800) 836-2211	D+ / 2.3	-2.86	2.82	8.97 /40	9.81 /26	2.86 /35	0.72	1.00
AA	MTB Mngd Alloc-Aggressive Gr B	VMABX	D+	(800) 836-2211	D / 2.1	-3.02	2.57	8.34 /35	9.18 /22	--	0.43	1.57
AA	MTB Mngd Alloc-Conserv Gr A	VMCGX	D+	(800) 836-2211	E- / 0.2	-0.40	1.08	2.67 / 6	3.19 / 1	2.79 /35	1.92	1.00
AA	MTB Mngd Alloc-Conserv Gr B	VMCBX	D+	(800) 836-2211	E- / 0.1	-0.54	0.89	2.20 / 5	2.62 / 1	--	1.44	1.56
AA	MTB Mngd Alloc-Moderate Gr A	VMMGX	D+	(800) 836-2211	E+ / 0.8	-1.93	1.90	5.73 /19	6.65 / 9	2.84 /35	0.95	1.00
AA	MTB Mngd Alloc-Moderate Gr B	VMMBX	D	(800) 836-2211	E+ / 0.6	-2.05	1.62	5.07 /15	5.88 / 6	--	0.55	1.75
GR	MTB Multi Cap Growth A	ARGAX	D-	(800) 836-2211	D- / 1.4	-4.52	1.60	7.51 /29	8.57 /18	-2.63 / 6	0.11	1.20
GR	MTB Multi Cap Growth B	ACPLX	D-	(800) 836-2211	D- / 1.2	-4.68	1.28	6.73 /25	7.83 /14	-3.31 / 5	0.00	1.90
GR	MTB Multi Cap Growth I	ARCGX	D	(800) 836-2211	D+ / 2.5	-4.51	1.71	7.63 /30	8.76 /19	-2.48 / 7	0.27	1.04
SC	MTB Small Cap Growth A	ARPAX	D	(800) 836-2211	C+ / 6.6	-5.77	11.43	22.05 /84	16.62 /66	3.85 /44	0.00	1.33
SC	MTB Small Cap Growth B	ASEBX	D	(800) 836-2211	C+ / 6.4	-5.91	11.00	21.10 /83	15.76 /62	4.25 /48	0.00	2.06
SC	MTB Small Cap Growth C	ARPCX	D+	(800) 836-2211	B- / 7.1	-5.69	11.53	22.28 /85	16.26 /65	4.46 /50	0.00	2.06
SC	MTB Small Cap Growth I	ARPEX	D+	(800) 836-2211	B- / 7.4	-5.72	11.51	22.17 /85	16.80 /67	5.19 /56	0.00	1.17
SC	MTB Small Cap Stock A	GVAGX	C-	(800) 836-2211	C+ / 5.9	-6.54	5.21	11.67 /58	16.27 /65	9.99 /80	0.00	1.30
SC	MTB Small Cap Stock B	VSCSX	D+	(800) 836-2211	C+ / 5.6	-6.60	4.90	10.90 /53	15.43 /61	9.15 /77	0.00	2.03
SC	MTB Small Cap Stock I	MSCIX	U	(800) 836-2211	U /	-6.45	5.33	11.82 /58	--	--	0.00	1.28
* GI	Muhlenkamp Fund	MUHLX	C	(800) 860-3863	C / 5.4	-5.47	-3.74	0.37 / 2	16.44 /65	8.70 /75	0.93	1.06
BA	Munder Asset Allocation Fd-Bal A	MUBAX	C-	(800) 438-5789	D / 2.2	-1.09	2.72	7.18 /27	10.16 /28	4.67 /52	1.12	1.52
BA	Munder Asset Allocation Fd-Bal B	MUBBX	C-	(800) 438-5789	D / 2.1	-1.29	2.37	6.36 /22	9.35 /23	3.91 /45	0.45	2.27
BA	Munder Asset Allocation Fd-Bal C	MUBCX	C	(800) 438-5789	D+ / 2.6	-1.28	2.36	6.34 /22	9.34 /23	3.91 /45	0.45	2.27
BA	Munder Asset Allocation Fd-Bal K	MUBKX	C	(800) 438-5789	C- / 3.1	-1.10	2.65	7.13 /27	10.15 /28	4.66 /51	1.19	1.52
BA	Munder Asset Allocation Fd-Bal Y	MUBYX	C	(800) 438-5789	C- / 3.3	-1.03	2.86	7.40 /29	10.45 /30	4.94 /54	1.43	1.27
HL	Munder Framlington Healthcare A	MFHAX	E	(800) 438-5789	D- / 1.0	-6.46	-7.53	-0.80 / 1	10.11 /28	-1.43 /10	0.00	1.78
HL	Munder Framlington Healthcare B	MFHBX	E	(800) 438-5789	E+ / 0.9	-6.63	-7.88	-1.52 / 1	9.29 /23	-2.16 / 8	0.00	2.53
HL	Munder Framlington Healthcare C	MFHCX	E	(800) 438-5789	D- / 1.4	-6.63	-7.85	-1.52 / 1	9.30 /23	-2.17 / 8	0.00	2.53
HL	Munder Framlington Healthcare K	MFHKX	D	(800) 438-5789	D / 2.0	-6.47	-7.54	-0.84 / 1	10.11 /28	-1.45 /10	0.00	1.78
HL	Munder Framlington Healthcare Y	MFHYX	E+	(800) 438-5789	D / 2.2	-6.40	-7.41	-0.58 / 1	10.39 /30	-1.18 /11	0.00	1.53
TC	Munder Future Technology A	MTFAX	E-	(800) 438-5789	E- / 0.1	-10.78	-7.61	2.82 / 7	3.74 / 2	-9.60 / 0	0.00	2.42
TC	Munder Future Technology B	MTFBX	E-	(800) 438-5789	E- / 0.0	-11.05	-8.22	1.76 / 4	2.96 / 1	-10.31 / 0	0.00	3.17
TC	Munder Future Technology C	MTFTX	E-	(800) 438-5789	E- / 0.1	-11.11	-8.24	1.63 / 3	2.94 / 1	-10.36 / 0	0.00	3.17
TC	Munder Future Technology Y	MTFYX	E-	(800) 438-5789	E- / 0.2	-10.86	-7.59	3.08 / 8	4.04 / 2	-9.36 / 0	0.00	2.17
IX	Munder Index 500 A	MUXAX	C-	(800) 438-5789	D+ / 2.9	-1.60	2.42	7.95 /32	10.52 /31	1.83 /26	1.28	0.67
IX	Munder Index 500 B	MUXBX	C-	(800) 438-5789	C- / 3.0	-1.66	2.29	7.72 /31	10.25 /29	1.56 /24	1.06	0.92

● Denotes fund is closed to new investors
* Denotes fund is included in Section II

RISK			NET ASSETS		ASSET					BULL / BEAR		FUND MANAGER		MINIMUMS		LOADS	
	3 Year		NAV						Portfolio	Last Bull	Last Bear	Manager	Manager	Initial	Additional	Front	Back
Risk Rating/Pts	Standard Deviation	Beta	As of 6/30/06	Total $(Mil)	Cash %	Stocks %	Bonds %	Other %	Turnover Ratio	Market Return	Market Return	Quality Pct	Tenure (Years)	Purch. $	Purch. $	End Load	End Load
B /8.4	7.6	0.99	10.56	5	N/A	100	0	N/A	12.0	60.9	-9.7	48	8	500	25	5.5	0.0
B /8.5	7.7	1.01	10.56	75	N/A	100	0	N/A	12.0	62.2	-9.7	51	N/A	100,000	150,000	0.0	0.0
C+ /6.4	9.7	0.92	11.67	11	1	98	0	1	107.0	106.7	-10.0	27	7	500	25	5.5	1.0
C+ /6.3	9.7	0.92	11.37	1	1	98	0	1	107.0	101.9	-10.3	23	7	500	25	0.0	5.0
U /	N/A	N/A	11.59	148	1	98	0	1	107.0	N/A	N/A	N/A	7	100,000	150,000	0.0	0.0
B- /7.6	8.4	1.01	7.97	3	0	99	0	1	26.0	34.6	-9.1	9	N/A	500	25	5.5	1.0
B- /7.5	8.4	1.02	7.57	1	0	99	0	1	26.0	31.3	-9.4	7	N/A	500	25	0.0	5.0
U /	N/A	N/A	7.97	45	0	99	0	1	26.0	N/A	N/A	N/A	N/A	100,000	150,000	0.0	0.0
C+ /6.4	8.3	1.04	8.27	33	1	98	0	1	28.0	49.4	-7.8	21	3	500	25	5.5	1.0
C+ /6.0	8.2	1.04	7.83	8	1	98	0	1	28.0	45.7	-7.9	16	3	500	25	0.0	5.0
C /4.7	8.2	1.04	8.22	260	1	98	0	1	28.0	49.9	-7.7	22	3	100,000	150,000	0.0	0.0
B /8.2	8.8	1.07	12.22	34	6	93	0	1	7.0	78.0	-9.7	74	3	500	25	5.5	0.0
B /8.2	8.8	1.07	12.06	1	6	93	0	1	7.0	73.2	-10.0	65	3	500	25	0.0	5.0
U /	N/A	N/A	12.22	120	6	93	0	1	7.0	N/A	N/A	N/A	3	100,000	150,000	0.0	0.0
C /5.5	13.1	1.16	15.18	7	1	98	0	1	38.0	96.8	-8.3	15	3	500	25	5.5	1.0
C /5.5	13.1	1.16	15.34	77	1	98	0	1	38.0	97.7	-8.2	16	3	100,000	150,000	0.0	0.0
C /5.1	11.0	1.00	15.78	64	1	98	0	1	22.0	80.5	-7.9	33	13	500	25	5.5	1.0
C /4.7	11.0	1.00	14.76	3	1	98	0	1	22.0	75.5	-8.1	26	6	500	25	0.0	5.0
U /	N/A	N/A	15.79	87	1	98	0	1	22.0	N/A	N/A	N/A	3	100,000	150,000	0.0	0.0
B- /7.8	8.2	1.58	10.20	20	3	96	0	1	1.0	59.1	-8.7	45	3	500	25	5.0	1.0
B- /7.7	8.2	1.59	9.97	9	3	96	0	1	1.0	55.9	-8.9	38	4	500	25	0.0	5.0
B+ /9.9	2.7	0.52	9.80	11	7	92	0	1	1.0	16.9	-1.3	36	4	500	25	4.0	1.0
B+ /9.9	2.7	0.52	9.78	3	7	92	0	1	1.0	14.6	-1.5	31	4	500	25	0.0	5.0
B /8.8	5.5	1.11	10.17	41	4	95	0	1	7.0	37.4	-5.2	38	4	500	25	4.5	1.0
B /8.8	5.5	1.11	10.05	22	4	95	0	1	7.0	33.9	-5.4	32	4	500	25	0.0	5.0
C+ /6.6	11.0	1.31	15.84	18	2	97	0	1	54.0	59.7	-7.3	14	3	500	25	5.5	1.0
C+ /6.5	11.0	1.31	15.07	7	2	97	0	1	54.0	56.2	-7.4	11	3	500	25	0.0	5.0
C+ /6.7	11.0	1.31	16.10	21	2	97	0	1	54.0	60.4	-7.1	15	3	100,000	150,000	0.0	0.0
D+ /2.4	21.0	1.32	19.60	54	1	98	0	1	219.0	110.7	-13.7	8	3	500	25	5.5	1.0
D+ /2.5	21.0	1.32	18.77	3	1	98	0	1	219.0	105.8	-13.8	6	3	500	25	0.0	5.0
D+ /2.5	21.0	1.32	19.05	N/A	1	98	0	1	219.0	108.1	-13.8	7	3	500	25	0.0	1.0
D+ /2.4	21.1	1.32	19.95	114	1	98	0	1	219.0	111.5	-13.5	8	3	100,000	150,000	0.0	0.0
C /4.6	16.0	1.08	9.29	5	2	97	0	1	28.0	120.4	-12.8	24	5	500	25	5.5	0.0
C /4.3	15.9	1.07	8.78	1	2	97	0	1	28.0	114.6	-12.9	20	5	500	25	0.0	5.0
U /	N/A	N/A	9.28	171	2	97	0	1	28.0	N/A	N/A	N/A	5	100,000	150,000	0.0	0.0
C+ /6.9	12.9	1.43	81.28	3,056	0	99	0	1	6.1	116.7	-10.3	68	18	1,500	50	0.0	2.0
B+ /9.0	6.6	1.27	12.19	47	0	65	47	0	28.0	53.7	-4.1	68	N/A	2,500	50	5.5	2.0
B+ /9.0	6.6	1.26	12.07	22	0	65	47	0	28.0	50.1	-4.3	60	N/A	2,500	50	0.0	5.0
B+ /9.0	6.6	1.26	12.12	18	0	65	47	0	28.0	50.1	-4.3	60	N/A	2,500	50	0.0	2.0
B+ /9.2	6.6	1.26	12.12	12	0	65	47	0	28.0	53.6	-4.2	68	N/A	0	0	0.0	2.0
B+ /9.0	6.5	1.25	12.13	34	0	65	47	0	28.0	55.0	-4.1	72	N/A	1,000,000	0	0.0	2.0
C /5.0	11.9	0.85	23.59	72	0	99	0	1	59.1	80.7	-11.4	59	N/A	2,500	50	5.5	2.0
C /5.0	11.9	0.85	21.98	46	0	99	0	1	59.1	76.6	-11.5	50	N/A	2,500	50	0.0	5.0
C /5.0	11.9	0.84	21.96	32	0	99	0	1	59.1	76.6	-11.5	50	N/A	2,500	50	0.0	1.0
B- /7.3	11.9	0.85	23.55	N/A	0	99	0	1	59.1	80.8	-11.4	60	N/A	0	0	0.0	0.0
C /5.1	11.9	0.85	24.13	11	0	99	0	1	59.1	82.2	-11.3	62	N/A	1,000,000	0	0.0	0.0
D+ /2.9	16.7	1.83	3.64	81	0	99	0	1	117.0	45.7	-11.4	0	N/A	2,500	50	5.5	2.0
D+ /2.9	16.8	1.84	3.46	20	0	99	0	1	117.0	42.5	-11.7	0	N/A	2,500	50	0.0	5.0
D+ /2.9	16.6	1.81	3.12	28	0	99	0	1	117.0	42.7	-11.8	0	N/A	2,500	50	0.0	2.0
D+ /2.9	16.6	1.82	4.02	1	0	99	0	1	117.0	47.4	-11.6	0	N/A	1,000,000	0	0.0	2.0
B- /7.8	7.7	1.00	26.42	472	3	96	0	1	5.4	61.6	-9.9	47	N/A	2,500	50	2.5	2.0
B- /7.8	7.7	1.00	26.43	80	3	96	0	1	5.4	60.3	-9.9	45	N/A	2,500	50	0.0	3.0

Fund Type	Fund Name	Ticker Symbol	Overall Weiss Investment Rating	Phone	Performance Rating/Pts	3 Mo	6 Mo	1Yr / Pct	Annualized 3Yr / Pct	Annualized 5Yr / Pct	Dividend Yield	Expense Ratio
IX	Munder Index 500 Y	MUXYX	C-	(800) 438-5789	C- / 3.5	-1.53	2.54	8.20 /34	10.79 /34	2.07 /28	1.55	0.42
MC	Munder Instl S&P MidCap Index K	MIMKX	B-	(800) 438-5789	C+ / 6.8	-3.35	3.90	12.11 /60	17.29 /69	8.45 /74	0.68	0.82
MC	Munder Instl S&P MidCap Index Y	MIMIX	B-	(800) 438-5789	B- / 7.0	-3.31	4.07	12.41 /62	17.55 /70	8.71 /75	0.80	0.57
SC	Munder Instl S&P SmCap Index K	MSIKX	B	(800) 438-5789	B / 7.6	-4.80	7.25	13.07 /65	19.49 /78	10.31 /82	0.29	0.79
FO	Munder International Equity A	MUIAX	A-	(800) 438-5789	B+ / 8.6	0.67	10.38	28.77 /93	22.67 /87	9.16 /77	0.79	1.57
FO	Munder International Equity B	MUIEX	A-	(800) 438-5789	B+ / 8.5	0.52	9.97	27.87 /92	21.78 /85	8.37 /73	0.29	2.32
FO	Munder International Equity C	MUICX	A	(800) 438-5789	B+ / 8.7	0.46	9.93	27.80 /92	21.79 /85	8.36 /73	0.28	2.32
FO	Munder International Equity Y	MUIYX	A	(800) 438-5789	A- / 9.0	0.72	10.48	29.11 /94	22.99 /87	9.46 /78	1.05	1.32
TC	Munder Internet Fund A	MNNAX	E-	(800) 438-5789	D- / 1.3	-10.24	-6.63	9.11 /41	9.78 /26	-4.79 / 3	0.00	2.17
TC	Munder Internet Fund B	MNNBX	E-	(800) 438-5789	D- / 1.3	-10.36	-6.96	8.35 /36	8.98 /21	-5.49 / 2	0.00	2.92
TC	Munder Internet Fund C	MNNCX	E-	(800) 438-5789	D / 1.7	-10.36	-6.96	8.34 /35	8.97 /21	-5.50 / 2	0.00	2.92
TC	Munder Internet Fund Y	MNNYX	E-	(800) 438-5789	D+ / 2.3	-10.11	-6.49	9.43 /43	10.06 /28	-4.56 / 3	0.00	1.92
GR	Munder Large Cap Core Growth A	MUSAX	D+	(800) 438-5789	D / 2.0	-3.67	-1.53	4.45 /13	10.77 /33	0.67 /19	0.00	1.53
GR	Munder Large Cap Core Growth B	MUSGX	D+	(800) 438-5789	D / 1.9	-3.84	-1.85	3.61 / 9	9.93 /27	-0.06 /15	0.00	2.28
GR	Munder Large Cap Core Growth C	MUSCX	C-	(800) 438-5789	D+ / 2.3	-3.94	-1.91	3.58 / 9	9.94 /27	-0.07 /15	0.00	2.28
GR	Munder Large Cap Core Growth K	MUSKX	C-	(800) 438-5789	D+ / 2.9	-3.66	-1.52	4.44 /12	10.77 /33	0.69 /19	0.00	1.53
GR	Munder Large Cap Core Growth Y	MUSYX	C-	(800) 438-5789	C- / 3.1	-3.66	-1.47	4.63 /13	11.04 /36	0.93 /20	0.00	1.28
GI	Munder Large Cap Value A	MUGAX	B-	(800) 438-5789	C / 5.1	0.26	4.46	10.08 /47	14.65 /57	5.83 /60	0.63	1.44
GI	Munder Large Cap Value B	MUGBX	B-	(800) 438-5789	C / 5.0	0.07	4.15	9.30 /42	13.84 /53	5.04 /55	0.21	2.19
GI	Munder Large Cap Value C	MUGCX	B	(800) 438-5789	C / 5.4	0.07	4.16	9.31 /42	13.82 /53	5.05 /55	0.21	2.19
GI	Munder Large Cap Value Y	MUGYX	B+	(800) 438-5789	C+ / 6.0	0.32	4.66	10.34 /49	14.95 /59	6.10 /62	0.85	1.19
SC	● Munder Micro-Cap Equity A	MMEAX	A	(800) 438-5789	B+ / 8.7	-2.81	4.97	15.14 /72	25.66 /92	13.18 /89	0.29	1.66
SC	● Munder Micro-Cap Equity B	MMEBX	A-	(800) 438-5789	B+ / 8.6	-2.98	4.58	14.29 /69	24.72 /90	12.35 /87	0.00	2.41
SC	● Munder Micro-Cap Equity C	MMECX	A	(800) 438-5789	B+ / 8.8	-2.98	4.58	14.28 /69	24.71 /90	12.35 /87	0.00	2.41
SC	● Munder Micro-Cap Equity K	MMEKX	A	(800) 438-5789	A- / 9.0	-2.81	4.95	15.11 /72	25.65 /92	13.20 /89	0.30	1.66
SC	● Munder Micro-Cap Equity Y	MMEYX	A	(800) 438-5789	A- / 9.0	-2.75	5.08	15.39 /73	25.97 /92	13.48 /89	0.52	1.41
MC	Munder MidCap Core Growth A	MGOAX	C+	(800) 438-5789	B- / 7.2	-4.43	6.11	12.10 /60	19.97 /79	10.48 /82	0.44	1.27
MC	Munder MidCap Core Growth B	MGROX	C+	(800) 438-5789	B- / 7.1	-4.60	5.74	11.32 /55	19.07 /76	9.66 /79	0.00	2.02
MC	Munder MidCap Core Growth II	MGOTX	B-	(800) 438-5789	B- / 7.4	-4.59	5.73	11.29 /55	19.10 /76	9.68 /79	0.00	2.02
MC	Munder MidCap Core Growth Y	MGOYX	B	(800) 438-5789	B / 7.8	-4.37	6.21	12.41 /62	20.28 /80	10.97 /84	0.70	1.02
EN	Munder Power Plus A	MPFAX	C	(800) 438-5789	A+ / 9.8	2.11	13.92	30.56 /95	36.92 /98	12.26 /87	0.00	1.55
EN	Munder Power Plus B	MPFBX	C	(800) 438-5789	A+ / 9.8	1.89	13.43	29.51 /94	35.91 /98	11.40 /85	0.00	2.30
EN	Munder Power Plus C	MPFTX	C	(800) 438-5789	A+ / 9.8	1.89	13.49	29.57 /94	35.90 /98	11.40 /85	0.00	2.30
RE	Munder Real Estate Equity A	MURAX	C+	(800) 438-5789	B+ / 8.7	-1.01	12.03	17.02 /77	24.47 /90	19.23 /95	2.61	1.49
RE	Munder Real Estate Equity B	MURBX	C+	(800) 438-5789	B+ / 8.6	-1.20	11.54	16.19 /75	23.54 /89	18.33 /95	2.08	2.24
RE	Munder Real Estate Equity C	MURCX	C+	(800) 438-5789	B+ / 8.8	-1.19	11.57	16.08 /75	23.52 /88	18.33 /95	2.07	2.24
RE	Munder Real Estate Equity Y	MURYX	C+	(800) 438-5789	A- / 9.0	-0.95	12.11	17.25 /78	24.77 /91	19.51 /96	2.97	1.24
SC	● Munder Small Cap Value A	MNVAX	B+	(800) 438-5789	B / 8.1	-2.76	6.99	14.10 /69	22.61 /86	15.35 /92	0.53	1.34
SC	● Munder Small Cap Value B	MCVBX	B+	(800) 438-5789	B / 8.0	-2.90	6.60	13.30 /65	21.82 /85	14.57 /91	0.26	2.09
SC	● Munder Small Cap Value C	MCVCX	A-	(800) 438-5789	B / 8.2	-2.95	6.59	13.26 /65	21.81 /85	14.57 /91	0.27	2.09
SC	● Munder Small Cap Value K	MCVKX	A	(800) 438-5789	B+ / 8.4	-2.76	6.99	14.12 /69	22.72 /87	15.43 /92	0.56	1.34
SC	● Munder Small Cap Value Y	MCVYX	A	(800) 438-5789	B+ / 8.5	-2.71	7.13	14.41 /70	23.04 /87	15.71 /93	0.79	1.59
GI	Mutual Beacon A	TEBIX	C+	(800) 342-5236	C+ / 6.0	-0.60	6.61	12.89 /64	15.59 /62	7.55 /69	1.37	1.18
GI	● Mutual Beacon B	TEBBX	C+	(800) 342-5236	C+ / 5.8	-0.73	6.31	12.23 /61	14.86 /58	6.86 /66	0.84	1.84
GI	Mutual Beacon C	TEMEX	B-	(800) 342-5236	C+ / 6.2	-0.78	6.28	12.19 /61	14.85 /58	6.85 /66	0.84	1.84
★ GI	Mutual Beacon Z	BEGRX	B-	(800) 321-8563	C+ / 6.9	-0.57	6.74	13.31 /65	16.00 /63	7.91 /71	1.73	0.84
★ GL	Mutual Discovery A	TEDIX	A+	(800) 342-5236	B / 8.0	-1.56	8.12	19.30 /81	20.58 /81	10.84 /83	1.00	1.42
GL	● Mutual Discovery B	TEDBX	A	(800) 342-5236	B / 7.8	-1.75	7.74	18.51 /80	19.78 /79	10.11 /81	0.49	2.04
GL	Mutual Discovery C	TEDSX	A+	(800) 342-5236	B / 8.1	-1.72	7.77	18.52 /80	19.79 /79	10.12 /81	0.55	2.04
GL	Mutual Discovery R	TEDRX	A+	(800) 342-5236	B+ / 8.3	-1.58	8.04	19.13 /81	20.40 /81	10.68 /83	0.97	1.54
GL	Mutual Discovery Z	MDISX	A+	(800) 321-8563	B+ / 8.4	-1.48	8.31	19.70 /81	20.98 /82	11.22 /84	1.31	1.04
FO	Mutual European A	TEMIX	A+	(800) 342-5236	B+ / 8.4	-2.04	9.02	23.69 /87	22.80 /87	11.96 /87	1.71	1.42

● Denotes fund is closed to new investors
★ Denotes fund is included in Section II

| RISK | | | NET ASSETS | | ASSET | | | | BULL / BEAR | | FUND MANAGER | | MINIMUMS | | LOADS | |
| | 3 Year | | NAV | | | | | | Portfolio | Last Bull | Last Bear | Manager | Manager | Initial | Additional | Front | Back |
Risk Rating/Pts	Standard Deviation	Beta	As of 6/30/06	Total $(Mil)	Cash %	Stocks %	Bonds %	Other %	Turnover Ratio	Market Return	Market Return	Quality Pct	Tenure (Years)	Purch. $	Purch. $	End Load	End Load
B- /7.8	7.6	1.00	26.47	75	3	96	0	1	5.4	62.9	-9.8	51	N/A	1,000,000	0	0.0	2.0
B- /7.8	10.8	1.00	11.02	65	3	96	0	1	17.0	100.1	-9.3	46	N/A	0	0	0.0	2.0
C+ /6.8	10.9	1.00	12.70	24	3	96	0	1	17.0	101.9	-9.3	49	8	1,000,000	0	0.0	2.0
C+ /6.9	13.6	0.92	17.09	113	2	97	0	1	17.0	115.9	-9.8	76	7	0	0	0.0	2.0
B- /7.0	10.4	1.01	17.97	15	0	99	0	1	20.0	126.9	-8.6	36	14	2,500	50	5.5	2.0
C+ /6.9	10.4	1.01	17.32	4	0	99	0	1	20.0	121.4	-8.8	30	14	2,500	50	0.0	5.0
C+ /6.9	10.5	1.02	17.49	4	0	99	0	1	20.0	121.5	-8.8	30	14	2,500	50	0.0	2.0
B- /7.0	10.5	1.02	18.14	102	0	99	0	1	20.0	128.6	-8.6	38	14	1,000,000	0	0.0	2.0
D /1.6	20.3	1.89	19.29	462	2	98	0	0	85.2	112.5	-14.0	3	N/A	2,500	50	5.5	2.0
D- /1.5	20.2	1.89	18.17	52	2	98	0	0	85.2	107.4	-14.1	2	N/A	2,500	50	0.0	5.0
D- /1.5	20.2	1.89	18.18	103	2	98	0	0	85.2	107.6	-14.2	2	N/A	2,500	50	0.0	2.0
D /1.6	20.2	1.89	19.73	6	2	98	0	0	85.2	114.2	-13.9	3	N/A	1,000,000	0	0.0	2.0
B /8.1	8.3	1.00	15.48	29	2	97	0	1	47.0	63.8	-9.7	51	N/A	2,500	50	5.5	2.0
B /8.0	8.2	1.00	13.79	3	2	97	0	1	47.0	59.9	-9.9	41	N/A	2,500	50	0.0	5.0
B /8.0	8.3	1.00	13.90	4	2	97	0	1	47.0	60.0	-9.9	41	N/A	2,500	50	0.0	2.0
B /8.2	8.3	1.00	15.52	49	2	97	0	1	47.0	63.9	-9.7	50	N/A	0	0	0.0	2.0
B /8.1	8.3	1.00	16.06	47	2	97	0	1	47.0	65.1	-9.7	54	N/A	1,000,000	0	0.0	2.0
B /8.8	8.0	0.99	15.89	13	4	95	0	1	48.5	80.2	-8.0	85	N/A	2,500	50	5.5	2.0
B /8.7	8.0	1.00	15.56	4	4	95	0	1	48.5	76.0	-8.1	80	N/A	2,500	50	0.0	5.0
B /8.8	8.0	0.99	15.55	3	4	95	0	1	48.5	76.1	-8.2	80	N/A	2,500	50	0.0	2.0
B /8.8	8.0	1.00	15.92	59	4	95	0	1	48.5	81.7	-7.9	87	N/A	1,000,000	0	0.0	2.0
C+ /6.9	13.9	0.87	45.38	393	3	96	0	1	26.9	162.3	-5.3	98	N/A	2,500	50	5.5	2.0
C+ /6.9	13.9	0.87	42.27	52	3	96	0	1	26.9	156.1	-5.5	97	N/A	2,500	50	0.0	5.0
C+ /6.9	13.9	0.87	42.28	103	3	96	0	1	26.9	156.2	-5.6	97	N/A	2,500	50	0.0	2.0
C+ /6.9	13.9	0.87	45.39	10	3	96	0	1	26.9	162.4	-5.4	98	N/A	0	0	0.0	2.0
B- /7.0	13.9	0.87	46.37	30	3	96	0	1	26.9	164.5	-5.3	98	N/A	1,000,000	0	0.0	2.0
C+ /6.3	12.0	1.06	23.95	1,006	1	98	0	1	65.2	112.8	-6.0	65	N/A	2,500	50	5.5	2.0
C+ /6.2	12.0	1.06	23.01	51	1	98	0	1	65.2	108.0	-6.2	56	N/A	2,500	50	0.0	5.0
C+ /6.2	12.0	1.06	23.06	254	1	98	0	1	65.2	107.9	-6.1	N/A	N/A	2,500	50	0.0	2.0
C+ /6.3	12.1	1.06	24.27	541	1	98	0	1	65.2	114.7	-5.9	67	N/A	1,000,000	0	0.0	2.0
D /2.2	19.9	0.94	17.43	56	0	100	0	0	26.8	194.4	1.3	92	N/A	2,500	50	5.5	2.0
D+ /2.3	19.8	0.94	16.72	43	0	100	0	0	26.8	187.5	1.0	90	N/A	2,500	50	0.0	5.0
D /2.2	19.9	0.94	16.74	23	0	100	0	0	26.8	187.8	1.0	89	N/A	2,500	50	0.0	2.0
C /4.3	16.4	0.98	23.77	10	1	98	0	1	25.9	117.6	0.9	63	N/A	2,500	50	5.5	2.0
C /4.3	16.4	0.98	23.70	3	1	98	0	1	25.9	112.6	0.7	54	N/A	2,500	50	0.0	5.0
C /4.3	16.4	0.98	23.85	3	1	98	0	1	25.9	112.5	0.7	55	N/A	2,500	50	0.0	2.0
C /4.3	16.3	0.98	23.78	58	1	98	0	1	25.9	119.4	0.9	66	N/A	1,000,000	0	0.0	2.0
B- /7.1	13.0	0.82	29.25	527	2	97	0	1	33.8	139.3	-1.7	96	N/A	2,500	50	5.5	2.0
B- /7.0	13.1	0.82	28.10	61	2	97	0	1	33.8	134.5	-1.9	94	N/A	2,500	50	0.0	5.0
B- /7.0	13.1	0.82	28.00	200	2	97	0	1	33.8	134.5	-1.9	94	N/A	2,500	50	0.0	2.0
B- /7.4	13.1	0.82	29.22	60	2	97	0	1	33.8	140.2	-1.7	96	N/A	0	0	0.0	2.0
B- /7.1	13.1	0.82	29.45	364	2	97	0	1	33.8	142.0	-1.7	96	N/A	1,000,000	0	0.0	2.0
B- /7.5	6.7	0.74	16.01	1,782	2	92	4	2	35.4	78.7	-3.9	96	2	1,000	50	5.8	0.0
B- /7.5	6.7	0.74	15.59	186	2	92	4	2	35.4	75.0	-4.1	95	2	1,000	50	0.0	4.0
B- /7.6	6.7	0.74	15.84	725	2	92	4	2	35.4	75.2	-4.1	95	2	1,000	50	0.0	1.0
B- /7.5	6.7	0.74	16.11	3,535	2	92	4	2	35.4	80.7	-3.9	97	2	1,000	50	0.0	0.0
B /8.1	7.6	0.65	27.63	4,695	6	90	2	2	25.7	108.2	-5.2	89	1	1,000	50	5.8	0.0
B /8.1	7.6	0.65	27.04	248	6	90	2	2	25.7	104.0	-5.4	85	1	1,000	50	0.0	4.0
B /8.1	7.6	0.65	27.39	1,803	6	90	2	2	25.7	104.0	-5.3	85	1	1,000	50	0.0	1.0
B /8.1	7.6	0.65	27.44	133	6	90	2	2	25.7	107.2	-5.2	88	1	1,000	50	0.0	0.0
B /8.1	7.6	0.65	27.92	3,396	6	90	2	2	25.7	110.6	-5.1	90	1	1,000	50	0.0	0.0
B /8.1	7.7	0.67	22.48	811	8	90	2	0	29.8	125.6	-6.8	94	N/A	1,000	50	5.8	0.0

								PERFORMANCE						
	99 Pct = Best				Overall				Total Return % through 6/30/06				Incl. in Returns	
	0 Pct = Worst				Weiss		Perfor-					Annualized		Dividend Expense
Fund			Ticker	Investment		mance								
Type	Fund Name		Symbol	Rating	Phone	Rating/Pts	3 Mo	6 Mo	1Yr / Pct	3Yr / Pct	5Yr / Pct	Yield	Ratio
FO	● Mutual European B	TEUBX	A+	(800) 342-5236	B+ / 8.3	-2.23	8.60	22.86 /86	21.99 /85	11.22 /84	1.24	2.04
FO	Mutual European C	TEURX	A+	(800) 342-5236	B+ / 8.5	-2.27	8.63	22.80 /85	21.99 /85	11.22 /84	1.23	2.04
FO	Mutual European Z	MEURX	A+	(800) 321-8563	B+ / 8.8	-1.98	9.15	24.06 /87	23.21 /88	12.34 /87	2.05	1.04
FS	Mutual Financial Svcs A	TFSIX	B-	(800) 342-5236	C+ / 6.7	-4.93	5.15	16.60 /76	17.42 /70	11.83 /86	1.95	1.44
FS	● Mutual Financial Svcs B	TBFSX	B-	(800) 342-5236	C+ / 6.5	-5.07	4.76	15.77 /74	16.65 /67	11.08 /84	1.45	2.11
FS	Mutual Financial Svcs C	TMFSX	B-	(800) 342-5236	C+ / 6.9	-5.06	4.78	15.80 /74	16.65 /67	11.09 /84	1.45	2.11
FS	Mutual Financial Svcs Z	TEFAX	B	(800) 321-8563	B- / 7.4	-4.83	5.31	16.96 /77	17.81 /72	12.19 /87	2.32	1.11
GI	Mutual Qualified A	TEQIX	B	(800) 342-5236	C+ / 6.6	-1.01	6.48	14.38 /70	16.98 /68	8.15 /72	1.49	1.17
GI	● Mutual Qualified B	TEBQX	B	(800) 342-5236	C+ / 6.5	-1.23	6.13	13.60 /67	16.22 /64	7.45 /69	1.00	1.81
GI	Mutual Qualified C	TEMQX	B	(800) 342-5236	C+ / 6.8	-1.16	6.16	13.63 /67	16.23 /64	7.44 /69	1.01	1.81
★ GI	Mutual Qualified Z	MQIFX	A	(800) 321-8563	B- / 7.4	-0.97	6.63	14.72 /71	17.39 /70	8.52 /74	1.87	0.81
AA	Mutual Recovery A	FMRAX	B+	(800) 342-5236	C / 5.4	0.70	6.90	9.59 /44	14.53 /56	--	0.00	3.15
AA	Mutual Recovery Adv	FMRVX	A	(800) 321-8563	C+ / 6.3	0.75	7.10	9.94 /47	14.90 /58	--	0.00	3.09
AA	● Mutual Recovery B		B	(800) 342-5236	C / 5.2	0.48	6.56	8.91 /39	13.83 /53	--	0.00	4.09
AA	Mutual Recovery C	FCMRX	B+	(800) 342-5236	C+ / 5.6	0.48	6.56	8.91 /39	13.82 /53	--	0.00	4.09
GI	Mutual Shares A	TESIX	B	(800) 342-5236	C / 5.5	-0.95	5.29	13.05 /64	14.57 /57	6.91 /66	1.65	1.16
GI	● Mutual Shares B	FMUBX	B	(800) 342-5236	C / 5.3	-1.12	4.94	12.30 /61	13.82 /53	6.22 /62	1.13	1.76
GI	Mutual Shares C	TEMTX	B+	(800) 342-5236	C+ / 5.7	-1.13	4.94	12.27 /61	13.81 /53	6.22 /62	1.21	1.76
GI	Mutual Shares R	TESRX	B+	(800) 342-5236	C+ / 6.1	-1.05	5.13	12.82 /63	14.37 /56	6.77 /65	1.63	1.26
★ GI	Mutual Shares Z	MUTHX	B+	(800) 321-8563	C+ / 6.4	-0.89	5.45	13.42 /66	14.96 /59	7.28 /68	2.01	0.76
GR	MUTUALS.com GenWave Growth	GWGFX	C+	(800) 688-8257	C / 5.3	-3.38	2.16	10.56 /51	13.59 /52	4.10 /47	0.28	1.50
GR	MUTUALS.com Vice Fund	VICEX	A+	(800) 688-8257	B / 8.1	-1.38	8.86	10.80 /52	20.74 /82	--	0.00	1.75
RE	Nations Mort & Asset Backed Port	NMTGX	D+	(800) 321-7854	E- / 0.2	0.04	0.08	0.47 / 2	2.75 / 1	--	4.41	N/A
GI	Navellier Fundamental A	NFMAX	U	(800) 887-8671	U /	-3.72	11.48	24.43 /88	--	--	0.11	1.49
FO	Navellier Millennium Intl Gr A	NAIMX	C+	(800) 887-8671	B / 8.0	-1.49	7.66	24.63 /88	19.57 /78	8.66 /75	0.47	1.50
GR	Navellier Millennium Top 20 A	NTGRX	E	(800) 887-8671	C- / 3.7	-7.74	3.24	15.79 /74	11.55 /40	-0.04 /15	0.00	1.50
SC	Navellier Performance Aggr Micro	NPMCX	D-	(800) 887-8671	C+ / 5.7	-4.65	4.57	13.72 /67	14.34 /56	3.81 /44	0.00	1.49
MC	Navellier Performance Mid Cap Gr Fd	NPMDX	D+	(800) 887-8671	C+ / 6.1	-5.97	6.02	16.10 /75	15.94 /63	5.81 /60	0.00	1.34
MC	Navellier Performance Mid Cap Gr I	NRFCX	C-	(800) 887-8671	C+ / 6.3	-5.89	6.22	16.50 /76	16.33 /65	6.20 /62	0.00	0.99
AG	Needham Aggressive Growth Fund	NEAGX	C	(800) 625-7071	C / 4.4	-4.21	2.77	14.07 /68	12.59 /46	--	0.00	2.50
GR	Needham Growth Fund	NEEGX	C	(800) 625-7071	B- / 7.4	-2.18	8.10	24.61 /88	17.18 /69	5.69 /59	0.00	1.91
SC	Needham Small Cap Gr Fund	NESGX	C	(800) 625-7071	C / 5.4	-6.86	3.34	8.39 /36	14.64 /57	--	0.00	2.44
BA	Neuberger Berman AMT Balanced	NBABX	C	(800) 877-9700	C- / 4.0	-2.23	4.99	13.10 /65	10.52 /31	2.83 /35	0.89	1.10
GR	Neuberger Berman Century Fd	NBCIX	D	(800) 877-9700	D / 1.9	-3.83	2.03	8.76 /39	7.99 /15	-2.71 / 6	0.10	1.50
SC	Neuberger Berman Fasciano Adv	NBFVX	C-	(800) 877-9700	C- / 4.1	-6.02	2.85	8.34 /35	11.60 /40	--	0.00	2.21
SC	Neuberger Berman Fasciano Inv	NBFSX	C-	(800) 877-9700	C / 4.4	-5.91	2.97	8.69 /38	11.97 /42	7.13 /67	0.00	1.88
GR	Neuberger Berman Focus Adv	NBFAX	D-	(800) 877-9700	C / 4.4	-4.04	5.59	5.95 /20	11.97 /42	0.25 /17	0.00	1.54
GR	Neuberger Berman Focus Inv	NBSSX	D-	(800) 877-9700	C / 4.7	-3.95	5.80	6.40 /23	12.39 /45	0.64 /18	0.61	1.16
GR	Neuberger Berman Focus Tr	NBFCX	D-	(800) 877-9700	C / 4.5	-4.00	5.71	6.19 /22	12.21 /44	0.46 /17	0.56	1.32
SC	● Neuberger Berman Genesis Adv	NBGAX	B	(800) 877-9700	B- / 7.4	-4.24	1.90	10.35 /49	18.83 /76	12.74 /88	0.00	1.36
SC	● Neuberger Berman Genesis Inv	NBGNX	B	(800) 877-9700	B- / 7.5	-4.17	2.06	10.71 /52	19.19 /77	13.07 /89	0.00	1.04
★ SC	● Neuberger Berman Genesis Tr	NBGEX	B	(800) 877-9700	B- / 7.5	-4.18	2.04	10.63 /51	19.12 /76	13.01 /89	0.00	1.11
GI	Neuberger Berman Guardian Adv	NBGUX	C+	(800) 877-9700	C / 5.1	-2.50	0.69	9.77 /45	13.17 /50	3.81 /44	0.00	2.37
GI	Neuberger Berman Guardian Inv	NGUAX	B-	(800) 877-9700	C / 5.5	-2.38	1.01	10.40 /49	13.80 /53	4.32 /49	0.66	1.71
GI	Neuberger Berman Guardian Tr	NBGTX	B-	(800) 877-9700	C / 5.4	-2.41	0.93	10.27 /49	13.65 /52	4.17 /48	0.55	1.85
FO	Neuberger Berman International Inv	NBISX	A+	(800) 877-9700	A+ / 9.6	-1.16	9.83	29.66 /94	31.39 /96	15.92 /93	0.52	1.54
FO	Neuberger Berman International Tr	NBITX	A+	(800) 877-9700	A+ / 9.6	-1.18	9.78	29.60 /94	31.14 /96	16.26 /93	0.29	1.62
GR	Neuberger Berman Manhattan Adv	NBMBX	C	(800) 877-9700	B- / 7.0	-3.94	6.86	18.79 /80	16.71 /67	1.21 /22	0.00	1.91
GR	Neuberger Berman Manhattan Inv	NMANX	C+	(800) 877-9700	B- / 7.2	-3.76	7.11	19.38 /81	17.30 /69	1.72 /25	0.00	1.47
GR	Neuberger Berman Manhattan Tr	NBMTX	C+	(800) 877-9700	B- / 7.1	-3.86	6.94	19.03 /81	17.12 /69	1.57 /24	0.00	1.73
SC	Neuberger Berman Millennium Adv	NBMVX	C+	(800) 877-9700	B- / 7.1	-4.64	3.63	18.88 /80	17.76 /71	-6.75 / 1	0.00	2.95
SC	Neuberger Berman Millennium Inv	NBMIX	C	(800) 877-9700	B- / 7.1	-4.57	3.79	19.14 /81	17.75 /71	-0.91 /12	0.00	2.73

● Denotes fund is closed to new investors
★ Denotes fund is included in Section II

RISK			NET ASSETS		ASSET					BULL / BEAR		FUND MANAGER		MINIMUMS		LOADS	
	3 Year		NAV						Portfolio	Last Bull	Last Bear	Manager	Manager	Initial	Additional	Front	Back
Risk Rating/Pts	Standard Deviation	Beta	As of 6/30/06	Total $(Mil)	Cash %	Stocks %	Bonds %	Other %	Turnover Ratio	Market Return	Market Return	Quality Pct	Tenure (Years)	Purch. $	Purch. $	End Load	End Load
B / 8.1	7.7	0.66	21.96	57	8	90	2	0	29.8	121.1	-7.0	92	N/A	1,000	50	0.0	4.0
B / 8.1	7.6	0.66	22.40	265	8	90	2	0	29.8	120.9	-6.9	92	N/A	1,000	50	0.0	1.0
B / 8.1	7.7	0.66	22.84	873	8	90	2	0	29.8	128.1	-6.7	95	N/A	1,000	50	0.0	0.0
B- / 7.2	8.8	0.74	22.26	448	8	90	0	2	31.7	96.6	-3.6	96	4	1,000	50	5.8	0.0
B- / 7.2	8.8	0.75	21.73	42	8	90	0	2	31.7	92.5	-3.7	94	4	1,000	50	0.0	4.0
B- / 7.2	8.8	0.74	22.09	190	8	90	0	2	31.7	92.5	-3.8	94	4	1,000	50	0.0	1.0
B- / 7.1	8.8	0.74	22.27	192	8	90	0	2	31.7	98.7	-3.5	96	4	1,000	50	0.0	0.0
B / 8.6	7.2	0.82	20.70	862	4	90	4	2	21.0	86.7	-4.2	97	6	1,000	50	5.8	0.0
B / 8.7	7.2	0.82	20.25	71	4	90	4	2	21.0	82.9	-4.4	96	6	1,000	50	0.0	4.0
B / 8.7	7.2	0.82	20.50	364	4	90	4	2	21.0	83.0	-4.4	96	6	1,000	50	0.0	1.0
B / 8.6	7.2	0.82	20.83	3,817	4	90	4	2	21.0	88.9	-4.2	97	6	1,000	50	0.0	0.0
B+ / 9.4	6.3	1.01	13.17	116	18	64	18	0	69.2	N/A	N/A	96	3	10,000	1,000	5.8	0.0
B+ / 9.4	6.3	1.01	13.25	77	18	64	18	0	69.2	N/A	N/A	97	3	5,000,000	50	0.0	0.0
B+ / 9.4	6.3	1.00	13.01	4	18	64	18	0	69.2	N/A	N/A	95	3	10,000	1,000	0.0	4.0
B+ / 9.3	6.3	1.01	13.01	57	18	64	18	0	69.2	N/A	N/A	95	3	10,000	1,000	0.0	1.0
B+ / 9.0	6.2	0.72	24.73	5,151	12	84	4	0	21.6	72.9	-3.3	94	13	1,000	50	5.8	0.0
B+ / 9.0	6.2	0.72	24.17	616	12	84	4	0	21.6	69.3	-3.4	93	13	1,000	50	0.0	4.0
B+ / 9.0	6.3	0.72	24.43	2,007	12	84	4	0	21.6	69.4	-3.5	93	13	1,000	50	0.0	1.0
B+ / 9.0	6.2	0.72	24.60	141	12	84	4	0	21.6	72.0	-3.3	94	13	1,000	50	0.0	0.0
B+ / 9.0	6.2	0.72	24.91	9,780	12	84	4	0	21.6	74.8	-3.2	95	13	1,000	50	0.0	0.0
B- / 7.9	8.9	1.04	12.29	53	0	98	0	2	6.6	84.6	-10.4	75	5	2,500	100	0.0	1.0
B / 8.0	10.5	1.08	17.83	54	1	98	0	1	65.8	125.4	-11.0	98	N/A	2,500	100	0.0	1.0
B+ / 9.9	2.8	0.05	9.73	96	0	0	0	100	N/A	9.3	2.0	49	3	1,000	100	0.0	0.0
U /	N/A	N/A	13.21	26	7	92	0	1	219.0	N/A	N/A	N/A	15	2,000	100	0.0	2.0
C / 5.0	12.3	1.12	9.28	1	3	96	0	1	74.0	114.0	-8.8	9	N/A	2,000	100	0.0	2.0
D- / 1.6	19.6	1.75	14.67	10	0	99	0	1	161.0	92.9	-9.5	10	N/A	2,000	100	0.0	2.0
D+ / 2.6	19.0	1.21	29.76	23	3	96	0	1	96.0	100.1	-13.3	7	N/A	2,000	100	0.0	2.0
C- / 3.8	14.9	1.27	31.01	166	1	98	0	1	104.0	101.2	-10.9	11	N/A	2,000	100	0.0	2.0
C / 4.4	15.0	1.27	31.77	63	1	98	0	1	104.0	103.5	-10.9	12	N/A	2,000	100	0.0	2.0
B- / 7.7	11.3	1.18	14.11	18	10	89	0	1	69.0	75.3	-11.5	52	5	5,000	500	0.0	2.0
C- / 4.0	15.7	1.62	38.58	231	7	88	0	5	16.0	102.9	-8.8	58	3	5,000	500	0.0	2.0
C+ / 6.1	15.6	0.95	17.66	18	3	96	0	1	104.0	111.6	-11.9	28	3	5,000	500	0.0	2.0
B- / 7.6	8.1	1.33	10.94	74	1	61	37	1	82.0	51.2	-4.2	68	17	1,000	100	0.0	0.0
B- / 7.6	9.2	1.10	6.53	11	0	100	0	0	107.0	50.7	-10.1	20	4	1,000	100	0.0	0.0
C+ / 6.9	10.8	0.70	11.55	34	0	99	0	1	22.0	74.1	-9.3	35	4	1,000	0	0.0	0.0
C+ / 6.9	10.8	0.70	43.65	519	0	99	0	1	22.0	76.1	-9.2	38	18	1,000	100	0.0	0.0
C- / 3.6	15.9	1.45	17.57	33	1	98	0	1	18.9	104.5	-17.3	26	3	1,000	0	0.0	0.0
C- / 3.6	15.9	1.45	34.29	1,168	1	98	0	1	18.9	107.0	-17.3	28	3	1,000	100	0.0	0.0
C- / 3.6	15.9	1.45	25.19	136	1	98	0	1	18.9	105.9	-17.3	27	N/A	1,000	0	0.0	0.0
C+ / 6.8	11.1	0.68	28.91	711	0	99	0	1	11.0	101.6	-6.0	93	9	1,000	0	0.0	0.0
C+ / 6.8	11.1	0.68	34.67	1,945	0	99	0	1	11.0	103.5	-5.9	94	12	1,000	100	0.0	0.0
C+ / 6.8	11.1	0.68	49.54	6,761	0	99	0	1	11.0	103.1	-5.9	94	N/A	1,000	0	0.0	0.0
B / 8.3	8.8	1.04	15.96	1	0	99	0	1	20.0	84.0	-8.2	72	4	1,000	100	0.0	0.0
B / 8.3	8.7	1.03	18.02	1,429	0	99	0	1	20.0	87.0	-8.0	77	4	1,000	100	0.0	0.0
B / 8.3	8.7	1.04	14.18	167	0	99	0	1	20.0	86.2	-8.0	76	4	1,000	0	0.0	0.0
C+ / 6.6	12.2	1.12	23.80	997	0	99	0	1	38.0	190.5	-6.8	86	3	1,000	100	0.0	2.0
B- / 7.7	12.2	1.12	26.05	844	0	99	0	1	38.0	189.4	-6.6	85	N/A	1,000	100	0.0	2.0
C / 5.4	13.8	1.49	13.40	1	N/A	100	0	N/A	65.0	94.7	-9.6	65	4	1,000	0	0.0	0.0
C / 5.5	13.7	1.48	8.44	370	N/A	100	0	N/A	65.0	98.2	-9.6	71	4	1,000	100	0.0	0.0
C / 5.5	13.8	1.50	12.95	8	N/A	100	0	N/A	65.0	97.1	-9.6	68	4	1,000	0	0.0	0.0
C / 5.5	16.2	1.02	11.71	2	0	99	0	1	204.0	105.6	-13.6	41	4	1,000	0	0.0	0.0
C / 4.4	16.2	1.02	15.87	51	0	99	0	1	204.0	105.6	-13.5	42	4	1,000	100	0.0	0.0

Fund Type	Fund Name	Ticker Symbol	Overall Weiss Investment Rating	Phone	Perfor-mance Rating/Pts	3 Mo	6 Mo	1Yr / Pct	3Yr / Pct	5Yr / Pct	Dividend Yield	Expense Ratio
SC	Neuberger Berman Millennium Tr	NBMOX	C	(800) 877-9700	B- / 7.1	-4.59	3.74	19.17 /81	17.72 /71	-0.95 /12	0.00	2.85
GR	Neuberger Berman Partners Adv	NBPBX	C+	(800) 877-9700	C+ / 6.9	-3.71	0.96	10.76 /52	17.35 /70	6.86 /66	0.06	2.24
★ GR	Neuberger Berman Partners Inv	NPRTX	B-	(800) 877-9700	B- / 7.1	-3.67	1.11	11.06 /54	17.80 /72	7.25 /68	0.91	1.70
GR	Neuberger Berman Partners Tr	NBPTX	B-	(800) 877-9700	B- / 7.0	-3.70	1.02	10.86 /53	17.61 /71	7.08 /67	0.55	1.90
RE	Neuberger Berman Real Estate Fund	NBRFX	C	(800) 877-9700	A / 9.4	-0.02	14.64	21.81 /84	28.08 /94	--	2.26	1.22
GR	Neuberger Berman Regency Inv	NBRVX	A	(800) 877-9700	B / 7.6	-2.95	2.26	11.15 /55	19.58 /78	10.74 /83	0.33	1.55
GR	Neuberger Berman Regency Tr	NBREX	B	(800) 877-9700	B / 7.6	-2.99	2.10	10.99 /53	19.45 /78	10.67 /83	0.15	1.73
GR	Neuberger Berman Socially Resp Inv	NBSRX	C+	(800) 877-9700	C / 5.1	-1.88	1.23	10.93 /53	12.73 /47	7.46 /69	0.60	1.38
GR	Neuberger Berman Socially Resp Tr	NBSTX	C+	(800) 877-9700	C / 4.9	-1.91	1.14	10.80 /52	12.53 /46	7.23 /68	0.37	1.54
GR	New Alternatives Fund	NALFX	B-	(800) 423-8383	B / 8.1	-1.40	18.86	22.46 /85	19.10 /76	2.42 /31	0.40	1.28
GL	New Century Aggressive	NCAPX	C-	(888) 639-0102	C / 4.8	-7.11	-0.44	9.84 /46	13.61 /52	0.74 /19	0.00	1.50
AA	New Century Alternative Strategies	NCHPX	C+	(888) 639-0102	C- / 4.0	0.40	1.79	10.85 /53	11.18 /37	--	2.62	1.01
BA	New Century Balanced	NCIPX	C	(888) 639-0102	C- / 3.2	-1.78	3.13	7.78 /31	10.24 /29	4.07 /47	1.37	1.32
GR	New Century Capital	NCCPX	C+	(888) 639-0102	C / 5.5	-3.36	3.93	12.10 /60	13.86 /53	3.08 /38	0.00	1.33
FO	New Century International	NCFPX	A	(888) 639-0102	A- / 9.0	-4.16	4.38	24.04 /87	24.80 /91	11.59 /86	0.36	1.50
GL	New Covenant Balanced Growth	NCBGX	C-	(800) 858-6127	D / 2.2	-1.65	1.11	5.93 /20	8.15 /16	3.76 /43	1.87	0.12
BA	New Covenant Balanced Income	NCBIX	C-	(800) 858-6127	E+ / 0.9	-1.02	0.43	3.26 / 8	5.54 / 5	4.17 /48	2.75	0.15
GL	New Covenant Growth	NCGFX	C+	(800) 858-6127	C / 4.8	-2.60	2.13	10.17 /48	12.33 /45	2.77 /35	0.61	1.07
GR	New Market Fund	AVMIX	D+	(800) 527-9500	D / 1.6	-0.86	2.19	3.03 / 7	8.85 /20	4.34 /49	0.25	1.49
SC	New River Small Cap Fund	NRVSX	U	(866) 672-3863	U /	-4.54	8.64	11.45 /56	--	--	0.47	1.50
GR	New York Equity Fund	NYSAX	E-	(888) 899-8344	E- / 0.1	-9.83	-6.16	1.25 / 3	3.78 / 2	-7.84 / 1	0.00	2.69
AA	NH 100% Equity Portfolio		C+	(800) 522-7297	C / 4.9	-3.37	1.96	11.47 /56	12.48 /46	3.01 /37	0.00	0.30
AA	NH 70% Equity Portfolio		C+	(800) 522-7297	C- / 3.3	-2.34	1.60	8.42 /36	9.88 /27	4.16 /47	0.00	0.30
AA	NH College Portfolio		C-	(800) 522-7297	E / 0.4	-0.42	0.64	2.62 / 6	3.54 / 2	3.45 /41	0.00	0.30
AA	NH Conservative Portfolio		D+	(800) 522-7297	E- / 0.1	0.44	0.61	1.23 / 3	1.67 / 0	--	0.00	0.30
AA	NH Portfolio 2006		C-	(800) 522-7297	D- / 1.0	-0.70	0.71	3.33 / 8	5.79 / 6	3.40 /40	0.00	0.30
AA	NH Portfolio 2009		C	(800) 522-7297	D / 1.8	-1.12	0.71	4.52 /13	7.49 /12	3.41 /40	0.00	0.30
AA	NH Portfolio 2012		C	(800) 522-7297	D+ / 2.5	-1.54	1.01	6.03 /21	8.72 /19	3.29 /39	0.00	0.30
AA	NH Portfolio 2015		C+	(800) 522-7297	C- / 3.4	-1.99	1.33	7.50 /29	10.24 /29	3.30 /39	0.00	0.30
AA	NH Portfolio 2018		C+	(800) 522-7297	C- / 3.7	-2.51	1.54	8.46 /36	10.66 /32	3.45 /41	0.00	0.30
AA	NH Portfolio 2021		C+	(800) 522-7297	C / 4.3	-2.80	1.99	10.03 /47	11.44 /39	--	0.00	0.30
SC	● NI Numeric Inv Emerging Growth	NIMCX	D	(800) 686-3742	B+ / 8.6	-3.75	10.64	21.24 /83	22.01 /85	13.19 /89	0.00	1.33
AG	● NI Numeric Inv Growth Fund	NISGX	C	(800) 686-3742	B- / 7.4	-3.65	5.95	13.75 /67	18.55 /75	8.33 /73	0.00	2.17
MC	NI Numeric Inv Mid Cap Fund	NIGVX	C	(800) 686-3742	B / 8.2	-1.59	6.13	18.95 /80	20.87 /82	10.34 /82	0.23	2.29
SC	● NI Numeric Inv Small Cap Value	NISVX	D	(800) 686-3742	B+ / 8.6	-1.22	9.95	16.54 /76	22.66 /87	19.05 /95	0.67	1.87
IN	Nicholas Equity Income Fund Fd	NSEIX	B	(800) 544-6547	C / 5.5	1.83	7.91	7.80 /31	13.04 /49	6.37 /63	2.36	0.90
IN	Nicholas Equity Income Fund N	NNEIX	C	(800) 544-6547	C / 5.4	1.83	7.75	7.43 /29	12.85 /48	6.26 /63	2.11	1.25
★ GR	Nicholas Fund	NICSX	C-	(800) 544-6547	C- / 3.3	-4.37	1.03	2.34 / 5	11.02 /36	2.89 /36	0.41	0.78
GR	Nicholas II Fund I	NCTWX	C-	(800) 544-6547	C / 4.4	-5.45	0.86	6.53 /23	12.40 /45	4.38 /49	0.09	0.70
GR	Nicholas II Fund N	NNTWX	D+	(800) 544-6547	C- / 4.2	-5.55	0.68	6.12 /21	12.22 /44	4.28 /49	0.00	1.06
SC	Nicholas Limited Edition	NCLEX	C	(800) 544-6547	C+ / 5.6	-7.80	1.40	6.68 /24	14.95 /59	6.13 /62	1.22	1.30
GL	Nicholas-Applegate Glb Select I	NACHX	B	(800) 551-8043	B / 7.9	-3.80	4.76	18.11 /79	19.35 /77	8.35 /73	0.14	1.15
GL	Nicholas-Applegate Glb Select II	NAGSX	B+	(800) 551-8043	B / 7.9	-3.74	4.82	18.17 /79	19.40 /77	8.37 /73	0.20	1.10
GR	Nicholas-Applegate Growth Equity A	NAPGX	C-	(800) 551-8043	C / 5.4	-5.59	3.39	13.31 /65	14.84 /58	-2.56 / 6	0.00	1.82
GR	Nicholas-Applegate Growth Equity B	NAGBX	C-	(800) 551-8043	C+ / 5.6	-5.78	3.04	12.39 /62	13.93 /54	-3.32 / 5	0.00	2.57
GR	Nicholas-Applegate Growth Equity C	PNACX	C-	(800) 551-8043	C / 5.5	-5.78	3.04	12.39 /62	13.93 /54	-3.32 / 5	0.00	2.57
GR	Nicholas-Applegate Growth Equity Z	PNAZX	C	(800) 551-8043	C+ / 6.2	-5.58	3.56	13.51 /66	15.08 /59	-2.35 / 7	0.00	1.57
FO	Nicholas-Applegate Intl Gr Oppty I	NAGPX	B	(800) 551-8043	A+ / 9.7	-3.35	11.96	38.69 /98	32.51 /97	14.79 /92	0.51	1.42
FO	Nicholas-Applegate Intl Gr Oppty II	NAIIX	A-	(800) 551-8043	A+ / 9.7	-3.30	12.05	38.90 /98	32.71 /97	14.89 /92	0.41	1.27
FO	Nicholas-Applegate Intl Gr Oppty IV	NAIVX	U	(800) 551-8043	U /	-3.27	12.10	--	--	--	0.00	1.17
FO	Nicholas-Applegate Intl Growth I	NACIX	C+	(800) 551-8043	B+ / 8.7	-2.38	5.47	29.50 /94	21.90 /85	7.47 /69	0.00	1.39
FO	Nicholas-Applegate Intl Growth R	NACRX	C+	(800) 551-8043	B+ / 8.6	-2.43	5.39	29.21 /94	21.51 /84	7.16 /68	0.00	1.64

● Denotes fund is closed to new investors
★ Denotes fund is included in Section II

RISK			NET ASSETS		ASSET				BULL / BEAR		FUND MANAGER		MINIMUMS		LOADS	
Risk Rating/Pts	3 Year Standard Deviation	Beta	NAV As of 6/30/06	Total $(Mil)	Cash %	Stocks %	Bonds %	Other %	Portfolio Turnover Ratio	Last Bull Market Return	Last Bear Market Return	Manager Quality Pct	Manager Tenure (Years)	Initial Purch. $	Additional Purch. $	Front End Load	Back End Load
C /4.4	16.2	1.02	17.47	3	0	99	0	1	204.0	105.5	-13.5	41	4	1,000	0	0.0	0.0
C+/6.9	11.9	1.29	18.96	607	0	99	0	1	61.0	107.4	-9.6	84	8	1,000	100	0.0	0.0
C+/6.9	11.9	1.30	28.36	2,136	0	99	0	1	61.0	110.1	-9.6	86	8	1,000	100	0.0	0.0
C+/6.9	11.9	1.29	21.87	934	0	99	0	1	61.0	109.0	-9.6	86	8	1,000	0	0.0	0.0
D+/2.9	16.3	0.98	14.51	69	5	94	0	1	129.0	136.4	1.5	88	4	1,000	100	0.0	1.0
B /8.0	11.2	1.24	16.76	113	N/A	100	0	N/A	91.0	108.1	-6.2	94	N/A	1,000	100	0.0	0.0
C+/6.7	11.3	1.25	14.61	67	N/A	100	0	N/A	91.0	107.6	-6.2	94	N/A	1,000	0	0.0	0.0
B /8.2	9.2	1.08	22.99	449	5	94	0	1	21.0	75.2	-4.7	64	5	1,000	100	0.0	0.0
B /8.2	9.2	1.08	15.92	213	5	94	0	1	21.0	74.2	-4.7	62	N/A	1,000	0	0.0	0.0
C+/5.9	11.1	1.00	40.96	91	23	76	0	1	52.1	101.5	-8.9	97	24	2,500	250	4.8	0.0
C+/6.4	14.0	1.06	9.15	13	0	100	0	0	19.0	88.9	-10.3	1	6	0	0	0.0	2.0
B+/9.1	7.2	1.09	12.54	91	2	90	6	2	11.0	51.2	-0.7	84	4	0	0	0.0	2.0
B /8.8	7.0	1.36	13.83	82	0	64	34	2	21.0	54.1	-4.6	64	11	0	0	0.0	2.0
B- /7.1	10.4	1.26	16.40	118	0	100	0	0	13.0	80.5	-10.0	58	11	0	0	0.0	2.0
C+/6.8	13.3	1.23	13.81	94	0	100	0	0	3.0	150.4	-6.7	18	6	0	0	0.0	2.0
B+/9.2	5.5	1.13	81.30	312	1	63	35	1	5.0	43.1	-5.4	55	N/A	500	100	0.0	0.0
B+/9.9	3.8	0.76	18.99	123	0	38	60	2	7.0	27.5	-1.9	47	N/A	500	100	0.0	0.0
B- /7.9	8.8	0.73	32.76	906	2	97	0	1	24.0	70.9	-10.3	14	N/A	500	100	0.0	0.0
B /8.4	7.0	0.76	14.91	6	2	97	0	1	76.5	53.0	-8.3	54	8	1,000	100	5.8	0.0
U /	N/A	N/A	15.34	38	4	95	0	1	6.0	N/A	N/A	N/A	N/A	1,000	250	0.0	2.0
D+/2.7	17.3	1.28	8.07	4	N/A	100	0	N/A	122.0	57.5	-14.7	2	9	1,000	0	4.8	0.0
B /8.5	8.8	1.70	11.47	364	0	100	0	0	3.0	73.3	-9.5	67	5	1,000	50	0.0	0.0
B+/9.3	6.4	1.31	12.10	197	0	70	29	1	2.0	55.9	-5.1	63	5	1,000	50	0.0	0.0
B+/9.9	2.3	0.42	14.11	140	40	19	40	1	21.0	16.6	-0.1	44	8	1,000	50	0.0	0.0
B+/9.9	2.3	0.12	11.54	70	54	0	45	1	8.0	6.5	2.4	41	5	1,000	50	0.0	0.0
B+/9.9	3.5	0.73	14.28	369	28	28	43	1	22.0	29.9	-3.1	52	8	1,000	50	0.0	0.0
B+/9.9	4.6	0.96	14.12	555	13	42	44	1	17.0	40.5	-4.5	58	8	1,000	50	0.0	0.0
B+/9.6	5.6	1.15	14.06	600	8	54	37	1	15.0	48.6	-5.5	60	8	1,000	50	0.0	0.0
B+/9.2	6.6	1.33	13.76	656	1	66	31	2	11.0	59.5	-7.0	66	8	1,000	50	0.0	0.0
B+/9.1	7.1	1.41	13.20	640	0	75	24	1	9.0	62.6	-7.2	65	7	1,000	50	0.0	0.0
B /8.8	7.9	1.41	12.83	365	0	85	14	1	0.3	67.4	-7.5	72	5	1,000	50	0.0	0.0
D- /1.0	16.5	1.10	15.39	142	0	100	0	0	318.4	140.1	-6.4	71	N/A	3,000	100	0.0	2.0
C /4.7	15.1	1.64	15.85	30	0	100	0	0	343.2	113.0	-6.1	69	N/A	3,000	100	0.0	2.0
C- /3.7	9.9	0.88	18.53	42	0	100	0	0	321.4	113.4	-6.3	90	N/A	3,000	100	0.0	2.0
E+/0.8	13.1	0.87	18.56	235	0	100	0	0	348.6	134.1	-4.3	94	N/A	3,000	100	0.0	2.0
B /8.6	7.0	0.79	13.83	30	5	94	0	1	18.9	66.0	-9.3	87	N/A	100,000	100	0.0	0.0
C+/6.5	7.0	0.79	13.80	N/A	5	94	0	1	18.9	65.2	-9.3	86	N/A	5,000	100	0.0	0.0
B- /7.5	8.1	0.89	57.68	2,373	1	98	0	1	25.5	69.7	-9.3	65	37	500	100	0.0	0.0
C+/6.6	9.5	1.10	22.39	543	3	96	0	1	20.8	75.6	-8.4	59	13	100,000	100	0.0	0.0
C+/5.9	9.5	1.10	22.30	1	3	96	0	1	20.8	74.8	-8.4	57	13	5,000	100	0.0	0.0
C+/6.0	11.6	0.75	19.50	176	7	92	0	1	37.3	98.1	-8.8	62	13	100,000	100	0.0	0.0
C+/6.4	11.8	1.02	18.25	72	1	98	0	1	66.0	115.8	-11.1	16	3	250,000	0	0.0	0.0
B- /7.2	11.8	1.02	18.26	79	1	98	0	1	66.0	116.0	-11.1	16	3	25,000,000	0	0.0	0.0
C /5.4	13.1	1.44	10.98	99	0	99	0	1	113.0	80.3	-10.1	50	N/A	1,000	100	5.5	0.0
C /5.4	12.9	1.42	8.80	24	0	99	0	1	113.0	75.7	-10.3	42	N/A	1,000	100	0.0	0.0
C /5.4	12.9	1.42	8.80	4	0	99	0	1	113.0	75.7	-10.3	42	N/A	2,500	100	1.0	0.0
C /5.4	13.1	1.44	11.34	3	0	99	0	1	113.0	81.4	-10.0	54	N/A	0	0	0.0	0.0
C /4.5	14.2	1.27	48.20	111	1	98	0	1	104.0	205.0	-6.4	68	N/A	250,000	0	0.0	0.0
C+/5.8	14.2	1.27	48.37	32	1	98	0	1	104.0	206.3	-6.4	69	N/A	10,000,000	0	0.0	0.0
U /	N/A	N/A	48.27	33	1	98	0	1	104.0	N/A	N/A	N/A	N/A	250,000	10,000	0.0	0.0
C /4.6	12.9	1.18	22.16	45	1	98	0	1	86.0	124.5	-8.5	11	N/A	250,000	0	0.0	0.0
C /4.5	12.9	1.18	21.72	2	1	98	0	1	86.0	122.3	-8.6	10	N/A	250,000	10,000	0.0	0.0

Fund Type	Fund Name	Ticker Symbol	Overall Weiss Investment Rating	Phone	Perfor-mance Rating/Pts	3 Mo	6 Mo	1Yr / Pct	3Yr / Pct	5Yr / Pct	Dividend Yield	Expense Ratio
CV	Nicholas-Applegate US Convertible	NIGIX	B-	(800) 551-8043	C / 5.5	-1.58	4.96	11.90 /59	13.21 /50	5.63 /59	2.15	1.02
SC	Nicholas-Applegate US Emerg Gr I	NAGQX	C	(800) 551-8043	B+ / 8.4	-5.32	13.45	28.87 /94	19.54 /78	3.74 /43	0.00	1.20
SC	Nicholas-Applegate US Emerg Gr R	NARRX	C	(800) 551-8043	B+ / 8.3	-5.33	13.29	28.54 /93	19.24 /77	3.50 /41	0.00	1.45
SC	Nicholas-Applegate US Grth Discov	NAMCX	D	(800) 551-8043	B / 7.7	-7.46	7.18	20.85 /83	19.78 /79	8.49 /74	0.00	1.56
GR	Nicholas-Applegate US Lg Cp Val I	NAVIX	B+	(800) 551-8043	C+ / 6.1	1.19	7.11	11.30 /55	14.07 /54	5.24 /56	1.70	0.81
GR	Nicholas-Applegate US Lg Cp Val R	NAVRX	B+	(800) 551-8043	C+ / 5.9	1.12	6.95	11.01 /54	13.77 /53	4.97 /54	1.04	1.06
SC	● Nicholas-Applegate US Sm Cap Val II	NASYX	U	(800) 551-8043	U /	-0.71	8.60	15.69 /74	--	--	1.69	1.20
GR	Nicholas-Applegate US Sys Lrg Gr I	NLCIX	D-	(800) 551-8043	D / 1.6	-3.58	3.24	9.13 /41	6.94 /10	-5.78 / 2	0.00	1.12
GR	Nicholas-Applegate US Sys Lrg Gr R	NLCRX	D-	(800) 551-8043	D- / 1.5	-3.64	3.16	8.93 /40	6.73 / 9	-5.99 / 2	0.00	1.37
SC	Nicholas-Applegate US Values Opp	NASVX	A-	(800) 551-8043	A- / 9.0	-0.71	8.54	15.59 /74	24.41 /90	16.96 /94	0.28	1.30
FS	North Track DJ US Fin 100+ A	NDUAX	D	(800) 826-4600	C- / 3.9	-0.39	3.04	11.46 /56	11.80 /41	4.82 /53	1.15	1.35
FS	North Track DJ US Fin 100+ B	NDUBX	C	(800) 826-4600	C- / 3.4	-0.54	2.65	10.59 /51	10.96 /35	4.06 /46	0.46	2.09
FS	North Track DJ US Fin 100+ C	NDUCX	C	(800) 826-4600	C- / 3.8	-0.55	2.58	10.57 /51	10.93 /35	4.05 /46	0.56	2.10
HL	North Track DJ US Hlthcare 100+ A	NDJAX	E+	(800) 826-4600	E / 0.4	-5.13	-4.33	-0.68 / 1	6.39 / 8	2.21 /29	0.00	1.34
HL	North Track DJ US Hlthcare 100+ B	NDJBX	E+	(800) 826-4600	E- / 0.2	-5.24	-4.57	-1.34 / 1	5.63 / 5	1.47 /23	0.00	2.09
HL	North Track DJ US Hlthcare 100+ C	NDJCX	E+	(800) 826-4600	E / 0.4	-5.32	-4.65	-1.42 / 1	5.59 / 5	1.47 /24	0.00	2.09
MC	North Track Geneva Growth A	PNMAX	C+	(800) 826-4600	C+ / 6.7	-5.08	3.66	13.81 /68	17.98 /72	8.39 /73	0.00	1.37
MC	North Track Geneva Growth B	PNMBX	C+	(800) 826-4600	C+ / 6.4	-5.24	3.31	13.02 /64	17.12 /69	8.50 /74	0.00	2.12
MC	North Track Geneva Growth C	MGPCX	C+	(800) 826-4600	C+ / 6.7	-5.23	3.33	13.00 /64	17.14 /69	7.59 /70	0.00	2.12
TC	North Track NYSE ArcaTech 100 Idx	PPTIX	E	(800) 826-4600	D / 1.9	-10.42	-6.50	4.63 /13	10.99 /35	1.01 /20	0.00	1.00
TC	North Track NYSE ArcaTech 100 Idx	PSEBX	E	(800) 826-4600	D- / 1.5	-10.62	-6.90	3.77 /10	10.16 /28	0.04 /16	0.00	1.75
TC	North Track NYSE ArcaTech 100 Idx	PTICX	E	(800) 826-4600	D / 2.0	-10.60	-6.86	3.80 /10	10.16 /28	0.05 /16	0.00	1.75
GR	North Track S&P 100 Index A	PPSPX	D	(800) 826-4600	E+ / 0.9	-1.09	2.25	4.99 /15	6.70 / 9	-1.03 /12	1.06	1.09
GR	North Track S&P 100 Index B	PSUBX	D	(800) 826-4600	E+ / 0.6	-1.30	1.88	4.18 /11	5.90 / 6	-1.77 / 9	0.27	1.84
GR	North Track S&P 100 Index C	SPPCX	D	(800) 826-4600	D- / 1.0	-1.29	1.87	4.19 /11	5.90 / 6	-1.76 / 9	0.14	1.84
AA	North Track Strategic Allocation A	NTSAX	U	(800) 826-4600	U /	-5.46	-2.85	4.45 /13	--	--	0.00	0.80
GR	Northeast Investors Growth	NTHFX	C+	(800) 225-6704	C / 5.0	-2.94	2.34	13.98 /68	12.95 /49	3.13 /38	0.00	1.18
GR	Northern Enhanced Lg Cap Retail	NOLCX	U	(800) 595-9111	U /	-1.36	2.45	--	--	--	0.00	0.60
BA	Northern Instl Balanced A	BBALX	D	(800) 637-1380	D- / 1.1	-2.55	-0.92	3.43 / 9	6.27 / 8	2.64 /33	1.90	0.61
BA	Northern Instl Balanced C	BBCCX	D	(800) 637-1380	E+ / 0.9	-2.61	-1.11	3.09 / 8	6.00 / 7	2.38 /31	1.67	0.85
BA	Northern Instl Balanced D	BBADX	D	(800) 637-1380	E+ / 0.9	-2.59	-1.10	2.97 / 7	5.83 / 6	2.24 /30	1.53	1.00
GR	Northern Instl Diversified Gr A	BDVAX	D-	(800) 637-1380	D+ / 2.9	-3.39	-0.67	6.01 /21	9.82 /26	0.67 /19	0.71	0.77
GR	Northern Instl Diversified Gr D	BDGDX	D-	(800) 637-1380	D+ / 2.6	-3.54	-0.98	5.57 /18	9.39 /23	0.23 /16	0.08	1.16
IX	Northern Instl Equity Index A	BEIAX	C	(800) 637-1380	C- / 4.0	-1.52	2.58	8.40 /36	11.00 /35	2.28 /30	1.62	0.21
IX	Northern Instl Equity Index C	BEICX	C	(800) 637-1380	C- / 3.8	-1.52	2.48	8.18 /34	10.76 /33	2.04 /28	1.40	0.45
IX	Northern Instl Equity Index D	BEIDX	C-	(800) 637-1380	C- / 3.7	-1.58	2.41	7.95 /32	10.57 /32	1.90 /26	1.25	0.60
GR	Northern Instl Focused Growth A	BFGAX	E+	(800) 637-1380	D- / 1.0	-5.63	-0.97	3.67 / 9	6.49 / 8	-2.82 / 6	0.29	0.86
GR	Northern Instl Focused Growth C	BFGCX	E	(800) 637-1380	E+ / 0.8	-5.69	-1.16	2.88 / 7	6.03 / 7	-3.15 / 5	0.30	1.10
GR	Northern Instl Focused Growth D	BFGDX	E	(800) 637-1380	E+ / 0.9	-5.74	-1.19	3.31 / 8	6.07 / 7	-3.20 / 5	0.31	1.25
FO	Northern Instl Intl Equity Index A	BIEIX	A+	(800) 637-1380	A- / 9.1	1.01	10.13	27.14 /91	24.16 /90	10.05 /81	1.69	0.43
FO	Northern Instl Intl Equity Index D	BIEDX	A	(800) 637-1380	B+ / 8.9	0.89	9.92	26.48 /91	23.49 /88	9.53 /79	1.38	0.82
FO	Northern Instl Int'l Growth A	BIGAX	B+	(800) 637-1380	B+ / 8.7	0.26	8.76	26.15 /90	22.59 /86	8.78 /75	1.09	1.07
FO	Northern Instl Int'l Growth D	BIGDX	B+	(800) 637-1380	B+ / 8.6	0.09	8.44	25.51 /89	22.08 /85	8.33 /73	0.75	1.46
MC	Northern Instl Mid Cap Growth A	BMGRX	D	(800) 637-1380	C- / 3.5	-7.10	-0.26	5.11 /16	11.43 /39	2.79 /35	0.00	0.92
MC	Northern Instl Mid Cap Growth C	BMDCX	D	(800) 637-1380	C- / 3.4	-7.11	-0.35	4.89 /15	11.19 /37	2.54 /32	0.00	1.16
MC	Northern Instl Mid Cap Growth D	BMCDX	D	(800) 637-1380	C- / 3.2	-7.17	-0.44	4.74 /14	11.00 /35	2.38 /31	0.00	1.31
SC	Northern Instl Small Co. Growth A	BSGRX	C-	(800) 637-1380	C+ / 6.1	-5.05	9.44	16.20 /75	14.22 /55	2.51 /32	0.00	0.92
SC	Northern Instl Small Co. Idx A	BSCAX	B-	(800) 637-1380	B / 7.6	-5.08	8.14	14.29 /69	18.54 /75	8.37 /73	1.06	0.31
SC	Northern Instl Small Co. Idx D	BSIDX	B-	(800) 637-1380	B- / 7.4	-5.20	7.90	13.83 /68	18.14 /73	8.00 /72	0.71	0.70
GR	Northern Trust Growth Equity	NOGEX	D	(800) 595-9111	D+ / 2.6	-3.66	-1.18	5.30 /17	9.48 /24	0.25 /17	0.49	1.00
CV	Northern Trust Income Equity	NOIEX	C-	(800) 595-9111	C- / 3.7	-0.43	3.58	7.64 /30	10.40 /30	6.79 /66	2.91	1.00
FO	Northern Trust Intl Growth Equity	NOIGX	B+	(800) 595-9111	B+ / 8.5	-0.16	8.34	25.59 /89	21.61 /84	7.77 /71	0.70	1.25

● Denotes fund is closed to new investors
* Denotes fund is included in Section II

300

RISK			NET ASSETS		ASSET				BULL / BEAR		FUND MANAGER		MINIMUMS		LOADS	
	3 Year		NAV						Last Bull	Last Bear	Manager	Manager	Initial	Additional	Front	Back
Risk Rating/Pts	Standard Deviation	Beta	As of 6/30/06	Total $(Mil)	Cash %	Stocks %	Bonds %	Other %	Portfolio Turnover Ratio	Market Return	Market Return	Quality Pct	Tenure (Years)	Purch. $	Purch. $	End Load	End Load
B /8.2	8.3	1.21	24.06	31	1	0	0	99	47.0	69.0	-3.0	91	N/A	250,000	0	0.0	0.0
C- /3.5	17.2	1.12	13.16	7	5	94	0	1	66.0	123.0	-12.1	43	N/A	250,000	0	0.0	0.0
C- /3.4	17.1	1.12	12.96	3	5	94	0	1	66.0	121.4	-12.2	41	N/A	250,000	10,000	0.0	0.0
D /1.8	18.8	1.20	16.13	78	1	98	0	1	101.0	163.5	-11.9	33	11	250,000	10,000	0.0	0.0
B /8.7	8.0	0.98	29.67	21	2	97	0	1	21.0	76.1	-8.1	83	N/A	250,000	0	0.0	0.0
B /8.7	8.0	0.98	29.68	5	2	97	0	1	21.0	74.7	-8.2	81	N/A	250,000	10,000	0.0	0.0
U /	N/A	N/A	19.69	43	9	90	0	1	25.0	N/A	N/A	N/A	N/A	20,000,000	10,000	0.0	0.0
C+ /6.9	9.9	1.12	17.22	1	0	99	0	1	86.0	45.2	-11.8	14	N/A	250,000	0	0.0	0.0
C+ /6.9	9.9	1.12	16.95	6	0	99	0	1	86.0	44.4	-11.9	13	N/A	250,000	10,000	0.0	0.0
C+ /6.4	13.0	0.86	19.71	113	7	92	0	1	25.0	150.2	-7.3	97	5	250,000	10,000	0.0	0.0
C /5.0	9.1	0.99	12.87	23	0	99	0	1	24.3	71.4	-9.9	36	4	1,000	50	5.3	0.0
B /8.1	9.2	1.00	12.78	9	0	99	0	1	24.3	67.3	-9.9	29	4	1,000	50	0.0	5.0
B /8.1	9.1	0.99	12.72	11	0	99	0	1	24.3	67.5	-10.0	30	4	1,000	50	1.0	1.0
C+ /6.7	8.6	0.65	11.28	26	0	99	0	1	31.5	43.8	-4.9	38	4	1,000	50	5.3	0.0
C+ /6.6	8.6	0.65	10.86	11	0	99	0	1	31.5	40.5	-5.1	31	4	1,000	50	0.0	5.0
C+ /6.6	8.6	0.66	10.86	11	0	99	0	1	31.5	40.6	-5.1	31	4	1,000	50	0.0	1.0
C+ /6.4	11.2	0.96	18.13	138	0	99	0	1	19.7	91.7	-9.5	61	N/A	1,000	50	5.3	0.0
C+ /6.3	11.2	0.96	17.19	26	0	99	0	1	19.7	87.2	-9.7	52	N/A	1,000	50	0.0	5.0
C+ /6.3	11.2	0.96	17.39	19	0	99	0	1	19.7	87.3	-9.7	52	N/A	1,000	50	1.0	1.0
C /4.4	14.7	1.66	22.60	273	0	99	0	1	16.5	87.2	-11.4	11	4	1,000	50	5.3	0.0
C /4.3	14.7	1.65	21.20	76	0	99	0	1	16.5	82.8	-11.5	8	4	1,000	50	0.0	5.0
C /4.3	14.7	1.65	21.59	28	0	99	0	1	16.5	82.6	-11.5	8	4	1,000	50	0.0	1.0
B /8.4	7.1	0.90	32.73	103	0	99	0	1	11.8	44.0	-11.0	24	4	1,000	50	5.3	0.0
B /8.3	7.1	0.90	31.99	31	0	99	0	1	11.8	40.6	-11.1	19	4	1,000	50	0.0	5.0
B /8.3	7.1	0.90	32.19	6	0	99	0	1	11.8	40.7	-11.1	19	4	1,000	50	0.0	1.0
U /	N/A	N/A	11.61	33	0	99	0	1	5.0	N/A	N/A	N/A	3	1,000	50	5.3	0.0
B- /7.6	9.5	1.14	18.83	133	0	99	0	1	57.0	74.2	-11.6	61	26	1,000	0	0.0	0.0
U /	N/A	N/A	10.05	49	3	96	0	1	22.1	N/A	N/A	N/A	1	2,500	50	0.0	0.0
B /8.3	5.5	1.09	11.86	118	4	63	31	2	119.6	32.6	-3.5	36	N/A	5,000,000	0	0.0	0.0
B /8.3	5.4	1.09	11.85	4	4	63	31	2	119.6	31.8	-3.5	34	N/A	5,000,000	0	0.0	0.0
B /8.3	5.5	1.10	11.77	N/A	4	63	31	2	119.6	31.1	-3.6	33	N/A	5,000,000	0	0.0	0.0
C+ /5.7	8.6	1.07	7.40	33	5	94	0	1	49.3	54.3	-8.9	35	N/A	5,000,000	0	0.0	0.0
C+ /5.7	8.7	1.07	7.08	N/A	5	94	0	1	49.3	52.3	-9.1	31	N/A	5,000,000	0	0.0	0.0
B- /7.7	7.7	1.00	15.58	697	0	99	0	1	18.7	63.9	-9.8	54	N/A	5,000,000	0	0.0	0.0
B- /7.7	7.6	1.00	15.51	24	0	99	0	1	18.7	62.7	-9.9	51	N/A	5,000,000	0	0.0	0.0
B- /7.7	7.6	1.00	15.48	7	0	99	0	1	18.7	61.8	-9.9	49	N/A	5,000,000	0	0.0	0.0
C /5.5	9.6	1.15	12.24	90	2	97	0	1	178.4	40.9	-9.9	11	4	5,000,000	0	0.0	0.0
C /5.5	9.6	1.15	11.93	N/A	2	97	0	1	178.4	39.1	-9.9	9	N/A	5,000,000	0	0.0	0.0
C /5.5	9.6	1.15	11.66	N/A	2	97	0	1	178.4	39.2	-10.0	10	N/A	5,000,000	0	0.0	0.0
B- /7.0	10.2	1.00	14.02	77	4	95	0	1	110.5	132.6	-9.6	53	N/A	5,000,000	0	0.0	2.0
B- /7.0	10.1	0.99	13.63	N/A	4	95	0	1	110.5	128.1	-9.8	47	N/A	5,000,000	0	1.0	2.0
C+ /6.3	10.9	1.05	11.67	187	3	96	0	1	85.6	122.4	-9.6	30	4	5,000,000	0	0.0	2.0
C+ /6.3	10.9	1.05	11.69	1	3	96	0	1	85.6	119.9	-9.9	27	4	5,000,000	0	0.0	2.0
C+ /6.0	13.1	1.13	11.51	7	3	96	0	1	98.8	67.2	-7.6	5	N/A	5,000,000	0	0.0	0.0
C+ /6.0	13.2	1.13	11.37	5	3	96	0	1	98.8	66.0	-7.6	4	N/A	5,000,000	0	0.0	0.0
C+ /6.0	13.1	1.13	11.27	N/A	3	96	0	1	98.8	65.1	-7.6	4	3	5,000,000	0	0.0	0.0
C /4.3	14.9	0.93	9.97	3	7	92	0	1	85.4	90.4	-9.4	27	N/A	5,000,000	0	0.0	0.0
C+ /6.3	14.6	1.00	16.07	72	2	98	0	0	34.0	119.4	-11.0	55	N/A	5,000,000	0	0.0	0.0
C+ /6.3	14.6	1.00	15.85	N/A	2	98	0	0	34.0	117.3	-11.2	50	N/A	5,000,000	0	0.0	0.0
C+ /6.5	8.6	1.06	15.61	628	3	96	0	1	60.2	52.8	-9.0	33	N/A	2,500	50	0.0	0.0
B- /7.1	6.2	0.86	11.91	353	6	45	0	49	74.7	49.5	-1.4	88	11	2,500	50	0.0	0.0
C+ /6.5	10.8	1.04	12.60	1,279	0	99	0	1	98.2	119.5	-9.6	26	N/A	2,500	50	0.0	2.0

					PERFORMANCE							
99 Pct = Best 0 Pct = Worst			Overall Weiss Investment Rating		Perfor-mance Rating/Pts	Total Return % through 6/30/06					Incl. in Returns	
									Annualized		Dividend Yield	Expense Ratio
Fund Type	Fund Name	Ticker Symbol		Phone		3 Mo	6 Mo	1Yr / Pct	3Yr / Pct	5Yr / Pct		
GR	Northern Trust Large Cap Value	NOLVX	C+	(800) 595-9111	C / 5.4	0.00	5.70	9.13 /41	13.01 /49	6.10 /62	1.59	1.10
MC	Northern Trust Midcap Growth	NOMCX	D	(800) 595-9111	C- / 3.3	-7.17	-0.29	4.64 /13	11.19 /37	2.63 /33	0.00	1.00
GR	Northern Trust Select Equity	NOEQX	E+	(800) 595-9111	E+ / 0.7	-5.70	-1.96	2.60 / 6	5.90 / 6	-1.64 / 9	0.18	1.00
SC	Northern Trust Small Cap Growth	NSGRX	C-	(800) 595-9111	C+ / 6.3	-5.03	9.55	16.07 /75	14.93 /58	2.81 /35	0.00	1.25
SC	Northern Trust Small Cap Index	NSIDX	C+	(800) 595-9111	B- / 7.4	-5.18	7.98	14.08 /68	18.04 /73	7.81 /71	0.65	0.35
SC	Northern Trust Small Cap Value	NOSGX	B+	(800) 595-9111	B+ / 8.5	-3.52	9.84	16.73 /76	22.00 /85	13.15 /89	0.43	1.00
IX	Northern Trust Stock Index	NOSIX	C	(800) 595-9111	C- / 3.8	-1.52	2.58	8.31 /35	10.76 /33	2.00 /27	1.64	0.25
TC	Northern Trust Technology	NTCHX	E-	(800) 595-9111	E+ / 0.9	-9.17	-4.48	1.83 / 4	7.08 /11	-4.95 / 3	0.00	1.25
GL	NorthPointe Small Cap Value Inst	NNSVX	D-	(800) 848-0920	B / 8.1	-3.92	9.54	15.42 /73	20.02 /79	11.11 /84	0.33	0.99
BA	Nuveen Balanced Muni & Stock A	NBMSX	C-	(800) 257-8787	D- / 1.1	-0.22	2.81	6.48 /23	7.51 /12	2.64 /33	2.52	1.22
BA	Nuveen Balanced Muni & Stock B	NMNBX	C-	(800) 257-8787	D- / 1.0	-0.36	2.41	5.73 /19	6.73 / 9	1.87 /26	1.29	1.97
BA	Nuveen Balanced Muni & Stock C	NBMCX	C-	(800) 257-8787	D- / 1.4	-0.36	2.45	5.70 /19	6.72 / 9	1.88 /26	1.29	1.97
BA	Nuveen Balanced Muni & Stock R	NMNRX	C	(800) 257-8787	D / 2.2	-0.14	2.92	6.75 /25	7.80 /14	2.91 /36	3.16	0.97
BA	Nuveen Balanced Stock & Bond A	NNSAX	D+	(800) 257-8787	D / 1.7	-0.21	3.30	7.57 /30	8.73 /19	3.84 /44	1.86	1.25
BA	Nuveen Balanced Stock & Bond B	NNSBX	D+	(800) 257-8787	D- / 1.5	-0.40	2.91	6.80 /25	7.93 /15	3.07 /38	1.81	2.00
BA	Nuveen Balanced Stock & Bond C	NUVCX	C-	(800) 257-8787	D / 2.1	-0.36	2.91	6.77 /25	7.94 /15	3.07 /38	1.26	2.00
BA	Nuveen Balanced Stock & Bond R	NNSRX	C-	(800) 257-8787	C- / 3.0	-0.15	3.43	7.84 /31	9.00 /21	4.11 /47	2.21	1.00
GR	Nuveen Large Cap Value A	NNGAX	B-	(800) 257-8787	C / 5.2	-0.33	6.08	13.97 /68	14.08 /54	4.08 /47	2.16	1.31
GR	Nuveen Large Cap Value B	NNGBX	C+	(800) 257-8787	C / 5.0	-0.52	5.67	13.13 /65	13.22 /50	3.31 /40	1.64	2.04
GR	Nuveen Large Cap Value C	NNGCX	B	(800) 257-8787	C+ / 5.6	-0.49	5.68	13.13 /65	13.23 /50	3.31 /40	0.13	2.04
GR	Nuveen Large Cap Value R	NNGRX	B+	(800) 257-8787	C+ / 6.3	-0.26	6.22	14.22 /69	14.36 /56	4.35 /49	1.03	1.04
FO	Nuveen NWQ International Value A	NAIGX	A	(800) 257-8787	B+ / 8.9	-1.36	5.72	20.66 /83	25.51 /92	12.72 /88	0.54	1.59
FO	Nuveen NWQ International Value B	NBIGX	A	(800) 257-8787	B+ / 8.7	-1.58	5.31	19.70 /81	24.47 /90	11.75 /86	0.00	2.33
FO	Nuveen NWQ International Value C	NCIGX	A	(800) 257-8787	A- / 9.0	-1.57	5.31	19.73 /81	24.50 /90	11.77 /86	0.00	2.35
FO	Nuveen NWQ International Value R	NGRRX	A+	(800) 257-8787	A- / 9.2	-1.32	5.84	20.92 /83	25.70 /92	12.88 /88	0.79	1.32
GI	Nuveen NWQ Multi-Cap Value Fund	NQVAX	B+	(800) 257-8787	B / 7.7	1.23	7.11	17.44 /78	19.88 /79	14.31 /91	0.22	1.31
GI	Nuveen NWQ Multi-Cap Value Fund	NQVBX	B+	(800) 257-8787	B- / 7.5	1.04	6.75	16.56 /76	18.98 /76	13.46 /89	0.00	2.06
GI	Nuveen NWQ Multi-Cap Value Fund	NQVCX	B+	(800) 257-8787	B / 7.8	1.04	6.70	16.56 /76	18.95 /76	13.46 /89	0.00	2.07
GI	● Nuveen NWQ Multi-Cap Value Fund	NQVRX	A-	(800) 257-8787	B / 8.2	1.32	7.27	17.76 /79	20.15 /80	14.62 /91	0.45	1.06
SC	Nuveen NWQ Small Cap Value A	NSCAX	U	(800) 257-8787	U /	-1.17	12.89	27.08 /91	--	--	0.28	1.25
GR	Nuveen NWQ Value Opportunities A	NVOAX	U	(800) 257-8787	U /	0.98	11.34	29.45 /94	--	--	0.24	1.31
GR	Nuveen NWQ Value Opportunities R	NVORX	U	(800) 257-8787	U /	1.01	11.46	29.80 /94	--	--	0.45	1.17
GR	Nuveen Rittenhouse Growth Fund A	NRGAX	D-	(800) 257-8787	E- / 0.2	-3.01	-0.77	2.90 / 7	4.52 / 3	-2.88 / 6	0.00	1.48
GR	Nuveen Rittenhouse Growth Fund B	NRGBX	D-	(800) 257-8787	E- / 0.2	-3.15	-1.12	2.11 / 5	3.74 / 2	-3.61 / 4	0.00	2.23
GR	Nuveen Rittenhouse Growth Fund C	NRGCX	D-	(800) 257-8787	E / 0.3	-3.15	-1.12	2.11 / 5	3.74 / 2	-3.60 / 4	0.00	2.23
GR	Nuveen Rittenhouse Growth Fund R	NRGRX	D-	(800) 257-8787	E / 0.5	-2.91	-0.66	3.14 / 8	4.78 / 4	-2.65 / 6	0.00	1.22
TC	Oak Assoc-Black Oak Emerging Tech	BOGSX	E-	(888) 462-5386	E+ / 0.9	-10.74	0.93	--	7.06 /11	-18.88 / 0	0.00	1.35
HL	Oak Assoc-Live Oak Health Sciences	LOGSX	E+	(888) 462-5386	E / 0.5	-12.80	-12.51	-6.59 / 0	7.69 /13	0.96 /20	0.00	1.22
SC	Oak Assoc-Pin Oak Aggressive Stock	POGSX	E-	(888) 462-5386	D- / 1.4	-9.25	-13.11	-2.41 / 1	9.83 /26	-8.61 / 0	0.00	1.22
TC	Oak Assoc-Red Oak Technology	ROGSX	E-	(888) 462-5386	E- / 0.2	-8.87	-8.08	0.79 / 2	4.26 / 3	-12.84 / 0	0.00	1.27
GR	Oak Assoc-White Oak Select Gr Fd	WOGSX	E-	(888) 462-5386	E- / 0.1	-7.51	-5.82	-0.76 / 1	2.51 / 1	-6.93 / 1	0.06	1.14
GR	Oak Value Fund	OAKVX	D-	(800) 680-4199	E+ / 0.6	0.49	-0.04	-1.66 / 1	5.82 / 6	0.13 /16	0.28	1.27
BA	● Oakmark Equity and Income I	OAKBX	B	(800) 625-6275	C / 4.3	1.57	3.60	10.13 /48	11.41 /39	9.44 /78	1.31	0.87
BA	Oakmark Equity and Income II	OARBX	B	(800) 625-6275	C / 4.4	1.46	3.41	9.80 /46	11.11 /36	9.17 /77	1.06	1.16
GR	Oakmark Fund (The) I	OAKMX	C-	(800) 625-6275	D / 2.0	-0.35	3.45	4.16 /11	8.41 /17	4.29 /49	0.82	1.07
GR	Oakmark Fund (The) II	OARMX	C-	(800) 625-6275	D / 2.1	-0.47	3.24	3.83 /10	8.06 /15	4.00 /46	0.54	1.37
GL	Oakmark Global I	OAKGX	A+	(800) 625-6275	B+ / 8.3	0.80	7.71	20.47 /82	20.73 /82	16.52 /94	1.01	1.19
GL	Oakmark Global II	OARGX	A+	(800) 625-6275	B+ / 8.4	0.69	7.50	20.00 /82	20.37 /81	--	0.84	1.55
FO	Oakmark International I	OAKIX	A+	(800) 625-6275	A- / 9.2	2.90	13.37	26.73 /91	24.30 /90	12.97 /89	2.24	1.09
FO	Oakmark International II	OARIX	A+	(800) 625-6275	A- / 9.2	2.80	13.12	26.28 /90	23.89 /89	12.60 /88	2.03	1.44
FO	● Oakmark International Small Cap I	OAKEX	A	(800) 625-6275	A+ / 9.7	-0.58	11.21	31.38 /95	32.72 /97	21.59 /97	2.73	1.38
FO	Oakmark International Small Cap II	OAREX	A+	(800) 625-6275	A+ / 9.7	-0.63	11.12	31.26 /95	32.65 /97	21.38 /97	2.67	1.46

● Denotes fund is closed to new investors
* Denotes fund is included in Section II

RISK			NET ASSETS		ASSET				Portfolio Turnover Ratio	BULL / BEAR		FUND MANAGER		MINIMUMS		LOADS	
Risk Rating/Pts	3 Year		NAV As of 6/30/06	Total $(Mil)	Cash %	Stocks %	Bonds %	Other %		Last Bull Market Return	Last Bear Market Return	Manager Quality Pct	Manager Tenure (Years)	Initial Purch. $	Additional Purch. $	Front End Load	Back End Load
	Standard Deviation	Beta															
B- /7.6	8.1	0.98	13.36	1,148	3	96	0	1	33.1	73.4	-11.1	75	N/A	2,500	50	0.0	0.0
C /5.3	13.1	1.13	13.98	258	0	99	0	1	149.6	65.7	-7.8	5	N/A	2,500	50	0.0	0.0
C+ /6.2	9.7	1.16	19.02	209	2	97	0	1	145.1	38.8	-9.0	9	N/A	2,500	50	0.0	0.0
C /4.6	14.9	0.94	12.28	60	0	99	0	1	150.8	92.4	-9.2	31	N/A	2,500	50	0.0	0.0
C+ /5.9	14.5	1.00	11.36	418	0	99	0	1	22.3	116.0	-11.2	49	N/A	2,500	50	0.0	0.0
C+ /6.7	12.6	0.85	16.97	580	3	96	0	1	31.6	127.2	-7.7	93	5	2,500	50	0.0	0.0
B- /7.8	7.6	1.00	15.67	495	1	98	0	1	4.9	62.4	-9.8	51	N/A	2,500	50	0.0	0.0
D+ /2.6	17.2	1.85	11.10	177	1	98	0	1	76.0	62.9	-13.4	1	N/A	2,500	50	0.0	0.0
E- /0.0	12.8	0.93	11.32	27	0	98	0	2	144.1	121.7	-9.8	31	6	1,000,000	0	0.0	0.0
B+ /9.9	3.6	0.71	23.85	58	1	41	57	1	22.0	33.6	-1.7	71	10	3,000	50	5.8	1.0
B+ /9.9	3.6	0.72	25.32	11	1	41	57	1	22.0	30.5	-1.8	64	10	3,000	50	0.0	5.0
B+ /9.9	3.6	0.72	25.29	8	1	41	57	1	22.0	30.5	-1.8	63	10	3,000	50	0.0	1.0
B+ /9.9	3.6	0.72	23.33	1	1	41	57	1	22.0	34.8	-1.6	74	10	3,000	50	0.0	0.0
B /8.4	4.7	0.94	25.40	31	2	62	35	1	33.0	42.7	-2.7	71	10	3,000	50	5.8	1.0
B /8.5	4.7	0.94	25.40	8	2	62	35	1	33.0	39.4	-2.9	64	10	3,000	50	0.0	5.0
B /8.5	4.7	0.94	25.42	7	2	62	35	1	33.0	39.3	-2.9	64	10	3,000	50	0.0	1.0
B /8.4	4.7	0.94	25.40	9	2	62	35	1	33.0	43.8	-2.7	74	10	3,000	50	0.0	0.0
B /8.5	7.6	0.93	27.23	441	2	98	0	0	44.0	74.2	-6.4	86	N/A	3,000	50	5.8	1.0
B /8.5	7.6	0.93	26.64	27	2	98	0	0	44.0	70.2	-6.6	80	N/A	3,000	50	0.0	5.0
B /8.5	7.6	0.93	26.60	29	2	98	0	0	44.0	70.2	-6.6	81	N/A	3,000	50	0.0	1.0
B /8.4	7.6	0.93	27.33	26	2	98	0	0	44.0	75.6	-6.3	87	N/A	3,000	50	0.0	0.0
B- /7.0	10.3	0.96	29.78	253	5	94	0	1	24.0	145.1	-4.2	74	4	3,000	50	5.8	1.0
C+ /6.9	10.3	0.96	28.74	16	5	94	0	1	24.0	138.1	-4.4	66	4	3,000	50	0.0	5.0
C+ /6.9	10.3	0.96	28.76	113	5	94	0	1	24.0	138.1	-4.4	67	4	3,000	50	0.0	1.0
B- /7.0	10.3	0.96	29.92	302	5	94	0	1	24.0	145.8	-4.1	76	4	3,000	50	0.0	1.0
B- /7.2	10.6	1.24	23.81	409	9	90	0	1	4.0	123.0	-6.2	95	9	3,000	50	5.8	1.0
B- /7.2	10.6	1.24	23.42	59	9	90	0	1	4.0	117.8	-6.4	93	9	3,000	50	0.0	5.0
B- /7.2	10.6	1.24	23.42	308	9	90	0	1	4.0	117.6	-6.3	93	9	3,000	50	0.0	1.0
B- /7.2	10.6	1.24	23.76	212	9	90	0	1	4.0	124.8	-6.2	95	9	3,000	50	0.0	1.0
U /	N/A	N/A	26.09	34	8	91	0	1	10.0	N/A	N/A	N/A	N/A	3,000	50	5.8	1.0
U /	N/A	N/A	26.90	73	16	69	0	15	15.0	N/A	N/A	N/A	N/A	3,000	50	5.8	1.0
U /	N/A	N/A	26.94	38	16	69	0	15	15.0	N/A	N/A	N/A	N/A	3,000	50	0.0	1.0
B- /7.8	7.4	0.88	20.61	37	3	96	0	1	25.0	33.4	-9.1	13	9	3,000	50	5.8	1.0
B- /7.9	7.4	0.88	19.35	44	3	96	0	1	25.0	30.3	-9.3	10	9	3,000	50	0.0	5.0
B- /7.9	7.4	0.88	19.36	43	3	96	0	1	25.0	30.4	-9.3	10	9	3,000	50	0.0	1.0
B /8.0	7.4	0.88	21.05	13	3	96	0	1	25.0	34.5	-9.1	14	9	3,000	50	0.0	1.0
E- /0.0	23.6	2.38	2.16	43	0	98	0	2	30.2	80.3	-15.4	0	6	2,000	50	0.0	0.0
C+ /6.8	13.3	1.06	10.49	29	0	99	0	1	15.7	53.7	-6.0	21	5	2,000	50	0.0	0.0
D+ /2.7	19.7	1.09	19.82	101	0	98	0	2	28.0	75.2	-13.2	3	N/A	2,000	50	0.0	0.0
D /1.6	18.1	1.97	6.37	119	1	98	0	1	40.5	51.9	-11.7	0	8	2,000	50	0.0	0.0
D+ /2.8	15.7	1.77	30.42	588	1	98	0	1	36.5	46.0	-15.2	0	N/A	2,000	50	0.0	0.0
B- /7.2	6.9	0.78	28.00	201	2	98	0	0	21.0	51.3	-11.9	25	N/A	2,500	100	0.0	2.0
B+ /9.7	5.3	0.78	25.88	9,851	4	62	33	1	31.0	55.8	-2.8	92	11	1,000	100	0.0	2.0
B+ /9.7	5.3	0.77	25.76	633	4	62	33	1	31.0	54.5	-3.1	92	6	1,000	100	0.0	0.0
B /8.7	6.4	0.74	42.29	5,426	4	94	0	2	3.0	52.6	-7.9	51	6	1,000	100	0.0	2.0
B /8.5	6.4	0.74	42.05	39	4	94	0	2	3.0	51.1	-8.0	46	5	1,000	100	0.0	0.0
B /8.4	8.8	0.79	25.28	2,172	0	99	0	1	24.0	139.1	-12.1	69	N/A	1,000	100	0.0	2.0
B /8.4	8.8	0.79	24.94	73	0	99	0	1	24.0	137.0	-12.3	65	N/A	1,000	100	0.0	0.0
B /8.3	8.9	0.83	25.53	6,884	4	95	0	1	19.0	141.7	-12.9	86	14	1,000	100	0.0	2.0
B /8.6	8.9	0.83	25.34	475	4	95	0	1	19.0	139.2	-13.1	84	14	1,000	100	0.0	0.0
C+ /6.2	10.8	0.91	22.22	1,186	7	92	0	1	22.0	214.2	-9.9	98	11	1,000	100	0.0	2.0
B /8.0	10.8	0.92	22.19	1	7	92	0	1	22.0	213.6	-10.0	98	5	1,000	100	0.0	0.0

99 Pct = Best　0 Pct = Worst					PERFORMANCE						Incl. in Returns	
			Overall Weiss Investment Rating		Perfor-mance Rating/Pts	Total Return % through 6/30/06			Annualized		Dividend Yield	Expense Ratio
Fund Type	Fund Name	Ticker Symbol		Phone		3 Mo	6 Mo	1Yr / Pct	3Yr / Pct	5Yr / Pct		
MC	Oakmark Select I	OAKLX	C-	(800) 625-6275	D+ / 2.6	-0.77	1.73	6.82 /25	9.30 /23	6.60 /65	0.83	1.00
MC	Oakmark Select II	OARLX	C-	(800) 625-6275	D+ / 2.7	-0.86	1.53	6.47 /23	9.02 /21	6.32 /63	0.57	1.33
AG	Oberweis Emerging Growth Portfolio	OBEGX	E	(800) 245-7311	C- / 3.8	-10.45	-0.11	8.21 /34	12.07 /43	4.95 /54	0.00	1.42
SC	● Oberweis Micro Cap Portfolio	OBMCX	E	(800) 245-7311	C+ / 5.6	-12.66	-5.55	10.24 /48	15.97 /63	14.21 /90	0.00	1.70
MC	Oberweis Mid Cap Growth Portfolio	OBMDX	D	(800) 245-7311	C+ / 6.1	-6.53	8.54	22.41 /85	13.92 /53	0.18 /16	0.00	2.00
FO	Oberwies China Opportunities Fund	OBCHX	U	(800) 245-7311	U /	-0.54	37.94	--	--	--	0.00	2.49
PM	OCM Gold Fund	OCMGX	D+	(800) 628-9403	A+ / 9.8	3.86	28.02	72.66 /99	27.15 /93	33.57 /99	0.28	2.14
IN	Old Mutual Analytic Dfns Eqty A	ANAEX	U	(888) 744-5050	U /	-1.22	0.62	3.82 /10	--	--	1.47	1.45
IN	Old Mutual Analytic Dfns Eqty C	ANCEX	U	(888) 744-5050	U /	-1.31	0.31	3.15 / 8	--	--	1.45	2.20
IN	● Old Mutual Analytic Dfns Eqty Z	ANDEX	C+	(888) 744-5050	C / 4.9	-1.15	0.86	4.39 /12	13.27 /50	6.29 /63	1.96	1.20
GI	Old Mutual Analytic U.S. Lng/Sht Z	OBDEX	C+	(888) 744-5050	C / 4.7	-0.09	3.82	8.11 /33	11.99 /42	2.17 /29	0.69	1.27
AA	Old Mutual Asset Alloc Bal Port A	OMABX	U	(888) 744-5050	U /	-1.30	2.98	8.23 /35	--	--	0.98	4.42
AA	Old Mutual Asset Alloc Bal Port C	OMBCX	U	(888) 744-5050	U /	-1.48	2.65	7.44 /29	--	--	0.40	4.92
AA	Old Mutual Asset Alloc Gr Prt A	OMGAX	U	(888) 744-5050	U /	-2.15	5.62	15.19 /72	--	--	0.12	5.02
AA	Old Mutual Asset Alloc Gr Prt C	OMCGX	U	(888) 744-5050	U /	-2.32	5.34	14.40 /70	--	--	0.00	5.63
AA	Old Mutual Asset Alloc Mod Gr Prt A	OMMAX	U	(888) 744-5050	U /	-1.79	4.31	11.20 /55	--	--	0.24	4.92
AA	Old Mutual Asset Alloc Mod Gr Prt C	OMMCX	U	(888) 744-5050	U /	-1.96	3.90	10.41 /50	--	--	0.00	5.44
GR	Old Mutual Barrow Hanley Value A	OAFOX	D	(888) 744-5050	E+ / 0.9	-0.48	0.98	1.87 / 4	7.36 /12	5.24 /56	0.43	1.59
GR	Old Mutual Barrow Hanley Value Adv	OCLFX	D+	(888) 744-5050	D / 1.6	-0.48	0.98	1.86 / 4	7.37 /12	--	0.50	1.59
GR	Old Mutual Barrow Hanley Value Z	OBFOX	D	(888) 744-5050	D / 1.7	-0.42	1.16	2.16 / 5	7.64 /13	5.12 /55	0.79	1.37
TC	Old Mutual Col Cir Tech & Comm Adv	OTNAX	E-	(888) 744-5050	D+ / 2.3	-8.54	-3.99	11.98 /59	10.46 /31	-11.43 / 0	0.00	1.87
TC	Old Mutual Col Cir Tech & Comm Z	OBTCX	E	(888) 744-5050	D+ / 2.5	-8.44	-3.86	12.22 /61	10.75 /33	-11.21 / 0	0.00	1.45
TC	Old Mutual Col Cir Tech&Comm Insur	OTECX	E	(888) 744-5050	C- / 3.1	-8.21	-3.53	12.84 /63	11.60 /40	-10.58 / 0	0.00	0.85
GR	Old Mutual Copper Rock Em Gr I	OMIRX	U	(888) 744-5050	U /	-8.98	5.44	--	--	--	0.00	1.10
SC	Old Mutual Emerging Growth Fd Z	OBEHX	E	(888) 744-5050	C- / 3.7	-9.48	1.49	8.64 /38	11.38 /38	-5.51 / 2	0.00	1.43
GR	Old Mutual Focused Fd Z	OBFVX	C+	(888) 744-5050	C / 5.1	0.15	3.61	6.55 /24	12.95 /49	1.93 /27	0.42	1.39
GR	Old Mutual Growth Fd Adv	OBGWX	D-	(888) 744-5050	C- / 3.8	-5.53	2.74	12.95 /64	11.39 /39	-3.33 / 5	0.00	1.61
GR	Old Mutual Growth Fd Z	OBHGX	D-	(888) 744-5050	C- / 4.1	-5.47	2.86	13.21 /65	11.71 /41	-3.07 / 5	0.00	1.35
RE	Old Mutual Heitman REIT Fund Adv	OBRAX	A	(888) 744-5050	A- / 9.2	-1.46	11.91	19.11 /81	26.22 /92	19.25 /95	1.81	1.56
RE	Old Mutual Heitman REIT Fund Z	OBRTX	B	(888) 744-5050	A / 9.3	-1.40	12.07	19.38 /81	26.55 /93	19.73 /96	2.02	1.31
SC	Old Mutual Ins Growth II Portfolio	OIIGX	D-	(888) 744-5050	C- / 3.8	-5.51	2.83	12.99 /64	11.23 /37	-2.71 / 6	0.00	1.04
GR	Old Mutual Ins Lg Cap Growth Portf	OLCGX	D+	(888) 744-5050	D+ / 2.3	-3.92	0.11	9.41 /43	9.25 /22	-1.76 / 9	0.00	0.96
GR	Old Mutual Ins Lg Cap Grth Concent	OSELX	D-	(888) 744-5050	C- / 3.4	-4.31	1.35	17.29 /78	9.65 /25	-1.81 / 9	0.00	0.89
MC	Old Mutual Ins Mid-Cap	OMCVX	B-	(888) 744-5050	C+ / 6.0	-4.71	1.74	10.46 /50	15.08 /59	6.48 /64	0.00	0.99
GR	Old Mutual Large Cap Fd Adv	OBLWX	C-	(888) 744-5050	D / 2.2	0.84	3.29	6.94 /26	7.59 /13	-1.13 /11	0.29	1.48
GR	Old Mutual Large Cap Fd Z	OLCVX	C-	(888) 744-5050	D+ / 2.3	0.84	3.36	7.21 /27	7.86 /14	-0.88 /12	0.56	1.23
GR	Old Mutual Large Cap Gr Con Adv	OLTAX	E+	(888) 744-5050	C- / 3.2	-4.44	1.02	16.54 /76	9.39 /23	-2.11 / 8	0.00	1.66
GR	Old Mutual Large Cap Gr Con Z	OLCPX	E+	(888) 744-5050	C- / 3.4	-4.39	1.19	16.92 /77	9.69 /25	-1.87 / 9	0.00	1.41
GR	Old Mutual Large Cap Growth Adv	OBLAX	D-	(888) 744-5050	D / 2.0	-4.17	-0.28	8.93 /40	8.79 /20	-2.30 / 7	0.00	1.56
GR	Old Mutual Large Cap Growth Z	OBHLX	D-	(888) 744-5050	D / 2.2	-4.12	-0.14	9.18 /41	9.05 /21	-2.04 / 8	0.00	1.31
MC	Old Mutual Mid-Cap Adv	OZZAX	C	(888) 744-5050	C+ / 6.0	-4.68	1.95	10.71 /52	14.94 /58	--	0.00	1.57
MC	Old Mutual Mid-Cap Z	OBMEX	C+	(888) 744-5050	C+ / 6.2	-4.57	2.15	11.03 /54	15.29 /60	6.22 /62	0.07	1.32
GR	Old Mutual Select Growth Fd Z	OBHEX	E	(888) 744-5050	C- / 3.0	-4.38	0.90	14.71 /71	9.47 /24	-4.90 / 3	0.00	1.46
SC	Old Mutual Small Cap Adv	OVAAX	C	(888) 744-5050	C+ / 5.8	-3.43	5.15	6.46 /23	14.70 /57	3.22 /39	0.00	1.67
SC	Old Mutual Small Cap Z	OBSWX	C	(888) 744-5050	C+ / 5.9	-3.39	5.26	6.70 /24	14.96 /59	3.45 /41	0.00	1.44
SC	Old Mutual Strategic Small Comp Adv	OBSSX	C-	(888) 744-5050	C / 5.2	-6.54	2.73	7.30 /28	13.92 /54	--	0.00	1.71
SC	Old Mutual Strategic Small Comp Z	OSSCX	D	(888) 744-5050	C / 5.4	-6.48	2.84	7.52 /29	14.18 /55	2.68 /34	0.00	1.46
SC	● Old Mutual TS&W Small Cap Value Z	OSMVX	U	(888) 744-5050	U /	-0.99	12.52	17.60 /78	--	--	0.00	1.46
SC	Old Mutual-Small Cap Growth	OSCGX	E	(888) 744-5050	C- / 3.6	-9.43	1.54	9.06 /40	11.19 /37	-2.95 / 6	0.00	1.07
FO	Old Westbury International	OWEIX	B+	(800) 607-2200	B+ / 8.5	-1.68	6.52	27.35 /92	21.23 /83	6.94 /66	0.64	1.25
GR	Olstein Financial Alert Adv	OFAFX	C	(800) 799-2113	C / 4.5	-4.82	0.12	5.40 /17	12.90 /48	4.89 /53	0.00	1.43
GR	Olstein Financial Alert C	OFALX	D	(800) 799-2113	C- / 3.7	-4.99	-0.24	4.58 /13	12.05 /43	4.10 /47	0.00	2.18

● Denotes fund is closed to new investors
* Denotes fund is included in Section II

RISK			NET ASSETS		ASSET				Portfolio Turnover Ratio	BULL / BEAR		FUND MANAGER		MINIMUMS		LOADS	
Risk Rating/Pts	3 Year		NAV As of 6/30/06	Total $(Mil)	Cash %	Stocks %	Bonds %	Other %		Last Bull Market Return	Last Bear Market Return	Manager Quality Pct	Manager Tenure (Years)	Initial Purch. $	Additional Purch. $	Front End Load	Back End Load
	Standard Deviation	Beta															
B /8.3	7.7	0.58	33.47	5,975	5	94	0	1	14.0	58.3	-6.2	36	6	1,000	100	0.0	2.0
B /8.4	7.7	0.58	33.26	70	5	94	0	1	14.0	57.0	-6.2	34	7	1,000	100	0.0	0.0
D /2.0	21.6	2.00	26.92	200	2	97	0	1	75.0	123.6	-16.3	5	N/A	1,000	100	0.0	1.0
E+ /0.8	24.3	1.41	16.35	73	2	97	0	1	76.0	158.1	-3.5	3	N/A	1,000	100	0.0	1.0
D+ /2.5	19.5	1.53	13.60	12	3	96	0	1	119.0	102.4	-10.2	1	N/A	1,000	100	0.0	1.0
U /	N/A	N/A	14.87	219	6	93	0	1	N/A	N/A	N/A	N/A	N/A	1,000	100	0.0	2.0
E- /0.0	32.9	1.58	18.55	112	4	95	0	1	5.0	132.2	21.0	14	10	1,000	100	4.5	1.5
U /	N/A	N/A	12.93	268	N/A	N/A	0	N/A	81.0	N/A	N/A	N/A	N/A	2,500	0	5.8	1.0
U /	N/A	N/A	12.85	192	N/A	N/A	0	N/A	81.0	N/A	N/A	N/A	N/A	2,500	0	0.0	1.0
B /8.6	6.3	0.62	12.93	141	N/A	N/A	0	N/A	81.0	61.5	-1.3	94	11	2,500	0	0.0	0.0
B /8.5	7.9	0.98	11.69	23	N/A	N/A	0	N/A	208.2	67.5	-9.8	67	N/A	2,500	0	0.0	0.0
U /	N/A	N/A	11.44	36	4	60	36	0	60.7	N/A	N/A	N/A	2	2,500	0	5.8	1.0
U /	N/A	N/A	11.42	60	4	60	36	0	60.7	N/A	N/A	N/A	2	2,500	0	0.0	1.0
U /	N/A	N/A	12.77	29	0	100	0	0	48.6	N/A	N/A	N/A	2	2,500	0	5.8	1.0
U /	N/A	N/A	12.63	48	0	100	0	0	48.6	N/A	N/A	N/A	2	2,500	0	0.0	1.0
U /	N/A	N/A	12.09	45	0	80	20	0	54.7	N/A	N/A	N/A	2	2,500	0	5.8	1.0
U /	N/A	N/A	11.98	93	0	80	20	0	54.7	N/A	N/A	N/A	2	2,500	0	0.0	1.0
B /8.2	8.9	0.89	16.50	4	N/A	100	0	N/A	26.9	52.1	-12.9	28	N/A	2,500	0	5.8	1.0
B /8.2	8.9	0.89	16.50	N/A	N/A	100	0	N/A	26.9	N/A	N/A	29	3	2,500	0	0.0	0.0
B- /7.8	8.9	0.89	16.54	221	N/A	100	0	N/A	26.9	53.1	-12.9	31	N/A	2,500	0	0.0	0.0
D+ /2.7	18.6	1.90	11.78	N/A	0	99	0	1	105.0	74.2	-15.6	4	N/A	2,500	0	0.0	0.0
D+ /2.7	18.5	1.89	11.94	192	0	99	0	1	105.0	75.6	-15.7	5	N/A	2,500	0	0.0	0.0
D+ /2.8	18.3	1.86	2.46	97	0	99	0	1	29.7	79.9	-15.3	7	N/A	2,500	0	0.0	0.0
U /	N/A	N/A	11.05	53	3	96	0	1	N/A	N/A	N/A	N/A	N/A	1,000,000	0	0.0	0.0
D /2.0	19.6	1.18	14.33	163	2	97	0	1	157.7	99.1	-19.0	3	N/A	2,500	0	0.0	0.0
B /8.0	8.8	1.01	20.39	16	3	96	0	1	110.5	70.2	-11.2	72	7	2,500	0	0.0	0.0
C /4.3	14.9	1.50	21.37	N/A	2	97	0	1	102.9	67.9	-9.0	19	N/A	2,500	0	0.0	0.0
C /4.3	14.9	1.50	21.94	587	2	97	0	1	102.9	69.4	-8.9	21	N/A	2,500	0	0.0	0.0
C+ /6.7	16.0	0.96	13.93	15	2	97	0	1	70.0	127.5	1.2	81	N/A	2,500	0	0.0	0.0
C /5.0	16.0	0.96	14.00	175	2	97	0	1	70.0	129.3	1.5	82	17	2,500	0	0.0	0.0
C /4.4	15.1	0.92	12.00	41	0	99	0	1	24.2	67.8	-9.1	12	9	2,500	0	0.0	0.0
B- /7.4	11.5	1.28	18.61	22	0	99	0	1	30.5	59.8	-7.0	19	N/A	2,500	0	0.0	0.0
C /4.4	14.9	1.50	9.77	72	0	99	0	1	28.4	64.7	-6.8	11	N/A	2,500	0	0.0	0.0
B- /7.6	11.1	0.97	16.98	48	2	97	0	1	89.1	88.6	-7.8	32	2	2,500	0	0.0	0.0
B /8.6	7.0	0.83	13.20	N/A	1	98	0	1	77.3	45.0	-9.8	34	N/A	2,500	0	0.0	0.0
B /8.7	7.0	0.83	13.24	75	1	98	0	1	77.3	46.1	-9.8	36	N/A	2,500	0	0.0	0.0
C- /3.5	14.9	1.50	16.77	N/A	0	99	0	1	128.6	63.7	-6.9	10	N/A	2,500	0	0.0	0.0
C- /3.5	14.9	1.50	17.00	126	0	99	0	1	128.6	65.1	-6.8	11	N/A	2,500	0	0.0	0.0
C+ /6.0	11.7	1.27	21.58	N/A	0	99	0	1	110.6	57.1	-7.2	16	N/A	2,500	0	0.0	0.0
C+ /6.1	11.7	1.29	21.88	98	0	99	0	1	110.6	58.4	-7.1	17	N/A	2,500	0	0.0	0.0
C+ /6.4	11.1	0.97	18.32	7	1	98	0	1	81.9	88.4	-8.4	31	7	2,500	0	0.0	0.0
C+ /6.5	11.1	0.97	18.57	354	1	98	0	1	81.9	90.1	-8.3	33	7	2,500	0	0.0	0.0
C- /3.3	15.3	1.48	23.55	135	0	99	0	1	157.8	62.0	-10.9	11	N/A	2,500	0	0.0	0.0
C+ /5.8	13.0	0.86	23.90	N/A	2	97	0	1	116.1	91.7	-12.6	40	2	2,500	0	0.0	0.0
C+ /5.9	13.0	0.86	24.20	45	2	97	0	1	116.1	93.1	-12.5	42	2	2,500	0	0.0	0.0
C+ /6.1	15.7	1.02	16.16	1	2	97	0	1	148.7	103.7	-14.4	17	N/A	2,500	0	0.0	0.0
C- /3.9	15.7	1.02	16.30	43	2	97	0	1	148.7	105.3	-14.6	18	N/A	2,500	0	0.0	0.0
U /	N/A	N/A	27.87	65	2	98	0	0	41.5	N/A	N/A	N/A	3	2,500	0	0.0	0.0
D- /1.5	20.8	1.26	8.55	3	1	98	0	1	64.4	99.0	-17.8	1	N/A	2,500	0	0.0	0.0
C+ /6.7	10.5	1.00	12.90	1,757	2	97	0	1	49.0	115.5	-10.4	28	N/A	1,000	100	0.0	0.0
B- /7.7	11.1	1.28	17.39	294	11	88	0	1	68.0	81.3	-15.2	45	7	1,000	100	0.0	0.0
C+ /5.9	11.1	1.28	16.37	1,398	11	88	0	1	68.0	77.1	-15.0	37	7	1,000	100	0.0	1.0

					PERFORMANCE							
	99 Pct = Best 0 Pct = Worst			Overall Weiss Investment Rating		Perfor- mance Rating/Pts	Total Return % through 6/30/06					Incl. in Returns	
										Annualized		Dividend	Expense
Fund Type	Fund Name	Ticker Symbol		Phone			3 Mo	6 Mo	1Yr / Pct	3Yr / Pct	5Yr / Pct	Yield	Ratio
AA	Oppenheimer Active Alloc Fd Cl A	OAAAX	U	(800) 525-7048	U /	-2.22	3.39	10.42 /50	--	--	1.75	1.27
AA	Oppenheimer Active Alloc Fd Cl B	OAABX	U	(800) 525-7048	U /	-2.41	3.02	9.55 /44	--	--	1.62	2.06
AA	Oppenheimer Active Alloc Fd Cl C	OAACX	U	(800) 525-7048	U /	-2.42	3.02	9.49 /43	--	--	1.65	2.03
AA	Oppenheimer Active Alloc Fd Cl N	OAANX	U	(800) 525-7048	U /	-2.23	3.39	10.19 /48	--	--	1.83	1.44
AG	Oppenheimer Agg Inv Fd Cl A	OAAIX	U	(800) 525-7048	U /	-3.48	2.89	13.08 /65	--	--	0.98	1.37
AG	Oppenheimer Agg Inv Fd Cl B	OBAIX	U	(800) 525-7048	U /	-3.67	2.54	12.15 /60	--	--	0.82	2.19
AG	Oppenheimer Agg Inv Fd Cl C	OCAIX	U	(800) 525-7048	U /	-3.67	2.54	12.21 /61	--	--	0.86	2.14
BA	Oppenheimer Balanced A	OPASX	D	(800) 525-7048	D- / 1.0	-2.39	-0.58	1.59 / 3	8.10 /16	3.94 /45	1.87	1.05
BA	Oppenheimer Balanced B	OASBX	D	(800) 525-7048	E+ / 0.7	-2.66	-1.08	0.61 / 2	7.08 /11	2.99 /37	1.11	1.98
BA	Oppenheimer Balanced C	OASCX	D	(800) 525-7048	D- / 1.1	-2.57	-1.04	0.76 / 2	7.16 /11	3.07 /38	1.18	1.91
BA	Oppenheimer Balanced N	OASNX	D	(800) 525-7048	D- / 1.3	-2.51	-0.83	1.20 / 3	7.59 /13	3.49 /41	1.61	1.46
★ GR	Oppenheimer Capital Appr A	OPTFX	D	(800) 525-7048	D- / 1.5	-4.72	-0.37	6.90 /26	8.80 /20	-0.57 /13	0.55	1.06
GR	Oppenheimer Capital Appr B	OTGBX	D	(800) 525-7048	D- / 1.1	-4.92	-0.78	6.00 /20	7.87 /14	-1.40 /10	0.00	1.93
GR	Oppenheimer Capital Appr C	OTFCX	D	(800) 525-7048	D / 1.7	-4.89	-0.74	6.08 /21	7.97 /15	-1.33 /11	0.00	1.84
GR	Oppenheimer Capital Appr N	OTCNX	D+	(800) 525-7048	D / 2.0	-4.78	-0.52	6.53 /23	8.42 /17	-0.87 /12	0.30	1.42
GR	Oppenheimer Capital Appr VA		D	(800) 525-7048	D+ / 2.8	-3.96	0.45	7.87 /32	9.37 /23	--	0.19	0.91
GR	Oppenheimer Capital Appr Y	OTCYX	C-	(800) 525-7048	D+ / 2.6	-4.61	-0.18	7.31 /28	9.22 /22	-0.21 /15	0.94	0.69
★ IN	Oppenheimer Capital Income Fd A	OPPEX	D+	(800) 525-7048	D / 1.8	1.40	2.48	4.43 /12	8.93 /20	4.25 /48	2.76	0.89
IN	Oppenheimer Capital Income Fd B	OPEBX	D+	(800) 525-7048	D- / 1.4	1.29	2.09	3.60 / 9	8.02 /15	3.38 /40	2.12	1.73
IN	Oppenheimer Capital Income Fd C	OPECX	C-	(800) 525-7048	D / 2.0	1.22	2.03	3.58 / 9	8.06 /15	3.41 /40	2.18	1.71
IN	Oppenheimer Capital Income Fd N	OCINX	C-	(800) 525-7048	D / 2.2	1.30	2.21	3.98 /10	8.52 /18	3.86 /44	2.58	1.24
AA	Oppenheimer Consrve Inv Fd Cl A	OACIX	U	(800) 525-7048	U /	-0.57	1.74	4.75 /14	--	--	1.63	1.17
AA	Oppenheimer Consrve Inv Fd Cl C	OCCIX	U	(800) 525-7048	U /	-0.67	1.46	3.99 /11	--	--	1.47	1.99
CV	Oppenheimer Convertible Sec A	RCVAX	D-	(800) 525-7048	D- / 1.3	0.03	2.95	9.07 /41	7.39 /12	4.61 /51	3.81	0.96
CV	Oppenheimer Convertible Sec B	RCVBX	D-	(800) 525-7048	D- / 1.0	-0.10	2.60	8.25 /35	6.55 / 9	3.81 /44	3.29	1.79
CV	Oppenheimer Convertible Sec C	RCVCX	D	(800) 525-7048	D- / 1.5	-0.10	2.62	8.30 /35	6.58 / 9	3.84 /44	3.33	1.74
CV	Oppenheimer Convertible Sec M	RCVGX	D	(800) 525-7048	D / 1.6	0.04	2.97	9.12 /41	7.31 /12	4.40 /50	3.95	0.91
CV	Oppenheimer Convertible Sec N	RCVNX	D	(800) 525-7048	D / 1.6	-0.21	2.59	8.43 /36	6.87 /10	4.18 /48	3.45	1.43
EM	Oppenheimer Developing Mkts A	ODMAX	B	(800) 525-7048	A+ / 9.8	-9.48	0.19	30.66 /95	39.19 /99	23.84 /98	1.14	1.43
EM	Oppenheimer Developing Mkts B	ODVBX	B	(800) 525-7048	A+ / 9.8	-9.64	-0.19	29.67 /94	38.06 /99	22.85 /98	0.64	2.24
EM	Oppenheimer Developing Mkts C	ODVCX	B	(800) 525-7048	A+ / 9.8	-9.65	-0.17	29.73 /94	38.17 /99	22.90 /98	0.82	2.17
EM	Oppenheimer Developing Mkts N	ODVNX	B	(800) 525-7048	A+ / 9.8	-9.57	0.00	30.23 /94	38.71 /99	23.48 /98	1.06	1.80
SC	Oppenheimer Discovery A	OPOCX	E-	(800) 525-7048	D / 1.8	-6.70	5.34	10.81 /52	10.00 /27	1.37 /23	0.00	1.31
SC	Oppenheimer Discovery B	ODIBX	E-	(800) 525-7048	D / 1.7	-6.89	4.93	9.90 /46	9.09 /21	0.56 /18	0.00	2.20
SC	Oppenheimer Discovery C	ODICX	E-	(800) 525-7048	D / 2.1	-6.90	4.93	9.93 /46	9.11 /21	0.57 /18	0.00	2.22
SC	Oppenheimer Discovery N	ODINX	E	(800) 525-7048	D+ / 2.5	-6.78	5.19	10.48 /50	9.68 /25	1.08 /21	0.00	1.68
SC	Oppenheimer Discovery Y	ODIYX	E	(800) 525-7048	D+ / 2.9	-6.66	5.45	11.05 /54	10.31 /29	1.66 /25	0.00	1.01
GR	Oppenheimer Dividend Growth Fund	OADGX	U	(800) 525-7048	U /	-0.54	2.44	6.64 /24	--	--	0.98	1.25
SC	Oppenheimer Emerging Growth A	OEGAX	E+	(800) 525-7048	C / 5.0	-5.49	8.45	19.88 /82	13.86 /53	3.75 /43	0.00	1.63
SC	Oppenheimer Emerging Growth B	OEGBX	E+	(800) 525-7048	C / 4.9	-5.66	7.97	18.90 /80	12.94 /48	2.94 /36	0.00	2.44
SC	Oppenheimer Emerging Growth C	OEGCX	E+	(800) 525-7048	C / 5.3	-5.65	7.96	18.87 /80	12.96 /49	2.95 /36	0.00	2.40
SC	Oppenheimer Emerging Growth N	OEGNX	E+	(800) 525-7048	C+ / 5.7	-5.57	8.31	19.56 /81	13.55 /52	3.45 /41	0.00	1.87
SC	Oppenheimer Emerging Growth Y	OEGYX	D-	(800) 525-7048	C+ / 6.2	-5.34	8.68	20.51 /82	14.50 /56	4.33 /49	0.00	0.97
TC	Oppenheimer Emerging Tech A	OETAX	E-	(800) 525-7048	E- / 0.2	-10.22	-0.34	9.85 /46	5.59 / 5	-11.47 / 0	0.00	1.66
TC	Oppenheimer Emerging Tech B	OETBX	E-	(800) 525-7048	E / 0.3	-10.29	-0.71	8.98 /40	4.71 / 3	-12.14 / 0	0.00	2.46
TC	Oppenheimer Emerging Tech C	OETCX	E-	(800) 525-7048	E / 0.3	-10.58	-0.71	8.98 /40	4.71 / 3	-12.14 / 0	0.00	2.40
TC	Oppenheimer Emerging Tech N	OETNX	E-	(800) 525-7048	E / 0.4	-10.31	-0.35	9.54 /44	5.35 / 5	-11.64 / 0	0.00	1.82
TC	Oppenheimer Emerging Tech Y	OETYX	E-	(800) 525-7048	E+ / 0.7	-9.91	0.00	10.70 /52	6.33 / 8	-10.85 / 0	0.00	0.97
AG	● Oppenheimer Enterprise A	OENAX	D-	(800) 525-7048	D / 1.9	-7.85	-1.18	7.73 /31	10.02 /28	-2.89 / 6	0.00	1.42
AG	● Oppenheimer Enterprise B	OENBX	D-	(800) 525-7048	D / 1.6	-7.99	-1.51	6.90 /26	9.20 /22	-3.62 / 4	0.00	2.18
AG	● Oppenheimer Enterprise C	OENCX	D-	(800) 525-7048	D / 2.2	-7.98	-1.51	6.98 /26	9.22 /22	-3.61 / 4	0.00	2.18
AG	● Oppenheimer Enterprise N	OENNX	D	(800) 525-7048	D+ / 2.5	-7.89	-1.27	7.52 /29	9.78 /26	-3.12 / 5	0.00	1.68

● Denotes fund is closed to new investors
★ Denotes fund is included in Section II

RISK			NET ASSETS		ASSET					Portfolio Turnover Ratio	BULL / BEAR		FUND MANAGER		MINIMUMS		LOADS	
Risk Rating/Pts	3 Year		NAV As of 6/30/06	Total $(Mil)	Cash %	Stocks %	Bonds %	Other %		Last Bull Market Return	Last Bear Market Return	Manager Quality Pct	Manager Tenure (Years)	Initial Purch. $	Additional Purch. $	Front End Load	Back End Load
	Standard Deviation	Beta															
U /	N/A	N/A	10.99	537	N/A	76	23	N/A	90.0	N/A	N/A	N/A	1	1,000	50	5.8	1.0
U /	N/A	N/A	10.92	210	N/A	76	23	N/A	90.0	N/A	N/A	N/A	1	1,000	50	0.0	5.0
U /	N/A	N/A	10.91	245	N/A	76	23	N/A	90.0	N/A	N/A	N/A	1	1,000	50	0.0	1.0
U /	N/A	N/A	10.97	52	N/A	76	23	N/A	90.0	N/A	N/A	N/A	1	1,000	50	0.0	1.0
U /	N/A	N/A	11.38	100	0	100	0	0	7.0	N/A	N/A	N/A	1	1,000	50	5.8	0.0
U /	N/A	N/A	11.30	35	0	100	0	0	7.0	N/A	N/A	N/A	1	1,000	50	0.0	5.0
U /	N/A	N/A	11.29	41	0	100	0	0	7.0	N/A	N/A	N/A	1	1,000	50	0.0	1.0
B / 8.1	5.3	1.01	13.33	791	9	50	40	1	73.0	45.5	-3.6	61	3	1,000	50	5.8	0.0
B / 8.2	5.3	1.01	13.04	98	9	50	40	1	73.0	41.2	-3.8	49	3	1,000	50	0.0	5.0
B / 8.2	5.3	1.02	13.11	93	9	50	40	1	73.0	41.5	-3.9	50	3	1,000	50	0.0	1.0
B / 8.2	5.3	1.01	13.20	15	9	50	40	1	73.0	43.3	-3.8	56	3	1,000	50	0.0	1.0
B- / 7.9	8.7	1.07	42.75	5,385	1	98	0	1	55.0	58.1	-11.2	27	1	1,000	50	5.8	0.0
B- / 7.8	8.7	1.07	39.22	889	1	98	0	1	55.0	53.8	-11.3	21	1	1,000	50	0.0	5.0
B- / 7.8	8.7	1.07	38.89	658	1	98	0	1	55.0	54.2	-11.3	22	1	1,000	50	0.0	1.0
B- / 7.9	8.7	1.07	42.19	257	1	98	0	1	55.0	56.3	-11.2	25	1	1,000	50	0.0	1.0
C+ / 5.8	8.8	1.08	38.33	417	1	98	0	1	55.0	60.3	-11.5	31	1	1,000	50	0.0	0.0
B- / 7.9	8.7	1.07	43.84	563	1	98	0	1	55.0	59.9	-11.1	30	1	1,000	50	0.0	0.0
B / 8.4	5.5	0.58	11.96	2,554	0	47	31	22	55.0	53.0	-1.0	72	7	1,000	50	5.8	0.0
B / 8.6	5.5	0.58	11.84	259	0	47	31	22	55.0	48.9	-1.2	63	7	1,000	50	0.0	5.0
B / 8.5	5.5	0.58	11.80	161	0	47	31	22	55.0	49.0	-1.2	64	7	1,000	50	0.0	1.0
B / 8.5	5.5	0.58	11.88	34	0	47	31	22	55.0	51.2	-1.1	68	7	1,000	50	0.0	1.0
U /	N/A	N/A	10.51	70	0	99	0	1	11.0	N/A	N/A	N/A	1	1,000	50	5.8	1.0
U /	N/A	N/A	10.44	32	0	99	0	1	11.0	N/A	N/A	N/A	1	1,000	50	0.0	1.0
B- / 7.1	6.5	0.97	13.49	235	6	18	0	76	50.0	39.0	0.8	59	13	1,000	50	5.8	0.0
B- / 7.4	6.4	0.97	13.51	48	6	18	0	76	50.0	35.4	0.5	49	13	1,000	50	0.0	5.0
B- / 7.4	6.4	0.96	13.48	56	6	18	0	76	50.0	35.5	0.6	49	13	1,000	50	0.0	1.0
B- / 7.4	6.5	0.97	13.48	72	6	18	0	76	50.0	38.5	0.6	58	13	1,000	50	3.3	0.0
B- / 7.4	6.5	0.97	13.49	3	6	18	0	76	50.0	36.7	0.6	53	13	1,000	50	0.0	1.0
C / 4.4	17.5	1.03	36.40	6,904	6	93	0	1	28.0	277.1	-2.6	73	2	50,000	50	5.8	2.0
C / 4.3	17.5	1.03	35.99	308	6	93	0	1	28.0	267.5	-2.7	65	2	5,000	50	0.0	5.0
C / 4.3	17.5	1.03	35.58	919	6	93	0	1	28.0	268.2	-2.8	65	2	50,000	50	0.0	2.0
C / 4.4	17.5	1.03	35.82	224	6	93	0	1	28.0	273.3	-2.6	69	2	50,000	50	0.0	2.0
C- / 3.0	17.5	1.13	46.34	582	1	98	0	1	162.0	75.6	-11.5	2	N/A	1,000	50	5.8	2.0
D+ / 2.9	17.5	1.13	41.08	82	1	98	0	1	162.0	71.2	-11.6	1	N/A	1,000	50	0.0	5.0
D+ / 2.9	17.5	1.13	41.96	39	1	98	0	1	162.0	71.3	-11.6	1	N/A	1,000	50	0.0	2.0
D+ / 2.9	17.5	1.13	45.63	11	1	98	0	1	162.0	74.1	-11.5	2	N/A	1,000	50	0.0	2.0
C- / 3.0	17.5	1.13	48.22	99	1	98	0	1	162.0	77.2	-11.4	2	N/A	1,000	50	0.0	2.0
U /	N/A	N/A	10.55	25	4	95	0	1	N/A	N/A	N/A	N/A	1	5,000	50	5.8	0.0
D / 1.7	20.0	1.23	12.06	75	2	97	0	1	207.0	116.5	-13.5	5	N/A	1,000	50	5.8	2.0
D / 1.7	20.0	1.23	11.51	24	2	97	0	1	207.0	111.2	-13.7	3	N/A	1,000	50	0.0	5.0
D / 1.7	20.0	1.23	11.53	21	2	97	0	1	207.0	111.3	-13.6	4	N/A	1,000	50	0.0	2.0
D / 1.7	20.0	1.24	11.86	7	2	97	0	1	207.0	114.9	-13.8	4	N/A	1,000	50	0.0	2.0
D / 1.8	20.0	1.23	12.40	3	2	97	0	1	207.0	120.5	-13.4	7	N/A	1,000	50	0.0	2.0
E / 0.4	22.8	2.15	2.90	73	4	95	0	1	147.0	76.3	-15.1	0	N/A	1,000	50	5.8	2.0
E / 0.4	22.8	2.16	2.79	44	4	95	0	1	147.0	72.4	-15.4	0	N/A	1,000	50	0.0	5.0
E / 0.4	22.7	2.16	2.79	17	4	95	0	1	147.0	72.4	-15.4	0	N/A	1,000	50	0.0	2.0
E / 0.4	22.9	2.15	2.87	4	4	95	0	1	147.0	75.0	-15.2	0	N/A	1,000	50	0.0	2.0
E / 0.5	22.8	2.16	3.00	2	4	95	0	1	147.0	80.1	-15.3	0	N/A	1,000	50	0.0	2.0
C+ / 6.2	12.3	1.32	14.21	122	5	94	0	1	59.0	80.3	-7.4	21	2	1,000	50	5.8	0.0
C+ / 6.1	12.3	1.32	13.01	38	5	94	0	1	59.0	76.0	-7.7	16	2	1,000	50	0.0	5.0
C+ / 6.1	12.3	1.32	13.03	14	5	94	0	1	59.0	76.0	-7.7	16	2	1,000	50	0.0	1.0
C+ / 6.2	12.3	1.31	14.01	34	5	94	0	1	59.0	78.9	-7.6	20	2	1,000	50	0.0	1.0

99 Pct = Best
0 Pct = Worst

Fund Type	Fund Name	Ticker Symbol	Overall Weiss Investment Rating	Phone	Perfor-mance Rating/Pts	3 Mo	6 Mo	1Yr / Pct	3Yr / Pct	5Yr / Pct	Dividend Yield	Expense Ratio
AG ●	Oppenheimer Enterprise Y	OENYX	D	(800) 525-7048	C- / 3.2	-7.71	-0.95	8.15 /34	10.47 /31	-2.52 / 6	0.00	1.05
★ GI	Oppenheimer Equity A	OEQAX	D-	(800) 525-7048	D+ / 2.5	-4.74	-0.57	6.46 /23	10.87 /34	3.27 /39	0.35	0.89
GI	Oppenheimer Equity B	OEQBX	D-	(800) 525-7048	D / 1.9	-4.95	-1.09	5.49 /18	9.84 /26	2.34 /30	0.00	1.79
GI	Oppenheimer Equity C	OEQCX	D-	(800) 525-7048	D+ / 2.6	-4.95	-0.99	5.59 /18	9.84 /26	2.35 /31	0.00	1.79
GI	Oppenheimer Equity N	OEQNX	D	(800) 525-7048	D+ / 2.9	-4.90	-0.87	6.00 /20	10.36 /30	2.85 /35	0.05	1.29
GI	Oppenheimer Equity Y	OEQYX	D	(800) 525-7048	C- / 3.5	-4.65	-0.48	6.70 /24	11.00 /36	3.39 /40	0.50	0.75
★ GL	Oppenheimer Global Fund A	OPPAX	A-	(800) 525-7048	B / 7.9	-3.45	3.70	18.77 /80	21.58 /84	8.33 /73	0.57	1.12
GL	Oppenheimer Global Fund B	OGLBX	A-	(800) 525-7048	B / 7.8	-3.63	3.30	17.83 /79	20.58 /81	7.46 /69	0.00	1.93
GL	Oppenheimer Global Fund C	OGLCX	A	(800) 525-7048	B / 8.1	-3.62	3.33	17.88 /79	20.65 /82	7.50 /69	0.00	1.87
GL	Oppenheimer Global Fund N	OGLNX	A	(800) 525-7048	B / 8.2	-3.55	3.52	18.32 /80	21.10 /83	7.99 /72	0.26	1.51
GL	Oppenheimer Global Fund Y	OGLYX	A+	(800) 525-7048	B+ / 8.5	-3.34	3.91	19.21 /81	21.92 /85	8.59 /75	0.93	0.81
★ GL	Oppenheimer Global Opportunities A	OPGIX	B-	(800) 525-7048	A / 9.3	-7.69	5.58	27.51 /92	29.23 /95	11.81 /86	1.65	1.13
GL	Oppenheimer Global Opportunities B	OGGIX	B-	(800) 525-7048	A / 9.3	-7.89	5.15	26.43 /90	28.16 /94	10.92 /84	1.02	1.95
GL	Oppenheimer Global Opportunities C	OGICX	B-	(800) 525-7048	A / 9.4	-7.88	5.18	26.51 /91	28.24 /94	10.96 /84	1.18	1.89
GL	Oppenheimer Global Opportunities N	OGINX	B-	(800) 525-7048	A / 9.4	-7.75	5.42	27.04 /91	28.78 /95	11.49 /85	1.53	1.49
GL	Oppenheimer Global Opportunities Y	OGIYX	B-	(800) 525-7048	A / 9.5	-7.60	5.77	27.92 /93	29.67 /95	12.26 /87	2.04	0.81
PM	Oppenheimer Gold/Spec Min A	OPGSX	C-	(800) 525-7048	A+ / 9.9	0.31	25.16	68.00 /99	36.49 /98	30.30 /99	0.00	1.23
PM	Oppenheimer Gold/Spec Min B	OGMBX	C-	(800) 525-7048	A+ / 9.9	0.07	24.63	66.67 /99	35.41 /98	29.28 /99	0.00	2.02
PM	Oppenheimer Gold/Spec Min C	OGMCX	C-	(800) 525-7048	A+ / 9.9	0.11	24.67	66.79 /99	35.47 /98	29.33 /99	0.00	1.96
PM	Oppenheimer Gold/Spec Min N	OGMNX	C-	(800) 525-7048	A+ / 9.9	0.24	25.02	67.62 /99	36.05 /98	29.90 /99	0.00	1.52
GR	Oppenheimer Growth A	OPPSX	E	(800) 525-7048	E- / 0.2	-8.68	-3.68	5.68 /19	5.65 / 6	-2.04 / 8	0.00	1.15
GR	Oppenheimer Growth B	OPSBX	E	(800) 525-7048	E- / 0.1	-8.88	-4.12	4.74 /14	4.70 / 3	-2.87 / 6	0.00	2.03
GR	Oppenheimer Growth C	OGRCX	E	(800) 525-7048	E- / 0.2	-8.90	-4.13	4.74 /14	4.72 / 3	-2.87 / 6	0.00	2.01
GR	Oppenheimer Growth N	OGRNX	E	(800) 525-7048	E / 0.3	-8.79	-3.87	5.27 /16	5.26 / 4	-2.13 / 8	0.00	1.51
GR	Oppenheimer Growth Y	OGRYX	E+	(800) 525-7048	E / 0.4	-8.67	-3.58	5.86 /20	5.84 / 6	-1.84 / 9	0.00	0.98
FO	Oppenheimer International Value A	OIVAX	U	(800) 525-7048	U /	1.28	9.26	21.19 /83	--	--	1.05	1.44
FO	Oppenheimer International Value C	OIVCX	U	(800) 525-7048	U /	1.07	8.79	20.19 /82	--	--	0.72	2.44
GR	Oppenheimer Intl Diversified A	OIDAX	U	(800) 525-7048	U /	-2.65	6.69	--	--	--	0.00	1.82
GR	Oppenheimer Intl Diversified C	OIDCX	U	(800) 525-7048	U /	-2.84	6.30		--	--	0.00	2.57
FO	Oppenheimer Intl Growth A	OIGAX	B+	(800) 525-7048	B+ / 8.5	-2.17	8.22	26.29 /90	23.89 /89	6.81 /66	0.61	1.41
FO	Oppenheimer Intl Growth B	IGRWX	B	(800) 525-7048	B+ / 8.5	-2.36	7.76	25.28 /89	22.92 /87	5.99 /61	0.00	2.19
FO	Oppenheimer Intl Growth C	OIGCX	B+	(800) 525-7048	B+ / 8.7	-2.36	7.76	25.33 /89	22.96 /87	6.00 /61	0.05	2.13
FO	Oppenheimer Intl Growth N	OIGNX	B+	(800) 525-7048	B+ / 8.8	-2.24	7.99	25.91 /90	23.55 /89	6.52 /64	0.43	1.67
FO	Oppenheimer Intl Growth VA		C+	(800) 525-7048	B+ / 8.5	-5.36	4.32	21.84 /84	21.88 /85	5.75 /59	0.39	1.40
FO	Oppenheimer Intl Growth Y	OIGYX	U	(800) 525-7048	U /	-2.09	8.43	--	--	--	0.00	0.85
FO	Oppenheimer Intl Small Comp A	OSMAX	B	(800) 525-7048	A+ / 9.9	-6.00	11.16	35.42 /97	41.31 /99	24.95 /98	0.00	1.31
FO	Oppenheimer Intl Small Comp B	OSMBX	B	(800) 525-7048	A+ / 9.9	-6.19	10.70	34.24 /96	40.01 /99	23.91 /98	0.00	2.23
FO	Oppenheimer Intl Small Comp C	OSMCX	B	(800) 525-7048	A+ / 9.9	-6.19	10.70	34.32 /96	40.13 /99	23.97 /98	0.00	2.14
FO	Oppenheimer Intl Small Comp N	OSMNX	B	(800) 525-7048	A+ / 9.9	-6.06	10.98	34.93 /97	40.77 /99	24.53 /98	0.00	1.68
FO	Oppenheimer Intl Small Comp Y	OSMYX	U	(800) 525-7048	U /	-5.87	11.35	--	--	--	0.00	1.07
★ GI	Oppenheimer Main St Fund A	MSIGX	C	(800) 525-7048	C- / 3.2	-1.92	3.02	9.58 /44	11.13 /37	3.11 /38	0.91	0.92
GI	Oppenheimer Main St Fund B	OMSBX	C-	(800) 525-7048	D+ / 2.7	-2.11	2.63	8.70 /38	10.22 /29	2.29 /30	0.08	1.72
GI	Oppenheimer Main St Fund C	MIGCX	C	(800) 525-7048	C- / 3.4	-2.09	2.63	8.77 /39	10.28 /29	2.33 /30	0.25	1.67
GI	Oppenheimer Main St Fund N	OMGNX	C	(800) 525-7048	C- / 3.7	-2.00	2.83	9.20 /41	10.73 /33	2.80 /35	0.74	1.26
GI	Oppenheimer Main St Fund Y	MIGYX	C+	(800) 525-7048	C / 4.5	-1.81	3.22	10.06 /47	11.52 /39	3.40 /40	1.38	0.53
★ GR	Oppenheimer Main St Oppty A	OMSOX	C+	(800) 525-7048	C / 5.4	-1.96	3.63	10.97 /53	14.95 /59	8.10 /72	0.48	1.11
GR	Oppenheimer Main St Oppty B	OMOBX	C+	(800) 525-7048	C / 4.9	-2.18	3.14	10.02 /47	13.99 /54	7.20 /68	0.00	1.95
GR	Oppenheimer Main St Oppty C	OMSCX	C+	(800) 525-7048	C+ / 5.6	-2.17	3.21	10.15 /48	14.11 /55	7.31 /68	0.00	1.85
GR	Oppenheimer Main St Oppty N	OMSNX	B-	(800) 525-7048	C+ / 6.0	-2.06	3.45	10.59 /51	14.51 /56	7.75 /70	0.19	1.54
GR	Oppenheimer Main St Oppty Y	OMSYX	B-	(800) 525-7048	C+ / 6.4	-1.94	3.73	11.38 /56	15.38 /61	8.49 /74	0.78	0.82
★ SC	Oppenheimer Main St Small Cap A	OPMSX	B-	(800) 525-7048	B / 8.0	-4.26	7.95	18.22 /79	21.13 /83	11.84 /86	0.00	1.17
SC	Oppenheimer Main St Small Cap B	OPMBX	C+	(800) 525-7048	B / 7.7	-4.47	7.55	17.28 /78	20.16 /80	10.97 /84	0.00	1.96

● Denotes fund is closed to new investors
★ Denotes fund is included in Section II

RISK			NET ASSETS		ASSET				BULL / BEAR		FUND MANAGER		MINIMUMS		LOADS	
	3 Year		NAV						Last Bull	Last Bear	Manager	Manager	Initial	Additional	Front	Back
	Standard		As of	Total	Cash	Stocks	Bonds	Other	Market	Market	Quality	Tenure	Purch.	Purch.	End	End
Risk Rating/Pts	Deviation	Beta	6/30/06	$(Mil)	%	%	%	%	Return	Return	Pct	(Years)	$	$	Load	Load
C+ / 6.3	12.2	1.31	14.60	12	5	94	0	1	59.0	82.4	-7.2	24	2	1,000	50	0.0	0.0
C+ / 5.9	8.8	1.08	10.45	2,249	0	99	0	1	75.0	66.8	-7.4	43	6	1,000	50	5.8	0.0
C+ / 5.8	8.8	1.09	9.98	177	0	99	0	1	75.0	61.9	-7.6	34	6	1,000	50	0.0	5.0
C+ / 5.8	8.9	1.09	9.99	77	0	99	0	1	75.0	62.1	-7.6	33	6	1,000	50	0.0	1.0
C+ / 5.9	8.8	1.09	10.29	22	0	99	0	1	75.0	64.4	-7.4	38	6	1,000	50	0.0	1.0
C+ / 5.9	8.8	1.09	10.46	56	0	99	0	1	75.0	67.3	-7.4	44	6	1,000	50	0.0	0.0
B- / 7.6	11.2	1.01	69.17	11,709	0	99	0	1	29.0	126.4	-12.4	30	2	1,000	50	5.8	2.0
B- / 7.6	11.2	1.01	64.42	1,403	0	99	0	1	29.0	120.7	-12.6	24	2	1,000	50	0.0	5.0
B- / 7.6	11.2	1.01	65.52	1,305	0	99	0	1	29.0	121.0	-12.6	24	2	1,000	50	0.0	1.0
B- / 7.6	11.2	1.01	68.55	406	0	99	0	1	29.0	123.7	-12.4	27	2	1,000	50	0.0	1.0
B- / 7.6	11.2	1.01	69.66	524	0	99	0	1	29.0	128.5	-12.4	32	2	1,000	50	0.0	0.0
C / 4.5	17.2	1.36	39.00	2,869	1	98	0	1	43.0	203.2	-18.9	23	11	1,000	50	5.8	2.0
C / 4.4	17.3	1.37	37.38	704	1	98	0	1	43.0	195.5	-19.0	18	11	1,000	50	0.0	5.0
C / 4.4	17.2	1.36	37.39	628	1	98	0	1	43.0	196.0	-19.0	19	11	1,000	50	0.0	1.0
C / 4.4	17.2	1.36	38.31	103	1	98	0	1	43.0	199.8	-18.9	21	11	1,000	50	0.0	2.0
C / 4.5	17.2	1.36	39.26	111	1	98	0	1	43.0	206.7	-18.8	26	11	1,000	50	0.0	2.0
E+ / 0.7	32.0	1.47	29.15	581	5	94	0	1	77.0	202.7	11.6	90	9	1,000	50	5.8	2.0
E+ / 0.7	32.0	1.47	28.13	104	5	94	0	1	77.0	195.3	11.5	86	9	1,000	50	0.0	5.0
E+ / 0.7	31.9	1.47	28.10	138	5	94	0	1	77.0	195.7	11.5	87	9	1,000	50	0.0	1.0
E+ / 0.7	31.9	1.47	28.68	18	5	94	0	1	77.0	199.8	11.5	89	9	1,000	50	0.0	1.0
C+ / 6.2	11.0	1.19	28.83	968	0	99	0	1	72.0	45.1	-7.8	8	2	1,000	50	5.8	0.0
C+ / 6.0	11.0	1.19	26.27	162	0	99	0	1	72.0	41.1	-7.9	5	2	1,000	50	0.0	5.0
C+ / 6.1	11.0	1.19	26.72	72	0	99	0	1	72.0	41.2	-8.0	5	2	1,000	50	0.0	1.0
C+ / 6.1	11.0	1.19	28.55	13	0	99	0	1	72.0	43.5	-7.8	6	2	1,000	50	0.0	1.0
C+ / 6.2	11.0	1.19	29.08	42	0	99	0	1	72.0	46.0	-7.7	8	2	1,000	50	0.0	0.0
U /	N/A	N/A	17.35	76	2	96	0	2	49.0	N/A	N/A	N/A	1	1,000	50	5.8	2.0
U /	N/A	N/A	17.08	26	2	96	0	2	49.0	N/A	N/A	N/A	1	1,000	50	0.0	2.0
U /	N/A	N/A	11.01	248	0	90	10	0	N/A	N/A	N/A	N/A	N/A	1,000	50	5.8	1.0
U /	N/A	N/A	10.96	115	0	90	10	0	N/A	N/A	N/A	N/A	N/A	1,000	50	0.0	1.0
C+ / 6.2	12.7	1.16	23.44	911	1	97	0	2	28.0	162.1	-15.7	22	10	1,000	50	5.8	2.0
C+ / 6.2	12.6	1.16	22.35	161	1	97	0	2	28.0	155.7	-15.8	17	10	1,000	50	0.0	5.0
C+ / 6.2	12.6	1.16	22.36	189	1	97	0	2	28.0	156.1	-15.9	17	10	1,000	50	0.0	2.0
C+ / 6.2	12.6	1.16	23.11	44	1	97	0	2	28.0	159.9	-15.8	20	10	1,000	50	0.0	2.0
C / 5.0	12.2	1.12	1.59	19	1	97	0	2	28.0	151.7	-15.3	17	10	1,000	50	0.0	0.0
U /	N/A	N/A	23.42	229	1	97	0	2	28.0	N/A	N/A	N/A	10	1,000	50	0.0	2.0
C / 4.4	17.2	1.34	22.41	1,295	3	96	0	1	51.0	327.2	-7.2	96	6	50,000	50	5.8	2.0
C / 4.3	17.2	1.34	21.52	123	3	96	0	1	51.0	315.0	-7.2	94	6	1,000	50	0.0	5.0
C / 4.3	17.2	1.34	21.52	233	3	96	0	1	51.0	316.2	-7.4	94	6	50,000	50	0.0	2.0
C / 4.4	17.2	1.34	21.84	50	3	96	0	1	51.0	322.1	-7.3	95	6	50,000	50	0.0	2.0
U /	N/A	N/A	22.47	70	3	96	0	1	51.0	N/A	N/A	N/A	6	50,000	50	0.0	0.0
B / 8.3	7.6	0.97	38.25	7,640	0	99	0	1	79.0	62.5	-8.8	58	8	1,000	50	5.8	0.0
B / 8.2	7.6	0.97	37.08	1,502	0	99	0	1	79.0	58.4	-9.0	47	8	1,000	50	0.0	5.0
B / 8.2	7.6	0.98	37.02	1,112	0	99	0	1	79.0	58.7	-9.0	48	8	1,000	50	0.0	1.0
B / 8.3	7.6	0.97	37.74	199	0	99	0	1	79.0	60.7	-8.9	53	8	1,000	50	0.0	1.0
B / 8.3	7.6	0.97	38.43	632	0	99	0	1	79.0	64.3	-8.7	62	8	1,000	50	0.0	0.0
B- / 7.7	8.9	1.10	13.98	2,234	1	98	0	1	107.0	87.9	-9.1	81	6	1,000	50	5.8	0.0
B- / 7.7	8.9	1.10	13.45	476	1	98	0	1	107.0	83.1	-9.4	74	6	1,000	50	0.0	5.0
B- / 7.7	8.9	1.10	13.51	532	1	98	0	1	107.0	83.6	-9.3	75	6	1,000	50	0.0	1.0
B- / 7.7	8.9	1.10	13.79	87	1	98	0	1	107.0	85.8	-9.2	78	6	1,000	50	0.0	0.0
B- / 7.7	8.9	1.10	14.18	138	1	98	0	1	107.0	90.4	-9.1	84	6	1,000	50	0.0	0.0
C+ / 6.0	13.8	0.93	22.27	2,576	1	98	0	1	57.0	130.7	-10.6	85	7	1,000	50	5.8	0.0
C+ / 5.8	13.8	0.93	20.94	502	1	98	0	1	57.0	124.9	-10.8	79	7	1,000	50	0.0	5.0

Fund Type	Fund Name	Ticker Symbol	Overall Weiss Investment Rating	Phone	Performance Rating/Pts	3 Mo	6 Mo	1Yr / Pct	3Yr / Pct	5Yr / Pct	Dividend Yield	Expense Ratio
SC	Oppenheimer Main St Small Cap C	OPMCX	B-	(800) 525-7048	B / 8.1	-4.46	7.58	17.35 /78	20.25 /80	11.02 /84	0.00	1.89
SC	Oppenheimer Main St Small Cap N	OPMNX	B	(800) 525-7048	B / 8.2	-4.33	7.79	17.79 /79	20.73 /82	11.51 /85	0.00	1.49
SC	Oppenheimer Main St Small Cap Y	OPMYX	B	(800) 525-7048	B+ / 8.5	-4.15	8.25	18.83 /80	21.72 /84	12.41 /87	0.00	0.67
MC	Oppenheimer Mid Cap A	OMDAX	C-	(800) 525-7048	C / 4.8	-5.51	1.85	11.38 /56	14.16 /55	1.38 /23	0.00	1.35
MC	Oppenheimer Mid Cap B	OMDBX	C-	(800) 525-7048	C / 4.4	-5.65	1.56	10.59 /51	13.29 /50	0.62 /18	0.00	2.14
MC	Oppenheimer Mid Cap C	OMDCX	C-	(800) 525-7048	C / 5.0	-5.65	1.56	10.59 /51	13.29 /50	0.62 /18	0.00	2.10
MC	Oppenheimer Mid Cap N	OMDNX	C	(800) 525-7048	C / 5.4	-5.52	1.82	11.20 /55	13.90 /53	1.14 /21	0.00	1.55
MC	Oppenheimer Mid Cap Y	OMDYX	C	(800) 525-7048	C+ / 5.9	-5.36	2.15	11.92 /59	14.62 /57	1.82 /26	0.00	0.89
AA	Oppenheimer Moderate Inv Fd Cl A	OAMIX	U	(800) 525-7048	U /	-1.01	2.29	7.14 /27	--	--	1.52	1.14
AA	Oppenheimer Moderate Inv Fd Cl B	OBMIX	U	(800) 525-7048	U /	-1.30	1.91	6.28 /22	--	--	1.37	1.97
AA	Oppenheimer Moderate Inv Fd Cl C	OCMIX	U	(800) 525-7048	U /	-1.30	1.91	6.31 /22	--	--	1.39	1.90
AA	● Oppenheimer Prin Prot Main St Fd A	OAPPX	D	(800) 525-7048	D- / 1.1	-2.21	2.57	7.26 /28	7.39 /12	--	0.83	1.04
AA	● Oppenheimer Prin Prot Main St Fd B	OBPPX	D-	(800) 525-7048	E+ / 0.9	-2.38	2.14	6.47 /23	6.59 / 9	--	0.13	1.80
AA	Oppenheimer Prin Prot Main St Fd C	OCPPX	D	(800) 525-7048	D- / 1.4	-2.37	2.22	6.51 /23	6.62 / 9	--	0.09	1.79
AA	Oppenheimer Prin Prot Main St Fd N	ONPPX	D	(800) 525-7048	D / 1.7	-2.29	2.40	7.08 /27	7.18 /11	--	0.71	1.22
AA	Oppenheimer Prin Prot Main St II A	OAPMX	U	(800) 525-7048	U /	-1.95	0.27	2.07 / 4	--	--	1.63	1.23
AA	Oppenheimer Prin Prot Main St II B	OBPMX	U	(800) 525-7048	U /	-2.12	-0.13	1.25 / 3	--	--	0.92	2.03
AA	Oppenheimer Prin Prot Main St II C	OCPMX	U	(800) 525-7048	U /	-2.12	-0.10	1.27 / 3	--	--	0.77	2.00
AA	Oppenheimer Prin Prot Main St III A	OAPRX	U	(800) 525-7048	U /	-2.19	0.13	2.55 / 6	--	--	1.68	1.20
★ BA	Oppenheimer Quest Balanced A	QVGIX	D	(800) 525-7048	D- / 1.3	-1.79	0.28	3.05 / 7	8.80 /20	2.73 /34	0.88	1.17
BA	Oppenheimer Quest Balanced B	QGRBX	D+	(800) 525-7048	D- / 1.1	-2.02	-0.13	2.18 / 5	7.94 /15	1.97 /27	0.34	1.96
BA	Oppenheimer Quest Balanced C	QGRCX	D+	(800) 525-7048	D / 1.6	-1.95	-0.10	2.30 / 5	8.00 /15	2.03 /28	0.40	1.89
BA	Oppenheimer Quest Balanced N	QGRNX	C-	(800) 525-7048	D / 1.8	-1.89	0.09	2.68 / 6	8.43 /17	2.47 /32	0.72	1.49
BA	Oppenheimer Quest Balanced Y	QGRYX	C-	(800) 525-7048	D+ / 2.4	-1.77	0.36	3.35 / 8	9.11 /21	3.12 /38	1.16	0.85
GR	Oppenheimer Quest Capital Val A	QCVAX	C+	(800) 525-7048	C / 5.5	-3.69	2.80	11.28 /55	15.59 /62	7.36 /69	0.00	1.34
GR	Oppenheimer Quest Capital Val B	QCVBX	C	(800) 525-7048	C / 5.1	-3.95	2.33	10.21 /48	14.56 /57	6.47 /64	0.00	2.25
GR	Oppenheimer Quest Capital Val C	QCVCX	C	(800) 525-7048	C+ / 5.7	-3.91	2.33	10.25 /48	14.55 /57	6.48 /64	0.00	2.24
GR	Oppenheimer Quest Capital Val N	QCVNX	C+	(800) 525-7048	C+ / 6.0	-3.86	2.54	10.82 /52	15.11 /59	7.00 /67	0.00	1.76
GL	Oppenheimer Quest Internatl Val A	QIVAX	B+	(800) 525-7048	B / 7.9	1.54	9.78	22.48 /85	20.24 /80	8.15 /72	1.52	1.38
GL	Oppenheimer Quest Internatl Val B	QIVBX	B	(800) 525-7048	B / 7.7	1.29	9.26	21.30 /83	19.17 /76	7.28 /68	0.95	2.28
GL	Oppenheimer Quest Internatl Val C	QIVCX	B+	(800) 525-7048	B / 8.0	1.29	9.31	21.40 /83	19.22 /77	7.29 /68	1.10	2.24
GL	Oppenheimer Quest Internatl Val N	QIVNX	B+	(800) 525-7048	B / 8.2	1.41	9.52	21.95 /84	19.79 /79	7.83 /71	1.42	1.74
GR	Oppenheimer Quest Opporty Val A	QVOPX	E	(800) 525-7048	E+ / 0.8	-2.99	-0.91	0.19 / 2	7.64 /13	1.11 /21	0.71	1.28
GR	Oppenheimer Quest Opporty Val B	QOPBX	E	(800) 525-7048	E+ / 0.6	-3.17	-1.27	-0.58 / 1	6.82 /10	0.37 /17	0.00	2.07
GR	Oppenheimer Quest Opporty Val C	QOPCX	E	(800) 525-7048	E+ / 0.9	-3.18	-1.28	-0.55 / 1	6.84 /10	0.39 /17	0.00	2.02
GR	Oppenheimer Quest Opporty Val N	QOPNX	E+	(800) 525-7048	D- / 1.1	-3.07	-1.07	-0.12 / 2	7.25 /11	0.81 /19	0.39	1.64
GR	Oppenheimer Quest Opporty Val Y	QOPYX	E+	(800) 525-7048	D- / 1.5	-2.95	-0.84	0.41 / 2	7.82 /14	1.33 /22	0.91	1.12
GR	Oppenheimer Quest Value A	QFVFX	D-	(800) 525-7048	C- / 3.5	-0.63	2.45	6.62 /24	12.05 /43	3.42 /41	0.58	1.24
GR	Oppenheimer Quest Value B	QFVBX	E+	(800) 525-7048	C- / 3.0	-0.90	1.98	5.67 /18	11.10 /36	2.60 /33	0.00	2.08
GR	Oppenheimer Quest Value C	QFVCX	D-	(800) 525-7048	C- / 3.6	-0.90	1.98	5.67 /18	11.10 /36	2.62 /33	0.00	2.06
GR	Oppenheimer Quest Value N	QFVNX	D-	(800) 525-7048	C- / 4.1	-0.74	2.30	6.27 /22	11.69 /40	3.14 /38	0.35	1.53
GR	Oppenheimer Quest Value Y	QFVYX	D	(800) 525-7048	C / 4.6	-0.57	2.57	6.87 /25	12.30 /44	3.67 /43	0.85	0.98
EN	● Oppenheimer Real Asset A	QRAAX	D-	(800) 525-7048	B / 8.0	6.50	5.60	14.88 /71	21.52 /84	14.97 /92	0.87	1.32
EN	● Oppenheimer Real Asset B	QRABX	D-	(800) 525-7048	B / 7.9	6.34	5.23	13.94 /68	20.48 /81	14.00 /90	0.57	2.19
EN	● Oppenheimer Real Asset C	QRACX	D-	(800) 525-7048	B / 8.2	6.24	5.16	13.94 /68	20.53 /81	14.01 /90	0.63	2.11
EN	● Oppenheimer Real Asset N	QRANX	D-	(800) 525-7048	B+ / 8.3	6.43	5.44	14.55 /70	21.08 /83	14.60 /91	0.78	1.68
EN	● Oppenheimer Real Asset Y	QRAYX	D-	(800) 525-7048	B+ / 8.5	6.60	5.92	15.31 /73	22.05 /85	15.44 /92	1.08	0.88
RE	Oppenheimer Real Estate A	OREAX	B+	(800) 525-7048	A / 9.4	-1.32	13.33	22.13 /84	28.83 /95	--	1.37	1.50
RE	Oppenheimer Real Estate B	OREBX	U	(800) 525-7048	U /	-1.51	12.86	21.20 /83	--	--	0.97	2.25
RE	Oppenheimer Real Estate C	ORECX	U	(800) 525-7048	U /	-1.50	12.91	21.21 /83	--	--	0.98	2.25
RE	Oppenheimer Real Estate Y	OREYX	U	(800) 525-7048	U /	-1.21	13.56	22.64 /85	--	--	1.75	1.08
GR	Oppenheimer Select Value A	OSVAX	B	(800) 525-7048	C+ / 6.1	-2.57	1.81	8.04 /33	17.11 /69	--	0.18	1.31

● Denotes fund is closed to new investors
* Denotes fund is included in Section II

RISK			NET ASSETS		ASSET					BULL / BEAR		FUND MANAGER		MINIMUMS		LOADS	
	3 Year		NAV						Portfolio	Last Bull	Last Bear	Manager	Manager	Initial	Additional	Front	Back
Risk Rating/Pts	Standard Deviation	Beta	As of 6/30/06	Total $(Mil)	Cash %	Stocks %	Bonds %	Other %	Turnover Ratio	Market Return	Market Return	Quality Pct	Tenure (Years)	Purch. $	Purch. $	End Load	End Load
C+ / 5.8	13.8	0.93	21.01	600	1	98	0	1	57.0	125.3	-10.8	80	7	1,000	50	0.0	1.0
C+ / 5.9	13.8	0.93	21.87	193	1	98	0	1	57.0	128.3	-10.6	83	7	1,000	50	0.0	1.0
C+ / 6.1	13.8	0.93	23.09	417	1	98	0	1	57.0	134.3	-10.5	88	7	1,000	50	0.0	0.0
C+ / 6.1	11.3	0.92	18.70	703	1	98	0	1	39.0	85.1	-9.1	30	3	1,000	50	5.8	0.0
C+ / 6.1	11.3	0.92	17.55	268	1	98	0	1	39.0	80.7	-9.2	25	3	1,000	50	0.0	5.0
C+ / 6.1	11.3	0.92	17.55	151	1	98	0	1	39.0	80.7	-9.2	26	3	1,000	50	0.0	1.0
C+ / 6.1	11.3	0.92	18.47	39	1	98	0	1	39.0	83.7	-9.1	29	3	1,000	50	0.0	1.0
C+ / 6.2	11.3	0.92	19.44	43	1	98	0	1	39.0	87.3	-9.0	34	3	1,000	50	0.0	0.0
U /	N/A	N/A	10.74	187	0	99	0	1	N/A	N/A	N/A	N/A	1	1,000	50	5.8	0.0
U /	N/A	N/A	10.66	64	0	99	0	1	N/A	N/A	N/A	N/A	1	1,000	50	0.0	5.0
U /	N/A	N/A	10.65	88	0	99	0	1	N/A	N/A	N/A	N/A	1	1,000	50	0.0	1.0
B / 8.0	6.4	1.28	11.97	56	0	99	0	1	122.0	N/A	N/A	37	3	1,000	50	5.8	1.0
B- / 7.4	6.4	1.28	11.92	111	0	99	0	1	122.0	N/A	N/A	31	3	1,000	50	0.0	5.0
B- / 7.3	6.4	1.27	11.95	37	0	99	0	1	122.0	N/A	N/A	31	3	1,000	50	0.0	1.0
B- / 7.7	6.4	1.27	11.96	5	0	99	0	1	122.0	N/A	N/A	36	3	1,000	50	0.0	1.0
U /	N/A	N/A	30.15	66	1	68	29	2	61.0	N/A	N/A	N/A	3	1,000	50	5.8	1.0
U /	N/A	N/A	30.00	78	1	68	29	2	61.0	N/A	N/A	N/A	3	1,000	50	0.0	5.0
U /	N/A	N/A	30.06	34	1	68	29	2	61.0	N/A	N/A	N/A	3	1,000	50	0.0	1.0
U /	N/A	N/A	30.31	34	11	69	19	1	37.0	N/A	N/A	N/A	2	1,000	50	5.8	1.0
B / 8.3	7.5	1.40	17.81	3,096	0	73	26	1	89.0	54.8	-5.5	44	14	1,000	50	5.8	1.0
B / 8.7	7.5	1.40	17.48	1,910	0	73	26	1	89.0	51.1	-5.7	36	14	1,000	50	0.0	5.0
B / 8.7	7.5	1.41	17.50	1,066	0	73	26	1	89.0	51.4	-5.6	36	14	1,000	50	0.0	1.0
B / 8.7	7.6	1.41	17.60	211	0	73	26	1	89.0	53.2	-5.5	41	14	1,000	50	0.0	1.0
B / 8.7	7.5	1.41	17.80	275	0	73	26	1	89.0	56.4	-5.3	48	14	1,000	50	0.0	0.0
B- / 7.2	9.7	1.14	27.18	379	1	98	0	1	89.0	87.8	-9.5	83	6	1,000	50	5.8	1.0
C+ / 6.7	9.7	1.14	24.56	75	1	98	0	1	89.0	82.7	-9.7	75	6	1,000	50	0.0	5.0
C+ / 6.8	9.7	1.14	24.60	52	1	98	0	1	89.0	82.7	-9.6	75	6	1,000	50	0.0	1.0
B- / 7.1	9.7	1.15	26.63	18	1	98	0	1	89.0	85.4	-9.5	79	6	1,000	50	0.0	1.0
C+ / 6.7	9.5	0.88	20.43	570	4	95	0	1	140.0	105.9	-6.6	42	1	1,000	50	5.8	2.0
C+ / 6.7	9.5	0.88	18.87	58	4	95	0	1	140.0	100.1	-6.8	33	1	1,000	50	0.0	5.0
C+ / 6.7	9.5	0.88	18.79	70	4	95	0	1	140.0	100.2	-6.7	33	1	1,000	50	0.0	2.0
C+ / 6.7	9.6	0.89	20.14	17	4	95	0	1	140.0	103.5	-6.6	37	1	1,000	50	0.0	2.0
C+ / 5.6	6.3	0.70	28.19	1,158	32	67	0	1	100.0	43.7	-4.9	46	1	1,000	50	5.8	0.0
C / 5.4	6.3	0.70	27.15	165	32	67	0	1	100.0	40.2	-5.1	38	1	1,000	50	0.0	5.0
C / 5.4	6.3	0.70	27.09	143	32	67	0	1	100.0	40.3	-5.1	38	1	1,000	50	0.0	1.0
C / 5.5	6.3	0.70	27.78	23	32	67	0	1	100.0	42.0	-4.9	42	1	1,000	50	0.0	1.0
C+ / 5.6	6.3	0.70	28.29	23	32	67	0	1	100.0	44.4	-4.8	48	1	1,000	50	0.0	0.0
C- / 4.2	7.4	0.84	18.82	631	1	98	0	1	129.0	70.0	-9.9	78	1	1,000	50	5.8	0.0
C- / 3.9	7.4	0.84	17.53	121	1	98	0	1	129.0	65.6	-10.0	70	1	1,000	50	0.0	5.0
C- / 3.9	7.4	0.84	17.53	85	1	98	0	1	129.0	65.6	-10.0	70	1	1,000	50	0.0	1.0
C- / 4.2	7.4	0.84	18.66	22	1	98	0	1	129.0	68.2	-9.9	75	1	1,000	50	0.0	1.0
C- / 4.2	7.4	0.84	19.13	28	1	98	0	1	129.0	71.1	-9.7	79	1	1,000	50	0.0	0.0
E- / 0.0	21.3	0.66	8.19	1,118	23	0	76	1	94.0	59.8	33.1	58	7	1,000	50	5.8	2.0
E- / 0.0	21.2	0.65	8.05	126	23	0	76	1	94.0	55.2	33.0	47	7	1,000	50	0.0	5.0
E- / 0.0	21.3	0.66	8.00	266	23	0	76	1	94.0	55.5	32.9	47	7	1,000	50	0.0	2.0
E- / 0.0	21.3	0.66	8.11	25	23	0	76	1	94.0	57.9	32.8	53	7	1,000	50	0.0	2.0
E- / 0.0	21.4	0.66	8.24	332	23	0	76	1	94.0	62.0	33.3	61	7	1,000	50	0.0	2.0
C+ / 5.8	16.8	1.01	21.65	190	2	97	0	1	77.0	145.4	-0.9	88	4	1,000	50	5.8	0.0
U /	N/A	N/A	21.59	30	2	97	0	1	77.0	N/A	N/A	N/A	4	1,000	50	0.0	5.0
U /	N/A	N/A	21.60	40	2	97	0	1	77.0	N/A	N/A	N/A	4	1,000	50	0.0	1.0
U /	N/A	N/A	21.68	130	2	97	0	1	77.0	N/A	N/A	N/A	4	1,000	50	0.0	0.0
B / 8.5	8.9	1.03	16.29	84	5	94	0	1	79.0	100.6	-5.9	93	4	1,000	50	5.8	0.0

Data as of June 30, 2006

Fund Type	Fund Name	Ticker Symbol	Overall Weiss Investment Rating	Phone	Perfor-mance Rating/Pts	3 Mo	6 Mo	1Yr / Pct	3Yr / Pct	5Yr / Pct	Dividend Yield	Expense Ratio
								Total Return % through 6/30/06	Annualized		Incl. in Returns	

99 Pct = Best
0 Pct = Worst

Fund Type	Fund Name	Ticker Symbol	Overall Weiss Investment Rating	Phone	Performance Rating/Pts	3 Mo	6 Mo	1Yr / Pct	3Yr / Pct	5Yr / Pct	Dividend Yield	Expense Ratio
* SC	Oppenheimer Small & Mid Cap Value	QVSCX	A	(800) 525-7048	B+ / 8.4	-1.95	4.84	12.81 /63	24.82 /91	14.51 /91	0.00	1.23
SC	Oppenheimer Small & Mid Cap Value	QSCBX	A-	(800) 525-7048	B+ / 8.4	-2.12	4.42	11.87 /59	23.78 /89	13.65 /90	0.00	2.09
SC	Oppenheimer Small & Mid Cap Value	QSCCX	A	(800) 525-7048	B+ / 8.6	-2.12	4.43	11.92 /59	23.83 /89	13.67 /90	0.00	2.03
SC	Oppenheimer Small & Mid Cap Value	QSCNX	A	(800) 525-7048	B+ / 8.7	-2.04	4.64	12.41 /62	24.32 /90	14.17 /90	0.00	1.57
GR	Oppenheimer Value A	CGRWX	C+	(800) 525-7048	C / 4.9	-0.58	2.49	7.05 /27	14.55 /57	6.77 /66	0.65	0.99
GR	Oppenheimer Value B	CGRBX	C+	(800) 525-7048	C / 4.4	-0.81	2.01	6.14 /21	13.52 /51	5.87 /60	0.00	1.87
GR	Oppenheimer Value C	CGRCX	C+	(800) 525-7048	C / 5.1	-0.78	2.09	6.23 /22	13.62 /52	5.92 /61	0.14	1.77
GR	Oppenheimer Value N	CGRNX	C+	(800) 525-7048	C / 5.4	-0.72	2.26	6.71 /24	14.14 /55	6.41 /64	0.49	1.30
GR	Oppenheimer Value Y	CGRYX	B	(800) 525-7048	C+ / 6.0	-0.49	2.65	7.40 /29	14.92 /58	7.11 /67	0.91	0.70
FO	Optimum Intl Equity C	OCIEX	U	(800) 523-4640	U /	1.18	10.67	25.11 /89	--	--	0.87	2.61
FO	Optimum Intl Equity I	OIIEX	U	(800) 523-4640	U /	1.40	11.16	26.39 /90	--	--	1.71	1.61
GR	Optimum Large Cap Growth A	OALGX	U	(800) 523-4640	U /	-3.85	-0.49	7.31 /28	--	--	0.00	1.69
GR	Optimum Large Cap Growth C	OCLGX	U	(800) 523-4640	U /	-4.01	-0.86	6.61 /24	--	--	0.00	2.34
GR	Optimum Large Cap Growth I	OILGX	U	(800) 523-4640	U /	-3.82	-0.40	7.64 /30	--	--	0.00	1.34
GR	Optimum Large Cap Value A	OALVX	U	(800) 523-4640	U /	0.46	4.72	9.13 /41	--	--	0.61	1.55
GR	Optimum Large Cap Value C	OCLVX	U	(800) 523-4640	U /	0.40	4.49	8.50 /37	--	--	0.03	2.20
GR	Optimum Large Cap Value I	OILVX	U	(800) 523-4640	U /	0.64	5.00	9.50 /43	--	--	0.97	1.20
SC	Optimum Small Cap Growth C	OCSGX	U	(800) 523-4640	U /	-6.77	2.30	9.45 /43	--	--	0.00	2.60
SC	Optimum Small Cap Growth I	OISGX	U	(800) 523-4640	U /	-6.53	2.78	10.59 /51	--	--	0.00	1.60
SC	Optimum Small Cap Value C	OCSVX	U	(800) 523-4640	U /	-6.74	0.65	7.08 /27	--	--	0.00	2.41
SC	Optimum Small Cap Value I	OISVX	U	(800) 523-4640	U /	-6.55	1.19	8.18 /34	--	--	0.00	1.41
GR	Osterweis Fund	OSTFX	C+	(866) 811-0215	C / 5.5	-3.59	0.50	5.24 /16	15.20 /60	6.61 /65	0.53	1.32
BA	Pacific Advisors Balanced A	PAABX	D+	(800) 282-6693	E+ / 0.9	-1.56	1.78	6.43 /23	7.53 /13	4.25 /48	0.77	2.53
BA	Pacific Advisors Balanced C	PGBCX	D+	(800) 282-6693	D- / 1.2	-1.72	1.36	5.61 /18	6.56 / 9	3.50 /41	0.17	3.30
GR	Pacific Advisors Growth A	PAGTX	C-	(800) 282-6693	C- / 3.5	-2.45	2.69	8.94 /40	12.44 /45	1.60 /24	0.00	2.63
GR	Pacific Advisors Growth C	PGCCX	C-	(800) 282-6693	C- / 3.8	-2.73	2.37	8.03 /33	11.52 /39	0.62 /18	0.00	3.40
GR	Pacific Advisors Multicap Value A	PAMVX	D	(800) 282-6693	D / 1.7	-6.32	-0.90	10.81 /52	10.73 /33	--	0.00	3.05
GR	Pacific Advisors Multicap Value C	PMVCX	D	(800) 282-6693	D / 2.0	-6.43	-1.26	9.97 /47	9.89 /27	--	0.00	3.82
SC	Pacific Advisors Small Cap Val A	PASMX	B+	(800) 282-6693	A+ / 9.9	0.19	20.68	43.78 /98	38.80 /99	16.51 /94	0.00	3.36
SC	Pacific Advisors Small Cap Val C	PGSCX	C+	(800) 282-6693	A+ / 9.9	0.00	20.15	42.45 /98	38.46 /99	15.27 /92	0.00	4.19
GI	Pacific Capital Gr & Inc A	PCIGX	D+	(800) 258-9232	D / 1.7	-4.01	0.58	5.52 /18	9.11 /21	-0.77 /12	0.18	1.38
GI	● Pacific Capital Gr & Inc B	PCBGX	D	(800) 258-9232	D- / 1.3	-4.24	0.16	4.64 /13	8.28 /17	-1.52 /10	0.00	2.13
GI	Pacific Capital Gr & Inc C	PGACX	D+	(800) 258-9232	D / 1.8	-4.17	0.16	4.73 /14	8.30 /17	-1.51 /10	0.00	2.14
GI	Pacific Capital Gr & Inc Y	PGNIX	C-	(800) 258-9232	D+ / 2.7	-3.99	0.91	5.99 /20	9.44 /24	-0.47 /14	0.69	1.13
GR	Pacific Capital Growth Stock A	PCGSX	E+	(800) 258-9232	E / 0.4	-5.56	-1.25	4.21 /11	5.70 / 6	-3.77 / 4	0.00	1.35
GR	● Pacific Capital Growth Stock B	PCGFX	E+	(800) 258-9232	E / 0.3	-5.72	-1.70	3.32 / 8	4.90 / 4	-4.48 / 3	0.00	2.10
GR	Pacific Capital Growth Stock Y	PGRSX	D-	(800) 258-9232	E+ / 0.9	-5.50	-1.11	4.44 /12	5.97 / 7	-3.51 / 4	0.00	1.13
FO	Pacific Capital Intl Stock A	PAISX	B	(800) 258-9232	B- / 7.5	-1.12	7.59	24.84 /88	19.02 /76	5.24 /56	0.45	1.69
FO	● Pacific Capital Intl Stock B	PBISX	B	(800) 258-9232	B- / 7.4	-1.26	7.26	23.97 /87	18.19 /73	4.60 /51	0.10	2.44
FO	Pacific Capital Intl Stock C	PIKCX	B+	(800) 258-9232	B / 7.7	-1.26	7.16	23.86 /87	18.15 /73	4.58 /51	0.11	2.39
FO	Pacific Capital Intl Stock Y	PCVSX	B+	(800) 258-9232	B / 8.0	-1.03	7.71	25.19 /89	19.27 /77	5.57 /58	0.66	1.43
MC	Pacific Capital MidCap Y	PMDYX	U	(800) 258-9232	U /	-2.25	3.90	11.77 /58	--	--	0.43	0.79
FO	Pacific Capital New Asia Gr A	PNAAX	B	(800) 258-9232	B+ / 8.7	-0.84	5.94	19.56 /81	24.95 /91	12.53 /88	0.26	1.92
FO	● Pacific Capital New Asia Gr B	PNABX	B	(800) 258-9232	B+ / 8.7	-1.01	5.57	18.67 /80	24.04 /89	11.83 /86	0.00	2.67
FO	Pacific Capital New Asia Gr Y	PCASX	B+	(800) 258-9232	A- / 9.1	-0.78	6.10	19.86 /82	25.29 /91	12.85 /88	0.55	1.67
SC	Pacific Capital Small Cap A	PCSAX	C+	(800) 258-9232	B+ / 8.5	-3.38	7.91	15.76 /74	23.57 /89	16.65 /94	0.00	1.60
SC	● Pacific Capital Small Cap B	PCSBX	C	(800) 258-9232	B+ / 8.3	-3.59	7.44	14.84 /71	22.60 /86	15.82 /93	0.00	2.30
SC	Pacific Capital Small Cap C	PCCCX	B+	(800) 258-9232	B+ / 8.5	-3.59	7.43	14.83 /71	22.62 /86	15.83 /93	0.00	2.38
SC	Pacific Capital Small Cap Y	PSCYX	C+	(800) 258-9232	B+ / 8.8	-3.34	7.99	16.01 /75	23.87 /89	16.97 /94	0.00	1.30
GI	Pacific Capital Value A	PCVVX	C+	(800) 258-9232	C / 4.8	-0.04	6.81	10.94 /53	13.68 /52	3.57 /42	0.84	1.31
GI	● Pacific Capital Value B	PCBVX	C+	(800) 258-9232	C / 4.6	-0.23	6.36	10.08 /47	12.81 /48	2.77 /35	0.16	2.06
GI	Pacific Capital Value C	PVLCX	B-	(800) 258-9232	C / 5.2	-0.22	6.46	10.07 /47	12.85 /48	2.80 /35	0.28	2.08

RISK			NET ASSETS		ASSET					BULL / BEAR		FUND MANAGER		MINIMUMS		LOADS	
	3 Year		NAV						Portfolio	Last Bull	Last Bear	Manager	Manager	Initial	Additional	Front	Back
Risk	Standard		As of	Total	Cash	Stocks	Bonds	Other	Turnover	Market	Market	Quality	Tenure	Purch.	Purch.	End	End
Rating/Pts	Deviation	Beta	6/30/06	$(Mil)	%	%	%	%	Ratio	Return	Return	Pct	(Years)	$	$	Load	Load
B- /7.4	12.2	0.77	34.65	2,061	2	97	0	1	121.0	142.7	-8.0	99	5	1,000	50	5.8	2.0
B- /7.1	12.2	0.77	31.39	317	2	97	0	1	121.0	136.4	-8.1	98	5	1,000	50	0.0	5.0
B- /7.1	12.2	0.77	31.36	474	2	97	0	1	121.0	136.6	-8.1	98	5	1,000	50	0.0	2.0
B- /7.3	12.2	0.77	34.02	189	2	97	0	1	121.0	139.8	-8.0	98	5	1,000	50	0.0	2.0
B /8.1	8.3	0.96	23.92	1,083	2	97	0	1	72.0	82.1	-7.2	87	6	1,000	50	5.8	0.0
B /8.1	8.3	0.96	23.30	135	2	97	0	1	72.0	77.0	-7.2	81	6	1,000	50	0.0	5.0
B /8.1	8.3	0.96	22.99	218	2	97	0	1	72.0	77.5	-7.3	81	6	1,000	50	0.0	1.0
B /8.1	8.3	0.96	23.48	102	2	97	0	1	72.0	80.1	-7.2	84	6	1,000	50	0.0	1.0
B /8.1	8.3	0.96	24.38	358	2	97	0	1	72.0	83.9	-6.6	88	6	1,000	50	0.0	0.0
U /	N/A	N/A	13.16	75	2	97	0	1	68.0	N/A	N/A	N/A	3	2,500	100	0.0	0.0
U /	N/A	N/A	13.42	108	2	97	0	1	68.0	N/A	N/A	N/A	3	0	0	0.0	0.0
U /	N/A	N/A	10.95	48	4	95	0	1	48.0	N/A	N/A	N/A	3	2,500	100	5.8	0.0
U /	N/A	N/A	10.74	171	4	95	0	1	48.0	N/A	N/A	N/A	3	2,500	100	0.0	0.0
U /	N/A	N/A	11.06	372	4	95	0	1	48.0	N/A	N/A	N/A	3	0	0	0.0	0.0
U /	N/A	N/A	11.22	48	4	95	0	1	52.0	N/A	N/A	N/A	1	2,500	100	5.8	0.0
U /	N/A	N/A	11.15	176	4	95	0	1	52.0	N/A	N/A	N/A	1	2,500	100	0.0	0.0
U /	N/A	N/A	11.24	351	4	95	0	1	52.0	N/A	N/A	N/A	1	0	0	0.0	0.0
U /	N/A	N/A	13.02	36	6	93	0	1	47.0	N/A	N/A	N/A	3	2,500	100	0.0	0.0
U /	N/A	N/A	13.39	67	6	93	0	1	47.0	N/A	N/A	N/A	3	0	0	0.0	0.0
U /	N/A	N/A	12.16	37	7	92	0	1	42.0	N/A	N/A	N/A	3	2,500	100	0.0	0.0
U /	N/A	N/A	12.54	54	7	92	0	1	42.0	N/A	N/A	N/A	3	0	0	0.0	0.0
B- /7.2	8.1	0.90	26.06	275	5	86	4	5	30.4	78.8	-3.7	92	13	5,000	500	0.0	2.0
B /8.8	5.0	0.93	17.70	6	13	62	23	2	25.4	41.6	-4.1	60	12	0	0	5.8	2.0
B+/9.0	5.1	0.94	17.15	35	13	62	23	2	25.4	39.2	-5.1	48	12	10,000	500	0.0	2.0
B- /7.6	11.4	1.14	8.77	2	8	91	0	1	30.5	64.7	-1.8	55	7	0	0	5.8	2.0
B- /7.6	11.4	1.15	8.21	2	8	91	0	1	30.5	58.4	-1.5	44	7	10,000	500	0.0	2.0
B- /7.0	12.7	1.47	12.16	3	0	99	0	1	49.0	79.6	-12.8	17	4	0	0	5.8	2.0
B- /7.0	12.7	1.47	11.78	9	0	99	0	1	49.0	75.5	-12.8	13	4	10,000	500	0.0	2.0
C /4.9	18.8	1.09	31.05	37	N/A	100	0	N/A	20.7	282.9	-17.6	99	13	0	0	5.8	2.0
C- /3.5	19.1	1.10	28.02	10	N/A	100	0	N/A	20.7	277.2	-18.6	99	13	10,000	500	0.0	2.0
B /8.0	8.4	1.06	13.47	5	0	100	0	0	81.8	56.9	-9.9	30	12	1,000	50	5.3	0.0
B /8.0	8.4	1.06	12.64	6	0	100	0	0	81.8	53.2	-10.0	25	3	1,000	50	0.0	5.0
B /8.1	8.3	1.06	12.63	2	0	100	0	0	81.8	53.3	-10.0	25	2	1,000	50	0.0	1.0
B /8.0	8.4	1.06	13.57	154	0	100	0	0	81.8	58.5	-9.8	32	12	1,000	50	0.0	0.0
C+/6.8	9.3	1.13	8.67	8	0	100	0	0	95.1	44.6	-9.9	9	3	1,000	50	5.3	0.0
C+/6.8	9.2	1.13	8.08	9	0	100	0	0	95.1	41.3	-10.1	7	N/A	1,000	50	0.0	5.0
C+/6.9	9.2	1.12	8.94	149	0	100	0	0	95.1	45.9	-9.9	10	3	1,000	50	0.0	0.0
C+/6.8	11.1	1.04	10.73	1	2	97	0	1	21.0	105.1	-8.8	12	N/A	1,000	50	5.3	2.0
C+/6.7	11.1	1.04	10.19	1	2	97	0	1	21.0	100.3	-8.7	10	N/A	1,000	50	0.0	5.0
B- /7.5	11.1	1.04	10.18	1	2	97	0	1	21.0	100.1	-8.7	9	N/A	1,000	50	0.0	2.0
C+/6.8	11.1	1.04	10.95	210	2	97	0	1	21.0	106.1	-8.5	13	N/A	1,000	50	0.0	2.0
U /	N/A	N/A	12.74	80	0	100	0	0	48.9	N/A	N/A	N/A	N/A	1,000	50	0.0	0.0
C+/5.7	14.8	1.10	16.42	2	2	96	0	2	21.4	128.3	-11.7	37	N/A	1,000	50	5.3	2.0
C+/5.7	14.7	1.10	15.72	1	2	96	0	2	21.4	123.1	-11.8	32	N/A	1,000	50	0.0	5.0
C+/5.6	14.8	1.10	16.65	85	2	96	0	2	21.4	130.2	-11.5	40	N/A	1,000	50	0.0	2.0
C /4.4	13.6	0.91	18.27	215	6	93	0	1	51.9	150.9	-7.5	94	8	1,000	50	5.3	0.0
C- /4.1	13.6	0.91	17.19	3	6	93	0	1	51.9	145.0	-7.6	92	8	1,000	50	0.0	5.0
C+/6.5	13.5	0.91	17.20	14	6	93	0	1	51.9	145.3	-7.6	92	2	1,000	50	0.0	1.0
C /4.5	13.5	0.91	18.52	187	6	93	0	1	51.9	152.9	-7.4	95	N/A	1,000	50	0.0	0.0
B /8.7	8.0	0.96	10.53	3	0	100	0	0	69.8	75.9	-10.1	82	8	1,000	50	5.3	2.0
B /8.7	8.0	0.96	10.33	1	0	100	0	0	69.8	71.6	-10.2	75	8	1,000	50	0.0	5.0
B /8.8	8.0	0.96	10.36	2	0	100	0	0	69.8	71.8	-10.2	76	2	1,000	50	0.0	1.0

Data as of June 30, 2006

99 Pct = Best / 0 Pct = Worst					PERFORMANCE							
						Total Return % through 6/30/06					Incl. in Returns	
			Overall Weiss Investment Rating		Perfor-mance Rating/Pts				Annualized		Dividend Expense	
Fund Type	Fund Name	Ticker Symbol		Phone		3 Mo	6 Mo	1Yr / Pct	3Yr / Pct	5Yr / Pct	Yield	Ratio
GI	Pacific Capital Value Y	PCVYX	B+	(800) 258-9232	C+ / 6.0	0.02	6.98	11.19 /55	13.88 /53	3.79 /44	1.12	1.06
GR	Paradigm Value Fund	PVFAX	B+	(877) 593-8637	A / 9.4	-4.68	6.27	18.47 /80	29.91 /95	--	0.00	2.06
GR	Parnassus Fund	PARNX	D-	(800) 999-3505	E- / 0.2	-6.28	0.82	5.67 /19	2.96 / 1	-1.17 /11	0.64	0.99
IN	Parnassus Income Fd-Equity Income	PRBLX	C-	(800) 999-3505	D / 2.2	-0.92	4.25	7.94 /32	7.79 /14	6.50 /64	3.11	0.99
BA	● Pax World Balanced Fd	PAXWX	C	(800) 767-1729	C- / 3.7	-1.50	2.88	7.91 /32	10.46 /31	4.73 /52	1.14	0.95
MC	Pax World Growth Fd	PXWGX	D+	(800) 767-1729	C / 4.7	-5.35	-1.95	6.80 /25	13.40 /51	2.61 /33	0.00	1.50
GI	Payden Market Return R	PYMRX	C	(888) 409-8007	C- / 3.7	-1.75	2.52	7.84 /31	11.21 /37	2.62 /33	4.33	0.45
SC	Payden Small Cap Leaders R	PSCLX	E	(888) 409-8007	D+ / 2.8	-7.36	1.70	11.32 /55	10.98 /35	0.77 /19	0.72	1.00
GR	Payden US Growth Leaders R	PUGLX	C	(888) 409-8007	C / 5.4	-4.40	1.25	9.74 /45	14.45 /56	2.70 /34	0.00	1.00
GI	Payden Value Leaders Fund	PYVLX	C	(888) 409-8007	C- / 3.0	0.77	6.50	8.52 /37	9.23 /22	1.50 /24	2.05	0.80
GR	Payson Total Return Fund	PBFDX	D+	(800) 805-8258	D- / 1.2	-2.88	0.03	2.14 / 5	6.76 / 9	1.24 /22	0.59	1.37
GI	Payson Value Fund	PVFDX	C-	(800) 805-8258	D+ / 2.4	-0.91	1.79	4.63 /13	8.69 /19	0.14 /16	0.29	1.74
GL	Pearl Aggressive Growth Fund	PFAGX	A-		B+ / 8.6	-5.19	4.15	21.64 /84	22.73 /87	--	1.87	0.98
GR	Penn Str Advisors Sector Rot Port A	PSRPX	C	(866) 207-5175	C+ / 6.6	-0.98	4.56	12.95 /64	17.24 /69	9.75 /80	0.00	1.75
GR	Penn Str Berkshire Advisors A	PBKAX	D+	(866) 207-5175	C / 4.3	0.08	9.12	15.02 /72	11.12 /36	--	0.24	2.00
GR	Performance Fds-Leaders Equity A	PILZX	C+	(800) 737-3676	C / 5.4	-4.93	4.67	16.14 /75	15.66 /62	4.84 /53	0.00	1.50
GR	Performance Fds-Leaders Equity B		C+	(800) 737-3676	C / 5.1	-5.14	4.30	15.25 /73	14.76 /58	4.02 /46	0.00	2.25
GR	Performance Fds-Leaders Equity Inst	PILEX	C-	(800) 737-3676	C+ / 6.4	-4.96	4.83	16.31 /75	15.93 /63	5.07 /55	0.00	N/A
GR	Performance Fds-Lrg Cap Eq A	PFECX	E	(800) 737-3676	D+ / 2.7	-3.54	2.94	8.69 /38	10.70 /33	1.79 /25	0.20	1.32
GR	Performance Fds-Lrg Cap Eq B		D+	(800) 737-3676	D+ / 2.4	-3.72	2.47	7.75 /31	9.90 /27	-2.34 / 7	0.02	1.98
GR	Performance Fds-Lrg Cap Eq Inst	PFEQX	D-	(800) 737-3676	C- / 3.9	-3.50	3.02	8.91 /39	10.96 /35	2.03 /28	0.30	1.04
MC	Performance Fds-Mid Cap Eq A	PCGCX	C-	(800) 737-3676	C+ / 5.9	-2.79	2.40	9.37 /42	16.61 /66	8.92 /76	0.00	1.32
MC	Performance Fds-Mid Cap Eq B		C+	(800) 737-3676	C+ / 5.6	-3.04	2.03	8.52 /37	15.76 /62	4.46 /50	0.00	2.07
MC	Performance Fds-Mid Cap Eq Inst	PCGIX	C-	(800) 737-3676	C+ / 6.7	-2.77	2.49	9.58 /44	16.88 /67	9.18 /77	0.01	1.17
AG	Permanent Portfolio Aggress Gr	PAGRX	C+	(800) 531-5142	B- / 7.1	-5.32	1.33	10.29 /49	18.25 /73	7.20 /68	0.00	1.41
AA	Permanent Portfolio Fund	PRPFX	B	(800) 531-5142	C+ / 6.1	1.31	7.70	14.42 /70	13.70 /52	13.32 /89	0.65	1.35
GR	Perritt Emerging Opportunities Fund	PREOX	U	(800) 331-8936	U /	-2.98	9.62	29.25 /94	--	--	1.56	2.22
SC	● Perritt Micro Cap Opportunities	PRCGX	A	(800) 331-8936	B+ / 8.9	-4.54	6.98	21.17 /83	24.47 /90	18.81 /95	0.00	1.29
FO	PF AllianceBern Intl Val A	PFAIX	C+	(800) 722-2333	C+ / 6.4	-0.83	7.69	18.57 /80	16.28 /65	--	0.60	1.80
FO	PF AllianceBern Intl Val AZ-529A	AZIAX	B-	(800) 722-2333	C+ / 6.5	-0.83	7.69	18.56 /80	16.28 /65	--	0.60	1.80
FO	PF AllianceBern Intl Val AZ-529B	AZIBX	B	(800) 722-2333	C+ / 6.3	-0.94	7.49	18.07 /79	15.75 /62	--	0.25	2.30
FO	PF AllianceBern Intl Val AZ-529C	AZICX	B-	(800) 722-2333	C+ / 6.7	-0.90	7.48	18.01 /79	15.68 /62	--	0.25	2.30
FO	PF AllianceBern Intl Val B	PFBIX	C+	(800) 722-2333	C+ / 6.3	-0.94	7.49	18.07 /79	15.75 /62	--	0.25	2.30
FO	PF AllianceBern Intl Val C	PCLIX	C+	(800) 722-2333	C+ / 6.7	-0.90	7.48	18.01 /79	15.67 /62	--	0.25	2.30
FO	PF AllianceBern Intl Val MT-529A	CPIAX	B-	(800) 722-2333	C+ / 6.5	-0.83	7.69	18.56 /80	16.28 /65	--	0.60	1.80
FO	PF AllianceBern Intl Val MT-529B	CPIBX	B	(800) 722-2333	C+ / 6.3	-0.94	7.49	18.07 /79	15.75 /62	--	0.25	2.30
FO	PF AllianceBern Intl Val MT-529C	CPICX	B-	(800) 722-2333	C+ / 6.7	-0.90	7.48	18.01 /79	15.68 /62	--	0.25	2.30
AG	PF Janus Growth LT A	PAJGX	D	(800) 722-2333	D / 2.0	-4.33	-0.59	8.43 /36	9.88 /27	--	0.00	1.70
AG	PF Janus Growth LT AZ-529A	AZGAX	D	(800) 722-2333	D / 2.2	-4.33	-0.59	8.43 /36	9.88 /27	--	0.00	1.70
AG	PF Janus Growth LT AZ-529B	AZGBX	D	(800) 722-2333	D / 1.9	-4.42	-0.87	7.91 /32	9.33 /23	--	0.00	2.20
AG	PF Janus Growth LT AZ-529C	AZGCX	D+	(800) 722-2333	D+ / 2.5	-4.44	-0.87	7.84 /31	9.28 /23	--	0.00	2.20
AG	PF Janus Growth LT B	PBJGX	D-	(800) 722-2333	D / 1.9	-4.42	-0.86	7.91 /32	9.33 /23	--	0.00	2.20
AG	PF Janus Growth LT C	PCJGX	D	(800) 722-2333	D+ / 2.5	-4.44	-0.87	7.84 /31	9.28 /23	--	0.00	2.20
AG	PF Janus Growth LT MT-529A	CPGAX	D	(800) 722-2333	D / 2.2	-4.33	-0.59	8.43 /36	9.88 /27	--	0.00	1.70
AG	PF Janus Growth LT MT-529B	CPGBX	D	(800) 722-2333	D / 1.9	-4.42	-0.87	7.91 /32	9.33 /23	--	0.00	2.20
AG	PF Janus Growth LT MT-529C	CPGCX	D+	(800) 722-2333	D+ / 2.5	-4.44	-0.87	7.84 /31	9.28 /23	--	0.00	2.20
MC	PF Lazard Mid Cap Value A	PFAVX	U	(800) 722-2333	U /	-0.67	2.64	9.10 /41	--	--	0.00	1.80
AG	PF Loomis Sayles Lg Cp Gr A	PFBAX	E-	(800) 722-2333	E- / 0.0	-10.74	-9.66	-4.77 / 0	2.25 / 1	--	0.00	1.90
AG	PF Loomis Sayles Lg Cp Gr AZ-529A	AZBAX	E+	(800) 722-2333	E- / 0.0	-10.74	-9.66	-4.77 / 0	2.25 / 1	--	0.00	1.90
AG	PF Loomis Sayles Lg Cp Gr AZ-529B	AZBBX	E+	(800) 722-2333	E- / 0.0	-10.88	-9.86	-5.26 / 0	1.81 / 1	--	0.00	2.40
AG	PF Loomis Sayles Lg Cp Gr AZ-529C	AZBCX	E+	(800) 722-2333	E- / 0.0	-10.80	-9.78	-5.26 / 0	1.73 / 0	--	0.00	2.40
AG	PF Loomis Sayles Lg Cp Gr B	PFBBX	E-	(800) 722-2333	E- / 0.0	-10.88	-9.86	-5.26 / 0	1.81 / 1	--	0.00	2.40

● Denotes fund is closed to new investors
* Denotes fund is included in Section II

RISK Rating/Pts	3 Year Standard Deviation	Beta	NAV As of 6/30/06	Total $(Mil)	Cash %	Stocks %	Bonds %	Other %	Portfolio Turnover Ratio	Last Bull Market Return	Last Bear Market Return	Manager Quality Pct	Manager Tenure (Years)	Initial Purch. $	Additional Purch. $	Front End Load	Back End Load
B /8.7	8.0	0.96	10.55	145	0	100	0	0	69.8	76.8	-10.1	83	N/A	1,000	50	0.0	0.0
C /5.2	12.4	1.28	45.59	41	2	97	0	1	67.4	204.8	N/A	99	3	25,000	1,000	0.0	0.0
B- /7.6	7.9	0.73	31.94	278	0	99	0	1	136.1	34.1	-13.8	12	22	2,000	50	0.0	0.0
B /8.3	6.4	0.73	24.87	818	1	90	0	9	109.5	41.8	-7.4	44	5	2,000	50	0.0	0.0
B /8.7	6.1	1.16	24.33	2,018	4	67	28	1	21.6	50.4	-3.3	76	8	250	50	0.0	0.0
C /4.9	13.9	1.10	12.57	107	6	93	0	1	105.4	83.1	-5.4	12	6	250	50	0.0	0.0
B /8.6	7.8	1.02	10.62	53	16	0	84	0	92.0	65.6	-9.4	54	11	5,000	1,000	0.0	2.0
C- /3.5	15.7	1.00	11.56	6	0	100	0	0	129.0	73.5	-18.0	8	7	5,000	1,000	0.0	2.0
C+ /6.8	13.2	1.19	8.90	63	0	100	0	0	150.0	89.5	-11.9	70	7	5,000	1,000	0.0	2.0
B /8.7	7.7	0.88	11.71	58	0	100	0	0	69.0	53.7	-11.0	45	N/A	5,000	1,000	0.0	2.0
B /8.5	6.6	0.80	12.49	18	0	99	0	1	85.0	40.1	-5.0	30	13	2,500	250	0.0	0.0
B /8.0	7.8	0.98	16.80	12	0	100	0	0	15.0	51.5	-11.0	33	11	2,500	250	0.0	0.0
C+ /6.8	13.4	1.17	14.06	40	1	98	0	1	44.0	158.7	-9.2	15	N/A	5,000	100	0.0	2.0
C+ /5.7	10.4	1.15	17.21	18	4	95	0	1	107.0	99.5	-5.4	90	N/A	2,000	100	5.5	0.0
C+ /5.6	10.1	1.12	12.56	2	2	97	0	1	247.0	N/A	N/A	43	N/A	2,000	100	5.5	0.0
B- /7.4	12.1	1.18	9.64	3	0	99	0	1	219.4	89.1	-4.3	81	N/A	1,000	100	5.3	1.0
B- /7.4	12.2	1.18	9.22	1	0	99	0	1	219.4	84.6	-4.3	74	N/A	1,000	100	0.0	5.0
C /5.1	12.6	1.21	9.77	51	0	99	0	1	219.4	90.6	-4.2	81	N/A	1,000,000	0	0.0	0.0
C- /3.6	8.8	1.01	14.13	26	0	99	0	1	79.0	61.4	-10.2	49	N/A	1,000	100	5.3	1.0
B- /7.6	8.4	0.99	13.39	2	0	99	0	1	79.0	57.5	-17.4	42	N/A	1,000	100	0.0	5.0
C- /3.7	8.4	0.99	14.26	53	0	99	0	1	79.0	62.9	-10.2	55	N/A	1,000,000	0	0.0	0.0
C /4.5	10.3	0.91	15.35	29	6	93	0	1	78.1	96.3	-7.1	55	12	1,000	100	5.3	1.0
B- /7.6	10.3	0.91	14.05	1	6	93	0	1	78.1	91.5	-7.1	46	8	1,000	100	0.0	5.0
C /4.6	10.3	0.91	15.73	75	6	93	0	1	78.1	97.6	-6.9	58	12	1,000,000	0	0.0	0.0
C+ /6.3	12.6	1.39	107.06	38	N/A	N/A	0	N/A	10.4	110.9	-9.2	84	15	1,000	100	0.0	0.0
B /8.0	8.1	0.99	30.91	559	0	64	34	2	0.7	59.2	4.2	95	15	1,000	100	0.0	0.0
U /	N/A	N/A	14.02	84	6	93	0	1	64.4	N/A	N/A	N/A	2	1,000	50	0.0	2.0
B- /7.0	13.4	0.85	31.57	537	25	74	0	1	24.1	159.0	-3.0	97	7	1,000	50	0.0	2.0
C+ /6.5	9.7	0.89	14.64	57	2	97	0	1	55.3	89.9	-9.1	16	5	1,000	50	5.5	1.0
B- /7.8	9.7	0.89	14.64	N/A	2	97	0	1	55.3	N/A	N/A	16	3	500	50	5.5	0.0
B- /7.8	9.7	0.89	14.39	N/A	2	97	0	1	55.3	N/A	N/A	13	3	500	50	0.0	5.0
B- /7.8	9.7	0.88	14.37	N/A	2	97	0	1	55.3	N/A	N/A	13	3	500	50	0.0	1.0
C+ /6.5	9.7	0.89	14.39	1	2	97	0	1	55.3	87.0	-9.2	13	5	1,000	50	0.0	5.0
C+ /6.5	9.7	0.88	14.37	2	2	97	0	1	55.3	86.7	-9.3	13	5	1,000	50	0.0	1.0
B- /7.8	9.7	0.89	14.64	1	2	97	0	1	55.3	89.9	-9.1	16	5	500	50	5.5	0.0
B- /7.8	9.7	0.89	14.39	N/A	2	97	0	1	55.3	87.0	-9.2	13	5	500	50	Front	5.0
B- /7.8	9.7	0.88	14.37	N/A	2	97	0	1	55.3	86.7	-9.3	13	5	500	50	0.0	1.0
C+ /6.7	9.3	1.12	11.70	47	6	93	0	1	69.5	63.7	-9.5	32	N/A	1,000	50	5.5	1.0
B- /7.3	9.3	1.12	11.70	N/A	6	93	0	1	69.5	N/A	N/A	32	3	500	50	5.5	0.0
B- /7.3	9.3	1.12	11.46	N/A	6	93	0	1	69.5	N/A	N/A	28	3	500	50	0.0	5.0
B- /7.3	9.3	1.12	11.42	N/A	6	93	0	1	69.5	N/A	N/A	27	3	500	50	0.0	1.0
C+ /6.7	9.3	1.12	11.46	N/A	6	93	0	1	69.5	61.1	-9.5	28	N/A	1,000	50	0.0	5.0
C+ /6.7	9.3	1.12	11.42	1	6	93	0	1	69.5	60.8	-9.4	27	N/A	1,000	50	0.0	1.0
B- /7.3	9.3	1.12	11.70	1	6	93	0	1	69.5	63.7	-9.5	32	5	500	50	5.5	0.0
B- /7.3	9.3	1.12	11.46	N/A	6	93	0	1	69.5	61.1	-9.5	28	5	500	50	0.0	5.0
B- /7.3	9.3	1.12	11.42	N/A	6	93	0	1	69.5	60.8	-9.4	28	5	500	50	0.0	1.0
U /	N/A	N/A	10.19	25	5	94	0	1	112.9	N/A	N/A	N/A	2	1,000	50	5.5	1.0
C /4.4	9.3	1.10	8.75	18	1	98	0	1	161.0	34.1	-9.0	2	N/A	1,000	50	5.5	1.0
B- /7.1	9.3	1.10	8.75	N/A	1	98	0	1	161.0	N/A	N/A	2	N/A	500	50	5.5	0.0
B- /7.1	9.3	1.10	8.53	N/A	1	98	0	1	161.0	N/A	N/A	2	N/A	500	50	0.0	5.0
B- /7.1	9.3	1.10	8.52	N/A	1	98	0	1	161.0	N/A	N/A	2	N/A	500	50	0.0	1.0
C /4.3	9.3	1.10	8.53	1	1	98	0	1	161.0	32.1	-9.1	2	N/A	1,000	50	0.0	5.0

Fund Type	Fund Name	Ticker Symbol	Overall Weiss Investment Rating	Phone	Perfor- mance Rating/Pts	3 Mo	6 Mo	1Yr / Pct	3Yr / Pct	5Yr / Pct	Dividend Yield	Expense Ratio
AG	PF Loomis Sayles Lg Cp Gr C	PFBCX	E-	(800) 722-2333	E- / 0.0	-10.80	-9.78	-5.26 / 0	1.73 / 0	--	0.00	2.40
AG	PF Loomis Sayles Lg Cp Gr MT-529A	CPBLX	E+	(800) 722-2333	E- / 0.0	-10.74	-9.66	-4.77 / 0	2.25 / 1	--	0.00	1.90
AG	PF Loomis Sayles Lg Cp Gr MT-529B	CPCBX	E+	(800) 722-2333	E- / 0.0	-10.88	-9.86	-5.26 / 0	1.81 / 1	--	0.00	2.40
AG	PF Loomis Sayles Lg Cp Gr MT-529C	CPBCX	E+	(800) 722-2333	E- / 0.0	-10.80	-9.78	-5.26 / 0	1.73 / 0	--	0.00	2.40
FO	PF MFS Intl Large Cap A	PAGGX	A-	(800) 722-2333	B / 8.1	0.98	10.73	27.00 / 91	19.81 / 79	--	0.18	2.00
FO	PF MFS Intl Large Cap AZ-529A	AZAGX	A+	(800) 722-2333	B / 8.2	0.98	10.73	27.00 / 91	19.80 / 79	--	0.18	2.00
FO	PF MFS Intl Large Cap AZ-529B	AZBGX	A+	(800) 722-2333	B / 8.0	0.87	10.43	26.31 / 90	19.22 / 77	--	0.00	2.50
FO	PF MFS Intl Large Cap AZ-529C	AZCGX	A+	(800) 722-2333	B+ / 8.3	0.87	10.41	26.37 / 90	19.21 / 77	--	0.00	2.50
FO	PF MFS Intl Large Cap B	PBGGX	B+	(800) 722-2333	B / 8.1	0.87	10.43	26.31 / 90	19.22 / 77	--	0.00	2.50
FO	PF MFS Intl Large Cap C	PFCGX	A-	(800) 722-2333	B+ / 8.3	0.87	10.41	26.37 / 90	19.22 / 77	--	0.00	2.50
FO	PF MFS Intl Large Cap MT-529A	CPAGX	A+	(800) 722-2333	B / 8.2	0.98	10.73	27.00 / 91	19.81 / 79	--	0.18	2.00
FO	PF MFS Intl Large Cap MT-529B	CPBGX	A+	(800) 722-2333	B / 8.1	0.87	10.43	26.31 / 90	19.22 / 77	--	0.00	2.50
FO	PF MFS Intl Large Cap MT-529C	CPCGX	A+	(800) 722-2333	B+ / 8.3	0.87	10.41	26.37 / 90	19.22 / 77	--	0.00	2.50
AG	PF NB Fasciano Small Eq A	PAAGX	E+	(800) 722-2333	D+ / 2.8	-4.53	4.19	7.37 / 28	11.18 / 37	--	0.00	1.95
AG	PF NB Fasciano Small Eq AZ-529A	AZAAX	D+	(800) 722-2333	C- / 3.0	-4.53	4.19	7.37 / 28	11.18 / 37	--	0.00	1.95
AG	PF NB Fasciano Small Eq AZ-529B	AZABX	D	(800) 722-2333	D+ / 2.7	-4.65	4.00	6.81 / 25	10.65 / 32	--	0.00	2.45
AG	PF NB Fasciano Small Eq AZ-529C	AZACX	D+	(800) 722-2333	C- / 3.4	-4.55	4.09	6.91 / 26	10.64 / 32	--	0.00	2.45
AG	PF NB Fasciano Small Eq B	PFBGX	E+	(800) 722-2333	D+ / 2.7	-4.65	4.00	6.81 / 25	10.65 / 32	--	0.00	2.45
AG	PF NB Fasciano Small Eq C	PCAGX	E+	(800) 722-2333	C- / 3.4	-4.55	4.09	6.91 / 26	10.64 / 32	--	0.00	2.45
AG	PF NB Fasciano Small Eq MT-529A	CPAAX	D+	(800) 722-2333	C- / 3.0	-4.53	4.19	7.37 / 28	11.18 / 37	--	0.00	1.95
AG	PF NB Fasciano Small Eq MT-529B	CPBAX	D	(800) 722-2333	D+ / 2.7	-4.65	4.00	6.81 / 25	10.65 / 32	--	0.00	2.45
AG	PF NB Fasciano Small Eq MT-529C	CPCAX	D+	(800) 722-2333	C- / 3.4	-4.55	4.09	6.91 / 26	10.64 / 32	--	0.00	2.45
GR	PF Optimization Model B Class A	POBAX	U	(800) 722-2333	U /	-0.70	1.35	5.17 / 16	--	--	1.73	0.02
GR	PF Optimization Model C Class A	POCAX	U	(800) 722-2333	U /	-1.40	2.31	8.30 / 35	--	--	1.39	1.73
GR	PF Optimization Model C Class B	POMBX	U	(800) 722-2333	U /	-1.52	2.03	7.87 / 32	--	--	1.04	0.50
GR	PF Optimization Model C Class C	POMCX	U	(800) 722-2333	U /	-1.52	2.03	7.88 / 32	--	--	1.05	0.50
GR	PF Optimization Model D Class A	PODAX	U	(800) 722-2333	U /	-1.90	2.98	10.78 / 52	--	--	1.07	1.80
GR	PF Optimization Model D Class B	PODBX	U	(800) 722-2333	U /	-1.99	2.82	10.40 / 49	--	--	0.83	0.50
GR	PF Optimization Model D Class C	PODCX	U	(800) 722-2333	U /	-1.99	2.82	10.42 / 50	--	--	0.84	0.50
GR	PF Optimization Model E Class A	POEAX	U	(800) 722-2333	U /	-1.88	4.62	14.55 / 70	--	--	0.84	1.85
GR	PF Optimization Model E Class C	POCEX	U	(800) 722-2333	U /	-1.97	4.46	14.17 / 69	--	--	0.59	0.50
GI	PF Salomon Bros Lrg-Cap Val A	PFALX	D+	(800) 722-2333	C- / 3.2	-0.34	4.27	10.44 / 50	10.86 / 34	--	0.20	1.80
GI	PF Salomon Bros Lrg-Cap Val	AZLAX	C-	(800) 722-2333	C- / 3.3	-0.34	4.27	10.44 / 50	10.86 / 34	--	0.20	1.80
GI	PF Salomon Bros Lrg-Cap Val	AZLBX	C-	(800) 722-2333	C- / 3.1	-0.51	3.98	9.94 / 47	10.38 / 30	--	0.14	2.30
GI	PF Salomon Bros Lrg-Cap Val	AZLCX	C-	(800) 722-2333	C- / 3.7	-0.51	3.99	9.83 / 46	10.32 / 30	--	0.10	2.30
GI	PF Salomon Bros Lrg-Cap Val B	PFBLX	D+	(800) 722-2333	C- / 3.1	-0.51	3.98	9.94 / 47	10.38 / 30	--	0.14	2.30
GI	PF Salomon Bros Lrg-Cap Val C	PFCLX	C-	(800) 722-2333	C- / 3.7	-0.51	3.99	9.83 / 46	10.32 / 30	--	0.10	2.30
GI	PF Salomon Bros Lrg-Cap Val	CPLAX	C-	(800) 722-2333	C- / 3.3	-0.34	4.27	10.44 / 50	10.86 / 34	--	0.20	1.80
GI	PF Salomon Bros Lrg-Cap Val	CPLBX	C-	(800) 722-2333	C- / 3.1	-0.51	3.98	9.94 / 47	10.38 / 30	--	0.14	2.30
GI	PF Salomon Bros Lrg-Cap Val	CPLCX	C-	(800) 722-2333	C- / 3.7	-0.51	3.99	9.83 / 46	10.32 / 30	--	0.10	2.30
GR	PF Van Kampen Comstock A	PFVAX	C	(800) 722-2333	C- / 3.9	0.60	3.24	8.27 / 35	12.59 / 46	--	0.45	1.90
GR	PF Van Kampen Comstock AZ-529A	AZCAX	C+	(800) 722-2333	C- / 4.1	0.60	3.24	8.27 / 35	12.59 / 46	--	0.46	1.90
GR	PF Van Kampen Comstock AZ-529B	AZCBX	C	(800) 722-2333	C- / 3.8	0.42	3.00	7.75 / 31	12.08 / 43	--	0.07	2.40
GR	PF Van Kampen Comstock AZ-529C	AZCCX	C+	(800) 722-2333	C / 4.5	0.49	3.00	7.75 / 31	12.04 / 43	--	0.06	2.40
GR	PF Van Kampen Comstock B	PFVBX	C	(800) 722-2333	C- / 3.8	0.42	3.00	7.75 / 31	12.08 / 43	--	0.07	2.40
GR	PF Van Kampen Comstock C	PFVCX	C+	(800) 722-2333	C / 4.5	0.49	3.00	7.75 / 31	12.04 / 43	--	0.06	2.40
GR	PF Van Kampen Comstock MT-529A	CPSAX	C+	(800) 722-2333	C- / 4.1	0.60	3.24	8.27 / 35	12.59 / 46	--	0.46	1.90
GR	PF Van Kampen Comstock MT-529B	CPSBX	C	(800) 722-2333	C- / 3.8	0.42	3.00	7.75 / 31	12.08 / 43	--	0.07	2.40
GR	PF Van Kampen Comstock MT-529C	CPSCX	C+	(800) 722-2333	C / 4.5	0.49	3.00	7.75 / 31	12.04 / 43	--	0.06	2.40
MC	PF Van Kampen Mid-Cp Gr A	PFAMX	C+	(800) 722-2333	B- / 7.0	-5.26	3.04	17.50 / 78	18.47 / 74	--	0.00	1.85
MC	PF Van Kampen Mid-Cp Gr AZ-529A	AZAMX	B-	(800) 722-2333	B- / 7.1	-5.26	3.04	17.50 / 78	18.47 / 74	--	0.00	1.85
MC	PF Van Kampen Mid-Cp Gr AZ-529B	AZBMX	C+	(800) 722-2333	C+ / 6.9	-5.27	3.01	17.13 / 77	18.01 / 73	--	0.00	2.35

● Denotes fund is closed to new investors
* Denotes fund is included in Section II

RISK			NET ASSETS		ASSET					Portfolio Turnover Ratio	BULL / BEAR		FUND MANAGER		MINIMUMS		LOADS	
Risk Rating/Pts	3 Year		NAV As of 6/30/06	Total $(Mil)	Cash %	Stocks %	Bonds %	Other %			Last Bull Market Return	Last Bear Market Return	Manager Quality Pct	Manager Tenure (Years)	Initial Purch. $	Additional Purch. $	Front End Load	Back End Load
	Standard Deviation	Beta																
C /4.3	9.3	1.10	8.52	1	1	98	0	1	161.0	31.9	-9.0	2	N/A	1,000	50	0.0	1.0
B- /7.1	9.3	1.10	8.75	1	1	98	0	1	161.0	34.1	-9.0	2	N/A	500	50	5.5	0.0
B- /7.1	9.3	1.10	8.53	N/A	1	98	0	1	161.0	32.1	-9.1	2	N/A	500	50	0.0	5.0
B- /7.1	9.3	1.10	8.52	N/A	1	98	0	1	161.0	31.9	-9.0	2	N/A	500	50	0.0	1.0
B- /7.2	9.5	0.90	15.12	55	2	97	0	1	63.1	103.4	-8.7	35	N/A	1,000	50	5.5	1.0
B /8.1	9.5	0.90	15.12	N/A	2	97	0	1	63.1	N/A	N/A	35	3	500	50	5.5	0.0
B /8.1	9.5	0.90	14.79	N/A	2	97	0	1	63.1	N/A	N/A	31	3	500	50	0.0	5.0
B /8.1	9.5	0.90	14.81	N/A	2	97	0	1	63.1	N/A	N/A	31	3	500	50	0.0	1.0
B- /7.2	9.5	0.90	14.79	1	2	97	0	1	63.1	100.2	-8.9	31	N/A	1,000	50	0.0	5.0
B- /7.2	9.5	0.90	14.81	1	2	97	0	1	63.1	100.2	-8.8	31	N/A	1,000	50	0.0	1.0
B /8.1	9.5	0.90	15.12	N/A	2	97	0	1	63.1	103.4	-8.7	35	4	500	50	5.5	0.0
B /8.1	9.5	0.90	14.79	N/A	2	97	0	1	63.1	100.2	-8.9	31	4	500	50	0.0	5.0
B /8.1	9.5	0.90	14.81	N/A	2	97	0	1	63.1	100.2	-8.8	31	4	500	50	0.0	1.0
C- /4.1	12.0	1.32	10.70	25	8	91	0	1	132.3	64.6	-8.2	28	5	1,000	50	5.5	1.0
C+ /6.6	12.0	1.32	10.70	N/A	8	91	0	1	132.3	N/A	N/A	28	3	500	50	5.5	0.0
C+ /6.6	12.1	1.32	10.43	N/A	8	91	0	1	132.3	N/A	N/A	25	3	500	50	0.0	5.0
C+ /6.6	12.1	1.33	10.45	N/A	8	91	0	1	132.3	N/A	N/A	24	3	500	50	0.0	1.0
C- /4.0	12.1	1.32	10.43	N/A	8	91	0	1	132.3	62.1	-8.4	25	5	1,000	50	0.0	5.0
C- /4.0	12.1	1.33	10.45	1	8	91	0	1	132.3	62.1	-8.4	24	5	1,000	50	0.0	1.0
C+ /6.6	12.0	1.32	10.70	N/A	8	91	0	1	132.3	64.6	-8.2	28	5	500	50	5.5	0.0
C+ /6.6	12.1	1.32	10.43	N/A	8	91	0	1	132.3	62.1	-8.4	25	5	500	50	0.0	5.0
C+ /6.6	12.1	1.33	10.45	N/A	8	91	0	1	132.3	62.1	-8.4	24	5	500	50	0.0	1.0
U /	N/A	N/A	10.63	28	6	37	55	2	37.9	N/A	N/A	N/A	N/A	1,000	50	5.5	1.0
U /	N/A	N/A	11.24	99	1	56	41	2	26.5	N/A	N/A	N/A	N/A	1,000	50	5.5	1.0
U /	N/A	N/A	11.19	33	1	56	41	2	26.5	N/A	N/A	N/A	N/A	1,000	50	0.0	5.0
U /	N/A	N/A	11.18	93	1	56	41	2	26.5	N/A	N/A	N/A	N/A	1,000	50	0.0	0.0
U /	N/A	N/A	11.64	100	0	71	28	1	28.0	N/A	N/A	N/A	N/A	1,000	50	5.5	1.0
U /	N/A	N/A	11.58	39	0	71	28	1	28.0	N/A	N/A	N/A	N/A	1,000	50	0.0	5.0
U /	N/A	N/A	11.56	95	0	71	28	1	28.0	N/A	N/A	N/A	N/A	1,000	50	0.0	0.0
U /	N/A	N/A	12.09	43	0	87	12	1	42.5	N/A	N/A	N/A	N/A	1,000	50	5.5	1.0
U /	N/A	N/A	12.02	31	0	87	12	1	42.5	N/A	N/A	N/A	N/A	1,000	50	0.0	0.0
C+ /6.8	7.9	0.98	11.81	34	4	95	0	1	77.1	66.4	-12.2	54	N/A	1,000	50	5.5	1.0
B- /7.5	7.9	0.98	11.81	N/A	4	95	0	1	77.1	N/A	N/A	54	3	500	50	5.5	0.0
B- /7.4	7.9	0.98	11.63	N/A	4	95	0	1	77.1	N/A	N/A	48	3	500	50	0.0	5.0
B- /7.4	7.9	0.98	11.60	N/A	4	95	0	1	77.1	N/A	N/A	48	3	500	50	0.0	1.0
C+ /6.7	7.9	0.98	11.63	1	4	95	0	1	77.1	64.3	-12.4	48	N/A	1,000	50	0.0	5.0
C+ /6.7	7.9	0.98	11.60	2	4	95	0	1	77.1	63.8	-12.2	48	N/A	1,000	50	0.0	1.0
B- /7.5	7.9	0.98	11.81	1	4	95	0	1	77.1	66.4	-12.2	54	4	500	50	5.5	0.0
B- /7.4	7.9	0.98	11.63	N/A	4	95	0	1	77.1	64.3	-12.4	48	4	500	50	0.0	5.0
B- /7.4	7.9	0.98	11.60	N/A	4	95	0	1	77.1	63.8	-12.2	48	4	500	50	0.0	1.0
B /8.1	7.1	0.83	12.74	66	8	91	0	1	22.4	72.0	-9.4	83	N/A	1,000	50	5.5	1.0
B /8.5	7.1	0.83	12.74	N/A	8	91	0	1	22.4	N/A	N/A	83	3	500	50	5.5	0.0
B /8.5	7.1	0.83	12.56	N/A	8	91	0	1	22.4	N/A	N/A	79	3	500	50	0.0	5.0
B /8.5	7.1	0.83	12.54	N/A	8	91	0	1	22.4	N/A	N/A	78	3	500	50	0.0	1.0
B /8.4	7.1	0.83	12.56	1	8	91	0	1	22.4	69.5	-9.5	79	N/A	1,000	50	0.0	5.0
B /8.3	7.1	0.83	12.54	1	8	91	0	1	22.4	69.3	-9.5	78	N/A	1,000	50	0.0	1.0
B /8.5	7.1	0.83	12.74	1	8	91	0	1	22.4	72.0	-9.4	83	4	500	50	5.5	0.0
B /8.5	7.1	0.83	12.56	N/A	8	91	0	1	22.4	69.5	-9.5	79	4	500	50	0.0	5.0
B /8.5	7.1	0.83	12.54	N/A	8	91	0	1	22.4	69.3	-9.5	78	4	500	50	0.0	1.0
C /5.5	12.1	1.04	10.33	38	2	97	0	1	107.6	100.9	-6.9	51	N/A	1,000	50	5.5	1.0
C+ /6.5	12.1	1.04	10.33	N/A	2	97	0	1	107.6	N/A	N/A	51	3	500	50	5.5	0.0
C+ /6.5	12.1	1.05	10.12	N/A	2	97	0	1	107.6	N/A	N/A	45	3	500	50	0.0	5.0

Fund Type	Fund Name	Ticker Symbol	Overall Weiss Investment Rating	Phone	Perfor-mance Rating/Pts	3 Mo	6 Mo	1Yr / Pct	3Yr / Pct	5Yr / Pct	Dividend Yield	Expense Ratio
MC	PF Van Kampen Mid-Cp Gr AZ-529C	AZCMX	B-	(800) 722-2333	B- / 7.3	-5.28	2.82	16.94 /77	17.90 /72	--	0.00	2.35
MC	PF Van Kampen Mid-Cp Gr B	PFBMX	C	(800) 722-2333	C+ / 6.9	-5.27	3.01	17.14 /77	18.01 /73	--	0.00	2.35
MC	PF Van Kampen Mid-Cp Gr C	PFCMX	C+	(800) 722-2333	B- / 7.3	-5.28	2.82	16.94 /77	17.90 /72	--	0.00	2.35
MC	PF Van Kampen Mid-Cp Gr MT-529A	CPMAX	B-	(800) 722-2333	B- / 7.1	-5.26	3.04	17.50 /78	18.47 /74	--	0.00	1.85
MC	PF Van Kampen Mid-Cp Gr MT-529B	CPMBX	C+	(800) 722-2333	C+ / 6.9	-5.27	3.01	17.13 /77	18.01 /73	--	0.00	2.35
MC	PF Van Kampen Mid-Cp Gr MT-529C	CPMCX	B-	(800) 722-2333	B- / 7.3	-5.28	2.82	16.94 /77	17.90 /72	--	0.00	2.35
RE	PF Van Kampen Real Est Fd A	PFARX	U	(800) 722-2333	U /	0.43	14.56	23.26 /86	--	--	0.94	2.05
GI	Philadelphia Fund	PHILX	C+	(800) 749-9933	C+ / 5.8	2.29	5.25	7.72 /31	13.95 /54	6.97 /67	1.57	1.52
GR	Phoenix All-Cap Growth A	PASGX	E+	(800) 243-4361	D- / 1.3	-8.45	-3.97	2.85 / 7	9.89 /27	2.29 /30	0.00	1.46
GR	Phoenix All-Cap Growth B	PGOBX	E	(800) 243-4361	D- / 1.1	-8.67	-4.35	2.12 / 5	9.06 /21	1.52 /24	0.00	2.21
GR	Phoenix All-Cap Growth C	PGOCX	E+	(800) 243-4361	D / 1.6	-8.67	-4.35	2.12 / 5	9.06 /21	1.54 /24	0.00	2.21
BA	Phoenix Balanced Fund Class A	PHBLX	D	(800) 243-4361	E+ / 0.8	-1.26	2.47	4.44 /12	6.96 /10	3.13 /38	1.96	1.05
BA	Phoenix Balanced Fund Class B	PBCBX	D	(800) 243-4361	E+ / 0.7	-1.51	2.04	3.63 / 9	6.14 / 7	2.35 /31	1.38	1.80
BA	Phoenix Balanced Fund Class C	PSBCX	U	(800) 243-4361	U /	-1.51	2.04	3.68 / 9	--	--	1.42	1.80
GR	Phoenix Capital Growth A	PHGRX	E+	(800) 243-4361	E- / 0.1	-8.04	-7.03	-0.44 / 1	4.65 / 3	-4.47 / 3	0.54	1.36
GR	Phoenix Capital Growth B	PGTBX	E+	(800) 243-4361	E- / 0.1	-8.17	-7.34	-1.19 / 1	3.88 / 2	-5.19 / 2	0.00	2.11
GR	Phoenix Earnings Driven Growth A	EDGEX	E-	(800) 243-4361	E+ / 0.9	-5.22	2.98	6.40 /23	7.38 /12	-3.29 / 5	0.00	1.45
GR	Phoenix Earnings Driven Growth B	EDBEX	E-	(800) 243-4361	E+ / 0.8	-5.34	2.62	5.58 /18	6.59 / 9	-4.01 / 4	0.00	2.20
GR	Phoenix Earnings Driven Growth C	EDBCX	E	(800) 243-4361	D- / 1.2	-5.34	2.62	5.58 /18	6.59 / 9	-4.00 / 4	0.00	2.20
GR	Phoenix Earnings Driven Growth X	EDGIX	E	(800) 243-4361	D / 1.9	-5.12	3.12	6.64 /24	7.67 /13	-3.04 / 5	0.00	1.20
MC	Phoenix Focused Value A	JVVAX	D	(800) 243-4361	E+ / 0.9	-0.82	0.45	1.41 / 3	7.93 /15	5.50 /58	0.88	1.25
MC	Phoenix Focused Value C	JVVCX	D	(800) 243-4361	D- / 1.2	-1.04	0.10	0.66 / 2	7.04 /10	--	0.14	2.00
FO	Phoenix Foreign Opportunities A	JVIAX	A+	(800) 243-4361	A- / 9.2	1.13	10.49	26.10 /90	26.10 /92	12.04 /87	1.08	1.25
GR	Phoenix Fundamental Growth A	PHFAX	U	(800) 243-4361	U /	-3.97	0.10	--	--	--	0.00	1.45
GI	Phoenix Gr & In Fund Class A	PDIAX	C	(800) 243-4361	D+ / 2.8	-1.09	3.08	7.30 /28	11.00 /36	1.91 /26	0.64	1.25
GI	Phoenix Gr & In Fund Class B	PBGIX	C-	(800) 243-4361	D+ / 2.6	-1.27	2.71	6.52 /23	10.19 /29	1.16 /21	0.16	2.00
GI	Phoenix Gr & In Fund Class C	PGICX	C	(800) 243-4361	C- / 3.2	-1.27	2.71	6.44 /23	10.19 /29	1.14 /21	0.16	2.00
AA	Phoenix In & Gr Fund Class A	NAINX	D	(800) 243-4361	E / 0.5	-0.77	0.86	2.82 / 7	6.24 / 7	3.59 /42	2.44	1.28
AA	Phoenix In & Gr Fund Class B	NBINX	D	(800) 243-4361	E / 0.5	-0.95	0.48	2.13 / 5	5.47 / 5	2.82 /35	1.81	2.03
AA	Phoenix In & Gr Fund Class C	POICX	D+	(800) 243-4361	E+ / 0.7	-0.95	0.48	2.11 / 5	5.47 / 5	2.80 /35	1.79	2.03
BA	Phoenix Insight Balanced A	HIBZX	D+	(800) 982-8782	D / 2.0	-2.61	1.07	4.86 /14	10.39 /30	5.67 /59	1.97	1.13
BA	Phoenix Insight Balanced Inst	HIBLX	C-	(800) 982-8782	C- / 3.1	-2.56	1.18	5.15 /16	10.64 /32	5.93 /61	2.29	0.88
GR	Phoenix Insight Core Equity A	HGRZX	C-	(800) 982-8782	C- / 3.8	-2.60	2.39	8.04 /33	13.07 /49	3.05 /37	0.62	1.11
GR	Phoenix Insight Core Equity Inst	HGRIX	C	(800) 982-8782	C / 4.9	-2.53	2.49	8.25 /35	13.34 /51	3.29 /39	0.98	0.86
EM	Phoenix Insight Emerging Mkt A	HEMZX	C	(800) 982-8782	A / 9.3	-4.15	6.01	35.83 /97	29.52 /95	19.69 /96	1.03	1.76
EM	Phoenix Insight Emerging Mkt Inst	HIEMX	C	(800) 982-8782	A / 9.5	-4.10	6.17	36.10 /97	29.84 /95	19.96 /96	1.45	1.51
GI	Phoenix Insight Equity Fund A	HIEZX	B-	(800) 982-8782	C+ / 6.7	-1.03	6.43	13.75 /67	17.74 /71	6.42 /64	0.86	1.06
GI	Phoenix Insight Equity Fund Inst	HEQIX	B+	(800) 982-8782	B- / 7.3	-1.01	6.56	14.06 /68	18.04 /73	6.69 /65	1.16	0.81
IX	Phoenix Insight Index A	HIDAX	D	(800) 982-8782	C- / 4.2	-0.51	3.69	10.35 /49	11.31 /38	2.32 /30	2.62	0.60
IX	Phoenix Insight Index Inst	HIDIX	D	(800) 982-8782	C / 4.3	-0.49	3.63	10.36 /49	11.52 /39	2.55 /32	2.67	0.45
FO	Phoenix Insight International A	HILZX	A	(800) 982-8782	B+ / 8.6	0.67	10.13	27.68 /92	22.96 /87	8.71 /75	1.25	1.65
FO	Phoenix Insight International Inst	HILIX	A+	(800) 982-8782	B+ / 8.9	0.75	10.29	27.97 /93	23.05 /87	9.83 /80	1.64	1.40
SC	Phoenix Insight Small Cap Oppt A	HSCZX	D	(800) 982-8782	B- / 7.0	-4.90	5.01	12.40 /62	19.43 /77	10.15 /81	0.13	1.17
SC	Phoenix Insight Small Cap Oppt Inst	HSCIX	D	(800) 982-8782	B / 7.6	-4.85	5.16	12.68 /63	19.73 /78	10.41 /82	0.31	0.92
SC	Phoenix Insight Small Cap Val A	HSVZX	C	(800) 982-8782	B- / 7.3	-5.35	3.46	10.44 /50	20.97 /82	10.95 /84	0.31	1.24
SC	Phoenix Insight Small Cap Val Inst	HSCVX	C+	(800) 982-8782	B / 7.9	-5.30	3.59	10.72 /52	21.27 /83	11.22 /84	0.54	0.99
SC	Phoenix Insight Sm-Cap Growth Inst	HSAIX	C	(800) 982-8782	C+ / 6.8	-5.45	3.40	11.22 /55	17.57 /71	7.00 /67	0.04	0.92
FO	Phoenix Intl strg Fund Class A	PHITX	B+	(800) 243-4361	B+ / 8.5	0.72	9.73	25.68 /89	22.40 /86	8.51 /74	1.28	1.42
FO	Phoenix Intl strg Fund Class B	PINBX	B+	(800) 243-4361	B+ / 8.7	0.53	9.34	24.76 /88	21.50 /84	7.72 /70	0.46	2.17
FO	Phoenix Intl strg Fund Class C	PAICX	B+	(800) 243-4361	B+ / 8.6	0.53	9.27	24.73 /88	21.55 /84	7.75 /70	0.46	2.17
GR	Phoenix Large Cap Growth A	SGCRX	E	(800) 243-4361	E- / 0.1	-4.92	-1.89	2.43 / 5	4.05 / 2	-3.63 / 4	0.00	1.48
GR	Phoenix Large Cap Growth B	SGBEX	E	(800) 243-4361	E- / 0.1	-5.05	-2.32	1.64 / 3	3.27 / 1	-4.36 / 3	0.00	2.23

● Denotes fund is closed to new investors
* Denotes fund is included in Section II

RISK			NET ASSETS		ASSET					Portfolio Turnover Ratio	BULL / BEAR		FUND MANAGER		MINIMUMS		LOADS	
Risk Rating/Pts	3 Year		NAV As of 6/30/06	Total $(Mil)	Cash %	Stocks %	Bonds %	Other %		Last Bull Market Return	Last Bear Market Return	Manager Quality Pct	Manager Tenure (Years)	Initial Purch. $	Additional Purch. $	Front End Load	Back End Load
	Standard Deviation	Beta															
C+ / 6.5	12.1	1.05	10.09	N/A	2	97	0	1	107.6	N/A	N/A	44	3	500	50	0.0	1.0
C / 5.5	12.1	1.05	10.12	1	2	97	0	1	107.6	98.1	-6.9	45	N/A	1,000	50	0.0	5.0
C / 5.5	12.1	1.05	10.09	2	2	97	0	1	107.6	97.9	-7.0	44	N/A	1,000	50	0.0	1.0
C+ / 6.5	12.1	1.04	10.33	1	2	97	0	1	107.6	100.9	-6.9	51	4	500	50	5.5	0.0
C+ / 6.5	12.1	1.05	10.12	N/A	2	97	0	1	107.6	98.1	-6.9	45	4	500	50	0.0	5.0
C+ / 6.5	12.1	1.05	10.09	N/A	2	97	0	1	107.6	97.9	-7.0	44	4	500	50	0.0	1.0
U /	N/A	N/A	12.81	25	3	96	0	1	9.8	N/A	N/A	N/A	2	1,000	50	5.5	1.0
C+ / 6.8	5.5	0.45	7.58	85	30	69	0	1	26.0	65.0	-2.5	97	19	1,000	0	0.0	0.0
C+ / 5.7	11.9	1.34	15.64	115	0	99	0	1	69.0	76.1	-8.9	19	N/A	500	25	5.8	1.0
C / 5.3	11.9	1.34	13.51	8	0	99	0	1	69.0	72.0	-9.2	15	N/A	500	25	0.0	5.0
C / 5.3	11.9	1.34	13.51	9	0	99	0	1	69.0	72.0	-9.2	15	N/A	500	25	0.0	1.0
B / 8.7	5.1	1.04	14.75	959	1	57	40	2	58.0	37.6	-4.3	46	N/A	500	25	5.8	1.0
B / 8.8	5.1	1.04	14.70	22	1	57	40	2	58.0	34.4	-4.5	37	N/A	500	25	0.0	5.0
U /	N/A	N/A	14.69	76	1	57	40	2	58.0	N/A	N/A	N/A	N/A	500	25	0.0	1.0
B- / 7.1	9.6	1.09	14.42	482	2	97	0	1	67.0	40.2	-9.0	7	N/A	500	25	5.8	1.0
B- / 7.0	9.5	1.08	13.26	9	2	97	0	1	67.0	36.9	-9.2	5	N/A	500	25	0.0	5.0
C- / 4.0	14.1	1.44	17.62	16	N/A	100	0	N/A	100.0	57.1	-10.8	6	N/A	500	25	5.8	1.0
C- / 3.9	14.1	1.44	16.47	12	N/A	100	0	N/A	100.0	53.2	-10.9	4	N/A	500	25	0.0	5.0
C- / 3.9	14.1	1.44	16.47	8	N/A	100	0	N/A	100.0	53.2	-10.9	4	N/A	500	25	0.0	1.0
C- / 4.0	14.1	1.44	18.16	5	N/A	100	0	N/A	100.0	58.2	-10.7	7	N/A	250,000	500	0.0	0.0
B / 8.6	6.3	0.40	18.47	51	20	79	0	1	34.0	44.2	-8.3	50	16	500	25	5.8	1.0
B- / 7.7	6.2	0.40	17.93	3	20	79	0	1	34.0	40.2	-8.5	40	16	500	25	0.0	1.0
B- / 7.1	9.7	0.87	21.74	153	4	95	0	1	52.0	136.2	-7.4	90	4	500	25	5.8	1.0
U /	N/A	N/A	10.40	26	3	96	0	1	N/A	N/A	N/A	N/A	N/A	500	25	5.8	1.0
B / 8.8	7.8	1.01	15.41	166	1	98	0	1	41.0	62.8	-10.1	53	9	500	25	5.8	1.0
B / 8.8	7.8	1.01	14.76	44	1	98	0	1	41.0	59.0	-10.1	43	9	500	25	0.0	5.0
B / 8.8	7.9	1.01	14.76	58	1	98	0	1	41.0	59.0	-10.2	43	9	500	25	0.0	1.0
B / 8.9	4.4	0.92	8.98	304	1	48	50	1	59.0	33.9	-3.4	45	N/A	500	25	5.8	1.0
B+ / 9.1	4.4	0.91	9.04	10	1	48	50	1	59.0	30.8	-3.6	37	N/A	500	25	0.0	5.0
B+ / 9.1	4.4	0.92	9.12	2	1	48	50	1	59.0	30.8	-3.5	37	N/A	500	25	0.0	1.0
B / 8.1	5.7	1.12	14.49	14	1	61	37	1	61.5	51.3	-2.6	77	N/A	1,000	50	5.5	2.0
B / 8.1	5.8	1.13	14.52	72	1	61	37	1	61.5	52.5	-2.6	79	9	100,000	0	0.0	2.0
C+ / 6.9	8.5	1.04	20.86	12	1	98	0	1	79.9	73.4	-6.3	71	1	1,000	50	5.5	2.0
C+ / 6.9	8.4	1.04	21.14	137	1	98	0	1	79.9	74.7	-6.2	73	10	100,000	0	0.0	2.0
D+ / 2.8	18.0	1.09	12.41	1	5	94	0	1	42.9	184.6	-4.2	6	N/A	1,000	50	5.5	2.0
D+ / 2.8	18.0	1.09	12.57	238	5	94	0	1	42.9	186.4	-4.2	6	N/A	100,000	0	0.0	2.0
B- / 7.8	7.9	0.95	14.59	27	2	97	0	1	62.7	90.6	-6.4	96	3	1,000	50	5.5	2.0
B- / 7.8	7.9	0.95	14.49	270	2	97	0	1	62.7	92.2	-6.4	97	10	100,000	0	0.0	2.0
C / 5.0	7.7	1.00	19.91	14	3	96	0	1	6.3	65.0	-10.0	57	N/A	1,000	50	0.0	2.0
C / 5.0	7.7	1.00	19.92	62	3	96	0	1	6.3	66.0	-9.8	59	N/A	100,000	0	0.0	2.0
B- / 7.4	10.5	0.98	18.68	N/A	3	96	0	1	44.0	126.1	-15.0	45	N/A	1,000	50	5.5	2.0
B- / 7.4	10.4	0.98	19.33	261	3	96	0	1	44.0	126.7	-10.3	46	N/A	100,000	0	0.0	2.0
D / 1.8	14.4	0.95	20.87	108	0	99	0	1	76.1	130.6	-8.6	72	10	1,000	50	5.5	2.0
D / 1.9	14.4	0.95	21.59	447	0	99	0	1	76.1	132.5	-8.5	74	10	100,000	0	0.0	2.0
C / 4.6	12.6	0.81	46.82	139	2	97	0	1	74.3	127.5	-6.1	93	N/A	1,000	50	5.5	2.0
C / 4.7	12.6	0.81	47.26	332	2	97	0	1	74.3	129.3	-6.0	93	N/A	100,000	0	0.0	2.0
C / 5.2	15.6	1.04	13.95	21	0	0	0	100	N/A	118.3	-11.5	37	1	100,000	0	0.0	2.0
C+ / 6.6	10.4	0.98	12.46	79	4	95	0	1	142.0	121.7	-12.9	40	8	500	25	5.8	1.0
C+ / 6.6	10.3	0.98	11.47	7	4	95	0	1	142.0	116.6	-13.2	34	8	500	25	0.0	0.0
C+ / 6.6	10.3	0.98	11.43	2	4	95	0	1	142.0	117.0	-13.1	34	8	500	25	0.0	1.0
C+ / 6.2	9.8	1.16	11.39	81	0	99	0	1	91.0	36.6	-10.8	4	N/A	500	25	5.8	1.0
C+ / 6.1	9.7	1.16	10.54	7	0	99	0	1	91.0	33.3	-10.9	3	N/A	500	25	0.0	5.0

Fund Type	Fund Name	Ticker Symbol	Overall Weiss Investment Rating	Phone	Performance Rating/Pts	3 Mo	6 Mo	1Yr / Pct	3Yr / Pct	5Yr / Pct	Dividend Yield	Expense Ratio
GR	Phoenix Large Cap Growth C	SGCCX	E	(800) 243-4361	E- / 0.2	-5.05	-2.23	1.64 / 3	3.31 / 2	-4.34 / 3	0.00	2.23
GR	Phoenix Large Cap Growth X	SGCIX	E+	(800) 243-4361	E / 0.4	-4.88	-1.82	2.67 / 6	4.33 / 3	-3.38 / 4	0.00	1.23
AG	Phoenix Mid Cap Growth A	PHSKX	E	(800) 243-4361	D- / 1.2	-9.71	-4.24	4.02 /11	9.63 /25	-1.40 /10	0.00	1.53
AG	Phoenix Mid Cap Growth B	PSKBX	E	(800) 243-4361	D- / 1.0	-9.85	-4.58	3.28 / 8	8.83 /20	-2.12 / 8	0.00	2.28
AG	Phoenix Mid Cap Growth C	PSKCX	E	(800) 243-4361	D- / 1.5	-9.87	-4.58	3.28 / 8	8.81 /20	-2.13 / 8	0.00	2.28
MC	Phoenix Mid Cap Value A	FMIVX	A+	(800) 243-4361	B / 8.0	2.40	8.44	11.07 /54	21.52 /84	12.50 /88	0.23	1.25
MC	Phoenix Mid Cap Value C	FMICX	U	(800) 243-4361	U /	2.23	8.08	10.26 /49	--	--	0.00	2.00
GR	Phoenix Mkt Neutral Fund Class A	EMNAX	U	(800) 243-4361	U /	0.89	-2.15	-5.80 / 0	--	1.56 /24	0.00	2.18
GR	Phoenix Mkt Neutral Fund Class B	EMNBX	D	(800) 243-4361	E- / 0.0	0.73	-2.48	-6.46 / 0	-0.72 / 0	0.84 /19	0.00	2.88
GR	Phoenix Mkt Neutral Fund Class C	EMNCX	D	(800) 243-4361	E- / 0.0	0.74	-2.41	-6.41 / 0	-0.69 / 0	0.87 /20	0.00	2.88
GR	Phoenix Nifty Fifty Fund A	PANFX	E+	(800) 243-4361	E- / 0.2	-7.78	-6.66	-0.51 / 1	5.62 / 5	-4.64 / 3	0.00	1.73
GR	Phoenix Nifty Fifty Fund B	PANBX	E+	(800) 243-4361	E- / 0.1	-7.98	-6.99	-1.20 / 1	4.83 / 4	-5.36 / 2	0.00	2.48
GR	Phoenix Nifty Fifty Fund C	PANCX	E+	(800) 243-4361	E- / 0.2	-8.04	-7.05	-1.32 / 1	4.81 / 4	-5.36 / 2	0.00	2.48
RE	Phoenix Real Estate Securities A	PHRAX	B	(800) 243-4361	A / 9.3	-1.71	14.10	24.37 /88	28.33 /94	22.03 /98	1.20	1.23
RE	Phoenix Real Estate Securities B	PHRBX	B-	(800) 243-4361	A / 9.3	-1.86	13.70	23.44 /87	27.37 /93	21.12 /97	0.64	1.98
RE	Phoenix Real Estate Securities C	PHRCX	U	(800) 243-4361	U /	-1.87	13.68	23.45 /87	--	--	0.63	1.98
GR	Phoenix Rising Dividends A	PKLAX	D-	(800) 243-4361	E- / 0.2	-1.63	-0.23	1.92 / 4	4.45 / 3	--	0.89	1.40
GR	Phoenix Rising Dividends B	PKLBX	D	(800) 243-4361	E- / 0.2	-1.78	-0.57	1.16 / 3	3.66 / 2	--	0.37	2.15
GR	Phoenix Rising Dividends C	PKLCX	D	(800) 243-4361	E / 0.3	-1.78	-0.57	1.16 / 3	3.68 / 2	--	0.37	2.15
GR	Phoenix Rising Dividends X	PKLFX	D	(800) 243-4361	E+ / 0.6	-1.56	-0.10	2.17 / 5	4.69 / 3	-0.11 /15	1.18	1.15
SC	Phoenix Small Cap Growth A	PAMAX	D-	(800) 243-4361	C- / 4.0	-8.51	0.80	8.93 /40	13.79 /53	0.44 /17	0.00	1.59
SC	Phoenix Small Cap Growth B	PSMGX	E+	(800) 243-4361	C- / 3.7	-8.70	0.40	8.10 /33	12.93 /48	-0.31 /14	0.00	2.34
SC	Phoenix Small Cap Growth C	PEMCX	D-	(800) 243-4361	C / 4.4	-8.70	0.43	8.10 /33	12.93 /48	-0.31 /14	0.00	2.34
SC	Phoenix Small Cap Value A	PDSAX	B-	(800) 243-4361	B- / 7.3	-3.39	8.27	14.44 /70	19.53 /78	9.87 /80	0.00	1.13
SC	Phoenix Small Cap Value B	PDSBX	B-	(800) 243-4361	B- / 7.2	-3.59	7.79	13.59 /67	18.65 /75	9.04 /76	0.00	2.15
SC	Phoenix Small Cap Value C	PDSCX	B-	(800) 243-4361	B- / 7.5	-3.54	7.86	13.59 /67	18.65 /75	9.06 /77	0.00	2.15
SC	Phoenix Small-Mid Cap Fund A	PKSAX	C-	(800) 243-4361	C- / 3.4	-3.48	3.23	11.11 /54	11.74 /41	--	0.00	1.50
SC	Phoenix Small-Mid Cap Fund B	PKSBX	D+	(800) 243-4361	C- / 3.2	-3.66	2.87	10.40 /49	10.99 /35	--	0.00	2.25
SC	Phoenix Small-Mid Cap Fund C	PKSCX	C-	(800) 243-4361	C- / 3.9	-3.70	2.86	10.33 /49	11.03 /36	--	0.00	2.25
SC	Phoenix Small-Mid Cap Fund X	PKSFX	C	(800) 243-4361	C / 4.7	-3.45	3.34	11.34 /56	12.01 /42	3.37 /40	0.00	1.25
GR	Phoenix Strategic Growth Fund A	PSTAX	E	(800) 243-4361	E- / 0.2	-6.85	-3.76	1.36 / 3	5.63 / 5	-5.84 / 2	0.00	1.74
GR	Phoenix Strategic Growth Fund B	PBTHX	E	(800) 243-4361	E- / 0.2	-7.00	-4.14	0.62 / 2	4.83 / 4	-6.55 / 1	0.00	2.49
GR	Phoenix Strategic Growth Fund C	SSTFX	E	(800) 243-4361	E / 0.3	-6.99	-4.13	0.62 / 2	4.87 / 4	-6.55 / 1	0.00	2.49
GR	Phoenix Total Value A	PTVAX	U	(800) 243-4361	U /	-0.91	5.35	--	--	--	0.00	1.40
GI	Phoenix Value Equity Fund Class A	PVEAX	C+	(800) 243-4361	C / 4.7	1.76	9.37	13.11 /65	12.45 /45	3.03 /37	0.76	1.25
GI	Phoenix Value Equity Fund Class B	PVEBX	C+	(800) 243-4361	C / 4.4	1.55	8.91	12.27 /61	11.59 /40	2.26 /30	0.19	2.00
GI	Phoenix Value Equity Fund Class C	PVECX	C+	(800) 243-4361	C / 5.0	1.55	8.91	12.26 /61	11.58 /40	2.25 /30	0.19	2.00
AA	Phoenix Wealth Builder PHOLIO A	PWBAX	U	(800) 243-4361	U /	-1.16	3.91	8.74 /38	--	--	1.18	N/A
AA	Phoenix Wealth Builder PHOLIO C	PWBCX	U	(800) 243-4361	U /	-1.45	3.45	7.86 /32	--	--	0.54	0.75
AA	Phoenix Wealth Guardian PHOLIO C	PSWCX	U	(800) 243-4361	U /	-1.18	2.30	5.45 /17	--	--	1.19	0.75
GL	Phoenix Worldwide Strg Fund Class	NWWOX	B-	(800) 243-4361	C+ / 6.6	-0.50	7.41	18.90 /80	16.99 /68	5.40 /57	0.93	1.67
GL	Phoenix Worldwide Strg Fund Class	WWOBX	B-	(800) 243-4361	C+ / 6.4	-0.66	7.03	17.92 /79	16.16 /64	4.63 /51	0.42	2.42
GL	Phoenix Worldwide Strg Fund Class	WWOCX	B-	(800) 243-4361	C+ / 6.9	-0.67	7.06	17.99 /79	16.10 /64	4.59 /51	0.43	2.42
AA	PIMCO All Asset A	PASAX	D+	(800) 227-7337	E+ / 0.7	-0.77	-1.15	1.26 / 3	7.19 /11	--	5.71	1.45
AA	PIMCO All Asset Admin	PAALX	C-	(800) 227-7337	D- / 1.3	-0.69	-0.99	1.67 / 4	7.59 /13	--	6.25	1.10
GR	PIMCO All Asset All Authority A	PAUAX	U	(800) 227-7337	U /	-1.39	-2.55	-0.35 / 1	--	--	5.39	1.59
GR	PIMCO All Asset All Authority C	PAUCX	U	(800) 227-7337	U /	-1.64	-3.02	-1.20 / 1	--	--	5.19	2.34
GR	PIMCO All Asset All Authority Inst	PAUIX	U	(800) 227-7337	U /	-1.36	-2.40	0.04 / 2	--	--	5.95	0.99
AA	PIMCO All Asset B	PASBX	D+	(800) 227-7337	E+ / 0.6	-0.94	-1.58	0.47 / 2	6.36 / 8	--	5.23	2.20
AA	PIMCO All Asset C	PASCX	D+	(800) 227-7337	E+ / 0.8	-0.94	-1.49	0.58 / 2	6.40 / 8	--	5.26	2.20
AA	PIMCO All Asset D	PASDX	D+	(800) 227-7337	D- / 1.1	-0.77	-1.16	1.26 / 3	7.19 /11	--	5.93	1.45
AA	PIMCO All Asset Inst	PAAIX	C-	(800) 227-7337	D- / 1.4	-0.55	-0.80	1.91 / 4	7.87 /14	--	6.49	0.85

● Denotes fund is closed to new investors
* Denotes fund is included in Section II

www.WeissRatings.com

Risk Rating/Pts	3 Year Standard Deviation	Beta	NAV As of 6/30/06	Total $(Mil)	Cash %	Stocks %	Bonds %	Other %	Portfolio Turnover Ratio	Last Bull Market Return	Last Bear Market Return	Manager Quality Pct	Manager Tenure (Years)	Initial Purch. $	Additional Purch. $	Front End Load	Back End Load
C+ / 6.1	9.8	1.16	10.52	4	0	99	0	1	91.0	33.4	-11.0	3	N/A	500	25	0.0	1.0
C+ / 6.2	9.8	1.16	11.90	11	0	99	0	1	91.0	37.7	-10.7	5	N/A	250,000	500	0.0	0.0
C- / 4.2	14.8	1.44	15.80	131	1	98	0	1	46.0	87.7	-12.0	13	N/A	500	25	5.8	1.0
C- / 4.1	14.7	1.43	14.18	11	1	98	0	1	46.0	83.4	-12.2	11	N/A	500	25	0.0	5.0
C- / 4.1	14.8	1.44	14.16	1	1	98	0	1	46.0	83.1	-12.1	10	N/A	500	25	0.0	1.0
B / 8.1	10.5	0.73	21.72	187	4	95	0	1	9.0	109.4	-10.4	97	9	500	25	5.8	0.0
U /	N/A	N/A	21.53	100	4	95	0	1	9.0	N/A	N/A	N/A	9	500	25	0.0	1.0
U /	2.9	-0.10	11.36	107	5	94	0	1	177.0	-2.9	5.0	N/A	6	500	25	5.8	1.0
B+ / 9.3	2.9	-0.10	11.00	5	5	94	0	1	177.0	-5.2	5.0	32	6	500	25	0.0	5.0
B+ / 9.3	2.9	-0.10	10.95	26	5	94	0	1	177.0	-5.0	4.9	32	6	500	25	0.0	1.3
C+ / 6.7	10.2	1.15	17.65	36	2	97	0	1	60.0	46.7	-9.7	8	N/A	500	25	5.8	1.0
C+ / 6.6	10.2	1.14	15.69	6	2	97	0	1	60.0	43.2	-9.8	6	N/A	500	25	0.0	5.0
C+ / 6.6	10.2	1.14	15.68	6	2	97	0	1	60.0	43.2	-9.8	6	N/A	500	25	0.0	1.0
C / 4.7	16.8	1.00	31.50	921	3	96	0	1	22.0	134.9	0.9	86	8	500	25	5.8	1.0
C / 4.7	16.8	1.00	31.19	62	3	96	0	1	22.0	129.4	0.8	81	8	500	25	0.0	5.0
U /	N/A	N/A	31.49	83	3	96	0	1	22.0	N/A	N/A	N/A	8	500	25	0.0	1.0
B / 8.1	6.6	0.76	15.41	10	0	99	0	1	33.0	31.3	-10.7	17	N/A	500	25	5.8	1.0
B / 8.6	6.6	0.77	15.26	2	0	99	0	1	33.0	28.1	-10.8	13	N/A	500	25	0.0	5.0
B / 8.6	6.6	0.77	15.27	2	0	99	0	1	33.0	28.1	-10.8	13	N/A	500	25	0.0	1.0
B / 8.6	6.6	0.77	15.45	79	0	99	0	1	33.0	32.2	-10.7	18	N/A	250,000	500	0.0	0.0
C- / 3.5	16.9	1.05	32.80	156	1	98	0	1	38.0	108.0	-12.7	13	N/A	500	25	5.8	1.0
C- / 3.5	16.9	1.05	30.43	33	1	98	0	1	38.0	103.0	-12.8	10	N/A	500	25	0.0	5.0
C- / 3.5	16.9	1.05	30.42	21	1	98	0	1	38.0	103.1	-12.8	10	N/A	500	25	0.0	1.0
C+ / 6.6	13.6	0.89	19.12	145	1	98	0	1	102.0	137.1	-11.7	80	N/A	500	25	5.8	1.0
C+ / 6.5	13.6	0.89	17.71	34	1	98	0	1	102.0	131.5	-11.8	73	N/A	500	25	0.0	5.0
C+ / 6.5	13.6	0.89	17.71	66	1	98	0	1	102.0	131.5	-11.8	74	N/A	500	25	0.0	1.0
B- / 7.1	10.9	0.70	21.16	35	0	99	0	1	22.0	70.7	-11.7	37	10	500	25	5.8	1.0
B- / 7.1	11.0	0.70	20.59	3	0	99	0	1	22.0	66.9	-11.8	31	10	500	25	0.0	5.0
B- / 7.1	11.0	0.70	20.61	13	0	99	0	1	22.0	67.1	-11.8	31	10	500	25	0.0	1.0
B- / 7.2	10.9	0.70	21.35	69	0	99	0	1	22.0	72.0	-11.6	40	10	250,000	500	0.0	0.0
C / 5.3	11.5	1.33	8.97	94	N/A	100	0	N/A	107.0	50.5	-10.0	5	N/A	500	25	5.8	1.0
C / 5.2	11.5	1.33	8.11	7	N/A	100	0	N/A	107.0	46.9	-10.1	3	N/A	500	25	0.0	5.0
C / 5.2	11.6	1.33	8.12	1	N/A	100	0	N/A	107.0	47.1	-10.1	3	N/A	500	25	0.0	1.0
U /	N/A	N/A	10.83	28	1	98	0	1	N/A	N/A	N/A	N/A	1	500	25	5.8	0.0
B / 8.4	8.6	1.01	15.06	28	0	99	0	1	69.0	70.3	-10.5	68	N/A	500	25	5.8	1.0
B / 8.3	8.5	1.00	14.42	9	0	99	0	1	69.0	66.1	-10.5	60	N/A	500	25	0.0	5.0
B / 8.3	8.5	1.00	14.43	9	0	99	0	1	69.0	66.2	-10.6	60	N/A	500	25	0.0	1.0
U /	N/A	N/A	11.88	52	N/A	100	0	N/A	4.0	N/A	N/A	N/A	N/A	500	25	5.8	1.0
U /	N/A	N/A	11.83	76	N/A	100	0	N/A	4.0	N/A	N/A	N/A	N/A	500	25	0.0	1.0
U /	N/A	N/A	11.28	34	0	99	0	1	5.0	N/A	N/A	N/A	N/A	500	25	0.0	1.0
B- / 7.2	9.1	0.85	9.86	103	2	97	0	1	49.0	94.8	-11.1	24	10	500	25	5.8	1.0
B- / 7.2	9.2	0.86	8.98	5	2	97	0	1	49.0	90.0	-11.4	19	10	500	25	0.0	5.0
B- / 7.2	9.2	0.85	8.95	3	2	97	0	1	49.0	90.2	-11.4	19	10	500	25	0.0	1.0
B+ / 9.2	6.9	0.85	12.34	1,591	7	9	83	1	84.0	29.1	8.5	61	N/A	5,000	100	3.8	2.0
B+ / 9.2	6.9	0.85	12.38	73	7	9	83	1	84.0	30.5	8.7	65	N/A	5,000,000	0	0.0	2.0
U /	N/A	N/A	10.39	259	3	27	68	2	104.0	N/A	N/A	N/A	N/A	5,000	100	3.8	2.0
U /	N/A	N/A	10.35	140	3	27	68	2	104.0	N/A	N/A	N/A	N/A	5,000	100	0.0	2.0
U /	N/A	N/A	10.39	346	3	27	68	2	104.0	N/A	N/A	N/A	N/A	5,000,000	0	0.0	2.0
B+ / 9.0	6.9	0.85	12.27	296	7	9	83	1	84.0	25.9	8.3	51	N/A	5,000	100	0.0	3.5
B+ / 9.0	6.8	0.85	12.26	1,475	7	9	83	1	84.0	25.9	8.3	52	N/A	5,000	100	0.0	2.0
B+ / 9.2	6.8	0.85	12.35	405	7	9	83	1	84.0	29.1	8.5	61	N/A	5,000	100	0.0	2.0
B+ / 9.1	6.9	0.86	12.40	7,561	7	9	83	1	84.0	31.6	8.7	68	N/A	5,000,000	0	0.0	2.0

Fund Type	Fund Name	Ticker Symbol	Overall Weiss Investment Rating	Phone	Performance Rating/Pts	3 Mo	6 Mo	1Yr / Pct	3Yr / Pct	5Yr / Pct	Dividend Yield	Expense Ratio
AA	PIMCO All Asset R	PATRX	D	(800) 227-7337	D- / 1.1	-1.02	-1.46	0.76 / 2	6.83 /10	--	6.24	1.75
* EN	PIMCO Commodity Real Ret Str A	PCRAX	C+	(800) 227-7337	C+ / 6.3	5.15	-0.83	10.40 /49	17.47 /70	--	16.13	1.24
EN	PIMCO Commodity Real Ret Str Adm	PCRRX	B-	(800) 227-7337	B- / 7.1	5.21	-0.69	10.66 /51	17.78 /72	--	17.30	0.99
EN	PIMCO Commodity Real Ret Str B	PCRBX	C+	(800) 227-7337	C+ / 6.2	5.01	-1.21	9.57 /44	16.61 /66	--	16.60	1.99
EN	PIMCO Commodity Real Ret Str C	PCRCX	C+	(800) 227-7337	C+ / 6.6	5.01	-1.22	9.59 /44	16.61 /66	--	16.64	1.99
EN	PIMCO Commodity Real Ret Str D	PCRDX	C+	(800) 227-7337	C+ / 6.9	5.14	-0.84	10.39 /49	17.46 /70	--	17.05	1.24
EN	PIMCO Commodity Real Ret Str Inst	PCRIX	B-	(800) 227-7337	B- / 7.2	5.31	-0.57	10.97 /53	18.06 /73	--	17.33	0.74
CV	PIMCO Convertible Bond Admin	PFCAX	C	(800) 227-7337	C- / 3.3	-0.14	3.83	8.12 /34	10.19 /29	5.94 /61	2.86	0.90
CV	PIMCO Convertible Bond Inst	PFCIX	C	(800) 227-7337	C- / 3.5	-0.08	3.96	8.40 /36	10.44 /30	6.27 /63	3.17	0.65
FO	PIMCO FarEast StksPLUS TR Str	PEJIX	U	(800) 227-7337	U /	-2.86	-0.20	12.14 /60	--	--	8.64	0.85
IN	PIMCO Fundamental IndexPLUS Inst	PFPIX	U	(800) 227-7337	U /	-0.52	4.74	9.56 /44	--	--	6.66	0.65
IN	PIMCO Fundamental IndexPLUS Tr	PXTIX	U	(800) 227-7337	U /	-1.91	1.86	5.47 /17	--	--	5.21	0.74
FO	PIMCO Intl StkPlus Tr Strat Inst	PISIX	U	(800) 227-7337	U /	-4.94	1.50	19.41 /81	--	--	13.32	0.85
FO	PIMCO Japanese StksPLUS TR Str	PJSIX	U	(800) 227-7337	U /	-8.24	-3.34	36.41 /97	--	--	21.10	0.85
RE	PIMCO RealEstate RlRetrn Str A	PETAX	U	(800) 227-7337	U /	-2.72	8.01	12.07 /60	--	--	35.72	1.19
RE	PIMCO RealEstate RlRetrn Str Inst	PRRSX	U	(800) 227-7337	U /	-2.53	8.23	12.60 /63	--	--	37.85	0.74
GR	PIMCO StocksPLUS A	PSPAX	D+	(800) 227-7337	D+ / 2.3	-1.90	1.80	6.46 /23	9.78 /26	2.19 /29	2.49	1.00
GR	PIMCO StocksPLUS Admin	PPLAX	C-	(800) 227-7337	D+ / 2.9	-1.68	1.97	6.66 /24	9.97 /27	2.34 /31	2.67	0.85
GR	PIMCO StocksPLUS B	PSPBX	D	(800) 227-7337	D / 1.8	-2.14	1.35	5.53 /18	8.90 /20	1.41 /23	2.04	1.75
GR	PIMCO StocksPLUS C	PSPCX	D+	(800) 227-7337	D+ / 2.4	-1.95	1.58	5.82 /19	9.22 /22	1.70 /25	2.23	1.50
GR	PIMCO StocksPLUS D	PSPDX	D+	(800) 227-7337	D+ / 2.8	-1.93	1.80	6.37 /22	9.76 /26	2.09 /28	2.57	1.00
GR	PIMCO StocksPLUS Inst	PSTKX	C-	(800) 227-7337	C- / 3.0	-1.78	1.94	6.81 /25	10.20 /29	2.68 /34	2.78	0.60
GR	PIMCO StocksPLUS R	PSPRX	C-	(800) 227-7337	D+ / 2.6	-1.94	1.65	6.06 /21	9.49 /24	2.00 /27	2.35	1.25
GI	PIMCO StocksPLUS Total Return A	PTOAX	D+	(800) 227-7337	D- / 1.5	-3.00	-0.64	2.48 / 6	9.29 /23	--	4.85	1.14
GI	PIMCO StocksPLUS Total Return B	PTOBX	D+	(800) 227-7337	D / 1.7	-3.21	-0.98	1.81 / 4	9.20 /22	--	4.42	1.89
GI	PIMCO StocksPLUS Total Return C	PSOCX	C-	(800) 227-7337	D / 1.9	-3.22	-1.00	1.77 / 4	9.21 /22	--	4.38	1.89
GI	PIMCO StocksPLUS Total Return D	PSTDX	C-	(800) 227-7337	D+ / 2.4	-3.02	-0.62	2.56 / 6	10.05 /28	--	5.11	1.14
GI	PIMCO StocksPLUS Total Return Inst	PSPTX	C-	(800) 227-7337	D+ / 2.6	-2.92	-0.45	2.96 / 7	10.41 /30	--	5.40	0.74
IX	PIMCO StocksPLUS TR Short Str	PSTIX	U	(800) 227-7337	U /	2.20	-1.50	-5.15 / 0	--	--	1.57	0.74
GR	Pioneer AmPac Growth A	PAPRX	E+	(800) 225-6292	E+ / 0.6	-2.60	0.37	5.79 /19	6.08 / 7	0.14 /16	0.02	1.25
GR	Pioneer AmPac Growth B	PRABX	D-	(800) 225-6292	E / 0.5	-2.76	-0.13	4.69 /14	5.16 / 4	-0.69 /13	0.00	2.32
GR	Pioneer AmPac Growth C	PRRCX	D-	(800) 225-6292	E+ / 0.7	-2.82	-0.13	4.69 /14	5.16 / 4	-0.69 /13	0.00	2.22
GR	Pioneer AmPac Growth R	PRFRX	D-	(800) 225-6292	E+ / 0.6	-2.61	0.13	4.12 /11	4.79 / 4	-0.80 /12	0.00	3.01
BA	Pioneer Balanced Fund A	MOMIX	D+	(800) 225-6292	E / 0.4	-2.47	0.00	3.67 / 9	4.82 / 4	1.46 /23	1.39	1.35
BA	Pioneer Balanced Fund B	PBMIX	D+	(800) 225-6292	E- / 0.2	-2.70	-0.41	2.73 / 6	3.82 / 2	0.54 /18	0.61	2.30
BA	Pioneer Balanced Fund C	PCMPX	D+	(800) 225-6292	E / 0.4	-2.68	-0.41	2.83 / 7	3.89 / 2	0.54 /18	0.63	2.12
GR	Pioneer Cullen Value Fund A	CVFCX	A	(800) 225-6292	B- / 7.4	-0.11	5.60	14.73 /71	19.20 /77	11.16 /84	0.31	1.18
GR	Pioneer Cullen Value Fund B	CVFBX	A	(800) 225-6292	B- / 7.3	-0.33	5.11	13.66 /67	18.73 /75	10.89 /84	0.09	2.11
GR	Pioneer Cullen Value Fund C	CVCFX	A	(800) 225-6292	B / 7.6	-0.28	5.23	13.81 /68	18.78 /75	10.92 /84	0.16	2.00
GR	Pioneer Cullen Value Fund Y	CVFYX	A+	(800) 225-6292	B / 7.9	0.00	5.83	15.12 /72	19.36 /77	11.25 /85	0.40	0.85
EM	Pioneer Emerging Markets A	PEMFX	B	(800) 225-6292	A+ / 9.7	-3.83	9.10	42.47 /98	34.50 /98	21.68 /97	0.37	2.15
EM	Pioneer Emerging Markets B	PBEFX	B-	(800) 225-6292	A+ / 9.7	-4.11	8.56	41.21 /98	33.43 /97	20.78 /97	0.01	2.94
EM	Pioneer Emerging Markets C	PCEFX	B	(800) 225-6292	A+ / 9.7	-4.08	8.58	41.46 /98	33.57 /97	20.86 /97	0.09	2.80
EM	Pioneer Emerging Markets R	PEMRX	B	(800) 225-6292	A+ / 9.8	-3.96	8.77	41.98 /98	34.21 /98	21.34 /97	0.53	2.37
EM	Pioneer Emerging Markets Y	PYEFX	B	(800) 225-6292	A+ / 9.8	-3.77	9.31	43.32 /98	35.52 /98	22.78 /98	0.94	1.40
IN	Pioneer Equity Income A	PEQIX	B+	(800) 225-6292	C+ / 5.9	2.56	8.30	12.18 /61	14.91 /58	5.72 /59	1.88	1.06
IN	Pioneer Equity Income B	PBEQX	B	(800) 225-6292	C+ / 5.6	2.34	7.81	11.19 /55	13.90 /53	4.83 /53	1.15	1.93
IN	Pioneer Equity Income C	PCEQX	B+	(800) 225-6292	C+ / 6.0	2.38	7.91	11.33 /56	14.01 /54	4.87 /53	1.26	1.86
IN	Pioneer Equity Income R	PQIRX	B	(800) 225-6292	C+ / 6.5	2.55	8.25	12.00 /60	14.78 /58	5.57 /58	1.84	1.26
IN	Pioneer Equity Income Y	PYEQX	B	(800) 225-6292	C+ / 6.8	2.69	8.52	12.64 /63	15.41 /61	6.20 /62	2.36	0.66
FO	Pioneer Europe Sel Eqty Fd A	PERAX	A+	(800) 225-6292	B+ / 8.5	0.78	12.16	22.57 /85	22.64 /86	14.76 /91	0.63	1.75
FO	Pioneer Europe Sel Eqty Fd B	PERBX	A+	(800) 225-6292	B+ / 8.5	0.55	11.63	21.47 /84	21.41 /84	13.68 /90	0.00	2.65

RISK			NET ASSETS		ASSET				BULL / BEAR		FUND MANAGER		MINIMUMS		LOADS	
Risk Rating/Pts	3 Year Standard Deviation	Beta	NAV As of 6/30/06	Total $(Mil)	Cash %	Stocks %	Bonds %	Other %	Portfolio Turnover Ratio	Last Bull Market Return	Last Bear Market Return	Manager Quality Pct	Manager Tenure (Years)	Initial Purch. $	Additional Purch. $	Front End Load	Back End Load
B /8.1	6.9	0.86	12.36	N/A	7	9	83	1	84.0	27.8	8.4	N/A	N/A	2,500	50	0.0	0.0
C+ /6.7	15.2	0.45	14.59	2,339	4	0	96	0	220.0	55.9	25.2	78	4	5,000	100	5.5	2.0
C+ /6.7	15.2	0.45	14.62	683	4	0	96	0	220.0	57.1	25.2	81	4	5,000,000	0	0.0	2.0
C+ /6.7	15.2	0.45	14.47	294	4	0	96	0	220.0	52.3	25.1	72	4	5,000	100	0.0	5.0
C+ /6.7	15.2	0.45	14.45	1,400	4	0	96	0	220.0	52.3	25.1	72	4	5,000	100	0.0	2.0
C+ /6.6	15.2	0.45	14.60	1,328	4	0	96	0	220.0	55.8	25.4	78	4	5,000	100	0.0	2.0
C+ /6.7	15.2	0.45	14.70	5,780	4	0	96	0	220.0	58.4	25.3	82	4	5,000,000	0	0.0	2.0
B /8.1	7.8	1.14	12.76	N/A	14	0	0	86	58.0	50.1	-0.1	77	N/A	5,000,000	0	0.0	2.0
B /8.1	7.8	1.13	12.49	53	14	0	0	86	58.0	51.1	0.4	79	N/A	5,000,000	0	0.0	2.0
U /	N/A	N/A	11.72	38	0	0	100	0	246.0	N/A	N/A	N/A	N/A	5,000,000	0	0.0	2.0
U /	N/A	N/A	10.25	153	48	0	50	2	N/A	N/A	N/A	N/A	N/A	5,000,000	0	0.0	2.0
U /	N/A	N/A	10.02	319	38	0	62	0	N/A	N/A	N/A	N/A	1	5,000,000	0	0.0	2.0
U /	N/A	N/A	11.66	716	N/A	0	N/A	N/A	90.0	N/A	N/A	N/A	3	5,000,000	0	0.0	2.0
U /	N/A	N/A	11.85	71	10	0	90	0	121.0	N/A	N/A	N/A	3	5,000,000	0	0.0	2.0
U /	N/A	N/A	8.57	36	2	0	98	0	286.0	N/A	N/A	N/A	N/A	5,000	100	5.5	2.0
U /	N/A	N/A	8.65	134	2	0	98	0	286.0	N/A	N/A	N/A	N/A	5,000,000	0	0.0	2.0
B- /7.5	7.7	1.00	9.88	131	24	0	76	0	402.0	59.1	-8.5	40	8	5,000	100	3.0	2.0
B- /7.5	7.7	1.01	9.91	33	24	0	76	0	402.0	60.0	-8.5	41	8	5,000,000	0	0.0	2.0
B- /7.5	7.8	1.01	9.64	49	24	0	76	0	402.0	55.2	-8.6	32	8	5,000	100	0.0	5.0
B- /7.5	7.7	1.00	9.73	100	24	0	76	0	402.0	56.5	-8.6	35	8	5,000	100	0.0	2.0
B- /7.5	7.7	1.00	9.84	12	24	0	76	0	402.0	58.9	-8.4	39	8	5,000	100	0.0	2.0
B- /7.6	7.7	1.00	10.12	637	24	0	76	0	402.0	61.1	-8.4	44	8	5,000,000	0	0.0	2.0
B /8.2	7.7	1.00	10.03	2	24	0	76	0	402.0	57.8	-8.5	37	8	2,500	50	0.0	2.0
B /8.5	8.2	0.98	11.33	39	28	0	72	0	422.0	64.7	-7.2	37	N/A	5,000	100	3.8	2.0
B /8.5	8.0	0.99	11.18	18	28	0	72	0	422.0	60.5	-7.4	35	N/A	5,000	100	0.0	3.5
B /8.5	8.1	1.00	11.19	24	28	0	72	0	422.0	60.7	-7.4	35	N/A	5,000	100	0.0	2.0
B /8.6	8.0	0.99	11.28	3	28	0	72	0	422.0	64.3	-7.2	43	N/A	5,000	100	0.0	2.0
B /8.6	8.0	0.99	11.31	145	28	0	72	0	422.0	66.3	-7.1	48	N/A	5,000,000	0	0.0	2.0
U /	N/A	N/A	9.05	170	48	0	50	2	436.0	N/A	N/A	N/A	N/A	5,000,000	0	0.0	0.0
C+ /6.6	9.3	1.09	16.14	14	0	99	0	1	16.0	40.7	-11.7	12	9	1,000	100	5.8	0.0
B- /7.1	9.2	1.09	15.85	1	0	99	0	1	16.0	36.8	-11.8	9	2	1,000	500	0.0	4.0
B- /7.1	9.3	1.09	15.85	2	0	99	0	1	16.0	36.9	-11.8	8	2	1,000	500	0.0	1.0
B- /7.1	9.2	1.08	15.66	N/A	0	99	0	1	16.0	35.3	-11.8	8	2	0	0	0.0	0.0
B+ /9.6	4.8	0.91	9.82	87	1	64	33	2	26.0	30.5	-2.7	32	11	1,000	100	4.5	0.0
B+ /9.7	4.8	0.92	9.70	14	1	64	33	2	26.0	26.7	-2.9	25	11	1,000	500	0.0	4.0
B+ /9.7	4.8	0.91	9.78	10	1	64	33	2	26.0	27.0	-2.9	26	10	1,000	500	0.0	1.0
B /8.4	9.0	1.04	18.28	806	10	89	0	1	49.0	101.2	-6.1	97	5	1,000	100	5.8	0.0
B /8.4	9.0	1.04	18.11	63	10	89	0	1	49.0	99.2	-6.1	96	1	1,000	500	0.0	4.0
B /8.4	9.0	1.04	18.12	238	10	89	0	1	49.0	99.3	-6.1	96	1	1,000	500	0.0	1.0
B /8.4	8.9	1.04	18.34	144	10	89	0	1	49.0	101.8	-6.1	97	1	5,000,000	0	0.0	0.0
C /4.4	18.3	1.10	27.34	191	2	98	0	0	69.0	229.4	-3.9	21	N/A	1,000	100	5.8	0.0
C /4.3	18.3	1.10	24.98	45	2	98	0	0	69.0	221.1	-4.0	16	N/A	1,000	500	0.0	4.0
C /4.3	18.3	1.10	24.92	52	2	98	0	0	69.0	222.4	-4.0	17	N/A	1,000	500	0.0	1.0
C /4.3	18.3	1.10	26.91	N/A	2	98	0	0	69.0	227.9	-4.1	20	N/A	0	0	0.0	0.0
C /4.4	18.3	1.10	28.87	38	2	98	0	0	69.0	237.8	-3.6	26	N/A	5,000,000	0	0.0	0.0
B /8.9	6.9	0.82	30.82	723	0	99	0	1	14.0	75.9	-8.8	93	5	1,000	100	5.8	0.0
B /8.9	6.9	0.82	30.65	148	0	99	0	1	14.0	71.2	-9.0	90	5	1,000	500	0.0	4.0
B /8.9	6.9	0.82	30.55	126	0	99	0	1	14.0	71.4	-8.9	90	5	1,000	500	0.0	1.0
B /8.9	6.9	0.82	31.02	16	0	99	0	1	14.0	76.2	-8.9	92	5	0	0	0.0	0.0
B /8.9	6.9	0.82	30.95	7	0	99	0	1	14.0	78.4	-8.7	94	N/A	5,000,000	0	0.0	0.0
B- /7.6	10.1	0.86	36.16	143	1	98	0	1	149.0	133.6	-10.3	70	6	1,000	100	5.8	2.0
B- /7.6	10.0	0.86	32.82	35	1	98	0	1	149.0	126.0	-10.6	59	6	1,000	500	0.0	2.0

						PERFORMANCE							
							Total Return % through 6/30/06					Incl. in Returns	
					Perfor-					Annualized		Dividend	Expense
Fund		Ticker	Overall Weiss Investment		mance							Yield	Ratio
Type	Fund Name	Symbol	Rating	Phone	Rating/Pts	3 Mo	6 Mo	1Yr / Pct	3Yr / Pct	5Yr / Pct		
FO	Pioneer Europe Sel Eqty Fd C	PERCX	A+	(800) 225-6292	B+ / 8.6	0.52	11.64	21.45 /84	21.74 /84	13.98 /90	0.22	2.65
FO	Pioneer Europe Sel Eqty Fd R	PESRX	B	(800) 225-6292	B+ / 8.8	0.76	12.11	22.37 /85	22.18 /86	14.27 /91	0.84	2.00
FO	Pioneer Europe Sel Eqty Fd Y	PEYSX	B	(800) 225-6292	B+ / 8.8	0.95	12.52	23.30 /86	22.88 /87	14.89 /92	1.09	1.27
IN	Pioneer Focused Equity A	ASECX	E	(800) 225-6292	E / 0.5	-1.56	1.85	2.06 / 4	6.26 / 7	5.33 /57	0.49	1.36
IN	Pioneer Focused Equity B	ASEDX	E	(800) 225-6292	E / 0.5	-1.78	1.44	1.23 / 3	5.46 / 5	4.54 /51	0.20	2.23
IN	Pioneer Focused Equity C	FETCX	E	(800) 225-6292	E+ / 0.6	-2.39	0.72	0.75 / 2	5.29 / 5	4.44 /50	0.13	2.21
IN	Pioneer Focused Equity Y	ASEPX	E+	(800) 225-6292	D- / 1.3	-1.41	2.15	2.60 / 6	6.59 / 9	5.58 /58	0.74	1.07
* GI	Pioneer Fund A	PIODX	C+	(800) 225-6292	C / 4.6	-0.21	4.66	12.40 /62	12.91 /48	3.05 /37	0.83	1.08
GI	Pioneer Fund B	PBODX	C+	(800) 225-6292	C- / 4.2	-0.44	4.17	11.32 /55	11.87 /42	2.12 /28	0.02	2.01
GI	Pioneer Fund C	PCODX	C+	(800) 225-6292	C / 4.8	-0.42	4.28	11.55 /57	12.01 /42	2.23 /29	0.16	1.87
GI	Pioneer Fund Inv	PFIOX	U	(800) 225-6292	U /	-0.19	4.82	12.76 /63	--	--	1.17	0.80
GI	Pioneer Fund R	PIORX	B-	(800) 225-6292	C / 5.4	-0.28	4.59	12.25 /61	12.82 /48	3.00 /37	0.76	1.21
GI	Pioneer Fund Y	PYODX	B	(800) 225-6292	C+ / 5.8	-0.13	4.88	12.88 /64	13.39 /51	3.50 /41	1.30	0.65
GR	Pioneer Fundamental Growth Fd A	PIGFX	E+	(800) 225-6292	D- / 1.1	-5.74	-1.99	3.90 /10	8.85 /20	--	0.47	1.30
GR	Pioneer Growth Leaders Fund A	LRPSX	E-	(800) 225-6292	E / 0.4	-2.07	-1.66	3.80 /10	5.69 / 6	-0.64 /13	0.01	1.25
GR	Pioneer Growth Leaders Fund B	LRPBX	D-	(800) 225-6292	E / 0.3	-2.40	-2.25	2.68 / 6	4.33 / 3	-1.71 / 9	0.00	2.33
GR	Pioneer Growth Leaders Fund C	LRPCX	D-	(800) 225-6292	E / 0.4	-2.42	-2.21	2.64 / 6	4.23 / 3	-1.77 / 9	0.00	2.32
GR	Pioneer Growth Leaders Fund R	LRPRX	D-	(800) 225-6292	E / 0.5	-2.11	-1.80	3.99 /11	4.18 / 3	-1.70 / 9	0.00	2.59
GR	Pioneer Growth Opportunities A	PGOFX	C-	(800) 225-6292	C / 4.8	-8.58	-0.90	5.25 /16	15.73 /62	2.04 /28	0.00	1.26
GR	Pioneer Growth Opportunities B	GOFBX	C-	(800) 225-6292	C / 4.5	-8.79	-1.38	4.12 /11	14.73 /58	1.21 /22	0.00	2.37
GR	Pioneer Growth Opportunities C	GOFCX	C-	(800) 225-6292	C / 5.1	-8.76	-1.21	4.48 /13	14.89 /58	1.31 /22	0.00	2.02
GR	● Pioneer Growth Opportunities Inv	PGIFX	C	(800) 225-6292	C+ / 5.9	-8.46	-0.66	5.65 /18	16.07 /64	2.32 /30	0.00	0.90
GR	Pioneer Growth Opportunities Y	GROYX	C-	(800) 225-6292	C+ / 5.8	-8.45	-0.64	5.62 /18	15.87 /63	2.12 /28	0.00	0.77
GR	Pioneer Growth Shares A	MOMGX	E+	(800) 225-6292	E / 0.3	-6.33	-3.04	2.38 / 5	5.63 / 5	-4.92 / 3	0.02	1.39
GR	Pioneer Growth Shares B	PBMGX	E+	(800) 225-6292	E / 0.4	-6.57	-3.52	1.30 / 3	4.59 / 3	-5.80 / 2	0.00	2.35
GR	Pioneer Growth Shares C	PCMGX	E+	(800) 225-6292	E / 0.4	-6.50	-3.48	1.37 / 3	4.71 / 3	-5.71 / 2	0.00	2.30
GR	Pioneer Growth Shares R	PGRRX	D-	(800) 225-6292	E+ / 0.6	-6.36	-3.13	2.04 / 4	5.53 / 5	-5.13 / 2	0.01	1.70
GR	Pioneer Growth Shares Y	PYMGX	E+	(800) 225-6292	E+ / 0.9	-6.14	-2.65	3.07 / 8	6.37 / 8	-4.27 / 3	0.02	0.72
AA	Pioneer Ibbotson Aggress Alloc Fd A	PIAAX	U	(800) 225-6292	U /	-2.28	3.23	11.99 /59	--	--	0.12	0.85
AA	Pioneer Ibbotson Aggress Alloc Fd B	IALBX	U	(800) 225-6292	U /	-2.46	2.85	11.09 /54	--	--	0.00	1.65
AA	Pioneer Ibbotson Gr Alloc A	GRAAX	U	(800) 225-6292	U /	-1.87	2.81	10.18 /48	--	--	0.38	0.76
AA	Pioneer Ibbotson Gr Alloc B	GRABX	U	(800) 225-6292	U /	-2.05	2.43	9.24 /42	--	--	0.17	1.73
AA	Pioneer Ibbotson Gr Alloc C	GRACX	U	(800) 225-6292	U /	-2.11	2.47	9.32 /42	--	--	0.00	1.47
AA	Pioneer Ibbotson Mod Alloc Fd A	PIALX	U	(800) 225-6292	U /	-1.47	2.15	7.87 /32	--	--	0.52	0.61
AA	Pioneer Ibbotson Mod Alloc Fd B	PIBLX	U	(800) 225-6292	U /	-1.62	1.67	6.86 /25	--	--	0.29	1.53
AA	Pioneer Ibbotson Mod Alloc Fd C	PIDCX	U	(800) 225-6292	U /	-1.63	1.78	6.95 /26	--	--	0.13	1.40
AA	Pioneer Ibbotson Mod Alloc Fd Y	IMOYX	U	(800) 225-6292	U /	-1.38	2.60	8.38 /36	--	--	0.66	0.26
GR	Pioneer Independence Fd A	INDAX	D	(800) 225-6292	C- / 3.5	-2.11	2.93	16.63 /76	11.43 /39	2.88 /36	0.08	1.25
GR	Pioneer Independence Fd P	PINDX	C	(800) 225-6292	C / 4.6	-2.11	2.85	16.54 /76	11.40 /39	2.86 /35	0.09	1.40
GR	Pioneer Independence Fd Y	INYDX	C-	(800) 225-6292	C / 4.7	-2.11	2.93	16.63 /76	11.43 /39	2.88 /36	0.09	1.00
FO	Pioneer International Core Equity A	IILAX	B+	(800) 225-6292	A / 9.3	-0.85	7.36	25.49 /89	27.72 /94	11.84 /86	0.77	1.59
FO	Pioneer International Core Equity B	IILBX	B+	(800) 225-6292	A- / 9.2	-1.14	6.81	24.42 /88	26.68 /93	11.08 /84	0.09	2.46
FO	Pioneer International Core Equity C	PCECX	B+	(800) 225-6292	A / 9.3	-1.13	7.08	24.93 /88	26.85 /93	11.17 /84	0.00	2.18
FO	Pioneer International Core Equity Y	IIEIX	B+	(800) 225-6292	A / 9.4	-0.85	7.49	25.84 /90	27.92 /94	12.11 /87	1.27	1.32
FO	Pioneer International Equity A	PIWEX	B+	(800) 225-6292	B+ / 8.6	-0.48	8.40	25.57 /89	23.49 /88	8.11 /72	0.03	1.60
FO	Pioneer International Equity B	PBWEX	B+	(800) 225-6292	B+ / 8.5	-0.70	7.96	24.45 /88	22.38 /86	7.13 /67	0.00	2.50
FO	Pioneer International Equity C	PCWEX	B+	(800) 225-6292	B+ / 8.6	-0.71	7.95	24.46 /88	22.31 /86	6.93 /66	0.00	2.45
FO	Pioneer International Equity Y	PIEYX	A+	(800) 225-6292	A- / 9.0	-0.32	8.71	26.31 /90	24.01 /89	8.38 /73	0.52	0.97
FO	Pioneer International Value A	PIIFX	B	(800) 225-6292	B+ / 8.4	-1.81	7.64	29.28 /94	21.77 /85	8.04 /72	0.28	1.70
FO	Pioneer International Value B	PBIFX	B	(800) 225-6292	B / 8.2	-1.98	7.24	28.15 /93	20.45 /81	6.87 /66	0.00	2.60
FO	Pioneer International Value C	PCITX	B	(800) 225-6292	B+ / 8.4	-2.00	7.21	28.22 /93	20.53 /81	6.83 /66	0.00	2.60
FO	Pioneer International Value R	MIVRX	A	(800) 225-6292	B+ / 8.7	-1.81	7.55	28.81 /94	21.64 /84	7.80 /71	0.24	1.95

● Denotes fund is closed to new investors
* Denotes fund is included in Section II

324

RISK Rating/Pts	3 Year Standard Deviation	Beta	NAV As of 6/30/06	Total $(Mil)	Cash %	Stocks %	Bonds %	Other %	Portfolio Turnover Ratio	Last Bull Market Return	Last Bear Market Return	Manager Quality Pct	Manager Tenure (Years)	Initial Purch. $	Additional Purch. $	Front End Load	Back End Load
B- / 7.6	10.1	0.87	32.70	15	1	98	0	1	149.0	128.4	-10.4	60	6	1,000	500	0.0	2.0
C+ / 5.7	10.1	0.86	35.73	N/A	1	98	0	1	149.0	130.8	-10.5	66	6	0	0	0.0	0.0
C+ / 5.7	10.1	0.86	37.30	4	1	98	0	1	149.0	134.8	-10.4	72	6	5,000,000	0	0.0	2.0
C+ / 5.8	8.3	0.86	13.23	14	4	95	0	1	8.0	39.7	-9.2	23	N/A	1,000	100	5.8	1.0
C+ / 5.8	8.3	0.87	12.72	11	4	95	0	1	8.0	36.5	-9.4	18	N/A	1,000	500	0.0	4.0
C+ / 5.7	8.3	0.88	12.67	N/A	4	95	0	1	8.0	36.7	-9.4	16	N/A	1,000	500	0.0	1.0
C+ / 5.9	8.4	0.87	13.33	50	4	95	0	1	8.0	40.9	-9.2	25	N/A	5,000,000	0	0.0	0.0
B / 8.4	8.2	1.03	46.06	5,708	0	99	0	1	13.0	69.2	-11.3	70	5	1,000	100	5.8	0.0
B / 8.4	8.2	1.03	45.00	424	0	99	0	1	13.0	64.4	-11.5	60	5	1,000	500	0.0	4.0
B / 8.4	8.2	1.03	44.57	288	0	99	0	1	13.0	65.0	-11.5	61	5	1,000	500	0.0	1.0
U /	N/A	N/A	46.05	499	0	99	0	1	13.0	N/A	N/A	N/A	2	1,000	500	0.0	0.0
B / 8.3	8.1	1.03	46.11	75	0	99	0	1	13.0	68.9	-11.3	69	3	0	0	0.0	0.0
B / 8.4	8.2	1.03	46.16	309	0	99	0	1	13.0	71.7	-11.3	74	5	5,000,000	0	0.0	0.0
C / 5.5	10.1	1.18	10.35	2	1	98	0	1	75.0	58.5	-8.2	21	N/A	1,000	100	5.8	1.0
D- / 1.4	7.6	0.81	18.90	48	0	100	0	0	3.0	39.9	-13.2	22	17	1,000	100	5.8	0.0
B- / 7.3	7.6	0.82	18.27	1	0	100	0	0	3.0	34.5	-13.4	14	2	1,000	500	0.0	4.0
B- / 7.3	7.6	0.81	18.18	N/A	0	100	0	0	3.0	34.2	-13.4	14	2	1,000	500	0.0	1.0
B- / 7.3	7.6	0.81	18.05	N/A	0	100	0	0	3.0	33.8	-13.4	14	2	0	0	0.0	0.0
C+ / 6.1	13.4	1.39	30.88	59	3	96	0	1	83.0	125.8	-18.0	65	N/A	1,000	100	5.8	0.0
C+ / 6.1	13.4	1.38	28.54	3	3	96	0	1	83.0	119.7	-18.1	55	N/A	1,000	500	0.0	4.0
C+ / 6.1	13.4	1.39	28.66	1	3	96	0	1	83.0	120.6	-18.1	57	N/A	1,000	500	0.0	1.0
C+ / 6.1	13.4	1.38	31.59	385	3	96	0	1	83.0	127.7	-17.9	68	N/A	1,000	500	0.0	0.0
C / 5.0	13.4	1.39	30.99	188	3	96	0	1	83.0	126.4	-18.0	67	N/A	5,000,000	0	0.0	0.0
C+ / 6.3	9.8	1.15	12.14	366	0	99	0	1	79.0	45.2	-9.5	8	N/A	1,000	100	5.8	0.0
C+ / 6.1	9.8	1.15	10.95	98	0	99	0	1	79.0	40.8	-9.8	6	N/A	1,000	500	0.0	0.0
C+ / 6.2	9.8	1.15	11.08	33	0	99	0	1	79.0	41.0	-9.7	6	N/A	1,000	500	0.0	1.0
B- / 7.3	9.8	1.15	12.08	N/A	0	99	0	1	79.0	44.9	-9.7	8	N/A	0	0	0.0	0.0
C+ / 6.3	9.8	1.15	12.84	3	0	99	0	1	79.0	48.3	-9.3	11	N/A	5,000,000	0	0.0	0.0
U /	N/A	N/A	12.45	83	0	90	9	1	56.0	N/A	N/A	N/A	2	1,000	100	5.8	0.0
U /	N/A	N/A	11.91	31	0	90	9	1	56.0	N/A	N/A	N/A	2	1,000	500	0.0	4.0
U /	N/A	N/A	12.08	113	0	75	24	1	31.0	N/A	N/A	N/A	2	1,000	100	5.8	0.0
U /	N/A	N/A	10.97	62	0	75	24	1	31.0	N/A	N/A	N/A	2	1,000	500	0.0	4.0
U /	N/A	N/A	11.62	33	0	75	24	1	31.0	N/A	N/A	N/A	2	1,000	500	0.0	1.0
U /	N/A	N/A	11.41	150	8	57	33	2	51.0	N/A	N/A	N/A	2	1,000	100	5.8	0.0
U /	N/A	N/A	10.95	55	8	57	33	2	51.0	N/A	N/A	N/A	2	1,000	500	0.0	4.0
U /	N/A	N/A	10.88	32	8	57	33	2	51.0	N/A	N/A	N/A	2	1,000	500	0.0	1.0
U /	N/A	N/A	11.45	28	8	57	33	2	51.0	N/A	N/A	N/A	2	5,000,000	0	0.0	0.0
C+ / 5.7	9.8	1.16	13.00	N/A	1	98	0	1	100.0	74.0	-10.3	42	N/A	1,000	100	5.8	1.0
B- / 7.3	9.8	1.16	12.99	435	1	98	0	1	100.0	74.0	-10.3	42	8	50	0	0.0	0.0
C+ / 5.7	9.8	1.16	13.00	N/A	1	98	0	1	100.0	74.0	-10.3	42	N/A	5,000,000	0	0.0	0.0
C / 5.4	11.1	1.06	15.17	39	0	99	0	1	187.0	163.2	-9.8	72	1	1,000	100	5.8	0.0
C / 5.4	11.1	1.06	14.74	5	0	99	0	1	187.0	156.9	-10.0	63	1	1,000	100	0.0	4.0
C / 5.4	11.1	1.06	14.82	1	0	99	0	1	187.0	158.0	-10.0	64	1	1,000	100	0.0	1.0
C / 5.4	11.1	1.06	15.21	452	0	99	0	1	187.0	164.3	-9.7	73	1	1,000	100	0.0	0.0
C+ / 6.6	10.2	0.97	24.78	38	3	96	0	1	97.0	127.5	-11.0	54	N/A	1,000	100	5.8	0.0
C+ / 6.5	10.2	0.97	22.66	14	3	96	0	1	97.0	121.1	-11.2	42	N/A	1,000	500	0.0	4.0
C+ / 6.5	10.2	0.97	22.40	9	3	96	0	1	97.0	120.6	-11.2	42	N/A	1,000	500	0.0	1.0
B- / 7.7	10.2	0.97	24.97	106	3	96	0	1	97.0	130.1	-11.0	59	N/A	5,000,000	0	0.0	0.0
C+ / 6.0	11.0	1.04	21.69	138	1	98	0	1	111.0	117.9	-10.1	26	N/A	1,000	100	5.8	0.0
C+ / 5.9	11.0	1.04	19.85	14	1	98	0	1	111.0	110.3	-10.3	18	N/A	1,000	500	0.0	4.0
C+ / 5.9	11.0	1.05	19.63	9	1	98	0	1	111.0	110.7	-10.4	19	N/A	1,000	500	0.0	1.0
B- / 7.3	11.0	1.05	21.65	1	1	98	0	1	111.0	117.4	-10.3	24	N/A	0	0	0.0	0.0

Fund Type	Fund Name	Ticker Symbol	Overall Weiss Investment Rating	Phone	Performance Rating/Pts	3 Mo	6 Mo	1Yr / Pct	3Yr / Pct	5Yr / Pct	Dividend Yield	Expense Ratio
MC	Pioneer Mid Cap Value A	PCGRX	C-	(800) 225-6292	C+ / 5.8	-3.44	1.07	4.53 /13	17.09 /68	9.29 /78	0.07	1.10
MC	Pioneer Mid Cap Value B	PBCGX	D+	(800) 225-6292	C / 5.4	-3.66	0.59	3.53 / 9	15.98 /63	8.33 /73	0.00	2.06
MC	Pioneer Mid Cap Value C	PCCGX	C-	(800) 225-6292	C+ / 5.9	-3.64	0.69	3.66 / 9	16.07 /64	8.36 /73	0.00	1.95
MC	Pioneer Mid Cap Value Inv	PGCIX	U	(800) 225-6292	U /	-3.39	1.20	4.74 /14	--	--	0.19	0.93
MC	Pioneer Mid Cap Value R	PCMRX	C	(800) 225-6292	C+ / 6.4	-3.47	0.99	4.28 /12	16.92 /68	9.14 /77	0.09	1.32
MC	Pioneer Mid Cap Value Y	PYCGX	C	(800) 225-6292	C+ / 6.7	-3.36	1.28	4.91 /15	17.65 /71	9.84 /80	0.39	0.67
MC	Pioneer Mid-Cap Growth Fd A	PITHX	E+	(800) 225-6292	D- / 1.4	-7.32	0.07	4.25 /12	9.15 /22	0.53 /18	0.00	0.90
MC	Pioneer Mid-Cap Growth Fd B	PBMDX	E	(800) 225-6292	D- / 1.0	-7.63	-0.63	2.93 / 7	7.77 /14	-0.80 /12	0.00	2.15
MC	Pioneer Mid-Cap Growth Fd C	PCMCX	E+	(800) 225-6292	D- / 1.4	-7.63	-0.53	3.06 / 7	7.88 /14	-0.80 /12	0.00	2.04
MC	Pioneer Mid-Cap Growth Fd Y	PMCYX	E+	(800) 225-6292	D+ / 2.3	-7.23	0.33	4.73 /14	9.35 /23	0.63 /18	0.00	0.51
GR	Pioneer Oak Ridge Lrg Cap Growth A	ORILX	D-	(800) 225-6292	D- / 1.0	-5.02	-4.46	3.99 /11	8.44 /17	0.81 /19	0.00	2.10
GR	Pioneer Oak Ridge Lrg Cap Growth B	ORLBX	D-	(800) 225-6292	E+ / 0.8	-5.19	-4.83	3.07 / 8	7.54 /13	--	0.00	2.10
GR	Pioneer Oak Ridge Lrg Cap Growth C	ORLCX	D-	(800) 225-6292	D- / 1.2	-5.17	-4.74	3.22 / 8	7.65 /13	0.07 /16	0.00	2.10
GR	Pioneer Oak Ridge Lrg Cap Growth R	ORLRX	D	(800) 225-6292	D- / 1.4	-5.04	-4.47	3.82 /10	7.64 /13	0.15 /16	0.00	1.45
GR	Pioneer Oak Ridge Lrg Cap Growth Y	PORYX	D	(800) 225-6292	D / 1.9	-4.85	-4.21	4.46 /13	8.68 /19	0.94 /20	0.00	0.89
SC	Pioneer Oak Ridge Sm Cap Growth A	ORIGX	C-	(800) 225-6292	C / 5.5	-6.42	2.97	8.82 /39	16.00 /63	6.99 /67	0.00	1.40
SC	Pioneer Oak Ridge Sm Cap Growth B	ORIBX	C-	(800) 225-6292	C / 5.2	-6.64	2.49	7.80 /31	15.06 /59	6.15 /62	0.00	2.30
SC	Pioneer Oak Ridge Sm Cap Growth C	ORICX	C-	(800) 225-6292	C+ / 5.7	-6.62	2.51	7.93 /32	15.07 /59	6.14 /62	0.00	2.30
BA	Pioneer Protected Principal + II A	PPFAX	D	(800) 225-6292	E- / 0.0	-0.31	-0.52	-0.89 / 1	0.67 / 0	--	1.48	1.94
BA	Pioneer Protected Principal + II B	PPFBX	D	(800) 225-6292	E- / 0.0	-0.52	-0.83	-1.70 / 1	-0.12 / 0	--	0.65	2.75
BA	Pioneer Protected Principal + II C	PPFCX	D	(800) 225-6292	E- / 0.0	-0.52	-0.83	-1.57 / 1	-0.03 / 0	--	0.67	2.66
AA	● Pioneer Protected Principal Plus A	PPPAX	D	(800) 225-6292	E- / 0.0	-0.21	0.41	0.54 / 2	1.06 / 0	--	1.51	2.10
AA	● Pioneer Protected Principal Plus B	PPPBX	D	(800) 225-6292	E- / 0.0	-0.41	0.10	-0.21 / 2	0.32 / 0	--	0.77	2.85
AA	● Pioneer Protected Principal Plus C	PPPCX	D	(800) 225-6292	E- / 0.1	-0.41	0.10	-0.15 / 2	0.32 / 0	--	0.62	2.85
RE	Pioneer Real Estate Shares A	PWREX	C+	(800) 225-6292	A / 9.4	-0.85	14.45	23.31 /86	28.56 /94	19.97 /96	2.15	1.50
RE	Pioneer Real Estate Shares B	PBREX	C+	(800) 225-6292	A / 9.3	-1.11	13.90	22.17 /85	27.45 /93	18.97 /95	1.45	2.42
RE	Pioneer Real Estate Shares C	PCREX	C+	(800) 225-6292	A / 9.4	-1.07	13.96	22.29 /85	27.55 /94	19.05 /95	1.53	2.32
RE	Pioneer Real Estate Shares Y	PYREX	C+	(800) 225-6292	A / 9.5	-0.78	14.70	23.94 /87	29.23 /95	20.62 /97	2.67	1.00
GR	Pioneer Research Fund A	PATMX	C	(800) 225-6292	C- / 4.2	-0.78	4.18	11.68 /58	12.30 /44	2.44 /32	0.28	1.25
GR	Pioneer Research Fund B	PBTMX	C	(800) 225-6292	C- / 3.8	-1.11	3.72	10.65 /51	11.35 /38	1.60 /24	0.00	2.15
GR	Pioneer Research Fund C	PCTMX	C	(800) 225-6292	C / 4.3	-1.11	3.70	10.59 /51	11.33 /38	1.66 /25	0.00	2.15
GR	Pioneer Research Fund Y	PRFYX	C+	(800) 225-6292	C / 5.1	-0.87	4.15	11.69 /58	12.37 /45	2.48 /32	0.17	1.12
MC	Pioneer Small & Mid Cap Gr A	PAPPX	D-	(800) 225-6292	D- / 1.5	-4.54	2.01	9.14 /41	9.11 /21	3.64 /42	0.00	1.25
MC	Pioneer Small & Mid Cap Gr B	MCSBX	D-	(800) 225-6292	D / 1.6	-4.77	1.56	8.14 /34	8.18 /16	2.80 /35	0.00	2.16
MC	Pioneer Small & Mid Cap Gr C	CGCPX	D	(800) 225-6292	D / 2.1	-4.72	1.63	8.25 /35	8.26 /16	2.84 /35	0.00	2.09
MC	Pioneer Small & Mid Cap Gr R	CGCRX	D	(800) 225-6292	D+ / 2.5	-4.62	1.77	8.56 /37	8.59 /18	3.14 /38	0.00	1.66
SC	Pioneer Small Cap Value Fund A	PIMCX	B-	(800) 225-6292	B / 7.6	-3.28	5.83	15.85 /74	20.16 /80	11.08 /84	0.00	1.48
SC	Pioneer Small Cap Value Fund B	PBMOX	C+	(800) 225-6292	B- / 7.4	-3.47	5.37	14.86 /71	19.20 /77	10.23 /81	0.00	2.29
SC	Pioneer Small Cap Value Fund C	PSVCX	B-	(800) 225-6292	B / 7.7	-3.46	5.42	14.93 /72	19.25 /77	--	0.00	2.25
SC	Pioneer Small Cap Value Fund Inv	CALLX	U	(800) 225-6292	U /	-3.23	5.93	16.14 /75	--	--	0.00	1.15
SC	Pioneer Small Cap Value Fund R	PSVRX	B	(800) 225-6292	B / 8.0	-3.31	5.75	15.63 /74	20.07 /79	10.84 /83	0.00	1.67
SC	Pioneer Small Cap Value Fund Y	PCAYX	B	(800) 225-6292	B / 8.2	-3.16	6.06	16.41 /76	20.56 /81	11.30 /85	0.00	0.94
★ GI	Pioneer Value Fund A	PIOTX	C-	(800) 225-6292	C / 4.3	0.47	3.98	9.43 /43	12.69 /47	4.67 /52	1.22	0.97
GI	Pioneer Value Fund B	PBOTX	D	(800) 225-6292	C- / 3.7	0.12	3.36	8.22 /35	11.44 /39	3.49 /41	0.11	2.02
GI	Pioneer Value Fund C	PCOTX	D+	(800) 225-6292	C / 4.3	0.18	3.43	8.29 /35	11.42 /39	3.49 /41	0.17	2.07
GI	● Pioneer Value Fund Inv	PIOIX	U	(800) 225-6292	U /	0.47	4.03	9.71 /45	--	--	1.53	0.74
GI	Pioneer Value Fund R	PVFRX	C	(800) 225-6292	C- / 3.8	-0.11	2.94	6.47 /23	10.81 /34	3.42 /41	0.00	3.03
GI	Pioneer Value Fund Y	PVFYX	B-	(800) 225-6292	C / 5.4	0.53	4.13	9.87 /46	13.02 /49	4.85 /53	1.26	0.59
IX	PMFM Managed Portfolio Trust Fd	ETFGX	E+	(800) 222-7636	E- / 0.1	0.53	1.60	1.23 / 3	1.53 / 0	--	0.00	1.30
GL	Polaris Global Value Fund	PGVFX	B+	(888) 263-5594	B+ / 8.8	-1.13	8.40	19.00 /80	23.15 /88	16.83 /94	0.90	1.34
GR	Polynous Growth Fund	PAGFX	D	(800) 924-3863	C- / 3.2	-6.71	1.67	14.33 /69	11.86 /41	6.25 /63	0.00	1.95
GL	Portfolio 21	PORTX	C+	(866) 811-0215	B- / 7.2	-1.82	8.07	20.21 /82	17.20 /69	7.17 /68	0.54	1.50

● Denotes fund is closed to new investors
★ Denotes fund is included in Section II

326

RISK			NET ASSETS		ASSET				BULL / BEAR		FUND MANAGER		MINIMUMS		LOADS	
Risk Rating/Pts	3 Year		NAV As of 6/30/06	Total $(Mil)	Cash %	Stocks %	Bonds %	Other %	Portfolio Turnover Ratio	Last Bull Market Return	Last Bear Market Return	Manager Quality Pct	Manager Tenure (Years)	Initial Purch. $	Additional Purch. $	Front End Load	Back End Load
	Standard Deviation	Beta															
C / 5.4	9.7	0.84	23.59	1,956	2	97	0	1	74.0	97.6	-8.3	71	4	1,000	100	5.8	0.0
C / 4.7	9.7	0.84	20.54	175	2	97	0	1	74.0	91.8	-8.5	61	4	1,000	500	0.0	4.0
C / 4.7	9.7	0.84	20.39	198	2	97	0	1	74.0	92.2	-8.6	62	4	1,000	500	0.0	1.0
U /	N/A	N/A	23.63	60	2	97	0	1	74.0	N/A	N/A	N/A	2	1,000	500	0.0	0.0
C+ / 5.8	9.7	0.84	23.37	35	2	97	0	1	74.0	96.6	-8.4	69	3	0	0	0.0	0.0
C / 5.5	9.8	0.85	24.45	304	2	97	0	1	74.0	100.8	-8.3	75	4	5,000,000	0	0.0	0.0
C / 5.3	12.6	1.11	14.94	457	0	99	0	1	115.0	67.9	-5.7	2	1	1,000	100	5.8	0.0
C / 5.2	12.6	1.11	12.71	22	0	99	0	1	115.0	61.2	-6.0	1	1	1,000	500	0.0	4.0
C / 5.2	12.6	1.10	13.19	11	0	99	0	1	115.0	61.7	-6.1	1	1	1,000	500	0.0	1.0
C / 4.8	12.6	1.10	15.02	29	0	99	0	1	115.0	68.6	-5.7	2	1	5,000,000	0	0.0	0.0
B- / 7.4	8.5	1.00	12.86	269	6	93	0	1	140.0	50.4	-8.0	29	12	1,000	100	5.8	0.0
B- / 7.3	8.5	1.00	12.61	36	6	93	0	1	140.0	46.6	-8.2	23	7	1,000	500	0.0	4.0
B- / 7.3	8.5	0.99	12.65	81	6	93	0	1	140.0	46.9	-8.1	25	7	1,000	500	0.0	1.0
B- / 7.3	8.5	0.99	12.62	2	6	93	0	1	140.0	46.7	-8.1	24	7	0	0	0.0	0.0
B- / 7.4	8.5	1.00	12.96	543	6	93	0	1	140.0	51.3	-8.0	31	7	5,000,000	0	0.0	0.0
C / 5.2	13.7	0.87	25.65	227	4	95	0	1	47.0	102.8	-5.5	51	12	1,000	100	5.8	0.0
C+ / 5.6	13.7	0.87	25.15	10	4	95	0	1	47.0	97.8	-5.7	41	12	1,000	500	0.0	4.0
C / 5.2	13.7	0.87	23.68	54	4	95	0	1	47.0	97.8	-5.7	41	12	1,000	500	0.0	1.0
B+ / 9.2	4.9	0.47	9.62	22	0	20	79	1	117.0	N/A	N/A	19	3	1,000	100	5.8	0.0
B+ / 9.2	4.9	0.47	9.56	34	0	20	79	1	117.0	N/A	N/A	15	3	1,000	500	0.0	4.0
B+ / 9.2	4.8	0.47	9.60	9	0	20	79	1	117.0	N/A	N/A	15	3	1,000	500	0.0	1.0
B / 8.7	4.7	0.53	9.73	16	0	31	68	1	31.0	7.6	0.6	20	4	1,000	100	5.8	0.0
B / 8.7	4.7	0.53	9.71	28	0	31	68	1	31.0	5.1	0.4	15	4	1,000	500	0.0	4.0
B / 8.8	4.6	0.52	9.76	7	0	31	68	1	31.0	5.0	0.4	16	4	1,000	500	0.0	1.0
C- / 3.4	15.9	0.95	29.29	128	2	97	0	1	24.0	134.0	-0.7	92	13	1,000	100	5.8	0.0
C- / 3.4	15.9	0.95	29.02	29	2	97	0	1	24.0	127.8	-0.9	88	10	1,000	500	0.0	4.0
C- / 3.4	15.9	0.95	29.07	21	2	97	0	1	24.0	128.5	-0.9	88	10	1,000	500	0.0	1.0
C- / 3.4	15.9	0.95	29.26	35	2	97	0	1	24.0	138.2	-0.6	93	8	5,000,000	0	0.0	0.0
B- / 7.9	8.3	1.05	10.21	7	2	97	0	1	89.0	68.3	-11.8	63	N/A	1,000	100	5.8	0.0
B- / 7.8	8.2	1.04	9.77	6	2	97	0	1	89.0	63.9	-12.0	53	N/A	1,000	500	0.0	4.0
B- / 7.8	8.3	1.05	9.82	3	2	97	0	1	89.0	64.1	-12.0	52	N/A	1,000	500	0.0	1.0
B / 8.0	8.3	1.05	10.28	78	2	97	0	1	89.0	68.7	-11.8	64	N/A	5,000,000	0	0.0	0.0
C+ / 6.8	9.9	0.81	27.94	48	0	99	0	1	13.0	60.0	-10.4	13	8	1,000	100	5.8	0.0
C+ / 6.7	9.9	0.81	27.37	5	0	99	0	1	13.0	55.9	-10.5	9	2	1,000	500	0.0	4.0
C+ / 6.7	9.9	0.81	27.43	10	0	99	0	1	13.0	56.2	-10.5	10	2	1,000	500	0.0	1.0
C+ / 6.7	9.9	0.81	27.64	2	0	99	0	1	13.0	57.6	-10.5	11	2	0	0	0.0	0.0
C+ / 6.1	12.3	0.81	33.35	559	9	90	0	1	42.0	123.3	-10.2	90	9	1,000	100	5.8	0.0
C+ / 5.8	12.3	0.81	30.57	149	9	90	0	1	42.0	117.8	-10.4	86	9	1,000	500	0.0	4.0
C+ / 5.9	12.3	0.81	32.06	133	9	90	0	1	42.0	118.1	-10.4	86	5	1,000	500	0.0	1.0
U /	N/A	N/A	33.52	45	9	90	0	1	42.0	N/A	N/A	N/A	2	0	0	0.0	0.0
C+ / 6.4	12.3	0.81	33.27	11	9	90	0	1	42.0	122.8	-10.4	90	3	0	0	0.0	0.0
C+ / 6.4	12.3	0.81	33.72	40	9	90	0	1	42.0	125.4	-10.2	92	2	5,000,000	0	0.0	0.0
C+ / 6.1	7.4	0.91	18.04	3,871	3	96	0	1	53.0	72.2	-10.1	77	N/A	1,000	100	5.8	0.0
C+ / 5.8	7.4	0.91	16.92	39	3	96	0	1	53.0	66.3	-10.4	67	N/A	1,000	500	0.0	4.0
C+ / 5.8	7.4	0.91	16.91	9	3	96	0	1	53.0	66.4	-10.4	67	N/A	1,000	500	0.0	1.0
U /	N/A	N/A	18.04	119	3	96	0	1	53.0	N/A	N/A	N/A	N/A	1,000	500	0.0	0.0
B / 8.4	7.5	0.92	17.48	N/A	3	96	0	1	53.0	64.2	-10.2	60	N/A	0	0	0.0	0.0
B / 8.5	7.4	0.91	18.14	329	3	96	0	1	53.0	73.6	-10.1	80	N/A	5,000,000	0	0.0	0.0
B- / 7.3	7.4	0.79	9.54	60	6	93	0	1	10.0	N/A	N/A	6	3	1,000	250	0.0	0.0
C+ / 6.0	10.2	0.87	17.56	443	0	93	6	1	10.0	137.6	-7.0	73	8	2,500	250	0.0	1.0
C+ / 5.6	15.4	1.43	14.04	12	26	73	0	1	148.5	105.0	5.4	26	10	2,500	200	4.5	0.0
C+ / 6.1	10.8	0.95	29.05	120	8	90	0	2	0.8	96.0	-12.4	14	N/A	5,000	100	0.0	2.0

Fund Type	Fund Name	Ticker Symbol	Overall Weiss Investment Rating	Phone	Performance Rating/Pts	3 Mo	6 Mo	1Yr / Pct	3Yr / Pct	5Yr / Pct	Dividend Yield	Expense Ratio
IN	Primary Income Fund	PINFX	C-	(800) 443-6544	D / 1.9	0.02	2.86	3.21 / 8	7.76 / 14	3.83 / 44	2.51	1.00
GI	Primary Trend Fund	PTFDX	C-	(800) 443-6544	C- / 3.0	1.55	4.70	6.26 / 22	9.05 / 21	4.81 / 53	0.84	1.48
GR	Principal Inv Disc LrgCp Bld A	PRMGX	C	(800) 247-4123	C- / 3.6	-2.24	1.78	8.22 / 35	12.46 / 45	--	0.29	1.17
GR	Principal Inv Disc LrgCp Bld AdvPfd		C+	(800) 247-4123	C / 4.5	-2.19	1.79	8.27 / 35	11.90 / 42	--	0.29	1.16
GR	Principal Inv Disc LrgCp Bld AdvSel		C+	(800) 247-4123	C / 4.3	-2.26	1.66	7.95 / 32	11.67 / 40	--	0.12	1.33
GR	Principal Inv Disc LrgCp Bld B	PBABX	C-	(800) 247-4123	D / 2.2	-2.50	1.23	7.38 / 29	8.47 / 18	2.51 / 32	0.00	2.11
GR	Principal Inv Disc LrgCp Bld Inst	PILBX	C-	(800) 247-4123	C / 4.8	-2.11	2.06	8.82 / 39	12.51 / 46	--	0.85	0.59
GL	Principal Inv Divers Intl A	PRWLX	A	(800) 247-4123	A / 9.3	-0.37	11.54	35.11 / 97	26.94 / 93	10.97 / 84	0.18	1.33
GL	Principal Inv Divers Intl AdvPfd	PINRX	A+	(800) 247-4123	A / 9.4	-0.45	11.41	34.99 / 97	26.74 / 93	10.87 / 83	0.16	1.47
GL	Principal Inv Divers Intl AdvSel	PINNX	A+	(800) 247-4123	A / 9.4	-0.45	11.39	34.90 / 97	26.58 / 93	10.65 / 83	0.00	1.65
GL	Principal Inv Divers Intl B	PRBWX	A	(800) 247-4123	A / 9.3	-0.59	11.12	34.32 / 96	25.87 / 92	9.89 / 80	0.00	2.22
GL	Principal Inv Divers Intl Inst	PIIIX	A+	(800) 247-4123	A / 9.5	-0.30	11.73	35.71 / 97	27.44 / 93	11.47 / 85	0.65	0.90
GL	Principal Inv Divers Intl J	PIIJX	A+	(800) 247-4123	A / 9.4	-0.45	11.37	34.96 / 97	26.42 / 93	10.51 / 82	0.00	1.61
GL	Principal Inv Divers Intl Pfd	PINPX	A+	(800) 247-4123	A / 9.5	-0.30	11.64	35.49 / 97	27.17 / 93	11.29 / 85	0.42	1.16
GL	Principal Inv Divers Intl Sel	PINLX	A+	(800) 247-4123	A / 9.5	-0.37	11.53	35.09 / 97	27.14 / 93	11.29 / 85	0.31	1.31
UT	Principal Inv Equity Income A	PUTLX	C	(800) 247-4123	C- / 4.2	-0.46	6.89	11.66 / 58	12.31 / 44	1.59 / 24	2.82	1.16
UT	Principal Inv Equity Income B	PRUBX	C	(800) 247-4123	C / 4.5	-0.74	6.43	10.54 / 51	11.31 / 38	0.69 / 19	1.97	2.19
EM	Principal Inv Intl Emrg Mkts A	PRIAX	C	(800) 247-4123	A+ / 9.8	-3.96	10.59	41.80 / 98	36.83 / 98	20.91 / 97	0.18	1.96
EM	Principal Inv Intl Emrg Mkts AdvPfd		B-	(800) 247-4123	A+ / 9.8	-3.95	10.59	41.85 / 98	36.92 / 99	21.14 / 97	0.24	1.93
EM	Principal Inv Intl Emrg Mkts AdvSel		B-	(800) 247-4123	A+ / 9.8	-3.97	10.54	41.64 / 98	36.51 / 98	20.77 / 97	0.10	2.11
EM	Principal Inv Intl Emrg Mkts B	PIEBX	C-	(800) 247-4123	A- / 9.2	-4.11	10.14	40.39 / 98	24.62 / 90	13.97 / 90	0.00	2.90
EM	Principal Inv Intl Emrg Mkts Inst		B-	(800) 247-4123	A+ / 9.8	-3.79	10.98	42.70 / 98	37.72 / 99	21.58 / 97	0.71	1.36
EM	Principal Inv Intl Emrg Mkts J	PIEJX	B-	(800) 247-4123	A+ / 9.8	-3.97	10.51	41.61 / 98	36.39 / 98	20.65 / 97	0.04	2.08
EM	Principal Inv Intl Emrg Mkts Pfd		B-	(800) 247-4123	A+ / 9.8	-3.88	10.82	42.30 / 98	37.35 / 99	21.52 / 97	0.49	1.62
EM	Principal Inv Intl Emrg Mkts Sel		B-	(800) 247-4123	A+ / 9.8	-3.88	10.79	42.32 / 98	37.25 / 99	21.39 / 97	0.40	1.76
GL	Principal Inv Intl Growth AdvPfd	PITMX	A+	(800) 247-4123	A / 9.4	0.47	10.46	31.06 / 95	26.44 / 93	12.67 / 88	0.33	1.57
GL	Principal Inv Intl Growth AdvSel	PITNX	A+	(800) 247-4123	A / 9.3	0.49	10.45	30.83 / 95	26.21 / 92	11.67 / 86	0.22	1.74
GL	Principal Inv Intl Growth Inst	PITIX	A+	(800) 247-4123	A / 9.4	0.64	10.85	31.85 / 96	27.16 / 93	12.32 / 87	0.83	0.99
GL	Principal Inv Intl Growth J	PITJX	A+	(800) 247-4123	A / 9.3	0.49	10.39	30.77 / 95	26.04 / 92	11.51 / 85	0.13	1.77
GL	Principal Inv Intl Growth Pfd	PITPX	A+	(800) 247-4123	A / 9.4	0.56	10.65	31.44 / 95	26.88 / 93	12.27 / 87	0.62	1.26
GL	Principal Inv Intl Growth Sel	PITSX	A+	(800) 247-4123	A / 9.4	0.65	10.68	31.39 / 95	26.76 / 93	12.17 / 87	0.52	1.37
GR	Principal Inv LgCap Growth A	PRGWX	E-	(800) 247-4123	C- / 3.5	-3.51	1.09	9.74 / 45	12.27 / 44	-0.45 / 14	0.00	1.10
GR	Principal Inv LgCap Growth AdvPfd		C+	(800) 247-4123	C / 4.6	-3.51	1.05	10.33 / 49	12.13 / 43	0.62 / 18	0.00	1.12
GR	Principal Inv LgCap Growth AdvSel		C+	(800) 247-4123	C / 4.5	-3.41	1.10	10.16 / 48	11.94 / 42	-0.20 / 15	0.00	1.30
GR	Principal Inv LgCap Growth B	PRGBX	E-	(800) 247-4123	C- / 3.9	-3.66	0.68	8.52 / 37	11.44 / 39	-1.17 / 11	0.00	2.01
GR	Principal Inv LgCap Growth Inst	PGLIX	C+	(800) 247-4123	C / 5.0	-3.25	1.36	11.00 / 53	12.74 / 47	0.53 / 18	0.12	0.54
GR	Principal Inv LgCap Growth J	PGLJX	C+	(800) 247-4123	C- / 4.2	-3.53	0.99	10.06 / 47	11.67 / 40	-0.43 / 14	0.00	1.38
GR	Principal Inv LgCap Growth Pfd		C+	(800) 247-4123	C / 4.8	-3.34	1.21	10.74 / 52	12.47 / 46	0.21 / 16	0.00	0.81
GR	Principal Inv LgCap Growth Sel		C+	(800) 247-4123	C / 5.0	-3.42	1.19	10.58 / 51	12.89 / 48	0.47 / 18	0.00	0.93
IX	Principal Inv LgCap S&P 500 A	PLSAX	C	(800) 247-4123	C- / 3.0	-1.52	2.37	4.84 / 14	10.25 / 29	1.57 / 24	1.03	0.66
IX	Principal Inv LgCap S&P 500 AdvPfd	PLFMX	C	(800) 247-4123	C- / 3.5	-1.63	2.37	7.83 / 31	10.33 / 30	1.66 / 25	0.97	0.72
IX	Principal Inv LgCap S&P 500 AdvSel	PLFNX	C	(800) 247-4123	C- / 3.4	-1.74	2.26	7.65 / 30	10.11 / 28	1.47 / 24	0.79	0.90
IX	Principal Inv LgCap S&P 500 Inst	PLFIX	C+	(800) 247-4123	C- / 4.0	-1.52	2.60	8.45 / 36	10.98 / 35	2.23 / 29	1.53	0.15
IX	Principal Inv LgCap S&P 500 J	PSPJX	C	(800) 247-4123	C- / 3.3	-1.64	2.28	7.77 / 31	10.17 / 28	1.36 / 23	0.85	0.84
IX	Principal Inv LgCap S&P 500 Pfd	PLFPX	C+	(800) 247-4123	C- / 3.8	-1.61	2.47	8.08 / 33	10.66 / 32	2.03 / 28	1.26	0.41
IX	Principal Inv LgCap S&P 500 Sel	PLFSX	C	(800) 247-4123	C- / 3.7	-1.62	2.36	8.00 / 33	10.53 / 31	1.83 / 26	1.15	0.53
GR	Principal Inv LgCap Val Fd A	PCACX	E	(800) 247-4123	C / 4.3	-0.08	5.88	11.08 / 54	12.56 / 46	4.96 / 54	0.77	0.87
GR	Principal Inv LgCap Val Fd AdvPfd	PLVMX	B-	(800) 247-4123	C / 5.2	-0.08	5.83	10.94 / 53	12.45 / 45	5.14 / 55	0.67	1.02
GR	Principal Inv LgCap Val Fd AdvSel	PLVNX	C+	(800) 247-4123	C / 5.2	-0.17	5.73	10.72 / 52	12.40 / 45	5.01 / 54	0.50	1.20
GR	Principal Inv LgCap Val Fd B	PCCBX	E	(800) 247-4123	C / 4.7	-0.25	5.43	10.37 / 49	11.90 / 42	4.25 / 48	0.46	1.89
GR	Principal Inv LgCap Val Fd Inst	PVLIX	B-	(800) 247-4123	C+ / 5.6	0.00	6.16	11.49 / 57	13.04 / 49	5.69 / 59	1.19	0.45
GR	Principal Inv LgCap Val Fd J	PVLJX	C+	(800) 247-4123	C / 4.8	-0.17	5.77	10.61 / 51	12.01 / 42	4.69 / 52	0.43	1.23

Summer 2006

I. Index of Stock Mutual Funds

RISK			NET ASSETS		ASSET				BULL / BEAR		FUND MANAGER		MINIMUMS		LOADS	
Risk Rating/Pts	3 Year Standard Deviation	Beta	NAV As of 6/30/06	Total $(Mil)	Cash %	Stocks %	Bonds %	Other %	Portfolio Turnover Ratio	Last Bull Market Return	Last Bear Market Return	Manager Quality Pct	Manager Tenure (Years)	Initial Purch. $	Additional Purch. $	Front End Load	Back End Load
B /8.7	5.7	0.60	12.99	4	4	88	0	8	17.0	43.6	-7.9	59	17	500	100	0.0	0.0
B- /7.5	6.5	0.76	13.14	17	17	80	0	3	20.0	52.2	-10.8	57	9	500	100	0.0	0.0
B /8.8	7.8	1.00	14.87	90	1	98	0	1	86.7	70.5	N/A	69	4	1,000	100	5.8	0.8
B /8.8	7.8	1.00	14.76	2	1	98	0	1	86.7	67.6	N/A	63	4	0	0	0.0	0.0
B /8.9	7.8	1.00	14.71	1	1	98	0	1	86.7	66.4	N/A	61	4	0	0	0.0	0.0
B /8.8	6.2	0.76	14.80	13	1	98	0	1	86.7	45.1	-4.5	49	4	1,000	100	0.0	1.0
C+ /6.2	7.8	1.00	14.87	842	1	98	0	1	86.7	70.5	N/A	69	4	0	0	0.0	0.0
C+ /6.3	11.7	1.12	13.44	345	2	97	0	1	202.7	148.5	-8.6	51	3	1,000	100	5.8	0.8
B- /7.4	11.8	1.12	13.38	35	2	97	0	1	202.7	147.4	-8.6	48	3	0	0	0.0	0.0
B- /7.4	11.7	1.12	13.30	17	2	97	0	1	202.7	146.3	-8.7	47	3	0	0	0.0	0.0
C+ /6.3	11.9	1.14	13.39	47	2	97	0	1	202.7	141.5	-8.7	37	3	1,000	100	0.0	1.0
B- /7.5	11.8	1.12	13.43	42	2	97	0	1	202.7	151.6	-8.5	56	3	0	0	0.0	0.0
B- /7.4	11.8	1.13	13.32	163	2	97	0	1	202.7	144.8	-8.6	45	3	1,000	100	0.0	1.0
B- /7.5	11.8	1.13	13.43	38	2	97	0	1	202.7	150.0	-8.5	53	3	0	0	0.0	0.0
B- /7.4	11.8	1.13	13.54	11	2	97	0	1	202.7	151.4	-8.5	51	3	0	0	0.0	0.0
B /8.0	8.8	0.44	12.13	95	0	96	3	1	88.4	63.0	-2.4	72	N/A	1,000	100	5.8	0.8
B /8.0	8.9	0.44	12.09	13	0	96	3	1	88.4	58.5	-2.5	62	N/A	1,000	100	0.0	1.0
D+ /2.5	18.9	1.15	22.34	70	0	99	0	1	181.2	236.2	-5.4	23	5	1,000	100	5.8	0.8
C- /3.9	18.7	1.14	22.13	5	0	99	0	1	181.2	236.0	-5.4	26	5	0	0	0.0	0.0
C- /3.9	18.7	1.13	22.02	3	0	99	0	1	181.2	232.3	-5.4	24	5	0	0	0.0	0.0
D /2.2	24.4	1.09	22.15	14	0	99	0	1	181.2	153.7	-5.6	1	5	1,000	100	0.0	4.0
C- /3.9	18.7	1.13	22.34	5	0	99	0	1	181.2	241.2	-5.3	30	5	0	0	0.0	0.0
C- /3.9	18.7	1.13	21.76	120	0	99	0	1	181.2	231.2	-5.5	23	5	1,000	100	0.0	1.0
C- /3.9	18.7	1.13	22.32	9	0	99	0	1	181.2	239.0	-5.4	28	5	0	0	0.0	0.0
C- /3.9	18.7	1.13	22.29	2	0	99	0	1	181.2	238.1	-5.4	28	5	0	0	0.0	0.0
B- /7.8	10.8	1.03	12.88	24	2	97	0	1	139.5	148.2	-6.7	69	1	0	0	0.0	0.0
B- /7.8	10.8	1.03	12.26	12	2	97	0	1	139.5	146.6	-6.7	67	1	0	0	0.0	0.0
B- /7.8	10.8	1.03	12.57	942	2	97	0	1	139.5	152.9	-6.5	74	1	0	0	0.0	0.0
B- /7.9	10.8	1.02	12.32	60	2	97	0	1	139.5	145.3	-6.8	67	1	1,000	100	0.0	1.0
B- /7.8	10.8	1.03	12.47	14	2	97	0	1	139.5	150.8	-6.5	72	1	0	0	0.0	0.0
B- /7.9	10.7	1.02	12.44	13	2	97	0	1	139.5	149.9	-6.6	73	1	0	0	0.0	0.0
E- /0.0	9.3	1.09	7.42	276	4	95	0	1	169.0	64.3	-9.2	58	1	1,000	100	5.8	0.8
B /8.4	9.1	1.08	7.69	30	4	95	0	1	169.0	62.1	-5.7	58	1	0	0	0.0	0.0
B /8.4	9.1	1.08	7.37	9	4	95	0	1	169.0	61.1	-8.8	56	1	0	0	0.0	0.0
E- /0.0	9.2	1.09	7.37	30	4	95	0	1	169.0	60.3	-9.5	49	1	1,000	100	0.0	1.0
B /8.4	9.1	1.08	7.45	414	4	95	0	1	169.0	65.0	-8.6	65	1	0	0	0.0	0.0
B /8.4	9.2	1.08	7.11	31	4	95	0	1	169.0	60.0	-8.8	53	1	1,000	100	0.0	1.0
B /8.4	9.2	1.08	7.53	25	4	95	0	1	169.0	63.7	-8.9	61	1	0	0	0.0	0.0
B /8.4	9.0	1.06	7.63	13	4	95	0	1	169.0	65.8	-8.7	68	1	0	0	0.0	0.0
B /8.8	7.6	0.94	9.06	73	1	98	0	1	11.5	60.3	-10.0	51	3	1,000	100	1.5	0.3
B /8.7	7.6	1.00	9.06	111	1	98	0	1	11.5	60.4	-9.9	46	3	0	0	0.0	0.0
B /8.7	7.7	1.00	9.04	61	1	98	0	1	11.5	59.5	-9.8	43	3	0	0	0.0	0.0
B /8.8	7.6	1.00	9.06	20	1	98	0	1	11.5	63.5	-9.8	54	3	0	0	0.0	0.0
B /8.7	7.7	1.00	8.97	339	1	98	0	1	11.5	59.4	-9.9	44	3	1,000	100	0.0	1.0
B /8.8	7.6	0.99	9.14	194	1	98	0	1	11.5	62.2	-9.9	51	3	0	0	0.0	0.0
B /8.7	7.6	0.99	9.09	32	1	98	0	1	11.5	61.6	-9.9	49	3	1,000	100	0.0	0.0
D- /1.5	8.2	0.99	12.06	279	0	99	0	1	181.1	67.8	-6.8	71	6	1,000	100	5.8	0.8
B /8.4	8.3	0.99	11.98	2	0	99	0	1	181.1	67.5	-6.6	69	6	0	0	0.0	0.0
B /8.4	8.2	0.98	12.00	4	0	99	0	1	181.1	67.1	-6.6	70	6	0	0	0.0	0.0
D- /1.5	8.2	0.99	12.03	23	0	99	0	1	181.1	64.5	-7.1	65	6	1,000	100	0.0	1.0
B /8.4	8.2	0.98	12.06	300	0	99	0	1	181.1	70.0	-6.5	75	N/A	0	0	0.0	0.0
B /8.4	8.2	0.99	11.92	40	0	99	0	1	181.1	65.2	-6.7	66	N/A	1,000	100	0.0	1.0

Fund Type	Fund Name	Ticker Symbol	Overall Weiss Investment Rating	Phone	Perfor-mance Rating/Pts	3 Mo	6 Mo	1Yr / Pct	3Yr / Pct	5Yr / Pct	Dividend Yield	Expense Ratio
GR	Principal Inv LgCap Val Fd Pfd	PLVPX	B-	(800) 247-4123	C / 5.5	0.00	6.06	11.29 /55	12.91 /48	5.48 /58	0.95	0.71
GR	Principal Inv LgCap Val Fd Sel	PLVSX	B-	(800) 247-4123	C / 5.3	0.00	6.01	11.12 /54	12.61 /46	5.29 /56	0.84	0.84
AA	Principal Inv LifeTime 2010 A	PENAX	D	(800) 247-4123	D / 2.0	-0.95	2.46	6.00 /20	9.69 /25	6.48 /64	1.16	0.50
AA	Principal Inv LifeTime 2010 AdvPfd	PTAMX	C+	(800) 247-4123	C- / 3.0	-0.96	2.49	6.35 /22	9.36 /23	6.07 /61	1.84	0.69
AA	Principal Inv LifeTime 2010 AdvSel	PTANX	C+	(800) 247-4123	D+ / 2.8	-1.04	2.41	6.08 /21	9.17 /22	5.88 /60	1.66	0.87
AA	Principal Inv LifeTime 2010 Inst	PTTIX	C+	(800) 247-4123	C- / 3.4	-0.80	2.80	6.90 /26	10.04 /28	6.68 /65	2.39	0.12
AA	Principal Inv LifeTime 2010 J	PTAJX	C+	(800) 247-4123	D+ / 2.8	-0.96	2.48	6.31 /22	9.31 /23	5.85 /60	1.81	0.70
AA	Principal Inv LifeTime 2010 Pfd	PTAPX	C+	(800) 247-4123	C- / 3.2	-0.88	2.64	6.65 /24	9.74 /25	6.40 /63	2.13	0.38
AA	Principal Inv LifeTime 2010 Sel	PTASX	C+	(800) 247-4123	C- / 3.1	-0.96	2.57	6.45 /23	9.56 /24	6.24 /63	2.02	0.50
AA	Principal Inv LifeTime 2020 AdvPfd	PTBMX	B-	(800) 247-4123	C- / 4.2	-1.40	3.17	8.73 /38	11.09 /36	6.64 /65	1.93	0.69
AA	Principal Inv LifeTime 2020 AdvSel	PTBNX	C+	(800) 247-4123	C- / 4.0	-1.48	3.01	8.47 /37	10.88 /34	6.44 /64	1.76	0.87
AA	Principal Inv LifeTime 2020 Inst	PLWIX	B-	(800) 247-4123	C / 4.5	-1.31	3.40	9.29 /42	11.72 /41	7.25 /68	2.48	0.12
AA	Principal Inv LifeTime 2020 J	PLFJX	C+	(800) 247-4123	C- / 3.9	-1.39	3.16	8.68 /38	10.98 /35	6.43 /64	1.90	0.70
AA	Principal Inv LifeTime 2020 Pfd	PTBPX	B-	(800) 247-4123	C / 4.4	-1.32	3.32	9.04 /40	11.41 /39	6.96 /66	2.23	0.38
AA	Principal Inv LifeTime 2020 Sel	PTBSX	B-	(800) 247-4123	C / 4.3	-1.32	3.24	8.91 /39	11.30 /38	6.82 /66	2.11	0.50
AA	Principal Inv LifeTime 2030 AdvPfd	PTCMX	B-	(800) 247-4123	C / 4.8	-1.56	3.52	10.05 /47	12.06 /43	6.33 /63	1.87	0.69
AA	Principal Inv LifeTime 2030 AdvSel	PTCNX	B-	(800) 247-4123	C / 4.7	-1.64	3.45	9.89 /46	11.89 /42	6.10 /62	1.70	0.87
AA	Principal Inv LifeTime 2030 Inst	PMTIX	B	(800) 247-4123	C / 5.2	-1.40	3.85	10.74 /52	12.74 /47	6.93 /66	2.42	0.12
AA	Principal Inv LifeTime 2030 J	PLTJX	B-	(800) 247-4123	C / 4.5	-1.56	3.52	10.04 /47	11.89 /42	6.04 /61	1.78	0.74
AA	Principal Inv LifeTime 2030 Pfd	PTCPX	B	(800) 247-4123	C / 5.0	-1.48	3.69	10.46 /50	12.45 /45	6.65 /65	2.17	0.38
AA	Principal Inv LifeTime 2030 Sel	PTCSX	B	(800) 247-4123	C / 5.3	-1.45	3.62	10.30 /49	12.96 /49	6.89 /66	2.01	0.50
AA	Principal Inv LifeTime 2040 AdvPfd	PTDMX	B	(800) 247-4123	C / 5.1	-1.69	3.57	10.78 /52	12.67 /47	6.44 /64	1.68	0.69
AA	Principal Inv LifeTime 2040 AdvSel	PTDNX	B	(800) 247-4123	C / 5.1	-1.77	3.49	10.68 /51	12.54 /46	6.29 /63	1.51	0.87
AA	Principal Inv LifeTime 2040 Inst	PTDIX	B	(800) 247-4123	C / 5.5	-1.61	3.88	11.43 /56	13.33 /50	7.06 /67	2.22	0.12
AA	Principal Inv LifeTime 2040 J	PTDJX	B-	(800) 247-4123	C / 4.8	-1.69	3.56	10.78 /52	12.39 /45	6.06 /61	1.44	0.75
AA	Principal Inv LifeTime 2040 Pfd	PTDPX	B	(800) 247-4123	C / 5.4	-1.61	3.80	11.17 /55	13.04 /49	6.79 /66	1.98	0.38
AA	Principal Inv LifeTime 2040 Sel	PTDSX	B	(800) 247-4123	C / 5.3	-1.69	3.65	10.99 /53	12.89 /48	6.62 /65	1.87	0.50
AA	Principal Inv LifeTime 2050 AdvPfd	PTERX	B	(800) 247-4123	C+ / 5.6	-1.82	3.86	11.95 /59	13.54 /52	5.63 /59	1.69	0.69
AA	Principal Inv LifeTime 2050 AdvSel	PTENX	B	(800) 247-4123	C+ / 5.6	-1.83	3.78	11.77 /58	13.38 /51	5.48 /58	1.51	0.87
AA	Principal Inv LifeTime 2050 Inst	PPLIX	B+	(800) 247-4123	C+ / 6.0	-1.66	4.18	12.62 /63	14.19 /55	6.21 /62	2.23	0.12
AA	Principal Inv LifeTime 2050 Pfd	PTEFX	B+	(800) 247-4123	C+ / 5.8	-1.82	3.93	12.25 /61	13.90 /53	5.96 /61	1.98	0.38
AA	Principal Inv LifeTime 2050 Sel	PTESX	B+	(800) 247-4123	C+ / 5.8	-1.74	3.93	12.13 /60	13.78 /53	5.84 /60	1.87	0.50
MC	Principal Inv MidCp Blend A	PEMGX	E+	(800) 247-4123	C+ / 5.7	-1.69	2.65	10.81 /52	15.82 /63	8.83 /76	0.17	1.02
MC	Principal Inv MidCp Blend AdvPfd	PMBMX	B-	(800) 247-4123	C+ / 6.2	-1.77	2.59	10.62 /51	15.26 /60	8.78 /75	0.00	1.21
MC	Principal Inv MidCp Blend AdvSel	PMBNX	B-	(800) 247-4123	C+ / 6.1	-1.71	2.53	10.44 /50	15.04 /59	8.58 /74	0.00	1.39
MC	Principal Inv MidCp Blend B	PRMBX	E+	(800) 247-4123	C+ / 6.2	-1.69	2.58	10.53 /51	15.49 /61	8.39 /73	0.00	1.32
MC	Principal Inv MidCp Blend Inst	PCBIX	B-	(800) 247-4123	C+ / 6.6	-1.55	2.88	11.27 /55	16.06 /64	9.09 /77	0.52	0.64
MC	Principal Inv MidCp Blend J	PMBJX	B-	(800) 247-4123	C+ / 6.0	-1.73	2.55	10.46 /50	14.95 /59	8.43 /74	0.00	1.37
MC	Principal Inv MidCp Blend Pfd	PMBPX	B	(800) 247-4123	C+ / 6.4	-1.62	2.80	10.98 /53	15.58 /62	9.10 /77	0.27	0.90
MC	Principal Inv MidCp Blend Sel	PMBSX	B-	(800) 247-4123	C+ / 6.5	-1.68	2.70	10.83 /53	15.87 /63	9.19 /77	0.16	1.03
MC	Principal Inv MidCp Grw AdvPfd		C	(800) 247-4123	C / 4.8	-7.41	0.44	11.53 /57	12.70 /47	-3.50 / 4	0.00	1.22
MC	Principal Inv MidCp Grw AdvSel		C-	(800) 247-4123	C / 4.6	-7.48	0.30	11.29 /55	12.55 /46	-3.70 / 4	0.00	1.40
MC	Principal Inv MidCp Grw Inst		C	(800) 247-4123	C / 5.2	-7.41	0.75	12.13 /60	13.39 /51	-2.97 / 5	0.00	0.67
MC	Principal Inv MidCp Grw J	PMGJX	C-	(800) 247-4123	C / 4.4	-7.51	0.31	11.11 /54	12.29 /44	-3.95 / 4	0.00	1.49
MC	Principal Inv MidCp Grw Pfd		C	(800) 247-4123	C / 5.0	-7.29	0.58	11.84 /59	13.03 /49	-3.19 / 5	0.00	0.91
MC	Principal Inv MidCp Grw Sel		C	(800) 247-4123	C / 4.8	-7.60	0.29	11.59 /57	12.87 /48	-3.38 / 4	0.00	1.03
MC	Principal Inv MidCp S&P 400 AdvPfd	PMFMX	B+	(800) 247-4123	B- / 7.0	-3.38	3.85	12.09 /60	17.17 /69	8.30 /73	0.44	0.72
MC	Principal Inv MidCp S&P 400 AdvSel	PMFNX	B-	(800) 247-4123	C+ / 6.9	-3.39	3.78	11.93 /59	16.97 /68	8.09 /72	0.28	0.90
MC	Principal Inv MidCp S&P 400 Inst		B+	(800) 247-4123	B- / 7.3	-3.14	4.19	12.76 /63	17.84 /72	8.38 /73	0.98	0.15
MC	Principal Inv MidCp S&P 400 J	PMFJX	B-	(800) 247-4123	C+ / 6.8	-3.40	3.80	11.90 /59	16.81 /67	7.89 /71	0.22	0.92
MC	Principal Inv MidCp S&P 400 Pfd	PMFPX	B+	(800) 247-4123	B- / 7.2	-3.23	4.06	12.45 /62	17.55 /70	8.62 /75	0.73	0.41
MC	Principal Inv MidCp S&P 400 Sel	PMFSX	B+	(800) 247-4123	B- / 7.1	-3.31	3.99	12.36 /61	17.40 /70	8.49 /74	0.62	0.53

● Denotes fund is closed to new investors
★ Denotes fund is included in Section II

RISK			NET ASSETS		ASSET				BULL / BEAR		FUND MANAGER		MINIMUMS		LOADS	
	3 Year		NAV						Last Bull	Last Bear	Manager	Manager	Initial	Additional	Front	Back
Risk	Standard		As of	Total	Cash	Stocks	Bonds	Other	Market	Market	Quality	Tenure	Purch.	Purch.	End	End
Rating/Pts	Deviation	Beta	6/30/06	$(Mil)	%	%	%	%	Return	Return	Pct	(Years)	$	$	Load	Load
B / 8.4	8.2	0.98	12.07	8	0	99	0	1	181.1	69.2	-6.5	74	6	0	0	0.0	0.0
B / 8.4	8.2	0.98	12.00	1	0	99	0	1	181.1	68.0	-6.5	71	6	1,000	100	0.0	0.8
C+ / 6.8	5.0	0.98	12.50	12	0	99	0	1	10.2	46.2	-2.2	77	1	1,000	100	5.8	0.8
B+ / 9.8	4.9	0.98	12.37	35	0	99	0	1	10.2	44.8	-2.4	75	5	0	0	0.0	0.0
B+ / 9.8	4.9	0.98	12.34	32	0	99	0	1	10.2	43.9	-2.5	73	5	0	0	0.0	0.0
B+ / 9.8	5.0	0.98	12.47	554	0	99	0	1	10.2	47.5	-2.2	80	5	0	0	0.0	0.0
B+ / 9.8	5.0	0.98	12.40	164	0	99	0	1	10.2	44.4	-2.6	75	5	1,000	100	0.0	1.0
B+ / 9.8	5.0	0.99	12.42	61	0	99	0	1	10.2	46.3	-2.4	78	5	0	0	0.0	0.0
B+ / 9.8	5.0	0.98	12.39	19	0	99	0	1	10.2	45.7	-2.4	77	5	1,000	100	0.0	0.0
B+ / 9.4	6.0	1.20	12.71	67	0	99	0	1	5.5	55.2	-3.6	79	5	0	0	0.0	0.0
B+ / 9.4	6.0	1.20	12.67	60	0	99	0	1	5.5	54.1	-3.7	77	5	0	0	0.0	0.0
B+ / 9.4	6.0	1.20	12.79	1,005	0	99	0	1	5.5	57.8	-3.5	83	5	0	0	0.0	0.0
B+ / 9.4	6.0	1.20	12.73	295	0	99	0	1	5.5	54.5	-3.7	78	5	1,000	100	0.0	1.0
B+ / 9.4	6.0	1.20	12.75	98	0	99	0	1	5.5	56.5	-3.5	81	5	0	0	0.0	0.0
B+ / 9.4	6.0	1.20	12.73	37	0	99	0	1	5.5	55.9	-3.6	81	5	1,000	100	0.0	0.0
B+ / 9.2	6.6	1.33	12.63	55	0	99	0	1	4.8	61.7	-5.0	81	5	0	0	0.0	0.0
B+ / 9.2	6.6	1.32	12.58	47	0	99	0	1	4.8	60.7	-5.1	80	5	0	0	0.0	0.0
B+ / 9.2	6.6	1.32	12.67	809	0	99	0	1	4.8	64.8	-4.9	85	5	0	0	0.0	0.0
B+ / 9.3	6.6	1.32	12.63	244	0	99	0	1	4.8	60.6	-5.0	80	5	1,000	100	0.0	1.0
B+ / 9.3	6.6	1.32	12.66	87	0	99	0	1	4.8	63.3	-4.9	84	5	0	0	0.0	0.0
B+ / 9.2	6.7	1.35	12.89	45	0	99	0	1	4.8	65.4	-4.9	86	5	1,000	100	0.0	0.0
B+ / 9.1	7.2	1.43	12.77	27	0	99	0	1	7.1	66.1	-6.2	81	5	0	0	0.0	0.0
B+ / 9.1	7.1	1.43	12.76	18	0	99	0	1	7.1	65.3	-6.2	80	5	0	0	0.0	0.0
B+ / 9.1	7.1	1.42	12.86	393	0	99	0	1	7.1	69.0	-6.1	86	5	0	0	0.0	0.0
B+ / 9.1	7.1	1.42	12.79	88	0	99	0	1	7.1	64.2	-6.5	79	5	1,000	100	0.0	1.0
B+ / 9.1	7.1	1.43	12.83	37	0	99	0	1	7.1	67.8	-6.2	84	5	0	0	0.0	0.0
B+ / 9.1	7.1	1.43	12.78	11	0	99	0	1	7.1	66.9	-6.2	83	5	1,000	100	0.0	0.0
B / 8.9	7.7	1.52	12.39	9	0	99	0	1	7.5	72.3	-7.7	83	5	0	0	0.0	0.0
B / 8.8	7.8	1.53	12.37	9	0	99	0	1	7.5	71.4	-7.6	82	5	0	0	0.0	0.0
B / 8.9	7.8	1.53	12.46	218	0	99	0	1	7.5	75.4	-7.3	87	6	0	0	0.0	0.0
B / 8.9	7.8	1.53	12.43	9	0	99	0	1	7.5	73.9	-7.5	85	5	0	0	0.0	0.0
B / 8.9	7.8	1.53	12.42	6	0	99	0	1	7.5	73.2	-7.5	84	5	0	0	0.0	0.0
D- / 1.1	8.4	0.75	13.93	529	0	99	0	1	133.8	84.4	-3.6	74	6	1,000	100	5.8	0.8
B- / 7.7	8.3	0.74	13.88	6	0	99	0	1	133.8	82.1	-3.4	70	6	0	0	0.0	0.0
B- / 7.7	8.3	0.74	13.79	3	0	99	0	1	133.8	80.8	-3.5	68	6	0	0	0.0	0.0
D- / 1.1	8.4	0.75	13.92	67	0	99	0	1	133.8	82.4	-3.6	71	6	1,000	100	0.0	1.0
B- / 7.7	8.3	0.75	13.94	N/A	0	99	0	1	133.8	85.9	-4.2	76	6	0	0	0.0	0.0
B- / 7.7	8.3	0.74	13.66	141	0	99	0	1	133.8	80.2	-3.6	67	6	1,000	100	0.0	1.0
B- / 7.7	8.3	0.74	13.94	17	0	99	0	1	133.8	83.4	-3.3	72	6	0	0	0.0	0.0
B- / 7.7	8.4	0.75	14.07	3	0	99	0	1	133.8	84.8	-3.4	74	6	0	0	0.0	0.0
C+ / 6.7	13.3	1.17	6.87	2	3	96	0	1	233.8	83.7	-8.4	6	1	0	0	0.0	0.0
C+ / 6.7	13.2	1.16	6.80	2	3	96	0	1	233.8	82.7	-8.4	6	1	0	0	0.0	0.0
C+ / 6.7	13.3	1.16	6.75	3	3	96	0	1	233.8	87.2	-8.2	8	1	0	0	0.0	0.0
C+ / 6.7	13.3	1.17	6.40	22	3	96	0	1	233.8	81.0	-8.4	5	1	1,000	100	0.0	1.0
C+ / 6.7	13.3	1.17	6.99	1	3	96	0	1	233.8	85.8	-8.3	7	1	0	0	0.0	0.0
C+ / 6.7	13.2	1.16	6.93	N/A	3	96	0	1	233.8	84.6	-8.3	7	1	0	0	0.0	0.0
B- / 7.9	10.8	1.00	14.30	27	1	98	0	1	52.1	99.7	-9.5	45	3	1,000	100	0.0	0.0
B- / 7.9	10.8	1.00	14.26	23	1	98	0	1	52.1	98.3	-9.4	43	3	1,000	100	0.0	0.0
B- / 7.9	10.8	1.00	14.17	8	1	98	0	1	52.1	103.0	-10.0	54	3	0	0	0.0	0.0
B- / 7.9	10.8	1.00	13.94	33	1	98	0	1	52.1	97.3	-9.5	42	3	1,000	100	0.0	1.0
B- / 7.9	10.8	1.00	14.37	46	1	98	0	1	52.1	101.6	-9.4	49	3	0	0	0.0	0.0
B- / 7.9	10.8	1.00	14.33	10	1	98	0	1	52.1	100.7	-9.4	48	3	0	0	0.0	0.0

					PERFORMANCE							
	99 Pct = Best 0 Pct = Worst		Overall Weiss		Perfor- mance	Total Return % through 6/30/06					Incl. in Returns	
		Ticker	Investment		Rating/Pts				Annualized		Dividend	Expense
Fund Type	Fund Name	Symbol	Rating	Phone		3 Mo	6 Mo	1Yr / Pct	3Yr / Pct	5Yr / Pct	Yield	Ratio
MC	Principal Inv MidCp Value AdvPfd		B	(800) 247-4123	C+ / 6.5	-0.52	3.96	10.23 /48	15.79 /63	9.32 /78	0.46	1.22
MC	Principal Inv MidCp Value AdvSel		B	(800) 247-4123	C+ / 6.4	-0.59	3.79	10.01 /47	15.43 /61	8.46 /74	0.31	1.40
MC	Principal Inv MidCp Value Inst	PVUIX	A-	(800) 247-4123	B- / 7.1	-0.43	4.22	10.81 /52	17.37 /70	9.42 /78	0.92	0.65
MC	Principal Inv MidCp Value J	PMCJX	B+	(800) 247-4123	C+ / 6.3	-0.60	3.83	9.98 /47	15.50 /61	8.95 /76	0.33	1.39
MC	Principal Inv MidCp Value Pfd		B	(800) 247-4123	C+ / 6.7	-0.52	4.04	10.47 /50	16.13 /64	9.52 /79	0.72	0.91
MC	Principal Inv MidCp Value Sel		B	(800) 247-4123	C+ / 6.6	-0.52	3.99	10.34 /49	15.97 /63	9.32 /78	0.63	1.04
GL	Principal Inv Prt Intl Inst	PINIX	U	(800) 247-4123	U /	0.14	9.88	25.74 /89	--	--	0.68	1.09
GR	Principal Inv Prt LgCp Bld I A	PBLCX	E-	(800) 247-4123	C- / 3.1	-1.78	1.97	9.27 /42	11.41 /39	0.97 /20	0.33	1.08
GR	Principal Inv Prt LgCp Bld I AdvPfd		C	(800) 247-4123	C- / 4.1	-1.78	1.96	9.31 /42	11.00 /36	1.02 /20	0.41	1.02
GR	Principal Inv Prt LgCp Bld I AdvSel		C	(800) 247-4123	C- / 3.9	-1.78	1.97	9.16 /41	10.75 /33	0.65 /18	0.24	1.20
GR	Principal Inv Prt LgCp Bld I B	PBLBX	E-	(800) 247-4123	C- / 3.5	-2.01	1.50	8.54 /37	10.52 /31	0.21 /16	0.00	2.03
GR	Principal Inv Prt LgCp Bld I Inst		C	(800) 247-4123	C / 4.5	-1.67	2.20	9.97 /47	11.65 /40	1.16 /21	0.97	0.44
GR	Principal Inv Prt LgCp Bld I J	PPXJX	C	(800) 247-4123	C- / 3.7	-1.80	1.98	9.25 /42	10.78 /34	0.73 /19	0.25	1.15
GR	Principal Inv Prt LgCp Bld I Pfd		C	(800) 247-4123	C / 4.3	-1.66	2.19	9.75 /45	11.35 /38	1.32 /22	0.71	0.71
GR	Principal Inv Prt LgCp Bld I Sel		C	(800) 247-4123	C- / 4.2	-1.67	2.08	9.51 /43	11.19 /37	1.18 /21	0.59	0.83
GR	Principal Inv Prt LgCp Blend A	PLRAX	D	(800) 247-4123	D- / 1.2	-1.87	2.24	4.90 /15	8.05 /15	1.67 /25	0.18	1.40
GR	Principal Inv Prt LgCp Blend AdvPfd	PPZMX	C	(800) 247-4123	C- / 3.1	-1.79	2.26	7.32 /28	9.65 /25	2.95 /36	0.30	1.31
GR	Principal Inv Prt LgCp Blend AdvSel	PPZNX	C	(800) 247-4123	C- / 3.0	-1.90	2.17	7.08 /27	9.41 /24	2.78 /35	0.13	1.49
GR	Principal Inv Prt LgCp Blend B	PLDBX	C-	(800) 247-4123	D+ / 2.6	-1.97	1.86	11.81 /58	8.78 /20	1.78 /25	0.00	1.99
GR	Principal Inv Prt LgCp Blend Inst	PLBIX	C	(800) 247-4123	C- / 3.5	-1.69	2.54	7.88 /32	10.25 /29	3.26 /39	0.84	0.74
GR	Principal Inv Prt LgCp Blend J	PLBJX	C-	(800) 247-4123	D+ / 2.8	-1.83	2.20	7.20 /27	9.41 /24	2.64 /33	0.16	1.44
GR	Principal Inv Prt LgCp Blend Pfd	PPZPX	C	(800) 247-4123	C- / 3.3	-1.79	2.46	7.64 /30	9.98 /27	3.26 /39	0.59	1.00
GR	Principal Inv Prt LgCp Blend Sel	PPZSX	C	(800) 247-4123	C- / 3.2	-1.79	2.35	7.39 /29	9.83 /26	3.19 /39	0.47	1.12
GR	Principal Inv Prt LgCp Gr Fd AdvPfd		D-	(800) 247-4123	E- / 0.1	-6.94	-5.95	-2.71 / 0	3.40 / 2	--	0.00	1.57
GR	Principal Inv Prt LgCp Gr Fd AdvSel		D-	(800) 247-4123	E- / 0.1	-7.06	-6.06	-2.89 / 0	3.23 / 1	--	0.00	1.75
GR	Principal Inv Prt LgCp Gr Fd J	PJPLX	D-	(800) 247-4123	E- / 0.1	-7.01	-6.08	-2.90 / 0	3.18 / 1	--	0.00	1.75
GR	Principal Inv Prt LgCp Gr Fd Pfd		D-	(800) 247-4123	E- / 0.2	-6.94	-5.80	-2.43 / 1	3.78 / 2	--	0.00	1.26
GR	Principal Inv Prt LgCp Gr Fd Sel		D-	(800) 247-4123	E- / 0.2	-6.89	-5.82	-2.52 / 0	3.66 / 2	--	0.00	1.39
GR	Principal Inv Prt LgCp Gr I A	PGGAX	D-	(800) 247-4123	E+ / 0.7	-5.20	-3.92	4.21 /11	7.60 /13	-1.53 /10	0.00	1.52
GR	Principal Inv Prt LgCp Gr I AdvPfd	PPUMX	D	(800) 247-4123	D- / 1.5	-5.11	-3.82	3.70 / 9	7.84 /14	-0.82 /12	0.00	1.31
GR	Principal Inv Prt LgCp Gr I AdvSel	PPUNX	D	(800) 247-4123	D- / 1.4	-5.12	-3.80	3.53 / 9	7.67 /13	-1.29 /11	0.00	1.49
GR	Principal Inv Prt LgCp Gr I B	PBAGX	D-	(800) 247-4123	E+ / 0.7	-5.35	-4.19	7.85 /32	6.79 /10	-2.29 / 7	0.00	2.36
GR	Principal Inv Prt LgCp Gr I Inst	PLGIX	D+	(800) 247-4123	D / 1.8	-4.93	-3.42	4.46 /13	8.50 /18	-0.55 /13	0.00	0.74
GR	Principal Inv Prt LgCp Gr I J	PLGJX	D	(800) 247-4123	D- / 1.2	-5.13	-3.78	3.63 / 9	7.50 /12	-1.50 /10	0.00	1.55
GR	Principal Inv Prt LgCp Gr I Pfd	PPUPX	D	(800) 247-4123	D / 1.7	-5.09	-3.69	3.96 /10	8.22 /16	-0.79 /12	0.00	1.00
GR	Principal Inv Prt LgCp Gr I Sel	PPUSX	D	(800) 247-4123	D / 1.6	-5.14	-3.73	3.87 /10	8.08 /16	-0.96 /12	0.00	1.12
GR	Principal Inv Prt LgCp Gr II AdvPfd	PPTMX	D+	(800) 247-4123	D / 1.7	-3.82	-1.59	5.00 /15	7.85 /14	-0.35 /14	0.00	1.56
GR	Principal Inv Prt LgCp Gr II AdvSel	PPTNX	D+	(800) 247-4123	D / 1.6	-3.86	-1.72	4.77 /14	7.66 /13	-0.52 /13	0.00	1.74
GR	Principal Inv Prt LgCp Gr II Inst	PPIIX	C-	(800) 247-4123	D / 2.1	-3.59	-1.30	5.59 /18	8.47 /18	0.23 /16	0.09	0.99
GR	Principal Inv Prt LgCp Gr II J	PPLJX	D+	(800) 247-4123	D- / 1.4	-3.94	-1.76	4.74 /14	7.62 /13	-0.63 /13	0.00	1.75
GR	Principal Inv Prt LgCp Gr II Pfd	PPTPX	D+	(800) 247-4123	D / 1.9	-3.76	-1.44	5.18 /16	8.15 /16	-0.05 /15	0.00	1.25
GR	Principal Inv Prt LgCp Gr II Sel	PPTSX	D+	(800) 247-4123	D / 1.8	-3.78	-1.45	5.21 /16	8.08 /16	-0.15 /15	0.00	1.37
GR	Principal Inv Prt LgCp Val A	PPVAX	C+	(800) 247-4123	C / 4.9	0.14	5.28	17.62 /78	13.12 /49	6.50 /64	0.58	1.39
GR	Principal Inv Prt LgCp Val AdvPfd	PPSFX	B	(800) 247-4123	C / 5.3	0.14	5.27	9.78 /45	12.83 /48	6.73 /65	0.70	1.34
GR	Principal Inv Prt LgCp Val AdvSel	PPSNX	B-	(800) 247-4123	C / 5.2	0.07	5.20	9.57 /44	12.65 /47	6.07 /62	0.57	1.52
GR	Principal Inv Prt LgCp Val B	PLVBX	B-	(800) 247-4123	C / 5.4	0.00	4.90	17.99 /79	12.29 /44	5.77 /60	0.00	1.97
GR	Principal Inv Prt LgCp Val Inst	PLVIX	B	(800) 247-4123	C+ / 5.7	0.21	5.52	10.34 /49	13.51 /51	6.84 /66	1.24	0.77
GR	Principal Inv Prt LgCp Val J	PLVJX	B-	(800) 247-4123	C / 5.0	0.07	5.12	9.58 /44	12.56 /46	5.91 /61	0.57	1.50
GR	Principal Inv Prt LgCp Val Pfd	PPSRX	B	(800) 247-4123	C / 5.5	0.21	5.45	10.15 /48	13.21 /50	6.62 /65	1.00	1.03
GR	Principal Inv Prt LgCp Val Sel	PPSSX	B	(800) 247-4123	C / 5.4	0.14	5.39	9.97 /47	13.04 /49	6.43 /64	0.89	1.15
GR	Principal Inv Prt LgCp VI I Inst		U	(800) 247-4123	U /	-0.39	4.29	12.34 /61	--	--	0.76	0.80
GR	Principal Inv Prt LgCp VI II Inst		U	(800) 247-4123	U /	0.38	4.22	8.91 /39	--	--	1.07	0.85

● Denotes fund is closed to new investors
* Denotes fund is included in Section II

Risk Rating/Pts	3 Year Standard Deviation	Beta	NAV As of 6/30/06	Total $(Mil)	Cash %	Stocks %	Bonds %	Other %	Portfolio Turnover Ratio	Last Bull Market Return	Last Bear Market Return	Manager Quality Pct	Manager Tenure (Years)	Initial Purch. $	Additional Purch. $	Front End Load	Back End Load
B / 8.4	9.1	0.79	13.40	1	1	98	0	1	167.8	81.7	-5.7	68	1	0	0	0.0	0.0
B / 8.4	9.1	0.78	13.43	1	1	98	0	1	167.8	80.2	-5.7	66	1	0	0	0.0	0.0
B / 8.4	9.2	0.79	13.82	6	1	98	0	1	167.8	89.4	-6.6	81	1	0	0	0.0	0.0
B / 8.4	9.1	0.78	13.28	123	1	98	0	1	167.8	80.2	-5.9	66	1	1,000	100	0.0	1.0
B / 8.4	9.1	0.78	13.38	1	1	98	0	1	167.8	83.4	-6.1	72	1	0	0	0.0	0.0
B / 8.4	9.1	0.79	13.29	1	1	98	0	1	167.8	82.7	-6.5	70	1	0	0	0.0	0.0
U /	N/A	N/A	14.35	689	1	98	0	1	60.1	N/A	N/A	N/A	3	0	0	0.0	0.0
D- / 1.1	8.0	1.03	8.82	130	1	98	0	1	148.8	64.8	-10.5	55	N/A	1,000	100	5.8	1.0
B- / 7.8	7.9	1.02	8.84	3	1	98	0	1	148.8	62.9	-10.0	51	N/A	0	0	0.0	0.0
B- / 7.8	7.9	1.02	8.81	3	1	98	0	1	148.8	61.7	-10.3	48	N/A	0	0	0.0	0.0
D- / 1.1	8.0	1.04	8.79	18	1	98	0	1	148.8	60.6	-10.7	44	N/A	1,000	100	0.0	1.0
B- / 7.9	7.9	1.03	8.82	N/A	1	98	0	1	148.8	65.9	-10.8	58	N/A	0	0	0.0	0.0
B- / 7.8	7.9	1.03	8.74	43	1	98	0	1	148.8	61.6	-10.1	48	N/A	1,000	100	0.0	1.0
B- / 7.8	8.0	1.03	8.88	4	1	98	0	1	148.8	64.6	-10.0	54	N/A	0	0	0.0	0.0
B- / 7.8	7.9	1.03	8.85	2	1	98	0	1	148.8	63.7	-10.0	53	N/A	0	0	0.0	0.0
B / 8.2	8.6	1.06	10.48	56	1	98	0	1	51.8	49.3	-9.5	23	2	1,000	100	5.8	1.0
B / 8.6	7.7	0.99	10.40	32	1	98	0	1	51.8	56.2	-9.4	39	2	0	0	0.0	0.0
B / 8.6	7.7	0.99	10.34	31	1	98	0	1	51.8	55.1	-9.2	37	2	0	0	0.0	0.0
B / 8.4	9.3	1.09	10.43	24	1	98	0	1	51.8	51.8	-9.5	26	2	1,000	100	0.0	1.0
B / 8.7	7.7	0.99	10.48	580	1	98	0	1	51.8	58.9	-9.6	46	2	0	0	0.0	0.0
B / 8.6	7.7	0.99	10.22	91	1	98	0	1	51.8	55.0	-9.4	37	2	1,000	100	0.0	1.0
B / 8.7	7.7	0.99	10.43	43	1	98	0	1	51.8	57.6	-9.2	43	2	0	0	0.0	0.0
B / 8.7	7.7	0.99	10.45	10	1	98	0	1	51.8	57.5	-9.3	41	2	0	0	0.0	0.0
B- / 7.6	9.0	1.08	11.39	2	3	96	0	1	87.9	32.5	N/A	4	2	0	0	0.0	0.0
B- / 7.6	9.0	1.08	11.32	2	3	96	0	1	87.9	31.9	N/A	4	2	0	0	0.0	0.0
B- / 7.6	9.0	1.08	11.28	10	3	96	0	1	87.9	31.4	N/A	4	2	1,000	100	0.0	1.0
B- / 7.6	9.0	1.08	11.53	N/A	3	96	0	1	87.9	34.0	N/A	5	2	0	0	0.0	0.0
B- / 7.6	9.0	1.08	11.49	N/A	3	96	0	1	87.9	33.5	N/A	5	2	0	0	0.0	0.0
B- / 7.0	9.9	1.09	7.84	48	4	95	0	1	66.5	47.6	-11.0	19	2	1,000	100	5.8	1.0
B- / 7.9	9.8	1.07	7.80	28	4	95	0	1	66.5	48.2	-10.7	21	2	0	0	0.0	0.0
B- / 7.9	9.7	1.07	7.60	20	4	95	0	1	66.5	47.4	-10.6	20	2	0	0	0.0	0.0
C+ / 6.9	11.2	1.17	7.78	14	4	95	0	1	66.5	44.1	-11.2	12	2	1,000	100	0.0	1.0
B- / 7.9	9.8	1.08	7.91	768	4	95	0	1	66.5	51.0	-10.6	25	2	0	0	0.0	0.0
B- / 7.8	9.8	1.08	7.39	34	4	95	0	1	66.5	46.3	-10.8	19	2	1,000	100	0.0	1.0
B- / 7.9	9.7	1.07	7.83	32	4	95	0	1	66.5	50.1	-10.6	24	2	0	0	0.0	0.0
B- / 7.9	9.8	1.08	7.75	4	4	95	0	1	66.5	49.2	-10.7	22	2	0	0	0.0	0.0
B / 8.2	8.5	1.03	8.06	8	1	98	0	1	124.7	48.9	-10.0	24	6	0	0	0.0	0.0
B / 8.1	8.5	1.03	7.98	14	1	98	0	1	124.7	48.2	-10.0	22	6	0	0	0.0	0.0
B / 8.3	8.5	1.03	8.32	789	1	98	0	1	124.7	52.0	-9.9	28	6	0	0	0.0	0.0
B / 8.2	8.4	1.02	7.81	12	1	98	0	1	124.7	47.9	-10.1	23	5	1,000	100	0.0	1.0
B / 8.2	8.5	1.03	8.19	21	1	98	0	1	124.7	50.4	-9.9	26	6	0	0	0.0	0.0
B / 8.2	8.5	1.03	8.15	19	1	98	0	1	124.7	50.2	-10.1	25	6	0	0	0.0	0.0
B / 8.5	10.2	1.11	14.15	59	2	97	0	1	28.1	73.3	-9.1	65	6	1,000	100	5.8	1.0
B / 8.8	7.9	0.98	14.38	78	2	97	0	1	28.1	70.9	-8.8	73	6	0	0	0.0	0.0
B / 8.8	7.9	0.98	13.97	51	2	97	0	1	28.1	69.8	-8.9	72	6	0	0	0.0	0.0
B / 8.5	10.8	1.14	14.14	22	2	97	0	1	28.1	69.1	-9.2	54	6	1,000	100	0.0	1.0
B / 8.8	7.9	0.98	14.14	1,750	2	97	0	1	28.1	74.0	-8.7	79	6	0	0	0.0	0.0
B / 8.8	7.9	0.98	13.96	86	2	97	0	1	28.1	69.4	-8.9	71	6	1,000	100	0.0	1.0
B / 8.8	7.9	0.99	14.13	85	2	97	0	1	28.1	72.4	-8.7	76	6	0	0	0.0	0.0
B / 8.8	7.9	0.98	14.07	34	2	97	0	1	28.1	71.7	-8.8	75	6	0	0	0.0	0.0
U /	N/A	N/A	12.63	419	2	97	0	1	58.9	N/A	N/A	N/A	2	0	0	0.0	0.0
U /	N/A	N/A	10.63	204	3	96	0	1	19.8	N/A	N/A	N/A	2	0	0	0.0	0.0

					PERFORMANCE							
99 Pct = Best 0 Pct = Worst			Overall Weiss Investment Rating		Perfor-mance Rating/Pts	Total Return % through 6/30/06			Annualized		Incl. in Returns	
Fund Type	Fund Name	Ticker Symbol		Phone		3 Mo	6 Mo	1Yr / Pct	3Yr / Pct	5Yr / Pct	Dividend Yield	Expense Ratio
MC	Principal Inv Prt MdCp Gr Fd A	PPMGX	D+	(800) 247-4123	C+ / 5.8	-7.38	3.58	14.14 /69	16.01 /64	1.32 /22	0.00	1.75
MC	Principal Inv Prt MdCp Gr Fd AdvPfd	PPQMX	C+	(800) 247-4123	C+ / 6.8	-7.28	3.70	14.75 /71	16.57 /66	2.32 /30	0.00	1.57
MC	Principal Inv Prt MdCp Gr Fd AdvSel	PPQNX	C+	(800) 247-4123	C+ / 6.7	-7.27	3.58	14.49 /70	16.37 /65	1.84 /26	0.00	1.75
MC	Principal Inv Prt MdCp Gr Fd B	PPGFX	C-	(800) 247-4123	C+ / 6.1	-7.51	3.27	13.43 /66	15.29 /60	0.75 /19	0.00	2.50
MC	Principal Inv Prt MdCp Gr Fd Inst		C+	(800) 247-4123	B- / 7.1	-7.14	4.00	15.34 /73	17.25 /69	2.60 /33	0.00	1.00
MC	Principal Inv Prt MdCp Gr Fd Pfd	PPQPX	C+	(800) 247-4123	B- / 7.0	-7.24	3.79	15.05 /72	17.06 /68	2.42 /31	0.00	1.26
MC	Principal Inv Prt MdCp Gr Fd Sel	PPQSX	C+	(800) 247-4123	C+ / 6.9	-7.31	3.72	14.82 /71	16.79 /67	2.21 /29	0.00	1.41
MC	Principal Inv Prt MdCp Gr I Inst	PMIIX	U	(800) 247-4123	U /	-4.12	2.66	14.09 /68	--	--	0.00	1.00
MC	Principal Inv Prt MdCp Gr II Inst		U	(800) 247-4123	U /	-6.56	3.59	13.75 /67	--	--	0.00	1.00
MC	Principal Inv Prt MdCp VI Fd AdvPf	PPPMX	A-	(800) 247-4123	B- / 7.5	-1.64	2.95	11.54 /57	18.75 /75	10.80 /83	0.00	1.57
MC	Principal Inv Prt MdCp VI Fd AdvSel	PPPNX	B+	(800) 247-4123	B- / 7.4	-1.68	2.89	11.38 /56	18.56 /75	10.34 /82	0.00	1.75
MC	Principal Inv Prt MdCp VI Fd Inst	PMVIX	A-	(800) 247-4123	B / 7.7	-1.49	3.26	12.23 /61	19.44 /78	11.16 /84	0.27	1.03
MC	Principal Inv Prt MdCp VI Fd J	PMVJX	B+	(800) 247-4123	B- / 7.3	-1.63	2.92	11.34 /56	18.41 /74	10.16 /81	0.00	1.77
MC	Principal Inv Prt MdCp VI Fd Pfd	PPPPX	A-	(800) 247-4123	B / 7.6	-1.50	3.15	11.93 /59	19.12 /76	10.87 /83	0.04	1.26
MC	Principal Inv Prt MdCp VI Fd Sel	PPPSX	A-	(800) 247-4123	B / 7.6	-1.58	3.10	11.81 /58	19.00 /76	10.75 /83	0.00	1.38
MC	Principal Inv Prt MdCp VI I Inst	PVMIX	U	(800) 247-4123	U /	-1.41	4.63	10.98 /53	--	--	0.38	1.00
SC	Principal Inv Prt SmCp Blend AdvPfd		B-	(800) 247-4123	B- / 7.0	-5.17	4.61	9.76 /45	17.62 /71	--	0.00	1.57
SC	Principal Inv Prt SmCp Blend AdvSel		C+	(800) 247-4123	C+ / 6.9	-5.20	4.51	9.62 /44	17.41 /70	--	0.00	1.75
SC	Principal Inv Prt SmCp Blend Inst	PSCIX	B-	(800) 247-4123	B- / 7.3	-5.01	4.91	10.38 /49	18.28 /74	--	0.04	1.00
SC	Principal Inv Prt SmCp Blend Sel		B-	(800) 247-4123	B- / 7.1	-5.07	4.71	10.04 /47	17.86 /72	--	0.00	1.37
SC	Principal Inv Prt SmCp Gr I AdvPfd	PPNMX	C+	(800) 247-4123	C+ / 6.7	-9.67	4.28	14.62 /70	16.57 /66	0.15 /16	0.00	1.68
SC	Principal Inv Prt SmCp Gr I AdvSel	PPNNX	C+	(800) 247-4123	C+ / 6.6	-9.66	4.21	14.36 /69	16.39 /65	-0.02 /15	0.00	1.85
SC	Principal Inv Prt SmCp Gr I Inst	PGRTX	C+	(800) 247-4123	B- / 7.0	-9.50	4.61	15.24 /72	17.26 /69	0.73 /19	0.00	1.08
SC	Principal Inv Prt SmCp Gr I J	PSIJX	C	(800) 247-4123	C+ / 6.4	-9.70	4.12	14.21 /69	16.16 /64	-0.22 /15	0.00	2.05
SC	Principal Inv Prt SmCp Gr I Pfd	PPNPX	C+	(800) 247-4123	C+ / 6.9	-9.57	4.42	14.96 /72	16.94 /68	0.54 /18	0.00	1.36
SC	Principal Inv Prt SmCp Gr I Sel	PPNSX	C+	(800) 247-4123	C+ / 6.8	-9.57	4.47	14.86 /71	16.79 /67	0.35 /17	0.00	1.51
SC	Principal Inv Prt SmCp Gr II A	PPSMX	C-	(800) 247-4123	C / 5.5	-6.59	5.64	13.00 /64	15.30 /60	-4.86 / 3	0.00	1.95
SC	Principal Inv Prt SmCp Gr II AdvPfd	PPMMX	C+	(800) 247-4123	C+ / 6.5	-6.53	5.77	13.24 /65	15.74 /62	3.73 /43	0.00	1.57
SC	Principal Inv Prt SmCp Gr II AdvSel	PPMNX	C+	(800) 247-4123	C+ / 6.5	-6.55	5.76	13.24 /65	15.62 /62	3.37 /40	0.00	1.75
SC	Principal Inv Prt SmCp Gr II B	PPSBX	C-	(800) 247-4123	C+ / 5.8	-6.73	5.33	11.70 /58	14.48 /56	-5.59 / 2	0.00	2.70
SC	Principal Inv Prt SmCp Gr II Inst	PSIIX	C+	(800) 247-4123	C+ / 6.8	-6.34	6.18	13.99 /68	16.45 /65	4.32 /49	0.00	1.00
SC	Principal Inv Prt SmCp Gr II J	PPMIX	C+	(800) 247-4123	C+ / 6.2	-6.61	5.64	13.00 /64	15.30 /60	3.26 /39	0.00	1.99
SC	Principal Inv Prt SmCp Gr II Pfd	PPMPX	C+	(800) 247-4123	C+ / 6.7	-6.43	6.03	13.80 /68	16.19 /64	4.02 /46	0.00	1.26
SC	Principal Inv Prt SmCp Gr II Sel	PPMSX	C+	(800) 247-4123	C+ / 6.7	-6.48	5.85	13.54 /66	16.08 /64	3.83 /44	0.00	1.38
SC	Principal Inv Prt SmCp Gr III Inst		U	(800) 247-4123	U /	-11.11	-0.51	15.30 /73	--	--	0.00	1.10
SC	Principal Inv Prt SmCp VI Fd AdvPfd		B-	(800) 247-4123	C+ / 6.6	-4.54	5.25	7.07 /27	16.82 /67	11.19 /84	0.00	1.57
SC	Principal Inv Prt SmCp VI Fd AdvSel		B-	(800) 247-4123	C+ / 6.5	-4.53	5.18	6.89 /26	16.58 /66	10.97 /84	0.00	1.75
SC	Principal Inv Prt SmCp VI Fd J	PCVJX	B	(800) 247-4123	C+ / 6.3	-4.58	5.11	6.69 /24	16.35 /65	10.74 /83	0.00	1.95
SC	Principal Inv Prt SmCp VI Fd Pfd		B-	(800) 247-4123	C+ / 6.8	-4.40	5.47	7.45 /29	17.17 /69	11.56 /86	0.00	1.26
SC	Principal Inv Prt SmCp VI Fd Sel		B-	(800) 247-4123	C+ / 6.7	-4.50	5.33	7.20 /27	17.00 /68	11.38 /85	0.00	1.38
SC	Principal Inv Prt SmCp VI I AdvPfd	PPKMX	A-	(800) 247-4123	B+ / 8.3	-3.83	8.66	13.00 /64	21.39 /83	--	0.00	1.57
SC	Principal Inv Prt SmCp VI I AdvSel	PPKNX	A-	(800) 247-4123	B / 8.2	-3.85	8.58	12.81 /63	21.19 /83	--	0.00	1.75
SC	Principal Inv Prt SmCp VI I Inst	PPKIX	A-	(800) 247-4123	B+ / 8.4	-3.68	8.99	13.69 /67	22.15 /86	--	0.37	1.01
SC	Principal Inv Prt SmCp VI I Pfd	PPKPX	A-	(800) 247-4123	B+ / 8.4	-3.75	8.83	13.40 /66	21.81 /85	--	0.15	1.26
SC	Principal Inv Prt SmCp VI I Sel	PPKSX	A-	(800) 247-4123	B+ / 8.4	-3.75	8.78	13.22 /65	21.68 /84	--	0.04	1.38
SC	Principal Inv Prt SmCp VI II Inst	PPVIX	U	(800) 247-4123	U /	-4.01	9.38	18.00 /79	--	--	0.00	1.00
RE	Principal Inv Real Estate A	PRRAX	C+	(800) 247-4123	A / 9.4	-0.79	15.20	24.45 /88	28.95 /95	21.70 /97	0.81	1.42
RE	Principal Inv Real Estate AdvPfd	PRERX	C+	(800) 247-4123	A / 9.5	-0.79	15.28	24.54 /88	28.96 /95	21.79 /98	0.92	1.41
RE	Principal Inv Real Estate AdvSel	PRENX	C+	(800) 247-4123	A / 9.5	-0.84	15.12	24.34 /88	28.72 /94	21.42 /97	0.81	1.59
RE	Principal Inv Real Estate B	PRLEX	C+	(800) 247-4123	A / 9.4	-0.90	14.90	23.58 /87	28.11 /94	20.86 /97	0.41	1.95
RE	Principal Inv Real Estate Inst	PIREX	C+	(800) 247-4123	A+ / 9.6	-0.64	15.54	25.20 /89	29.67 /95	22.41 /98	1.28	0.84
RE	Principal Inv Real Estate J	PREJX	C+	(800) 247-4123	A / 9.5	-0.83	15.16	24.29 /88	28.65 /94	21.25 /97	0.79	1.56

● Denotes fund is closed to new investors
* Denotes fund is included in Section II

RISK			NET ASSETS		ASSET				BULL / BEAR		FUND MANAGER		MINIMUMS		LOADS	
	3 Year		NAV						Last Bull	Last Bear	Manager	Manager	Initial	Additional	Front	Back
Risk Rating/Pts	Standard Deviation	Beta	As of 6/30/06	Total $(Mil)	Cash %	Stocks %	Bonds %	Other %	Portfolio Turnover Ratio	Market Return	Market Return	Quality Pct	Tenure (Years)	Purch. $	Purch. $	End Load	End Load
C /4.5	15.4	1.34	9.54	30	1	98	0	1	185.7	106.2	-10.8	7	6	1,000	100	5.8	0.8
C+ /6.2	15.2	1.33	9.80	26	1	98	0	1	185.7	109.1	-10.2	9	6	0	0	0.0	0.0
C+ /6.2	15.2	1.33	9.56	13	1	98	0	1	185.7	108.1	-10.4	9	6	0	0	0.0	0.0
C /4.4	15.4	1.35	9.48	11	1	98	0	1	185.7	103.3	-11.0	5	6	1,000	100	0.0	1.0
C+ /6.2	15.1	1.32	9.62	305	1	98	0	1	185.7	113.1	-10.2	12	6	0	0	0.0	0.0
C+ /6.2	15.2	1.33	9.86	27	1	98	0	1	185.7	111.9	-10.3	11	6	0	0	0.0	0.0
C+ /6.2	15.2	1.33	9.76	18	1	98	0	1	185.7	110.4	-10.1	10	6	0	0	0.0	0.0
U /	N/A	N/A	12.34	266	0	99	0	1	84.5	N/A	N/A	N/A	3	0	0	0.0	0.0
U /	N/A	N/A	11.82	556	0	99	0	1	126.4	N/A	N/A	N/A	2	0	0	0.0	0.0
B- /7.8	10.9	0.94	15.00	28	3	96	0	1	87.9	98.5	-5.8	72	1	0	0	0.0	0.0
B- /7.8	10.8	0.94	14.62	22	3	96	0	1	87.9	97.4	-5.9	70	1	0	0	0.0	0.0
B- /7.8	10.9	0.94	15.22	465	3	96	0	1	87.9	102.2	-5.8	77	1	0	0	0.0	0.0
B- /7.8	10.8	0.94	14.47	90	3	96	0	1	87.9	96.6	-5.9	69	1	1,000	100	0.0	1.0
B- /7.8	10.8	0.94	15.07	22	3	96	0	1	87.9	100.3	-5.8	75	1	0	0	0.0	0.0
B- /7.8	10.9	0.94	14.97	16	3	96	0	1	87.9	99.8	-5.9	73	1	0	0	0.0	0.0
U /	N/A	N/A	13.33	632	2	97	0	1	59.4	N/A	N/A	N/A	N/A	0	0	0.0	0.0
C+ /6.8	14.0	0.94	16.34	3	1	98	0	1	110.2	112.9	N/A	55	1	0	0	0.0	0.0
C+ /6.8	14.0	0.94	16.23	1	1	98	0	1	110.2	111.6	N/A	53	1	0	0	0.0	0.0
C+ /6.8	14.0	0.95	16.67	240	1	98	0	1	110.2	116.6	N/A	62	1	0	0	0.0	0.0
C+ /6.8	14.0	0.94	16.46	1	1	98	0	1	110.2	114.3	N/A	58	1	0	0	0.0	0.0
C+ /5.9	16.3	1.08	9.25	2	1	98	0	1	91.5	113.7	-13.2	26	N/A	0	0	0.0	0.0
C+ /5.9	16.3	1.08	9.16	1	1	98	0	1	91.5	112.5	-13.2	25	N/A	0	0	0.0	0.0
C+ /5.9	16.4	1.09	9.53	77	1	98	0	1	91.5	117.7	-13.0	29	N/A	0	0	0.0	0.0
C+ /5.9	16.4	1.08	8.84	10	1	98	0	1	91.5	111.4	-13.4	23	6	1,000	100	0.0	1.0
C+ /5.9	16.4	1.08	9.45	6	1	98	0	1	91.5	116.0	-13.2	28	N/A	0	0	0.0	0.0
C+ /5.9	16.4	1.09	9.35	N/A	1	98	0	1	91.5	115.1	-13.1	27	N/A	0	0	0.0	0.0
C /4.9	14.7	0.97	9.36	16	3	96	0	1	53.4	99.9	-10.6	29	N/A	1,000	100	5.8	0.8
C+ /6.4	14.8	0.98	9.16	15	3	96	0	1	53.4	102.6	-10.3	31	4	0	0	0.0	0.0
C+ /6.4	14.9	0.99	8.99	13	3	96	0	1	53.4	101.3	-10.6	30	4	0	0	0.0	0.0
C /5.3	14.6	0.97	9.29	8	3	96	0	1	53.4	95.2	-10.8	25	N/A	1,000	100	0.0	1.0
C+ /6.4	14.8	0.98	9.45	525	3	96	0	1	53.4	105.9	-10.1	36	4	0	0	0.0	0.0
C+ /6.4	14.9	0.99	8.62	16	3	96	0	1	53.4	99.2	-10.4	28	N/A	1,000	100	0.0	1.0
C+ /6.4	14.8	0.98	9.32	27	3	96	0	1	53.4	104.6	-10.3	34	4	0	0	0.0	0.0
C+ /6.4	14.9	0.98	9.23	6	3	96	0	1	53.4	103.6	-10.3	34	4	0	0	0.0	0.0
U /	N/A	N/A	11.60	197	1	98	0	1	84.0	N/A	N/A	N/A	N/A	0	0	0.0	0.0
B- /7.8	10.9	0.71	16.83	9	3	96	0	1	51.3	101.2	-7.1	83	N/A	0	0	0.0	0.0
B- /7.8	11.0	0.71	16.64	3	3	96	0	1	51.3	99.7	-7.1	81	N/A	0	0	0.0	0.0
B- /7.8	10.9	0.71	16.47	11	3	96	0	1	51.3	98.5	-7.1	80	N/A	1,000	100	0.0	1.0
B- /7.8	10.9	0.71	17.15	20	3	96	0	1	51.3	103.1	-7.0	85	N/A	0	0	0.0	0.0
B- /7.8	10.9	0.71	16.99	1	3	96	0	1	51.3	102.1	-7.1	84	N/A	0	0	0.0	0.0
B- /7.1	13.1	0.89	17.82	20	4	95	0	1	43.1	132.8	N/A	90	N/A	0	0	0.0	0.0
B- /7.1	13.1	0.89	17.71	18	4	95	0	1	43.1	131.6	N/A	89	N/A	0	0	0.0	0.0
B- /7.1	13.1	0.89	18.07	315	4	95	0	1	43.1	137.3	N/A	92	4	0	0	0.0	0.0
B- /7.1	13.1	0.89	17.99	16	4	95	0	1	43.1	135.2	N/A	91	N/A	0	0	0.0	0.0
B- /7.1	13.1	0.89	17.96	4	4	95	0	1	43.1	134.5	N/A	91	N/A	0	0	0.0	0.0
U /	N/A	N/A	13.18	340	0	99	0	1	50.8	N/A	N/A	N/A	N/A	0	0	0.0	0.0
C- /3.3	17.4	1.04	24.14	104	1	98	0	1	26.7	135.9	1.8	85	6	1,000	100	5.8	0.8
C- /3.5	17.4	1.04	23.89	44	1	98	0	1	26.7	135.0	1.9	85	6	0	0	0.0	0.0
C- /3.5	17.3	1.04	23.66	27	1	98	0	1	26.7	133.8	1.8	84	6	0	0	0.0	0.0
C- /3.2	17.4	1.04	24.13	26	1	98	0	1	26.7	131.0	1.6	80	6	1,000	100	0.0	1.0
C- /3.5	17.3	1.04	24.13	602	1	98	0	1	26.7	139.5	1.9	89	6	0	0	0.0	0.0
C- /3.5	17.3	1.04	23.84	191	1	98	0	1	26.7	133.1	1.7	84	6	1,000	100	0.0	1.0

Fund Type	Fund Name	Ticker Symbol	Overall Weiss Investment Rating	Phone	PERFORMANCE Perfor- mance Rating/Pts	Total Return % through 6/30/06 3 Mo	6 Mo	1Yr / Pct	Annualized 3Yr / Pct	5Yr / Pct	Incl. in Returns Dividend Yield	Expense Ratio
RE	Principal Inv Real Estate Pfd	PREPX	C+	(800) 247-4123	A / 9.5	-0.67	15.44	24.95 /88	29.36 /95	22.01 /98	1.13	1.10
RE	Principal Inv Real Estate Sel	PRETX	C+	(800) 247-4123	A / 9.5	-0.74	15.37	24.80 /88	29.20 /95	21.84 /98	1.05	1.22
SC	Principal Inv SmCap Blend A	PLLAX	C+	(800) 247-4123	C+ / 6.8	-5.28	6.37	12.66 /63	18.55 /75	4.44 /50	0.00	1.36
SC	Principal Inv SmCap Blend AdvPfd	PSBMX	B	(800) 247-4123	B- / 7.2	-5.31	6.41	12.69 /63	17.68 /71	10.31 /82	0.00	1.33
SC	Principal Inv SmCap Blend AdvSel	PSBNX	B	(800) 247-4123	B- / 7.1	-5.34	6.26	12.50 /62	17.47 /70	10.16 /81	0.00	1.50
SC	Principal Inv SmCap Blend B	PLLBX	C+	(800) 247-4123	B- / 7.1	-5.48	5.95	11.75 /58	17.64 /71	3.63 /42	0.00	2.15
SC	Principal Inv SmCap Blend Inst	PSLIX	B	(800) 247-4123	B- / 7.5	-5.14	6.73	13.41 /66	18.40 /74	10.84 /83	0.00	0.75
SC	Principal Inv SmCap Blend J	PSBJX	B-	(800) 247-4123	B- / 7.0	-5.29	6.34	12.59 /63	17.44 /70	10.01 /80	0.00	1.46
SC	Principal Inv SmCap Blend Pfd	PSBPX	B	(800) 247-4123	B- / 7.4	-5.22	6.56	13.11 /65	18.05 /73	10.70 /83	0.00	1.01
SC	Principal Inv SmCap Blend Sel	PSBSX	B	(800) 247-4123	B- / 7.4	-5.25	7.01	13.50 /66	18.10 /73	10.56 /82	0.00	1.15
SC	Principal Inv SmCap S&P 600 AdvPfd	PSSMX	B+	(800) 247-4123	B / 7.8	-4.75	7.24	13.06 /64	19.44 /78	10.13 /81	0.16	0.72
SC	Principal Inv SmCap S&P 600 AdvSel	PSSNX	B+	(800) 247-4123	B / 7.7	-4.78	7.17	12.82 /63	19.26 /77	9.98 /80	0.00	0.90
SC	Principal Inv SmCap S&P 600 Inst	PSSIX	B+	(800) 247-4123	B / 8.0	-4.59	7.59	13.66 /67	20.13 /80	10.51 /82	0.69	0.15
SC	Principal Inv SmCap S&P 600 Pfd	PSSPX	B+	(800) 247-4123	B / 7.9	-4.66	7.44	13.45 /66	19.85 /79	10.48 /82	0.44	0.41
SC	Principal Inv SmCap S&P 600 Sel	PSSSX	B+	(800) 247-4123	B / 7.8	-4.67	7.39	13.33 /66	19.68 /78	10.34 /82	0.33	0.53
SC	Principal Inv SmCap Value A	PUSAX	C+	(800) 247-4123	B / 7.8	-1.45	9.16	16.06 /75	20.67 /82	14.50 /91	0.00	1.46
SC	Principal Inv SmCap Value AdvPfd	PSVMX	A-	(800) 247-4123	B+ / 8.3	-1.45	9.28	16.41 /76	20.70 /82	14.52 /91	0.00	1.32
SC	Principal Inv SmCap Value AdvSel	PSVNX	A-	(800) 247-4123	B+ / 8.3	-1.46	9.24	16.21 /75	20.48 /81	14.29 /91	0.00	1.50
SC	Principal Inv SmCap Value Inst	PVSIX	A	(800) 247-4123	B+ / 8.5	-1.29	9.64	17.05 /77	21.58 /84	14.92 /92	0.47	0.75
SC	Principal Inv SmCap Value Pfd	PSVPX	A-	(800) 247-4123	B+ / 8.4	-1.33	9.51	16.78 /77	21.07 /83	14.86 /92	0.25	1.01
SC	Principal Inv SmCap Value Sel	PSVSX	A-	(800) 247-4123	B+ / 8.4	-1.39	9.43	16.65 /76	20.90 /82	14.72 /91	0.15	1.14
SC	Principal Inv SmCp Gr Fd AdvPfd		C	(800) 247-4123	C+ / 6.1	-5.92	5.94	13.59 /67	14.47 /56	-0.02 /15	0.00	1.32
SC	Principal Inv SmCp Gr Fd AdvSel		C	(800) 247-4123	C+ / 5.9	-6.07	5.74	13.43 /66	14.21 /55	-0.21 /15	0.00	1.53
SC	Principal Inv SmCp Gr Fd Inst		C+	(800) 247-4123	C+ / 6.4	-5.85	6.11	14.25 /69	15.07 /59	-0.33 /14	0.00	0.76
SC	Principal Inv SmCp Gr Fd J	PSGJX	C	(800) 247-4123	C+ / 5.7	-6.04	5.77	13.41 /66	14.05 /54	-0.37 /14	0.00	1.53
SC	Principal Inv SmCp Gr Fd Pfd		C+	(800) 247-4123	C+ / 6.2	-5.91	6.07	14.00 /68	14.85 /58	0.29 /17	0.00	1.01
SC	Principal Inv SmCp Gr Fd Sel		C+	(800) 247-4123	C+ / 6.2	-6.04	5.85	13.79 /68	14.69 /57	0.19 /16	0.00	1.16
GR	Pro-Conscience Women's Equity	FEMMX	D+	(866) 811-0215	D / 2.0	-2.45	0.48	4.26 /12	8.77 /19	3.76 /43	0.39	1.50
GI	Profit Fund	PVALX	C		C- / 3.5	-3.47	0.99	4.31 /12	11.12 /36	1.96 /27	0.00	2.45
FS	ProFunds-Bank UltraSector Inv	BKPIX	C	(888) 776-3637	C+ / 5.8	1.91	4.28	9.90 /46	13.86 /53	--	0.80	1.68
FS	ProFunds-Bank UltraSector Svc	BKPSX	C-	(888) 776-3637	C / 5.2	1.68	3.78	8.80 /39	12.71 /47	--	0.15	2.68
GR	ProFunds-Basic Mat UltraSector Inv	BMPIX	C-	(888) 776-3637	A- / 9.1	-0.72	11.25	29.29 /94	23.15 /88	--	0.09	1.68
GR	ProFunds-Basic Mat UltraSector Svc	BMPSX	C-	(888) 776-3637	B+ / 8.8	-0.97	10.72	28.16 /93	21.96 /85	--	0.00	2.68
AG	ProFunds-Bear Fund Inv	BRPIX	E-	(888) 776-3637	E- / 0.0	3.06	0.40	-2.79 / 0	-8.28 / 0	-2.94 / 6	2.12	1.56
AG	ProFunds-Bear Fund Svc	BRPSX	E-	(888) 776-3637	E- / 0.0	2.85	-0.07	-3.71 / 0	-9.18 / 0	-3.92 / 4	0.00	2.56
AG	ProFunds-Biotech Ultra Sector Inv	BIPIX	E-	(888) 776-3637	D / 2.0	-13.03	-12.88	15.60 /74	11.53 /39	-3.73 / 4	0.00	1.58
AG	ProFunds-Biotech Ultra Sector Svc	BIPSX	E-	(888) 776-3637	D- / 1.4	-13.23	-13.31	14.44 /70	10.43 /30	-4.67 / 3	0.00	2.58
AG	ProFunds-Bull Fund Inv	BLPIX	C	(888) 776-3637	D+ / 2.8	-1.88	1.78	6.52 /23	9.25 /22	-0.06 /15	0.32	1.45
AG	ProFunds-Bull Fund Svc	BLPSX	C-	(888) 776-3637	D / 2.1	-2.13	1.26	5.43 /17	8.14 /16	-1.01 /12	0.00	2.45
FO	ProFunds-Europe 30 Inv	UEPIX	B+	(888) 776-3637	B / 7.7	-1.04	6.69	16.44 /76	18.42 /74	2.06 /28	0.07	1.51
FO	ProFunds-Europe 30 Svc	UEPSX	B	(888) 776-3637	B- / 7.4	-1.25	6.19	15.38 /73	17.38 /70	2.83 /35	0.00	2.51
AG	ProFunds-Financial UltraSector Inv	FNPIX	C	(888) 776-3637	C+ / 6.5	-1.88	3.19	13.59 /67	15.54 /61	3.34 /40	0.22	1.68
AG	ProFunds-Financial UltraSector Svc	FNPSX	C	(888) 776-3637	C+ / 6.0	-2.13	2.70	12.53 /62	14.44 /56	2.36 /31	0.00	2.68
AG	ProFunds-HlthCare UltraSector Inv	HCPIX	E-	(888) 776-3637	E- / 0.1	-8.44	-7.54	-4.66 / 0	2.93 / 1	-3.71 / 4	0.00	1.68
AG	ProFunds-HlthCare UltraSector Svc	HCPSX	E-	(888) 776-3637	E- / 0.0	-8.56	-7.93	-5.52 / 0	2.03 / 1	-4.58 / 3	0.00	2.68
AG	ProFunds-Internet UltraSector Inv	INPIX	E	(888) 776-3637	C+ / 6.3	-11.01	-8.11	19.85 /82	18.73 /75	-6.08 / 2	0.00	1.52
AG	ProFunds-Internet UltraSector Svc	INPSX	E	(888) 776-3637	C+ / 5.7	-11.24	-8.57	18.67 /80	17.56 /70	-6.92 / 1	0.00	2.52
GR	ProFunds-Large Cap Growth Inv	LGPIX	D-	(888) 776-3637	E / 0.5	-4.07	-1.99	2.66 / 6	4.66 / 3	--	0.00	1.55
GR	ProFunds-Large Cap Growth Svc	LGPSX	D-	(888) 776-3637	E / 0.3	-4.30	-2.42	1.63 / 3	3.66 / 2	--	0.00	2.55
GR	ProFunds-Large Cap Value Inv	LVPIX	B-	(888) 776-3637	C / 5.2	0.13	5.51	10.43 /50	12.44 /45	--	0.45	1.57
GR	ProFunds-Large Cap Value Svc	LVPSX	C+	(888) 776-3637	C / 4.5	-0.13	4.99	9.32 /42	11.34 /38	--	0.00	2.57
AG	ProFunds-Mble Telcm UltraSector Inv	WCPIX	C	(888) 776-3637	B+ / 8.9	-15.07	-3.37	-6.04 / 0	29.82 /95	-16.82 / 0	0.00	1.50

● Denotes fund is closed to new investors
* Denotes fund is included in Section II

Risk Rating/Pts	3 Year Standard Deviation	Beta	NAV As of 6/30/06	Total $(Mil)	Cash %	Stocks %	Bonds %	Other %	Portfolio Turnover Ratio	Last Bull Market Return	Last Bear Market Return	Manager Quality Pct	Manager Tenure (Years)	Initial Purch. $	Additional Purch. $	Front End Load	Back End Load
C- /3.5	17.3	1.04	23.79	81	1	98	0	1	26.7	137.5	1.9	87	6	0	0	0.0	0.0
C- /3.5	17.3	1.04	23.77	12	1	98	0	1	26.7	136.5	1.8	86	6	0	0	0.0	0.0
C+ /5.7	14.4	0.98	16.70	108	1	98	0	1	137.4	116.3	-11.8	59	3	1,000	100	5.8	0.8
C+ /6.9	13.6	0.91	16.60	2	1	98	0	1	137.4	111.0	-8.5	62	3	0	0	0.0	0.0
C+ /6.9	13.6	0.91	16.47	3	1	98	0	1	137.4	109.9	-8.4	60	3	0	0	0.0	0.0
C+ /5.7	14.4	0.98	16.56	25	1	98	0	1	137.4	111.2	-11.9	49	3	1,000	100	0.0	1.0
C+ /6.9	13.6	0.91	16.81	38	1	98	0	1	137.4	114.9	-8.3	68	3	0	0	0.0	0.0
C+ /6.9	13.6	0.91	16.10	143	1	98	0	1	137.4	109.6	-8.6	59	3	1,000	100	0.0	1.0
C+ /6.9	13.6	0.91	16.90	7	1	98	0	1	137.4	113.3	-8.4	65	3	0	0	0.0	0.0
C+ /6.9	13.6	0.91	16.80	1	1	98	0	1	137.4	113.5	-8.4	66	3	0	0	0.0	0.0
B- /7.2	13.5	0.92	18.06	31	0	99	0	1	43.2	115.4	-9.9	76	3	0	0	0.0	0.0
B- /7.2	13.5	0.92	17.94	21	0	99	0	1	43.2	114.1	-9.7	74	3	0	0	0.0	0.0
B- /7.2	13.5	0.92	17.86	163	0	99	0	1	43.2	119.2	-10.2	81	3	0	0	0.0	0.0
B- /7.2	13.5	0.92	18.19	74	0	99	0	1	43.2	117.6	-9.9	79	3	0	0	0.0	0.0
B- /7.2	13.5	0.92	18.17	11	0	99	0	1	43.2	116.7	-9.9	78	3	1,000	100	0.0	0.0
C /5.1	12.8	0.87	18.36	6	1	98	0	1	133.7	123.0	-9.0	89	1	1,000	100	5.8	1.0
B- /7.1	12.9	0.87	18.37	8	1	98	0	1	133.7	123.2	-9.0	88	6	0	0	0.0	0.0
B- /7.2	12.9	0.87	18.21	5	1	98	0	1	133.7	121.9	-9.0	87	6	0	0	0.0	0.0
B- /7.2	12.8	0.87	18.42	82	1	98	0	1	133.7	128.6	-9.4	92	N/A	0	0	0.0	0.0
B- /7.1	12.9	0.87	18.54	14	1	98	0	1	133.7	125.4	-8.8	90	6	0	0	0.0	0.0
B- /7.2	12.8	0.86	18.46	3	1	98	0	1	133.7	124.7	-9.0	89	6	0	0	0.0	0.0
C+ /6.4	14.8	0.99	8.74	N/A	3	96	0	1	181.7	111.9	-12.9	23	1	0	0	0.0	0.0
C+ /6.4	14.8	0.99	8.66	1	3	96	0	1	181.7	110.7	-12.9	21	1	0	0	0.0	0.0
C+ /6.4	14.8	0.99	8.69	6	3	96	0	1	181.7	115.6	-12.9	26	1	0	0	0.0	0.0
C+ /6.4	14.8	0.99	8.25	35	3	96	0	1	181.7	109.9	-13.1	20	1	1,000	100	0.0	1.0
C+ /6.4	14.8	0.99	8.91	N/A	3	96	0	1	181.7	114.3	-12.9	25	1	0	0	0.0	0.0
C+ /6.4	14.8	0.99	8.87	N/A	3	96	0	1	181.7	113.5	-12.9	24	1	0	0	0.0	0.0
B /8.0	7.5	0.91	20.72	34	3	96	0	1	22.1	52.3	-9.5	38	11	1,000	100	0.0	2.0
B /8.6	8.1	0.97	19.46	970	N/A	100	0	N/A	65.0	66.9	-7.8	59	10	2,500	50	0.0	0.0
C+ /5.7	14.4	1.37	39.98	2	27	72	0	1	1,038.0	93.7	-6.4	20	5	15,000	100	0.0	0.0
C /5.5	14.4	1.37	40.64	2	27	72	0	1	1,038.0	87.7	-6.5	14	5	15,000	100	0.0	0.0
D /1.6	24.6	2.42	42.92	6	24	75	0	1	677.0	138.1	-19.5	37	N/A	15,000	100	0.0	0.0
D- /1.5	24.6	2.42	41.83	1	24	75	0	1	677.0	130.9	-19.5	29	N/A	5,000	100	0.0	0.0
C- /3.3	7.8	-1.00	29.96	64	100	0	0	0	1,299.0	-37.0	9.5	29	9	15,000	100	0.0	0.0
C- /3.2	7.8	-1.00	28.85	8	100	0	0	0	1,299.0	-39.0	9.3	22	9	5,000	100	0.0	0.0
D+ /2.4	23.7	1.43	51.27	29	28	71	0	1	724.0	108.0	-2.4	24	N/A	15,000	100	0.0	0.0
D+ /2.3	23.7	1.43	48.41	3	28	71	0	1	724.0	101.7	-2.6	17	N/A	5,000	100	0.0	0.0
B /8.7	7.7	1.01	57.33	54	5	94	0	1	358.0	55.6	-10.1	35	9	15,000	100	0.0	0.0
B /8.6	7.7	1.01	53.19	8	5	94	0	1	358.0	50.7	-10.4	27	9	5,000	100	0.0	0.0
B- /7.0	11.5	1.02	17.07	7	0	99	0	1	800.0	103.8	-11.0	12	7	15,000	100	0.0	0.0
B- /7.0	11.4	1.02	17.33	2	0	99	0	1	800.0	97.8	-3.6	9	7	5,000	100	0.0	0.0
C+ /5.7	13.9	1.36	28.13	5	24	75	0	1	652.0	105.8	-14.5	66	6	15,000	100	0.0	0.0
C+ /5.6	14.0	1.36	26.67	1	24	75	0	1	652.0	99.6	-14.6	54	6	5,000	100	0.0	0.0
C- /4.2	13.2	0.92	14.11	9	22	77	0	1	636.0	37.8	-9.7	6	6	15,000	100	0.0	0.0
C- /4.1	13.1	0.91	13.35	2	22	77	0	1	636.0	33.9	-9.8	4	6	5,000	100	0.0	0.0
E- /0.0	33.6	3.12	80.66	29	26	74	0	0	568.0	215.5	-15.0	1	6	15,000	100	0.0	0.0
E- /0.0	33.6	3.12	75.21	8	26	74	0	0	568.0	205.7	-15.2	1	6	5,000	100	0.0	0.0
B- /7.8	7.8	0.98	37.48	2	2	97	0	1	1,287.0	35.5	-9.5	10	4	15,000	100	0.0	0.0
B- /7.6	7.8	0.98	36.24	8	2	97	0	1	1,287.0	31.6	-9.8	7	4	5,000	100	0.0	0.0
B /8.8	8.0	1.01	48.03	17	0	100	0	0	644.0	70.7	-10.8	68	4	15,000	100	0.0	0.0
B /8.8	8.0	1.01	46.69	7	0	100	0	0	644.0	65.6	-11.1	57	4	5,000	100	0.0	0.0
C- /3.0	23.1	2.05	18.94	21	24	75	0	1	520.0	244.0	-26.9	97	6	15,000	100	0.0	0.0

			Overall Weiss Investment Rating		PERFORMANCE						Incl. in Returns	
					Perfor- mance Rating/Pts	Total Return % through 6/30/06			Annualized		Dividend	Expense
Fund Type	Fund Name	Ticker Symbol		Phone		3 Mo	6 Mo	1Yr / Pct	3Yr / Pct	5Yr / Pct	Yield	Ratio
AG	ProFunds-Mble Telcm UltraSector	WCPSX	C	(888) 776-3637	B+ / 8.7	-15.24	-3.81	-6.97 / 0	28.52 /94	-17.63 / 0	0.00	2.50
GR	ProFunds-Mid Cap Growth Inv	MGPIX	C	(888) 776-3637	C / 4.7	-4.92	0.64	9.30 /42	12.71 /47	--	0.00	1.59
GR	ProFunds-Mid Cap Growth Svc	MGPSX	C-	(888) 776-3637	C- / 3.9	-5.17	0.11	8.19 /34	11.53 /39	--	0.00	2.59
MC	ProFunds-Mid Cap Inv	MDPIX	B-	(888) 776-3637	C+ / 6.6	-3.81	3.35	11.02 /54	16.20 /64	--	0.12	1.47
MC	ProFunds-Mid Cap Svc	MDPSX	C+	(888) 776-3637	C+ / 6.0	-4.06	2.84	9.87 /46	15.03 /59	--	0.00	2.47
MC	ProFunds-Mid Cap Value Inv	MLPIX	B+	(888) 776-3637	B- / 7.5	-2.47	5.83	12.28 /61	18.58 /75	--	0.11	1.50
MC	ProFunds-Mid Cap Value Svc	MLPSX	B	(888) 776-3637	B- / 7.1	-2.68	5.34	11.23 /55	17.41 /70	--	0.00	2.50
AG	ProFunds-Oil & Gas UltraSector Inv	ENPIX	C	(888) 776-3637	A+ / 9.9	4.59	16.92	32.82 /96	44.73 /99	16.43 /93	0.00	1.43
AG	ProFunds-Oil & Gas UltraSector Svc	ENPSX	C	(888) 776-3637	A+ / 9.9	4.37	16.35	31.49 /95	43.29 /99	15.34 /92	0.00	2.43
AG	ProFunds-OTC Inv	OTPIX	E+	(888) 776-3637	D / 1.7	-7.78	-4.70	4.66 /14	8.42 /17	-4.13 / 3	0.30	1.40
AG	ProFunds-OTC Svc	OTPSX	E	(888) 776-3637	D- / 1.1	-8.03	-5.20	3.56 / 9	7.32 /12	-5.11 / 2	0.00	2.40
AG	ProFunds-Pharm UltraSector Inv	PHPIX	E-	(888) 776-3637	E- / 0.0	-2.46	0.89	-6.33 / 0	-8.43 / 0	-11.09 / 0	0.56	1.68
AG	ProFunds-Pharm UltraSector Svc	PHPSX	E-	(888) 776-3637	E- / 0.0	-2.80	0.35	-7.37 / 0	-9.33 / 0	-11.86 / 0	0.00	2.68
PM	ProFunds-Precious Metals Ultra Inv	PMPIX	D+	(888) 776-3637	A+ / 9.8	1.24	12.39	74.31 /99	26.82 /93	--	0.00	1.44
PM	ProFunds-Precious Metals Ultra Svc	PMPSX	D+	(888) 776-3637	A+ / 9.8	0.99	11.87	72.67 /99	26.46 /93	--	0.00	2.44
RE	ProFunds-Real Est UltraSector Inv	REPIX	D+	(888) 776-3637	A+ / 9.7	-3.52	17.42	20.10 /82	32.96 /97	19.56 /96	2.12	1.73
RE	ProFunds-Real Est UltraSector Svc	REPSX	D	(888) 776-3637	A+ / 9.6	-3.73	16.90	18.93 /80	31.61 /96	18.35 /95	1.66	2.73
OT	ProFunds-Rising Rates Opport Inv	RRPIX	D-	(888) 776-3637	D+ / 2.3	6.21	17.10	23.78 /87	0.51 / 0	--	1.70	1.43
OT	ProFunds-Rising Rates Opport Svc	RRPSX	E+	(888) 776-3637	E+ / 0.6	5.91	16.53	22.56 /85	-0.48 / 0	--	0.64	2.43
TC	ProFunds-Semicond UltraSector Inv	SMPIX	E-	(888) 776-3637	E- / 0.0	-15.40	-17.07	-9.21 / 0	1.47 / 0	-17.94 / 0	0.00	1.58
TC	ProFunds-Semicond UltraSector Svc	SMPSX	E-	(888) 776-3637	E- / 0.0	-15.60	-17.49	-10.13 / 0	0.48 / 0	-18.77 / 0	0.00	2.58
OT	ProFunds-Short OTC Inv	SOPIX	E	(888) 776-3637	E- / 0.0	9.50	6.74	-0.91 / 1	-8.65 / 0	--	1.28	1.52
OT	ProFunds-Short OTC Svc	SOPSX	E	(888) 776-3637	E- / 0.0	9.22	6.35	-1.82 / 1	-9.54 / 0	--	0.00	2.52
SC	ProFunds-Short Small Cap Inv	SHPIX	E	(888) 776-3637	E- / 0.0	6.22	-5.83	-9.67 / 0	-15.67 / 0	--	3.71	1.51
SC	ProFunds-Short Small Cap Svc	SHPSX	E	(888) 776-3637	E- / 0.0	6.05	-6.34	-10.55 / 0	-16.45 / 0	--	0.00	2.51
SC	ProFunds-Small Cap Growth Inv	SGPIX	B-	(888) 776-3637	B- / 7.1	-5.49	4.72	11.32 /55	17.66 /71	--	0.00	1.55
SC	ProFunds-Small Cap Growth Svc	SGPSX	C+	(888) 776-3637	C+ / 6.6	-5.74	4.19	10.18 /48	16.50 /66	--	0.00	2.55
SC	ProFunds-Small Cap Inv	SLPIX	C+	(888) 776-3637	B- / 7.1	-4.83	7.61	13.12 /65	17.20 /69	--	0.00	1.37
SC	ProFunds-Small Cap Svc	SLPSX	C+	(888) 776-3637	C+ / 6.6	-5.09	7.06	11.99 /59	16.00 /63	--	0.00	2.37
SC	ProFunds-Small Cap Value Inv	SVPIX	B	(888) 776-3637	B- / 7.5	-4.49	8.47	12.04 /60	18.53 /74	--	0.00	1.59
SC	ProFunds-Small Cap Value Svc	SVPSX	B-	(888) 776-3637	B- / 7.1	-4.73	7.91	10.94 /53	17.37 /70	--	0.00	2.59
AG	ProFunds-Tech UltraSector Inv	TEPIX	E-	(888) 776-3637	E / 0.4	-14.60	-9.33	0.69 / 2	6.34 / 8	-13.75 / 0	0.30	1.68
AG	ProFunds-Tech UltraSector Svc	TEPSX	E-	(888) 776-3637	E- / 0.2	-14.84	-9.79	-0.39 / 1	5.29 / 5	-14.46 / 0	0.00	2.68
AG	ProFunds-Telecom UltraSector Inv	TCPIX	D-	(888) 776-3637	C / 4.3	-2.61	18.30	14.13 /69	9.21 /22	-13.29 / 0	2.76	1.68
AG	ProFunds-Telecom UltraSector Svc	TCPSX	E+	(888) 776-3637	C- / 3.5	-2.88	17.72	12.77 /63	8.12 /16	-14.05 / 0	2.31	2.68
AG	ProFunds-Ultra Bear Fund Inv	URPIX	E-	(888) 776-3637	E- / 0.0	5.02	-1.36	-8.74 / 0	-17.43 / 0	-8.43 / 0	2.26	1.41
AG	ProFunds-Ultra Bear Fund Svc	URPSX	E-	(888) 776-3637	E- / 0.0	4.72	-1.82	-9.63 / 0	-18.18 / 0	-9.26 / 0	0.83	2.41
AG	ProFunds-Ultra Bull Fund Inv	ULPIX	C	(888) 776-3637	C+ / 6.5	-5.11	1.15	9.02 /40	16.56 /66	-3.11 / 5	0.25	1.44
AG	ProFunds-Ultra Bull Fund Svc	ULPSX	C-	(888) 776-3637	C+ / 5.9	-5.36	0.65	7.94 /32	15.48 /61	-3.94 / 4	0.00	2.44
GR	ProFunds-Ultra Dow 30 Inv	UDPIX	D+	(888) 776-3637	C+ / 5.7	-0.59	5.97	12.01 /60	13.28 /50	--	0.87	1.49
GR	ProFunds-Ultra Dow 30 Svc	UDPSX	D	(888) 776-3637	C / 5.1	-0.85	5.45	10.96 /53	12.24 /44	--	0.16	2.49
FO	ProFunds-Ultra Japan Inv	UJPIX	D+	(888) 776-3637	A+ / 9.9	-17.57	-7.98	77.87 /99	37.70 /99	0.91 /20	0.00	1.55
FO	ProFunds-Ultra Japan Svc	UJPSX	D+	(888) 776-3637	A+ / 9.8	-17.77	-8.46	76.05 /99	36.35 /98	-0.07 /15	0.00	2.55
AG	ProFunds-Ultra Mid Cap Inv	UMPIX	C	(888) 776-3637	A / 9.5	-8.56	4.24	17.88 /79	30.82 /96	8.44 /74	0.01	1.49
AG	ProFunds-Ultra Mid Cap Svc	UMPSX	C	(888) 776-3637	A / 9.4	-8.76	3.73	16.69 /76	29.53 /95	7.45 /69	0.00	2.49
AG	ProFunds-Ultra OTC Fund Inv	UOPIX	E-	(888) 776-3637	D+ / 2.8	-16.28	-11.82	3.81 /10	12.32 /45	-16.81 / 0	0.00	1.38
AG	ProFunds-Ultra OTC Fund Svc	UOPSX	E-	(888) 776-3637	D+ / 2.3	-16.48	-12.28	2.77 / 7	11.68 /40	-17.40 / 0	0.00	2.38
TC	ProFunds-Ultra Short OTC Fund Inv	USPIX	E-	(888) 776-3637	E- / 0.0	18.01	10.91	-6.47 / 0	-19.71 / 0	-13.70 / 0	1.99	1.39
TC	ProFunds-Ultra Short OTC Fund Svc	USPSX	E-	(888) 776-3637	E- / 0.0	17.70	10.37	-7.38 / 0	-20.49 / 0	-14.48 / 0	0.90	2.39
SC	ProFunds-Ultra Short Small-Cap Inv	UCPIX	U	(888) 776-3637	U /	11.08	-13.35	-22.40 / 0	--	--	2.67	1.43
SC	ProFunds-Ultra Small Cap Inv	UAPIX	D+	(888) 776-3637	A / 9.5	-11.91	11.95	19.84 /82	30.72 /96	6.82 /66	0.42	1.41
SC	ProFunds-Ultra Small Cap Svc	UAPSX	D+	(888) 776-3637	A / 9.4	-12.20	11.35	18.60 /80	29.43 /95	5.73 /59	0.00	2.41

● Denotes fund is closed to new investors
★ Denotes fund is included in Section II

RISK			NET ASSETS		ASSET				BULL / BEAR		FUND MANAGER		MINIMUMS		LOADS	
	3 Year		NAV						Portfolio	Last Bull	Last Bear	Manager	Manager	Initial	Additional	Front	Back
Risk Rating/Pts	Standard Deviation	Beta	As of 6/30/06	Total $(Mil)	Cash %	Stocks %	Bonds %	Other %	Turnover Ratio	Market Return	Market Return	Quality Pct	Tenure (Years)	Purch. $	Purch. $	End Load	End Load
D+ / 2.9	23.1	2.05	17.69	3	24	75	0	1	520.0	233.1	-27.4	95	6	5,000	100	0.0	0.0
C+ / 6.9	10.8	1.19	37.71	8	0	99	0	1	918.0	76.8	-10.2	53	5	15,000	100	0.0	0.0
C+ / 6.8	10.8	1.19	35.93	9	0	99	0	1	918.0	71.2	-10.5	40	5	5,000	100	0.0	0.0
B- / 7.2	10.8	1.00	42.62	90	17	82	0	1	500.0	94.7	-10.0	36	5	15,000	100	0.0	0.0
B- / 7.2	10.8	1.00	40.91	5	17	82	0	1	500.0	88.4	-10.2	28	5	5,000	100	0.0	0.0
B- / 7.3	11.2	1.02	43.37	23	1	98	0	1	520.0	103.1	-10.1	58	5	15,000	100	0.0	0.0
B- / 7.2	11.2	1.02	41.43	6	1	98	0	1	520.0	97.1	-10.4	44	5	5,000	100	0.0	0.0
D / 2.0	30.0	1.66	38.28	129	25	74	0	1	352.0	244.8	-1.5	99	6	15,000	100	0.0	0.0
D / 2.0	30.0	1.66	36.08	14	25	74	0	1	352.0	234.1	-1.7	99	6	5,000	100	0.0	0.0
C / 5.2	14.9	1.68	59.75	44	3	96	0	1	671.0	63.4	-9.9	4	6	15,000	100	0.0	0.0
C / 5.1	14.9	1.68	56.48	11	3	96	0	1	671.0	58.2	-10.2	2	6	5,000	100	0.0	0.0
D- / 1.1	18.0	0.76	9.11	9	25	74	0	1	576.0	-7.9	-12.9	0	6	15,000	100	0.0	0.0
D- / 1.0	18.0	0.77	8.67	1	25	74	0	1	576.0	-10.5	-13.2	0	6	5,000	100	0.0	0.0
E- / 0.0	50.5	2.27	46.61	92	100	0	0	0	N/A	166.5	18.6	0	N/A	15,000	100	0.0	0.0
E- / 0.0	50.6	2.27	44.86	17	100	0	0	0	N/A	158.5	18.3	0	N/A	5,000	100	0.0	0.0
E- / 0.0	25.7	1.53	44.96	16	23	76	0	1	1,411.0	179.7	-4.5	23	6	15,000	100	0.0	0.0
E- / 0.0	25.7	1.53	45.66	2	23	76	0	1	1,411.0	170.8	-4.8	16	6	5,000	100	0.0	0.0
C+ / 6.0	15.8	0.38	22.39	479	96	0	3	1	N/A	-4.2	-8.7	14	4	15,000	100	0.0	0.0
C+ / 6.0	15.7	0.38	21.85	47	96	0	3	1	N/A	-7.2	-8.9	10	4	5,000	100	0.0	0.0
E- / 0.0	43.5	3.89	17.25	24	24	75	0	1	681.0	68.1	-29.0	0	6	15,000	100	0.0	0.0
E- / 0.0	43.5	3.89	16.23	2	24	75	0	1	681.0	62.9	-29.1	0	6	5,000	100	0.0	0.0
C+ / 6.4	15.1	-1.69	19.95	20	100	0	0	0	N/A	-42.5	8.2	83	4	15,000	100	0.0	0.0
C+ / 6.4	15.2	-1.69	19.43	4	100	0	0	0	N/A	-44.3	7.9	75	4	5,000	100	0.0	0.0
C+ / 6.4	14.7	-1.00	17.94	59	99	0	0	1	N/A	-55.4	11.4	16	4	15,000	100	0.0	0.0
C+ / 6.3	14.7	-1.00	17.89	2	99	0	0	1	N/A	-56.6	11.2	12	4	5,000	100	0.0	0.0
C+ / 6.6	13.7	0.91	40.81	35	0	99	0	1	628.0	103.5	-9.7	61	N/A	15,000	100	0.0	0.0
C+ / 6.5	13.7	0.92	39.06	11	0	99	0	1	628.0	97.4	-10.0	48	N/A	5,000	100	0.0	0.0
C+ / 5.9	14.6	1.00	41.98	83	27	72	0	1	475.0	107.1	-12.1	39	N/A	15,000	100	0.0	0.0
C+ / 5.8	14.6	1.00	39.88	22	27	72	0	1	475.0	100.4	-12.3	30	N/A	5,000	100	0.0	0.0
C+ / 6.6	13.7	0.92	44.84	10	1	98	0	1	761.0	110.2	-11.5	68	N/A	15,000	100	0.0	0.0
C+ / 6.5	13.7	0.92	42.71	3	1	98	0	1	761.0	103.6	-11.8	57	N/A	5,000	100	0.0	0.0
E / 0.4	24.4	2.60	24.10	19	24	75	0	1	634.0	75.3	-21.3	0	N/A	15,000	100	0.0	0.0
E / 0.3	24.4	2.60	23.13	1	24	75	0	1	634.0	70.0	-20.9	0	N/A	5,000	100	0.0	0.0
C- / 3.6	18.4	1.31	21.27	2	24	74	0	2	1,212.0	66.3	-31.1	17	N/A	15,000	100	0.0	0.0
C- / 3.4	18.4	1.30	20.26	N/A	24	74	0	2	1,212.0	61.2	-31.2	12	N/A	5,000	100	0.0	0.0
E+ / 0.9	15.7	-2.00	17.35	148	8	91	0	1	1,300.0	-62.5	19.1	15	N/A	15,000	100	0.0	0.0
E+ / 0.9	15.6	-1.99	17.29	11	8	91	0	1	1,300.0	-63.6	18.9	11	N/A	5,000	100	0.0	0.0
C / 5.4	15.7	2.02	57.91	140	8	91	0	1	648.0	125.4	-20.2	20	N/A	15,000	100	0.0	0.0
C / 5.3	15.7	2.02	53.84	17	8	91	0	1	648.0	118.7	-20.1	15	N/A	5,000	100	0.0	0.0
C- / 3.9	16.8	2.01	33.56	40	0	100	0	0	458.0	94.3	-22.6	8	N/A	15,000	100	0.0	0.0
C- / 3.9	16.8	2.01	32.69	5	0	100	0	0	458.0	88.6	-22.7	5	N/A	5,000	100	0.0	0.0
E- / 0.2	31.7	1.85	59.48	123	87	12	0	1	299.9	253.7	-16.5	8	N/A	15,000	100	0.0	0.0
E- / 0.2	31.7	1.85	56.81	15	87	12	0	1	299.9	243.1	-16.8	5	N/A	5,000	100	0.0	0.0
D+ / 2.7	22.1	2.53	45.51	174	12	87	0	1	402.0	240.5	-20.0	87	N/A	15,000	100	0.0	0.0
D+ / 2.6	22.2	2.54	42.79	9	12	87	0	1	402.0	229.9	-20.1	81	N/A	5,000	100	0.0	0.0
E- / 0.0	30.6	3.37	21.55	354	10	89	0	1	157.0	129.0	-21.1	0	N/A	15,000	100	0.0	0.0
E- / 0.0	30.7	3.38	20.07	22	10	89	0	1	157.0	124.6	-21.0	0	N/A	5,000	100	0.0	0.0
E- / 0.0	30.6	-3.35	16.97	182	100	0	0	0	1,300.0	-70.9	14.0	89	N/A	15,000	100	0.0	0.0
E- / 0.0	30.6	-3.35	17.56	8	100	0	0	0	1,300.0	-71.8	13.8	82	N/A	15,000	100	0.0	0.0
U /	N/A	N/A	16.74	175	100	0	0	0	N/A	N/A	N/A	N/A	2	15,000	100	0.0	0.0
E+ / 0.6	29.9	2.01	28.39	141	29	70	0	1	481.0	279.9	-22.0	12	6	15,000	100	0.0	0.0
E+ / 0.6	29.9	2.01	26.78	8	29	70	0	1	481.0	267.8	-22.2	9	6	5,000	100	0.0	0.0

Fund Type	Fund Name	Ticker Symbol	Overall Weiss Investment Rating	Phone	PERFORMANCE							
	99 Pct = Best / 0 Pct = Worst				Perfor-mance Rating/Pts	Total Return % through 6/30/06			Annualized		Incl. in Returns	
						3 Mo	6 Mo	1Yr / Pct	3Yr / Pct	5Yr / Pct	Dividend Yield	Expense Ratio
UT	ProFunds-Utilities UltraSector Inv	UTPIX	B-	(888) 776-3637	B / 8.1	6.72	4.68	2.92 / 7	21.15 /83	-1.09 /12	0.00	1.48
UT	ProFunds-Utilities UltraSector Svc	UTPSX	C+	(888) 776-3637	B / 7.6	6.38	4.09	1.80 / 4	19.84 /79	-2.03 / 8	0.00	2.48
GR	Progressive Capital Accumulation	PCATX	D-		E / 0.5	-2.85	0.28	3.26 / 8	4.18 / 3	-1.46 /10	0.00	2.25
MC	Provident Inv Counsel Flexible Gr I	PFLEX	E+	(800) 618-7643	D+ / 2.5	-6.67	-5.72	4.08 /11	10.51 /31	-0.88 /12	0.00	0.95
SC	Provident Inv Counsel Sm Cap Gr I	PISCX	D	(800) 618-7643	C+ / 5.9	-5.27	8.48	12.33 /61	14.36 /56	1.99 /27	0.00	1.00
SC	Provident Inv Counsel Sm Co Gr A	PINSX	D-	(800) 618-7643	C / 4.8	-5.37	8.27	11.82 /58	13.82 /53	1.46 /23	0.00	1.40
FO	Pru Target-Intl Equity	TAIEX	A	(800) 778-5970	B+ / 8.7	0.17	11.42	29.16 /94	20.47 /81	8.15 /72	1.26	0.99
GR	Pru Target-Large Cap Gr Portf	TALGX	E+	(800) 778-5970	D+ / 2.6	-4.10	-0.03	10.17 /48	9.73 /25	-1.25 /11	0.17	0.76
GI	Pru Target-Large Cap Val Portf	TALVX	C+	(800) 778-5970	B- / 7.0	0.56	5.29	9.30 /42	17.02 /68	8.71 /75	1.40	0.74
SC	Pru Target-Small Cap Gr Portf	TASGX	D+	(800) 778-5970	C / 5.1	-7.18	3.19	10.65 /51	13.17 /50	-1.02 /12	0.00	0.91
SC	Pru Target-Small Cap Val Portf	TASVX	C+	(800) 778-5970	B+ / 8.8	-1.82	8.16	12.96 /64	23.79 /89	15.98 /93	0.69	0.79
GR	Prudent Bear C	PBRCX	D	(800) 711-1848	E- / 0.2	5.33	9.56	13.98 /68	-0.92 / 0	8.33 /73	0.77	3.47
GR	Prudent Bear Fd	BEARX	E-	(800) 711-1848	E / 0.3	5.51	10.00	14.80 /71	-0.23 / 0	9.16 /77	0.98	2.72
AA	Purisima Total Return Fund	PURIX	C+	(800) 841-0199	C+ / 6.7	-1.70	6.96	19.25 /81	14.99 /59	6.60 /65	1.32	1.47
BA	Putnam Asset Alloc-Balanced A	PABAX	C	(800) 354-2228	D+ / 2.6	-0.66	3.30	8.33 /35	9.96 /27	4.37 /49	1.82	1.12
BA	Putnam Asset Alloc-Balanced B	PABBX	C	(800) 354-2228	D / 2.1	-0.86	2.91	7.47 /29	9.15 /22	3.59 /42	1.19	1.87
BA	Putnam Asset Alloc-Balanced C	AABCX	C	(800) 354-2228	D+ / 2.8	-0.86	2.88	7.38 /29	9.10 /21	3.56 /42	1.24	2.00
BA	Putnam Asset Alloc-Balanced M	PABMX	C	(800) 354-2228	D+ / 2.6	-0.79	3.04	7.81 /31	9.43 /24	3.84 /44	1.39	1.75
BA	Putnam Asset Alloc-Balanced R	PAARX	C+	(800) 354-2228	C- / 3.3	-0.71	3.19	8.03 /33	9.59 /25	4.06 /46	1.72	1.50
BA	Putnam Asset Alloc-Balanced Y	PABYX	C+	(800) 354-2228	C- / 3.7	-0.51	3.51	8.59 /37	10.26 /29	4.64 /51	2.17	1.00
AA	Putnam Asset Alloc-Conserv A	PACAX	C-	(800) 354-2228	E+ / 0.6	-0.53	1.51	4.01 /11	6.08 / 7	4.75 /52	3.22	1.20
AA	Putnam Asset Alloc-Conserv B	PACBX	C-	(800) 354-2228	E / 0.4	-0.73	1.03	3.15 / 8	5.18 / 4	3.84 /44	2.68	1.95
AA	Putnam Asset Alloc-Conserv C	PACCX	C-	(800) 354-2228	E+ / 0.7	-0.72	1.04	3.19 / 8	5.23 / 4	3.89 /45	2.71	2.00
AA	Putnam Asset Alloc-Conserv M	PACMX	C-	(800) 354-2228	E+ / 0.6	-0.56	1.26	3.51 / 9	5.51 / 5	4.13 /47	2.82	1.75
AA	Putnam Asset Alloc-Conserv R	PUTRX	C-	(800) 354-2228	D- / 1.2	-0.37	1.48	4.18 /11	6.12 / 7	4.69 /52	3.13	1.50
AA	Putnam Asset Alloc-Conserv Y	PACYX	C-	(800) 354-2228	D- / 1.3	-0.47	1.53	4.29 /12	6.33 / 8	4.95 /54	3.67	1.00
AA	Putnam Asset Alloc-Growth A	PAEAX	B-	(800) 354-2228	C / 5.5	-1.01	4.76	13.23 /65	14.45 /56	6.42 /64	0.74	1.25
AA	Putnam Asset Alloc-Growth B	PAEBX	C+	(800) 354-2228	C / 5.0	-1.26	4.33	12.31 /61	13.56 /52	5.61 /59	0.10	2.00
AA	Putnam Asset Alloc-Growth C	PAECX	B-	(800) 354-2228	C+ / 5.6	-1.28	4.31	12.31 /61	13.60 /52	5.61 /59	0.19	2.00
AA	Putnam Asset Alloc-Growth M	PAGMX	C+	(800) 354-2228	C / 5.4	-1.18	4.49	12.63 /63	13.87 /53	5.89 /60	0.32	1.75
AA	Putnam Asset Alloc-Growth R	PASRX	B	(800) 354-2228	C+ / 6.0	-1.10	4.64	12.98 /64	14.12 /55	6.15 /62	0.70	1.50
AA	Putnam Asset Alloc-Growth Y	PAGYX	B+	(800) 354-2228	C+ / 6.3	-1.00	4.89	13.45 /66	14.71 /57	6.68 /65	0.97	1.00
GR	Putnam Capital Appreciation A	PCAPX	C-	(800) 354-2228	C- / 4.1	-3.15	2.39	8.99 /40	12.78 /47	2.66 /33	0.29	1.28
GR	Putnam Capital Appreciation B	PCABX	C-	(800) 354-2228	C- / 3.5	-3.34	2.00	8.21 /34	11.93 /42	1.90 /26	0.00	2.16
GR	Putnam Capital Appreciation C		C	(800) 354-2228	C / 4.3	-3.32	2.01	8.20 /34	11.91 /42	1.89 /26	0.00	2.16
GR	Putnam Capital Appreciation M	PCAMX	C-	(800) 354-2228	C- / 4.1	-3.28	2.17	8.51 /37	12.22 /44	2.16 /29	0.00	1.91
GR	Putnam Capital Appreciation R	PCPRX	C	(800) 354-2228	C / 4.8	-3.21	2.30	8.75 /38	12.53 /46	2.41 /31	0.25	1.66
GR	Putnam Capital Appreciation Y		C-	(800) 354-2228	C / 5.0	-3.10	2.53	9.19 /41	12.85 /48	2.70 /34	0.35	1.16
SC	Putnam Capital Opportunities A	PCOAX	C	(800) 354-2228	B- / 7.2	-3.82	6.90	17.40 /78	18.27 /73	5.77 /60	0.50	1.23
SC	Putnam Capital Opportunities B	POPBX	C-	(800) 354-2228	C+ / 6.8	-4.06	6.38	16.45 /76	17.39 /70	4.97 /54	0.00	1.98
SC	Putnam Capital Opportunities C	PCOCX	C	(800) 354-2228	B- / 7.2	-4.03	6.42	16.41 /76	17.38 /70	4.97 /54	0.00	1.98
SC	Putnam Capital Opportunities M	POPMX	C	(800) 354-2228	B- / 7.1	-3.98	6.54	16.71 /76	17.68 /71	5.22 /56	0.13	1.73
SC	Putnam Capital Opportunities R	PCORX	C	(800) 354-2228	B- / 7.5	-3.85	6.68	17.09 /77	17.94 /72	5.50 /58	0.49	1.48
SC	Putnam Capital Opportunities Y	PYCOX	B+	(800) 354-2228	B / 7.7	-3.76	6.97	17.61 /78	18.57 /75	6.02 /61	0.74	1.18
GI	Putnam Classic Equity A	PXGIX	D+	(800) 354-2228	D / 2.1	-1.82	1.69	5.96 /20	9.63 /25	1.98 /27	0.85	1.15
GI	Putnam Classic Equity B	PGIIX	D	(800) 354-2228	D / 1.7	-2.05	1.30	5.17 /16	8.80 /20	1.22 /22	0.11	1.90
GI	Putnam Classic Equity C	PGTCX	D+	(800) 354-2228	D+ / 2.3	-2.02	1.31	5.21 /16	8.82 /20	1.21 /22	0.18	1.90
GI	Putnam Classic Equity M	PGIMX	D+	(800) 354-2228	D / 2.1	-2.03	1.37	5.37 /17	9.06 /21	1.46 /23	0.38	1.65
GI	Putnam Classic Equity R	PCERX	C-	(800) 354-2228	D+ / 2.8	-1.88	1.59	5.76 /19	9.38 /23	1.72 /25	0.70	1.40
GI	Putnam Classic Equity Y		C-	(800) 354-2228	C- / 3.2	-1.83	1.75	6.23 /22	9.88 /27	2.24 /30	1.15	0.90
GI	Putnam Col Adv US LCV Grwth & Inc		C	(800) 354-2228	D+ / 2.9	-1.07	2.73	7.68 /30	10.66 /32	--	0.00	0.64
GI	Putnam Col Adv US LCV Grwth & Inc		C-	(800) 354-2228	D+ / 2.3	-1.27	2.28	6.78 /25	9.80 /26	--	0.00	1.39

● Denotes fund is closed to new investors
* Denotes fund is included in Section II

RISK			NET ASSETS		ASSET				BULL / BEAR		FUND MANAGER		MINIMUMS		LOADS	
	3 Year		NAV						Last Bull	Last Bear	Manager	Manager	Initial	Additional	Front	Back
Risk	Standard		As of	Total	Cash	Stocks	Bonds	Other	Market	Market	Quality	Tenure	Purch.	Purch.	End	End
Rating/Pts	Deviation	Beta	6/30/06	$(Mil)	%	%	%	%	Return	Return	Pct	(Years)	$	$	Load	Load
C+ / 5.7	14.3	1.23	20.79	27	28	71	0	1	615.0	131.7	-8.3	13	N/A	15,000	100	0.0	0.0
C+ / 5.6	14.3	1.23	19.84	6	28	71	0	1	615.0	124.2	-8.7	8	N/A	5,000	100	0.0	0.0
B- / 7.5	6.7	0.78	18.06	7	21	78	0	1	0.1	31.7	-7.3	15	10	500	0	0.0	0.0
C / 4.4	13.1	1.10	20.42	3	1	98	0	1	60.0	77.8	-9.8	4	N/A	1,000,000	250	0.0	1.0
C- / 3.0	16.1	1.04	18.68	130	5	94	0	1	59.6	100.6	-12.2	17	N/A	1,000,000	250	0.0	1.0
C- / 3.0	16.1	1.04	16.75	11	5	94	0	1	59.6	97.8	-12.4	14	N/A	2,000	250	5.8	1.0
C+ / 6.9	10.0	0.95	15.55	244	0	99	0	1	123.0	111.1	-8.2	30	N/A	10,000	250	0.0	0.0
C- / 4.2	12.4	1.42	14.44	292	N/A	100	0	N/A	246.0	63.5	-10.9	14	N/A	10,000	250	0.0	0.0
C+ / 5.7	8.3	1.01	14.71	364	1	98	0	1	90.0	96.3	-9.4	94	N/A	10,000	250	0.0	0.0
C / 5.2	15.1	1.00	11.64	139	2	97	0	1	147.0	90.0	-12.2	15	N/A	10,000	250	0.0	0.0
C- / 3.9	11.7	0.77	20.19	289	2	97	0	1	118.0	137.7	-8.1	98	N/A	10,000	250	0.0	0.0
B / 8.6	8.4	-0.58	5.73	31	0	21	78	1	129.1	-19.0	10.3	73	N/A	2,000	100	0.0	1.0
C- / 3.1	8.5	-0.58	5.94	640	0	21	78	1	129.1	-17.1	10.5	79	N/A	2,000	100	0.0	1.0
C+ / 6.0	10.6	1.84	21.37	382	0	99	0	1	16.7	86.9	-10.7	81	N/A	25,000	1,000	0.0	0.0
B+ / 9.5	5.2	1.05	11.43	1,230	9	65	24	2	144.4	52.8	-5.3	77	12	500	50	5.3	0.0
B+ / 9.6	5.2	1.04	11.35	323	9	65	24	2	144.4	49.2	-5.5	70	12	500	50	0.0	5.0
B+ / 9.5	5.2	1.05	11.24	119	9	65	24	2	144.4	49.3	-5.5	69	12	500	50	0.0	1.0
B+ / 9.5	5.2	1.05	11.41	35	9	65	24	2	144.4	50.4	-5.4	72	11	500	50	3.3	0.0
B+ / 9.5	5.2	1.05	11.37	9	9	65	24	2	144.4	51.3	-5.3	73	11	500	50	0.0	0.0
B+ / 9.7	5.2	1.04	11.45	162	9	65	24	2	144.4	54.2	-5.3	79	12	150,000,000	0	0.0	0.0
B+ / 9.9	3.4	0.61	9.32	391	22	34	42	2	209.1	32.1	0.3	63	12	500	50	5.3	0.0
B+ / 9.9	3.4	0.62	9.23	93	22	34	42	2	209.1	28.9	N/A	52	12	500	50	0.0	5.0
B+ / 9.9	3.4	0.62	9.22	44	22	34	42	2	209.1	28.9	N/A	52	12	500	50	0.0	1.0
B+ / 9.9	3.4	0.63	9.24	12	22	34	42	2	209.1	29.8	N/A	56	11	500	50	3.3	0.0
B+ / 9.9	3.4	0.62	9.40	1	22	34	42	2	209.1	32.1	0.3	63	11	500	50	0.0	0.0
B+ / 9.9	3.4	0.61	9.30	365	22	34	42	2	209.1	33.1	0.1	66	12	150,000,000	0	0.0	0.0
B / 8.1	7.4	1.43	12.77	1,006	6	83	10	1	111.9	80.0	-7.0	90	12	500	50	5.3	0.0
B / 8.1	7.4	1.43	12.52	343	6	83	10	1	111.9	75.7	-7.2	86	12	500	50	0.0	5.0
B / 8.1	7.5	1.43	12.34	133	6	83	10	1	111.9	75.8	-7.2	86	12	500	50	0.0	1.0
B / 8.1	7.5	1.43	12.56	38	6	83	10	1	111.9	77.2	-7.2	88	11	500	50	3.3	0.0
B / 8.1	7.4	1.42	12.64	5	6	83	10	1	111.9	78.5	-7.0	89	11	500	50	0.0	0.0
B / 8.5	7.5	1.43	12.87	151	6	83	10	1	111.9	81.5	-7.0	91	12	150,000,000	0	0.0	0.0
B- / 7.2	10.4	1.23	20.60	527	0	99	0	1	121.0	77.1	-10.2	49	N/A	500	50	5.3	0.0
B- / 7.2	10.4	1.23	19.38	101	0	99	0	1	121.0	72.9	-10.3	40	N/A	500	50	0.0	5.0
B- / 7.2	10.4	1.23	19.79	4	0	99	0	1	121.0	72.9	-10.3	39	N/A	500	50	0.0	1.0
B- / 7.2	10.4	1.23	19.77	14	0	99	0	1	121.0	74.4	-10.3	43	N/A	500	50	3.3	0.0
B- / 7.3	10.4	1.23	20.48	N/A	0	99	0	1	121.0	75.8	-10.2	46	N/A	500	50	0.0	0.0
C+ / 5.6	10.4	1.24	20.63	7	0	99	0	1	121.0	77.4	-10.2	50	N/A	150,000,000	0	0.0	0.0
C / 4.7	12.7	0.85	12.09	454	2	97	0	1	70.9	111.3	-12.8	76	7	500	50	5.3	0.0
C / 4.5	12.7	0.85	11.33	210	2	97	0	1	70.9	106.4	-13.0	69	7	500	50	0.0	5.0
C / 4.5	12.7	0.85	11.44	33	2	97	0	1	70.9	106.2	-12.9	69	7	500	50	0.0	1.0
C / 4.6	12.7	0.85	11.57	16	2	97	0	1	70.9	107.9	-12.9	72	7	500	50	3.3	0.0
C / 4.6	12.7	0.85	11.98	1	2	97	0	1	70.9	109.6	-12.8	74	7	500	50	0.0	0.0
B- / 7.2	12.7	0.85	12.28	382	2	97	0	1	70.9	112.7	-12.7	78	7	150,000,000	0	0.0	0.0
B- / 7.8	7.9	1.01	13.41	603	0	99	0	1	67.3	59.1	-10.2	38	2	500	50	5.3	0.0
B- / 7.7	7.9	1.01	13.31	116	0	99	0	1	67.3	55.3	-10.4	31	2	500	50	0.0	5.0
B- / 7.7	8.0	1.01	13.39	14	0	99	0	1	67.3	55.3	-10.3	31	2	500	50	0.0	1.0
B- / 7.7	8.0	1.01	13.35	28	0	99	0	1	67.3	56.5	-10.3	33	2	500	50	3.3	0.0
B- / 7.9	7.9	1.01	13.39	N/A	0	99	0	1	67.3	57.8	-10.2	36	2	500	50	0.0	0.0
B- / 7.9	8.0	1.01	13.41	5	0	99	0	1	67.3	60.3	-10.2	40	2	150,000,000	0	0.0	0.0
B / 8.9	7.6	0.96	12.06	32	4	80	15	1	10.5	64.7	-10.0	54	N/A	25	25	5.3	0.0
B / 8.7	7.6	0.97	11.65	28	4	80	15	1	10.5	60.9	-10.2	43	N/A	25	25	0.0	5.0

99 Pct = Best
0 Pct = Worst

Fund Type	Fund Name	Ticker Symbol	Overall Weiss Investment Rating	Phone	Performance Rating/Pts	3 Mo	6 Mo	1Yr / Pct	Annualized 3Yr / Pct	Annualized 5Yr / Pct	Dividend Yield	Expense Ratio
GI	Putnam Col Adv US LCV Grwth & Inc		C	(800) 354-2228	C- / 3.0	-1.27	2.28	6.78 / 25	9.80 / 26	--	0.00	1.39
GI	Putnam Col Adv US LCV Grwth & Inc		C+	(800) 354-2228	C- / 4.0	-0.97	2.93	8.18 / 34	11.26 / 38	--	0.00	0.09
AA	Putnam College Adv Agg Gr A		C+	(800) 354-2228	C- / 4.1	-3.20	2.13	11.12 / 54	12.45 / 45	--	0.00	0.64
AA	Putnam College Adv Agg Gr AX		C	(800) 354-2228	C- / 3.8	-3.12	2.13	11.01 / 54	12.45 / 45	--	0.00	0.64
AA	Putnam College Adv Agg Gr B		C	(800) 354-2228	C- / 3.5	-3.39	1.74	10.20 / 48	11.59 / 40	--	0.00	1.39
AA	Putnam College Adv Agg Gr BX		C	(800) 354-2228	C- / 3.6	-3.28	1.91	10.45 / 50	11.82 / 41	--	0.00	1.19
AA	Putnam College Adv Agg Gr C		C+	(800) 354-2228	C / 4.3	-3.37	1.73	10.35 / 49	11.65 / 40	--	0.00	1.39
AA	Putnam College Adv Agg Gr CX		C+	(800) 354-2228	C / 4.5	-3.24	1.98	10.63 / 51	12.15 / 43	--	0.00	0.89
AA	Putnam College Adv Agg Gr O		C+	(800) 354-2228	C / 5.1	-3.06	2.35	11.60 / 57	12.94 / 49	--	0.00	0.20
AA	Putnam College Adv Bal A		C-	(800) 354-2228	D / 1.7	-1.59	1.55	6.62 / 24	8.69 / 19	3.42 / 41	0.00	0.64
AA	Putnam College Adv Bal AX		C-	(800) 354-2228	D / 1.6	-1.59	1.55	6.62 / 24	8.69 / 19	3.42 / 41	0.00	0.64
AA	Putnam College Adv Bal B		C-	(800) 354-2228	D- / 1.3	-1.83	1.13	5.82 / 19	7.87 / 14	2.64 / 33	0.00	1.39
AA	Putnam College Adv Bal BX		C-	(800) 354-2228	D- / 1.4	-1.82	1.13	6.00 / 20	8.07 / 15	2.84 / 35	0.00	1.19
AA	Putnam College Adv Bal C		C	(800) 354-2228	D / 1.8	-1.82	1.12	5.78 / 19	7.85 / 14	2.64 / 33	0.00	1.39
AA	Putnam College Adv Bal CX		C	(800) 354-2228	D / 2.2	-1.79	1.29	6.30 / 22	8.38 / 17	3.14 / 38	0.00	0.89
AA	Putnam College Adv Bal George Put		C-	(800) 354-2228	D- / 1.0	-0.55	1.61	4.20 / 11	7.13 / 11	--	0.00	0.64
AA	Putnam College Adv Bal George Put		C-	(800) 354-2228	E+ / 0.7	-0.72	1.23	3.43 / 9	6.34 / 8	--	0.00	1.39
AA	Putnam College Adv Bal George Put		C-	(800) 354-2228	D- / 1.1	-0.72	1.23	3.43 / 9	6.34 / 8	--	0.00	1.39
AA	Putnam College Adv Bal George Put		C	(800) 354-2228	D / 1.8	-0.39	1.90	4.81 / 14	7.71 / 13	--	0.00	0.09
AA	Putnam College Adv Bal O		C	(800) 354-2228	D+ / 2.6	-1.57	1.62	6.99 / 26	9.05 / 21	3.77 / 44	0.00	0.30
AA	Putnam College Adv Growth A		C+	(800) 354-2228	C- / 4.2	-2.17	3.05	10.99 / 53	12.46 / 46	3.66 / 42	0.00	0.64
AA	Putnam College Adv Growth AX		C+	(800) 354-2228	C- / 4.0	-2.26	3.05	10.99 / 53	12.46 / 46	3.66 / 42	0.00	0.64
AA	Putnam College Adv Growth B		C	(800) 354-2228	C- / 3.6	-2.43	2.66	10.14 / 48	11.67 / 40	2.92 / 36	0.00	1.39
AA	Putnam College Adv Growth BX		C+	(800) 354-2228	C- / 3.7	-2.33	2.74	10.30 / 49	11.83 / 41	3.11 / 38	0.00	1.19
AA	Putnam College Adv Growth C		C+	(800) 354-2228	C / 4.4	-2.41	2.74	10.17 / 48	11.66 / 40	2.90 / 36	0.00	1.39
AA	Putnam College Adv Growth CX		C+	(800) 354-2228	C / 4.7	-2.29	2.99	10.68 / 51	12.22 / 44	3.42 / 41	0.00	0.89
AA	Putnam College Adv Growth O		B-	(800) 354-2228	C / 5.1	-2.13	3.27	11.40 / 56	12.91 / 48	4.06 / 46	0.00	0.26
GL	Putnam College Adv Intl Cap Opp A		A+	(800) 354-2228	A / 9.5	1.01	13.11	33.20 / 96	30.64 / 96	--	0.00	0.64
GL	Putnam College Adv Intl Cap Opp B		A+	(800) 354-2228	A / 9.5	0.83	12.62	32.24 / 96	29.67 / 95	--	0.00	1.39
GL	Putnam College Adv Intl Cap Opp C		A+	(800) 354-2228	A+ / 9.6	0.83	12.68	32.22 / 96	29.64 / 95	--	0.00	1.39
GL	Putnam College Adv Intl Cap Opp O		A+	(800) 354-2228	A+ / 9.7	1.18	13.38	33.96 / 96	31.35 / 96	--	0.00	0.09
GL	Putnam College Adv Intl Equity A		A	(800) 354-2228	B / 8.1	0.20	10.14	25.31 / 89	19.81 / 79	--	0.00	0.64
GL	Putnam College Adv Intl Equity B		A-	(800) 354-2228	B / 7.8	0.00	9.77	24.34 / 88	18.91 / 76	--	0.00	1.39
GL	Putnam College Adv Intl Equity C		A	(800) 354-2228	B / 8.1	0.00	9.69	24.36 / 88	18.93 / 76	--	0.00	1.39
GL	Putnam College Adv Intl Equity O		A+	(800) 354-2228	B+ / 8.5	0.26	10.35	25.90 / 90	20.48 / 81	--	0.00	0.09
AA	Putnam College Adv Mod 1985 A		D+	(800) 354-2228	E- / 0.2	-0.09	0.75	2.47 / 6	3.47 / 2	1.84 / 26	0.00	0.70
AA	Putnam College Adv Mod 1985 AX		D+	(800) 354-2228	E- / 0.1	-0.09	0.75	2.47 / 6	3.47 / 2	1.84 / 26	0.00	N/A
AA	Putnam College Adv Mod 1985 C		D+	(800) 354-2228	E- / 0.2	-0.29	0.38	1.65 / 4	2.72 / 1	1.08 / 21	0.00	0.70
AA	Putnam College Adv Mod 1985 CX		D+	(800) 354-2228	E / 0.3	-0.09	0.66	2.21 / 5	3.24 / 1	1.62 / 24	0.00	N/A
AA	Putnam College Adv Mod 1985 O		C-	(800) 354-2228	E / 0.5	0.00	0.92	2.63 / 6	3.71 / 2	2.08 / 28	0.00	N/A
AA	Putnam College Adv Mod 1986 A		D+	(800) 354-2228	E- / 0.2	-0.19	0.75	2.57 / 6	3.90 / 2	1.97 / 27	0.00	0.72
AA	Putnam College Adv Mod 1986 AX		D+	(800) 354-2228	E- / 0.2	-0.19	0.75	2.57 / 6	3.90 / 2	1.97 / 27	0.00	N/A
AA	Putnam College Adv Mod 1986 B		D+	(800) 354-2228	E- / 0.1	-0.38	0.29	1.76 / 4	3.14 / 1	1.22 / 22	0.00	0.70
AA	Putnam College Adv Mod 1986 BX		D+	(800) 354-2228	E- / 0.2	-0.29	0.48	1.95 / 4	3.34 / 2	1.40 / 23	0.00	N/A
AA	Putnam College Adv Mod 1986 C		D+	(800) 354-2228	E / 0.3	-0.38	0.38	1.75 / 4	3.15 / 1	1.21 / 22	0.00	0.70
AA	Putnam College Adv Mod 1986 CX		D+	(800) 354-2228	E / 0.4	-0.28	0.66	2.31 / 5	3.64 / 2	1.70 / 25	0.00	N/A
AA	Putnam College Adv Mod 1986 O		C-	(800) 354-2228	E / 0.5	-0.09	0.83	2.82 / 7	4.17 / 2	2.21 / 29	0.00	N/A
AA	Putnam College Adv Mod 1987 A		D+	(800) 354-2228	E / 0.3	-0.37	0.56	2.58 / 6	4.33 / 3	2.02 / 27	0.00	0.73
AA	Putnam College Adv Mod 1987 AX		D+	(800) 354-2228	E- / 0.2	-0.37	0.56	2.58 / 6	4.33 / 3	2.02 / 27	0.00	N/A
AA	Putnam College Adv Mod 1987 B		D+	(800) 354-2228	E- / 0.2	-0.58	0.19	1.77 / 4	3.53 / 2	1.27 / 22	0.00	0.73
AA	Putnam College Adv Mod 1987 BX		D+	(800) 354-2228	E- / 0.2	-0.48	0.39	2.06 / 4	3.76 / 2	1.47 / 24	0.00	N/A
AA	Putnam College Adv Mod 1987 C		D+	(800) 354-2228	E / 0.3	-0.57	0.29	1.86 / 4	3.57 / 2	1.30 / 22	0.00	0.73

RISK			NET ASSETS		ASSET					BULL / BEAR		FUND MANAGER		MINIMUMS		LOADS	
	3 Year		NAV						Portfolio	Last Bull	Last Bear	Manager	Manager	Initial	Additional	Front	Back
Risk Rating/Pts	Standard Deviation	Beta	As of 6/30/06	Total $(Mil)	Cash %	Stocks %	Bonds %	Other %	Turnover Ratio	Market Return	Market Return	Quality Pct	Tenure (Years)	Purch. $	Purch. $	End Load	End Load
B / 8.7	7.7	0.97	11.65	11	4	80	15	1	10.5	60.9	-10.2	43	N/A	25	25	0.0	1.0
B / 8.9	7.6	0.96	12.30	5	4	80	15	1	10.5	67.7	-10.0	60	N/A	25	25	0.0	1.0
B / 8.4	9.0	1.72	11.49	27	0	99	0	1	48.1	75.1	-10.4	66	N/A	25	25	5.3	0.0
B / 8.5	9.0	1.71	11.49	79	0	99	0	1	48.1	75.1	-10.4	66	N/A	25	25	5.3	1.0
B / 8.4	9.0	1.73	11.13	10	0	99	0	1	48.1	71.1	-10.6	57	N/A	25	25	0.0	5.0
B / 8.5	9.0	1.71	11.20	44	0	99	0	1	48.1	72.0	-10.4	60	N/A	25	25	0.0	5.0
B / 8.4	9.0	1.72	11.19	9	0	99	0	1	48.1	71.3	-10.5	58	N/A	25	25	0.0	1.0
B / 8.4	9.0	1.72	11.34	33	0	99	0	1	48.1	73.7	-10.4	63	N/A	25	25	0.0	1.0
B / 8.4	9.0	1.72	11.74	24	0	99	0	1	48.1	77.7	-10.2	70	N/A	25	25	0.0	1.0
B+ / 9.7	5.3	1.10	11.12	45	5	88	5	2	28.5	47.5	-5.4	62	N/A	25	25	5.3	0.0
B+ / 9.7	5.4	1.11	11.12	190	5	88	5	2	28.5	47.5	-5.4	62	N/A	25	25	5.3	1.0
B+ / 9.7	5.3	1.09	10.72	19	5	88	5	2	28.5	44.0	-5.5	54	N/A	25	25	0.0	5.0
B+ / 9.7	5.3	1.10	10.78	97	5	88	5	2	28.5	44.9	-5.5	56	N/A	25	25	0.0	5.0
B+ / 9.7	5.4	1.11	10.80	20	5	88	5	2	28.5	44.1	-5.5	52	N/A	25	25	0.0	1.0
B+ / 9.7	5.4	1.11	10.96	84	5	88	5	2	28.5	46.3	-5.5	59	N/A	25	25	0.0	1.0
B+ / 9.8	4.9	1.02	12.64	9	0	0	0	100	11.3	N/A	N/A	49	N/A	25	25	5.3	0.0
B+ / 9.8	4.9	1.02	12.35	5	0	0	0	100	11.3	N/A	N/A	40	N/A	25	25	0.0	5.0
B+ / 9.8	4.9	1.02	12.35	5	0	0	0	100	11.3	N/A	N/A	41	N/A	25	25	0.0	1.0
B+ / 9.8	4.9	1.02	12.86	1	0	0	0	100	11.3	N/A	N/A	57	N/A	25	25	0.0	1.0
B+ / 9.7	5.3	1.10	11.32	37	5	88	5	2	28.5	49.1	-5.3	67	N/A	25	25	0.0	1.0
B / 8.8	7.8	1.53	10.81	70	0	100	0	0	25.8	72.2	-8.8	75	N/A	25	25	5.3	0.0
B / 8.8	7.8	1.53	10.81	369	0	100	0	0	25.8	72.2	-8.8	75	N/A	25	25	5.3	1.0
B / 8.8	7.8	1.53	10.43	26	0	100	0	0	25.8	68.5	-9.0	68	N/A	25	25	0.0	5.0
B / 8.9	7.8	1.53	10.49	193	0	100	0	0	25.8	69.1	-8.9	70	N/A	25	25	0.0	5.0
B / 8.8	7.8	1.54	10.51	29	0	100	0	0	25.8	68.4	-9.1	68	N/A	25	25	0.0	1.0
B / 8.8	7.8	1.53	10.67	160	0	100	0	0	25.8	70.7	-8.8	73	N/A	25	25	0.0	1.0
B / 8.8	7.8	1.53	11.04	67	0	100	0	0	25.8	74.1	-8.6	79	N/A	25	25	0.0	1.0
B- / 7.2	12.6	1.16	20.02	9	0	0	0	100	12.7	179.5	-10.5	74	N/A	25	25	5.3	0.0
B- / 7.2	12.6	1.16	19.36	6	0	0	0	100	12.7	172.8	-10.7	68	N/A	25	25	0.0	5.0
B- / 7.2	12.6	1.16	19.37	4	0	0	0	100	12.7	172.9	-10.7	67	N/A	25	25	0.0	1.0
B- / 7.2	12.6	1.16	20.51	2	0	0	0	100	12.7	184.2	-10.3	79	N/A	25	25	0.0	0.0
B- / 7.7	10.4	1.01	15.10	13	0	100	0	0	18.2	108.2	-10.7	20	N/A	25	25	5.3	0.0
B- / 7.6	10.4	1.01	14.61	8	0	100	0	0	18.2	103.2	-10.9	15	N/A	25	25	0.0	5.0
B- / 7.6	10.4	1.01	14.60	7	0	100	0	0	18.2	103.2	-10.8	15	N/A	25	25	0.0	1.0
B- / 7.7	10.4	1.00	15.46	5	0	100	0	0	18.2	111.9	-10.6	24	N/A	25	25	0.0	0.0
B+ / 9.9	2.0	0.39	10.79	1	0	14	84	2	29.5	16.8	-1.5	45	N/A	25	25	5.3	0.0
B+ / 9.9	2.0	0.39	10.79	4	0	14	84	2	29.5	16.8	-1.5	45	N/A	25	25	5.3	1.0
B+ / 9.9	2.0	0.39	10.48	1	0	14	84	2	29.5	14.1	-1.6	37	N/A	25	25	0.0	1.0
B+ / 9.9	2.0	0.39	10.64	4	0	14	84	2	29.5	16.0	-1.6	43	N/A	25	25	0.0	1.0
B+ / 9.9	2.0	0.39	10.92	1	0	14	84	2	29.5	17.7	-1.5	48	N/A	25	25	0.0	0.0
B+ / 9.9	2.3	0.46	10.78	2	0	26	74	0	29.6	19.4	-1.9	46	N/A	25	25	5.3	0.0
B+ / 9.9	2.3	0.46	10.78	14	0	26	74	0	29.6	19.4	-1.9	46	N/A	25	25	5.3	1.0
B+ / 9.9	2.3	0.46	10.38	N/A	0	26	74	0	29.6	16.6	-2.2	38	N/A	25	25	0.0	5.0
B+ / 9.9	2.3	0.45	10.45	2	0	26	74	0	29.6	17.3	-2.1	40	N/A	25	25	0.0	5.0
B+ / 9.9	2.3	0.46	10.46	1	0	26	74	0	29.6	16.6	-2.1	38	N/A	25	25	0.0	1.0
B+ / 9.9	2.3	0.46	10.62	13	0	26	74	0	29.6	18.4	-2.0	43	N/A	25	25	0.0	1.0
B+ / 9.9	2.3	0.46	10.92	2	0	26	74	0	29.6	20.3	-1.8	49	N/A	25	25	0.0	0.0
B+ / 9.9	2.6	0.53	10.73	4	0	26	74	0	25.5	22.0	-2.4	47	N/A	25	25	5.3	0.0
B+ / 9.9	2.6	0.52	10.73	22	0	26	74	0	25.5	21.9	-2.4	47	N/A	25	25	5.3	1.0
B+ / 9.9	2.5	0.52	10.33	1	0	26	74	0	25.5	19.2	-2.6	38	N/A	25	25	0.0	5.0
B+ / 9.9	2.6	0.53	10.40	8	0	26	74	0	25.5	19.9	-2.6	41	N/A	25	25	0.0	5.0
B+ / 9.9	2.6	0.53	10.42	4	0	26	74	0	25.5	19.2	-2.5	38	N/A	25	25	0.0	1.0

					PERFORMANCE							
99 Pct = Best 0 Pct = Worst			Overall Weiss				Total Return % through 6/30/06				Incl. in Returns	
					Perfor- mance				Annualized		Dividend	Expense
Fund Type	Fund Name	Ticker Symbol	Investment Rating	Phone	Rating/Pts	3 Mo	6 Mo	1Yr / Pct	3Yr / Pct	5Yr / Pct	Yield	Ratio
AA	Putnam College Adv Mod 1987 CX		C-	(800) 354-2228	E / 0.4	-0.47	0.47	2.32 / 5	4.06 / 2	1.77 / 25	0.00	N/A
AA	Putnam College Adv Mod 1987 O		C-	(800) 354-2228	E+ / 0.6	-0.37	0.74	2.84 / 7	4.59 / 3	2.28 / 30	0.00	N/A
AA	Putnam College Adv Mod 1988 A		D+	(800) 354-2228	E / 0.3	-0.56	0.47	2.69 / 6	4.75 / 3	2.07 / 28	0.00	0.74
AA	Putnam College Adv Mod 1988 AX		D+	(800) 354-2228	E / 0.3	-0.56	0.47	2.69 / 6	4.75 / 3	2.07 / 28	0.00	N/A
AA	Putnam College Adv Mod 1988 B		D+	(800) 354-2228	E- / 0.2	-0.77	0.10	1.88 / 4	3.95 / 2	1.29 / 22	0.00	0.74
AA	Putnam College Adv Mod 1988 BX		D+	(800) 354-2228	E- / 0.2	-0.67	0.29	2.17 / 5	4.18 / 3	1.53 / 24	0.00	N/A
AA	Putnam College Adv Mod 1988 C		C-	(800) 354-2228	E / 0.4	-0.76	0.19	1.96 / 4	3.99 / 2	1.32 / 22	0.00	0.74
AA	Putnam College Adv Mod 1988 CX		C-	(800) 354-2228	E / 0.5	-0.66	0.38	2.43 / 5	4.49 / 3	1.82 / 26	0.00	N/A
AA	Putnam College Adv Mod 1988 O		C-	(800) 354-2228	E+ / 0.7	-0.55	0.56	2.94 / 7	5.05 / 4	2.35 / 31	0.00	N/A
AA	Putnam College Adv Mod 1989 A		C-	(800) 354-2228	E / 0.4	-0.75	0.57	3.00 / 7	5.27 / 4	2.16 / 29	0.00	0.76
AA	Putnam College Adv Mod 1989 AX		C-	(800) 354-2228	E / 0.4	-0.75	0.57	3.00 / 7	5.27 / 4	2.16 / 29	0.00	N/A
AA	Putnam College Adv Mod 1989 B		D+	(800) 354-2228	E / 0.3	-0.87	0.20	2.30 / 5	4.51 / 3	1.40 / 23	0.00	0.76
AA	Putnam College Adv Mod 1989 BX		D+	(800) 354-2228	E / 0.3	-0.87	0.19	2.39 / 5	4.68 / 3	1.61 / 24	0.00	N/A
AA	Putnam College Adv Mod 1989 C		C-	(800) 354-2228	E / 0.5	-0.96	0.10	2.18 / 5	4.51 / 3	1.41 / 23	0.00	0.76
AA	Putnam College Adv Mod 1989 CX		C-	(800) 354-2228	E+ / 0.6	-0.76	0.38	2.74 / 6	5.01 / 4	1.92 / 27	0.00	N/A
AA	Putnam College Adv Mod 1989 O		C-	(800) 354-2228	E+ / 0.9	-0.64	0.65	3.25 / 8	5.57 / 5	2.43 / 32	0.00	N/A
AA	Putnam College Adv Mod 1990 A		C-	(800) 354-2228	E / 0.5	-0.93	0.57	3.31 / 8	5.80 / 6	2.23 / 29	0.00	0.77
AA	Putnam College Adv Mod 1990 AX		C-	(800) 354-2228	E / 0.5	-0.93	0.57	3.31 / 8	5.80 / 6	2.23 / 29	0.00	N/A
AA	Putnam College Adv Mod 1990 B		C-	(800) 354-2228	E / 0.4	-1.06	0.20	2.61 / 6	5.03 / 4	1.49 / 24	0.00	0.77
AA	Putnam College Adv Mod 1990 BX		C-	(800) 354-2228	E / 0.4	-0.96	0.29	2.80 / 7	5.23 / 4	1.67 / 25	0.00	N/A
AA	Putnam College Adv Mod 1990 C		C-	(800) 354-2228	E+ / 0.6	-1.06	0.19	2.48 / 6	5.02 / 4	1.46 / 23	0.00	0.77
AA	Putnam College Adv Mod 1990 CX		C-	(800) 354-2228	E+ / 0.8	-0.95	0.48	3.05 / 7	5.56 / 5	1.98 / 27	0.00	N/A
AA	Putnam College Adv Mod 1990 O		C-	(800) 354-2228	D- / 1.1	-0.83	0.75	3.65 / 9	6.12 / 7	2.56 / 32	0.00	N/A
AA	Putnam College Adv Mod 1991 A		C-	(800) 354-2228	E+ / 0.7	-1.03	0.57	3.74 / 10	6.35 / 8	2.29 / 30	0.00	0.79
AA	Putnam College Adv Mod 1991 AX		C-	(800) 354-2228	E+ / 0.6	-1.03	0.67	3.74 / 10	6.35 / 8	2.29 / 30	0.00	N/A
AA	Putnam College Adv Mod 1991 B		C-	(800) 354-2228	E / 0.5	-1.26	0.20	2.94 / 7	5.54 / 5	1.54 / 24	0.00	0.79
AA	Putnam College Adv Mod 1991 BX		C-	(800) 354-2228	E / 0.5	-1.25	0.29	3.13 / 8	5.75 / 6	1.75 / 25	0.00	N/A
AA	Putnam College Adv Mod 1991 C		C-	(800) 354-2228	E+ / 0.8	-1.25	0.20	2.91 / 7	5.54 / 5	1.53 / 24	0.00	0.79
AA	Putnam College Adv Mod 1991 CX		C-	(800) 354-2228	D- / 1.0	-1.14	0.48	3.38 / 8	6.09 / 7	2.04 / 28	0.00	N/A
AA	Putnam College Adv Mod 1991 O		C-	(800) 354-2228	D- / 1.4	-1.02	0.75	3.98 / 10	6.68 / 9	2.62 / 33	0.00	N/A
AA	Putnam College Adv Mod 1992 A		C-	(800) 354-2228	E+ / 0.9	-1.13	0.76	4.25 / 12	6.97 / 10	2.38 / 31	0.00	0.80
AA	Putnam College Adv Mod 1992 AX		C-	(800) 354-2228	E+ / 0.8	-1.22	0.67	4.15 / 11	6.94 / 10	2.36 / 31	0.00	N/A
AA	Putnam College Adv Mod 1992 B		C-	(800) 354-2228	E+ / 0.6	-1.46	0.30	3.36 / 8	6.14 / 7	1.61 / 24	0.00	0.80
AA	Putnam College Adv Mod 1992 BX		C-	(800) 354-2228	E+ / 0.7	-1.26	0.49	3.65 / 9	6.38 / 8	1.82 / 26	0.00	N/A
AA	Putnam College Adv Mod 1992 C		C-	(800) 354-2228	D- / 1.0	-1.45	0.29	3.34 / 8	6.13 / 7	1.60 / 24	0.00	0.80
AA	Putnam College Adv Mod 1992 CX		C-	(800) 354-2228	D- / 1.2	-1.33	0.58	3.90 / 10	6.68 / 9	2.11 / 28	0.00	N/A
AA	Putnam College Adv Mod 1992 O		C	(800) 354-2228	D / 1.7	-1.11	0.94	4.49 / 13	7.30 / 12	2.71 / 34	0.00	N/A
AA	Putnam College Adv Mod 1993 A		C-	(800) 354-2228	D- / 1.1	-1.31	0.86	4.68 / 14	7.54 / 13	2.45 / 32	0.00	0.81
AA	Putnam College Adv Mod 1993 AX		C-	(800) 354-2228	D- / 1.0	-1.31	0.86	4.68 / 14	7.54 / 13	2.45 / 32	0.00	N/A
AA	Putnam College Adv Mod 1993 B		C-	(800) 354-2228	E+ / 0.8	-1.56	0.50	3.90 / 10	6.70 / 9	1.68 / 25	0.00	0.81
AA	Putnam College Adv Mod 1993 BX		C-	(800) 354-2228	E+ / 0.9	-1.45	0.59	4.09 / 11	6.91 / 10	1.89 / 26	0.00	N/A
AA	Putnam College Adv Mod 1993 C		C-	(800) 354-2228	D- / 1.2	-1.45	0.59	3.98 / 10	6.73 / 9	1.71 / 25	0.00	0.81
AA	Putnam College Adv Mod 1993 CX		C-	(800) 354-2228	D- / 1.5	-1.33	0.78	4.44 / 12	7.28 / 12	2.23 / 29	0.00	N/A
AA	Putnam College Adv Mod 1993 O		C	(800) 354-2228	D / 2.0	-1.20	1.04	5.01 / 15	7.90 / 15	2.80 / 35	0.00	N/A
AA	Putnam College Adv Mod 1994 A		C-	(800) 354-2228	D- / 1.4	-1.41	1.06	5.22 / 16	8.12 / 16	2.53 / 32	0.00	0.64
AA	Putnam College Adv Mod 1994 AX		C-	(800) 354-2228	D- / 1.2	-1.41	1.06	5.22 / 16	8.12 / 16	2.53 / 32	0.00	0.64
AA	Putnam College Adv Mod 1994 B		C-	(800) 354-2228	D- / 1.0	-1.56	0.70	4.44 / 12	7.27 / 11	1.77 / 25	0.00	1.39
AA	Putnam College Adv Mod 1994 BX		C-	(800) 354-2228	D- / 1.1	-1.64	0.69	4.63 / 13	7.48 / 12	1.98 / 27	0.00	1.19
AA	Putnam College Adv Mod 1994 C		C-	(800) 354-2228	D- / 1.5	-1.64	0.69	4.41 / 12	7.30 / 12	1.78 / 25	0.00	1.39
AA	Putnam College Adv Mod 1994 CX		C	(800) 354-2228	D / 1.8	-1.53	0.88	4.98 / 15	7.83 / 14	2.26 / 30	0.00	0.89
AA	Putnam College Adv Mod 1994 O		C	(800) 354-2228	D+ / 2.3	-1.39	1.14	5.54 / 18	8.47 / 18	2.88 / 36	0.00	0.30
AA	Putnam College Adv Mod 1995 A		C-	(800) 354-2228	D / 1.7	-1.50	1.26	5.97 / 20	8.70 / 19	2.64 / 33	0.00	0.64

Risk Rating/Pts	Standard Deviation	Beta	NAV As of 6/30/06	Total $(Mil)	Cash %	Stocks %	Bonds %	Other %	Portfolio Turnover Ratio	Last Bull Market Return	Last Bear Market Return	Manager Quality Pct	Manager Tenure (Years)	Initial Purch. $	Additional Purch. $	Front End Load	Back End Load
B+ / 9.9	2.6	0.53	10.58	17	0	26	74	0	25.5	21.0	-2.4	44	N/A	25	25	0.0	1.0
B+ / 9.9	2.6	0.53	10.87	3	0	26	74	0	25.5	22.9	-2.3	50	N/A	25	25	0.0	0.0
B+ / 9.9	2.9	0.59	10.69	7	0	26	74	0	26.0	24.6	-2.7	48	N/A	25	25	5.3	0.0
B+ / 9.9	2.9	0.59	10.69	30	0	26	74	0	26.0	24.6	-2.7	48	N/A	25	25	5.3	1.0
B+ / 9.9	2.9	0.60	10.30	1	0	26	74	0	26.0	21.6	-2.8	38	N/A	25	25	0.0	5.0
B+ / 9.9	2.9	0.59	10.37	17	0	26	74	0	26.0	22.4	-2.8	41	N/A	25	25	0.0	5.0
B+ / 9.9	2.9	0.59	10.38	5	0	26	74	0	26.0	21.7	-2.8	39	N/A	25	25	0.0	1.0
B+ / 9.9	2.9	0.61	10.54	19	0	26	74	0	26.0	23.7	-2.9	44	N/A	25	25	0.0	1.0
B+ / 9.9	2.9	0.60	10.84	5	0	26	74	0	26.0	25.7	-2.7	51	N/A	25	25	0.0	0.0
B+ / 9.9	3.2	0.67	10.64	9	0	38	62	0	25.9	27.6	-3.2	50	N/A	25	25	5.3	0.0
B+ / 9.9	3.2	0.67	10.64	34	0	38	62	0	25.9	27.6	-3.2	50	N/A	25	25	5.3	1.0
B+ / 9.9	3.2	0.68	10.24	3	0	38	62	0	25.9	24.8	-3.4	40	N/A	25	25	0.0	5.0
B+ / 9.9	3.2	0.67	10.30	24	0	38	62	0	25.9	25.5	-3.4	42	N/A	25	25	0.0	5.0
B+ / 9.9	3.2	0.67	10.33	6	0	38	62	0	25.9	24.8	-3.3	41	N/A	25	25	0.0	1.0
B+ / 9.9	3.3	0.68	10.49	19	0	38	62	0	25.9	26.7	-3.3	46	N/A	25	25	0.0	1.0
B+ / 9.9	3.2	0.67	10.80	5	0	38	62	0	25.9	28.9	-3.2	53	N/A	25	25	0.0	0.0
B+ / 9.9	3.5	0.74	10.61	10	0	38	62	0	26.6	30.9	-3.7	52	N/A	25	25	5.3	0.0
B+ / 9.9	3.5	0.74	10.61	38	0	38	62	0	26.6	30.9	-3.7	52	N/A	25	25	5.3	1.0
B+ / 9.9	3.5	0.74	10.23	5	0	38	62	0	26.6	27.8	-3.9	42	N/A	25	25	0.0	5.0
B+ / 9.9	3.6	0.75	10.29	25	0	38	62	0	26.6	28.5	-3.9	44	N/A	25	25	0.0	5.0
B+ / 9.9	3.5	0.74	10.31	5	0	38	62	0	26.6	27.7	-3.9	42	N/A	25	25	0.0	1.0
B+ / 9.9	3.5	0.74	10.47	16	0	38	62	0	26.6	29.8	-3.8	48	N/A	25	25	0.0	1.0
B+ / 9.9	3.6	0.75	10.78	7	0	38	62	0	26.6	32.3	-3.7	55	N/A	25	25	0.0	0.0
B+ / 9.9	3.9	0.82	10.55	12	0	38	62	0	25.2	34.3	-4.3	53	N/A	25	25	5.3	0.0
B+ / 9.9	3.9	0.82	10.55	38	0	38	62	0	25.2	34.3	-4.3	53	N/A	25	25	5.3	1.0
B+ / 9.9	3.9	0.82	10.17	5	0	38	62	0	25.2	31.1	-4.5	43	N/A	25	25	0.0	5.0
B+ / 9.9	3.9	0.82	10.23	28	0	38	62	0	25.2	31.9	-4.4	45	N/A	25	25	0.0	5.0
B+ / 9.9	3.9	0.82	10.24	5	0	38	62	0	25.2	31.0	-4.4	43	N/A	25	25	0.0	1.0
B+ / 9.9	3.9	0.82	10.40	17	0	38	62	0	25.2	33.0	-4.2	50	N/A	25	25	0.0	1.0
B+ / 9.9	3.9	0.82	10.72	6	0	38	62	0	25.2	35.5	-4.2	57	N/A	25	25	0.0	0.0
B+ / 9.9	4.2	0.89	10.54	12	0	50	50	0	27.4	37.8	-4.9	56	N/A	25	25	5.3	0.0
B+ / 9.9	4.2	0.89	10.53	39	0	50	50	0	27.4	37.8	-4.9	56	N/A	25	25	5.3	1.0
B+ / 9.9	4.2	0.89	10.14	6	0	50	50	0	27.4	34.7	-5.1	46	N/A	25	25	0.0	5.0
B+ / 9.9	4.3	0.90	10.21	27	0	50	50	0	27.4	35.3	-4.9	48	N/A	25	25	0.0	5.0
B+ / 9.9	4.2	0.89	10.22	5	0	50	50	0	27.4	34.5	-5.0	46	N/A	25	25	0.0	1.0
B+ / 9.9	4.3	0.90	10.38	13	0	50	50	0	27.4	36.8	-4.9	52	N/A	25	25	0.0	1.0
B+ / 9.9	4.3	0.90	10.71	7	0	50	50	0	27.4	39.1	-4.6	59	N/A	25	25	0.0	0.0
B+ / 9.9	4.6	0.97	10.51	12	0	50	50	0	28.2	41.1	-5.2	58	N/A	25	25	5.3	0.0
B+ / 9.9	4.6	0.97	10.51	37	0	50	50	0	28.2	41.1	-5.2	58	N/A	25	25	5.3	1.0
B+ / 9.9	4.6	0.97	10.12	6	0	50	50	0	28.2	38.0	-5.4	48	N/A	25	25	0.0	5.0
B+ / 9.9	4.6	0.97	10.18	26	0	50	50	0	28.2	38.8	-5.4	50	N/A	25	25	0.0	5.0
B+ / 9.9	4.6	0.97	10.20	4	0	50	50	0	28.2	37.9	-5.4	47	N/A	25	25	0.0	1.0
B+ / 9.9	4.6	0.96	10.36	14	0	50	50	0	28.2	40.1	-5.4	56	N/A	25	25	0.0	1.0
B+ / 9.9	4.6	0.96	10.69	7	0	50	50	0	28.2	42.8	-5.2	62	N/A	25	25	0.0	0.0
B+ / 9.8	5.0	1.04	10.49	12	0	50	50	0	27.6	44.9	-5.8	60	N/A	25	25	5.3	0.0
B+ / 9.8	5.0	1.04	10.49	38	0	50	50	0	27.6	44.9	-5.8	60	N/A	25	25	5.3	1.0
B+ / 9.8	4.9	1.04	10.11	7	0	50	50	0	27.6	41.5	-6.0	50	N/A	25	25	0.0	5.0
B+ / 9.8	5.0	1.04	10.17	27	0	50	50	0	27.6	42.4	-6.0	52	N/A	25	25	0.0	5.0
B+ / 9.8	5.0	1.04	10.18	4	0	50	50	0	27.6	41.5	-6.0	50	N/A	25	25	0.0	1.0
B+ / 9.8	4.9	1.04	10.33	14	0	50	50	0	27.6	43.7	-6.0	57	N/A	25	25	0.0	1.0
B+ / 9.8	5.0	1.04	10.67	7	0	50	50	0	27.6	46.3	-5.7	64	N/A	25	25	0.0	0.0
B+ / 9.7	5.3	1.10	10.48	12	0	66	34	0	26.1	48.4	-6.2	63	N/A	25	25	5.3	0.0

99 Pct = Best
0 Pct = Worst

Fund Type	Fund Name	Ticker Symbol	Overall Weiss Investment Rating	Phone	Perfor-mance Rating/Pts	3 Mo	6 Mo	1Yr / Pct	3Yr / Pct	5Yr / Pct	Dividend Yield	Expense Ratio
									Annualized		Incl. in Returns	
AA	Putnam College Adv Mod 1995 AX		C-	(800) 354-2228	D- / 1.5	-1.60	1.16	5.86 /20	8.66 /19	2.62 /33	0.00	0.64
AA	Putnam College Adv Mod 1995 B		C-	(800) 354-2228	D- / 1.3	-1.75	0.80	5.10 /16	7.90 /15	1.86 /26	0.00	1.39
AA	Putnam College Adv Mod 1995 BX		C-	(800) 354-2228	D- / 1.4	-1.74	0.89	5.28 /16	8.11 /16	2.07 /28	0.00	1.19
AA	Putnam College Adv Mod 1995 C		C	(800) 354-2228	D / 1.8	-1.74	0.79	5.07 /15	7.85 /14	1.85 /26	0.00	1.39
AA	Putnam College Adv Mod 1995 CX		C	(800) 354-2228	D / 2.1	-1.62	1.08	5.63 /18	8.41 /17	2.37 /31	0.00	0.89
AA	Putnam College Adv Mod 1995 O		C	(800) 354-2228	D+ / 2.7	-1.39	1.43	6.38 /23	9.08 /21	2.99 /37	0.00	0.29
AA	Putnam College Adv Mod 1996 A		C	(800) 354-2228	D / 2.0	-1.60	1.45	6.62 /24	9.29 /23	2.73 /34	0.00	0.64
AA	Putnam College Adv Mod 1996 AX		C-	(800) 354-2228	D / 1.8	-1.60	1.45	6.62 /24	9.29 /23	2.73 /34	0.00	0.64
AA	Putnam College Adv Mod 1996 B		C-	(800) 354-2228	D / 1.6	-1.75	1.10	5.88 /20	8.46 /18	1.95 /27	0.00	1.39
AA	Putnam College Adv Mod 1996 BX		C-	(800) 354-2228	D / 1.7	-1.74	1.30	6.06 /21	8.71 /19	2.19 /29	0.00	1.19
AA	Putnam College Adv Mod 1996 C		C	(800) 354-2228	D / 2.2	-1.74	1.20	5.83 /19	8.47 /18	1.98 /27	0.00	1.39
AA	Putnam College Adv Mod 1996 CX		C	(800) 354-2228	D+ / 2.5	-1.62	1.38	6.39 /23	9.04 /21	2.48 /32	0.00	0.89
AA	Putnam College Adv Mod 1996 O		C+	(800) 354-2228	C- / 3.1	-1.48	1.62	7.03 /26	9.68 /25	3.08 /38	0.00	0.28
AA	Putnam College Adv Mod 1997 A		C	(800) 354-2228	D+ / 2.3	-1.69	1.65	7.16 /27	9.83 /26	2.82 /35	0.00	0.64
AA	Putnam College Adv Mod 1997 AX		C	(800) 354-2228	D / 2.2	-1.69	1.65	7.16 /27	9.83 /26	2.82 /35	0.00	0.64
AA	Putnam College Adv Mod 1997 B		C-	(800) 354-2228	D / 1.9	-1.85	1.30	6.43 /23	9.04 /21	2.06 /28	0.00	1.39
AA	Putnam College Adv Mod 1997 BX		C-	(800) 354-2228	D / 2.0	-1.84	1.40	6.61 /24	9.21 /22	2.25 /30	0.00	1.19
AA	Putnam College Adv Mod 1997 C		C	(800) 354-2228	D+ / 2.5	-1.83	1.39	6.49 /23	9.05 /21	2.07 /28	0.00	1.39
AA	Putnam College Adv Mod 1997 CX		C	(800) 354-2228	D+ / 2.9	-1.71	1.57	7.04 /26	9.57 /24	2.57 /33	0.00	0.89
AA	Putnam College Adv Mod 1997 O		C+	(800) 354-2228	C- / 3.5	-1.57	1.91	7.65 /30	10.28 /29	3.21 /39	0.00	0.27
AA	Putnam College Adv Mod 1998 A		C	(800) 354-2228	D+ / 2.7	-1.78	1.94	7.91 /32	10.36 /30	2.90 /36	0.00	0.64
AA	Putnam College Adv Mod 1998 AX		C	(800) 354-2228	D+ / 2.5	-1.78	1.94	7.91 /32	10.36 /30	2.90 /36	0.00	0.64
AA	Putnam College Adv Mod 1998 B		C	(800) 354-2228	D / 2.1	-1.94	1.50	6.98 /26	9.49 /24	2.10 /28	0.00	1.39
AA	Putnam College Adv Mod 1998 BX		C	(800) 354-2228	D+ / 2.3	-1.92	1.70	7.26 /28	9.74 /25	2.36 /31	0.00	1.19
AA	Putnam College Adv Mod 1998 C		C	(800) 354-2228	D+ / 2.8	-1.93	1.50	7.05 /27	9.47 /24	2.09 /28	0.00	1.39
AA	Putnam College Adv Mod 1998 CX		C+	(800) 354-2228	C- / 3.2	-1.80	1.77	7.58 /30	10.06 /28	2.65 /33	0.00	0.89
AA	Putnam College Adv Mod 1998 O		C+	(800) 354-2228	C- / 3.8	-1.65	2.10	8.29 /35	10.77 /33	3.27 /39	0.00	0.27
AA	Putnam College Adv Mod 1999 A		C	(800) 354-2228	C- / 3.0	-1.78	2.14	8.48 /37	10.86 /34	3.00 /37	0.00	0.64
AA	Putnam College Adv Mod 1999 AX		C	(800) 354-2228	D+ / 2.8	-1.78	2.14	8.48 /37	10.86 /34	3.00 /37	0.00	0.64
AA	Putnam College Adv Mod 1999 B		C	(800) 354-2228	D+ / 2.5	-2.03	1.71	7.67 /30	9.98 /27	2.22 /29	0.00	1.39
AA	Putnam College Adv Mod 1999 BX		C	(800) 354-2228	D+ / 2.6	-2.02	1.90	7.85 /32	10.20 /29	2.43 /32	0.00	1.19
AA	Putnam College Adv Mod 1999 C		C	(800) 354-2228	C- / 3.1	-2.12	1.70	7.61 /30	9.99 /27	2.22 /29	0.00	1.39
AA	Putnam College Adv Mod 1999 CX		C+	(800) 354-2228	C- / 3.5	-1.99	1.97	8.16 /34	10.57 /32	2.72 /34	0.00	0.89
AA	Putnam College Adv Mod 1999 O		C+	(800) 354-2228	C- / 4.2	-1.75	2.30	8.86 /39	11.27 /38	3.36 /40	0.00	0.27
AA	Putnam College Adv Mod 2000 A		C	(800) 354-2228	C- / 3.3	-1.95	2.33	8.99 /40	11.26 /38	3.09 /38	0.00	0.64
AA	Putnam College Adv Mod 2000 AX		C	(800) 354-2228	C- / 3.1	-1.95	2.33	8.99 /40	11.26 /38	3.09 /38	0.00	0.64
AA	Putnam College Adv Mod 2000 B		C	(800) 354-2228	D+ / 2.8	-2.12	2.01	8.19 /34	10.44 /30	2.32 /30	0.00	1.39
AA	Putnam College Adv Mod 2000 BX		C	(800) 354-2228	D+ / 2.9	-2.11	2.10	8.37 /36	10.66 /32	2.53 /32	0.00	1.19
AA	Putnam College Adv Mod 2000 C		C+	(800) 354-2228	C- / 3.4	-2.10	1.99	8.12 /34	10.44 /30	2.32 /30	0.00	1.39
AA	Putnam College Adv Mod 2000 CX		C+	(800) 354-2228	C- / 3.8	-1.98	2.26	8.78 /39	11.01 /36	2.86 /35	0.00	0.89
AA	Putnam College Adv Mod 2000 O		B-	(800) 354-2228	C / 4.5	-1.82	2.48	9.46 /43	11.70 /40	3.48 /41	0.00	0.26
AA	Putnam College Adv Mod 2001 A		C+	(800) 354-2228	C- / 3.5	-2.09	2.45	9.42 /43	11.59 /40	3.20 /39	0.00	0.64
AA	Putnam College Adv Mod 2001 AX		C	(800) 354-2228	C- / 3.3	-2.09	2.45	9.42 /43	11.59 /40	3.20 /39	0.00	0.64
AA	Putnam College Adv Mod 2001 B		C	(800) 354-2228	C- / 3.0	-2.15	2.16	8.67 /38	10.77 /33	2.42 /31	0.00	1.39
AA	Putnam College Adv Mod 2001 BX		C	(800) 354-2228	C- / 3.2	-2.14	2.24	8.94 /40	11.01 /36	2.64 /33	0.00	1.19
AA	Putnam College Adv Mod 2001 C		C+	(800) 354-2228	C- / 3.6	-2.23	2.14	8.62 /38	10.74 /33	2.41 /31	0.00	1.39
AA	Putnam College Adv Mod 2001 CX		C+	(800) 354-2228	C- / 4.1	-2.11	2.39	9.22 /41	11.31 /38	2.94 /36	0.00	0.89
AA	Putnam College Adv Mod 2001 O		B-	(800) 354-2228	C / 4.7	-1.88	2.68	9.96 /47	12.05 /43	3.58 /42	0.00	0.26
AA	Putnam College Adv Mod 2002 A		C+	(800) 354-2228	C- / 3.7	-2.02	2.68	10.01 /47	11.95 /42	--	0.00	0.64
AA	Putnam College Adv Mod 2002 AX		C+	(800) 354-2228	C- / 3.5	-2.09	2.68	9.92 /46	11.92 /42	--	0.00	0.64
AA	Putnam College Adv Mod 2002 B		C	(800) 354-2228	C- / 3.2	-2.23	2.34	9.16 /41	11.09 /36	--	0.00	1.39
AA	Putnam College Adv Mod 2002 BX		C	(800) 354-2228	C- / 3.3	-2.22	2.41	9.31 /42	11.27 /38	--	0.00	1.19

● Denotes fund is closed to new investors
★ Denotes fund is included in Section II

RISK			NET ASSETS		ASSET				BULL / BEAR		FUND MANAGER		MINIMUMS		LOADS	
	3 Year		NAV						Last Bull	Last Bear	Manager	Manager	Initial	Additional	Front	Back
Risk Rating/Pts	Standard Deviation	Beta	As of 6/30/06	Total $(Mil)	Cash %	Stocks %	Bonds %	Other %	Portfolio Turnover Ratio	Market Return	Market Return	Quality Pct	Tenure (Years)	Purch. $	Purch. $	End Load	End Load
B+ / 9.7	5.3	1.10	10.47	38	0	66	34	0	26.1	48.4	-6.2	62	N/A	25	25	5.3	1.0
B+ / 9.7	5.3	1.09	10.10	6	0	66	34	0	26.1	44.8	-6.4	54	N/A	25	25	0.0	5.0
B+ / 9.7	5.3	1.10	10.16	27	0	66	34	0	26.1	46.0	-6.4	N/A	N/A	25	25	0.0	5.0
B+ / 9.7	5.3	1.10	10.16	4	0	66	34	0	26.1	44.7	-6.4	53	N/A	25	25	0.0	1.0
B+ / 9.7	5.3	1.10	10.32	14	0	66	34	0	26.1	47.2	-6.4	59	N/A	25	25	0.0	1.0
B+ / 9.7	5.3	1.10	10.67	8	0	66	34	0	26.1	50.2	-6.2	67	N/A	25	25	0.0	0.0
B+ / 9.5	5.7	1.17	10.47	11	0	66	34	0	26.4	52.1	-6.7	65	N/A	25	25	5.3	0.0
B+ / 9.6	5.7	1.17	10.47	38	0	66	34	0	26.4	52.1	-6.7	65	N/A	25	25	5.3	1.0
B+ / 9.6	5.7	1.17	10.08	6	0	66	34	0	26.4	48.4	-6.9	56	N/A	25	25	0.0	5.0
B+ / 9.5	5.7	1.18	10.15	26	0	66	34	0	26.4	49.6	-6.9	58	N/A	25	25	0.0	5.0
B+ / 9.6	5.7	1.17	10.16	3	0	66	34	0	26.4	48.5	-6.9	56	N/A	25	25	0.0	1.0
B+ / 9.6	5.7	1.17	10.32	12	0	66	34	0	26.4	51.0	-6.9	62	N/A	25	25	0.0	1.0
B+ / 9.6	5.7	1.17	10.66	8	0	66	34	0	26.4	53.9	-6.7	68	N/A	25	25	0.0	0.0
B+ / 9.4	6.0	1.23	10.48	12	0	66	34	0	26.2	55.7	-7.2	67	N/A	25	25	5.3	0.0
B+ / 9.4	6.0	1.23	10.48	38	0	66	34	0	26.2	55.7	-7.2	67	N/A	25	25	5.3	1.0
B+ / 9.4	6.0	1.23	10.10	6	0	66	34	0	26.2	52.0	-7.4	59	N/A	25	25	0.0	5.0
B+ / 9.4	6.1	1.25	10.16	25	0	66	34	0	26.2	52.8	-7.3	59	N/A	25	25	0.0	5.0
B+ / 9.4	6.0	1.23	10.18	3	0	66	34	0	26.2	51.9	-7.4	59	N/A	25	25	0.0	1.0
B+ / 9.4	6.0	1.24	10.34	13	0	66	34	0	26.2	54.4	-7.3	64	N/A	25	25	0.0	1.0
B+ / 9.4	6.0	1.23	10.69	7	0	66	34	0	26.2	57.4	-7.2	71	N/A	25	25	0.0	0.0
B+ / 9.3	6.4	1.30	10.51	12	0	78	20	2	25.4	58.8	-7.7	68	N/A	25	25	5.3	0.0
B+ / 9.3	6.4	1.30	10.51	42	0	78	20	2	25.4	58.8	-7.7	68	N/A	25	25	5.3	1.0
B+ / 9.3	6.3	1.29	10.12	6	0	78	20	2	25.4	55.0	-7.9	60	N/A	25	25	0.0	5.0
B+ / 9.3	6.3	1.29	10.19	25	0	78	20	2	25.4	55.9	-7.7	63	N/A	25	25	0.0	5.0
B+ / 9.3	6.3	1.28	10.18	3	0	78	20	2	25.4	54.8	-7.9	60	N/A	25	25	0.0	1.0
B+ / 9.3	6.3	1.28	10.36	13	0	78	20	2	25.4	57.5	-7.7	67	N/A	25	25	0.0	1.0
B+ / 9.3	6.3	1.29	10.71	8	0	78	20	2	25.4	60.8	-7.5	72	N/A	25	25	0.0	0.0
B+ / 9.2	6.7	1.35	10.49	11	0	78	20	2	24.9	61.9	-8.0	70	N/A	25	25	5.3	0.0
B+ / 9.2	6.7	1.34	10.49	40	0	78	20	2	24.9	61.9	-8.0	71	N/A	25	25	5.3	1.0
B+ / 9.2	6.7	1.35	10.11	6	0	78	20	2	24.9	58.1	-8.2	62	N/A	25	25	0.0	5.0
B+ / 9.2	6.7	1.35	10.17	28	0	78	20	2	24.9	59.0	-8.0	64	N/A	25	25	0.0	5.0
B+ / 9.2	6.7	1.34	10.18	3	0	78	20	2	24.9	58.1	-8.1	62	N/A	25	25	0.0	1.0
B+ / 9.2	6.6	1.34	10.34	12	0	78	20	2	24.9	60.5	-7.9	68	N/A	25	25	0.0	1.0
B+ / 9.2	6.7	1.35	10.69	8	0	78	20	2	24.9	63.6	-7.8	74	N/A	25	25	0.0	0.0
B+ / 9.1	6.9	1.39	10.55	10	0	78	20	2	22.9	64.5	-8.3	72	N/A	25	25	5.3	0.0
B+ / 9.1	6.9	1.39	10.55	49	0	78	20	2	22.9	64.5	-8.3	72	N/A	25	25	5.3	1.0
B+ / 9.1	7.0	1.40	10.17	6	0	78	20	2	22.9	60.7	-8.5	63	N/A	25	25	0.0	5.0
B+ / 9.1	7.0	1.40	10.23	32	0	78	20	2	22.9	61.6	-8.4	66	N/A	25	25	0.0	5.0
B+ / 9.1	7.0	1.40	10.25	2	0	78	20	2	22.9	60.9	-8.6	64	N/A	25	25	0.0	1.0
B+ / 9.1	7.0	1.40	10.41	14	0	78	20	2	22.9	63.1	-8.2	69	N/A	25	25	0.0	1.0
B+ / 9.1	7.0	1.40	10.76	11	0	78	20	2	22.9	66.6	-8.1	75	N/A	25	25	0.0	0.0
B+ / 9.1	7.2	1.43	11.27	11	0	84	14	2	24.8	66.8	-8.4	73	N/A	25	25	5.3	0.0
B+ / 9.1	7.2	1.43	11.27	51	0	84	14	2	24.8	66.8	-8.4	73	N/A	25	25	5.3	1.0
B+ / 9.1	7.1	1.43	10.90	6	0	84	14	2	24.8	62.8	-8.5	66	N/A	25	25	0.0	5.0
B+ / 9.0	7.2	1.45	10.97	32	0	84	14	2	24.8	64.2	-8.7	67	N/A	25	25	0.0	5.0
B+ / 9.0	7.2	1.44	10.96	2	0	84	14	2	24.8	62.9	-8.6	65	N/A	25	25	0.0	1.0
B+ / 9.0	7.2	1.45	11.13	14	0	84	14	2	24.8	65.5	-8.5	70	N/A	25	25	0.0	1.0
B+ / 9.0	7.2	1.44	11.48	10	0	84	14	2	24.8	69.1	-8.4	76	N/A	25	25	0.0	0.0
B+ / 9.0	7.4	1.48	12.64	14	0	84	14	2	18.8	68.9	-8.6	73	N/A	25	25	5.3	0.0
B+ / 9.0	7.4	1.48	12.63	25	0	84	14	2	18.8	68.9	-8.6	73	N/A	25	25	5.3	1.0
B+ / 9.0	7.4	1.47	12.27	8	0	84	14	2	18.8	64.9	-8.7	66	N/A	25	25	0.0	5.0
B+ / 9.0	7.4	1.46	12.33	15	0	84	14	2	18.8	65.9	-8.7	68	N/A	25	25	0.0	5.0

Fund Type	Fund Name	Ticker Symbol	Overall Weiss Investment Rating	Phone	Perfor- mance Rating/Pts	3 Mo	6 Mo	1Yr / Pct	3Yr / Pct	5Yr / Pct	Dividend Yield	Expense Ratio
AA	Putnam College Adv Mod 2002 C		C+	(800) 354-2228	C- / 3.9	-2.30	2.24	9.03 /40	11.09 /36	--	0.00	1.39
AA	Putnam College Adv Mod 2002 CX		C+	(800) 354-2228	C / 4.3	-2.19	2.54	9.65 /45	11.65 /40	--	0.00	0.89
AA	Putnam College Adv Mod 2002 O		B-	(800) 354-2228	C / 4.9	-1.98	2.88	10.39 /49	12.38 /45	--	0.00	0.26
AA	Putnam College Adv Mod 2003 A		C+	(800) 354-2228	C- / 3.9	-2.17	2.75	10.31 /49	12.17 /43	--	0.00	0.64
AA	Putnam College Adv Mod 2003 AX		C+	(800) 354-2228	C- / 3.7	-2.11	2.82	10.38 /49	12.20 /44	--	0.00	0.64
AA	Putnam College Adv Mod 2003 B		C	(800) 354-2228	C- / 3.4	-2.29	2.47	9.53 /44	11.35 /38	--	0.00	1.39
AA	Putnam College Adv Mod 2003 BX		C	(800) 354-2228	C- / 3.5	-2.28	2.52	9.71 /45	11.58 /40	--	0.00	1.19
AA	Putnam College Adv Mod 2003 C		C+	(800) 354-2228	C- / 4.1	-2.29	2.47	9.52 /44	11.34 /38	--	0.00	1.39
AA	Putnam College Adv Mod 2003 CX		C+	(800) 354-2228	C / 4.5	-2.19	2.70	10.07 /47	11.90 /42	--	0.00	0.89
AA	Putnam College Adv Mod 2003 O		B-	(800) 354-2228	C / 4.9	-2.02	3.05	10.86 /53	12.64 /47	--	0.00	0.25
AA	Putnam College Adv Mod Grad A		D+	(800) 354-2228	E- / 0.1	-0.09	0.80	2.45 / 5	2.87 / 1	2.15 /28	0.00	0.64
AA	Putnam College Adv Mod Grad AX		D+	(800) 354-2228	E- / 0.1	-0.09	0.80	2.45 / 5	2.87 / 1	2.15 /29	0.00	0.64
AA	Putnam College Adv Mod Grad B		D+	(800) 354-2228	E- / 0.1	-0.27	0.46	1.68 / 4	2.07 / 1	1.35 /23	0.00	1.39
AA	Putnam College Adv Mod Grad BX		D+	(800) 354-2228	E- / 0.1	-0.18	0.55	1.95 / 4	2.29 / 1	1.58 /24	0.00	1.19
AA	Putnam College Adv Mod Grad C		D+	(800) 354-2228	E- / 0.1	-0.27	0.37	1.67 / 4	2.06 / 1	1.35 /23	0.00	1.39
AA	Putnam College Adv Mod Grad CX		D+	(800) 354-2228	E- / 0.2	-0.18	0.63	2.20 / 5	2.61 / 1	1.90 /26	0.00	0.89
AA	Putnam College Adv Mod Grad O		D+	(800) 354-2228	E / 0.3	0.00	0.88	2.70 / 6	3.07 / 1	2.35 /31	0.00	0.43
AG	Putnam College Adv New Opps A		C-	(800) 354-2228	C- / 3.0	-6.29	0.00	9.49 /43	11.26 /38	--	0.00	0.64
AG	Putnam College Adv New Opps B		D+	(800) 354-2228	D+ / 2.5	-6.39	-0.29	8.79 /39	10.49 /31	--	0.00	1.39
AG	Putnam College Adv New Opps C		C-	(800) 354-2228	C- / 3.1	-6.49	-0.38	8.69 /38	10.42 /30	--	0.00	1.39
AG	Putnam College Adv New Opps O		C	(800) 354-2228	C / 4.3	-6.14	0.27	10.11 /48	11.90 /42	--	0.00	0.09
BA	Putnam College Adv New Value A		C+	(800) 354-2228	C / 4.9	-0.43	3.27	8.94 /40	13.90 /53	--	0.00	0.64
BA	Putnam College Adv New Value B		C+	(800) 354-2228	C / 4.4	-0.66	2.91	8.12 /34	13.05 /49	--	0.00	1.39
BA	Putnam College Adv New Value C		B-	(800) 354-2228	C / 5.0	-0.67	2.84	8.14 /34	13.04 /49	--	0.00	1.39
BA	Putnam College Adv New Value O		B+	(800) 354-2228	C+ / 6.0	-0.35	3.50	9.58 /44	14.55 /57	--	0.00	0.09
AA	Putnam College Adv US Eqty Inc A		C+	(800) 354-2228	C- / 3.9	-0.07	4.06	8.95 /40	12.03 /43	--	0.00	0.64
AA	Putnam College Adv US Eqty Inc B		C	(800) 354-2228	C- / 3.4	-0.21	3.71	8.19 /34	11.20 /37	--	0.00	1.39
AA	Putnam College Adv US Eqty Inc C		C+	(800) 354-2228	C- / 4.1	-0.21	3.70	8.18 /34	11.21 /37	--	0.00	1.39
AA	Putnam College Adv US Eqty Inc O		B-	(800) 354-2228	C / 5.0	0.13	4.35	9.59 /44	12.63 /47	--	0.00	0.09
GR	Putnam College Adv US SCB Cap		B	(800) 354-2228	B- / 7.0	-3.91	6.67	16.92 /77	17.76 /71	--	0.00	0.64
GR	Putnam College Adv US SCB Cap		B-	(800) 354-2228	C+ / 6.7	-4.04	6.31	16.06 /75	16.93 /68	--	0.00	1.39
GR	Putnam College Adv US SCB Cap		B	(800) 354-2228	B- / 7.1	-4.04	6.31	16.04 /75	16.91 /68	--	0.00	1.39
GR	Putnam College Adv US SCB Cap		B+	(800) 354-2228	B / 7.6	-3.76	7.00	17.54 /78	18.48 /74	--	0.00	0.09
AG	Putnam College Adv Voyager A		D-	(800) 354-2228	E / 0.3	-6.02	-4.03	2.58 / 6	5.74 / 6	--	0.00	0.64
AG	Putnam College Adv Voyager B		D-	(800) 354-2228	E- / 0.2	-6.21	-4.36	1.77 / 4	4.94 / 4	--	0.00	1.39
AG	Putnam College Adv Voyager C		D-	(800) 354-2228	E / 0.4	-6.21	-4.36	1.88 / 4	4.94 / 4	--	0.00	1.39
AG	Putnam College Adv Voyager O		D-	(800) 354-2228	E+ / 0.8	-5.98	-3.85	3.07 / 8	6.29 / 8	--	0.00	0.09
CV	Putnam Convertible Inc & Gr A	PCONX	C	(800) 354-2228	C- / 3.6	-0.08	4.96	11.08 /54	11.14 /37	7.36 /69	2.77	1.03
CV	Putnam Convertible Inc & Gr B	PCNBX	C	(800) 354-2228	C- / 3.1	-0.24	4.62	10.32 /49	10.32 /30	6.56 /65	2.19	1.78
CV	Putnam Convertible Inc & Gr C		C	(800) 354-2228	C- / 3.8	-0.27	4.60	10.28 /49	10.32 /30	6.57 /65	2.23	1.78
CV	Putnam Convertible Inc & Gr M	PCNMX	C	(800) 354-2228	C- / 3.6	-0.22	4.73	10.54 /51	10.59 /32	6.83 /66	2.37	1.53
CV	Putnam Convertible Inc & Gr R	PCVRX	C+	(800) 354-2228	C- / 3.8	-0.13	4.89	10.82 /52	10.89 /35	7.10 /67	2.71	1.28
CV	Putnam Convertible Inc & Gr Y	PCGYX	B-	(800) 354-2228	C / 4.7	-0.02	5.16	11.43 /56	11.43 /39	7.63 /70	3.18	0.78
AG	Putnam Discovery Growth Fund A	PVIIX	E+	(800) 354-2228	D+ / 2.7	-5.03	2.44	10.28 /49	10.35 /30	-1.49 /10	0.00	1.54
AG	Putnam Discovery Growth Fund B	PVYBX	E+	(800) 354-2228	D / 2.2	-5.25	2.00	9.41 /43	9.53 /24	-2.22 / 8	0.00	2.29
AG	Putnam Discovery Growth Fund C	PVYCX	E+	(800) 354-2228	D+ / 2.9	-5.20	2.06	9.50 /43	9.53 /24	-2.22 / 8	0.00	2.29
AG	Putnam Discovery Growth Fund M	PVYMX	E+	(800) 354-2228	D+ / 2.7	-5.15	2.17	9.77 /45	9.81 /26	-1.97 / 8	0.00	2.04
AG	Putnam Discovery Growth Fund R	PDGRX	D	(800) 354-2228	C- / 3.4	-5.11	2.29	9.96 /47	10.09 /28	-1.73 / 9	0.00	1.79
AG	Putnam Discovery Growth Fund Y		D	(800) 354-2228	C- / 3.8	-4.98	2.53	10.54 /51	10.63 /32	-1.28 /11	0.00	1.29
★ IN	Putnam Equity Income A	PEYAX	C	(800) 354-2228	C- / 4.2	0.05	4.24	9.38 /43	12.47 /46	5.80 /60	1.30	0.98
IN	Putnam Equity Income B	PEQNX	C	(800) 354-2228	C- / 3.7	-0.09	3.92	8.61 /38	11.65 /40	5.02 /54	0.66	1.73
IN	Putnam Equity Income C	PEQCX	C+	(800) 354-2228	C / 4.4	-0.08	3.87	8.56 /37	11.64 /40	5.01 /54	0.68	1.73

● Denotes fund is closed to new investors
★ Denotes fund is included in Section II

| RISK | 3 Year | | NET ASSETS | | ASSET | | | | Portfolio | BULL / BEAR | | FUND MANAGER | | MINIMUMS | | LOADS | |
Risk Rating/Pts	Standard Deviation	Beta	NAV As of 6/30/06	Total $(Mil)	Cash %	Stocks %	Bonds %	Other %	Turnover Ratio	Last Bull Market Return	Last Bear Market Return	Manager Quality Pct	Manager Tenure (Years)	Initial Purch. $	Additional Purch. $	Front End Load	Back End Load
B+ / 9.0	7.4	1.47	12.31	3	0	84	14	2	18.8	65.1	-8.8	66	N/A	25	25	0.0	1.0
B+ / 9.0	7.5	1.48	12.50	6	0	84	14	2	18.8	67.4	-8.7	71	N/A	25	25	0.0	1.0
B+ / 9.0	7.4	1.46	12.86	9	0	84	14	2	18.8	71.0	-8.5	78	N/A	25	25	0.0	0.0
B / 8.9	7.6	1.50	15.30	21	0	84	14	2	19.7	70.5	N/A	74	N/A	25	25	5.3	0.0
B / 8.9	7.6	1.50	15.31	2	0	84	14	2	19.7	70.5	N/A	75	N/A	25	25	5.3	1.0
B / 8.9	7.6	1.50	14.94	11	0	84	14	2	19.7	66.5	N/A	67	N/A	25	25	0.0	5.0
B / 8.9	7.6	1.50	15.03	1	0	84	14	2	19.7	67.4	N/A	70	N/A	25	25	0.0	5.0
B / 8.9	7.6	1.50	14.96	4	0	84	14	2	19.7	66.7	N/A	67	N/A	25	25	0.0	1.0
B / 8.9	7.6	1.50	15.19	N/A	0	84	14	2	19.7	69.1	N/A	72	N/A	25	25	0.0	1.0
B / 8.9	7.6	1.49	15.52	5	0	84	14	2	19.7	72.4	N/A	78	N/A	25	25	0.0	1.0
B+ / 9.9	1.5	0.30	11.31	2	0	0	0	100	56.7	12.7	-0.7	44	N/A	25	25	5.3	0.0
B+ / 9.9	1.5	0.30	11.31	11	0	0	0	100	56.7	12.7	-0.7	43	N/A	25	25	5.3	1.0
B+ / 9.9	1.5	0.30	10.91	N/A	0	0	0	100	56.7	9.9	-0.9	35	N/A	25	25	0.0	5.0
B+ / 9.9	1.5	0.31	10.98	N/A	0	0	0	100	56.7	10.7	-0.9	37	N/A	25	25	0.0	5.0
B+ / 9.9	1.5	0.30	10.97	1	0	0	0	100	56.7	10.0	-0.9	35	N/A	25	25	0.0	1.0
B+ / 9.9	1.5	0.30	11.15	10	0	0	0	100	56.7	11.9	-0.8	41	N/A	25	25	0.0	1.0
B+ / 9.9	1.5	0.30	11.42	1	0	0	0	100	56.7	13.5	-0.7	46	N/A	25	25	0.0	1.0
B- / 7.5	11.5	1.29	10.73	11	0	0	0	100	15.9	74.7	-9.9	30	N/A	25	25	5.3	0.0
B- / 7.4	11.6	1.30	10.40	10	0	0	0	100	15.9	70.8	-10.0	25	N/A	25	25	0.0	5.0
B- / 7.4	11.5	1.29	10.38	4	0	0	0	100	15.9	70.8	-10.1	25	N/A	25	25	0.0	1.0
B- / 7.5	11.5	1.30	11.00	3	0	0	0	100	15.9	77.8	-9.7	34	N/A	25	25	0.0	0.0
B / 8.7	8.4	1.65	13.89	21	0	100	0	0	19.6	80.7	-10.3	81	N/A	25	25	5.3	0.0
B / 8.7	8.4	1.65	13.45	20	0	100	0	0	19.6	76.6	-10.6	75	N/A	25	25	0.0	5.0
B / 8.7	8.3	1.64	13.42	8	0	100	0	0	19.6	76.5	-10.5	75	N/A	25	25	0.0	1.0
B / 8.7	8.4	1.65	14.19	8	0	100	0	0	19.6	84.0	-10.3	85	N/A	25	25	0.0	0.0
B / 8.9	7.7	1.52	14.61	9	0	0	0	100	12.2	N/A	N/A	72	N/A	25	25	5.3	0.0
B / 8.9	7.7	1.52	14.26	4	0	0	0	100	12.2	N/A	N/A	65	N/A	25	25	0.0	5.0
B / 8.9	7.7	1.53	14.29	4	0	0	0	100	12.2	N/A	N/A	64	N/A	25	25	0.0	1.0
B / 8.9	7.7	1.52	14.86	5	0	0	0	100	12.2	N/A	N/A	77	N/A	25	25	0.0	1.0
B- / 7.2	12.7	1.39	13.75	15	0	100	0	0	18.2	108.3	-12.8	81	N/A	25	25	5.3	0.0
B- / 7.2	12.7	1.39	13.30	14	0	100	0	0	18.2	103.7	-13.0	75	N/A	25	25	0.0	5.0
B- / 7.2	12.7	1.39	13.31	7	0	100	0	0	18.2	103.5	-13.0	75	N/A	25	25	0.0	1.0
B- / 7.2	12.7	1.39	14.07	6	0	100	0	0	18.2	112.2	-12.8	85	N/A	25	25	0.0	1.0
B- / 7.7	9.6	1.15	9.53	20	0	100	0	0	17.2	44.3	-9.7	9	N/A	25	25	5.3	0.0
B- / 7.6	9.6	1.14	9.21	17	0	100	0	0	17.2	41.0	-9.9	7	N/A	25	25	0.0	5.0
B- / 7.6	9.6	1.14	9.21	8	0	100	0	0	17.2	41.0	-9.9	7	N/A	25	25	0.0	1.0
B- / 7.8	9.5	1.14	9.74	3	0	100	0	0	17.2	46.8	-9.6	11	N/A	25	25	0.0	0.0
B / 8.0	7.1	1.08	18.08	567	1	1	1	97	66.5	57.0	1.1	85	4	500	50	5.3	0.0
B / 8.6	7.1	1.08	17.81	51	1	1	1	97	66.5	53.4	0.9	80	4	500	50	0.0	5.0
B / 8.5	7.1	1.08	17.97	19	1	1	1	97	66.5	53.4	0.9	80	4	500	50	0.0	1.0
B / 8.3	7.1	1.08	17.95	5	1	1	1	97	66.5	54.6	0.9	82	4	500	50	3.3	0.0
B+ / 9.1	7.1	1.08	18.05	1	1	1	1	97	66.5	55.9	1.1	84	4	500	50	3.3	0.0
B+ / 9.1	7.1	1.08	18.08	24	1	1	1	97	66.5	58.3	1.2	87	4	150,000,000	0	0.0	0.0
C / 4.6	13.0	1.40	18.88	548	0	98	0	2	141.1	71.7	-11.0	19	N/A	500	50	5.3	0.0
C / 4.5	12.9	1.40	17.32	280	0	98	0	2	141.1	67.5	-11.2	14	N/A	500	50	0.0	5.0
C / 4.5	13.0	1.40	17.87	36	0	98	0	2	141.1	67.6	-11.3	14	N/A	500	50	0.0	1.0
C / 4.5	13.0	1.40	17.86	21	0	98	0	2	141.1	68.9	-11.1	16	N/A	500	50	3.3	0.0
C+ / 5.7	13.0	1.40	18.76	N/A	0	98	0	2	141.1	70.4	-11.1	17	N/A	500	50	0.0	0.0
C+ / 5.7	12.9	1.40	19.08	10	0	98	0	2	141.1	72.9	-11.0	20	N/A	150,000,000	0	0.0	0.0
B / 8.1	7.8	0.97	17.35	2,473	1	94	0	5	52.3	69.1	-8.8	71	8	500	50	5.3	0.0
B / 8.1	7.8	0.97	17.22	611	1	94	0	5	52.3	65.1	-8.9	63	8	500	50	0.0	5.0
B / 8.1	7.7	0.97	17.27	89	1	94	0	5	52.3	65.0	-9.0	64	7	500	50	0.0	1.0

Data as of June 30, 2006

					PERFORMANCE							
99 Pct = Best			**Overall Weiss Investment Rating**				Total Return % through 6/30/06				Incl. in Returns	
0 Pct = Worst					**Perfor- mance Rating/Pts**				Annualized		Dividend	Expense
Fund Type	Fund Name	Ticker Symbol		Phone		3 Mo	6 Mo	1Yr / Pct	3Yr / Pct	5Yr / Pct	Yield	Ratio
IN	Putnam Equity Income M	PEIMX	C	(800) 354-2228	C- / 4.2	-0.02	4.01	8.83 /39	11.92 /42	5.28 /56	0.88	1.48
IN	Putnam Equity Income R	PEIRX	C+	(800) 354-2228	C / 4.9	0.05	4.13	9.09 /41	12.19 /44	5.55 /58	1.16	1.23
IN	Putnam Equity Income Y	PEIYX	B-	(800) 354-2228	C / 5.2	0.12	4.38	9.66 /45	12.78 /47	6.08 /62	1.60	0.73
FO	Putnam Europe Equity A	PEUGX	A-	(800) 354-2228	B+ / 8.5	1.27	12.54	24.54 /88	21.55 /84	7.92 /71	1.03	1.49
FO	Putnam Europe Equity B	PEUBX	A-	(800) 354-2228	B+ / 8.3	1.06	12.13	23.65 /87	20.64 /82	7.10 /67	0.32	2.24
FO	Putnam Europe Equity C		A	(800) 354-2228	B+ / 8.5	1.08	12.13	23.66 /87	20.63 /82	7.10 /67	0.42	2.24
FO	Putnam Europe Equity M	PEUMX	A-	(800) 354-2228	B+ / 8.4	1.16	12.30	23.97 /87	20.94 /82	7.36 /69	0.58	1.99
FO	Putnam Europe Equity R	PEERX	A+	(800) 354-2228	B+ / 8.7	1.23	12.51	24.52 /88	21.34 /83	7.71 /70	1.01	1.74
FO	Putnam Europe Equity Y		B	(800) 354-2228	B+ / 8.8	1.31	12.67	24.75 /88	21.62 /84	7.95 /71	1.13	1.24
★ GI	Putnam Fund for Gr & Inc A	PGRWX	C-	(800) 354-2228	C- / 3.2	-1.00	2.84	7.98 /33	11.06 /36	3.20 /39	1.15	0.89
GI	Putnam Fund for Gr & Inc B	PGIBX	C-	(800) 354-2228	D+ / 2.6	-1.23	2.45	7.12 /27	10.23 /29	2.42 /31	0.45	1.64
GI	Putnam Fund for Gr & Inc C	PGRIX	C	(800) 354-2228	C- / 3.3	-1.20	2.45	7.12 /27	10.21 /29	2.43 /32	0.47	1.64
GI	Putnam Fund for Gr & Inc M	PGRMX	C-	(800) 354-2228	C- / 3.1	-1.14	2.58	7.41 /29	10.50 /31	2.69 /34	0.69	1.39
GI	Putnam Fund for Gr & Inc R	PATNX	C	(800) 354-2228	C- / 3.8	-1.07	2.68	7.65 /30	10.78 /34	2.94 /36	1.00	1.14
GI	Putnam Fund for Gr & Inc Y	PGIYX	C+	(800) 354-2228	C / 4.3	-0.93	2.97	8.23 /35	11.33 /38	3.46 /41	1.46	0.64
★ AA	Putnam George Fund A	PGEOX	C-	(800) 354-2228	D- / 1.2	-0.49	1.78	4.57 /13	7.53 /13	4.05 /46	2.58	0.99
AA	Putnam George Fund B	PGEBX	C-	(800) 354-2228	E+ / 0.8	-0.64	1.40	3.79 /10	6.73 / 9	3.28 /39	1.96	1.74
AA	Putnam George Fund C	PGPCX	C-	(800) 354-2228	D- / 1.3	-0.69	1.41	3.75 /10	6.72 / 9	3.27 /39	1.99	1.74
AA	Putnam George Fund M	PGEMX	C-	(800) 354-2228	D- / 1.1	-0.63	1.48	4.02 /11	6.98 /10	3.54 /42	2.17	1.49
AA	Putnam George Fund R	PUTNX	C	(800) 354-2228	D / 1.7	-0.55	1.65	4.25 /12	7.27 /11	3.80 /44	2.53	1.24
AA	Putnam George Fund Y	PGEYX	C	(800) 354-2228	D / 2.0	-0.43	1.91	4.82 /14	7.80 /14	4.33 /49	2.97	0.75
GL	Putnam Global Equity Fd A	PEQUX	C+	(800) 354-2228	C+ / 6.3	-0.30	7.79	16.89 /77	15.85 /63	4.72 /52	0.72	1.26
GL	Putnam Global Equity Fd B	PEQBX	C	(800) 354-2228	C+ / 5.9	-0.56	7.31	15.99 /75	15.01 /59	3.96 /46	0.05	2.01
GL	Putnam Global Equity Fd C	PUGCX	C+	(800) 354-2228	C+ / 6.4	-0.42	7.39	16.06 /75	15.05 /59	3.98 /46	0.07	2.01
GL	Putnam Global Equity Fd M	PEQMX	C	(800) 354-2228	C+ / 6.2	-0.42	7.48	16.27 /75	15.30 /60	4.22 /48	0.30	1.76
GL	Putnam Global Equity Fd R	PGLRX	C+	(800) 354-2228	C+ / 6.7	-0.41	7.72	16.61 /76	15.59 /62	4.51 /50	0.69	1.51
GL	Putnam Global Equity Fd Y	PEQYX	C+	(800) 354-2228	C+ / 6.9	-0.30	7.89	17.13 /77	16.15 /64	4.91 /53	0.97	1.01
EN	Putnam Global Natural Resources A	EBERX	B	(800) 354-2228	A+ / 9.7	3.42	13.86	31.53 /95	32.24 /97	17.57 /94	0.08	1.22
EN	Putnam Global Natural Resources B	PNRBX	B	(800) 354-2228	A+ / 9.6	3.21	13.40	30.52 /95	31.25 /96	16.68 /94	0.00	1.97
EN	Putnam Global Natural Resources C	PGLCX	B	(800) 354-2228	A+ / 9.7	3.23	13.43	30.56 /95	31.24 /96	16.68 /94	0.00	1.97
EN	Putnam Global Natural Resources M	PGLMX	B	(800) 354-2228	A+ / 9.6	3.30	13.57	30.87 /95	31.57 /96	16.98 /94	0.00	1.72
EN	Putnam Global Natural Resources R	PGNRX	B-	(800) 354-2228	A+ / 9.7	3.38	13.72	31.21 /95	31.93 /97	17.29 /94	0.08	1.47
EN	Putnam Global Natural Resources Y		C	(800) 354-2228	A+ / 9.7	3.49	13.96	31.75 /95	32.31 /97	17.61 /94	0.12	N/A
GR	Putnam Growth Opportunities A	POGAX	E	(800) 354-2228	E- / 0.2	-4.14	-1.27	5.17 /16	5.00 / 4	-5.06 / 2	0.84	1.37
GR	Putnam Growth Opportunities B	POGBX	E	(800) 354-2228	E- / 0.1	-4.37	-1.66	4.41 /12	4.20 / 3	-5.77 / 2	0.06	2.12
GR	Putnam Growth Opportunities C	POGCX	E	(800) 354-2228	E / 0.3	-4.32	-1.64	4.36 /12	4.20 / 3	-5.77 / 2	0.06	2.12
GR	Putnam Growth Opportunities M	PGOMX	E	(800) 354-2228	E- / 0.2	-4.30	-1.55	4.60 /13	4.45 / 3	-5.54 / 2	0.31	1.87
GR	Putnam Growth Opportunities R	PGORX	E	(800) 354-2228	E / 0.4	-4.17	-1.36	4.97 /15	4.74 / 3	-5.29 / 2	0.90	1.62
GR	Putnam Growth Opportunities Y	PGOYX	E+	(800) 354-2228	E / 0.5	-4.07	-1.18	5.44 /17	5.27 / 5	-4.82 / 3	1.15	1.12
HL	Putnam Health Sciences Trust A	PHSTX	E	(800) 354-2228	E+ / 0.7	-5.03	-4.18	4.29 /12	7.24 /11	0.98 /20	0.00	1.10
HL	Putnam Health Sciences Trust B	PHSBX	E	(800) 354-2228	E / 0.5	-5.21	-4.53	3.53 / 9	6.45 / 8	0.23 /16	0.00	1.85
HL	Putnam Health Sciences Trust C	PCHSX	E	(800) 354-2228	E+ / 0.8	-5.19	-4.53	3.54 / 9	6.45 / 8	0.23 /16	0.00	1.85
HL	Putnam Health Sciences Trust M	PHLMX	E	(800) 354-2228	E+ / 0.7	-5.14	-4.42	3.77 /10	6.71 / 9	0.48 /18	0.00	1.60
HL	Putnam Health Sciences Trust R	PHSRX	E+	(800) 354-2228	D- / 1.1	-5.08	-4.30	4.05 /11	6.98 /10	0.74 /19	0.00	1.35
HL	Putnam Health Sciences Trust Y	PHSYX	D-	(800) 354-2228	D- / 1.4	-4.96	-4.06	4.55 /13	7.51 /12	1.24 /22	0.00	0.85
FO	Putnam International Capital Opp A	PNVAX	A	(800) 354-2228	A+ / 9.6	1.09	13.24	33.70 /96	31.16 /96	13.90 /90	1.17	1.60
FO	Putnam International Capital Opp B	PVNBX	A	(800) 354-2228	A / 9.5	0.89	12.81	32.70 /96	30.16 /96	13.02 /89	0.60	2.35
FO	Putnam International Capital Opp C	PUVCX	A	(800) 354-2228	A+ / 9.6	0.88	12.82	32.70 /96	30.19 /96	13.04 /89	0.61	2.35
FO	Putnam International Capital Opp M	PIVMX	A	(800) 354-2228	A+ / 9.6	0.94	12.98	33.04 /96	30.51 /96	13.33 /89	0.83	2.10
FO	Putnam International Capital Opp R	PICRX	A	(800) 354-2228	A+ / 9.6	1.00	13.10	33.38 /96	30.90 /96	13.66 /90	1.24	1.85
FO	Putnam International Capital Opp Y	PIVYX	A+	(800) 354-2228	A+ / 9.7	1.15	13.39	34.05 /96	31.48 /96	14.16 /90	1.44	1.40
★ FO	Putnam International Equity A	POVSX	B+	(800) 354-2228	B / 8.2	0.24	10.29	25.70 /89	20.30 /80	7.44 /69	1.74	1.30

● Denotes fund is closed to new investors
★ Denotes fund is included in Section II

RISK			NET ASSETS		ASSET				BULL / BEAR		FUND MANAGER		MINIMUMS		LOADS	
	3 Year		NAV						Portfolio	Last Bull	Last Bear	Manager	Manager	Initial	Additional	Front	Back
Risk Rating/Pts	Standard Deviation	Beta	As of 6/30/06	Total $(Mil)	Cash %	Stocks %	Bonds %	Other %	Turnover Ratio	Market Return	Market Return	Quality Pct	Tenure (Years)	Purch. $	Purch. $	End Load	End Load
B /8.1	7.8	0.97	17.24	51	1	94	0	5	52.3	66.5	-8.9	67	8	500	50	3.3	0.0
B /8.1	7.8	0.97	17.31	3	1	94	0	5	52.3	67.7	-8.8	69	6	500	50	0.0	0.0
B /8.4	7.7	0.97	17.35	320	1	94	0	5	52.3	70.4	-8.8	74	6	150,000,000	0	0.0	0.0
B- /7.1	10.5	0.97	25.58	341	0	99	0	1	56.4	116.9	-11.2	36	N/A	500	50	5.3	0.0
B- /7.1	10.4	0.96	24.68	127	0	99	0	1	56.4	111.8	-11.3	30	N/A	500	50	0.0	5.0
B- /7.2	10.5	0.97	25.33	6	0	99	0	1	56.4	111.8	-11.4	30	N/A	500	50	0.0	1.0
B- /7.1	10.5	0.97	25.38	14	0	99	0	1	56.4	113.4	-11.3	32	N/A	500	50	3.3	1.0
B- /7.7	10.5	0.97	25.55	N/A	0	99	0	1	56.4	115.9	-11.3	34	N/A	500	50	0.0	1.0
C /5.5	10.5	0.97	25.61	6	0	99	0	1	56.4	117.2	-11.2	36	N/A	150,000,000	0	0.0	0.0
B /8.1	7.7	0.97	20.18	11,525	1	98	0	1	52.8	66.9	-10.0	58	1	500	50	5.3	0.0
B /8.2	7.6	0.97	19.89	1,786	1	98	0	1	52.8	62.8	-10.1	48	1	500	50	0.0	5.0
B /8.2	7.7	0.97	20.11	94	1	98	0	1	52.8	62.9	-10.1	48	1	500	50	0.0	1.0
B /8.2	7.7	0.97	20.05	110	1	98	0	1	52.8	64.2	-10.0	51	1	500	50	3.3	0.0
B /8.2	7.7	0.97	20.12	1	1	98	0	1	52.8	65.5	-10.0	55	1	500	50	0.0	0.0
B /8.3	7.7	0.97	20.22	1,253	1	98	0	1	52.8	68.2	-9.9	61	1	150,000,000	0	0.0	0.0
B+ /9.5	4.8	1.01	18.04	3,153	N/A	60	38	N/A	169.0	40.6	-5.1	55	6	500	50	5.3	0.0
B+ /9.8	4.9	1.02	17.87	643	N/A	60	38	N/A	169.0	37.4	-5.4	45	6	500	50	0.0	5.0
B+ /9.8	4.9	1.02	17.94	70	N/A	60	38	N/A	169.0	37.4	-5.4	45	7	500	50	0.0	1.0
B+ /9.8	4.9	1.02	17.86	194	N/A	60	38	N/A	169.0	38.5	-5.3	48	6	500	50	3.3	0.0
B+ /9.8	4.9	1.02	17.99	2	N/A	60	38	N/A	169.0	39.6	-5.2	51	6	500	50	0.0	0.0
B+ /9.8	4.9	1.02	18.09	492	N/A	60	38	N/A	169.0	41.8	-5.1	58	4	150,000,000	0	0.0	0.0
C+ /6.3	9.1	0.84	9.82	1,601	1	98	0	1	82.1	89.8	-9.9	19	4	500	50	5.3	0.0
C+ /6.2	9.2	0.84	8.95	310	1	98	0	1	82.1	84.9	-9.8	14	4	500	50	0.0	5.0
C+ /6.2	9.1	0.84	9.44	31	1	98	0	1	82.1	84.7	-9.7	15	4	500	50	0.0	1.0
C+ /6.2	9.1	0.84	9.48	31	1	98	0	1	82.1	86.1	-9.7	16	4	500	50	3.3	1.0
C+ /6.3	9.1	0.84	9.77	1	1	98	0	1	82.1	88.5	-9.9	18	4	500	50	0.0	1.0
C+ /6.8	9.1	0.84	10.12	25	1	98	0	1	82.1	91.6	-10.0	21	N/A	150,000,000	0	0.0	1.0
C /4.7	17.1	0.85	31.71	466	0	99	0	1	81.2	158.1	-0.6	88	N/A	500	50	5.3	0.0
C /4.6	17.1	0.85	29.88	130	0	99	0	1	81.2	152.0	-0.8	83	N/A	500	50	0.0	5.0
C /4.6	17.1	0.85	30.32	26	0	99	0	1	81.2	152.2	-0.8	83	N/A	500	50	0.0	1.0
C /4.6	17.1	0.85	30.96	8	0	99	0	1	81.2	154.1	-0.7	85	N/A	500	50	3.3	1.0
C /4.3	17.1	0.85	31.50	2	0	99	0	1	81.2	156.2	-0.6	86	N/A	500	50	0.0	1.0
D+ /2.6	17.1	0.85	31.75	15	0	99	0	1	81.2	158.5	-0.6	88	N/A	150,000,000	0	0.0	0.0
C+ /5.7	8.8	1.09	13.21	363	0	99	0	1	114.0	39.2	-9.7	8	N/A	500	50	5.3	0.0
C+ /5.7	8.9	1.09	12.46	282	0	99	0	1	114.0	36.0	-9.9	6	N/A	500	50	0.0	5.0
C+ /5.7	8.9	1.09	12.62	28	0	99	0	1	114.0	35.9	-9.9	6	N/A	500	50	0.0	1.0
C+ /5.7	8.8	1.09	12.69	10	0	99	0	1	114.0	37.0	-9.8	7	N/A	500	50	3.3	0.0
C+ /5.7	8.8	1.09	13.10	N/A	0	99	0	1	114.0	38.1	-9.7	8	N/A	500	50	0.0	0.0
C+ /6.4	8.9	1.09	13.44	8	0	99	0	1	114.0	40.3	-9.7	9	N/A	150,000,000	0	0.0	0.0
C /5.5	8.1	0.52	59.81	1,695	2	97	0	1	31.0	46.7	-4.6	61	N/A	500	50	5.3	0.0
C /5.3	8.1	0.52	53.72	595	2	97	0	1	31.0	43.3	-4.8	51	N/A	500	50	0.0	5.0
C /5.4	8.1	0.52	56.84	38	2	97	0	1	31.0	43.3	-4.8	51	N/A	500	50	0.0	1.0
C /5.4	8.1	0.52	56.61	26	2	97	0	1	31.0	44.4	-4.7	54	N/A	500	50	3.3	0.0
C /5.5	8.1	0.52	59.18	1	2	97	0	1	31.0	45.6	-4.7	58	N/A	500	50	0.0	0.0
C+ /6.6	8.1	0.52	60.70	24	2	97	0	1	31.0	47.9	-4.5	63	N/A	150,000,000	0	0.0	0.0
C+ /6.3	12.7	1.17	32.51	923	2	97	0	1	63.9	183.2	-10.3	77	7	500	50	5.3	0.0
C+ /6.2	12.6	1.16	31.71	438	2	97	0	1	63.9	176.8	-10.6	70	N/A	500	50	0.0	5.0
C+ /6.2	12.6	1.16	32.13	80	2	97	0	1	63.9	176.7	-10.5	71	7	500	50	0.0	1.0
C+ /6.2	12.6	1.16	32.12	24	2	97	0	1	63.9	178.9	-10.5	73	N/A	500	50	3.3	1.0
C+ /6.3	12.7	1.17	32.30	1	2	97	0	1	63.9	181.8	-10.4	76	N/A	500	50	0.0	0.0
B- /7.3	12.6	1.16	32.60	73	2	97	0	1	63.9	185.7	-10.3	80	N/A	150,000,000	0	0.0	1.0
C+ /6.6	10.4	1.01	28.82	3,602	1	98	0	1	74.8	110.9	-10.6	22	N/A	500	50	5.3	0.0

					PERFORMANCE						Incl. in Returns	
			Overall Weiss Investment Rating		Perfor-mance Rating/Pts	Total Return % through 6/30/06			Annualized		Dividend Yield	Expense Ratio
Fund Type	Fund Name	Ticker Symbol		Phone		3 Mo	6 Mo	1Yr / Pct	3Yr / Pct	5Yr / Pct		
FO	Putnam International Equity B	POVBX	B	(800) 354-2228	B / 8.0	0.04	9.87	24.77 /88	19.39 /77	6.64 /65	1.15	2.05
FO	Putnam International Equity C	PIGCX	B+	(800) 354-2228	B / 8.2	0.04	9.88	24.77 /88	19.40 /77	6.65 /65	1.16	2.05
FO	Putnam International Equity M	POVMX	B+	(800) 354-2228	B / 8.1	0.11	10.01	25.12 /89	19.69 /78	6.90 /66	1.33	1.80
FO	Putnam International Equity R	PIERX	B+	(800) 354-2228	B+ / 8.4	0.18	10.12	25.42 /89	20.00 /79	7.19 /68	1.75	1.55
FO	Putnam International Equity Y	POVYX	A	(800) 354-2228	B+ / 8.5	0.31	10.42	26.05 /90	20.60 /81	7.72 /70	2.04	0.97
FO	Putnam Intl Growth & Inc A	PNGAX	A+	(800) 354-2228	B+ / 8.9	0.54	9.96	28.23 /93	24.17 /90	10.63 /83	1.03	1.43
FO	Putnam Intl Growth & Inc B	PGNBX	A	(800) 354-2228	B+ / 8.8	0.35	9.50	27.31 /92	23.26 /88	9.79 /80	0.30	2.18
FO	Putnam Intl Growth & Inc C	PIGRX	A+	(800) 354-2228	A- / 9.0	0.41	9.49	27.29 /92	23.26 /88	9.81 /80	0.48	2.18
FO	Putnam Intl Growth & Inc M	PIGMX	A	(800) 354-2228	B+ / 8.9	0.41	9.61	27.67 /92	23.57 /89	10.06 /81	0.61	1.93
FO	Putnam Intl Growth & Inc R	PIIRX	A+	(800) 354-2228	A- / 9.1	0.48	9.77	28.03 /93	23.87 /89	10.36 /82	1.05	1.68
FO	Putnam Intl Growth & Inc Y		A+	(800) 354-2228	A- / 9.2	0.68	10.07	28.69 /93	24.52 /90	10.97 /84	1.28	0.55
FO	Putnam Intl New Opportunities A	PINOX	B-	(800) 354-2228	B+ / 8.5	0.20	10.75	27.19 /92	21.67 /84	9.34 /78	1.41	1.70
FO	Putnam Intl New Opportunities B	PINWX	B-	(800) 354-2228	B+ / 8.3	0.00	10.39	26.30 /90	20.80 /82	8.51 /74	0.74	2.45
FO	Putnam Intl New Opportunities C	PIOCX	B-	(800) 354-2228	B+ / 8.5	0.07	10.40	26.29 /90	20.77 /82	8.55 /74	0.91	2.45
FO	Putnam Intl New Opportunities M	PINMX	B-	(800) 354-2228	B+ / 8.4	0.07	10.52	26.65 /91	21.07 /83	8.80 /76	1.06	2.20
FO	Putnam Intl New Opportunities R	PNPRX	B+	(800) 354-2228	B+ / 8.7	0.13	10.64	26.91 /91	21.44 /84	9.11 /77	1.42	1.95
FO	Putnam Intl New Opportunities Y		B-	(800) 354-2228	B+ / 8.8	0.20	10.90	27.43 /92	21.75 /85	9.38 /78	1.53	N/A
★ GR	Putnam Investors Fund A	PINVX	C	(800) 354-2228	C- / 3.8	-2.98	0.88	8.48 /37	12.55 /46	1.32 /22	0.97	1.07
GR	Putnam Investors Fund B	PNVBX	C-	(800) 354-2228	C- / 3.3	-3.17	0.56	7.70 /30	11.73 /41	0.57 /18	0.32	1.82
GR	Putnam Investors Fund C	PCINX	C	(800) 354-2228	C- / 3.9	-3.22	0.46	7.57 /30	11.69 /40	0.56 /18	0.33	1.82
GR	Putnam Investors Fund M	PNVMX	C	(800) 354-2228	C- / 3.8	-3.11	0.62	7.90 /32	12.02 /43	0.81 /19	0.53	1.57
GR	Putnam Investors Fund R	PIVRX	C+	(800) 354-2228	C / 4.5	-3.07	0.74	8.19 /34	12.28 /44	1.10 /21	1.10	1.32
GR	Putnam Investors Fund Y	PNVYX	C+	(800) 354-2228	C / 4.9	-2.94	1.02	8.71 /38	12.82 /48	1.56 /24	1.26	0.41
MC	Putnam Mid Cap Value Fund A	PMVAX	B-	(800) 354-2228	B- / 7.1	-1.99	5.46	15.38 /73	18.24 /73	10.19 /81	0.07	1.30
MC	Putnam Mid Cap Value Fund B	PMVBX	C+	(800) 354-2228	C+ / 6.7	-2.25	5.11	14.52 /70	17.37 /70	9.36 /78	0.00	2.05
MC	Putnam Mid Cap Value Fund C	PMPCX	B-	(800) 354-2228	B- / 7.2	-2.18	5.11	14.52 /70	17.39 /70	9.37 /78	0.00	2.05
MC	Putnam Mid Cap Value Fund M		B-	(800) 354-2228	B- / 7.1	-2.16	5.20	14.77 /71	17.67 /71	9.64 /79	0.00	1.80
MC	Putnam Mid Cap Value Fund R	PMVRX	A-	(800) 354-2228	B- / 7.5	-2.07	5.37	15.09 /72	17.95 /72	9.93 /80	0.11	1.55
MC	Putnam Mid Cap Value Fund Y	PMVYX	A	(800) 354-2228	B / 7.7	-1.92	5.67	15.68 /74	18.55 /75	10.43 /82	0.28	0.54
★ GR	Putnam New Opportunities A	PNOPX	D-	(800) 354-2228	C- / 3.2	-6.20	0.13	9.90 /46	11.72 /41	-0.96 /12	0.00	1.12
GR	Putnam New Opportunities B	PNOBX	D-	(800) 354-2228	D+ / 2.7	-6.37	-0.24	9.05 /40	10.88 /34	-1.70 / 9	0.00	1.87
GR	Putnam New Opportunities C	PNOCX	D-	(800) 354-2228	C- / 3.4	-6.37	-0.23	9.09 /41	10.88 /34	-1.70 / 9	0.00	1.87
GR	Putnam New Opportunities M	PNOMX	D-	(800) 354-2228	C- / 3.2	-6.33	-0.12	9.33 /42	11.16 /37	-1.45 /10	0.00	1.62
GR	Putnam New Opportunities R	PNORX	D	(800) 354-2228	C- / 4.0	-6.26	0.00	9.62 /44	11.46 /39	-1.19 /11	0.00	1.37
GR	Putnam New Opportunities Y	PNOYX	C-	(800) 354-2228	C / 4.4	-6.15	0.25	10.15 /48	11.99 /42	-0.71 /13	0.00	0.87
GR	Putnam New Value Fund A	PANVX	C+	(800) 354-2228	C / 5.1	-0.43	3.45	9.32 /42	14.34 /56	6.13 /62	0.96	1.13
GR	Putnam New Value Fund B	PBNVX	C+	(800) 354-2228	C / 4.6	-0.54	3.10	8.57 /37	13.49 /51	5.33 /57	0.23	1.88
GR	Putnam New Value Fund C	PNVCX	C+	(800) 354-2228	C / 5.3	-0.55	3.11	8.58 /37	13.49 /51	5.35 /57	0.43	1.88
GR	Putnam New Value Fund M	PMNVX	C+	(800) 354-2228	C / 5.1	-0.48	3.17	8.81 /39	13.79 /53	5.62 /59	0.46	1.63
GR	Putnam New Value Fund R	PNLRX	B-	(800) 354-2228	C+ / 5.7	-0.49	3.30	9.04 /40	14.08 /54	5.87 /60	0.98	1.38
GR	Putnam New Value Fund Y	PYNVX	B	(800) 354-2228	C+ / 6.0	-0.32	3.56	9.61 /44	14.63 /57	6.40 /63	1.22	0.88
MC	Putnam OTC Emerging Growth A	POEGX	E+	(800) 354-2228	C- / 3.7	-5.13	5.18	13.95 /68	12.12 /43	-2.64 / 6	0.00	1.40
MC	Putnam OTC Emerging Growth B	POTBX	E+	(800) 354-2228	C- / 3.2	-5.30	4.87	13.14 /65	11.29 /38	-3.37 / 5	0.00	2.15
MC	Putnam OTC Emerging Growth C	POECX	E+	(800) 354-2228	C- / 3.9	-5.28	4.78	13.20 /65	11.32 /38	-3.38 / 5	0.00	2.15
MC	Putnam OTC Emerging Growth M	POEMX	E+	(800) 354-2228	C- / 3.7	-5.15	5.02	13.49 /66	11.59 /40	-3.12 / 5	0.00	1.90
MC	Putnam OTC Emerging Growth R	POTRX	D	(800) 354-2228	C / 4.5	-5.15	5.08	13.74 /67	11.83 /41	-2.87 / 6	0.00	1.65
MC	Putnam OTC Emerging Growth Y	POEYX	D+	(800) 354-2228	C / 4.8	-5.07	5.39	14.34 /69	12.42 /45	-2.38 / 7	0.00	1.15
GR	Putnam Research Fund A	PNRAX	D	(800) 354-2228	D / 1.9	-2.32	1.66	6.04 /21	9.30 /23	0.23 /16	0.26	1.19
GR	Putnam Research Fund B	PRFBX	D	(800) 354-2228	D- / 1.5	-2.52	1.24	5.21 /16	8.45 /17	-0.52 /13	0.00	1.94
GR	Putnam Research Fund C	PRACX	D	(800) 354-2228	D / 2.1	-2.57	1.23	5.18 /16	8.46 /18	-0.52 /13	0.00	1.94
GR	Putnam Research Fund M	PRFMX	D	(800) 354-2228	D / 1.9	-2.54	1.35	5.49 /18	8.71 /19	-0.28 /14	0.00	1.69
GR	Putnam Research Fund R	PRSRX	D+	(800) 354-2228	D+ / 2.6	-2.46	1.45	5.71 /19	9.02 /21	-0.03 /15	0.09	1.44

● Denotes fund is closed to new investors
★ Denotes fund is included in Section II

Risk Rating/Pts	3 Year Standard Deviation	Beta	NAV As of 6/30/06	Total $(Mil)	Cash %	Stocks %	Bonds %	Other %	Portfolio Turnover Ratio	Last Bull Market Return	Last Bear Market Return	Manager Quality Pct	Manager Tenure (Years)	Initial Purch. $	Additional Purch. $	Front End Load	Back End Load
C+ / 6.5	10.4	1.01	27.71	1,164	1	98	0	1	74.8	105.9	-10.8	18	N/A	500	50	0.0	5.0
C+ / 6.5	10.4	1.01	28.25	264	1	98	0	1	74.8	105.9	-10.8	18	N/A	500	50	0.0	1.0
C+ / 6.5	10.4	1.01	28.35	90	1	98	0	1	74.8	107.5	-10.7	19	N/A	500	50	3.3	1.0
C+ / 6.5	10.4	1.01	28.61	3	1	98	0	1	74.8	109.3	-10.7	20	N/A	500	50	0.0	1.0
B- / 7.4	10.4	1.01	29.03	1,256	1	98	0	1	74.8	112.5	-10.6	24	N/A	150,000,000	0	0.0	1.0
B- / 7.2	10.0	0.98	14.80	624	1	98	0	1	62.4	133.6	-8.8	59	N/A	500	50	5.3	0.0
B- / 7.1	10.0	0.98	14.53	179	1	98	0	1	62.4	128.1	-9.0	49	N/A	500	50	0.0	5.0
B- / 7.1	10.0	0.98	14.65	35	1	98	0	1	62.4	128.3	-9.1	49	N/A	500	50	0.0	1.0
B- / 7.1	10.0	0.98	14.72	18	1	98	0	1	62.4	129.9	-8.9	53	N/A	500	50	3.3	1.0
B / 8.1	10.0	0.98	14.72	N/A	1	98	0	1	62.4	131.9	-8.9	56	N/A	500	50	0.0	0.0
B / 8.1	10.0	0.98	14.86	20	1	98	0	1	62.4	135.6	-8.9	62	N/A	150,000,000	0	0.0	1.0
C / 5.3	11.5	1.10	15.04	581	0	99	0	1	92.1	123.1	-8.9	18	7	500	50	5.3	0.0
C / 5.3	11.6	1.10	14.03	129	0	99	0	1	92.1	117.8	-9.1	14	N/A	500	50	0.0	5.0
C / 5.3	11.5	1.09	14.44	17	0	99	0	1	92.1	117.7	-9.1	14	N/A	500	50	0.0	1.0
C / 5.3	11.6	1.10	14.39	19	0	99	0	1	92.1	119.6	-9.0	15	N/A	500	50	3.3	1.0
C+ / 6.2	11.5	1.09	14.98	N/A	0	99	0	1	92.1	121.8	-9.0	18	7	500	50	0.0	0.0
C / 5.2	11.6	1.10	15.06	16	0	99	0	1	92.1	123.4	-8.9	19	N/A	150,000,000	0	0.0	0.0
B / 8.1	8.9	1.12	13.68	2,193	0	99	0	1	112.5	75.0	-10.4	58	4	500	50	5.3	0.0
B / 8.0	8.9	1.13	12.54	901	0	99	0	1	112.5	70.9	-10.5	48	4	500	50	0.0	5.0
B / 8.0	8.9	1.12	13.22	56	0	99	0	1	112.5	70.8	-10.5	48	4	500	50	0.0	1.0
B / 8.0	8.9	1.13	13.07	43	0	99	0	1	112.5	72.2	-10.5	52	4	500	50	3.3	0.0
B / 8.0	8.9	1.13	13.58	N/A	0	99	0	1	112.5	73.9	-10.4	55	4	500	50	0.0	0.0
B / 8.1	8.9	1.12	13.86	632	0	99	0	1	112.5	76.2	-10.3	62	4	150,000,000	0	0.0	0.0
C+ / 6.9	10.3	0.90	15.25	595	0	99	0	1	N/A	99.3	-9.3	73	7	500	50	5.3	0.0
C+ / 6.8	10.3	0.90	14.80	251	0	99	0	1	N/A	94.5	-9.5	66	7	500	50	0.0	5.0
C+ / 6.8	10.3	0.90	14.81	38	0	99	0	1	N/A	94.6	-9.5	65	5	500	50	0.0	1.0
C+ / 6.9	10.3	0.90	14.96	13	0	99	0	1	N/A	96.2	-9.4	68	5	500	50	3.3	0.0
B / 8.0	10.3	0.90	15.11	3	0	99	0	1	N/A	97.9	-9.4	71	7	500	50	0.0	0.0
B / 8.0	10.3	0.90	15.29	45	0	99	0	1	N/A	100.7	-9.2	75	7	150,000,000	0	0.0	0.0
C / 5.2	11.5	1.30	45.72	3,691	0	99	0	1	97.3	77.1	-9.8	33	1	500	50	5.3	0.0
C / 5.2	11.6	1.30	40.84	612	0	99	0	1	97.3	73.0	-10.0	27	1	500	50	0.0	5.0
C / 5.2	11.5	1.30	43.34	40	0	99	0	1	97.3	73.0	-10.0	27	1	500	50	0.0	1.0
C / 5.2	11.5	1.29	42.79	80	0	99	0	1	97.3	74.4	-9.9	29	1	500	50	3.3	0.0
C / 5.2	11.6	1.30	45.36	1	0	99	0	1	97.3	75.8	-9.8	31	1	500	50	0.0	0.0
C+ / 6.1	11.6	1.30	47.33	414	0	99	0	1	97.3	78.5	-9.8	35	1	150,000,000	0	0.0	0.0
B / 8.2	8.4	1.05	18.60	1,298	2	98	0	0	52.0	83.2	-10.3	80	11	500	50	5.3	0.0
B / 8.2	8.4	1.05	18.29	444	2	98	0	0	52.0	78.8	-10.4	73	10	500	50	0.0	5.0
B / 8.2	8.4	1.05	18.23	66	2	98	0	0	52.0	78.8	-10.4	73	7	500	50	0.0	1.0
B / 8.3	8.4	1.05	18.53	32	2	98	0	0	52.0	80.3	-10.4	76	10	500	50	3.3	0.0
B / 8.3	8.4	1.05	18.46	1	2	98	0	0	52.0	81.8	-10.4	78	11	500	50	0.0	0.0
B / 8.3	8.4	1.05	18.63	115	2	98	0	0	52.0	84.6	-10.2	82	11	150,000,000	0	0.0	0.0
C- / 3.6	15.1	1.30	8.33	511	4	93	0	3	163.5	83.3	-11.2	2	2	500	50	5.3	0.0
C- / 3.5	15.1	1.30	7.32	146	4	93	0	3	163.5	78.7	-11.4	1	2	500	50	0.0	5.0
C- / 3.5	15.1	1.30	7.89	13	4	93	0	3	163.5	79.0	-11.5	1	2	500	50	0.0	1.0
C- / 3.5	15.0	1.29	7.74	16	4	93	0	3	163.5	80.4	-11.3	2	2	500	50	3.3	0.0
C / 4.9	15.0	1.29	8.28	N/A	4	93	0	3	163.5	81.7	-11.2	2	2	500	50	0.0	0.0
C / 4.9	15.0	1.29	8.61	45	4	93	0	3	163.5	84.7	-11.3	2	2	150,000,000	0	0.0	0.0
B- / 7.6	8.6	1.09	14.72	495	0	99	0	1	113.0	59.0	-11.6	30	N/A	500	50	5.3	0.0
B- / 7.5	8.6	1.09	13.93	251	0	99	0	1	113.0	55.3	-11.8	24	N/A	500	50	0.0	5.0
B- / 7.5	8.6	1.09	14.01	31	0	99	0	1	113.0	55.3	-11.8	24	N/A	500	50	0.0	1.0
B- / 7.6	8.6	1.09	14.22	13	0	99	0	1	113.0	56.5	-11.7	26	N/A	500	50	3.3	0.0
B- / 7.6	8.6	1.09	14.66	N/A	0	99	0	1	113.0	57.8	-11.6	28	N/A	500	50	0.0	0.0

			Overall Weiss Investment Rating	Phone	Perfor-mance Rating/Pts	3 Mo	6 Mo	1Yr / Pct	Annualized 3Yr / Pct	Annualized 5Yr / Pct	Dividend Yield	Expense Ratio

99 Pct = Best
0 Pct = Worst

PERFORMANCE — Total Return % through 6/30/06 — Incl. in Returns

Fund Type	Fund Name	Ticker Symbol	Overall Weiss Investment Rating	Phone	Perfor-mance Rating/Pts	3 Mo	6 Mo	1Yr / Pct	3Yr / Pct	5Yr / Pct	Dividend Yield	Expense Ratio
GR	Putnam Research Fund Y	PURYX	C-	(800) 354-2228	D+ / 2.9	-2.30	1.78	6.28 /22	9.54 /24	0.48 /18	0.55	0.94
AA	Putnam Retirement Ready 2010 A		U	(800) 354-2228	U /	-0.98	0.67	3.74 /10	--	--	2.42	1.07
AA	Putnam Retirement Ready 2010 Y		U	(800) 354-2228	U /	-0.92	0.79	3.98 /10	--	--	2.65	N/A
AA	Putnam Retirement Ready 2015 A		U	(800) 354-2228	U /	-1.54	1.40	6.25 /22	--	--	2.23	1.12
AA	Putnam Retirement Ready 2015 Y		U	(800) 354-2228	U /	-1.47	1.52	6.53 /23	--	--	2.55	N/A
AA	Putnam Retirement Ready 2020 A		U	(800) 354-2228	U /	-1.76	2.03	8.20 /34	--	--	1.84	1.15
AA	Putnam Retirement Ready 2020 Y		U	(800) 354-2228	U /	-1.71	2.14	8.45 /36	--	--	2.00	N/A
AA	Putnam Retirement Ready 2025 A		U	(800) 354-2228	U /	-1.85	2.82	10.09 /48	--	--	1.71	1.18
AA	Putnam Retirement Ready 2025 Y		U	(800) 354-2228	U /	-1.77	2.96	10.37 /49	--	--	1.99	N/A
AA	Putnam Retirement Ready 2030 A		U	(800) 354-2228	U /	-1.96	3.05	10.83 /53	--	--	1.68	1.20
AA	Putnam Retirement Ready 2030 Y		U	(800) 354-2228	U /	-1.91	3.17	11.09 /54	--	--	1.82	N/A
AA	Putnam Retirement Ready 2035 A		U	(800) 354-2228	U /	-2.07	3.23	11.54 /57	--	--	1.61	1.21
AA	Putnam Retirement Ready 2035 Y		U	(800) 354-2228	U /	-2.02	3.36	11.82 /58	--	--	1.74	N/A
AA	Putnam Retirement Ready Maturity A		U	(800) 354-2228	U /	-0.79	0.36	2.30 / 5	--	--	2.98	1.04
SC	Putnam Small Cap Growth A	PNSAX	D+	(800) 354-2228	C+ / 5.8	-8.47	1.80	10.17 /48	16.57 /66	4.45 /50	0.00	1.55
SC	Putnam Small Cap Growth B	PNSBX	D	(800) 354-2228	C / 5.3	-8.66	1.44	9.36 /42	15.72 /62	3.68 /43	0.00	2.30
SC	Putnam Small Cap Growth C		D+	(800) 354-2228	C+ / 5.9	-8.66	1.39	9.31 /42	15.70 /62	3.67 /43	0.00	2.30
SC	Putnam Small Cap Growth M	PSGMX	D+	(800) 354-2228	C+ / 5.7	-8.61	1.56	9.61 /44	15.99 /63	3.94 /45	0.00	2.05
SC	Putnam Small Cap Growth R	PSGRX	C	(800) 354-2228	C+ / 6.3	-8.52	1.68	9.92 /46	16.29 /65	4.19 /48	0.00	1.80
SC	Putnam Small Cap Growth Y	PSYGX	C+	(800) 354-2228	C+ / 6.5	-8.46	1.93	10.46 /50	16.81 /67	4.58 /51	0.00	1.30
SC	● Putnam Small Capital Value Fund A	PSLAX	C-	(800) 354-2228	B / 8.2	-4.40	7.39	13.91 /68	22.61 /86	12.51 /88	0.00	1.23
SC	● Putnam Small Capital Value Fund B	PSLBX	D+	(800) 354-2228	B / 8.0	-4.55	7.01	13.07 /65	21.69 /84	11.68 /86	0.00	1.98
SC	● Putnam Small Capital Value Fund C	PSLCX	C-	(800) 354-2228	B / 8.2	-4.59	6.99	13.05 /64	21.68 /84	11.67 /86	0.00	1.98
SC	● Putnam Small Capital Value Fund M	PSLMX	C-	(800) 354-2228	B / 8.2	-4.52	7.12	13.35 /66	21.97 /85	11.96 /87	0.00	1.73
SC	● Putnam Small Capital Value Fund Y	PYSVX	A-	(800) 354-2228	B+ / 8.6	-4.33	7.50	14.17 /69	22.91 /87	12.80 /88	0.00	0.98
GR	Putnam Tax Smart Equity A	PATSX	C	(800) 354-2228	C- / 3.4	-3.17	0.27	7.30 /28	12.04 /43	2.99 /37	0.16	1.21
GR	Putnam Tax Smart Equity B	PBTSX	C-	(800) 354-2228	D+ / 2.9	-3.33	-0.10	6.52 /23	11.23 /37	2.23 /29	0.00	1.96
GR	Putnam Tax Smart Equity C	PCSMX	C	(800) 354-2228	C- / 3.5	-3.33	-0.10	6.41 /23	11.19 /37	2.23 /29	0.00	1.96
GR	Putnam Tax Smart Equity M		C	(800) 354-2228	C- / 3.3	-3.26	0.00	6.70 /24	11.49 /39	2.48 /32	0.00	1.71
UT	Putnam Utilities Gr & Inc A	PUGIX	B-	(800) 354-2228	C+ / 5.6	4.53	5.04	7.23 /28	14.90 /58	2.77 /35	1.97	1.22
UT	Putnam Utilities Gr & Inc B	PUTBX	C+	(800) 354-2228	C / 5.1	4.35	4.74	6.43 /23	14.05 /54	2.01 /27	1.32	1.97
UT	Putnam Utilities Gr & Inc C		B	(800) 354-2228	C+ / 5.7	4.35	4.65	6.36 /22	14.06 /54	2.00 /27	1.34	1.97
UT	Putnam Utilities Gr & Inc M	PUTMX	B-	(800) 354-2228	C / 5.5	4.40	4.77	6.68 /24	14.33 /56	2.27 /30	1.52	1.72
UT	Putnam Utilities Gr & Inc R	PULRX	B	(800) 354-2228	C+ / 6.1	4.47	4.92	6.99 /26	14.63 /57	2.53 /32	1.85	1.47
UT	Putnam Utilities Gr & Inc Y		C+	(800) 354-2228	C+ / 6.3	4.60	5.17	7.42 /29	14.97 /59	2.81 /35	2.25	0.97
MC	Putnam Vista Fund A	PVISX	C	(800) 354-2228	C+ / 6.0	-7.03	1.78	14.33 /69	16.29 /65	1.36 /23	0.00	1.10
MC	Putnam Vista Fund B	PVTBX	C-	(800) 354-2228	C / 5.5	-7.19	1.40	13.49 /66	15.40 /61	0.61 /18	0.00	1.85
MC	Putnam Vista Fund C	PCVFX	C	(800) 354-2228	C+ / 6.1	-7.23	1.38	13.48 /66	15.42 /61	0.61 /18	0.00	1.85
MC	Putnam Vista Fund M	PVIMX	C	(800) 354-2228	C+ / 5.9	-7.12	1.52	13.83 /68	15.65 /62	0.86 /20	0.00	1.60
MC	Putnam Vista Fund R	PVIRX	C	(800) 354-2228	C+ / 6.5	-7.07	1.70	14.07 /68	16.04 /64	1.15 /21	0.00	1.35
MC	Putnam Vista Fund Y	PVIYX	C+	(800) 354-2228	C+ / 6.7	-6.92	1.89	14.60 /70	16.59 /66	1.63 /24	0.00	0.85
★ GR	Putnam Voyager A	PVOYX	E+	(800) 354-2228	E / 0.4	-5.96	-3.91	2.92 / 7	6.12 / 7	-2.64 / 6	0.71	1.08
GR	Putnam Voyager B	PVOBX	E+	(800) 354-2228	E / 0.3	-6.12	-4.20	2.24 / 5	5.35 / 5	-3.36 / 5	0.00	1.83
GR	Putnam Voyager C	PVFCX	E+	(800) 354-2228	E / 0.5	-6.16	-4.25	2.17 / 5	5.33 / 5	-3.37 / 5	0.00	1.83
GR	Putnam Voyager M	PVOMX	E+	(800) 354-2228	E / 0.4	-6.04	-4.09	2.45 / 5	5.60 / 5	-3.12 / 5	0.17	1.58
GR	Putnam Voyager R	PVYRX	E+	(800) 354-2228	E+ / 0.7	-6.00	-3.99	2.70 / 6	5.87 / 6	-2.86 / 6	0.63	1.33
GR	Putnam Voyager Y	PVYYX	D-	(800) 354-2228	E+ / 0.9	-5.94	-3.79	3.15 / 8	6.38 / 8	-2.39 / 7	1.00	0.83
HL	Quaker Biotech Pharma-Hlthcare A	QBPAX	D-	(800) 220-8888	E / 0.4	-11.22	-2.34	2.13 / 5	6.43 / 8	--	0.00	2.16
HL	● Quaker Biotech Pharma-Hlthcare B	QBPBX	D-	(800) 220-8888	E / 0.3	-11.31	-2.64	1.43 / 3	5.67 / 6	--	0.00	2.91
HL	Quaker Biotech Pharma-Hlthcare C	CBPCX	D-	(800) 220-8888	E / 0.5	-11.31	-2.64	1.43 / 3	5.67 / 6	--	0.00	2.91
GR	Quaker Capital Opportunities A	QUKTX	C+	(800) 220-8888	C / 4.7	-3.32	0.00	7.04 /26	14.49 /56	--	0.00	1.72
GR	● Quaker Capital Opportunities B	QCOBX	C+	(800) 220-8888	C / 4.3	-3.40	-0.37	6.31 /22	13.69 /52	--	0.00	2.47

● Denotes fund is closed to new investors
★ Denotes fund is included in Section II

www.WeissRatings.com

RISK Risk Rating/Pts	3 Year Standard Deviation	Beta	NAV As of 6/30/06	Total $(Mil)	Cash %	Stocks %	Bonds %	Other %	Portfolio Turnover Ratio	Last Bull Market Return	Last Bear Market Return	Manager Quality Pct	Manager Tenure (Years)	Initial Purch. $	Additional Purch. $	Front End Load	Back End Load
B- /7.9	8.6	1.09	14.84	84	0	99	0	1	113.0	60.3	-11.6	32	N/A	150,000,000	0	0.0	0.0
U /	N/A	N/A	58.65	43	25	33	40	2	N/A	N/A	N/A	N/A	N/A	500	50	5.3	0.0
U /	N/A	N/A	61.34	41	25	33	40	2	N/A	N/A	N/A	N/A	N/A	500	50	0.0	0.0
U /	N/A	N/A	65.92	63	15	53	30	2	N/A	N/A	N/A	N/A	N/A	500	50	5.3	0.0
U /	N/A	N/A	66.14	63	15	53	30	2	N/A	N/A	N/A	N/A	N/A	500	50	0.0	0.0
U /	N/A	N/A	66.50	79	9	66	23	2	N/A	N/A	N/A	N/A	N/A	500	50	5.3	0.0
U /	N/A	N/A	71.25	73	9	66	23	2	N/A	N/A	N/A	N/A	N/A	500	50	0.0	0.0
U /	N/A	N/A	73.38	59	7	76	15	2	N/A	N/A	N/A	N/A	N/A	500	50	5.3	0.0
U /	N/A	N/A	73.67	59	7	76	15	2	N/A	N/A	N/A	N/A	N/A	500	50	0.0	0.0
U /	N/A	N/A	69.91	44	4	81	13	2	N/A	N/A	N/A	N/A	2	500	50	5.3	0.0
U /	N/A	N/A	75.57	43	4	81	13	2	N/A	N/A	N/A	N/A	2	500	50	0.0	0.0
U /	N/A	N/A	70.86	30	3	86	9	2	N/A	N/A	N/A	N/A	2	500	50	5.3	0.0
U /	N/A	N/A	77.22	26	3	86	9	2	N/A	N/A	N/A	N/A	2	500	50	0.0	0.0
U /	N/A	N/A	56.00	31	30	25	44	1	N/A	N/A	N/A	N/A	N/A	500	50	5.3	0.0
C- /4.1	16.3	1.08	22.58	375	1	98	0	1	92.0	124.1	-12.3	26	N/A	500	50	5.3	0.0
C- /4.0	16.3	1.08	21.83	69	1	98	0	1	92.0	118.8	-12.5	21	N/A	500	50	0.0	5.0
C- /4.0	16.3	1.08	21.82	22	1	98	0	1	92.0	119.0	-12.5	20	N/A	500	50	0.0	1.0
C- /4.0	16.3	1.08	22.09	6	1	98	0	1	92.0	120.6	-12.4	22	N/A	500	50	3.3	0.0
C+ /5.9	16.3	1.08	22.44	10	1	98	0	1	92.0	122.5	-12.4	24	N/A	500	50	0.0	0.0
C+ /5.9	16.3	1.08	22.73	35	1	98	0	1	92.0	125.5	-12.3	27	N/A	150,000,000	0	0.0	0.0
C- /3.0	13.9	0.93	18.02	475	0	99	0	1	28.7	140.9	-8.9	91	7	500	50	5.3	0.0
D+ /2.3	13.9	0.93	16.80	218	0	99	0	1	28.7	135.4	-9.1	88	7	500	50	0.0	5.0
D+ /2.3	13.9	0.93	16.83	41	0	99	0	1	28.7	135.2	-9.1	88	7	500	50	0.0	1.0
D+ /2.6	13.9	0.93	17.31	7	0	99	0	1	28.7	137.2	-9.0	89	4	500	50	3.3	0.0
C+ /6.8	13.9	0.93	18.35	47	0	99	0	1	28.7	142.9	-8.8	92	4	150,000,000	0	0.0	0.0
B /8.3	8.9	1.13	10.98	134	0	99	0	1	135.5	71.1	-9.0	52	3	500	50	5.3	0.0
B /8.2	9.0	1.13	10.46	98	0	99	0	1	135.5	67.2	-9.2	42	3	500	50	0.0	5.0
B /8.2	8.9	1.13	10.46	32	0	99	0	1	135.5	67.2	-9.2	42	3	500	50	0.0	1.0
B /8.2	9.0	1.13	10.67	4	0	99	0	1	135.5	68.6	-9.2	45	3	500	50	3.3	0.0
B /8.3	7.5	0.61	11.37	447	4	91	4	1	38.8	81.8	-5.9	63	N/A	500	50	5.3	0.0
B /8.4	7.5	0.61	11.32	62	4	91	4	1	38.8	77.6	-6.1	54	N/A	500	50	0.0	5.0
B /8.5	7.5	0.61	11.31	4	4	91	4	1	38.8	77.7	-6.1	55	N/A	500	50	0.0	1.0
B /8.4	7.5	0.61	11.36	3	4	91	4	1	38.8	78.9	-6.1	57	N/A	500	50	3.3	0.0
B /8.4	7.5	0.61	11.36	N/A	4	91	4	1	38.8	80.5	-6.1	61	N/A	500	50	0.0	0.0
C+ /6.4	7.5	0.61	11.37	3	4	91	4	1	38.8	82.1	-5.9	64	N/A	150,000,000	0	0.0	0.0
C+ /5.7	13.5	1.18	10.85	1,905	1	98	0	1	73.8	102.2	-9.8	18	1	500	50	5.3	0.0
C+ /5.7	13.4	1.17	9.42	405	1	98	0	1	73.8	97.5	-9.9	15	1	500	50	0.0	5.0
C+ /5.7	13.4	1.17	10.27	41	1	98	0	1	73.8	97.5	-10.0	14	1	500	50	0.0	1.0
C+ /5.7	13.5	1.18	10.04	32	1	98	0	1	73.8	98.9	-9.9	15	1	500	50	3.3	0.0
C+ /5.7	13.4	1.17	10.78	1	1	98	0	1	73.8	100.9	-9.8	18	1	500	50	0.0	0.0
C+ /6.7	13.5	1.17	11.30	226	1	98	0	1	73.8	103.8	-9.8	20	1	150,000,000	0	0.0	0.0
C+ /6.7	9.6	1.15	16.72	5,812	N/A	100	0	N/A	93.3	46.1	-9.6	10	N/A	500	50	5.3	0.0
C+ /6.7	9.6	1.15	14.58	1,175	N/A	100	0	N/A	93.3	42.7	-9.8	8	N/A	500	50	0.0	5.0
C+ /6.7	9.6	1.15	16.00	77	N/A	100	0	N/A	93.3	42.7	-9.9	8	N/A	500	50	0.0	1.0
C+ /6.7	9.6	1.15	15.72	64	N/A	100	0	N/A	93.3	43.8	-9.7	8	N/A	500	50	3.3	0.0
C+ /6.7	9.6	1.15	16.61	2	N/A	100	0	N/A	93.3	44.9	-9.6	9	N/A	500	50	0.0	0.0
B- /7.2	9.6	1.14	17.27	1,592	N/A	100	0	N/A	93.3	47.2	-9.6	11	N/A	150,000,000	0	0.0	0.0
B- /7.8	12.1	0.71	12.50	15	20	79	0	1	272.8	59.4	-2.6	34	4	2,000	100	5.5	0.0
B- /7.7	12.1	0.70	12.15	1	20	79	0	1	272.8	55.6	-2.8	29	4	2,000	100	0.0	5.0
B- /7.7	12.1	0.71	12.16	4	20	79	0	1	272.8	55.6	-2.7	28	4	2,000	100	0.0	1.0
B /8.4	9.1	0.94	11.07	13	9	90	0	1	226.6	69.6	0.1	87	4	2,000	100	5.5	0.0
B /8.4	9.1	0.94	10.81	1	9	90	0	1	226.6	65.9	-0.1	83	4	2,000	100	0.0	5.0

Fund Type	Fund Name	Ticker Symbol	Overall Weiss Investment Rating	Phone	Performance Rating/Pts	Total Return % through 6/30/06			Annualized		Incl. in Returns	
	99 Pct = Best 0 Pct = Worst					3 Mo	6 Mo	1Yr / Pct	3Yr / Pct	5Yr / Pct	Dividend Yield	Expense Ratio
GR	Quaker Capital Opportunities C	QCOCX	C+	(800) 220-8888	C / 4.9	-3.40	-0.28	6.32 /22	13.69 /52	--	0.00	2.47
GR	Quaker Core Equity A	QUCEX	D	(800) 220-8888	D / 1.9	-3.30	4.05	9.57 /44	9.12 /22	0.18 /16	0.00	1.76
GR	● Quaker Core Equity B	QCEBX	D+	(800) 220-8888	D- / 1.5	-3.52	3.69	8.74 /38	8.31 /17	-0.57 /13	0.00	2.51
GR	Quaker Core Equity C	QCECX	C-	(800) 220-8888	D / 2.1	-3.46	3.72	8.79 /39	8.33 /17	-0.56 /13	0.00	2.51
GR	Quaker Core Equity Inst	QCEIX	C-	(800) 220-8888	D+ / 2.9	-3.28	4.13	9.81 /46	9.41 /24	0.44 /17	0.00	1.51
GR	Quaker Geewax Terker Core Value A	QUGTX	A	(800) 220-8888	B- / 7.4	-2.97	8.72	21.42 /83	19.00 /76	--	0.59	2.09
MC	Quaker Mid Cap Value A	QMCVX	C+	(800) 220-8888	B / 8.0	-5.75	3.45	10.32 /49	22.80 /87	13.59 /90	0.00	1.61
MC	● Quaker Mid Cap Value B	QMCBX	B+	(800) 220-8888	B / 7.7	-6.00	3.05	9.47 /43	21.88 /85	12.85 /88	0.00	2.36
MC	Quaker Mid Cap Value C	QMCCX	A-	(800) 220-8888	B / 8.0	-5.97	3.10	9.47 /43	21.86 /85	12.73 /88	0.00	2.36
MC	Quaker Mid Cap Value Inst	QMVIX	A	(800) 220-8888	B+ / 8.4	-5.74	3.56	10.56 /51	23.10 /88	13.87 /90	0.00	1.36
SC	Quaker Small Cap Growth A	QSGAX	C+	(800) 220-8888	C+ / 6.2	-7.30	5.64	12.32 /61	16.72 /67	3.69 /43	0.00	1.81
SC	● Quaker Small Cap Growth B	QSGBX	C+	(800) 220-8888	C+ / 5.7	-7.59	5.25	11.32 /55	15.67 /62	2.82 /35	0.00	2.56
SC	Quaker Small Cap Growth C	QSGCX	C+	(800) 220-8888	C+ / 6.2	-7.54	5.32	11.47 /57	15.76 /62	--	0.00	2.56
SC	Quaker Small Cap Growth Inst	QSGIX	B-	(800) 220-8888	C+ / 6.9	-7.35	5.79	12.51 /62	16.94 /68	4.20 /48	0.00	1.56
SC	Quaker Small Cap Value A	QUSVX	C+	(800) 220-8888	B / 7.8	-3.80	7.73	16.76 /76	20.61 /82	12.53 /88	0.00	1.75
SC	● Quaker Small Cap Value B	QSVBX	B+	(800) 220-8888	B / 7.6	-3.99	7.36	15.95 /75	19.72 /78	11.67 /86	0.00	2.50
SC	Quaker Small Cap Value C	QSVCX	B+	(800) 220-8888	B / 7.9	-4.00	7.34	15.91 /74	19.78 /79	11.73 /86	0.00	2.50
SC	Quaker Small Cap Value Inst	QSVIX	A-	(800) 220-8888	B+ / 8.3	-3.73	7.87	17.12 /77	20.92 /82	12.80 /88	0.00	1.50
AG	Quaker Strategic Growth A	QUAGX	B	(800) 220-8888	C+ / 6.4	-2.58	2.46	13.66 /67	16.98 /68	7.43 /69	0.00	1.85
AG	● Quaker Strategic Growth B	QAGBX	B	(800) 220-8888	C+ / 6.0	-2.77	2.12	12.78 /63	16.14 /64	6.64 /65	0.00	2.60
AG	Quaker Strategic Growth C	QAGCX	B	(800) 220-8888	C+ / 6.5	-2.78	2.08	12.78 /63	16.12 /64	6.64 /65	0.00	2.60
AG	Quaker Strategic Growth Inst	QAGIX	A-	(800) 220-8888	B- / 7.1	-2.55	2.60	13.91 /68	17.28 /69	7.69 /70	0.00	1.60
EM	Quant Emg-Markets Inst	QEMAX	B-	(800) 326-2151	A+ / 9.9	-6.12	7.21	35.63 /97	40.07 /99	25.20 /98	1.40	1.37
EM	Quant Emg-Markets Ord	QFFOX	B-	(800) 326-2151	A+ / 9.9	-6.15	7.07	35.26 /97	39.44 /99	24.63 /98	1.14	1.87
GI	Quant Gr & Inc Inst	QGIAX	C+	(800) 326-2151	C / 4.4	-0.97	2.14	11.74 /58	11.78 /41	0.83 /19	0.45	1.16
GI	Quant Gr & Inc Ord	USBOX	C+	(800) 326-2151	C- / 4.2	-1.15	1.89	11.19 /55	11.23 /37	0.34 /17	0.06	1.69
SC	Quant Small Cap Inst	QBNAX	B	(800) 326-2151	B+ / 8.8	-0.83	10.88	18.69 /80	23.34 /88	8.09 /72	0.00	1.40
SC	Quant Small Cap Ord	USBNX	B	(800) 326-2151	B+ / 8.7	-0.96	10.59	18.15 /79	22.73 /87	7.55 /70	0.00	1.91
FO	Quantitative Foreign Value Ord	QFVOX	A+	(800) 326-2151	A / 9.5	-1.71	11.13	27.46 /92	29.00 /95	18.45 /95	0.66	1.72
SC	Queens Road Small Cap Value Fund	QRSVX	B-		C+ / 6.9	-3.26	3.93	3.99 /11	18.08 /73	--	0.17	1.35
IN	Queens Road Value Fund	QRVLX	C+		C / 5.0	-0.42	3.44	8.56 /37	12.57 /46	--	0.39	0.95
BA	Rainier Balanced Fd	RIMBX	C-	(800) 280-6111	D+ / 2.3	-1.04	1.95	7.44 /29	8.05 /15	3.97 /46	1.27	1.19
BA	Rainier Balanced Inst	RAIBX	C	(800) 280-6111	D+ / 2.5	-0.97	2.08	7.72 /31	8.32 /17	--	1.50	1.19
IN	Rainier Core Equity Fd	RIMEX	C+	(800) 280-6111	C / 5.4	-1.50	3.45	12.52 /62	12.94 /49	3.42 /41	0.43	1.14
IN	Rainier Core Equity Inst	RAIEX	B	(800) 280-6111	C+ / 5.6	-1.43	3.56	12.84 /64	13.22 /50	--	0.66	1.13
GR	Rainier Growth Equity Portfolio	RGROX	C	(800) 280-6111	C / 4.7	-5.30	-1.63	10.53 /51	12.69 /47	2.66 /33	0.00	1.19
★ SC	● Rainier Small-Mid Cap Equity Fd	RIMSX	B	(800) 280-6111	B+ / 8.7	-4.29	9.08	25.40 /89	22.65 /86	11.36 /85	0.00	1.21
SC	● Rainier Small-Mid Cap Equity Inst	RAISX	A-	(800) 280-6111	B+ / 8.7	-4.22	9.17	25.71 /89	22.96 /87	--	0.00	0.95
RE	REMS Real Estate Value Opp Fd	HLRRX	C+	(800) 527-9500	C+ / 6.8	0.07	8.65	11.22 /55	15.99 /63	--	2.68	2.23
GR	Reynolds Blue Chip Growth Fund	RBCGX	E-	(800) 773-9665	E / 0.5	-6.40	0.70	6.58 /24	5.01 / 4	-5.23 / 2	0.00	1.97
GR	Reynolds Fund	REYFX	E-	(800) 773-9665	D / 2.0	-12.63	8.94	14.69 /71	7.52 /12	-0.64 /13	0.00	1.97
GR	Reynolds Opportunity Fund	ROPPX	E-	(800) 773-9665	D- / 1.0	-14.16	2.04	5.39 /17	6.75 / 9	-4.31 / 3	0.00	2.00
SC	● Rice Hall James Micro Cap Port	RHJSX	C	(866) 777-7818	B / 7.7	-6.83	3.56	14.18 /69	20.10 /80	9.89 /80	0.00	1.18
SC	Rice Hall James Small/Mid Cap Port	RHJMX	D-	(866) 777-7818	C / 4.5	-3.87	4.27	7.59 /30	11.94 /42	3.60 /42	0.00	1.05
BA	RMK Sel Balanced A	FPALX	C-	(800) 366-7426	D- / 1.4	-0.32	2.37	10.04 /47	7.86 /14	4.34 /49	1.10	1.28
BA	RMK Sel Balanced C	RMKBX	C-	(800) 366-7426	D / 1.6	-0.45	2.00	9.23 /42	7.06 /11	--	0.31	2.03
GR	RMK Sel Growth A	RGRAX	D-	(800) 366-7426	D- / 1.2	-1.66	1.40	9.33 /42	7.92 /15	1.86 /26	0.04	1.23
GR	RMK Sel Growth C	RMKGX	D-	(800) 366-7426	D- / 1.4	-1.88	1.03	8.72 /38	7.22 /11	--	0.00	1.98
GR	RMK Sel Growth I	RGRIX	U	(800) 366-7426	U /	-1.60	1.53	9.60 /44	--	--	0.29	0.98
GI	RMK Sel LEADER Gr & Inc A	MGIFX	D-	(800) 366-7426	D / 1.6	-3.21	0.30	6.79 /25	8.98 /21	1.71 /25	0.77	1.43
GI	RMK Sel LEADER Gr & Inc Inst	MAGIX	D	(800) 366-7426	D+ / 2.7	-3.15	0.40	7.04 /26	9.27 /23	1.98 /27	1.08	1.18
MC	RMK Sel Mid Cap Growth A	RAGAX	C+	(800) 366-7426	C+ / 6.7	-0.05	6.62	20.00 /82	16.76 /67	8.58 /74	0.00	1.26

● Denotes fund is closed to new investors
★ Denotes fund is included in Section II

356

RISK			NET ASSETS		ASSET				BULL / BEAR		FUND MANAGER		MINIMUMS		LOADS	
	3 Year		NAV						Last Bull	Last Bear	Manager	Manager	Initial	Additional	Front	Back
Risk Rating/Pts	Standard Deviation	Beta	As of 6/30/06	Total $(Mil)	Cash %	Stocks %	Bonds %	Other %	Portfolio Turnover Ratio	Market Return	Market Return	Quality Pct	Tenure (Years)	Purch. $	Purch. $	End Load	End Load
B /8.4	9.1	0.94	10.81	12	9	90	0	1	226.6	66.0	-0.1	83	4	2,000	100	0.0	1.0
B- /7.6	9.6	1.13	12.59	9	1	98	0	1	88.8	57.4	-8.8	26	10	2,000	100	5.5	0.0
B /8.3	9.6	1.13	12.07	N/A	1	98	0	1	88.8	53.6	-8.9	21	10	2,000	100	0.0	5.0
B /8.3	9.6	1.13	12.00	N/A	1	98	0	1	88.8	53.6	-8.9	21	10	2,000	100	0.0	1.0
B /8.4	9.6	1.13	12.09	3	1	98	0	1	88.8	58.6	-8.7	28	10	1,000,000	0	0.0	0.0
B /8.3	10.5	1.14	13.09	3	0	99	0	1	86.6	103.7	-6.2	95	4	2,000	100	5.5	0.0
C /5.5	13.7	1.16	15.89	64	3	96	0	1	186.7	148.1	-11.7	73	1	2,000	100	5.5	0.0
B- /7.2	13.7	1.16	15.20	2	3	96	0	1	186.7	142.3	-11.8	65	1	2,000	100	0.0	5.0
B- /7.2	13.7	1.16	14.96	16	3	96	0	1	186.7	142.2	-11.8	65	1	2,000	100	0.0	1.0
B- /7.2	13.7	1.16	16.27	2	3	96	0	1	186.7	149.9	-11.5	75	1	1,000,000	0	0.0	0.0
B- /7.2	14.7	0.92	10.67	1	1	98	0	1	115.8	105.9	-12.7	50	6	2,000	100	5.5	0.0
B- /7.2	14.7	0.92	10.23	N/A	1	98	0	1	115.8	100.4	-12.8	39	6	2,000	100	0.0	5.0
B- /7.2	14.8	0.92	10.30	N/A	1	98	0	1	115.8	100.9	-12.9	39	6	2,000	100	0.0	1.0
B- /7.2	14.8	0.93	10.97	3	1	98	0	1	115.8	107.4	-11.7	51	6	1,000,000	0	0.0	0.0
C /5.2	13.4	0.90	19.51	35	1	98	0	1	127.2	132.9	-6.7	85	10	2,000	100	5.5	0.0
B- /7.2	13.4	0.90	18.52	1	1	98	0	1	127.2	127.3	-6.9	80	10	2,000	100	0.0	5.0
B- /7.2	13.3	0.90	17.99	10	1	98	0	1	127.2	127.6	-6.8	81	10	2,000	100	0.0	1.0
B- /7.2	13.4	0.90	19.88	29	1	98	0	1	127.2	134.6	-6.7	87	10	1,000,000	0	0.0	0.0
B- /7.7	9.8	1.01	24.12	897	12	74	13	1	204.6	97.7	-8.3	93	10	2,000	100	5.5	0.0
B /8.2	9.9	1.01	23.16	17	12	74	13	1	204.6	93.2	-8.5	91	10	2,000	100	0.0	5.0
B /8.2	9.8	1.01	23.07	98	12	74	13	1	204.6	93.2	-8.5	91	10	2,000	100	0.0	1.0
B /8.2	9.9	1.01	24.47	42	12	74	13	1	204.6	99.3	-8.3	94	10	1,000,000	0	0.0	0.0
C- /4.0	21.3	1.25	18.88	2	2	97	0	1	26.0	274.3	-3.6	19	4	1,000,000	0	0.0	2.0
C- /4.0	21.4	1.26	18.63	146	2	97	0	1	26.0	268.7	-3.8	15	4	2,500	0	0.0	1.0
B /8.4	8.0	0.95	15.25	1	0	98	0	2	109.0	58.8	-10.7	67	15	1,000,000	0	0.0	2.0
B /8.3	8.0	0.95	14.59	59	0	98	0	2	109.0	56.4	-10.8	61	15	2,500	0	0.0	1.0
C+ /5.7	13.4	0.88	25.18	12	2	97	0	1	60.0	138.1	-12.2	95	10	1,000,000	0	0.0	2.0
C /5.4	13.7	0.89	22.77	97	2	97	0	1	60.0	134.3	-12.4	93	10	2,500	0	0.0	1.0
C+ /6.6	12.4	1.06	19.57	475	2	96	0	2	4.0	167.6	-7.0	80	8	2,500	0	0.0	1.0
B- /7.7	11.5	0.74	17.19	8	8	91	0	1	47.0	101.9	-3.2	87	4	10,000	1,000	0.0	0.0
B /8.6	7.5	0.91	14.13	5	1	98	0	1	13.3	69.7	-8.4	77	N/A	10,000	1,000	0.0	0.0
B /8.7	5.4	1.09	17.69	94	21	65	13	1	66.0	42.7	-3.8	N/A	N/A	25,000	1,000	0.0	0.0
B+ /9.1	5.4	1.09	17.78	22	21	65	13	1	66.0	43.9	-3.8	59	N/A	500,000	1,000	0.0	0.0
B /8.1	8.7	1.09	27.58	403	1	98	0	1	71.3	73.5	-9.3	66	N/A	25,000	1,000	0.0	0.0
B /8.5	8.8	1.09	27.65	208	1	98	0	1	71.3	74.9	-9.2	68	N/A	500,000	1,000	0.0	0.0
B- /7.1	11.9	1.38	18.06	19	N/A	N/A	0	N/A	96.0	79.3	-10.6	35	N/A	25,000	1,000	0.0	0.0
C+ /5.8	15.2	0.97	36.16	2,509	1	98	0	1	94.1	141.0	-9.1	89	N/A	25,000	1,000	0.0	0.0
C+ /6.7	15.2	0.97	36.54	1,051	1	98	0	1	94.1	142.9	-9.0	90	N/A	500,000	1,000	0.0	0.0
C+ /6.7	9.0	0.52	15.02	54	N/A	N/A	0	N/A	57.1	66.3	N/A	82	4	50,000	5,000	0.0	0.0
D- /1.0	20.2	1.99	30.13	43	0	99	0	1	167.6	50.5	-14.6	0	18	1,000	100	0.0	0.0
E- /0.0	33.7	3.18	6.09	22	N/A	N/A	0	N/A	142.9	123.9	-24.7	0	7	1,000	100	0.0	0.0
E- /0.0	25.1	2.45	17.04	11	N/A	100	0	N/A	97.5	83.9	-17.8	0	14	1,000	100	0.0	0.0
C /4.7	13.7	0.88	19.79	201	4	95	0	1	99.0	134.9	-10.0	84	12	2,500	100	0.0	2.0
C- /3.8	12.1	0.79	14.66	101	4	95	0	1	61.0	75.5	-11.5	28	10	2,500	100	0.0	0.0
B+ /9.1	5.9	1.00	15.68	174	4	68	27	1	22.0	38.2	-5.0	60	N/A	1,000	50	5.5	1.0
B+ /9.0	6.0	1.01	15.69	1	4	68	27	1	22.0	34.9	-5.2	49	N/A	1,000	50	1.0	1.0
C+ /6.6	8.5	1.00	17.18	377	1	98	0	1	53.0	50.5	-9.2	26	N/A	1,000	50	5.5	1.0
C+ /6.5	8.7	1.01	16.71	4	1	98	0	1	53.0	47.6	-9.4	21	N/A	1,000	50	1.0	1.0
U /	N/A	N/A	17.18	28	1	98	0	1	53.0	N/A	N/A	N/A	N/A	0	0	0.0	0.0
C+ /6.9	9.0	1.03	27.89	6	2	97	0	1	6.0	55.0	-6.6	31	N/A	1,000	50	5.5	1.0
C+ /6.9	9.1	1.03	27.90	101	2	97	0	1	6.0	56.4	-6.5	33	N/A	0	0	0.0	0.0
C+ /5.9	12.1	1.02	18.35	362	5	94	0	1	73.0	103.7	-11.4	38	6	1,000	50	5.5	1.0

Fund Type	Fund Name	Ticker Symbol	Overall Weiss Investment Rating	Phone	Perfor-mance Rating/Pts	3 Mo	6 Mo	1Yr / Pct	3Yr / Pct	5Yr / Pct	Dividend Yield	Expense Ratio
MC	RMK Sel Mid Cap Growth C	RMKAX	C+	(800) 366-7426	C+ / 6.9	-0.22	6.45	19.66 /81	16.18 /64	--	0.00	2.01
MC	RMK Sel Mid Cap Value A	RSEAX	E+	(800) 366-7426	C / 4.8	-2.29	1.99	6.56 /24	14.76 /58	--	0.00	1.25
MC	RMK Sel Mid Cap Value C	RSECX	E+	(800) 366-7426	C / 5.2	-2.43	1.62	5.95 /20	14.08 /54	--	0.00	2.00
IN	RMK Sel Value A	RVLAX	C-	(800) 366-7426	C- / 3.6	-1.10	2.83	12.61 /63	12.22 /44	3.58 /42	0.62	1.25
IN	RMK Sel Value C	RMKVX	C-	(800) 366-7426	C- / 4.0	-1.29	2.44	11.83 /59	11.41 /39	--	0.00	2.00
AG	Robeco WPG Tudor Fund Inst	WPGTX	C	(888) 261-4073	C+ / 6.7	-1.20	8.54	9.61 /44	16.73 /67	5.35 /57	0.00	1.44
FO	Rochdale Atlas Portfolio	RIMAX	B-		A / 9.3	-0.95	12.59	32.24 /96	27.31 /93	13.89 /90	0.54	1.95
IN	Rochdale Dividend & Income Port	RIMHX	D+		C- / 3.9	-0.04	7.07	6.49 /23	12.56 /46	0.64 /18	4.46	1.35
SC	Rockland Small Cap Growth	RKGRX	E-	(800) 497-3933	E+ / 0.7	-11.21	2.69	10.17 /48	6.45 / 8	-1.11 /11	0.00	1.73
SC	Roxbury Small Cap Growth Fund Inst	RSCIX	C+	(800) 336-9970	C+ / 6.8	-7.80	6.92	18.17 /79	17.34 /69	--	0.00	1.05
GR	Royce 100 Fund Svc	RYOHX	B+	(800) 221-4268	B- / 7.5	-7.35	5.59	20.96 /83	19.54 /78	--	0.00	1.49
SC	Royce Capital Micro-Cap Port	RCMCX	A-	(800) 221-4268	B+ / 8.7	-3.45	11.38	28.09 /93	21.75 /85	13.75 /90	0.46	1.33
SC	Royce Heritage Cons	RYGCX	A	(800) 221-4268	B+ / 8.5	-3.92	12.93	28.69 /93	20.64 /82	--	0.00	2.49
SC	Royce Heritage Svc	RGFAX	C+	(800) 221-4268	B+ / 8.8	-3.67	13.63	30.07 /94	21.93 /85	10.88 /84	0.00	1.43
★ SC ●	Royce Low Priced Stock Svc	RYLPX	B-	(800) 221-4268	B / 8.0	-5.45	9.40	25.03 /88	19.28 /77	10.71 /83	0.00	1.49
SC ●	Royce Micro-Cap Cons	RYMCX	B-	(800) 221-4268	B+ / 8.7	-3.36	11.35	27.78 /92	21.69 /84	12.73 /88	0.00	1.49
SC ●	Royce Micro-Cap Fd	RYOTX	B	(800) 221-4268	B+ / 8.9	-3.16	11.89	29.03 /94	22.95 /87	13.79 /90	0.66	2.49
SC ●	Royce Micro-Cap Svc	RMCFX	B	(800) 221-4268	B+ / 8.9	-3.22	11.80	28.89 /94	22.84 /87	13.71 /90	0.66	1.66
SC ●	Royce Opportunity Fd	RYPNX	B	(800) 221-4268	B+ / 8.8	-5.93	9.76	18.92 /80	23.54 /89	13.73 /90	0.00	1.14
SC ●	Royce Opportunity Inst	ROFIX	B	(800) 221-4268	B+ / 8.9	-5.90	9.81	19.02 /81	23.65 /89	13.81 /90	0.00	1.04
SC ●	Royce Opportunity Svc	RYOFX	B	(800) 221-4268	B+ / 8.7	-5.94	9.65	18.72 /80	23.34 /88	13.52 /89	0.00	1.29
SC	Royce PA Mutual Fd Cons	RYPCX	B+	(800) 221-4268	B / 7.8	-5.58	5.56	15.16 /72	19.91 /79	11.63 /86	0.00	1.89
★ SC	Royce PA Mutual Fd Inv	PENNX	B+	(800) 221-4268	B / 8.2	-5.22	6.12	16.40 /76	21.11 /83	12.76 /88	0.00	0.90
SC ●	Royce Premier Cons	RPRCX	A-	(800) 221-4268	B / 8.0	-5.86	4.41	21.82 /84	21.21 /83	13.52 /89	0.00	2.17
★ SC ●	Royce Premier Fd	RYPRX	B+	(800) 221-4268	B+ / 8.4	-5.55	4.98	23.14 /86	22.60 /86	14.34 /91	0.00	1.13
SC ●	Royce Premier Inst	RPFIX	A-	(800) 221-4268	B+ / 8.4	-5.59	4.97	23.23 /86	22.71 /87	14.40 /91	0.00	1.02
SC ●	Royce Premier Svc	RPFFX	B+	(800) 221-4268	B+ / 8.3	-5.63	4.89	22.90 /86	22.40 /86	14.21 /91	0.00	1.29
SC	Royce Select Fd	RYSFX	B+	(800) 221-4268	B / 7.7	-4.45	5.43	20.24 /82	20.15 /80	13.04 /89	0.00	1.67
SC	Royce Small-Cap Premier	RCPFX	A-	(800) 221-4268	B / 7.9	-6.30	4.65	9.01 /40	21.35 /83	11.87 /86	0.00	1.11
SC ●	Royce Special Equity Cons	RSQCX	C-	(800) 221-4268	C- / 3.4	-3.97	4.42	5.20 /16	10.73 /33	13.24 /89	0.00	2.26
SC ●	Royce Special Equity Fd	RYSEX	C	(800) 221-4268	C / 4.3	-3.68	4.97	6.38 /23	11.97 /42	14.02 /90	1.08	1.14
SC	Royce Technology Value Svc	RYTVX	E-	(800) 221-4268	D- / 1.2	-11.73	2.76	10.77 /52	8.16 /16	--	0.00	1.99
SC	Royce Total Return Cons	RYTCX	B	(800) 221-4268	C+ / 6.2	-3.64	5.09	11.45 /56	15.15 /60	10.60 /83	0.15	2.10
★ SC	Royce Total Return Fd	RYTRX	B-	(800) 221-4268	C+ / 6.7	-3.48	5.56	12.59 /63	16.28 /65	11.57 /86	1.13	1.12
SC	Royce Total Return Inst	RTRIX	B	(800) 221-4268	C+ / 6.9	-3.37	5.71	12.75 /63	16.46 /66	11.70 /86	1.29	1.00
SC	Royce Total Return Svc	RYTFX	B-	(800) 221-4268	C+ / 6.6	-3.52	5.50	12.34 /61	16.14 /64	--	0.88	1.29
SC	Royce Value Fd Svc	RYVFX	A+	(800) 221-4268	A- / 9.2	-5.86	6.31	22.15 /84	26.43 /93	17.16 /94	0.00	1.28
SC	Royce Value Plus Svc	RYVPX	A	(800) 221-4268	A / 9.4	-5.84	8.65	30.00 /94	28.78 /95	22.73 /98	0.00	1.17
MC	RS Diversified Growth Fund	RSDGX	E	(800) 766-3863	D+ / 2.3	-7.62	0.49	5.06 /15	9.10 /21	-1.42 /10	0.00	1.63
SC ●	RS Emerging Growth Fund	RSEGX	D	(800) 766-3863	C / 5.1	-7.42	3.04	9.06 /40	13.53 /51	-1.45 /10	0.00	1.54
EN	RS Global Natural Resources Fund	RSNRX	A-	(800) 766-3863	A+ / 9.9	2.12	10.54	42.46 /98	37.80 /99	26.74 /99	1.81	1.49
AG	RS Growth Fund	RSGRX	D+	(800) 766-3863	C+ / 6.0	-4.31	0.76	11.69 /58	14.87 /58	3.95 /45	0.00	1.37
TC	RS Internet Age Fund	RIAFX	E	(800) 766-3863	C / 4.3	-12.97	-8.38	5.65 /18	13.99 /54	3.66 /42	0.00	1.69
GL	RS Investors Fund	RSINX	U	(800) 766-3863	U /	-4.32	1.72	--	--	--	0.00	1.69
GI	RS MidCap Opportunities Fund	RSMOX	C+	(800) 766-3863	B- / 7.0	-4.57	4.79	15.52 /73	16.53 /66	4.49 /50	0.00	1.34
★ SC ●	RS Partners Fund	RSPFX	B	(800) 766-3863	A- / 9.1	-3.21	4.97	12.98 /64	26.02 /92	20.09 /96	0.00	1.49
SC	RS Smaller Company Growth Fund	RSSGX	C-	(800) 766-3863	C+ / 6.8	-8.46	0.99	8.77 /39	17.92 /72	5.23 /56	0.00	1.55
MC	RS Value Fund	RSVAX	A+	(800) 766-3863	A- / 9.0	-0.39	4.11	10.68 /51	25.93 /92	17.59 /94	0.03	1.39
GR	RSI Retirement Tr-Core Equity	RSICX	D	(800) 772-3615	D+ / 2.8	-2.98	-0.54	7.33 /28	9.39 /23	--	0.00	1.19
GI	Russell Diversified Equity Fund C	RDECX	C	(800) 832-6688	C- / 4.0	-2.48	2.23	8.56 /37	11.09 /36	1.70 /25	0.07	1.97
GI	Russell Diversified Equity Fund E	RDEEX	C+	(800) 832-6688	C / 4.6	-2.29	2.61	9.37 /42	11.93 /42	2.44 /32	0.42	1.22
★ GI	Russell Diversified Equity Fund S	RDESX	C+	(800) 832-6688	C / 4.7	-2.24	2.72	9.63 /44	12.21 /44	2.72 /34	0.64	0.97

● Denotes fund is closed to new investors
★ Denotes fund is included in Section II

358

RISK			NET ASSETS		ASSET				Portfolio Turnover Ratio	BULL / BEAR		FUND MANAGER		MINIMUMS		LOADS	
	3 Year		NAV							Last Bull	Last Bear	Manager	Manager	Initial	Additional	Front	Back
Risk Rating/Pts	Standard Deviation	Beta	As of 6/30/06	Total $(Mil)	Cash %	Stocks %	Bonds %	Other %		Market Return	Market Return	Quality Pct	Tenure (Years)	Purch. $	Purch. $	End Load	End Load
C+ / 5.7	12.3	1.04	17.83	9	5	94	0	1	73.0	100.5	-11.6	32	N/A	1,000	50	1.0	1.0
D / 2.0	8.8	0.73	10.24	76	1	98	0	1	68.0	76.5	N/A	68	4	1,000	50	5.5	1.0
D- / 1.3	8.8	0.73	10.02	1	1	98	0	1	68.0	73.7	N/A	60	4	1,000	50	0.0	1.0
B- / 7.0	10.1	1.04	16.88	247	1	98	0	1	58.0	70.7	-12.5	63	N/A	1,000	50	5.5	1.0
B- / 7.0	10.1	1.04	16.82	3	1	98	0	1	58.0	66.9	-12.5	54	N/A	1,000	50	0.0	1.0
C / 4.9	12.7	1.38	16.53	49	4	95	0	1	135.9	100.2	-11.7	74	3	100,000	100	0.0	2.0
C / 4.6	14.1	1.30	49.19	202	N/A	100	0	N/A	77.3	159.6	-4.9	22	20	1,000	100	5.8	1.0
C+ / 6.1	8.2	0.79	26.71	52	0	99	0	1	1.0	65.6	-4.0	84	N/A	1,000	100	5.8	1.0
D / 2.1	17.9	1.13	16.79	47	N/A	100	0	N/A	246.2	90.8	-10.3	0	10	2,000	250	0.0	2.0
C+ / 6.1	16.7	1.07	19.62	199	3	96	0	1	146.0	134.0	N/A	32	3	1,000	0	0.0	1.0
B- / 7.3	12.1	1.21	7.94	26	5	94	0	1	60.0	N/A	N/A	95	3	2,000	50	0.0	1.0
C+ / 6.8	14.1	0.91	14.00	492	0	84	14	2	2.0	142.4	-10.7	90	5	2,000	50	0.0	1.0
B- / 7.2	13.0	0.82	12.75	3	12	87	0	1	142.0	118.6	-11.9	91	5	2,000	50	0.0	1.0
C / 4.5	13.0	0.82	14.17	70	12	87	0	1	142.0	126.0	-11.7	94	5	5,000	50	0.0	1.0
C+ / 5.7	14.3	0.92	16.99	4,077	12	87	0	1	N/A	129.1	-10.4	74	6	2,000	50	0.0	1.0
C / 5.3	14.2	0.91	16.68	214	16	83	0	1	31.0	142.7	-10.8	89	5	2,000	50	0.0	1.0
C / 5.5	14.3	0.92	17.79	638	16	83	0	1	31.0	150.6	-10.5	93	5	2,000	50	0.0	1.0
C / 5.5	14.3	0.91	17.72	5	16	83	0	1	31.0	149.8	-10.5	93	5	2,000	50	0.0	1.0
C / 5.4	17.0	1.13	13.49	1,699	6	93	0	1	44.0	165.7	-10.8	77	6	2,000	50	0.0	1.0
C / 5.4	17.0	1.14	13.55	216	6	93	0	1	44.0	166.2	-10.8	78	6	1,000,000	0	0.0	0.0
C / 5.3	17.0	1.13	13.30	237	6	93	0	1	44.0	164.2	-10.9	76	6	2,000	50	0.0	1.0
C+ / 6.8	12.5	0.83	10.82	1,050	5	94	0	1	26.0	118.7	-8.6	88	9	2,000	50	0.0	1.0
C+ / 6.9	12.5	0.83	11.44	2,445	5	94	0	1	26.0	125.9	-7.7	92	9	2,000	50	0.0	1.0
B- / 7.4	12.4	0.78	17.03	53	14	85	0	1	20.0	124.3	-8.6	94	3	2,000	50	0.0	1.0
C+ / 6.9	12.4	0.78	17.70	3,790	14	85	0	1	20.0	132.0	-8.6	97	3	2,000	50	0.0	1.0
C+ / 6.9	12.4	0.78	17.75	265	14	85	0	1	20.0	132.6	-8.6	97	4	1,000,000	0	0.0	0.0
C+ / 6.9	12.3	0.78	17.59	193	14	85	0	1	20.0	130.8	-8.6	96	4	2,000	50	0.0	1.0
B- / 7.3	11.7	0.76	20.20	23	10	88	0	2	83.0	114.7	-6.3	93	8	50,000	100	0.0	2.0
B- / 7.6	12.1	0.80	10.12	244	12	87	0	1	45.0	129.9	-8.7	94	5	2,000	50	0.0	1.0
B- / 7.9	11.0	0.68	19.37	16	4	95	0	1	22.0	62.8	-5.5	32	3	2,000	50	0.0	1.0
B- / 7.2	10.9	0.68	19.63	450	4	95	0	1	22.0	68.2	-5.5	43	3	2,000	50	0.0	1.0
E / 0.5	22.8	1.27	6.32	25	7	92	0	1	94.0	94.5	-5.4	0	5	2,000	50	0.0	2.0
B- / 7.9	9.5	0.64	13.20	651	7	86	6	1	24.0	84.7	-6.6	79	5	2,000	50	0.0	1.0
B- / 7.9	9.5	0.64	13.22	4,446	7	86	6	1	24.0	90.4	-6.4	86	5	2,000	50	0.0	1.0
B / 8.2	9.5	0.64	13.26	227	7	86	6	1	24.0	91.4	-6.4	87	3	2,000	50	0.0	0.0
B- / 7.9	9.6	0.64	13.08	352	7	86	6	1	24.0	89.7	-6.4	85	5	2,000	50	0.0	1.0
B- / 7.1	13.1	0.83	10.28	366	10	89	0	1	44.0	174.4	-8.8	99	N/A	2,000	50	0.0	1.0
C+ / 6.6	14.7	0.91	13.07	755	8	91	0	1	62.0	214.1	-5.6	99	5	2,000	50	0.0	1.0
C- / 3.0	18.0	1.52	22.44	294	2	97	0	1	184.0	99.5	-18.1	0	9	5,000	1,000	0.0	0.0
C- / 3.9	17.6	1.14	33.57	817	0	98	0	2	95.0	104.4	-16.5	8	10	5,000	1,000	0.0	0.0
C+ / 5.7	19.9	0.89	36.09	2,032	24	75	0	1	62.0	204.9	6.5	97	11	5,000	1,000	0.0	0.0
C- / 3.7	12.4	1.42	15.97	198	2	96	0	2	159.0	97.0	-10.1	53	5	5,000	1,000	0.0	0.0
D- / 1.5	24.5	2.31	7.11	70	6	93	0	1	129.0	144.3	-16.5	4	N/A	5,000	1,000	0.0	0.0
U /	N/A	N/A	10.62	63	5	94	0	1	5.0	N/A	N/A	N/A	1	5,000	1,000	0.0	0.0
C+ / 6.2	13.8	1.50	13.99	260	1	98	0	1	207.0	107.0	-9.1	62	11	5,000	1,000	0.0	0.0
C / 5.5	12.1	0.71	34.65	2,422	20	79	0	1	77.0	164.2	2.3	99	11	5,000	1,000	0.0	0.0
C / 4.5	15.6	1.01	21.32	301	5	94	0	1	122.0	140.9	-14.4	46	5	5,000	1,000	0.0	0.0
B / 8.2	11.8	0.90	25.56	1,714	12	87	0	1	83.0	149.1	1.3	98	8	5,000	1,000	0.0	0.0
C+ / 6.1	7.7	0.95	8.87	127	0	98	0	2	18.7	52.5	-8.4	40	2	0	0	0.0	0.0
B / 8.1	8.4	1.08	44.44	142	0	100	0	0	110.7	65.2	-10.0	46	10	0	0	0.0	0.0
B / 8.1	8.4	1.08	46.05	61	0	100	0	0	110.7	69.2	-9.8	56	N/A	0	0	0.0	0.0
B / 8.1	8.4	1.08	46.07	3,091	0	100	0	0	110.7	70.5	-9.7	59	10	0	0	0.0	0.0

					PERFORMANCE							
99 Pct = Best *0 Pct = Worst*			Overall Weiss Investment Rating		Perfor-mance	Total Return % through 6/30/06					Incl. in Returns	
									Annualized		Dividend	Expense
Fund Type	Fund Name	Ticker Symbol		Phone	Rating/Pts	3 Mo	6 Mo	1Yr / Pct	3Yr / Pct	5Yr / Pct	Yield	Ratio
EM	Russell Emerging Markets C	REMCX	C	(800) 832-6688	A+ / 9.7	-6.89	5.85	32.09 /96	33.30 /97	19.44 /96	1.47	2.72
EM	Russell Emerging Markets E	REMEX	C	(800) 832-6688	A+ / 9.7	-6.74	6.23	33.01 /96	34.26 /98	20.25 /96	2.22	1.97
EM	Russell Emerging Markets S	REMSX	C	(800) 832-6688	A+ / 9.8	-6.65	6.40	33.46 /96	34.54 /98	20.50 /97	2.51	1.72
IX	Russell Inst Equity I Fd E	REAEX	C+	(800) 832-6688	C / 4.8	-2.14	2.80	9.67 /45	12.36 /45	2.81 /35	0.68	0.95
IX	Russell Inst Equity I Fd I	REASX	C+	(800) 832-6688	C / 5.0	-2.09	2.89	9.87 /46	12.61 /46	3.05 /37	0.89	0.75
SC	Russell Inst Equity II Fd E	REBEX	D	(800) 832-6688	B- / 7.3	-4.99	7.37	15.25 /73	17.37 /70	8.55 /74	0.00	1.11
SC	Russell Inst Equity II Fd I	REBSX	D	(800) 832-6688	B- / 7.4	-4.97	7.48	15.50 /73	17.61 /71	8.76 /75	0.20	0.91
GI	Russell Inst Equity Q Fd E	REQEX	C	(800) 832-6688	C- / 4.1	-2.17	2.01	8.93 /40	11.22 /37	2.50 /32	0.87	0.94
GI	Russell Inst Equity Q Fd I	REDSX	C	(800) 832-6688	C / 4.3	-2.12	2.15	9.19 /41	11.50 /39	2.73 /34	1.10	0.69
FO	Russell Inst International E	RIFEX	A-	(800) 832-6688	B+ / 8.9	-0.28	9.53	26.65 /91	22.83 /87	9.23 /78	1.44	1.17
FO	Russell Inst International I	RINSX	A	(800) 832-6688	A- / 9.0	-0.19	9.66	26.97 /91	23.11 /88	9.45 /78	1.65	0.95
FO	Russell International Securities C	RCISX	B+	(800) 832-6688	B+ / 8.6	-0.42	8.99	25.24 /89	21.27 /83	7.97 /72	0.36	2.23
FO	Russell International Securities E	REISX	A-	(800) 832-6688	B+ / 8.8	-0.25	9.39	26.17 /90	22.18 /86	8.79 /75	0.91	1.48
★ FO	Russell International Securities S	RISSX	A-	(800) 832-6688	B+ / 8.8	-0.18	9.53	26.49 /91	22.49 /86	9.05 /76	1.10	1.23
GL	Russell LifePoints Bal Strat A	RBLAX	C+	(800) 832-6688	D+ / 2.9	-1.18	3.04	8.92 /40	10.89 /35	6.27 /63	1.89	0.25
GL	Russell LifePoints Bal Strat C	RBLCX	C+	(800) 832-6688	C- / 3.5	-1.36	2.69	8.09 /33	10.10 /28	5.50 /58	1.32	1.00
GL	Russell LifePoints Bal Strat D	RBLDX	C+	(800) 832-6688	C- / 3.8	-1.24	2.97	8.62 /38	10.63 /32	6.01 /61	1.75	0.50
GL	Russell LifePoints Bal Strat E	RBLEX	C+	(800) 832-6688	C- / 4.1	-1.18	3.03	8.88 /39	10.90 /35	6.27 /63	1.99	0.25
GL	Russell LifePoints Bal Strat S	RBLSX	C+	(800) 832-6688	C / 4.3	-1.11	3.26	9.20 /41	11.17 /37	6.55 /64	2.22	N/A
GL	Russell LifePoints Cons Strat A	RCLAX	D+	(800) 832-6688	E- / 0.2	-0.07	1.14	2.90 / 7	3.93 / 2	4.00 /46	2.64	0.25
GL	Russell LifePoints Cons Strat C	RCLCX	D+	(800) 832-6688	E / 0.3	-0.37	0.75	2.13 / 5	3.14 / 1	3.23 /39	2.06	1.00
GL	Russell LifePoints Cons Strat D	RCLDX	C-	(800) 832-6688	E / 0.4	-0.23	0.97	2.63 / 6	3.64 / 2	3.74 /43	2.54	0.50
GL	Russell LifePoints Cons Strat E	RCLEX	C-	(800) 832-6688	E / 0.5	-0.14	1.16	2.92 / 7	3.90 / 2	4.00 /46	2.72	0.25
GL	Russell LifePoints Cons Strat S	RCLSX	C-	(800) 832-6688	E+ / 0.6	-0.01	1.29	3.14 / 8	4.20 / 3	4.26 /48	3.03	N/A
AA	Russell LifePoints Eq Gr Strat A	REAAX	B+	(800) 832-6688	C+ / 6.3	-1.98	5.27	15.41 /73	16.60 /66	6.70 /65	0.82	0.25
AA	Russell LifePoints Eq Gr Strat C	RELCX	B-	(800) 832-6688	C+ / 6.7	-2.24	4.84	14.43 /70	15.74 /62	5.52 /58	0.51	1.00
AA	Russell LifePoints Eq Gr Strat D	RELDX	B+	(800) 832-6688	B- / 7.0	-2.00	5.10	15.04 /72	16.33 /65	6.05 /61	0.70	0.50
AA	Russell LifePoints Eq Gr Strat E	RELEX	B+	(800) 832-6688	B- / 7.1	-2.02	5.26	15.34 /73	16.61 /66	6.33 /63	0.87	0.25
AA	Russell LifePoints Eq Gr Strat S	RELSX	B+	(800) 832-6688	B- / 7.2	-1.94	5.44	15.67 /74	16.90 /68	6.61 /65	1.04	N/A
GL	Russell LifePoints Gr Strat A	RALAX	B-	(800) 832-6688	C / 4.7	-1.57	4.19	12.02 /60	13.73 /53	6.34 /63	1.41	0.25
GL	Russell LifePoints Gr Strat C	RALCX	B-	(800) 832-6688	C / 5.3	-1.76	3.76	11.11 /54	12.85 /48	5.52 /58	0.82	1.00
GL	Russell LifePoints Gr Strat D	RALDX	B	(800) 832-6688	C+ / 5.6	-1.72	3.93	11.61 /57	13.38 /51	6.04 /61	1.24	0.50
GL	Russell LifePoints Gr Strat E	RALEX	B	(800) 832-6688	C+ / 5.7	-1.66	4.09	11.89 /59	13.68 /52	6.32 /63	1.48	0.25
GL	Russell LifePoints Gr Strat S	RALSX	B	(800) 832-6688	C+ / 5.9	-1.59	4.22	12.20 /61	13.97 /54	6.57 /65	1.70	N/A
GL	Russell LifePoints Mod Strategy A	RMLAX	C-	(800) 832-6688	D- / 1.0	-0.60	2.21	5.89 /20	7.20 /11	5.11 /55	2.19	0.25
GL	Russell LifePoints Mod Strategy C	RMLCX	C-	(800) 832-6688	D- / 1.4	-0.79	1.84	5.14 /16	6.40 / 8	4.30 /49	1.60	1.00
GL	Russell LifePoints Mod Strategy D	RMLDX	C	(800) 832-6688	D / 1.7	-0.67	2.14	5.70 /19	6.95 /10	4.83 /53	2.05	0.50
GL	Russell LifePoints Mod Strategy E	RMLEX	C	(800) 832-6688	D / 1.8	-0.61	2.20	5.88 /20	7.20 /11	5.07 /55	2.30	0.25
GL	Russell LifePoints Mod Strategy R2	RMLTX	C	(800) 832-6688	D / 1.8	-0.63	2.18	5.85 /19	7.19 /11	5.07 /55	2.37	0.25
GL	Russell LifePoints Mod Strategy S	RMLSX	C	(800) 832-6688	D / 2.0	-0.54	2.35	6.21 /22	7.48 /12	5.35 /57	2.53	N/A
GR	● Russell Multi-Mngr Prncpl-Prtctd A	RMPAX	D+	(800) 832-6688	E- / 0.1	-0.39	0.39	1.20 / 3	1.33 / 0	--	0.00	2.10
GR	● Russell Multi-Mngr Prncpl-Prtctd B	RMPBX	D+	(800) 832-6688	E- / 0.0	-0.70	0.00	0.43 / 2	0.56 / 0	--	0.00	2.85
GI	Russell Quantitative Equity C	RQECX	C	(800) 832-6688	C- / 3.3	-2.49	1.38	7.54 /29	9.99 /27	1.33 /22	0.09	1.97
GI	Russell Quantitative Equity E	RQEEX	C	(800) 832-6688	C- / 3.8	-2.31	1.74	8.32 /35	10.80 /34	2.08 /28	0.61	1.22
★ GI	Russell Quantitative Equity S	RQESX	C	(800) 832-6688	C- / 4.0	-2.25	1.88	8.59 /37	11.09 /36	2.35 /31	0.84	0.97
RE	Russell Real Estate Securities C	RRSCX	B-	(800) 832-6688	A / 9.3	-0.89	13.24	20.03 /82	26.74 /93	18.79 /95	0.70	2.08
RE	Russell Real Estate Securities E	RREEX	B-	(800) 832-6688	A / 9.4	-0.70	13.65	20.90 /83	27.70 /94	19.66 /96	1.20	1.33
RE	Russell Real Estate Securities S	RRESX	B-	(800) 832-6688	A / 9.4	-0.65	13.79	21.21 /83	28.00 /94	19.97 /96	1.39	1.08
GR	Russell Select Growth Fund C	RSGCX	D-	(800) 832-6688	D / 1.6	-5.97	-2.45	5.44 /17	7.89 /14	-1.39 /10	0.00	2.20
GR	Russell Select Growth Fund E	RSGEX	D-	(800) 832-6688	D / 2.2	-5.71	-1.98	6.44 /23	8.90 /20	-0.50 /14	0.00	1.36
GR	Russell Select Growth Fund I	RSGIX	D+	(800) 832-6688	D+ / 2.5	-5.70	-1.82	6.72 /25	9.32 /23	-0.15 /15	0.00	0.95
GR	Russell Select Growth Fund S	RSGSX	D-	(800) 832-6688	D+ / 2.4	-5.74	-1.83	6.62 /24	9.15 /22	-0.22 /15	0.00	1.13

● Denotes fund is closed to new investors
★ Denotes fund is included in Section II

RISK			NET ASSETS		ASSET				Portfolio	BULL / BEAR		FUND MANAGER		MINIMUMS		LOADS	
Risk Rating/Pts	3 Year Standard Deviation	Beta	NAV As of 6/30/06	Total $(Mil)	Cash %	Stocks %	Bonds %	Other %	Turnover Ratio	Last Bull Market Return	Last Bear Market Return	Manager Quality Pct	Manager Tenure (Years)	Initial Purch. $	Additional Purch. $	Front End Load	Back End Load
D+ / 2.5	19.0	1.15	19.18	43	0	100	0	0	71.9	226.0	-6.5	9	N/A	0	0	0.0	0.0
D+ / 2.6	19.0	1.15	19.78	26	0	100	0	0	71.9	232.5	-6.2	12	N/A	0	0	0.0	0.0
D+ / 2.6	19.0	1.15	19.78	964	0	100	0	0	71.9	234.6	-6.2	13	N/A	0	0	0.0	0.0
B- / 7.6	8.5	1.09	31.51	40	7	92	0	1	109.7	71.6	-9.8	60	10	0	0	0.0	0.0
B- / 7.7	8.4	1.09	31.50	980	7	92	0	1	109.7	72.8	-9.8	62	10	100,000	0	0.0	0.0
D- / 1.5	13.6	0.92	32.78	39	6	93	0	1	156.4	112.4	-9.1	57	6	0	0	0.0	0.0
D- / 1.5	13.6	0.92	32.89	496	6	93	0	1	156.4	113.7	-9.1	59	N/A	100,000	0	0.0	0.0
B- / 7.7	8.2	1.05	36.46	51	2	97	0	1	117.3	66.4	-9.0	51	N/A	0	0	0.0	0.0
B- / 7.7	8.2	1.05	36.48	1,090	2	97	0	1	117.3	67.8	-9.0	54	N/A	100,000	0	0.0	0.0
C+ / 6.7	10.4	1.02	47.13	48	6	93	0	1	80.4	128.8	-9.7	36	6	0	0	0.0	0.0
C+ / 6.7	10.4	1.02	47.13	1,346	6	93	0	1	80.4	130.1	-9.6	38	6	100,000	0	0.0	0.0
C+ / 6.7	10.4	1.02	70.53	149	0	100	0	0	79.5	119.2	-9.8	27	6	0	0	0.0	0.0
C+ / 6.7	10.4	1.02	73.15	64	0	100	0	0	79.5	124.5	-9.6	32	6	0	0	0.0	0.0
C+ / 6.7	10.4	1.02	73.92	2,845	0	100	0	0	79.5	126.3	-9.6	34	6	0	0	0.0	0.0
B+ / 9.6	5.6	1.14	11.54	825	0	60	40	0	0.6	55.1	-3.7	80	N/A	0	0	5.8	1.0
B+ / 9.3	5.6	1.13	11.47	1,187	0	60	40	0	0.6	51.5	-3.8	74	N/A	0	0	0.0	0.0
B+ / 9.3	5.6	1.14	11.56	1,003	0	60	40	0	0.6	53.9	-3.7	78	N/A	0	0	0.0	0.0
B+ / 9.2	5.6	1.15	11.56	550	0	60	40	0	0.6	55.1	-3.7	80	N/A	0	0	0.0	0.0
B+ / 9.3	5.6	1.14	11.62	619	0	60	40	0	0.6	56.5	-3.7	82	N/A	0	0	0.0	0.0
B+ / 9.9	2.4	0.41	10.72	42	0	20	80	0	9.5	17.8	0.1	50	N/A	0	0	5.8	1.0
B+ / 9.9	2.3	0.41	10.66	80	0	20	80	0	9.5	15.1	-0.1	41	N/A	0	0	0.0	0.0
B+ / 9.9	2.4	0.42	10.76	172	0	20	80	0	9.5	16.8	0.1	45	N/A	0	0	0.0	0.0
B+ / 9.9	2.4	0.42	10.74	74	0	20	80	0	9.5	17.7	0.1	48	N/A	0	0	0.0	0.0
B+ / 9.9	2.4	0.41	10.78	43	0	20	80	0	9.5	18.7	0.2	53	N/A	0	0	0.0	0.0
B / 8.4	9.0	1.75	11.64	165	0	100	0	0	3.4	97.0	-8.8	91	N/A	0	0	5.8	1.0
B- / 7.7	9.1	1.76	11.14	377	0	100	0	0	3.4	89.0	-8.9	88	N/A	0	0	0.0	0.0
B- / 7.7	9.1	1.75	11.44	375	0	100	0	0	3.4	92.2	-8.8	90	N/A	0	0	0.0	0.0
B- / 7.7	9.1	1.76	11.45	211	0	100	0	0	3.4	93.7	-8.8	91	N/A	0	0	0.0	0.0
B- / 7.7	9.1	1.76	11.60	184	0	100	0	0	3.4	95.4	-8.8	92	N/A	0	0	0.0	0.0
B+ / 9.0	7.3	1.46	11.70	542	0	80	20	0	0.7	74.6	-6.4	87	N/A	0	0	5.8	1.0
B / 8.5	7.3	1.46	11.61	745	0	80	20	0	0.7	70.4	-6.6	82	N/A	0	0	0.0	0.0
B / 8.5	7.3	1.45	11.72	730	0	80	20	0	0.7	73.1	-6.4	85	N/A	0	0	0.0	0.0
B / 8.5	7.3	1.46	11.71	450	0	80	20	0	0.7	74.4	-6.4	86	N/A	0	0	0.0	0.0
B / 8.5	7.3	1.44	11.77	372	0	80	20	0	0.7	76.0	-6.4	88	N/A	0	0	0.0	0.0
B+ / 9.9	3.8	0.77	11.12	148	0	40	60	0	4.5	34.4	-1.7	66	N/A	0	0	5.8	1.0
B+ / 9.9	3.8	0.76	11.06	199	0	40	60	0	4.5	31.2	-2.0	58	N/A	0	0	0.0	0.0
B+ / 9.9	3.7	0.76	11.15	334	0	40	60	0	4.5	33.2	-1.7	64	N/A	0	0	0.0	0.0
B+ / 9.9	3.7	0.75	11.12	170	0	40	60	0	4.5	34.2	-1.7	67	N/A	0	0	0.0	0.0
B+ / 9.9	3.7	0.75	11.11	1	0	40	60	0	4.5	34.2	-1.7	67	N/A	0	0	0.0	0.0
B+ / 9.9	3.8	0.76	11.16	122	0	40	60	0	4.5	35.4	-1.8	69	N/A	0	0	0.0	0.0
B+ / 9.9	3.5	0.25	10.27	2	6	34	59	1	19.6	9.1	N/A	26	N/A	1,000	50	5.0	0.0
B+ / 9.9	3.5	0.26	10.00	47	6	34	59	1	19.6	6.5	N/A	20	N/A	1,000	50	0.0	5.0
B / 8.2	8.1	1.04	37.60	144	4	95	0	1	108.5	60.8	-9.2	38	N/A	0	0	0.0	0.0
B / 8.2	8.1	1.04	38.69	65	4	95	0	1	108.5	64.7	-9.1	46	N/A	0	0	0.0	0.0
B / 8.2	8.1	1.04	38.82	3,182	4	95	0	1	108.5	66.0	-9.0	50	N/A	0	0	0.0	0.0
C / 4.3	16.1	0.97	48.93	93	2	96	0	2	64.0	125.7	0.2	83	N/A	0	0	0.0	0.0
C / 4.3	16.1	0.97	49.71	46	2	96	0	2	64.0	131.3	0.4	87	N/A	0	0	0.0	0.0
C / 4.3	16.1	0.97	50.22	1,585	2	96	0	2	64.0	133.0	0.5	89	N/A	0	0	0.0	0.0
C+ / 5.9	11.2	1.33	7.56	10	6	93	0	1	127.7	61.2	-11.4	10	N/A	0	0	0.0	0.0
C+ / 5.9	11.1	1.32	7.93	6	6	93	0	1	127.7	65.7	-11.1	15	N/A	0	0	0.0	0.0
C+ / 6.0	11.1	1.32	8.10	107	6	93	0	1	127.7	67.9	-11.1	17	N/A	100,000	0	0.0	0.0
C+ / 6.0	11.2	1.33	8.05	70	6	93	0	1	127.7	67.3	-11.2	16	N/A	0	0	0.0	0.0

			Overall Weiss		PERFORMANCE						Incl. in Returns	
	99 Pct = Best 0 Pct = Worst				Perfor-mance	Total Return % through 6/30/06			Annualized		Dividend	Expense
Fund Type	Fund Name	Ticker Symbol	Investment Rating	Phone	Rating/Pts	3 Mo	6 Mo	1Yr / Pct	3Yr / Pct	5Yr / Pct	Yield	Ratio
IN	Russell Select Value C	RSVCX	B	(800) 832-6688	C+ / 5.8	-1.71	3.70	10.02 /47	14.24 /55	4.82 /53	0.11	2.10
IN	Russell Select Value E	RSVEX	B	(800) 832-6688	C+ / 6.3	-1.54	4.06	10.87 /53	15.24 /60	5.76 /60	0.73	1.28
IN	Russell Select Value I	RSVIX	B	(800) 832-6688	C+ / 6.5	-1.46	4.22	11.25 /55	15.70 /62	6.11 /62	1.07	0.95
IN	Russell Select Value S	RSVSX	B	(800) 832-6688	C+ / 6.4	-1.49	4.19	11.07 /54	15.51 /61	6.02 /61	0.90	1.10
SC	Russell Special Growth C	RSPCX	C	(800) 832-6688	C+ / 6.8	-5.19	6.58	14.06 /68	16.30 /65	7.36 /69	0.00	2.24
SC	Russell Special Growth E	RSPEX	C	(800) 832-6688	B- / 7.2	-4.99	7.00	14.90 /71	17.18 /69	8.17 /72	0.00	1.49
SC	Russell Special Growth S	RSPSX	C+	(800) 832-6688	B- / 7.3	-4.92	7.14	15.20 /72	17.48 /70	8.45 /74	0.00	1.24
GL	Russell Tax Managed Global Eq C	RTGCX	C+	(800) 832-6688	C+ / 5.7	-2.97	2.74	11.55 /57	13.89 /53	3.83 /44	0.00	1.00
GL	Russell Tax Managed Global Eq S	RTGSX	B-	(800) 832-6688	C+ / 6.2	-2.80	3.17	12.67 /63	15.01 /59	4.89 /53	0.74	N/A
GI	Russell Tax-Managed Large Cap C	RTLCX	C-	(800) 832-6688	D+ / 2.4	-3.08	-0.71	4.89 /15	9.16 /22	0.20 /16	0.00	1.93
GI	Russell Tax-Managed Large Cap E	RTLEX	C	(800) 832-6688	C- / 3.0	-2.92	-0.37	5.64 /18	9.96 /27	0.97 /20	0.55	1.18
GI	Russell Tax-Managed Large Cap S	RETSX	C	(800) 832-6688	C- / 3.2	-2.86	-0.27	5.90 /20	10.24 /29	1.22 /22	0.77	0.93
SC	Russell Tax-Managed Mid-Sm Cap C	RTSCX	C+	(800) 832-6688	C+ / 6.5	-6.01	4.97	12.12 /60	15.99 /63	6.22 /62	0.00	2.25
SC	Russell Tax-Managed Mid-Sm Cap E	RTSEX	B-	(800) 832-6688	C+ / 6.9	-5.87	5.38	12.98 /64	16.84 /67	7.02 /67	0.00	1.50
SC	Russell Tax-Managed Mid-Sm Cap S	RTSSX	B	(800) 832-6688	B- / 7.1	-5.73	5.55	13.35 /66	17.18 /69	7.30 /68	0.00	1.25
AG	RVS Aggressive Growth Fund A	ASGFX	C-	(800) 328-8300	C+ / 6.2	-5.13	5.03	15.23 /72	16.32 /65	--	0.00	1.44
AG	RVS Aggressive Growth Fund B	ARGBX	C-	(800) 328-8300	C+ / 5.8	-5.35	4.61	14.51 /70	15.45 /61	--	0.00	2.21
AG	RVS Aggressive Growth Fund I	APAIX	U	(800) 328-8300	U /	-5.08	5.24	15.69 /74	--	--	0.00	1.27
BA	RVS Balanced Fund Class A	INMUX	C-	(800) 328-8300	D- / 1.4	-0.47	2.72	5.26 /16	8.22 /16	2.17 /29	2.24	1.01
BA	RVS Balanced Fund Class B	IDMBX	C-	(800) 328-8300	D- / 1.1	-0.68	2.21	4.43 /12	7.37 /12	1.36 /23	1.57	1.78
BA	RVS Balanced Fund Class C		D-	(800) 328-8300	D / 1.7	-0.58	2.32	4.49 /13	7.38 /12	1.36 /23	1.63	1.78
BA	RVS Balanced Fund Class Y	IDMYX	C	(800) 328-8300	D+ / 2.4	-0.43	2.81	5.44 /17	8.41 /17	2.34 /31	2.55	0.83
GR	RVS Disciplined Equity Fund A	AQEAX	D	(800) 328-8300	C- / 3.1	-2.19	3.31	9.89 /46	10.97 /35	--	0.79	1.27
GR	RVS Disciplined Equity Fund I	ALEIX	U	(800) 328-8300	U /	-2.18	3.38	10.20 /48	--	--	1.16	0.91
★ IN	RVS Diversified Equity Income A	INDZX	A+	(800) 328-8300	B+ / 8.3	0.32	8.55	21.05 /83	21.53 /84	10.38 /82	1.29	1.06
IN	RVS Diversified Equity Income B	IDEBX	A+	(800) 328-8300	B / 8.1	0.12	8.20	20.06 /82	20.60 /81	9.54 /79	0.28	1.82
IN	RVS Diversified Equity Income C	ADECX	A+	(800) 328-8300	B+ / 8.3	0.13	8.15	20.05 /82	20.58 /81	9.53 /79	0.33	1.82
IN	RVS Diversified Equity Income I	ADIIX	U	(800) 328-8300	U /	0.42	8.77	21.47 /84	--	--	1.94	0.66
IN	RVS Diversified Equity Income Y	IDQYX	A+	(800) 328-8300	B+ / 8.7	0.36	8.63	21.22 /83	21.75 /85	10.58 /82	1.52	0.89
IN	RVS Dividend Opportunity A	INUTX	C+	(800) 328-8300	C- / 3.7	1.50	6.31	10.34 /49	11.23 /37	0.42 /17	2.60	1.14
IN	RVS Dividend Opportunity B	IUTBX	C	(800) 328-8300	C- / 3.2	1.31	6.06	9.55 /44	10.38 /30	-0.34 /14	2.01	1.90
IN	RVS Dividend Opportunity C	ACUIX	C+	(800) 328-8300	C- / 3.9	1.31	5.94	9.47 /43	10.37 /30	-0.36 /14	2.06	1.91
IN	RVS Dividend Opportunity Y		C-	(800) 328-8300	C / 4.8	1.54	6.55	10.55 /51	11.50 /39	0.62 /18	2.97	0.77
EM	RVS Emerging Markets Fund A	IDEAX	C+	(800) 328-8300	A / 9.5	-5.14	6.74	36.04 /97	32.55 /97	19.30 /95	0.19	1.77
EM	RVS Emerging Markets Fund B	IEMBX	C+	(800) 328-8300	A / 9.5	-5.35	6.23	35.08 /97	31.60 /96	18.36 /95	0.00	2.53
EM	RVS Emerging Markets Fund C		A-	(800) 328-8300	A+ / 9.6	-5.34	6.22	34.98 /97	31.51 /96	18.43 /95	0.00	2.54
EM	RVS Emerging Markets Fund Y		C-	(800) 328-8300	A+ / 9.6	-5.16	6.74	36.29 /97	32.80 /97	19.48 /96	0.00	1.57
IN	RVS Equity Value A	IEVAX	A-	(800) 328-8300	B- / 7.4	-0.61	7.59	18.69 /80	18.71 /75	5.37 /57	0.87	1.17
IN	RVS Equity Value B	INEGX	B	(800) 328-8300	C+ / 6.6	-0.81	7.24	17.79 /79	16.63 /66	3.96 /46	0.14	1.93
IN	RVS Equity Value C		A	(800) 328-8300	B- / 7.1	-0.79	7.16	18.10 /79	16.76 /67	3.98 /46	0.44	1.93
IN	RVS Equity Value Y	AEVYX	C+	(800) 328-8300	B- / 7.5	-0.57	7.69	18.89 /80	17.77 /71	4.91 /53	1.10	0.99
FO	RVS European Equity Fund A	AXEAX	A	(800) 328-8300	B+ / 8.5	2.87	15.97	28.15 /93	20.14 /80	7.66 /70	1.26	1.50
FO	RVS European Equity Fund B	AEEBX	A-	(800) 328-8300	B+ / 8.4	2.70	15.65	27.12 /91	19.24 /77	6.86 /66	0.58	2.27
FO	RVS European Equity Fund C		A+	(800) 328-8300	B+ / 8.6	2.70	15.42	27.01 /91	19.18 /77	6.83 /66	0.68	2.27
GR	RVS Fundamental Growth Fund A	AXPAX	E+	(800) 328-8300	E- / 0.2	-5.04	-2.11	3.57 / 9	4.71 / 3	--	0.00	1.40
GR	RVS Fundamental Growth Fund B		E+	(800) 328-8300	E- / 0.1	-5.31	-2.49	2.76 / 6	3.90 / 2	--	0.00	2.17
GR	RVS Fundamental Growth Fund C		E+	(800) 328-8300	E / 0.3	-5.31	-2.49	2.76 / 6	3.90 / 2	--	0.00	2.18
GR	RVS Fundamental Growth Fund Y		D-	(800) 328-8300	E+ / 0.6	-5.16	-2.10	3.73 /10	4.94 / 4	--	0.00	1.22
GR	RVS Fundamental Value Fund A	AFVAX	B-	(800) 328-8300	C / 4.6	0.49	3.04	10.68 /51	13.30 /50	4.93 /54	0.31	1.27
GR	RVS Fundamental Value Fund B	AFVBX	C+	(800) 328-8300	C- / 4.2	0.34	2.60	9.81 /46	12.45 /45	4.15 /47	0.00	2.03
GR	RVS Fundamental Value Fund C	AFVCX	B-	(800) 328-8300	C / 4.8	0.34	2.59	9.78 /45	12.40 /45	4.22 /48	0.00	2.04
GL	RVS Global Equity Fund A	IGLGX	B	(800) 328-8300	B / 7.6	-1.25	6.92	24.40 /88	19.16 /76	5.30 /56	0.22	1.59

● Denotes fund is closed to new investors
★ Denotes fund is included in Section II

RISK			NET ASSETS		ASSET						BULL / BEAR		FUND MANAGER		MINIMUMS		LOADS	
	3 Year		NAV						Portfolio	Last Bull	Last Bear	Manager	Manager	Initial	Additional	Front	Back
Risk	Standard		As of	Total	Cash	Stocks	Bonds	Other	Turnover	Market	Market	Quality	Tenure	Purch.	Purch.	End	End
Rating/Pts	Deviation	Beta	6/30/06	$(Mil)	%	%	%	%	Ratio	Return	Return	Pct	(Years)	$	$	Load	Load
B /8.2	8.4	1.08	11.50	24	5	94	0	1	84.7	80.2	-9.7	77	N/A	0	0	0.0	0.0
B /8.3	8.4	1.07	11.71	9	5	94	0	1	84.7	85.3	-9.5	84	N/A	0	0	0.0	0.0
B /8.3	8.4	1.07	11.74	121	5	94	0	1	84.7	87.6	-9.4	87	N/A	100,000	0	0.0	0.0
B /8.3	8.4	1.07	11.72	227	5	94	0	1	84.7	86.5	-9.4	86	N/A	0	0	0.0	0.0
C /4.8	13.6	0.92	48.27	65	5	94	0	1	153.6	105.0	-9.3	44	6	0	0	0.0	0.0
C /5.0	13.6	0.92	51.83	24	5	94	0	1	153.6	109.9	-9.1	55	6	0	0	0.0	0.0
C /5.2	13.6	0.92	53.87	982	5	94	0	1	153.6	111.7	-9.1	58	6	0	0	0.0	0.0
B- /7.7	8.8	0.77	10.14	19	0	100	0	0	12.5	81.4	-9.3	17	N/A	0	0	0.0	0.0
B- /7.8	8.8	0.77	10.41	49	0	100	0	0	12.5	87.5	-9.2	23	N/A	0	0	0.0	0.0
B /8.6	7.7	0.99	18.23	18	6	93	0	1	42.9	57.5	-9.9	35	N/A	0	0	0.0	0.0
B /8.6	7.7	0.99	18.64	11	6	93	0	1	42.9	61.2	-9.6	43	N/A	0	0	0.0	0.0
B /8.6	7.7	0.99	18.71	423	6	93	0	1	42.9	62.5	-9.6	46	N/A	0	0	0.0	0.0
B- /7.0	12.7	0.86	12.67	11	7	92	0	1	57.9	97.7	-8.3	53	N/A	0	0	0.0	0.0
B- /7.1	12.8	0.86	13.32	2	7	92	0	1	57.9	102.3	-8.0	62	N/A	0	0	0.0	0.0
B- /7.1	12.8	0.87	13.50	185	7	92	0	1	57.9	104.0	-8.0	65	N/A	0	0	0.0	0.0
C /4.7	14.4	1.54	8.33	410	2	97	0	1	218.0	N/A	N/A	N/A	N/A	2,000	100	5.8	0.0
C /4.7	14.5	1.54	8.14	116	2	97	0	1	218.0	N/A	N/A	46	N/A	2,000	100	0.0	5.0
U /	N/A	N/A	8.41	76	2	97	0	1	218.0	N/A	N/A	N/A	N/A	10,000,000	0	0.0	0.0
B+ /9.5	4.9	1.01	10.04	938	0	64	35	1	70.0	45.4	-5.5	63	N/A	2,000	100	5.8	0.0
B+ /9.7	4.9	1.02	9.97	90	0	64	35	1	70.0	41.9	-5.7	52	N/A	2,000	100	0.0	5.0
C+ /6.2	5.0	1.03	9.97	4	0	64	35	1	70.0	42.1	-5.8	52	N/A	2,000	100	0.0	1.0
B+ /9.8	4.9	1.02	10.04	143	0	64	35	1	70.0	46.2	-5.4	64	N/A	10,000,000	0	0.0	0.0
C+ /5.9	8.5	1.06	6.70	1,360	0	100	0	0	28.0	N/A	N/A	46	N/A	2,000	100	5.8	0.0
U /	N/A	N/A	6.74	225	0	100	0	0	28.0	N/A	N/A	N/A	N/A	10,000,000	0	0.0	0.0
B /8.0	10.5	1.27	12.83	4,949	1	98	0	1	7.0	127.1	-9.8	97	6	2,000	100	5.8	0.0
B /8.0	10.5	1.27	12.84	1,338	1	98	0	1	7.0	121.7	-9.8	95	6	2,000	100	0.0	5.0
B /8.0	10.6	1.27	12.82	80	1	98	0	1	7.0	121.6	-9.8	95	6	2,000	100	0.0	1.0
U /	N/A	N/A	12.82	173	1	98	0	1	7.0	N/A	N/A	N/A	N/A	10,000,000	0	0.0	0.0
B /8.1	10.6	1.27	12.84	83	1	98	0	1	7.0	128.2	-9.6	97	6	10,000,000	0	0.0	0.0
B /8.9	7.2	0.63	7.83	907	0	99	0	1	11.0	63.7	-5.2	85	2	2,000	100	5.8	0.0
B /8.9	7.2	0.64	7.78	275	0	99	0	1	11.0	59.7	-5.3	79	2	2,000	100	0.0	5.0
B+ /9.0	7.1	0.63	7.77	15	0	99	0	1	11.0	59.7	-5.4	80	2	2,000	100	0.0	1.0
C+ /6.4	7.1	0.63	7.85	1	0	99	0	1	11.0	64.5	-5.2	87	2	10,000,000	0	0.0	0.0
C- /3.4	19.1	1.16	10.14	379	0	100	0	0	124.0	190.0	-4.3	7	6	2,000	100	5.8	0.0
C- /3.4	19.1	1.16	9.55	92	0	100	0	0	124.0	182.8	-4.3	5	6	2,000	100	0.0	5.0
C+ /5.9	19.1	1.16	9.57	4	0	100	0	0	124.0	183.8	-4.5	5	6	2,000	100	0.0	1.0
D /1.7	19.1	1.16	10.29	6	0	100	0	0	124.0	191.4	-4.0	7	6	10,000,000	0	0.0	0.0
B /8.1	10.1	1.18	12.05	910	0	98	0	2	28.0	106.5	-10.5	94	6	2,000	100	5.8	0.0
B /8.1	9.7	1.15	12.08	218	0	98	0	2	28.0	95.8	-10.7	88	6	2,000	100	0.0	5.0
B /8.8	9.7	1.16	11.98	4	0	98	0	2	28.0	96.2	-10.7	88	6	2,000	100	0.0	1.0
C+ /5.8	9.7	1.15	12.06	13	0	98	0	2	28.0	101.7	-10.5	92	6	10,000,000	0	0.0	0.0
B- /7.2	10.7	0.95	5.01	78	0	100	0	0	56.0	106.2	-11.1	29	3	2,000	100	5.8	0.0
B- /7.2	10.7	0.96	4.95	31	0	100	0	0	56.0	101.7	-11.4	23	3	2,000	100	0.0	5.0
B /8.8	10.9	0.96	4.94	1	0	100	0	0	56.0	101.4	-11.4	22	3	2,000	100	0.0	1.0
B- /7.0	9.8	1.18	6.03	20	2	96	0	2	122.0	N/A	N/A	5	3	2,000	100	5.8	0.0
C+ /6.9	9.8	1.18	5.88	7	2	96	0	2	122.0	N/A	N/A	4	3	2,000	100	0.0	5.0
C+ /6.9	9.8	1.18	5.88	1	2	96	0	2	122.0	N/A	N/A	4	3	2,000	100	0.0	1.0
B- /7.0	9.9	1.19	6.07	N/A	2	96	0	2	122.0	N/A	N/A	6	3	10,000,000	0	0.0	0.0
B+ /9.1	7.0	0.84	6.10	736	N/A	N/A	0	N/A	2.0	70.0	-6.8	86	5	2,000	100	5.8	0.0
B+ /9.1	7.0	0.83	5.93	278	N/A	N/A	0	N/A	2.0	66.0	-6.9	81	5	2,000	100	0.0	5.0
B+ /9.0	6.9	0.83	5.95	18	N/A	N/A	0	N/A	2.0	66.1	-7.2	81	5	2,000	100	0.0	1.0
C+ /6.7	10.3	0.94	7.11	561	0	100	0	0	93.0	100.7	-9.0	25	3	2,000	100	5.8	0.0

99 Pct = Best
0 Pct = Worst

Fund Type	Fund Name	Ticker Symbol	Overall Weiss Investment Rating	Phone	Perfor-mance Rating/Pts	3 Mo	6 Mo	1Yr / Pct	3Yr / Pct	5Yr / Pct	Dividend Yield	Expense Ratio
GL	RVS Global Equity Fund B	IDGBX	B-	(800) 328-8300	B- / 7.3	-1.47	6.53	23.43 /86	18.21 /73	4.49 /50	0.00	2.36
GL	RVS Global Equity Fund C		A+	(800) 328-8300	B / 7.7	-1.34	6.57	23.64 /87	18.27 /73	4.46 /50	0.03	2.35
GL	RVS Global Equity Fund Y	IDGYX	A	(800) 328-8300	B / 8.1	-1.38	7.01	24.71 /88	19.32 /77	5.46 /58	0.34	1.40
TC	RVS Global Technology A	AXIAX	E	(800) 328-8300	C- / 3.9	-9.13	-0.48	9.42 /43	13.48 /51	-1.46 /10	0.00	1.75
TC	RVS Global Technology B	INVBX	E	(800) 328-8300	C- / 3.4	-9.50	-1.09	8.38 /36	12.54 /46	-2.27 / 7	0.00	2.53
* GR	RVS Growth Fund A	INIDX	D	(800) 328-8300	E+ / 0.7	-6.25	-1.08	3.41 / 9	7.34 /12	-2.11 / 8	0.03	1.20
GR	RVS Growth Fund B	IGRBX	D-	(800) 328-8300	E / 0.5	-6.45	-1.44	2.64 / 6	6.52 / 8	-2.87 / 6	0.04	1.98
GR	RVS Growth Fund C	AXGCX	D	(800) 328-8300	E+ / 0.8	-6.45	-1.44	2.64 / 6	6.52 / 8	-2.88 / 6	0.04	1.98
GR	RVS Growth Fund I	AGWIX	U	(800) 328-8300	U /	-6.17	-0.85	3.87 /10	--	--	0.13	0.69
GR	RVS Growth Fund Y	IGRYX	D+	(800) 328-8300	D- / 1.4	-6.24	-0.99	3.59 / 9	7.52 /12	-1.95 / 8	0.06	0.97
GL	RVS International Aggressive Gr A	AXGAX	A-	(800) 328-8300	B+ / 8.9	-1.67	10.36	27.96 /93	24.84 /91	--	0.68	1.79
GL	RVS International Aggressive Gr B	APIBX	A-	(800) 328-8300	B+ / 8.8	-1.83	9.86	27.00 /91	23.86 /89	--	0.12	2.56
GL	RVS International Aggressive Gr C		A+	(800) 328-8300	A- / 9.0	-1.83	9.86	27.02 /91	23.86 /89	--	0.11	2.55
FO	RVS International Equity Fund A	AAICX	A+	(800) 328-8300	B+ / 8.3	-1.37	7.90	27.87 /92	21.28 /83	--	0.69	1.58
FO	RVS International Equity Fund B	APCBX	B	(800) 328-8300	B / 8.1	-1.51	7.43	26.83 /91	20.30 /80	--	0.09	2.36
FO	RVS International Equity Fund C		A+	(800) 328-8300	B+ / 8.3	-1.51	7.42	26.88 /91	20.30 /80	--	0.04	2.36
FO	RVS International Equity Fund Y		A+	(800) 328-8300	B+ / 8.6	-1.50	7.78	27.67 /92	21.32 /83	--	0.98	1.41
FO	RVS International Opportunity A	INIFX	B+	(800) 328-8300	B+ / 8.4	-0.55	10.33	29.25 /94	20.79 /82	6.32 /63	0.98	1.49
FO	RVS International Opportunity B	IWWGX	B+	(800) 328-8300	B / 8.2	-0.68	9.94	28.26 /93	19.82 /79	5.51 /58	0.34	2.25
FO	RVS International Opportunity C		A+	(800) 328-8300	B+ / 8.4	-0.80	9.90	28.11 /93	19.82 /79	5.49 /58	0.54	2.25
FO	RVS International Opportunity I	ATNIX	U	(800) 328-8300	U /	-0.44	10.50	29.81 /94	--	--	1.53	1.07
FO	RVS International Opportunity Y	IDIYX	A+	(800) 328-8300	B+ / 8.7	-0.44	10.39	29.46 /94	20.94 /82	6.55 /64	0.00	1.32
FO	RVS International Select Value A	APIAX	A+	(800) 328-8300	A- / 9.1	-1.66	9.79	29.86 /94	25.41 /91	--	2.02	1.49
FO	RVS International Select Value B	AXIBX	A+	(800) 328-8300	B+ / 8.9	-2.01	9.28	28.84 /94	24.41 /90	--	1.58	2.26
FO	RVS International Select Value C	APICX	A+	(800) 328-8300	A- / 9.1	-1.91	9.29	28.80 /94	24.47 /90	--	1.64	2.26
FO	RVS International Small Cap A	AISCX	B-	(800) 328-8300	B+ / 8.3	-5.04	5.73	19.40 /81	22.67 /87	--	0.88	1.82
FO	RVS International Small Cap B	APNBX	C+	(800) 328-8300	B / 8.1	-5.15	5.36	18.42 /80	21.76 /85	--	0.27	2.59
FO	RVS International Small Cap C		A	(800) 328-8300	B+ / 8.4	-5.25	5.35	18.43 /80	21.74 /85	--	0.38	2.60
FO	RVS International Small Cap Y		A+	(800) 328-8300	B+ / 8.7	-4.91	5.95	19.64 /81	22.97 /87	--	1.04	1.65
* GR	RVS Large Cap Equity A	ALEAX	D	(800) 328-8300	D- / 1.2	-3.07	1.39	5.55 /18	7.88 /14	--	0.78	1.18
GR	RVS Large Cap Equity B	ALEBX	D	(800) 328-8300	E+ / 0.9	-3.31	0.96	4.58 /13	6.99 /10	--	0.00	1.95
GR	RVS Large Cap Equity C	ARQCX	D	(800) 328-8300	D- / 1.3	-3.31	0.96	4.57 /13	6.98 /10	--	0.00	1.95
GR	RVS Large Cap Equity I	ALRIX	U	(800) 328-8300	U /	-2.88	1.59	5.90 /20	--	--	1.58	0.75
GR	RVS Large Cap Equity Y	ALEYX	C-	(800) 328-8300	D / 2.0	-3.22	1.29	5.49 /18	7.96 /15	--	0.43	0.87
GI	RVS Large Cap Value A	ALVAX	C	(800) 328-8300	C- / 3.3	-0.86	4.14	7.97 /32	11.35 /38	--	1.17	1.28
GI	RVS Large Cap Value B	ALVBX	C	(800) 328-8300	D+ / 2.9	-1.04	3.80	7.28 /28	10.48 /31	--	0.40	2.04
GI	RVS Large Cap Value C		C	(800) 328-8300	C- / 3.5	-1.21	3.62	7.12 /27	10.47 /31	--	0.45	2.05
GI	RVS Large Cap Value I	ALCIX	U	(800) 328-8300	U /	-0.85	4.31	8.44 /36	--	--	1.68	0.73
GI	RVS Large Cap Value Y		C+	(800) 328-8300	C / 4.4	-0.85	4.13	8.10 /33	11.55 /40	--	1.41	0.99
MC	RVS Mid Cap Growth Fd Cl A	INVPX	D-	(800) 328-8300	D / 1.9	-7.14	-2.93	7.23 /28	10.05 /28	4.24 /48	0.00	1.10
MC	RVS Mid Cap Growth Fd Cl B	IDQBX	E+	(800) 328-8300	D- / 1.5	-7.30	-3.27	6.36 /22	9.20 /22	3.43 /41	0.00	1.87
MC	RVS Mid Cap Growth Fd Cl C	AESCX	D-	(800) 328-8300	D / 2.1	-7.30	-3.27	6.45 /23	9.22 /22	3.44 /41	0.00	1.88
MC	RVS Mid Cap Value A	AMVAX	A+	(800) 328-8300	A- / 9.0	-0.11	8.47	21.00 /83	25.84 /92	--	0.31	1.34
MC	RVS Mid Cap Value B	AMVBX	A+	(800) 328-8300	B+ / 8.9	-0.22	8.03	20.18 /82	24.90 /91	--	0.00	2.11
MC	RVS Mid Cap Value C	AMVCX	A+	(800) 328-8300	A- / 9.1	-0.34	8.03	20.18 /82	24.90 /91	--	0.00	2.11
MC	RVS Mid Cap Value Y		A+	(800) 328-8300	A / 9.3	0.00	8.66	21.45 /84	26.08 /92	--	0.44	1.19
AG	RVS Portfolio Bldr Aggressive A	AXBAX	U	(800) 328-8300	U /	-2.10	3.84	11.43 /56	--	--	1.34	1.38
AG	RVS Portfolio Bldr Aggressive B	AXPBX	U	(800) 328-8300	U /	-2.37	3.32	10.48 /50	--	--	0.85	2.16
AA	RVS Portfolio Bldr Conservative A	ABDAX	U	(800) 328-8300	U /	-0.47	0.87	2.83 / 7	--	--	2.96	1.20
AA	RVS Portfolio Bldr Conservative B	ABBDX	U	(800) 328-8300	U /	-0.65	0.49	2.13 / 5	--	--	2.32	1.95
AG	RVS Portfolio Bldr Mod Agg A	AXMAX	U	(800) 328-8300	U /	-1.63	3.05	9.09 /41	--	--	2.32	1.32
AG	RVS Portfolio Bldr Mod Agg B	ABMBX	U	(800) 328-8300	U /	-1.82	2.76	8.28 /35	--	--	1.70	2.08

● Denotes fund is closed to new investors
* Denotes fund is included in Section II

www.WeissRatings.com

RISK			NET ASSETS		ASSET					BULL / BEAR		FUND MANAGER		MINIMUMS		LOADS	
	3 Year		NAV						Portfolio	Last Bull	Last Bear	Manager	Manager	Initial	Additional	Front	Back
Risk	Standard		As of	Total	Cash	Stocks	Bonds	Other	Turnover	Market	Market	Quality	Tenure	Purch.	Purch.	End	End
Rating/Pts	Deviation	Beta	6/30/06	$(Mil)	%	%	%	%	Ratio	Return	Return	Pct	(Years)	$	$	Load	Load
C+ / 6.7	10.2	0.93	6.69	126	0	100	0	0	93.0	95.8	-9.2	21	3	2,000	100	0.0	5.0
B / 8.5	10.3	0.94	6.65	5	0	100	0	0	93.0	95.7	-9.2	20	3	2,000	100	0.0	1.0
B- / 7.7	10.3	0.94	7.17	9	0	100	0	0	93.0	102.1	-9.2	26	3	10,000,000	0	0.0	0.0
D+ / 2.5	19.0	2.02	2.09	110	2	97	0	1	115.0	111.8	-10.6	8	4	2,000	100	5.8	0.0
D+ / 2.3	18.9	2.03	1.81	42	2	97	0	1	115.0	106.1	-10.9	6	4	2,000	100	0.0	5.0
B / 8.0	7.2	0.75	28.50	2,297	19	80	0	1	72.0	53.5	-9.4	38	4	2,000	100	5.8	0.0
B- / 7.9	7.2	0.75	25.98	541	19	80	0	1	72.0	49.8	-9.6	32	4	2,000	100	0.0	5.0
B- / 7.9	7.2	0.75	25.98	19	19	80	0	1	72.0	49.8	-9.6	32	4	2,000	100	0.0	1.0
U /	N/A	N/A	29.18	220	19	80	0	1	72.0	N/A	N/A	N/A	2	10,000,000	0	0.0	0.0
B / 8.2	7.2	0.75	29.01	285	19	80	0	1	72.0	54.3	-9.4	40	4	10,000,000	0	0.0	0.0
C+ / 6.5	11.0	1.05	8.84	265	0	100	0	0	67.0	140.5	-7.6	47	N/A	2,000	100	5.8	0.0
C+ / 6.5	11.0	1.05	8.58	68	0	100	0	0	67.0	135.0	-7.9	38	N/A	2,000	100	0.0	5.0
B / 8.6	11.0	1.05	8.58	4	0	100	0	0	67.0	135.0	-7.7	38	N/A	2,000	100	0.0	1.0
B- / 7.9	10.3	0.99	7.92	95	0	100	0	0	110.0	120.2	-11.2	30	4	2,000	100	5.8	0.0
C+ / 6.4	10.3	0.99	7.81	27	0	100	0	0	110.0	115.1	-11.4	24	4	2,000	100	0.0	5.0
B- / 7.8	10.2	0.99	7.82	2	0	100	0	0	110.0	114.8	-11.4	25	4	2,000	100	0.0	1.0
B- / 7.8	10.3	0.99	7.90	N/A	0	100	0	0	110.0	121.4	-11.1	30	4	10,000,000	0	0.0	0.0
C+ / 6.6	10.7	1.03	8.97	437	0	100	0	0	93.0	109.2	-10.2	22	3	2,000	100	5.8	0.0
C+ / 6.5	10.7	1.03	8.74	88	0	100	0	0	93.0	104.1	-10.3	18	3	2,000	100	0.0	5.0
B- / 7.7	10.7	1.03	8.66	3	0	100	0	0	93.0	103.9	-10.4	18	3	2,000	100	0.0	1.0
U /	N/A	N/A	9.05	60	0	100	0	0	93.0	N/A	N/A	N/A	N/A	10,000,000	0	0.0	0.0
B- / 7.7	10.7	1.03	9.14	1	0	100	0	0	93.0	110.6	-10.2	23	3	10,000,000	0	0.0	0.0
B- / 7.4	9.7	0.90	10.09	1,338	0	100	0	0	22.0	146.2	-5.4	82	N/A	2,000	100	5.8	0.0
B- / 7.3	9.7	0.90	9.77	382	0	100	0	0	22.0	140.3	-5.6	77	N/A	2,000	100	0.0	5.0
B- / 7.3	9.7	0.91	9.76	23	0	100	0	0	22.0	140.3	-5.6	76	N/A	2,000	100	0.0	1.0
C / 5.3	10.7	0.96	8.86	71	0	100	0	0	80.0	147.6	-4.6	48	4	2,000	100	5.8	0.0
C / 5.3	10.8	0.97	8.65	19	0	100	0	0	80.0	141.3	-4.6	37	4	2,000	100	0.0	5.0
B- / 7.5	10.8	0.96	8.66	1	0	100	0	0	80.0	141.1	-4.8	38	4	2,000	100	0.0	1.0
B- / 7.5	10.8	0.96	8.91	N/A	0	100	0	0	80.0	148.6	-4.6	50	4	10,000,000	0	0.0	0.0
B- / 7.8	7.4	0.90	5.36	5,325	0	100	0	0	53.0	54.5	-9.1	32	1	2,000	100	5.8	0.0
B- / 7.7	7.3	0.89	5.25	1,409	0	100	0	0	53.0	50.7	-9.5	26	1	2,000	100	0.0	5.0
B / 8.0	7.4	0.90	5.26	35	0	100	0	0	53.0	50.5	-9.5	26	1	2,000	100	0.0	1.0
U /	N/A	N/A	5.39	124	0	100	0	0	53.0	N/A	N/A	N/A	N/A	10,000,000	0	0.0	0.0
B / 8.4	7.0	0.82	5.41	1,183	0	100	0	0	53.0	55.3	-9.1	38	1	10,000,000	0	0.0	0.0
B / 8.5	7.4	0.93	5.78	61	0	100	0	0	29.0	68.3	-10.2	64	4	2,000	100	5.8	0.0
B / 8.6	7.4	0.93	5.73	21	0	100	0	0	29.0	64.1	-10.4	55	4	2,000	100	0.0	5.0
B / 8.9	7.4	0.93	5.72	1	0	100	0	0	29.0	64.0	-10.4	55	4	2,000	100	0.0	1.0
U /	N/A	N/A	5.81	26	0	100	0	0	29.0	N/A	N/A	N/A	2	10,000,000	0	0.0	0.0
B / 8.9	7.4	0.92	5.80	N/A	0	100	0	0	29.0	69.1	-10.2	67	4	10,000,000	0	0.0	0.0
C+ / 5.9	12.5	1.08	13.92	1,217	0	100	0	0	27.0	59.3	-7.2	4	6	2,000	100	5.8	0.0
C+ / 5.8	12.5	1.08	12.70	277	0	100	0	0	27.0	55.3	-7.3	3	6	2,000	100	0.0	5.0
C+ / 5.8	12.6	1.08	12.70	11	0	100	0	0	27.0	55.4	-7.3	3	6	2,000	100	0.0	1.0
B- / 7.8	11.1	0.94	9.09	1,303	1	97	0	2	13.0	158.9	-12.0	97	N/A	2,000	100	5.8	0.0
B- / 7.8	11.0	0.94	8.88	321	1	97	0	2	13.0	152.8	-12.2	96	N/A	2,000	100	0.0	5.0
B- / 7.8	11.1	0.95	8.88	25	1	97	0	2	13.0	153.0	-12.2	96	N/A	2,000	100	0.0	1.0
B- / 7.8	11.2	0.95	9.16	25	1	97	0	2	13.0	160.4	-11.8	98	N/A	10,000,000	0	0.0	0.0
U /	N/A	N/A	11.63	319	5	79	15	1	24.0	N/A	N/A	N/A	2	2,000	100	5.8	0.0
U /	N/A	N/A	11.51	87	5	79	15	1	24.0	N/A	N/A	N/A	2	2,000	100	0.0	5.0
U /	N/A	N/A	10.19	76	19	22	58	1	23.0	N/A	N/A	N/A	2	2,000	100	4.8	0.0
U /	N/A	N/A	10.17	38	19	22	58	1	23.0	N/A	N/A	N/A	2	2,000	100	0.0	5.0
U /	N/A	N/A	11.21	631	5	64	29	2	20.0	N/A	N/A	N/A	2	2,000	100	5.8	0.0
U /	N/A	N/A	11.18	175	5	64	29	2	20.0	N/A	N/A	N/A	2	2,000	100	0.0	5.0

Fund Type	Fund Name	Ticker Symbol	Overall Weiss Investment Rating	Phone	Performance Rating/Pts	3 Mo	6 Mo	1Yr / Pct	3Yr / Pct	5Yr / Pct	Dividend Yield	Expense Ratio
AA	RVS Portfolio Bldr Mod Cons A	AUCAX	U	(800) 328-8300	U /	-0.82	1.70	5.03 /15	--	--	2.91	1.23
AA	RVS Portfolio Bldr Mod Cons B	AMDBX	U	(800) 328-8300	U /	-1.01	1.31	4.22 /11	--	--	2.31	1.98
AA	RVS Portfolio Bldr Moderate A	ABUAX	U	(800) 328-8300	U /	-1.24	2.50	7.17 /27	--	--	2.78	1.26
AA	RVS Portfolio Bldr Moderate B	AURBX	U	(800) 328-8300	U /	-1.44	2.12	6.36 /22	--	--	2.18	2.02
GR	RVS Portfolio Bldr Total Equity A	AXTAX	U	(800) 328-8300	U /	-2.61	4.46	13.59 /67	--	--	1.02	1.42
GR	RVS Portfolio Bldr Total Equity B	AXTBX	U	(800) 328-8300	U /	-2.88	3.96	12.66 /63	--	--	0.53	2.20
PM	RVS Precious Metals Fund A	INPMX	D+	(800) 328-8300	A+ / 9.8	0.14	25.11	69.54 /99	28.74 /95	27.13 /99	0.00	1.43
PM	RVS Precious Metals Fund B	INPBX	D+	(800) 328-8300	A+ / 9.8	0.00	24.71	68.24 /99	27.79 /94	26.15 /99	0.00	2.19
RE	RVS Real Estate Fund A	ARLAX	U	(800) 328-8300	U /	0.18	14.87	24.02 /87	--	--	0.81	1.50
RE	RVS Real Estate Fund B	AESBX	U	(800) 328-8300	U /	-0.07	14.46	23.06 /86	--	--	0.26	2.28
RE	RVS Real Estate Fund I	AESIX	U	(800) 328-8300	U /	0.27	15.10	24.55 /88	--	--	1.20	1.08
IX	RVS S&P 500 Index Fund D	ADIDX	C	(800) 328-8300	C- / 3.7	-1.40	2.50	8.13 /34	10.49 /31	1.86 /26	1.30	0.59
IX	RVS S&P 500 Index Fund E	ADIEX	C	(800) 328-8300	C- / 3.8	-1.59	2.49	8.15 /34	10.71 /33	2.11 /28	1.56	0.34
GI	RVS Select Value Fund A	AXVAX	C+	(800) 328-8300	C / 4.9	1.11	8.47	9.57 /44	13.33 /50	--	0.09	1.33
GI	RVS Select Value Fund B	AXVBX	C+	(800) 328-8300	C / 4.5	1.00	8.24	8.75 /38	12.54 /46	--	0.00	2.10
GI	RVS Select Value Fund C	ACSVX	C+	(800) 328-8300	C / 5.1	1.00	8.24	8.75 /38	12.54 /46	--	0.00	2.10
GI	RVS Select Value Fund Y		B-	(800) 328-8300	C+ / 5.8	1.10	8.73	9.91 /46	13.55 /52	--	0.17	1.16
SC	RVS Small Cap Advantage A	ASAAX	C-	(800) 328-8300	B- / 7.0	-5.67	6.23	12.42 /62	18.80 /76	9.48 /79	0.00	1.28
SC	RVS Small Cap Advantage B	ASABX	D+	(800) 328-8300	C+ / 6.7	-5.91	5.64	11.35 /56	17.87 /72	8.63 /75	0.00	2.05
SC	RVS Small Cap Advantage C	ADVCX	C-	(800) 328-8300	B- / 7.1	-5.91	5.64	11.35 /56	17.87 /72	8.63 /75	0.00	2.05
SC	RVS Small Cap Equity Fund A	AXSAX	C+	(800) 328-8300	C+ / 6.9	-7.36	3.83	11.77 /58	19.08 /76	--	0.00	1.58
SC	RVS Small Cap Equity Fund B	AXSBX	C+	(800) 328-8300	C+ / 6.6	-7.63	3.42	10.82 /52	18.13 /73	--	0.00	2.34
SC	RVS Small Cap Equity Fund C		B-	(800) 328-8300	B- / 7.0	-7.64	3.24	10.84 /53	18.16 /73	--	0.00	2.34
SC	RVS Small Cap Equity Fund Y		B	(800) 328-8300	B- / 7.5	-7.44	3.79	11.85 /59	19.26 /77	--	0.00	1.42
SC	RVS Small Cap Growth Fund A	AXSCX	D-	(800) 328-8300	C / 4.4	-7.38	6.36	16.03 /75	13.41 /51	0.35 /17	0.00	1.54
SC	RVS Small Cap Growth Fund B	ASGBX	E+	(800) 328-8300	C- / 4.0	-7.49	6.17	15.14 /72	12.66 /47	-0.38 /14	0.00	2.31
SC	RVS Small Cap Growth Fund C	APRCX	D-	(800) 328-8300	C / 4.7	-7.49	6.17	15.14 /72	12.66 /47	-0.38 /14	0.00	2.31
SC	RVS Small Cap Value Fund A	ASVAX	C	(800) 328-8300	B- / 7.5	-1.90	8.90	15.38 /73	19.50 /78	11.54 /85	0.00	1.47
SC	RVS Small Cap Value Fund B	ASVBX	C	(800) 328-8300	B- / 7.5	-2.10	9.03	15.19 /72	19.15 /76	11.00 /84	0.00	2.24
SC	RVS Small Cap Value Fund C	APVCX	C+	(800) 328-8300	B / 7.8	-1.95	9.18	15.34 /73	19.18 /77	11.06 /84	0.00	2.24
SC	RVS Small Cap Value Fund Y		C+	(800) 328-8300	B / 8.0	-1.88	9.00	15.45 /73	19.67 /78	11.68 /86	0.00	1.29
SC	RVS Small Company Index Fund A	ISIAX	C+	(800) 328-8300	B- / 7.3	-4.72	7.25	13.01 /64	19.38 /77	10.09 /81	0.00	0.89
SC	RVS Small Company Index Fund B	ISIBX	C+	(800) 328-8300	B- / 7.0	-4.95	6.89	12.17 /60	18.52 /74	9.25 /78	0.00	1.65
SC	RVS Small Company Index Fund Y	ISCYX	B-	(800) 328-8300	B / 7.8	-4.74	7.36	13.17 /65	19.61 /78	10.26 /81	0.00	0.72
AA	RVS Strategic Allocation A	IMRFX	C	(800) 328-8300	C- / 3.6	-2.21	3.71	10.80 /52	11.68 /40	5.20 /56	1.32	1.11
AA	RVS Strategic Allocation B	IMRBX	C-	(800) 328-8300	C- / 3.2	-2.32	3.36	9.97 /47	10.86 /34	4.41 /50	0.69	1.88
AA	RVS Strategic Allocation C		C	(800) 328-8300	C- / 3.9	-2.29	3.43	10.01 /47	10.89 /35	4.41 /50	0.80	1.88
AA	RVS Strategic Allocation Y	IDRYX	C+	(800) 328-8300	C / 4.8	-2.08	3.90	11.10 /54	11.91 /42	5.42 /57	1.57	0.94
GI	RVS Value Fund A	AVLAX	C-	(800) 328-8300	C- / 4.2	-0.56	5.10	11.37 /56	12.29 /44	4.53 /50	0.49	1.24
GI	RVS Value Fund B	AVFBX	C-	(800) 328-8300	C- / 3.7	-0.76	4.41	10.40 /50	11.42 /39	3.71 /43	0.00	2.00
GI	RVS Value Fund C	AVUCX	C+	(800) 328-8300	C / 4.5	-0.76	4.60	10.59 /51	11.47 /39	3.84 /44	0.00	2.00
GI	RVS Value Fund I	AUEIX	U	(800) 328-8300	U /	-0.37	5.26	11.98 /59	--	--	0.92	0.78
GI	RVS Value Fund Y		C-	(800) 328-8300	C / 5.2	-0.55	5.28	11.37 /56	12.43 /45	4.65 /51	0.62	1.06
AG	Rydex Dynamics-Dow H	RYCVX	U	(800) 820-0888	U /	-0.23	6.39	14.24 /69	--	--	0.02	1.65
AG	Rydex Dynamics-Inv Dyn Dow H	RYCWX	U	(800) 820-0888	U /	0.05	-5.94	-12.96 / 0	--	--	0.16	1.66
AG	Rydex Dynamics-Inv Dyn OTC C	RYCDX	E-	(800) 820-0888	E- / 0.0	17.56	10.37	-7.37 / 0	-20.39 / 0	-13.90 / 0	0.00	2.40
AG	Rydex Dynamics-Inv Dyn OTC H	RYVNX	E-	(800) 820-0888	E- / 0.0	17.79	10.76	-6.71 / 0	-19.78 / 0	-13.32 / 0	1.64	1.66
AG	Rydex Dynamics-Inv Dyn S&P 500 C	RYCBX	E-	(800) 820-0888	E- / 0.0	4.81	-1.52	-9.27 / 0	-18.11 / 0	-9.37 / 0	1.84	2.41
AG	Rydex Dynamics-Inv Dyn S&P 500 H	RYTPX	E-	(800) 820-0888	E- / 0.0	5.00	-1.16	-8.57 / 0	-17.45 / 0	-8.67 / 0	1.76	1.66
AG	Rydex Dynamics-OTC C	RYCCX	E-	(800) 820-0888	D / 1.8	-16.46	-12.17	2.87 / 7	11.00 /36	-17.67 / 0	0.69	2.40
AG	Rydex Dynamics-OTC H	RYVYX	E-	(800) 820-0888	D+ / 2.5	-16.29	-11.82	3.76 /10	11.89 /42	-16.66 / 0	0.64	1.65
AG	Rydex Dynamics-S&P 500 C	RYCTX	C-	(800) 820-0888	C+ / 6.1	-5.08	1.10	8.88 /39	15.84 /63	-4.35 / 3	1.10	2.41

● Denotes fund is closed to new investors
* Denotes fund is included in Section II

www.WeissRatings.com

99 Pct = Best
0 Pct = Worst

RISK			NET ASSETS		ASSET				Portfolio Turnover Ratio	BULL / BEAR		FUND MANAGER		MINIMUMS		LOADS	
Risk Rating/Pts	3 Year		NAV As of 6/30/06	Total $(Mil)	Cash %	Stocks %	Bonds %	Other %		Last Bull Market Return	Last Bear Market Return	Manager Quality Pct	Manager Tenure (Years)	Initial Purch. $	Additional Purch. $	Front End Load	Back End Load
	Standard Deviation	Beta															
U /	N/A	N/A	10.52	166	11	36	52	1	19.0	N/A	N/A	N/A	2	2,000	100	5.8	0.0
U /	N/A	N/A	10.50	70	11	36	52	1	19.0	N/A	N/A	N/A	2	2,000	100	0.0	5.0
U /	N/A	N/A	10.91	469	5	50	43	2	15.0	N/A	N/A	N/A	2	2,000	100	5.8	0.0
U /	N/A	N/A	10.88	170	5	50	43	2	15.0	N/A	N/A	N/A	2	2,000	100	0.0	5.0
U /	N/A	N/A	11.94	276	3	95	0	2	17.0	N/A	N/A	N/A	2	2,000	100	5.8	0.0
U /	N/A	N/A	11.82	81	3	95	0	2	17.0	N/A	N/A	N/A	2	2,000	100	0.0	5.0
E- /0.0	33.3	1.50	14.75	87	1	98	0	1	111.0	150.0	17.4	32	7	2,000	100	5.8	0.0
E- /0.0	33.4	1.50	13.93	20	1	98	0	1	111.0	143.9	17.4	26	7	2,000	100	0.0	5.0
U /	N/A	N/A	15.30	107	1	98	0	1	27.0	N/A	N/A	N/A	1	2,000	100	5.8	0.0
U /	N/A	N/A	15.20	27	1	98	0	1	27.0	N/A	N/A	N/A	1	2,000	100	0.0	5.0
U /	N/A	N/A	15.33	57	1	98	0	1	27.0	N/A	N/A	N/A	1	10,000,000	0	0.0	0.0
B /8.6	7.6	1.00	4.92	56	0	100	0	0	7.0	61.3	-9.9	48	5	2,000	100	0.0	0.0
B /8.6	7.5	0.98	4.94	185	0	100	0	0	7.0	62.6	-10.0	53	5	2,000	100	0.0	0.0
B /8.2	8.5	1.01	7.30	454	2	98	0	0	12.0	74.3	-9.0	76	4	2,000	100	5.8	0.0
B /8.1	8.5	1.01	7.09	147	2	98	0	0	12.0	70.3	-9.3	69	4	2,000	100	0.0	5.0
B /8.1	8.5	1.01	7.09	9	2	98	0	0	12.0	70.3	-9.4	69	4	2,000	100	0.0	1.0
B /8.2	8.5	1.00	7.35	N/A	2	98	0	0	12.0	75.0	-8.8	77	4	10,000,000	0	0.0	0.0
C- /3.7	14.5	0.99	6.82	534	0	99	0	1	110.0	118.8	-10.0	59	N/A	2,000	100	5.8	0.0
C- /3.3	14.5	0.99	6.37	176	0	99	0	1	110.0	113.7	-10.0	49	N/A	2,000	100	0.0	5.0
C- /3.3	14.5	0.99	6.37	11	0	99	0	1	110.0	113.7	-10.0	49	N/A	2,000	100	0.0	1.0
C+ /6.8	13.7	0.92	5.92	294	2	97	0	1	88.0	124.8	-12.2	73	N/A	2,000	100	5.8	0.0
C+ /6.8	13.7	0.92	5.69	59	2	97	0	1	88.0	119.3	-12.3	65	N/A	2,000	100	0.0	5.0
C+ /6.8	13.4	0.89	5.68	4	2	97	0	1	88.0	119.6	-12.3	69	N/A	2,000	100	0.0	1.0
C+ /6.8	13.7	0.92	5.97	4	2	97	0	1	88.0	125.9	-12.0	74	N/A	10,000,000	0	0.0	0.0
C- /3.2	17.5	1.17	5.02	132	1	98	0	1	152.0	97.1	-14.2	7	5	2,000	100	5.8	0.0
C- /3.1	17.4	1.16	4.82	55	1	98	0	1	152.0	93.0	-14.7	5	5	2,000	100	0.0	5.0
C- /3.5	17.4	1.16	4.82	5	1	98	0	1	152.0	93.0	-14.7	5	5	2,000	100	0.0	1.0
C /4.5	12.1	0.81	6.73	676	5	94	0	1	70.0	111.9	-9.9	87	5	2,000	100	5.8	0.0
C- /4.2	12.4	0.84	6.52	292	5	94	0	1	70.0	110.4	-10.4	83	5	2,000	100	0.0	5.0
C /5.3	12.4	0.83	6.54	19	5	94	0	1	70.0	109.7	-10.2	84	5	2,000	100	0.0	1.0
C /5.3	12.0	0.81	6.78	N/A	5	94	0	1	70.0	112.7	-9.9	88	5	10,000,000	0	0.0	0.0
C+ /6.2	13.5	0.92	8.88	813	0	100	0	0	14.0	115.6	-10.0	75	5	2,000	100	5.8	0.0
C+ /5.9	13.6	0.92	8.07	314	0	100	0	0	14.0	110.4	-10.2	68	5	2,000	100	0.0	5.0
C+ /6.2	13.5	0.92	9.04	11	0	100	0	0	14.0	116.6	-9.9	77	5	10,000,000	0	0.0	0.0
B /8.1	7.6	1.48	10.41	1,106	1	80	18	1	57.0	59.3	-3.8	71	4	2,000	100	5.8	0.0
B /8.0	7.7	1.50	10.33	145	1	80	18	1	57.0	55.5	-4.0	62	4	2,000	100	0.0	5.0
B /8.5	7.7	1.50	10.30	18	1	80	18	1	57.0	55.5	-3.8	62	4	2,000	100	0.0	1.0
B /8.4	7.7	1.49	10.42	13	1	80	18	1	57.0	60.2	-3.7	72	4	10,000,000	0	0.0	0.0
B- /7.1	8.7	1.07	5.36	214	1	98	0	1	40.0	72.3	-11.1	61	N/A	2,000	100	5.8	0.0
B- /7.2	8.6	1.07	5.21	103	1	98	0	1	40.0	68.3	-11.5	51	N/A	2,000	100	0.0	5.0
B /8.1	8.7	1.07	5.23	7	1	98	0	1	40.0	68.1	-11.4	51	N/A	2,000	100	0.0	1.0
U /	N/A	N/A	5.40	89	1	98	0	1	40.0	N/A	N/A	N/A	N/A	10,000,000	0	0.0	0.0
C /5.3	11.7	1.24	5.38	N/A	1	98	0	1	40.0	72.9	-11.1	45	N/A	10,000,000	0	0.0	0.0
U /	N/A	N/A	25.96	57	14	85	0	1	410.0	N/A	N/A	N/A	N/A	25,000	0	0.0	0.0
U /	N/A	N/A	42.92	56	100	0	0	0	N/A	N/A	N/A	N/A	N/A	25,000	0	0.0	0.0
E- /0.0	30.5	-3.33	20.75	38	100	0	0	0	N/A	-71.7	13.3	82	N/A	2,500	0	0.0	1.0
E- /0.0	30.6	-3.34	21.52	415	100	0	0	0	N/A	-71.0	13.5	87	N/A	25,000	0	0.0	0.0
E+ /0.9	15.6	-1.99	37.47	47	100	0	0	0	N/A	-63.5	18.8	11	N/A	2,500	0	0.0	1.0
E+ /0.9	15.6	-1.98	39.05	377	100	0	0	0	N/A	-62.6	19.1	14	N/A	25,000	0	0.0	0.0
E- /0.0	30.5	3.37	17.97	47	13	86	0	1	133.0	120.5	-21.4	0	N/A	2,500	0	0.0	1.0
E- /0.0	30.5	3.37	19.32	413	13	86	0	1	133.0	126.3	-21.3	0	N/A	25,000	0	0.0	0.0
C /5.3	15.5	1.99	37.78	49	7	92	0	1	77.0	119.8	-20.7	18	N/A	2,500	0	0.0	1.0

					PERFORMANCE							
99 Pct = Best							Total Return % through 6/30/06				Incl. in Returns	
0 Pct = Worst			Overall Weiss Investment Rating		Perfor-mance Rating/Pts					Annualized		Dividend Expense
Fund Type	Fund Name	Ticker Symbol		Phone		3 Mo	6 Mo	1Yr / Pct	3Yr / Pct	5Yr / Pct	Yield	Ratio
AG	Rydex Dynamics-S&P 500 H	RYTNX	C	(800) 820-0888	C+ / 6.6	-4.88	1.49	9.74 /45	16.70 /67	-3.58 / 4	1.05	1.67
IN	Rydex Series-Ablt Ret St H	RYMSX	U	(800) 820-0888	U /	0.59	3.09	--	--	--	0.00	1.83
FS	Rydex Series-Banking Adv	RYKAX	D+	(800) 820-0888	D+ / 2.8	-0.78	2.20	3.42 / 9	9.61 /25	6.27 /63	1.59	1.84
FS	Rydex Series-Banking C	RYKCX	D	(800) 820-0888	D+ / 2.3	-0.78	2.12	3.14 / 8	8.99 /21	5.68 /59	1.61	2.35
FS	Rydex Series-Banking Inv	RYKIX	C-	(800) 820-0888	C- / 3.4	-0.46	2.76	4.42 /12	10.31 /29	6.97 /67	1.50	1.34
GR	Rydex Series-Basic Materials Adv	RYBAX	C+	(800) 820-0888	B / 8.2	-2.15	9.36	22.29 /85	20.22 /80	8.53 /74	0.57	1.85
GR	Rydex Series-Basic Materials C	RYBCX	B-	(800) 820-0888	B / 8.0	-2.27	9.07	21.73 /84	19.64 /78	7.93 /71	0.58	2.36
GR	Rydex Series-Basic Materials Inv	RYBIX	B	(800) 820-0888	B+ / 8.4	-2.04	9.59	22.89 /86	20.82 /82	9.01 /76	0.55	1.35
HL	Rydex Series-Biotechnology Adv	RYOAX	E-	(800) 820-0888	E / 0.5	-9.89	-6.13	10.86 /53	6.12 / 7	-5.19 / 2	0.00	1.86
HL	Rydex Series-Biotechnology C	RYCFX	E-	(800) 820-0888	E / 0.4	-9.97	-6.35	10.29 /49	5.55 / 5	-5.70 / 2	0.00	2.36
HL	Rydex Series-Biotechnology Inv	RYOIX	E-	(800) 820-0888	E+ / 0.7	-9.77	-5.87	11.37 /56	6.64 / 9	-4.72 / 3	0.00	1.34
OT	Rydex Series-Commodities Fund H	RYMBX	U	(800) 820-0888	U /	6.89	4.59	10.45 /50	--	--	0.00	1.57
GR	Rydex Series-Consumer Products	RYCAX	C	(800) 820-0888	C- / 3.6	2.67	6.33	6.07 /21	9.95 /27	7.65 /70	1.35	1.82
GR	Rydex Series-Consumer Products C	RYCPX	C-	(800) 820-0888	C- / 3.1	2.57	6.05	5.51 /18	9.34 /23	--	1.37	2.33
GR	Rydex Series-Consumer Products Inv	RYCIX	C	(800) 820-0888	C- / 4.1	2.77	6.55	6.58 /24	10.50 /31	8.12 /72	1.30	1.32
IN	Rydex Series-Dyn Strgth Dollar H	RYSBX	U	(800) 820-0888	U /	-8.48	-10.33	-4.40 / 0	--	--	0.51	1.66
IN	Rydex Series-Dyn Weakening Dollar	RYWBX	U	(800) 820-0888	U /	10.36	13.35	7.15 /27	--	--	0.54	1.68
TC	Rydex Series-Electronics Adv	RYSAX	E-	(800) 820-0888	E / 0.5	-11.71	2.05	11.05 /54	4.72 / 3	-9.15 / 0	0.00	1.84
TC	Rydex Series-Electronics C	RYSCX	E-	(800) 820-0888	E / 0.4	-11.74	1.89	10.73 /52	4.24 / 3	-9.60 / 0	0.00	2.36
TC	Rydex Series-Electronics Inv	RYSIX	E-	(800) 820-0888	E+ / 0.7	-11.46	2.40	11.87 /59	5.27 / 5	-8.68 / 0	0.00	1.34
EN	Rydex Series-Energy Adv	RYEAX	B	(800) 820-0888	A+ / 9.7	4.34	12.15	28.14 /93	32.47 /97	14.93 /92	0.12	1.84
EN	Rydex Series-Energy C	RYECX	B	(800) 820-0888	A+ / 9.7	4.22	11.87	27.56 /92	31.76 /97	14.36 /91	0.12	2.35
EN	Rydex Series-Energy Inv	RYEIX	B	(800) 820-0888	A+ / 9.7	4.47	12.41	28.88 /94	33.09 /97	15.48 /92	0.13	1.34
EN	Rydex Series-Energy Services Adv	RYVAX	C+	(800) 820-0888	A+ / 9.8	2.88	17.04	46.30 /98	33.46 /97	13.65 /90	0.00	1.85
EN	Rydex Series-Energy Services C	RYVCX	C+	(800) 820-0888	A+ / 9.8	2.75	16.76	45.59 /98	32.78 /97	13.08 /89	0.00	2.36
EN	Rydex Series-Energy Services Inv	RYVIX	C+	(800) 820-0888	A+ / 9.8	2.97	17.32	47.04 /99	34.07 /98	14.17 /90	0.00	1.35
FO	Rydex Series-Europe Advantage C	RYCEX	B+	(800) 820-0888	B+ / 8.4	1.92	11.54	22.42 /85	20.36 /81	4.79 /52	0.00	2.41
FO	Rydex Series-Europe Advantage H	RYEUX	B+	(800) 820-0888	B+ / 8.7	2.14	12.03	23.45 /87	21.35 /83	5.64 /59	0.00	1.63
FS	Rydex Series-Financial Service Adv	RYFAX	C+	(800) 820-0888	C / 5.3	-2.17	3.62	9.58 /44	13.13 /50	4.56 /51	0.95	1.83
FS	Rydex Series-Financial Service C	RYFCX	C	(800) 820-0888	C / 4.7	-2.29	3.34	8.90 /39	12.56 /46	4.00 /46	0.97	2.34
FS	Rydex Series-Financial Service Inv	RYFIX	C+	(800) 820-0888	C+ / 5.7	-1.96	3.92	10.28 /49	13.83 /53	4.96 /54	0.92	1.34
HL	Rydex Series-Health Care Adv	RYHAX	D-	(800) 820-0888	D- / 1.4	-5.52	-3.94	2.41 / 5	7.98 /15	3.31 /40	0.00	1.84
HL	Rydex Series-Health Care C	RYHCX	D-	(800) 820-0888	D- / 1.0	-5.66	-4.20	1.88 / 4	7.37 /12	2.73 /34	0.00	2.34
HL	Rydex Series-Health Care Inv	RYHIX	D	(800) 820-0888	D / 1.8	-5.43	-3.64	3.00 / 7	8.58 /18	3.82 /44	0.00	1.33
TC	Rydex Series-Internet Adv	RYIAX	E	(800) 820-0888	C- / 3.2	-8.71	-2.63	9.99 /47	10.61 /32	-5.53 / 2	0.00	1.85
TC	Rydex Series-Internet C	RYICX	E-	(800) 820-0888	D+ / 2.7	-8.80	-2.86	9.40 /43	10.03 /28	-5.99 / 2	0.00	2.35
TC	Rydex Series-Internet Inv	RYIIX	E	(800) 820-0888	C- / 3.6	-8.60	-2.39	10.49 /50	11.12 /36	-5.06 / 2	0.00	1.34
MC	Rydex Series-Inverse Mid-Cap H	RYMHX	U	(800) 820-0888	U /	4.45	-1.48	-7.26 / 0	--	--	1.69	1.64
AG	Rydex Series-Inverse OTC C	RYACX	E-	(800) 820-0888	E- / 0.0	9.21	6.32	-2.01 / 1	-9.46 / 0	-3.59 / 4	1.47	2.39
AG	Rydex Series-Inverse OTC Inv	RYAIX	E-	(800) 820-0888	E- / 0.0	9.50	6.85	-1.01 / 1	-8.53 / 0	-2.57 / 6	1.39	1.38
SC	Rydex Series-Inverse Russell 2000 H	RYSHX	U	(800) 820-0888	U /	6.17	-5.65	-9.78 / 0	--	--	1.83	1.65
AG	Rydex Series-Inverse S&P 500 Adv	RYUAX	E-	(800) 820-0888	E- / 0.0	3.11	0.38	-2.82 / 0	-8.36 / 0	-2.67 / 6	1.55	1.88
AG	Rydex Series-Inverse S&P 500 C	RYUCX	E-	(800) 820-0888	E- / 0.0	2.88	0.13	-3.32 / 0	-8.87 / 0	-3.17 / 5	1.56	2.38
AG	Rydex Series-Inverse S&P 500 Inv	RYURX	E-	(800) 820-0888	E- / 0.0	3.23	0.60	-2.36 / 1	-7.91 / 0	-2.18 / 8	1.48	1.38
FO	Rydex Series-Japan Advantage C	RYCJX	C-	(800) 820-0888	B+ / 8.5	-6.46	-0.57	37.15 /97	21.73 /84	--	0.00	2.42
FO	Rydex Series-Japan Advantage H	RYJPX	C-	(800) 820-0888	B+ / 8.8	-6.27	-0.18	38.21 /97	22.72 /87	1.17 /21	0.00	1.66
GR	Rydex Series-Large Cap Value H	RYZAX	U	(800) 820-0888	U /	1.75	6.01	10.94 /53	--	--	0.00	1.49
GR	Rydex Series-Leisure Adv	RYLAX	C-	(800) 820-0888	C / 5.1	-3.82	6.39	4.75 /14	13.35 /51	0.73 /19	0.00	1.80
GR	Rydex Series-Leisure C	RYLCX	C-	(800) 820-0888	C / 4.5	-3.93	6.08	4.23 /12	12.75 /47	0.11 /16	0.00	2.32
GR	Rydex Series-Leisure Inv	RYLIX	C	(800) 820-0888	C / 5.4	-3.69	6.63	5.31 /17	13.89 /53	1.13 /21	0.00	1.34
MC	Rydex Series-Mid Cap Advantage C	RYDCX	C+	(800) 820-0888	B+ / 8.3	-6.16	3.79	13.34 /66	22.32 /86	--	0.00	2.40
MC	Rydex Series-Mid Cap Advantage H	RYMDX	C+	(800) 820-0888	B+ / 8.6	-5.97	4.16	14.20 /69	23.23 /88	--	0.00	1.64

RISK			NET ASSETS		ASSET				BULL / BEAR		FUND MANAGER		MINIMUMS		LOADS	
	3 Year		NAV						Last Bull	Last Bear	Manager	Manager	Initial	Additional	Front	Back
Risk	Standard		As of	Total	Cash	Stocks	Bonds	Other	Market	Market	Quality	Tenure	Purch.	Purch.	End	End
Rating/Pts	Deviation	Beta	6/30/06	$(Mil)	%	%	%	%	Return	Return	Pct	(Years)	$	$	Load	Load
C / 5.5	15.5	1.99	39.56	227	7	92	0	1	77.0	125.0	-20.6	23	N/A	25,000	0	0.0	0.0
U /	N/A	N/A	25.67	52	50	49	0	1	127.0	N/A	N/A	N/A	N/A	25,000	0	0.0	1.0
B- / 7.3	9.7	0.95	10.22	3	0	100	0	0	1,834.4	53.8	-3.0	25	N/A	25,000	0	0.0	0.0
B- / 7.1	9.7	0.95	10.12	2	0	100	0	0	1,834.4	51.0	-3.3	21	N/A	2,500	0	0.0	1.0
B- / 7.4	9.8	0.95	10.81	8	0	100	0	0	1,834.4	56.8	-2.9	29	N/A	25,000	0	0.0	0.0
C / 5.3	16.3	1.73	33.30	6	0	99	0	1	826.0	107.1	-13.0	74	N/A	25,000	0	0.0	0.0
C+ / 6.0	16.3	1.73	32.72	8	0	99	0	1	826.0	104.1	-13.1	70	N/A	2,500	0	0.0	1.0
C+ / 6.0	16.4	1.74	34.51	23	0	99	0	1	826.0	110.0	-12.7	78	N/A	25,000	0	0.0	0.0
D+ / 2.5	14.8	1.04	20.22	12	0	99	0	1	338.0	67.8	-14.1	14	N/A	25,000	0	0.0	0.0
D+ / 2.4	14.8	1.04	20.05	4	0	99	0	1	338.0	65.1	-14.3	11	N/A	2,500	0	0.0	1.0
D+ / 2.5	14.7	1.04	21.16	77	0	99	0	1	338.0	70.7	-14.0	16	N/A	25,000	0	0.0	0.0
U /	N/A	N/A	29.17	36	100	0	0	0	N/A	N/A	N/A	N/A	1	25,000	0	0.0	0.0
B / 8.1	8.0	0.66	30.76	7	0	99	0	1	813.0	50.7	-7.9	74	N/A	25,000	0	0.0	0.0
B / 8.0	8.0	0.66	30.31	2	0	99	0	1	813.0	48.0	-8.1	69	N/A	2,500	0	0.0	1.0
B / 8.2	8.0	0.66	31.89	38	0	99	0	1	813.0	52.9	-7.8	79	N/A	25,000	0	0.0	0.0
U /	N/A	N/A	25.36	42	100	0	0	0	N/A	N/A	N/A	N/A	1	25,000	0	0.0	0.0
U /	N/A	N/A	25.04	127	100	0	0	0	N/A	N/A	N/A	N/A	1	25,000	0	0.0	0.0
E- / 0.0	30.5	2.88	11.46	3	0	99	0	1	911.0	62.7	-22.9	0	N/A	25,000	0	0.0	0.0
E- / 0.0	30.5	2.89	11.35	6	0	99	0	1	911.0	60.2	-23.0	0	N/A	2,500	0	0.0	1.0
E- / 0.0	30.6	2.89	11.97	25	0	99	0	1	911.0	65.4	-22.8	0	N/A	25,000	0	0.0	0.0
C / 4.8	19.7	0.98	21.87	17	0	99	0	1	415.0	160.3	-0.5	59	N/A	25,000	0	0.0	0.0
C / 4.8	19.7	0.98	21.49	23	0	99	0	1	415.0	156.2	-0.6	53	N/A	2,500	0	0.0	1.0
C / 4.9	19.7	0.98	22.65	85	0	99	0	1	415.0	164.1	-0.3	65	N/A	25,000	0	0.0	0.0
C- / 3.5	24.0	1.09	44.71	33	0	99	0	1	324.0	160.1	-0.3	35	N/A	25,000	0	0.0	0.0
C- / 3.4	24.0	1.09	44.10	31	0	99	0	1	324.0	156.0	-0.5	31	N/A	2,500	0	0.0	1.0
C- / 3.5	24.0	1.09	46.39	156	0	99	0	1	324.0	164.0	-0.3	39	N/A	25,000	0	0.0	0.0
C+ / 6.3	13.1	1.16	19.62	7	20	78	0	2	454.0	125.5	-15.3	8	N/A	2,500	0	0.0	1.0
C+ / 6.4	13.1	1.16	20.49	32	20	78	0	2	454.0	131.4	-15.1	11	N/A	25,000	0	0.0	0.0
B- / 7.7	9.7	1.00	12.60	6	0	100	0	0	821.0	74.1	-7.6	50	N/A	25,000	0	0.0	0.0
B- / 7.7	9.7	1.00	12.38	1	0	100	0	0	821.0	71.3	-7.8	43	N/A	2,500	0	0.0	1.0
B- / 7.8	9.7	1.00	13.00	9	0	100	0	0	821.0	76.8	-7.7	58	N/A	25,000	0	0.0	0.0
B- / 7.1	8.6	0.75	13.17	15	0	99	0	1	568.0	53.8	-4.4	45	N/A	25,000	0	0.0	0.0
B- / 7.0	8.6	0.75	13.01	6	0	99	0	1	568.0	51.1	-4.5	39	N/A	2,500	0	0.0	1.0
B- / 7.1	8.6	0.75	13.75	31	0	99	0	1	568.0	56.3	-4.3	52	N/A	25,000	0	0.0	0.0
D+ / 2.3	19.3	1.94	35.55	2	0	99	0	1	1,371.0	91.4	-18.2	4	N/A	25,000	0	0.0	0.0
D / 2.2	19.3	1.93	34.93	1	0	99	0	1	1,371.0	88.2	-18.2	3	N/A	2,500	0	0.0	1.0
D+ / 2.4	19.3	1.94	36.76	4	0	99	0	1	1,371.0	94.3	-18.1	5	N/A	25,000	0	0.0	0.0
U /	N/A	N/A	38.69	51	100	0	0	0	N/A	N/A	N/A	N/A	N/A	25,000	0	0.0	0.0
D / 1.7	15.0	-1.68	22.53	18	100	0	0	0	N/A	-44.0	7.7	75	N/A	2,500	0	0.0	1.0
D / 1.8	15.0	-1.67	23.87	179	100	0	0	0	N/A	-42.2	8.1	83	N/A	25,000	0	0.0	0.0
U /	N/A	N/A	39.26	109	100	0	0	0	N/A	N/A	N/A	N/A	N/A	25,000	0	0.0	0.0
D+ / 2.9	7.9	-1.01	7.95	64	100	0	0	0	N/A	-37.2	9.6	28	N/A	25,000	0	0.0	0.0
D+ / 2.8	7.8	-1.00	7.87	50	100	0	0	0	N/A	-38.2	7.5	24	N/A	2,500	0	0.0	1.0
D+ / 2.9	7.8	-1.00	8.32	503	100	0	0	0	N/A	-36.1	9.6	32	N/A	25,000	0	0.0	0.0
D+ / 2.4	21.0	1.45	36.92	11	100	0	0	0	N/A	112.4	-7.6	1	N/A	2,500	0	0.0	1.0
D+ / 2.3	21.0	1.45	38.09	51	100	0	0	0	N/A	117.6	-7.7	1	N/A	25,000	0	0.0	0.0
U /	N/A	N/A	29.63	122	0	99	0	1	1,054.0	N/A	N/A	N/A	N/A	25,000	0	0.0	0.0
C+ / 6.2	11.7	1.21	29.97	3	0	99	0	1	734.0	87.9	-14.2	58	N/A	25,000	0	0.0	0.0
C+ / 6.1	11.7	1.21	29.83	1	0	99	0	1	734.0	84.8	-14.4	51	N/A	2,500	0	0.0	1.0
C+ / 6.3	11.7	1.21	31.36	5	0	99	0	1	734.0	90.6	-14.2	63	N/A	25,000	0	0.0	0.0
C / 4.6	16.5	1.51	36.42	21	19	80	0	1	528.0	152.3	-14.8	20	N/A	2,500	0	0.0	1.0
C / 4.7	16.5	1.51	37.77	49	19	80	0	1	528.0	158.3	-14.7	25	N/A	25,000	0	0.0	0.0

Data as of June 30, 2006

					PERFORMANCE							
	99 Pct = Best						Total Return % through 6/30/06				Incl. in Returns	
	0 Pct = Worst		Overall Weiss		Perfor-					Annualized	Dividend	Expense
Fund		Ticker	Investment		mance							
Type	Fund Name	Symbol	Rating	Phone	Rating/Pts	3 Mo	6 Mo	1Yr / Pct	3Yr / Pct	5Yr / Pct	Yield	Ratio
MC	Rydex Series-Mid Cap Value H	RYAVX	U	(800) 820-0888	U /	0.28	6.23	11.72 /58	--	--	0.01	1.48
AG	Rydex Series-Nova Adv	RYNAX	C	(800) 820-0888	C / 5.3	-3.64	1.48	8.32 /35	13.82 /53	-0.54 /13	3.18	1.74
AG	Rydex Series-Nova C	RYNCX	C	(800) 820-0888	C / 4.9	-3.76	1.23	7.83 /31	13.28 /50	-1.01 /12	3.22	2.24
AG	Rydex Series-Nova Inv	RYNVX	C+	(800) 820-0888	C+ / 5.7	-3.53	1.72	8.87 /39	14.42 /56	--	3.05	1.23
AG	Rydex Series-OTC Adv	RYAOX	E	(800) 820-0888	D- / 1.3	-7.80	-5.01	4.06 /11	7.88 /14	-4.69 / 3	0.36	1.70
AG	Rydex Series-OTC C	RYCOX	E	(800) 820-0888	D- / 1.0	-7.92	-5.27	3.48 / 9	7.27 /11	-5.20 / 2	0.36	2.21
AG	Rydex Series-OTC Inv	RYOCX	E+	(800) 820-0888	D / 1.7	-7.67	-4.82	4.51 /13	8.43 /17	-4.16 / 3	0.34	1.20
PM	Rydex Series-Precious Metal C	RYZCX	D	(800) 820-0888	A- / 9.1	-2.88	13.84	50.76 /99	18.99 /76	20.23 /96	0.00	2.25
PM	Rydex Series-Precious Metal Inv	RYPMX	D	(800) 820-0888	A / 9.3	-2.64	14.43	52.30 /99	20.20 /80	21.41 /97	0.00	1.24
GR	Rydex Series-Retailing Adv	RYRAX	D-	(800) 820-0888	D+ / 2.5	-4.44	0.81	--	9.94 /27	3.85 /44	0.00	1.82
GR	Rydex Series-Retailing C	RYRCX	E+	(800) 820-0888	D / 2.0	-4.53	0.58	-0.41 / 1	9.37 /23	3.16 /38	0.00	2.34
GR	Rydex Series-Retailing Inv	RYRIX	D-	(800) 820-0888	D+ / 2.8	-4.30	1.02	0.62 / 2	10.39 /30	4.26 /48	0.00	1.33
AG	Rydex Series-Russell 2000 Adv C	RYCMX	C	(800) 820-0888	B+ / 8.7	-8.85	9.02	15.89 /74	23.85 /89	6.89 /66	0.00	2.40
AG	Rydex Series-Russell 2000 Adv H	RYMKX	C	(800) 820-0888	B+ / 8.9	-8.65	9.44	16.79 /77	24.82 /91	7.71 /70	0.00	1.64
AG	Rydex Series-Sector Rotation A	RYAMX	U	(800) 820-0888	U /	-6.08	3.75	15.16 /72	--	--	0.00	1.67
AG	Rydex Series-Sector Rotation C	RYISX	D+	(800) 820-0888	C / 5.1	-6.25	3.45	14.36 /69	13.99 /54	--	0.00	2.41
AG	Rydex Series-Sector Rotation H	RYSRX	C-	(800) 820-0888	C+ / 5.7	-6.06	3.82	15.22 /72	14.86 /58	--	0.00	1.66
TC	Rydex Series-Technology Adv	RYTAX	E-	(800) 820-0888	D- / 1.0	-9.63	-3.66	4.44 /12	6.93 /10	-5.02 / 2	0.29	1.84
TC	Rydex Series-Technology C	RYCHX	E-	(800) 820-0888	E+ / 0.7	-9.74	-3.88	3.89 /10	6.46 / 8	-5.56 / 2	0.30	2.35
TC	Rydex Series-Technology Inv	RYTIX	E-	(800) 820-0888	D- / 1.2	-9.55	-3.46	4.97 /15	7.40 /12	-4.72 / 3	0.28	1.33
TC	Rydex Series-Telecomm Adv	RYMAX	D-	(800) 820-0888	C- / 3.6	-6.96	5.71	11.48 /57	10.99 /35	-4.65 / 3	2.54	1.82
TC	Rydex Series-Telecomm C	RYCSX	E+	(800) 820-0888	C- / 3.1	-7.10	5.37	10.87 /53	10.42 /30	-5.25 / 2	2.58	2.31
TC	Rydex Series-Telecomm Inv	RYMIX	D-	(800) 820-0888	C- / 3.9	-6.88	5.90	11.98 /59	11.49 /39	-4.33 / 3	2.45	1.38
GR	Rydex Series-Transportation Adv	RYPAX	B+	(800) 820-0888	A- / 9.2	5.72	15.24	40.77 /98	20.38 /81	8.15 /72	0.00	1.86
GR	Rydex Series-Transportation C	RYCNX	B+	(800) 820-0888	A- / 9.1	5.56	14.97	40.10 /98	19.71 /78	7.60 /70	0.00	2.38
GR	Rydex Series-Transportation Inv	RYPIX	B+	(800) 820-0888	A / 9.3	5.83	15.55	41.47 /98	20.90 /82	8.56 /74	0.00	1.37
UT	Rydex Series-Utilities Adv	RYAUX	C	(800) 820-0888	C / 4.5	4.15	4.33	2.16 / 5	12.05 /43	-2.45 / 7	1.74	1.83
UT	Rydex Series-Utilities C	RYCUX	C-	(800) 820-0888	C- / 3.9	4.06	4.06	1.64 / 3	11.50 /39	-2.99 / 5	1.79	2.34
UT	Rydex Series-Utilities Inv	RYUIX	C+	(800) 820-0888	C / 4.9	4.34	4.63	2.69 / 6	12.63 /47	-1.87 / 9	1.68	1.33
AG	Rydex Ser-Multi-Cap Core Eq C	RYQCX	C+	(800) 820-0888	C / 5.4	-3.69	3.23	9.54 /44	13.94 /54	--	0.00	2.40
AG	Rydex Ser-Multi-Cap Core Eq H	RYQMX	B	(800) 820-0888	C+ / 6.0	-3.47	3.66	10.39 /49	14.83 /58	--	0.00	1.64
BA	Salomon Brothers Balanced A	STRAX	D+	(800) 725-6666	E+ / 0.7	-0.74	2.78	6.59 /24	6.44 / 8	4.86 /53	2.43	1.26
BA	Salomon Brothers Balanced B	STRBX	D+	(800) 725-6666	E / 0.5	-0.90	2.35	5.71 /19	5.56 / 5	4.04 /46	1.80	2.11
BA	Salomon Brothers Balanced C	STRCX	C-	(800) 725-6666	E+ / 0.9	-0.87	2.39	5.91 /20	5.65 / 6	4.07 /47	1.84	1.98
BA	Salomon Brothers Balanced O	STROX	C-	(800) 725-6666	D- / 1.5	-0.67	2.74	6.74 /25	6.62 / 9	5.08 /55	2.81	0.97
GR	Salomon Brothers Capital A	SCCAX	D	(800) 725-6666	D+ / 2.9	-6.35	-2.70	3.39 / 8	12.83 /48	4.58 /51	0.00	1.11
GR	Salomon Brothers Capital B	SPABX	D-	(800) 725-6666	D+ / 2.6	-6.56	-3.13	2.48 / 6	11.86 /42	3.71 /43	0.00	1.97
GR	Salomon Brothers Capital C	SCCCX	D	(800) 725-6666	C- / 3.3	-6.55	-3.12	2.55 / 6	11.89 /42	3.73 /43	0.00	1.94
GR	Salomon Brothers Capital O	SACPX	D+	(800) 725-6666	C / 4.4	-6.28	-2.53	3.83 /10	13.26 /50	5.02 /54	0.00	0.67
GR	Salomon Brothers Capital Y	SACYX	C	(800) 725-6666	C / 5.5	-6.30	-2.56	3.34 / 8	15.47 /61	6.25 /63	0.00	1.06
GR	Salomon Brothers Investors Value A	SINAX	C	(800) 725-6666	C- / 4.0	-0.16	4.74	11.61 /57	12.22 /44	4.03 /46	0.94	0.93
GR	Salomon Brothers Investors Value B	SBINX	C-	(800) 725-6666	C- / 3.6	-0.48	4.15	10.56 /51	11.18 /37	3.02 /37	0.13	1.89
GR	Salomon Brothers Investors Value C	SINOX	C	(800) 725-6666	C / 4.3	-0.40	4.27	10.49 /50	11.25 /37	3.10 /38	0.19	1.81
GR	Salomon Brothers Investors Value O	SAIFX	C+	(800) 725-6666	C / 5.3	-0.13	4.87	11.50 /57	12.57 /46	4.30 /49	1.31	0.58
GR	Salomon Brothers Investors Value Y	SIVYX	C+	(800) 725-6666	C / 5.3	-0.13	4.89	11.92 /59	12.61 /46	--	1.34	0.54
MC	Salomon Brothers Mid Cap A	SMDAX	C	(800) 725-6666	C- / 4.2	-5.08	2.02	9.22 /41	13.63 /52	--	0.06	1.50
MC	Salomon Brothers Mid Cap B	SMDBX	C-	(800) 725-6666	C- / 3.9	-5.24	1.67	8.40 /36	12.79 /47	--	0.00	2.25
MC	Salomon Brothers Mid Cap C	SMDZX	C	(800) 725-6666	C / 4.6	-5.22	1.66	8.42 /36	12.80 /48	--	0.00	2.25
MC	Salomon Brothers Mid Cap O	SMDOX	C-	(800) 725-6666	C / 5.5	-4.97	2.25	9.64 /44	14.13 /55	5.50 /58	0.46	1.08
GR	Salomon Brothers Opportunity	SAOPX	A-	(800) 725-6666	B- / 7.0	-0.72	7.88	15.67 /74	15.99 /63	5.92 /61	0.81	0.97
SC	Salomon Brothers Small Cap Gr A	SASMX	C	(800) 725-6666	C / 5.4	-10.27	2.72	8.03 /33	16.52 /66	3.70 /43	0.00	1.15
SC	Salomon Brothers Small Cap Gr B	SBSMX	C-	(800) 725-6666	C / 5.0	-10.45	2.23	6.94 /26	15.43 /61	2.74 /34	0.00	2.17

● Denotes fund is closed to new investors
★ Denotes fund is included in Section II

www.WeissRatings.com

RISK			NET ASSETS		ASSET				Portfolio Turnover Ratio	BULL / BEAR		FUND MANAGER		MINIMUMS		LOADS	
Risk Rating/Pts	3 Year		NAV As of 6/30/06	Total $(Mil)	Cash %	Stocks %	Bonds %	Other %		Last Bull Market Return	Last Bear Market Return	Manager Quality Pct	Manager Tenure (Years)	Initial Purch. $	Additional Purch. $	Front End Load	Back End Load
	Standard Deviation	Beta															
U /	N/A	N/A	31.91	31	0	99	0	1	558.0	N/A	N/A	N/A	N/A	25,000	0	0.0	0.0
C+ / 6.9	11.8	1.53	26.72	26	11	88	0	1	192.0	91.9	-15.5	33	N/A	25,000	0	0.0	0.0
B- / 7.0	11.9	1.53	26.36	41	11	88	0	1	192.0	89.1	-15.6	29	N/A	2,500	0	0.0	1.0
B- / 7.0	11.9	1.53	27.87	98	11	88	0	1	192.0	95.2	-15.4	37	N/A	25,000	0	0.0	0.0
C / 5.1	14.9	1.68	10.05	11	1	98	0	1	122.0	60.5	-10.2	3	N/A	25,000	0	0.0	0.0
C / 5.0	14.9	1.68	9.88	11	1	98	0	1	122.0	57.7	-10.3	2	N/A	2,500	0	0.0	1.0
C / 5.2	14.9	1.67	10.47	641	1	98	0	1	122.0	63.3	-10.2	4	9	25,000	0	0.0	0.0
E- / 0.0	35.6	1.60	50.52	23	0	99	0	1	277.0	102.7	11.5	1	N/A	2,500	0	0.0	1.0
E- / 0.0	35.6	1.60	53.06	169	0	99	0	1	277.0	109.2	11.8	1	N/A	25,000	0	0.0	0.0
C / 5.2	15.2	1.33	12.49	2	0	99	0	1	1,163.0	72.1	-15.4	20	N/A	25,000	0	0.0	0.0
C / 5.2	15.2	1.32	12.22	1	0	99	0	1	1,163.0	69.3	-17.5	17	N/A	2,500	0	0.0	1.0
C / 5.3	15.1	1.32	12.90	5	0	99	0	1	1,163.0	74.1	-15.4	23	N/A	25,000	0	0.0	0.0
D+ / 2.8	22.4	2.44	32.75	20	27	72	0	1	441.0	185.9	-18.1	40	N/A	2,500	0	0.0	1.0
D+ / 2.9	22.4	2.44	34.09	74	27	72	0	1	441.0	192.7	-18.0	50	N/A	25,000	0	0.0	0.0
U /	N/A	N/A	13.29	45	1	98	0	1	263.0	N/A	N/A	N/A	N/A	2,500	0	4.8	1.0
C / 4.9	13.5	1.44	12.90	130	1	98	0	1	263.0	89.2	-10.6	41	N/A	2,500	0	0.0	1.0
C / 4.9	13.5	1.44	13.32	231	1	98	0	1	263.0	93.8	-10.4	51	N/A	25,000	0	0.0	0.0
D / 1.8	17.9	1.85	10.79	4	0	99	0	1	666.0	69.7	-16.6	1	N/A	25,000	0	0.0	0.0
D / 1.8	18.0	1.86	10.66	1	0	99	0	1	666.0	67.1	-16.7	1	N/A	2,500	0	0.0	1.0
D / 1.8	17.9	1.86	11.17	14	0	99	0	1	666.0	71.8	-16.4	1	N/A	25,000	0	0.0	0.0
C- / 4.2	14.5	1.52	15.91	3	0	99	0	1	820.0	74.1	-16.7	16	N/A	25,000	0	0.0	0.0
C- / 4.1	14.5	1.52	15.70	2	0	99	0	1	820.0	71.6	-16.6	13	N/A	2,500	0	0.0	1.0
C / 4.3	14.5	1.52	16.52	10	0	99	0	1	820.0	76.8	-16.6	19	N/A	25,000	0	0.0	0.0
C+ / 5.8	14.3	1.23	28.28	13	0	99	0	1	669.0	92.4	-14.0	96	N/A	25,000	0	0.0	0.0
C+ / 5.7	14.4	1.23	28.65	6	0	99	0	1	669.0	88.7	-14.9	95	N/A	2,500	0	0.0	1.0
C+ / 5.8	14.3	1.23	29.95	36	0	99	0	1	669.0	94.9	-14.1	97	N/A	25,000	0	0.0	0.0
B- / 7.5	8.7	0.70	25.08	6	0	100	0	0	728.0	73.3	-5.0	22	N/A	25,000	0	0.0	0.0
B- / 7.4	8.7	0.70	24.37	4	0	100	0	0	728.0	70.8	-5.3	19	N/A	2,500	0	0.0	1.0
B- / 7.6	8.7	0.70	25.98	22	0	100	0	0	728.0	76.2	-5.0	26	N/A	25,000	0	0.0	0.0
B / 8.1	10.0	1.19	15.64	31	5	94	0	1	168.0	80.5	-9.4	66	4	2,500	0	0.0	1.0
B / 8.1	10.0	1.19	16.14	45	5	94	0	1	168.0	85.0	-9.2	73	N/A	25,000	0	0.0	0.0
B+ / 9.0	4.6	0.91	13.16	53	10	45	44	1	199.0	35.5	-2.6	48	11	250	50	5.8	1.0
B+ / 9.5	4.5	0.90	13.04	15	10	45	44	1	199.0	32.0	-2.9	39	11	250	50	0.0	5.0
B+ / 9.5	4.5	0.90	13.10	22	10	45	44	1	199.0	32.2	-2.8	40	11	250	50	0.0	1.0
B+ / 9.5	4.5	0.89	13.26	2	10	45	44	1	199.0	36.3	-2.5	52	11	250	50	0.0	0.0
C+ / 5.8	10.2	1.20	27.79	339	4	94	0	2	265.0	85.1	-7.9	53	N/A	250	50	5.8	1.0
C / 5.4	10.2	1.20	25.94	343	4	94	0	2	265.0	80.1	-8.1	42	N/A	250	50	0.0	5.0
C / 5.5	10.2	1.20	26.02	460	4	94	0	2	265.0	80.3	-8.1	42	N/A	250	50	0.0	1.0
C+ / 5.9	10.2	1.20	28.56	384	4	94	0	2	265.0	87.4	-7.7	58	N/A	250	50	0.0	0.0
C+ / 6.0	11.3	1.21	30.57	5	4	94	0	2	265.0	98.6	-7.7	77	N/A	2,500,000	1,000	0.0	0.0
B- / 7.7	8.1	1.00	21.20	264	3	96	0	1	53.0	73.1	-11.9	67	N/A	250	50	5.8	1.0
B- / 7.7	8.1	1.00	20.71	32	3	96	0	1	53.0	68.1	-12.1	56	N/A	250	50	0.0	5.0
B- / 7.7	8.1	1.00	20.80	49	3	96	0	1	53.0	68.4	-12.1	57	N/A	250	50	0.0	1.0
B- / 7.7	8.1	1.00	21.16	543	3	96	0	1	53.0	74.8	-11.8	70	N/A	250	50	0.0	0.0
B / 8.2	8.1	1.00	21.17	890	3	96	0	1	53.0	74.9	-11.8	70	N/A	2,500,000	1,000	0.0	0.0
B- / 7.5	11.0	0.98	20.17	3	5	94	0	1	34.0	80.6	-9.4	22	N/A	250	50	5.8	1.0
B- / 7.5	11.0	0.98	19.52	1	5	94	0	1	34.0	76.5	-9.6	17	N/A	250	50	0.0	5.0
B- / 7.5	11.0	0.98	19.60	N/A	5	94	0	1	34.0	76.3	-9.5	17	N/A	250	50	0.0	1.0
C / 5.4	11.0	0.98	20.47	20	5	94	0	1	34.0	83.2	-9.4	25	N/A	250	50	0.0	0.0
B / 8.5	8.4	0.94	55.14	143	0	99	0	1	N/A	78.0	-9.1	93	N/A	1,000	100	0.0	0.0
C+ / 6.3	15.4	1.00	15.38	412	8	92	0	0	117.0	119.6	-12.8	35	N/A	250	50	5.8	1.0
C+ / 6.3	15.4	0.99	14.14	25	8	92	0	0	117.0	113.1	-13.0	28	N/A	250	50	0.0	5.0

99 Pct = Best
0 Pct = Worst

Fund Type	Fund Name	Ticker Symbol	Overall Weiss Investment Rating	Phone	Perfor-mance Rating/Pts	3 Mo	6 Mo	1Yr / Pct	3Yr / Pct	5Yr / Pct	Dividend Yield	Expense Ratio
SC	Salomon Brothers Small Cap Gr O	SOSMX	C-	(800) 725-6666	C+ / 6.4	-10.18	2.87	8.36 /36	16.78 /67	3.93 /45	0.00	0.88
SC	Salomon Brothers Small Cap Gr Y	SBPYX	U	(800) 725-6666	U /	-10.16	2.98	8.49 /37	--	--	0.00	0.81
★ EM	Sanford Bernstein Emerg Markets Val	SNEMX	C+		A+ / 9.9	-6.11	6.36	32.19 /96	40.32 /99	27.00 /99	1.29	1.68
★ FO	Sanford Bernstein Internatl Val II	SIMTX	A+		B+ / 8.7	-1.35	9.16	27.63 /92	21.24 /83	11.26 /85	1.17	1.26
★ GL	Sanford Bernstein T/M Intl Val	SNIVX	B		B+ / 8.6	-1.61	9.10	27.28 /92	20.92 /82	11.12 /84	1.13	1.16
GR	Santa Barbara Fds-Bender Growth A	BEGAX	E-	(800) 723-8637	D / 1.6	-9.35	-2.47	6.17 /21	9.78 /26	-1.14 /11	0.00	1.85
GR	Santa Barbara Fds-Bender Growth C	BEGCX	E-	(800) 723-8637	D- / 1.5	-9.64	-3.09	4.80 /14	8.48 /18	-2.35 / 7	0.00	3.11
GR	Santa Barbara Fds-Bender Growth Y	BEGYX	E	(800) 723-8637	D+ / 2.3	-9.46	-2.61	5.87 /20	9.59 /25	-1.32 /11	0.00	2.07
GR	Santa Barbara Fds-Montecito A	MONAX	D	(800) 723-8637	D- / 1.3	0.28	4.54	7.80 /31	7.18 /11	--	1.36	1.19
EN	Saratoga Adv Tr-Energy&Basic Mat I	SEPIX	C	(800) 807-3863	A+ / 9.7	0.81	11.51	39.86 /98	32.80 /97	--	0.00	2.93
FS	Saratoga Adv Tr-Financial Service I	SFPIX	C+	(800) 807-3863	C / 5.4	-2.84	5.08	15.09 /72	13.80 /53	--	0.00	2.93
HL	Saratoga Adv Tr-Health & Biotech A	SHPAX	E+	(800) 807-3863	E- / 0.0	-10.56	-11.30	-6.33 / 0	2.33 / 1	-7.01 / 1	0.00	2.84
HL	Saratoga Adv Tr-Health & Biotech B	SHPBX	E-	(800) 807-3863	E- / 0.0	-10.65	-11.55	-6.80 / 0	1.73 / 1	-7.55 / 1	0.00	3.30
HL	Saratoga Adv Tr-Health & Biotech C	SHPCX	E+	(800) 807-3863	E- / 0.0	-10.72	-11.61	-6.87 / 0	1.71 / 0	-7.56 / 1	0.00	3.44
HL	Saratoga Adv Tr-Health & Biotech I	SBHIX	D-	(800) 807-3863	E- / 0.0	-10.54	-11.15	-5.94 / 0	2.76 / 1	--	0.00	2.45
MC	Saratoga Adv Tr-Mid Cap I	SMIPX	C+	(800) 807-3863	C / 5.5	-3.93	2.65	7.49 /29	14.72 /57	--	0.00	1.89
TC	Saratoga Adv Tr-Technology &	STPIX	E-	(800) 807-3863	D- / 1.0	-8.71	-3.89	8.82 /39	8.44 /17	--	0.00	2.75
SC	Satuit Capital Micro Cap Fd A	SATMX	B	(800) 527-9500	B / 8.2	-7.32	7.22	28.67 /93	22.88 /87	16.01 /93	0.00	1.95
FO	Schroder International Alpha Inv	SCIEX	A-	(800) 464-3108	B+ / 8.8	-1.22	8.21	29.04 /94	23.10 /88	7.69 /70	1.70	1.25
GL	Schroder North American Equity Inv	SNAEX	U	(800) 464-3108	U /	-1.52	2.73	9.38 /43	--	--	0.87	0.35
SC	Schroder US Opportunities Inv	SCUIX	B	(800) 464-3108	B+ / 8.3	-3.12	9.90	16.78 /77	21.53 /84	11.10 /84	0.00	1.13
★ GI	Schwab 1000 Inv	SNXFX	C	(866) 855-9102	C- / 4.1	-1.56	2.84	9.00 /40	11.66 /40	2.95 /36	1.23	0.51
GI	Schwab 1000 Sel	SNXSX	C	(866) 855-9102	C / 4.3	-1.53	2.90	9.16 /41	11.82 /41	3.08 /38	1.38	0.36
GR	Schwab Core Equity Fd	SWANX	C+	(866) 855-9102	C / 5.4	-1.29	2.62	10.29 /49	13.89 /53	3.87 /45	0.54	0.75
IN	Schwab Dividend Eqty Fund Inv	SWDIX	U	(866) 855-9102	U /	0.44	5.31	8.92 /40	--	--	1.78	1.07
IN	Schwab Dividend Eqty Fund Sel	SWDSX	U	(866) 855-9102	U /	0.48	5.33	9.04 /40	--	--	2.02	0.95
FS	Schwab Financial Services Focus	SWFFX	B-	(866) 855-9102	B- / 7.2	-0.94	4.22	15.34 /73	17.76 /71	8.50 /74	0.69	1.10
HL	Schwab Health Care Focus	SWHFX	B+	(866) 855-9102	B / 7.6	-6.15	-4.44	4.64 /13	21.79 /85	9.35 /78	0.00	0.89
IN	Schwab Hedged Equity Inv	SWHIX	U	(866) 855-9102	U /	2.44	3.91	10.91 /53	--	--	0.28	1.77
IN	Schwab Hedged Equity Sel	SWHEX	C+	(866) 855-9102	C+ / 6.3	2.57	3.98	11.18 /55	15.36 /61	--	0.32	2.21
GR	Schwab Instl Select S&P 500 Sel	ISLCX	C+	(866) 855-9102	C- / 3.7	-1.47	2.76	8.57 /37	11.14 /37	2.41 /31	1.33	0.10
FO	Schwab International Index Inv	SWINX	A	(866) 855-9102	B+ / 8.7	1.24	10.01	25.65 /89	22.28 /86	8.91 /76	1.78	0.69
FO	Schwab International Index Sel	SWISX	A+	(866) 855-9102	B+ / 8.8	1.24	10.07	25.87 /90	22.52 /86	9.07 /77	1.95	0.50
GR	Schwab Large-Cap Growth Inv	SWLNX	U	(866) 855-9102	U /	-4.91	-0.98	--	--	--	0.00	1.20
GR	Schwab Large-Cap Growth Sel	SWLSX	U	(866) 855-9102	U /	-4.81	-0.88	--	--	--	0.00	0.99
GR	Schwab MarketTrack All Equity Port	SWEGX	B	(866) 855-9102	C+ / 6.5	-1.40	5.86	14.30 /69	15.59 /62	5.11 /55	1.05	0.80
BA	Schwab MarketTrack Balanced Port	SWBGX	C+	(866) 855-9102	D+ / 2.9	-0.99	3.02	7.76 /31	9.69 /25	4.82 /53	2.11	0.86
AA	Schwab MarketTrack Consv Port	SWCGX	C-	(866) 855-9102	D- / 1.4	-0.59	1.82	4.89 /15	7.04 /10	4.72 /52	2.87	0.91
AA	Schwab MarketTrack Growth Port	SWHGX	C+	(866) 855-9102	C / 4.7	-1.21	4.31	10.71 /52	12.37 /45	4.81 /53	1.57	0.80
IN	● Schwab Premier Equity Fund Inv	SWPNX	U	(866) 855-9102	U /	-2.41	3.17	13.51 /66	--	--	0.34	1.23
IN	● Schwab Premier Equity Fund Sel	SWPSX	U	(866) 855-9102	U /	-2.41	3.26	13.68 /67	--	--	0.39	1.08
GI	Schwab Retirement Income Fund	SWARX	U	(866) 855-9102	U /	0.29	1.58	--	--	--	0.00	0.70
IX	Schwab S&P 500 E	SWPEX	C	(866) 855-9102	C- / 3.7	-1.45	2.66	8.53 /37	11.00 /36	2.29 /30	1.69	0.22
★ IX	Schwab S&P 500 Inv	SWPIX	C-	(866) 855-9102	C- / 3.6	-1.50	2.60	8.37 /36	10.90 /35	2.19 /29	1.53	0.37
IX	Schwab S&P 500 Sel	SWPPX	C	(866) 855-9102	C- / 3.7	-1.45	2.70	8.55 /37	11.09 /36	2.36 /31	1.72	0.19
SC	Schwab Small-Cap Equity Inv	SWSIX	A	(866) 855-9102	A- / 9.0	-2.92	6.60	16.68 /76	25.36 /91	--	0.01	1.30
SC	Schwab Small-Cap Equity Sel	SWSCX	A+	(866) 855-9102	A- / 9.0	-2.91	6.63	16.87 /77	25.52 /92	--	0.10	1.12
SC	Schwab Small-Cap Index Inv	SWSMX	C+	(866) 855-9102	C+ / 6.9	-4.41	6.98	12.73 /63	17.24 /69	6.69 /65	0.56	0.60
SC	Schwab Small-Cap Index Sel	SWSSX	B-	(866) 855-9102	B- / 7.0	-4.36	7.06	12.90 /64	17.46 /70	6.85 /66	0.72	0.42
GR	Schwab Target 2010 Fund	SWBRX	U	(866) 855-9102	U /	-1.19	3.06	--	--	--	0.00	0.06
GR	Schwab Target 2020 Fund	SWCRX	U	(866) 855-9102	U /	-1.27	3.42	--	--	--	0.00	0.04
GR	Schwab Target 2030 Fund	SWDRX	U	(866) 855-9102	U /	-1.26	3.88	--	--	--	0.00	0.03

● Denotes fund is closed to new investors
★ Denotes fund is included in Section II

RISK			NET ASSETS		ASSET				BULL / BEAR		FUND MANAGER		MINIMUMS		LOADS	
	3 Year		NAV						Portfolio	Last Bull	Last Bear	Manager	Manager	Initial	Additional	Front	Back
Risk	Standard		As of	Total	Cash	Stocks	Bonds	Other	Turnover	Market	Market	Quality	Tenure	Purch.	Purch.	End	End
Rating/Pts	Deviation	Beta	6/30/06	$(Mil)	%	%	%	%	Ratio	Return	Return	Pct	(Years)	$	$	Load	Load
C / 4.6	15.4	1.00	15.71	3	8	92	0	0	117.0	120.9	-12.7	37	N/A	250	50	0.0	0.0
U /	N/A	N/A	15.48	78	8	92	0	0	117.0	N/A	N/A	N/A	N/A	2,500,000	1,000	0.0	0.0
D+ / 2.9	19.7	1.14	37.31	2,040	2	97	0	1	54.0	281.1	-0.1	45	N/A	25,000	5,000	0.0	0.0
B / 8.0	10.0	0.96	26.23	3,255	1	98	0	1	61.0	125.4	-4.9	35	N/A	25,000	5,000	0.0	0.0
C+ / 6.0	10.0	0.97	26.25	7,193	2	97	0	1	32.0	123.5	-4.9	32	N/A	25,000	5,000	0.0	0.0
D / 2.2	17.4	1.81	25.31	3	0	99	0	1	27.0	84.1	-16.1	4	8	2,500	1,000	5.8	0.0
D+ / 2.8	17.5	1.81	24.46	12	0	99	0	1	27.0	77.2	-16.3	2	8	2,500	1,000	0.0	1.0
D+ / 2.9	17.5	1.81	26.89	7	0	99	0	1	27.0	83.1	-16.1	4	8	2,500	1,000	0.0	0.0
B- / 7.3	11.7	1.00	10.71	8	4	71	24	1	68.1	41.9	-10.5	21	3	2,500	1,000	5.8	0.0
D+ / 2.5	19.4	0.90	32.35	4	3	96	0	1	22.0	169.2	N/A	83	N/A	10,000	100	0.0	2.0
B- / 7.8	11.1	1.06	13.66	1	0	99	0	1	79.0	84.0	N/A	47	N/A	10,000	100	0.0	2.0
C+ / 6.8	8.2	0.46	12.87	13	0	99	0	1	5.0	28.0	-10.0	20	N/A	2,500	250	5.8	2.0
C+ / 6.7	8.2	0.46	12.33	20	0	99	0	1	5.0	25.6	-10.2	17	N/A	2,500	250	0.0	2.0
C+ / 6.7	8.2	0.46	12.33	5	0	99	0	1	5.0	25.6	-10.2	17	N/A	2,500	250	0.0	2.0
B / 8.2	8.2	0.46	12.99	2	0	99	0	1	5.0	29.1	N/A	23	N/A	10,000	100	0.0	2.0
B- / 7.3	11.7	1.03	11.24	11	2	97	0	1	40.0	92.9	N/A	24	N/A	10,000	100	0.0	2.0
D- / 1.0	21.6	2.15	7.65	2	0	99	0	1	50.0	66.3	N/A	1	N/A	10,000	100	0.0	2.0
C+ / 6.3	14.8	0.95	24.80	62	1	98	0	1	183.6	153.9	-6.7	91	6	1,000	250	5.8	2.0
C+ / 6.6	10.8	1.02	9.75	21	1	98	0	1	126.0	128.5	-15.0	38	1	250,000	1,000	0.0	2.0
U /	N/A	N/A	11.66	1,350	5	94	0	1	30.0	N/A	N/A	N/A	N/A	250,000	1,000	0.0	0.0
C+ / 5.9	11.6	0.77	21.75	192	9	90	0	1	107.0	122.9	-10.2	95	N/A	250,000	1,000	0.0	2.0
B- / 7.8	7.7	1.01	37.26	4,080	1	98	0	1	6.0	66.8	-9.6	60	N/A	2,500	1	0.0	2.0
B- / 7.8	7.8	1.01	37.27	2,427	1	98	0	1	6.0	67.6	-9.6	62	N/A	50,000	1	0.0	2.0
B- / 7.8	8.3	1.03	16.86	856	1	98	0	1	48.0	75.9	-9.2	78	N/A	2,500	1	0.0	2.0
U /	N/A	N/A	13.48	543	0	99	0	1	26.0	N/A	N/A	N/A	3	2,500	1	0.0	2.0
U /	N/A	N/A	13.46	537	0	99	0	1	26.0	N/A	N/A	N/A	3	50,000	1	0.0	2.0
C+ / 6.5	9.9	1.00	14.83	75	0	99	0	1	74.0	102.7	-8.2	88	N/A	2,500	1	0.0	2.0
B- / 7.4	10.3	0.81	14.20	561	N/A	100	0	N/A	42.0	115.4	-7.0	99	N/A	2,500	1	0.0	2.0
U /	N/A	N/A	15.14	104	0	99	0	1	87.0	N/A	N/A	N/A	1	2,500	500	0.0	2.0
C+ / 6.5	6.5	0.65	15.16	563	0	99	0	1	87.0	65.5	-3.4	97	N/A	50,000	1,000	0.0	2.0
B+ / 9.0	7.6	0.99	10.07	1,628	2	97	0	1	3.0	64.3	-9.8	N/A	N/A	75,000	1	0.0	2.0
B- / 7.2	9.7	0.95	19.57	667	0	99	0	1	10.0	120.6	-9.0	45	N/A	2,500	1	0.0	2.0
B- / 7.7	9.8	0.95	19.57	890	0	99	0	1	10.0	121.9	-9.0	47	N/A	50,000	1	0.0	2.0
U /	N/A	N/A	10.08	53	0	0	0	100	N/A	N/A	N/A	N/A	N/A	2,500	1	0.0	2.0
U /	N/A	N/A	10.09	41	0	0	0	100	N/A	N/A	N/A	N/A	N/A	50,000	1	0.0	2.0
B / 8.0	9.1	1.13	12.64	497	0	99	0	1	49.0	90.0	-10.4	83	N/A	1,000	1	0.0	2.0
B+ / 9.6	5.4	1.11	16.03	514	4	60	34	2	25.0	50.7	-5.1	72	14	1,000	100	0.0	2.0
B+ / 9.9	3.9	0.80	13.67	225	3	41	55	1	9.0	34.9	-2.2	62	N/A	1,000	1	0.0	2.0
B- / 7.8	7.1	1.41	17.90	575	0	83	16	1	33.0	67.9	-7.7	80	N/A	1,000	1	0.0	2.0
U /	N/A	N/A	11.72	674	0	99	0	1	2.0	N/A	N/A	N/A	N/A	2,500	1	0.0	2.0
U /	N/A	N/A	11.73	858	0	99	0	1	2.0	N/A	N/A	N/A	N/A	50,000	1	0.0	2.0
U /	N/A	N/A	9.91	32	8	20	71	1	N/A	N/A	N/A	N/A	N/A	2,500	1	0.0	0.0
B- / 7.9	7.6	1.00	19.71	218	0	99	0	1	4.0	63.7	-9.7	54	N/A	1,000	1	0.0	2.0
B- / 7.8	7.6	1.00	19.70	3,623	0	99	0	1	4.0	63.2	-9.8	53	N/A	2,500	1	0.0	2.0
B- / 7.9	7.6	1.00	19.77	3,849	0	99	0	1	4.0	64.2	-9.8	55	N/A	50,000	1	0.0	2.0
B- / 7.0	13.2	0.86	16.97	356	1	98	0	1	90.0	N/A	N/A	98	N/A	2,500	1	0.0	2.0
B- / 7.0	13.2	0.87	17.04	165	1	98	0	1	90.0	N/A	N/A	98	N/A	50,000	1	0.0	2.0
C+ / 6.2	14.1	0.96	24.51	835	0	99	0	1	40.0	113.2	-12.5	47	N/A	2,500	1	0.0	2.0
C+ / 6.7	14.1	0.96	24.55	821	0	99	0	1	40.0	114.2	-12.5	50	N/A	50,000	1	0.0	2.0
U /	N/A	N/A	10.77	48	4	62	33	1	N/A	N/A	N/A	N/A	N/A	2,500	1	0.0	2.0
U /	N/A	N/A	10.88	63	1	70	27	2	N/A	N/A	N/A	N/A	N/A	2,500	1	0.0	2.0
U /	N/A	N/A	10.98	40	1	77	20	2	N/A	N/A	N/A	N/A	N/A	2,500	1	0.0	2.0

			99 Pct = Best 0 Pct = Worst		PERFORMANCE						Incl. in Returns	
			Overall Weiss Investment Rating		Perfor- mance Rating/Pts	Total Return % through 6/30/06			Annualized		Dividend Yield	Expense Ratio
Fund Type	Fund Name	Ticker Symbol		Phone		3 Mo	6 Mo	1Yr / Pct	3Yr / Pct	5Yr / Pct		
TC	Schwab Technology Focus	SWTFX	E	(866) 855-9102	C- / 4.1	-7.32	-3.89	7.86 /32	12.93 /48	-1.36 /11	0.00	1.10
GR	Schwab Total Stock Market Inv	SWTIX	C+	(866) 855-9102	C / 4.7	-1.87	3.23	9.39 /43	12.64 /47	3.81 /44	1.12	0.58
GR	Schwab Total Stock Market Sel	SWTSX	C+	(866) 855-9102	C / 4.8	-1.82	3.27	9.59 /44	12.84 /48	3.97 /46	1.28	0.39
BA	Schwab Viewpoints Fund Inv	SWOBX	C-	(866) 855-9102	D / 2.2	-2.97	0.55	4.05 /11	9.23 /22	4.78 /52	1.23	1.10
GR	Schwartz Ave Maria Catholic Values	AVEMX	B+	(888) 726-0753	B- / 7.0	-3.93	5.44	10.12 /48	17.43 /70	10.71 /83	0.00	1.50
GR	Schwartz Ave Maria Growth Fund	AVEGX	B+	(888) 726-0753	B- / 7.1	1.29	10.07	16.83 /77	15.80 /63	--	0.00	1.50
GR	Schwartz Value Fund	RCMFX	C	(888) 726-0753	B- / 7.1	-2.96	5.50	8.27 /35	18.12 /73	10.73 /83	0.00	1.36
GR	Security Equity Fund A	SECEX	D-	(800) 888-2461	E+ / 0.9	-2.06	1.52	8.01 /33	7.79 /14	-0.25 /15	0.54	1.36
GR	Security Equity Fund B	SEQBX	D-	(800) 888-2461	D- / 1.2	-2.16	1.20	7.26 /28	6.99 /10	-1.06 /12	0.00	2.11
GR	Security Equity Fund C	SFECX	D-	(800) 888-2461	D- / 1.2	-2.20	1.14	7.21 /27	6.97 /10	-1.04 /12	0.00	2.11
GL	Security Equity Fund-Global A	SEQAX	B-	(800) 888-2461	B / 7.6	-3.58	3.23	17.59 /78	20.77 /82	6.95 /66	0.00	1.77
GL	Security Equity Fund-Global B	SGOBX	B	(800) 888-2461	B / 7.9	-3.54	3.38	17.70 /78	20.20 /80	6.54 /64	0.00	2.53
GL	Security Equity Fund-Global C	SFGCX	B	(800) 888-2461	B / 7.9	-3.76	2.85	16.72 /76	19.88 /79	6.14 /62	0.00	2.53
GR	Security Equity Select 25 A	SEFAX	D	(800) 888-2461	D+ / 2.8	-4.20	0.51	14.75 /71	10.87 /34	0.99 /20	0.00	1.99
GR	Security Equity Select 25 B	SEFBX	D	(800) 888-2461	D+ / 2.8	-4.53	0.11	13.73 /67	10.01 /27	0.22 /16	0.00	2.74
GR	Security Equity Select 25 C	SSSCX	D+	(800) 888-2461	C- / 3.2	-4.41	0.22	13.94 /68	10.06 /28	0.24 /17	0.00	2.73
GI	Security Large Cap Value A	SECIX	B+	(800) 888-2461	B- / 7.0	3.81	10.60	22.39 /85	15.91 /63	4.63 /51	0.47	1.58
GI	Security Large Cap Value B	SECBX	B-	(800) 888-2461	C+ / 6.9	3.61	10.31	21.53 /84	15.04 /59	3.77 /44	0.00	2.34
GI	Security Large Cap Value C	SEGIX	B+	(800) 888-2461	B- / 7.2	3.55	10.27	21.46 /84	15.08 /59	3.79 /44	0.00	2.33
AG	Security Mid Cap Growth A	SECUX	E	(800) 888-2461	C- / 4.2	-9.41	1.83	12.52 /62	13.53 /51	4.59 /51	0.00	1.40
AG	Security Mid Cap Growth B	SEUBX	E	(800) 888-2461	C- / 3.9	-9.56	1.48	11.86 /59	12.73 /47	3.80 /44	0.00	2.15
AG	Security Mid Cap Growth C	SUFCX	E+	(800) 888-2461	C / 4.6	-9.58	1.52	11.78 /58	12.77 /47	3.83 /44	0.00	2.15
MC	Security Mid Cap Value A	SEVAX	B+	(800) 888-2461	B+ / 8.9	-1.69	9.24	23.29 /86	25.16 /91	15.36 /92	0.00	1.36
MC	Security Mid Cap Value B	SVSBX	B+	(800) 888-2461	B+ / 8.8	-1.91	8.79	22.32 /85	24.22 /90	14.44 /91	0.00	2.11
MC	Security Mid Cap Value C	SEVSX	B+	(800) 888-2461	A- / 9.0	-1.90	8.81	22.33 /85	24.23 /90	14.45 /91	0.00	2.10
SC	Security Small Cap Growth A	SSCAX	D	(800) 888-2461	C+ / 5.8	-8.36	1.06	8.57 /37	17.34 /69	4.61 /51	0.00	2.02
SC	Security Small Cap Growth B	SEPBX	D	(800) 888-2461	C+ / 5.6	-8.51	0.67	7.79 /31	16.48 /66	3.81 /44	0.00	2.77
AA	SEI Asset Alloc-Divers Conserv A	SACNX	C	(800) 342-5734	D / 1.6	-0.91	1.33	4.82 /14	7.07 /11	4.75 /52	2.78	0.12
AA	SEI Asset Alloc-Divers Conserv D	SEADX	C-	(800) 342-5734	D- / 1.1	-1.19	0.90	3.80 /10	6.00 / 7	3.72 /43	1.80	1.12
AA	SEI Asset Alloc-Divers Consv Inc A	SACIX	C-	(800) 342-5734	E+ / 0.6	-0.53	0.81	2.81 / 7	4.71 / 3	3.77 /44	3.07	0.12
AA	SEI Asset Alloc-Divers Consv Inc D	SDCDX	C-	(800) 342-5734	E / 0.4	-0.71	0.30	1.84 / 4	3.69 / 2	2.76 /34	2.03	1.12
GL	SEI Asset Alloc-Dvrs Glb Growth A	SAGRX	B-	(800) 342-5734	C / 5.3	-1.69	3.59	11.71 /58	12.86 /48	4.95 /54	1.56	0.12
GL	SEI Asset Alloc-Dvrs Glb Growth D	SAGDX	C+	(800) 342-5734	C / 4.6	-1.92	3.14	10.63 /51	11.76 /41	3.91 /45	0.61	1.12
GL	SEI Asset Alloc-Dvrs Glb Mod Gr A	SAGMX	C+	(800) 342-5734	C- / 3.9	-1.34	2.63	8.84 /39	10.72 /33	5.65 /59	2.30	0.12
GL	SEI Asset Alloc-Dvrs Glb Mod Gr D	SDMDX	C	(800) 342-5734	C- / 3.1	-1.60	2.18	7.73 /31	9.46 /24	4.41 /50	1.31	1.12
GL	SEI Asset Alloc-Dvrs Glb Stock A	SAGSX	B	(800) 342-5734	C+ / 6.4	-1.98	4.55	14.54 /70	15.04 /59	4.30 /49	0.87	0.12
GL	SEI Asset Alloc-Dvrs Glb Stock D	SDGDX	B-	(800) 342-5734	C+ / 5.9	-2.27	4.05	13.36 /66	13.87 /53	3.26 /39	0.31	1.12
AA	SEI Asset Alloc-Dvrs Mod Gr A	SAMGX	C+	(800) 342-5734	C- / 3.1	-1.28	2.30	7.77 /31	9.49 /24	4.44 /50	2.10	0.12
AA	SEI Asset Alloc-Dvrs Mod Gr D	SMGDX	C	(800) 342-5734	D+ / 2.4	-1.51	1.83	6.67 /24	8.41 /17	3.40 /40	1.14	1.12
GR	SEI Asset Alloc-Dvrs US Stock A	SAUSX	C+	(800) 342-5734	C / 4.8	-2.58	2.99	10.24 /48	12.28 /44	2.63 /33	0.49	0.12
GR	SEI Asset Alloc-Dvrs US Stock D	SADDX	C	(800) 342-5734	C- / 4.1	-2.81	2.45	9.12 /41	11.16 /37	1.58 /24	0.00	1.12
IX	SEI Index Fds-S&P 500 Idx Fd A	SSPIX	C-	(800) 342-5734	C- / 3.7	-1.54	2.52	7.85 /32	10.65 /32	2.02 /27	1.04	0.40
IX	SEI Index Fds-S&P 500 Idx Fd E	TRQIX	C-	(800) 342-5734	C- / 3.9	-1.48	2.61	7.97 /32	10.82 /34	2.17 /29	1.17	0.25
EM	SEI Instl Managed Tr-Intl Eq I	SEEIX	B	(800) 342-5734	B+ / 8.9	-0.15	9.32	27.10 /91	22.48 /86	--	1.86	1.49
GR	SEI Instl Managed Tr-Lg Cap Gr A	SELCX	D	(800) 342-5734	D / 2.2	-4.54	-1.16	7.60 /30	8.55 /18	-1.88 / 9	0.12	0.86
GR	SEI Instl Managed Tr-Lg Cap Val A	TRMVX	B	(800) 342-5734	C+ / 6.4	0.27	5.72	11.38 /56	14.96 /59	5.91 /61	1.56	0.86
GR	SEI Instl Managed Tr-LgCp Dvf Alp A	SDAAX	U	(800) 342-5734	U /	-2.05	2.63	--	--	--	0.00	1.05
MC	SEI Instl Managed Tr-MidCap Portf A	SEMCX	B+	(800) 342-5734	B+ / 8.4	-2.30	5.23	15.69 /74	21.85 /85	11.94 /87	0.44	1.01
RE	SEI Instl Managed Tr-Real Est A	SETAX	U	(800) 342-5734	U /	-0.86	14.80	25.57 /89	--	--	1.70	2.93
SC	SEI Instl Managed Tr-Sm Cap Gr A	SSCGX	D	(800) 342-5734	C+ / 5.8	-8.98	4.03	12.46 /62	14.42 /56	1.46 /23	0.00	1.11
SC	SEI Instl Managed Tr-Sm Cap Val A	SESVX	C+	(800) 342-5734	B / 8.1	-3.48	7.26	12.47 /62	20.71 /82	12.56 /88	0.27	1.11
GR	SEI Instl Managed Tr-T/M Lg Cap A	TMLCX	C+	(800) 342-5734	C / 4.5	-2.16	2.28	9.28 /42	11.77 /41	2.45 /32	0.85	0.86

● Denotes fund is closed to new investors
★ Denotes fund is included in Section II

374

Risk Rating/Pts	3 Year Standard Deviation	Beta	NAV As of 6/30/06	Total $(Mil)	Cash %	Stocks %	Bonds %	Other %	Portfolio Turnover Ratio	Last Bull Market Return	Last Bear Market Return	Manager Quality Pct	Manager Tenure (Years)	Initial Purch. $	Additional Purch. $	Front End Load	Back End Load
D /1.7	19.7	2.01	4.94	77	0	99	0	1	89.0	88.5	-13.6	7	6	2,500	1	0.0	2.0
B /8.7	8.1	1.05	22.03	612	0	99	0	1	2.0	72.7	-9.4	66	7	2,500	1	0.0	2.0
B /8.7	8.2	1.05	22.08	668	0	99	0	1	2.0	73.6	-9.3	68	7	50,000	1	0.0	2.0
B /8.9	6.4	1.28	12.74	127	36	45	18	1	283.0	51.0	-2.6	58	N/A	2,500	500	0.0	2.0
B /8.0	10.4	1.10	15.88	238	1	98	0	1	61.0	103.5	-12.4	92	3	1,000	0	0.0	0.0
B /8.1	10.0	1.09	16.51	72	3	96	0	1	29.0	N/A	N/A	87	3	1,000	0	0.0	0.0
C /4.7	10.6	1.13	26.84	69	3	96	0	1	78.0	107.8	-12.2	93	13	1,000	0	0.0	1.0
B- /7.5	6.9	0.87	6.66	343	0	99	0	1	32.0	45.9	-10.2	33	2	100	100	5.8	2.0
B- /7.3	6.9	0.87	5.88	31	0	99	0	1	32.0	42.5	-10.5	27	2	100	100	0.0	2.0
B- /7.4	7.0	0.87	6.22	6	0	99	0	1	32.0	42.4	-10.3	27	2	100	100	0.0	2.0
C+ /6.3	11.3	1.02	18.85	111	0	99	0	1	31.0	120.1	-12.5	23	2	100	100	5.8	2.0
C+ /6.3	11.3	1.02	17.42	30	0	99	0	1	31.0	116.8	-12.4	20	2	100	100	0.0	2.0
C+ /6.3	11.3	1.02	17.66	10	0	99	0	1	31.0	115.1	-12.7	18	2	100	100	0.0	0.0
C+ /6.6	10.7	1.18	9.80	13	5	94	0	1	12.7	59.5	-11.8	35	2	100	100	5.8	0.0
C+ /6.5	10.6	1.17	9.28	10	5	94	0	1	12.7	56.0	-12.1	29	2	100	100	0.0	2.0
C+ /6.5	10.6	1.17	9.32	6	5	94	0	1	12.7	56.0	-12.1	30	2	100	100	0.0	0.0
B- /7.8	8.7	1.01	7.62	75	2	97	0	1	110.0	76.9	-10.4	90	N/A	100	100	5.8	1.0
B- /7.8	8.6	1.01	7.17	10	2	97	0	1	110.0	72.9	-10.9	87	N/A	100	100	0.0	5.0
B- /7.8	8.6	1.00	7.30	3	2	97	0	1	110.0	72.7	-10.7	87	N/A	100	100	0.0	1.0
D /2.0	17.6	1.85	12.23	206	4	95	0	1	30.6	107.0	-8.6	13	8	100	100	5.8	1.0
D /1.9	17.6	1.85	10.31	25	4	95	0	1	30.6	102.4	-8.9	11	8	100	100	0.0	5.0
D /1.9	17.6	1.86	11.33	16	4	95	0	1	30.6	102.5	-8.8	11	8	100	100	0.0	1.0
C+ /6.3	13.2	1.09	39.03	532	3	95	0	2	19.0	159.1	-5.4	92	9	100	100	5.8	1.0
C+ /6.2	13.2	1.09	35.51	113	3	95	0	2	19.0	152.9	-5.6	89	9	100	100	0.0	5.0
C+ /6.2	13.2	1.09	36.20	144	3	95	0	2	19.0	153.1	-5.7	89	9	100	100	0.0	1.0
C- /3.4	15.5	1.00	16.22	27	2	97	0	1	133.8	134.5	-14.4	41	4	100	100	5.8	1.0
C- /3.3	15.6	1.01	14.95	9	2	97	0	1	133.8	129.0	-14.5	34	4	100	100	0.0	5.0
B+ /9.8	3.9	0.79	10.87	92	0	40	59	1	43.0	34.7	-2.0	63	N/A	150,000	1,000	0.0	0.0
B+ /9.9	3.9	0.80	10.83	9	0	40	59	1	43.0	30.5	-2.3	50	N/A	150,000	1,000	0.0	0.0
B+ /9.9	2.8	0.54	11.22	51	20	24	54	2	41.0	22.2	-0.6	51	N/A	150,000	1,000	0.0	0.0
B+ /9.9	2.8	0.54	11.13	8	20	24	54	2	41.0	18.5	-1.0	39	N/A	150,000	1,000	0.0	0.0
B /8.7	7.2	1.43	13.38	232	0	80	19	1	69.0	69.6	-7.6	82	N/A	150,000	1,000	0.0	0.0
B /8.7	7.2	1.44	13.26	14	0	80	19	1	69.0	64.2	-7.8	74	N/A	150,000	1,000	0.0	0.0
B /8.9	5.6	1.15	11.80	177	1	60	38	1	58.0	55.9	-4.6	78	N/A	150,000	1,000	0.0	0.0
B+ /9.0	5.6	1.15	11.66	8	1	60	38	1	58.0	49.7	-4.8	68	N/A	150,000	1,000	0.0	0.0
B /8.0	8.8	0.77	12.85	141	0	98	0	2	86.0	83.7	-10.1	23	N/A	150,000	1,000	0.0	0.0
B- /7.9	8.8	0.78	12.08	6	0	98	0	2	86.0	77.8	-10.2	16	N/A	150,000	1,000	0.0	0.0
B+ /9.6	5.3	1.10	13.12	325	0	60	38	2	52.0	49.0	-5.0	70	N/A	150,000	1,000	0.0	0.0
B+ /9.6	5.3	1.10	13.04	19	0	60	38	2	52.0	44.3	-5.2	60	N/A	150,000	1,000	0.0	0.0
B /8.3	8.6	1.10	15.12	83	0	99	0	1	101.0	71.8	-10.0	58	N/A	150,000	1,000	0.0	0.0
B /8.3	8.7	1.11	14.19	13	0	99	0	1	101.0	66.3	-10.3	44	N/A	150,000	1,000	0.0	0.0
B- /7.5	7.7	1.00	37.79	578	0	97	7	0	12.0	62.2	-9.8	49	N/A	100,000	1,000	0.0	0.0
B- /7.5	7.7	1.00	37.91	1,495	0	97	7	0	12.0	63.0	-9.8	51	N/A	5,000,000	1,000	0.0	0.0
C+ /5.6	10.6	0.54	13.49	13	0	86	16	0	41.0	120.1	-11.3	82	N/A	100,000	1,000	0.0	0.0
C+ /6.5	9.2	1.11	19.55	3,416	0	97	8	0	58.0	54.5	-10.6	23	12	100,000	1,000	0.0	0.0
B /8.1	7.9	0.99	22.31	3,661	0	98	5	0	38.0	82.7	-9.4	87	N/A	100,000	1,000	0.0	0.0
U /	N/A	N/A	10.04	1,002	0	84	14	2	23.0	N/A	N/A	N/A	N/A	100,000	1,000	0.0	0.0
C+ /6.6	11.0	0.98	20.43	87	0	96	15	0	43.0	123.4	-6.5	87	N/A	100,000	1,000	0.0	0.0
U /	N/A	N/A	17.30	144	53	45	0	2	1,502.0	N/A	N/A	N/A	N/A	100,000	1,000	0.0	0.0
D+ /2.9	18.2	1.21	18.86	1,106	0	95	27	0	52.0	114.3	-15.6	7	12	100,000	1,000	0.0	0.0
C /4.6	12.3	0.83	20.83	1,117	0	96	20	0	37.0	121.6	-7.5	91	12	100,000	1,000	0.0	0.0
B /8.7	8.0	1.04	12.22	2,287	0	97	6	0	52.0	68.9	-10.2	59	N/A	100,000	1,000	0.0	0.0

Fund Type	Fund Name	Ticker Symbol	Overall Weiss Investment Rating	Phone	Performance Rating/Pts	3 Mo	6 Mo	1Yr / Pct	3Yr / Pct	5Yr / Pct	Dividend Yield	Expense Ratio
								Total Return % through 6/30/06	Annualized		Incl. in Returns	
SC	SEI Instl Managed Tr-T/M Sm Cap A	STMSX	C+	(800) 342-5734	B- / 7.1	-6.50	3.89	11.35 /56	17.74 /71	8.43 /74	0.00	1.11
EM	SEI Instl Mgd Tr-US Mgd Volty A	SVOAX	U	(800) 342-5734	U /	-0.34	4.10	7.88 /32	--	--	0.82	1.11
EM	SEI Intl Tr-Emerging Mkts Eq Tr	SIEMX	B-	(800) 342-5734	A+ / 9.6	-6.08	4.53	30.37 /95	31.60 /96	18.23 /95	0.54	1.96
FO	SEI Intl Tr-International Eq Tr	SEITX	A	(800) 342-5734	B+ / 8.9	-0.07	9.40	27.33 /92	22.74 /87	7.98 /72	2.05	1.24
GR	Select Air Transport	FSAIX	A	(800) 544-8888	A- / 9.1	1.00	15.09	38.63 /98	20.92 /82	7.24 /68	0.00	1.13
GR	Select Automotive Fund	FSAVX	D	(800) 544-8888	C- / 3.2	-4.35	0.47	5.17 /16	10.71 /33	8.47 /74	0.20	1.25
FS	Select Banking Port	FSRBX	D	(800) 544-8888	C- / 3.7	-0.18	3.29	7.61 /30	10.62 /32	6.58 /65	1.68	0.92
HL	Select Biotech Port	FBIOX	E-	(800) 522-7297	D / 1.8	-8.36	-2.81	11.78 /58	9.14 /22	-2.33 / 7	0.00	0.93
FS	Select Brokerage & Invtmt Mmgt	FSLBX	C	(800) 544-8888	B / 7.7	-8.96	1.94	24.53 /88	20.32 /81	10.75 /83	0.71	0.92
GR	Select Business Services & Outsrcng	FBSOX	C-	(800) 544-8888	C+ / 6.5	-1.08	6.48	19.04 /81	14.68 /57	4.59 /51	0.00	1.19
GR	Select Chemicals Portfolio	FSCHX	B-	(800) 544-8888	B+ / 8.3	-1.57	4.67	9.92 /46	22.12 /85	12.81 /88	0.98	1.03
TC	Select Computers Portfolio	FDCPX	E-	(800) 544-8888	E+ / 0.6	-9.42	-5.43	1.22 / 3	6.65 / 9	-4.63 / 3	0.00	1.00
GR	Select Construction & Housing	FSHOX	C-	(800) 544-8888	C+ / 6.7	-9.25	-3.11	-2.45 / 1	19.89 /79	14.38 /91	0.00	1.01
GR	Select Consumer Industries	FSCPX	D	(800) 544-8888	D+ / 2.5	-2.15	2.29	5.74 /19	8.97 /21	2.72 /34	0.00	1.12
GR	Select Cyclical Industries	FCYIX	A-	(800) 544-8888	A- / 9.1	-2.34	9.44	22.55 /85	24.51 /90	11.01 /84	0.22	1.10
GR	Select Defense & Aerospace	FSDAX	A	(800) 544-8888	B+ / 8.8	-5.64	6.75	15.07 /72	24.30 /90	15.31 /92	0.16	0.94
TC	Select Developing Communications	FSDCX	D-	(800) 544-8888	C+ / 6.0	-14.45	-0.85	11.34 /56	16.43 /65	-2.50 / 7	0.00	1.02
★ TC	Select Electronics Port	FSELX	E-	(800) 544-8888	D+ / 2.9	-9.32	-3.93	7.25 /28	10.85 /34	-4.71 / 3	0.00	0.91
★ EN	Select Energy	FSENX	B+	(800) 544-8888	A+ / 9.9	3.82	15.97	39.92 /98	37.96 /99	19.05 /95	0.16	0.91
EN	Select Energy Svcs	FSESX	B-	(800) 544-8888	A+ / 9.8	2.36	15.03	45.23 /98	34.37 /98	19.12 /95	0.00	0.90
EN	Select Environmental	FSLEX	C	(800) 544-8888	C+ / 6.4	-7.06	9.46	17.42 /78	15.50 /61	4.50 /50	0.00	1.25
FS	Select Financial Services	FIDSX	C-	(800) 544-8888	C / 5.0	-2.98	1.78	12.24 /61	12.74 /47	5.90 /60	1.12	0.94
GR	Select Food & Agriculture	FDFAX	B-	(800) 544-8888	C+ / 5.9	2.23	7.26	13.74 /67	13.39 /51	8.17 /72	0.85	1.01
PM	Select Gold	FSAGX	C-	(800) 544-8888	A+ / 9.7	-1.94	15.03	69.56 /99	26.01 /92	27.74 /99	0.05	0.94
★ HL	Select Health Care	FSPHX	E-	(800) 544-8888	D / 1.7	-5.48	-3.75	5.44 /17	8.36 /17	3.49 /41	0.00	0.89
FS	Select Home Finance	FSVLX	E	(800) 544-8888	C- / 3.2	0.60	2.88	4.93 /15	10.04 /28	7.10 /67	1.97	0.94
GR	Select Ind Equipment	FSCGX	B+	(800) 544-8888	B+ / 8.5	-2.22	10.76	23.68 /87	21.54 /84	7.60 /70	0.13	1.02
GR	Select Ind Materials	FSDPX	B	(800) 544-8888	A+ / 9.6	3.25	13.43	38.77 /98	27.67 /94	17.93 /94	0.60	1.02
FS	Select Insurance	FSPCX	C	(800) 544-8888	C / 4.7	-2.20	-2.26	7.70 /30	13.17 /50	7.94 /71	0.84	1.00
GR	Select Leisure	FDLSX	C	(800) 544-8888	C+ / 6.1	-4.11	5.58	14.15 /69	14.62 /57	5.67 /59	0.00	0.96
HL	Select Medical Delivery	FSHCX	B	(800) 544-8888	A- / 9.1	-8.78	-8.51	1.42 / 3	30.03 /96	14.68 /91	0.00	0.92
GR	Select Medical Eqpmnt Sys	FSMEX	E+	(800) 544-8888	D / 1.8	-6.44	-5.98	-2.19 / 1	9.87 /26	9.84 /80	0.00	0.92
GR	Select Multimedia	FBMPX	E+	(800) 544-8888	D+ / 2.5	-1.16	0.17	9.36 /42	9.14 /22	4.11 /47	0.00	1.04
EN	Select Natural Gas	FSNGX	C+	(800) 544-8888	A+ / 9.8	2.54	8.56	30.94 /95	35.68 /98	17.75 /94	0.00	0.91
EN	Select Natural Resources	FNARX	B+	(800) 544-8888	A+ / 9.9	4.09	18.47	46.83 /99	36.47 /98	18.21 /95	0.14	0.96
TC	Select Networking & Infrastructure	FNINX	E-	(800) 544-8888	E / 0.4	-16.91	-1.70	9.48 /43	6.54 / 9	-8.39 / 0	0.00	1.11
EN	Select Paper/Forest	FSPFX	E-	(800) 544-8888	D- / 1.0	-6.23	-1.29	10.62 /51	6.65 / 9	2.97 /37	2.17	1.25
HL	Select Pharmaceuticals	FPHAX	D	(800) 544-8888	D+ / 2.8	-2.05	4.76	17.41 /78	7.41 /12	1.34 /22	0.19	1.07
GR	Select Retailing	FSRPX	C-	(800) 544-8888	C / 5.4	-2.36	4.81	5.45 /17	14.24 /55	5.34 /57	0.00	1.05
TC	Select Software & Computer Svcs	FSCSX	E	(800) 544-8888	D+ / 2.6	-4.10	3.39	10.17 /48	9.28 /23	0.83 /19	0.00	0.92
TC	Select Technology	FSPTX	E-	(800) 544-8888	D / 1.6	-8.49	-3.37	4.65 /13	8.48 /18	-2.88 / 6	0.00	0.96
TC	Select Telecommunications	FSTCX	C	(800) 544-8888	C+ / 5.9	-4.86	8.71	17.50 /78	13.99 /54	0.99 /20	0.79	1.01
GR	Select Transportation	FSRFX	A	(800) 544-8888	A / 9.3	2.01	14.18	38.48 /98	23.56 /89	12.74 /88	0.22	1.10
UT	Select Utilities Growth	FSUTX	A	(800) 544-8888	B- / 7.5	2.31	10.98	14.82 /71	17.43 /70	2.15 /29	1.80	0.94
TC	Select Wireless Fund	FWRLX	B-	(800) 544-8888	A- / 9.2	-9.78	-2.00	8.47 /37	29.04 /95	0.25 /17	0.00	0.97
GI	Selected American Shares D	SLADX	U	(800) 279-0279	U /	0.46	3.53	12.40 /62	--	--	0.93	0.69
★ GI	Selected American Shares S	SLASX	B+	(800) 279-0279	C+ / 6.0	0.36	3.35	12.06 /60	14.26 /55	5.71 /59	0.67	0.94
GR	Selected Special Shares D	SLSDX	U	(800) 279-0279	U /	-2.58	5.94	13.65 /67	--	--	1.14	0.96
GR	Selected Special Shares S	SLSSX	C+	(800) 279-0279	C+ / 6.6	-2.66	5.69	13.25 /65	15.63 /62	6.64 /65	0.89	1.21
MC	Seligman Capital Fund A	SCFIX	D	(800) 221-2783	C- / 4.0	-7.28	-1.31	7.30 /28	13.46 /51	-1.01 /12	0.00	1.52
MC	Seligman Capital Fund B	SLCBX	D-	(800) 221-2783	C- / 3.4	-7.45	-1.68	6.51 /23	12.62 /46	-1.76 / 9	0.00	2.27
MC	Seligman Capital Fund C	SCLCX	D	(800) 221-2783	C- / 3.8	-7.49	-1.68	6.43 /23	12.59 /46	-1.76 / 9	0.00	2.27

99 Pct = Best
0 Pct = Worst

● Denotes fund is closed to new investors
★ Denotes fund is included in Section II

www.WeissRatings.com

RISK			NET ASSETS		ASSET				BULL / BEAR		FUND MANAGER		MINIMUMS		LOADS	
	3 Year		NAV						Portfolio	Last Bull	Last Bear	Manager	Manager	Initial	Additional	Front	Back
Risk Rating/Pts	Standard Deviation	Beta	As of 6/30/06	Total $(Mil)	Cash %	Stocks %	Bonds %	Other %	Turnover Ratio	Market Return	Market Return	Quality Pct	Tenure (Years)	Purch. $	Purch. $	End Load	End Load
C /5.5	13.8	0.94	13.10	305	N/A	94	6	N/A	38.0	116.0	-9.7	58	6	100,000	1,000	0.0	0.0
U /	N/A	N/A	11.63	244	5	94	0	1	65.0	N/A	N/A	N/A	N/A	100,000	1,000	0.0	0.0
C- /4.2	17.6	1.08	15.91	1,285	2	98	0	0	69.0	199.2	-6.8	12	N/A	100,000	1,000	0.0	0.0
C+ /6.8	10.6	1.04	13.50	3,395	N/A	98	2	N/A	80.0	121.5	-11.2	32	N/A	100,000	1,000	0.0	0.0
C+ /6.9	12.5	1.15	45.82	99	5	94	0	1	93.0	145.8	-13.4	98	1	2,500	250	0.0	0.8
C+ /6.2	14.0	1.36	34.30	14	2	97	0	1	206.0	69.3	-12.8	23	2	2,500	250	0.0	0.8
C /5.5	8.9	0.91	36.09	362	1	98	0	1	70.0	61.3	-5.8	34	N/A	2,500	250	0.0	0.8
D /2.0	16.4	0.88	60.94	1,554	0	99	0	1	63.0	62.4	-6.6	44	1	2,500	250	0.0	0.8
C /4.6	15.0	1.34	67.78	909	0	99	0	1	112.0	148.5	-16.7	77	N/A	2,500	250	0.0	0.8
C /4.9	10.7	1.12	16.86	42	4	95	0	1	73.0	85.8	-12.9	77	N/A	2,500	250	0.0	0.8
C /5.5	15.3	1.43	66.86	98	0	99	0	1	141.0	108.8	-10.2	95	N/A	2,500	250	0.0	0.8
D /1.7	20.6	2.11	34.12	436	1	98	0	1	112.0	70.1	-12.6	0	N/A	2,500	250	0.0	0.8
C /4.7	16.9	1.67	44.41	184	1	98	0	1	154.0	130.7	-9.6	76	N/A	2,500	250	0.0	0.8
C+ /6.3	9.7	1.07	25.10	53	3	96	0	1	71.0	54.6	-10.4	29	2	2,500	250	0.0	0.8
C+ /6.5	12.5	1.43	20.90	105	1	98	0	1	168.0	135.2	-9.8	98	1	2,500	250	0.0	0.8
C+ /6.8	12.5	1.23	76.44	918	8	91	0	1	50.0	142.6	-9.2	99	1	2,500	250	0.0	0.8
D /1.7	24.4	2.37	19.84	409	1	98	0	1	167.0	125.4	-10.0	7	3	2,500	250	0.0	0.8
D- /1.2	24.8	2.43	42.01	2,286	1	98	0	1	80.0	91.9	-19.4	1	2	2,500	250	0.0	0.8
C /5.2	20.0	0.99	51.82	2,782	1	98	0	1	128.0	190.0	1.7	91	2	2,500	250	0.0	0.8
C- /3.8	23.8	1.08	74.02	1,928	1	98	0	1	58.0	164.8	1.6	46	1	2,500	250	0.0	0.8
C /5.3	13.6	0.24	17.12	88	4	95	0	1	166.0	92.6	-10.7	96	2	2,500	250	0.0	0.8
C+ /5.7	9.6	1.02	113.42	465	0	99	0	1	47.0	77.4	-9.1	42	1	2,500	250	0.0	0.8
B- /7.9	7.1	0.61	53.74	152	1	98	0	1	75.0	61.6	-8.0	94	2	2,500	250	0.0	0.8
D /1.7	31.3	1.46	34.45	1,457	14	85	0	1	108.0	127.2	19.7	21	3	2,500	250	0.0	0.8
C- /3.0	9.0	0.61	118.91	2,074	0	99	0	1	120.0	48.8	-5.0	64	1	2,500	250	0.0	0.8
D+ /2.9	11.3	1.09	51.63	284	4	95	0	1	76.0	56.2	-3.2	17	2	2,500	250	0.0	0.8
C+ /6.2	14.4	1.62	29.52	85	2	97	0	1	40.0	115.9	-12.3	89	3	2,500	250	0.0	0.8
C /4.5	17.1	1.55	48.57	225	2	97	0	1	124.0	127.4	2.0	99	3	2,500	250	0.0	0.8
B- /7.0	10.1	0.85	66.34	188	0	99	0	1	44.0	81.9	-12.3	69	N/A	2,500	250	0.0	0.8
C+ /5.7	11.3	1.20	80.16	217	4	95	0	1	107.0	98.6	-8.4	71	1	2,500	250	0.0	0.8
C /5.3	14.9	0.95	48.57	796	0	99	0	1	106.0	134.7	-4.7	99	1	2,500	250	0.0	0.8
C+ /5.6	9.8	0.81	21.92	829	0	99	0	1	99.0	65.0	1.8	61	N/A	2,500	250	0.0	0.8
C /4.8	12.0	1.20	44.89	85	1	98	0	1	48.0	73.7	-14.1	22	2	2,500	250	0.0	0.8
D+ /2.9	22.6	1.07	40.97	1,404	0	98	0	2	148.0	179.0	6.9	61	1	2,500	250	0.0	0.8
C /4.9	19.6	0.96	28.04	1,180	2	98	0	0	119.0	184.3	1.2	90	N/A	2,500	250	0.0	0.8
E- /0.0	26.0	2.42	2.31	111	3	96	0	1	201.0	79.0	-12.1	0	2	2,500	250	0.0	0.8
C- /3.0	17.0	0.38	29.48	21	0	99	0	1	207.0	33.3	-9.7	10	N/A	2,500	250	0.0	0.8
C+ /6.0	11.4	0.68	10.08	161	0	99	0	1	207.0	53.7	-6.2	46	1	2,500	250	0.0	0.8
C /5.2	13.1	1.19	49.50	65	0	99	0	1	114.0	97.0	-17.4	68	1	2,500	250	0.0	0.8
C- /3.0	15.7	1.40	54.27	526	1	98	0	1	59.0	61.2	-8.3	13	N/A	2,500	250	0.0	0.8
D /1.9	18.8	1.97	61.02	1,675	1	98	0	1	100.0	74.7	-12.9	1	1	2,500	250	0.0	0.8
C+ /6.0	13.5	1.39	42.06	399	0	99	0	1	148.0	89.6	-15.9	46	4	2,500	250	0.0	0.8
C+ /6.7	13.8	1.29	52.26	138	5	94	0	1	142.0	136.6	-8.0	98	N/A	2,500	250	0.0	0.8
B /8.4	8.7	0.44	47.77	335	1	98	0	1	101.0	100.3	-8.6	95	3	2,500	250	0.0	0.8
C /4.6	16.5	1.73	6.31	397	0	98	0	2	162.0	207.3	-15.7	99	3	2,500	250	0.0	0.8
U /	N/A	N/A	41.65	3,642	2	97	0	1	4.0	N/A	N/A	N/A	N/A	10,000	250	0.0	0.0
B+ /9.1	7.1	0.87	41.59	6,767	2	97	0	1	4.0	76.5	-7.8	89	9	1,000	25	0.0	0.0
U /	N/A	N/A	13.20	83	2	97	0	1	53.0	N/A	N/A	N/A	N/A	10,000	250	0.0	0.0
C+ /6.9	10.8	1.24	13.18	51	2	97	0	1	53.0	99.7	-11.4	76	5	1,000	25	0.0	0.0
C /5.0	13.3	1.16	21.02	329	2	97	0	1	176.4	77.5	-9.1	8	8	1,000	100	4.8	0.0
C /5.0	13.3	1.16	17.51	52	2	97	0	1	176.4	73.3	-9.3	6	8	1,000	100	0.0	5.0
C /5.0	13.3	1.16	17.54	45	2	97	0	1	176.4	73.2	-9.2	6	6	1,000	100	1.0	1.0

| | | | Overall Weiss | | PERFORMANCE | | | | | | Incl. in Returns | |
| | 99 Pct = Best
0 Pct = Worst | | Investment | | Perfor-
mance | Total Return % through 6/30/06 | | | Annualized | | Dividend | Expense |
Fund Type	Fund Name	Ticker Symbol	Rating	Phone	Rating/Pts	3 Mo	6 Mo	1Yr / Pct	3Yr / Pct	5Yr / Pct	Yield	Ratio
MC	Seligman Capital Fund D	SLCDX	D	(800) 221-2783	C- / 4.1	-7.44	-1.68	6.50 /23	12.62 /46	-1.75 / 9	0.00	2.27
MC	Seligman Capital Fund I	SCLIX	C-	(800) 221-2783	C / 5.1	-7.21	-1.10	7.83 /31	14.04 /54	--	0.00	1.00
MC	Seligman Capital Fund R	SCFRX	C-	(800) 221-2783	C / 4.5	-7.35	-1.41	7.07 /27	13.32 /50	--	0.00	1.77
GI	Seligman Common Stock Fund A	SCSFX	D	(800) 221-2783	D / 1.8	-3.44	0.94	4.56 /13	9.32 /23	-0.72 /13	0.46	1.28
GI	Seligman Common Stock Fund B	SBCSX	D	(800) 221-2783	D- / 1.4	-3.60	0.61	3.88 /10	8.51 /18	-1.46 /10	0.00	2.04
GI	Seligman Common Stock Fund C	SCKCX	D	(800) 221-2783	D / 1.8	-3.60	0.61	3.88 /10	8.55 /18	-1.46 /10	0.00	2.04
GI	Seligman Common Stock Fund D	SCSDX	D	(800) 221-2783	D / 1.9	-3.60	0.61	3.79 /10	8.51 /18	-1.48 /10	0.00	2.04
GI	Seligman Common Stock Fund R	SCSRX	D+	(800) 221-2783	D+ / 2.3	-3.52	0.86	4.31 /12	9.12 /22	--	0.24	1.54
★ TC	Seligman Communications/Info A	SLMCX	D-	(800) 221-2783	C / 4.4	-6.91	4.62	16.82 /77	13.11 /49	0.66 /18	0.00	1.49
TC	Seligman Communications/Info B	SLMBX	D-	(800) 221-2783	C- / 3.7	-7.09	4.25	15.89 /74	12.23 /44	-0.11 /15	0.00	2.24
TC	Seligman Communications/Info C	SCICX	D-	(800) 221-2783	C / 4.3	-7.05	4.25	15.93 /74	12.26 /44	-0.09 /15	0.00	2.24
TC	Seligman Communications/Info D	SLMDX	D-	(800) 221-2783	C / 4.4	-7.09	4.26	15.89 /74	12.26 /44	-0.10 /15	0.00	2.24
TC	Seligman Communications/Info I	SCMIX	C-	(800) 221-2783	C / 5.5	-6.80	4.89	17.37 /78	13.66 /52	--	0.00	1.08
TC	Seligman Communications/Info R	SCIRX	D+	(800) 221-2783	C / 4.8	-6.94	4.50	16.55 /76	12.79 /47	--	0.00	1.74
EM	Seligman Emerging Markets A	SHEMX	C+	(800) 221-2783	A / 9.5	-5.88	5.77	30.42 /95	30.83 /96	19.45 /96	0.00	2.58
EM	Seligman Emerging Markets B	SHEBX	C+	(800) 221-2783	A / 9.4	-6.03	5.34	29.51 /94	29.74 /95	18.51 /95	0.00	3.33
EM	Seligman Emerging Markets C	SHECX	C+	(800) 221-2783	A / 9.5	-6.09	5.33	29.55 /94	29.85 /95	18.52 /95	0.00	3.33
EM	Seligman Emerging Markets D	SHEDX	C+	(800) 221-2783	A / 9.5	-6.09	5.33	29.55 /94	29.85 /95	18.52 /95	0.00	3.33
EM	Seligman Emerging Markets R	SERRX	B-	(800) 221-2783	A+ / 9.6	-5.90	5.69	30.23 /95	30.72 /96	--	0.00	2.83
SC	Seligman Frontier Fund A	SLFRX	D	(800) 221-2783	C- / 4.1	-5.91	7.39	10.49 /50	12.27 /44	2.23 /29	0.00	1.98
SC	Seligman Frontier Fund B	SLFBX	D-	(800) 221-2783	C- / 3.5	-6.05	6.98	9.70 /45	11.43 /39	1.45 /23	0.00	2.73
SC	Seligman Frontier Fund C	SLFCX	D-	(800) 221-2783	C- / 4.1	-6.12	6.98	9.70 /45	11.47 /39	1.47 /24	0.00	2.73
SC	Seligman Frontier Fund D	SLFDX	D	(800) 221-2783	C- / 4.2	-6.13	6.89	9.71 /45	11.44 /39	1.45 /23	0.00	2.73
SC	Seligman Frontier Fund R	SFFRX	D+	(800) 221-2783	C / 4.6	-5.95	7.18	10.12 /48	12.03 /43	--	0.00	2.22
GL	Seligman Global Growth A	SHGOX	C-	(800) 221-2783	C / 4.9	-1.77	4.91	15.53 /73	13.35 /51	0.28 /17	0.00	2.10
GL	Seligman Global Growth B	SHOBX	C-	(800) 221-2783	C / 4.3	-1.94	4.54	14.80 /71	12.48 /46	-0.45 /14	0.00	2.85
GL	Seligman Global Growth C	SHOCX	C-	(800) 221-2783	C / 4.8	-1.81	4.68	14.61 /70	12.46 /46	-0.43 /14	0.00	2.85
GL	Seligman Global Growth D	SHODX	C-	(800) 221-2783	C / 4.9	-1.94	4.54	14.63 /70	12.41 /45	-0.45 /14	0.00	2.85
GL	Seligman Global Growth R	SGGRX	C	(800) 221-2783	C / 5.3	-1.78	4.81	15.16 /72	13.12 /49	--	0.00	2.35
GL	Seligman Global Small Co A	SHGAX	B+	(800) 221-2783	B+ / 8.8	-4.47	7.67	21.24 /83	24.31 /90	7.84 /71	0.00	1.98
GL	Seligman Global Small Co B	SHGBX	B+	(800) 221-2783	B+ / 8.5	-4.67	7.27	20.31 /82	23.35 /88	7.00 /67	0.00	2.73
GL	Seligman Global Small Co C	SHGCX	B+	(800) 221-2783	B+ / 8.7	-4.65	7.25	20.41 /82	23.42 /88	7.04 /67	0.00	2.73
GL	Seligman Global Small Co D	SHGDX	B+	(800) 221-2783	B+ / 8.8	-4.66	7.25	20.34 /82	23.40 /88	7.03 /67	0.00	2.73
GL	Seligman Global Small Co R	SGSRX	A+	(800) 221-2783	B+ / 8.9	-4.55	7.47	20.89 /83	24.03 /89	--	0.00	2.23
TC	Seligman Global Tech A	SHGTX	E+	(800) 221-2783	C- / 3.6	-7.94	2.49	16.35 /76	12.30 /44	-1.34 /11	0.00	1.83
TC	Seligman Global Tech B	SHTBX	E	(800) 221-2783	C- / 3.0	-8.14	2.05	15.53 /73	11.46 /39	-2.11 / 8	0.00	2.58
TC	Seligman Global Tech C	SHTCX	E+	(800) 221-2783	C- / 3.5	-8.13	2.14	15.52 /73	11.49 /39	-2.10 / 8	0.00	2.58
TC	Seligman Global Tech D	SHTDX	E+	(800) 221-2783	C- / 3.6	-8.15	2.06	15.46 /73	11.48 /39	-2.12 / 8	0.00	2.58
TC	Seligman Global Tech R	SGTRX	D+	(800) 221-2783	C- / 4.1	-7.99	2.35	16.08 /75	12.06 /43	--	0.00	2.08
GR	Seligman Growth Fund A	SGRFX	D-	(800) 221-2783	D- / 1.4	-3.57	-1.22	4.92 /15	8.62 /19	-3.50 / 4	0.00	1.38
GR	Seligman Growth Fund B	SGBTX	D-	(800) 221-2783	D- / 1.0	-4.12	-1.81	4.15 /11	7.83 /14	-4.24 / 3	0.00	2.14
GR	Seligman Growth Fund C	SGRCX	D-	(800) 221-2783	D- / 1.5	-3.82	-1.51	4.47 /13	7.94 /15	-4.18 / 3	0.00	2.14
GR	Seligman Growth Fund D	SGRDX	D-	(800) 221-2783	D- / 1.5	-3.82	-1.51	4.14 /11	7.80 /14	-4.23 / 3	0.00	2.14
GR	Seligman Growth Fund R	SGFRX	D	(800) 221-2783	D / 1.8	-3.83	-1.47	4.69 /14	8.35 /17	--	0.00	1.64
AA	Seligman Harvester A	SATVX	C	(800) 221-2783	D+ / 2.3	-2.15	2.81	6.94 /26	9.61 /25	1.90 /26	1.98	0.31
AA	Seligman Harvester B	STVBX	C-	(800) 221-2783	D / 1.8	-2.34	2.43	6.14 /21	8.81 /20	1.23 /22	1.34	1.07
AA	Seligman Harvester C	STVCX	C	(800) 221-2783	D / 2.2	-2.34	2.43	6.14 /21	8.81 /20	1.23 /22	1.33	1.07
AA	Seligman Harvester D	STVDX	C	(800) 221-2783	D+ / 2.4	-2.34	2.43	6.14 /21	8.81 /20	1.23 /22	1.34	1.07
AA	Seligman Income & Growth A	SINFX	D+	(800) 221-2783	E+ / 0.8	-0.50	2.21	4.30 /12	6.39 / 8	2.21 /29	2.06	1.42
AA	Seligman Income & Growth B	SIBBX	D+	(800) 221-2783	E / 0.5	-0.70	1.90	3.51 / 9	5.61 / 5	1.45 /23	1.31	2.17
AA	Seligman Income & Growth D	SINDX	C-	(800) 221-2783	E+ / 0.9	-0.70	1.81	3.51 / 9	5.59 / 5	1.44 /23	1.31	2.17
AA	Seligman Income & Growth I	SINIX	C-	(800) 221-2783	D- / 1.4	-0.32	2.79	4.65 /13	6.50 / 8	--	2.03	1.40

● Denotes fund is closed to new investors
★ Denotes fund is included in Section II

www.WeissRatings.com

RISK			NET ASSETS		ASSET				Portfolio Turnover Ratio	BULL / BEAR		FUND MANAGER		MINIMUMS		LOADS	
Risk Rating/Pts	3 Year		NAV As of 6/30/06	Total $(Mil)	Cash %	Stocks %	Bonds %	Other %		Last Bull Market Return	Last Bear Market Return	Manager Quality Pct	Manager Tenure (Years)	Initial Purch. $	Additional Purch. $	Front End Load	Back End Load
	Standard Deviation	Beta															
C / 5.0	13.3	1.16	17.54	42	2	97	0	1	176.4	73.2	-9.3	6	8	1,000	100	0.0	1.0
C+ / 5.9	13.3	1.16	21.49	21	2	97	0	1	176.4	80.4	-9.0	10	8	1,000	100	0.0	0.0
C+ / 5.9	13.3	1.16	20.91	2	2	97	0	1	176.4	N/A	N/A	8	8	1,000	100	0.0	1.0
B- / 7.6	7.9	1.01	11.78	213	3	96	0	1	68.3	55.8	-8.8	35	N/A	1,000	100	4.8	0.0
B- / 7.5	7.8	1.01	11.50	7	3	96	0	1	68.3	52.1	-9.0	29	N/A	1,000	100	0.0	5.0
B- / 7.5	7.9	1.01	11.51	4	3	96	0	1	68.3	52.0	-9.0	29	N/A	1,000	100	1.0	1.0
B- / 7.5	7.8	1.00	11.50	13	3	96	0	1	68.3	52.0	-9.0	30	N/A	1,000	100	0.0	1.0
B- / 7.5	7.9	1.01	11.77	N/A	3	96	0	1	68.3	N/A	N/A	33	N/A	1,000	100	0.0	1.0
C- / 4.0	16.3	1.69	28.55	2,372	4	95	0	1	136.1	99.7	-12.5	19	17	2,500	100	4.8	0.0
C- / 4.0	16.3	1.70	24.51	407	4	95	0	1	136.1	95.0	-12.7	14	10	2,500	100	0.0	5.0
C- / 4.0	16.3	1.69	24.52	190	4	95	0	1	136.1	95.1	-12.7	14	7	2,500	100	1.0	1.0
C- / 4.0	16.3	1.69	24.50	499	4	95	0	1	136.1	95.1	-12.7	14	13	2,500	100	0.0	1.0
C / 5.5	16.3	1.70	29.19	19	4	95	0	1	136.1	102.9	-12.4	22	17	2,500	100	0.0	1.0
C / 5.5	16.3	1.69	28.31	8	4	95	0	1	136.1	N/A	N/A	17	17	2,500	100	0.0	1.0
C- / 4.0	18.1	1.09	11.36	57	0	100	0	0	129.3	206.5	-3.7	9	N/A	1,000	100	4.8	0.0
C- / 3.9	18.1	1.09	10.45	9	0	100	0	0	129.3	198.8	-3.9	6	N/A	1,000	100	0.0	5.0
C- / 3.9	18.1	1.09	10.48	6	0	100	0	0	129.3	199.8	-3.9	6	N/A	1,000	100	1.0	1.0
C- / 3.9	18.0	1.09	10.48	18	0	100	0	0	129.3	199.8	-3.9	7	N/A	1,000	100	0.0	1.0
C- / 4.0	18.1	1.09	11.33	2	0	100	0	0	129.3	N/A	N/A	8	N/A	1,000	100	0.0	1.0
C / 4.5	15.6	1.03	13.37	48	0	99	0	1	96.0	80.6	-11.5	10	N/A	1,000	100	4.8	0.0
C / 4.4	15.6	1.03	11.65	5	0	99	0	1	96.0	76.1	-11.6	7	N/A	1,000	100	0.0	5.0
C / 4.4	15.6	1.03	11.65	2	0	99	0	1	96.0	76.3	-11.6	7	N/A	1,000	100	1.0	1.0
C / 4.4	15.6	1.03	11.64	19	0	99	0	1	96.0	76.3	-11.6	7	N/A	1,000	100	0.0	1.0
C+ / 5.7	15.7	1.04	13.28	N/A	0	99	0	1	96.0	N/A	N/A	8	N/A	1,000	100	0.0	1.0
C+ / 6.0	12.4	0.98	8.33	28	0	100	0	0	269.1	76.2	-9.0	3	N/A	1,000	100	4.8	0.0
C+ / 6.0	12.4	0.98	7.60	5	0	100	0	0	269.1	72.0	-9.0	2	N/A	1,000	100	0.0	5.0
C+ / 6.0	12.4	0.98	7.61	3	0	100	0	0	269.1	72.2	-9.2	2	N/A	1,000	100	1.0	1.0
C+ / 6.0	12.5	0.99	7.60	10	0	100	0	0	269.1	72.2	-9.2	2	N/A	1,000	100	0.0	1.0
C+ / 6.7	12.4	0.98	8.28	N/A	0	100	0	0	269.1	N/A	N/A	3	N/A	1,000	100	0.0	1.0
C+ / 6.2	12.8	1.05	17.96	123	0	99	0	1	76.4	146.9	-10.9	42	N/A	1,000	100	4.8	0.0
C+ / 6.1	12.7	1.05	15.93	14	0	99	0	1	76.4	140.8	-11.0	35	N/A	1,000	100	0.0	5.0
C+ / 6.1	12.7	1.05	15.98	8	0	99	0	1	76.4	141.1	-10.9	35	N/A	1,000	100	1.0	1.0
C+ / 6.1	12.7	1.05	15.97	51	0	99	0	1	76.4	141.0	-10.9	35	N/A	1,000	100	0.0	1.0
B- / 7.3	12.7	1.05	17.84	N/A	0	99	0	1	76.4	N/A	N/A	40	N/A	1,000	100	0.0	1.0
C- / 3.3	16.7	1.76	14.02	246	2	97	0	1	150.8	81.2	-10.5	12	N/A	1,000	100	4.8	0.0
C- / 3.2	16.7	1.77	12.42	36	2	97	0	1	150.8	77.1	-10.8	9	N/A	1,000	100	0.0	5.0
C- / 3.2	16.7	1.76	12.43	20	2	97	0	1	150.8	77.1	-10.9	9	N/A	1,000	100	1.0	1.0
C- / 3.2	16.8	1.76	12.40	67	2	97	0	1	150.8	77.1	-10.8	9	N/A	1,000	100	0.0	1.0
C+ / 5.7	16.8	1.77	13.93	N/A	2	97	0	1	150.8	N/A	N/A	11	N/A	1,000	100	0.0	1.0
C+ / 6.6	8.6	1.04	4.05	366	1	98	0	1	132.6	55.0	-10.2	28	7	1,000	100	4.8	0.0
C+ / 6.5	8.6	1.03	3.26	17	1	98	0	1	132.6	50.9	-10.3	23	7	1,000	100	0.0	5.0
C+ / 6.5	8.6	1.03	3.27	16	1	98	0	1	132.6	50.9	-10.3	24	N/A	1,000	100	1.0	1.0
C+ / 6.5	8.7	1.05	3.27	18	1	98	0	1	132.6	51.3	-10.3	22	8	1,000	100	0.0	1.0
B- / 7.0	8.6	1.02	4.02	N/A	1	98	0	1	132.6	N/A	N/A	27	7	1,000	100	0.0	1.0
B+ / 9.4	6.2	1.25	5.77	7	N/A	69	30	N/A	18.4	49.3	-4.6	64	14	1,000	100	4.8	0.0
B+ / 9.2	6.2	1.25	5.77	3	N/A	69	30	N/A	18.4	45.9	-4.8	55	14	1,000	100	0.0	5.0
B+ / 9.2	6.2	1.25	5.77	6	N/A	69	30	N/A	18.4	45.9	-4.8	55	14	1,000	100	1.0	1.0
B+ / 9.2	6.2	1.25	5.77	2	N/A	69	30	N/A	18.4	45.9	-4.8	55	14	1,000	100	0.0	1.0
B+ / 9.3	5.0	1.04	12.75	62	4	67	28	1	219.1	33.5	-3.8	40	N/A	1,000	100	4.8	0.0
B+ / 9.7	4.9	1.03	12.70	7	4	67	28	1	219.1	30.3	-4.0	33	N/A	1,000	100	0.0	5.0
B+ / 9.7	5.0	1.04	12.69	9	4	67	28	1	219.1	30.3	-4.0	33	N/A	1,000	100	0.0	1.0
B+ / 9.8	5.1	1.05	12.80	1	4	67	28	1	219.1	N/A	N/A	40	N/A	1,000	100	0.0	0.0

Fund Type	Fund Name	Ticker Symbol	Overall Weiss Investment Rating	Phone	PERFORMANCE Perfor-mance Rating/Pts	Total Return % through 6/30/06 3 Mo	6 Mo	1Yr / Pct	Annualized 3Yr / Pct	5Yr / Pct	Incl. in Returns Dividend Yield	Expense Ratio
AA	Seligman Income & Growth R	SIFRX	C-	(800) 221-2783	D- / 1.1	-0.58	2.22	4.16 /11	6.20 / 7	--	1.87	1.67
FO	Seligman International Growth A	SHIFX	C+	(800) 221-2783	B- / 7.3	-2.13	6.84	21.91 /84	18.27 /73	5.11 /55	0.00	2.08
FO	Seligman International Growth B	SHBIX	C	(800) 221-2783	C+ / 6.9	-2.29	6.53	21.08 /83	17.42 /70	4.30 /49	0.00	2.83
FO	Seligman International Growth D	SHIDX	C+	(800) 221-2783	B- / 7.3	-2.29	6.52	21.02 /83	17.41 /70	4.33 /49	0.00	2.83
FO	Seligman International Growth R	SIGRX	B	(800) 221-2783	B- / 7.5	-2.21	6.79	21.61 /84	18.11 /73	--	0.00	2.33
GR	Seligman Large-Cap Value A	SLVAX	B+	(800) 221-2783	C+ / 6.4	-0.53	3.21	10.37 /49	16.87 /67	2.73 /34	0.01	1.61
GR	Seligman Large-Cap Value B	SLVBX	B+	(800) 221-2783	C+ / 5.9	-0.71	2.76	9.41 /43	16.00 /64	1.94 /27	0.00	2.36
GR	Seligman Large-Cap Value D	SLVDX	B+	(800) 221-2783	C+ / 6.4	-0.71	2.76	9.52 /44	15.97 /63	1.94 /27	0.00	2.36
GR	Seligman Large-Cap Value R	SLVRX	B	(800) 221-2783	C+ / 6.7	-0.60	3.06	10.04 /47	16.62 /66	--	0.00	1.86
GR	Seligman LaSalle Div Real Estate A	SREAX	U	(800) 221-2783	U /	-0.91	13.54	14.53 /70	--	--	3.62	1.60
SC	Seligman Small-Cap Value A	SSCVX	C	(800) 221-2783	C+ / 6.0	-6.54	6.57	11.17 /55	16.00 /64	10.28 /82	0.00	1.76
SC	Seligman Small-Cap Value B	SSCBX	C-	(800) 221-2783	C / 5.4	-6.77	6.22	10.36 /49	15.10 /59	9.45 /78	0.00	2.51
SC	Seligman Small-Cap Value D	SSVDX	C	(800) 221-2783	C+ / 6.0	-6.77	6.22	10.36 /49	15.10 /59	9.45 /78	0.00	2.51
SC	Seligman Small-Cap Value R	SSVRX	C+	(800) 221-2783	C+ / 6.4	-6.58	6.49	10.89 /53	15.94 /63	--	0.00	2.01
AA	Seligman Time Horizon 10 A	SANAX	C+	(800) 221-2783	C / 5.4	-4.03	4.07	12.54 /62	14.49 /56	3.74 /43	0.75	0.30
AA	Seligman Time Horizon 10 B	SANBX	C+	(800) 221-2783	C / 4.8	-4.23	3.66	11.69 /58	13.64 /52	2.94 /36	0.17	1.06
AA	Seligman Time Horizon 10 C	STNCX	C+	(800) 221-2783	C / 5.3	-4.23	3.66	11.69 /58	13.64 /52	2.94 /36	0.17	1.06
AA	Seligman Time Horizon 10 D	STNDX	C+	(800) 221-2783	C / 5.4	-4.23	3.66	11.69 /58	13.64 /52	2.94 /36	0.17	1.06
AA	Seligman Time Horizon 20 A	SATWX	B-	(800) 221-2783	C+ / 6.5	-5.09	3.90	14.59 /70	16.98 /68	4.50 /50	0.00	0.42
AA	Seligman Time Horizon 20 B	STWBX	C+	(800) 221-2783	C+ / 6.0	-5.35	3.36	13.64 /67	16.14 /64	3.73 /43	0.00	1.18
AA	Seligman Time Horizon 20 C	STWCX	B-	(800) 221-2783	C+ / 6.4	-5.35	3.36	13.64 /67	16.14 /64	3.73 /43	0.00	1.18
AA	Seligman Time Horizon 20 D	STWDX	B-	(800) 221-2783	C+ / 6.5	-5.35	3.36	13.64 /67	16.14 /64	3.73 /43	0.00	1.18
AA	Seligman Time Horizon 30 A	STHAX	C+	(800) 221-2783	C+ / 6.7	-5.74	4.14	15.27 /73	17.53 /70	5.17 /55	0.00	0.42
AA	Seligman Time Horizon 30 B	SBTHX	C+	(800) 221-2783	C+ / 6.3	-5.87	3.74	14.44 /70	16.67 /67	4.38 /49	0.00	1.18
AA	Seligman Time Horizon 30 C	STHCX	B-	(800) 221-2783	C+ / 6.7	-5.87	3.74	14.44 /70	16.76 /67	4.38 /49	0.00	1.18
AA	Seligman Time Horizon 30 D	STHDX	B-	(800) 221-2783	C+ / 6.8	-5.87	3.74	14.44 /70	16.76 /67	4.38 /49	0.00	1.18
BA	Sentinel Balanced A	SEBLX	C	(800) 282-3863	D / 2.2	-0.77	2.19	6.74 /25	9.51 /24	4.73 /52	1.94	1.12
BA	● Sentinel Balanced B	SEBBX	C-	(800) 282-3863	D / 1.8	-0.98	1.75	5.87 /20	8.58 /18	3.87 /45	1.20	1.94
BA	Sentinel Balanced C	SBACX	C	(800) 282-3863	D / 2.2	-1.00	1.66	5.75 /19	8.43 /17	3.75 /43	1.14	2.04
BA	● Sentinel Balanced D	SBLDX	C-	(800) 282-3863	D / 1.8	-0.80	2.02	6.45 /23	8.99 /21	3.97 /46	1.72	1.46
GR	Sentinel Capital Growth Fund A	BRGRX	E+	(800) 282-3863	D- / 1.3	-2.34	2.40	9.95 /47	8.02 /15	0.50 /18	0.00	1.20
GR	Sentinel Capital Opportunity A	SIDAX	D	(800) 282-3863	E / 0.5	-3.98	-1.32	3.83 /10	6.00 / 7	-0.23 /15	0.86	1.30
GR	● Sentinel Capital Opportunity B	SBGRX	D-	(800) 282-3863	E / 0.4	-4.23	-1.83	2.74 / 6	5.02 / 4	-1.19 /11	0.04	2.35
GR	Sentinel Capital Opportunity C	SGICX	D-	(800) 282-3863	E / 0.4	-4.31	-1.92	2.45 / 5	4.53 / 3	-2.06 / 8	0.00	2.42
GI	Sentinel Common Stock A	SENCX	C	(800) 282-3863	C / 4.5	-1.19	3.39	11.01 /54	12.85 /48	4.40 /50	0.72	1.10
GI	● Sentinel Common Stock B	SNCBX	C-	(800) 282-3863	C- / 3.9	-1.44	2.90	9.94 /47	11.79 /41	3.42 /41	0.00	2.09
GI	Sentinel Common Stock C	SCSCX	C-	(800) 282-3863	C / 4.4	-1.44	2.84	9.83 /46	11.65 /40	3.30 /39	0.00	2.16
GR	Sentinel Growth Leaders Fund A	BRFOX	D-	(800) 282-3863	D+ / 2.5	-2.58	4.85	13.75 /67	9.39 /23	1.17 /21	0.00	1.75
FO	Sentinel International Equity A	SWRLX	A-	(800) 282-3863	B+ / 8.4	0.00	10.41	24.40 /88	21.89 /85	9.24 /78	1.09	1.43
FO	● Sentinel International Equity B	SEWBX	B+	(800) 282-3863	B / 8.2	-0.25	9.79	23.03 /86	20.44 /81	7.94 /71	0.15	2.57
FO	Sentinel International Equity C	SWFCX	B+	(800) 282-3863	B+ / 8.3	-0.35	9.68	22.84 /85	20.38 /81	7.73 /70	0.00	2.66
MC	Sentinel Mid Cap Growth A	SNTNX	D-	(800) 282-3863	C- / 3.2	-7.32	0.25	6.48 /23	12.24 /44	1.56 /24	0.00	1.33
MC	● Sentinel Mid Cap Growth B	SMGBX	D-	(800) 282-3863	D+ / 2.8	-7.52	-0.27	5.45 /17	11.35 /38	0.64 /18	0.00	2.30
MC	Sentinel Mid Cap Growth C	SMGCX	D-	(800) 282-3863	D+ / 2.9	-7.60	-0.41	5.22 /16	10.75 /33	0.19 /16	0.00	2.56
SC	Sentinel Small Company Fd A	SAGWX	C+	(800) 282-3863	C+ / 6.1	-4.90	5.58	12.84 /64	16.06 /64	10.58 /82	0.00	1.16
SC	● Sentinel Small Company Fd B	SESBX	C	(800) 282-3863	C+ / 5.7	-5.12	5.21	11.85 /59	15.08 /59	9.58 /79	0.00	2.08
SC	Sentinel Small Company Fd C	SSCOX	C	(800) 282-3863	C+ / 6.1	-5.15	5.29	11.93 /59	15.14 /59	--	0.00	1.97
★ GR	● Sequoia Fund	SEQUX	D-	(800) 686-6884	D / 1.6	-1.82	0.78	4.44 /13	7.11 /11	5.74 /59	0.00	1.00
GR	Sextant Growth Fund	SSGFX	C	(800) 728-8762	C+ / 5.8	-4.61	-1.60	17.13 /77	15.28 /60	7.41 /69	0.23	1.28
FO	Sextant International Fund	SSIFX	B	(800) 728-8762	B+ / 8.8	-2.66	4.50	19.01 /80	23.33 /88	10.08 /81	0.46	1.36
GR	Shaker Fund A	SHKAX	E-	(888) 314-9048	D / 1.6	-10.78	-1.79	--	10.74 /33	-6.01 / 2	0.00	1.65
GR	Shaker Fund B	SHKBX	E-	(888) 314-9048	D- / 1.3	-10.97	-2.20	-0.53 / 1	10.08 /28	-6.38 / 1	0.00	2.25

● Denotes fund is closed to new investors
★ Denotes fund is included in Section II

www.WeissRatings.com

RISK			NET ASSETS		ASSET					BULL / BEAR		FUND MANAGER		MINIMUMS		LOADS	
	3 Year		NAV						Portfolio	Last Bull	Last Bear	Manager	Manager	Initial	Additional	Front	Back
Risk	Standard		As of	Total	Cash	Stocks	Bonds	Other	Turnover	Market	Market	Quality	Tenure	Purch.	Purch.	End	End
Rating/Pts	Deviation	Beta	6/30/06	$(Mil)	%	%	%	%	Ratio	Return	Return	Pct	(Years)	$	$	Load	Load
B+ / 9.8	5.0	1.04	12.77	N/A	4	67	28	1	219.1	N/A	N/A	38	N/A	1,000	100	0.0	1.0
C / 5.3	12.9	1.10	14.69	43	2	98	0	0	189.2	104.6	-8.3	7	N/A	1,000	100	4.8	0.0
C / 5.3	12.9	1.10	13.21	8	2	98	0	0	189.2	99.7	-8.6	5	N/A	1,000	100	0.0	5.0
C / 5.3	12.8	1.10	13.24	19	2	98	0	0	189.2	99.9	-8.6	5	N/A	1,000	100	0.0	1.0
C+ / 6.8	12.9	1.10	14.63	N/A	2	98	0	0	189.2	N/A	N/A	6	N/A	1,000	100	0.0	1.0
B+ / 9.0	8.2	0.98	13.20	126	0	100	0	0	29.9	94.5	-11.9	94	9	1,000	100	4.8	0.0
B+ / 9.0	8.2	0.97	12.67	43	0	100	0	0	29.9	89.7	-12.0	92	9	1,000	100	0.0	5.0
B+ / 9.0	8.2	0.97	12.66	34	0	100	0	0	29.9	89.6	-11.9	92	9	1,000	100	0.0	1.0
B / 8.7	8.2	0.98	13.15	2	0	100	0	0	29.9	N/A	N/A	93	9	1,000	100	0.0	1.0
U /	N/A	N/A	9.68	36	0	98	0	2	41.1	N/A	N/A	N/A	3	1,000	100	4.8	0.0
C+ / 5.8	15.1	0.98	16.86	177	N/A	100	0	N/A	25.1	115.9	-14.0	34	9	1,000	100	4.8	0.0
C+ / 5.7	15.1	0.97	15.71	48	N/A	100	0	N/A	25.1	111.0	-14.3	28	9	1,000	100	0.0	5.0
C+ / 5.7	15.1	0.97	15.71	55	N/A	100	0	N/A	25.1	111.0	-14.3	28	9	1,000	100	0.0	1.0
C+ / 6.4	15.2	0.98	16.74	4	N/A	100	0	N/A	25.1	N/A	N/A	33	9	1,000	100	0.0	1.0
B / 8.1	10.0	1.83	6.91	13	0	90	10	0	3.5	83.1	-7.7	78	14	1,000	100	4.8	0.0
B / 8.1	10.0	1.83	6.79	6	0	90	10	0	3.5	79.1	-8.1	71	14	1,000	100	0.0	5.0
B / 8.1	9.9	1.82	6.79	12	0	90	10	0	3.5	79.1	-8.1	72	14	1,000	100	1.0	1.0
B / 8.1	10.0	1.83	6.79	3	0	90	10	0	3.5	79.1	-8.1	71	14	1,000	100	0.0	1.0
B- / 7.4	12.0	2.13	7.46	11	0	99	0	1	5.4	104.1	-10.1	83	14	1,000	100	4.8	0.0
B- / 7.4	12.1	2.14	7.08	5	0	99	0	1	5.4	99.7	-10.4	77	14	1,000	100	0.0	5.0
B- / 7.4	12.1	2.14	7.08	10	0	99	0	1	5.4	99.7	-10.4	77	14	1,000	100	1.0	1.0
B- / 7.4	12.1	2.14	7.08	2	0	99	0	1	5.4	99.7	-10.4	77	14	1,000	100	0.0	1.0
C+ / 6.7	14.2	2.40	7.55	7	0	99	0	1	2.3	110.1	-10.4	76	14	1,000	100	4.8	0.0
B- / 7.2	12.8	2.22	7.21	4	0	99	0	1	2.3	105.0	-10.6	77	14	1,000	100	0.0	5.0
B- / 7.2	12.8	2.22	7.21	4	0	99	0	1	2.3	105.0	-10.6	78	14	1,000	100	1.0	1.0
B- / 7.2	12.8	2.22	7.21	1	0	99	0	1	2.3	105.0	-10.6	78	14	1,000	100	0.0	1.0
B+ / 9.3	5.0	0.98	16.68	239	0	62	36	2	187.0	49.8	-4.9	76	N/A	1,000	50	5.0	0.0
B+ / 9.4	5.1	0.98	16.77	25	0	62	36	2	187.0	45.7	-5.1	68	N/A	1,000	50	0.0	4.0
B+ / 9.4	5.0	0.98	16.71	7	0	62	36	2	187.0	45.1	-5.1	67	N/A	1,000	50	0.0	1.0
B+ / 9.3	5.0	0.98	16.67	22	0	62	36	2	187.0	47.6	-5.2	72	N/A	1,000	50	0.0	6.0
C+ / 5.8	9.3	1.08	18.80	132	2	97	0	1	28.0	44.1	-7.8	22	12	1,000	50	5.0	1.0
B / 8.2	7.7	0.96	14.96	61	0	98	0	2	30.0	42.8	-9.3	16	7	1,000	50	5.0	0.0
B / 8.1	7.7	0.97	14.49	11	0	98	0	2	30.0	38.6	-9.5	12	7	1,000	50	0.0	4.0
B / 8.0	7.7	0.96	13.78	3	0	98	0	2	30.0	35.2	-9.8	10	7	1,000	50	0.0	1.0
B- / 7.0	8.0	0.98	30.76	1,077	1	98	0	1	26.0	73.4	-9.5	74	N/A	1,000	50	5.0	0.0
B- / 7.0	8.0	0.98	30.21	50	1	98	0	1	26.0	68.4	-9.7	65	N/A	1,000	50	0.0	4.0
B- / 7.0	8.0	0.98	30.08	11	1	98	0	1	26.0	67.6	-9.7	63	N/A	1,000	50	0.0	1.0
C+ / 5.6	12.6	1.35	10.59	6	1	98	0	1	71.0	49.3	-6.8	16	7	1,000	50	5.0	1.0
C+ / 6.9	9.9	0.95	20.05	133	2	97	0	1	23.0	117.0	-9.2	41	N/A	1,000	50	5.0	0.0
C+ / 6.9	9.9	0.95	19.62	14	2	97	0	1	23.0	108.8	-9.5	30	N/A	1,000	50	0.0	4.0
C+ / 6.9	9.9	0.96	19.71	4	2	97	0	1	23.0	108.2	-9.6	30	N/A	1,000	50	0.0	1.0
C / 5.0	13.7	1.20	15.95	154	0	99	0	1	160.0	81.5	-8.4	4	13	1,000	50	5.0	0.0
C / 5.0	13.7	1.20	14.52	21	0	99	0	1	160.0	76.8	-8.7	3	13	1,000	50	0.0	4.0
C / 4.9	13.7	1.20	14.71	5	0	99	0	1	160.0	73.8	-8.7	2	6	1,000	50	0.0	1.0
C+ / 6.4	11.3	0.74	7.76	1,183	5	94	0	1	64.0	100.9	-5.8	74	N/A	1,000	50	5.0	0.0
C+ / 6.1	11.3	0.74	6.67	148	5	94	0	1	64.0	94.9	-5.8	66	N/A	1,000	50	0.0	4.0
C+ / 6.3	11.3	0.74	7.37	158	5	94	0	1	64.0	95.5	-5.9	66	N/A	1,000	50	0.0	1.0
C+ / 6.9	8.8	0.55	156.61	3,562	0	95	4	1	8.0	41.7	-10.6	56	1	0	50	0.0	0.0
C+ / 6.1	11.2	1.18	17.12	13	4	96	0	0	4.0	85.7	-7.0	78	11	1,000	25	0.0	0.0
C+ / 5.7	12.6	1.08	12.08	8	12	87	0	1	5.0	135.6	-8.7	30	11	1,000	25	0.0	0.0
D+ / 2.5	19.2	1.94	7.70	3	0	100	0	0	85.0	88.7	-10.8	4	5	3,000	250	5.8	0.0
D+ / 2.4	19.2	1.93	7.55	1	0	100	0	0	85.0	85.3	-10.8	3	5	3,000	250	0.0	5.0

Fund Type	Fund Name	Ticker Symbol	Overall Weiss Investment Rating	Phone	Perfor-mance Rating/Pts	Total Return % through 6/30/06			Annualized		Incl. in Returns	
						3 Mo	6 Mo	1Yr / Pct	3Yr / Pct	5Yr / Pct	Dividend Yield	Expense Ratio
GR	Shaker Fund C	SHKCX	E-	(888) 314-9048	D / 1.9	-10.95	-2.20	-0.53 / 1	10.13 /28	-6.36 / 1	0.00	2.20
GR	Shaker Fund I	SHKIX	E	(888) 314-9048	D+ / 2.6	-10.83	-1.76	0.26 / 2	10.99 /35	-5.76 / 2	0.00	1.45
GR	Shepherd Large Cap Growth Fund	DOIGX	D	(800) 416-2053	C- / 4.0	-4.35	8.37	21.88 /84	9.95 /27	-4.36 / 3	0.00	2.25
GR	Shepherd Street Equity Fund	SSEFX	D-	(888) 575-4800	E+ / 0.8	-6.72	-2.87	-1.07 / 1	6.84 /10	0.12 /16	0.00	1.15
BA	Sierra Club Equity Income Fund	SCFLX	D-	(800) 222-5852	D- / 1.0	-4.24	0.35	5.81 /19	6.51 / 8	--	0.07	0.90
GI	Sierra Club Stock Fund	SCFSX	D	(800) 222-5852	D+ / 2.4	-5.26	-1.85	5.62 /18	9.96 /27	2.18 /29	0.00	1.69
GR	Signal Large Cap Growth A	SLLAX	D+	(888) 426-9709	C- / 3.0	-3.81	-0.43	5.38 /17	11.62 /40	--	0.00	1.43
GR	Signal Large Cap Growth I	SLLGX	C+	(888) 426-9709	C- / 4.0	-3.84	-0.41	5.58 /18	11.90 /42	--	0.05	1.18
BA	Sit Balanced Fund	SIBAX	C-	(800) 332-5580	D+ / 2.3	-1.89	0.25	6.03 /21	8.57 /18	1.94 /27	1.73	1.00
EM	Sit Developing Mkts Growth Fund	SDMGX	C+	(800) 332-5580	A / 9.5	-3.12	8.56	34.47 /96	29.32 /95	13.88 /90	0.32	2.00
FO	Sit International Growth Fund	SNGRX	B	(800) 332-5580	B / 7.9	-1.46	7.50	26.37 /90	18.73 /75	1.47 /24	0.46	1.50
GI	Sit Large Cap Growth	SNIGX	C-	(800) 332-5580	C / 4.3	-2.24	1.24	9.91 /46	12.01 /42	-0.41 /14	0.18	1.00
MC	Sit Mid Cap Growth Fund	NBNGX	C	(800) 332-5580	C+ / 6.9	-4.06	1.96	15.34 /73	17.30 /69	1.53 /24	0.00	1.15
TC	Sit Science & Technology Growth	SISTX	E+	(800) 332-5580	E+ / 0.8	-7.99	-5.11	9.63 /44	7.57 /13	-7.93 / 1	0.00	1.35
SC	Sit Small Cap Growth Fund	SSMGX	C-	(800) 332-5580	C+ / 6.4	-5.08	5.62	20.62 /83	15.64 /62	3.02 /37	0.00	1.50
SC	Skyline-Special Equities	SKSEX	C	(800) 458-5222	B / 8.0	-3.87	8.34	17.26 /78	19.91 /79	13.12 /89	0.00	1.47
BA	SM&R Balanced Fund T	ANTRX	D	(800) 231-4639	E+ / 0.7	-0.05	2.32	3.70 / 9	6.49 / 8	3.00 /37	1.66	1.24
IN	SM&R Equity Income	AMNIX	C-	(800) 231-4639	D+ / 2.7	0.36	4.26	7.24 /28	10.25 /29	2.37 /31	1.56	1.14
GR	SM&R Growth Fund T	AMRNX	C-	(800) 231-4639	D+ / 2.4	0.14	3.69	7.10 /27	9.87 /26	-0.89 /12	0.67	1.19
★ GR	Sound Shore Fund	SSHFX	C	(800) 754-8758	C / 5.3	-1.60	1.54	9.78 /45	13.30 /50	6.55 /64	0.34	0.93
GR	Sparrow Growth Fd C		D+	(888) 569-6161	C- / 3.4	-3.32	3.24	10.49 /50	10.52 /31	2.07 /28	0.00	2.75
AG	SSgA Aggressive Equity Fd	SSAEX	C	(800) 647-7327	C- / 4.2	-1.08	3.20	10.70 /52	10.88 /34	3.82 /44	0.14	1.10
AG	SSgA Aggressive Equity R	SAERX	C	(800) 647-7327	C- / 4.1	-1.09	3.02	10.35 /49	10.74 /33	3.73 /43	0.00	1.60
GR	SSgA Core Opportunities Fd	SSGWX	D	(800) 647-7327	D- / 1.4	-4.11	-1.73	4.82 /14	7.28 /12	-0.69 /13	0.41	1.10
GR	SSgA Core Opportunities R	SCPRX	D	(800) 647-7327	D- / 1.3	-4.24	-1.97	4.27 /12	7.01 /10	-0.89 /12	0.03	1.56
GI	SSgA Disciplined Equity	SSMTX	C+	(800) 647-7327	C- / 3.8	-1.49	2.98	8.11 /33	10.69 /33	2.57 /33	1.03	0.46
EM	SSgA Emerging Markets I	SSEMX	C+	(800) 647-7327	A+ / 9.8	-4.66	9.06	39.40 /98	35.96 /98	21.69 /97	2.24	1.25
GR	SSgA IAM Shares Fd	SIAMX	C	(800) 647-7327	C- / 3.7	-1.27	3.11	8.27 /35	10.49 /31	1.83 /26	1.10	0.46
FO	SSgA Intl Stock Selection Fd	SSAIX	A+	(800) 647-7327	A / 9.4	1.81	11.97	31.18 /95	26.56 /93	12.41 /87	1.18	1.00
FO	SSgA Intl Stock Selection R	SSARX	A+	(800) 647-7327	A / 9.3	1.66	11.64	30.45 /95	25.95 /92	11.82 /86	0.68	1.58
FO	SSgA Intnl Growth Oppty Fd	SINGX	B+	(800) 647-7327	B / 8.2	-0.25	6.90	25.36 /89	19.76 /79	5.34 /57	1.28	1.10
BA	SSgA Life Solutions Balance Fd	SSLBX	C	(800) 647-7327	D+ / 2.8	-0.88	1.90	7.53 /29	8.92 /20	5.22 /56	1.48	0.33
BA	SSgA Life Solutions Balance R	SLBRX	C	(800) 647-7327	D+ / 2.5	-0.97	1.58	6.85 /25	8.47 /18	4.72 /52	1.33	0.81
GR	SSgA Life Solutions Growth Fd	SSLGX	C+	(800) 647-7327	C / 4.4	-1.03	2.97	10.55 /51	11.30 /38	5.33 /57	0.79	0.45
GR	SSgA Life Solutions Growth R	SLRRX	C+	(800) 647-7327	C- / 4.2	-1.12	2.65	10.00 /47	10.91 /35	4.85 /53	0.84	0.74
GI	SSgA Life Solutions Inc & Gr Fd	SSLIX	C-	(800) 647-7327	D- / 1.2	-0.74	0.92	4.37 /12	6.29 / 8	4.80 /53	2.09	0.45
GI	SSgA Life Solutions Inc & Gr R	SLIRX	C-	(800) 647-7327	D- / 1.1	-0.83	0.59	3.74 /10	5.90 / 6	4.33 /49	1.99	0.74
IX	SSgA S&P 500 Index	SVSPX	C+	(800) 647-7327	C- / 4.1	-1.50	2.63	8.45 /36	11.05 /36	2.32 /30	1.74	0.16
SC	SSgA SmallCap Fd	SVSCX	B-	(800) 647-7327	B- / 7.4	-5.58	5.26	12.33 /61	18.34 /74	9.89 /80	0.01	1.05
SC	SSgA SmallCap R	SSCRX	B	(800) 647-7327	B- / 7.4	-5.26	5.52	12.34 /61	18.30 /74	9.77 /80	0.00	1.54
RE	SSgA Tuckerman Active REIT	SSREX	B-	(800) 647-7327	A / 9.5	-1.52	14.17	23.05 /86	28.74 /95	20.23 /96	1.20	1.00
BA	State Farm Balanced Fund	STFBX	C+	(877) 734-2265	D+ / 2.8	0.36	4.58	8.34 /36	8.52 /18	4.88 /53	3.02	0.13
IN	State Farm Equity & Bond Inst	SEBIX	C	(877) 734-2265	D / 2.0	0.10	2.37	6.70 /24	7.46 /12	--	2.44	0.82
IN	State Farm Equity Inst	SLEIX	C	(877) 734-2265	C / 4.4	0.24	4.25	11.70 /58	11.23 /37	--	1.29	0.93
IN	● State Farm Equity LegA	SLEAX	C-	(877) 734-2265	C- / 3.6	0.23	4.14	11.44 /56	10.73 /33	3.04 /37	0.91	1.18
IN	● State Farm Equity LegB	SLEBX	C-	(877) 734-2265	C- / 3.3	0.00	3.80	10.86 /53	10.35 /30	2.60 /33	0.60	1.58
★ GR	State Farm Growth Fund	STFGX	C+	(877) 734-2265	C / 5.0	-0.15	6.27	11.56 /57	11.89 /42	4.37 /49	1.93	0.12
FO	State Farm Intl Equity Inst	SFIIX	B+	(877) 734-2265	B+ / 8.4	-1.05	6.18	26.50 /91	20.46 /81	--	1.53	1.09
FO	● State Farm Intl Equity LegA	SFFAX	B+	(877) 734-2265	B / 8.1	-1.22	5.96	26.30 /90	19.97 /79	7.43 /69	1.22	1.50
FO	● State Farm Intl Equity LegB	SFFBX	B+	(877) 734-2265	B / 7.9	-1.40	5.71	25.84 /90	19.55 /78	7.01 /67	0.93	1.90
FO	State Farm Intl Index Inst	SFFFX	A	(877) 734-2265	B+ / 8.9	0.48	9.51	25.47 /89	23.17 /88	--	1.71	0.74
FO	● State Farm Intl Index LegA	SIIAX	A	(877) 734-2265	B+ / 8.7	0.32	9.37	25.17 /89	22.65 /86	8.84 /76	1.44	1.15

RISK	3 Year		NET ASSETS		ASSET				Portfolio	BULL / BEAR		FUND MANAGER		MINIMUMS		LOADS	
Risk Rating/Pts	Standard Deviation	Beta	NAV As of 6/30/06	Total $(Mil)	Cash %	Stocks %	Bonds %	Other %	Turnover Ratio	Last Bull Market Return	Last Bear Market Return	Manager Quality Pct	Manager Tenure (Years)	Initial Purch. $	Additional Purch. $	Front End Load	Back End Load
D+ / 2.4	19.2	1.93	7.56	1	0	100	0	0	85.0	86.1	-11.0	3	5	3,000	250	0.0	1.0
D+ / 2.6	19.2	1.94	7.82	8	0	100	0	0	85.0	90.1	-10.8	4	5	3,000	250	0.0	0.0
C / 5.1	15.7	1.41	4.40	7	N/A	N/A	0	N/A	487.3	65.8	-6.0	16	4	1,000	100	4.8	0.0
B- / 7.7	9.8	1.13	13.88	27	0	99	0	1	76.0	44.8	-8.2	13	8	1,000	500	0.0	0.5
B- / 7.0	7.5	1.36	11.52	31	4	78	16	2	52.0	38.7	N/A	27	N/A	4,000	100	0.0	2.0
C+ / 6.3	11.3	1.31	11.70	26	2	97	0	1	46.0	62.5	-7.8	21	3	4,000	100	0.0	2.0
B- / 7.3	8.1	0.98	11.62	1	3	96	0	1	36.4	60.8	-10.0	62	4	1,000	25	4.8	0.0
B / 8.7	8.1	0.99	11.71	39	3	96	0	1	36.4	62.2	-9.9	65	4	1,000	25	0.0	0.0
B+ / 9.0	5.7	1.10	15.14	12	2	65	31	2	22.3	45.9	-4.6	61	13	5,000	100	0.0	0.0
C- / 3.8	16.3	0.97	17.38	13	2	97	0	1	4.3	181.7	-8.9	19	12	5,000	100	0.0	2.0
C+ / 6.2	11.0	1.04	15.48	35	0	99	0	1	10.8	103.3	-11.1	12	15	5,000	100	0.0	2.0
C+ / 6.8	8.4	1.01	37.60	102	5	94	0	1	12.9	69.7	-9.2	64	24	5,000	100	0.0	2.0
C / 5.2	13.3	1.12	13.01	192	6	94	0	0	17.2	101.4	-6.5	29	24	5,000	100	0.0	2.0
C+ / 5.8	16.1	1.63	10.02	13	0	99	0	1	20.6	60.2	-9.9	3	N/A	5,000	100	0.0	2.0
C- / 4.1	15.3	0.96	33.46	107	5	94	0	1	20.6	102.0	-10.9	33	12	5,000	100	0.0	2.0
C- / 3.6	11.7	0.78	27.55	572	5	94	0	1	51.0	123.2	-10.0	91	N/A	1,000	100	0.0	2.0
B / 8.3	4.8	0.99	18.24	23	3	66	30	1	14.2	35.5	-5.0	44	6	100	20	5.8	0.0
B- / 7.8	6.8	0.85	23.03	90	2	97	0	1	18.5	54.3	-7.8	60	6	100	20	5.8	0.0
B / 8.4	7.5	0.95	4.37	95	2	97	0	1	9.5	55.1	-8.9	46	5	100	20	5.8	0.0
B- / 7.1	8.6	1.02	37.11	2,502	0	100	0	0	62.0	84.3	-9.1	74	21	10,000	0	0.0	0.0
C+ / 6.3	8.0	0.90	13.69	1	3	91	4	2	137.0	65.1	-8.6	59	N/A	10,000	500	0.0	2.5
B- / 7.4	10.0	1.20	5.49	48	0	100	0	0	147.6	68.9	-9.1	33	N/A	1,000	100	0.0	0.0
B / 8.2	10.0	1.21	5.46	N/A	0	100	0	0	147.6	67.9	-8.8	32	N/A	1,000	100	0.0	0.0
B- / 7.8	7.8	0.98	19.70	123	0	99	0	1	59.0	47.4	-10.0	23	N/A	1,000	100	0.0	0.0
B / 8.2	7.9	0.98	19.65	N/A	0	99	0	1	59.0	46.2	-10.1	21	N/A	1,000	250	0.0	0.0
B / 8.7	7.7	0.99	10.11	227	0	100	0	0	33.6	62.3	-9.0	51	N/A	1,000	100	0.0	0.0
C- / 3.5	19.0	1.16	20.47	1,347	1	98	0	1	52.6	235.1	-7.0	17	N/A	1,000	100	0.0	2.0
B / 8.6	7.9	1.03	9.69	203	0	100	0	0	13.2	61.0	-10.6	44	N/A	1,000	100	0.0	0.0
B- / 7.1	10.8	1.05	12.35	753	0	100	0	0	59.4	146.7	-7.9	65	N/A	100	100	0.0	2.0
B / 8.2	10.7	1.04	12.28	N/A	0	100	0	0	59.4	143.4	-7.9	61	N/A	1,000	100	0.0	2.0
C+ / 6.8	10.8	1.01	12.09	56	0	100	0	0	82.0	107.8	-12.8	19	N/A	1,000	100	0.0	2.0
B+ / 9.5	5.6	1.15	12.34	79	3	60	35	2	31.9	49.9	-5.2	62	N/A	1,000	100	0.0	0.0
B+ / 9.6	5.6	1.14	12.24	1	3	60	35	2	31.9	48.5	-5.4	58	N/A	1,000	100	0.0	0.0
B / 8.7	7.2	0.90	12.48	50	3	80	15	2	25.4	65.9	-7.6	67	N/A	1,000	100	0.0	0.0
B+ / 9.1	7.2	0.89	12.39	1	3	80	15	2	25.4	65.4	-7.9	64	N/A	1,000	100	0.0	0.0
B+ / 9.8	4.3	0.45	12.10	28	3	40	55	2	35.4	34.5	-2.9	57	N/A	1,000	100	0.0	0.0
B+ / 9.9	4.3	0.44	12.01	N/A	3	40	55	2	35.4	33.3	-3.0	53	N/A	1,000	100	0.0	0.0
B / 8.8	7.7	1.00	20.91	1,921	0	100	0	0	10.4	64.1	-9.7	54	N/A	10,000	100	0.0	0.0
C+ / 6.3	15.0	1.01	30.63	129	0	100	0	0	83.6	115.0	-10.5	51	N/A	1,000	100	0.0	0.0
C+ / 6.9	15.0	1.01	30.60	2	0	100	0	0	83.6	114.8	-10.6	51	N/A	1,000	100	0.0	0.0
C / 4.5	17.2	1.03	19.28	175	0	100	0	0	34.9	137.6	-1.8	85	N/A	1,000	100	0.0	0.0
B+ / 9.8	4.7	0.92	51.94	1,161	4	62	33	1	3.0	42.0	-4.4	70	N/A	100	50	0.0	0.0
B+ / 9.9	4.2	0.49	9.86	10	0	62	37	1	1.0	36.4	-3.7	66	N/A	250	50	0.0	0.0
B- / 7.3	7.0	0.85	8.34	134	1	98	0	1	90.0	59.6	-9.1	70	N/A	250	50	0.0	0.0
B- / 7.4	7.0	0.86	8.55	104	1	98	0	1	90.0	57.4	-9.2	65	N/A	250	50	3.0	0.0
B- / 7.5	7.0	0.86	8.47	40	1	98	0	1	90.0	55.6	-9.2	61	N/A	250	50	0.0	3.0
B- / 7.8	7.3	0.89	52.04	3,194	1	98	0	1	1.0	62.6	-9.5	72	N/A	50	50	0.0	0.0
C+ / 6.7	10.2	0.98	11.34	11	4	95	0	1	27.0	110.3	-10.9	27	6	250	50	0.0	0.0
C+ / 6.7	10.2	0.97	11.38	51	4	95	0	1	27.0	107.4	-10.9	25	6	250	50	3.0	0.0
C+ / 6.7	10.2	0.98	11.29	18	4	95	0	1	27.0	105.0	-11.0	22	6	250	50	0.0	3.0
B- / 7.0	10.2	1.00	12.55	27	5	94	0	1	1.0	127.9	-9.7	43	N/A	250	50	0.0	0.0
C+ / 6.9	10.2	1.00	12.49	110	5	94	0	1	1.0	124.9	-9.9	39	N/A	250	50	3.0	0.0

Fund Type	Fund Name	Ticker Symbol	Overall Weiss Investment Rating	Phone	Performance Rating/Pts	3 Mo	6 Mo	1Yr / Pct	3Yr / Pct	5Yr / Pct	Dividend Yield	Expense Ratio
FO	● State Farm Intl Index LegB	SIIBX	A-	(877) 734-2265	B+ / 8.6	0.24	9.19	24.75 /88	22.26 /86	8.47 /74	1.14	1.55
AA	State Farm LifePath 2010 Inst	SATIX	C	(877) 734-2265	D / 2.0	-0.57	2.01	6.08 /21	7.62 /13	--	2.10	1.02
AA	● State Farm LifePath 2010 LegA	SATAX	C-	(877) 734-2265	D- / 1.4	-0.58	1.94	5.76 /19	7.19 /11	--	1.81	1.27
AA	● State Farm LifePath 2010 LegB	SATBX	C-	(877) 734-2265	D- / 1.2	-0.66	1.78	5.49 /18	6.78 /10	--	1.51	1.67
AA	State Farm LifePath 2020 Inst	SAWIX	C+	(877) 734-2265	C- / 3.6	-0.75	3.12	8.93 /40	10.06 /28	--	1.59	1.00
AA	● State Farm LifePath 2020 LegA	SAWAX	C	(877) 734-2265	D+ / 2.8	-0.76	3.15	8.74 /38	9.62 /25	--	1.32	1.25
AA	● State Farm LifePath 2020 LegB	SAWBX	C	(877) 734-2265	D+ / 2.5	-0.91	2.92	8.31 /35	9.22 /22	--	1.03	1.65
AA	State Farm LifePath 2030 Inst	SAYIX	B-	(877) 734-2265	C / 4.7	-0.78	4.03	11.21 /55	11.69 /40	--	1.26	0.99
AA	● State Farm LifePath 2030 LegA	SAYAX	C+	(877) 734-2265	C- / 3.9	-0.86	3.90	10.85 /53	11.26 /38	--	1.01	1.30
AA	● State Farm LifePath 2030 LegB	SAYBX	C+	(877) 734-2265	C- / 3.6	-1.01	3.77	10.48 /50	10.83 /34	--	0.73	1.70
AA	● State Farm LifePath 2040 Inst	SAUIX	B	(877) 734-2265	C+ / 5.6	-0.95	4.66	12.68 /63	13.07 /49	--	0.94	0.99
AA	● State Farm LifePath 2040 LegA	SAUAX	B-	(877) 734-2265	C / 4.8	-1.02	4.61	12.51 /62	12.68 /47	--	0.71	1.30
AA	● State Farm LifePath 2040 LegB	SAUBX	C+	(877) 734-2265	C / 4.6	-1.10	4.41	12.05 /60	12.28 /44	--	0.45	1.70
GI	State Farm LifePath Income Inst	SLRIX	C-	(877) 734-2265	D- / 1.1	-0.40	1.44	4.32 /12	5.92 / 7	--	3.10	1.05
GI	● State Farm LifePath Income LegA	SLRAX	C-	(877) 734-2265	E+ / 0.6	-0.48	1.34	4.14 /11	5.54 / 5	--	2.84	1.30
GI	● State Farm LifePath Income LegB	SLRBX	C-	(877) 734-2265	E+ / 0.6	-0.59	1.15	3.67 / 9	5.11 / 4	--	2.38	1.70
GR	State Farm S&P 500 Index Inst	SFXIX	C+	(877) 734-2265	C- / 3.8	-1.52	2.42	8.08 /33	10.78 /34	--	1.29	0.53
GR	● State Farm S&P 500 Index LegA	SLIAX	C	(877) 734-2265	C- / 3.1	-1.63	2.33	7.79 /31	10.31 /29	1.66 /25	0.96	0.78
GR	● State Farm S&P 500 Index LegB	SLIBX	C	(877) 734-2265	D+ / 2.8	-1.73	2.11	7.41 /29	10.00 /27	1.31 /22	0.62	1.18
SC	State Farm Small Cap Equity Inst	SFEIX	E+	(877) 734-2265	C- / 3.2	-6.42	2.34	5.72 /19	10.40 /30	--	0.00	0.99
SC	● State Farm Small Cap Equity LegA	SFSAX	E	(877) 734-2265	D+ / 2.4	-6.52	2.08	5.49 /18	9.95 /27	1.21 /22	0.00	1.40
SC	● State Farm Small Cap Equity LegB	SFSBX	E	(877) 734-2265	D / 2.1	-6.65	1.92	4.98 /15	9.53 /24	0.82 /19	0.00	1.80
SC	State Farm Small Cap Index Inst	SMIIX	C+	(877) 734-2265	B- / 7.4	-5.31	7.62	13.59 /67	17.95 /72	--	0.35	0.54
SC	● State Farm Small Cap Index LegA	SMIAX	C+	(877) 734-2265	C+ / 6.9	-5.37	7.55	13.33 /66	17.49 /70	7.36 /69	0.08	0.95
SC	● State Farm Small Cap Index LegB	SMIBX	C	(877) 734-2265	C+ / 6.7	-5.49	7.31	12.94 /64	17.08 /68	6.98 /67	0.00	1.35
GR	State Street Equity 500 Index A	STFAX	D+	(800) 882-0052	C- / 4.0	-1.48	2.59	8.39 /36	10.97 /35	--	0.96	0.25
GR	State Street Equity 500 Index B	STBIX	D+	(800) 882-0052	C- / 3.9	-1.57	2.50	8.23 /35	10.85 /34	--	0.90	0.25
SC	Stephens Small Cap Growth Fund A	STSGX	U	(866) 811-0215	U /	-7.07	5.48	--	--	--	0.00	N/A
GR	Steward Domestic All-Cap Equity I	SEECX	U	(800) 262-6631	U /	-2.75	3.72	10.34 /49	--	--	0.76	1.02
GR	Steward SmallCap Equity Fund	TRDFX	D	(800) 262-6631	C- / 3.7	-4.60	7.12	12.26 /61	10.27 /29	0.72 /19	0.00	1.67
AA	STI Classic Aggressive Gr Stock I	SCATX	U	(888) 784-3863	U /	-6.70	-0.35	12.07 /60	--	--	0.00	1.19
BA	STI Classic Balanced A	STBLX	D-	(888) 784-3863	E- / 0.1	-2.54	-0.71	1.61 / 3	3.21 / 1	0.90 /20	1.60	1.25
BA	STI Classic Balanced C	SCBFX	D-	(888) 784-3863	E- / 0.1	-2.65	-1.00	0.88 / 2	2.47 / 1	0.17 /16	0.98	1.97
BA	STI Classic Balanced I	SBATX	D-	(888) 784-3863	E / 0.3	-2.49	-0.57	1.84 / 4	3.52 / 2	1.21 /22	1.99	0.97
GR	STI Classic Capital Appreciation A	STCIX	D-	(888) 784-3863	E- / 0.2	-4.05	0.13	3.79 /10	4.82 / 4	-1.91 / 9	0.04	1.50
GR	STI Classic Capital Appreciation C	STCFX	D-	(888) 784-3863	E / 0.4	-4.19	-0.18	3.13 / 8	4.32 / 3	-2.38 / 7	0.00	2.07
GR	STI Classic Capital Appreciation I	STCAX	D-	(888) 784-3863	E+ / 0.8	-3.95	0.29	4.20 /11	5.39 / 5	-1.33 /11	0.29	1.06
AG	STI Classic Emerging Gr Stk I	SEGTX	U	(888) 784-3863	U /	-6.78	5.19	17.60 /78	--	--	0.00	1.20
FO	STI Classic Intl Eq Index A	SIIIX	B+	(888) 784-3863	B+ / 8.7	0.00	9.74	27.05 /91	23.58 /89	8.77 /75	0.93	1.09
FO	STI Classic Intl Eq Index C	SIIFX	A-	(888) 784-3863	B+ / 8.8	-0.20	9.23	25.99 /90	22.73 /87	8.07 /72	0.13	1.77
FO	STI Classic Intl Eq Index I	SIEIX	A-	(888) 784-3863	A- / 9.0	0.00	9.79	27.24 /92	24.06 /89	9.21 /77	1.35	0.76
FO	STI Classic Intl Equity A	SCIIX	A	(888) 784-3863	B+ / 8.5	0.84	9.97	27.26 /92	22.35 /86	8.81 /76	0.72	1.62
FO	STI Classic Intl Equity C	SIEFX	A	(888) 784-3863	B+ / 8.7	0.66	9.62	26.34 /90	21.60 /84	8.07 /72	0.00	2.31
FO	STI Classic Intl Equity I	STITX	A+	(888) 784-3863	B+ / 8.9	0.97	10.17	27.63 /92	22.84 /87	9.20 /77	1.07	1.31
GI	STI Classic Large Cap Val Equity A	SVIIX	B	(888) 784-3863	C / 5.2	-0.01	7.96	12.59 /63	13.95 /54	5.43 /57	1.25	1.16
GI	STI Classic Large Cap Val Equity C	SVIFX	B	(888) 784-3863	C+ / 5.6	-0.10	7.67	11.82 /58	13.18 /50	4.67 /52	0.65	1.85
GI	STI Classic Large Cap Val Equity I	STVTX	B+	(888) 784-3863	C+ / 6.3	0.13	8.18	12.90 /64	14.31 /55	5.81 /60	1.62	0.85
GI	STI Classic LgCp Relative Val A	CFVIX	B-	(888) 784-3863	C / 5.1	-0.77	3.72	10.12 /48	14.61 /57	5.01 /54	0.86	1.15
GI	STI Classic LgCp Relative Val C	CVIBX	B-	(888) 784-3863	C / 5.4	-0.96	3.36	9.26 /42	13.76 /53	4.23 /48	0.22	1.90
GI	STI Classic LgCp Relative Val I	CRVAX	B+	(888) 784-3863	C+ / 6.2	-0.66	3.88	10.42 /50	14.86 /58	5.24 /56	1.16	0.90
AG	STI Classic Life Vision Aggr Gr A	SLAAX	C+	(888) 784-3863	C- / 4.2	-2.19	3.78	10.91 /53	12.86 /48	4.17 /48	0.93	0.52
AG	● STI Classic Life Vision Aggr Gr B	SLABX	C+	(888) 784-3863	C- / 4.1	-2.38	3.48	10.29 /49	12.32 /45	3.81 /44	0.71	0.99

● Denotes fund is closed to new investors
★ Denotes fund is included in Section II

www.WeissRatings.com

RISK			NET ASSETS		ASSET				BULL / BEAR		FUND MANAGER		MINIMUMS		LOADS	
	3 Year		NAV						Last Bull	Last Bear	Manager	Manager	Initial	Additional	Front	Back
Risk	Standard		As of	Total	Cash	Stocks	Bonds	Other	Market	Market	Quality	Tenure	Purch.	Purch.	End	End
Rating/Pts	Deviation	Beta	6/30/06	$(Mil)	%	%	%	%	Return	Return	Pct	(Years)	$	$	Load	Load
C+ / 6.9	10.2	1.00	12.47	35	5	94	0	1	1.0	122.2	-9.9	35	N/A	250	50	0.0	3.0
B+ / 9.9	4.3	0.88	12.16	28	28	28	43	1	12.0	N/A	N/A	64	3	250	50	0.0	0.0
B+ / 9.9	4.3	0.87	12.07	254	28	28	43	1	12.0	N/A	N/A	60	N/A	250	50	3.0	0.0
B+ / 9.9	4.3	0.89	12.02	46	28	28	43	1	12.0	N/A	N/A	54	N/A	250	50	0.0	3.0
B+ / 9.6	5.5	1.13	13.20	52	33	39	27	1	17.0	N/A	N/A	74	3	250	50	0.0	0.0
B+ / 9.6	5.5	1.13	13.10	391	33	39	27	1	17.0	N/A	N/A	70	N/A	250	50	3.0	0.0
B+ / 9.6	5.6	1.14	13.05	84	33	39	27	1	17.0	N/A	N/A	66	N/A	250	50	0.0	3.0
B+ / 9.3	6.6	1.33	13.93	51	36	47	16	1	24.0	N/A	N/A	78	3	250	50	0.0	0.0
B+ / 9.0	7.4	1.46	13.84	257	36	47	16	1	24.0	N/A	N/A	68	N/A	250	50	3.0	0.0
B+ / 9.2	6.6	1.33	13.76	65	36	47	16	1	24.0	N/A	N/A	71	N/A	250	50	0.0	3.0
B / 8.9	7.5	1.50	14.59	43	38	53	7	2	38.0	N/A	N/A	81	N/A	250	50	0.0	0.0
B / 8.9	7.5	1.50	14.51	170	38	53	7	2	38.0	N/A	N/A	78	N/A	250	50	3.0	0.5
B / 8.9	7.5	1.50	14.45	45	38	53	7	2	38.0	N/A	N/A	75	N/A	250	50	0.0	3.0
B+ / 9.9	3.6	0.35	11.29	10	27	21	51	1	11.0	N/A	N/A	62	3	250	50	0.0	0.0
B+ / 9.9	3.6	0.35	11.26	110	27	21	51	1	11.0	N/A	N/A	58	N/A	250	50	3.0	0.5
B+ / 9.9	3.6	0.35	11.26	12	27	21	51	1	11.0	N/A	N/A	53	N/A	250	50	0.0	3.0
B+ / 9.0	7.6	0.99	9.72	59	1	98	0	1	14.0	62.7	-9.8	52	N/A	250	50	0.0	0.0
B / 8.9	7.6	1.00	9.68	346	1	98	0	1	14.0	60.8	-10.0	46	N/A	250	50	0.0	0.0
B / 8.9	7.7	1.00	9.66	130	1	98	0	1	14.0	59.1	-10.1	42	N/A	250	50	0.0	3.0
C- / 3.4	15.8	1.04	10.49	14	2	97	0	1	61.0	79.8	-12.1	5	N/A	250	50	0.0	0.0
C- / 3.4	15.7	1.04	10.33	67	2	97	0	1	61.0	77.6	-12.4	4	N/A	250	50	3.0	0.0
C- / 3.3	15.8	1.04	10.10	24	2	97	0	1	61.0	75.3	-12.3	3	N/A	250	50	0.0	3.0
C / 5.5	14.6	1.00	14.26	39	2	97	0	1	3.0	115.1	-10.9	47	N/A	50	50	0.0	0.0
C+ / 5.7	14.6	1.00	14.10	175	2	97	0	1	3.0	112.6	-11.4	43	N/A	250	50	3.0	0.0
C+ / 5.7	14.5	0.99	13.94	63	2	97	0	1	3.0	110.3	-11.4	40	N/A	250	50	0.0	3.0
C+ / 6.2	7.7	1.00	10.68	195	2	97	0	1	8.0	N/A	N/A	53	N/A	25,000,000	0	0.0	0.0
C+ / 6.2	7.7	1.01	10.66	41	2	97	0	1	8.0	N/A	N/A	51	N/A	25,000,000	0	0.0	0.0
U /	N/A	N/A	10.39	46	2	97	0	1	N/A	N/A	N/A	N/A	2	2,500	100	5.3	2.0
U /	N/A	N/A	29.19	87	0	99	0	1	3.3	N/A	N/A	N/A	N/A	25,000	0	0.0	0.0
C+ / 5.7	9.6	1.11	12.64	43	5	94	0	1	113.0	58.2	-9.5	35	N/A	200	0	0.0	0.0
U /	N/A	N/A	11.42	314	1	98	0	1	30.0	N/A	N/A	N/A	N/A	0	0	0.0	0.0
B- / 7.6	4.6	0.92	11.58	5	5	56	38	1	133.0	19.3	-1.8	21	6	2,000	1,000	5.8	1.0
B- / 7.8	4.7	0.91	11.43	27	5	56	38	1	133.0	16.6	-2.0	17	6	5,000	1,000	0.0	1.0
B- / 7.8	4.6	0.91	11.52	61	5	56	38	1	133.0	20.6	-1.8	23	6	0	0	0.0	0.0
B- / 7.6	8.1	1.01	11.70	90	2	97	0	1	74.0	33.0	-8.3	10	6	2,000	1,000	5.8	1.0
B- / 7.5	8.2	1.01	10.98	44	2	97	0	1	74.0	31.1	-8.4	8	6	5,000	1,000	0.0	1.0
B- / 7.6	8.1	1.01	12.30	1,204	2	97	0	1	74.0	35.4	-8.1	12	6	0	0	0.0	0.0
U /	N/A	N/A	11.96	54	0	99	0	1	107.0	N/A	N/A	N/A	2	0	0	0.0	0.0
C+ / 6.5	10.5	1.02	15.66	5	4	95	0	1	7.0	129.2	-8.5	42	7	2,000	1,000	5.8	1.0
C+ / 6.4	10.5	1.02	15.26	5	4	95	0	1	7.0	124.8	-8.6	35	7	5,000	1,000	0.0	1.0
C+ / 6.5	10.5	1.02	15.81	812	4	95	0	1	7.0	132.4	-8.4	46	7	0	0	0.0	2.0
B- / 7.4	10.2	1.00	14.45	13	3	96	0	1	59.0	121.6	-9.0	37	6	2,000	1,000	5.8	1.0
B- / 7.3	10.2	1.00	13.67	8	3	96	0	1	59.0	116.9	-9.1	32	6	5,000	1,000	0.0	1.0
B- / 7.4	10.3	1.00	14.62	999	3	96	0	1	59.0	124.3	-8.9	41	6	0	0	0.0	2.0
B / 8.9	7.6	0.94	13.78	61	1	98	0	1	104.0	72.3	-9.9	84	11	2,000	1,000	5.8	1.0
B / 8.8	7.6	0.94	13.65	42	1	98	0	1	104.0	68.2	-10.1	79	11	5,000	1,000	0.0	1.0
B / 8.9	7.6	0.94	13.82	762	1	98	0	1	104.0	74.0	-9.8	86	13	0	0	0.0	0.0
B / 8.6	7.4	0.93	17.17	45	1	98	0	1	55.0	78.5	-9.1	88	13	2,000	1,000	5.8	1.0
B / 8.6	7.4	0.93	16.81	73	1	98	0	1	55.0	74.3	-9.2	84	11	5,000	1,000	0.0	1.0
B / 8.6	7.3	0.93	17.02	1,438	1	98	0	1	55.0	79.8	-9.1	89	14	0	0	0.0	0.0
B / 8.7	8.3	1.05	12.01	3	4	95	0	1	31.0	70.3	-8.6	68	N/A	2,000	1,000	5.8	1.0
B / 8.7	8.3	1.05	11.90	6	4	95	0	1	31.0	67.6	-8.6	63	N/A	5,000	1,000	0.0	5.0

Fund Type	Fund Name	Ticker Symbol	Overall Weiss Investment Rating	Phone	Perfor-mance Rating/Pts	3 Mo	6 Mo	1Yr / Pct	Annualized 3Yr / Pct	5Yr / Pct	Dividend Yield	Expense Ratio
AG	STI Classic Life Vision Aggr Gr I	CVMGX	B-	(888) 784-3863	C / 5.4	-2.12	3.91	11.18 /55	13.18 /50	4.35 /49	1.34	0.21
AA	STI Classic Life Vision Conserv A	SVCAX	D+	(888) 784-3863	E / 0.3	-0.57	0.45	2.17 / 5	4.71 / 3	--	3.07	0.53
AA ●	STI Classic Life Vision Conserv B	SCCBX	D+	(888) 784-3863	E / 0.3	-0.76	0.22	1.69 / 4	4.29 / 3	--	2.74	0.97
AA	STI Classic Life Vision Conserv I	SCCTX	C-	(888) 784-3863	E+ / 0.7	-0.59	0.51	2.39 / 5	4.96 / 4	--	3.54	0.20
AA	STI Classic Life Vision Gr&Inc A	SGIAX	C	(888) 784-3863	D+ / 2.6	-1.58	2.74	8.21 /34	10.52 /31	4.89 /53	1.67	0.51
AA ●	STI Classic Life Vision Gr&Inc B	SGIBX	C	(888) 784-3863	D+ / 2.5	-1.69	2.50	7.70 /30	9.97 /27	4.56 /51	1.30	0.96
AA	STI Classic Life Vision Gr&Inc C	SGILX	C+	(888) 784-3863	C- / 3.2	-1.80	2.31	7.42 /29	10.05 /28	4.65 /51	1.29	1.15
AA	STI Classic Life Vision Gr&Inc I	CLVGX	C+	(888) 784-3863	C- / 3.9	-1.60	2.88	8.53 /37	10.81 /34	5.06 /55	2.07	0.19
AA	STI Classic Life Vision Mod Gr A	SVMAX	C-	(888) 784-3863	D- / 1.4	-1.18	1.76	5.67 /19	8.54 /18	4.59 /51	2.29	0.47
AA ●	STI Classic Life Vision Mod Gr B	SVGBX	C-	(888) 784-3863	D- / 1.3	-1.29	1.46	5.10 /16	7.98 /15	4.21 /48	1.98	0.92
AA	STI Classic Life Vision Mod Gr I	CLVBX	C	(888) 784-3863	D+ / 2.5	-1.12	1.83	5.90 /20	8.78 /20	4.72 /52	2.74	0.18
GR	STI Classic Lrg Cap Quant Eqty I	SQETX	U	(888) 784-3863	U /	-1.74	3.48	7.08 /27	--	--	0.10	1.06
MC	STI Classic Mid Cap Value Eq C	SMVFX	C+	(888) 784-3863	B / 7.7	-0.75	7.57	16.53 /76	18.56 /75	--	0.17	2.03
MC	STI Classic Mid Cap Value Eq I	SMVTX	A+	(888) 784-3863	B / 8.1	-0.51	8.14	17.65 /78	19.46 /78	--	0.98	1.13
MC	STI Classic Mid-Cap Equity A	SCAIX	B-	(888) 784-3863	C+ / 6.2	-2.39	3.50	11.01 /54	17.14 /69	4.31 /49	0.25	1.47
MC	STI Classic Mid-Cap Equity C	SCMEX	B-	(888) 784-3863	C+ / 6.5	-2.55	3.14	10.12 /48	16.43 /65	3.64 /42	0.00	2.13
MC	STI Classic Mid-Cap Equity I	SAGTX	B+	(888) 784-3863	B- / 7.2	-2.30	3.67	11.32 /56	17.60 /71	4.72 /52	0.55	1.12
GR	STI Classic Quality Gr Stk A	SXSAX	D-	(888) 784-3863	E / 0.4	-4.25	-2.27	1.94 / 4	6.02 / 7	-1.18 /11	0.11	1.39
GR	STI Classic Quality Gr Stk C	STTFX	D-	(888) 784-3863	E / 0.5	-4.44	-2.62	1.19 / 3	5.25 / 4	-2.03 / 8	0.00	2.07
GR	STI Classic Quality Gr Stk I	STTAX	D	(888) 784-3863	E+ / 0.9	-4.18	-2.10	2.22 / 5	6.34 / 8	-1.00 /12	0.21	1.07
SC	STI Classic Sm Cap Gr Stock A	SCGIX	C-	(888) 784-3863	C+ / 6.3	-9.00	2.55	12.15 /60	17.87 /72	6.92 /66	0.00	1.51
SC	STI Classic Sm Cap Gr Stock C	SSCFX	C-	(888) 784-3863	C+ / 6.6	-9.15	2.14	11.35 /56	17.13 /69	6.19 /62	0.00	2.18
SC	STI Classic Sm Cap Gr Stock I	SSCTX	C	(888) 784-3863	B- / 7.2	-8.96	2.67	12.46 /62	18.29 /74	7.29 /68	0.00	1.17
SC ●	STI Classic Small Cap Val Eq A	SASVX	C	(888) 784-3863	C+ / 5.6	-3.37	10.08	2.17 / 5	16.55 /66	12.46 /88	1.57	1.45
SC ●	STI Classic Small Cap Val Eq C	STCEX	D+	(888) 784-3863	C+ / 5.9	-3.39	10.12	0.17 / 2	15.63 /62	11.45 /85	0.26	1.45
SC ●	STI Classic Small Cap Val Eq I	SCETX	C+	(888) 784-3863	A- / 9.2	-3.29	10.27	24.62 /88	24.84 /91	17.20 /94	0.38	1.20
FO	STI Classic Var Tr-Intl Eq Inst		A-	(888) 784-3863	A- / 9.0	0.83	10.01	27.14 /92	23.00 /87	8.97 /76	2.13	4.97
GI	STI Classic Var Tr-Large Cap Val Eq		B-	(888) 784-3863	C+ / 6.1	0.13	8.13	11.96 /59	14.03 /54	5.09 /55	0.69	0.95
MC	STI Classic Var Tr-Mid Cap Eq Inst		B	(888) 784-3863	B / 7.9	-2.43	3.51	16.29 /75	19.52 /78	5.90 /60	0.23	1.36
SC ●	STI Classic Var Tr-Sm Cap Val Eq I		A+	(888) 784-3863	A- / 9.1	-3.31	11.04	25.17 /89	24.77 /91	17.15 /94	0.41	1.34
GI	Stonebridge Growth Fund	SBGFX	D+	(800) 639-3935	D- / 1.0	-3.80	-1.62	1.11 / 3	7.37 /12	-1.35 /11	0.00	2.22
AG	Stonebridge Small-Cap Growth Fund	SBAGX	D-	(800) 639-3935	C / 4.9	-8.28	7.65	2.68 / 6	14.33 /56	5.23 /56	0.00	2.90
BA	Strategic Partners Balanced Fund C	ACBCX	C-	(800) 778-8769	D- / 1.3	-0.68	1.01	3.54 / 9	6.91 /10	2.98 /37	0.72	2.15
BA ●	Strategic Partners Balanced Fund L	AACBX	C-	(800) 778-8769	E+ / 0.9	-0.51	1.18	3.98 /10	7.42 /12	3.49 /41	1.14	1.65
BA ●	Strategic Partners Balanced Fund M	ACBBX	C-	(800) 778-8769	E+ / 0.8	-0.68	0.94	3.47 / 9	6.87 /10	2.97 /37	0.72	2.15
BA ●	Strategic Partners Balanced Fund X	ACBZX	C-	(800) 778-8769	E+ / 0.8	-0.68	0.94	3.47 / 9	6.88 /10	2.97 /37	0.72	2.15
GR	Strategic Partners Cap Gr Fund A		D+	(800) 778-8769	D+ / 2.6	-4.22	-1.00	5.72 /19	11.47 /39	3.79 /44	0.00	1.55
GR	Strategic Partners Cap Gr Fund B		D	(800) 778-8769	D+ / 2.3	-4.40	-1.36	4.90 /15	10.68 /33	3.14 /38	0.00	2.30
GR	Strategic Partners Cap Gr Fund C	MARCX	D+	(800) 778-8769	C- / 3.0	-4.35	-1.30	4.91 /15	10.64 /32	3.12 /38	0.00	2.30
GR ●	Strategic Partners Cap Gr Fund L	MARAX	D	(800) 778-8769	D+ / 2.4	-4.24	-1.07	5.48 /18	11.21 /37	3.65 /42	0.00	1.80
GR ●	Strategic Partners Cap Gr Fund M	MARBX	D	(800) 778-8769	D / 2.2	-4.41	-1.36	4.91 /15	10.63 /32	3.12 /38	0.00	2.30
GR ●	Strategic Partners Cap Gr Fund X	MARZX	D	(800) 778-8769	D / 2.2	-4.35	-1.30	4.91 /15	10.65 /32	3.14 /38	0.00	2.30
GR	Strategic Partners Conc Gr Fund C	CCGSX	E+	(800) 778-8769	E / 0.5	-6.07	-1.61	4.65 /13	4.76 / 4	-5.75 / 2	0.00	2.25
GR ●	Strategic Partners Conc Gr Fund L	CAGSX	E+	(800) 778-8769	E / 0.3	-5.98	-1.30	5.21 /16	5.31 / 5	-5.25 / 2	0.00	1.75
GR ●	Strategic Partners Conc Gr Fund M	CBGSX	E	(800) 778-8769	E- / 0.2	-6.06	-1.61	4.63 /13	4.75 / 3	-5.74 / 2	0.00	2.25
GR ●	Strategic Partners Conc Gr Fund X	CZGSX	E	(800) 778-8769	E- / 0.2	-6.14	-1.61	4.63 /13	4.74 / 3	-5.74 / 2	0.00	2.25
AA	Strategic Partners Consv Alloc A	PCGAX	D-	(800) 778-8769	D- / 1.0	-1.51	0.68	3.27 / 8	7.83 /14	5.32 /57	2.53	1.44
AA	Strategic Partners Consv Alloc B	PBCFX	D-	(800) 778-8769	E+ / 0.8	-1.61	0.30	2.47 / 6	7.04 /10	4.56 /51	1.92	2.19
AA	Strategic Partners Consv Alloc C	PCCFX	D	(800) 778-8769	D- / 1.3	-1.61	0.30	2.56 / 6	7.04 /10	4.56 /51	1.92	2.19
AA	Strategic Partners Consv Alloc Z	PDCZX	D	(800) 778-8769	D / 2.0	-1.35	0.84	3.54 / 9	8.12 /16	5.61 /59	2.90	1.19
GR	Strategic Partners Core Val Fd C	SBVCX	C+	(800) 778-8769	C / 5.0	-0.23	4.92	9.60 /44	12.68 /47	6.67 /65	0.19	2.20
GR ●	Strategic Partners Core Val Fd L	SOVAX	C+	(800) 778-8769	C / 4.5	-0.15	5.16	10.14 /48	13.21 /50	7.17 /68	0.63	1.70

RISK			NET ASSETS		ASSET					BULL / BEAR		FUND MANAGER		MINIMUMS		LOADS	
	3 Year		NAV						Portfolio	Last Bull	Last Bear	Manager	Manager	Initial	Additional	Front	Back
Risk Rating/Pts	Standard Deviation	Beta	As of 6/30/06	Total $(Mil)	Cash %	Stocks %	Bonds %	Other %	Turnover Ratio	Market Return	Market Return	Quality Pct	Tenure (Years)	Purch. $	Purch. $	End Load	End Load
B / 8.3	8.3	1.05	12.04	54	4	95	0	1	31.0	71.7	-8.6	71	N/A	0	0	0.0	0.0
B+ / 9.9	2.9	0.55	11.05	1	9	20	70	1	29.0	N/A	N/A	50	N/A	2,000	1,000	4.8	1.0
B+ / 9.9	2.9	0.54	11.05	5	9	20	70	1	29.0	N/A	N/A	46	N/A	5,000	1,000	0.0	5.0
B+ / 9.9	2.9	0.55	11.04	3	9	20	70	1	29.0	N/A	N/A	54	N/A	0	0	0.0	0.0
B+ / 9.4	6.3	1.27	12.17	6	7	70	21	2	34.0	56.8	-6.3	71	N/A	2,000	1,000	5.8	1.0
B+ / 9.4	6.2	1.26	12.17	17	7	70	21	2	34.0	54.4	-6.3	67	N/A	5,000	1,000	0.0	5.0
B+ / 9.3	6.3	1.27	12.13	4	7	70	21	2	34.0	55.2	-6.3	67	N/A	5,000	1,000	0.0	1.0
B+ / 9.3	6.2	1.26	12.18	101	7	70	21	2	34.0	57.9	-6.3	74	N/A	0	0	0.0	0.0
B+ / 9.8	4.8	1.00	10.65	6	6	50	42	2	34.0	44.3	-4.3	67	N/A	2,000	1,000	5.8	1.0
B+ / 9.8	4.8	1.01	10.62	13	6	50	42	2	34.0	41.9	-4.3	60	N/A	5,000	1,000	0.0	5.0
B+ / 9.8	4.9	1.01	10.65	160	6	50	42	2	34.0	45.3	-4.4	68	N/A	0	0	0.0	0.0
U /	N/A	N/A	13.50	319	1	98	0	1	217.0	N/A	N/A	N/A	3	0	0	0.0	0.0
C+ / 5.7	10.0	0.89	12.96	6	2	97	0	1	169.0	98.7	-13.1	77	N/A	5,000	1,000	0.0	1.0
B / 8.2	10.1	0.89	13.04	261	2	97	0	1	169.0	103.6	-10.9	83	N/A	0	0	0.0	0.0
B- / 7.6	10.6	0.94	12.80	12	2	96	0	2	138.0	89.4	-10.1	56	N/A	2,000	1,000	5.8	1.0
B- / 7.5	10.5	0.94	11.84	12	2	96	0	2	138.0	85.8	-10.2	49	N/A	5,000	1,000	0.0	1.0
B- / 7.6	10.6	0.94	13.34	431	2	96	0	2	138.0	91.8	-10.0	61	N/A	0	0	0.0	0.0
B- / 7.8	8.0	1.01	24.58	1	1	98	0	1	82.0	39.6	-9.0	14	N/A	2,000	1,000	5.8	1.0
B- / 7.9	8.0	1.01	23.04	41	1	98	0	1	82.0	36.2	-9.3	11	N/A	5,000	1,000	0.0	1.0
B- / 7.9	8.1	1.02	24.75	64	1	98	0	1	82.0	40.8	-9.0	16	N/A	0	0	0.0	0.0
C / 4.3	15.7	1.05	20.94	60	2	97	0	1	98.0	126.2	-12.4	38	N/A	2,000	1,000	5.8	1.0
C- / 4.1	15.7	1.05	19.55	31	2	97	0	1	98.0	121.7	-12.6	33	N/A	5,000	1,000	0.0	1.0
C / 4.4	15.7	1.05	21.53	1,561	2	97	0	1	98.0	129.0	-12.4	42	N/A	25,000	0	0.0	0.0
C+ / 6.1	16.9	0.85	20.06	6	1	98	0	1	58.0	93.2	-7.1	61	3	2,000	1,000	5.8	1.0
C- / 4.1	17.8	0.86	19.67	42	1	98	0	1	58.0	87.9	-7.3	48	9	5,000	1,000	0.0	1.0
C- / 4.2	12.0	0.79	20.20	724	1	98	0	1	58.0	137.4	-7.1	99	9	25,000	0	0.0	0.0
C+ / 6.3	13.9	1.20	13.41	5	3	96	0	1	57.0	126.0	-9.2	13	N/A	0	0	0.0	0.0
B- / 7.6	7.7	0.94	15.70	37	0	99	0	1	100.0	72.8	-10.3	85	11	0	0	0.0	0.0
C+ / 6.5	11.2	0.94	13.95	14	1	98	0	1	115.0	102.0	-10.1	77	N/A	25,000	0	0.0	0.0
B- / 7.4	12.0	0.79	20.20	23	1	98	0	1	57.0	135.2	-6.7	98	N/A	500,000	1,000	0.0	0.0
B / 8.8	7.3	0.89	9.11	20	0	99	0	1	39.3	49.5	-6.1	29	22	1,000	100	0.0	2.0
C- / 3.1	16.3	1.55	10.41	7	0	99	0	1	116.2	100.2	-10.7	35	N/A	1,000	100	0.0	2.0
B+ / 9.7	5.2	1.06	13.60	12	0	62	39	0	196.0	36.7	-4.0	44	9	2,500	100	0.0	1.0
B+ / 9.4	5.2	1.05	13.61	13	0	62	39	0	196.0	38.9	-3.9	51	9	1,000	100	5.8	1.0
B+ / 9.7	5.2	1.05	13.60	46	0	62	39	0	196.0	36.7	-4.1	44	9	1,000	100	0.0	6.0
B+ / 9.7	5.2	1.05	13.59	11	0	62	39	0	196.0	36.7	-4.1	44	9	1,000	100	0.0	6.0
B- / 7.3	10.0	1.14	15.90	39	N/A	N/A	0	N/A	60.0	72.3	-8.8	44	8	1,000	100	5.5	1.0
B- / 7.3	10.0	1.14	15.20	10	N/A	N/A	0	N/A	60.0	68.6	-8.9	36	8	1,000	100	0.0	5.0
B- / 7.0	10.0	1.14	15.17	130	N/A	N/A	0	N/A	60.0	68.4	-8.9	36	8	2,500	100	0.0	1.0
B- / 7.0	10.0	1.14	15.79	89	N/A	N/A	0	N/A	60.0	71.1	-8.8	41	8	1,000	100	5.8	1.0
B- / 7.0	10.0	1.14	15.18	253	N/A	N/A	0	N/A	60.0	68.3	-8.9	36	8	1,000	100	0.0	6.0
B- / 7.0	10.0	1.14	15.16	46	N/A	N/A	0	N/A	60.0	68.5	-8.9	36	8	1,000	100	0.0	6.0
C+ / 6.6	9.9	1.15	10.36	37	0	100	0	0	16.0	44.7	-12.8	6	N/A	2,500	100	0.0	1.0
C+ / 6.5	10.0	1.16	12.11	42	0	100	0	0	16.0	47.2	-12.8	7	N/A	1,000	100	5.8	1.0
C+ / 6.1	9.9	1.15	10.39	127	0	100	0	0	16.0	44.8	-12.9	6	N/A	1,000	100	0.0	6.0
C+ / 6.1	10.0	1.16	10.40	24	0	100	0	0	16.0	44.8	-12.9	6	N/A	1,000	100	0.0	6.0
B- / 7.4	4.5	0.92	10.35	59	0	43	56	1	379.0	40.7	-1.7	64	N/A	1,000	100	5.5	1.0
B- / 7.6	4.4	0.91	10.32	95	0	43	56	1	379.0	37.5	-1.8	56	N/A	1,000	100	0.0	5.0
B- / 7.5	4.4	0.91	10.32	36	0	43	56	1	379.0	37.5	-1.8	56	N/A	2,500	100	0.0	1.0
B- / 7.5	4.5	0.92	10.37	5	0	43	56	1	379.0	41.9	-1.6	67	N/A	0	0	0.0	0.0
B / 8.3	8.0	0.99	13.21	9	1	98	0	1	27.0	72.0	-8.3	71	5	2,500	100	0.0	1.0
B / 8.3	8.0	1.00	13.24	6	1	98	0	1	27.0	74.6	-8.1	76	5	1,000	100	5.8	1.0

Data as of June 30, 2006

					PERFORMANCE							
	99 Pct = Best					Total Return % through 6/30/06					Incl. in Returns	
	0 Pct = Worst		Overall Weiss		Perfor-				Annualized			
Fund		Ticker	Investment		mance						Dividend	Expense
Type	Fund Name	Symbol	Rating	Phone	Rating/Pts	3 Mo	6 Mo	1Yr / Pct	3Yr / Pct	5Yr / Pct	Yield	Ratio
GR	● Strategic Partners Core Val Fd M	SVCBX	C+	(800) 778-8769	C- / 4.2	-0.23	4.85	9.51 /43	12.64 /47	6.67 /65	0.19	2.20
GR	● Strategic Partners Core Val Fd X		C+	(800) 778-8769	C / 4.3	-0.23	4.84	9.51 /43	12.68 /47	6.69 /65	0.19	2.20
IN	Strategic Partners Eqty Inc Fund C	AGOCX	C	(800) 778-8769	C- / 3.2	-1.16	2.85	7.04 /26	9.96 /27	1.10 /21	0.00	2.15
IN	● Strategic Partners Eqty Inc Fund L	AGOAX	C-	(800) 778-8769	D+ / 2.6	-1.06	3.12	7.62 /30	10.52 /31	1.63 /24	0.02	1.65
IN	● Strategic Partners Eqty Inc Fund M	AGOBX	C-	(800) 778-8769	D+ / 2.3	-1.16	2.77	7.11 /27	9.98 /27	1.12 /21	0.00	2.15
IN	● Strategic Partners Eqty Inc Fund X	AXGOX	C-	(800) 778-8769	D+ / 2.3	-1.23	2.78	7.05 /27	9.97 /27	1.12 /21	0.00	2.15
GR	Strategic Partners Growth Alloc A	PHGAX	C+	(800) 778-8769	C+ / 6.0	-1.91	4.55	13.14 /65	16.06 /64	5.80 /60	0.00	1.38
GR	Strategic Partners Growth Alloc B	PIHGX	C+	(800) 778-8769	C+ / 5.7	-2.10	4.22	12.22 /61	15.20 /60	4.99 /54	0.00	2.13
GR	Strategic Partners Growth Alloc C	PHGCX	C+	(800) 778-8769	C+ / 6.2	-2.10	4.22	12.22 /61	15.20 /60	4.99 /54	0.00	2.13
GR	Strategic Partners Growth Alloc Z	PDHZX	B-	(800) 778-8769	C+ / 6.9	-1.88	4.70	13.41 /66	16.37 /65	6.08 /62	0.00	1.13
FO	Strategic Partners Internatl Val A	PISAX	B+	(800) 778-8769	B+ / 8.5	0.20	11.41	28.48 /93	21.49 /84	6.89 /66	1.49	1.57
FO	Strategic Partners Internatl Val B	PISBX	B+	(800) 778-8769	B+ / 8.3	0.00	10.94	27.42 /92	20.55 /81	6.07 /62	0.86	2.37
FO	Strategic Partners Internatl Val C	PCISX	B+	(800) 778-8769	B+ / 8.6	-0.04	10.88	27.39 /92	20.55 /81	6.06 /61	0.86	2.37
FO	Strategic Partners Internatl Val Z	PISZX	A-	(800) 778-8769	B+ / 8.9	0.16	11.40	28.69 /93	21.75 /85	7.13 /67	1.78	1.37
FO	Strategic Partners Intl Gr Fund A		B+	(800) 778-8769	B / 7.7	-3.95	4.64	23.25 /86	21.30 /83	5.70 /59	0.00	1.80
FO	Strategic Partners Intl Gr Fund B		B+	(800) 778-8769	B / 7.6	-4.14	4.23	22.36 /85	20.39 /81	5.01 /54	0.00	2.60
FO	Strategic Partners Intl Gr Fund C	WBCIX	C+	(800) 778-8769	B / 7.9	-4.13	4.29	22.38 /85	20.40 /81	5.03 /54	0.00	2.60
FO	● Strategic Partners Intl Gr Fund L	WBAIX	C+	(800) 778-8769	B / 7.7	-3.97	4.58	23.06 /86	21.07 /83	5.57 /58	0.00	2.10
FO	● Strategic Partners Intl Gr Fund M	WBBIX	C+	(800) 778-8769	B- / 7.5	-4.08	4.30	22.36 /85	20.39 /81	5.01 /54	0.00	2.60
FO	● Strategic Partners Intl Gr Fund X	WBZIX	C+	(800) 778-8769	B- / 7.5	-4.08	4.30	22.34 /85	20.41 /81	5.03 /54	0.00	2.60
GR	Strategic Partners Large Cap Val A	PLVAX	B-	(800) 778-8769	C+ / 5.9	0.29	4.76	8.60 /38	16.24 /64	7.96 /71	0.51	1.41
GR	Strategic Partners Large Cap Val B	TLCBX	C+	(800) 778-8769	C+ / 5.6	0.15	4.40	7.67 /30	15.37 /61	7.14 /67	0.00	2.21
GR	Strategic Partners Large Cap Val C	TLCCX	B	(800) 778-8769	C+ / 6.1	0.07	4.40	7.67 /30	15.36 /61	7.14 /67	0.00	2.21
GR	Strategic Partners Lrg Cp Core C	MCIFX	D	(800) 778-8769	D- / 1.5	-3.28	-0.84	4.06 /11	7.76 /14	0.62 /18	0.09	2.00
GR	● Strategic Partners Lrg Cp Core L	MAIFX	D-	(800) 778-8769	D- / 1.1	-3.20	-0.62	4.58 /13	8.27 /16	1.07 /21	0.56	1.50
GR	● Strategic Partners Lrg Cp Core M	MBIFX	D	(800) 778-8769	E+ / 0.9	-3.28	-0.84	4.17 /11	7.76 /14	0.60 /18	0.09	2.00
GR	● Strategic Partners Lrg Cp Core X	MXIFX	D	(800) 778-8769	E+ / 0.9	-3.29	-0.95	3.95 /10	7.70 /13	0.56 /18	0.09	2.00
MC	Strategic Partners Mid Cap Gr A		D	(800) 778-8769	D+ / 2.3	-7.50	-1.23	5.48 /18	11.33 /38	-1.81 / 9	0.00	1.55
MC	Strategic Partners Mid Cap Gr B		D-	(800) 778-8769	D / 2.1	-7.54	-1.69	4.48 /13	10.60 /32	-2.36 / 7	0.00	2.40
MC	Strategic Partners Mid Cap Gr C	GCMGX	D-	(800) 778-8769	D+ / 2.7	-7.57	-1.49	4.74 /14	10.49 /31	-2.44 / 7	0.00	2.40
MC	● Strategic Partners Mid Cap Gr L	GAMGX	D-	(800) 778-8769	D / 2.1	-7.38	-1.45	5.07 /15	10.98 /35	-1.97 / 8	0.00	1.90
MC	● Strategic Partners Mid Cap Gr M	GBMGX	D-	(800) 778-8769	D / 1.9	-7.55	-1.69	4.73 /14	10.57 /32	-2.40 / 7	0.00	2.40
MC	● Strategic Partners Mid Cap Gr X		D-	(800) 778-8769	D / 1.9	-7.57	-1.49	4.74 /14	10.49 /31	-2.44 / 7	0.00	2.40
MC	Strategic Partners Mid Cap Val Fd C	NCBVX	C-	(800) 778-8769	B- / 7.0	-3.25	1.64	9.70 /45	18.31 /74	9.73 /79	0.00	2.35
MC	Strategic Partners Mid Cap Val Fd L	NABVX	C-	(800) 778-8769	C+ / 6.7	-3.15	1.92	10.19 /48	18.87 /76	10.27 /81	0.00	1.85
MC	Strategic Partners Mid Cap Val Fd M	NBBVX	D+	(800) 778-8769	C+ / 6.6	-3.25	1.65	9.63 /44	18.29 /74	9.74 /80	0.00	2.35
MC	Strategic Partners Mid Cap Val Fd X	NBVZX	C-	(800) 778-8769	C+ / 6.7	-3.02	2.14	10.14 /48	18.46 /74	9.83 /80	0.00	2.35
AA	Strategic Partners Moderate Alloc A	PAMGX	C-	(800) 778-8769	C- / 3.2	-1.40	2.91	8.14 /34	11.56 /40	5.61 /59	1.46	1.32
AA	Strategic Partners Moderate Alloc B	DMGBX	C-	(800) 778-8769	D+ / 2.9	-1.49	2.49	7.44 /29	10.75 /33	4.84 /53	0.83	2.07
AA	Strategic Partners Moderate Alloc C	PIMGX	C-	(800) 778-8769	C- / 3.6	-1.49	2.49	7.36 /28	10.75 /33	4.84 /53	0.83	2.07
AA	Strategic Partners Moderate Alloc Z	PDMZX	C	(800) 778-8769	C / 4.5	-1.23	3.08	8.48 /37	11.86 /42	5.88 /60	1.76	1.07
GR	Strategic Partners New Era Gr A	SNGAX	D	(800) 778-8769	C / 5.1	-8.21	-3.07	11.56 /57	15.70 /62	0.87 /20	0.00	1.68
GR	Strategic Partners New Era Gr B	SNGBX	D	(800) 778-8769	C / 4.8	-8.33	-3.30	10.69 /52	14.84 /58	0.11 /16	0.00	2.43
GR	Strategic Partners New Era Gr C	SNGCX	D	(800) 778-8769	C / 5.4	-8.33	-3.30	10.69 /52	14.84 /58	0.11 /16	0.00	2.43
GR	Strategic Partners New Era Gr Z	SNGZX	D+	(800) 778-8769	C+ / 6.2	-8.19	-2.82	11.90 /59	16.03 /64	1.13 /21	0.00	1.43
RE	Strategic Partners Real Est Sec A	PURAX	B-	(800) 778-8769	A / 9.5	-1.15	13.34	23.61 /87	31.50 /96	23.87 /98	1.06	1.40
RE	Strategic Partners Real Est Sec B	PURBX	B-	(800) 778-8769	A / 9.5	-1.33	12.90	22.69 /85	30.54 /96	22.94 /98	0.50	2.15
RE	Strategic Partners Real Est Sec C		B	(800) 778-8769	A+ / 9.6	-1.33	12.90	22.69 /85	30.54 /96	22.94 /98	0.50	2.15
RE	Strategic Partners Real Est Sec Z		B	(800) 778-8769	A+ / 9.7	-1.06	13.51	23.94 /87	31.85 /97	24.19 /98	1.31	1.15
SC	Strategic Partners Sm Cap Gr C	DCAMX	E+	(800) 778-8769	D+ / 2.4	-7.80	2.70	6.22 /22	9.36 /23	-1.59 /10	0.00	2.40
SC	● Strategic Partners Sm Cap Gr L	DAMAX	E	(800) 778-8769	D / 1.9	-7.72	2.80	6.82 /25	9.94 /27	-1.08 /12	0.00	1.90
SC	● Strategic Partners Sm Cap Gr M	DAMBX	E	(800) 778-8769	D / 1.7	-7.80	2.70	6.22 /22	9.36 /23	-1.55 /10	0.00	2.40

● Denotes fund is closed to new investors
* Denotes fund is included in Section II

www.WeissRatings.com

RISK			NET ASSETS		ASSET				BULL / BEAR		FUND MANAGER		MINIMUMS		LOADS	
	3 Year		NAV						Last Bull	Last Bear	Manager	Manager	Initial	Additional	Front	Back
Risk Rating/Pts	Standard Deviation	Beta	As of 6/30/06	Total $(Mil)	Cash %	Stocks %	Bonds %	Other %	Portfolio Turnover Ratio	Market Return	Market Return	Quality Pct	Tenure (Years)	Purch. $	Purch. $	End Load	End Load
B /8.3	8.0	0.99	13.20	19	1	98	0	1	27.0	72.0	-8.3	71	5	1,000	100	0.0	6.0
B /8.4	8.0	0.99	13.21	4	1	98	0	1	27.0	72.0	-8.3	71	5	1,000	100	0.0	6.0
B /8.6	7.3	0.90	14.44	47	1	98	0	1	54.0	63.2	-8.4	52	N/A	2,500	100	0.0	1.0
B /8.5	7.3	0.90	14.87	39	1	98	0	1	54.0	65.8	-8.3	59	N/A	1,000	100	5.8	1.0
B /8.6	7.2	0.90	14.46	122	1	98	0	1	54.0	63.2	-8.4	53	N/A	1,000	100	0.0	6.0
B /8.6	7.2	0.90	14.43	34	1	98	0	1	54.0	63.2	-8.4	53	N/A	1,000	100	0.0	6.0
B- /7.0	9.5	1.15	13.33	100	0	100	0	0	200.0	92.9	-10.0	85	N/A	1,000	100	5.5	1.0
C+ /6.9	9.5	1.15	12.60	101	0	100	0	0	200.0	88.4	-10.2	79	N/A	1,000	100	0.0	5.0
C+ /6.9	9.5	1.16	12.60	89	0	100	0	0	200.0	88.3	-10.0	78	N/A	2,500	100	0.0	1.0
B- /7.0	9.5	1.16	13.60	8	0	100	0	0	200.0	94.5	-9.9	86	N/A	0	0	0.0	0.0
C+ /6.6	10.2	0.97	25.09	70	0	99	0	1	24.0	120.4	-13.5	34	N/A	1,000	100	5.5	1.0
C+ /6.6	10.2	0.97	24.34	19	0	99	0	1	24.0	115.0	-13.7	28	N/A	1,000	100	0.0	5.0
C+ /6.6	10.2	0.98	24.36	16	0	99	0	1	24.0	115.2	-13.7	28	N/A	2,500	100	0.0	1.0
C+ /6.6	10.2	0.98	25.21	167	0	99	0	1	24.0	122.0	-13.5	36	N/A	0	0	0.0	0.0
B- /7.2	11.8	1.11	15.80	24	1	98	0	1	87.0	125.8	-8.6	15	N/A	1,000	100	5.5	1.0
B- /7.2	11.8	1.11	15.27	4	1	98	0	1	87.0	120.7	-8.7	12	N/A	1,000	100	0.0	5.0
C /5.5	11.8	1.11	15.31	48	1	98	0	1	87.0	120.9	-8.7	12	N/A	2,500	100	0.0	1.0
C+ /5.6	11.8	1.11	15.74	40	1	98	0	1	87.0	124.5	-8.6	14	N/A	1,000	100	5.8	1.0
C /5.5	11.8	1.11	15.27	102	1	98	0	1	87.0	120.8	-8.8	12	N/A	1,000	100	0.0	6.0
C+ /5.6	11.8	1.11	15.28	30	1	98	0	1	87.0	120.7	-8.6	12	N/A	1,000	100	0.0	6.0
B- /7.9	8.2	1.00	13.86	32	29	70	0	1	47.0	92.7	-9.5	92	N/A	1,000	100	5.5	1.0
B- /7.9	8.3	1.01	13.53	25	29	70	0	1	47.0	88.1	-9.7	88	N/A	1,000	100	0.0	5.0
B- /7.9	8.3	1.01	13.53	22	29	70	0	1	47.0	88.1	-9.7	88	N/A	2,500	100	0.0	1.0
B- /7.7	8.2	1.06	9.44	22	N/A	100	0	N/A	29.0	50.3	-8.9	22	N/A	2,500	100	0.0	1.0
B- /7.5	8.2	1.06	9.69	17	N/A	100	0	N/A	29.0	52.3	-8.8	25	N/A	1,000	100	5.8	1.0
B- /7.7	8.2	1.06	9.44	61	N/A	100	0	N/A	29.0	50.3	-8.9	21	N/A	1,000	100	0.0	6.0
B- /7.7	8.3	1.06	9.41	7	N/A	100	0	N/A	29.0	50.1	-8.9	21	N/A	1,000	100	0.0	6.0
C+ /6.5	11.1	0.98	4.81	13	N/A	100	0	N/A	98.0	75.8	-10.2	11	N/A	1,000	100	5.5	1.0
C+ /6.4	11.1	0.98	4.66	2	N/A	100	0	N/A	98.0	72.5	-10.3	9	N/A	1,000	100	0.0	5.0
C+ /5.9	11.0	0.97	4.64	18	N/A	100	0	N/A	98.0	71.8	-10.5	9	N/A	2,500	100	0.0	1.0
C+ /5.9	11.0	0.97	4.77	20	N/A	100	0	N/A	98.0	74.2	-10.1	10	N/A	1,000	100	5.8	1.0
C+ /5.9	11.0	0.97	4.65	50	N/A	100	0	N/A	98.0	71.6	-10.2	9	N/A	1,000	100	0.0	6.0
C+ /5.9	11.0	0.97	4.64	10	N/A	100	0	N/A	98.0	71.8	-10.2	9	N/A	1,000	100	0.0	6.0
C- /3.7	11.6	0.99	16.69	86	1	98	0	1	80.0	101.2	-6.4	59	8	2,500	100	1.0	1.0
C- /4.0	11.5	0.99	17.53	42	1	98	0	1	80.0	104.3	-6.2	65	8	1,000	100	5.5	1.0
C- /3.7	11.6	0.99	16.68	122	1	98	0	1	80.0	101.1	-6.3	59	8	1,000	100	0.0	6.0
C- /3.7	11.5	0.99	16.70	23	1	98	0	1	80.0	101.8	-6.4	61	8	1,000	100	0.0	6.0
B- /7.7	6.4	1.27	12.01	136	0	69	30	1	285.0	62.7	-5.0	79	N/A	1,000	100	5.5	1.0
B- /7.8	6.4	1.26	11.93	172	0	69	30	1	285.0	58.8	-5.3	73	N/A	1,000	100	0.0	5.0
B- /7.8	6.4	1.26	11.93	123	0	69	30	1	285.0	58.9	-5.3	73	N/A	2,500	100	0.0	1.0
B- /7.5	6.4	1.26	12.05	14	0	69	30	1	285.0	63.9	-5.0	82	N/A	0	0	0.0	0.0
C- /4.1	15.4	1.67	9.17	15	0	99	0	1	116.0	108.8	-9.6	36	1	1,000	100	5.5	1.0
C- /4.0	15.4	1.67	8.80	35	0	99	0	1	116.0	104.0	-9.8	30	1	1,000	100	0.0	5.0
C- /4.0	15.4	1.67	8.80	24	0	99	0	1	116.0	104.0	-9.8	30	1	2,500	100	0.0	1.0
C- /4.1	15.5	1.68	9.31	4	0	99	0	1	116.0	110.6	-9.6	38	1	0	0	0.0	0.0
C- /4.2	15.9	0.95	24.61	130	3	96	0	1	35.0	163.2	2.6	97	N/A	1,000	100	5.5	1.0
C- /4.2	15.9	0.95	24.48	22	3	96	0	1	35.0	157.2	2.4	96	N/A	1,000	100	0.0	5.0
C /4.9	15.9	0.95	24.48	25	3	96	0	1	35.0	157.1	2.4	96	N/A	2,500	100	0.0	1.0
C /4.9	15.9	0.95	24.67	28	3	96	0	1	35.0	165.2	2.8	97	N/A	0	0	0.0	0.0
C- /4.1	16.5	1.10	5.32	19	2	97	0	1	288.0	75.7	-10.0	2	N/A	2,500	100	0.0	1.0
C- /4.2	16.4	1.09	5.50	14	2	97	0	1	288.0	78.7	-9.8	3	N/A	1,000	100	5.8	1.0
C- /4.1	16.3	1.09	5.32	36	2	97	0	1	288.0	75.7	-10.0	2	N/A	1,000	100	0.0	6.0

					PERFORMANCE								
	99 Pct = Best 0 Pct = Worst			Overall Weiss Investment Rating		Perfor- mance Rating/Pts	Total Return % through 6/30/06					Incl. in Returns	
										Annualized		Dividend	Expense
Fund Type	Fund Name	Ticker Symbol	Phone				3 Mo	6 Mo	1Yr / Pct	3Yr / Pct	5Yr / Pct	Yield	Ratio
SC	● Strategic Partners Sm Cap Gr X	DAMZX	(800) 778-8769	E		D / 1.7	-7.79	2.70	6.21 /22	9.34 /23	-1.55 /10	0.00	2.40
SC	Strategic Partners Small Cap Val A	PZVAX	(800) 778-8769	C+		B / 8.1	-1.56	8.52	11.13 /54	22.47 /86	14.64 /91	0.00	2.31
SC	Strategic Partners Small Cap Val B	PZVBX	(800) 778-8769	C		B / 7.9	-1.78	8.08	10.32 /49	21.54 /84	13.80 /90	0.00	2.20
SC	Strategic Partners Small Cap Val C	PZVCX	(800) 778-8769	C+		B / 8.2	-1.78	8.08	10.32 /49	21.54 /84	13.80 /90	0.00	2.20
SC	● Strategic Partners Small Cap Val L		(800) 778-8769	U		U /	-1.61	8.46	--	--	--	0.00	1.70
SC	● Strategic Partners Small Cap Val M		(800) 778-8769	U		U /	-1.78	8.22	--	--	--	0.00	2.20
GR	Stratton Growth Fund	STRGX	(800) 634-5726	B+		B+ / 8.3	-3.19	2.95	12.58 /62	22.21 /86	10.73 /83	0.24	1.08
RE	Stratton Monthly Dividend Reit Shs	STMDX	(800) 634-5726	C		B- / 7.5	-2.06	11.53	11.06 /54	18.57 /75	14.87 /92	4.56	0.95
SC	Stratton Small-Cap Value Fund	STSCX	(800) 634-5726	A		A- / 9.1	-3.18	10.55	16.21 /75	25.53 /92	16.72 /94	0.00	1.28
IN	Summit Apex Everest I	SAEVX	(888) 259-7565	B-		C+ / 6.5	1.46	7.29	13.14 /65	14.72 /57	6.69 /65	0.98	0.97
GR	Summit Apex Nasdaq 100 Index I	SANIX	(888) 259-7565	D-		D+ / 2.8	-7.57	-4.31	5.37 /17	10.46 /31	-2.80 / 6	0.34	0.90
GR	SunAmerica 2010 High Watermark A	HWIAX	(800) 858-8850	U		U /	-1.64	-0.39	0.28 / 2	--		1.58	1.65
GR	SunAmerica 2010 High Watermark C	HWICX	(800) 858-8850	U		U /	-1.84	-0.78	-0.41 / 1	--	--	1.08	2.30
BA	SunAmerica Bal Assets A	SBAAX	(800) 858-8850	D-		E / 0.3	-1.58	0.24	2.82 / 7	4.95 / 4	-0.66 /13	1.60	1.62
BA	SunAmerica Bal Assets B	SBABX	(800) 858-8850	D		E / 0.3	-1.77	-0.14	2.10 / 5	4.24 / 3	-1.32 /11	0.98	2.27
BA	SunAmerica Bal Assets C	SBDTX	(800) 858-8850	D		E / 0.4	-1.69	-0.06	2.17 / 5	4.26 / 3	-1.31 /11	0.98	2.26
GR	SunAmerica Blue Chip Growth A	SVLAX	(800) 858-8850	E+		E / 0.3	-4.68	-2.65	2.45 / 5	5.57 / 5	-3.42 / 4	0.00	1.59
GR	SunAmerica Blue Chip Growth B	SVLBX	(800) 858-8850	E+		E / 0.3	-4.83	-3.04	1.75 / 4	4.83 / 4	-4.12 / 3	0.00	2.32
GR	SunAmerica Blue Chip Growth C	NGECX	(800) 858-8850	E+		E / 0.4	-4.85	-3.05	1.68 / 4	4.71 / 3	-4.20 / 3	0.00	2.49
BA	SunAmerica Foc Balanced Strat A	FBAAX	(800) 858-8850	D+		D- / 1.3	-2.76	0.63	6.31 /22	8.56 /18	--	2.34	0.19
BA	SunAmerica Foc Balanced Strat B	FBABX	(800) 858-8850	D+		D- / 1.3	-2.93	0.31	5.62 /18	7.85 /14	--	1.83	0.84
BA	SunAmerica Foc Balanced Strat C	FBACX	(800) 858-8850	C-		D / 1.8	-2.86	0.37	5.68 /19	7.86 /14	--	1.83	0.82
GI	SunAmerica Foc Div Strategy A	FDSAX	(800) 858-8850	D		D+ / 2.6	-4.10	4.95	11.66 /58	10.75 /33	6.00 /61	0.92	0.95
GI	SunAmerica Foc Div Strategy B	FDSBX	(800) 858-8850	D		D+ / 2.6	-4.26	4.66	11.00 /53	10.03 /28	5.31 /56	0.67	1.60
GI	SunAmerica Foc Div Strategy C	FDSTX	(800) 858-8850	D+		C- / 3.1	-4.26	4.66	11.00 /53	10.03 /28	5.31 /56	0.67	1.60
GR	SunAmerica Foc Equity Strat A	FESAX	(800) 858-8850	C-		C- / 3.4	-3.57	1.58	9.89 /46	12.00 /42	--	1.57	0.19
GR	SunAmerica Foc Equity Strat B	FESBX	(800) 858-8850	C-		C- / 3.3	-3.76	1.21	9.14 /41	11.27 /38	--	1.07	0.86
GR	SunAmerica Foc Equity Strat C	FESTX	(800) 858-8850	C		C- / 3.9	-3.71	1.26	9.20 /41	11.31 /38	--	1.07	0.83
GI	SunAmerica Foc Fix Inc&Eq Strat A	FFEAX	(800) 858-8850	D+		E / 0.3	-1.63	-0.08	3.67 / 9	5.08 / 4	--	3.31	0.22
GI	SunAmerica Foc Fix Inc&Eq Strat B		(800) 858-8850	D+		E / 0.3	-1.95	-0.42	2.84 / 7	4.37 / 3	--	2.85	0.90
GI	SunAmerica Foc Fix Inc&Eq Strat C	FFICX	(800) 858-8850	C-		E / 0.5	-1.80	-0.41	2.99 / 7	4.35 / 3	--	2.85	0.89
GI	SunAmerica Foc Gr & Inc A	FOGAX	(800) 858-8850	D		D- / 1.4	-1.33	3.01	9.44 /43	8.18 /16	3.53 /42	0.56	1.70
GI	SunAmerica Foc Gr & Inc B	FOGBX	(800) 858-8850	D-		D- / 1.4	-1.46	2.67	8.75 /38	7.50 /12	2.87 /36	0.00	2.35
GI	SunAmerica Foc Gr & Inc C	FOGTX	(800) 858-8850	D		D / 1.8	-1.46	2.74	8.75 /38	7.51 /12	2.87 /36	0.00	2.35
FO	SunAmerica Foc Intl Eqty A	SFINX	(800) 858-8850	A		B / 7.9	-0.60	8.95	24.31 /88	20.15 /80	--	1.32	1.81
FO	SunAmerica Foc Intl Eqty B		(800) 858-8850	A		B / 7.9	-0.76	8.64	23.52 /87	19.37 /77	--	0.85	2.38
FO	SunAmerica Foc Intl Eqty C	FINTX	(800) 858-8850	A		B / 8.1	-0.82	8.59	23.50 /87	19.33 /77	--	0.85	2.41
GR	SunAmerica Foc Lrg-Cp Gr A	SSFAX	(800) 858-8850	E		E / 0.3	-7.50	-6.12	3.76 /10	6.34 / 8	0.96 /20	0.00	1.47
GR	SunAmerica Foc Lrg-Cp Gr B	SSFBX	(800) 858-8850	E		E / 0.3	-7.68	-6.44	3.08 / 8	5.62 / 5	0.30 /17	0.00	2.14
GR	SunAmerica Foc Lrg-Cp Gr C	SSFTX	(800) 858-8850	E		E / 0.5	-7.67	-6.43	3.14 / 8	5.64 / 6	0.31 /17	0.00	2.12
GR	SunAmerica Foc Lrg-Cp Val A	SSLAX	(800) 858-8850	C-		D+ / 2.9	-0.52	4.32	12.55 /62	10.42 /30	3.94 /45	0.27	1.65
GR	SunAmerica Foc Lrg-Cp Val B	SELBX	(800) 858-8850	C-		D+ / 2.8	-0.73	3.94	11.72 /58	9.65 /25	3.24 /39	0.00	2.37
GR	SunAmerica Foc Lrg-Cp Val C	SSLTX	(800) 858-8850	C		C- / 3.3	-0.67	3.99	11.77 /58	9.66 /25	3.26 /39	0.00	2.37
GR	SunAmerica Foc Multi-Asset Strat A	FASAX	(800) 858-8850	C		C- / 3.2	-2.65	3.09	8.93 /40	11.62 /40	--	1.62	0.19
GR	SunAmerica Foc Multi-Asset Strat B	FMABX	(800) 858-8850	C		C- / 3.2	-2.78	2.77	8.22 /35	10.88 /34	--	1.15	0.84
GR	SunAmerica Foc Multi-Asset Strat C	FMATX	(800) 858-8850	C		C- / 3.7	-2.83	2.77	8.22 /35	10.88 /34	--	1.15	0.82
AG	SunAmerica Foc Multi-Cp Gr A	SSAAX	(800) 858-8850	C-		C / 4.7	-8.67	-1.99	5.79 /19	15.79 /63	3.97 /46	0.00	1.72
AG	SunAmerica Foc Multi-Cp Gr B	SSABX	(800) 858-8850	C-		C / 4.6	-8.83	-2.32	5.09 /16	15.01 /59	3.29 /39	0.00	2.37
AG	SunAmerica Foc Multi-Cp Gr C	SSACX	(800) 858-8850	C-		C / 5.1	-8.79	-2.27	5.14 /16	15.04 /59	3.30 /40	0.00	2.37
GR	SunAmerica Foc Multi-Cp Val A	SFVAX	(800) 858-8850	C+		C+ / 6.3	2.04	9.99	12.67 /63	15.99 /63	5.93 /61	0.00	1.70
GR	SunAmerica Foc Multi-Cp Val B	SFDBX	(800) 858-8850	C+		C+ / 6.2	1.92	9.68	12.00 /60	15.27 /60	5.26 /56	0.00	2.35
GR	SunAmerica Foc Multi-Cp Val C	SFVTX	(800) 858-8850	B-		C+ / 6.6	1.93	9.64	12.02 /60	15.26 /60	5.25 /56	0.00	2.35

● Denotes fund is closed to new investors
* Denotes fund is included in Section II

RISK Rating/Pts	3 Year Standard Deviation	Beta	NAV As of 6/30/06	Total $(Mil)	Cash %	Stocks %	Bonds %	Other %	Portfolio Turnover Ratio	Last Bull Market Return	Last Bear Market Return	Manager Quality Pct	Manager Tenure (Years)	Initial Purch. $	Additional Purch. $	Front End Load	Back End Load
C- /4.1	16.3	1.09	5.33	9	2	97	0	1	288.0	75.5	-9.9	2	N/A	1,000	100	0.0	6.0
C /4.6	11.6	0.76	17.71	106	2	97	0	1	106.0	128.9	-8.1	97	N/A	1,000	100	5.5	1.0
C- /4.2	11.6	0.76	16.58	33	2	97	0	1	106.0	123.5	-8.3	96	N/A	1,000	100	0.0	5.0
C- /4.2	11.6	0.76	16.58	102	2	97	0	1	106.0	123.5	-8.3	96	N/A	2,500	100	0.0	1.0
U /	N/A	N/A	17.70	26	2	97	0	1	106.0	N/A	N/A	N/A	N/A	1,000	100	0.0	1.0
U /	N/A	N/A	16.58	67	2	97	0	1	106.0	N/A	N/A	N/A	N/A	1,000	100	0.0	6.0
C+ /6.7	13.4	1.44	44.60	126	N/A	N/A	0	N/A	29.2	128.4	-7.7	95	34	2,000	100	0.0	1.5
C- /4.1	15.8	0.95	36.59	147	4	95	0	1	5.4	87.6	-1.4	22	N/A	2,000	100	0.0	1.5
C+ /6.8	14.6	0.92	47.56	523	6	93	0	1	15.5	154.3	-6.6	97	N/A	2,000	100	0.0	1.5
B- /7.2	7.3	0.90	60.60	73	5	94	0	1	58.0	86.7	-10.7	90	7	250,000	0	0.0	0.0
C /4.9	15.2	1.73	20.65	16	0	100	0	0	10.6	72.6	-9.7	7	N/A	250,000	0	0.0	0.0
U /	N/A	N/A	10.17	131	30	0	69	1	4.3	N/A	N/A	N/A	N/A	500	100	5.8	0.0
U /	N/A	N/A	10.13	135	30	0	69	1	4.3	N/A	N/A	N/A	N/A	500	100	0.0	1.0
B /8.0	5.0	1.04	13.68	129	0	64	34	2	67.0	27.6	-5.5	28	11	500	100	5.8	1.0
B /8.3	5.0	1.05	13.63	23	0	64	34	2	67.0	25.0	-5.7	23	11	500	100	0.0	4.0
B /8.6	5.0	1.04	13.66	16	0	64	34	2	67.0	25.0	-5.7	23	11	500	100	0.0	1.0
C+ /6.4	9.1	1.12	15.07	50	N/A	N/A	0	N/A	51.0	40.0	-10.2	9	N/A	500	100	5.8	1.0
C+ /6.3	9.2	1.13	13.41	19	N/A	N/A	0	N/A	51.0	36.9	-10.4	7	11	500	100	0.0	4.0
C+ /6.6	9.2	1.12	13.33	5	N/A	N/A	0	N/A	51.0	36.5	-10.5	7	N/A	500	100	0.0	1.0
B /8.9	6.7	1.32	16.01	144	0	67	32	1	9.8	49.8	-4.1	47	4	500	100	5.8	1.0
B /8.6	6.7	1.32	15.99	113	0	67	32	1	9.8	46.8	-4.2	39	4	500	100	0.0	4.0
B /8.6	6.7	1.33	16.02	213	0	67	32	1	9.8	46.9	-4.2	39	4	500	100	0.0	1.0
C+ /6.8	9.5	0.99	13.79	62	N/A	100	0	N/A	310.0	65.4	-12.9	51	N/A	500	100	5.8	1.0
C+ /6.8	9.5	0.99	13.71	44	N/A	100	0	N/A	310.0	62.0	-13.0	43	N/A	500	100	0.0	4.0
C+ /6.8	9.5	0.99	13.71	89	N/A	100	0	N/A	310.0	61.9	-13.0	43	N/A	500	100	0.0	1.0
B /8.0	9.9	1.21	18.64	204	0	100	0	0	22.0	75.8	-8.2	43	4	500	100	5.8	1.0
B /8.0	10.0	1.21	18.41	125	0	100	0	0	22.0	72.0	-8.3	36	4	500	100	0.0	4.0
B /8.0	9.9	1.21	18.42	322	0	100	0	0	22.0	72.3	-8.4	36	4	500	100	0.0	1.0
B+ /9.9	4.4	0.40	13.60	22	0	36	63	1	37.6	28.2	-0.5	47	4	500	100	5.8	1.0
B+ /9.9	4.4	0.40	13.59	15	0	36	63	1	37.6	25.4	-0.8	39	4	500	100	0.0	4.0
B+ /9.9	4.3	0.39	13.59	26	0	36	63	1	37.6	25.4	-0.9	40	4	500	100	0.0	1.0
B- /7.3	9.0	1.02	17.81	166	2	92	0	6	74.0	60.2	-7.6	26	9	500	100	5.8	1.0
B- /7.2	9.0	1.02	16.91	64	2	92	0	6	74.0	57.0	-7.9	22	9	500	100	0.0	4.0
B- /7.2	9.0	1.02	16.90	96	2	92	0	6	74.0	56.9	-7.8	22	9	500	100	0.0	1.0
B /8.0	9.8	0.92	19.96	294	9	90	0	1	280.0	110.7	-10.1	34	N/A	500	100	5.8	1.0
B- /7.9	9.9	0.92	19.50	18	9	90	0	1	280.0	106.5	-10.2	29	N/A	500	100	0.0	4.0
B- /7.9	9.9	0.92	19.46	41	9	90	0	1	280.0	106.4	-10.2	29	N/A	500	100	0.0	1.0
C /5.4	12.4	1.40	17.64	273	3	96	0	1	78.1	55.2	-8.3	5	8	500	100	5.8	1.0
C /5.3	12.4	1.40	16.72	347	3	96	0	1	78.1	52.0	-8.4	3	8	500	100	0.0	4.0
C /5.3	12.4	1.40	16.73	80	3	96	0	1	78.1	52.0	-8.4	3	8	500	100	0.0	1.0
B /8.3	8.9	0.90	17.14	484	2	97	0	1	62.0	69.1	-9.3	58	9	500	100	5.8	1.0
B /8.3	8.9	0.90	16.37	32	2	97	0	1	62.0	65.5	-9.5	48	9	500	100	0.0	4.0
B /8.3	8.9	0.90	16.40	69	2	97	0	1	62.0	65.5	-9.4	49	9	500	100	0.0	1.0
B /8.7	8.1	0.98	18.34	261	0	83	16	1	1.2	66.8	-6.3	63	4	500	100	5.8	1.0
B /8.7	8.1	0.98	18.20	156	0	83	16	1	1.2	63.4	-6.4	54	4	500	100	0.0	4.0
B /8.7	8.1	0.98	18.20	403	0	83	16	1	1.2	63.4	-6.4	55	4	500	100	0.0	1.0
C+ /5.8	12.7	1.34	22.65	287	10	89	0	1	40.0	103.7	-10.3	70	10	500	100	5.8	1.0
C+ /5.7	12.6	1.34	21.07	77	10	89	0	1	40.0	99.7	-10.5	63	10	500	100	0.0	4.0
C+ /5.7	12.7	1.33	21.07	62	10	89	0	1	40.0	99.7	-10.5	63	10	500	100	0.0	1.0
B- /7.2	9.9	1.09	22.02	241	1	98	0	1	10.0	81.4	-8.5	87	7	500	100	5.8	1.0
B- /7.1	9.9	1.09	21.18	161	1	98	0	1	10.0	77.7	-8.6	83	7	500	100	0.0	4.0
B- /7.1	9.9	1.09	21.16	188	1	98	0	1	10.0	77.7	-8.7	83	7	500	100	0.0	1.0

Fund Type	Fund Name	Ticker Symbol	Overall Weiss Investment Rating	Phone	Perfor-mance Rating/Pts	3 Mo	6 Mo	1Yr / Pct	Annualized 3Yr / Pct	5Yr / Pct	Dividend Yield	Expense Ratio
SC	SunAmerica Foc Small Cap Growth A	NSKAX	C	(800) 858-8850	B / 7.6	-2.94	9.30	17.70 /78	19.69 /78	8.84 /76	0.00	1.71
SC	SunAmerica Foc Small Cap Growth B	NBSCX	C	(800) 858-8850	B- / 7.5	-3.08	8.96	16.89 /77	18.94 /76	8.25 /73	0.00	2.36
SC	SunAmerica Foc Small Cap Growth C	NCSCX	C	(800) 858-8850	B / 7.8	-3.09	8.99	16.88 /77	18.92 /76	8.18 /72	0.00	2.36
SC	SunAmerica Foc Small Cap Value A	SSSAX	D-	(800) 858-8850	C+ / 6.0	-3.70	4.47	4.43 /12	17.53 /70	10.28 /82	0.00	1.63
SC	SunAmerica Foc Small Cap Value B	SSSBX	E+	(800) 858-8850	C+ / 5.9	-3.84	4.09	3.68 / 9	16.75 /67	9.55 /79	0.00	2.32
SC	SunAmerica Foc Small Cap Value C	SSSTX	D-	(800) 858-8850	C+ / 6.3	-3.82	4.14	3.74 /10	16.76 /67	9.59 /79	0.00	2.32
TC	SunAmerica Foc Technology A	STNAX	E+	(800) 858-8850	C- / 4.1	-10.59	-8.02	7.61 /30	15.17 /60	-1.21 /11	0.00	1.95
TC	SunAmerica Foc Technology B	STNBX	E+	(800) 858-8850	C- / 4.1	-10.67	-8.29	6.93 /26	14.44 /56	-1.84 / 9	0.00	2.60
TC	SunAmerica Foc Technology C	STNTX	D-	(800) 858-8850	C / 4.5	-10.81	-8.29	6.93 /26	14.44 /56	-1.81 / 9	0.00	2.61
GI	SunAmerica Growth & Income A	SEIAX	D	(800) 858-8850	D / 1.8	-0.85	2.65	4.95 /15	8.96 /21	-1.37 /10	0.62	1.55
GI	SunAmerica Growth & Income B	SEIBX	D	(800) 858-8850	D / 1.6	-1.07	2.21	4.24 /12	8.26 /16	-2.03 / 8	0.00	2.20
GI	SunAmerica Growth & Income C	SEICX	D	(800) 858-8850	D / 2.0	-1.07	2.30	4.25 /12	8.26 /16	-2.00 / 8	0.00	2.18
GI	SunAmerica Growth & Income I	NARIX	D+	(800) 858-8850	D+ / 2.8	-0.78	2.73	5.20 /16	9.17 /22	--	0.99	1.32
GR	SunAmerica Growth Opportunities A	SGWAX	E	(800) 858-8850	D- / 1.2	-6.43	1.91	9.08 /41	8.59 /18	-4.42 / 3	0.00	1.65
GR	SunAmerica Growth Opportunities B	SGWBX	E	(800) 858-8850	D- / 1.0	-6.54	1.59	8.31 /35	7.86 /14	-5.08 / 2	0.00	2.32
GR	SunAmerica Growth Opportunities C	SGWTX	D-	(800) 858-8850	D- / 1.4	-6.61	1.59	8.33 /35	7.81 /14	-5.11 / 2	0.00	2.39
GR	SunAmerica Growth Opportunities I	NISIX	D-	(800) 858-8850	D / 2.1	-6.31	2.13	9.38 /43	8.93 /20	--	0.00	1.33
FO	SunAmerica Intl Equity A	SIEAX	A-	(800) 858-8850	B+ / 8.8	0.45	9.72	31.21 /95	23.78 /89	7.90 /71	0.00	1.90
FO	SunAmerica Intl Equity B	SSIBX	A-	(800) 858-8850	B+ / 8.9	0.35	9.41	30.43 /95	23.04 /87	7.27 /68	0.00	2.55
FO	SunAmerica Intl Equity C	SIETX	A-	(800) 858-8850	A- / 9.0	0.28	9.34	30.37 /95	22.99 /87	7.24 /68	0.00	2.55
FO	SunAmerica Intl Equity I	NAOIX	A+	(800) 858-8850	A- / 9.2	0.52	9.80	31.37 /95	23.94 /89	--	0.00	1.80
HL	SunAmerica New Biotech/Health A	SBHAX	E	(800) 858-8850	E- / 0.0	-9.31	-8.06	-1.81 / 1	-1.71 / 0	-6.62 / 1	0.00	1.55
HL	SunAmerica New Biotech/Health B	SHFBX	E	(800) 858-8850	E- / 0.0	-9.36	-8.36	-2.46 / 1	-2.36 / 0	-7.23 / 1	0.00	2.20
HL	SunAmerica New Biotech/Health C	SBHTX	E	(800) 858-8850	E- / 0.0	-9.34	-8.34	-2.34 / 1	-2.32 / 0	-7.20 / 1	0.00	2.20
SC	SunAmerica New Century A	SEGAX	D	(800) 858-8850	C- / 3.2	-6.17	1.11	5.25 /16	12.41 /45	0.08 /16	0.00	1.58
SC	SunAmerica New Century B	SEGBX	D	(800) 858-8850	C- / 3.0	-6.37	0.69	4.50 /13	11.60 /40	-0.64 /13	0.00	2.32
SC	SunAmerica New Century C	SEGCX	D	(800) 858-8850	C- / 3.6	-6.34	0.81	4.68 /14	11.81 /41	-0.48 /14	0.00	2.80
GR	SunAmerica New Tax Mngd Equity A	TXMAX	C-	(800) 858-8850	C / 4.7	-3.00	11.68	17.21 /77	11.93 /42	1.97 /27	0.39	1.45
GR	SunAmerica New Tax Mngd Equity B	TXMBX	C	(800) 858-8850	C / 4.6	-3.19	11.33	16.50 /76	11.22 /37	1.31 /22	0.01	2.10
GR	SunAmerica New Tax Mngd Equity C	TXMTX	C	(800) 858-8850	C / 5.0	-3.18	11.22	16.38 /76	11.17 /37	1.31 /22	0.01	2.10
IN	SunAmerica Value A	SSVAX	C-	(800) 858-8850	C- / 4.2	0.80	4.65	7.84 /31	12.73 /47	8.21 /72	0.67	1.63
IN	SunAmerica Value B	SSVBX	C-	(800) 858-8850	C- / 4.0	0.60	4.30	7.10 /27	12.02 /43	7.51 /69	0.14	2.28
IN	SunAmerica Value C	SVPCX	C-	(800) 858-8850	C / 4.5	0.66	4.30	7.11 /27	11.99 /42	7.51 /69	0.14	2.28
GR	Synovus Large Cap Core Eq A	SYEAX	E+	(866) 777-7818	D- / 1.0	-2.76	0.65	5.56 /18	7.54 /13	--	0.64	1.11
GR	Synovus Large Cap Core Eq B	SYEBX	E+	(866) 777-7818	E+ / 0.8	-2.99	0.28	4.70 /14	6.74 / 9	--	0.29	1.86
GR	Synovus Large Cap Core Eq C	SYECX	E+	(866) 777-7818	D- / 1.2	-2.90	0.28	4.69 /14	6.77 / 9	--	0.29	1.86
GR	Synovus Large Cap Core Eq Inst	SYEIX	D-	(866) 777-7818	D / 1.9	-2.71	0.84	5.76 /19	7.80 /14	--	0.88	N/A
MC	Synovus Mid Cap Value A	SYVAX	C	(866) 777-7818	C+ / 5.6	-4.04	1.40	6.98 /26	16.36 /65	--	0.00	1.35
MC	Synovus Mid Cap Value B	SYVBX	C-	(866) 777-7818	C / 5.2	-4.28	0.93	6.05 /21	15.44 /61	--	0.00	2.10
MC	Synovus Mid Cap Value C	SYVCX	C	(866) 777-7818	C+ / 5.8	-4.27	1.00	6.12 /21	15.46 /61	--	0.00	2.10
MC	Synovus Mid Cap Value Inst	SYVIX	C+	(866) 777-7818	C+ / 6.4	-4.01	1.46	7.18 /27	16.59 /66	--	0.02	N/A
★ BA	T. Rowe Price Balanced Fd	RPBAX	C+	(800) 638-5660	C- / 3.4	-0.39	2.58	7.50 /29	9.90 /27	5.55 /58	2.41	0.67
GR	T. Rowe Price Blue Chip Growth Adv	PABGX	C-	(800) 638-5660	D+ / 2.4	-4.01	-1.22	6.32 /22	9.07 /21	1.38 /23	0.00	0.95
★ GR	T. Rowe Price Blue Chip Growth Fd	TRBCX	C-	(800) 638-5660	D+ / 2.5	-3.98	-1.16	6.51 /23	9.19 /22	1.46 /23	0.25	0.83
GR	T. Rowe Price Blue Chip Growth R	RRBGX	D+	(800) 638-5660	D / 2.2	-4.08	-1.36	6.04 /21	8.74 /19	1.15 /21	0.00	1.23
AA	T. Rowe Price Cap Appreciation Adv	PACLX	U	(800) 638-5660	U /	-0.96	2.90	8.74 /38	--	--	1.38	1.02
★ AA	T. Rowe Price Cap Appreciation Fd	PRWCX	B+	(800) 638-5660	C / 5.3	-0.86	3.09	9.09 /41	13.22 /50	10.12 /81	1.42	0.74
GR	T. Rowe Price Cap Opportunity Fd	PRCOX	C+	(800) 638-5660	C- / 4.1	-1.66	2.45	7.71 /31	11.26 /38	2.87 /36	0.49	0.84
TC	T. Rowe Price Developing Tech	PRDTX	E	(800) 638-5660	D+ / 2.8	-10.93	-1.59	8.27 /35	10.41 /30	-4.47 / 3	0.00	1.50
MC	T. Rowe Price Diversified MidCap Gr	PRDMX	U	(800) 638-5660	U /	-4.95	1.77	12.50 /62	--	--	0.00	1.25
SC	T. Rowe Price Diversified Sm-Cap Gr	PRDSX	D+	(800) 638-5660	C / 4.4	-9.03	-0.07	8.53 /37	13.01 /49	3.13 /38	0.00	1.25
IN	T. Rowe Price Dividend Growth Fd	PRDGX	C+	(800) 638-5660	C- / 4.0	-1.14	3.64	8.14 /34	10.86 /34	3.91 /45	1.24	0.75

Risk Rating/Pts	3 Year Standard Deviation	Beta	NAV As of 6/30/06	Total $(Mil)	Cash %	Stocks %	Bonds %	Other %	Portfolio Turnover Ratio	Last Bull Market Return	Last Bear Market Return	Manager Quality Pct	Manager Tenure (Years)	Initial Purch. $	Additional Purch. $	Front End Load	Back End Load
C /4.7	16.2	1.04	19.50	209	2	97	0	1	37.0	123.3	-8.9	60	N/A	500	100	5.8	1.0
C /4.6	16.2	1.04	18.25	41	2	97	0	1	37.0	118.8	-8.9	51	N/A	500	100	0.0	4.0
C /4.6	16.2	1.04	18.19	83	2	97	0	1	37.0	118.8	-9.0	51	N/A	500	100	0.0	1.0
D /2.1	11.7	0.77	18.47	231	6	93	0	1	78.5	100.6	-10.1	81	9	500	100	5.8	1.0
D- /1.3	11.8	0.77	17.05	56	6	93	0	1	78.5	96.5	-10.2	75	9	500	100	0.0	4.0
D- /1.4	11.8	0.77	17.10	106	6	93	0	1	78.5	96.5	-10.2	75	9	500	100	0.0	1.0
C- /3.1	18.0	1.85	6.08	44	3	96	0	1	45.0	142.7	-13.5	22	6	500	100	5.8	1.0
C- /3.1	17.8	1.83	5.86	23	3	96	0	1	45.0	137.2	-13.4	19	6	500	100	0.0	4.0
C- /3.1	17.9	1.84	5.86	28	3	96	0	1	45.0	138.4	-13.8	18	6	500	100	0.0	1.0
B- /7.6	7.3	0.91	12.77	61	1	98	0	1	83.3	49.5	-10.7	40	N/A	500	100	5.8	0.0
B- /7.5	7.3	0.91	12.04	30	1	98	0	1	83.3	46.5	-10.9	34	N/A	500	100	0.0	4.0
B- /7.6	7.3	0.92	12.03	28	1	98	0	1	83.3	46.7	-10.9	33	N/A	500	100	0.0	1.0
B- /7.5	7.3	0.91	12.80	N/A	1	98	0	1	83.3	50.2	-10.6	42	N/A	5,000,000	100	0.0	0.0
C- /4.1	12.9	1.35	16.58	41	9	90	0	1	112.6	67.0	-10.0	12	N/A	500	100	5.8	0.0
C- /4.0	12.9	1.34	14.73	24	9	90	0	1	112.6	63.3	-10.2	10	N/A	500	100	0.0	4.0
C+ /6.2	12.8	1.34	14.70	10	9	90	0	1	112.6	63.1	-10.2	10	N/A	500	100	0.0	1.0
C+ /6.3	12.8	1.34	16.79	1	9	90	0	1	112.6	68.5	-10.0	14	N/A	5,000,000	100	0.0	0.0
C+ /6.5	11.3	1.07	15.47	61	1	98	0	1	70.0	129.1	-7.2	35	N/A	500	100	5.8	2.0
C+ /6.5	11.4	1.07	14.53	22	1	98	0	1	70.0	124.7	-7.5	29	N/A	500	100	0.0	4.0
C+ /6.5	11.3	1.07	14.51	22	1	98	0	1	70.0	124.8	-7.3	30	N/A	500	100	0.0	1.0
B- /7.5	11.4	1.07	15.58	10	1	98	0	1	70.0	129.8	-7.1	35	N/A	5,000,000	100	0.0	0.0
C+ /6.3	13.9	0.98	8.67	11	1	98	0	1	63.0	27.9	-10.5	1	N/A	500	100	5.8	0.0
C+ /6.3	13.9	0.98	8.33	9	1	98	0	1	63.0	25.1	-10.7	0	N/A	500	100	0.0	4.0
C+ /6.3	13.8	0.97	8.35	6	1	98	0	1	63.0	25.2	-10.6	0	N/A	500	100	0.0	1.0
C+ /5.8	12.2	0.77	18.25	81	7	92	0	1	102.0	79.3	-7.8	33	N/A	500	100	5.8	0.0
C+ /5.7	12.2	0.78	16.01	9	7	92	0	1	102.0	75.2	-8.0	27	N/A	500	100	0.0	4.0
C+ /5.7	12.2	0.78	16.09	2	7	92	0	1	102.0	76.3	-8.0	28	N/A	500	100	0.0	1.0
C+ /6.6	12.5	1.15	13.58	18	N/A	N/A	0	N/A	484.0	71.9	-9.8	48	N/A	500	100	5.8	0.0
B- /7.2	12.6	1.15	13.07	12	N/A	N/A	0	N/A	484.0	68.4	-10.0	40	N/A	500	100	0.0	4.0
B- /7.2	12.5	1.15	13.08	19	N/A	N/A	0	N/A	484.0	68.4	-10.0	40	N/A	500	100	0.0	1.0
C+ /6.9	6.3	0.75	17.57	116	0	99	0	1	71.0	66.0	-7.1	87	N/A	500	100	5.8	0.0
C+ /6.9	6.3	0.75	16.73	47	0	99	0	1	71.0	62.7	-7.2	83	N/A	500	100	0.0	4.0
C+ /6.9	6.3	0.74	16.73	35	0	99	0	1	71.0	62.6	-7.2	84	N/A	500	100	0.0	1.0
C+ /5.9	7.4	0.95	10.60	4	4	95	0	1	34.8	44.6	-7.7	27	N/A	2,500	10	5.8	0.0
C+ /5.8	7.5	0.95	10.44	1	4	95	0	1	34.8	41.2	-7.9	21	N/A	2,500	10	0.0	5.0
C+ /5.8	7.4	0.95	10.45	2	4	95	0	1	34.8	41.3	-7.9	21	N/A	2,500	10	0.0	1.0
C+ /6.0	7.4	0.94	10.64	191	4	95	0	1	34.8	45.7	-7.6	28	N/A	2,500	0	0.0	0.0
C+ /6.0	9.4	0.74	14.50	4	7	92	0	1	N/A	100.1	-3.5	79	N/A	2,500	10	5.8	0.0
C+ /6.0	9.4	0.74	14.10	6	7	92	0	1	N/A	95.4	-3.7	72	N/A	2,500	10	0.0	5.0
C+ /6.1	9.3	0.74	14.12	10	7	92	0	1	N/A	95.5	-3.7	72	N/A	2,500	10	0.0	1.0
C+ /6.1	9.3	0.74	14.59	80	7	92	0	1	N/A	101.6	-3.4	81	N/A	2,500	0	0.0	0.0
B+ /9.3	5.2	1.08	19.76	2,609	1	64	34	1	27.4	51.5	-4.6	75	14	2,500	100	0.0	0.0
B /8.0	8.7	1.09	32.32	737	0	99	0	1	40.9	59.4	-9.2	28	13	2,500	100	0.0	0.0
B /8.1	8.7	1.09	32.30	8,002	0	99	0	1	40.9	59.9	-9.3	29	13	2,500	100	0.0	0.0
B /8.0	8.7	1.09	31.97	67	0	99	0	1	40.9	57.9	-9.3	26	N/A	2,500	100	0.0	0.0
U /	N/A	N/A	20.60	31	19	61	0	20	59.2	N/A	N/A	N/A	2	2,500	100	0.0	0.0
B+ /9.7	6.4	1.23	20.68	7,929	19	61	0	20	59.2	66.6	-3.6	90	5	2,500	100	0.0	0.0
B /8.9	7.8	1.01	14.19	186	0	99	0	1	58.6	67.1	-9.1	55	N/A	2,500	100	0.0	0.0
D+ /2.4	20.1	2.16	4.32	46	4	95	0	1	128.9	91.1	-13.8	1	N/A	2,500	100	0.0	1.0
U /	N/A	N/A	12.67	85	0	99	0	1	29.3	N/A	N/A	N/A	3	2,500	100	0.0	0.0
C+ /5.6	14.0	0.92	14.00	96	1	98	0	1	37.4	98.1	-12.1	21	N/A	2,500	100	0.0	1.0
B /8.9	7.0	0.90	23.25	786	2	97	0	1	20.6	63.2	-9.7	62	6	2,500	100	0.0	0.0

Fund Type	Fund Name	Ticker Symbol	Overall Weiss Investment Rating	Phone	PERFORMANCE Perfor-mance Rating/Pts	Total Return % through 6/30/06 3 Mo	6 Mo	1Yr / Pct	Annualized 3Yr / Pct	5Yr / Pct	Incl. in Returns Dividend Yield	Expense Ratio
EM	T. Rowe Price Emer Europe & Mdtr	TREMX	C+	(800) 638-5660	A+ / 9.9	-9.07	1.47	31.62 /95	41.50 /99	31.16 /99	0.16	1.21
★ EM	T. Rowe Price Emerging Mkts Stk	PRMSX	B-	(800) 638-5660	A+ / 9.7	-7.75	2.88	32.34 /96	34.64 /98	20.50 /97	0.66	1.25
IN	T. Rowe Price Equity Income Adv	PAFDX	B	(800) 638-5660	C / 5.3	-0.29	4.99	9.66 /45	12.81 /48	6.21 /62	1.50	0.90
★ IN	T. Rowe Price Equity Income Fd	PRFDX	B	(800) 638-5660	C / 5.4	-0.29	5.06	9.85 /46	13.03 /49	6.39 /63	1.71	0.70
IN	T. Rowe Price Equity Income R	RRFDX	B-	(800) 638-5660	C / 5.1	-0.40	4.80	9.34 /42	12.50 /46	6.04 /61	1.28	1.18
★ IX	T. Rowe Price Equity Index 500	PREIX	C+	(800) 638-5660	C- / 3.8	-1.51	2.54	8.30 /35	10.88 /34	2.23 /29	1.73	0.35
FO	T. Rowe Price European Stk	PRESX	C	(800) 638-5660	B / 8.0	-1.11	9.21	20.86 /83	19.58 /78	8.30 /73	1.40	1.05
MC	T. Rowe Price Extended Eq Mkt Indx	PEXMX	B+	(800) 638-5660	B / 7.6	-3.47	5.60	13.70 /67	18.84 /76	8.69 /75	0.65	0.40
FS	T. Rowe Price Financial Services	PRISX	C	(800) 638-5660	C+ / 5.8	-1.39	4.26	14.70 /71	14.00 /54	7.86 /71	1.26	0.94
GL	T. Rowe Price Global Stock Fd	PRGSX	B	(800) 638-5660	B / 7.9	-3.03	4.18	25.38 /89	19.80 /79	7.32 /68	0.10	1.00
TC	T. Rowe Price Global Technology	PRGTX	C-	(800) 638-5660	C / 5.2	-7.49	-2.79	7.62 /30	14.41 /56	1.12 /21	0.00	1.30
GI	T. Rowe Price Growth & Inc	PRGIX	D+	(800) 638-5660	C- / 3.4	-2.13	1.90	7.02 /26	10.35 /30	2.41 /31	1.06	0.74
GR	T. Rowe Price Growth Stock Adv	TRSAX	C	(800) 638-5660	C- / 3.5	-3.11	0.67	8.40 /36	10.50 /31	2.93 /36	0.00	0.93
★ GR	T. Rowe Price Growth Stock Fd	PRGFX	C	(800) 638-5660	C- / 3.7	-3.01	0.81	8.69 /38	10.73 /33	3.12 /38	0.07	0.71
GR	T. Rowe Price Growth Stock R	RRGSX	C-	(800) 638-5660	C- / 3.3	-3.13	0.57	8.13 /34	10.20 /29	2.75 /34	0.00	1.19
HL	T. Rowe Price Health Sciences	PRHSX	D+	(800) 638-5660	C / 4.6	-6.02	-1.04	15.40 /73	13.14 /50	6.07 /62	0.00	0.89
EM	T. Rowe Price Instl Emer Mkt Eqty	IEMFX	B-	(800) 638-5660	A+ / 9.7	-7.93	2.65	31.63 /95	34.58 /98	--	0.69	1.10
FO	T. Rowe Price Instl Foreign Eq	PRFEX	B-	(800) 638-5660	B- / 7.5	-3.37	3.79	22.92 /86	19.02 /76	6.99 /67	2.70	0.81
GR	T. Rowe Price Instl Lrg Cap Core Gr	TPLGX	U	(800) 638-5660	U /	-4.00	-1.88	4.30 /12	--	--	0.58	0.65
GR	T. Rowe Price Instl Lrg Cap Gr	TRLGX	D+	(800) 638-5660	D+ / 2.7	-4.98	-3.47	4.29 /12	10.23 /29	--	0.08	0.58
GI	T. Rowe Price Instl Lrg Cap Val	TILCX	B+	(800) 638-5660	C+ / 5.9	0.52	5.60	11.31 /55	13.92 /54	6.79 /66	1.37	0.65
MC	T. Rowe Price Instl Mid-Cap Eq Gr	PMEGX	B	(800) 638-5660	B- / 7.3	-4.85	1.24	14.73 /71	17.99 /72	8.82 /76	0.00	0.65
SC ●	T. Rowe Price Instl Small Cap Stk	TRSSX	B+	(800) 638-5660	B / 7.6	-5.07	5.80	16.59 /76	18.38 /74	10.04 /81	0.00	0.69
FO	T. Rowe Price Intl Discovery	PRIDX	A-	(800) 638-5660	A+ / 9.7	-3.88	9.74	37.15 /97	33.50 /97	15.67 /93	0.33	1.26
GL	T. Rowe Price Intl Equity Index Fd	PIEQX	A+	(800) 638-5660	B+ / 8.9	0.46	10.03	26.55 /91	23.10 /88	9.47 /78	1.30	0.50
FO	T. Rowe Price Intl Gr & Inc Adv	PAIGX	A+	(800) 638-5660	A- / 9.2	0.96	11.17	28.13 /93	25.16 /91	12.76 /88	1.39	1.07
FO	T. Rowe Price Intl Gr & Inc Fd	TRIGX	A+	(800) 638-5660	A- / 9.2	0.96	11.24	28.25 /93	25.18 /91	12.75 /88	1.32	0.93
FO	T. Rowe Price Intl Gr & Inc R	RRIGX	A+	(800) 638-5660	A- / 9.2	0.90	11.00	27.86 /92	24.84 /91	12.53 /88	1.20	1.40
FO	T. Rowe Price Intl Stock Adv	PAITX	B-	(800) 638-5660	B- / 7.4	-3.36	3.67	22.85 /86	18.52 /74	6.38 /63	1.18	1.07
★ FO	T. Rowe Price Intl Stock Fd	PRITX	B-	(800) 638-5660	B- / 7.5	-3.34	3.79	23.05 /86	18.74 /75	6.59 /65	1.30	0.88
FO	T. Rowe Price Intl Stock R	RRITX	C+	(800) 638-5660	B- / 7.3	-3.50	3.41	22.32 /85	18.13 /73	6.19 /62	0.92	1.40
FO	T. Rowe Price Japan Fund	PRJPX	B	(800) 638-5660	A- / 9.1	-7.48	-5.84	32.65 /96	28.53 /94	6.93 /66	0.00	1.00
FO	T. Rowe Price Latin America	PRLAX	C+	(800) 638-5660	A+ / 9.9	-0.17	16.75	60.67 /99	50.63 /99	24.93 /98	0.68	1.21
TC	T. Rowe Price Media & Telecomm	PRMTX	A	(800) 638-5660	A / 9.3	-0.63	7.62	23.59 /87	26.47 /93	10.79 /83	0.00	0.89
MC ●	T. Rowe Price Mid-Cap Growth Adv	PAMCX	B-	(800) 638-5660	C+ / 6.9	-4.76	1.12	13.95 /68	16.96 /68	8.12 /72	0.00	1.03
★ MC ●	T. Rowe Price Mid-Cap Growth Fd	RPMGX	B	(800) 638-5660	B- / 7.0	-4.69	1.24	14.20 /69	17.25 /69	8.38 /73	0.00	0.79
MC ●	T. Rowe Price Mid-Cap Growth R	RRMGX	B-	(800) 638-5660	C+ / 6.8	-4.80	0.99	13.68 /67	16.69 /68	8.00 /72	0.00	1.29
MC ●	T. Rowe Price Mid-Cap Value Adv	TAMVX	A-	(800) 638-5660	B- / 7.5	-1.01	4.85	12.23 /61	18.50 /74	--	0.43	1.05
MC ●	T. Rowe Price Mid-Cap Value Fd	TRMCX	A	(800) 638-5660	B / 7.6	-1.01	4.92	12.50 /62	18.74 /75	13.34 /89	0.62	0.81
MC ●	T. Rowe Price Mid-Cap Value R	RRMVX	A-	(800) 638-5660	B- / 7.4	-1.14	4.67	11.95 /59	18.18 /73	12.93 /88	0.24	1.28
GR	T. Rowe Price New Amer Growth Fd	PRWAX	D	(800) 638-5660	D+ / 2.5	-4.67	-1.47	4.74 /14	9.63 /25	0.80 /19	0.00	0.90
FO	T. Rowe Price New Asia Fd	PRASX	B	(800) 638-5660	A / 9.3	-8.20	3.21	23.01 /86	28.98 /95	16.51 /94	0.93	1.05
★ EN	T. Rowe Price New Era	PRNEX	A	(800) 638-5660	A+ / 9.8	3.35	13.36	33.59 /96	33.38 /97	18.52 /95	0.76	0.67
★ SC	T. Rowe Price New Horizons	PRNHX	C+	(800) 638-5660	C+ / 6.9	-8.83	1.80	10.36 /49	17.83 /72	7.48 /69	0.00	0.82
BA	T. Rowe Price Personal Strategy Bal	TRPBX	C+	(800) 638-5660	C- / 4.1	-1.49	2.03	8.12 /34	11.27 /38	6.86 /66	1.98	0.89
GR	T. Rowe Price Personal Strategy Gr	TRSGX	B	(800) 638-5660	C+ / 5.6	-1.98	2.69	10.43 /50	13.79 /53	7.02 /67	0.88	0.99
AA	T. Rowe Price Personal Strategy Inc	PRSIX	C	(800) 638-5660	D+ / 2.5	-0.90	1.60	6.07 /21	8.68 /19	6.37 /63	2.62	0.78
RE	T. Rowe Price Real Estate Adv	PAREX	U	(800) 638-5660	U /	-0.38	15.55	24.21 /87	--	--	2.20	1.02
RE	T. Rowe Price Real Estate Fd	TRREX	C+	(800) 638-5660	A / 9.5	-0.38	15.70	24.44 /88	29.33 /95	21.13 /97	3.03	0.80
AA	T. Rowe Price Retirement 2005 Fd	TRRFX	U	(800) 638-5660	U /	-1.16	2.21	7.59 /30	--	--	1.88	0.64
FO	T. Rowe Price Retirement 2010 Adv	PARAX	U	(800) 638-5660	U /	-1.32	2.48	8.60 /38	--	--	1.60	N/A
FO	T. Rowe Price Retirement 2010 Fd	TRRAX	C+	(800) 638-5660	C- / 4.0	-1.32	2.61	8.87 /39	10.82 /34	--	1.73	0.68

● Denotes fund is closed to new investors
★ Denotes fund is included in Section II

www.WeissRatings.com

RISK			NET ASSETS		ASSET				BULL / BEAR		FUND MANAGER		MINIMUMS		LOADS	
	3 Year		NAV						Last Bull	Last Bear	Manager	Manager	Initial	Additional	Front	Back
Risk Rating/Pts	Standard Deviation	Beta	As of 6/30/06	Total $(Mil)	Cash %	Stocks %	Bonds %	Other %	Portfolio Turnover Ratio	Market Return	Market Return	Quality Pct	Tenure (Years)	Purch. $	Purch. $	End Load	End Load
C- /3.2	22.0	1.18	25.58	1,346	5	94	0	1	3.0	316.0	-3.1	44	6	2,500	100	0.0	2.0
C- /3.9	18.9	1.15	26.42	2,067	4	90	0	6	38.5	233.1	-7.7	14	11	2,500	100	0.0	2.0
B /8.9	7.3	0.92	26.88	1,965	4	95	0	1	13.6	71.6	-10.1	78	6	2,500	100	0.0	0.0
B /8.9	7.3	0.92	26.92	18,666	4	95	0	1	13.6	72.6	-9.9	79	21	2,500	100	0.0	0.0
B /8.9	7.3	0.92	26.85	215	4	95	0	1	13.6	70.2	-10.2	76	4	2,500	100	0.0	0.0
B /8.8	7.7	1.00	34.09	6,274	1	98	0	1	2.3	63.3	-9.8	52	N/A	2,500	100	0.0	0.5
C- /4.1	11.1	1.03	18.74	866	0	98	0	2	88.3	118.3	-11.2	16	N/A	2,500	100	0.0	2.0
B- /7.4	11.6	1.05	15.28	297	4	95	0	1	26.2	114.5	-8.9	54	N/A	2,500	100	0.0	0.5
C+ /6.2	10.5	1.05	22.04	402	N/A	100	0	N/A	63.7	89.1	-11.5	51	N/A	2,500	100	0.0	0.0
C+ /6.6	10.4	0.90	20.18	321	1	96	0	3	169.1	112.6	-9.5	35	N/A	2,500	100	0.0	2.0
C /5.1	15.9	1.72	5.93	130	5	94	0	1	204.8	100.0	-11.7	25	N/A	2,500	100	0.0	0.0
C+ /6.7	8.0	1.03	20.55	1,573	1	97	0	2	39.6	60.0	-9.3	43	N/A	2,500	100	0.0	0.0
B /8.1	8.7	1.09	28.39	1,636	2	97	0	1	47.7	65.0	-8.8	39	5	2,500	100	0.0	0.0
B /8.1	8.7	1.08	28.63	12,377	2	97	0	1	47.7	66.0	-8.7	42	5	2,500	100	0.0	0.0
B /8.1	8.7	1.08	28.20	475	2	97	0	1	47.7	63.5	-8.8	37	4	2,500	100	0.0	0.0
C /5.3	12.3	0.95	24.81	1,556	2	97	0	1	34.0	84.8	-4.7	78	6	2,500	100	0.0	0.0
C- /4.0	18.9	1.15	25.55	173	3	90	0	7	37.4	234.0	-9.1	13	4	1,000,000	100,000	0.0	2.0
C+ /6.4	10.9	1.04	18.09	236	2	97	0	1	70.9	111.8	-11.2	12	17	1,000,000	100,000	0.0	2.0
U /	N/A	N/A	12.00	35	1	98	0	1	42.5	N/A	N/A	N/A	3	1,000,000	100,000	0.0	0.0
B- /7.5	9.8	1.09	13.35	364	4	96	0	0	76.4	67.7	-7.8	36	N/A	1,000,000	100,000	0.0	0.0
B+ /9.0	7.5	0.93	13.57	195	2	97	0	1	21.7	81.6	-11.1	85	N/A	1,000,000	100,000	0.0	0.0
B- /7.0	11.2	0.97	26.09	456	0	99	0	1	32.9	112.8	-8.4	60	10	1,000,000	100,000	0.0	0.0
B- /7.3	12.8	0.86	14.97	470	2	97	0	1	17.4	107.4	-9.4	76	N/A	1,000,000	100,000	0.0	0.0
C+ /5.9	13.5	1.17	45.39	1,967	7	92	0	1	98.7	224.1	-3.0	89	18	2,500	100	0.0	2.0
B- /7.5	9.9	0.98	13.05	205	0	99	0	1	41.1	128.4	-9.5	48	N/A	2,500	100	0.0	2.0
B- /7.4	10.3	0.99	15.73	339	1	98	0	1	44.6	146.1	-7.5	65	4	2,500	100	0.0	2.0
B- /7.4	10.2	0.99	15.73	1,272	1	98	0	1	44.6	146.3	-7.7	66	N/A	2,500	100	0.0	2.0
B- /7.4	10.3	0.99	15.64	23	1	98	0	1	44.6	144.0	-7.7	61	4	2,500	100	0.0	2.0
C+ /6.3	10.8	1.04	15.26	69	1	97	0	2	70.0	109.0	-11.5	11	6	2,500	100	0.0	2.0
C+ /6.3	10.9	1.05	15.35	6,080	1	97	0	2	70.0	110.4	-11.5	11	6	2,500	100	0.0	2.0
C+ /6.2	10.9	1.05	15.15	5	1	97	0	2	70.0	107.1	-11.6	9	N/A	2,500	100	0.0	2.0
C /5.2	18.0	1.02	11.13	643	4	95	0	1	172.1	158.3	-7.4	84	15	2,500	100	0.0	2.0
C- /3.1	22.7	1.66	29.56	1,628	2	80	0	18	19.9	393.0	-7.4	96	10	2,500	100	0.0	2.0
C+ /6.5	12.6	1.48	36.15	1,173	0	98	0	2	80.6	173.1	-11.0	99	N/A	2,500	100	0.0	0.0
B- /7.4	10.7	0.94	54.26	554	4	95	0	1	33.0	105.2	-8.1	56	14	2,500	100	0.0	0.0
B- /7.4	10.7	0.93	54.81	15,600	4	95	0	1	33.0	106.7	-8.1	58	14	2,500	100	0.0	0.0
B- /7.4	10.7	0.94	53.90	181	4	95	0	1	33.0	103.6	-8.2	52	4	2,500	100	0.0	0.0
B /8.0	9.7	0.83	24.41	448	8	90	0	2	61.5	105.7	-8.8	83	4	2,500	100	0.0	0.0
B /8.0	9.7	0.83	24.53	5,613	8	90	0	2	61.5	107.0	-8.7	84	5	2,500	100	0.0	0.0
B /8.0	9.8	0.83	24.22	319	8	90	0	2	61.5	103.8	-8.8	81	4	2,500	100	0.0	0.0
C+ /6.7	9.2	1.10	31.41	821	0	99	0	1	55.1	64.7	-8.3	31	N/A	2,500	100	0.0	0.0
C /5.0	16.5	1.29	12.21	1,689	3	93	0	4	56.1	176.5	-9.2	33	16	2,500	100	0.0	2.0
C+ /6.1	16.6	0.78	46.59	4,512	4	94	0	2	4.0	167.8	-1.6	96	9	2,500	100	0.0	0.0
C+ /5.8	14.1	0.92	32.31	6,888	2	97	0	1	26.5	128.7	-10.2	61	19	2,500	100	0.0	0.0
B+ /9.1	5.8	1.21	18.94	1,292	4	67	28	1	49.9	59.5	-4.2	80	8	2,500	100	0.0	0.0
B /8.7	7.4	0.94	23.71	985	1	85	12	2	36.3	76.0	-6.6	83	8	2,500	100	0.0	0.0
B+ /9.5	4.3	0.90	15.09	534	15	46	38	1	55.7	43.2	-2.1	73	12	2,500	100	0.0	0.0
U /	N/A	N/A	22.09	29	4	95	0	1	20.4	N/A	N/A	N/A	2	2,500	100	0.0	1.0
C- /3.8	16.0	0.95	22.11	1,275	4	95	0	1	20.4	138.8	0.5	93	9	2,500	100	0.0	1.0
U /	N/A	N/A	11.11	476	11	56	31	2	4.6	N/A	N/A	N/A	2	2,500	100	0.0	0.0
U /	N/A	N/A	14.90	78	8	66	24	2	6.1	N/A	N/A	N/A	3	2,500	100	0.0	0.0
B+ /9.5	5.9	0.51	14.95	1,832	8	66	24	2	6.1	57.8	-5.6	34	4	2,500	100	0.0	0.0

Fund Type	Fund Name	Ticker Symbol	Overall Weiss Investment Rating	Phone	Performance Rating/Pts	3 Mo	6 Mo	1Yr / Pct	3Yr / Pct	5Yr / Pct	Dividend Yield	Expense Ratio
	99 Pct = Best				PERFORMANCE			Total Return % through 6/30/06	Annualized		Incl. in Returns	
FO	T. Rowe Price Retirement 2010 R	RRTAX	U	(800) 638-5660	U /	-1.46	2.34	8.25 /35	--	--	1.47	2.47
AA	T. Rowe Price Retirement 2015 Fd	TRRGX	U	(800) 638-5660	U /	-1.54	2.76	9.54 /44	--	--	1.47	0.72
IN	T. Rowe Price Retirement 2020 Adv	PARBX	U	(800) 638-5660	U /	-1.72	2.89	10.22 /48	--	--	1.24	1.30
★ IN	T. Rowe Price Retirement 2020 Fd	TRRBX	B	(800) 638-5660	C / 5.1	-1.65	3.01	10.47 /50	12.60 /46	--	1.36	0.76
IN	T. Rowe Price Retirement 2020 R	RRTBX	U	(800) 638-5660	U /	-1.78	2.70	9.90 /46	--	--	1.18	2.44
AA	T. Rowe Price Retirement 2025 Fd	TRRHX	U	(800) 638-5660	U /	-1.74	3.31	11.29 /55	--	--	1.09	0.78
IN	T. Rowe Price Retirement 2030 Adv	PARCX	U	(800) 638-5660	U /	-2.02	3.47	12.12 /60	--	--	0.82	1.30
IN	T. Rowe Price Retirement 2030 Fd	TRRCX	B	(800) 638-5660	C+ / 6.0	-1.95	3.58	12.42 /62	14.23 /55	--	0.93	0.80
IN	T. Rowe Price Retirement 2030 R	RRTCX	U	(800) 638-5660	U /	-2.02	3.35	11.87 /59	--	--	0.70	2.50
AA	T. Rowe Price Retirement 2035 Fd	TRRJX	U	(800) 638-5660	U /	-1.95	3.61	12.47 /62	--	--	0.91	0.80
IN	T. Rowe Price Retirement 2040 Adv	PARDX	U	(800) 638-5660	U /	-2.01	3.51	12.12 /60	--	--	0.81	1.30
IN	T. Rowe Price Retirement 2040 Fd	TRRDX	B	(800) 638-5660	C+ / 6.0	-1.94	3.62	12.42 /62	14.26 /55	--	0.93	0.80
IN	T. Rowe Price Retirement 2045	TRRKX	U	(800) 638-5660	U /	-1.92	3.60	12.41 /62	--	--	0.62	0.81
FO	T. Rowe Price Retirement Income Fd	TRRIX	C	(800) 638-5660	D / 2.0	-0.57	2.09	6.47 /23	7.48 /12	--	3.11	0.57
TC	T. Rowe Price Science & Tech Adv	PASTX	E	(800) 638-5660	E+ / 0.7	-9.99	-5.57	-0.11 / 2	6.80 /10	-6.49 / 1	0.00	1.05
★ TC	T. Rowe Price Science & Tech Fd	PRSCX	E	(800) 638-5660	E+ / 0.7	-9.99	-5.57	-0.05 / 2	6.82 /10	-6.51 / 1	0.00	0.99
SC ●	T. Rowe Price Small Cap Stock Adv	PASSX	B	(800) 638-5660	B- / 7.2	-4.90	5.63	15.57 /73	17.30 /69	9.27 /78	0.00	1.13
★ SC ●	T. Rowe Price Small Cap Stock Fd	OTCFX	B	(800) 638-5660	B- / 7.3	-4.85	5.76	15.85 /74	17.57 /71	9.50 /79	0.00	0.91
SC ●	T. Rowe Price Small Cap Value Adv	PASVX	A	(800) 638-5660	B+ / 8.5	-4.06	10.10	18.83 /80	21.94 /85	15.43 /92	0.21	1.01
★ SC ●	T. Rowe Price Small Cap Value Fd	PRSVX	A	(800) 638-5660	B+ / 8.6	-4.03	10.19	19.02 /81	22.16 /86	15.64 /93	0.40	0.83
★ GI	T. Rowe Price Spectrum Growth	PRSGX	B	(800) 638-5660	C+ / 6.5	-3.09	3.18	12.76 /63	15.59 /62	6.37 /63	0.74	0.82
FO	T. Rowe Price Spectrum Intl	PSILX	B	(800) 638-5660	B+ / 8.4	-3.49	4.97	25.44 /89	22.24 /86	9.43 /78	0.16	1.00
BA	T. Rowe Price Tax Eff Balanced	PRTEX	D	(800) 638-5660	E / 0.5	-1.27	0.07	2.73 / 6	4.55 / 3	2.60 /33	2.60	1.04
GR	T. Rowe Price Tax Eff Growth	PTEGX	D-	(800) 638-5660	E+ / 0.8	-4.28	-1.80	3.67 / 9	6.09 / 7	-0.18 /15	0.20	1.05
MC	T. Rowe Price Tax Eff Mult-Cap Gr	PREFX	C-	(800) 638-5660	C- / 4.2	-5.25	0.71	8.17 /34	12.19 /44	3.29 /39	0.00	1.25
GR	T. Rowe Price Total Eq Mkt Index	POMIX	B-	(800) 638-5660	C / 5.0	-1.98	3.35	9.88 /46	12.77 /47	3.73 /43	1.30	0.40
GR	T. Rowe Price Value Adv	PAVLX	B	(800) 638-5660	C+ / 6.5	-0.45	5.34	11.76 /58	15.26 /60	6.14 /62	0.99	1.01
★ GR	T. Rowe Price Value Fd	TRVLX	B	(800) 638-5660	C+ / 6.5	-0.44	5.39	11.93 /59	15.40 /61	6.26 /63	0.99	0.89
FO	TA IDEX Alliancebernstein Int Val I		U	(888) 233-4339	U /	0.53	12.85	--	--	--	0.00	1.05
GI ●	TA IDEX American Century Lg Co VI	IAIAX	C+	(888) 233-4339	C- / 3.8	0.36	4.15	8.27 /35	12.08 /43	3.87 /45	0.96	1.32
GI ●	TA IDEX American Century Lg Co VI	IAIBX	C+	(888) 233-4339	C / 4.3	0.28	3.90	7.57 /30	11.30 /38	3.11 /38	0.20	1.29
GI ●	TA IDEX American Century Lg Co VI	IAILX	C+	(888) 233-4339	C / 4.3	0.37	4.00	7.75 /31	11.26 /38	--	0.25	1.21
GI ●	TA IDEX American Century Lg Co VI I		U	(888) 233-4339	U /	0.44	4.34	--	--	--	0.00	0.90
AA	TA IDEX Asset Allocation-Consv Pt A	ICLAX	D	(888) 233-4339	D / 1.9	-0.91	2.61	7.58 /30	9.08 /21	--	2.68	1.48
AA	TA IDEX Asset Allocation-Consv Pt B	ICLBX	C-	(888) 233-4339	D / 1.7	-1.10	2.31	6.78 /25	8.34 /17	--	2.18	2.13
AA	TA IDEX Asset Allocation-Consv Pt C	ICLLX	D+	(888) 233-4339	D+ / 2.3	-0.99	2.33	6.84 /25	8.36 /17	--	2.23	2.10
AA	TA IDEX Asset Allocation-Grth Pt A	IAAAX	C+	(888) 233-4339	C / 5.2	-2.67	4.85	15.70 /74	14.73 /58	--	0.78	1.61
AA	TA IDEX Asset Allocation-Grth Pt B	IAABX	C	(888) 233-4339	C / 4.9	-2.87	4.42	14.94 /72	13.99 /54	--	0.29	2.26
AA	TA IDEX Asset Allocation-Grth Pt C	IAALX	C+	(888) 233-4339	C+ / 5.6	-2.79	4.50	14.98 /72	14.06 /54	--	0.33	2.20
AA	TA IDEX Asset Allocation-Md Gr Pt A	IMLAX	C	(888) 233-4339	C- / 3.9	-1.82	4.36	12.84 /64	12.68 /47	--	1.48	0.63
AA	TA IDEX Asset Allocation-Md Gr Pt B	IMLBX	C-	(888) 233-4339	C- / 3.6	-2.06	3.95	11.96 /59	11.94 /42	--	1.01	1.30
AA	TA IDEX Asset Allocation-Md Gr Pt C	IMLLX	C+	(888) 233-4339	C / 4.4	-1.98	4.04	12.09 /60	12.01 /42	--	1.05	1.25
AA	TA IDEX Asset Allocation-Md Pt A	IMOAX	C	(888) 233-4339	C- / 3.0	-1.47	3.42	9.76 /45	10.94 /35	--	2.17	1.48
AA	TA IDEX Asset Allocation-Md Pt B	IMOBX	C-	(888) 233-4339	D+ / 2.8	-1.72	3.00	8.93 /40	10.21 /29	--	1.69	2.14
AA	TA IDEX Asset Allocation-Md Pt C	IMOLX	C	(888) 233-4339	C- / 3.5	-1.64	3.09	9.08 /41	10.26 /29	--	1.74	2.11
RE ●	TA IDEX Clarion Glb Real Estate A	ICRAX	A	(888) 233-4339	A- / 9.2	-1.39	13.48	22.45 /85	26.34 /92	--	1.23	1.17
RE ●	TA IDEX Clarion Glb Real Estate B	ICRBX	A	(888) 233-4339	A- / 9.2	-1.45	13.31	21.71 /84	25.56 /92	--	1.07	1.16
RE ●	TA IDEX Clarion Glb Real Estate C	ICRLX	A	(888) 233-4339	A- / 9.2	-1.38	13.38	21.92 /84	25.42 /91	--	1.15	1.06
RE ●	TA IDEX Clarion Glb Real Estate I		U	(888) 233-4339	U /	-1.23	13.75	--	--	--	0.00	0.89
GI	TA IDEX Federated Market Opp I		U	(888) 233-4339	U /	3.00	3.76	--	--	--	0.00	1.05
GR	TA IDEX Great Companies America	IGAAX	D-	(888) 233-4339	E- / 0.2	-3.25	-1.75	3.37 / 8	4.59 / 3	0.04 /16	0.00	1.52
GR	TA IDEX Great Companies America	IGABX	D-	(888) 233-4339	E- / 0.2	-3.48	-2.14	2.70 / 6	3.90 / 2	-0.64 /13	0.00	2.14

● Denotes fund is closed to new investors
★ Denotes fund is included in Section II

www.WeissRatings.com

| RISK | 3 Year | | NET ASSETS | | ASSET | | | | | BULL / BEAR | | FUND MANAGER | | MINIMUMS | | LOADS | |
Risk Rating/Pts	Standard Deviation	Beta	NAV As of 6/30/06	Total $(Mil)	Cash %	Stocks %	Bonds %	Other %	Portfolio Turnover Ratio	Last Bull Market Return	Last Bear Market Return	Manager Quality Pct	Manager Tenure (Years)	Initial Purch. $	Additional Purch. $	Front End Load	Back End Load
U /	N/A	N/A	14.84	76	8	66	24	2	6.1	N/A	N/A	N/A	3	2,500	100	0.0	0.0
U /	N/A	N/A	11.53	1,254	4	72	22	2	1.8	N/A	N/A	N/A	2	2,500	100	0.0	0.0
U /	N/A	N/A	16.04	108	4	75	19	2	0.8	N/A	N/A	N/A	3	2,500	100	0.0	0.0
B+ / 9.1	6.9	0.88	16.10	2,455	4	75	19	2	0.8	69.6	-7.2	79	4	2,500	100	0.0	0.0
U /	N/A	N/A	15.97	78	4	75	19	2	0.8	N/A	N/A	N/A	3	2,500	100	0.0	0.0
U /	N/A	N/A	11.85	1,109	0	85	14	1	2.2	N/A	N/A	N/A	2	2,500	100	0.0	0.0
U /	N/A	N/A	17.01	70	3	89	6	2	1.3	N/A	N/A	N/A	3	2,500	100	0.0	0.0
B / 8.6	8.0	1.02	17.08	1,604	3	89	6	2	1.3	80.4	-8.7	82	4	2,500	100	0.0	0.0
U /	N/A	N/A	16.97	58	3	89	6	2	1.3	N/A	N/A	N/A	3	2,500	100	0.0	0.0
U /	N/A	N/A	12.04	529	0	93	6	1	6.2	N/A	N/A	N/A	2	2,500	100	0.0	0.0
U /	N/A	N/A	17.10	33	3	89	6	2	1.3	N/A	N/A	N/A	3	2,500	100	0.0	0.0
B / 8.5	8.0	1.02	17.17	744	3	89	6	2	1.3	80.6	-8.9	82	4	2,500	100	0.0	0.0
U /	N/A	N/A	11.23	103	0	93	6	1	N/A	N/A	N/A	N/A	N/A	2,500	100	0.0	0.0
B+ / 9.9	3.9	0.33	12.52	633	27	42	29	2	21.2	37.0	-2.2	36	4	2,500	100	0.0	0.0
C / 4.3	15.6	1.69	18.47	457	3	96	0	1	99.0	62.4	-11.8	2	4	2,500	100	0.0	0.0
C / 4.3	15.6	1.69	18.48	2,863	3	96	0	1	99.0	62.5	-11.8	2	4	2,500	100	0.0	0.0
B- / 7.0	12.2	0.82	34.51	600	7	92	0	1	18.3	98.9	-8.9	72	6	2,500	100	0.0	0.0
B- / 7.0	12.2	0.82	34.70	7,222	7	92	0	1	18.3	100.4	-9.0	74	14	2,500	100	0.0	0.0
B- / 7.2	11.7	0.79	40.44	735	6	92	0	2	8.2	127.0	-7.2	95	6	2,500	100	0.0	1.0
B- / 7.1	11.8	0.79	40.67	5,244	6	92	0	2	8.2	128.2	-7.1	96	15	2,500	100	0.0	1.0
B / 8.0	9.1	1.15	18.80	3,068	2	96	0	2	4.6	93.0	-9.8	82	N/A	2,500	100	0.0	0.0
C+ / 5.7	11.3	1.09	12.45	227	2	96	0	2	29.0	132.5	-10.0	22	N/A	2,500	100	0.0	2.0
B+ / 9.0	4.3	0.87	13.82	39	0	48	50	2	11.9	27.3	-3.9	32	9	2,500	100	0.0	1.0
B- / 7.6	9.0	1.11	9.83	64	0	99	0	1	18.4	46.1	-11.4	11	7	2,500	100	0.0	1.0
B- / 7.0	11.1	0.96	11.38	35	0	99	0	1	29.4	79.6	-10.5	15	6	2,500	100	0.0	1.0
B / 8.6	8.4	1.08	13.87	404	2	97	0	1	6.1	73.7	-9.7	65	N/A	2,500	100	0.0	0.5
B / 8.9	8.1	1.02	24.48	798	3	94	0	3	12.0	85.3	-11.9	87	N/A	2,500	100	0.0	0.0
B / 8.9	8.1	1.02	24.64	3,878	3	94	0	3	12.0	85.9	-11.9	88	N/A	2,500	100	0.0	0.0
U /	N/A	N/A	11.42	253	0	98	0	2	N/A	N/A	N/A	N/A	N/A	0	0	0.0	0.0
B+ / 9.0	6.9	0.86	11.30	8	5	94	0	1	28.0	68.4	-9.7	77	N/A	1,000	50	5.5	0.0
B+ / 9.1	6.9	0.87	10.93	14	5	94	0	1	28.0	64.6	-9.8	69	N/A	1,000	50	0.0	0.0
B+ / 9.1	6.9	0.86	10.91	5	5	94	0	1	28.0	64.3	-9.8	69	N/A	1,000	50	0.0	0.0
U /	N/A	N/A	11.30	237	5	94	0	1	28.0	N/A	N/A	N/A	N/A	0	0	0.0	0.0
B- / 7.0	5.1	1.01	11.39	143	10	34	54	2	32.0	46.7	-2.3	71	N/A	1,000	50	5.5	1.0
B / 8.9	5.1	1.01	11.36	106	10	34	54	2	32.0	43.5	-2.4	64	N/A	1,000	50	0.0	5.0
B- / 7.8	5.1	1.02	11.36	230	10	34	54	2	32.0	43.6	-2.4	64	N/A	1,000	50	0.0	1.0
B- / 7.3	9.6	1.76	12.76	417	0	100	0	0	35.0	84.5	-10.6	83	N/A	1,000	50	5.5	1.0
B- / 7.3	9.6	1.76	12.53	263	0	100	0	0	35.0	81.0	-10.7	77	N/A	1,000	50	0.0	5.0
B- / 7.3	9.6	1.75	12.54	753	0	100	0	0	35.0	81.3	-10.7	78	N/A	1,000	50	0.0	1.0
B / 8.0	7.8	1.48	12.44	770	4	70	24	2	26.0	69.1	-7.3	79	N/A	1,000	50	5.5	1.0
B- / 7.7	7.8	1.49	12.36	508	4	70	24	2	26.0	65.7	-7.5	73	N/A	1,000	50	0.0	5.0
B / 8.2	7.8	1.49	12.37	1,309	4	70	24	2	26.0	65.9	-7.5	73	N/A	1,000	50	0.0	1.0
B / 8.9	6.3	1.22	12.08	409	4	50	44	2	19.0	58.2	-5.0	77	N/A	1,000	50	5.5	1.0
B / 8.0	6.2	1.21	12.01	322	4	50	44	2	19.0	55.0	-5.1	71	N/A	1,000	50	0.0	5.0
B / 8.9	6.2	1.22	12.01	810	4	50	44	2	19.0	55.2	-5.1	71	N/A	1,000	50	0.0	1.0
C+ / 6.7	16.5	0.96	17.61	7	7	92	0	1	66.0	130.4	N/A	82	4	1,000	50	5.5	0.0
C+ / 6.7	16.5	0.96	17.56	6	7	92	0	1	66.0	125.8	N/A	77	3	1,000	50	0.0	0.0
C+ / 6.7	16.5	0.96	17.43	3	7	92	0	1	66.0	125.0	N/A	76	3	1,000	50	0.0	0.0
U /	N/A	N/A	17.66	239	7	92	0	1	66.0	N/A	N/A	N/A	N/A	0	0	0.0	0.0
U /	N/A	N/A	10.20	77	0	100	0	0	N/A	N/A	N/A	N/A	N/A	0	0	0.0	0.0
B- / 7.7	7.0	0.79	9.52	25	4	95	0	1	100.0	40.0	-11.0	17	6	1,000	50	5.5	1.0
B- / 7.6	7.0	0.80	9.14	33	4	95	0	1	100.0	37.2	-11.2	13	6	1,000	50	0.0	5.0

	99 Pct = Best 0 Pct = Worst				PERFORMANCE							
			Overall Weiss Investment Rating					Total Return % through 6/30/06			Incl. in Returns	
					Perfor-mance Rating/Pts				Annualized		Dividend Yield	Expense Ratio
Fund Type	Fund Name	Ticker Symbol		Phone		3 Mo	6 Mo	1Yr / Pct	3Yr / Pct	5Yr / Pct		
GR	TA IDEX Great Companies America	IGALX	D-	(888) 233-4339	E / 0.3	-3.38	-2.14	2.70 / 6	3.90 / 2	--	0.00	2.17
TC	TA IDEX Great Companies Tech A	IGTAX	E-	(888) 233-4339	E / 0.4	-10.12	-6.75	3.78 /10	7.22 /11	-4.12 / 4	0.67	1.53
TC	TA IDEX Great Companies Tech B	IGTBX	E-	(888) 233-4339	E / 0.4	-10.28	-7.01	3.18 / 8	6.46 / 8	-4.86 / 3	0.00	2.18
TC	TA IDEX Great Companies Tech C	IGTLX	E-	(888) 233-4339	E+ / 0.6	-10.05	-6.77	3.48 / 9	6.46 / 8	--	0.00	2.18
TC	TA IDEX Great Companies Tech I		U	(888) 233-4339	U /	-9.86	-6.25	--	--	--	0.00	0.91
GR	TA IDEX Janus Growth A	IDETX	D	(888) 233-4339	D / 2.2	-4.04	-3.75	6.42 /23	10.80 /34	-1.14 /11	0.00	1.51
GR	TA IDEX Janus Growth B	IDEWX	D-	(888) 233-4339	D / 1.9	-4.23	-4.15	5.54 /18	9.98 /27	-1.92 / 8	0.00	2.30
GR	TA IDEX Janus Growth C	IDELX	D	(888) 233-4339	D+ / 2.5	-4.28	-4.20	5.49 /18	9.95 /27	--	0.00	2.30
GR	TA IDEX Janus Growth I		U	(888) 233-4339	U /	-3.92	-3.51	--	--	--	0.00	0.86
GR	● TA IDEX Janus Growth T	TIDEX	D	(888) 233-4339	D / 2.1	-3.94	-3.55	6.90 /26	11.17 /37	-0.75 /13	0.00	1.01
GR	● TA IDEX Jennison Growth A	ICASX	D	(888) 233-4339	D+ / 2.4	-7.94	-6.98	5.43 /17	11.77 /41	3.78 /44	0.00	1.36
GR	● TA IDEX Jennison Growth B	ICSBX	D	(888) 233-4339	D+ / 2.9	-7.93	-7.07	5.04 /15	11.11 /36	3.12 /38	0.00	1.26
GR	● TA IDEX Jennison Growth C	IJOLX	D+	(888) 233-4339	C- / 3.0	-7.91	-7.06	5.03 /15	11.18 /37	--	0.00	1.32
GR	● TA IDEX Jennison Growth I		U	(888) 233-4339	U /	-7.84	-6.71	--	--	--	0.00	0.86
GR	● TA IDEX Marsico Growth A	IDGSX	D	(888) 233-4339	D / 2.1	-4.72	-1.38	6.67 /24	10.17 /28	0.19 /16	0.00	1.23
GR	● TA IDEX Marsico Growth B	IGSBX	D+	(888) 233-4339	D+ / 2.6	-4.68	-1.45	6.04 /21	9.47 /24	-0.52 /13	0.00	1.21
GR	● TA IDEX Marsico Growth C	IGSLX	D+	(888) 233-4339	D+ / 2.6	-4.69	-1.36	6.16 /21	9.43 /24	--	0.00	1.10
GR	● TA IDEX Marsico Growth I		U	(888) 233-4339	U /	-4.61	-1.10	--	--	--	0.00	0.90
GL	TA IDEX Mercury Global Markets I		U	(888) 233-4339	U /	7.33	13.52	--	--	--	0.00	0.90
GR	TA IDEX Mercury Large Cap Value I		U	(888) 233-4339	U /	-0.09	6.30	--	--	--	0.00	0.84
FO	● TA IDEX MFS International Equity A	ICIAX	E+	(888) 233-4339	B- / 7.0	-1.70	8.21	22.01 /84	17.21 /69	3.05 /37	0.79	1.88
FO	● TA IDEX MFS International Equity B	ICIBX	E+	(888) 233-4339	B- / 7.3	-1.69	8.05	21.52 /84	16.64 /66	2.41 /31	0.68	1.77
FO	● TA IDEX MFS International Equity C	ICILX	E+	(888) 233-4339	B- / 7.3	-1.57	8.15	21.63 /84	16.58 /66	--	0.69	1.66
FO	TA IDEX Neuberger Berman Intl I		U	(888) 233-4339	U /	-0.62	10.45	--	--	--	0.00	1.05
GL	TA IDEX Oppenheimer Devlp Market		U	(888) 233-4339	U /	-9.12	-0.20	--	--	--	0.00	1.26
GI	TA IDEX Protected Principal Stck A	IPPAX	C-	(888) 233-4339	E+ / 0.7	0.43	2.80	6.24 /22	6.10 / 7	--	0.00	2.02
GI	TA IDEX Protected Principal Stck B	IPPBX	C-	(888) 233-4339	E+ / 0.7	0.26	2.48	5.56 /18	5.61 / 5	--	0.00	2.59
GI	TA IDEX Protected Principal Stck C2	IPPCX	C-	(888) 233-4339	D- / 1.1	0.26	2.48	5.67 /19	5.55 / 5	--	0.00	2.59
GR	TA IDEX Salomon All Cap A	IALAX	C-	(888) 233-4339	C- / 3.5	-1.22	4.63	12.05 /60	11.86 /42	2.89 /36	0.04	1.55
GR	TA IDEX Salomon All Cap B	IACBX	C-	(888) 233-4339	C- / 3.3	-1.35	4.34	11.26 /55	11.13 /37	2.18 /29	0.02	2.20
GR	TA IDEX Salomon All Cap C	ILLLX	C-	(888) 233-4339	C- / 4.0	-1.35	4.34	11.33 /56	11.13 /37	--	0.02	2.20
GR	● TA IDEX Salomon Investors Value A	IVEAX	E	(888) 233-4339	C- / 3.7	-0.29	4.26	10.87 /53	11.50 /39	3.57 /42	0.84	1.20
GR	● TA IDEX Salomon Investors Value B	IVEQX	E	(888) 233-4339	C / 4.3	-0.31	4.28	10.34 /49	10.79 /34	2.88 /36	0.17	1.20
GR	● TA IDEX Salomon Investors Value C	IVELX	E	(888) 233-4339	C- / 4.2	-0.32	4.19	10.36 /49	10.71 /33	--	0.25	1.20
GR	● TA IDEX Salomon Investors Value I		U	(888) 233-4339	U /	-0.19	4.58	--	--	--	0.00	0.88
SC	TA IDEX Small/Mid Cap Value A	IIVAX	B	(888) 233-4339	B+ / 8.6	-2.34	8.35	16.99 /77	24.19 /90	12.16 /87	0.37	1.44
SC	TA IDEX Small/Mid Cap Value B	IIVBX	B	(888) 233-4339	B+ / 8.5	-2.48	7.98	16.04 /75	23.33 /88	11.38 /85	0.17	2.12
SC	TA IDEX Small/Mid Cap Value C	IIVLX	B	(888) 233-4339	B+ / 8.7	-2.48	8.07	16.07 /75	23.28 /88	--	0.17	2.13
SC	TA IDEX Small/Mid Cap Value I		U	(888) 233-4339	U /	-2.22	8.65	--	--	--	0.00	0.87
HL	● TA IDEX T.Rowe Price Health Sci A	IRHAX	D+	(888) 233-4339	C / 4.8	-2.98	3.67	19.08 /81	13.06 /49	--	0.00	1.28
HL	● TA IDEX T.Rowe Price Health Sci B	IRHBX	D+	(888) 233-4339	C / 5.2	-3.30	3.78	18.58 /80	12.30 /44	--	0.00	1.24
HL	● TA IDEX T.Rowe Price Health Sci C	IRHLX	C	(888) 233-4339	C / 5.2	-3.30	3.71	18.63 /80	12.22 /44	--	0.00	1.18
SC	● TA IDEX T.Rowe Price Small Cap A	IPSAX	E-	(888) 233-4339	C- / 3.4	-9.26	-0.25	8.26 /35	12.56 /46	2.45 /32	0.00	1.35
SC	● TA IDEX T.Rowe Price Small Cap B	IPSBX	E	(888) 233-4339	C- / 3.9	-9.19	-0.27	7.69 /30	11.88 /42	1.75 /25	0.00	1.35
SC	● TA IDEX T.Rowe Price Small Cap C	IPSLX	E	(888) 233-4339	C- / 3.8	-9.23	-0.40	7.65 /30	11.77 /41	--	0.00	1.35
GI	● TA IDEX T.Rowe Price Tax-Eff Gr A	IPGAX	E+	(888) 233-4339	E- / 0.2	-4.57	-2.97	1.69 / 4	4.81 / 4	-0.04 /15	0.03	1.35
GI	● TA IDEX T.Rowe Price Tax-Eff Gr B	IDGRX	D-	(888) 233-4339	E / 0.4	-4.54	-3.07	1.32 / 3	4.23 / 3	-0.67 /13	0.02	1.35
GI	● TA IDEX T.Rowe Price Tax-Eff Gr C	IPGLX	D-	(888) 233-4339	E / 0.4	-4.45	-3.07	1.32 / 3	4.23 / 3	--	0.02	1.35
GL	TA IDEX Templeton Great Cmp Glb A	IGLBX	D+	(888) 233-4339	C- / 3.3	-0.81	4.15	14.43 /70	10.92 /35	-1.30 /11	0.84	1.55
GL	TA IDEX Templeton Great Cmp Glb B	IGLWX	D	(888) 233-4339	C- / 3.1	-0.94	3.83	13.72 /67	10.20 /29	-2.01 / 8	0.01	2.20
GL	TA IDEX Templeton Great Cmp Glb	IGLLX	D+	(888) 233-4339	C- / 3.7	-0.94	3.83	13.70 /67	10.16 /28	--	0.02	2.20
GL	TA IDEX Templeton Great Cmp Glb I		U	(888) 233-4339	U /	-0.66	4.45	--	--	--	0.00	0.89

● Denotes fund is closed to new investors
* Denotes fund is included in Section II

www.WeissRatings.com

RISK			NET ASSETS		ASSET				Portfolio Turnover Ratio	BULL / BEAR		FUND MANAGER		MINIMUMS		LOADS	
	3 Year		NAV							Last Bull Market Return	Last Bear Market Return	Manager Quality Pct	Manager Tenure (Years)	Initial Purch. $	Additional Purch. $	Front End Load	Back End Load
Risk Rating/Pts	Standard Deviation	Beta	As of 6/30/06	Total $(Mil)	Cash %	Stocks %	Bonds %	Other %									
B- / 7.6	7.0	0.79	9.14	14	4	95	0	1	100.0	37.2	-11.2	13	5	1,000	50	0.0	1.0
C / 4.4	13.5	1.47	3.73	6	4	95	0	1	73.0	60.6	-9.7	5	6	1,000	50	5.5	1.0
C / 4.3	13.7	1.49	3.58	5	4	95	0	1	73.0	57.5	-10.2	3	6	1,000	50	0.0	5.0
C / 4.3	13.7	1.49	3.58	2	4	95	0	1	73.0	57.2	-10.2	4	6	1,000	50	0.0	1.0
U /	N/A	N/A	3.75	55	4	95	0	1	73.0	N/A	N/A	N/A	N/A	0	0	0.0	0.0
C+ / 6.6	10.1	1.10	25.18	400	6	93	0	1	57.0	64.9	-6.8	41	N/A	1,000	50	5.5	1.0
C+ / 6.6	10.2	1.11	23.07	155	6	93	0	1	57.0	61.2	-7.1	33	N/A	1,000	50	0.0	5.0
C+ / 6.6	10.1	1.10	23.05	54	6	93	0	1	57.0	61.1	-7.1	33	N/A	1,000	50	0.0	1.0
U /	N/A	N/A	25.27	147	6	93	0	1	57.0	N/A	N/A	N/A	N/A	0	0	0.0	0.0
C+ / 6.6	10.1	1.10	26.34	209	6	93	0	1	57.0	66.5	-6.7	44	N/A	1,000	50	8.5	0.0
C+ / 6.4	11.7	1.39	10.66	13	8	91	0	1	86.0	77.7	-13.0	28	N/A	1,000	50	5.5	0.0
C+ / 6.4	11.7	1.39	9.99	23	8	91	0	1	86.0	74.3	-13.2	24	N/A	1,000	50	0.0	0.0
B- / 7.3	11.7	1.39	10.01	7	8	91	0	1	86.0	74.7	-13.2	24	N/A	1,000	50	0.0	0.0
U /	N/A	N/A	10.70	92	8	91	0	1	86.0	N/A	N/A	N/A	N/A	0	0	0.0	0.0
B- / 7.2	9.5	1.09	10.71	10	8	91	0	1	74.0	62.0	-8.1	36	N/A	1,000	50	5.5	0.0
B- / 7.2	9.5	1.10	10.18	17	8	91	0	1	74.0	58.8	-8.4	30	N/A	1,000	50	0.0	0.0
B- / 7.2	9.5	1.09	10.17	9	8	91	0	1	74.0	58.6	-8.4	30	4	1,000	50	0.0	0.0
U /	N/A	N/A	10.75	98	8	91	0	1	74.0	N/A	N/A	N/A	N/A	0	0	0.0	0.0
U /	N/A	N/A	11.42	313	10	64	25	1	N/A	N/A	N/A	N/A	N/A	0	0	0.0	0.0
U /	N/A	N/A	11.47	475	9	90	0	1	N/A	N/A	N/A	N/A	N/A	0	0	0.0	0.0
E- / 0.0	10.5	1.00	7.51	13	1	98	0	1	82.0	91.5	-10.4	10	4	1,000	50	5.5	0.0
E- / 0.0	10.6	1.00	6.98	18	1	98	0	1	82.0	88.5	-10.7	8	4	1,000	50	0.0	0.0
E- / 0.0	10.5	1.00	6.90	7	1	98	0	1	82.0	88.1	-10.8	8	N/A	1,000	50	0.0	0.0
U /	N/A	N/A	11.20	441	3	96	0	1	N/A	N/A	N/A	N/A	N/A	0	0	0.0	0.0
U /	N/A	N/A	10.17	309	0	100	0	0	N/A	N/A	N/A	N/A	N/A	0	0	0.0	0.0
B+ / 9.8	2.5	0.29	11.74	6	N/A	N/A	0	N/A	3.0	29.2	-4.8	69	N/A	1,000	50	5.5	1.0
B+ / 9.9	2.5	0.30	11.58	31	N/A	N/A	0	N/A	3.0	27.6	-4.8	64	4	1,000	50	0.0	5.0
B+ / 9.9	2.5	0.30	11.56	4	N/A	N/A	0	N/A	3.0	27.5	-4.8	63	4	1,000	50	0.0	0.0
B- / 7.5	9.6	1.17	16.95	57	1	98	0	1	27.0	78.5	-14.2	45	4	1,000	50	5.5	1.0
B- / 7.4	9.6	1.18	16.12	115	1	98	0	1	27.0	74.7	-14.4	37	4	1,000	50	0.0	5.0
B- / 7.4	9.6	1.17	16.12	43	1	98	0	1	27.0	74.7	-14.4	37	4	1,000	50	0.0	1.0
D / 1.7	8.1	1.00	10.27	11	6	93	0	1	47.0	68.3	-11.9	60	N/A	1,000	50	5.5	0.0
D / 1.7	8.1	1.00	9.51	15	6	93	0	1	47.0	64.8	-12.0	52	N/A	1,000	50	0.0	0.0
D / 1.7	8.1	1.00	9.45	3	6	93	0	1	47.0	64.4	-12.0	50	N/A	1,000	50	0.0	0.0
U /	N/A	N/A	10.28	61	6	93	0	1	47.0	N/A	N/A	N/A	N/A	0	0	0.0	0.0
C+ / 6.0	13.4	0.85	17.52	47	7	92	0	1	42.0	157.2	-14.9	97	N/A	1,000	50	5.5	1.0
C+ / 5.9	13.4	0.85	16.91	50	7	92	0	1	42.0	151.6	-15.1	96	N/A	1,000	50	0.0	5.0
C+ / 5.9	13.4	0.85	16.88	26	7	92	0	1	42.0	151.2	-15.1	96	N/A	1,000	50	0.0	1.0
U /	N/A	N/A	17.58	445	7	92	0	1	42.0	N/A	N/A	N/A	N/A	0	0	0.0	0.0
C / 5.0	11.3	0.89	13.01	4	N/A	93	7	N/A	59.0	81.5	-4.9	82	N/A	1,000	50	5.5	0.0
C / 5.0	11.2	0.89	12.62	5	N/A	93	7	N/A	59.0	78.4	-5.0	76	N/A	1,000	50	0.0	0.0
B- / 7.1	11.3	0.89	12.59	2	N/A	93	7	N/A	59.0	78.0	-5.0	75	N/A	1,000	50	0.0	0.0
D- / 1.4	14.0	0.92	8.04	9	17	82	0	1	22.0	93.6	-12.1	19	6	1,000	50	5.5	0.0
D- / 1.4	14.0	0.92	7.41	9	17	82	0	1	22.0	89.6	-12.3	15	6	1,000	50	0.0	0.0
D- / 1.4	14.0	0.92	7.38	3	17	82	0	1	22.0	89.1	-12.3	14	6	1,000	50	0.0	0.0
B- / 7.2	8.7	1.07	10.45	4	5	94	0	1	6.0	42.8	-11.4	8	N/A	1,000	50	5.5	0.0
B- / 7.2	8.8	1.08	10.10	7	5	94	0	1	6.0	40.3	-11.6	6	N/A	1,000	50	0.0	0.0
B- / 7.2	8.8	1.08	10.10	2	5	94	0	1	6.0	40.3	-11.6	6	N/A	1,000	50	0.0	0.0
C+ / 6.3	9.2	0.81	26.87	116	3	96	0	1	87.0	62.4	-11.8	5	N/A	1,000	50	5.5	1.0
C+ / 6.3	9.2	0.81	25.21	81	3	96	0	1	87.0	59.2	-12.0	3	N/A	1,000	50	0.0	5.0
C+ / 6.3	9.2	0.81	25.18	34	3	96	0	1	87.0	59.0	-12.0	4	N/A	1,000	50	0.0	1.0
U /	N/A	N/A	26.98	39	3	96	0	1	87.0	N/A	N/A	N/A	N/A	0	0	0.0	0.0

Data as of June 30, 2006

			99 Pct = Best / 0 Pct = Worst		PERFORMANCE							
			Overall Weiss Investment Rating		Perfor-mance Rating/Pts	Total Return % through 6/30/06			Annualized		Incl. in Returns	
Fund Type	Fund Name	Ticker Symbol		Phone		3 Mo	6 Mo	1Yr / Pct	3Yr / Pct	5Yr / Pct	Dividend Yield	Expense Ratio
BA	TA IDEX Transamerica Balanced A	IBALX	D+	(888) 233-4339	D- / 1.5	-1.76	2.41	10.45 /50	8.45 /17	4.29 /49	0.27	1.59
BA	TA IDEX Transamerica Balanced B	IBABX	D+	(888) 233-4339	D- / 1.4	-1.90	2.16	9.92 /46	7.83 /14	3.64 /42	0.08	2.14
BA	TA IDEX Transamerica Balanced C	IBLLX	C-	(888) 233-4339	D / 2.0	-1.86	2.17	10.01 /47	7.81 /14	--	0.09	2.13
CV	TA IDEX Transamerica Convertb Sec	ICVAX	D+	(888) 233-4339	C- / 4.0	-0.42	6.91	15.35 /73	11.19 /37	--	0.96	1.35
CV	TA IDEX Transamerica Convertb Sec	ICVBX	D	(888) 233-4339	C- / 3.5	-0.61	6.55	14.48 /70	10.38 /30	--	0.50	2.01
CV	TA IDEX Transamerica Convertb Sec	ICVLX	C-	(888) 233-4339	C / 4.3	-0.52	6.66	14.59 /70	10.31 /29	--	0.63	1.94
IN	TA IDEX Transamerica Equity A	ITQAX	C+	(888) 233-4339	C+ / 5.7	-3.76	2.49	18.46 /80	15.99 /63	4.30 /49	0.00	1.52
IN	TA IDEX Transamerica Equity B	ITQBX	C	(888) 233-4339	C / 5.4	-3.84	2.15	17.67 /78	15.14 /59	3.52 /42	0.00	2.17
IN	TA IDEX Transamerica Equity C	ITQLX	C+	(888) 233-4339	C+ / 5.9	-3.94	2.04	17.52 /78	15.14 /59	--	0.00	2.17
IN	TA IDEX Transamerica Equity I		U	(888) 233-4339	U /	-3.55	2.81	--	--	--	0.00	0.82
SC	TA IDEX Transamerica Growth Opp	ITSAX	B-	(888) 233-4339	B- / 7.2	-2.89	5.94	25.21 /89	18.29 /74	10.52 /82	0.00	1.75
SC	TA IDEX Transamerica Growth Opp	ITCBX	C+	(888) 233-4339	B- / 7.0	-3.04	5.73	23.88 /87	17.32 /69	9.68 /79	0.00	2.21
SC	TA IDEX Transamerica Growth Opp	ITSLX	B-	(888) 233-4339	B- / 7.4	-3.03	5.59	24.22 /87	17.37 /70	--	0.00	2.40
SC	TA IDEX Transamerica Growth Opp I		U	(888) 233-4339	U /	-2.66	6.42	--	--	--	0.00	0.88
BA	TA IDEX Transamerica Value Bal A	ITAPX	C-	(888) 233-4339	D / 2.0	-0.53	3.38	9.64 /44	9.34 /23	3.43 /41	1.67	1.45
BA	TA IDEX Transamerica Value Bal B	ITABX	D+	(888) 233-4339	D / 1.8	-0.71	3.07	8.91 /39	8.63 /19	2.73 /34	1.09	2.10
BA	TA IDEX Transamerica Value Bal C	ITALX	C-	(888) 233-4339	D+ / 2.4	-0.71	3.00	8.91 /39	8.63 /19	--	1.17	2.20
SC	Tamarack Enterprise Fund A	TETAX	B+	(800) 422-2766	B- / 7.4	-2.33	10.47	16.99 /77	19.43 /77	15.18 /92	0.00	1.33
SC	Tamarack Enterprise Fund C	TETCX	B+	(800) 422-2766	B / 7.7	-2.57	10.00	16.07 /75	18.76 /75	14.80 /92	0.00	2.08
SC	Tamarack Enterprise Fund I	TETIX	C	(800) 422-2766	B / 8.0	-2.32	10.59	17.23 /78	19.64 /78	15.31 /92	0.00	1.08
SC	Tamarack Enterprise Fund R	TETRX	A-	(800) 422-2766	B / 7.8	-2.42	10.30	16.66 /76	19.19 /77	15.04 /92	0.00	1.58
SC	Tamarack Enterprise Fund S	TETSX	B	(800) 422-2766	B / 8.0	-2.32	10.59	17.27 /78	19.65 /78	15.31 /92	0.00	1.08
SC	Tamarack Enterprise Small Cap S	TEESX	C	(800) 422-2766	B- / 7.5	-5.20	11.37	15.23 /72	18.49 /74	10.16 /81	0.00	1.30
GR	Tamarack Large Cap Growth A	TLEAX	D-	(800) 422-2766	E / 0.4	-5.51	-3.62	3.00 / 7	6.45 / 8	-1.66 / 9	0.00	1.25
GR	Tamarack Large Cap Growth I	TLEIX	E	(800) 422-2766	E+ / 0.8	-5.45	-3.50	3.30 / 8	6.69 / 9	-1.54 /10	0.04	1.00
GR	Tamarack Large Cap Growth S	TLESX	U	(800) 422-2766	U /	-5.45	-3.58	3.31 / 8	--	--	0.05	1.00
SC	Tamarack Micro Cap Value S	TMVSX	A	(800) 422-2766	B+ / 8.6	-2.88	9.44	17.46 /78	22.97 /87	14.82 /92	0.33	1.10
MC	Tamarack Mid Cap Growth A	TMCAX	D-	(800) 422-2766	C- / 3.6	-6.48	1.76	12.44 /62	12.62 /46	5.69 /59	0.00	1.35
MC	Tamarack Mid Cap Growth I	TMCIX	D+	(800) 422-2766	C / 4.8	-6.44	1.87	12.81 /63	12.88 /48	5.95 /61	0.00	1.10
SC	Tamarack Small Cap Growth C	TSMCX	C+	(800) 422-2766	C+ / 5.8	-7.85	2.99	9.88 /46	15.45 /61	6.92 /66	0.00	2.43
GI	Tamarack Value Fund A	TVAAX	C	(800) 422-2766	C- / 3.1	-0.28	3.43	6.39 /23	11.83 /41	3.91 /45	1.04	1.32
GI	Tamarack Value Fund S	TVASX	D-	(800) 422-2766	C / 4.3	-0.23	3.56	6.67 /24	11.99 /42	4.10 /47	1.30	1.06
GR	TCM Small Cap Growth Fund	TCMSX	U	(866) 811-0215	U /	-3.57	12.26	28.09 /93	--	--	0.00	0.95
AG	TCW Aggressive Gr Eq I	TGMCX	E-	(800) 386-3829	D- / 1.3	-8.45	-2.82	9.62 /44	8.37 /17	-2.32 / 7	0.00	1.35
AG	TCW Aggressive Gr Eq N	TGANX	E-	(800) 386-3829	D- / 1.2	-8.45	-2.89	9.50 /43	8.05 /15	-2.64 / 6	0.00	1.67
FO	TCW Asia Pacific Equities I	TGAPX	C+	(800) 386-3829	B+ / 8.7	0.09	8.87	24.54 /88	22.79 /87	12.55 /88	1.01	1.97
CV	TCW Convertible Sec I	TGCVX	D-	(800) 386-3829	E+ / 0.8	-2.92	-0.01	3.33 / 8	5.34 / 5	-0.42 /14	2.26	1.37
GR	TCW Diversified Value I	TGDIX	U	(800) 386-3829	U /	0.34	6.28	11.36 /56	--	--	0.33	1.01
GR	TCW Diversified Value N	TGDVX	A+	(800) 386-3829	B- / 7.5	0.20	6.08	10.94 /53	18.50 /74	7.41 /69	0.01	1.40
MC	TCW Dividend Focused Fd	TGIGX	B+	(800) 386-3829	C+ / 6.2	0.17	4.45	6.99 /26	15.36 /61	9.20 /77	1.26	1.25
EM	TCW Emerging Markets Eq I	TGEMX	B-	(800) 386-3829	A / 9.4	-5.51	6.49	31.84 /96	29.45 /95	17.32 /94	1.53	2.03
GR	TCW Equities I	TGLVX	B+	(800) 386-3829	B- / 7.1	-0.18	5.91	14.91 /71	16.37 /65	6.05 /61	0.85	0.77
GR	TCW Equities K	TGLKX	B+	(800) 386-3829	B- / 7.0	-0.18	5.85	14.72 /71	16.26 /65	--	0.00	1.67
GR	TCW Equities N	TGLNX	B	(800) 386-3829	C+ / 6.7	-0.24	5.64	14.21 /69	15.64 /62	5.39 /57	0.00	1.42
GR	TCW Focused Equities Fund N	TGFVX	C+	(800) 386-3829	B / 7.6	-0.87	5.75	14.57 /70	18.41 /74	6.03 /61	0.07	1.38
FO	TCW Global Alpha Fund I	TGIEX	B+	(800) 386-3829	B+ / 8.3	0.16	7.84	27.11 /91	19.55 /78	4.33 /49	0.00	1.63
MC	TCW Growth Equities I	TGGEX	U	(800) 386-3829	U /	-7.08	-1.06	15.16 /72	--	--	0.00	1.62
SC	TCW Opportunity I	TGOIX	C+	(800) 386-3829	B- / 7.0	-7.12	5.66	11.82 /58	17.42 /70	-1.70 / 9	0.00	0.92
SC	TCW Opportunity K	TGOKX	C+	(800) 386-3829	C+ / 6.8	-7.32	5.30	11.12 /54	16.99 /68	--	0.00	1.75
SC	TCW Opportunity N	TGONX	C+	(800) 386-3829	C+ / 6.9	-7.20	5.51	11.48 /57	17.06 /68	9.45 /78	0.00	1.27
* GR	TCW Select Equities I	TGCEX	E+	(800) 386-3829	D / 1.9	-5.32	-7.04	3.11 / 8	9.25 /22	1.29 /22	0.00	0.90
GR	TCW Select Equities N	TGCNX	E+	(800) 386-3829	D / 1.8	-5.39	-7.15	2.79 / 7	8.92 /20	0.96 /20	0.00	1.21

● Denotes fund is closed to new investors
* Denotes fund is included in Section II

RISK Risk Rating/Pts	3 Year Standard Deviation	Beta	NET ASSETS NAV As of 6/30/06	Total $(Mil)	ASSET Cash %	Stocks %	Bonds %	Other %	Portfolio Turnover Ratio	BULL / BEAR Last Bull Market Return	Last Bear Market Return	FUND MANAGER Manager Quality Pct	Manager Tenure (Years)	MINIMUMS Initial Purch. $	Additional Purch. $	LOADS Front End Load	Back End Load
B / 8.3	7.1	1.32	21.18	57	3	69	26	2	27.0	40.8	-3.2	46	N/A	1,000	50	5.5	1.0
B / 8.4	7.1	1.32	21.12	127	3	69	26	2	27.0	38.3	-3.6	39	N/A	1,000	50	0.0	5.0
B / 8.4	7.1	1.31	21.06	39	3	69	26	2	27.0	38.2	-3.6	39	N/A	1,000	50	0.0	1.0
C+ / 5.8	9.8	1.40	12.69	6	0	9	0	91	87.0	62.3	0.1	74	N/A	1,000	50	4.8	1.0
C+ / 5.8	9.7	1.40	12.64	7	0	9	0	91	87.0	58.5	-0.1	67	N/A	1,000	50	0.0	5.0
C+ / 6.5	9.8	1.41	12.60	4	0	9	0	91	87.0	58.2	-0.1	66	N/A	1,000	50	0.0	1.0
C+ / 6.8	10.1	1.16	9.46	83	1	98	0	1	39.0	86.7	-8.5	84	N/A	1,000	50	5.5	1.0
C+ / 6.8	10.2	1.17	9.02	52	1	98	0	1	39.0	82.4	-8.5	77	N/A	1,000	50	0.0	5.0
C+ / 6.8	10.2	1.17	9.02	26	1	98	0	1	39.0	82.4	-8.5	78	N/A	1,000	50	0.0	1.0
U /	N/A	N/A	9.50	509	1	98	0	1	39.0	N/A	N/A	N/A	N/A	0	0	0.0	0.0
C+ / 6.5	11.3	0.66	8.74	60	2	97	0	1	34.0	97.8	-11.5	93	N/A	1,000	50	5.5	1.0
C+ / 6.4	11.2	0.66	8.30	74	2	97	0	1	34.0	92.6	-11.6	89	N/A	1,000	50	0.0	5.0
C+ / 6.4	11.2	0.66	8.31	25	2	97	0	1	34.0	92.8	-11.6	90	N/A	1,000	50	0.0	1.0
U /	N/A	N/A	8.79	220	2	97	0	1	34.0	N/A	N/A	N/A	N/A	0	0	0.0	0.0
B / 8.4	5.5	1.06	12.44	31	5	67	27	1	57.0	48.8	-4.4	71	5	1,000	50	5.5	1.0
B / 8.5	5.5	1.06	12.41	22	5	67	27	1	57.0	45.8	-4.8	64	5	1,000	50	0.0	5.0
B / 8.5	5.5	1.06	12.40	11	5	67	27	1	57.0	46.0	-4.8	65	N/A	1,000	50	0.0	1.0
B- / 7.5	12.0	0.76	25.54	17	4	94	1	1	13.0	110.9	-3.9	91	2	1,000	100	5.8	2.0
B- / 7.5	12.0	0.76	25.07	2	4	94	1	1	13.0	107.8	-3.9	88	2	1,000	100	0.0	2.0
C / 4.5	15.7	0.61	25.70	34	4	94	1	1	13.0	112.0	-3.9	97	2	250,000	0	0.0	2.0
B- / 7.5	12.0	0.76	25.37	N/A	4	94	1	1	13.0	109.8	-3.9	90	2	1,000	100	0.0	2.0
C+ / 6.1	12.0	0.76	25.70	324	4	94	1	1	13.0	112.1	-3.9	92	7	1,000	100	0.0	2.0
C / 4.8	13.8	0.89	31.15	65	1	98	0	1	19.1	106.7	-8.6	72	2	1,000	100	0.0	2.0
B- / 7.1	8.8	1.02	10.64	5	0	99	0	1	15.0	45.9	-11.6	16	N/A	1,000	100	5.8	2.0
C+ / 5.6	8.8	1.01	10.76	1	0	99	0	1	15.0	47.2	-12.2	18	N/A	250,000	0	0.0	2.0
U /	N/A	N/A	10.76	127	0	99	0	1	15.0	N/A	N/A	N/A	N/A	1,000	100	0.0	2.0
B- / 7.0	12.9	0.86	21.91	235	0	97	1	2	4.3	144.6	-9.1	95	N/A	1,000	100	0.0	2.0
C / 4.8	12.0	1.01	12.71	46	2	97	0	1	11.0	80.9	-9.0	14	N/A	1,000	100	5.8	2.0
C / 4.9	12.0	1.00	13.08	77	2	97	0	1	11.0	82.1	-8.9	16	N/A	250,000	0	0.0	2.0
C+ / 6.9	13.4	0.86	10.33	N/A	2	97	0	1	10.0	90.6	-7.2	46	2	1,000	100	0.0	2.0
B / 8.9	7.5	0.89	39.80	1	2	97	0	1	20.0	67.6	-9.2	72	N/A	1,000	100	5.8	2.0
C / 4.3	7.5	0.89	39.90	291	2	97	0	1	20.0	68.3	-9.2	74	N/A	1,000	100	0.0	2.0
U /	N/A	N/A	30.22	356	2	97	0	1	138.5	N/A	N/A	N/A	2	100,000	2,500	0.0	1.0
C- / 3.5	17.5	1.91	13.11	18	0	99	0	1	57.2	73.0	-8.4	2	N/A	2,000	250	0.0	0.0
C- / 3.4	17.5	1.90	12.79	10	0	99	0	1	57.2	71.2	-8.5	1	N/A	2,000	250	0.0	0.0
C / 4.8	16.7	1.20	11.54	21	2	97	0	1	192.3	125.5	-10.5	12	N/A	2,000	250	0.0	2.0
B- / 7.4	7.8	1.16	8.62	16	0	0	0	100	81.4	36.6	-2.8	29	9	2,000	250	0.0	0.0
U /	N/A	N/A	14.89	415	9	90	0	1	34.7	N/A	N/A	N/A	7	2,000	250	0.0	0.0
B / 8.9	9.0	1.07	14.84	49	9	90	0	1	34.7	101.1	-11.3	95	7	2,000	250	0.0	0.0
B / 8.8	8.8	0.71	12.03	1,004	5	94	0	1	31.1	81.3	-8.3	75	5	2,000	250	0.0	0.0
C / 4.4	18.0	1.08	15.10	13	2	97	0	1	84.2	186.7	-7.6	6	3	2,000	250	0.0	2.0
B / 8.0	10.1	1.17	16.49	86	0	99	0	1	32.3	92.6	-11.7	85	21	2,000	250	0.0	0.0
B / 8.0	9.9	1.16	16.83	N/A	0	99	0	1	32.3	91.9	-12.5	86	8	2,000	500	0.0	0.0
B / 8.0	10.0	1.17	16.48	5	0	99	0	1	32.3	88.6	-11.8	81	21	2,000	250	0.0	0.0
C / 5.4	11.4	1.28	13.62	22	1	98	0	1	29.3	101.5	-11.8	90	N/A	2,000	250	0.0	0.0
C+ / 6.8	12.1	1.10	12.66	59	1	98	0	1	114.7	106.1	-14.8	9	14	2,000	500	0.0	0.0
U /	N/A	N/A	12.08	25	1	98	0	1	58.0	N/A	N/A	N/A	N/A	2,000	250	0.0	0.0
C+ / 6.0	15.1	0.99	14.75	35	4	95	0	1	44.6	116.6	-10.6	44	11	2,000	250	0.0	0.0
C+ / 6.0	14.9	0.98	14.69	4	4	95	0	1	44.6	114.4	-10.6	42	11	2,000	250	0.0	0.0
C+ / 5.9	15.1	0.99	14.56	78	4	95	0	1	44.6	114.6	-10.7	41	11	2,000	250	0.0	0.0
C / 5.5	14.6	1.55	18.88	2,838	1	98	0	1	16.3	71.8	-11.0	8	2	2,000	250	0.0	0.0
C / 5.5	14.6	1.55	18.44	1,082	1	98	0	1	16.3	70.1	-11.0	8	2	2,000	250	0.0	0.0

Fund Type	Fund Name	Ticker Symbol	Overall Weiss Investment Rating	Phone	Perfor-mance Rating/Pts	3 Mo	6 Mo	1Yr / Pct	Annualized 3Yr / Pct	5Yr / Pct	Dividend Yield	Expense Ratio
SC	TCW Small Cap Growth I	TGSCX	D+	(800) 386-3829	B- / 7.2	-5.70	8.48	23.01 /86	16.52 /66	-4.71 / 3	0.00	1.40
SC	TCW Small Cap Growth N	TGSNX	D+	(800) 386-3829	B- / 7.0	-5.78	8.32	22.80 /85	16.05 /64	-5.03 / 2	0.00	1.75
SC	TCW Value Added I	TGSVX	D	(800) 386-3829	C+ / 5.9	-6.35	6.94	11.06 /54	14.50 /56	5.31 /57	0.00	1.62
SC	TCW Value Added K	TGDKX	D+	(800) 386-3829	C+ / 5.7	-5.41	5.78	9.60 /44	14.09 /54	--	0.00	1.87
SC	TCW Value Added N	TGSSX	D+	(800) 386-3829	C+ / 5.6	-5.46	5.64	9.60 /44	14.02 /54	--	0.00	1.62
MC	TCW Value Opportunities I	TGVOX	C+	(800) 386-3829	C+ / 6.6	-3.43	4.91	11.76 /58	15.88 /63	8.23 /72	0.17	0.92
MC	TCW Value Opportunities K	TGVKX	C+	(800) 386-3829	C+ / 6.3	-3.60	4.49	10.89 /53	15.33 /60	--	0.00	1.75
MC	TCW Value Opportunities N	TGVNX	C+	(800) 386-3829	C+ / 6.4	-3.49	4.70	11.35 /56	15.49 /61	7.86 /71	0.00	1.27
AA	Teberg Fund (The)	TEBRX	D	(866) 209-1964	E+ / 0.7	-1.27	1.57	5.92 /20	4.61 / 3	--	0.00	2.25
FO	Templeton China World A	TCWAX	A-	(800) 342-5236	A- / 9.2	2.94	10.17	22.41 /85	27.07 /93	19.65 /96	1.18	2.08
FO	Templeton China World Adv	TACWX	A	(800) 321-8563	A / 9.4	3.05	10.35	22.86 /86	27.53 /94	20.09 /96	1.42	1.73
FO	● Templeton China World B	TCWBX	A-	(800) 342-5236	A- / 9.2	2.83	9.87	21.71 /84	26.25 /92	18.87 /95	0.68	3.00
FO	Templeton China World C	TCWCX	A-	(800) 342-5236	A / 9.3	2.80	9.85	21.68 /84	26.27 /92	18.88 /95	0.95	3.00
★ EM	Templeton Developing Markets A	TEDMX	B+	(800) 342-5236	A / 9.5	-4.63	6.14	27.90 /93	31.66 /96	19.91 /96	1.11	2.03
EM	Templeton Developing Markets Adv	TDADX	B+	(800) 321-8563	A+ / 9.6	-4.56	6.23	28.24 /93	32.06 /97	20.37 /96	1.43	1.71
EM	● Templeton Developing Markets B	TDMBX	B+	(800) 342-5236	A / 9.5	-4.80	5.76	27.02 /91	30.80 /96	19.15 /95	0.66	2.62
EM	Templeton Developing Markets C	TDMTX	B+	(800) 342-5236	A / 9.5	-4.77	5.77	27.05 /91	30.78 /96	19.14 /95	0.70	2.71
EM	Templeton Developing Markets R	TDMRX	B+	(800) 342-5236	A+ / 9.6	-4.68	5.98	27.62 /92	31.42 /96	19.70 /96	1.18	2.21
FO	Templeton Foreign A	TEMFX	B+	(800) 342-5236	B- / 7.4	-0.30	6.15	18.40 /80	19.22 /77	9.78 /80	1.42	1.00
FO	Templeton Foreign Adv	TFFAX	A-	(800) 321-8563	B / 8.1	-0.30	6.17	18.65 /80	19.47 /78	10.01 /81	1.73	0.90
FO	● Templeton Foreign B	TFRBX	B+	(800) 342-5236	B- / 7.4	-0.53	5.68	17.57 /78	18.31 /74	8.96 /76	0.85	2.00
FO	Templeton Foreign C	TEFTX	B+	(800) 342-5236	B / 7.6	-0.45	5.75	17.56 /78	18.33 /74	8.97 /76	0.87	2.00
FO	Templeton Foreign R	TEFRX	B+	(800) 342-5236	B / 7.9	-0.37	5.95	18.13 /79	18.90 /76	9.49 /79	1.33	1.00
FO	Templeton Foreign Smaller Co A	FINEX	B	(800) 342-5236	B+ / 8.3	-2.83	7.16	17.47 /78	22.74 /87	13.68 /90	2.02	2.00
FO	Templeton Foreign Smaller Co Adv	FTFAX	B+	(800) 321-8563	B+ / 8.7	-2.75	7.33	17.81 /79	23.07 /87	14.00 /90	2.46	1.00
FO	● Templeton Foreign Smaller Co B		B	(800) 342-5236	B / 8.2	-2.96	6.77	16.59 /76	21.83 /85	12.80 /88	1.87	2.00
FO	Templeton Foreign Smaller Co C	FCFSX	B	(800) 342-5236	B+ / 8.4	-2.96	6.81	16.58 /76	21.82 /85	12.81 /88	1.89	2.00
GL	Templeton Global Long-Short A	TLSAX	C-	(800) 342-5236	D+ / 2.4	0.56	6.21	11.38 /56	9.03 /21	--	1.16	1.00
GL	Templeton Global Long-Short Adv		D	(800) 321-8563	C- / 3.6	0.56	6.39	11.74 /58	9.26 /22	--	1.53	1.00
GL	● Templeton Global Long-Short B	TLSBX	C-	(800) 342-5236	D+ / 2.3	0.33	5.77	10.51 /50	8.29 /17	--	0.49	2.00
GL	Templeton Global Opportunities A	TEGOX	A-	(800) 342-5236	B / 7.9	-0.17	8.53	21.01 /83	20.79 /82	7.92 /71	0.99	1.44
GL	● Templeton Global Opportunities B		A-	(800) 342-5236	B / 7.8	-0.39	8.12	20.11 /82	19.90 /79	7.12 /67	0.40	2.19
GL	Templeton Global Opportunities C	TEGPX	A	(800) 342-5236	B / 8.0	-0.39	8.09	20.06 /82	19.85 /79	7.10 /67	0.41	2.13
GL	Templeton Global Smaller Co Gr A	TEMGX	C	(800) 342-5236	B+ / 8.5	-4.80	7.08	14.10 /69	24.51 /90	14.71 /91	1.31	1.00
GL	Templeton Global Smaller Co Gr Adv	TGSAX	C	(800) 321-8563	B+ / 8.9	-4.79	7.19	14.28 /69	24.81 /91	15.02 /92	1.53	1.10
GL	● Templeton Global Smaller Co Gr B		C	(800) 342-5236	B+ / 8.4	-4.99	6.72	13.24 /65	23.60 /89	13.83 /90	0.98	2.00
GL	Templeton Global Smaller Co Gr C	TESGX	C	(800) 342-5236	B+ / 8.6	-5.01	6.73	13.23 /65	23.60 /89	13.86 /90	1.05	2.00
★ GL	Templeton Growth A	TEPLX	B-	(800) 342-5236	C+ / 6.7	0.83	6.41	15.13 /72	17.16 /69	10.39 /82	1.51	1.00
GL	Templeton Growth Adv	TGADX	B+	(800) 321-8563	B- / 7.4	0.87	6.54	15.44 /73	17.45 /70	10.68 /83	1.81	0.81
GL	● Templeton Growth B	TMGBX	B-	(800) 342-5236	C+ / 6.6	0.63	5.98	14.25 /69	16.29 /65	9.58 /79	0.94	2.00
GL	Templeton Growth C	TEGTX	B-	(800) 342-5236	C+ / 6.9	0.63	6.01	14.25 /69	16.28 /65	9.57 /79	1.01	2.00
GL	Templeton Growth R	TEGRX	B+	(800) 342-5236	B- / 7.2	0.75	6.28	14.82 /71	16.87 /67	10.11 /81	1.46	1.00
GL	Templeton Income Fund A	TINCX	U	(800) 342-5236	U /	1.23	7.30	--	--	--	0.00	1.20
GL	Templeton Income Fund C	TCINX	U	(800) 342-5236	U /	1.13	7.14	--	--	--	0.00	1.60
EM	Templeton Inst-Emerg Markets Mkt	TEEMX	B+	(800) 321-8563	A+ / 9.6	-4.48	6.22	28.42 /93	32.01 /97	20.52 /97	1.79	1.42
FO	Templeton Inst-Foreign Eq Prim	TFEQX	A+	(800) 321-8563	A- / 9.1	0.25	8.07	22.82 /85	24.45 /90	11.27 /85	2.23	0.81
FO	Templeton International (ex EM) A	TEGEX	A	(800) 342-5236	B / 7.9	1.65	9.41	19.83 /82	20.24 /80	9.16 /77	1.24	1.63
FO	Templeton International (ex EM) Adv		A+	(800) 321-8563	B+ / 8.5	1.76	9.57	20.19 /82	20.68 /82	9.52 /79	1.60	1.32
FO	Templeton International (ex EM) C	TGEFX	A	(800) 342-5236	B / 8.1	1.50	9.02	18.99 /80	19.47 /78	8.48 /74	0.73	2.23
★ GL	Templeton World A	TEMWX	C+	(800) 342-5236	B- / 7.2	0.27	5.75	16.77 /77	18.55 /75	9.43 /78	1.24	1.00
GL	● Templeton World B	TWDBX	C+	(800) 342-5236	B- / 7.1	0.05	5.38	15.88 /74	17.66 /71	8.62 /75	0.79	2.00
GL	Templeton World C	TEWTX	B-	(800) 342-5236	B- / 7.4	0.05	5.38	15.89 /74	17.66 /71	8.62 /75	0.81	2.00

● Denotes fund is closed to new investors
★ Denotes fund is included in Section II

RISK			NET ASSETS		ASSET				BULL / BEAR		FUND MANAGER		MINIMUMS		LOADS	
	3 Year		NAV						Last Bull	Last Bear	Manager	Manager	Initial	Additional	Front	Back
Risk Rating/Pts	Standard Deviation	Beta	As of 6/30/06	Total $(Mil)	Cash %	Stocks %	Bonds %	Other %	Portfolio Turnover Ratio	Market Return	Market Return	Quality Pct	Tenure (Years)	Purch. $	Purch. $	End Load	End Load
C- / 3.0	18.2	1.14	19.19	27	1	98	0	1	90.9	114.8	-16.3	20	N/A	2,000	250	0.0	0.0
C- / 3.0	18.2	1.14	18.74	31	1	98	0	1	90.9	112.4	-16.4	18	N/A	2,000	250	0.0	0.0
C- / 3.1	18.7	1.23	13.56	29	1	98	0	1	62.8	102.4	-13.4	7	24	2,000	250	0.0	0.0
C / 4.3	18.0	1.17	16.10	N/A	1	98	0	1	62.8	98.0	-13.4	8	6	2,000	500	0.0	0.0
C / 4.3	18.0	1.17	16.10	N/A	1	98	0	1	62.8	98.2	-13.4	8	6	2,000	250	0.0	0.0
C+ / 6.2	12.9	1.09	23.09	819	7	92	0	1	59.5	102.2	-10.7	24	24	2,000	250	0.0	0.0
C+ / 6.2	12.9	1.09	22.79	7	7	92	0	1	59.5	99.6	-10.7	21	24	2,000	250	0.0	0.0
C+ / 6.2	12.9	1.09	22.70	202	7	92	0	1	59.5	100.0	-10.7	22	24	2,000	250	0.0	0.0
B / 8.3	5.2	0.94	11.63	34	2	48	49	1	113.6	33.2	-1.8	29	4	25,000	1,000	0.0	0.0
C+ / 6.3	15.4	1.11	25.23	252	8	90	0	2	9.7	134.4	10.6	54	N/A	1,000	50	5.8	1.0
C+ / 6.3	15.4	1.11	25.38	242	8	90	0	2	9.7	137.2	10.7	59	N/A	5,000,000	50	0.0	0.0
C+ / 6.3	15.4	1.11	25.04	15	8	90	0	2	9.7	129.6	10.4	46	N/A	1,000	50	0.0	4.0
C+ / 6.3	15.4	1.12	24.99	101	8	90	0	2	9.7	129.8	10.4	46	N/A	1,000	50	0.0	1.0
C / 5.2	15.7	0.94	24.71	4,225	2	96	0	2	34.8	197.7	-3.5	38	15	1,000	50	5.8	1.0
C / 5.2	15.7	0.94	24.72	367	2	96	0	2	34.8	200.9	-3.5	41	15	5,000,000	50	0.0	0.0
C / 5.2	15.7	0.94	24.21	49	2	96	0	2	34.8	191.5	-3.7	32	7	1,000	50	0.0	4.0
C / 5.2	15.7	0.94	24.18	414	2	96	0	2	34.8	191.5	-3.8	33	11	1,000	50	0.0	1.0
C / 5.2	15.7	0.94	24.44	27	2	96	0	2	34.8	195.6	-3.6	36	4	1,000	50	0.0	0.0
B- / 7.3	9.7	0.92	13.46	14,656	10	88	0	2	34.0	101.1	-9.4	28	17	1,000	50	5.8	1.0
B- / 7.3	9.7	0.92	13.43	2,188	10	88	0	2	34.0	102.2	-9.2	29	17	5,000,000	50	0.0	0.0
B- / 7.3	9.7	0.92	13.22	231	10	88	0	2	34.0	96.3	-9.5	22	7	1,000	50	0.0	4.0
B- / 7.3	9.7	0.92	13.25	1,503	10	88	0	2	34.0	96.3	-9.5	22	11	1,000	50	0.0	1.0
B- / 7.3	9.7	0.92	13.35	220	10	88	0	2	34.0	99.4	-9.5	26	17	1,000	50	0.0	0.0
C+ / 5.9	11.1	1.00	21.76	330	10	90	0	0	36.9	140.5	-7.1	40	N/A	1,000	50	5.8	1.0
C+ / 5.9	11.1	1.00	21.80	35	10	90	0	0	36.9	142.5	-7.0	43	N/A	5,000,000	50	0.0	0.0
C+ / 5.8	11.1	1.00	21.28	8	10	90	0	0	36.9	134.7	-7.3	33	N/A	1,000	50	0.0	4.0
C+ / 5.8	11.1	1.00	21.33	29	10	90	0	0	36.9	134.2	-7.3	33	N/A	1,000	50	0.0	1.0
B+ / 9.1	6.3	0.56	12.49	120	N/A	N/A	0	N/A	111.5	34.0	-4.8	15	5	10,000	50	5.8	1.0
C / 5.1	6.3	0.56	12.48	3	N/A	N/A	0	N/A	111.5	34.8	-4.8	17	5	5,000,000	50	0.0	0.0
B+ / 9.0	6.4	0.57	12.28	35	N/A	N/A	0	N/A	111.5	31.0	-4.9	12	5	10,000	50	0.0	4.0
B- / 7.7	10.2	0.96	18.03	415	0	98	0	2	10.2	117.0	-11.8	32	N/A	1,000	50	5.8	1.0
B- / 7.7	10.2	0.96	17.81	2	0	98	0	2	10.2	111.8	-11.9	27	N/A	1,000	50	0.0	4.0
B- / 7.7	10.2	0.96	17.74	22	0	98	0	2	10.2	111.8	-11.9	27	N/A	1,000	50	0.0	1.0
C- / 3.6	12.1	1.05	8.92	1,105	6	94	0	0	41.6	165.9	-10.1	43	7	1,000	50	5.8	1.0
C- / 3.5	12.1	1.05	8.94	55	6	94	0	0	41.6	168.2	-10.1	46	7	5,000,000	50	0.0	0.0
C- / 3.6	12.1	1.05	8.57	8	6	94	0	0	41.6	159.5	-10.3	36	7	1,000	50	0.0	4.0
C- / 3.6	12.2	1.06	8.72	71	6	94	0	0	41.6	160.0	-10.3	34	7	1,000	50	0.0	1.0
B- / 7.7	8.3	0.79	24.41	23,116	6	92	0	2	20.0	94.0	-9.6	34	N/A	1,000	50	5.8	1.0
B- / 7.6	8.3	0.79	24.45	3,693	6	92	0	2	20.0	95.4	-9.4	37	N/A	5,000,000	50	0.0	0.0
B- / 7.8	8.3	0.79	23.92	572	6	92	0	2	20.0	89.5	-9.7	29	N/A	1,000	50	0.0	4.0
B- / 7.7	8.3	0.79	23.80	2,279	6	92	0	2	20.0	89.4	-9.7	29	N/A	1,000	50	0.0	1.0
B- / 7.7	8.3	0.79	24.20	389	6	92	0	2	20.0	92.4	-9.6	33	N/A	1,000	50	0.0	0.0
U /	N/A	N/A	2.67	112	8	56	34	2	N/A	N/A	N/A	N/A	N/A	1,000	50	4.3	1.0
U /	N/A	N/A	2.67	55	8	56	34	2	N/A	N/A	N/A	N/A	N/A	1,000	50	0.0	1.0
C / 5.2	15.8	0.95	20.05	2,802	0	99	0	1	36.4	199.4	-3.2	39	N/A	5,000,000	50	0.0	0.0
B- / 7.6	10.7	1.02	23.89	6,323	4	95	0	1	13.0	133.9	-10.1	52	N/A	5,000,000	50	0.0	0.0
B- / 7.8	9.5	0.91	17.39	53	2	97	0	1	18.9	108.6	-9.9	37	11	1,000	50	5.8	1.0
B- / 7.8	9.5	0.91	17.45	1	2	97	0	1	18.9	111.3	-9.9	39	11	5,000,000	50	0.0	0.0
B- / 7.8	9.5	0.91	17.15	32	2	97	0	1	18.9	104.4	-9.9	31	11	1,000	50	0.0	1.0
C+ / 6.3	9.8	0.91	18.76	8,388	4	94	0	2	24.1	101.6	-11.6	26	5	1,000	50	5.8	1.0
C+ / 6.4	9.8	0.91	18.42	63	4	94	0	2	24.1	96.9	-11.8	21	5	1,000	50	0.0	4.0
C+ / 6.4	9.8	0.91	18.21	396	4	94	0	2	24.1	96.9	-11.9	20	5	1,000	50	0.0	1.0

Fund Type	Fund Name	Ticker Symbol	Overall Weiss Investment Rating	Phone	Performance Rating/Pts	3 Mo	6 Mo	1Yr / Pct	3Yr / Pct	5Yr / Pct	Dividend Yield	Expense Ratio
	99 Pct = Best / 0 Pct = Worst				PERFORMANCE — Total Return % through 6/30/06 / Annualized — Incl. in Returns							
SC	Texas Capital-Value & Growth	TCVGX	B+	(800) 880-0324	B / 8.2	-2.14	5.09	12.37 /61	23.39 /88	14.31 /91	0.00	1.78
FO	The Boston Co Intl Core Eq	SDIEX	A+	(800) 221-4795	A / 9.4	0.60	11.17	29.86 /94	27.99 /94	15.01 /92	1.70	1.12
FO	● The Boston Co Intl Small Cap Fd	SDISX	A+	(800) 221-4795	A+ / 9.8	-1.18	12.80	38.73 /98	37.08 /99	23.17 /98	0.77	1.27
GR	The Boston Co Large Cap Core Fd	SDEQX	D+	(800) 221-4795	C- / 3.7	-2.21	2.40	8.59 /37	11.15 /37	3.74 /43	0.96	0.84
SC	The Boston Co Small Cap Eq Fd	SDSCX	B	(800) 221-4795	B / 8.0	-3.94	6.45	15.28 /73	20.51 /81	6.75 /65	0.00	1.33
SC	The Boston Co Small Cap Growth	SSETX	B-	(800) 221-4795	B- / 7.5	-4.71	6.48	15.08 /72	18.90 /76	5.10 /55	0.00	1.37
SC	The Boston Co Sml Cp Tx Sensitve	SDCEX	C+	(800) 221-4795	B / 7.6	-4.68	6.60	15.27 /73	18.99 /76	5.56 /58	0.00	1.03
SC	The Boston Company Small Cap Val	STSVX	A+	(800) 221-4795	B+ / 8.9	-1.05	10.55	16.77 /77	24.52 /90	16.01 /93	0.12	1.18
TC	The Information Age Fund	RSIFX	E-	(800) 766-3863	C- / 3.2	-13.41	-4.46	4.20 /11	12.06 /43	0.77 /19	0.00	1.62
FO	● The Japan Fund CL S	SJPNX	C-	(800) 544-8888	B / 7.9	-8.79	-7.48	25.51 /89	23.21 /88	7.14 /67	0.00	1.59
★ FO	● Third Avenue International Value	TAVIX	A+	(800) 443-1021	A / 9.4	-0.82	8.27	20.50 /82	29.35 /95	--	2.00	N/A
★ RE	● Third Avenue Real Estate Value	TAREX	A+	(800) 443-1021	B+ / 8.8	-1.48	8.82	13.44 /66	23.93 /89	18.81 /95	1.35	1.11
★ SC	● Third Avenue Sm Cap Value Fund	TASCX	A+	(800) 443-1021	B / 8.0	-0.89	4.99	12.21 /61	20.52 /81	11.67 /86	1.16	1.11
★ GR	Third Avenue Value Fund	TAVFX	A+	(800) 443-1021	B+ / 8.7	-1.21	5.44	14.72 /71	23.58 /89	12.34 /87	2.61	1.05
EM	Third Millennium Russia Fund	TMRFX	D+	(800) 527-9500	A+ / 9.8	-7.23	12.21	52.26 /99	37.00 /99	32.97 /99	0.00	2.75
MC	Thomas White American Oppor	TWAOX	C	(800) 811-0535	C+ / 6.9	-2.30	3.13	9.94 /47	17.68 /71	11.04 /84	0.00	1.35
FO	Thomas White International	TWWDX	B	(800) 811-0535	A / 9.5	-0.72	12.50	37.93 /97	28.81 /95	13.83 /90	0.94	1.50
GR	Thompson Plumb Growth	THPGX	D-	(800) 999-0887	E+ / 0.6	-2.59	-0.52	1.62 / 3	5.14 / 4	3.05 /37	0.60	1.09
GR	Thornburg Core Growth A	THCGX	C	(800) 847-0200	C+ / 6.9	-5.04	3.44	21.65 /84	18.63 /75	9.58 /79	0.00	1.43
GR	Thornburg Core Growth C	TCGCX	C	(800) 847-0200	B- / 7.0	-5.21	3.04	20.67 /83	17.74 /71	8.62 /75	0.00	2.19
GR	Thornburg Core Growth I	THIGX	U	(800) 847-0200	U /	-4.90	3.79	22.26 /85	--	--	0.00	0.99
GR	Thornburg Core Growth R1	THCRX	U	(800) 847-0200	U /	-5.02	3.43	21.57 /84	--	--	0.00	1.50
★ FO	Thornburg Intl Value A	TGVAX	A+	(800) 847-0200	A- / 9.0	0.00	9.87	27.43 /92	24.82 /91	12.15 /87	0.64	1.32
FO	Thornburg Intl Value B	THGBX	A	(800) 847-0200	B+ / 8.8	-0.16	9.38	26.41 /90	23.78 /89	11.19 /84	0.08	2.12
FO	Thornburg Intl Value C	THGCX	A+	(800) 847-0200	A- / 9.0	-0.16	9.48	26.51 /91	23.90 /89	11.24 /84	0.16	2.04
FO	Thornburg Intl Value I	TGVIX	A+	(800) 847-0200	A- / 9.2	0.11	10.06	27.94 /93	25.37 /91	12.68 /88	1.04	0.93
FO	Thornburg Intl Value R1	TGVRX	U	(800) 847-0200	U /	0.00	9.79	27.32 /92	--	--	0.74	1.45
GL	Thornburg Investment Inc Builder A	TIBAX	B	(800) 847-0200	C+ / 6.6	-0.21	9.00	14.80 /71	16.60 /66	--	3.21	1.39
GL	Thornburg Investment Inc Builder C	TIBCX	B	(800) 847-0200	C+ / 6.9	-0.30	8.82	14.35 /69	16.07 /64	--	3.00	1.90
GL	Thornburg Investment Inc Builder I	TIBIX	U	(800) 847-0200	U /	-0.22	9.15	15.18 /72	--	--	3.55	0.99
GI	Thornburg Value Fund A	TVAFX	C-	(800) 847-0200	C- / 4.1	-1.20	5.51	14.44 /70	11.83 /41	3.47 /41	0.62	1.35
GI	Thornburg Value Fund B	TVBFX	C-	(800) 847-0200	C- / 3.5	-1.36	5.10	13.55 /66	10.93 /35	2.63 /33	0.03	2.16
GI	Thornburg Value Fund C	TVCFX	C-	(800) 847-0200	C / 4.3	-1.38	5.11	13.60 /67	10.97 /35	2.68 /34	0.05	2.10
GI	Thornburg Value Fund I	TVIFX	C	(800) 847-0200	C / 5.1	-1.11	5.70	14.91 /71	12.27 /44	3.92 /45	1.04	0.95
GI	Thornburg Value Fund R1	TVRFX	U	(800) 847-0200	U /	-1.21	5.48	14.40 /70	--	--	0.75	1.35
GL	Thrivent Aggressive Allocation A	TAAAX	U	(800) 847-4836	U /	-2.69	4.17	13.66 /67	--	--	1.10	1.35
GL	Thrivent Aggressive Allocation I	TAAIX	U	(800) 847-4836	U /	-2.51	4.45	14.20 /69	--	--	1.28	0.60
BA	Thrivent Balanced A	AABFX	D+	(800) 847-4836	E+ / 0.7	-2.19	0.74	6.64 /24	6.66 / 9	3.04 /37	1.51	1.08
BA	● Thrivent Balanced B	BBBFX	D+	(800) 847-4836	E / 0.5	-2.38	0.23	5.71 /19	5.64 / 6	2.11 /28	0.63	2.03
BA	Thrivent Balanced I	IBBFX	C-	(800) 847-4836	D- / 1.5	-2.00	1.06	7.24 /28	7.17 /11	3.53 /42	2.06	0.62
GR	Thrivent Large Cap Growth A	AAAGX	E-	(800) 847-4836	D- / 1.2	-5.13	-2.35	5.59 /18	8.66 /19	-1.57 /10	0.09	0.76
GR	● Thrivent Large Cap Growth B	BBAGX	E-	(800) 847-4836	E+ / 0.9	-5.25	-2.90	4.45 /13	7.57 /13	-2.46 / 7	0.00	1.87
GR	Thrivent Large Cap Growth I	THLCX	E-	(800) 847-4836	D+ / 2.6	-4.85	-2.03	6.33 /22	9.56 /24	-0.57 /13	0.52	0.03
GR	Thrivent Large Cap Index A	AALCX	C-	(800) 847-4836	D+ / 2.6	-1.57	2.46	8.02 /33	10.61 /32	1.88 /26	1.17	0.60
GR	Thrivent Large Cap Index I	IILCX	C+	(800) 847-4836	C- / 3.7	-1.59	2.36	8.10 /33	10.65 /32	2.00 /27	1.35	0.56
★ GR	Thrivent Large Cap Stock A	AALGX	E-	(800) 847-4836	D- / 1.3	-2.21	0.80	6.77 /25	8.25 /16	0.39 /17	0.59	1.00
GR	● Thrivent Large Cap Stock B	BBLGX	E-	(800) 847-4836	D- / 1.0	-2.42	0.37	5.81 /19	7.20 /11	-0.64 /13	0.00	1.89
GR	Thrivent Large Cap Stock I	IILGX	E-	(800) 847-4836	D+ / 2.5	-2.08	1.02	7.25 /28	8.74 /19	0.84 /19	1.07	0.56
GI	Thrivent Large Cap Value A	AAUTX	C+	(800) 847-4836	C / 5.3	0.19	6.39	12.78 /63	14.28 /55	3.82 /44	1.04	1.01
GI	● Thrivent Large Cap Value B	BBEIX	C+	(800) 847-4836	C / 4.8	-0.06	5.75	11.48 /57	13.10 /49	2.87 /36	0.00	2.12
GI	Thrivent Large Cap Value I	TLVIX	B-	(800) 847-4836	C+ / 6.5	0.38	6.71	13.42 /66	14.98 /59	4.60 /51	1.57	0.51
MC	Thrivent Mid Cap Growth A	LBMGX	D+	(800) 847-4836	C- / 3.8	-6.50	1.56	12.09 /60	12.66 /47	2.71 /34	0.00	1.21

● Denotes fund is closed to new investors
★ Denotes fund is included in Section II

RISK			NET ASSETS		ASSET					BULL / BEAR		FUND MANAGER		MINIMUMS		LOADS	
	3 Year		NAV						Portfolio	Last Bull	Last Bear	Manager	Manager	Initial	Additional	Front	Back
	Standard		As of	Total	Cash	Stocks	Bonds	Other	Turnover	Market	Market	Quality	Tenure	Purch.	Purch.	End	End
Risk Rating/Pts	Deviation	Beta	6/30/06	$(Mil)	%	%	%	%	Ratio	Return	Return	Pct	(Years)	$	$	Load	Load
C+ / 6.6	14.0	0.82	34.70	101	3	96	0	1	130.0	170.4	-11.5	97	11	5,000	100	5.8	1.0
B- / 7.3	10.8	1.04	37.51	1,556	4	95	0	1	58.0	156.3	-5.2	77	9	100,000	5,000	0.0	2.0
C+ / 6.3	12.2	1.11	23.61	745	6	93	0	1	50.0	231.4	-3.1	98	6	100,000	5,000	0.0	2.0
C+ / 6.3	7.7	0.99	35.85	49	4	96	0	0	85.0	65.9	-8.0	57	N/A	100,000	5,000	0.0	2.0
C+ / 6.4	13.5	0.89	14.86	21	2	96	0	2	167.0	122.1	-11.4	86	N/A	100,000	5,000	0.0	2.0
C+ / 6.3	13.9	0.92	49.61	38	4	95	0	1	135.0	116.9	-11.4	71	5	100,000	5,000	0.0	2.0
C+ / 5.9	13.8	0.92	42.16	160	2	97	0	1	137.0	117.5	-11.5	72	5	100,000	5,000	0.0	2.0
B- / 7.5	12.9	0.87	23.47	436	2	96	0	2	70.0	144.4	-10.7	97	6	100,000	5,000	0.0	2.0
D- / 1.0	24.8	2.38	15.62	80	2	97	0	1	141.0	130.3	-15.5	1	5	5,000	1,000	0.0	0.0
D+ / 2.6	20.9	1.27	12.25	458	1	98	0	1	90.0	132.0	-8.0	9	4	2,500	250	0.0	2.0
B / 8.4	9.0	0.78	22.91	2,315	31	68	0	1	14.0	160.9	-0.8	99	5	10,000	1,000	0.0	2.0
B- / 7.5	8.9	0.49	31.95	2,930	12	86	0	2	13.0	125.0	0.1	99	8	10,000	1,000	0.0	1.0
B / 8.6	9.8	0.64	25.67	2,409	39	60	0	1	11.0	110.7	-8.9	97	9	10,000	1,000	0.0	1.0
B- / 7.6	8.9	0.88	57.76	8,371	15	84	0	1	17.0	130.0	-7.3	99	3	10,000	1,000	0.0	1.0
E- / 0.0	26.0	1.19	53.12	126	3	96	0	1	63.8	279.2	4.9	17	8	1,000	100	5.8	2.0
C / 5.4	10.3	0.90	16.16	22	1	98	0	1	41.9	93.0	-6.2	69	7	2,500	100	0.0	2.0
C / 4.6	12.1	1.15	17.91	119	2	97	0	1	35.7	166.7	-10.0	63	12	2,500	100	0.0	2.0
B- / 7.2	8.3	0.91	44.05	802	0	100	0	0	20.5	47.4	-13.6	14	14	2,500	100	0.0	0.0
C / 4.9	12.8	1.28	15.65	448	1	98	0	1	115.4	140.2	-6.8	91	6	5,000	100	4.5	1.0
C / 4.8	12.8	1.27	14.92	153	1	98	0	1	115.4	134.1	-7.1	87	6	5,000	100	0.0	1.0
U /	N/A	N/A	15.90	181	1	98	0	1	115.4	N/A	N/A	N/A	6	2,500,000	5,000	0.0	1.0
U /	N/A	N/A	15.70	69	1	98	0	1	115.4	N/A	N/A	N/A	6	5,000	100	0.0	0.0
B- / 7.1	10.4	0.97	25.72	3,823	3	96	0	1	34.2	142.2	-10.3	67	8	5,000	100	4.5	1.0
B- / 7.1	10.4	0.97	24.49	77	3	96	0	1	34.2	136.1	-10.5	58	8	5,000	100	0.0	5.0
B- / 7.1	10.4	0.97	24.59	1,170	3	96	0	1	34.2	136.6	-10.5	59	8	5,000	100	0.0	1.0
B- / 7.1	10.4	0.97	26.20	1,699	3	96	0	1	34.2	146.0	-10.2	71	8	2,500,000	5,000	0.0	1.0
U /	N/A	N/A	25.79	362	3	96	0	1	34.2	N/A	N/A	N/A	8	5,000	100	0.0	0.0
B / 8.8	7.7	1.34	18.92	736	1	90	8	1	76.8	92.8	N/A	96	N/A	5,000	100	4.5	1.0
B / 8.9	7.6	1.31	18.93	517	1	90	8	1	76.8	90.0	N/A	96	N/A	5,000	100	0.0	1.0
U /	N/A	N/A	19.04	220	1	90	8	1	76.8	N/A	N/A	N/A	N/A	2,500,000	5,000	0.0	1.0
B- / 7.1	8.5	1.04	35.33	1,039	0	96	3	1	58.9	78.0	-9.2	59	11	5,000	100	4.5	1.0
B- / 7.1	8.5	1.04	34.01	92	0	96	3	1	58.9	73.4	-9.4	49	11	5,000	100	0.0	5.0
B- / 7.1	8.5	1.04	34.36	461	0	96	3	1	58.9	73.6	-9.3	49	11	5,000	100	0.0	1.0
B- / 7.1	8.5	1.04	35.81	879	0	96	3	1	58.9	80.2	-9.0	64	11	2,500,000	5,000	0.0	1.0
U /	N/A	N/A	35.19	32	0	96	3	1	58.9	N/A	N/A	N/A	11	5,000	100	0.0	0.0
U /	N/A	N/A	11.23	131	2	97	0	1	3.9	N/A	N/A	N/A	N/A	1,000	50	5.5	1.0
U /	N/A	N/A	11.27	27	2	97	0	1	3.9	N/A	N/A	N/A	N/A	50,000	0	0.0	0.0
B / 8.9	5.5	1.10	12.28	254	0	69	35	0	120.0	36.4	-3.4	39	N/A	1,000	50	5.5	1.0
B+ / 9.2	5.5	1.10	12.24	11	0	69	35	0	120.0	32.5	-3.7	31	N/A	1,000	50	0.0	5.0
B+ / 9.1	5.5	1.10	12.27	87	0	69	35	0	120.0	38.6	-3.4	45	N/A	50,000	0	0.0	0.0
E- / 0.0	9.7	1.18	4.99	130	1	98	0	1	106.0	56.9	-10.4	20	4	1,000	50	5.5	1.0
E- / 0.0	9.7	1.18	4.69	13	1	98	0	1	106.0	52.0	-10.5	14	4	1,000	50	0.0	5.0
E- / 0.0	9.7	1.19	5.30	150	1	98	0	1	106.0	61.4	-10.0	25	4	50,000	0	0.0	0.0
B / 8.6	7.7	1.00	8.75	90	2	97	0	1	13.0	62.2	-9.8	49	4	1,000	50	5.5	1.0
B / 8.9	7.6	1.00	8.68	31	2	97	0	1	13.0	62.0	-9.8	50	4	50,000	0	0.0	0.0
D / 1.9	7.3	0.93	26.61	3,086	1	98	0	1	18.0	48.1	-8.0	32	11	1,000	50	5.5	1.0
D- / 1.5	7.3	0.93	24.62	73	1	98	0	1	18.0	43.4	-8.4	25	11	1,000	50	0.0	5.0
D / 2.0	7.3	0.93	26.78	201	1	98	0	1	18.0	50.2	-8.0	36	11	50,000	0	0.0	0.0
B- / 7.3	7.3	0.92	15.64	322	5	94	0	1	23.0	75.7	-9.1	87	2	1,000	50	5.5	1.0
B- / 7.7	7.2	0.92	15.44	15	5	94	0	1	23.0	70.3	-9.3	80	2	1,000	50	0.0	5.0
B- / 7.5	7.3	0.92	15.74	121	5	94	0	1	23.0	79.4	-8.9	90	2	50,000	0	0.0	0.0
C+ / 5.9	12.6	1.13	15.67	272	3	96	0	1	82.0	83.0	-9.3	8	9	1,000	50	5.5	1.0

					PERFORMANCE							
99 Pct = Best 0 Pct = Worst			Overall Weiss Investment Rating		Perfor- mance Rating/Pts	Total Return % through 6/30/06			Annualized		Incl. in Returns	
Fund Type	Fund Name	Ticker Symbol		Phone		3 Mo	6 Mo	1Yr / Pct	3Yr / Pct	5Yr / Pct	Dividend Yield	Expense Ratio
MC	● Thrivent Mid Cap Growth B	LUGBX	D	(800) 847-4836	C- / 3.3	-6.79	1.04	10.90 /53	11.59 /40	1.78 /25	0.00	2.26
MC	Thrivent Mid Cap Growth I	LBMIX	C-	(800) 847-4836	C / 5.4	-6.40	1.90	12.87 /64	13.55 /52	3.60 /42	0.00	0.47
MC	Thrivent Mid Cap Index A	AAMIX	C+	(800) 847-4836	C+ / 6.2	-3.36	3.76	12.02 /60	17.02 /68	8.11 /72	0.38	0.90
MC	Thrivent Mid Cap Index I	AALMX	B-	(800) 847-4836	B- / 7.1	-3.27	3.82	12.15 /60	17.29 /69	8.72 /75	0.48	0.64
MC	Thrivent Mid Cap Stock A	AASCX	C+	(800) 847-4836	B- / 7.0	-4.24	3.47	15.99 /75	18.57 /75	6.37 /63	0.00	1.17
MC	● Thrivent Mid Cap Stock B	BBSCX	C	(800) 847-4836	C+ / 6.6	-4.48	2.98	14.86 /71	17.28 /69	5.17 /55	0.00	2.22
MC	Thrivent Mid Cap Stock I	TMSIX	B-	(800) 847-4836	B / 7.8	-4.09	3.75	16.58 /76	19.19 /77	6.97 /67	0.00	0.70
GL	Thrivent Moder Aggressive Alloc A	TMAAX	U	(800) 847-4836	U /	-1.95	3.56	11.73 /58	--	--	1.10	0.11
GL	Thrivent Moder Aggressive Alloc I	TMAFX	U	(800) 847-4836	U /	-1.86	3.84	12.25 /61	--	--	1.26	0.84
GL	Thrivent Moderate Allocation A	THMAX	U	(800) 847-4836	U /	-1.45	3.07	9.79 /46	--	--	2.07	0.01
GL	Thrivent Moderate Conser Alloc A	TCAAX	U	(800) 847-4836	U /	-0.90	2.48	7.27 /28	--	--	2.38	1.10
FO	Thrivent Partner International St A	AAITX	C+	(800) 847-4836	B- / 7.4	-1.31	6.73	24.27 /88	18.53 /74	6.07 /62	0.88	1.36
FO	● Thrivent Partner International St B	BBITX	C+	(800) 847-4836	B- / 7.1	-1.52	6.21	22.94 /86	17.31 /69	5.10 /55	0.00	2.45
FO	Thrivent Partner International St I	TISFX	B-	(800) 847-4836	B / 8.2	-1.13	7.07	25.13 /89	19.44 /78	7.01 /67	1.48	0.73
SC	Thrivent Partner Small Cap Value A	AALVX	C+	(800) 847-4836	B+ / 8.5	-0.90	13.81	20.42 /82	22.45 /86	--	0.23	0.99
SC	● Thrivent Partner Small Cap Value B	BBSVX	C	(800) 847-4836	B+ / 8.3	-1.15	13.24	19.28 /81	21.33 /83	--	0.00	1.93
SC	Thrivent Partner Small Cap Value I	TPSIX	B-	(800) 847-4836	A- / 9.0	-0.75	14.15	21.20 /83	23.35 /88	--	0.76	0.31
RE	Thrivent Real Estate Securities I	TREIX	U	(800) 847-4836	U /	-0.51	13.84	20.79 /83	--	--	3.26	0.11
SC	Thrivent Small Cap Index Fund A	AALSX	B-	(800) 847-4836	B- / 7.1	-4.78	7.18	12.99 /64	19.21 /77	9.84 /80	0.13	0.95
SC	Thrivent Small Cap Stock A	AASMX	C+	(800) 847-4836	B- / 7.4	-4.90	6.88	14.33 /69	19.93 /79	9.39 /78	0.00	1.29
SC	● Thrivent Small Cap Stock B	BBSMX	C	(800) 847-4836	B- / 7.1	-5.18	6.34	13.19 /65	18.72 /75	8.29 /73	0.00	2.27
SC	Thrivent Small Cap Stock I	TSCSX	B-	(800) 847-4836	B / 8.1	-4.78	7.12	14.94 /72	20.64 /82	10.08 /81	0.00	0.72
TC	Thrivent Technology Stock A	AATSX	E-	(800) 847-4836	E+ / 0.7	-10.03	-4.89	5.11 /16	8.11 /16	-6.70 / 1	0.00	1.45
TC	● Thrivent Technology Stock B	BBTSX	E-	(800) 847-4836	E+ / 0.7	-9.95	-5.10	5.02 /15	7.59 /13	-7.32 / 1	0.00	1.95
TC	Thrivent Technology Stock I	THTIX	E	(800) 847-4836	D / 1.7	-9.80	-4.66	5.75 /19	8.64 /19	-5.98 / 2	0.00	0.95
GR	● TIAA-CREF Equity Index Fund	TCEIX	C+	(800) 842-2252	C / 4.8	-2.01	3.12	9.27 /42	12.28 /44	3.33 /40	1.44	0.26
GI	● TIAA-CREF Growth & Income	TIGIX	C	(800) 842-2252	C- / 4.1	-2.48	2.66	9.48 /43	11.06 /36	1.54 /24	1.16	0.43
GR	● TIAA-CREF Growth Equity	TIGEX	D-	(800) 842-2252	D- / 1.3	-5.66	-2.91	4.68 /14	7.25 /11	-2.39 / 7	0.44	0.45
GI	TIAA-CREF Inst Growth & Inc Retire	TRGIX	C		C- / 3.5	-2.49	2.62	7.82 /31	10.33 /30	--	1.01	0.46
FO	TIAA-CREF Inst Intl Eq Index Retire	TRIEX	A+		A- / 9.0	0.69	10.01	26.37 /90	23.27 /88	--	0.43	0.50
FO	TIAA-CREF Inst Intl Equity Retire	TRERX	A+		A- / 9.0	-1.21	10.03	28.29 /93	23.57 /89	--	1.01	0.56
GR	TIAA-CREF Inst LgCap Growth Idx	TILIX	D+		D / 2.0	-3.96	-0.96	5.93 /20	8.17 /16	--	0.79	0.08
GR	TIAA-CREF Inst LgCap Val Idx Retail	TILVX	B		C+ / 6.7	0.60	6.53	12.03 /60	15.53 /61	--	1.90	0.80
GR	TIAA-CREF Inst LgCap Val Idx Retire	TRCVX	B		C+ / 6.5	0.53	6.39	11.61 /57	15.11 /59	--	0.74	0.44
GR	TIAA-CREF Inst LgCap Value Retail	TCLCX	A-		B- / 7.1	-0.81	6.08	11.74 /58	16.97 /68	--	1.89	0.44
GR	TIAA-CREF Inst LgCap Value Retire	TRLCX	A-		B- / 7.1	-0.79	6.16	11.82 /59	16.96 /68	--	1.60	0.48
MC	TIAA-CREF Inst MdCap Val Idx	TRVUX	A+		B+ / 8.4	-0.63	6.80	13.80 /68	21.59 /84	--	0.29	0.44
MC	TIAA-CREF Inst Mid Cap Growth	TRPWX	C+		C+ / 6.2	-7.41	1.91	9.03 /40	16.05 /64	--	0.10	0.55
MC	TIAA-CREF Inst Mid Cap Value Retail	TCMVX	A+		B+ / 8.6	-0.67	6.36	14.22 /69	22.80 /87	--	1.16	0.55
RE	TIAA-CREF Inst Real Est Sec Instl	TIREX	A		B+ / 8.9	-0.94	11.51	12.74 /63	24.12 /90	--	3.47	0.17
RE	TIAA-CREF Inst Real Est Sec Retail	TCREX	A		B+ / 8.9	-1.05	11.31	12.68 /63	24.15 /90	--	3.05	0.46
GR	TIAA-CREF Inst S&P 500 Idx Retire	TRSPX	C+		C- / 3.8	-1.56	2.48	8.16 /34	10.68 /33	--	1.43	0.44
SC	TIAA-CREF Inst Sm Cap Equity	TCSEX	B		B / 7.8	-4.33	8.88	14.80 /71	19.04 /76	--	0.71	0.30
SC	TIAA-CREF Inst Sm Cap Equity	TRSEX	B		B / 7.7	-4.31	8.83	14.63 /70	18.86 /76	--	0.63	0.48
SC	TIAA-CREF Inst Sm Cp Blend Idx	TISBX	B		B / 7.6	-5.03	8.18	14.48 /70	18.56 /75	--	0.85	1.39
SC	TIAA-CREF Inst Sm Cp Val Idx Retire	TRSVX	A-		B / 8.2	-2.79	10.18	14.18 /69	20.60 /81	--	0.68	0.44
IN	TIAA-CREF Inst Social Ch Eq Retire	TRSCX	C+		C / 4.7	-2.21	2.51	10.17 /48	12.02 /43	--	1.04	0.44
FO	● TIAA-CREF International Equity	TIINX	B+	(800) 842-2252	A- / 9.1	-0.89	10.65	29.55 /94	24.12 /90	9.92 /80	1.27	0.49
AA	● TIAA-CREF Managed Allocation	TIMAX	C+	(800) 842-2252	C- / 3.3	-1.60	2.25	7.52 /29	9.93 /27	4.61 /51	3.08	0.62
GR	● TIAA-CREF Social Choice Equity	TCSCX	C+	(800) 842-2252	C / 4.8	-2.27	2.59	10.23 /48	12.25 /44	3.84 /44	1.22	0.27
AG	Timothy Plan Aggressive Growth A	TAAGX	C-	(800) 846-7526	C / 4.4	-6.30	4.88	16.73 /76	13.16 /50	1.06 /21	0.00	1.60
AG	● Timothy Plan Aggressive Growth B	TBAGX	D+	(800) 846-7526	C- / 3.8	-6.44	4.51	15.78 /74	12.32 /45	0.31 /17	0.00	2.35

● Denotes fund is closed to new investors
* Denotes fund is included in Section II

RISK Rating/Pts	3 Year Standard Deviation	3 Year Beta	NAV As of 6/30/06	Total $(Mil)	Cash %	Stocks %	Bonds %	Other %	Portfolio Turnover Ratio	Last Bull Market Return	Last Bear Market Return	Manager Quality Pct	Manager Tenure (Years)	Initial Purch. $	Additional Purch. $	Front End Load	Back End Load
C+ / 5.7	12.7	1.13	14.55	29	3	96	0	1	82.0	77.5	-9.5	5	9	1,000	50	0.0	5.0
C+ / 5.9	12.6	1.13	16.66	26	3	96	0	1	82.0	87.8	-9.0	10	9	50,000	0	0.0	0.0
B- / 7.0	10.7	0.99	14.09	64	3	96	0	1	11.0	98.2	-9.3	45	4	1,000	50	5.5	1.0
B- / 7.0	10.8	0.99	13.59	23	3	96	0	1	11.0	100.0	-9.2	47	4	50,000	0	0.0	0.0
C+ / 5.7	11.2	1.01	17.61	968	3	96	0	1	46.0	102.9	-7.2	60	2	1,000	50	5.5	1.0
C / 5.3	11.3	1.01	15.57	20	3	96	0	1	46.0	95.7	-7.6	45	2	1,000	50	0.0	5.0
C+ / 5.8	11.2	1.00	18.52	93	3	96	0	1	46.0	106.3	-7.1	66	2	50,000	0	0.0	0.0
U /	N/A	N/A	11.04	301	3	96	0	1	6.0	N/A	N/A	N/A	N/A	1,000	50	5.5	1.0
U /	N/A	N/A	11.08	29	3	96	0	1	6.0	N/A	N/A	N/A	N/A	50,000	0	0.0	0.0
U /	N/A	N/A	10.74	316	6	93	0	1	4.2	N/A	N/A	N/A	N/A	1,000	50	5.5	1.0
U /	N/A	N/A	10.46	112	9	90	0	1	5.2	N/A	N/A	N/A	N/A	1,000	50	5.5	1.0
C+ / 6.0	10.8	1.04	12.06	329	3	96	0	1	19.0	103.5	-11.9	11	9	1,000	50	5.5	1.0
C+ / 6.3	10.6	1.03	11.63	15	3	96	0	1	19.0	97.4	-12.1	8	9	1,000	50	0.0	5.0
C+ / 5.7	10.7	1.03	12.27	150	3	96	0	1	19.0	108.8	-11.5	15	9	50,000	0	0.0	0.0
C / 4.3	12.4	0.83	15.33	80	4	95	0	1	30.0	127.8	-8.6	95	2	1,000	50	5.5	1.0
C- / 4.1	12.4	0.83	14.63	6	4	95	0	1	30.0	121.3	-8.8	93	2	1,000	50	0.0	5.0
C / 4.7	12.4	0.83	15.89	37	4	95	0	1	30.0	133.5	-8.3	97	2	50,000	0	0.0	0.0
U /	N/A	N/A	11.67	30	3	96	0	1	10.4	N/A	N/A	N/A	1	50,000	0	0.0	0.0
C+ / 6.4	13.5	0.92	15.53	49	3	96	0	1	9.0	113.9	-9.9	74	4	1,000	50	5.5	1.0
C / 5.2	13.1	0.88	17.86	466	4	95	0	1	52.0	116.7	-10.1	84	3	1,000	50	5.5	1.0
C / 4.9	13.1	0.88	15.94	18	4	95	0	1	52.0	110.0	-10.3	76	3	1,000	50	0.0	5.0
C+ / 5.8	13.1	0.88	19.11	65	4	95	0	1	52.0	121.2	-9.9	87	3	50,000	0	0.0	0.0
D+ / 2.6	16.9	1.91	3.50	40	2	97	0	1	23.0	69.6	-13.2	1	6	1,000	50	5.5	1.0
D+ / 2.6	16.9	1.90	3.35	3	2	97	0	1	23.0	66.5	-13.2	1	6	1,000	50	0.0	5.0
C / 4.7	16.8	1.89	3.68	2	2	97	0	1	23.0	72.6	-13.2	2	6	50,000	0	0.0	0.0
B / 8.6	8.3	1.07	9.24	368	0	99	0	1	8.0	71.1	-9.5	61	N/A	2,500	50	0.0	0.0
B- / 7.5	7.8	1.00	13.07	511	0	99	0	1	183.0	62.7	-9.9	55	6	2,500	50	0.0	0.0
C+ / 6.3	9.2	1.12	9.33	518	0	99	0	1	78.0	50.4	-9.3	16	6	2,500	50	0.0	0.0
B / 8.7	7.9	1.01	8.34	76	0	99	0	1	223.0	60.0	N/A	45	4	2,500	50	0.0	0.0
B / 8.0	10.2	1.01	18.91	42	0	99	0	1	32.0	127.9	-9.6	42	4	2,500	50	0.0	0.0
B- / 7.6	11.1	1.08	13.06	444	0	99	0	1	147.0	130.6	-8.5	31	4	2,500	50	0.0	0.0
B / 8.1	8.7	1.08	11.39	545	N/A	100	0	N/A	18.9	53.0	-9.6	23	4	2,500	50	0.0	0.0
B / 8.9	7.7	0.96	15.00	521	3	96	0	1	154.0	84.4	-9.1	91	4	2,500	50	0.0	0.0
B / 8.9	7.7	0.96	15.16	11	3	96	0	1	154.0	82.3	-9.1	89	4	2,500	50	0.0	0.0
B / 8.5	8.9	1.10	14.66	190	0	99	0	1	113.0	95.9	-9.6	91	4	2,500	50	0.0	0.0
B / 8.5	8.9	1.10	14.99	201	0	99	0	1	113.0	95.6	-8.8	91	4	2,500	50	0.0	0.0
B / 8.3	9.4	0.82	15.86	10	0	99	0	1	43.0	115.7	-6.7	95	5	2,500	50	0.0	0.0
B- / 7.0	12.7	1.13	17.11	24	0	99	0	1	115.0	105.1	-6.6	21	4	2,500	50	0.0	0.0
B- / 7.9	10.5	0.92	17.73	118	0	99	0	1	110.0	125.0	-6.8	94	4	2,500	50	0.0	0.0
C+ / 6.8	14.0	0.82	14.29	244	1	98	0	1	244.0	119.7	2.0	87	4	2,500	50	0.0	0.0
C+ / 6.7	14.1	0.82	14.19	163	1	98	0	1	244.0	119.8	2.7	87	4	2,500	100	0.0	0.0
B / 8.8	7.6	0.99	14.48	123	N/A	100	0	N/A	38.0	62.1	-9.7	51	4	2,500	50	0.0	0.0
C+ / 6.6	14.4	0.99	15.70	86	0	99	0	1	273.0	121.1	-11.1	62	N/A	2,500	100	0.0	0.0
C+ / 6.6	14.4	0.99	15.77	227	0	99	0	1	273.0	120.1	-10.9	61	N/A	2,500	50	0.0	0.0
C+ / 6.6	14.5	1.00	15.48	187	0	100	0	0	63.0	119.0	-11.5	56	4	2,500	50	0.0	0.0
B- / 7.1	13.1	0.89	14.29	13	0	99	0	1	60.0	123.9	N/A	86	4	2,500	50	0.0	0.0
B / 8.7	8.3	1.06	10.63	71	0	99	0	1	17.0	69.5	-9.0	59	4	2,500	50	0.0	0.0
C+ / 6.0	11.3	1.09	13.30	484	0	99	0	1	151.0	134.6	-8.7	33	6	2,500	50	0.0	0.0
B+ / 9.4	5.7	1.16	11.51	539	0	60	39	1	33.0	52.0	-4.4	71	6	2,500	50	0.0	0.0
B / 8.7	8.3	1.06	9.92	166	0	99	0	1	7.0	71.1	-9.2	61	N/A	2,500	50	0.0	0.0
C+ / 6.1	14.5	1.50	7.74	22	1	98	0	1	102.6	92.1	-9.8	30	N/A	1,000	0	5.3	0.0
C+ / 6.1	14.4	1.50	7.41	1	1	98	0	1	102.6	87.8	-9.7	24	N/A	1,000	0	0.0	5.0

					PERFORMANCE							
99 Pct = Best 0 Pct = Worst			Overall Weiss Investment Rating		Perfor- mance Rating/Pts	Total Return % through 6/30/06			Annualized		Incl. in Returns	
Fund Type	Fund Name	Ticker Symbol		Phone		3 Mo	6 Mo	1Yr / Pct	3Yr / Pct	5Yr / Pct	Dividend Yield	Expense Ratio
AA	Timothy Plan Conservative Growth A	TCGAX	C-	(800) 846-7526	D / 2.0	-1.85	2.86	8.79 /39	8.81 /20	3.74 /43	0.00	1.15
AA	● Timothy Plan Conservative Growth B	TCGBX	C-	(800) 846-7526	D / 1.6	-2.02	2.49	7.98 /33	8.02 /15	2.94 /36	0.00	1.90
GR	● Timothy Plan Large Mid Cap Growth	TLGBX	D-	(800) 846-7526	E+ / 0.6	-6.04	-2.25	4.48 /13	6.74 / 9	-2.58 / 6	0.00	2.35
GR	Timothy Plan Large/Mid Cap Val A	TLVAX	B-	(800) 846-7526	B- / 7.3	0.43	8.47	21.76 /84	17.60 /71	7.90 /71	0.02	1.10
GR	● Timothy Plan Large/Mid Cap Val B	TLVBX	A-	(800) 846-7526	B- / 7.0	0.23	8.10	20.82 /83	16.71 /67	7.06 /67	0.00	1.00
SC	Timothy Plan Small Cap Value A	TPLNX	C-	(800) 846-7526	C+ / 5.8	-2.06	9.23	16.10 /75	14.87 /58	6.54 /64	0.00	1.10
SC	● Timothy Plan Small Cap Value B	TIMBX	C-	(800) 846-7526	C / 5.4	-2.23	8.87	15.28 /73	14.02 /54	5.72 /59	0.00	1.00
GR	Timothy Plan Strategic Growth A	TSGAX	C-	(800) 846-7526	C- / 3.2	-3.74	3.70	12.27 /61	11.34 /38	1.84 /26	0.00	1.15
GR	● Timothy Plan Strategic Growth B	TSGBX	C-	(800) 846-7526	D+ / 2.6	-3.89	3.28	11.47 /57	10.54 /31	1.12 /21	0.00	1.90
GR	Tocqueville Alexis Fund	TOCAX	D	(800) 697-3863	D- / 1.0	-5.03	-2.57	-1.56 / 1	7.91 /15	3.44 /41	0.36	1.22
GR	Tocqueville Fund	TOCQX	B+	(800) 697-3863	B / 7.6	-3.22	4.78	16.72 /76	18.95 /76	9.03 /76	0.43	1.29
PM	Tocqueville Gold Fund	TGLDX	D+	(800) 697-3863	A+ / 9.9	-0.42	23.06	63.28 /99	31.54 /96	35.70 /99	0.00	1.48
FO	Tocqueville Intl Value Fund	TIVFX	A+	(800) 697-3863	A / 9.4	-1.46	5.81	25.20 /89	29.19 /95	16.47 /93	0.29	1.61
SC	Tocqueville Small Cap Val Fund	TSCVX	E-	(800) 697-3863	D / 1.9	-8.03	1.59	13.45 /66	8.77 /19	5.50 /58	0.00	1.36
GR	Torray Fund	TORYX	D	(800) 443-3036	D- / 1.5	-4.17	0.46	6.61 /24	6.89 /10	3.75 /43	0.26	1.07
GR	Torray Institutional Fd	TORRX	E+	(800) 443-3036	D- / 1.1	-5.07	-0.11	4.45 /13	6.54 / 9	4.38 /49	0.59	0.85
GR	Touchstone Growth Opps A	TGVFX	E	(800) 638-8194	D- / 1.2	-8.48	-3.99	5.56 /18	9.34 /23	-2.19 / 8	0.00	1.64
GR	Touchstone Growth Opps B	TGVBX	E	(800) 638-8194	D- / 1.0	-9.17	-4.73	4.57 /13	8.52 /18	-3.17 / 5	0.00	2.97
GR	Touchstone Growth Opps C	TGVCX	E	(800) 638-8194	D / 1.7	-9.08	-4.58	4.93 /15	8.81 /20	-2.95 / 6	0.00	2.57
GR	Touchstone Large Cap Core Equity A	TENAX	C-	(800) 638-8194	D+ / 2.3	-1.33	3.40	9.03 /40	9.73 /25	3.37 /40	0.07	1.00
GR	Touchstone Large Cap Core Equity B	TETBX	C-	(800) 638-8194	D / 2.0	-1.55	2.93	8.25 /35	8.93 /20	2.61 /33	0.07	1.75
GR	Touchstone Large Cap Core Equity C	TENCX	C-	(800) 638-8194	D+ / 2.7	-1.54	2.92	8.22 /35	8.89 /20	2.71 /34	0.07	1.75
GR	Touchstone Large Cap Growth A	TEQAX	D+	(800) 638-8194	C / 4.3	-7.57	-4.57	7.72 /31	14.94 /58	5.46 /58	0.00	1.17
GR	Touchstone Large Cap Growth B	TEQBX	U	(800) 638-8194	U /	-7.88	-5.06	6.91 /26	--	--	0.00	2.08
GR	Touchstone Large Cap Growth C	TEQCX	U	(800) 638-8194	U /	-7.87	-5.00	7.00 /26	--	--	0.00	1.98
GR	Touchstone Large Cap Growth I	TIQIX	U	(800) 638-8194	U /	-7.46	-4.38	8.00 /33	--	--	0.00	0.93
SC	Touchstone Micro Cap Growth A	TAMCX	U	(800) 638-8194	U /	-10.96	-0.74	3.62 / 9	--	--	0.00	1.95
SC	Touchstone Micro Cap Growth C	TCMCX	U	(800) 638-8194	U /	-11.18	-1.17	2.78 / 7	--	--	0.00	2.70
SC	Touchstone Mid Cap Growth A	TEGAX	C	(800) 638-8194	C+ / 6.6	-2.87	5.95	16.52 /76	17.14 /69	8.26 /73	0.00	1.50
SC	Touchstone Mid Cap Growth B	TBEGX	C	(800) 638-8194	C+ / 6.5	-3.02	5.57	15.67 /74	16.66 /67	7.49 /69	0.00	2.25
SC	Touchstone Mid Cap Growth C	TOECX	C	(800) 638-8194	B- / 7.0	-3.02	5.57	15.66 /74	16.65 /67	7.51 /69	0.00	2.25
SC	Touchstone Small Cap Gr A	TESAX	E-	(800) 638-8194	D- / 1.3	-13.06	-1.90	1.59 / 3	10.48 /31	--	0.00	1.95
SC	Touchstone Small Cap Gr B	TESBX	E-	(800) 638-8194	D- / 1.2	-13.50	-2.26	0.84 / 2	9.69 /25	--	0.00	2.70
SC	Touchstone Small Cap Gr C	TESCX	E-	(800) 638-8194	D / 1.7	-13.49	-2.26	0.84 / 2	9.74 /25	--	0.00	2.70
SC	Touchstone Small Cap Gr I	THSIX	U	(800) 638-8194	U /	-12.93	-1.71	1.96 / 4	--	--	0.00	1.55
GR	Touchstone Value Plus A	TVPAX	D+	(800) 638-8194	D / 2.2	-1.12	2.96	7.22 /28	9.84 /26	1.35 /23	0.11	1.30
GR	Touchstone Value Plus B	TVPBX	D+	(800) 638-8194	D / 2.0	-1.27	2.65	6.39 /23	9.00 /21	0.60 /18	0.12	2.05
GR	Touchstone Value Plus C	TVPCX	C-	(800) 638-8194	D+ / 2.6	-1.27	2.63	6.46 /23	9.01 /21	0.59 /18	0.12	2.05
BA	Transamerica Premier Balanced Inv	TBAIX	C+	(800) 892-7587	C / 5.0	-1.52	4.02	13.55 /66	12.59 /46	5.85 /60	0.50	1.10
GR	Transamerica Premier Divers Eq Inv	TPVIX	C+	(800) 892-7587	C / 5.5	-1.80	3.65	16.60 /76	13.84 /53	3.12 /38	0.00	1.15
GR	Transamerica Premier Equity Inst	TPIEX	U	(800) 892-7587	U /	-3.88	2.10	19.28 /81	--	--	0.00	0.75
GR	Transamerica Premier Equity Inv	TEQUX	C+	(800) 892-7587	C+ / 6.3	-4.43	1.86	18.35 /80	16.33 /65	4.48 /50	0.00	1.09
AG	Transamerica Premier Focus Fund	TPAGX	D+	(800) 892-7587	C / 5.3	-6.42	-3.60	12.85 /64	14.56 /57	2.86 /35	0.00	1.24
SC	Transamerica Premier Growth Opp	TPSCX	C+	(800) 892-7587	B / 7.9	-2.40	6.43	24.66 /88	19.48 /78	9.49 /79	0.00	1.23
GR	TravelersUnivWstrnAstMgtStratBdOp	TLGAX	D-	(800) 846-7526	E+ / 0.9	-5.82	-1.73	5.26 /16	7.52 /12	-1.86 / 9	0.00	1.60
GR	TrendStar American Endeavor Fund	TREAX	U	(888) 747-4872	U /	-6.55	-3.97	1.73 / 4	--	--	0.08	1.40
SC	TrendStar Small Cap Fund	TRESX	U	(888) 747-4872	U /	-5.34	5.36	8.67 /38	--	--	0.00	1.36
GR	Turnaround Fund	TURNX	D-		D / 2.0	-6.70	1.85	-3.09 / 0	9.62 /25	--	0.00	1.75
GR	Turner Core Growth Fund	TTMEX	C-	(800) 224-6312	C+ / 5.8	-3.78	1.87	14.37 /69	14.64 /57	2.02 /28	0.29	0.59
GR	Turner Disciplined Large Cap Growth	TSGEX	D	(800) 224-6312	D / 1.8	-4.87	-1.09	6.06 /21	7.84 /14	-1.91 / 9	0.25	0.75
SC	● Turner Micro Cap Growth Fund	TMCGX	B+	(800) 224-6312	A- / 9.1	-2.58	10.76	20.51 /82	24.97 /91	13.32 /89	0.00	1.40
MC	Turner Midcap Growth I	TMGFX	C	(800) 224-6312	B- / 7.1	-6.73	4.24	15.79 /74	17.12 /69	2.10 /28	0.00	1.18

● Denotes fund is closed to new investors
* Denotes fund is included in Section II

RISK			NET ASSETS		ASSET				BULL / BEAR		FUND MANAGER		MINIMUMS		LOADS	
	3 Year		NAV						Last Bull	Last Bear	Manager	Manager	Initial	Additional	Front	Back
Risk Rating/Pts	Standard Deviation	Beta	As of 6/30/06	Total $(Mil)	Cash %	Stocks %	Bonds %	Other %	Portfolio Turnover Ratio	Market Return	Market Return	Quality Pct	Tenure (Years)	Purch. $	Purch. $	End Load	End Load
B+ / 9.2	6.6	1.20	11.14	31	5	94	0	1	3.6	47.7	-6.0	58	N/A	1,000	0	5.3	0.0
B / 8.9	6.6	1.21	10.69	11	5	94	0	1	3.6	44.4	-6.1	47	N/A	1,000	0	0.0	5.0
B- / 7.7	9.8	1.14	6.53	2	0	0	0	100	60.3	41.9	-8.2	12	N/A	1,000	0	0.0	5.0
C+ / 6.5	16.5	1.27	14.09	68	3	96	0	1	129.2	94.1	-8.7	87	N/A	1,000	0	5.3	0.0
B / 8.5	9.2	1.00	13.08	7	3	96	0	1	129.2	89.6	-8.8	93	N/A	1,000	0	0.0	5.0
C / 4.9	13.1	0.84	16.68	56	4	95	0	1	44.2	87.8	-13.3	44	N/A	1,000	0	5.3	0.0
C / 4.9	13.0	0.84	15.34	16	4	95	0	1	44.2	83.3	-13.4	36	N/A	1,000	0	0.0	5.0
B- / 7.9	10.5	1.15	9.52	36	0	99	0	1	1.6	67.5	-9.8	41	N/A	1,000	0	5.3	0.0
B- / 7.8	10.4	1.21	9.14	17	0	99	0	1	1.6	63.7	-10.0	31	N/A	1,000	0	0.0	5.0
B / 8.4	7.4	0.91	13.18	74	0	99	0	1	43.0	51.7	-9.2	31	12	1,000	100	0.0	2.0
B- / 7.5	11.6	1.34	24.33	235	4	92	2	2	45.0	107.2	-7.7	90	15	1,000	100	0.0	2.0
E- / 0.0	29.8	1.42	50.21	828	11	87	0	2	27.0	167.9	20.1	71	8	1,000	100	0.0	2.0
B- / 7.0	10.9	0.99	16.20	259	3	96	0	1	35.0	171.7	-4.9	90	12	1,000	100	0.0	2.0
D / 1.7	17.5	0.98	17.29	59	5	94	0	1	30.0	88.2	-12.6	4	12	1,000	100	0.0	2.0
B / 8.0	8.0	0.97	38.96	1,163	0	96	0	4	33.2	50.3	-9.4	21	16	10,000	500	0.0	0.0
C+ / 5.8	8.1	0.98	111.33	229	0	93	0	7	53.7	49.8	-9.1	18	N/A	5,000,000	0	0.0	0.0
C / 4.9	13.3	1.49	19.74	52	0	99	0	1	80.0	72.2	-6.8	10	N/A	1,000	50	5.8	1.0
C / 4.6	14.0	1.56	18.52	3	0	99	0	1	80.0	70.3	-7.4	6	N/A	1,000	50	0.0	5.0
C / 4.6	13.9	1.55	18.73	19	0	99	0	1	80.0	71.5	-7.4	7	N/A	1,000	50	0.0	1.0
B / 8.2	8.0	0.97	10.35	25	2	97	0	1	6.0	61.6	-10.1	42	6	1,000	50	5.8	1.0
B / 8.4	8.1	0.98	10.19	2	2	97	0	1	6.0	57.9	-10.2	34	5	1,000	50	0.0	5.0
B / 8.4	8.0	0.98	10.23	1	2	97	0	1	6.0	57.8	-10.2	34	6	1,000	50	0.0	1.0
C+ / 5.7	11.9	1.24	21.50	862	3	96	0	1	104.0	90.6	-6.9	71	9	1,000	50	5.8	1.0
U /	N/A	N/A	21.03	28	3	96	0	1	104.0	N/A	N/A	N/A	9	1,000	50	0.0	5.0
U /	N/A	N/A	21.08	202	3	96	0	1	104.0	N/A	N/A	N/A	9	1,000	50	0.0	1.0
U /	N/A	N/A	21.59	58	3	96	0	1	104.0	N/A	N/A	N/A	9	1,000	50	0.0	0.0
U /	N/A	N/A	12.02	55	0	99	0	1	90.0	N/A	N/A	N/A	2	10,000	50	5.8	1.0
U /	N/A	N/A	11.84	32	0	99	0	1	90.0	N/A	N/A	N/A	2	10,000	50	0.0	1.0
C / 5.5	12.5	0.79	23.33	616	2	97	0	1	69.0	105.0	-9.1	76	12	1,000	50	5.8	1.0
C / 5.4	12.7	0.80	20.84	75	2	97	0	1	69.0	106.1	-10.1	71	N/A	1,000	50	0.0	5.0
C / 5.4	12.6	0.79	20.86	318	2	97	0	1	69.0	106.1	-10.1	71	12	1,000	50	0.0	1.0
C- / 3.0	18.3	1.17	15.97	42	0	99	0	1	109.0	96.9	-11.2	2	4	1,000	50	5.8	1.0
D+ / 2.8	18.5	1.19	15.57	8	0	99	0	1	109.0	93.2	-11.4	1	4	1,000	50	0.0	5.0
D+ / 2.8	18.6	1.19	15.58	18	0	99	0	1	109.0	93.3	-11.4	1	4	1,000	50	0.0	1.0
U /	N/A	N/A	16.10	363	0	99	0	1	109.0	N/A	N/A	N/A	4	10,000	50	0.0	0.0
B- / 7.7	7.8	0.99	11.47	71	1	98	0	1	57.0	61.3	-9.2	41	7	1,000	50	5.8	1.0
B- / 7.8	7.8	0.98	10.86	1	1	98	0	1	57.0	57.5	-9.3	35	7	1,000	50	0.0	5.0
B- / 7.8	7.8	0.98	10.92	2	1	98	0	1	57.0	57.3	-9.4	34	7	1,000	50	0.0	1.0
B / 8.5	8.0	1.42	24.58	329	1	72	25	2	53.0	60.7	-3.6	81	8	1,000	50	0.0	0.0
B- / 7.4	9.4	1.07	14.19	182	1	98	0	1	35.0	72.4	-8.7	75	N/A	1,000	50	0.0	2.0
U /	N/A	N/A	11.65	46	1	98	0	1	122.0	N/A	N/A	N/A	2	250,000	0	0.0	0.0
C+ / 6.5	10.2	1.17	22.46	473	1	98	0	1	122.0	90.6	-8.6	85	7	1,000	50	0.0	2.0
C / 4.9	10.7	1.01	17.92	94	0	99	0	1	67.0	101.1	-11.5	84	N/A	1,000	50	0.0	2.0
C / 5.1	11.4	0.67	24.01	160	4	95	0	1	52.0	104.5	-12.6	95	N/A	1,000	50	0.0	2.0
B- / 7.2	9.9	1.14	6.80	62	3	96	0	1	38.6	45.1	-8.1	16	N/A	1,000	0	5.3	0.0
U /	N/A	N/A	10.41	26	1	98	0	1	11.7	N/A	N/A	N/A	N/A	2,000	100	0.0	0.0
U /	N/A	N/A	12.77	264	2	97	0	1	12.0	N/A	N/A	N/A	N/A	2,000	100	0.0	0.0
C+ / 6.0	15.7	1.57	12.68	9	6	93	0	1	121.8	N/A	N/A	9	3	2,500	250	0.0	0.0
C+ / 5.6	10.8	1.27	11.46	66	2	97	0	1	61.4	86.1	-9.5	65	N/A	2,500	50	0.0	2.0
B- / 7.4	10.3	1.19	5.47	16	6	93	0	1	92.8	58.5	-10.3	15	6	2,500	50	0.0	0.0
C+ / 5.8	15.1	1.00	58.87	609	9	90	0	1	37.7	149.4	-9.7	94	8	2,500	50	0.0	0.0
C / 4.9	15.6	1.36	28.53	1,146	2	97	0	1	57.4	112.0	-10.7	9	10	2,500	50	0.0	0.0

			Overall Weiss Investment Rating		PERFORMANCE							
	99 Pct = Best				Perfor-	Total Return % through 6/30/06					Incl. in Returns	
	0 Pct = Worst				mance				Annualized		Dividend	Expense
Fund Type	Fund Name	Ticker Symbol		Phone	Rating/Pts	3 Mo	6 Mo	1Yr / Pct	3Yr / Pct	5Yr / Pct	Yield	Ratio
MC	Turner Midcap Growth II	TMIIX	C+	(800) 224-6312	C+ / 6.8	-6.85	3.99	15.21 /72	16.55 /66	1.63 /24	0.00	1.68
AG	Turner New Enterprise Fund	TBTBX	D-	(800) 224-6312	C+ / 6.8	-12.40	2.25	22.07 /84	18.94 /76	0.48 /18	0.00	1.61
SC	● Turner Small Cap Equity Inst	TSEIX	B+	(800) 224-6312	B / 8.0	-5.76	8.56	15.36 /73	20.53 /81	--	0.00	1.28
SC	● Turner Small Cap Growth Fund	TSCEX	C	(800) 224-6312	B- / 7.1	-8.08	7.65	18.38 /80	17.93 /72	4.48 /50	0.00	1.25
GR	Turner Strategic Growth Fund	TLCGX	C-	(800) 224-6312	C / 4.6	-7.58	-0.08	10.81 /52	12.67 /47	1.26 /22	0.00	1.25
TC	Turner Technology Fund	TTECX	E	(800) 224-6312	C / 4.8	-18.63	-5.41	11.41 /56	14.53 /56	-6.07 / 2	0.00	1.52
AG	Turner Top 20 Fund	TTOPX	E	(800) 224-6312	C- / 3.1	-10.31	-1.06	14.37 /69	11.34 /38	-2.89 / 6	0.00	1.41
GR	● Tweedy Browne American Value	TWEBX	C-	(800) 432-4789	C- / 3.2	0.04	2.15	6.12 /21	9.76 /26	1.79 /25	1.26	1.36
★ GL	● Tweedy Browne Global Value	TBGVX	A+	(800) 432-4789	B / 7.9	-2.87	5.08	14.00 /68	20.28 /80	8.27 /73	1.32	1.38
GL	UBS Dynamic Alpha A	BNAAX	U	(888) 793-8637	U /	0.00	2.32	9.02 /40	--	--	0.85	1.22
GL	UBS Dynamic Alpha B	BNABX	U	(888) 793-8637	U /	-0.27	1.86	8.09 /33	--	--	0.40	1.98
GL	UBS Dynamic Alpha C	BNACX	U	(888) 793-8637	U /	-0.18	1.95	8.15 /34	--	--	0.45	1.98
GL	UBS Dynamic Alpha Y	BNAYX	U	(888) 793-8637	U /	0.00	2.41	9.27 /42	--	--	1.05	0.94
★ GL	UBS Global Allocation A	BNGLX	C+	(888) 793-8637	C / 4.3	-0.36	3.43	9.72 /45	12.91 /48	9.76 /80	0.93	1.17
GL	UBS Global Allocation B	BNPBX	C+	(888) 793-8637	C- / 3.8	-0.58	3.03	8.80 /39	12.02 /43	--	0.11	1.98
GL	UBS Global Allocation C	BNPCX	B-	(888) 793-8637	C / 4.6	-0.59	3.03	8.82 /39	12.07 /43	--	0.33	1.94
GL	UBS Global Allocation Y	BPGLX	B	(888) 793-8637	C / 5.3	-0.28	3.53	9.98 /47	13.20 /50	9.95 /80	1.19	0.89
GL	UBS Global Equity A	BNGEX	C+	(888) 793-8637	C / 5.1	-1.07	4.09	12.35 /61	14.10 /54	5.96 /61	0.54	1.25
GL	UBS Global Equity B	BNEBX	C+	(888) 793-8637	C / 4.7	-1.25	3.59	11.41 /56	13.22 /50	--	0.00	2.00
GL	UBS Global Equity C	BNECX	C+	(888) 793-8637	C / 5.3	-1.33	3.60	11.45 /56	13.23 /50	--	0.00	2.00
GL	UBS Global Equity Y	BPGEX	B	(888) 793-8637	C+ / 6.0	-0.97	4.17	12.66 /63	14.47 /56	6.33 /63	0.71	1.00
FO	UBS International Equity A	BNIEX	B-	(888) 793-8637	B- / 7.5	-0.36	7.77	20.93 /83	19.07 /76	7.77 /71	0.84	1.25
FO	UBS International Equity B	BNIBX	B-	(888) 793-8637	B- / 7.2	-0.55	7.25	19.86 /82	18.16 /73	--	0.00	2.00
FO	UBS International Equity C	BNICX	B	(888) 793-8637	B / 7.7	-0.56	7.29	19.93 /82	18.57 /75	--	0.16	2.00
FO	UBS International Equity Y	BNUEX	B	(888) 793-8637	B / 8.1	-0.27	7.91	21.22 /83	19.76 /79	8.00 /72	1.05	1.00
EM	UBS PACE Intertl Emg Mkts Eq Inve	PWEAX	C+	(888) 793-8637	A / 9.4	-5.99	5.13	27.94 /93	29.80 /95	15.66 /93	0.75	1.96
EM	UBS PACE Intertl Emg Mkts Eq Inve	PWEBX	C+	(888) 793-8637	A / 9.3	-6.11	4.77	26.81 /91	28.67 /94	14.63 /91	0.00	2.95
EM	UBS PACE Intertl Emg Mkts Eq Inve	PWECX	C+	(888) 793-8637	A / 9.4	-6.16	4.70	26.89 /91	28.79 /95	14.70 /91	0.16	2.76
EM	UBS PACE Intertl Emg Mkts Eq Inve	PCEMX	C+	(888) 793-8637	A / 9.5	-6.00	5.15	27.89 /93	29.92 /95	15.84 /93	0.82	1.97
EM	UBS PACE Intertl Emg Mkts Eq Inve	PWEYX	C	(888) 793-8637	A / 9.5	-5.88	5.37	28.46 /93	30.33 /96	16.06 /93	1.09	1.57
FO	UBS PACE Intrntl Eq Inve A	PWGAX	A	(888) 793-8637	B+ / 8.9	0.86	11.07	27.70 /92	23.95 /89	8.40 /73	1.15	1.53
FO	UBS PACE Intrntl Eq Inve B	PWGBX	A-	(888) 793-8637	B+ / 8.7	0.65	10.55	26.55 /91	22.71 /87	7.32 /68	0.13	2.50
FO	UBS PACE Intrntl Eq Inve C	PWGCX	A	(888) 793-8637	B+ / 8.9	0.65	10.58	26.70 /91	22.94 /87	7.49 /69	0.48	2.33
FO	UBS PACE Intrntl Eq Inve P	PCIEX	A+	(888) 793-8637	A- / 9.2	0.96	11.27	28.11 /93	24.33 /90	8.70 /75	1.51	1.18
FO	UBS PACE Intrntl Eq Inve Y	PWIYX	A+	(888) 793-8637	A- / 9.2	1.02	11.31	28.27 /93	24.48 /90	8.81 /76	1.59	1.07
GR	UBS PACE Large Co Gr Eq Inve A	PLAAX	D	(888) 793-8637	D / 1.6	-3.95	-0.43	6.49 /23	9.06 /21	-1.59 /10	0.00	1.25
GR	UBS PACE Large Co Gr Eq Inve B	PLABX	D	(888) 793-8637	D- / 1.2	-4.18	-0.84	5.50 /18	8.07 /15	-2.43 / 7	0.00	2.13
GR	UBS PACE Large Co Gr Eq Inve C	PLACX	D	(888) 793-8637	D / 1.8	-4.11	-0.84	5.56 /18	8.14 /16	-2.39 / 7	0.00	2.10
GR	UBS PACE Large Co Gr Eq Inve P	PCLCX	D+	(888) 793-8637	D+ / 2.6	-3.84	-0.25	6.80 /25	9.39 /23	-1.31 /11	0.11	0.95
GR	UBS PACE Large Co Gr Eq Inve Y	PLAYX	D+	(888) 793-8637	D+ / 2.6	-3.88	-0.24	6.88 /26	9.47 /24	-1.23 /11	0.16	0.85
GI	UBS PACE Large Co Val Eq Inve A	PCPAX	B	(888) 793-8637	C+ / 5.8	0.32	6.07	14.45 /70	14.83 /58	6.05 /61	0.85	1.13
GI	UBS PACE Large Co Val Eq Inve B	PCPBX	B	(888) 793-8637	C / 5.4	0.14	5.66	13.48 /66	13.87 /53	5.17 /55	0.00	2.04
GI	UBS PACE Large Co Val Eq Inve C	PLVCX	B+	(888) 793-8637	C+ / 5.9	0.14	5.68	13.52 /66	13.93 /54	5.21 /56	0.10	1.92
GI	UBS PACE Large Co Val Eq Inve P	PCLVX	B	(888) 793-8637	C+ / 6.6	0.41	6.27	14.76 /71	15.13 /59	6.31 /63	1.12	0.86
GI	UBS PACE Large Co Val Eq Inve Y	PLVYX	B	(888) 793-8637	C+ / 6.6	0.45	6.30	14.89 /71	15.23 /60	6.40 /64	1.12	0.77
MC	UBS PACE Smal/Med Co Val Eq Inve	PEVAX	E	(888) 793-8637	C- / 4.1	-4.92	1.79	2.64 / 6	14.19 /55	8.88 /76	0.00	1.33
MC	UBS PACE Smal/Med Co Val Eq Inve	PEVBX	E	(888) 793-8637	C- / 3.6	-5.07	1.34	1.81 / 4	13.28 /50	8.01 /72	0.00	2.14
MC	UBS PACE Smal/Med Co Val Eq Inve	PEVCX	E	(888) 793-8637	C / 4.4	-5.12	1.34	1.86 / 4	13.33 /50	8.04 /72	0.00	2.08
MC	UBS PACE Smal/Med Co Val Eq Inve	PCSVX	E+	(888) 793-8637	C / 5.1	-4.91	1.83	2.76 / 6	14.37 /56	9.13 /77	0.00	1.16
MC	UBS PACE Smal/Med Co Val Eq Inve	PVEYX	E+	(888) 793-8637	C / 5.1	-4.84	1.94	3.02 / 7	14.57 /57	9.21 /77	0.00	0.98
MC	UBS PACE Smal/Med Comp Gr Eq	PQUAX	E	(888) 793-8637	D+ / 2.8	-8.67	2.03	6.77 /25	11.63 /40	3.59 /42	0.00	1.33
MC	UBS PACE Smal/Med Comp Gr Eq	PUMBX	E	(888) 793-8637	D+ / 2.3	-8.87	1.56	5.75 /19	10.63 /32	2.69 /34	0.00	2.13

● Denotes fund is closed to new investors
★ Denotes fund is included in Section II

RISK			NET ASSETS		ASSET				BULL / BEAR		FUND MANAGER		MINIMUMS		LOADS	
	3 Year		NAV						Portfolio	Last Bull	Last Bear	Manager	Manager	Initial	Additional	Front	Back
Risk Rating/Pts	Standard Deviation	Beta	As of 6/30/06	Total $(Mil)	Cash %	Stocks %	Bonds %	Other %	Turnover Ratio	Market Return	Market Return	Quality Pct	Tenure (Years)	Purch. $	Purch. $	End Load	End Load
C+ / 6.1	15.6	1.36	27.88	3	2	97	0	1	57.4	108.6	-10.7	8	10	2,500	50	0.0	0.0
E+ / 0.7	24.5	2.37	6.36	16	1	98	0	1	75.2	174.7	-18.5	15	6	2,500	50	0.0	2.0
C+ / 6.9	14.3	0.93	17.50	83	3	96	0	1	71.7	123.6	-6.9	82	4	2,500	50	0.0	2.0
C / 4.7	17.4	1.14	27.31	253	2	96	0	2	69.0	132.6	-11.5	28	N/A	2,500	50	0.0	0.0
C+ / 6.5	14.2	1.57	12.20	12	2	98	0	0	77.5	89.5	-10.2	23	N/A	2,500	50	0.0	0.0
D- / 1.2	25.8	2.40	6.64	12	N/A	100	0	N/A	62.7	133.1	-19.9	3	7	2,500	50	0.0	0.0
D+ / 2.9	18.5	1.85	7.48	38	0	99	0	1	329.5	97.1	-14.3	7	7	2,500	50	0.0	0.0
B- / 7.5	6.6	0.81	24.28	522	10	89	0	1	5.0	48.8	-5.0	59	13	2,500	200	0.0	0.0
B / 8.5	7.1	0.49	27.74	7,526	20	79	0	1	13.0	106.5	-8.0	97	13	2,500	200	0.0	2.0
U /	N/A	N/A	11.04	1,773	8	92	0	0	18.0	N/A	N/A	N/A	1	1,000	100	5.5	0.5
U /	N/A	N/A	10.97	30	8	92	0	0	18.0	N/A	N/A	N/A	1	1,000	100	0.0	5.0
U /	N/A	N/A	10.97	520	8	92	0	0	18.0	N/A	N/A	N/A	1	1,000	100	0.0	1.0
U /	N/A	N/A	11.06	292	8	92	0	0	18.0	N/A	N/A	N/A	1	5,000,000	100	0.0	1.0
B+ / 9.2	6.1	1.19	13.86	2,245	20	58	21	1	39.0	68.7	-4.9	90	N/A	1,000	100	5.5	0.5
B+ / 9.3	6.1	1.19	13.60	162	20	58	21	1	39.0	64.3	-5.0	85	N/A	1,000	100	0.0	5.0
B+ / 9.3	6.1	1.19	13.58	1,045	20	58	21	1	39.0	64.5	-5.0	86	N/A	1,000	100	0.0	1.0
B+ / 9.2	6.0	1.18	14.06	463	20	58	21	1	39.0	69.9	-4.8	91	N/A	10,000,000	100	0.0	1.0
B / 8.1	7.7	0.73	12.99	173	11	88	0	1	23.0	80.4	-9.9	24	N/A	1,000	100	5.5	0.5
B / 8.0	7.8	0.73	12.69	14	11	88	0	1	23.0	76.1	-10.0	18	N/A	1,000	100	0.0	5.0
B / 8.0	7.8	0.73	12.65	57	11	88	0	1	23.0	76.0	-10.0	19	N/A	1,000	100	0.0	1.0
B / 8.1	7.7	0.73	13.23	181	11	88	0	1	23.0	82.1	-9.7	26	N/A	10,000,000	100	0.0	1.0
C+ / 6.5	9.5	0.93	10.96	23	4	95	0	1	24.0	106.4	-10.6	26	N/A	1,000	100	5.5	0.5
C+ / 6.5	9.6	0.93	10.80	1	4	95	0	1	24.0	101.4	-10.7	20	N/A	1,000	100	0.0	5.0
C+ / 6.5	9.5	0.93	10.74	2	4	95	0	1	24.0	101.4	-10.8	23	N/A	1,000	100	0.0	1.0
C+ / 6.5	9.6	0.93	11.05	168	4	95	0	1	24.0	108.1	-10.6	29	N/A	10,000,000	100	0.0	1.0
C- / 3.4	18.2	1.11	18.04	22	1	98	0	1	42.0	192.8	-8.7	5	6	1,000	100	5.5	0.5
C- / 3.4	18.2	1.11	17.36	1	1	98	0	1	42.0	184.9	-9.0	3	N/A	1,000	100	0.0	5.0
C- / 3.3	18.2	1.11	17.38	6	1	98	0	1	42.0	185.8	-9.0	4	6	1,000	100	0.0	1.0
C- / 3.4	18.2	1.11	18.18	257	1	98	0	1	42.0	193.8	-8.7	5	N/A	10,000	500	0.0	0.5
D+ / 2.3	18.2	1.11	18.26	22	1	98	0	1	42.0	197.9	-9.0	6	N/A	10,000,000	100	0.0	1.0
C+ / 6.9	10.7	1.04	18.86	112	2	97	0	1	23.0	132.4	-11.9	40	6	1,000	100	5.5	0.5
C+ / 6.8	10.7	1.05	18.45	1	2	97	0	1	23.0	124.9	-12.1	31	6	1,000	100	0.0	5.0
C+ / 6.8	10.7	1.05	18.50	8	2	97	0	1	23.0	126.2	-12.0	33	6	1,000	100	0.0	1.0
C+ / 6.9	10.7	1.05	18.86	883	2	97	0	1	23.0	134.4	-11.7	43	11	10,000	500	0.0	0.5
C+ / 6.9	10.7	1.05	18.89	54	2	97	0	1	23.0	135.3	-11.8	45	5	10,000,000	100	0.0	1.0
B- / 7.5	9.0	1.10	16.07	86	3	96	0	1	36.0	56.7	-8.7	27	N/A	1,000	100	5.5	0.5
B- / 7.4	8.9	1.10	15.35	2	3	96	0	1	36.0	52.3	-8.9	21	N/A	1,000	100	0.0	5.0
B- / 7.4	8.9	1.09	15.39	8	3	96	0	1	36.0	52.7	-9.0	22	N/A	1,000	100	0.0	1.0
B- / 7.6	9.0	1.10	16.29	948	3	96	0	1	36.0	58.2	-8.7	29	N/A	10,000	500	0.0	0.5
B- / 7.6	9.0	1.10	16.36	24	3	96	0	1	36.0	58.7	-8.7	30	N/A	10,000,000	100	0.0	1.0
B / 8.7	7.9	0.97	22.01	293	1	98	0	1	37.0	76.8	-7.3	87	6	1,000	100	5.5	0.5
B / 8.7	7.9	0.97	22.02	6	1	98	0	1	37.0	72.2	-7.5	82	6	1,000	100	0.0	5.0
B / 8.7	7.9	0.97	21.97	36	1	98	0	1	37.0	72.5	-7.5	82	6	1,000	100	0.0	1.0
B / 8.7	7.9	0.97	22.04	1,040	1	98	0	1	37.0	78.4	-7.3	89	11	10,000	500	0.0	0.5
B / 8.7	8.0	0.97	22.10	43	1	98	0	1	37.0	78.8	-7.2	89	5	10,000,000	100	0.0	1.0
D / 2.0	10.7	0.95	17.59	49	2	97	0	1	55.0	92.0	-10.5	29	N/A	1,000	100	5.5	0.5
D- / 1.5	10.7	0.95	16.66	2	2	97	0	1	55.0	87.1	-10.7	23	N/A	1,000	100	0.0	5.0
D- / 1.5	10.7	0.95	16.69	13	2	97	0	1	55.0	87.3	-10.7	23	N/A	1,000	100	0.0	1.0
D / 2.2	10.7	0.94	17.83	399	2	97	0	1	55.0	93.0	-10.5	30	N/A	10,000	500	0.0	0.5
D+ / 2.3	10.7	0.95	17.91	5	2	97	0	1	55.0	94.0	-10.5	31	N/A	10,000,000	100	0.0	1.0
C- / 3.6	13.9	1.21	15.07	53	4	95	0	1	60.0	84.0	-9.5	3	6	1,000	100	5.5	0.5
C- / 3.2	13.9	1.21	14.28	1	4	95	0	1	60.0	78.8	-9.7	2	6	1,000	100	0.0	5.0

	99 Pct = Best 0 Pct = Worst		Overall Weiss Investment Rating		PERFORMANCE							
					Perfor-mance Rating/Pts	Total Return % through 6/30/06			Annualized		Incl. in Returns	
Fund Type	Fund Name	Ticker Symbol		Phone		3 Mo	6 Mo	1Yr / Pct	3Yr / Pct	5Yr / Pct	Dividend Yield	Expense Ratio
MC	UBS PACE Smal/Med Comp Gr Eq	PUMCX	E	(888) 793-8637	C- / 3.0	-8.89	1.63	5.87 /20	10.74 /33	2.77 /35	0.00	2.13
MC	UBS PACE Smal/Med Comp Gr Eq	PCSGX	D-	(888) 793-8637	C- / 3.8	-8.66	2.14	6.95 /26	11.85 /41	3.84 /44	0.00	1.13
MC	UBS PACE Smal/Med Comp Gr Eq	PUMYX	D-	(888) 793-8637	C- / 3.9	-8.58	2.20	7.14 /27	12.05 /43	3.82 /44	0.00	0.96
GR	UBS S&P 500 Index Fund A	PSPIX	C-	(888) 793-8637	C- / 3.2	-1.60	2.42	7.99 /33	10.54 /31	1.84 /26	1.16	0.70
GR	UBS S&P 500 Index Fund C	PWSPX	D+	(888) 793-8637	C- / 3.0	-1.81	2.02	7.18 /27	9.69 /25	1.07 /21	0.37	1.45
GR	UBS S&P 500 Index Fund Y	PSPYX	C-	(888) 793-8637	C- / 3.7	-1.52	2.55	8.20 /34	10.77 /33	2.08 /28	1.43	0.45
AA	UBS US Allocation A	PWTAX	C	(888) 793-8637	D+ / 2.9	-1.62	0.97	6.02 /21	11.29 /38	2.15 /29	1.94	0.91
AA	UBS US Allocation B	PWTBX	C	(888) 793-8637	D+ / 2.4	-1.82	0.56	5.15 /16	10.42 /30	1.35 /23	0.81	1.74
AA	UBS US Allocation C	KPAAX	C+	(888) 793-8637	C- / 3.2	-1.82	0.60	5.23 /16	10.47 /31	1.39 /23	1.25	1.66
AA	UBS US Allocation Y	PWTYX	B-	(888) 793-8637	C- / 4.0	-1.56	1.13	6.37 /22	11.68 /40	2.50 /32	2.38	0.55
GI	UBS US Large Cap Eq A	BNEQX	C	(888) 793-8637	C- / 3.9	-2.30	1.22	8.62 /38	12.85 /48	5.94 /61	0.54	1.15
GI	UBS US Large Cap Eq B	BNQBX	C	(888) 793-8637	C- / 3.5	-2.46	0.79	7.73 /31	11.97 /42	--	0.00	1.96
GI	UBS US Large Cap Eq C	BNQCX	C+	(888) 793-8637	C- / 4.2	-2.46	0.79	7.79 /31	11.99 /42	--	0.05	1.89
GI	UBS US Large Cap Eq Y	BPEQX	C+	(888) 793-8637	C / 5.0	-2.23	1.32	8.91 /39	13.17 /50	6.24 /63	0.69	0.87
GR	UBS US Large Cap Growth Fund A	BNLGX	D	(888) 793-8637	D+ / 2.3	-7.94	-6.28	7.33 /28	11.31 /38	-0.08 /15	0.02	1.05
GR	UBS US Large Cap Growth Fund B	BNWBX	D-	(888) 793-8637	D / 1.9	-8.09	-6.68	6.50 /23	10.47 /31	--	0.00	1.80
GR	UBS US Large Cap Growth Fund C	BNWCX	D	(888) 793-8637	D+ / 2.6	-7.98	-6.47	6.62 /24	10.51 /31	--	0.00	1.80
GR	UBS US Large Cap Growth Fund Y	BLGIX	D+	(888) 793-8637	C- / 3.3	-7.87	-6.14	7.72 /31	11.63 /40	0.20 /16	0.09	0.80
SC	UBS US Small Cap Growth A	BNSCX	D+	(888) 793-8637	C / 5.2	-7.09	3.89	9.88 /46	15.14 /59	6.22 /62	0.00	1.28
SC	UBS US Small Cap Growth B	BNMBX	D	(888) 793-8637	C / 4.8	-7.20	3.50	9.08 /41	14.28 /55	--	0.00	2.03
SC	UBS US Small Cap Growth C	BNMCX	D+	(888) 793-8637	C / 5.4	-7.28	3.50	9.05 /40	14.26 /55	--	0.00	2.03
SC	UBS US Small Cap Growth Y	BISCX	C-	(888) 793-8637	C+ / 6.0	-7.06	3.95	10.10 /48	15.42 /61	6.50 /64	0.00	1.03
IN	UBS US Value Equity A	BNVAX	C-	(888) 793-8637	C / 5.5	-0.47	4.15	12.13 /60	14.86 /58	--	1.01	1.10
IN	UBS US Value Equity B	BNVBX	D+	(888) 793-8637	C / 5.2	-0.67	3.90	11.25 /55	14.01 /54	--	0.00	1.85
IN	UBS US Value Equity C	BNVCX	C-	(888) 793-8637	C+ / 5.7	-0.67	3.82	11.26 /55	14.01 /54	--	0.35	1.85
IN	UBS US Value Equity Y	BUSVX	C-	(888) 793-8637	C+ / 6.3	-0.47	4.34	12.37 /62	15.14 /60	7.63 /70	1.30	0.85
SC	UMB Scout Small Cap Fund	UMBHX	B+	(800) 996-2862	B / 8.1	-2.36	9.78	16.16 /75	20.30 /80	12.37 /87	0.00	1.02
GR	UMB Scout Stock Fund	UMBSX	D	(800) 996-2862	C- / 4.2	-0.58	4.25	13.05 /64	10.54 /31	3.59 /42	0.84	0.90
★ FO	UMB Scout WorldWide Fund	UMBWX	B+	(800) 996-2862	B+ / 8.4	-1.52	6.28	23.36 /86	21.85 /85	9.97 /80	0.87	1.00
GR	Undiscovered Mgrs Behavior Gr A	UBGAX	E	(800) 358-4782	D+ / 2.8	-9.74	-1.19	5.68 /19	12.00 /42	5.98 /61	0.00	1.65
GR	Undiscovered Mgrs Behavior Gr B	UMGBX	E	(800) 358-4782	D+ / 2.6	-9.83	-1.43	5.19 /16	11.62 /40	5.76 /60	0.00	2.15
GR	Undiscovered Mgrs Behavior Gr C	UBGCX	E	(800) 358-4782	C- / 3.3	-9.83	-1.43	5.19 /16	11.62 /40	5.76 /60	0.00	2.15
GR	Undiscovered Mgrs Behavior Gr Inst	UBRLX	E+	(800) 358-4782	C- / 4.0	-9.63	-0.99	6.12 /21	12.39 /45	6.29 /63	0.00	1.29
GR	Undiscovered Mgrs Behavior Gr Inv	UBRRX	E	(800) 358-4782	C- / 3.7	-9.73	-1.19	5.72 /19	12.02 /43	5.99 /61	0.00	1.58
GR	Undiscovered Mgrs Behavior Val A	UBVAX	B-	(800) 358-4782	B- / 7.2	-6.81	3.31	9.89 /46	19.91 /79	11.88 /86	0.00	1.60
GR	Undiscovered Mgrs Behavior Val B	UBVBX	C+	(800) 358-4782	B- / 7.0	-6.90	3.06	9.34 /42	19.51 /78	11.65 /86	0.00	2.10
GR	Undiscovered Mgrs Behavior Val C	UBVCX	B-	(800) 358-4782	B- / 7.4	-6.91	3.03	9.34 /42	19.49 /78	11.65 /86	0.00	2.10
GR	Undiscovered Mgrs Behavior Val Inst	UBVLX	C+	(800) 358-4782	B / 7.7	-6.75	3.40	10.11 /48	20.08 /80	11.98 /87	0.00	1.40
SC ●	Undiscovered Mgrs Sm Cap Gr A	USRAX	E-	(800) 358-4782	D / 1.9	-12.84	-0.69	8.46 /37	10.08 /28	-0.15 /15	0.00	1.60
SC ●	Undiscovered Mgrs Sm Cap Gr Inst	USRLX	E-	(800) 358-4782	D+ / 2.9	-12.76	-0.49	8.96 /40	10.36 /30	0.01 /15	0.00	1.20
GR	Unified Srs Tr Marathon Val port	MVPFX	C-	(800) 408-4682	C / 4.7	-3.02	2.29	10.21 /48	12.11 /43	7.02 /67	0.65	1.27
IX	United Assoc S&P 500 Index I	UASPX	C+	(888) 766-8043	C- / 4.0	-1.32	2.87	8.80 /39	10.92 /35	2.17 /29	1.90	1.47
FO	Universal Inst Emer Markets Eqty II	UEMBX	C	(800) 869-6397	A+ / 9.7	-5.01	8.23	37.31 /97	33.60 /97	--	0.29	0.66
EM	Universal Inst Emerging Markets Eq	UEMEX	C	(800) 869-6397	A+ / 9.7	-4.95	8.21	37.27 /97	33.67 /97	18.81 /95	0.30	1.65
EM	Universal Inst Emerg-Mrkts Debt	UEMDX	C	(800) 869-6397	D+ / 2.8	-3.25	-1.33	4.64 /13	9.87 /26	12.34 /87	8.01	1.09
IN	Universal Inst Eq & Inc II	UEIIX	C+	(800) 869-6397	C- / 3.9	-0.14	2.19	8.40 /36	10.79 /34	--	0.61	0.83
GL	Universal Inst Global II	UGIIX	B-	(800) 869-6397	B- / 7.4	2.27	7.98	16.12 /75	16.78 /67	--	0.00	1.20
GL	Universal Inst Global Value Equity	UGEPX	C	(800) 869-6397	C+ / 6.3	-0.13	4.71	12.15 /60	14.88 /58	5.18 /56	0.93	1.02
FO	Universal Inst Intl Magnum	UIMPX	B-	(800) 869-6397	B+ / 8.3	-0.22	8.40	23.01 /86	20.04 /79	6.53 /64	1.05	1.15
MC	Universal Inst Mid Cap Gr 1	UMGPX	C+	(800) 869-6397	B / 8.2	-5.12	3.37	18.10 /79	20.87 /82	4.26 /48	0.00	1.05
RE	Universal Inst Real Estate Fd	UUSRX	B	(800) 869-6397	A+ / 9.6	0.49	14.77	24.27 /88	30.25 /96	20.50 /97	0.97	1.03
SC	Universal Inst Small Comp Grwth II	USIIX	D	(800) 869-6397	C / 5.2	-8.45	3.00	10.75 /52	13.47 /51	--	0.00	1.25

● Denotes fund is closed to new investors
★ Denotes fund is included in Section II

412

RISK Risk Rating/Pts	3 Year Standard Deviation	Beta	NET ASSETS NAV As of 6/30/06	Total $(Mil)	ASSET Cash %	Stocks %	Bonds %	Other %	Portfolio Turnover Ratio	BULL/BEAR Last Bull Market Return	Last Bear Market Return	FUND MANAGER Manager Quality Pct	Manager Tenure (Years)	MINIMUMS Initial Purch. $	Additional Purch. $	LOADS Front End Load	Back End Load
C- / 3.2	14.0	1.22	14.34	7	4	95	0	1	60.0	79.5	-9.7	2	6	1,000	100	0.0	1.0
C- / 3.7	13.9	1.21	15.30	399	4	95	0	1	60.0	85.4	-9.5	3	11	10,000	500	0.0	0.5
C / 4.6	13.9	1.21	15.35	5	4	95	0	1	60.0	86.3	-9.5	4	6	10,000,000	100	0.0	1.0
B- / 7.3	7.6	1.00	14.80	139	0	99	0	1	2.0	61.6	-9.9	48	N/A	1,000	100	2.5	0.5
B- / 7.2	7.7	1.00	14.63	30	0	99	0	1	2.0	57.8	-10.0	39	N/A	1,000	100	0.0	1.0
B- / 7.3	7.7	1.00	14.88	29	0	99	0	1	2.0	62.7	-9.9	51	N/A	1,000	100	0.0	1.0
B+ / 9.5	5.9	1.16	29.20	481	8	63	28	1	42.0	63.3	-9.9	82	13	1,000	100	5.5	0.5
B+ / 9.5	6.0	1.17	28.55	89	8	63	28	1	42.0	59.2	-10.1	75	10	1,000	100	0.0	5.0
B+ / 9.8	5.9	1.15	28.58	234	8	63	28	1	42.0	59.5	-10.1	77	14	1,000	100	0.0	1.0
B+ / 9.9	5.9	1.16	29.62	116	8	63	28	1	42.0	65.1	-9.9	84	13	1,000	100	0.0	1.0
B / 8.4	7.3	0.91	18.24	89	5	94	0	1	41.0	74.7	-9.6	79	9	1,000	100	5.5	0.5
B / 8.4	7.3	0.92	17.84	1	5	94	0	1	41.0	70.4	-9.7	71	5	1,000	100	0.0	5.0
B / 8.4	7.3	0.91	17.83	6	5	94	0	1	41.0	70.7	-9.8	72	5	1,000	100	0.0	1.0
B / 8.4	7.3	0.91	18.43	543	5	94	0	1	41.0	76.4	-9.5	81	12	10,000,000	100	0.0	1.0
C+ / 6.4	10.5	1.22	8.81	7	3	96	0	1	53.0	69.3	-8.4	35	N/A	1,000	100	5.5	0.5
C+ / 6.4	10.5	1.23	8.52	N/A	3	96	0	1	53.0	65.3	-8.6	29	N/A	1,000	100	0.0	5.0
C+ / 6.4	10.4	1.22	8.53	1	3	96	0	1	53.0	65.5	-8.4	30	N/A	1,000	100	0.0	1.0
C+ / 6.5	10.5	1.23	9.02	5	3	96	0	1	53.0	70.9	-8.4	38	N/A	10,000,000	100	0.0	1.0
C / 4.8	14.9	0.98	14.41	153	2	97	0	1	25.0	97.7	-10.8	27	N/A	1,000	100	5.5	0.5
C / 4.7	14.8	0.98	13.91	6	2	97	0	1	25.0	93.3	-11.1	23	N/A	1,000	100	0.0	5.0
C / 4.7	14.9	0.98	13.89	8	2	97	0	1	25.0	93.0	-11.0	22	N/A	1,000	100	0.0	1.0
C / 4.8	14.9	0.98	14.75	270	2	97	0	1	25.0	99.2	-10.8	29	N/A	5,000,000	100	0.0	1.0
C / 4.8	7.3	0.88	10.54	106	0	99	0	1	49.0	83.0	-8.1	91	5	1,000	100	5.5	0.5
C / 5.1	7.2	0.88	10.39	2	0	99	0	1	49.0	78.5	-8.3	88	5	1,000	100	0.0	5.0
C / 5.0	7.3	0.88	10.34	16	0	99	0	1	49.0	78.5	-8.3	88	5	1,000	100	0.0	1.0
C / 4.8	7.3	0.88	10.58	7	0	99	0	1	49.0	84.5	-8.1	92	5	10,000,000	100	0.0	1.0
C+ / 6.9	12.8	0.80	17.40	585	10	90	0	0	157.0	110.4	-1.4	91	6	1,000	100	0.0	2.0
C / 5.3	7.7	0.93	15.09	116	0	98	0	2	62.0	60.9	-7.9	56	7	1,000	100	0.0	0.0
C+ / 6.6	10.6	0.99	29.80	2,669	5	94	0	1	18.0	120.5	-7.2	34	13	1,000	100	0.0	2.0
D+ / 2.6	18.8	1.82	22.34	2	1	98	0	1	53.0	103.4	-8.7	9	N/A	1,000	25	5.3	0.0
D+ / 2.6	18.8	1.82	22.11	1	1	98	0	1	53.0	101.5	-8.7	8	N/A	1,000	25	0.0	5.0
D+ / 2.6	18.8	1.82	22.11	1	1	98	0	1	53.0	101.5	-8.7	8	N/A	1,000	25	0.0	1.0
D+ / 2.7	18.8	1.81	22.90	118	1	98	0	1	53.0	105.4	-8.6	11	9	3,000,000	0	0.0	0.0
D+ / 2.6	18.8	1.81	22.35	12	1	98	0	1	53.0	103.5	-8.7	9	8	10,000	1,000	0.0	0.0
C+ / 6.6	14.7	1.66	30.26	37	4	95	0	1	8.0	150.7	-14.9	77	N/A	1,000	25	5.3	0.0
C+ / 6.6	14.7	1.66	29.94	4	4	95	0	1	8.0	148.4	-14.9	74	N/A	1,000	25	0.0	5.0
C+ / 6.6	14.6	1.66	29.93	18	4	95	0	1	8.0	148.3	-14.9	74	N/A	1,000	25	0.0	1.0
C+ / 5.6	14.6	1.66	30.40	172	4	95	0	1	8.0	151.8	-14.9	79	N/A	3,000,000	0	0.0	0.0
E+ / 0.7	22.1	1.42	10.11	N/A	1	98	0	1	56.0	112.9	-21.5	0	N/A	1,000	25	5.3	0.0
E+ / 0.7	22.2	1.43	10.19	320	1	98	0	1	56.0	114.5	-21.5	0	N/A	3,000,000	0	0.0	0.0
C+ / 6.6	6.9	0.83	14.76	24	3	82	14	1	28.0	67.8	-5.6	79	6	2,500	100	0.0	0.0
B / 8.7	7.6	0.99	9.19	405	1	98	0	1	10.0	64.3	-9.7	54	N/A	500,000	0	0.0	0.0
D / 1.9	18.9	1.55	15.92	151	2	97	0	1	53.0	211.1	N/A	21	3	0	0	0.0	0.0
D / 1.8	18.9	1.15	15.94	740	2	97	0	1	53.0	212.1	-8.2	10	N/A	0	0	0.0	0.0
B / 8.9	7.0	0.28	8.92	146	6	0	92	2	63.0	54.5	7.1	46	N/A	0	0	0.0	0.0
B+ / 9.6	5.5	0.66	13.99	477	5	67	27	1	46.0	N/A	N/A	81	N/A	0	0	0.0	0.0
C+ / 6.4	7.8	0.56	16.65	180	6	93	0	1	15.0	N/A	N/A	80	N/A	0	0	0.0	0.0
C+ / 5.9	8.0	0.75	15.57	131	2	97	0	1	26.0	85.3	-12.7	25	9	0	0	0.0	0.0
C+ / 5.7	9.9	0.97	13.42	152	7	92	0	1	34.0	104.4	-10.3	26	9	0	0	0.0	0.0
C / 5.2	12.4	1.09	12.59	124	2	97	0	1	103.0	126.2	-8.8	68	N/A	0	0	0.0	0.0
C / 4.6	14.9	0.89	26.49	1,129	4	95	0	1	26.0	147.2	-0.3	97	N/A	0	0	0.0	0.0
C / 4.4	15.5	0.79	17.88	87	2	97	0	1	72.0	N/A	N/A	38	N/A	0	0	0.0	0.0

			Overall Weiss Investment Rating		Perfor-mance Rating/Pts	PERFORMANCE					Incl. in Returns	
	99 Pct = Best 0 Pct = Worst					Total Return % through 6/30/06						
									Annualized		Dividend Yield	Expense Ratio
Fund Type	Fund Name	Ticker Symbol		Phone		3 Mo	6 Mo	1Yr / Pct	3Yr / Pct	5Yr / Pct		
MC	Universal Inst US MidCap Value II	UMCCX	C+	(800) 869-6397	B- / 7.3	-2.06	4.44	14.43 /70	17.55 /70	--	0.23	1.11
RE	Universal Inst US Real Estate II	USRBX	B	(800) 869-6397	A+ / 9.6	0.46	14.62	23.96 /87	29.93 /95	--	0.91	1.28
GR	Universal Inst Value	UVAPX	C	(800) 869-6397	C+ / 6.0	1.07	4.00	9.63 /44	14.54 /56	5.54 /58	1.25	0.85
EM	US Global Accolade East European	EUROX	C-	(800) 873-8637	A+ / 9.9	-9.89	4.23	42.73 /98	44.58 /99	38.97 /99	0.00	1.85
GR	US Global Accolade Holmes Growth	ACBGX	C+	(800) 873-8637	B- / 7.2	-4.18	6.61	16.23 /75	17.21 /69	5.36 /57	0.00	1.75
GR	US Global Accolade MegaTrends	MEGAX	B	(800) 873-8637	C+ / 5.7	-1.48	-0.09	11.10 /54	14.24 /55	1.45 /23	0.00	2.60
GR	US Global Inv All American Equity	GBTFX	C-	(800) 873-8637	C / 5.5	-4.50	5.43	15.25 /73	13.77 /53	2.09 /28	0.00	1.75
GL	US Global Inv China Region Opport	USCOX	B	(800) 873-8637	A+ / 9.6	-3.65	12.69	29.88 /94	30.20 /96	13.34 /89	2.23	2.33
EN	US Global Inv Global Resources	PSPFX	C+	(800) 873-8637	A+ / 9.9	2.68	20.50	48.91 /99	58.13 /99	38.92 /99	1.72	0.97
PM	US Global Inv Gold Shares	USERX	C	(800) 873-8637	A+ / 9.9	7.27	44.77	104.28 /99	45.05 /99	41.06 /99	0.76	1.60
PM	US Global Inv World Prec Minerals	UNWPX	C-	(800) 873-8637	A+ / 9.9	3.07	42.03	96.21 /99	53.24 /99	46.82 /99	2.29	1.36
AG	USAA Aggressive Growth Fund	USAUX	D	(800) 382-8722	C- / 3.3	-4.40	-1.56	5.69 /19	10.78 /34	-1.93 / 8	0.04	1.02
BA	USAA Balanced Strategy	USBSX	D+	(800) 382-8722	D / 1.6	-1.92	-0.16	3.51 / 9	7.38 /12	4.19 /48	2.17	1.00
GR	USAA Capital Growth	USCGX	B	(800) 382-8722	B / 8.0	-1.96	6.52	15.88 /74	19.78 /79	5.99 /61	0.00	0.95
GL	USAA Cornerstone Strategy Fund	USCRX	C	(800) 382-8722	C- / 4.2	-1.19	2.51	8.46 /36	11.18 /37	6.01 /61	0.79	1.18
EM	USAA Emerging Markets	USEMX	B	(800) 382-8722	A+ / 9.6	-4.73	6.09	28.91 /94	30.70 /96	19.19 /95	0.65	1.80
GR	USAA Extended Market Index	USMIX	C+	(800) 382-8722	B- / 7.5	-3.70	5.29	13.52 /66	18.57 /75	8.75 /75	0.66	0.50
GR	USAA First Start Growth Fund	UFSGX	D-	(800) 382-8722	D- / 1.5	-7.92	-8.00	1.24 / 3	8.88 /20	-3.56 / 4	0.00	1.45
PM	USAA Gold Fund	USAGX	C-	(800) 382-8722	A+ / 9.9	3.60	27.67	81.81 /99	37.42 /99	37.98 /99	0.00	1.26
GI	USAA Growth & Income Fund	USGRX	C-	(800) 382-8722	C- / 3.8	-3.38	0.20	7.14 /27	11.19 /37	2.88 /36	0.53	1.00
AA	USAA Growth & Tax Strategy	USBLX	D	(800) 382-8722	D / 2.1	-0.89	0.74	5.49 /18	7.98 /15	3.73 /43	2.35	0.81
GR	USAA Growth Fund	USAAX	E+	(800) 382-8722	D / 1.7	-8.31	-6.44	2.37 / 5	8.97 /21	-2.53 / 6	0.00	1.00
★ IN	USAA Income Stock Fund	USISX	C	(800) 382-8722	C / 5.3	-0.74	4.52	8.41 /36	13.10 /49	4.12 /47	1.71	0.78
FO	USAA International Fund	USIFX	A+	(800) 382-8722	A- / 9.0	1.48	11.44	28.63 /93	21.95 /85	11.48 /85	0.76	1.24
GR	USAA Nasdaq 100 Index	USNQX	E	(800) 382-8722	D / 1.9	-7.74	-4.49	4.94 /15	8.91 /20	-3.34 / 5	0.00	0.80
IX	USAA S&P 500 Index Members	USSPX	C+	(800) 382-8722	C- / 4.0	-1.49	2.61	8.45 /36	10.94 /35	2.24 /30	1.70	0.19
IX	USAA S&P 500 Index Reward	USPRX	C-	(800) 382-8722	C- / 4.1	-1.46	2.67	8.56 /37	11.07 /36	--	1.80	0.09
TC	USAA Science & Technology Fund	USSCX	E+	(800) 382-8722	C- / 3.7	-7.05	-1.42	12.91 /64	12.30 /44	-2.38 / 7	0.00	1.59
SC	USAA Small Cap Stock Fund	USCAX	C+	(800) 382-8722	C+ / 6.5	-3.57	5.37	9.48 /43	16.05 /64	8.58 /74	0.00	1.34
GR	USAA Value Fund	UVALX	C+	(800) 382-8722	C+ / 6.4	-0.36	4.48	8.28 /35	15.60 /62	--	0.88	1.15
GL	USAA World Growth Fund	USAWX	A+	(800) 382-8722	B / 7.8	1.78	9.03	20.42 /82	17.84 /72	7.15 /67	0.39	1.31
GR	Valley Forge Fund	VAFGX	D	(800) 548-1942	D / 1.9	-2.29	0.90	5.13 /16	7.79 /14	5.65 /59	1.98	1.30
AA	Value Line Asset Allocation	VLAAX	C+	(800) 223-0818	C / 5.2	-2.80	3.87	10.11 /48	12.87 /48	5.33 /57	0.38	1.14
CV	Value Line Convertible Fund	VALCX	C-	(800) 223-0818	D / 1.9	-1.57	3.49	8.71 /38	7.30 /12	3.80 /44	1.64	1.52
SC	Value Line Emerging Opportunities	VLEOX	B	(800) 223-0818	B- / 7.5	-3.72	8.81	16.05 /75	17.65 /71	9.80 /80	0.00	1.10
GR	Value Line Fund	VLIFX	E	(800) 223-0818	C- / 3.8	-6.65	2.59	10.40 /50	10.81 /34	0.64 /18	0.00	1.13
IN	Value Line Income & Growth Fund	VALIX	C+	(800) 223-0818	C+ / 5.8	-1.47	3.89	11.58 /57	13.89 /53	6.80 /66	1.89	1.11
AG	Value Line Leveraged Growth	VALLX	E-	(800) 223-0818	C- / 3.4	-5.00	4.18	12.94 /64	10.23 /29	-0.21 /15	0.00	1.16
AG	Value Line Premier Growth	VALSX	B	(800) 223-0818	B / 7.6	-2.96	6.45	16.04 /75	18.26 /73	7.40 /69	0.00	1.15
EM	Van Eck Emerging Mkts A	GBFAX	C+	(800) 221-2220	A+ / 9.7	-5.07	10.93	35.63 /97	35.38 /98	14.82 /92	0.00	2.10
EN	Van Eck Global Hard Assets A	GHAAX	B	(800) 221-2220	A+ / 9.9	2.35	15.25	49.36 /99	41.65 /99	25.01 /98	0.00	1.56
EN	Van Eck Global Hard Assets C	GHACX	B	(800) 221-2220	A+ / 9.9	2.20	14.89	48.60 /99	40.71 /99	24.05 /98	0.00	2.07
PM	Van Eck Intl Investors Gold A	INIVX	C	(800) 221-2220	A+ / 9.9	2.54	30.42	85.61 /99	35.18 /98	37.22 /99	0.11	1.69
GI	Van Eck Mid Cap Value A	CHGIX	C+	(800) 221-2220	C+ / 6.1	-1.66	3.41	9.89 /46	16.60 /66	4.07 /47	0.00	1.92
AG	Van Kampen Aggressive Growth A	VAGAX	C-	(800) 421-5666	C / 5.3	-6.50	2.29	12.51 /62	15.09 /59	0.46 /18	0.00	1.37
AG	Van Kampen Aggressive Growth B	VAGBX	D+	(800) 421-5666	C / 4.9	-6.71	1.94	11.68 /58	14.24 /55	-0.30 /14	0.00	2.12
AG	Van Kampen Aggressive Growth C	VAGCX	C-	(800) 421-5666	C / 5.5	-6.70	1.93	11.64 /58	14.23 /55	-0.32 /14	0.00	2.13
IN	Van Kampen American Franchise A	VAFAX	U	(800) 421-5666	U /	1.21	4.41	10.38 /49	--	--	0.49	3.97
SC	Van Kampen American Value A	MSAVX	B	(800) 421-5666	C+ / 6.9	-2.00	4.48	14.25 /69	17.98 /72	7.89 /71	0.00	1.33
SC	Van Kampen American Value B	MGAVX	B	(800) 421-5666	C+ / 6.8	-1.77	4.83	14.39 /70	17.44 /70	7.26 /68	0.00	2.09
SC	Van Kampen American Value C	MSVCX	B+	(800) 421-5666	B- / 7.0	-2.20	4.10	13.39 /66	17.10 /68	7.21 /68	0.00	2.09
★ GI	Van Kampen Comstock A	ACSTX	C+	(800) 421-5666	C / 4.8	0.83	3.75	9.17 /41	13.76 /53	4.46 /50	1.74	0.84

● Denotes fund is closed to new investors
★ Denotes fund is included in Section II

414

RISK	3 Year		NET ASSETS		ASSET				Portfolio	BULL / BEAR		FUND MANAGER		MINIMUMS		LOADS	
Risk Rating/Pts	Standard Deviation	Beta	NAV As of 6/30/06	Total $(Mil)	Cash %	Stocks %	Bonds %	Other %	Portfolio Turnover Ratio	Last Bull Market Return	Last Bear Market Return	Manager Quality Pct	Manager Tenure (Years)	Initial Purch. $	Additional Purch. $	Front End Load	Back End Load
C+ / 5.8	10.1	0.84	19.53	87	6	93	0	1	77.0	N/A	N/A	75	N/A	0	0	0.0	0.0
C / 4.6	14.9	0.89	26.27	759	4	95	0	1	26.0	145.2	-0.4	97	4	0	0	0.0	0.0
C+ / 6.2	7.8	0.93	15.07	67	2	97	0	1	32.0	84.5	-10.0	88	N/A	0	0	0.0	0.0
E+ / 0.7	25.3	1.39	41.17	1,830	3	96	0	1	92.0	339.4	-0.2	14	6	5,000	50	0.0	2.0
C+ / 5.9	13.4	1.39	18.55	71	10	88	0	2	268.0	75.0	-9.4	77	N/A	5,000	50	0.0	0.3
B / 8.5	9.7	1.05	10.63	17	3	96	0	1	54.0	75.8	-2.6	79	15	5,000	50	0.0	0.3
C+ / 5.9	12.5	1.32	27.59	23	9	90	0	1	184.0	79.2	-6.6	51	13	5,000	50	0.0	0.1
C / 4.5	19.4	1.56	8.70	76	9	90	0	1	90.0	171.2	-1.3	8	N/A	5,000	50	0.0	1.0
C- / 3.1	24.5	0.94	17.22	145	12	86	0	2	71.0	362.5	25.3	99	14	5,000	50	0.0	0.3
D- / 1.5	36.6	1.65	15.49	209	22	77	0	1	28.0	235.7	25.0	98	N/A	5,000	50	0.0	0.5
D- / 1.5	35.7	1.56	28.86	100	24	75	0	1	24.0	293.8	32.1	99	8	5,000	50	0.0	0.5
C+ / 6.0	9.7	1.10	30.85	1,143	4	94	0	2	71.3	67.6	-7.0	41	4	3,000	50	0.0	0.0
B / 8.0	5.4	1.12	14.90	631	2	52	44	2	63.5	41.0	-5.1	46	2	3,000	50	0.0	0.0
C+ / 6.5	14.9	1.53	8.50	149	2	96	0	2	165.8	126.7	-8.4	85	N/A	3,000	50	0.0	0.0
B- / 7.6	6.7	1.33	26.54	1,717	2	58	38	2	75.0	60.4	-6.6	74	N/A	3,000	50	0.0	0.0
C / 4.6	16.6	1.00	16.72	296	4	96	0	0	18.1	199.8	-6.1	20	4	3,000	50	0.0	0.0
C+ / 5.8	11.6	1.33	12.74	214	16	84	0	0	18.1	114.2	-8.7	88	N/A	3,000	50	0.0	0.0
B- / 7.0	9.7	1.04	9.77	229	8	68	22	2	149.5	60.4	-7.0	30	N/A	3,000	20	0.0	0.0
D- / 1.5	31.4	1.47	27.04	589	6	92	0	2	7.1	211.7	14.4	93	N/A	3,000	50	0.0	0.0
C+ / 6.8	8.9	1.12	18.43	1,404	2	98	0	0	81.3	68.3	-10.6	43	N/A	3,000	50	0.0	0.0
B- / 7.4	5.2	1.00	14.27	191	1	43	54	2	43.8	39.1	-2.5	61	7	3,000	50	0.0	0.0
C / 5.5	10.7	1.24	14.24	899	2	96	0	2	128.0	60.5	-8.2	19	N/A	3,000	50	0.0	0.0
C+ / 6.3	8.5	1.03	15.75	2,119	0	98	0	2	72.8	68.8	-8.4	72	N/A	3,000	50	0.0	0.0
B- / 7.3	9.6	0.92	26.01	1,011	2	98	0	0	22.5	116.2	-7.5	50	4	3,000	50	0.0	0.0
C / 4.4	14.9	1.68	4.89	121	0	98	0	2	1.8	65.4	-9.6	5	1	3,000	50	0.0	0.0
B / 8.8	7.6	1.00	19.03	2,034	0	98	0	2	1.0	63.2	-9.8	53	1	3,000	50	0.0	0.0
C+ / 6.2	7.7	1.00	19.03	815	0	98	0	2	1.0	64.0	-9.8	55	1	100,000	50	0.0	0.0
C- / 3.5	15.3	1.65	10.41	345	0	98	0	2	130.8	88.0	-12.3	17	N/A	3,000	50	0.0	0.0
C+ / 6.6	11.9	0.80	14.32	382	2	98	0	0	69.1	90.2	-6.7	66	N/A	3,000	50	0.0	0.0
C+ / 6.2	8.4	0.99	13.75	340	6	94	0	0	21.7	82.2	-5.1	90	N/A	3,000	50	0.0	0.0
B / 8.3	7.7	0.72	19.44	413	2	96	0	2	21.4	92.9	-9.0	58	4	3,000	50	0.0	0.0
B- / 7.1	10.1	1.17	8.97	10	14	86	0	0	18.0	46.7	-8.2	16	35	1,000	100	0.0	0.0
B- / 7.4	7.6	1.28	21.49	140	15	72	12	1	45.0	65.6	-4.6	87	N/A	1,000	100	0.0	0.0
B / 8.8	6.7	1.01	12.35	35	15	11	0	74	134.0	38.0	-1.2	55	16	1,000	250	0.0	0.0
C+ / 6.8	12.0	0.81	30.52	684	8	90	0	2	40.0	98.7	-5.2	77	N/A	1,000	100	0.0	0.0
D+ / 2.3	13.8	1.47	13.48	214	3	96	0	1	297.0	65.4	-6.0	18	N/A	1,000	100	0.0	0.0
C+ / 6.7	6.4	0.75	8.60	331	8	59	27	6	103.0	71.4	-3.6	92	N/A	1,000	100	0.0	0.0
D- / 1.1	13.1	1.39	23.17	304	0	100	0	0	200.0	61.9	-8.5	18	N/A	1,000	100	0.0	0.0
B- / 7.0	10.7	1.17	27.25	473	5	94	0	1	54.0	95.7	-5.9	93	N/A	1,000	100	0.0	0.0
C- / 3.3	17.8	1.03	12.18	46	9	90	0	1	101.0	243.2	-8.1	42	4	1,000	100	5.8	0.0
C / 4.7	19.5	0.83	38.31	341	6	93	0	1	51.0	217.9	5.4	99	N/A	1,000	100	5.8	0.0
C / 4.7	19.5	0.83	36.66	129	6	93	0	1	51.0	210.4	5.2	99	N/A	1,000	100	0.0	1.0
D / 1.9	33.0	1.61	16.12	389	6	92	0	2	29.0	175.5	22.5	66	8	1,000	100	5.8	0.0
B- / 7.0	11.3	1.26	23.67	18	0	99	0	1	103.0	101.6	-8.7	82	3	1,000	100	5.8	0.0
C / 5.1	14.1	1.54	16.10	540	0	99	0	1	129.0	100.0	-8.5	42	10	0	0	5.8	0.0
C / 5.0	14.2	1.54	14.73	378	0	99	0	1	129.0	95.2	-8.6	35	10	0	0	0.0	5.0
C / 5.0	14.1	1.54	14.77	61	0	99	0	1	129.0	95.2	-8.7	35	10	0	0	0.0	1.0
U /	N/A	N/A	10.88	142	6	93	0	1	N/A	N/A	N/A	N/A	1	0	0	5.8	0.0
B / 8.0	10.1	0.62	28.46	390	6	93	0	1	82.0	109.4	-10.2	94	3	0	0	5.8	0.0
B / 8.0	10.0	0.62	26.71	85	6	93	0	1	82.0	105.4	-10.3	93	3	0	0	0.0	5.0
B / 8.0	10.1	0.62	26.67	57	6	93	0	1	82.0	104.5	-9.8	91	3	0	0	0.0	1.0
B / 8.3	7.2	0.84	17.81	12,404	7	92	0	1	30.0	76.7	-8.4	88	12	0	0	5.8	0.0

Data as of June 30, 2006

Fund Type	Fund Name	Ticker Symbol	Overall Weiss Investment Rating	Phone	Performance Rating/Pts	3 Mo	6 Mo	1Yr / Pct	3Yr / Pct	5Yr / Pct	Dividend Yield	Expense Ratio
	99 Pct = Best *0 Pct = Worst*							Total Return % through 6/30/06	Annualized		Incl. in Returns	
GI	Van Kampen Comstock B	ACSWX	C+	(800) 421-5666	C / 4.4	0.63	3.41	8.36 /36	12.91 /48	3.68 /43	1.14	1.59
GI	Van Kampen Comstock C	ACSYX	C+	(800) 421-5666	C / 5.0	0.63	3.41	8.36 /36	12.93 /48	3.69 /43	1.14	1.59
GI	Van Kampen Comstock I	ACSDX	U	(800) 421-5666	U /	0.90	3.94	9.45 /43	--	--	2.07	0.56
GI	Van Kampen Comstock R	ACSRX	B-	(800) 421-5666	C / 5.5	0.76	3.68	8.90 /39	13.47 /51	--	1.60	1.09
★ GR	Van Kampen Emerging Growth A	ACEGX	E+	(800) 421-5666	D- / 1.4	-4.98	-0.96	7.48 /29	8.67 /19	-3.35 / 5	0.00	1.12
GR	Van Kampen Emerging Growth B	ACEMX	E+	(800) 421-5666	D- / 1.1	-5.15	-1.32	6.67 /24	7.85 /14	-4.09 / 4	0.00	1.88
GR	Van Kampen Emerging Growth C	ACEFX	E+	(800) 421-5666	D / 1.7	-5.15	-1.32	6.65 /24	7.84 /14	-4.08 / 4	0.00	1.88
GR	Van Kampen Emerging Growth I	ACEDX	D-	(800) 421-5666	D+ / 2.4	-4.91	-0.83	7.75 /31	8.93 /20	-3.11 / 5	0.00	0.87
EM	Van Kampen Emerging Markets A	MSRAX	C	(800) 421-5666	A+ / 9.6	-5.35	7.97	36.73 /97	34.47 /98	20.56 /97	0.43	2.15
EM	Van Kampen Emerging Markets B	MSRBX	C	(800) 421-5666	A+ / 9.6	-5.56	7.56	35.67 /97	33.43 /97	19.69 /96	0.00	2.90
EM	Van Kampen Emerging Markets C	MSRCX	C	(800) 421-5666	A+ / 9.7	-5.54	7.53	35.61 /97	33.40 /97	19.71 /96	0.00	2.90
GR	Van Kampen Enterprise A	ACENX	D-	(800) 421-5666	E+ / 0.9	-5.45	-1.44	5.60 /18	7.58 /13	-1.55 /10	0.00	1.11
GR	Van Kampen Enterprise B	ACEOX	D-	(800) 421-5666	E+ / 0.7	-5.60	-1.83	4.88 /14	6.78 /10	-2.30 / 7	0.00	1.88
GR	Van Kampen Enterprise C	ACEPX	D-	(800) 421-5666	D- / 1.1	-5.61	-1.89	4.73 /14	6.76 / 9	-2.31 / 7	0.00	1.88
★ BA	Van Kampen Equity & Income A	ACEIX	C	(800) 421-5666	C- / 3.1	0.01	2.27	8.19 /34	11.10 /36	6.41 /64	1.98	0.80
BA	Van Kampen Equity & Income B	ACEQX	C	(800) 421-5666	D+ / 2.7	-0.19	1.80	7.40 /29	10.28 /29	5.61 /59	1.41	1.55
★ BA	Van Kampen Equity & Income C	ACERX	C+	(800) 421-5666	C- / 3.4	-0.07	1.90	7.36 /28	10.28 /29	5.64 /59	1.40	1.55
BA	Van Kampen Equity & Income I	ACETX	U	(800) 421-5666	U /	0.07	2.28	8.45 /36	--	--	2.33	0.55
BA	Van Kampen Equity & Income R	ACESX	C+	(800) 421-5666	C- / 3.9	-0.06	2.01	7.89 /32	10.84 /34	--	1.85	1.05
GR	Van Kampen Equity Growth A	VEGAX	D-	(800) 421-5666	D / 1.8	-3.76	-3.33	11.40 /56	10.08 /28	-0.02 /15	0.00	1.34
GR	Van Kampen Equity Growth B	VEGBX	D-	(800) 421-5666	D- / 1.4	-3.99	-3.81	10.49 /50	9.22 /22	-0.77 /12	0.00	2.09
GR	Van Kampen Equity Growth C	VEGCX	D-	(800) 421-5666	D / 1.9	-3.97	-3.79	10.45 /50	9.22 /22	-0.68 /13	0.00	2.09
GI	● Van Kampen Exchange	ACEHX	C-	(800) 421-5666	C- / 3.9	0.35	4.53	8.49 /37	11.11 /36	2.27 /30	0.42	0.54
GL	Van Kampen Global Eqty Allocatn A	MSGAX	C	(800) 421-5666	C / 5.5	-2.10	4.55	17.07 /77	15.43 /61	5.01 /54	0.73	1.90
GL	Van Kampen Global Eqty Allocatn B	MSGBX	C+	(800) 421-5666	C+ / 5.9	-1.85	4.81	17.29 /78	15.53 /61	4.77 /52	0.79	2.65
GL	Van Kampen Global Eqty Allocatn C	MSGCX	C	(800) 421-5666	C+ / 5.8	-2.25	4.23	16.27 /75	14.58 /57	4.25 /48	0.07	2.65
GL	● Van Kampen Global Franchise A	VGFAX	B+	(800) 421-5666	C+ / 6.8	2.01	7.85	16.34 /75	17.47 /70	13.21 /89	1.40	1.28
GL	● Van Kampen Global Franchise B	VGFBX	B+	(800) 421-5666	C+ / 6.7	1.81	7.43	15.45 /73	16.58 /66	12.34 /87	0.87	2.03
GL	● Van Kampen Global Franchise C	VGFCX	A+	(800) 421-5666	B- / 7.1	1.79	7.44	15.49 /73	16.59 /66	12.35 /87	0.86	2.03
GL	Van Kampen Global Value Equity A	MGEAX	C+	(800) 421-5666	C / 5.2	-0.16	4.59	11.89 /59	14.65 /57	4.40 /50	0.60	1.38
GL	Van Kampen Global Value Equity B	MGEBX	C+	(800) 421-5666	C / 5.1	-0.40	4.15	11.10 /54	13.82 /53	3.66 /43	0.00	2.15
GL	Van Kampen Global Value Equity C	MGECX	C+	(800) 421-5666	C / 5.5	-0.40	4.14	10.97 /53	13.77 /53	3.71 /43	0.00	2.15
★ GI	Van Kampen Growth & Income A	ACGIX	C+	(800) 421-5666	C / 5.1	0.01	2.91	10.53 /51	14.19 /55	6.22 /63	1.26	0.81
GI	Van Kampen Growth & Income B	ACGJX	C+	(800) 421-5666	C / 4.8	0.30	2.99	10.19 /48	13.51 /51	5.51 /58	0.81	1.57
GI	Van Kampen Growth & Income C	ACGKX	B-	(800) 421-5666	C / 5.3	-0.18	2.54	9.75 /45	13.36 /51	5.44 /57	0.64	1.57
GI	Van Kampen Growth & Income I	ACGMX	U	(800) 421-5666	U /	0.08	3.04	10.86 /53	--	--	1.56	0.57
GI	Van Kampen Growth & Income R	ACGLX	B	(800) 421-5666	C+ / 5.7	0.00	2.83	10.31 /49	13.92 /54	--	1.09	1.07
CV	Van Kampen Harbor A	ACHBX	D	(800) 421-5666	D / 2.0	-1.32	3.84	8.27 /35	8.85 /20	2.79 /35	3.24	1.04
CV	Van Kampen Harbor B	ACHAX	D	(800) 421-5666	D / 1.6	-1.51	3.46	7.47 /29	8.03 /15	2.01 /27	2.69	1.80
CV	Van Kampen Harbor C	ACHCX	D+	(800) 421-5666	D / 2.2	-1.50	3.42	7.47 /29	8.03 /15	2.00 /27	2.65	1.80
FO	Van Kampen International Growth A	VIFAX	U	(800) 421-5666	U /	-0.88	9.56	--	--	--	0.00	1.52
FO	Van Kampen International Growth I	VIFIX	B+	(800) 421-5666	A- / 9.1	-0.77	9.69	28.16 /93	24.93 /91	9.99 /80	0.27	1.25
FO	Van Kampen Intl Advantage A	VKIAX	C+	(800) 421-5666	C+ / 6.5	-3.77	5.32	21.55 /84	17.63 /71	--	0.68	1.65
FO	Van Kampen Intl Advantage B	VKIBX	C+	(800) 421-5666	C+ / 6.5	-3.97	4.95	20.68 /83	16.88 /67	--	0.16	2.40
FO	Van Kampen Intl Advantage C	VKICX	C+	(800) 421-5666	B- / 7.0	-3.93	4.98	20.63 /83	17.28 /69	--	0.23	2.40
GR	Van Kampen Mid Cap Gr A	VGRAX	C+	(800) 421-5666	B- / 7.2	-5.17	3.07	17.83 /79	18.99 /76	5.96 /61	0.00	1.32
GR	Van Kampen Mid Cap Gr B	VGRBX	C+	(800) 421-5666	C+ / 6.9	-5.38	2.70	16.93 /77	18.07 /73	5.16 /55	0.00	2.08
GR	Van Kampen Mid Cap Gr C	VGRCX	C+	(800) 421-5666	B- / 7.3	-5.38	2.70	16.93 /77	18.07 /73	5.17 /55	0.00	2.08
GR	Van Kampen Pace A	ACPAX	D-	(800) 421-5666	D- / 1.5	-3.87	-3.42	11.50 /57	9.44 /24	0.43 /17	0.00	0.99
GR	Van Kampen Pace B	ACPBX	E+	(800) 421-5666	D- / 1.2	-4.04	-3.75	10.67 /51	8.61 /19	-0.33 /14	0.00	1.76
GR	Van Kampen Pace C	ACPCX	D-	(800) 421-5666	D / 1.7	-4.02	-3.74	10.63 /51	8.63 /19	-0.32 /14	0.00	1.76
RE	Van Kampen Real Estate Sec A	ACREX	B+	(800) 421-5666	A / 9.4	0.52	14.71	23.95 /87	29.83 /95	20.12 /96	1.18	1.36

RISK			NET ASSETS		ASSET				BULL / BEAR		FUND MANAGER		MINIMUMS		LOADS	
	3 Year		NAV						Last Bull	Last Bear	Manager	Manager	Initial	Additional	Front	Back
Risk	Standard		As of	Total	Cash	Stocks	Bonds	Other	Market	Market	Quality	Tenure	Purch.	Purch.	End	End
Rating/Pts	Deviation	Beta	6/30/06	$(Mil)	%	%	%	%	Return	Return	Pct	(Years)	$	$	Load	Load
B / 8.4	7.2	0.84	17.82	2,441	7	92	0	1	30.0	72.6	-8.7	84	12	0	0	0.0	5.0
B / 8.4	7.2	0.84	17.83	1,414	7	92	0	1	30.0	72.5	-8.6	84	12	0	0	0.0	1.0
U /	N/A	N/A	17.81	1,474	7	92	0	1	30.0	N/A	N/A	N/A	N/A	0	0	0.0	0.0
B / 8.3	7.2	0.84	17.82	229	7	92	0	1	30.0	75.3	-8.6	87	12	0	0	0.0	0.0
C+ / 5.9	12.0	1.35	41.24	2,937	4	95	0	1	100.0	57.3	-8.8	12	17	0	0	5.8	0.0
C+ / 5.8	12.0	1.35	35.02	1,395	4	95	0	1	100.0	53.5	-9.0	9	17	0	0	0.0	5.0
C+ / 5.8	12.0	1.35	35.92	265	4	95	0	1	100.0	53.6	-9.0	9	17	0	0	0.0	1.0
C / 5.1	12.0	1.35	41.83	60	4	95	0	1	100.0	58.5	-8.8	14	N/A	0	0	0.0	0.0
D+ / 2.3	18.9	1.16	20.87	331	2	96	0	2	60.0	224.9	-8.3	12	5	0	0	5.8	2.0
D+ / 2.3	18.9	1.16	19.36	73	2	96	0	2	60.0	217.2	-8.5	9	N/A	0	0	0.0	5.0
D+ / 2.3	18.9	1.16	19.42	58	2	96	0	2	60.0	217.3	-8.5	9	N/A	0	0	0.0	1.0
B- / 7.1	9.7	1.16	13.01	1,080	1	98	0	1	42.0	51.2	-9.9	15	N/A	0	0	5.8	0.0
B- / 7.0	9.7	1.16	11.81	222	1	98	0	1	42.0	47.7	-10.1	12	N/A	0	0	0.0	5.0
B- / 7.0	9.7	1.17	11.95	23	1	98	0	1	42.0	47.7	-10.2	12	N/A	0	0	0.0	1.0
B+ / 9.1	5.3	1.05	8.64	11,126	6	60	17	17	38.0	56.7	-3.6	85	16	0	0	5.8	0.0
B+ / 9.2	5.3	1.05	8.50	3,135	6	60	17	17	38.0	53.3	-3.9	79	4	0	0	0.0	5.0
B+ / 9.2	5.3	1.05	8.54	2,061	6	60	17	17	38.0	53.1	-3.8	79	4	0	0	0.0	1.0
U /	N/A	N/A	8.64	86	6	60	17	17	38.0	N/A	N/A	N/A	N/A	0	0	0.0	0.0
B+ / 9.7	5.4	1.06	8.67	118	6	60	17	17	38.0	56.2	-3.8	83	N/A	0	0	0.0	0.0
C+ / 6.4	11.3	1.28	10.75	184	0	99	0	1	154.0	59.9	-10.8	24	N/A	0	0	5.8	0.0
C+ / 6.4	11.2	1.27	10.11	85	0	99	0	1	154.0	56.2	-11.0	19	N/A	0	0	0.0	5.0
C+ / 6.4	11.2	1.27	10.15	30	0	99	0	1	154.0	56.3	-10.6	19	N/A	0	0	0.0	1.0
B- / 7.2	9.5	1.04	381.88	67	4	96	0	0	N/A	57.7	-10.2	51	16	0	0	0.0	2.0
C+ / 6.6	9.2	0.89	15.84	220	3	96	0	1	20.0	85.4	-8.7	12	13	0	0	5.8	2.0
C+ / 6.6	9.3	0.89	14.82	82	3	96	0	1	20.0	85.0	-8.8	12	11	0	0	0.0	5.0
C+ / 6.6	9.3	0.89	14.79	34	3	96	0	1	20.0	81.0	-8.8	9	13	0	0	0.0	2.0
B+ / 9.1	8.0	0.58	25.43	1,399	2	97	0	1	14.0	87.5	-5.3	81	4	0	0	5.8	2.0
B+ / 9.1	8.0	0.58	24.74	486	2	97	0	1	14.0	83.1	-5.5	74	4	0	0	0.0	5.0
B+ / 9.1	8.0	0.58	24.97	338	2	97	0	1	14.0	83.1	-5.5	74	4	0	0	0.0	2.0
B- / 7.8	7.9	0.75	12.75	299	2	97	0	1	28.0	84.0	-13.1	24	9	0	0	5.8	2.0
B- / 7.8	7.9	0.75	12.31	53	2	97	0	1	28.0	79.8	-13.2	19	9	0	0	0.0	5.0
B- / 7.8	8.0	0.75	12.34	29	2	97	0	1	28.0	79.7	-13.0	19	9	0	0	0.0	2.0
B / 8.3	7.2	0.87	20.67	6,907	6	93	0	1	43.0	76.8	-7.0	89	N/A	0	0	5.8	0.0
B / 8.4	7.1	0.87	20.54	853	6	93	0	1	43.0	72.9	-7.1	86	N/A	0	0	0.0	5.0
B / 8.3	7.2	0.88	20.53	579	6	93	0	1	43.0	72.7	-7.1	84	N/A	0	0	0.0	1.0
U /	N/A	N/A	20.68	885	6	93	0	1	43.0	N/A	N/A	N/A	N/A	0	0	0.0	0.0
B / 8.3	7.2	0.88	20.69	95	6	93	0	1	43.0	75.5	-7.0	87	N/A	0	0	0.0	0.0
B- / 7.1	6.7	1.03	14.79	301	2	3	0	95	69.0	39.9	N/A	70	8	0	0	5.8	0.0
B- / 7.6	6.7	1.03	14.76	28	2	3	0	95	69.0	36.5	-0.2	62	8	0	0	0.0	5.0
B- / 7.6	6.7	1.03	14.89	10	2	3	0	95	69.0	36.6	-0.2	62	8	0	0	0.0	1.0
U /	N/A	N/A	18.10	167	N/A	100	0	N/A	17.0	N/A	N/A	N/A	N/A	0	0	5.8	2.0
C / 5.5	10.6	1.02	18.12	38	N/A	100	0	N/A	17.0	138.2	-8.7	56	1	0	0	0.0	2.0
C+ / 6.1	11.0	1.05	14.05	98	4	95	0	1	69.0	111.3	-11.5	8	5	0	0	5.8	2.0
C+ / 6.1	11.0	1.05	13.78	24	4	95	0	1	69.0	106.9	-11.7	6	5	0	0	0.0	5.0
C+ / 6.1	11.0	1.04	13.92	9	4	95	0	1	69.0	109.0	-11.7	7	5	0	0	0.0	2.0
C+ / 6.1	12.2	1.31	25.85	860	3	96	0	1	86.0	106.6	-8.9	91	N/A	0	0	5.8	0.0
C+ / 6.0	12.2	1.31	23.58	175	3	96	0	1	86.0	101.7	-9.1	87	N/A	0	0	0.0	5.0
C+ / 6.0	12.2	1.31	23.58	80	3	96	0	1	86.0	101.7	-9.1	87	N/A	0	0	0.0	1.0
C+ / 6.3	11.0	1.21	10.18	1,380	0	99	0	1	154.0	56.7	-7.7	23	N/A	0	0	5.8	0.0
C+ / 6.3	11.0	1.22	9.75	52	0	99	0	1	154.0	53.0	-8.0	18	6	0	0	0.0	5.0
C+ / 6.3	11.0	1.22	9.78	9	0	99	0	1	154.0	53.0	-8.0	18	6	0	0	0.0	1.0
C+ / 5.6	15.0	0.90	27.64	634	4	95	0	1	25.0	145.2	-0.5	97	9	0	0	4.8	2.0

Fund Type	Fund Name	Ticker Symbol	Overall Weiss Investment Rating	Phone	Perfor- mance Rating/Pts	Total Return % through 6/30/06			Annualized		Incl. in Returns	
						3 Mo	6 Mo	1Yr / Pct	3Yr / Pct	5Yr / Pct	Dividend Yield	Expense Ratio
RE	Van Kampen Real Estate Sec B	ACRBX	B+	(800) 421-5666	A / 9.4	0.38	14.33	23.08 /86	28.89 /95	19.24 /95	0.57	2.11
RE	Van Kampen Real Estate Sec C	ACRCX	B+	(800) 421-5666	A / 9.5	0.38	14.30	23.08 /86	28.96 /95	19.29 /95	0.57	2.11
GR	Van Kampen Select Growth A	VSGAX	E+	(800) 421-5666	D- / 1.4	-4.85	-1.67	6.64 /24	8.85 /20	-1.38 /10	0.00	1.69
GR	Van Kampen Select Growth B	VBSGX	E+	(800) 421-5666	D- / 1.1	-5.24	-2.13	5.86 /20	7.97 /15	-2.15 / 8	0.00	2.45
GR	Van Kampen Select Growth C	VSGCX	E+	(800) 421-5666	D / 1.6	-5.24	-2.13	5.86 /20	7.97 /15	-2.15 / 8	0.00	2.45
SC	Van Kampen Small Cap Growth A	VASCX	C+	(800) 421-5666	B / 7.8	-7.51	8.36	20.97 /83	21.10 /83	4.84 /53	0.00	1.61
SC	Van Kampen Small Cap Growth B	VBSCX	C+	(800) 421-5666	B / 7.8	-7.70	8.00	20.18 /82	20.29 /80	4.09 /47	0.00	2.36
SC	Van Kampen Small Cap Growth C	VCSCX	C+	(800) 421-5666	B / 8.0	-7.71	8.00	20.05 /82	20.25 /80	4.09 /47	0.00	2.36
SC	● Van Kampen Small Cap Value A	VSCAX	C+	(800) 421-5666	C+ / 6.9	-2.63	8.50	13.30 /65	18.52 /74	10.08 /81	0.00	1.38
SC	● Van Kampen Small Cap Value B	VSMBX	C+	(800) 421-5666	C+ / 6.8	-2.83	8.10	12.46 /62	17.60 /71	9.22 /77	0.00	2.15
SC	● Van Kampen Small Cap Value C	VSMCX	C+	(800) 421-5666	B- / 7.1	-2.83	8.09	12.43 /62	17.62 /71	9.26 /78	0.00	2.12
TC	Van Kampen Technology A	VTFAX	E	(800) 421-5666	D / 1.7	-11.09	-7.98	4.65 /13	11.42 /39	-8.09 / 0	0.00	2.42
TC	Van Kampen Technology B	VTFBX	E	(800) 421-5666	D- / 1.5	-11.29	-8.38	3.94 /10	10.50 /31	-8.80 / 0	0.00	3.19
TC	Van Kampen Technology C	VTFCX	E	(800) 421-5666	D / 2.0	-11.09	-8.18	4.18 /11	10.59 /32	-8.76 / 0	0.00	3.19
UT	Van Kampen Utility A	VKUAX	B-	(800) 421-5666	C / 5.5	3.54	4.66	8.18 /34	15.63 /62	4.13 /47	2.52	1.30
UT	Van Kampen Utility B	VKUBX	B-	(800) 421-5666	C+ / 5.6	3.39	4.30	7.38 /29	14.74 /58	3.35 /40	2.08	2.06
UT	Van Kampen Utility C	VKUCX	B	(800) 421-5666	C+ / 5.8	3.34	4.25	7.33 /28	14.75 /58	3.34 /40	2.08	2.06
GI	Van Kampen Value Opportunities A	VVOAX	B-	(800) 421-5666	C / 5.4	-1.20	2.50	10.95 /53	15.05 /59	6.55 /64	0.46	1.41
GI	Van Kampen Value Opportunities B	VVOBX	C+	(800) 421-5666	C / 5.0	-1.39	2.03	10.02 /47	14.22 /55	5.77 /60	0.00	2.17
GI	Van Kampen Value Opportunities C	VVOCX	B-	(800) 421-5666	C+ / 5.6	-1.39	2.03	10.02 /47	14.22 /55	5.77 /60	0.00	2.17
EM	Van Wagoner Emerging Growth Fund	VWEGX	E-	(800) 228-2121	E- / 0.0	-10.65	9.16	5.35 /17	-4.62 / 0	-22.53 / 0	0.00	3.53
GR	Van Wagoner Growth Opportunities	VWGOX	E-	(800) 228-2121	E- / 0.0	-12.05	3.31	1.21 / 3	-0.65 / 0	--	0.00	5.01
SC	Van Wagoner Small-Cap Growth	VWMCX	E-	(800) 228-2121	E- / 0.0	-12.14	6.17	5.02 /15	-2.06 / 0	-8.87 / 0	0.00	3.32
IX	Vanguard 500 Index Adm	VFIAX	C+	(800) 662-7447	C- / 4.2	-1.45	2.70	8.59 /37	11.16 /37	2.45 /32	1.89	0.09
★ IX	Vanguard 500 Index Inv	VFINX	C+	(800) 662-7447	C- / 4.1	-1.48	2.64	8.49 /37	11.06 /36	2.37 /31	1.80	0.18
AA	Vanguard Asset Allocation Adm	VAARX	C+	(800) 662-7447	C- / 4.2	-0.97	3.13	8.93 /40	11.01 /36	--	2.08	0.28
★ AA	Vanguard Asset Allocation Inv	VAAPX	C+	(800) 662-7447	C- / 4.1	-1.00	3.10	8.83 /39	10.90 /35	5.01 /54	1.97	0.38
BA	Vanguard Balanced Index Adm	VBIAX	C	(800) 662-7447	D+ / 2.4	-1.20	1.71	5.55 /18	8.56 /18	4.55 /51	2.96	0.11
BA	Vanguard Balanced Index Inst	VBAIX	C	(800) 662-7447	D+ / 2.4	-1.20	1.73	5.58 /18	8.59 /18	4.59 /51	2.99	0.08
★ BA	Vanguard Balanced Index Inv	VBINX	C	(800) 662-7447	D+ / 2.3	-1.27	1.67	5.40 /17	8.45 /17	4.46 /50	2.87	0.20
GR	Vanguard Capital Opportunity Adm	VHCAX	C+	(800) 662-7447	B- / 7.5	-6.07	3.25	13.36 /66	19.30 /77	--	0.22	0.51
★ GR	● Vanguard Capital Opportunity Inv	VHCOX	C+	(800) 662-7447	B- / 7.5	-6.09	3.21	13.25 /65	19.19 /77	6.18 /62	0.16	N/A
GR	Vanguard Capital Value Inv	VCVLX	C+	(800) 662-7447	C+ / 5.9	-2.11	3.43	8.71 /38	14.65 /57	--	0.80	0.59
CV	Vanguard Convertible Securities	VCVSX	C	(800) 662-7447	C / 4.7	-2.83	5.22	15.99 /75	11.70 /41	7.17 /68	2.44	0.86
★ FO	Vanguard Developed Markets Index	VDMIX	A+	(800) 662-7447	A- / 9.0	0.81	10.19	26.81 /91	23.84 /89	9.90 /80	1.95	N/A
IN	Vanguard Diversified Equity Inv	VDEQX	U	(800) 662-7447	U /	-3.22	1.64	9.24 /42	--	--	0.69	0.43
GI	Vanguard Dividend Growth Fd	VDIGX	B-	(800) 662-7447	C / 4.7	-0.90	4.29	9.88 /46	11.87 /42	1.29 /22	1.95	0.37
★ EM	Vanguard Emerging Mkts Stk Idx Fd	VEIEX	B	(800) 662-7447	A+ / 9.7	-4.57	6.14	33.25 /96	34.08 /98	20.35 /96	1.56	0.45
EM	Vanguard Emerging Mkts Stk Idx Inst	VEMIX	B	(800) 662-7447	A+ / 9.8	-4.52	6.18	33.44 /96	34.34 /98	20.56 /97	1.69	0.45
EN	Vanguard Energy Adm	VGELX	A+	(800) 662-7447	A+ / 9.9	4.55	16.51	37.33 /97	39.83 /99	--	1.17	0.27
EN	Vanguard Energy Index Adm	VENAX	U	(800) 662-7447	U /	4.34	13.58	29.76 /94	--	--	0.86	0.28
★ EN	Vanguard Energy Inv	VGENX	A+	(800) 662-7447	A+ / 9.9	4.54	16.47	37.25 /97	39.76 /99	25.08 /98	1.13	0.33
IN	Vanguard Equity Income Adm	VEIRX	B	(800) 662-7447	C+ / 5.7	1.27	6.34	10.73 /52	13.19 /50	--	2.99	0.19
★ IN	Vanguard Equity Income Inv	VEIPX	B-	(800) 662-7447	C+ / 5.6	1.24	6.25	10.54 /51	13.04 /49	5.67 /59	2.85	0.30
FO	Vanguard European Stock Index Adm	VEUSX	A+	(800) 662-7447	A- / 9.0	2.71	13.59	25.06 /89	23.39 /88	--	2.27	0.18
FO	Vanguard European Stock Index Inst	VESIX	A+	(800) 662-7447	A- / 9.1	2.71	13.60	25.14 /89	23.47 /88	10.59 /83	2.34	0.18
★ FO	Vanguard European Stock Index Inv	VEURX	A+	(800) 662-7447	A- / 9.0	2.68	13.54	24.96 /88	23.28 /88	10.43 /82	2.23	0.27
SC	● Vanguard Explorer Fund Adm	VEXRX	C	(800) 662-7447	C+ / 6.9	-6.61	4.13	13.32 /65	16.98 /68	--	0.44	0.41
★ SC	● Vanguard Explorer Fund Inv	VEXPX	C	(800) 662-7447	C+ / 6.8	-6.67	4.02	13.11 /65	16.81 /67	6.64 /65	0.27	0.56
GR	Vanguard Extended Market Index	VEXAX	B	(800) 662-7447	B / 7.7	-3.88	5.57	14.25 /69	19.23 /77	9.00 /76	1.10	0.10
GR	Vanguard Extended Market Index Inst	VIEIX	B	(800) 662-7447	B / 7.7	-3.88	5.57	14.28 /69	19.29 /77	9.09 /77	1.16	0.07
★ GR	Vanguard Extended Market Index Inv	VEXMX	B	(800) 662-7447	B / 7.7	-3.94	5.48	14.07 /68	19.08 /76	8.91 /76	0.99	0.25

RISK			NET ASSETS		ASSET				Portfolio	BULL / BEAR		FUND MANAGER		MINIMUMS		LOADS	
	3 Year		NAV							Last Bull	Last Bear	Manager	Manager	Initial	Additional	Front	Back
Risk Rating/Pts	Standard Deviation	Beta	As of 6/30/06	Total $(Mil)	Cash %	Stocks %	Bonds %	Other %	Turnover Ratio	Market Return	Market Return	Quality Pct	Tenure (Years)	Purch. $	Purch. $	End Load	End Load
C+ / 5.6	15.0	0.90	27.66	137	4	95	0	1	25.0	139.5	-0.7	95	9	0	0	0.0	4.0
C+ / 5.6	15.0	0.90	27.71	94	4	95	0	1	25.0	139.9	-0.7	95	9	0	0	0.0	2.0
C+ / 5.7	11.9	1.31	5.30	32	2	97	0	1	154.0	56.9	-9.9	15	6	0	0	5.8	0.0
C+ / 5.6	11.8	1.31	5.06	113	2	97	0	1	154.0	53.1	-10.0	11	6	0	0	0.0	5.0
C+ / 5.6	11.8	1.31	5.06	23	2	97	0	1	154.0	53.1	-10.0	11	6	0	0	0.0	1.0
C / 5.2	15.7	1.01	9.98	176	5	94	0	1	277.0	136.1	-8.3	76	6	0	0	5.8	2.0
C / 5.2	15.7	1.01	9.59	55	5	94	0	1	277.0	130.6	-8.4	69	6	0	0	0.0	5.0
C / 5.2	15.7	1.01	9.58	28	5	94	0	1	277.0	130.4	-8.2	69	6	0	0	0.0	2.0
C+ / 6.1	11.6	0.74	17.75	155	2	97	0	1	40.0	107.2	-8.2	89	N/A	0	0	5.8	2.0
C+ / 5.9	11.6	0.73	16.81	110	2	97	0	1	40.0	102.2	-8.3	85	N/A	0	0	0.0	5.0
C+ / 5.8	11.6	0.74	16.84	35	2	97	0	1	40.0	102.4	-8.3	85	N/A	0	0	0.0	2.0
C / 4.5	16.7	1.72	4.73	99	0	99	0	1	93.0	85.6	-13.2	10	N/A	0	0	5.8	2.0
C / 4.3	16.8	1.74	4.48	115	0	99	0	1	93.0	81.2	-13.2	7	N/A	0	0	0.0	5.0
C / 4.3	16.8	1.73	4.49	25	0	99	0	1	93.0	81.2	-13.2	8	N/A	0	0	0.0	2.0
B / 8.4	8.1	0.65	19.44	131	2	96	0	2	27.0	79.0	-4.3	63	N/A	0	0	5.8	2.0
B / 8.3	8.2	0.65	19.39	43	2	96	0	2	27.0	74.9	-4.6	53	N/A	0	0	0.0	4.0
B / 8.3	8.1	0.65	19.38	15	2	96	0	2	27.0	74.8	-4.5	53	N/A	0	0	0.0	2.0
B / 8.2	8.2	0.97	12.30	178	10	89	0	1	46.0	87.8	-8.4	89	5	0	0	5.8	0.0
B / 8.2	8.2	0.96	12.05	33	10	89	0	1	46.0	83.5	-8.4	85	5	0	0	0.0	5.0
B / 8.2	8.2	0.96	12.05	27	10	89	0	1	46.0	83.5	-8.6	85	5	0	0	0.0	1.0
E- / 0.1	24.7	0.81	4.53	40	0	100	0	0	468.0	20.6	-20.3	0	11	5,000	50	0.0	0.0
E- / 0.0	23.3	2.11	10.00	14	0	100	0	0	570.0	35.8	N/A	0	3	2,500	50	0.0	0.0
E / 0.3	25.6	1.48	9.63	15	6	93	0	1	440.0	30.4	-11.6	0	11	5,000	50	0.0	0.0
B / 8.6	7.6	1.00	117.00	40,452	0	100	0	0	6.4	64.6	-9.7	56	N/A	100,000	100	0.0	0.0
B / 8.6	7.6	1.00	116.99	66,855	0	100	0	0	6.4	64.1	-9.8	55	N/A	3,000	100	0.0	0.0
B / 8.8	6.8	1.40	58.03	1,778	0	100	0	0	6.0	63.0	-8.8	69	5	100,000	100	0.0	0.0
B / 8.8	6.8	1.39	25.85	9,477	0	100	0	0	6.0	62.4	-8.9	69	18	3,000	100	0.0	0.0
B+ / 9.2	5.0	1.06	19.88	1,953	0	60	39	1	31.0	45.1	-4.4	63	N/A	100,000	100	0.0	0.0
B+ / 9.2	5.0	1.06	19.88	2,185	0	60	39	1	31.0	45.3	-4.4	63	N/A	5,000,000	0	0.0	0.0
B+ / 9.2	5.0	1.06	19.87	4,137	0	60	39	1	31.0	44.7	-4.4	62	N/A	3,000	100	0.0	0.0
C+ / 5.9	13.5	1.52	78.79	3,596	3	96	0	1	12.0	125.2	-10.8	83	N/A	100,000	100	0.0	1.0
C+ / 5.9	13.5	1.51	34.09	4,894	3	96	0	1	12.0	124.4	-10.8	82	N/A	25,000	100	0.0	1.0
B- / 7.1	10.0	1.18	12.07	435	1	98	0	1	46.0	94.4	-9.7	72	5	3,000	100	0.0	0.0
B- / 7.5	7.8	1.14	13.93	632	21	0	0	79	86.0	60.4	1.0	87	10	10,000	100	0.0	1.0
B / 8.0	10.2	1.01	11.25	2,131	0	99	0	1	10.0	131.0	-9.5	48	6	3,000	100	0.0	2.0
U /	N/A	N/A	21.64	107	4	95	0	1	1.0	N/A	N/A	N/A	N/A	3,000	100	0.0	0.0
B / 8.9	6.9	0.87	12.82	985	1	98	0	1	16.0	67.4	-9.9	74	N/A	3,000	100	0.0	0.0
C / 4.3	18.5	1.12	20.24	7,454	0	99	0	1	15.0	224.7	-6.8	15	N/A	3,000	100	0.0	0.5
C / 4.3	18.6	1.13	20.28	528	0	99	0	1	15.0	226.7	-6.8	15	N/A	5,000,000	100	0.0	0.0
C+ / 6.2	18.3	0.91	122.47	3,706	4	95	0	1	10.0	213.4	4.0	98	N/A	100,000	100	0.0	1.0
U /	N/A	N/A	40.89	82	0	100	0	0	35.0	N/A	N/A	N/A	N/A	100,000	100	0.0	1.0
C+ / 6.2	18.3	0.91	65.20	6,796	4	95	0	1	10.0	212.7	4.0	98	N/A	25,000	100	0.0	1.0
B / 8.9	7.2	0.88	50.06	1,614	0	99	0	1	42.0	70.3	-8.6	83	N/A	100,000	100	0.0	0.0
B / 8.4	7.2	0.88	23.88	2,756	0	99	0	1	42.0	69.7	-8.6	83	N/A	3,000	100	0.0	0.0
B / 8.2	10.5	0.97	73.89	1,888	0	100	0	0	5.0	131.8	-11.2	54	N/A	100,000	100	0.0	2.0
B- / 7.9	10.5	0.97	31.49	2,429	0	100	0	0	5.0	132.3	-11.2	55	N/A	5,000,000	100	0.0	2.0
B- / 7.9	10.5	0.96	31.45	14,457	0	100	0	0	5.0	131.1	-11.2	53	N/A	3,000	100	0.0	2.0
C / 4.9	14.1	0.95	72.80	3,314	1	98	0	1	80.0	113.1	-11.6	46	N/A	100,000	100	0.0	0.0
C / 4.9	14.1	0.95	78.13	8,659	1	98	0	1	80.0	112.0	-11.7	45	N/A	3,000	100	0.0	0.0
C+ / 6.5	11.8	1.36	36.16	2,788	0	99	0	1	28.0	118.0	-9.0	90	N/A	100,000	100	0.0	0.0
C+ / 6.5	11.8	1.36	36.17	2,518	0	99	0	1	28.0	118.4	-8.9	90	N/A	5,000,000	100	0.0	0.0
C+ / 6.5	11.8	1.36	36.11	6,125	0	99	0	1	28.0	117.2	-9.0	89	N/A	3,000	100	0.0	0.0

Fund Type	Fund Name	Ticker Symbol	Overall Weiss Investment Rating	Phone	Perfor-mance Rating/Pts	3 Mo	6 Mo	1Yr / Pct	3Yr / Pct	5Yr / Pct	Dividend Yield	Expense Ratio
GR	Vanguard FTSE Social Index Inst	VFTNX	D+	(800) 662-7447	C- / 3.1	-2.34	1.09	8.47 /37	9.55 /24	--	1.32	0.25
GR	Vanguard FTSE Social Index Inv	VFTSX	D+	(800) 662-7447	C- / 3.0	-2.46	0.85	8.22 /35	9.41 /24	1.07 /21	1.20	0.25
★ GL	Vanguard Global Equity Fund	VHGEX	A+	(800) 662-7447	B+ / 8.9	0.42	9.02	22.33 /85	22.96 /87	13.54 /89	1.11	0.74
GI	Vanguard Growth & Income Adm	VGIAX	C+	(800) 662-7447	C / 4.4	-1.95	1.74	7.80 /31	11.91 /42	2.94 /36	1.82	0.23
★ GI	Vanguard Growth & Income Inv	VQNPX	C+	(800) 662-7447	C / 4.3	-2.01	1.65	7.63 /30	11.73 /41	2.79 /35	1.62	0.25
GR	Vanguard Growth Equity	VGEQX	D	(800) 662-7447	C- / 3.2	-5.97	-0.29	9.73 /45	10.06 /28	-0.65 /13	0.01	0.88
GR	Vanguard Growth Index Adm	VIGAX	D	(800) 662-7447	D / 2.1	-3.95	-0.72	5.95 /20	8.50 /18	1.13 /21	0.98	0.11
GR	Vanguard Growth Index Inst	VIGIX	D	(800) 662-7447	D / 2.2	-3.94	-0.70	5.99 /20	8.53 /18	1.17 /21	1.01	0.08
★ GR	Vanguard Growth Index Inv	VIGRX	D	(800) 662-7447	D / 2.1	-3.94	-0.77	5.88 /20	8.39 /17	1.03 /20	0.86	0.22
HL	● Vanguard Health Care Adm	VGHAX	C+	(800) 662-7447	C / 5.4	-0.41	2.44	12.21 /61	13.30 /50	--	1.27	0.16
★ HL	● Vanguard Health Care Inv	VGHCX	C+	(800) 662-7447	C / 5.3	-0.43	2.40	12.10 /60	13.20 /50	7.93 /71	1.20	0.23
HL	Vanguard HealthCare Index Adm	VHCIX	U	(800) 662-7447	U /	-5.15	-3.19	0.52 / 2	--	--	0.71	0.28
GL	Vanguard Instl Developd Mkts Idx Fd	VIDMX	A+	(800) 662-7447	A- / 9.0	0.90	10.18	26.95 /91	23.99 /89	10.03 /81	2.05	0.13
GI	Vanguard Instl Index Fd	VINIX	C+	(800) 662-7447	C- / 4.2	-1.44	2.71	8.62 /38	11.20 /37	2.50 /32	1.89	0.05
GI	Vanguard Instl Index Plus	VIIIX	C+	(800) 662-7447	C- / 4.2	-1.43	2.73	8.65 /38	11.23 /37	2.53 /32	1.91	0.03
GI	Vanguard Instl Total Stock Mkt Plus	VITPX	C+	(800) 662-7447	C / 5.2	-1.93	3.38	9.94 /47	12.99 /49	4.09 /47	1.60	0.05
★ FO	● Vanguard International Explorer Fd	VINEX	A	(800) 662-7447	A+ / 9.7	-1.86	11.61	29.34 /94	32.45 /97	16.19 /93	1.87	0.50
FO	Vanguard International Growth Adm	VWILX	A	(800) 662-7447	B+ / 8.9	-0.07	9.88	28.52 /93	23.05 /87	--	1.73	0.40
★ FO	Vanguard International Growth Inv	VWIGX	A	(800) 662-7447	B+ / 8.9	-0.13	9.76	28.27 /93	22.82 /87	9.39 /78	1.58	0.60
★ FO	Vanguard International Value Fund	VTRIX	A+	(800) 662-7447	A / 9.3	0.03	11.11	31.03 /95	26.79 /93	12.93 /89	1.41	0.50
GR	Vanguard Large Cap Index Adm	VLCAX	U	(800) 662-7447	U /	-1.49	2.77	9.18 /41	--	--	1.65	0.12
GR	Vanguard Large Cap Index Inst	VLISX	U	(800) 662-7447	U /	-1.48	2.79	9.24 /42	--	--	1.68	0.08
GR	Vanguard Large Cap Index Inv	VLACX	U	(800) 662-7447	U /	-1.54	2.72	9.11 /41	--	--	1.57	0.20
★ AA	Vanguard LifeStrategy Conserv Gr Fd	VSCGX	C	(800) 662-7447	D / 1.9	-0.49	1.95	5.64 /18	7.51 /12	4.98 /54	3.15	0.25
★ AA	Vanguard LifeStrategy Growth Fd	VASGX	B	(800) 662-7447	C / 5.3	-1.20	3.78	11.04 /54	12.99 /49	5.43 /57	2.08	0.26
AA	Vanguard LifeStrategy Income Fd	VASIX	C-	(800) 662-7447	E+ / 0.7	-0.28	0.82	2.69 / 6	4.77 / 4	4.63 /51	3.82	0.25
★ AA	Vanguard LifeStrategy Mod Growth	VSMGX	C+	(800) 662-7447	C- / 3.5	-0.92	2.68	7.97 /33	10.21 /29	5.35 /57	2.67	0.25
MC	Vanguard Mid-Cap Growth Fd	VMGRX	D+	(800) 662-7447	C+ / 6.0	-5.52	5.48	17.15 /77	14.77 /58	2.03 /28	0.03	0.48
MC	Vanguard Mid-Cap Index Adm	VIMAX	A-	(800) 662-7447	B / 8.0	-2.87	4.50	14.57 /70	20.11 /80	--	1.09	0.13
MC	Vanguard Mid-Cap Index Inst	VMCIX	A-	(800) 662-7447	B / 8.0	-2.89	4.53	14.58 /70	20.16 /80	10.23 /81	1.14	0.08
★ MC	Vanguard Mid-Cap Index Inv	VIMSX	B+	(800) 662-7447	B / 8.0	-2.90	4.42	14.43 /70	20.01 /79	10.08 /81	1.04	0.22
GR	Vanguard Morgan Growth Adm	VMRAX	C	(800) 662-7447	C / 4.9	-3.79	1.27	10.88 /53	12.51 /46	2.85 /35	0.72	0.24
★ GR	Vanguard Morgan Growth Inv	VMRGX	C	(800) 662-7447	C / 4.7	-3.86	1.19	10.66 /51	12.33 /45	2.72 /34	0.53	0.41
FO	Vanguard Pacific Stock Index Adm	VPADX	A	(800) 662-7447	A- / 9.1	-2.78	3.58	31.50 /95	25.43 /91	--	1.44	0.20
FO	Vanguard Pacific Stock Index Inst	VPKIX	B+	(800) 662-7447	A- / 9.1	-2.81	3.61	31.66 /95	25.49 /92	8.90 /76	1.50	0.14
★ FO	Vanguard Pacific Stock Index Inv	VPACX	B+	(800) 662-7447	A- / 9.1	-2.81	3.53	31.40 /95	25.30 /91	8.71 /75	1.36	0.32
★ PM	● Vanguard Prec. Metals & Mining Fd	VGPMX	C-	(800) 662-7447	A+ / 9.9	4.44	26.92	72.86 /99	44.17 /99	35.20 /99	0.87	0.45
GR	● Vanguard PRIMECAP Adm	VPMAX	B	(800) 662-7447	B- / 7.0	-2.82	3.88	16.19 /75	16.74 /67	--	0.65	0.31
GR	Vanguard PRIMECAP Core Inv	VPCCX	U	(800) 662-7447	U /	-2.16	3.33	13.71 /67	--	--	0.42	0.63
★ GR	● Vanguard PRIMECAP Inv	VPMCX	B-	(800) 662-7447	C+ / 6.9	-2.85	3.80	16.02 /75	16.57 /66	5.26 /56	0.55	0.45
AG	Vanguard PRIMECAP Odyssey Agg	POAGX	U	(800) 662-7447	U /	-2.68	6.27	20.36 /82	--	--	0.00	1.82
GR	Vanguard PRIMECAP Odyssey	POGRX	U	(800) 662-7447	U /	-2.66	4.58	15.81 /74	--	--	0.00	1.79
GR	Vanguard PRIMECAP Odyssey Stock	POSKX	U	(800) 662-7447	U /	-2.33	3.96	14.71 /71	--	--	0.04	1.80
RE	Vanguard REIT Index Adm	VGSLX	C	(800) 662-7447	A- / 9.2	-1.38	13.24	19.32 /81	25.66 /92	--	4.35	0.16
RE	Vanguard REIT Index Inst	VGSNX	U	(800) 662-7447	U /	-1.36	13.25	19.38 /81	--	--	4.38	0.13
★ RE	Vanguard REIT Index Inv	VGSIX	C	(800) 662-7447	A- / 9.2	-1.37	13.21	19.23 /81	25.60 /92	18.92 /95	4.28	0.21
★ MC	Vanguard Selected Value Fund	VASVX	A-	(800) 662-7447	B- / 7.2	0.31	2.97	5.93 /20	18.58 /75	10.53 /82	1.43	0.51
★ SC	Vanguard Small-Cap Grwth Index Fd	VISGX	C	(800) 662-7447	B- / 7.5	-6.72	5.67	14.80 /71	18.46 /74	9.83 /80	0.24	0.23
SC	Vanguard Small-Cap Grwth Index Inst	VSGIX	C	(800) 662-7447	B- / 7.5	-6.70	5.73	14.92 /72	18.65 /75	10.02 /81	0.38	0.08
SC	Vanguard Small-Cap Index Adm	VSMAX	B	(800) 662-7447	B / 7.9	-4.72	6.92	13.90 /68	19.87 /79	9.06 /77	1.04	0.13
SC	Vanguard Small-Cap Index Inst	VSCIX	B	(800) 662-7447	B / 7.9	-4.65	6.99	14.00 /68	19.95 /79	9.19 /77	1.09	0.08
★ SC	Vanguard Small-Cap Index Inv	NAESX	B	(800) 662-7447	B / 7.9	-4.72	6.89	13.78 /68	19.76 /79	9.00 /76	0.96	0.23

● Denotes fund is closed to new investors
★ Denotes fund is included in Section II

www.WeissRatings.com

RISK			NET ASSETS		ASSET				Portfolio	BULL / BEAR		FUND MANAGER		MINIMUMS		LOADS	
	3 Year		NAV						Turnover	Last Bull	Last Bear	Manager	Manager	Initial	Additional	Front	Back
Risk	Standard		As of	Total	Cash	Stocks	Bonds	Other	Ratio	Market	Market	Quality	Tenure	Purch.	Purch.	End	End
Rating/Pts	Deviation	Beta	6/30/06	$(Mil)	%	%	%	%		Return	Return	Pct	(Years)	$	$	Load	Load
C+ / 6.7	8.8	1.10	8.34	69	0	100	0	0	53.0	59.8	N/A	31	N/A	5,000,000	100	0.0	0.0
C+ / 6.7	8.8	1.10	8.32	396	0	100	0	0	53.0	59.1	-10.0	29	6	3,000	100	0.0	0.0
B- / 7.5	10.5	0.99	21.27	3,791	1	98	0	1	83.0	125.6	-7.0	43	11	3,000	100	0.0	0.0
B / 8.7	8.1	1.04	52.51	2,235	0	99	0	1	84.0	67.4	-9.7	60	5	100,000	100	0.0	0.0
B / 8.7	8.1	1.04	32.16	4,937	0	99	0	1	84.0	66.6	-9.7	58	N/A	3,000	100	0.0	0.0
C / 5.4	11.4	1.33	10.39	771	1	98	0	1	22.0	70.0	-10.3	20	14	10,000	100	0.0	0.0
B- / 7.3	8.8	1.10	27.21	2,139	0	99	0	1	24.0	51.3	-9.1	24	N/A	100,000	100	0.0	0.0
B- / 7.3	8.8	1.10	27.21	1,691	0	99	0	1	24.0	51.4	-9.2	24	N/A	5,000,000	100	0.0	0.0
B- / 7.3	8.8	1.10	27.21	6,432	0	99	0	1	24.0	50.8	-9.2	23	N/A	3,000	100	0.0	0.0
B- / 7.8	7.6	0.60	58.76	9,510	10	89	0	1	14.0	71.8	-6.6	94	N/A	100,000	100	0.0	1.0
B- / 7.8	7.6	0.60	139.17	16,020	10	89	0	1	14.0	71.3	-6.6	94	22	25,000	100	0.0	1.0
U /	N/A	N/A	26.14	100	0	99	0	1	13.0	N/A	N/A	N/A	N/A	100,000	100	0.0	2.0
B / 8.0	10.2	1.01	11.15	2,725	0	99	0	1	6.0	132.0	-9.5	49	6	5,000,000	100	0.0	2.0
B / 8.6	7.7	1.00	116.07	40,290	0	100	0	0	8.1	64.8	-9.7	N/A	N/A	5,000,000	100	0.0	0.0
B / 8.6	7.7	1.00	116.08	17,067	0	100	0	0	8.1	64.9	-9.7	57	N/A	200,000,000	100	0.0	0.0
B / 8.2	8.4	1.08	27.67	3,918	0	99	0	1	25.0	75.3	-9.4	67	N/A	200,000,000	100	0.0	0.0
C+ / 6.3	11.5	1.04	20.00	2,527	2	97	0	1	38.0	214.4	-7.0	94	10	25,000	100	0.0	2.0
C+ / 6.8	10.6	1.02	73.42	3,318	0	99	0	1	54.0	127.4	-11.1	37	N/A	100,000	100	0.0	2.0
C+ / 6.8	10.5	1.02	23.06	10,026	0	99	0	1	54.0	125.9	-11.1	35	3	3,000	100	0.0	2.0
B- / 7.2	11.4	1.07	38.69	5,908	2	97	0	1	32.0	149.5	-10.1	62	N/A	3,000	100	0.0	2.0
U /	N/A	N/A	28.53	121	0	100	0	0	11.0	N/A	N/A	N/A	N/A	100,000	100	0.0	0.0
U /	N/A	N/A	117.41	61	0	100	0	0	11.0	N/A	N/A	N/A	N/A	5,000,000	100	0.0	0.0
U /	N/A	N/A	22.82	141	0	100	0	0	11.0	N/A	N/A	N/A	N/A	3,000	100	0.0	0.0
B+ / 9.9	4.0	0.84	15.56	4,678	19	50	30	1	7.0	37.8	-3.1	65	12	3,000	100	0.0	0.0
B / 8.9	7.2	1.45	21.60	7,585	0	90	9	1	4.0	71.6	-8.0	83	12	3,000	100	0.0	0.0
B+ / 9.9	3.0	0.54	13.35	1,604	19	29	50	2	6.0	23.2	-0.5	52	12	3,000	100	0.0	0.0
B+ / 9.5	5.5	1.15	18.73	8,540	0	70	29	1	8.0	54.0	-5.5	74	12	3,000	100	0.0	0.0
C- / 3.9	14.6	1.23	18.47	758	0	98	0	2	80.0	99.9	-9.1	9	N/A	10,000	100	0.0	0.0
B- / 7.3	11.1	1.00	83.58	3,584	0	100	0	0	21.0	111.5	-9.2	73	N/A	100,000	100	0.0	0.0
B- / 7.3	11.0	1.00	18.47	3,602	0	100	0	0	21.0	111.8	-9.1	74	N/A	5,000,000	100	0.0	0.0
B- / 7.3	11.1	1.01	18.41	7,111	0	100	0	0	21.0	111.0	-9.2	72	N/A	3,000	100	0.0	0.0
B- / 7.1	10.2	1.21	55.62	1,507	0	99	0	1	89.0	77.6	-9.6	48	N/A	100,000	100	0.0	0.0
B- / 7.1	10.2	1.22	17.92	5,013	0	99	0	1	89.0	76.9	-9.7	45	N/A	3,000	100	0.0	0.0
C+ / 6.7	14.2	1.10	76.88	1,076	0	99	0	1	7.0	130.8	-5.3	42	N/A	100,000	100	0.0	2.0
C+ / 5.7	14.2	1.10	11.76	1,522	0	99	0	1	7.0	131.4	-5.3	43	N/A	5,000,000	100	0.0	2.0
C+ / 5.7	14.2	1.10	11.74	7,190	0	99	0	1	7.0	130.0	-5.3	41	N/A	3,000	100	0.0	2.0
D- / 1.2	24.6	1.10	29.16	3,386	2	97	0	1	20.0	237.7	9.7	99	10	10,000	100	0.0	1.0
B- / 7.3	10.4	1.25	70.40	8,154	4	95	0	1	8.0	98.9	-10.1	83	5	100,000	100	0.0	1.0
U /	N/A	N/A	11.79	1,952	12	87	0	1	1.0	N/A	N/A	N/A	2	10,000	100	0.0	1.0
B- / 7.3	10.4	1.25	67.79	21,260	4	95	0	1	8.0	97.9	-10.1	82	22	25,000	100	0.0	1.0
U /	N/A	N/A	12.71	63	11	88	0	1	7.4	N/A	N/A	N/A	N/A	2,000	150	0.0	2.0
U /	N/A	N/A	12.80	130	17	82	0	1	8.8	N/A	N/A	N/A	N/A	2,000	150	0.0	2.0
U /	N/A	N/A	12.60	58	11	88	0	1	12.4	N/A	N/A	N/A	2	2,000	150	0.0	2.0
C- / 3.0	16.4	0.99	94.12	2,265	2	97	0	1	17.0	122.4	-0.2	72	N/A	100,000	100	0.0	1.0
U /	N/A	N/A	14.57	676	2	97	0	1	17.0	N/A	N/A	N/A	N/A	5,000,000	100	0.0	1.0
C- / 3.0	16.4	0.99	22.06	4,952	2	97	0	1	17.0	121.8	-0.2	71	N/A	3,000	100	0.0	1.0
B / 8.2	8.4	0.64	19.42	3,892	5	94	0	1	28.0	99.5	-7.3	95	N/A	25,000	100	0.0	1.0
C / 4.6	15.1	1.02	17.36	2,127	0	100	0	0	39.0	115.8	-9.3	50	N/A	3,000	100	0.0	0.0
C / 4.6	15.1	1.02	17.40	179	0	100	0	0	39.0	116.8	-9.2	52	N/A	5,000,000	100	0.0	0.0
C+ / 6.3	13.2	0.91	30.50	2,835	0	100	0	0	18.0	123.8	-11.0	80	N/A	100,000	100	0.0	0.0
C+ / 6.3	13.2	0.90	30.53	2,608	0	100	0	0	18.0	124.3	-11.0	81	N/A	5,000,000	100	0.0	0.0
C+ / 6.3	13.2	0.90	30.48	6,529	0	100	0	0	18.0	123.0	-11.0	79	N/A	3,000	100	0.0	0.0

	Fund Type	Fund Name	Ticker Symbol	Overall Weiss Investment Rating	Phone	Performance Rating/Pts	3 Mo	6 Mo	1Yr / Pct	3Yr / Pct	5Yr / Pct	Dividend Yield	Expense Ratio
★	SC	Vanguard Small-Cap Value Index Fd	VISVX	A	(800) 662-7447	B / 8.2	-2.72	8.03	12.64 /63	20.92 /82	11.06 /84	1.71	0.23
★	GI	Vanguard STAR Fund	VGSTX	C+	(800) 662-7447	C- / 3.8	-1.36	1.91	7.82 /31	10.85 /34	6.07 /62	2.58	0.36
★	AG ●	Vanguard Strategic Equity Fd	VSEQX	B+	(800) 662-7447	B / 7.8	-2.93	5.93	13.01 /64	19.65 /78	11.63 /86	0.85	0.40
	BA	Vanguard Target Retirement 2005 Fd	VTOVX	U	(800) 662-7447	U /	-0.82	0.09	2.07 / 5	--	--	2.83	0.20
	BA	Vanguard Target Retirement 2015 Fd	VTXVX	U	(800) 662-7447	U /	-1.11	1.31	5.18 /16	--	--	2.24	0.20
	BA	Vanguard Target Retirement 2025 Fd	VTTVX	U	(800) 662-7447	U /	-1.32	1.87	6.58 /24	--	--	2.00	0.20
	BA	Vanguard Target Retirement 2035 Fd	VTTHX	U	(800) 662-7447	U /	-1.41	3.02	9.32 /42	--	--	1.66	0.21
	BA	Vanguard Target Retirement 2045 Fd	VTIVX	U	(800) 662-7447	U /	-1.44	3.74	11.13 /54	--	--	1.46	0.21
	BA	Vanguard Target Retirement Income	VTINX	U	(800) 662-7447	U /	-0.47	-0.28	1.00 / 3	--	--	4.20	0.20
	BA	Vanguard Tax-Managed Balanced Fd	VTMFX	C-	(800) 662-7447	D- / 1.4	-1.04	1.11	4.65 /13	7.03 /10	3.97 /46	2.79	0.12
	GR	Vanguard Tax-Managed Cap Appr	VTCLX	C+	(800) 662-7447	C / 4.8	-2.15	2.25	9.40 /43	12.65 /47	--	1.21	0.10
	GR	Vanguard Tax-Managed Cap Appr	VTCIX	C+	(800) 662-7447	C / 4.8	-2.15	2.26	9.42 /43	12.67 /47	2.85 /35	1.25	0.07
	GR	Vanguard Tax-Managed Cap Appr	VMCAX	C+	(800) 662-7447	C / 4.7	-2.18	2.23	9.34 /42	12.60 /46	2.76 /34	1.18	0.14
	GI	Vanguard Tax-Managed Gr & Inc	VTGLX	C+	(800) 662-7447	C- / 4.0	-1.44	2.71	8.63 /38	11.21 /37	--	1.84	0.10
	GI	Vanguard Tax-Managed Gr & Inc Inst	VTMIX	C+	(800) 662-7447	C- / 4.0	-1.46	2.73	8.63 /38	11.24 /37	2.58 /33	1.88	0.07
	GI	Vanguard Tax-Managed Gr & Inc Inv	VTGIX	C+	(800) 662-7447	C- / 4.0	-1.45	2.69	8.55 /37	11.16 /37	2.49 /32	1.80	0.14
	FO	Vanguard Tax-Managed Intl Fd	VTMGX	A+	(800) 662-7447	A- / 9.1	0.96	10.31	27.26 /92	24.04 /89	10.02 /81	2.05	0.20
	FO	Vanguard Tax-Managed Intl Inst	VTMNX	A+	(800) 662-7447	A- / 9.1	0.96	10.40	27.31 /92	24.16 /90	10.13 /81	2.10	0.14
	SC	Vanguard Tax-Managed Small-Cap	VTMSX	B+	(800) 662-7447	B / 8.0	-4.84	7.33	13.50 /66	20.38 /81	11.07 /84	0.82	0.14
★	FO	Vanguard Total Intl Stock Index Fd	VGTSX	A	(800) 662-7447	A- / 9.1	0.06	9.53	27.60 /92	24.93 /91	10.89 /84	1.88	0.31
	GR	Vanguard Total Stock Mkt Index Adm	VTSAX	C+	(800) 662-7447	C / 5.2	-1.96	3.32	9.85 /46	12.86 /48	3.91 /45	1.81	0.09
★	GR	Vanguard Total Stock Mkt Index Inv	VTSMX	C+	(800) 662-7447	C / 5.1	-1.99	3.27	9.74 /45	12.77 /47	3.84 /44	1.70	0.19
	AG	Vanguard US Growth Adm	VWUAX	D-	(800) 662-7447	D / 1.8	-7.61	-5.92	5.39 /17	8.74 /19	--	0.41	0.36
★	AG	Vanguard US Growth Inv	VWUSX	D-	(800) 662-7447	D / 1.7	-7.72	-6.07	5.12 /16	8.48 /18	-3.57 / 4	0.21	0.59
	GR	Vanguard US Value Fd	VUVLX	C+	(800) 662-7447	C / 4.7	-2.78	1.34	5.34 /17	12.92 /48	5.95 /61	1.93	0.39
	UT	Vanguard Utilities Index Adm	VUIAX	U	(800) 662-7447	U /	5.45	5.27	5.75 /19	--	--	3.01	0.28
	GI	Vanguard Value Index Adm	VVIAX	B+	(800) 662-7447	C+ / 6.6	0.94	6.30	12.46 /62	15.29 /60	4.48 /50	2.60	0.11
	GI	Vanguard Value Index Inst	VIVIX	B+	(800) 662-7447	C+ / 6.6	0.95	6.32	12.44 /62	15.33 /60	4.52 /50	2.63	0.08
★	GI	Vanguard Value Index Inv	VIVAX	B+	(800) 662-7447	C+ / 6.5	0.91	6.25	12.34 /61	15.18 /60	4.39 /50	2.50	0.21
	AA	Vanguard Wellesley Income Adm	VWIAX	D+	(800) 662-7447	D- / 1.0	1.02	2.06	2.95 / 7	5.52 / 5	6.15 /62	4.26	0.24
★	AA	Vanguard Wellesley Income Inv	VWINX	C-	(800) 662-7447	E+ / 0.9	1.01	2.01	2.86 / 7	5.42 / 5	6.08 /62	4.14	0.14
	BA	Vanguard Wellington Adm	VWENX	B-	(800) 662-7447	C / 4.4	0.72	3.75	9.65 /45	11.12 /36	7.04 /67	3.11	0.18
★	BA ●	Vanguard Wellington Inv	VWELX	C+	(800) 662-7447	C / 4.3	0.69	3.71	9.50 /43	10.98 /35	6.91 /66	2.97	0.31
	GI	Vanguard Windsor-I Adm	VWNEX	C+	(800) 662-7447	C+ / 5.8	-0.80	3.93	9.41 /43	14.13 /55	--	1.49	0.28
	GI	Vanguard Windsor-I Inv	VWNDX	C+	(800) 662-7447	C+ / 5.7	-0.88	3.86	9.29 /42	14.00 /54	5.61 /59	1.38	0.39
	GI	Vanguard Windsor-II Adm	VWNAX	A-	(800) 662-7447	C+ / 6.1	0.73	4.33	8.70 /38	14.84 /58	6.38 /63	2.29	0.23
★	GI	Vanguard Windsor-II Inv	VWNFX	A-	(800) 662-7447	C+ / 6.1	0.70	4.30	8.57 /37	14.72 /57	6.28 /63	2.17	0.35
	IX	Vantagepoint 500 Stock Index I	VPFIX	C+	(800) 669-7400	C- / 3.8	-1.56	2.43	8.10 /33	10.74 /33	2.04 /28	1.36	0.46
	IX	Vantagepoint 500 Stock Index II	VPSKX	C+	(800) 669-7400	C- / 4.0	-1.44	2.67	8.43 /36	10.90 /35	2.24 /30	1.65	0.26
	AG	Vantagepoint Aggressive Opport	VPAOX	B+	(800) 669-7400	B- / 7.2	-5.84	2.67	12.48 /62	18.01 /73	0.86 /20	2.36	1.22
	AA	Vantagepoint Asset Allocation	VPAAX	C+	(800) 669-7400	C- / 3.7	-1.02	2.93	8.49 /37	10.44 /30	4.62 /51	1.51	0.75
	GR	Vantagepoint Broad Market Index I	VPMIX	B-	(800) 669-7400	C / 4.9	-1.93	3.28	9.50 /43	12.54 /46	3.04 /37	1.28	0.44
	GR	Vantagepoint Broad Market Index II	VPBMX	B-	(800) 669-7400	C / 5.1	-1.94	3.37	9.73 /45	12.74 /47	3.74 /43	1.58	0.24
	IN	Vantagepoint Equity Income	VPEIX	B+	(800) 669-7400	C+ / 6.1	-0.21	5.30	9.17 /41	14.71 /57	7.16 /68	1.65	0.90
	GI	Vantagepoint Growth & Income	VPGIX	C+	(800) 669-7400	C- / 4.1	-1.36	2.54	9.47 /43	10.88 /34	3.07 /38	0.83	0.82
★	GR	Vantagepoint Growth Fund	VPGRX	D	(800) 669-7400	D / 1.6	-4.41	-0.23	9.36 /42	7.75 /14	0.01 /15	0.16	0.93
	FO	Vantagepoint International	VPINX	A+	(800) 669-7400	B+ / 8.7	-0.79	8.13	29.08 /94	21.50 /84	8.06 /72	1.59	1.14
	MC	Vantagepoint Mid-Small Comp Indx I	VPSIX	B+	(800) 669-7400	B- / 7.5	-3.71	5.47	13.65 /67	18.37 /74	8.23 /72	0.89	0.52
	MC	Vantagepoint Mid-Small Comp Indx II	VPMSX	B+	(800) 669-7400	B- / 7.5	-3.68	5.57	13.84 /68	18.56 /75	8.44 /74	1.10	0.32
	AA	Vantagepoint Milestone 2010 Fund	VPRQX	U	(800) 669-7400	U /	-0.57	1.65	5.85 /19	--	--	1.71	0.15
	AA	Vantagepoint Milestone 2015 Fund	VPRPX	U	(800) 669-7400	U /	-1.02	2.30	8.15 /34	--	--	1.42	0.15
	AA	Vantagepoint Milestone 2020 Fund	VPROX	U	(800) 669-7400	U /	-1.19	2.76	9.31 /42	--	--	1.34	0.15

● Denotes fund is closed to new investors
★ Denotes fund is included in Section II

RISK Risk Rating/Pts	3 Year Standard Deviation	Beta	NET ASSETS NAV As of 6/30/06	Total $(Mil)	ASSET Cash %	Stocks %	Bonds %	Other %	Portfolio Turnover Ratio	BULL/BEAR Last Bull Market Return	Last Bear Market Return	FUND MANAGER Manager Quality Pct	Manager Tenure (Years)	MINIMUMS Initial Purch. $	Additional Purch. $	LOADS Front End Load	Back End Load
B- /7.5	11.9	0.79	15.72	3,763	0	99	0	1	28.0	116.3	-10.1	93	N/A	3,000	100	0.0	0.0
B+ /9.4	5.6	0.67	19.75	12,798	12	62	24	2	6.0	57.1	-4.4	80	21	1,000	100	0.0	0.0
C+ /6.9	12.2	1.38	23.23	6,943	0	100	0	0	75.0	116.6	-6.0	91	N/A	3,000	100	0.0	0.0
U /	N/A	N/A	10.94	902	1	31	67	1	4.0	N/A	N/A	N/A	N/A	3,000	100	0.0	0.0
U /	N/A	N/A	11.61	3,257	0	47	52	1	1.0	N/A	N/A	N/A	N/A	3,000	100	0.0	0.0
U /	N/A	N/A	11.99	3,524	0	56	43	1	2.0	N/A	N/A	N/A	N/A	3,000	100	0.0	0.0
U /	N/A	N/A	12.63	2,248	0	75	24	1	N/A	N/A	N/A	N/A	N/A	3,000	100	0.0	0.0
U /	N/A	N/A	13.04	1,019	0	87	11	2	7.0	N/A	N/A	N/A	N/A	3,000	100	0.0	0.0
U /	N/A	N/A	10.22	797	4	20	74	2	N/A	N/A	N/A	N/A	N/A	3,000	100	0.0	0.0
B+ /9.4	4.1	0.87	18.84	619	0	48	50	2	10.0	36.5	-3.0	58	N/A	10,000	100	0.0	1.0
B /8.3	8.3	1.07	61.34	2,560	0	100	0	0	8.0	73.3	-9.6	64	N/A	100,000	100	0.0	1.0
B /8.3	8.3	1.07	30.48	197	0	100	0	0	8.0	73.5	-9.6	64	N/A	5,000,000	100	0.0	1.0
B /8.2	8.3	1.07	30.46	800	0	100	0	0	8.0	73.1	-9.6	64	N/A	10,000	100	0.0	1.0
B /8.6	7.6	1.00	56.85	1,682	0	100	0	0	9.7	64.8	-9.7	57	N/A	100,000	100	0.0	1.0
B /8.6	7.7	1.00	27.66	328	0	100	0	0	9.7	65.0	-9.7	57	N/A	5,000,000	100	0.0	1.0
B /8.6	7.6	1.00	27.66	747	0	100	0	0	9.7	64.6	-9.7	56	N/A	10,000	100	0.0	1.0
B- /7.4	10.3	1.01	12.66	1,342	0	100	0	0	5.0	131.8	-9.5	49	N/A	10,000	100	0.0	1.0
B- /7.4	10.2	1.01	12.67	222	0	100	0	0	5.0	132.5	-9.5	51	N/A	5,000,000	100	0.0	1.0
C+ /6.8	13.5	0.92	24.36	1,641	0	100	0	0	20.0	121.0	-9.6	83	N/A	10,000	100	0.0	1.0
C+ /6.6	10.9	1.08	15.63	15,924	0	100	0	0	3.0	140.1	-9.3	42	N/A	3,000	100	0.0	2.0
B /8.2	8.4	1.08	30.74	22,728	0	100	0	0	12.0	74.6	-9.5	66	N/A	100,000	100	0.0	0.0
B /8.2	8.3	1.08	30.74	33,798	0	100	0	0	12.0	74.2	-9.5	65	N/A	3,000	100	0.0	0.0
C+ /6.4	11.0	1.27	43.73	1,256	0	99	0	1	43.0	58.4	-10.5	16	N/A	100,000	100	0.0	0.0
C+ /6.4	10.9	1.27	16.86	4,561	0	99	0	1	43.0	57.2	-10.5	15	N/A	3,000	100	0.0	0.0
B /8.7	8.6	1.05	13.66	1,237	1	98	0	1	50.0	75.3	-8.8	69	N/A	3,000	100	0.0	0.0
U /	N/A	N/A	33.87	47	0	100	0	0	4.0	N/A	N/A	N/A	N/A	100,000	100	0.0	2.0
B+ /9.0	7.5	0.93	23.42	2,066	0	100	0	0	21.0	87.1	-10.3	91	N/A	100,000	100	0.0	0.0
B+ /9.0	7.5	0.93	23.42	1,445	0	100	0	0	21.0	87.3	-10.3	91	N/A	5,000,000	100	0.0	0.0
B+ /9.0	7.5	0.93	23.42	3,502	0	100	0	0	21.0	86.6	-10.4	90	N/A	3,000	100	0.0	0.0
B /8.7	4.2	0.58	51.04	4,331	0	38	61	1	18.0	26.9	-0.6	59	N/A	100,000	100	0.0	0.0
B+ /9.7	4.2	0.58	21.07	7,305	0	38	61	1	18.0	26.5	-0.7	57	24	3,000	100	0.0	0.0
B+ /9.3	5.4	1.09	53.56	13,933	3	65	31	1	24.0	56.3	-5.1	83	N/A	100,000	100	0.0	0.0
B+ /9.3	5.4	1.08	31.01	27,000	3	65	31	1	24.0	55.7	-5.2	83	12	10,000	100	0.0	0.0
B- /7.6	8.6	1.08	59.67	8,479	2	97	0	1	33.0	85.3	-9.2	77	3	100,000	100	0.0	0.0
B- /7.6	8.6	1.09	17.68	13,227	2	97	0	1	33.0	84.6	-9.3	75	3	3,000	100	0.0	0.0
B+ /9.2	7.1	0.84	57.33	14,147	1	98	0	1	31.0	82.9	-7.1	92	5	100,000	100	0.0	0.0
B+ /9.2	7.0	0.83	32.30	28,523	1	98	0	1	31.0	82.3	-7.1	92	21	10,000	100	0.0	0.0
B /8.8	7.6	1.00	10.11	100	2	97	0	1	5.0	62.6	-9.8	51	N/A	0	0	0.0	0.0
B /8.9	7.6	1.00	9.61	252	2	97	0	1	5.0	63.5	-9.8	53	N/A	0	0	0.0	0.0
B- /7.5	11.3	1.24	11.94	1,279	2	97	0	1	45.0	118.9	-10.1	90	N/A	0	0	0.0	0.0
B+ /9.1	6.8	1.39	7.73	721	10	89	0	1	9.0	60.1	-9.0	64	N/A	0	0	0.0	0.0
B /8.7	8.4	1.08	10.69	194	0	99	0	1	2.0	72.8	-9.6	63	N/A	0	0	0.0	0.0
B /8.7	8.3	1.07	10.13	410	0	99	0	1	2.0	74.1	-9.6	65	N/A	0	0	0.0	0.0
B+ /9.0	7.4	0.92	9.34	1,283	4	94	0	2	16.0	84.8	-9.8	89	N/A	0	0	0.0	0.0
B /8.6	8.1	1.05	10.91	1,041	2	97	0	1	27.0	65.2	-9.8	47	N/A	0	0	0.0	0.0
B- /7.8	9.6	1.16	8.68	2,678	2	97	0	1	85.0	52.0	-10.7	16	N/A	0	0	0.0	0.0
B /8.0	10.5	1.00	12.50	923	4	95	0	1	42.0	121.0	-12.8	30	N/A	0	0	0.0	0.0
B- /7.5	11.8	1.07	15.81	73	1	98	0	1	12.0	112.1	-8.9	46	N/A	0	0	0.0	0.0
B- /7.5	11.7	1.06	15.16	107	1	98	0	1	12.0	113.4	-8.9	49	N/A	0	0	0.0	0.0
U /	N/A	N/A	10.45	35	0	48	52	0	18.0	N/A	N/A	N/A	N/A	0	0	0.0	0.0
U /	N/A	N/A	10.68	59	N/A	63	36	N/A	8.0	N/A	N/A	N/A	N/A	0	0	0.0	0.0
U /	N/A	N/A	10.79	43	0	71	28	1	6.0	N/A	N/A	N/A	N/A	0	0	0.0	0.0

Fund Type	Fund Name	Ticker Symbol	Overall Weiss Investment Rating	Phone	Perfor-mance Rating/Pts	3 Mo	6 Mo	1Yr / Pct	3Yr / Pct	5Yr / Pct	Dividend Yield	Expense Ratio
AA	Vantagepoint Milestone 2025 Fund	VPRNX	U	(800) 669-7400	U /	-1.36	3.02	10.53 /51	--	--	1.24	0.15
GR	Vantagepoint Model Port All Eq Gr	VPAGX	B-	(800) 669-7400	C+ / 5.7	-2.87	3.18	12.95 /64	13.57 /52	3.20 /39	1.05	1.16
GR	Vantagepoint Model Port Cons Grwth	VPCGX	C	(800) 669-7400	D- / 1.5	-0.72	1.51	5.15 /16	6.75 / 9	3.84 /44	2.62	0.90
GR	Vantagepoint Model Port Long-Trm	VPLGX	C+	(800) 669-7400	C / 4.3	-2.15	2.48	10.01 /47	11.23 /37	3.79 /44	1.69	1.01
AA	Vantagepoint Model Port Savings Ori	VPSOX	C-	(800) 669-7400	E+ / 0.8	0.00	1.20	3.14 / 8	5.08 / 4	3.90 /45	2.95	0.85
GR	Vantagepoint Model Port Traditnl Gr	VPTGX	C+	(800) 669-7400	D+ / 2.8	-1.42	2.09	7.81 /31	9.00 /21	3.78 /44	2.04	0.97
FO	Vantagepoint Overseas Eqty Index I	VPOIX	A+	(800) 669-7400	A- / 9.0	0.41	9.77	26.10 /90	23.11 /88	9.29 /78	1.67	0.89
FO	Vantagepoint Overseas Eqty Index II	VPOEX	A+	(800) 669-7400	A- / 9.0	0.34	9.84	26.25 /90	23.43 /88	9.56 /79	1.94	0.69
SC	Veracity Small Cap Value	VSCVX	U	(866) 896-9292	U /	-2.57	10.15	18.21 /79	--	--	0.00	1.49
BA	Victory Balanced A	SBALX	C-	(800) 539-3863	D- / 1.2	-1.80	0.76	6.01 /21	7.91 /15	3.11 /38	1.53	1.21
BA	Victory Balanced C	VBFCX	C-	(800) 539-3863	D- / 1.5	-1.99	0.45	5.16 /16	7.23 /11	--	0.74	2.00
BA	Victory Balanced R	VBFGX	C-	(800) 539-3863	D / 1.8	-1.89	0.56	5.59 /18	7.56 /13	2.77 /35	1.23	1.60
CV	Victory Convertible A	SBFCX	C-	(800) 539-3863	D / 1.7	-0.15	3.13	8.14 /34	7.32 /12	3.28 /39	1.22	1.33
★ GR	Victory Diversified Stk A	SRVEX	C+	(800) 539-3863	C / 4.4	-2.60	1.56	10.35 /49	13.25 /50	4.37 /49	0.40	1.07
GR	Victory Diversified Stk R	GRINX	C+	(800) 539-3863	C / 5.0	-2.70	1.41	10.01 /47	12.83 /48	3.93 /45	0.11	1.43
GR	Victory Established Value A	VETAX	B-	(800) 539-3863	B- / 7.0	-2.20	5.14	14.56 /70	18.34 /74	9.04 /76	0.44	1.24
GR	Victory Established Value R	GETGX	B	(800) 539-3863	B- / 7.5	-2.20	5.12	14.46 /70	18.15 /73	8.81 /76	0.35	1.36
SC	Victory Sm Co Opportunity A	SSGSX	C+	(800) 539-3863	B- / 7.4	-1.29	9.18	14.30 /69	19.01 /76	10.65 /83	0.08	1.13
SC	Victory Sm Co Opportunity R	GOGFX	B-	(800) 539-3863	B / 7.7	-1.35	9.02	13.91 /68	18.71 /75	10.30 /82	0.01	1.49
MC	Victory Special Value A	SSVSX	C	(800) 539-3863	B- / 7.5	-4.33	4.31	16.06 /75	20.12 /80	11.16 /84	0.23	1.24
MC	Victory Special Value R	VSVGX	C	(800) 539-3863	B / 7.9	-4.41	4.11	15.65 /74	19.74 /78	10.81 /83	0.13	1.52
IX	Victory Stock Index Fund A	SSTIX	D+	(800) 539-3863	D+ / 2.7	-1.61	2.43	7.91 /32	10.53 /31	1.84 /26	1.16	0.70
IX	Victory Stock Index Fund R	VINGX	C-	(800) 539-3863	C- / 3.5	-1.66	2.33	7.72 /31	10.26 /29	1.62 /24	1.04	0.90
GR	Victory Value Fund A	SVLSX	C+	(800) 539-3863	C+ / 5.8	-0.15	7.02	17.51 /78	14.55 /57	3.87 /45	0.50	1.24
GR	Victory Value Fund R	VVFGX	B-	(800) 539-3863	C+ / 6.3	-0.25	6.82	17.03 /77	14.21 /55	3.55 /42	0.14	1.60
BA	Villere Balanced Fund	VILLX	C+	(866) 811-0215	C / 5.1	-2.44	3.69	5.13 /16	13.42 /51	6.92 /66	0.42	1.28
GR	Volumetric Fund	VOLMX	C-	(800) 541-3863	C+ / 6.2	-4.11	8.26	14.12 /69	14.23 /55	7.69 /70	6.86	1.93
FO	Vontobel Eastern European Eq A	VEEEX	A+	(800) 527-9500	A+ / 9.8	3.22	9.28	24.85 /88	36.91 /98	29.41 /99	0.00	2.54
GR	Waddell & Reed Adv Accumulative A	UNACX	D	(888) 923-3355	D+ / 2.3	-2.15	0.89	8.82 /39	9.90 /27	0.82 /19	0.06	1.15
GR	Waddell & Reed Adv Accumulative B	WAABX	D	(888) 923-3355	D / 1.7	-2.41	0.31	7.63 /30	8.65 /19	-0.32 /14	0.00	2.23
GR	Waddell & Reed Adv Accumulative C	WAACX	D	(888) 923-3355	D+ / 2.3	-2.54	0.31	7.59 /30	8.75 /19	-0.20 /15	0.00	2.18
GR	Waddell & Reed Adv Accumulative Y	WAAYX	C-	(888) 923-3355	C- / 3.4	-2.14	1.03	9.13 /41	10.15 /28	1.11 /21	0.21	0.89
AA	Waddell & Reed Adv Asset Strat A	UNASX	B+	(888) 923-3355	B+ / 8.9	3.35	15.78	38.80 /98	20.37 /81	12.68 /88	0.29	1.29
AA	Waddell & Reed Adv Asset Strat B	WBASX	B+	(888) 923-3355	B+ / 8.8	3.17	15.15	37.60 /97	19.32 /77	11.67 /86	0.00	2.15
AA	Waddell & Reed Adv Asset Strat C	WCASX	B+	(888) 923-3355	A- / 9.0	3.07	15.15	37.60 /97	19.35 /77	11.71 /86	0.00	2.13
AA	Waddell & Reed Adv Asset Strat Y	WYASX	A-	(888) 923-3355	A- / 9.2	3.44	15.88	39.30 /98	20.83 /82	13.12 /89	0.44	0.96
BA	Waddell & Reed Adv Cntinentl Inc A	UNCIX	C-	(888) 923-3355	D / 2.0	0.28	3.65	7.90 /32	8.94 /20	3.98 /46	1.02	1.25
BA	Waddell & Reed Adv Cntinentl Inc B	WACBX	C-	(888) 923-3355	D / 1.6	0.01	3.25	6.96 /26	7.94 /15	2.97 /37	0.10	2.22
BA	Waddell & Reed Adv Cntinentl Inc C	WACCX	C	(888) 923-3355	D / 2.2	0.03	3.28	6.99 /26	7.94 /15	2.96 /36	0.13	2.21
BA	Waddell & Reed Adv Cntinentl Inc Y	WACYX	C+	(888) 923-3355	C- / 3.2	0.36	3.81	8.22 /35	9.27 /23	4.30 /49	1.37	0.96
★ GR	Waddell & Reed Adv Core Invest A	UNCMX	C+	(888) 923-3355	C / 5.4	2.29	8.98	16.10 /75	13.04 /49	2.67 /33	0.27	1.11
GR	Waddell & Reed Adv Core Invest B	UNIBX	C	(888) 923-3355	C / 4.7	1.93	8.39	14.88 /71	11.72 /41	1.48 /24	0.00	2.21
GR	Waddell & Reed Adv Core Invest C	WCCIX	C+	(888) 923-3355	C / 5.3	1.93	8.36	14.83 /71	11.75 /41	1.55 /24	0.00	2.18
GR	Waddell & Reed Adv Core Invest Y	UNIYX	B-	(888) 923-3355	C+ / 6.3	2.37	9.13	16.43 /76	13.38 /51	2.98 /37	0.56	0.82
GI	Waddell & Reed Adv Div Inc A	WDVAX	U	(888) 923-3355	U /	2.18	8.53	19.31 /81	--	--	1.00	1.29
FO	Waddell & Reed Adv Intl Gr A	UNCGX	B-	(888) 923-3355	B / 7.6	-1.19	7.67	27.74 /92	18.18 /73	4.78 /52	0.78	1.58
FO	Waddell & Reed Adv Intl Gr B	WAIBX	C+	(888) 923-3355	B- / 7.2	-1.38	7.08	26.16 /90	16.74 /67	3.40 /40	0.00	2.77
FO	Waddell & Reed Adv Intl Gr C	WAICX	B-	(888) 923-3355	B / 7.6	-1.35	7.20	26.42 /90	17.08 /68	3.78 /44	0.00	2.57
FO	Waddell & Reed Adv Intl Gr Y	WAIYX	B	(888) 923-3355	B / 8.2	-1.07	7.93	28.26 /93	18.75 /75	5.31 /57	1.25	1.11
MC	Waddell & Reed Adv New Concepts	UNECX	C-	(888) 923-3355	C+ / 5.9	-4.74	2.76	14.35 /69	15.88 /63	3.68 /43	0.00	1.47
MC	Waddell & Reed Adv New Concepts	UNEBX	C-	(888) 923-3355	C / 5.3	-4.95	2.24	13.21 /65	14.59 /57	2.45 /32	0.00	2.53
MC	Waddell & Reed Adv New Concepts	WNCCX	C-	(888) 923-3355	C+ / 5.9	-4.92	2.33	13.36 /66	14.75 /58	2.58 /33	0.00	2.39

● Denotes fund is closed to new investors
★ Denotes fund is included in Section II

RISK			NET ASSETS		ASSET				BULL / BEAR		FUND MANAGER		MINIMUMS		LOADS	
	3 Year		NAV						Last Bull	Last Bear	Manager	Manager	Initial	Additional	Front	Back
Risk Rating/Pts	Standard Deviation	Beta	As of 6/30/06	Total $(Mil)	Cash %	Stocks %	Bonds %	Other %	Portfolio Turnover Ratio	Market Return	Market Return	Quality Pct	Tenure (Years)	Purch. $	Purch. $	End Load	End Load
U /	N/A	N/A	10.90	32	0	79	20	1	N/A	N/A	N/A	N/A	N/A	0	0	0.0	0.0
B /8.3	8.9	1.11	23.69	378	5	94	0	1	2.0	82.1	-10.7	70	N/A	0	0	0.0	0.0
B+ /9.9	3.4	0.42	23.59	517	5	37	56	2	7.0	33.6	-3.5	65	N/A	0	0	0.0	0.0
B /8.5	6.9	0.86	22.71	1,296	4	75	19	2	7.0	64.3	-7.8	69	N/A	0	0	0.0	0.0
B+ /9.9	2.2	0.43	24.52	278	5	23	70	2	9.0	23.1	-1.8	62	N/A	0	0	0.0	0.0
B+ /9.7	5.1	0.65	22.93	1,205	5	56	37	2	4.0	48.4	-5.8	67	N/A	0	0	0.0	0.0
B /8.2	10.1	0.99	12.36	39	8	91	0	1	8.0	127.3	-9.7	45	N/A	0	0	0.0	0.0
B /8.3	10.0	0.98	11.72	74	8	91	0	1	8.0	129.0	-9.7	51	N/A	0	0	0.0	0.0
U /	N/A	N/A	26.49	57	6	93	0	1	146.0	N/A	N/A	N/A	N/A	25,000	1,000	0.0	2.0
B+ /9.3	5.9	1.18	13.09	120	0	67	32	1	127.0	40.9	-5.6	48	N/A	2,500	250	5.8	0.0
B+ /9.5	5.8	1.16	13.07	N/A	0	67	32	1	127.0	38.0	N/A	42	N/A	2,500	250	0.0	1.0
B+ /9.5	5.9	1.18	13.10	4	0	67	32	1	127.0	39.5	-5.6	44	N/A	2,500	250	0.0	0.0
B /8.8	6.4	0.97	12.92	62	2	0	0	98	44.0	34.6	-0.3	58	10	2,500	250	2.0	0.0
B /8.2	9.3	1.15	17.16	3,134	3	96	0	1	93.0	78.6	-11.3	63	17	2,500	250	5.8	0.0
B /8.2	9.4	1.15	17.03	212	3	96	0	1	93.0	76.5	-11.4	58	17	2,500	250	0.0	0.0
C+ /6.8	9.5	1.11	28.99	10	2	97	0	1	22.0	98.5	-6.1	94	8	2,500	250	5.8	0.0
C+ /6.8	9.5	1.11	28.83	275	2	97	0	1	22.0	97.5	-6.1	94	8	2,500	250	0.0	0.0
C+ /6.0	11.5	0.75	29.79	75	5	94	0	1	62.0	106.6	-7.2	90	8	2,500	250	5.8	0.0
C+ /5.9	11.5	0.75	29.15	93	5	94	0	1	62.0	105.0	-7.3	89	8	2,500	250	0.0	0.0
C- /4.0	12.0	1.03	16.00	312	3	96	0	1	196.0	108.0	-7.2	70	4	2,500	250	5.8	0.0
C- /3.9	12.0	1.03	15.74	32	3	96	0	1	196.0	105.8	-7.2	67	4	2,500	250	0.0	0.0
B- /7.5	7.7	1.01	18.79	65	1	98	0	1	8.0	62.0	-10.0	47	7	2,500	250	5.8	0.0
B- /7.8	7.7	1.01	18.77	20	1	98	0	1	8.0	60.8	-10.0	44	7	2,500	250	0.0	0.0
B- /7.6	9.3	1.05	15.53	211	1	98	0	1	110.0	82.0	-10.2	82	1	2,500	250	5.8	0.0
B- /7.6	9.3	1.04	15.52	5	1	98	0	1	110.0	80.4	-10.3	79	1	2,500	250	0.0	0.0
B /8.2	9.8	1.55	16.00	61	10	59	29	2	17.8	66.7	-1.0	82	N/A	2,000	500	0.0	0.0
C /4.9	10.9	1.23	18.20	24	3	96	0	1	160.0	82.4	-8.8	65	19	500	200	0.0	0.0
B- /7.2	14.5	1.08	24.97	69	25	74	0	1	92.0	199.3	1.8	98	5	2,500	50	5.8	1.0
B- /7.2	8.9	1.05	6.83	1,879	1	98	0	1	19.0	53.5	-7.0	37	N/A	500	0	5.8	0.0
B- /7.0	8.9	1.05	6.49	59	1	98	0	1	19.0	48.2	-7.4	28	N/A	500	0	0.0	5.0
B- /7.1	8.9	1.05	6.52	17	1	98	0	1	19.0	48.6	-7.4	28	N/A	500	0	0.0	1.0
B- /7.2	8.8	1.04	6.85	6	1	98	0	1	19.0	54.9	-7.1	40	N/A	0	0	0.0	0.0
C+ /6.2	12.3	1.51	10.49	1,407	7	84	7	2	41.0	85.4	2.5	99	9	500	0	5.8	0.0
C+ /6.1	12.3	1.52	10.41	120	7	84	7	2	41.0	80.1	2.2	98	7	500	0	0.0	5.0
C+ /6.1	12.3	1.52	10.41	64	7	84	7	2	41.0	80.4	2.2	98	7	500	0	0.0	1.0
C+ /6.2	12.3	1.53	10.51	7	7	84	7	2	41.0	87.4	2.6	99	9	0	0	0.0	0.0
B+ /9.4	5.5	1.08	7.69	464	1	74	23	2	33.0	42.5	-3.6	67	13	500	0	5.8	0.0
B+ /9.5	5.5	1.06	7.69	16	1	74	23	2	33.0	38.3	-4.0	57	7	500	0	0.0	5.0
B+ /9.5	5.5	1.07	7.69	6	1	74	23	2	33.0	38.3	-4.0	N/A	7	500	0	0.0	1.0
B+ /9.5	5.5	1.07	7.69	1	1	74	23	2	33.0	43.9	-3.7	70	10	0	0	0.0	0.0
B- /7.6	8.2	0.91	6.69	3,976	4	95	0	1	30.0	62.7	-9.0	81	9	500	0	5.8	0.0
B- /7.5	8.2	0.91	6.33	80	4	95	0	1	30.0	56.7	-9.3	70	7	500	0	0.0	5.0
B- /7.5	8.1	0.90	6.35	20	4	95	0	1	30.0	57.2	-9.3	71	7	500	0	0.0	1.0
B- /7.5	8.2	0.91	6.69	47	4	95	0	1	30.0	64.2	-8.9	83	9	0	0	0.0	0.0
U /	N/A	N/A	14.76	364	5	94	0	1	10.0	N/A	N/A	N/A	3	500	0	5.8	0.0
C+ /6.2	10.9	1.03	8.28	715	2	97	0	1	40.0	92.0	-8.0	10	10	500	0	5.8	0.0
C+ /6.2	11.0	1.04	7.86	22	2	97	0	1	40.0	84.3	-8.3	6	7	500	0	0.0	5.0
C+ /6.2	11.1	1.04	8.04	7	2	97	0	1	40.0	86.0	-8.1	7	7	500	0	0.0	1.0
C+ /6.2	11.0	1.05	8.30	33	2	97	0	1	40.0	95.3	-7.8	11	10	0	0	0.0	0.0
C /5.5	10.4	0.87	10.44	1,253	4	95	0	1	6.0	93.1	-5.7	55	5	500	0	5.8	0.0
C /5.5	10.4	0.87	9.60	55	4	95	0	1	6.0	86.5	-6.1	41	5	500	0	0.0	5.0
C /5.5	10.5	0.88	9.67	19	4	95	0	1	6.0	87.1	-5.9	42	5	500	0	0.0	1.0

Fund Type	Fund Name	Ticker Symbol	Overall Weiss Investment Rating	Phone	Performance Rating/Pts	3 Mo	6 Mo	1Yr / Pct	3Yr / Pct	5Yr / Pct	Dividend Yield	Expense Ratio
MC	Waddell & Reed Adv New Concepts	UNEYX	C	(888) 923-3355	C+ / 6.8	-4.68	2.96	14.77 /71	16.39 /65	4.19 /48	0.00	1.06
GI	Waddell & Reed Adv Retirement A	UNFDX	D	(888) 923-3355	D+ / 2.8	-3.06	0.43	12.70 /63	11.20 /37	3.41 /40	0.27	1.26
GI	Waddell & Reed Adv Retirement B	WRRBX	D-	(888) 923-3355	D / 2.1	-3.44	-0.13	11.47 /57	9.97 /27	2.30 /30	0.00	2.27
GI	Waddell & Reed Adv Retirement C	WARCX	D	(888) 923-3355	D+ / 2.8	-3.43	-0.13	11.60 /57	10.06 /28	2.38 /31	0.00	2.19
GI	Waddell & Reed Adv Retirement Y	WARYX	D+	(888) 923-3355	C- / 4.0	-3.01	0.53	12.98 /64	11.51 /39	3.76 /43	0.60	0.94
★ TC	Waddell & Reed Adv Sci & Tech A	UNSCX	C	(888) 923-3355	C+ / 6.7	-5.20	0.27	13.16 /65	18.42 /74	6.09 /62	0.00	1.36
TC	Waddell & Reed Adv Sci & Tech B	USTBX	C-	(888) 923-3355	C+ / 6.1	-5.47	-0.30	11.83 /59	16.91 /68	4.66 /52	0.00	2.51
TC	Waddell & Reed Adv Sci & Tech C	WCSTX	C-	(888) 923-3355	C+ / 6.6	-5.46	-0.30	11.80 /58	16.96 /68	4.70 /52	0.00	2.50
TC	Waddell & Reed Adv Sci & Tech Y	USTFX	C	(888) 923-3355	B- / 7.4	-5.07	0.52	13.54 /66	18.86 /76	6.51 /64	0.00	1.04
SC	Waddell & Reed Adv Small Cap A	UNSAX	C-	(888) 923-3355	C / 5.0	-5.96	2.27	9.14 /41	14.90 /58	6.59 /65	0.00	1.56
SC	Waddell & Reed Adv Small Cap B	WRSBX	D+	(888) 923-3355	C / 4.4	-6.21	1.77	8.12 /34	13.80 /53	5.52 /58	0.00	2.49
SC	Waddell & Reed Adv Small Cap C	WSCCX	C-	(888) 923-3355	C / 5.1	-6.14	1.82	8.24 /35	13.94 /54	5.70 /59	0.00	2.40
SC	Waddell & Reed Adv Small Cap Y	WRSYX	C	(888) 923-3355	C+ / 6.1	-5.80	2.54	9.68 /45	15.54 /62	7.18 /68	0.00	1.07
GR	Waddell & Reed Adv Tax Managed A	WTEAX	D	(888) 923-3355	D / 2.1	-4.21	-2.41	6.64 /24	10.36 /30	2.53 /32	0.00	1.35
GR	Waddell & Reed Adv Tax Managed B	WBTMX	D-	(888) 923-3355	D / 1.7	-4.43	-2.75	5.73 /19	9.34 /23	1.61 /24	0.00	2.29
GR	Waddell & Reed Adv Tax Managed C	WCTMX	D	(888) 923-3355	D+ / 2.3	-4.33	-2.75	5.75 /19	9.31 /23	1.57 /24	0.00	2.32
GR	Waddell & Reed Adv Tax Managed Y	WYTMX	D+	(888) 923-3355	C- / 3.1	-4.41	-2.61	6.39 /23	10.38 /30	2.60 /33	0.00	1.17
GR	Waddell & Reed Adv Value A	WVAAX	C	(888) 923-3355	C- / 3.5	-1.01	2.73	5.40 /17	12.19 /44	5.15 /55	1.02	1.35
GR	Waddell & Reed Adv Value B	WVABX	C-	(888) 923-3355	D+ / 2.9	-1.34	2.21	4.41 /12	11.13 /37	4.12 /47	0.14	2.29
GR	Waddell & Reed Adv Value C	WVACX	C	(888) 923-3355	C- / 3.6	-1.26	2.28	4.53 /13	11.23 /37	4.25 /48	0.20	2.24
GR	Waddell & Reed Adv Value Y	WVAYX	C+	(888) 923-3355	C / 4.8	-0.93	2.97	5.83 /19	12.72 /47	5.63 /59	1.48	0.94
GR	Waddell & Reed Adv Vanguard Adv A	UNVGX	D	(888) 923-3355	C- / 3.6	-1.85	1.17	12.96 /64	12.43 /45	3.42 /41	0.00	1.21
GR	Waddell & Reed Adv Vanguard Adv B	WRVBX	D-	(888) 923-3355	C- / 3.0	-2.01	0.69	11.81 /58	11.21 /37	2.18 /29	0.00	2.31
GR	Waddell & Reed Adv Vanguard Adv C	WAVCX	D	(888) 923-3355	C- / 3.7	-2.00	0.69	11.77 /58	11.28 /38	2.27 /30	0.00	2.24
GR	Waddell & Reed Adv Vanguard Adv Y	WAVYX	C-	(888) 923-3355	C / 4.9	-1.71	1.35	13.28 /65	12.80 /48	3.80 /44	0.00	0.88
BA	Waddell & Reed InvestEd Balanced A	WBLAX	C	(888) 923-3355	D / 2.2	-0.08	3.77	9.88 /46	9.29 /23	--	1.13	0.71
GR	Waddell & Reed InvestEd Conserv A	WICAX	D+	(888) 923-3355	E- / 0.2	0.66	1.92	3.40 / 8	3.14 / 1	--	1.56	0.85
GR	Waddell & Reed InvestEd Growth A	WAGRX	C+	(888) 923-3355	C- / 3.9	-0.81	4.57	12.65 /63	12.17 /43	--	0.68	0.74
BA	Walden Social Balanced	WSBFX	C-	(877) 792-5336	D- / 1.3	-1.73	0.53	4.51 /13	6.53 / 9	4.00 /46	1.48	1.00
GI	Walden Social Equity Fund	WSEFX	C-	(877) 792-5336	D+ / 2.9	-1.24	1.70	7.12 /27	9.28 /23	4.52 /50	0.66	1.00
GR	Wall Street Fund	WALLX	D-	(800) 443-4693	C / 4.7	-5.34	1.07	10.38 /49	12.54 /46	-0.44 /14	0.00	1.71
GR	● Wasatch Core Growth Fund	WGROX	D+	(800) 551-1700	C / 4.3	-8.03	0.10	1.16 / 3	13.98 /54	5.58 /58	1.42	1.16
TC	Wasatch Global Sci & Tech	WAGTX	D-	(800) 551-1700	C / 5.5	-7.93	4.22	19.39 /81	14.47 /56	5.63 /59	0.00	1.88
GR	Wasatch Heritage Growth Fund	WAHGX	U	(800) 551-1700	U /	-5.21	-2.20	1.81 / 4	--	--	0.12	0.92
FO	● Wasatch International Growth	WAIGX	A+	(800) 551-1700	A / 9.3	-2.91	9.22	28.82 /94	27.38 /93	--	0.00	1.76
FO	● Wasatch International Opp Fund	WAIOX	U	(800) 551-1700	U /	-2.17	12.92	37.56 /97	--	--	0.00	2.25
SC	● Wasatch Micro Cap Fund	WMICX	D	(800) 551-1700	B- / 7.1	-5.31	6.45	12.53 /62	17.88 /72	15.30 /92	0.00	2.14
SC	● Wasatch Micro Cap Value Fund	WAMVX	U	(800) 551-1700	U /	-1.67	15.69	31.29 /95	--	--	0.00	2.25
SC	● Wasatch Small Cap Growth	WAAEX	E+	(800) 551-1700	D+ / 2.9	-8.01	0.08	1.29 / 3	11.45 /39	6.97 /67	0.00	1.17
SC	● Wasatch Small Cap Value	WMCVX	C	(800) 551-1700	B / 8.0	-2.69	8.38	12.11 /60	20.64 /82	12.13 /87	1.12	1.68
MC	● Wasatch Ultra Growth	WAMCX	E-	(800) 551-1700	D- / 1.3	-9.64	0.17	3.87 /10	8.02 /15	5.52 /58	0.00	1.46
BA	Weitz Balanced Fund	WBALX	U	(800) 232-4161	U /	0.31	2.95	3.24 / 8	--	--	1.20	1.15
GR	Weitz Partners-Partners Value	WPVLX	C	(800) 232-4161	C- / 3.3	2.36	5.74	5.22 /16	9.58 /25	3.06 /37	0.57	1.14
GR	Weitz Series-Hickory Fund	WEHIX	B-	(800) 232-4161	C+ / 6.4	0.84	5.46	4.91 /15	16.02 /64	4.78 /52	0.27	1.20
★ MC	Weitz Series-Value	WVALX	C-	(800) 232-4161	C- / 3.4	2.56	5.19	4.70 /14	9.87 /26	3.75 /43	0.75	1.12
AG	Wells Fargo Avtg Agg Allc Adm	NWBEX	C	(800) 222-8222	C- / 4.1	-2.39	2.72	9.76 /45	11.04 /36	3.44 /41	1.34	1.00
FO	Wells Fargo Avtg Asia Pac Inv	SASPX	B	(800) 222-8222	A+ / 9.6	-3.30	8.42	34.54 /96	32.43 /97	18.56 /95	0.44	1.65
AA	Wells Fargo Avtg Ast Allc A	SFAAX	D+	(800) 222-8222	D- / 1.3	-1.78	0.58	4.51 /13	8.57 /18	3.72 /43	1.95	1.15
AA	Wells Fargo Avtg Ast Allc Adm	WFAIX	C-	(800) 222-8222	D+ / 2.4	-1.75	0.67	4.74 /14	8.85 /20	3.93 /45	2.34	0.90
AA	Wells Fargo Avtg Ast Allc B	SASBX	D+	(800) 222-8222	D- / 1.1	-1.96	0.20	3.75 /10	7.77 /14	2.94 /36	1.28	1.90
AA	Wells Fargo Avtg Ast Allc C	WFALX	C-	(800) 222-8222	D / 1.6	-1.96	0.12	3.68 / 9	7.77 /14	2.93 /36	1.29	1.90
BA	Wells Fargo Avtg Bal Inv	STAAX	C-	(800) 222-8222	D- / 1.2	-1.07	0.50	3.54 / 9	6.27 / 8	1.60 /24	2.12	1.25

● Denotes fund is closed to new investors
★ Denotes fund is included in Section II

426

RISK			NET ASSETS		ASSET					BULL / BEAR		FUND MANAGER		MINIMUMS		LOADS	
	3 Year		NAV						Portfolio	Last Bull	Last Bear	Manager	Manager	Initial	Additional	Front	Back
Risk Rating/Pts	Standard Deviation	Beta	As of 6/30/06	Total $(Mil)	Cash %	Stocks %	Bonds %	Other %	Turnover Ratio	Market Return	Market Return	Quality Pct	Tenure (Years)	Purch. $	Purch. $	End Load	End Load
C+ / 5.6	10.5	0.87	10.80	25	4	95	0	1	6.0	96.2	-5.6	60	5	0	0	0.0	0.0
C+ / 6.1	11.3	1.21	7.90	573	3	80	15	2	117.0	62.4	-4.3	35	7	500	0	5.8	0.0
C+ / 6.1	11.3	1.20	7.58	23	3	80	15	2	117.0	57.1	-4.7	27	7	500	0	0.0	5.0
C+ / 6.1	11.4	1.22	7.60	6	3	80	15	2	117.0	57.7	-4.7	27	7	500	0	0.0	1.0
C+ / 6.2	11.4	1.21	7.94	7	3	80	15	2	117.0	63.9	-4.2	38	7	0	0	0.0	0.0
C / 4.8	13.7	1.42	11.13	2,313	5	94	0	1	52.0	89.2	-3.8	83	5	500	0	5.8	0.0
C / 4.6	13.7	1.42	10.02	80	5	94	0	1	52.0	81.7	-4.1	73	5	500	0	0.0	5.0
C / 4.6	13.7	1.42	10.05	15	5	94	0	1	52.0	81.7	-4.1	73	5	500	0	0.0	1.0
C / 4.8	13.7	1.42	11.60	17	5	94	0	1	52.0	91.5	-3.7	85	5	0	0	0.0	0.0
C+ / 5.6	13.5	0.86	15.31	647	9	90	0	1	37.0	83.3	-4.0	41	N/A	500	0	5.8	0.0
C / 5.4	13.5	0.86	14.34	75	9	90	0	1	37.0	77.9	-4.3	32	N/A	500	0	0.0	5.0
C / 5.4	13.5	0.86	14.53	23	9	90	0	1	37.0	78.6	-4.3	33	N/A	500	0	0.0	1.0
C+ / 5.7	13.6	0.86	15.74	233	9	90	0	1	37.0	86.7	-3.9	47	N/A	0	0	0.0	0.0
C+ / 6.8	10.4	1.20	9.32	65	3	96	0	1	24.0	59.9	-5.6	30	N/A	500	0	5.8	0.0
C+ / 6.7	10.5	1.21	8.85	4	3	96	0	1	24.0	55.2	-5.7	23	N/A	500	0	0.0	5.0
C+ / 6.7	10.4	1.20	8.83	3	3	96	0	1	24.0	55.1	-5.7	23	N/A	500	0	0.0	1.0
C+ / 6.8	10.4	1.20	9.32	N/A	3	96	0	1	24.0	59.9	-5.4	30	N/A	0	0	0.0	0.0
B / 8.3	7.3	0.92	12.80	436	0	99	0	1	20.0	63.8	-7.9	73	N/A	500	0	5.8	0.0
B / 8.5	7.3	0.92	12.47	47	0	99	0	1	20.0	58.8	-8.2	63	N/A	500	0	0.0	5.0
B / 8.5	7.3	0.92	12.55	20	0	99	0	1	20.0	59.3	-8.3	64	N/A	500	0	0.0	1.0
B / 8.3	7.3	0.92	12.83	30	0	99	0	1	20.0	66.1	-7.8	77	N/A	0	0	0.0	0.0
C+ / 5.6	12.0	1.19	9.54	1,719	3	96	0	1	33.0	63.9	-5.1	49	9	500	0	5.8	0.0
C / 5.4	12.0	1.19	8.77	57	3	96	0	1	33.0	58.2	-5.6	37	7	500	0	0.0	5.0
C / 5.4	12.0	1.18	8.80	19	3	96	0	1	33.0	58.9	-5.6	38	7	500	0	0.0	1.0
C+ / 5.6	12.0	1.18	9.76	49	3	96	0	1	33.0	65.8	-5.0	55	9	0	0	0.0	0.0
B+ / 9.6	5.2	1.00	12.40	80	0	99	0	1	5.0	42.7	-2.4	73	4	500	0	5.8	0.0
B+ / 9.9	1.9	0.17	10.64	29	0	99	0	1	22.0	11.9	0.5	48	4	500	50	4.3	0.0
B+ / 9.0	7.4	0.90	13.51	116	0	99	0	1	5.0	60.3	-4.0	74	N/A	500	50	5.8	0.0
B+ / 9.7	5.1	0.91	11.38	29	2	72	25	1	41.1	34.4	-3.7	49	7	2,000	500	0.0	0.0
B / 8.1	7.8	0.95	11.94	48	0	99	0	1	29.1	52.7	-7.9	39	7	2,000	500	0.0	0.0
C- / 3.4	14.3	1.61	8.51	17	0	98	0	2	115.9	88.3	-8.4	20	N/A	1,000	100	0.0	0.0
C+ / 5.6	13.3	1.45	40.80	1,541	5	94	0	1	38.0	108.4	-13.5	40	7	2,000	100	0.0	2.0
D+ / 2.4	19.5	1.94	13.82	130	7	92	0	1	67.0	119.0	-21.4	14	6	2,000	100	0.0	2.0
U /	N/A	N/A	11.09	267	2	97	0	1	53.0	N/A	N/A	N/A	2	2,000	100	0.0	2.0
B- / 7.4	12.4	1.09	21.68	390	2	97	0	1	57.0	173.2	-10.5	63	N/A	2,000	100	0.0	2.0
U /	N/A	N/A	2.71	37	2	96	0	2	28.9	N/A	N/A	N/A	1	2,000	100	0.0	2.0
D / 1.9	15.0	0.93	6.77	592	4	94	0	2	51.0	131.5	-14.0	61	11	2,000	100	0.0	2.0
U /	N/A	N/A	2.95	97	6	94	0	0	84.8	N/A	N/A	N/A	3	2,000	100	0.0	2.0
C- / 3.9	14.6	0.93	36.73	1,299	1	98	0	1	41.0	94.7	-16.1	12	20	2,000	100	0.0	2.0
C- / 4.0	13.3	0.86	5.43	711	2	97	0	1	42.0	135.6	-9.9	89	7	2,000	100	0.0	2.0
D- / 1.2	17.8	1.45	24.09	340	1	98	0	1	81.0	83.3	-17.7	0	14	2,000	100	0.0	2.0
U /	N/A	N/A	11.12	63	11	59	28	2	36.0	N/A	N/A	N/A	3	10,000	0	0.0	0.0
B / 8.2	6.7	0.67	23.12	1,816	9	90	0	1	36.0	55.9	-7.8	70	12	10,000	0	0.0	0.0
B- / 7.5	9.3	0.97	34.48	314	4	95	0	1	65.0	99.1	-11.8	92	3	10,000	0	0.0	0.0
B- / 7.8	6.7	0.45	36.78	2,816	12	87	0	1	40.0	58.5	-6.8	63	20	10,000	0	0.0	0.0
B / 8.2	8.2	1.04	14.72	215	0	79	19	2	43.0	64.2	-10.6	50	9	1,000,000	0	0.0	0.0
C / 4.5	15.6	1.23	12.62	367	4	94	0	2	117.0	206.6	-4.4	75	N/A	2,500	100	0.0	0.0
B / 8.9	6.3	1.33	19.92	857	6	58	35	1	1.0	49.1	-7.9	46	N/A	1,000	100	5.8	1.0
B+ / 9.0	6.3	1.33	19.94	72	6	58	35	1	1.0	50.2	-7.9	50	N/A	1,000,000	0	0.0	0.0
B+ / 9.0	6.3	1.33	12.11	127	6	58	35	1	1.0	45.5	-8.0	38	N/A	1,000	100	0.0	5.0
B+ / 9.0	6.3	1.33	12.12	36	6	58	35	1	1.0	45.5	-8.1	38	N/A	1,000	100	0.0	1.0
B+ / 9.8	4.9	0.99	19.73	130	4	56	38	2	87.0	35.8	-5.7	41	N/A	2,500	100	0.0	0.0

Fund Type	Fund Name	Ticker Symbol	Overall Weiss Investment Rating	Phone	Perfor-mance Rating/Pts	3 Mo	6 Mo	1Yr / Pct	3Yr / Pct	5Yr / Pct	Dividend Yield	Expense Ratio
	99 Pct = Best							Total Return % through 6/30/06	Annualized		Incl. in Returns	
GR	Wells Fargo Avtg Cap Gr Adm	WFCDX	D+	(800) 222-8222	C- / 4.1	-4.53	-2.78	5.80 / 19	12.26 / 44	5.05 / 55	0.00	0.94
GR	Wells Fargo Avtg Cap Gr I	WWCIX	D+	(800) 222-8222	C- / 4.1	-4.46	-2.72	5.92 / 20	12.32 / 45	5.09 / 55	0.00	0.80
GR	Wells Fargo Avtg Cap Gr Inv	SLGIX	D	(800) 222-8222	C- / 3.5	-4.65	-3.05	5.21 / 16	11.68 / 40	4.72 / 52	0.00	1.42
GR	Wells Fargo Avtg CB Lg Cp VI A	CBEAX	C	(800) 222-8222	C- / 3.5	0.22	5.49	7.41 / 29	11.96 / 42	8.30 / 73	0.45	1.20
GR	Wells Fargo Avtg CB Lg Cp VI Adm	CBLLX	B-	(800) 222-8222	C / 4.9	0.33	5.72	7.75 / 31	12.15 / 43	8.40 / 73	0.68	0.95
GR	Wells Fargo Avtg CB Lg Cp VI B	CBEBX	B	(800) 222-8222	C / 5.4	0.00	5.16	6.56 / 24	15.11 / 59	10.02 / 81	0.00	1.95
GR	Wells Fargo Avtg CB Lg Cp VI D	CBEQX	B-	(800) 222-8222	C / 4.7	0.22	5.49	7.40 / 29	11.96 / 42	8.29 / 73	0.47	1.20
GR	Wells Fargo Avtg CB Lg Cp VI I	CBLSX	B-	(800) 222-8222	C / 5.0	0.33	5.70	7.92 / 32	12.36 / 45	8.52 / 74	0.85	0.70
MC	Wells Fargo Avtg CB MdCp VI A	CBMAX	C+	(800) 222-8222	C+ / 5.6	-2.86	7.91	10.81 / 52	15.33 / 60	11.83 / 86	0.00	1.39
MC	Wells Fargo Avtg CB MdCp VI Adm	CBMIX	C+	(800) 222-8222	C+ / 6.5	-2.80	8.09	11.10 / 54	15.52 / 61	11.94 / 87	0.01	1.15
MC	Wells Fargo Avtg CB MdCp VI B	CBMBX	C	(800) 222-8222	C / 5.2	-3.03	7.49	8.79 / 39	14.37 / 56	11.27 / 85	0.00	2.14
MC	Wells Fargo Avtg CB MdCp VI D	CBMDX	C+	(800) 222-8222	C+ / 6.5	-2.81	8.00	10.95 / 53	15.43 / 61	11.89 / 86	0.00	1.25
MC	Wells Fargo Avtg CB MdCp VI I	CBMSX	C+	(800) 222-8222	C+ / 6.6	-2.75	8.17	11.34 / 56	15.69 / 62	12.04 / 87	0.19	0.90
BA	Wells Fargo Avtg Cnsrv Allc Adm	NVCBX	D+	(800) 222-8222	E / 0.5	-0.42	0.74	2.72 / 6	4.20 / 3	3.50 / 41	3.24	0.85
MC	Wells Fargo Avtg Comm Stk A	SCSAX	C-	(800) 222-8222	C / 5.5	-2.28	5.64	15.73 / 74	15.45 / 61	7.19 / 68	0.00	1.31
MC	Wells Fargo Avtg Comm Stk B	SCSKX	C-	(800) 222-8222	C / 5.3	-2.44	5.26	14.88 / 71	14.58 / 57	6.37 / 63	0.00	2.06
MC	Wells Fargo Avtg Comm Stk C	STSAX	C-	(800) 222-8222	C+ / 5.8	-2.48	5.26	14.84 / 71	14.57 / 57	6.36 / 63	0.00	2.06
MC	● Wells Fargo Avtg Comm Stk Z	STCSX	C	(800) 222-8222	C+ / 6.5	-2.25	5.70	15.81 / 74	15.63 / 62	7.37 / 69	0.00	1.29
GR	Wells Fargo Avtg Discovery Adm	WFDDX	C	(800) 222-8222	B- / 7.2	-4.11	5.75	15.04 / 72	17.35 / 70	8.70 / 75	0.00	1.15
GR	Wells Fargo Avtg Discovery Inv	STDIX	C	(800) 222-8222	B- / 7.2	-4.12	5.67	14.81 / 71	17.21 / 69	8.63 / 75	0.00	1.38
GR	Wells Fargo Avtg Divers Eqty A	NVDAX	D	(800) 222-8222	C- / 3.3	-2.96	2.16	9.58 / 44	11.83 / 41	2.79 / 35	0.25	1.25
GR	Wells Fargo Avtg Divers Eqty Adm	NVDEX	C-	(800) 222-8222	C / 4.7	-2.88	2.30	9.89 / 46	12.12 / 43	3.06 / 37	0.47	1.00
GR	Wells Fargo Avtg Divers Eqty B	NVDBX	D	(800) 222-8222	C- / 3.1	-3.14	1.79	8.76 / 39	11.00 / 36	2.03 / 28	0.00	2.00
GR	Wells Fargo Avtg Divers Eqty C	WFDEX	D+	(800) 222-8222	C- / 3.7	-3.14	1.79	8.77 / 39	11.00 / 36	2.02 / 28	0.00	2.00
SC	Wells Fargo Avtg Divers Sm Cp Adm	NVDSX	C+	(800) 222-8222	B- / 7.4	-6.45	5.17	12.49 / 62	18.65 / 75	9.79 / 80	0.00	1.19
GI	Wells Fargo Avtg Dividend Inc Adm	WWIDX	C	(800) 222-8222	C+ / 5.6	0.59	3.56	8.95 / 40	13.76 / 53	3.84 / 44	1.81	0.96
GI	Wells Fargo Avtg Dividend Inc Inv	SDVIX	C+	(800) 222-8222	C / 5.2	0.48	3.36	8.50 / 37	13.31 / 50	3.46 / 41	1.38	1.37
EM	Wells Fargo Avtg Emg Mkt Foc A	MFFAX	C	(800) 222-8222	A / 9.5	-3.52	13.11	41.87 / 98	29.55 / 95	19.00 / 95	1.47	1.90
EM	Wells Fargo Avtg Emg Mkt Foc Adm	MNEFX	C	(800) 222-8222	A+ / 9.6	-3.44	13.28	42.27 / 98	29.93 / 95	19.22 / 95	1.80	1.60
EM	Wells Fargo Avtg Emg Mkt Foc B	MFFBX	C	(800) 222-8222	A / 9.5	-3.71	12.71	40.84 / 98	28.62 / 94	18.35 / 95	1.11	2.65
EM	Wells Fargo Avtg Emg Mkt Foc C	MFFCX	C	(800) 222-8222	A / 9.5	-3.69	12.69	40.73 / 98	28.56 / 94	--	0.91	2.65
GR	Wells Fargo Avtg Endeavor Lg Cp A	STALX	D-	(800) 222-8222	C- / 3.1	-4.74	-2.97	5.02 / 15	12.68 / 47	--	0.00	1.25
OT	Wells Fargo Avtg Endeavor Sel A	STAEX	D+	(800) 222-8222	C / 4.7	-4.12	-2.36	6.66 / 24	15.39 / 61	3.25 / 39	0.00	1.25
OT	Wells Fargo Avtg Endeavor Sel Adm	WECDX	C-	(800) 222-8222	C+ / 5.8	-4.02	-2.25	6.87 / 25	15.51 / 61	3.32 / 40	0.00	1.00
OT	Wells Fargo Avtg Endeavor Sel B	WECBX	D	(800) 222-8222	C / 4.5	-4.30	-2.67	5.86 / 20	14.56 / 57	2.48 / 32	0.00	2.00
OT	Wells Fargo Avtg Endeavor Sel C	WECCX	D+	(800) 222-8222	C / 5.1	-4.31	-2.67	5.75 / 19	14.46 / 56	2.46 / 32	0.00	2.00
OT	Wells Fargo Avtg Endeavor Sel I	WFCIX	C-	(800) 222-8222	C+ / 5.9	-4.01	-2.15	7.09 / 27	15.59 / 62	3.36 / 40	0.00	0.80
MC	Wells Fargo Avtg Enterprise Adv	SENAX	C-	(800) 222-8222	B- / 7.0	-3.83	5.98	15.20 / 72	16.38 / 65	3.45 / 41	0.00	1.40
MC	Wells Fargo Avtg Enterprise I	WFEIX	C	(800) 222-8222	B- / 7.2	-3.70	6.25	15.79 / 74	17.05 / 68	3.75 / 43	0.00	0.90
MC	Wells Fargo Avtg Enterprise Inv	SENTX	C-	(800) 222-8222	C+ / 6.8	-3.85	5.90	15.03 / 72	16.10 / 64	3.25 / 39	0.00	1.57
MC	Wells Fargo Avtg Entprs-Adm	SEPKX	C	(800) 222-8222	B- / 7.1	-3.80	6.11	15.45 / 73	16.75 / 67	3.72 / 43	0.00	1.15
IN	Wells Fargo Avtg Eqty Inc A	NVAEX	E+	(800) 222-8222	C- / 3.0	0.12	2.77	7.32 / 28	11.30 / 38	3.46 / 41	1.37	1.10
IN	Wells Fargo Avtg Eqty Inc Adm	NVIEX	D-	(800) 222-8222	C / 4.4	0.15	2.86	7.56 / 30	11.57 / 40	3.71 / 43	1.71	0.85
IN	Wells Fargo Avtg Eqty Inc B	NVBEX	E+	(800) 222-8222	D+ / 2.8	-0.09	2.36	6.48 / 23	10.45 / 30	2.68 / 34	0.55	1.85
IN	Wells Fargo Avtg Eqty Inc C	WFEEX	D-	(800) 222-8222	C- / 3.4	-0.09	2.34	6.48 / 23	10.45 / 30	2.69 / 34	0.50	1.85
IN	Wells Fargo Avtg Eqty Indx A	SFCSX	D+	(800) 222-8222	D+ / 2.5	-1.58	2.40	8.01 / 33	10.51 / 31	1.84 / 26	1.07	0.62
IN	Wells Fargo Avtg Eqty Indx B	SQIBX	D+	(800) 222-8222	D+ / 2.3	-1.78	2.02	7.19 / 27	9.68 / 25	1.08 / 21	0.27	1.37
GR	Wells Fargo Avtg Eqty Val Adm	WLVIX	U	(800) 222-8222	U /	-0.27	5.07	12.86 / 64	--	--	0.30	1.00
GR	Wells Fargo Avtg Gr & Inc Adm	SGIKX	E+	(800) 222-8222	E+ / 0.9	-3.65	-1.96	2.09 / 5	6.21 / 7	-0.81 / 12	0.74	0.96
GR	Wells Fargo Avtg Gr & Inc Adv	SGNAX	D	(800) 222-8222	E+ / 0.8	-3.74	-2.10	1.90 / 4	5.87 / 6	-1.12 / 11	0.54	1.14
GR	Wells Fargo Avtg Gr & Inc I	SGNIX	E+	(800) 222-8222	D- / 1.0	-3.58	-1.79	2.39 / 5	6.51 / 8	-0.48 / 14	1.04	0.66
GR	Wells Fargo Avtg Gr & Inc Inv	SGRIX	E	(800) 222-8222	E+ / 0.6	-3.76	-2.17	1.69 / 4	5.80 / 6	-1.18 / 11	0.35	1.31

● Denotes fund is closed to new investors

★ Denotes fund is included in Section II

RISK			NET ASSETS		ASSET				Portfolio	BULL / BEAR		FUND MANAGER		MINIMUMS		LOADS	
	3 Year		NAV							Last Bull	Last Bear	Manager	Manager	Initial	Additional	Front	Back
Risk	Standard		As of	Total	Cash	Stocks	Bonds	Other	Turnover	Market	Market	Quality	Tenure	Purch.	Purch.	End	End
Rating/Pts	Deviation	Beta	6/30/06	$(Mil)	%	%	%	%	Ratio	Return	Return	Pct	(Years)	$	$	Load	Load
C+ / 5.7	10.0	1.13	16.45	382	0	99	0	1	99.3	74.1	-10.0	55	N/A	1,000,000	0	0.0	0.0
C+ / 5.7	9.9	1.11	16.48	99	0	99	0	1	99.3	74.4	-10.0	57	N/A	5,000,000	0	0.0	0.0
C+ / 5.6	10.0	1.13	16.19	245	0	99	0	1	99.3	71.6	-10.0	47	N/A	2,500	100	0.0	1.0
B / 8.7	8.2	0.98	9.03	54	4	95	0	1	30.0	75.9	-11.9	66	2	1,000	100	5.8	1.0
B / 8.7	8.2	0.99	9.05	221	4	95	0	1	30.0	76.5	-11.9	67	2	1,000,000	0	0.0	0.0
B / 8.6	8.6	0.73	8.96	24	4	95	0	1	30.0	90.9	-11.2	95	2	1,000	100	0.0	5.0
B / 8.9	8.1	0.98	9.03	153	4	95	0	1	30.0	75.9	-11.9	66	2	2,500	100	0.0	0.0
B / 8.7	8.1	0.99	9.08	67	4	95	0	1	30.0	77.7	-11.9	69	2	5,000,000	0	0.0	0.0
C+ / 6.9	11.9	0.99	21.41	35	3	96	0	1	30.4	95.8	-9.5	31	N/A	1,000	100	5.8	1.0
C+ / 6.9	11.9	0.99	21.52	137	3	96	0	1	30.4	96.8	-9.5	33	N/A	1,000,000	0	0.0	0.0
C+ / 6.9	12.0	0.99	21.09	14	3	96	0	1	30.4	91.4	-9.5	25	N/A	1,000	100	0.0	5.0
C+ / 6.3	11.9	0.99	21.47	524	3	96	0	1	30.4	96.3	-9.5	32	N/A	2,500	100	0.0	0.0
C+ / 7.0	11.8	0.99	21.58	53	3	96	0	1	30.4	97.6	-9.5	34	N/A	5,000,000	0	0.0	0.0
B+ / 9.2	2.3	0.47	19.11	481	0	20	79	1	94.0	19.9	-1.5	49	12	1,000,000	0	0.0	0.0
C / 5.5	11.4	1.00	22.68	65	8	91	0	1	47.9	90.6	-8.8	31	N/A	1,000	100	5.8	1.0
C / 5.5	11.4	1.00	21.63	34	8	91	0	1	47.9	86.1	-9.0	26	N/A	1,000	100	0.0	5.0
C / 5.5	11.4	1.00	21.62	19	8	91	0	1	47.9	86.1	-9.0	26	N/A	1,000	100	0.0	1.0
C / 5.5	11.4	1.00	23.01	1,071	8	91	0	1	47.9	91.6	-8.8	32	N/A	2,500	100	0.0	0.0
C / 4.3	16.0	1.69	21.71	48	1	98	0	1	110.0	98.9	-8.0	52	N/A	1,000,000	0	0.0	0.0
C / 4.3	16.0	1.69	21.63	215	1	98	0	1	110.0	98.3	-8.0	50	N/A	2,500	100	0.0	0.0
C+ / 6.1	8.5	1.09	38.70	116	N/A	100	0	N/A	17.0	70.6	-10.6	54	10	1,000	100	5.8	1.0
C+ / 6.0	8.5	1.09	38.77	1,147	N/A	100	0	N/A	17.0	72.0	-10.6	57	10	1,000,000	0	0.0	0.0
C+ / 6.0	8.5	1.09	37.01	53	N/A	100	0	N/A	17.0	66.6	-10.8	44	10	1,000	100	0.0	5.0
C+ / 6.0	8.5	1.09	37.59	6	N/A	100	0	N/A	17.0	66.6	-10.9	44	10	1,000	100	0.0	1.0
C / 5.5	13.8	0.93	14.65	639	4	94	0	2	75.0	119.7	-9.9	67	9	1,000,000	0	0.0	0.0
C+ / 6.3	7.5	0.86	16.35	10	0	99	0	1	15.6	76.0	-7.8	87	N/A	1,000,000	0	0.0	0.0
B / 8.1	7.5	0.87	16.58	192	0	99	0	1	15.6	73.8	-7.9	85	N/A	2,500	100	0.0	1.0
D+ / 2.9	21.8	1.27	32.62	165	3	96	0	1	184.0	208.2	-7.9	1	5	1,000	100	5.8	2.0
D+ / 2.5	21.8	1.27	32.58	93	3	96	0	1	184.0	211.2	-7.8	1	9	1,000,000	0	0.0	2.0
D+ / 2.9	21.8	1.27	31.92	6	3	96	0	1	184.0	201.4	-8.0	0	5	1,000	100	0.0	2.0
D+ / 2.9	21.8	1.27	31.80	3	3	96	0	1	184.0	201.2	-8.2	0	5	1,000	100	0.0	2.0
C / 5.3	11.4	1.29	10.44	39	0	99	0	1	120.5	77.0	-9.1	42	N/A	1,000	100	5.8	1.0
C / 5.0	13.1	1.42	9.53	151	1	98	0	1	100.0	86.2	-10.0	58	N/A	1,000	100	5.8	1.0
C / 5.0	13.1	1.42	9.56	76	1	98	0	1	100.0	86.8	-10.0	60	N/A	1,000,000	0	0.0	0.0
C / 4.9	13.1	1.43	9.12	12	1	98	0	1	100.0	81.7	-10.3	48	N/A	1,000	100	0.0	5.0
C / 5.0	13.1	1.42	9.11	7	1	98	0	1	100.0	81.2	-10.1	48	N/A	1,000	100	0.0	1.0
C / 5.0	13.1	1.42	9.58	512	1	98	0	1	100.0	87.1	-10.0	61	N/A	5,000,000	0	0.0	0.0
C / 4.3	15.4	1.31	28.88	2	2	97	0	1	116.0	98.5	-9.7	10	6	1,000	100	0.0	0.0
C / 4.4	15.4	1.31	29.41	26	2	97	0	1	116.0	101.5	-9.8	12	N/A	5,000,000	0	0.0	0.0
C / 4.3	15.3	1.31	28.70	202	2	97	0	1	116.0	96.8	-9.8	9	N/A	2,500	100	0.0	0.0
C / 4.3	15.4	1.31	29.36	3	2	97	0	1	116.0	100.5	-9.6	11	N/A	1,000,000	0	0.0	0.0
C- / 4.1	7.2	0.89	30.03	166	0	99	0	1	20.0	65.3	-10.9	68	10	1,000	100	5.8	1.0
C- / 4.1	7.2	0.89	29.98	531	0	99	0	1	20.0	66.6	-10.9	70	12	1,000,000	0	0.0	0.0
C- / 4.1	7.2	0.89	30.04	43	0	99	0	1	20.0	61.4	-11.1	59	10	1,000	100	0.0	5.0
C / 4.3	7.2	0.89	31.35	5	0	99	0	1	20.0	61.5	-11.1	59	8	1,000	100	0.0	1.0
B- / 7.2	7.7	1.00	48.63	331	1	98	0	1	3.0	61.5	-9.8	48	7	1,000	100	5.8	1.0
B- / 7.4	7.6	1.00	48.59	32	1	98	0	1	3.0	57.7	-10.0	39	7	1,000	100	0.0	5.0
U /	N/A	N/A	14.72	64	1	98	0	1	145.0	N/A	N/A	N/A	3	1,000,000	0	0.0	0.0
C+ / 5.6	8.6	1.09	20.22	41	1	98	0	1	11.6	44.6	-10.0	12	1	1,000,000	0	0.0	0.0
B- / 7.9	8.6	1.09	20.25	3	1	98	0	1	11.6	43.1	-10.1	11	1	1,000	100	0.0	0.0
C+ / 5.6	8.6	1.08	20.45	29	1	98	0	1	11.6	45.9	-9.9	13	N/A	5,000,000	0	0.0	0.0
C / 5.5	8.6	1.09	20.37	231	1	98	0	1	11.6	42.8	-10.2	11	N/A	2,500	100	0.0	1.0

			99 Pct = Best 0 Pct = Worst Overall Weiss		PERFORMANCE							
					Perfor- mance	Total Return % through 6/30/06					Incl. in Returns	
									Annualized			
Fund Type	Fund Name	Ticker Symbol	Investment Rating	Phone	Rating/Pts	3 Mo	6 Mo	1Yr / Pct	3Yr / Pct	5Yr / Pct	Dividend Yield	Expense Ratio
BA	Wells Fargo Avtg Gr Bal A	WFGBX	D+	(800) 222-8222	D / 1.9	-2.04	2.09	7.85 /32	9.35 /23	3.41 /40	1.26	1.20
BA	Wells Fargo Avtg Gr Bal Adm	NVGBX	C-	(800) 222-8222	C- / 3.2	-1.97	2.23	8.14 /34	9.62 /25	3.66 /43	1.70	0.95
BA	Wells Fargo Avtg Gr Bal B	NVGRX	D+	(800) 222-8222	D / 1.7	-2.21	1.74	7.11 /27	8.53 /18	2.64 /33	0.76	1.95
BA	Wells Fargo Avtg Gr Bal C	WFGWX	C-	(800) 222-8222	D+ / 2.3	-2.21	1.74	7.06 /27	8.52 /18	2.64 /33	0.73	1.95
GR	Wells Fargo Avtg Gr Eqty A	NVEAX	D	(800) 222-8222	C / 4.5	-5.20	2.10	11.95 /59	13.87 /53	3.94 /45	0.01	1.50
GR	Wells Fargo Avtg Gr Eqty Adm	NVGEX	C-	(800) 222-8222	C+ / 5.7	-5.16	2.18	12.19 /61	14.15 /55	4.19 /48	0.19	1.25
GR	Wells Fargo Avtg Gr Eqty B	NVEBX	D	(800) 222-8222	C / 4.3	-5.40	1.72	11.11 /54	13.01 /49	3.14 /38	0.00	2.25
GR	Wells Fargo Avtg Gr Eqty C	WFGGX	D	(800) 222-8222	C / 4.7	-5.38	1.72	11.14 /55	13.02 /49	3.14 /38	0.00	2.25
GR	Wells Fargo Avtg Gr Eqty I	WGEIX	C-	(800) 222-8222	C+ / 5.8	-5.10	2.33	12.44 /62	14.25 /55	4.24 /48	0.36	1.05
GR	Wells Fargo Avtg Growth Adm	SGRKX	C-	(800) 222-8222	C+ / 5.7	-4.20	4.78	16.69 /76	13.93 /54	2.02 /28	0.00	0.96
GR	Wells Fargo Avtg Growth Adv	SGRAX	C-	(800) 222-8222	C / 5.5	-4.23	4.63	16.27 /75	13.39 /51	1.52 /24	0.00	1.30
GR	Wells Fargo Avtg Growth Instl	SGRNX	C-	(800) 222-8222	C+ / 5.8	-4.17	4.84	16.84 /77	14.03 /54	2.23 /29	0.00	0.85
GR	Wells Fargo Avtg Growth Inv	SGROX	D+	(800) 222-8222	C / 5.2	-4.30	4.50	16.06 /75	13.36 /51	1.53 /24	0.00	1.47
GR	Wells Fargo Avtg Gwth-C	WGFCX	D+	(800) 222-8222	C / 4.8	-4.44	4.22	15.41 /73	12.57 /46	--	0.00	2.05
OT	Wells Fargo Avtg Indx Adm	NVINX	C+	(800) 222-8222	C- / 4.0	-1.50	2.58	8.37 /36	10.94 /35	2.31 /30	1.47	0.25
OT	Wells Fargo Avtg Indx Inv	WFVEX	U	(800) 222-8222	U /	-1.54	2.48	8.15 /34	--	--	1.36	0.45
EM	Wells Fargo Avtg Inst Emg Mkt I	MIEMX	C+	(800) 222-8222	A+ / 9.6	-6.30	9.36	34.77 /97	31.92 /97	19.47 /96	2.45	1.25
FO	Wells Fargo Avtg Intl Core A	WFIAX	C+	(800) 222-8222	B- / 7.3	-0.65	7.56	18.46 /80	19.00 /76	--	0.72	1.50
FO	Wells Fargo Avtg Intl Core B	WFIBX	C+	(800) 222-8222	B / 7.7	-0.81	7.16	17.58 /78	18.68 /75	--	0.93	2.25
FO	Wells Fargo Avtg Intl Core C	WFICX	C+	(800) 222-8222	B / 7.7	-0.88	7.14	17.48 /78	18.71 /75	--	0.59	2.25
FO	Wells Fargo Avtg Intl Eqty A	SILAX	B	(800) 222-8222	B- / 7.5	-0.26	9.45	23.87 /87	18.74 /75	4.28 /49	0.95	1.50
FO	Wells Fargo Avtg Intl Eqty Adm	WFIEX	B+	(800) 222-8222	B / 8.1	-0.20	9.54	24.24 /88	18.93 /76	4.49 /50	1.25	1.25
FO	Wells Fargo Avtg Intl Eqty B	SILBX	B+	(800) 222-8222	B / 7.7	-0.41	9.06	23.02 /86	17.79 /72	3.46 /41	0.36	2.25
FO	Wells Fargo Avtg Intl Eqty C	WFECX	B+	(800) 222-8222	B / 7.6	-0.48	9.00	23.02 /86	17.77 /71	3.46 /41	0.39	2.25
GR	Wells Fargo Avtg Lg Co Core A	SLGAX	E	(800) 222-8222	E / 0.4	-3.78	-1.87	1.74 / 4	6.16 / 7	1.75 /25	0.00	1.25
GR	Wells Fargo Avtg Lg Co Core Adm	SLCKX	E+	(800) 222-8222	D- / 1.0	-3.64	-1.74	2.03 / 4	6.59 / 9	2.08 /28	0.53	0.95
GR	Wells Fargo Avtg Lg Co Core B	WLCBX	E-	(800) 222-8222	E- / 0.0	-4.03	-2.28	0.86 / 2	0.27 / 0	-1.68 / 9	0.00	2.00
GR	● Wells Fargo Avtg Lg Co Core Z	WLCZX	U	(800) 222-8222	U /	-3.90	-1.99	1.46 / 3	--	--	0.17	1.42
GR	Wells Fargo Avtg Lg Co Gr A	NVLAX	E	(800) 222-8222	E- / 0.1	-8.64	-7.51	1.51 / 3	4.40 / 3	-2.80 / 6	0.13	1.20
GR	Wells Fargo Avtg Lg Co Gr Adm	NVLCX	E+	(800) 222-8222	E / 0.3	-8.58	-7.39	1.75 / 4	4.66 / 3	-2.58 / 6	0.23	0.95
GR	Wells Fargo Avtg Lg Co Gr B	NVLOX	E	(800) 222-8222	E- / 0.1	-8.83	-7.87	0.73 / 2	3.61 / 2	-3.48 / 4	0.00	1.95
GR	Wells Fargo Avtg Lg Co Gr C	WFLCX	E	(800) 222-8222	E- / 0.1	-8.83	-7.88	0.73 / 2	3.62 / 2	-3.46 / 4	0.00	1.95
GR	Wells Fargo Avtg Lg Co Gr I	WLCSX	U	(800) 222-8222	U /	-8.55	-7.31	1.95 / 4	--	--	0.33	0.75
GR	● Wells Fargo Avtg Lg Co Gr Z	WFLZX	U	(800) 222-8222	U /	-8.68	-7.58	1.34 / 3	--	--	0.29	1.37
GR	Wells Fargo Avtg Lg Cp App A	WFAPX	C-	(800) 222-8222	C- / 3.4	-3.90	1.98	9.69 /45	12.02 /43	--	0.00	1.25
GR	Wells Fargo Avtg Lg Cp App Adm	WFAKX	C	(800) 222-8222	C / 4.7	-3.87	2.05	9.93 /46	12.24 /44	--	0.20	1.00
GR	Wells Fargo Avtg Lg Cp App B	WFABX	C-	(800) 222-8222	C- / 3.1	-4.12	1.58	8.89 /39	11.18 /37	--	0.00	2.00
GR	Wells Fargo Avtg Lg Cp App C	WFACX	C-	(800) 222-8222	C- / 3.7	-4.12	1.48	8.88 /39	11.18 /37	--	0.00	2.00
GR	Wells Fargo Avtg Lg Cp Gr Inv	STRFX	E+	(800) 222-8222	D / 2.0	-5.16	-2.57	6.22 /22	8.42 /17	-1.76 / 9	0.00	1.19
AG	Wells Fargo Avtg Life Stg Aggr Inv	SAGGX	D+	(800) 222-8222	C- / 3.6	-1.53	2.16	7.87 /32	10.42 /30	2.70 /34	1.82	1.45
IN	Wells Fargo Avtg Life Stg Cons Inv	SCONX	C-	(800) 222-8222	D- / 1.2	-0.40	1.51	4.74 /14	6.05 / 7	2.63 /33	3.33	1.25
AA	Wells Fargo Avtg Life Stg Mod Inv	SMDPX	C	(800) 222-8222	D / 2.2	-1.03	1.74	6.12 /21	8.15 /16	2.85 /35	2.47	1.35
MC	Wells Fargo Avtg Mid Cp Discp Adm	WFMDX	B	(800) 222-8222	B / 8.1	1.06	7.26	14.73 /71	19.87 /79	13.53 /89	0.10	1.15
MC	Wells Fargo Avtg Mid Cp Discp I	WFMIX	B	(800) 222-8222	B / 8.1	1.10	7.40	14.99 /72	19.99 /79	13.60 /90	0.19	0.90
MC	Wells Fargo Avtg Mid Cp Discp Inv	SMCDX	A+	(800) 222-8222	B / 8.1	1.06	7.17	14.52 /70	19.79 /79	13.48 /89	0.00	1.31
GR	Wells Fargo Avtg Mid Cp Gr A	WFMCX	C-	(800) 222-8222	C+ / 6.7	-3.92	7.83	16.68 /76	17.35 /70	3.29 /39	0.00	1.40
GR	Wells Fargo Avtg Mid Cp Gr B	WFMBX	C-	(800) 222-8222	C+ / 6.5	-4.10	7.50	15.92 /74	16.50 /66	--	0.00	2.15
GR	Wells Fargo Avtg Mid Cp Gr C	WFMHX	C-	(800) 222-8222	C+ / 6.9	-4.11	7.51	15.73 /74	16.44 /65	--	0.00	2.15
GR	● Wells Fargo Avtg Mid Cp Gr Z	WFMZX	U	(800) 222-8222	U /	-3.93	7.84	16.52 /76	--	--	0.00	1.57
BA	Wells Fargo Avtg Mod Bal Adm	NVMBX	D+	(800) 222-8222	D- / 1.5	-1.07	1.52	5.32 /17	6.73 / 9	3.71 /43	2.48	0.90
GR	Wells Fargo Avtg Oppty Adm	WOFDX	U	(800) 222-8222	U /	-2.72	2.21	9.03 /40	--	--	0.00	1.03
GR	Wells Fargo Avtg Oppty Adv	SOPVX	B-	(800) 222-8222	C+ / 5.9	-2.79	2.06	8.80 /39	14.93 /58	4.15 /47	0.00	1.40

● Denotes fund is closed to new investors
* Denotes fund is included in Section II

RISK Risk Rating/Pts	3 Year Standard Deviation	Beta	NET ASSETS NAV As of 6/30/06	Total $(Mil)	ASSET Cash %	Stocks %	Bonds %	Other %	Portfolio Turnover Ratio	BULL/BEAR Last Bull Market Return	Last Bear Market Return	FUND MANAGER Manager Quality Pct	Manager Tenure (Years)	MINIMUMS Initial Purch. $	Additional Purch. $	LOADS Front End Load	Back End Load
B / 8.3	6.8	1.29	32.23	63	0	64	34	2	80.0	52.9	-8.9	59	8	1,000	100	5.8	1.0
B / 8.1	6.8	1.29	29.78	1,840	0	64	34	2	80.0	54.1	-8.9	62	12	1,000,000	0	0.0	0.0
B / 8.2	6.8	1.29	29.20	76	0	64	34	2	80.0	49.3	-9.1	49	8	1,000	100	0.0	5.0
B / 8.2	6.8	1.29	29.27	16	0	64	34	2	80.0	49.3	-9.1	48	8	1,000	100	0.0	1.0
C / 4.9	10.5	1.27	27.72	25	N/A	100	0	N/A	50.0	85.3	-11.1	57	10	1,000	100	5.8	1.0
C / 5.0	10.5	1.27	28.10	395	N/A	100	0	N/A	50.0	86.7	-11.0	60	10	1,000,000	0	0.0	0.0
C / 4.4	10.5	1.27	24.87	8	N/A	100	0	N/A	50.0	80.9	-11.2	47	10	1,000	100	0.0	5.0
C / 4.6	10.5	1.27	26.02	1	N/A	100	0	N/A	50.0	80.8	-11.2	47	10	1,000	100	1.0	1.0
C+ / 5.6	10.5	1.27	28.12	138	N/A	100	0	N/A	50.0	87.1	-11.0	61	1	5,000,000	0	0.0	0.0
C / 4.9	13.2	1.42	22.58	124	0	99	0	1	125.9	85.5	-10.3	43	N/A	1,000,000	0	0.0	0.0
C / 4.9	13.2	1.42	21.94	15	0	99	0	1	125.9	82.6	-10.4	37	N/A	1,000	100	0.0	0.0
C / 4.9	13.2	1.42	22.97	190	0	99	0	1	125.9	85.9	-10.3	43	N/A	5,000,000	0	0.0	0.0
C / 4.9	13.2	1.42	22.04	1,059	0	99	0	1	125.9	82.5	-10.5	37	N/A	2,500	100	0.0	1.0
C / 4.9	13.1	1.41	21.50	N/A	0	99	0	1	76.0	78.3	N/A	32	N/A	1,000	100	0.0	1.0
B / 8.7	7.6	1.00	51.36	1,535	0	99	0	1	8.0	63.5	-9.8	53	10	1,000,000	0	0.0	0.0
U /	N/A	N/A	51.29	140	0	99	0	1	8.0	N/A	N/A	N/A	N/A	2,500	100	0.0	0.0
C- / 3.8	18.8	1.13	80.85	28	9	90	0	1	109.0	216.6	-6.6	8	N/A	5,000,000	0	0.0	2.0
C+ / 5.7	9.7	0.93	13.66	3	4	94	0	2	37.0	101.8	-6.0	25	N/A	1,000	100	5.8	2.0
C+ / 5.7	9.7	0.93	13.47	3	4	94	0	2	37.0	100.2	-6.7	23	N/A	1,000	100	0.0	2.0
C+ / 5.7	9.8	0.94	13.50	1	4	94	0	2	37.0	100.5	-6.7	23	N/A	1,000	100	0.0	2.0
B- / 7.1	10.3	1.00	15.29	52	2	96	0	2	46.0	99.2	-12.0	15	N/A	1,000	100	5.8	2.0
B- / 7.1	10.3	1.00	15.27	676	2	96	0	2	46.0	100.3	-11.8	16	N/A	1,000,000	0	0.0	1.0
B- / 7.0	10.3	1.00	14.57	15	2	96	0	2	46.0	94.2	-12.1	11	N/A	1,000	100	0.0	2.0
B- / 7.0	10.3	1.00	14.54	2	2	96	0	2	46.0	94.1	-12.0	11	N/A	1,000	100	0.0	2.0
C / 5.5	9.1	1.05	8.92	17	1	98	0	1	75.0	44.6	-8.8	13	N/A	1,000	100	5.8	1.0
C+ / 5.6	9.1	1.06	9.01	18	1	98	0	1	75.0	46.6	-8.6	15	N/A	1,000,000	0	0.0	0.0
C / 4.4	14.2	1.31	8.58	5	1	98	0	1	75.0	22.1	-8.8	0	N/A	1,000	100	0.0	5.0
U /	N/A	N/A	8.88	33	1	98	0	1	75.0	N/A	N/A	N/A	N/A	2,500	100	0.0	0.0
C+ / 6.3	11.1	1.23	47.89	485	1	98	0	1	18.0	42.7	-12.3	4	24	1,000	100	5.8	1.0
C+ / 6.3	11.1	1.23	45.60	1,496	1	98	0	1	18.0	43.8	-12.2	4	24	1,000,000	0	0.0	0.0
C+ / 6.2	11.1	1.23	42.85	115	1	98	0	1	18.0	39.3	-12.4	3	24	1,000	100	0.0	5.0
C+ / 6.2	11.1	1.23	42.93	15	1	98	0	1	18.0	39.3	-12.4	3	24	1,000	100	1.0	1.0
U /	N/A	N/A	45.66	103	1	98	0	1	18.0	N/A	N/A	N/A	2	5,000,000	0	0.0	0.0
U /	N/A	N/A	45.34	106	1	98	0	1	18.0	N/A	N/A	N/A	N/A	2,500	100	0.0	0.0
B- / 7.7	10.2	1.19	11.34	37	1	98	0	1	133.0	70.9	-6.4	45	5	1,000	100	5.8	1.0
B- / 7.7	10.2	1.19	11.44	19	1	98	0	1	133.0	71.9	-6.2	48	5	1,000,000	0	Front	Back
B- / 7.7	10.1	1.18	10.95	4	1	98	0	1	133.0	66.7	-6.4	37	5	1,000	100	0.0	5.0
B- / 7.7	10.1	1.18	10.95	1	1	98	0	1	133.0	66.7	-6.4	37	5	1,000	100	0.0	1.0
C / 5.4	10.7	1.23	23.91	413	2	97	0	1	50.0	56.2	-10.7	16	N/A	2,500	100	0.0	0.0
C+ / 6.6	7.3	0.91	10.92	26	6	76	17	1	42.0	57.8	-7.2	57	N/A	2,500	100	0.0	0.0
B+ / 9.9	3.7	0.43	9.94	14	10	37	52	1	42.0	29.9	-2.3	56	N/A	2,500	100	0.0	0.0
B+ / 9.6	5.5	1.09	10.58	36	8	56	34	2	38.0	43.5	-4.9	58	N/A	2,500	100	0.0	0.0
C+ / 6.2	7.8	0.59	22.00	82	1	98	0	1	94.0	112.1	-8.9	98	N/A	1,000,000	0	0.0	0.0
C+ / 6.2	7.8	0.59	22.05	135	1	98	0	1	94.0	112.8	-8.9	98	N/A	5,000,000	0	0.0	0.0
B / 8.9	7.8	0.59	21.98	601	1	98	0	1	94.0	111.8	-8.9	98	5	2,500	100	0.0	0.0
C / 4.5	13.7	1.34	6.61	111	1	98	0	1	143.0	109.9	-10.1	81	N/A	1,000	100	5.8	1.0
C / 4.4	13.6	1.33	6.31	8	1	98	0	1	143.0	N/A	N/A	76	N/A	1,000	100	0.0	5.0
C / 4.4	13.7	1.35	6.30	2	1	98	0	1	143.0	N/A	N/A	74	N/A	1,000	100	0.0	1.0
U /	N/A	N/A	6.60	40	1	98	0	1	143.0	N/A	N/A	N/A	N/A	2,500	100	0.0	0.0
B / 8.4	4.2	0.85	21.32	554	9	32	58	1	91.0	34.7	-5.0	56	12	1,000,000	0	0.0	0.0
U /	N/A	N/A	46.22	172	10	89	0	1	18.0	N/A	N/A	N/A	N/A	1,000,000	0	0.0	0.0
B- / 7.7	10.1	1.19	45.02	55	10	89	0	1	18.0	92.2	-10.0	74	15	1,000	100	0.0	0.0

						PERFORMANCE						
	99 Pct = Best			Overall Weiss Investment Rating		Perfor-mance Rating/Pts	Total Return % through 6/30/06					Incl. in Returns	
	0 Pct = Worst									Annualized		Dividend	Expense
Fund Type	Fund Name	Ticker Symbol	Phone				3 Mo	6 Mo	1Yr / Pct	3Yr / Pct	5Yr / Pct	Yield	Ratio
GR	Wells Fargo Avtg Oppty Inv	SOPFX	C	(800) 222-8222		C+ / 6.0	-2.80	2.03	8.74 /38	15.04 /59	4.30 /49	0.00	1.35
AA	Wells Fargo Avtg Otlk 2010 A	STNRX	D+	(800) 222-8222		E+ / 0.7	-0.69	1.79	4.92 /15	6.49 / 8	3.27 /39	1.71	1.25
AA	Wells Fargo Avtg Otlk 2010 Adm	WFLGX	C	(800) 222-8222		D / 1.6	-0.54	1.92	5.29 /17	6.82 /10	3.59 /42	2.10	0.95
AA	Wells Fargo Avtg Otlk 2010 B	SPTBX	C-	(800) 222-8222		E+ / 0.6	-0.88	1.41	4.11 /11	5.68 / 6	2.61 /33	1.04	2.00
AA	Wells Fargo Avtg Otlk 2010 C	WFOCX	C-	(800) 222-8222		E+ / 0.9	-0.79	1.40	4.23 /12	5.72 / 6	2.61 /33	1.03	2.00
AA	Wells Fargo Avtg Otlk 2020 A	STTRX	C-	(800) 222-8222		D / 1.7	-0.88	2.78	7.67 /30	8.68 /19	3.09 /38	1.38	1.25
AA	Wells Fargo Avtg Otlk 2020 Adm	WFLPX	C	(800) 222-8222		D+ / 2.9	-0.80	2.90	7.99 /33	9.02 /21	3.40 /40	1.75	0.95
AA	Wells Fargo Avtg Otlk 2020 B	STPBX	C-	(800) 222-8222		D- / 1.5	-1.00	2.43	6.91 /26	7.88 /14	2.43 /32	0.72	2.00
AA	Wells Fargo Avtg Otlk 2020 C	WFLAX	C	(800) 222-8222		D / 2.0	-0.99	2.41	6.87 /25	7.90 /15	2.42 /31	0.73	2.00
AA	Wells Fargo Avtg Otlk 2020 I	WFOBX	U	(800) 222-8222		U /	-0.68	3.07	8.27 /35	--	--	1.94	0.75
AA	Wells Fargo Avtg Otlk 2030 A	STHRX	C	(800) 222-8222		D+ / 2.4	-1.44	2.83	8.73 /38	10.17 /29	3.07 /38	1.09	1.25
AA	Wells Fargo Avtg Otlk 2030 Adm	WFLIX	C+	(800) 222-8222		C- / 3.8	-1.36	3.03	9.06 /40	10.52 /31	3.40 /40	1.44	0.95
AA	Wells Fargo Avtg Otlk 2030 B	SGPBX	C-	(800) 222-8222		D / 2.2	-1.65	2.44	7.90 /32	9.33 /23	2.40 /31	0.43	2.00
AA	Wells Fargo Avtg Otlk 2030 C	WFDMX	C	(800) 222-8222		D+ / 2.9	-1.65	2.42	7.90 /32	9.34 /23	2.41 /31	0.44	2.00
AA	Wells Fargo Avtg Otlk 2030 I	WFOOX	C+	(800) 222-8222		C- / 3.9	-1.31	3.12	9.35 /42	10.67 /33	3.48 /41	1.63	0.75
AA	Wells Fargo Avtg Otlk 2040 A	STFRX	C	(800) 222-8222		C- / 3.6	-1.56	3.70	10.78 /52	11.87 /42	3.07 /38	0.90	1.25
AA	Wells Fargo Avtg Otlk 2040 Adm	WFLWX	B-	(800) 222-8222		C / 4.9	-1.50	3.81	11.12 /54	12.21 /44	3.37 /40	1.25	0.95
AA	Wells Fargo Avtg Otlk 2040 B	SLPBX	C	(800) 222-8222		C- / 3.3	-1.79	3.33	9.90 /46	11.03 /36	2.39 /31	0.23	2.00
AA	Wells Fargo Avtg Otlk 2040 C	WFOFX	C+	(800) 222-8222		C- / 4.0	-1.74	3.33	9.92 /46	11.02 /36	2.39 /31	0.24	2.00
AA	Wells Fargo Avtg Otlk 2040 I	WFOSX	B	(800) 222-8222		C / 5.1	-1.43	3.97	11.32 /56	12.39 /45	3.47 /41	1.43	0.75
AA	Wells Fargo Avtg Otlk Today A	STWRX	D+	(800) 222-8222		E / 0.3	-0.45	1.30	3.53 / 9	4.73 / 3	3.63 /42	1.97	1.25
AA	Wells Fargo Avtg Otlk Today Adm	WFLOX	C-	(800) 222-8222		E+ / 0.8	-0.27	1.42	3.88 /10	5.07 / 4	3.93 /45	2.35	0.95
AA	Wells Fargo Avtg Otlk Today B	WFOKX	D+	(800) 222-8222		E- / 0.2	-0.63	0.89	2.65 / 6	3.93 / 2	2.93 /36	1.26	2.00
AA	Wells Fargo Avtg Otlk Today C	WFODX	C-	(800) 222-8222		E / 0.4	-0.63	0.89	2.66 / 6	3.94 / 2	2.94 /36	1.27	2.00
GL	Wells Fargo Avtg Overseas Inv	SOVRX	C+	(800) 222-8222		B / 7.9	-0.62	7.45	18.21 /79	18.64 /75	5.98 /61	1.35	1.46
SC	● Wells Fargo Avtg Sm Co Gr Adm	NVSCX	D+	(800) 222-8222		C+ / 6.0	-10.27	2.83	13.56 /67	15.09 /59	3.73 /43	0.00	1.20
SC	● Wells Fargo Avtg Sm Co Val A	SCVAX	B+	(800) 222-8222		B / 7.6	-4.71	4.84	10.49 /50	21.42 /84	13.50 /89	0.04	1.45
SC	● Wells Fargo Avtg Sm Co Val Adm	SCVIX	A-	(800) 222-8222		B / 8.2	-4.67	4.94	10.78 /52	21.71 /84	13.75 /90	0.20	1.20
SC	● Wells Fargo Avtg Sm Co Val B	SCVBX	B	(800) 222-8222		B- / 7.4	-4.82	4.45	9.63 /44	20.49 /81	12.64 /88	0.00	2.20
SC	● Wells Fargo Avtg Sm Co Val C	SCVFX	B+	(800) 222-8222		B / 7.7	-4.88	4.38	9.63 /44	20.47 /81	12.63 /88	0.00	2.20
SC	Wells Fargo Avtg Sm Cp Discp Adm	WFSDX	C+	(800) 222-8222		B+ / 8.5	-3.94	10.59	12.45 /62	22.29 /86	--	0.00	1.24
SC	Wells Fargo Avtg Sm Cp Discp I	WFSSX	B-	(800) 222-8222		B+ / 8.5	-3.93	10.71	12.57 /62	22.36 /86	--	0.00	1.00
SC	Wells Fargo Avtg Sm Cp Discp Inv	SCOVX	C+	(800) 222-8222		B+ / 8.4	-4.06	10.37	11.95 /59	22.08 /85	--	0.00	1.61
SC	Wells Fargo Avtg Sm Cp Gr A	MNSCX	D	(800) 222-8222		B- / 7.1	-4.37	11.91	22.77 /85	17.76 /71	4.43 /50	0.00	1.40
SC	Wells Fargo Avtg Sm Cp Gr Adm	WMNIX	C	(800) 222-8222		B / 7.8	-4.28	12.02	22.94 /86	17.93 /72	4.54 /51	0.00	1.20
SC	Wells Fargo Avtg Sm Cp Gr B	WMNBX	C-	(800) 222-8222		C+ / 6.9	-4.55	11.48	21.78 /84	16.84 /67	--	0.00	2.15
SC	Wells Fargo Avtg Sm Cp Gr C	WMNCX	C	(800) 222-8222		B- / 7.3	-4.47	11.46	21.86 /84	16.90 /68	--	0.00	2.15
SC	Wells Fargo Avtg Sm Cp Gr I	WFSIX	U	(800) 222-8222		U /	-4.26	12.16	23.28 /86	--	--	0.00	0.90
SC	● Wells Fargo Avtg Sm Cp Gr Z	WFSZX	U	(800) 222-8222		U /	-4.38	11.75	22.51 /85	--	--	0.00	1.57
SC	● Wells Fargo Avtg Sm Cp Opp Adm	NVSOX	C+	(800) 222-8222		B+ / 8.5	-3.10	10.20	17.10 /77	21.65 /84	11.30 /85	0.00	1.20
SC	● Wells Fargo Avtg Sm Cp Val A	SMVAX	B	(800) 222-8222		B+ / 8.7	-1.23	7.37	22.71 /85	24.32 /90	14.54 /91	0.00	1.44
SC	● Wells Fargo Avtg Sm Cp Val B	SMVBX	C+	(800) 222-8222		B+ / 8.6	-1.45	6.94	21.74 /84	23.37 /88	13.66 /90	0.00	2.19
SC	● Wells Fargo Avtg Sm Cp Val C	SMVCX	B	(800) 222-8222		B+ / 8.9	-1.45	6.96	21.76 /84	23.38 /88	13.67 /90	0.00	2.19
★ SC	● Wells Fargo Avtg Sm Cp Val Z	SSMVX	B-	(800) 222-8222		A- / 9.1	-1.25	7.36	22.76 /85	24.48 /90	14.68 /91	0.00	1.36
SC	Wells Fargo Avtg Sm/MdCp Vl Adm	WWMDX	C+	(800) 222-8222		A- / 9.0	-3.19	7.07	21.75 /84	24.40 /90	--	0.00	1.15
SC	Wells Fargo Avtg Sm/MdCp Vl Inv	SMMVX	C+	(800) 222-8222		A- / 9.0	-3.27	6.82	21.33 /83	24.19 /90	--	0.00	1.62
FS	● Wells Fargo Avtg Spc Fin Svc A	SIFEX	E	(800) 222-8222		D / 2.1	-1.25	2.24	11.10 /54	9.76 /26	4.36 /49	1.05	1.35
FS	Wells Fargo Avtg Spc Fin Svc B	SIFBX	E	(800) 222-8222		D / 1.9	-1.46	1.84	9.94 /47	8.90 /20	3.52 /42	0.35	2.10
FS	Wells Fargo Avtg Spc Fin Svc C	SIFCX	E	(800) 222-8222		D+ / 2.5	-1.46	1.87	10.35 /49	8.91 /20	3.52 /42	0.40	2.10
HL	Wells Fargo Avtg Spc Hlth Sci A	WFHAX	E+	(800) 222-8222		E- / 0.1	-7.27	-4.63	0.36 / 2	4.27 / 3	0.24 /17	0.00	1.65
HL	Wells Fargo Avtg Spc Hlth Sci B	WFHBX	E+	(800) 222-8222		E- / 0.1	-7.47	-5.08	-0.49 / 1	3.47 / 2	-0.54 /13	0.00	2.40
HL	Wells Fargo Avtg Spc Hlth Sci C	WFHCX	E+	(800) 222-8222		E- / 0.1	-7.55	-5.07	-0.49 / 1	3.46 / 2	-0.52 /13	0.00	2.40

● Denotes fund is closed to new investors
★ Denotes fund is included in Section II

RISK			NET ASSETS		ASSET				Portfolio Turnover Ratio	BULL / BEAR		FUND MANAGER		MINIMUMS		LOADS	
Risk Rating/Pts	3 Year		NAV As of 6/30/06	Total $(Mil)	Cash %	Stocks %	Bonds %	Other %		Last Bull Market Return	Last Bear Market Return	Manager Quality Pct	Manager Tenure (Years)	Initial Purch. $	Additional Purch. $	Front End Load	Back End Load
	Standard Deviation	Beta															
C+ / 6.0	10.1	1.19	45.78	1,831	10	89	0	1	18.0	92.9	-10.0	75	N/A	2,500	100	0.0	0.0
B+ / 9.5	4.1	0.86	12.79	73	0	45	53	2	38.0	34.2	-4.6	52	N/A	1,000	100	5.8	1.0
B+ / 9.9	4.0	0.85	12.89	86	0	45	53	2	38.0	35.4	-4.6	57	N/A	1,000,000	0	0.0	0.0
B+ / 9.9	4.1	0.85	12.82	18	0	45	53	2	38.0	31.1	-4.8	43	N/A	1,000	100	0.0	5.0
B+ / 9.9	4.1	0.85	12.94	5	0	45	53	2	38.0	31.1	-4.8	43	N/A	1,000	100	0.0	1.0
B+ / 9.2	5.4	1.12	14.17	150	0	63	35	2	30.0	46.2	-6.5	62	N/A	1,000	100	5.8	1.0
B+ / 9.5	5.3	1.10	14.32	154	0	63	35	2	30.0	47.5	-6.4	66	N/A	1,000,000	0	0.0	0.0
B+ / 9.5	5.4	1.11	14.07	19	0	63	35	2	30.0	42.8	-6.6	53	N/A	1,000	100	0.0	5.0
B+ / 9.5	5.4	1.11	14.18	4	0	63	35	2	30.0	43.0	-6.7	53	N/A	1,000	100	0.0	1.0
U /	N/A	N/A	14.34	50	0	63	35	2	30.0	N/A	N/A	N/A	N/A	5,000,000	0	0.0	0.0
B+ / 9.0	6.4	1.31	14.93	108	0	77	21	2	24.0	56.2	-7.5	66	N/A	1,000	100	5.8	1.0
B+ / 9.0	6.4	1.31	15.06	88	0	77	21	2	24.0	57.7	-7.4	69	N/A	1,000,000	0	0.0	0.0
B+ / 9.0	6.4	1.31	14.69	12	0	77	21	2	24.0	52.6	-7.5	57	N/A	1,000	100	0.0	5.0
B+ / 9.0	6.4	1.31	14.72	3	0	77	21	2	24.0	52.6	-7.6	57	N/A	1,000	100	0.0	1.0
B+ / 9.3	6.4	1.31	15.06	28	0	77	21	2	24.0	58.3	-7.4	70	N/A	5,000,000	0	0.0	0.0
B / 8.7	7.4	1.49	16.62	157	0	88	10	2	11.0	66.6	-8.5	72	N/A	1,000	100	5.8	1.0
B / 8.7	7.4	1.50	16.83	65	0	88	10	2	11.0	68.3	-8.5	75	N/A	1,000,000	0	0.0	0.0
B / 8.6	7.4	1.49	16.04	18	0	88	10	2	11.0	62.8	-8.6	64	N/A	1,000	100	0.0	5.0
B / 8.6	7.4	1.49	16.02	3	0	88	10	2	11.0	62.7	-8.6	64	N/A	1,000	100	0.0	1.0
B+ / 9.0	7.4	1.49	16.83	16	0	88	10	2	11.0	69.0	-8.5	77	N/A	5,000,000	0	0.0	0.0
B+ / 9.6	3.3	0.66	10.18	37	0	35	63	2	36.0	24.6	-2.8	44	N/A	1,000	100	5.8	1.0
B+ / 9.9	3.3	0.66	10.35	15	0	35	63	2	36.0	25.7	-2.6	47	N/A	2,000,000	0	0.0	0.0
B+ / 9.9	3.3	0.66	10.39	14	0	35	63	2	36.0	21.8	-2.9	36	N/A	1,000	100	0.0	5.0
B+ / 9.9	3.3	0.66	10.36	9	0	35	63	2	36.0	21.7	-2.8	36	N/A	1,000	100	0.0	1.0
C / 5.5	10.0	0.96	11.25	62	2	97	0	1	111.0	99.4	-6.1	19	N/A	2,500	100	0.0	0.0
C- / 3.9	16.1	1.05	30.57	537	2	97	0	1	142.0	110.1	-7.9	20	2	1,000,000	0	0.0	0.0
B- / 7.2	12.7	0.84	15.59	90	4	95	0	1	70.0	133.5	-11.9	93	N/A	1,000	100	5.8	1.0
B- / 7.2	12.7	0.84	15.72	265	4	95	0	1	70.0	135.4	-11.7	93	N/A	1,000,000	0	0.0	0.0
B- / 7.0	12.7	0.84	15.01	15	4	95	0	1	70.0	128.1	-12.0	90	N/A	1,000	100	0.0	5.0
B- / 7.0	12.7	0.84	15.00	5	4	95	0	1	70.0	128.0	-12.0	90	N/A	1,000	100	0.0	1.0
C / 5.1	12.9	0.73	17.33	3	3	96	0	1	56.0	157.5	-9.2	97	1	1,000,000	0	0.0	0.0
C / 5.1	12.9	0.73	17.36	57	3	96	0	1	56.0	158.0	-9.2	97	4	5,000,000	0	0.0	0.0
C / 5.1	12.9	0.73	17.24	278	3	96	0	1	56.0	156.6	-9.2	97	4	2,500	100	0.0	0.0
D / 2.2	16.6	1.03	13.34	108	0	99	0	1	10.0	121.4	-10.1	40	3	1,000	100	5.8	1.0
C / 4.3	16.7	1.04	13.42	55	0	99	0	1	10.0	122.7	-10.1	41	3	1,000,000	0	0.0	0.0
C- / 4.2	16.7	1.04	13.01	21	0	99	0	1	10.0	N/A	N/A	33	3	1,000	100	0.0	5.0
C- / 4.2	16.7	1.03	13.03	6	0	99	0	1	10.0	N/A	N/A	33	3	1,000	100	0.0	1.0
U /	N/A	N/A	13.47	50	0	99	0	1	10.0	N/A	N/A	N/A	N/A	5,000,000	0	0.0	0.0
U /	N/A	N/A	13.31	38	0	99	0	1	10.0	N/A	N/A	N/A	13	2,500	100	0.0	0.0
C / 4.6	11.7	0.78	36.20	764	10	89	0	1	7.0	122.9	-9.9	95	3	2,000,000	0	0.0	0.0
C+ / 5.7	15.2	0.90	32.07	670	10	89	0	1	40.2	137.8	-5.5	96	9	1,000	100	5.8	1.0
C / 4.8	15.2	0.90	30.49	135	10	89	0	1	40.2	132.0	-5.7	94	9	1,000	100	0.0	5.0
C+ / 5.7	15.2	0.90	30.57	149	10	89	0	1	40.2	132.2	-5.7	94	9	1,000	100	0.0	1.0
C / 4.8	15.2	0.90	32.39	2,499	10	89	0	1	40.2	138.8	-5.4	96	N/A	2,500	100	0.0	0.0
C / 4.3	16.3	0.98	16.06	71	4	95	0	1	80.0	149.4	-4.2	93	N/A	1,000,000	0	0.0	0.0
C / 4.3	16.3	0.98	15.98	124	4	95	0	1	80.0	148.2	-4.2	93	N/A	2,500	100	0.0	0.0
C- / 3.6	8.4	0.88	3.85	341	0	99	0	1	49.0	63.8	-7.6	31	N/A	1,000	100	5.8	1.0
C- / 3.6	8.4	0.89	3.84	4	0	99	0	1	49.0	59.8	-7.8	25	N/A	1,000	100	0.0	5.0
C- / 3.6	8.5	0.89	3.82	1	0	99	0	1	49.0	59.9	-7.9	25	N/A	1,000	100	0.0	1.0
B- / 7.3	8.7	0.56	10.72	9	5	94	0	1	200.0	44.8	-2.1	27	N/A	1,000	100	5.8	1.0
B- / 7.2	8.7	0.56	10.28	12	5	94	0	1	200.0	41.5	-2.3	22	N/A	1,000	100	0.0	5.0
B- / 7.2	8.7	0.56	10.29	1	5	94	0	1	200.0	41.4	-2.3	22	N/A	1,000	100	0.0	1.0

							PERFORMANCE							
99 Pct = Best									Total Return % through 6/30/06				Incl. in Returns	
0 Pct = Worst				Overall Weiss Investment Rating		Perfor-mance Rating/Pts					Annualized		Dividend	Expense
Fund Type	Fund Name	Ticker Symbol			Phone			3 Mo	6 Mo	1Yr / Pct	3Yr / Pct	5Yr / Pct	Yield	Ratio
TC	Wells Fargo Avtg Spc Tech A	WFSTX	E		(800) 222-8222	C- / 3.6		-12.56	-6.62	8.32 /35	14.32 /56	2.50 /32	0.00	1.75
TC	Wells Fargo Avtg Spc Tech B	WFTBX	E		(800) 222-8222	C- / 3.3		-12.75	-7.07	7.52 /29	13.43 /51	1.73 /25	0.00	2.50
TC	Wells Fargo Avtg Spc Tech C	WFTCX	E		(800) 222-8222	C- / 4.0		-12.77	-7.09	7.54 /29	13.47 /51	1.69 /25	0.00	2.50
TC	● Wells Fargo Avtg Spc Tech Z	WFTZX	U		(800) 222-8222	U /		-12.59	-6.80	8.10 /33	--	--	0.00	1.90
GR	Wells Fargo Avtg US Val A	WFUAX	D+		(800) 222-8222	C- / 3.6		0.67	4.59	7.35 /28	12.07 /43	2.21 /29	0.95	1.25
GR	Wells Fargo Avtg US Val Adm	SEQKX	C		(800) 222-8222	C / 5.2		0.75	4.80	7.70 /30	12.78 /47	4.82 /53	1.31	0.96
GR	● Wells Fargo Avtg US Val Z	SEQIX	C-		(800) 222-8222	C / 4.9		0.70	4.58	7.28 /28	12.35 /45	4.28 /49	0.68	1.32
GR	● Wells Fargo Avtg Value Fund A	CBTTX	C		(800) 222-8222	C- / 3.3		0.32	5.77	7.62 /30	11.41 /39	7.91 /71	0.57	1.20
GR	Wells Fargo Avtg Value Fund Adm	CBTIX	C		(800) 222-8222	A+ / 9.9		0.42	5.90	7.92 /32	44.80 /99	26.36 /99	0.80	0.95
GR	Wells Fargo Avtg Value Fund D	CBTAX	C+		(800) 222-8222	C / 4.3		0.32	5.73	7.62 /30	11.33 /38	7.87 /71	0.58	1.20
AA	Wells Fargo Avtg VT Ast Allc		C-		(800) 222-8222	D+ / 2.3		-1.73	0.61	4.66 /14	8.60 /18	3.82 /44	2.20	1.00
IN	Wells Fargo Avtg VT CB Lg Cp Val		C-		(800) 222-8222	C / 4.5		0.23	5.61	7.53 /29	11.48 /39	1.79 /25	0.83	1.00
GR	Wells Fargo Avtg VT Dscvry		C		(800) 222-8222	B- / 7.5		-3.96	6.49	16.21 /75	18.04 /73	9.20 /77	0.00	1.15
IN	Wells Fargo Avtg VT Eqty Inc		C-		(800) 222-8222	C- / 4.2		0.14	2.84	7.40 /29	11.24 /37	3.72 /43	1.48	1.00
FO	Wells Fargo Avtg VT Intl Core		C+		(800) 222-8222	B- / 7.3		-0.64	7.85	19.44 /81	16.88 /68	4.26 /48	1.71	1.00
GI	Wells Fargo Avtg VT Lg Co Core		E		(800) 222-8222	E+ / 0.7		-3.77	-2.21	1.72 / 4	5.67 / 6	-2.73 / 6	0.59	1.00
GL	Wells Fargo Avtg VT Lg Co Gwth		E		(800) 222-8222	E / 0.3		-8.21	-6.94	2.16 / 5	4.70 / 3	-2.43 / 7	0.18	1.00
GR	Wells Fargo Avtg VT Multi Cp Val		C+		(800) 222-8222	B+ / 8.5		-2.89	8.05	23.31 /86	22.03 /85	9.12 /77	0.00	1.14
GR	Wells Fargo Avtg VT Opp		C		(800) 222-8222	C+ / 6.0		-2.96	1.57	8.90 /39	15.18 /60	4.57 /51	0.00	1.07
SC	Wells Fargo Avtg VT Sm Cp Gwth		C		(800) 222-8222	B / 7.8		-4.30	11.99	22.89 /86	18.10 /73	1.88 /26	0.00	1.20
AA	Wells Fargo Avtg Wlth Bld Cons Allc	WBCAX	U		(800) 222-8222	U /		-1.05	0.41	2.24 / 5	--	--	2.18	1.50
GI	Wells Fargo Avtg Wlth Bld Eqty	WBGIX	C		(800) 222-8222	C / 5.0		-3.66	2.54	11.40 /56	13.13 /50	2.25 /30	0.00	1.50
AA	Wells Fargo Avtg Wlth Bld Gr Allc	WBGGX	U		(800) 222-8222	U /		-3.03	2.42	10.38 /49	--	--	0.24	1.50
AA	Wells Fargo Avtg Wlth Bld Gr Bal	WBGBX	C		(800) 222-8222	C- / 3.5		-2.60	2.66	9.23 /42	10.48 /31	3.45 /41	1.05	1.50
AA	Wells Fargo Avtg Wlth Bld Mod Bal	WBBBX	U		(800) 222-8222	U /		-1.65	1.34	5.40 /17	--	--	1.37	1.50
AA	Wells Fargo Avtg Wlth Bld Tact Eqty	WBGAX	B		(800) 222-8222	B- / 7.2		-2.36	4.93	16.58 /76	17.40 /70	4.21 /48	0.00	1.50
RE	Wells S&P REIT Index A	WSPAX	B-		(800) 282-1581	B+ / 8.8		-1.96	12.55	17.36 /78	24.08 /90	17.85 /94	3.47	0.99
RE	Wells S&P REIT Index B	WSPBX	C+		(800) 282-1581	B+ / 8.5		-2.18	12.10	16.47 /76	23.14 /88	16.98 /94	2.86	1.74
RE	Wells S&P REIT Index C	WSPCX	B-		(800) 282-1581	B+ / 8.8		-2.11	12.15	16.54 /76	23.16 /88	16.98 /94	2.87	1.74
BA	WesMark Balanced Fund	WMBLX	D+		(800) 341-7400	D- / 1.0		-1.53	2.54	6.89 /26	5.44 / 5	0.09 /16	1.40	1.12
GR	WesMark Growth Fund	WMKGX	D		(800) 341-7400	D+ / 2.5		-3.26	1.42	8.30 /35	8.61 /19	0.94 /20	0.08	1.28
SC	WesMark Small Company Growth	WMKSX	D+		(800) 341-7400	C+ / 6.6		-7.57	4.33	15.14 /72	15.89 /63	0.96 /20	0.00	1.52
GI	Westcore Blue Chip Fund	WTMVX	C		(800) 392-2673	C / 4.5		-3.76	0.85	8.02 /33	12.82 /48	2.81 /35	0.48	1.15
GI	Westcore Growth and Income	WTEIX	D+		(800) 392-2673	C- / 3.2		-6.37	-1.81	7.44 /29	11.21 /37	1.24 /22	0.02	1.13
EM	Westcore International Frontier	WTIFX	A		(800) 392-2673	B / 8.2		-3.47	7.04	19.74 /82	20.75 /82	9.56 /79	0.22	1.50
MC	Westcore Mid-Cap Value	WTMCX	A		(800) 392-2673	B / 7.7		-2.47	1.94	11.57 /57	20.36 /81	8.78 /75	0.21	1.25
AG	Westcore MIDCO Growth	WTMGX	D		(800) 392-2673	C- / 3.3		-6.22	2.30	11.68 /58	11.48 /39	5.84 /60	0.00	1.11
GR	Westcore Select Fund	WTSLX	C+		(800) 392-2673	C+ / 6.1		-4.36	6.27	16.30 /75	15.41 /61	2.50 /32	0.00	1.15
SC	Westcore Small-Cap Opportunity	WTSCX	C+		(800) 392-2673	B / 7.7		-4.18	6.60	15.60 /74	19.61 /78	10.12 /81	0.00	1.30
SC	Westcore Small-Cap Value Fund	WTSVX	U		(800) 392-2673	U /		0.00	10.14	13.36 /66	--	--	0.97	1.30
MC	Westport Fund I	WPFIX	B-		(888) 593-7878	C+ / 6.7		-3.03	3.72	8.28 /35	16.74 /67	8.01 /72	0.00	1.41
MC	Westport Fund R	WPFRX	B-		(888) 593-7878	C+ / 6.7		-3.07	3.66	8.25 /35	16.70 /67	8.08 /72	0.00	1.49
SC	● Westport Select Cap I	WPSCX	C		(888) 593-7878	C / 5.0		-3.65	2.16	4.64 /13	13.55 /52	6.90 /66	0.00	1.09
SC	● Westport Select Cap R	WPSRX	C		(888) 593-7878	C / 4.8		-3.71	2.03	4.35 /12	13.27 /50	6.65 /65	0.00	1.33
EM	William Blair Emrg Mkts Gr I	WBEIX	U		(800) 742-7272	U /		-6.29	5.99	47.44 /99	--	--	0.07	1.40
EM	William Blair Emrg Mkts Gr inst	BIEMX	U		(800) 742-7272	U /		-6.28	6.13	47.45 /99	--	--	0.00	1.25
EM	William Blair Emrg Mkts Gr N	WBENX	U		(800) 742-7272	U /		-6.43	5.86	47.05 /99	--	--	0.07	1.55
FO	William Blair Inst Intl SmallCap Gr	WIISX	U		(800) 742-7272	U /		-4.71	8.78	--	--	--	0.00	1.25
FO	William Blair Instl Int Eqty Fd	WIIEX	U		(800) 742-7272	U /		-3.45	4.65	23.52 /87	--	--	0.16	1.10
FO	William Blair Instl Intl Gr	WBIIX	B		(800) 742-7272	A- / 9.1		-3.66	6.02	28.00 /93	25.25 /91	--	0.71	1.05
FO	William Blair Intl Equity I	WIEIX	U		(800) 742-7272	U /		-3.56	4.79	20.53 /83	--	--	0.00	1.23
FO	William Blair Intl Equity N	WIENX	U		(800) 742-7272	U /		-3.65	4.67	20.18 /82	--	--	0.00	1.48

● Denotes fund is closed to new investors
* Denotes fund is included in Section II

RISK			NET ASSETS		ASSET					BULL / BEAR		FUND MANAGER		MINIMUMS		LOADS	
	3 Year		NAV						Portfolio	Last Bull	Last Bear	Manager	Manager	Initial	Additional	Front	Back
Risk	Standard		As of	Total	Cash	Stocks	Bonds	Other	Turnover	Market	Market	Quality	Tenure	Purch.	Purch.	End	End
Rating/Pts	Deviation	Beta	6/30/06	$(Mil)	%	%	%	%	Ratio	Return	Return	Pct	(Years)	$	$	Load	Load
D+ / 2.3	19.0	1.74	5.08	106	5	94	0	1	270.0	135.0	-14.6	23	6	1,000	100	5.8	1.0
D+ / 2.3	18.9	1.73	4.86	24	5	94	0	1	270.0	128.9	-14.5	19	6	1,000	100	0.0	5.0
D+ / 2.3	19.0	1.75	4.85	5	5	94	0	1	270.0	128.5	-14.5	18	6	1,000	100	0.0	1.0
U /	N/A	N/A	5.07	80	5	94	0	1	270.0	N/A	N/A	N/A	6	2,500	100	0.0	0.0
C+ / 6.4	7.4	0.91	16.85	3	5	94	0	1	42.3	69.7	-11.2	73	N/A	1,000	100	5.8	1.0
C+ / 6.5	7.2	0.89	16.70	243	5	94	0	1	42.3	73.0	-10.7	79	N/A	1,000,000	0	0.0	0.0
C+ / 6.5	7.2	0.89	17.04	40	5	94	0	1	42.3	70.7	-11.0	76	N/A	2,500	100	0.0	0.0
B / 8.7	8.0	0.97	19.06	4	2	97	0	1	18.0	70.2	-12.6	61	N/A	1,000	100	5.8	1.0
D / 1.7	44.0	-0.82	19.04	2	2	97	0	1	18.0	279.8	-11.9	99	N/A	1,000,000	0	0.0	1.0
B / 8.8	8.0	0.97	19.01	18	2	97	0	1	18.0	69.8	-12.6	61	N/A	2,500	100	0.0	1.0
B / 8.4	6.2	1.32	12.98	286	7	55	36	2	1.0	49.1	-7.7	48	N/A	2,000	100	0.0	0.0
C+ / 6.5	7.2	0.87	9.82	29	4	95	0	1	106.0	64.9	-10.3	71	8	2,000	100	0.0	0.0
C / 4.3	16.0	1.69	15.27	247	2	97	0	1	144.0	103.7	-8.0	59	N/A	2,500	100	0.0	0.0
C+ / 6.4	7.0	0.86	17.31	103	0	99	0	1	23.0	64.9	-10.5	69	10	2,000	100	0.0	0.0
C / 5.4	10.1	0.97	9.34	42	1	98	0	1	53.0	92.0	-11.1	10	N/A	2,000	100	0.0	0.0
C / 5.5	9.3	1.10	13.28	24	1	98	0	1	112.0	37.9	-7.4	10	N/A	1,000	100	0.0	0.0
C / 5.1	10.9	0.56	8.72	111	2	97	0	1	11.0	43.3	-12.0	3	7	2,000	100	0.0	0.0
C- / 4.2	16.3	1.59	14.76	24	0	99	0	1	112.0	127.0	-6.5	92	N/A	2,500	100	0.0	0.0
C+ / 6.1	10.0	1.17	24.60	923	15	84	0	1	41.0	94.5	-10.1	78	N/A	2,500	100	0.0	0.0
C- / 4.1	16.5	1.03	9.34	177	0	99	0	1	128.0	119.3	-12.3	44	N/A	2,000	100	0.0	0.0
U /	N/A	N/A	10.25	41	1	24	74	1	93.0	N/A	N/A	N/A	2	1,000	100	1.5	0.0
B- / 7.4	9.6	1.20	12.90	157	0	99	0	1	52.0	78.7	-11.4	57	9	1,000	100	1.5	0.0
U /	N/A	N/A	11.85	71	0	94	4	2	60.0	N/A	N/A	N/A	2	1,000	100	1.5	0.0
B / 8.2	7.7	1.45	12.37	455	0	64	35	1	74.0	59.5	-9.0	61	9	1,000	100	1.5	0.0
U /	N/A	N/A	10.87	75	0	49	49	2	79.0	N/A	N/A	N/A	2	1,000	100	1.5	0.0
B- / 7.3	9.6	1.77	15.33	279	0	99	0	1	57.0	98.4	-11.5	93	9	1,000	100	1.5	0.0
C / 4.9	16.5	0.99	12.90	229	0	99	0	1	15.0	115.1	-0.7	57	8	2,500	0	4.0	0.0
C / 4.9	16.6	0.99	13.12	61	0	99	0	1	15.0	109.9	-0.9	46	N/A	2,500	0	0.0	5.0
C / 4.9	16.5	0.99	13.07	79	0	99	0	1	15.0	110.1	-0.9	47	N/A	2,500	0	0.0	1.0
B+ / 9.0	5.4	1.06	9.37	53	7	59	30	4	76.0	34.4	-6.0	31	8	1,000	100	0.0	0.0
C+ / 6.9	9.3	1.15	13.37	260	6	93	0	1	76.0	57.6	-9.0	21	9	1,000	100	0.0	0.0
C- / 3.4	16.3	1.02	8.67	35	12	87	0	1	84.0	100.7	-11.3	27	6	1,000	100	0.0	0.0
B- / 7.8	8.3	1.02	13.05	64	3	96	0	1	46.7	72.6	-9.9	71	N/A	2,500	100	0.0	2.0
C+ / 6.7	10.6	1.27	12.50	255	0	99	0	1	98.9	67.5	-9.5	31	N/A	2,500	100	0.0	2.0
B- / 7.5	12.4	0.50	13.08	36	3	96	0	1	33.0	145.5	-8.2	81	7	2,500	100	0.0	2.0
B / 8.0	10.5	0.88	18.94	71	4	95	0	1	49.2	112.6	-8.6	88	N/A	2,500	100	0.0	2.0
C / 5.4	12.9	1.45	7.99	194	1	98	0	1	118.8	80.9	-5.8	22	1	2,500	100	0.0	2.0
B- / 7.0	12.4	1.26	14.91	10	5	94	0	1	127.2	84.1	-11.5	73	4	2,500	100	0.0	2.0
C / 5.4	15.0	0.98	36.18	21	2	97	0	1	79.2	117.1	-11.0	69	N/A	2,500	100	0.0	2.0
U /	N/A	N/A	11.40	38	3	96	0	1	21.1	N/A	N/A	N/A	N/A	2,500	100	0.0	2.0
B- / 7.5	9.8	0.79	19.50	12	0	98	0	2	45.1	96.1	-10.1	75	5	250,000	0	0.0	0.0
B- / 7.4	9.8	0.80	19.56	39	0	98	0	2	45.1	96.0	-10.1	74	8	2,500	0	0.0	0.0
C+ / 6.7	9.4	0.60	25.05	743	4	95	0	1	2.0	78.0	-8.4	72	8	250,000	0	0.0	0.0
C+ / 6.7	9.4	0.60	24.65	432	4	95	0	1	2.0	76.6	-8.5	70	8	5,000	0	0.0	0.0
U /	N/A	N/A	15.04	59	5	94	0	1	131.2	N/A	N/A	N/A	1	5,000	1,000	0.0	1.0
U /	N/A	N/A	15.07	340	5	94	0	1	131.2	N/A	N/A	N/A	1	5,000,000	0	0.0	0.0
U /	N/A	N/A	15.00	37	5	94	0	1	131.2	N/A	N/A	N/A	1	5,000	1,000	0.0	1.0
U /	N/A	N/A	12.14	47	5	94	0	1	N/A	N/A	N/A	N/A	1	5,000,000	0	0.0	0.0
U /	N/A	N/A	12.60	342	4	95	0	1	127.0	N/A	N/A	N/A	N/A	5,000,000	0	0.0	0.0
C / 5.2	11.9	1.12	19.20	1,686	2	97	0	1	70.0	147.7	-8.6	35	4	5,000,000	0	0.0	0.0
U /	N/A	N/A	13.56	209	6	93	0	1	75.1	N/A	N/A	N/A	2	5,000	1,000	0.0	1.0
U /	N/A	N/A	13.46	35	6	93	0	1	75.1	N/A	N/A	N/A	2	5,000	1,000	0.0	2.0

Fund Type	Fund Name	Ticker Symbol	Overall Weiss Investment Rating	Phone	Performance Rating/Pts	3 Mo	6 Mo	1Yr / Pct	3Yr / Pct	5Yr / Pct	Dividend Yield	Expense Ratio
GR	William Blair Mutual-Growth I	BGFIX	C	(800) 742-7272	C- / 3.7	-4.29	2.52	13.48 /66	11.19 /37	1.61 /24	0.00	0.90
GR	William Blair Mutual-Growth N	WBGSX	C-	(800) 742-7272	C- / 3.5	-4.37	2.38	13.21 /65	10.88 /34	1.34 /22	0.00	1.15
FO	● William Blair Mutual-Intl Grwth I	BIGIX	A+	(800) 742-7272	A- / 9.0	-3.49	6.03	27.31 /92	25.34 /91	11.93 /86	0.57	1.17
★ FO	● William Blair Mutual-Intl Grwth N	WBIGX	B+	(800) 742-7272	B+ / 8.9	-3.57	5.91	26.95 /91	25.01 /91	11.65 /86	0.40	1.17
SC	● William Blair Mutual-Small Cap Gr I	WBSIX	B	(800) 742-7272	B / 8.0	-5.43	5.96	12.04 /60	21.11 /83	14.43 /91	0.00	1.24
SC	● William Blair Mutual-Small Cap Gr N	WBSNX	C+	(800) 742-7272	B / 8.0	-5.49	5.85	11.75 /58	20.82 /82	13.95 /90	0.00	1.46
SC	● William Blair Mutual-Val Discvry I	BVDIX	B-	(800) 742-7272	C+ / 6.6	-2.61	8.73	14.72 /71	15.47 /61	9.16 /77	0.00	1.09
SC	William Blair Mutual-Val Discvry N	WBVDX	D-	(800) 742-7272	C+ / 6.5	-2.70	8.56	14.43 /70	15.25 /60	8.92 /76	0.00	1.39
MC	William Blair Small-Mid Cap Gr I	WSMDX	U	(800) 742-7272	U /	-6.09	5.14	17.17 /77	--	--	0.00	1.20
GR	Wilmington Large Cap Core Inst	WLRIX	C-	(800) 336-9970	D+ / 2.5	-4.30	0.73	6.41 /23	9.38 /23	-0.34 /14	1.52	0.80
MC	Wilmington Mlti Mgr Mid Cap Inst	WMMIX	U	(800) 336-9970	U /	-5.35	2.38	9.93 /46	--	--	0.01	1.15
SC	Wilmington Mlti Mgr Sm Cap Inst	WMSIX	U	(800) 336-9970	U /	-6.39	5.34	9.83 /46	--	--	0.00	1.25
GI	Wilmington Multi Mgr Lg Cap Inst	WMLIX	U	(800) 336-9970	U /	-1.65	2.00	6.47 /23	--	--	0.64	1.00
RE	Wilmington Real Estate Inst	WREIX	U	(800) 336-9970	U /	-3.42	9.90	16.48 /76	--	--	1.90	1.17
GR	Wilshire 5000 Index Inst	WINDX	C+	(888) 200-6796	C / 4.7	-2.06	2.92	9.14 /41	12.08 /43	3.35 /40	0.92	0.54
GR	Wilshire 5000 Index Inv	WFIVX	C+	(888) 200-6796	C / 4.5	-2.16	2.74	8.84 /39	11.78 /41	3.03 /37	0.63	0.82
GR	Wilshire Large Co Growth Inst	WLCGX	D+	(888) 200-6796	D+ / 2.7	-4.77	-1.14	9.12 /41	9.20 /22	1.94 /27	0.00	1.01
GR	Wilshire Large Co Growth Inv	DTLGX	D+	(888) 200-6796	D+ / 2.4	-4.84	-1.33	8.72 /38	8.81 /20	1.60 /24	0.00	1.38
GR	Wilshire Large Co Val Inst	WLCVX	C+	(888) 200-6796	C+ / 6.2	-0.76	4.81	12.24 /61	14.54 /57	5.91 /61	0.84	1.20
GR	Wilshire Large Co Val Inv	DTLVX	C+	(888) 200-6796	C+ / 6.0	-0.81	4.63	11.95 /59	14.20 /55	5.62 /59	0.57	1.49
SC	Wilshire Small Co Growth Inst	WSMGX	D+	(888) 200-6796	C+ / 6.2	-6.79	4.23	9.72 /45	15.70 /62	8.06 /72	0.00	1.19
SC	Wilshire Small Co Growth Inv	DTSGX	D+	(888) 200-6796	C+ / 6.1	-6.89	4.15	9.43 /43	15.34 /60	7.80 /71	0.00	1.50
SC	Wilshire Small Co Val Inst	WSMVX	D+	(888) 200-6796	B+ / 8.4	-2.30	11.10	16.82 /77	21.06 /83	14.26 /91	0.00	1.16
SC	Wilshire Small Co Val Inv	DTSVX	D+	(888) 200-6796	B+ / 8.3	-2.37	10.94	16.51 /76	20.68 /82	13.93 /90	0.00	1.48
GR	Winslow Green Growth Fund	WGGFX	D	(888) 314-9049	B / 7.6	-9.20	8.63	21.56 /84	19.66 /78	8.19 /72	0.00	1.45
GR	Wireless Fund (The)	WIREX	E	(800) 590-0898	C+ / 6.0	-6.68	7.45	26.63 /91	12.49 /46	-7.47 / 1	0.00	1.95
GI	Wisdom Fund B	WSDBX	D	(877) 352-0020	E+ / 0.8	-1.87	-0.25	0.92 / 2	5.83 / 6	3.94 /45	0.68	1.75
GI	Wisdom Fund C	WSDCX	D	(877) 352-0020	E+ / 0.8	-1.86	-0.25	0.87 / 2	5.81 / 6	3.95 /45	0.62	1.75
GI	Wisdom Fund Inst	WSDIX	D	(877) 352-0020	D- / 1.3	-1.63	0.24	1.92 / 4	6.89 /10	5.00 /54	0.58	1.23
GI	Wisdom Fund Inv	WSDVX	D-	(877) 352-0020	E+ / 0.6	-1.73	0.16	1.65 / 4	6.62 / 9	4.73 /52	0.59	1.48
★ AA	WM Balanced Portfolio A	SABPX	C-	(800) 222-5852	D / 1.6	-1.98	1.32	5.91 /20	8.89 /20	4.63 /51	1.92	1.35
AA	WM Balanced Portfolio B	SBBPX	C-	(800) 222-5852	D- / 1.3	-2.18	0.86	5.03 /15	8.05 /15	3.82 /44	1.27	2.13
AA	WM Balanced Portfolio C	SCBPX	C-	(800) 222-5852	D / 1.9	-2.17	0.90	5.04 /15	8.08 /16	--	1.33	2.11
BA	WM Conservative Balanced A	SAIPX	D+	(800) 222-5852	E+ / 0.6	-1.21	1.08	4.07 /11	6.53 / 9	4.84 /53	2.66	1.30
BA	WM Conservative Balanced B	SBIPX	C-	(800) 222-5852	E / 0.5	-1.31	0.68	3.28 / 8	5.73 / 6	4.04 /46	2.04	2.08
BA	WM Conservative Balanced C	SCIPX	C-	(800) 222-5852	E+ / 0.8	-1.40	0.61	3.23 / 8	5.70 / 6	--	2.09	2.06
AA	WM Conservative Gr Portfolio A	SAGPX	C-	(800) 222-5852	D+ / 2.7	-2.60	1.65	7.62 /30	11.02 /36	4.05 /46	0.84	1.39
AA	WM Conservative Gr Portfolio B	SBGPX	C-	(800) 222-5852	D+ / 2.4	-2.75	1.29	6.75 /25	10.17 /29	3.24 /39	0.79	2.17
AA	WM Conservative Gr Portfolio C	SCGPX	C	(800) 222-5852	C- / 3.1	-2.83	1.23	6.74 /25	10.18 /29	--	0.81	2.15
IN	WM Equity Income A	CMPBX	B+	(800) 222-5852	C+ / 6.1	0.03	5.42	10.81 /52	16.49 /66	9.40 /78	1.47	0.90
IN	WM Equity Income B	CMBBX	B+	(800) 222-5852	C+ / 5.8	-0.18	4.96	9.80 /46	15.48 /61	8.43 /74	0.76	1.78
IN	WM Equity Income C	CMPCX	B+	(800) 222-5852	C+ / 6.4	-0.15	5.02	9.95 /47	15.59 /62	--	0.93	1.68
AA	WM Flexible Inc Portfolio A	SAUPX	D+	(800) 222-5852	E / 0.3	-0.62	0.57	2.13 / 5	4.59 / 3	4.65 /51	3.42	1.26
AA	WM Flexible Inc Portfolio B	SBUPX	E	(800) 222-5852	E- / 0.2	-0.82	0.17	1.41 / 3	3.77 / 2	3.86 /44	2.77	2.03
AA	WM Flexible Inc Portfolio C	SCUPX	D+	(800) 222-5852	E / 0.4	-0.90	0.10	1.37 / 3	3.78 / 2	--	2.82	2.02
GI	WM Growth & Income Fd A	CMPFX	D+	(800) 222-5852	D- / 1.1	-2.20	0.16	3.03 / 7	8.19 /16	1.05 /20	1.14	0.89
GI	WM Growth & Income Fd B	CMFBX	D	(800) 222-5852	E+ / 0.8	-2.48	-0.37	1.95 / 4	7.09 /11	0.03 /15	0.12	1.92
GI	WM Growth & Income Fd C	CMGCX	D+	(800) 222-5852	D- / 1.2	-2.40	-0.29	2.21 / 5	7.20 /11	--	0.47	1.88
GR	WM Growth Fd A	SRGFX	D-	(800) 222-5852	E+ / 0.8	-5.96	-4.13	3.88 /10	8.00 /15	-4.18 / 3	0.00	1.36
GR	WM Growth Fd B	SQGRX	D-	(800) 222-5852	E+ / 0.6	-6.21	-4.55	2.93 / 7	7.00 /10	-5.04 / 2	0.00	2.31
GR	WM Growth Fd C	SGWCX	D-	(800) 222-5852	D- / 1.0	-6.15	-4.51	3.05 / 7	7.22 /11	--	0.00	2.08
FO	WM International Gr A	SRIGX	B	(800) 222-5852	B / 7.7	-1.78	4.74	26.05 /90	20.05 /79	7.71 /70	1.24	1.39

● Denotes fund is closed to new investors
★ Denotes fund is included in Section II

www.WeissRatings.com

Risk Rating/Pts	Standard Deviation	Beta	NAV As of 6/30/06	Total $(Mil)	Cash %	Stocks %	Bonds %	Other %	Portfolio Turnover Ratio	Last Bull Market Return	Last Bear Market Return	Manager Quality Pct	Manager Tenure (Years)	Initial Purch. $	Additional Purch. $	Front End Load	Back End Load
B- / 7.8	9.2	1.06	11.81	199	1	98	0	1	61.5	69.3	-11.5	50	5	5,000	1,000	0.0	1.0
B- / 7.1	9.2	1.05	11.60	45	1	98	0	1	61.5	68.0	-11.6	46	5	5,000	1,000	0.0	1.0
B- / 7.4	11.9	1.12	27.09	1,643	4	95	0	1	69.8	146.9	-7.2	36	10	5,000	1,000	0.0	2.0
C+ / 6.1	11.9	1.12	26.71	3,728	4	95	0	1	69.8	144.9	-8.5	34	10	5,000	1,000	0.0	2.0
C+ / 6.5	15.0	0.97	25.60	483	2	97	0	1	104.6	155.5	-9.2	81	7	5,000	1,000	0.0	1.0
C / 4.8	15.0	0.97	25.15	668	2	97	0	1	104.6	153.5	-9.3	79	7	5,000	1,000	0.0	1.0
B- / 7.1	14.0	0.90	16.44	40	3	96	0	1	133.8	95.7	-10.0	40	7	5,000	1,000	0.0	1.0
D / 1.7	14.0	0.90	16.23	9	3	96	0	1	133.8	94.6	-10.1	38	10	5,000	1,000	0.0	1.0
U /	N/A	N/A	13.10	68	2	98	0	0	69.5	N/A	N/A	N/A	N/A	500,000	0	0.0	1.0
B / 8.2	8.8	1.05	16.36	52	0	99	0	1	113.0	57.9	-8.4	33	N/A	500,000	0	0.0	1.0
U /	N/A	N/A	12.91	50	2	97	0	1	32.0	N/A	N/A	N/A	N/A	500,000	0	0.0	1.0
U /	N/A	N/A	14.20	55	0	98	0	2	44.0	N/A	N/A	N/A	N/A	500,000	0	0.0	1.0
U /	N/A	N/A	12.33	128	1	98	0	1	42.0	N/A	N/A	N/A	3	500,000	0	0.0	1.0
U /	N/A	N/A	15.06	279	5	94	0	1	75.0	N/A	N/A	N/A	3	500,000	0	0.0	1.0
B / 8.2	8.2	1.06	10.91	24	0	99	0	1	46.0	70.5	-9.7	59	N/A	250,000	100,000	0.0	0.0
B / 8.2	8.2	1.06	10.88	127	0	99	0	1	46.0	68.7	-9.6	57	7	2,500	100	0.0	0.0
B- / 7.2	9.5	1.14	34.57	206	0	99	0	1	58.0	57.5	-9.7	26	10	250,000	100,000	0.0	0.0
B- / 7.2	9.5	1.14	34.03	381	0	99	0	1	58.0	55.8	-9.8	23	14	2,500	100	0.0	0.0
B- / 7.1	7.8	0.97	22.21	8	1	98	0	1	43.0	79.7	-7.2	86	10	250,000	100,000	0.0	0.0
B- / 7.1	7.8	0.97	22.15	59	1	98	0	1	43.0	78.2	-7.2	84	14	2,500	100	0.0	0.0
C- / 4.1	15.6	1.05	17.99	N/A	1	98	0	1	71.0	102.3	-11.2	24	10	250,000	100,000	0.0	0.0
C- / 4.0	15.6	1.05	17.58	14	1	98	0	1	71.0	100.5	-11.2	21	14	2,500	100	0.0	0.0
D- / 1.5	13.5	0.90	19.51	1	1	98	0	1	68.0	120.6	-7.9	88	10	250,000	100,000	0.0	0.0
D- / 1.5	13.5	0.89	19.37	18	1	98	0	1	68.0	118.5	-8.0	86	14	2,500	100	0.0	0.0
D- / 1.3	22.9	1.98	19.14	279	0	100	0	0	103.0	196.2	-14.2	45	5	5,000	250	0.0	2.0
E- / 0.1	26.5	2.46	4.47	7	5	94	0	1	56.2	114.5	-18.4	1	6	5,000	100	0.0	0.0
B / 8.0	5.9	0.69	12.05	13	5	94	0	1	42.0	35.3	-7.0	30	7	2,500	250	0.0	0.0
B / 8.0	5.8	0.68	12.11	8	5	94	0	1	42.0	35.3	-6.9	31	7	2,500	250	0.0	0.0
B / 8.3	5.9	0.69	12.64	4	5	94	0	1	42.0	39.7	-6.8	38	7	25,000	250	0.0	0.0
B / 8.0	5.8	0.69	12.51	10	5	94	0	1	42.0	38.6	-6.8	36	7	2,500	250	5.8	0.0
B+ / 9.4	5.4	1.12	13.71	2,312	0	66	32	2	6.0	47.2	-3.6	64	6	1,000	100	5.5	1.0
B+ / 9.4	5.4	1.13	13.68	1,406	0	66	32	2	6.0	43.8	-3.8	54	6	1,000	100	0.0	5.0
B+ / 9.4	5.4	1.12	13.61	849	0	66	32	2	6.0	43.7	-3.7	55	4	1,000	100	0.0	1.0
B+ / 9.7	4.0	0.81	10.62	309	2	44	52	2	7.0	33.2	-1.0	56	6	1,000	100	5.5	1.0
B+ / 9.9	4.0	0.81	10.61	167	2	44	52	2	7.0	29.9	-1.1	46	6	1,000	100	0.0	5.0
B+ / 9.9	4.0	0.81	10.56	167	2	44	52	2	7.0	30.0	-1.1	46	4	1,000	100	0.0	1.0
B / 8.4	7.0	1.41	15.38	1,754	2	84	12	2	8.0	61.6	-5.9	69	6	1,000	100	5.5	1.0
B / 8.3	6.9	1.40	14.88	1,077	2	84	12	2	8.0	57.7	-6.1	61	6	1,000	100	0.0	5.0
B / 8.3	7.0	1.41	14.77	864	2	84	12	2	8.0	57.8	-6.1	61	4	1,000	100	0.0	1.0
B+ / 9.0	7.0	0.86	20.91	1,316	4	94	0	2	56.0	88.9	-6.8	95	1	1,000	100	5.5	1.0
B+ / 9.0	7.1	0.86	20.77	293	4	94	0	2	56.0	83.7	-7.1	93	1	1,000	100	0.0	5.0
B+ / 9.0	7.0	0.86	20.61	215	4	94	0	2	56.0	84.2	-6.9	94	1	1,000	100	0.0	1.0
B+ / 9.9	3.1	0.57	11.13	412	2	24	70	4	11.0	22.8	0.6	47	6	1,000	100	4.5	1.0
C+ / 6.1	3.2	0.58	11.12	334	2	24	70	4	11.0	19.9	0.4	38	6	1,000	100	0.0	5.0
B+ / 9.9	3.1	0.57	11.06	156	2	24	70	4	11.0	20.0	0.5	38	4	1,000	100	0.0	1.0
B / 8.7	7.0	0.84	25.29	556	2	98	0	0	29.0	54.4	-8.0	38	7	1,000	100	5.5	1.0
B / 8.7	7.0	0.84	24.37	67	2	98	0	0	29.0	49.5	-8.3	30	7	1,000	100	0.0	5.0
B / 8.7	7.0	0.84	24.01	2	2	98	0	0	29.0	49.9	-8.3	31	4	1,000	100	0.0	1.0
B- / 7.6	9.1	1.11	15.78	133	2	96	0	2	46.0	53.6	-10.6	20	4	1,000	100	5.5	1.0
B- / 7.5	9.1	1.11	14.04	81	2	96	0	2	46.0	49.2	-10.9	15	4	1,000	100	0.0	5.0
B- / 7.5	9.0	1.10	14.18	3	2	96	0	2	46.0	50.4	-10.8	16	4	1,000	100	0.0	1.0
C+ / 6.6	10.6	1.00	12.16	106	2	98	0	0	64.0	109.2	-10.9	22	N/A	1,000	100	5.5	1.0

Fund Type	Fund Name	Ticker Symbol	Overall Weiss Investment Rating	Phone	PERFORMANCE Perfor-mance Rating/Pts	Total Return % through 6/30/06 3 Mo	6 Mo	1Yr / Pct	Annualized 3Yr / Pct	5Yr / Pct	Incl. in Returns Dividend Yield	Expense Ratio
FO	WM International Gr B	SQIGX	B-	(800) 222-5852	B- / 7.4	-2.11	4.22	24.66 /88	18.68 /75	6.56 /65	0.56	2.51
FO	WM International Gr C	SIGCX	B	(800) 222-5852	B / 7.8	-1.97	4.38	24.98 /88	18.94 /76	--	1.12	2.29
MC	WM Mid Cap Stock A	WMCAX	B	(800) 222-5852	C+ / 6.3	-2.33	5.74	13.87 /68	16.61 /66	8.90 /76	1.18	1.12
MC	WM Mid Cap Stock B	WMCBX	B-	(800) 222-5852	C+ / 5.9	-2.56	5.19	12.78 /63	15.47 /61	7.59 /70	0.52	2.11
MC	WM Mid Cap Stock C	WMCCX	B	(800) 222-5852	C+ / 6.4	-2.56	5.26	12.92 /64	15.54 /61	--	0.91	1.99
RE	WM REIT Fund A	WMRAX	B	(800) 222-5852	B+ / 8.7	-2.17	11.32	16.19 /75	24.54 /90	--	2.00	1.31
RE	WM REIT Fund B	WMRBX	B	(800) 222-5852	B+ / 8.5	-2.32	10.73	15.06 /72	23.51 /88	--	1.20	2.09
RE	WM REIT Fund C	WMRCX	B	(800) 222-5852	B+ / 8.8	-2.31	10.77	15.18 /72	23.63 /89	--	1.29	2.00
SC	WM Small Cap Growth Fund A	SREMX	E	(800) 222-5852	C- / 3.1	-9.84	1.53	9.80 /46	11.75 /41	-5.55 / 2	0.00	1.51
SC	WM Small Cap Growth Fund B	SQEMX	E-	(800) 222-5852	D+ / 2.4	-10.13	0.96	8.62 /38	10.53 /31	-6.58 / 1	0.00	2.65
SC	WM Small Cap Growth Fund C	SSKCX	E	(800) 222-5852	C- / 3.4	-10.04	1.18	8.93 /40	10.87 /34	--	0.00	2.33
AA	WM Strategic Gr Portfolio A	SACAX	C	(800) 222-5852	C- / 3.7	-2.98	1.87	8.70 /38	12.61 /46	3.27 /39	0.50	1.43
AA	WM Strategic Gr Portfolio B	SBCAX	C	(800) 222-5852	C- / 3.4	-3.13	1.52	7.97 /33	11.73 /41	2.49 /32	0.44	2.20
AA	WM Strategic Gr Portfolio C	SWHCX	C	(800) 222-5852	C- / 4.1	-3.19	1.45	7.88 /32	11.77 /41	--	0.44	2.18
GR	WM West Coast Equity Fd A	CMNWX	C+	(800) 222-5852	C+ / 5.7	-3.27	3.44	13.38 /66	15.66 /62	4.20 /48	0.29	0.91
GR	WM West Coast Equity Fd B	CMNBX	C+	(800) 222-5852	C / 5.3	-3.48	2.96	12.34 /61	14.58 /57	3.20 /39	0.00	1.85
GR	WM West Coast Equity Fd C	CMNCX	C+	(800) 222-5852	C+ / 5.9	-3.47	3.03	12.43 /62	14.67 /57	--	0.00	1.78
GR	WP Stewart & Co Growth Fund	WPSGX	D-	(212) 750-8585	D+ / 2.5	-4.64	-3.70	6.71 /24	9.49 /24	3.06 /37	0.70	1.88
GI	WPG Large Cap Growth	WPGLX	E-	(888) 261-4073	E / 0.3	-2.83	0.83	-2.27 / 1	4.68 / 3	-2.63 / 6	0.00	1.40
FO	Wright Intl Blue Chip Eq Fd	WIBCX	A	(800) 232-0013	A- / 9.2	1.42	11.72	30.77 /95	23.96 /89	10.71 /83	0.75	1.62
GI	Wright Major Blue Chip Eq Fd	WQCEX	C-	(800) 232-0013	C- / 4.1	-2.47	1.65	9.53 /44	11.05 /36	1.16 /21	0.58	1.25
GI	Wright Selected Blue Chip Eq Fd	WSBEX	C-	(800) 232-0013	C+ / 6.3	-2.17	1.92	7.37 /28	16.09 /64	5.73 /59	0.00	1.25
GI	Yacktman Focused Fund	YAFFX	D	(800) 525-8258	D+ / 2.5	-0.38	4.08	3.68 / 9	9.28 /23	14.51 /91	1.39	1.25
GI	Yacktman Fund	YACKX	C-	(800) 525-8258	D+ / 2.8	-0.26	3.82	3.82 /10	9.82 /26	13.47 /89	1.82	1.20

RISK			NET ASSETS		ASSET					BULL / BEAR		FUND MANAGER		MINIMUMS		LOADS	
	3 Year		NAV						Portfolio	Last Bull	Last Bear	Manager	Manager	Initial	Additional	Front	Back
Risk	Standard		As of	Total	Cash	Stocks	Bonds	Other	Turnover	Market	Market	Quality	Tenure	Purch.	Purch.	End	End
Rating/Pts	Deviation	Beta	6/30/06	$(Mil)	%	%	%	%	Ratio	Return	Return	Pct	(Years)	$	$	Load	Load
C+ / 6.6	10.6	1.00	11.60	11	2	98	0	0	64.0	102.0	-11.2	14	N/A	1,000	100	0.0	5.0
C+ / 6.6	10.6	1.00	11.44	5	2	98	0	0	64.0	103.3	-11.0	16	N/A	1,000	100	0.0	1.0
B / 8.0	9.0	0.78	19.70	190	4	94	0	2	27.0	84.0	-4.6	75	4	1,000	100	5.5	1.0
B / 8.0	9.0	0.78	18.63	29	4	94	0	2	27.0	78.3	-4.9	66	4	1,000	100	0.0	5.0
B / 8.0	9.0	0.78	18.62	8	4	94	0	2	27.0	78.8	-4.8	67	4	1,000	100	0.0	1.0
C / 5.5	16.0	0.96	19.14	26	4	94	0	2	26.0	115.5	N/A	68	3	1,000	100	5.5	1.0
C+ / 5.6	15.9	0.96	19.09	11	4	94	0	2	26.0	110.1	N/A	59	4	1,000	100	0.0	5.0
C / 5.5	16.0	0.96	19.09	6	4	94	0	2	26.0	110.8	N/A	60	3	1,000	100	0.0	1.0
D+ / 2.3	19.9	1.28	14.57	108	4	96	0	0	140.0	99.1	-14.3	2	8	1,000	100	5.5	0.0
D / 2.2	19.9	1.28	12.60	9	4	96	0	0	140.0	92.2	-14.5	1	8	1,000	100	0.0	5.0
D / 2.2	19.9	1.28	12.81	1	4	96	0	0	140.0	94.2	-14.4	1	4	1,000	100	0.0	0.0
B / 8.3	8.0	1.59	16.92	1,019	0	95	4	1	11.0	72.8	-8.0	74	6	1,000	100	5.5	1.0
B / 8.2	8.0	1.59	16.08	698	0	95	4	1	11.0	68.7	-8.2	66	6	1,000	100	0.0	5.0
B / 8.2	8.0	1.59	16.11	513	0	95	4	1	11.0	68.9	-8.1	66	4	1,000	100	0.0	1.0
B- / 7.7	10.8	1.31	41.16	849	2	96	0	2	12.0	89.6	-8.6	71	4	1,000	100	5.5	1.0
B- / 7.6	10.8	1.31	36.56	183	2	96	0	2	12.0	84.0	-8.9	61	4	1,000	100	0.0	5.0
B- / 7.6	10.8	1.31	36.69	20	2	96	0	2	12.0	84.6	-8.8	62	4	1,000	100	0.0	1.0
C+ / 5.7	10.0	1.06	185.47	100	4	95	0	1	49.0	53.1	-8.6	33	N/A	50,000	0	0.0	0.0
C / 4.7	12.1	1.30	21.95	19	0	99	0	1	100.0	35.9	-11.6	3	2	100,000	100	0.0	2.0
C+ / 6.5	11.0	1.03	20.02	171	0	99	0	1	99.0	130.1	-8.2	43	17	1,000	0	0.0	2.0
C+ / 6.9	8.4	1.04	12.61	64	0	99	0	1	82.0	61.1	-9.4	50	7	1,000	0	0.0	0.0
C / 5.0	11.2	1.27	12.60	45	0	99	0	1	110.0	89.0	-8.3	78	23	1,000	0	0.0	0.0
C+ / 6.7	8.6	0.85	15.57	72	30	68	0	2	5.6	57.2	-5.7	50	9	2,500	100	0.0	2.0
B- / 7.7	7.9	0.80	15.23	364	28	69	1	2	8.6	59.6	-6.4	61	14	2,500	100	0.0	2.0

Data as of June 30, 2006

Section II

Analysis of Largest Stock Mutual Funds

A summary analysis of the 300 largest retail

Equity Mutual Funds

receiving a Weiss Investment Rating.

Funds are listed in alphabetical order.

Section II Contents

1. Fund Name The name of the mutual fund as stated in its prospectus, which can sometimes differ slightly from the name that the company uses for advertising. If you cannot find the paritcular mutual fund you are interested in, or if you have any doubts regarding the precise name, verify the information with your broker or on your account statement. Also, use the fund's ticker symbol for confirmation.

2. Ticker Symbol The unique alphabetic symbol used for identifying and trading a specific mutual fund. No two funds can have the same ticker symbol, and the ticker symbol for mutual funds always ends with an "X".

A handful of funds currently show no associated ticker symbol. This means that the fund is either small or new since the NASD only assigns a ticker symbol to funds with at least $25 million in assets or 1,000 shareholders.

3. Weiss Investment Rating Our overall rating is measured on a scale from A to E based on each fund's risk-adjusted performance. Please see page 10 for specific descriptions of each letter grade. Also refer to page 7 for information on how our ratings are derived. Most important, when using this rating, please be sure to consider the warnings beginning on page 11 regarding the ratings' limitations and the underlying assumptions.

4. Major Rating Factors A synopsis of the key ratios and sub-factors that have most influenced the rating of a particular mutual fund, including an examination of the fund's performance, risk, and managerial performance. There may be additional factors which have influenced the rating but do not appear due to space limitations.

5. Services Offered Services and/or benefits offered by the fund.

6. Address The address of the company managing the fund.

7. Phone The telephone number of the company managing the fund. Call this number to receive a prospectus or other information about the fund.

8. Fund Family The umbrella group of mutual funds to which the fund belongs. In many cases, investors may move their assets from one fund to another within the same family at little or no cost.

9. Fund Type   The mutual fund's peer category based on an analysis of its investment portfolio.

AG	Aggressive Growth	HL	Health
AA	Asset Allocation	IN	Income
BA	Balanced	IX	Index
CV	Convertible	MC	Mid Cap
EM	Emerging Market	OT	Other
EN	Energy/Natural Resources	PM	Precious Metals
FS	Financial Services	RE	Real Estate
FO	Foreign	SC	Small Cap
GL	Global	TC	Technology
GR	Growth	UT	Utilities
GI	Growth and Income		

A blank fund type means that the mutual fund has not yet been categorized.

How to Read the Historical Data Table

NAV:
The fund's share price as of the date indicated. A fund's NAV is computed by dividing the value of the fund's asset holdings, less accrued fees and expenses, by the number of its shares outstanding.

Risk Rating/Pts:
A letter grade rating based solely on the mutual fund's risk as determined by its monthly performance volatility over the trailing three years. Pts is a points rank where 0=worst and 10=best.

Data Date:
The quarter-end or year-end as of date used for evaluating the mutual fund.

Data Date	Weiss Investment Rating	Net Assets ($Mil)	NAV	Performance Rating/Pts	Total Return Y-T-D	Risk Rating/Pts
6-06	D	55	36.50	C- / 3.7	25.01%	C- / 4.1
2005	D+	66	35.69	C+ / 5.9	19.98%	D+ / 2.0
2004	C	823	14.46	C+ / 6.1	4.18%	C / 4.8
2003	B+	760	20.11	B / 7.8	-3.28%	B / 8.5
2002	B-	155	41.31	C+ / 6.4	-1.41%	C+ / 5.2
2001	C+	105	38.99	C+ / 6.3	20.69%	D+ / 2.9

Weiss Investment Rating:
Our overall opinion of the fund's risk-adjusted performance at the specified time period.

Net Assets $(Mil):
The total value of all of the fund's asset holdings (in millions) including stocks, bonds, cash, and other financial instruments, less accrued expenses and fees.

Performance Rating/Pts:
A letter grade rating based solely on the mutual fund's return to shareholders over the trailing three years, without any consideration for the amount of risk the fund poses. Pts is a points rank where 0=worst and 10=best.

Total Return Y-T-D:
The fund's total return to shareholders since the beginning of the calendar year specified.

AIM Basic Value A (GTVLX)   C-   Fair

Fund Family: AIM Investments   **Phone:** (800) 347-4246
Address: 11 Greenway Plaza, Houston, TX 77046
Fund Type: GR - Growth

Major Rating Factors: Middle of the road best describes AIM Basic Value A whose Weiss Investment Rating is currently a C- (Fair). The fund currently has a performance rating of C- (Fair) based on an average return of 11.72% over the last three years and 0.96% over the last six months. Factored into the performance evaluation is an expense ratio of 1.14% (low) and a 5.5% front-end load that is levied at the time of purchase.

The fund's risk rating is currently B (Good). It carries a beta of 1.10, meaning it is expected to move 11.0% for every 10% move in the market. Volatility, as measured by both the semi-deviation and a drawdown factor, is considered low.

Bret W. Stanley has been running the fund for 8 years and currently receives a manager quality ranking of 51 (0=worst, 99=best). If you desire an average level of risk, then this fund may be an option.

Services Offered: Automated phone transactions, check writing, bank draft capabilities, an IRA investment plan, a 401K investment plan, wire transfers and a systematic withdrawal plan.

Data Date	Weiss Investment Rating	Net Assets ($Mil)	NAV	Performance Rating/Pts	Total Return Y-T-D	Risk Rating/Pts
6-06	C-	3,354	34.55	C- / 3.1	0.96%	B / 8.1
2005	C-	3,742	34.22	C- / 3.9	5.55%	B- / 7.0
2004	D+	4,428	32.42	C- / 3.1	10.88%	C / 4.9
2003	B-	3,545	29.24	B- / 7.1	33.76%	C+ / 6.2
2002	B-	2,682	21.86	B- / 7.2	-23.14%	B- / 7.0
2001	B	1,864	28.44	A- / 9.2	0.13%	C- / 3.3

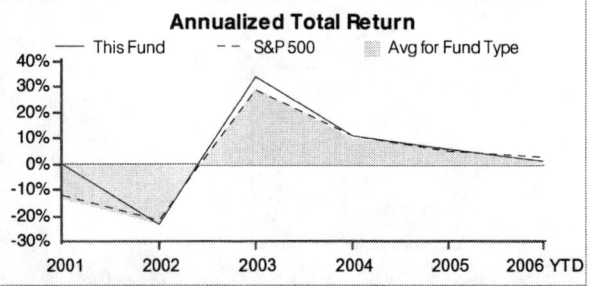

AIM Charter Fund A (CHTRX)   C   Fair

Fund Family: AIM Investments   **Phone:** (800) 347-4246
Address: 11 Greenway Plaza, Houston, TX 77046
Fund Type: GI - Growth and Income

Major Rating Factors: Disappointing performance is the major factor driving the C (Fair) Weiss Investment Rating for AIM Charter Fund A. The fund currently has a performance rating of D+ (Weak) based on an average return of 10.28% over the last three years and 3.75% over the last six months. Factored into the performance evaluation is an expense ratio of 1.20% (average) and a 5.5% front-end load that is levied at the time of purchase.

The fund's risk rating is currently B+ (Good). It carries a beta of 0.87, meaning the fund's expected move will be 8.7% for every 10% move in the market. Volatility, as measured by both the semi-deviation and a drawdown factor, is considered very low.

Ronald S. Sloan has been running the fund for 4 years and currently receives a manager quality ranking of 59 (0=worst, 99=best). This fund offers only a moderate level of risk but investors looking for strong performance are still waiting.

Services Offered: Automated phone transactions, check writing, bank draft capabilities, an IRA investment plan, a 401K investment plan, wire transfers and a systematic withdrawal plan.

Data Date	Weiss Investment Rating	Net Assets ($Mil)	NAV	Performance Rating/Pts	Total Return Y-T-D	Risk Rating/Pts
6-06	C	4,701	13.82	D+ / 2.9	3.75%	B+ / 9.0
2005	D+	1,664	13.32	D / 1.6	4.93%	B / 8.0
2004	C	1,871	12.81	C- / 3.0	8.67%	B- / 7.0
2003	C-	2,005	11.89	D / 1.8	23.99%	C+ / 5.7
2002	C-	2,162	9.61	C- / 3.0	-16.14%	C / 5.0
2001	E+	3,407	11.46	D- / 1.3	-23.09%	E- / 0.0

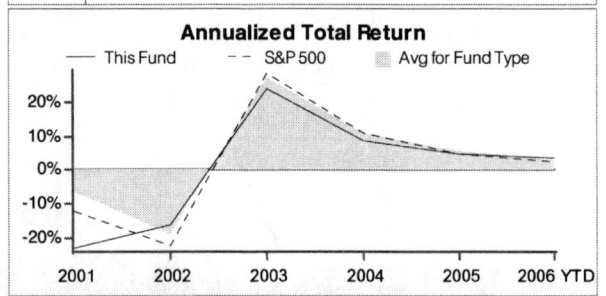

AIM Constellation Fund A (CSTGX)   D-   Weak

Fund Family: AIM Investments   **Phone:** (800) 347-4246
Address: 11 Greenway Plaza, Houston, TX 77046
Fund Type: GR - Growth

Major Rating Factors: Disappointing performance is the major factor driving the D- (Weak) Weiss Investment Rating for AIM Constellation Fund A. The fund currently has a performance rating of D (Weak) based on an average return of 9.96% over the last three years and -0.65% over the last six months. Factored into the performance evaluation is an expense ratio of 1.26% (average) and a 5.5% front-end load that is levied at the time of purchase.

The fund's risk rating is currently C+ (Fair). It carries a beta of 1.30, meaning it is expected to move 13.0% for every 10% move in the market. Volatility, as measured by both the semi-deviation and a drawdown factor, is considered low.

Lanny H. Sachnowitz has been running the fund for 1 year and currently receives a manager quality ranking of 21 (0=worst, 99=best). This fund offers only a moderate level of risk but investors looking for strong performance are still waiting.

Services Offered: Automated phone transactions, check writing, bank draft capabilities, an IRA investment plan, a 401K investment plan, wire transfers and a systematic withdrawal plan.

Data Date	Weiss Investment Rating	Net Assets ($Mil)	NAV	Performance Rating/Pts	Total Return Y-T-D	Risk Rating/Pts
6-06	D-	6,657	24.61	D / 1.7	-0.65%	C+ / 6.7
2005	C-	4,569	24.77	C- / 3.3	8.45%	B- / 7.0
2004	D	5,768	22.84	D- / 1.4	6.18%	C / 5.5
2003	D	6,854	21.51	D- / 1.5	29.34%	C / 4.6
2002	D	6,947	16.63	D / 2.0	-24.75%	C- / 3.4
2001	D-	10,584	22.10	D+ / 2.7	-23.61%	E- / 0.0

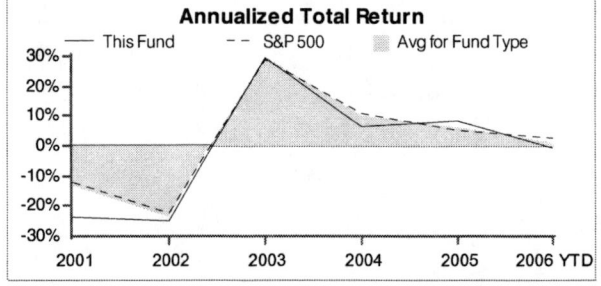

AllianceBernstein Gr & Inc A (CABDX)

D+   Weak

Fund Family: Alliance Bernstein   **Phone:** (800) 221-5672
Address: 1345 Avenue of the Americas, New York, NY 10105
Fund Type: GI - Growth and Income

Major Rating Factors: Disappointing performance is the major factor driving the D+ (Weak) Weiss Investment Rating for AllianceBernstein Gr & Inc A. The fund currently has a performance rating of D+ (Weak) based on an average return of 10.70% over the last three years and 1.30% over the last six months. Factored into the performance evaluation is an expense ratio of 1.06% (low), a 4.3% front-end load that is levied at the time of purchase and a 1.0% back-end load levied at the time of sale.

The fund's risk rating is currently B- (Good). It carries a beta of 0.91, meaning that its performance tracks fairly well with that of the overall stock market. Volatility, as measured by both the semi-deviation and a drawdown factor, is considered low.

Frank Caruso has been running the fund for 8 years and currently receives a manager quality ranking of 60 (0=worst, 99=best). This fund offers only a moderate level of risk but investors looking for strong performance are still waiting.

Services Offered: Automated phone transactions, bank draft capabilities, an IRA investment plan, a 401K investment plan, a Keogh investment plan and a systematic withdrawal plan.

Data Date	Weiss Investment Rating	Net Assets ($Mil)	NAV	Perfor- mance Rating/Pts	Total Return Y-T-D	Risk Rating/Pts
6-06	D+	2,345	3.89	D+ / 2.6	1.30%	B- / 7.7
2005	D+	2,556	3.84	C- / 3.3	3.78%	C+ / 6.8
2004	D+	3,045	3.74	C- / 3.3	11.92%	C / 4.3
2003	C	3,055	3.38	C / 5.1	31.76%	C / 5.2
2002	C+	2,501	2.60	C+ / 6.2	-26.56%	C+ / 6.5
2001	B-	3,287	3.59	B- / 7.5	-1.84%	C- / 3.7

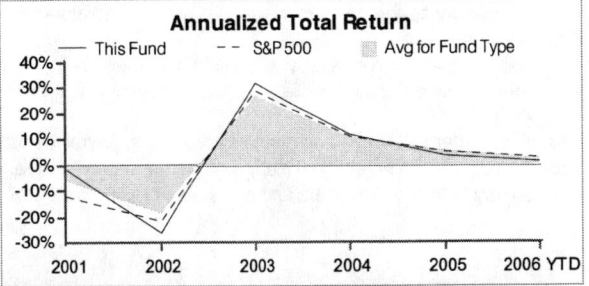
Annualized Total Return

AllianceBernstein Intl Value A (ABIAX)

A+   Excellent

Fund Family: Alliance Bernstein   **Phone:** (800) 221-5672
Address: 1345 Avenue of the Americas, New York, NY 10105
Fund Type: FO - Foreign

Major Rating Factors: Exceptional performance is the major factor driving the A+ (Excellent) Weiss Investment Rating for AllianceBernstein Intl Value A. The fund currently has a performance rating of A (Excellent) based on an average return of 27.12% over the last three years and 13.66% over the last six months. Factored into the performance evaluation is an expense ratio of 1.20% (average), a 4.3% front-end load that is levied at the time of purchase and a 1.0% back-end load levied at the time of sale.

The fund's risk rating is currently C+ (Fair). It carries a beta of 1.00, meaning that its performance tracks fairly well with that of the overall stock market. Volatility, as measured by both the semi-deviation and a drawdown factor, is considered low.

This fund has been team managed for 6 years and currently receives a manager quality ranking of 77 (0=worst, 99=best). If you desire only a moderate level of risk and strong performance, then this fund is an excellent option.

Services Offered: Automated phone transactions, bank draft capabilities, an IRA investment plan, a 401K investment plan, wire transfers and a systematic withdrawal plan.

Data Date	Weiss Investment Rating	Net Assets ($Mil)	NAV	Perfor- mance Rating/Pts	Total Return Y-T-D	Risk Rating/Pts
6-06	A+	2,107	20.30	A / 9.4	13.66%	C+ / 6.8
2005	A+	1,370	17.86	A- / 9.1	16.75%	B- / 7.2
2004	A-	521	16.36	A / 9.4	24.49%	C+ / 5.8
2003	U	180	13.58	U / --	42.50%	U / --
2002	U	74	9.53	U / --	-4.22%	U / --

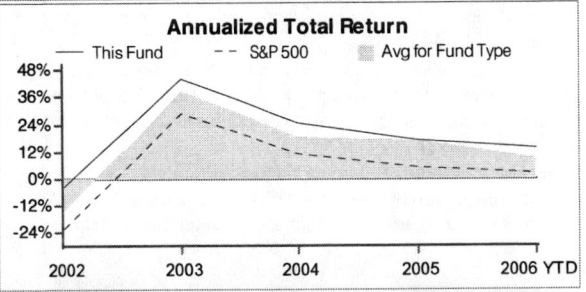
Annualized Total Return

American Century Equity Growth Inv (BEQGX)

C+   Fair

Fund Family: American Century Investments   **Phone:** (800) 345-6488
Address: 4500 Main Street, Kansas City, MO 64141
Fund Type: GR - Growth

Major Rating Factors: Middle of the road best describes American Century Equity Growth Inv whose Weiss Investment Rating is currently a C+ (Fair). The fund currently has a performance rating of C (Fair) based on an average return of 13.29% over the last three years and 2.95% over the last six months. Factored into the performance evaluation is an expense ratio of 0.67% (very low).

The fund's risk rating is currently B (Good). It carries a beta of 1.04, meaning that its performance tracks fairly well with that of the overall stock market. Volatility, as measured by both the semi-deviation and a drawdown factor, is considered low.

William Martin has been running the fund for 9 years and currently receives a manager quality ranking of 72 (0=worst, 99=best). If you desire an average level of risk, then this fund may be an option.

Services Offered: Automated phone transactions, payroll deductions, bank draft capabilities, an IRA investment plan, a 401K investment plan, a Keogh investment plan, wire transfers and a systematic withdrawal plan.

Data Date	Weiss Investment Rating	Net Assets ($Mil)	NAV	Perfor- mance Rating/Pts	Total Return Y-T-D	Risk Rating/Pts
6-06	C+	2,211	23.93	C / 5.3	2.95%	B / 8.3
2005	C+	1,926	23.37	C / 5.2	7.30%	B- / 7.4
2004	C+	1,484	22.08	C+ / 6.0	13.98%	C+ / 5.7
2003	C+	1,144	19.60	C / 5.2	30.27%	C+ / 6.1
2002	C	1,064	15.19	C / 4.7	-20.32%	C+ / 6.1
2001	C-	1,481	19.24	C- / 3.4	-11.14%	C- / 3.5

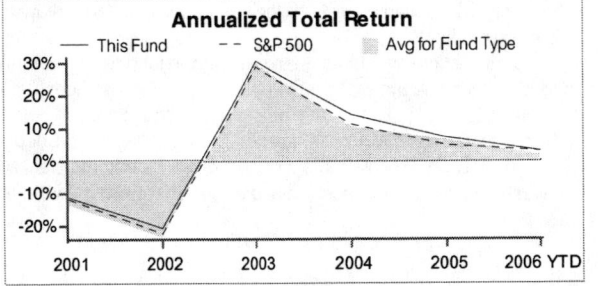
Annualized Total Return

American Century Equity Income Inv (TWEIX)   C+   Fair

Fund Family: American Century Investments   **Phone:** (800) 345-6488
Address: 4500 Main Street, Kansas City, MO 64141
Fund Type: IN - Income
Major Rating Factors: Middle of the road best describes American Century Equity Income Inv whose Weiss Investment Rating is currently a C+ (Fair). The fund currently has a performance rating of C (Fair) based on an average return of 11.46% over the last three years and 5.31% over the last six months. Factored into the performance evaluation is an expense ratio of 0.99% (low).

The fund's risk rating is currently B (Good). It carries a beta of 0.70, meaning the fund's expected move will be 7.0% for every 10% move in the market. Volatility, as measured by both the semi-deviation and a drawdown factor, is considered low.

Kevin Toney, CFA currently receives a manager quality ranking of 83 (0=worst, 99=best). If you desire an average level of risk, then this fund may be an option.

Services Offered: Automated phone transactions, payroll deductions, bank draft capabilities, an IRA investment plan, a 401K investment plan, a Keogh investment plan, wire transfers and a systematic withdrawal plan.

Data Date	Weiss Investment Rating	Net Assets ($Mil)	NAV	Performance Rating/Pts	Total Return Y-T-D	Risk Rating/Pts
6-06	C+	3,580	8.16	C / 4.5	5.31%	B / 8.5
2005	D+	3,840	7.82	D / 2.2	2.46%	B- / 7.5
2004	B+	2,822	8.11	B- / 7.0	12.53%	B- / 7.4
2003	A	1,935	7.78	B / 8.2	24.25%	B / 8.3
2002	A+	1,208	6.53	A / 9.5	-5.00%	B+ / 9.5
2001	A+	766	7.14	A- / 9.1	10.51%	B- / 7.3

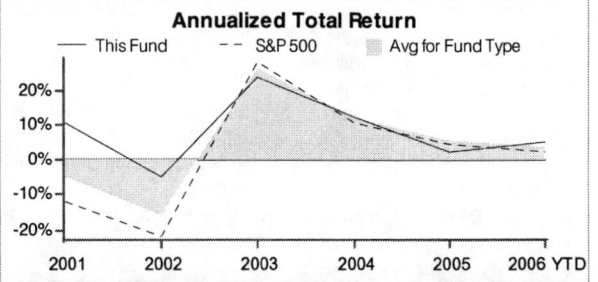

Annualized Total Return

American Century Growth Inv (TWCGX)   D   Weak

Fund Family: American Century Investments   **Phone:** (800) 345-6488
Address: 4500 Main Street, Kansas City, MO 64141
Fund Type: GR - Growth
Major Rating Factors: Disappointing performance is the major factor driving the D (Weak) Weiss Investment Rating for American Century Growth Inv. The fund currently has a performance rating of D (Weak) based on an average return of 8.77% over the last three years and -1.21% over the last six months. Factored into the performance evaluation is an expense ratio of 1.00% (low).

The fund's risk rating is currently B- (Good). It carries a beta of 1.03, meaning that its performance tracks fairly well with that of the overall stock market. Volatility, as measured by both the semi-deviation and a drawdown factor, is considered low.

Gregory Woodhams, CFA has been running the fund for 9 years and currently receives a manager quality ranking of 30 (0=worst, 99=best). This fund offers only a moderate level of risk but investors looking for strong performance are still waiting.

Services Offered: Automated phone transactions, payroll deductions, bank draft capabilities, an IRA investment plan, a 401K investment plan, a Keogh investment plan, wire transfers and a systematic withdrawal plan.

Data Date	Weiss Investment Rating	Net Assets ($Mil)	NAV	Performance Rating/Pts	Total Return Y-T-D	Risk Rating/Pts
6-06	D	3,841	20.33	D / 2.2	-1.21%	B- / 7.3
2005	D	4,166	20.58	D+ / 2.9	4.84%	C+ / 6.6
2004	D+	4,264	19.71	D+ / 2.7	9.91%	C / 4.8
2003	D+	4,367	17.94	D / 1.7	24.41%	C / 4.8
2002	D+	4,116	14.42	D+ / 2.4	-26.13%	C / 4.4
2001	D	6,280	19.52	D+ / 2.9	-18.67%	D- / 1.0

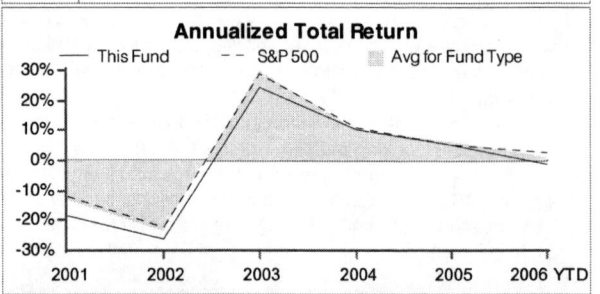

Annualized Total Return

American Century Inc & Gr Inv (BIGRX)   C+   Fair

Fund Family: American Century Investments   **Phone:** (800) 345-6488
Address: 4500 Main Street, Kansas City, MO 64141
Fund Type: GI - Growth and Income
Major Rating Factors: Middle of the road best describes American Century Inc & Gr Inv whose Weiss Investment Rating is currently a C+ (Fair). The fund currently has a performance rating of C (Fair) based on an average return of 12.05% over the last three years and 2.82% over the last six months. Factored into the performance evaluation is an expense ratio of 0.67% (very low).

The fund's risk rating is currently B (Good). It carries a beta of 1.06, meaning that its performance tracks fairly well with that of the overall stock market. Volatility, as measured by both the semi-deviation and a drawdown factor, is considered low.

John Schniedwind has been running the fund for 9 years and currently receives a manager quality ranking of 59 (0=worst, 99=best). If you desire an average level of risk, then this fund may be an option.

Services Offered: Automated phone transactions, payroll deductions, bank draft capabilities, an IRA investment plan, a 401K investment plan, a Keogh investment plan, wire transfers and a systematic withdrawal plan.

Data Date	Weiss Investment Rating	Net Assets ($Mil)	NAV	Performance Rating/Pts	Total Return Y-T-D	Risk Rating/Pts
6-06	C+	3,439	30.74	C / 4.6	2.82%	B / 8.1
2005	C	3,754	30.33	C- / 4.1	4.79%	B- / 7.5
2004	C	3,870	30.67	C+ / 5.8	12.98%	C+ / 5.6
2003	C+	3,636	27.70	C+ / 5.7	29.62%	C+ / 6.3
2002	C+	3,345	21.74	C / 5.1	-19.37%	C+ / 6.7
2001	C+	4,405	27.35	C- / 4.1	-8.61%	C+ / 5.9

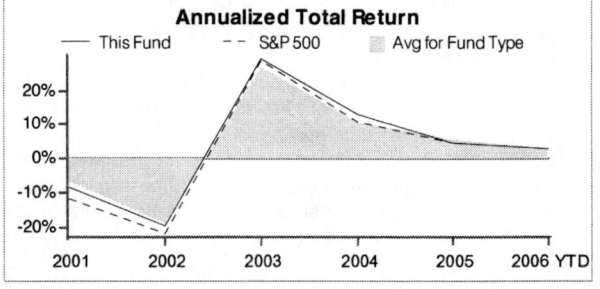

Annualized Total Return

American Century Intl Gr Inv (TWIEX)

B-   Good

Fund Family: American Century Investments   **Phone:** (800) 345-6488
Address: 4500 Main Street, Kansas City, MO 64141
Fund Type: FO - Foreign

Major Rating Factors: Strong performance is the major factor driving the B- (Good) Weiss Investment Rating for American Century Intl Gr Inv. The fund currently has a performance rating of B (Good) based on an average return of 18.72% over the last three years and 7.73% over the last six months. Factored into the performance evaluation is an expense ratio of 1.23% (average) and a 2.0% back-end load levied at the time of sale.

The fund's risk rating is currently C+ (Fair). It carries a beta of 1.01, meaning that its performance tracks fairly well with that of the overall stock market. Volatility, as measured by both the semi-deviation and a drawdown factor, is considered low.

Michael M. Perelstein has been running the fund for 2 years and currently receives a manager quality ranking of 14 (0=worst, 99=best). If you desire only a moderate level of risk and strong performance, then this fund is an excellent option.

Services Offered: Automated phone transactions, payroll deductions, bank draft capabilities, an IRA investment plan, a 401K investment plan, a Keogh investment plan, wire transfers and a systematic withdrawal plan. However, the fund is currently closed to new investors.

Data Date	Weiss Investment Rating	Net Assets ($Mil)	NAV	Performance Rating/Pts	Total Return Y-T-D	Risk Rating/Pts
6-06	B-	2,195	10.87	B / 7.8	7.73%	C+ / 6.3
2005	C+	2,257	10.09	C+ / 6.4	13.34%	C+ / 6.2
2004	C+	2,404	9.06	C+ / 6.5	15.31%	C / 5.5
2003	D+	2,505	7.94	D / 2.0	25.38%	C / 5.1
2002	C-	2,417	6.38	D+ / 2.4	-19.25%	C / 4.8
2001	D	3,317	7.97	C- / 3.1	-26.79%	E / 0.5

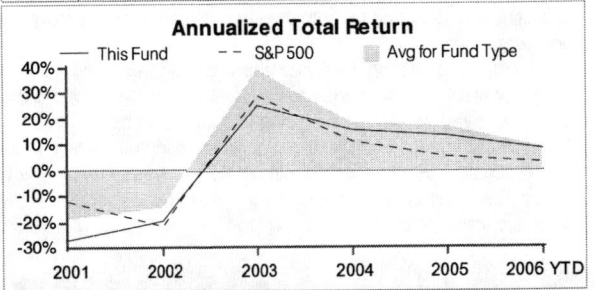

American Century Select Inv (TWCIX)

E+   Very Weak

Fund Family: American Century Investments   **Phone:** (800) 345-6488
Address: 4500 Main Street, Kansas City, MO 64141
Fund Type: GR - Growth

Major Rating Factors: Very poor performance is the major factor driving the E+ (Very Weak) Weiss Investment Rating for American Century Select Inv. The fund currently has a performance rating of E- (Very Weak) based on an average return of 3.48% over the last three years and -7.16% over the last six months. Factored into the performance evaluation is an expense ratio of 1.00% (low).

The fund's risk rating is currently C+ (Fair). It carries a beta of 1.02, meaning that its performance tracks fairly well with that of the overall stock market. Volatility, as measured by both the semi-deviation and a drawdown factor, is considered low.

John Sykora, CFA currently receives a manager quality ranking of 5 (0=worst, 99=best). This fund offers only a moderate level of risk but investors looking for strong performance are still waiting.

Services Offered: Automated phone transactions, payroll deductions, bank draft capabilities, an IRA investment plan, a 401K investment plan, a Keogh investment plan, wire transfers and a systematic withdrawal plan. However, the fund is currently closed to new investors.

Data Date	Weiss Investment Rating	Net Assets ($Mil)	NAV	Performance Rating/Pts	Total Return Y-T-D	Risk Rating/Pts
6-06	E+	2,770	35.42	E- / 0.1	-7.16%	C+ / 6.7
2005	D-	3,426	38.15	D- / 1.3	0.86%	B- / 7.1
2004	D+	3,694	38.08	D / 2.0	7.35%	C+ / 5.7
2003	C-	3,845	35.55	D / 2.1	24.74%	C+ / 5.8
2002	C	3,657	28.50	C- / 3.6	-22.77%	C+ / 6.0
2001	C	4,989	37.00	D+ / 2.3	-18.16%	C+ / 5.8

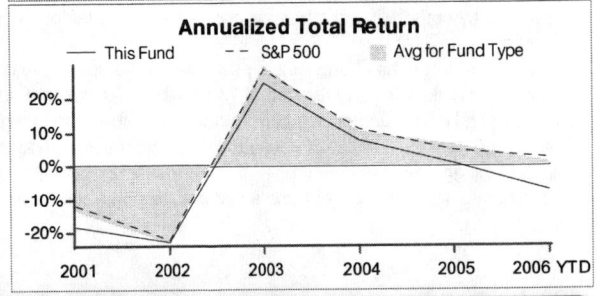

American Century Ultra Inv (TWCUX)

E+   Very Weak

Fund Family: American Century Investments   **Phone:** (800) 345-6488
Address: 4500 Main Street, Kansas City, MO 64141
Fund Type: GR - Growth

Major Rating Factors: Very poor performance is the major factor driving the E+ (Very Weak) Weiss Investment Rating for American Century Ultra Inv. The fund currently has a performance rating of E (Very Weak) based on an average return of 5.93% over the last three years and -6.02% over the last six months. Factored into the performance evaluation is an expense ratio of 0.99% (low).

The fund's risk rating is currently C+ (Fair). It carries a beta of 1.12, meaning it is expected to move 11.2% for every 10% move in the market. Volatility, as measured by both the semi-deviation and a drawdown factor, is considered low.

Bruce A. Wimberly has been running the fund for 10 years and currently receives a manager quality ranking of 10 (0=worst, 99=best). This fund offers only a moderate level of risk but investors looking for strong performance are still waiting.

Services Offered: Automated phone transactions, payroll deductions, bank draft capabilities, an IRA investment plan, a 401K investment plan, a Keogh investment plan, wire transfers and a systematic withdrawal plan.

Data Date	Weiss Investment Rating	Net Assets ($Mil)	NAV	Performance Rating/Pts	Total Return Y-T-D	Risk Rating/Pts
6-06	E+	14,912	28.28	E / 0.5	-6.02%	C+ / 6.7
2005	D	19,570	30.09	D+ / 2.5	2.12%	C+ / 6.9
2004	C-	21,456	29.50	C- / 3.6	10.69%	C / 5.1
2003	C-	21,427	26.65	D+ / 2.8	25.83%	C / 5.3
2002	C-	19,210	21.18	D+ / 2.7	-23.15%	C / 4.7
2001	D	26,453	27.64	C- / 3.7	-14.61%	E- / 0.1

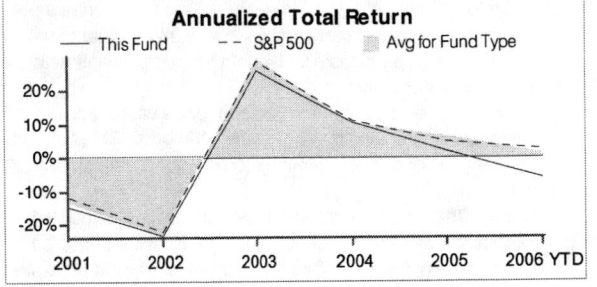

American Century Value Inv (TWVLX)   C-   Fair

Fund Family: American Century Investments   **Phone:** (800) 345-6488
Address: 4500 Main Street, Kansas City, MO 64141
Fund Type: GI - Growth and Income
Major Rating Factors: Middle of the road best describes American Century Value Inv whose Weiss Investment Rating is currently a C- (Fair). The fund currently has a performance rating of C (Fair) based on an average return of 13.37% over the last three years and 2.88% over the last six months. Factored into the performance evaluation is an expense ratio of 0.99% (low).

The fund's risk rating is currently C+ (Fair). It carries a beta of 0.87, meaning the fund's expected move will be 8.7% for every 10% move in the market. Volatility, as measured by both the semi-deviation and a drawdown factor, is considered low.

Phillip N. Davidson, CFA has been running the fund for 13 years and currently receives a manager quality ranking of 85 (0=worst, 99=best). If you desire an average level of risk, then this fund may be an option.
Services Offered: Automated phone transactions, payroll deductions, bank draft capabilities, an IRA investment plan, a 401K investment plan, a Keogh investment plan, wire transfers and a systematic withdrawal plan. However, the fund is currently closed to new investors.

Data Date	Weiss Investment Rating	Net Assets ($Mil)	NAV	Performance Rating/Pts	Total Return Y-T-D	Risk Rating/Pts
6-06	C-	2,227	7.10	C / 5.3	2.88%	C+ / 6.1
2005	C-	2,302	6.95	C / 4.6	5.03%	C+ / 5.6
2004	C+	2,322	7.39	C+ / 6.9	14.36%	C+ / 5.9
2003	B+	1,926	7.50	B+ / 8.4	29.06%	B- / 7.3
2002	A	1,767	5.95	A- / 9.2	-12.69%	B / 8.3
2001	B	1,809	7.00	B+ / 8.9	12.44%	C- / 3.2

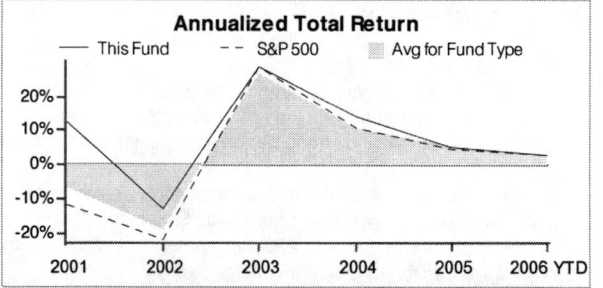

American Century Vista Inv (TWCVX)   C-   Fair

Fund Family: American Century Investments   **Phone:** (800) 345-6488
Address: 4500 Main Street, Kansas City, MO 64141
Fund Type: GR - Growth
Major Rating Factors: Strong performance is the major factor driving the C- (Fair) Weiss Investment Rating for American Century Vista Inv. The fund currently has a performance rating of B- (Good) based on an average return of 17.47% over the last three years and 6.64% over the last six months. Factored into the performance evaluation is an expense ratio of 1.00% (low).

The fund's risk rating is currently C- (Fair). It carries a beta of 1.46, meaning it is expected to move 14.6% for every 10% move in the market. Volatility, as measured by both the semi-deviation and a drawdown factor, is considered average.

Glenn A. Fogle has been running the fund for 13 years and currently receives a manager quality ranking of 74 (0=worst, 99=best). If you desire an average level of risk and strong performance, then this fund is a good option.
Services Offered: Automated phone transactions, payroll deductions, bank draft capabilities, an IRA investment plan, a 401K investment plan, a Keogh investment plan, wire transfers and a systematic withdrawal plan.

Data Date	Weiss Investment Rating	Net Assets ($Mil)	NAV	Performance Rating/Pts	Total Return Y-T-D	Risk Rating/Pts
6-06	C-	2,118	16.86	B- / 7.4	6.64%	C- / 3.8
2005	C+	1,987	15.81	B / 7.7	8.88%	C / 4.6
2004	C+	1,501	14.52	B- / 7.2	15.79%	C / 5.3
2003	C	1,293	12.54	C / 4.6	42.82%	C+ / 5.6
2002	D+	983	8.78	C- / 3.0	-20.90%	C- / 3.1
2001	C	1,240	11.10	B+ / 8.6	-27.59%	E- / 0.0

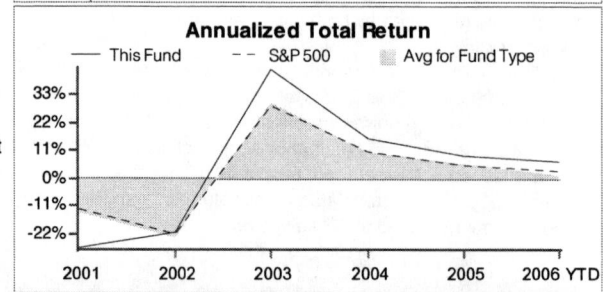

American Funds AMCAP A (AMCPX)   D   Weak

Fund Family: American Funds   **Phone:** (800) 421-4120
Address: 333 South Hope Street, Los Angeles, CA 90071
Fund Type: GR - Growth
Major Rating Factors: Disappointing performance is the major factor driving the D (Weak) Weiss Investment Rating for American Funds AMCAP A. The fund currently has a performance rating of D (Weak) based on an average return of 10.14% over the last three years and 0.57% over the last six months. Factored into the performance evaluation is an expense ratio of 0.65% (very low), a 5.8% front-end load that is levied at the time of purchase and a 1.0% back-end load levied at the time of sale.

The fund's risk rating is currently B- (Good). It carries a beta of 0.95, meaning that its performance tracks fairly well with that of the overall stock market. Volatility, as measured by both the semi-deviation and a drawdown factor, is considered low.

This fund has been team managed for 39 years and currently receives a manager quality ranking of 49 (0=worst, 99=best). This fund offers only a moderate level of risk but investors looking for strong performance are still waiting.
Services Offered: Automated phone transactions, check writing, bank draft capabilities, an IRA investment plan, a 401K investment plan, a Keogh investment plan, wire transfers and a systematic withdrawal plan.

Data Date	Weiss Investment Rating	Net Assets ($Mil)	NAV	Performance Rating/Pts	Total Return Y-T-D	Risk Rating/Pts
6-06	D	15,986	19.06	D / 2.2	0.57%	B- / 7.3
2005	C-	15,364	19.12	C- / 3.4	6.98%	B- / 7.0
2004	C-	12,782	18.33	C- / 3.7	9.80%	C+ / 5.9
2003	C+	9,842	16.85	C+ / 6.5	29.64%	C+ / 6.1
2002	C+	7,077	13.00	C+ / 6.6	-18.66%	C+ / 6.9
2001	B+	7,437	16.12	B- / 7.4	-5.01%	C+ / 6.3

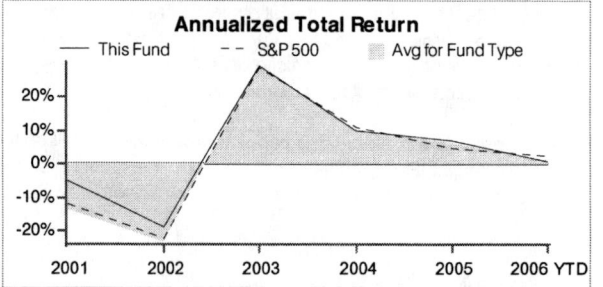

American Funds AMCAP F (AMPFX) | C- Fair

Fund Family: American Funds   **Phone:** (800) 421-4120
Address: 333 South Hope Street, Los Angeles, CA 90071
Fund Type: GR - Growth
Major Rating Factors: Middle of the road best describes American Funds
AMCAP F whose Weiss Investment Rating is currently a C- (Fair). The fund
currently has a performance rating of C- (Fair) based on an average return of
10.11% over the last three years and 0.63% over the last six months. Factored
into the performance evaluation is an expense ratio of 0.68% (very low).

The fund's risk rating is currently B- (Good). It carries a beta of 0.95,
meaning that its performance tracks fairly well with that of the overall stock
market. Volatility, as measured by both the semi-deviation and a drawdown
factor, is considered low.

This fund has been team managed for 5 years and currently receives a
manager quality ranking of 49 (0=worst, 99=best). If you desire an average level
of risk, then this fund may be an option.

Services Offered: Automated phone transactions, check writing, bank draft
capabilities, an IRA investment plan, a 401K investment plan, a Keogh
investment plan, wire transfers and a systematic withdrawal plan.

Data Date	Weiss Investment Rating	Net Assets ($Mil)	NAV	Perfor-mance Rating/Pts	Total Return Y-T-D	Risk Rating/Pts
6-06	C-	2,144	18.98	C- / 3.3	0.63%	B- / 7.4
2005	C	2,010	19.03	C / 4.4	6.94%	B- / 7.0
2004	C	1,361	18.25	C / 4.8	9.71%	C+ / 5.9
2003	C	770	16.77	C+ / 6.0	29.54%	C- / 3.7
2002	C	274	12.95	B- / 7.0	-18.71%	C- / 3.4
2001	U	74	16.08	U / --	0.00%	U / --

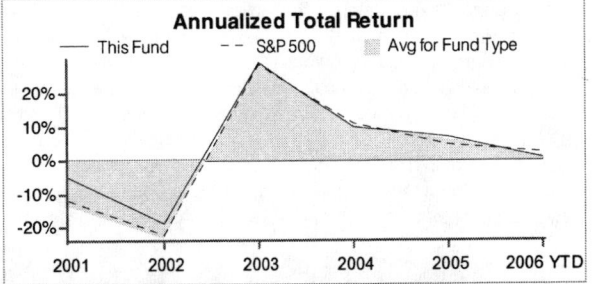

American Funds Amer Balancd Fd A (ABALX) | D+ Weak

Fund Family: American Funds   **Phone:** (800) 421-4120
Address: 333 South Hope Street, Los Angeles, CA 90071
Fund Type: BA - Balanced
Major Rating Factors: Disappointing performance is the major factor driving the
D+ (Weak) Weiss Investment Rating for American Funds Amer Balancd Fd A.
The fund currently has a performance rating of D- (Weak) based on an average
return of 8.63% over the last three years and 2.24% over the last six months.
Factored into the performance evaluation is an expense ratio of 0.59% (very
low), a 5.8% front-end load that is levied at the time of purchase and a 1.0%
back-end load levied at the time of sale.

The fund's risk rating is currently B (Good). It carries a beta of 1.04, meaning
that its performance tracks fairly well with that of the overall stock market.
Volatility, as measured by both the semi-deviation and a drawdown factor, is
considered low.

This fund has been team managed for 31 years and currently receives a
manager quality ranking of 65 (0=worst, 99=best). This fund offers only a
moderate level of risk but investors looking for strong performance are still
waiting.

Services Offered: Automated phone transactions, check writing, bank draft
capabilities, an IRA investment plan, a 401K investment plan, a Keogh
investment plan, wire transfers and a systematic withdrawal plan.

Data Date	Weiss Investment Rating	Net Assets ($Mil)	NAV	Perfor-mance Rating/Pts	Total Return Y-T-D	Risk Rating/Pts
6-06	D+	33,072	18.00	D- / 1.5	2.24%	B / 8.8
2005	D	32,947	17.82	D- / 1.0	3.12%	B / 8.4
2004	C+	28,004	18.00	C / 5.0	8.92%	B- / 7.5
2003	A	18,520	17.29	B- / 7.4	22.82%	B / 8.8
2002	A+	12,511	14.42	A- / 9.2	-6.27%	B+ / 9.5
2001	A+	8,512	15.85	B / 8.2	8.19%	B / 8.4

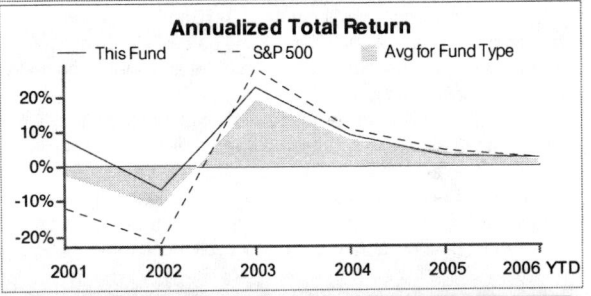

American Funds Amer Mutual Fd A (AMRMX) | C Fair

Fund Family: American Funds   **Phone:** (800) 421-4120
Address: 333 South Hope Street, Los Angeles, CA 90071
Fund Type: GI - Growth and Income
Major Rating Factors: Middle of the road best describes American Funds Amer
Mutual Fd A whose Weiss Investment Rating is currently a C (Fair). The fund
currently has a performance rating of C- (Fair) based on an average return of
11.12% over the last three years and 4.23% over the last six months. Factored
into the performance evaluation is an expense ratio of 0.56% (very low) and a
5.8% front-end load that is levied at the time of purchase.

The fund's risk rating is currently B+ (Good). It carries a beta of 0.76,
meaning the fund's expected move will be 7.6% for every 10% move in the
market. Volatility, as measured by both the semi-deviation and a drawdown
factor, is considered very low.

Alan N. Berro currently receives a manager quality ranking of 76 (0=worst,
99=best). If you desire an average level of risk, then this fund may be an option.

Services Offered: Automated phone transactions, check writing, bank draft
capabilities, an IRA investment plan, a 401K investment plan, a Keogh
investment plan, wire transfers and a systematic withdrawal plan.

Data Date	Weiss Investment Rating	Net Assets ($Mil)	NAV	Perfor-mance Rating/Pts	Total Return Y-T-D	Risk Rating/Pts
6-06	C	14,808	27.10	C- / 3.3	4.23%	B+ / 9.0
2005	D+	14,283	26.27	D / 1.7	4.94%	B / 8.0
2004	C	12,567	26.48	C / 4.6	10.74%	C+/ 6.3
2003	B+	9,853	24.38	B- / 7.1	23.32%	B- / 7.8
2002	A-	8,235	20.32	B+ / 8.4	-12.18%	B / 8.5
2001	A-	8,836	24.05	B- / 7.1	6.67%	B- / 7.4

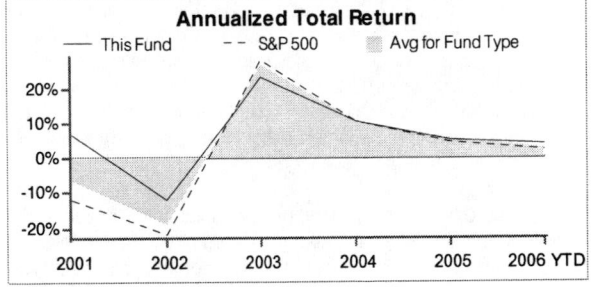

American Funds Cap Inc Builder A (CAIBX)

B   **Good**

Fund Family: American Funds   **Phone:** (800) 421-4120
Address: 333 South Hope Street, Los Angeles, CA 90071
Fund Type: GL - Global

Major Rating Factors: American Funds Cap Inc Builder A receives a Weiss Investment Rating of B (Good). The fund currently has a performance rating of C (Fair) based on an average return of 13.89% over the last three years and 6.66% over the last six months. Factored into the performance evaluation is an expense ratio of 0.57% (very low), a 5.8% front-end load that is levied at the time of purchase and a 1.0% back-end load levied at the time of sale.

The fund's risk rating is currently B+ (Good). It carries a beta of 1.05, meaning that its performance tracks fairly well with that of the overall stock market. Volatility, as measured by both the semi-deviation and a drawdown factor, is considered very low.

Joyce E. Gordon currently receives a manager quality ranking of 95 (0=worst, 99=best). If you desire an average level of risk, then this fund may be an option.

Services Offered: Automated phone transactions, check writing, bank draft capabilities, an IRA investment plan, a 401K investment plan, a Keogh investment plan, wire transfers and a systematic withdrawal plan.

Data Date	Weiss Investment Rating	Net Assets ($Mil)	NAV	Performance Rating/Pts	Total Return Y-T-D	Risk Rating/Pts
6-06	B	49,729	55.59	C / 5.1	6.66%	B+ / 9.3
2005	C	43,361	53.03	D / 2.2	4.02%	B+ / 9.4
2004	A+	30,346	53.26	B / 8.0	17.40%	B / 8.7
2003	A+	19,022	47.87	B / 7.6	21.57%	B+ / 9.6
2002	A+	10,590	41.33	A / 9.3	0.65%	B+ / 9.9
2001	B	8,234	43.59	C+ / 6.8	4.75%	B / 8.9

Annualized Total Return

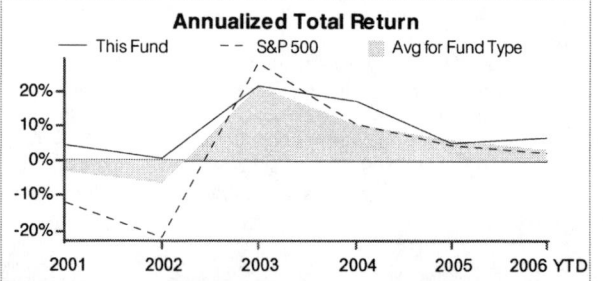

American Funds Cap Wld Gr&Inc A (CWGIX)

A   **Excellent**

Fund Family: American Funds   **Phone:** (800) 421-4120
Address: 333 South Hope Street, Los Angeles, CA 90071
Fund Type: GL - Global

Major Rating Factors: Strong performance is the major factor driving the A (Excellent) Weiss Investment Rating for American Funds Cap Wld Gr&Inc A. The fund currently has a performance rating of B+ (Good) based on an average return of 22.16% over the last three years and 6.57% over the last six months. Factored into the performance evaluation is an expense ratio of 0.73% (very low), a 5.8% front-end load that is levied at the time of purchase and a 1.0% back-end load levied at the time of sale.

The fund's risk rating is currently B- (Good). It carries a beta of 0.85, meaning the fund's expected move will be 8.5% for every 10% move in the market. Volatility, as measured by both the semi-deviation and a drawdown factor, is considered low.

Andrew B. Suzman currently receives a manager quality ranking of 68 (0=worst, 99=best). If you desire only a moderate level of risk and strong performance, then this fund is an excellent option.

Services Offered: Automated phone transactions, check writing, bank draft capabilities, an IRA investment plan, a 401K investment plan, a Keogh investment plan, wire transfers and a systematic withdrawal plan.

Data Date	Weiss Investment Rating	Net Assets ($Mil)	NAV	Performance Rating/Pts	Total Return Y-T-D	Risk Rating/Pts
6-06	A	50,226	38.51	B+ / 8.3	6.57%	B- / 7.7
2005	A	39,841	36.57	B+ / 8.3	14.72%	B- / 7.8
2004	A-	25,137	33.89	B+ / 8.8	19.42%	C+ / 6.4
2003	A-	14,703	29.88	B+ / 8.5	39.07%	B- / 7.4
2002	B	10,016	22.25	B / 7.7	-7.15%	B- / 7.6
2001	B+	10,346	24.50	B- / 7.0	-4.96%	B- / 7.2

Annualized Total Return

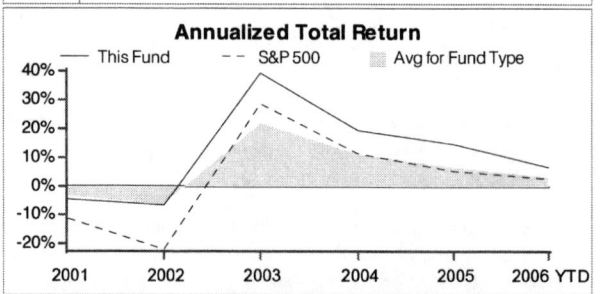

American Funds EuroPacific Gr A (AEPGX)

B+   **Good**

Fund Family: American Funds   **Phone:** (800) 421-4120
Address: 333 South Hope Street, Los Angeles, CA 90071
Fund Type: FO - Foreign

Major Rating Factors: Strong performance is the major factor driving the B+ (Good) Weiss Investment Rating for American Funds EuroPacific Gr A. The fund currently has a performance rating of B+ (Good) based on an average return of 24.53% over the last three years and 6.81% over the last six months. Factored into the performance evaluation is an expense ratio of 0.76% (very low), a 5.8% front-end load that is levied at the time of purchase and a 1.0% back-end load levied at the time of sale.

The fund's risk rating is currently C+ (Fair). It carries a beta of 0.99, meaning that its performance tracks fairly well with that of the overall stock market. Volatility, as measured by both the semi-deviation and a drawdown factor, is considered low.

Multiple Portfolio Counselors has been running the fund for 22 years and currently receives a manager quality ranking of 60 (0=worst, 99=best). If you desire only a moderate level of risk and strong performance, then this fund is an excellent option.

Services Offered: Automated phone transactions, check writing, bank draft capabilities, an IRA investment plan, a 401K investment plan, a Keogh investment plan, wire transfers and a systematic withdrawal plan.

Data Date	Weiss Investment Rating	Net Assets ($Mil)	NAV	Performance Rating/Pts	Total Return Y-T-D	Risk Rating/Pts
6-06	B+	49,564	43.90	B+ / 8.8	6.81%	C+ / 6.4
2005	A-	43,140	41.10	B+ / 8.8	21.12%	C+ / 6.7
2004	B+	35,639	35.63	B / 7.9	19.69%	C+ / 6.2
2003	B-	27,987	30.21	B- / 7.1	32.91%	C+ / 6.5
2002	C	23,439	22.97	C- / 4.2	-13.61%	C+ / 5.8
2001	C	26,819	26.87	C / 5.5	-12.17%	C- / 3.6

Annualized Total Return

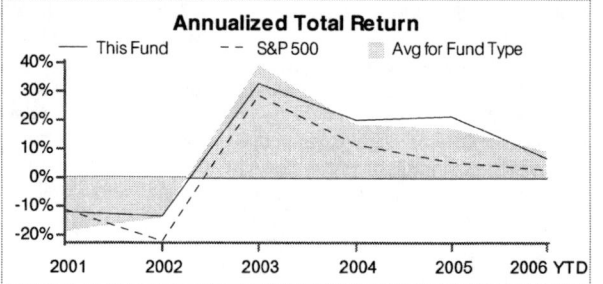

American Funds Fundamentl Invs A (ANCFX)   B+   Good

Fund Family: American Funds   **Phone:** (800) 421-4120
Address: 333 South Hope Street, Los Angeles, CA 90071
Fund Type: GI - Growth and Income
Major Rating Factors: Strong performance is the major factor driving the B+ (Good) Weiss Investment Rating for American Funds Fundamentl Invs A. The fund currently has a performance rating of B- (Good) based on an average return of 18.63% over the last three years and 8.82% over the last six months. Factored into the performance evaluation is an expense ratio of 0.62% (very low) and a 5.8% front-end load that is levied at the time of purchase.

The fund's risk rating is currently B- (Good). It carries a beta of 1.14, meaning it is expected to move 11.4% for every 10% move in the market. Volatility, as measured by both the semi-deviation and a drawdown factor, is considered low.

This fund has been team managed for 28 years and currently receives a manager quality ranking of 94 (0=worst, 99=best). If you desire only a moderate level of risk and strong performance, then this fund is an excellent option.

Services Offered: Automated phone transactions, check writing, payroll deductions, bank draft capabilities, an IRA investment plan, a 401K investment plan, a Keogh investment plan, wire transfers and a systematic withdrawal plan.

Data Date	Weiss Investment Rating	Net Assets ($Mil)	NAV	Performance Rating/Pts	Total Return Y-T-D	Risk Rating/Pts
6-06	B+	27,883	38.30	B- / 7.5	8.82%	B- / 7.6
2005	C+	23,717	35.40	C+ / 5.9	11.68%	B- / 7.0
2004	C+	21,080	32.25	C+ / 6.0	13.91%	C+ / 6.6
2003	C+	17,932	28.85	C+ / 5.9	31.96%	C+ / 6.0
2002	C+	15,961	22.23	C+ / 6.0	-17.34%	C+ / 6.9
2001	C+	19,100	27.45	C+ / 6.3	-9.55%	C+ / 6.4

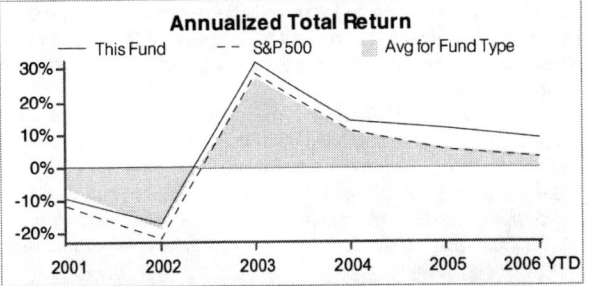
Annualized Total Return

American Funds Gr Fnd of Amer A (AGTHX)   C+   Fair

Fund Family: American Funds   **Phone:** (800) 421-4120
Address: 333 South Hope Street, Los Angeles, CA 90071
Fund Type: GR - Growth
Major Rating Factors: Middle of the road best describes American Funds Gr Fnd of Amer A whose Weiss Investment Rating is currently a C+ (Fair). The fund currently has a performance rating of C (Fair) based on an average return of 15.16% over the last three years and 2.72% over the last six months. Factored into the performance evaluation is an expense ratio of 0.66% (very low) and a 5.8% front-end load that is levied at the time of purchase.

The fund's risk rating is currently B- (Good). It carries a beta of 1.11, meaning it is expected to move 11.1% for every 10% move in the market. Volatility, as measured by both the semi-deviation and a drawdown factor, is considered low.

Multiple Portfolio Counselors has been running the fund for 33 years and currently receives a manager quality ranking of 82 (0=worst, 99=best). If you desire an average level of risk, then this fund may be an option.

Services Offered: Automated phone transactions, check writing, payroll deductions, bank draft capabilities, an IRA investment plan, a 401K investment plan, a Keogh investment plan, wire transfers and a systematic withdrawal plan.

Data Date	Weiss Investment Rating	Net Assets ($Mil)	NAV	Performance Rating/Pts	Total Return Y-T-D	Risk Rating/Pts
6-06	C+	77,843	31.70	C / 5.4	2.72%	B- / 7.2
2005	B-	71,536	30.86	C+ / 6.5	14.23%	B- / 7.0
2004	C-	58,164	27.38	C / 4.4	11.95%	C / 5.4
2003	C	45,421	24.54	C / 4.4	32.90%	C / 5.1
2002	C	33,482	18.47	C / 5.4	-22.02%	C / 5.5
2001	C+	35,402	23.71	B / 8.0	-12.28%	D- / 1.1

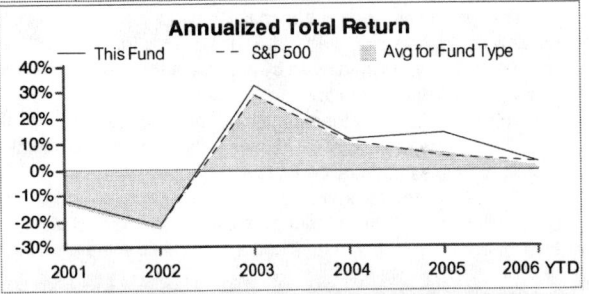
Annualized Total Return

American Funds Gr Fnd of Amer R2 (RGABX)   C+   Fair

Fund Family: American Funds   **Phone:** (800) 421-4120
Address: 333 South Hope Street, Los Angeles, CA 90071
Fund Type: GR - Growth
Major Rating Factors: Middle of the road best describes American Funds Gr Fnd of Amer R2 whose Weiss Investment Rating is currently a C+ (Fair). The fund currently has a performance rating of C+ (Fair) based on an average return of 14.25% over the last three years and 2.31% over the last six months. Factored into the performance evaluation is an expense ratio of 1.45% (average).

The fund's risk rating is currently B- (Good). It carries a beta of 1.11, meaning it is expected to move 11.1% for every 10% move in the market. Volatility, as measured by both the semi-deviation and a drawdown factor, is considered low.

Multiple Portfolio Counselors has been running the fund for 33 years and currently receives a manager quality ranking of 75 (0=worst, 99=best). If you desire an average level of risk, then this fund may be an option.

Services Offered: Automated phone transactions, check writing, payroll deductions, bank draft capabilities, an IRA investment plan, a 401K investment plan, a Keogh investment plan, wire transfers and a systematic withdrawal plan.

Data Date	Weiss Investment Rating	Net Assets ($Mil)	NAV	Performance Rating/Pts	Total Return Y-T-D	Risk Rating/Pts
6-06	C+	2,080	30.98	C+ / 5.7	2.31%	B- / 7.1
2005	B-	1,752	30.28	C+ / 6.8	13.32%	B- / 7.2
2004	C	1,052	26.92	C / 4.8	11.06%	C+ / 5.9
2003	D	420	24.24	C / 4.8	31.88%	D- / 1.3

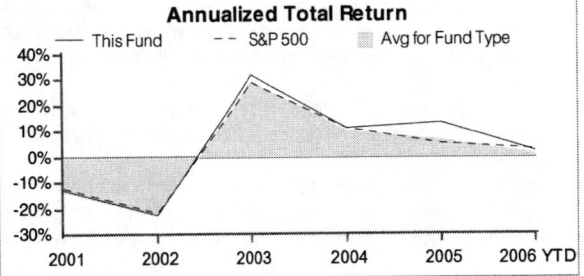
Annualized Total Return

American Funds Inc Fnd of Amer A (AMECX)
C+   **Fair**

Fund Family: American Funds   **Phone:** (800) 421-4120
Address: 333 South Hope Street, Los Angeles, CA 90071
Fund Type: AA - Asset Allocation

Major Rating Factors: Middle of the road best describes American Funds Inc Fnd of Amer A whose Weiss Investment Rating is currently a C+ (Fair). The fund currently has a performance rating of C- (Fair) based on an average return of 12.35% over the last three years and 6.77% over the last six months. Factored into the performance evaluation is an expense ratio of 0.54% (very low), a 5.8% front-end load that is levied at the time of purchase and a 1.0% back-end load levied at the time of sale.

The fund's risk rating is currently B+ (Good). It carries a beta of 1.10, meaning it is expected to move 11.0% for every 10% move in the market. Volatility, as measured by both the semi-deviation and a drawdown factor, is considered very low.

This fund has been team managed for 33 years and currently receives a manager quality ranking of 89 (0=worst, 99=best). If you desire an average level of risk, then this fund may be an option.

Services Offered: Automated phone transactions, check writing, bank draft capabilities, an IRA investment plan, a 401K investment plan, a Keogh investment plan, wire transfers and a systematic withdrawal plan.

Data Date	Weiss Investment Rating	Net Assets ($Mil)	NAV	Performance Rating/Pts	Total Return Y-T-D	Risk Rating/Pts
6-06	C+	51,236	18.97	C- / 4.1	6.77%	B+ / 9.2
2005	C-	48,075	18.11	D- / 1.5	2.45%	B+ / 9.3
2004	B-	40,768	18.56	C+/ 6.6	11.99%	B- / 7.9
2003	A	29,562	17.18	B / 7.7	25.27%	B / 8.8
2002	A+	20,836	14.35	A- / 9.0	-4.37%	B+ / 9.4
2001	A+	19,746	15.82	B- / 7.0	5.41%	B / 8.8

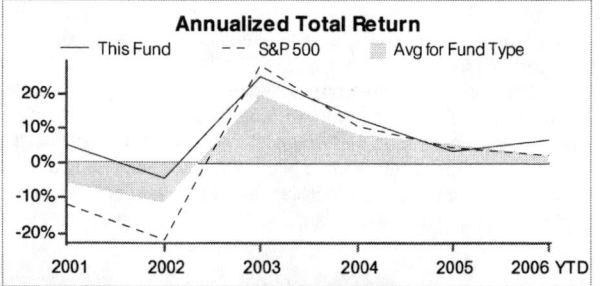
Annualized Total Return

American Funds Inv Co of Amer A (AIVSX)
C+   **Fair**

Fund Family: American Funds   **Phone:** (800) 421-4120
Address: 333 South Hope Street, Los Angeles, CA 90071
Fund Type: GI - Growth and Income

Major Rating Factors: Middle of the road best describes American Funds Inv Co of Amer A whose Weiss Investment Rating is currently a C+ (Fair). The fund currently has a performance rating of C (Fair) based on an average return of 12.71% over the last three years and 5.72% over the last six months. Factored into the performance evaluation is an expense ratio of 0.57% (very low), a 5.8% front-end load that is levied at the time of purchase and a 1.0% back-end load levied at the time of sale.

The fund's risk rating is currently B+ (Good). It carries a beta of 0.86, meaning the fund's expected move will be 8.6% for every 10% move in the market. Volatility, as measured by both the semi-deviation and a drawdown factor, is considered very low.

This fund has been team managed for 73 years and currently receives a manager quality ranking of 82 (0=worst, 99=best). If you desire an average level of risk, then this fund may be an option.

Services Offered: Automated phone transactions, check writing, bank draft capabilities, an IRA investment plan, a 401K investment plan, a Keogh investment plan, wire transfers and a systematic withdrawal plan.

Data Date	Weiss Investment Rating	Net Assets ($Mil)	NAV	Performance Rating/Pts	Total Return Y-T-D	Risk Rating/Pts
6-06	C+	68,759	32.85	C / 4.4	5.72%	B+ / 9.0
2005	C-	66,546	31.36	D+ / 2.7	6.87%	B / 8.0
2004	C	63,633	30.75	C / 4.4	9.78%	C+ / 6.2
2003	B-	55,087	28.84	C+ / 6.7	26.31%	B- / 7.0
2002	B	48,006	23.48	C+ / 6.9	-14.47%	B- / 7.8
2001	B-	54,008	28.53	C+ / 6.3	-4.59%	B- / 7.3

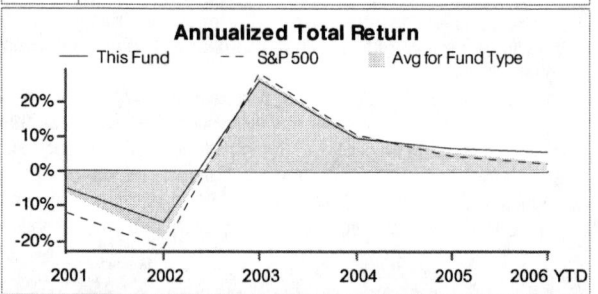
Annualized Total Return

American Funds New Economy A (ANEFX)
C   **Fair**

Fund Family: American Funds   **Phone:** (800) 421-4120
Address: 333 South Hope Street, Los Angeles, CA 90071
Fund Type: GR - Growth

Major Rating Factors: Middle of the road best describes American Funds New Economy A whose Weiss Investment Rating is currently a C (Fair). The fund currently has a performance rating of C (Fair) based on an average return of 14.47% over the last three years and 0.55% over the last six months. Factored into the performance evaluation is an expense ratio of 0.83% (very low), a 5.8% front-end load that is levied at the time of purchase and a 1.0% back-end load levied at the time of sale.

The fund's risk rating is currently B- (Good). It carries a beta of 1.26, meaning it is expected to move 12.6% for every 10% move in the market. Volatility, as measured by both the semi-deviation and a drawdown factor, is considered low.

Gordon Crawford currently receives a manager quality ranking of 65 (0=worst, 99=best). If you desire an average level of risk, then this fund may be an option.

Services Offered: Automated phone transactions, check writing, bank draft capabilities, an IRA investment plan, a 401K investment plan, a Keogh investment plan, wire transfers and a systematic withdrawal plan.

Data Date	Weiss Investment Rating	Net Assets ($Mil)	NAV	Performance Rating/Pts	Total Return Y-T-D	Risk Rating/Pts
6-06	C	7,086	23.57	C / 5.0	0.55%	B- / 7.2
2005	B-	7,061	23.44	B- / 7.1	12.17%	C+ / 6.2
2004	D	6,938	21.03	C- / 3.6	12.45%	C- / 3.8
2003	C-	6,671	18.77	C- / 3.8	38.71%	C- / 3.7
2002	D+	5,882	13.54	D / 2.1	-26.01%	C- / 4.1
2001	D	8,086	18.30	C- / 3.3	-17.34%	E- / 0.2

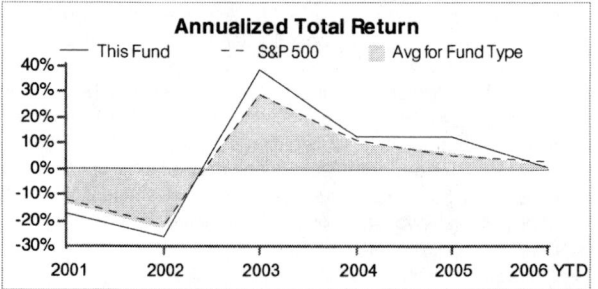
Annualized Total Return

American Funds New Perspective A (ANWPX)   B+   Good

Fund Family: American Funds   **Phone:** (800) 421-4120
Address: 333 South Hope Street, Los Angeles, CA 90071
Fund Type: GL - Global
Major Rating Factors: Strong performance is the major factor driving the B+ (Good) Weiss Investment Rating for American Funds New Perspective A. The fund currently has a performance rating of B- (Good) based on an average return of 18.78% over the last three years and 6.15% over the last six months. Factored into the performance evaluation is an expense ratio of 0.77% (very low), a 5.8% front-end load that is levied at the time of purchase and a 1.0% back-end load levied at the time of sale.

The fund's risk rating is currently B- (Good). It carries a beta of 0.92, meaning that its performance tracks fairly well with that of the overall stock market. Volatility, as measured by both the semi-deviation and a drawdown factor, is considered low.

Gregg E. Ireland currently receives a manager quality ranking of 25 (0=worst, 99=best). If you desire only a moderate level of risk and strong performance, then this fund is an excellent option.

Services Offered: Automated phone transactions, check writing, bank draft capabilities, an IRA investment plan, a 401K investment plan, a Keogh investment plan, wire transfers and a systematic withdrawal plan.

Data Date	Weiss Investment Rating	Net Assets ($Mil)	NAV	Performance Rating/Pts	Total Return Y-T-D	Risk Rating/Pts
6-06	B+	38,995	30.39	B- / 7.3	6.15%	B- / 7.6
2005	B-	35,791	28.63	C+ / 6.8	11.28%	B- / 7.2
2004	C+	32,600	27.72	C+ / 6.9	14.27%	C+ / 5.8
2003	B-	27,244	24.49	B- / 7.5	36.76%	C+ / 6.2
2002	C+	23,358	18.04	C / 5.3	-16.05%	C+ / 6.2
2001	C+	27,394	21.69	C+ / 6.4	-8.30%	C+ / 6.1

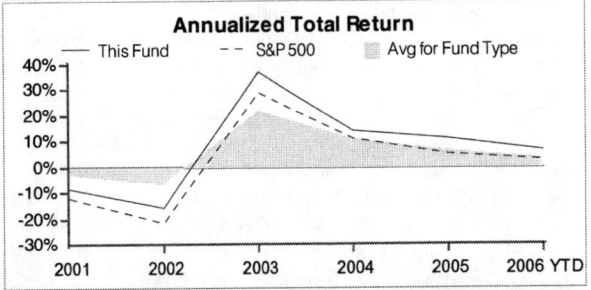

Annualized Total Return

American Funds New World A (NEWFX)   B+   Good

Fund Family: American Funds   **Phone:** (800) 421-4120
Address: 333 South Hope Street, Los Angeles, CA 90071
Fund Type: GL - Global
Major Rating Factors: Exceptional performance is the major factor driving the B+ (Good) Weiss Investment Rating for American Funds New World A. The fund currently has a performance rating of A- (Excellent) based on an average return of 26.60% over the last three years and 8.35% over the last six months. Factored into the performance evaluation is an expense ratio of 1.18% (low), a 5.8% front-end load that is levied at the time of purchase and a 1.0% back-end load levied at the time of sale.

The fund's risk rating is currently C+ (Fair). It carries a beta of 1.08, meaning that its performance tracks fairly well with that of the overall stock market. Volatility, as measured by both the semi-deviation and a drawdown factor, is considered low.

This is team managed and currently receives a manager quality ranking of 57 (0=worst, 99=best). If you desire only a moderate level of risk and strong performance, then this fund is an excellent option.

Services Offered: Automated phone transactions, check writing, bank draft capabilities, an IRA investment plan, a 401K investment plan, a Keogh investment plan, wire transfers and a systematic withdrawal plan.

Data Date	Weiss Investment Rating	Net Assets ($Mil)	NAV	Performance Rating/Pts	Total Return Y-T-D	Risk Rating/Pts
6-06	B+	6,626	41.93	A- / 9.0	8.35%	C+ / 5.8
2005	A+	4,580	38.70	A / 9.3	22.20%	B- / 7.1
2004	A+	2,414	32.27	A- / 9.2	20.79%	B- / 7.2
2003	A	1,562	27.18	B+ / 8.9	43.36%	B- / 7.7
2002	C+	1,123	19.38	C+ / 6.0	-4.62%	C+ / 6.9
2001	U	1,118	20.58	U / --	-3.96%	U / --

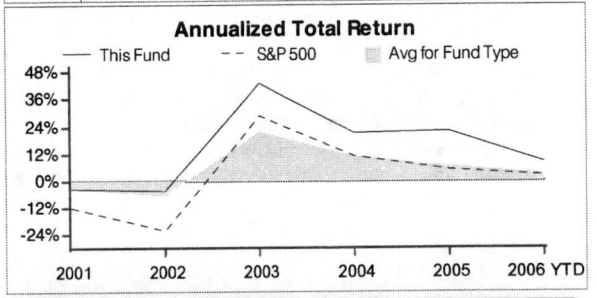

Annualized Total Return

American Funds SMALLCAP World A (SMCWX)   B+   Good

Fund Family: American Funds   **Phone:** (800) 421-4120
Address: 333 South Hope Street, Los Angeles, CA 90071
Fund Type: GL - Global
Major Rating Factors: Strong performance is the major factor driving the B+ (Good) Weiss Investment Rating for American Funds SMALLCAP World A. The fund currently has a performance rating of B+ (Good) based on an average return of 23.76% over the last three years and 7.83% over the last six months. Factored into the performance evaluation is an expense ratio of 1.04% (low), a 5.8% front-end load that is levied at the time of purchase and a 1.0% back-end load levied at the time of sale.

The fund's risk rating is currently C+ (Fair). It carries a beta of 1.04, meaning that its performance tracks fairly well with that of the overall stock market. Volatility, as measured by both the semi-deviation and a drawdown factor, is considered low.

This is team managed and currently receives a manager quality ranking of 40 (0=worst, 99=best). If you desire only a moderate level of risk and strong performance, then this fund is an excellent option.

Services Offered: Automated phone transactions, check writing, bank draft capabilities, an IRA investment plan, a 401K investment plan, a Keogh investment plan, wire transfers and a systematic withdrawal plan.

Data Date	Weiss Investment Rating	Net Assets ($Mil)	NAV	Performance Rating/Pts	Total Return Y-T-D	Risk Rating/Pts
6-06	B+	15,140	38.03	B+ / 8.6	7.83%	C+ / 6.2
2005	A	12,776	35.27	A- / 9.0	16.53%	B- / 7.0
2004	B-	10,625	31.20	B / 7.8	17.76%	C / 5.5
2003	C+	8,894	26.77	C+ / 6.6	50.40%	C / 4.9
2002	D+	6,543	17.82	D+ / 2.3	-22.25%	C- / 3.7
2001	D+	8,422	22.92	C+ / 5.6	-17.35%	E- / 0.0

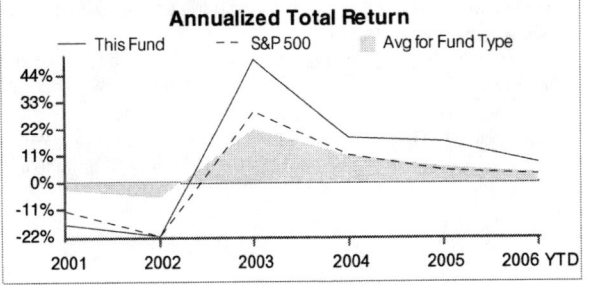

Annualized Total Return

American Funds Wash Mutl Invs A (AWSHX)   C   Fair

Fund Family: American Funds   **Phone:** (800) 421-4120
Address: 333 South Hope Street, Los Angeles, CA 90071
Fund Type: GI - Growth and Income

Major Rating Factors: Middle of the road best describes American Funds Wash Mutl Invs A whose Weiss Investment Rating is currently a C (Fair). The fund currently has a performance rating of C- (Fair) based on an average return of 10.96% over the last three years and 5.16% over the last six months. Factored into the performance evaluation is an expense ratio of 0.60% (very low), a 5.8% front-end load that is levied at the time of purchase and a 1.0% back-end load levied at the time of sale.

The fund's risk rating is currently B (Good). It carries a beta of 0.86, meaning the fund's expected move will be 8.6% for every 10% move in the market. Volatility, as measured by both the semi-deviation and a drawdown factor, is considered low.

Multiple Portfolio Counselors has been running the fund for 54 years and currently receives a manager quality ranking of 68 (0=worst, 99=best). If you desire an average level of risk, then this fund may be an option.

Services Offered: Automated phone transactions, check writing, bank draft capabilities, an IRA investment plan, a 401K investment plan, a Keogh investment plan, wire transfers and a systematic withdrawal plan.

Data Date	Weiss Investment Rating	Net Assets ($Mil)	NAV	Performance Rating/Pts	Total Return Y-T-D	Risk Rating/Pts
6-06	C	62,498	32.11	C- / 3.1	5.16%	B / 8.5
2005	D-	62,684	30.84	D- / 1.5	3.55%	B- / 7.4
2004	C-	61,398	30.78	C- / 4.0	9.92%	C+ / 6.0
2003	B-	52,127	28.78	C+ / 6.9	25.83%	B- / 7.0
2002	B	44,159	23.51	B / 7.7	-14.85%	B- / 7.9
2001	C+	48,135	28.25	C+ / 6.3	1.51%	C+ / 6.6

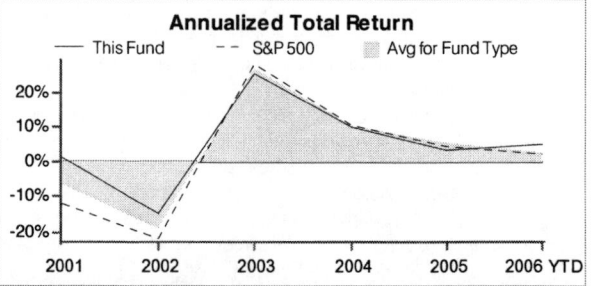

Annualized Total Return

Ariel Appreciation Fund (CAAPX)   C-   Fair

Fund Family: Ariel   **Phone:** (800) 292-7435
Address: 200 E. Randolph Drive, Chicago, IL 60601
Fund Type: MC - Mid Cap

Major Rating Factors: Disappointing performance is the major factor driving the C- (Fair) Weiss Investment Rating for Ariel Appreciation Fund. The fund currently has a performance rating of D+ (Weak) based on an average return of 9.97% over the last three years and -1.22% over the last six months. Factored into the performance evaluation is an expense ratio of 1.13% (low).

The fund's risk rating is currently B (Good). It carries a beta of 0.66, meaning the fund's expected move will be 6.6% for every 10% move in the market. Volatility, as measured by both the semi-deviation and a drawdown factor, is considered low.

John W. Rogers, Jr. currently receives a manager quality ranking of 32 (0=worst, 99=best). This fund offers only a moderate level of risk but investors looking for strong performance are still waiting.

Services Offered: Automated phone transactions, check writing, bank draft capabilities, an IRA investment plan, a 401K investment plan, wire transfers and a systematic withdrawal plan.

Data Date	Weiss Investment Rating	Net Assets ($Mil)	NAV	Performance Rating/Pts	Total Return Y-T-D	Risk Rating/Pts
6-06	C-	2,900	46.15	D+ / 2.6	-1.22%	B / 8.3
2005	C-	3,389	46.72	C- / 3.8	2.92%	C+ / 6.7
2004	B	2,190	47.67	B- / 7.3	13.11%	C+ / 6.2
2003	B+	2,345	43.30	B+ / 8.6	30.97%	C+ / 6.9
2002	A	1,472	33.06	A / 9.3	-10.36%	B / 8.3
2001	A-	771	37.02	A- / 9.1	16.23%	C+ / 5.9

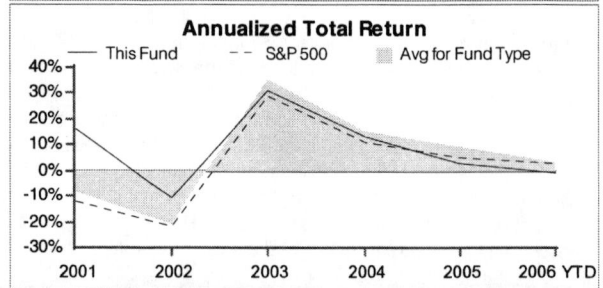

Annualized Total Return

Ariel Fund (ARGFX)   C   Fair

Fund Family: Ariel   **Phone:** (800) 292-7435
Address: 200 E. Randolph Drive, Chicago, IL 60601
Fund Type: SC - Small Cap

Major Rating Factors: Middle of the road best describes Ariel Fund whose Weiss Investment Rating is currently a C (Fair). The fund currently has a performance rating of C- (Fair) based on an average return of 12.87% over the last three years and 1.40% over the last six months. Factored into the performance evaluation is an expense ratio of 1.05% (low).

The fund's risk rating is currently B- (Good). It carries a beta of 0.57, meaning the fund's expected move will be 5.7% for every 10% move in the market. Volatility, as measured by both the semi-deviation and a drawdown factor, is considered low.

John W. Rogers, Jr. has been running the fund for 20 years and currently receives a manager quality ranking of 70 (0=worst, 99=best). If you desire an average level of risk, then this fund may be an option.

Services Offered: Automated phone transactions, check writing, bank draft capabilities, an IRA investment plan, a 401K investment plan, wire transfers and a systematic withdrawal plan.

Data Date	Weiss Investment Rating	Net Assets ($Mil)	NAV	Performance Rating/Pts	Total Return Y-T-D	Risk Rating/Pts
6-06	C	4,600	50.77	C- / 4.2	1.40%	B- / 7.5
2005	C	4,920	50.07	C- / 4.0	0.92%	B- / 7.4
2004	A	3,380	53.17	B+ / 8.6	21.97%	B- / 7.0
2003	A-	2,268	45.12	B+ / 8.6	28.04%	B- / 7.5
2002	A+	1,190	35.24	A+ / 9.6	-5.18%	B / 8.9
2001	B+	620	37.72	A- / 9.2	14.21%	C- / 3.6

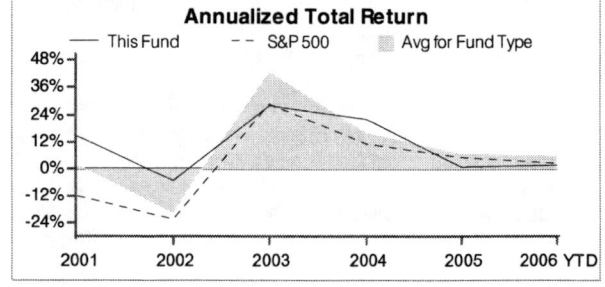

Annualized Total Return

Artisan International Fund Inv (ARTIX)

A- Excellent

Fund Family: Artisan Funds   **Phone:** (800) 344-1770
Address: 1000 North Water Street, Milwaukee, WI 53202
Fund Type: FO - Foreign

Major Rating Factors: Strong performance is the major factor driving the A- (Excellent) Weiss Investment Rating for Artisan International Fund Inv. The fund currently has a performance rating of B+ (Good) based on an average return of 22.36% over the last three years and 9.48% over the last six months. Factored into the performance evaluation is an expense ratio of 1.19% (average) and a 2.0% back-end load levied at the time of sale.

The fund's risk rating is currently C+ (Fair). It carries a beta of 1.05, meaning that its performance tracks fairly well with that of the overall stock market. Volatility, as measured by both the semi-deviation and a drawdown factor, is considered low.

Mark L. Yockey, CFA has been running the fund for 11 years and currently receives a manager quality ranking of 27 (0=worst, 99=best). If you desire only a moderate level of risk and strong performance, then this fund is an excellent option.

Services Offered: Automated phone transactions, bank draft capabilities, an IRA investment plan, a 401K investment plan, a Keogh investment plan and a systematic withdrawal plan.

Data Date	Weiss Investment Rating	Net Assets ($Mil)	NAV	Perfor- mance Rating/Pts	Total Return Y-T-D	Risk Rating/Pts
6-06	A-	9,288	27.71	B+ / 8.8	9.48%	C+ / 6.7
2005	B	7,662	25.31	B / 8.0	16.27%	C+ / 5.8
2004	C+	9,728	22.14	B- / 7.3	17.76%	C / 5.1
2003	C	5,688	18.91	C / 4.9	29.14%	C+ / 5.9
2002	C-	7,221	14.79	C- / 4.0	-18.90%	C / 4.7
2001	C	4,059	18.36	B+ / 8.9	-11.13%	E- / 0.0

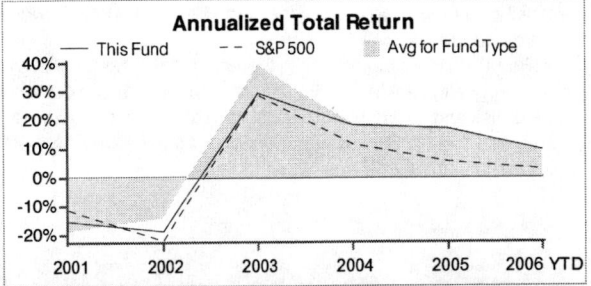

Artisan Mid Cap Fund (ARTMX)

C Fair

Fund Family: Artisan Funds   **Phone:** (800) 344-1770
Address: 1000 North Water Street, Milwaukee, WI 53202
Fund Type: MC - Mid Cap

Major Rating Factors: Middle of the road best describes Artisan Mid Cap Fund whose Weiss Investment Rating is currently a C (Fair). The fund currently has a performance rating of C+ (Fair) based on an average return of 14.76% over the last three years and 2.20% over the last six months. Factored into the performance evaluation is an expense ratio of 1.18% (low).

The fund's risk rating is currently C+ (Fair). It carries a beta of 1.07, meaning that its performance tracks fairly well with that of the overall stock market. Volatility, as measured by both the semi-deviation and a drawdown factor, is considered low.

Andrew C. Stephens has been running the fund for 9 years and currently receives a manager quality ranking of 19 (0=worst, 99=best). If you desire an average level of risk, then this fund may be an option.

Services Offered: An IRA investment plan and a 401K investment plan. However, the fund is currently closed to new investors.

Data Date	Weiss Investment Rating	Net Assets ($Mil)	NAV	Perfor- mance Rating/Pts	Total Return Y-T-D	Risk Rating/Pts
6-06	C	5,756	31.60	C+ / 6.0	2.20%	C+ / 6.4
2005	C+	5,021	30.92	C+ / 6.3	9.11%	C+ / 6.3
2004	C	5,080	29.56	C+ / 5.8	14.66%	C / 4.8
2003	C+	3,032	25.78	C+ / 6.0	31.80%	C / 5.4
2002	B-	1,721	19.56	B / 7.7	-24.16%	C+ / 5.8
2001	C+	1,470	25.79	A+ / 9.8	-3.05%	E- / 0.0

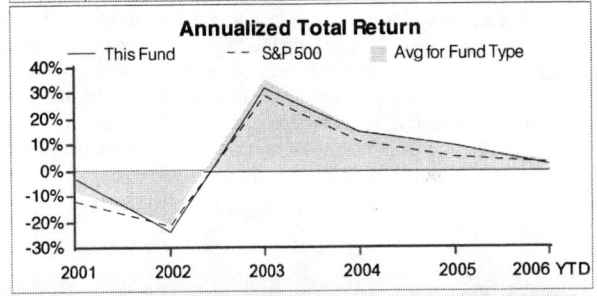

Artisan Mid Cap Value Inv (ARTQX)

A+ Excellent

Fund Family: Artisan Funds   **Phone:** (800) 344-1770
Address: 1000 North Water Street, Milwaukee, WI 53202
Fund Type: MC - Mid Cap

Major Rating Factors: Strong performance is the major factor driving the A+ (Excellent) Weiss Investment Rating for Artisan Mid Cap Value Inv. The fund currently has a performance rating of B (Good) based on an average return of 21.61% over the last three years and 3.04% over the last six months. Factored into the performance evaluation is an expense ratio of 1.22% (average).

The fund's risk rating is currently B (Good). It carries a beta of 0.81, meaning the fund's expected move will be 8.1% for every 10% move in the market. Volatility, as measured by standard deviation, is considered low for equity funds at 10.13.

James C. Kieffer, CFA has been running the fund for 5 years and currently receives a manager quality ranking of 95 (0=worst, 99=best). If you desire only a moderate level of risk and strong performance, then this fund is an excellent option.

Services Offered: Automated phone transactions, bank draft capabilities, an IRA investment plan, a 401K investment plan, a Keogh investment plan and wire transfers.

Data Date	Weiss Investment Rating	Net Assets ($Mil)	NAV	Perfor- mance Rating/Pts	Total Return Y-T-D	Risk Rating/Pts
6-06	A+	2,773	19.32	B / 8.1	3.04%	B / 8.4
2005	A+	2,727	18.75	B+ / 8.8	15.46%	B / 8.2
2004	B+	309	16.96	A / 9.4	26.20%	C / 4.9

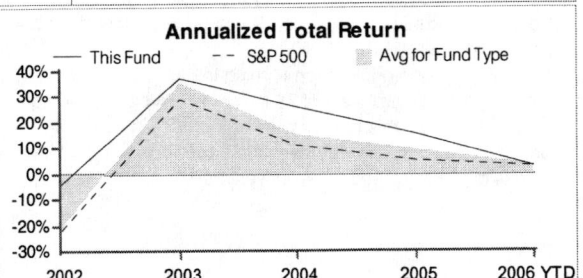

Baron Asset Fund (BARAX)   B   Good

Fund Family: Baron Funds   **Phone:** (800) 992-2766
Address: 767 Fifth Avenue, New York, NY 10153
Fund Type: SC - Small Cap
Major Rating Factors: Strong performance is the major factor driving the B
(Good) Weiss Investment Rating for Baron Asset Fund. The fund currently has a
performance rating of B+ (Good) based on an average return of 21.01% over the
last three years and 6.47% over the last six months. Factored into the
performance evaluation is an expense ratio of 1.34% (average).

The fund's risk rating is currently C+ (Fair). It carries a beta of 0.63, meaning
the fund's expected move will be 6.3% for every 10% move in the market.
Volatility, as measured by both the semi-deviation and a drawdown factor, is
considered low.

Ron Baron has been running the fund for 19 years and currently receives a
manager quality ranking of 98 (0=worst, 99=best). If you desire only a moderate
level of risk and strong performance, then this fund is an excellent option.
Services Offered: Bank draft capabilities, an IRA investment plan and a 401K
investment plan.

Data Date	Weiss Investment Rating	Net Assets ($Mil)	NAV	Perfor-mance Rating/Pts	Total Return Y-T-D	Risk Rating/Pts
6-06	B	3,207	59.93	B+ / 8.3	6.47%	C+/ 5.7
2005	B-	2,509	56.29	B / 8.1	12.46%	C / 5.2
2004	C+	2,040	52.52	B+ / 8.4	27.13%	C- / 3.8
2003	C-	1,009	43.83	C / 4.9	27.34%	C- / 3.8
2002	C	2,058	34.42	C / 5.3	-19.99%	C / 5.3
2001	C-	2,691	44.46	C+/ 6.0	-10.12%	E- / 0.0

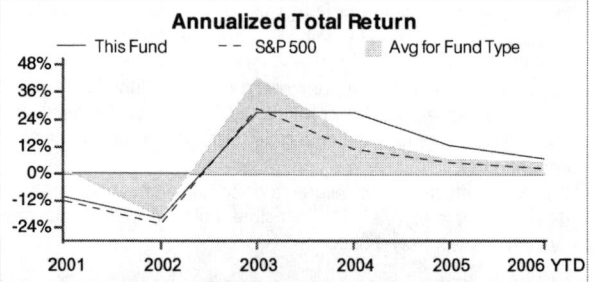

Annualized Total Return

Baron Growth Fund (BGRFX)   C+   Fair

Fund Family: Baron Funds   **Phone:** (800) 992-2766
Address: 767 Fifth Avenue, New York, NY 10153
Fund Type: GR - Growth
Major Rating Factors: Strong performance is the major factor driving the C+
(Fair) Weiss Investment Rating for Baron Growth Fund. The fund currently has a
performance rating of B- (Good) based on an average return of 17.90% over the
last three years and 6.92% over the last six months. Factored into the
performance evaluation is an expense ratio of 1.31% (average).

The fund's risk rating is currently C+ (Fair). It carries a beta of 1.11, meaning
it is expected to move 11.1% for every 10% move in the market. Volatility, as
measured by both the semi-deviation and a drawdown factor, is considered low.

Ron Baron has been running the fund for 12 years and currently receives a
manager quality ranking of 93 (0=worst, 99=best). If you desire only a moderate
level of risk and strong performance, then this fund is an excellent option.
Services Offered: Automated phone transactions, bank draft capabilities, an
IRA investment plan and a 401K investment plan. However, the fund is currently
closed to new investors.

Data Date	Weiss Investment Rating	Net Assets ($Mil)	NAV	Perfor-mance Rating/Pts	Total Return Y-T-D	Risk Rating/Pts
6-06	C+	5,584	48.54	B- / 7.2	6.92%	C+/ 5.9
2005	C+	4,906	45.40	B- / 7.0	5.71%	C+/ 6.0
2004	B+	3,020	44.87	A- / 9.1	26.61%	C / 5.5
2003	B+	2,002	35.44	B+ / 8.3	31.75%	C+/ 6.5
2002	B+	1,029	26.90	B / 8.0	-12.29%	B- / 7.6
2001	C+	510	30.67	A+/ 9.6	12.67%	D- / 1.0

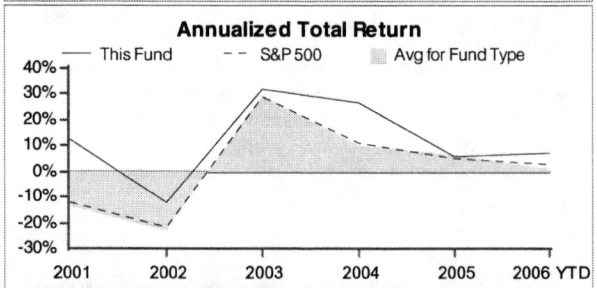

Annualized Total Return

Baron Small Cap (BSCFX)   C+   Fair

Fund Family: Baron Funds   **Phone:** (800) 992-2766
Address: 767 Fifth Avenue, New York, NY 10153
Fund Type: SC - Small Cap
Major Rating Factors: Middle of the road best describes Baron Small Cap
whose Weiss Investment Rating is currently a C+ (Fair). The fund currently has a
performance rating of C+ (Fair) based on an average return of 16.48% over the
last three years and 3.06% over the last six months. Factored into the
performance evaluation is an expense ratio of 1.33% (average).

The fund's risk rating is currently C+ (Fair). It carries a beta of 0.75, meaning
the fund's expected move will be 7.5% for every 10% move in the market.
Volatility, as measured by both the semi-deviation and a drawdown factor, is
considered low.

Cliff Greenberg has been running the fund for 9 years and currently receives
a manager quality ranking of 76 (0=worst, 99=best). If you desire an average
level of risk, then this fund may be an option.
Services Offered: An IRA investment plan and wire transfers. However, the
fund is currently closed to new investors.

Data Date	Weiss Investment Rating	Net Assets ($Mil)	NAV	Perfor-mance Rating/Pts	Total Return Y-T-D	Risk Rating/Pts
6-06	C+	3,185	23.88	C+/ 6.3	3.06%	C+/ 6.2
2005	B	2,716	23.17	B / 7.8	8.34%	C+/ 6.5
2004	A-	1,840	22.08	A- / 9.1	22.16%	C+/ 6.2
2003	A-	1,002	18.56	B+/ 8.6	38.82%	B- / 7.2
2002	B-	719	13.37	C+/ 6.5	-9.66%	B- / 7.1
2001	C+	586	15.21	A / 9.3	5.19%	E- / 0.0

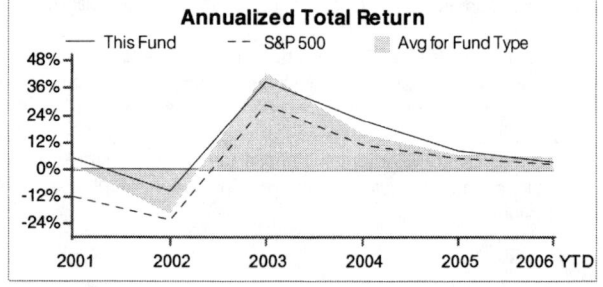

Annualized Total Return

Brandywine Fund Inc. (BRWIX)

C+ **Fair**

Fund Family: Brandywine
Phone: (800) 656-3017
Address: 3711 Kennett Pike, Greenville, DE 19807
Fund Type: GR - Growth

Major Rating Factors: Middle of the road best describes Brandywine Fund Inc. whose Weiss Investment Rating is currently a C+ (Fair). The fund currently has a performance rating of C+ (Fair) based on an average return of 15.57% over the last three years and 3.57% over the last six months. Factored into the performance evaluation is an expense ratio of 1.07% (low).

The fund's risk rating is currently C+ (Fair). It carries a beta of 1.45, meaning it is expected to move 14.5% for every 10% move in the market. Volatility, as measured by both the semi-deviation and a drawdown factor, is considered low.

D' Alonzo currently receives a manager quality ranking of 57 (0=worst, 99=best). If you desire an average level of risk, then this fund may be an option.

Services Offered: Automated phone transactions, wire transfers and a systematic withdrawal plan.

Data Date	Weiss Investment Rating	Net Assets ($Mil)	NAV	Performance Rating/Pts	Total Return Y-T-D	Risk Rating/Pts
6-06	C+	4,128	32.20	C+ / 6.5	3.57%	C+ / 6.3
2005	B-	3,963	31.09	B- / 7.0	14.39%	C+ / 6.4
2004	C+	3,822	27.18	C+ / 6.1	13.11%	C+ / 5.6
2003	C	3,796	24.03	C- / 3.4	31.46%	C+ / 6.2
2002	C-	2,997	18.28	C / 4.5	-21.71%	C- / 3.6
2001	C	4,265	23.35	B- / 7.2	-20.55%	D / 1.6

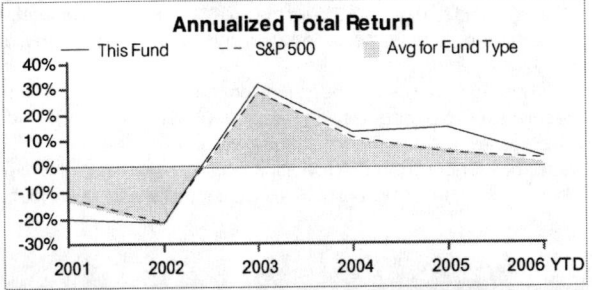

Calamos Growth & Income A (CVTRX)

C- **Fair**

Fund Family: Calamos
Phone: (800) 823-7386
Address: 1111 East Warrenville Road, Naperville, IL 60563
Fund Type: GI - Growth and Income

Major Rating Factors: Middle of the road best describes Calamos Growth & Income A whose Weiss Investment Rating is currently a C- (Fair). The fund currently has a performance rating of C- (Fair) based on an average return of 11.05% over the last three years and 2.30% over the last six months. Factored into the performance evaluation is an expense ratio of 1.06% (low), a 4.8% front-end load that is levied at the time of purchase and a 0.5% back-end load levied at the time of sale.

The fund's risk rating is currently B- (Good). It carries a beta of 0.96, meaning that its performance tracks fairly well with that of the overall stock market. Volatility, as measured by both the semi-deviation and a drawdown factor, is considered low.

John P. Calamos Sr. has been running the fund for 18 years and currently receives a manager quality ranking of 59 (0=worst, 99=best). If you desire an average level of risk, then this fund may be an option.

Services Offered: Automated phone transactions, check writing, payroll deductions, bank draft capabilities, an IRA investment plan, a 401K investment plan, wire transfers and a systematic withdrawal plan.

Data Date	Weiss Investment Rating	Net Assets ($Mil)	NAV	Performance Rating/Pts	Total Return Y-T-D	Risk Rating/Pts
6-06	C-	3,384	31.17	C- / 3.2	2.30%	B- / 7.8
2005	C	2,930	30.83	C- / 3.5	8.06%	B / 8.1
2004	B	2,395	29.82	C+ / 6.3	9.67%	B / 8.7
2003	A+	1,634	27.78	B- / 7.5	27.57%	B+ / 9.3
2002	B+	435	22.21	B+ / 8.5	-4.11%	B / 8.0
2001	B	173	23.60	A- / 9.2	-2.38%	D+ / 2.7

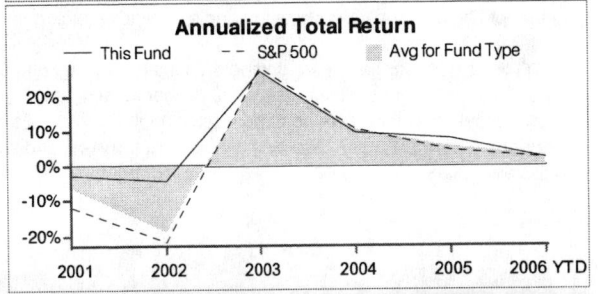

Calamos Growth & Income C (CVTCX)

C- **Fair**

Fund Family: Calamos
Phone: (800) 823-7386
Address: 1111 East Warrenville Road, Naperville, IL 60563
Fund Type: GI - Growth and Income

Major Rating Factors: Middle of the road best describes Calamos Growth & Income C whose Weiss Investment Rating is currently a C- (Fair). The fund currently has a performance rating of C- (Fair) based on an average return of 10.21% over the last three years and 1.91% over the last six months. Factored into the performance evaluation is an expense ratio of 1.81% (above average) and a 1.0% back-end load levied at the time of sale.

The fund's risk rating is currently B- (Good). It carries a beta of 0.96, meaning that its performance tracks fairly well with that of the overall stock market. Volatility, as measured by both the semi-deviation and a drawdown factor, is considered low.

John P. Calamos, Sr. has been running the fund for 10 years and currently receives a manager quality ranking of 49 (0=worst, 99=best). If you desire an average level of risk, then this fund may be an option.

Services Offered: Automated phone transactions, check writing, payroll deductions, bank draft capabilities, an IRA investment plan, a 401K investment plan, wire transfers and a systematic withdrawal plan.

Data Date	Weiss Investment Rating	Net Assets ($Mil)	NAV	Performance Rating/Pts	Total Return Y-T-D	Risk Rating/Pts
6-06	C-	2,082	31.36	C- / 3.3	1.91%	B- / 7.8
2005	C	1,861	31.02	C- / 3.7	7.24%	B / 8.1
2004	B	1,517	30.01	C+ / 6.4	8.80%	B / 8.7
2003	A+	1,035	27.98	B- / 7.5	26.61%	B+ / 9.4
2002	B+	263	22.39	B+ / 8.7	-4.79%	B / 8.1
2001	B	71	23.83	A / 9.3	-3.05%	D+ / 2.7

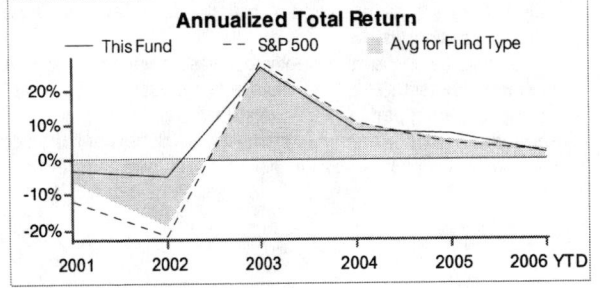

Calamos Growth Fund A (CVGRX)   D+   Weak

Fund Family: Calamos   **Phone:** (800) 823-7386
Address: 1111 East Warrenville Road, Naperville, IL 60563
Fund Type: MC - Mid Cap

Major Rating Factors: Calamos Growth Fund A receives a Weiss Investment Rating of D+ (Weak). The fund currently has a performance rating of C (Fair) based on an average return of 15.55% over the last three years and -1.47% over the last six months. Factored into the performance evaluation is an expense ratio of 1.20% (average), a 4.8% front-end load that is levied at the time of purchase and a 0.5% back-end load levied at the time of sale.

The fund's risk rating is currently C (Fair). It carries a beta of 1.35, meaning it is expected to move 13.5% for every 10% move in the market. Volatility, as measured by both the semi-deviation and a drawdown factor, is considered average.

Nick P. Calamos has been running the fund for 16 years and currently receives a manager quality ranking of 6 (0=worst, 99=best). If you desire an average level of risk, then this fund may be an option.

Services Offered: An IRA investment plan, a 401K investment plan, a Keogh investment plan, wire transfers and a systematic withdrawal plan.

Data Date	Weiss Investment Rating	Net Assets ($Mil)	NAV	Performance Rating/Pts	Total Return Y-T-D	Risk Rating/Pts
6-06	D+	13,291	54.25	C / 5.3	-1.47%	C / 4.8
2005	B-	12,615	55.06	B / 7.7	8.47%	C+/ 5.9
2004	B+	9,010	52.98	B / 7.9	18.65%	C+/ 6.7
2003	B+	4,458	44.78	B / 7.8	42.34%	B- / 7.7
2002	B-	1,535	31.46	B / 7.8	-15.88%	C+/ 5.9
2001	C+	642	37.40	A+/ 9.8	-7.68%	E- / 0.0

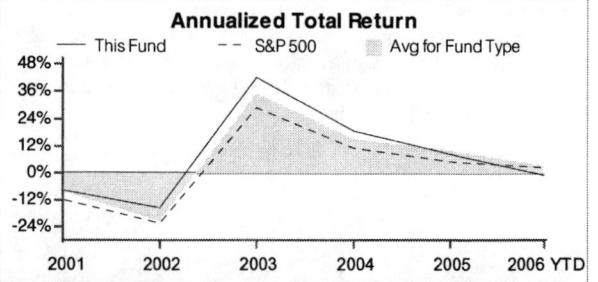

Annualized Total Return

CGM Focus Fund (CGMFX)   C+   Fair

Fund Family: CGM   **Phone:** (800) 345-4048
Address: One International Place, Boston, MA 02110
Fund Type: AG - Aggressive Growth

Major Rating Factors: Exceptional performance is the major factor driving the C+ (Fair) Weiss Investment Rating for CGM Focus Fund. The fund currently has a performance rating of A+ (Excellent) based on an average return of 29.43% over the last three years and 15.32% over the last six months. Factored into the performance evaluation is an expense ratio of 1.07% (low).

The fund's risk rating is currently C- (Fair). It carries a beta of 1.43, meaning it is expected to move 14.3% for every 10% move in the market. Volatility, as measured by both the semi-deviation and a drawdown factor, is considered average.

G. Ken Heebner has been running the fund for 9 years and currently receives a manager quality ranking of 99 (0=worst, 99=best). If you desire an average level of risk and strong performance, then this fund is a good option.

Services Offered: An IRA investment plan, wire transfers and a systematic withdrawal plan.

Data Date	Weiss Investment Rating	Net Assets ($Mil)	NAV	Performance Rating/Pts	Total Return Y-T-D	Risk Rating/Pts
6-06	C+	2,270	38.53	A+/ 9.6	15.32%	C- / 3.8
2005	B-	1,590	33.41	A / 9.5	25.37%	C- / 4.1
2004	C	852	29.49	B+/ 8.4	12.33%	D / 2.0
2003	B+	694	29.93	A+/ 9.9	66.46%	C+/ 5.6
2002	B+	428	17.98	A+/ 9.8	-17.79%	C+/ 6.0
2001	C+	250	21.87	A+/ 9.9	47.65%	E- / 0.0

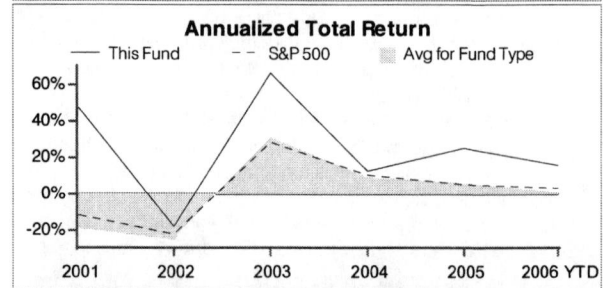

Annualized Total Return

Clipper Fund (CFIMX)   D   Weak

Fund Family: Clipper   **Phone:** (800) 432-2504
Address: 9601 Wilshire Boulevard, Beverly Hills, CA 90210
Fund Type: GR - Growth

Major Rating Factors: Disappointing performance is the major factor driving the D (Weak) Weiss Investment Rating for Clipper Fund. The fund currently has a performance rating of D- (Weak) based on an average return of 6.62% over the last three years and 1.33% over the last six months. Factored into the performance evaluation is an expense ratio of 0.70% (very low).

The fund's risk rating is currently B- (Good). It carries a beta of 0.65, meaning the fund's expected move will be 6.5% for every 10% move in the market. Volatility, as measured by both the semi-deviation and a drawdown factor, is considered low.

Christopher C.Davis currently receives a manager quality ranking of 40 (0=worst, 99=best). This fund offers only a moderate level of risk but investors looking for strong performance are still waiting.

Services Offered: Automated phone transactions, bank draft capabilities, an IRA investment plan, a 401K investment plan, wire transfers and a systematic withdrawal plan.

Data Date	Weiss Investment Rating	Net Assets ($Mil)	NAV	Performance Rating/Pts	Total Return Y-T-D	Risk Rating/Pts
6-06	D	3,250	84.88	D- / 1.3	1.33%	B- / 7.9
2005	E	4,400	88.15	E / 0.5	-0.28%	C+/ 6.7
2004	C	6,819	89.68	C / 4.5	5.87%	C+/ 6.5
2003	B+	6,556	87.97	B / 7.6	19.35%	B- / 7.7
2002	A+	5,017	75.73	A+/ 9.7	-5.51%	B / 8.7
2001	A+	2,685	83.53	A / 9.3	10.26%	B- / 7.7

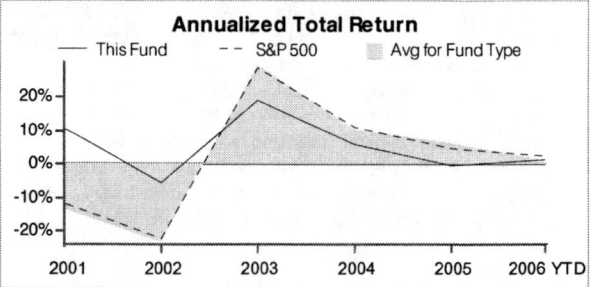

Annualized Total Return

Cohen & Steers Realty Shrs Fd (CSRSX) B Good

Fund Family: Cohen & Steers **Phone:** (800) 437-9912
Address: 757 Third Avenue, New York, NY 10017
Fund Type: RE - Real Estate
Major Rating Factors: Exceptional performance is the major factor driving the B (Good) Weiss Investment Rating for Cohen & Steers Realty Shrs Fd. The fund currently has a performance rating of A (Excellent) based on an average return of 30.16% over the last three years and 14.54% over the last six months. Factored into the performance evaluation is an expense ratio of 0.97% (low) and a 1.0% back-end load levied at the time of sale.

The fund's risk rating is currently C (Fair). It carries a beta of 0.97, meaning that its performance tracks fairly well with that of the overall stock market. Volatility, as measured by both the semi-deviation and a drawdown factor, is considered average.

Martin Cohen has been running the fund for 15 years and currently receives a manager quality ranking of 94 (0=worst, 99=best). If you desire an average level of risk and strong performance, then this fund is a good option.
Services Offered: Automated phone transactions, check writing, bank draft capabilities, a 401K investment plan and wire transfers.

Data Date	Weiss Investment Rating	Net Assets ($Mil)	NAV	Performance Rating/Pts	Total Return Y-T-D	Risk Rating/Pts
6-06	B	2,464	82.00	A / 9.5	14.54%	C / 4.8
2005	B	1,260	72.59	A / 9.3	14.90%	C / 4.9
2004	A+	1,260	69.66	A+ / 9.9	38.48%	C+ / 6.9
2003	A+	1,625	55.64	A- / 9.2	38.09%	B / 8.4
2002	A+	1,257	43.34	A+ / 9.6	2.79%	B+ / 9.6
2001	A	1,372	44.41	B+ / 8.8	5.70%	C+ / 6.7

Annualized Total Return

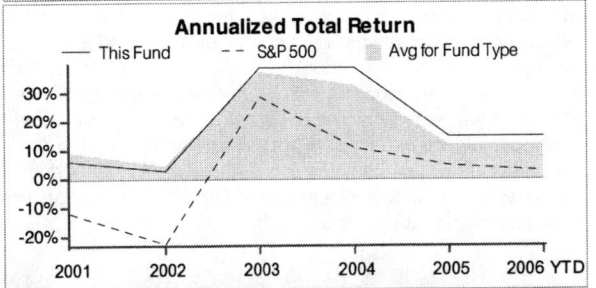

Columbia Acorn International Fund Z (ACINX) B+ Good

Fund Family: Columbia Funds **Phone:** (800) 426-3750
Address: One Financial Center, Boston, MA 02111
Fund Type: FO - Foreign
Major Rating Factors: Exceptional performance is the major factor driving the B+ (Good) Weiss Investment Rating for Columbia Acorn International Fund Z. The fund currently has a performance rating of A+ (Excellent) based on an average return of 32.82% over the last three years and 14.27% over the last six months. Factored into the performance evaluation is an expense ratio of 0.94% (low) and a 2.0% back-end load levied at the time of sale.

The fund's risk rating is currently C (Fair). It carries a beta of 1.15, meaning it is expected to move 11.5% for every 10% move in the market. Volatility, as measured by both the semi-deviation and a drawdown factor, is considered average.

Louis J. Mendes, CFA has been running the fund for 3 years and currently receives a manager quality ranking of 88 (0=worst, 99=best). If you desire an average level of risk and strong performance, then this fund is a good option.
Services Offered: Automated phone transactions, bank draft capabilities, an IRA investment plan, a 401K investment plan, wire transfers and a systematic withdrawal plan.

Data Date	Weiss Investment Rating	Net Assets ($Mil)	NAV	Performance Rating/Pts	Total Return Y-T-D	Risk Rating/Pts
6-06	B+	3,221	37.58	A+ / 9.7	14.27%	C / 5.2
2005	A+	2,467	33.44	A+ / 9.6	21.81%	B- / 7.7
2004	A	1,919	29.03	A / 9.5	29.47%	C+ / 6.4
2003	C+	1,564	22.66	B- / 7.0	47.80%	C+ / 6.0
2002	C-	1,242	15.40	C- / 3.1	-16.15%	C- / 4.0
2001	C-	1,675	18.47	C+ / 6.1	-19.59%	E- / 0.0

Annualized Total Return

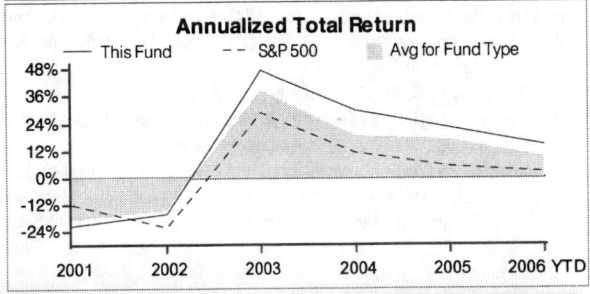

Columbia Marsico Focused Eq Fd A (NFEAX) C- Fair

Fund Family: Columbia Funds **Phone:** (800) 426-3750
Address: One Financial Center, Boston, MA 02111
Fund Type: GR - Growth
Major Rating Factors: Middle of the road best describes Columbia Marsico Focused Eq Fd A whose Weiss Investment Rating is currently a C- (Fair). The fund currently has a performance rating of C- (Fair) based on an average return of 11.42% over the last three years and -0.59% over the last six months. Factored into the performance evaluation is an expense ratio of 1.22% (average) and a 5.8% front-end load that is levied at the time of purchase.

The fund's risk rating is currently B- (Good). It carries a beta of 1.16, meaning it is expected to move 11.6% for every 10% move in the market. Volatility, as measured by both the semi-deviation and a drawdown factor, is considered low.

Thomas F. Marsico has been running the fund for 9 years and currently receives a manager quality ranking of 41 (0=worst, 99=best). If you desire an average level of risk, then this fund may be an option.
Services Offered: Automated phone transactions, bank draft capabilities, an IRA investment plan, a 401K investment plan, wire transfers and a systematic withdrawal plan.

Data Date	Weiss Investment Rating	Net Assets ($Mil)	NAV	Performance Rating/Pts	Total Return Y-T-D	Risk Rating/Pts
6-06	C-	2,060	20.11	C- / 3.1	-0.59%	B- / 7.3
2005	C+	1,729	20.23	C / 4.8	9.59%	B- / 7.3
2004	C	1,113	18.46	C / 5.0	10.67%	C+ / 5.8
2003	C	859	16.68	C- / 3.8	31.34%	C+ / 6.5
2002	C-	569	12.70	D+ / 2.7	-15.73%	C+ / 6.2
2001	D	476	15.07	C- / 3.3	-19.11%	E- / 0.0

Annualized Total Return

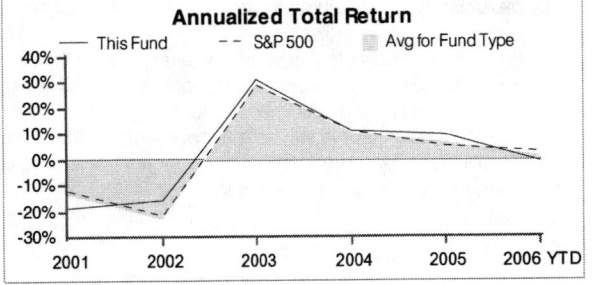

Columbia Marsico Growth Fund A (NMGIX)

C-   **Fair**

Fund Family: Columbia Funds   **Phone:** (800) 426-3750
Address: One Financial Center, Boston, MA 02111
Fund Type: GR - Growth

Major Rating Factors: Disappointing performance is the major factor driving the C- (Fair) Weiss Investment Rating for Columbia Marsico Growth Fund A. The fund currently has a performance rating of D+ (Weak) based on an average return of 11.48% over the last three years and -0.85% over the last six months. Factored into the performance evaluation is an expense ratio of 1.21% (average) and a 5.8% front-end load that is levied at the time of purchase.

The fund's risk rating is currently B- (Good). It carries a beta of 1.10, meaning it is expected to move 11.0% for every 10% move in the market. Volatility, as measured by both the semi-deviation and a drawdown factor, is considered low.

Thomas F. Marsico currently receives a manager quality ranking of 49 (0=worst, 99=best). This fund offers only a moderate level of risk but investors looking for strong performance are still waiting.

Services Offered: Automated phone transactions, payroll deductions, bank draft capabilities, an IRA investment plan, a 401K investment plan, wire transfers and a systematic withdrawal plan.

Data Date	Weiss Investment Rating	Net Assets ($Mil)	NAV	Performance Rating/Pts	Total Return Y-T-D	Risk Rating/Pts
6-06	C-	2,066	18.65	D+ / 2.8	-0.85%	B- / 7.6
2005	C	1,585	18.81	C- / 4.0	5.85%	B- / 7.7
2004	C+	722	17.77	C+ / 6.6	15.39%	C+ / 6.7
2003	C	449	15.40	C- / 3.2	28.65%	C+ / 6.5
2002	C	280	11.97	C- / 3.0	-15.29%	C+ / 6.2
2001	D	195	14.13	C- / 3.3	-19.76%	E / 0.5

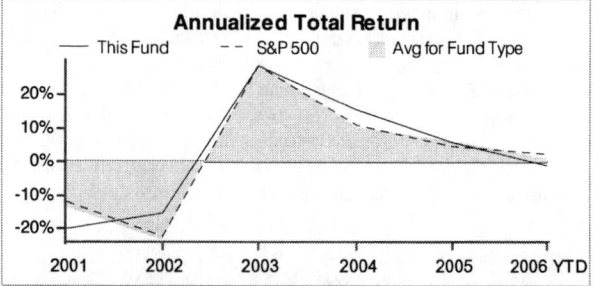

Annualized Total Return

Davis New York Venture Fund A (NYVTX)

B   **Good**

Fund Family: Davis Funds   **Phone:** (800) 279-0279
Address: 2949 East Elvira St, Tuscon, AZ 85706
Fund Type: GR - Growth

Major Rating Factors: Davis New York Venture Fund A receives a Weiss Investment Rating of B (Good). The fund currently has a performance rating of C+ (Fair) based on an average return of 14.89% over the last three years and 3.20% over the last six months. Factored into the performance evaluation is an expense ratio of 0.89% (low), a 4.8% front-end load that is levied at the time of purchase and a 0.8% back-end load levied at the time of sale.

The fund's risk rating is currently B+ (Good). It carries a beta of 0.91, meaning that its performance tracks fairly well with that of the overall stock market. Volatility, as measured by both the semi-deviation and a drawdown factor, is considered very low.

Christopher C. Davis has been running the fund for 11 years and currently receives a manager quality ranking of 90 (0=worst, 99=best). If you desire an average level of risk, then this fund may be an option.

Services Offered: Automated phone transactions, payroll deductions, bank draft capabilities, an IRA investment plan, a 401K investment plan, a Keogh investment plan, wire transfers and a systematic withdrawal plan.

Data Date	Weiss Investment Rating	Net Assets ($Mil)	NAV	Performance Rating/Pts	Total Return Y-T-D	Risk Rating/Pts
6-06	B	22,272	34.78	C+ / 5.6	3.20%	B+ / 9.0
2005	B-	18,904	33.70	C+ / 5.6	10.68%	B- / 7.8
2004	C+	14,494	30.69	C+ / 5.6	12.37%	C+ / 6.4
2003	C+	10,899	27.52	C+ / 5.7	32.34%	B- / 7.1
2002	C+	8,258	20.94	C+ / 6.5	-17.16%	C+ / 6.8
2001	C+	10,463	25.43	C+ / 6.0	-11.41%	C+ / 6.2

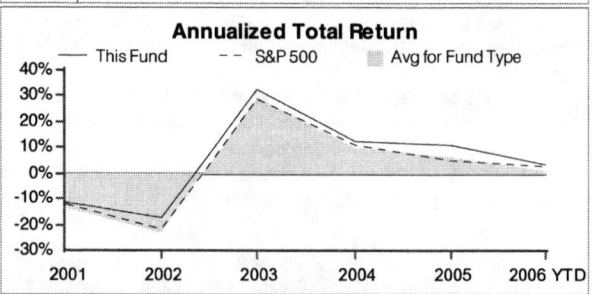

Annualized Total Return

Dodge & Cox Balanced Fund (DODBX)

B+   **Good**

Fund Family: Dodge & Cox   **Phone:** (800) 621-3979
Address: 555 California Street, San Francisco, CA 94104
Fund Type: BA - Balanced

Major Rating Factors: Dodge & Cox Balanced Fund receives a Weiss Investment Rating of B+ (Good). The fund currently has a performance rating of C (Fair) based on an average return of 12.76% over the last three years and 4.09% over the last six months. Factored into the performance evaluation is an expense ratio of 0.53% (very low).

The fund's risk rating is currently B+ (Good). It carries a beta of 1.09, meaning that its performance tracks fairly well with that of the overall stock market. Volatility, as measured by both the semi-deviation and a drawdown factor, is considered very low.

Fixed-Income Strategy Committe has been running the fund for 75 years and currently receives a manager quality ranking of 91 (0=worst, 99=best). If you desire an average level of risk, then this fund may be an option.

Services Offered: Automated phone transactions, an IRA investment plan, a 401K investment plan, wire transfers and a systematic withdrawal plan. However, the fund is currently closed to new investors.

Data Date	Weiss Investment Rating	Net Assets ($Mil)	NAV	Performance Rating/Pts	Total Return Y-T-D	Risk Rating/Pts
6-06	B+	24,683	83.57	C / 5.3	4.09%	B+ / 9.7
2005	C+	23,629	81.34	C / 4.0	6.59%	B / 8.4
2004	A	20,091	79.35	B- / 7.5	13.30%	B / 8.1
2003	A+	12,280	73.04	B+ / 8.3	24.44%	B+ / 9.1
2002	A+	7,885	60.75	A / 9.4	-2.94%	B+ / 9.4
2001	A+	6,040	65.42	A- / 9.1	10.05%	B / 8.1

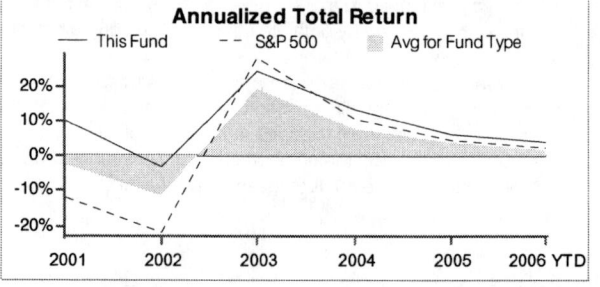

Annualized Total Return

Dodge & Cox International Stock (DODFX)

A+ Excellent

Fund Family: Dodge & Cox **Phone:** (800) 621-3979
Address: 555 California Street, San Francisco, CA 94104
Fund Type: FO - Foreign

Major Rating Factors: Exceptional performance is the major factor driving the A+ (Excellent) Weiss Investment Rating for Dodge & Cox International Stock. The fund currently has a performance rating of A+ (Excellent) based on an average return of 33.39% over the last three years and 11.22% over the last six months. Factored into the performance evaluation is an expense ratio of 0.70% (very low).

The fund's risk rating is currently B- (Good). It carries a beta of 1.06, meaning that its performance tracks fairly well with that of the overall stock market. Volatility, as measured by standard deviation, is considered low for equity funds at 11.73.

International Investment Polic currently receives a manager quality ranking of 95 (0=worst, 99=best). If you desire only a moderate level of risk and strong performance, then this fund is an excellent option.

Services Offered: Automated phone transactions, bank draft capabilities, an IRA investment plan, a 401K investment plan and wire transfers.

Data Date	Weiss Investment Rating	Net Assets ($Mil)	NAV	Performance Rating/Pts	Total Return Y-T-D	Risk Rating/Pts
6-06	A+	20,665	38.96	A+ / 9.7	11.22%	B- / 7.7
2005	A+	12,056	35.03	A / 9.5	16.75%	B- / 7.3
2004	C	3,376	30.64	A+ / 9.6	32.46%	D / 1.6

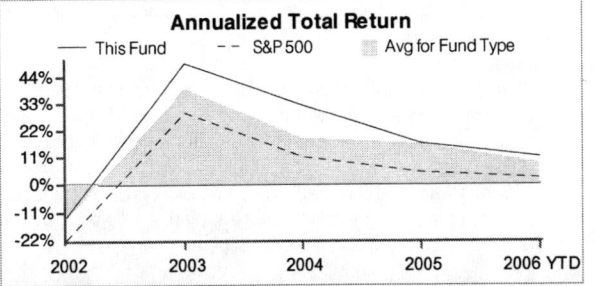

Dodge & Cox Stock Fund (DODGX)

A+ Excellent

Fund Family: Dodge & Cox **Phone:** (800) 621-3979
Address: 555 California Street, San Francisco, CA 94104
Fund Type: GI - Growth and Income

Major Rating Factors: Strong performance is the major factor driving the A+ (Excellent) Weiss Investment Rating for Dodge & Cox Stock Fund. The fund currently has a performance rating of B (Good) based on an average return of 18.36% over the last three years and 6.15% over the last six months. Factored into the performance evaluation is an expense ratio of 0.52% (very low).

The fund's risk rating is currently B (Good). It carries a beta of 1.03, meaning that its performance tracks fairly well with that of the overall stock market. Volatility, as measured by both the semi-deviation and a drawdown factor, is considered low.

Investment Policy Committee has been running the fund for 41 years and currently receives a manager quality ranking of 96 (0=worst, 99=best). If you desire only a moderate level of risk and strong performance, then this fund is an excellent option.

Services Offered: Automated phone transactions, bank draft capabilities, an IRA investment plan, a 401K investment plan, wire transfers and a systematic withdrawal plan. However, the fund is currently closed to new investors.

Data Date	Weiss Investment Rating	Net Assets ($Mil)	NAV	Performance Rating/Pts	Total Return Y-T-D	Risk Rating/Pts
6-06	A+	57,086	144.48	B / 7.7	6.15%	B / 8.8
2005	B+	51,035	137.22	B- / 7.0	9.37%	B- / 7.5
2004	B+	41,436	130.22	B+ / 8.4	19.17%	C+ / 6.4
2003	A	26,408	113.78	B+ / 8.6	32.34%	B- / 7.7
2002	A-	14,036	88.05	A- / 9.1	-10.54%	B / 8.2
2001	A	9,396	100.51	A / 9.4	9.33%	C+ / 6.1

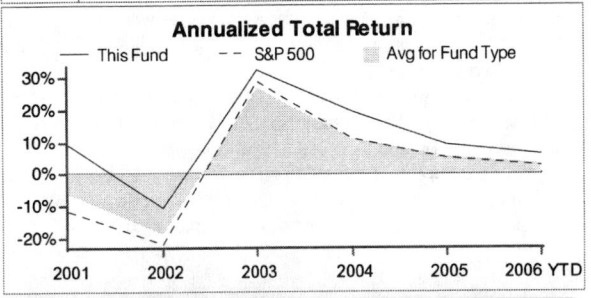

Dreyfus Appreciation Fund (DGAGX)

C- Fair

Fund Family: Dreyfus **Phone:** (800) 242-8671
Address: 200 Park Avenue, New York, NY 10166
Fund Type: GR - Growth

Major Rating Factors: Disappointing performance is the major factor driving the C- (Fair) Weiss Investment Rating for Dreyfus Appreciation Fund. The fund currently has a performance rating of D (Weak) based on an average return of 7.88% over the last three years and 2.57% over the last six months. Factored into the performance evaluation is an expense ratio of 0.91% (low).

The fund's risk rating is currently B+ (Good). It carries a beta of 0.75, meaning the fund's expected move will be 7.5% for every 10% move in the market. Volatility, as measured by both the semi-deviation and a drawdown factor, is considered very low.

Fayez Sarofim & Co. has been running the fund for 16 years and currently receives a manager quality ranking of 44 (0=worst, 99=best). This fund offers only a moderate level of risk but investors looking for strong performance are still waiting.

Services Offered: Automated phone transactions, bank draft capabilities, an IRA investment plan, a 401K investment plan, a Keogh investment plan, wire transfers and a systematic withdrawal plan.

Data Date	Weiss Investment Rating	Net Assets ($Mil)	NAV	Performance Rating/Pts	Total Return Y-T-D	Risk Rating/Pts
6-06	C-	4,015	40.72	D / 2.2	2.57%	B+ / 9.1
2005	E+	4,536	39.75	D- / 1.1	4.14%	B- / 7.0
2004	D+	4,307	38.69	D / 2.0	5.57%	C+ / 6.0
2003	C	3,779	37.14	C- / 3.7	20.39%	C+ / 6.6
2002	B-	3,275	31.20	C+ / 6.2	-17.14%	B- / 7.4
2001	B-	3,428	38.02	C / 4.3	-10.75%	B- / 7.0

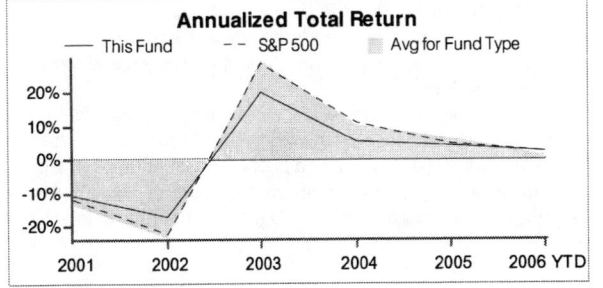

Dreyfus MidCap Index Fund (PESPX)   B-   Good

Fund Family: Dreyfus
Phone: (800) 242-8671
Address: 200 Park Avenue, New York, NY 10166
Fund Type: MC - Mid Cap

Major Rating Factors: Strong performance is the major factor driving the B- (Good) Weiss Investment Rating for Dreyfus MidCap Index Fund. The fund currently has a performance rating of B- (Good) based on an average return of 17.61% over the last three years and 4.08% over the last six months. Factored into the performance evaluation is an expense ratio of 0.50% (very low) and a 1.0% back-end load levied at the time of sale.

The fund's risk rating is currently C+ (Fair). It carries a beta of 1.00, meaning that its performance tracks fairly well with that of the overall stock market. Volatility, as measured by both the semi-deviation and a drawdown factor, is considered low.

The Dreyfus Corporation has been running the fund for 11 years and currently receives a manager quality ranking of 50 (0=worst, 99=best). If you desire only a moderate level of risk and strong performance, then this fund is an excellent option.

Services Offered: Automated phone transactions, bank draft capabilities, an IRA investment plan, a 401K investment plan, a Keogh investment plan, wire transfers and a systematic withdrawal plan.

Data Date	Weiss Investment Rating	Net Assets ($Mil)	NAV	Performance Rating/Pts	Total Return Y-T-D	Risk Rating/Pts
6-06	B-	2,267	29.08	B- / 7.1	4.08%	C+ / 6.8
2005	B	2,173	27.94	B- / 7.4	12.05%	C+ / 6.6
2004	B-	1,637	26.19	B / 7.6	15.92%	C+ / 5.6
2003	B	1,197	23.36	B / 8.1	35.61%	C+ / 6.5
2002	B	752	17.47	B+ / 8.3	-15.02%	C+ / 6.8
2001	B-	591	21.06	B+ / 8.6	-1.01%	D+ / 2.3

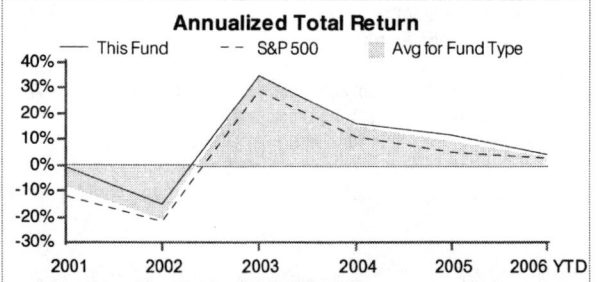

Annualized Total Return

Dreyfus S&P 500 Index Fund (PEOPX)   C-   Fair

Fund Family: Dreyfus
Phone: (800) 242-8671
Address: 200 Park Avenue, New York, NY 10166
Fund Type: IX - Index

Major Rating Factors: Middle of the road best describes Dreyfus S&P 500 Index Fund whose Weiss Investment Rating is currently a C- (Fair). The fund currently has a performance rating of C- (Fair) based on an average return of 10.69% over the last three years and 2.48% over the last six months. Factored into the performance evaluation is an expense ratio of 0.50% (very low) and a 1.0% back-end load levied at the time of sale.

The fund's risk rating is currently B- (Good). It carries a beta of 1.00, meaning that its performance tracks fairly well with that of the overall stock market. Volatility, as measured by both the semi-deviation and a drawdown factor, is considered low.

Dreyfus Corporation has been running the fund for 11 years and currently receives a manager quality ranking of 50 (0=worst, 99=best). If you desire an average level of risk, then this fund may be an option.

Services Offered: Automated phone transactions, bank draft capabilities, an IRA investment plan, a 401K investment plan, a Keogh investment plan, wire transfers and a systematic withdrawal plan.

Data Date	Weiss Investment Rating	Net Assets ($Mil)	NAV	Performance Rating/Pts	Total Return Y-T-D	Risk Rating/Pts
6-06	C-	3,368	37.25	C- / 3.6	2.48%	B- / 7.7
2005	D+	3,428	36.35	C- / 3.1	4.42%	C+ / 6.7
2004	C-	3,231	35.27	C- / 3.9	10.38%	C / 5.1
2003	C	2,838	32.43	C / 4.4	29.44%	C / 5.5
2002	C	2,326	25.60	C- / 4.1	-22.51%	C+ / 6.3
2001	C-	2,732	33.42	C- / 3.4	-12.36%	C- / 3.6

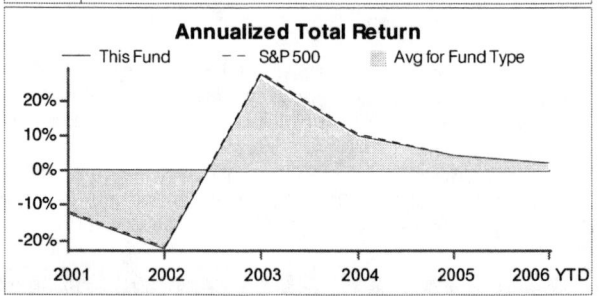

Annualized Total Return

DWS Dreman High Ret Eqty A (KDHAX)   C+   Fair

Fund Family: DWS Scudder
Phone: (800) 621-1048
Address: Two International Place, Boston, MA 02110
Fund Type: GR - Growth

Major Rating Factors: Middle of the road best describes DWS Dreman High Ret Eqty A whose Weiss Investment Rating is currently a C+ (Fair). The fund currently has a performance rating of C (Fair) based on an average return of 13.84% over the last three years and 4.03% over the last six months. Factored into the performance evaluation is an expense ratio of 1.12% (low), a 5.8% front-end load that is levied at the time of purchase and a 1.0% back-end load levied at the time of sale.

The fund's risk rating is currently B (Good). It carries a beta of 0.86, meaning the fund's expected move will be 8.6% for every 10% move in the market. Volatility, as measured by both the semi-deviation and a drawdown factor, is considered low.

David Dreman currently receives a manager quality ranking of 88 (0=worst, 99=best). If you desire an average level of risk, then this fund may be an option.

Services Offered: Automated phone transactions, payroll deductions, bank draft capabilities, an IRA investment plan, a 401K investment plan, a Keogh investment plan, wire transfers and a systematic withdrawal plan.

Data Date	Weiss Investment Rating	Net Assets ($Mil)	NAV	Performance Rating/Pts	Total Return Y-T-D	Risk Rating/Pts
6-06	C+	5,201	46.81	C / 4.7	4.03%	B / 8.7
2005	C+	4,768	45.31	C / 4.5	7.72%	B- / 7.7
2004	C	4,365	42.67	C+ / 5.8	13.48%	C / 5.0
2003	B-	3,190	38.18	B- / 7.3	31.34%	C+ / 6.6
2002	B+	2,043	29.58	B+ / 8.9	-18.52%	B- / 7.4
2001	B-	2,126	36.91	B- / 7.4	1.23%	C- / 3.4

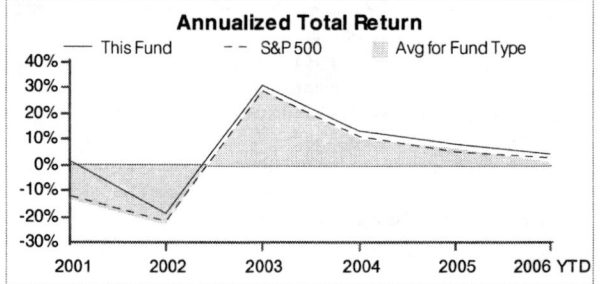

Annualized Total Return

DWS Growth & Income AARP (ACDGX)

C-   Fair

Fund Family: DWS Scudder   **Phone:** (800) 621-1048
Address: Two International Place, Boston, MA 02110
Fund Type: GI - Growth and Income
Major Rating Factors: Middle of the road best describes DWS Growth & Income AARP whose Weiss Investment Rating is currently a C- (Fair). The fund currently has a performance rating of C- (Fair) based on an average return of 9.98% over the last three years and -0.18% over the last six months. Factored into the performance evaluation is an expense ratio of 0.64% (very low).

The fund's risk rating is currently B- (Good). It carries a beta of 1.03, meaning that its performance tracks fairly well with that of the overall stock market. Volatility, as measured by both the semi-deviation and a drawdown factor, is considered low.

This is team managed and currently receives a manager quality ranking of 39 (0=worst, 99=best). If you desire an average level of risk, then this fund may be an option.

Services Offered: Automated phone transactions, payroll deductions, bank draft capabilities, an IRA investment plan, a 401K investment plan, a Keogh investment plan, wire transfers and a systematic withdrawal plan.

Data Date	Weiss Investment Rating	Net Assets ($Mil)	NAV	Perfor-mance Rating/Pts	Total Return Y-T-D	Risk Rating/Pts
6-06	C-	2,298	21.67	C- / 3.0	-0.18%	B- / 7.5
2005	C	2,572	21.83	C- / 3.6	5.95%	B- / 7.6
2004	C-	2,730	21.93	C- / 3.5	9.86%	C / 5.3
2003	C	2,754	20.17	C- / 3.7	26.99%	C+ / 6.0
2002	U	2,360	15.98	U / --	-23.52%	U / --
2001	U	3,653	21.06	U / --	-12.08%	U / --

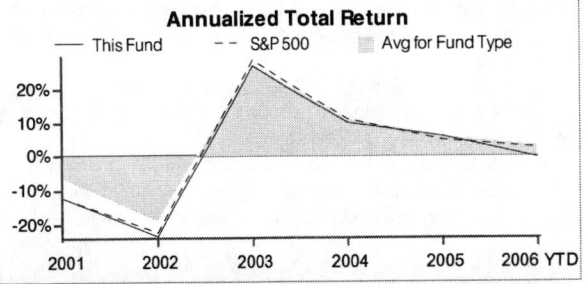

Eaton Vance Large Cap Value A (EHSTX)

B   Good

Fund Family: Eaton Vance   **Phone:** (800) 225-6265
Address: The Eaton Vance Building, Boston, MA 02109
Fund Type: GI - Growth and Income
Major Rating Factors: Eaton Vance Large Cap Value A receives a Weiss Investment Rating of B (Good). The fund currently has a performance rating of C+ (Fair) based on an average return of 16.14% over the last three years and 5.89% over the last six months. Factored into the performance evaluation is an expense ratio of 1.07% (low) and a 5.8% front-end load that is levied at the time of purchase.

The fund's risk rating is currently B (Good). It carries a beta of 0.90, meaning the fund's expected move will be 9.0% for every 10% move in the market. Volatility, as measured by both the semi-deviation and a drawdown factor, is considered low.

Michael R. Mach has been running the fund for 6 years and currently receives a manager quality ranking of 94 (0=worst, 99=best). If you desire an average level of risk, then this fund may be an option.

Services Offered: Automated phone transactions, bank draft capabilities, an IRA investment plan, a 401K investment plan, a Keogh investment plan and a systematic withdrawal plan.

Data Date	Weiss Investment Rating	Net Assets ($Mil)	NAV	Perfor-mance Rating/Pts	Total Return Y-T-D	Risk Rating/Pts
6-06	B	2,331	19.22	C+ / 6.3	5.89%	B / 8.9
2005	C+	1,472	18.42	C / 4.7	11.47%	B- / 7.7
2004	C+	669	16.88	C+ / 5.8	15.68%	C+ / 6.4
2003	B-	307	14.76	C+ / 6.7	23.31%	B- / 7.6
2002	B+	186	12.11	B / 8.0	-15.78%	B / 8.3
2001	B+	168	14.53	B- / 7.4	1.83%	C+ / 6.6

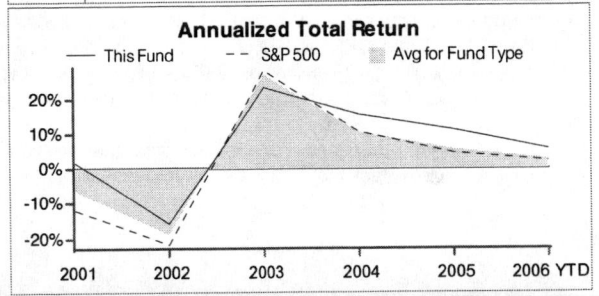

Elfun Trusts (ELFNX)

E+   Very Weak

Fund Family: GE Investment   **Phone:** (800) 242-0134
Address: 3003 Summer Street, Stamford, CT 06905
Fund Type: GR - Growth
Major Rating Factors: Disappointing performance is the major factor driving the E+ (Very Weak) Weiss Investment Rating for Elfun Trusts. The fund currently has a performance rating of D- (Weak) based on an average return of 6.73% over the last three years and 0.89% over the last six months. Factored into the performance evaluation is an expense ratio of 0.11% (very low).

The fund's risk rating is currently C+ (Fair). It carries a beta of 0.85, meaning the fund's expected move will be 8.5% for every 10% move in the market. Volatility, as measured by both the semi-deviation and a drawdown factor, is considered low.

David B. Carlson has been running the fund for 18 years and currently receives a manager quality ranking of 27 (0=worst, 99=best). This fund offers only a moderate level of risk but investors looking for strong performance are still waiting.

Services Offered: Automated phone transactions, payroll deductions, an IRA investment plan, a 401K investment plan and a systematic withdrawal plan.

Data Date	Weiss Investment Rating	Net Assets ($Mil)	NAV	Perfor-mance Rating/Pts	Total Return Y-T-D	Risk Rating/Pts
6-06	E+	2,233	51.19	D- / 1.3	0.89%	C+ / 6.1
2005	E+	2,355	50.74	D- / 1.1	0.80%	C+ / 6.4
2004	D+	2,391	55.13	D+ / 2.5	7.94%	C+ / 5.9
2003	C	2,300	55.28	C / 4.4	22.95%	C+ / 6.4
2002	C+	2,140	46.47	C+ / 6.6	-19.91%	C+ / 6.8
2001	B+	2,547	60.19	B- / 7.5	-5.98%	C+ / 6.6

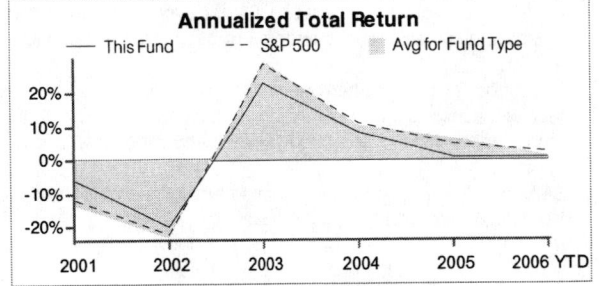

Evergreen Asset Allocation C (EACFX) — C+ — Fair

Fund Family: Evergreen Investments
Phone: (800) 343-2898
Address: 200 Berkeley St, Boston, MA 02116
Fund Type: GL - Global

Major Rating Factors: Middle of the road best describes Evergreen Asset Allocation C whose Weiss Investment Rating is currently a C+ (Fair). The fund currently has a performance rating of C- (Fair) based on an average return of 11.15% over the last three years and 2.13% over the last six months. Factored into the performance evaluation is an expense ratio of 1.63% (above average) and a 1.0% back-end load levied at the time of sale.

The fund's risk rating is currently B+ (Good). It carries a beta of 1.17, meaning it is expected to move 11.7% for every 10% move in the market. Volatility, as measured by both the semi-deviation and a drawdown factor, is considered very low.

This fund has been team managed for 10 years and currently receives a manager quality ranking of 81 (0=worst, 99=best). If you desire an average level of risk, then this fund may be an option.

Services Offered: Automated phone transactions, check writing, payroll deductions, bank draft capabilities, an IRA investment plan, a 401K investment plan, a Keogh investment plan, wire transfers and a systematic withdrawal plan.

Data Date	Weiss Investment Rating	Net Assets ($Mil)	NAV	Performance Rating/Pts	Total Return Y-T-D	Risk Rating/Pts
6-06	C+	3,619	13.80	C- / 3.8	2.13%	B+ / 9.0
2005	C+	2,871	13.71	C- / 3.4	7.09%	B+ / 9.2
2004	A	1,465	13.28	B- / 7.2	11.26%	B / 8.8
2003	A	378	12.18	B / 7.9	24.18%	B / 8.7

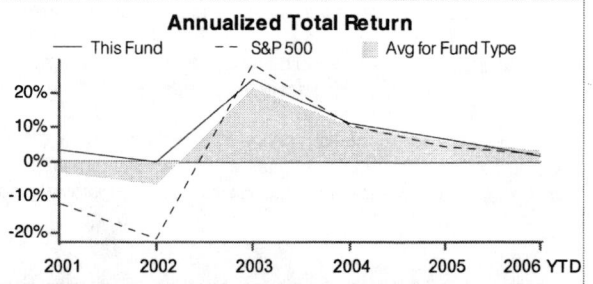

Excelsior Value & Restructg Fd (UMBIX) — B+ — Good

Fund Family: Excelsior Funds
Phone: (800) 446-1012
Address: 6 St. James Avenue, Boston, MA 02116
Fund Type: GR - Growth

Major Rating Factors: Strong performance is the major factor driving the B+ (Good) Weiss Investment Rating for Excelsior Value & Restructg Fd. The fund currently has a performance rating of B (Good) based on an average return of 20.05% over the last three years and 5.44% over the last six months. Factored into the performance evaluation is an expense ratio of 1.04% (low).

The fund's risk rating is currently C+ (Fair). It carries a beta of 1.34, meaning it is expected to move 13.4% for every 10% move in the market. Volatility, as measured by both the semi-deviation and a drawdown factor, is considered low.

David J. Williams, CFA has been running the fund for 14 years and currently receives a manager quality ranking of 93 (0=worst, 99=best). If you desire only a moderate level of risk and strong performance, then this fund is an excellent option.

Services Offered: Automated phone transactions, check writing, bank draft capabilities, an IRA investment plan, a 401K investment plan and wire transfers.

Data Date	Weiss Investment Rating	Net Assets ($Mil)	NAV	Performance Rating/Pts	Total Return Y-T-D	Risk Rating/Pts
6-06	B+	6,581	48.43	B / 8.0	5.44%	C+ / 6.7
2005	A	4,859	46.18	B+ / 8.5	9.96%	B- / 7.5
2004	B	4,115	42.43	B / 8.1	19.36%	C / 5.3
2003	B	2,827	35.86	B+ / 8.5	47.33%	C+ / 6.1
2002	C+	1,682	24.46	C+ / 6.2	-23.32%	C+ / 6.8
2001	C+	2,221	32.06	A- / 9.0	-5.02%	D / 1.7

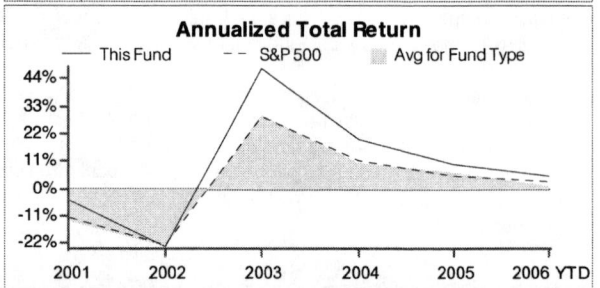

Fairholme Fund (FAIRX) — A+ — Excellent

Fund Family: Fairholme Capital Management, LLC
Phone: (800) 417-5525
Address: 51 JFK Parkway, Short Hills, NJ 07078
Fund Type: MC - Mid Cap

Major Rating Factors: Strong performance is the major factor driving the A+ (Excellent) Weiss Investment Rating for Fairholme Fund. The fund currently has a performance rating of B+ (Good) based on an average return of 21.49% over the last three years and 8.93% over the last six months. Factored into the performance evaluation is an expense ratio of 1.00% (low) and a 2.0% back-end load levied at the time of sale.

The fund's risk rating is currently B (Good). It carries a beta of 0.50, meaning the fund's expected move will be 5.0% for every 10% move in the market. Volatility, as measured by standard deviation, is considered low for equity funds at 7.71.

Bruce R Berkowitz has been running the fund for 7 years and currently receives a manager quality ranking of 99 (0=worst, 99=best). If you desire only a moderate level of risk and strong performance, then this fund is an excellent option.

Services Offered: Automated phone transactions, bank draft capabilities and an IRA investment plan.

Data Date	Weiss Investment Rating	Net Assets ($Mil)	NAV	Performance Rating/Pts	Total Return Y-T-D	Risk Rating/Pts
6-06	A+	2,629	27.44	B+ / 8.4	8.93%	B / 8.9
2005	B	1,439	25.19	B- / 7.4	13.68%	B- / 7.0
2004	A-	235	22.77	A- / 9.1	24.93%	C+ / 6.3

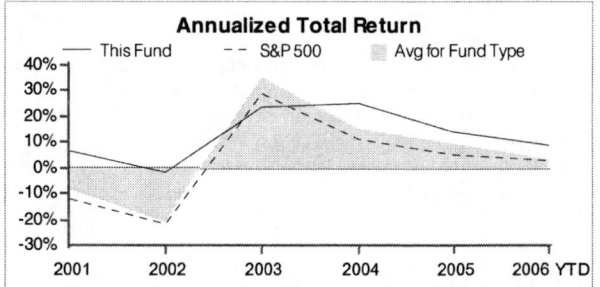

Federated Kaufmann K (KAUFX)   C+   Fair

Fund Family: Federated Investors   **Phone:** (800) 341-7400
Address: 5800 Corporate Drive, Pittsburgh, PA 15237
Fund Type: MC - Mid Cap

Major Rating Factors: Middle of the road best describes Federated Kaufmann K whose Weiss Investment Rating is currently a C+ (Fair). The fund currently has a performance rating of C+ (Fair) based on an average return of 15.98% over the last three years and 2.86% over the last six months. Factored into the performance evaluation is an expense ratio of 1.95% (above average) and a 0.2% back-end load levied at the time of sale.

The fund's risk rating is currently C+ (Fair). It carries a beta of 1.04, meaning that its performance tracks fairly well with that of the overall stock market. Volatility, as measured by both the semi-deviation and a drawdown factor, is considered low.

This fund has been team managed for 20 years and currently receives a manager quality ranking of 30 (0=worst, 99=best). If you desire an average level of risk, then this fund may be an option.

Services Offered: Automated phone transactions, payroll deductions, bank draft capabilities, an IRA investment plan, a 401K investment plan, a Keogh investment plan, wire transfers and a systematic withdrawal plan.

Data Date	Weiss Investment Rating	Net Assets ($Mil)	NAV	Performance Rating/Pts	Total Return Y-T-D	Risk Rating/Pts
6-06	C+	4,178	5.76	C+ / 6.5	2.86%	C+ / 6.5
2005	B+	4,088	5.60	B / 8.1	10.84%	C+ / 6.5
2004	C+	3,881	5.36	C+ / 6.8	14.29%	C / 5.5
2003	B+	3,560	4.96	B+ / 8.5	45.08%	C+ / 6.7
2002	C+	2,512	3.45	B / 7.6	-21.41%	C- / 3.7
2001	C+	3,365	4.39	A / 9.4	7.85%	E- / 0.0

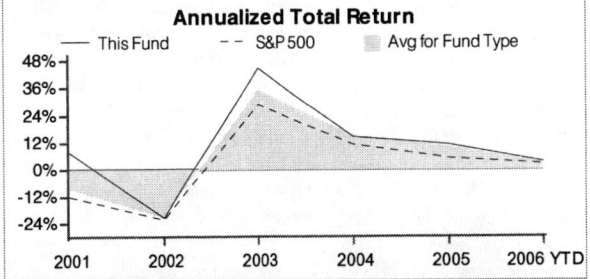

Fidelity Adv Diversified Intl A (FDVAX)   B   Good

Fund Family: Fidelity Advisor   **Phone:** (800) 522-7297
Address: 82 Devonshire Street, Boston, MA 02109
Fund Type: FO - Foreign

Major Rating Factors: Strong performance is the major factor driving the B (Good) Weiss Investment Rating for Fidelity Adv Diversified Intl A. The fund currently has a performance rating of B+ (Good) based on an average return of 23.35% over the last three years and 5.88% over the last six months. Factored into the performance evaluation is an expense ratio of 1.20% (average), a 5.8% front-end load that is levied at the time of purchase and a 1.0% back-end load levied at the time of sale.

The fund's risk rating is currently C+ (Fair). It carries a beta of 1.08, meaning that its performance tracks fairly well with that of the overall stock market. Volatility, as measured by both the semi-deviation and a drawdown factor, is considered low.

Penelope A. Dobkin has been running the fund for 2 years and currently receives a manager quality ranking of 30 (0=worst, 99=best). If you desire only a moderate level of risk and strong performance, then this fund is an excellent option.

Services Offered: Automated phone transactions, check writing, bank draft capabilities, an IRA investment plan, a 401K investment plan, a Keogh investment plan, wire transfers and a systematic withdrawal plan.

Data Date	Weiss Investment Rating	Net Assets ($Mil)	NAV	Performance Rating/Pts	Total Return Y-T-D	Risk Rating/Pts
6-06	B	4,237	22.34	B+ / 8.3	5.88%	C+ / 6.2
2005	A+	2,970	21.10	B+ / 8.9	18.99%	B- / 7.9
2004	A	1,593	18.68	B+ / 8.7	19.02%	B- / 7.0
2003	B+	313	15.81	B / 8.0	41.02%	B- / 7.7
2002	C+	56	11.30	C+ / 5.6	-9.19%	C+ / 6.3

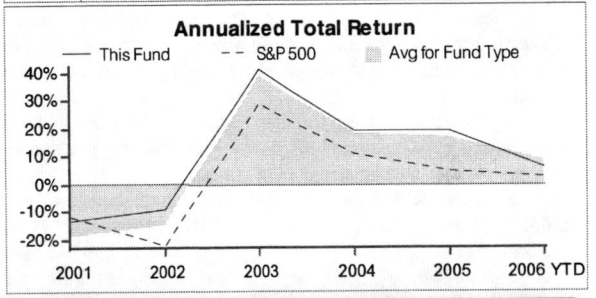

Fidelity Adv Diversified Intl T (FADIX)   B   Good

Fund Family: Fidelity Advisor   **Phone:** (800) 522-7297
Address: 82 Devonshire Street, Boston, MA 02109
Fund Type: FO - Foreign

Major Rating Factors: Strong performance is the major factor driving the B (Good) Weiss Investment Rating for Fidelity Adv Diversified Intl T. The fund currently has a performance rating of B+ (Good) based on an average return of 23.04% over the last three years and 5.74% over the last six months. Factored into the performance evaluation is an expense ratio of 1.45% (average), a 3.5% front-end load that is levied at the time of purchase and a 1.0% back-end load levied at the time of sale.

The fund's risk rating is currently C+ (Fair). It carries a beta of 1.08, meaning that its performance tracks fairly well with that of the overall stock market. Volatility, as measured by both the semi-deviation and a drawdown factor, is considered low.

Penelope A. Dobkin has been running the fund for 2 years and currently receives a manager quality ranking of 28 (0=worst, 99=best). If you desire only a moderate level of risk and strong performance, then this fund is an excellent option.

Services Offered: Automated phone transactions, check writing, bank draft capabilities, an IRA investment plan, a 401K investment plan, a Keogh investment plan, wire transfers and a systematic withdrawal plan.

Data Date	Weiss Investment Rating	Net Assets ($Mil)	NAV	Performance Rating/Pts	Total Return Y-T-D	Risk Rating/Pts
6-06	B	3,407	22.11	B+ / 8.4	5.74%	C+ / 6.2
2005	A+	2,565	20.91	B+ / 8.9	18.70%	B- / 7.9
2004	A	1,718	18.56	B+ / 8.7	18.68%	C+ / 6.8
2003	B+	633	15.71	B / 8.1	40.54%	B- / 7.5
2002	C+	221	11.23	C+ / 5.7	-9.42%	B- / 7.5

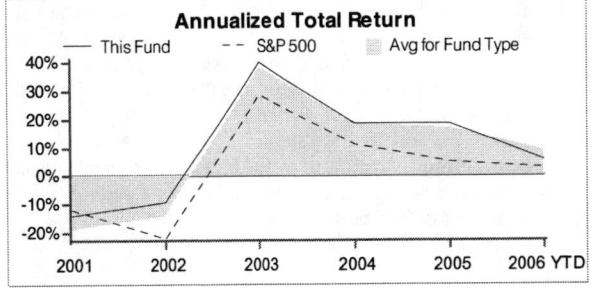

Fidelity Adv Equity Growth T (FAEGX)

D-   Weak

Fund Family: Fidelity Advisor   **Phone:** (800) 522-7297
Address: 82 Devonshire Street, Boston, MA 02109
Fund Type: GR - Growth

Major Rating Factors: Disappointing performance is the major factor driving the D- (Weak) Weiss Investment Rating for Fidelity Adv Equity Growth T. The fund currently has a performance rating of D- (Weak) based on an average return of 7.90% over the last three years and -0.25% over the last six months. Factored into the performance evaluation is an expense ratio of 1.33% (average), a 3.5% front-end load that is levied at the time of purchase and a 0.2% back-end load levied at the time of sale.

The fund's risk rating is currently C+ (Fair). It carries a beta of 1.25, meaning it is expected to move 12.5% for every 10% move in the market. Volatility, as measured by both the semi-deviation and a drawdown factor, is considered low.

Jennifer Uhrig has been running the fund for 9 years and currently receives a manager quality ranking of 13 (0=worst, 99=best). This fund offers only a moderate level of risk but investors looking for strong performance are still waiting.

Services Offered: Automated phone transactions, check writing, bank draft capabilities, an IRA investment plan, a 401K investment plan and a systematic withdrawal plan.

Data Date	Weiss Investment Rating	Net Assets ($Mil)	NAV	Performance Rating/Pts	Total Return Y-T-D	Risk Rating/Pts
6-06	D-	3,206	47.96	D- / 1.4	-0.25%	C+ / 6.2
2005	D-	3,858	48.08	D / 2.1	5.18%	C+ / 6.4
2004	E+	5,092	45.71	E / 0.5	2.67%	C- / 3.7
2003	D	5,428	44.52	D / 1.9	31.83%	C / 4.3
2002	D+	4,821	33.77	D / 1.8	-30.64%	C / 4.7
2001	D	7,153	48.69	C- / 3.3	-18.19%	E+ / 0.7

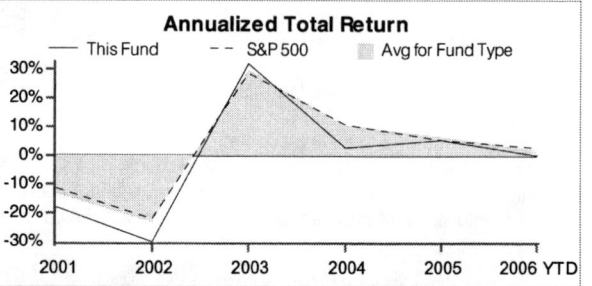

Annualized Total Return

Fidelity Adv Equity Income T (FEIRX)

C+   Fair

Fund Family: Fidelity Advisor   **Phone:** (800) 522-7297
Address: 82 Devonshire Street, Boston, MA 02109
Fund Type: IN - Income

Major Rating Factors: Middle of the road best describes Fidelity Adv Equity Income T whose Weiss Investment Rating is currently a C+ (Fair). The fund currently has a performance rating of C (Fair) based on an average return of 12.79% over the last three years and 3.44% over the last six months. Factored into the performance evaluation is an expense ratio of 1.22% (average), a 3.5% front-end load that is levied at the time of purchase and a 0.3% back-end load levied at the time of sale.

The fund's risk rating is currently B (Good). It carries a beta of 1.04, meaning that its performance tracks fairly well with that of the overall stock market. Volatility, as measured by both the semi-deviation and a drawdown factor, is considered low.

Robert Chow has been running the fund for 10 years and currently receives a manager quality ranking of 69 (0=worst, 99=best). If you desire an average level of risk, then this fund may be an option.

Services Offered: Automated phone transactions, check writing, bank draft capabilities, an IRA investment plan, a 401K investment plan and a systematic withdrawal plan.

Data Date	Weiss Investment Rating	Net Assets ($Mil)	NAV	Performance Rating/Pts	Total Return Y-T-D	Risk Rating/Pts
6-06	C+	2,848	29.06	C / 4.6	3.44%	B / 8.5
2005	C-	3,010	28.34	C- / 3.7	6.17%	B- / 7.2
2004	C	3,025	28.33	C / 5.3	11.89%	C+ / 5.6
2003	B-	2,238	25.85	B- / 7.1	28.41%	C+ / 6.7
2002	B	1,915	20.31	B- / 7.5	-15.64%	B- / 7.5
2001	C+	2,123	24.27	C+ / 6.1	-2.43%	C+ / 6.4

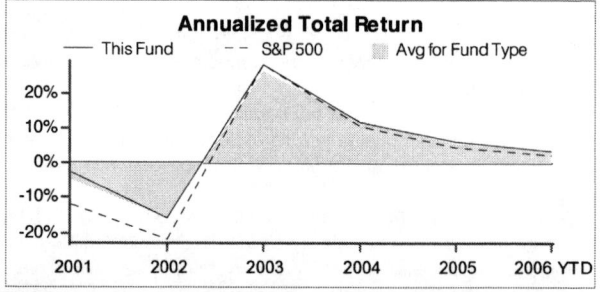

Annualized Total Return

Fidelity Adv Gr Opportunity T (FAGOX)

D-   Weak

Fund Family: Fidelity Advisor   **Phone:** (800) 522-7297
Address: 82 Devonshire Street, Boston, MA 02109
Fund Type: GR - Growth

Major Rating Factors: Disappointing performance is the major factor driving the D- (Weak) Weiss Investment Rating for Fidelity Adv Gr Opportunity T. The fund currently has a performance rating of D- (Weak) based on an average return of 8.24% over the last three years and -4.59% over the last six months. Factored into the performance evaluation is an expense ratio of 1.26% (average) and a 3.5% front-end load that is levied at the time of purchase.

The fund's risk rating is currently C+ (Fair). It carries a beta of 1.16, meaning it is expected to move 11.6% for every 10% move in the market. Volatility, as measured by both the semi-deviation and a drawdown factor, is considered low.

John Porter has been running the fund for 1 year and currently receives a manager quality ranking of 19 (0=worst, 99=best). This fund offers only a moderate level of risk but investors looking for strong performance are still waiting.

Services Offered: Automated phone transactions, bank draft capabilities, an IRA investment plan, a 401K investment plan, a Keogh investment plan and a systematic withdrawal plan.

Data Date	Weiss Investment Rating	Net Assets ($Mil)	NAV	Performance Rating/Pts	Total Return Y-T-D	Risk Rating/Pts
6-06	D-	2,285	31.59	D- / 1.2	-4.59%	C+ / 6.3
2005	C-	3,151	33.11	C- / 3.9	8.44%	B- / 7.0
2004	D+	3,815	30.54	D / 2.0	6.95%	C / 5.4
2003	C-	4,586	28.64	C- / 3.2	29.25%	C+ / 5.7
2002	C-	4,901	22.19	D+ / 2.8	-22.43%	C / 5.3
2001	D	8,056	28.76	E / 0.5	-15.14%	C- / 3.1

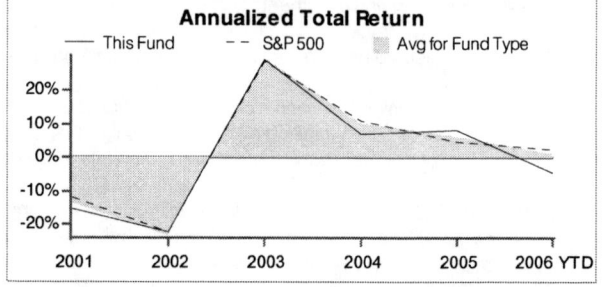

Annualized Total Return

Fidelity Adv Mid Cap Fund T (FMCAX)　　　　　　C-　　　Fair

Fund Family: Fidelity Advisor　　　　　**Phone:** (800) 522-7297
Address: 82 Devonshire Street, Boston, MA 02109
Fund Type: MC - Mid Cap

Major Rating Factors: Middle of the road best describes Fidelity Adv Mid Cap Fund T whose Weiss Investment Rating is currently a C- (Fair). The fund currently has a performance rating of C (Fair) based on an average return of 15.31% over the last three years and 1.32% over the last six months. Factored into the performance evaluation is an expense ratio of 1.25% (average), a 3.5% front-end load that is levied at the time of purchase and a 0.3% back-end load levied at the time of sale.

The fund's risk rating is currently C (Fair). It carries a beta of 1.13, meaning it is expected to move 11.3% for every 10% move in the market. Volatility, as measured by both the semi-deviation and a drawdown factor, is considered average.

Peter Saperstone has been running the fund for 5 years and currently receives a manager quality ranking of 17 (0=worst, 99=best). If you desire an average level of risk, then this fund may be an option.

Services Offered: Automated phone transactions, bank draft capabilities, an IRA investment plan, a 401K investment plan and a systematic withdrawal plan. However, the fund is currently closed to new investors.

Data Date	Weiss Investment Rating	Net Assets ($Mil)	NAV	Performance Rating/Pts	Total Return Y-T-D	Risk Rating/Pts
6-06	C-	4,019	23.82	C / 5.5	1.32%	C / 4.9
2005	B-	4,193	24.27	B- / 7.3	8.21%	C+ / 6.0
2004	C+	4,879	25.22	B / 7.7	15.88%	C / 4.9
2003	B-	3,227	22.41	B / 7.6	43.75%	C+ / 5.9
2002	B-	1,714	15.59	B / 7.6	-18.72%	C+ / 6.2
2001	C+	1,539	19.18	A- / 9.1	-13.19%	E- / 0.0

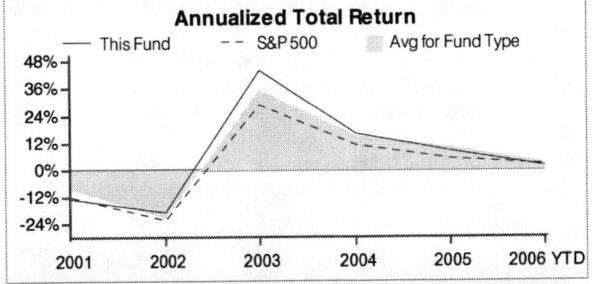

Annualized Total Return

Fidelity Aggressive Growth Fund (FDEGX)　　　　　D-　　　Weak

Fund Family: Fidelity Investments　　　　　**Phone:** (800) 544-8888
Address: 82 Devonshire Street, Boston, MA 02109
Fund Type: AG - Aggressive Growth

Major Rating Factors: Disappointing performance is the major factor driving the D- (Weak) Weiss Investment Rating for Fidelity Aggressive Growth Fund. The fund currently has a performance rating of D+ (Weak) based on an average return of 10.61% over the last three years and -2.70% over the last six months. Factored into the performance evaluation is an expense ratio of 0.70% (very low) and a 1.5% back-end load levied at the time of sale.

The fund's risk rating is currently C (Fair). It carries a beta of 1.36, meaning it is expected to move 13.6% for every 10% move in the market. Volatility, as measured by both the semi-deviation and a drawdown factor, is considered average.

Steven Calhoun has been running the fund for 1 year and currently receives a manager quality ranking of 22 (0=worst, 99=best). This fund offers an average level of risk but investors looking for strong performance will be frustrated.

Services Offered: Automated phone transactions, bank draft capabilities, an IRA investment plan, a 401K investment plan, wire transfers and a systematic withdrawal plan.

Data Date	Weiss Investment Rating	Net Assets ($Mil)	NAV	Performance Rating/Pts	Total Return Y-T-D	Risk Rating/Pts
6-06	D-	3,798	17.32	D+ / 2.7	-2.70%	C / 5.2
2005	C-	4,349	17.80	C / 5.2	7.23%	C / 5.0
2004	E	5,054	16.60	E / 0.5	11.19%	D- / 1.4
2003	E-	5,241	14.93	E- / 0.0	33.42%	E+ / 0.7
2002	E	4,492	11.19	E- / 0.1	-41.17%	E+ / 0.8
2001	E-	7,410	19.02	E / 0.3	-47.27%	E- / 0.0

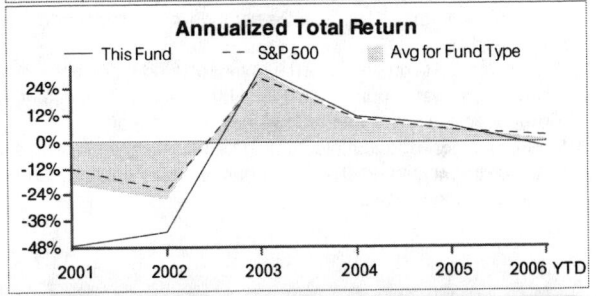

Annualized Total Return

Fidelity Asset Manager (FASMX)　　　　　　　　　C-　　　Fair

Fund Family: Fidelity Investments　　　　　**Phone:** (800) 544-8888
Address: 82 Devonshire Street, Boston, MA 02109
Fund Type: AA - Asset Allocation

Major Rating Factors: Disappointing performance is the major factor driving the C- (Fair) Weiss Investment Rating for Fidelity Asset Manager. The fund currently has a performance rating of D- (Weak) based on an average return of 5.90% over the last three years and 1.49% over the last six months. Factored into the performance evaluation is an expense ratio of 0.72% (very low).

The fund's risk rating is currently B+ (Good). It carries a beta of 0.91, meaning that its performance tracks fairly well with that of the overall stock market. Volatility, as measured by both the semi-deviation and a drawdown factor, is considered very low.

Dick Habermann has been running the fund for 10 years and currently receives a manager quality ranking of 42 (0=worst, 99=best). This fund offers only a moderate level of risk but investors looking for strong performance are still waiting.

Services Offered: Automated phone transactions, bank draft capabilities, an IRA investment plan, a 401K investment plan, a Keogh investment plan and a systematic withdrawal plan.

Data Date	Weiss Investment Rating	Net Assets ($Mil)	NAV	Performance Rating/Pts	Total Return Y-T-D	Risk Rating/Pts
6-06	C-	9,283	16.19	D- / 1.2	1.49%	B+ / 9.6
2005	C-	10,134	16.05	E+ / 0.8	4.16%	B+ / 9.3
2004	C	10,955	16.21	C- / 3.1	5.40%	B- / 7.4
2003	B	11,002	15.76	C+ / 6.1	17.18%	B / 8.3
2002	B+	10,496	13.80	B / 8.2	-8.05%	B / 8.0
2001	B	11,924	15.50	C+ / 6.6	-3.93%	B / 8.1

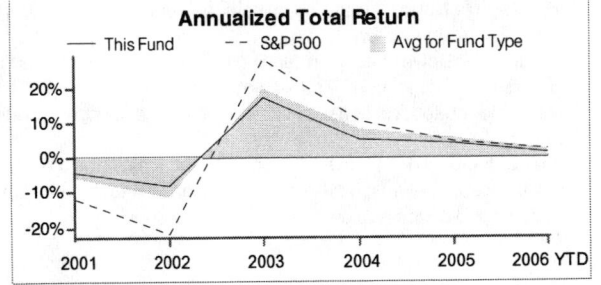

Annualized Total Return

Fidelity Asset Manager Growth (FASGX)

C- **Fair**

Fund Family: Fidelity Investments **Phone:** (800) 544-8888
Address: 82 Devonshire Street, Boston, MA 02109
Fund Type: AA - Asset Allocation

Major Rating Factors: Disappointing performance is the major factor driving the C- (Fair) Weiss Investment Rating for Fidelity Asset Manager Growth. The fund currently has a performance rating of D- (Weak) based on an average return of 6.76% over the last three years and 1.46% over the last six months. Factored into the performance evaluation is an expense ratio of 0.81% (very low).

The fund's risk rating is currently B+ (Good). It carries a beta of 1.19, meaning it is expected to move 11.9% for every 10% move in the market. Volatility, as measured by both the semi-deviation and a drawdown factor, is considered very low.

Richard Habermann has been running the fund for 10 years and currently receives a manager quality ranking of 36 (0=worst, 99=best). This fund offers only a moderate level of risk but investors looking for strong performance are still waiting.

Services Offered: Automated phone transactions, bank draft capabilities, an IRA investment plan, a 401K investment plan and a systematic withdrawal plan.

Data Date	Weiss Investment Rating	Net Assets ($Mil)	NAV	Performance Rating/Pts	Total Return Y-T-D	Risk Rating/Pts
6-06	C-	3,107	15.30	D- / 1.3	1.46%	B+ / 9.1
2005	D+	3,301	15.08	D- / 1.4	3.77%	B / 8.5
2004	C-	3,733	14.82	D+ / 2.9	6.05%	C+ / 6.3
2003	C+	3,617	14.28	C / 5.0	21.93%	B- / 7.1
2002	C+	3,535	11.97	C+ / 6.7	-14.05%	C+ / 6.3
2001	C+	4,234	14.34	C / 5.2	-7.22%	C+ / 6.8

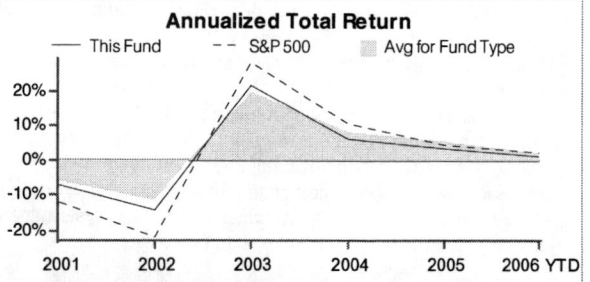

Fidelity Balanced Fund (FBALX)

B- **Good**

Fund Family: Fidelity Investments **Phone:** (800) 544-8888
Address: 82 Devonshire Street, Boston, MA 02109
Fund Type: GI - Growth and Income

Major Rating Factors: Fidelity Balanced Fund receives a Weiss Investment Rating of B- (Good). The fund currently has a performance rating of C (Fair) based on an average return of 12.93% over the last three years and 3.14% over the last six months. Factored into the performance evaluation is an expense ratio of 0.64% (very low).

The fund's risk rating is currently B (Good). It carries a beta of 0.90, meaning the fund's expected move will be 9.0% for every 10% move in the market. Volatility, as measured by both the semi-deviation and a drawdown factor, is considered low.

Lawrence Rakers has been running the fund for 4 years and currently receives a manager quality ranking of 80 (0=worst, 99=best). If you desire an average level of risk, then this fund may be an option.

Services Offered: Automated phone transactions, bank draft capabilities, an IRA investment plan, a 401K investment plan, a Keogh investment plan and a systematic withdrawal plan.

Data Date	Weiss Investment Rating	Net Assets ($Mil)	NAV	Performance Rating/Pts	Total Return Y-T-D	Risk Rating/Pts
6-06	B-	19,707	19.27	C / 5.3	3.14%	B / 8.5
2005	B	15,999	18.76	C / 5.4	10.68%	B / 8.7
2004	B-	12,577	17.82	C+ / 6.8	10.94%	B- / 7.1
2003	A-	9,224	16.75	B / 7.8	28.24%	B / 8.3
2002	A	6,714	13.29	B+ / 8.6	-8.49%	B+ / 9.0
2001	A+	7,005	14.90	B- / 7.5	2.25%	B / 8.4

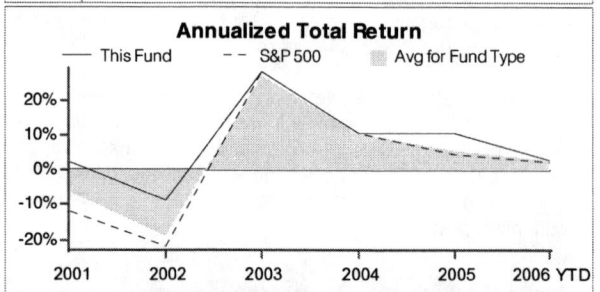

Fidelity Blue Chip Growth (FBGRX)

D **Weak**

Fund Family: Fidelity Investments **Phone:** (800) 544-8888
Address: 82 Devonshire Street, Boston, MA 02109
Fund Type: GR - Growth

Major Rating Factors: Disappointing performance is the major factor driving the D (Weak) Weiss Investment Rating for Fidelity Blue Chip Growth. The fund currently has a performance rating of D- (Weak) based on an average return of 6.45% over the last three years and -2.80% over the last six months. Factored into the performance evaluation is an expense ratio of 0.64% (very low).

The fund's risk rating is currently B- (Good). It carries a beta of 1.03, meaning that its performance tracks fairly well with that of the overall stock market. Volatility, as measured by both the semi-deviation and a drawdown factor, is considered low.

John McDowell has been running the fund for 10 years and currently receives a manager quality ranking of 15 (0=worst, 99=best). This fund offers only a moderate level of risk but investors looking for strong performance are still waiting.

Services Offered: Automated phone transactions, bank draft capabilities, an IRA investment plan, a 401K investment plan, a Keogh investment plan and a systematic withdrawal plan.

Data Date	Weiss Investment Rating	Net Assets ($Mil)	NAV	Performance Rating/Pts	Total Return Y-T-D	Risk Rating/Pts
6-06	D	20,139	41.95	D- / 1.0	-2.80%	B- / 7.7
2005	D+	22,577	43.16	D / 1.9	4.03%	B- / 7.8
2004	D	23,578	41.71	D- / 1.4	6.26%	C+ / 5.6
2003	C-	21,426	39.63	D / 2.1	24.80%	C+ / 5.6
2002	C-	17,730	31.94	C- / 3.2	-25.32%	C / 5.4
2001	D+	21,959	42.94	D+ / 2.8	-16.55%	D / 2.0

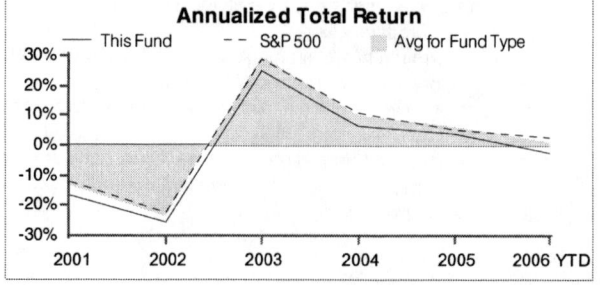

Fidelity Canada Fund (FICDX)   A   Excellent

Fund Family: Fidelity Investments   **Phone:** (800) 544-8888
Address: 82 Devonshire Street, Boston, MA 02109
Fund Type: FO - Foreign
Major Rating Factors: Exceptional performance is the major factor driving the A (Excellent) Weiss Investment Rating for Fidelity Canada Fund. The fund currently has a performance rating of A (Excellent) based on an average return of 27.87% over the last three years and 5.77% over the last six months. Factored into the performance evaluation is an expense ratio of 1.04% (low) and a 1.5% back-end load levied at the time of sale.

The fund's risk rating is currently C+ (Fair). It carries a beta of 1.04, meaning that its performance tracks fairly well with that of the overall stock market. Volatility, as measured by both the semi-deviation and a drawdown factor, is considered low.

Maxime Lemieux has been running the fund for 4 years and currently receives a manager quality ranking of 76 (0=worst, 99=best). If you desire only a moderate level of risk and strong performance, then this fund is an excellent option.

Services Offered: Automated phone transactions, bank draft capabilities, an IRA investment plan, a 401K investment plan, a Keogh investment plan and a systematic withdrawal plan.

Data Date	Weiss Investment Rating	Net Assets ($Mil)	NAV	Performance Rating/Pts	Total Return Y-T-D	Risk Rating/Pts
6-06	A	2,826	45.62	A / 9.4	5.77%	C+ / 6.3
2005	A	1,915	43.13	A+ / 9.6	27.89%	C+ / 6.3
2004	A+	646	33.86	A+ / 9.6	23.92%	C+ / 6.8
2003	A	185	27.39	A- / 9.2	51.91%	B- / 7.3
2002	B+	79	18.12	B+ / 8.4	-4.27%	B- / 7.2
2001	C+	86	18.97	B+ / 8.5	-9.61%	D- / 1.5

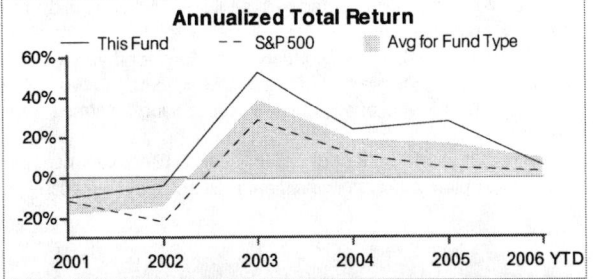

Fidelity Capital Appreciation (FDCAX)   C+   Fair

Fund Family: Fidelity Investments   **Phone:** (800) 544-8888
Address: 82 Devonshire Street, Boston, MA 02109
Fund Type: GR - Growth
Major Rating Factors: Middle of the road best describes Fidelity Capital Appreciation whose Weiss Investment Rating is currently a C+ (Fair). The fund currently has a performance rating of C+ (Fair) based on an average return of 15.36% over the last three years and 5.70% over the last six months. Factored into the performance evaluation is an expense ratio of 0.90% (low).

The fund's risk rating is currently C+ (Fair). It carries a beta of 1.33, meaning it is expected to move 13.3% for every 10% move in the market. Volatility, as measured by both the semi-deviation and a drawdown factor, is considered low.

J. Fergus Shiel has been running the fund for 1 year and currently receives a manager quality ranking of 67 (0=worst, 99=best). If you desire an average level of risk, then this fund may be an option.

Services Offered: Automated phone transactions, bank draft capabilities, an IRA investment plan, a 401K investment plan, a Keogh investment plan and a systematic withdrawal plan.

Data Date	Weiss Investment Rating	Net Assets ($Mil)	NAV	Performance Rating/Pts	Total Return Y-T-D	Risk Rating/Pts
6-06	C+	8,018	26.53	C+ / 6.6	5.70%	C+ / 6.1
2005	C+	7,284	25.10	B- / 7.4	5.80%	C+ / 5.7
2004	C+	6,452	26.03	B- / 7.1	11.26%	C / 4.8
2003	B-	4,031	24.51	B+ / 8.5	51.68%	C / 5.2
2002	C	1,958	16.18	C- / 4.1	-21.27%	C / 5.0
2001	C-	2,311	20.55	C+ / 6.4	-7.56%	E- / 0.0

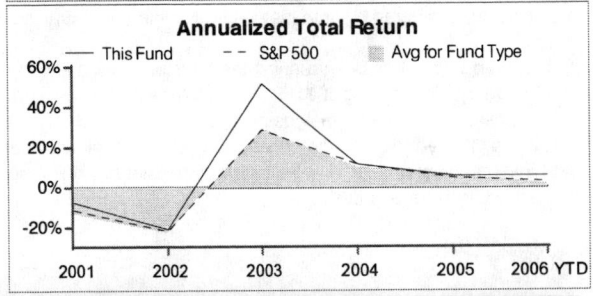

Fidelity Contrafund (FCNTX)   B+   Good

Fund Family: Fidelity Investments   **Phone:** (800) 544-8888
Address: 82 Devonshire Street, Boston, MA 02109
Fund Type: GR - Growth
Major Rating Factors: Strong performance is the major factor driving the B+ (Good) Weiss Investment Rating for Fidelity Contrafund. The fund currently has a performance rating of B- (Good) based on an average return of 17.58% over the last three years and 3.95% over the last six months. Factored into the performance evaluation is an expense ratio of 0.91% (low).

The fund's risk rating is currently B- (Good). It carries a beta of 1.04, meaning that its performance tracks fairly well with that of the overall stock market. Volatility, as measured by both the semi-deviation and a drawdown factor, is considered low.

William Danoff has been running the fund for 16 years and currently receives a manager quality ranking of 94 (0=worst, 99=best). If you desire only a moderate level of risk and strong performance, then this fund is an excellent option.

Services Offered: Automated phone transactions, bank draft capabilities, an IRA investment plan, a 401K investment plan, a Keogh investment plan and a systematic withdrawal plan. However, the fund is currently closed to new investors.

Data Date	Weiss Investment Rating	Net Assets ($Mil)	NAV	Performance Rating/Pts	Total Return Y-T-D	Risk Rating/Pts
6-06	B+	64,904	66.03	B- / 7.4	3.95%	B- / 7.4
2005	A-	58,486	64.76	B- / 7.5	16.23%	B / 8.1
2004	B+	44,485	56.74	B- / 7.3	15.07%	C+ / 6.8
2003	B	35,008	49.35	B- / 7.0	27.95%	B- / 7.3
2002	C+	27,963	38.60	C+ / 5.9	-9.63%	B- / 7.3
2001	C+	32,321	42.77	C- / 4.2	-12.57%	C+ / 6.6

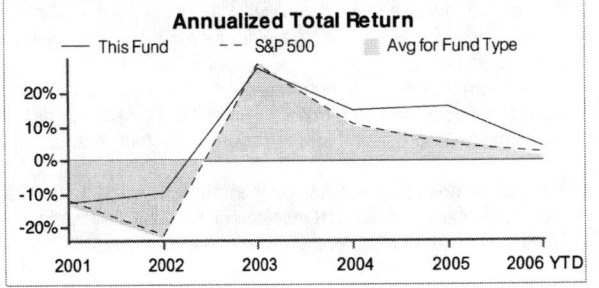

Fidelity Destiny II Class O (FDETX)

D+ **Weak**

Fund Family: Fidelity Advisor **Phone:** (800) 522-7297
Address: 82 Devonshire Street, Boston, MA 02109
Fund Type: GR - Growth
Major Rating Factors: Disappointing performance is the major factor driving the D+ (Weak) Weiss Investment Rating for Fidelity Destiny II Class O. The fund currently has a performance rating of D (Weak) based on an average return of 8.38% over the last three years and 1.68% over the last six months. Factored into the performance evaluation is an expense ratio of 0.61% (very low).

The fund's risk rating is currently B- (Good). It carries a beta of 0.91, meaning that its performance tracks fairly well with that of the overall stock market. Volatility, as measured by both the semi-deviation and a drawdown factor, is considered low.

Adam Hetnarski has been running the fund for 6 years and currently receives a manager quality ranking of 35 (0=worst, 99=best). This fund offers only a moderate level of risk but investors looking for strong performance are still waiting.

Services Offered: Bank draft capabilities, an IRA investment plan, a 401K investment plan, a Keogh investment plan and a systematic withdrawal plan.

Data Date	Weiss Investment Rating	Net Assets ($Mil)	NAV	Performance Rating/Pts	Total Return Y-T-D	Risk Rating/Pts
6-06	D+	4,807	12.09	D / 2.0	1.68%	B- / 7.8
2005	D-	4,994	11.89	E+ / 0.7	2.37%	B / 8.0
2004	C-	5,405	11.92	C- / 3.5	10.60%	C+ / 6.3
2003	C-	4,791	10.93	D+ / 2.8	20.23%	C+ / 6.4
2002	C	4,378	9.16	C / 4.7	-15.37%	C+ / 5.6
2001	D+	4,938	10.93	D+ / 2.8	-9.35%	D+ / 2.5

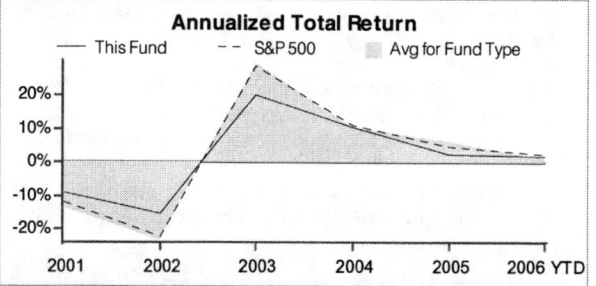

Fidelity Disciplined Equity (FDEQX)

B- **Good**

Fund Family: Fidelity Investments **Phone:** (800) 544-8888
Address: 82 Devonshire Street, Boston, MA 02109
Fund Type: GR - Growth
Major Rating Factors: Fidelity Disciplined Equity receives a Weiss Investment Rating of B- (Good). The fund currently has a performance rating of C (Fair) based on an average return of 13.39% over the last three years and 3.54% over the last six months. Factored into the performance evaluation is an expense ratio of 0.87% (low) and a 0.8% back-end load levied at the time of sale.

The fund's risk rating is currently B (Good). It carries a beta of 1.06, meaning that its performance tracks fairly well with that of the overall stock market. Volatility, as measured by both the semi-deviation and a drawdown factor, is considered low.

Steven Snider has been running the fund for 6 years and currently receives a manager quality ranking of 71 (0=worst, 99=best). If you desire an average level of risk, then this fund may be an option.

Services Offered: Automated phone transactions, bank draft capabilities, an IRA investment plan, a 401K investment plan, a Keogh investment plan and a systematic withdrawal plan.

Data Date	Weiss Investment Rating	Net Assets ($Mil)	NAV	Performance Rating/Pts	Total Return Y-T-D	Risk Rating/Pts
6-06	B-	6,925	28.69	C / 5.5	3.54%	B / 8.5
2005	C+	6,083	27.71	C / 5.2	10.27%	B- / 7.4
2004	C+	4,951	25.29	C / 5.5	12.02%	C+ / 6.4
2003	C	3,805	22.74	C / 4.3	27.18%	C+ / 6.6
2002	C+	2,870	17.97	C / 5.1	-18.56%	C+ / 6.3
2001	C+	2,992	22.10	C / 4.4	-14.21%	C+ / 6.1

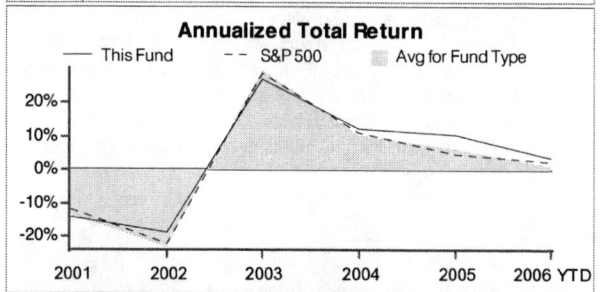

Fidelity Diversified Intl Fund (FDIVX)

A **Excellent**

Fund Family: Fidelity Investments **Phone:** (800) 544-8888
Address: 82 Devonshire Street, Boston, MA 02109
Fund Type: FO - Foreign
Major Rating Factors: Exceptional performance is the major factor driving the A (Excellent) Weiss Investment Rating for Fidelity Diversified Intl Fund. The fund currently has a performance rating of A- (Excellent) based on an average return of 24.21% over the last three years and 8.27% over the last six months. Factored into the performance evaluation is an expense ratio of 1.07% (low) and a 1.0% back-end load levied at the time of sale.

The fund's risk rating is currently C+ (Fair). It carries a beta of 1.03, meaning that its performance tracks fairly well with that of the overall stock market. Volatility, as measured by both the semi-deviation and a drawdown factor, is considered low.

William Bower has been running the fund for 5 years and currently receives a manager quality ranking of 45 (0=worst, 99=best). If you desire only a moderate level of risk and strong performance, then this fund is an excellent option.

Services Offered: Automated phone transactions, bank draft capabilities, an IRA investment plan, a 401K investment plan and a systematic withdrawal plan. However, the fund is currently closed to new investors.

Data Date	Weiss Investment Rating	Net Assets ($Mil)	NAV	Performance Rating/Pts	Total Return Y-T-D	Risk Rating/Pts
6-06	A	39,868	35.23	A- / 9.0	8.27%	C+ / 6.7
2005	A+	31,026	32.54	A- / 9.1	17.23%	B- / 7.7
2004	A	23,420	28.64	A- / 9.1	19.66%	B- / 7.0
2003	A-	12,078	24.12	B+ / 8.4	42.38%	B- / 7.4
2002	B-	7,107	17.16	C+ / 6.0	-9.37%	B- / 7.3
2001	C+	6,379	19.08	C+ / 6.9	-12.99%	C- / 3.5

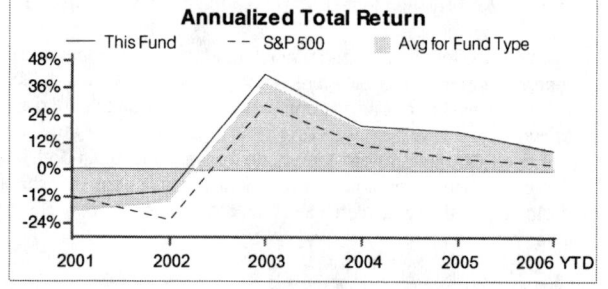

Fidelity Dividend Growth Fund (FDGFX)   D   Weak

Fund Family: Fidelity Investments   **Phone:** (800) 544-8888
Address: 82 Devonshire Street, Boston, MA 02109
Fund Type: GR - Growth

Major Rating Factors: Disappointing performance is the major factor driving the D (Weak) Weiss Investment Rating for Fidelity Dividend Growth Fund. The fund currently has a performance rating of D- (Weak) based on an average return of 6.97% over the last three years and 1.22% over the last six months. Factored into the performance evaluation is an expense ratio of 0.66% (very low).

The fund's risk rating is currently B- (Good). It carries a beta of 0.91, meaning that its performance tracks fairly well with that of the overall stock market. Volatility, as measured by both the semi-deviation and a drawdown factor, is considered low.

Charles Mangum has been running the fund for 9 years and currently receives a manager quality ranking of 25 (0=worst, 99=best). This fund offers only a moderate level of risk but investors looking for strong performance are still waiting.

Services Offered: Automated phone transactions, bank draft capabilities, an IRA investment plan, a 401K investment plan and a systematic withdrawal plan.

Data Date	Weiss Investment Rating	Net Assets ($Mil)	NAV	Perfor-mance Rating/Pts	Total Return Y-T-D	Risk Rating/Pts
6-06	D	15,540	29.14	D- / 1.3	1.22%	B- / 7.6
2005	D-	16,565	28.79	D- / 1.5	3.50%	C+ / 6.8
2004	D	19,422	28.49	D / 1.9	5.84%	C / 5.1
2003	C	16,954	27.30	C / 4.8	23.36%	C+ / 6.1
2002	B-	14,176	22.32	B- / 7.4	-20.44%	B- / 7.0
2001	B+	15,210	28.33	B- / 7.4	-3.74%	C+ / 6.3

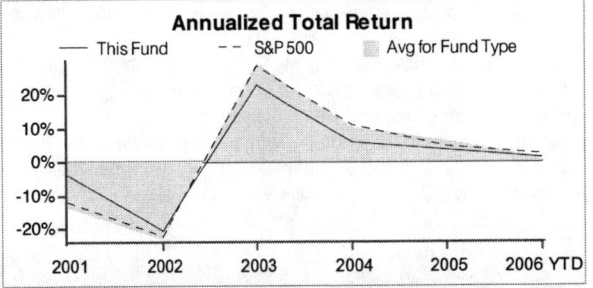

Fidelity Emerging Markets (FEMKX)   B-   Good

Fund Family: Fidelity Investments   **Phone:** (800) 544-8888
Address: 82 Devonshire Street, Boston, MA 02109
Fund Type: EM - Emerging Market

Major Rating Factors: Exceptional performance is the major factor driving the B- (Good) Weiss Investment Rating for Fidelity Emerging Markets. The fund currently has a performance rating of A+ (Excellent) based on an average return of 36.75% over the last three years and 8.30% over the last six months. Factored into the performance evaluation is an expense ratio of 1.07% (low) and a 1.5% back-end load levied at the time of sale.

The fund's risk rating is currently C- (Fair). It carries a beta of 1.19, meaning it is expected to move 11.9% for every 10% move in the market. Volatility, as measured by both the semi-deviation and a drawdown factor, is considered average.

Robert Von Rekowsky has been running the fund for 2 years and currently receives a manager quality ranking of 15 (0=worst, 99=best). If you desire an average level of risk and strong performance, then this fund is a good option.

Services Offered: Automated phone transactions, bank draft capabilities, an IRA investment plan, a 401K investment plan and a systematic withdrawal plan.

Data Date	Weiss Investment Rating	Net Assets ($Mil)	NAV	Perfor-mance Rating/Pts	Total Return Y-T-D	Risk Rating/Pts
6-06	B-	2,700	19.97	A+ / 9.8	8.30%	C- / 3.9
2005	B+	1,690	18.44	A+ / 9.9	44.31%	C / 4.9
2004	A	760	12.93	A / 9.4	22.94%	C+ / 6.1
2003	A	444	10.61	A / 9.4	48.80%	C+ / 6.8
2002	C	277	7.21	C / 4.5	-6.93%	C / 5.4
2001	C-	243	7.80	C+ / 6.9	-2.48%	E- / 0.0

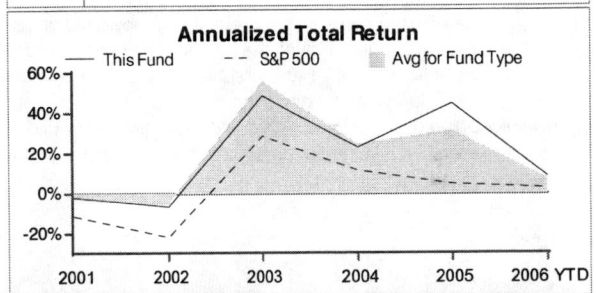

Fidelity Europe (FIEUX)   A+   Excellent

Fund Family: Fidelity Investments   **Phone:** (800) 544-8888
Address: 82 Devonshire Street, Boston, MA 02109
Fund Type: FO - Foreign

Major Rating Factors: Exceptional performance is the major factor driving the A+ (Excellent) Weiss Investment Rating for Fidelity Europe. The fund currently has a performance rating of A (Excellent) based on an average return of 28.65% over the last three years and 9.34% over the last six months. Factored into the performance evaluation is an expense ratio of 1.07% (low) and a 1.0% back-end load levied at the time of sale.

The fund's risk rating is currently C+ (Fair). It carries a beta of 1.09, meaning that its performance tracks fairly well with that of the overall stock market. Volatility, as measured by both the semi-deviation and a drawdown factor, is considered low.

Frederic Gautier has been running the fund for 3 years and currently receives a manager quality ranking of 73 (0=worst, 99=best). If you desire only a moderate level of risk and strong performance, then this fund is an excellent option.

Services Offered: Automated phone transactions, bank draft capabilities, an IRA investment plan, a 401K investment plan, a Keogh investment plan and a systematic withdrawal plan.

Data Date	Weiss Investment Rating	Net Assets ($Mil)	NAV	Perfor-mance Rating/Pts	Total Return Y-T-D	Risk Rating/Pts
6-06	A+	3,373	39.33	A / 9.4	9.34%	C+ / 6.7
2005	B+	2,624	35.97	A / 9.5	18.17%	C / 5.0
2004	B-	2,208	34.15	A- / 9.2	28.95%	C- / 3.7
2003	C	1,386	26.62	C+ / 6.5	46.91%	C / 4.3
2002	C-	955	18.32	C- / 3.3	-25.46%	C / 4.5
2001	D+	1,153	24.76	C- / 3.0	-16.03%	D / 1.9

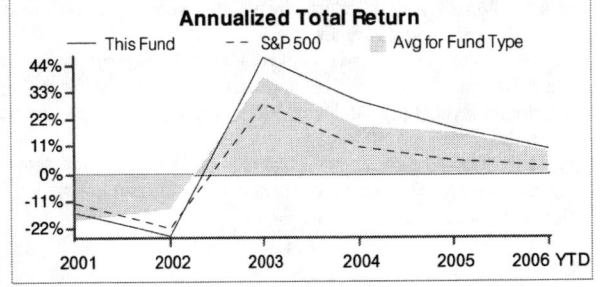

Fidelity Export Fund (FEXPX)

B-   Good

Fund Family: Fidelity Investments **Phone:** (800) 544-8888
Address: 82 Devonshire Street, Boston, MA 02109
Fund Type: GR - Growth

Major Rating Factors: Fidelity Export Fund receives a Weiss Investment Rating of B- (Good). The fund currently has a performance rating of C+ (Fair) based on an average return of 15.82% over the last three years and 1.51% over the last six months. Factored into the performance evaluation is an expense ratio of 0.82% (very low) and a 0.8% back-end load levied at the time of sale.

The fund's risk rating is currently B- (Good). It carries a beta of 1.21, meaning it is expected to move 12.1% for every 10% move in the market. Volatility, as measured by both the semi-deviation and a drawdown factor, is considered low.

Victor Thay has been running the fund for 1 year and currently receives a manager quality ranking of 80 (0=worst, 99=best). If you desire an average level of risk, then this fund may be an option.

Services Offered: Automated phone transactions, payroll deductions, bank draft capabilities, an IRA investment plan, a 401K investment plan, a Keogh investment plan and a systematic withdrawal plan.

Data Date	Weiss Investment Rating	Net Assets ($Mil)	NAV	Performance Rating/Pts	Total Return Y-T-D	Risk Rating/Pts
6-06	B-	4,661	21.56	C+ / 6.6	1.51%	B- / 7.0
2005	B	3,837	21.24	B / 7.7	15.29%	C+ / 6.7
2004	C+	1,643	19.64	C+ / 6.3	13.59%	C / 5.2
2003	B-	947	18.16	B- / 7.5	32.62%	C+ / 6.4
2002	C+	708	13.75	B- / 7.2	-18.66%	C+ / 5.6
2001	B	673	16.97	A- / 9.1	0.72%	C- / 3.2

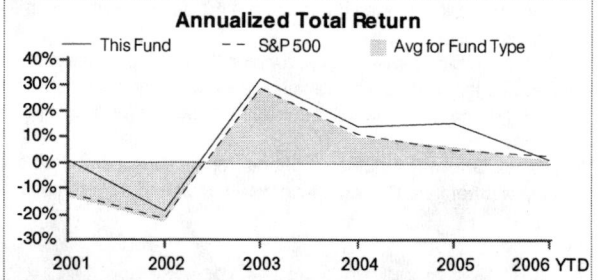

Annualized Total Return

Fidelity Freedom 2020 Fd (FFFDX)

C   Fair

Fund Family: Fidelity Investments **Phone:** (800) 544-8888
Address: 82 Devonshire Street, Boston, MA 02109
Fund Type: AA - Asset Allocation

Major Rating Factors: Middle of the road best describes Fidelity Freedom 2020 Fd whose Weiss Investment Rating is currently a C (Fair). The fund currently has a performance rating of C- (Fair) based on an average return of 10.78% over the last three years and 2.27% over the last six months. Factored into the performance evaluation is an expense ratio of 0.75% (very low).

The fund's risk rating is currently B (Good). It carries a beta of 1.32, meaning it is expected to move 13.2% for every 10% move in the market. Volatility, as measured by both the semi-deviation and a drawdown factor, is considered low.

Ren Cheng has been running the fund for 10 years and currently receives a manager quality ranking of 71 (0=worst, 99=best). If you desire an average level of risk, then this fund may be an option.

Services Offered: Automated phone transactions, payroll deductions, bank draft capabilities, an IRA investment plan, a 401K investment plan and a Keogh investment plan.

Data Date	Weiss Investment Rating	Net Assets ($Mil)	NAV	Performance Rating/Pts	Total Return Y-T-D	Risk Rating/Pts
6-06	C	14,282	14.77	C- / 3.9	2.27%	B / 8.4
2005	C+	11,971	14.71	C- / 3.8	7.75%	B+ / 9.2
2004	C+	9,338	13.96	C / 5.3	9.55%	B- / 7.4
2003	C+	6,319	13.02	C / 5.5	24.90%	B- / 7.2
2002	B-	3,742	10.64	C+ / 6.5	-13.71%	B- / 7.1
2001	C+	2,796	12.58	C+ / 6.2	-9.07%	C+ / 6.8

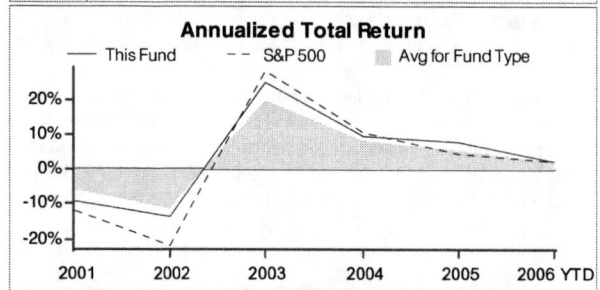

Annualized Total Return

Fidelity Freedom Income Fd (FFFAX)

C-   Fair

Fund Family: Fidelity Advisor **Phone:** (800) 522-7297
Address: 82 Devonshire Street, Boston, MA 02109
Fund Type: BA - Balanced

Major Rating Factors: Very poor performance is the major factor driving the C- (Fair) Weiss Investment Rating for Fidelity Freedom Income Fd. The fund currently has a performance rating of E (Very Weak) based on an average return of 4.02% over the last three years and 1.14% over the last six months. Factored into the performance evaluation is an expense ratio of 0.56% (very low).

The fund's risk rating is currently B+ (Good). It carries a beta of 0.44, meaning the fund's expected move will be 4.4% for every 10% move in the market. Volatility, as measured by both the semi-deviation and a drawdown factor, is considered very low.

Ren Cheng has been running the fund for 10 years and currently receives a manager quality ranking of 49 (0=worst, 99=best). This fund offers only a moderate level of risk but investors looking for strong performance are still waiting.

Services Offered: Automated phone transactions, payroll deductions, bank draft capabilities, an IRA investment plan, a 401K investment plan and a Keogh investment plan.

Data Date	Weiss Investment Rating	Net Assets ($Mil)	NAV	Performance Rating/Pts	Total Return Y-T-D	Risk Rating/Pts
6-06	C-	2,167	11.32	E / 0.5	1.14%	B+ / 9.9
2005	C-	2,055	11.37	E- / 0.2	3.78%	B+ / 9.9
2004	C+	1,900	11.27	D+ / 2.6	3.89%	B+ / 9.9
2003	B+	1,566	11.09	C / 5.5	7.33%	B+ / 9.9
2002	A+	1,079	10.60	A- / 9.2	-0.26%	B+ / 9.9
2001	A+	862	10.93	B- / 7.4	2.22%	B+ / 9.9

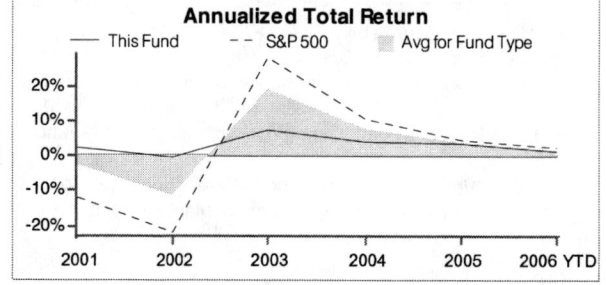

Annualized Total Return

Fidelity Fund (FFIDX)   C   Fair

Fund Family: Fidelity Investments   **Phone:** (800) 544-8888
Address: 82 Devonshire Street, Boston, MA 02109
Fund Type: GI - Growth and Income

Major Rating Factors: Middle of the road best describes Fidelity Fund whose Weiss Investment Rating is currently a C (Fair). The fund currently has a performance rating of C- (Fair) based on an average return of 11.11% over the last three years and 2.51% over the last six months. Factored into the performance evaluation is an expense ratio of 0.60% (very low).

The fund's risk rating is currently B- (Good). It carries a beta of 1.00, meaning that its performance tracks fairly well with that of the overall stock market. Volatility, as measured by both the semi-deviation and a drawdown factor, is considered low.

John Avery has been running the fund for 4 years and currently receives a manager quality ranking of 55 (0=worst, 99=best). If you desire an average level of risk, then this fund may be an option.

Services Offered: Automated phone transactions, bank draft capabilities, an IRA investment plan, a 401K investment plan, a Keogh investment plan and a systematic withdrawal plan.

Data Date	Weiss Investment Rating	Net Assets ($Mil)	NAV	Perfor-mance Rating/Pts	Total Return Y-T-D	Risk Rating/Pts
6-06	C	8,297	32.55	C- / 4.2	2.51%	B- / 7.9
2005	C	9,671	31.82	C- / 3.9	7.52%	B- / 7.2
2004	C-	10,812	29.88	D+ / 2.9	7.84%	C / 5.5
2003	C	9,854	28.08	C / 4.3	27.26%	C+ / 5.7
2002	C	9,256	22.26	C- / 4.2	-22.25%	C+ / 5.6
2001	C-	12,452	28.88	C- / 4.1	-11.20%	D+ / 2.3

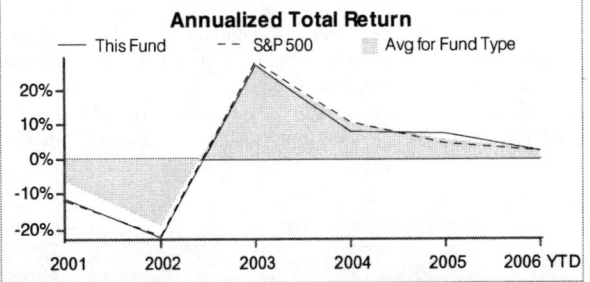

Fidelity Growth & Income (FGRIX)   D-   Weak

Fund Family: Fidelity Investments   **Phone:** (800) 544-8888
Address: 82 Devonshire Street, Boston, MA 02109
Fund Type: GI - Growth and Income

Major Rating Factors: Disappointing performance is the major factor driving the D- (Weak) Weiss Investment Rating for Fidelity Growth & Income. The fund currently has a performance rating of D (Weak) based on an average return of 7.89% over the last three years and 0.95% over the last six months. Factored into the performance evaluation is an expense ratio of 0.69% (very low).

The fund's risk rating is currently C+ (Fair). It carries a beta of 0.85, meaning the fund's expected move will be 8.5% for every 10% move in the market. Volatility, as measured by both the semi-deviation and a drawdown factor, is considered low.

Tim Cohen has been running the fund for 1 year and currently receives a manager quality ranking of 35 (0=worst, 99=best). This fund offers only a moderate level of risk but investors looking for strong performance are still waiting.

Services Offered: Automated phone transactions, bank draft capabilities, an IRA investment plan, a 401K investment plan, a Keogh investment plan and a systematic withdrawal plan. However, the fund is currently closed to new investors.

Data Date	Weiss Investment Rating	Net Assets ($Mil)	NAV	Perfor-mance Rating/Pts	Total Return Y-T-D	Risk Rating/Pts
6-06	D-	29,366	34.66	D / 1.9	0.95%	C+ / 6.2
2005	E+	31,527	34.40	D- / 1.3	2.71%	C+ / 6.6
2004	C-	32,106	38.21	C- / 3.5	9.84%	C+ / 6.2
2003	C	29,167	35.63	C- / 3.3	19.01%	C+ / 6.6
2002	C+	27,196	30.31	C+ / 5.9	-18.08%	B- / 7.2
2001	B-	34,255	37.38	C- / 4.2	-9.35%	B- / 7.3

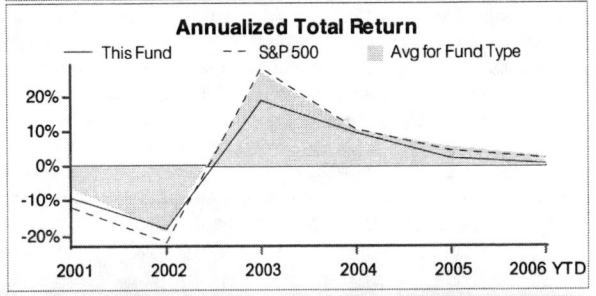

Fidelity Growth Company (FDGRX)   C   Fair

Fund Family: Fidelity Investments   **Phone:** (800) 544-8888
Address: 82 Devonshire Street, Boston, MA 02109
Fund Type: GR - Growth

Major Rating Factors: Middle of the road best describes Fidelity Growth Company whose Weiss Investment Rating is currently a C (Fair). The fund currently has a performance rating of C+ (Fair) based on an average return of 15.06% over the last three years and 0.71% over the last six months. Factored into the performance evaluation is an expense ratio of 0.96% (low).

The fund's risk rating is currently C (Fair). It carries a beta of 1.36, meaning it is expected to move 13.6% for every 10% move in the market. Volatility, as measured by both the semi-deviation and a drawdown factor, is considered average.

Steven Wymer has been running the fund for 9 years and currently receives a manager quality ranking of 61 (0=worst, 99=best). If you desire an average level of risk, then this fund may be an option.

Services Offered: Automated phone transactions, bank draft capabilities, an IRA investment plan, a 401K investment plan, a Keogh investment plan and a systematic withdrawal plan. However, the fund is currently closed to new investors.

Data Date	Weiss Investment Rating	Net Assets ($Mil)	NAV	Perfor-mance Rating/Pts	Total Return Y-T-D	Risk Rating/Pts
6-06	C	28,297	64.08	C+ / 6.2	0.71%	C / 5.3
2005	B-	26,818	63.63	B / 8.2	13.50%	C / 5.3
2004	D-	25,180	56.07	D+ / 2.8	12.12%	D+ / 2.9
2003	D-	22,374	50.07	D / 2.1	41.36%	C- / 3.0
2002	D	16,411	35.42	D / 1.7	-33.45%	D+ / 2.9
2001	C-	22,742	53.22	B- / 7.2	-25.31%	E- / 0.0

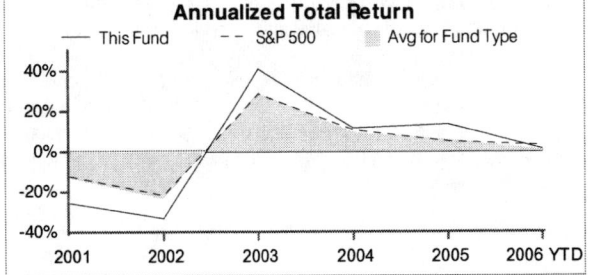

Fidelity Independence Fund (FDFFX)

C **Fair**

Fund Family: Fidelity Investments   **Phone:** (800) 544-8888
Address: 82 Devonshire Street, Boston, MA 02109
Fund Type: GR - Growth

Major Rating Factors: Middle of the road best describes Fidelity Independence Fund whose Weiss Investment Rating is currently a C (Fair). The fund currently has a performance rating of C (Fair) based on an average return of 13.02% over the last three years and 4.48% over the last six months. Factored into the performance evaluation is an expense ratio of 0.72% (very low).

The fund's risk rating is currently C+ (Fair). It carries a beta of 1.35, meaning it is expected to move 13.5% for every 10% move in the market. Volatility, as measured by both the semi-deviation and a drawdown factor, is considered low.

Jason Weiner has been running the fund for 3 years and currently receives a manager quality ranking of 39 (0=worst, 99=best). If you desire an average level of risk, then this fund may be an option.

Services Offered: Automated phone transactions, bank draft capabilities, an IRA investment plan, a 401K investment plan, a Keogh investment plan and a systematic withdrawal plan.

Data Date	Weiss Investment Rating	Net Assets ($Mil)	NAV	Perfor-mance Rating/Pts	Total Return Y-T-D	Risk Rating/Pts
6-06	C	4,468	20.53	C / 5.5	4.48%	C+ / 6.8
2005	C	4,656	19.65	C / 5.1	10.55%	C+ / 6.4
2004	C	4,705	17.83	C / 5.5	11.65%	C / 5.0
2003	D	4,604	16.06	D / 1.7	23.66%	C / 4.5
2002	C-	4,444	13.07	C / 4.9	-15.82%	C- / 3.7
2001	D+	5,486	15.77	C / 4.7	-27.22%	E- / 0.0

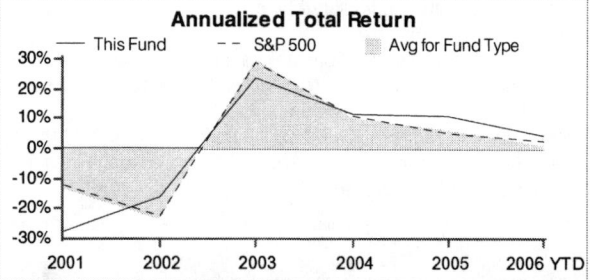

Fidelity International Discovery Fd (FIGRX)

A **Excellent**

Fund Family: Fidelity Investments   **Phone:** (800) 544-8888
Address: 82 Devonshire Street, Boston, MA 02109
Fund Type: FO - Foreign

Major Rating Factors: Exceptional performance is the major factor driving the A (Excellent) Weiss Investment Rating for Fidelity International Discovery Fd. The fund currently has a performance rating of A- (Excellent) based on an average return of 25.46% over the last three years and 7.99% over the last six months. Factored into the performance evaluation is an expense ratio of 1.01% (low) and a 1.0% back-end load levied at the time of sale.

The fund's risk rating is currently C+ (Fair). It carries a beta of 1.13, meaning it is expected to move 11.3% for every 10% move in the market. Volatility, as measured by both the semi-deviation and a drawdown factor, is considered low.

William Kennedy has been running the fund for 2 years and currently receives a manager quality ranking of 35 (0=worst, 99=best). If you desire only a moderate level of risk and strong performance, then this fund is an excellent option.

Services Offered: Automated phone transactions, bank draft capabilities, an IRA investment plan, a 401K investment plan, a Keogh investment plan, wire transfers and a systematic withdrawal plan.

Data Date	Weiss Investment Rating	Net Assets ($Mil)	NAV	Perfor-mance Rating/Pts	Total Return Y-T-D	Risk Rating/Pts
6-06	A	6,835	34.19	A- / 9.1	7.99%	C+ / 6.5
2005	A	4,219	31.66	A- / 9.2	18.55%	B- / 7.0
2004	A-	2,504	28.20	A- / 9.1	19.05%	C+ / 6.4
2003	B+	1,300	23.92	B+ / 8.4	43.34%	C+ / 6.7
2002	C+	932	16.82	C / 5.0	-9.87%	C+ / 6.0
2001	C	941	18.76	C / 5.5	-17.43%	D+ / 2.7

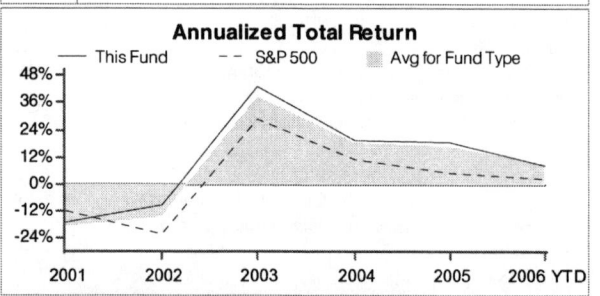

Fidelity International Small Cap (FISMX)

B **Good**

Fund Family: Fidelity Investments   **Phone:** (800) 544-8888
Address: 82 Devonshire Street, Boston, MA 02109
Fund Type: FO - Foreign

Major Rating Factors: Exceptional performance is the major factor driving the B (Good) Weiss Investment Rating for Fidelity International Small Cap. The fund currently has a performance rating of A+ (Excellent) based on an average return of 37.11% over the last three years and 7.34% over the last six months. Factored into the performance evaluation is an expense ratio of 1.25% (average) and a 2.0% back-end load levied at the time of sale.

The fund's risk rating is currently C (Fair). It carries a beta of 1.33, meaning it is expected to move 13.3% for every 10% move in the market. Volatility, as measured by both the semi-deviation and a drawdown factor, is considered average.

Tokuya Sano has been running the fund for 4 years and currently receives a manager quality ranking of 86 (0=worst, 99=best). If you desire an average level of risk and strong performance, then this fund is a good option.

Services Offered: An IRA investment plan. However, the fund is currently closed to new investors.

Data Date	Weiss Investment Rating	Net Assets ($Mil)	NAV	Perfor-mance Rating/Pts	Total Return Y-T-D	Risk Rating/Pts
6-06	B	2,250	28.95	A+ / 9.8	7.34%	C / 4.7
2005	A+	2,154	26.97	A+ / 9.9	29.47%	C+ / 6.8
2004	U	1,412	23.28	U / --	29.43%	U / --
2003	U	616	18.67	U / --	80.25%	U / --

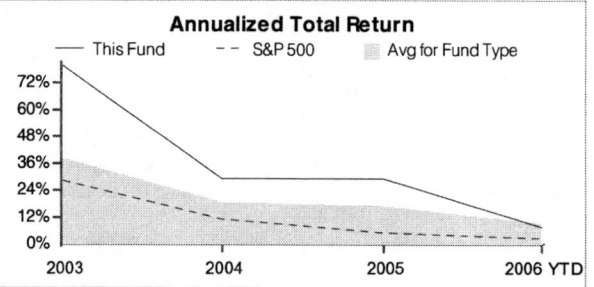

Fidelity Latin American Fund (FLATX) | C+ | Fair

Fund Family: Fidelity Investments **Phone:** (800) 544-8888
Address: 82 Devonshire Street, Boston, MA 02109
Fund Type: EM - Emerging Market
Major Rating Factors: Exceptional performance is the major factor driving the C+ (Fair) Weiss Investment Rating for Fidelity Latin American Fund. The fund currently has a performance rating of A+ (Excellent) based on an average return of 50.37% over the last three years and 13.35% over the last six months. Factored into the performance evaluation is an expense ratio of 1.04% (low) and a 1.5% back-end load levied at the time of sale.

The fund's risk rating is currently C- (Fair). It carries a beta of 1.27, meaning it is expected to move 12.7% for every 10% move in the market. Volatility, as measured by both the semi-deviation and a drawdown factor, is considered average.

Adam Kutas currently receives a manager quality ranking of 83 (0=worst, 99=best). If you desire an average level of risk and strong performance, then this fund is a good option.

Services Offered: Automated phone transactions, bank draft capabilities, an IRA investment plan, a 401K investment plan and a systematic withdrawal plan.

Data Date	Weiss Investment Rating	Net Assets ($Mil)	NAV	Performance Rating/Pts	Total Return Y-T-D	Risk Rating/Pts
6-06	C+	2,545	36.25	A+ / 9.9	13.35%	C- / 3.3
2005	B+	1,691	31.98	A+ / 9.9	55.17%	C / 4.6
2004	B-	502	21.15	A+ / 9.8	41.11%	C- / 3.4
2003	B	234	15.22	A / 9.5	65.78%	C / 4.8
2002	C-	144	9.33	C / 4.3	-20.85%	C / 4.6
2001	C-	210	12.01	B- / 7.2	-6.04%	E- / 0.0

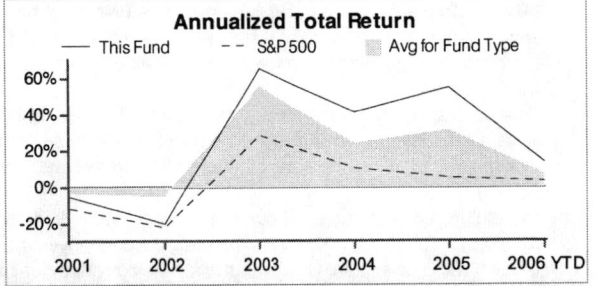

Fidelity Leveraged Company Stock (FLVCX) | A | Excellent

Fund Family: Fidelity Investments **Phone:** (800) 544-8888
Address: 82 Devonshire Street, Boston, MA 02109
Fund Type: GR - Growth
Major Rating Factors: Exceptional performance is the major factor driving the A (Excellent) Weiss Investment Rating for Fidelity Leveraged Company Stock. The fund currently has a performance rating of A (Excellent) based on an average return of 27.77% over the last three years and 9.30% over the last six months. Factored into the performance evaluation is an expense ratio of 0.86% (very low) and a 1.5% back-end load levied at the time of sale.

The fund's risk rating is currently C+ (Fair). It carries a beta of 1.51, meaning it is expected to move 15.1% for every 10% move in the market. Volatility, as measured by both the semi-deviation and a drawdown factor, is considered low.

Thomas Soviero has been running the fund for 3 years and currently receives a manager quality ranking of 99 (0=worst, 99=best). If you desire only a moderate level of risk and strong performance, then this fund is an excellent option.

Services Offered: Automated phone transactions, payroll deductions, bank draft capabilities, an IRA investment plan, a 401K investment plan, a Keogh investment plan, wire transfers and a systematic withdrawal plan.

Data Date	Weiss Investment Rating	Net Assets ($Mil)	NAV	Performance Rating/Pts	Total Return Y-T-D	Risk Rating/Pts
6-06	A	4,177	28.44	A / 9.3	9.30%	C+ / 6.4
2005	A+	3,454	26.02	A+ / 9.8	17.47%	C+ / 6.7
2004	B+	2,142	22.68	A+ / 9.9	24.33%	C / 4.6
2003	B+	1,026	19.33	A+ / 9.9	96.31%	C / 5.4
2002	U	65	10.00	U / --	-1.77%	U / --
2001	U	60	10.18	U / --	3.23%	U / --

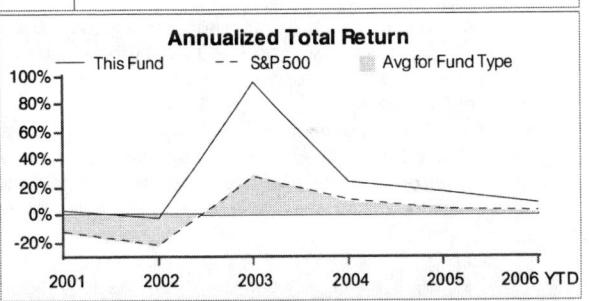

Fidelity Low-Priced Stock (FLPSX) | A- | Excellent

Fund Family: Fidelity Investments **Phone:** (800) 544-8888
Address: 82 Devonshire Street, Boston, MA 02109
Fund Type: SC - Small Cap
Major Rating Factors: Strong performance is the major factor driving the A- (Excellent) Weiss Investment Rating for Fidelity Low-Priced Stock. The fund currently has a performance rating of B (Good) based on an average return of 19.92% over the last three years and 5.07% over the last six months. Factored into the performance evaluation is an expense ratio of 0.85% (very low) and a 1.5% back-end load levied at the time of sale.

The fund's risk rating is currently B- (Good). It carries a beta of 0.73, meaning the fund's expected move will be 7.3% for every 10% move in the market. Volatility, as measured by both the semi-deviation and a drawdown factor, is considered low.

Joel Tillinghast has been running the fund for 17 years and currently receives a manager quality ranking of 94 (0=worst, 99=best). If you desire only a moderate level of risk and strong performance, then this fund is an excellent option.

Services Offered: Automated phone transactions, bank draft capabilities, an IRA investment plan, a 401K investment plan, a Keogh investment plan and a systematic withdrawal plan. However, the fund is currently closed to new investors.

Data Date	Weiss Investment Rating	Net Assets ($Mil)	NAV	Performance Rating/Pts	Total Return Y-T-D	Risk Rating/Pts
6-06	A-	36,659	42.91	B / 7.7	5.07%	B- / 7.8
2005	A-	36,517	40.84	B / 8.0	8.65%	B- / 7.3
2004	A	35,976	40.25	A / 9.3	22.24%	C+ / 6.7
2003	A+	25,016	34.98	A+ / 9.6	40.85%	B- / 7.6
2002	A	15,540	25.17	A+ / 9.6	-6.18%	B / 8.3
2001	A+	12,429	27.42	A+ / 9.7	26.73%	B- / 7.2

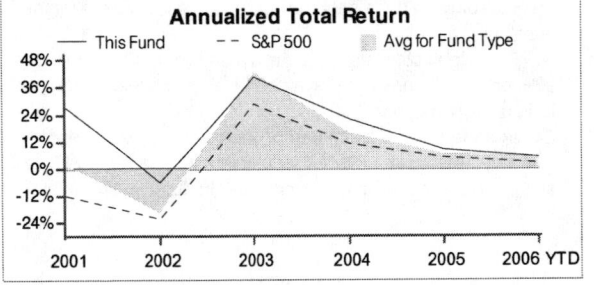

Fidelity Magellan Fund (FMAGX)   E-   Very Weak

Fund Family: Fidelity Investments   **Phone:** (800) 544-8888
Address: 82 Devonshire Street, Boston, MA 02109
Fund Type: GR - Growth

Major Rating Factors: Fidelity Magellan Fund has adopted a very risky asset allocation strategy and currently receives an overall Weiss Investment Rating of E- (Very Weak). The fund has a high level of volatility, as measured by both semi-deviation and drawdown factors. It carries a beta of 1.03, meaning that its performance tracks fairly well with that of the overall stock market. Unfortunately, the high level of risk (D, Weak) failed to pay off as investors endured poor performance.

The fund's performance rating is currently D+ (Weak). It has registered an average return of 9.40% over the last three years and is up 1.75% over the last six months. Factored into the performance evaluation is an expense ratio of 0.59% (very low).

Robert Stansky has been running the fund for 10 years and currently receives a manager quality ranking of 34 (0=worst, 99=best). If you can tolerate very high levels of risk in the hope of improved future returns, holding this fund may be an option.

Services Offered: Automated phone transactions, bank draft capabilities, an IRA investment plan, a 401K investment plan, a Keogh investment plan and a systematic withdrawal plan. However, the fund is currently closed to new investors.

Data Date	Weiss Investment Rating	Net Assets ($Mil)	NAV	Perfor-mance Rating/Pts	Total Return Y-T-D	Risk Rating/Pts
6-06	E-	46,615	87.61	D+/ 2.6	1.75%	D / 2.0
2005	D	51,337	106.44	C-/ 3.0	6.42%	C+/ 6.1
2004	D-	63,296	103.79	D / 1.6	7.49%	C / 4.5
2003	D+	64,989	97.74	D+/ 2.7	24.82%	C / 4.8
2002	C	60,873	78.96	C-/ 3.9	-23.66%	C+/ 6.0
2001	C-	79,515	104.22	C-/ 3.9	-11.65%	C-/ 3.2

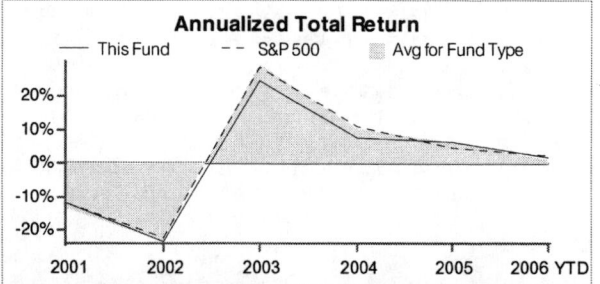

Fidelity Mid-Cap Stock Fund (FMCSX)   C+   Fair

Fund Family: Fidelity Investments   **Phone:** (800) 544-8888
Address: 82 Devonshire Street, Boston, MA 02109
Fund Type: MC - Mid Cap

Major Rating Factors: Strong performance is the major factor driving the C+ (Fair) Weiss Investment Rating for Fidelity Mid-Cap Stock Fund. The fund currently has a performance rating of B (Good) based on an average return of 17.83% over the last three years and 9.21% over the last six months. Factored into the performance evaluation is an expense ratio of 0.62% (very low) and a 0.8% back-end load levied at the time of sale.

The fund's risk rating is currently C+ (Fair). It carries a beta of 1.17, meaning it is expected to move 11.7% for every 10% move in the market. Volatility, as measured by both the semi-deviation and a drawdown factor, is considered low.

Shep Perkins has been running the fund for 1 year and currently receives a manager quality ranking of 27 (0=worst, 99=best). If you desire only a moderate level of risk and strong performance, then this fund is an excellent option.

Services Offered: Automated phone transactions, bank draft capabilities, an IRA investment plan, a 401K investment plan, wire transfers and a systematic withdrawal plan. However, the fund is currently closed to new investors.

Data Date	Weiss Investment Rating	Net Assets ($Mil)	NAV	Perfor-mance Rating/Pts	Total Return Y-T-D	Risk Rating/Pts
6-06	C+	12,027	28.40	B / 7.7	9.21%	C+/ 5.8
2005	B-	9,684	26.57	B-/ 7.3	16.07%	C+/ 6.0
2004	D	9,093	23.45	D+/ 2.5	9.05%	C / 4.5
2003	C	7,856	21.57	C-/ 4.1	33.26%	C / 5.4
2002	C+	5,440	16.26	C+/ 6.6	-27.59%	C+/ 5.6
2001	C+	6,547	22.57	A / 9.3	-12.80%	E-/ 0.0

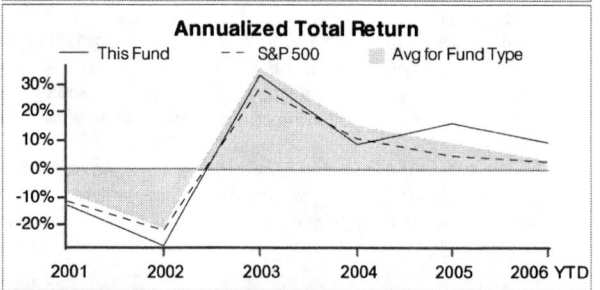

Fidelity New Millennium (FMILX)   C   Fair

Fund Family: Fidelity Investments   **Phone:** (800) 544-8888
Address: 82 Devonshire Street, Boston, MA 02109
Fund Type: AG - Aggressive Growth

Major Rating Factors: Strong performance is the major factor driving the C (Fair) Weiss Investment Rating for Fidelity New Millennium. The fund currently has a performance rating of B- (Good) based on an average return of 14.90% over the last three years and 10.00% over the last six months. Factored into the performance evaluation is an expense ratio of 0.86% (very low).

The fund's risk rating is currently C (Fair). It carries a beta of 1.63, meaning it is expected to move 16.3% for every 10% move in the market. Volatility, as measured by both the semi-deviation and a drawdown factor, is considered average.

Roth John currently receives a manager quality ranking of 34 (0=worst, 99=best). If you desire an average level of risk and strong performance, then this fund is a good option.

Services Offered: Automated phone transactions, bank draft capabilities, an IRA investment plan, a 401K investment plan, a Keogh investment plan and a systematic withdrawal plan. However, the fund is currently closed to new investors.

Data Date	Weiss Investment Rating	Net Assets ($Mil)	NAV	Perfor-mance Rating/Pts	Total Return Y-T-D	Risk Rating/Pts
6-06	C	2,763	37.56	B-/ 7.2	10.00%	C / 4.5
2005	C-	3,411	34.89	C+/ 5.7	10.10%	C / 4.5
2004	D+	3,618	31.69	C-/ 3.1	4.28%	C / 5.0
2003	C	3,620	30.39	C / 5.2	37.31%	C / 4.4
2002	C-	2,715	22.14	C-/ 4.1	-19.87%	C-/ 3.1
2001	C+	2,939	27.63	A / 9.3	-18.15%	E-/ 0.0

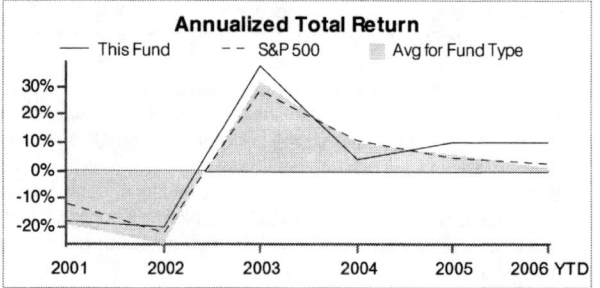

Fidelity OTC Portfolio (FOCPX)   D-   Weak

Fund Family: Fidelity Investments   **Phone:** (800) 544-8888
Address: 82 Devonshire Street, Boston, MA 02109
Fund Type: SC - Small Cap
Major Rating Factors: Fidelity OTC Portfolio receives a Weiss Investment Rating of D- (Weak). The fund currently has a performance rating of C- (Fair) based on an average return of 11.07% over the last three years and -3.76% over the last six months. Factored into the performance evaluation is an expense ratio of 0.72% (very low).

The fund's risk rating is currently C (Fair). It carries a beta of 0.92, meaning that its performance tracks fairly well with that of the overall stock market. Volatility, as measured by both the semi-deviation and a drawdown factor, is considered average.

Sonu Kalra currently receives a manager quality ranking of 12 (0=worst, 99=best). If you desire an average level of risk, then this fund may be an option.
Services Offered: Automated phone transactions, bank draft capabilities, an IRA investment plan, a 401K investment plan, a Keogh investment plan and a systematic withdrawal plan.

Data Date	Weiss Investment Rating	Net Assets ($Mil)	NAV	Perfor- mance Rating/Pts	Total Return Y-T-D	Risk Rating/Pts
6-06	D-	7,795	36.37	C- / 3.1	-3.76%	C / 4.4
2005	D+	8,209	37.79	C+ / 5.7	8.94%	C- / 4.0
2004	D	8,144	34.69	C- / 3.7	8.12%	C- / 3.6
2003	D+	7,827	32.47	C- / 3.4	35.80%	C- / 3.2
2002	D-	6,510	23.91	D- / 1.5	-23.29%	D / 2.0
2001	D	8,070	31.17	C- / 3.4	-24.07%	E- / 0.0

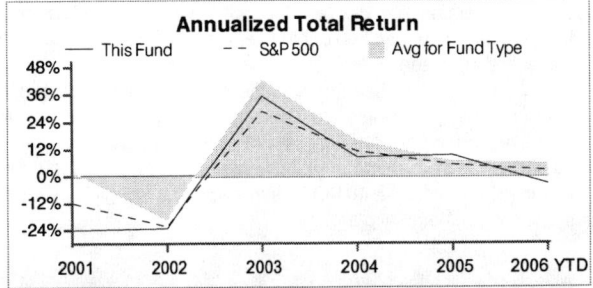

Fidelity Overseas Fund (FOSFX)   B+   Good

Fund Family: Fidelity Investments   **Phone:** (800) 544-8888
Address: 82 Devonshire Street, Boston, MA 02109
Fund Type: FO - Foreign
Major Rating Factors: Strong performance is the major factor driving the B+ (Good) Weiss Investment Rating for Fidelity Overseas Fund. The fund currently has a performance rating of B+ (Good) based on an average return of 23.35% over the last three years and 6.42% over the last six months. Factored into the performance evaluation is an expense ratio of 0.86% (very low) and a 1.0% back-end load levied at the time of sale.

The fund's risk rating is currently C+ (Fair). It carries a beta of 1.15, meaning it is expected to move 11.5% for every 10% move in the market. Volatility, as measured by both the semi-deviation and a drawdown factor, is considered low.

Ian Hart currently receives a manager quality ranking of 20 (0=worst, 99=best). If you desire only a moderate level of risk and strong performance, then this fund is an excellent option.
Services Offered: Automated phone transactions, bank draft capabilities, an IRA investment plan, a 401K investment plan, a Keogh investment plan and a systematic withdrawal plan.

Data Date	Weiss Investment Rating	Net Assets ($Mil)	NAV	Perfor- mance Rating/Pts	Total Return Y-T-D	Risk Rating/Pts
6-06	B+	6,492	44.28	B+ / 8.9	6.42%	C+ / 6.3
2005	A-	5,002	41.61	A- / 9.1	19.29%	C+ / 6.3
2004	C+	4,687	35.38	B- / 7.1	13.54%	C / 5.2
2003	C+	3,660	31.43	C+ / 6.5	44.30%	C / 5.4
2002	C-	3,059	22.00	D+ / 2.7	-19.45%	C / 5.2
2001	D+	3,481	27.42	D+ / 2.4	-20.22%	C- / 3.0

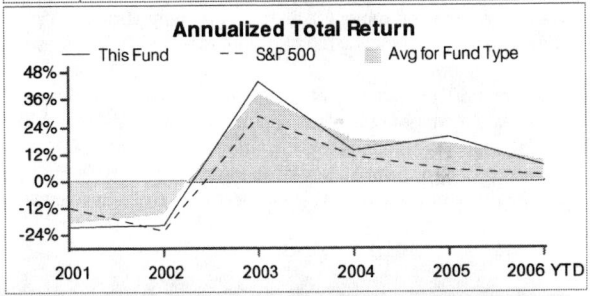

Fidelity Puritan Fund (FPURX)   C   Fair

Fund Family: Fidelity Investments   **Phone:** (800) 544-8888
Address: 82 Devonshire Street, Boston, MA 02109
Fund Type: GI - Growth and Income
Major Rating Factors: Middle of the road best describes Fidelity Puritan Fund whose Weiss Investment Rating is currently a C (Fair). The fund currently has a performance rating of C- (Fair) based on an average return of 9.89% over the last three years and 3.26% over the last six months. Factored into the performance evaluation is an expense ratio of 0.62% (very low).

The fund's risk rating is currently B (Good). It carries a beta of 0.70, meaning the fund's expected move will be 7.0% for every 10% move in the market. Volatility, as measured by both the semi-deviation and a drawdown factor, is considered low.

Stephen Petersen has been running the fund for 6 years and currently receives a manager quality ranking of 71 (0=worst, 99=best). If you desire an average level of risk, then this fund may be an option.
Services Offered: Automated phone transactions, bank draft capabilities, an IRA investment plan, a 401K investment plan, a Keogh investment plan and a systematic withdrawal plan.

Data Date	Weiss Investment Rating	Net Assets ($Mil)	NAV	Perfor- mance Rating/Pts	Total Return Y-T-D	Risk Rating/Pts
6-06	C	23,404	19.21	C- / 3.5	3.26%	B / 8.9
2005	C-	24,180	18.73	D / 2.1	4.67%	B / 8.0
2004	B-	23,935	18.95	C+ / 5.7	9.28%	B- / 7.5
2003	B+	20,776	18.47	B- / 7.1	22.20%	B / 8.3
2002	A	18,468	15.79	B+ / 8.6	-7.91%	B / 8.9
2001	B	20,315	17.67	C+ / 6.5	-1.05%	B / 8.7

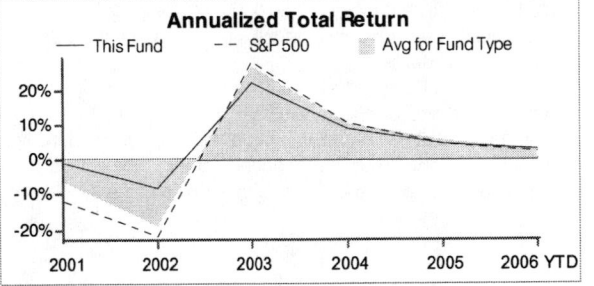

Fidelity Real Estate Investment (FRESX)   C   Fair

Fund Family: Fidelity Investments   **Phone:** (800) 544-8888
Address: 82 Devonshire Street, Boston, MA 02109
Fund Type: RE - Real Estate

Major Rating Factors: Exceptional performance is the major factor driving the C (Fair) Weiss Investment Rating for Fidelity Real Estate Investment. The fund currently has a performance rating of A (Excellent) based on an average return of 27.47% over the last three years and 12.11% over the last six months. Factored into the performance evaluation is an expense ratio of 0.81% (very low) and a 0.8% back-end load levied at the time of sale.

The fund's risk rating is currently C- (Fair). It carries a beta of 0.95, meaning that its performance tracks fairly well with that of the overall stock market. Volatility, as measured by both the semi-deviation and a drawdown factor, is considered average.

Steve Buller has been running the fund for 8 years and currently receives a manager quality ranking of 88 (0=worst, 99=best). If you desire an average level of risk and strong performance, then this fund is a good option.

Services Offered: Automated phone transactions, bank draft capabilities, an IRA investment plan, a 401K investment plan, a Keogh investment plan and a systematic withdrawal plan.

Data Date	Weiss Investment Rating	Net Assets ($Mil)	NAV	Perfor- mance Rating/Pts	Total Return Y-T-D	Risk Rating/Pts
6-06	C	6,659	34.82	A / 9.3	12.11%	C- / 3.1
2005	B	5,791	31.16	A- / 9.1	14.87%	C / 5.0
2004	A+	4,557	29.54	A+ / 9.8	34.15%	B- / 7.4
2003	A+	2,586	23.71	A- / 9.2	33.78%	B / 8.8
2002	A+	1,697	18.39	A+ / 9.8	5.77%	B+ / 9.8
2001	A+	1,245	18.52	A- / 9.1	9.50%	B- / 7.0

Annualized Total Return

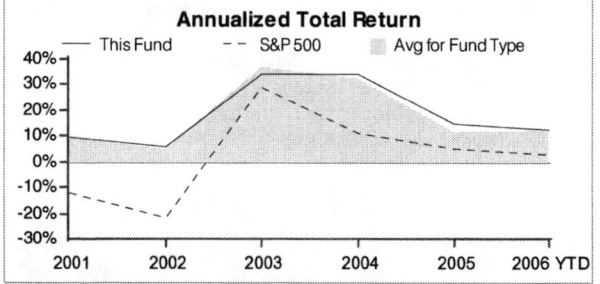

Fidelity Small Cap Independence (FDSCX)   C+   Fair

Fund Family: Fidelity Investments   **Phone:** (800) 544-8888
Address: 82 Devonshire Street, Boston, MA 02109
Fund Type: SC - Small Cap

Major Rating Factors: Middle of the road best describes Fidelity Small Cap Independence whose Weiss Investment Rating is currently a C+ (Fair). The fund currently has a performance rating of C+ (Fair) based on an average return of 17.21% over the last three years and 4.93% over the last six months. Factored into the performance evaluation is an expense ratio of 0.75% (very low) and a 1.5% back-end load levied at the time of sale.

The fund's risk rating is currently C+ (Fair). It carries a beta of 0.85, meaning the fund's expected move will be 8.5% for every 10% move in the market. Volatility, as measured by both the semi-deviation and a drawdown factor, is considered low.

Richard Thompson has been running the fund for 1 year and currently receives a manager quality ranking of 68 (0=worst, 99=best). If you desire an average level of risk, then this fund may be an option.

Services Offered: Automated phone transactions, bank draft capabilities, an IRA investment plan, a 401K investment plan and a systematic withdrawal plan.

Data Date	Weiss Investment Rating	Net Assets ($Mil)	NAV	Perfor- mance Rating/Pts	Total Return Y-T-D	Risk Rating/Pts
6-06	C+	2,509	21.49	C+ / 6.9	4.93%	C+ / 5.6
2005	C+	1,769	20.48	C+ / 6.8	10.96%	C+ / 6.5
2004	C+	1,093	19.72	C+ / 6.7	15.02%	C+ / 5.6
2003	B+	963	17.94	B / 8.0	34.89%	C+ / 6.9
2002	B	886	13.30	C+ / 6.9	-20.83%	B- / 7.9
2001	B-	958	16.80	B+ / 8.7	6.29%	D+ / 2.7

Annualized Total Return

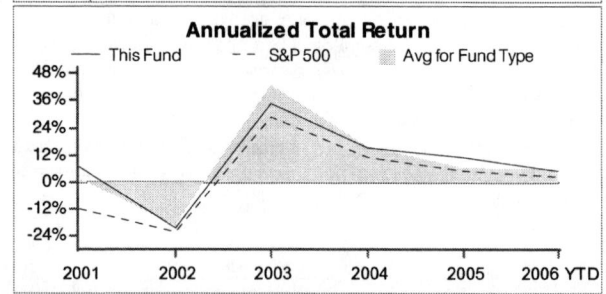

Fidelity Small Cap Stock Fund (FSLCX)   C   Fair

Fund Family: Fidelity Investments   **Phone:** (800) 544-8888
Address: 82 Devonshire Street, Boston, MA 02109
Fund Type: SC - Small Cap

Major Rating Factors: Strong performance is the major factor driving the C (Fair) Weiss Investment Rating for Fidelity Small Cap Stock Fund. The fund currently has a performance rating of B- (Good) based on an average return of 19.27% over the last three years and 5.95% over the last six months. Factored into the performance evaluation is an expense ratio of 1.00% (low) and a 2.0% back-end load levied at the time of sale.

The fund's risk rating is currently C (Fair). It carries a beta of 0.86, meaning the fund's expected move will be 8.6% for every 10% move in the market. Volatility, as measured by both the semi-deviation and a drawdown factor, is considered average.

Katherine Collins has been running the fund for 1 year and currently receives a manager quality ranking of 82 (0=worst, 99=best). If you desire an average level of risk and strong performance, then this fund is a good option.

Services Offered: Automated phone transactions, bank draft capabilities, an IRA investment plan, a 401K investment plan and a systematic withdrawal plan.

Data Date	Weiss Investment Rating	Net Assets ($Mil)	NAV	Perfor- mance Rating/Pts	Total Return Y-T-D	Risk Rating/Pts
6-06	C	4,789	18.17	B- / 7.5	5.95%	C / 4.6
2005	B-	4,290	18.30	B- / 7.4	8.09%	C+ / 6.2
2004	C+	4,159	18.16	B / 7.7	14.57%	C / 4.7
2003	B+	2,294	17.10	A- / 9.1	45.04%	C+ / 6.4
2002	B+	1,469	11.84	B / 8.2	-15.73%	B- / 7.4
2001	B-	1,354	14.36	A+ / 9.7	6.44%	D- / 1.4

Annualized Total Return

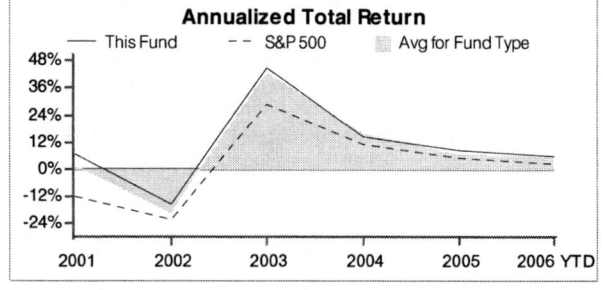

Fidelity Spartan 500 Idx Fd (FSMKX)

C+   **Fair**

Fund Family: Fidelity Investments   **Phone:** (800) 544-8888
Address: 82 Devonshire Street, Boston, MA 02109
Fund Type: IX - Index
Major Rating Factors: Middle of the road best describes Fidelity Spartan 500 Idx Fd whose Weiss Investment Rating is currently a C+ (Fair). The fund currently has a performance rating of C- (Fair) based on an average return of 11.10% over the last three years and 2.68% over the last six months. Factored into the performance evaluation is an expense ratio of 0.10% (very low) and a 0.5% back-end load levied at the time of sale.

The fund's risk rating is currently B (Good). It carries a beta of 1.00, meaning that its performance tracks fairly well with that of the overall stock market. Volatility, as measured by both the semi-deviation and a drawdown factor, is considered low.

Geode Capital Management has been running the fund for 3 years and currently receives a manager quality ranking of 55 (0=worst, 99=best). If you desire an average level of risk, then this fund may be an option.

Services Offered: Bank draft capabilities, an IRA investment plan, a 401K investment plan, a Keogh investment plan and a systematic withdrawal plan.

Data Date	Weiss Investment Rating	Net Assets ($Mil)	NAV	Perfor-mance Rating/Pts	Total Return Y-T-D	Risk Rating/Pts
6-06	C+	6,928	87.89	C- / 4.0	2.68%	B / 8.7
2005	C-	7,235	86.02	C- / 3.6	4.86%	B- / 7.0
2004	C-	12,113	83.36	C / 4.3	10.73%	C / 5.2
2003	C	9,240	76.60	C / 4.3	28.49%	C+ / 5.6
2002	C	7,245	60.47	C / 4.4	-22.17%	C+ / 6.3
2001	C-	8,602	78.89	C- / 3.7	-12.05%	C- / 3.6

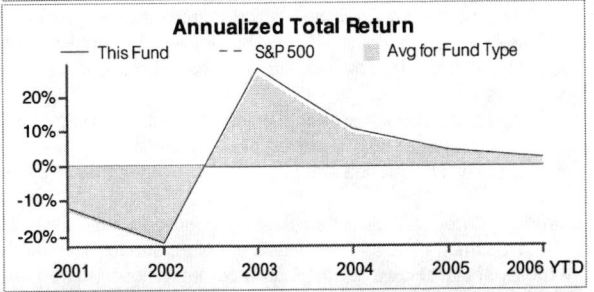

Annualized Total Return

Fidelity Spartan Total Mkt Idx Inv (FSTMX)

C+   **Fair**

Fund Family: Fidelity Investments   **Phone:** (800) 544-8888
Address: 82 Devonshire Street, Boston, MA 02109
Fund Type: GR - Growth
Major Rating Factors: Middle of the road best describes Fidelity Spartan Total Mkt Idx Inv whose Weiss Investment Rating is currently a C+ (Fair). The fund currently has a performance rating of C (Fair) based on an average return of 12.82% over the last three years and 3.40% over the last six months. Factored into the performance evaluation is an expense ratio of 0.07% (very low) and a 0.5% back-end load levied at the time of sale.

The fund's risk rating is currently B (Good). It carries a beta of 1.07, meaning that its performance tracks fairly well with that of the overall stock market. Volatility, as measured by both the semi-deviation and a drawdown factor, is considered low.

Geode Capital Mgmt has been running the fund for 3 years and currently receives a manager quality ranking of 66 (0=worst, 99=best). If you desire an average level of risk, then this fund may be an option.

Services Offered: An IRA investment plan, a 401K investment plan, a Keogh investment plan and wire transfers.

Data Date	Weiss Investment Rating	Net Assets ($Mil)	NAV	Perfor-mance Rating/Pts	Total Return Y-T-D	Risk Rating/Pts
6-06	C+	2,123	35.73	C / 5.1	3.40%	B / 8.4
2005	C+	1,974	34.66	C / 4.8	6.42%	B- / 7.6
2004	C	2,774	33.05	C / 5.5	12.11%	C / 5.3
2003	C+	1,835	29.91	C / 5.3	31.24%	C+ / 5.8
2002	C	1,083	23.05	C / 4.5	-20.99%	C+ / 6.2
2001	C-	1,103	29.56	C- / 4.2	-10.79%	C- / 3.1

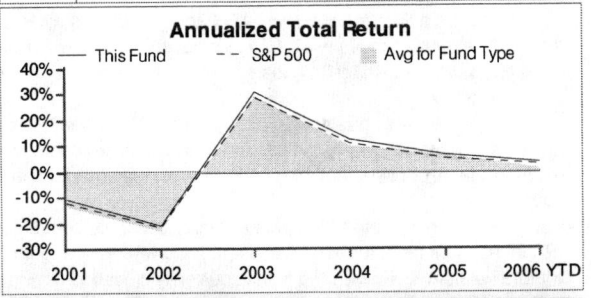

Annualized Total Return

Fidelity Value Fund (FDVLX)

A-   **Excellent**

Fund Family: Fidelity Investments   **Phone:** (800) 544-8888
Address: 82 Devonshire Street, Boston, MA 02109
Fund Type: GI - Growth and Income
Major Rating Factors: Strong performance is the major factor driving the A- (Excellent) Weiss Investment Rating for Fidelity Value Fund. The fund currently has a performance rating of B (Good) based on an average return of 19.82% over the last three years and 3.58% over the last six months. Factored into the performance evaluation is an expense ratio of 0.72% (very low).

The fund's risk rating is currently B- (Good). It carries a beta of 1.24, meaning it is expected to move 12.4% for every 10% move in the market. Volatility, as measured by both the semi-deviation and a drawdown factor, is considered low.

Richard Fentin has been running the fund for 10 years and currently receives a manager quality ranking of 95 (0=worst, 99=best). If you desire only a moderate level of risk and strong performance, then this fund is an excellent option.

Services Offered: Automated phone transactions, bank draft capabilities, an IRA investment plan, a 401K investment plan, a Keogh investment plan, wire transfers and a systematic withdrawal plan.

Data Date	Weiss Investment Rating	Net Assets ($Mil)	NAV	Perfor-mance Rating/Pts	Total Return Y-T-D	Risk Rating/Pts
6-06	A-	15,805	78.60	B / 7.8	3.58%	B- / 7.7
2005	A-	13,896	75.88	B+ / 8.4	14.27%	B- / 7.1
2004	B+	10,279	71.29	B+ / 8.7	21.21%	C+ / 5.8
2003	A-	6,526	62.07	B+ / 8.9	34.43%	B- / 7.1
2002	A-	5,287	46.39	A- / 9.0	-9.25%	B / 8.0
2001	B-	5,238	51.51	B+ / 8.8	12.25%	D+ / 2.4

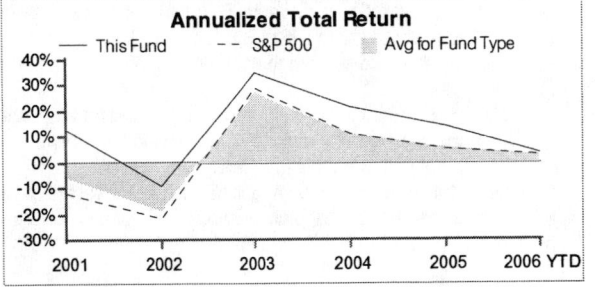

Annualized Total Return

First Eagle Global Fund A (SGENX)

A+   Excellent

Fund Family: First Eagle **Phone:** (800) 334-2143
Address: 1345 Avenue of the Americas, New York, NY 10105
Fund Type: GL - Global

Major Rating Factors: Strong performance is the major factor driving the A+ (Excellent) Weiss Investment Rating for First Eagle Global Fund A. The fund currently has a performance rating of B (Good) based on an average return of 21.75% over the last three years and 9.18% over the last six months. Factored into the performance evaluation is an expense ratio of 1.20% (average), a 5.0% front-end load that is levied at the time of purchase and a 2.0% back-end load levied at the time of sale.

The fund's risk rating is currently B (Good). It carries a beta of 0.66, meaning the fund's expected move will be 6.6% for every 10% move in the market. Volatility, as measured by both the semi-deviation and a drawdown factor, is considered low.

Charles de Vaulx has been running the fund for 7 years and currently receives a manager quality ranking of 92 (0=worst, 99=best). If you desire only a moderate level of risk and strong performance, then this fund is an excellent option.

Services Offered: Automated phone transactions, bank draft capabilities, an IRA investment plan, a 401K investment plan, wire transfers and a systematic withdrawal plan. However, the fund is currently closed to new investors.

Data Date	Weiss Investment Rating	Net Assets ($Mil)	NAV	Performance Rating/Pts	Total Return Y-T-D	Risk Rating/Pts
6-06	A+	11,148	45.92	B / 8.2	9.18%	B / 8.8
2005	A+	10,038	42.06	B / 7.9	14.91%	B+ / 9.4
2004	A+	6,651	38.81	A- / 9.2	18.37%	B / 8.9
2003	A+	3,738	33.32	A / 9.5	37.64%	B+ / 9.5
2002	A+	1,976	25.35	A+ / 9.7	10.23%	B+ / 9.4
2001	A+	1,518	23.82	A- / 9.1	10.21%	B / 8.3

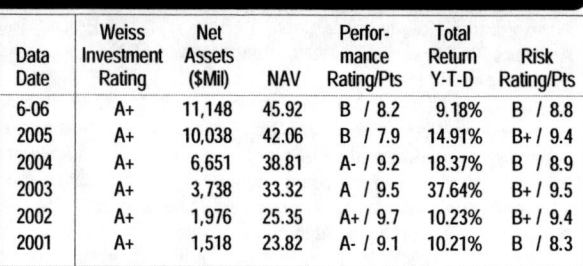

Annualized Total Return

First Eagle Overseas Fund A (SGOVX)

A+   Excellent

Fund Family: First Eagle **Phone:** (800) 334-2143
Address: 1345 Avenue of the Americas, New York, NY 10105
Fund Type: FO - Foreign

Major Rating Factors: Exceptional performance is the major factor driving the A+ (Excellent) Weiss Investment Rating for First Eagle Overseas Fund A. The fund currently has a performance rating of A- (Excellent) based on an average return of 25.26% over the last three years and 11.59% over the last six months. Factored into the performance evaluation is an expense ratio of 1.18% (low), a 5.0% front-end load that is levied at the time of purchase and a 2.0% back-end load levied at the time of sale.

The fund's risk rating is currently B (Good). It carries a beta of 0.71, meaning the fund's expected move will be 7.1% for every 10% move in the market. Volatility, as measured by both the semi-deviation and a drawdown factor, is considered low.

Charles de Vaulx has been running the fund for 7 years and currently receives a manager quality ranking of 96 (0=worst, 99=best). If you desire only a moderate level of risk and strong performance, then this fund is an excellent option.

Services Offered: Automated phone transactions, bank draft capabilities, an IRA investment plan, a 401K investment plan, wire transfers and a systematic withdrawal plan. However, the fund is currently closed to new investors.

Data Date	Weiss Investment Rating	Net Assets ($Mil)	NAV	Performance Rating/Pts	Total Return Y-T-D	Risk Rating/Pts
6-06	A+	5,646	25.71	A- / 9.0	11.59%	B / 8.0
2005	A+	5,110	23.04	B+ / 8.8	16.92%	B / 8.8
2004	A+	4,085	21.77	A / 9.5	21.83%	B / 8.3
2003	A+	2,944	18.17	A / 9.5	41.41%	B+ / 9.2
2002	A	912	13.30	A+ / 9.6	12.53%	B / 8.0
2001	A+	428	12.02	A- / 9.1	5.35%	B- / 7.4

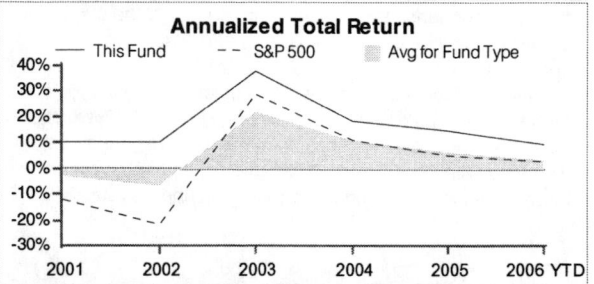

Annualized Total Return

FPA Capital Fund Inc (FPPTX)

C+   Fair

Fund Family: FPA Funds **Phone:** (800) 982-4372
Address: 11400 West Olympic Boulevard, Los Angeles, CA 90064
Fund Type: GR - Growth

Major Rating Factors: Middle of the road best describes FPA Capital Fund Inc whose Weiss Investment Rating is currently a C+ (Fair). The fund currently has a performance rating of C+ (Fair) based on an average return of 17.22% over the last three years and 1.14% over the last six months. Factored into the performance evaluation is an expense ratio of 0.83% (very low), a 5.3% front-end load that is levied at the time of purchase and a 2.0% back-end load levied at the time of sale.

The fund's risk rating is currently B- (Good). It carries a beta of 1.16, meaning it is expected to move 11.6% for every 10% move in the market. Volatility, as measured by both the semi-deviation and a drawdown factor, is considered low.

Robert L. Rodriguez has been running the fund for 22 years and currently receives a manager quality ranking of 90 (0=worst, 99=best). If you desire an average level of risk, then this fund may be an option.

Services Offered: Bank draft capabilities, an IRA investment plan, wire transfers and a systematic withdrawal plan. However, the fund is currently closed to new investors.

Data Date	Weiss Investment Rating	Net Assets ($Mil)	NAV	Performance Rating/Pts	Total Return Y-T-D	Risk Rating/Pts
6-06	C+	2,240	43.37	C+ / 6.0	1.14%	B- / 7.1
2005	B-	2,088	42.88	B- / 7.4	16.53%	C+ / 5.8
2004	B-	1,670	39.98	B- / 7.5	12.62%	C / 5.1
2003	A	1,067	36.85	A+ / 9.7	38.54%	C+ / 6.7
2002	B+	642	26.86	A / 9.4	-3.86%	C+ / 6.4
2001	C+	510	28.26	A+ / 9.8	38.13%	E- / 0.0

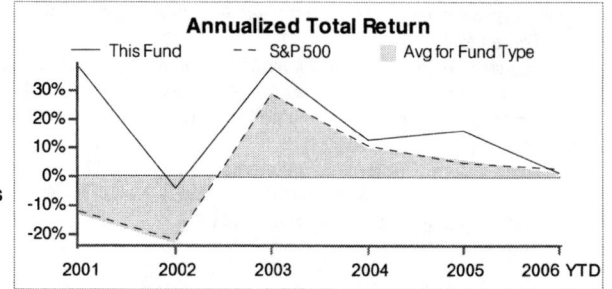

Annualized Total Return

Franklin Balance Sheet Investmt A (FRBSX) — A+ Excellent

Fund Family: Franklin Templeton Investments   **Phone:** (800) 342-5236
Address: 777 Mariners Island Blvd., San Mateo, CA 94404
Fund Type: GI - Growth and Income
Major Rating Factors: Strong performance is the major factor driving the A+ (Excellent) Weiss Investment Rating for Franklin Balance Sheet Investmt A. The fund currently has a performance rating of B (Good) based on an average return of 21.91% over the last three years and 8.73% over the last six months. Factored into the performance evaluation is an expense ratio of 1.00% (low), a 5.8% front-end load that is levied at the time of purchase and a 1.0% back-end load levied at the time of sale.

The fund's risk rating is currently B (Good). It carries a beta of 1.15, meaning it is expected to move 11.5% for every 10% move in the market. Volatility, as measured by both the semi-deviation and a drawdown factor, is considered low.

This is team managed and currently receives a manager quality ranking of 98 (0=worst, 99=best). If you desire only a moderate level of risk and strong performance, then this fund is an excellent option.

Services Offered: Automated phone transactions, payroll deductions, bank draft capabilities, an IRA investment plan, a 401K investment plan, a Keogh investment plan and a systematic withdrawal plan. However, the fund is currently closed to new investors.

Data Date	Weiss Investment Rating	Net Assets ($Mil)	NAV	Performance Rating/Pts	Total Return Y-T-D	Risk Rating/Pts
6-06	A+	4,421	67.12	B / 8.2	8.73%	B / 8.3
2005	B-	4,193	61.73	C+ / 5.7	6.75%	B / 8.0
2004	A+	4,219	58.26	B+ / 8.9	25.30%	B- / 7.6
2003	B-	3,112	47.57	B+ / 8.7	29.58%	C / 4.9
2002	B-	2,460	37.09	A / 9.4	-5.96%	C / 4.6
2001	A+	1,778	40.02	A- / 9.2	17.70%	B- / 7.0

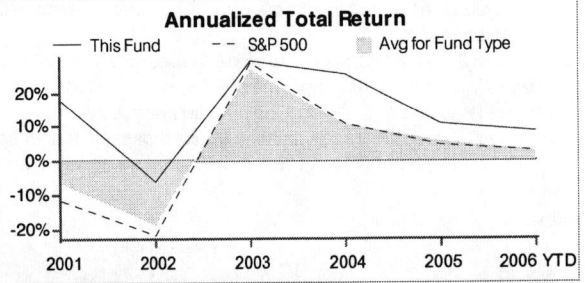

Annualized Total Return

Franklin Income A (FKINX) — C Fair

Fund Family: Franklin Templeton Investments   **Phone:** (800) 342-5236
Address: 777 Mariners Island Blvd., San Mateo, CA 94404
Fund Type: IN - Income
Major Rating Factors: Middle of the road best describes Franklin Income A whose Weiss Investment Rating is currently a C (Fair). The fund currently has a performance rating of C- (Fair) based on an average return of 11.16% over the last three years and 6.42% over the last six months. Factored into the performance evaluation is an expense ratio of 0.64% (very low), a 4.3% front-end load that is levied at the time of purchase and a 1.0% back-end load levied at the time of sale.

The fund's risk rating is currently B (Good). It carries a beta of 0.50, meaning the fund's expected move will be 5.0% for every 10% move in the market. Volatility, as measured by both the semi-deviation and a drawdown factor, is considered low.

Charles B. Johnson has been running the fund for 49 years and currently receives a manager quality ranking of 91 (0=worst, 99=best). If you desire an average level of risk, then this fund may be an option.

Services Offered: Automated phone transactions, payroll deductions, bank draft capabilities, an IRA investment plan, a 401K investment plan, a Keogh investment plan, wire transfers and a systematic withdrawal plan.

Data Date	Weiss Investment Rating	Net Assets ($Mil)	NAV	Performance Rating/Pts	Total Return Y-T-D	Risk Rating/Pts
6-06	C	23,999	2.48	C- / 3.4	6.42%	B / 8.8
2005	C-	21,907	2.40	D / 2.1	1.85%	B / 8.8
2004	A-	16,135	2.52	B- / 7.5	12.17%	B- / 7.9
2003	A	10,657	2.41	B / 8.1	30.96%	B / 8.5
2002	A+	6,429	1.99	A / 9.4	-1.06%	B+ / 9.2
2001	A+	6,243	2.18	B- / 7.2	0.65%	B / 8.9

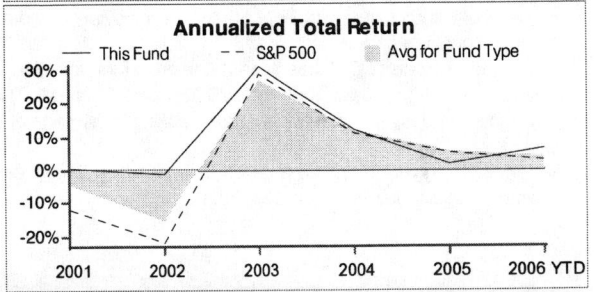

Annualized Total Return

Franklin Small-Mid Cap Growth A (FRSGX) — C- Fair

Fund Family: Franklin Templeton Investments   **Phone:** (800) 342-5236
Address: 777 Mariners Island Blvd., San Mateo, CA 94404
Fund Type: MC - Mid Cap
Major Rating Factors: Middle of the road best describes Franklin Small-Mid Cap Growth A whose Weiss Investment Rating is currently a C- (Fair). The fund currently has a performance rating of C (Fair) based on an average return of 14.46% over the last three years and 1.06% over the last six months. Factored into the performance evaluation is an expense ratio of 0.97% (low), a 5.8% front-end load that is levied at the time of purchase and a 1.0% back-end load levied at the time of sale.

The fund's risk rating is currently C+ (Fair). It carries a beta of 1.11, meaning it is expected to move 11.1% for every 10% move in the market. Volatility, as measured by both the semi-deviation and a drawdown factor, is considered low.

Edward B. Jamieson has been running the fund for 14 years and currently receives a manager quality ranking of 15 (0=worst, 99=best). If you desire an average level of risk, then this fund may be an option.

Services Offered: Automated phone transactions, payroll deductions, bank draft capabilities, an IRA investment plan, a 401K investment plan, a Keogh investment plan, wire transfers and a systematic withdrawal plan.

Data Date	Weiss Investment Rating	Net Assets ($Mil)	NAV	Performance Rating/Pts	Total Return Y-T-D	Risk Rating/Pts
6-06	C-	5,937	38.12	C / 4.7	1.06%	C+ / 6.6
2005	B-	6,899	37.72	C+ / 6.3	10.55%	B- / 7.0
2004	D	7,729	34.16	D+ / 2.7	13.04%	C- / 3.6
2003	D	7,736	30.22	D+ / 2.4	37.68%	C- / 3.3
2002	D	6,023	21.95	D / 1.8	-29.58%	C- / 3.2
2001	C	8,526	31.17	B / 8.1	-20.53%	E- / 0.0

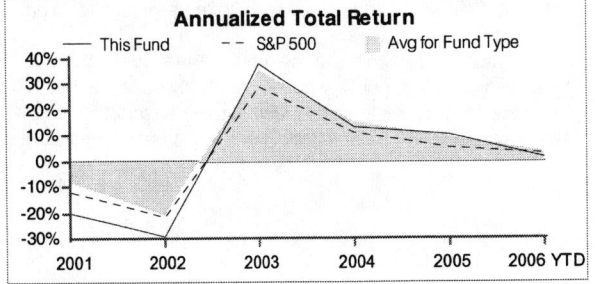

Annualized Total Return

Gabelli Asset Fd (GABAX)   B   Good

Fund Family: Gabelli Funds   **Phone:** (800) 422-3554
Address: One Corporate Center, Rye, NY 10580
Fund Type: GR - Growth
Major Rating Factors: Gabelli Asset Fd receives a Weiss Investment Rating of B (Good). The fund currently has a performance rating of C+ (Fair) based on an average return of 15.56% over the last three years and 8.29% over the last six months. Factored into the performance evaluation is an expense ratio of 1.38% (average) and a 2.0% back-end load levied at the time of sale.

The fund's risk rating is currently B (Good). It carries a beta of 1.06, meaning that its performance tracks fairly well with that of the overall stock market. Volatility, as measured by both the semi-deviation and a drawdown factor, is considered low.

Mario J. Gabelli has been running the fund for 20 years and currently receives a manager quality ranking of 87 (0=worst, 99=best). If you desire an average level of risk, then this fund may be an option.

Services Offered: Automated phone transactions, bank draft capabilities, an IRA investment plan, a 401K investment plan, wire transfers and a systematic withdrawal plan.

Data Date	Weiss Investment Rating	Net Assets ($Mil)	NAV	Performance Rating/Pts	Total Return Y-T-D	Risk Rating/Pts
6-06	B	2,331	44.54	C+ / 6.5	8.29%	B / 8.3
2005	C	2,260	41.13	C / 4.4	4.42%	C+/ 6.9
2004	B	2,000	41.45	B / 7.6	16.50%	C+/ 5.8
2003	B	1,960	36.26	B / 7.7	30.57%	C+/ 6.8
2002	B-	1,503	28.25	B- / 7.3	-14.27%	B- / 7.0
2001	A-	1,911	32.97	B / 8.0	0.16%	C+/ 6.9

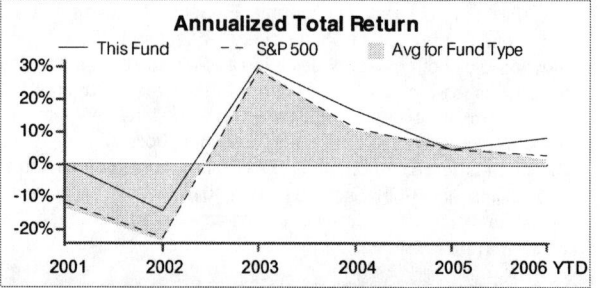

Annualized Total Return

Gateway Fund (GATEX)   C-   Fair

Fund Family: Gateway Funds   **Phone:** (800) 354-6339
Address: 3805 Edwards Road, Cincinnati, OH 45209
Fund Type: GI - Growth and Income
Major Rating Factors: Disappointing performance is the major factor driving the C- (Fair) Weiss Investment Rating for Gateway Fund. The fund currently has a performance rating of D (Weak) based on an average return of 7.13% over the last three years and 4.15% over the last six months. Factored into the performance evaluation is an expense ratio of 0.95% (low).

The fund's risk rating is currently B+ (Good). It carries a beta of 0.32, meaning the fund's expected move will be 3.2% for every 10% move in the market. Volatility, as measured by both the semi-deviation and a drawdown factor, is considered very low.

J. Patrick Rogers, CFA has been running the fund for 12 years and currently receives a manager quality ranking of 76 (0=worst, 99=best). This fund offers only a moderate level of risk but investors looking for strong performance are still waiting.

Services Offered: Automated phone transactions, an IRA investment plan, wire transfers and a systematic withdrawal plan.

Data Date	Weiss Investment Rating	Net Assets ($Mil)	NAV	Performance Rating/Pts	Total Return Y-T-D	Risk Rating/Pts
6-06	C-	2,934	25.91	D / 1.9	4.15%	B+/ 9.3
2005	D	2,632	25.00	E / 0.5	4.66%	B / 8.5
2004	C	1,950	24.31	C- / 3.4	6.95%	B / 8.0
2003	B-	1,385	23.00	C / 5.3	11.61%	B- / 7.8
2002	A	1,019	20.76	B+ / 8.8	-4.86%	B / 8.8
2001	A+	1,295	21.98	B- / 7.0	-3.53%	B+/ 9.3

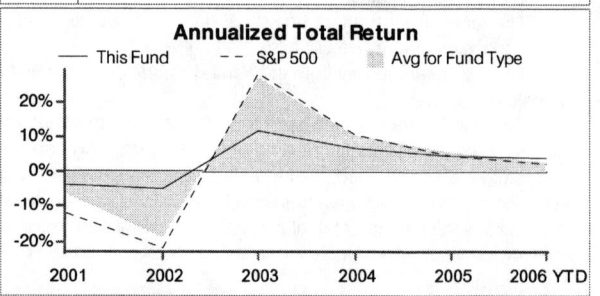

Annualized Total Return

GE S&S Program Mutual Fund (GESSX)   C-   Fair

Fund Family: GE Investment   **Phone:** (800) 242-0134
Address: 3003 Summer Street, Stamford, CT 06905
Fund Type: GI - Growth and Income
Major Rating Factors: Middle of the road best describes GE S&S Program Mutual Fund whose Weiss Investment Rating is currently a C- (Fair). The fund currently has a performance rating of C- (Fair) based on an average return of 9.12% over the last three years and 3.59% over the last six months. Factored into the performance evaluation is an expense ratio of 0.09% (very low).

The fund's risk rating is currently B- (Good). It carries a beta of 0.87, meaning the fund's expected move will be 8.7% for every 10% move in the market. Volatility, as measured by both the semi-deviation and a drawdown factor, is considered low.

Eugene K. Bolton has been running the fund for 26 years and currently receives a manager quality ranking of 46 (0=worst, 99=best). If you desire an average level of risk, then this fund may be an option.

Services Offered: Payroll deductions and a 401K investment plan.

Data Date	Weiss Investment Rating	Net Assets ($Mil)	NAV	Performance Rating/Pts	Total Return Y-T-D	Risk Rating/Pts
6-06	C-	3,934	44.39	C- / 3.0	3.59%	B- / 7.7
2005	D	4,103	42.85	D / 1.7	2.95%	B- / 7.2
2004	D+	4,034	45.36	D / 2.0	5.64%	C+/ 6.1
2003	C	3,738	42.94	C / 4.5	23.77%	C+/ 6.6
2002	C+	3,337	35.13	C+ / 6.0	-18.91%	C+/ 6.8
2001	C+	3,909	44.03	C+ / 6.1	-8.73%	C+/ 6.6

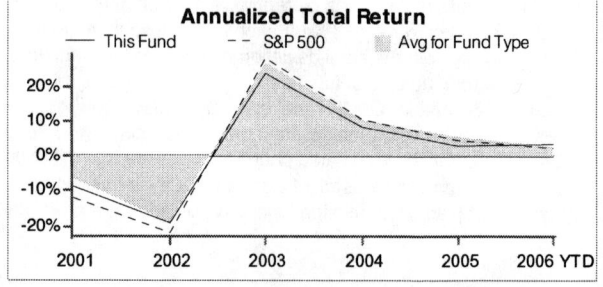

Annualized Total Return

Goldman Sachs Mid Cap Value A (GCMAX)   A-   Excellent

Fund Family: Goldman Sachs   **Phone:** (800) 292-4726
Address: 1 New York Plaza, New York, NY 10004
Fund Type: MC - Mid Cap
Major Rating Factors: Strong performance is the major factor driving the A-
(Excellent) Weiss Investment Rating for Goldman Sachs Mid Cap Value A. The
fund currently has a performance rating of B- (Good) based on an average return
of 20.27% over the last three years and 4.49% over the last six months.
Factored into the performance evaluation is an expense ratio of 1.17% (low), a
5.5% front-end load that is levied at the time of purchase and a 1.0% back-end
load levied at the time of sale.

The fund's risk rating is currently B- (Good). It carries a beta of 0.80,
meaning the fund's expected move will be 8.0% for every 10% move in the
market. Volatility, as measured by both the semi-deviation and a drawdown
factor, is considered low.

This is team managed and currently receives a manager quality ranking of
92 (0=worst, 99=best). If you desire only a moderate level of risk and strong
performance, then this fund is an excellent option.

Services Offered: Automated phone transactions, check writing, bank draft
capabilities, an IRA investment plan, a 401K investment plan, a Keogh
investment plan, wire transfers and a systematic withdrawal plan. However, the
fund is currently closed to new investors.

Data Date	Weiss Investment Rating	Net Assets ($Mil)	NAV	Performance Rating/Pts	Total Return Y-T-D	Risk Rating/Pts
6-06	A-	3,375	36.57	B- / 7.4	4.49%	B- / 7.9
2005	B+	2,989	35.00	B- / 7.0	12.44%	B- / 7.4
2004	B+	1,383	33.38	B- / 7.2	16.91%	B- / 7.3
2003	A+	638	28.64	B+ / 8.4	27.52%	B / 8.5
2002	A+	331	22.60	A / 9.5	-5.11%	B+ / 9.1
2001	B	169	24.48	A- / 9.2	11.84%	C- / 3.4

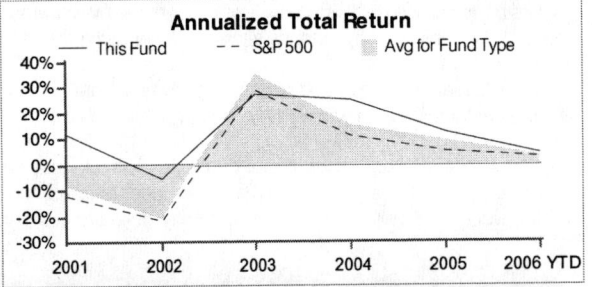

Annualized Total Return

Hartford Capital Apprec A (ITHAX)   B+   Good

Fund Family: Hartford Funds, The   **Phone:** (800) 523-7798
Address: P.O. Box 8416, Boston, MA 02266
Fund Type: GR - Growth
Major Rating Factors: Strong performance is the major factor driving the B+
(Good) Weiss Investment Rating for Hartford Capital Apprec A. The fund
currently has a performance rating of B (Good) based on an average return of
20.27% over the last three years and 3.50% over the last six months. Factored
into the performance evaluation is an expense ratio of 1.26% (average), a 5.5%
front-end load that is levied at the time of purchase and a 1.0% back-end load
levied at the time of sale.

The fund's risk rating is currently B- (Good). It carries a beta of 1.33,
meaning it is expected to move 13.3% for every 10% move in the market.
Volatility, as measured by both the semi-deviation and a drawdown factor, is
considered low.

Saul J. Pannell,CFA has been running the fund for 10 years and currently
receives a manager quality ranking of 94 (0=worst, 99=best). If you desire only a
moderate level of risk and strong performance, then this fund is an excellent
option.

Services Offered: Automated phone transactions, bank draft capabilities, an
IRA investment plan, a 401K investment plan, a Keogh investment plan, wire
transfers and a systematic withdrawal plan.

Data Date	Weiss Investment Rating	Net Assets ($Mil)	NAV	Performance Rating/Pts	Total Return Y-T-D	Risk Rating/Pts
6-06	B+	8,089	36.96	B / 7.7	3.50%	B- / 7.6
2005	A-	6,760	35.71	B+ / 8.4	15.10%	B- / 7.2
2004	C+	4,592	34.14	C+ / 6.9	17.93%	C+ / 5.9
2003	C+	2,545	28.95	B- / 7.5	40.40%	C / 5.4
2002	C+	1,851	20.62	C+ / 5.9	-22.89%	C / 5.2
2001	C+	1,764	26.74	A / 9.3	-6.86%	E- / 0.0

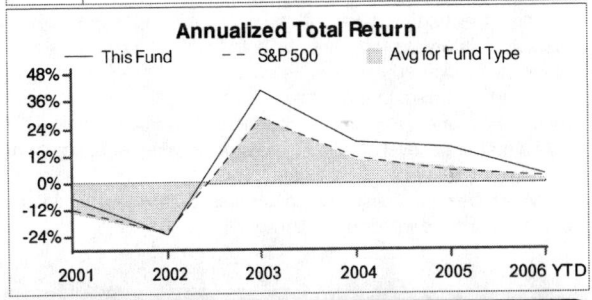

Annualized Total Return

Hartford Dividend & Growth A (IHGIX)   C+   Fair

Fund Family: Hartford Funds, The   **Phone:** (800) 523-7798
Address: P.O. Box 8416, Boston, MA 02266
Fund Type: IN - Income
Major Rating Factors: Middle of the road best describes Hartford Dividend &
Growth A whose Weiss Investment Rating is currently a C+ (Fair). The fund
currently has a performance rating of C (Fair) based on an average return of
12.82% over the last three years and 5.13% over the last six months. Factored
into the performance evaluation is an expense ratio of 1.17% (low), a 5.5%
front-end load that is levied at the time of purchase and a 1.0% back-end load
levied at the time of sale.

The fund's risk rating is currently B+ (Good). It carries a beta of 0.94,
meaning that its performance tracks fairly well with that of the overall stock
market. Volatility, as measured by both the semi-deviation and a drawdown
factor, is considered very low.

Edward P. Bousa, CFA has been running the fund for 5 years and currently
receives a manager quality ranking of 77 (0=worst, 99=best). If you desire an
average level of risk, then this fund may be an option.

Services Offered: Automated phone transactions, bank draft capabilities, an
IRA investment plan, a 401K investment plan, a Keogh investment plan, wire
transfers and a systematic withdrawal plan.

Data Date	Weiss Investment Rating	Net Assets ($Mil)	NAV	Performance Rating/Pts	Total Return Y-T-D	Risk Rating/Pts
6-06	C+	2,362	19.77	C / 4.5	5.13%	B+ / 9.0
2005	C-	2,181	18.94	D+ / 2.6	5.42%	B- / 7.8
2004	C+	1,929	18.92	C / 5.3	12.01%	C+ / 6.4
2003	B-	1,421	17.25	C+ / 6.7	25.66%	B- / 7.3
2002	B	884	13.85	B- / 7.4	-14.19%	B / 8.0
2001	B-	581	16.25	C+ / 5.6	-4.57%	B- / 7.1

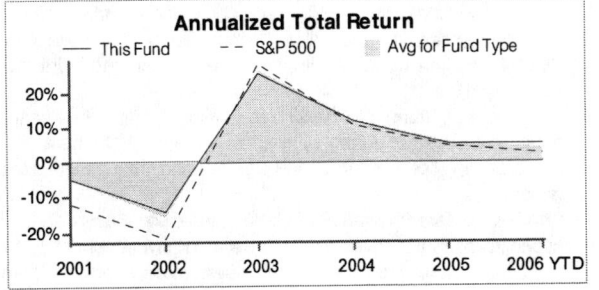

Annualized Total Return

Hotchkis and Wiley Large Cap Val A (HWLAX) | B Good

Fund Family: Hotchkis & Wiley **Phone:** (800) 796-5606
Address: 725 S. Figueroa St., Los Angeles, CA 90017
Fund Type: GI - Growth and Income

Major Rating Factors: Hotchkis and Wiley Large Cap Val A receives a Weiss Investment Rating of B (Good). The fund currently has a performance rating of C+ (Fair) based on an average return of 17.12% over the last three years and -0.09% over the last six months. Factored into the performance evaluation is an expense ratio of 1.18% (low) and a 5.3% front-end load that is levied at the time of purchase.

The fund's risk rating is currently B (Good). It carries a beta of 1.06, meaning that its performance tracks fairly well with that of the overall stock market. Volatility, as measured by both the semi-deviation and a drawdown factor, is considered low.

This is team managed and currently receives a manager quality ranking of 93 (0=worst, 99=best). If you desire an average level of risk, then this fund may be an option.

Services Offered: Automated phone transactions, bank draft capabilities, an IRA investment plan, a 401K investment plan, wire transfers and a systematic withdrawal plan. However, the fund is currently closed to new investors.

Data Date	Weiss Investment Rating	Net Assets ($Mil)	NAV	Performance Rating/Pts	Total Return Y-T-D	Risk Rating/Pts
6-06	B	2,956	23.32	C+ / 5.7	-0.09%	B / 8.8
2005	B-	2,875	23.34	C+ / 6.9	6.12%	B- / 7.4
2004	A	820	22.68	A- / 9.0	21.70%	C+ / 6.8
2003	U	120	18.79	U / --	42.32%	U / --
2002	U	15	13.34	U / --	-7.58%	U / --

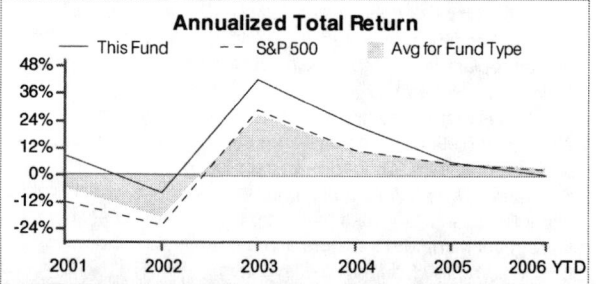

Hussman Strategic Growth (HSGFX) | C- Fair

Fund Family: Hussman Investment Trust **Phone:** (800) 487-7626
Address: 3525 Ellicot Mill Drive, Ellicot, MD 21043
Fund Type: GR - Growth

Major Rating Factors: Disappointing performance is the major factor driving the C- (Fair) Weiss Investment Rating for Hussman Strategic Growth. The fund currently has a performance rating of D (Weak) based on an average return of 8.30% over the last three years and 2.87% over the last six months. Factored into the performance evaluation is an expense ratio of 1.16% (low) and a 1.5% back-end load levied at the time of sale.

The fund's risk rating is currently B+ (Good). It carries a beta of 0.42, meaning the fund's expected move will be 4.2% for every 10% move in the market. Volatility, as measured by both the semi-deviation and a drawdown factor, is considered very low.

John P. Hussman, Ph.D has been running the fund for 6 years and currently receives a manager quality ranking of 78 (0=worst, 99=best). This fund offers only a moderate level of risk but investors looking for strong performance are still waiting.

Services Offered: Bank draft capabilities, an IRA investment plan, wire transfers and a systematic withdrawal plan.

Data Date	Weiss Investment Rating	Net Assets ($Mil)	NAV	Performance Rating/Pts	Total Return Y-T-D	Risk Rating/Pts
6-06	C-	2,816	16.13	D / 2.2	2.87%	B+ / 9.2
2005	C-	2,243	15.68	D- / 1.1	5.71%	B+ / 9.2
2004	A+	1,462	15.36	B- / 7.0	5.16%	B+ / 9.1
2003	A+	707	15.32	B+ / 8.8	21.08%	B+ / 9.3
2002	U	443	12.66	U / --	14.02%	U / --
2001	U	44	11.94	U / --	14.67%	U / --

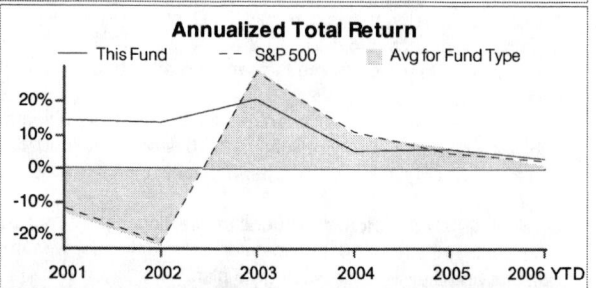

Ivy Fund-Global Nat Resource A (IGNAX) | A Excellent

Fund Family: Ivy Funds **Phone:** (800) 777-6472
Address: P.O. Box 5007, Boca Raton, FL 33431
Fund Type: EN - Energy/Natural Resources

Major Rating Factors: Exceptional performance is the major factor driving the A (Excellent) Weiss Investment Rating for Ivy Fund-Global Nat Resource A. The fund currently has a performance rating of A+ (Excellent) based on an average return of 39.05% over the last three years and 20.23% over the last six months. Factored into the performance evaluation is an expense ratio of 1.37% (average), a 5.8% front-end load that is levied at the time of purchase and a 2.0% back-end load levied at the time of sale.

The fund's risk rating is currently C+ (Fair). It carries a beta of 0.72, meaning the fund's expected move will be 7.2% for every 10% move in the market. Volatility, as measured by both the semi-deviation and a drawdown factor, is considered low.

Frederick Sturm, CFA has been running the fund for 9 years and currently receives a manager quality ranking of 99 (0=worst, 99=best). If you desire only a moderate level of risk and strong performance, then this fund is an excellent option.

Services Offered: Automated phone transactions, payroll deductions, bank draft capabilities, an IRA investment plan, a 401K investment plan, a Keogh investment plan, wire transfers and a systematic withdrawal plan.

Data Date	Weiss Investment Rating	Net Assets ($Mil)	NAV	Performance Rating/Pts	Total Return Y-T-D	Risk Rating/Pts
6-06	A	2,645	31.32	A+ / 9.9	20.23%	C+ / 5.7
2005	A	1,527	26.05	A+ / 9.6	29.11%	C+ / 6.4
2004	A-	539	21.35	A+ / 9.6	27.94%	C / 5.4
2003	A	67	16.69	A+ / 9.7	45.61%	C+ / 6.6
2002	A-	17	11.50	A / 9.5	4.67%	B- / 7.5
2001	C+	8	11.05	A+ / 9.7	15.39%	E- / 0.0

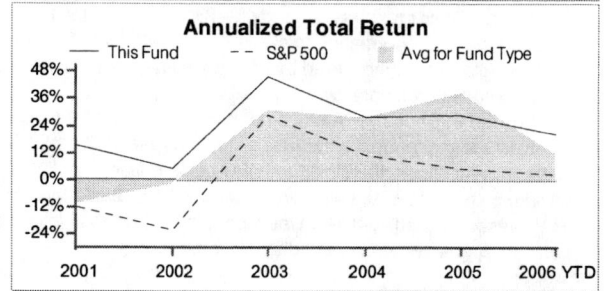

Janus Contrarian Fund (JSVAX)

B-   **Good**

Fund Family: Janus Fund   **Phone:** (800) 525-3713

Address: 100 Fillmore Street, Denver, CO 80206

Fund Type: GR - Growth

Major Rating Factors: Strong performance is the major factor driving the B- (Good) Weiss Investment Rating for Janus Contrarian Fund. The fund currently has a performance rating of B+ (Good) based on an average return of 23.56% over the last three years and 5.28% over the last six months. Factored into the performance evaluation is an expense ratio of 0.93% (low).

The fund's risk rating is currently C (Fair). It carries a beta of 1.35, meaning it is expected to move 13.5% for every 10% move in the market. Volatility, as measured by both the semi-deviation and a drawdown factor, is considered average.

David Decker has been running the fund for 6 years and currently receives a manager quality ranking of 98 (0=worst, 99=best). If you desire an average level of risk and strong performance, then this fund is a good option.

Services Offered: Automated phone transactions, payroll deductions, bank draft capabilities, an IRA investment plan, a 401K investment plan, a Keogh investment plan, wire transfers and a systematic withdrawal plan.

Data Date	Weiss Investment Rating	Net Assets ($Mil)	NAV	Perfor-mance Rating/Pts	Total Return Y-T-D	Risk Rating/Pts
6-06	B-	3,642	15.94	B+ / 8.9	5.28%	C / 5.2
2005	A	3,042	15.14	A / 9.4	16.01%	C+/ 6.8
2004	B	2,602	13.24	A- / 9.0	22.61%	C / 4.9
2003	B-	2,524	10.82	B+ / 8.4	53.26%	C / 5.3
2002	U	1,375	7.06	U / --	-23.70%	U / --
2001	U	2,079	9.26	U / --	-11.74%	U / --

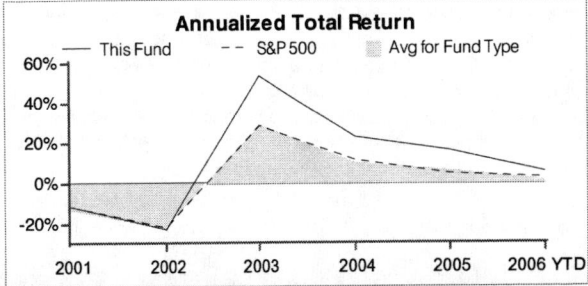

Annualized Total Return

Janus Fd Inc-Balanced Fund (JABAX)

C-   **Fair**

Fund Family: Janus Fund   **Phone:** (800) 525-3713

Address: 100 Fillmore Street, Denver, CO 80206

Fund Type: BA - Balanced

Major Rating Factors: Disappointing performance is the major factor driving the C- (Fair) Weiss Investment Rating for Janus Fd Inc-Balanced Fund. The fund currently has a performance rating of D+ (Weak) based on an average return of 8.47% over the last three years and 1.70% over the last six months. Factored into the performance evaluation is an expense ratio of 0.79% (very low).

The fund's risk rating is currently B (Good). It carries a beta of 1.05, meaning that its performance tracks fairly well with that of the overall stock market. Volatility, as measured by both the semi-deviation and a drawdown factor, is considered low.

Gibson Smith currently receives a manager quality ranking of 63 (0=worst, 99=best). This fund offers only a moderate level of risk but investors looking for strong performance are still waiting.

Services Offered: Automated phone transactions, payroll deductions, bank draft capabilities, an IRA investment plan, a 401K investment plan, a Keogh investment plan, wire transfers and a systematic withdrawal plan.

Data Date	Weiss Investment Rating	Net Assets ($Mil)	NAV	Perfor-mance Rating/Pts	Total Return Y-T-D	Risk Rating/Pts
6-06	C-	2,474	22.68	D+ / 2.5	1.70%	B / 8.5
2005	D+	2,571	22.48	D / 1.6	7.75%	B / 8.4
2004	B-	2,871	21.25	C- / 4.1	7.97%	B / 8.6
2003	B	3,807	19.94	C+/ 5.6	13.74%	B / 8.8
2002	B+	3,994	17.88	B / 7.8	-6.56%	B / 8.8
2001	B-	4,472	19.63	C+/ 6.8	-5.04%	B- / 7.8

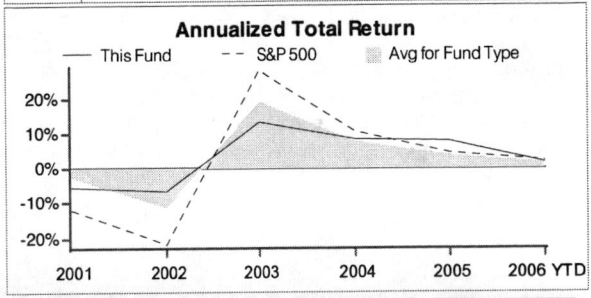

Annualized Total Return

Janus Fd Inc-Growth & Income (JAGIX)

C   **Fair**

Fund Family: Janus Fund   **Phone:** (800) 525-3713

Address: 100 Fillmore Street, Denver, CO 80206

Fund Type: GI - Growth and Income

Major Rating Factors: Middle of the road best describes Janus Fd Inc-Growth & Income whose Weiss Investment Rating is currently a C (Fair). The fund currently has a performance rating of C (Fair) based on an average return of 13.34% over the last three years and 1.35% over the last six months. Factored into the performance evaluation is an expense ratio of 0.87% (low).

The fund's risk rating is currently C+ (Fair). It carries a beta of 1.17, meaning it is expected to move 11.7% for every 10% move in the market. Volatility, as measured by both the semi-deviation and a drawdown factor, is considered low.

Minyoung (Min) Sohn currently receives a manager quality ranking of 62 (0=worst, 99=best). If you desire an average level of risk, then this fund may be an option.

Services Offered: Automated phone transactions, payroll deductions, bank draft capabilities, an IRA investment plan, a 401K investment plan, a Keogh investment plan, wire transfers and a systematic withdrawal plan.

Data Date	Weiss Investment Rating	Net Assets ($Mil)	NAV	Perfor-mance Rating/Pts	Total Return Y-T-D	Risk Rating/Pts
6-06	C	6,867	36.16	C / 5.3	1.35%	C+/ 6.3
2005	C	6,022	36.01	C / 5.5	12.48%	C+/ 5.7
2004	C-	5,422	32.19	C- / 3.6	11.89%	C+/ 5.8
2003	C-	5,913	28.91	C- / 3.2	24.65%	C+/ 5.8
2002	C	5,576	23.34	C- / 3.9	-21.51%	C+/ 5.7
2001	C	7,148	29.97	C+/ 6.3	-14.36%	D+/ 2.3

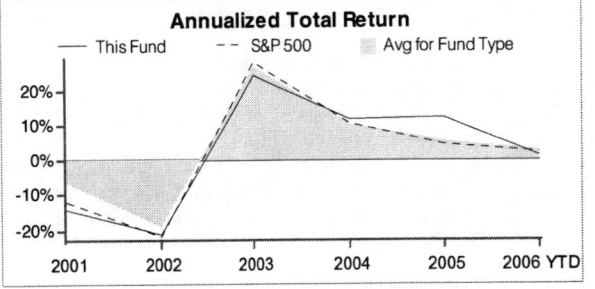

Annualized Total Return

Janus Fd Inc-Janus Fund (JANSX)   D   Weak

Fund Family: Janus Fund   **Phone:** (800) 525-3713
Address: 100 Fillmore Street, Denver, CO 80206
Fund Type: GR - Growth

Major Rating Factors: Disappointing performance is the major factor driving the D (Weak) Weiss Investment Rating for Janus Fd Inc-Janus Fund. The fund currently has a performance rating of D+ (Weak) based on an average return of 8.80% over the last three years and 0.63% over the last six months. Factored into the performance evaluation is an expense ratio of 0.87% (low).

The fund's risk rating is currently C+ (Fair). It carries a beta of 1.23, meaning it is expected to move 12.3% for every 10% move in the market. Volatility, as measured by both the semi-deviation and a drawdown factor, is considered low.

David Corkins currently receives a manager quality ranking of 18 (0=worst, 99=best). This fund offers only a moderate level of risk but investors looking for strong performance are still waiting.

Services Offered: Automated phone transactions, payroll deductions, an IRA investment plan, a 401K investment plan, a Keogh investment plan, wire transfers and a systematic withdrawal plan.

Data Date	Weiss Investment Rating	Net Assets ($Mil)	NAV	Performance Rating/Pts	Total Return Y-T-D	Risk Rating/Pts
6-06	D	10,967	25.69	D+ / 2.4	0.63%	C+ / 6.2
2005	D-	11,389	25.53	D+ / 2.7	3.98%	C+ / 6.1
2004	D-	13,519	24.57	D- / 1.4	4.69%	C / 4.6
2003	D-	17,223	23.47	D / 1.7	31.71%	C- / 3.4
2002	D	17,001	17.82	D- / 1.5	-27.56%	C- / 3.8
2001	D-	25,622	24.60	D / 1.9	-26.10%	E- / 0.0

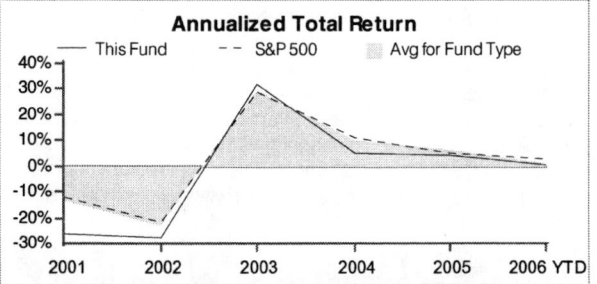

Annualized Total Return

Janus Fd Inc-Mercury Fund (JAMRX)   D   Weak

Fund Family: Janus Fund   **Phone:** (800) 525-3713
Address: 100 Fillmore Street, Denver, CO 80206
Fund Type: GR - Growth

Major Rating Factors: Janus Fd Inc-Mercury Fund receives a Weiss Investment Rating of D (Weak). The fund currently has a performance rating of C- (Fair) based on an average return of 10.27% over the last three years and -1.96% over the last six months. Factored into the performance evaluation is an expense ratio of 0.92% (low).

The fund's risk rating is currently C+ (Fair). It carries a beta of 1.22, meaning it is expected to move 12.2% for every 10% move in the market. Volatility, as measured by both the semi-deviation and a drawdown factor, is considered low.

Jim Goff currently receives a manager quality ranking of 28 (0=worst, 99=best). If you desire an average level of risk, then this fund may be an option.

Services Offered: Automated phone transactions, payroll deductions, bank draft capabilities, an IRA investment plan, a 401K investment plan, a Keogh investment plan, wire transfers and a systematic withdrawal plan.

Data Date	Weiss Investment Rating	Net Assets ($Mil)	NAV	Performance Rating/Pts	Total Return Y-T-D	Risk Rating/Pts
6-06	D	3,767	22.53	C- / 3.1	-1.96%	C+ / 5.8
2005	C	4,607	22.98	C / 5.1	6.82%	C+ / 6.4
2004	D	4,601	21.57	D+ / 2.4	10.62%	C / 4.7
2003	D-	5,280	19.50	D- / 1.2	32.11%	C- / 3.4
2002	D-	5,327	14.76	E+ / 0.9	-29.00%	C- / 3.0
2001	D	8,438	20.79	C- / 3.7	-29.78%	E- / 0.0

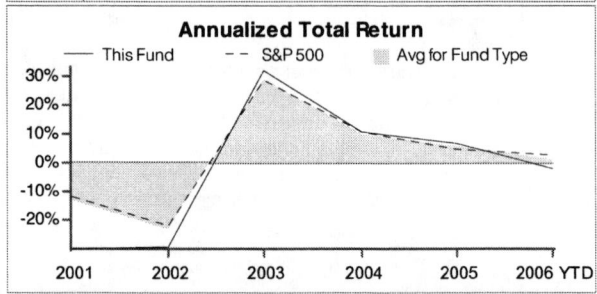

Annualized Total Return

Janus Fd Inc-Mid Cap Value Inv (JMCVX)   B   Good

Fund Family: Janus Fund   **Phone:** (800) 525-3713
Address: 100 Fillmore Street, Denver, CO 80206
Fund Type: MC - Mid Cap

Major Rating Factors: Strong performance is the major factor driving the B (Good) Weiss Investment Rating for Janus Fd Inc-Mid Cap Value Inv. The fund currently has a performance rating of B- (Good) based on an average return of 18.54% over the last three years and 4.03% over the last six months. Factored into the performance evaluation is an expense ratio of 0.92% (low).

The fund's risk rating is currently C+ (Fair). It carries a beta of 0.80, meaning the fund's expected move will be 8.0% for every 10% move in the market. Volatility, as measured by both the semi-deviation and a drawdown factor, is considered low.

Robert H. Perkins has been running the fund for 8 years and currently receives a manager quality ranking of 86 (0=worst, 99=best). If you desire only a moderate level of risk and strong performance, then this fund is an excellent option.

Services Offered: Automated phone transactions, payroll deductions, bank draft capabilities, an IRA investment plan, a 401K investment plan, a Keogh investment plan, wire transfers and a systematic withdrawal plan.

Data Date	Weiss Investment Rating	Net Assets ($Mil)	NAV	Performance Rating/Pts	Total Return Y-T-D	Risk Rating/Pts
6-06	B	4,891	23.22	B- / 7.5	4.03%	C+ / 6.7
2005	B+	4,408	22.32	B / 7.9	10.36%	C+ / 6.8
2004	C+	3,278	22.09	C+ / 5.8	8.34%	C+ / 6.2
2003	A	1,596	20.39	A / 9.3	39.33%	B- / 7.4
2002	A	963	14.71	A / 9.5	-13.09%	B / 8.3
2001	B+	211	16.96	A+ / 9.9	20.52%	C- / 3.0

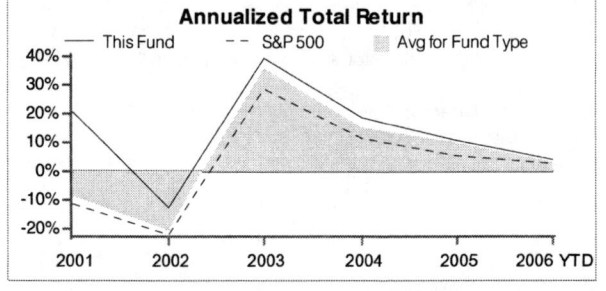

Annualized Total Return

Janus Fd Inc-Olympus Fund (JAOLX)　　　　　D　　Weak

Fund Family: Janus Fund　　　　**Phone:** (800) 525-3713
Address: 100 Fillmore Street, Denver, CO 80206
Fund Type: GR - Growth
Major Rating Factors: Janus Fd Inc-Olympus Fund receives a Weiss Investment Rating of D (Weak). The fund currently has a performance rating of C- (Fair) based on an average return of 12.05% over the last three years and -2.54% over the last six months. Factored into the performance evaluation is an expense ratio of 0.96% (low).

The fund's risk rating is currently C (Fair). It carries a beta of 1.27, meaning it is expected to move 12.7% for every 10% move in the market. Volatility, as measured by both the semi-deviation and a drawdown factor, is considered average.

Claire Young has been running the fund for 9 years and currently receives a manager quality ranking of 37 (0=worst, 99=best). If you desire an average level of risk, then this fund may be an option.

Services Offered: Automated phone transactions, payroll deductions, bank draft capabilities, an IRA investment plan, a 401K investment plan, a Keogh investment plan, wire transfers and a systematic withdrawal plan.

Data Date	Weiss Investment Rating	Net Assets ($Mil)	NAV	Perfor- mance Rating/Pts	Total Return Y-T-D	Risk Rating/Pts
6-06	D	2,229	31.86	C- / 4.2	-2.54%	C / 4.5
2005	C	2,334	32.69	C+ / 6.7	14.21%	C / 5.2
2004	D	2,424	28.63	D / 2.1	8.74%	C / 4.8
2003	D-	2,780	26.33	D- / 1.0	31.65%	C- / 3.4
2002	D-	2,188	20.00	E+ / 0.7	-28.19%	C- / 3.3
2001	D	3,437	27.85	C- / 4.2	-32.05%	E- / 0.0

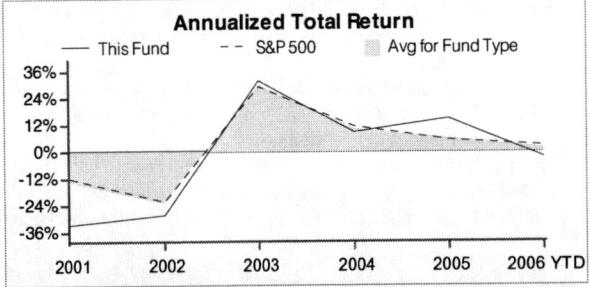

Janus Fd Inc-Overseas Fund (JAOSX)　　　　　C+　　Fair

Fund Family: Janus Fund　　　　**Phone:** (800) 525-3713
Address: 100 Fillmore Street, Denver, CO 80206
Fund Type: FO - Foreign
Major Rating Factors: Janus Fd Inc-Overseas Fund has adopted a risky asset allocation strategy and currently receives an overall Weiss Investment Rating of C+ (Fair). The fund has shown an above average level of volatility, as measured by both semi-deviation and drawdown factors. It carries a beta of 1.34, meaning it is expected to move 13.4% for every 10% move in the market. The high level of risk (D+, Weak) did however, reward investors with excellent performance.

The fund's performance rating is currently A+ (Excellent). It has registered an average return of 33.29% over the last three years and is up 17.34% over the last six months. Factored into the performance evaluation is an expense ratio of 0.89% (low) and a 2.0% back-end load levied at the time of sale.

Brent A. Lynn has been running the fund for 6 years and currently receives a manager quality ranking of 58 (0=worst, 99=best). If you are comfortable owning a high risk investment, this fund may be an option.

Services Offered: Automated phone transactions, payroll deductions, bank draft capabilities, an IRA investment plan, a 401K investment plan, a Keogh investment plan, wire transfers and a systematic withdrawal plan.

Data Date	Weiss Investment Rating	Net Assets ($Mil)	NAV	Perfor- mance Rating/Pts	Total Return Y-T-D	Risk Rating/Pts
6-06	C+	4,241	37.35	A+ / 9.8	17.34%	D+ / 2.9
2005	B+	2,779	31.83	A+ / 9.6	32.39%	C / 5.3
2004	C+	2,252	24.26	C+ / 6.6	17.43%	C / 5.1
2003	C-	2,724	20.66	C / 4.4	36.79%	C / 4.5
2002	D+	3,364	15.29	D / 1.9	-23.89%	C- / 3.9
2001	C-	5,279	20.30	C+ / 6.1	-23.11%	E- / 0.0

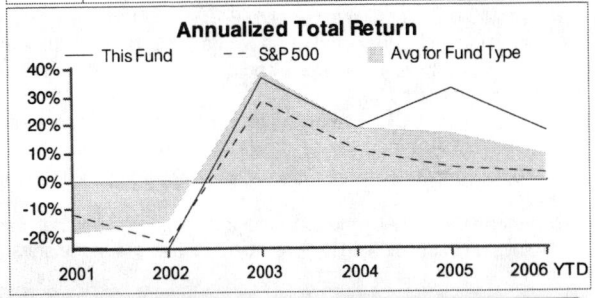

Janus Fd Inc-Twenty Fund (JAVLX)　　　　　C　　Fair

Fund Family: Janus Fund　　　　**Phone:** (800) 525-3713
Address: 100 Fillmore Street, Denver, CO 80206
Fund Type: GR - Growth
Major Rating Factors: Middle of the road best describes Janus Fd Inc-Twenty Fund whose Weiss Investment Rating is currently a C (Fair). The fund currently has a performance rating of C+ (Fair) based on an average return of 15.13% over the last three years and 0.86% over the last six months. Factored into the performance evaluation is an expense ratio of 0.86% (very low).

The fund's risk rating is currently C+ (Fair). It carries a beta of 1.17, meaning it is expected to move 11.7% for every 10% move in the market. Volatility, as measured by both the semi-deviation and a drawdown factor, is considered low.

Scott Schoelzel has been running the fund for 9 years and currently receives a manager quality ranking of 77 (0=worst, 99=best). If you desire an average level of risk, then this fund may be an option.

Services Offered: Automated phone transactions, payroll deductions, bank draft capabilities, an IRA investment plan, a 401K investment plan, a Keogh investment plan, wire transfers and a systematic withdrawal plan. However, the fund is currently closed to new investors.

Data Date	Weiss Investment Rating	Net Assets ($Mil)	NAV	Perfor- mance Rating/Pts	Total Return Y-T-D	Risk Rating/Pts
6-06	C	9,218	49.34	C+ / 6.2	0.86%	C+ / 5.8
2005	C+	9,817	48.92	C+ / 6.8	9.42%	C+ / 6.2
2004	C+	9,590	44.80	B- / 7.2	23.89%	C / 4.7
2003	D-	9,628	36.17	E+ / 0.9	25.31%	C- / 4.1
2002	D-	10,238	29.01	E+ / 0.7	-24.02%	C- / 3.5
2001	E	15,082	38.46	E+ / 0.6	-29.20%	E- / 0.0

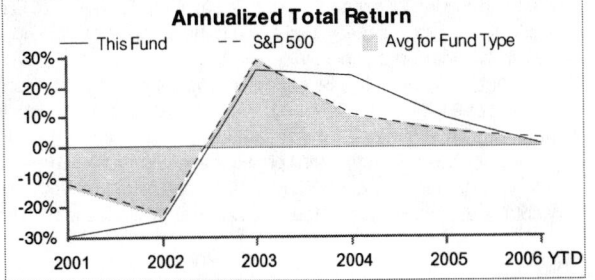

Janus Fd Inc-Worldwide Fund (JAWWX)   D   Weak

Fund Family: Janus Fund   **Phone:** (800) 525-3713
Address: 100 Fillmore Street, Denver, CO 80206
Fund Type: GL - Global

Major Rating Factors: Disappointing performance is the major factor driving the D (Weak) Weiss Investment Rating for Janus Fd Inc-Worldwide Fund. The fund currently has a performance rating of D+ (Weak) based on an average return of 9.60% over the last three years and 1.13% over the last six months. Factored into the performance evaluation is an expense ratio of 0.85% (very low) and a 2.0% back-end load levied at the time of sale.

The fund's risk rating is currently C+ (Fair). It carries a beta of 0.78, meaning the fund's expected move will be 7.8% for every 10% move in the market. Volatility, as measured by both the semi-deviation and a drawdown factor, is considered low.

Jason Yee currently receives a manager quality ranking of 4 (0=worst, 99=best). This fund offers only a moderate level of risk but investors looking for strong performance are still waiting.

Services Offered: Automated phone transactions, payroll deductions, bank draft capabilities, an IRA investment plan, a 401K investment plan, a Keogh investment plan, wire transfers and a systematic withdrawal plan.

Data Date	Weiss Investment Rating	Net Assets ($Mil)	NAV	Performance Rating/Pts	Total Return Y-T-D	Risk Rating/Pts
6-06	D	4,424	43.83	D+ / 2.4	1.13%	C+/ 6.5
2005	D-	5,000	43.34	D / 2.0	5.84%	C+/ 6.7
2004	D	7,119	41.41	D- / 1.4	5.54%	C / 5.2
2003	D	10,965	39.54	D- / 1.4	24.23%	C / 4.4
2002	D+	13,793	32.13	D / 1.8	-26.01%	C- / 4.2
2001	D	21,679	43.84	C / 4.3	-22.88%	E- / 0.0

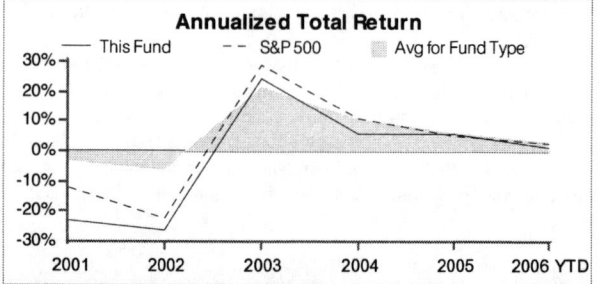

JennDry Jennison Utility A (PRUAX)   A+   Excellent

Fund Family: JennisonDryden   **Phone:** (800) 257-3893
Address: Gateway Center Three, Newark, NJ 07102
Fund Type: UT - Utilities

Major Rating Factors: Exceptional performance is the major factor driving the A+ (Excellent) Weiss Investment Rating for JennDry Jennison Utility A. The fund currently has a performance rating of A (Excellent) based on an average return of 28.91% over the last three years and 11.38% over the last six months. Factored into the performance evaluation is an expense ratio of 0.80% (very low), a 5.5% front-end load that is levied at the time of purchase and a 1.0% back-end load levied at the time of sale.

The fund's risk rating is currently B- (Good). It carries a beta of 0.63, meaning the fund's expected move will be 6.3% for every 10% move in the market. Volatility, as measured by both the semi-deviation and a drawdown factor, is considered low.

Shaun Hong, CFA has been running the fund for 6 years and currently receives a manager quality ranking of 99 (0=worst, 99=best). If you desire only a moderate level of risk and strong performance, then this fund is an excellent option.

Services Offered: Automated phone transactions, bank draft capabilities, an IRA investment plan, a 401K investment plan and wire transfers.

Data Date	Weiss Investment Rating	Net Assets ($Mil)	NAV	Performance Rating/Pts	Total Return Y-T-D	Risk Rating/Pts
6-06	A+	3,595	15.42	A / 9.4	11.38%	B- / 7.9
2005	A+	3,336	14.11	A / 9.5	30.32%	B- / 7.1
2004	C+	2,667	11.68	B / 8.2	31.11%	C / 4.3
2003	D+	2,151	9.06	D / 2.1	31.25%	C / 4.4
2002	C+	1,925	7.05	C+/ 6.5	-26.04%	C / 5.1
2001	C+	2,979	9.75	C / 5.1	-19.18%	C+/ 6.2

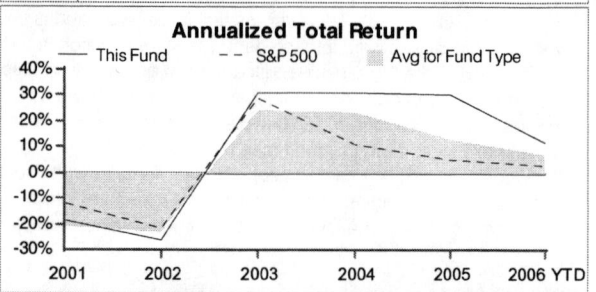

JPMorgan Mid Cap Value A (JAMCX)   B+   Good

Fund Family: JPMorgan Funds   **Phone:** (800) 358-4782
Address: 522 Fifth Avenue, New York, NY 10036
Fund Type: MC - Mid Cap

Major Rating Factors: JPMorgan Mid Cap Value A receives a Weiss Investment Rating of B+ (Good). The fund currently has a performance rating of C+ (Fair) based on an average return of 17.30% over the last three years and 6.23% over the last six months. Factored into the performance evaluation is an expense ratio of 1.25% (average) and a 5.3% front-end load that is levied at the time of purchase.

The fund's risk rating is currently B+ (Good). It carries a beta of 0.60, meaning the fund's expected move will be 6.0% for every 10% move in the market. Volatility, as measured by both the semi-deviation and a drawdown factor, is considered very low.

Jonathan Simon & Lawrence Play currently receives a manager quality ranking of 94 (0=worst, 99=best). If you desire an average level of risk, then this fund may be an option.

Services Offered: Automated phone transactions, bank draft capabilities, an IRA investment plan, a 401K investment plan, wire transfers and a systematic withdrawal plan. However, the fund is currently closed to new investors.

Data Date	Weiss Investment Rating	Net Assets ($Mil)	NAV	Performance Rating/Pts	Total Return Y-T-D	Risk Rating/Pts
6-06	B+	3,006	24.73	C+/ 6.6	6.23%	B+/ 9.1
2005	B+	2,843	23.28	C+/ 5.7	8.87%	B / 8.8
2004	A+	1,322	22.05	B+/ 8.9	20.31%	B / 8.2
2003	A	230	18.62	B+/ 8.7	30.07%	B- / 7.7
2002	U	21	14.44	U / --	2.69%	U / --

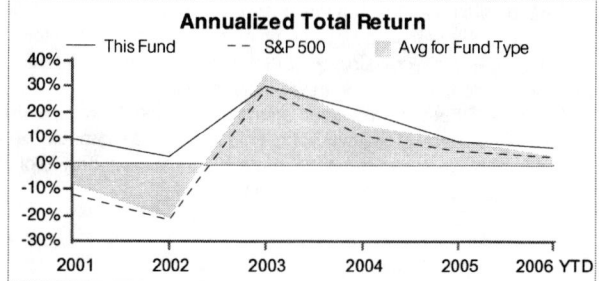

Julius Baer International Equity A (BJBIX)

A-   Excellent

Fund Family: Julius Baer Funds   **Phone:** (800) 435-4659
Address: c/o Unified Fund Services, Inc, Indianapolis, IN 46204
Fund Type: FO - Foreign

Major Rating Factors: Exceptional performance is the major factor driving the A- (Excellent) Weiss Investment Rating for Julius Baer International Equity A. The fund currently has a performance rating of A (Excellent) based on an average return of 26.73% over the last three years and 11.65% over the last six months. Factored into the performance evaluation is an expense ratio of 1.31% (average) and a 2.0% back-end load levied at the time of sale.

The fund's risk rating is currently C+ (Fair). It carries a beta of 1.18, meaning it is expected to move 11.8% for every 10% move in the market. Volatility, as measured by both the semi-deviation and a drawdown factor, is considered low.

Rudolph-Riad Younes, CFA has been running the fund for 13 years and currently receives a manager quality ranking of 36 (0=worst, 99=best). If you desire only a moderate level of risk and strong performance, then this fund is an excellent option.

Services Offered: Automated phone transactions, check writing, payroll deductions, bank draft capabilities, an IRA investment plan, a 401K investment plan, a Keogh investment plan, wire transfers and a systematic withdrawal plan. However, the fund is currently closed to new investors.

Data Date	Weiss Investment Rating	Net Assets ($Mil)	NAV	Performance Rating/Pts	Total Return Y-T-D	Risk Rating/Pts
6-06	A-	8,467	39.57	A / 9.3	11.65%	C+ / 6.1
2005	A	7,245	35.44	B+ / 8.9	17.05%	B- / 7.2
2004	A+	4,217	31.61	A / 9.4	23.22%	B- / 7.5
2003	B+	1,905	26.50	B / 8.0	35.92%	B- / 7.5
2002	C+	694	19.74	C+ / 6.4	-3.60%	C+ / 6.7
2001	C	310	20.81	B / 7.7	-18.93%	D- / 1.1

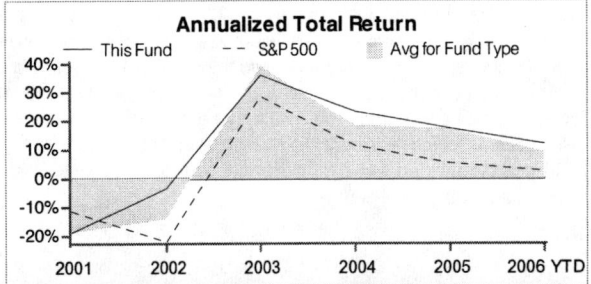

Keeley Small Cap Value Fund (KSCVX)

A   Excellent

Fund Family: Keeley   **Phone:** (800) 533-5344
Address: 401 South La Salle, Chicago, IL 60605
Fund Type: SC - Small Cap

Major Rating Factors: Exceptional performance is the major factor driving the A (Excellent) Weiss Investment Rating for Keeley Small Cap Value Fund. The fund currently has a performance rating of A (Excellent) based on an average return of 29.79% over the last three years and 14.00% over the last six months. Factored into the performance evaluation is an expense ratio of 1.52% (average) and a 4.5% front-end load that is levied at the time of purchase.

The fund's risk rating is currently C+ (Fair). It carries a beta of 0.86, meaning the fund's expected move will be 8.6% for every 10% move in the market. Volatility, as measured by both the semi-deviation and a drawdown factor, is considered low.

John L. Keeley, Jr. has been running the fund for 13 years and currently receives a manager quality ranking of 99 (0=worst, 99=best). If you desire only a moderate level of risk and strong performance, then this fund is an excellent option.

Services Offered: Automated phone transactions, bank draft capabilities, an IRA investment plan, a 401K investment plan and wire transfers.

Data Date	Weiss Investment Rating	Net Assets ($Mil)	NAV	Performance Rating/Pts	Total Return Y-T-D	Risk Rating/Pts
6-06	A	2,377	49.74	A / 9.5	14.00%	C+ / 6.3
2005	A-	1,001	43.63	A- / 9.2	16.12%	C+ / 6.4
2004	A-	277	37.95	A / 9.5	32.94%	C / 5.5
2003	A-	103	29.52	A- / 9.2	39.31%	B- / 7.0
2002	A	74	21.19	A- / 9.0	-8.47%	B / 8.5
2001	A	66	24.59	B+ / 8.9	13.65%	C+ / 6.3

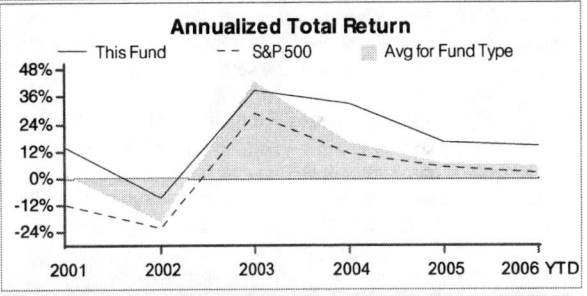

Legg Mason Opport Tr Prim (LMOPX)

D   Weak

Fund Family: Legg Mason   **Phone:** (800) 822-5544
Address: 100 Light Street, Baltimore, MD 21203
Fund Type: GR - Growth

Major Rating Factors: Legg Mason Opport Tr Prim receives a Weiss Investment Rating of D (Weak). The fund currently has a performance rating of C (Fair) based on an average return of 12.71% over the last three years and 0.88% over the last six months. Factored into the performance evaluation is an expense ratio of 2.18% (high) and a 1.0% back-end load levied at the time of sale.

The fund's risk rating is currently C (Fair). It carries a beta of 1.82, meaning it is expected to move 18.2% for every 10% move in the market. Volatility, as measured by both the semi-deviation and a drawdown factor, is considered average.

Bill Miller, CFA currently receives a manager quality ranking of 12 (0=worst, 99=best). If you desire an average level of risk, then this fund may be an option.

Services Offered: Automated phone transactions, bank draft capabilities, an IRA investment plan, wire transfers and a systematic withdrawal plan.

Data Date	Weiss Investment Rating	Net Assets ($Mil)	NAV	Performance Rating/Pts	Total Return Y-T-D	Risk Rating/Pts
6-06	D	4,291	16.86	C / 4.6	0.88%	C / 4.4
2005	B-	3,743	16.72	B+ / 8.8	6.70%	C / 4.6
2004	C+	3,357	15.67	B+ / 8.9	13.80%	C- / 3.0
2003	B-	2,644	13.77	A+ / 9.6	67.95%	C / 4.3
2002	B-	1,534	8.23	B / 7.7	-15.52%	C+ / 5.8
2001	U	1,714	9.80	U / --	1.94%	U / --

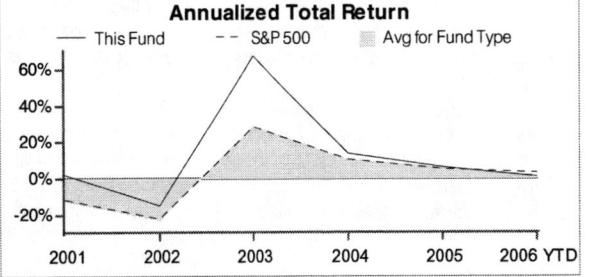

Legg Mason Prt Aggr Growth A (SHRAX)

D+ **Weak**

Fund Family: Legg Mason Partners **Phone:** (866) 890-4247
Address: c/o BFDS 66 Brooks Dr, Massachusetts, MA 02205
Fund Type: AG - Aggressive Growth

Major Rating Factors: Legg Mason Prt Aggr Growth A receives a Weiss
Investment Rating of D+ (Weak). The fund currently has a performance rating of
C- (Fair) based on an average return of 12.41% over the last three years and
-0.07% over the last six months. Factored into the performance evaluation is an
expense ratio of 1.16% (low), a 5.0% front-end load that is levied at the time of
purchase and a 1.0% back-end load levied at the time of sale.

The fund's risk rating is currently C+ (Fair). It carries a beta of 1.19, meaning
it is expected to move 11.9% for every 10% move in the market. Volatility, as
measured by both the semi-deviation and a drawdown factor, is considered low.

Richie Freeman has been running the fund for 23 years and currently
receives a manager quality ranking of 49 (0=worst, 99=best). If you desire an
average level of risk, then this fund may be an option.

Services Offered: Automated phone transactions, bank draft capabilities, an
IRA investment plan, a 401K investment plan, a Keogh investment plan and a
systematic withdrawal plan.

Data Date	Weiss Investment Rating	Net Assets ($Mil)	NAV	Performance Rating/Pts	Total Return Y-T-D	Risk Rating/Pts
6-06	D+	4,214	107.03	C- / 3.4	-0.07%	C+ / 6.8
2005	C	3,906	107.11	C+ / 6.4	12.55%	C / 5.5
2004	D-	3,265	95.17	D / 2.1	10.61%	C- / 3.2
2003	C-	2,788	86.04	C- / 3.9	36.57%	C- / 4.0
2002	C	1,855	63.00	C / 5.5	-32.75%	C / 5.5
2001	C+	2,106	93.68	A+ / 9.7	-5.00%	E- / 0.0

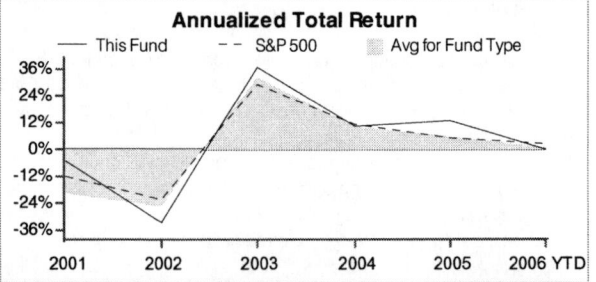

Annualized Total Return

Legg Mason Prt Fundamental Value A (SHFVX)

C- **Fair**

Fund Family: Legg Mason Partners **Phone:** (866) 890-4247
Address: c/o BFDS 66 Brooks Dr, Massachusetts, MA 02205
Fund Type: GR - Growth

Major Rating Factors: Middle of the road best describes Legg Mason Prt
Fundamental Value A whose Weiss Investment Rating is currently a C- (Fair).
The fund currently has a performance rating of C- (Fair) based on an average
return of 11.82% over the last three years and 4.10% over the last six months.
Factored into the performance evaluation is an expense ratio of 1.05% (low), a
5.0% front-end load that is levied at the time of purchase and a 1.0% back-end
load levied at the time of sale.

The fund's risk rating is currently B- (Good). It carries a beta of 1.22,
meaning it is expected to move 12.2% for every 10% move in the market.
Volatility, as measured by both the semi-deviation and a drawdown factor, is
considered low.

John G. Goode has been running the fund for 16 years and currently
receives a manager quality ranking of 39 (0=worst, 99=best). If you desire an
average level of risk, then this fund may be an option.

Services Offered: Automated phone transactions, bank draft capabilities, an
IRA investment plan, a 401K investment plan and a systematic withdrawal plan.

Data Date	Weiss Investment Rating	Net Assets ($Mil)	NAV	Performance Rating/Pts	Total Return Y-T-D	Risk Rating/Pts
6-06	C-	2,293	15.22	C- / 3.7	4.10%	B- / 7.3
2005	D+	2,252	14.62	C- / 3.6	3.99%	C+ / 6.2
2004	D	2,289	15.06	D / 2.1	7.42%	C- / 4.2
2003	C+	1,997	14.02	C+ / 5.9	38.95%	C / 5.3
2002	C+	1,405	10.09	C+ / 5.9	-26.51%	C+ / 6.2
2001	B	1,541	13.73	B+ / 8.6	-6.26%	C- / 3.7

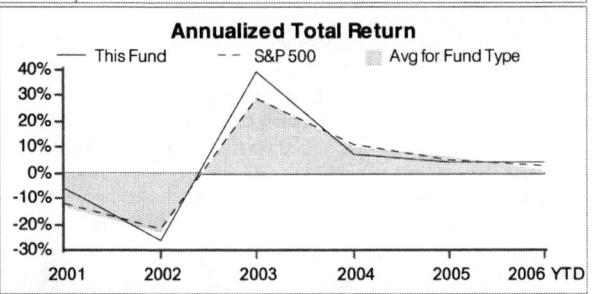

Annualized Total Return

Legg Mason Prt Large Cap Growth A (SBLGX)

E **Very Weak**

Fund Family: Legg Mason Partners **Phone:** (866) 890-4247
Address: c/o BFDS 66 Brooks Dr, Massachusetts, MA 02205
Fund Type: GR - Growth

Major Rating Factors: Very poor performance is the major factor driving the E
(Very Weak) Weiss Investment Rating for Legg Mason Prt Large Cap Growth A.
The fund currently has a performance rating of E- (Very Weak) based on an
average return of 5.43% over the last three years and -6.66% over the last six
months. Factored into the performance evaluation is an expense ratio of 1.17%
(low), a 5.0% front-end load that is levied at the time of purchase and a 1.0%
back-end load levied at the time of sale.

The fund's risk rating is currently C (Fair). It carries a beta of 1.33, meaning
it is expected to move 13.3% for every 10% move in the market. Volatility, as
measured by both the semi-deviation and a drawdown factor, is considered
average.

Alan J. Blake has been running the fund for 9 years and currently receives a
manager quality ranking of 4 (0=worst, 99=best). This fund offers an average
level of risk but investors looking for strong performance will be frustrated.

Services Offered: Automated phone transactions, bank draft capabilities, an
IRA investment plan, a 401K investment plan and a systematic withdrawal plan.

Data Date	Weiss Investment Rating	Net Assets ($Mil)	NAV	Performance Rating/Pts	Total Return Y-T-D	Risk Rating/Pts
6-06	E	2,045	21.46	E- / 0.2	-6.66%	C / 5.4
2005	D	2,039	22.99	C- / 3.9	5.12%	C+ / 5.7
2004	D-	1,281	21.87	D / 1.6	0.23%	C- / 4.2
2003	C+	1,177	21.82	C+ / 6.1	46.74%	C / 5.1
2002	C	722	14.87	C- / 3.4	-25.58%	C+ / 5.7
2001	C-	912	19.98	C / 4.7	-12.79%	D- / 1.4

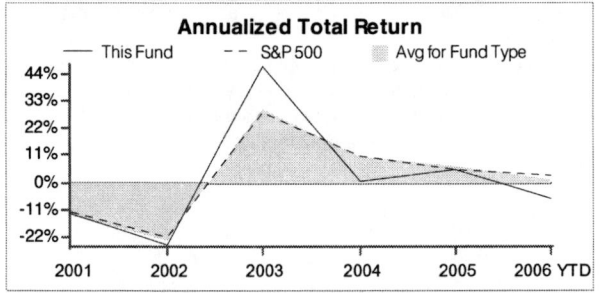

Annualized Total Return

Legg Mason Special Invest Prim (LMASX)   E+   Very Weak

Fund Family: Legg Mason   **Phone:** (800) 822-5544
Address: 100 Light Street, Baltimore, MD 21203
Fund Type: MC - Mid Cap

Major Rating Factors: Legg Mason Special Invest Prim has adopted a risky asset allocation strategy and currently receives an overall Weiss Investment Rating of E+ (Very Weak). The fund has an above average level of volatility, as measured by both semi-deviation and drawdown factors. It carries a beta of 1.23, meaning it is expected to move 12.3% for every 10% move in the market. Unfortunately, the high level of risk (D+, Weak) has only provided investors with average performance.

The fund's performance rating is currently C- (Fair). It has registered an average return of 12.86% over the last three years but is down -2.95% over the last six months. Factored into the performance evaluation is an expense ratio of 1.76% (above average).

Sam Peters currently receives a manager quality ranking of 5 (0=worst, 99=best). If you are comfortable owning a high risk investment, then this fund may be an option.

Services Offered: Automated phone transactions, check writing, payroll deductions, bank draft capabilities, an IRA investment plan, a 401K investment plan, a Keogh investment plan, wire transfers and a systematic withdrawal plan.

Data Date	Weiss Investment Rating	Net Assets ($Mil)	NAV	Performance Rating/Pts	Total Return Y-T-D	Risk Rating/Pts
6-06	E+	3,388	39.56	C- / 4.2	-2.95%	D+ / 2.4
2005	C+	3,584	44.59	B+ / 8.3	8.34%	C / 4.7
2004	B-	3,445	46.48	B+ / 8.7	13.05%	C / 4.4
2003	B+	3,148	44.49	A / 9.4	54.36%	C / 5.4
2002	B-	1,985	29.63	B / 7.7	-8.74%	C+ / 6.3
2001	C	2,242	33.73	B / 8.2	2.26%	E- / 0.0

Annualized Total Return
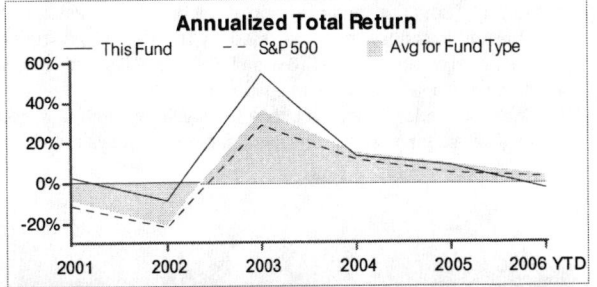

Legg Mason Value Trust Prim (LMVTX)   D   Weak

Fund Family: Legg Mason   **Phone:** (800) 822-5544
Address: 100 Light Street, Baltimore, MD 21203
Fund Type: GR - Growth

Major Rating Factors: Disappointing performance is the major factor driving the D (Weak) Weiss Investment Rating for Legg Mason Value Trust Prim. The fund currently has a performance rating of D (Weak) based on an average return of 9.67% over the last three years and -5.07% over the last six months. Factored into the performance evaluation is an expense ratio of 1.68% (above average).

The fund's risk rating is currently C+ (Fair). It carries a beta of 1.39, meaning it is expected to move 13.9% for every 10% move in the market. Volatility, as measured by both the semi-deviation and a drawdown factor, is considered low.

Bill Miller, CFA currently receives a manager quality ranking of 16 (0=worst, 99=best). This fund offers only a moderate level of risk but investors looking for strong performance are still waiting.

Services Offered: Automated phone transactions, bank draft capabilities, an IRA investment plan, a 401K investment plan, a Keogh investment plan, wire transfers and a systematic withdrawal plan.

Data Date	Weiss Investment Rating	Net Assets ($Mil)	NAV	Performance Rating/Pts	Total Return Y-T-D	Risk Rating/Pts
6-06	D	11,192	65.22	D / 2.2	-5.07%	C+ / 6.4
2005	C+	11,794	68.70	C+ / 6.5	5.32%	C+ / 6.0
2004	C	11,272	65.23	C+ / 6.8	11.96%	C- / 4.2
2003	C+	10,193	58.26	B / 7.9	43.53%	C / 5.0
2002	C+	7,853	40.59	C+ / 5.7	-18.92%	C / 5.2
2001	C-	9,789	50.06	C / 5.3	-9.29%	D / 1.6

Annualized Total Return
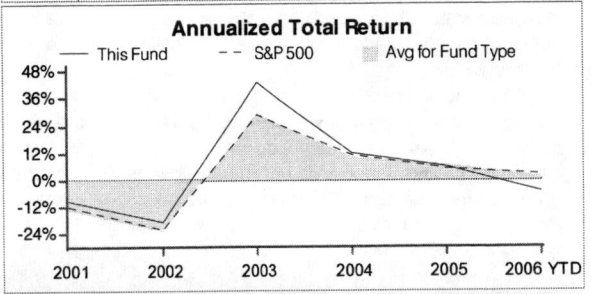

Lord Abbett Affiliated Fund A (LAFFX)   C   Fair

Fund Family: Lord Abbett   **Phone:** (800) 201-6984
Address: 90 Hudson Street 10th Flr, Jersey City, NJ 07302
Fund Type: GI - Growth and Income

Major Rating Factors: Middle of the road best describes Lord Abbett Affiliated Fund A whose Weiss Investment Rating is currently a C (Fair). The fund currently has a performance rating of C (Fair) based on an average return of 12.78% over the last three years and 5.31% over the last six months. Factored into the performance evaluation is an expense ratio of 0.82% (very low) and a 5.8% front-end load that is levied at the time of purchase.

The fund's risk rating is currently B- (Good). It carries a beta of 1.06, meaning that its performance tracks fairly well with that of the overall stock market. Volatility, as measured by both the semi-deviation and a drawdown factor, is considered low.

This fund has been team managed for 10 years and currently receives a manager quality ranking of 67 (0=worst, 99=best). If you desire an average level of risk, then this fund may be an option.

Services Offered: Automated phone transactions, bank draft capabilities, an IRA investment plan, a 401K investment plan and a systematic withdrawal plan.

Data Date	Weiss Investment Rating	Net Assets ($Mil)	NAV	Performance Rating/Pts	Total Return Y-T-D	Risk Rating/Pts
6-06	C	15,078	14.72	C / 4.6	5.31%	B- / 7.6
2005	D	14,837	14.05	C- / 3.0	3.33%	C+ / 6.5
2004	C	15,002	14.78	C / 5.3	12.60%	C / 5.1
2003	C+	12,600	13.55	C / 5.5	30.89%	C+ / 6.1
2002	C+	8,883	10.53	C+ / 6.8	-18.79%	C+ / 6.9
2001	B+	10,292	13.69	B- / 7.2	-7.94%	C+ / 6.5

Annualized Total Return
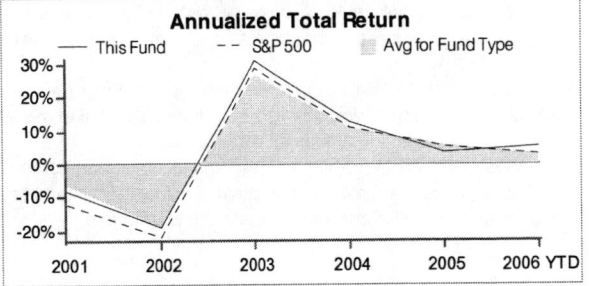

Lord Abbett All Value A (LDFVX)

B-   **Good**

Fund Family: Lord Abbett   **Phone:** (800) 201-6984
Address: 90 Hudson Street 10th Flr, Jersey City, NJ 07302
Fund Type: GI - Growth and Income

Major Rating Factors: Lord Abbett All Value A receives a Weiss Investment Rating of B- (Good). The fund currently has a performance rating of C+ (Fair) based on an average return of 15.50% over the last three years and 7.38% over the last six months. Factored into the performance evaluation is an expense ratio of 1.17% (low) and a 5.8% front-end load that is levied at the time of purchase.

The fund's risk rating is currently B (Good). It carries a beta of 1.16, meaning it is expected to move 11.6% for every 10% move in the market. Volatility, as measured by both the semi-deviation and a drawdown factor, is considered low.

This fund has been team managed for 10 years and currently receives a manager quality ranking of 81 (0=worst, 99=best). If you desire an average level of risk, then this fund may be an option.

Services Offered: Automated phone transactions, bank draft capabilities, an IRA investment plan, a 401K investment plan and a systematic withdrawal plan.

Data Date	Weiss Investment Rating	Net Assets ($Mil)	NAV	Performance Rating/Pts	Total Return Y-T-D	Risk Rating/Pts
6-06	B-	2,068	12.66	C+ / 6.0	7.38%	B / 8.0
2005	C	1,863	11.79	C / 4.5	5.48%	B- / 7.1
2004	C+	1,480	12.02	C+ / 6.8	15.61%	C+ / 6.4
2003	B	676	10.56	B- / 7.3	31.93%	C+ / 6.9
2002	B	198	8.09	B- / 7.3	-14.41%	B- / 7.8
2001	A-	187	9.66	B- / 7.5	-4.20%	B- / 7.1

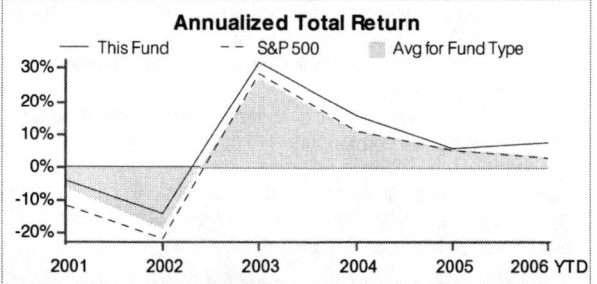

Annualized Total Return

Lord Abbett Mid-Cap Value A (LAVLX)

C   **Fair**

Fund Family: Lord Abbett   **Phone:** (800) 201-6984
Address: 90 Hudson Street 10th Flr, Jersey City, NJ 07302
Fund Type: MC - Mid Cap

Major Rating Factors: Middle of the road best describes Lord Abbett Mid-Cap Value A whose Weiss Investment Rating is currently a C (Fair). The fund currently has a performance rating of C+ (Fair) based on an average return of 16.67% over the last three years and 0.70% over the last six months. Factored into the performance evaluation is an expense ratio of 1.02% (low) and a 5.8% front-end load that is levied at the time of purchase.

The fund's risk rating is currently C+ (Fair). It carries a beta of 0.81, meaning the fund's expected move will be 8.1% for every 10% move in the market. Volatility, as measured by both the semi-deviation and a drawdown factor, is considered low.

This fund has been team managed for 11 years and currently receives a manager quality ranking of 72 (0=worst, 99=best). If you desire an average level of risk, then this fund may be an option.

Services Offered: Automated phone transactions, bank draft capabilities, an IRA investment plan, a 401K investment plan and a systematic withdrawal plan. However, the fund is currently closed to new investors.

Data Date	Weiss Investment Rating	Net Assets ($Mil)	NAV	Performance Rating/Pts	Total Return Y-T-D	Risk Rating/Pts
6-06	C	6,858	21.85	C+ / 5.7	0.70%	C+ / 6.7
2005	C	7,435	22.41	C / 5.4	8.16%	C+ / 6.3
2004	B+	6,355	22.63	B+ / 8.3	24.10%	C+ / 6.3
2003	B+	4,224	18.83	B / 7.6	24.94%	B- / 7.5
2002	A+	2,230	15.39	A+ / 9.6	-9.75%	B / 8.6
2001	A+	1,246	17.41	A+ / 9.6	8.00%	C+ / 6.4

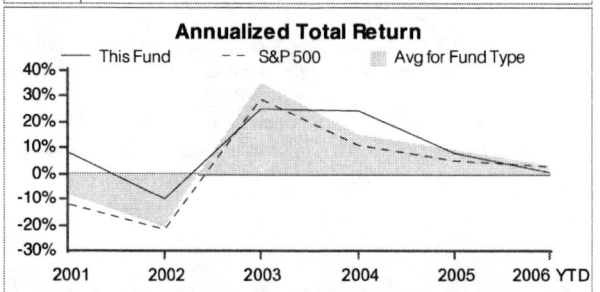

Annualized Total Return

Lord Abbett Small Cap Value A (LRSCX)

B+   **Good**

Fund Family: Lord Abbett   **Phone:** (800) 201-6984
Address: 90 Hudson Street 10th Flr, Jersey City, NJ 07302
Fund Type: SC - Small Cap

Major Rating Factors: Exceptional performance is the major factor driving the B+ (Good) Weiss Investment Rating for Lord Abbett Small Cap Value A. The fund currently has a performance rating of A- (Excellent) based on an average return of 25.30% over the last three years and 14.32% over the last six months. Factored into the performance evaluation is an expense ratio of 1.30% (average) and a 5.8% front-end load that is levied at the time of purchase.

The fund's risk rating is currently C+ (Fair). It carries a beta of 0.91, meaning that its performance tracks fairly well with that of the overall stock market. Volatility, as measured by both the semi-deviation and a drawdown factor, is considered low.

Gerard S.E.Heffernan currently receives a manager quality ranking of 97 (0=worst, 99=best). If you desire only a moderate level of risk and strong performance, then this fund is an excellent option.

Services Offered: Automated phone transactions, bank draft capabilities, an IRA investment plan, a 401K investment plan and a systematic withdrawal plan. However, the fund is currently closed to new investors.

Data Date	Weiss Investment Rating	Net Assets ($Mil)	NAV	Performance Rating/Pts	Total Return Y-T-D	Risk Rating/Pts
6-06	B+	2,182	32.42	A- / 9.1	14.32%	C+ / 5.7
2005	B+	1,726	28.36	B+ / 8.7	13.21%	C+ / 5.8
2004	B+	1,066	27.54	B+ / 8.8	22.39%	C+ / 5.6
2003	A-	537	24.72	A- / 9.1	44.94%	B- / 7.0
2002	A	301	18.21	A / 9.3	-11.09%	B / 8.2
2001	B	407	21.96	A / 9.3	7.93%	D+ / 2.8

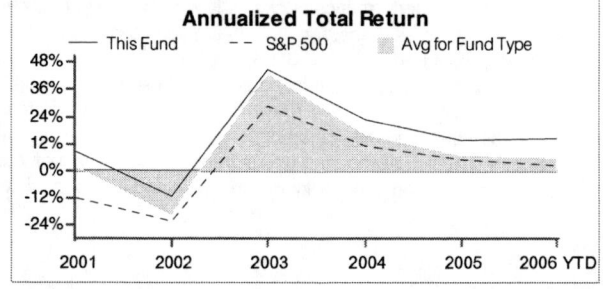

Annualized Total Return

Mairs & Power Growth Fund (MPGFX)   B-   Good

Fund Family: Mairs & Power   **Phone:** (800) 304-7404
Address: West 1420 First Natl Bank Bldg, St. Paul, MN 55101
Fund Type: GR - Growth
Major Rating Factors: Mairs & Power Growth Fund receives a Weiss Investment Rating of B- (Good). The fund currently has a performance rating of C (Fair) based on an average return of 13.14% over the last three years and 2.52% over the last six months. Factored into the performance evaluation is an expense ratio of 0.70% (very low).

The fund's risk rating is currently B (Good). It carries a beta of 0.86, meaning the fund's expected move will be 8.6% for every 10% move in the market. Volatility, as measured by both the semi-deviation and a drawdown factor, is considered low.

William B. Frels has been running the fund for 7 years and currently receives a manager quality ranking of 84 (0=worst, 99=best). If you desire an average level of risk, then this fund may be an option.

Services Offered: An IRA investment plan, a 401K investment plan, a Keogh investment plan and a systematic withdrawal plan.

Data Date	Weiss Investment Rating	Net Assets ($Mil)	NAV	Performance Rating/Pts	Total Return Y-T-D	Risk Rating/Pts
6-06	B-	2,589	73.19	C / 5.1	2.52%	B / 8.8
2005	C+	2,515	71.69	C / 4.8	4.37%	B / 8.3
2004	B+	1,934	70.33	B / 7.8	18.44%	B- / 7.1
2003	C	1,253	60.90	B / 7.9	26.33%	D+ / 2.4
2002	C+	872	49.26	A / 9.4	-8.12%	C- / 3.2
2001	A+	677	54.36	A- / 9.2	6.48%	B- / 7.0

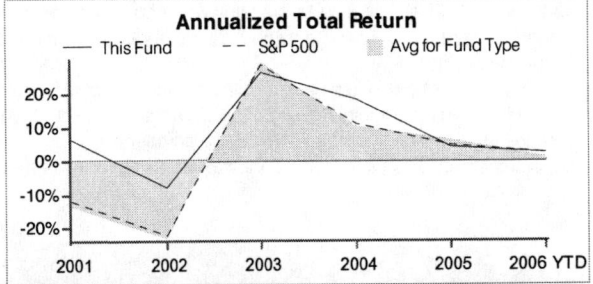

Managers Special Equity Fd (MGSEX)   C+   Fair

Fund Family: Managers Funds, LLC   **Phone:** (800) 835-3879
Address: 40 Richards Avenue, Norwalk, CT 06854
Fund Type: SC - Small Cap
Major Rating Factors: Middle of the road best describes Managers Special Equity Fd whose Weiss Investment Rating is currently a C+ (Fair). The fund currently has a performance rating of C+ (Fair) based on an average return of 16.66% over the last three years and 5.14% over the last six months. Factored into the performance evaluation is an expense ratio of 1.40% (average).

The fund's risk rating is currently C+ (Fair). It carries a beta of 0.92, meaning that its performance tracks fairly well with that of the overall stock market. Volatility, as measured by both the semi-deviation and a drawdown factor, is considered low.

This fund has been team managed for 21 years and currently receives a manager quality ranking of 49 (0=worst, 99=best). If you desire an average level of risk, then this fund may be an option.

Services Offered: Automated phone transactions, check writing, bank draft capabilities, an IRA investment plan, a 401K investment plan, wire transfers and a systematic withdrawal plan.

Data Date	Weiss Investment Rating	Net Assets ($Mil)	NAV	Performance Rating/Pts	Total Return Y-T-D	Risk Rating/Pts
6-06	C+	2,789	91.23	C+ / 6.8	5.14%	C+ / 6.0
2005	C+	3,004	86.77	C+ / 6.3	4.00%	C+ / 6.0
2004	C+	3,343	90.41	B- / 7.3	15.19%	C / 5.1
2003	B-	3,158	78.49	B / 8.0	42.50%	C+ / 5.6
2002	C	2,080	55.08	C / 5.3	-21.98%	C / 4.6
2001	C	2,159	70.60	B+ / 8.6	-8.07%	E- / 0.0

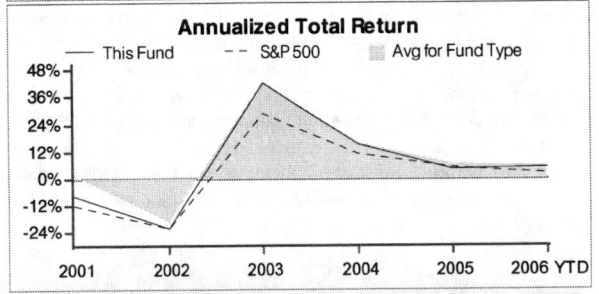

Marsico Focus Fund (MFOCX)   C-   Fair

Fund Family: Marsico Investment Fund   **Phone:** (888) 860-8686
Address: 1200 17th Street, Denver, CO 80202
Fund Type: GR - Growth
Major Rating Factors: Middle of the road best describes Marsico Focus Fund whose Weiss Investment Rating is currently a C- (Fair). The fund currently has a performance rating of C- (Fair) based on an average return of 11.93% over the last three years and -0.49% over the last six months. Factored into the performance evaluation is an expense ratio of 1.20% (average) and a 2.0% back-end load levied at the time of sale.

The fund's risk rating is currently B- (Good). It carries a beta of 1.16, meaning it is expected to move 11.6% for every 10% move in the market. Volatility, as measured by both the semi-deviation and a drawdown factor, is considered low.

Thomas F. Marsico has been running the fund for 9 years and currently receives a manager quality ranking of 47 (0=worst, 99=best). If you desire an average level of risk, then this fund may be an option.

Services Offered: An IRA investment plan, a 401K investment plan and wire transfers.

Data Date	Weiss Investment Rating	Net Assets ($Mil)	NAV	Performance Rating/Pts	Total Return Y-T-D	Risk Rating/Pts
6-06	C-	4,485	18.13	C- / 4.1	-0.49%	B- / 7.2
2005	C+	3,961	18.22	C+ / 5.6	9.69%	B- / 7.3
2004	C+	3,791	16.61	C+ / 5.9	11.70%	C+ / 6.3
2003	C	2,533	14.87	C- / 4.2	31.24%	C+ / 6.1
2002	C-	1,349	11.33	D+ / 2.9	-16.69%	C / 5.5
2001	D	1,401	13.60	C- / 3.9	-20.81%	E- / 0.0

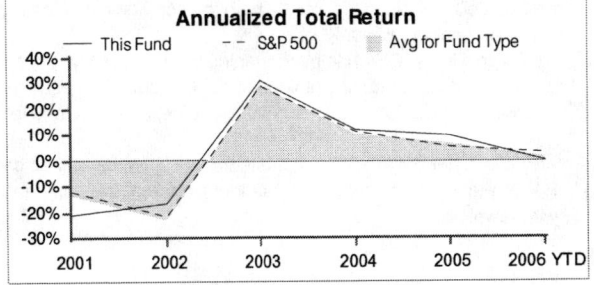

Marsico Growth Fund (MGRIX)

C-   Fair

Fund Family: Marsico Investment Fund   **Phone:** (888) 860-8686
Address: 1200 17th Street, Denver, CO 80202
Fund Type: GR - Growth
Major Rating Factors: Middle of the road best describes Marsico Growth Fund whose Weiss Investment Rating is currently a C- (Fair). The fund currently has a performance rating of C- (Fair) based on an average return of 11.74% over the last three years and -1.27% over the last six months. Factored into the performance evaluation is an expense ratio of 1.24% (average) and a 2.0% back-end load levied at the time of sale.

The fund's risk rating is currently B- (Good). It carries a beta of 1.08, meaning that its performance tracks fairly well with that of the overall stock market. Volatility, as measured by both the semi-deviation and a drawdown factor, is considered low.

Thomas F. Marsico has been running the fund for 9 years and currently receives a manager quality ranking of 53 (0=worst, 99=best). If you desire an average level of risk, then this fund may be an option.
Services Offered: An IRA investment plan and a 401K investment plan.

Data Date	Weiss Investment Rating	Net Assets ($Mil)	NAV	Performance Rating/Pts	Total Return Y-T-D	Risk Rating/Pts
6-06	C-	2,420	18.61	C- / 3.5	-1.27%	B- / 7.3
2005	C+	2,245	18.85	C / 5.3	6.74%	B- / 7.4
2004	C+	1,517	17.66	C+ / 6.8	14.38%	C+ / 6.4
2003	C	944	15.44	C / 4.4	31.97%	C+ / 6.3
2002	C	622	11.70	C- / 3.2	-16.79%	C+ / 6.0
2001	D	604	14.06	C- / 4.1	-20.33%	E- / 0.1

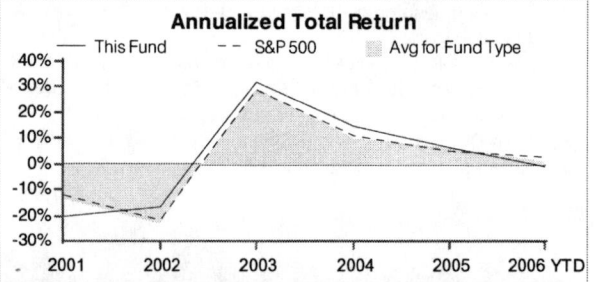

Matthews Pacific Tiger Fund (MAPTX)

B+   Good

Fund Family: Matthews Asian Funds   **Phone:** (800) 892-0382
Address: 456 Montgomery Street, San Francisco, CA 94104
Fund Type: FO - Foreign
Major Rating Factors: Exceptional performance is the major factor driving the B+ (Good) Weiss Investment Rating for Matthews Pacific Tiger Fund. The fund currently has a performance rating of A (Excellent) based on an average return of 29.64% over the last three years and 4.05% over the last six months. Factored into the performance evaluation is an expense ratio of 1.31% (average) and a 2.0% back-end load levied at the time of sale.

The fund's risk rating is currently C+ (Fair). It carries a beta of 1.23, meaning it is expected to move 12.3% for every 10% move in the market. Volatility, as measured by both the semi-deviation and a drawdown factor, is considered low.

Mark W. Headley has been running the fund for 12 years and currently receives a manager quality ranking of 50 (0=worst, 99=best). If you desire only a moderate level of risk and strong performance, then this fund is an excellent option.
Services Offered: Automated phone transactions, bank draft capabilities, an IRA investment plan and a 401K investment plan. However, the fund is currently closed to new investors.

Data Date	Weiss Investment Rating	Net Assets ($Mil)	NAV	Performance Rating/Pts	Total Return Y-T-D	Risk Rating/Pts
6-06	B+	2,736	20.05	A / 9.4	4.05%	C+ / 5.8
2005	A-	1,927	19.27	A+ / 9.6	22.51%	C+ / 6.0
2004	A	764	15.90	A+ / 9.6	23.34%	C+ / 6.5
2003	A+	456	13.15	A+ / 9.8	60.10%	B- / 7.0
2002	C+	107	8.24	C+ / 6.3	-6.47%	C / 5.2
2001	C+	87	8.81	A / 9.4	7.91%	E- / 0.0

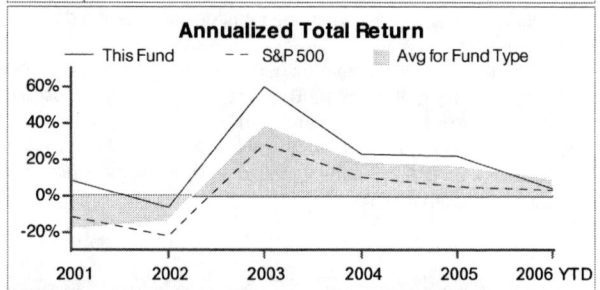

Mellon International M (MPITX)

A   Excellent

Fund Family: Mellon Funds   **Phone:** (800) 499-3327
Address: One Mellon Center, Pittsburgh, PA 15258
Fund Type: FO - Foreign
Major Rating Factors: Strong performance is the major factor driving the A (Excellent) Weiss Investment Rating for Mellon International M. The fund currently has a performance rating of B+ (Good) based on an average return of 23.28% over the last three years and 9.74% over the last six months. Factored into the performance evaluation is an expense ratio of 1.09% (low).

The fund's risk rating is currently B- (Good). It carries a beta of 0.92, meaning that its performance tracks fairly well with that of the overall stock market. Volatility, as measured by both the semi-deviation and a drawdown factor, is considered low.

D Kirk Henry, CFA has been running the fund for 4 years and currently receives a manager quality ranking of 64 (0=worst, 99=best). If you desire only a moderate level of risk and strong performance, then this fund is an excellent option.
Services Offered: Automated phone transactions, bank draft capabilities, an IRA investment plan, a 401K investment plan, wire transfers and a systematic withdrawal plan.

Data Date	Weiss Investment Rating	Net Assets ($Mil)	NAV	Performance Rating/Pts	Total Return Y-T-D	Risk Rating/Pts
6-06	A	2,436	17.24	B+ / 8.9	9.74%	B- / 7.0
2005	A	1,962	15.71	B+ / 8.4	11.16%	B- / 7.6
2004	B+	1,475	15.70	B+ / 8.9	20.29%	C+ / 6.1
2003	C	967	13.76	B / 8.2	39.29%	D+ / 2.4

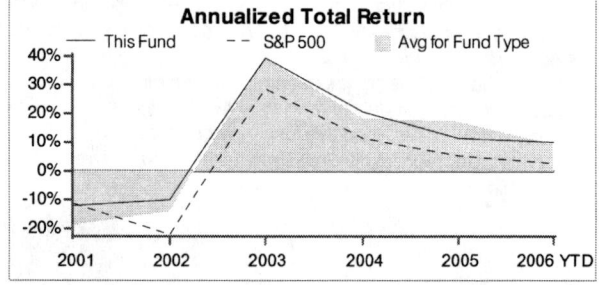

Merrill Lynch Basic Value A (MDBAX)   C   Fair

Fund Family: Merrill Lynch Investment Managers   **Phone:** (800) 543-6217
Address: PO Box 9011, Princeton, NJ 08543
Fund Type: GI - Growth and Income

Major Rating Factors: Middle of the road best describes Merrill Lynch Basic Value A whose Weiss Investment Rating is currently a C (Fair). The fund currently has a performance rating of C (Fair) based on an average return of 13.09% over the last three years and 5.72% over the last six months. Factored into the performance evaluation is an expense ratio of 0.82% (very low) and a 5.3% front-end load that is levied at the time of purchase.

The fund's risk rating is currently B- (Good). It carries a beta of 1.14, meaning it is expected to move 11.4% for every 10% move in the market. Volatility, as measured by both the semi-deviation and a drawdown factor, is considered low.

Kevin Redino has been running the fund for 7 years and currently receives a manager quality ranking of 62 (0=worst, 99=best). If you desire an average level of risk, then this fund may be an option.

Services Offered: Automated phone transactions, bank draft capabilities, an IRA investment plan, a 401K investment plan, a Keogh investment plan, wire transfers and a systematic withdrawal plan.

Data Date	Weiss Investment Rating	Net Assets ($Mil)	NAV	Performance Rating/Pts	Total Return Y-T-D	Risk Rating/Pts
6-06	C	2,294	32.69	C / 4.8	5.72%	B- / 7.3
2005	D	2,277	30.92	D+ / 2.9	3.60%	C+ / 6.3
2004	C-	2,284	31.70	C / 4.8	10.17%	C / 4.4
2003	C+	1,905	30.46	B- / 7.5	32.43%	C / 5.1
2002	C+	1,635	23.28	C+ / 6.9	-17.03%	C+ / 6.0
2001	C+	1,751	29.19	C+ / 6.5	-0.73%	C+ / 6.3

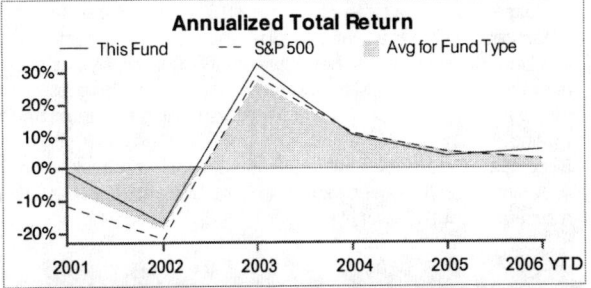

Annualized Total Return

Merrill Lynch Glbl Allocation A (MDLOX)   B   Good

Fund Family: Merrill Lynch Investment Managers   **Phone:** (800) 543-6217
Address: PO Box 9011, Princeton, NJ 08543
Fund Type: GL - Global

Major Rating Factors: Merrill Lynch Glbl Allocation A receives a Weiss Investment Rating of B (Good). The fund currently has a performance rating of C+ (Fair) based on an average return of 16.45% over the last three years and 6.63% over the last six months. Factored into the performance evaluation is an expense ratio of 1.09% (low), a 5.3% front-end load that is levied at the time of purchase and a 2.0% back-end load levied at the time of sale.

The fund's risk rating is currently B (Good). It carries a beta of 1.20, meaning it is expected to move 12.0% for every 10% move in the market. Volatility, as measured by both the semi-deviation and a drawdown factor, is considered low.

Dan Chamby currently receives a manager quality ranking of 97 (0=worst, 99=best). If you desire an average level of risk, then this fund may be an option.

Services Offered: Automated phone transactions, bank draft capabilities, an IRA investment plan, a 401K investment plan, a Keogh investment plan, wire transfers and a systematic withdrawal plan.

Data Date	Weiss Investment Rating	Net Assets ($Mil)	NAV	Performance Rating/Pts	Total Return Y-T-D	Risk Rating/Pts
6-06	B	5,334	18.01	C+ / 6.4	6.63%	B / 8.6
2005	B	4,625	16.89	C+ / 6.6	12.48%	B / 8.6
2004	B+	3,653	16.47	B / 7.7	14.27%	B- / 7.0
2003	A-	2,730	14.97	B / 8.2	35.98%	B- / 7.9
2002	A-	2,191	11.41	B+ / 8.5	-7.96%	B / 8.4
2001	A+	1,996	12.83	B+ / 8.5	0.47%	B- / 7.8

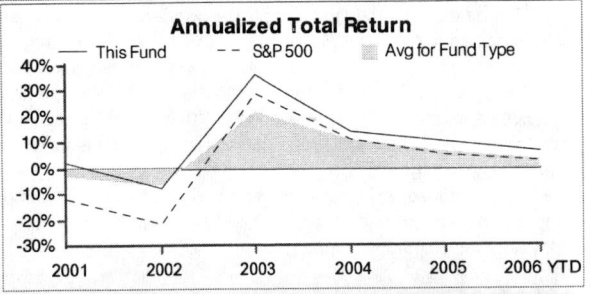

Annualized Total Return

Merrill Lynch Glbl Allocation B (MBLOX)   B   Good

Fund Family: Merrill Lynch Investment Managers   **Phone:** (800) 543-6217
Address: PO Box 9011, Princeton, NJ 08543
Fund Type: GL - Global

Major Rating Factors: Merrill Lynch Glbl Allocation B receives a Weiss Investment Rating of B (Good). The fund currently has a performance rating of C+ (Fair) based on an average return of 15.57% over the last three years and 6.22% over the last six months. Factored into the performance evaluation is an expense ratio of 1.86% (above average) and a 2.0% back-end load levied at the time of sale.

The fund's risk rating is currently B (Good). It carries a beta of 1.19, meaning it is expected to move 11.9% for every 10% move in the market. Volatility, as measured by both the semi-deviation and a drawdown factor, is considered low.

Dennis Stattman has been running the fund for 17 years and currently receives a manager quality ranking of 96 (0=worst, 99=best). If you desire an average level of risk, then this fund may be an option.

Services Offered: Automated phone transactions, bank draft capabilities, an IRA investment plan, a 401K investment plan, a Keogh investment plan, wire transfers and a systematic withdrawal plan.

Data Date	Weiss Investment Rating	Net Assets ($Mil)	NAV	Performance Rating/Pts	Total Return Y-T-D	Risk Rating/Pts
6-06	B	2,100	17.60	C+ / 6.6	6.22%	B / 8.6
2005	B	2,061	16.57	C+ / 6.8	11.29%	B / 8.6
2004	B+	2,238	16.17	B- / 7.3	13.36%	B- / 7.0
2003	A-	2,115	14.71	B / 8.1	34.97%	B- / 7.9
2002	A-	1,875	11.22	B+ / 8.4	-8.66%	B / 8.4
2001	A+	2,646	12.61	B+ / 8.4	0.02%	B- / 7.8

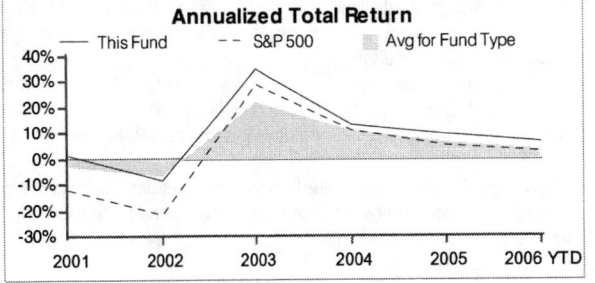

Annualized Total Return

MFS Emerging Growth Fund A (MFEGX)
D-   **Weak**

Fund Family: MFS   **Phone:** (800) 343-2829

Address: 500 Boylston Street, Boston, MA 02116

Fund Type: GR - Growth

Major Rating Factors: Disappointing performance is the major factor driving the D- (Weak) Weiss Investment Rating for MFS Emerging Growth Fund A. The fund currently has a performance rating of D+ (Weak) based on an average return of 10.67% over the last three years and -1.21% over the last six months. Factored into the performance evaluation is an expense ratio of 1.27% (average) and a 5.8% front-end load that is levied at the time of purchase.

The fund's risk rating is currently C+ (Fair). It carries a beta of 1.34, meaning it is expected to move 13.4% for every 10% move in the market. Volatility, as measured by both the semi-deviation and a drawdown factor, is considered low.

Eric B. Fischman has been running the fund for 4 years and currently receives a manager quality ranking of 24 (0=worst, 99=best). This fund offers only a moderate level of risk but investors looking for strong performance are still waiting.

Services Offered: Automated phone transactions, check writing, bank draft capabilities, an IRA investment plan, a 401K investment plan, wire transfers and a systematic withdrawal plan.

Data Date	Weiss Investment Rating	Net Assets ($Mil)	NAV	Perfor- mance Rating/Pts	Total Return Y-T-D	Risk Rating/Pts
6-06	D-	2,208	34.31	D+ / 2.4	-1.21%	C+ / 5.9
2005	C	2,366	34.73	C / 5.1	8.67%	C+ / 6.5
2004	E+	2,470	31.96	D- / 1.1	13.05%	C- / 3.3
2003	E+	2,677	28.27	E / 0.5	31.79%	D / 1.9
2002	D-	2,304	21.45	E / 0.4	-35.43%	D+ / 2.4
2001	E	4,625	33.22	E+ / 0.9	-25.82%	E- / 0.0

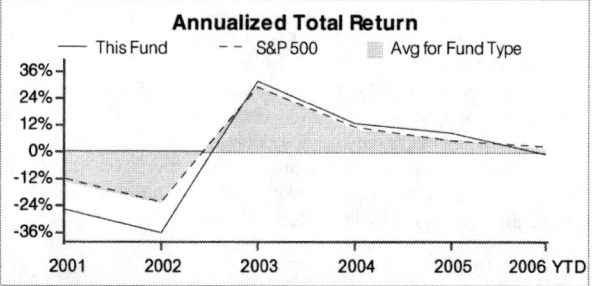

MFS Intl New Discovery A (MIDAX)
A-   **Excellent**

Fund Family: MFS   **Phone:** (800) 343-2829

Address: 500 Boylston Street, Boston, MA 02116

Fund Type: FO - Foreign

Major Rating Factors: Exceptional performance is the major factor driving the A- (Excellent) Weiss Investment Rating for MFS Intl New Discovery A. The fund currently has a performance rating of A (Excellent) based on an average return of 29.05% over the last three years and 7.72% over the last six months. Factored into the performance evaluation is an expense ratio of 1.58% (above average), a 5.8% front-end load that is levied at the time of purchase and a 1.0% back-end load levied at the time of sale.

The fund's risk rating is currently C+ (Fair). It carries a beta of 1.12, meaning it is expected to move 11.2% for every 10% move in the market. Volatility, as measured by both the semi-deviation and a drawdown factor, is considered low.

David A. Antonelli has been running the fund for 9 years and currently receives a manager quality ranking of 70 (0=worst, 99=best). If you desire only a moderate level of risk and strong performance, then this fund is an excellent option.

Services Offered: Automated phone transactions, check writing, bank draft capabilities, an IRA investment plan, a 401K investment plan, wire transfers and a systematic withdrawal plan.

Data Date	Weiss Investment Rating	Net Assets ($Mil)	NAV	Perfor- mance Rating/Pts	Total Return Y-T-D	Risk Rating/Pts
6-06	A-	2,644	25.68	A / 9.4	7.72%	C+ / 5.9
2005	A+	2,072	23.84	A / 9.4	20.21%	B- / 7.9
2004	A+	1,243	21.34	A / 9.3	24.30%	B- / 7.1
2003	A+	514	18.10	A- / 9.0	48.57%	B- / 7.8
2002	C	155	12.26	B / 7.6	-7.05%	C- / 3.1
2001	B-	34	13.19	A- / 9.2	-7.95%	D / 2.2

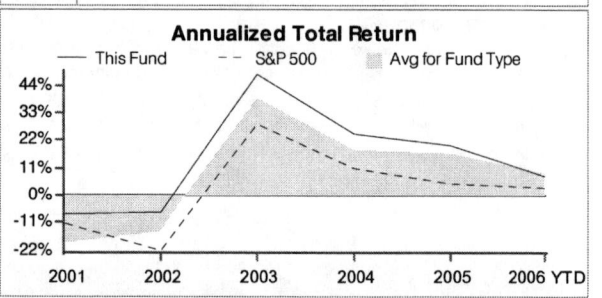

MFS Mass Investors Gr Stk A (MIGFX)
D-   **Weak**

Fund Family: MFS   **Phone:** (800) 343-2829

Address: 500 Boylston Street, Boston, MA 02116

Fund Type: GR - Growth

Major Rating Factors: Very poor performance is the major factor driving the D- (Weak) Weiss Investment Rating for MFS Mass Investors Gr Stk A. The fund currently has a performance rating of E+ (Very Weak) based on an average return of 7.00% over the last three years and -1.17% over the last six months. Factored into the performance evaluation is an expense ratio of 0.92% (low) and a 5.8% front-end load that is levied at the time of purchase.

The fund's risk rating is currently B- (Good). It carries a beta of 1.07, meaning that its performance tracks fairly well with that of the overall stock market. Volatility, as measured by both the semi-deviation and a drawdown factor, is considered low.

Stephen Pesek has been running the fund for 7 years and currently receives a manager quality ranking of 16 (0=worst, 99=best). This fund offers only a moderate level of risk but investors looking for strong performance are still waiting.

Services Offered: Automated phone transactions, check writing, bank draft capabilities, an IRA investment plan, a 401K investment plan, wire transfers and a systematic withdrawal plan.

Data Date	Weiss Investment Rating	Net Assets ($Mil)	NAV	Perfor- mance Rating/Pts	Total Return Y-T-D	Risk Rating/Pts
6-06	D-	4,152	12.69	E+ / 0.7	-1.17%	B- / 7.5
2005	D	4,777	12.84	D- / 1.3	3.88%	B- / 7.7
2004	D-	5,553	12.36	E+ / 0.9	9.63%	C / 4.9
2003	D-	7,082	11.32	E / 0.4	22.64%	C / 4.3
2002	D+	5,864	9.23	D / 1.7	-28.39%	C / 4.7
2001	D-	8,425	12.89	D / 2.2	-24.80%	E / 0.5

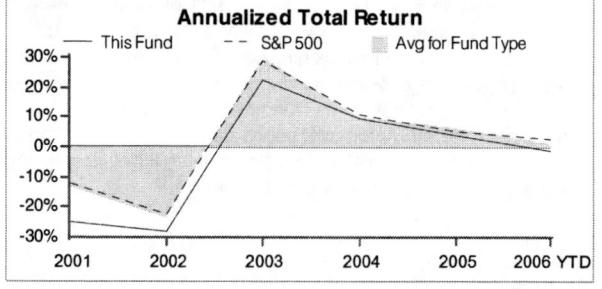

MFS Mass Investors Trust A (MITTX)

C-   **Fair**

Fund Family: MFS   **Phone:** (800) 343-2829

Address: 500 Boylston Street, Boston, MA 02116

Fund Type: GI - Growth and Income

Major Rating Factors: Disappointing performance is the major factor driving the C- (Fair) Weiss Investment Rating for MFS Mass Investors Trust A. The fund currently has a performance rating of D+ (Weak) based on an average return of 10.65% over the last three years and 0.79% over the last six months. Factored into the performance evaluation is an expense ratio of 0.93% (low) and a 5.8% front-end load that is levied at the time of purchase.

The fund's risk rating is currently B- (Good). It carries a beta of 0.94, meaning that its performance tracks fairly well with that of the overall stock market. Volatility, as measured by both the semi-deviation and a drawdown factor, is considered low.

Nicole Zatlyn currently receives a manager quality ranking of 56 (0=worst, 99=best). This fund offers only a moderate level of risk but investors looking for strong performance are still waiting.

Services Offered: Automated phone transactions, check writing, bank draft capabilities, an IRA investment plan, a 401K investment plan, wire transfers and a systematic withdrawal plan.

Data Date	Weiss Investment Rating	Net Assets ($Mil)	NAV	Perfor-mance Rating/Pts	Total Return Y-T-D	Risk Rating/Pts
6-06	C-	3,227	18.59	D+ / 2.7	0.79%	B- / 7.7
2005	D	3,308	18.45	D+ / 2.5	7.29%	B- / 7.0
2004	C-	3,425	17.26	C- / 3.1	11.51%	C+ / 6.4
2003	C-	3,624	15.62	D / 1.7	22.14%	C+ / 6.4
2002	C+	3,565	12.87	C- / 4.2	-22.00%	C+ / 6.7
2001	C	5,732	16.58	D / 1.6	-16.24%	C+ / 6.6

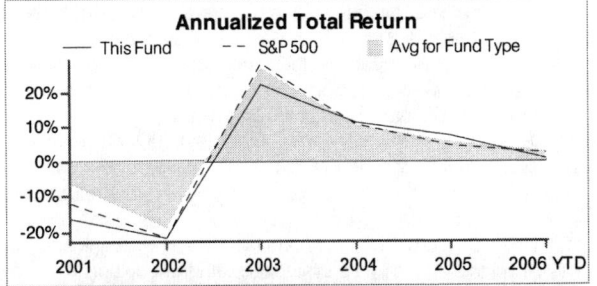

Annualized Total Return

MFS Total Return Fund A (MSFRX)

C-   **Fair**

Fund Family: MFS   **Phone:** (800) 343-2829

Address: 500 Boylston Street, Boston, MA 02116

Fund Type: BA - Balanced

Major Rating Factors: Disappointing performance is the major factor driving the C- (Fair) Weiss Investment Rating for MFS Total Return Fund A. The fund currently has a performance rating of D (Weak) based on an average return of 8.41% over the last three years and 1.79% over the last six months. Factored into the performance evaluation is an expense ratio of 0.91% (low) and a 4.8% front-end load that is levied at the time of purchase.

The fund's risk rating is currently B+ (Good). It carries a beta of 0.97, meaning that its performance tracks fairly well with that of the overall stock market. Volatility, as measured by both the semi-deviation and a drawdown factor, is considered very low.

Brooks Taylor currently receives a manager quality ranking of 67 (0=worst, 99=best). This fund offers only a moderate level of risk but investors looking for strong performance are still waiting.

Services Offered: Automated phone transactions, check writing, bank draft capabilities, an IRA investment plan, a 401K investment plan, wire transfers and a systematic withdrawal plan.

Data Date	Weiss Investment Rating	Net Assets ($Mil)	NAV	Perfor-mance Rating/Pts	Total Return Y-T-D	Risk Rating/Pts
6-06	C-	7,182	15.46	D / 1.6	1.79%	B+ / 9.1
2005	D+	6,995	15.37	E+ / 0.8	3.31%	B+ / 9.2
2004	B	6,492	16.00	C / 5.3	11.14%	B / 8.6
2003	B+	5,931	15.10	C+ / 6.3	16.85%	B+ / 9.2
2002	A+	4,772	13.27	A- / 9.0	-5.56%	B+ / 9.7
2001	A+	4,541	14.48	B- / 7.2	-0.62%	B / 8.5

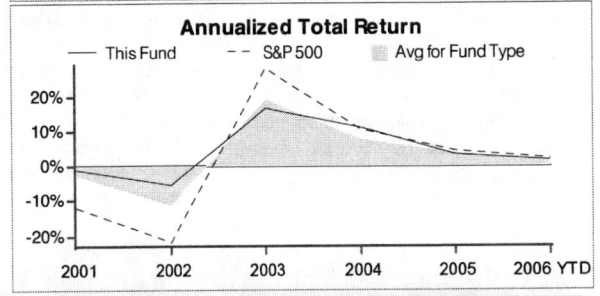

Annualized Total Return

MFS Value Fund A (MEIAX)

B   **Good**

Fund Family: MFS   **Phone:** (800) 343-2829

Address: 500 Boylston Street, Boston, MA 02116

Fund Type: IN - Income

Major Rating Factors: MFS Value Fund A receives a Weiss Investment Rating of B (Good). The fund currently has a performance rating of C (Fair) based on an average return of 14.62% over the last three years and 6.03% over the last six months. Factored into the performance evaluation is an expense ratio of 1.19% (average) and a 5.8% front-end load that is levied at the time of purchase.

The fund's risk rating is currently B (Good). It carries a beta of 0.84, meaning the fund's expected move will be 8.4% for every 10% move in the market. Volatility, as measured by both the semi-deviation and a drawdown factor, is considered low.

Steven R. Gorham has been running the fund for 4 years and currently receives a manager quality ranking of 91 (0=worst, 99=best). If you desire an average level of risk, then this fund may be an option.

Services Offered: Automated phone transactions, check writing, bank draft capabilities, an IRA investment plan, a 401K investment plan, wire transfers and a systematic withdrawal plan.

Data Date	Weiss Investment Rating	Net Assets ($Mil)	NAV	Perfor-mance Rating/Pts	Total Return Y-T-D	Risk Rating/Pts
6-06	B	4,819	24.41	C / 5.5	6.03%	B / 8.9
2005	C-	4,627	23.15	C- / 3.1	6.22%	B- / 7.4
2004	C+	3,859	23.14	C+ / 6.1	15.08%	C+ / 6.4
2003	C+	3,303	20.34	C / 5.3	24.70%	B- / 7.5
2002	B+	2,049	16.52	B+ / 8.3	-13.70%	B / 8.3
2001	B+	1,284	19.42	B- / 7.4	-7.79%	C+ / 6.7

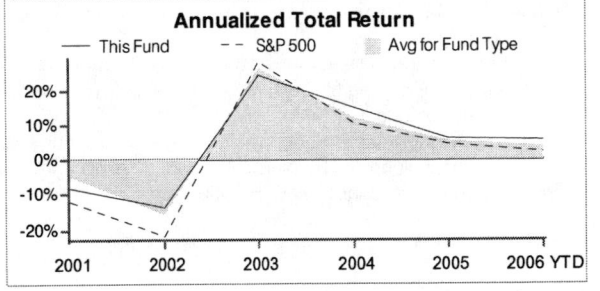

Annualized Total Return

Morgan Stanley Dividend Gr Sec A (DIVAX)   E-   Very Weak

Fund Family: Morgan Stanley   **Phone:** (800) 869-6397
Address: 1221 Avenue of the Americas, New York, NY 10020
Fund Type: GI - Growth and Income

Major Rating Factors: Morgan Stanley Dividend Gr Sec A has adopted a very risky asset allocation strategy and currently receives an overall Weiss Investment Rating of E- (Very Weak). The fund has a high level of volatility, as measured by both semi-deviation and drawdown factors. It carries a beta of 0.93, meaning that its performance tracks fairly well with that of the overall stock market. Unfortunately, the high level of risk (D-, Weak) failed to pay off as investors endured poor performance.

The fund's performance rating is currently D (Weak). It has registered an average return of 9.27% over the last three years but is down -0.25% over the last six months. Factored into the performance evaluation is an expense ratio of 0.80% (very low), a 5.3% front-end load that is levied at the time of purchase and a 1.0% back-end load levied at the time of sale.

Sean Aurigemma has been running the fund for 3 years and currently receives a manager quality ranking of 41 (0=worst, 99=best). If you can tolerate very high levels of risk in the hope of improved future returns, holding this fund may be an option.

Services Offered: Automated phone transactions, bank draft capabilities, an IRA investment plan and a systematic withdrawal plan.

Data Date	Weiss Investment Rating	Net Assets ($Mil)	NAV	Performance Rating/Pts	Total Return Y-T-D	Risk Rating/Pts
6-06	E-	3,114	27.61	D / 1.7	-0.25%	D- / 1.0
2005	E-	3,536	33.04	D / 2.1	5.13%	C- / 3.7
2004	D+	102	36.97	C- / 3.2	8.54%	C / 4.5
2003	C	122	41.14	C / 4.7	27.63%	C+ / 5.7
2002	C+	115	35.82	C+ / 6.0	-18.72%	C+ / 6.5
2001	C+	152	45.93	C- / 3.0	-8.51%	C+ / 6.1

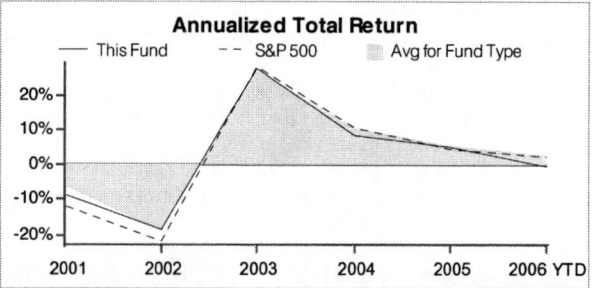

Annualized Total Return

Muhlenkamp Fund (MUHLX)   C   Fair

Fund Family: Muhlenkamp   **Phone:** (800) 860-3863
Address: P.O. Box 598, Wexford, PA 15090
Fund Type: GI - Growth and Income

Major Rating Factors: Middle of the road best describes Muhlenkamp Fund whose Weiss Investment Rating is currently a C (Fair). The fund currently has a performance rating of C (Fair) based on an average return of 16.44% over the last three years and -3.74% over the last six months. Factored into the performance evaluation is an expense ratio of 1.06% (low) and a 2.0% back-end load levied at the time of sale.

The fund's risk rating is currently C+ (Fair). It carries a beta of 1.43, meaning it is expected to move 14.3% for every 10% move in the market. Volatility, as measured by both the semi-deviation and a drawdown factor, is considered low.

Ronald Muhlenkamp has been running the fund for 18 years and currently receives a manager quality ranking of 68 (0=worst, 99=best). If you desire an average level of risk, then this fund may be an option.

Services Offered: Bank draft capabilities, an IRA investment plan, a 401K investment plan, a Keogh investment plan and a systematic withdrawal plan.

Data Date	Weiss Investment Rating	Net Assets ($Mil)	NAV	Performance Rating/Pts	Total Return Y-T-D	Risk Rating/Pts
6-06	C	3,056	81.28	C / 5.4	-3.74%	C+ / 6.9
2005	A-	3,022	84.44	B+ / 8.5	7.88%	C+ / 6.9
2004	B	1,758	78.97	A- / 9.1	24.51%	C / 4.8
2003	B+	1,157	63.51	A- / 9.1	48.08%	C+ / 6.1
2002	B	642	42.89	B+ / 8.8	-19.92%	C+ / 6.7
2001	C+	539	53.56	A / 9.5	9.35%	E- / 0.0

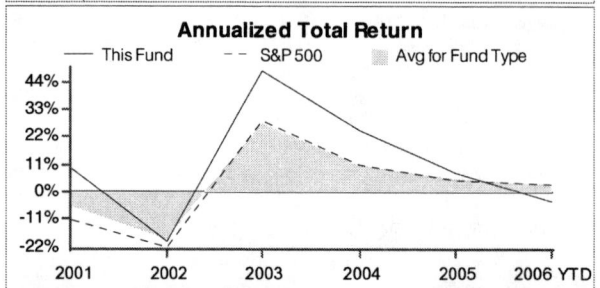

Annualized Total Return

Mutual Beacon Z (BEGRX)   B-   Good

Fund Family: Franklin Templeton Institutional Gr   **Phone:** (800) 321-8563
Address: 777 Mariners Island Blvd., San Mateo, CA 94403
Fund Type: GI - Growth and Income

Major Rating Factors: Mutual Beacon Z receives a Weiss Investment Rating of B- (Good). The fund currently has a performance rating of C+ (Fair) based on an average return of 16.00% over the last three years and 6.74% over the last six months. Factored into the performance evaluation is an expense ratio of 0.84% (very low).

The fund's risk rating is currently B- (Good). It carries a beta of 0.74, meaning the fund's expected move will be 7.4% for every 10% move in the market. Volatility, as measured by both the semi-deviation and a drawdown factor, is considered low.

Charles Lahr has been running the fund for 2 years and currently receives a manager quality ranking of 97 (0=worst, 99=best). If you desire an average level of risk, then this fund may be an option.

Services Offered: Automated phone transactions, bank draft capabilities, an IRA investment plan, a 401K investment plan, a Keogh investment plan, wire transfers and a systematic withdrawal plan.

Data Date	Weiss Investment Rating	Net Assets ($Mil)	NAV	Performance Rating/Pts	Total Return Y-T-D	Risk Rating/Pts
6-06	B-	3,535	16.11	C+ / 6.9	6.74%	B- / 7.5
2005	B-	3,434	15.52	C+ / 5.7	9.25%	B- / 7.7
2004	B+	3,360	15.94	B- / 7.4	14.52%	B- / 7.2
2003	A-	3,012	14.39	B / 8.1	29.44%	B- / 7.8
2002	A	2,619	11.31	B+ / 8.9	-11.05%	B / 8.5
2001	A+	3,092	13.05	B+ / 8.9	6.11%	B- / 7.3

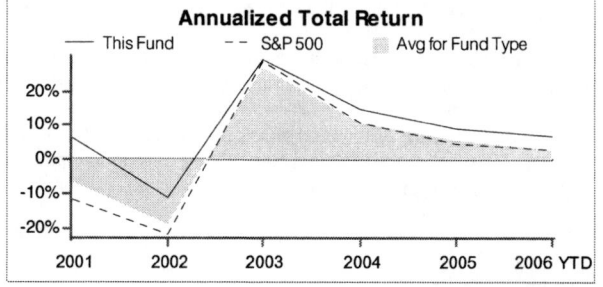

Annualized Total Return

Mutual Discovery A (TEDIX)

A+   Excellent

Fund Family: Franklin Templeton Investments   **Phone:** (800) 342-5236
Address: 777 Mariners Island Blvd., San Mateo, CA 94404
Fund Type: GL - Global

Major Rating Factors: Strong performance is the major factor driving the A+ (Excellent) Weiss Investment Rating for Mutual Discovery A. The fund currently has a performance rating of B (Good) based on an average return of 20.58% over the last three years and 8.12% over the last six months. Factored into the performance evaluation is an expense ratio of 1.42% (average) and a 5.8% front-end load that is levied at the time of purchase.

The fund's risk rating is currently B (Good). It carries a beta of 0.65, meaning the fund's expected move will be 6.5% for every 10% move in the market. Volatility, as measured by both the semi-deviation and a drawdown factor, is considered low.

Anne E. Gudefin, CFA has been running the fund for 1 year and currently receives a manager quality ranking of 89 (0=worst, 99=best). If you desire only a moderate level of risk and strong performance, then this fund is an excellent option.

Services Offered: Automated phone transactions, bank draft capabilities, an IRA investment plan, a 401K investment plan, wire transfers and a systematic withdrawal plan.

Data Date	Weiss Investment Rating	Net Assets ($Mil)	NAV	Performance Rating/Pts	Total Return Y-T-D	Risk Rating/Pts
6-06	A+	4,695	27.63	B / 8.0	8.12%	B / 8.1
2005	A	3,545	26.04	B- / 7.5	15.29%	B / 8.2
2004	A-	2,108	24.08	B / 8.1	18.98%	B- / 7.3
2003	A-	1,341	20.66	B / 7.8	31.13%	B / 8.3
2002	B+	931	16.06	B+ / 8.3	-9.39%	B / 8.2
2001	A+	913	18.08	B+ / 8.6	0.87%	B / 8.1

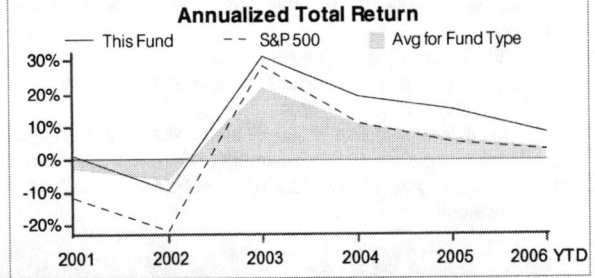

Mutual Qualified Z (MQIFX)

A   Excellent

Fund Family: Franklin Templeton Institutional Gr   **Phone:** (800) 321-8563
Address: 777 Mariners Island Blvd., San Mateo, CA 94403
Fund Type: GI - Growth and Income

Major Rating Factors: Strong performance is the major factor driving the A (Excellent) Weiss Investment Rating for Mutual Qualified Z. The fund currently has a performance rating of B- (Good) based on an average return of 17.39% over the last three years and 6.63% over the last six months. Factored into the performance evaluation is an expense ratio of 0.81% (very low).

The fund's risk rating is currently B (Good). It carries a beta of 0.82, meaning the fund's expected move will be 8.2% for every 10% move in the market. Volatility, as measured by both the semi-deviation and a drawdown factor, is considered low.

Anne E, CFA has been running the fund for 6 years and currently receives a manager quality ranking of 97 (0=worst, 99=best). If you desire only a moderate level of risk and strong performance, then this fund is an excellent option.

Services Offered: Automated phone transactions, bank draft capabilities, an IRA investment plan, a 401K investment plan, a Keogh investment plan, wire transfers and a systematic withdrawal plan.

Data Date	Weiss Investment Rating	Net Assets ($Mil)	NAV	Performance Rating/Pts	Total Return Y-T-D	Risk Rating/Pts
6-06	A	3,817	20.83	B- / 7.4	6.63%	B / 8.6
2005	B	3,650	19.81	C+ / 6.8	11.26%	B / 8.5
2004	A-	3,420	19.49	B / 7.7	16.64%	B- / 7.4
2003	A-	2,984	17.87	B / 8.2	30.50%	B / 7.6
2002	A-	2,558	13.95	B+ / 8.8	-12.70%	B / 8.3
2001	A+	3,022	16.49	B+ / 8.9	8.21%	C+ / 6.9

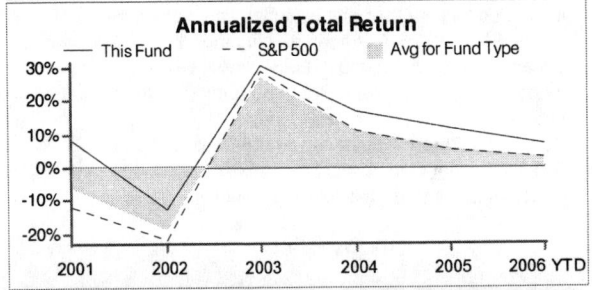

Mutual Shares Z (MUTHX)

B+   Good

Fund Family: Franklin Templeton Institutional Gr   **Phone:** (800) 321-8563
Address: 777 Mariners Island Blvd., San Mateo, CA 94403
Fund Type: GI - Growth and Income

Major Rating Factors: Mutual Shares Z receives a Weiss Investment Rating of B+ (Good). The fund currently has a performance rating of C+ (Fair) based on an average return of 14.96% over the last three years and 5.45% over the last six months. Factored into the performance evaluation is an expense ratio of 0.76% (very low).

The fund's risk rating is currently B+ (Good). It carries a beta of 0.72, meaning the fund's expected move will be 7.2% for every 10% move in the market. Volatility, as measured by both the semi-deviation and a drawdown factor, is considered very low.

Debbie Turner, CFA has been running the fund for 13 years and currently receives a manager quality ranking of 95 (0=worst, 99=best). If you desire an average level of risk, then this fund may be an option.

Services Offered: Automated phone transactions, bank draft capabilities, an IRA investment plan, a 401K investment plan, a Keogh investment plan, wire transfers and a systematic withdrawal plan.

Data Date	Weiss Investment Rating	Net Assets ($Mil)	NAV	Performance Rating/Pts	Total Return Y-T-D	Risk Rating/Pts
6-06	B+	9,780	24.91	C+ / 6.4	5.45%	B+ / 9.0
2005	B+	8,950	23.95	C / 5.5	10.39%	B+ / 9.2
2004	B+	7,240	23.05	B- / 7.0	13.89%	B- / 7.7
2003	A-	5,465	20.98	B / 7.8	26.62%	B / 8.0
2002	A	4,664	16.84	B+ / 8.9	-10.89%	B / 8.5
2001	A+	5,465	19.44	B+ / 8.8	6.32%	B- / 7.0

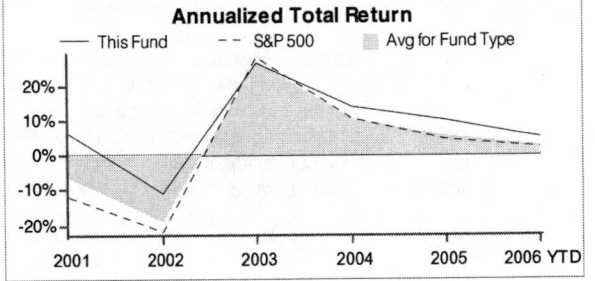

Neuberger Berman Genesis Tr (NBGEX)

B   **Good**

Fund Family: Neuberger Berman   **Phone:** (800) 877-9700
Address: 605 Third Avenue, New York, NY 10158
Fund Type: SC - Small Cap

Major Rating Factors: Strong performance is the major factor driving the B (Good) Weiss Investment Rating for Neuberger Berman Genesis Tr. The fund currently has a performance rating of B- (Good) based on an average return of 19.12% over the last three years and 2.04% over the last six months. Factored into the performance evaluation is an expense ratio of 1.11% (low).

The fund's risk rating is currently C+ (Fair). It carries a beta of 0.68, meaning the fund's expected move will be 6.8% for every 10% move in the market. Volatility, as measured by both the semi-deviation and a drawdown factor, is considered low.

Judith M. Vale currently receives a manager quality ranking of 94 (0=worst, 99=best). If you desire only a moderate level of risk and strong performance, then this fund is an excellent option.

Services Offered: Automated phone transactions, bank draft capabilities, an IRA investment plan, a 401K investment plan, a Keogh investment plan, wire transfers and a systematic withdrawal plan. However, the fund is currently closed to new investors.

Data Date	Weiss Investment Rating	Net Assets ($Mil)	NAV	Performance Rating/Pts	Total Return Y-T-D	Risk Rating/Pts
6-06	B	6,761	49.54	B- / 7.5	2.04%	C+ / 6.8
2005	A+	6,698	48.55	B / 8.1	16.30%	B / 8.5
2004	A	4,773	42.67	B+ / 8.6	18.68%	B- / 7.1
2003	A+	3,373	37.03	A- / 9.0	31.65%	B- / 7.8
2002	A+	2,305	28.14	A+ / 9.7	-2.99%	B+ / 9.3
2001	A+	1,624	29.11	A / 9.5	12.08%	C+ / 6.5

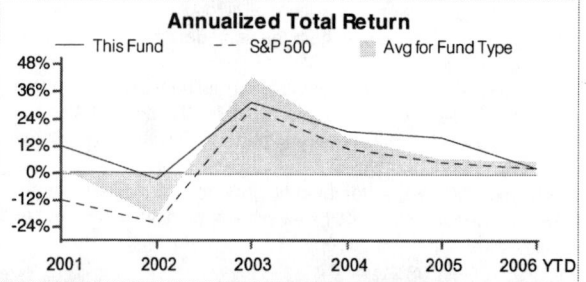

Annualized Total Return

Neuberger Berman Partners Inv (NPRTX)

B-   **Good**

Fund Family: Neuberger Berman   **Phone:** (800) 877-9700
Address: 605 Third Avenue, New York, NY 10158
Fund Type: GR - Growth

Major Rating Factors: Strong performance is the major factor driving the B- (Good) Weiss Investment Rating for Neuberger Berman Partners Inv. The fund currently has a performance rating of B- (Good) based on an average return of 17.80% over the last three years and 1.11% over the last six months. Factored into the performance evaluation is an expense ratio of 1.70% (above average).

The fund's risk rating is currently C+ (Fair). It carries a beta of 1.30, meaning it is expected to move 13.0% for every 10% move in the market. Volatility, as measured by both the semi-deviation and a drawdown factor, is considered low.

S. Basu Mullick has been running the fund for 8 years and currently receives a manager quality ranking of 86 (0=worst, 99=best). If you desire only a moderate level of risk and strong performance, then this fund is an excellent option.

Services Offered: Automated phone transactions, bank draft capabilities, an IRA investment plan, a 401K investment plan, a Keogh investment plan, wire transfers and a systematic withdrawal plan.

Data Date	Weiss Investment Rating	Net Assets ($Mil)	NAV	Performance Rating/Pts	Total Return Y-T-D	Risk Rating/Pts
6-06	B-	2,136	28.36	B- / 7.1	1.11%	C+ / 6.9
2005	A+	1,995	28.05	B+ / 8.7	17.99%	B- / 7.8
2004	C+	1,138	25.09	B- / 7.2	19.21%	C / 5.2
2003	C+	1,288	21.19	C+ / 6.4	35.87%	C+ / 6.2
2002	C+	1,185	15.60	C / 5.5	-24.82%	C+ / 6.4
2001	C+	1,655	20.79	C+ / 6.2	-3.02%	C+ / 5.9

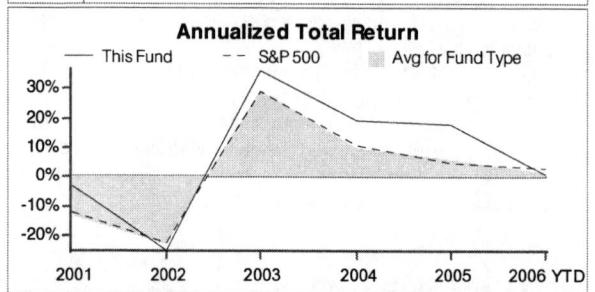

Annualized Total Return

Nicholas Fund (NICSX)

C-   **Fair**

Fund Family: Nicholas Funds   **Phone:** (800) 544-6547
Address: 700 North Water Street, Milwaukee, WI 53202
Fund Type: GR - Growth

Major Rating Factors: Middle of the road best describes Nicholas Fund whose Weiss Investment Rating is currently a C- (Fair). The fund currently has a performance rating of C- (Fair) based on an average return of 11.02% over the last three years and 1.03% over the last six months. Factored into the performance evaluation is an expense ratio of 0.78% (very low).

The fund's risk rating is currently B- (Good). It carries a beta of 0.89, meaning the fund's expected move will be 8.9% for every 10% move in the market. Volatility, as measured by both the semi-deviation and a drawdown factor, is considered low.

Albert O. Nicholas,CFA has been running the fund for 37 years and currently receives a manager quality ranking of 65 (0=worst, 99=best). If you desire an average level of risk, then this fund may be an option.

Services Offered: Automated phone transactions, bank draft capabilities, an IRA investment plan, a 401K investment plan, a Keogh investment plan, wire transfers and a systematic withdrawal plan.

Data Date	Weiss Investment Rating	Net Assets ($Mil)	NAV	Performance Rating/Pts	Total Return Y-T-D	Risk Rating/Pts
6-06	C-	2,373	57.68	C- / 3.3	1.03%	B- / 7.5
2005	C	2,400	58.20	C- / 3.8	5.60%	B- / 7.3
2004	C	2,425	60.42	C / 4.9	11.80%	C+ / 6.5
2003	C+	2,437	54.47	C / 4.6	28.66%	C+ / 6.5
2002	C	2,255	42.41	C / 5.1	-21.85%	C+ / 5.7
2001	C	3,141	54.47	D+ / 2.9	-10.98%	C+ / 5.9

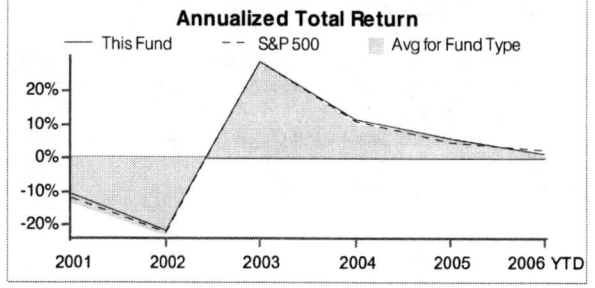

Annualized Total Return

Oppenheimer Capital Appr A (OPTFX) D Weak

Fund Family: OppenheimerFunds **Phone:** (800) 525-7048
Address: P.O. Box 5270, Denver, CO 80217
Fund Type: GR - Growth
Major Rating Factors: Disappointing performance is the major factor driving the D (Weak) Weiss Investment Rating for Oppenheimer Capital Appr A. The fund currently has a performance rating of D- (Weak) based on an average return of 8.80% over the last three years and -0.37% over the last six months. Factored into the performance evaluation is an expense ratio of 1.06% (low) and a 5.8% front-end load that is levied at the time of purchase.

The fund's risk rating is currently B- (Good). It carries a beta of 1.07, meaning that its performance tracks fairly well with that of the overall stock market. Volatility, as measured by both the semi-deviation and a drawdown factor, is considered low.

Marc L. Baylin, CFA has been running the fund for 1 year and currently receives a manager quality ranking of 27 (0=worst, 99=best). This fund offers only a moderate level of risk but investors looking for strong performance are still waiting.

Services Offered: Automated phone transactions, bank draft capabilities, an IRA investment plan, a 401K investment plan and a systematic withdrawal plan.

Data Date	Weiss Investment Rating	Net Assets ($Mil)	NAV	Perfor-mance Rating/Pts	Total Return Y-T-D	Risk Rating/Pts
6-06	D	5,385	42.75	D- / 1.5	-0.37%	B- / 7.9
2005	D	5,711	42.91	D / 2.0	4.70%	C+ / 6.9
2004	D-	5,678	41.22	D- / 1.1	6.46%	C / 4.8
2003	D+	4,925	38.72	D+ / 2.7	29.46%	C / 4.7
2002	C-	3,504	29.91	C- / 3.8	-26.26%	C / 5.2
2001	C-	3,345	40.56	C+ / 6.7	-12.69%	E+ / 0.8

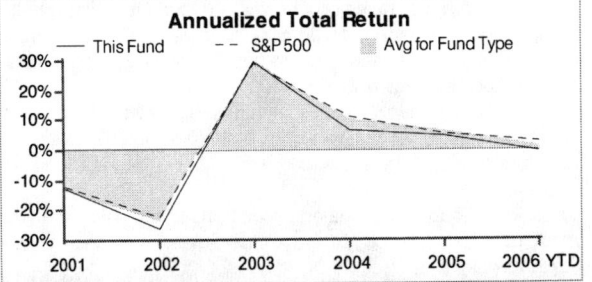

Oppenheimer Capital Income Fd A (OPPEX) D+ Weak

Fund Family: OppenheimerFunds **Phone:** (800) 525-7048
Address: P.O. Box 5270, Denver, CO 80217
Fund Type: IN - Income
Major Rating Factors: Disappointing performance is the major factor driving the D+ (Weak) Weiss Investment Rating for Oppenheimer Capital Income Fd A. The fund currently has a performance rating of D (Weak) based on an average return of 8.93% over the last three years and 2.48% over the last six months. Factored into the performance evaluation is an expense ratio of 0.89% (low) and a 5.8% front-end load that is levied at the time of purchase.

The fund's risk rating is currently B (Good). It carries a beta of 0.58, meaning the fund's expected move will be 5.8% for every 10% move in the market. Volatility, as measured by both the semi-deviation and a drawdown factor, is considered low.

Michael S. Levine has been running the fund for 7 years and currently receives a manager quality ranking of 72 (0=worst, 99=best). This fund offers only a moderate level of risk but investors looking for strong performance are still waiting.

Services Offered: Automated phone transactions, bank draft capabilities, an IRA investment plan, a 401K investment plan, wire transfers and a systematic withdrawal plan.

Data Date	Weiss Investment Rating	Net Assets ($Mil)	NAV	Perfor-mance Rating/Pts	Total Return Y-T-D	Risk Rating/Pts
6-06	D+	2,554	11.96	D / 1.8	2.48%	B / 8.4
2005	C-	2,649	11.82	D / 2.2	2.43%	B / 8.6
2004	C+	2,534	12.46	C / 5.5	10.28%	C+ / 5.9
2003	B-	2,377	12.14	B- / 7.2	33.47%	C+ / 6.5
2002	B+	1,802	9.52	B / 8.1	-16.16%	B- / 7.6
2001	B-	2,377	11.89	C+ / 5.7	-0.19%	B- / 7.2

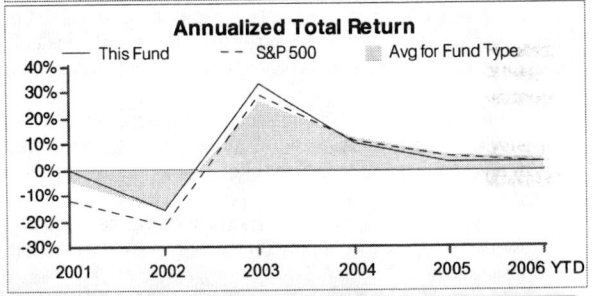

Oppenheimer Equity A (OEQAX) D- Weak

Fund Family: OppenheimerFunds **Phone:** (800) 525-7048
Address: P.O. Box 5270, Denver, CO 80217
Fund Type: GI - Growth and Income
Major Rating Factors: Disappointing performance is the major factor driving the D- (Weak) Weiss Investment Rating for Oppenheimer Equity A. The fund currently has a performance rating of D+ (Weak) based on an average return of 10.87% over the last three years and -0.57% over the last six months. Factored into the performance evaluation is an expense ratio of 0.89% (low) and a 5.8% front-end load that is levied at the time of purchase.

The fund's risk rating is currently C+ (Fair). It carries a beta of 1.08, meaning that its performance tracks fairly well with that of the overall stock market. Volatility, as measured by both the semi-deviation and a drawdown factor, is considered low.

Chris Leavy has been running the fund for 6 years and currently receives a manager quality ranking of 43 (0=worst, 99=best). This fund offers only a moderate level of risk but investors looking for strong performance are still waiting.

Services Offered: Automated phone transactions, bank draft capabilities, an IRA investment plan, a 401K investment plan, wire transfers and a systematic withdrawal plan.

Data Date	Weiss Investment Rating	Net Assets ($Mil)	NAV	Perfor-mance Rating/Pts	Total Return Y-T-D	Risk Rating/Pts
6-06	D-	2,249	10.45	D+ / 2.5	-0.57%	C+ / 5.9
2005	D	2,317	10.51	C- / 3.2	8.16%	C+ / 6.2
2004	C	2,296	10.84	C / 4.3	10.73%	C+ / 6.6
2003	C	2,287	10.77	C- / 4.1	26.26%	C+ / 6.6
2002	C+	1,934	8.53	C / 5.0	-17.80%	C+ / 6.6
2001	C+	2,667	10.40	C- / 3.7	-10.43%	C+ / 5.9

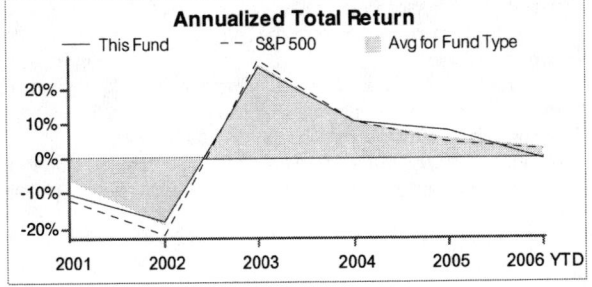

Oppenheimer Global Fund A (OPPAX)

A-   Excellent

Fund Family: OppenheimerFunds   **Phone:** (800) 525-7048
Address: P.O. Box 5270, Denver, CO 80217
Fund Type: GL - Global

Major Rating Factors: Strong performance is the major factor driving the A-(Excellent) Weiss Investment Rating for Oppenheimer Global Fund A. The fund currently has a performance rating of B (Good) based on an average return of 21.58% over the last three years and 3.70% over the last six months. Factored into the performance evaluation is an expense ratio of 1.12% (low), a 5.8% front-end load that is levied at the time of purchase and a 2.0% back-end load levied at the time of sale.

The fund's risk rating is currently B- (Good). It carries a beta of 1.01, meaning that its performance tracks fairly well with that of the overall stock market. Volatility, as measured by both the semi-deviation and a drawdown factor, is considered low.

Rajeev Bhaman, CFA has been running the fund for 2 years and currently receives a manager quality ranking of 30 (0=worst, 99=best). If you desire only a moderate level of risk and strong performance, then this fund is an excellent option.

Services Offered: Automated phone transactions, bank draft capabilities, an IRA investment plan, a 401K investment plan, wire transfers and a systematic withdrawal plan.

Data Date	Weiss Investment Rating	Net Assets ($Mil)	NAV	Perfor-mance Rating/Pts	Total Return Y-T-D	Risk Rating/Pts
6-06	A-	11,709	69.17	B / 7.9	3.70%	B- / 7.6
2005	A	10,609	66.70	B+ / 8.3	13.83%	B- / 7.4
2004	C+	9,291	60.77	B- / 7.5	18.67%	C / 5.1
2003	C+	7,182	51.50	C+ / 6.5	43.07%	C+ / 5.7
2002	C	4,681	36.24	C / 4.8	-22.45%	C / 5.2
2001	C+	5,807	46.73	B+ / 8.6	-11.80%	D- / 1.1

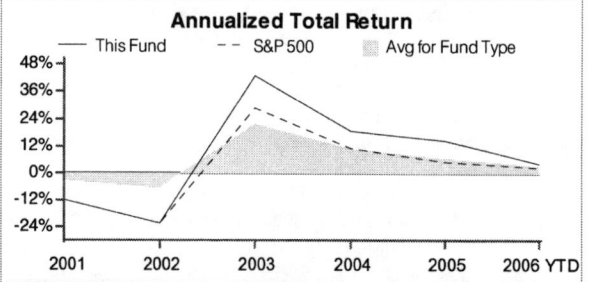

Oppenheimer Global Opportunities A (OPGIX)

B-   Good

Fund Family: OppenheimerFunds   **Phone:** (800) 525-7048
Address: P.O. Box 5270, Denver, CO 80217
Fund Type: GL - Global

Major Rating Factors: Exceptional performance is the major factor driving the B- (Good) Weiss Investment Rating for Oppenheimer Global Opportunities A. The fund currently has a performance rating of A (Excellent) based on an average return of 29.23% over the last three years and 5.58% over the last six months. Factored into the performance evaluation is an expense ratio of 1.13% (low), a 5.8% front-end load that is levied at the time of purchase and a 2.0% back-end load levied at the time of sale.

The fund's risk rating is currently C (Fair). It carries a beta of 1.36, meaning it is expected to move 13.6% for every 10% move in the market. Volatility, as measured by both the semi-deviation and a drawdown factor, is considered average.

Frank V. Jennings, PhD has been running the fund for 11 years and currently receives a manager quality ranking of 23 (0=worst, 99=best). If you desire an average level of risk and strong performance, then this fund is a good option.

Services Offered: Automated phone transactions, bank draft capabilities, an IRA investment plan, a 401K investment plan, wire transfers and a systematic withdrawal plan.

Data Date	Weiss Investment Rating	Net Assets ($Mil)	NAV	Perfor-mance Rating/Pts	Total Return Y-T-D	Risk Rating/Pts
6-06	B-	2,869	39.00	A / 9.3	5.58%	C / 4.5
2005	B	2,183	36.94	A+ / 9.6	17.43%	C / 4.6
2004	B-	1,885	33.25	A- / 9.2	29.88%	C- / 3.7
2003	C	1,400	25.60	C+ / 6.9	57.25%	C- / 4.1
2002	C-	916	16.28	D+ / 2.9	-26.99%	C- / 4.1
2001	C	1,353	22.59	B+ / 8.8	-16.32%	E- / 0.0

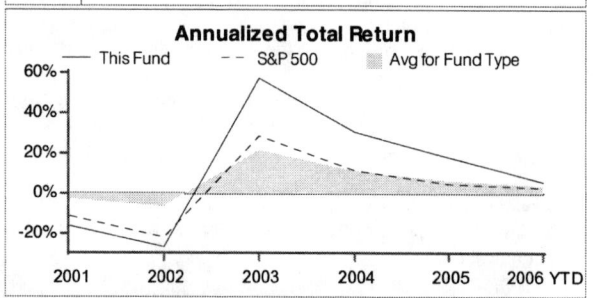

Oppenheimer Main St Fund A (MSIGX)

C   Fair

Fund Family: OppenheimerFunds   **Phone:** (800) 525-7048
Address: P.O. Box 5270, Denver, CO 80217
Fund Type: GI - Growth and Income

Major Rating Factors: Middle of the road best describes Oppenheimer Main St Fund A whose Weiss Investment Rating is currently a C (Fair). The fund currently has a performance rating of C- (Fair) based on an average return of 11.13% over the last three years and 3.02% over the last six months. Factored into the performance evaluation is an expense ratio of 0.92% (low) and a 5.8% front-end load that is levied at the time of purchase.

The fund's risk rating is currently B (Good). It carries a beta of 0.97, meaning that its performance tracks fairly well with that of the overall stock market. Volatility, as measured by both the semi-deviation and a drawdown factor, is considered low.

Nikolaos Monoyios has been running the fund for 8 years and currently receives a manager quality ranking of 58 (0=worst, 99=best). If you desire an average level of risk, then this fund may be an option.

Services Offered: Automated phone transactions, bank draft capabilities, an IRA investment plan, a 401K investment plan and a systematic withdrawal plan.

Data Date	Weiss Investment Rating	Net Assets ($Mil)	NAV	Perfor-mance Rating/Pts	Total Return Y-T-D	Risk Rating/Pts
6-06	C	7,640	38.25	C- / 3.2	3.02%	B / 8.3
2005	D+	7,946	37.13	D+ / 2.4	5.74%	B- / 7.6
2004	C-	7,764	35.46	C- / 3.3	9.39%	C+ / 6.1
2003	C	7,886	32.80	C- / 4.0	26.95%	C+ / 6.6
2002	C+	6,043	26.00	C / 4.4	-19.42%	C+ / 6.6
2001	C	7,426	32.50	C- / 3.0	-10.46%	C+ / 6.0

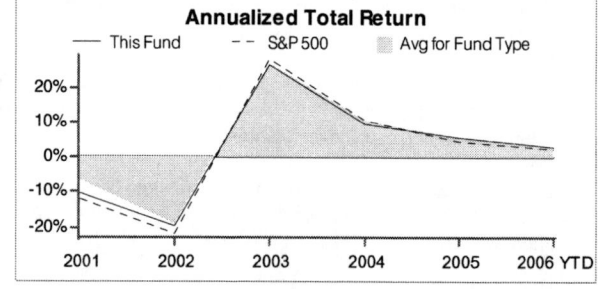

Oppenheimer Main St Oppty A (OMSOX)   C+   Fair

Fund Family: OppenheimerFunds   **Phone:** (800) 525-7048
Address: P.O. Box 5270, Denver, CO 80217
Fund Type: GR - Growth
Major Rating Factors: Middle of the road best describes Oppenheimer Main St Oppty A whose Weiss Investment Rating is currently a C+ (Fair). The fund currently has a performance rating of C (Fair) based on an average return of 14.95% over the last three years and 3.63% over the last six months. Factored into the performance evaluation is an expense ratio of 1.11% (low) and a 5.8% front-end load that is levied at the time of purchase.

The fund's risk rating is currently B- (Good). It carries a beta of 1.10, meaning it is expected to move 11.0% for every 10% move in the market. Volatility, as measured by both the semi-deviation and a drawdown factor, is considered low.

Nikolaos Monoyios has been running the fund for 6 years and currently receives a manager quality ranking of 81 (0=worst, 99=best). If you desire an average level of risk, then this fund may be an option.

Services Offered: Automated phone transactions, bank draft capabilities, an IRA investment plan, a 401K investment plan, wire transfers and a systematic withdrawal plan.

Data Date	Weiss Investment Rating	Net Assets ($Mil)	NAV	Performance Rating/Pts	Total Return Y-T-D	Risk Rating/Pts
6-06	C+	2,234	13.98	C / 5.4	3.63%	B- / 7.7
2005	C+	1,991	13.49	C / 5.5	6.84%	B- / 7.3
2004	C+	1,435	13.13	C+/ 6.7	12.66%	C+/ 6.0
2003	A	718	12.65	B+ / 8.8	40.56%	B- / 7.7
2002	U	335	9.00	U / --	-16.04%	U / --
2001	U	233	10.72	U / --	16.14%	U / --

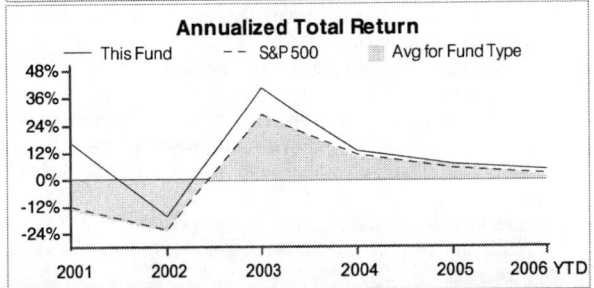

Oppenheimer Main St Small Cap A (OPMSX)   B-   Good

Fund Family: OppenheimerFunds   **Phone:** (800) 525-7048
Address: P.O. Box 5270, Denver, CO 80217
Fund Type: SC - Small Cap
Major Rating Factors: Strong performance is the major factor driving the B- (Good) Weiss Investment Rating for Oppenheimer Main St Small Cap A. The fund currently has a performance rating of B (Good) based on an average return of 21.13% over the last three years and 7.95% over the last six months. Factored into the performance evaluation is an expense ratio of 1.17% (low) and a 5.8% front-end load that is levied at the time of purchase.

The fund's risk rating is currently C+ (Fair). It carries a beta of 0.93, meaning that its performance tracks fairly well with that of the overall stock market. Volatility, as measured by both the semi-deviation and a drawdown factor, is considered low.

Mark Zavanelli, CFA has been running the fund for 7 years and currently receives a manager quality ranking of 85 (0=worst, 99=best). If you desire only a moderate level of risk and strong performance, then this fund is an excellent option.

Services Offered: Automated phone transactions, bank draft capabilities, an IRA investment plan, a 401K investment plan, wire transfers and a systematic withdrawal plan.

Data Date	Weiss Investment Rating	Net Assets ($Mil)	NAV	Performance Rating/Pts	Total Return Y-T-D	Risk Rating/Pts
6-06	B-	2,576	22.27	B / 8.0	7.95%	C+/ 6.0
2005	B-	1,819	20.63	B / 8.1	10.00%	C+/ 5.6
2004	B+	1,361	20.08	B+ / 8.5	19.18%	C+/ 5.7
2003	A	911	18.56	A- / 9.1	46.49%	B- / 7.4
2002	B+	492	12.67	B / 8.2	-15.98%	B- / 7.9
2001	U	381	15.08	U / --	12.93%	U / --

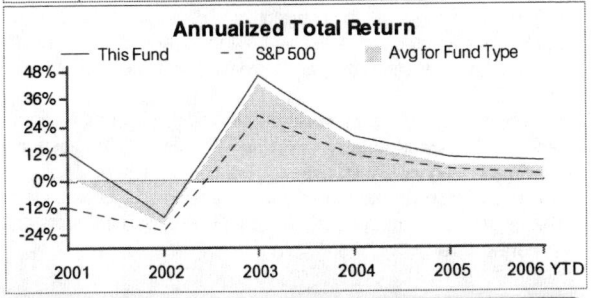

Oppenheimer Quest Balanced A (QVGIX)   D   Weak

Fund Family: OppenheimerFunds   **Phone:** (800) 525-7048
Address: P.O. Box 5270, Denver, CO 80217
Fund Type: BA - Balanced
Major Rating Factors: Disappointing performance is the major factor driving the D (Weak) Weiss Investment Rating for Oppenheimer Quest Balanced A. The fund currently has a performance rating of D- (Weak) based on an average return of 8.80% over the last three years and 0.28% over the last six months. Factored into the performance evaluation is an expense ratio of 1.17% (low), a 5.8% front-end load that is levied at the time of purchase and a 1.0% back-end load levied at the time of sale.

The fund's risk rating is currently B (Good). It carries a beta of 1.40, meaning it is expected to move 14.0% for every 10% move in the market. Volatility, as measured by both the semi-deviation and a drawdown factor, is considered low.

Colin Glinsman, CPA has been running the fund for 14 years and currently receives a manager quality ranking of 44 (0=worst, 99=best). This fund offers only a moderate level of risk but investors looking for strong performance are still waiting.

Services Offered: Automated phone transactions, bank draft capabilities, an IRA investment plan, a 401K investment plan and a systematic withdrawal plan.

Data Date	Weiss Investment Rating	Net Assets ($Mil)	NAV	Performance Rating/Pts	Total Return Y-T-D	Risk Rating/Pts
6-06	D	3,096	17.81	D- / 1.3	0.28%	B / 8.3
2005	D+	3,391	17.86	D / 2.1	2.76%	B- / 7.8
2004	C-	3,177	18.04	C- / 3.4	10.29%	C / 5.1
2003	C+	2,484	16.37	C+/ 6.9	30.56%	C+/ 6.4
2002	B	1,733	12.63	B- / 7.3	-19.92%	B- / 7.5
2001	A	1,989	16.01	B- / 7.4	3.20%	B- / 7.9

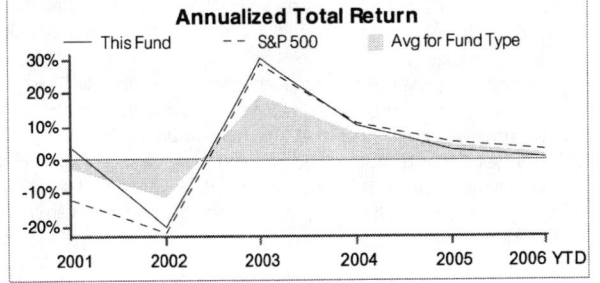

Oppenheimer Small & Mid Cap Value A (QVSCX)   A   Excellent

Fund Family: OppenheimerFunds   **Phone:** (800) 525-7048
Address: P.O. Box 5270, Denver, CO 80217
Fund Type: SC - Small Cap
Major Rating Factors: Strong performance is the major factor driving the A (Excellent) Weiss Investment Rating for Oppenheimer Small & Mid Cap Value A. The fund currently has a performance rating of B+ (Good) based on an average return of 24.82% over the last three years and 4.84% over the last six months. Factored into the performance evaluation is an expense ratio of 1.23% (average), a 5.8% front-end load that is levied at the time of purchase and a 2.0% back-end load levied at the time of sale.

The fund's risk rating is currently B- (Good). It carries a beta of 0.77, meaning the fund's expected move will be 7.7% for every 10% move in the market. Volatility, as measured by both the semi-deviation and a drawdown factor, is considered low.

Christopher Leavy has been running the fund for 5 years and currently receives a manager quality ranking of 99 (0=worst, 99=best). If you desire only a moderate level of risk and strong performance, then this fund is an excellent option.

Services Offered: Automated phone transactions, bank draft capabilities, an IRA investment plan, a 401K investment plan, wire transfers and a systematic withdrawal plan.

Data Date	Weiss Investment Rating	Net Assets ($Mil)	NAV	Performance Rating/Pts	Total Return Y-T-D	Risk Rating/Pts
6-06	A	2,061	34.65	B+ / 8.4	4.84%	B- / 7.4
2005	A-	1,415	33.05	B+ / 8.7	11.73%	C+ / 6.9
2004	A	622	31.26	A / 9.4	28.30%	C+ / 6.2
2003	A+	379	27.00	A / 9.4	46.06%	B- / 7.4
2002	A-	228	19.40	A- / 9.0	-10.52%	B / 8.0
2001	C+	204	21.68	B+ / 8.5	12.20%	D- / 1.3

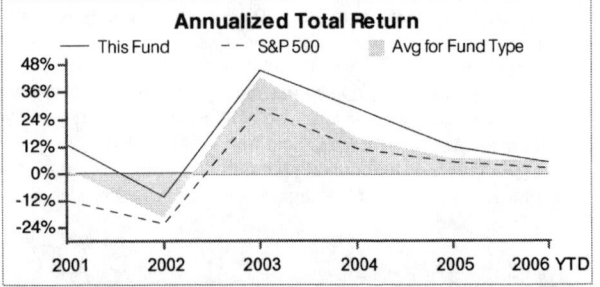

PIMCO Commodity Real Ret Str A (PCRAX)   C+   Fair

Fund Family: PIMCO Funds   **Phone:** (800) 227-7337
Address: 840 Newport Center Drive, Newport Beach, CA 92660
Fund Type: EN - Energy/Natural Resources
Major Rating Factors: Middle of the road best describes PIMCO Commodity Real Ret Str A whose Weiss Investment Rating is currently a C+ (Fair). The fund currently has a performance rating of C+ (Fair) based on an average return of 17.47% over the last three years and -0.83% over the last six months. Factored into the performance evaluation is an expense ratio of 1.24% (average), a 5.5% front-end load that is levied at the time of purchase and a 2.0% back-end load levied at the time of sale.

The fund's risk rating is currently C+ (Fair). It carries a beta of 0.45, meaning the fund's expected move will be 4.5% for every 10% move in the market. Volatility, as measured by standard deviation, is considered low for equity funds at 15.19.

John B. Brynjolfsson has been running the fund for 4 years and currently receives a manager quality ranking of 78 (0=worst, 99=best). If you desire an average level of risk, then this fund may be an option.

Services Offered: Automated phone transactions, bank draft capabilities, an IRA investment plan, a 401K investment plan, wire transfers and a systematic withdrawal plan.

Data Date	Weiss Investment Rating	Net Assets ($Mil)	NAV	Performance Rating/Pts	Total Return Y-T-D	Risk Rating/Pts
6-06	C+	2,339	14.59	C+ / 6.3	-0.83%	C+ / 6.7
2005	C	2,491	14.77	B- / 7.2	19.92%	C- / 3.8
2004	U	1,412	14.78	U / --	15.78%	U / --
2003	U	286	13.62	U / --	29.09%	U / --

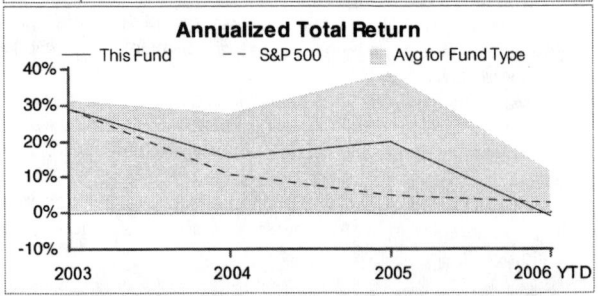

Pioneer Fund A (PIODX)   C+   Fair

Fund Family: Pioneer Investments   **Phone:** (800) 225-6292
Address: 60 State Street, Boston, MA 02109
Fund Type: GI - Growth and Income
Major Rating Factors: Middle of the road best describes Pioneer Fund A whose Weiss Investment Rating is currently a C+ (Fair). The fund currently has a performance rating of C (Fair) based on an average return of 12.91% over the last three years and 4.66% over the last six months. Factored into the performance evaluation is an expense ratio of 1.08% (low) and a 5.8% front-end load that is levied at the time of purchase.

The fund's risk rating is currently B (Good). It carries a beta of 1.03, meaning that its performance tracks fairly well with that of the overall stock market. Volatility, as measured by both the semi-deviation and a drawdown factor, is considered low.

Walter Hunnewell, Jr has been running the fund for 5 years and currently receives a manager quality ranking of 70 (0=worst, 99=best). If you desire an average level of risk, then this fund may be an option.

Services Offered: Automated phone transactions, check writing, payroll deductions, bank draft capabilities, an IRA investment plan, a 401K investment plan, a Keogh investment plan, wire transfers and a systematic withdrawal plan.

Data Date	Weiss Investment Rating	Net Assets ($Mil)	NAV	Performance Rating/Pts	Total Return Y-T-D	Risk Rating/Pts
6-06	C+	5,708	46.06	C / 4.6	4.66%	B / 8.4
2005	D	5,647	44.21	D+ / 2.7	6.39%	C+ / 6.9
2004	C-	5,471	42.06	C- / 3.7	11.63%	C / 5.4
2003	C-	5,131	38.00	C- / 3.3	24.58%	C+ / 5.9
2002	C+	4,864	30.76	C / 5.1	-20.26%	C+ / 6.5
2001	C+	6,089	38.91	C- / 4.0	-11.04%	C+ / 6.6

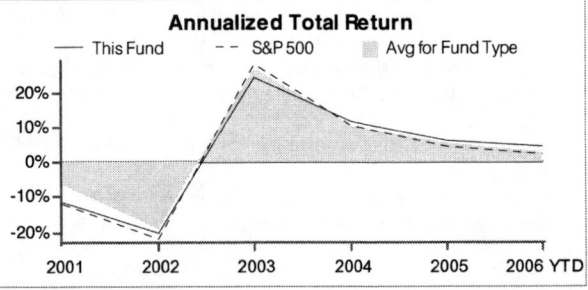

Pioneer Value Fund A (PIOTX)   C-   Fair

Fund Family: Pioneer Investments   **Phone:** (800) 225-6292
Address: 60 State Street, Boston, MA 02109
Fund Type: GI - Growth and Income

Major Rating Factors: Middle of the road best describes Pioneer Value Fund A whose Weiss Investment Rating is currently a C- (Fair). The fund currently has a performance rating of C (Fair) based on an average return of 12.69% over the last three years and 3.98% over the last six months. Factored into the performance evaluation is an expense ratio of 0.97% (low) and a 5.8% front-end load that is levied at the time of purchase.

The fund's risk rating is currently C+ (Fair). It carries a beta of 0.91, meaning that its performance tracks fairly well with that of the overall stock market. Volatility, as measured by both the semi-deviation and a drawdown factor, is considered low.

Aaron C.Clark currently receives a manager quality ranking of 77 (0=worst, 99=best). If you desire an average level of risk, then this fund may be an option.

Services Offered: Automated phone transactions, check writing, payroll deductions, bank draft capabilities, an IRA investment plan, a 401K investment plan, a Keogh investment plan, wire transfers and a systematic withdrawal plan.

Data Date	Weiss Investment Rating	Net Assets ($Mil)	NAV	Perfor-mance Rating/Pts	Total Return Y-T-D	Risk Rating/Pts
6-06	C-	3,871	18.04	C / 4.3	3.98%	C+ 6.1
2005	D	3,951	17.48	C- / 3.0	5.66%	C+ 6.0
2004	C-	3,863	17.73	C / 4.7	12.26%	C / 4.5
2003	C+	3,633	18.29	C+ 6.7	28.54%	C+ 5.9
2002	B	3,387	14.38	B- / 7.3	-18.79%	B- / 7.1
2001	C+	4,190	20.47	C+ 6.4	-3.09%	C+ 6.7

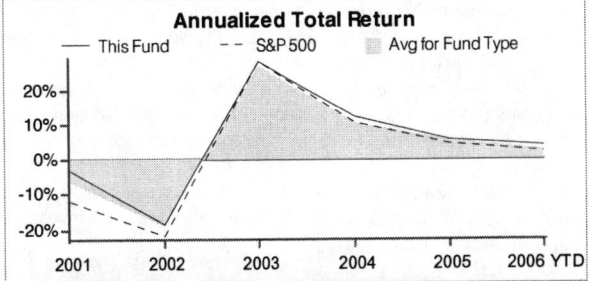

Annualized Total Return

Putnam Equity Income A (PEYAX)   C   Fair

Fund Family: Putnam Funds   **Phone:** (800) 354-2228
Address: One Post Office Square, Boston, MA 02109
Fund Type: IN - Income

Major Rating Factors: Middle of the road best describes Putnam Equity Income A whose Weiss Investment Rating is currently a C (Fair). The fund currently has a performance rating of C- (Fair) based on an average return of 12.47% over the last three years and 4.24% over the last six months. Factored into the performance evaluation is an expense ratio of 0.98% (low) and a 5.3% front-end load that is levied at the time of purchase.

The fund's risk rating is currently B (Good). It carries a beta of 0.97, meaning that its performance tracks fairly well with that of the overall stock market. Volatility, as measured by both the semi-deviation and a drawdown factor, is considered low.

This fund has been team managed for 8 years and currently receives a manager quality ranking of 71 (0=worst, 99=best). If you desire an average level of risk, then this fund may be an option.

Services Offered: Automated phone transactions, bank draft capabilities, an IRA investment plan, a 401K investment plan, a Keogh investment plan and a systematic withdrawal plan.

Data Date	Weiss Investment Rating	Net Assets ($Mil)	NAV	Perfor-mance Rating/Pts	Total Return Y-T-D	Risk Rating/Pts
6-06	C	2,473	17.35	C- / 4.2	4.24%	B / 8.1
2005	D+	2,390	16.77	D+/ 2.8	5.68%	B- / 7.1
2004	C+	2,021	17.43	C+/ 5.8	12.18%	C+/ 6.2
2003	B	1,762	15.74	B- / 7.0	26.61%	B- / 7.5
2002	B+	1,369	12.62	B / 8.0	-12.87%	B / 8.2
2001	B-	1,289	14.71	C+/ 6.1	-1.57%	B- / 7.1

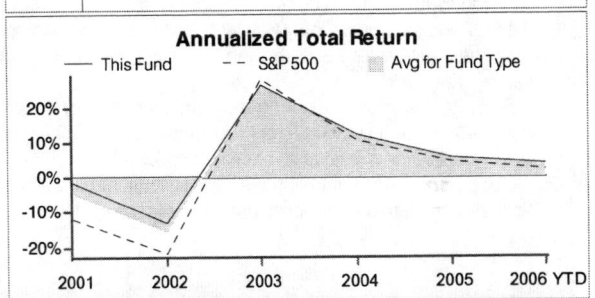

Annualized Total Return

Putnam Fund for Gr & Inc A (PGRWX)   C-   Fair

Fund Family: Putnam Funds   **Phone:** (800) 354-2228
Address: One Post Office Square, Boston, MA 02109
Fund Type: GI - Growth and Income

Major Rating Factors: Middle of the road best describes Putnam Fund for Gr & Inc A whose Weiss Investment Rating is currently a C- (Fair). The fund currently has a performance rating of C- (Fair) based on an average return of 11.06% over the last three years and 2.84% over the last six months. Factored into the performance evaluation is an expense ratio of 0.89% (low) and a 5.3% front-end load that is levied at the time of purchase.

The fund's risk rating is currently B (Good). It carries a beta of 0.97, meaning that its performance tracks fairly well with that of the overall stock market. Volatility, as measured by both the semi-deviation and a drawdown factor, is considered low.

Joshua H Brooks has been running the fund for 1 year and currently receives a manager quality ranking of 58 (0=worst, 99=best). If you desire an average level of risk, then this fund may be an option.

Services Offered: Automated phone transactions, check writing, payroll deductions, bank draft capabilities, an IRA investment plan, a 401K investment plan, a Keogh investment plan and a systematic withdrawal plan.

Data Date	Weiss Investment Rating	Net Assets ($Mil)	NAV	Perfor-mance Rating/Pts	Total Return Y-T-D	Risk Rating/Pts
6-06	C-	11,525	20.18	C- / 3.2	2.84%	B / 8.1
2005	D	11,876	19.73	D+/ 2.5	5.15%	C+/ 6.9
2004	C-	12,532	19.40	C- / 3.9	10.97%	C / 5.3
2003	C+	13,457	17.70	C / 4.9	27.22%	C+/ 6.3
2002	B-	14,196	14.14	C+/ 6.4	-19.13%	B- / 7.2
2001	C+	19,023	17.72	C- / 4.1	-6.37%	C+/ 6.6

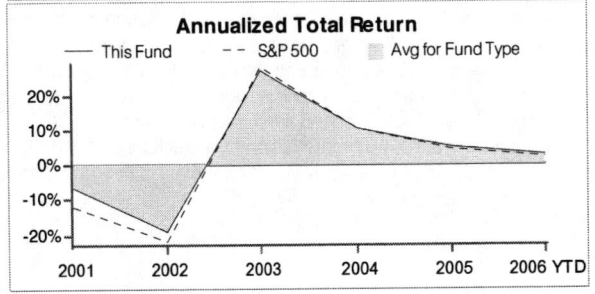

Annualized Total Return

Putnam George Fund A (PGEOX)   C-   Fair

Fund Family: Putnam Funds   **Phone:** (800) 354-2228
Address: One Post Office Square, Boston, MA 02109
Fund Type: AA - Asset Allocation

Major Rating Factors: Disappointing performance is the major factor driving the C- (Fair) Weiss Investment Rating for Putnam George Fund A. The fund currently has a performance rating of D- (Weak) based on an average return of 7.53% over the last three years and 1.78% over the last six months. Factored into the performance evaluation is an expense ratio of 0.99% (low) and a 5.3% front-end load that is levied at the time of purchase.

The fund's risk rating is currently B+ (Good). It carries a beta of 1.01, meaning that its performance tracks fairly well with that of the overall stock market. Volatility, as measured by both the semi-deviation and a drawdown factor, is considered very low.

Jeanne L. Mockard has been running the fund for 6 years and currently receives a manager quality ranking of 55 (0=worst, 99=best). This fund offers only a moderate level of risk but investors looking for strong performance are still waiting.

Services Offered: Automated phone transactions, bank draft capabilities, an IRA investment plan, a 401K investment plan, a Keogh investment plan and a systematic withdrawal plan.

Data Date	Weiss Investment Rating	Net Assets ($Mil)	NAV	Performance Rating/Pts	Total Return Y-T-D	Risk Rating/Pts
6-06	C-	3,153	18.04	D- / 1.2	1.78%	B+ / 9.5
2005	D+	3,321	17.92	E+ / 0.6	4.04%	B+ / 9.0
2004	C	3,407	18.06	C- / 3.6	8.32%	B- / 7.8
2003	B+	3,511	16.98	C+ / 6.2	17.40%	B / 8.8
2002	A	3,576	14.80	B+ / 8.4	-8.42%	B+ / 9.3
2001	B	3,267	16.74	C+ / 5.9	0.51%	B / 8.5

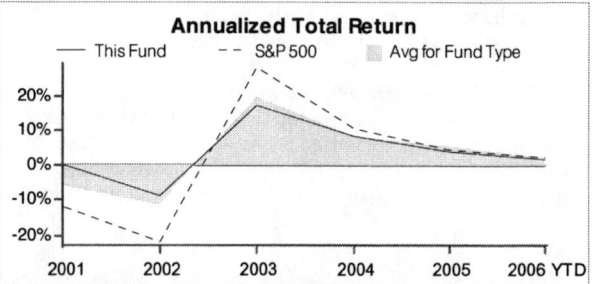

Putnam International Equity A (POVSX)   B+   Good

Fund Family: Putnam Funds   **Phone:** (800) 354-2228
Address: One Post Office Square, Boston, MA 02109
Fund Type: FO - Foreign

Major Rating Factors: Strong performance is the major factor driving the B+ (Good) Weiss Investment Rating for Putnam International Equity A. The fund currently has a performance rating of B (Good) based on an average return of 20.30% over the last three years and 10.29% over the last six months. Factored into the performance evaluation is an expense ratio of 1.30% (average) and a 5.3% front-end load that is levied at the time of purchase.

The fund's risk rating is currently C+ (Fair). It carries a beta of 1.01, meaning that its performance tracks fairly well with that of the overall stock market. Volatility, as measured by both the semi-deviation and a drawdown factor, is considered low.

Joshua L. Byrne currently receives a manager quality ranking of 22 (0=worst, 99=best). If you desire only a moderate level of risk and strong performance, then this fund is an excellent option.

Services Offered: Automated phone transactions, bank draft capabilities, an IRA investment plan, a 401K investment plan and a systematic withdrawal plan.

Data Date	Weiss Investment Rating	Net Assets ($Mil)	NAV	Performance Rating/Pts	Total Return Y-T-D	Risk Rating/Pts
6-06	B+	3,602	28.82	B / 8.2	10.29%	C+ / 6.6
2005	C+	3,251	26.13	C+ / 6.0	12.62%	C+ / 6.6
2004	C+	3,518	23.68	C+ / 6.9	16.23%	C+ / 5.8
2003	C-	5,501	20.66	C- / 3.3	28.14%	C+ / 5.9
2002	C	6,220	16.41	C- / 3.7	-17.03%	C+ / 5.9
2001	C	6,562	19.82	C / 5.5	-19.76%	D+ / 2.3

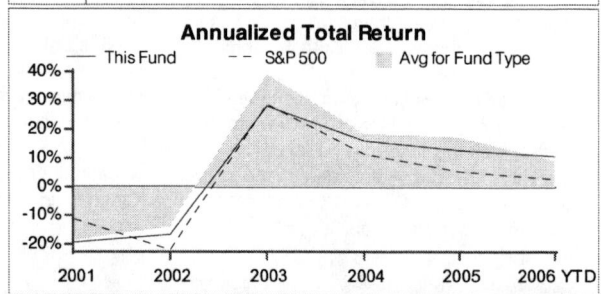

Putnam Investors Fund A (PINVX)   C   Fair

Fund Family: Putnam Funds   **Phone:** (800) 354-2228
Address: One Post Office Square, Boston, MA 02109
Fund Type: GR - Growth

Major Rating Factors: Middle of the road best describes Putnam Investors Fund A whose Weiss Investment Rating is currently a C (Fair). The fund currently has a performance rating of C- (Fair) based on an average return of 12.55% over the last three years and 0.88% over the last six months. Factored into the performance evaluation is an expense ratio of 1.07% (low) and a 5.3% front-end load that is levied at the time of purchase.

The fund's risk rating is currently B (Good). It carries a beta of 1.12, meaning it is expected to move 11.2% for every 10% move in the market. Volatility, as measured by both the semi-deviation and a drawdown factor, is considered low.

Richard Cervone has been running the fund for 4 years and currently receives a manager quality ranking of 58 (0=worst, 99=best). If you desire an average level of risk, then this fund may be an option.

Services Offered: Automated phone transactions, bank draft capabilities, an IRA investment plan, a 401K investment plan, a Keogh investment plan and a systematic withdrawal plan.

Data Date	Weiss Investment Rating	Net Assets ($Mil)	NAV	Performance Rating/Pts	Total Return Y-T-D	Risk Rating/Pts
6-06	C	2,193	13.68	C- / 3.8	0.88%	B / 8.1
2005	C	2,201	13.56	C / 4.4	8.81%	B- / 7.3
2004	C-	2,252	12.59	C- / 3.9	12.76%	C / 5.5
2003	D+	2,632	11.18	D- / 1.3	27.62%	C / 5.4
2002	D+	3,026	8.80	D / 1.6	-23.81%	C / 4.9
2001	E+	5,064	11.55	E / 0.5	-24.80%	E+ / 0.9

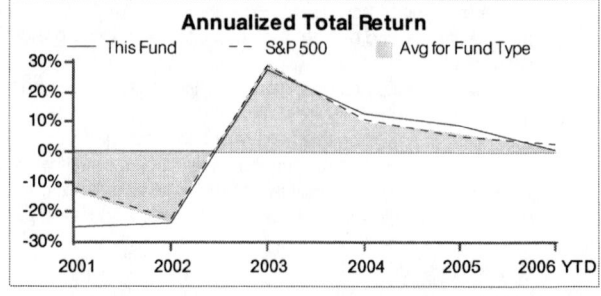

Putnam New Opportunities A (PNOPX)

D-   Weak

Fund Family: Putnam Funds **Phone:** (800) 354-2228
Address: One Post Office Square, Boston, MA 02109
Fund Type: GR - Growth

Major Rating Factors: Putnam New Opportunities A receives a Weiss Investment Rating of D- (Weak). The fund currently has a performance rating of C- (Fair) based on an average return of 11.72% over the last three years and 0.13% over the last six months. Factored into the performance evaluation is an expense ratio of 1.12% (low) and a 5.3% front-end load that is levied at the time of purchase.

The fund's risk rating is currently C (Fair). It carries a beta of 1.30, meaning it is expected to move 13.0% for every 10% move in the market. Volatility, as measured by both the semi-deviation and a drawdown factor, is considered average.

Brian DeChristopher has been running the fund for 1 year and currently receives a manager quality ranking of 33 (0=worst, 99=best). If you desire an average level of risk, then this fund may be an option.

Services Offered: Automated phone transactions, payroll deductions, bank draft capabilities, an IRA investment plan, a 401K investment plan, a Keogh investment plan, wire transfers and a systematic withdrawal plan.

Data Date	Weiss Investment Rating	Net Assets ($Mil)	NAV	Perfor-mance Rating/Pts	Total Return Y-T-D	Risk Rating/Pts
6-06	D-	3,691	45.72	C- / 3.2	0.13%	C / 5.2
2005	C-	4,606	45.65	C / 5.1	9.92%	C / 5.5
2004	D-	4,967	41.53	D- / 1.5	10.13%	C- / 3.7
2003	E+	6,111	37.72	E+ / 0.6	32.68%	D+ / 2.4
2002	E+	6,290	28.43	E / 0.5	-30.62%	D / 2.1
2001	E+	10,572	40.98	D- / 1.0	-30.09%	E- / 0.0

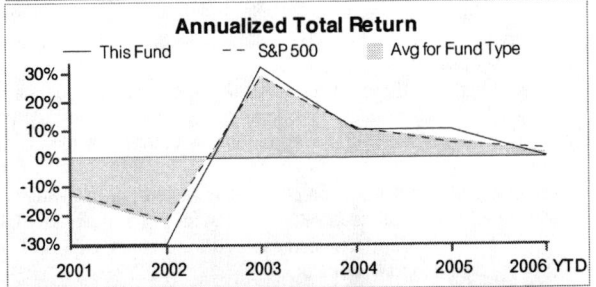

Annualized Total Return

Putnam Voyager A (PVOYX)

E+   Very Weak

Fund Family: Putnam Funds **Phone:** (800) 354-2228
Address: One Post Office Square, Boston, MA 02109
Fund Type: GR - Growth

Major Rating Factors: Very poor performance is the major factor driving the E+ (Very Weak) Weiss Investment Rating for Putnam Voyager A. The fund currently has a performance rating of E (Very Weak) based on an average return of 6.12% over the last three years and -3.91% over the last six months. Factored into the performance evaluation is an expense ratio of 1.08% (low) and a 5.3% front-end load that is levied at the time of purchase.

The fund's risk rating is currently C+ (Fair). It carries a beta of 1.15, meaning it is expected to move 11.5% for every 10% move in the market. Volatility, as measured by both the semi-deviation and a drawdown factor, is considered low.

Kelly A. Morgan currently receives a manager quality ranking of 10 (0=worst, 99=best). This fund offers only a moderate level of risk but investors looking for strong performance are still waiting.

Services Offered: Automated phone transactions, bank draft capabilities, an IRA investment plan, a 401K investment plan, a Keogh investment plan and a systematic withdrawal plan.

Data Date	Weiss Investment Rating	Net Assets ($Mil)	NAV	Perfor-mance Rating/Pts	Total Return Y-T-D	Risk Rating/Pts
6-06	E+	5,812	16.72	E / 0.4	-3.91%	C+ / 6.7
2005	D-	6,944	17.40	D- / 1.3	5.50%	C+ / 6.9
2004	D-	8,511	16.61	E+ / 0.6	4.79%	C / 5.0
2003	D	11,204	15.85	E+ / 0.9	24.70%	C / 5.0
2002	D	11,026	12.71	D- / 1.5	-26.53%	C- / 4.2
2001	D-	15,953	17.30	D+ / 2.7	-22.46%	E- / 0.0

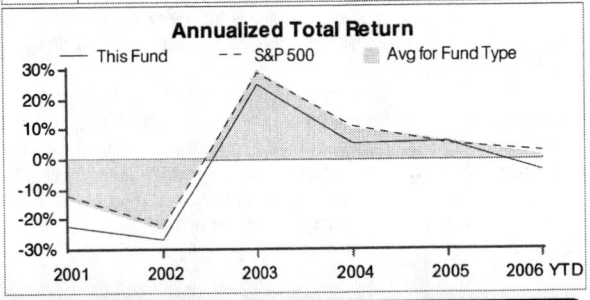

Annualized Total Return

Rainier Small-Mid Cap Equity Fd (RIMSX)

B   Good

Fund Family: RIM Funds **Phone:** (800) 280-6111
Address: 601 Union Street, Seattle, WA 98101
Fund Type: SC - Small Cap

Major Rating Factors: Strong performance is the major factor driving the B (Good) Weiss Investment Rating for Rainier Small-Mid Cap Equity Fd. The fund currently has a performance rating of B+ (Good) based on an average return of 22.65% over the last three years and 9.08% over the last six months. Factored into the performance evaluation is an expense ratio of 1.21% (average).

The fund's risk rating is currently C+ (Fair). It carries a beta of 0.97, meaning that its performance tracks fairly well with that of the overall stock market. Volatility, as measured by both the semi-deviation and a drawdown factor, is considered low.

Daniel M. Brewer, CFA currently receives a manager quality ranking of 89 (0=worst, 99=best). If you desire only a moderate level of risk and strong performance, then this fund is an excellent option.

Services Offered: Automated phone transactions, an IRA investment plan, a 401K investment plan, a Keogh investment plan and a systematic withdrawal plan. However, the fund is currently closed to new investors.

Data Date	Weiss Investment Rating	Net Assets ($Mil)	NAV	Perfor-mance Rating/Pts	Total Return Y-T-D	Risk Rating/Pts
6-06	B	2,509	36.16	B+ / 8.7	9.08%	C+ / 5.8
2005	A-	1,434	33.15	A- / 9.1	17.53%	C+ / 6.6
2004	B	487	29.04	B / 8.1	17.36%	C+ / 5.8
2003	B+	259	25.65	B+ / 8.5	46.24%	C+ / 6.7
2002	C+	167	17.54	C+ / 6.7	-20.02%	C+ / 6.2
2001	C	308	21.93	B / 7.8	-3.92%	E+ / 0.9

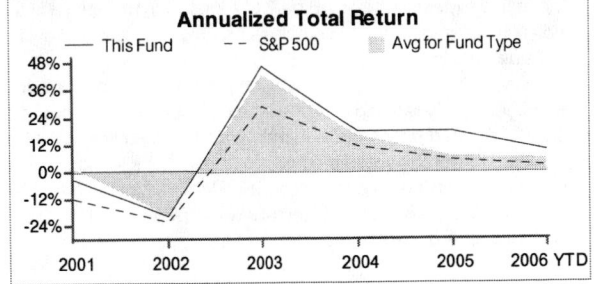

Annualized Total Return

Royce Low Priced Stock Svc (RYLPX)

B-   **Good**

Fund Family: Royce Funds   **Phone:** (800) 221-4268
Address: 1414 Avenue of the Americas, New York, NY 10019
Fund Type: SC - Small Cap

Major Rating Factors: Strong performance is the major factor driving the B- (Good) Weiss Investment Rating for Royce Low Priced Stock Svc. The fund currently has a performance rating of B (Good) based on an average return of 19.28% over the last three years and 9.40% over the last six months. Factored into the performance evaluation is an expense ratio of 1.49% (average) and a 1.0% back-end load levied at the time of sale.

The fund's risk rating is currently C+ (Fair). It carries a beta of 0.92, meaning that its performance tracks fairly well with that of the overall stock market. Volatility, as measured by both the semi-deviation and a drawdown factor, is considered low.

W. Whitney George has been running the fund for 6 years and currently receives a manager quality ranking of 74 (0=worst, 99=best). If you desire only a moderate level of risk and strong performance, then this fund is an excellent option.

Services Offered: Automated phone transactions, check writing, payroll deductions, bank draft capabilities, an IRA investment plan, a 401K investment plan, wire transfers and a systematic withdrawal plan. However, the fund is currently closed to new investors.

Data Date	Weiss Investment Rating	Net Assets ($Mil)	NAV	Perfor- mance Rating/Pts	Total Return Y-T-D	Risk Rating/Pts
6-06	B-	4,077	16.99	B / 8.0	9.40%	C+ / 5.7
2005	C-	3,932	15.53	C / 5.2	1.30%	C+ / 5.7
2004	C+	4,735	15.33	B- / 7.3	13.64%	C / 4.7
2003	A-	2,926	13.98	A / 9.4	44.02%	C+ / 6.4
2002	B+	1,843	9.75	A / 9.4	-16.28%	B- / 7.2
2001	C+	852	11.67	A+ / 9.9	25.07%	E+ / 0.8

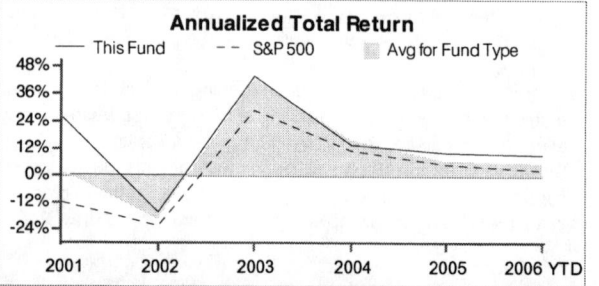

Annualized Total Return

Royce PA Mutual Fd Inv (PENNX)

B+   **Good**

Fund Family: Royce Funds   **Phone:** (800) 221-4268
Address: 1414 Avenue of the Americas, New York, NY 10019
Fund Type: SC - Small Cap

Major Rating Factors: Strong performance is the major factor driving the B+ (Good) Weiss Investment Rating for Royce PA Mutual Fd Inv. The fund currently has a performance rating of B (Good) based on an average return of 21.11% over the last three years and 6.12% over the last six months. Factored into the performance evaluation is an expense ratio of 0.90% (low) and a 1.0% back-end load levied at the time of sale.

The fund's risk rating is currently C+ (Fair). It carries a beta of 0.83, meaning the fund's expected move will be 8.3% for every 10% move in the market. Volatility, as measured by both the semi-deviation and a drawdown factor, is considered low.

Chuck Royce has been running the fund for 9 years and currently receives a manager quality ranking of 92 (0=worst, 99=best). If you desire only a moderate level of risk and strong performance, then this fund is an excellent option.

Services Offered: Automated phone transactions, check writing, payroll deductions, bank draft capabilities, an IRA investment plan, a 401K investment plan, wire transfers and a systematic withdrawal plan.

Data Date	Weiss Investment Rating	Net Assets ($Mil)	NAV	Perfor- mance Rating/Pts	Total Return Y-T-D	Risk Rating/Pts
6-06	B+	2,445	11.44	B / 8.2	6.12%	C+ / 6.9
2005	A-	1,803	10.78	B+ / 8.4	12.50%	B- / 7.1
2004	A-	1,196	10.14	B+ / 8.8	20.23%	C+ / 6.2
2003	A+	800	8.88	A / 9.3	40.29%	B- / 7.4
2002	A-	473	6.59	A / 9.4	-9.22%	B- / 7.9
2001	A	410	7.39	A / 9.5	17.36%	C+ / 6.1

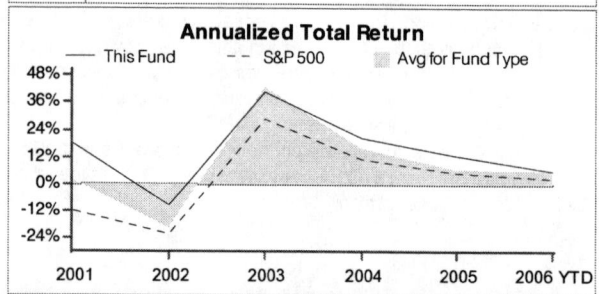

Annualized Total Return

Royce Premier Fd (RYPRX)

B+   **Good**

Fund Family: Royce Funds   **Phone:** (800) 221-4268
Address: 1414 Avenue of the Americas, New York, NY 10019
Fund Type: SC - Small Cap

Major Rating Factors: Strong performance is the major factor driving the B+ (Good) Weiss Investment Rating for Royce Premier Fd. The fund currently has a performance rating of B+ (Good) based on an average return of 22.60% over the last three years and 4.98% over the last six months. Factored into the performance evaluation is an expense ratio of 1.13% (low) and a 1.0% back-end load levied at the time of sale.

The fund's risk rating is currently C+ (Fair). It carries a beta of 0.78, meaning the fund's expected move will be 7.8% for every 10% move in the market. Volatility, as measured by both the semi-deviation and a drawdown factor, is considered low.

Chuck Royce has been running the fund for 3 years and currently receives a manager quality ranking of 97 (0=worst, 99=best). If you desire only a moderate level of risk and strong performance, then this fund is an excellent option.

Services Offered: Automated phone transactions, check writing, payroll deductions, bank draft capabilities, an IRA investment plan, a 401K investment plan, wire transfers and a systematic withdrawal plan. However, the fund is currently closed to new investors.

Data Date	Weiss Investment Rating	Net Assets ($Mil)	NAV	Perfor- mance Rating/Pts	Total Return Y-T-D	Risk Rating/Pts
6-06	B+	3,790	17.70	B+ / 8.4	4.98%	C+ / 6.9
2005	A	3,276	16.86	A- / 9.1	17.07%	C+ / 6.9
2004	A-	2,864	15.12	B+ / 8.9	22.82%	C+ / 6.3
2003	A	1,697	12.90	A- / 9.0	38.72%	B- / 7.6
2002	A	874	9.39	A / 9.3	-7.75%	B / 8.5
2001	B	749	10.54	A- / 9.2	9.61%	C- / 3.5

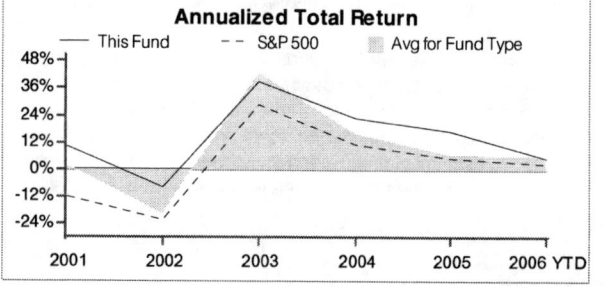

Annualized Total Return

Royce Total Return Fd (RYTRX)   B-   Good

Fund Family: Royce Funds   **Phone:** (800) 221-4268
Address: 1414 Avenue of the Americas, New York, NY 10019
Fund Type: SC - Small Cap

Major Rating Factors: Royce Total Return Fd receives a Weiss Investment
Rating of B- (Good). The fund currently has a performance rating of C+ (Fair)
based on an average return of 16.28% over the last three years and 5.56% over
the last six months. Factored into the performance evaluation is an expense ratio
of 1.12% (low) and a 1.0% back-end load levied at the time of sale.

The fund's risk rating is currently B- (Good). It carries a beta of 0.64,
meaning the fund's expected move will be 6.4% for every 10% move in the
market. Volatility, as measured by both the semi-deviation and a drawdown
factor, is considered low.

Chuck Royce has been running the fund for 5 years and currently receives a
manager quality ranking of 86 (0=worst, 99=best). If you desire an average level
of risk, then this fund may be an option.

Services Offered: Automated phone transactions, check writing, payroll
deductions, bank draft capabilities, an IRA investment plan, a 401K investment
plan, wire transfers and a systematic withdrawal plan.

Data Date	Weiss Investment Rating	Net Assets ($Mil)	NAV	Performance Rating/Pts	Total Return Y-T-D	Risk Rating/Pts
6-06	B-	4,446	13.22	C+ / 6.7	5.56%	B- / 7.9
2005	B-	4,274	12.60	C+ / 6.0	8.23%	B- / 7.7
2004	A	3,584	12.26	B+ / 8.6	17.52%	B- / 7.4
2003	A+	2,569	10.69	B+ / 8.8	29.99%	B / 8.5
2002	A+	1,052	8.37	A / 9.5	-1.60%	B+ / 9.2
2001	A+	466	8.59	A- / 9.0	11.94%	B- / 7.1

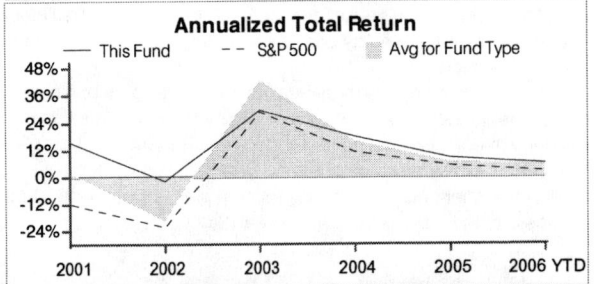

Annualized Total Return

RS Partners Fund (RSPFX)   B   Good

Fund Family: RS Funds   **Phone:** (800) 766-3863
Address: 388 Market Street, San Francisco, CA 94111
Fund Type: SC - Small Cap

Major Rating Factors: Exceptional performance is the major factor driving the B
(Good) Weiss Investment Rating for RS Partners Fund. The fund currently has a
performance rating of A- (Excellent) based on an average return of 26.02% over
the last three years and 4.97% over the last six months. Factored into the
performance evaluation is an expense ratio of 1.49% (average).

The fund's risk rating is currently C (Fair). It carries a beta of 0.71, meaning
the fund's expected move will be 7.1% for every 10% move in the market.
Volatility, as measured by both the semi-deviation and a drawdown factor, is
considered average.

Andrew P. Pilara, Jr. has been running the fund for 11 years and currently
receives a manager quality ranking of 99 (0=worst, 99=best). If you desire an
average level of risk and strong performance, then this fund is a good option.

Services Offered: Automated phone transactions, bank draft capabilities, an
IRA investment plan, a 401K investment plan, wire transfers and a systematic
withdrawal plan. However, the fund is currently closed to new investors.

Data Date	Weiss Investment Rating	Net Assets ($Mil)	NAV	Performance Rating/Pts	Total Return Y-T-D	Risk Rating/Pts
6-06	B	2,422	34.65	A- / 9.1	4.97%	C / 5.5
2005	B+	2,163	33.01	A / 9.5	11.94%	C+ / 5.6
2004	A+	2,045	34.77	A+ / 9.9	31.81%	B / 8.0
2003	A+	711	27.70	A+ / 9.9	65.63%	B / 8.6
2002	A+	111	17.82	A+ / 9.8	1.23%	B+ / 9.2
2001	B	69	17.67	A+ / 9.6	15.19%	D+ / 2.4

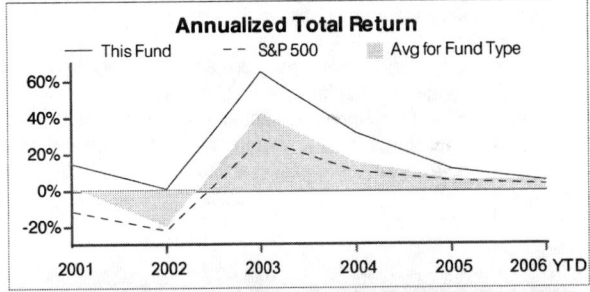

Annualized Total Return

Russell Diversified Equity Fund S (RDESX)   C+   Fair

Fund Family: Russell Funds   **Phone:** (800) 832-6688
Address: 909 A Street, Tacoma, WA 98402
Fund Type: GI - Growth and Income

Major Rating Factors: Middle of the road best describes Russell Diversified
Equity Fund S whose Weiss Investment Rating is currently a C+ (Fair). The fund
currently has a performance rating of C (Fair) based on an average return of
12.21% over the last three years and 2.72% over the last six months. Factored
into the performance evaluation is an expense ratio of 0.97% (low).

The fund's risk rating is currently B (Good). It carries a beta of 1.08, meaning
that its performance tracks fairly well with that of the overall stock market.
Volatility, as measured by both the semi-deviation and a drawdown factor, is
considered low.

Dennis J. Trittin has been running the fund for 10 years and currently
receives a manager quality ranking of 59 (0=worst, 99=best). If you desire an
average level of risk, then this fund may be an option.

Services Offered: Automated phone transactions, bank draft capabilities, an
IRA investment plan, a 401K investment plan, a Keogh investment plan, wire
transfers and a systematic withdrawal plan.

Data Date	Weiss Investment Rating	Net Assets ($Mil)	NAV	Performance Rating/Pts	Total Return Y-T-D	Risk Rating/Pts
6-06	C+	3,091	46.07	C / 4.7	2.72%	B / 8.1
2005	C+	2,673	44.87	C / 4.6	7.65%	B- / 7.6
2004	C	2,054	43.14	C / 4.7	11.23%	C+ / 5.9
2003	C	1,507	39.05	C- / 3.7	28.30%	C+ / 6.2
2002	C	1,014	30.58	C- / 3.7	-22.27%	C+ / 6.3
2001	D+	1,194	39.60	D+ / 2.4	-14.84%	C- / 3.4

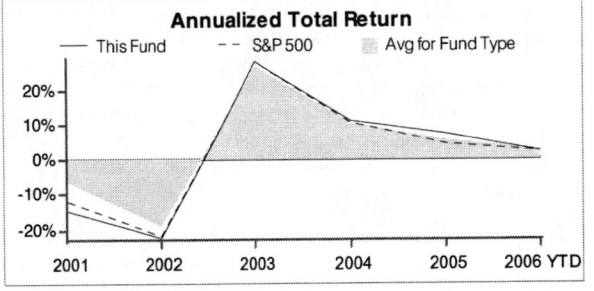

Annualized Total Return

Russell International Securities S (RISSX)

A- **Excellent**

Fund Family: Russell Funds   **Phone:** (800) 832-6688
Address: 909 A Street, Tacoma, WA 98402
Fund Type: FO - Foreign

Major Rating Factors: Strong performance is the major factor driving the A- (Excellent) Weiss Investment Rating for Russell International Securities S. The fund currently has a performance rating of B+ (Good) based on an average return of 22.49% over the last three years and 9.53% over the last six months. Factored into the performance evaluation is an expense ratio of 1.23% (average).

The fund's risk rating is currently C+ (Fair). It carries a beta of 1.02, meaning that its performance tracks fairly well with that of the overall stock market. Volatility, as measured by both the semi-deviation and a drawdown factor, is considered low.

Jim Jornlin has been running the fund for 6 years and currently receives a manager quality ranking of 34 (0=worst, 99=best). If you desire only a moderate level of risk and strong performance, then this fund is an excellent option.

Services Offered: Automated phone transactions, bank draft capabilities, an IRA investment plan, a 401K investment plan, a Keogh investment plan, wire transfers and a systematic withdrawal plan.

Data Date	Weiss Investment Rating	Net Assets ($Mil)	NAV	Performance Rating/Pts	Total Return Y-T-D	Risk Rating/Pts
6-06	A-	2,845	73.92	B+ / 8.8	9.53%	C+/ 6.7
2005	A-	2,389	67.49	B+ / 8.5	14.18%	C+/ 6.9
2004	B	1,792	61.82	B / 8.2	16.94%	C / 5.5
2003	C+	1,329	53.74	C+/ 6.0	38.12%	C+/ 5.6
2002	C	799	39.70	C- / 3.8	-15.94%	C+/ 6.2
2001	C	841	47.84	D / 1.9	-21.98%	C+/ 6.1

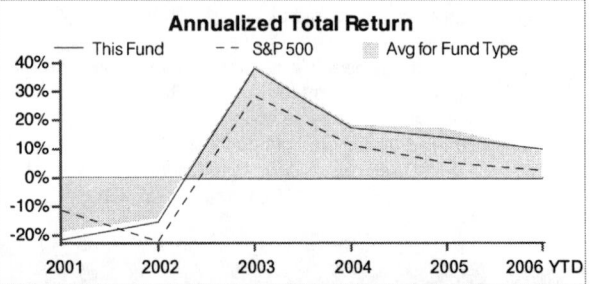

Russell Quantitative Equity S (RQESX)

C **Fair**

Fund Family: Russell Funds   **Phone:** (800) 832-6688
Address: 909 A Street, Tacoma, WA 98402
Fund Type: GI - Growth and Income

Major Rating Factors: Middle of the road best describes Russell Quantitative Equity S whose Weiss Investment Rating is currently a C (Fair). The fund currently has a performance rating of C- (Fair) based on an average return of 11.09% over the last three years and 1.88% over the last six months. Factored into the performance evaluation is an expense ratio of 0.97% (low).

The fund's risk rating is currently B (Good). It carries a beta of 1.04, meaning that its performance tracks fairly well with that of the overall stock market. Volatility, as measured by both the semi-deviation and a drawdown factor, is considered low.

Tom Monroe currently receives a manager quality ranking of 50 (0=worst, 99=best). If you desire an average level of risk, then this fund may be an option.

Services Offered: Automated phone transactions, bank draft capabilities, an IRA investment plan, a 401K investment plan, a Keogh investment plan, wire transfers and a systematic withdrawal plan.

Data Date	Weiss Investment Rating	Net Assets ($Mil)	NAV	Performance Rating/Pts	Total Return Y-T-D	Risk Rating/Pts
6-06	C	3,182	38.82	C- / 4.0	1.88%	B / 8.2
2005	C	2,770	38.17	C / 4.3	6.25%	B- / 7.6
2004	C	2,165	37.79	C / 4.4	10.72%	C+/ 5.7
2003	C	1,625	34.42	C / 4.5	29.26%	C+/ 6.3
2002	C	1,124	26.78	C / 4.6	-23.10%	C+/ 6.2
2001	C	1,290	35.11	C / 4.6	-10.58%	C- / 3.3

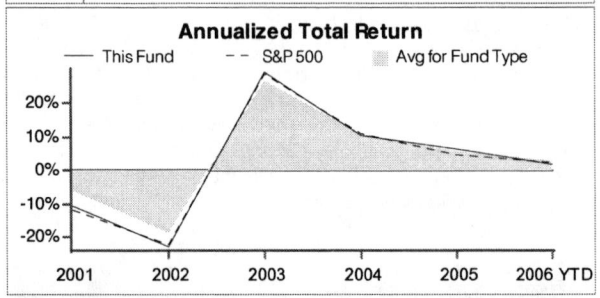

RVS Diversified Equity Income A (INDZX)

A+ **Excellent**

Fund Family: Ameriprise Financial   **Phone:** (800) 328-8300
Address: 430 AXP Financial Center, Minneapolis, MN 55474
Fund Type: IN - Income

Major Rating Factors: Strong performance is the major factor driving the A+ (Excellent) Weiss Investment Rating for RVS Diversified Equity Income A. The fund currently has a performance rating of B+ (Good) based on an average return of 21.53% over the last three years and 8.55% over the last six months. Factored into the performance evaluation is an expense ratio of 1.06% (low) and a 5.8% front-end load that is levied at the time of purchase.

The fund's risk rating is currently B (Good). It carries a beta of 1.27, meaning it is expected to move 12.7% for every 10% move in the market. Volatility, as measured by both the semi-deviation and a drawdown factor, is considered low.

Warren Spitz has been running the fund for 6 years and currently receives a manager quality ranking of 97 (0=worst, 99=best). If you desire only a moderate level of risk and strong performance, then this fund is an excellent option.

Services Offered: Automated phone transactions, check writing, bank draft capabilities, an IRA investment plan, a 401K investment plan, a Keogh investment plan and wire transfers.

Data Date	Weiss Investment Rating	Net Assets ($Mil)	NAV	Performance Rating/Pts	Total Return Y-T-D	Risk Rating/Pts
6-06	A+	4,949	12.83	B+ / 8.3	8.55%	B / 8.0
2005	B+	3,936	11.89	B / 8.2	13.33%	B- / 7.0
2004	C+	2,729	11.13	B / 7.8	18.23%	C / 4.6
2003	B	1,761	9.56	B+ / 8.4	41.89%	C+/ 5.9
2002	B-	1,313	6.84	C+/ 6.4	-18.39%	B- / 7.0
2001	C+	1,652	8.51	C+/ 6.2	2.69%	C+/ 6.2

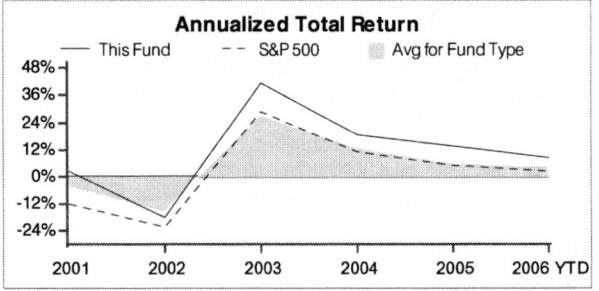

RVS Growth Fund A (INIDX)

D **Weak**

Fund Family: Ameriprise Financial **Phone:** (800) 328-8300
Address: 430 AXP Financial Center, Minneapolis, MN 55474
Fund Type: GR - Growth

Major Rating Factors: Very poor performance is the major factor driving the D (Weak) Weiss Investment Rating for RVS Growth Fund A. The fund currently has a performance rating of E+ (Very Weak) based on an average return of 7.34% over the last three years and -1.08% over the last six months. Factored into the performance evaluation is an expense ratio of 1.20% (average) and a 5.8% front-end load that is levied at the time of purchase.

The fund's risk rating is currently B (Good). It carries a beta of 0.75, meaning the fund's expected move will be 7.5% for every 10% move in the market. Volatility, as measured by both the semi-deviation and a drawdown factor, is considered low.

Nick Thakore has been running the fund for 4 years and currently receives a manager quality ranking of 38 (0=worst, 99=best). This fund offers only a moderate level of risk but investors looking for strong performance are still waiting.

Services Offered: Automated phone transactions, check writing, payroll deductions, bank draft capabilities, an IRA investment plan, a 401K investment plan, a Keogh investment plan, wire transfers and a systematic withdrawal plan.

Data Date	Weiss Investment Rating	Net Assets ($Mil)	NAV	Perfor- mance Rating/Pts	Total Return Y-T-D	Risk Rating/Pts
6-06	D	2,297	28.50	E+ / 0.7	-1.08%	B / 8.0
2005	D	2,266	28.81	D / 1.6	8.42%	B / 8.0
2004	D-	2,083	26.58	D- / 1.1	8.49%	C / 4.4
2003	E+	2,302	24.50	E / 0.3	20.75%	C- / 3.1
2002	D	2,017	20.29	D- / 1.0	-24.09%	C- / 3.4
2001	E-	3,254	26.73	E / 0.4	-31.30%	E- / 0.0

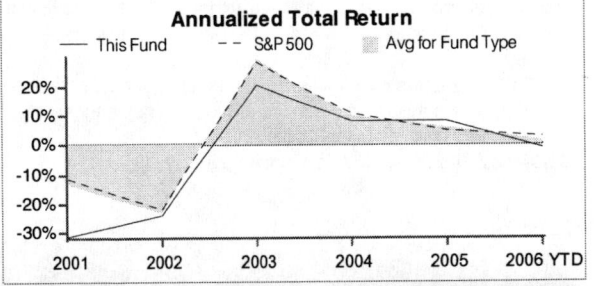

RVS Large Cap Equity A (ALEAX)

D **Weak**

Fund Family: Ameriprise Financial **Phone:** (800) 328-8300
Address: 430 AXP Financial Center, Minneapolis, MN 55474
Fund Type: GR - Growth

Major Rating Factors: Disappointing performance is the major factor driving the D (Weak) Weiss Investment Rating for RVS Large Cap Equity A. The fund currently has a performance rating of D- (Weak) based on an average return of 7.88% over the last three years and 1.39% over the last six months. Factored into the performance evaluation is an expense ratio of 1.18% (low) and a 5.8% front-end load that is levied at the time of purchase.

The fund's risk rating is currently B- (Good). It carries a beta of 0.90, meaning the fund's expected move will be 9.0% for every 10% move in the market. Volatility, as measured by both the semi-deviation and a drawdown factor, is considered low.

Bob Ewing has been running the fund for 1 year and currently receives a manager quality ranking of 32 (0=worst, 99=best). This fund offers only a moderate level of risk but investors looking for strong performance are still waiting.

Services Offered: Automated phone transactions, check writing, payroll deductions, bank draft capabilities, an IRA investment plan, a 401K investment plan, a Keogh investment plan, wire transfers and a systematic withdrawal plan.

Data Date	Weiss Investment Rating	Net Assets ($Mil)	NAV	Perfor- mance Rating/Pts	Total Return Y-T-D	Risk Rating/Pts
6-06	D	5,325	5.36	D- / 1.2	1.39%	B- / 7.8
2005	D+	1,011	5.31	D- / 1.5	5.76%	B / 8.3
2004	U	1,215	5.04	U / --	8.24%	U / --
2003	U	157	4.93	U / --	29.88%	U / --

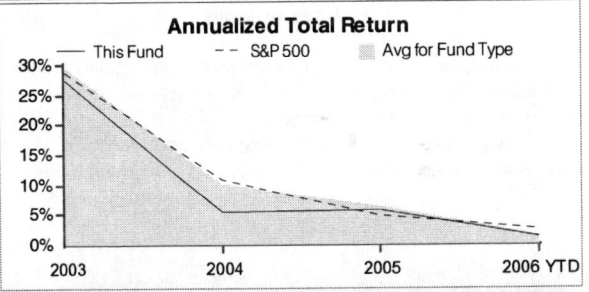

Sanford Bernstein Emerg Markets Val (SNEMX)

C+ **Fair**

Fund Family: Bernstein Funds **Phone:** N/A
Address: 767 Fifth Avenue, New York, NY 10153
Fund Type: EM - Emerging Market

Major Rating Factors: Sanford Bernstein Emerg Markets Val has adopted a risky asset allocation strategy and currently receives an overall Weiss Investment Rating of C+ (Fair). The fund has shown an above average level of volatility, as measured by both semi-deviation and drawdown factors. It carries a beta of 1.14, meaning it is expected to move 11.4% for every 10% move in the market. The high level of risk (D+, Weak) did however, reward investors with excellent performance.

The fund's performance rating is currently A+ (Excellent). It has registered an average return of 40.32% over the last three years and is up 6.36% over the last six months. Factored into the performance evaluation is an expense ratio of 1.68% (above average).

Drew Demakis currently receives a manager quality ranking of 45 (0=worst, 99=best). If you are comfortable owning a high risk investment, this fund may be an option.

Services Offered: A 401K investment plan, wire transfers and a systematic withdrawal plan.

Data Date	Weiss Investment Rating	Net Assets ($Mil)	NAV	Perfor- mance Rating/Pts	Total Return Y-T-D	Risk Rating/Pts
6-06	C+	2,040	37.31	A+ / 9.9	6.36%	D+ / 2.9
2005	B	1,890	35.08	A+ / 9.9	28.78%	C- / 3.8
2004	A+	1,698	35.17	A+ / 9.9	39.18%	B- / 7.3
2003	A+	1,021	25.92	A+ / 9.9	76.89%	B / 8.0
2002	C+	574	14.79	C+ / 6.8	3.84%	C+ / 6.7
2001	C	561	14.32	B- / 7.4	-4.47%	E / 0.5

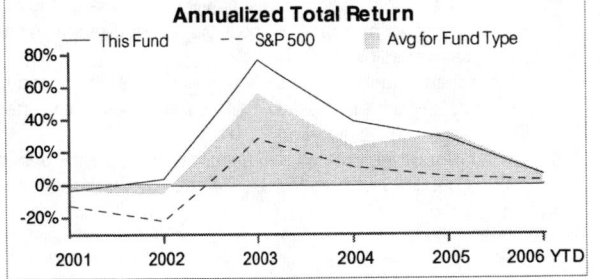

Sanford Bernstein Internatl Val II (SIMTX)   A+   Excellent

Fund Family: Bernstein Funds   **Phone:** N/A
Address: 767 Fifth Avenue, New York, NY 10153
Fund Type: FO - Foreign

Major Rating Factors: Strong performance is the major factor driving the A+ (Excellent) Weiss Investment Rating for Sanford Bernstein Internatl Val II. The fund currently has a performance rating of B+ (Good) based on an average return of 21.24% over the last three years and 9.16% over the last six months. Factored into the performance evaluation is an expense ratio of 1.26% (average).

The fund's risk rating is currently B (Good). It carries a beta of 0.96, meaning that its performance tracks fairly well with that of the overall stock market. Volatility, as measured by standard deviation, is considered low for equity funds at 9.99.

Seth J. Masters currently receives a manager quality ranking of 35 (0=worst, 99=best). If you desire only a moderate level of risk and strong performance, then this fund is an excellent option.

Services Offered: An IRA investment plan.

Data Date	Weiss Investment Rating	Net Assets ($Mil)	NAV	Performance Rating/Pts	Total Return Y-T-D	Risk Rating/Pts
6-06	A+	3,255	26.23	B+ / 8.7	9.16%	B / 8.0
2005	A	2,928	24.03	B+ / 8.7	14.67%	B- / 7.4
2004	B-	2,458	21.23	B+ / 8.9	18.48%	C- / 4.1

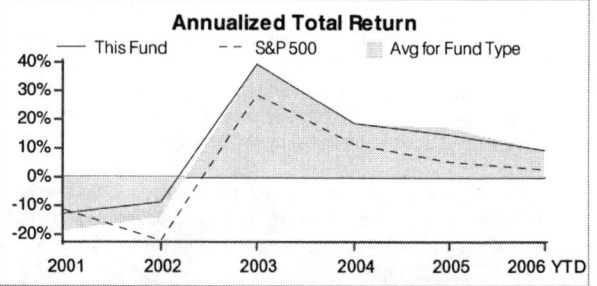

Sanford Bernstein T/M Intl Val (SNIVX)   B   Good

Fund Family: Bernstein Funds   **Phone:** N/A
Address: 767 Fifth Avenue, New York, NY 10153
Fund Type: GL - Global

Major Rating Factors: Strong performance is the major factor driving the B (Good) Weiss Investment Rating for Sanford Bernstein T/M Intl Val. The fund currently has a performance rating of B+ (Good) based on an average return of 20.92% over the last three years and 9.10% over the last six months. Factored into the performance evaluation is an expense ratio of 1.16% (low).

The fund's risk rating is currently C+ (Fair). It carries a beta of 0.97, meaning that its performance tracks fairly well with that of the overall stock market. Volatility, as measured by both the semi-deviation and a drawdown factor, is considered low.

Drew Demakis currently receives a manager quality ranking of 32 (0=worst, 99=best). If you desire only a moderate level of risk and strong performance, then this fund is an excellent option.

Services Offered: Automated phone transactions, an IRA investment plan, a 401K investment plan, a Keogh investment plan and a systematic withdrawal plan.

Data Date	Weiss Investment Rating	Net Assets ($Mil)	NAV	Performance Rating/Pts	Total Return Y-T-D	Risk Rating/Pts
6-06	B	7,193	26.25	B+ / 8.6	9.10%	C+ / 6.0
2005	B+	6,402	24.06	B+ / 8.6	14.44%	C+ / 6.5
2004	B+	5,281	22.58	B+ / 8.8	17.58%	C / 5.5
2003	B	3,841	19.61	B / 8.1	38.83%	C+ / 6.2
2002	C+	2,707	14.35	C+ / 6.6	-8.51%	C+ / 6.8
2001	C	1,505	15.90	D / 2.2	-14.05%	C+ / 6.7

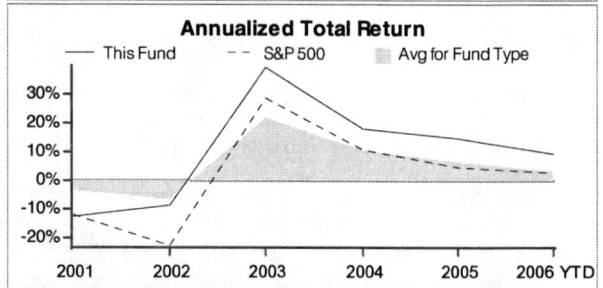

Schwab 1000 Inv (SNXFX)   C   Fair

Fund Family: Schwab Funds   **Phone:** (866) 855-9102
Address: 101 Montgomery Street, San Francisco, CA 94104
Fund Type: GI - Growth and Income

Major Rating Factors: Middle of the road best describes Schwab 1000 Inv whose Weiss Investment Rating is currently a C (Fair). The fund currently has a performance rating of C- (Fair) based on an average return of 11.66% over the last three years and 2.84% over the last six months. Factored into the performance evaluation is an expense ratio of 0.51% (very low) and a 2.0% back-end load levied at the time of sale.

The fund's risk rating is currently B- (Good). It carries a beta of 1.01, meaning that its performance tracks fairly well with that of the overall stock market. Volatility, as measured by both the semi-deviation and a drawdown factor, is considered low.

This is team managed and currently receives a manager quality ranking of 60 (0=worst, 99=best). If you desire an average level of risk, then this fund may be an option.

Services Offered: Automated phone transactions, payroll deductions, bank draft capabilities, an IRA investment plan, a 401K investment plan and a Keogh investment plan.

Data Date	Weiss Investment Rating	Net Assets ($Mil)	NAV	Performance Rating/Pts	Total Return Y-T-D	Risk Rating/Pts
6-06	C	4,080	37.26	C- / 4.1	2.84%	B- / 7.8
2005	C-	4,283	36.23	C- / 3.8	6.05%	B- / 7.0
2004	C	4,524	34.59	C / 4.8	10.82%	C / 5.3
2003	C	4,211	31.65	C / 4.6	28.74%	C+ / 5.7
2002	C+	3,191	24.86	C / 4.7	-21.19%	C+ / 6.4
2001	C-	4,163	31.95	C- / 4.0	-12.26%	C- / 3.5

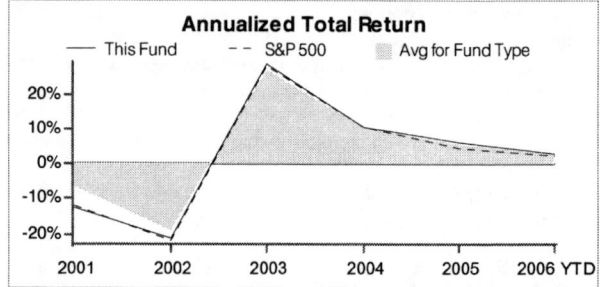

Schwab S&P 500 Inv (SWPIX)

C-   Fair

Fund Family: Schwab Funds   **Phone:** (866) 855-9102
Address: 101 Montgomery Street, San Francisco, CA 94104
Fund Type: IX - Index

Major Rating Factors: Middle of the road best describes Schwab S&P 500 Inv whose Weiss Investment Rating is currently a C- (Fair). The fund currently has a performance rating of C- (Fair) based on an average return of 10.90% over the last three years and 2.60% over the last six months. Factored into the performance evaluation is an expense ratio of 0.37% (very low) and a 2.0% back-end load levied at the time of sale.

The fund's risk rating is currently B- (Good). It carries a beta of 1.00, meaning that its performance tracks fairly well with that of the overall stock market. Volatility, as measured by both the semi-deviation and a drawdown factor, is considered low.

Jeffrey Mortimer currently receives a manager quality ranking of 53 (0=worst, 99=best). If you desire an average level of risk, then this fund may be an option.

Services Offered: Automated phone transactions, bank draft capabilities, an IRA investment plan, a 401K investment plan and a Keogh investment plan.

Data Date	Weiss Investment Rating	Net Assets ($Mil)	NAV	Performance Rating/Pts	Total Return Y-T-D	Risk Rating/Pts
6-06	C-	3,623	19.70	C- / 3.6	2.60%	B- / 7.8
2005	D+	3,776	19.20	C- / 3.1	4.66%	C+ / 6.9
2004	C-	4,061	18.63	C- / 4.2	10.53%	C / 5.1
2003	C	3,760	17.13	C- / 4.2	28.15%	C+ / 5.6
2002	C	2,755	13.54	C / 4.4	-22.28%	C+ / 6.4
2001	C-	3,384	17.68	C- / 3.7	-12.15%	C- / 3.6

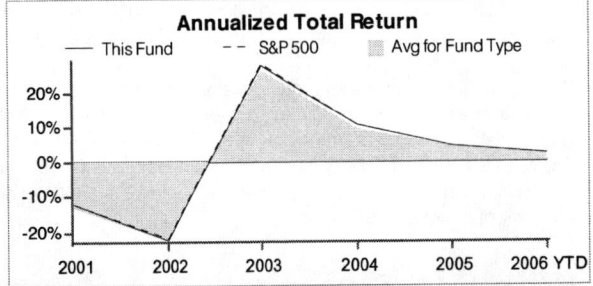

Select Electronics Port (FSELX)

E-   Very Weak

Fund Family: Fidelity Select   **Phone:** (800) 544-8888
Address: 82 Devonshire Street, Boston, MA 02109
Fund Type: TC - Technology

Major Rating Factors: Select Electronics Port has adopted a very risky asset allocation strategy and currently receives an overall Weiss Investment Rating of E- (Very Weak). The fund has a high level of volatility, as measured by both semi-deviation and drawdown factors. It carries a beta of 2.43, meaning it is expected to move 24.3% for every 10% move in the market. Unfortunately, the high level of risk (D-, Weak) failed to pay off as investors endured poor performance.

The fund's performance rating is currently D+ (Weak). It has registered an average return of 10.85% over the last three years but is down -3.93% over the last six months. Factored into the performance evaluation is an expense ratio of 0.91% (low) and a 0.8% back-end load levied at the time of sale.

James Morrow has been running the fund for 2 years and currently receives a manager quality ranking of 1 (0=worst, 99=best). If you can tolerate very high levels of risk in the hope of improved future returns, holding this fund may be an option.

Services Offered: Automated phone transactions, bank draft capabilities, an IRA investment plan and a 401K investment plan.

Data Date	Weiss Investment Rating	Net Assets ($Mil)	NAV	Performance Rating/Pts	Total Return Y-T-D	Risk Rating/Pts
6-06	E-	2,286	42.01	D+ / 2.9	-3.93%	D- / 1.2
2005	D	2,673	43.73	B / 8.0	15.75%	D- / 1.5
2004	E-	2,921	37.78	E- / 0.9	-9.81%	E+ / 0.9
2003	D+	4,000	41.89	C / 5.5	71.89%	D- / 1.0
2002	E-	2,861	24.37	E / 0.3	-50.54%	E- / 0.0
2001	C	5,106	49.27	A- / 9.0	-14.73%	E- / 0.0

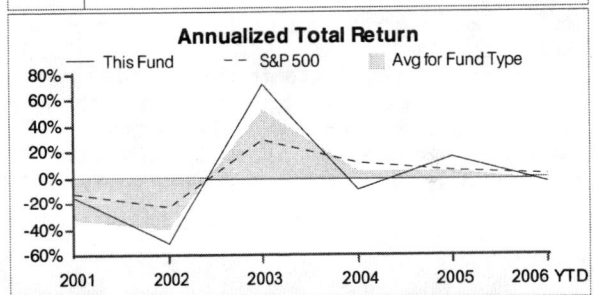

Select Energy (FSENX)

B+   Good

Fund Family: Fidelity Select   **Phone:** (800) 544-8888
Address: 82 Devonshire Street, Boston, MA 02109
Fund Type: EN - Energy/Natural Resources

Major Rating Factors: Exceptional performance is the major factor driving the B+ (Good) Weiss Investment Rating for Select Energy. The fund currently has a performance rating of A+ (Excellent) based on an average return of 37.96% over the last three years and 15.97% over the last six months. Factored into the performance evaluation is an expense ratio of 0.91% (low) and a 0.8% back-end load levied at the time of sale.

The fund's risk rating is currently C (Fair). It carries a beta of 0.99, meaning that its performance tracks fairly well with that of the overall stock market. Volatility, as measured by both the semi-deviation and a drawdown factor, is considered average.

Matthew Friedman has been running the fund for 2 years and currently receives a manager quality ranking of 91 (0=worst, 99=best). If you desire an average level of risk and strong performance, then this fund is a good option.

Services Offered: Automated phone transactions, bank draft capabilities, an IRA investment plan, a 401K investment plan, a Keogh investment plan and wire transfers.

Data Date	Weiss Investment Rating	Net Assets ($Mil)	NAV	Performance Rating/Pts	Total Return Y-T-D	Risk Rating/Pts
6-06	B+	2,782	51.82	A+ / 9.9	15.97%	C / 5.2
2005	A	2,229	46.76	A+ / 9.8	52.02%	C+ / 6.3
2004	A-	570	32.53	B+ / 8.8	31.70%	C+ / 6.2
2003	C+	187	25.06	C / 5.2	22.87%	C+ / 6.7
2002	B+	186	20.52	B+ / 8.5	-11.48%	B- / 7.3
2001	C	226	23.33	B+ / 8.9	-11.99%	E- / 0.0

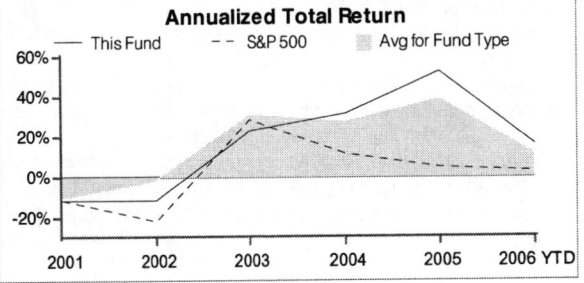

Select Health Care (FSPHX)   E-   Very Weak

Fund Family: Fidelity Select   **Phone:** (800) 544-8888
Address: 82 Devonshire Street, Boston, MA 02109
Fund Type: HL - Health

Major Rating Factors: Disappointing performance is the major factor driving the E- (Very Weak) Weiss Investment Rating for Select Health Care. The fund currently has a performance rating of D (Weak) based on an average return of 8.36% over the last three years and -3.75% over the last six months. Factored into the performance evaluation is an expense ratio of 0.89% (low) and a 0.8% back-end load levied at the time of sale.

The fund's risk rating is currently C- (Fair). It carries a beta of 0.61, meaning the fund's expected move will be 6.1% for every 10% move in the market. Volatility, as measured by both the semi-deviation and a drawdown factor, is considered average.

Harlan Carere has been running the fund for 1 year and currently receives a manager quality ranking of 64 (0=worst, 99=best). This fund offers an average level of risk but investors looking for strong performance will be frustrated.

Services Offered: Automated phone transactions, check writing, bank draft capabilities, an IRA investment plan, a 401K investment plan, a Keogh investment plan and wire transfers.

Data Date	Weiss Investment Rating	Net Assets ($Mil)	NAV	Performance Rating/Pts	Total Return Y-T-D	Risk Rating/Pts
6-06	E-	2,074	118.91	D / 1.7	-3.75%	C- / 3.0
2005	C-	2,316	136.09	C / 4.7	16.86%	C / 5.5
2004	D	1,970	128.09	D / 2.2	8.66%	C / 5.0
2003	D+	1,879	118.01	D / 1.6	15.91%	C / 5.5
2002	B	1,922	101.98	B / 7.9	-18.04%	C+ / 6.9
2001	C+	2,511	127.26	C+ / 5.6	-15.01%	C+ / 6.2

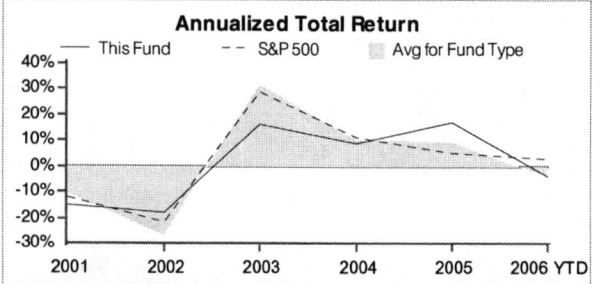

Selected American Shares S (SLASX)   B+   Good

Fund Family: Davis Funds   **Phone:** (800) 279-0279
Address: 2949 East Elvira St, Tuscon, AZ 85706
Fund Type: GI - Growth and Income

Major Rating Factors: Selected American Shares S receives a Weiss Investment Rating of B+ (Good). The fund currently has a performance rating of C+ (Fair) based on an average return of 14.26% over the last three years and 3.35% over the last six months. Factored into the performance evaluation is an expense ratio of 0.94% (low).

The fund's risk rating is currently B+ (Good). It carries a beta of 0.87, meaning the fund's expected move will be 8.7% for every 10% move in the market. Volatility, as measured by both the semi-deviation and a drawdown factor, is considered very low.

Christopher C. Davis has been running the fund for 9 years and currently receives a manager quality ranking of 89 (0=worst, 99=best). If you desire an average level of risk, then this fund may be an option.

Services Offered: Check writing, bank draft capabilities, an IRA investment plan, a 401K investment plan, wire transfers and a systematic withdrawal plan.

Data Date	Weiss Investment Rating	Net Assets ($Mil)	NAV	Performance Rating/Pts	Total Return Y-T-D	Risk Rating/Pts
6-06	B+	6,767	41.59	C+ / 6.0	3.35%	B+ / 9.1
2005	B	7,780	40.24	C+ / 5.8	9.90%	B- / 7.9
2004	C+	6,603	36.87	C+ / 6.0	11.99%	C+ / 6.4
2003	C+	5,614	33.17	C+ / 6.0	30.90%	C+ / 6.6
2002	C+	4,569	25.51	C+ / 6.9	-17.06%	C+ / 6.8
2001	C+	5,457	30.99	C+ / 6.8	-11.17%	C+ / 6.3

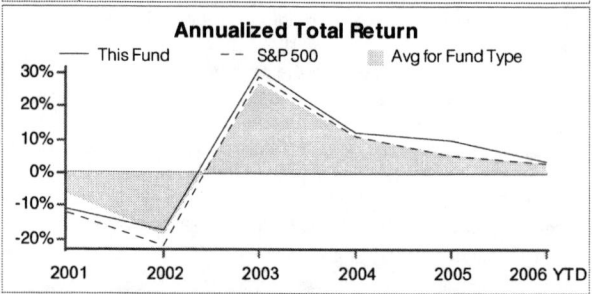

Seligman Communications/Info A (SLMCX)   D-   Weak

Fund Family: Seligman Group   **Phone:** (800) 221-2783
Address: 100 Park Avenue, New York, NY 10017
Fund Type: TC - Technology

Major Rating Factors: Seligman Communications/Info A receives a Weiss Investment Rating of D- (Weak). The fund currently has a performance rating of C (Fair) based on an average return of 13.11% over the last three years and 4.62% over the last six months. Factored into the performance evaluation is an expense ratio of 1.49% (average) and a 4.8% front-end load that is levied at the time of purchase.

The fund's risk rating is currently C- (Fair). It carries a beta of 1.69, meaning it is expected to move 16.9% for every 10% move in the market. Volatility, as measured by both the semi-deviation and a drawdown factor, is considered average.

Paul H. Wick has been running the fund for 17 years and currently receives a manager quality ranking of 19 (0=worst, 99=best). If you desire an average level of risk, then this fund may be an option.

Services Offered: Automated phone transactions, check writing, payroll deductions, bank draft capabilities, an IRA investment plan, a 401K investment plan, a Keogh investment plan and a systematic withdrawal plan.

Data Date	Weiss Investment Rating	Net Assets ($Mil)	NAV	Performance Rating/Pts	Total Return Y-T-D	Risk Rating/Pts
6-06	D-	2,372	28.55	C / 4.4	4.62%	C- / 4.0
2005	D+	2,260	27.29	C+ / 5.8	7.36%	C- / 4.2
2004	E	2,307	25.42	D- / 1.5	10.57%	D / 1.8
2003	C-	2,398	22.99	C / 5.5	42.35%	D+ / 2.7
2002	E+	2,106	16.15	E+ / 0.8	-36.82%	D- / 1.4
2001	C-	3,447	25.56	B- / 7.3	3.58%	E- / 0.0

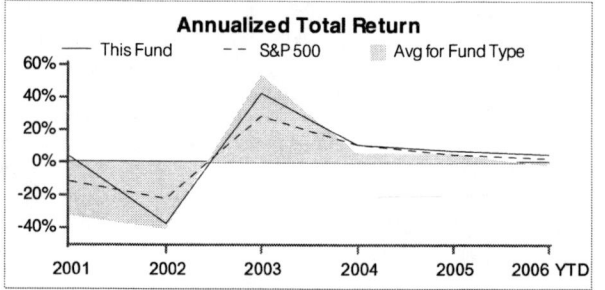

Sequoia Fund (SEQUX)

D- **Weak**

Fund Family: Sequoia **Phone:** (800) 686-6884
Address: 767 Fifth Avenue, New York, NY 10153
Fund Type: GR - Growth

Major Rating Factors: Disappointing performance is the major factor driving the D- (Weak) Weiss Investment Rating for Sequoia Fund. The fund currently has a performance rating of D (Weak) based on an average return of 7.11% over the last three years and 0.78% over the last six months. Factored into the performance evaluation is an expense ratio of 1.00% (low).

The fund's risk rating is currently C+ (Fair). It carries a beta of 0.55, meaning the fund's expected move will be 5.5% for every 10% move in the market. Volatility, as measured by both the semi-deviation and a drawdown factor, is considered low.

David M. Poppe has been running the fund for 1 year and currently receives a manager quality ranking of 56 (0=worst, 99=best). This fund offers only a moderate level of risk but investors looking for strong performance are still waiting.

Services Offered: Bank draft capabilities, an IRA investment plan, a 401K investment plan, wire transfers and a systematic withdrawal plan. However, the fund is currently closed to new investors.

Data Date	Weiss Investment Rating	Net Assets ($Mil)	NAV	Performance Rating/Pts	Total Return Y-T-D	Risk Rating/Pts
6-06	D-	3,562	156.61	D / 1.6	0.78%	C+ / 6.9
2005	E+	3,590	155.45	E+ / 0.6	3.05%	C+ / 6.9
2004	C	4,370	154.27	C- / 3.7	4.51%	B- / 7.6
2003	A	3,959	147.61	B / 7.7	17.12%	B / 8.6
2002	A	3,990	126.63	A / 9.5	-2.64%	B / 8.6
2001	B-	4,230	130.24	B / 7.9	10.52%	C- / 3.0

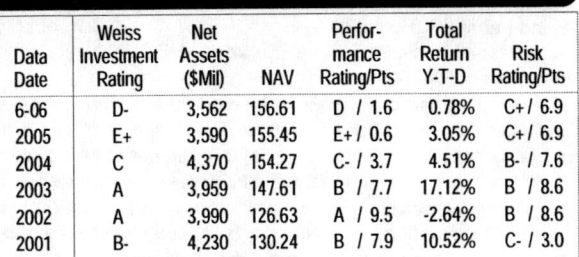

Annualized Total Return

Sound Shore Fund (SSHFX)

C **Fair**

Fund Family: Sound Shore **Phone:** (800) 754-8758
Address: 2 Portland Square, Portland, ME 04101
Fund Type: GR - Growth

Major Rating Factors: Middle of the road best describes Sound Shore Fund whose Weiss Investment Rating is currently a C (Fair). The fund currently has a performance rating of C (Fair) based on an average return of 13.30% over the last three years and 1.54% over the last six months. Factored into the performance evaluation is an expense ratio of 0.93% (low).

The fund's risk rating is currently B- (Good). It carries a beta of 1.02, meaning that its performance tracks fairly well with that of the overall stock market. Volatility, as measured by both the semi-deviation and a drawdown factor, is considered low.

Harry Burn, III/T. has been running the fund for 21 years and currently receives a manager quality ranking of 74 (0=worst, 99=best). If you desire an average level of risk, then this fund may be an option.

Services Offered: Automated phone transactions, an IRA investment plan, a 401K investment plan, wire transfers and a systematic withdrawal plan.

Data Date	Weiss Investment Rating	Net Assets ($Mil)	NAV	Performance Rating/Pts	Total Return Y-T-D	Risk Rating/Pts
6-06	C	2,502	37.11	C / 5.3	1.54%	B- / 7.1
2005	C	2,265	36.63	C / 5.5	6.80%	C+ / 6.2
2004	B-	1,698	36.70	B- / 7.1	15.34%	C+ / 5.6
2003	B	1,017	33.51	B / 7.6	31.74%	C+ / 6.6
2002	B+	759	25.81	B+ / 8.6	-15.43%	B- / 7.5
2001	B+	1,052	30.58	B- / 7.5	-0.81%	C+ / 6.5

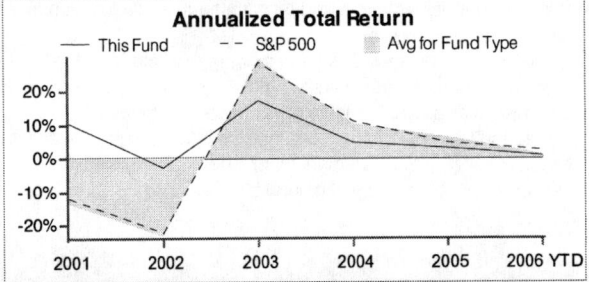

Annualized Total Return

State Farm Growth Fund (STFGX)

C+ **Fair**

Fund Family: State Farm **Phone:** (877) 734-2265
Address: Three State Farm Plaza, Bloomington, IL 61710
Fund Type: GR - Growth

Major Rating Factors: Middle of the road best describes State Farm Growth Fund whose Weiss Investment Rating is currently a C+ (Fair). The fund currently has a performance rating of C (Fair) based on an average return of 11.89% over the last three years and 6.27% over the last six months. Factored into the performance evaluation is an expense ratio of 0.12% (very low).

The fund's risk rating is currently B- (Good). It carries a beta of 0.89, meaning the fund's expected move will be 8.9% for every 10% move in the market. Volatility, as measured by both the semi-deviation and a drawdown factor, is considered low.

Duncan Funk currently receives a manager quality ranking of 72 (0=worst, 99=best). If you desire an average level of risk, then this fund may be an option.

Services Offered: Automated phone transactions, payroll deductions, an IRA investment plan, a 401K investment plan, a Keogh investment plan, wire transfers and a systematic withdrawal plan.

Data Date	Weiss Investment Rating	Net Assets ($Mil)	NAV	Performance Rating/Pts	Total Return Y-T-D	Risk Rating/Pts
6-06	C+	3,194	52.04	C / 5.0	6.27%	B- / 7.8
2005	D	3,068	49.46	D+ / 2.5	4.60%	B- / 7.1
2004	C-	2,941	48.20	C- / 4.2	8.47%	C+ / 5.8
2003	C+	2,700	44.98	C / 4.9	24.22%	C+ / 6.2
2002	C+	2,228	36.51	C+ / 5.8	-16.09%	C+ / 6.9
2001	C+	2,537	44.23	C / 4.5	-10.82%	C+ / 6.2

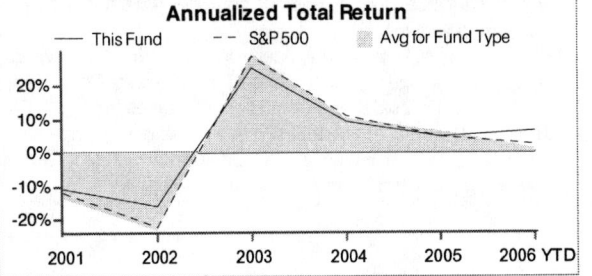

Annualized Total Return

T. Rowe Price Balanced Fd (RPBAX)

C+   **Fair**

Fund Family: T. Rowe Price   **Phone:** (800) 638-5660
Address: 100 East Pratt Street, Baltimore, MD 21202
Fund Type: BA - Balanced

Major Rating Factors: Middle of the road best describes T. Rowe Price Balanced Fd whose Weiss Investment Rating is currently a C+ (Fair). The fund currently has a performance rating of C- (Fair) based on an average return of 9.90% over the last three years and 2.58% over the last six months. Factored into the performance evaluation is an expense ratio of 0.67% (very low).

The fund's risk rating is currently B+ (Good). It carries a beta of 1.08, meaning that its performance tracks fairly well with that of the overall stock market. Volatility, as measured by both the semi-deviation and a drawdown factor, is considered very low.

Richard T. Whitney has been running the fund for 14 years and currently receives a manager quality ranking of 75 (0=worst, 99=best). If you desire an average level of risk, then this fund may be an option.

Services Offered: Automated phone transactions, payroll deductions, bank draft capabilities, an IRA investment plan, a 401K investment plan, a Keogh investment plan and a systematic withdrawal plan.

Data Date	Weiss Investment Rating	Net Assets ($Mil)	NAV	Performance Rating/Pts	Total Return Y-T-D	Risk Rating/Pts
6-06	C+	2,609	19.76	C- / 3.4	2.58%	B+ / 9.3
2005	C	2,502	19.77	D+ / 2.4	5.52%	B+ / 9.3
2004	B	2,270	19.70	C+ / 5.9	10.32%	B / 8.2
2003	B	1,960	18.41	C+ / 6.8	21.71%	B / 8.4
2002	B+	1,618	15.51	B / 8.0	-8.54%	B / 8.7
2001	B	1,791	17.49	C+ / 6.1	-3.98%	B / 8.4

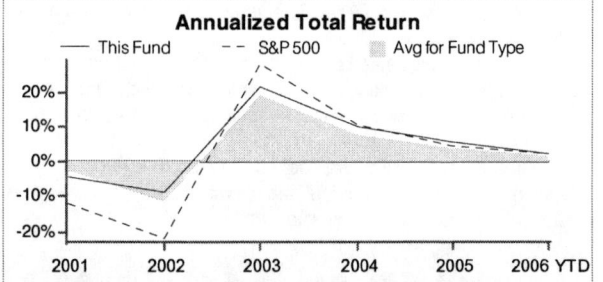

Annualized Total Return

T. Rowe Price Blue Chip Growth Fd (TRBCX)

C-   **Fair**

Fund Family: T. Rowe Price   **Phone:** (800) 638-5660
Address: 100 East Pratt Street, Baltimore, MD 21202
Fund Type: GR - Growth

Major Rating Factors: Disappointing performance is the major factor driving the C- (Fair) Weiss Investment Rating for T. Rowe Price Blue Chip Growth Fd. The fund currently has a performance rating of D+ (Weak) based on an average return of 9.19% over the last three years and -1.16% over the last six months. Factored into the performance evaluation is an expense ratio of 0.83% (very low).

The fund's risk rating is currently B (Good). It carries a beta of 1.09, meaning that its performance tracks fairly well with that of the overall stock market. Volatility, as measured by both the semi-deviation and a drawdown factor, is considered low.

Larry J. Puglia has been running the fund for 13 years and currently receives a manager quality ranking of 29 (0=worst, 99=best). This fund offers only a moderate level of risk but investors looking for strong performance are still waiting.

Services Offered: Automated phone transactions, payroll deductions, bank draft capabilities, an IRA investment plan, a 401K investment plan, a Keogh investment plan, wire transfers and a systematic withdrawal plan.

Data Date	Weiss Investment Rating	Net Assets ($Mil)	NAV	Performance Rating/Pts	Total Return Y-T-D	Risk Rating/Pts
6-06	C-	8,002	32.30	D+ / 2.5	-1.16%	B / 8.1
2005	C	7,842	32.68	C- / 4.2	5.95%	B- / 7.7
2004	D+	7,057	30.92	D+ / 2.7	9.25%	C+ / 5.6
2003	C	6,031	28.45	C- / 3.6	29.75%	C+ / 5.8
2002	C	4,868	21.95	C / 4.5	-24.23%	C+ / 5.8
2001	C-	6,242	28.97	C / 4.5	-14.42%	D+ / 2.7

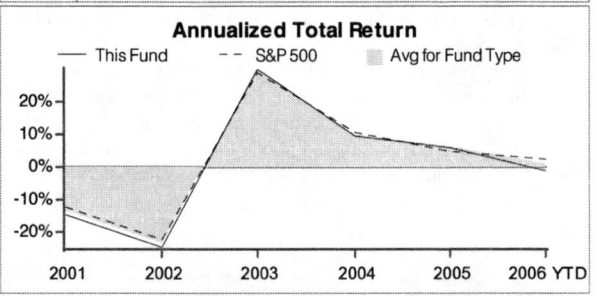

Annualized Total Return

T. Rowe Price Cap Appreciation Fd (PRWCX)

B+   **Good**

Fund Family: T. Rowe Price   **Phone:** (800) 638-5660
Address: 100 East Pratt Street, Baltimore, MD 21202
Fund Type: AA - Asset Allocation

Major Rating Factors: T. Rowe Price Cap Appreciation Fd receives a Weiss Investment Rating of B+ (Good). The fund currently has a performance rating of C (Fair) based on an average return of 13.22% over the last three years and 3.09% over the last six months. Factored into the performance evaluation is an expense ratio of 0.74% (very low).

The fund's risk rating is currently B+ (Good). It carries a beta of 1.23, meaning it is expected to move 12.3% for every 10% move in the market. Volatility, as measured by both the semi-deviation and a drawdown factor, is considered very low.

Stephen W. Boessel has been running the fund for 5 years and currently receives a manager quality ranking of 90 (0=worst, 99=best). If you desire an average level of risk, then this fund may be an option.

Services Offered: Automated phone transactions, payroll deductions, bank draft capabilities, an IRA investment plan, a 401K investment plan, a Keogh investment plan and a systematic withdrawal plan.

Data Date	Weiss Investment Rating	Net Assets ($Mil)	NAV	Performance Rating/Pts	Total Return Y-T-D	Risk Rating/Pts
6-06	B+	7,929	20.68	C / 5.3	3.09%	B+ / 9.7
2005	B	7,280	20.06	C / 4.6	6.85%	B+ / 9.1
2004	A+	4,693	19.49	B / 8.2	15.29%	B / 8.5
2003	A+	2,737	17.50	B+ / 8.6	25.47%	B+ / 9.5
2002	A+	1,856	14.21	A+ / 9.6	0.54%	B+ / 9.9
2001	A+	1,405	14.64	A- / 9.2	10.26%	B / 8.3

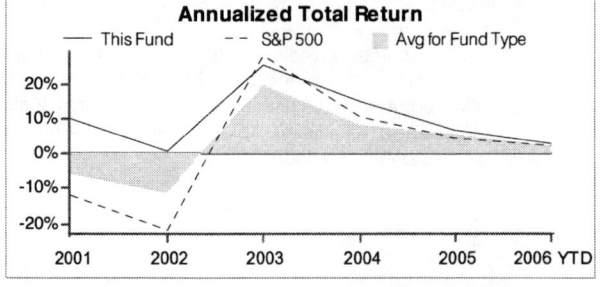

Annualized Total Return

T. Rowe Price Emerging Mkts Stk (PRMSX)

B-   **Good**

Fund Family: T. Rowe Price   **Phone:** (800) 638-5660
Address: 100 East Pratt Street, Baltimore, MD 21202
Fund Type: EM - Emerging Market

Major Rating Factors: Exceptional performance is the major factor driving the B- (Good) Weiss Investment Rating for T. Rowe Price Emerging Mkts Stk. The fund currently has a performance rating of A+ (Excellent) based on an average return of 34.64% over the last three years and 2.88% over the last six months. Factored into the performance evaluation is an expense ratio of 1.25% (average) and a 2.0% back-end load levied at the time of sale.

The fund's risk rating is currently C- (Fair). It carries a beta of 1.15, meaning it is expected to move 11.5% for every 10% move in the market. Volatility, as measured by both the semi-deviation and a drawdown factor, is considered average.

This fund has been team managed for 11 years and currently receives a manager quality ranking of 14 (0=worst, 99=best). If you desire an average level of risk and strong performance, then this fund is a good option.

Services Offered: Automated phone transactions, payroll deductions, bank draft capabilities, an IRA investment plan, a 401K investment plan, a Keogh investment plan and a systematic withdrawal plan.

Data Date	Weiss Investment Rating	Net Assets ($Mil)	NAV	Performance Rating/Pts	Total Return Y-T-D	Risk Rating/Pts
6-06	B-	2,067	26.42	A+ / 9.7	2.88%	C- / 3.9
2005	A-	1,465	25.68	A+ / 9.9	38.77%	C+ / 5.7
2004	A+	684	19.41	A+ / 9.6	26.98%	C+ / 6.6
2003	A-	373	15.47	A / 9.5	52.30%	C+ / 6.7
2002	C+	173	10.22	C+ / 5.6	-4.93%	C / 5.3
2001	C	155	10.77	B+ / 8.4	-5.69%	E- / 0.0

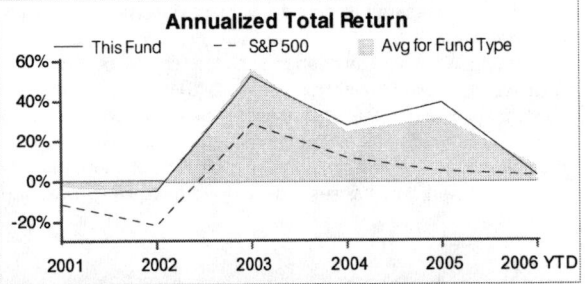
Annualized Total Return

T. Rowe Price Equity Income Fd (PRFDX)

B   **Good**

Fund Family: T. Rowe Price   **Phone:** (800) 638-5660
Address: 100 East Pratt Street, Baltimore, MD 21202
Fund Type: IN - Income

Major Rating Factors: T. Rowe Price Equity Income Fd receives a Weiss Investment Rating of B (Good). The fund currently has a performance rating of C (Fair) based on an average return of 13.03% over the last three years and 5.06% over the last six months. Factored into the performance evaluation is an expense ratio of 0.70% (very low).

The fund's risk rating is currently B (Good). It carries a beta of 0.92, meaning that its performance tracks fairly well with that of the overall stock market. Volatility, as measured by both the semi-deviation and a drawdown factor, is considered low.

Brian C. Rogers has been running the fund for 21 years and currently receives a manager quality ranking of 79 (0=worst, 99=best). If you desire an average level of risk, then this fund may be an option.

Services Offered: Automated phone transactions, payroll deductions, bank draft capabilities, an IRA investment plan, a 401K investment plan, a Keogh investment plan, wire transfers and a systematic withdrawal plan.

Data Date	Weiss Investment Rating	Net Assets ($Mil)	NAV	Performance Rating/Pts	Total Return Y-T-D	Risk Rating/Pts
6-06	B	18,666	26.92	C / 5.4	5.06%	B / 8.9
2005	C	17,958	25.92	C- / 3.8	4.26%	B- / 7.2
2004	C+	15,276	26.59	C+ / 6.9	15.05%	C+ / 6.3
2003	B+	11,407	24.16	B- / 7.4	25.78%	B- / 7.5
2002	B+	9,383	19.79	B+ / 8.5	-13.04%	B- / 7.9
2001	B+	10,128	23.65	B / 7.7	1.64%	C+ / 6.5

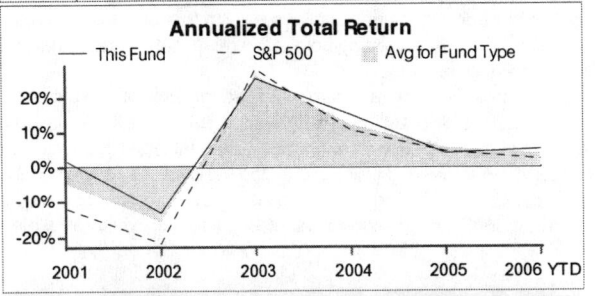
Annualized Total Return

T. Rowe Price Equity Index 500 (PREIX)

C+   **Fair**

Fund Family: T. Rowe Price   **Phone:** (800) 638-5660
Address: 100 East Pratt Street, Baltimore, MD 21202
Fund Type: IX - Index

Major Rating Factors: Middle of the road best describes T. Rowe Price Equity Index 500 whose Weiss Investment Rating is currently a C+ (Fair). The fund currently has a performance rating of C- (Fair) based on an average return of 10.88% over the last three years and 2.54% over the last six months. Factored into the performance evaluation is an expense ratio of 0.35% (very low) and a 0.5% back-end load levied at the time of sale.

The fund's risk rating is currently B (Good). It carries a beta of 1.00, meaning that its performance tracks fairly well with that of the overall stock market. Volatility, as measured by both the semi-deviation and a drawdown factor, is considered low.

E. Frederick Bair currently receives a manager quality ranking of 52 (0=worst, 99=best). If you desire an average level of risk, then this fund may be an option.

Services Offered: Automated phone transactions, check writing, payroll deductions, bank draft capabilities, an IRA investment plan, a 401K investment plan, a Keogh investment plan and a systematic withdrawal plan.

Data Date	Weiss Investment Rating	Net Assets ($Mil)	NAV	Performance Rating/Pts	Total Return Y-T-D	Risk Rating/Pts
6-06	C+	6,274	34.09	C- / 3.8	2.54%	B / 8.8
2005	C	5,683	33.55	C- / 3.4	4.62%	B- / 7.8
2004	C	4,590	32.56	C / 4.3	10.51%	C+ / 5.8
2003	C	3,662	29.95	C / 4.3	28.31%	C+ / 6.1
2002	C	2,865	23.67	C / 4.4	-22.21%	C+ / 6.3
2001	C-	3,473	30.84	C- / 3.7	-12.17%	C- / 3.6

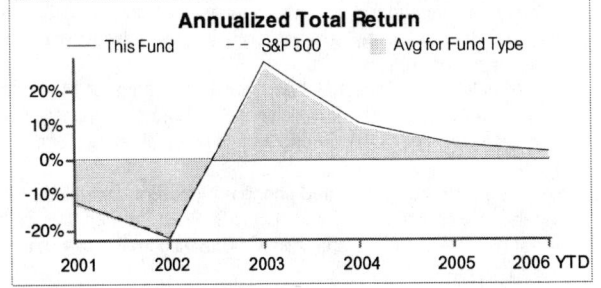
Annualized Total Return

T. Rowe Price Growth Stock Fd (PRGFX)   C   Fair

Fund Family: T. Rowe Price   **Phone:** (800) 638-5660
Address: 100 East Pratt Street, Baltimore, MD 21202
Fund Type: GR - Growth
Major Rating Factors: Middle of the road best describes T. Rowe Price Growth Stock Fd whose Weiss Investment Rating is currently a C (Fair). The fund currently has a performance rating of C- (Fair) based on an average return of 10.73% over the last three years and 0.81% over the last six months. Factored into the performance evaluation is an expense ratio of 0.71% (very low).

The fund's risk rating is currently B (Good). It carries a beta of 1.08, meaning that its performance tracks fairly well with that of the overall stock market. Volatility, as measured by both the semi-deviation and a drawdown factor, is considered low.

Robert W. Smith has been running the fund for 5 years and currently receives a manager quality ranking of 42 (0=worst, 99=best). If you desire an average level of risk, then this fund may be an option.
Services Offered: Automated phone transactions, payroll deductions, bank draft capabilities, an IRA investment plan, a 401K investment plan, a Keogh investment plan, wire transfers and a systematic withdrawal plan.

Data Date	Weiss Investment Rating	Net Assets ($Mil)	NAV	Perfor-mance Rating/Pts	Total Return Y-T-D	Risk Rating/Pts
6-06	C	12,377	28.63	C- / 3.7	0.81%	B / 8.1
2005	C+	10,749	28.40	C / 4.8	6.56%	B- / 7.7
2004	C-	7,714	26.67	D+ / 2.8	10.24%	C+ / 6.6
2003	C-	5,266	24.33	C / 5.1	31.23%	C- / 3.4
2002	C-	3,941	18.58	C / 5.4	-23.00%	D- / 1.5
2001	C	4,685	24.18	C+ / 6.4	-9.79%	D+ / 2.6

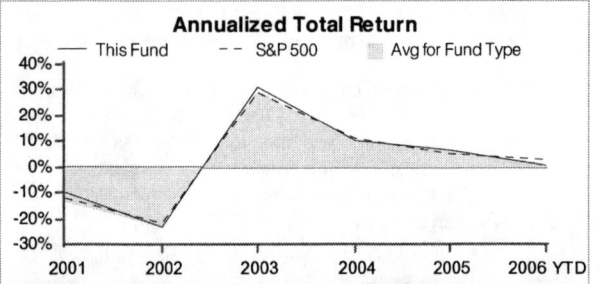

T. Rowe Price Intl Stock Fd (PRITX)   B-   Good

Fund Family: T. Rowe Price   **Phone:** (800) 638-5660
Address: 100 East Pratt Street, Baltimore, MD 21202
Fund Type: FO - Foreign
Major Rating Factors: Strong performance is the major factor driving the B- (Good) Weiss Investment Rating for T. Rowe Price Intl Stock Fd. The fund currently has a performance rating of B- (Good) based on an average return of 18.74% over the last three years and 3.79% over the last six months. Factored into the performance evaluation is an expense ratio of 0.88% (low) and a 2.0% back-end load levied at the time of sale.

The fund's risk rating is currently C+ (Fair). It carries a beta of 1.05, meaning that its performance tracks fairly well with that of the overall stock market. Volatility, as measured by both the semi-deviation and a drawdown factor, is considered low.

This fund has been team managed for 6 years and currently receives a manager quality ranking of 11 (0=worst, 99=best). If you desire only a moderate level of risk and strong performance, then this fund is an excellent option.
Services Offered: Automated phone transactions, payroll deductions, bank draft capabilities, an IRA investment plan, a 401K investment plan, a Keogh investment plan, wire transfers and a systematic withdrawal plan.

Data Date	Weiss Investment Rating	Net Assets ($Mil)	NAV	Perfor-mance Rating/Pts	Total Return Y-T-D	Risk Rating/Pts
6-06	B-	6,080	15.35	B- / 7.5	3.79%	C+ / 6.3
2005	B	5,427	14.79	B / 7.8	16.27%	C+ / 6.6
2004	C+	5,085	12.93	C+ / 6.1	13.89%	C+ / 5.7
2003	C	4,947	11.49	C- / 4.2	31.28%	C / 5.4
2002	C-	4,751	8.88	C- / 3.0	-18.18%	C / 5.3
2001	D+	6,507	10.99	D / 1.7	-22.02%	D+ / 2.8

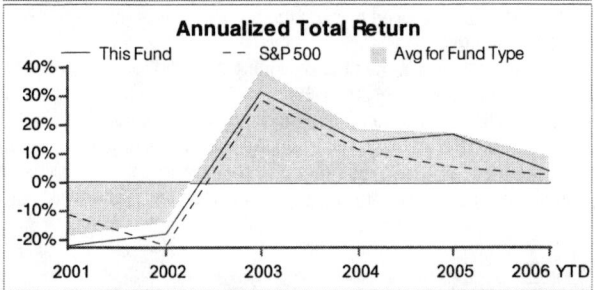

T. Rowe Price Mid-Cap Growth Fd (RPMGX)   B   Good

Fund Family: T. Rowe Price   **Phone:** (800) 638-5660
Address: 100 East Pratt Street, Baltimore, MD 21202
Fund Type: MC - Mid Cap
Major Rating Factors: Strong performance is the major factor driving the B (Good) Weiss Investment Rating for T. Rowe Price Mid-Cap Growth Fd. The fund currently has a performance rating of B- (Good) based on an average return of 17.25% over the last three years and 1.24% over the last six months. Factored into the performance evaluation is an expense ratio of 0.79% (very low).

The fund's risk rating is currently B- (Good). It carries a beta of 0.93, meaning that its performance tracks fairly well with that of the overall stock market. Volatility, as measured by both the semi-deviation and a drawdown factor, is considered low.

Brian W.H. Berghuis has been running the fund for 14 years and currently receives a manager quality ranking of 58 (0=worst, 99=best). If you desire only a moderate level of risk and strong performance, then this fund is an excellent option.
Services Offered: Automated phone transactions, payroll deductions, bank draft capabilities, an IRA investment plan, a 401K investment plan, a Keogh investment plan and a systematic withdrawal plan. However, the fund is currently closed to new investors.

Data Date	Weiss Investment Rating	Net Assets ($Mil)	NAV	Perfor-mance Rating/Pts	Total Return Y-T-D	Risk Rating/Pts
6-06	B	15,600	54.81	B- / 7.0	1.24%	B- / 7.4
2005	A	14,892	54.14	B+ / 8.6	14.82%	B- / 7.3
2004	B-	12,178	49.88	B- / 7.5	18.39%	C / 5.5
2003	B	9,517	42.90	B / 7.7	38.21%	C+ / 6.4
2002	C+	5,975	31.04	C+ / 6.9	-21.22%	C+ / 6.6
2001	C+	6,739	39.40	B+ / 8.6	-0.98%	D- / 1.2

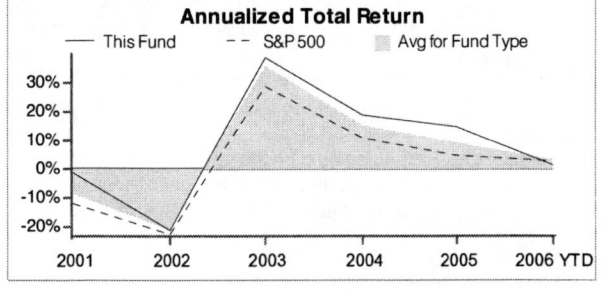

T. Rowe Price New Era (PRNEX)

A   Excellent

Fund Family: T. Rowe Price   **Phone:** (800) 638-5660
Address: 100 East Pratt Street, Baltimore, MD 21202
Fund Type: EN - Energy/Natural Resources

Major Rating Factors: Exceptional performance is the major factor driving the A (Excellent) Weiss Investment Rating for T. Rowe Price New Era. The fund currently has a performance rating of A+ (Excellent) based on an average return of 33.38% over the last three years and 13.36% over the last six months. Factored into the performance evaluation is an expense ratio of 0.67% (very low).

The fund's risk rating is currently C+ (Fair). It carries a beta of 0.78, meaning the fund's expected move will be 7.8% for every 10% move in the market. Volatility, as measured by both the semi-deviation and a drawdown factor, is considered low.

Charles M. Ober has been running the fund for 9 years and currently receives a manager quality ranking of 96 (0=worst, 99=best). If you desire only a moderate level of risk and strong performance, then this fund is an excellent option.

Services Offered: Automated phone transactions, payroll deductions, bank draft capabilities, an IRA investment plan, a 401K investment plan, a Keogh investment plan, wire transfers and a systematic withdrawal plan.

Data Date	Weiss Investment Rating	Net Assets ($Mil)	NAV	Perfor- mance Rating/Pts	Total Return Y-T-D	Risk Rating/Pts
6-06	A	4,512	46.59	A+ / 9.8	13.36%	C+ / 6.1
2005	A+	3,616	41.10	A+ / 9.6	29.88%	B- / 7.2
2004	A+	2,145	33.68	A / 9.4	30.09%	C+ / 6.9
2003	B+	1,168	27.22	B+ / 8.5	33.20%	B- / 7.2
2002	A-	984	20.63	A- / 9.0	-6.34%	B- / 7.9
2001	C+	1,070	22.24	B+ / 8.7	-4.35%	D / 1.8

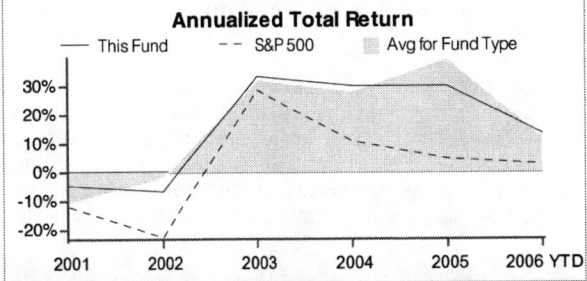

Annualized Total Return

T. Rowe Price New Horizons (PRNHX)

C+   Fair

Fund Family: T. Rowe Price   **Phone:** (800) 638-5660
Address: 100 East Pratt Street, Baltimore, MD 21202
Fund Type: SC - Small Cap

Major Rating Factors: Middle of the road best describes T. Rowe Price New Horizons whose Weiss Investment Rating is currently a C+ (Fair). The fund currently has a performance rating of C+ (Fair) based on an average return of 17.83% over the last three years and 1.80% over the last six months. Factored into the performance evaluation is an expense ratio of 0.82% (very low).

The fund's risk rating is currently C+ (Fair). It carries a beta of 0.92, meaning that its performance tracks fairly well with that of the overall stock market. Volatility, as measured by both the semi-deviation and a drawdown factor, is considered low.

John H. Laporte has been running the fund for 19 years and currently receives a manager quality ranking of 61 (0=worst, 99=best). If you desire an average level of risk, then this fund may be an option.

Services Offered: Automated phone transactions, payroll deductions, bank draft capabilities, an IRA investment plan, a 401K investment plan, a Keogh investment plan, wire transfers and a systematic withdrawal plan.

Data Date	Weiss Investment Rating	Net Assets ($Mil)	NAV	Perfor- mance Rating/Pts	Total Return Y-T-D	Risk Rating/Pts
6-06	C+	6,888	32.31	C+ / 6.9	1.80%	C+ / 5.8
2005	B+	6,530	31.74	B+ / 8.8	11.90%	C+ / 6.1
2004	C	5,565	29.24	B / 7.6	17.90%	C- / 3.6
2003	C+	4,949	24.80	B+ / 8.3	49.31%	C- / 4.0
2002	C	3,616	16.61	C / 5.2	-26.60%	C / 4.3
2001	C	5,583	22.63	B+ / 8.4	-2.84%	E- / 0.0

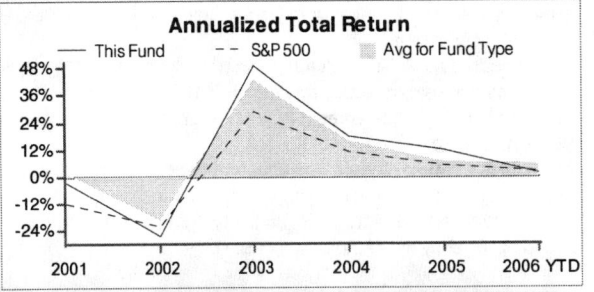

Annualized Total Return

T. Rowe Price Retirement 2020 Fd (TRRBX)

B   Good

Fund Family: T. Rowe Price   **Phone:** (800) 638-5660
Address: 100 East Pratt Street, Baltimore, MD 21202
Fund Type: IN - Income

Major Rating Factors: T. Rowe Price Retirement 2020 Fd receives a Weiss Investment Rating of B (Good). The fund currently has a performance rating of C (Fair) based on an average return of 12.60% over the last three years and 3.01% over the last six months. Factored into the performance evaluation is an expense ratio of 0.76% (very low).

The fund's risk rating is currently B+ (Good). It carries a beta of 0.88, meaning the fund's expected move will be 8.8% for every 10% move in the market. Volatility, as measured by both the semi-deviation and a drawdown factor, is considered very low.

Jerome A. Clark has been running the fund for 4 years and currently receives a manager quality ranking of 79 (0=worst, 99=best). If you desire an average level of risk, then this fund may be an option.

Services Offered: Payroll deductions, bank draft capabilities, an IRA investment plan, a 401K investment plan, a Keogh investment plan, wire transfers and a systematic withdrawal plan.

Data Date	Weiss Investment Rating	Net Assets ($Mil)	NAV	Perfor- mance Rating/Pts	Total Return Y-T-D	Risk Rating/Pts
6-06	B	2,455	16.10	C / 5.1	3.01%	B+ / 9.1
2005	B-	1,636	15.63	C / 4.7	7.17%	B / 8.8
2004	U	791	14.89	U / --	12.82%	U / --
2003	U	146	13.45	U / --	27.41%	U / --

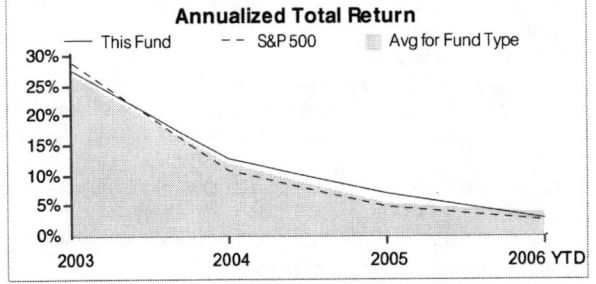

Annualized Total Return

T. Rowe Price Science & Tech Fd (PRSCX)   E   Very Weak

Fund Family: T. Rowe Price   **Phone:** (800) 638-5660
Address: 100 East Pratt Street, Baltimore, MD 21202
Fund Type: TC - Technology

Major Rating Factors: Very poor performance is the major factor driving the E
(Very Weak) Weiss Investment Rating for T. Rowe Price Science & Tech Fd.
The fund currently has a performance rating of E+ (Very Weak) based on an
average return of 6.82% over the last three years and -5.57% over the last six
months. Factored into the performance evaluation is an expense ratio of 0.99%
(low).

The fund's risk rating is currently C (Fair). It carries a beta of 1.69, meaning
it is expected to move 16.9% for every 10% move in the market. Volatility, as
measured by both the semi-deviation and a drawdown factor, is considered
average.

Michael F. Sola has been running the fund for 4 years and currently receives
a manager quality ranking of 2 (0=worst, 99=best). This fund offers an average
level of risk but investors looking for strong performance will be frustrated.

Services Offered: Automated phone transactions, payroll deductions, bank draft
capabilities, an IRA investment plan, a 401K investment plan, a Keogh
investment plan, wire transfers and a systematic withdrawal plan.

Data Date	Weiss Investment Rating	Net Assets ($Mil)	NAV	Performance Rating/Pts	Total Return Y-T-D	Risk Rating/Pts
6-06	E	2,863	18.48	E+ / 0.7	-5.57%	C / 4.3
2005	D	3,394	19.57	C / 4.6	2.46%	C / 4.5
2004	E	3,866	19.10	E+ / 0.6	1.60%	D / 1.7
2003	E	4,309	18.80	E+ / 0.7	51.25%	E+ / 0.9
2002	E-	3,307	12.43	E- / 0.2	-40.58%	E- / 0.2
2001	E	5,209	20.92	E+ / 0.6	-41.19%	E- / 0.0

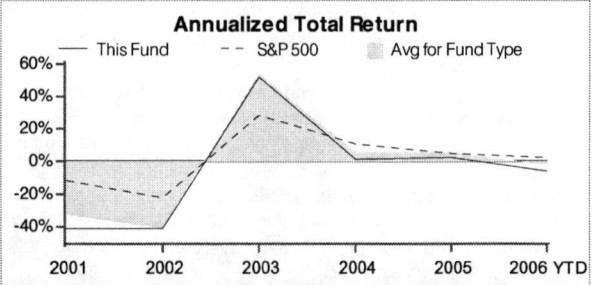

T. Rowe Price Small Cap Stock Fd (OTCFX)   B   Good

Fund Family: T. Rowe Price   **Phone:** (800) 638-5660
Address: 100 East Pratt Street, Baltimore, MD 21202
Fund Type: SC - Small Cap

Major Rating Factors: Strong performance is the major factor driving the B
(Good) Weiss Investment Rating for T. Rowe Price Small Cap Stock Fd. The
fund currently has a performance rating of B- (Good) based on an average return
of 17.57% over the last three years and 5.76% over the last six months.
Factored into the performance evaluation is an expense ratio of 0.91% (low).

The fund's risk rating is currently B- (Good). It carries a beta of 0.82,
meaning the fund's expected move will be 8.2% for every 10% move in the
market. Volatility, as measured by both the semi-deviation and a drawdown
factor, is considered low.

Gregory A. McCrickard has been running the fund for 14 years and currently
receives a manager quality ranking of 74 (0=worst, 99=best). If you desire only a
moderate level of risk and strong performance, then this fund is an excellent
option.

Services Offered: Automated phone transactions, payroll deductions, bank draft
capabilities, an IRA investment plan, a 401K investment plan, a Keogh
investment plan, wire transfers and a systematic withdrawal plan. However, the
fund is currently closed to new investors.

Data Date	Weiss Investment Rating	Net Assets ($Mil)	NAV	Performance Rating/Pts	Total Return Y-T-D	Risk Rating/Pts
6-06	B	7,222	34.70	B- / 7.3	5.76%	B- / 7.0
2005	B-	6,966	32.81	C+ / 6.8	8.44%	B- / 7.0
2004	B	6,176	31.82	B / 8.0	18.77%	C+ / 6.0
2003	B+	4,779	27.98	B+ / 8.3	32.35%	B- / 7.3
2002	B+	3,408	21.50	B+ / 8.8	-14.21%	B / 8.0
2001	B	3,158	25.34	A- / 9.2	6.81%	D+ / 2.8

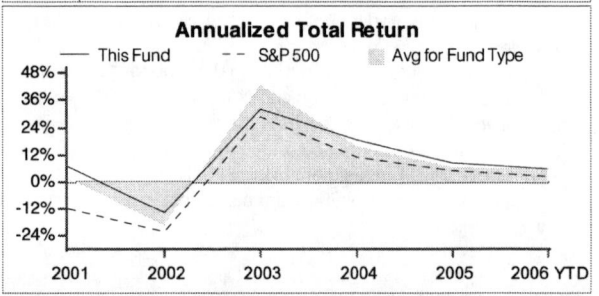

T. Rowe Price Small Cap Value Fd (PRSVX)   A   Excellent

Fund Family: T. Rowe Price   **Phone:** (800) 638-5660
Address: 100 East Pratt Street, Baltimore, MD 21202
Fund Type: SC - Small Cap

Major Rating Factors: Strong performance is the major factor driving the A
(Excellent) Weiss Investment Rating for T. Rowe Price Small Cap Value Fd. The
fund currently has a performance rating of B+ (Good) based on an average
return of 22.16% over the last three years and 10.19% over the last six months.
Factored into the performance evaluation is an expense ratio of 0.83% (very low)
and a 1.0% back-end load levied at the time of sale.

The fund's risk rating is currently B- (Good). It carries a beta of 0.79,
meaning the fund's expected move will be 7.9% for every 10% move in the
market. Volatility, as measured by both the semi-deviation and a drawdown
factor, is considered low.

Preston G. Athey has been running the fund for 15 years and currently
receives a manager quality ranking of 96 (0=worst, 99=best). If you desire only a
moderate level of risk and strong performance, then this fund is an excellent
option.

Services Offered: Automated phone transactions, payroll deductions, bank draft
capabilities, an IRA investment plan, a 401K investment plan, a Keogh
investment plan, wire transfers and a systematic withdrawal plan. However, the
fund is currently closed to new investors.

Data Date	Weiss Investment Rating	Net Assets ($Mil)	NAV	Performance Rating/Pts	Total Return Y-T-D	Risk Rating/Pts
6-06	A	5,244	40.67	B+ / 8.6	10.19%	B- / 7.1
2005	A-	4,800	36.91	B / 8.0	8.74%	B- / 7.6
2004	A+	4,355	35.65	A / 9.4	25.58%	C+ / 6.7
2003	A+	3,192	29.39	A / 9.5	36.43%	B / 8.0
2002	A+	2,435	21.94	A+ / 9.7	-1.76%	B / 8.8
2001	A+	2,012	22.66	A+ / 9.6	21.94%	C+ / 6.9

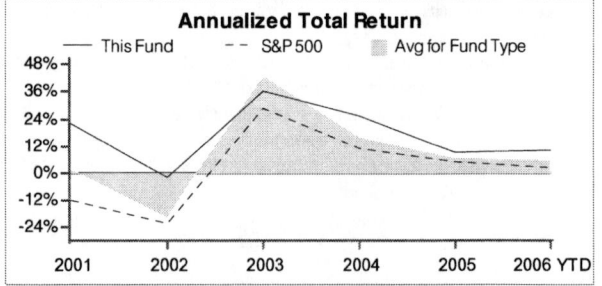

T. Rowe Price Spectrum Growth (PRSGX)   B   Good

Fund Family: T. Rowe Price   **Phone:** (800) 638-5660
Address: 100 East Pratt Street, Baltimore, MD 21202
Fund Type: GI - Growth and Income

Major Rating Factors: T. Rowe Price Spectrum Growth receives a Weiss Investment Rating of B (Good). The fund currently has a performance rating of C+ (Fair) based on an average return of 15.59% over the last three years and 3.18% over the last six months. Factored into the performance evaluation is an expense ratio of 0.82% (very low).

The fund's risk rating is currently B (Good). It carries a beta of 1.15, meaning it is expected to move 11.5% for every 10% move in the market. Volatility, as measured by both the semi-deviation and a drawdown factor, is considered low.

Edmund M. Notzon III currently receives a manager quality ranking of 82 (0=worst, 99=best). If you desire an average level of risk, then this fund may be an option.

Services Offered: Automated phone transactions, payroll deductions, bank draft capabilities, an IRA investment plan, a 401K investment plan, a Keogh investment plan, wire transfers and a systematic withdrawal plan.

Data Date	Weiss Investment Rating	Net Assets ($Mil)	NAV	Perfor-mance Rating/Pts	Total Return Y-T-D	Risk Rating/Pts
6-06	B	3,068	18.80	C+/ 6.5	3.18%	B / 8.0
2005	B-	2,816	18.22	C+/ 6.7	9.47%	B- / 7.9
2004	C+	2,496	16.87	C+/ 6.9	15.16%	C+/ 6.2
2003	C+	2,156	14.80	C+/ 6.4	34.09%	C+/ 6.7
2002	C+	1,840	11.13	C+/ 6.0	-19.83%	C+/ 6.2
2001	C+	2,373	14.07	C+/ 6.7	-7.63%	C- / 3.6

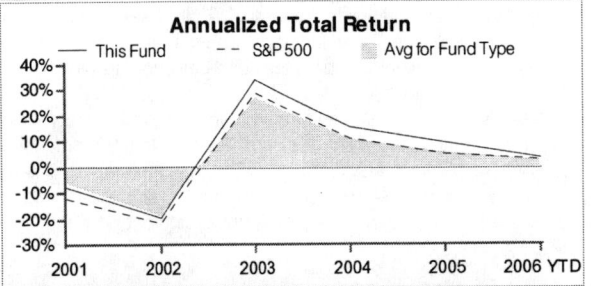

Annualized Total Return

T. Rowe Price Value Fd (TRVLX)   B   Good

Fund Family: T. Rowe Price   **Phone:** (800) 638-5660
Address: 100 East Pratt Street, Baltimore, MD 21202
Fund Type: GR - Growth

Major Rating Factors: T. Rowe Price Value Fd receives a Weiss Investment Rating of B (Good). The fund currently has a performance rating of C+ (Fair) based on an average return of 15.40% over the last three years and 5.39% over the last six months. Factored into the performance evaluation is an expense ratio of 0.89% (low).

The fund's risk rating is currently B (Good). It carries a beta of 1.02, meaning that its performance tracks fairly well with that of the overall stock market. Volatility, as measured by both the semi-deviation and a drawdown factor, is considered low.

John Linehan currently receives a manager quality ranking of 88 (0=worst, 99=best). If you desire an average level of risk, then this fund may be an option.

Services Offered: Automated phone transactions, payroll deductions, bank draft capabilities, an IRA investment plan, a 401K investment plan, a Keogh investment plan and a systematic withdrawal plan.

Data Date	Weiss Investment Rating	Net Assets ($Mil)	NAV	Perfor-mance Rating/Pts	Total Return Y-T-D	Risk Rating/Pts
6-06	B	3,878	24.64	C+/ 6.5	5.39%	B / 8.9
2005	C+	3,072	23.38	C / 5.3	6.30%	B- / 7.0
2004	C+	2,310	22.90	C+/ 6.9	15.36%	C+/ 5.6
2003	B	1,367	20.01	B / 7.7	30.00%	C+/ 6.7
2002	B+	1,199	15.56	B+/ 8.3	-16.58%	B- / 7.3
2001	B	1,322	18.88	B+/ 8.3	1.60%	C- / 3.4

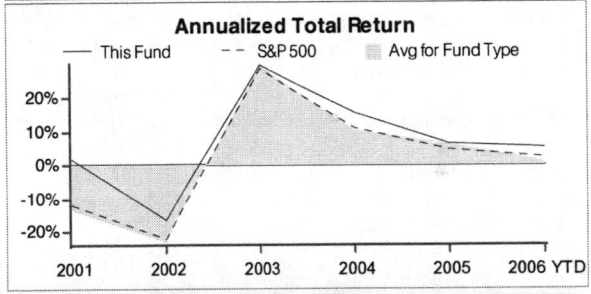

Annualized Total Return

TCW Select Equities I (TGCEX)   E+   Very Weak

Fund Family: TCW   **Phone:** (800) 386-3829
Address: 865 S Figueroa Street, Los Angeles, CA 90017
Fund Type: GR - Growth

Major Rating Factors: Disappointing performance is the major factor driving the E+ (Very Weak) Weiss Investment Rating for TCW Select Equities I. The fund currently has a performance rating of D (Weak) based on an average return of 9.25% over the last three years and -7.04% over the last six months. Factored into the performance evaluation is an expense ratio of 0.90% (low).

The fund's risk rating is currently C (Fair). It carries a beta of 1.55, meaning it is expected to move 15.5% for every 10% move in the market. Volatility, as measured by both the semi-deviation and a drawdown factor, is considered average.

Craig C. Blum has been running the fund for 2 years and currently receives a manager quality ranking of 8 (0=worst, 99=best). This fund offers an average level of risk but investors looking for strong performance will be frustrated.

Services Offered: Automated phone transactions, bank draft capabilities, an IRA investment plan and a 401K investment plan.

Data Date	Weiss Investment Rating	Net Assets ($Mil)	NAV	Perfor-mance Rating/Pts	Total Return Y-T-D	Risk Rating/Pts
6-06	E+	2,838	18.88	D / 1.9	-7.04%	C / 5.5
2005	C+	3,313	20.31	B- / 7.2	3.73%	C+/ 5.6
2004	C-	2,742	19.58	C+/ 5.8	12.92%	C- / 3.2
2003	C-	1,978	17.34	C / 5.4	50.26%	C- / 3.3
2002	D+	1,126	11.54	D+/ 2.7	-30.36%	C- / 3.8
2001	D+	1,139	16.57	C+/ 5.8	-19.25%	E- / 0.0

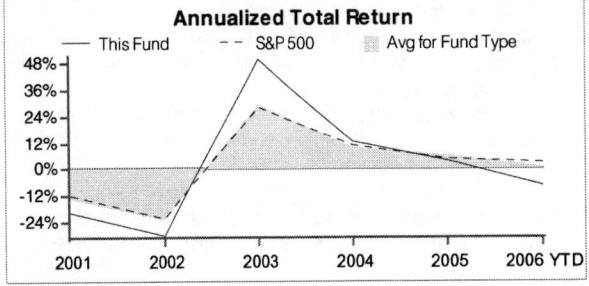

Annualized Total Return

Templeton Developing Markets A (TEDMX)

B+   Good

Fund Family: Franklin Templeton Investments   **Phone:** (800) 342-5236
Address: 777 Mariners Island Blvd., San Mateo, CA 94404
Fund Type: EM - Emerging Market

Major Rating Factors: Exceptional performance is the major factor driving the B+ (Good) Weiss Investment Rating for Templeton Developing Markets A. The fund currently has a performance rating of A (Excellent) based on an average return of 31.66% over the last three years and 6.14% over the last six months. Factored into the performance evaluation is an expense ratio of 2.03% (high), a 5.8% front-end load that is levied at the time of purchase and a 1.0% back-end load levied at the time of sale.

The fund's risk rating is currently C (Fair). It carries a beta of 0.94, meaning that its performance tracks fairly well with that of the overall stock market. Volatility, as measured by both the semi-deviation and a drawdown factor, is considered average.

Mark Mobius, Ph.D. has been running the fund for 15 years and currently receives a manager quality ranking of 38 (0=worst, 99=best). If you desire an average level of risk and strong performance, then this fund is a good option.

Services Offered: Payroll deductions, bank draft capabilities, an IRA investment plan, a 401K investment plan, a Keogh investment plan and a systematic withdrawal plan.

Data Date	Weiss Investment Rating	Net Assets ($Mil)	NAV	Performance Rating/Pts	Total Return Y-T-D	Risk Rating/Pts
6-06	B+	4,225	24.71	A / 9.5	6.14%	C / 5.2
2005	A+	3,428	23.42	A+ / 9.6	28.20%	C+ / 6.7
2004	A+	2,307	18.52	A+ / 9.7	25.45%	B- / 7.5
2003	A+	1,712	14.99	A+ / 9.6	53.14%	B- / 7.7
2002	C+	1,227	10.00	C / 5.5	1.68%	C+ / 6.2
2001	D	1,228	9.88	C- / 3.6	-5.76%	E- / 0.0

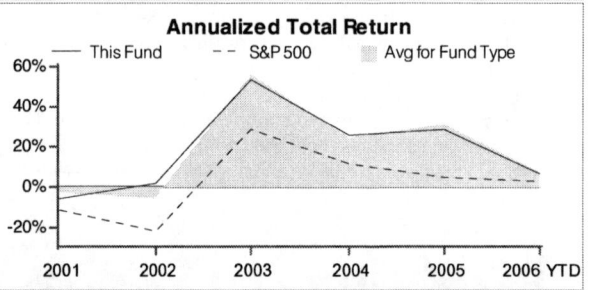

Templeton Growth A (TEPLX)

B-   Good

Fund Family: Franklin Templeton Investments   **Phone:** (800) 342-5236
Address: 777 Mariners Island Blvd., San Mateo, CA 94404
Fund Type: GL - Global

Major Rating Factors: Templeton Growth A receives a Weiss Investment Rating of B- (Good). The fund currently has a performance rating of C+ (Fair) based on an average return of 17.16% over the last three years and 6.41% over the last six months. Factored into the performance evaluation is an expense ratio of 1.00% (low), a 5.8% front-end load that is levied at the time of purchase and a 1.0% back-end load levied at the time of sale.

The fund's risk rating is currently B- (Good). It carries a beta of 0.79, meaning the fund's expected move will be 7.9% for every 10% move in the market. Volatility, as measured by both the semi-deviation and a drawdown factor, is considered low.

Jeffrey A. Everett, CFA currently receives a manager quality ranking of 34 (0=worst, 99=best). If you desire an average level of risk, then this fund may be an option.

Services Offered: Payroll deductions, bank draft capabilities, an IRA investment plan, a 401K investment plan, a Keogh investment plan, wire transfers and a systematic withdrawal plan.

Data Date	Weiss Investment Rating	Net Assets ($Mil)	NAV	Performance Rating/Pts	Total Return Y-T-D	Risk Rating/Pts
6-06	B-	23,116	24.41	C+ / 6.7	6.41%	B- / 7.7
2005	C+	20,500	22.94	C / 5.5	8.10%	C+ / 6.5
2004	B+	16,210	22.89	B / 7.8	17.00%	C+ / 6.5
2003	A-	14,036	20.67	B / 8.0	32.85%	B- / 7.9
2002	B+	11,584	15.93	B / 7.7	-9.48%	B / 8.6
2001	A-	12,108	18.00	B+ / 8.3	0.54%	C+ / 6.5

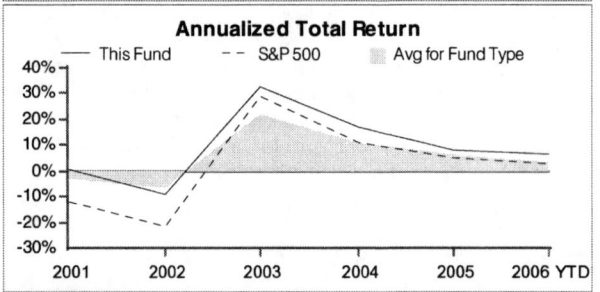

Templeton World A (TEMWX)

C+   Fair

Fund Family: Franklin Templeton Investments   **Phone:** (800) 342-5236
Address: 777 Mariners Island Blvd., San Mateo, CA 94404
Fund Type: GL - Global

Major Rating Factors: Strong performance is the major factor driving the C+ (Fair) Weiss Investment Rating for Templeton World A. The fund currently has a performance rating of B- (Good) based on an average return of 18.55% over the last three years and 5.75% over the last six months. Factored into the performance evaluation is an expense ratio of 1.00% (low), a 5.8% front-end load that is levied at the time of purchase and a 1.0% back-end load levied at the time of sale.

The fund's risk rating is currently C+ (Fair). It carries a beta of 0.91, meaning that its performance tracks fairly well with that of the overall stock market. Volatility, as measured by both the semi-deviation and a drawdown factor, is considered low.

Jeffrey A. Everett, CFA has been running the fund for 5 years and currently receives a manager quality ranking of 26 (0=worst, 99=best). If you desire only a moderate level of risk and strong performance, then this fund is an excellent option.

Services Offered: Payroll deductions, bank draft capabilities, an IRA investment plan, a 401K investment plan, a Keogh investment plan, wire transfers and a systematic withdrawal plan.

Data Date	Weiss Investment Rating	Net Assets ($Mil)	NAV	Performance Rating/Pts	Total Return Y-T-D	Risk Rating/Pts
6-06	C+	8,388	18.76	B- / 7.2	5.75%	C+ / 6.3
2005	C	8,201	17.74	C+ / 6.3	11.67%	C / 5.5
2004	B	7,786	17.75	B- / 7.5	15.63%	C+ / 6.2
2003	B	6,767	16.87	B- / 7.4	33.38%	B- / 7.1
2002	B-	6,147	12.89	C+ / 6.1	-12.15%	B- / 7.4
2001	C+	7,060	14.86	C+ / 6.1	-8.10%	C+ / 6.1

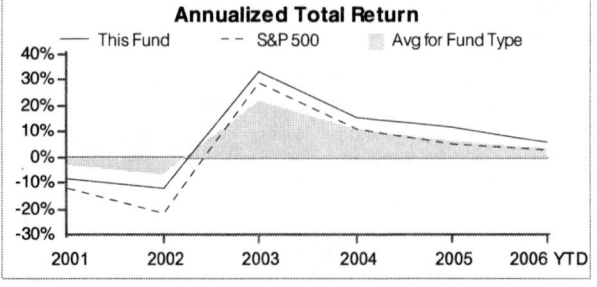

Third Avenue International Value (TAVIX)

A+   Excellent

Fund Family: Third Avenue **Phone:** (800) 443-1021
Address: 767 Third Avenue, New York, NY 10017
Fund Type: FO - Foreign

Major Rating Factors: Exceptional performance is the major factor driving the A+ (Excellent) Weiss Investment Rating for Third Avenue International Value. The fund currently has a performance rating of A (Excellent) based on an average return of 29.35% over the last three years and 8.27% over the last six months. Factored into the performance evaluation is a 2.0% back-end load levied at the time of sale.

The fund's risk rating is currently B (Good). It carries a beta of 0.78, meaning the fund's expected move will be 7.8% for every 10% move in the market. Volatility, as measured by standard deviation, is considered low for equity funds at 9.04.

Amit B.Wadhwaney has been running the fund for 5 years and currently receives a manager quality ranking of 99 (0=worst, 99=best). If you desire only a moderate level of risk and strong performance, then this fund is an excellent option.

Services Offered: Automated phone transactions, bank draft capabilities, an IRA investment plan, a 401K investment plan, a Keogh investment plan, wire transfers and a systematic withdrawal plan. However, the fund is currently closed to new investors.

Data Date	Weiss Investment Rating	Net Assets ($Mil)	NAV	Performance Rating/Pts	Total Return Y-T-D	Risk Rating/Pts
6-06	A+	2,315	22.91	A / 9.4	8.27%	B / 8.4
2005	A+	2,073	21.16	A / 9.5	18.00%	B / 8.4
2004	A+	667	18.41	A+ / 9.7	27.70%	B- / 7.8
2003	U	140	14.59	U / --	54.68%	U / --

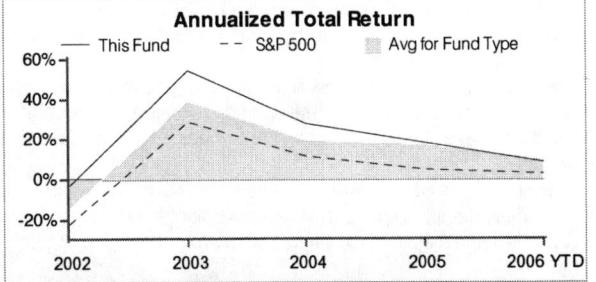

Annualized Total Return

Third Avenue Real Estate Value (TAREX)

A+   Excellent

Fund Family: Third Avenue **Phone:** (800) 443-1021
Address: 767 Third Avenue, New York, NY 10017
Fund Type: RE - Real Estate

Major Rating Factors: Strong performance is the major factor driving the A+ (Excellent) Weiss Investment Rating for Third Avenue Real Estate Value. The fund currently has a performance rating of B+ (Good) based on an average return of 23.93% over the last three years and 8.82% over the last six months. Factored into the performance evaluation is an expense ratio of 1.11% (low) and a 1.0% back-end load levied at the time of sale.

The fund's risk rating is currently B- (Good). It carries a beta of 0.49, meaning the fund's expected move will be 4.9% for every 10% move in the market. Volatility, as measured by both the semi-deviation and a drawdown factor, is considered low.

Michael H.Winer has been running the fund for 8 years and currently receives a manager quality ranking of 99 (0=worst, 99=best). If you desire only a moderate level of risk and strong performance, then this fund is an excellent option.

Services Offered: Automated phone transactions, bank draft capabilities, an IRA investment plan, a 401K investment plan, a Keogh investment plan, wire transfers and a systematic withdrawal plan. However, the fund is currently closed to new investors.

Data Date	Weiss Investment Rating	Net Assets ($Mil)	NAV	Performance Rating/Pts	Total Return Y-T-D	Risk Rating/Pts
6-06	A+	2,930	31.95	B+ / 8.8	8.82%	B- / 7.5
2005	A+	2,910	29.36	B+ / 8.9	14.38%	B- / 7.8
2004	A+	2,029	26.96	A+ / 9.6	28.16%	B / 8.3
2003	A+	787	21.38	A+ / 9.6	37.34%	B+ / 9.9
2002	A+	337	15.96	A+ / 9.8	4.24%	B+ / 9.9

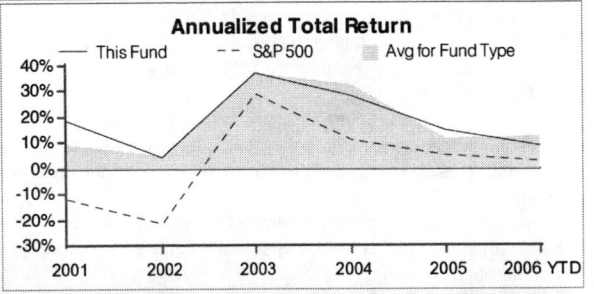

Annualized Total Return

Third Avenue Sm Cap Value Fund (TASCX)

A+   Excellent

Fund Family: Third Avenue **Phone:** (800) 443-1021
Address: 767 Third Avenue, New York, NY 10017
Fund Type: SC - Small Cap

Major Rating Factors: Strong performance is the major factor driving the A+ (Excellent) Weiss Investment Rating for Third Avenue Sm Cap Value Fund. The fund currently has a performance rating of B (Good) based on an average return of 20.52% over the last three years and 4.99% over the last six months. Factored into the performance evaluation is an expense ratio of 1.11% (low) and a 1.0% back-end load levied at the time of sale.

The fund's risk rating is currently B (Good). It carries a beta of 0.64, meaning the fund's expected move will be 6.4% for every 10% move in the market. Volatility, as measured by both the semi-deviation and a drawdown factor, is considered low.

Curtis R.Jensen has been running the fund for 9 years and currently receives a manager quality ranking of 97 (0=worst, 99=best). If you desire only a moderate level of risk and strong performance, then this fund is an excellent option.

Services Offered: Automated phone transactions, bank draft capabilities, an IRA investment plan, a 401K investment plan, a Keogh investment plan, wire transfers and a systematic withdrawal plan. However, the fund is currently closed to new investors.

Data Date	Weiss Investment Rating	Net Assets ($Mil)	NAV	Performance Rating/Pts	Total Return Y-T-D	Risk Rating/Pts
6-06	A+	2,409	25.67	B / 8.0	4.99%	B / 8.6
2005	A	2,069	24.45	B / 8.1	11.09%	B- / 7.7
2004	B+	1,134	22.57	B+ / 8.7	21.27%	C+ / 5.8
2003	A	602	18.75	A- / 9.1	39.08%	B- / 7.4
2002	A	414	13.56	A / 9.3	-10.89%	B / 8.3
2001	B+	332	15.37	A / 9.4	15.26%	C- / 3.6

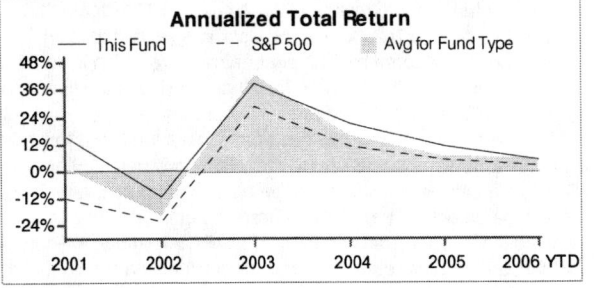

Annualized Total Return

Third Avenue Value Fund (TAVFX)

A+ Excellent

Fund Family: Third Avenue **Phone:** (800) 443-1021
Address: 767 Third Avenue, New York, NY 10017
Fund Type: GR - Growth
Major Rating Factors: Strong performance is the major factor driving the A+ (Excellent) Weiss Investment Rating for Third Avenue Value Fund. The fund currently has a performance rating of B+ (Good) based on an average return of 23.58% over the last three years and 5.44% over the last six months. Factored into the performance evaluation is an expense ratio of 1.05% (low) and a 1.0% back-end load levied at the time of sale.

The fund's risk rating is currently B- (Good). It carries a beta of 0.88, meaning the fund's expected move will be 8.8% for every 10% move in the market. Volatility, as measured by both the semi-deviation and a drawdown factor, is considered low.

Martin J.Whitman has been running the fund for 3 years and currently receives a manager quality ranking of 99 (0=worst, 99=best). If you desire only a moderate level of risk and strong performance, then this fund is an excellent option.

Services Offered: Automated phone transactions, bank draft capabilities, an IRA investment plan, a 401K investment plan, a Keogh investment plan, wire transfers and a systematic withdrawal plan.

Data Date	Weiss Investment Rating	Net Assets ($Mil)	NAV	Performance Rating/Pts	Total Return Y-T-D	Risk Rating/Pts
6-06	A+	8,371	57.76	B+ / 8.7	5.44%	B- / 7.6
2005	A+	6,891	54.78	A- / 9.0	16.50%	B- / 7.5
2004	B+	4,321	51.70	B+ / 8.9	26.60%	C+ / 5.9
2003	B+	3,098	41.45	B+ / 8.3	37.20%	B- / 7.3
2002	B+	2,134	30.47	B+ / 8.7	-15.19%	B- / 7.4
2001	A	2,632	36.43	B+ / 8.9	2.82%	C+ / 6.2

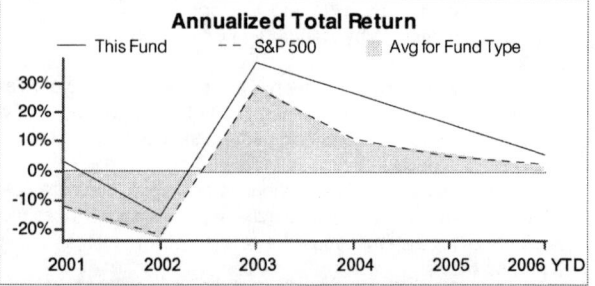

Thornburg Intl Value A (TGVAX)

A+ Excellent

Fund Family: Thornburg Funds **Phone:** (800) 847-0200
Address: 119 E. Marcy Street, Santa Fe, NM 87501
Fund Type: FO - Foreign
Major Rating Factors: Exceptional performance is the major factor driving the A+ (Excellent) Weiss Investment Rating for Thornburg Intl Value A. The fund currently has a performance rating of A- (Excellent) based on an average return of 24.82% over the last three years and 9.87% over the last six months. Factored into the performance evaluation is an expense ratio of 1.32% (average), a 4.5% front-end load that is levied at the time of purchase and a 1.0% back-end load levied at the time of sale.

The fund's risk rating is currently B- (Good). It carries a beta of 0.97, meaning that its performance tracks fairly well with that of the overall stock market. Volatility, as measured by both the semi-deviation and a drawdown factor, is considered low.

William V. Fries, CFA has been running the fund for 8 years and currently receives a manager quality ranking of 67 (0=worst, 99=best). If you desire only a moderate level of risk and strong performance, then this fund is an excellent option.

Services Offered: Automated phone transactions, bank draft capabilities, an IRA investment plan, a 401K investment plan, wire transfers and a systematic withdrawal plan.

Data Date	Weiss Investment Rating	Net Assets ($Mil)	NAV	Performance Rating/Pts	Total Return Y-T-D	Risk Rating/Pts
6-06	A+	3,823	25.72	A- / 9.0	9.87%	B- / 7.1
2005	A	2,434	23.46	B+ / 8.9	19.73%	B- / 7.2
2004	B+	1,113	20.40	B+ / 8.5	17.72%	C+ / 6.5
2003	B+	169	17.39	B / 8.2	40.02%	B- / 7.4
2002	B-	79	12.42	C+ / 6.3	-10.45%	B- / 7.6
2001	B-	64	13.87	B+ / 8.4	-10.53%	C- / 3.2

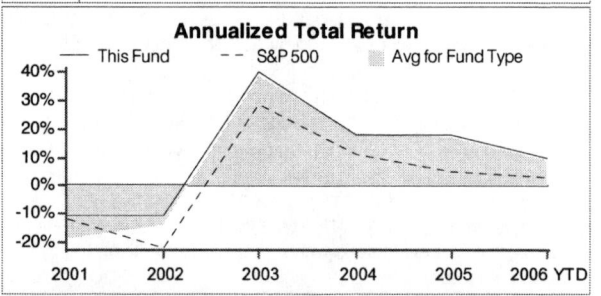

Thrivent Large Cap Stock A (AALGX)

E- Very Weak

Fund Family: Thrivent Financial for Lutherans **Phone:** (800) 847-4836
Address: 625 Fourth Avenue S., Minneapolis, MN 55415
Fund Type: GR - Growth
Major Rating Factors: Thrivent Large Cap Stock A has adopted a very risky asset allocation strategy and currently receives an overall Weiss Investment Rating of E- (Very Weak). The fund has a high level of volatility, as measured by both semi-deviation and drawdown factors. It carries a beta of 0.93, meaning that its performance tracks fairly well with that of the overall stock market. Unfortunately, the high level of risk (D, Weak) failed to pay off as investors endured poor performance.

The fund's performance rating is currently D- (Weak). It has registered an average return of 8.25% over the last three years and is up 0.80% over the last six months. Factored into the performance evaluation is an expense ratio of 1.00% (low), a 5.5% front-end load that is levied at the time of purchase and a 1.0% back-end load levied at the time of sale.

Frederick L. Plautz has been running the fund for 11 years and currently receives a manager quality ranking of 32 (0=worst, 99=best). If you can tolerate very high levels of risk in the hope of improved future returns, holding this fund may be an option. **Services Offered:** Automated phone transactions, payroll deductions, bank draft capabilities, an IRA investment plan, a 401K investment plan, a Keogh investment plan and a systematic withdrawal plan.

Data Date	Weiss Investment Rating	Net Assets ($Mil)	NAV	Performance Rating/Pts	Total Return Y-T-D	Risk Rating/Pts
6-06	E-	3,086	26.61	D- / 1.3	0.80%	D / 1.9
2005	E-	3,450	26.40	D- / 1.1	5.10%	D / 1.9
2004	D-	3,630	25.54	D- / 1.3	8.21%	C- / 3.8
2003	D+	2,776	29.29	D / 1.6	21.13%	C / 5.4
2002	C+	2,639	24.27	C / 4.5	-22.75%	C+ / 6.7
2001	C+	3,555	31.51	C / 4.4	-13.95%	C+ / 6.6

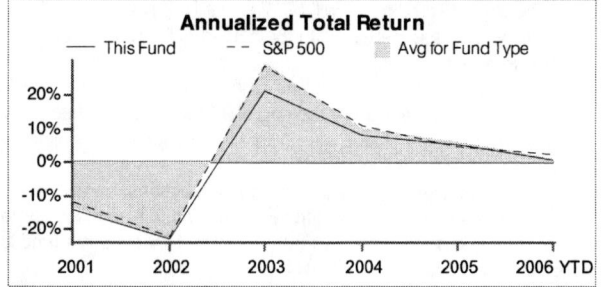

Tweedy Browne Global Value (TBGVX)   A+   Excellent

Fund Family: Tweedy Browne   **Phone:** (800) 432-4789
Address: 350 Park Avenue, New York, NY 10022
Fund Type: GL - Global
Major Rating Factors: Strong performance is the major factor driving the A+ (Excellent) Weiss Investment Rating for Tweedy Browne Global Value. The fund currently has a performance rating of B (Good) based on an average return of 20.28% over the last three years and 5.08% over the last six months. Factored into the performance evaluation is an expense ratio of 1.38% (average) and a 2.0% back-end load levied at the time of sale.

The fund's risk rating is currently B (Good). It carries a beta of 0.49, meaning the fund's expected move will be 4.9% for every 10% move in the market. Volatility, as measured by both the semi-deviation and a drawdown factor, is considered low.

Christopher H. Browne has been running the fund for 13 years and currently receives a manager quality ranking of 97 (0=worst, 99=best). If you desire only a moderate level of risk and strong performance, then this fund is an excellent option.

Services Offered: Automated phone transactions, an IRA investment plan, a 401K investment plan, a Keogh investment plan and wire transfers. However, the fund is currently closed to new investors.

Data Date	Weiss Investment Rating	Net Assets ($Mil)	NAV	Perfor-mance Rating/Pts	Total Return Y-T-D	Risk Rating/Pts
6-06	A+	7,526	27.74	B / 7.9	5.08%	B / 8.5
2005	B+	7,272	26.40	B- / 7.2	15.42%	B- / 7.7
2004	B	6,144	23.19	B- / 7.2	20.01%	C+ / 6.3
2003	B	4,834	19.55	B- / 7.1	24.93%	B- / 7.4
2002	B+	4,237	15.81	B / 8.1	-12.14%	B / 8.0
2001	A+	3,915	18.53	B / 8.2	-4.69%	B / 8.0

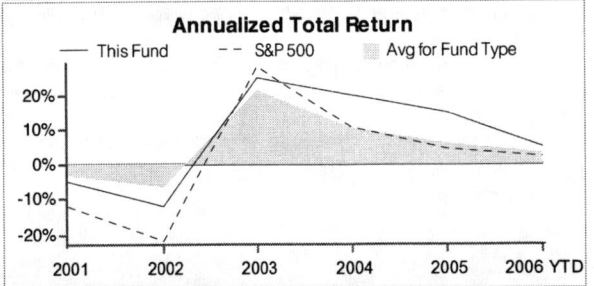
Annualized Total Return

UBS Global Allocation A (BNGLX)   C+   Fair

Fund Family: UBS Global Asset Management   **Phone:** (888) 793-8637
Address: 51 West 52nd Street, New York, NY 10019
Fund Type: GL - Global
Major Rating Factors: Middle of the road best describes UBS Global Allocation A whose Weiss Investment Rating is currently a C+ (Fair). The fund currently has a performance rating of C (Fair) based on an average return of 12.91% over the last three years and 3.43% over the last six months. Factored into the performance evaluation is an expense ratio of 1.17% (low), a 5.5% front-end load that is levied at the time of purchase and a 0.5% back-end load levied at the time of sale.

The fund's risk rating is currently B+ (Good). It carries a beta of 1.19, meaning it is expected to move 11.9% for every 10% move in the market. Volatility, as measured by both the semi-deviation and a drawdown factor, is considered very low.

Brian D. Singer currently receives a manager quality ranking of 90 (0=worst, 99=best). If you desire an average level of risk, then this fund may be an option.

Services Offered: Automated phone transactions, payroll deductions, an IRA investment plan, a 401K investment plan, a Keogh investment plan, wire transfers and a systematic withdrawal plan.

Data Date	Weiss Investment Rating	Net Assets ($Mil)	NAV	Perfor-mance Rating/Pts	Total Return Y-T-D	Risk Rating/Pts
6-06	C+	2,245	13.86	C / 4.3	3.43%	B+ / 9.2
2005	C+	1,865	13.40	C- / 3.4	6.16%	B / 8.7
2004	A	1,152	13.32	B / 7.6	14.15%	B / 8.2
2003	B+	411	12.12	B / 7.8	27.48%	B- / 7.6
2002	B+	23	9.63	B+ / 8.8	-2.99%	B- / 7.8
2001	B	6	10.37	C / 5.3	1.94%	B / 8.3

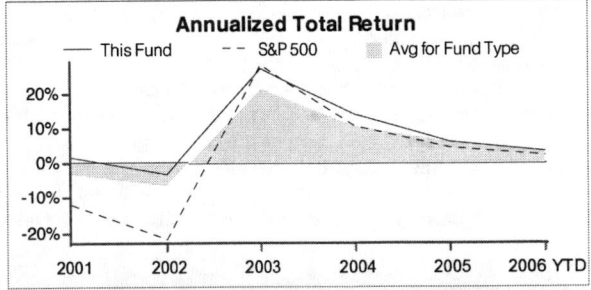
Annualized Total Return

UMB Scout WorldWide Fund (UMBWX)   B+   Good

Fund Family: UMB Scout Funds   **Phone:** (800) 996-2862
Address: 2440 Pershing Road, Kansas City, MO 64108
Fund Type: FO - Foreign
Major Rating Factors: Strong performance is the major factor driving the B+ (Good) Weiss Investment Rating for UMB Scout WorldWide Fund. The fund currently has a performance rating of B+ (Good) based on an average return of 21.85% over the last three years and 6.28% over the last six months. Factored into the performance evaluation is an expense ratio of 1.00% (low) and a 2.0% back-end load levied at the time of sale.

The fund's risk rating is currently C+ (Fair). It carries a beta of 0.99, meaning that its performance tracks fairly well with that of the overall stock market. Volatility, as measured by both the semi-deviation and a drawdown factor, is considered low.

James L. Moffett, CFA has been running the fund for 13 years and currently receives a manager quality ranking of 34 (0=worst, 99=best). If you desire only a moderate level of risk and strong performance, then this fund is an excellent option.

Services Offered: Automated phone transactions, bank draft capabilities, an IRA investment plan, a 401K investment plan and a systematic withdrawal plan.

Data Date	Weiss Investment Rating	Net Assets ($Mil)	NAV	Perfor-mance Rating/Pts	Total Return Y-T-D	Risk Rating/Pts
6-06	B+	2,669	29.80	B+ / 8.4	6.28%	C+ / 6.6
2005	A	1,820	28.26	B+ / 8.6	19.58%	B- / 7.3
2004	B+	878	24.10	B / 7.9	18.02%	C+ / 6.3
2003	C+	557	20.58	C+ / 6.5	33.10%	C+ / 6.8
2002	C+	354	15.58	C / 5.5	-15.85%	B- / 7.2
2001	C+	358	18.67	C+ / 5.6	-11.00%	C+ / 6.8

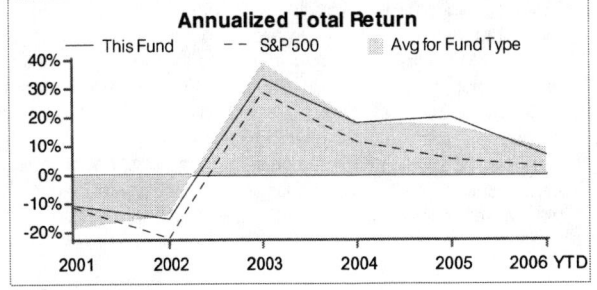
Annualized Total Return

USAA Income Stock Fund (USISX)

C   Fair

Fund Family: USAA Group   **Phone:** (800) 382-8722
Address: 9800 Fredericksburg Road, San Antonio, TX 78288
Fund Type: IN - Income

Major Rating Factors: Middle of the road best describes USAA Income Stock Fund whose Weiss Investment Rating is currently a C (Fair). The fund currently has a performance rating of C (Fair) based on an average return of 13.10% over the last three years and 4.52% over the last six months. Factored into the performance evaluation is an expense ratio of 0.78% (very low).

The fund's risk rating is currently C+ (Fair). It carries a beta of 1.03, meaning that its performance tracks fairly well with that of the overall stock market. Volatility, as measured by both the semi-deviation and a drawdown factor, is considered low.

This is team managed and currently receives a manager quality ranking of 72 (0=worst, 99=best). If you desire an average level of risk, then this fund may be an option.

Services Offered: Automated phone transactions, bank draft capabilities, an IRA investment plan, a 401K investment plan, wire transfers and a systematic withdrawal plan.

Data Date	Weiss Investment Rating	Net Assets ($Mil)	NAV	Performance Rating/Pts	Total Return Y-T-D	Risk Rating/Pts
6-06	C	2,119	15.75	C / 5.3	4.52%	C+/ 6.3
2005	D+	2,069	15.20	C- / 3.5	5.79%	C+/ 6.3
2004	C-	1,944	16.66	C / 4.9	11.57%	C / 5.0
2003	C+	1,675	15.27	C+/ 5.9	25.76%	C+/ 6.2
2002	B-	1,508	12.37	B- / 7.1	-19.00%	B- / 7.2
2001	C+	1,831	16.83	C+/ 6.1	-4.18%	C+/ 6.8

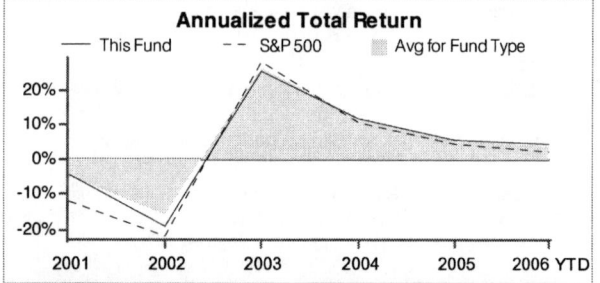
Annualized Total Return

Van Kampen Comstock A (ACSTX)

C+   Fair

Fund Family: Van Kampen   **Phone:** (800) 421-5666
Address: One Parkview Plaza, Oakbrook Terrace, IL 60181
Fund Type: GI - Growth and Income

Major Rating Factors: Middle of the road best describes Van Kampen Comstock A whose Weiss Investment Rating is currently a C+ (Fair). The fund currently has a performance rating of C (Fair) based on an average return of 13.76% over the last three years and 3.75% over the last six months. Factored into the performance evaluation is an expense ratio of 0.84% (very low) and a 5.8% front-end load that is levied at the time of purchase.

The fund's risk rating is currently B (Good). It carries a beta of 0.84, meaning the fund's expected move will be 8.4% for every 10% move in the market. Volatility, as measured by both the semi-deviation and a drawdown factor, is considered low.

B. Robert Baker, Jr. has been running the fund for 12 years and currently receives a manager quality ranking of 88 (0=worst, 99=best). If you desire an average level of risk, then this fund may be an option.

Services Offered: Automated phone transactions, check writing, bank draft capabilities, an IRA investment plan, a 401K investment plan, a Keogh investment plan, wire transfers and a systematic withdrawal plan.

Data Date	Weiss Investment Rating	Net Assets ($Mil)	NAV	Performance Rating/Pts	Total Return Y-T-D	Risk Rating/Pts
6-06	C+	12,404	17.81	C / 4.8	3.75%	B / 8.3
2005	C	12,065	17.81	C / 4.3	4.19%	B- / 7.6
2004	C	10,023	18.51	C+/ 6.2	17.57%	C / 5.1
2003	C+	6,734	15.95	C+/ 6.9	30.98%	C+/ 6.0
2002	B	4,195	12.34	B+/ 8.4	-19.59%	C+/ 6.5
2001	B-	3,797	15.68	B / 7.9	-1.79%	C- / 3.3

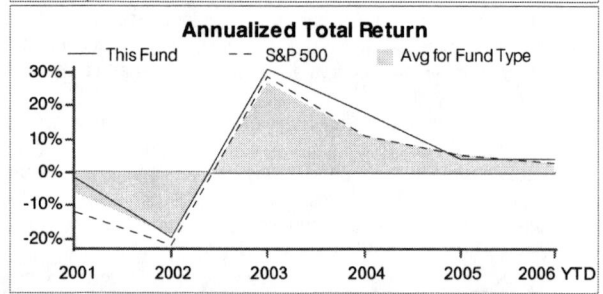
Annualized Total Return

Van Kampen Emerging Growth A (ACEGX)

E+   Very Weak

Fund Family: Van Kampen   **Phone:** (800) 421-5666
Address: One Parkview Plaza, Oakbrook Terrace, IL 60181
Fund Type: GR - Growth

Major Rating Factors: Disappointing performance is the major factor driving the E+ (Very Weak) Weiss Investment Rating for Van Kampen Emerging Growth A. The fund currently has a performance rating of D- (Weak) based on an average return of 8.67% over the last three years and -0.96% over the last six months. Factored into the performance evaluation is an expense ratio of 1.12% (low) and a 5.8% front-end load that is levied at the time of purchase.

The fund's risk rating is currently C+ (Fair). It carries a beta of 1.35, meaning it is expected to move 13.5% for every 10% move in the market. Volatility, as measured by both the semi-deviation and a drawdown factor, is considered low.

Gary M. Lewis, CFA has been running the fund for 17 years and currently receives a manager quality ranking of 12 (0=worst, 99=best). This fund offers only a moderate level of risk but investors looking for strong performance are still waiting.

Services Offered: Automated phone transactions, check writing, payroll deductions, bank draft capabilities, an IRA investment plan, a 401K investment plan, a Keogh investment plan, wire transfers and a systematic withdrawal plan.

Data Date	Weiss Investment Rating	Net Assets ($Mil)	NAV	Performance Rating/Pts	Total Return Y-T-D	Risk Rating/Pts
6-06	E+	2,937	41.24	D- / 1.4	-0.96%	C+/ 5.9
2005	D	3,224	41.64	D+/ 2.7	7.71%	C+/ 6.7
2004	D-	3,769	38.66	E / 0.4	7.00%	C / 4.8
2003	D-	4,354	36.13	E- / 0.2	27.85%	C- / 4.2
2002	D-	3,778	28.26	E+/ 0.6	-33.22%	D+/ 2.6
2001	D+	6,067	42.32	C / 5.0	-32.59%	E- / 0.0

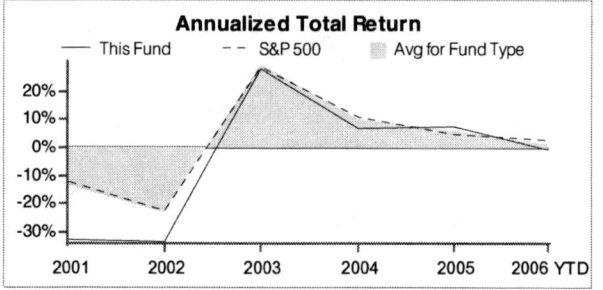
Annualized Total Return

Van Kampen Equity & Income A (ACEIX)   C   Fair

Fund Family: Van Kampen   **Phone:** (800) 421-5666
Address: One Parkview Plaza, Oakbrook Terrace, IL 60181
Fund Type: BA - Balanced
Major Rating Factors: Middle of the road best describes Van Kampen Equity & Income A whose Weiss Investment Rating is currently a C (Fair). The fund currently has a performance rating of C- (Fair) based on an average return of 11.10% over the last three years and 2.27% over the last six months. Factored into the performance evaluation is an expense ratio of 0.80% (very low) and a 5.8% front-end load that is levied at the time of purchase.

The fund's risk rating is currently B+ (Good). It carries a beta of 1.05, meaning that its performance tracks fairly well with that of the overall stock market. Volatility, as measured by both the semi-deviation and a drawdown factor, is considered very low.

This fund has been team managed for 16 years and currently receives a manager quality ranking of 85 (0=worst, 99=best). If you desire an average level of risk, then this fund may be an option.

Services Offered: Automated phone transactions, check writing, bank draft capabilities, an IRA investment plan, a 401K investment plan, a Keogh investment plan, wire transfers and a systematic withdrawal plan.

Data Date	Weiss Investment Rating	Net Assets ($Mil)	NAV	Perfor-mance Rating/Pts	Total Return Y-T-D	Risk Rating/Pts
6-06	C	11,126	8.64	C- / 3.1	2.27%	B+ / 9.1
2005	C	10,372	8.68	D+ / 2.5	7.81%	B / 8.9
2004	B-	7,363	8.62	C / 5.5	11.77%	B- / 7.7
2003	B	5,192	7.90	C+ / 6.6	22.16%	B / 8.4
2002	A	2,833	6.62	B+ / 8.8	-8.32%	B / 8.7
2001	A+	2,261	7.46	B / 7.7	-2.23%	B / 8.1

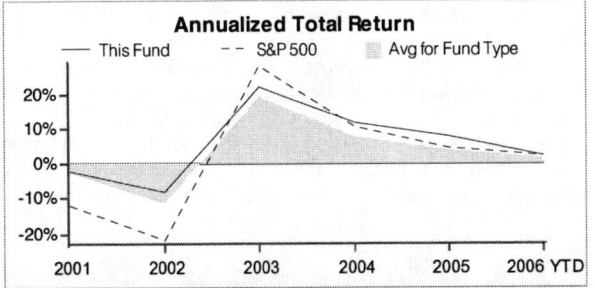

Van Kampen Equity & Income C (ACERX)   C+   Fair

Fund Family: Van Kampen   **Phone:** (800) 421-5666
Address: One Parkview Plaza, Oakbrook Terrace, IL 60181
Fund Type: BA - Balanced
Major Rating Factors: Middle of the road best describes Van Kampen Equity & Income C whose Weiss Investment Rating is currently a C+ (Fair). The fund currently has a performance rating of C- (Fair) based on an average return of 10.28% over the last three years and 1.90% over the last six months. Factored into the performance evaluation is an expense ratio of 1.55% (average) and a 1.0% back-end load levied at the time of sale.

The fund's risk rating is currently B+ (Good). It carries a beta of 1.05, meaning that its performance tracks fairly well with that of the overall stock market. Volatility, as measured by both the semi-deviation and a drawdown factor, is considered very low.

This fund has been team managed for 4 years and currently receives a manager quality ranking of 79 (0=worst, 99=best). If you desire an average level of risk, then this fund may be an option.

Services Offered: Automated phone transactions, check writing, bank draft capabilities, an IRA investment plan, a 401K investment plan, a Keogh investment plan, wire transfers and a systematic withdrawal plan.

Data Date	Weiss Investment Rating	Net Assets ($Mil)	NAV	Perfor-mance Rating/Pts	Total Return Y-T-D	Risk Rating/Pts
6-06	C+	2,061	8.54	C- / 3.4	1.90%	B+ / 9.2
2005	C	1,968	8.58	D+ / 2.8	7.12%	B / 8.9
2004	B-	1,494	8.52	C+ / 5.8	10.81%	B- / 7.7
2003	B	1,068	7.82	C+ / 6.8	21.40%	B / 8.4
2002	A	529	6.55	B+ / 8.9	-9.12%	B / 8.7
2001	A+	365	7.39	B / 7.8	-2.88%	B / 8.1

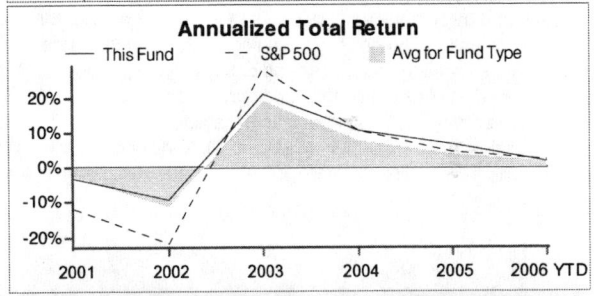

Van Kampen Growth & Income A (ACGIX)   C+   Fair

Fund Family: Van Kampen   **Phone:** (800) 421-5666
Address: One Parkview Plaza, Oakbrook Terrace, IL 60181
Fund Type: GI - Growth and Income
Major Rating Factors: Middle of the road best describes Van Kampen Growth & Income A whose Weiss Investment Rating is currently a C+ (Fair). The fund currently has a performance rating of C (Fair) based on an average return of 14.19% over the last three years and 2.91% over the last six months. Factored into the performance evaluation is an expense ratio of 0.81% (very low) and a 5.8% front-end load that is levied at the time of purchase.

The fund's risk rating is currently B (Good). It carries a beta of 0.87, meaning the fund's expected move will be 8.7% for every 10% move in the market. Volatility, as measured by both the semi-deviation and a drawdown factor, is considered low.

This is team managed and currently receives a manager quality ranking of 89 (0=worst, 99=best). If you desire an average level of risk, then this fund may be an option.

Services Offered: Automated phone transactions, check writing, payroll deductions, bank draft capabilities, an IRA investment plan, a 401K investment plan, a Keogh investment plan, wire transfers and a systematic withdrawal plan.

Data Date	Weiss Investment Rating	Net Assets ($Mil)	NAV	Perfor-mance Rating/Pts	Total Return Y-T-D	Risk Rating/Pts
6-06	C+	6,907	20.67	C / 5.1	2.91%	B / 8.3
2005	C+	6,539	20.54	C / 4.7	9.87%	B- / 7.5
2004	C+	5,443	20.19	C+ / 6.0	13.94%	C+ / 6.2
2003	B-	3,647	18.04	C+ / 6.7	27.57%	B- / 7.3
2002	B	2,071	14.29	B / 7.8	-14.71%	B- / 7.5
2001	B+	1,744	17.01	B- / 7.3	-6.06%	C+ / 6.9

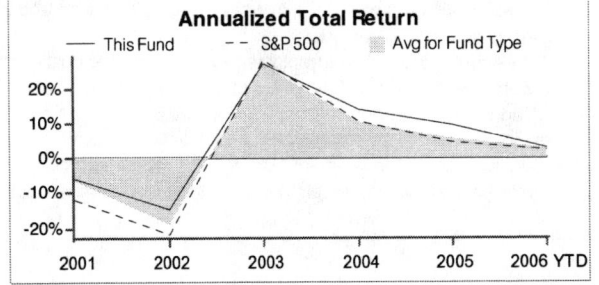

Vanguard 500 Index Inv (VFINX)   C+   Fair

Fund Family: Vanguard   **Phone:** (800) 662-7447
Address: Vanguard Financial Center, Valley Forge, PA 19482
Fund Type: IX - Index
Major Rating Factors: Middle of the road best describes Vanguard 500 Index Inv whose Weiss Investment Rating is currently a C+ (Fair). The fund currently has a performance rating of C- (Fair) based on an average return of 11.06% over the last three years and 2.64% over the last six months. Factored into the performance evaluation is an expense ratio of 0.18% (very low).

The fund's risk rating is currently B (Good). It carries a beta of 1.00, meaning that its performance tracks fairly well with that of the overall stock market. Volatility, as measured by both the semi-deviation and a drawdown factor, is considered low.

Michael H. Buek, CFA currently receives a manager quality ranking of 55 (0=worst, 99=best). If you desire an average level of risk, then this fund may be an option.

Services Offered: Automated phone transactions, payroll deductions, bank draft capabilities, an IRA investment plan, a 401K investment plan, a Keogh investment plan, wire transfers and a systematic withdrawal plan.

Data Date	Weiss Investment Rating	Net Assets ($Mil)	NAV	Perfor- mance Rating/Pts	Total Return Y-T-D	Risk Rating/Pts
6-06	C+	66,855	116.99	C- / 4.1	2.64%	B / 8.6
2005	C	69,916	114.92	C- / 3.6	4.77%	B- / 7.6
2004	C-	84,167	111.64	C / 4.4	10.74%	C / 5.5
2003	C	71,893	102.67	C / 4.4	28.50%	C+ / 5.9
2002	C	59,672	81.15	C / 4.4	-22.15%	C+ / 6.3
2001	C-	73,151	105.89	C- / 3.9	-12.02%	C- / 3.6

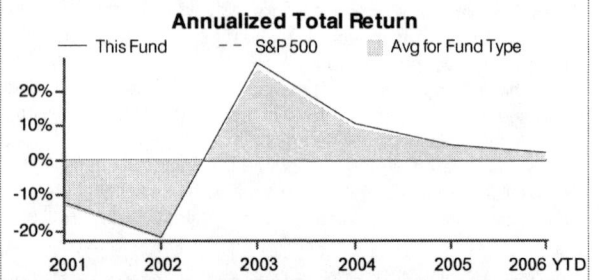

Vanguard Asset Allocation Inv (VAAPX)   C+   Fair

Fund Family: Vanguard   **Phone:** (800) 662-7447
Address: Vanguard Financial Center, Valley Forge, PA 19482
Fund Type: AA - Asset Allocation
Major Rating Factors: Middle of the road best describes Vanguard Asset Allocation Inv whose Weiss Investment Rating is currently a C+ (Fair). The fund currently has a performance rating of C- (Fair) based on an average return of 10.90% over the last three years and 3.10% over the last six months. Factored into the performance evaluation is an expense ratio of 0.38% (very low).

The fund's risk rating is currently B (Good). It carries a beta of 1.39, meaning it is expected to move 13.9% for every 10% move in the market. Volatility, as measured by both the semi-deviation and a drawdown factor, is considered low.

Thomas F. Loeb has been running the fund for 18 years and currently receives a manager quality ranking of 69 (0=worst, 99=best). If you desire an average level of risk, then this fund may be an option.

Services Offered: Automated phone transactions, payroll deductions, bank draft capabilities, an IRA investment plan, a 401K investment plan, a Keogh investment plan, wire transfers and a systematic withdrawal plan.

Data Date	Weiss Investment Rating	Net Assets ($Mil)	NAV	Perfor- mance Rating/Pts	Total Return Y-T-D	Risk Rating/Pts
6-06	C+	9,477	25.85	C- / 4.1	3.10%	B / 8.8
2005	C	9,424	25.33	C- / 3.4	5.00%	B- / 7.8
2004	C+	9,724	24.56	C+ / 5.6	11.09%	C+ / 6.3
2003	B-	8,088	22.56	C+ / 6.8	26.49%	B- / 7.1
2002	B	6,871	18.07	B- / 7.3	-15.43%	B- / 7.7
2001	B-	7,751	21.81	C+ / 5.7	-5.30%	B- / 7.8

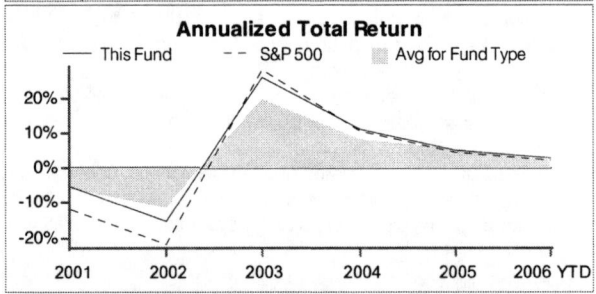

Vanguard Balanced Index Inv (VBINX)   C   Fair

Fund Family: Vanguard   **Phone:** (800) 662-7447
Address: Vanguard Financial Center, Valley Forge, PA 19482
Fund Type: BA - Balanced
Major Rating Factors: Disappointing performance is the major factor driving the C (Fair) Weiss Investment Rating for Vanguard Balanced Index Inv. The fund currently has a performance rating of D+ (Weak) based on an average return of 8.45% over the last three years and 1.67% over the last six months. Factored into the performance evaluation is an expense ratio of 0.20% (very low).

The fund's risk rating is currently B+ (Good). It carries a beta of 1.06, meaning that its performance tracks fairly well with that of the overall stock market. Volatility, as measured by both the semi-deviation and a drawdown factor, is considered very low.

Gregory Davis, CFA currently receives a manager quality ranking of 62 (0=worst, 99=best). This fund offers only a moderate level of risk but investors looking for strong performance are still waiting.

Services Offered: Automated phone transactions, payroll deductions, bank draft capabilities, an IRA investment plan, a 401K investment plan, a Keogh investment plan, wire transfers and a systematic withdrawal plan.

Data Date	Weiss Investment Rating	Net Assets ($Mil)	NAV	Perfor- mance Rating/Pts	Total Return Y-T-D	Risk Rating/Pts
6-06	C	4,137	19.87	D+ / 2.3	1.67%	B+ / 9.2
2005	C-	4,091	19.81	D / 1.7	4.65%	B+ / 9.0
2004	B-	4,674	19.45	C / 5.1	9.33%	B- / 7.8
2003	B+	3,772	18.27	C+ / 6.5	19.87%	B / 8.3
2002	B+	3,061	15.65	B / 7.7	-9.52%	B / 8.5
2001	B-	3,117	17.86	C+ / 6.2	-3.02%	B- / 7.9

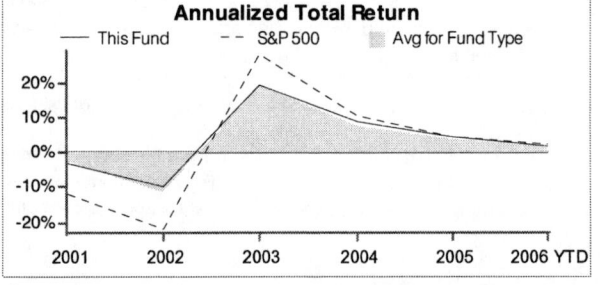

Vanguard Capital Opportunity Inv (VHCOX)

C+ **Fair**

Fund Family: Vanguard **Phone:** (800) 662-7447
Address: Vanguard Financial Center, Valley Forge, PA 19482
Fund Type: GR - Growth

Major Rating Factors: Strong performance is the major factor driving the C+ (Fair) Weiss Investment Rating for Vanguard Capital Opportunity Inv. The fund currently has a performance rating of B- (Good) based on an average return of 19.19% over the last three years and 3.21% over the last six months. Factored into the performance evaluation is a 1.0% back-end load levied at the time of sale.

The fund's risk rating is currently C+ (Fair). It carries a beta of 1.51, meaning it is expected to move 15.1% for every 10% move in the market. Volatility, as measured by both the semi-deviation and a drawdown factor, is considered low.

This is team managed and currently receives a manager quality ranking of 82 (0=worst, 99=best). If you desire only a moderate level of risk and strong performance, then this fund is an excellent option.

Services Offered: Automated phone transactions, payroll deductions, bank draft capabilities, an IRA investment plan, a 401K investment plan, a Keogh investment plan, wire transfers and a systematic withdrawal plan. However, the fund is currently closed to new investors.

Data Date	Weiss Investment Rating	Net Assets ($Mil)	NAV	Perfor- mance Rating/Pts	Total Return Y-T-D	Risk Rating/Pts
6-06	C+	4,894	34.09	B- / 7.5	3.21%	C+ / 5.9
2005	B	5,182	33.03	B+ / 8.7	8.27%	C+ / 5.7
2004	C	6,963	30.77	B / 7.8	21.65%	C- / 3.4
2003	C	5,294	25.41	C+ / 6.8	49.55%	C- / 3.0
2002	C+	3,578	17.00	C+ / 6.1	-27.97%	C / 5.0
2001	C+	4,846	23.62	A+ / 9.8	-9.64%	E- / 0.0

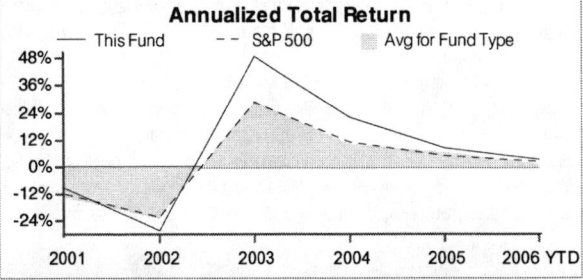
Annualized Total Return

Vanguard Developed Markets Index Fd (VDMIX)

A+ **Excellent**

Fund Family: Vanguard **Phone:** (800) 662-7447
Address: Vanguard Financial Center, Valley Forge, PA 19482
Fund Type: FO - Foreign

Major Rating Factors: Exceptional performance is the major factor driving the A+ (Excellent) Weiss Investment Rating for Vanguard Developed Markets Index Fd. The fund currently has a performance rating of A- (Excellent) based on an average return of 23.84% over the last three years and 10.19% over the last six months. Factored into the performance evaluation is a 2.0% back-end load levied at the time of sale.

The fund's risk rating is currently B (Good). It carries a beta of 1.01, meaning that its performance tracks fairly well with that of the overall stock market. Volatility, as measured by standard deviation, is considered low for equity funds at 10.21.

George U. Sauter has been running the fund for 6 years and currently receives a manager quality ranking of 48 (0=worst, 99=best). If you desire only a moderate level of risk and strong performance, then this fund is an excellent option.

Services Offered: Automated phone transactions, payroll deductions, bank draft capabilities, an IRA investment plan, a 401K investment plan, wire transfers and a systematic withdrawal plan.

Data Date	Weiss Investment Rating	Net Assets ($Mil)	NAV	Perfor- mance Rating/Pts	Total Return Y-T-D	Risk Rating/Pts
6-06	A+	2,131	11.25	A- / 9.0	10.19%	B / 8.0
2005	A	1,679	10.21	B+ / 8.5	13.34%	B- / 7.6
2004	B-	1,198	9.20	B+ / 8.6	20.25%	C- / 4.2

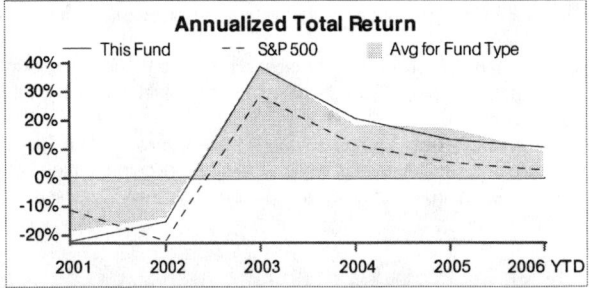
Annualized Total Return

Vanguard Emerging Mkts Stk Idx Fd (VEIEX)

B **Good**

Fund Family: Vanguard **Phone:** (800) 662-7447
Address: Vanguard Financial Center, Valley Forge, PA 19482
Fund Type: EM - Emerging Market

Major Rating Factors: Exceptional performance is the major factor driving the B (Good) Weiss Investment Rating for Vanguard Emerging Mkts Stk Idx Fd. The fund currently has a performance rating of A+ (Excellent) based on an average return of 34.08% over the last three years and 6.14% over the last six months. Factored into the performance evaluation is an expense ratio of 0.45% (very low) and a 0.5% back-end load levied at the time of sale.

The fund's risk rating is currently C (Fair). It carries a beta of 1.12, meaning it is expected to move 11.2% for every 10% move in the market. Volatility, as measured by both the semi-deviation and a drawdown factor, is considered average.

Duane F. Kelly currently receives a manager quality ranking of 15 (0=worst, 99=best). If you desire an average level of risk and strong performance, then this fund is a good option.

Services Offered: Automated phone transactions, payroll deductions, bank draft capabilities, an IRA investment plan, a 401K investment plan, a Keogh investment plan, wire transfers and a systematic withdrawal plan.

Data Date	Weiss Investment Rating	Net Assets ($Mil)	NAV	Perfor- mance Rating/Pts	Total Return Y-T-D	Risk Rating/Pts
6-06	B	7,454	20.24	A+ / 9.7	6.14%	C / 4.3
2005	A-	5,515	19.07	A+ / 9.8	32.05%	C+ / 5.7
2004	A	3,140	14.68	A+ / 9.6	26.12%	C+ / 6.2
2003	A	1,669	11.85	A+ / 9.7	57.65%	C+ / 6.9
2002	C+	915	7.63	C / 5.5	-7.43%	C+ / 5.8
2001	C-	801	8.37	B- / 7.4	-2.88%	E- / 0.0

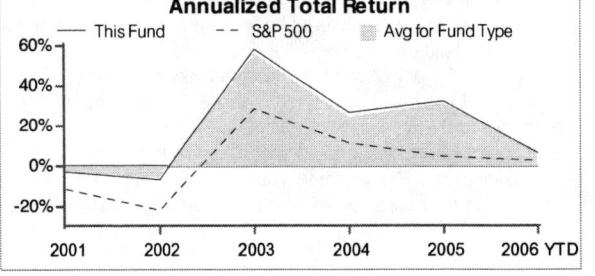
Annualized Total Return

Vanguard Energy Inv (VGENX)   A+   Excellent

Fund Family: Vanguard   **Phone:** (800) 662-7447
Address: Vanguard Financial Center, Valley Forge, PA 19482
Fund Type: EN - Energy/Natural Resources

Major Rating Factors: Exceptional performance is the major factor driving the
A+ (Excellent) Weiss Investment Rating for Vanguard Energy Inv. The fund
currently has a performance rating of A+ (Excellent) based on an average return
of 39.76% over the last three years and 16.47% over the last six months.
Factored into the performance evaluation is an expense ratio of 0.33% (very low)
and a 1.0% back-end load levied at the time of sale.

The fund's risk rating is currently C+ (Fair). It carries a beta of 0.91, meaning
that its performance tracks fairly well with that of the overall stock market.
Volatility, as measured by both the semi-deviation and a drawdown factor, is
considered low.

James A. Bevilacqua currently receives a manager quality ranking of 98
(0=worst, 99=best). If you desire only a moderate level of risk and strong
performance, then this fund is an excellent option.

Services Offered: Automated phone transactions, payroll deductions, bank draft
capabilities, an IRA investment plan, a 401K investment plan, a Keogh
investment plan, wire transfers and a systematic withdrawal plan.

Data Date	Weiss Investment Rating	Net Assets ($Mil)	NAV	Performance Rating/Pts	Total Return Y-T-D	Risk Rating/Pts
6-06	A+	6,796	65.20	A+ / 9.9	16.47%	C+ / 6.2
2005	A+	5,438	56.05	A+ / 9.8	44.60%	B- / 7.1
2004	A+	4,706	40.00	A+ / 9.6	36.52%	B- / 7.3
2003	A	1,921	29.85	B+ / 8.6	33.80%	B- / 7.6
2002	A	1,269	23.20	A / 9.5	-0.62%	B / 8.0
2001	C+	1,282	25.29	A / 9.4	-2.55%	E- / 0.0

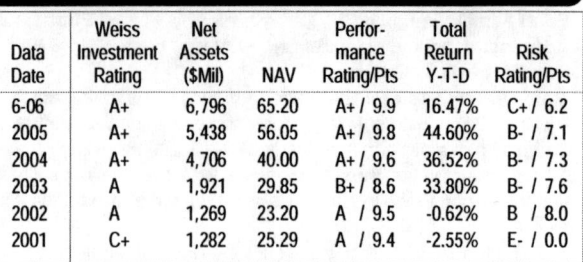

Vanguard Equity Income Inv (VEIPX)   B-   Good

Fund Family: Vanguard   **Phone:** (800) 662-7447
Address: Vanguard Financial Center, Valley Forge, PA 19482
Fund Type: IN - Income

Major Rating Factors: Vanguard Equity Income Inv receives a Weiss
Investment Rating of B- (Good). The fund currently has a performance rating of
C+ (Fair) based on an average return of 13.04% over the last three years and
6.25% over the last six months. Factored into the performance evaluation is an
expense ratio of 0.30% (very low).

The fund's risk rating is currently B (Good). It carries a beta of 0.88, meaning
the fund's expected move will be 8.8% for every 10% move in the market.
Volatility, as measured by both the semi-deviation and a drawdown factor, is
considered low.

James P. Stetler currently receives a manager quality ranking of 83
(0=worst, 99=best). If you desire an average level of risk, then this fund may be
an option.

Services Offered: Automated phone transactions, payroll deductions, bank draft
capabilities, an IRA investment plan, a 401K investment plan, a Keogh
investment plan, wire transfers and a systematic withdrawal plan.

Data Date	Weiss Investment Rating	Net Assets ($Mil)	NAV	Performance Rating/Pts	Total Return Y-T-D	Risk Rating/Pts
6-06	B-	2,756	23.88	C+ / 5.6	6.25%	B / 8.4
2005	C-	2,836	22.79	C- / 3.3	4.37%	B- / 7.3
2004	C+	3,162	23.50	C+ / 6.2	13.57%	C+ / 6.2
2003	B	2,404	22.31	B- / 7.0	25.14%	B- / 7.4
2002	B+	1,997	18.70	B / 8.0	-15.65%	B- / 7.9
2001	B-	2,250	22.71	C+ / 6.6	-2.34%	B- / 7.0

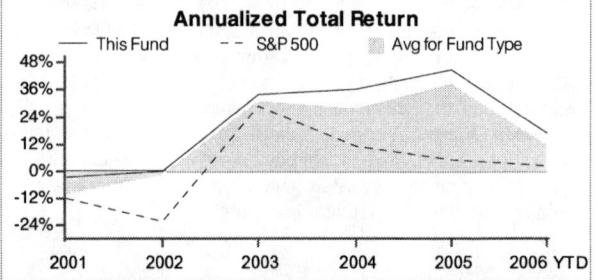

Vanguard European Stock Index Inv (VEURX)   A+   Excellent

Fund Family: Vanguard   **Phone:** (800) 662-7447
Address: Vanguard Financial Center, Valley Forge, PA 19482
Fund Type: FO - Foreign

Major Rating Factors: Exceptional performance is the major factor driving the
A+ (Excellent) Weiss Investment Rating for Vanguard European Stock Index Inv.
The fund currently has a performance rating of A- (Excellent) based on an
average return of 23.28% over the last three years and 13.54% over the last six
months. Factored into the performance evaluation is an expense ratio of 0.27%
(very low) and a 2.0% back-end load levied at the time of sale.

The fund's risk rating is currently B- (Good). It carries a beta of 0.96,
meaning that its performance tracks fairly well with that of the overall stock
market. Volatility, as measured by both the semi-deviation and a drawdown
factor, is considered low.

Duane F. Kelly currently receives a manager quality ranking of 53 (0=worst,
99=best). If you desire only a moderate level of risk and strong performance,
then this fund is an excellent option.

Services Offered: Automated phone transactions, payroll deductions, bank draft
capabilities, an IRA investment plan, a 401K investment plan, a Keogh
investment plan, wire transfers and a systematic withdrawal plan.

Data Date	Weiss Investment Rating	Net Assets ($Mil)	NAV	Performance Rating/Pts	Total Return Y-T-D	Risk Rating/Pts
6-06	A+	14,457	31.45	A- / 9.0	13.54%	B- / 7.9
2005	B	11,052	27.70	B / 7.8	9.26%	C+ / 6.6
2004	B	9,220	25.99	B+ / 8.6	20.86%	C / 5.3
2003	C	5,688	22.00	C+ / 6.1	38.70%	C / 4.7
2002	C	4,102	16.21	C- / 4.2	-17.95%	C+ / 6.1
2001	C	4,405	20.25	D / 1.6	-20.30%	C+ / 6.1

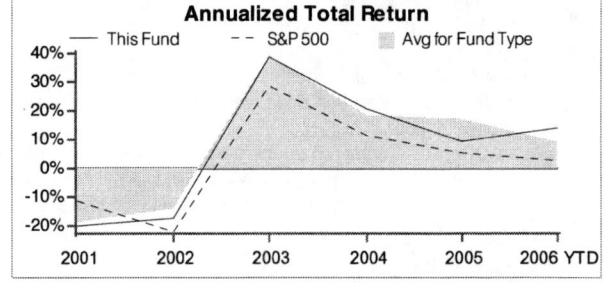

Vanguard Explorer Fund Inv (VEXPX)   C   Fair

Fund Family: Vanguard   **Phone:** (800) 662-7447
Address: Vanguard Financial Center, Valley Forge, PA 19482
Fund Type: SC - Small Cap

Major Rating Factors: Middle of the road best describes Vanguard Explorer Fund Inv whose Weiss Investment Rating is currently a C (Fair). The fund currently has a performance rating of C+ (Fair) based on an average return of 16.81% over the last three years and 4.02% over the last six months. Factored into the performance evaluation is an expense ratio of 0.56% (very low).

The fund's risk rating is currently C (Fair). It carries a beta of 0.95, meaning that its performance tracks fairly well with that of the overall stock market. Volatility, as measured by both the semi-deviation and a drawdown factor, is considered average.

This is team managed and currently receives a manager quality ranking of 45 (0=worst, 99=best). If you desire an average level of risk, then this fund may be an option.

Services Offered: Automated phone transactions, payroll deductions, bank draft capabilities, an IRA investment plan, a 401K investment plan, a Keogh investment plan, wire transfers and a systematic withdrawal plan. However, the fund is currently closed to new investors.

Data Date	Weiss Investment Rating	Net Assets ($Mil)	NAV	Performance Rating/Pts	Total Return Y-T-D	Risk Rating/Pts
6-06	C	8,659	78.13	C+ / 6.8	4.02%	C / 4.9
2005	C+	8,303	75.11	B / 7.7	9.29%	C / 5.3
2004	C	8,230	74.57	C+ / 6.1	13.75%	C- / 4.2
2003	B-	5,943	65.62	B / 8.2	44.25%	C / 4.8
2002	C+	3,764	45.49	C+ / 6.6	-24.56%	C / 5.2
2001	C+	4,648	60.31	A / 9.4	0.54%	E- / 0.0

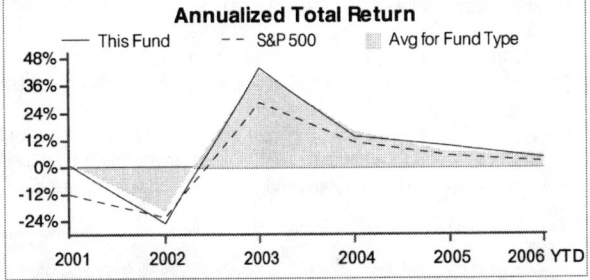

Annualized Total Return

Vanguard Extended Market Index Inv (VEXMX)   B   Good

Fund Family: Vanguard   **Phone:** (800) 662-7447
Address: Vanguard Financial Center, Valley Forge, PA 19482
Fund Type: GR - Growth

Major Rating Factors: Strong performance is the major factor driving the B (Good) Weiss Investment Rating for Vanguard Extended Market Index Inv. The fund currently has a performance rating of B (Good) based on an average return of 19.08% over the last three years and 5.48% over the last six months. Factored into the performance evaluation is an expense ratio of 0.25% (very low).

The fund's risk rating is currently C+ (Fair). It carries a beta of 1.36, meaning it is expected to move 13.6% for every 10% move in the market. Volatility, as measured by both the semi-deviation and a drawdown factor, is considered low.

Donald M. Butler, CFA currently receives a manager quality ranking of 89 (0=worst, 99=best). If you desire only a moderate level of risk and strong performance, then this fund is an excellent option.

Services Offered: Automated phone transactions, payroll deductions, bank draft capabilities, an IRA investment plan, a 401K investment plan, a Keogh investment plan, wire transfers and a systematic withdrawal plan.

Data Date	Weiss Investment Rating	Net Assets ($Mil)	NAV	Performance Rating/Pts	Total Return Y-T-D	Risk Rating/Pts
6-06	B	6,125	36.11	B / 7.7	5.48%	C+ / 6.5
2005	B+	5,275	34.26	B+ / 8.3	10.29%	C+ / 6.4
2004	B-	5,484	31.36	B+ / 8.4	18.71%	C / 4.7
2003	B-	4,097	26.66	B / 8.1	43.43%	C / 5.2
2002	C-	2,686	18.74	C / 4.7	-18.06%	C- / 4.2
2001	D+	3,115	23.09	C+ / 5.7	-9.17%	E- / 0.0

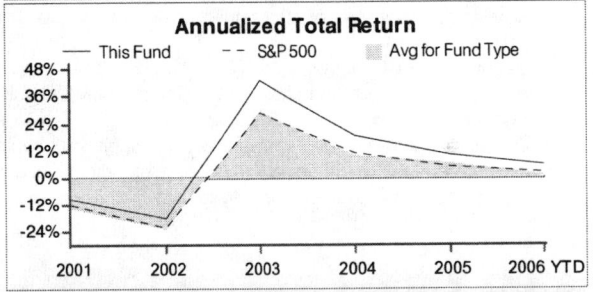

Annualized Total Return

Vanguard Global Equity Fund (VHGEX)   A+   Excellent

Fund Family: Vanguard   **Phone:** (800) 662-7447
Address: Vanguard Financial Center, Valley Forge, PA 19482
Fund Type: GL - Global

Major Rating Factors: Strong performance is the major factor driving the A+ (Excellent) Weiss Investment Rating for Vanguard Global Equity Fund. The fund currently has a performance rating of B+ (Good) based on an average return of 22.96% over the last three years and 9.02% over the last six months. Factored into the performance evaluation is an expense ratio of 0.74% (very low).

The fund's risk rating is currently B- (Good). It carries a beta of 0.99, meaning that its performance tracks fairly well with that of the overall stock market. Volatility, as measured by both the semi-deviation and a drawdown factor, is considered low.

Jeremy J. Hosking has been running the fund for 11 years and currently receives a manager quality ranking of 43 (0=worst, 99=best). If you desire only a moderate level of risk and strong performance, then this fund is an excellent option.

Services Offered: Automated phone transactions, payroll deductions, bank draft capabilities, an IRA investment plan, a 401K investment plan, a Keogh investment plan, wire transfers and a systematic withdrawal plan.

Data Date	Weiss Investment Rating	Net Assets ($Mil)	NAV	Performance Rating/Pts	Total Return Y-T-D	Risk Rating/Pts
6-06	A+	3,791	21.27	B+ / 8.9	9.02%	B- / 7.5
2005	A+	2,479	19.51	B+ / 8.7	11.77%	B- / 7.9
2004	A-	1,143	18.06	A / 9.3	20.09%	C+ / 6.1
2003	A-	744	15.45	A- / 9.1	44.51%	B- / 7.0
2002	B+	245	10.83	B / 8.1	-5.61%	B- / 7.8
2001	B+	158	11.58	B- / 7.4	-3.73%	C+ / 6.6

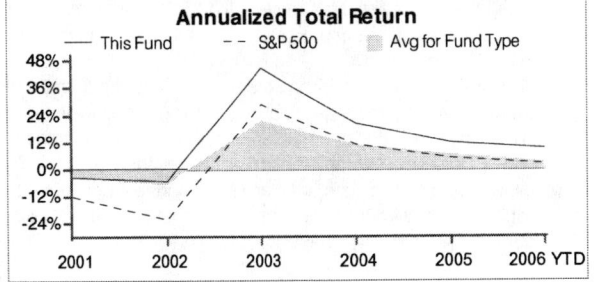

Annualized Total Return

Vanguard Growth & Income Inv (VQNPX)

C+   Fair

Fund Family: Vanguard   **Phone:** (800) 662-7447
Address: Vanguard Financial Center, Valley Forge, PA 19482
Fund Type: GI - Growth and Income

Major Rating Factors: Middle of the road best describes Vanguard Growth &
Income Inv whose Weiss Investment Rating is currently a C+ (Fair). The fund
currently has a performance rating of C (Fair) based on an average return of
11.73% over the last three years and 1.65% over the last six months. Factored
into the performance evaluation is an expense ratio of 0.25% (very low).

The fund's risk rating is currently B (Good). It carries a beta of 1.04, meaning
that its performance tracks fairly well with that of the overall stock market.
Volatility, as measured by both the semi-deviation and a drawdown factor, is
considered low.

John S. Cone, CFA currently receives a manager quality ranking of 58
(0=worst, 99=best). If you desire an average level of risk, then this fund may be
an option.

Services Offered: Automated phone transactions, payroll deductions, bank draft
capabilities, an IRA investment plan, a 401K investment plan, a Keogh
investment plan, wire transfers and a systematic withdrawal plan.

Data Date	Weiss Investment Rating	Net Assets ($Mil)	NAV	Perfor- mance Rating/Pts	Total Return Y-T-D	Risk Rating/Pts
6-06	C+	4,937	32.16	C / 4.3	1.65%	B / 8.7
2005	C+	5,223	31.89	C / 4.4	5.82%	B- / 7.9
2004	C	6,091	30.61	C / 4.8	11.11%	C+/ 6.0
2003	C+	5,506	27.94	C / 5.0	30.15%	C+/ 6.4
2002	C+	4,870	21.75	C / 4.5	-21.92%	C+/ 6.4
2001	C	6,925	28.20	C / 4.8	-11.13%	C- / 3.3

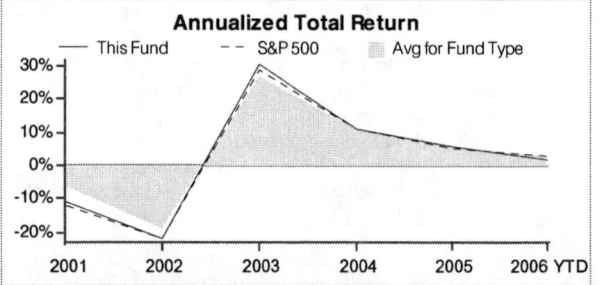

Annualized Total Return

Vanguard Growth Index Inv (VIGRX)

D   Weak

Fund Family: Vanguard   **Phone:** (800) 662-7447
Address: Vanguard Financial Center, Valley Forge, PA 19482
Fund Type: GR - Growth

Major Rating Factors: Disappointing performance is the major factor driving the
D (Weak) Weiss Investment Rating for Vanguard Growth Index Inv. The fund
currently has a performance rating of D (Weak) based on an average return of
8.39% over the last three years and -0.77% over the last six months. Factored
into the performance evaluation is an expense ratio of 0.22% (very low).

The fund's risk rating is currently B- (Good). It carries a beta of 1.10,
meaning it is expected to move 11.0% for every 10% move in the market.
Volatility, as measured by both the semi-deviation and a drawdown factor, is
considered low.

Gerard C. O Reilly currently receives a manager quality ranking of 23
(0=worst, 99=best). This fund offers only a moderate level of risk but investors
looking for strong performance are still waiting.

Services Offered: Automated phone transactions, payroll deductions, bank draft
capabilities, an IRA investment plan, a 401K investment plan, a Keogh
investment plan, wire transfers and a systematic withdrawal plan.

Data Date	Weiss Investment Rating	Net Assets ($Mil)	NAV	Perfor- mance Rating/Pts	Total Return Y-T-D	Risk Rating/Pts
6-06	D	6,432	27.21	D / 2.1	-0.77%	B- / 7.3
2005	D+	6,757	27.54	D+/ 2.6	5.09%	B- / 7.2
2004	D	7,522	26.41	D / 1.9	7.20%	C / 5.0
2003	C-	7,415	24.92	C- / 3.2	25.92%	C / 5.2
2002	C-	6,566	19.95	D+/ 2.8	-23.65%	C / 5.3
2001	D	8,445	26.41	D+/ 2.4	-12.96%	D- / 1.3

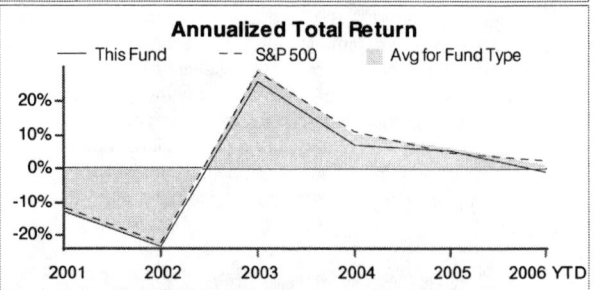

Annualized Total Return

Vanguard Health Care Inv (VGHCX)

C+   Fair

Fund Family: Vanguard   **Phone:** (800) 662-7447
Address: Vanguard Financial Center, Valley Forge, PA 19482
Fund Type: HL - Health

Major Rating Factors: Middle of the road best describes Vanguard Health Care
Inv whose Weiss Investment Rating is currently a C+ (Fair). The fund currently
has a performance rating of C (Fair) based on an average return of 13.20% over
the last three years and 2.40% over the last six months. Factored into the
performance evaluation is an expense ratio of 0.23% (very low) and a 1.0%
back-end load levied at the time of sale.

The fund's risk rating is currently B- (Good). It carries a beta of 0.60,
meaning the fund's expected move will be 6.0% for every 10% move in the
market. Volatility, as measured by both the semi-deviation and a drawdown
factor, is considered low.

Edward P. Owens, CFA has been running the fund for 22 years and
currently receives a manager quality ranking of 94 (0=worst, 99=best). If you
desire an average level of risk, then this fund may be an option.

Services Offered: Automated phone transactions, payroll deductions, bank draft
capabilities, an IRA investment plan, a 401K investment plan, a Keogh
investment plan, wire transfers and a systematic withdrawal plan. However, the
fund is currently closed to new investors.

Data Date	Weiss Investment Rating	Net Assets ($Mil)	NAV	Perfor- mance Rating/Pts	Total Return Y-T-D	Risk Rating/Pts
6-06	C+	16,020	139.17	C / 5.3	2.40%	B- / 7.8
2005	C+	16,340	139.45	C+/ 5.9	15.41%	B- / 7.2
2004	C+	18,819	126.79	C / 5.5	9.51%	C+/ 6.2
2003	B-	16,746	120.57	C+/ 6.9	26.58%	B- / 7.0
2002	A	14,115	96.16	A / 9.5	-11.36%	B / 8.2
2001	A+	16,241	116.84	A / 9.3	-6.87%	B- / 7.2

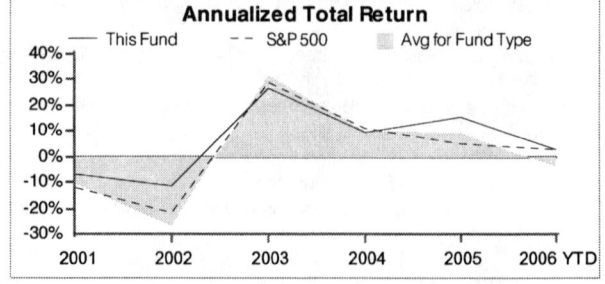

Annualized Total Return

Vanguard International Explorer Fd (VINEX)

A   Excellent

Fund Family: Vanguard   **Phone:** (800) 662-7447
Address: Vanguard Financial Center, Valley Forge, PA 19482
Fund Type: FO - Foreign

Major Rating Factors: Exceptional performance is the major factor driving the A (Excellent) Weiss Investment Rating for Vanguard International Explorer Fd. The fund currently has a performance rating of A+ (Excellent) based on an average return of 32.45% over the last three years and 11.61% over the last six months. Factored into the performance evaluation is an expense ratio of 0.50% (very low) and a 2.0% back-end load levied at the time of sale.

The fund's risk rating is currently C+ (Fair). It carries a beta of 1.04, meaning that its performance tracks fairly well with that of the overall stock market. Volatility, as measured by both the semi-deviation and a drawdown factor, is considered low.

Matthew Dobbs has been running the fund for 10 years and currently receives a manager quality ranking of 94 (0=worst, 99=best). If you desire only a moderate level of risk and strong performance, then this fund is an excellent option.

Services Offered: Automated phone transactions, payroll deductions, bank draft capabilities, an IRA investment plan, a 401K investment plan, wire transfers and a systematic withdrawal plan. However, the fund is currently closed to new investors.

Data Date	Weiss Investment Rating	Net Assets ($Mil)	NAV	Perfor-mance Rating/Pts	Total Return Y-T-D	Risk Rating/Pts
6-06	A	2,527	20.00	A+ / 9.7	11.61%	C+ / 6.3
2005	A+	2,181	17.92	A+ / 9.6	20.49%	B / 8.0
2004	A+	1,729	16.34	A+ / 9.7	31.77%	C+ / 6.4
2003	C	500	12.82	B+ / 8.6	57.37%	D- / 1.5

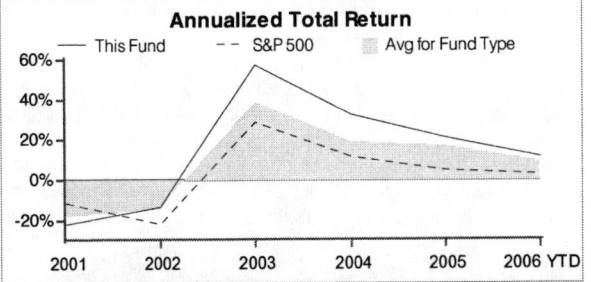

Annualized Total Return

Vanguard International Growth Inv (VWIGX)

A   Excellent

Fund Family: Vanguard   **Phone:** (800) 662-7447
Address: Vanguard Financial Center, Valley Forge, PA 19482
Fund Type: FO - Foreign

Major Rating Factors: Strong performance is the major factor driving the A (Excellent) Weiss Investment Rating for Vanguard International Growth Inv. The fund currently has a performance rating of B+ (Good) based on an average return of 22.82% over the last three years and 9.76% over the last six months. Factored into the performance evaluation is an expense ratio of 0.60% (very low) and a 2.0% back-end load levied at the time of sale.

The fund's risk rating is currently C+ (Fair). It carries a beta of 1.02, meaning that its performance tracks fairly well with that of the overall stock market. Volatility, as measured by both the semi-deviation and a drawdown factor, is considered low.

James K. Anderson has been running the fund for 3 years and currently receives a manager quality ranking of 35 (0=worst, 99=best). If you desire only a moderate level of risk and strong performance, then this fund is an excellent option.

Services Offered: Automated phone transactions, payroll deductions, bank draft capabilities, an IRA investment plan, a 401K investment plan, a Keogh investment plan, wire transfers and a systematic withdrawal plan.

Data Date	Weiss Investment Rating	Net Assets ($Mil)	NAV	Perfor-mance Rating/Pts	Total Return Y-T-D	Risk Rating/Pts
6-06	A	10,026	23.06	B+ / 8.9	9.76%	C+ / 6.8
2005	A-	8,410	21.00	B+ / 8.3	14.95%	B- / 7.2
2004	B	7,725	18.86	B / 8.0	18.95%	C+ / 5.8
2003	C	6,024	16.13	C / 5.5	34.45%	C / 5.5
2002	C	5,089	12.16	C / 4.3	-17.79%	C+ / 5.8
2001	C	6,088	15.01	D+ / 2.9	-18.92%	C+ / 5.9

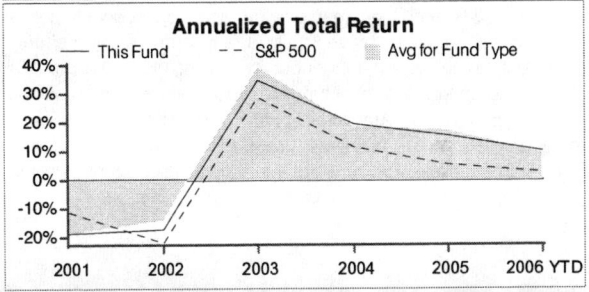

Annualized Total Return

Vanguard International Value Fund (VTRIX)

A+   Excellent

Fund Family: Vanguard   **Phone:** (800) 662-7447
Address: Vanguard Financial Center, Valley Forge, PA 19482
Fund Type: FO - Foreign

Major Rating Factors: Exceptional performance is the major factor driving the A+ (Excellent) Weiss Investment Rating for Vanguard International Value Fund. The fund currently has a performance rating of A (Excellent) based on an average return of 26.79% over the last three years and 11.11% over the last six months. Factored into the performance evaluation is an expense ratio of 0.50% (very low) and a 2.0% back-end load levied at the time of sale.

The fund's risk rating is currently B- (Good). It carries a beta of 1.07, meaning that its performance tracks fairly well with that of the overall stock market. Volatility, as measured by both the semi-deviation and a drawdown factor, is considered low.

Aureole L. W. Foong currently receives a manager quality ranking of 62 (0=worst, 99=best). If you desire only a moderate level of risk and strong performance, then this fund is an excellent option.

Services Offered: Automated phone transactions, payroll deductions, bank draft capabilities, an IRA investment plan, a 401K investment plan, a Keogh investment plan, wire transfers and a systematic withdrawal plan.

Data Date	Weiss Investment Rating	Net Assets ($Mil)	NAV	Perfor-mance Rating/Pts	Total Return Y-T-D	Risk Rating/Pts
6-06	A+	5,908	38.69	A / 9.3	11.11%	B- / 7.2
2005	A+	3,818	34.82	A- / 9.1	17.96%	B- / 7.2
2004	B+	2,463	30.93	B+ / 8.8	19.77%	C+ / 5.9
2003	B	1,564	26.24	B+ / 8.3	41.90%	C+ / 5.9
2002	C+	1,155	18.83	C / 5.5	-13.35%	B- / 7.0
2001	C-	895	22.07	C- / 3.8	-14.05%	C- / 3.5

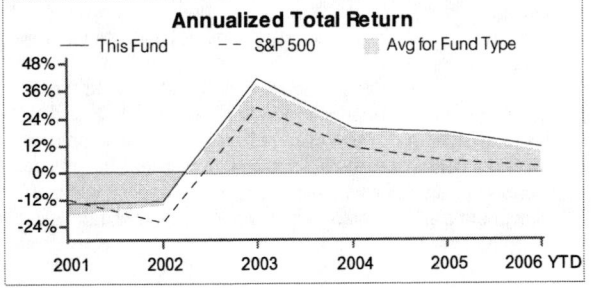

Annualized Total Return

Vanguard LifeStrategy Conserv Gr Fd (VSCGX)   C   Fair

Fund Family: Vanguard   **Phone:** (800) 662-7447
Address: Vanguard Financial Center, Valley Forge, PA 19482
Fund Type: AA - Asset Allocation

Major Rating Factors: Disappointing performance is the major factor driving the C (Fair) Weiss Investment Rating for Vanguard LifeStrategy Conserv Gr Fd. The fund currently has a performance rating of D (Weak) based on an average return of 7.51% over the last three years and 1.95% over the last six months. Factored into the performance evaluation is an expense ratio of 0.25% (very low).

The fund's risk rating is currently B+ (Good). It carries a beta of 0.84, meaning the fund's expected move will be 8.4% for every 10% move in the market. Volatility, as measured by both the semi-deviation and a drawdown factor, is considered very low.

Vanguard Quantitative Equity G has been running the fund for 12 years and currently receives a manager quality ranking of 65 (0=worst, 99=best). This fund offers only a moderate level of risk but investors looking for strong performance are still waiting.

Services Offered: Automated phone transactions, payroll deductions, bank draft capabilities, an IRA investment plan, a 401K investment plan, a Keogh investment plan, wire transfers and a systematic withdrawal plan.

Data Date	Weiss Investment Rating	Net Assets ($Mil)	NAV	Perfor- mance Rating/Pts	Total Return Y-T-D	Risk Rating/Pts
6-06	C	4,678	15.56	D / 1.9	1.95%	B+ / 9.9
2005	C	4,254	15.49	D- / 1.1	4.45%	B+ / 9.9
2004	B	3,569	15.26	C / 4.9	8.02%	B / 8.9
2003	A-	2,854	14.54	C+ / 6.6	16.57%	B+ / 9.3
2002	A+	2,210	12.82	B+ / 8.6	-5.37%	B+ / 9.6
2001	B+	2,026	14.06	C+ / 6.7	-0.01%	B+ / 9.1

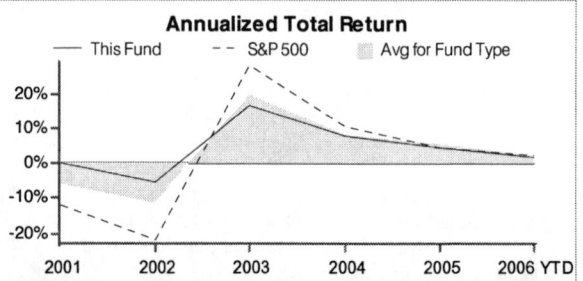

Annualized Total Return

Vanguard LifeStrategy Growth Fd (VASGX)   B   Good

Fund Family: Vanguard   **Phone:** (800) 662-7447
Address: Vanguard Financial Center, Valley Forge, PA 19482
Fund Type: AA - Asset Allocation

Major Rating Factors: Vanguard LifeStrategy Growth Fd receives a Weiss Investment Rating of B (Good). The fund currently has a performance rating of C (Fair) based on an average return of 12.99% over the last three years and 3.78% over the last six months. Factored into the performance evaluation is an expense ratio of 0.26% (very low).

The fund's risk rating is currently B (Good). It carries a beta of 1.45, meaning it is expected to move 14.5% for every 10% move in the market. Volatility, as measured by both the semi-deviation and a drawdown factor, is considered low.

Vanguard Quantitative Equity G has been running the fund for 12 years and currently receives a manager quality ranking of 83 (0=worst, 99=best). If you desire an average level of risk, then this fund may be an option.

Services Offered: Automated phone transactions, payroll deductions, bank draft capabilities, an IRA investment plan, a 401K investment plan, a Keogh investment plan, wire transfers and a systematic withdrawal plan.

Data Date	Weiss Investment Rating	Net Assets ($Mil)	NAV	Perfor- mance Rating/Pts	Total Return Y-T-D	Risk Rating/Pts
6-06	B	7,585	21.60	C / 5.3	3.78%	B / 8.9
2005	C+	6,938	21.00	C / 4.7	6.88%	B / 8.2
2004	C+	5,828	20.04	C+ / 6.3	12.58%	C+ / 6.4
2003	C+	4,553	18.16	C+ / 6.0	28.52%	C+ / 6.7
2002	C+	3,405	14.36	C+ / 6.0	-15.84%	B- / 7.2
2001	C+	3,726	17.43	C / 4.9	-8.86%	C+ / 6.8

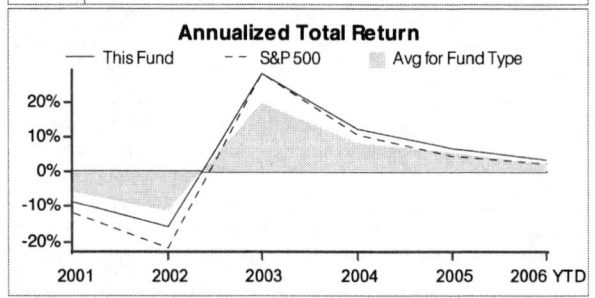

Annualized Total Return

Vanguard LifeStrategy Mod Growth Fd (VSMGX)   C+   Fair

Fund Family: Vanguard   **Phone:** (800) 662-7447
Address: Vanguard Financial Center, Valley Forge, PA 19482
Fund Type: AA - Asset Allocation

Major Rating Factors: Middle of the road best describes Vanguard LifeStrategy Mod Growth Fd whose Weiss Investment Rating is currently a C+ (Fair). The fund currently has a performance rating of C- (Fair) based on an average return of 10.21% over the last three years and 2.68% over the last six months. Factored into the performance evaluation is an expense ratio of 0.25% (very low).

The fund's risk rating is currently B+ (Good). It carries a beta of 1.15, meaning it is expected to move 11.5% for every 10% move in the market. Volatility, as measured by both the semi-deviation and a drawdown factor, is considered very low.

Vanguard Quantitative Equity G has been running the fund for 12 years and currently receives a manager quality ranking of 74 (0=worst, 99=best). If you desire an average level of risk, then this fund may be an option.

Services Offered: Automated phone transactions, payroll deductions, bank draft capabilities, an IRA investment plan, a 401K investment plan, a Keogh investment plan, wire transfers and a systematic withdrawal plan.

Data Date	Weiss Investment Rating	Net Assets ($Mil)	NAV	Perfor- mance Rating/Pts	Total Return Y-T-D	Risk Rating/Pts
6-06	C+	8,540	18.73	C- / 3.5	2.68%	B+ / 9.5
2005	C	8,062	18.47	D+ / 2.7	5.69%	B+ / 9.2
2004	B-	6,818	17.91	C+ / 5.8	10.57%	B- / 7.7
2003	B	5,408	16.61	C+ / 6.7	22.40%	B / 8.1
2002	B+	4,075	13.87	B / 7.6	-10.32%	B / 8.4
2001	B	4,243	15.93	C+ / 5.9	-4.42%	B / 8.0

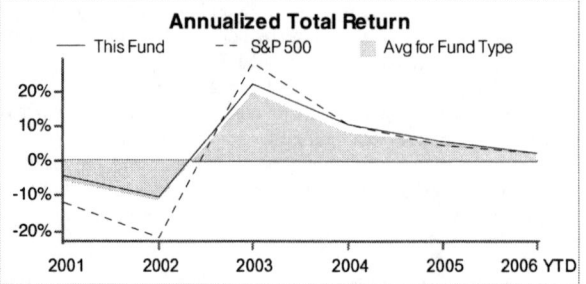

Annualized Total Return

Vanguard Mid-Cap Index Inv (VIMSX)   B+   Good

Fund Family: Vanguard   **Phone:** (800) 662-7447
Address: Vanguard Financial Center, Valley Forge, PA 19482
Fund Type: MC - Mid Cap

Major Rating Factors: Strong performance is the major factor driving the B+ (Good) Weiss Investment Rating for Vanguard Mid-Cap Index Inv. The fund currently has a performance rating of B (Good) based on an average return of 20.01% over the last three years and 4.42% over the last six months. Factored into the performance evaluation is an expense ratio of 0.22% (very low).

    The fund's risk rating is currently B- (Good). It carries a beta of 1.01, meaning that its performance tracks fairly well with that of the overall stock market. Volatility, as measured by both the semi-deviation and a drawdown factor, is considered low.

    Donald M. Butler, CFA currently receives a manager quality ranking of 72 (0=worst, 99=best). If you desire only a moderate level of risk and strong performance, then this fund is an excellent option.

Services Offered: Automated phone transactions, payroll deductions, bank draft capabilities, an IRA investment plan, a 401K investment plan, a Keogh investment plan and a systematic withdrawal plan.

Data Date	Weiss Investment Rating	Net Assets ($Mil)	NAV	Performance Rating/Pts	Total Return Y-T-D	Risk Rating/Pts
6-06	B+	7,111	18.41	B / 8.0	4.42%	B- / 7.3
2005	B+	6,237	17.63	B / 8.2	13.93%	B- / 7.0
2004	B+	4,925	15.64	B+ / 8.5	20.35%	C+ / 6.3
2003	C+	3,451	13.13	B / 8.1	34.14%	C- / 3.3
2002	C	2,333	9.88	B+ / 8.4	-14.61%	D / 1.8

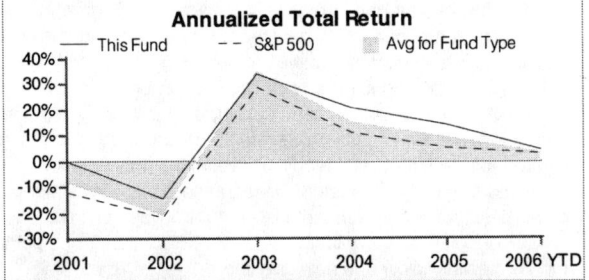

Annualized Total Return

Vanguard Morgan Growth Inv (VMRGX)   C   Fair

Fund Family: Vanguard   **Phone:** (800) 662-7447
Address: Vanguard Financial Center, Valley Forge, PA 19482
Fund Type: GR - Growth

Major Rating Factors: Middle of the road best describes Vanguard Morgan Growth Inv whose Weiss Investment Rating is currently a C (Fair). The fund currently has a performance rating of C (Fair) based on an average return of 12.33% over the last three years and 1.19% over the last six months. Factored into the performance evaluation is an expense ratio of 0.41% (very low).

    The fund's risk rating is currently B- (Good). It carries a beta of 1.22, meaning it is expected to move 12.2% for every 10% move in the market. Volatility, as measured by both the semi-deviation and a drawdown factor, is considered low.

    Paul E. Marrkand, CFA currently receives a manager quality ranking of 45 (0=worst, 99=best). If you desire an average level of risk, then this fund may be an option.

Services Offered: Automated phone transactions, payroll deductions, bank draft capabilities, an IRA investment plan, a 401K investment plan, a Keogh investment plan, wire transfers and a systematic withdrawal plan.

Data Date	Weiss Investment Rating	Net Assets ($Mil)	NAV	Performance Rating/Pts	Total Return Y-T-D	Risk Rating/Pts
6-06	C	5,013	17.92	C / 4.7	1.19%	B- / 7.1
2005	C+	4,681	17.71	C+ / 5.8	9.09%	B- / 7.0
2004	C-	4,389	16.32	C- / 3.8	10.47%	C / 5.2
2003	C	3,673	14.87	C / 4.9	33.73%	C / 5.1
2002	C-	2,739	11.15	C- / 3.6	-23.52%	C / 4.8
2001	D+	3,493	14.63	C / 4.6	-13.60%	E+ / 0.6

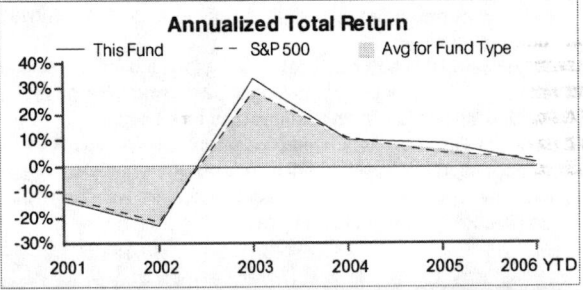

Annualized Total Return

Vanguard Pacific Stock Index Inv (VPACX)   B+   Good

Fund Family: Vanguard   **Phone:** (800) 662-7447
Address: Vanguard Financial Center, Valley Forge, PA 19482
Fund Type: FO - Foreign

Major Rating Factors: Exceptional performance is the major factor driving the B+ (Good) Weiss Investment Rating for Vanguard Pacific Stock Index Inv. The fund currently has a performance rating of A- (Excellent) based on an average return of 25.30% over the last three years and 3.53% over the last six months. Factored into the performance evaluation is an expense ratio of 0.32% (very low) and a 2.0% back-end load levied at the time of sale.

    The fund's risk rating is currently C+ (Fair). It carries a beta of 1.10, meaning it is expected to move 11.0% for every 10% move in the market. Volatility, as measured by both the semi-deviation and a drawdown factor, is considered low.

    Michael H. Buek, CFA currently receives a manager quality ranking of 41 (0=worst, 99=best). If you desire only a moderate level of risk and strong performance, then this fund is an excellent option.

Services Offered: Automated phone transactions, payroll deductions, bank draft capabilities, an IRA investment plan, a 401K investment plan, a Keogh investment plan, wire transfers and a systematic withdrawal plan.

Data Date	Weiss Investment Rating	Net Assets ($Mil)	NAV	Performance Rating/Pts	Total Return Y-T-D	Risk Rating/Pts
6-06	B+	7,190	11.74	A- / 9.1	3.53%	C+ / 5.7
2005	A-	5,473	11.34	A / 9.3	22.59%	C+ / 6.1
2004	A-	3,732	9.38	B+ / 8.7	18.83%	C+ / 6.5
2003	C+	2,275	8.03	C+ / 6.2	38.42%	C+ / 5.6
2002	C-	1,445	5.88	D+ / 2.6	-9.32%	C+ / 5.8
2001	D-	1,327	6.56	E+ / 0.8	-26.34%	D / 1.8

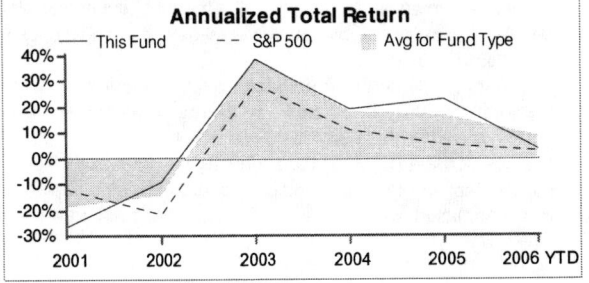

Annualized Total Return

Vanguard Prec. Metals & Mining Fd (VGPMX)   C-   Fair

Fund Family: Vanguard   **Phone:** (800) 662-7447
Address: Vanguard Financial Center, Valley Forge, PA 19482
Fund Type: PM - Precious Metals

Major Rating Factors: Vanguard Prec. Metals & Mining Fd has adopted a very risky asset allocation strategy and currently receives an overall Weiss Investment Rating of C- (Fair). The fund has shown a high level of volatility, as measured by both semi-deviation and drawdown factors. It carries a beta of 1.10, meaning it is expected to move 11.0% for every 10% move in the market. The high level of risk (D-, Weak) did however, reward investors with excellent performance.

The fund's performance rating is currently A+ (Excellent). It has registered an average return of 44.17% over the last three years and is up 26.92% over the last six months. Factored into the performance evaluation is an expense ratio of 0.45% (very low) and a 1.0% back-end load levied at the time of sale.

Graham E. French has been running the fund for 10 years and currently receives a manager quality ranking of 99 (0=worst, 99=best). If you are comfortable owning a very high risk investment, this fund may be an option.
Services Offered: Automated phone transactions, payroll deductions, bank draft capabilities, an IRA investment plan, a 401K investment plan, a Keogh investment plan, wire transfers and a systematic withdrawal plan. However, the fund is currently closed to new investors.

Data Date	Weiss Investment Rating	Net Assets ($Mil)	NAV	Perfor-mance Rating/Pts	Total Return Y-T-D	Risk Rating/Pts
6-06	C-	3,386	29.16	A+ / 9.9	26.92%	D- / 1.2
2005	C+	2,222	23.20	A+ / 9.8	43.79%	D / 2.1
2004	B	885	16.69	A+ / 9.8	8.09%	C- / 4.1
2003	A-	679	16.38	A+ / 9.9	59.45%	C+ / 6.1
2002	A-	480	10.89	A+ / 9.9	33.35%	B- / 7.4
2001	C+	371	8.55	A / 9.3	18.33%	E- / 0.0

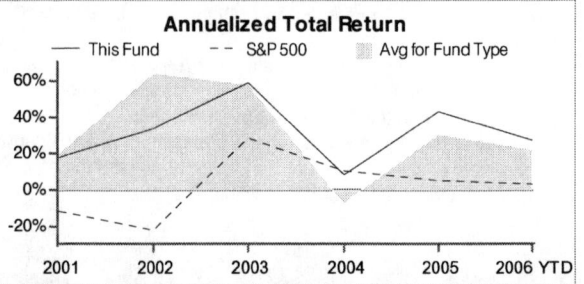

Vanguard PRIMECAP Inv (VPMCX)   B-   Good

Fund Family: Vanguard   **Phone:** (800) 662-7447
Address: Vanguard Financial Center, Valley Forge, PA 19482
Fund Type: GR - Growth

Major Rating Factors: Vanguard PRIMECAP Inv receives a Weiss Investment Rating of B- (Good). The fund currently has a performance rating of C+ (Fair) based on an average return of 16.57% over the last three years and 3.80% over the last six months. Factored into the performance evaluation is an expense ratio of 0.45% (very low) and a 1.0% back-end load levied at the time of sale.

The fund's risk rating is currently B- (Good). It carries a beta of 1.25, meaning it is expected to move 12.5% for every 10% move in the market. Volatility, as measured by both the semi-deviation and a drawdown factor, is considered low.

Howard B. Schow has been running the fund for 22 years and currently receives a manager quality ranking of 82 (0=worst, 99=best). If you desire an average level of risk, then this fund may be an option.
Services Offered: Automated phone transactions, payroll deductions, bank draft capabilities, an IRA investment plan, a 401K investment plan, a Keogh investment plan, wire transfers and a systematic withdrawal plan. However, the fund is currently closed to new investors.

Data Date	Weiss Investment Rating	Net Assets ($Mil)	NAV	Perfor-mance Rating/Pts	Total Return Y-T-D	Risk Rating/Pts
6-06	B-	21,260	67.79	C+ / 6.9	3.80%	B- / 7.3
2005	B+	20,762	65.31	B- / 7.5	8.49%	B- / 7.0
2004	C	22,226	62.30	C+ / 6.8	18.31%	C- / 4.2
2003	C	18,163	53.04	C / 5.5	37.75%	C- / 4.2
2002	C	14,054	38.66	C / 5.2	-24.56%	C / 5.3
2001	C	18,096	51.52	B / 7.9	-13.35%	E+ / 0.7

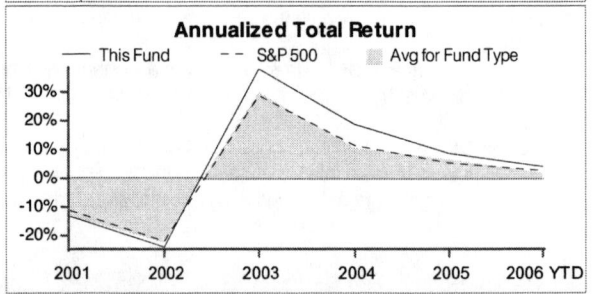

Vanguard REIT Index Inv (VGSIX)   C   Fair

Fund Family: Vanguard   **Phone:** (800) 662-7447
Address: Vanguard Financial Center, Valley Forge, PA 19482
Fund Type: RE - Real Estate

Major Rating Factors: Exceptional performance is the major factor driving the C (Fair) Weiss Investment Rating for Vanguard REIT Index Inv. The fund currently has a performance rating of A- (Excellent) based on an average return of 25.60% over the last three years and 13.21% over the last six months. Factored into the performance evaluation is an expense ratio of 0.21% (very low) and a 1.0% back-end load levied at the time of sale.

The fund's risk rating is currently C- (Fair). It carries a beta of 0.99, meaning that its performance tracks fairly well with that of the overall stock market. Volatility, as measured by both the semi-deviation and a drawdown factor, is considered average.

Gerard C. O'Reilly currently receives a manager quality ranking of 71 (0=worst, 99=best). If you desire an average level of risk and strong performance, then this fund is a good option.
Services Offered: Automated phone transactions, payroll deductions, bank draft capabilities, an IRA investment plan, a 401K investment plan, a Keogh investment plan, wire transfers and a systematic withdrawal plan.

Data Date	Weiss Investment Rating	Net Assets ($Mil)	NAV	Perfor-mance Rating/Pts	Total Return Y-T-D	Risk Rating/Pts
6-06	C	4,952	22.06	A- / 9.2	13.21%	C- / 3.0
2005	C	4,444	19.80	B+ / 8.7	11.95%	C- / 3.1
2004	A	4,381	18.78	A+ / 9.7	30.69%	C+ / 6.2
2003	A+	2,891	15.18	A / 9.3	35.65%	B / 8.7
2002	A+	1,765	11.84	A+ / 9.7	3.75%	B+ / 9.7
2001	A+	1,230	12.13	B+ / 8.9	12.35%	B- / 7.2

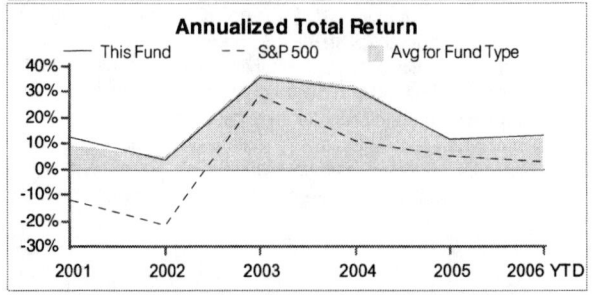

Vanguard Selected Value Fund (VASVX)   A-   Excellent

Fund Family: Vanguard   **Phone:** (800) 662-7447
Address: Vanguard Financial Center, Valley Forge, PA 19482
Fund Type: MC - Mid Cap

Major Rating Factors: Strong performance is the major factor driving the A- (Excellent) Weiss Investment Rating for Vanguard Selected Value Fund. The fund currently has a performance rating of B- (Good) based on an average return of 18.58% over the last three years and 2.97% over the last six months. Factored into the performance evaluation is an expense ratio of 0.51% (very low) and a 1.0% back-end load levied at the time of sale.

The fund's risk rating is currently B (Good). It carries a beta of 0.64, meaning the fund's expected move will be 6.4% for every 10% move in the market. Volatility, as measured by both the semi-deviation and a drawdown factor, is considered low.

James P. Barrow currently receives a manager quality ranking of 95 (0=worst, 99=best). If you desire only a moderate level of risk and strong performance, then this fund is an excellent option.

Services Offered: Automated phone transactions, payroll deductions, bank draft capabilities, an IRA investment plan, a 401K investment plan, a Keogh investment plan, wire transfers and a systematic withdrawal plan.

Data Date	Weiss Investment Rating	Net Assets ($Mil)	NAV	Perfor-mance Rating/Pts	Total Return Y-T-D	Risk Rating/Pts
6-06	A-	3,892	19.42	B- / 7.2	2.97%	B / 8.2
2005	B+	3,867	18.86	B- / 7.5	10.67%	B- / 7.3
2004	B+	2,111	18.07	B+ / 8.7	20.38%	C+ / 5.7
2003	A-	1,322	15.23	A- / 9.0	35.21%	B- / 7.1
2002	A-	1,118	11.46	A / 9.3	-9.79%	B / 8.0
2001	B	995	12.97	B+ / 8.8	15.09%	C- / 3.0

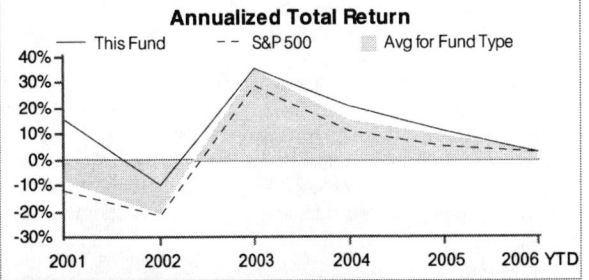

Vanguard Small-Cap Grwth Index Fd (VISGX)   C   Fair

Fund Family: Vanguard   **Phone:** (800) 662-7447
Address: Vanguard Financial Center, Valley Forge, PA 19482
Fund Type: SC - Small Cap

Major Rating Factors: Strong performance is the major factor driving the C (Fair) Weiss Investment Rating for Vanguard Small-Cap Grwth Index Fd. The fund currently has a performance rating of B- (Good) based on an average return of 18.46% over the last three years and 5.67% over the last six months. Factored into the performance evaluation is an expense ratio of 0.23% (very low).

The fund's risk rating is currently C (Fair). It carries a beta of 1.02, meaning that its performance tracks fairly well with that of the overall stock market. Volatility, as measured by both the semi-deviation and a drawdown factor, is considered average.

Gerard C. O'Reilly currently receives a manager quality ranking of 50 (0=worst, 99=best). If you desire an average level of risk and strong performance, then this fund is a good option.

Services Offered: Automated phone transactions, payroll deductions, bank draft capabilities, an IRA investment plan, a 401K investment plan and a Keogh investment plan.

Data Date	Weiss Investment Rating	Net Assets ($Mil)	NAV	Perfor-mance Rating/Pts	Total Return Y-T-D	Risk Rating/Pts
6-06	C	2,127	17.36	B- / 7.5	5.67%	C / 4.6
2005	C+	1,696	16.43	B / 7.7	8.64%	C / 5.0
2004	C	1,348	15.16	B / 8.2	16.06%	D+ / 2.8
2003	C	872	13.08	B+ / 8.6	42.88%	D- / 1.5
2002	C-	403	9.17	B- / 7.2	-15.41%	E- / 0.0

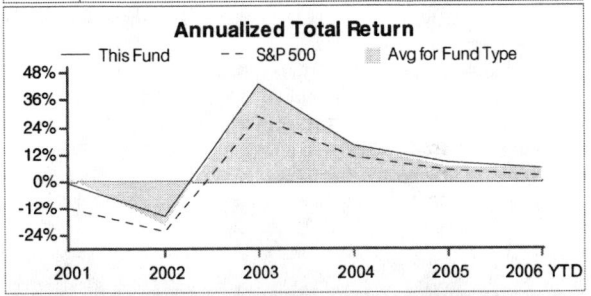

Vanguard Small-Cap Index Inv (NAESX)   B   Good

Fund Family: Vanguard   **Phone:** (800) 662-7447
Address: Vanguard Financial Center, Valley Forge, PA 19482
Fund Type: SC - Small Cap

Major Rating Factors: Strong performance is the major factor driving the B (Good) Weiss Investment Rating for Vanguard Small-Cap Index Inv. The fund currently has a performance rating of B (Good) based on an average return of 19.76% over the last three years and 6.89% over the last six months. Factored into the performance evaluation is an expense ratio of 0.23% (very low).

The fund's risk rating is currently C+ (Fair). It carries a beta of 0.90, meaning the fund's expected move will be 9.0% for every 10% move in the market. Volatility, as measured by both the semi-deviation and a drawdown factor, is considered low.

Michael H. Buek, CFA currently receives a manager quality ranking of 79 (0=worst, 99=best). If you desire only a moderate level of risk and strong performance, then this fund is an excellent option.

Services Offered: Automated phone transactions, payroll deductions, bank draft capabilities, an IRA investment plan, a 401K investment plan, a Keogh investment plan, wire transfers and a systematic withdrawal plan.

Data Date	Weiss Investment Rating	Net Assets ($Mil)	NAV	Perfor-mance Rating/Pts	Total Return Y-T-D	Risk Rating/Pts
6-06	B	6,529	30.48	B / 7.9	6.89%	C+ / 6.3
2005	B+	5,869	28.52	B / 8.0	7.40%	C+ / 6.7
2004	C+	5,996	26.82	B+ / 8.4	19.85%	C- / 4.2
2003	B	4,698	22.60	B+ / 8.8	45.63%	C+ / 5.8
2002	C+	3,142	15.66	C+ / 6.4	-20.02%	C+ / 5.6
2001	C	3,545	19.82	B / 8.2	3.10%	E- / 0.2

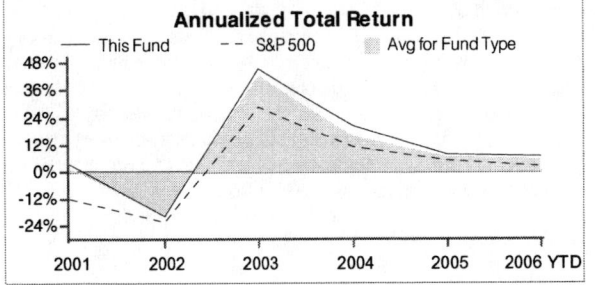

Vanguard Small-Cap Value Index Fd (VISVX)   A   Excellent

Fund Family: Vanguard   **Phone:** (800) 662-7447
Address: Vanguard Financial Center, Valley Forge, PA 19482
Fund Type: SC - Small Cap
Major Rating Factors: Strong performance is the major factor driving the A (Excellent) Weiss Investment Rating for Vanguard Small-Cap Value Index Fd. The fund currently has a performance rating of B (Good) based on an average return of 20.92% over the last three years and 8.03% over the last six months. Factored into the performance evaluation is an expense ratio of 0.23% (very low).

    The fund's risk rating is currently B- (Good). It carries a beta of 0.79, meaning the fund's expected move will be 7.9% for every 10% move in the market. Volatility, as measured by both the semi-deviation and a drawdown factor, is considered low.

    Michael H. Buek, CFA currently receives a manager quality ranking of 93 (0=worst, 99=best). If you desire only a moderate level of risk and strong performance, then this fund is an excellent option.

Services Offered: Automated phone transactions, payroll deductions, bank draft capabilities, an IRA investment plan, a 401K investment plan, a Keogh investment plan, wire transfers and a systematic withdrawal plan.

Data Date	Weiss Investment Rating	Net Assets ($Mil)	NAV	Perfor-mance Rating/Pts	Total Return Y-T-D	Risk Rating/Pts
6-06	A	3,763	15.72	B / 8.2	8.03%	B- / 7.5
2005	B	3,473	14.56	B- / 7.3	6.07%	C+ / 6.5
2004	B	2,753	13.97	B+ / 8.9	23.55%	C / 4.9
2003	B+	1,622	11.49	A- / 9.0	37.19%	C+ / 6.3
2002	B+	1,217	8.52	A- / 9.1	-14.20%	B- / 7.3
2001	B	803	10.29	A / 9.4	13.70%	D+ / 2.5

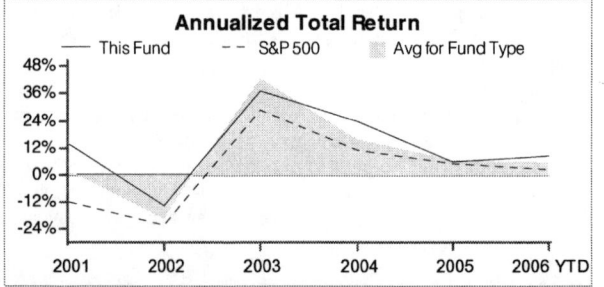

Vanguard STAR Fund (VGSTX)   C+   Fair

Fund Family: Vanguard   **Phone:** (800) 662-7447
Address: Vanguard Financial Center, Valley Forge, PA 19482
Fund Type: GI - Growth and Income
Major Rating Factors: Middle of the road best describes Vanguard STAR Fund whose Weiss Investment Rating is currently a C+ (Fair). The fund currently has a performance rating of C- (Fair) based on an average return of 10.85% over the last three years and 1.91% over the last six months. Factored into the performance evaluation is an expense ratio of 0.36% (very low).

    The fund's risk rating is currently B+ (Good). It carries a beta of 0.67, meaning the fund's expected move will be 6.7% for every 10% move in the market. Volatility, as measured by both the semi-deviation and a drawdown factor, is considered very low.

    Vanguard Quantitative Equity G has been running the fund for 21 years and currently receives a manager quality ranking of 80 (0=worst, 99=best). If you desire an average level of risk, then this fund may be an option.

Services Offered: Automated phone transactions, payroll deductions, bank draft capabilities, an IRA investment plan, a 401K investment plan, a Keogh investment plan, wire transfers and a systematic withdrawal plan.

Data Date	Weiss Investment Rating	Net Assets ($Mil)	NAV	Perfor-mance Rating/Pts	Total Return Y-T-D	Risk Rating/Pts
6-06	C+	12,798	19.75	C- / 3.8	1.91%	B+ / 9.4
2005	C+	11,858	19.60	C- / 3.6	7.44%	B+ / 9.5
2004	B-	10,435	18.74	C+ / 6.1	11.60%	B- / 7.9
2003	B+	8,822	17.20	B- / 7.0	22.70%	B / 8.2
2002	A	7,498	14.35	B+ / 8.6	-9.86%	B / 8.8
2001	A+	8,242	16.44	B / 7.6	0.50%	B / 8.3

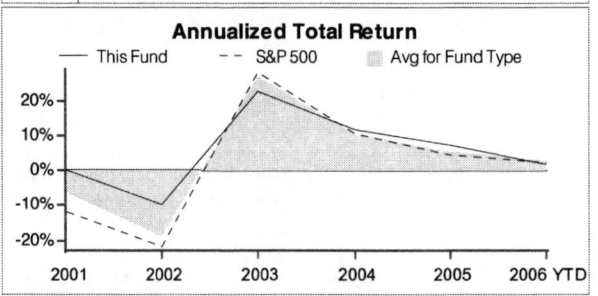

Vanguard Strategic Equity Fd (VSEQX)   B+   Good

Fund Family: Vanguard   **Phone:** (800) 662-7447
Address: Vanguard Financial Center, Valley Forge, PA 19482
Fund Type: AG - Aggressive Growth
Major Rating Factors: Strong performance is the major factor driving the B+ (Good) Weiss Investment Rating for Vanguard Strategic Equity Fd. The fund currently has a performance rating of B (Good) based on an average return of 19.65% over the last three years and 5.93% over the last six months. Factored into the performance evaluation is an expense ratio of 0.40% (very low).

    The fund's risk rating is currently C+ (Fair). It carries a beta of 1.38, meaning it is expected to move 13.8% for every 10% move in the market. Volatility, as measured by both the semi-deviation and a drawdown factor, is considered low.

    James D Troyer, CFA, currently receives a manager quality ranking of 91 (0=worst, 99=best). If you desire only a moderate level of risk and strong performance, then this fund is an excellent option.

Services Offered: Automated phone transactions, payroll deductions, bank draft capabilities, an IRA investment plan, a 401K investment plan, a Keogh investment plan, wire transfers and a systematic withdrawal plan. However, the fund is currently closed to new investors.

Data Date	Weiss Investment Rating	Net Assets ($Mil)	NAV	Perfor-mance Rating/Pts	Total Return Y-T-D	Risk Rating/Pts
6-06	B+	6,943	23.23	B / 7.8	5.93%	C+ / 6.9
2005	A-	5,484	21.93	B+ / 8.3	9.97%	B- / 7.3
2004	A	3,467	21.43	B+ / 8.9	20.49%	C+ / 6.7
2003	A+	1,861	18.71	B+ / 8.9	43.83%	B- / 7.8
2002	B-	932	13.10	C+ / 6.8	-13.14%	B- / 7.4
2001	C+	880	15.23	C+ / 6.8	-1.34%	C+ / 5.8

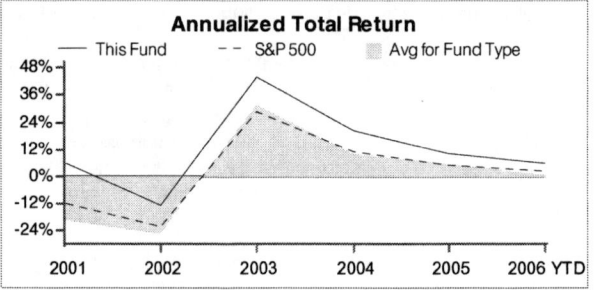

Vanguard Total Intl Stock Index Fd (VGTSX) A Excellent

Fund Family: Vanguard **Phone:** (800) 662-7447
Address: Vanguard Financial Center, Valley Forge, PA 19482
Fund Type: FO - Foreign

Major Rating Factors: Exceptional performance is the major factor driving the A (Excellent) Weiss Investment Rating for Vanguard Total Intl Stock Index Fd. The fund currently has a performance rating of A- (Excellent) based on an average return of 24.93% over the last three years and 9.53% over the last six months. Factored into the performance evaluation is an expense ratio of 0.31% (very low) and a 2.0% back-end load levied at the time of sale.

The fund's risk rating is currently C+ (Fair). It carries a beta of 1.08, meaning that its performance tracks fairly well with that of the overall stock market. Volatility, as measured by both the semi-deviation and a drawdown factor, is considered low.

George U.Sauter currently receives a manager quality ranking of 42 (0=worst, 99=best). If you desire only a moderate level of risk and strong performance, then this fund is an excellent option.

Services Offered: Automated phone transactions, payroll deductions, bank draft capabilities, an IRA investment plan, a 401K investment plan, a Keogh investment plan, wire transfers and a systematic withdrawal plan.

Data Date	Weiss Investment Rating	Net Assets ($Mil)	NAV	Perfor-mance Rating/Pts	Total Return Y-T-D	Risk Rating/Pts
6-06	A	15,924	15.63	A- / 9.1	9.53%	C+ / 6.6
2005	A	11,889	14.27	B+ / 8.9	15.57%	C+ / 6.9
2004	B+	7,986	12.60	B+ / 8.8	20.84%	C+ / 5.6
2003	C+	4,786	10.64	C+ / 6.6	40.34%	C / 5.5
2002	C	3,069	7.72	C- / 3.8	-15.08%	C+ / 6.2
2001	C	2,900	9.28	D / 1.7	-20.15%	C+ / 5.9

Annualized Total Return

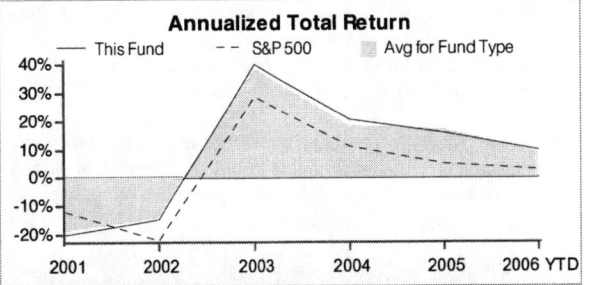

Vanguard Total Stock Mkt Index Inv (VTSMX) C+ Fair

Fund Family: Vanguard **Phone:** (800) 662-7447
Address: Vanguard Financial Center, Valley Forge, PA 19482
Fund Type: GR - Growth

Major Rating Factors: Middle of the road best describes Vanguard Total Stock Mkt Index Inv whose Weiss Investment Rating is currently a C+ (Fair). The fund currently has a performance rating of C (Fair) based on an average return of 12.77% over the last three years and 3.27% over the last six months. Factored into the performance evaluation is an expense ratio of 0.19% (very low).

The fund's risk rating is currently B (Good). It carries a beta of 1.08, meaning that its performance tracks fairly well with that of the overall stock market. Volatility, as measured by both the semi-deviation and a drawdown factor, is considered low.

Gerard C. O Reilly currently receives a manager quality ranking of 65 (0=worst, 99=best). If you desire an average level of risk, then this fund may be an option.

Services Offered: Automated phone transactions, payroll deductions, bank draft capabilities, an IRA investment plan, a 401K investment plan, a Keogh investment plan, wire transfers and a systematic withdrawal plan.

Data Date	Weiss Investment Rating	Net Assets ($Mil)	NAV	Perfor-mance Rating/Pts	Total Return Y-T-D	Risk Rating/Pts
6-06	C+	33,798	30.74	C / 5.1	3.27%	B / 8.2
2005	C+	29,339	30.00	C / 4.9	5.98%	B- / 7.6
2004	C	30,433	28.77	C+ / 5.7	12.52%	C / 5.5
2003	C+	22,735	25.99	C / 5.4	31.35%	C+ / 5.9
2002	C	14,917	20.07	C / 4.6	-20.96%	C+ / 6.1
2001	C-	15,782	25.74	C / 4.3	-10.97%	C- / 3.1

Annualized Total Return

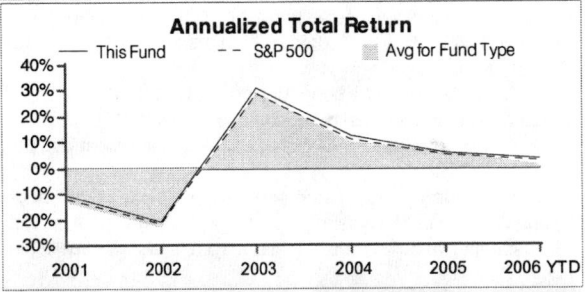

Vanguard US Growth Inv (VWUSX) D- Weak

Fund Family: Vanguard **Phone:** (800) 662-7447
Address: Vanguard Financial Center, Valley Forge, PA 19482
Fund Type: AG - Aggressive Growth

Major Rating Factors: Disappointing performance is the major factor driving the D- (Weak) Weiss Investment Rating for Vanguard US Growth Inv. The fund currently has a performance rating of D (Weak) based on an average return of 8.48% over the last three years and -6.07% over the last six months. Factored into the performance evaluation is an expense ratio of 0.59% (very low).

The fund's risk rating is currently C+ (Fair). It carries a beta of 1.27, meaning it is expected to move 12.7% for every 10% move in the market. Volatility, as measured by both the semi-deviation and a drawdown factor, is considered low.

Alan Levi currently receives a manager quality ranking of 15 (0=worst, 99=best). This fund offers only a moderate level of risk but investors looking for strong performance are still waiting.

Services Offered: Automated phone transactions, payroll deductions, bank draft capabilities, an IRA investment plan, a 401K investment plan, a Keogh investment plan, wire transfers and a systematic withdrawal plan.

Data Date	Weiss Investment Rating	Net Assets ($Mil)	NAV	Perfor-mance Rating/Pts	Total Return Y-T-D	Risk Rating/Pts
6-06	D-	4,561	16.86	D / 1.7	-6.07%	C+ / 6.4
2005	C	5,075	17.95	C / 4.9	11.15%	C+ / 6.4
2004	E+	5,357	16.18	E / 0.4	7.03%	C- / 3.4
2003	E+	6,081	15.16	E / 0.3	26.10%	D+ / 2.6
2002	E+	5,480	12.06	E / 0.5	-35.80%	D / 2.1
2001	E-	9,180	18.85	E- / 0.2	-31.70%	E- / 0.0

Annualized Total Return

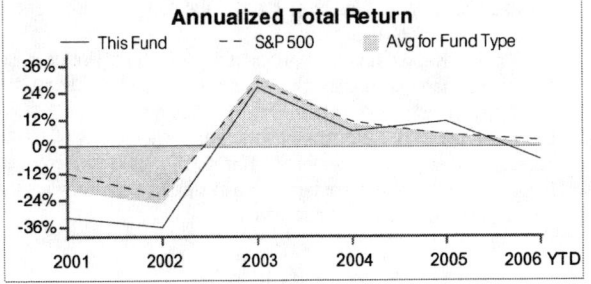

Vanguard Value Index Inv (VIVAX)

B+   Good

Fund Family: Vanguard   **Phone:** (800) 662-7447
Address: Vanguard Financial Center, Valley Forge, PA 19482
Fund Type: GI - Growth and Income

Major Rating Factors: Vanguard Value Index Inv receives a Weiss Investment Rating of B+ (Good). The fund currently has a performance rating of C+ (Fair) based on an average return of 15.18% over the last three years and 6.25% over the last six months. Factored into the performance evaluation is an expense ratio of 0.21% (very low).

The fund's risk rating is currently B+ (Good). It carries a beta of 0.93, meaning that its performance tracks fairly well with that of the overall stock market. Volatility, as measured by both the semi-deviation and a drawdown factor, is considered very low.

Gerard C. O Reilly currently receives a manager quality ranking of 90 (0=worst, 99=best). If you desire an average level of risk, then this fund may be an option.

Services Offered: Automated phone transactions, payroll deductions, bank draft capabilities, an IRA investment plan, a 401K investment plan, a Keogh investment plan, wire transfers and a systematic withdrawal plan.

Data Date	Weiss Investment Rating	Net Assets ($Mil)	NAV	Performance Rating/Pts	Total Return Y-T-D	Risk Rating/Pts
6-06	B+	3,502	23.42	C+ / 6.5	6.25%	B+ / 9.0
2005	C+	3,360	22.29	C+ / 5.6	7.09%	B- / 7.5
2004	C+	3,455	21.35	C+ / 6.5	15.29%	C / 5.3
2003	C+	2,727	18.95	C / 5.4	32.25%	C+ / 5.7
2002	C+	2,353	14.65	C+ / 5.9	-20.91%	C+ / 6.3
2001	C+	3,018	18.90	C / 4.9	-11.88%	C+ / 6.0

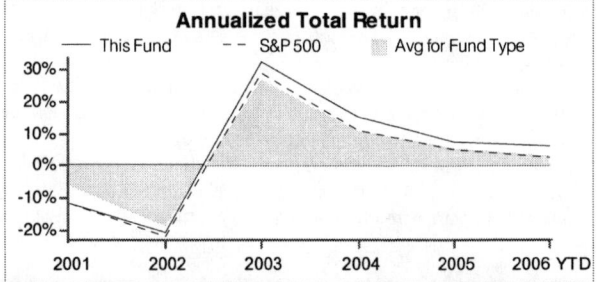

Vanguard Wellesley Income Inv (VWINX)

C-   Fair

Fund Family: Vanguard   **Phone:** (800) 662-7447
Address: Vanguard Financial Center, Valley Forge, PA 19482
Fund Type: AA - Asset Allocation

Major Rating Factors: Very poor performance is the major factor driving the C- (Fair) Weiss Investment Rating for Vanguard Wellesley Income Inv. The fund currently has a performance rating of E+ (Very Weak) based on an average return of 5.42% over the last three years and 2.01% over the last six months. Factored into the performance evaluation is an expense ratio of 0.14% (very low).

The fund's risk rating is currently B+ (Good). It carries a beta of 0.58, meaning the fund's expected move will be 5.8% for every 10% move in the market. Volatility, as measured by both the semi-deviation and a drawdown factor, is considered very low.

Earl E. McEvoy has been running the fund for 24 years and currently receives a manager quality ranking of 57 (0=worst, 99=best). This fund offers only a moderate level of risk but investors looking for strong performance are still waiting.

Services Offered: Automated phone transactions, payroll deductions, bank draft capabilities, an IRA investment plan, a 401K investment plan, a Keogh investment plan, wire transfers and a systematic withdrawal plan.

Data Date	Weiss Investment Rating	Net Assets ($Mil)	NAV	Performance Rating/Pts	Total Return Y-T-D	Risk Rating/Pts
6-06	C-	7,305	21.07	E+ / 0.9	2.01%	B+ / 9.7
2005	D+	7,632	21.07	E / 0.3	3.48%	B+ / 9.3
2004	B+	9,087	21.58	C / 5.3	7.57%	B+ / 9.0
2003	A	8,199	20.91	C+ / 6.8	9.66%	B+ / 9.8
2002	A+	7,402	19.90	A+ / 9.6	4.64%	B+ / 9.9
2001	A+	6,495	19.91	B / 7.8	7.39%	B+ / 9.5

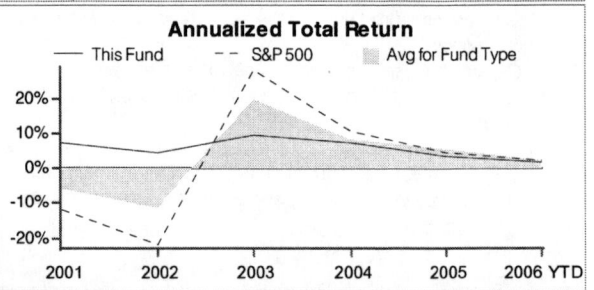

Vanguard Wellington Inv (VWELX)

C+   Fair

Fund Family: Vanguard   **Phone:** (800) 662-7447
Address: Vanguard Financial Center, Valley Forge, PA 19482
Fund Type: BA - Balanced

Major Rating Factors: Middle of the road best describes Vanguard Wellington Inv whose Weiss Investment Rating is currently a C+ (Fair). The fund currently has a performance rating of C (Fair) based on an average return of 10.98% over the last three years and 3.71% over the last six months. Factored into the performance evaluation is an expense ratio of 0.31% (very low).

The fund's risk rating is currently B+ (Good). It carries a beta of 1.08, meaning that its performance tracks fairly well with that of the overall stock market. Volatility, as measured by both the semi-deviation and a drawdown factor, is considered very low.

Paul D. Kaplan has been running the fund for 12 years and currently receives a manager quality ranking of 83 (0=worst, 99=best). If you desire an average level of risk, then this fund may be an option.

Services Offered: Automated phone transactions, payroll deductions, bank draft capabilities, an IRA investment plan, a 401K investment plan, a Keogh investment plan, wire transfers and a systematic withdrawal plan. However, the fund is currently closed to new investors.

Data Date	Weiss Investment Rating	Net Assets ($Mil)	NAV	Performance Rating/Pts	Total Return Y-T-D	Risk Rating/Pts
6-06	C+	27,000	31.01	C / 4.3	3.71%	B+ / 9.3
2005	C	26,074	30.35	D+ / 2.9	6.82%	B / 8.8
2004	B-	27,503	30.19	C+ / 6.2	11.17%	B- / 7.9
2003	A-	23,108	28.81	B- / 7.3	20.75%	B / 8.5
2002	A	20,007	24.56	A- / 9.0	-6.90%	B+ / 9.1
2001	A+	21,724	27.26	B / 7.8	4.19%	B / 8.1

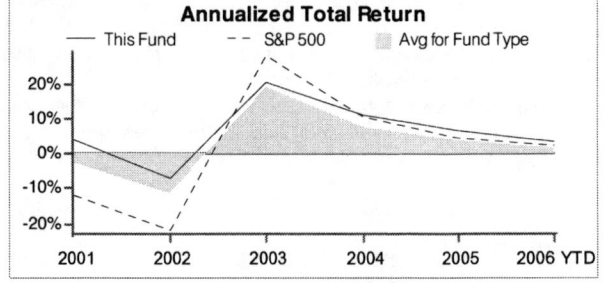

Vanguard Windsor-II Inv (VWNFX)

A-   Excellent

Fund Family: Vanguard   **Phone:** (800) 662-7447
Address: Vanguard Financial Center, Valley Forge, PA 19482
Fund Type: GI - Growth and Income
Major Rating Factors: Vanguard Windsor-II Inv receives a Weiss Investment Rating of A- (Excellent). The fund currently has a performance rating of C+ (Fair) based on an average return of 14.72% over the last three years and 4.30% over the last six months. Factored into the performance evaluation is an expense ratio of 0.35% (very low).

The fund's risk rating is currently B+ (Good). It carries a beta of 0.83, meaning the fund's expected move will be 8.3% for every 10% move in the market. Volatility, as measured by both the semi-deviation and a drawdown factor, is considered very low.

James P. Barrow has been running the fund for 21 years and currently receives a manager quality ranking of 92 (0=worst, 99=best). If you desire an average level of risk, then this fund may be an option.

Services Offered: Automated phone transactions, payroll deductions, bank draft capabilities, an IRA investment plan, a 401K investment plan, a Keogh investment plan, wire transfers and a systematic withdrawal plan.

Data Date	Weiss Investment Rating	Net Assets ($Mil)	NAV	Performance Rating/Pts	Total Return Y-T-D	Risk Rating/Pts
6-06	A-	28,523	32.30	C+ / 6.1	4.30%	B+ / 9.2
2005	B	28,868	31.33	C+ / 5.6	7.01%	B / 8.1
2004	B	27,919	30.73	B- / 7.3	18.31%	C+ / 6.1
2003	B	21,370	26.49	B- / 7.2	30.08%	B- / 7.1
2002	B	18,494	20.80	B / 7.9	-16.86%	B- / 7.6
2001	C+	22,429	25.59	C+ / 5.8	-3.40%	C+ / 6.3

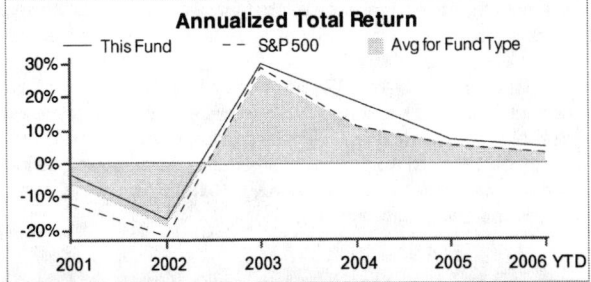

Annualized Total Return

Vantagepoint Growth Fund (VPGRX)

D   Weak

Fund Family: Vantagepoint Funds   **Phone:** (800) 669-7400
Address: 777 North Capital Street NE, Washington,, DC 20002
Fund Type: GR - Growth
Major Rating Factors: Disappointing performance is the major factor driving the D (Weak) Weiss Investment Rating for Vantagepoint Growth Fund. The fund currently has a performance rating of D (Weak) based on an average return of 7.75% over the last three years and -0.23% over the last six months. Factored into the performance evaluation is an expense ratio of 0.93% (low).

The fund's risk rating is currently B- (Good). It carries a beta of 1.16, meaning it is expected to move 11.6% for every 10% move in the market. Volatility, as measured by standard deviation, is considered low for equity funds at 9.57.

Multiple Subadvisors currently receives a manager quality ranking of 16 (0=worst, 99=best). This fund offers only a moderate level of risk but investors looking for strong performance are still waiting.

Services Offered: Automated phone transactions, payroll deductions, bank draft capabilities, an IRA investment plan, a 401K investment plan and wire transfers.

Data Date	Weiss Investment Rating	Net Assets ($Mil)	NAV	Performance Rating/Pts	Total Return Y-T-D	Risk Rating/Pts
6-06	D	2,678	8.68	D / 1.6	-0.23%	B- / 7.8
2005	D+	2,830	8.70	D+ / 2.4	4.86%	B- / 7.3
2004	D-	2,942	8.31	D- / 1.4	3.27%	C- / 4.2

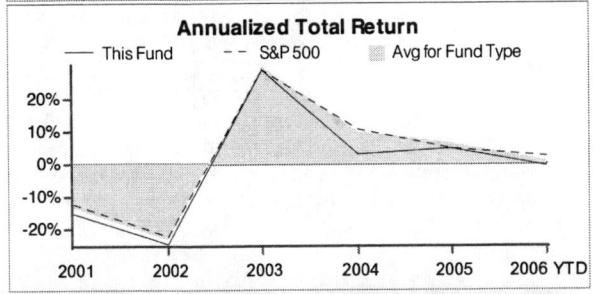

Annualized Total Return

Victory Diversified Stk A (SRVEX)

C+   Fair

Fund Family: Victory Funds   **Phone:** (800) 539-3863
Address: 3435 Stelzer Road, Columbus, OH 43219
Fund Type: GR - Growth
Major Rating Factors: Middle of the road best describes Victory Diversified Stk A whose Weiss Investment Rating is currently a C+ (Fair). The fund currently has a performance rating of C (Fair) based on an average return of 13.25% over the last three years and 1.56% over the last six months. Factored into the performance evaluation is an expense ratio of 1.07% (low) and a 5.8% front-end load that is levied at the time of purchase.

The fund's risk rating is currently B (Good). It carries a beta of 1.15, meaning it is expected to move 11.5% for every 10% move in the market. Volatility, as measured by both the semi-deviation and a drawdown factor, is considered low.

Lawrence G. Babin has been running the fund for 17 years and currently receives a manager quality ranking of 63 (0=worst, 99=best). If you desire an average level of risk, then this fund may be an option.

Services Offered: Automated phone transactions, payroll deductions, bank draft capabilities, an IRA investment plan, a 401K investment plan, a Keogh investment plan, wire transfers and a systematic withdrawal plan.

Data Date	Weiss Investment Rating	Net Assets ($Mil)	NAV	Performance Rating/Pts	Total Return Y-T-D	Risk Rating/Pts
6-06	C+	3,134	17.16	C / 4.4	1.56%	B / 8.2
2005	C+	2,834	16.94	C / 5.1	9.38%	C+ / 6.9
2004	D+	2,037	16.24	C- / 3.7	10.23%	C / 4.7
2003	B-	1,132	14.87	B- / 7.4	35.60%	C+ / 5.7
2002	C+	874	11.04	C+ / 5.9	-22.78%	C+ / 5.9
2001	C+	1,117	14.37	B / 7.6	0.93%	C- / 3.1

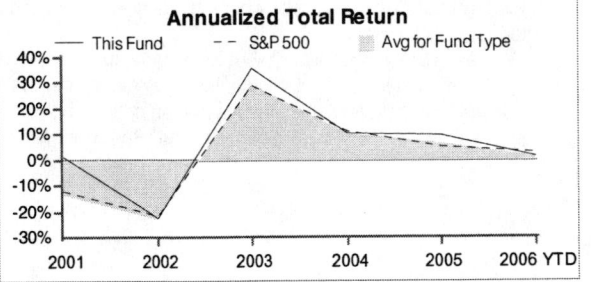

Annualized Total Return

Waddell & Reed Adv Core Invest A (UNCMX)

C+   Fair

Fund Family: Waddell & Reed
Phone: (888) 923-3355
Address: 6300 Lamar Avenue, Shawnee Mission, KS 66201
Fund Type: GR - Growth

Major Rating Factors: Middle of the road best describes Waddell & Reed Adv Core Invest A whose Weiss Investment Rating is currently a C+ (Fair). The fund currently has a performance rating of C (Fair) based on an average return of 13.04% over the last three years and 8.98% over the last six months. Factored into the performance evaluation is an expense ratio of 1.11% (low) and a 5.8% front-end load that is levied at the time of purchase.

The fund's risk rating is currently B- (Good). It carries a beta of 0.91, meaning that its performance tracks fairly well with that of the overall stock market. Volatility, as measured by both the semi-deviation and a drawdown factor, is considered low.

James D. Wineland, CFA has been running the fund for 9 years and currently receives a manager quality ranking of 81 (0=worst, 99=best). If you desire an average level of risk, then this fund may be an option.

Services Offered: Automated phone transactions, payroll deductions, bank draft capabilities, an IRA investment plan, a 401K investment plan, wire transfers and a systematic withdrawal plan.

Data Date	Weiss Investment Rating	Net Assets ($Mil)	NAV	Performance Rating/Pts	Total Return Y-T-D	Risk Rating/Pts
6-06	C+	3,976	6.69	C / 5.4	8.98%	B- / 7.6
2005	D-	3,941	6.15	D / 1.6	8.83%	C+ / 6.7
2004	D	4,092	5.66	D / 2.0	9.83%	C / 5.4
2003	D+	4,251	5.18	D- / 1.3	17.49%	C / 5.4
2002	C	4,386	4.44	C / 5.2	-22.06%	C / 5.3
2001	C+	6,492	5.72	C / 4.7	-15.30%	C+ / 6.2

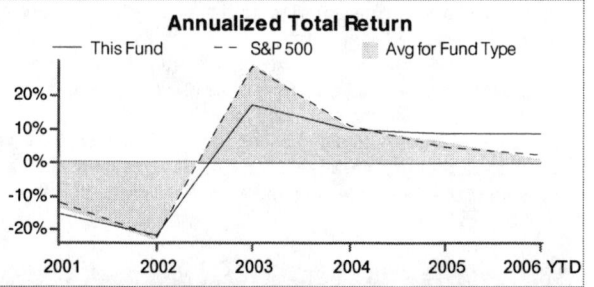

Annualized Total Return

Waddell & Reed Adv Sci & Tech A (UNSCX)

C   Fair

Fund Family: Waddell & Reed
Phone: (888) 923-3355
Address: 6300 Lamar Avenue, Shawnee Mission, KS 66201
Fund Type: TC - Technology

Major Rating Factors: Middle of the road best describes Waddell & Reed Adv Sci & Tech A whose Weiss Investment Rating is currently a C (Fair). The fund currently has a performance rating of C+ (Fair) based on an average return of 18.42% over the last three years and 0.27% over the last six months. Factored into the performance evaluation is an expense ratio of 1.36% (average) and a 5.8% front-end load that is levied at the time of purchase.

The fund's risk rating is currently C (Fair). It carries a beta of 1.42, meaning it is expected to move 14.2% for every 10% move in the market. Volatility, as measured by both the semi-deviation and a drawdown factor, is considered average.

Zachary H. Shafran has been running the fund for 5 years and currently receives a manager quality ranking of 83 (0=worst, 99=best). If you desire an average level of risk, then this fund may be an option.

Services Offered: Automated phone transactions, payroll deductions, bank draft capabilities, an IRA investment plan, a 401K investment plan, wire transfers and a systematic withdrawal plan.

Data Date	Weiss Investment Rating	Net Assets ($Mil)	NAV	Performance Rating/Pts	Total Return Y-T-D	Risk Rating/Pts
6-06	C	2,313	11.13	C+ / 6.7	0.27%	C / 4.8
2005	C+	133	11.10	B / 7.6	17.20%	C / 5.0
2004	C-	2,134	10.40	C / 5.1	16.20%	C / 4.9
2003	C-	1,994	8.95	C- / 3.3	32.01%	C / 5.0
2002	D	1,646	6.78	D+ / 2.4	-26.78%	D+ / 2.7
2001	C	2,570	9.26	B+ / 8.9	-13.42%	E- / 0.0

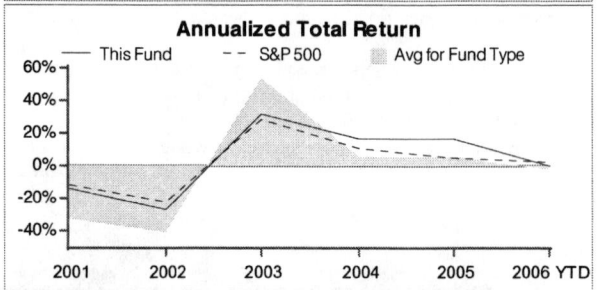

Annualized Total Return

Weitz Series-Value (WVALX)

C-   Fair

Fund Family: Weitz Series
Phone: (800) 232-4161
Address: 1125 South 103 Street, Omaha, NE 68124
Fund Type: MC - Mid Cap

Major Rating Factors: Middle of the road best describes Weitz Series-Value whose Weiss Investment Rating is currently a C- (Fair). The fund currently has a performance rating of C- (Fair) based on an average return of 9.87% over the last three years and 5.19% over the last six months. Factored into the performance evaluation is an expense ratio of 1.12% (low).

The fund's risk rating is currently B- (Good). It carries a beta of 0.45, meaning the fund's expected move will be 4.5% for every 10% move in the market. Volatility, as measured by both the semi-deviation and a drawdown factor, is considered low.

Wallace R. Weitz, CFA has been running the fund for 20 years and currently receives a manager quality ranking of 63 (0=worst, 99=best). If you desire an average level of risk, then this fund may be an option.

Services Offered: Bank draft capabilities, an IRA investment plan and wire transfers.

Data Date	Weiss Investment Rating	Net Assets ($Mil)	NAV	Performance Rating/Pts	Total Return Y-T-D	Risk Rating/Pts
6-06	C-	2,816	36.78	C- / 3.4	5.19%	B- / 7.8
2005	D+	3,338	35.42	D / 2.0	-2.77%	B- / 7.7
2004	C+	4,370	37.70	C+ / 6.7	15.74%	C+ / 5.6
2003	B	4,062	35.78	B- / 7.2	28.73%	C+ / 6.8
2002	B+	3,589	27.92	B+ / 8.5	-17.10%	B- / 7.5
2001	A	4,150	34.29	A- / 9.0	0.24%	C+ / 6.6

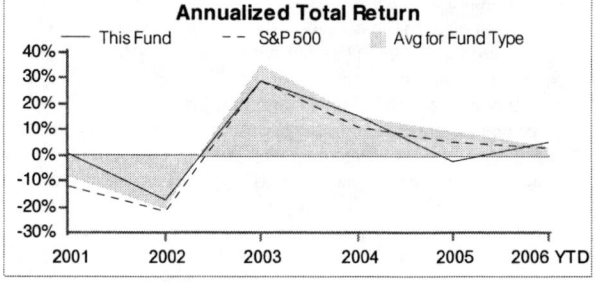

Annualized Total Return

Wells Fargo Avtg Sm Cp Val Z (SSMVX)   B-   Good

Fund Family: Wells Fargo Advantage Funds   **Phone:** (800) 222-8222
Address: PO Box 8266, Boston, MA 02266
Fund Type: SC - Small Cap

Major Rating Factors: Exceptional performance is the major factor driving the B- (Good) Weiss Investment Rating for Wells Fargo Avtg Sm Cp Val Z. The fund currently has a performance rating of A- (Excellent) based on an average return of 24.48% over the last three years and 7.36% over the last six months. Factored into the performance evaluation is an expense ratio of 1.36% (average).

The fund's risk rating is currently C (Fair). It carries a beta of 0.90, meaning the fund's expected move will be 9.0% for every 10% move in the market. Volatility, as measured by standard deviation, is considered average for equity funds at 15.15.

I. Charles Rinaldi currently receives a manager quality ranking of 96 (0=worst, 99=best). If you desire an average level of risk and strong performance, then this fund is a good option.

Services Offered: Payroll deductions, bank draft capabilities, an IRA investment plan, a 401K investment plan, a Keogh investment plan, wire transfers and a systematic withdrawal plan. However, the fund is currently closed to new investors.

Data Date	Weiss Investment Rating	Net Assets ($Mil)	NAV	Perfor- mance Rating/Pts	Total Return Y-T-D	Risk Rating/Pts
6-06	B-	2,499	32.39	A- / 9.1	7.36%	C / 4.8
2005	B	2,075	30.17	A- / 9.1	15.03%	C / 4.7

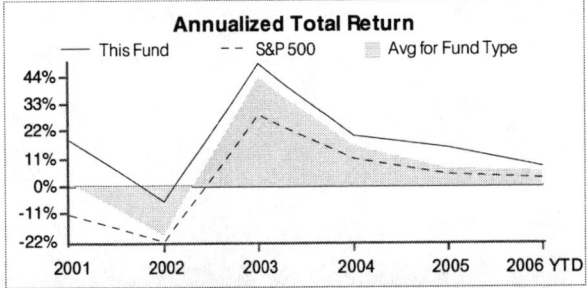

William Blair Mutual-Intl Grwth N (WBIGX)   B+   Good

Fund Family: William Blair Funds   **Phone:** (800) 742-7272
Address: 222 West Adams Street, Chicago, IL 60606
Fund Type: FO - Foreign

Major Rating Factors: Strong performance is the major factor driving the B+ (Good) Weiss Investment Rating for William Blair Mutual-Intl Grwth N. The fund currently has a performance rating of B+ (Good) based on an average return of 25.01% over the last three years and 5.91% over the last six months. Factored into the performance evaluation is an expense ratio of 1.17% (low) and a 2.0% back-end load levied at the time of sale.

The fund's risk rating is currently C+ (Fair). It carries a beta of 1.12, meaning it is expected to move 11.2% for every 10% move in the market. Volatility, as measured by both the semi-deviation and a drawdown factor, is considered low.

W. George Greig has been running the fund for 10 years and currently receives a manager quality ranking of 34 (0=worst, 99=best). If you desire only a moderate level of risk and strong performance, then this fund is an excellent option.

Services Offered: Automated phone transactions, check writing, bank draft capabilities, an IRA investment plan, a 401K investment plan, wire transfers and a systematic withdrawal plan. However, the fund is currently closed to new investors.

Data Date	Weiss Investment Rating	Net Assets ($Mil)	NAV	Perfor- mance Rating/Pts	Total Return Y-T-D	Risk Rating/Pts
6-06	B+	3,728	26.71	B+ / 8.9	5.91%	C+ / 6.1
2005	A+	2,832	25.22	A / 9.3	21.65%	B- / 7.2
2004	A-	1,953	22.09	B+ / 8.7	18.48%	C+ / 6.7
2003	B+	1,167	18.65	B / 8.1	42.14%	B- / 7.1
2002	C	396	13.13	C / 5.1	-15.18%	C / 5.5
2001	C+	167	15.48	A- / 9.1	-13.66%	D- / 1.0

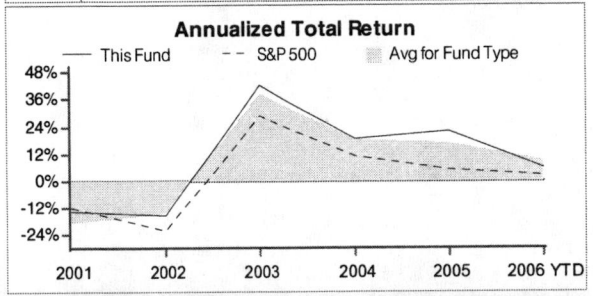

WM Balanced Portfolio A (SABPX)   C-   Fair

Fund Family: WM Funds   **Phone:** (800) 222-5852
Address: West 601 Main Street, Spokane, WA 99201
Fund Type: AA - Asset Allocation

Major Rating Factors: Disappointing performance is the major factor driving the C- (Fair) Weiss Investment Rating for WM Balanced Portfolio A. The fund currently has a performance rating of D (Weak) based on an average return of 8.89% over the last three years and 1.32% over the last six months. Factored into the performance evaluation is an expense ratio of 1.35% (average), a 5.5% front-end load that is levied at the time of purchase and a 1.0% back-end load levied at the time of sale.

The fund's risk rating is currently B+ (Good). It carries a beta of 1.12, meaning it is expected to move 11.2% for every 10% move in the market. Volatility, as measured by both the semi-deviation and a drawdown factor, is considered very low.

Randall L. Yoakum, CFA has been running the fund for 6 years and currently receives a manager quality ranking of 64 (0=worst, 99=best). This fund offers only a moderate level of risk but investors looking for strong performance are still waiting.

Services Offered: Automated phone transactions, check writing, payroll deductions, bank draft capabilities, an IRA investment plan, a 401K investment plan, wire transfers and a systematic withdrawal plan.

Data Date	Weiss Investment Rating	Net Assets ($Mil)	NAV	Perfor- mance Rating/Pts	Total Return Y-T-D	Risk Rating/Pts
6-06	C-	2,312	13.71	D / 1.6	1.32%	B+ / 9.4
2005	C-	2,219	13.63	D- / 1.3	5.21%	B+ / 9.6
2004	C+	1,697	13.21	C / 4.4	9.23%	B / 8.2
2003	B	953	12.30	C+ / 6.6	21.35%	B / 8.4
2002	B+	450	10.33	B / 7.7	-9.41%	B / 8.5
2001	A	404	11.71	B / 7.6	-0.52%	B- / 7.7

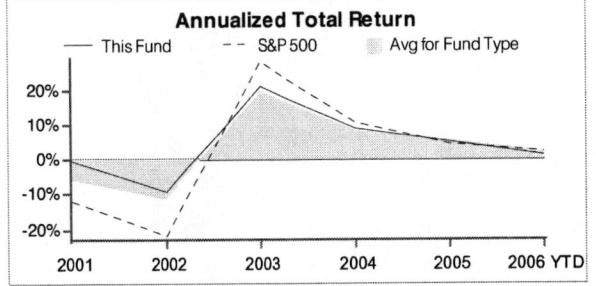

Section III

Top 200
Stock Mutual Funds

A compilation of those

Equity Mutual Funds

receiving the highest Weiss Investment Ratings.

Funds are listed in order by Overall Weiss Investment Rating.

Section III Contents

This section contains a summary analysis of each of the top 200 equity mutual funds as determined by their overall Weiss Investment Rating. You can use this section to identify those mutual funds that have achieved the best possible combination of total return on investment and reduced volatility over the past three years. Consult each fund's individual Performance Rating and Risk Rating to find the fund that best matches your investing style.

1. **Fund Type**   The mutual fund's peer category based on an analysis of its investment portfolio.

AG	Aggressive Growth	HL	Health
AA	Asset Allocation	IN	Income
BA	Balanced	IX	Index
CV	Convertible	MC	Mid Cap
EM	Emerging Market	OT	Other
EN	Energy/Natural Resources	PM	Precious Metals
FS	Financial Services	RE	Real Estate
FO	Foreign	SC	Small Cap
GL	Global	TC	Technology
GR	Growth	UT	Utilities
GI	Growth and Income		

A blank fund type means that the mutual fund has not yet been categorized.

2. **Fund Name**   The name of the mutual fund as stated in its prospectus, which can sometimes differ slightly from the name that the company uses for advertising. If you cannot find the particular mutual fund you are interested in, or if you have any doubts regarding the precise name, verify the information with your broker or on your account statement. Also, use the fund's ticker symbol for confirmation. (See column 3.)

3. **Ticker Symbol**   The unique alphabetic symbol used for identifying and trading a specific mutual fund. No two funds can have the same ticker symbol, and the ticker symbol for mutual funds always ends with an "X".

A handful of funds currently show no associated ticker symbol. This means that the fund is either small or new since the NASD only assigns a ticker symbol to funds with at least $25 million in assets or 1,000 shareholders.

4. **Overall Weiss Investment Rating**   Our overall rating is measured on a scale from A to E based on each fund's risk-adjusted performance. Please see page 10 for specific descriptions of each letter grade. Also, refer to page 7 for information on how our ratings are derived. Most important, when using this rating, please be sure to consider the warnings beginning on page 11 regarding the ratings' limitations and the underlying assumptions.

5. Phone

The telephone number of the company managing the fund. Call this number to receive a prospectus or other information about the fund.

6. Net Asset Value (NAV)

The fund's share price as of the date indicated. A fund's NAV is computed by dividing the value of the fund's asset holdings, less accrued fees and expenses, by the number of its shares outstanding.

7. Performance Rating/Points

A letter grade rating based solely on the mutual fund's financial performance over the trailing three years, without any consideration for the amount of risk the fund poses. Like the overall Weiss Investment Rating, the Performance Rating is measured on a scale from A to E for ease of interpretation. The points score indicates where the Performance Rating falls on a scale of 0 to 10.

8. 1-Year Total Return

The total return the fund has provided investors over the preceeding twelve months. This total return figure is computed based on the fund's dividend distributions and share price appreciation/depreciation during the period, net of the expenses and fees it imposes on its shareholders. Although the total return figure does not reflect an adjustment for any loads the fund may carry, such adjustments have been made in deriving the Weiss Investment Ratings.

9. 1-Year Total Return Percentile

The fund's percentile rank based on its one-year performance compared to that of all other equity funds in existence for at least one year. A score of 99 is the best possible, indicating that the fund outperformed 99% of the other mutual funds. Zero is the worst possible percentile score.

10. 3-Year Total Return

The total annual return the fund has provided investors over the preceeding three years.

11. 3-Year Total Return Percentile

The fund's percentile rank based on its three-year performance compared to that of all other equity funds in existence for at least three years. A score of 99 is the best possible, indicating that the fund outperformed 99% of the other mutual funds. Zero is the worst possible percentile score.

12. 5-Year Total Return

The total annual return the fund has provided investors over the preceeding five years.

13. 5-Year Total Return Percentile

The fund's percentile rank based on its five-year performance compared to that of all other equity funds in existence for at least five years. A score of 99 is the best possible, indicating that the fund outperformed 99% of the other mutual funds. Zero is the worst possible percentile score.

14. Risk Rating/Points

A letter grade rating based solely on the mutual fund's risk as determined by its monthly performance volatility over the trailing three years. The risk rating does not take into consideration the overall financial performance the fund has achieved or the total return it has provided to its shareholders. Like the overall Weiss Investment Rating, the Risk Rating is measured on a scale from A to E for ease of interpretation. The points score indicates where the Risk Rating falls on a scale of 0 to 10.

15. Manager Quality Percentile

The manager quality percentile is based on a ranking of the fund's alpha, a statistical measure representing the difference between a fund's actual returns and its expected performance given its level of risk. Fund managers who have been able to exceed the fund's statistically expected performance receive a high percentile rank with 99 representing the highest possible score. At the other end of the spectrum, fund managers who have actually detracted from the fund's expected performance receive a low percentile rank with 0 representing the lowest possible score.

16. Manager Tenure

The number of years the current manager has been managing the fund. Since fund managers who deliver substandard returns are usually replaced, a long tenure is usually a good sign that shareholders are satisfied that the fund is achieving its stated objectives.

Fund Type	Fund Name	Ticker Symbol	Overall Weiss Investment Rating	Phone	Net Asset Value As of 6/30/06	PERFORMANCE				RISK	FUND MGR	
	99 Pct = Best / 0 Pct = Worst					Performance Rating/Pts	Annualized Total Return Through 6/30/06			Risk Rating/Pts	Mgr. Quality Pct	Mgr. Tenure (Years)
							1Yr / Pct	3Yr / Pct	5Yr / Pct			
FO	● AIM European Small Company C	ESMCX	A+	(800) 347-4246	26.16	A+ /9.9	48.74 /99	48.83 /99	31.59 /99	C+ / 6.5	99	6
FO	● AIM European Small Company A	ESMAX	A+	(800) 347-4246	27.07	A+ /9.9	49.80 /99	49.86 /99	32.52 /99	C+ / 6.6	99	6
FO	● AIM European Small Company B	ESMBX	A+	(800) 347-4246	26.15	A+ /9.9	48.69 /99	48.76 /99	31.58 /99	C+ / 6.5	99	6
EM	● AIM International Small Co C	IEGCX	A+	(800) 347-4246	23.71	A+ /9.9	45.88 /98	43.45 /99	29.33 /99	C+ / 6.2	99	6
EM	● AIM International Small Co A	IEGAX	A+	(800) 347-4246	24.48	A+ /9.9	47.00 /99	44.51 /99	30.21 /99	C+ / 6.2	99	6
EM	● AIM International Small Co B	IEGBX	A+	(800) 347-4246	23.72	A+ /9.9	45.85 /98	43.47 /99	29.30 /99	C+ / 6.2	99	6
EN	● Ivy Fund-Global Nat Resource Adv	IGNVX	A+	(800) 777-6472	31.12	A+ /9.9	46.95 /99	39.19 /99	24.29 /98	C+ / 6.2	99	8
EN	Vanguard Energy Adm	VGELX	A+	(800) 662-7447	122.47	A+ /9.9	37.33 /97	39.83 /99	--	C+ / 6.2	98	N/A
EN	Vanguard Energy Inv	VGENX	A+	(800) 662-7447	65.20	A+ /9.9	37.25 /97	39.76 /99	25.08 /98	C+ / 6.2	98	N/A
FO	Eaton Vance Tax-Mgd Emg Mkt Fd	EITEX	A+	(800) 225-6265	31.61	A+ /9.8	35.45 /97	37.77 /99	25.58 /99	C+ / 6.7	85	8
FO	American Century Intl Opport Inst	ACIOX	A+	(800) 345-6488	10.81	A+ /9.8	34.51 /96	38.09 /99	--	C+ / 6.2	89	N/A
FO	American Century Intl Opport Inv	AIOIX	A+	(800) 345-6488	10.77	A+ /9.8	34.22 /96	37.77 /99	25.47 /99	C+ / 6.3	89	N/A
FO	● The Boston Co Intl Small Cap Fd	SDISX	A+	(800) 221-4795	23.61	A+ /9.8	38.73 /98	37.08 /99	23.17 /98	C+ / 6.3	98	6
FO	● Dreyfus Premier Intl Small Cap R	DSMRX	A+	(800) 782-6620	26.38	A+ /9.8	37.95 /97	36.13 /98	22.58 /98	C+ / 6.4	98	3
RE	MSIF Inc. Intl Real Estate A	MSUAX	A+	(800) 354-8185	27.44	A+ /9.8	29.15 /94	35.81 /98	27.26 /99	B- / 7.5	99	7
RE	MSIF Inc. Intl Real Estate B	IERBX	A+	(800) 354-8185	27.46	A+ /9.8	28.87 /94	35.44 /98	26.95 /99	B- / 7.6	99	7
FO	Vontobel Eastern European Eq A	VEEEX	A+	(800) 527-9500	24.97	A+ /9.8	24.85 /88	36.91 /98	29.41 /99	B- / 7.2	98	5
FO	● Dreyfus Premier Intl Small Cap C	DSMCX	A+	(800) 782-6620	25.62	A+ /9.8	36.45 /97	34.74 /98	21.72 /97	C+ / 6.3	96	3
FO	● Dreyfus Premier Intl Small Cap T	DSMTX	A+	(800) 782-6620	26.00	A+ /9.8	37.16 /97	35.34 /98	22.11 /98	C+ / 6.3	97	3
FO	● Dreyfus Premier Intl Small Cap A	DSMAX	A+	(800) 782-6620	26.14	A+ /9.8	37.42 /97	35.64 /98	22.32 /98	C+ / 6.4	97	3
FO	Dodge & Cox International Stock	DODFX	A+	(800) 621-3979	38.96	A+ /9.7	27.64 /92	33.39 /97	16.39 /93	B- / 7.7	95	N/A
FO	● Dreyfus Premier Intl Small Cap B	DSMBX	A+	(800) 782-6620	25.62	A+ /9.7	36.45 /97	34.71 /98	21.72 /97	C+ / 6.3	96	3
FO	DFA International Small Cap Value	DISVX	A+	(800) 984-9472	19.30	A+ /9.7	28.16 /93	33.59 /97	23.77 /98	C+ / 6.7	98	N/A
FO	Oakmark International Small Cap II	OAREX	A+	(800) 625-6275	22.19	A+ /9.7	31.26 /95	32.65 /97	21.38 /97	B / 8.0	98	5
FO	Allianz NACM International I	NAISX	A+	(800) 628-1237	22.01	A+ /9.7	39.76 /98	31.33 /96	16.20 /93	C+ / 6.8	89	N/A
GR	Bruce Fund		A+	(800) 872-7823	408.85	A+ /9.7	18.36 /80	33.71 /97	29.74 /99	B / 8.4	99	23
FO	GMO Foreign Small Companies IV	GFSFX	A+		18.78	A+ /9.7	30.86 /95	31.51 /96	--	B- / 7.8	93	N/A
FO	Allianz NACM International D	PNIDX	A+	(800) 628-1237	21.84	A+ /9.7	39.19 /98	31.01 /96	16.01 /93	B- / 7.7	87	N/A
GL	Putnam College Adv Intl Cap Opp		A+	(800) 354-2228	20.51	A+ /9.7	33.96 /96	31.35 /96	--	B- / 7.2	79	N/A
FO	Allianz NFJ Intl Value Inst	ANJIX	A+	(800) 628-1237	19.43	A+ /9.7	28.63 /93	32.44 /97	--	B- / 7.2	61	N/A
FO	● AIM European Growth Inv	EGINX	A+	(800) 347-4246	36.61	A+ /9.7	31.71 /95	30.70 /96	16.53 /94	B- / 7.9	92	9
FO	Putnam International Capital Opp Y	PIVYX	A+	(800) 354-2228	32.60	A+ /9.7	34.05 /96	31.48 /96	14.16 /90	B- / 7.3	80	N/A
FO	Allianz NACM International C	PNICX	A+	(800) 628-1237	21.65	A+ /9.7	38.19 /97	30.07 /96	15.14 /92	B- / 7.7	83	N/A
FO	● Artisan International Small Cap Inv	ARTJX	A+	(800) 344-1770	21.83	A+ /9.6	34.99 /97	32.51 /97	--	B- / 7.2	70	5
FO	Neuberger Berman International	NBISX	A+	(800) 877-9700	23.80	A+ /9.6	29.66 /94	31.39 /96	15.92 /93	C+ / 6.6	86	3
FO	Allianz NACM International A	PNIAX	A+	(800) 628-1237	21.84	A+ /9.6	39.18 /98	30.99 /96	16.00 /93	B- / 7.7	87	N/A
FO	Neuberger Berman International Tr	NBITX	A+	(800) 877-9700	26.05	A+ /9.6	29.60 /94	31.14 /96	16.26 /93	B- / 7.7	85	N/A
FO	AIM European Growth C	AEDCX	A+	(800) 347-4246	34.74	A+ /9.6	30.64 /95	29.73 /95	15.69 /93	B- / 7.0	88	9
FO	DFA International Value IV	DFVFX	A+	(800) 984-9472	16.41	A+ /9.6	31.38 /95	30.29 /96	15.88 /93	B / 8.0	89	N/A
FO	DFA International Small Company	DFISX	A+	(800) 984-9472	17.55	A+ /9.6	27.97 /93	30.60 /96	20.00 /96	B- / 7.6	94	N/A
FO	JPMorgan Intl Value Inst	JNUSX	A+	(800) 358-4782	15.41	A+ /9.6	35.15 /97	29.53 /95	12.79 /88	B- / 7.3	91	9
FO	DFA International Value I	DFIVX	A+	(800) 984-9472	20.01	A+ /9.6	31.08 /95	30.05 /96	15.74 /93	B- / 7.0	89	N/A
FO	JPMorgan Intl Value Sel	JIESX	A+	(800) 358-4782	15.35	A+ /9.6	34.87 /97	29.07 /95	12.45 /87	B- / 7.3	90	9
GL	Putnam College Adv Intl Cap Opp		A+	(800) 354-2228	19.37	A+ /9.6	32.22 /96	29.64 /95	--	B- / 7.2	67	N/A
FO	AIM European Growth A	AEDAX	A+	(800) 347-4246	36.66	A+ /9.6	31.66 /95	30.63 /96	16.49 /93	B- / 7.0	91	9
GL	Putnam College Adv Intl Cap Opp		A+	(800) 354-2228	20.02	A /9.5	33.20 /96	30.64 /96	--	B- / 7.2	74	N/A
UT	JennDry Jennison Utility Z	PRUZX	A+	(800) 257-3893	15.42	A /9.5	25.94 /90	29.17 /95	10.13 /81	B- / 7.9	99	6
FO	AIM European Growth B	AEDBX	A+	(800) 347-4246	34.72	A /9.5	30.66 /95	29.73 /95	15.70 /93	B- / 7.0	89	9
FO	DFA Tax Managed Intl Value	DTMIX	A+	(800) 984-9472	17.58	A /9.5	31.05 /95	29.32 /95	14.73 /91	B / 8.0	86	N/A
FO	Gartmore Intl Growth Inst	GIGIX	A+	(800) 848-0920	12.17	A /9.5	38.94 /98	28.54 /94	11.67 /86	B- / 7.0	46	N/A
FO	AllianceBernstein Intl Value Adv	ABIYX	A+	(800) 221-5672	20.59	A /9.5	34.32 /96	27.51 /94	18.15 /95	C+ / 6.8	80	6
FO	Quantitative Foreign Value Ord	QFVOX	A+	(800) 326-2151	19.57	A /9.5	27.46 /92	29.00 /95	18.45 /95	C+ / 6.6	80	8

● Denotes fund is closed to new investors

Fund Type	Fund Name	Ticker Symbol	Overall Weiss Investment Rating	Phone	Net Asset Value As of 6/30/06	Performance Rating/Pts	1Yr / Pct	3Yr / Pct	5Yr / Pct	Risk Rating/Pts	Mgr. Quality Pct	Mgr. Tenure (Years)
	99 Pct = Best 0 Pct = Worst							Annualized Total Return Through 6/30/06				
FO	Artisan International Value Inv	ARTKX	A+	(800) 344-1770	25.32	A /9.5	30.13 /94	28.71 /94	--	B /8.1	91	4
GR	Baron Partners Fund	BPTRX	A+	(800) 992-2766	20.24	A /9.5	20.06 /82	29.89 /95	14.37 /91	B- /7.2	99	14
GL	Putnam College Adv Intl Cap Opp		A+	(800) 354-2228	19.36	A /9.5	32.24 /96	29.67 /95	--	B- /7.2	68	N/A
SC	Gartmore Small Cap Fd Inst	GSCIX	A+	(800) 848-0920	19.66	A /9.5	27.15 /92	29.43 /95	14.85 /92	C+ /6.9	99	N/A
GL	Principal Inv Divers Intl Inst	PIIIX	A+	(800) 247-4123	13.43	A /9.5	35.71 /97	27.44 /93	11.47 /85	B- /7.5	56	3
GL	Principal Inv Divers Intl Pfd	PINPX	A+	(800) 247-4123	13.43	A /9.5	35.49 /97	27.17 /93	11.29 /85	B- /7.5	53	3
GL	Principal Inv Divers Intl Sel	PINLX	A+	(800) 247-4123	13.54	A /9.5	35.09 /97	27.14 /93	11.29 /85	B- /7.4	51	3
FO	JPMorgan Intl Value A	JFEAX	A+	(800) 358-4782	15.27	A /9.5	34.50 /96	28.89 /95	12.25 /87	B- /7.3	89	9
FO	JPMorgan Intl Value B	JFEBX	A+	(800) 358-4782	15.03	A /9.5	33.84 /96	28.26 /94	11.75 /86	B- /7.3	86	9
FO	MFS Intl New Discovery R3	MIDRX	A+	(800) 343-2829	25.34	A /9.4	27.62 /92	28.60 /94	16.33 /93	B- /7.4	67	3
FO	Fidelity Europe	FIEUX	A+	(800) 544-8888	39.33	A /9.4	25.28 /89	28.65 /94	12.56 /88	C+ /6.7	73	3
FO	DFA United Kingdom Small Co	DFUKX	A+	(800) 984-9472	27.37	A /9.4	28.30 /93	27.28 /93	17.47 /94	B- /7.2	91	N/A
SC	Gartmore Small Cap Fd R	GNSRX	A+	(800) 848-0920	18.53	A /9.4	26.75 /91	28.85 /95	14.13 /90	C+ /6.9	99	N/A
FO	Tocqueville Intl Value Fund	TIVFX	A+	(800) 697-3863	16.20	A /9.4	25.20 /89	29.19 /95	16.47 /93	B- /7.0	90	12
UT	JennDry Jennison Utility C	PCUFX	A+	(800) 257-3893	15.40	A /9.4	24.75 /88	27.91 /94	9.06 /77	B- /7.9	99	6
FO	ICAP International Fund	ICEUX	A+	(888) 221-4227	36.05	A /9.4	31.53 /95	28.02 /94	13.98 /90	B- /7.5	83	9
GL	Principal Inv Divers Intl AdvPfd	PINRX	A+	(800) 247-4123	13.38	A /9.4	34.99 /97	26.74 /93	10.87 /83	B- /7.4	48	3
FO	● Third Avenue International Value	TAVIX	A+	(800) 443-1021	22.91	A /9.4	20.50 /82	29.35 /95	--	B /8.4	99	5
FO	Gartmore Intl Growth C	GIGCX	A+	(800) 848-0920	11.63	A /9.4	37.73 /97	27.32 /93	10.58 /82	C+ /6.9	36	N/A
GL	Principal Inv Intl Growth Inst	PITIX	A+	(800) 247-4123	12.57	A /9.4	31.85 /96	27.16 /93	12.32 /87	B- /7.8	74	1
GL	Principal Inv Divers Intl AdvSel	PINNX	A+	(800) 247-4123	13.30	A /9.4	34.90 /97	26.58 /93	10.65 /83	B- /7.4	47	3
UT	JennDry Jennison Utility A	PRUAX	A+	(800) 257-3893	15.42	A /9.4	25.73 /89	28.91 /95	9.90 /80	B- /7.9	99	6
FO	The Boston Co Intl Core Eq	SDIEX	A+	(800) 221-4795	37.51	A /9.4	29.86 /94	27.99 /94	15.01 /92	B- /7.3	77	9
GL	Principal Inv Intl Growth Pfd	PITPX	A+	(800) 247-4123	12.47	A /9.4	31.44 /95	26.88 /93	12.27 /87	B- /7.8	72	1
FO	MFS Intl New Discovery 529C	ECIDX	A+	(800) 343-2829	24.59	A /9.4	26.95 /91	27.90 /94	15.57 /93	B- /7.4	60	4
FO	MFS Intl New Discovery 529B	EBIDX	A+	(800) 343-2829	24.62	A /9.4	26.91 /91	27.88 /94	15.56 /93	B- /7.4	60	4
GL	Principal Inv Intl Growth Sel	PITSX	A+	(800) 247-4123	12.44	A /9.4	31.39 /95	26.76 /93	12.17 /87	B- /7.9	73	1
GL	Principal Inv Divers Intl J	PIIJX	A+	(800) 247-4123	13.32	A /9.4	34.96 /97	26.42 /93	10.51 /82	B- /7.4	45	3
FO	AllianceBernstein Intl Value C	ABICX	A+	(800) 221-5672	19.99	A /9.4	32.96 /96	26.23 /92	16.97 /94	C+ /6.7	71	6
FO	AllianceBernstein Intl Value A	ABIAX	A+	(800) 221-5672	20.30	A /9.4	33.85 /96	27.12 /93	17.74 /94	C+ /6.8	77	6
FO	SSgA Intl Stock Selection Fd	SSAIX	A+	(800) 647-7327	12.35	A /9.4	31.18 /95	26.56 /93	12.41 /87	B- /7.1	65	N/A
UT	JennDry Jennison Utility B	PRUTX	A+	(800) 257-3893	15.41	A /9.4	24.82 /88	27.93 /94	9.07 /77	B- /7.9	99	6
GL	Principal Inv Intl Growth AdvPfd	PITMX	A+	(800) 247-4123	12.88	A /9.4	31.06 /95	26.44 /93	12.67 /88	B- /7.8	69	1
FO	● Julius Baer International Equity I	JIEIX	A+	(800) 435-4659	40.35	A /9.3	31.22 /95	27.08 /93	15.84 /93	B- /7.2	38	13
GR	Hodges Fund	HDPMX	A+	(877) 232-1222	24.86	A /9.3	23.29 /86	28.05 /94	16.52 /94	C+ /6.8	99	14
GL	GMO International Eq Alloc III	GIEAX	A+		17.64	A /9.3	27.70 /92	27.38 /93	18.12 /95	B- /7.6	99	10
FO	Dreyfus Premier Intl Equity R	DIERX	A+	(800) 782-6620	39.05	A /9.3	28.26 /93	26.78 /93	14.08 /90	B- /7.3	73	3
GL	Principal Inv Intl Growth AdvSel	PITNX	A+	(800) 247-4123	12.26	A /9.3	30.83 /95	26.21 /92	11.67 /86	B- /7.8	67	1
FO	● ING International Value I	NIIVX	A+	(800) 992-0180	19.82	A /9.3	28.16 /93	26.70 /93	11.98 /87	B- /7.4	69	N/A
FO	MFS Intl New Discovery 529A	EAIDX	A+	(800) 343-2829	25.47	A /9.3	27.75 /92	28.73 /94	16.35 /93	B- /7.4	67	4
FO	Vanguard International Value Fund	VTRIX	A+	(800) 662-7447	38.69	A /9.3	31.03 /95	26.79 /93	12.93 /89	B- /7.2	62	N/A
FO	● ING International Value Q	NQGVX	A+	(800) 992-0180	19.83	A /9.3	27.88 /92	26.41 /93	11.71 /86	B- /7.4	66	N/A
FO	GMO Tax Managed Intl Equities III	GTMIX	A+		19.10	A /9.3	28.56 /93	26.24 /92	15.83 /93	B /8.1	68	N/A
FO	Brandes Instl Intl Equity Fund	BIIEX	A+	(800) 237-7119	23.48	A /9.3	25.82 /89	26.07 /92	12.09 /87	B- /7.3	76	N/A
GL	Principal Inv Intl Growth J	PITJX	A+	(800) 247-4123	12.32	A /9.3	30.77 /95	26.04 /92	11.51 /85	B- /7.9	67	1
FO	SSgA Intl Stock Selection R	SSARX	A+	(800) 647-7327	12.28	A /9.3	30.45 /95	25.95 /92	11.82 /86	B /8.2	61	N/A
UT	Evergreen Utility and Telecom I	EVUYX	A+	(800) 343-2898	12.85	A /9.3	16.95 /77	26.25 /92	6.93 /66	B /8.1	99	N/A
FO	● Wasatch International Growth	WAIGX	A+	(800) 551-1700	21.68	A /9.3	28.82 /94	27.38 /93	--	B- /7.4	63	N/A
FO	MFS Inst Intl Research Equity Fund	MIREX	A+	(800) 343-2829	16.13	A /9.3	32.87 /96	24.88 /91	--	B- /7.9	57	N/A
MC	RVS Mid Cap Value Y		A+	(800) 328-8300	9.16	A /9.3	21.45 /84	26.08 /92	--	B- /7.8	98	N/A
FO	Henderson Internatl Opport C	HFOCX	A+	(866) 443-6337	20.96	A- /9.2	31.27 /95	25.09 /91	--	C+ /6.8	64	N/A
FO	GMO International Intrinsic Val IV	GMCFX	A+		34.07	A- /9.2	26.76 /91	25.53 /92	16.13 /93	B /8.4	74	N/A

● Denotes fund is closed to new investors

Data as of June 30, 2006

Fund Type	Fund Name	Ticker Symbol	Overall Weiss Investment Rating	Phone	Net Asset Value As of 6/30/06	Perform-ance Rating/Pts	Annualized Total Return Through 6/30/06 1Yr / Pct	3Yr / Pct	5Yr / Pct	Risk Rating/Pts	Mgr. Quality Pct	Mgr. Tenure (Years)
FO	● First Eagle Overseas Fund I	SGOIX	A+	(800) 334-2143	25.93	A- /9.2	26.68 /91	25.58 /92	20.66 /97	B /8.1	97	7
FO	JennDry Dryden Intl Equity Z	PJIZX	A+	(800) 257-3893	8.02	A- /9.2	26.45 /90	25.47 /92	8.02 /72	B- /7.0	63	3
FO	MFS Research International I	MRSIX	A+	(800) 343-2829	19.02	A- /9.2	32.09 /96	24.53 /90	11.04 /84	B- /7.9	56	10
FO	Thornburg Intl Value I	TGVIX	A+	(800) 847-0200	26.20	A- /9.2	27.94 /93	25.37 /91	12.68 /88	B- /7.1	71	8
FO	Dreyfus Premier Intl Equity C	DIECX	A+	(800) 782-6620	38.02	A- /9.2	27.02 /91	25.49 /92	13.29 /89	B- /7.3	64	3
FO	Merrill Lynch Intl Value I	MAIVX	A+	(800) 543-6217	30.50	A- /9.2	26.97 /91	24.92 /91	11.05 /84	B- /7.1	63	5
FO	T. Rowe Price Intl Gr & Inc Fd	TRIGX	A+	(800) 638-5660	15.73	A- /9.2	28.25 /93	25.18 /91	12.75 /88	B- /7.4	66	N/A
SC	Royce Value Fd Svc	RYVFX	A+	(800) 221-4268	10.28	A- /9.2	22.15 /84	26.43 /93	17.16 /94	B- /7.1	99	N/A
FO	Henderson Internatl Opport A	HFOAX	A+	(866) 443-6337	21.66	A- /9.2	32.31 /96	26.03 /92	--	C+ /6.8	72	N/A
FO	T. Rowe Price Intl Gr & Inc Adv	PAIGX	A+	(800) 638-5660	15.73	A- /9.2	28.13 /93	25.16 /91	12.76 /88	B- /7.4	65	4
FO	MFS Intl Value Fund C	MGICX	A+	(800) 343-2829	27.51	A- /9.2	27.26 /92	24.76 /91	12.48 /88	B- /7.2	81	N/A
FO	Goldman Sachs Stru Intl Eq Inst	GCIIX	A+	(800) 292-4726	14.01	A- /9.2	27.59 /92	25.41 /91	11.07 /84	C+ /6.9	56	N/A
FO	● ING International Value C	NIVCX	A+	(800) 992-0180	19.34	A- /9.2	26.79 /91	25.34 /91	10.73 /83	C+ /6.9	56	N/A
FO	SunAmerica Intl Equity I	NAOIX	A+	(800) 858-8850	15.58	A- /9.2	31.37 /95	23.94 /89	--	B- /7.5	35	N/A
FO	Oakmark International II	OARIX	A+	(800) 625-6275	25.34	A- /9.2	26.28 /90	23.89 /89	12.60 /88	B /8.6	84	14
FO	Dreyfus Premier Intl Equity T	DIETX	A+	(800) 782-6620	38.57	A- /9.2	27.59 /92	26.15 /92	13.69 /90	B- /7.3	69	3
FO	UBS PACE Intrntl Eq Inve Y	PWIYX	A+	(888) 793-8637	18.89	A- /9.2	28.27 /93	24.48 /90	8.81 /76	C+ /6.9	45	5
FO	Dreyfus Inv Founders Intl Eqty I		A+	(800) 242-8671	17.85	A- /9.2	26.25 /90	24.95 /91	5.87 /60	B- /7.9	54	3
FO	UBS PACE Intrntl Eq Inve P	PCIEX	A+	(888) 793-8637	18.86	A- /9.2	28.11 /93	24.33 /90	8.70 /75	C+ /6.9	43	11
FO	Oakmark International I	OAKIX	A+	(800) 625-6275	25.53	A- /9.2	26.73 /91	24.30 /90	12.97 /89	B /8.3	86	14
FO	Dreyfus Premier Intl Equity A	DIEAX	A+	(800) 782-6620	38.58	A- /9.2	27.94 /93	26.31 /92	13.77 /90	B- /7.3	71	3
FO	Phoenix Foreign Opportunities A	JVIAX	A+	(800) 243-4361	21.74	A- /9.2	26.10 /90	26.10 /92	12.04 /87	B- /7.1	90	4
FO	T. Rowe Price Intl Gr & Inc R	RRIGX	A+	(800) 638-5660	15.64	A- /9.2	27.86 /92	24.84 /91	12.53 /88	B- /7.4	61	4
FO	Putnam Intl Growth & Inc Y		A+	(800) 354-2228	14.86	A- /9.2	28.69 /93	24.52 /90	10.97 /84	B /8.1	62	N/A
FO	GMO Foreign Fund IV	GMFFX	A+		17.37	A- /9.2	27.87 /92	24.46 /90	14.19 /90	B- /7.1	58	8
FO	● ING International Value A	NIVAX	A+	(800) 992-0180	19.79	A- /9.2	27.69 /92	26.23 /92	11.51 /85	C+ /6.9	65	N/A
FO	Nuveen NWQ International Value	NGRRX	A+	(800) 257-8787	29.92	A- /9.2	20.92 /83	25.70 /92	12.88 /88	B- /7.0	76	4
FO	GMO Foreign Fund III	GMOFX	A+		17.36	A- /9.1	27.80 /92	24.36 /90	14.10 /90	B- /7.1	57	10
FO	MFS Intl Value Fund A	MGIAX	A+	(800) 343-2829	29.01	A- /9.1	28.10 /93	25.50 /92	13.11 /89	B- /7.3	86	N/A
FO	Fidelity Adv International Disc I	FIADX	A+	(800) 522-7297	34.23	A- /9.1	27.15 /92	25.54 /92	13.15 /89	B- /7.5	36	1
FO	Merrill Lynch Intl Value R	MRIVX	A+	(800) 543-6217	30.20	A- /9.1	26.36 /90	24.34 /90	--	B- /7.8	58	3
UT	Evergreen Utility and Telecom C	EVUCX	A+	(800) 343-2898	12.85	A- /9.1	15.76 /74	25.01 /91	5.85 /60	B /8.1	99	N/A
FO	MFS Research International R3	MRSRX	A+	(800) 343-2829	18.27	A- /9.1	31.20 /95	23.64 /89	10.41 /82	B- /7.9	47	3
FO	Goldman Sachs Stru Intl Eq Svc	GCISX	A+	(800) 292-4726	13.76	A- /9.1	27.12 /91	24.88 /91	10.55 /82	C+ /6.9	51	N/A
FO	Delaware Global Value C	DABCX	A+	(800) 362-3863	11.74	A- /9.1	20.81 /83	24.85 /91	--	C+ /6.9	89	N/A
FO	Merrill Lynch Eurofund I	MAEFX	A+	(800) 543-6217	21.00	A- /9.1	25.93 /90	23.17 /88	11.61 /86	B- /7.3	49	6
FO	Templeton Inst-Foreign Eq Prim	TFEQX	A+	(800) 321-8563	23.89	A- /9.1	22.82 /85	24.45 /90	11.27 /85	B- /7.6	52	N/A
FO	Dreyfus Premier Intl Equity B	DIEBX	A+	(800) 782-6620	38.02	A- /9.1	27.00 /91	25.53 /92	13.31 /89	B- /7.3	64	3
FO	● Columbia FS Intl Value Port C		A+	(800) 426-3750	17.43	A- /9.1	25.76 /89	24.74 /90	--	B /8.2	55	N/A
FO	JPMorgan Intl Equity Index Sel	OIEAX	A+	(800) 358-4782	24.67	A- /9.1	27.74 /92	25.09 /91	10.20 /81	B- /7.1	42	N/A
FO	Vanguard Tax-Managed Intl Inst	VTMNX	A+	(800) 662-7447	12.67	A- /9.1	27.31 /92	24.16 /90	10.13 /81	B- /7.4	51	N/A
FO	Putnam Intl Growth & Inc R	PIIRX	A+	(800) 354-2228	14.72	A- /9.1	28.03 /93	23.87 /89	10.36 /82	B /8.1	56	N/A
FO	GMO Foreign Fund M	GMFMX	A+		17.34	A- /9.1	27.46 /92	24.03 /89	--	B- /7.1	54	3
FO	MFS Intl Value Fund B	MGIBX	A+	(800) 343-2829	28.03	A- /9.1	27.29 /92	24.76 /91	12.48 /88	B- /7.3	81	N/A
GR	Fidelity Adv Cyclical Indust I	FCLIX	A+	(800) 522-7297	23.94	A- /9.1	22.78 /85	24.68 /90	11.85 /86	B- /7.2	98	N/A
FO	American Beacon Intl Eq Index Inst	AIIIX	A+	(800) 967-9009	11.39	A- /9.1	26.58 /91	23.88 /89	9.96 /80	B /8.1	50	6
FO	Vanguard Tax-Managed Intl Fd	VTMGX	A+	(800) 662-7447	12.66	A- /9.1	27.26 /92	24.04 /89	10.02 /81	B- /7.4	49	N/A
FO	● First Eagle Overseas Fund C	FESOX	A+	(800) 334-2143	25.42	A- /9.1	25.40 /89	24.36 /90	19.50 /96	B /8.1	95	7
FO	RVS International Select Value C	APICX	A+	(800) 328-8300	9.76	A- /9.1	28.80 /94	24.47 /90	--	B- /7.3	76	N/A
MC	RVS Mid Cap Value C	AMVCX	A+	(800) 328-8300	8.88	A- /9.1	20.18 /82	24.90 /91	--	B- /7.8	96	N/A
SC	● STI Classic Var Tr-Sm Cap Val Eq		A+	(888) 784-3863	20.20	A- /9.1	25.17 /89	24.77 /91	17.15 /94	B- /7.4	98	N/A
SC	Constellation TIP Sm Cap Val opp	TSVOX	A+	(800) 224-6312	19.55	A- /9.1	17.30 /78	25.87 /92	--	B- /7.1	98	4

● Denotes fund is closed to new investors

Fund Type	Fund Name	Ticker Symbol	Overall Weiss Investment Rating	Phone	Net Asset Value As of 6/30/06	Perform-ance Rating/Pts	Annualized Total Return Through 6/30/06 1Yr / Pct	3Yr / Pct	5Yr / Pct	Risk Rating/Pts	Mgr. Quality Pct	Mgr. Tenure (Years)
	99 Pct = Best *0 Pct = Worst*											
FO	American Beacon Intl Eq Inst	AAIEX	A+	(800) 967-9009	22.96	A- /9.1	25.22 /89	24.47 /90	11.41 /85	B- /7.8	70	N/A
FO	JPMorgan Intl Opps Inst	JPIOX	A+	(800) 358-4782	14.05	A- /9.1	29.81 /94	23.25 /88	8.84 /76	B- /7.1	35	9
FO	Northern Instl Intl Equity Index A	BIEIX	A+	(800) 637-1380	14.02	A- /9.1	27.14 /91	24.16 /90	10.05 /81	B- /7.0	53	N/A
UT	Evergreen Utility and Telecom A	EVUAX	A+	(800) 343-2898	12.84	A- /9.1	16.61 /76	25.92 /92	6.62 /65	B /8.1	99	N/A
FO	Vanguard European Stock Index	VESIX	A+	(800) 662-7447	31.49	A- /9.1	25.14 /89	23.47 /88	10.59 /83	B- /7.9	55	N/A
FO	RVS International Select Value A	APIAX	A+	(800) 328-8300	10.09	A- /9.1	29.86 /94	25.41 /91	--	B- /7.4	82	N/A
MC	RVS Mid Cap Value A	AMVAX	A+	(800) 328-8300	9.09	A- /9.0	21.00 /83	25.84 /92	--	B- /7.8	97	N/A
FO	TIAA-CREF Inst Intl Equity Retire	TRERX	A+		13.06	A- /9.0	28.29 /93	23.57 /89	--	B- /7.6	31	4
FO	● Delaware Pooled Tr-Intl Equity	DPIEX	A+	(800) 362-3863	22.91	A- /9.0	24.51 /88	23.20 /88	13.26 /89	B /8.4	73	N/A
FO	Vanguard European Stock Index	VEUSX	A+	(800) 662-7447	73.89	A- /9.0	25.06 /89	23.39 /88	--	B /8.2	54	N/A
FO	Pioneer International Equity Y	PIEYX	A+	(800) 225-6292	24.97	A- /9.0	26.31 /90	24.01 /89	8.38 /73	B- /7.7	59	N/A
GL	Vanguard Instl Developd Mkts Idx	VIDMX	A+	(800) 662-7447	11.15	A- /9.0	26.95 /91	23.99 /89	10.03 /81	B /8.0	49	6
FO	● Masters Select International Fund	MSILX	A+	(800) 960-0188	18.86	A- /9.0	29.63 /94	24.09 /90	11.49 /85	B- /7.6	43	N/A
FO	● Columbia FS Intl Value Port A		A+	(800) 426-3750	18.71	A- /9.0	26.68 /91	25.66 /92	--	B /8.2	63	N/A
FO	● First Eagle Overseas Fund A	SGOVX	A+	(800) 334-2143	25.71	A- /9.0	26.35 /90	25.26 /91	20.35 /96	B /8.0	96	7
MC	RS Value Fund	RSVAX	A+	(800) 766-3863	25.56	A- /9.0	10.68 /51	25.93 /92	17.59 /94	B /8.2	98	8
FO	Vanguard European Stock Index	VEURX	A+	(800) 662-7447	31.45	A- /9.0	24.96 /88	23.28 /88	10.43 /82	B- /7.9	53	N/A
FO	American Beacon Intl Eq PlanAhd	AAIPX	A+	(800) 967-9009	22.73	A- /9.0	24.88 /88	24.18 /90	11.23 /84	B- /7.8	67	N/A
SC	DWS Dreman Small Cap Val R	KDSRX	A+	(800) 621-1048	36.86	A- /9.0	20.94 /83	24.11 /90	14.25 /91	B- /7.5	98	4
FO	Vanguard Developed Markets	VDMIX	A+	(800) 662-7447	11.25	A- /9.0	26.81 /91	23.84 /89	9.90 /80	B /8.0	48	6
SC	Schwab Small-Cap Equity Sel	SWSCX	A+	(866) 855-9102	17.04	A- /9.0	16.87 /77	25.52 /92	--	B- /7.0	98	N/A
FO	Vantagepoint Overseas Eqty Index	VPOEX	A+	(800) 669-7400	11.72	A- /9.0	26.25 /90	23.43 /88	9.56 /79	B /8.3	51	N/A
FO	Thornburg Intl Value C	THGCX	A+	(800) 847-0200	24.59	A- /9.0	26.51 /91	23.90 /89	11.24 /84	B- /7.1	59	8
FO	TIAA-CREF Inst Intl Eq Index	TRIEX	A+		18.91	A- /9.0	26.37 /90	23.27 /88	--	B /8.0	42	4
FO	Fidelity Adv International Disc C	FCADX	A+	(800) 522-7297	33.87	A- /9.0	25.67 /89	24.83 /91	12.76 /88	B- /7.4	31	1
FO	JPMorgan Intl Opps Sel	JIOSX	A+	(800) 358-4782	13.97	A- /9.0	29.43 /94	22.92 /87	8.52 /74	B- /7.1	32	N/A
FO	Fidelity Adv International Disc B	FADDX	A+	(800) 522-7297	33.82	A- /9.0	25.61 /89	24.76 /91	12.73 /88	B- /7.4	30	1
FO	Fidelity Spartan Intl Index Inv	FSIIX	A+	(800) 544-8888	39.15	A- /9.0	26.64 /91	23.51 /88	9.66 /79	B- /7.3	47	3
FO	Glenmede Philadelphia Intl Fund	GTIIX	A+	(800) 442-8299	20.95	A- /9.0	26.84 /91	23.02 /87	10.47 /82	B- /7.3	60	14
FO	● William Blair Mutual-Intl Grwth I	BIGIX	A+	(800) 742-7272	27.09	A- /9.0	27.31 /92	25.34 /91	11.93 /86	B- /7.4	36	10
FO	Merrill Lynch Eurofund R	MREFX	A+	(800) 543-6217	18.04	A- /9.0	25.35 /89	22.89 /87	--	B- /7.3	45	6
RE	Columbia Real Estate Equity Fd		A+	(800) 426-3750	19.71	A- /9.0	17.25 /78	23.91 /89	--	B- /7.4	84	N/A
FO	MFS Research International 529C	ECRIX	A+	(800) 343-2829	17.61	A- /9.0	30.44 /95	22.99 /87	9.34 /78	B- /7.8	40	4
FO	Causeway International Value Inst	CIVIX	A+	(866) 947-7000	18.31	A- /9.0	20.08 /82	24.04 /89	--	B /8.2	77	5
GL	RVS International Aggressive Gr C		A+	(800) 328-8300	8.58	A- /9.0	27.02 /91	23.86 /89	--	B /8.6	38	N/A
FO	E*TRADE International Index Fund	ETINX	A+	(800) 786-2575	11.78	A- /9.0	26.75 /91	23.38 /88	9.48 /79	B- /7.1	50	N/A
FO	MFS Inst Intl Equity Fund	MIEIX	A+	(800) 343-2829	19.22	A- /9.0	28.80 /94	22.05 /85	11.94 /86	B /8.2	53	N/A
FO	Merrill Lynch Intl Value A	MDIVX	A+	(800) 543-6217	30.40	A- /9.0	26.67 /91	24.62 /90	10.78 /83	B- /7.1	61	5
UT	Evergreen Utility and Telecom B	EVUBX	A+	(800) 343-2898	12.84	A- /9.0	15.77 /74	24.98 /91	5.85 /60	B /8.1	99	N/A
FO	● MFS International Growth Fund I	MQGIX	A+	(800) 343-2829	25.68	A- /9.0	27.82 /92	23.19 /88	10.89 /84	B- /7.6	34	9
FO	Thornburg Intl Value A	TGVAX	A+	(800) 847-0200	25.72	A- /9.0	27.43 /92	24.82 /91	12.15 /87	B- /7.1	67	8
FO	Putnam Intl Growth & Inc C	PIGRX	A+	(800) 354-2228	14.65	A- /9.0	27.29 /92	23.26 /88	9.81 /80	B- /7.1	49	N/A
FO	Vantagepoint Overseas Eqty Index	VPOIX	A+	(800) 669-7400	12.36	A- /9.0	26.10 /90	23.11 /88	9.29 /78	B /8.2	45	N/A
SC	Kinetics Small Cap Opport NL	KSCOX	A+	(800) 930-3828	23.20	A- /9.0	20.95 /83	24.32 /90	11.91 /86	B- /7.2	99	N/A

● Denotes fund is closed to new investors

Section IV

Bottom 200
Stock Mutual Funds

A compilation of those

Equity Mutual Funds

receiving the lowest Weiss Investment Ratings.

Funds are listed in order by Overall Weiss Investment Rating.

Section IV Contents

This section contains a summary analysis of each of the bottom 200 equity mutual funds as determined by their overall Weiss Investment Rating. Typically, these funds have invested in stocks that are currently out of favor, presenting a risky investment proposition. As such, these are the funds that you should generally avoid since they have historically underperformed most other mutual funds given the level of risk in their underlying investments.

1. **Fund Type**

The mutual fund's peer category based on an analysis of its investment portfolio.

AG	Aggressive Growth	HL	Health
AA	Asset Allocation	IN	Income
BA	Balanced	IX	Index
CV	Convertible	MC	Mid Cap
EM	Emerging Market	OT	Other
EN	Energy/Natural Resources	PM	Precious Metals
FS	Financial Services	RE	Real Estate
FO	Foreign	SC	Small Cap
GL	Global	TC	Technology
GR	Growth	UT	Utilities
GI	Growth and Income		

A blank fund type means that the mutual fund has not yet been categorized.

2. **Fund Name**

The name of the mutual fund as stated in its prospectus, which can sometimes differ slightly from the name that the company uses for advertising. If you cannot find the particular mutual fund you are interested in, or if you have any doubts regarding the precise name, verify the information with your broker or on your account statement. Also, use the fund's ticker symbol for confirmation. (See column 3.)

3. **Ticker Symbol**

The unique alphabetic symbol used for identifying and trading a specific mutual fund. No two funds can have the same ticker symbol, and the ticker symbol for mutual funds always ends with an "X".

A handful of funds currently show no associated ticker symbol. This means that the fund is either small or new since the NASD only assigns a ticker symbol to funds with at least $25 million in assets or 1,000 shareholders.

4. **Overall Weiss Investment Rating**

Our overall rating is measured on a scale from A to E based on each fund's risk-adjusted performance. Please see page 10 for specific descriptions of each letter grade. Also, refer to page 7 for information on how our ratings are derived. Most important, when using this rating, please be sure to consider the warnings beginning on page 11 regarding the ratings' limitations and the underlying assumptions.

5. Phone

The telephone number of the company managing the fund. Call this number to receive a prospectus or other information about the fund.

6. Net Asset Value (NAV)

The fund's share price as of the date indicated. A fund's NAV is computed by dividing the value of the fund's asset holdings, less accrued fees and expenses, by the number of its shares outstanding.

7. Performance Rating/Points

A letter grade rating based solely on the mutual fund's financial performance over the trailing three years, without any consideration for the amount of risk the fund poses. Like the overall Weiss Investment Rating, the Performance Rating is measured on a scale from A to E for ease of interpretation. The points score indicates where the Performance Rating falls on a scale of 0 to 10.

8. 1-Year Total Return

The total return the fund has provided investors over the preceeding twelve months. This total return figure is computed based on the fund's dividend distributions and share price appreciation/depreciation during the period, net of the expenses and fees it imposes on its shareholders. Although the total return figure does not reflect an adjustment for any loads the fund may carry, such adjustments have been made in deriving the Weiss Investment Ratings.

9. 1-Year Total Return Percentile

The fund's percentile rank based on its one-year performance compared to that of all other equity funds in existence for at least one year. A score of 99 is the best possible, indicating that the fund outperformed 99% of the other mutual funds. Zero is the worst possible percentile score.

10. 3-Year Total Return

The total annual return the fund has provided investors over the preceeding three years.

11. 3-Year Total Return Percentile

The fund's percentile rank based on its three-year performance compared to that of all other equity funds in existence for at least three years. A score of 99 is the best possible, indicating that the fund outperformed 99% of the other mutual funds. Zero is the worst possible percentile score.

12. 5-Year Total Return

The total annual return the fund has provided investors over the preceeding five years.

13. 5-Year Total Return Percentile

The fund's percentile rank based on its five-year performance compared to that of all other equity funds in existence for at least five years. A score of 99 is the best possible, indicating that the fund outperformed 99% of the other mutual funds. Zero is the worst possible percentile score.

14. Risk Rating/Points

A letter grade rating based solely on the mutual fund's risk as determined by its monthly performance volatility over the trailing three years. The risk rating does not take into consideration the overall financial performance the fund has achieved or the total return it has provided to its shareholders. Like the overall Weiss Investment Rating, the Risk Rating is measured on a scale from A to E for ease of interpretation. The points score indicates where the Risk Rating falls on a scale of 0 to 10.

15. Manager Quality Percentile

The manager quality percentile is based on a ranking of the fund's alpha, a statistical measure representing the difference between a fund's actual returns and its expected performance given its level of risk. Fund managers who have been able to exceed the fund's statistically expected performance receive a high percentile rank with 99 representing the highest possible score. At the other end of the spectrum, fund managers who have actually detracted from the fund's expected performance receive a low percentile rank with 0 representing the lowest possible score.

16. Manager Tenure

The number of years the current manager has been managing the fund. Since fund managers who deliver substandard returns are usually replaced, a long tenure is usually a good sign that shareholders are satisfied that the fund is achieving its stated objectives.

Fund Type	Fund Name	Ticker Symbol	Overall Weiss Investment Rating	Phone	Net Asset Value As of 6/30/06	Performance Rating/Pts	Annualized Total Return Through 6/30/06 1Yr / Pct	3Yr / Pct	5Yr / Pct	Risk Rating/Pts	Mgr. Quality Pct	Mgr. Tenure (Years)
	99 Pct = Best 0 Pct = Worst											
AG	Ameritor Investment	AIVTX	E-	(800) 424-8570	0.03	E- /0.0	-75.00 / 0	-56.72 / 0	-47.61 / 0	D- / 1.3	0	9
SC	Direxion Small Cp Bear 2.5X	DXRSX	E-	(800) 851-0511	15.86	E- /0.0	-24.02 / 0	-22.65 / 0	-14.36 / 0	E- / 0.2	11	7
SC	Frontier Fund-Equity	FEFPX	E-	(800) 231-2901	0.19	E- /0.0	-17.39 / 0	-15.06 / 0	-35.18 / 0	E / 0.5	0	4
AG	Rydex Dynamics-Inv Dyn S&P 500	RYCBX	E-	(800) 820-0888	37.47	E- /0.0	-9.27 / 0	-18.11 / 0	-9.37 / 0	E+ / 0.9	11	N/A
AG	ProFunds-Ultra Bear Fund Svc	URPSX	E-	(888) 776-3637	17.29	E- /0.0	-9.63 / 0	-18.18 / 0	-9.26 / 0	E+ / 0.9	11	N/A
AG	Rydex Dynamics-Inv Dyn OTC C	RYCDX	E-	(800) 820-0888	20.75	E- /0.0	-7.37 / 0	-20.39 / 0	-13.90 / 0	E- / 0.0	82	N/A
TC	ProFunds-Ultra Short OTC Fund	USPSX	E-	(888) 776-3637	17.56	E- /0.0	-7.38 / 0	-20.49 / 0	-14.48 / 0	E- / 0.0	82	N/A
AG	ProFunds-Ultra Bear Fund Inv	URPIX	E-	(888) 776-3637	17.35	E- /0.0	-8.74 / 0	-17.43 / 0	-8.43 / 0	E+ / 0.9	15	N/A
AG	Rydex Dynamics-Inv Dyn S&P 500	RYTPX	E-	(800) 820-0888	39.05	E- /0.0	-8.57 / 0	-17.45 / 0	-8.67 / 0	E+ / 0.9	14	N/A
AG	Rydex Dynamics-Inv Dyn OTC H	RYVNX	E-	(800) 820-0888	21.52	E- /0.0	-6.71 / 0	-19.78 / 0	-13.32 / 0	E- / 0.0	87	N/A
TC	ProFunds-Ultra Short OTC Fund	USPIX	E-	(888) 776-3637	16.97	E- /0.0	-6.47 / 0	-19.71 / 0	-13.70 / 0	E- / 0.0	89	N/A
AG	Gabelli Comstck Partners Cap Val	DCVBX	E-	(800) 422-3554	2.38	E- /0.0	-9.35 / 0	-14.59 / 0	-5.27 / 2	D+ / 2.3	5	10
AG	Gabelli Comstck Partners Cap Val	DRCVX	E-	(800) 422-3554	2.44	E- /0.0	-8.86 / 0	-13.99 / 0	-4.56 / 3	D+ / 2.3	7	10
AG	Gabelli Comstck Partners Cap Val	CPCCX	E-	(800) 422-3554	2.28	E- /0.0	-9.35 / 0	-14.59 / 0	-5.27 / 2	D+ / 2.3	4	10
AG	Gabelli Comstock Partners Strat A	CPFAX	E-	(800) 422-3554	2.77	E- /0.0	-10.77 / 0	-11.71 / 0	-5.88 / 2	C- / 3.2	2	10
AG	Gabelli Comstock Partners Strat C	CPFCX	E-	(800) 422-3554	2.80	E- /0.0	-11.71 / 0	-12.47 / 0	-6.61 / 1	C- / 3.2	1	10
AG	Gabelli Comstck Partners Cap Val	CPCRX	E-	(800) 422-3554	2.44	E- /0.0	-8.67 / 0	-13.78 / 0	-4.44 / 3	D+ / 2.3	7	10
AG	Leuthold Grizzly Short Fund	GRZZX	E-	(888) 200-0409	6.08	E- /0.0	-10.38 / 0	-12.67 / 0	-6.49 / 1	D / 2.2	14	6
AG	● Gabelli Comstock Partners Strat O	CPSFX	E-	(800) 422-3554	2.69	E- /0.0	-10.66 / 0	-11.47 / 0	-5.62 / 2	C- / 3.2	2	10
AG	ProFunds-Pharm UltraSector Svc	PHPSX	E-	(888) 776-3637	8.67	E- /0.0	-7.37 / 0	-9.33 / 0	-11.86 / 0	D- / 1.0	0	6
GR	Direxion U.S. Short Inv	PSPSX	E-	(800) 851-0511	27.46	E- /0.0	-3.48 / 0	-9.61 / 0	-4.46 / 3	C- / 3.2	19	9
AG	ProFunds-Pharm UltraSector Inv	PHPIX	E-	(888) 776-3637	9.11	E- /0.0	-6.33 / 0	-8.43 / 0	-11.09 / 0	D- / 1.1	0	6
AG	ProFunds-Bear Fund Svc	BRPSX	E-	(888) 776-3637	28.85	E- /0.0	-3.71 / 0	-9.18 / 0	-3.92 / 4	C- / 3.2	22	9
AG	Rydex Series-Inverse S&P 500 C	RYUCX	E-	(800) 820-0888	7.87	E- /0.0	-3.32 / 0	-8.87 / 0	-3.17 / 5	D+ / 2.8	24	N/A
AG	Rydex Series-Inverse OTC C	RYACX	E-	(800) 820-0888	22.53	E- /0.0	-2.01 / 1	-9.46 / 0	-3.59 / 4	D / 1.7	75	N/A
AG	Rydex Series-Inverse S&P 500 Adv	RYUAX	E-	(800) 820-0888	7.95	E- /0.0	-2.82 / 0	-8.36 / 0	-2.67 / 6	D+ / 2.9	28	N/A
AG	ProFunds-Bear Fund Inv	BRPIX	E-	(888) 776-3637	29.96	E- /0.0	-2.79 / 0	-8.28 / 0	-2.94 / 6	C- / 3.3	29	9
AG	Rydex Series-Inverse S&P 500 Inv	RYURX	E-	(800) 820-0888	8.32	E- /0.0	-2.36 / 1	-7.91 / 0	-2.18 / 8	D+ / 2.9	32	N/A
AG	Rydex Series-Inverse OTC Inv	RYAIX	E-	(800) 820-0888	23.87	E- /0.0	-1.01 / 1	-8.53 / 0	-2.57 / 6	D / 1.8	83	N/A
TC	ProFunds-Semicond UltraSector	SMPSX	E-	(888) 776-3637	16.23	E- /0.0	-10.13 / 0	0.48 / 0	-18.77 / 0	E- / 0.0	0	6
MC	Apex Mid-Cap Growth Fund	BMCGX	E-	(877) 593-8637	1.35	E- /0.0	2.27 / 5	-3.24 / 0	-1.82 / 9	E- / 0.0	0	13
EM	Van Wagoner Emerging Growth	VWEGX	E-	(800) 228-2121	4.53	E- /0.0	5.35 / 17	-4.62 / 0	-22.53 / 0	E- / 0.1	0	11
GR	Jundt Twenty Five Fund B	JTFBX	E-	(800) 370-0612	7.40	E- /0.0	-1.46 / 1	-0.49 / 0	-7.35 / 1	C / 4.7	3	9
GR	Columbia Growth Stock Fund 529B		E-	(800) 426-3750	10.28	E- /0.0	-3.11 / 0	-0.10 / 0	--	C / 5.0	1	N/A
GR	Jundt Twenty Five Fund A	JTFHX	E-	(800) 370-0612	8.01	E- /0.0	-0.74 / 1	0.25 / 0	-6.64 / 1	C / 4.7	4	9
GR	Managers 20 Fund B	MTWBX	E-	(800) 835-3879	4.29	E- /0.0	-3.60 / 0	0.39 / 0	-10.64 / 0	D+ / 2.5	0	6
TC	ProFunds-Semicond UltraSector	SMPIX	E-	(888) 776-3637	17.25	E- /0.0	-9.21 / 0	1.47 / 0	-17.94 / 0	E- / 0.0	0	6
GR	Managers 20 Fund A	MTWAX	E-	(800) 835-3879	4.53	E- /0.0	-2.79 / 0	0.98 / 0	-10.11 / 0	D+ / 2.6	0	6
GR	Columbia Growth Stock Fund 529C		E-	(800) 426-3750	10.28	E- /0.0	-3.02 / 0	-0.10 / 0	--	C / 5.0	1	N/A
GR	Jundt Twenty Five Fund C	JTFCX	E-	(800) 370-0612	7.45	E- /0.0	-1.59 / 1	-0.53 / 0	-7.36 / 1	C / 4.6	3	9
AG	PF Loomis Sayles Lg Cp Gr B	PFBBX	E-	(800) 722-2333	8.53	E- /0.0	-5.26 / 0	1.81 / 1	--	C / 4.3	2	N/A
AG	PF Loomis Sayles Lg Cp Gr A	PFBAX	E-	(800) 722-2333	8.75	E- /0.0	-4.77 / 0	2.25 / 1	--	C / 4.4	2	N/A
HL	Allianz RCM Biotechnology B	RBBTX	E-	(800) 628-1237	22.53	E- /0.0	-6.05 / 0	2.34 / 1	-5.55 / 2	D / 2.1	4	N/A
GR	Wells Fargo Avtg Lg Co Core B	WLCBX	E-	(800) 222-8222	8.58	E- /0.0	0.86 / 2	0.27 / 0	-1.68 / 9	C / 4.4	0	N/A
GR	Managers 20 Fund C	MTWCX	E-	(800) 835-3879	4.31	E- /0.0	-3.58 / 0	0.39 / 0	-10.63 / 0	D+ / 2.5	0	6
SC	Van Wagoner Small-Cap Growth	VWMCX	E-	(800) 228-2121	9.63	E- /0.0	5.02 / 15	-2.06 / 0	-8.87 / 0	E / 0.3	0	11
HL	Allianz RCM Biotechnology A	RABTX	E-	(800) 628-1237	23.30	E- /0.0	-5.28 / 0	3.13 / 1	-4.81 / 3	D / 2.1	6	N/A
TC	J Hancock Technology B	FGTBX	E-	(800) 257-3336	3.01	E- /0.0	-0.66 / 1	1.48 / 0	-12.89 / 0	D- / 1.4	0	N/A
AG	Ameritor Security Trust 1	ASTRX	E-	(800) 424-8570	0.41	E- /0.0	10.81 / 52	-3.06 / 0	-10.15 / 0	D+ / 2.7	0	9
AG	PF Loomis Sayles Lg Cp Gr C	PFBCX	E-	(800) 722-2333	8.52	E- /0.0	-5.26 / 0	1.73 / 0	--	C / 4.3	2	N/A
GR	Van Wagoner Growth	VWGOX	E-	(800) 228-2121	10.00	E- /0.0	1.21 / 3	-0.65 / 0	--	E- / 0.0	0	3
HL	Allianz RCM Biotechnology C	RCBTX	E-	(800) 628-1237	22.54	E- /0.0	-6.01 / 0	2.35 / 1	-5.54 / 2	D / 2.1	4	N/A

● Denotes fund is closed to new investors

Fund Type	Fund Name	Ticker Symbol	Overall Weiss Investment Rating	Phone	Net Asset Value As of 6/30/06	PERFORMANCE Perform-ance Rating/Pts	Annualized Total Return Through 6/30/06 1Yr / Pct	3Yr / Pct	5Yr / Pct	RISK Risk Rating/Pts	FUND MGR Mgr. Quality Pct	Mgr. Tenure (Years)
TC	J Hancock Technology A	NTTFX	E-	(800) 257-3336	3.32	E- /0.0	--	2.09 / 1	-12.30 / 0	D- / 1.4	0	N/A
GR	Managers 20 Fund Y	MTWYX	E-	(800) 835-3879	4.62	E- /0.0	-2.74 / 0	1.41 / 0	-9.74 / 0	D+ / 2.6	0	6
TC	J Hancock Technology C	JHTCX	E-	(800) 257-3336	3.01	E- /0.0	-0.66 / 1	1.48 / 0	-12.89 / 0	D- / 1.4	0	N/A
TC	Monetta Trust-Select Technology A	MSCEX	E-	(800) 666-3882	7.19	E- /0.0	-3.23 / 0	2.69 / 1	-9.83 / 0	D- / 1.4	0	9
HL	Allianz RCM Biotechnology D	DRBNX	E-	(800) 628-1237	23.28	E- /0.0	-5.33 / 0	3.10 / 1	-4.64 / 3	D / 1.6	6	N/A
AG	ProFunds-HlthCare UltraSector	HCPSX	E-	(888) 776-3637	13.35	E- /0.0	-5.52 / 0	2.03 / 1	-4.58 / 3	C- / 4.1	4	6
TC	Munder Future Technology B	MTFBX	E-	(800) 438-5789	3.46	E- /0.0	1.76 / 4	2.96 / 1	-10.31 / 0	D+ / 2.9	0	N/A
GR	Jundt US Emerging Growth B	JEGBX	E-	(800) 370-0612	11.70	E- /0.1	2.36 / 5	2.96 / 1	-1.47 /10	C- / 3.0	5	10
TC	Munder Future Technology A	MTFAX	E-	(800) 438-5789	3.64	E- /0.1	2.82 / 7	3.74 / 2	-9.60 / 0	D+ / 2.9	0	N/A
IN	Kelmoore Strategy Eagle A	KSEAX	E-	(877) 328-9456	11.17	E- /0.1	-0.87 / 1	4.38 / 3	-3.59 / 4	D- / 1.3	1	6
TC	Munder Future Technology C	MTFTX	E-	(800) 438-5789	3.12	E- /0.1	1.63 / 3	2.94 / 1	-10.36 / 0	D+ / 2.9	0	N/A
AG	ProFunds-HlthCare UltraSector Inv	HCPIX	E-	(888) 776-3637	14.11	E- /0.1	-4.66 / 0	2.93 / 1	-3.71 / 4	C- / 4.2	6	6
TC	DWS Technology Fd B	KTCBX	E-	(800) 621-1048	8.82	E- /0.1	-1.45 / 1	4.45 / 3	-7.25 / 1	D+ / 2.6	0	N/A
GR	New York Equity Fund	NYSAX	E-	(888) 899-8344	8.07	E- /0.1	1.25 / 3	3.78 / 2	-7.84 / 1	D+ / 2.7	2	9
GR	Jundt US Emerging Growth A	JEGHX	E-	(800) 370-0612	12.69	E- /0.1	3.09 / 8	3.73 / 2	-0.74 /13	C- / 3.1	7	10
TC	DWS Technology Fd A	KTCAX	E-	(800) 621-1048	10.48	E- /0.1	-0.38 / 1	5.64 / 5	-6.25 / 1	D+ / 2.7	1	N/A
GR	Oak Assoc-White Oak Select Gr Fd	WOGSX	E-	(888) 462-5386	30.42	E- /0.1	-0.76 / 1	2.51 / 1	-6.93 / 1	D+ / 2.8	0	N/A
GR	American Growth Fund B	AMRBX	E-	(800) 525-2406	2.72	E- /0.1	6.25 /22	4.12 / 2	-7.10 / 1	D+ / 2.6	1	10
TC	Gartmore Glob Tech & Comm A	GAGTX	E-	(800) 848-0920	3.71	E- /0.1	6.61 /24	6.17 / 7	-7.61 / 1	D+ / 2.5	0	N/A
TC	Morgan Stanley Information Fd B	IFOBX	E-	(800) 869-6397	8.83	E- /0.1	-2.00 / 1	5.17 / 4	-9.27 / 0	D / 1.6	0	N/A
GR	BNY Hamilton Lrg Cap Gr A	BLCGX	E-	(800) 426-9363	7.44	E- /0.1	1.38 / 3	4.01 / 2	-2.75 / 6	C- / 3.1	8	N/A
IN	Kelmoore Strategy Eagle C	KSECX	E-	(877) 328-9456	10.33	E- /0.1	-1.63 / 1	3.46 / 2	-4.35 / 3	D- / 1.1	1	6
TC	Firsthand-Global Technology	GTFQX	E-	(888) 884-2675	3.89	E- /0.1	4.01 /11	3.10 / 1	-6.69 / 1	E / 0.3	0	6
HL	Eaton Vance WW Health Sciences	EMHSX	E-	(800) 225-6265	11.29	E- /0.1	6.01 /20	4.90 / 4	0.43 /17	C / 4.4	21	10
GR	American Growth Fund A	AMRAX	E-	(800) 525-2406	2.95	E- /0.1	7.27 /28	4.98 / 4	-6.24 / 2	D+ / 2.9	1	10
AG	American Heritage Fund	AHERX	E-	(212) 397-3900	0.08	E- /0.1	-11.11 / 0	4.55 / 3	-12.94 / 0	D / 1.9	3	16
TC	Morgan Stanley Information Fd A	IFOAX	E-	(800) 869-6397	9.53	E- /0.1	-1.14 / 1	6.05 / 7	-8.50 / 0	D / 1.6	0	N/A
GR	American Growth Fund D	AMRGX	E-	(800) 525-2406	3.02	E- /0.1	7.47 /29	5.12 / 4	-6.03 / 2	C- / 3.0	1	10
GR	Jundt US Emerging Growth C	JEGCX	E-	(800) 370-0612	11.69	E- /0.1	2.36 / 5	2.96 / 1	-1.47 /10	C- / 3.0	5	10
TC	DWS Technology Fd C	KTCCX	E-	(800) 621-1048	9.07	E- /0.1	-1.20 / 1	4.67 / 3	-7.10 / 1	D+ / 2.6	0	N/A
TC	Munder Future Technology Y	MTFYX	E-	(800) 438-5789	4.02	E- /0.2	3.08 / 8	4.04 / 2	-9.36 / 0	D+ / 2.9	0	N/A
HL	Eaton Vance WW Health Sciences	ETHSX	E-	(800) 225-6265	10.75	E- /0.2	6.86 /25	5.67 / 6	1.19 /21	C / 4.4	26	17
TC	Gartmore Glob Tech & Comm B	GBGTX	E-	(800) 848-0920	3.55	E- /0.2	5.97 /20	5.42 / 5	-8.22 / 0	D+ / 2.4	0	N/A
TC	Gartmore Glob Tech & Comm C	GCGTX	E-	(800) 848-0920	3.58	E- /0.2	5.92 /20	5.49 / 5	-8.13 / 0	D+ / 2.4	0	N/A
SC	KOPP Emerging Growth Fund A	KOPPX	E-	(888) 533-5677	9.23	E- /0.2	13.81 /68	6.46 / 8	-8.33 / 0	E- / 0.0	0	9
GR	American Growth Fund C	AMRCX	E-	(800) 525-2406	2.72	E- /0.2	6.25 /22	4.12 / 2	-7.10 / 1	D+ / 2.9	0	10
TC	Morgan Stanley Information Fd C	IFOCX	E-	(800) 869-6397	8.83	E- /0.2	-1.89 / 1	5.17 / 4	-9.22 / 0	D / 1.6	0	N/A
TC	Oppenheimer Emerging Tech A	OETAX	E-	(800) 525-7048	2.90	E- /0.2	9.85 /46	5.59 / 5	-11.47 / 0	E / 0.4	0	N/A
SC	KOPP Emerging Growth Fund C	KEGCX	E-	(888) 533-5677	8.80	E- /0.2	13.11 /65	5.80 / 6	-8.92 / 0	E- / 0.0	0	9
TC	Legg Mason Prt Technology B	SBTBX	E-	(866) 890-4247	3.78	E- /0.2	-1.05 / 1	5.38 / 5	-7.23 / 1	C- / 3.8	1	N/A
TC	J Hancock Technology I	JHTIX	E-	(800) 257-3336	3.62	E- /0.2	0.84 / 2	4.09 / 2	-10.83 / 0	D- / 1.4	0	N/A
TC	Oak Assoc-Red Oak Technology	ROGSX	E-	(888) 462-5386	6.37	E- /0.2	0.79 / 2	4.26 / 3	-12.84 / 0	D / 1.6	0	8
TC	Dreyfus Premier Tech Growth B	DTGBX	E-	(800) 782-6620	21.60	E- /0.2	5.83 /19	5.82 / 6	-4.73 / 3	D+ / 2.4	1	7
AG	ProFunds-Tech UltraSector Svc	TEPSX	E-	(888) 776-3637	23.13	E- /0.2	-0.39 / 1	5.29 / 5	-14.46 / 0	E / 0.3	0	N/A
HL	Eaton Vance WW Health Sciences	ECHSX	E-	(800) 225-6265	11.29	E- /0.2	5.99 /20	4.90 / 4	0.43 /17	C / 4.4	21	8
TC	Gartmore Glob Tech & Comm R	GGTRX	E-	(800) 848-0920	3.60	E- /0.2	6.83 /25	5.91 / 6	-7.96 / 0	D+ / 2.8	0	N/A
TC	Firsthand-Technology Innovators	TIFQX	E	(888) 884-2675	9.66	E /0.3	14.86 /71	1.27 / 0	-10.52 / 0	E / 0.3	0	8
TC	Dreyfus Premier Tech Growth T	DPTGX	E	(800) 782-6620	22.39	E /0.3	6.57 /24	6.43 / 8	-4.23 / 3	D+ / 2.5	2	7
TC	Oppenheimer Emerging Tech C	OETCX	E	(800) 525-7048	2.79	E /0.3	8.98 /40	4.71 / 3	-12.14 / 0	E / 0.4	0	N/A
GR	Prudent Bear Fd	BEARX	E	(800) 711-1848	5.94	E /0.3	14.80 /71	-0.23 / 0	9.16 /77	C- / 3.1	79	N/A
TC	Oppenheimer Emerging Tech B	OETBX	E	(800) 525-7048	2.79	E /0.3	8.98 /40	4.71 / 3	-12.14 / 0	E / 0.4	0	N/A
TC	Gartmore Glob Tech & Comm	GIGTX	E	(800) 848-0920	3.78	E /0.3	6.78 /25	6.27 / 8	-7.33 / 1	D+ / 2.5	0	N/A

● Denotes fund is closed to new investors

Data as of June 30, 2006

Fund Type	Fund Name	Ticker Symbol	Overall Weiss Investment Rating	Phone	Net Asset Value As of 6/30/06	Perform-ance Rating/Pts	Annualized Total Return Through 6/30/06			Risk Rating/Pts	Mgr. Quality Pct	Mgr. Tenure (Years)
	99 Pct = Best 0 Pct = Worst						1Yr / Pct	3Yr / Pct	5Yr / Pct			
GR	BNY Hamilton Lrg Cap Gr Inst	BNLIX	E-	(800) 426-9363	7.52	E /0.3	1.47 / 3	3.84 / 2	-2.75 / 6	C- / 3.2	8	N/A
TC	Legg Mason Prt Technology A	SBTAX	E-	(866) 890-4247	3.97	E /0.3	-0.25 / 2	6.14 / 7	-6.52 / 1	C- / 3.9	1	N/A
TC	Dreyfus Premier Tech Growth A	DTGRX	E-	(800) 782-6620	23.08	E /0.3	7.00 /26	6.91 /10	-3.80 / 4	D+ / 2.5	2	9
GI	WPG Large Cap Growth	WPGLX	E-	(888) 261-4073	21.95	E /0.3	-2.27 / 1	4.68 / 3	-2.63 / 6	C / 4.7	3	2
TC	Gartmore Glob Tech & Comm Inst	GGTIX	E-	(800) 848-0920	3.80	E /0.3	7.34 /28	6.45 / 8	-7.23 / 1	D+ / 2.8	0	N/A
SC	KOPP Emerging Growth Fund I	KEGIX	E-	(888) 533-5677	9.56	E /0.3	14.22 /69	6.84 /10	-7.99 / 0	E- / 0.0	0	9
TC	Rydex Series-Electronics C	RYSCX	E-	(800) 820-0888	11.35	E /0.4	10.73 /52	4.24 / 3	-9.60 / 0	E- / 0.0	0	N/A
HL	Rydex Series-Biotechnology C	RYCFX	E-	(800) 820-0888	20.05	E /0.4	10.29 /49	5.55 / 5	-5.70 / 2	D+ / 2.4	11	N/A
TC	TA IDEX Great Companies Tech B	IGTBX	E-	(888) 233-4339	3.58	E /0.4	3.18 / 8	6.46 / 8	-4.86 / 3	C / 4.3	3	6
TC	Morgan Stanley Information Fd D	IFODX	E-	(800) 869-6397	9.74	E /0.4	-0.92 / 1	6.30 / 8	-8.33 / 0	D / 1.6	1	N/A
TC	Dreyfus Premier Tech Growth C	DTGCX	E-	(800) 782-6620	21.65	E /0.4	5.97 /20	5.88 / 6	-4.68 / 3	D+ / 2.4	1	7
TC	Legg Mason Prt Technology C	SBQLX	E-	(866) 890-4247	3.78	E /0.4	-1.05 / 1	5.38 / 5	-7.23 / 1	C- / 3.8	1	N/A
TC	Select Networking & Infrastructure	FNINX	E-	(800) 544-8888	2.31	E /0.4	9.48 /43	6.54 / 9	-8.39 / 0	E- / 0.0	0	2
GR	Atlantic Whitehall Growth Dist	WHGFX	E-	(800) 994-2533	12.14	E /0.4	1.50 / 3	4.65 / 3	-3.25 / 5	D / 1.6	7	N/A
BA	Dreyfus Premier Balanced Opport	DBOCX	E-	(800) 782-6620	18.84	E /0.4	0.17 / 2	4.45 / 3	3.68 /43	E- / 0.0	19	19
TC	Oppenheimer Emerging Tech N	OETNX	E-	(800) 525-7048	2.87	E /0.4	9.54 /44	5.35 / 5	-11.64 / 0	E / 0.4	0	N/A
AG	ProFunds-Tech UltraSector Inv	TEPIX	E-	(888) 776-3637	24.10	E /0.4	0.69 / 2	6.34 / 8	-13.75 / 0	E / 0.4	0	N/A
GR	Pioneer Growth Leaders Fund A	LRPSX	E-	(800) 225-6292	18.90	E /0.4	3.80 /10	5.69 / 6	-0.64 /13	D- / 1.4	22	17
TC	TA IDEX Great Companies Tech A	IGTAX	E-	(888) 233-4339	3.73	E /0.4	3.78 /10	7.22 /11	-4.12 / 4	C / 4.4	5	6
TC	Federated Technology B	FCTEX	E-	(800) 341-7400	4.85	E /0.5	-0.61 / 1	7.63 /13	-7.08 / 1	D / 2.2	1	6
TC	Merrill Lynch Global Technology A	MDGTX	E-	(800) 543-6217	7.44	E /0.5	5.38 /17	6.96 /10	-7.25 / 1	D / 1.7	1	N/A
TC	Rydex Series-Electronics Adv	RYSAX	E-	(800) 820-0888	11.46	E /0.5	11.05 /54	4.72 / 3	-9.15 / 0	E- / 0.0	0	N/A
TC	ICON Information Technology	ICTEX	E-	(800) 764-0442	8.47	E /0.5	2.29 / 5	5.27 / 4	-5.43 / 2	D+ / 2.4	0	9
HL	Rydex Series-Biotechnology Adv	RYOAX	E-	(800) 820-0888	20.22	E /0.5	10.86 /53	6.12 / 7	-5.19 / 2	D+ / 2.5	14	N/A
GR	Reynolds Blue Chip Growth Fund	RBCGX	E-	(800) 773-9665	30.13	E /0.5	6.58 /24	5.01 / 4	-5.23 / 2	D- / 1.0	0	18
TC	Merrill Lynch Global Technology C	MCGTX	E-	(800) 543-6217	6.96	E /0.5	4.35 /12	5.96 / 7	-8.09 / 0	D / 1.7	0	N/A
TC	Merrill Lynch Global Technology B	MBGTX	E-	(800) 543-6217	6.98	E /0.5	4.49 /13	6.00 / 7	-8.03 / 0	D / 1.8	0	N/A
TC	Federated Technology A	FCTAX	E-	(800) 341-7400	5.10	E+ /0.6	--	8.34 /17	-6.38 / 1	D+ / 2.4	1	6
HL	Franklin Biotechnology Discovery A	FBDIX	E-	(800) 342-5236	52.86	E+ /0.6	4.67 /14	8.21 /16	-3.46 / 4	D / 2.2	24	9
TC	TA IDEX Great Companies Tech C	IGTLX	E-	(888) 233-4339	3.58	E+ /0.6	3.48 / 9	6.46 / 8	--	C / 4.3	4	6
HL	Morgan Stanley Health Sci Tr B	HCRBX	E-	(800) 869-6397	15.37	E+ /0.6	8.34 /35	7.23 /11	2.18 /29	C- / 3.2	28	1
TC	Select Computers Portfolio	FDCPX	E-	(800) 544-8888	34.12	E+ /0.6	1.22 / 3	6.65 / 9	-4.63 / 3	D / 1.7	0	N/A
TC	Rydex Series-Electronics Inv	RYSIX	E-	(800) 820-0888	11.97	E+ /0.7	11.87 /59	5.27 / 5	-8.68 / 0	E- / 0.0	0	N/A
TC	Oppenheimer Emerging Tech Y	OETYX	E-	(800) 525-7048	3.00	E+ /0.7	10.70 /52	6.33 / 8	-10.85 / 0	E / 0.5	0	N/A
HL	Rydex Series-Biotechnology Inv	RYOIX	E-	(800) 820-0888	21.16	E+ /0.7	11.37 /56	6.64 / 9	-4.72 / 3	D+ / 2.5	16	N/A
GR	Boyle Marathon Fund	BFUNX	E-	(888) 882-6953	7.47	E+ /0.7	-0.80 / 1	6.52 / 8	-4.33 / 3	C- / 4.2	2	8
GR	Legg Mason Growth Tr Prim	LMGTX	E-	(800) 822-5544	27.98	E+ /0.7	0.97 / 2	6.81 /10	7.14 /67	C- / 4.2	2	N/A
TC	Federated Technology C	FCTYX	E-	(800) 341-7400	4.85	E+ /0.7	-0.61 / 1	7.63 /13	-7.08 / 1	D / 2.2	1	6
TC	● Thrivent Technology Stock B	BBTSX	E-	(800) 847-4836	3.35	E+ /0.7	5.02 /15	7.59 /13	-7.32 / 1	D+ / 2.6	1	6
HL	Morgan Stanley Health Sci Tr A	HCRAX	E-	(800) 869-6397	16.88	E+ /0.7	9.16 /41	8.04 /15	2.96 /36	C- / 3.9	34	1
TC	Rydex Series-Technology C	RYCHX	E-	(800) 820-0888	10.66	E+ /0.7	3.89 /10	6.46 / 8	-5.56 / 2	D / 1.8	1	N/A
SC	Rockland Small Cap Growth	RKGRX	E-	(800) 497-3933	16.79	E+ /0.7	10.17 /48	6.45 / 8	-1.11 /11	D / 2.1	0	10
TC	Thrivent Technology Stock A	AATSX	E-	(800) 847-4836	3.50	E+ /0.7	5.11 /16	8.11 /16	-6.70 / 1	D+ / 2.6	1	6
GR	ICON Leisure & Consumer Staple	ICLEX	E-	(800) 764-0442	8.91	E+ /0.7	-8.00 / 0	7.17 /11	6.05 /61	D- / 1.4	13	N/A
AG	Jundt Opportunity Fund B	JOPBX	E-	(800) 370-0612	12.32	E+ /0.8	5.12 /16	7.31 /12	-1.28 /11	C- / 4.2	36	10
GR	AXA Enterprise Equity Fund B	ENEBX	E-	(800) 432-4320	6.00	E+ /0.8	1.35 / 3	8.17 /16	0.84 /19	C- / 4.2	6	N/A
HL	Merrill Lynch Healthcare B	MBHCX	E-	(800) 543-6217	4.75	E+ /0.8	6.15 /21	7.20 /11	2.27 /30	D+ / 2.8	32	14
GR	Phoenix Earnings Driven Growth B	EDBEX	E-	(800) 243-4361	16.47	E+ /0.8	5.58 /18	6.59 / 9	-4.01 / 4	C- / 3.9	4	N/A
HL	Fidelity Adv Biotechnology A	FBTAX	E-	(800) 522-7297	6.93	E+ /0.8	11.24 /55	8.60 /18	-2.41 / 7	D+ / 2.9	39	1
TC	Merrill Lynch Global Technology R	MRGTX	E-	(800) 543-6217	7.20	E+ /0.8	5.11 /16	6.86 /10	--	D / 1.9	1	N/A
TC	AllianceBernstein Glb Tech B	ATEBX	E-	(800) 221-5672	51.11	E+ /0.8	3.67 / 9	7.86 /14	-6.63 / 1	D / 2.0	2	3
SC	Allegiant Small Cap Growth B	ASGRX	E-	(800) 622-3863	8.94	E+ /0.8	8.63 /38	6.84 /10	-5.50 / 2	D- / 1.5	0	N/A

● Denotes fund is closed to new investors

Fund Type	Fund Name	Ticker Symbol	Overall Weiss Investment Rating	Phone	Net Asset Value As of 6/30/06	Perform-ance Rating/Pts	1Yr / Pct	3Yr / Pct	5Yr / Pct	Risk Rating/Pts	Mgr. Quality Pct	Mgr. Tenure (Years)
TC	Dreyfus Premier Tech Growth R	DGVRX	E-	(800) 782-6620	23.74	E+ /0.8	7.37 /28	7.35 /12	-3.36 / 5	D+ / 2.6	2	7
GR	Constellation HLAM Lg Cp Qty Gr	HLGRX	E-	(800) 444-1854	15.66	E+ /0.9	7.11 /27	6.16 / 7	-1.50 /10	D- / 1.3	13	N/A
SC	Allegiant Small Cap Growth A	ASMGX	E-	(800) 622-3863	9.48	E+ /0.9	9.34 /42	7.55 /13	-4.86 / 3	D- / 1.5	0	N/A
GR	● Thrivent Large Cap Growth B	BBAGX	E-	(800) 847-4836	4.69	E+ /0.9	4.45 /13	7.57 /13	-2.46 / 7	E- / 0.0	14	4
HL	Merrill Lynch Healthcare A	MDHCX	E-	(800) 543-6217	6.45	E+ /0.9	6.92 /26	8.03 /15	3.06 /37	C- / 3.0	37	12
HL	J Hancock Health Sciences B	JHRBX	E-	(800) 257-3336	39.08	E+ /0.9	2.46 / 5	8.30 /17	2.83 /35	C- / 3.9	40	N/A
FO	Amidex 35 Israel Fund A	AMDAX	E-	(888) 876-3566	8.32	E+ /0.9	10.49 /50	9.43 /24	-2.29 / 7	C- / 4.0	1	N/A
HL	Fidelity Adv Biotechnology T	FBTTX	E-	(800) 522-7297	6.83	E+ /0.9	11.06 /54	8.28 /17	-2.67 / 6	D+ / 2.9	36	1
TC	Northern Trust Technology	NTCHX	E-	(800) 595-9111	11.10	E+ /0.9	1.83 / 4	7.08 /11	-4.95 / 3	D+ / 2.6	1	N/A
HL	Morgan Stanley Health Sci Tr C	HCRCX	E-	(800) 869-6397	15.40	E+ /0.9	8.40 /36	7.27 /11	2.21 /29	C- / 3.2	28	1
GR	Phoenix Earnings Driven Growth A	EDGEX	E-	(800) 243-4361	17.62	E+ /0.9	6.40 /23	7.38 /12	-3.29 / 5	C- / 4.0	6	N/A
TC	Fifth Third Technology B	FTCBX	E-	(800) 282-5706	10.06	E+ /0.9	13.29 /65	8.67 /19	--	D- / 1.0	0	6
TC	Oak Assoc-Black Oak Emerging	BOGSX	E-	(888) 462-5386	2.16	E+ /0.9	--	7.06 /11	-18.88 / 0	E- / 0.0	0	6
TC	E*TRADE Technology Index Fund	ETTIX	E-	(800) 786-2575	5.09	E+ /0.9	3.67 / 9	7.35 /12	-5.31 / 2	C- / 3.2	1	7
GR	AllianceBernstein Growth Fund B	AGBBX	E-	(800) 221-5672	23.30	D- /1.0	-0.55 / 1	9.62 /25	-0.62 /13	C- / 3.9	9	5
TC	Merrill Lynch Global Technology I	MAGTX	E-	(800) 543-6217	7.58	D- /1.0	5.57 /18	7.22 /11	-7.02 / 1	D / 1.7	1	N/A
TC	Saratoga Adv Tr-Technology &	STPIX	E-	(800) 807-3863	7.65	D- /1.0	8.82 /39	8.44 /17	--	D- / 1.0	1	N/A
SC	Legg Mason Prt Sm Cp Core B	SBDBX	E-	(866) 890-4247	13.53	D- /1.0	-6.27 / 0	8.54 /18	2.70 /34	C- / 3.8	2	N/A
TC	Rydex Series-Technology Adv	RYTAX	E-	(800) 820-0888	10.79	D- /1.0	4.44 /12	6.93 /10	-5.02 / 2	D / 1.8	1	N/A
GR	● Thrivent Large Cap Stock B	BBLGX	E-	(800) 847-4836	24.62	D- /1.0	5.81 /19	7.20 /11	-0.64 /13	D- / 1.5	25	11
EN	Select Paper/Forest	FSPFX	E-	(800) 544-8888	29.48	D- /1.0	10.62 /51	6.65 / 9	2.97 /37	C- / 3.0	10	N/A
GR	Reynolds Opportunity Fund	ROPPX	E-	(800) 773-9665	17.04	D- /1.0	5.39 /17	6.75 / 9	-4.31 / 3	E- / 0.0	0	14
TC	AIM Technology B	ITYBX	E-	(800) 347-4246	25.19	D- /1.0	7.51 /29	7.73 /13	--	C- / 3.0	1	N/A
TC	AllianceBernstein Glb Tech A	ALTFX	E-	(800) 221-5672	57.02	D- /1.0	4.49 /13	8.70 /19	-5.91 / 2	D / 2.1	3	3
HL	Fidelity Adv Biotechnology C	FBTCX	E-	(800) 522-7297	6.64	D- /1.1	10.48 /50	7.74 /14	-3.17 / 5	D+ / 2.8	32	1
HL	Fidelity Adv Biotechnology B	FBTBX	E-	(800) 522-7297	6.64	D- /1.1	10.48 /50	7.74 /14	-3.17 / 5	D+ / 2.9	33	1
MC	Managers Essex Growth	MEAGX	E-	(800) 835-3879	9.86	D- /1.1	10.04 /47	6.34 / 8	-2.41 / 7	C- / 3.6	0	N/A
HL	Merrill Lynch Healthcare C	MCHCX	E-	(800) 543-6217	4.74	D- /1.1	6.22 /22	7.15 /11	2.24 /30	D+ / 2.7	30	12
TC	Fifth Third Technology A	FTTAX	E-	(800) 282-5706	10.51	D- /1.2	14.12 /69	9.48 /24	-1.54 /10	D- / 1.0	0	6
TC	AllianceBernstein Glb Tech C	ATECX	E-	(800) 221-5672	51.19	D- /1.2	3.73 /10	7.92 /15	-6.60 / 1	D / 2.0	3	3
SC	Touchstone Small Cap Gr B	TESBX	E-	(800) 638-8194	15.57	D- /1.2	0.84 / 2	9.69 /25	--	D+ / 2.8	1	4
GR	Thrivent Large Cap Growth A	AAAGX	E-	(800) 847-4836	4.99	D- /1.2	5.59 /18	8.66 /19	-1.57 /10	E- / 0.0	20	4
TC	Rydex Series-Technology Inv	RYTIX	E-	(800) 820-0888	11.17	D- /1.2	4.97 /15	7.40 /12	-4.72 / 3	D / 1.8	1	N/A
AG	TCW Aggressive Gr Eq N	TGANX	E-	(800) 386-3829	12.79	D- /1.2	9.50 /43	8.05 /15	-2.64 / 6	C- / 3.4	1	N/A
SC	Royce Technology Value Svc	RYTVX	E-	(800) 221-4268	6.32	D- /1.2	10.77 /52	8.16 /16	--	E / 0.5	0	5
TC	Munder Internet Fund B	MNNBX	E-	(800) 438-5789	18.17	D- /1.3	8.35 /36	8.98 /21	-5.49 / 2	D- / 1.5	2	N/A
MC	● Wasatch Ultra Growth	WAMCX	E-	(800) 551-1700	24.09	D- /1.3	3.87 /10	8.02 /15	5.52 /58	D- / 1.2	0	14
SC	Allegiant Small Cap Growth C	ASGCX	E-	(800) 622-3863	8.96	D- /1.3	8.74 /38	6.83 /10	-5.49 / 2	D- / 1.5	0	N/A
TC	Fidelity Adv Technology A	FADTX	E-	(800) 522-7297	16.63	D- /1.3	9.12 /41	9.56 /24	-2.60 / 6	D- / 1.2	2	1
GR	Thrivent Large Cap Stock A	AALGX	E-	(800) 847-4836	26.61	D- /1.3	6.77 /25	8.25 /16	0.39 /17	D / 1.9	32	11
TC	AIM Technology A	ITYAX	E-	(800) 347-4246	26.03	D- /1.3	8.37 /36	8.48 /18	--	C- / 3.1	2	N/A
TC	Fidelity Adv Electronics A	FELAX	E-	(800) 522-7297	7.90	D- /1.3	5.90 /20	9.48 /24	-4.62 / 3	E / 0.5	0	2
TC	Fifth Third Technology Adv	FTTVX	E-	(800) 282-5706	10.37	D- /1.3	13.71 /67	9.17 /22	--	D- / 1.0	0	5
TC	Munder Internet Fund A	MNNAX	E-	(800) 438-5789	19.29	D- /1.3	9.11 /41	9.78 /26	-4.79 / 3	D / 1.6	3	N/A

Data as of June 30, 2006

Section V

Performance:
100 Best and Worst
Stock Mutual Funds

A compilation of those

Equity Mutual Funds

receiving the highest and lowest Performance Ratings.

Funds are listed in order by Performance Rating.

Section V Contents

This section contains a summary analysis of each of the top 100 and bottom 100 equity mutual funds as determined by their Weiss Performance Rating. Since the Performance Rating does not take into consideration the amount of risk a fund poses, the selection of funds presented here is based solely on each fund's financial performance over the past three years.

You can use this section to identify those funds that have historically given shareholders the highest returns on their investments. A word of caution though: past performance is not necessarily indicative of future results. While these funds have provided the highest returns, some of them may be currently overvalued and due for a correction.

1. Fund Type   The mutual fund's peer category based on an analysis of its investment portfolio.

AG	Aggressive Growth	HL	Health
AA	Asset Allocation	IN	Income
BA	Balanced	IX	Index
CV	Convertible	MC	Mid Cap
EM	Emerging Market	OT	Other
EN	Energy/Natural Resources	PM	Precious Metals
FS	Financial Services	RE	Real Estate
FO	Foreign	SC	Small Cap
GL	Global	TC	Technology
GR	Growth	UT	Utilities
GI	Growth and Income		

A blank fund type means that the mutual fund has not yet been categorized.

2. Fund Name   The name of the mutual fund as stated in its prospectus, which can sometimes differ slightly from the name that the company uses for advertising. If you cannot find the particular mutual fund you are interested in, or if you have any doubts regarding the precise name, verify the information with your broker or on your account statement. Also, use the fund's ticker symbol for confirmation. (See column 3.)

3. Ticker Symbol   The unique alphabetic symbol used for identifying and trading a specific mutual fund. No two funds can have the same ticker symbol, and the ticker symbol for mutual funds always ends with an "X".

A handful of funds currently show no associated ticker symbol. This means that the fund is either small or new since the NASD only assigns a ticker symbol to funds with at least $25 million in assets or 1,000 shareholders.

4.	**Overall Weiss Investment Rating**	Our overall rating is measured on a scale from A to E based on each fund's risk-adjusted performance. Please see page 10 for specific descriptions of each letter grade. Also, refer to page 7 for information on how our ratings are derived. Most important, when using this rating, please be sure to consider the warnings beginning on page 11 regarding the ratings' limitations and the underlying assumptions.
5.	**Phone**	The telephone number of the company managing the fund. Call this number to receive a prospectus or other information about the fund.
6.	**Net Asset Value (NAV)**	The fund's share price as of the date indicated. A fund's NAV is computed by dividing the value of the fund's asset holdings, less accrued fees and expenses, by the number of its shares outstanding.
7.	**Performance Rating/Points**	A letter grade rating based solely on the mutual fund's financial performance over the trailing three years, without any consideration for the amount of risk the fund poses. Like the overall Weiss Investment Rating, the Performance Rating is measured on a scale from A to E for ease of interpretation. The points score indicates where the Performance Rating falls on a scale of 0 to 10.
8.	**1-Year Total Return**	The total return the fund has provided investors over the preceeding twelve months. This total return figure is computed based on the fund's dividend distributions and share price appreciation/depreciation during the period, net of the expenses and fees it imposes on its shareholders. Although the total return figure does not reflect an adjustment for any loads the fund may carry, such adjustments have been made in deriving the Weiss Investment Ratings.
9.	**1-Year Total Return Percentile**	The fund's percentile rank based on its one-year performance compared to that of all other equity funds in existence for at least one year. A score of 99 is the best possible, indicating that the fund outperformed 99% of the other mutual funds. Zero is the worst possible percentile score.
10.	**3-Year Total Return**	The total annual return the fund has provided investors over the preceeding three years.
11.	**3-Year Total Return Percentile**	The fund's percentile rank based on its three-year performance compared to that of all other equity funds in existence for at least three years. A score of 99 is the best possible, indicating that the fund outperformed 99% of the other mutual funds. Zero is the worst possible percentile score.
12.	**5-Year Total Return**	The total annual return the fund has provided investors over the preceeding five years.

13.	**5-Year Total Return Percentile**	The fund's percentile rank based on its five-year performance compared to that of all other equity funds in existence for at least five years. A score of 99 is the best possible, indicating that the fund outperformed 99% of the other mutual funds. Zero is the worst possible percentile score.
14.	**Risk Rating/Points**	A letter grade rating based solely on the mutual fund's risk as determined by its monthly performance volatility over the trailing three years. The risk rating does not take into consideration the overall financial performance the fund has achieved or the total return it has provided to its shareholders. Like the overall Weiss Investment Rating, the Risk Rating is measured on a scale from A to E for ease of interpretation. The points score indicates where the Risk Rating falls on a scale of 0 to 10.
15.	**Manager Quality Percentile**	The manager quality percentile is based on a ranking of the fund's alpha, a statistical measure representing the difference between a fund's actual returns and its expected performance given its level of risk. Fund managers who have been able to exceed the fund's statistically expected performance receive a high percentile rank with 99 representing the highest possible score. At the other end of the spectrum, fund managers who have actually detracted from the fund's expected performance receive a low percentile rank with 0 representing the lowest possible score.
16.	**Manager Tenure**	The number of years the current manager has been managing the fund. Since fund managers who deliver substandard returns are usually replaced, a long tenure is usually a good sign that shareholders are satisfied that the fund is achieving its stated objectives.

						PERFORMANCE				RISK	FUND MGR	
99 Pct = Best 0 Pct = Worst					Net Asset Value As of 6/30/06	Perform-ance Rating/Pts	Annualized Total Return Through 6/30/06			Risk Rating/Pts	Mgr. Quality Pct	Mgr. Tenure (Years)
Fund Type	Fund Name	Ticker Symbol	Overall Weiss Investment Rating	Phone			1Yr / Pct	3Yr / Pct	5Yr / Pct			
FO	● AIM European Small Company A	ESMAX	A+	(800) 347-4246	27.07	A+ /9.9	49.80 /99	49.86 /99	32.52 /99	C+ / 6.6	99	6
FO	● AIM European Small Company C	ESMCX	A+	(800) 347-4246	26.16	A+ /9.9	48.74 /99	48.83 /99	31.59 /99	C+ / 6.5	99	6
FO	● AIM European Small Company B	ESMBX	A+	(800) 347-4246	26.15	A+ /9.9	48.69 /99	48.76 /99	31.58 /99	C+ / 6.5	99	6
EN	● Ivy Fund-Global Nat Resource Adv	IGNVX	A+	(800) 777-6472	31.12	A+ /9.9	46.95 /99	39.19 /99	24.29 /98	C+ / 6.2	99	8
EM	● AIM International Small Co C	IEGCX	A+	(800) 347-4246	23.71	A+ /9.9	45.88 /98	43.45 /99	29.33 /99	C+ / 6.2	99	6
EM	● AIM International Small Co A	IEGAX	A+	(800) 347-4246	24.48	A+ /9.9	47.00 /99	44.51 /99	30.21 /99	C+ / 6.2	99	6
EM	● AIM International Small Co B	IEGBX	A+	(800) 347-4246	23.72	A+ /9.9	45.85 /99	43.47 /99	29.30 /99	C+ / 6.2	99	6
EN	Vanguard Energy Inv	VGENX	A+	(800) 662-7447	65.20	A+ /9.9	37.25 /97	39.76 /99	25.08 /98	C+ / 6.2	98	N/A
EN	Vanguard Energy Adm	VGELX	A+	(800) 662-7447	122.47	A+ /9.9	37.33 /97	39.83 /99	--	C+ / 6.2	98	N/A
EN	RS Global Natural Resources Fund	RSNRX	A-	(800) 766-3863	36.09	A+ /9.9	42.46 /98	37.80 /99	26.74 /99	C+ / 5.7	97	11
EN	● AIM Energy Inv	FSTEX	A-	(800) 347-4246	45.48	A+ /9.9	38.47 /98	38.02 /99	20.95 /97	C+ / 5.7	89	9
EN	Ivy Fund-Global Nat Resource A	IGNAX	A	(800) 777-6472	31.32	A+ /9.9	46.52 /99	39.05 /99	24.20 /98	C+ / 5.7	99	9
EN	Ivy Fund-Global Nat Resource B	IGNBX	A-	(800) 777-6472	29.64	A+ /9.9	45.42 /98	37.92 /99	23.17 /98	C+ / 5.7	99	9
EN	Ivy Fund-Global Nat Resource C	IGNCX	A-	(800) 777-6472	29.10	A+ /9.9	45.48 /98	38.01 /99	23.19 /98	C+ / 5.7	99	9
EN	Select Energy	FSENX	B+	(800) 544-8888	51.82	A+ /9.9	39.92 /98	37.96 /99	19.05 /95	C / 5.2	91	2
SC	Pacific Advisors Small Cap Val A	PASMX	B+	(800) 282-6693	31.05	A+ /9.9	43.78 /98	38.80 /99	16.51 /94	C / 4.9	99	13
FO	Franklin Intl Smaller Co Grw Adv	FKSCX	B+	(800) 321-8563	26.43	A+ /9.9	53.40 /99	40.64 /99	--	C / 4.9	99	4
EM	● AIM International Small Co Inst	IEGIX	B+	(800) 347-4246	24.52	A+ /9.9	47.30 /99	44.61 /99	30.26 /99	C / 4.9	99	N/A
EN	Select Natural Resources	FNARX	B+	(800) 544-8888	28.04	A+ /9.9	46.83 /99	36.47 /98	18.21 /95	C / 4.9	90	N/A
FO	FTI European Smaller Companies	FESCX	B+	(888) 343-8242	14.65	A+ /9.9	45.14 /98	34.94 /98	13.74 /90	C / 4.8	75	5
EN	Fidelity Adv Natural Resources I	FANIX	B+	(800) 522-7297	48.14	A+ /9.9	46.62 /99	36.85 /98	18.75 /95	C / 4.8	90	N/A
EN	Fidelity Adv Natural Resources C	FNRCX	B+	(800) 522-7297	46.00	A+ /9.9	45.09 /98	35.39 /98	17.49 /94	C / 4.8	84	N/A
EN	Fidelity Adv Natural Resources T	FAGNX	B+	(800) 522-7297	47.86	A+ /9.9	45.80 /98	36.07 /98	18.08 /95	C / 4.8	87	N/A
EN	JennDry Jennison Nat Resources	PNRCX	B	(800) 257-3893	42.66	A+ /9.9	53.54 /99	41.66 /99	27.71 /99	C / 4.7	98	3
EN	JennDry Jennison Nat Resources Z	PNRZX	B	(800) 257-3893	49.14	A+ /9.9	55.09 /99	43.11 /99	29.00 /99	C / 4.7	99	3
EN	Van Eck Global Hard Assets A	GHAAX	B	(800) 221-2220	38.31	A+ /9.9	49.36 /99	41.65 /99	25.01 /98	C / 4.7	99	N/A
EN	Van Eck Global Hard Assets C	GHACX	B	(800) 221-2220	36.66	A+ /9.9	48.60 /99	40.71 /99	24.05 /98	C / 4.7	99	N/A
EN	JennDry Jennison Nat Resources	PGNAX	B	(800) 257-3893	48.25	A+ /9.9	54.75 /99	42.75 /99	28.68 /99	C / 4.7	98	3
EN	JennDry Jennison Nat Resources	PRGNX	B	(800) 257-3893	42.67	A+ /9.9	53.57 /99	41.67 /99	27.72 /99	C / 4.7	98	3
FO	Oppenheimer Intl Small Comp A	OSMAX	B	(800) 525-7048	22.41	A+ /9.9	35.42 /97	41.31 /99	24.95 /98	C / 4.4	96	6
FO	Oppenheimer Intl Small Comp N	OSMNX	B	(800) 525-7048	21.84	A+ /9.9	34.93 /97	40.77 /99	24.53 /98	C / 4.4	95	6
FO	Oppenheimer Intl Small Comp B	OSMBX	B	(800) 525-7048	21.52	A+ /9.9	34.24 /96	40.01 /99	23.91 /98	C / 4.3	94	6
FO	Oppenheimer Intl Small Comp C	OSMCX	B	(800) 525-7048	21.52	A+ /9.9	34.32 /96	40.13 /99	23.97 /98	C / 4.3	94	6
EM	DFA Emerging Markets Value	DFEVX	B	(800) 984-9472	25.82	A+ /9.9	37.52 /97	41.16 /99	28.82 /99	C- / 4.2	70	N/A
EM	GMO Emerging Markets Fund IV	GMEFX	B-		21.80	A+ /9.9	37.75 /97	39.36 /99	26.52 /99	C- / 4.1	43	N/A
EM	GMO Emerging Markets Fund VI	GEMMX	B-		21.81	A+ /9.9	37.82 /97	39.46 /99	--	C- / 4.0	43	N/A
EM	Quant Emg-Markets Ord	QFFOX	B-	(800) 326-2151	18.63	A+ /9.9	35.26 /97	39.44 /99	24.63 /98	C- / 4.0	15	4
EM	Quant Emg-Markets Inst	QEMAX	B-	(800) 326-2151	18.88	A+ /9.9	35.63 /97	40.07 /99	25.20 /98	C- / 4.0	19	4
EM	● Adv Inn Cir Acadian Emg Mkt I	AEMGX	B-	(866) 777-7818	28.61	A+ /9.9	43.02 /98	42.26 /99	30.72 /99	C- / 3.9	43	N/A
EN	● BlackRock-Global Resources A	SSGRX	B-	(888) 825-2257	75.84	A+ /9.9	50.16 /99	52.19 /99	33.45 /99	C- / 3.8	99	1
EM	Metzler/Payden European Emrg	MPYMX	C+	(888) 409-8007	27.36	A+ /9.9	50.99 /99	45.63 /99	--	C- / 3.6	86	N/A
EN	● BlackRock-Global Resources C	SSGDX	B-	(888) 825-2257	68.07	A+ /9.9	49.09 /99	51.16 /99	32.57 /99	C- / 3.6	99	1
EN	● BlackRock-Global Resources B	SSGPX	B-	(888) 825-2257	68.13	A+ /9.9	49.06 /99	51.19 /99	32.57 /99	C- / 3.6	99	1
SC	Pacific Advisors Small Cap Val C	PGSCX	C+	(800) 282-6693	28.02	A+ /9.9	42.45 /98	38.46 /99	15.27 /92	C- / 3.5	99	13
EM	Fidelity Latin American Fund	FLATX	C+	(800) 544-8888	36.25	A+ /9.9	56.63 /99	50.37 /99	24.99 /98	C- / 3.3	83	N/A
EN	ICON Energy	ICENX	C+	(800) 764-0442	36.31	A+ /9.9	38.56 /98	40.72 /99	23.86 /98	C- / 3.3	89	N/A
FO	Fidelity Adv Latin America A	FLTAX	C+	(800) 522-7297	33.45	A+ /9.9	56.82 /99	49.18 /99	23.94 /98	C- / 3.3	94	1
FO	Fidelity Adv Latin America B	FLTBX	C+	(800) 522-7297	32.66	A+ /9.9	55.53 /99	48.10 /99	23.02 /98	C- / 3.3	91	1
FO	Fidelity Adv Latin America C	FLACX	C+	(800) 522-7297	32.55	A+ /9.9	55.72 /99	48.10 /99	23.03 /98	C- / 3.3	91	1
FO	Fidelity Adv Latin America I	FLNIX	C+	(800) 522-7297	34.05	A+ /9.9	57.17 /99	49.53 /99	24.28 /98	C- / 3.3	94	1
FO	Fidelity Adv Latin America T	FLTTX	C+	(800) 522-7297	33.22	A+ /9.9	56.36 /99	48.81 /99	23.63 /98	C- / 3.3	93	1
EM	T. Rowe Price Emer Europe & Mdtr	TREMX	C+	(800) 638-5660	25.58	A+ /9.9	31.62 /95	41.50 /99	31.16 /99	C- / 3.2	44	6

● Denotes fund is closed to new investors

Fund Type	Fund Name	Ticker Symbol	Overall Weiss Investment Rating	Phone	Net Asset Value As of 6/30/06	Performance Rating/Pts	Annualized Total Return Through 6/30/06			Risk Rating/Pts	Mgr. Quality Pct	Mgr. Tenure (Years)
	99 Pct = Best 0 Pct = Worst						1Yr / Pct	3Yr / Pct	5Yr / Pct			
FO	T. Rowe Price Latin America	PRLAX	C+	(800) 638-5660	29.56	A+ /9.9	60.67 /99	50.63 /99	24.93 /98	C- / 3.1	96	10
EN	US Global Inv Global Resources	PSPFX	C+	(800) 873-8637	17.22	A+ /9.9	48.91 /99	58.13 /99	38.92 /99	C- / 3.1	99	14
FO	Merrill Lynch Latin America I	MALTX	C+	(800) 543-6217	42.19	A+ /9.9	55.80 /99	51.91 /99	25.37 /99	C- / 3.0	96	N/A
EM	Driehaus Emerging Markets	DREGX	C+	(800) 560-6111	32.21	A+ /9.9	55.77 /99	38.46 /99	24.86 /98	C- / 3.0	41	9
FO	Merrill Lynch Latin America A	MDLTX	C+	(800) 543-6217	41.82	A+ /9.9	55.40 /99	51.54 /99	25.05 /99	C- / 3.0	96	N/A
FO	Merrill Lynch Latin America C	MCLTX	C+	(800) 543-6217	39.63	A+ /9.9	54.28 /99	50.38 /99	24.07 /98	D+ / 2.9	94	N/A
EM	Sanford Bernstein Emerg Markets	SNEMX	C+		37.31	A+ /9.9	32.19 /96	40.32 /99	27.00 /99	D+ / 2.9	45	N/A
FO	Merrill Lynch Latin America B	MBLTX	C+	(800) 543-6217	40.14	A+ /9.9	54.23 /99	50.38 /99	24.07 /98	D+ / 2.9	94	N/A
EN	● BlackRock-Global Resources Inst	SGLSX	C+	(888) 825-2257	80.06	A+ /9.9	50.63 /99	52.62 /99	33.96 /99	D+ / 2.7	99	1
AG	ProFunds-Oil & Gas UltraSector	ENPIX	C	(888) 776-3637	38.28	A+ /9.9	32.82 /96	44.73 /99	16.43 /93	D / 2.0	99	6
AG	ProFunds-Oil & Gas UltraSector	ENPSX	C	(888) 776-3637	36.08	A+ /9.9	31.49 /95	43.29 /99	15.34 /92	D / 2.0	99	6
PM	Van Eck Intl Investors Gold A	INIVX	C	(800) 221-2220	16.12	A+ /9.9	85.61 /99	35.18 /98	37.22 /99	D / 1.9	66	8
GR	Wells Fargo Avtg Value Fund Adm	CBTIX	C	(800) 222-8222	19.04	A+ /9.9	7.92 /32	44.80 /99	26.36 /99	D / 1.7	99	N/A
EM	ING Russia A	LETRX	C	(800) 992-0180	50.15	A+ /9.9	91.70 /99	41.58 /99	42.61 /99	D / 1.6	42	5
PM	USAA Gold Fund	USAGX	C-	(800) 382-8722	27.04	A+ /9.9	81.81 /99	37.42 /99	37.98 /99	D- / 1.5	93	N/A
PM	US Global Inv Gold Shares	USERX	C	(800) 873-8637	15.49	A+ /9.9	104.28 /99	45.05 /99	41.06 /99	D- / 1.5	98	N/A
PM	US Global Inv World Prec Minerals	UNWPX	C-	(800) 873-8637	28.86	A+ /9.9	96.21 /99	53.24 /99	46.82 /99	D- / 1.5	99	8
FO	DWS Latin America Eq Fund AARP	SLAMX	C-	(800) 621-1048	51.62	A+ /9.9	52.61 /99	43.70 /99	22.00 /98	D- / 1.4	65	6
FO	DWS Latin America Eq Fund C	SLAPX	C-	(800) 621-1048	50.85	A+ /9.9	51.13 /99	42.29 /99	20.69 /97	D- / 1.4	52	5
FO	DWS Latin America Eq Fund B	SLAOX	C-	(800) 621-1048	50.89	A+ /9.9	51.00 /99	42.21 /99	20.70 /97	D- / 1.4	52	5
FO	DWS Latin America Eq Fund A	SLANX	C-	(800) 621-1048	51.35	A+ /9.9	52.33 /99	43.41 /99	21.67 /97	D- / 1.4	63	5
FO	● DWS Latin America Eq Fund S	SLAFX	C-	(800) 621-1048	51.48	A+ /9.9	52.65 /99	43.72 /99	21.97 /98	D- / 1.4	66	10
FO	Eaton Vance Greater India A	ETGIX	C-	(800) 225-6265	20.55	A+ /9.9	39.32 /98	47.36 /99	28.71 /99	D- / 1.2	80	1
FO	Eaton Vance Greater India B	EMGIX	C-	(800) 225-6265	19.27	A+ /9.9	38.64 /98	47.04 /99	28.24 /99	D- / 1.2	78	1
PM	● Vanguard Prec. Metals & Mining Fd	VGPMX	C-	(800) 662-7447	29.16	A+ /9.9	72.86 /99	44.17 /99	35.20 /99	D- / 1.2	99	10
PM	Midas Fund	MIDSX	C-	(800) 400-6432	4.05	A+ /9.9	104.55 /99	39.25 /99	35.70 /99	D- / 1.1	90	N/A
PM	Oppenheimer Gold/Spec Min B	OGMBX	C-	(800) 525-7048	28.13	A+ /9.9	66.67 /99	35.41 /98	29.28 /99	E+ / 0.7	86	9
PM	Oppenheimer Gold/Spec Min C	OGMCX	C-	(800) 525-7048	28.10	A+ /9.9	66.79 /99	35.47 /98	29.33 /99	E+ / 0.7	87	9
PM	Oppenheimer Gold/Spec Min A	OPGSX	C-	(800) 525-7048	29.15	A+ /9.9	68.00 /99	36.49 /98	30.30 /99	E+ / 0.7	90	9
EM	US Global Accolade East	EUROX	C-	(800) 873-8637	41.17	A+ /9.9	42.73 /98	44.58 /99	38.97 /99	E+ / 0.7	14	6
PM	Oppenheimer Gold/Spec Min N	OGMNX	C-	(800) 525-7048	28.68	A+ /9.9	67.62 /99	36.05 /98	29.90 /99	E+ / 0.7	89	9
PM	Evergreen Precious Metals B	EKWBX	D+	(800) 343-2898	53.26	A+ /9.9	74.33 /99	36.66 /98	36.06 /99	E- / 0.2	83	N/A
PM	Evergreen Precious Metals A	EKWAX	D+	(800) 343-2898	55.56	A+ /9.9	75.57 /99	37.63 /99	37.06 /99	E- / 0.2	87	N/A
PM	Evergreen Precious Metals C	EKWCX	D+	(800) 343-2898	52.96	A+ /9.9	74.33 /99	36.68 /98	36.05 /99	E- / 0.2	83	N/A
PM	Evergreen Precious Metals I	EKWYX	D+	(800) 343-2898	55.24	A+ /9.9	76.08 /99	38.03 /99	37.41 /99	E- / 0.2	89	N/A
FO	ProFunds-Ultra Japan Inv	UJPIX	D+	(888) 776-3637	59.48	A+ /9.9	77.87 /99	37.70 /99	0.91 /20	E- / 0.2	8	N/A
PM	GAMCO Gold A	GLDAX	D+	(800) 422-3554	25.94	A+ /9.9	76.43 /99	30.54 /96	35.10 /99	E- / 0.0	35	12
PM	GAMCO Gold B	GLDBX	D+	(800) 422-3554	25.67	A+ /9.9	75.03 /99	29.52 /95	34.38 /99	E- / 0.0	29	12
PM	GAMCO Gold C	GLDCX	D+	(800) 422-3554	25.66	A+ /9.9	75.05 /99	29.56 /95	34.40 /99	E- / 0.0	29	12
PM	GAMCO Gold AAA	GOLDX	D+	(800) 422-3554	25.96	A+ /9.9	76.37 /99	30.54 /96	35.10 /99	E- / 0.0	35	12
PM	Franklin Gold & Prec Metals C	FRGOX	D+	(800) 342-5236	30.13	A+ /9.9	70.95 /99	32.29 /97	26.51 /99	E- / 0.0	66	9
PM	Franklin Gold & Prec Metals A	FKRCX	D+	(800) 342-5236	30.88	A+ /9.9	72.23 /99	33.32 /97	27.46 /99	E- / 0.0	73	9
PM	Franklin Gold & Prec Metals Adv	FGADX	D+	(800) 321-8563	31.71	A+ /9.9	72.57 /99	33.63 /97	27.75 /99	E- / 0.0	75	9
PM	DWS Gold & Prec Metals Fund	SGLDX	D+	(800) 621-1048	23.36	A+ /9.9	57.98 /99	35.10 /98	34.70 /99	E- / 0.0	71	5
PM	Tocqueville Gold Fund	TGLDX	D+	(800) 697-3863	50.21	A+ /9.9	63.28 /99	31.54 /96	35.70 /99	E- / 0.0	71	8
PM	● DWS Gold & Prec Metals Fund S	SCGDX	D+	(800) 621-1048	23.33	A+ /9.9	58.04 /99	35.10 /98	34.68 /99	E- / 0.0	71	5
PM	● Franklin Gold & Prec Metals B	FAGPX	D+	(800) 342-5236	29.85	A+ /9.9	70.90 /99	32.30 /97	26.49 /99	E- / 0.0	66	9
PM	DWS Gold & Prec Metals Fund C	SGDCX	D+	(800) 621-1048	23.03	A+ /9.9	56.47 /99	33.80 /97	33.38 /99	E- / 0.0	61	5

● Denotes fund is closed to new investors

Fund Type	Fund Name	Ticker Symbol	Overall Weiss Investment Rating	Phone	Net Asset Value As of 6/30/06	Perform-ance Rating/Pts	Annualized Total Return Through 6/30/06			Risk Rating/Pts	Mgr. Quality Pct	Mgr. Tenure (Years)
	99 Pct = Best 0 Pct = Worst						1Yr / Pct	3Yr / Pct	5Yr / Pct			
GR	Van Wagoner Growth	VWGOX	E-	(800) 228-2121	10.00	E- /0.0	1.21 / 3	-0.65 / 0	--	E- / 0.0	0	3
MC	Apex Mid-Cap Growth Fund	BMCGX	E-	(877) 593-8637	1.35	E- /0.0	2.27 / 5	-3.24 / 0	-1.82 / 9	E- / 0.0	0	13
TC	ProFunds-Ultra Short OTC Fund	USPSX	E-	(888) 776-3637	17.56	E- /0.0	-7.38 / 0	-20.49 / 0	-14.48 / 0	E- / 0.0	82	N/A
TC	ProFunds-Semicond UltraSector	SMPSX	E-	(888) 776-3637	16.23	E- /0.0	-10.13 / 0	0.48 / 0	-18.77 / 0	E- / 0.0	0	6
TC	ProFunds-Semicond UltraSector	SMPIX	E-	(888) 776-3637	17.25	E- /0.0	-9.21 / 0	1.47 / 0	-17.94 / 0	E- / 0.0	0	6
TC	ProFunds-Ultra Short OTC Fund	USPIX	E-	(888) 776-3637	16.97	E- /0.0	-6.47 / 0	-19.71 / 0	-13.70 / 0	E- / 0.0	89	N/A
AG	Rydex Dynamics-Inv Dyn OTC H	RYVNX	E-	(800) 820-0888	21.52	E- /0.0	-6.71 / 0	-19.78 / 0	-13.32 / 0	E- / 0.0	87	N/A
AG	Rydex Dynamics-Inv Dyn OTC C	RYCDX	E-	(800) 820-0888	20.75	E- /0.0	-7.37 / 0	-20.39 / 0	-13.90 / 0	E- / 0.0	82	N/A
EM	Van Wagoner Emerging Growth	VWEGX	E-	(800) 228-2121	4.53	E- /0.0	5.35 / 17	-4.62 / 0	-22.53 / 0	E- / 0.1	0	11
SC	Direxion Small Cp Bear 2.5X	DXRSX	E-	(800) 851-0511	15.86	E- /0.0	-24.02 / 0	-22.65 / 0	-14.36 / 0	E- / 0.2	11	7
SC	Van Wagoner Small-Cap Growth	VWMCX	E-	(800) 228-2121	9.63	E- /0.0	5.02 / 15	-2.06 / 0	-8.87 / 0	E / 0.3	0	11
SC	Frontier Fund-Equity	FEFPX	E-	(800) 231-2901	0.19	E- /0.0	-17.39 / 0	-15.06 / 0	-35.18 / 0	E / 0.5	0	4
AG	ProFunds-Ultra Bear Fund Inv	URPIX	E-	(888) 776-3637	17.35	E- /0.0	-8.74 / 0	-17.43 / 0	-8.43 / 0	E+ / 0.9	15	N/A
AG	ProFunds-Ultra Bear Fund Svc	URPSX	E-	(888) 776-3637	17.29	E- /0.0	-9.63 / 0	-18.18 / 0	-9.26 / 0	E+ / 0.9	11	N/A
AG	Rydex Dynamics-Inv Dyn S&P 500	RYTPX	E-	(800) 820-0888	39.05	E- /0.0	-8.57 / 0	-17.45 / 0	-8.67 / 0	E+ / 0.9	14	N/A
AG	Rydex Dynamics-Inv Dyn S&P 500	RYCBX	E-	(800) 820-0888	37.47	E- /0.0	-9.27 / 0	-18.11 / 0	-9.37 / 0	E+ / 0.9	11	N/A
AG	ProFunds-Pharm UltraSector Svc	PHPSX	E-	(888) 776-3637	8.67	E- /0.0	-7.37 / 0	-9.33 / 0	-11.86 / 0	D- / 1.0	0	6
AG	ProFunds-Pharm UltraSector Inv	PHPIX	E-	(888) 776-3637	9.11	E- /0.0	-6.33 / 0	-8.43 / 0	-11.09 / 0	D- / 1.1	0	6
AG	Ameritor Investment	AIVTX	E-	(800) 424-8570	0.03	E- /0.0	-75.00 / 0	-56.72 / 0	-47.61 / 0	D- / 1.3	0	9
TC	J Hancock Technology B	FGTBX	E-	(800) 257-3336	3.01	E- /0.0	-0.66 / 1	1.48 / 0	-12.89 / 0	D- / 1.4	0	N/A
TC	J Hancock Technology A	NTTFX	E-	(800) 257-3336	3.32	E- /0.0	--	2.09 / 1	-12.30 / 0	D- / 1.4	0	N/A
TC	Monetta Trust-Select Technology A	MSCEX	E-	(800) 666-3882	7.19	E- /0.0	-3.23 / 0	2.69 / 1	-9.83 / 0	D- / 1.4	0	9
TC	J Hancock Technology C	JHTCX	E-	(800) 257-3336	3.01	E- /0.0	-0.66 / 1	1.48 / 0	-12.89 / 0	D- / 1.4	0	N/A
HL	Allianz RCM Biotechnology D	DRBNX	E-	(800) 628-1237	23.28	E- /0.0	-5.33 / 0	3.10 / 1	-4.64 / 3	D / 1.6	6	N/A
AG	Rydex Series-Inverse OTC C	RYACX	E-	(800) 820-0888	22.53	E- /0.0	-2.01 / 1	-9.46 / 0	-3.59 / 4	D / 1.7	75	N/A
AG	Rydex Series-Inverse OTC Inv	RYAIX	E-	(800) 820-0888	23.87	E- /0.0	-1.01 / 1	-8.53 / 0	-2.57 / 6	D / 1.8	83	N/A
HL	Allianz RCM Biotechnology A	RABTX	E-	(800) 628-1237	23.30	E- /0.0	-5.28 / 0	3.13 / 1	-4.81 / 3	D / 2.1	6	N/A
HL	Allianz RCM Biotechnology B	RBBTX	E-	(800) 628-1237	22.53	E- /0.0	-6.05 / 0	2.34 / 1	-5.55 / 2	D / 2.1	4	N/A
HL	Allianz RCM Biotechnology C	RCBTX	E-	(800) 628-1237	22.54	E- /0.0	-6.01 / 0	2.35 / 1	-5.54 / 2	D / 2.1	4	N/A
AG	Leuthold Grizzly Short Fund	GRZZX	E-	(888) 200-0409	6.08	E- /0.0	-10.38 / 0	-12.67 / 0	-6.49 / 1	D / 2.2	14	6
AG	Gabelli Comstck Partners Cap Val	CPCCX	E-	(800) 422-3554	2.28	E- /0.0	-9.35 / 0	-14.59 / 0	-5.27 / 2	D+ / 2.3	4	10
AG	Gabelli Comstck Partners Cap Val	CPCRX	E-	(800) 422-3554	2.44	E- /0.0	-8.67 / 0	-13.78 / 0	-4.44 / 3	D+ / 2.3	7	10
AG	Gabelli Comstck Partners Cap Val	DRCVX	E-	(800) 422-3554	2.44	E- /0.0	-8.86 / 0	-13.99 / 0	-4.56 / 3	D+ / 2.3	7	10
AG	Gabelli Comstck Partners Cap Val	DCVBX	E-	(800) 422-3554	2.38	E- /0.0	-9.35 / 0	-14.59 / 0	-5.27 / 2	D+ / 2.3	5	10
GR	Managers 20 Fund B	MTWBX	E-	(800) 835-3879	4.29	E- /0.0	-3.60 / 0	0.39 / 0	-10.64 / 0	D+ / 2.5	0	6
GR	Managers 20 Fund C	MTWCX	E-	(800) 835-3879	4.31	E- /0.0	-3.58 / 0	0.39 / 0	-10.63 / 0	D+ / 2.5	0	6
GR	Managers 20 Fund Y	MTWYX	E-	(800) 835-3879	4.62	E- /0.0	-2.74 / 0	1.41 / 0	-9.74 / 0	D+ / 2.6	0	6
GR	Managers 20 Fund A	MTWAX	E-	(800) 835-3879	4.53	E- /0.0	-2.79 / 0	0.98 / 0	-10.11 / 0	D+ / 2.6	0	6
AG	Ameritor Security Trust 1	ASTRX	E-	(800) 424-8570	0.41	E- /0.0	10.81 / 52	-3.06 / 0	-10.15 / 0	D+ / 2.7	0	9
AG	Rydex Series-Inverse S&P 500 C	RYUCX	E-	(800) 820-0888	7.87	E- /0.0	-3.32 / 0	-8.87 / 0	-3.17 / 5	D+ / 2.8	24	N/A
AG	Rydex Series-Inverse S&P 500 Inv	RYURX	E-	(800) 820-0888	8.32	E- /0.0	-2.36 / 1	-7.91 / 0	-2.18 / 8	D+ / 2.9	32	N/A
TC	Munder Future Technology B	MTFBX	E-	(800) 438-5789	3.46	E- /0.0	1.76 / 4	2.96 / 1	-10.31 / 0	D+ / 2.9	0	N/A
AG	Rydex Series-Inverse S&P 500 Adv	RYUAX	E-	(800) 820-0888	7.95	E- /0.0	-2.82 / 0	-8.36 / 0	-2.67 / 6	D+ / 2.9	28	N/A
GR	Direxion U.S. Short Inv	PSPSX	E-	(800) 851-0511	27.46	E- /0.0	-3.48 / 0	-9.61 / 0	-4.46 / 3	C- / 3.2	19	9
AG	Gabelli Comstock Partners Strat C	CPFCX	E-	(800) 422-3554	2.80	E- /0.0	-11.71 / 0	-12.47 / 0	-6.61 / 1	C- / 3.2	1	10
AG	ProFunds-Bear Fund Svc	BRPSX	E-	(888) 776-3637	28.85	E- /0.0	-3.71 / 0	-9.18 / 0	-3.92 / 4	C- / 3.2	22	9
AG	● Gabelli Comstock Partners Strat O	CPSFX	E-	(800) 422-3554	2.69	E- /0.0	-10.66 / 0	-11.47 / 0	-5.62 / 2	C- / 3.2	2	10
AG	Gabelli Comstock Partners Strat A	CPFAX	E-	(800) 422-3554	2.77	E- /0.0	-10.77 / 0	-11.71 / 0	-5.88 / 2	C- / 3.2	2	10
AG	ProFunds-Bear Fund Inv	BRPIX	E-	(888) 776-3637	29.96	E- /0.0	-2.79 / 0	-8.28 / 0	-2.94 / 6	C- / 3.3	29	9
AG	ProFunds-HlthCare UltraSector	HCPSX	E-	(888) 776-3637	13.35	E- /0.0	-5.52 / 0	2.03 / 1	-4.58 / 3	C- / 4.1	4	6
AG	PF Loomis Sayles Lg Cp Gr B	PFBBX	E-	(800) 722-2333	8.53	E- /0.0	-5.26 / 0	1.81 / 1	--	C / 4.3	2	N/A
AG	PF Loomis Sayles Lg Cp Gr C	PFBCX	E-	(800) 722-2333	8.52	E- /0.0	-5.26 / 0	1.73 / 0	--	C / 4.3	2	N/A

● Denotes fund is closed to new investors

Fund Type	Fund Name	Ticker Symbol	Overall Weiss Investment Rating	Phone	Net Asset Value As of 6/30/06	Performance Rating/Pts	Annualized Total Return Through 6/30/06			Risk Rating/Pts	Mgr. Quality Pct	Mgr. Tenure (Years)
							1Yr / Pct	3Yr / Pct	5Yr / Pct			
GR	Wells Fargo Avtg Lg Co Core B	WLCBX	E-	(800) 222-8222	8.58	E- /0.0	0.86 / 2	0.27 / 0	-1.68 / 9	C /4.4	0	N/A
AG	PF Loomis Sayles Lg Cp Gr A	PFBAX	E-	(800) 722-2333	8.75	E- /0.0	-4.77 / 0	2.25 / 1	--	C /4.4	2	N/A
GR	Jundt Twenty Five Fund C	JTFCX	E-	(800) 370-0612	7.45	E- /0.0	-1.59 / 1	-0.53 / 0	-7.36 / 1	C /4.6	3	9
GR	Jundt Twenty Five Fund A	JTFHX	E-	(800) 370-0612	8.01	E- /0.0	-0.74 / 1	0.25 / 0	-6.64 / 1	C /4.7	4	9
GR	Jundt Twenty Five Fund B	JTFBX	E-	(800) 370-0612	7.40	E- /0.0	-1.46 / 1	-0.49 / 0	-7.35 / 1	C /4.7	3	9
GR	Columbia Growth Stock Fund 529B		E-	(800) 426-3750	10.28	E- /0.0	-3.11 / 0	-0.10 / 0	--	C /5.0	1	N/A
GR	Columbia Growth Stock Fund 529C		E-	(800) 426-3750	10.28	E- /0.0	-3.02 / 0	-0.10 / 0	--	C /5.0	1	N/A
GR	Columbia Growth Stock Fund 529A		E	(800) 426-3750	10.95	E- /0.0	1.67 / 4	1.99 / 1	--	C /5.1	2	N/A
GR	Columbia Growth Stock Fund B	CGSBX	E	(800) 426-3750	10.28	E- /0.0	2.29 / 5	1.68 / 0	--	C+ /6.0	1	3
GR	Columbia Growth Stock Fund A	CGSAX	E	(800) 426-3750	10.95	E- /0.0	3.11 / 8	2.46 / 1	-1.51 / 10	C+ /6.1	2	N/A
AA	Caldwell & Orkin Mkt Opportunity	COAGX	E	(800) 237-7073	16.82	E- /0.0	0.51 / 2	-1.24 / 0	-0.65 / 13	C+ /6.3	36	14
GR	Jundt Growth Fund B	JGFBX	E	(800) 370-0612	6.39	E- /0.0	2.73 / 6	1.39 / 0	-4.03 / 4	C+ /6.3	10	11
HL	SunAmerica New Biotech/Health A	SBHAX	E	(800) 858-8850	8.67	E- /0.0	-1.81 / 1	-1.71 / 0	-6.62 / 1	C+ /6.3	1	N/A
HL	SunAmerica New Biotech/Health B	SHFBX	E	(800) 858-8850	8.33	E- /0.0	-2.46 / 1	-2.36 / 0	-7.23 / 1	C+ /6.3	0	N/A
HL	SunAmerica New Biotech/Health C	SBHTX	E	(800) 858-8850	8.35	E- /0.0	-2.34 / 1	-2.32 / 0	-7.20 / 1	C+ /6.3	0	N/A
SC	ProFunds-Short Small Cap Svc	SHPSX	E	(888) 776-3637	17.89	E- /0.0	-10.55 / 0	-16.45 / 0	--	C+ /6.3	12	4
GR	Jundt Growth Fund A	JGFHX	E	(800) 370-0612	7.11	E- /0.0	3.49 / 9	2.15 / 1	-3.31 / 5	C+ /6.4	13	11
GR	Jundt Growth Fund I	JGFIX	E	(800) 370-0612	7.36	E- /0.0	3.66 / 9	2.37 / 1	-3.07 / 5	C+ /6.4	13	11
SC	ProFunds-Short Small Cap Inv	SHPIX	E	(888) 776-3637	17.94	E- /0.0	-9.67 / 0	-15.67 / 0	--	C+ /6.4	16	4
OT	ProFunds-Short OTC Svc	SOPSX	E	(888) 776-3637	19.43	E- /0.0	-1.82 / 1	-9.54 / 0	--	C+ /6.4	75	4
OT	ProFunds-Short OTC Inv	SOPIX	E	(888) 776-3637	19.95	E- /0.0	-0.91 / 1	-8.65 / 0	--	C+ /6.4	83	4
GR	American Century Select A	AASLX	E+	(800) 345-6488	35.26	E- /0.0	-3.46 / 0	3.21 / 1	--	C+ /6.6	5	N/A
HL	Saratoga Adv Tr-Health & Biotech	SHPBX	E+	(800) 807-3863	12.33	E- /0.0	-6.80 / 0	1.73 / 1	-7.55 / 1	C+ /6.7	17	N/A
HL	Saratoga Adv Tr-Health & Biotech	SHPCX	E+	(800) 807-3863	12.33	E- /0.0	-6.87 / 0	1.71 / 0	-7.56 / 1	C+ /6.7	17	N/A
HL	Saratoga Adv Tr-Health & Biotech	SHPAX	E+	(800) 807-3863	12.87	E- /0.0	-6.33 / 0	2.33 / 1	-7.01 / 1	C+ /6.8	20	N/A
AG	PF Loomis Sayles Lg Cp Gr	AZBAX	E+	(800) 722-2333	8.75	E- /0.0	-4.77 / 0	2.25 / 1	--	B- /7.1	2	N/A
AG	PF Loomis Sayles Lg Cp Gr	AZBBX	E+	(800) 722-2333	8.53	E- /0.0	-5.26 / 0	1.81 / 1	--	B- /7.1	2	N/A
AG	PF Loomis Sayles Lg Cp Gr	AZBCX	E+	(800) 722-2333	8.52	E- /0.0	-5.26 / 0	1.73 / 0	--	B- /7.1	2	N/A
AG	PF Loomis Sayles Lg Cp Gr	CPBLX	E+	(800) 722-2333	8.75	E- /0.0	-4.77 / 0	2.25 / 1	--	B- /7.1	2	N/A
AG	PF Loomis Sayles Lg Cp Gr	CPCBX	E+	(800) 722-2333	8.53	E- /0.0	-5.26 / 0	1.81 / 1	--	B- /7.1	2	N/A
AG	PF Loomis Sayles Lg Cp Gr	CPBCX	E+	(800) 722-2333	8.52	E- /0.0	-5.26 / 0	1.73 / 0	--	B- /7.1	2	N/A
GR	American Century Select B	ABSLX	E+	(800) 345-6488	34.54	E- /0.0	-4.16 / 0	2.44 / 1	--	B- /7.2	4	N/A
AA	● DWS Target 2010	KRFAX	D-	(800) 621-1048	8.95	E- /0.0	-1.28 / 1	1.93 / 1	3.51 / 41	B- /7.7	25	1
HL	Saratoga Adv Tr-Health & Biotech I	SBHIX	D-	(800) 807-3863	12.99	E- /0.0	-5.94 / 0	2.76 / 1	--	B /8.2	23	N/A
AA	● Pioneer Protected Principal Plus A	PPPAX	D	(800) 225-6292	9.73	E- /0.0	0.54 / 2	1.06 / 0	--	B /8.7	20	4
AA	● Pioneer Protected Principal Plus B	PPPBX	D	(800) 225-6292	9.71	E- /0.0	-0.21 / 2	0.32 / 0	--	B /8.7	15	4
GR	Franklin U.S. Long-Short A	FUSLX	D	(800) 342-5236	16.06	E- /0.0	0.63 / 2	0.56 / 0	-1.33 / 11	B /8.7	18	6
IN	● Legg Mason Prt Cp Pres II A	SMPRX	D	(866) 890-4247	11.23	E- /0.0	1.98 / 4	0.99 / 0	--	B /8.8	27	N/A
BA	● DWS Target 2008 Fd A	KRFGX	D	(800) 621-1048	10.47	E- /0.0	0.62 / 2	1.57 / 0	3.12 / 38	B /8.8	26	N/A
BA	Pioneer Protected Principal + II C	PPFCX	D	(800) 225-6292	9.60	E- /0.0	-1.57 / 1	-0.03 / 0	--	B+ /9.2	15	3
BA	Pioneer Protected Principal + II B	PPFBX	D	(800) 225-6292	9.56	E- /0.0	-1.70 / 1	-0.12 / 0	--	B+ /9.2	15	3
BA	Pioneer Protected Principal + II A	PPFAX	D	(800) 225-6292	9.62	E- /0.0	-0.89 / 1	0.67 / 0	--	B+ /9.2	19	3
GR	Phoenix Mkt Neutral Fund Class C	EMNCX	D	(800) 243-4361	10.95	E- /0.0	-6.41 / 0	-0.69 / 0	0.87 /20	B+ /9.3	32	6
GR	Phoenix Mkt Neutral Fund Class B	EMNBX	D	(800) 243-4361	11.00	E- /0.0	-6.46 / 0	-0.72 / 0	0.84 / 19	B+ /9.3	32	6
IN	● Legg Mason Prt Cp Pres A	SPNAX	D	(866) 890-4247	10.95	E- /0.0	1.15 / 3	0.21 / 0	--	B+ /9.5	28	N/A
IN	● Legg Mason Prt Cp Pres B	SPRBX	D	(866) 890-4247	10.90	E- /0.0	0.45 / 2	-0.52 / 0	--	B+ /9.5	23	N/A
IN	● Legg Mason Prt Cp Pres C	SPRLX	D	(866) 890-4247	10.90	E- /0.0	0.44 / 2	-0.53 / 0	--	B+ /9.5	23	N/A
IN	● Legg Mason Prt Cp Pres II B	SPCBX	D+	(866) 890-4247	11.12	E- /0.0	1.21 / 3	0.25 / 0	--	B+ /9.6	22	N/A

● Denotes fund is closed to new investors

Data as of June 30, 2006

Section VI

Risk:
100 Best and Worst
Stock Mutual Funds

A compilation of those

Equity Mutual Funds

receiving the highest and lowest Risk Ratings.

Funds are listed in order by Risk Rating.

Section VI Contents

This section contains a summary analysis of each of the top 100 and bottom 100 mutual funds as determined by their Weiss Risk Rating. Since the Risk Rating does not take into consideration a fund's overall financial performance, the selection of funds presented here is based solely on each fund's performance volatility over the past three years.

You can use this section to identify those funds that have historically given shareholders the most consistent returns on their investments. A word of caution though: consistency in the past is not necessarily indicative of future results. While these funds have provided the most stable returns, it is possible for a fund manager – especially a newly appointed fund manager – to suddenly shift the fund's investment focus which could lead to greater volatility.

1.	**Fund Type**	The mutual fund's peer category based on an analysis of its investment portfolio.

AG	Aggressive Growth	HL	Health
AA	Asset Allocation	IN	Income
BA	Balanced	IX	Index
CV	Convertible	MC	Mid Cap
EM	Emerging Market	OT	Other
EN	Energy/Natural Resources	PM	Precious Metals
FS	Financial Services	RE	Real Estate
FO	Foreign	SC	Small Cap
GL	Global	TC	Technology
GR	Growth	UT	Utilities
GI	Growth and Income		

A blank fund type means that the mutual fund has not yet been categorized.

2.	**Fund Name**	The name of the mutual fund as stated in its prospectus, which can sometimes differ slightly from the name that the company uses for advertising. If you cannot find the particular mutual fund you are interested in, or if you have any doubts regarding the precise name, verify the information with your broker or on your account statement. Also, use the fund's ticker symbol for confirmation. (See column 3.)

3.	**Ticker Symbol**	The unique alphabetic symbol used for identifying and trading a specific mutual fund. No two funds can have the same ticker symbol, and the ticker symbol for mutual funds always ends with an "X".

A handful of funds currently show no associated ticker symbol. This means that the fund is either small or new since the NASD only assigns a ticker symbol to funds with at least $25 million in assets or 1,000 shareholders.

4.	**Overall Weiss Investment Rating**	Our overall rating is measured on a scale from A to E based on each fund's risk-adjusted performance. Please see page 10 for specific descriptions of each letter grade. Also, refer to page 7 for information on how our ratings are derived. Most important, when using this rating, please be sure to consider the warnings beginning on page 11 regarding the ratings' limitations and the underlying assumptions.
5.	**Phone**	The telephone number of the company managing the fund. Call this number to receive a prospectus or other information about the fund.
6.	**Net Asset Value (NAV)**	The fund's share price as of the date indicated. A fund's NAV is computed by dividing the value of the fund's asset holdings, less accrued fees and expenses, by the number of its shares outstanding.
7.	**Performance Rating/Points**	A letter grade rating based solely on the mutual fund's financial performance over the trailing three years, without any consideration for the amount of risk the fund poses. Like the overall Weiss Investment Rating, the Performance Rating is measured on a scale from A to E for ease of interpretation. The points score indicates where the Performance Rating falls on a scale of 0 to 10.
8.	**1-Year Total Return**	The total return the fund has provided investors over the preceeding twelve months. This total return figure is computed based on the fund's dividend distributions and share price appreciation/depreciation during the period, net of the expenses and fees it imposes on its shareholders. Although the total return figure does not reflect an adjustment for any loads the fund may carry, such adjustments have been made in deriving the Weiss Investment Ratings.
9.	**1-Year Total Return Percentile**	The fund's percentile rank based on its one-year performance compared to that of all other equity funds in existence for at least one year. A score of 99 is the best possible, indicating that the fund outperformed 99% of the other mutual funds. Zero is the worst possible percentile score.
10.	**3-Year Total Return**	The total annual return the fund has provided investors over the preceeding three years.
11.	**3-Year Total Return Percentile**	The fund's percentile rank based on its three-year performance compared to that of all other equity funds in existence for at least three years. A score of 99 is the best possible, indicating that the fund outperformed 99% of the other mutual funds. Zero is the worst possible percentile score.
12.	**5-Year Total Return**	The total annual return the fund has provided investors over the preceeding five years.

13. 5-Year Total Return Percentile

The fund's percentile rank based on its five-year performance compared to that of all other equity funds in existence for at least five years. A score of 99 is the best possible, indicating that the fund outperformed 99% of the other mutual funds. Zero is the worst possible percentile score.

14. Risk Rating/Points

A letter grade rating based solely on the mutual fund's risk as determined by its monthly performance volatility over the trailing three years. The risk rating does not take into consideration the overall financial performance the fund has achieved or the total return it has provided to its shareholders. Like the overall Weiss Investment Rating, the Risk Rating is measured on a scale from A to E for ease of interpretation. The points score indicates where the Risk Rating falls on a scale of 0 to 10.

15. Manager Quality Percentile

The manager quality percentile is based on a ranking of the fund's alpha, a statistical measure representing the difference between a fund's actual returns and its expected performance given its level of risk. Fund managers who have been able to exceed the fund's statistically expected performance receive a high percentile rank with 99 representing the highest possible score. At the other end of the spectrum, fund managers who have actually detracted from the fund's expected performance receive a low percentile rank with 0 representing the lowest possible score.

16. Manager Tenure

The number of years the current manager has been managing the fund. Since fund managers who deliver substandard returns are usually replaced, a long tenure is usually a good sign that shareholders are satisfied that the fund is achieving its stated objectives.

Fund Type	Fund Name	Ticker Symbol	Overall Weiss Investment Rating	Phone	Net Asset Value As of 6/30/06	PERFORMANCE Performance Rating/Pts	Annualized Total Return Through 6/30/06 1Yr / Pct	3Yr / Pct	5Yr / Pct	RISK Risk Rating/Pts	FUND MGR Mgr. Quality Pct	Mgr. Tenure (Years)
	99 Pct = Best *0 Pct = Worst*											
AA	UBS US Allocation Y	PWTYX	B-	(888) 793-8637	29.62	C- /4.0	6.37 /22	11.68 /40	2.50 /32	B+ / 9.9	84	13
BA	Mairs & Power Balanced Fund	MAPOX	B-	(800) 304-7404	60.66	C- /3.9	8.95 /40	10.48 /31	7.08 /67	B+ / 9.9	82	14
BA	Bridgeway Balanced Fund	BRBPX	C+	(800) 661-3550	12.65	C- /3.2	7.83 /31	9.33 /23	5.87 /60	B+ / 9.9	86	5
RE	Fidelity Real Estate Income	FRIFX	C+	(800) 544-8888	11.67	D+ /2.9	5.40 /17	9.41 /24	--	B+ / 9.9	84	3
BA	Accessor Fd-Balanced Alloc Adv	ABAAX	C+	(800) 759-3504	16.05	D+ /2.8	6.96 /26	9.10 /21	4.82 /53	B+ / 9.9	76	6
GL	Franklin Templeton Conserv Tgt		C+	(800) 321-8563	12.91	D+ /2.6	7.98 /33	8.49 /18	5.46 /58	B+ / 9.9	72	10
AA	JPMorgan Investor Balanced Sel	OIBFX	C	(800) 358-4782	12.36	D+ /2.5	6.52 /23	8.46 /18	4.88 /53	B+ / 9.9	72	10
BA	MFS Total Return Fund I	MTRIX	C	(800) 343-2829	15.46	D+ /2.5	4.54 /13	8.79 /20	5.59 /58	B+ / 9.9	70	N/A
BA	Accessor Fd-Balanced Alloc Inv	ACBIX	C	(800) 759-3504	16.04	D+ /2.5	6.47 /23	8.56 /18	4.30 /49	B+ / 9.9	72	6
BA	Columbia FS Balanced Portfolio Dir		C	(800) 426-3750	12.57	D+ /2.4	6.80 /25	8.28 /16	--	B+ / 9.9	68	N/A
BA	MFS Total Return Fund R5	MSFJX	C	(800) 343-2829	15.46	D+ /2.3	4.37 /12	8.52 /18	5.29 /56	B+ / 9.9	68	N/A
BA	Goldman Sachs Balanced Inst	GSBIX	C	(800) 292-4726	20.27	D+ /2.3	6.10 /21	8.30 /17	4.11 /47	B+ / 9.9	66	9
GR	CM Advisers Fund	CMAFX	C	(800) 664-4888	12.07	D /2.2	7.20 /27	8.14 /16	--	B+ / 9.9	83	3
BA	MFS Total Return Fund R4	MSFHX	C	(800) 343-2829	15.47	D /2.2	4.14 /11	8.41 /17	5.23 /56	B+ / 9.9	67	N/A
IN	ING MFS Total Return I	IMTIX	C	(800) 992-0180	18.62	D /2.2	4.28 /12	8.31 /17	--	B+ / 9.9	70	2
BA	Nuveen Balanced Muni & Stock R	NMNRX	C	(800) 257-8787	23.33	D /2.2	6.75 /25	7.80 /14	2.91 /36	B+ / 9.9	74	10
IN	ING MFS Total Return S	IMSRX	C	(800) 992-0180	18.57	D /2.1	3.99 /11	8.04 /15	5.26 /56	B+ / 9.9	69	2
FO	T. Rowe Price Retirement Income	TRRIX	C	(800) 638-5660	12.52	D /2.0	6.47 /23	7.48 /12	--	B+ / 9.9	36	4
BA	Accessor Fd-Balanced Alloc C	ABAFX	C	(800) 759-3504	16.01	D /2.0	5.86 /19	8.00 /15	--	B+ / 9.9	67	6
GI	Columbia Thermostat C	CTFDX	C	(800) 426-3750	12.52	D /2.0	5.55 /18	8.00 /15	--	B+ / 9.9	66	N/A
AA	State Farm LifePath 2010 Inst	SATIX	C	(877) 734-2265	12.16	D /2.0	6.08 /21	7.62 /13	--	B+ / 9.9	64	3
BA	MFS Total Return Fund R3	MTRRX	C	(800) 343-2829	15.50	D /2.0	3.77 /10	8.01 /15	4.72 /52	B+ / 9.9	63	3
AA	Putnam College Adv Mod 1993 O		C	(800) 354-2228	10.69	D /2.0	5.01 /15	7.90 /15	2.80 /35	B+ / 9.9	62	N/A
IN	ING MFS Total Return S2	IMTRX	C	(800) 992-0180	18.45	D /2.0	3.83 /10	7.88 /14	--	B+ / 9.9	66	2
GL	Russell LifePoints Mod Strategy S	RMLSX	C	(800) 832-6688	11.16	D /2.0	6.21 /22	7.48 /12	5.35 /57	B+ / 9.9	69	N/A
IN	State Farm Equity & Bond Inst	SEBIX	C	(877) 734-2265	9.86	D /2.0	6.70 /24	7.46 /12	--	B+ / 9.9	66	N/A
AA	Vanguard LifeStrategy Conserv Gr	VSCGX	C	(800) 662-7447	15.56	D /1.9	5.64 /18	7.51 /12	4.98 /54	B+ / 9.9	65	12
BA	MFS Total Return Fund R2	MSFKX	C	(800) 343-2829	15.44	D /1.9	3.59 / 9	7.76 /14	4.57 /51	B+ / 9.9	61	N/A
BA	Calvert Social-Balanced Portf I	CBAIX	C	(800) 368-2745	28.69	D /1.9	4.66 /13	7.82 /14	2.82 /35	B+ / 9.9	62	11
BA	MassMutual Premier Balanced Y	MBAYX	C	(800) 542-6767	10.05	D /1.9	5.38 /17	7.69 /13	3.27 /39	B+ / 9.9	58	12
GI	Columbia Thermostat A	CTFAX	C	(800) 426-3750	12.53	D /1.8	6.29 /22	8.77 /19	--	B+ / 9.9	73	N/A
AA	NH Portfolio 2009		C	(800) 522-7297	14.12	D /1.8	4.52 /13	7.49 /12	3.41 /40	B+ / 9.9	58	8
AA	Barclays Gbl Inv LifePath 2010 Fd	LPRBX	C	(800) 474-2737	12.83	D /1.8	5.94 /20	7.28 /12	3.89 /45	B+ / 9.9	60	N/A
BA	MFS Total Return Fund R1	MSFFX	C	(800) 343-2829	15.46	D /1.8	3.37 / 8	7.65 /13	4.51 /50	B+ / 9.9	59	N/A
GL	Russell LifePoints Mod Strategy R2	RMLTX	C	(800) 832-6688	11.11	D /1.8	5.85 /19	7.19 /11	5.07 /55	B+ / 9.9	67	N/A
BA	Goldman Sachs Balanced Svc	GSBSX	C	(800) 292-4726	20.04	D /1.8	4.41 /12	7.36 /12	3.38 /40	B+ / 9.9	57	9
GL	Russell LifePoints Mod Strategy E	RMLEX	C	(800) 832-6688	11.12	D /1.8	5.88 /20	7.20 /11	5.07 /55	B+ / 9.9	67	N/A
BA	Legg Mason Prt Div & Inc C	SBBLX	C	(866) 890-4247	12.69	D /1.8	5.44 /17	7.33 /12	2.18 /29	B+ / 9.9	63	N/A
AA	American Century Str Alloc:Con	ACCIX	C	(800) 345-6488	5.51	D /1.7	5.00 /15	7.11 /11	4.69 /52	B+ / 9.9	62	N/A
AA	DE Portfolio 2009		C	(800) 522-7297	13.86	D /1.7	4.76 /14	7.23 /11	2.98 /37	B+ / 9.9	57	8
AA	Putnam College Adv Mod 1992 O		C	(800) 354-2228	10.71	D /1.7	4.49 /13	7.30 /12	2.71 /34	B+ / 9.9	59	N/A
GI	Columbia FS Inc & Gr Port Z		C	(800) 426-3750	12.87	D /1.7	6.63 /24	6.78 /10	--	B+ / 9.9	68	N/A
AA	● DWS Conserv Alloc Fd S	SCPCX	C	(800) 621-1048	11.90	D /1.7	5.72 /19	6.99 /10	3.95 /45	B+ / 9.9	62	N/A
GL	Russell LifePoints Mod Strategy D	RMLDX	C	(800) 832-6688	11.15	D /1.7	5.70 /19	6.95 /10	4.83 /53	B+ / 9.9	64	N/A
AA	DWS Conserv Alloc Fd AARP	APWCX	C	(800) 621-1048	11.90	D /1.7	5.72 /19	7.00 /10	3.96 /46	B+ / 9.9	63	N/A
GL	Gartmore Inv Dest Mod Conserv	GMIMX	C	(800) 848-0920	10.30	D /1.6	5.01 /15	6.93 /10	4.31 /49	B+ / 9.9	64	N/A
AA	Wells Fargo Avtg Otlk 2010 Adm	WFLGX	C	(800) 222-8222	12.89	D /1.6	5.29 /17	6.82 /10	3.59 /42	B+ / 9.9	57	N/A
GI	Columbia Thermostat B	CTFBX	C-	(800) 426-3750	12.53	D- /1.5	5.71 /19	8.10 /16	--	B+ / 9.9	66	N/A
AA	MA Portfolio 2009		C	(800) 522-7297	12.64	D- /1.5	4.12 /11	7.03 /10	3.14 /38	B+ / 9.9	54	7
AA	Putnam College Adv Mod 1993 CX		C-	(800) 354-2228	10.36	D- /1.5	4.44 /12	7.28 /12	2.23 /29	B+ / 9.9	56	N/A
GR	Vantagepoint Model Port Cons	VPCGX	C	(800) 669-7400	23.59	D- /1.5	5.15 /16	6.75 / 9	3.84 /44	B+ / 9.9	65	N/A
BA	MFS Total Return Fund 529C	ECTRX	C-	(800) 343-2829	15.52	D- /1.5	3.17 / 8	7.42 /12	4.35 /49	B+ / 9.9	57	4

● Denotes fund is closed to new investors

Fund Type	Fund Name	Ticker Symbol	Overall Weiss Investment Rating	Phone	Net Asset Value As of 6/30/06	PERFORMANCE Perform-ance Rating/Pts	Annualized Total Return Through 6/30/06 1Yr / Pct	3Yr / Pct	5Yr / Pct	RISK Risk Rating/Pts	FUND MGR Mgr. Quality Pct	Mgr. Tenure (Years)
	99 Pct = Best *0 Pct = Worst*											
BA	MassMutual Premier Balanced N	MMBNX	C-	(800) 542-6767	9.55	D- /1.4	4.52 /13	6.91 /10	--	B+ / 9.9	47	N/A
AA	● State Farm LifePath 2010 LegA	SATAX	C-	(877) 734-2265	12.07	D- /1.4	5.76 /19	7.19 /11	--	B+ / 9.9	60	N/A
GL	Gartmore Inv Dest Mod Conserv	NSDCX	C-	(800) 848-0920	10.28	D- /1.4	4.72 /14	6.69 / 9	4.17 /47	B+ / 9.9	62	N/A
GL	Gartmore Inv Dest Mod Conserv R	GMMRX	C-	(800) 848-0920	10.29	D- /1.4	4.69 /14	6.68 / 9	3.89 /45	B+ / 9.9	62	N/A
AA	Putnam College Adv Mod 1991 O		C-	(800) 354-2228	10.72	D- /1.4	3.98 /10	6.68 / 9	2.62 /33	B+ / 9.9	57	N/A
GI	Columbia FS Inc & Gr Port CX		C-	(800) 426-3750	11.93	D- /1.4	6.04 /21	6.24 / 7	--	B+ / 9.9	62	N/A
GI	Columbia FS Inc & Gr Port E		C-	(800) 426-3750	12.60	D- /1.4	6.06 /21	6.23 / 7	--	B+ / 9.9	61	N/A
AA	Schwab MarketTrack Consv Port	SWCGX	C-	(866) 855-9102	13.67	D- /1.4	4.89 /15	7.04 /10	4.72 /52	B+ / 9.9	62	N/A
BA	Nuveen Balanced Muni & Stock C	NBMCX	C-	(800) 257-8787	25.29	D- /1.4	5.70 /19	6.72 / 9	1.88 /26	B+ / 9.9	63	10
GL	Russell LifePoints Mod Strategy C	RMLCX	C-	(800) 832-6688	11.06	D- /1.4	5.14 /16	6.40 / 8	4.30 /49	B+ / 9.9	58	N/A
BA	MFS Conservative Alloc I	MACIX	C-	(800) 343-2829	11.77	D- /1.4	5.05 /15	6.57 / 9	--	B+ / 9.9	63	4
BA	MFS Total Return Fund 529A	EATRX	C-	(800) 343-2829	15.43	D- /1.4	3.85 /10	8.12 /16	4.99 /54	B+ / 9.9	64	4
AA	JPMorgan Multi-Cap Mrkt Netral	OGNIX	C-	(800) 358-4782	11.04	D- /1.3	5.36 /17	5.33 / 5	--	B+ / 9.9	77	N/A
BA	MFS Conservative Alloc R4	MACNX	C-	(800) 343-2829	11.67	D- /1.3	4.72 /14	6.24 / 7	--	B+ / 9.9	59	N/A
BA	MFS Conservative Alloc R5	MACJX	C-	(800) 343-2829	11.70	D- /1.3	4.99 /15	6.36 / 8	--	B+ / 9.9	61	N/A
AA	Columbia Bal Ass Alloc 529Z		C-	(800) 426-3750	12.39	D- /1.3	5.36 /17	6.25 / 7	--	B+ / 9.9	50	3
AA	ING VP Strt Alloc Consv Port I		C-	(800) 992-0180	12.65	D- /1.3	3.78 /10	6.58 / 9	3.90 /45	B+ / 9.9	55	5
BA	Goldman Sachs Balanced C	GSBCX	C-	(800) 292-4726	19.88	D- /1.3	3.85 /10	6.72 / 9	2.72 /34	B+ / 9.9	49	N/A
BA	Legg Mason Prt Div & Inc B	SLSUX	C-	(866) 890-4247	12.68	D- /1.3	5.66 /18	7.57 /13	2.43 /31	B+ / 9.9	66	N/A
AA	Putnam Asset Alloc-Conserv Y	PACYX	C-	(800) 354-2228	9.30	D- /1.3	4.29 /12	6.33 / 8	4.95 /54	B+ / 9.9	66	12
GL	Accessor Fd-Inc & Gr Alloc Adv	AIGAX	C-	(800) 759-3504	15.55	D- /1.3	4.69 /14	6.27 / 7	4.38 /49	B+ / 9.9	66	N/A
BA	MFS Conservative Alloc R	MACRX	C-	(800) 343-2829	11.64	D- /1.2	4.57 /13	6.09 / 7	--	B+ / 9.9	57	4
AA	Putnam Asset Alloc-Conserv R	PUTRX	C-	(800) 354-2228	9.40	D- /1.2	4.18 /11	6.12 / 7	4.69 /52	B+ / 9.9	63	11
AA	● State Farm LifePath 2010 LegB	SATBX	C-	(877) 734-2265	12.02	D- /1.2	5.49 /18	6.78 /10	--	B+ / 9.9	54	N/A
AA	Putnam College Adv Mod 1992 CX		C-	(800) 354-2228	10.38	D- /1.2	3.90 /10	6.68 / 9	2.11 /28	B+ / 9.9	52	N/A
AA	Putnam College Adv Mod 1993 C		C-	(800) 354-2228	10.20	D- /1.2	3.98 /10	6.73 / 9	1.71 /25	B+ / 9.9	47	N/A
IN	Wells Fargo Avtg Life Stg Cons Inv	SCONX	C-	(800) 222-8222	9.94	D- /1.2	4.74 /14	6.05 / 7	2.63 /33	B+ / 9.9	56	N/A
GI	State Farm LifePath Income Inst	SLRIX	C-	(877) 734-2265	11.29	D- /1.1	4.32 /12	5.92 / 7	--	B+ / 9.9	62	3
IN	ING MFS Total Return A	IMTAX	C-	(800) 992-0180	18.35	D- /1.1	3.27 / 8	7.68 /13	--	B+ / 9.9	65	2
GI	Delaware Conservative Alloc Port	DFIRX	C-	(800) 362-3863	8.93	D- /1.1	3.60 / 9	6.25 / 7	--	B+ / 9.9	56	2
BA	MFS Conservative Alloc R3	MCARX	C-	(800) 343-2829	11.53	D- /1.1	4.36 /12	5.77 / 6	--	B+ / 9.9	54	3
AA	Putnam College Adv Mod 1990 O		C-	(800) 354-2228	10.78	D- /1.1	3.65 / 9	6.12 / 7	2.56 /32	B+ / 9.9	55	N/A
AA	Putnam College Adv Mod 1993 A		C-	(800) 354-2228	10.51	D- /1.1	4.68 /14	7.54 /13	2.45 /32	B+ / 9.9	58	N/A
GI	SSgA Life Solutions Inc & Gr R	SLIRX	C-	(800) 647-7327	12.01	D- /1.1	3.74 /10	5.90 / 6	4.33 /49	B+ / 9.9	53	N/A
GI	Columbia FS Inc & Gr Port Dir		C-	(800) 426-3750	11.95	D- /1.1	4.92 /15	5.73 / 6	--	B+ / 9.9	62	N/A
AA	SEI Asset Alloc-Divers Conserv D	SEADX	C-	(800) 342-5734	10.83	D- /1.1	3.80 /10	6.00 / 7	3.72 /43	B+ / 9.9	50	N/A
BA	Nuveen Balanced Muni & Stock A	NBMSX	C-	(800) 257-8787	23.85	D- /1.1	6.48 /23	7.51 /12	2.64 /33	B+ / 9.9	71	10
AA	JPMorgan Investor Conserv Gr Sel	ONCFX	C-	(800) 358-4782	11.01	D- /1.1	3.97 /10	5.73 / 6	4.44 /50	B+ / 9.9	62	10
AA	First American Strat-Inc Alloc Y	FSFYX	C-	(800) 677-3863	11.09	D- /1.1	4.04 /11	6.09 / 7	--	B+ / 9.9	59	8
GL	Accessor Fd-Inc & Gr Alloc Inv	ACIGX	C-	(800) 759-3504	15.55	D- /1.1	4.33 /12	5.77 / 6	3.88 /45	B+ / 9.9	61	6
GI	TA IDEX Protected Principal Stck	IPPCX	C-	(888) 233-4339	11.56	D- /1.1	5.67 /19	5.55 / 5	--	B+ / 9.9	63	4
BA	MFS Total Return Fund 529B	EBTRX	C-	(800) 343-2829	15.46	D- /1.1	3.24 / 8	7.42 /12	4.35 /49	B+ / 9.9	57	4
GL	Russell LifePoints Mod Strategy A	RMLAX	C-	(800) 832-6688	11.12	D- /1.0	5.89 /20	7.20 /11	5.11 /55	B+ / 9.9	66	N/A
AA	● Fidelity Adv 529 2007 D		C-	(800) 522-7297	11.55	D- /1.0	4.05 /11	5.81 / 6	--	B+ / 9.9	45	1
AA	NH Portfolio 2006		C-	(800) 522-7297	14.28	D- /1.0	3.33 / 8	5.79 / 6	3.40 /40	B+ / 9.9	52	8
AA	Putnam College Adv Mod 1991 CX		C-	(800) 354-2228	10.40	D- /1.0	3.38 / 8	6.09 / 7	2.04 /28	B+ / 9.9	50	N/A
AA	Putnam College Adv Mod 1992 C		C-	(800) 354-2228	10.22	D- /1.0	3.34 / 8	6.13 / 7	1.60 /24	B+ / 9.9	46	N/A
AA	Putnam College Adv Mod 1993 AX		C-	(800) 354-2228	10.51	D- /1.0	4.68 /14	7.54 /13	2.45 /32	B+ / 9.9	58	N/A

● Denotes fund is closed to new investors

Data as of June 30, 2006

Fund Type	Fund Name	Ticker Symbol	Overall Weiss Investment Rating	Phone	Net Asset Value As of 6/30/06	PERFORMANCE Perform-ance Rating/Pts	Annualized Total Return Through 6/30/06 1Yr / Pct	3Yr / Pct	5Yr / Pct	RISK Risk Rating/Pts	FUND MGR Mgr. Quality Pct	Mgr. Tenure (Years)
	99 Pct = Best											
	0 Pct = Worst											
GR	Van Wagoner Growth	VWGOX	E-	(800) 228-2121	10.00	E- /0.0	1.21 / 3	-0.65 / 0	--	E- / 0.0	0	3
MC	Apex Mid-Cap Growth Fund	BMCGX	E-	(877) 593-8637	1.35	E- /0.0	2.27 / 5	-3.24 / 0	-1.82 / 9	E- / 0.0	0	13
TC	ProFunds-Ultra Short OTC Fund	USPSX	E-	(888) 776-3637	17.56	E- /0.0	-7.38 / 0	-20.49 / 0	-14.48 / 0	E- / 0.0	82	N/A
TC	ProFunds-Semicond UltraSector	SMPSX	E-	(888) 776-3637	16.23	E- /0.0	-10.13 / 0	0.48 / 0	-18.77 / 0	E- / 0.0	0	6
TC	ProFunds-Semicond UltraSector	SMPIX	E-	(888) 776-3637	17.25	E- /0.0	-9.21 / 0	1.47 / 0	-17.94 / 0	E- / 0.0	0	6
TC	ProFunds-Ultra Short OTC Fund	USPIX	E-	(888) 776-3637	16.97	E- /0.0	-6.47 / 0	-19.71 / 0	-13.70 / 0	E- / 0.0	89	N/A
AG	Rydex Dynamics-Inv Dyn OTC H	RYVNX	E-	(800) 820-0888	21.52	E- /0.0	-6.71 / 0	-19.78 / 0	-13.32 / 0	E- / 0.0	87	N/A
AG	Rydex Dynamics-Inv Dyn OTC C	RYCDX	E-	(800) 820-0888	20.75	E- /0.0	-7.37 / 0	-20.39 / 0	-13.90 / 0	E- / 0.0	82	N/A
SC	KOPP Emerging Growth Fund A	KOPPX	E-	(888) 533-5677	9.23	E- /0.2	13.81 / 68	6.46 / 8	-8.33 / 0	E- / 0.0	0	9
SC	KOPP Emerging Growth Fund C	KEGCX	E-	(888) 533-5677	8.80	E- /0.2	13.11 / 65	5.80 / 6	-8.92 / 0	E- / 0.0	0	9
SC	KOPP Emerging Growth Fund I	KEGIX	E-	(888) 533-5677	9.56	E /0.3	14.22 / 69	6.84 / 10	-7.99 / 0	E- / 0.0	0	9
BA	Dreyfus Premier Balanced Opport	DBOCX	E-	(800) 782-6620	18.84	E /0.4	0.17 / 2	4.45 / 3	3.68 /43	E- / 0.0	19	19
TC	Rydex Series-Electronics C	RYSCX	E-	(800) 820-0888	11.35	E /0.4	10.73 / 52	4.24 / 3	-9.60 / 0	E- / 0.0	0	N/A
TC	Select Networking & Infrastructure	FNINX	E-	(800) 544-8888	2.31	E /0.4	9.48 /43	6.54 / 9	-8.39 / 0	E- / 0.0	0	2
TC	Rydex Series-Electronics Adv	RYSAX	E-	(800) 820-0888	11.46	E /0.5	11.05 /54	4.72 / 3	-9.15 / 0	E- / 0.0	0	N/A
TC	Rydex Series-Electronics Inv	RYSIX	E-	(800) 820-0888	11.97	E+ /0.7	11.87 / 59	5.27 / 5	-8.68 / 0	E- / 0.0	0	N/A
TC	Oak Assoc-Black Oak Emerging	BOGSX	E-	(888) 462-5386	2.16	E+ /0.9	--	7.06 /11	-18.88 / 0	E- / 0.0	0	6
GR	● Thrivent Large Cap Growth B	BBAGX	E-	(800) 847-4836	4.69	E+ /0.9	4.45 /13	7.57 /13	-2.46 / 7	E- / 0.0	14	4
GR	Reynolds Opportunity Fund	ROPPX	E-	(800) 773-9665	17.04	D- /1.0	5.39 /17	6.75 / 9	-4.31 / 3	E- / 0.0	0	14
GR	Thrivent Large Cap Growth A	AAAGX	E-	(800) 847-4836	4.99	D- /1.2	5.59 /18	8.66 /19	-1.57 /10	E- / 0.0	20	4
BA	Eaton Vance Balanced B	EMIFX	E-	(800) 225-6265	7.04	D /1.6	7.79 /31	8.10 /16	3.65 /42	E- / 0.0	44	6
AG	Rydex Dynamics-OTC C	RYCCX	E-	(800) 820-0888	17.97	D /1.8	2.87 / 7	11.00 /36	-17.67 / 0	E- / 0.0	0	N/A
GR	Reynolds Fund	REYFX	E-	(800) 773-9665	6.09	D /2.0	14.69 /71	7.52 /12	-0.64 /13	E- / 0.0	0	7
BA	Eaton Vance Balanced C	ECIFX	E-	(800) 225-6265	7.06	D /2.1	7.88 /32	8.11 /16	3.66 /42	E- / 0.0	44	6
GR	Gartmore Long-Short Equity Plus C	MLSCX	E-	(800) 848-0920	7.45	D /2.1	7.37 /28	8.48 /18	0.96 /20	E- / 0.0	70	N/A
AG	ProFunds-Ultra OTC Fund Svc	UOPSX	E-	(888) 776-3637	20.07	D+ /2.3	2.77 / 7	11.68 /40	-17.40 / 0	E- / 0.0	0	N/A
AG	Rydex Dynamics-OTC H	RYVYX	E-	(800) 820-0888	19.32	D+ /2.5	3.76 /10	11.89 /42	-16.66 / 0	E- / 0.0	0	N/A
GR	Thrivent Large Cap Growth I	THLCX	E-	(800) 847-4836	5.30	D+ /2.6	6.33 /22	9.56 /24	-0.57 /13	E- / 0.0	25	4
AG	ProFunds-Ultra OTC Fund Inv	UOPIX	E-	(888) 776-3637	21.55	D+ /2.8	3.81 /10	12.32 /45	-16.81 / 0	E- / 0.0	0	N/A
GR	Berkshire Focus Fund	BFOCX	E-	(877) 526-0707	7.12	C- /3.0	18.86 /80	11.69 /40	-13.99 / 0	E- / 0.0	0	9
GR	Principal Inv LgCap Growth A	PRGWX	E-	(800) 247-4123	7.42	C- /3.5	9.74 /45	12.27 /44	-0.45 /14	E- / 0.0	58	1
GR	Principal Inv LgCap Growth B	PRGBX	E-	(800) 247-4123	7.37	C- /3.9	8.52 /37	11.44 /39	-1.17 /11	E- / 0.0	49	1
AG	ProFunds-Internet UltraSector Svc	INPSX	E	(888) 776-3637	75.21	C+ /5.7	18.67 /80	17.56 /70	-6.92 / 1	E- / 0.0	1	6
AG	ProFunds-Internet UltraSector Inv	INPIX	E	(888) 776-3637	80.66	C+ /6.3	19.85 /82	18.73 /75	-6.08 / 2	E- / 0.0	1	6
SC	● BlackRock-Small Cap Val B	CCVBX	E+	(888) 825-2257	11.06	C+ /6.9	8.19 /34	17.84 /72	9.07 /77	E- / 0.0	76	4
SC	● BlackRock-Small Cap Val C	BSCCX	E+	(888) 825-2257	11.07	C+ /6.9	8.29 /35	17.87 /72	9.06 /77	E- / 0.0	76	4
RE	Gabelli Westwood Income AAA	WESRX	E+	(800) 422-3554	11.71	B- /7.0	3.07 / 7	18.33 /74	14.79 /92	E- / 0.0	45	9
FO	● TA IDEX MFS International Equity	ICIAX	E+	(888) 233-4339	7.51	B- /7.0	22.01 /84	17.21 /69	3.05 /37	E- / 0.0	10	4
SC	● Managers Small Cap Fund	MSSCX	E+	(800) 835-3879	14.83	B- /7.1	17.23 /78	17.00 /68	0.19 /16	E- / 0.0	93	N/A
FO	● TA IDEX MFS International Equity	ICILX	E+	(888) 233-4339	6.90	B- /7.3	21.63 /84	16.58 /66	--	E- / 0.0	8	N/A
FO	● TA IDEX MFS International Equity	ICIBX	E+	(888) 233-4339	6.98	B- /7.3	21.52 /84	16.64 /66	2.41 /31	E- / 0.0	8	4
EN	● Oppenheimer Real Asset B	QRABX	D-	(800) 525-7048	8.05	B /7.9	13.94 /68	20.48 /81	14.00 /90	E- / 0.0	47	7
EN	● Oppenheimer Real Asset A	QRAAX	D-	(800) 525-7048	8.19	B /8.0	14.88 /71	21.52 /84	14.97 /92	E- / 0.0	58	7
GL	NorthPointe Small Cap Value Inst	NNSVX	D-	(800) 848-0920	11.32	B /8.1	15.42 /73	20.02 /79	11.11 /84	E- / 0.0	31	6
EN	● Oppenheimer Real Asset C	QRACX	D-	(800) 525-7048	8.00	B /8.2	13.94 /68	20.53 /81	14.01 /90	E- / 0.0	47	7
EN	● Oppenheimer Real Asset N	QRANX	D-	(800) 525-7048	8.11	B+ /8.3	14.55 /70	21.08 /83	14.60 /91	E- / 0.0	53	7
EN	● Oppenheimer Real Asset Y	QRAYX	D-	(800) 525-7048	8.24	B+ /8.5	15.31 /73	22.05 /85	15.44 /92	E- / 0.0	61	7
PM	Rydex Series-Precious Metal C	RYZCX	D	(800) 820-0888	50.52	A- /9.1	50.76 /99	18.99 /76	20.23 /96	E- / 0.0	1	N/A
PM	Rydex Series-Precious Metal Inv	RYPMX	D	(800) 820-0888	53.06	A /9.3	52.30 /99	20.20 /80	21.41 /97	E- / 0.0	1	N/A
PM	● First Eagle Gold Fund C	FEGOX	D	(800) 334-2143	23.50	A /9.5	53.69 /99	24.13 /90	--	E- / 0.0	21	7
RE	JPMorgan Realty Income Fund Cl I	URTLX	D	(800) 358-4782	17.30	A /9.5	22.99 /86	28.38 /94	20.66 /97	E- / 0.0	90	N/A
PM	● First Eagle Gold Fund I	FEGIX	D	(800) 334-2143	23.88	A+ /9.6	55.27 /99	25.32 /91	--	E- / 0.0	27	7

● Denotes fund is closed to new investors

Fund Type	Fund Name	Ticker Symbol	Overall Weiss Investment Rating	Phone	Net Asset Value As of 6/30/06	PERFORMANCE				RISK	FUND MGR	
	99 Pct = Best *0 Pct = Worst*					Perform-ance Rating/Pts	Annualized Total Return Through 6/30/06			Risk Rating/Pts	Mgr. Quality Pct	Mgr. Tenure (Years)
							1Yr / Pct	3Yr / Pct	5Yr / Pct			
RE	ProFunds-Real Est UltraSector Svc	REPSX	D	(888) 776-3637	45.66	A+ /9.6	18.93 /80	31.61 /96	18.35 /95	E- / 0.0	16	6
PM	ING Precious Metals A	LEXMX	D+	(800) 992-0180	10.69	A+ /9.7	67.59 /99	27.11 /93	30.19 /99	E- / 0.0	21	8
RE	ProFunds-Real Est UltraSector Inv	REPIX	D+	(888) 776-3637	44.96	A+ /9.7	20.10 /82	32.96 /97	19.56 /96	E- / 0.0	23	6
PM	American Century Global Gold Adv	ACGGX	D+	(800) 345-6488	18.60	A+ /9.8	65.85 /99	27.39 /93	31.64 /99	E- / 0.0	9	15
PM	RVS Precious Metals Fund B	INPBX	D+	(800) 328-8300	13.93	A+ /9.8	68.24 /99	27.79 /94	26.15 /99	E- / 0.0	26	7
PM	RVS Precious Metals Fund A	INPMX	D+	(800) 328-8300	14.75	A+ /9.8	69.54 /99	28.74 /95	27.13 /99	E- / 0.0	32	7
EM	Third Millennium Russia Fund	TMRFX	D+	(800) 527-9500	53.12	A+ /9.8	52.26 /99	37.00 /99	32.97 /99	E- / 0.0	17	8
PM	OCM Gold Fund	OCMGX	D+	(800) 628-9403	18.55	A+ /9.8	72.66 /99	27.15 /93	33.57 /99	E- / 0.0	14	10
PM	American Century Global Gold Inv	BGEIX	D+	(800) 345-6488	18.62	A+ /9.8	66.31 /99	27.65 /94	31.93 /99	E- / 0.0	10	15
PM	DWS Gold & Prec Metals Fund A	SGDAX	D+	(800) 621-1048	23.30	A+ /9.8	57.64 /99	34.79 /98	34.41 /99	E- / 0.0	69	5
PM	DWS Gold & Prec Metals Fund B	SGDBX	D+	(800) 621-1048	23.06	A+ /9.8	56.42 /99	33.76 /97	33.35 /99	E- / 0.0	61	5
PM	ProFunds-Precious Metals Ultra	PMPSX	D+	(888) 776-3637	44.86	A+ /9.8	72.67 /99	26.46 /93	--	E- / 0.0	0	N/A
PM	ProFunds-Precious Metals Ultra Inv	PMPIX	D+	(888) 776-3637	46.61	A+ /9.8	74.31 /99	26.82 /93	--	E- / 0.0	0	N/A
PM	GAMCO Gold A	GLDAX	D+	(800) 422-3554	25.94	A+ /9.9	76.43 /99	30.54 /96	35.10 /99	E- / 0.0	35	12
PM	GAMCO Gold B	GLDBX	D+	(800) 422-3554	25.67	A+ /9.9	75.03 /99	29.52 /95	34.38 /99	E- / 0.0	29	12
PM	GAMCO Gold C	GLDCX	D+	(800) 422-3554	25.66	A+ /9.9	75.05 /99	29.56 /95	34.40 /99	E- / 0.0	29	12
PM	GAMCO Gold AAA	GOLDX	D+	(800) 422-3554	25.96	A+ /9.9	76.37 /99	30.54 /96	35.10 /99	E- / 0.0	35	12
PM	Franklin Gold & Prec Metals C	FRGOX	D+	(800) 342-5236	30.13	A+ /9.9	70.95 /99	32.29 /97	26.51 /99	E- / 0.0	66	9
PM	Franklin Gold & Prec Metals A	FKRCX	D+	(800) 342-5236	30.88	A+ /9.9	72.23 /99	33.32 /97	27.46 /99	E- / 0.0	73	9
PM	Franklin Gold & Prec Metals Adv	FGADX	D+	(800) 321-8563	31.71	A+ /9.9	72.57 /99	33.63 /97	27.75 /99	E- / 0.0	75	9
PM	DWS Gold & Prec Metals Fund	SGLDX	D+	(800) 621-1048	23.36	A+ /9.9	57.98 /99	35.10 /98	34.70 /99	E- / 0.0	71	5
PM	Tocqueville Gold Fund	TGLDX	D+	(800) 697-3863	50.21	A+ /9.9	63.28 /99	31.54 /96	35.70 /99	E- / 0.0	71	8
PM	● DWS Gold & Prec Metals Fund S	SCGDX	D+	(800) 621-1048	23.33	A+ /9.9	58.04 /99	35.10 /98	34.68 /99	E- / 0.0	71	5
PM	● Franklin Gold & Prec Metals B	FAGPX	D+	(800) 342-5236	29.85	A+ /9.9	70.90 /99	32.30 /97	26.49 /99	E- / 0.0	66	9
PM	DWS Gold & Prec Metals Fund C	SGDCX	D+	(800) 621-1048	23.03	A+ /9.9	56.47 /99	33.80 /97	33.38 /99	E- / 0.0	61	5
EM	Van Wagoner Emerging Growth	VWEGX	E-	(800) 228-2121	4.53	E- /0.0	5.35 /17	-4.62 / 0	-22.53 / 0	E- / 0.1	0	11
GR	Wireless Fund (The)	WIREX	E	(800) 590-0898	4.47	C+ /6.0	26.63 /91	12.49 /46	-7.47 / 1	E- / 0.1	1	6
SC	● BlackRock-Small Cap Val A	PSEIX	E+	(888) 825-2257	12.81	C+ /6.7	9.10 /41	18.76 /75	9.89 /80	E- / 0.1	83	4
SC	● BlackRock-Small Cap Val Svc	PSESX	E+	(888) 825-2257	12.90	B- /7.3	9.15 /41	18.81 /76	10.00 /80	E- / 0.1	82	4
SC	Direxion Small Cp Bear 2.5X	DXRSX	E-	(800) 851-0511	15.86	E- /0.0	-24.02 / 0	-22.65 / 0	-14.36 / 0	E- / 0.2	11	7
SC	● BlackRock-Small Cap Val Inst	PNSEX	D-	(888) 825-2257	13.17	B- /7.4	9.51 /43	19.21 /77	10.35 /82	E- / 0.2	85	4
FO	ProFunds-Ultra Japan Svc	UJPSX	D+	(888) 776-3637	56.81	A+ /9.8	76.05 /99	36.35 /98	-0.07 /15	E- / 0.2	5	N/A
PM	Evergreen Precious Metals B	EKWBX	D+	(800) 343-2898	53.26	A+ /9.9	74.33 /99	36.66 /98	36.06 /99	E- / 0.2	83	N/A
PM	Evergreen Precious Metals A	EKWAX	D+	(800) 343-2898	55.56	A+ /9.9	75.57 /99	37.63 /99	37.06 /99	E- / 0.2	87	N/A
PM	Evergreen Precious Metals C	EKWCX	D+	(800) 343-2898	52.96	A+ /9.9	74.33 /99	36.68 /98	36.05 /99	E- / 0.2	83	N/A
PM	Evergreen Precious Metals I	EKWYX	D+	(800) 343-2898	55.24	A+ /9.9	76.08 /99	38.03 /99	37.41 /99	E- / 0.2	89	N/A
FO	ProFunds-Ultra Japan Inv	UJPIX	D+	(888) 776-3637	59.48	A+ /9.9	77.87 /99	37.70 /99	0.91 /20	E- / 0.2	8	N/A
SC	Van Wagoner Small-Cap Growth	VWMCX	E-	(800) 228-2121	9.63	E- /0.0	5.02 /15	-2.06 / 0	-8.87 / 0	E / 0.3	0	11
TC	Firsthand-Global Technology	GTFQX	E-	(888) 884-2675	3.89	E- /0.1	4.01 /11	3.10 / 1	-6.69 / 1	E / 0.3	0	6
AG	ProFunds-Tech UltraSector Svc	TEPSX	E-	(888) 776-3637	23.13	E- /0.2	-0.39 / 1	5.29 / 5	-14.46 / 0	E / 0.3	0	N/A
TC	Firsthand-Technology Innovators	TIFQX	E-	(888) 884-2675	9.66	E /0.3	14.86 /71	1.27 / 0	-10.52 / 0	E / 0.3	0	8
TC	Oppenheimer Emerging Tech A	OETAX	E-	(800) 525-7048	2.90	E- /0.2	9.85 /46	5.59 / 5	-11.47 / 0	E / 0.4	0	N/A
TC	Oppenheimer Emerging Tech B	OETBX	E-	(800) 525-7048	2.79	E /0.3	8.98 /40	4.71 / 3	-12.14 / 0	E / 0.4	0	N/A
TC	Oppenheimer Emerging Tech C	OETCX	E-	(800) 525-7048	2.79	E /0.3	8.98 /40	4.71 / 3	-12.14 / 0	E / 0.4	0	N/A
AG	ProFunds-Tech UltraSector Inv	TEPIX	E-	(888) 776-3637	24.10	E /0.4	0.69 / 2	6.34 / 8	-13.75 / 0	E / 0.4	0	N/A
TC	Oppenheimer Emerging Tech N	OETNX	E-	(800) 525-7048	2.87	E /0.4	9.54 /44	5.35 / 5	-11.64 / 0	E / 0.4	0	N/A
TC	Fidelity Adv Electronics C	FELCX	E-	(800) 522-7297	7.59	D /1.7	4.98 /15	8.70 /19	-5.31 / 2	E / 0.4	0	2
TC	Fidelity Adv Electronics B	FELBX	E-	(800) 522-7297	7.60	D /1.7	5.12 /16	8.68 /19	-5.32 / 2	E / 0.4	0	2

● Denotes fund is closed to new investors

Data as of June 30, 2006

Section VII

Top-Rated
Stock Mutual Funds
by Risk Category

A compilation of those

Equity Mutual Funds

receiving the highest Weiss Investment Ratings

within each risk grade.

Funds are listed in order by Overall Weiss Investment Rating.

Section VII Contents

This section contains a summary analysis of the top 100 rated stock mutual funds within each risk grade. Based on your personal risk tolerance, each page shows those funds that have achieved the best financial performance over the past three years.

Take the Investor Profile Quiz on page 631 of the Appendix for assistance in determining your own risk tolerance level. Then you can use this section to identify those funds that are most appropriate for your investing style.

Note that increased risk does not always mean increased performance. Most of the riskiest mutual funds in the E (Very Weak) Risk Rating category have also provided very poor returns to their shareholders. Funds in the D and E Risk Rating categories generally represent speculative ventures that should not be entered into lightly.

1. **Fund Type**   The mutual fund's peer category based on an analysis of its investment portfolio.

AG	Aggressive Growth	HL	Health
AA	Asset Allocation	IN	Income
BA	Balanced	IX	Index
CV	Convertible	MC	Mid Cap
EM	Emerging Market	OT	Other
EN	Energy/Natural Resources	PM	Precious Metals
FS	Financial Services	RE	Real Estate
FO	Foreign	SC	Small Cap
GL	Global	TC	Technology
GR	Growth	UT	Utilities
GI	Growth and Income		

A blank fund type means that the mutual fund has not yet been categorized.

2. **Fund Name**   The name of the mutual fund as stated in its prospectus, which can sometimes differ slightly from the name that the company uses for advertising. If you cannot find the particular mutual fund you are interested in, or if you have any doubts regarding the precise name, verify the information with your broker or on your account statement. Also, use the fund's ticker symbol for confirmation. (See column 3.)

3. **Ticker Symbol**   The unique alphabetic symbol used for identifying and trading a specific mutual fund. No two funds can have the same ticker symbol, and the ticker symbol for mutual funds always ends with an "X".

A handful of funds currently show no associated ticker symbol. This means that the fund is either small or new since the NASD only assigns a ticker symbol to funds with at least $25 million in assets or 1,000 shareholders.

4. **Overall Weiss Investment Rating**

    Our overall rating is measured on a scale from A to E based on each fund's risk-adjusted performance. Please see page 10 for specific descriptions of each letter grade. Also, refer to page 7 for information on how our ratings are derived. Most important, when using this rating, please be sure to consider the warnings beginning on page 11 regarding the ratings' limitations and the underlying assumptions.

5. **Phone**

    The telephone number of the company managing the fund. Call this number to receive a prospectus or other information about the fund.

6. **Net Asset Value (NAV)**

    The fund's share price as of the date indicated. A fund's NAV is computed by dividing the value of the fund's asset holdings, less accrued fees and expenses, by the number of its shares outstanding.

7. **Performance Rating/Points**

    A letter grade rating based solely on the mutual fund's financial performance over the trailing three years, without any consideration for the amount of risk the fund poses. Like the overall Weiss Investment Rating, the Performance Rating is measured on a scale from A to E for ease of interpretation. The points score indicates where the Performance Rating falls on a scale of 0 to 10.

8. **1-Year Total Return**

    The total return the fund has provided investors over the preceeding twelve months. This total return figure is computed based on the fund's dividend distributions and share price appreciation/depreciation during the period, net of the expenses and fees it imposes on its shareholders. Although the total return figure does not reflect an adjustment for any loads the fund may carry, such adjustments have been made in deriving the Weiss Investment Ratings.

9. **1-Year Total Return Percentile**

    The fund's percentile rank based on its one-year performance compared to that of all other equity funds in existence for at least one year. A score of 99 is the best possible, indicating that the fund outperformed 99% of the other mutual funds. Zero is the worst possible percentile score.

10. **3-Year Total Return**

    The total annual return the fund has provided investors over the preceeding three years.

11. **3-Year Total Return Percentile**

    The fund's percentile rank based on its three-year performance compared to that of all other equity funds in existence for at least three years. A score of 99 is the best possible, indicating that the fund outperformed 99% of the other mutual funds. Zero is the worst possible percentile score.

12. **5-Year Total Return**

    The total annual return the fund has provided investors over the preceeding five years.

13. **5-Year Total Return Percentile**

The fund's percentile rank based on its five-year performance compared to that of all other equity funds in existence for at least five years. A score of 99 is the best possible, indicating that the fund outperformed 99% of the other mutual funds. Zero is the worst possible percentile score.

14. **Risk Rating/Points**

A letter grade rating based solely on the mutual fund's risk as determined by its monthly performance volatility over the trailing three years. The risk rating does not take into consideration the overall financial performance the fund has achieved or the total return it has provided to its shareholders. Like the overall Weiss Investment Rating, the Risk Rating is measured on a scale from A to E for ease of interpretation. The points score indicates where the Risk Rating falls on a scale of 0 to 10.

15. **Manager Quality Percentile**

The manager quality percentile is based on a ranking of the fund's alpha, a statistical measure representing the difference between a fund's actual returns and its expected performance given its level of risk. Fund managers who have been able to exceed the fund's statistically expected performance receive a high percentile rank with 99 representing the highest possible score. At the other end of the spectrum, fund managers who have actually detracted from the fund's expected performance receive a low percentile rank with 0 representing the lowest possible score.

16. **Manager Tenure**

The number of years the current manager has been managing the fund. Since fund managers who deliver substandard returns are usually replaced, a long tenure is usually a good sign that shareholders are satisfied that the fund is achieving its stated objectives.

Fund Type	Fund Name	Ticker Symbol	Overall Weiss Investment Rating	Phone	Net Asset Value As of 6/30/06	Perform-ance Rating/Pts	Annualized Total Return Through 6/30/06			Risk Rating/Pts	Mgr. Quality Pct	Mgr. Tenure (Years)
							1Yr / Pct	3Yr / Pct	5Yr / Pct			
RE	MSIF Inc. Intl Real Estate B	IERBX	A+	(800) 354-8185	27.46	A+ /9.8	28.87 /94	35.44 /98	26.95 /99	B- / 7.6	99	7
RE	MSIF Inc. Intl Real Estate A	MSUAX	A+	(800) 354-8185	27.44	A+ /9.8	29.15 /94	35.81 /98	27.26 /99	B- / 7.5	99	7
FO	Vontobel Eastern European Eq A	VEEEX	A+	(800) 527-9500	24.97	A+ /9.8	24.85 /88	36.91 /98	29.41 /99	B- / 7.2	98	5
GR	Bruce Fund		A+	(800) 872-7823	408.85	A+ /9.7	18.36 /80	33.71 /97	29.74 /99	B / 8.4	99	23
FO	Oakmark International Small Cap II	OAREX	A+	(800) 625-6275	22.19	A+ /9.7	31.26 /95	32.65 /97	21.38 /97	B / 8.0	98	5
FO	● AIM European Growth Inv	EGINX	A+	(800) 347-4246	36.61	A+ /9.7	31.71 /95	30.70 /96	16.53 /94	B- / 7.9	92	9
FO	GMO Foreign Small Companies IV	GFSFX	A+		18.78	A+ /9.7	30.86 /95	31.51 /96	--	B- / 7.8	93	N/A
FO	Allianz NACM International C	PNICX	A+	(800) 628-1237	21.65	A+ /9.7	38.19 /97	30.07 /96	15.14 /92	B- / 7.7	83	N/A
FO	Allianz NACM International D	PNIDX	A+	(800) 628-1237	21.84	A+ /9.7	39.19 /98	31.01 /96	16.01 /93	B- / 7.7	87	N/A
FO	Dodge & Cox International Stock	DODFX	A+	(800) 621-3979	38.96	A+ /9.7	27.64 /92	33.39 /97	16.39 /93	B- / 7.7	95	N/A
FO	Putnam International Capital Opp Y	PIVYX	A+	(800) 354-2228	32.60	A+ /9.7	34.05 /96	31.48 /96	14.16 /90	B- / 7.3	80	N/A
FO	Allianz NFJ Intl Value Inst	ANJIX	A+	(800) 628-1237	19.43	A+ /9.7	28.63 /93	32.44 /97	--	B- / 7.2	61	N/A
GL	Putnam College Adv Intl Cap Opp		A+	(800) 354-2228	20.51	A+ /9.7	33.96 /96	31.35 /96	--	B- / 7.2	79	N/A
FO	DFA International Value IV	DFVFX	A+	(800) 984-9472	16.41	A+ /9.6	31.38 /95	30.29 /96	15.88 /93	B / 8.0	89	N/A
FO	Allianz NACM International A	PNIAX	A+	(800) 628-1237	21.84	A+ /9.6	39.18 /98	30.99 /96	16.00 /93	B- / 7.7	87	N/A
FO	Neuberger Berman International Tr	NBITX	A+	(800) 877-9700	26.05	A+ /9.6	29.60 /94	31.14 /96	16.26 /93	B- / 7.7	85	N/A
FO	DFA International Small Company	DFISX	A+	(800) 984-9472	17.55	A+ /9.6	27.97 /93	30.60 /96	20.00 /96	B- / 7.6	94	N/A
FO	JPMorgan Intl Value Inst	JNUSX	A+	(800) 358-4782	15.41	A+ /9.6	35.15 /97	29.53 /95	12.79 /88	B- / 7.3	91	9
FO	JPMorgan Intl Value Sel	JIESX	A+	(800) 358-4782	15.35	A+ /9.6	34.87 /97	29.07 /95	12.45 /87	B- / 7.3	90	9
GL	Putnam College Adv Intl Cap Opp		A+	(800) 354-2228	19.37	A+ /9.6	32.22 /96	29.64 /95	--	B- / 7.2	67	N/A
FO	● Artisan International Small Cap Inv	ARTJX	A+	(800) 344-1770	21.83	A+ /9.6	34.99 /97	32.51 /97	--	B- / 7.2	70	5
FO	DFA International Value I	DFIVX	A+	(800) 984-9472	20.01	A+ /9.6	31.08 /95	30.05 /96	15.74 /93	B- / 7.0	89	N/A
FO	AIM European Growth A	AEDAX	A+	(800) 347-4246	36.66	A+ /9.6	31.66 /95	30.63 /96	16.49 /93	B- / 7.0	91	9
FO	AIM European Growth C	AEDCX	A+	(800) 347-4246	34.74	A+ /9.6	30.64 /95	29.73 /95	15.69 /93	B- / 7.0	88	9
FO	Artisan International Value Inv	ARTKX	A+	(800) 344-1770	25.32	A /9.5	30.13 /94	28.71 /94	--	B / 8.1	91	4
FO	DFA Tax Managed Intl Value	DTMIX	A+	(800) 984-9472	17.58	A /9.5	31.05 /95	29.32 /95	14.73 /91	B / 8.0	86	N/A
UT	JennDry Jennison Utility Z	PRUZX	A+	(800) 257-3893	15.42	A /9.5	25.94 /90	29.17 /95	10.13 /81	B- / 7.9	99	6
GL	Principal Inv Divers Intl Inst	PIIIX	A+	(800) 247-4123	13.43	A /9.5	35.71 /97	27.44 /93	11.47 /85	B- / 7.5	56	3
GL	Principal Inv Divers Intl Pfd	PINPX	A+	(800) 247-4123	13.43	A /9.5	35.49 /97	27.17 /93	11.29 /85	B- / 7.5	53	3
GL	Principal Inv Divers Intl Sel	PINLX	A+	(800) 247-4123	13.54	A /9.5	35.09 /97	27.14 /93	11.29 /85	B- / 7.4	51	3
FO	JPMorgan Intl Value B	JFEBX	A+	(800) 358-4782	15.03	A /9.5	33.84 /96	28.26 /94	11.75 /86	B- / 7.3	86	9
FO	JPMorgan Intl Value A	JFEAX	A+	(800) 358-4782	15.27	A /9.5	34.50 /96	28.89 /95	12.25 /87	B- / 7.3	89	9
GR	Baron Partners Fund	BPTRX	A+	(800) 992-2766	20.24	A /9.5	20.06 /82	29.89 /95	14.37 /91	B- / 7.2	99	14
GL	Putnam College Adv Intl Cap Opp		A+	(800) 354-2228	20.02	A /9.5	33.20 /96	30.64 /96	--	B- / 7.2	74	N/A
GL	Putnam College Adv Intl Cap Opp		A+	(800) 354-2228	19.36	A /9.5	32.24 /96	29.67 /95	--	B- / 7.2	68	N/A
FO	Gartmore Intl Growth Inst	GIGIX	A+	(800) 848-0920	12.17	A /9.5	38.94 /98	28.54 /94	11.67 /86	B- / 7.0	46	N/A
FO	AIM European Growth B	AEDBX	A+	(800) 347-4246	34.72	A /9.5	30.66 /95	29.73 /95	15.70 /93	B- / 7.0	89	9
FO	● Third Avenue International Value	TAVIX	A+	(800) 443-1021	22.91	A /9.4	20.50 /82	29.35 /95	--	B / 8.4	99	5
GL	Principal Inv Intl Growth Sel	PITSX	A+	(800) 247-4123	12.44	A /9.4	31.39 /95	26.76 /93	12.17 /87	B- / 7.9	73	1
UT	JennDry Jennison Utility C	PCUFX	A+	(800) 257-3893	15.40	A /9.4	24.75 /88	27.91 /94	9.06 /77	B- / 7.9	99	6
UT	JennDry Jennison Utility B	PRUTX	A+	(800) 257-3893	15.41	A /9.4	24.82 /88	27.93 /94	9.07 /77	B- / 7.9	99	6
UT	JennDry Jennison Utility A	PRUAX	A+	(800) 257-3893	15.42	A /9.4	25.73 /89	28.91 /95	9.90 /80	B- / 7.9	99	6
GL	Principal Inv Intl Growth AdvPfd	PITMX	A+	(800) 247-4123	12.88	A /9.4	31.06 /95	26.44 /93	12.67 /88	B- / 7.8	69	1
GL	Principal Inv Intl Growth Pfd	PITPX	A+	(800) 247-4123	12.47	A /9.4	31.44 /95	26.88 /93	12.27 /87	B- / 7.8	72	1
GL	Principal Inv Intl Growth Inst	PITIX	A+	(800) 247-4123	12.57	A /9.4	31.85 /96	27.16 /93	12.32 /87	B- / 7.8	74	1
FO	ICAP International Fund	ICEUX	A+	(888) 221-4227	36.05	A /9.4	31.53 /95	28.02 /94	13.98 /90	B- / 7.5	83	9
GL	Principal Inv Divers Intl J	PIIJX	A+	(800) 247-4123	13.32	A /9.4	34.96 /97	26.42 /93	10.51 /82	B- / 7.4	45	3
GL	Principal Inv Divers Intl AdvSel	PINNX	A+	(800) 247-4123	13.30	A /9.4	34.90 /97	26.58 /93	10.65 /83	B- / 7.4	47	3
GL	Principal Inv Divers Intl AdvPfd	PINRX	A+	(800) 247-4123	13.38	A /9.4	34.99 /97	26.74 /93	10.87 /83	B- / 7.4	48	3
FO	MFS Intl New Discovery R3	MIDRX	A+	(800) 343-2829	25.34	A /9.4	27.62 /92	28.60 /94	16.33 /93	B- / 7.4	67	3
FO	MFS Intl New Discovery 529C	ECIDX	A+	(800) 343-2829	24.59	A /9.4	26.95 /91	27.90 /94	15.57 /93	B- / 7.4	60	4
FO	MFS Intl New Discovery 529B	EBIDX	A+	(800) 343-2829	24.62	A /9.4	26.91 /91	27.88 /94	15.56 /93	B- / 7.4	60	4

● Denotes fund is closed to new investors

Fund Type	Fund Name	Ticker Symbol	Overall Weiss Investment Rating	Phone	Net Asset Value As of 6/30/06	PERFORMANCE Perform-ance Rating/Pts	Annualized Total Return Through 6/30/06 1Yr / Pct	3Yr / Pct	5Yr / Pct	RISK Risk Rating/Pts	FUND MGR Mgr. Quality Pct	Mgr. Tenure (Years)
	99 Pct = Best 0 Pct = Worst											
FO	The Boston Co Intl Core Eq	SDIEX	A+	(800) 221-4795	37.51	A /9.4	29.86 /94	27.99 /94	15.01 /92	B- /7.3	77	9
FO	DFA United Kingdom Small Co	DFUKX	A+	(800) 984-9472	27.37	A /9.4	28.30 /93	27.28 /93	17.47 /94	B- /7.2	91	N/A
FO	SSgA Intl Stock Selection Fd	SSAIX	A+	(800) 647-7327	12.35	A /9.4	31.18 /95	26.56 /93	12.41 /87	B- /7.1	65	N/A
FO	Tocqueville Intl Value Fund	TIVFX	A+	(800) 697-3863	16.20	A /9.4	25.20 /89	29.19 /95	16.47 /93	B- /7.0	90	12
FO	SSgA Intl Stock Selection R	SSARX	A+	(800) 647-7327	12.28	A /9.3	30.45 /95	25.95 /92	11.82 /86	B /8.2	61	N/A
UT	Evergreen Utility and Telecom I	EVUYX	A+	(800) 343-2898	12.85	A /9.3	16.95 /77	26.25 /92	6.93 /66	B /8.1	99	N/A
FO	GMO Tax Managed Intl Equities III	GTMIX	A+		19.10	A /9.3	28.56 /93	26.24 /92	15.83 /93	B /8.1	68	N/A
FO	MFS Inst Intl Research Equity Fund	MIREX	A+	(800) 343-2829	16.13	A /9.3	32.87 /96	24.88 /91	--	B- /7.9	57	N/A
GL	Principal Inv Intl Growth J	PITJX	A+	(800) 247-4123	12.32	A /9.3	30.77 /95	26.04 /92	11.51 /85	B- /7.9	67	1
GL	Principal Inv Intl Growth AdvSel	PITNX	A+	(800) 247-4123	12.26	A /9.3	30.83 /95	26.21 /92	11.67 /86	B- /7.8	67	1
MC	RVS Mid Cap Value Y		A+	(800) 328-8300	9.16	A /9.3	21.45 /84	26.08 /92	--	B- /7.8	98	N/A
GL	GMO International Eq Alloc III	GIEAX	A+		17.64	A /9.3	27.70 /92	27.38 /93	18.12 /95	B- /7.6	99	10
FO ●	ING International Value I	NIIVX	A+	(800) 992-0180	19.82	A /9.3	28.16 /93	26.70 /93	11.98 /87	B- /7.4	69	N/A
FO ●	ING International Value Q	NQGVX	A+	(800) 992-0180	19.83	A /9.3	27.88 /92	26.41 /93	11.71 /86	B- /7.4	66	N/A
FO ●	Wasatch International Growth	WAIGX	A+	(800) 551-1700	21.68	A /9.3	28.82 /94	27.38 /93	--	B- /7.4	63	N/A
FO	MFS Intl New Discovery 529A	EAIDX	A+	(800) 343-2829	25.47	A /9.3	27.75 /92	28.73 /94	16.35 /93	B- /7.4	67	4
FO	Dreyfus Premier Intl Equity R	DIERX	A+	(800) 782-6620	39.05	A /9.3	28.26 /93	26.78 /93	14.08 /90	B- /7.3	73	3
FO	Brandes Instl Intl Equity Fund	BIIEX	A+	(800) 237-7119	23.48	A /9.3	25.82 /89	26.07 /92	12.09 /87	B- /7.3	76	N/A
FO	Vanguard International Value Fund	VTRIX	A+	(800) 662-7447	38.69	A /9.3	31.03 /95	26.79 /93	12.93 /89	B- /7.2	62	N/A
FO ●	Julius Baer International Equity I	JIEIX	A+	(800) 435-4659	40.35	A /9.3	31.22 /95	27.08 /93	15.84 /93	B- /7.2	38	13
FO	Oakmark International II	OARIX	A+	(800) 625-6275	25.34	A- /9.2	26.28 /90	23.89 /89	12.60 /88	B /8.6	84	14
FO	GMO International Intrinsic Val IV	GMCFX	A+		34.07	A- /9.2	26.76 /91	25.53 /92	16.13 /93	B /8.4	74	N/A
FO	Oakmark International I	OAKIX	A+	(800) 625-6275	25.53	A- /9.2	26.73 /91	24.30 /90	12.97 /89	B /8.3	86	14
FO ●	First Eagle Overseas Fund I	SGOIX	A+	(800) 334-2143	25.93	A- /9.2	26.68 /91	25.58 /92	20.66 /97	B /8.1	97	7
FO	Putnam Intl Growth & Inc Y		A+	(800) 354-2228	14.86	A- /9.2	28.69 /93	24.52 /90	10.97 /84	B /8.1	62	N/A
FO	Dreyfus Inv Founders Intl Eqty I		A+	(800) 242-8671	17.85	A- /9.2	26.25 /90	24.95 /91	5.87 /60	B- /7.9	54	3
FO	MFS Research International I	MRSIX	A+	(800) 343-2829	19.02	A- /9.2	32.09 /96	24.53 /90	11.04 /84	B- /7.9	56	10
FO	SunAmerica Intl Equity I	NAOIX	A+	(800) 858-8850	15.58	A- /9.2	31.37 /95	23.94 /89	--	B- /7.5	35	N/A
FO	T. Rowe Price Intl Gr & Inc R	RRIGX	A+	(800) 638-5660	15.64	A- /9.2	27.86 /92	24.84 /91	12.53 /88	B- /7.4	61	4
FO	T. Rowe Price Intl Gr & Inc Adv	PAIGX	A+	(800) 638-5660	15.73	A- /9.2	28.13 /93	25.16 /91	12.76 /88	B- /7.4	65	4
FO	T. Rowe Price Intl Gr & Inc Fd	TRIGX	A+	(800) 638-5660	15.73	A- /9.2	28.25 /93	25.18 /91	12.75 /88	B- /7.4	66	N/A
FO	Dreyfus Premier Intl Equity A	DIEAX	A+	(800) 782-6620	38.58	A- /9.2	27.94 /93	26.31 /92	13.77 /90	B- /7.3	71	3
FO	Dreyfus Premier Intl Equity C	DIECX	A+	(800) 782-6620	38.02	A- /9.2	27.02 /91	25.49 /92	13.29 /89	B- /7.3	64	3
FO	Dreyfus Premier Intl Equity T	DIETX	A+	(800) 782-6620	38.57	A- /9.2	27.59 /92	26.15 /92	13.69 /90	B- /7.3	69	3
FO	MFS Intl Value Fund C	MGICX	A+	(800) 343-2829	27.51	A- /9.2	27.26 /92	24.76 /91	12.48 /88	B- /7.2	81	N/A
FO	Phoenix Foreign Opportunities A	JVIAX	A+	(800) 243-4361	21.74	A- /9.2	26.10 /90	26.10 /92	12.04 /87	B- /7.1	90	4
FO	GMO Foreign Fund IV	GMFFX	A+		17.37	A- /9.2	27.87 /92	24.46 /90	14.19 /90	B- /7.1	58	8
FO	Merrill Lynch Intl Value I	MAIVX	A+	(800) 543-6217	30.50	A- /9.2	26.97 /91	24.92 /91	11.05 /84	B- /7.1	63	5
FO	Thornburg Intl Value I	TGVIX	A+	(800) 847-0200	26.20	A- /9.2	27.94 /93	25.37 /91	12.68 /88	B- /7.1	71	8
SC	Royce Value Fd Svc	RYVFX	A+	(800) 221-4268	10.28	A- /9.2	22.15 /84	26.43 /93	17.16 /94	B- /7.1	99	N/A
FO	JennDry Dryden Intl Equity Z	PJIZX	A+	(800) 257-3893	8.02	A- /9.2	26.45 /90	25.47 /92	8.02 /72	B- /7.0	63	3
FO	Nuveen NWQ International Value	NGRRX	A+	(800) 257-8787	29.92	A- /9.2	20.92 /83	25.70 /92	12.88 /88	B- /7.0	76	4
FO ●	Columbia FS Intl Value Port C		A+	(800) 426-3750	17.43	A- /9.1	25.76 /89	24.74 /90	--	B /8.2	55	N/A
UT	Evergreen Utility and Telecom A	EVUAX	A+	(800) 343-2898	12.84	A- /9.1	16.61 /76	25.92 /92	6.62 /65	B /8.1	99	N/A
UT	Evergreen Utility and Telecom C	EVUCX	A+	(800) 343-2898	12.85	A- /9.1	15.76 /74	25.01 /91	5.85 /60	B /8.1	99	N/A
FO	Putnam Intl Growth & Inc R	PIIRX	A+	(800) 354-2228	14.72	A- /9.1	28.03 /93	23.87 /89	10.36 /82	B /8.1	56	N/A
FO ●	First Eagle Overseas Fund C	FESOX	A+	(800) 334-2143	25.42	A- /9.1	25.40 /89	24.36 /90	19.50 /96	B /8.1	95	7
FO	American Beacon Intl Eq Index Inst	AIIIX	A+	(800) 967-9009	11.39	A- /9.1	26.58 /91	23.88 /89	9.96 /80	B /8.1	50	6

● Denotes fund is closed to new investors

Fund Type	Fund Name	Ticker Symbol	Overall Weiss Investment Rating	Phone	Net Asset Value As of 6/30/06	PERFORMANCE				RISK	FUND MGR	
	99 Pct = Best / 0 Pct = Worst					Perform-ance Rating/Pts	Annualized Total Return Through 6/30/06			Risk Rating/Pts	Mgr. Quality Pct	Mgr. Tenure (Years)
							1Yr / Pct	3Yr / Pct	5Yr / Pct			
FO	● AIM European Small Company A	ESMAX	A+	(800) 347-4246	27.07	A+ /9.9	49.80 /99	49.86 /99	32.52 /99	C+ / 6.6	99	6
FO	● AIM European Small Company C	ESMCX	A+	(800) 347-4246	26.16	A+ /9.9	48.74 /99	48.83 /99	31.59 /99	C+ / 6.5	99	6
FO	● AIM European Small Company B	ESMBX	A+	(800) 347-4246	26.15	A+ /9.9	48.69 /99	48.76 /99	31.58 /99	C+ / 6.5	99	6
EN	● Ivy Fund-Global Nat Resource Adv	IGNVX	A+	(800) 777-6472	31.12	A+ /9.9	46.95 /99	39.19 /99	24.29 /98	C+ / 6.2	99	8
EM	● AIM International Small Co C	IEGCX	A+	(800) 347-4246	23.71	A+ /9.9	45.88 /98	43.45 /99	29.33 /99	C+ / 6.2	99	6
EM	● AIM International Small Co A	IEGAX	A+	(800) 347-4246	24.48	A+ /9.9	47.00 /99	44.51 /99	30.21 /99	C+ / 6.2	99	6
EM	● AIM International Small Co B	IEGBX	A+	(800) 347-4246	23.72	A+ /9.9	45.85 /99	43.47 /99	29.30 /99	C+ / 6.2	99	6
EN	Vanguard Energy Inv	VGENX	A+	(800) 662-7447	65.20	A+ /9.9	37.25 /97	39.76 /99	25.08 /98	C+ / 6.2	98	N/A
EN	Vanguard Energy Adm	VGELX	A+	(800) 662-7447	122.47	A+ /9.9	37.33 /97	39.83 /99	--	C+ / 6.2	98	N/A
FO	Eaton Vance Tax-Mgd Emg Mkt Fd	EITEX	A+	(800) 225-6265	31.61	A+ /9.8	35.45 /97	37.77 /99	25.58 /99	C+ / 6.7	85	8
FO	● Dreyfus Premier Intl Small Cap A	DSMAX	A+	(800) 782-6620	26.14	A+ /9.8	37.42 /97	35.64 /98	22.32 /98	C+ / 6.4	97	3
FO	● Dreyfus Premier Intl Small Cap R	DSMRX	A+	(800) 782-6620	26.38	A+ /9.8	37.95 /97	36.13 /98	22.58 /98	C+ / 6.4	98	3
FO	● Dreyfus Premier Intl Small Cap C	DSMCX	A+	(800) 782-6620	25.62	A+ /9.8	36.45 /97	34.74 /98	21.72 /97	C+ / 6.3	96	3
FO	● Dreyfus Premier Intl Small Cap T	DSMTX	A+	(800) 782-6620	26.00	A+ /9.8	37.16 /97	35.34 /98	22.11 /98	C+ / 6.3	97	3
FO	● The Boston Co Intl Small Cap Fd	SDISX	A+	(800) 221-4795	23.61	A+ /9.8	38.73 /98	37.08 /99	23.17 /98	C+ / 6.3	98	6
FO	American Century Intl Opport Inv	AIOIX	A+	(800) 345-6488	10.77	A+ /9.8	34.22 /96	37.77 /99	25.47 /99	C+ / 6.3	89	N/A
FO	American Century Intl Opport Inst	ACIOX	A+	(800) 345-6488	10.81	A+ /9.8	34.51 /96	38.09 /99	--	C+ / 6.2	89	N/A
FO	Allianz NACM International I	NAISX	A+	(800) 628-1237	22.01	A+ /9.7	39.76 /98	31.33 /96	16.20 /93	C+ / 6.8	89	N/A
FO	DFA International Small Cap Value	DISVX	A+	(800) 984-9472	19.30	A+ /9.7	28.16 /93	33.59 /97	23.77 /98	C+ / 6.7	98	N/A
FO	● Dreyfus Premier Intl Small Cap B	DSMBX	A+	(800) 782-6620	25.62	A+ /9.7	36.45 /97	34.71 /98	21.72 /97	C+ / 6.3	96	3
FO	Neuberger Berman International	NBISX	A+	(800) 877-9700	23.80	A+ /9.6	29.66 /94	31.39 /96	15.92 /93	C+ / 6.6	86	3
SC	Gartmore Small Cap Fd Inst	GSCIX	A+	(800) 848-0920	19.66	A /9.5	27.15 /92	29.43 /95	14.85 /92	C+ / 6.9	99	N/A
FO	AllianceBernstein Intl Value Adv	ABIYX	A+	(800) 221-5672	20.59	A /9.5	34.32 /96	27.51 /94	18.15 /95	C+ / 6.8	80	6
FO	Quantitative Foreign Value Ord	QFVOX	A+	(800) 326-2151	19.57	A /9.5	27.46 /92	29.00 /95	18.45 /95	C+ / 6.6	80	8
SC	Gartmore Small Cap Fd R	GNSRX	A+	(800) 848-0920	18.53	A /9.4	26.75 /91	28.85 /95	14.13 /90	C+ / 6.9	99	N/A
FO	Gartmore Intl Growth C	GIGCX	A+	(800) 848-0920	11.63	A /9.4	37.73 /97	27.32 /93	10.58 /82	C+ / 6.9	36	N/A
FO	AllianceBernstein Intl Value A	ABIAX	A+	(800) 221-5672	20.30	A /9.4	33.85 /96	27.12 /93	17.74 /94	C+ / 6.8	77	6
FO	Fidelity Europe	FIEUX	A+	(800) 544-8888	39.33	A /9.4	25.28 /89	28.65 /94	12.56 /88	C+ / 6.7	73	3
FO	AllianceBernstein Intl Value C	ABICX	A+	(800) 221-5672	19.99	A /9.4	32.96 /96	26.23 /92	16.97 /94	C+ / 6.7	71	6
GR	Hodges Fund	HDPMX	A+	(877) 232-1222	24.86	A /9.3	23.29 /86	28.05 /94	16.52 /94	C+ / 6.8	99	14
FO	UBS PACE Intrntl Eq Inve P	PCIEX	A+	(888) 793-8637	18.86	A- /9.2	28.11 /93	24.33 /90	8.70 /75	C+ / 6.9	43	11
FO	● ING International Value A	NIVAX	A+	(800) 992-0180	19.79	A- /9.2	27.69 /92	26.23 /92	11.51 /85	C+ / 6.9	65	N/A
FO	● ING International Value C	NIVCX	A+	(800) 992-0180	19.34	A- /9.2	26.79 /91	25.34 /91	10.73 /83	C+ / 6.9	56	N/A
FO	UBS PACE Intrntl Eq Inve Y	PWIYX	A+	(888) 793-8637	18.89	A- /9.2	28.27 /93	24.48 /90	8.81 /76	C+ / 6.9	45	5
FO	Goldman Sachs Stru Intl Eq Inst	GCIIX	A+	(800) 292-4726	14.01	A- /9.2	27.59 /92	25.41 /91	11.07 /84	C+ / 6.9	56	N/A
FO	Henderson Internatl Opport A	HFOAX	A+	(866) 443-6337	21.66	A- /9.2	32.31 /96	26.03 /92	--	C+ / 6.8	72	N/A
FO	Henderson Internatl Opport C	HFOCX	A+	(866) 443-6337	20.96	A- /9.2	31.27 /95	25.09 /91	--	C+ / 6.8	64	N/A
FO	Delaware Global Value C	DABCX	A+	(800) 362-3863	11.74	A- /9.1	20.81 /83	24.85 /91	--	C+ / 6.9	89	N/A
FO	Goldman Sachs Stru Intl Eq Svc	GCISX	A+	(800) 292-4726	13.76	A- /9.1	27.12 /91	24.88 /91	10.55 /82	C+ / 6.9	51	N/A
EN	Ivy Fund-Global Nat Resource A	IGNAX	A	(800) 777-6472	31.32	A+ /9.9	46.52 /99	39.05 /99	24.20 /98	C+ / 5.7	99	9
EN	T. Rowe Price New Era	PRNEX	A	(800) 638-5660	46.59	A+ /9.8	33.59 /96	33.38 /97	18.52 /95	C+ / 6.1	96	9
FO	● Vanguard International Explorer Fd	VINEX	A	(800) 662-7447	20.00	A+ /9.7	29.34 /94	32.45 /97	16.19 /93	C+ / 6.3	94	10
FO	● Oakmark International Small Cap I	OAKEX	A	(800) 625-6275	22.22	A+ /9.7	31.38 /95	32.72 /97	21.59 /97	C+ / 6.2	98	11
FO	● Laudus Rosenberg Intl SmCp Inst	ICSIX	A	(800) 447-3332	20.50	A+ /9.7	30.92 /95	33.13 /97	20.57 /97	C+ / 6.1	96	10
FO	● Laudus Rosenberg Intl SmCp Inv	RISIX	A	(800) 447-3332	20.26	A+ /9.7	30.50 /95	32.70 /97	20.26 /96	C+ / 6.1	95	10
FO	● Ivy Fund-European Opport Adv	IEOVX	A	(800) 777-6472	33.63	A+ /9.7	24.07 /87	33.07 /97	19.78 /96	C+ / 6.0	90	7
FO	JPMorgan Intrepid Euro Inst	JFEIX	A	(800) 358-4782	25.87	A+ /9.6	35.87 /97	29.19 /95	19.11 /95	C+ / 6.4	82	N/A
FO	JPMorgan Intrepid Euro Sel	JFESX	A	(800) 358-4782	25.56	A+ /9.6	35.61 /97	28.78 /95	18.67 /95	C+ / 6.4	79	N/A
FO	Putnam International Capital Opp	PICRX	A	(800) 354-2228	32.30	A+ /9.6	33.38 /96	30.90 /96	13.66 /90	C+ / 6.3	76	N/A
FO	Putnam International Capital Opp A	PNVAX	A	(800) 354-2228	32.51	A+ /9.6	33.70 /96	31.16 /96	13.90 /90	C+ / 6.3	77	7
FO	Putnam International Capital Opp	PIVMX	A	(800) 354-2228	32.12	A+ /9.6	33.04 /96	30.51 /96	13.33 /89	C+ / 6.2	73	N/A
FO	Putnam International Capital Opp	PUVCX	A	(800) 354-2228	32.13	A+ /9.6	32.70 /96	30.19 /96	13.04 /89	C+ / 6.2	71	7

● Denotes fund is closed to new investors

Fund Type	Fund Name	Ticker Symbol	Overall Weiss Investment Rating	Phone	Net Asset Value As of 6/30/06	Performance Rating/Pts	1Yr / Pct	3Yr / Pct	5Yr / Pct	Risk Rating/Pts	Mgr. Quality Pct	Mgr. Tenure (Years)
RE	Cohen & Steers Realty Shrs Inst	CSRIX	A	(800) 437-9912	51.30	A+ /9.6	22.64 /85	30.21 /96	20.76 /97	C+ / 6.1	94	15
FO	JPMorgan Intrepid Euro A	VEUAX	A	(800) 358-4782	25.40	A /9.5	35.29 /97	28.38 /94	18.39 /95	C+ / 6.4	76	6
RE	Alpine Intl Real Estate Y	EGLRX	A	(888) 785-5578	33.18	A /9.5	18.73 /80	31.05 /96	22.11 /98	C+ / 6.4	99	17
FO	JPMorgan Intrepid Euro B	VEUBX	A	(800) 358-4782	23.67	A /9.5	34.49 /96	27.70 /94	17.65 /94	C+ / 6.3	71	6
SC	Keeley Small Cap Value Fund	KSCVX	A	(800) 533-5344	49.74	A /9.5	31.10 /95	29.79 /95	18.02 /94	C+ / 6.3	99	13
FO	JPMorgan Intrepid Euro C	VEUCX	A	(800) 358-4782	23.62	A /9.5	34.61 /97	27.74 /94	17.66 /94	C+ / 6.3	72	6
FO	Putnam International Capital Opp B	PVNBX	A	(800) 354-2228	31.71	A /9.5	32.70 /96	30.16 /96	13.02 /89	C+ / 6.2	70	N/A
SC	Royce Value Plus Svc	RYVPX	A	(800) 221-4268	13.07	A /9.4	30.00 /94	28.78 /95	22.73 /98	C+ / 6.6	99	5
FO	Templeton China World Adv	TACWX	A	(800) 321-8563	25.38	A /9.4	22.86 /86	27.53 /94	20.09 /96	C+ / 6.3	59	N/A
FO	Fidelity Canada Fund	FICDX	A	(800) 544-8888	45.62	A /9.4	27.34 /92	27.87 /94	18.98 /95	C+ / 6.3	76	4
FO	Columbia Acorn Intl Select Fund Z	ACFFX	A	(800) 426-3750	23.16	A /9.4	30.10 /94	27.82 /94	11.83 /86	C+ / 6.3	66	5
FO	Harbor International Retire	HRINX	A	(800) 422-1050	55.09	A /9.4	35.16 /97	26.83 /93	--	C+ / 6.2	50	19
FO	Harbor International Inst	HAINX	A	(800) 422-1050	55.31	A /9.4	35.48 /97	27.13 /93	15.12 /92	C+ / 6.8	53	19
FO	● Ivy Fund-International Value Adv	IVIVX	A	(800) 777-6472	15.48	A /9.3	33.22 /96	24.98 /91	9.94 /80	C+ / 6.8	41	4
GR	Fidelity Adv Leveraged Co Stk I	FLVIX	A	(800) 522-7297	31.29	A /9.3	19.03 /81	27.54 /94	25.00 /98	C+ / 6.7	99	3
GR	Select Transportation	FSRFX	A	(800) 544-8888	52.26	A /9.3	38.48 /98	23.56 /89	12.74 /88	C+ / 6.7	98	N/A
FO	AllianceBernstein Intl Value B	ABIBX	A	(800) 221-5672	19.99	A /9.3	32.96 /96	26.23 /92	16.94 /94	C+ / 6.7	71	6
FO	Delaware Global Value I	DABIX	A	(800) 362-3863	11.89	A /9.3	22.04 /84	26.11 /92	13.95 /90	C+ / 6.7	92	N/A
FO	HSBC Investor Intl Equity Adv	RINEX	A	(800) 782-8183	20.23	A /9.3	31.44 /95	25.35 /91	9.74 /80	C+ / 6.6	56	N/A
FO	● Columbia International Value Fd Z	EMIEX	A	(800) 426-3750	23.62	A /9.3	27.28 /92	26.30 /92	12.46 /88	C+ / 6.5	69	N/A
TC	T. Rowe Price Media & Telecomm	PRMTX	A	(800) 638-5660	36.15	A /9.3	23.59 /87	26.47 /93	10.79 /83	C+ / 6.5	99	N/A
GR	Fidelity Leveraged Company Stock	FLVCX	A	(800) 544-8888	28.44	A /9.3	20.58 /83	27.77 /94	24.27 /98	C+ / 6.4	99	3
FO	Columbia Acorn Intl Select Fund A	LAFAX	A	(800) 426-3750	22.95	A /9.3	29.75 /94	27.47 /93	11.45 /85	C+ / 6.3	62	5
FO	Columbia Acorn Intl Select Fund C	LFFCX	A	(800) 426-3750	22.23	A /9.3	28.79 /94	26.51 /93	10.69 /83	C+ / 6.3	54	5
GL	Principal Inv Divers Intl B	PRBWX	A	(800) 247-4123	13.39	A /9.3	34.32 /96	25.87 /92	9.89 /80	C+ / 6.3	37	3
FO	Excelsior Instl Intl Equity I	EXIIX	A	(800) 446-1012	9.70	A /9.3	26.82 /91	26.70 /93	9.10 /77	C+ / 6.3	57	N/A
GL	Principal Inv Divers Intl A	PRWLX	A	(800) 247-4123	13.44	A /9.3	35.11 /97	26.94 /93	10.97 /84	C+ / 6.3	51	3
FO	Henderson Internatl Opport B	HFOBX	A	(866) 443-6337	20.97	A- /9.2	31.24 /95	25.11 /91	--	C+ / 6.8	65	N/A
SC	DWS Dreman Small Cap Val Inst	KDSIX	A	(800) 621-1048	36.89	A- /9.2	21.61 /84	24.86 /91	--	C+ / 6.8	98	N/A
RE	● TA IDEX Clarion Glb Real Estate A	ICRAX	A	(888) 233-4339	17.61	A- /9.2	22.45 /85	26.34 /92	--	C+ / 6.7	82	4
RE	● TA IDEX Clarion Glb Real Estate B	ICRBX	A	(888) 233-4339	17.56	A- /9.2	21.71 /84	25.56 /92	--	C+ / 6.7	77	3
RE	● TA IDEX Clarion Glb Real Estate C	ICRLX	A	(888) 233-4339	17.43	A- /9.2	21.92 /84	25.42 /91	--	C+ / 6.7	76	3
RE	Old Mutual Heitman REIT Fund	OBRAX	A	(888) 744-5050	13.93	A- /9.2	19.11 /81	26.22 /92	19.25 /95	C+ / 6.7	81	N/A
GR	Fidelity Adv Leveraged Co Stk C	FLSCX	A	(800) 522-7297	30.11	A- /9.2	17.85 /79	26.25 /92	23.76 /98	C+ / 6.6	99	3
GR	Fidelity Adv Leveraged Co Stk T	FLSTX	A	(800) 522-7297	30.61	A- /9.2	18.36 /80	26.78 /93	24.29 /98	C+ / 6.6	99	3
GR	ICON Industrials	ICTRX	A	(800) 764-0442	14.70	A- /9.2	29.19 /94	23.24 /88	8.49 /74	C+ / 6.6	98	9
FO	GE Institutional Intl Equity Inv	GIEIX	A	(800) 242-0134	14.72	A- /9.2	31.20 /95	24.32 /90	9.30 /78	C+ / 6.6	33	9
FO	Elfun International Fund	EGLBX	A	(800) 242-0134	23.98	A- /9.2	31.75 /95	24.91 /91	9.72 /79	C+ / 6.6	37	15
GL	DWS Global Thematic Fund AARP	ACOBX	A	(800) 621-1048	33.78	A- /9.2	33.36 /96	24.45 /90	9.58 /79	C+ / 6.5	45	N/A
GL	● DWS Global Thematic Fund S	SCOBX	A	(800) 621-1048	33.73	A- /9.2	33.54 /96	24.58 /90	9.65 /79	C+ / 6.5	47	N/A
FO	Excelsior International Fd	UMINX	A	(800) 446-1012	16.29	A- /9.2	25.75 /89	26.15 /92	8.70 /75	C+ / 6.5	54	N/A
FO	Wright Intl Blue Chip Eq Fd	WIBCX	A	(800) 232-0013	20.02	A- /9.2	30.77 /95	23.96 /89	10.71 /83	C+ / 6.5	43	17
FO	Adv Inn Cir McKee Intl Eqty I	MKIEX	A	(866) 777-7818	14.64	A- /9.1	26.03 /90	24.00 /89	10.54 /82	C+ / 6.9	57	6
FO	● ING International Value B	NIVBX	A	(800) 992-0180	19.42	A- /9.1	26.76 /91	25.34 /91	10.74 /83	C+ / 6.9	56	N/A
GR	Select Air Transport	FSAIX	A	(800) 544-8888	45.82	A- /9.1	38.63 /98	20.92 /82	7.24 /68	C+ / 6.9	98	1
FO	Gartmore Internatl Index Inst	GIXIX	A	(800) 848-0920	9.87	A- /9.1	27.03 /91	23.72 /89	9.19 /77	C+ / 6.9	48	7
FO	JennDry Dryden Intl Equity C	PJRCX	A	(800) 257-3893	7.67	A- /9.1	25.33 /89	24.25 /90	6.98 /67	C+ / 6.9	49	3
SC	Stratton Small-Cap Value Fund	STSCX	A	(800) 634-5726	47.56	A- /9.1	16.21 /75	25.53 /92	16.72 /94	C+ / 6.8	97	N/A

● Denotes fund is closed to new investors

Data as of June 30, 2006

Fund Type	Fund Name	Ticker Symbol	Overall Weiss Investment Rating	Phone	Net Asset Value As of 6/30/06	Perform-ance Rating/Pts	Annualized Total Return Through 6/30/06			Risk Rating/Pts	Mgr. Quality Pct	Mgr. Tenure (Years)
							1Yr / Pct	3Yr / Pct	5Yr / Pct			
FO	Merrill Lynch Latin America C	MCLTX	C+	(800) 543-6217	39.63	A+ /9.9	54.28 /99	50.38 /99	24.07 /98	D+ / 2.9	94	N/A
EM	Sanford Bernstein Emerg Markets	SNEMX	C+		37.31	A+ /9.9	32.19 /96	40.32 /99	27.00 /99	D+ / 2.9	45	N/A
FO	Merrill Lynch Latin America B	MBLTX	C+	(800) 543-6217	40.14	A+ /9.9	54.23 /99	50.38 /99	24.07 /98	D+ / 2.9	94	N/A
EN	● BlackRock-Global Resources Inst	SGLSX	C+	(888) 825-2257	80.06	A+ /9.9	50.63 /99	52.62 /99	33.96 /99	D+ / 2.7	99	1
FO	Janus Fd Inc-Overseas Fund	JAOSX	C+	(800) 525-3713	37.35	A+ /9.8	52.33 /99	33.29 /97	11.83 /86	D+ / 2.9	58	6
EN	Select Natural Gas	FSNGX	C+	(800) 544-8888	40.97	A+ /9.8	30.94 /95	35.68 /98	17.75 /94	D+ / 2.9	61	1
EN	Excelsior Energy & Nat Resrc Fd	UMESX	C+	(800) 446-1012	25.94	A+ /9.8	34.61 /97	36.56 /98	19.13 /95	D+ / 2.9	84	11
EM	CG Cap Mkt Fds-Emerging Mkts	TEMUX	C+	(800) 446-1013	13.18	A+ /9.7	35.28 /97	32.92 /97	19.75 /96	D+ / 2.9	9	N/A
FO	Matthews Korea Fund	MAKOX	C+	(800) 892-0382	6.29	A+ /9.6	40.57 /98	32.77 /97	29.71 /99	D+ / 2.9	78	11
AG	ProFunds-Oil & Gas UltraSector	ENPIX	C	(888) 776-3637	38.28	A+ /9.9	32.82 /96	44.73 /99	16.43 /93	D / 2.0	99	6
AG	ProFunds-Oil & Gas UltraSector	ENPSX	C	(888) 776-3637	36.08	A+ /9.9	31.49 /95	43.29 /99	15.34 /92	D / 2.0	99	6
PM	Van Eck Intl Investors Gold A	INIVX	C	(800) 221-2220	16.12	A+ /9.9	85.61 /99	35.18 /98	37.22 /99	D / 1.9	66	8
GR	Wells Fargo Avtg Value Fund Adm	CBTIX	C	(800) 222-8222	19.04	A+ /9.9	7.92 /32	44.80 /99	26.36 /99	D / 1.7	99	N/A
EM	ING Russia A	LETRX	C	(800) 992-0180	50.15	A+ /9.9	91.70 /99	41.58 /99	42.61 /99	D / 1.6	42	5
PM	US Global Inv Gold Shares	USERX	C	(800) 873-8637	15.49	A+ /9.9	104.28 /99	45.05 /99	41.06 /99	D- / 1.5	98	N/A
EM	Russell Emerging Markets S	REMSX	C	(800) 832-6688	19.78	A+ /9.8	33.46 /96	34.54 /98	20.50 /97	D+ / 2.6	13	N/A
EM	Legg Mason Emerg Mkts Prim	LMEMX	C	(800) 822-5544	20.81	A+ /9.8	41.98 /98	36.95 /99	21.19 /97	D+ / 2.5	13	10
EM	Principal Inv Intl Emrg Mkts A	PRIAX	C	(800) 247-4123	22.34	A+ /9.8	41.80 /98	36.83 /98	20.91 /97	D+ / 2.5	23	5
EM	AIM Developing Markets Fd Inst	GTDIX	C	(800) 347-4246	20.99	A+ /9.8	39.76 /98	36.36 /98	21.82 /98	D+ / 2.4	29	N/A
EN	Munder Power Plus B	MPFBX	C	(800) 438-5789	16.72	A+ /9.8	29.51 /94	35.91 /98	11.40 /85	D+ / 2.3	90	N/A
EN	Munder Power Plus A	MPFAX	C	(800) 438-5789	17.43	A+ /9.8	30.56 /95	36.92 /98	12.26 /87	D / 2.2	92	N/A
EN	Munder Power Plus C	MPFTX	C	(800) 438-5789	16.74	A+ /9.8	29.57 /94	35.90 /98	11.40 /85	D / 2.2	89	N/A
RE	CGM Realty Fund	CGMRX	C	(800) 345-4048	30.69	A+ /9.8	31.65 /95	37.79 /99	31.43 /99	D / 1.9	99	12
EM	● Delaware Pooled Tr-Emerging	DPEMX	C	(800) 362-3863	13.87	A+ /9.8	23.89 /87	36.76 /98	24.45 /98	D / 1.9	84	9
FO	Fidelity Adv Korea I	FKRIX	C	(800) 522-7297	23.34	A+ /9.8	53.42 /99	34.89 /98	26.46 /99	D / 1.9	60	N/A
EN	Putnam Global Natural Resources		C	(800) 354-2228	31.75	A+ /9.7	31.75 /95	32.31 /97	17.61 /94	D+ / 2.6	88	N/A
EM	Russell Emerging Markets E	REMEX	C	(800) 832-6688	19.78	A+ /9.7	33.01 /96	34.26 /98	20.25 /96	D+ / 2.6	12	N/A
EN	Saratoga Adv Tr-Energy&Basic	SEPIX	C	(800) 807-3863	32.35	A+ /9.7	39.86 /98	32.80 /97	--	D+ / 2.5	83	N/A
EM	Russell Emerging Markets C	REMCX	C	(800) 832-6688	19.18	A+ /9.7	32.09 /96	33.30 /97	19.44 /96	D+ / 2.5	9	N/A
EM	Van Kampen Emerging Markets C	MSRCX	C	(800) 421-5666	19.42	A+ /9.7	35.61 /97	33.40 /97	19.71 /96	D+ / 2.3	9	N/A
EM	JPMorgan Emerg Mkt Eq C	JEMCX	C	(800) 358-4782	14.48	A+ /9.7	30.33 /95	33.95 /97	18.68 /95	D / 2.2	17	N/A
FO	Fidelity Adv Korea T	FAKTX	C	(800) 522-7297	22.65	A+ /9.7	52.59 /99	34.16 /98	25.79 /99	D / 1.9	54	N/A
FO	Universal Inst Emer Markets Eqty II	UEMBX	C	(800) 869-6397	15.92	A+ /9.7	37.31 /97	33.60 /97	--	D / 1.9	21	3
EM	Forward Global Emerg Markets Inv	PGERX	C	(800) 999-6809	19.49	A+ /9.7	30.96 /95	34.55 /98	--	D / 1.9	18	N/A
FO	Fidelity Adv Korea A	FAKAX	C	(800) 522-7297	22.99	A+ /9.7	53.08 /99	34.48 /98	26.14 /99	D / 1.9	57	N/A
EM	Universal Inst Emerging Markets	UEMEX	C	(800) 869-6397	15.94	A+ /9.7	37.27 /97	33.67 /97	18.81 /95	D / 1.8	10	N/A
FO	Fidelity Adv Korea B	FAKBX	C	(800) 522-7297	22.00	A+ /9.7	51.83 /99	33.48 /97	25.21 /98	D / 1.8	46	N/A
FO	Fidelity Adv Korea C	FAKCX	C	(800) 522-7297	22.00	A+ /9.7	51.76 /99	33.45 /97	25.18 /98	D / 1.8	46	N/A
EM	Wells Fargo Avtg Emg Mkt Foc	MNEFX	C	(800) 222-8222	32.58	A+ /9.6	42.27 /98	29.93 /95	19.22 /95	D+ / 2.5	1	9
EM	Van Kampen Emerging Markets A	MSRAX	C	(800) 421-5666	20.87	A+ /9.6	36.73 /97	34.47 /98	20.56 /97	D+ / 2.3	12	5
EM	Van Kampen Emerging Markets B	MSRBX	C	(800) 421-5666	19.36	A+ /9.6	35.67 /97	33.43 /97	19.69 /96	D+ / 2.3	9	N/A
EM	ING JPMorgan Emrg Mkt Eq Port	IJPTX	C	(800) 992-0180	15.72	A+ /9.6	36.83 /97	30.62 /96	--	D / 2.2	6	1
EM	ING JPMorgan Emrg Mkt Eq Port S	IJPIX	C	(800) 992-0180	15.82	A+ /9.6	36.96 /97	30.81 /96	16.94 /94	D / 2.2	6	1
GR	● CGM Capital Development	LOMCX	C	(800) 345-4048	31.75	A+ /9.6	27.79 /92	30.60 /96	13.19 /89	D / 2.0	99	30
EM	Wells Fargo Avtg Emg Mkt Foc C	MFFCX	C	(800) 222-8222	31.80	A /9.5	40.73 /98	28.56 /94	--	D+ / 2.9	0	5
EM	Wells Fargo Avtg Emg Mkt Foc B	MFFBX	C	(800) 222-8222	31.92	A /9.5	40.84 /98	28.62 /94	18.35 /95	D+ / 2.9	0	5
EM	Wells Fargo Avtg Emg Mkt Foc A	MFFAX	C	(800) 222-8222	32.62	A /9.5	41.87 /98	29.55 /95	19.00 /95	D+ / 2.9	1	5
EM	Phoenix Insight Emerging Mkt Inst	HIEMX	C	(800) 982-8782	12.57	A /9.5	36.10 /97	29.84 /95	19.96 /96	D+ / 2.8	6	N/A
AG	ProFunds-Ultra Mid Cap Inv	UMPIX	C	(888) 776-3637	45.51	A /9.5	17.88 /79	30.82 /96	8.44 /74	D+ / 2.7	87	N/A
EM	UBS PACE Intertl Emg Mkts Eq	PWEYX	C	(888) 793-8637	18.26	A /9.5	28.46 /93	30.33 /96	16.06 /93	D+ / 2.3	6	N/A
RE	Neuberger Berman Real Estate	NBRFX	C	(800) 877-9700	14.51	A /9.4	21.81 /84	28.08 /94	--	D+ / 2.9	88	4
RE	ING Real Estate Fd I	CRARX	C	(800) 992-0180	18.30	A /9.4	23.83 /87	27.77 /94	19.97 /96	D+ / 2.7	84	N/A

● Denotes fund is closed to new investors

Fund Type	Fund Name	Ticker Symbol	Overall Weiss Investment Rating	Phone	Net Asset Value As of 6/30/06	PERFORMANCE Perform-ance Rating/Pts	Annualized Total Return Through 6/30/06 1Yr / Pct	3Yr / Pct	5Yr / Pct	RISK Risk Rating/Pts	FUND MGR Mgr. Quality Pct	Mgr. Tenure (Years)
AG	ProFunds-Ultra Mid Cap Svc	UMPSX	C	(888) 776-3637	42.79	A /9.4	16.69 /76	29.53 /95	7.45 /69	D+ / 2.6	81	N/A
FS	Merrill Lynch Global Finan Svc I	MAFNX	C	(800) 543-6217	16.81	A /9.3	25.75 /89	27.05 /93	16.83 /94	D+ / 2.9	98	N/A
EM	Phoenix Insight Emerging Mkt A	HEMZX	C	(800) 982-8782	12.41	A /9.3	35.83 /97	29.52 /95	19.69 /96	D+ / 2.8	6	N/A
TC	Columbia Technology D	CTCDX	C	(800) 426-3750	9.65	A- /9.1	29.43 /94	26.88 /93	--	D+ / 2.9	88	1
FS	Merrill Lynch Global Finan Svc C	MCFNX	C	(800) 543-6217	16.33	A- /9.1	24.49 /88	25.77 /92	15.60 /93	D+ / 2.9	97	N/A
FS	Merrill Lynch Global Finan Svc A	MDFNX	C	(800) 543-6217	16.70	A- /9.1	25.39 /89	26.72 /93	16.50 /94	D+ / 2.9	98	N/A
FS	Merrill Lynch Global Finan Svc B	MBFNX	C	(800) 543-6217	16.42	A- /9.1	24.47 /88	25.74 /92	15.61 /93	D+ / 2.8	97	N/A
TC	Columbia Technology B	CTCBX	C	(800) 426-3750	9.59	A- /9.0	29.49 /94	26.89 /93	--	D+ / 2.9	88	1
AG	Rydex Series-Russell 2000 Adv H	RYMKX	C	(800) 820-0888	34.09	B+ /8.9	16.79 /77	24.82 /91	7.71 /70	D+ / 2.9	50	N/A
AG	ProFunds-Mble Telcm UltraSector	WCPSX	C	(888) 776-3637	17.69	B+ /8.7	-6.97 / 0	28.52 /94	-17.63 / 0	D+ / 2.9	95	6
AG	Rydex Series-Russell 2000 Adv C	RYCMX	C	(800) 820-0888	32.75	B+ /8.7	15.89 /74	23.85 /89	6.89 /66	D+ / 2.8	40	N/A
PM	USAA Gold Fund	USAGX	C-	(800) 382-8722	27.04	A+ /9.9	81.81 /99	37.42 /99	37.98 /99	D- / 1.5	93	N/A
PM	US Global Inv World Prec Minerals	UNWPX	C-	(800) 873-8637	28.86	A+ /9.9	96.21 /99	53.24 /99	46.82 /99	D- / 1.5	99	8
FO	DWS Latin America Eq Fund AARP	SLAMX	C-	(800) 621-1048	51.62	A+ /9.9	52.61 /99	43.70 /99	22.00 /98	D- / 1.4	65	6
FO	DWS Latin America Eq Fund C	SLAPX	C-	(800) 621-1048	50.85	A+ /9.9	51.13 /99	42.29 /99	20.69 /97	D- / 1.4	52	5
FO	DWS Latin America Eq Fund B	SLAOX	C-	(800) 621-1048	50.89	A+ /9.9	51.00 /99	42.21 /99	20.70 /97	D- / 1.4	52	5
FO	DWS Latin America Eq Fund A	SLANX	C-	(800) 621-1048	51.35	A+ /9.9	52.33 /99	43.41 /99	21.67 /97	D- / 1.4	63	5
FO	● DWS Latin America Eq Fund S	SLAFX	C-	(800) 621-1048	51.48	A+ /9.9	52.65 /99	43.72 /99	21.97 /98	D- / 1.4	66	10
FO	Eaton Vance Greater India B	EMGIX	C-	(800) 225-6265	19.27	A+ /9.9	38.64 /98	47.04 /99	28.24 /99	D- / 1.2	78	1
FO	Eaton Vance Greater India A	ETGIX	C-	(800) 225-6265	20.55	A+ /9.9	39.32 /98	47.36 /99	28.71 /99	D- / 1.2	80	1
PM	● Vanguard Prec. Metals & Mining Fd	VGPMX	C-	(800) 662-7447	29.16	A+ /9.9	72.86 /99	44.17 /99	35.20 /99	D- / 1.2	99	10
PM	Midas Fund	MIDSX	C-	(800) 400-6432	4.05	A+ /9.9	104.55 /99	39.25 /99	35.70 /99	D- / 1.1	90	N/A
PM	● AIM Gold & Prec Met Inv	FGLDX	C-	(800) 347-4246	5.71	A+ /9.8	59.50 /99	29.76 /95	29.72 /99	D- / 1.2	65	7
PM	AIM Gold & Prec Met C	IGDCX	C-	(800) 347-4246	5.94	A+ /9.8	58.40 /99	28.87 /95	28.40 /99	D- / 1.2	58	7
PM	AIM Gold & Prec Met A	IGDAX	C-	(800) 347-4246	5.67	A+ /9.8	59.27 /99	29.65 /95	--	D- / 1.2	65	7
PM	Select Gold	FSAGX	C-	(800) 544-8888	34.45	A+ /9.7	69.56 /99	26.01 /92	27.74 /99	D / 1.7	21	3
PM	AIM Gold & Prec Met B	IGDBX	C-	(800) 347-4246	5.60	A+ /9.7	58.19 /99	28.87 /95	--	D- / 1.2	57	7
EM	RVS Emerging Markets Fund Y		C-	(800) 328-8300	10.29	A+ /9.6	36.29 /97	32.80 /97	19.48 /96	D / 1.7	7	6
SC	● Bridgeway Ultra Small Company	BRUSX	C-	(800) 661-3550	42.42	A /9.4	25.58 /89	26.85 /93	25.83 /99	D- / 1.0	88	12
FO	Fidelity Japan Small Companies	FJSCX	C-	(800) 544-8888	14.49	A /9.3	19.40 /81	30.39 /96	14.18 /90	D / 2.0	89	10
EM	Principal Inv Intl Emrg Mkts B	PIEBX	C-	(800) 247-4123	22.15	A- /9.2	40.39 /98	24.62 /90	13.97 /90	D / 2.2	1	5
GR	ProFunds-Basic Mat UltraSector	BMPIX	C-	(888) 776-3637	42.92	A- /9.1	29.29 /94	23.15 /88	--	D / 1.6	37	N/A
FO	DWS Internatl Sel Eqty Inv	MGIVX	C-	(800) 621-1048	12.13	B+ /8.9	29.53 /94	23.03 /87	9.55 /79	D / 1.9	23	N/A
FO	Rydex Series-Japan Advantage H	RYJPX	C-	(800) 820-0888	38.09	B+ /8.8	38.21 /97	22.72 /87	1.17 /21	D+ / 2.3	1	N/A
FO	DWS Internatl Sel Eqty Prem	MGIPX	C-	(800) 621-1048	12.16	B+ /8.8	27.68 /92	22.79 /87	9.63 /79	D / 1.9	25	N/A
GR	ProFunds-Basic Mat UltraSector	BMPSX	C-	(888) 776-3637	41.83	B+ /8.8	28.16 /93	21.96 /85	--	D- / 1.5	29	N/A
FO	DWS Internatl Sel Eqty Inst	MGINX	C-	(800) 621-1048	12.15	B+ /8.7	27.37 /92	22.53 /86	9.37 /78	D / 1.9	23	N/A
FO	Rydex Series-Japan Advantage C	RYCJX	C-	(800) 820-0888	36.92	B+ /8.5	37.15 /97	21.73 /84	--	D+ / 2.4	1	N/A
UT	Eaton Vance Utilities C	ECTMX	C-	(800) 225-6265	12.03	B+ /8.4	16.24 /75	21.10 /83	9.05 /76	D+ / 2.3	96	7
SC	● Putnam Small Capital Value Fund	PSLMX	C-	(800) 354-2228	17.31	B /8.2	13.35 /66	21.97 /85	11.96 /87	D+ / 2.6	89	4
SC	● Putnam Small Capital Value Fund	PSLCX	C-	(800) 354-2228	16.83	B /8.2	13.05 /64	21.68 /84	11.67 /86	D+ / 2.3	88	7
SC	Adv Inn Cir FMA Sm Co I	FMACX	C-	(866) 777-7818	21.70	B /8.0	16.74 /76	19.11 /76	9.20 /77	D+ / 2.8	87	N/A
FO	● The Japan Fund CL S	SJPNX	C-	(800) 544-8888	12.25	B /7.9	25.51 /89	23.21 /88	7.14 /67	D+ / 2.6	9	4
SC	● DWS Small Cap Value S	SCSUX	C-	(800) 621-1048	26.40	B /7.6	10.73 /52	19.51 /78	12.69 /88	D+ / 2.9	80	N/A
TC	Jacob Internet Fund	JAMFX	D+	(888) 522-6239	2.48	A- /9.0	28.50 /93	26.33 /92	14.69 /91	D- / 1.2	91	10
FO	JPMorgan Japan Fund Sel	JPNSX	D+	(800) 358-4782	9.82	B+ /8.8	33.62 /96	25.74 /92	8.41 /74	D- / 1.3	32	N/A
FO	JPMorgan Japan Fund C	JPCNX	D+	(800) 358-4782	9.19	B+ /8.6	32.82 /96	24.89 /91	7.58 /70	D- / 1.4	28	N/A
FO	Delaware Intl Value Equity I	DEQIX	D+	(800) 362-3863	14.42	B+ /8.4	19.04 /81	21.03 /83	11.48 /85	D / 1.7	38	N/A

● Denotes fund is closed to new investors

Data as of June 30, 2006

Fund Type	Fund Name	Ticker Symbol	Overall Weiss Investment Rating	Phone	Net Asset Value As of 6/30/06	Perform-ance Rating/Pts	Annualized Total Return Through 6/30/06 1Yr / Pct	3Yr / Pct	5Yr / Pct	Risk Rating/Pts	Mgr. Quality Pct	Mgr. Tenure (Years)
	99 Pct = Best *0 Pct = Worst*											
PM	Oppenheimer Gold/Spec Min A	OPGSX	C-	(800) 525-7048	29.15	A+ /9.9	68.00 /99	36.49 /98	30.30 /99	E+ / 0.7	90	9
EM	US Global Accolade East	EUROX	C-	(800) 873-8637	41.17	A+ /9.9	42.73 /98	44.58 /99	38.97 /99	E+ / 0.7	14	6
PM	Oppenheimer Gold/Spec Min C	OGMCX	C-	(800) 525-7048	28.10	A+ /9.9	66.79 /99	35.47 /98	29.33 /99	E+ / 0.7	87	9
PM	Oppenheimer Gold/Spec Min B	OGMBX	C-	(800) 525-7048	28.13	A+ /9.9	66.67 /99	35.41 /98	29.28 /99	E+ / 0.7	86	9
PM	Oppenheimer Gold/Spec Min N	OGMNX	C-	(800) 525-7048	28.68	A+ /9.9	67.62 /99	36.05 /98	29.90 /99	E+ / 0.7	89	9
EN	ING VP Natural Resources Trust		C-	(800) 992-0180	27.53	A+ /9.8	45.72 /98	31.59 /96	17.37 /94	E+ / 0.7	42	6
FO	● Eaton Vance Asian Small Co B	EBASX	C-	(800) 225-6265	25.26	A+ /9.7	40.10 /98	33.48 /97	25.00 /98	E+ / 0.6	92	2
FO	● Eaton Vance Asian Small Co A	EVASX	C-	(800) 225-6265	25.34	A+ /9.7	40.82 /98	34.16 /98	25.65 /99	E+ / 0.6	93	2
PM	Evergreen Precious Metals I	EKWYX	D+	(800) 343-2898	55.24	A+ /9.9	76.08 /99	38.03 /99	37.41 /99	E- / 0.2	89	N/A
PM	Evergreen Precious Metals C	EKWCX	D+	(800) 343-2898	52.96	A+ /9.9	74.33 /99	36.68 /98	36.05 /99	E- / 0.2	83	N/A
PM	Evergreen Precious Metals A	EKWAX	D+	(800) 343-2898	55.56	A+ /9.9	75.57 /99	37.63 /99	37.06 /99	E- / 0.2	87	N/A
PM	Evergreen Precious Metals B	EKWBX	D+	(800) 343-2898	53.26	A+ /9.9	74.33 /99	36.66 /98	36.06 /99	E- / 0.2	83	N/A
FO	ProFunds-Ultra Japan Inv	UJPIX	D+	(888) 776-3637	59.48	A+ /9.9	77.87 /99	37.70 /99	0.91 /20	E- / 0.2	8	N/A
PM	GAMCO Gold C	GLDCX	D+	(800) 422-3554	25.66	A+ /9.9	75.05 /99	29.56 /95	34.40 /99	E- / 0.0	29	12
PM	GAMCO Gold B	GLDBX	D+	(800) 422-3554	25.67	A+ /9.9	75.03 /99	29.52 /95	34.38 /99	E- / 0.0	29	12
PM	GAMCO Gold A	GLDAX	D+	(800) 422-3554	25.94	A+ /9.9	76.43 /99	30.54 /96	35.10 /99	E- / 0.0	35	12
PM	Franklin Gold & Prec Metals A	FKRCX	D+	(800) 342-5236	30.88	A+ /9.9	72.23 /99	33.32 /97	27.46 /99	E- / 0.0	73	9
PM	Franklin Gold & Prec Metals C	FRGOX	D+	(800) 342-5236	30.13	A+ /9.9	70.95 /99	32.29 /97	26.51 /99	E- / 0.0	66	9
PM	GAMCO Gold AAA	GOLDX	D+	(800) 422-3554	25.96	A+ /9.9	76.37 /99	30.54 /96	35.10 /99	E- / 0.0	35	12
PM	Tocqueville Gold Fund	TGLDX	D+	(800) 697-3863	50.21	A+ /9.9	63.28 /99	31.54 /96	35.70 /99	E- / 0.0	71	8
PM	Franklin Gold & Prec Metals Adv	FGADX	D+	(800) 321-8563	31.71	A+ /9.9	72.57 /99	33.63 /97	27.75 /99	E- / 0.0	75	9
PM	DWS Gold & Prec Metals Fund	SGLDX	D+	(800) 621-1048	23.36	A+ /9.9	57.98 /99	35.10 /98	34.70 /99	E- / 0.0	71	5
PM	● DWS Gold & Prec Metals Fund S	SCGDX	D+	(800) 621-1048	23.33	A+ /9.9	58.04 /99	35.10 /98	34.68 /99	E- / 0.0	71	5
PM	● Franklin Gold & Prec Metals B	FAGPX	D+	(800) 342-5236	29.85	A+ /9.9	70.90 /99	32.30 /97	26.49 /99	E- / 0.0	66	9
PM	DWS Gold & Prec Metals Fund C	SGDCX	D+	(800) 621-1048	23.03	A+ /9.9	56.47 /99	33.80 /97	33.38 /99	E- / 0.0	61	5
FO	ProFunds-Ultra Japan Svc	UJPSX	D+	(888) 776-3637	56.81	A+ /9.8	76.05 /99	36.35 /98	-0.07 /15	E- / 0.2	5	N/A
EM	Third Millennium Russia Fund	TMRFX	D+	(800) 527-9500	53.12	A+ /9.8	52.26 /99	37.00 /99	32.97 /99	E- / 0.0	17	8
PM	American Century Global Gold Inv	BGEIX	D+	(800) 345-6488	18.62	A+ /9.8	66.31 /99	27.65 /94	31.93 /99	E- / 0.0	10	15
PM	OCM Gold Fund	OCMGX	D+	(800) 628-9403	18.55	A+ /9.8	72.66 /99	27.15 /93	33.57 /99	E- / 0.0	14	10
PM	American Century Global Gold Adv	ACGGX	D+	(800) 345-6488	18.60	A+ /9.8	65.85 /99	27.39 /93	31.64 /99	E- / 0.0	9	15
PM	RVS Precious Metals Fund B	INPBX	D+	(800) 328-8300	13.93	A+ /9.8	68.24 /99	27.79 /94	26.15 /99	E- / 0.0	26	7
PM	RVS Precious Metals Fund A	INPMX	D+	(800) 328-8300	14.75	A+ /9.8	69.54 /99	28.74 /95	27.13 /99	E- / 0.0	32	7
PM	DWS Gold & Prec Metals Fund A	SGDAX	D+	(800) 621-1048	23.30	A+ /9.8	57.64 /99	34.79 /98	34.41 /99	E- / 0.0	69	5
PM	DWS Gold & Prec Metals Fund B	SGDBX	D+	(800) 621-1048	23.06	A+ /9.8	56.42 /99	33.76 /97	33.35 /99	E- / 0.0	61	5
PM	ProFunds-Precious Metals Ultra	PMPSX	D+	(888) 776-3637	44.86	A+ /9.8	72.67 /99	26.46 /93	--	E- / 0.0	0	N/A
PM	ProFunds-Precious Metals Ultra Inv	PMPIX	D+	(888) 776-3637	46.61	A+ /9.8	74.31 /99	26.82 /93	--	E- / 0.0	0	N/A
PM	ING Precious Metals A	LEXMX	D+	(800) 992-0180	10.69	A+ /9.7	67.59 /99	27.11 /93	30.19 /99	E- / 0.0	21	8
RE	ProFunds-Real Est UltraSector Inv	REPIX	D+	(888) 776-3637	44.96	A+ /9.7	20.10 /82	32.96 /97	19.56 /96	E- / 0.0	23	6
RE	Morgan Stanley Real Estate D	REFDX	D+	(800) 869-6397	16.75	A+ /9.6	24.36 /88	30.63 /96	20.70 /97	E+ / 0.6	97	7
PM	● First Eagle Gold Fund A	SGGDX	D+	(800) 334-2143	23.75	A /9.5	54.82 /99	25.01 /91	35.05 /99	E+ / 0.7	26	7
RE	Morgan Stanley Real Estate A	REFAX	D+	(800) 869-6397	16.73	A /9.5	24.02 /87	30.33 /96	20.41 /96	E+ / 0.6	97	7
RE	Morgan Stanley Real Estate C	REFCX	D+	(800) 869-6397	16.66	A /9.5	23.05 /86	29.33 /95	19.52 /96	E+ / 0.6	95	7
SC	ProFunds-Ultra Small Cap Inv	UAPIX	D+	(888) 776-3637	28.39	A /9.5	19.84 /82	30.72 /96	6.82 /66	E+ / 0.6	12	7
RE	Morgan Stanley Real Estate B	REFBX	D+	(800) 869-6397	16.66	A /9.4	22.99 /86	29.32 /95	19.49 /96	E+ / 0.6	95	7
SC	ProFunds-Ultra Small Cap Svc	UAPSX	D+	(888) 776-3637	26.78	A /9.4	18.60 /80	29.43 /95	5.73 /59	E+ / 0.6	9	6
RE	ProFunds-Real Est UltraSector Svc	REPSX	D	(888) 776-3637	45.66	A+ /9.6	18.93 /80	31.61 /96	18.35 /95	E- / 0.0	16	6
PM	● First Eagle Gold Fund I	FEGIX	D	(800) 334-2143	23.88	A+ /9.6	55.27 /99	25.32 /91	--	E- / 0.0	27	7
PM	● First Eagle Gold Fund C	FEGOX	D	(800) 334-2143	23.50	A /9.5	53.69 /99	24.13 /90	--	E- / 0.0	21	7
RE	JPMorgan Realty Income Fund Cl I	URTLX	D	(800) 358-4782	17.30	A /9.5	22.99 /86	28.38 /94	20.66 /97	E- / 0.0	90	N/A
PM	Rydex Series-Precious Metal Inv	RYPMX	D	(800) 820-0888	53.06	A /9.3	52.30 /99	20.20 /80	21.41 /97	E- / 0.0	1	N/A
PM	Rydex Series-Precious Metal C	RYZCX	D	(800) 820-0888	50.52	A- /9.1	50.76 /99	18.99 /76	20.23 /96	E- / 0.0	1	N/A
SC	● NI Numeric Inv Small Cap Value	NISVX	D	(800) 686-3742	18.56	B+ /8.6	16.54 /76	22.66 /87	19.05 /95	E+ / 0.8	94	N/A

● Denotes fund is closed to new investors

Fund Type	Fund Name	Ticker Symbol	Overall Weiss Investment Rating	Phone	Net Asset Value As of 6/30/06	Performance Rating/Pts	1Yr / Pct	3Yr / Pct	5Yr / Pct	Risk Rating/Pts	Mgr. Quality Pct	Mgr. Tenure (Years)
	99 Pct = Best *0 Pct = Worst*							Annualized Total Return Through 6/30/06				
SC	CG Cap Mkt Fds-Small Cap Val Eq	TSVUX	D	(800) 446-1013	14.04	B+ /8.6	15.38 /73	22.66 /86	13.16 /89	E / 0.5	94	13
EN	● Oppenheimer Real Asset Y	QRAYX	D-	(800) 525-7048	8.24	B+ /8.5	15.31 /73	22.05 /85	15.44 /92	E- / 0.0	61	7
EN	● Oppenheimer Real Asset N	QRANX	D-	(800) 525-7048	8.11	B+ /8.3	14.55 /70	21.08 /83	14.60 /91	E- / 0.0	53	7
EN	● Oppenheimer Real Asset C	QRACX	D-	(800) 525-7048	8.00	B /8.2	13.94 /68	20.53 /81	14.01 /90	E- / 0.0	47	7
GL	NorthPointe Small Cap Value Inst	NNSVX	D-	(800) 848-0920	11.32	B /8.1	15.42 /73	20.02 /79	11.11 /84	E- / 0.0	31	6
EN	● Oppenheimer Real Asset A	QRAAX	D-	(800) 525-7048	8.19	B /8.0	14.88 /71	21.52 /84	14.97 /92	E- / 0.0	58	7
EN	● Oppenheimer Real Asset B	QRABX	D-	(800) 525-7048	8.05	B /7.9	13.94 /68	20.48 /81	14.00 /90	E- / 0.0	47	7
SC	● BlackRock-Small Cap Val Inst	PNSEX	D-	(888) 825-2257	13.17	B- /7.4	9.51 /43	19.21 /77	10.35 /82	E- / 0.2	85	4
AG	Turner New Enterprise Fund	TBTBX	D-	(800) 224-6312	6.36	C+ /6.8	22.07 /84	18.94 /76	0.48 /18	E+ / 0.7	15	6
SC	● BlackRock-Small Cap Val Svc	PSESX	E+	(888) 825-2257	12.90	B- /7.3	9.15 /41	18.81 /76	10.00 /80	E- / 0.1	82	4
FO	● TA IDEX MFS International Equity	ICILX	E+	(888) 233-4339	6.90	B- /7.3	21.63 /84	16.58 /66	--	E- / 0.0	8	N/A
FO	● TA IDEX MFS International Equity	ICIBX	E+	(888) 233-4339	6.98	B- /7.3	21.52 /84	16.64 /66	2.41 /31	E- / 0.0	8	4
SC	● Managers Small Cap Fund	MSSCX	E+	(800) 835-3879	14.83	B- /7.1	17.23 /78	17.00 /68	0.19 /16	E- / 0.0	93	N/A
RE	Gabelli Westwood Income AAA	WESRX	E+	(800) 422-3554	11.71	B- /7.0	3.07 / 7	18.33 /74	14.79 /92	E- / 0.0	45	9
FO	● TA IDEX MFS International Equity	ICIAX	E+	(888) 233-4339	7.51	B- /7.0	22.01 /84	17.21 /69	3.05 /37	E- / 0.0	10	4
SC	● BlackRock-Small Cap Val C	BSCCX	E+	(888) 825-2257	11.07	C+ /6.9	8.29 /35	17.87 /72	9.06 /77	E- / 0.0	76	4
SC	● BlackRock-Small Cap Val B	CCVBX	E+	(888) 825-2257	11.06	C+ /6.9	8.19 /34	17.84 /72	9.07 /77	E- / 0.0	76	4
SC	● BlackRock-Small Cap Val A	PSEIX	E+	(888) 825-2257	12.81	C+ /6.7	9.10 /41	18.76 /75	9.89 /80	E- / 0.1	83	4
AG	ProFunds-Internet UltraSector Inv	INPIX	E	(888) 776-3637	80.66	C+ /6.3	19.85 /82	18.73 /75	-6.08 / 2	E- / 0.0	1	6
GR	Wireless Fund (The)	WIREX	E	(800) 590-0898	4.47	C+ /6.0	26.63 /91	12.49 /46	-7.47 / 1	E- / 0.1	1	6
TC	Firsthand-Technology Value Fund	TVFQX	E	(888) 884-2675	34.63	C+ /5.7	24.17 /87	13.46 /51	-6.56 / 1	E+ / 0.7	5	12
AG	ProFunds-Internet UltraSector Svc	INPSX	E	(888) 776-3637	75.21	C+ /5.7	18.67 /80	17.56 /70	-6.92 / 1	E- / 0.0	1	6
SC	● Oberweis Micro Cap Portfolio	OBMCX	E	(800) 245-7311	16.35	C+ /5.6	10.24 /48	15.97 /63	14.21 /90	E+ / 0.8	3	N/A
TC	Fidelity Adv Developing Comm I	FDMIX	E	(800) 522-7297	8.15	C /5.5	10.43 /50	15.57 /62	-1.59 /10	E+ / 0.8	6	3
TC	Fidelity Adv Developing Comm B	FDMBX	E	(800) 522-7297	7.71	C /4.8	9.36 /42	14.40 /56	-2.59 / 6	E+ / 0.8	4	3
TC	Fidelity Adv Developing Comm C	FDMCX	E	(800) 522-7297	7.71	C /4.8	9.36 /42	14.40 /56	-2.59 / 6	E+ / 0.7	3	3
TC	Fidelity Adv Developing Comm T	FDMTX	E	(800) 522-7297	7.93	C /4.6	9.99 /47	14.96 /59	-2.10 / 8	E+ / 0.8	4	3
TC	Fidelity Adv Developing Comm A	FDMAX	E	(800) 522-7297	8.03	C /4.5	10.15 /48	15.29 /60	-1.86 / 9	E+ / 0.8	5	3
SC	MassMutual Select Small Comp Gr	MMCYX	E	(800) 542-6767	10.28	C /4.3	11.32 /55	11.69 /40	--	E+ / 0.9	1	3
SC	MassMutual Select Small Comp Gr	MMCLX	E	(800) 542-6767	10.21	C- /4.2	11.17 /55	11.50 /39	--	E+ / 0.9	1	N/A
GR	Principal Inv LgCap Growth B	PRGBX	E-	(800) 247-4123	7.37	C- /3.9	8.52 /37	11.44 /39	-1.17 /11	E- / 0.0	49	1
GR	Principal Inv LgCap Growth A	PRGWX	E-	(800) 247-4123	7.42	C- /3.5	9.74 /45	12.27 /44	-0.45 /14	E- / 0.0	58	1
GR	Berkshire Focus Fund	BFOCX	E-	(877) 526-0707	7.12	C- /3.0	18.86 /80	11.69 /40	-13.99 / 0	E- / 0.0	0	9
SC	● Undiscovered Mgrs Sm Cap Gr Inst	USRLX	E-	(800) 358-4782	10.19	D+ /2.9	8.96 /40	10.36 /30	0.01 /15	E+ / 0.7	0	N/A
AG	ProFunds-Ultra OTC Fund Inv	UOPIX	E-	(888) 776-3637	21.55	D+ /2.8	3.81 /10	12.32 /45	-16.81 / 0	E- / 0.0	0	N/A
SC	First American Sm Cap Gr Opp B	FROBX	E-	(800) 677-3863	18.18	D+ /2.6	7.73 /31	11.32 /38	3.35 /40	E+ / 0.9	5	2
GR	Eaton Vance Growth Fund C	ECGFX	E-	(800) 225-6265	7.82	D+ /2.6	11.56 /57	10.06 /28	2.18 /29	E+ / 0.7	8	6
GR	Thrivent Large Cap Growth I	THLCX	E-	(800) 847-4836	5.30	D+ /2.6	6.33 /22	9.56 /24	-0.57 /13	E- / 0.0	25	4
AG	Rydex Dynamics-OTC H	RYVYX	E-	(800) 820-0888	19.32	D+ /2.5	3.76 /10	11.89 /42	-16.66 / 0	E- / 0.0	0	N/A
TC	Fidelity Adv Electronics I	FELIX	E-	(800) 522-7297	8.04	D+ /2.4	6.21 /22	9.88 /27	-4.31 / 3	E / 0.5	0	2
AG	ProFunds-Ultra OTC Fund Svc	UOPSX	E-	(888) 776-3637	20.07	D+ /2.3	2.77 / 7	11.68 /40	-17.40 / 0	E- / 0.0	0	N/A
TC	American Century Technology Inst	ATYIX	E-	(800) 345-6488	20.15	D /2.2	18.18 /79	9.12 /21	-4.37 / 3	E+ / 0.8	1	N/A
TC	American Century Technology Fd	ATCIX	E-	(800) 345-6488	19.89	D /2.1	17.97 /79	8.93 /20	-4.62 / 3	E+ / 0.8	0	4
GR	Gartmore Long-Short Equity Plus B	MLSBX	E-	(800) 848-0920	9.82	D /2.1	7.51 /29	8.51 /18	2.18 /29	E+ / 0.7	70	N/A
BA	Eaton Vance Balanced C	ECIFX	E-	(800) 225-6265	7.06	D /2.1	7.88 /32	8.11 /16	3.66 /42	E- / 0.0	44	6
GR	Gartmore Long-Short Equity Plus C	MLSCX	E-	(800) 848-0920	7.45	D /2.1	7.37 /28	8.48 /18	0.96 /20	E- / 0.0	70	N/A
GR	Eaton Vance Growth Fund B	EMGFX	E-	(800) 225-6265	7.82	D /2.0	11.57 /57	10.09 /28	2.18 /29	E+ / 0.7	8	6
GR	Reynolds Fund	REYFX	E-	(800) 773-9665	6.09	D /2.0	14.69 /71	7.52 /12	-0.64 /13	E- / 0.0	0	7

● Denotes fund is closed to new investors

Data as of June 30, 2006

Section VIII

Top-Rated
Stock Mutual Funds
by Fund Type

A compilation of those

Equity Mutual Funds

receiving the highest Weiss Investment Rating

within each type of fund.

Funds are listed in order by Overall Weiss Investment Rating.

Section VIII Contents

This section contains a summary analysis of the top 100 rated mutual funds within each fund type. If you are looking for a particular type of mutual fund, these pages show those funds that have achieved the best combination of risk and financial performance over the past three years.

1.	**Fund Type**	The mutual fund's peer category based on an analysis of its investment portfolio.	

AG	Aggressive Growth	HL	Health
AA	Asset Allocation	IN	Income
BA	Balanced	IX	Index
CV	Convertible	MC	Mid Cap
EM	Emerging Market	OT	Other
EN	Energy/Natural Resources	PM	Precious Metals
FS	Financial Services	RE	Real Estate
FO	Foreign	SC	Small Cap
GL	Global	TC	Technology
GR	Growth	UT	Utilities
GI	Growth and Income		

A blank fund type means that the mutual fund has not yet been categorized.

2. **Fund Name**   The name of the mutual fund as stated in its prospectus, which can sometimes differ slightly from the name that the company uses for advertising. If you cannot find the particular mutual fund you are interested in, or if you have any doubts regarding the precise name, verify the information with your broker or on your account statement. Also, use the fund's ticker symbol for confirmation. (See column 3.)

3. **Ticker Symbol**   The unique alphabetic symbol used for identifying and trading a specific mutual fund. No two funds can have the same ticker symbol, and the ticker symbol for mutual funds always ends with an "X".

A handful of funds currently show no associated ticker symbol. This means that the fund is either small or new since the NASD only assigns a ticker symbol to funds with at least $25 million in assets or 1,000 shareholders.

4. **Overall Weiss Investment Rating**   Our overall rating is measured on a scale from A to E based on each fund's risk-adjusted performance. Please see page 10 for specific descriptions of each letter grade. Also, refer to page 7 for information on how our ratings are derived. Most important, when using this rating, please be sure to consider the warnings beginning on page 11 regarding the ratings' limitations and the underlying assumptions.

5.   Phone   The telephone number of the company managing the fund. Call this number to receive a prospectus or other information about the fund.

6.   Net Asset Value (NAV)   The fund's share price as of the date indicated. A fund's NAV is computed by dividing the value of the fund's asset holdings, less accrued fees and expenses, by the number of its shares outstanding.

7.   Performance Rating/Points   A letter grade rating based solely on the mutual fund's financial performance over the trailing three years, without any consideration for the amount of risk the fund poses. Like the overall Weiss Investment Rating, the Performance Rating is measured on a scale from A to E for ease of interpretation. The points score indicates where the Performance Rating falls on a scale of 0 to 10.

8.   1-Year Total Return   The total return the fund has provided investors over the preceeding twelve months. This total return figure is computed based on the fund's dividend distributions and share price appreciation/depreciation during the period, net of the expenses and fees it imposes on its shareholders. Although the total return figure does not reflect an adjustment for any loads the fund may carry, such adjustments have been made in deriving the Weiss Investment Ratings.

9.   1-Year Total Return Percentile   The fund's percentile rank based on its one-year performance compared to that of all other equity funds in existence for at least one year. A score of 99 is the best possible, indicating that the fund outperformed 99% of the other mutual funds. Zero is the worst possible percentile score.

10. 3-Year Total Return   The total annual return the fund has provided investors over the preceeding three years.

11. 3-Year Total Return Percentile   The fund's percentile rank based on its three-year performance compared to that of all other equity funds in existence for at least three years. A score of 99 is the best possible, indicating that the fund outperformed 99% of the other mutual funds. Zero is the worst possible percentile score.

12. 5-Year Total Return   The total annual return the fund has provided investors over the preceeding five years.

13. 5-Year Total Return Percentile   The fund's percentile rank based on its five-year performance compared to that of all other equity funds in existence for at least five years. A score of 99 is the best possible, indicating that the fund outperformed 99% of the other mutual funds. Zero is the worst possible percentile score.

14. **Risk Rating/Points**

A letter grade rating based solely on the mutual fund's risk as determined by its monthly performance volatility over the trailing three years. The risk rating does not take into consideration the overall financial performance the fund has achieved or the total return it has provided to its shareholders. Like the overall Weiss Investment Rating, the Risk Rating is measured on a scale from A to E for ease of interpretation. The points score indicates where the Risk Rating falls on a scale of 0 to 10.

15. **Manager Quality Percentile**

The manager quality percentile is based on a ranking of the fund's alpha, a statistical measure representing the difference between a fund's actual returns and its expected performance given its level of risk. Fund managers who have been able to exceed the fund's statistically expected performance receive a high percentile rank with 99 representing the highest possible score. At the other end of the spectrum, fund managers who have actually detracted from the fund's expected performance receive a low percentile rank with 0 representing the lowest possible score.

16. **Manager Tenure**

The number of years the current manager has been managing the fund. Since fund managers who deliver substandard returns are usually replaced, a long tenure is usually a good sign that shareholders are satisfied that the fund is achieving its stated objectives.

Fund Type	Fund Name	Ticker Symbol	Overall Weiss Investment Rating	Phone	Net Asset Value As of 6/30/06	Performance Rating/Pts	Annualized Total Return Through 6/30/06			Risk Rating/Pts	Mgr. Quality Pct	Mgr. Tenure (Years)
							1Yr / Pct	3Yr / Pct	5Yr / Pct			
AG	Allianz NACM Flex-Cap Value Inst		A	(800) 628-1237	17.61	B- /7.3	15.14 /72	17.18 /69	--	B /8.4	91	4
AG	Allianz NACM Flex-Cap Value		A	(800) 628-1237	17.52	B- /7.2	14.90 /71	16.89 /68	--	B /8.4	90	4
AG	BlackRock-U.S Opportunities Inst	BMCIX	A-	(888) 825-2257	29.28	B+ /8.9	24.60 /88	24.15 /90	4.58 /51	C+ /6.5	97	N/A
AG	BlackRock-U.S Opportunities Svc	BMCSX	A-	(888) 825-2257	28.52	B+ /8.8	24.22 /87	23.78 /89	4.35 /49	C+ /6.5	96	N/A
AG	Quaker Strategic Growth Inst	QAGIX	A-	(800) 220-8888	24.47	B- /7.1	13.91 /68	17.28 /69	7.69 /70	B /8.2	94	10
AG	BlackRock-U.S Opportunities B	BRMBX	B+	(888) 825-2257	26.63	B+ /8.6	23.17 /86	22.74 /87	3.35 /40	C+ /6.5	95	N/A
AG	BlackRock-U.S Opportunities C	BMECX	B+	(888) 825-2257	26.61	B+ /8.6	23.19 /86	22.74 /87	3.34 /40	C+ /6.5	95	8
AG	BlackRock-U.S Opportunities A	BMEAX	B+	(888) 825-2257	28.27	B+ /8.4	24.05 /87	23.66 /89	4.13 /47	C+ /6.5	96	8
AG	ICON Long/Short I	IOLIX	B+	(800) 764-0442	17.57	B /7.8	17.06 /77	18.51 /74	--	B- /7.5	91	N/A
AG ●	Vanguard Strategic Equity Fd	VSEQX	B+	(800) 662-7447	23.23	B /7.8	13.01 /64	19.65 /78	11.63 /86	C+ /6.9	91	N/A
AG	ICON Long/Short C	IOLCX	B+	(800) 764-0442	17.09	B- /7.4	16.18 /75	17.63 /71	--	B- /7.5	88	N/A
AG	Dreyfus Premier Strategic Value R	DRGVX	B+	(800) 782-6620	30.08	B- /7.3	14.17 /69	17.24 /69	7.24 /68	B- /7.4	91	3
AG	Vantagepoint Aggressive Opport	VPAOX	B+	(800) 669-7400	11.94	B- /7.2	12.48 /62	18.01 /73	0.86 /20	B- /7.5	90	N/A
AG	Allianz NACM Flex-Cap Value D	PNFDX	B+	(800) 628-1237	17.41	B- /7.0	14.74 /71	16.68 /67	--	B /8.3	89	4
AG	Columbia FS Agg Gr Portfolio BX		B+	(800) 426-3750	12.46	C+ /6.3	15.16 /72	15.25 /60	--	B /8.7	79	N/A
AG	Columbia FS Agg Gr Portfolio C		B+	(800) 426-3750	16.44	C+ /6.3	14.80 /71	14.89 /58	--	B /8.7	77	N/A
AG	Columbia FS Agg Gr Portfolio Dir		B+	(800) 426-3750	13.25	C+ /6.2	12.67 /63	14.79 /58	--	B /8.8	80	N/A
AG	Columbia FS Agg Gr Portfolio A		B+	(800) 426-3750	12.77	C+ /6.0	15.67 /74	15.77 /62	--	B /8.7	83	N/A
AG	Value Line Premier Growth	VALSX	B	(800) 223-0818	27.25	B /7.6	16.04 /75	18.26 /73	7.40 /69	B- /7.0	93	N/A
AG	Columbia FS Agg Gr Portfolio Z		B	(800) 426-3750	16.66	C+ /6.9	15.94 /74	16.05 /64	--	B /8.7	85	N/A
AG	Columbia FS Agg Gr Portfolio CX		B	(800) 426-3750	12.45	C+ /6.7	15.38 /73	15.50 /61	--	B /8.7	82	N/A
AG	Columbia FS Agg Gr Portfolio E		B	(800) 426-3750	16.87	C+ /6.7	15.31 /73	15.60 /62	--	B /8.7	83	N/A
AG	Allianz NACM Flex-Cap Value C	PNFCX	B	(800) 628-1237	16.90	C+ /6.7	13.78 /67	15.80 /63	--	B /8.2	85	4
AG	Quaker Strategic Growth C	QAGCX	B	(800) 220-8888	23.07	C+ /6.5	12.78 /63	16.12 /64	6.64 /65	B /8.2	91	10
AG	Allianz NACM Flex-Cap Value A	PNFAX	B	(800) 628-1237	17.36	C+ /6.5	14.70 /71	16.68 /67	--	B /8.1	89	4
AG	Quaker Strategic Growth A	QUAGX	B	(800) 220-8888	24.12	C+ /6.4	13.66 /67	16.98 /68	7.43 /69	B- /7.7	93	10
AG	Allianz NACM Flex-Cap Value B	PNFBX	B	(800) 628-1237	16.90	C+ /6.2	13.78 /67	15.80 /63	--	B /8.2	85	4
AG ●	Quaker Strategic Growth B	QAGBX	B	(800) 220-8888	23.16	C+ /6.0	12.78 /63	16.14 /64	6.64 /65	B /8.2	91	10
AG	Rydex Ser-Multi-Cap Core Eq H	RYQMX	B	(800) 820-0888	16.14	C+ /6.0	10.39 /49	14.83 /58	--	B /8.1	73	N/A
AG	Columbia FS Agg Gr Portfolio B		B	(800) 426-3750	16.74	C+ /5.8	14.74 /71	14.88 /58	--	B /8.7	77	N/A
AG	Accessor Fd-Aggress Gr Alloc C	ACAGX	B	(800) 759-3504	16.43	C+ /5.7	11.54 /57	14.10 /54	--	B /8.6	79	N/A
AG	Morgan Stanley Aggr Equity D	AEQDX	B-	(800) 869-6397	12.39	B- /7.3	23.28 /86	17.49 /70	4.00 /46	C+ /6.4	78	N/A
AG	Dreyfus Premier Strategic Value C	DCGVX	B-	(800) 782-6620	29.02	C+ /6.7	13.07 /65	16.19 /64	6.47 /64	B- /7.4	87	3
AG	Dreyfus Premier Strategic Value A	DAGVX	B-	(800) 782-6620	30.06	C+ /6.6	13.82 /68	17.02 /68	7.18 /68	B- /7.4	91	3
AG	Dreyfus Premier Strategic Value T	DTGVX	B-	(800) 782-6620	29.38	C+ /6.6	13.57 /67	16.67 /67	6.72 /65	B- /7.4	89	3
AG	Dreyfus Premier Strategic Value B	DBGVX	B-	(800) 782-6620	28.99	C+ /6.4	12.99 /64	16.17 /64	6.44 /64	B- /7.4	87	3
AG	MFS Aggressive Gr Alloc I	MIAGX	B-	(800) 343-2829	14.53	C+ /5.9	11.43 /56	14.52 /56	--	B /8.1	68	4
AG	MFS Aggressive Gr Alloc R3	MAWAX	B-	(800) 343-2829	14.24	C /5.5	10.68 /51	13.85 /53	--	B /8.1	61	3
AG	STI Classic Life Vision Aggr Gr I	CVMGX	B-	(888) 784-3863	12.04	C /5.4	11.18 /55	13.18 /50	4.35 /49	B /8.3	71	N/A
AG	BB&T Capital Manager Eqty Tr	BCATX	B-	(800) 228-1872	11.30	C /4.8	10.58 /51	12.59 /46	3.00 /37	B /8.9	73	N/A
AG	CGM Focus Fund	CGMFX	C+	(800) 345-4048	38.53	A+ /9.6	26.45 /90	29.43 /95	21.11 /97	C- /3.8	99	9
AG	Permanent Portfolio Aggress Gr	PAGRX	C+	(800) 531-5142	107.06	B- /7.1	10.29 /49	18.25 /73	7.20 /68	C+ /6.3	84	15
AG	Janus Aspen Mid Cap Gr Inst	JAAGX	C+	(800) 525-3713	29.77	B- /7.1	14.68 /71	17.37 /70	2.22 /29	C+ /5.6	83	13
AG	Franklin Aggressive Growth Fd Adv	FRAAX	C+	(800) 321-8563	17.44	B- /7.0	18.72 /80	18.28 /73	2.72 /34	C+ /5.8	72	7
AG	Morgan Stanley Aggr Equity C	AEQCX	C+	(800) 869-6397	11.50	C+ /6.8	22.08 /84	16.36 /65	2.99 /37	C+ /6.3	69	N/A
AG	Franklin Aggressive Growth Fd R	FKARX	C+	(800) 342-5236	16.90	C+ /6.8	18.18 /79	17.68 /71	2.21 /29	C+ /5.8	68	7
AG	Morgan Stanley Aggr Equity A	AEQAX	C+	(800) 869-6397	12.17	C+ /6.5	22.93 /86	17.20 /69	3.75 /43	C+ /6.4	76	N/A
AG	Morgan Stanley Aggr Equity B	AEQBX	C+	(800) 869-6397	11.49	C+ /6.3	22.10 /84	16.32 /65	2.98 /37	C+ /6.3	68	N/A
AG	Rydex Series-Nova Inv	RYNVX	C+	(800) 820-0888	27.87	C+ /5.7	8.87 /39	14.42 /56	--	B- /7.0	37	N/A
AG	MFS Aggressive Gr Alloc R	MAARX	C+	(800) 343-2829	14.35	C+ /5.6	10.87 /53	13.99 /54	--	B- /7.2	63	4
AG	Fifth Third LifeModel Agg Inst	LASIX	C+	(800) 282-5706	14.75	C /5.5	10.99 /53	13.29 /50	--	B- /7.4	57	4
AG	Rydex Ser-Multi-Cap Core Eq C	RYQCX	C+	(800) 820-0888	15.64	C /5.4	9.54 /44	13.94 /54	--	B /8.1	66	4

● Denotes fund is closed to new investors

Fund Type	Fund Name	Ticker Symbol	Overall Weiss Investment Rating	Phone	Net Asset Value As of 6/30/06	Performance Rating/Pts	Annualized Total Return Through 6/30/06			Risk Rating/Pts	Mgr. Quality Pct	Mgr. Tenure (Years)
							1Yr / Pct	3Yr / Pct	5Yr / Pct			
AA	Goldman Sachs Aggr Gr Strat Inst	GAPIX	A	(800) 292-4726	14.90	B+ /8.4	20.06 /82	20.78 /82	8.89 /76	B- /7.4	98	8
AA	Goldman Sachs Aggr Gr Strat Svc	GAPSX	A	(800) 292-4726	14.67	B /8.2	19.57 /81	20.16 /80	8.34 /73	B- /7.4	98	8
AA	Goldman Sachs Growth Strategy	GGSIX	A	(800) 292-4726	13.77	B- /7.6	16.37 /76	18.29 /74	8.31 /73	B /8.4	97	8
AA	Goldman Sachs Growth Strategy	GGSSX	A	(800) 292-4726	13.66	B- /7.4	15.76 /74	17.71 /71	7.73 /70	B /8.3	96	8
AA	Mutual Recovery Adv	FMRVX	A	(800) 321-8563	13.25	C+ /6.3	9.94 /47	14.90 /58	--	B+ /9.4	97	3
AA	Waddell & Reed Adv Asset Strat Y	WYASX	A-	(888) 923-3355	10.51	A- /9.2	39.30 /98	20.83 /82	13.12 /89	C+ /6.2	99	9
AA	Goldman Sachs Aggr Gr Strat C	GAXCX	A-	(800) 292-4726	14.24	B /8.0	18.67 /80	19.40 /77	7.64 /70	B- /7.4	97	8
AA	Goldman Sachs Growth Strategy C	GGSCX	A-	(800) 292-4726	13.61	B- /7.1	14.96 /72	16.96 /68	7.05 /67	B /8.3	95	8
AA	Goldman Sachs Gr & Inc Strat Inst	GOIIX	A-	(800) 292-4726	12.62	C+ /6.3	12.94 /64	14.88 /58	7.85 /71	B+ /9.1	94	N/A
AA	Ivy Fund-Asset Strategy Y	WASYX	B+	(800) 777-6472	19.44	A- /9.1	37.07 /97	19.85 /79	12.55 /88	C+ /5.7	99	9
AA	Waddell & Reed Adv Asset Strat C	WCASX	B+	(888) 923-3355	10.41	A- /9.0	37.60 /97	19.35 /77	11.71 /86	C+ /6.1	98	7
AA	Waddell & Reed Adv Asset Strat A	UNASX	B+	(888) 923-3355	10.49	B+ /8.9	38.80 /98	20.37 /81	12.68 /88	C+ /6.2	99	9
AA	Ivy Fund-Asset Strategy A	WASAX	B+	(800) 777-6472	19.42	B+ /8.8	37.01 /97	19.78 /79	12.46 /88	C+ /6.2	99	7
AA	Waddell & Reed Adv Asset Strat B	WBASX	B+	(888) 923-3355	10.41	B+ /8.8	37.60 /97	19.32 /77	11.67 /86	C+ /6.1	98	7
AA	Ivy Fund-Asset Strategy B	WASBX	B+	(800) 777-6472	19.13	B+ /8.6	35.95 /97	18.75 /75	11.47 /85	C+ /6.2	98	7
AA	Goldman Sachs Aggr Gr Strat A	GAPAX	B+	(800) 292-4726	14.75	B /7.8	19.64 /81	20.31 /80	8.46 /74	B- /7.4	98	8
AA	Goldman Sachs Aggr Gr Strat B	GAPBX	B+	(800) 292-4726	14.27	B /7.6	18.82 /80	19.42 /77	7.65 /70	B- /7.4	97	8
AA	Russell LifePoints Eq Gr Strat S	RELSX	B+	(800) 832-6688	11.60	B- /7.2	15.67 /74	16.90 /68	6.61 /65	B- /7.7	92	N/A
AA	Russell LifePoints Eq Gr Strat E	RELEX	B+	(800) 832-6688	11.45	B- /7.1	15.34 /73	16.61 /66	6.33 /63	B- /7.7	91	N/A
AA	Russell LifePoints Eq Gr Strat D	RELDX	B+	(800) 832-6688	11.44	B- /7.0	15.04 /72	16.33 /65	6.05 /61	B- /7.7	90	N/A
AA	Putnam Asset Alloc-Growth Y	PAGYX	B+	(800) 354-2228	12.87	C+ /6.3	13.45 /66	14.71 /57	6.68 /65	B /8.5	91	12
AA	Russell LifePoints Eq Gr Strat A	REAAX	B+	(800) 832-6688	11.64	C+ /6.3	15.41 /73	16.60 /66	6.70 /65	B /8.4	91	N/A
AA	Goldman Sachs Gr & Inc Strat Svc	GOISX	B+	(800) 292-4726	12.57	C+ /6.1	12.46 /62	14.31 /55	7.32 /68	B+ /9.0	93	N/A
AA	Principal Inv LifeTime 2050 Inst	PPLIX	B+	(800) 247-4123	12.46	C+ /6.0	12.62 /63	14.19 /55	6.21 /62	B /8.9	87	6
AA	ING T. Rowe Price Cap App I	ITRIX	B+	(800) 992-0180	25.99	C+ /5.9	10.02 /47	14.38 /56	--	B+ /9.1	92	5
AA	Principal Inv LifeTime 2050 Pfd	PTEFX	B+	(800) 247-4123	12.43	C+ /5.8	12.25 /61	13.90 /53	5.96 /61	B /8.9	85	5
AA	Principal Inv LifeTime 2050 Sel	PTESX	B+	(800) 247-4123	12.42	C+ /5.8	12.13 /60	13.78 /53	5.84 /60	B /8.9	84	5
AA	ING T. Rowe Price Cap App S2		B+	(800) 992-0180	25.80	C+ /5.7	9.60 /44	13.97 /54	--	B+ /9.1	91	5
AA	Mutual Recovery C	FCMRX	B+	(800) 342-5236	13.01	C+ /5.6	8.91 /39	13.82 /53	--	B+ /9.3	95	3
AA	Morgan Stanley Strategist Fund D	SRTDX	B+	(800) 869-6397	19.66	C /5.5	12.50 /62	12.74 /47	5.40 /57	B+ /9.4	88	9
AA	Mutual Recovery A	FMRAX	B+	(800) 342-5236	13.17	C /5.4	9.59 /44	14.53 /56	--	B+ /9.4	96	3
AA	American Funds Inc Fnd of Amer	RIDFX	B+	(800) 421-4120	18.97	C /5.4	9.89 /46	12.59 /46	8.64 /75	B+ /9.4	90	33
AA	T. Rowe Price Cap Appreciation Fd	PRWCX	B+	(800) 638-5660	20.68	C /5.3	9.09 /41	13.22 /50	10.12 /81	B+ /9.7	90	5
AA	American Funds Inc Fnd of Amer	CIMFX	B+	(800) 421-4120	18.95	C /5.2	9.75 /45	12.27 /44	8.29 /73	B+ /9.4	89	33
AA	Ivy Fund-Asset Strategy C	WASCX	B	(800) 777-6472	19.17	B+ /8.9	36.08 /97	18.88 /76	11.60 /86	C+ /5.7	98	7
AA	Wells Fargo Avtg Wlth Bld Tact	WBGAX	B	(800) 222-8222	15.33	B- /7.2	16.58 /76	17.40 /70	4.21 /48	B- /7.3	93	9
AA	Lifetime Achievement Fund	LFTAX	B	(414) 299-2120	21.22	B- /7.1	23.52 /87	16.16 /64	8.15 /72	B- /7.3	80	6
AA	Goldman Sachs Growth Strategy A	GGSAX	B	(800) 292-4726	13.72	C+ /6.9	15.85 /74	17.82 /72	7.86 /71	B /8.3	96	8
AA	Goldman Sachs Growth Strategy B	GGSBX	B	(800) 292-4726	13.69	C+ /6.7	15.02 /72	16.96 /68	7.05 /67	B /8.3	95	8
AA	First American Strat-Agg Gr Alloc Y	FSAYX	B	(800) 677-3863	11.67	C+ /6.1	12.96 /64	14.54 /56	--	B /8.1	86	N/A
AA	Permanent Portfolio Fund	PRPFX	B	(800) 531-5142	30.91	C+ /6.1	14.42 /70	13.70 /52	13.32 /89	B /8.0	95	15
AA	Putnam Asset Alloc-Growth R	PASRX	B	(800) 354-2228	12.64	C+ /6.0	12.98 /64	14.12 /55	6.15 /62	B /8.1	89	11
AA	State Farm LifePath 2040 Inst	SAUIX	B	(877) 734-2265	14.59	C+ /5.6	12.68 /63	13.07 /49	--	B /8.9	81	N/A
AA	Principal Inv LifeTime 2050 AdvPfd	PTERX	B	(800) 247-4123	12.39	C+ /5.6	11.95 /59	13.54 /52	5.63 /59	B /8.9	83	5
AA	Principal Inv LifeTime 2050 AdvSel	PTENX	B	(800) 247-4123	12.37	C+ /5.6	11.77 /58	13.38 /51	5.48 /58	B /8.8	82	5
AA	Principal Inv LifeTime 2040 Inst	PTDIX	B	(800) 247-4123	12.86	C /5.5	11.43 /56	13.33 /50	7.06 /67	B+ /9.1	86	5
AA	Goldman Sachs Gr & Inc Strat C	GOICX	B	(800) 292-4726	12.55	C /5.5	11.74 /58	13.57 /52	6.61 /65	B+ /9.0	91	N/A
AA	Principal Inv LifeTime 2040 Pfd	PTDPX	B	(800) 247-4123	12.83	C /5.4	11.17 /55	13.04 /49	6.79 /66	B+ /9.1	84	5
AA	Principal Inv LifeTime 2030 Sel	PTCSX	B	(800) 247-4123	12.89	C /5.3	10.30 /49	12.96 /49	6.89 /66	B+ /9.2	86	5
AA	Principal Inv LifeTime 2040 Sel	PTDSX	B	(800) 247-4123	12.78	C /5.3	10.99 /53	12.89 /48	6.62 /65	B+ /9.1	83	5
AA	Accessor Fd-Growth Alloc Adv	ACGAX	B	(800) 759-3504	16.54	C /5.3	10.28 /49	13.23 /50	5.05 /55	B+ /9.1	86	6
AA	Vanguard LifeStrategy Growth Fd	VASGX	B	(800) 662-7447	21.60	C /5.3	11.04 /54	12.99 /49	5.43 /57	B /8.9	83	12

● Denotes fund is closed to new investors

Data as of June 30, 2006

Fund Type	Fund Name	Ticker Symbol	Overall Weiss Investment Rating	Phone	Net Asset Value As of 6/30/06	Perform-ance Rating/Pts	Annualized Total Return Through 6/30/06			Risk Rating/Pts	Mgr. Quality Pct	Mgr. Tenure (Years)
							1Yr / Pct	3Yr / Pct	5Yr / Pct			
BA	Putnam College Adv New Value O		B+	(800) 354-2228	14.19	C+ /6.0	9.58 /44	14.55 /57	--	B /8.7	85	N/A
BA	Buffalo Balanced Fund	BUFBX	B+	(800) 492-8332	10.96	C+ /5.6	11.82 /58	13.24 /50	5.76 /59	B+ /9.7	96	N/A
BA	J Hancock Balanced I	SVBIX	B+	(800) 257-3336	13.25	C /5.5	14.82 /71	12.26 /44	--	B+ /9.5	92	3
BA	● FPA Crescent Fund	FPACX	B+	(800) 982-4372	26.62	C /5.5	12.35 /61	13.29 /50	13.08 /89	B+ /9.4	95	13
BA	● Dodge & Cox Balanced Fund	DODBX	B+	(800) 621-3979	83.57	C /5.3	9.88 /46	12.76 /47	9.27 /78	B+ /9.7	91	75
BA	AFBA 5Star Balanced I	AFBAX	B+	(800) 243-9865	13.25	C /5.2	11.22 /55	12.70 /47	5.95 /61	B+ /9.8	95	N/A
BA	AFBA 5Star Balanced R	ASBRX	B+	(800) 243-9865	13.13	C /4.9	10.64 /51	12.27 /44	5.51 /58	B+ /9.8	94	N/A
BA	Columbia FS Bal Gr Portfolio Z		B	(800) 426-3750	15.72	C /5.2	11.73 /58	12.54 /46	--	B+ /9.3	83	N/A
BA	MDT Balanced Growth Instl	QIBGX	B	(866) 784-6867	13.29	C /5.0	9.56 /44	13.02 /49	--	B+ /9.3	89	16
BA	Columbia FS Bal Gr Portfolio CX		B	(800) 426-3750	12.76	C /5.0	11.64 /57	12.13 /43	--	B+ /9.3	81	N/A
BA	MDT Balanced Growth C	QCBGX	B	(866) 784-6867	13.22	C /4.9	8.73 /38	12.74 /47	--	B+ /9.3	87	N/A
BA	Columbia FS Bal Gr Portfolio E		B	(800) 426-3750	15.53	C /4.9	11.41 /56	12.05 /43	--	B+ /9.3	79	N/A
BA	AFBA 5Star Balanced C	AFSCX	B	(800) 243-9865	13.53	C /4.6	10.16 /48	11.58 /40	5.17 /55	B+ /9.8	92	N/A
BA	Oakmark Equity and Income II	OARBX	B	(800) 625-6275	25.76	C /4.4	9.80 /46	11.11 /36	9.17 /77	B+ /9.7	92	6
BA	● Oakmark Equity and Income I	OAKBX	B	(800) 625-6275	25.88	C /4.3	10.13 /48	11.41 /39	9.44 /78	B+ /9.7	92	11
BA	CGM Mutual Fund	LOMMX	B-	(800) 345-4048	29.61	B /7.7	13.62 /67	18.67 /75	9.11 /77	C+ /6.1	95	25
BA	Putnam College Adv New Value C		B-	(800) 354-2228	13.42	C /5.0	8.14 /34	13.04 /49	--	B /8.7	75	N/A
BA	J Hancock Balanced C	SVBCX	B-	(800) 257-3336	13.24	C /4.5	13.38 /66	10.86 /34	3.32 /40	B+ /9.5	86	3
BA	Columbia FS Bal Gr Portfolio BX		B-	(800) 426-3750	12.66	C /4.4	11.35 /56	11.88 /42	--	B+ /9.3	78	N/A
BA	Columbia FS Bal Gr Portfolio C		B-	(800) 426-3750	15.01	C /4.4	10.94 /53	11.53 /39	--	B+ /9.3	76	N/A
BA	Vanguard Wellington Adm	VWENX	B-	(800) 662-7447	53.56	C /4.4	9.65 /45	11.12 /36	7.04 /67	B+ /9.3	83	N/A
BA	AFBA 5Star Balanced A	AFSAX	B-	(800) 243-9865	13.70	C /4.3	11.06 /54	12.47 /46	5.87 /60	B+ /9.8	95	N/A
BA	J Hancock Balanced A	SVBAX	B-	(800) 257-3336	13.24	C /4.3	14.18 /69	11.63 /40	4.05 /46	B+ /9.5	90	3
BA	MDT Balanced Growth A	QABGX	B-	(866) 784-6867	13.28	C /4.3	9.40 /43	12.97 /49	--	B+ /9.3	88	N/A
BA	James Advantage Bal Goldn	GLRBX	B-	(888) 426-7640	17.32	C- /4.2	6.48 /23	11.39 /38	8.71 /75	B+ /9.7	91	9
BA	Columbia FS Bal Gr Portfolio Dir		B-	(800) 426-3750	12.98	C- /4.2	9.26 /42	11.00 /35	--	B+ /9.5	76	N/A
BA	AFBA 5Star Balanced B	AFSBX	B-	(800) 243-9865	13.52	C- /4.1	10.26 /48	11.63 /40	5.20 /56	B+ /9.8	92	N/A
BA	Mairs & Power Balanced Fund	MAPOX	B-	(800) 304-7404	60.66	C- /3.9	8.95 /40	10.48 /31	7.08 /67	B+ /9.9	82	14
BA	Villere Balanced Fund	VILLX	C+	(866) 811-0215	16.00	C /5.1	5.13 /16	13.42 /51	6.92 /66	B /8.2	82	N/A
BA	Transamerica Premier Balanced	TBAIX	C+	(800) 892-7587	24.58	C /5.0	13.55 /66	12.59 /46	5.85 /60	B /8.5	81	8
BA	Greenspring Fund	GRSPX	C+	(800) 366-3863	22.94	C /5.0	13.55 /66	12.52 /46	8.85 /76	B /8.3	92	19
BA	Putnam College Adv New Value A		C+	(800) 354-2228	13.89	C /4.9	8.94 /40	13.90 /53	--	B /8.7	81	N/A
BA	Putnam College Adv New Value B		C+	(800) 354-2228	13.45	C /4.4	8.12 /34	13.05 /49	--	B /8.7	75	N/A
BA	● Vanguard Wellington Inv	VWELX	C+	(800) 662-7447	31.01	C /4.3	9.50 /43	10.98 /35	6.91 /66	B+ /9.3	83	12
BA	First Focus Balanced Fund Inst	FOBAX	C+	(800) 662-4203	13.74	C /4.3	8.08 /33	11.63 /40	7.88 /71	B /8.6	68	10
BA	Columbia FS Bal Gr Portfolio A		C+	(800) 426-3750	12.96	C- /4.1	11.82 /58	12.43 /45	--	B+ /9.3	82	N/A
BA	T. Rowe Price Personal Strategy	TRPBX	C+	(800) 638-5660	18.94	C- /4.1	8.12 /34	11.27 /38	6.86 /66	B+ /9.1	80	8
BA	American Beacon Balance Inst	AADBX	C+	(800) 967-9009	14.65	C- /4.1	5.70 /19	11.53 /39	7.53 /69	B /8.6	85	N/A
BA	Gabelli Westwood Balanced Fd	WEBAX	C+	(800) 422-3554	12.48	C- /4.0	10.53 /50	10.36 /30	5.32 /57	B /8.8	84	15
BA	Van Kampen Equity & Income R	ACESX	C+	(800) 421-5666	8.67	C- /3.9	7.89 /32	10.84 /34	--	B+ /9.7	83	N/A
BA	MainStay Balanced R1	MBNRX	C+	(800) 624-6782	26.82	C- /3.9	5.94 /20	10.96 /35	8.60 /75	B+ /9.2	78	17
BA	MainStay Balanced I	MBAIX	C+	(800) 624-6782	26.83	C- /3.9	6.04 /21	11.08 /36	8.71 /75	B /8.7	79	17
BA	Columbia FS Bal Gr Portfolio B		C+	(800) 426-3750	15.07	C- /3.8	11.05 /54	11.57 /40	--	B+ /9.3	76	N/A
BA	Putnam Asset Alloc-Balanced Y	PABYX	C+	(800) 354-2228	11.45	C- /3.7	8.59 /37	10.26 /29	4.64 /51	B+ /9.7	79	12
BA	American Beacon Balance Ser	ABLSX	C+	(800) 967-9009	13.75	C- /3.7	4.86 /14	10.94 /35	7.13 /67	B+ /9.6	82	N/A
BA	J Hancock Balanced B	SVBBX	C+	(800) 257-3336	13.24	C- /3.7	13.38 /66	10.87 /34	3.32 /40	B+ /9.5	86	3
BA	MainStay Balanced R2	MBCRX	C+	(800) 624-6782	26.80	C- /3.7	5.65 /18	10.68 /33	8.33 /73	B+ /9.2	76	17
BA	Columbia FS Balanced Portfolio Z		C+	(800) 426-3750	14.42	C- /3.5	9.57 /44	9.81 /26	--	B+ /9.8	76	N/A
BA	Morgan Stanley Balance Growth D	BGRDX	C+	(800) 869-6397	14.05	C- /3.5	7.03 /26	10.26 /29	4.83 /53	B+ /9.0	81	4
BA	T. Rowe Price Balanced Fd	RPBAX	C+	(800) 638-5660	19.76	C- /3.4	7.50 /29	9.90 /27	5.55 /58	B+ /9.3	75	14
BA	Van Kampen Equity & Income C	ACERX	C+	(800) 421-5666	8.54	C- /3.4	7.36 /28	10.28 /29	5.64 /59	B+ /9.2	79	4
BA	American Performance Balanced	APBAX	C+	(800) 762-7085	13.60	C- /3.4	9.23 /41	9.77 /26	4.90 /53	B+ /9.2	71	N/A

● Denotes fund is closed to new investors

Fund Type	Fund Name	Ticker Symbol	Overall Weiss Investment Rating	Phone	Net Asset Value As of 6/30/06	Performance Rating/Pts	Annualized Total Return Through 6/30/06			Risk Rating/Pts	Mgr. Quality Pct	Mgr. Tenure (Years)
	99 Pct = Best *0 Pct = Worst*						1Yr / Pct	3Yr / Pct	5Yr / Pct			
CV	Nicholas-Applegate US Convertible	NIGIX	B-	(800) 551-8043	24.06	C /5.5	11.90 /59	13.21 /50	5.63 /59	B /8.2	91	N/A
CV	Davis Appreciation & Income Y	DCSYX	B-	(800) 279-0279	29.53	C /5.4	10.33 /49	12.71 /47	8.46 /74	B /8.3	96	13
CV	Putnam Convertible Inc & Gr Y	PCGYX	B-	(800) 354-2228	18.08	C /4.7	11.43 /56	11.43 /39	7.63 /70	B+ /9.1	87	4
CV	Fidelity Convertible Securities	FCVSX	C+	(800) 544-8888	23.93	C /5.3	15.64 /74	11.63 /40	6.36 /63	B /8.0	84	N/A
CV	Franklin Convertible Securities C	FROTX	C+	(800) 342-5236	16.30	C /4.9	8.24 /35	12.88 /48	6.98 /67	B- /7.9	93	8
CV	Davis Appreciation & Income A	RPFCX	C+	(800) 279-0279	29.40	C /4.5	10.06 /47	12.46 /45	8.27 /73	B /8.3	96	13
CV	Davis Appreciation & Income C	DCSCX	C+	(800) 279-0279	29.46	C /4.4	9.10 /41	11.45 /39	7.29 /68	B /8.3	94	13
CV	Columbia Convertible Sec Fund Z	NCIAX	C+	(800) 426-3750	16.40	C- /4.0	9.37 /42	10.71 /33	5.73 /59	B+ /9.2	85	1
CV	Putnam Convertible Inc & Gr R	PCVRX	C+	(800) 354-2228	18.05	C- /3.8	10.82 /52	10.89 /35	7.10 /67	B+ /9.1	84	4
CV	Vanguard Convertible Securities	VCVSX	C	(800) 662-7447	13.93	C /4.7	15.99 /75	11.70 /41	7.17 /68	B- /7.5	87	10
CV	Franklin Convertible Securities A	FISCX	C	(800) 342-5236	16.43	C /4.6	9.02 /40	13.73 /52	7.79 /71	B- /7.4	95	8
CV	Davis Appreciation & Income B	DCSBX	C	(800) 279-0279	29.05	C- /3.9	9.09 /41	11.44 /39	7.27 /68	B /8.3	94	13
CV	Putnam Convertible Inc & Gr C		C	(800) 354-2228	17.97	C- /3.8	10.28 /49	10.32 /30	6.57 /65	B /8.5	80	4
CV	Putnam Convertible Inc & Gr M	PCNMX	C	(800) 354-2228	17.95	C- /3.6	10.54 /51	10.59 /32	6.83 /66	B /8.3	82	4
CV	Putnam Convertible Inc & Gr A	PCONX	C	(800) 354-2228	18.08	C- /3.6	11.08 /54	11.14 /37	7.36 /69	B /8.0	85	4
CV	PIMCO Convertible Bond Inst	PFCIX	C	(800) 227-7337	12.49	C- /3.5	8.40 /36	10.44 /30	6.27 /63	B /8.1	79	N/A
CV	PIMCO Convertible Bond Admin	PFCAX	C	(800) 227-7337	12.76	C- /3.3	8.12 /34	10.19 /29	5.94 /61	B /8.1	77	N/A
CV	GAMCO Global Convertible C		C	(800) 422-3554	6.09	C- /3.2	13.36 /66	9.78 /26	--	B /8.9	81	N/A
CV	Putnam Convertible Inc & Gr B	PCNBX	C	(800) 354-2228	17.81	C- /3.1	10.32 /49	10.32 /30	6.56 /65	B /8.6	80	4
CV	GAMCO Global Convertible A		C	(800) 422-3554	6.36	D+ /2.8	14.13 /69	10.62 /32	5.52 /58	B /8.9	86	N/A
CV	Lord Abbett Convertible Fund Y	LCFYX	C	(800) 201-6984	11.98	D+ /2.7	9.31 /42	8.97 /21	--	B+ /9.1	71	3
CV	Columbia Convertible Sec Fund B	NCVBX	C	(800) 426-3750	16.20	D+ /2.4	8.33 /35	9.61 /25	4.69 /52	B+ /9.2	78	1
CV	Lord Abbett Convertible Fund P	LCFPX	C	(800) 201-6984	11.98	D+ /2.4	8.88 /39	8.49 /18	--	B+ /9.1	66	3
CV	TA IDEX Transamerica Convertb	ICVLX	C-	(888) 233-4339	12.60	C /4.3	14.59 /70	10.31 /29	--	C+ /6.5	66	N/A
CV	Legg Mason Prt Con SmB Cl Y	SCVYX	C-	(866) 890-4247	17.03	C- /4.0	8.98 /40	10.95 /35	7.62 /70	B- /7.1	81	N/A
CV	Northern Trust Income Equity	NOIEX	C-	(800) 595-9111	11.91	C- /3.7	7.64 /30	10.40 /30	6.79 /66	B- /7.1	88	11
CV	ING Convertible Q	NAIQX	C-	(800) 992-0180	18.76	C- /3.2	10.99 /53	8.75 /19	5.03 /54	B- /7.9	66	N/A
CV	Columbia Convertible Sec Fund C	PHIKX	C-	(800) 426-3750	16.39	C- /3.1	8.30 /35	9.60 /25	4.68 /52	B- /7.5	78	1
CV	Legg Mason Prt Con SmB Cl C	SMCLX	C-	(866) 890-4247	16.90	C- /3.0	7.74 /31	9.70 /25	6.43 /64	B- /7.5	71	N/A
CV	Columbia FS Convertible Sec Port		C-	(800) 426-3750	13.59	D+ /2.9	7.94 /32	9.29 /23	--	B /8.1	75	N/A
CV	GAMCO Global Convertible B		C-	(800) 422-3554	6.01	D+ /2.5	13.35 /66	9.77 /26	4.72 /52	B /8.9	81	N/A
CV	Morgan Stanley Convertbl Sec Tr D	CNSDX	C-	(800) 869-6397	16.86	D+ /2.5	9.06 /40	8.41 /17	5.59 /58	B /8.7	66	5
CV	ING Convertible C	NRTLX	C-	(800) 992-0180	19.87	D+ /2.4	10.06 /47	7.84 /14	4.07 /46	B /8.0	57	N/A
CV	Lord Abbett Convertible Fund C	LACCX	C-	(800) 201-6984	11.91	D /1.9	8.18 /34	7.80 /14	--	B+ /9.1	59	3
CV	Value Line Convertible Fund	VALCX	C-	(800) 223-0818	12.35	D /1.9	8.71 /38	7.30 /12	3.80 /44	B /8.8	55	16
CV	Lord Abbett Convertible Fund A	LACFX	C-	(800) 201-6984	11.95	D /1.7	8.94 /40	8.53 /18	--	B+ /9.1	67	3
CV	Victory Convertible A	SBFCX	C-	(800) 539-3863	12.92	D /1.7	8.14 /34	7.32 /12	3.28 /39	B /8.8	58	10
CV	Morgan Stanley Convertbl Sec Tr C	CNSCX	C-	(800) 869-6397	16.78	D /1.7	8.15 /34	7.39 /12	4.58 /51	B /8.6	55	5
CV	Lord Abbett Convertible Fund B	LBCFX	C-	(800) 201-6984	11.92	D- /1.3	8.27 /35	7.81 /14	--	B+ /9.1	59	3
CV	TA IDEX Transamerica Convertb	ICVAX	D+	(888) 233-4339	12.69	C- /4.0	15.35 /73	11.19 /37	--	C+ /5.8	74	N/A
CV	Columbia Convertible Sec Fund A	PACIX	D+	(800) 426-3750	16.41	D+ /2.9	9.17 /41	10.44 /30	5.48 /58	C+ /6.9	84	1
CV	Legg Mason Prt Con SmB Cl A	SCRAX	D+	(866) 890-4247	16.89	D+ /2.7	8.58 /37	10.52 /31	7.18 /68	B- /7.1	78	N/A
CV	MainStay Convertible Fund C	MCCVX	D+	(800) 624-6782	14.08	D+ /2.4	9.82 /46	8.59 /18	4.07 /47	B- /7.6	69	7
CV	Columbia FS Convertible Sec Port		D+	(800) 426-3750	13.77	D /2.2	7.92 /32	9.28 /23	--	B /8.1	75	N/A
CV	Van Kampen Harbor C	ACHCX	D+	(800) 421-5666	14.89	D /2.2	7.47 /29	8.03 /15	2.00 /27	B- /7.6	62	8
CV	Columbia FS Convertible Sec Port		D+	(800) 426-3750	13.97	D /2.0	8.80 /39	9.23 /22	--	B /8.0	74	N/A
CV	MainStay Convertible Fund A	MCOAX	D+	(800) 624-6782	14.05	D /2.0	10.60 /51	9.37 /23	4.85 /53	B- /7.6	76	7
CV	ING Convertible B	NANBX	D+	(800) 992-0180	21.41	D /1.8	10.06 /47	7.83 /14	4.08 /47	B /8.1	57	N/A
CV	Morgan Stanley Convertbl Sec Tr B	CNSBX	D+	(800) 869-6397	16.89	D- /1.2	8.05 /33	7.34 /12	4.55 /51	B /8.6	54	5
CV	GAMCO Global Convertible AAA	GAGCX	D	(800) 422-3554	6.35	C- /3.9	14.17 /69	10.61 /32	5.48 /58	C /4.9	86	N/A
CV	TA IDEX Transamerica Convertb	ICVBX	D	(888) 233-4339	12.64	C- /3.5	14.48 /70	10.38 /30	--	C+ /5.8	67	N/A
CV	Calamos Convertible Fund I	CICVX	D	(800) 823-7386	18.37	D+ /2.8	9.08 /41	9.03 /21	6.36 /63	C+ /6.0	66	9

• Denotes fund is closed to new investors

Data as of June 30, 2006

Fund Type	Fund Name	Ticker Symbol	Overall Weiss Investment Rating	Phone	Net Asset Value As of 6/30/06	Performance Rating/Pts	Annualized Total Return Through 6/30/06			Risk Rating/Pts	Mgr. Quality Pct	Mgr. Tenure (Years)
							1Yr / Pct	3Yr / Pct	5Yr / Pct			
EM	● AIM International Small Co C	IEGCX	A+	(800) 347-4246	23.71	A+ /9.9	45.88 /98	43.45 /99	29.33 /99	C+ / 6.2	99	6
EM	● AIM International Small Co A	IEGAX	A+	(800) 347-4246	24.48	A+ /9.9	47.00 /99	44.51 /99	30.21 /99	C+ / 6.2	99	6
EM	● AIM International Small Co B	IEGBX	A+	(800) 347-4246	23.72	A+ /9.9	45.85 /98	43.47 /99	29.30 /99	C+ / 6.2	99	6
EM	Westcore International Frontier	WTIFX	A	(800) 392-2673	13.08	B /8.2	19.74 /82	20.75 /82	9.56 /79	B- / 7.5	81	7
EM	RVS Emerging Markets Fund C		A-	(800) 328-8300	9.57	A+ /9.6	34.98 /97	31.51 /96	18.43 /95	C+ / 5.9	5	6
EM	● AIM International Small Co Inst	IEGIX	B+	(800) 347-4246	24.52	A+ /9.9	47.30 /99	44.61 /99	30.26 /99	C / 4.9	99	N/A
EM	Lazard Emerging Markets Inst	LZEMX	B+	(800) 823-6300	18.61	A+ /9.8	35.04 /97	38.12 /99	23.42 /98	C / 4.8	62	12
EM	Lazard Emerging Markets Open	LZOEX	B+	(800) 823-6300	18.74	A+ /9.8	34.65 /97	37.87 /99	23.14 /98	C / 4.8	61	9
EM	● Delaware Emerging Markets I	DEMIX	B+	(800) 362-3863	18.13	A+ /9.7	23.10 /86	34.51 /98	22.60 /98	C / 5.5	70	10
EM	● Delaware Emerging Markets A	DEMAX	B+	(800) 362-3863	18.06	A+ /9.6	22.77 /85	34.18 /98	22.30 /98	C / 5.5	68	10
EM	● Delaware Emerging Markets B	DEMBX	B+	(800) 362-3863	17.73	A+ /9.6	21.86 /84	33.18 /97	21.39 /97	C / 5.5	59	10
EM	● Delaware Emerging Markets C	DEMCX	B+	(800) 362-3863	17.71	A+ /9.6	21.89 /84	33.19 /97	21.40 /97	C / 5.5	59	10
EM	Templeton Developing Markets	TDADX	B+	(800) 321-8563	24.72	A+ /9.6	28.24 /93	32.06 /97	20.37 /96	C / 5.2	41	15
EM	Templeton Developing Markets R	TDMRX	B+	(800) 342-5236	24.44	A+ /9.6	27.62 /92	31.42 /96	19.70 /96	C / 5.2	36	4
EM	Templeton Inst-Emerg Markets Mkt	TEEMX	B+	(800) 321-8563	20.05	A+ /9.6	28.42 /93	32.01 /97	20.52 /97	C / 5.2	39	N/A
EM	Templeton Developing Markets C	TDMTX	B+	(800) 342-5236	24.18	A /9.5	27.05 /91	30.78 /96	19.14 /95	C / 5.2	33	11
EM	● Templeton Developing Markets B	TDMBX	B+	(800) 342-5236	24.21	A /9.5	27.02 /91	30.80 /96	19.15 /95	C / 5.2	32	7
EM	Templeton Developing Markets A	TEDMX	B+	(800) 342-5236	24.71	A /9.5	27.90 /93	31.66 /96	19.91 /96	C / 5.2	38	15
EM	ING Emerging Countries M		B+	(800) 992-0180	26.43	B+ /8.5	19.27 /81	23.32 /88	--	C+ / 6.5	5	N/A
EM	DFA Emerging Markets Value	DFEVX	B	(800) 984-9472	25.82	A+ /9.9	37.52 /97	41.16 /99	28.82 /99	C- / 4.2	70	N/A
EM	JPMorgan Emerg Mkt Eq Inst	JMIEX	B	(800) 358-4782	14.91	A+ /9.8	31.62 /95	35.26 /98	19.85 /96	C / 4.7	23	N/A
EM	JPMorgan Emerg Mkt Eq Sel	JEMSX	B	(800) 358-4782	14.77	A+ /9.8	31.32 /95	34.97 /98	19.47 /96	C / 4.6	22	N/A
EM	● MFS Emerging Mkt Equity Fund I	MEMIX	B	(800) 343-2829	33.59	A+ /9.8	35.34 /97	35.38 /98	21.52 /97	C / 4.5	30	9
EM	Oppenheimer Developing Mkts A	ODMAX	B	(800) 525-7048	36.40	A+ /9.8	30.66 /95	39.19 /99	23.84 /98	C / 4.4	73	2
EM	Oppenheimer Developing Mkts N	ODVNX	B	(800) 525-7048	35.82	A+ /9.8	30.23 /94	38.71 /99	23.48 /98	C / 4.4	69	2
EM	Pioneer Emerging Markets Y	PYEFX	B	(800) 225-6292	28.87	A+ /9.8	43.32 /98	35.52 /98	22.78 /98	C / 4.4	26	N/A
EM	Guardian Baillie Giff Emerg Mkts C		B	(800) 343-0817	18.64	A+ /9.8	41.65 /98	35.61 /98	21.00 /97	C / 4.3	18	6
EM	Pioneer Emerging Markets R	PEMRX	B	(800) 225-6292	26.91	A+ /9.8	41.98 /98	34.21 /98	21.34 /97	C / 4.3	20	N/A
EM	Vanguard Emerging Mkts Stk Idx	VEMIX	B	(800) 662-7447	20.28	A+ /9.8	33.44 /96	34.34 /98	20.56 /97	C / 4.3	15	N/A
EM	Oppenheimer Developing Mkts B	ODVBX	B	(800) 525-7048	35.99	A+ /9.8	29.67 /94	38.06 /99	22.85 /98	C / 4.3	65	2
EM	Oppenheimer Developing Mkts C	ODVCX	B	(800) 525-7048	35.58	A+ /9.8	29.73 /94	38.17 /99	22.90 /98	C / 4.3	65	2
EM	Guardian Baillie Giff Emerg Mkts B		B	(800) 343-0817	18.56	A+ /9.8	41.58 /98	35.55 /98	20.91 /97	C / 4.3	18	9
EM	Forward Global Emerg Markets Inst	PTEMX	B	(800) 999-6809	19.56	A+ /9.7	31.25 /95	34.91 /98	24.37 /98	C / 4.6	20	11
EM	JPMorgan Emerg Mkt Eq B	JFBMX	B	(800) 358-4782	14.49	A+ /9.7	30.42 /95	33.98 /98	18.70 /95	C / 4.6	18	N/A
EM	JPMorgan Emerg Mkt Eq A	JFAMX	B	(800) 358-4782	14.60	A+ /9.7	30.94 /95	34.58 /98	19.18 /95	C / 4.6	20	N/A
EM	AIM Developing Markets Fd A	GTDDX	B	(800) 347-4246	20.94	A+ /9.7	39.34 /98	36.22 /98	21.75 /98	C / 4.5	28	3
EM	American Beacon Emerg Mkts Inst	AEMFX	B	(800) 967-9009	15.67	A+ /9.7	32.27 /96	32.43 /97	21.18 /97	C / 4.5	16	N/A
EM	MFS Emerging Mkt Equity Fund B	MEMBX	B	(800) 343-2829	31.19	A+ /9.7	34.05 /96	34.06 /98	20.33 /96	C / 4.4	23	N/A
EM	MFS Emerging Mkt Equity Fund C	MEMCX	B	(800) 343-2829	30.86	A+ /9.7	34.01 /96	34.04 /98	20.31 /96	C / 4.4	23	N/A
EM	AIM Developing Markets Fd B	GTDBX	B	(800) 347-4246	20.40	A+ /9.7	38.21 /97	35.37 /98	21.04 /97	C+ / 4.4	23	3
EM	AIM Developing Markets Fd C	GTDCX	B	(800) 347-4246	20.39	A+ /9.7	38.33 /98	35.40 /98	21.06 /97	C / 4.4	24	3
EM	Pioneer Emerging Markets A	PEMFX	B	(800) 225-6292	27.34	A+ /9.7	42.47 /98	34.50 /98	21.68 /97	B- / 4.4	21	N/A
EM	Vanguard Emerging Mkts Stk Idx	VEIEX	B	(800) 662-7447	20.24	A+ /9.7	33.25 /96	34.08 /98	20.35 /96	C / 4.3	15	N/A
EM	Pioneer Emerging Markets C	PCEFX	B	(800) 225-6292	24.92	A+ /9.7	41.46 /98	33.57 /97	20.86 /97	C / 4.3	17	N/A
EM	USAA Emerging Markets	USEMX	B	(800) 382-8722	16.72	A+ /9.6	28.91 /94	30.70 /96	19.19 /95	C / 4.6	20	4
EM	● Dreyfus Premier Emerging Mrkts R	DRPEX	B	(800) 782-6620	22.92	A+ /9.6	28.65 /93	30.81 /96	--	C / 4.5	19	10
EM	American Beacon Emerg Mkts	AAEPX	B	(800) 967-9009	15.53	A+ /9.6	32.06 /96	32.16 /97	20.95 /97	C / 4.5	15	N/A
EM	MFS Emerging Mkt Equity Fund A	MEMAX	B	(800) 343-2829	32.49	A+ /9.6	34.86 /97	34.84 /98	20.99 /97	C / 4.4	27	N/A
EM	SEI Instl Managed Tr-Intl Eq I	SEEIX	B	(800) 342-5734	13.49	B+ /8.9	27.10 /91	22.48 /86	--	C+ / 5.6	82	N/A
EM	GMO Emerging Markets Fund IV	GMEFX	B-		21.80	A+ /9.9	37.75 /97	39.36 /99	26.52 /99	C- / 4.1	43	N/A
EM	GMO Emerging Markets Fund VI	GEMMX	B-		21.81	A+ /9.9	37.82 /97	39.46 /99	--	C- / 4.0	43	N/A
EM	Quant Emg-Markets Ord	QFFOX	B-	(800) 326-2151	18.63	A+ /9.9	35.26 /97	39.44 /99	24.63 /98	C- / 4.0	15	4

● Denotes fund is closed to new investors

Fund Type	Fund Name	Ticker Symbol	Overall Weiss Investment Rating	Phone	Net Asset Value As of 6/30/06	PERFORMANCE Perform-ance Rating/Pts	Annualized Total Return Through 6/30/06 1Yr/Pct	3Yr/Pct	5Yr/Pct	RISK Risk Rating/Pts	FUND MGR Mgr. Quality Pct	Mgr. Tenure (Years)
EN	Vanguard Energy Inv	VGENX	A+	(800) 662-7447	65.20	A+ /9.9	37.25 /97	39.76 /99	25.08 /98	C+ / 6.2	98	N/A
EN	● Ivy Fund-Global Nat Resource Adv	IGNVX	A+	(800) 777-6472	31.12	A+ /9.9	46.95 /99	39.19 /99	24.29 /98	C+ / 6.2	99	8
EN	Vanguard Energy Adm	VGELX	A+	(800) 662-7447	122.47	A+ /9.9	37.33 /97	39.83 /99	--	C+ / 6.2	98	N/A
EN	Ivy Fund-Global Nat Resource A	IGNAX	A	(800) 777-6472	31.32	A+ /9.9	46.52 /99	39.05 /99	24.20 /98	C+ / 5.7	99	9
EN	T. Rowe Price New Era	PRNEX	A	(800) 638-5660	46.59	A+ /9.8	33.59 /96	33.38 /97	18.52 /95	C+ / 6.1	96	9
EN	Ivy Fund-Global Nat Resource C	IGNCX	A-	(800) 777-6472	29.10	A+ /9.9	45.48 /98	38.01 /99	23.19 /98	C+ / 5.7	99	9
EN	Ivy Fund-Global Nat Resource B	IGNBX	A-	(800) 777-6472	29.64	A+ /9.9	45.42 /98	37.92 /99	23.17 /98	C+ / 5.7	99	9
EN	RS Global Natural Resources Fund	RSNRX	A-	(800) 766-3863	36.09	A+ /9.9	42.46 /98	37.80 /99	26.74 /99	C+ / 5.7	97	11
EN	● AIM Energy Inv	FSTEX	A-	(800) 347-4246	45.48	A+ /9.9	38.47 /98	38.02 /99	20.95 /97	C+ / 5.7	89	9
EN	AIM Energy B	IENBX	A-	(800) 347-4246	44.16	A+ /9.8	37.49 /97	37.06 /99	--	C+ / 5.7	85	9
EN	AIM Energy A	IENAX	A-	(800) 347-4246	45.59	A+ /9.8	38.51 /98	38.00 /99	--	C+ / 5.7	89	9
EN	AIM Energy C	IEFCX	A-	(800) 347-4246	43.44	A+ /9.8	37.48 /97	37.06 /99	20.12 /96	C+ / 5.6	85	9
EN	Select Energy	FSENX	B+	(800) 544-8888	51.82	A+ /9.9	39.92 /98	37.96 /99	19.05 /95	C / 5.2	91	2
EN	Select Natural Resources	FNARX	B+	(800) 544-8888	28.04	A+ /9.9	46.83 /99	36.47 /98	18.21 /95	C / 4.9	90	N/A
EN	Fidelity Adv Natural Resources I	FANIX	B+	(800) 522-7297	48.14	A+ /9.9	46.62 /99	36.85 /98	18.75 /95	C / 4.8	90	N/A
EN	Fidelity Adv Natural Resources C	FNRCX	B+	(800) 522-7297	46.00	A+ /9.9	45.09 /98	35.39 /98	17.49 /94	C / 4.8	84	N/A
EN	Fidelity Adv Natural Resources T	FAGNX	B+	(800) 522-7297	47.86	A+ /9.9	45.80 /98	36.07 /98	18.08 /95	C / 4.8	87	N/A
EN	Fidelity Adv Natural Resources A	FANAX	B+	(800) 522-7297	47.03	A+ /9.8	46.08 /98	36.31 /98	18.29 /95	C / 4.8	88	N/A
EN	Fidelity Adv Natural Resources B	FANRX	B+	(800) 522-7297	45.77	A+ /9.8	45.02 /98	35.33 /98	17.44 /94	C / 4.8	83	N/A
EN	ICON Materials	ICBMX	B+	(800) 764-0442	12.48	A+ /9.7	35.29 /97	31.37 /96	16.63 /94	C / 5.1	98	9
EN	FBR Gas Utility Index Fund	GASFX	B+	(888) 888-0025	18.19	B- /7.0	7.49 /29	17.17 /69	5.38 /57	B / 8.2	97	N/A
EN	JennDry Jennison Nat Resources Z	PNRZX	B	(800) 257-3893	49.14	A+ /9.9	55.09 /99	43.11 /99	29.00 /99	C / 4.7	99	3
EN	JennDry Jennison Nat Resources	PNRCX	B	(800) 257-3893	42.66	A+ /9.9	53.54 /99	41.66 /99	27.71 /99	C / 4.7	98	3
EN	Van Eck Global Hard Assets C	GHACX	B	(800) 221-2220	36.66	A+ /9.9	48.60 /99	40.71 /99	24.05 /98	C / 4.7	99	N/A
EN	Van Eck Global Hard Assets A	GHAAX	B	(800) 221-2220	38.31	A+ /9.9	49.36 /99	41.65 /99	25.01 /98	C / 4.7	99	N/A
EN	JennDry Jennison Nat Resources	PGNAX	B	(800) 257-3893	48.25	A+ /9.9	54.75 /99	42.75 /99	28.68 /99	C / 4.7	98	3
EN	JennDry Jennison Nat Resources	PRGNX	B	(800) 257-3893	42.67	A+ /9.9	53.57 /99	41.67 /99	27.72 /99	C / 4.7	98	3
EN	Merrill Lynch Natural Resource A	MDGRX	B	(800) 543-6217	54.66	A+ /9.8	35.07 /97	35.94 /98	22.64 /98	C / 4.6	80	N/A
EN	Merrill Lynch Natural Resource I	MAGRX	B	(800) 543-6217	55.55	A+ /9.8	35.40 /97	36.28 /98	22.95 /98	C / 4.6	82	N/A
EN	Merrill Lynch Natural Resource C	MCGRX	B	(800) 543-6217	51.34	A+ /9.8	34.06 /96	34.89 /98	21.69 /97	C / 4.5	73	N/A
EN	Merrill Lynch Natural Resource B	MBGRX	B	(800) 543-6217	52.00	A+ /9.8	34.07 /96	34.89 /98	21.70 /97	C / 4.5	73	9
EN	Morgan Stanley Natural Res Dev D	NREDX	B	(800) 869-6397	27.19	A+ /9.8	37.22 /97	35.03 /98	15.37 /92	C / 4.4	75	1
EN	Rydex Series-Energy Inv	RYEIX	B	(800) 820-0888	22.65	A+ /9.7	28.88 /94	33.09 /97	15.48 /92	C / 4.9	65	N/A
EN	Rydex Series-Energy Adv	RYEAX	B	(800) 820-0888	21.87	A+ /9.7	28.14 /93	32.47 /97	14.93 /92	C / 4.8	59	N/A
EN	Rydex Series-Energy C	RYECX	B	(800) 820-0888	21.49	A+ /9.7	27.56 /92	31.76 /97	14.36 /91	C / 4.8	53	N/A
EN	Putnam Global Natural Resources	EBERX	B	(800) 354-2228	31.71	A+ /9.7	31.53 /95	32.24 /97	17.57 /94	C / 4.7	88	N/A
EN	Putnam Global Natural Resources	PGLCX	B	(800) 354-2228	30.32	A+ /9.7	30.56 /95	31.24 /96	16.68 /94	C / 4.6	83	N/A
EN	Morgan Stanley Natural Res Dev A	NREAX	B	(800) 869-6397	26.76	A+ /9.7	36.93 /97	34.71 /98	15.15 /92	C / 4.4	72	1
EN	Putnam Global Natural Resources	PGLMX	B	(800) 354-2228	30.96	A+ /9.6	30.87 /95	31.57 /96	16.98 /94	C / 4.6	85	N/A
EN	Putnam Global Natural Resources	PNRBX	B	(800) 354-2228	29.88	A+ /9.6	30.52 /95	31.25 /96	16.68 /94	C / 4.6	83	N/A
EN	● BlackRock-Global Resources A	SSGRX	B-	(888) 825-2257	75.84	A+ /9.9	50.16 /99	52.19 /99	33.45 /99	C- / 3.8	99	1
EN	● BlackRock-Global Resources C	SSGDX	B-	(888) 825-2257	68.07	A+ /9.9	49.09 /99	51.16 /99	32.57 /99	C- / 3.6	99	1
EN	● BlackRock-Global Resources B	SSGPX	B-	(888) 825-2257	68.13	A+ /9.9	49.06 /99	51.19 /99	32.57 /99	C- / 3.6	99	1
EN	Franklin Natural Resources Adv	FNRAX	B-	(800) 321-8563	36.29	A+ /9.8	35.01 /97	33.70 /97	16.60 /94	C- / 4.2	69	N/A
EN	Select Energy Svcs	FSESX	B-	(800) 544-8888	74.02	A+ /9.8	45.23 /98	34.37 /98	19.12 /95	C- / 3.8	46	1
EN	Morgan Stanley Natural Res Dev C	NRECX	B-	(800) 869-6397	24.89	A+ /9.7	35.82 /97	33.69 /97	14.21 /90	C / 4.3	65	1
EN	Morgan Stanley Natural Res Dev B	NREBX	B-	(800) 869-6397	24.96	A+ /9.7	35.90 /97	33.69 /97	14.22 /91	C / 4.3	65	1
EN	Putnam Global Natural Resources	PGNRX	B-	(800) 354-2228	31.50	A+ /9.7	31.21 /95	31.93 /97	17.29 /94	C / 4.3	86	N/A
EN	Franklin Natural Resources A	FRNRX	B-	(800) 342-5236	34.67	A+ /9.7	34.56 /96	33.23 /97	16.17 /93	C- / 4.1	65	11
EN	PIMCO Commodity Real Ret Str	PCRIX	B-	(800) 227-7337	14.70	B- /7.2	10.97 /53	18.06 /73	--	C+ / 6.7	82	4
EN	PIMCO Commodity Real Ret Str	PCRRX	B-	(800) 227-7337	14.62	B- /7.1	10.66 /51	17.78 /72	--	C+ / 6.7	81	4
EN	ICON Energy	ICENX	C+	(800) 764-0442	36.31	A+ /9.9	38.56 /98	40.72 /99	23.86 /98	C- / 3.3	89	N/A

● Denotes fund is closed to new investors

Data as of June 30, 2006

Fund Type	Fund Name	Ticker Symbol	Overall Weiss Investment Rating	Phone	Net Asset Value As of 6/30/06	PERFORMANCE				RISK	FUND MGR	
	99 Pct = Best / 0 Pct = Worst					Perform-ance Rating/Pts	Annualized Total Return Through 6/30/06			Risk Rating/Pts	Mgr. Quality Pct	Mgr. Tenure (Years)
							1Yr / Pct	3Yr / Pct	5Yr / Pct			
FS	Gartmore Global Finan Svc Inst	GLFIX	A+	(800) 848-0920	14.62	B /8.2	21.83 /84	21.22 /83	--	B /8.6	98	2
FS	Gartmore Global Finan Svc	GFISX	A+	(800) 848-0920	14.62	B /8.2	21.83 /84	21.22 /83	--	B /8.0	98	4
FS	Gartmore Global Finan Svc R	GLFRX	A+	(800) 848-0920	14.30	B /8.0	21.43 /84	20.59 /81	--	B /8.6	97	3
FS	Gartmore Global Finan Svc B	GLFBX	A+	(800) 848-0920	14.26	B /7.9	20.68 /83	20.01 /79	--	B /8.6	97	4
FS	AXA Entp-Global Financial Serv Y	EGFYX	A	(800) 432-4320	8.87	B /8.1	24.24 /88	19.92 /79	11.44 /85	B- /7.6	97	N/A
FS	Gartmore Global Finan Svc C	GLFCX	A	(800) 848-0920	14.25	B /7.8	20.62 /83	20.00 /79	--	B /8.0	97	4
FS	Gartmore Global Finan Svc A	GLFAX	A	(800) 848-0920	14.54	B /7.7	21.48 /84	20.91 /82	--	B /8.0	98	4
FS	AXA Entp-Global Financial Serv C	EGFCX	A-	(800) 432-4320	8.70	B /7.7	22.96 /86	18.65 /75	10.31 /82	B- /7.7	95	N/A
FS	Hartford Global Finan Serv Y	HGFYX	A-	(800) 523-7798	13.12	B- /7.1	18.73 /80	16.30 /65	5.39 /57	B /8.2	83	N/A
FS	AXA Entp-Global Financial Serv A	EGFAX	B+	(800) 432-4320	8.83	B- /7.5	23.79 /87	19.44 /77	10.95 /84	B- /7.7	96	N/A
FS	AXA Entp-Global Financial Serv B	EGFBX	B+	(800) 432-4320	8.73	B- /7.3	22.47 /85	18.54 /75	10.23 /81	B- /7.7	94	N/A
FS	Mutual Financial Svcs Z	TEFAX	B	(800) 321-8563	22.27	B- /7.4	16.96 /77	17.81 /72	12.19 /87	B- /7.1	96	4
FS	Delaware American Services Fund	DASIX	B	(800) 362-3863	17.50	B- /7.2	11.61 /57	17.58 /71	14.66 /91	B- /7.1	87	N/A
FS	Hartford Global Finan Serv C	HGFCX	B	(800) 523-7798	12.77	C+ /6.3	17.37 /78	14.93 /58	4.17 /48	B /8.2	74	N/A
FS	Hartford Global Finan Serv A	HGFAX	B	(800) 523-7798	13.00	C+ /6.1	18.28 /80	15.78 /63	4.92 /53	B /8.2	80	N/A
FS	Schwab Financial Services Focus	SWFFX	B-	(866) 855-9102	14.83	B- /7.2	15.34 /73	17.76 /71	8.50 /74	C+ /6.5	88	N/A
FS	Mutual Financial Svcs C	TMFSX	B-	(800) 342-5236	22.09	C+ /6.9	15.80 /74	16.65 /67	11.09 /84	B- /7.2	94	4
FS	Mutual Financial Svcs A	TFSIX	B-	(800) 342-5236	22.26	C+ /6.7	16.60 /76	17.42 /70	11.83 /86	B- /7.2	96	4
FS	Delaware American Services Fund	DAMCX	B-	(800) 362-3863	16.57	C+ /6.6	10.47 /50	16.42 /65	13.53 /89	B- /7.1	80	N/A
FS	● Mutual Financial Svcs B	TBFSX	B-	(800) 342-5236	21.73	C+ /6.5	15.77 /74	16.65 /67	11.08 /84	B- /7.2	94	4
FS	Hartford Global Finan Serv B	HGFBX	B-	(800) 523-7798	12.77	C+ /5.8	17.36 /78	14.96 /59	4.19 /48	B /8.2	74	N/A
FS	Davis Financial Y	DVFYX	B-	(800) 279-0279	43.69	C+ /5.8	13.15 /65	13.92 /53	5.01 /54	B- /7.8	77	15
FS	Merrill Lynch Global Finan Svc R	MRFNX	C+	(800) 543-6217	16.41	A- /9.2	25.11 /89	26.44 /93	--	C- /4.2	97	N/A
FS	ICON Financial	ICFSX	C+	(800) 764-0442	13.81	C+ /6.7	13.56 /66	15.77 /62	7.27 /68	C+ /6.0	53	9
FS	Delaware American Services Fund	DASAX	C+	(800) 362-3863	17.27	C+ /6.3	11.35 /56	17.32 /69	14.37 /91	B- /7.1	86	N/A
FS	Emerald Select Banking & Finance	HSSAX	C+	(800) 232-0224	28.71	C+ /6.2	9.50 /43	17.37 /70	16.50 /94	B- /7.1	94	9
FS	Delaware American Services Fund	DASBX	C+	(800) 362-3863	16.57	C+ /6.2	10.47 /50	16.42 /65	13.53 /89	B- /7.1	80	N/A
FS	Rydex Series-Financial Service Inv	RYFIX	C+	(800) 820-0888	13.00	C+ /5.7	10.28 /49	13.83 /53	4.96 /54	B- /7.8	58	N/A
FS	Saratoga Adv Tr-Financial Service I	SFPIX	C+	(800) 807-3863	13.66	C /5.4	15.09 /72	13.80 /53	--	B- /7.8	47	N/A
FS	Rydex Series-Financial Service	RYFAX	C+	(800) 820-0888	12.60	C /5.3	9.58 /44	13.13 /50	4.56 /51	B- /7.7	50	N/A
FS	J Hancock Financial Indust I	FIDIX	C+	(800) 257-3336	19.97	C /5.0	13.82 /68	12.84 /48	3.91 /45	B /8.0	55	5
FS	Davis Financial A	RPFGX	C+	(800) 279-0279	42.95	C /5.0	12.99 /64	13.74 /53	4.82 /53	B- /7.8	76	15
FS	Davis Financial C	DFFCX	C+	(800) 279-0279	39.80	C /5.0	12.00 /59	12.73 /47	3.92 /45	B- /7.7	68	15
FS	Dreyfus Premier Financial Svcs A	DFSFX	C+	(800) 782-6620	15.41	C /4.6	9.78 /45	13.49 /51	--	B /8.1	35	4
FS	Merrill Lynch Global Finan Svc I	MAFNX	C	(800) 543-6217	16.81	A /9.3	25.75 /89	27.05 /93	16.83 /94	D+ /2.9	98	N/A
FS	Merrill Lynch Global Finan Svc C	MCFNX	C	(800) 543-6217	16.33	A- /9.1	24.49 /88	25.77 /92	15.60 /93	D+ /2.9	97	N/A
FS	Merrill Lynch Global Finan Svc A	MDFNX	C	(800) 543-6217	16.70	A- /9.1	25.39 /89	26.72 /93	16.50 /94	D+ /2.9	98	N/A
FS	Merrill Lynch Global Finan Svc B	MBFNX	C	(800) 543-6217	16.42	A- /9.1	24.47 /88	25.74 /92	15.61 /93	D+ /2.8	97	N/A
FS	Select Brokerage & Invtmt Mmgt	FSLBX	C	(800) 544-8888	67.78	B /7.7	24.53 /88	20.32 /81	10.75 /83	C /4.6	77	N/A
FS	T. Rowe Price Financial Services	PRISX	C	(800) 638-5660	22.04	C+ /5.8	14.70 /71	14.00 /54	7.86 /71	C+ /6.2	51	N/A
FS	ProFunds-Bank UltraSector Inv	BKPIX	C	(888) 776-3637	39.98	C+ /5.8	9.90 /46	13.86 /53	--	C+ /5.7	20	5
FS	Legg Mason Prt Financial Svc C	SFSLX	C	(866) 890-4247	15.94	C+ /5.6	13.18 /65	13.59 /52	5.54 /58	C+ /6.4	66	N/A
FS	Legg Mason Prt Financial Svc A	SBFAX	C	(866) 890-4247	16.39	C /5.3	13.78 /68	14.38 /56	6.30 /63	C+ /6.3	72	N/A
FS	Fidelity Adv Financial Serv I	FFSIX	C	(800) 522-7297	23.27	C /5.1	12.28 /61	13.00 /49	6.25 /63	C+ /6.8	44	N/A
FS	Rydex Series-Financial Service C	RYFCX	C	(800) 820-0888	12.38	C /4.7	8.90 /39	12.56 /46	4.00 /46	B- /7.7	43	N/A
FS	Select Insurance	FSPCX	C	(800) 544-8888	66.34	C /4.7	7.70 /30	13.17 /50	7.94 /71	B- /7.0	69	N/A
FS	ING Financial Services A	PBTAX	C	(800) 992-0180	23.08	C /4.7	10.97 /53	13.75 /53	7.36 /68	B- /7.0	55	5
FS	Davis Financial B	DFIBX	C	(800) 279-0279	39.16	C /4.5	11.99 /59	12.74 /47	3.92 /45	B- /7.6	68	15
FS	ING Financial Services B	PBTBX	C	(800) 992-0180	22.70	C /4.3	10.15 /48	12.89 /48	6.53 /64	B- /7.2	45	5
FS	J Hancock Financial Indust C	FIDCX	C	(800) 257-3336	18.69	C- /4.2	12.35 /61	11.56 /40	2.66 /33	B- /7.8	39	7
FS	North Track DJ US Fin 100+ C	NDUCX	C	(800) 826-4600	12.72	C- /3.8	10.57 /51	10.93 /35	4.05 /46	B /8.1	30	4
FS	J Hancock Financial Indust A	FIDAX	C	(800) 257-3336	19.61	C- /3.8	13.15 /65	12.35 /45	3.38 /40	B- /7.8	48	10

● Denotes fund is closed to new investors

Fund Type	Fund Name	Ticker Symbol	Overall Weiss Investment Rating	Phone	Net Asset Value As of 6/30/06	Perform-ance Rating/Pts	Annualized Total Return Through 6/30/06			Risk Rating/Pts	Mgr. Quality Pct	Mgr. Tenure (Years)
	99 Pct = Best / 0 Pct = Worst						1Yr / Pct	3Yr / Pct	5Yr / Pct			
FO	● AIM European Small Company A	ESMAX	A+	(800) 347-4246	27.07	A+ /9.9	49.80 /99	49.86 /99	32.52 /99	C+ / 6.6	99	6
FO	● AIM European Small Company C	ESMCX	A+	(800) 347-4246	26.16	A+ /9.9	48.74 /99	48.83 /99	31.59 /99	C+ / 6.5	99	6
FO	● AIM European Small Company B	ESMBX	A+	(800) 347-4246	26.15	A+ /9.9	48.69 /99	48.76 /99	31.58 /99	C+ / 6.5	99	6
FO	Vontobel Eastern European Eq A	VEEEX	A+	(800) 527-9500	24.97	A+ /9.8	24.85 /88	36.91 /98	29.41 /99	B- / 7.2	98	5
FO	Eaton Vance Tax-Mgd Emg Mkt Fd	EITEX	A+	(800) 225-6265	31.61	A+ /9.8	35.45 /97	37.77 /99	25.58 /99	C+ / 6.7	85	8
FO	● Dreyfus Premier Intl Small Cap A	DSMAX	A+	(800) 782-6620	26.14	A+ /9.8	37.42 /97	35.64 /98	22.32 /98	C+ / 6.4	97	3
FO	● Dreyfus Premier Intl Small Cap R	DSMRX	A+	(800) 782-6620	26.38	A+ /9.8	37.95 /97	36.13 /98	22.58 /98	C+ / 6.4	98	3
FO	● Dreyfus Premier Intl Small Cap C	DSMCX	A+	(800) 782-6620	25.62	A+ /9.8	36.45 /97	34.74 /98	21.72 /97	C+ / 6.3	96	3
FO	● Dreyfus Premier Intl Small Cap T	DSMTX	A+	(800) 782-6620	26.00	A+ /9.8	37.16 /97	35.34 /98	22.11 /98	C+ / 6.3	97	3
FO	● The Boston Co Intl Small Cap Fd	SDISX	A+	(800) 221-4795	23.61	A+ /9.8	38.73 /98	37.08 /99	23.17 /98	C+ / 6.3	98	6
FO	American Century Intl Opport Inv	AIOIX	A+	(800) 345-6488	10.77	A+ /9.8	34.22 /96	37.77 /99	25.47 /99	C+ / 6.3	89	N/A
FO	American Century Intl Opport Inst	ACIOX	A+	(800) 345-6488	10.81	A+ /9.8	34.51 /96	38.09 /99	--	C+ / 6.2	89	N/A
FO	Oakmark International Small Cap II	OAREX	A+	(800) 625-6275	22.19	A+ /9.7	31.26 /95	32.65 /97	21.38 /97	B / 8.0	98	5
FO	● AIM European Growth Inv	EGINX	A+	(800) 347-4246	36.61	A+ /9.7	31.71 /95	30.70 /96	16.53 /94	B- / 7.9	92	9
FO	GMO Foreign Small Companies IV	GFSFX	A+		18.78	A+ /9.7	30.86 /95	31.51 /96	--	B- / 7.8	93	N/A
FO	Allianz NACM International C	PNICX	A+	(800) 628-1237	21.65	A+ /9.7	38.19 /97	30.07 /96	15.14 /92	B- / 7.7	83	N/A
FO	Allianz NACM International D	PNIDX	A+	(800) 628-1237	21.84	A+ /9.7	39.19 /98	31.01 /96	16.01 /93	B- / 7.7	87	N/A
FO	Dodge & Cox International Stock	DODFX	A+	(800) 621-3979	38.96	A+ /9.7	27.64 /92	33.39 /97	16.39 /93	B- / 7.7	95	N/A
FO	Putnam International Capital Opp Y	PIVYX	A+	(800) 354-2228	32.60	A+ /9.7	34.05 /96	31.48 /96	14.16 /90	B- / 7.3	80	N/A
FO	Allianz NFJ Intl Value Inst	ANJIX	A+	(800) 628-1237	19.43	A+ /9.7	28.63 /93	32.44 /97	--	B- / 7.2	61	N/A
FO	Allianz NACM International I	NAISX	A+	(800) 628-1237	22.01	A+ /9.7	39.76 /98	31.33 /96	16.20 /93	C+ / 6.8	89	N/A
FO	DFA International Small Cap Value	DISVX	A+	(800) 984-9472	19.30	A+ /9.7	28.16 /93	33.59 /97	23.77 /98	C+ / 6.7	98	N/A
FO	● Dreyfus Premier Intl Small Cap B	DSMBX	A+	(800) 782-6620	25.62	A+ /9.7	36.45 /97	34.71 /98	21.72 /97	C+ / 6.3	96	3
FO	DFA International Value IV	DFVFX	A+	(800) 984-9472	16.41	A+ /9.6	31.38 /95	30.29 /96	15.88 /93	B / 8.0	89	N/A
FO	Allianz NACM International A	PNIAX	A+	(800) 628-1237	21.84	A+ /9.6	39.18 /98	30.99 /96	16.00 /93	B- / 7.7	87	N/A
FO	Neuberger Berman International Tr	NBITX	A+	(800) 877-9700	26.05	A+ /9.6	29.60 /94	31.14 /96	16.26 /93	B- / 7.7	85	N/A
FO	DFA International Small Company	DFISX	A+	(800) 984-9472	17.55	A+ /9.6	27.97 /93	30.60 /96	20.00 /96	B- / 7.6	94	N/A
FO	JPMorgan Intl Value Inst	JNUSX	A+	(800) 358-4782	15.41	A+ /9.6	35.15 /97	29.53 /95	12.79 /88	B- / 7.3	91	9
FO	JPMorgan Intl Value Sel	JIESX	A+	(800) 358-4782	15.35	A+ /9.6	34.87 /97	29.07 /95	12.45 /87	B- / 7.3	90	9
FO	● Artisan International Small Cap Inv	ARTJX	A+	(800) 344-1770	21.83	A+ /9.6	34.99 /97	32.51 /97	--	B- / 7.2	70	5
FO	DFA International Value I	DFIVX	A+	(800) 984-9472	20.01	A+ /9.6	31.08 /95	30.05 /96	15.74 /93	B- / 7.0	89	N/A
FO	AIM European Growth A	AEDAX	A+	(800) 347-4246	36.66	A+ /9.6	31.66 /95	30.63 /96	16.49 /93	B- / 7.0	91	9
FO	AIM European Growth C	AEDCX	A+	(800) 347-4246	34.74	A+ /9.6	30.64 /95	29.73 /95	15.69 /93	B- / 7.0	88	9
FO	Neuberger Berman International	NBISX	A+	(800) 877-9700	23.80	A+ /9.6	29.66 /94	31.39 /96	15.92 /93	C+ / 6.6	86	3
FO	Artisan International Value Inv	ARTKX	A+	(800) 344-1770	25.32	A /9.5	30.13 /94	28.71 /94	--	B / 8.1	91	4
FO	DFA Tax Managed Intl Value	DTMIX	A+	(800) 984-9472	17.58	A /9.5	31.05 /95	29.32 /95	14.73 /91	B / 8.0	86	N/A
FO	JPMorgan Intl Value B	JFEBX	A+	(800) 358-4782	15.03	A /9.5	33.84 /96	28.26 /94	11.75 /86	B- / 7.3	86	9
FO	JPMorgan Intl Value A	JFEAX	A+	(800) 358-4782	15.27	A /9.5	34.50 /96	28.89 /95	12.25 /87	B- / 7.3	89	9
FO	Gartmore Intl Growth Inst	GIGIX	A+	(800) 848-0920	12.17	A /9.5	38.94 /98	28.54 /94	11.67 /86	B- / 7.0	46	N/A
FO	AIM European Growth B	AEDBX	A+	(800) 347-4246	34.72	A /9.5	30.66 /95	29.73 /95	15.70 /93	B- / 7.0	89	9
FO	AllianceBernstein Intl Value Adv	ABIYX	A+	(800) 221-5672	20.59	A /9.5	34.32 /96	27.51 /94	18.15 /95	C+ / 6.8	80	6
FO	Quantitative Foreign Value Ord	QFVOX	A+	(800) 326-2151	19.57	A /9.5	27.46 /92	29.00 /95	18.45 /95	C+ / 6.6	80	8
FO	● Third Avenue International Value	TAVIX	A+	(800) 443-1021	22.91	A /9.4	20.50 /82	29.35 /95	--	B / 8.4	99	5
FO	ICAP International Fund	ICEUX	A+	(888) 221-4227	36.05	A /9.4	31.53 /95	28.02 /94	13.98 /90	B- / 7.5	83	9
FO	MFS Intl New Discovery R3	MIDRX	A+	(800) 343-2829	25.34	A /9.4	27.62 /92	28.60 /94	16.33 /93	B- / 7.4	67	3
FO	MFS Intl New Discovery 529C	ECIDX	A+	(800) 343-2829	24.59	A /9.4	26.95 /91	27.90 /94	15.57 /93	B- / 7.4	60	4
FO	MFS Intl New Discovery 529B	EBIDX	A+	(800) 343-2829	24.62	A /9.4	26.91 /91	27.88 /94	15.56 /93	B- / 7.4	60	4
FO	The Boston Co Intl Core Eq	SDIEX	A+	(800) 221-4795	37.51	A /9.4	29.86 /94	27.99 /94	15.01 /92	B- / 7.3	77	9
FO	DFA United Kingdom Small Co	DFUKX	A+	(800) 984-9472	27.37	A /9.4	28.30 /93	27.28 /93	17.47 /94	B- / 7.2	91	N/A
FO	SSgA Intl Stock Selection Fd	SSAIX	A+	(800) 647-7327	12.35	A /9.4	31.18 /95	26.56 /93	12.41 /87	B- / 7.1	65	N/A
FO	Tocqueville Intl Value Fund	TIVFX	A+	(800) 697-3863	16.20	A /9.4	25.20 /89	29.19 /95	16.47 /93	B- / 7.0	90	12
FO	Gartmore Intl Growth C	GIGCX	A+	(800) 848-0920	11.63	A /9.4	37.73 /97	27.32 /93	10.58 /82	C+ / 6.9	36	N/A

● Denotes fund is closed to new investors   Data as of June 30, 2006

Fund Type	Fund Name	Ticker Symbol	Overall Weiss Investment Rating	Phone	Net Asset Value As of 6/30/06	Perform-ance Rating/Pts	Annualized Total Return Through 6/30/06			Risk Rating/Pts	Mgr. Quality Pct	Mgr. Tenure (Years)
	99 Pct = Best 0 Pct = Worst						1Yr / Pct	3Yr / Pct	5Yr / Pct			
GL	Putnam College Adv Intl Cap Opp		A+	(800) 354-2228	20.51	A+ /9.7	33.96 /96	31.35 /96	--	B- /7.2	79	N/A
GL	Putnam College Adv Intl Cap Opp		A+	(800) 354-2228	19.37	A+ /9.6	32.22 /96	29.64 /95	--	B- /7.2	67	N/A
GL	Principal Inv Divers Intl Inst	PIIIX	A+	(800) 247-4123	13.43	A /9.5	35.71 /97	27.44 /93	11.47 /85	B- /7.5	56	3
GL	Principal Inv Divers Intl Pfd	PINPX	A+	(800) 247-4123	13.43	A /9.5	35.49 /97	27.17 /93	11.29 /85	B- /7.5	53	3
GL	Principal Inv Divers Intl Sel	PINLX	A+	(800) 247-4123	13.54	A /9.5	35.09 /97	27.14 /93	11.29 /85	B- /7.4	51	3
GL	Putnam College Adv Intl Cap Opp		A+	(800) 354-2228	20.02	A /9.5	33.20 /96	30.64 /96	--	B- /7.2	74	N/A
GL	Putnam College Adv Intl Cap Opp		A+	(800) 354-2228	19.36	A /9.5	32.24 /96	29.67 /95	--	B- /7.2	68	N/A
GL	Principal Inv Intl Growth Sel	PITSX	A+	(800) 247-4123	12.44	A /9.4	31.39 /95	26.76 /93	12.17 /87	B- /7.9	73	1
GL	Principal Inv Intl Growth AdvPfd	PITMX	A+	(800) 247-4123	12.88	A /9.4	31.06 /95	26.44 /93	12.67 /88	B- /7.8	69	1
GL	Principal Inv Intl Growth Pfd	PITPX	A+	(800) 247-4123	12.47	A /9.4	31.44 /95	26.88 /93	12.27 /87	B- /7.8	72	1
GL	Principal Inv Intl Growth Inst	PITIX	A+	(800) 247-4123	12.57	A /9.4	31.85 /96	27.16 /93	12.32 /87	B- /7.8	74	1
GL	Principal Inv Divers Intl J	PIIJX	A+	(800) 247-4123	13.32	A /9.4	34.96 /97	26.42 /93	10.51 /82	B- /7.4	45	3
GL	Principal Inv Divers Intl AdvSel	PINNX	A+	(800) 247-4123	13.30	A /9.4	34.90 /97	26.58 /93	10.65 /83	B- /7.4	47	3
GL	Principal Inv Divers Intl AdvPfd	PINRX	A+	(800) 247-4123	13.38	A /9.4	34.99 /97	26.74 /93	10.87 /83	B- /7.4	48	3
GL	Principal Inv Intl Growth J	PITJX	A+	(800) 247-4123	12.32	A /9.3	30.77 /95	26.04 /92	11.51 /85	B- /7.9	67	1
GL	Principal Inv Intl Growth AdvSel	PITNX	A+	(800) 247-4123	12.26	A /9.3	30.83 /95	26.21 /92	11.67 /86	B- /7.8	67	1
GL	GMO International Eq Alloc III	GIEAX	A+		17.64	A /9.3	27.70 /92	27.38 /93	18.12 /95	B- /7.6	99	10
GL	RVS International Aggressive Gr C		A+	(800) 328-8300	8.58	A- /9.0	27.02 /91	23.86 /89	--	B /8.6	38	N/A
GL	Vanguard Instl Developd Mkts Idx	VIDMX	A+	(800) 662-7447	11.15	A- /9.0	26.95 /91	23.99 /89	10.03 /81	B /8.0	49	6
GL	Vanguard Global Equity Fund	VHGEX	A+	(800) 662-7447	21.27	B+ /8.9	22.33 /85	22.96 /87	13.54 /89	B- /7.5	43	11
GL	T. Rowe Price Intl Equity Index Fd	PIEQX	A+	(800) 638-5660	13.05	B+ /8.9	26.55 /91	23.10 /88	9.47 /78	B- /7.5	48	N/A
GL	Seligman Global Small Co R	SGSRX	A+	(800) 221-2783	17.84	B+ /8.9	20.89 /83	24.03 /89	--	B- /7.3	40	N/A
GL	American Funds Cap Wld Gr&Inc	RWIFX	A+	(800) 421-4120	38.52	B+ /8.8	21.80 /84	22.44 /86	12.63 /88	B- /7.7	70	N/A
GL	American Funds Cap Wld Gr&Inc F	CWGFX	A+	(800) 421-4120	38.46	B+ /8.7	21.46 /84	22.08 /85	12.28 /87	B- /7.7	67	N/A
GL	American Funds Cap Wld Gr&Inc	CWIFX	A+	(800) 421-4120	38.47	B+ /8.7	21.70 /84	22.09 /85	12.26 /87	B- /7.7	67	N/A
GL	American Funds Cap Wld Gr&Inc	RWIEX	A+	(800) 421-4120	38.46	B+ /8.7	21.40 /83	22.04 /85	12.29 /87	B- /7.6	67	N/A
GL	● First Eagle Global Fund I	SGIIX	A+	(800) 334-2143	46.07	B+ /8.6	22.62 /85	22.04 /85	18.42 /95	B /8.8	93	7
GL	American Funds Cap Wld Gr&Inc	CWIEX	A+	(800) 421-4120	38.42	B+ /8.6	21.03 /83	21.65 /84	11.92 /86	B- /7.6	63	N/A
GL	American Funds Cap Wld Gr&Inc	RWICX	A+	(800) 421-4120	38.37	B+ /8.6	21.00 /83	21.64 /84	11.89 /86	B- /7.6	63	N/A
GL	Putnam College Adv Intl Equity O		A+	(800) 354-2228	15.46	B+ /8.5	25.90 /90	20.48 /81	--	B- /7.7	24	N/A
GL	Oppenheimer Global Fund Y	OGLYX	A+	(800) 525-7048	69.66	B+ /8.5	19.21 /81	21.92 /85	8.59 /75	B- /7.6	32	2
GL	AllianceBernstein Global Value Adv	ABGYX	A+	(800) 221-5672	14.97	B+ /8.5	23.95 /87	20.89 /82	10.77 /83	B- /7.6	55	5
GL	American Funds Cap Wld Gr&Inc	RWIBX	A+	(800) 421-4120	38.25	B+ /8.5	20.50 /82	21.11 /83	11.44 /85	B- /7.6	58	N/A
GL	American Funds Cap Wld Gr&Inc	RWIAX	A+	(800) 421-4120	38.34	B+ /8.5	20.47 /82	21.11 /83	11.41 /85	B- /7.6	58	N/A
GL	Legg Mason Prt Intl Lg Cp Y	SMYIX	A+	(866) 890-4247	13.02	B+ /8.4	23.49 /87	20.26 /80	--	B /8.4	37	N/A
GL	Oakmark Global II	OARGX	A+	(800) 625-6275	24.94	B+ /8.4	20.00 /82	20.37 /81	--	B /8.4	65	N/A
GL	Mutual Discovery Z	MDISX	A+	(800) 321-8563	27.92	B+ /8.4	19.70 /81	20.98 /82	11.22 /84	B /8.1	90	1
GL	American Funds Cap Wld Gr&Inc C	CWGCX	A+	(800) 421-4120	38.25	B+ /8.4	20.51 /82	21.15 /83	11.42 /85	B- /7.6	59	N/A
GL	● First Eagle Global Fund C	FESGX	A+	(800) 334-2143	45.53	B+ /8.3	21.43 /83	20.84 /82	17.26 /94	B /8.8	89	7
GL	Oakmark Global I	OAKGX	A+	(800) 625-6275	25.28	B+ /8.3	20.47 /82	20.73 /82	16.52 /94	B /8.4	69	N/A
GL	Mutual Discovery R	TEDRX	A+	(800) 342-5236	27.44	B+ /8.3	19.13 /81	20.40 /81	10.68 /83	B /8.1	88	1
GL	Columbia Oppenheimer Global		A+	(800) 426-3750	19.39	B+ /8.3	18.52 /80	21.35 /83	--	B /8.0	28	3
GL	● First Eagle Global Fund A	SGENX	A+	(800) 334-2143	45.92	B /8.2	22.33 /85	21.75 /85	18.11 /95	B /8.8	92	7
GL	Mutual Discovery C	TEDSX	A+	(800) 342-5236	27.39	B /8.1	18.52 /80	19.79 /79	10.12 /81	B /8.1	85	1
GL	Mutual Discovery A	TEDIX	A+	(800) 342-5236	27.63	B /8.0	19.30 /81	20.58 /81	10.84 /83	B /8.1	89	1
GL	● Tweedy Browne Global Value	TBGVX	A+	(800) 432-4789	27.74	B /7.9	14.00 /68	20.28 /80	8.27 /73	B /8.5	97	13
GL	MFS Global Equity Fund I	MWEIX	A+	(800) 343-2829	28.71	B /7.9	20.86 /83	18.12 /73	8.97 /76	B /8.4	58	9
GL	Legg Mason Prt Intl Lg Cp C	SILLX	A+	(866) 890-4247	13.11	B /7.9	21.64 /84	18.86 /76	6.95 /66	B /8.3	29	N/A
GL	MFS Global Equity Fund R3	MEQRX	A+	(800) 343-2829	27.81	B /7.9	20.01 /82	18.35 /74	8.68 /75	B /8.2	51	3
GL	● Ivy Fund-Cundill Global Value Adv	ICDVX	A+	(800) 777-6472	15.25	B /7.9	14.96 /72	20.03 /79	9.89 /80	B /8.2	98	6
GL	USAA World Growth Fund	USAWX	A+	(800) 382-8722	19.44	B /7.8	20.42 /82	17.84 /72	7.15 /67	B /8.3	58	4
GL	American Funds New Perspective	CNPFX	A+	(800) 421-4120	30.25	B /7.8	20.73 /83	18.71 /75	7.85 /71	B /8.3	24	N/A

● Denotes fund is closed to new investors

Fund Type	Fund Name	Ticker Symbol	Overall Weiss Investment Rating	Phone	Net Asset Value As of 6/30/06	PERFORMANCE				RISK	FUND MGR	
	99 Pct = Best 0 Pct = Worst					Perform-ance Rating/Pts	Annualized Total Return Through 6/30/06			Risk Rating/Pts	Mgr. Quality Pct	Mgr. Tenure (Years)
							1Yr / Pct	3Yr / Pct	5Yr / Pct			
GR	Bruce Fund		A+	(800) 872-7823	408.85	A+ /9.7	18.36 /80	33.71 /97	29.74 /99	B /8.4	99	23
GR	Baron Partners Fund	BPTRX	A+	(800) 992-2766	20.24	A /9.5	20.06 /82	29.89 /95	14.37 /91	B- /7.2	99	14
GR	Hodges Fund	HDPMX	A+	(877) 232-1222	24.86	A /9.3	23.29 /86	28.05 /94	16.52 /94	C+ /6.8	99	14
GR	Fidelity Adv Cyclical Indust I	FCLIX	A+	(800) 522-7297	23.94	A- /9.1	22.78 /85	24.68 /90	11.85 /86	B- /7.2	98	N/A
GR	James Advantage Equity A	JALCX	A+	(888) 426-7640	11.04	B+/8.7	24.45 /88	21.58 /84	7.90 /71	B- /7.6	97	7
GR	Third Avenue Value Fund	TAVFX	A+	(800) 443-1021	57.76	B+/8.7	14.72 /71	23.58 /89	12.34 /87	B- /7.6	99	3
GR	DFA Large Cap Value I	DFLVX	A+	(800) 984-9472	23.38	B /8.1	15.77 /74	19.45 /78	8.87 /76	B /8.7	95	N/A
GR	MUTUALS.com Vice Fund	VICEX	A+	(800) 688-8257	17.83	B /8.1	10.80 /52	20.74 /82	--	B /8.0	98	N/A
GR	Pioneer Cullen Value Fund Y	CVFYX	A+	(800) 225-6292	18.34	B /7.9	15.12 /72	19.36 /77	11.25 /85	B /8.4	97	1
GR	Diamond Hill Large Cap C	DHLCX	A+		14.80	B /7.9	15.93 /74	19.50 /78	8.36 /73	B /8.3	97	4
GR	Diamond Hill Long-Short Fd Cl C	DHFCX	A+		17.03	B /7.8	20.70 /83	18.33 /74	7.44 /69	B /8.9	99	6
GR	JPMorgan Intrepid Value Sel	JPIVX	A+	(800) 358-4782	24.82	B /7.8	15.87 /74	18.53 /74	--	B /8.8	96	3
GR	Diamond Hill Large Cap A	DHLAX	A+		15.16	B /7.8	16.76 /74	20.40 /81	9.24 /78	B /8.3	98	4
GR	Diamond Hill Long-Short Fd Cl A	DIAMX	A+		17.68	B /7.7	21.57 /84	19.23 /77	8.28 /73	B /8.9	96	6
GR	JPMorgan Intrepid Value C	JIVCX	A+	(800) 358-4782	24.69	B /7.6	15.04 /72	18.12 /73	--	B /8.8	96	3
GR	Allianz NFJ Large Cap Value Inst		A+	(800) 628-1237	17.79	B- /7.5	15.77 /74	17.64 /71	10.94 /84	B+ /9.1	96	N/A
GR	TCW Diversified Value N	TGDVX	A+	(800) 386-3829	14.84	B- /7.5	10.94 /53	18.50 /74	7.41 /69	B /8.9	95	7
GR	ICAP Select Equity Fund	ICSLX	A+	(888) 221-4227	38.25	B- /7.4	12.86 /64	17.95 /72	7.03 /67	B /8.8	95	9
GR	American Beacon Lg Cap Val Inst	AADEX	A+	(800) 967-9009	21.84	B- /7.4	11.93 /59	18.20 /73	9.05 /76	B /8.8	96	N/A
GR	Allianz NFJ Large Cap Value D	PNBDX	A+	(800) 628-1237	17.73	B- /7.3	15.22 /72	17.12 /69	10.40 /82	B+ /9.1	96	N/A
GR	American Beacon Lg Cap Val	AAGPX	A+	(800) 967-9009	20.91	B- /7.3	11.62 /57	17.90 /72	8.75 /75	B /8.8	95	N/A
GR	JPMorgan Intrepid Value A	JIVAX	A+	(800) 358-4782	24.78	B- /7.3	15.64 /74	18.40 /74	--	B /8.8	96	3
GR	Allianz NFJ Large Cap Value C	PNBCX	A+	(800) 628-1237	17.58	B- /7.1	14.45 /70	16.24 /64	9.60 /79	B+ /9.1	94	N/A
GR	Fidelity Adv Leveraged Co Stk I	FLVIX	A	(800) 522-7297	31.29	A /9.3	19.03 /81	27.54 /94	25.00 /98	C+ /6.7	99	3
GR	Select Transportation	FSRFX	A	(800) 544-8888	52.26	A /9.3	38.48 /98	23.56 /89	12.74 /88	C+ /6.7	98	N/A
GR	Fidelity Leveraged Company Stock	FLVCX	A	(800) 544-8888	28.44	A /9.3	20.58 /83	27.77 /94	24.27 /98	C+ /6.4	99	3
GR	Fidelity Adv Leveraged Co Stk C	FLSCX	A	(800) 522-7297	30.11	A- /9.2	17.85 /79	26.25 /92	23.76 /98	C+ /6.6	99	3
GR	Fidelity Adv Leveraged Co Stk T	FLSTX	A	(800) 522-7297	30.61	A- /9.2	18.36 /80	26.78 /93	24.29 /98	C+ /6.6	99	3
GR	ICON Industrials	ICTRX	A	(800) 764-0442	14.70	A- /9.2	29.19 /94	23.24 /88	8.49 /74	C+ /6.7	98	9
GR	Select Air Transport	FSAIX	A	(800) 544-8888	45.82	A- /9.1	38.63 /98	20.92 /82	7.24 /68	C+ /6.9	98	1
GR	Fidelity Adv Leveraged Co Stk B	FLCBX	A	(800) 522-7297	30.14	A- /9.1	17.73 /79	26.15 /92	23.78 /98	C+ /6.6	99	3
GR	Fidelity Adv Leveraged Co Stk A	FLSAX	A	(800) 522-7297	31.02	A- /9.1	18.65 /80	27.14 /93	24.67 /98	C+ /6.6	99	3
GR	Fidelity Adv Cyclical Indust B	FCLBX	A	(800) 522-7297	22.12	B+/8.9	21.38 /83	23.37 /88	10.70 /83	B- /7.1	97	N/A
GR	Fidelity Adv Cyclical Indust C	FCLCX	A	(800) 522-7297	22.27	B+/8.9	21.52 /84	23.43 /88	10.73 /83	B- /7.1	97	N/A
GR	Fidelity Adv Cyclical Indust A	FCLAX	A	(800) 522-7297	23.30	B+/8.8	22.33 /85	24.34 /90	11.55 /86	B- /7.2	98	N/A
GR	Fidelity Adv Cyclical Indust T	FCLTX	A	(800) 522-7297	22.99	B+/8.8	22.10 /84	24.04 /89	11.29 /85	B- /7.1	98	N/A
GR	Select Defense & Aerospace	FSDAX	A	(800) 544-8888	76.44	B+/8.8	15.07 /72	24.30 /90	15.31 /92	C+ /6.8	99	1
GR	Hartford Capital Apprec Y	HCAYX	A	(800) 523-7798	39.25	B+/8.3	20.50 /82	20.88 /82	7.31 /68	B- /7.6	95	10
GR	Merrill Lynch Large Cap Value R	MRLVX	A	(800) 543-6217	17.48	B /8.2	16.10 /75	20.21 /80	--	B- /7.5	96	N/A
GR	Adv Inn Cir LSV Value Equity	LSVEX	A	(866) 777-7818	17.43	B /8.1	15.03 /72	19.76 /78	11.26 /85	B- /7.8	97	7
GR	Excelsior Value & Restructg I	EXBIX	A	(800) 446-1012	48.40	B /8.1	13.47 /66	20.33 /81	--	B- /7.6	94	14
GR	JennDry Jennison Value Z	PEIZX	A	(800) 257-3893	21.18	B /7.7	19.11 /81	18.68 /75	6.92 /66	B /8.1	96	3
GR	Pioneer Cullen Value Fund C	CVCFX	A	(800) 225-6292	18.12	B /7.6	13.81 /68	18.78 /75	10.92 /84	B /8.4	96	1
GR	DF Dent Premier Growth	DFDPX	A	(866) 233-3368	15.11	B /7.6	15.77 /74	18.46 /74	--	B /8.3	95	5
GR	Neuberger Berman Regency Inv	NBRVX	A	(800) 877-9700	16.76	B /7.6	11.15 /55	19.58 /78	10.74 /83	B /8.0	94	N/A
GR	Pioneer Cullen Value Fund A	CVFCX	A	(800) 225-6292	18.28	B- /7.4	14.73 /71	19.20 /77	11.16 /84	B /8.4	97	5
GR	Quaker Geewax Terker Core Value	QUGTX	A	(800) 220-8888	13.09	B- /7.4	21.42 /83	19.00 /76	--	B /8.3	95	4
GR	Pioneer Cullen Value Fund B	CVFBX	A	(800) 225-6292	18.11	B- /7.3	13.66 /67	18.73 /75	10.89 /84	B /8.4	96	1
GR	Boston Ptrs All Cap Value Inst	BPAIX	A	(800) 261-4073	15.32	B- /7.2	8.40 /36	18.29 /74	--	B /8.7	96	4
GR	Gabelli Westwood Equity Fund	WESWX	A	(800) 422-3554	12.04	B- /7.0	16.49 /76	16.04 /64	5.30 /56	B /8.9	92	19
GR	Boston Ptrs All Cap Value Inv	BPAVX	A	(800) 261-4073	15.26	B- /7.0	8.03 /33	18.00 /72	--	B /8.7	95	4
GR	Select Cyclical Industries	FCYIX	A-	(800) 544-8888	20.90	A- /9.1	22.55 /85	24.51 /90	11.01 /84	C+ /6.5	98	1

● Denotes fund is closed to new investors

Data as of June 30, 2006

Fund Type	Fund Name	Ticker Symbol	Overall Weiss Investment Rating	Phone	Net Asset Value As of 6/30/06	Performance Rating/Pts	1Yr / Pct	3Yr / Pct	5Yr / Pct	Risk Rating/Pts	Mgr. Quality Pct	Mgr. Tenure (Years)
GI	● Franklin Balance Sheet Investmt	FBSAX	A+	(800) 321-8563	67.22	B+ /8.6	17.39 /78	22.20 /86	13.81 /90	B /8.3	99	N/A
GI	FMC Strategic Value Fund		A+	(866) 777-7818	22.32	B+ /8.6	19.52 /81	21.41 /83	15.28 /92	B- /7.7	98	8
GI	Franklin Balance Sheet Investmt R	FBSRX	A+	(800) 342-5236	66.73	B+ /8.5	16.79 /77	21.58 /84	13.25 /89	B /8.3	98	N/A
GI	● Franklin Balance Sheet Investmt C	FCBSX	A+	(800) 342-5236	66.25	B+ /8.3	16.22 /75	20.98 /82	12.69 /88	B /8.3	98	N/A
GI	● Franklin Balance Sheet Investmt A	FRBSX	A+	(800) 342-5236	67.12	B /8.2	17.11 /77	21.91 /85	13.55 /90	B /8.3	98	N/A
GI	● Franklin Balance Sheet Investmt B	FBSBX	A+	(800) 342-5236	66.16	B /8.1	16.23 /75	20.98 /82	12.68 /88	B /8.3	98	N/A
GI	● Dodge & Cox Stock Fund	DODGX	A+	(800) 621-3979	144.48	B /7.7	15.30 /73	18.36 /74	10.58 /82	B /8.8	96	41
GI	Loomis Sayles Core Value Inst	LSGIX	A+	(800) 633-3330	19.69	B- /7.3	17.92 /79	16.98 /68	6.92 /66	B /8.8	96	6
GI	American Funds Fundamentl Invs	RFNFX	A	(800) 421-4120	38.31	B /8.1	20.83 /83	18.90 /76	7.63 /70	B- /7.5	95	28
GI	Mutual Qualified Z	MQIFX	A	(800) 321-8563	20.83	B- /7.4	14.72 /71	17.39 /70	8.52 /74	B /8.6	97	6
GI	ING Corp Leaders Trust A	LEXCX	A	(800) 992-0180	19.79	B- /7.4	13.65 /67	17.36 /70	8.32 /73	B /8.4	96	N/A
GI	Goldman Sachs Stru Lrg Cp Val	GCVIX	A	(800) 292-4726	13.53	B- /7.2	14.52 /70	17.21 /69	6.83 /66	B /8.7	95	N/A
GI	Homestead Funds-Value Fund	HOVLX	A	(800) 258-3030	35.12	B- /7.1	15.76 /74	16.64 /66	9.14 /77	B /8.7	95	16
GI	Eaton Vance Large Cap Value I	EILVX	A	(800) 225-6265	19.22	B- /7.0	14.13 /69	16.19 /64	7.06 /67	B /8.8	94	2
GI	Goldman Sachs Stru Lrg Cp Val	GCLSX	A	(800) 292-4726	13.60	B- /7.0	13.94 /68	16.62 /66	6.33 /63	B /8.7	93	N/A
GI	Ameriprime Adv Monteagle Value	MVRGX	A-	(800) 934-5550	17.13	B+ /8.5	18.65 /80	21.05 /83	9.15 /77	C+ /6.9	94	N/A
GI	● Nuveen NWQ Multi-Cap Value	NQVRX	A-	(800) 257-8787	23.76	B /8.2	17.76 /79	20.15 /80	14.62 /91	B- /7.2	95	9
GI	American Funds Fundamentl Invs	AFIFX	A-	(800) 421-4120	38.29	B /8.0	20.60 /83	18.58 /75	7.32 /68	B- /7.6	94	5
GI	American Funds Fundamentl Invs	RFNEX	A-	(800) 421-4120	38.26	B /8.0	20.51 /82	18.55 /75	7.30 /68	B- /7.6	94	28
GI	American Funds Fundamentl Invs	CFNFX	A-	(800) 421-4120	38.26	B /8.0	20.74 /83	18.56 /75	7.26 /68	B- /7.5	94	28
GI	Fidelity Value Fund	FDVLX	A-	(800) 544-8888	78.60	B /7.8	13.28 /65	19.82 /79	11.92 /86	B- /7.7	95	10
GI	American Funds Fundamentl Invs	CFNEX	A-	(800) 421-4120	38.27	B /7.8	20.14 /82	18.15 /73	6.93 /66	B- /7.6	93	28
GI	American Funds Fundamentl Invs	RFNCX	A-	(800) 421-4120	38.25	B /7.8	20.10 /82	18.14 /73	6.93 /66	B- /7.6	93	28
GI	● Leuthold Core Investment Fund	LCORX	A-	(888) 200-0409	17.79	B- /7.5	17.40 /78	17.51 /70	9.99 /80	B- /7.8	97	11
GI	ABN AMRO Value N	RVALX	A-	(800) 443-4725	12.89	C+ /6.3	11.35 /56	14.77 /58	4.66 /51	B+ /9.2	92	4
GI	Goldman Sachs Growth & Income	GSIIX	A-	(800) 292-4726	27.31	C+ /6.2	9.69 /45	14.64 /57	6.89 /66	B+ /9.2	93	10
GI	Vanguard Windsor-II Inv	VWNFX	A-	(800) 662-7447	32.30	C+ /6.1	8.57 /37	14.72 /57	6.28 /63	B+ /9.2	92	21
GI	Vanguard Windsor-II Adm	VWNAX	A-	(800) 662-7447	57.33	C+ /6.1	8.70 /38	14.84 /58	6.38 /63	B+ /9.2	92	5
GI	Fidelity Value Discovery Fund	FVDFX	B+	(800) 544-8888	16.58	B /7.8	19.55 /81	19.09 /76	--	B- /7.3	92	4
GI	Nuveen NWQ Multi-Cap Value	NQVCX	B+	(800) 257-8787	23.42	B /7.8	16.56 /76	18.95 /76	13.46 /89	B- /7.2	93	9
GI	American Funds Fundamentl Invs	RFNBX	B+	(800) 421-4120	38.19	B /7.7	19.56 /81	17.66 /71	6.50 /64	B- /7.6	92	28
GI	Nuveen NWQ Multi-Cap Value	NQVAX	B+	(800) 257-8787	23.81	B /7.7	17.44 /78	19.88 /79	14.31 /91	B- /7.2	95	9
GI	American Funds Fundamentl Invs	AFICX	B+	(800) 421-4120	38.19	B /7.6	19.57 /81	17.64 /71	6.47 /64	B- /7.6	92	28
GI	American Funds Fundamentl Invs	RFNAX	B+	(800) 421-4120	38.21	B /7.6	19.56 /81	17.63 /71	6.46 /64	B- /7.6	92	28
GI	American Funds Fundamentl Invs	ANCFX	B+	(800) 421-4120	38.30	B- /7.5	20.56 /83	18.63 /75	7.36 /68	B- /7.6	94	28
GI	American Funds Fundamentl Invs	CFNAX	B+	(800) 421-4120	38.28	B- /7.5	20.51 /82	18.54 /75	7.28 /68	B- /7.6	94	28
GI	American Funds Fundamentl Invs	CFNCX	B+	(800) 421-4120	38.27	B- /7.5	19.53 /81	17.54 /70	6.43 /64	B- /7.6	92	28
GI	Nuveen NWQ Multi-Cap Value	NQVBX	B+	(800) 257-8787	23.42	B- /7.5	16.56 /76	18.98 /76	13.46 /89	B- /7.2	93	9
GI	Phoenix Insight Equity Fund Inst	HEQIX	B+	(800) 982-8782	14.49	B- /7.3	14.06 /68	18.04 /73	6.69 /65	B- /7.8	97	10
GI	Fifth Third Multi Cap Value Inst	MXEIX	B+	(800) 282-5706	25.62	B- /7.3	13.08 /65	17.44 /70	10.16 /81	B- /7.7	88	3
GI	Security Large Cap Value C	SEGIX	B+	(800) 888-2461	7.30	B- /7.2	21.46 /84	15.08 /59	3.79 /44	B- /7.8	87	N/A
GI	American Funds Fundamentl Invs	CFNBX	B+	(800) 421-4120	38.28	B- /7.2	19.51 /81	17.53 /70	6.42 /64	B- /7.6	92	28
GI	American Funds Fundamentl Invs	AFIBX	B+	(800) 421-4120	38.23	B- /7.2	19.65 /81	17.72 /71	6.55 /64	B- /7.6	92	28
GI	MainStay MAP Fund I	MUBFX	B+	(800) 624-6782	36.84	B- /7.0	14.12 /69	16.55 /66	7.62 /70	B- /7.8	87	4
GI	Security Large Cap Value A	SECIX	B+	(800) 888-2461	7.62	B- /7.0	22.39 /85	15.91 /63	4.63 /51	B- /7.8	90	N/A
GI	Vanguard Value Index Inst	VIVIX	B+	(800) 662-7447	23.42	C+ /6.6	12.44 /62	15.33 /60	4.52 /50	B+ /9.0	91	N/A
GI	Vanguard Value Index Adm	VVIAX	B+	(800) 662-7447	23.42	C+ /6.6	12.46 /62	15.29 /60	4.48 /50	B+ /9.0	91	N/A
GI	Vanguard Value Index Inv	VIVAX	B+	(800) 662-7447	23.42	C+ /6.5	12.34 /61	15.18 /60	4.39 /50	B+ /9.0	90	N/A
GI	Mutual Shares Z	MUTHX	B+	(800) 321-8563	24.91	C+ /6.4	13.42 /66	14.96 /59	7.28 /68	B+ /9.0	95	13
GI	STI Classic Large Cap Val Equity I	STVTX	B+	(888) 784-3863	13.82	C+ /6.3	12.90 /64	14.31 /55	5.81 /60	B /8.9	86	13
GI	● Hotchkis and Wiley Large Cap Val	HWLRX	B+	(800) 796-5606	23.47	C+ /6.3	2.59 / 6	17.05 /68	10.67 /83	B /8.6	92	N/A
GI	Ivy Fund-Dividend Income A	IVDAX	B+	(800) 777-6472	14.67	C+ /6.2	18.96 /80	14.68 /57	--	B /8.8	91	3

● Denotes fund is closed to new investors

Fund Type	Fund Name	Ticker Symbol	Overall Weiss Investment Rating	Phone	Net Asset Value As of 6/30/06	Perform-ance Rating/Pts	Annualized Total Return Through 6/30/06 1Yr / Pct	3Yr / Pct	5Yr / Pct	Risk Rating/Pts	Mgr. Quality Pct	Mgr. Tenure (Years)
HL	Schwab Health Care Focus	SWHFX	B+	(866) 855-9102	14.20	B /7.6	4.64 /13	21.79 /85	9.35 /78	B- /7.4	99	N/A
HL	Select Medical Delivery	FSHCX	B	(800) 544-8888	48.57	A- /9.1	1.42 / 3	30.03 /96	14.68 /91	C /5.3	99	1
HL	BlackRock-Health Sciences B	SHSPX	B	(888) 825-2257	23.17	C+ /6.3	11.13 /54	16.76 /67	11.64 /86	B- /7.8	95	1
HL	BlackRock-Health Sciences C	SHSCX	B	(888) 825-2257	23.13	C+ /6.3	11.16 /55	16.78 /67	11.65 /86	B- /7.8	96	1
HL	BlackRock-Health Sciences Inst	SHSSX	B-	(888) 825-2257	24.53	C+ /6.9	12.31 /61	17.93 /72	12.76 /88	B- /7.8	97	1
HL	BlackRock-Health Sciences A	SHSAX	B-	(888) 825-2257	24.13	C+ /6.0	11.97 /59	17.60 /71	12.44 /87	B- /7.8	97	1
HL	● JennDry Jennison Health Sciences	PHSZX	C+	(800) 257-3893	20.16	B- /7.5	9.12 /41	20.32 /80	9.41 /78	C /5.0	99	7
HL	● Vanguard Health Care Adm	VGHAX	C+	(800) 662-7447	58.76	C /5.4	12.21 /61	13.30 /50	--	B- /7.8	94	N/A
HL	● Vanguard Health Care Inv	VGHCX	C+	(800) 662-7447	139.17	C /5.3	12.10 /60	13.20 /50	7.93 /71	B- /7.8	94	22
HL	● JennDry Jennison Health Sciences	PHLCX	C	(800) 257-3893	18.47	C+ /6.9	7.95 /32	19.08 /76	8.29 /73	C /4.9	99	7
HL	BlackRock-Health Sciences Svc	SHISX	C	(888) 825-2257	24.18	C+ /6.7	12.05 /60	17.68 /71	12.49 /88	C+ /5.6	97	1
HL	● JennDry Jennison Health Sciences	PHLAX	C	(800) 257-3893	19.70	C+ /6.7	8.82 /39	19.99 /79	9.12 /77	C /5.0	99	7
HL	Janus Aspen Global Life Sci Inst	JGLIX	C	(800) 525-3713	9.31	C+ /6.0	12.99 /64	14.76 /58	3.52 /41	C+ /5.6	93	6
HL	● TA IDEX T.Rowe Price Health Sci	IRHLX	C	(888) 233-4339	12.59	C /5.2	18.63 /80	12.22 /44	--	B- /7.1	75	N/A
HL	Hartford Global Health Y	HGHYX	C	(800) 523-7798	17.30	C /4.9	15.23 /72	12.61 /46	7.76 /70	C+ /6.9	88	N/A
HL	● JennDry Jennison Health Sciences	PHLBX	C-	(800) 257-3893	18.48	C+ /6.5	8.01 /33	19.10 /76	8.31 /73	C /4.9	99	7
HL	Alger Fund-Health Sciences C	AHSCX	C-	(800) 992-3863	15.69	C /5.0	4.39 /12	14.96 /59	--	C+ /5.8	94	N/A
HL	Alger Fund-Health Sciences A	AHSAX	C-	(800) 992-3863	16.20	C /4.7	5.26 /16	15.83 /63	--	C+ /5.9	95	N/A
HL	Evergreen Health Care Fund I	EHCYX	C-	(800) 343-2898	19.94	C /4.6	11.47 /56	12.09 /43	7.73 /70	C+ /6.2	78	7
HL	ICON Healthcare	ICHCX	C-	(800) 764-0442	17.43	C /4.6	1.56 / 3	14.10 /54	7.96 /71	C+ /6.1	90	9
HL	Alger Fund-Health Sciences B	AHSBX	C-	(800) 992-3863	15.69	C /4.5	4.39 /12	14.96 /59	--	C+ /5.8	93	N/A
HL	Hartford Global Health C	HGHCX	C-	(800) 523-7798	15.83	C- /3.8	13.73 /67	11.24 /37	6.35 /63	C+ /6.7	80	N/A
HL	● TA IDEX T.Rowe Price Health Sci	IRHBX	D+	(888) 233-4339	12.62	C /5.2	18.58 /80	12.30 /44	--	C /5.0	76	N/A
HL	● TA IDEX T.Rowe Price Health Sci	IRHAX	D+	(888) 233-4339	13.01	C /4.8	19.08 /81	13.06 /49	--	C /5.0	82	N/A
HL	T. Rowe Price Health Sciences	PRHSX	D+	(800) 638-5660	24.81	C /4.6	15.40 /73	13.14 /50	6.07 /62	C /5.3	78	6
HL	Evergreen Health Care Fund C	EHCCX	D+	(800) 343-2898	18.49	C- /3.7	10.30 /49	10.96 /35	6.65 /65	C+ /6.1	68	7
HL	Hartford Global Health A	HGHAX	D+	(800) 523-7798	16.65	C- /3.4	14.58 /70	12.06 /43	7.13 /67	C+ /6.8	86	N/A
HL	Hartford Global Health B	HGHBX	D+	(800) 523-7798	15.84	C- /3.2	13.88 /68	11.29 /38	6.37 /63	C+ /6.7	81	N/A
HL	AXA Enterprise Multimgr Hlth Care	AEAYX	D+	(800) 432-4320	10.71	D /2.1	7.03 /26	9.22 /22	--	B- /7.8	68	N/A
HL	AllianceBernstein Glb Hlth Care	AHLDX	D+	(800) 221-5672	13.51	D /1.9	6.21 /22	8.46 /17	3.53 /42	B /8.2	61	7
HL	Evergreen Health Care Fund A	EHABX	D	(800) 343-2898	19.56	C- /3.3	11.09 /54	11.75 /41	7.42 /69	C+ /6.2	75	7
HL	Evergreen Health Care Fund B	EHCBX	D	(800) 343-2898	18.50	C- /3.0	10.29 /49	10.95 /35	6.64 /65	C+ /6.1	68	7
HL	Select Pharmaceuticals	FPHAX	D	(800) 544-8888	10.08	D+ /2.8	17.41 /78	7.41 /12	1.34 /22	C+ /6.0	46	1
HL	Munder Framlington Healthcare K	MFHKX	D	(800) 438-5789	23.55	D /2.0	-0.84 / 1	10.11 /28	-1.45 /10	B- /7.3	60	N/A
HL	Constellation TIP Hlth & Bio Fd II	THBCX	D	(800) 224-6312	14.80	D /2.0	-0.84 / 1	10.79 /34	7.02 /67	B- /7.2	66	N/A
HL	Rydex Series-Health Care Inv	RYHIX	D	(800) 820-0888	13.75	D /1.8	3.00 / 7	8.58 /18	3.82 /44	B- /7.1	52	N/A
HL	AIM Global Health Care C	GTHCX	D	(800) 347-4246	26.35	D /1.7	6.57 /24	8.27 /16	0.91 /20	B- /7.4	53	N/A
HL	Fidelity Adv Health Care I	FHCIX	D	(800) 522-7297	23.62	D /1.6	5.33 /17	8.27 /16	3.51 /41	B- /7.0	63	1
HL	AXA Enterprise Multimgr Hlth Care	AEACX	D	(800) 432-4320	10.29	D- /1.5	5.93 /20	8.13 /16	--	B- /7.6	57	N/A
HL	AIM Global Health Care A	GGHCX	D	(800) 347-4246	29.28	D- /1.4	7.38 /28	8.93 /20	1.48 /24	B- /7.4	61	N/A
HL	Kinetics Medical Fund NL	MEDRX	D	(800) 930-3828	17.53	D- /1.2	13.17 /65	5.31 / 5	-1.59 /10	B- /7.8	32	N/A
HL	AXA Enterprise Multimgr Hlth Care	AEAPX	D	(800) 432-4320	10.60	D- /1.2	6.79 /25	8.90 /20	--	B- /7.8	65	N/A
HL	AXA Enterprise Multimgr Hlth Care	AEABX	D	(800) 432-4320	10.29	D- /1.1	6.04 /21	8.15 /16	--	B- /7.6	57	N/A
HL	Janus Fd Inc-Global Life Sciences	JAGLX	D-	(800) 525-3713	19.79	C- /4.1	6.63 /24	12.77 /47	2.08 /28	C /4.3	85	8
HL	AIM Global Health Care Inv	GTHIX	D-	(800) 347-4246	29.28	D /2.2	7.38 /29	8.93 /20	1.48 /24	C+ /5.9	61	N/A
HL	● DWS Health Care Fund S	SCHLX	D-	(800) 621-1048	24.04	D /1.7	3.71 / 9	8.56 /18	2.93 /36	C+ /6.2	56	6
HL	DWS Health Care Fund Inst	SUHIX	D-	(800) 621-1048	24.24	D /1.6	3.81 /10	8.67 /19	3.10 /38	C+ /6.3	57	6
HL	DWS Health Care Fund AARP	SHCAX	D-	(800) 621-1048	24.03	D- /1.5	3.67 / 9	8.53 /18	2.94 /36	C+ /6.2	55	6
HL	Rydex Series-Health Care Adv	RYHAX	D-	(800) 820-0888	13.17	D- /1.4	2.41 / 5	7.98 /15	3.31 /40	B- /7.1	45	N/A
HL	Putnam Health Sciences Trust Y	PHSYX	D-	(800) 354-2228	60.70	D- /1.4	4.55 /13	7.51 /12	1.24 /22	C+ /6.6	63	N/A
HL	Dreyfus Premier Health Care R	DHCRX	D-	(800) 782-6620	14.83	D- /1.2	1.47 / 3	7.65 /13	--	C+ /6.9	44	N/A
HL	AllianceBernstein Glb Hlth Care C	AHLCX	D-	(800) 221-5672	12.49	D- /1.2	5.13 /16	7.37 /12	2.48 /32	C+ /6.4	47	7

● Denotes fund is closed to new investors

Data as of June 30, 2006

99 Pct = Best
0 Pct = Worst

Fund Type	Fund Name	Ticker Symbol	Overall Weiss Investment Rating	Phone	Net Asset Value As of 6/30/06	Perform-ance Rating/Pts	Annualized Total Return Through 6/30/06			Risk Rating/Pts	Mgr. Quality Pct	Mgr. Tenure (Years)
							1Yr / Pct	3Yr / Pct	5Yr / Pct			
IN	RVS Diversified Equity Income Y	IDQYX	A+	(800) 328-8300	12.84	B+ /8.7	21.22 /83	21.75 /85	10.58 /82	B /8.1	97	6
IN	RVS Diversified Equity Income A	INDZX	A+	(800) 328-8300	12.83	B+ /8.3	21.05 /83	21.53 /84	10.38 /82	B /8.0	97	6
IN	Amana Mutual Fund-Income Fund	AMANX	A+	(800) 728-8762	25.54	B+ /8.3	19.65 /81	20.62 /82	8.77 /75	B /8.0	98	16
IN	RVS Diversified Equity Income C	ADECX	A+	(800) 328-8300	12.82	B+ /8.3	20.05 /82	20.58 /81	9.53 /79	B /8.0	95	6
IN	Hancock Horizon Value Tr	HHGTX	A+	(888) 346-6300	25.29	B /8.2	16.12 /75	20.12 /80	11.80 /86	B- /7.8	98	6
IN	RVS Diversified Equity Income B	IDEBX	A+	(800) 328-8300	12.84	B /8.1	20.06 /82	20.60 /81	9.54 /79	B /8.0	95	6
IN	Allianz NFJ Dividend Value Admin		A+	(800) 628-1237	15.56	B /7.7	16.89 /77	17.73 /71	10.60 /83	B+ /9.1	97	N/A
IN	Allianz NFJ Dividend Value Inst	NFJEX	A+	(800) 628-1237	15.51	B /7.6	17.21 /77	18.07 /73	10.90 /84	B+ /9.1	97	N/A
IN	BB&T Special Opport Eqty Inst	BOPIX	A+	(800) 228-1872	15.70	B /7.6	8.84 /39	18.89 /76	--	B /8.7	98	3
IN	Allianz NFJ Dividend Value D	PEIDX	A+	(800) 628-1237	15.38	B- /7.4	16.72 /76	17.53 /70	10.36 /82	B+ /9.4	96	5
IN	Allianz NFJ Dividend Value R	PNERX	A+	(800) 628-1237	15.33	B- /7.3	16.44 /76	17.24 /69	10.10 /81	B+ /9.1	96	N/A
IN	Allianz NFJ Dividend Value C	PNECX	A+	(800) 628-1237	15.23	B- /7.2	15.84 /74	16.65 /66	9.54 /79	B+ /9.4	95	5
IN	Allianz NFJ Dividend Value A	PNEAX	A+	(800) 628-1237	15.35	B- /7.0	16.73 /76	17.52 /70	10.37 /82	B+ /9.4	96	5
IN	Merrill Lynch Equity Dividend R	MRDVX	A	(800) 543-6217	17.19	B /7.7	17.43 /78	17.65 /71	--	B /8.2	97	N/A
IN	Merrill Lynch Equity Dividend C	MCDVX	A	(800) 543-6217	16.80	B- /7.4	16.77 /77	16.93 /68	8.36 /73	B /8.2	96	N/A
IN	Merrill Lynch Equity Dividend I	MADVX	A	(800) 543-6217	17.11	B- /7.4	18.07 /79	18.13 /73	9.47 /78	B /8.2	97	N/A
IN	RVS Equity Value C		A	(800) 328-8300	11.98	B- /7.1	18.10 /79	16.76 /67	3.98 /46	B /8.8	88	6
IN	BB&T Special Opport Eqty C	BOPCX	A	(800) 228-1872	15.21	B- /7.1	7.79 /31	17.69 /71	--	B /8.7	97	3
IN	Hancock Horizon Value C	HHGCX	A-	(888) 346-6300	24.85	B /7.8	14.97 /72	18.93 /76	10.72 /83	B- /7.8	97	4
IN	Hancock Horizon Value A	HHGAX	A-	(888) 346-6300	25.23	B /7.8	15.80 /74	19.84 /79	11.53 /85	B- /7.8	98	6
IN	RVS Equity Value A	IEVAX	A-	(800) 328-8300	12.05	B- /7.4	18.69 /80	18.71 /75	5.37 /57	B /8.1	94	6
IN	Merrill Lynch Equity Dividend A	MDDVX	A-	(800) 543-6217	17.09	B- /7.3	17.74 /79	17.84 /72	9.19 /77	B /8.2	97	N/A
IN	HighMark Large Cap Value Fid	HMIEX	A-	(800) 433-6884	13.46	B- /7.1	12.74 /63	16.93 /68	4.86 /53	B /8.4	94	15
IN	Merrill Lynch Equity Dividend B	MBDVX	A-	(800) 543-6217	17.13	B- /7.1	16.87 /77	16.96 /68	8.49 /74	B /8.2	96	N/A
IN	Hancock Horizon Burnkenroad D	HYBUX	B+	(888) 346-6300	29.37	B+ /8.3	17.76 /79	20.68 /82	--	C+ /6.7	96	6
IN	Hancock Horizon Burnkenroad A	HHBUX	B+	(888) 346-6300	29.61	B /8.1	17.92 /79	20.94 /82	--	C+ /6.7	96	5
IN	Allianz NFJ Dividend Value B	PNEBX	B+	(800) 628-1237	15.25	C+ /6.8	15.94 /74	16.64 /66	9.56 /79	B+ /9.4	95	5
IN	● MFS Value Fund I	MEIIX	B+	(800) 343-2829	24.50	C+ /6.4	11.84 /59	15.01 /59	6.48 /64	B+ /9.1	93	4
IN	WM Equity Income C	CMPCX	B+	(800) 222-5852	20.61	C+ /6.4	9.95 /47	15.59 /62	--	B+ /9.0	94	1
IN	MFS Value Fund R	MFVRX	B+	(800) 343-2829	24.36	C+ /6.2	11.27 /55	14.45 /56	6.01 /61	B /8.9	91	4
IN	MFS Value Fund R3	MVRRX	B+	(800) 343-2829	24.30	C+ /6.1	11.12 /54	14.23 /55	5.91 /61	B+ /9.1	90	3
IN	WM Equity Income A	CMPBX	B+	(800) 222-5852	20.91	C+ /6.1	10.81 /52	16.49 /66	9.40 /78	B+ /9.0	95	1
IN	Vantagepoint Equity Income	VPEIX	B+	(800) 669-7400	9.34	C+ /6.1	9.17 /41	14.71 /57	7.16 /68	B+ /9.0	89	N/A
IN	MassMutual Select Fundamental	MVUSX	B+	(800) 542-6767	12.00	C+ /6.1	14.40 /70	13.74 /53	--	B /8.7	79	N/A
IN	Gabelli Equity Income Fd	GABEX	B+	(800) 422-3554	19.51	C+ /6.0	11.62 /57	13.82 /53	8.16 /72	B+ /9.2	88	3
IN	Pioneer Equity Income C	PCEQX	B+	(800) 225-6292	30.55	C+ /6.0	11.33 /56	14.01 /54	4.87 /53	B /8.9	90	5
IN	MassMutual Select Fundamental	MFUYX	B+	(800) 542-6767	11.99	C+ /6.0	14.39 /70	13.68 /52	--	B /8.8	79	4
IN	MassMutual Select Fundamental	MFULX	B+	(800) 542-6767	11.97	C+ /6.0	14.33 /69	13.51 /51	--	B /8.7	77	4
IN	Delaware Value I	DDVIX	B+	(800) 362-3863	11.96	C+ /5.9	10.76 /52	13.79 /53	5.29 /56	B+ /9.1	84	N/A
IN	Pioneer Equity Income A	PEQIX	B+	(800) 225-6292	30.82	C+ /5.9	12.18 /61	14.91 /58	5.72 /59	B /8.9	93	5
IN	WM Equity Income B	CMBBX	B+	(800) 222-5852	20.77	C+ /5.8	9.80 /46	15.48 /61	8.43 /74	B+ /9.0	93	1
IN	Hartford Dividend & Growth Y	HDGYX	B+	(800) 523-7798	19.99	C+ /5.8	12.45 /62	13.35 /51	5.92 /61	B+ /9.0	80	5
IN	MFS Value Fund C	MEICX	B+	(800) 343-2829	24.25	C+ /5.8	10.74 /52	13.87 /53	5.43 /57	B /8.9	89	4
IN	MFS Value Fund 529C	ECVLX	B+	(800) 343-2829	24.11	C+ /5.6	10.42 /50	13.59 /52	5.37 /57	B+ /9.1	87	4
IN	Dreyfus Premier Small Co Growth	DSGRX	B	(800) 782-6620	19.01	B /7.7	14.16 /69	19.05 /76	--	C+ /6.8	85	3
IN	1st Source Monogram Income	FMIEX	B	(800) 766-8938	13.98	B /7.7	15.55 /73	18.42 /74	10.10 /81	C+ /6.8	94	10
IN	Evergreen Disciplined Value I	EDSIX	B	(800) 343-2898	16.36	C+ /6.9	11.16 /55	16.27 /65	5.81 /60	B /8.9	92	1
IN	BB&T Special Opport Eqty A	BOPAX	B	(800) 228-1872	15.58	C+ /6.9	8.55 /37	18.60 /75	--	B /8.7	98	3
IN	Pioneer Equity Income Y	PYEQX	B	(800) 225-6292	30.95	C+ /6.8	12.64 /63	15.41 /61	6.20 /62	B /8.9	94	N/A
IN	BB&T Special Opport Eqty B	BOPBX	B	(800) 228-1872	15.20	C+ /6.7	7.79 /31	17.67 /71	--	B /8.7	97	3
IN	HighMark Large Cap Value Ret C	HIECX	B	(800) 433-6884	13.26	C+ /6.6	11.70 /58	15.95 /63	3.93 /45	B /8.4	91	15
IN	RVS Equity Value B	INEGX	B	(800) 328-8300	12.08	C+ /6.6	17.79 /79	16.63 /66	3.96 /46	B /8.1	88	6

● Denotes fund is closed to new investors

Fund Type	Fund Name	Ticker Symbol	Overall Weiss Investment Rating	Phone	Net Asset Value As of 6/30/06	Performance Rating/Pts	Annualized Total Return Through 6/30/06			Risk Rating/Pts	Mgr. Quality Pct	Mgr. Tenure (Years)
							1Yr / Pct	3Yr / Pct	5Yr / Pct			
IX	Russell Inst Equity I Fd I	REASX	C+	(800) 832-6688	31.50	C /5.0	9.87 /46	12.61 /46	3.05 /37	B- /7.7	62	10
IX	Russell Inst Equity I Fd E	REAEX	C+	(800) 832-6688	31.51	C /4.8	9.67 /45	12.36 /45	2.81 /35	B- /7.6	60	10
IX	Catholic Equity Fund I	CTHRX	C+	(877) 222-2402	10.41	C /4.3	9.76 /45	11.20 /37	--	B /8.9	57	N/A
IX	Vanguard 500 Index Adm	VFIAX	C+	(800) 662-7447	117.00	C- /4.2	8.59 /37	11.16 /37	2.45 /32	B /8.6	56	N/A
IX	SSgA S&P 500 Index	SVSPX	C+	(800) 647-7327	20.91	C- /4.1	8.45 /36	11.05 /36	2.32 /30	B /8.8	54	N/A
IX	DFA US Large Company	DFLCX	C+	(800) 984-9472	37.28	C- /4.1	8.58 /37	11.10 /36	2.37 /31	B /8.7	55	15
IX	Vanguard 500 Index Inv	VFINX	C+	(800) 662-7447	116.99	C- /4.1	8.49 /37	11.06 /36	2.37 /31	B /8.6	55	N/A
IX	Fidelity Spartan US Equity Idx Inv	FUSEX	C+	(800) 544-8888	45.15	C- /4.1	8.57 /37	11.11 /36	2.32 /30	B /8.6	55	3
IX	JennDry Dryden Stock Index I	PDSIX	C+	(800) 257-3893	28.49	C- /4.0	8.40 /36	10.94 /35	2.24 /30	B /8.9	53	N/A
IX	Vantagepoint 500 Stock Index II	VPSKX	C+	(800) 669-7400	9.61	C- /4.0	8.43 /36	10.90 /35	2.24 /30	B /8.9	53	N/A
IX	Principal Inv LgCap S&P 500 Inst	PLFIX	C+	(800) 247-4123	9.06	C- /4.0	8.45 /36	10.98 /35	2.23 /29	B /8.8	54	3
IX	USAA S&P 500 Index Members	USSPX	C+	(800) 382-8722	19.03	C- /4.0	8.45 /36	10.94 /35	2.24 /30	B /8.8	53	1
IX	JPMorgan Equity Index Sel	HLEIX	C+	(800) 358-4782	28.90	C- /4.0	8.45 /36	10.93 /35	2.21 /29	B /8.8	53	12
IX	GE Institutional S&P 500 Index Inv	GIDIX	C+	(800) 242-0134	12.13	C- /4.0	8.43 /36	11.02 /36	2.27 /30	B /8.7	54	9
IX	Barclays Gbl Inv S&P500 Stock Fd	WFSPX	C+	(800) 474-2737	152.25	C- /4.0	8.43 /36	11.01 /36	2.29 /30	B /8.7	54	N/A
IX	Fidelity Spartan 500 Idx Fd	FSMKX	C+	(800) 544-8888	87.89	C- /4.0	8.55 /37	11.10 /36	2.33 /30	B /8.7	55	3
IX	Dreyfus Basic S&P 500 Stock Idx	DSPIX	C+	(800) 242-8671	26.48	C- /4.0	8.40 /36	11.00 /35	2.28 /30	B /8.7	53	11
IX	United Assoc S&P 500 Index I	UASPX	C+	(888) 766-8043	9.19	C- /4.0	8.80 /39	10.92 /35	2.17 /29	B /8.7	54	N/A
IX	Gartmore S&P 500 Index Inst	GRMIX	C+	(800) 848-0920	10.87	C- /4.0	8.43 /36	11.01 /36	2.29 /30	B /8.4	54	N/A
IX	JennDry Dryden Stock Index Z	PSIFX	C+	(800) 257-3893	28.48	C- /3.9	8.33 /35	10.85 /34	2.15 /28	B /8.9	52	N/A
IX	American Beacon S&P 500 Index	AASPX	C+	(800) 967-9009	17.27	C- /3.9	7.98 /33	10.86 /34	2.19 /29	B /8.7	51	N/A
IX	First American Eqty Indx Y	FEIIX	C+	(800) 677-3863	23.78	C- /3.9	8.39 /36	10.87 /34	2.21 /29	B /8.7	53	N/A
IX	Evergreen Equity Index Fund I	EVIIX	C+	(800) 343-2898	47.48	C- /3.9	8.32 /35	10.88 /34	2.16 /29	B /8.6	52	6
IX	Gartmore S&P 500 Index L	GRMLX	C+	(800) 848-0920	10.89	C- /3.9	8.34 /35	10.90 /35	2.19 /29	B /8.5	52	N/A
IX	Morgan Stanley S&P 500 Index D	SPIDX	C+	(800) 869-6397	13.90	C- /3.8	8.18 /34	10.75 /33	2.04 /28	B /8.9	51	8
IX	Principal Inv LgCap S&P 500 Pfd	PLFPX	C+	(800) 247-4123	9.14	C- /3.8	8.08 /33	10.66 /32	2.03 /28	B /8.8	51	3
IX	Vantagepoint 500 Stock Index I	VPFIX	C+	(800) 669-7400	10.11	C- /3.8	8.10 /33	10.74 /33	2.04 /28	B /8.8	51	N/A
IX	T. Rowe Price Equity Index 500	PREIX	C+	(800) 638-5660	34.09	C- /3.8	8.30 /35	10.88 /34	2.23 /29	B /8.8	52	N/A
IX	Columbia Large Cap Index Fund A	NEIAX	C+	(800) 426-3750	24.47	C- /3.8	8.22 /34	10.78 /33	2.00 /27	B /8.7	51	N/A
IX	California Inv Tr-S&P 500 Index Fd	SPFIX	C	(800) 225-8778	25.55	C- /4.0	8.29 /35	10.97 /35	2.40 /31	B- /7.7	53	4
IX	Northern Instl Equity Index A	BEIAX	C	(800) 637-1380	15.58	C- /4.0	8.40 /36	11.00 /35	2.28 /30	B- /7.7	54	N/A
IX	Diversified Inst Stock Index	DISFX	C	(800) 926-0044	8.48	C- /3.9	8.24 /35	10.92 /35	2.19 /29	B /8.2	53	N/A
IX	E*TRADE S & P 500 Index Fund	ETSPX	C	(800) 786-2575	10.07	C- /3.8	8.45 /36	10.98 /35	2.22 /29	B /8.6	53	7
IX	RVS S&P 500 Index Fund E	ADIEX	C	(800) 328-8300	4.94	C- /3.8	8.15 /34	10.71 /33	2.11 /28	B /8.6	53	5
IX	Gartmore S&P 500 Index Instl-Svc	GRISX	C	(800) 848-0920	10.86	C- /3.8	8.17 /34	10.69 /33	2.01 /27	B /8.4	50	N/A
IX	Northern Trust Stock Index	NOSIX	C	(800) 595-9111	15.67	C- /3.8	8.31 /35	10.76 /33	2.00 /27	B- /7.8	51	N/A
IX	Northern Instl Equity Index C	BEICX	C	(800) 637-1380	15.51	C- /3.8	8.18 /34	10.76 /33	2.04 /28	B- /7.7	51	N/A
IX	Principal Inv LgCap S&P 500 Sel	PLFSX	C	(800) 247-4123	9.09	C- /3.7	8.00 /33	10.53 /31	1.83 /26	B /8.7	49	3
IX	Evergreen Equity Index Fund IS	EVISX	C	(800) 343-2898	47.45	C- /3.7	8.05 /33	10.60 /32	1.90 /26	B /8.6	49	6
IX	AIM S&P 500 Inst	ISIIX	C	(800) 347-4246	12.76	C- /3.7	8.28 /35	10.86 /34	1.93 /27	B /8.6	52	3
IX	DWS Equity 500 Index Inst	BTIIX	C	(800) 621-1048	143.86	C- /3.7	8.57 /37	11.11 /36	2.39 /31	B /8.6	55	7
IX	BlackRock-Index Eq Inst	PNIEX	C	(888) 825-2257	24.42	C- /3.7	8.56 /37	11.09 /36	2.35 /31	B /8.6	55	8
IX	RVS S&P 500 Index Fund D	ADIDX	C	(800) 328-8300	4.92	C- /3.7	8.13 /34	10.49 /31	1.86 /26	B /8.6	48	5
IX	Gartmore S&P 500 Index Svc	GRMSX	C	(800) 848-0920	10.82	C- /3.7	7.94 /32	10.54 /31	1.86 /26	B /8.6	49	N/A
IX	Schwab S&P 500 Sel	SWPPX	C	(866) 855-9102	19.77	C- /3.7	8.55 /37	11.09 /36	2.36 /31	B- /7.9	55	N/A
IX	Schwab S&P 500 E	SWPEX	C	(866) 855-9102	19.71	C- /3.7	8.53 /37	11.00 /36	2.29 /30	B- /7.9	54	N/A
IX	American Beacon S&P 500	AAFPX	C	(800) 967-9009	17.03	C- /3.6	7.55 /30	10.51 /31	1.81 /26	B /8.7	47	6
IX	First American Eqty Indx R	FADSX	C	(800) 677-3863	23.77	C- /3.6	7.88 /32	10.40 /30	--	B /8.7	47	N/A
IX	DWS Equity 500 Index Inv	BTIEX	C	(800) 621-1048	142.38	C- /3.6	8.40 /36	10.95 /35	2.25 /30	B /8.6	53	7
IX	Merrill Lynch S & P Index I	MASRX	C	(800) 543-6217	15.69	C- /3.6	8.31 /35	10.34 /30	1.81 /26	B /8.2	48	N/A
IX	Diversified Inv Stock Index	DSKIX	C	(800) 926-0044	9.88	C- /3.6	7.87 /32	10.53 /31	1.83 /26	B /8.2	48	7
IX	● MainStay Equity Index A	MCSEX	C	(800) 624-6782	43.22	C- /3.6	9.46 /43	11.36 /38	3.93 /45	B- /7.9	N/A	10

● Denotes fund is closed to new investors

Fund Type	Fund Name	Ticker Symbol	Overall Weiss Investment Rating	Phone	Net Asset Value As of 6/30/06	Performance Rating/Pts	1Yr / Pct	3Yr / Pct	5Yr / Pct	Risk Rating/Pts	Mgr. Quality Pct	Mgr. Tenure (Years)
MC	RVS Mid Cap Value Y		A+	(800) 328-8300	9.16	A /9.3	21.45 /84	26.08 /92	--	B- / 7.8	98	N/A
MC	RVS Mid Cap Value C	AMVCX	A+	(800) 328-8300	8.88	A- /9.1	20.18 /82	24.90 /91	--	B- / 7.8	96	N/A
MC	RS Value Fund	RSVAX	A+	(800) 766-3863	25.56	A- /9.0	10.68 /51	25.93 /92	17.59 /94	B / 8.2	98	8
MC	RVS Mid Cap Value A	AMVAX	A+	(800) 328-8300	9.09	A- /9.0	21.00 /83	25.84 /92	--	B- / 7.8	97	N/A
MC	RVS Mid Cap Value B	AMVBX	A+	(800) 328-8300	8.88	B+ /8.9	20.18 /82	24.90 /91	--	B- / 7.8	96	N/A
MC	TIAA-CREF Inst Mid Cap Value	TCMVX	A+		17.73	B+ /8.6	14.22 /69	22.80 /87	--	B- / 7.9	94	4
MC	Fairholme Fund	FAIRX	A+	(800) 417-5525	27.44	B+ /8.4	16.90 /77	21.49 /84	14.55 /91	B / 8.9	99	7
MC	TIAA-CREF Inst MdCap Val Idx	TRVUX	A+		15.86	B+ /8.4	13.80 /68	21.59 /84	--	B / 8.3	95	5
MC	Columbia Mid Cap Value Fund Z	NAMAX	A+	(800) 426-3750	13.87	B+ /8.4	15.78 /74	21.76 /85	--	B / 8.3	94	N/A
MC	First American Mid Cap Val Y	FSEIX	A+	(800) 677-3863	25.66	B+ /8.3	14.69 /71	21.15 /83	12.58 /88	B / 8.5	93	N/A
MC	DFA Tax Managed US MktWide	DTMMX	A+	(800) 984-9472	16.34	B+ /8.3	17.94 /79	20.18 /80	6.17 /62	B / 8.3	87	8
MC ●	Hotchkis and Wiley Mid-Cap Val R	HWMRX	A+	(800) 796-5606	29.05	B+ /8.3	7.99 /33	22.77 /87	15.36 /92	B / 8.0	92	N/A
MC ●	Hotchkis and Wiley Mid-Cap Val I	HWMIX	A+	(800) 796-5606	28.91	B+ /8.3	8.53 /37	22.79 /87	15.61 /93	B / 8.0	92	N/A
MC	First American Mid Cap Val R	FMVSX	A+	(800) 677-3863	25.47	B /8.2	14.16 /69	20.66 /82	--	B / 8.5	92	2
MC	Allegiant Mid Cap Value C	ARVCX	A+	(800) 622-3863	13.41	B /8.2	17.41 /78	20.56 /81	--	B / 8.2	90	N/A
MC	Wells Fargo Avtg Mid Cp Discp Inv	SMCDX	A+	(800) 222-8222	21.98	B /8.1	14.52 /70	19.79 /79	13.48 /89	B / 8.9	98	5
MC	Artisan Mid Cap Value Inv	ARTQX	A+	(800) 344-1770	19.32	B /8.1	7.32 /28	21.61 /84	13.56 /90	B / 8.4	95	5
MC	STI Classic Mid Cap Value Eq I	SMVTX	A+	(888) 784-3863	13.04	B /8.1	17.65 /78	19.46 /78	--	B / 8.2	83	N/A
MC ●	CRM Mid Cap Value Instl	CRIMX	A+	(800) 276-2883	28.47	B /8.0	11.82 /58	20.44 /81	12.73 /88	B / 8.1	94	3
MC	Phoenix Mid Cap Value A	FMIVX	A+	(800) 243-4361	21.72	B /8.0	11.07 /54	21.52 /84	12.50 /88	B / 8.1	97	9
MC	First American Mid Cap Val C	FACSX	A+	(800) 677-3863	24.97	B /7.9	13.55 /66	19.93 /79	11.46 /85	B / 8.5	90	2
MC	Allegiant Mid Cap Value B	ARVBX	A+	(800) 622-3863	13.35	B /7.9	17.50 /78	20.60 /81	--	B / 8.2	91	N/A
MC	First American Mid Cap Val A	FASEX	A+	(800) 677-3863	25.55	B /7.8	14.41 /70	20.85 /82	12.30 /87	B / 8.5	93	7
MC	First American Mid Cap Val B	FAESX	A+	(800) 677-3863	24.47	B /7.6	13.56 /66	19.95 /79	11.46 /85	B / 8.4	90	2
MC ●	JPMorgan Mid Cap Value Inst	FLMVX	A+	(800) 358-4782	25.10	B- /7.3	10.71 /52	17.87 /72	13.99 /90	B+ / 9.2	95	N/A
MC	ING JPMorgan MidCap Val Port I	IJMIX	A+	(800) 992-0180	14.90	B- /7.2	10.23 /48	17.60 /71	--	B+ / 9.1	94	3
MC ●	JPMorgan Mid Cap Value Sel	JMVSX	A+	(800) 358-4782	24.92	B- /7.2	10.42 /50	17.57 /70	13.72 /90	B+ / 9.1	94	N/A
MC	ING JPMorgan MidCap Val Port	IJMAX	A+	(800) 992-0180	14.73	B- /7.0	9.66 /45	17.03 /68	--	B+ / 9.1	93	4
MC	Dreyfus Premier S&P STARS Opp	DSORX	A	(800) 782-6620	21.83	B+ /8.6	23.81 /87	22.74 /87	--	B- / 7.3	82	2
MC	Quaker Mid Cap Value Inst	QMVIX	A	(800) 220-8888	16.27	B+ /8.4	10.56 /51	23.10 /88	13.87 /90	B- / 7.2	75	1
MC	Fidelity Structured Mid Cap Value	FSMVX	A	(800) 522-7297	15.75	B /8.2	15.50 /73	20.70 /82	--	B- / 7.8	91	N/A
MC ●	Goldman Sachs Mid Cap Value	GSMCX	A	(800) 292-4726	36.88	B /8.1	11.31 /55	20.75 /82	13.54 /89	B- / 7.9	93	11
MC	Heartland Select Value Fd	HRSVX	A	(888) 505-5180	27.37	B /8.0	16.35 /76	19.81 /79	12.65 /88	B- / 7.9	82	N/A
MC ●	CRM Mid Cap Value Inv A	CRMMX	A	(800) 276-2883	28.07	B /7.9	11.55 /57	20.12 /80	12.44 /87	B / 8.1	93	3
MC ●	Hotchkis and Wiley Mid-Cap Val C	HWMCX	A	(800) 796-5606	27.83	B /7.9	7.46 /29	21.56 /84	14.48 /91	B / 8.0	88	N/A
MC ●	Goldman Sachs Mid Cap Value	GSMSX	A	(800) 292-4726	36.30	B /7.9	10.74 /52	20.21 /80	13.00 /89	B- / 7.9	92	9
MC ●	Hotchkis and Wiley Mid-Cap Val A	HWMAX	A	(800) 796-5606	28.77	B /7.8	8.27 /35	22.47 /86	15.36 /92	B / 8.0	91	N/A
MC	Putnam Mid Cap Value Fund Y	PMVYX	A	(800) 354-2228	15.29	B /7.7	15.68 /74	18.55 /75	10.43 /82	B / 8.0	75	7
MC	Westcore Mid-Cap Value	WTMCX	A	(800) 392-2673	18.94	B /7.7	11.57 /57	20.36 /81	8.78 /75	B / 8.0	88	N/A
MC	MSIF Trust Mid Cap Value Inst	MPMVX	A	(800) 354-8185	27.68	B /7.6	16.11 /75	18.31 /74	5.74 /59	B / 8.1	79	12
MC	MSIF Trust Mid Cap Value Inv	MPMIX	A	(800) 354-8185	27.54	B /7.6	15.94 /74	18.13 /73	5.56 /58	B / 8.1	78	10
MC ●	T. Rowe Price Mid-Cap Value Fd	TRMCX	A	(800) 638-5660	24.53	B /7.6	12.50 /62	18.74 /75	13.34 /89	B / 8.0	84	5
MC	Diversified Inst Mid-Cap Value	DIMVX	A-	(800) 926-0044	15.77	B+ /8.4	14.04 /68	21.56 /84	--	B- / 7.0	95	5
MC	Diversified Inv Mid-Cap Value	DVMVX	A-	(800) 926-0044	14.57	B+ /8.3	13.60 /67	21.12 /83	--	B- / 7.2	95	5
MC	Dreyfus Premier S&P STARS Opp	DPOAX	A-	(800) 782-6620	21.37	B /8.1	23.38 /86	22.20 /86	--	B- / 7.3	79	2
MC	Vanguard Mid-Cap Index Inst	VMCIX	A-	(800) 662-7447	18.47	B /8.0	14.58 /70	20.16 /80	10.23 /81	B- / 7.3	74	N/A
MC	Vanguard Mid-Cap Index Adm	VIMAX	A-	(800) 662-7447	83.58	B /8.0	14.57 /70	20.11 /80	--	B- / 7.3	73	N/A
MC	Quaker Mid Cap Value C	QMCCX	A-	(800) 220-8888	14.96	B /8.0	9.47 /43	21.86 /85	12.73 /88	B- / 7.2	65	1
MC ●	Hartford MidCap Value Y	HMVYX	A-	(800) 523-7798	14.16	B /7.9	15.42 /73	19.18 /77	10.79 /83	B- / 7.5	67	N/A
MC	Mellon Mid Cap Stock Inv	MIMSX	A-	(800) 499-3327	14.47	B /7.9	17.20 /77	19.38 /77	--	B- / 7.5	59	2
MC	Principal Inv Prt MdCp VI Fd Inst	PMVIX	A-	(800) 247-4123	15.22	B /7.7	12.23 /61	19.44 /78	11.16 /84	B- / 7.8	77	1
MC	Principal Inv Prt MdCp VI Fd Pfd	PPPPX	A-	(800) 247-4123	15.07	B /7.6	11.93 /59	19.12 /76	10.87 /83	B- / 7.8	75	1

● Denotes fund is closed to new investors

Fund Type	Fund Name	Ticker Symbol	Overall Weiss Investment Rating	Phone	Net Asset Value As of 6/30/06	Perform-ance Rating/Pts	Annualized Total Return Through 6/30/06			Risk Rating/Pts	Mgr. Quality Pct	Mgr. Tenure (Years)
							1Yr / Pct	3Yr / Pct	5Yr / Pct			
OT	Wells Fargo Avtg Indx Adm	NVINX	C+	(800) 222-8222	51.36	C- /4.0	8.37 /36	10.94 /35	2.31 /30	B /8.7	53	10
OT	Wells Fargo Avtg Endeavor Sel I	WFCIX	C-	(800) 222-8222	9.58	C+ /5.9	7.09 /27	15.59 /62	3.36 /40	C /5.0	61	N/A
OT	Wells Fargo Avtg Endeavor Sel	WECDX	C-	(800) 222-8222	9.56	C+ /5.8	6.87 /25	15.51 /61	3.32 /40	C /5.0	60	N/A
OT	● Davis Research Fund Class A		C-	(800) 279-0279	13.27	C /5.0	7.19 /27	14.81 /58	--	C+ /5.9	90	5
OT	● Davis Research Fund Class C		C-	(800) 279-0279	12.87	C /4.6	5.54 /18	13.08 /49	--	C+ /5.9	81	5
OT	Wells Fargo Avtg Endeavor Sel C	WECCX	D+	(800) 222-8222	9.11	C /5.1	5.75 /19	14.46 /56	2.46 /32	C /5.0	48	N/A
OT	Wells Fargo Avtg Endeavor Sel A	STAEX	D+	(800) 222-8222	9.53	C /4.7	6.66 /24	15.39 /61	3.25 /39	C /5.0	58	N/A
OT	● Davis Research Fund Class B		D+	(800) 279-0279	12.85	C- /4.1	5.47 /17	13.03 /49	--	C+ /5.9	81	5
OT	Diversified Inst Money Market	DFINX	D+	(800) 926-0044	10.06	E /0.3	3.85 /10	2.08 / 1	1.92 /26	B+ /9.9	53	N/A
OT	Diversified Inv Money Market	DVMKX	D+	(800) 926-0044	10.64	E- /0.2	3.43 / 9	1.76 / 1	1.63 /24	B+ /9.9	49	N/A
OT	Wells Fargo Avtg Endeavor Sel B	WECBX	D	(800) 222-8222	9.12	C /4.5	5.86 /20	14.56 /57	2.48 /32	C /4.9	48	N/A
OT	ProFunds-Rising Rates Opport Inv	RRPIX	D-	(888) 776-3637	22.39	D+ /2.3	23.78 /87	0.51 / 0	--	C+ /6.0	14	4
OT	ProFunds-Rising Rates Opport Svc	RRPSX	E+	(888) 776-3637	21.85	E+ /0.6	22.56 /85	-0.48 / 0	--	C+ /6.0	10	4
OT	ProFunds-Short OTC Inv	SOPIX	E	(888) 776-3637	19.95	E- /0.0	-0.91 / 1	-8.65 / 0	--	C+ /6.4	83	4
OT	ProFunds-Short OTC Svc	SOPSX	E	(888) 776-3637	19.43	E- /0.0	-1.82 / 1	-9.54 / 0	--	C+ /6.4	75	4

● Denotes fund is closed to new investors

Data as of June 30, 2006

						PERFORMANCE				RISK	FUND MGR	
	99 Pct = Best 0 Pct = Worst			Overall Weiss		Net Asset Value As of 6/30/06	Perform- ance Rating/Pts	Annualized Total Return Through 6/30/06				Mgr. Quality Pct	Mgr. Tenure (Years)
Fund Type	Fund Name	Ticker Symbol	Investment Rating	Phone				1Yr / Pct	3Yr / Pct	5Yr / Pct	Risk Rating/Pts		
PM	Van Eck Intl Investors Gold A	INIVX	C	(800) 221-2220	16.12	A+ /9.9	85.61 /99	35.18 /98	37.22 /99	D / 1.9	66	8
PM	US Global Inv Gold Shares	USERX	C	(800) 873-8637	15.49	A+ /9.9	104.28 /99	45.05 /99	41.06 /99	D- / 1.5	98	N/A
PM	US Global Inv World Prec Minerals	UNWPX	C-	(800) 873-8637	28.86	A+ /9.9	96.21 /99	53.24 /99	46.82 /99	D- / 1.5	99	8
PM	USAA Gold Fund	USAGX	C-	(800) 382-8722	27.04	A+ /9.9	81.81 /99	37.42 /99	37.98 /99	D- / 1.5	93	N/A
PM	● Vanguard Prec. Metals & Mining Fd	VGPMX	C-	(800) 662-7447	29.16	A+ /9.9	72.86 /99	44.17 /99	35.20 /99	D- / 1.2	99	10
PM	Midas Fund	MIDSX	C-	(800) 400-6432	4.05	A+ /9.9	104.55 /99	39.25 /99	35.70 /99	D- / 1.1	90	N/A
PM	Oppenheimer Gold/Spec Min C	OGMCX	C-	(800) 525-7048	28.10	A+ /9.9	66.79 /99	35.47 /98	29.33 /99	E+ / 0.7	87	9
PM	Oppenheimer Gold/Spec Min B	OGMBX	C-	(800) 525-7048	28.13	A+ /9.9	66.67 /99	35.41 /98	29.28 /99	E+ / 0.7	86	9
PM	Oppenheimer Gold/Spec Min A	OPGSX	C-	(800) 525-7048	29.15	A+ /9.9	68.00 /99	36.49 /98	30.30 /99	E+ / 0.7	90	9
PM	Oppenheimer Gold/Spec Min N	OGMNX	C-	(800) 525-7048	28.68	A+ /9.9	67.62 /99	36.05 /98	29.90 /99	E+ / 0.7	89	9
PM	AIM Gold & Prec Met A	IGDAX	C-	(800) 347-4246	5.67	A+ /9.8	59.27 /99	29.65 /95	--	D- / 1.2	65	7
PM	AIM Gold & Prec Met C	IGDCX	C-	(800) 347-4246	5.94	A+ /9.8	58.40 /99	28.87 /95	28.40 /99	D- / 1.2	58	7
PM	● AIM Gold & Prec Met Inv	FGLDX	C-	(800) 347-4246	5.71	A+ /9.8	59.50 /99	29.76 /95	29.72 /99	D- / 1.2	65	7
PM	Select Gold	FSAGX	C-	(800) 544-8888	34.45	A+ /9.7	69.56 /99	26.01 /92	27.74 /99	D / 1.7	21	3
PM	AIM Gold & Prec Met B	IGDBX	C-	(800) 347-4246	5.60	A+ /9.7	58.19 /99	28.87 /95	--	D- / 1.2	57	7
PM	Evergreen Precious Metals I	EKWYX	D+	(800) 343-2898	55.24	A+ /9.9	76.08 /99	38.03 /99	37.41 /99	E- / 0.2	89	N/A
PM	Evergreen Precious Metals C	EKWCX	D+	(800) 343-2898	52.96	A+ /9.9	74.33 /99	36.68 /98	36.05 /99	E- / 0.2	83	N/A
PM	Evergreen Precious Metals A	EKWAX	D+	(800) 343-2898	55.56	A+ /9.9	75.57 /99	37.63 /99	37.06 /99	E- / 0.2	87	N/A
PM	Evergreen Precious Metals B	EKWBX	D+	(800) 343-2898	53.26	A+ /9.9	74.33 /99	36.66 /98	36.06 /99	E- / 0.2	83	N/A
PM	Franklin Gold & Prec Metals A	FKRCX	D+	(800) 342-5236	30.88	A+ /9.9	72.23 /99	33.32 /97	27.46 /99	E- / 0.0	73	9
PM	Franklin Gold & Prec Metals C	FRGOX	D+	(800) 342-5236	30.13	A+ /9.9	70.95 /99	32.29 /97	26.51 /99	E- / 0.0	66	9
PM	GAMCO Gold AAA	GOLDX	D+	(800) 422-3554	25.96	A+ /9.9	76.37 /99	30.54 /96	35.10 /99	E- / 0.0	35	12
PM	GAMCO Gold C	GLDCX	D+	(800) 422-3554	25.66	A+ /9.9	75.05 /99	29.56 /95	34.40 /99	E- / 0.0	29	12
PM	GAMCO Gold B	GLDBX	D+	(800) 422-3554	25.67	A+ /9.9	75.03 /99	29.52 /95	34.38 /99	E- / 0.0	29	12
PM	GAMCO Gold A	GLDAX	D+	(800) 422-3554	25.94	A+ /9.9	76.43 /99	30.54 /96	35.10 /99	E- / 0.0	35	12
PM	DWS Gold & Prec Metals Fund	SGLDX	D+	(800) 621-1048	23.36	A+ /9.9	57.98 /99	35.10 /98	34.70 /99	E- / 0.0	71	5
PM	Franklin Gold & Prec Metals Adv	FGADX	D+	(800) 321-8563	31.71	A+ /9.9	72.57 /99	33.63 /97	27.75 /99	E- / 0.0	75	9
PM	● Franklin Gold & Prec Metals B	FAGPX	D+	(800) 342-5236	29.85	A+ /9.9	70.90 /99	32.30 /97	26.49 /99	E- / 0.0	66	9
PM	● DWS Gold & Prec Metals Fund S	SCGDX	D+	(800) 621-1048	23.33	A+ /9.9	58.04 /99	35.10 /98	34.68 /99	E- / 0.0	71	5
PM	Tocqueville Gold Fund	TGLDX	D+	(800) 697-3863	50.21	A+ /9.9	63.28 /99	31.54 /96	35.70 /99	E- / 0.0	71	8
PM	DWS Gold & Prec Metals Fund C	SGDCX	D+	(800) 621-1048	23.03	A+ /9.9	56.47 /99	33.80 /97	33.38 /99	E- / 0.0	61	5
PM	DWS Gold & Prec Metals Fund B	SGDBX	D+	(800) 621-1048	23.06	A+ /9.8	56.42 /99	33.76 /97	33.35 /99	E- / 0.0	61	5
PM	DWS Gold & Prec Metals Fund A	SGDAX	D+	(800) 621-1048	23.30	A+ /9.8	57.64 /99	34.79 /98	34.41 /99	E- / 0.0	69	5
PM	ProFunds-Precious Metals Ultra Inv	PMPIX	D+	(888) 776-3637	46.61	A+ /9.8	74.31 /99	26.82 /93	--	E- / 0.0	0	N/A
PM	ProFunds-Precious Metals Ultra	PMPSX	D+	(888) 776-3637	44.86	A+ /9.8	72.67 /99	26.46 /93	--	E- / 0.0	0	N/A
PM	American Century Global Gold Inv	BGEIX	D+	(800) 345-6488	18.62	A+ /9.8	66.31 /99	27.65 /94	31.93 /99	E- / 0.0	10	15
PM	OCM Gold Fund	OCMGX	D+	(800) 628-9403	18.55	A+ /9.8	72.66 /99	27.15 /93	33.57 /99	E- / 0.0	14	10
PM	RVS Precious Metals Fund B	INPBX	D+	(800) 328-8300	13.93	A+ /9.8	68.24 /99	27.79 /94	26.15 /99	E- / 0.0	26	7
PM	American Century Global Gold Adv	ACGGX	D+	(800) 345-6488	18.60	A+ /9.8	65.85 /99	27.39 /93	31.64 /99	E- / 0.0	9	15
PM	RVS Precious Metals Fund A	INPMX	D+	(800) 328-8300	14.75	A+ /9.8	69.54 /99	28.74 /95	27.13 /99	E- / 0.0	32	7
PM	ING Precious Metals A	LEXMX	D+	(800) 992-0180	10.69	A+ /9.7	67.59 /99	27.11 /93	30.19 /99	E- / 0.0	21	8
PM	● First Eagle Gold Fund A	SGGDX	D+	(800) 334-2143	23.75	A /9.5	54.82 /99	25.01 /91	35.05 /99	E+ / 0.7	26	7
PM	● First Eagle Gold Fund I	FEGIX	D	(800) 334-2143	23.88	A+ /9.6	55.27 /99	25.32 /91	--	E- / 0.0	27	7
PM	● First Eagle Gold Fund C	FEGOX	D	(800) 334-2143	23.50	A /9.5	53.69 /99	24.13 /90	--	E- / 0.0	21	7
PM	Rydex Series-Precious Metal Inv	RYPMX	D	(800) 820-0888	53.06	A /9.3	52.30 /99	20.20 /80	21.41 /97	E- / 0.0	1	N/A
PM	Rydex Series-Precious Metal C	RYZCX	D	(800) 820-0888	50.52	A- /9.1	50.76 /99	18.99 /76	20.23 /96	E- / 0.0	1	N/A

● Denotes fund is closed to new investors

Fund Type	Fund Name	Ticker Symbol	Overall Weiss Investment Rating	Phone	Net Asset Value As of 6/30/06	PERFORMANCE				RISK	FUND MGR	
	99 Pct = Best 0 Pct = Worst					Perform-ance Rating/Pts	Annualized Total Return Through 6/30/06			Risk Rating/Pts	Mgr. Quality Pct	Mgr. Tenure (Years)
							1Yr / Pct	3Yr / Pct	5Yr / Pct			
RE	MSIF Inc. Intl Real Estate B	IERBX	A+	(800) 354-8185	27.46	A+ /9.8	28.87 /94	35.44 /98	26.95 /99	B- / 7.6	99	7
RE	MSIF Inc. Intl Real Estate A	MSUAX	A+	(800) 354-8185	27.44	A+ /9.8	29.15 /94	35.81 /98	27.26 /99	B- / 7.5	99	7
RE	Columbia Real Estate Equity Fd		A+	(800) 426-3750	19.71	A- /9.0	17.25 /78	23.91 /89	--	B- / 7.4	84	N/A
RE	● Third Avenue Real Estate Value	TAREX	A+	(800) 443-1021	31.95	B+ /8.8	13.44 /66	23.93 /89	18.81 /95	B- / 7.5	99	8
RE	Columbia Real Estate Equity Fd		A+	(800) 426-3750	19.07	B+ /8.7	16.00 /75	22.63 /86	--	B- / 7.4	75	N/A
RE	Cohen & Steers Realty Shrs Inst	CSRIX	A	(800) 437-9912	51.30	A+ /9.6	22.64 /85	30.21 /96	20.76 /97	C+ / 6.1	94	15
RE	Alpine Intl Real Estate Y	EGLRX	A	(888) 785-5578	33.18	A /9.5	18.73 /80	31.05 /96	22.11 /98	C+ / 6.4	99	17
RE	● TA IDEX Clarion Glb Real Estate C	ICRLX	A	(888) 233-4339	17.43	A- /9.2	21.92 /84	25.42 /91	--	C+ / 6.7	76	3
RE	● TA IDEX Clarion Glb Real Estate B	ICRBX	A	(888) 233-4339	17.56	A- /9.2	21.71 /84	25.56 /92	--	C+ / 6.7	77	3
RE	● TA IDEX Clarion Glb Real Estate A	ICRAX	A	(888) 233-4339	17.61	A- /9.2	22.45 /85	26.34 /92	--	C+ / 6.7	82	4
RE	Old Mutual Heitman REIT Fund	OBRAX	A	(888) 744-5050	13.93	A- /9.2	19.11 /81	26.22 /92	19.25 /95	C+ / 6.7	81	N/A
RE	TIAA-CREF Inst Real Est Sec Instl	TIREX	A		14.29	B+ /8.9	12.74 /63	24.12 /90	--	C+ / 6.8	87	4
RE	TIAA-CREF Inst Real Est Sec	TCREX	A		14.19	B+ /8.9	12.68 /63	24.15 /90	--	C+ / 6.7	87	4
RE	Columbia Real Estate Equity Fd		A	(800) 426-3750	19.53	B+ /8.5	16.88 /77	23.53 /88	--	B- / 7.4	82	N/A
RE	Columbia Real Estate Equity Fd		A	(800) 426-3750	19.08	B+ /8.4	16.06 /75	22.62 /86	--	B- / 7.4	75	N/A
RE	JPMorgan Realty Income Fund Cl	URTCX	A-	(800) 358-4782	17.22	A /9.4	21.92 /84	27.59 /94	20.21 /96	C+ / 6.1	87	N/A
RE	JPMorgan Realty Income Fund Cl	URTAX	A-	(800) 358-4782	17.31	A /9.3	22.50 /85	28.03 /94	20.46 /96	C+ / 6.1	89	N/A
RE	JPMorgan Realty Income Fund Cl	URTBX	A-	(800) 358-4782	17.26	A /9.3	21.87 /84	27.58 /94	20.21 /96	C+ / 6.1	87	N/A
RE	AssetMark Real Estate Securities	AFREX	A-	(800) 664-5345	18.29	A /9.3	21.81 /84	26.33 /92	19.36 /95	C+ / 6.0	80	5
RE	Ivy Fund-Real Estate Securities A	IRSAX	A-	(800) 777-6472	22.88	A- /9.1	17.64 /78	26.47 /93	20.51 /97	C+ / 6.4	88	N/A
RE	Alpine Realty Inc & Growth Y	AIGYX	A-	(888) 785-5578	24.74	B+ /8.8	14.94 /72	23.66 /89	20.36 /96	C+ / 6.6	89	7
RE	Cohen & Steers Reality Income I	CSDIX	A-	(800) 437-9912	16.89	B+ /8.4	13.21 /65	21.26 /83	16.64 /94	B- / 7.0	52	N/A
RE	MSIF Inc. US Real Estate A	MSUSX	B+	(800) 354-8185	26.88	A+ /9.6	25.08 /89	30.91 /96	21.16 /97	C / 5.5	98	11
RE	MSIF Inc. US Real Estate B	MUSDX	B+	(800) 354-8185	26.63	A+ /9.6	24.77 /88	30.59 /96	20.81 /97	C / 5.5	97	10
RE	● AIM Real Estate Fund Inv	REINX	B+	(800) 347-4246	31.83	A+ /9.6	24.72 /88	29.64 /95	22.80 /98	C / 5.3	95	N/A
RE	ING Global Real Estate C	IGCAX	B+	(800) 992-0180	17.58	A /9.5	25.02 /88	28.49 /94	--	C+ / 5.7	99	N/A
RE	Van Kampen Real Estate Sec C	ACRCX	B+	(800) 421-5666	27.71	A /9.5	23.08 /86	28.96 /95	19.29 /95	C+ / 5.6	95	9
RE	Cohen & Steers Realty Focus I	CSSPX	B+	(800) 437-9912	64.79	A /9.5	17.59 /78	30.22 /96	22.16 /98	C+ / 5.6	98	9
RE	JPMorgan US Real Estate A	SUSIX	B+	(800) 358-4782	22.10	A /9.5	26.77 /91	29.99 /95	20.34 /96	C / 5.3	95	N/A
RE	Oppenheimer Real Estate A	OREAX	B+	(800) 525-7048	21.65	A /9.4	22.13 /84	28.83 /95	--	C+ / 5.8	88	4
RE	ING Global Real Estate A	IGLAX	B+	(800) 992-0180	19.44	A /9.4	25.96 /90	29.35 /95	--	C+ / 5.8	99	N/A
RE	ING Global Real Estate B	IGBAX	B+	(800) 992-0180	16.80	A /9.4	25.02 /88	28.39 /94	--	C+ / 5.7	99	N/A
RE	Van Kampen Real Estate Sec B	ACRBX	B+	(800) 421-5666	27.66	A /9.4	23.08 /86	28.89 /95	19.24 /95	C+ / 5.6	95	9
RE	Van Kampen Real Estate Sec A	ACREX	B+	(800) 421-5666	27.64	A /9.4	23.95 /87	29.83 /95	20.12 /96	C+ / 5.6	97	9
RE	Delaware REIT R	DPRRX	B+	(800) 362-3863	21.02	B+ /8.6	12.77 /63	22.57 /86	--	C+ / 6.4	44	9
RE	Strategic Partners Real Est Sec Z		B	(800) 778-8769	24.67	A+ /9.7	23.94 /87	31.85 /97	24.19 /98	C / 4.9	97	N/A
RE	Strategic Partners Real Est Sec C		B	(800) 778-8769	24.48	A+ /9.6	22.69 /85	30.54 /96	22.94 /98	C / 4.9	96	N/A
RE	ING Van Kampen Real Estate S2	IVRTX	B	(800) 992-0180	35.52	A+ /9.6	24.75 /88	30.54 /96	--	C / 4.7	98	5
RE	ING Van Kampen Real Estate S	IVRSX	B	(800) 992-0180	35.62	A+ /9.6	24.91 /88	30.71 /96	20.98 /97	C / 4.7	98	5
RE	ING Van Kampen Real Estate I	IVRIX	B	(800) 992-0180	35.81	A+ /9.6	25.25 /89	31.05 /96	--	C / 4.7	98	5
RE	Universal Inst US Real Estate II	USRBX	B	(800) 869-6397	26.27	A+ /9.6	23.96 /87	29.93 /95	--	C / 4.6	97	4
RE	Universal Inst Real Estate Fd	UUSRX	B	(800) 869-6397	26.49	A+ /9.6	24.27 /88	30.25 /96	20.50 /97	C / 4.6	97	N/A
RE	● AIM Real Estate Fund Inst	IARIX	B	(800) 347-4246	31.85	A+ /9.6	25.32 /89	30.04 /96	23.03 /98	C / 4.5	96	N/A
RE	Cohen & Steers Realty Shrs Fd	CSRSX	B	(800) 437-9912	82.00	A /9.5	22.77 /85	30.16 /96	20.65 /97	C / 4.8	94	15
RE	Goldman Sachs Real Estate Sec	GREIX	B	(800) 292-4726	20.37	A /9.5	21.96 /84	28.40 /94	20.01 /96	C / 4.7	93	N/A
RE	First American Real Est Secs Y	FARCX	B	(800) 677-3863	22.97	A /9.5	26.21 /90	29.04 /95	21.74 /98	C / 4.6	92	7
RE	First American Real Est Secs R	FRSSX	B	(800) 677-3863	23.03	A /9.5	25.60 /89	28.48 /94	--	C / 4.6	90	7
RE	Old Mutual Heitman REIT Fund Z	OBRTX	B	(888) 744-5050	14.00	A /9.3	19.38 /81	26.55 /93	19.73 /96	C / 5.0	82	17
RE	Phoenix Real Estate Securities A	PHRAX	B	(800) 243-4361	31.50	A /9.3	24.37 /88	28.33 /94	22.03 /98	C / 4.7	86	8
RE	GMO Real Estate III	GMORX	B		10.94	A- /9.1	18.37 /80	24.88 /91	17.38 /94	C / 5.2	66	N/A
RE	WM REIT Fund C	WMRCX	B	(800) 222-5852	19.09	B+ /8.8	15.18 /72	23.63 /89	--	C / 5.5	60	3
RE	WM REIT Fund A	WMRAX	B	(800) 222-5852	19.14	B+ /8.7	16.19 /75	24.54 /90	--	C / 5.5	68	3

● Denotes fund is closed to new investors

Fund Type	Fund Name	Ticker Symbol	Overall Weiss Investment Rating	Phone	Net Asset Value As of 6/30/06	PERFORMANCE				RISK	FUND MGR	
						Perform-ance Rating/Pts	Annualized Total Return Through 6/30/06			Risk Rating/Pts	Mgr. Quality Pct	Mgr. Tenure (Years)
							1Yr / Pct	3Yr / Pct	5Yr / Pct			
SC	Gartmore Small Cap Fd Inst	GSCIX	A+	(800) 848-0920	19.66	A /9.5	27.15 /92	29.43 /95	14.85 /92	C+ / 6.9	99	N/A
SC	Gartmore Small Cap Fd R	GNSRX	A+	(800) 848-0920	18.53	A /9.4	26.75 /91	28.85 /95	14.13 /90	C+ / 6.9	99	N/A
SC	Royce Value Fd Svc	RYVFX	A+	(800) 221-4268	10.28	A- /9.2	22.15 /84	26.43 /93	17.16 /94	B- / 7.1	99	N/A
SC •	STI Classic Var Tr-Sm Cap Val Eq		A+	(888) 784-3863	20.20	A- /9.1	25.17 /89	24.77 /91	17.15 /94	B- / 7.4	98	N/A
SC	Constellation TIP Sm Cap Val opp	TSVOX	A+	(800) 224-6312	19.55	A- /9.1	17.30 /78	25.87 /92	--	B- / 7.1	98	4
SC	DWS Dreman Small Cap Val R	KDSRX	A+	(800) 621-1048	36.86	A- /9.0	20.94 /83	24.11 /90	14.25 /91	B- / 7.5	98	4
SC	Kinetics Small Cap Opport NL	KSCOX	A+	(800) 930-3828	23.20	A- /9.0	20.95 /83	24.32 /90	11.91 /86	B- / 7.2	99	N/A
SC	Schwab Small-Cap Equity Sel	SWSCX	A+	(866) 855-9102	17.04	A- /9.0	16.87 /77	25.52 /92	--	B- / 7.0	98	N/A
SC	The Boston Company Small Cap	STSVX	A+	(800) 221-4795	23.47	B+ /8.9	16.77 /77	24.52 /90	16.01 /93	B- / 7.5	97	6
SC •	Dreyfus Premier Small Cap Eqty R	DSERX	A+	(800) 782-6620	30.47	B+ /8.9	15.96 /75	23.84 /89	15.66 /93	B- / 7.3	96	3
SC •	Franklin MicroCap Value A	FRMCX	A+	(800) 342-5236	40.47	B+ /8.3	19.63 /81	22.28 /86	16.26 /93	B / 8.7	99	11
SC •	Allianz NFJ Small Cap Value D	PNVDX	A+	(800) 628-1237	32.07	B /8.1	14.51 /70	20.54 /81	15.19 /92	B / 8.0	96	N/A
SC •	Third Avenue Sm Cap Value Fund	TASCX	A+	(800) 443-1021	25.67	B /8.0	12.21 /61	20.52 /81	11.67 /86	B / 8.6	97	9
SC	Keeley Small Cap Value Fund	KSCVX	A	(800) 533-5344	49.74	A /9.5	31.10 /95	29.79 /95	18.02 /94	C+ / 6.3	99	13
SC	Royce Value Plus Svc	RYVPX	A	(800) 221-4268	13.07	A /9.4	30.00 /94	28.78 /95	22.73 /98	C+ / 6.6	99	5
SC	DWS Dreman Small Cap Val Inst	KDSIX	A	(800) 621-1048	36.89	A- /9.2	21.61 /84	24.86 /91	--	C+ / 6.8	98	N/A
SC	Stratton Small-Cap Value Fund	STSCX	A	(800) 634-5726	47.56	A- /9.1	16.21 /75	25.53 /92	16.72 /94	C+ / 6.8	97	N/A
SC	Schwab Small-Cap Equity Inv	SWSIX	A	(866) 855-9102	16.97	A- /9.0	16.68 /76	25.36 /91	--	B- / 7.0	98	N/A
SC •	Munder Micro-Cap Equity Y	MMEYX	A	(800) 438-5789	46.37	A- /9.0	15.39 /73	25.97 /92	13.48 /89	B- / 7.0	98	N/A
SC •	Munder Micro-Cap Equity K	MMEKX	A	(800) 438-5789	45.39	A- /9.0	15.11 /72	25.65 /92	13.20 /89	C+ / 6.9	98	N/A
SC	DFA Tax Mgd Sm Cap Val Fd	DTMVX	A	(800) 984-9472	25.68	A- /9.0	19.23 /81	23.95 /89	13.68 /90	C+ / 6.9	92	8
SC •	Perritt Micro Cap Opportunities	PRCGX	A	(800) 331-8936	31.57	B+ /8.9	21.17 /83	24.47 /90	18.81 /95	B- / 7.0	97	7
SC •	Munder Micro-Cap Equity C	MMECX	A	(800) 438-5789	42.28	B+ /8.8	14.28 /69	24.71 /90	12.35 /87	C+ / 6.9	97	N/A
SC	Franklin Small Cap Value Adv	FVADX	A	(800) 321-8563	45.56	B+ /8.7	18.39 /80	22.41 /86	13.04 /89	B- / 7.3	96	10
SC	Oppenheimer Small & Mid Cap	QSCNX	A	(800) 525-7048	34.02	B+ /8.7	12.41 /62	24.32 /90	14.17 /90	B- / 7.3	98	5
SC	DWS Dreman Small Cap Val I		A	(800) 621-1048	36.89	B+ /8.7	16.49 /76	23.06 /87	13.94 /90	B- / 7.1	96	4
SC •	Munder Micro-Cap Equity A	MMEAX	A	(800) 438-5789	45.38	B+ /8.7	15.14 /72	25.66 /92	13.18 /89	C+ / 6.9	98	N/A
SC •	Diamond Hill Small Cap A	DHSCX	A		24.75	B+ /8.6	14.06 /68	24.58 /90	15.20 /92	B- / 7.4	99	6
SC •	Diamond Hill Small Cap C	DHSMX	A		23.76	B+ /8.6	13.22 /65	23.68 /89	14.33 /91	B- / 7.4	99	5
SC •	Dreyfus Premier Small Cap Eqty C	DSECX	A	(800) 782-6620	29.39	B+ /8.6	14.79 /71	22.57 /86	14.85 /92	B- / 7.3	94	3
SC	Franklin Small Cap Value R	FVFRX	A	(800) 342-5236	44.28	B+ /8.6	17.79 /79	21.81 /85	12.47 /88	B- / 7.3	95	10
SC	Oppenheimer Small & Mid Cap	QSCCX	A	(800) 525-7048	31.36	B+ /8.6	11.92 /59	23.83 /89	13.67 /90	B- / 7.1	98	5
SC •	T. Rowe Price Small Cap Value Fd	PRSVX	A	(800) 638-5660	40.67	B+ /8.6	19.02 /81	22.16 /86	15.64 /93	B- / 7.1	96	15
SC	Kinetics Small Cap Opport A	KSOAX	A	(800) 930-3828	23.02	B+ /8.6	20.52 /82	23.97 /89	--	B- / 7.1	99	N/A
SC	Tamarack Micro Cap Value S	TMVSX	A	(800) 422-2766	21.91	B+ /8.6	17.46 /78	22.97 /87	14.82 /92	B- / 7.0	95	N/A
SC •	Dreyfus Premier Small Cap Eqty A	DSEAX	A	(800) 782-6620	30.21	B+ /8.5	15.73 /74	23.54 /88	15.47 /92	B- / 7.3	96	3
SC •	Dreyfus Premier Small Cap Eqty T	DSETX	A	(800) 782-6620	29.91	B+ /8.5	15.42 /73	23.17 /88	15.25 /92	B- / 7.3	96	3
SC	Principal Inv SmCap Value Inst	PVSIX	A	(800) 247-4123	18.42	B+ /8.5	17.05 /77	21.58 /84	14.92 /92	B- / 7.2	92	N/A
SC •	T. Rowe Price Small Cap Value	PASVX	A	(800) 638-5660	40.44	B+ /8.5	18.83 /80	21.94 /85	15.43 /92	B- / 7.2	95	6
SC	Royce Heritage Cons	RYGCX	A	(800) 221-4268	12.75	B+ /8.5	28.69 /93	20.64 /82	--	B- / 7.2	91	5
SC •	Munder Small Cap Value Y	MCVYX	A	(800) 438-5789	29.45	B+ /8.5	14.41 /70	23.04 /87	15.71 /93	B- / 7.1	96	N/A
SC •	Munder Small Cap Value K	MCVKX	A	(800) 438-5789	29.22	B+ /8.4	14.12 /69	22.72 /87	15.43 /92	B- / 7.4	96	N/A
SC	Oppenheimer Small & Mid Cap	QVSCX	A	(800) 525-7048	34.65	B+ /8.4	12.81 /63	24.82 /91	14.51 /91	B- / 7.4	99	5
SC •	Dreyfus Premier Small Cap Eqty B	DSEBX	A	(800) 782-6620	29.41	B+ /8.4	14.83 /71	22.60 /86	14.87 /92	B- / 7.3	95	3
SC	Franklin Small Cap Value C	FRVFX	A	(800) 342-5236	42.31	B+ /8.4	17.23 /78	21.20 /83	11.91 /86	B- / 7.3	94	10
SC	Credit Suisse Small Cap Val Tr	CUSVX	A	(800) 222-8977	15.92	B+ /8.3	23.41 /86	21.44 /84	--	B- / 7.5	98	3
SC •	Harbor Small Cap Value Retire	HSVRX	A	(800) 422-1050	20.70	B /8.2	6.92 /26	21.99 /85	--	B- / 7.6	96	5
SC •	Evergreen Special Values R	ESPRX	A	(800) 343-2898	28.99	B /8.2	15.49 /73	20.52 /81	13.44 /89	B- / 7.6	93	3
SC •	Harbor Small Cap Value Inst	HASCX	A	(800) 422-1050	20.76	B /8.2	7.23 /28	22.14 /85	--	B- / 7.6	96	5
SC	Vanguard Small-Cap Value Index	VISVX	A	(800) 662-7447	15.72	B /8.2	12.64 /63	20.92 /82	11.06 /84	B- / 7.5	93	N/A
SC	American Beacon Sm Cap Val	AASVX	A	(800) 967-9009	21.47	B /8.1	10.20 /48	21.31 /83	16.04 /93	B- / 7.7	93	N/A
SC •	American Beacon Sm Cap Val Inst	AVFIX	A	(800) 967-9009	21.54	B /8.1	9.91 /46	21.00 /83	15.73 /93	B- / 7.7	92	N/A

• Denotes fund is closed to new investors

Fund Type	Fund Name	Ticker Symbol	Overall Weiss Investment Rating	Phone	Net Asset Value As of 6/30/06	Perform-ance Rating/Pts	1Yr / Pct	3Yr / Pct	5Yr / Pct	Risk Rating/Pts	Mgr. Quality Pct	Mgr. Tenure (Years)
								Annualized Total Return Through 6/30/06				
TC	T. Rowe Price Media & Telecomm	PRMTX	A	(800) 638-5660	36.15	A /9.3	23.59 /87	26.47 /93	10.79 /83	C+ / 6.5	99	N/A
TC	Select Wireless Fund	FWRLX	B-	(800) 544-8888	6.31	A- /9.2	8.47 /37	29.04 /95	0.25 /17	C / 4.6	99	3
TC	GAMCO Global Telecom AAA	GABTX	B-	(800) 422-3554	18.41	C+ /6.4	10.51 /50	15.38 /61	2.85 /35	B- / 7.4	84	6
TC	GAMCO Global Telecom C	GTCCX	B-	(800) 422-3554	17.82	C+ /5.9	9.66 /45	14.51 /56	2.07 /28	B / 8.1	78	6
TC	GAMCO Global Telecom A	GTCAX	B-	(800) 422-3554	18.39	C+ /5.6	10.56 /51	15.39 /61	2.85 /35	B / 8.1	84	6
TC	Matthews Asian Technology Fund	MATFX	C+	(800) 892-0382	6.62	B+ /8.8	21.02 /83	24.29 /90	10.09 /81	C / 4.7	98	7
TC	Huntington New Economy Tr	HNETX	C+	(800) 253-0412	16.27	B- /7.1	12.21 /61	17.87 /72	9.45 /78	C+ / 5.9	83	5
TC	DWS Communication Fund Inst	FLICX	C+	(800) 621-1048	20.60	C+ /6.8	16.32 /75	16.38 /65	-1.72 / 9	C+ / 6.3	83	4
TC	AFBA 5Star Science & Tech I	AFITX	C+	(800) 243-9865	12.69	C+ /6.4	13.22 /65	16.50 /66	--	C+ / 6.3	57	9
TC	DWS Communication Fund C	FTICX	C+	(800) 621-1048	18.75	C+ /6.3	15.10 /72	15.21 /60	-2.88 / 6	C+ / 6.2	74	11
TC	GAMCO Global Telecom B	GTCBX	C+	(800) 422-3554	17.90	C /5.3	9.68 /45	14.51 /56	2.08 /28	B / 8.1	78	6
TC	Columbia Technology Z	CMTFX	C	(800) 426-3750	9.92	A /9.3	30.68 /95	28.11 /94	7.64 /70	C- / 3.0	92	1
TC	Columbia Technology A	CTCAX	C	(800) 426-3750	9.82	A- /9.1	30.29 /95	27.78 /94	--	C- / 3.0	91	1
TC	Columbia Technology D	CTCDX	C	(800) 426-3750	9.65	A- /9.1	29.43 /94	26.88 /93	--	D+ / 2.9	88	1
TC	Columbia Technology B	CTCBX	C	(800) 426-3750	9.59	A- /9.0	29.49 /94	26.89 /93	--	D+ / 2.9	88	1
TC	Baron iOpportunity Fund	BIOPX	C	(800) 992-2766	9.80	B /7.6	15.02 /72	19.66 /78	8.29 /73	C / 4.5	77	N/A
TC	Waddell & Reed Adv Sci & Tech Y	USTFX	C	(888) 923-3355	11.60	B- /7.4	13.54 /66	18.86 /76	6.51 /64	C / 4.8	85	5
TC	Ivy Fund-Science & Tech Y	WSTYX	C	(800) 777-6472	26.48	B- /7.2	13.07 /65	18.24 /73	6.19 /62	C / 4.8	84	5
TC	Franklin Global Communications C	FRUTX	C	(800) 342-5236	10.05	C+ /6.9	22.16 /84	16.71 /67	0.62 /18	C / 5.2	66	N/A
TC	Buffalo Science & Technology	BUFTX	C	(800) 492-8332	12.13	C+ /6.9	13.59 /67	17.79 /72	3.35 /40	C / 4.7	73	5
TC	Franklin Global Communications A	FRGUX	C	(800) 342-5236	10.53	C+ /6.7	23.17 /86	17.61 /71	1.40 /23	C / 5.3	73	N/A
TC	Waddell & Reed Adv Sci & Tech A	UNSCX	C	(888) 923-3355	11.13	C+ /6.7	13.16 /65	18.42 /74	6.09 /62	C / 4.8	83	5
TC	● Franklin Global Communications B		C	(800) 342-5236	10.04	C+ /6.6	22.25 /85	16.70 /67	0.65 /18	C / 5.2	66	N/A
TC	Ivy Fund-Science & Tech A	WSTAX	C	(800) 777-6472	25.68	C+ /6.5	12.93 /64	17.97 /72	5.89 /60	C+ / 5.6	82	5
TC	Guinness Atkinson Glob Innov	IWIRX	C	(800) 915-6565	15.97	C+ /6.4	20.17 /82	14.93 /58	0.72 /19	C+ / 5.9	52	N/A
TC	Huntington New Economy A	HNEAX	C	(800) 253-0412	16.07	C+ /6.3	11.84 /59	17.55 /70	9.22 /77	C+ / 5.9	81	5
TC	AFBA 5Star Science & Tech R	ASNRX	C	(800) 243-9865	12.43	C+ /6.2	12.64 /63	16.07 /64	--	C+ / 6.2	50	2
TC	DWS Communication Fund B	FTEBX	C	(800) 621-1048	18.73	C+ /6.1	15.12 /72	15.20 /60	-2.88 / 6	C+ / 6.2	74	11
TC	Huntington New Economy B	HNEBX	C	(800) 253-0412	15.62	C+ /6.1	11.26 /55	16.96 /68	8.57 /74	C+ / 5.9	77	5
TC	DWS Communication Fund A	TISHX	C	(800) 621-1048	20.19	C+ /6.0	15.97 /75	16.07 /64	-2.02 / 8	C+ / 6.3	81	22
TC	Ivy Fund-Science & Tech B	WSTBX	C	(800) 777-6472	24.04	C+ /6.0	11.71 /58	16.64 /66	4.70 /52	C+ / 5.6	72	5
TC	Select Telecommunications	FSTCX	C	(800) 544-8888	42.06	C+ /5.9	17.50 /78	13.99 /54	0.99 /20	C+ / 6.0	46	4
TC	AFBA 5Star Science & Tech C	AFCTX	C	(800) 243-9865	12.07	C+ /5.8	12.05 /60	15.39 /61	--	C+ / 6.2	45	9
TC	AFBA 5Star Science & Tech A	AFATX	C	(800) 243-9865	12.54	C /5.5	12.90 /64	16.26 /65	--	C+ / 6.3	55	9
TC	AFBA 5Star Science & Tech B	AFBTX	C	(800) 243-9865	12.06	C /5.4	12.06 /60	15.36 /60	--	C+ / 6.2	44	9
TC	Ivy Fund-Science & Tech C	WSTCX	C-	(800) 777-6472	24.45	C+ /6.6	11.95 /59	16.96 /68	5.01 /54	C / 4.7	75	5
TC	Waddell & Reed Adv Sci & Tech C	WCSTX	C-	(888) 923-3355	10.05	C+ /6.6	11.80 /58	16.96 /68	4.70 /52	C / 4.6	73	5
TC	Waddell & Reed Adv Sci & Tech B	USTBX	C-	(888) 923-3355	10.02	C+ /6.1	11.83 /59	16.91 /68	4.66 /52	C / 4.6	73	5
TC	Seligman Communications/Info I	SCMIX	C-	(800) 221-2783	29.19	C /5.5	17.37 /78	13.66 /52	--	C / 5.5	22	17
TC	T. Rowe Price Global Technology	PRGTX	C-	(800) 638-5660	5.93	C /5.2	7.62 /30	14.41 /56	1.12 /21	C / 5.1	25	N/A
TC	FBR Large Cap Technology Fd	FBRTX	C-	(888) 888-0025	10.94	C /4.8	12.41 /62	13.13 /49	--	C+ / 6.5	21	4
TC	Jacob Internet Fund	JAMFX	D+	(888) 522-6239	2.48	A- /9.0	28.50 /93	26.33 /92	14.69 /91	D- / 1.2	91	10
TC	Seligman Communications/Info R	SCIRX	D+	(800) 221-2783	28.31	C /4.8	16.55 /76	12.79 /47	--	C / 5.5	17	17
TC	Kinetics Internet Fund NL	WWWFX	D+	(800) 930-3828	27.30	C /4.3	17.13 /77	9.80 /26	2.61 /33	C+ / 5.8	49	7
TC	Seligman Global Tech R	SGTRX	D+	(800) 221-2783	13.93	C- /4.1	16.08 /75	12.06 /43	--	C+ / 5.7	11	N/A
TC	Integrity Technology Fund A	ITKAX	D+	(701) 852-5292	8.94	C- /4.0	6.68 /24	14.03 /54	-5.30 / 2	C+ / 5.9	24	N/A
TC	Henderson Global Technology C	HFGCX	D	(866) 443-6337	12.50	C+ /5.7	17.64 /78	15.82 /63	--	C- / 3.1	26	5
TC	Kinetics Internet Fund A	KINAX	D	(800) 930-3828	26.98	C- /3.3	17.28 /78	9.64 /25	2.14 /28	C+ / 5.9	47	N/A
TC	Emerald Select Technology C	HSYCX	D-	(800) 232-0224	8.63	B- /7.0	25.62 /89	15.78 /62	-5.72 / 2	D- / 1.4	9	1
TC	Select Developing	FSDCX	D-	(800) 544-8888	19.84	C+ /6.0	11.34 /56	16.43 /65	-2.50 / 7	D / 1.7	7	3
TC	First American Sm Mid Cap Core Y	FATCX	D-	(800) 677-3863	9.68	C+ /5.7	15.10 /72	13.16 /50	-5.15 / 2	D+ / 2.7	8	1
TC	Wasatch Global Sci & Tech	WAGTX	D-	(800) 551-1700	13.82	C /5.5	19.39 /81	14.47 /56	5.63 /59	D+ / 2.4	14	6

● Denotes fund is closed to new investors

Data as of June 30, 2006

Fund Type	Fund Name	Ticker Symbol	Overall Weiss Investment Rating	Phone	Net Asset Value As of 6/30/06	Perform-ance Rating/Pts	Annualized Total Return Through 6/30/06			Risk Rating/Pts	Mgr. Quality Pct	Mgr. Tenure (Years)
							1Yr / Pct	3Yr / Pct	5Yr / Pct			
UT	JennDry Jennison Utility Z	PRUZX	A+	(800) 257-3893	15.42	A /9.5	25.94 /90	29.17 /95	10.13 /81	B- /7.9	99	6
UT	JennDry Jennison Utility B	PRUTX	A+	(800) 257-3893	15.41	A /9.4	24.82 /88	27.93 /94	9.07 /77	B- /7.9	99	6
UT	JennDry Jennison Utility C	PCUFX	A+	(800) 257-3893	15.40	A /9.4	24.75 /88	27.91 /94	9.06 /77	B- /7.9	99	6
UT	JennDry Jennison Utility A	PRUAX	A+	(800) 257-3893	15.42	A /9.4	25.73 /89	28.91 /95	9.90 /80	B- /7.9	99	6
UT	Evergreen Utility and Telecom I	EVUYX	A+	(800) 343-2898	12.85	A /9.3	16.95 /77	26.25 /92	6.93 /66	B /8.1	99	N/A
UT	Evergreen Utility and Telecom C	EVUCX	A+	(800) 343-2898	12.85	A- /9.1	15.76 /74	25.01 /91	5.85 /60	B /8.1	99	N/A
UT	Evergreen Utility and Telecom A	EVUAX	A+	(800) 343-2898	12.84	A- /9.1	16.61 /76	25.92 /92	6.62 /65	B /8.1	99	N/A
UT	Evergreen Utility and Telecom B	EVUBX	A+	(800) 343-2898	12.84	A- /9.0	15.77 /74	24.98 /91	5.85 /60	B /8.1	99	N/A
UT	MFS Utilities Fund I	MMUIX	A+	(800) 343-2829	13.65	B+ /8.9	17.24 /78	22.95 /87	7.47 /69	B /8.1	98	14
UT	MFS Utilities Fund R	MMURX	A+	(800) 343-2829	13.61	B+ /8.7	16.53 /76	22.32 /86	6.97 /67	B /8.3	98	14
UT	MFS Utilities Fund R3	MURRX	A+	(800) 343-2829	13.61	B+ /8.7	16.43 /76	22.09 /85	6.56 /64	B /8.1	98	3
UT	MFS Utilities Fund C	MMUCX	A+	(800) 343-2829	13.60	B+ /8.5	16.07 /75	21.78 /85	6.40 /63	B /8.3	97	12
UT	MFS Utilities Fund A	MMUFX	A+	(800) 343-2829	13.63	B+ /8.5	16.88 /77	22.69 /87	7.19 /68	B /8.3	98	14
UT	MFS Utilities Fund B	MMUBX	A+	(800) 343-2829	13.58	B+ /8.4	15.99 /75	21.77 /85	6.39 /63	B /8.3	97	13
UT	Eaton Vance Utilities A	EVTMX	A+	(800) 225-6265	12.02	B+ /8.3	17.10 /77	22.03 /85	9.88 /80	B /8.4	97	7
UT	Gartmore Global Utilities Inst	GLUIX	A+	(800) 848-0920	11.40	B /8.2	14.97 /72	20.42 /81	--	B /8.4	97	N/A
UT	Gartmore Global Utilities R	GLURX	A+	(800) 848-0920	11.23	B /8.1	14.45 /70	19.81 /79	--	B /8.4	96	N/A
UT	● AIM Utilities Fund Inv	FSTUX	A+	(800) 347-4246	14.67	B /8.0	14.12 /69	19.21 /77	2.71 /34	B /8.3	77	3
UT	AIM Utilities Fund C	IUTCX	A	(800) 347-4246	14.71	B /7.6	13.22 /65	18.25 /73	1.81 /25	B /8.3	69	3
UT	AllianceBernstein Utility Inc Adv	AUIYX	A	(800) 221-5672	18.69	B /7.6	10.80 /52	18.80 /75	5.21 /56	B /8.1	87	5
UT	Select Utilities Growth	FSUTX	A	(800) 544-8888	47.77	B- /7.5	14.82 /71	17.43 /70	2.15 /29	B /8.4	95	3
UT	AIM Utilities Fund A	IAUTX	A	(800) 347-4246	14.55	B- /7.5	14.14 /69	19.12 /76	--	B /8.3	76	3
UT	Fidelity Adv Telecom & Util Gr I	FUGIX	A	(800) 522-7297	16.67	B- /7.4	15.20 /72	17.12 /69	3.52 /41	B /8.2	96	3
UT	AIM Utilities Fund B	IBUTX	A	(800) 347-4246	14.60	B- /7.3	13.24 /65	18.27 /73	--	B /8.3	69	3
UT	Merrill Lynch Utilities/Telecom I	MAGUX	A-	(800) 543-6217	12.73	B /7.7	11.83 /59	18.61 /75	6.26 /63	B- /7.6	81	4
UT	American Century Utilities Inv	BULIX	A-	(800) 345-6488	13.99	B- /7.3	8.84 /39	17.84 /72	3.33 /40	B /8.1	78	9
UT	American Century Utilities Adv	ACUTX	A-	(800) 345-6488	13.97	B- /7.2	8.50 /37	17.53 /70	3.04 /37	B /8.1	75	N/A
UT	Fidelity Adv Telecom & Util Gr C	FUGCX	A-	(800) 522-7297	16.23	B- /7.0	13.86 /68	15.87 /63	2.36 /31	B /8.3	93	3
UT	MFS Utilities Fund R4	MMUHX	B+	(800) 343-2829	13.62	B+ /8.8	16.63 /76	22.58 /86	7.13 /67	C+ /6.2	98	1
UT	MFS Utilities Fund R5	MMUJX	B+	(800) 343-2829	13.63	B+ /8.8	17.07 /77	22.76 /87	7.23 /68	C+ /6.2	98	1
UT	Eaton Vance Utilities I	EIUTX	B+	(800) 225-6265	12.02	B+ /8.7	17.39 /78	22.13 /85	9.94 /80	C+ /6.0	97	1
UT	MFS Utilities Fund R2	MMUKX	B+	(800) 343-2829	13.58	B+ /8.6	16.34 /75	21.87 /85	6.44 /64	C+ /6.2	98	1
UT	MFS Utilities Fund R1	MMUGX	B+	(800) 343-2829	13.59	B+ /8.6	16.04 /75	21.74 /84	6.37 /63	C+ /6.2	97	1
UT	Merrill Lynch Utilities/Telecom C	MCGUX	B+	(800) 543-6217	12.57	B- /7.3	10.99 /53	17.66 /71	5.39 /57	B- /7.7	74	4
UT	Merrill Lynch Utilities/Telecom A	MDGUX	B+	(800) 543-6217	12.74	B- /7.2	11.64 /58	18.30 /74	6.01 /61	B- /7.6	78	4
UT	AllianceBernstein Utility Inc A	AUIAX	B+	(800) 221-5672	18.60	B- /7.1	10.42 /50	18.42 /74	4.90 /53	B /8.1	85	5
UT	AllianceBernstein Utility Inc C	AUICX	B+	(800) 221-5672	18.44	B- /7.1	9.58 /44	17.59 /71	4.15 /47	B /8.1	80	10
UT	Fidelity Utilities Fund	FIUIX	B+	(800) 544-8888	16.14	B- /7.0	14.71 /71	15.59 /62	2.84 /35	B /8.1	78	2
UT	Merrill Lynch Utilities/Telecom B	MBGUX	B+	(800) 543-6217	12.69	B- /7.0	10.97 /53	17.66 /71	5.44 /57	B- /7.7	73	4
UT	Gabelli Utilities AAA	GABUX	B+	(800) 422-3554	8.44	C+ /6.2	7.65 /30	14.45 /56	6.41 /64	B+ /9.0	71	N/A
UT	Franklin Utilities R	FRURX	B+	(800) 342-5236	12.19	C+ /6.2	4.97 /15	15.20 /60	7.73 /70	B /8.8	54	4
UT	Fidelity Adv Telecom & Util Gr B	FAUBX	B	(800) 522-7297	16.22	C+ /6.9	13.80 /68	15.76 /62	2.29 /30	B /8.3	92	3
UT	Fidelity Adv Telecom & Util Gr T	FAUFX	B	(800) 522-7297	16.48	C+ /6.8	14.37 /69	16.35 /65	2.77 /35	B /8.3	94	3
UT	AllianceBernstein Utility Inc B	AUIBX	B	(800) 221-5672	18.40	C+ /6.8	9.60 /44	17.58 /71	4.15 /47	B /8.1	79	5
UT	Flex-funds Total Return Utilities	FLRUX	B	(800) 325-3539	19.99	C+ /6.8	10.90 /53	16.03 /64	1.61 /24	B /8.0	89	11
UT	Fidelity Adv Telecom & Util Gr A	FUGAX	B	(800) 522-7297	16.51	C+ /6.7	14.68 /71	16.66 /67	3.04 /37	B /8.2	95	3
UT	Morgan Stanley Glbl Utilities D	GUTDX	B	(800) 869-6397	15.84	C+ /6.5	6.85 /25	16.35 /65	4.09 /47	B /8.5	68	9
UT	Franklin Utilities Adv	FRUAX	B	(800) 321-8563	12.27	C+ /6.5	5.56 /18	15.75 /62	8.27 /73	B /8.3	60	14
UT	Columbia Utilities Fund Z	LUFZX	B	(800) 426-3750	14.21	C+ /6.4	7.39 /29	15.22 /60	-1.28 /11	B /8.8	66	N/A
UT	Columbia World Equity Fund C	CGUCX	B	(800) 426-3750	13.40	C+ /6.3	16.66 /76	14.75 /58	2.72 /34	B- /7.9	99	1
UT	Putnam Utilities Gr & Inc R	PULRX	B	(800) 354-2228	11.36	C+ /6.1	6.99 /26	14.63 /57	2.53 /32	B /8.4	61	N/A
UT	Columbia World Equity Fund A	CGUAX	B	(800) 426-3750	13.97	C+ /6.1	17.56 /78	15.60 /62	3.52 /41	B /8.0	99	1

● Denotes fund is closed to new investors

Appendix

What is a Mutual Fund?

Picking individual stocks is difficult and buying individual bonds can be expensive. Mutual funds were introduced to allow the small investor to participate in the stock and bond market for just a small initial investment. Mutual funds are pools of stocks or bonds that are managed by investment professionals. First, an investment company organizes the fund and collects the money from investors. The company then takes that money and pays a portfolio manager to invest it in stocks, bonds, money market instruments and other types of securities.

Most funds fit within one of two main categories, open-ended funds or closed-end funds. Open-ended funds issue new shares when investors put in money and redeem shares when investors withdraw money. The price of a share is determined by dividing the total net assets of the fund by the number of shares outstanding.

On the other hand, closed-end funds issue a fixed number of shares in an initial public offering, trading thereafter in the open market like a stock. Open-end funds are the most common type of mutual fund. Investing in either class of funds means you own a share of the portfolio, so you participate in the fund's gains and losses.

There are more than 11,000 different mutual funds, each with a stated investment objective. Here are descriptions for five of the most popular types of funds:

Stock funds: A mutual fund which invests mainly in stocks. These funds are more actively traded than other more conservative funds. The stocks chosen may vary widely according to the fund's investment strategy.

Bond funds: A mutual fund which invests in bonds, in an effort to provide stable income while preserving principal as much as possible. These funds invest in medium- to long-term bonds issued by corporations and governments.

Index funds: A mutual fund that aims to match the performance of a specific index, such as the S&P 500. Index funds tend to have fewer expenses than other funds because portfolio decisions are automatic and transactions are infrequent.

Balanced funds: A mutual fund that buys a combination of stocks and bonds, in order to supply both income and capital growth while ensuring a minimal amount of risk for investors.

Money market funds: An open-end mutual fund which invests only in stable, short-term securities. The fund's value remains at a constant $1 per share, but only those administered by banks are government insured.

Investing in a mutual fund has several advantages over owning a single stock or bond. For example, funds offer instant portfolio diversification by giving you ownership of many stocks or bonds simultaneously. This diversification protects you in case a part of your investment takes a sudden downturn. You also get the benefit of having a professional handling your investment, though a management fee is charged for these services, typically 1% or 2% a year. You should be aware that the fund may also levy other fees and that you will likely have to pay a sales commission (known as a load) if you purchase the fund from a financial adviser.

The fund manager's strategy is laid out in the fund's prospectus, which is the official name for the legal document that contains financial information about the fund, including its history, its officers and its performance. Mutual fund investments are fully liquid so you can easily get in or out by just placing an order through a broker.

Investor Profile Quiz

We recognize that each person approaches his or her investment decisions from a unique perspective. A mutual fund that is perfect for someone else may be totally inappropriate for you due to factors such as:

- How much risk you are comfortable taking
- Your age and the number of years you have before retirement
- Your income level and tax rate
- Your other existing investments and personal net worth
- Preconceived expectations about investment performance

The following quiz will help you quantify your tolerance for risk based on your own personal life situation. As you read through each question, circle the letter next to the single answer that you feel most accurately describes your current position. Keep in mind that there are no "correct" answers to this quiz, only answers that are helpful in assessing your investment style. So don't worry about how your answer might be perceived by others; just try to be as honest and accurate as possible.

Then at the end of the quiz, use the point totals listed on the right side of the page to compute your test score. Once you've added up your total points, refer to the corresponding investor profile for an evaluation of your personal risk tolerance. Each profile also lists the page number where you will find the top performing mutual funds matching your risk profile.

		Points	Your Score
1.	I am currently investing to pay for:		
	a. Retirement	0 pts	
	b. College	0 pts	
	c. A house	0 pts	
2.	I expect I will need to liquidate some or all of this investment in:		
	a. 2 years or less	0 pts	
	b. 2 to 5 years	5 pts	
	c. 5 to 10 years	8 pts	
	d. 10 years or more	10 pts	
3.	My age group is		
	a. Under 30	10 pts	
	b. 30 to 44	9 pts	
	c. 45 to 60	7 pts	
	d. 60 to 74	5 pts	
	e. 75 and older	1 pts	
4.	I am currently looking to invest money through:		
	a. An IRA or other tax-deferred account	0 pts	
	b. A fully taxable account	0 pts	

5.	I have a cash reserve equal to 3 to 6 months expenses.		
	a. Yes	10 pts	
	b. No	1 pts	
6.	My primary source of income is:		
	a. Salary and other earnings from my primary occupation	7 pts	
	b. Earnings from my investment portfolio	5 pts	
	c. Retirement pension and/or Social Security	3 pts	
7.	I will need regular income from this investment now or in the near future.		
	a. Yes	6 pts	
	b. No	10 pts	
8.	Over the long run, I expect this investment to average returns of:		
	a. 8% annually or less	0 pts	
	b. 8% to 12% annually	6 pts	
	c. 12% to 15% annually	8 pts	
	d. 15% to 20% annually	10 pts	
	e. Over 20% annually	18 pts	
9.	The worst loss I would be comfortable accepting on my investment is:		
	a. Less than 5%. Stability of principal is very important to me.	1 pts	
	b. 5% to 10%. Modest periodic declines are acceptable.	3 pts	
	c. 10% to 15%. I understand that there may be losses in the short run but over the long term, higher risk investments will offer highest returns.	8 pts	
	d. Over 15%. You don't get high returns without taking risk. I'm looking for maximum capital gains and understand that my funds can substantially decline.	15 pts	
10.	If the stock market were to suddenly decline by 15%, which of the following would most likely be your reaction?		
	a. I should have left the market long ago, at the first sign of trouble.	3 pts	
	b. I should have substantially exited the stock market by now to limit my exposure.	5 pts	
	c. I'm still in the stock market but I've got my finger on the trigger.	7 pts	
	d. I'm staying fully invested so I'll be ready for the next bull market.	10 pts	
11.	The best defense against a bear market is:		
	a. A defensive market timing system that avoids large losses.	4 pts	
	b. A potent offense that will make big gains in the next bull market.	10 pts	
12.	The best strategy to employ during bear markets is:		
	a. Move to cash. It's the only safe hiding place.	5 pts	
	b. Short the market and try to make a profit as it declines.	10 pts	
	c. Wait it out because the market will eventually recover.	8 pts	

13.	I would classify myself as:			
	a. A buy-and-hold investor who rides out all the peaks and valleys.	10 pts		
	b. A market timer who wants to capture the major bull markets.	7 pts		
	c. A market timer who wants to avoid the major bear markets.	5 pts		
14.	My attitude regarding trading activity is:			
	a. Active trading is costly and unproductive.	0 pts		
	b. I don't mind frequent trades as long as I'm making money	2 pts		
	c. Occasional trading is okay but too much activity is not good.	1 pts		
15.	If the S&P 500 advanced strongly over the last 12 months, my investment should have:			
	a. Grown even more than the market.	10 pts		
	b. Approximated the performance of the broad market.	5 pts		
	c. Focused on reducing the risk of loss in a bear market, even if it meant giving up some upside potential in the bull market.	2 pts		

		Exten-sive	Some	None	
16.	I have experience (extensive, some, or none) with the following types of investments.				
	a. U.S. stocks or stock mutual funds	2 pts	1 pts	0 pts	
	b. International stock funds	2 pts	1 pts	0 pts	
	c. Bonds or bond funds	1 pts	0 pts	0 pts	
	d. Futures and/or options	5 pts	3 pts	0 pts	
	e. Managed futures or funds	3 pts	1 pts	0 pts	
	f. Real estate	2 pts	1 pts	0 pts	
	g. Private hedge funds	3 pts	1 pts	0 pts	
	h. Privately managed accounts	2 pts	1 pts	0 pts	

17.	Excluding my primary residence, this investment represents ___% of my investment holdings.		
	a. Less than 5%	10 pts	
	b. 5% to 10%	7 pts	
	c. 10% to 20%	5 pts	
	d. 20% to 30%	3 pts	
	e. 30% or more	1 pts	
		TOTAL	

Under 58 pts   **Very Conservative.** You appear to be very risk averse with capital preservation as your primary goal. As such, most equity mutual funds may be a little too risky for your taste, especially in a turbulent market environment. We recommend you stick to the safest bond funds and money market mutual funds where your income stream is predictable and more secure. Those funds are not covered in this publication, but you can easily find them in Section VII of *Weiss Ratings' Guide to Bond and Money Market Mutual Funds.*

58 to 77 pts   **Conservative.** Based on your responses, it appears that you are more concerned about minimizing the risk to your principal than you are about maximizing your returns. Don't worry, there are plenty of good mutual funds that offer strong returns with very little volatility. As a starting point, we recommend you turn to page 592 where you will find a list of the top-rated funds receiving the best risk rating we issue to equity mutual funds (B– or better, meaning Good).

78 to 108 pts   **Moderate.** You are prepared to take on a little added risk in order to enhance your investment returns. This is probably the most common approach to mutual fund investing. To select a mutual fund matching your style, we recommend you turn to page 594. There you can easily pick from the top-rated mutual funds receiving a risk rating in the C (Fair) range.

109 to 129 pts   **Aggressive.** You appear to be ready to ride out almost any financial storm on your way toward maximizing your investment returns. You understand that the only way to make large returns on your investments is by taking on added risk, and your personal situation seems to allow for that approach. We recommend you use pages 594 - 597 as a starting point for selecting a top-rated mutual fund with a risk rating in the C (Fair) or D (Weak) range.

Over 129 pts   **Very Aggressive.** Based on your responses, you appear to be leaning heavily toward speculation. Your primary concern is maximizing your investment growth, and you are prepared to take on as much risk as necessary in order to do so. To this end, turn to page 598 where you'll find the top-rated mutual funds with a risk rating in the E (Very Weak) range. These investments have historically been extremely volatile, oftentimes investing in stocks that are currently out of favor. As such, they are highly speculative investments that could provide superior results if you can stomach the volatility and uncertainty. For a list of the top performing mutual funds regardless of risk category, turn to page 572. Also see section VI of *Weiss Ratings' Guide to Common Stocks.*

Performance Benchmarks

The following benchmarks represent the average performance for all mutual funds within each stock fund type category. Comparing an individual mutual fund's returns to these benchmarks is yet another way to assess its performance. For the top performing funds within each of the following categories, turn to Section VIII, Top-Rated Stock Mutual Funds By Fund Type, beginning on page 606. You can also use this information to compare the average performance of one category of funds to another (updated through June 30, 2006).

		3 Month Total Return %	1 Year Total Return %	Refer to page:
AG	Aggressive Growth	-4.44%	8.46%	606
AA	Asset Allocation	-1.47%	7.62%	607
BA	Balanced	-1.21%	5.60%	608
CV	Convertible	-1.27%	9.37%	609
EM	Emerging Market	-4.89%	34.84%	610
EN	Energy/Natural Resources	3.29%	34.03%	611
FS	Financial Services	-1.44%	12.20%	612
FO	Foreign	-1.16%	27.52%	613
GL	Global	-1.57%	16.92%	614
GR	Growth	-3.05%	8.68%	615
GI	Growth & Income	-1.20%	9.09%	616
HL	Health	-6.73%	4.77%	617
IN	Income	-0.64%	9.11%	618
IX	Index	-1.68%	7.80%	619
MC	Mid Cap	-4.08%	11.73%	620
OT	Other	0.05%	8.91%	621
PM	Precious Metals	1.48%	68.80%	622
RE	Real Estate	-0.98%	19.68%	623
SC	Small Cap	-5.13%	13.05%	624
TC	Technology	-8.90%	9.73%	625
UT	Utilities	3.40%	10.90%	626

Fund Type Descriptions

<u>AG - Aggressive Growth</u> - Seeks maximum capital appreciation, by investing primarily in common stocks of companies that are believed to offer rapid growth potential. These funds tend to employ greater-than-average risk strategies than a typical growth fund in an attempt to gain a higher rate of return. Aggressive Growth funds have the flexibility to invest in companies with any capitalization.

<u>AA - Asset Allocation</u> - Seeks both income and capital appreciation by determining the optimal percentage of assets to place in stocks, bonds, and cash.

<u>BA - Balanced</u> - Seeks both income and capital appreciation by determining the optimal proportion of assets to place in stocks, bonds, and cash. The allocation across asset classes will remain relatively stable.

<u>CV - Convertible</u> - Invests at least 65% in convertible securities. Convertible securities are bonds or preferred stocks that are exchangeable for a set number of shares of common stock.

<u>EM - Emerging Market</u> - Seeks long term capital appreciation by investing primarily in emerging market equity securities. Income is usually incidental.

<u>EN - Energy/Natural Resources</u> - Invests primarily in equity securities of companies involved in the exploration, distribution, or processing of natural resources.

<u>FS - Financial</u> - Seeks capital appreciation by investing in equity securities of companies engaged in providing financial services. Typically, securities are from commercial banks, S&Ls, finance companies, securities brokerages, investment managers, insurance companies, and leasing companies.

<u>FO - Foreign</u> - Invests primarily in non-U.S. equity securities of any market capitalization. Income is usually incidental.

<u>GL - Global</u> - Invests primarily in domestic and foreign equity securities of any market capitalization. Income is usually incidental.

<u>GR - Growth</u> - Seeks long term capital appreciation by investing primarily in equity securities of any market capitalization. Income is usually incidental.

<u>GI - Growth and Income</u> - Seeks both capital appreciation and income primarily by investing in equities with a level or rising dividend stream.

<u>HL - Health</u> - Seeks capital appreciation by investing primarily in equities of companies engaged in the design, manufacture, or sale of products or services connected with health care or medicine.

<u>IN - Income</u> - Seeks current income by investing a minimum of 65% of its assets in income-producing equity securities.

<u>IX - Index</u> - Seeks to provide investment results comparable to that of a particular index by investing substantially in the securities of, or characteristically similar to those of, the index.

<u>MC - Mid Cap</u> - Seeks long term capital appreciation by investing in stocks of medium size companies, as determined by market capitalization. Typically, capitalizations between $1 billion and $5 billion are ranked as medium capitalization companies.

<u>OT - Other</u> - Funds which have a specific focus that do not fit into any of the existing categories.

<u>PM - Precious Metals</u> - Seeks capital appreciation by investing primarily in equity securities of companies involved in mining, distribution, processing, or dealing in gold, silver, platinum, diamonds, or other precious metals and minerals.

<u>RE - Real Estate</u> - Seeks capital appreciation and income by investing in equity securities of real estate investment trusts and other real estate industry companies.

<u>SC - Small Cap</u> - Seeks maximum capital appreciation, by investing primarily in stocks of small companies, as determined by market capitalization. Typically, capitalizations under $1 billion are classified as small capitalization companies.

<u>TC - Technology</u> - Seeks capital appreciation by investing a minimum of 65% of its assets in the technology sector.

<u>UT - Utilities</u> - Seeks a high level of current income by investing primarily in the equity securities of utility companies.

Share Class Descriptions

Many mutual funds have several classes of shares, each with different fees and associated sales charges. While there is no official standardization of mutual fund classes we have compiled a list of those most frequently seen. Ultimately you must consult a fund's prospectus for particular share class designations and what they mean. Federal regulation requires that the load, or sales charge, not exceed 8.5% of the investment purchase.

Class	Description
A	**Front End Load.** Sales charge is paid at the time of purchase and is deducted from the investment amount.
B	**Back End Load.** Also know as contingent deferred sales charge (CDSC); the sales charge is imposed if the fund is sold. Class B shares usually convert to Class A shares after six to eight years from the date of purchase.
C	**Level Load.** A set sales charge paid annually for as long as the fund is held. This class is especially beneficial to the short–term investor.
D	**Flexible.** Class D shares can be anything a fund company wants. Check the fund prospectus for the details regarding a specific fund's fee structure.
I	**Institutional.** No sales charge is collected due to the size of the order. This class usually requires a minimum investment of $100,000.
M	**Mid Load.** Similar to Class A, but with a lower front end load and higher expense ratio (see page 17 for more information on expense ratios).
N	**No Load.** No sales fee is imposed.
R	**No Load.** No sales fee is imposed and fund must be held in a qualified retirement account.
T	**Mid Load.** Similar to Class A, but with a lower front end load and higher expense ratio (see page 17 for more information on expense ratios).
Y	**Institutional.** No sales charge is collected due to the size of the order. This class usually requires a minimum investment of $100,000.
Z	**No Load.** Fund is only available for purchase to employees of the mutual fund company, as an employee benefit. No sales fee is imposed.

Weiss Ratings'

WEISS RATINGS' SAFETY GUIDES

Weiss Ratings' comprehensive industry-wide guides provide the most accurate, complete source of safety ratings on more than 15,000 financial institutions including banks and insurance companies.

Issued Quarterly. Price: $499 + $19.95 s/h for 4 quarterly issues, or $249 + $8.95 s/h for a single edition.

Guide to Life, Health, and Annuity Insurers covers more than 1,500 U.S. life, health and annuity insurers.

Guide to Property and Casualty Insurers covers more than 2,500 property and casualty insurers in the U.S.

Guide to HMOs and Health Insurers is the only source covering more than 1,200 U.S. health insurers including all Blue Cross/Blue Shield plans and over 500 HMOs.

Guide to Banks and Thrifts covers more than 9,000 banks and thrifts in the U.S.

WEISS RATINGS' INVESTMENT GUIDES

Weiss Ratings' comprehensive investment guides provide the most accurate, complete information for more than 20,000 investment choices.

Issued Quarterly. Price: $499 + $19.95 s/h for 4 quarterly issues, or $249 + $8.95 s/h for a single edition.

Ultimate Guided Tour of Stock Investing is a must-have, easy-to-understand guide presented in a friendly, fun format complete with our "Wise Guide" who leads you on an informative safari through the stock market jungle. Complete with how-to information on stock investing, useful worksheets, examples on common topics such as diversification, the Weiss Performance and Risk Ratings, and much more! This guide will help you learn to invest and successfully manage your stock portfolio. Covers every stock on the American Stock Exchange, New York Stock Exchange, and the NASDAQ.

Guide to Stock Mutual Funds covers more than 7,000 equity mutual funds, including balanced funds, international funds, and individual sector funds.

Guide to Bond and Money Market Mutual Funds covers more than 4,200 fixed-income mutual funds, including government bond funds, municipal bond funds, and corporate bond funds.

Guide to Closed-End Mutual Funds covers more than 600 closed-end mutual funds, including growth funds, sector funds, international funds, municipal bond funds and other closed-end funds.

Guide to Common Stocks covers stocks on the American Stock Exchange, New York Stock Exchange, and the NASDAQ, plus more.

WEISS RATINGS' SHOPPER'S GUIDES

Weiss Ratings' Shopper's Guides come packed with customized information needed to make sound purchasing decisions.

Fully Customized Reports. Price: $49 + $4.95 s/h

Shopper's Guide to Medicare Supplement Insurance has price comparisons for Medigap insurance based on your age, gender, and zip code. Insurance companies are listed by Weiss rating to provide price and financial safety comparisons.

Shopper's Guide to Term Life Insurance has price comparisons for term life insurance based on your age, gender, zip code and other unique information. You'll find the insurers who are currently offering the best rates.

WEISS RATINGS' CONSUMER GUIDES

Weiss Ratings' Consumer Guides provide the critical information needed to make sound financial decisions including step-by-step instructions, worksheets, sample rates and more.

Price: $119 + $7.95 s/h for 4 quarterly issues, or $49 + $4.95 s/h for a single edition.
Consumer Guide Box Set Price: $399 + $19.95 s/h includes one full year of updates.

Consumer Guide to Variable Annuities leads you step by step through understanding when variable annuities make sense and how they actually work. This easy-to-use guide looks at the 20 best and worst variable annuities on the market today, all the costs to look for, and the advantages and disadvantages of variable annuities versus other investments.

Consumer Guide to Elder Care Choices is designed to educate you on the many care options available and to provide you with the necessary tools to make informed decisions on Continuing Care Retirement Communities, Assisted Living Facilities, Home Health Care Agencies, Adult Day Care, Nursing Homes, and more.

Consumer Guide to Long-Term Care Insurance gives you how-to information on how to select the right long-term care policy for you, with worksheets, definitions and sample policy information.

Consumer Guide to Medicare Supplement Insurance is a must have for anyone considering the purchase of Medigap insurance. This how-to guide leads you through the process showing where the gaps are, how to fill them, and how you determine what type of policy is best for you.

Consumer Guide to Medicare Prescription Drug Coverage helps you through the decision making process of adding Medicare prescription drug coverage to your health benefits. You'll learn how the benefit works and what happens after enrollment. The guide also includes a listing of all Medicare-approved prescription drug plans.

Consumer Guide to Term Life Insurance walks you through the decision of whether or not to purchase term life insurance, providing easy-to-understand information and guidance, including an overview of other life insurance options. You'll learn how to determine if you need a term life policy and how to calculate the amount of insurance to buy. The guide includes a list of Weiss recommended insurers with their Weiss rating.

Consumer Guide to Auto Insurance can help you save hundreds of dollars on auto insurance. The guide can help you understand the coverage required in your state, get the right insurance for your vehicle, save money on your premiums, and so much more.

Consumer Guide to Homeowners Insurance provides a complete how-to guide on purchasing homeowner's insurance including types of coverage, how to save money, choosing the right company, and more.

For a consumer-friendly guide on Stock Investing, see the "Weiss Ratings' Investment Guides" category on the previous page for our *Ultimate Guided Tour of Stock Investing*.

WEISS RATINGS' REPORTS AND SERVICES

See pricing below for each report and service.

Ratings Online — An on-line summary covering an individual company's Weiss Safety Rating or an investment's unique Weiss Investment Rating with the factors contributing to that rating; available 24 hours a day by visiting www.WeissRatings.com. Price: $14.99 each.

Ratings Over the Phone — Call our customer hotline at 1-800-289-9222 to receive a rating over the telephone. Price: $19 each.

Unlimited Ratings Research — The ultimate research tool providing fast, easy online access to the very latest Weiss Safety Ratings and Weiss Investment Ratings (includes 4 quarterly editions of one guide). Price: $559 per industry, + $19.95 s/h.

WEISS RATINGS' REPORTS AND SERVICES continued

See pricing below for each report and service.

Rating Analysis Report — A detailed report on an individual company or investment including the rating and an in-depth analysis of each of the factors contributing to the rating. Price: $49 + $4.95 s/h.

Weiss Watchdog Service — An e-mail notification service for stocks, mutual funds, banks and insurance companies that immediately notifies you of any upgrades and downgrades in the Weiss investment or safety rating. Additionally, you get 24/7 online access to the rating of each company being watched. Price: starting as low as $8 per month for up to 20 companies. Free trial available – go to www.weisswatchdog.com.

WEISS RATINGS' CUSTOM REPORTS

Weiss Ratings is pleased to offer two customized options for receiving our data. Each taps into our vast data repositories and is designed to provide exactly the data you need. Choose from a variety of industries, companies, data variables, and delivery formats including print, Excel, SQL, Text or Access.

Call 1-800-289-9222 today for pricing.

Customized Reports - get right to the heart of your company's research and data needs with a report customized with just the data you need.

Complete Database Download - we design and deliver the database; you're then free to sort it, recalculate it, and format your results to suit your specific needs.

2 EASY WAYS TO ORDER

❶ **Call our Customer Hotline at 1-800-289-9222**

❷ **Order Online at www.WeissRatings.com**